THE

NEW TESTAMENT

OF OUR

LORD AND SAVIOUR JESUS CHRIST

THE TEXT

CAREFULLY PRINTED FROM THE MOST CORRECT COPIES OF THE PRESENT

AUTHORIZED TRANSLATION,

INCLUDING THE

MARGINAL READINGS AND PARALLEL TEXTS:

WITH

A COMMENTARY AND CRITICAL NOTES;

DESIGNED AS A HELP TO A BETTER UNDERSTANDING OF THE SACRED WRITINGS

BY ADAM CLARKE, LL.D., F.S.A., &c.

A NEW EDITION, WITH THE AUTHOR'S FINAL CORRECTIONS.

FOR WHATSOEVER THINGS WERE WRITTEN AFORETIME WERE WRITTEN FOR OUR LEARNING; THAT WE
THROUGH PATIENCE AND COMFORT OF THE SCRIPTURES, MIGHT HAVE HOPE.—ROM. xv, 4.

VOLUME II.—ROMANS TO THE REVELATIONS.

ABINGDON PRESS
NEW YORK ● NASHVILLE

Printed in the United States of America

PREFACE

EPISTLE TO THE ROMANS.

THAT St. Paul was the author of this epistle, and that it possesses every evidence of *authenticity* that any work of the kind can possess, or that even the most fastidious skepticism can require, has been most amply proved by Dr. W. Paley, Archdeacon of Carlisle, in his work entitled "*Horæ Paulinæ;* or, the Truth of the Scripture History of St. Paul evinced, by a comparison of the Epistles which bear his name with the Acts of the Apostles, and with one another."

Of this apostle I have spoken at large in the notes on the preceding book, and especially in the observa tions at the close of the ninth chapter, to which I beg leave to refer the reader. It will be sufficient to state here, that *Saul*, (afterwards called *Paul*,) was born in Tarsus, a city of ·Cilicia, of Jewish parents, who pos- sessed the right of Roman citizens; (see the note on Acts xxii. 28;) that, when young, he was sent to Jeru- salem for the purpose of receiving a Jewish education; that he was there put under the tuition of the famous Rabbi *Gamaliel*, and was incorporated with the sect of the Pharisees, of whose system he imbibed all the pride, self-confidence, and intolerance; and distinguished himself as one of the most inveterate enemies of the Christian cause; but, being converted by a most singular interposition of Divine Providence and grace, he became one of the most zealous promoters and successful defenders of the cause which he had before so inveterately persecuted.

Though this epistle is directed *to the Romans*, yet we are not to suppose that *Romans*, in the proper sense of the word, are meant; but rather those who *dwelt at Rome*, and composed the Christian Church in that city: that there were among these *Romans*, properly such, that is heathens who had been converted to the Christian faith, there can be no doubt; but the principal part of the Church in that city seems to have been formed from *Jews*, sojourners at Rome, and from such as were *proselytes* to the Jewish religion.

When, or by *whom*, the Gospel was first preached at Rome cannot be ascertained. Those who assert that St. *Peter* was its founder, can produce no solid reason for the support of their opinion. Had this apostle first preached the Gospel in that city, it is not likely that such an event would have been unnoticed in the *Acts of the Apostles*, where the labours of St. Peter are particularly detailed with those of St. Paul, which indeed form the chief subject of this book. Nor is it likely that the author of this epistle should have made no reference to this circumstance, had it been true. Those who say that this Church was founded by these two apostles conjointly, have still less reason on their side; for it is evident, from chap. i. 8, &c., that St. Paul had *never been at Rome* previously to his writing this epistle. It is most likely that no *apostle* was employed in this important work, and that the Gospel was first preached there by some of those persons who were converted at Jerusalem on the day of pentecost; for we find, from Acts ii. 10, that there were at Jerusalem *strangers of Rome, Jews, and proselytes;* and these, on their return, would naturally declare the wonders they had witnessed, and proclaim that truth by which they themselves had received salvation. Of ROME itself, then the metropolis of the world, a particular account has been given in the note on Acts xxviii. 16; to which the reader is requested to refer.

The *occasion* of writing this epistle may be easily collected from the epistle itself. It appears that St. Paul had been made acquainted with all the circumstances of the Christians at Rome, by Aquila and Priscilla, (see chap. xvi. 3,) and by other Jews who had been expelled from Rome by the decree of Claudius, (men tioned Acts xviii. 2;) and, finding that they consisted partly of *heathens* converted to Christianity, and partly of *Jews* who had, with many remaining prejudices, believed in Jesus as the true Messiah, and that many con- tentions arose from the claims of the Gentile converts to equal privileges with the Jews, and from the abso- lute refusal of the Jews to admit these claims unless the Gentile converts became circumcised, he wrote to adjust and settle these differences.

Dr. Paley, with his usual perspicuity, has shown that the principal object of the argumentative part of the epistle is "to place the Gentile convert upon a parity of situation with the Jewish, in respect of his religious condition, and his rank in the Divine favour." The epistle supports this point by a variety of arguments; such as, that no man of either description was justified by the works of the law—for this plain reason, that no man had performed them; that it became therefore necessary to appoint *another medium*, or condition of justification, in which *new medium* the Jewish peculiarity was merged and lost; that Abraham's own justification was *antecedent* to the *law*, and *independent of it*; that the Jewish converts were to consider the law as now dead, and themselves as married to another; that what the law in truth could not do, in that it was weak through the flesh, God had done by sending his Son; that God had rejected the unbelieving Jews, and had substituted in their place a society of believers in Christ, collected indifferently from Jews and Gentiles. Therefore, in an epistle directed to Roman believers, the point to be endeavoured after by St. Paul was to reconcile the Jewish converts to the opinion that the Gentiles were admitted by God to a parity of religious situation with themselves, and that without their being obliged to keep the law of Moses. In this epistle, though directed to the Roman Church in general, it is, in truth, a Jew writing to Jews. Accordingly, as often as his argument leads him to say any thing derogatory from the Jewish institution, he constantly follows it by a softening clause. Having, chap. ii. 28, 29, pronounced " that he is not a Jew who is one outwardly, nor that circumcision which is outward in the flesh," he adds immediately, " What advantage then hath the Jew ? or what profit is there in circumcision ? *Much every way.*" Having in chap. iii. 28, brought his argument to this formal conclusion, " that a man is justified by faith, without the deeds of the law," he presently subjoins, ver. 31, " Do we then make void the law through faith ? God forbid ! *Yea, we establish the law.*" In the seventh chapter, when in ver. 6 he had advanced the bold assertion, " that now we are delivered from the law, that being dead wherein we were held ;" in the next verse he comes in with this healing question, " What shall we say then ? Is the law sin ? God forbid ! Nay, I had not known sin but by the law." Having, in the following words, more than insinuated the inefficacy of the Jewish law, chap. viii. 3 : " For what the law could not do, in that it was weak through the flesh, God, sending his own Son in the likeness of sinful flesh, and for sin, condemned sin in the flesh ;" after a digression indeed, but that sort of a digression which he could never resist, a rapturous contemplation of his Christian hope, and which occupies the latter part of this chapter; we find him in the next, as if sensible that he had said something which would give offence, returning to his Jewish brethren in terms of the warmest affection and respect : " I say the truth in Christ Jesus, I lie not ; my conscience also bearing me witness in the Holy Ghost, that I have great heaviness and continual sorrow in my heart ; for I could wish that myself were accursed from Christ for my brethren, my kinsmen according to the flesh, who are Israelites, to whom pertaineth the adoption, and the glory, and the covenants, and the giving of the law, and the service of God, and the promises ; whose are the fathers ; and of whom, as concerning the flesh, Christ came." When, in the 31st and 32d verses of the ninth chapter, he represented to the Jews the error of even the best of their nation, by telling them that " Israel, which followed after the law of righteousness, had not attained to the law of righteousness, because they sought it not by faith, but as it were by the works of the law, for they stumbled at that stumbling-stone ;" he takes care to annex to this declaration these conciliating expressions : " Brethren, my heart's desire and prayer to God for Israel is, that they might be saved ; for I bear them record, that they have a zeal of God, but not according to knowledge." Lastly, having, chap. x. 20, 21, by the application of a passage in Isaiah, insinuated the most ungrateful of all propositions to a Jewish ear, the rejection of the Jewish nation as God's peculiar people ; he hastens, as it were, to qualify the intelligence of their fall by this interesting exposition : " I say then, hath God cast away his people, (i. e. wholly and entirely ?) God forbid ! For I also am an Israelite, of the seed of Abraham, of the tribe of Benjamin. God hath not cast away his people which he foreknew ;" and follows this throughout the whole of the eleventh chapter, in a series of reflections calculated to soothe the Jewish converts, as well as to procure from their Gentile brethren respect to the Jewish institution. Dr. Paley, drawing an argument from this manner of writing, in behalf of the genuineness of this epistle, adds, " Now all this is perfectly natural. In a *real* St. Paul writing to *real* converts, it is what anxiety to bring them over to his persuasion would naturally produce ; but there is an *earnestness* and a *personality*, if I may so call it, in the manner, which a cold forgery, I apprehend, would neither have conceived nor supported." *Horæ Paulinæ*, p. 49, &c.

From a proper consideration of the *design* of the apostle in writing this epistle, and from the *nature* and *circumstances* of the persons to whom it was directed, much light may be derived for a proper understanding of the epistle itself. When the reader considers that the Church at Rome was composed of *heathens* and *Jews*, that the latter were taught to consider themselves the only people on earth to whom the Divine favour extended ; that *these* alone had a right to all the blessings of the Messiah's kingdom ; that the giving *them* the law and the prophets, which had not been given to any other people, was the fullest proof that these privileges did not extend to the nations of the earth ; and that, though it was possible for the Gentiles to be saved, yet it must be *in consequence* of their becoming *circumcised*, and taking on them the *yoke of the law* :—when, on the other hand, the reader considers the Roman Gentiles, who formed the other part of the Church at Rome, as educated in the most perfect contempt of *Judaism* and of the *Jews*, who were deemed to be haters of all mankind, and degraded with the silliest superstitions, and now evidently rejected and abandoned by that God in whom they professed to trust ; it is no wonder if, from these causes, many contentions and scandals arose, especially at a time when the spirit of Christianity was but little understood, and among a people, too, who do not appear to have had any apostolic authority established among them to compose feuds and settle religious differences.

That the apostle had these things particularly in his eye is evident from the epistle itself. His first object is to confound the *pride* of the *Jews* and the *Gentiles ;* and this he does by showing the *former* that they had *broken their own law*, and, consequently, *forfeited* all the privileges which the obedient had a right to expect

He shows the *latter* that, however they might boast of eminent men, who had been an honour to their country, nevertheless, the Gentiles, *as a people*, were degraded by the basest of crimes, and the lowest idolatry; that, in a word, the Gentiles had as little cause to boast in their *philosophers* as the Jews had to boast in the faith and piety of their *ancestors;* "for all had sinned and come short of the glory of God." This subject is particularly handled in the *five* first chapters, and often referred to in other places.

Concerning the *time* in which this epistle was written, there is not much difference of opinion: it is most likely that it was written about A. D. 58, when Paul was at Corinth: see chap. xvi. 23, conferred with 1 Cor. i. 14; and Rom. xvi. 1, conferred with 2 Tim. iv. 20. It appears, from chap. xvi. 22, that Paul did not write this epistle with his *own* hand, but used a person called *Tertius* as his amanuensis; and that it was sent by the hands of *Phœbe*, a deaconess, (δια Φοιβης της διακυνου,) of the Church of Cenchrea, which was the eastern port on the Isthmus of Corinth.

From internal evidence Dr. Paley has demonstrated the authenticity of this epistle; and its existence in the ancient *Antehieronymian* versions and the *Syriac*, as well as its being mentioned by the *Apostolic Fathers*, *Barnabas*, chap. xii. 13; *Clemens Romanus*, Ep. i. c. i. 30, 32, 35, 46; *Ignatius*, Epist. ad Ephes. 20, ad Smyrn. 1, ad Trall. 8; and *Polycarp*, 3 and 6, and by all *succeeding* writers, puts it beyond all dispute.

Of the fourteen epistles attributed to St. Paul, (thirteen only of which bear his name,) this has been reckoned the first in importance, though certainly not in order of time; for there is every reason to believe that both the epistles to the *Thessalonians*, that to the *Galatians*, those to the *Corinthians*, the first to *Timothy*, and that to *Titus*, were all written before the epistle to the Romans. See the dates of the books of the New Testament at the end of the introduction to the Gospels, &c.

In the arrangement of the epistles nothing seems to have been consulted besides the length of the epistle, the character of the writer, and the importance of the place to which it was sent. ROME, being the mistress of the world, the epistle to that city was placed first. Those to the *Corinthians*, because of the great importance of their city, next. *Galatia, Ephesus, Philippi, Colosse*, and *Thessalonica*, follow in graduated order. *Timothy, Titus*, and *Philemon* succeed in the same way: and the epistle to the *Hebrews*, because the author of it was long in dispute, was placed at the end of the epistles of Paul, as being *probably* written by him. *James*, as Bp. of Jerusalem, precedes Peter; *Peter* precedes *John*, as the supposed chief of the apostles; and *John* the beloved disciple, *Jude*. The book of the *Revelation*, as being long disputed in the Christian Church, was thrown to the conclusion of the New Testament Scriptures. The *surats* or chapters of the *Koran* were disposed in the same sort of order; the *longest* being put first, and all the *short ones* thrown to the end, without any regard to the *times* in which it was pretended they were revealed.

There have been some doubts concerning the *language* in which this epistle was written. *John Adrian Bolten* endeavoured to prove that St. Paul wrote it in *Syriac*, and that it was translated into *Greek* by *Tertius :* but this supposition has been amply refuted by *Griesbach*. Others think that it must have been written originally in *Latin*, the language of the people to whom it was addressed; "for although the Greek tongue was well known in Rome, yet it was the language of the *great* and the *learned ;* and it is more natural to suppose that the apostle would write in the language of the *common people*, as those were most likely to be his chief readers, than that of the *great* and the *learned*." This argument is more specious than solid.—1. It is certain that at this time the Greek language was very generally cultivated in Rome, as it was in most parts of the Roman empire. *Cicer., pro Arch.* 10, says *Græca leguntur in omnibus fere gentibus: Latina, suis finibus, exiguis sane continentur.* "The Greek writings are read in almost all nations: those of the Latin within their own narrow limits." *Tacitus*, Orator. 29, observes, *Nunc natus infans delegatur Græculæ alicui ancillæ.* " Now the new-born child is put under the care of some Greek maid;" and this undoubtedly for the purpose of its learning to speak the Greek tongue. And Juvenal, Sat. vi. ver. 184, ridicules this affectation of his countrymen, which in his time appears to have been carried to a most extravagant excess.

> *Nam quid rancidius, quam quod se non putat ulla*
> *Formosam, nisi quæ de Tusca Græcula facta est?*
> *De Sulmonensi mera Cecropis?* OMNIA GRÆCE,
> *Cum sit turpe magis nostris nescire Latine.*
> *Hoc sermone pavent, hoc Iram, Gaudia, Curas,*
> *Hoc cuncta effundunt animi secreta.* Quid ultrâ

> " For what so nauseous and affected too,
> As those that think they due perfection want
> Who have not learned to lisp the *Grecian cant?*
> In *Greece* their whole accomplishments they seek:
> Their fashion, breeding, *language* must be *Greek*,
> But raw in all that does to *Rome* belong,
> They scorn to cultivate their *mother-tongue*,
> In *Greek* they flatter, all their fears they speak,
> Tell all their secrets, nay they scold in *Greek*." DRYDEN.

From these testimonies it is evident that the Greek was a common language in Rome in the days of the apostle; and that in writing in this language, which he probably understood better than he did Latin, he consulted the *taste* and propensity of the Romans, as well as the probability of his epistle being more extensively read in consequence of its being written in *Greek*.

2. But were these arguments wanting, there are others of great weight that evince the propriety of choosing this language in preference to any other. The sacred writings of the Old Testament were, at that time,

confined to two languages, the *Hebrew* and the *Greek*. The former was known only within the confines of Palestine; the latter over the whole Roman empire: and the *Latin* tongue appears to have been as much confined to *Italy* as the *Hebrew* was to *Judea*. The epistle, therefore, being designed by the Spirit of God to be of general use to the Christian Churches, not only in *Italy*, but through *Greece* and all *Asia Minor*, where the Greek language was spoken and understood, it was requisite that the instructions to be conveyed by it should be put in a language the most generally known; and a language too which was then in high and in daily increasing credit.

3. As the Jews were the principal objects of the epistle, and they must be convinced of the truth of Christianity from the evidence of their *own Scriptures*; and as the *Greek version* of the *Septuagint* was then their universal text-book, in all their dispersions, it was absolutely requisite that the epistle should be written in a tongue with which they were best acquainted, and in which their acknowledged Scriptures were contained These arguments seem conclusive for a *Greek* and not a *Latin* original of this epistle.

From the manner in which this epistle has been interpreted and applied, various most discordant and conflicting opinions have originated. Many commentators, forgetting the scope and design of it, have applied that to men in general which most obviously belongs to the Jews, as distinguished from the Gentiles, and to them only. From this one mistake the principal controversies that have agitated and divided the Church of Christ concerning the doctrines of unconditional *reprobation* and *election* have arisen. Men, eminent for their talents, learning, and piety, have interpreted and applied the whole on this mistaken ground. They have been opposed by others, not at all their inferiors either in religion or learning, who, not attending properly to the scope of the apostle, have rather argued from the perfections of the Divine nature, and the general concurrent sense of Scripture, and thus proved that such doctrines cannot comport with those perfections, nor with the analogy of faith; and that the apostle is to be interpreted according to these, and not according to the apparent grammatical import of the phraseology which he employs. On both sides the disputes have run high; the cause of truth has gained little, and Christian charity and candour have been nearly lost. Dispassionate men, on seeing this, have been obliged to exclaim—

————tantæne animis cœlestibus iræ !
Can such fierce zeal in *heavenly* bosoms dwell!

To compose these differences, and do justice to the apostle, and set an important portion of the word of God in its true and genuine light, Dr. John Taylor of Norwich, a divine who yielded to few in command of temper, benevolent feeling, and deep acquaintance with the Hebrew and Greek Scriptures, undertook the elucidation of this much-controverted epistle. The result of his labours was a paraphrase and notes on the whole book, to which is prefixed "A KEY to the Apostolic Writings; or, an essay to explain the Gospel scheme, and the principal words and phrases the apostles have used in describing it." 4to. 1769, fourth edition. This KEY, in the main, is a most invaluable work, and has done great justice to the subject. Christians, whether advocates for general or particular redemption, might have derived great service from this work, in explaining the Epistle to the Romans; but the author's creed, who was an *Arian*, (for he certainly cannot be ranked with modern Unitarians,) has prevented many from consulting his book.

To bring the subject of this epistle before the reader, into the fairest and most luminous point of view in my power, I think it right to make a large extract from this *Key*, steering as clear as possible of those points in which my own creed is certainly at variance with that of my author; especially in the articles of *Original Sin*, the *Atonement*, and *Deity of Christ;* but as these points are seldom directly touched in this introductory key, the reader need be under no apprehension that he shall meet with any thing in hostility to the orthodoxy of his own creed.

A KEY TO THE APOSTOLIC WRITINGS; or, an Essay to explain the Gospel Scheme, and the principal words and phrases which the apostles have used in describing it.

§ 1. *On the Original and Nature of the Jewish Constitution of Religion.*

1. God, the Father of the universe, who has exercised his boundless wisdom, power, and goodness, in producing various beings of different capacities; who created the earth, and appointed divers climates, soils, and situations in it; hath, from the beginning of the world, introduced several schemes and dispensations for promoting the virtue and happiness of his rational creatures, for curing their corruption, and preserving among them the knowledge and worship of himself, the true God, the possessor of all being, and the fountain of all good.

2. In pursuance of this grand and gracious design, when, about four hundred years after the flood, the generality of mankind were fallen into idolatry, (a vice which in those times made its first appearance in the world,) and served *other gods*, thereby renouncing allegiance to the one God, the maker and governor of heaven and earth, He, to counteract this new and prevailing corruption, was pleased, in his infinite wisdom, to select *one family* of the earth to be a repository of true knowledge and the pattern of obedience and reward among the nations; that, as mankind were propagated, and idolatry took its rise and was dispersed from one part of the world into various countries, so also the knowledge, worship, and obedience of the true God might be propagated and spread from nearly the same quarter; or, however, from those parts which then were most

famous and distinguished. To this family he particularly revealed himself, visited them with several public and remarkable dispensations of providence, and at last formed them into a *nation* under his special protection, and governed them by laws delivered from himself; placing them in the open view of the world, first in *Egypt*, and afterwards in the land of *Canaan*.

3. The head or root of this family was *Abraham*, the son of *Terah*, who lived in *Ur* of the *Chaldees*, beyond *Euphrates*. His family was infected with the common contagion of idolatry, as appears from Joshua xxiv. 2, 3 : "And Joshua said unto all the people, Thus saith the Lord God of Israel, your fathers dwelt on the other side of the flood (or river *Euphrates*) in old time; even Terah, the father of *Abraham*, and the father of Nachor: and they served other gods. And I took your father *Abraham* from the other side of the flood, &c." And the Apostle Paul intimates as much, Rom. iv. 3, 4, 5 : "For what saith the Scripture? Abraham believed God, and it was counted unto him for righteousness. Now to him that worketh is the reward not reckoned of grace, but of debt. But to him that worketh not, but believeth on him that justifieth the ungodly, his faith is counted for righteousness." *Abraham* is the person he is discoursing about; and he plainly hints, though he did not care to speak out, that even *Abraham* was chargeable with not paying due reverence and worship to God; as the word ΑΣΕΒΗΣ, which we render *ungodly*, properly imports.

4. But, though *Abraham* had been an idolater, God was pleased, in his infinite wisdom and goodness, to single him out to be the head or root of that family or nation which he intended to separate to himself from the rest of mankind for the forementioned purposes. Accordingly he appeared to him in his native country, and ordered him to leave it and his idolatrous kindred, and to remove into a distant land to which he would direct and conduct him, declaring at the same time his covenant or grant of mercy to him, in these words, Gen. xii. 1, 2, 3 : "I will make of thee a great nation, and I will bless thee, and make thy name great, and thou shalt be a blessing. And I will bless them that bless thee, and curse him that curseth thee: and in thee shall all the families of the earth be blessed." So certainly did God make himself known to *Abraham*, that he was satisfied this was a revelation from the one true God, and that it was his duty to pay an implicit obedience to it. Accordingly, upon the foot of this faith, he went out, though he did not know whither he was to go. The same covenant, or promise of blessings, God afterwards at sundry times repeated to him; particularly when it is said, Gen. xv. 5 : "And the Lord brought him forth abroad, and said, Look now towards heaven, and tell the stars, if thou be able to number them : and he said unto him, so shall thy seed be." Here again he believed in the Lord, and he counted it to him for *righteousness*. Also, Gen. xvii. 1–8, he repeats and establishes the same covenant, to be a God unto *him* and *his seed* after him; promising him the land of *Canaan* for an everlasting possession, and appointing *circumcision* as a perpetual token of the certainty and perpetuity of this covenant. Thus *Abraham* was taken into God's covenant, and became entitled to the blessings it conveyed; not because he was not chargeable before God with impiety, irreligion, and idolatry; but because God, on his part, freely forgave his prior transgressions, and because *Abraham*, on his part, believed in the power and goodness of God; without which belief or persuasion that God was both true and able to perform what he had promised, he could have paid no regard to the Divine manifestations; and consequently must have been rejected as a person altogether improper to be the head of that family which God intended to set apart to himself.

5. And as *Abraham*, so likewise his seed or posterity, were at the same time, and before they had a being, taken into God's covenant, and entitled to the blessings of it. Gen. xvii. 7 : "I will establish my covenant between me and thee, and thy SEED AFTER thee, &c." Not all his posterity, but only those whom God intended in the promise; namely, first, the nation of the *Jews*, who hereby became particularly related to God, and invested in sundry invaluable privileges; and, after them, the believing *Gentiles*, who were reckoned the children of *Abraham*, as they should believe in God as *Abraham* did.

6. For about two hundred and fifteen years from the time God ordered *Abraham* to leave his native country, he, and his son *Isaac* and grandson *Jacob*, sojourned in the land of *Canaan*, under the special protection of Heaven, till infinite wisdom thought fit to send the family into *Egypt*, the then head-quarters of idolatry, with a design they should there increase into a nation; and there, notwithstanding the cruel oppression they long groaned under, they multiplied to a surprising number. At length God delivered them from the servitude of *Egypt*, by the most dreadful displays of his almighty power; whereby he demonstrated himself to be the one true God, in a signal and complete triumph over idols, even in their metropolis, and in a country of fame and eminence among all the nations round about. Thus freed from the vilest bondage, God formed them into a *kingdom*, of which he himself was *king;* gave them a revelation of his nature and will; instituted sundry ordinances of worship; taught them the way of truth and life; set before them various motives to duty, promising singular blessings to their obedience and fidelity, and threatening disobedience and apostasy, or revolt from his government, with very heavy judgments, especially that of being expelled from the land of *Canaan* and "scattered among all people from one end of the earth unto the other," in a wretched, persecuted state; Deut. xxviii. 63–68 ; Lev. xxvi. 3, 4, &c. Having settled their constitution, he led them through the wilderness, where he disciplined them for forty years together, made all opposition fall before them, and at last brought them to the promised land.

7. Here I may observe that God did not *choose* the *Israelites* out of any *partial-regard* to that nation, nor because they were *better* than other people, (Deut. ix. 4, 5,) and would always observe his laws. It is plain he knew the contrary, (Deut. xxxi. 29 ; xxxii. 5, 6, 15.) It was indeed with great propriety that, among other advantages, he gave them also that of being descended from progenitors illustrious for piety and virtue

and that he grounded the extraordinary favours they enjoyed upon *Abraham's* faith and obedience; Gen. xxii. 16, 17, 18. But it was not out of regard to the moral character of the *Jewish* nation that God chose them; any other nation would have served as well on that account; but, as he thought fit to select one nation of the world, he selected *them* out of respect to the piety and virtue of their ancestors; Exod. iii. 15; vi. 3, 4, 5, Deut. iv. 37.

8. It should also be carefully observed that God selected the *Israelitish* nation, and manifested himself to them by various displays of his power and goodness, not principally for their *own sakes*, to make them a happy and flourishing people, but to be subservient to his own high and great designs with regard to *all mankind*. And we shall entertain a very wrong, low, and narrow idea of this select nation, and of the dispensations of God towards it, if we do not consider it as a *beacon*, or a *light* set upon a hill, as raised up to be a public voucher of the being and providence of God, and of the truth of the revelation delivered to them in all ages and in all parts of the world; and, consequently, that the Divine scheme, in relation to the *Jewish* polity, had reference to other people, and even to *us* at this day, as well as to the *Jews* themselves. The situation of this nation, lying upon the borders of *Asia, Europe,* and *Africa,* was very convenient for such a general purpose.

9. It is farther observable that this scheme was wisely calculated to answer great ends under all events. If this nation continued *obedient,* their visible prosperity, under the guardianship of an extraordinary Providence, would be a very proper and extensive instruction to the nations of the earth; and no doubt was so; for, as they were obedient, and favoured with the signal interpositions of the Divine power, their case was very useful to their neighbours. On the other hand, if they were *disobedient,* then their *calamities,* and especially their dispersions, would nearly answer the same purpose, by spreading the knowledge of the true God and of revelation in the countries where before they were not known. And so wisely was this scheme laid at first, with regard to the laws of the nation, both civil and religious, and so carefully has it all along been conducted by the Divine providence, that it still holds good, even at this day, full 3600 years from the time when it first took place, and is still of public use for confirming the truth of revelation. I mean, not only as the Christian profession spread over a great part of the world has grown out of this scheme, but as the *Jews* themselves, in virtue thereof, after a dispersion of about 1700 years over all the face of the earth, every where in a state of ignominy and contempt, have, notwithstanding, subsisted in great numbers, distinct and separate from all other nations. This seems to me a *standing miracle;* nor can I assign it to any other cause but the will and the extraordinary interposal of Heaven, when I consider that, of all the famous nations of the world who might have been distinguished from others with great advantage, and the most illustrious marks of honour and renown, as the *Assyrians, Persians, Macedonians, Romans,* who all, in their turns, held the empire of the world, and were, with great ambition, the lords of mankind, yet *these,* even in their own countries, the seat of their ancient glory, are quite dissolved and sunk into the body of mankind; nor is there a person upon earth can boast he is descended from those renowned and imperial ancestors. Whereas a small nation, generally despised, and which was, both by *Pagans* and *pretended Christians,* for many ages harassed, persecuted, butchered, and distressed, as the most detestable of all people upon the face of the earth, (according to the prophecy of Moses, Deut. xxviii. 63, &c.; see Dr. Patrick's commentary upon that place,) and which, therefore, one would imagine, every soul that belonged to it should have gladly disowned, and have been willing the odious name should be entirely extinguished; yet, I say, this hated nation has continued in a body quite *distinct* and *separate* from all other people, even in a state of dispersion and grievous persecution, for about 1700 years; agreeably to the prediction, Jer. xlvi. 28: "I will make a full end *of all* the nations whither I have driven thee; but I will not make a full end of thee." This demonstrates that the wisdom which so formed them into a peculiar body, and the providence which has so preserved them that they have almost ever since the *deluge* subsisted in a state divided from the rest of mankind, and are still likely to do so, is not *human* but *Divine.* For, no human wisdom nor power could form, or, however, could execute such a vast, extensive design. Thus the very being of the *Jews,* in their present circumstances, is a standing public proof of the truth of revelation.

§ II. *The peculiar Honours and Privileges of the* Jewish *Nation, while they were the peculiar People of God, and the Terms signifying those Honours explained.*

10. The nature and dignity of the foregoing scheme, and the state and privileges of the *Jewish* nation will be better understood if we carefully observe the particular *phrases* by which their relation to God and his favours to them are expressed in Scripture.

11. As God, in his infinite wisdom and goodness, was pleased to prefer them before any other nation, and to single them out for the purposes of revelation, and preserving the knowledge, worship, and obedience of the true God, he is said to *choose* them, and they are represented as his *chosen* or *elect* people. Deut. iv. 37; vii. 6; x. 15: "The Lord had a delight in thy fathers—and he *chose* their seed after them, even you above all people." 1 Kings iii. 8: "Thy servant is in the midst of thy people which thou hast *chosen,* a great people that cannot be numbered." 1 Chron. xvi. 13: "O ye seed of Israel his servant, ye children of Jacob his *chosen* ones;" Psa. cv. 6; xxxiii. 12: "Blessed is the nation whose God is the Lord; and the people whom he hath *chosen* for his own inheritance;" cv. 43; cvi. 5: "That I may see the good of thy *chosen* or *elect,* that I may rejoice in the goodness of thy nation;" cxxxv. 4; Isa. xli. 8, 9; xliii. 20; xliv.

1, 2 ; xlv. 4 : " For Jacob my servant's sake, and Israel mine *elect*, I have even called thee by thy name."
Ezek. xx. 5 : " Thus saith the Lord, in the day when I *chose* Israel, and lifted my hand unto the seed of the
house of Jacob, and made myself known unto them in the land of Egypt." Hence, reinstating them in their
former privileges is expressed by *choosing them again*. Isa. xiv. 1 : " For the Lord will have mercy on
Jacob, and will yet *choose* Israel, and set them in their own land ;" Zech. i. 17 ; ii. 12.

12. The first step he took in execution of his purpose of *election*, was to rescue them from their wretched
situation, in the servitude and idolatry of *Egypt ;* and to carry them, through all enemies and dangers, to the
liberty and happy state to which he intended to advance them. With regard to which the language of Scripture is : 1. That he delivered ; 2. Saved ; 3. Bought, or purchased ; 4. Redeemed them. Exod. iii. 8 :
" And I am come down to *deliver* them out of the hand of the Egyptians, and to bring them unto a good
land." So Exod. xviii. 8, 9, 10 ; Judg. vi. 8, 9 ; Exod. vi. 6 : " I am the Lord, and I will bring you from
under the burdens of the Egyptians, and I will rid (*deliver*) you out of their bondage. So Exod. v. 23 ; 1
Sam. x. 18.

13. As God brought them out of *Egypt*, invited them to the honours and happiness of his people, and by
many express declarations and acts of mercy engaged them to adhere to him as their God, he is said to *call*
them, and they were his *called*. Isa. xli. 8, 9 : " But thou, Israel, art my servant,—thou whom I have
taken from the ends of the earth, and *called* thee from the chief men thereof." See ver. 2 ; chap. li. 2 ; Hos.
xi. 1 : " When Israel was a child, then I loved him, and *called* my son out of Egypt." Isa. xlviii. 12 :
" Hearken unto me, O Jacob, and Israel my *called*."

14. And as he brought them out of the most abject slavery, and advanced them to a new and happy state
of being, attended with distinguishing privileges, enjoyments, and marks of honour, he is said—1. to *create*,
make, and *form* them ; 2. to give them *life ;* 3. to have *begotten* them. Isa. xliii. 1 : " But thus saith the
Lord that *created* thee, O Jacob, and he that *formed* thee, O Israel, Fear not." Ver. 5 : " Fear not, for I am
with thee : I will bring thy seed from the east, and will gather thee from the west." Ver. 7 : " Even every one
that is called by my name ; for I have *created* him for my glory ; I have *formed* him ; yea I have *made* him."
Ver. 15 : " I am the Lord, your Holy One ; the *creator* of Israel, your king." Deut. xxxii. 6 : " Do ye thus
requite the Lord, O foolish people ?—Hath he not *made* thee, and established thee ?" Ver. 15 ; Psa. cxlix. 2.
Isa. xxvii. 11 : " It is a people of no understanding ; therefore, he that *made* them will have no mercy on
them ; and he that *formed* them will show them no favour ;" xliii. 21. xliv. 1, 2 : " Yet hear now, O Jacob
my servant ; and Israel, whom I have chosen.: Thus saith the Lord that *made* thee, and *formed* thee from the
womb." Ver. 21, 24 : " Thus saith the Lord thy *Redeemer*, and he that *formed* thee from the womb," &c.

15. Thus, as God *created* the whole body of the *Jews*, and made them to *live*, they received a being or
existence. Isa. lxiii. 19 : " We are ; thou hast never ruled over them ; (*the heathen ;*) they were not called
by thy name." Or rather thus : " We are of old ; thou hast not ruled over them ; thy name hath not been
called upon them." It is in the *Hebrew*, היינו מעולם לא משלת בם *hayinu me-ólam, lo mashalta bam ;* and are
therefore called by the apostle, " things that *are*," in opposition to the *Gentiles*, who, as they were not formerly *created* in the same *manner*, were, " the things which *are not ;*" 1 Cor. i. 28 : " God has chosen things
which *are not*, to bring to nought things that *are*." Farther—

16. As he made them *live*, and *begat* them, (1) He sustains the character of a *Father ;* and (2) they are
his *children*, his *sons* and *daughters*, which were born to him. Deut. xxxii. 6 : " Do ye thus requite the
Lord, O foolish people ?—Is he not thy *father* that hath *bought* thee ?" Isa. lxiii. 16 : " Doubtless thou art
our *father*, though Abraham be ignorant of us, and Israel acknowledge us not. Thou, O Lord, art our *Father*,
our *Redeemer*," &c. Jer. xxxi. 9 : " For I am a *Father* to Israel, and Ephraim is my *first-born*." Mal. ii.
10 : " Have we not all one *father ?* hath not one God *created* us ?"

17. And, as the whole body of the *Jews* were the children of one father, even of God, this naturally established among themselves the mutual and endearing relation of *brethren*, (including that of *sisters*,) and they
were obliged to consider and to deal with each other accordingly. Lev. xxv. 46 ; Deut i. 16 ; ii. 8 ; xv. 7 :
" If there be among you a poor man of one of thy *brethren*—thou shalt not harden thy heart, nor shut thine
hand against thy poor *brother ;*" xvii. 15 ; xviii. 15 ; xix. 19 ; xxii. 1 ; xxiii. 19 ; xxiv. 14 ; Judg. xx. 13 ; 1
Kings xii. 24 ; [Acts xxiii. 1.] And in many other places.

18. And the relation of God, as a *father* to the *Jewish* nation, and they his *children*, will lead our thoughts
to a clear idea of their being, as they are frequently called, the *house* or *family* of God. Num. xii. 7 : " My
servant Moses is not so, who is faithful in all my *house*." 1 Chron. xvii. 14 : " I will settle him in my *house*,
and in my kingdom for ever." Jer. xii. 7 : " I have forsaken my *house*, I have left my *heritage*." Hos.
ix. 15 : " For the wickedness of their (*Ephraim's*) doings, I will drive them out of my *house*, I will love them
no more : all their princes are revolters ; Zech. ix. 8 ; Psa. xciii. 5. And in other places ; and, perhaps, frequently in the *Psalms*. See xxiii. 6 ; xxvii. 4, &c.

19. Farther ; the Scripture directs us to consider the land of Canaan as the *estate* or *inheritance* belonging
to this *house* or family. Num. xxvi. 53 : " Unto these, (namely, all the children of *Israel*,) the land shall be
divided for an *inheritance*." Deut. xxi. 23 : " That thy land be not defiled, which the Lord thy God giveth
thee for an *inheritance*." See the same in many other places.

20. Here it may not be improper to take notice that the land of *Canaan*, in reference to their trials, wanderings, and fatigues in the wilderness, is represented as their *rest*. Exod. xxxiii. 14 : " My presence shall
go with thee, and I will give thee *rest*." Deut. iii. 20 ; xii. 9 : " For ye are not yet come to the *rest* and to

the *inheritance* which the Lord your God giveth you ;" ver. 10 ; xxv. 19. Psa. xcv. 11 : " Unto whom I sware in my wrath that they should not enter into my *rest*."

21. Thus the *Israelites* were the *house* or family of God. Or we may conceive them formed into a nation, having the Lord *Jehovah*, the true God, at their head; who, on this account, is styled their God, governor, protector, or king ; and they his people, *subjects*, or servants. Exod. xix. 6 : " Ye shall be unto me a *kingdom of priests*, and a holy *nation*." Deut. iv. 34 : " Hath God essayed to go and take him a *nation* from the midst of another nation ?" Isa. li. 4 : " Hearken unto me my people, and give ear unto me my *nation*."

22. And it is in reference to their being a society peculiarly appropriated to God and under his special protection and government, that they are sometimes called the *city*, the *holy city*, the *city* of the Lord, of God Psa. xlvi. 4 : " There is a river, the streams whereof shall make glad the *city* of our God, the holy place of the tabernacles of the Most High." ci. 8 : " I will early destroy all the wicked of the land, that I may cut off all wicked doers from the *city* of the Lord." Isa. xlviii. 1, 2 : " Hear ye this, O house of Jacob, which are called by the name of Israel ; for they call themselves of the *holy city*, and stay themselves upon the God of Israel."

23. Hence the whole community, or Church, is denoted by the *city Jerusalem*, and sometimes by *Zion*, *Mount Zion*, the *city of David*. Isa. lxii. 1, 6, 7 : " I have set watchmen upon thy walls, O *Jerusalem*, which shall never hold their peace—and give him no rest, till he establish, and till he make *Jerusalem* a praise in the earth." lxv. 18, 19 : " I will rejoice in *Jerusalem*, and joy in my people ;" lxvi. 10 ; Ezek. xvi. 2, 3 ; Joel iii. 17 ; Zech. i. 14 ; viii. 3, &c. ; xiii. 1. Isa. xxviii. 16 : " Thus saith the Lord God, Behold, I lay in *Zion* for a foundation," &c.; lxi. 3 ; Joel ii. 32. Obad. 17 : " But upon *Mount Zion* shall be deliverance," &c. ; ver. 21.

24. Hence, also, they are said to be *written* or *enrolled* in the book of God, as being citizens invested in the privileges and immunities of his kingdom. Exod. xxxii. 32 : " Yet now, if thou wilt, forgive their sin ; and, if not, blot me, I pray thee, out of the *book* thou hast written." Ver. 33 : " And the Lord said—Whosoevei hath sinned against me, him will I blot out of my *book* ;" Ezek. xiii. 9.

25. And it deserves our notice that, as the other nations of the world did not belong to this *city*, *commonwealth*, or *kingdom* of God, and so were not his *subjects* and *people* in the same peculiar sense as the *Jews*, for these reasons they are frequently represented as *strangers* and *aliens*, and as being *not a people*. And, as they served other gods, and were generally corrupt in their morals, they have the character of enemies. Exod. xx. 10 ; Lev. xxv. 47 : " And if a sojourner, or a *stranger*, wax rich by thee, and thy brother sell himself to the *stranger*." Deut. xiv. 21 : " Thou mayest sell it to an *alien*." Isa. lxi. 5 : " And *strangers* shall stand and feed your flocks, and the sons of the *alien* shall be your plowmen." And in many other places Deut. xxxii. 21 : " I will move them to jealousy with those which are *not a people* ;" Isa. vii. 8 ; Hos. i. 10, ii. 23 : " I will say to them which were *not my people*, Thou art my people : and they shall say, Thou art *my God*." Psa. lxxiv. 4 : " Thine *enemies* roar in the midst of thy *congregation* ;" lxxviii. 66 ; lxxxiii. 2 ; lxxxix. 10 ; Isa. xlii. 13 ; lix. 18. Rom. v. 10 : " When we were *enemies*, we were reconciled to God ;" Col. i. 21.

26. The kind and particular regards of God for the *Israelites*, and their special relation to him, are also signified by that of *husband* and *wife ;* and his making a covenant with them to be their God, is called *espousals.* Jer. xxxi. 32 : " Not according to the covenant that I made with their fathers, in the day that I took them by the hand to bring them out of the land of Egypt, (which my covenant they broke, although I was a *husband* unto them, saith the Lord ;") iii. 20 ; Ezek. xvi. 31, 32. Hos. ii. 2 : " Plead (*ye children of* Judah, *and children of* Israel, chap. i. 11) with your mother ; plead, for she is not my *wife*, neither am I her *husband ;*" that is, for her wickedness I have *divorced* her, (Isa. lxii. 4, 5.) Jer. ii. 2 : " Go and cry in the ears of Jerusalem, saying, Thus saith the Lord, I remember thee, the kindness of thy youth, the love of thine *espousals ;* when thou wentest after me in the wilderness, in the land that was not sown." iii. 14 : " Turn, O backsliding children, saith the Lord, for I am *married* unto you ;" Isa. lxii. 4, 5.

27. Hence it is that the *Jewish* Church, or community, is represented as a *mother ;* and particular members as her *children.* Isa. l. 1 : " Thus saith the Lord, where is the bill of your *mother's* divorcement ?" &c. Hos. ii. 2, 5 : " For their *mother* hath played the harlot." Isa. xlix. 17 : " Thy *children* (O Zion) shall make haste," &c.; ver. 22, 25 ; Jer. v. 7 ; Ezek. xvi. 35, 36. Hos. iv. 6 : " My people are destroyed for lack of knowledge—seeing thou hast forgotten the law of God, I will also forget thy *children*."

28. Hence, also, from the notion of the *Jewish* Church being a *wife* to God her *husband*, her idolatry, or worshipping of strange gods, comes under the name of *adultery* and *whoredom*, and she takes the character of a *harlot*. Jer. iii. 8 : " And I saw, when for all the causes whereby backsliding Israel committed *adultery*." Ver. 9 : " And it came to pass, through the lightness of her *whoredom*, that she defiled the land, and committed *adultery* with stones and with stocks ;" xiii. 27 ; Ezek. xvi. 15 ; xxiii. 43 ; Jer. iii. 6 : " Backsliding Israel is gone up upon every high mountain, and under every green tree, and there has played the *harlot*."

29. As God exercised a singular providence over them in supplying, guiding, and protecting them, he was their *shepherd*, and they his *flock*, his *sheep*. Psa. lxxvii. 20 ; lxxviii. 52 ; lxxx. 1 : " Give ear, O *shepherd* of Israel." Isa. xl. 11 : " He shall feed his *flock* like a *shepherd*." Psa. lxxiv. 1 : " O God, why hast thou cast us off for ever ? Why doth thine anger smoke against the *sheep* of thy pasture ?" lxxix. 13 ; xcv. 7 ; Jer. xiii. 17 : " Mine eye shall weep sore—because the Lord's *flock* is carried captive." See Ezek. xxxiv. throughout ; and in many other places.

30. Upon nearly the same account, as God established them, provided proper means for their happiness, and improvement in knowledge and virtue, they are compared to a *vine* and a *vineyard*, and God to the *husbandman* who *planted* and *dressed* it; and particular members of the community are compared to *branches*. Psa. lxxx. 8 : " Thou hast brought a *vine* out of Egypt; thou hast cast out the heathen and *planted* it." Ver. 14 : " Return, we beseech thee, O Lord of hosts; look down from heaven; behold and visit this *vine*, and the *vineyard* which thy right hand has *planted*." Isa. v. 1, 2 : " Now will I sing to my well-beloved a song, touching his *vineyard*. My well-beloved has a *vineyard* in a very fruitful hill; and he fenced it," &c. Ver. 7 : " For the *vineyard* of the Lord—is the house of Israel ;" Exod. xv. 17 ; Jer. ii. 21. Psa. lxxx. 11 : " She sent out her *boughs* unto the sea, and her *branches* unto the river." Isa. xxvii. 9, 10, 11 : " By this shall the iniquity of Jacob be purged ;—yet the defenced city shall be desolate,—there shall the calf feed,— and consume the *branches* thereof. When the *boughs* thereof are withered, they shall be broken off : the women come, and set them on fire : for it is a *people* of no understanding ; therefore, he that *made* them will have no mercy on them." Jer. xi. 16 : " The Lord hath called thy name a green *olive tree*, fair and of goodly fruit," &c. ; Ezek. xvii. 6 ; Hos. xiv. 5, 6 ; Nahum ii. 2 ; and in many other places. Rom. xi. 17, 18, 19 : " And if some of the *branches* were broken off," &c. " Thou wilt say then, the *branches* were broken off that I might be grafted in."

31. As they were, by the will of God, *set apart*, and appropriated in a special manner to his honour and obedience, and furnished with extraordinary means and motives to holiness, so God is said to *sanctify* or *hallow* them. Exod. xxxi. 13 : " Speak unto the children of Israel, saying, Verily my Sabbaths ye shall keep ; for it is a sign between me and you, throughout your generations ; that ye may know that I am the Lord that doth *sanctify* you ;" Ezek. xx. 12 ; Lev. xx. 8 : " And ye shall keep my statutes, and do them ; for I am the Lord which *sanctify* you ;" xxi. 8 ; xxii. 9, 16, 32 ; Ezek. xxxvii. 28.

32. Hence it is that they are styled a *holy* nation, or people, and *saints*. Exod. xix. 6 : " And ye shall be to me—a *holy* nation." Deut. vii. 6 : " For thou art a *holy* people unto the Lord thy God ;" xiv. 2 ; xxvi. 19 ; xxxiii. 3. 2 Chron. vi. 41 : " Let thy priests, O Lord God, be clothed with salvation, and let thy *saints* rejoice in goodness." Psa. xxxiv. 9 : " O fear the Lord, ye his *saints*." l. 5 : " Gather my *saints* together unto me." Ver. 7 : " Hear, O my people," &c. ; lxxix. 2 ; cxlviii. 14 : " He also exalteth the horn of his people, the praise of his *saints ;* even of the children of Israel," &c.

33. Farther, by his presence among them, and their being consecrated to him, they were made his *house* or *building*, the sanctuary which he built. And this is implied by his *dwelling* and *walking* amongst them. Psa. cxiv. 2 : " Judah was his sanctuary, and Israel his dominion." Isa. lvi. 3, 4, 5 : " Neither let the son of the *stranger*, that hath joined himself to the Lord, speak, saying, The Lord hath utterly separated me from his *people :*—for thus saith the Lord—Even unto them will I give in my *house*, and within my walls, a place and a name." Jer. xxxiii. 7 : " And I will cause the captivity of Judah and of Israel to return,—and will *build* them as at the first." Amos ix. 11 : " I will raise up the tabernacle of David—I will raise up its ruins, and I will *build* it as in the days of old." Exod. xxv. 8 : " And let them, (the children of Israel,) make me a sanctuary ; that I may *dwell* among them." xxix. 45, 46 : " And I will *dwell* among the children of Israel, and I will be their God," &c. Lev. xxvi. 11, 12 : " And I will set my tabernacle among you :—And I will *walk* among you, and will be your God, and ye shall be my people ;" Num. xxxv. 34 ; 2 Sam. vii. 7. Ezek. xliii. 7, 9 : " And he said unto me—the place of my *throne*, and the place of the soles of my feet, where I *dwell* in the midst of the children of Israel," &c. Hence we may gather that *dwell*, in such places, imports to *reign*, and may be applied figuratively to whatever *governs* in our hearts ; Rom. vii. 17, 20 ; viii. 9, 11.

34. And not only did God, as their king, dwell among them, as in his *house*, *temple*, or palace ; but he also conferred upon them the honour of *kings*, as he redeemed them from servitude, and made them *lords* of themselves, and raised them above other nations, to reign over them ; and of priests, too, as they were to attend upon God, from time to time, continually, in the solemn offices of religion, which he had appointed. Exod. xix. 6 : " And ye shall be unto me a *kingdom of priests*, or a *kingly priesthood*." Deut. xxvi. 19 : " And to make thee *high above* all nations—in praise, and in name, and in honour ; and that thou mayest be a *holy* people unto the Lord thy God ;" xxviii. 1 ; xv. 6 : " For the Lord thy God blesseth thee—and thou shalt *reign* over many nations." Isa. lxi. 6 : " But ye, (the seed of Jacob,) shall be named the *priests* of the Lord ; men shall call you the *ministers* of our God."

35. Thus the whole body of the *Jewish* nation were *separated* unto God ; and, as they were more nearly related to him than any other people, as they were joined to him in covenant, and felt access to him in the ordinances of worship, and, in virtue of his promise, had a particular title to his regards and blessings, he is said to be near unto them, and they unto him ; Exod. xxxiii. 16. Lev. xx. 24 : " I am the Lord your God, who have *separated* you from other people ;" ver. 26 ; 1 Kings viii. 52, 53. Deut. iv. 7 : " For what nation is there so great, that hath God so *near* unto them, as the Lord our God is in all things that we call upon him for ?" Psa. cxlviii. 14 : " The children of Israel, a people *near* unto him."

36. And here I may observe that, as the *Gentiles* were not then taken into the same peculiar covenant with the *Jews*, nor stood in the same special relation to God, nor enjoyed their extraordinary religious privileges, but lay out of the commonwealth of *Israel*, they are, on the other hand said to be *far off*. Isa. lvii. 19 : " I create the fruit of the lips : peace, peace to him that is *far off*, and to him that is *near*, saith the Lord, and I will heal him." Zech. vi. 15 : " And they that are *far off* shall come and build in the *temple*." Eph. ii. 17 : " And came and preached to you, (*Gentiles*,) which were *afar off*, and to them that were *nigh*, (the Jews.)

37. And as God had, in all these respects, distinguished them from all other nations, and sequestered them unto himself, they are styled his *peculiar people.* Deut. vii. 6 : " The Lord has chosen thee to be a special (or peculiar) *people* unto himself." xiv. 2 : " The Lord hath chosen thee to be a *peculiar people* unto himself, above all the nations that are upon the earth ;" xxvi. 18.

38. As they were a body of men particularly related to God, instructed by him in the rules of wisdom, devoted to his service, and employed in his true worship, they are called his *congregation* or *Church.* Num. xvi. 3 ; xxvii. 17 ; Josh. xxii. 17. 1 Chron. xxviii. 8 : " Now therefore, in the sight of all Israel the *congregation, the Church,* of the Lord ;" Psa. lxxiv. 2.

39. For the same reason they are considered as God's *possession, inheritance,* or *heritage.* Deut. ix. 26 : " O Lord, destroy not thy people and thine *inheritance ;*" ver. 29 ; Psa. xxxiii. 12 ; cvi. 40 ; Jer. x. 16. xii. 7 : " I have forsaken my *house,* I have left my *heritage.* I have given the dearly beloved of my soul into the hands of her enemies " And in many other places.

§ III. *Reflections on the foregoing Privileges and Honours.*

40. Whether I have ranged the foregoing particulars in proper order, or given an exact account of each, let the studious of Scripture knowledge consider. What ought to be specially observed is this ; that all the forementioned privileges, benefits, relations, and honours, did belong to ALL the children of *Israel,* without exception. The Lord Jehovah was the *God, King, Saviour, Father, Husband, Shepherd, &c.,* to them ALL. He *saved, bought, redeemed ;* he *created,* he *begot,* he *made,* he *planted,* &c., them ALL. And they were ALL his *people, nation, heritage ;* his *children, spouse, flock, vineyard, &c.* They *all* had a right to the *ordinances* of worship, to the *promises* of God's blessing, and especially to the promise of the land of *Canaan ;* ALL enjoyed the protection and special favours of God in the wilderness, till they had forfeited them ; ALL ate of the *manna,* and ALL drank of the *water* out of the *rock, &c.* That these privileges and benefits belonged to the *whole body* of the *Israelitish* nation is evident from all the texts I have already quoted ; which he, who observes carefully, will find do all of them speak of the whole nation, the whole community, without exception.

41. And that all these privileges, honours, and advantages were *common* to the whole nation, is confirmed by this farther consideration ; that they were the effect of God's *free grace,* without regard to any *prior* righteousness of theirs ; and therefore they are assigned to God's love as the *spring* from whence they flowed ; and the donation of those benefits is expressed by God's loving them : they are also assigned to God's mercy, and the bestowing of them is expressed by God's showing them mercy. Deut. ix. 4, 5, 6 : " Speak not thou in thy heart, after that the Lord hath cast them out before thee, saying, For my *righteousness* the Lord hath brought me in to possess this land.—Not for thy *righteousness* or the *uprightness* of thy heart dost thou go to possess their land," &c. " Understand, therefore, that the Lord thy God giveth thee not this good land to possess it for thy *righteousness ;* for thou art a stiff-necked people."

42. Deut. vii. 7, 8 : " The Lord did not set his love upon you, nor *choose* you, because ye were more in number than any people ; but because the Lord *loved* you, and because he would keep the oath which he had sworn unto your fathers, hath the Lord brought you out" (*of Egypt.*) xxxiii. 3 : " He *loved* the people ;" Isa. xliii. 3, 4 ; Jer. xxxi. 3 ; Hos. iii. 1 ; ix. 15.

43. It is on account of this general love to the *Israelites,* that they are honoured with the title of *Beloved.* Psa. lx. 5 : " That thy *beloved* may be delivered, save with thy right hand, and hear me ;" Psa. cviii. 6. Jer. xi. 15 : " What hath my *beloved* to do in my house, seeing she hath wrought lewdness with many ?" xii. 7 : " I have forsaken my *house,* I have given the dearly *beloved* of my soul into the hands of my enemies," (and in their present condition at this day the Jews are still, in a sense, beloved, Rom. xi. 28.) 44. Exod. xv. 13 : " Thou, in thy *mercy,* hast led forth the people which thou hast redeemed," &c. ; Psa. xcviii. 3 ; Isa. liv. 10. Mic. vii. 20 : " Thou shalt perform the truth to Jacob, and the *mercy* to Abraham, which thou hast sworn unto our fathers from the days of old." Luke i. 54, 55 : " He hath holpen his servant Israel, in remembrance of his *mercy,* as he spake to our fathers, to Abraham and his seed for ever." Agreeably to this, he *showed* them mercy, as he continued them to be his people, when he might have cut them off. Exod. xxxiii. 19 : " I will be gracious to whom I will be gracious, and I will *show mercy* on whom I will *show mercy.*" And when, after their present state of rejection, they shall again be taken into the Church, this too is expressed by their " obtaining mercy," Rom. xi. 31.

45. In these texts, and others of the same kind, it is evident the *love* and *mercy* of God hath respect not to *particular persons* among the *Jews,* but to the *whole nation ;* and therefore it is to be understood of that general love and mercy whereby he singled them out to be a peculiar nation to himself, favoured with extraordinary blessings.

46. And it is with regard to this sentiment and manner of speech, that the GENTILES, who were not distinguished in the same manner, are said not to have obtained mercy. Hos. ii. 23 : " And I will sow her unto me in the earth, and I will have *mercy* upon her that had not *obtained mercy,* and I will say to them which were not my people, Thou art my people ; and they shall say, Thou art my God."

47. Farther, it should be noted, as a very material and important circumstance, that all this mercy and love was granted and confirmed to the *Israelites* under the sanction of a *covenant ;* the most solemn declaration and assurance, sworn to and ratified by the oath of God. Gen. xvii. 7, 8 : " And I will establish my cove-

nant between me and thee, and thy seed after thee, in their generations, for an everlasting *covenant; to be a* God unto thee, and to thy seed after thee. And I will give unto thee, and to thy seed after thee, the land wherein thou art a stranger, all the land of Canaan, for an everlasting possession; and I will be their God." Gen. xxii. 16, 17, 18: "By myself have I sworn, saith the Lord, for because thou hast done this thing, that in blessing I will bless thee, and in multiplying I will multiply thy seed as the stars of the heaven, and as the sand which is upon the sea-shore, and thy seed shall possess the gate of his enemies; and in thy seed shall all the nations of the earth be blessed; because thou hast obeyed my voice." This covenant with *Abraham* was the *Magna Charta*, the *basis* of the *Jewish* constitution, which was renewed afterwards with the whole nation; and is frequently referred to as the ground and security of all their blessings. Exod. vi. 3-7: "I appeared unto Abraham, Isaac," &c. "And I have also established my *covenant* with them, to give them the land of Canaan. I have also heard the groaning of the children of Israel, and I have remembered my *covenant*, and will take you to me for a people, and I will be to you a God;" Deut. vii. 8. Psa. cv. 8, 9, 10: "He hath remembered his *covenant* for ever, the word which he commanded to a thousand generations: Which *covenant* he made with Abraham, and his *oath* unto Isaac, and confirmed the same unto Jacob for a law, and to Israel for an everlasting COVENANT;" Jer. xi. 5; Ezek. xvi. 8; xx. 5.

48. But, what most of all deserves our attention is this,—that the Jewish constitution was *a scheme for promoting virtue*, true religion, or a good and pious life. In all the forementioned instances they were very happy. But were they to rest in them? Because these blessings were the gift of love and mercy, without respect to their righteousness or obedience, was it therefore needless for them to be obedient? or, were they, purely on account of benefits already received, secure of the favour and blessing of God for ever? By no means. And that I may explain this important point more clearly, I shall distinguish their blessings into *antecedent* and *consequent*, and show, from the Scriptures, how both stand in relation to their duty.

49. *Antecedent blessings* are all the benefits hitherto mentioned, which were given by the mere grace of God, *antecedently* to their obedience, and without respect to it; but *yet so* that they were intended to be *motives* to obedience. Which effect if they produced, then their *election, redemption,* and *calling* were confirmed, and they were entitled to all their blessings, promised in the covenant; which blessings I therefore call *consequent*, because they were given only in *consequence* of their obedience. But, on the other hand, if the *antecedent* blessings did not produce obedience to the will of God; if his *chosen people*, his *children*, did not obey his voice, then they forfeited all their privileges, all their honours, and relations to God, all his favours and promises, and fell under the severest threatenings of his wrath and displeasure. Thus life itself may be distinguished into—I. *Antecedent*, which God gives freely to all his creatures of his mere good will and liberality, before they can have done any thing to deserve it. II. *Consequent* life; which is the continuance of life in happy circumstances, and has relation to the good conduct of a rational creature. As he improves life *antecedent*, so he shall, through the favour of God, enjoy life *consequent*.

50. And that this was the very *end* and *design* of the dispensation of God's extraordinary favours to the *Jews*, namely, to engage them to duty and obedience; or, that it was a *scheme for promoting virtue*, is clear, beyond all dispute, from every part of the Old Testament. Note: I shall make ANT. stand for *antecedent* love or motives; CONS. for *consequent* love or *reward*; and THR. for *threatening*. (Ant.) Gen. xvii. 1: "I am God, all-sufficient; (Duty) Walk before me, and be thou perfect." Verse 7, 8, 9: (Ant.) "I will be a God unto thee, and thy seed after thee. And I will give unto thee, and unto thy seed, the land of Canaan; and I will be their God. (Duty) Thou shalt keep my covenant therefore, thou and thy seed after thee." Gen. xxii. 16, 18: (Duty) "Because thou hast done this thing, and hast not withheld thy son, thine only son; because thou hast obeyed my voice;" Verse 16–18: (Cons.) "By myself have I sworn, saith the Lord, that in blessing I will bless thee, and in multiplying I will multiply thy seed as the stars of heaven, and thy seed shall possess the gate of his enemies; and in thy seed shall all the nations of the earth be blessed."

51. Here let it be noted, that the same blessings may be both *consequent* and *antecedent* with regard to different persons. With regard to *Abraham*, the blessings promised in this place (Gen. xxii. 16, 17, 18) are *consequent*, as they were the reward of his *obedience*, "because thou hast obeyed my voice." But with regard to his posterity these same blessings were of the *antecedent* kind; because, though they had respect to *Abraham's* obedience, yet, with regard to the *Jews*, they were given freely or *antecedently* to any obedience *they* had performed. So the blessings of redemption, with regard to our Lord's obedience, are *consequent;* but, with regard to us, they are of *free grace* and *antecedent*, not owing to any obedience of ours, though granted in *consequence* of *Christ's* obedience; Phil. ii. 8, 9, &c.; Eph. i. 7; Heb. v. 8, 9. Nor doth the donation of blessings upon *many*, in consequence of the obedience of *one*, at all diminish the grace, but very much recommends the wisdom that bestows them.

52. Isa. xliii. 7, 21: (Ant.) "This people have I made for myself: (Duty) They shall show forth my praise;" Jer. xiii. 11; Lev. xx. 7, 8:

(Ant.) "I am the Lord your God; I am the Lord which sanctify you. (Duty) Sanctify yourselves therefore, and be ye holy; and ye shall keep my statutes and do them." Deut. iv. 7, 8, 9:

(Ant.) "What nation is there so great, who hath God so nigh them, as the Lord our God is? And what nation is there so great, that hath statutes and judgments so righteous," &c. (Duty) "Only take heed to thyself, and keep thy soul diligently, lest thou forget the things which thine eyes have seen." Verse 20:

(Ant.) "The Lord hath taken you forth out of the iron furnace, even out of Egypt, to be unto him a people of inheritance, as ye are at this day." Verse 23: (Duty) "Take heed unto yourselves, lest ye forget the covenant of the Lord your God." Verse 24 : (Thr.) " For the Lord thy God is a consuming fire." Verse 25 : " When ye shall corrupt yourselves, and do evil in the sight of the Lord thy God." Verse 26 : " I call heaven and earth to witness, that ye shall soon utterly perish from off the land." Verse 34 :

(Ant.) " Hath God assayed to go, and take him a nation from the midst of another nation, by signs and wonders," &c., &c. Verse 39, 40 : (Duty) " Know therefore this day, and consider it in thy heart, that the Lord he is God in heaven above," &c. " Thou shalt keep, therefore, his statutes and his commandments, (Cons.) that it may go well with thee, and with thy children after thee," &c. Deut. v. 6, 7 :

(Ant.) " I am the Lord thy God, which brought thee out of the land of Egypt, from the house of bondage." (Duty) " Thou shalt have no other gods before me," &c. Verse 29 : " O that there were such a heart in them that they would fear me and keep all my commandments always, (Cons.) that it might be well with them, and with their children for ever." Verse 33 : (Duty) " You shall walk in all the ways which the Lord your God hath commanded you, (Cons.) that ye may live, and that it may be well with you," &c. Chap. vi. 21 :

(Ant.) " We were Pharaoh's bondmen, and the Lord brought us out of Egypt," &c. Verse 24 : (Duty) " And the Lord commanded us to do all these statutes, to fear the Lord our God, (Cons.) for our good always, that he might preserve us alive," &c. Chap. vii. 6, 7, 8 :

(Ant.) " Thou art a holy people unto the Lord thy God : the Lord thy God hath chosen thee to be a special people unto himself : the Lord loved you and redeemed you out of the house of bondmen." Verse 9 : (Duty) " Know therefore that the Lord thy God, he is God," &c. Verse 11: " Thou shalt therefore keep the commandments, and the statutes, and the judgments which I command thee this day, to do them." Verse 12, 13, 18 : (Cons.) " Wherefore it shall come to pass, if ye hearken to these judgments, and keep and do them, that the Lord thy God shall keep unto thee the covenant and the mercy which he sware unto thy fathers. And he will love thee, and bless thee, and multiply thee," &c. Chap. viii. 2 :

(Ant.) " Thou shalt remember all the way which the Lord thy God led thee," &c. Verse 5 : " Thou shalt also consider in thine heart, that as a man chasteneth his son, so the Lord thy God chasteneth thee." Verse 6 : (Duty) " Therefore thou shalt keep the commandments of the Lord thy God, to walk in his ways, and to fear him." Verse 11: " Beware that thou forget not the Lord thy God," &c. Verse 19 : (Thr.) " And it shall be, if thou do at all forget the Lord thy God, and walk after other gods, I testify against you this day, that ye shall surely perish." Chap. x. 15 :

(Ant.) " The Lord hath a delight in thy fathers to love them, and he chose their seed after them, even you above all people." Verse 12, 16 : (Duty) " Circumcise therefore the foreskin of your heart," &c. Verse 22 :

(Ant.) " Thy fathers went down into Egypt with threescore and ten persons, and now the Lord thy God hath made thee as the stars of heaven for multitude." Chap. xi. 1, 8 : (Duty) " Therefore shalt thou love the Lord thy God, and keep his charge," &c. Verse 13, 14 : " And it shall come to pass, if ye shall hearken diligently unto my commandments," &c., (Cons.) " that I will give you the rain of your land," &c. Verse 26 : " Behold, I set before you this day a *blessing* and a curse. A *blessing*, if you obey the commandments of the Lord ; and a *curse*, if ye will not obey," &c. Chap. xii. 28 : (Duty) " Observe and hear all these words which I command thee, (Cons.) that it may go well with thee and thy children after thee for ever, when thou hast done that which is good and right in the sight of the Lord thy God ;" Chap. xiii. 17, 18 ; xv. 4, 5. xxvii. 9, 10 :

(Ant.) " Take heed and hearken, O Israel : this day thou art become the people of the Lord thy God. (Duty) Thou shalt therefore obey the voice of the Lord thy God, and do his commandments," &c. Chap. xxviii. 1: " And it shall come to pass, if thou hearken diligently unto the voice of the Lord thy God, to observe and to do his commandments, (Cons.) that the Lord will set thee on high above all nations of the earth. And all these *blessings* shall come on thee and overtake thee, if thou shalt hearken unto the voice of the Lord thy God. Blessed shalt thou be in the city," &c. Verse 15: (Thr.) " But it shall come to pass, if thou wilt not hearken unto the voice of the Lord thy God, to observe and to do all his commandments and his statutes, that all these *curses* shall come upon thee and overtake thee," &c. Verse 45 : " Moreover, all these curses shall come upon thee till thou be destroyed, because thou hearkenedst not unto the voice of the Lord thy God ;" Chap. xxix. 2, 10. xxx. 15–18 : (Duty) " See, I have set before you this day life and good, and death and evil ; in that I command thee this day to love the Lord thy God, to walk in his ways, and to keep his commandments, and his statutes, and his judgments, (Cons.) that thou mayest live and multiply ; and the Lord thy God shall bless thee in the land whither thou goest to possess it. (Thr.) But if thine heart turn away, so that thou wilt not hear, but shalt be drawn away and worship other gods, and serve them, I denounce unto you this day that ye shall surely perish."

53. Whosoever peruses the first sixteen, and the twenty-eighth, twenty-ninth, thirtieth, thirty-first, and thirty-second chapters of *Deuteronomy*, will clearly see that all the privileges, honours, instructions, protections, &c., which were given them as a select body of men, were intended as *motives* to obedience ; which, if thus wisely improved, would bring upon them still farther blessings. Thus God *drew* them to duty and virtue *by his loving-kindness.* Jer. xxxi. 3 : " He drew them with cords of a man, (*such considerations as are apt to influence the rational nature,*) and with the bands of love ;" Hos. xi. 4. But if they were disobedient, and did not make a right use of God's benefits and favours, then they were subjected to a curse, and should perish. And this is so evident from this single book that I shall not need to heap together the numerous quotations which might be collected from other parts of Scripture, particularly the prophetic writings. Only I may farther establish this point by observing,—that, in *fact*, though all the *Israelites* in the

2

wilderness were the *people, children,* and *chosen* of God ; all entitled to the Divine blessing, and partakers of the several instances of his goodness ; yet, notwithstanding all their advantages and honours, when they were *disobedient* to his will, distrustful of his power and providence, or revolted to the worship of idol gods, great numbers of them fell under the Divine vengeance ; Exod. xxxii. 8, 27, 28 ; Num. xi. 4, 5, 6, 33 ; xvi. 2, 3, 32, 35, 41, 49 ; xxi. 5, 6. And though they had *all* a promise of entering into the land of *Canaan,* yet the then generation, from twenty years old and upwards, for their unbelief, were, by the righteous judgment of God, excluded from the benefit of that promise : they forfeited their inheritance, and died in the wilderness ; Num. xiv. 28—36 ; Heb. iii. 7, &c.

54. From all this it appears that all the high privileges of the *Jews* before mentioned, and all the singular relations in which they stood to God, as they were *saved, bought, redeemed* by him ; as they were his *called* and *elect ;* as they were his *children* whom he *begot, created, made,* and *formed ;* his *sons* and *daughters, born to him ;* his *heritage, church, house,* and *kingdom ;* his *saints,* whom he sanctified ; his *vine* or *vineyard,* which he *planted ;* his *sheep* and *flock ;*—I say these, and such like honours, advantages, and relations, as they are assigned to the whole body, do not import an *absolute final state of happiness and favour of any kind ;* but are to be considered as displays, instances, and descriptions of God's love and goodness to them, which were to operate as a *mean,* a moral mean, upon their hearts. They were, in truth, motives to oblige and excite to obedience ; and only when so improved, became *final* and *permanent* blessings ; but neglected, or misimproved, they were enjoyed *in vain,* they vanished and came to nothing ; and wicked *Israelites* were no more the objects of God's favour than wicked *heathens.* Amos ix. 7, speaking of the corrupt *Jews :* "Are ye not as children of the Ethiopians unto me, O children of Israel ? saith the Lord."

55. And upon the whole, we may from the clearest evidence conclude that the selecting the *Jewish* nation from the rest of the world, and taking them into a peculiar relation to God, was a scheme for promoting true religion and virtue in all its principles and branches, upon motives adapted to rational nature ; which principles and branches of true religion are particularly specified in their law. And to this end, no doubt, every part of their constitution, even the *ceremonial,* was wisely adapted, considering their circumstances, and the then state of the world.

56. The love of God, as it was the *foundation* and *original* of this scheme, so it was the prime *motive* in it. God began the work of salvation among them, antecedently to any thing which they might do, on their part, to engage his goodness. They did not *first* love God ; but God *first* loved them : their *obedience* did not *first* advance towards God ; but his *mercy first* advanced towards them, and *saved, bought, redeemed* them ; took them for his people, and gave them a part in the blessings of his covenant. And as for his *displeasure,* they were under that only *consequentially ;* or after they had neglected his goodness, and abused the mercy and means, the privileges and honours, which they enjoyed. This, I think, must appear very evident to any one who closely and maturely deliberates upon the true state of the *Jewish* Church.

Thus, and for those ends, not excluding others before or afterwards mentioned, the *Jewish* constitution was erected.

§ IV. *The Jewish peculiarity not prejudicial to the rest of Mankind ; the Jewish Economy being established for the Benefit of the World in general.*

57. But although the Father of mankind was pleased, in his wisdom to erect the foregoing scheme, for promoting virtue and preserving true religion in one nation of the world, upon which he conferred particular blessings and privileges ; this was no injury nor prejudice to the rest of mankind. For, as to original favours, or external advantages, God, who may do what he pleases with his own, bestows them in any kind or degree, as he thinks fit. Thus he makes a variety of creatures ; some *angels* in a higher sphere of being, some *men* in a lower. And, among men, he distributes different faculties, stations, and opportunities in life. To one he gives *ten talents,* to another *five,* to another *two,* and to another *one,* severally as he pleases ; without any impeachment of his justice, and to the glorious display and illustration of his wisdom. And so he may bestow different advantages and favours upon different nations, with as much justice and wisdom as he has placed them in different climates, or vouchsafed them various accommodations and conveniencies of life. But, whatever advantages some nations may enjoy above others, still God is the God and *Father of all ;* and his extraordinary blessings to some are not intended to diminish his regards to others. He erected a scheme of polity and religion for promoting the knowledge of God, and the practice of virtue in one nation ; but not with a design to withdraw his goodness or providential regards from the rest. God has made a variety of soils and situations ; yet he cares for every part of the globe ; and the inhabitants of the *North Cape,* where they conflict a good part of the year with *night* and extreme *cold,* are no more neglected by the universal Lord, than those who enjoy the perpetual summer and pleasures of the *Canary Isles.* At the same time God chose the children of *Israel* to be his peculiar people in a special covenant, he was the God of the rest of mankind, and regarded them as the objects of his care and benevolence. Exod. xix. 5 : "Now, therefore, if ye will obey my voice indeed, and keep my covenant, then ye shall be a *peculiar treasure unto me* above all people ; כי לי כל הארץ, *although* all the earth is mine." So it should be rendered. Deut. x. 14, 15 : "Behold the heaven and the heaven of heavens is the Lord's thy God, the *earth* with *all* that therein *are.* Only the Lord had a delight in thy fathers to *love* them, and he *chose* their seed after them, even you above all people, as it is this day." Verse 17, 18 : "For the Lord your God is God of gods, and Lord of lords, a great God, a

mighty and a terrible, which *regardeth not persons*, (or is no respecter of persons, Acts x. 34, through partiality to one person or one nation more than another,) nor taketh reward. He doth execute the judgment of the fatherless and widow, and *loveth the stranger*, in giving him food and raiment." A *stranger* was one who was of any other nation beside the *Jewish*. Psa. cxlvi. 9 : " The Lord preserveth the *strangers ;*" viii. 1 ; xix. 1, 2, 3, 4 ; xxiv. 1, xxxiii. 5 : " The *earth* is full of the goodness of the Lord." Verse 8 : " Let *all* the earth fear the Lord ; let *all* the inhabitants of the world stand in awe of him." Ver. 12 : " Blessed is the nation whose God is the Lord, and the people whom he hath *chosen* for his own *inheritance*." Verse 13 : " The Lord looketh from heaven ; he beholdeth *all* the sons of men. From the place of his habitation he looketh upon *all* the inhabitants of the earth ; he fashioneth their hearts alike ; he considereth all their works." xlvii. 2, 8 ;, " The Lord most high is a great king over *all* the earth. God reigneth over the heathen;" lxvi. 7 ; cvii. 8, 15, 21. cxlv. 9 : " The Lord is good to *all*, and his tender mercies are over *all* his *works*." Many more passages might be brought out of the Scriptures of the Old Testament to show that *all the nations of the earth* were the object of the Divine care and goodness ; at the same time that he vouchsafed a *particular* and extraordinary providence towards the *Jewish* nation.

58. And, agreeably to this, the *Israelites* were required to exercise all benevolence to the *Gentiles*, or *strangers ;* to abstain from all injurious treatment ; to permit them to dwell peaceably and comfortably among them ; to partake of their blessings ; to incorporate into the same happy body, if they thought fit ; and to join in their religious solemnities. Exod. xxii. 21 : " Thou shalt neither vex a *stranger* nor oppress him ;" xxii. 9, 12. Lev. xix. 10 : " Thou shalt not glean thy vineyard, neither shalt thou gather every grape of thy vineyard ; thou shalt leave them for the poor and *stranger ;* I am the Lord your God ;" xxiii. 22. xix. 33, 34 : " And if a *stranger* sojourn with thee in your land, ye shall not vex him. But the *stranger* that dwelleth with you shall be unto you as one born amongst you, and thou shalt love him as thyself." xxv. 35 : " And if thy brother be waxen poor, and fallen in decay with thee, then thou shalt relieve him ; yea, though he be a *stranger* or a *sojourner ;* that he may live with thee." Num. xv. 14, 15 : " And if a *stranger* sojourn with you, or *whosoever* be among you in your generations, and will offer an offering made by fire, of a sweet savour unto the Lord ; as ye do, so shall he do. One ordinance shall be both for *you* of the congregation and also for the *stranger* that sojourneth with you, an ordinance for ever in your generations ; as ye are, so shall the *stranger* be, before the Lord." Deut. xxvi. 11, 12 : " And thou shalt rejoice in every good thing which the Lord thy God hath given unto thee, and unto thy house, thou, and the Levite, and the *stranger* that is among you;" Ezek. xxii. 7, 29.

59. And not only were they required to treat *strangers*, or men of other nations, with *kindness* and *humanity ;* but it appears from several parts of Scripture that the whole *Jewish* dispensation had respect to the nations of the world. Not, indeed, to bring them all into the *Jewish* Church, (that would have been impracticable as to the greatest part of the world,) but to spread the knowledge and obedience of God in the earth. Or, it was a scheme which was intended to have its good effects beyond the pale of the *Jewish* enclosure, and was established for the benefit of all mankind. Gen. xii. 3 : " And in thee (*Abraham*) shall all families of the earth be blessed." xxii. 18 : " And in thy seed shall all the nations of the earth be blessed." Exod. vii. 5 : " And the Egyptians shall know that I am the Lord, when I stretch forth my hand upon Egypt, and bring out the children of Israel." ix. 16 : " And indeed for this very cause have I raised thee (*Pharaoh*) up, for to show in thee my power, and that my name shall be declared throughout all the earth ;" xv. 14 ; Lev. xxvi. 45 ; Num. xiv. 13, 14, 15.

60. But though the *Jewish* peculiarity did not exclude the rest of the world from the care and beneficence of the universal Father ; and though the *Jews* were commanded to exercise benevolence towards persons of other nations ; yet, about the time when the Gospel was promulgated, the *Jews* were greatly elevated on account of their distinguishing privileges : they looked upon themselves as the only favourites of Heaven, and regarded the rest of mankind with a sovereign contempt, as nothing, as abandoned of God, and without a possibility of salvation, unless they should incorporate, in some degree or other, with their nation. Their constitution, they supposed, was established for ever, never to be altered, or in any respect abolished. They were the true and only Church, out of which no man could be accepted of God ; and consequently, unless a man submitted to the law of *Moses*, how virtuous or good soever he were, it was their belief he could not be saved. He had no right to a place in the Church, nor could hereafter obtain life.

§ V. *The Jewish peculiarity was to receive its perfection from the Gospel.*

61. But the *Jewish* dispensation, as peculiar to that people, though *superior* to the mere light of nature, which it supposed and included, was but of a temporary duration, and of an inferior and imperfect kind, in comparison of that which was to follow, and which God from the beginning (when he entered into covenant with *Abraham*, and made the promise to him) intended to erect, and which he made several declarations under the Old Testament that he would erect, in the proper time, as successive to the *Jewish* dispensation, and, as a superstructure, perfective of it. And as the *Jewish* dispensation was erected by the ministry of a much nobler hand, even that of the Son *of* God, the Messiah, foreordained before the world was made, promised to *Abraham*, foretold by the *prophets*, and even expected by the *Jews* themselves, though under no just conceptions of the end of his coming into the world. He was to assume and live in a human body, to declare the truth and grace of God more clearly and expressly to the *Jews*, to exhibit a pattern of the most perfect *obedience*, and

to be obedient even unto death in compliance with the will of God.* When Christ came into the world, the *Jews* were ripe for destruction : but he published a general indemnity for the transgressions of the former covenant, upon their repentance ; and openly revealed a future state, as the true land of promise, even eternal life in heaven. Thus he confirmed the former covenant with the *Jews* as to the favour and blessing of God ; and enlarged, or more clearly explained it, as to the blessings therein bestowed ; instead of an earthly *Canaan*, revealing the resurrection from the dead, and everlasting happiness and glory in the world to come.

62. That the Gospel is the *Jewish* scheme *enlarged* and *improved*, will evidently appear, if we consider that we, *Gentiles*, believing *in Christ*, are said to be incorporated into the same body with the *Jews ;* and that believing *Jews* and *Gentiles* are now become *one, one flock, one body* in Christ. John x. 16 : " And other sheep I have which are not of this (*the Jewish*) fold ; them also I must bring, and they shall hear my voice, and there shall be one *flock*, (so the word ποιμνη signifies, and so our translators have rendered it in all the other places where it is used in the New Testament. See Matt. xxvi. 31 ; Luke ii. 8 ; 1 Cor. ix. 7. And here also it should have been translated *flock*, not *fold*,) *and one shepherd*." 1 Cor. xii. 13 : " By one Spirit are we all baptized in *one body*, whether we be Jews or Gentiles." Gal. iii. 28 : " There is neither Jew nor Greek, there is neither bond nor free, there is neither male nor female ; for ye are all ONE in Christ Jesus ;" that is, under the Gospel dispensation. Ephes. ii. 14, 15, 16 : " For he is our peace, who has made both (*Jews* and *Gentiles*) *one*, and has broken down the middle wall of partition between us, (*Jews* and *Gentiles*.) Having abolished by his flesh the enmity, even the law of commandments, contained in ordinances, for to make in himself of twain one new man, so making peace ; and that he might reconcile both unto God in one body by the cross, having slain the enmity thereby."

63. And that this union or coalition between believing *Jews* and *Gentiles* is to be understood of the believing *Gentiles* being taken into that Church and covenant in which the Jews were before the Gospel dispensation was erected, and out of which the unbelieving Jews were cast, is evident from the following considerations.

64. *First*, that *Abraham*, the head or root of the *Jewish* nation, is the father of us all. Rom. iv. 16, 17 : " Therefore it is of faith, that it might be by grace ; to the end that the promise might be sure to all the seed ; not to that only which is of the law, (the *Jews*,) but to that also which is of the faith of Abraham, (the believing *Gentiles*,) who is *the father of us all*, (as it is written, I have made thee a father of many nations,) before him whom he believed ;" that is to say, in the account and purpose of God, whom he believed, he is the father of US ALL. *Abraham*, when he stood before God and received the promise, did not, in the account of God, appear as a *private* person, but *as the father of us all ;* as the *head* and *father* of the whole future Church of God, from whom we were all, believing *Jews* and *Gentiles*, to descend ; as we were to be accepted and interested in the Divine blessing and covenant after the same manner as he was, namely, by faith. Gal. iii. 6, &c. : " Even as Abraham believed God, and it was accounted to him for righteousness. Know ye, therefore, that they which are of faith, the same are the children of Abraham. For the Scripture, foreseeing that God would justify (would take into his Church and covenant) the heathen through faith, preached before the Gospel unto Abraham, saying, In thee shall all nations be blessed. So then they which be of faith (of what country soever they are, heathens as well as Jews) are blessed, (justified, taken into the kingdom and covenant of God,) together with believing Abraham," (and into that very covenant which was made with him and his seed.)†
In this covenant were the *Jews* during the whole period from *Abraham* to *Moses*, and from *Moses* to *Christ*. For the covenant with *Abraham* was with him, and with his *seed after him*," Gen. xvii. 7. " To Abraham and his seed were the promises made," Gal. iii. 16. And the apostle in the next verse tells us that (the promises or) the covenant, that was confirmed before of God in Christ, the law which was (given *by Moses*) four hundred and thirty years after *could* not disannul, that it should make the promise (or covenant with *Abraham*) of none effect ; consequently the *Jews*, during the whole period of the law, or *Mosaical* dispensation, were under the covenant with *Abraham ;* and into that same covenant the apostle argues, Rom. iv. and Gal. iii., that the believing *Gentiles* are taken. For which reason he affirms that they are *no more strangers and foreigners, but fellow-citizens with the saints*, that is, the patriarchs, &c. And that the great mystery, not understood in other ages, was this, *That the Gentiles should be fellow-heirs, and of the same body* with his Church and children, the *Jews*, Eph. ii. 19 ; iii. 5, 6.

65. *Secondly.* Agreeably to this sentiment, the believing *Gentiles* are said to partake of all the spiritual privileges which the *Jews* enjoyed, and from which the unbelieving *Jews* fell ; and to be taken into that kingdom and Church of God out of which they were cast. Several of the parables of our Lord are intended to point out this fact ; and many passages in the epistles directly prove it.

66. Matt. xx. 1–16. In this parable the vineyard is the *kingdom of heaven*, into which God, *the householder*, hired the Jews early in the *morning ;* and into the *same* vineyard he hired the *Gentiles* at the *eleventh* hour, or an hour before sun-set.

67. Matt. xxi. 33, 34. The *husbandmen* to whom the vineyard was first let were the *Jews ;* to whom God first sent *his servants*, the prophets, ver. 34–36, and at last he sent his Son, whom they slew, ver. 37—

---

* Yes, and thus to become a sacrifice for sin, that those who believe in him might have redemption in his blood. This is the light in which the New Testament places the death of Christ.—A. C.

† Being *justified* does not merely signify *being taken into covenant*, so as to be incorporated with the visible Church of God ; it is used repeatedly by St. Paul to signify that act of God's mercy whereby a penitent sinner, believing on Christ as a sacrifice for sin, has his transgressions forgiven for Christ's sake. Rom. v. 1, &c.

39, and then the vineyard was let out to *other husbandmen;* which our Saviour clearly explains, ver. 43 : "Therefore I say unto you, (*Jews,*) the kingdom of God shall be taken from you, and given to a nation (the believing *Gentiles*) bringing forth the fruits thereof." Hence it appears that the very same *kingdom of God,* which the *Jews* once possessed, and in which the ancient prophets exercised their ministry, one after another, is now in *our* possession ; for it was taken from *them* and given to *us.*

68. Rom. xi. 17–24. The Church or *kingdom of God* is compared to an *olive-tree,* and the membres of it to the *branches.* "And if some of the branches (the unbelieving *Jews*) be broken off, and thou (*Gentile Christian*) wert grafted in among them, and with them partakest of the root and fatness of the olive-tree ;" *that is, the* Jewish *Church and covenant.* Ver. 24 : "For if thou (*Gentile Christian*) wert cut out of the olive-tree, which is wild by nature, and wert grafted, contrary to nature, into the good olive-tree," &c.

69. 1 Pet. ii. 7, 8, 9, 10 : "Unto *you* Gentiles who believe, he (*Christ*) is an honour, τιμη, but unto *them* which be disobedient, (the unbelieving *Jews,*) the stone which the builders disallowed, the same is made the head of the corner, and also a stone of stumbling, and a rock of offence.* They stumbled at the word, being disobedient, whereunto also they were appointed, (they are fallen from their privileges and honour, as God appointed they should, in case of their unbelief.) But *ye* (*Gentiles,* are raised into the high degree from which they are fallen, and so) are a chosen generation, a royal priesthood, a holy nation, a peculiar people ; that ye should show forth the praises of him who hath called you out of the *heathenish* darkness into his marvellous light."

70. *Thirdly.* The *Jews* vehemently opposed the admission of the uncircumcised *Gentiles* into the kingdom and covenant of God, at the first preaching of the Gospel. But if the *Gentiles* were not taken into the same Church and covenant in which the *Jewish* nation had so long gloried, why should they so zealously oppose their being admitted into it ? Or why so strenuously insist that they ought to be circumcised in order to their being admitted ? For what was it to them, if the *Gentiles* were called, and taken into another kingdom and covenant, distinct and quite different from that which they would have confined wholly to themselves, or to such only as were circumcised ? It is plain the *Gentiles* might have been admitted into *another* kingdom and covenant without any offence to the *Jews,* as they would still have been left in the sole possession of their ancient privileges. And the apostles could not have failed in using this as an argument to pacify their incensed brethren, had they so understood it. But, seeing they never gave the least intimation of this, it shows they understood the affair as the unbelieving *Jews* did, namely, that the *Gentiles,* without being circumcised, were taken into the kingdom of God, in which they and their forefathers had so long stood.

71. *Fourthly.* It is upon this foundation, namely, that the believing *Gentiles* are taken into that Church and kingdom in which the *Jews* once stood, that the apostles drew parallels, for caution and instruction, between the state of the ancient *Jews* and that of the Christians. 1 Cor. x. 1–13 : "Moreover, brethren, I would not that ye should be ignorant, how that all our fathers were under the cloud, and all passed through the sea, and were all baptized unto Moses, and did all eat of the same spiritual meat, and did all drink of the same spiritual drink ; but with many of them God was not well pleased ; for they were overthrown in the wilderness. Now those things were *our examples,* to the intent *we* should not lust after evil things as *they* also lusted. Neither be ye idolaters, as were some of *them;* neither let us provoke Christ, as some of *them* provoked," &c. Heb. iii. 7, &c. : "Wherefore, as the Holy Ghost saith, To-day,† when *or* while you hear his voice, harden not your hearts, as in the day of temptation in the wilderness, when your fathers tempted me : wherefore I was grieved with that generation, and sware in my wrath, They shall not enter into my rest. Take heed, brethren, lest there be in any of *you* an evil heart of unbelief." Chap. iv. 1, 2 : "Let us therefore fear, lest a promise being left *us* of entering into his rest, any of *you* should seem to come short of it. For unto *us* hath the Gospel been preached, as well as to them," that is, we have the joyful promise of a happy state, or of *entering into rest,* as well as the *Jews* of old. Ver. 11 : "Let us labour, therefore, to enter into that rest, lest any man fall after the same example of unbelief."

72. *Fifthly.* Hence also the scriptures of the Old Testament are represented as being written for our use and instruction, and to explain *our* dispensation as well as *theirs.* Matt. v. 17 : "Think not that I am come to destroy the *law* and the prophets ; I am not come to destroy, but to fulfil." And when our Saviour taught his disciples the things pertaining to his kingdom, he *opened to them the Scriptures,* which were then no other than the *Old Testament;* Luke iv. 17–22 ; xviii. 31. xxiv. 27 : "And beginning at Moses and all the prophets, he expounded unto them in all the Scriptures, the things concerning himself." Verse 45 : "Then opened he their understandings, that they might understand the Scriptures." Thus the apostles were instructed in the things pertaining to the Gospel dispensation. And always, in their sermons in the *Acts,* they confirm their doctrine from the Scriptures of the Old Testament. And in their *Epistles* they not only do the same,

---

* We render this passage thus : *A stone of stumbling and rock of offence, even to them which stumble at the word, being disobedient, &c.,* as if it were one continued sentence. But, thus, violence is done to the text, and the apostle's sense is thrown into obscurity and disorder, which is restored by putting a period after *offence,* and beginning a new sentence, thus : *They stumble* at the word, &c. For observe, the apostle runs a double *antithesis* between the unbelieving *Jews* and believing *Gentiles.*

† Σημερον, ε αν της φωνης αυτου ακουσητε. EAN, *if,* should here have been rendered *when,* as it is rendered, 1 John iii. 2, and should have been rendered, John xii. 32 ; xiv. 3 ; xvi. 7 ; 2 Cor. v. 1. In like manner the particle ᴆᴺ, Psa. xcv. 7, (whence the place is quoted,) should have been translated WHEN or WHILE. For it is translated *when,* 1 Sam. xv. 17 ; Prov. iii. 24 ; iv. 12 ; Job vii. 4 ; xvii. 16 : Psa. l. 18 ; and might have been so translated in other places.

but also expressly declare that those Scriptures were written as well for the benefit of the *Christian* as the *Jewish* Church. Rom. xv. 4: After a quotation out of the Old Testament, the apostle adds :—" For whatsoever things were written *aforetime* were written for our learning ; that *we* through patience and comfort of the Scriptures might have hope." 1 Cor. ix. 9 : " It is written in the law of Moses; that thou shalt not muzzle the mouth of the ox that treadeth out the corn." Verse 10 : " For *our* sakes, no doubt, this is written." 1 Cor. x. 11 : " Now all these things (namely, the before-mentioned privileges, sins, and punishments of the ancient *Jews*) happened unto them for ensamples ; and they are written for *our* admonition, upon whom the ends of the earth are come." 2 Tim. iii. 16, 17 : " All Scripture is given by inspiration of God, and is profitable for doctrine, for reproof, for correction, for instruction in righteousness ; that the man of God may be perfect, thoroughly furnished unto all good works."

73. *Sixthly.* Agreeably to this notion, that the believing *Gentiles* are taken into that Church or kingdom; out of which the unbelieving *Jews* are cast, the Christian Church, considered in a body, is called by the same general names as the Church under the Old Testament. *Israel* was the general name of the *Jewish* Church; so also of the *Christian*. Gal. vi. 16 : " As many as walk according to this rule, peace be on them, and mercy, and upon the *Israel* of God." Rev. vii. 3, 4 : Speaking of the Christian Church, the angel said, " Hurt not the earth, neither the sea, nor the trees, till we have sealed the *servants* of our God in their foreheads. And I heard the number of them that were sealed : and there were sealed a hundred and forty-four thousand, of all the tribes of the children of Israel." Rev. xxi. 10–14 : " He showed me that great city, the holy Jerusalem, (the Christian Church,) having the glory of God—and had a wall great and high, and had twelve gates, and at the gates twelves angels, and names written thereon, which are the names of the twelve tribes of *Israel*, (as comprehending the whole Church.) And the wall of the city had twelve founda-tions, and in them the names of the twelve *apostles* of the *Lamb*." *Jews* was another running title of the Church in our Saviour's time, and this is also applied to *Christians*. Rev. ii. 8, 9 : " And unto the angel of the (Christian) Church in Smyrna, write, I know thy works, and tribulation, and poverty ; and I know the blasphemy of them who say they are *Jews* (members of the Church of *Christ*) and are not, but are the synagogue of Satan." And again, chap. iii. 9.

§ VI. *The particular honours and privileges of Christians, and the terms signifying these honours explained*

74. *Seventhly.* In conformity to this sentiment, (namely, that the believing *Gentiles* are taken into that Church, covenant, and kingdom, out of which the unbelieving *Jews* were cast,) the state, membership, privileges, honours, and relations of professed *Christians*, particularly of believing *Gentiles*, are expressed by the same phrases with those of the ancient Jewish Church ; and therefore, unless we admit a very strange abuse of words, must convey the same general ideas of our *present* state, membership, honours, and relations to God, as we are professed Christians. For instance :—

75. I. As God *chose* his ancient people the *Jews*, and they were his *chosen* and *elect*, so now the whole body of Christians, *Gentiles* as well as *Jews*, are admitted to the same honour, as they are selected from the rest of the world, and taken into the kingdom of God, for the knowledge, worship, and obedience of God, in hopes of eternal life. Rom. viii. 33 : " Who shall lay any thing to the charge of God's *elect?*" &c. Eph. i. 4 : " According as he hath *chosen* us (*Gentiles*, chap. ii. 11) in him before the foundation of the world, that we should be holy, and without blame before him in love." Col. iii. 12 : " Put on, therefore, as the *elect* of God, holy and beloved, bowels of mercies," &c. 2 Thess. ii. 13 : " But we are bound to give thanks to God always for you, brethren, beloved of the Lord, because God hath from the beginning *chosen* you to salvation ; through sanctification of the Spirit, and belief of the truth." Tit. i. 1 : " Paul, a servant of God, and an apostle of Jesus Christ, according to the faith of God's *elect*, and the acknowledging of the truth which is after godliness." 2 Tim. ii. 10 : " Therefore I endure all things for the *elect's* sake, that they also may obtain the salvation which is in Christ Jesus, with eternal glory." 1 Pet. i. 1, 2 : " Peter to the strangers scattered throughout Pontus, Galatia, Cappadocia, Asia, and Bithynia, *elect*, according to the fore-knowledge of God the Father, through sanctification of the Spirit, unto obedience." ii. 9 : " Ye (*Gentiles*) are a *chosen* generation," &c. v. 13 : " The Church that is at Babylon, *elected* together with you, saluteth you."

76. II. The first step which the goodness of God took in execution of his purpose of *election*, with regard to the *Gentile world*, was to rescue them from their wretched situation in the sin and idolatry of their heathen state (by sending his son Jesus Christ into the world to die for mankind, and thus) to bring them into the light and privileges of the Gospel. With regard to which the language of Scripture is : 1st, that he delivered; 2nd, saved ; 3rd, bought or purchased ; 4th, redeemed them. Gal. i. 4 : " Who gave himself for our sins, that he might *deliver* us from this present evil world," the vices and lusts in which the world is involved. Col. i. 12, 13 : " Giving thanks to the Father, who has *delivered* us from the power of (heathenish) darkness, (Acts xxvi. 18 ; 1 Pet. ii. 9 ; Eph. iv. 18 ; v. 8,) and translated us into the kingdom of his dear Son." And thus, consequentially, we are " *delivered* from the wrath to come ;" 1 Thess i. 10.*

---

* That is, through the redemption that is in Jesus we receive the remission of all our sins, and the gift of the Holy Ghost to cleanse, purify, and refine our souls, and thus render them capable of enjoying the inheritance of the saints in light. Our justification, adoption, and sanctification, and finally our admission into the kingdom of glory, are

77. 1 Cor. i. 18 : " For the preaching of the cross is to them that perish foolishness, but unto us which are *saved* it is the power of God." vii. 16 : " What knowest thou, O wife, whether thou shalt *save* thy husband ? or how knowest thou, O man, whether thou shalt *save* thy wife ?" *that is, convert her to the Christian faith.* x. 33 : " Even as I please all men in all things, not seeking mine own profit, but the profit of many, that they may be *saved.*" Eph. ii. 8 : " For by grace are ye *saved,* through faith." 1 Thess. ii. 16 : " Forbidding us to speak to the Gentiles that they might be *saved.*" 1 Tim. ii. 4 : " Who will have all men to be *saved,* and to come unto the knowledge of the truth." 2 Tim. i. 9 : " Who hath *saved* us, and called us with a holy calling, not according to our works, but according to his own purpose and grace." In this general sense, *saved* is in other places applied to both *Jews* and *Gentiles ;* particularly to the *Jews,* Rom. ix. 27 ; x. 1 ; xi. 26. Hence God is styled *our* Saviour. Tit. iii. 4, 5 : " But after that the kindness and love of God our Saviour toward man appeared, not by works of righteousness which we have done, but according to his mercy he *saved* us." 1 Tim. i. 1 : " Paul, an apostle of Jesus Christ, by the command-ment of God our *Saviour ;*" ii. 3 ; Tit. i. 3. Rom. xi. 11 : " Through their (*the Jews'*) fall, *salvation* is come to the Gentiles." And as this *salvation* is by *Jesus Christ,* he also is frequently called our *Saviour.*

78. Acts xx. 28 : " Feed the Church of God, which he has *purchased* with his own blood." 1 Cor. vi. 19, 20 : " And ye are not your own ; for ye are *bought* with a price." vii. 23 : " Ye are *bought* with a price." 2 Pet. ii. 1 : " False prophets shall bring in damnable heresies, even denying the Lord that *bought* them." Rev. v. 9 : " Thou wast slain, and hast redeemed (*bought*) us to God by thy blood, out of every kindred, and tongue, and people, and nation."

79. Tit. ii. 14 : " Who gave himself for us, that he might *redeem* us from all iniquity." 1 Pet. i. 18 : " Ye were not *redeemed* with corruptible things, as silver and gold, from your vain (heathenish) conversation, received by tradition from your fathers ; but with the precious blood of Christ." And at the same time he *redeemed* or bought us from death, or *the curse of the law ;* Gal. iii. 13 ; and the *Jews,* in particular, from the law, and the condemnation to which it subjected them ; Gal. iv. 5. Hence frequent mention is made of the *redemption* which is in Jesus Christ ; Rom. iii. 24 ; 1 Cor. i. 30 ; Eph. i. 7 ; Col. i. 14 ; Heb. ix. 12, 15. Hence also *Christ* is said to give himself a *ransom* for us ; Matt. xx. 28 ; Mark x. 45. 1 Tim. ii. 6 : " Who gave himself a *ransom* for all." That is, that he might redeem them unto God by the *sacrificial* shedding of his blood.—See the note under 76.

80. III. As God sent the Gospel to bring *Gentiles, Christians,* out of heathenism, and invited and made them welcome to the honours and privileges of his people, he is said to *call* them, and they are his *called.* Rom. i. 6, 7 : " Among whom are ye also *called* of Jesus Christ. To all that are at Rome *called* saints ;" viii. 28. 1 Cor. i. 9 : " God is faithful, by whom ye were *called* into the fellowship of his Son ;" vii. 20. Gal. i, 6 : " I marvel that ye are so soon removed from him that *called* you ;" v. 13. Eph. iv. 1 : " I be-seech you, that ye walk worthy of the vocation wherewith ye are *called ;*" iv. 4. 1 Thess. ii. 12 : " That ye walk worthy of God, who hath *called* you unto his kingdom and glory." iv. 7 : " God hath not *called* us unto uncleanness, but unto holiness." 2 Tim. i. 9 : " Who hath saved us, and *called* us with a holy calling ; not according to our works," &c. 1 Pet. i. 15 : " But as he which hath *called* you is holy, so be ye holy in all manner of conversation." ii. 9 : " Ye (Gentile Christians) are a chosen generation—to show forth the praises of him who hath *called* you out of darkness into his marvellous light."

81. Note—The *Jews* also were *called.* Rom. ix. 24 : " Even us, whom he has *called,* not of the *Jews* only, but also of the *Gentiles.*" 1 Cor. i. 24 ; vii. 18 : " Is any man *called* being circumcised ;" Heb. ix. 15. But the calling of the *Jews* must be different from that of the *Gentiles.* The *Gentiles* were called into the kingdom of God as *strangers* and *foreigners,* who had never been in it before. But the *Jews* were then subjects of God's kingdom, under the old form ; and therefore could be *called* only to submit to it, as it was now modelled under the *Messiah.* Or they were *called* to repentance, to the faith, allegiance, and obedience of the Son of God, and to the hope of eternal life through him ; whom rejecting, they were cast out of God's peculiar kingdom.

82. IV. And as we stand in the relation of children to the God and Father of our Lord *Jesus Christ,* hence it is that we are his brethren, and he is considered as the first born among us. Matt. xxviii. 10 ; John xx. 17 : " Jesus saith—Go to my *brethren,* and say unto them, I ascend unto my Father and your Father, and to my God and your God ;" Heb. ii. 11, 17. Rom. viii. 29 : " That he might be the *first-born* among many *brethren.*"

83. V. And the relation of God, as a *Father,* to us *Christians,* who are his *children,* will lead our thoughts to a clear idea of our being, as we are called, the *house* or *family* of God or of Christ. 1 Tim. iii. 15 : " But if I tarry long, that thou mayest know how to behave thyself in the *house* of God, which is the Church of the living God." Heb. iii. 6 : " But Christ, as a Son over his own *house,* whose *house* are we, (*Chris-tians,*) if we hold fast the confidence and rejoicing of the hope firm unto the end." Heb. x. 21 : " And having a great high priest over the *house* of God," &c. 1 Pet. iv. 17 : " For the time is come that judg-ment must begin at the *house* of God, (that is, when the *Christian* Church shall undergo sharp trials and sufferings ;) and if it first begin at us, (Christians, who are the *house* or *family* of God,) what shall the end

most positively attributed to the sacrificial passion and death of Jesus : and we are not *consequentially delivered from the wrath to come,* till our sins are blotted out and our hearts purified from sin ; and these blessings we receive from God *through Christ,* i. e. for his *sake,* his *worth* or *merit ;* for he has bought these blessings for mankind by his *sacrificial* passion and death. *Justice* required these to make way for mercy.—A. C. See No. 79.

be of them that obey not *the Gospel?*" that is, of the infidel world, who lie out of the Church. See Rom. i. 5; xv. 18; 1 Pet. i. 22. Eph. ii. 19: "We are of the *household* (domestics) of God." iii. 14, 15: "I bow my knees unto the Father of our Lord Jesus Christ, of whom the whole *family* in heaven and earth is named," &c.

84. VI. Farther, as the land of *Canaan* was the *estate* or *inheritance* belonging to the *Jewish family* or *house*, so the *heavenly country* is given to the *Christan house* or *family* for their inheritance. Acts xx. 32: "And now, brethren, I commend you to God, and to the word of his grace, which is able to build you up, and to give you an *inheritance* among all them which are sanctified." Col. iii. 24: "Knowing that of the Lord ye shall receive the reward of the *inheritance.*" Heb. ix. 15: "He is the mediator of the New Testament, that they which are called might receive the promise of eternal *inheritance.*" 1 Pet. i. 3, 4: "God has begotten us again—to an *inheritance* incorruptible, undefiled, and that fadeth not away, reserved in heaven for us." Hence we have the title of *heirs.* Tit. iii. 7: "That being justified by his grace, we should be made *heirs* according to the hope of eternal life." James ii. 5: "Hath not God chosen the poor of this world, rich in faith, and *heirs* of the kingdom which he has promised to them that love him?" See Rom. viii. 17; 1 Pet. iii. 7.

85. And as *Canaan* was considered as the *rest* of the *Jews*, so, in reference to our trials and afflictions in this world, heaven is considered as the *rest* of *Christians.* 2 Thess. i. 7: "And to you who are troubled, (he will give) *rest* with us, when the Lord Jesus shall be revealed from heaven." Heb. iv. 1: "Let us therefore fear, lest a promise being left us of entering into his *rest*, any of you should seem to come short of it. For unto us hath the Gospel been preached, as well as to them;" that is, we have the joyful promise of *entering into rest* as well as the *Jews* of old. Verse 9: "There remains, therefore, a *rest* for the people of God;" that is, for *Christians* now in this world, as well as for the *Jews* formerly in the wilderness, which is the point the apostle is proving, from ver. 3 to 10.

86. VII. Thus *Christians*, as well as the ancient *Jews*, are the *house* or *family* of God: or we may conceive the whole body of *Christians* formed into a nation, having God at their head; who, on this account, is styled our God, governor, protector, or king; and we his people, subjects, or servants.

87. VIII. And it is in reference to our being a *society* peculiarly appropriated to God, and under his special protection and government, that we are called the *city of God*, the *holy city.* Heb. xii. 22: "Ye are come unto—the *city* of the living God." Rev. xi. 2: "And the *holy city* shall they tread under foot forty and two months." This city is described in some future happy state; Rev. xxi. and xxvi.

88. Hence the whole *Christian* community or Church is denoted by the *city Jerusalem*, and sometimes by *Mount Zion.* Gal. iv. 26: "But *Jerusalem*, which is above, is free, which is the mother of us all."—In her reformed, or future happy state, she is the New Jerusalem; Rev. iii. 12; xxi. 2. Heb. xii. 22: "Ye are come unto *Mount Zion*," &c.; Rev. xiv. 1.

89. Hence also we are said to be *written* or *enrolled* in the *book of God*, or, which comes to the same thing, *of the Lamb*, the Son of God. Rev. iii. 5: "He that overcometh, the same shall be clothed in white raiment; and I will not blot out his name out of the *book of life.*" xxii. 19: "And if any man take away from the words of the book of this prophecy, God shall take away his part out of the *book of life*, and out of the holy city," &c.; which shows that the names of such as are in *the book of life* may be blotted out, consequently, that to be enrolled there is the privilege of all professed *Christians.*

90. And whereas the believing *Gentiles* were once *strangers, aliens, not a people, enemies*; now (Eph. ii. 19) "they are no more *strangers* and *foreigners*, but *fellow-citizens* with the saints." 1 Pet. ii. 10: "Which in time past were *not a people*, but are now the *people of God.*" *Now* "we are at *peace* with God;" Rom. v. 1. *Now* "we are *reconciled* and become the servants of God," the *subjects* of his kingdom; Rom. v. 10; 1 Thess. i. 9; 2 Cor. v. 18, 19.—[That is, all those who have turned to God by true repentance have received remission of sin, and are walking in the way of righteousness, with a believing, obedient, loving, and grateful heart.—A. C.]

91. On the other hand, the body of the *Jewish* nation, (having, through unbelief, *rejected* the *Messiah*, and the Gospel, and being therefore *cast out* of the city and kingdom of God,) are, in their turn, at present represented under the name and notion of *enemies.* Rom. xi. 28: "As concerning the Gospel, they are *enemies* for your sake."

92. IX. The kind and particular regards of God to the converted *Gentiles*, and their relation to *Jesus Christ*, is also signified by that of a *husband* and *wife;* and his taking them into his covenant is represented by his *espousing* them. 2 Cor. xi. 2: "For I am jealous over you with godly jealousy; for I have *espoused* you to one *husband*, that I may present you as a chaste virgin to Christ."

93. Hence the *Christian* Church or community is represented as a mother, and particular members as her children. Gal. iv. 26, 27, 28: "But Jerusalem, which is above, is free, which is the *mother* of us all. For it is written, Rejoice, thou barren that bearest not; break forth and cry, thou that travailest not; for the desolate hath many more *children* than she which hath a husband. Now we, brethren, as Israel was, are the *children* of promise." Verse 31: "So then, brethren, we are not *children* of the bond-woman, but of the free."

94. Hence also, from the notion of the *Christian* Church being the *spouse* of God in *Christ*, her *corruption* and her *idolatry* come under the name of *fornication* and *adultery.*

95. X. As God, by *Christ*, exercises a particular providence over the *Christian* Church, in supplying them

2   21

with all spiritual blessings, guiding them through all difficulties, and guarding them in all spiritual dangers, He is their *shepherd*, and they his *flock*, his *sheep*. John x. 11: " I am the good *shepherd*." Verse 16: " And other *sheep* I have which are not of this fold ; them also I must bring, and they shall hear my voice ; and there shall be one *flock*, and one *shepherd*;" Acts xx. 28, 29; Heb. xiii. 20. 1 Pet. ii. 25 : " For ye were as *sheep* going astray ; but are now returned to the shepherd and bishop (overseer) of your souls." v. 2, 3, 4 : " Feed the *flock* of God," &c.

96. XI. Nearly on the same account as God, by *Christ*, has established the *Christian* Church, and provided all means for our happiness and improvement in knowledge and virtue, we are compared to a *vine* and a *vineyard*, and God to the *husbandman*, who planted and dresses it ; and particular members of the community are compared to *branches*. John xv. 1, 2 : " I am the true *vine*, and my Father is the *husbandman*. Every *branch* in me that beareth not fruit, he taketh away ; and every *branch* that beareth fruit, he purgeth it," &c. ver. 5: " I am the *vine*, ye are the *branches*." Matt. xv. 13 : " Every *plant* which my heavenly Father hath not planted shall be rooted up." Rom. vi. 5 : " If we have been *planted* together in the likeness of his death, we shall be also in the likeness of his resurrection." Matt. xx. 1. The *vineyard* into which *labourers* were hired is the *Christian* as well as the *Jewish* Church : and so chap. xxi. 33 ; Mark xii. 1 ; Luke xx. 9. 1 Cor. iii. 9 : " Ye are God's *husbandry*." Rom. xi. 17 : " And if some of the *branches* (*Jews*) be broken off, and thou, being a wild olive-tree, wert grafted in among them, and with them partakest of the root and fatness of the olive-tree," &c. See also ver. 24.

97. XII. As *Christians* are, by the will of God, *set apart* and appropriated in a special manner to his honour, service, and obedience, and furnished with extraordinary means and motives to holiness, so they are said to be *sanctified*. 1 Cor. i. 2 : " Unto the Church of God which is at Corinth, to them that are *sanctified* in Christ Jesus." vi. 11 : " And such were some of you ; but ye are washed, but ye are *sanctified*, but ye are justified, in the name of the Lord Jesus, and by the Spirit of our God." Heb. ii. 11 : " For both he that *sanctifieth*, and they who are *sanctified*, are all of one ;" x. 10.

98. XIII. Farther ; by the presence of God in the *Christian* Church, and our being by profession *consecrated* to him, *we*, as well as the ancient *Jews*, are made his *house* or *temple*, which God has built, and in which he dwells, or walks. 1 Pet. ii. 5 : " Ye also, as lively stones, are built up a spiritual house," &c. 1 Cor. iii. 9 : " Ye are God's *building*." Ver. 16, 17 : " Know ye not that ye (*Christians*) are the *temple* of God, and that the Spirit of God *dwelleth* in you : if any man defile the *temple* of God, him shall God destroy ; for the *temple* of God is holy, which *temple* ye are." 2 Cor. vi. 16 : " And what agreement hath the *temple* of God (the Christian Church) with idols ? For ye are the *temple* of the living God, as God hath said : I will *dwell* in them, and *walk* in them." Eph. ii. 20, 21, 22 : " And are *built* upon the foundation of the apostles, &c., Christ Jesus being the chief corner-stone ; in whom all the building fitly framed together groweth unto a holy *temple* in the Lord ; in whom ye also are builded together, for a habitation of God through the Spirit." 2 Thess. ii. 4 : " So that he, as God, sitteth in the *temple* of God, SHOWING HIMSELF that he is God."

99. XIV. And not only does God, as our king, dwell in the *Christian* Church, as in his *house* or *temple* ; but he has also conferred on *Christians* the honours of *kings* ; as he has redeemed us from the servitude of sin, made us lords of ourselves, and raised us above others, to *sit on thrones*, and to *judge* and *reign over* them. And he has made us *priests* too, as we are peculiarly consecrated to God, and obliged to attend upon him, from time to time continually, in the solemn offices of religion which he has appointed. 1 Pet. ii. 5: " Ye also, as lively stones, are built up a spiritual house, a holy *priesthood*." Ver. 9: " But ye (*Gentile Christians*) are a chosen generation, a royal (or kingly) *priesthood*." Rev. i. 5, 6 : " Unto him that loved us, and washed us from our sins in his own blood, and hath made us *kings* and *priests* unto God and his Father," &c.

100. XV. Thus the whole body of the *Christian* Church is separated unto God from the rest of the world. And whereas, before, the Gentile believers were *afar off*, lying out of the commonwealth of *Israel*, now they are *nigh*, as they are joined to God in covenant, have full access to him in the ordinances of worship, and, in virtue of his promise, a particular title to his regards and blessing. 2 Cor. vi. 17 : " Wherefore come out from among them, and be *separate*, saith the Lord, and touch not the unclean thing ; and I will receive you." Eph. ii. 13 : " But now, in Christ Jesus, ye, who sometimes were *afar off*, are made *nigh*, by the blood of Christ."

101. XVI. And as God, in all these respects, has distinguished the *Christian* Church, and sequestered them unto himself, they are styled his *peculiar people*. Tit. ii. 14 : " Who gave himself for us, that he might redeem us from all iniquity, and purify unto himself a *peculiar people*, zealous of good works." 1 Pet. ii. 9 : " But ye are a *chosen generation*, a *royal priesthood*, a *holy nation*, a *peculiar people*."

102. XVII. As Christians are a body of men particularly related to God, instructed by him in the rules of wisdom, devoted to his service, and employed in his true worship, they are called his *Church* or *congregation*. Acts xx. 28 : " Feed the *Church* of God." 1 Cor. x. 32 : " Giving none offence to the *Church* of God ;" xv. 9 ; Gal. i. 13 ; and elsewhere. Eph. i. 22 : " Head over all things to the *Church* :"—and particular societies are *Churches*. Rom. xvi. 16 : " The *Churches* of Christ salute you :"—and so in several other places.

103. XVIII. For the same reason they are considered as God's *possession* or *heritage*. 1 Pet. v. 3 : " Neither as being lords over God's *heritage*, but being ensamples to the flock." The reader cannot well

avoid observing that the words and phrases by which our *Christian* privileges are expressed in the *New Testament* are the *very same* with the words and phrases by which the privileges of the *Jewish* Church are expressed in the *Old Testament*; which makes good what St. Paul says concerning the language in which the apostles *declared the things that are freely given to us of God.* 1 Cor. ii. 12, 13 : "We (*apostles*) have received, not the spirit of the world, but the Spirit which is of God, that we might know the things that are given to us of God;" namely, the fore-recited privileges and blessings. "Which things we speak, not in the words which man's wisdom teacheth," not in .philosophic terms of human invention, "but which the Holy Spirit teacheth," in the writings of the Old Testament, the only Scriptures from which they took their ideas and arguments, "comparing spiritual things" under the Gospel.

Whence we may conclude : 1. That the holy Scriptures are admirably calculated to be understood in those things which we are most of all concerned to understand. Seeing the same language runs through the whole, and is set in such a variety of lights, that one part is well adapted to illustrate another : an advantage I reckon peculiar to the sacred writings above all others. 2. It follows that, to understand the *sense* of the Spirit in the *New*, it is essentially necessary that we understand its sense in the Old Testament.

§ VII. *Reflections on the foregoing Honours and Privileges of the Christian Church.*

From what has been said it appears,—

104. I. That the believing *Gentiles* are taken into that kingdom and covenant in which the *Jews* once stood, and out of which they were cast for their unbelief and rejection of the Son of God ; and that we *Christians* ought to have the same general ideas of our present religious state, membership, privileges, honours, and relation to God, as the *Jews* had while they were in possession of the kingdom. Only in some things the kingdom of God under the Gospel dispensation differs much from the kingdom of God under the Mosaical. As, 1. That it is now so constituted that it admits, and is adapted to, men of *all nations* upon the earth, who believe in *Christ*. 2. That the *law*, as a *ministration of condemnation*, which was an appendage to the Jewish dispensation, is removed and annulled under the Gospel. [But the *moral law*, as a rule of life, is still in force.] 3. And so is the polity or civil state of the *Jews*, which was interwoven with their religion, but has no connection with the Christian religion. 4. The *ceremonial* part of the Jewish constitution is likewise abolished, for we are taught the spirit and duties of religion, not by figures and symbols, as sacrifices, offerings, watchings, &c., but by express and clear precepts. 5. The kingdom of God is now put under the special government of the Son of God, who is the head and king of the Church, to whom we owe faith and allegiance.*

105. II. From the above recited particulars it appears that the Christian Church is happy, and highly honoured with privileges of the most excellent nature ; of which the *apostles*, who well understood this new constitution, were deeply sensible. Rom. i. 16 : "I am not ashamed of the Gospel of Christ, for it is the power of God unto salvation to every one that believeth." v. 1, 2, 3, &c. : "Therefore, being justified by faith, we have peace with God through our Lord Jesus Christ ; by whom also we have access, by faith, into this grace wherein we stand, and rejoice (*glory*) in hope of the glory of God. And not only so, but we *glory* in tribulation also," &c. Ver. 11 : "And not only so, but we also joy (*glory*) in God through our Lord Jesus Christ," &c. viii. 31 : "What shall we then say to these things ? If God be for us, who can be against us ! He that spared not his own Son, but delivered him up for us all, how shall he not with him also freely give us all things ? Who shall lay any thing to the charge of God's elect ! Who is he that condemneth ? Who shall separate us from the love of Christ ?" ix. 23, 24 : "He has made known the riches of his glory on the vessels of mercy, which he had afore prepared unto glory, even on us whom he has called, not of the Jews only, but also of the Gentiles." 2 Cor. iii. 18 : "But we all, with open face, beholding, as in a glass, the glory of the Lord, are changed into the same image, from glory to glory, as by the Spirit of the Lord." Eph. i. 3, 4, &c. : "Blessed be the God and Father of our Lord Jesus Christ, who hath blessed us with all spiritual blessings in heavenly places in Christ ; according as he hath chosen us in him," &c., &c.

106. And it is the duty of the whole body of *Christians* to rejoice in the goodness of God, to *thank* and *praise* him for all the benefits conferred upon them in the Gospel. Rom. xv. 10 : "*Rejoice*, ye Gentiles, with his people." Phil. iii. 1 : "My brethren, *rejoice* in the Lord." iv. 4 : "*Rejoice* in the Lord alway ; again I say, *rejoice*." 1 Thess. v. 16 : "*Rejoice* evermore ;" James i. 9 ; 1 Pet. i. 6, 8. Col. i. 12 : "Giving *thanks* unto the Father, which hath made us meet to be partakers of the inheritance of the saints in light." ii. 7 : "Rooted and built up in him, and established in the faith, abounding therein with *thanksgiving*;" 1 Thess. v. 18. Heb. xiii. 15 : "By him, therefore, let us offer the sacrifice of *praise* to God continually, that is, the fruit of our lips, giving *thanks* to his name." Eph. i. 6 : "To the *praise* of the glory of his grace, wherein he has made us accepted in the Beloved ;" ver. 12, 14.

107. Farther, it is to be observed that all the foregoing privileges, benefits, relations, and honours *belong to all* professed *Christians*, without exception. God is the God, King, Saviour, Father, Husband, Shepherd, &c., of them *all*. He created, saved, bought, redeemed ; he begot, he made, he planted, &c., them *all*. And they are *all* as *created*, *redeemed*, and *begotten* by him ; his people, nation, heritage ; his children, spouse, flock, vineyard, &c. We are *all enriched* with the blessings of the Gospel, Rom. xi. 12, 13, 14 ; *all recon-*

---

* Add to this, that all the privileges under the Gospel are abundantly more *spiritual* than they were under the law—THAT being the *shadow*, THIS the *substance*. Hence, while we consider these privileges the same in *kind*, we must view them as differing widely in *degree*.—A. C.

2

ciled to God, ver. 15 ; *all* the *seed* of *Abraham*, and *heirs* according to the *promise*, Gal. iii. 29 ; *all* partake of the *root* and *fatness* of the *good olive*, the Jewish Church ; *all* the brethren of *Christ* and members of his body ; *all* are under grace ; *all* have a right to the ordinances of worship ; *all* are golden candlesticks in the temple of God, Rev. i. 12, 13, 20 ; even those who, by reason of their misimprovement of their privileges, are threatened with having the candlestick removed out of its place, ii. 5. Either *every* professed *Christian* is not in the Church, or all the forementioned privileges belong to *every* professed *Christian ;* which will appear more evidently if we consider,—

108. III. That all the aforementioned privileges, honours, and advantages are the effects of God's free grace, without regard to any prior righteousness, which deserved or procured the donation of them. It was not for any goodness or worthiness which God found in the *heathen* world, when the Gospel was first preached to them ; not for any works of obedience or righteousness which we, in our *Gentile* state, had performed, whereby we had rendered ourselves deserving of the blessings of the Gospel, namely, to be taken into the family, kingdom, or Church of God ; by no means. It was not thus of ourselves that we are saved, justified, &c. So far from that, the Gospel, when first preached to us *Gentiles*, found us sinners, dead in trespasses and sins, enemies *through wicked works*, disobedient ; therefore, I say, all the forementioned *privileges, blessings, honours,* &c., are the effects of God's free grace or favour, without regard to *any* prior works or righteousness in the *Gentile* world, which procured the donation of them. Accordingly, they are always in Scripture, assigned to the *love, grace,* and *mercy* of God, as the sole spring from whence they flow. John iii. 16 : " For God so *loved* the world, that he gave his only begotten Son, that whosoever believeth on him should not perish, but have everlasting life." Rom. v. 8 : " But God commendeth his *love* to us, in that, while we were *sinners,* Christ died for us." Eph. ii. 4–9, 10 : " But God, who is rich in *mercy,* for his great *love* wherewith he has *loved* us, even when we were *dead in sins,* hath quickened us together with Christ, (by *grace* ye are saved,) and hath raised us up together, and made us sit together in heavenly places in Christ Jesus : that in the ages to come he might show the exceeding riches of his *grace* in his *kindness* towards us, through Jesus Christ. For by *grace* are ye saved, through faith, and that (salvation is) not of yourselves, it is the *gift* of God ; not of works, so that* no man (nor *Gentile* nor *Jew*) can boast. For we (Christians, converted from heathenism) are his workmanship, created in Christ Jesus unto good works, which God hath before ordained, that we should walk in them."

109. It is on account of this general love that Christians are honoured with the title of *beloved.* Rom. i. 7 : " To all that are in Rome, *beloved* of God, called *saints.*" ix. 25 : " I will call her (the *Gentile* Church) *beloved,* which was not beloved." Col. iii. 12 : " Put on, therefore, as the elect of God, holy and *beloved,* bowels of mercies," &c.

110. Rom. iii. 23, 24 : " For all have sinned and come short of the glory of God ; being justified freely by his *grace,* through the redemption which is in Christ Jesus ;" v. 2. 1 Cor. i. 4 : " I thank my God—for the *grace* of God which is given you by Jesus Christ." Eph. i. 6, 7 : " To the praise of the glory of his *grace,* whereby he has made us accepted in the beloved, in whom we have redemption through his blood, the forgiveness of sins, according to the riches of his *grace ;*" Col. i. 6 ; 2 Thess. i. 12. 2 Tim. i. 9 : " Who hath saved us, and called us with a holy calling, not according to our works, but according to his own *purpose* and *grace,* which was given us in Jesus Christ before the world began ;" Tit. ii. 11 ; Heb. xii. 15. Hence *grace,* and *the grace of God,* is sometimes put for the *whole Gospel,* and all its blessings. Acts xiii. 43 : " Paul and Barnabas persuaded them to continue in the *grace* of God ;" 2 Cor. vi. 1. 1 Pet. v. 12 : " Testifying that this is the true *grace* of God in which ye stand ;" 1 Cor. i. 4 ; Rom. v. 2 ; 2 Cor. vi. 1 ; Tit. ii. 11 ; Jude 4. Rom. xii. 1 : " I beseech you, therefore, brethren by the *mercies* of God, that ye present your bodies," &c. xv. 9 : " And that the Gentiles might glorify God for his *mercy.*" 1 Pet. i. 3 : " Blessed be the God and Father of our Lord Jesus Christ, who, according to his abundant *mercy,* hath begotten us again to a lively hope," &c.

111. In these texts, and others of the same kind, it is evident that the love, grace, and mercy of God hath respect, not to *particular persons* in the Christian Church, but to the *whole body,* or whole societies, and therefore are to be understood of that general love, grace, and mercy whereby the whole body of *Christians* is separated unto God, to be his peculiar people, favoured with extraordinary blessings. And it is with regard to this sentiment and mode of speech that the *Gentiles,* who before lay out of the Church, and had not obtained mercy, are said now *to have obtained mercy,* Rom. xi. 30.

112. Hence also we may conclude that all the privileges and blessings of the Gospel, even the whole of our redemption and salvation, are the effect of God's pure, free, original love and grace, to which he was inclined of his own motion, without any other motive besides his own goodness, in mere kindness and good will to a sinful, perishing world. These are *the things that are* freely *given to us of God,* 1 Cor. ii. 12.

* Ἵνα μη τις καυχησηται, *lest any man should boast.* So we render it ; as if the Gospel salvation were appointed to be *not of works,* to prevent our boasting ; which supposes we might have boasted, had not God taken this method to preclude it. Whereas, in truth, we had nothing to boast of. Neither *Jew* nor *Gentile* could pretend to any prior righteousness, which might make them worthy to be taken into the house and kingdom of God under his Son ; therefore the apostle's meaning is : " We are not saved from heathenism, and translated into the Church and kingdom of *Christ,* for any prior goodness, obedience, or righteousness we had performed. For which reason, no man can boast, as if he had merited the blessing, &c." This is the apostle's sense ; and the place should have been translated, *so that no man can boast.* For *Ἵνα* signifies *so that.* See Rom. iii. 19 ; 1 Cor. vii. 29 ; 2 Cor. i. 17 ; vii. 9 ; Gal. v. 17 ; Heb. ii. 17 ; vi. 18 ; Mark iv. 12.

GOSPEL BLESSINGS DISPENSED THROUGH CHRIST.

§ VIII. *All the grace of the Gospel is dispensed to us* by, in, or through *Christ Jesus.*

113. Nevertheless, all the forementioned *love, grace,* and *mercy* is dispensed or conveyed to us, *in, by, or through* the Son of God, Jesus Christ, *our Lord.* To quote all the places to this purpose would be to transcribe a great part of the New Testament. But it may suffice, at present, to review the texts under the numbers 108 and 110. From which texts it is evident that " the *grace* (or favour) of God is given unto us *by* Jesus Christ ;" that he has " shown the exceeding riches of his *grace* in his kindness to us *through* Jesus Christ ;" that he has " sent his Son into the world that we might live *through* him ;" to be " the propitiation (or mercy seat) for our sins ;" that he " died for us ;" that " we who were afar off are made nigh *by* his blood ;" that God has " made us accepted *in* the Beloved, (*in* his beloved Son,) *in* whom we have redemption *through* his blood, the forgiveness of sins ;" that " we are his workmanship, created *in* Christ Jesus ;" that, " before the world began, the purpose and *grace* of God (relating to our calling and salvation) was given us *in* Christ Jesus ;" " Before the foundation of the world God chose us *in* Christ," Eph. i. 4. " We have peace with God *through* our Lord Jesus Christ, *by* whom also we have access into this grace wherein we stand," Rom. v. 1, 2. " God hath given to us eternal life, and this life is *in* his Son," 1 John v. 11. Nothing is clearer, from the whole current of Scripture, than that all the mercy and love of God, and all the blessings of the Gospel, from first to last, from the *original* purpose and grace of God to our *final* salvation in the possession of eternal life, are *in, by,* or *through* Christ ; and particularly *by his blood,* by the redemption which is *in him,* as he is the propitiation (or atonement) for the sins of the whole world, 1 John ii. 2. This can bear no dispute among *Christians.* The only difference that can be must relate to the *manner*—how these blessings are conveyed to us *in, by,* or *through* Christ. Doubtless they are conveyed through his hands, as he is the *minister* or *agent,* appointed of God to put us in possession of them. But his *blood, death,* and *cross* could be no *ministering* cause of blessings assigned to his *blood,* &c., before we were put in possession of them.— See Rom. v. 6, 8, 10, 19 ; Eph. ii. 13, 16 ; Col. i. 20, 21, 22. Nor truly can his *blood* be possibly considered as a *ministering* or *instrumental* cause in any sense at all ; for it is not an *agent* but an *object,* and therefore, though it may be a *moving* cause, or a reason for bestowing blessings, yet it can be no *active* or *instrumental* cause in conferring them. His *blood* and *death* is indeed to us an *assurance* of pardon ; but it is evidently something more ; for it is also considered as an *offering* and *sacrifice* to God, highly pleasing to him, to *put away* our *sin,* and to obtain eternal redemption ; Heb. ix. 12, 14, 26 ; Eph. v. 2.

114 *But why should God choose to communicate his grace in this mediate way, by the interposition, obedience, and agency of his Son, who again employs subordinate agents and instruments under him?* I answer : For the display of the glory of his nature and perfections. The Sovereign Disposer of all things may communicate his blessings by what means and in any way he thinks fit. But whatever he effects by the interposition of means, and a train of intermediate causes, he could produce by his own immediate power. He wants not clouds to distil rain ; nor rain nor human industry to make the earth fruitful ; nor the fruitfulness of the earth to supply food ; nor food to sustain our life. He could do this by his own immediate power ; but he chooses to manifest his providence, power, wisdom, and goodness in a variety of ways and dispositions ; and yet his power and goodness are not only as much concerned and exercised in this way, as if he produced the end without the intervention of means, but even much more, because his power, wisdom and goodness are as much exerted and illustrated in every single intermediate step, as if he had done the thing at once, without any intermediate step at all. There is as much power and wisdom exercised in producing rain, or in making the earth fruitful, or in adapting food to the nourishment of our bodies—I say there is as much power in any one of these steps as there would be in nourishing our bodies by one immediate act without those intermediate means. Therefore, in this method of procedure, the displays of the Divine providence and perfections are multiplied and beautifully diversified, to arrest our attention, exercise our contemplation, and excite our admiration and thankfulness ; for thus we see God in a surprising variety of instances. Nor, indeed, can we turn our eyes to any part of the visible creation, but we see his power, wisdom, and goodness in perpetual exercise, every where. In like manner, in the *moral world,* he chooses to work by means, the mediation of his Son, the influences of his Spirit, the teachings of his word, the endeavours of apostles and ministers ; not to supply any defects of his power, wisdom, or goodness ; but to multiply the instances of them ; to show himself to us in a varied display of his glorious dispensations ; to exercise the moral powers and virtues of all the subordinate agents employed in carrying on his great designs, and to set before our thoughts the most engaging subjects of meditation, and the most powerful motives of action. And this method, in the *moral world,* is still more necessary ; because, without the attention of our minds, the end proposed, our sanctification, cannot be obtained.*

115. *But how is it agreeable to the infinite distance there is between the most high God and creatures so low and imperfect, who are of no consideration when compared to the immensity of his nature, that he should*

* But it certainly was not merely to display the various operations of Divine Providence, and to multiply the displays of the Divine perfections, that God required the sacrifice and death of his Son : as he was a sacrifice for sin—and the true notion of sacrifice is redeeming the life of a guilty creature by the death of one that is *innocent*— therefore Christ died, the just for the unjust, that he might bring us to God, 1 Pet. iii. 18. Consequently the justice and righteousness of God required this sacrifice : and *justice* must have required it, else such a sacrifice could not have taken place ; for had not *justice* required it, no attribute of God could, without injustice, have demanded it.—A. C.

2

25

so greatly concern himself about our redemption? Answer:—He who is all-present, all-knowing, all-powerful, attends to all the minutest affairs in the whole universe without the least confusion or difficulty. And, if it was not below his infinite greatness to *make* mankind, it cannot be so to *take care* of them, when created. For *kind*, he can produce no beings *more excellent* than the *rational* and *intelligent;* consequently, those must be most worthy of his regard. And when they are corrupted, as thereby the end of their being is frustrated, it must be as agreeable to his *greatness* to endeavour (when he sees fit) their reformation, or to restore them to the true ends for which they were created, as it was originally to create them.

116. And as for mankind being a *mean* and *inconsiderable* part of the creation, it may not be so easy to demonstrate as we may imagine. The *sin* that is or hath been in the world will not do it; for then the beings which we know stand in a much higher, and, perhaps, in a very high rank of *natural* perfection, will be proved to be as mean and inconsiderable as ourselves; seeing they in great numbers have sinned. Neither will our *natural weakness* and *imperfection* prove that we are a mean and inconsiderable part of God's creation : for the Son of God, when clothed in our flesh, and encompassed with all our infirmities and temptations, lost nothing of the real excellency and worth he possessed when in a state of glory with the Father before the world was. Still he was the beloved Son of God, in whom he was well pleased. Besides, since God may bestow honours and privileges as he pleases, who will tell me what *pre-eminence*, in the purpose of God, this world may possibly have above any other part of the universe; or what relation it bears to the rest of the creation? We know that even *angels* have been ministering spirits to some part at least of mankind. Who will determine how far the scheme of *redemption* may exceed any scheme of Divine wisdom in other parts of the universe; or how far it may affect the improvement and happiness of other beings in the remotest regions? Eph. iii. 10, 11 : "To the intent that now unto the principalities and powers in heavenly places might be known by the Church, the manifold wisdom of God, according to the eternal purpose which he purposed in Christ Jesus our Lord." 1 Pet. i. 12 : "Which things (that are reported by them that have preached the Gospel) the angels desire to look into." It is therefore the sense of revelation, that the heavenly principalities and powers study the wisdom and grace of redemption, and even increase their stock of wisdom from the displays of the Divine love in the Gospel. Who can say how much our virtue is, more or less, severely proved, than in other worlds; or how far our virtue may excel that of other beings, who are not subjected to our long and heavy trials? May not a virtue, firm and steady under our present clogs, inconveniences, discouragements, persecutions, trials, and temptations, possibly *surpass* the virtue of the *highest angel*, whose state is not attended with such embarrassments? Do ye know how far such as shall have honourably passed through the trials of this life shall hereafter be dispersed through the creation? How much their capacities will be enlarged? How highly they shall be exalted? What power and trusts will be put into their hands? How far their influence shall extend, and how much they shall contribute to the *good order and happiness of the universe?* Possibly, the faithful soul, when disengaged from our present incumbrances, may *blaze out into a degree of excellency* equal to the *highest honours*, the most important and extensive services. Our Lord has made us *kings* and *priests* unto God and the Father, and we shall sit together in *heavenly places,* and *reign with him. To him that overcomes* the trials of this present state, he will give *to sit with him in his throne.* True, many from among mankind shall perish among the vile and worthless for ever : and so shall many of the *angels.* These considerations may satisfy us that, possibly, mankind are not so despicable as to be below the interposition of the *Son of God.* Rather, the surprising condescensions and sufferings of a being so glorious should be an argument that the scheme of redemption is of the utmost importance; and that, in the estimate of God, who alone confers dignity, we are creatures of *very great consequence.* Lastly: *God by Christ created the world;* and if it was not below his dignity to *create*, it is much less below his dignity to *redeem* the world, which, of the two, is the more honourable.

117. It is farther to be observed, that the whole scheme of the Gospel *in Christ*, and as it stands in relation to his *blood, or obedience unto death*, was formed in the council of God, before the calling of *Abraham*, and even before the beginning of the world. Acts xv. 18 : "Known unto God are all his works (the dispensations which he intended to advance) from the beginning of the world." Eph. i. 4 : "According as he hath *chosen* us in him (*Christ*) before the foundation of the world" (προ καταβολης κοσμου.) 2 Tim. i. 9 : "Who hath saved us and called us, according to his own purpose and grace, which was given us *in Christ Jesus* before the world began." 1 Pet. i. 20 : "Who (*Christ*) verily was foreordained before the foundation of the world, (προ καταβολης κοσμου,) but was manifest in these last times for you" (Gentiles.) Hence it appears that the whole plan of the Divine mercy in the Gospel, in relation to the method of communicating it, and the person through whose obedience it was to be dispensed, and by whose ministry it was to be executed, was formed in the mind and purpose of God before this earth was created. God, by his perfect and unerring knowledge, foreknew the future state of mankind, and so before appointed the means which he judged proper for their recovery : which foreknowledge is fully confirmed by the promise to *Abraham*, and very copiously by the repeated predictions of the prophets, in relation to our Lord's work, and particularly to his death, with the end and design of it.

118. Again : it is to be noted, that all the forementioned *mercy* and *love*, privileges and blessings, are granted and confirmed to the *Christian* Church under the sanction of a *covenant;* which is *a grant or donation of blessings confirmed by a proper authority.* The Gospel covenant is established by the promise and oath of God, and ratified by the blood of *Christ*, as a pledge and assurance that it is a reality, and will certainly be made good. Matt. xxvi. 28 : "This is my blood of the new *testament*" (or *covenant.*) Luke xxii. 20 :

" This cup is the new *testament* (*covenant*) in my blood." 2 Cor. iii. 6 : " Made us able ministers of the new *testament*" (*covenant*.) Heb. vii. 22 : " Jesus made a surety of a better *testament*." Heb. viii. 6 : " He is the mediator of a better *covenant*, established upon better promises ;" viii. 8 ; ix. 15 ; xii. 24 ; xiii. 20. Here observe : 1. Jesus is the *surety*, (Εγγυος,) sponsor, and mediator (Μεσιτης) of the new *covenant*, as he is the great agent appointed of God to negotiate, transact, secure, and execute all the blessings which are conferred by this covenant. Obs. 2. That as the covenant is a donation or grant of blessing, hence it is that the *promise* or *promiser*, is sometimes put for *the covenant ;* as, Gal. iii. 17, 18 : " The *covenant* that was confirmed before (to Abraham) of God in Christ, the law, which was four hundred and thirty years after, cannot disannul, that it should make the *promise* of none effect : for if the inheritance be of the law, it is no more of *promise*. But God gave it to Abraham by *promise ;*" and so, ver. 19. Again ver. 21 : " Is the law then against the *promises* of God ?" ver. 22. Obs. 3. That the Gospel covenant was included in that made with *Abraham*, Gen. xvii. 1, &c. ; xxii. 16, 17, 18 ; as appears from Gal. iii. 17 ; and from Heb. vi. 13 : " When God made *the promise* to Abraham, because he could swear by no greater, he *sware* by himself," &c. Ver. 17, 18 : " He confirmed (εμεσιτευσεν, he mediatored) it by an *oath ;* that by two immutable things (the promise and oath of God) we (*Christians*) might have strong consolation, who have fled for refuge to lay hold on the hope set before us."

119. But what should carefully and specially be observed is this, that the Gospel constitution is a scheme, and the most perfect and effectual scheme, for restoring true religion, and for promoting virtue and happiness, that the world has ever yet seen. Upon faith in *Christ*, men of all nations were admitted into the Church, family, kingdom, and covenant of God by *baptism ;* were all numbered among the *justified, regenerate or born again, sanctified, saved, chosen, called, saints, and beloved ; were all of the flock, Church, house, vine,* and *vineyard* of God ; and were entitled to the *ordinances* and *privileges* of the Church ; had *exceeding great and precious promises given unto them*, especially that of entering into the *rest* of heaven. And in all these blessings and honours we are certainly very happy, as they are *the things which are* freely *given to us of God*, 1 Cor. ii. 12. But because these things are *freely* given, without respect to any *obedience* or *righteousness* of ours, prior to the donation of them, is our *obedience* and *personal righteousness* therefore unnecessary ! Or are we, on account of benefits already received, secure of the favour and blessing of God in a future world and for ever ? By no means.

120. To explain this important point more clearly, I shall proceed as before, and show that these privileges and blessings, given in general to the Christian Church, are ANTECEDENT blessings ; given indeed *freely*, without any respect to the prior obedience of the *Gentile* world, before they were taken into the Church ; but intended to be motives to the most upright obedience for the future, after they were joined to the family and kingdom of God. Which effect if they produce, then our *election* and *calling*, our *redemption, adoption*, &c., are made good : upon which account I shall call them CONSEQUENT blessings ; because they are secured to us, and made ours for ever, only in consequence of our obedience. But, on the other hand, if the *antecedent* blessings do not produce obedience to the will of God ; if we, his *chosen* people and *children*, do not obey the laws and rules of the Gospel ; then we, as well as any other wicked persons, may expect *tribulation and wrath ;* then we forfeit all our privileges, and all our honours and relations to God ; all the favour and promises given freely to us are of no avail ; we *receive the grace of God in vain*, and everlasting death will certainly be our wretched portion.

121. That this is the great end of the dispensation of God's grace to the *Christian* Church—namely, to engage us to duty and obedience, and that it is a *scheme for promoting virtue* and true religion, is clear from every part of the New Testament, and requires a large and particular proof ; not because the thing in itself is difficult or intricate, but because it is of great importance to the right understanding of the Gospel and the apostolic writings, and serves to explain several points which stand in close relation to it ; as, particularly, that all the forementioned privileges belong to all professed *Christians*, even to those that shall perish eternally. For—

1. If the apostles affirm them of *all* Christians, to whom they write ;

2. If they declare some of those *Christians* who were favoured with those privileges to be wicked, or suppose they might be wicked ;

3. If they declare those privileges are conferred by mere grace, without regard to prior *works of righteousness ;*

4. If they plainly intimate those privileges are conferred in order to produce true holiness ;

5. If they exhort all to use them to that purpose, as they will answer it to God at the last day ;

6. If they declare they shall perish, if they do not improve them to the purifying their hearts, and the right ordering of their conversation ; then it must be true that these privileges belong to all *Christians*, and are intended to induce them to a holy life. And the truth of all those six particulars will sufficiently appear, if we attend to the Gospels and epistles.

§ IX. *Conclusions from the preceding Discourse.*

122. Though, in the foregoing collection I have faithfully and impartially endeavoured to give the true sense of every text, yet possibly, in some few that are doubtful, I may have erred. But there are so many indisputably plain and full to the purpose as will, I am persuaded, sufficiently justify the following conclusions :—

123. I. That the Gospel is a scheme for restoring true religion, and for promoting virtue and happiness.

124. II. That *election, adoption, vocation, salvation, justification, sanctification, regeneration,* and the other blessings, honours, and privileges, which come under the head of ANTECEDENT *blessings,* do, in a sense, be long at present to all *Christians,* even those who, for their wickedness, may perish eternally.

125. III. That those *antecedent blessings,* as they are offered and assigned to the whole body of *Christians,* do not import an absolute final state of favour and happiness, but are to be considered as displays, instances, and descriptions of God's love and goodness to us, which are to operate as a moral mean upon our hearts. They are a display of the love of God, who is the FATHER of the universe, who cannot but delight in the well-being of his creatures, and, being perfect in goodness, possessed of all power, and the only original of all life and happiness, must be the *prime* author of all blessedness, and bestow his favours in the most free, generous, and disinterested manner; and therefore those blessings, as freely bestowed antecedently to our obedience, are perfectly consonant to the nature and moral character of God. He has freely, in our first birth and creation, given us a distinguished and eminent degree of being, and all the noble powers and advantage of reason : and what should stop the course of his liberality, or hinder his conferring new and higher blessings, even when we could pretend no title or claim to them? And as the blessings of the Gospel are of the most noble kind, raising us to high dignity, and the most delightful prospects of immortality, they are well adapted to engage the attention of men, to give the most pleasing ideas of God, to demonstrate most clearly, what nature itself discovers, that he is our FATHER, and to win and engage our hearts to him in love, who has, in a manner so surprising, loved us. By promising the remission of sins, protection and guidance through this world, and the hope of eternal life, every cloud, discouragement, and obstacle is removed ; and the *grace of God,* in its brightest glory, shines full upon our minds, and is divinely powerful to support our patience and animate our obedience under temptations, trials, and difficulties ; and to inspire peace of conscience, comfort, and joy.

126. IV. These principles ought to be admitted and claimed by all *Christians,* and firmly established in their hearts, as containing privileges and blessings in which they are all undoubtedly interested ; otherwise it is evident they will be defective in the true principles of their religion, the only ground of their *Christian* joy and peace, and the proper motives of their *Christian* obedience. Now those principles (namely, our *election, vocation, justification, regeneration, sanctification,* &c., in *Christ,* through the free *grace* of God) are ad mitted and duly established in our hearts by FAITH. *Faith,* then, as exercised upon the blessings which God has gratuitously bestowed upon us, is, in our hearts, the foundation of the Christian life ; and retaining and exercising this *Christian* virtue of *faith* is called *tasting that the Lord is gracious,* 1 Pet. ii. 3. *Having** (or holding fast) grace,* Heb. xii. 28. *Growing in grace,* 2 Pet. iii. 18. *Being strong in the grace of Jesus Christ,* 2 Tim. ii. 1. *Holding faith,* 1 Tim. i. 19 ; iii. 9. *Continuing in the faith, grounded and settled, and not being moved away from the hope of the Gospel,* Col. i. 23. *Holding fast the confidence and rejoicing of hope,* Heb. iii. 6. *Holding the beginning of our confidence steadfast,* Heb. iii. 14. *Having* (holding) *hope,* 1 John iii. 3. *Hoping perfectly for the grace that is to be brought unto us at the revelation of Jesus Christ,* 1 Pet. i. 13. *Giving earnest heed to the things we have heard,* Heb. ii. 1. *Having* (holding) *the Son,* or *Christ,* 1 John v. 12. By *these,* and such-like phrases, the apostles express our being thoroughly persuaded of, and duly affected with, the blessings included in our *election, vocation, justification,* &c. : or, their being firmly established in our hearts as principles of obedience, to secure our perseverance and final happiness, *through the mighty working of God's power ;* to purify our hearts, and to guard us through all our spiritual dangers and conflicts ; which power will always assuredly attend every one who *holds faith, grace, and hope,* 1 Pet. i. 5. Here note, that the *primary object* of faith is not in ourselves, but in God. Not our own obedience or goodness, but the *free grace of God,* is the primary object of faith. But the *fruit* of faith must be in ourselves. The grace or free gift of God is the foundation of faith ; and faith is the foundation of the whole life of a true Christian. 2 Pet. i. 5, 6, 7 : " Giving all diligence, add to your FAITH virtue," &c. Jude 20 : " Building up yourselves on your most holy FAITH," &c.

127. These *antecedent blessings* are the first *principles* of the *Christian* religion ; but the first principles of religion must be free from all doubt or scruple, otherwise the religion which is built upon them must sink, as having no foundation. The principles of *natural* religion—that I am endowed with a rational nature, that there is a God in whom I live, move, and have my being, and to whom I am accountable for my actions, are perfectly evident ; otherwise the obligations of natural religion would be necessarily doubtful and uncertain. In like manner, the first principles of the *Christian* religion must be free from all perplexity, otherwise its obligations must be doubtful and perplexed. If it be doubtful whether ever *Christ* came into the world to redeem it, the whole Gospel is doubtful ; and it is the same thing, if it be doubtful *who* are *redeemed* by him ; for, if he has redeemed we know not *whom,* it is nearly the same thing, with regard to our improvement of redemption, as if he had redeemed no body at all.

128. Faith is the first act of the *Christian* life to which every *Christian* is obliged, and therefore it must have a *sure* and *certain object* to work upon ; but if the *love of God* in our *election, calling, adoption, justification,* redemption, &c., be in itself *uncertain* to *any persons* in the *Christian* Church, then faith has no sure nor certain object to work upon with respect to some *Christians ;* and consequently, some *Christians* are not obliged to believe ; which is false.

---

* Εχειν, *to have,* in such passages signifies to *keep* or *hold,* as a property or principle for use. Matt. xiii. 12 ; xxv. 29 ; John iii. 29 ; v. 42 ; viii. 12 ; Rom. i. 28 ; xv. 4 ; 1 Thess. iii. 6 ; 1 Tim. i. 19 ; iii. 9 ; Heb. vi. 9 ; ix. 4 ; 1 John ii. 23 ; iii. 3 ; v. 12 ; 2 John ver. 9.

129. Farther, the apostles make our *election, calling, adoption,* &c., motives to obedience and holiness. And therefore these (our *election, calling, adoption,* &c.) must have an existence antecedent to our obedience; otherwise they can be no motive to it. And if only an *uncertain, unknown number* of men be elected to eternal life, no *individual* can certainly know that *he* is of that number; and so, *election* can be no motive to obedience to any person in the *Christian* Church. To confine *election, adoption,* &c., to some *few* is unchurching the greatest part of the Church, and robbing them of common motives and comforts.

130. Our *election, adoption,* and other *antecedent* blessings, are not of *works;* consequently we are not to work *for* them, but *upon* them. They are not the *effect* of our good works, but our good works are the *effect* of *them;* they are not founded upon our *holiness,* but our *holiness* is founded upon *them.* We do not procure them by our *obedience,* for they are the effect of *free grace;* but they are *motives* and *reasons* exciting and encouraging our obedience; therefore our *election* is not proved by our *sanctification,* or real holiness. Our real holiness proves that our *election is made sure;* but our *election* itself is proved by the free grace of God.

131. From all this it follows that *we,* as well as the *Christians* of the first times, may claim and appropriate to ourselves all the forementioned *antecedent* blessings without any doubt or scruple. In confidence of hope and full assurance of faith we may boldly say, " the Lord is my helper," and come with boldness to the throne of grace. Our life, even eternal life, is sure to every one of us in the promise of God, and the hands of our *Lord Jesus Christ.* And the business of every Christian is, not to perplex himself with doubts and fears, and gloomy apprehensions, but to rejoice in the Lord, and to do the duties of his place cheerfully and faithfully, in the assured hope of eternal life through *Jesus Christ,* to whom be everlasting glory and praise. Amen.*

132. V. From the preceding collection of texts we may gather that some of the expressions whereby the *antecedent* blessings are signified, such as *elect, justify, sanctify,* &c., may be used in a double sense; namely, either as they are applied to all *Christians* in general, in relation to their being translated into the kingdom of God, and made his peculiar people, enjoying the privileges of the Gospel; or, as they signify the *effects* of those privileges. Wherever any blessing is assigned to all *Christians,* without exception; wherever it is said not to be of *works;* wherever Christians are expected to make a due improvement of it, and threatened with the loss of God's blessing and of eternal life if they do not; there, the expressions which signify that blessing are to be understood in a general sense, as denoting a Gospel privilege, profession, or obligation. And in this general sense, *saved, elect, chosen, justified, sanctified,* are *sometimes* used; and *calling, called, election,* are, I think, *always* used in the New Testament. But when any blessing denotes real holiness as actually existing in the subject, then it *may* be understood in the *special* and *eminent* sense, and always *must* be understood in this sense when it implies the actual possession of eternal life; and in this sense, *saved, elect, chosen, justify, sanctify, born of God,* are *sometimes* used. Matt. xx. 16: " Many are *called,* but few are *chosen*" (who make a worthy use of their calling.) Matt. xxiv. 31: " He shall send his angels with a great sound of a trumpet, and they shall gather together his *elect.*" xii. 36, 37: " In the day of judgment, by thy words thou shalt be *justified,* and by thy words thou shalt be condemned." 1 Thess. v. 25: " The God of peace *sanctify* you wholly," &c. 1 John ii. 29: " Every one that doth righteousness is *born of him.*" iv. 7: " Every one that loveth is *born of God,*" in the *eminent* sense.

133. The *faith* which gave a person a place or standing in the Christian Church was a *profession* considered simply and separately from the *fruits* and *effects* of it; but it included a profession of repentance, of forsaking sin and idolatry, and of bringing forth the fruits of righteousness. And it is the *continued* profession of this faith in Christ which gives us a continued right to a place in the Church: for, if we cast off our first faith, we renounce our *profession,* we cease to be *Christians,* or we no longer continue to be the *peculiar family* of God.

134. Here it should be carefully observed that it is very common in the sacred writings to express not only our Christian privileges, but also the duty to which they oblige in the *present* or *preterperfect* tense; or to speak of that as *done,* which only *ought to be done,* and which, in fact, may possibly *never* be done. Mal. i. 6: " A son honours (ought to honour) his father." Matt. v. 13: " Ye are (ought to be) the salt of the earth; but if the salt have lost his savour," &c. Rom. ii. 4: " The goodness of God leads (ought to lead) thee to repentance;" Rom. vi. 2, 11; viii. 9; Col. iii. 3. 1 Pet. i. 6: " Wherein ye (ought) greatly (to) rejoice." 2 Cor. iii. 18: " We all with open face (enjoying the means of) beholding as in a glass the glory of the Lord, are (ought to be—enjoy the means of being) changed into the same image, from glory to glory." 1 Cor. v. 7: " Purge out the old leaven, that ye may be a new lump, as ye are (obliged by the Christian profession to be) unleavened." Heb. xiii. 14: " We seek (we ought to seek, or, according to our profession, we seek) a city to come;" 1 John ii. 12, 15; iii. 9; v. 4, 18, and in various other places.

135. The man of true goodness, courage, and greatness of soul, is he who has that *faith which worketh by love;* who lives the life he now lives by *faith in the Son of God.* Such a man is happy under all events. This is he, who while he despises a vain life, has the truest and highest enjoyment of all that can be enjoyed in it. This is the man who alone properly *lives,* for he has nothing but *life* and *immortality* before him; *death* itself giving no interruption to his life. Blessed, unspeakably blessed is this man. *Such* the Gospel is

---

* This is all right, when the sinner has been led, by a deep knowledge of his lost estate, to seek and find redemption in the blood of the Lamb: then it is his business to rejoice in the Lord and to do the duties of his place cheerfully and faithfully, in the assured hope of eternal life through Jesus Christ. But he must not presume, because he is in a Christian Church, and believes the doctrines of Christianity, that therefore he is safe. He cannot be safe unless Christ be formed in his heart, the hope of glory.—A. C.

designed to make us all ; and such we all may be, if we do not shamefully neglect the grace of God and our own happiness. But the knowledge and sense of these things are generally lost among those called Christians, to whom the words of the psalmist may be too truly applied : *They are a people that do err in their hearts, for they have not known my ways*, Psa. xcv. 10.

136. From all the preceding observations and arguments we may clearly see what is implied in *preaching Christ*. It is not teaching that only a *small, uncertain* number among *Christians* are ARBITRARILY *redeemed, elected, called, adopted, born again*, or *regenerated ;* and that all the rest are, by a *sovereign, absolute, eternal* DECREE, *passed by*, or *reprobated*. These are no principles of Christianity, but stand in direct contradiction to them, and have drawn a dark veil over the grace of the Gospel, sunk the Christian world into an abject state of fear and a false superstitious humility ; and thrown ministers into endless absurdities.——"It is such doctrines as these that have misrepresented the Christian religion, harassed the Christian world endlessly, by blending and confounding men's understandings and embittering their spirits ; and have been the reason of, calling in a false kind of learning, *logic, metaphysics*, and *school divinity*, in order to give a colour of reason to the grossest absurdities, and to enable divines to make a plausible show of supporting and defending palpable contradictions."——See Dr. *Taylor's* Key to the Apostolical Writings.

30   2

A GENERAL SURVEY

OF THE

EPISTLE TO THE ROMANS.

PAUL had never been at *Rome* when he wrote this letter, and therefore it cannot turn upon some *particular points*, to revive the remembrance of what he had more largely taught in *person*, or to satisfy the scrupulous in some things he might not have touched upon at all; but in it we may expect a full account of his Gospel, or those glad tidings of salvation which he preached among the *Gentiles*, seeing this epistle was intended to supply the total want of his preaching at *Rome*.

He understood perfectly well the system of religion he taught, for he was instructed in it by the immediate *revelation of Jesus Christ*, Gal. i. 11; Eph. iii. 3; 1 Cor. xi. 23; and being also endowed with the most eminent gifts of the Holy Spirit; a man disinterested and quite unbiassed by any temporal considerations, we may be sure he has given us the truth, as he received it from our Lord, after his ascension. On the other hand, he was also well acquainted with the sentiments and system of religion which he opposed, for he was well skilled in *Jewish* literature, having had the best education his country could afford, and having been once a most zealous advocate for *Judaism*. Having frequently disputed with the *Jews* he was thoroughly versed in the controversy, and knew very well what would be retorted upon every point: and therefore we may very reasonably suppose that the queries and objections, which the apostle in this epistle puts into the mouth of the *Jews*, were really such as *had been advanced* in opposition to his arguments.

He was a great genius and a fine writer; and he seems to have exercised all his talents, as well as the most perfect *Christian* temper, in drawing up this epistle. The plan of it is very extensive; and it is surprising to see what a spacious field of knowledge he has comprised, and how many various designs, arguments, explications, instructions, and exhortations, he has executed in so small a compass.

This letter was sent to the world's *metropolis*, where it might be exposed to all sorts of persons, *Heathens, Jews, Christians, philosophers, magistrates,* and the *emperor* himself: and I make no doubt that the apostle kept this in view while he was writing, and guarded and adapted it accordingly.

However, it is plain enough it was designed to confute the *unbelieving* and to instruct the *believing Jew;* to confirm the *Christian* and to convert the idolatrous *Gentile.* Those several designs he reduces to one scheme, by opposing and arguing with the *infidel* or *unbelieving Jew* in favour of the *Christian* or *believing Gentile.*

Upon this plan, if the *unbelieving Jew* escaped and remained unconvinced, yet the *Christian Jew* would be more inoffensively and more effectually instructed in the nature of the Gospel, and the kind brotherly regards he ought to have to the *believing Gentiles*, than if he had directed his discourse plainly and immediately to him. But if his arguments should fail in reference to the *believing Jew*, yet the *believing Gentile* would see his interest in the covenant and kingdom of God as solidly established, by a full confutation of the Jewish objections, (which were the only objections that could, with any show of reason, be advanced against it,) as if the epistle had been written for no other purpose. And thus it is of the greatest use to us at this day.

It is also at present exceeding useful, as it entirely demolishes the engrossing pretensions and imposing principles of the Church of *Rome.* For, a professed faith in *Christ*, and a subjection to *him*, is, in this epistle, fully shown to be the only Gospel condition of a place in his Church, an interest in the covenant of God, and of Christian fellowship. By this extensive principle God broke down the pales of his own ancient inclosure, the *Jewish* Church; and therefore, by the same principle, more strongly forbids the building any other partition wall of schemes and terms of Christian fellowship, devised by human wisdom or imposed by human authority. He then who professes faith in *Christ* and subjection to him is, by the apostle, allowed and demonstrated to be a member of the true visible Church, and to have a right to all its privileges.

Both ancients and moderns make heavy complaints of the obscurity of this epistle, though all agree it is a great and useful performance. *Origen*, one of the fathers, compares our apostle to a person who leads a stranger into a magnificent palace, but, perplexed with various cross and intricate passages, and many remote and secret apartments, shows him some things at a distance, out of an opulent treasury; brings some things near to his view; conceals others from it; often enters in at one door, and comes out at another; so that the stranger is surprised, and wonders *whence* he came, *where* he is, and *how* he shall get out. But we shall have a tolerable idea of this princely structure if we observe that it consists of four grand parts or divisions. The *first* division contains the five first chapters; the *second*, the sixth, seventh, and eighth; the *third*, the ninth, tenth, and eleventh; the *fourth*, the five last chapters.

PART I.—Displays the riches of Divine grace, as free to all mankind. *Jews* and *Gentiles* are equally sinful and obnoxious to wrath; and, therefore, there was no way for the *Jew* to be continued in the kingdom of God, but *by* GRACE, *through* FAITH; and by grace and *faith* the Gentile might be admitted into it. To reject this way of justification was to reject the very method in which *Abraham* himself was justified, or interested in the covenant made with him: in which covenant believing *Gentiles* were included, as well as believing *Jews*, and had as great or greater privileges to glory in. But if the Jew should pertinaciously deny that, he could not deny that all mankind are interested in the grace of God, which removes the consequences of *Adam's* offence. Through that offence all mankind were subjected to death; and through *Christ's* obedience all mankind should be restored to life at the last day. The resurrection from the dead is, therefore, a part of the grace of God in the Redeemer; and if all mankind have an interest in this part of the grace of God, why not in the whole of it? If all mankind were subjected to death through *Adam's* one offence, is it not much more reasonable that, through the opposite nobler cause, the obedience of the Son of God, all mankind should be interested in the whole of the grace which God has established upon it? And as for *law*, or the rule of right action, it was absurd for any part of mankind to expect pardon or any blessedness upon the foot of that, seeing all mankind had broken it; and it was still more absurd to seek pardon and life by the law of *Moses*, which condemned those that were under it to death for *every* transgression.

PART II.—Having proved that believing *Jews* and *Gentiles* were pardoned, and interested in all the privileges and blessings of the Gospel, through mere grace, he next shows the obligations laid upon them to a life of virtue and piety under the new dispensation. And upon this subject he adapts this discourse to the *Gentile Christians* in the sixth chapter; and in the seventh, and part of the eighth, he turns himself to the *Jewish Christians*; then, from verse 12 to the end of the eighth chapter, he addresses himself upon the same head to both *Christian Jews* and *Gentiles*; particularly giving them right notions of the sufferings to which they were exposed, and by which they might be deterred from the duties required in the Gospel; and concluding with a very strong and lively assertion of the certain perseverance of all who love God, notwithstanding any infirmities or trials in this world.

PART III.—Gives right sentiments concerning the rejection of the *Jews*, which was a matter of great moment to the due establishment of the *Gentile* converts.

PART IV.—Is filled with exhortations to several instances of *Christian* duty; and concludes with salutations to and from particular persons. It will be an advantage to the reader to have this sketch of the epistle ready in his thoughts.

Farther; we cannot enter into the spirit of this epistle unless we enter into the spirit of a *Jew* in those times, and have some just notion of his utter aversion to the *Gentiles*; his valuing and raising himself high upon his relation to God, and to *Abraham*; upon his law and pompous worship, circumcision, &c., as if the *Jews* were the only people in the world who had any manner of right to the favour of God.

And let it also be well noted, that the apostle in this epistle disputes with the whole body of the *Jews*, without respect to any particular sect or party among them, such as *Pharisees, Sadducees*, &c.; for the grand proposition or question in debate is, Are WE Jews *better than* THEY *Gentiles?* (chap. iii. 9.) And one argument in proof of the negative which the apostle espouses is this (chap. iii. 29:) "Is God the God of the *Jews* only? Is he not also of the *Gentiles?* Yes, of the Gentiles also." These are the two points through which the line of the apostle's discourse in the third chapter, and consequently in all the argumentative part of the epistle, must necessarily run: and as, both in the *proposition* and in the *argument*, he evidently means the whole body of the *Jews*, in opposition to the whole body of the *Gentiles*, he who doth not give such a sense of the apostle's discourse throughout the argumentative part of the epistle as exactly hits and suits this general, collective notion of *Jews* and *Gentiles*, certainly misses his aim, and shoots wide of the mark.

Lastly, the whole epistle is to be taken in connection, or considered as one continued discourse; and the sense of every part must be taken from the drift of the whole. Every sentence, or verse, is not to be regarded as a distinct mathematical proposition or theorem, or as a sentence in the book of *Proverbs*, whose sense is absolute and independent of what goes before or comes after: but we must remember that every sentence, especially in the argumentative part, bears relation to, and is dependent upon, the whole discourse, and cannot be understood unless we understand the scope and drift of the *whole*; and therefore the whole epistle, or at least the eleven first chapters of it, ought to be read over at *once*, without stopping.

As to the use and excellency of this epistle, I shall leave it to speak for itself when the reader has studied and well digested the contents of it. And methinks curiosity, if nothing else, should invite us to examine carefully the doctrine by which (accompanied with the gifts and operations of the Spirit of God) a few men, otherwise naked, weak, and contemptible, in opposition to the power, learning, and deep-rooted prejudices of the world, confronted and overthrew the *Pagan* religion and idolatry throughout the *Roman empire*: a victory far more difficult and surprising than all the achievements of *Alexander* and *Cæsar*. The fact cannot be denied. And surely the dignity and virtue of the cause must be proportionable to such an unusual and wonderful event. It is certain the world never, either before or since, has seen any thing equal to the writings of the *New Testament*. Never was the love of God, and the dignity to which he has raised the human nature, so clearly shown and demonstrated; never were motives so Divine and powerful proposed to induce us to the practice of all virtue and goodness. In short, there we find whatever ennobles and adorns the mind; whatever gives solid peace and joy; whatever renders us the most excellent and happy creatures; taught, recommended, and enforced by light and authority derived from the only fountain of truth and of all good.

As to the apostle's *manner of writing*, it is with great spirit and force, I may add, perspicuity too; for it will not be difficult to understand him if our minds are unprejudiced and at liberty to attend to the subject he is upon, and to the current Scriptural sense of the words he uses; for he keeps very strictly to the standard of Scripture phraseology. He takes great care to guard and explain every part of his subject; and I may venture to say he has left no part of it unexplained or unguarded. Never was author more exact and cautious in this than he. Sometimes he writes notes upon a sentence liable to exception and wanting explanation, as Rom. ii. 12—16; here the 13th and 15th verses are a comment upon the former part of it. Sometimes he comments upon a single word, as chap. x. 11, 12, 13; the 12th and 13th verses are a comment upon πας *every one*, in the 11th.

He was studious of a perspicuous brevity. Chap. v. 13, 14: "For until the law, sin was in the world; but sin is not imputed when law is not in being. Nevertheless death reigned from *Adam* to *Moses*, even over them that had not sinned after the likeness of *Adam's* transgression." Surely never was a greater variety of useful sentiments crowded into a smaller compass, and yet so skilfully, that one part very clearly explains another. Hence we learn: 1. That here *imputing* of *sin* means, men's being subject to death for sin; for it follows, *Nevertheless death reigned*. 2. That *law* is the constitution that subjects the sinner to death; for he saith, *Sin is not imputed when law is not in being*. 3. That *until the law*, is the times before the law of *Moses* was given; for he saith, *Nevertheless death reigned from* Adam to Moses. *Until the law*, is the same as *until* Moses. 4. That law was not in being from *Adam* to *Moses*; for having said, *when law is not in being*, he immediately adds, *nevertheless death reigned from* Adam *to* Moses. 5. That *Adam* was under the law; for if the law was not in being from *Adam*, or after the dispensation he was under, it is plain it was in being before; or, that law was the dispensation under which God placed *Adam*. 6. That the clause, *even over those that had not sinned after the likeness of* Adam's *transgression*, is not to be understood only of some particular persons, as *infants*, but of all that lived from *Adam* to *Moses*; because none that lived from *Adam* to *Moses* were under the law, and so none could *sin after the likeness of* Adam's transgression. 7. That the law was in being after *Moses*; for it was not in being from *Adam* to *Moses*, which evidently supposes it was in being *afterwards*; and that the *Jews*, from that time, sinned after the likeness of *Adam's* transgression, or were by the law condemned to death for every transgression. 8. Lastly, from the whole it is evident that from *Adam* to *Moses* men did not die for their own personal transgressions, but in consequence of Adam's one transgression, which is the point to be proved. One shall hardly find in any other author an *argument* so justly managed, so fully established, attended with such a variety of instructive sentiments in the compass of thirty words; for setting aside the articles, there are no more in the *Greek*. It is by this unparalleled art that the apostle has brought such a variety of arguments, instructions, and sentiments, all stated, proved, and sufficiently guarded, explained, and defended, within the limits of this letter; which has made it a magazine of the most real, extensive, useful, and profitable knowledge.

He treats his countrymen, the *Jews*, with great caution and tenderness. He had a natural affection for them, was very desirous of winning them over to the Gospel; he knew that their passions and prejudices were very strong for their own constitution; therefore, in his debates with them he avoids every thing harsh, introduces every kind and endearing sentiment, and is very nice in choosing soft and inoffensive expressions, *so far as he honestly could*, for he never flatters, nor dissembles the truth.

His transitions and advances to an ungrateful subject are very dexterous and apposite, as chap. ii. 1—17; viii. 17.

He often carries on a complicated design, and while he is teaching one thing, gives us an opportunity of learning one or two more. So, chap. xiii. 1—8, he teaches the duty of *subjects*, and at the same time instructs *magistrates* in their duty, and shows the true grounds of their authority.

He is a nervous reasoner and a close writer, who never loses sight of his subject, and who throws in every colour that may enliven it.

He writes under a deep and lively sense of the truth and importance of the Gospel, as a man who clearly understood it, and in whose heart and affections it reigned far superior to all temporal considerations. See DR. TAYLOR's Preface to the Romans.

There is so much good sense and sound criticism in the above remarks, that I cannot help considering them of high importance to a proper understanding of this epistle. The apostle's *manner* of writing is here well vindicated, and proved to be *close*, *nervous*, and *conclusive*; and such a testimony from such a man as Dr. Taylor must, with every unprejudiced reader, outweigh the miserable sentiment of that philosopher who, while professing to hold the same creed with the above writer, has had the awful temerity to say that St. Paul was "an inconclusive reasoner." By such a saying, a man fixes the broad seal to his own incompetency to judge either of the apostle's writings or doctrine.

In the preceding pages I have borrowed largely from the work of Dr. Taylor, on a full conviction that it is the best ever written upon this subject, that it is indispensably necessary to a proper understanding of the apostolic writings; and that I could not hope to equal it by any production of my own. Those parts of his *Key* which did not fall in with my plan I have taken the liberty to pass by; the rest I have greatly abridged, and only added a few notes where I thought there might be any danger of misapprehending the subject.*

May 21, 1814.

A. C.

* On this subject a learned and judicious friend wrote as follows:—

"I find there is a hue and cry raised about Dr. Taylor. I have not yielded to my antagonists, and I will still dare to think for myself. I tell them I would go as far as I can with the pope, or any man; yea, with the devil, when he speaks truth, (which he sometimes does.) If these persons alluded to would attentively read and compare the texts in the Old Testament quoted by Dr. Taylor in his *Key*, it would lead them to a more clear understanding of St. Paul in his Epistle to the Romans than they ever had before. And I think this *Key* is better than any thing my friend himself could have written upon the subject. But the cry is, 'An Arian, an Arian!' Prejudice shuts up the mind against truth; but let truth be defended wherever it may be found. It is easy to perceive that a certain class of men would reject Dr. Taylor's *Key* because it cuts up the very foundation of their system. Go on in the strength of God; and in all things act with a single eye to his glory. Vive valeque.

J. C.

"13th March, 1815."

(3**)

THE

EPISTLE OF PAUL THE APOSTLE

TO

THE ROMANS.

Year of the Constantinopolitan Æra of the World, 5566.—Year of the Alexandrian Æra of the World, 5560.—Year of the Antiochian Æra of the World, 5550.—Year of the Julian Period, 4768.—Year of the Usherian Æra of the World, 4062.—Year of the two hundred and ninth Olympiad, 2.—Year from the building of Rome, according to the Roman account, 811.—Year of the Æra of the Seleucidæ, 370.—Year of the Cæsarean Æra of Antioch, 106.—Year of the Julian Æra, 103.—Year of the Spanish Æra, 96.—Year from the birth of Christ, 62.—Year of the vulgar Æra of Christ's nativity, 58.—Year of the Dionysian Period, or Easter Cycle, 59.—Year of the Grecian Cycle of nineteen years, 2, or the first embolismic.—Year of the Jewish Cycle of nineteen years, 18.—Year of the Solar Cycle, 11.—Dominical Letter, A.—Epact, or the Moon's age at the commencement of the year, 11.—Jewish Passover, Saturday, March 25.—Easter Sunday, March 26.—Year after Bissextile, or Leap-year, 2.—Year of the reign of the Emperor Nero Cæsar, 5.—Year of Claudius Felix, the Jewish Governor, 6.—Year of the reign of Vologesus, king of the Parthians, 9.—Year of Caius Numidius Quadratus, Governor of Syria, 8.—High Priest of the Jews, Joseph.—Consuls, Nero Augustus the third time, and Valerius Messala.

CHAPTER I.

St. Paul shows the Romans his Divine call to the apostleship, and for what end he was thus called, 1–6. His salutation to the Church at Rome, and his commendation of their faith, 7, 8. His earnest desire to see them, that he might impart to them some spiritual gifts, 9–15. His description of the Gospel of Christ, 16, 17. The crimes and profligacy of the Gentile world, which called aloud for the judgments of God, 18–32.

A. M. cir. 4062.
A. D. cir. 58.
An. Olymp.
cir. CCIX. 2.
A. U. C. cir. 811.

PAUL, a servant of Jesus Christ, [a] called *to be* an apostle, [b] separated unto the Gospel of God,

2 ([c] Which he had promised afore [d] by his prophets in the holy Scriptures,)

3 Concerning his Son Jesus

A. M. cir. 4062.
A. D. cir. 58.
An. Olymp.
cir. CCIX. 2.
A. U. C. cir. 811.

---

[a] Acts xxii. 21; 1 Cor. i. 1; Gal. i. 1; 1 Tim. i. 11; ii. 7; 2 Tim. i. 11.

[b] Acts ix. 15; xiii. 2; Gal. i. 15.——[c] See on Acts xxvi. 6; Tit. i. 2.——[d] Chap. iii. 21; xvi. 26; Gal. iii. 8.

PRELIMINARY OBSERVATIONS.

DIFFERENT interpreters have divided this epistle into certain parts or divisions, by which they suppose its subject and matter may be the better understood. Some of these divisions have been mentioned in the preceding *preface.*

The epistle contains *three* grand divisions.

I. The PREFACE, chap. i. 1–17.

II. The TRACTATION, or setting forth of the main subject, including two sections : 1. *Dogmatic,* or what relates to *doctrine.* 2. *Parænetic,* or what relates to the necessity and importance of the *virtues* and *duties* of the Christian life. The *dogmatic* part is included in the first *eleven chapters,* the grand object of which is to show that eternal salvation cannot be procured by any *observance* of the *Jewish law,* and can be hoped for only on the *Christian scheme;* for by the *works of*

the law no man can be justified ; but *what the law could not do, in that it was weak through the flesh,* God has accomplished by *sending his Son* into the world, who, becoming an *offering for sin, condemned sin in the flesh.* The *parænetic* part commences with chap. xii. 1 : *I beseech you, therefore, brethren, by the mercies of God, that ye present your bodies a living sacrifice, holy, acceptable unto God, which is your reasonable service, &c.;* and extends to chap. xv. 14.

III. The *peroration* or *epilogue,* which contains the author's apology for writing; his commendation of his apostolical office ; his promise to visit them; his request of an interest in their prayers; his commendations of certain persons, and his salutations to others. These points are contained in the succeeding parts of the epistle, from chap. xv. 14 to chap. xvi. 24. The 25th, 26th, and 27th verses of this chapter evidently

2

| A. M. cir. 4062.
 A. D. cir. 58.
 An. Olymp.
 cir. CCIX. 2.
 A. U. C. cir.
 811. | Christ our Lord, ^e which was ^f made of the seed of David according to the flesh;

 4 And ^g declared ^h *to be* the | Son of God with power, according ⁱ to the spirit of holiness, by the resurrection from the dead: | A. M. cir. 4062.
 A. D. cir. 58.
 An. Olymp.
 cir. CCIX. 2.
 A. U. C. cir.
 811. |

---

^e Matt. i. 6, 16; Luke i. 32; Acts ii. 30; 2 Tim. ii. 8.——^f John i. 14; | Gal. iv. 4.——^g Gr. *determined.*——^h Acts xiii. 33.——ⁱ Heb. ix. 14.

belong to another part of the epistle, and should come in, as they do in a vast majority of the best MSS., after the 23d verse of chap. xiv.

For every thing necessary to *a general knowledge* of the epistle itself, see the preceding *preface.*

The inscriptions to this epistle are various in the different MSS. and versions. The following are the principal:—*To the Romans*—*The Epistle of Paul to the Romans*—*The Epistle of Paul the Apostle to the Romans*—*The Epistle of the Holy Apostle Paul to the Romans.* The word ἁγιος, *holy*, we have translated *saint;* and thus, instead of saying *the holy Paul*, &c., we say *Saint Paul*, &c.; and this is now brought into general use. The older the MSS. are, the more simple the appellatives given to *apostles* and *apostolic men.*

NOTES ON CHAP. I.

Verse 1. *Paul, a servant of Jesus Christ*] The word δουλος, which we translate *servant*, properly means a *slave*, one who is the *entire property* of his master; and is used here by the apostle with great propriety. He felt he was not *his* own, and that his *life* and *powers* belonged to his heavenly *owner*, and that he had no right to dispose of or employ them but in the strictest subserviency to the will of his Lord. In this sense, and in this spirit, he is the *willing slave* of Jesus Christ; and this is, perhaps, the highest character which any soul of man can attain on this side eternity. " I am wholly the Lord's ; and wholly devoted to the spirit of sacrificial obedience, to the constant, complete, and energetic performance of the Divine will." A *friend* of God is high; a *son* of God is higher; but the *servant*, or, in the above sense, the *slave* of God, is higher than all;—in a word, he is a person who feels he has no property in himself, and that God is all and in all.

Called to be an apostle] The word αποστολος, *apostle*, from αποστελλειν, *to send*, signifies simply a *messenger* or *envoy;* one sent on a confidential errand : but here it means an *extraordinary messenger;* one sent by God himself to deliver the most important message on behalf of his Maker ;—in a word, one sent by the *Divine authority* to preach the Gospel to the nations. The word κλητος, *called*, signifies here the same as *constituted*, and should be joined with αποστολος, as it is in the Greek, and translated thus : *Paul, a servant of Jesus Chist, constituted an apostle*, &c. This sense the word *called* has in many places of the sacred writings; *e. g. Behold what manner of love the Father hath bestowed on us, that we should be called*, κληθωμεν, CONSTITUTED, *or made the sons of God.* As it is likely that no apostle had been employed in founding the Church of Rome, and there was need of much *authority* to settle the matters that were there in dispute, it was necessary he should show them that he derived his authority from *God*, and was immediately delegated by him to *preach* and *write* as he was now doing.

Separated unto the Gospel] Set apart and appointed to this work, and to this only ; as the Israelites were *separate* from all the people of the earth, to be the servants of God : see Lev. xx. 26. St. Paul may here refer to his former state as a *Pharisee*, which literally signifies a *separatist*, or one *separated. Before* he was separated unto the service of his own *sect ;* now he is separated unto the Gospel of God. On the word GOSPEL, and its meaning, see the preface to the notes on St. Matthew ; and for the meaning of the word *Pharisee*, see the same Gospel, chap. iii. at the end.

Verse 2. *Which he had promised afore*] Both in the *law* and in the *prophets* God showed his purpose to introduce into the world a more *perfect* and *glorious* state of things ; which state was to take place by and under the influence of the Messiah, who should bring life and immortality to light by his Gospel.

Verse 3. *Concerning his Son*] That is, the Gospel relates every thing concerning the *conception, birth, preaching, miracles, passion, death, resurrection,* and *ascension* of Jesus Christ, who was of the *seed-royal*, being, as far as his *humanity* was considered, the *son of David*, and *then* the only *rightful heir* to the Israelitish throne.

Verse 4. *And declared* to be *the Son of God*] See the note on Acts xiii. 33, where this subject is considered at large. The word ὁρισθεντος, which we render *declared*, comes from ὁριζω, to *bound, define, determine*, or *limit*, and hence our word *horizon*, the *line* that *determines* the farthest visible part of the earth, in reference to the heavens. In this place the word signifies such a *manifest* and *complete exhibition* of the subject as to render it *indubitable.* The resurrection of Christ from the dead was such a *manifest proof* of our Lord's innocence, the *truth* of his *doctrine*, and the fulfilment of all that the prophets had spoken, as to leave no doubt on any considerate and candid mind.

With power] Εν δυναμει, With a *miraculous* display of Divine energy ; for, how could his body be raised again, but by the miraculous energy of God ? Some apply the word here to the *proof* of Christ's *sonship ;* as if it were said that he was most manifestly declared to be the Son of God, with such powerful evidence and argument as to render the truth irresistible.

According to the spirit of holiness] There are many differences of sentiment relative to the meaning of this phrase in this place ; some supposing that the spirit of holiness implies the *Divine nature* of Jesus Christ ; others, his *immaculate sanctity*, &c. To me it seems that the apostle simply means that the person called Jesus, lately crucified at Jerusalem, and in whose name salvation was preached to the world, was the *Son of God*, the very Messiah promised before in the holy Scriptures ; and that he was this Messiah was amply demonstrated. 1st, By his resurrection from the dead, the irrefragable proof of his purity, innocence, and the

A. M. cir. 4062.
A. D. cir. 58.
An. Olymp.
cir. CCIX. 2.
A. U. C. cir.
811.

5 By whom ᵏ we have received grace and apostleship, ¹ for ᵐ obedience to the faith among all nations, ⁿ for his name :

6 Among whom are ye also the called of Jesus Christ :

7 To all that be in Rome, beloved of God, ° called *to be*

A. M. cir. 4062.
A. D. cir. 58.
An. Olymp.
cir. CCIX. 2.
A. U. C. cir.
811.

ᵏ Chap. xii. 3; xv. 15; 1 Cor. xv. 10; Gal. i. 15; ii. 9: Eph. iii. 8.——¹ Or, *to the obedience of faith.*

ᵐ Acts vi. 7; chap. xvi. 26.——ⁿ Acts ix. 15.——° Chap. ix. 24; 1 Cor. i. 2; 1 Thess. iv. 7.

Divine approbation ; for, had he been a *malefactor*, as the Jews pretended, the miraculous power of God would not have been exerted in raising his body from the dead. 2d, He was proved to be the Son of God, the promised Messiah, by the Holy Spirit, (called here the *spirit of holiness*,) which he sent down upon his apostles, and not on them only, but on all that believed on his name ; by whose influence multitudes were convinced of sin, righteousness, and judgment, and multitudes sanctified unto God ; and it was by the peculiar unction of this *spirit of holiness*, that the apostles gave witness of the resurrection of the Lord Jesus, Acts iv. 33. Thus, then, Christ was proved to be the *true Messiah*, the *son of David according to the flesh*, having the *sole right* to the throne of Israel ; and God recognized this character, and this right, by his resurrection from the dead, and sending forth the various gifts and graces of the Spirit of holiness in his name.

Verse 5. *Grace and apostleship*] The peculiar influence and the essential qualifications which such an *office* requires. Without the GRACE, *favour*, and peculiar help of God, he could not have been an apostle : he had an extraordinary conversion, and an extraordinary call to preach the Gospel. Probably χαριν και αποστολην, *grace and apostleship*, mean the same as χαριν της αποστολης, the *apostolical office* ; for so the word χαρις means in chap. xii. 3 ; xv. 15 ; 1 Cor. iii. 10 ; Eph. iii. 8. See the various acceptations of the word *grace*, on ver. 7.

For obedience to the faith] That by this *office*, which I have received from God, and the *power* by which it is accompanied, I might proclaim the *faith*, the Gospel of Jesus ; and show all nations the necessity of believing in it, in order to their salvation. Here is : 1. The Gospel of the Son of God. 2. An apostle divinely commissioned and empowered to preach it. 3. The necessity of faith in the name of Jesus, as the only Saviour of the world. 4. Of obedience, as the necessary consequence of genuine faith. And, 5. This is to be proclaimed among all nations ; that all might have the opportunity of believing and being saved.

Verse 8. *Ye are the called*] Ye Romans are all *invited* to believe in Christ Jesus, for the salvation of your souls ; and to you, with the rest, my apostolical mission extends. This appears to be the most obvious sense of the word *called* in this place—to be *called by the Gospel* is to be *invited* to believe in Christ Jesus, and become his disciples. The word sometimes means *constituted*, or *made*, as in verse 1

Verse 7. *Called to be saints*] Invited to become holy persons, by believing the Gospel and receiving the gifts of the Holy Ghost. Or, here, the word may have the meaning of *made* or *constituted*, as above ; κλητοις αγιοις, *to all that be in Rome*, CONSTITUTED *saints*, for they had already received the Gospel grace, and were formed into a Christian Church.

Grace to you] Χαρις ὑμιν ; May you be partakers of the *Divine favour*, the *source* whence every blessing *is* derived.

I think it necessary, once for all, to give the several acceptations of this word *grace* which occur in the sacred writings.

1. The word χαριν signifies in general *favour* or *benevolence*, but especially that *favour* which is *powerful* and *active*, and loads its objects with *benefits*. Luke i. 30 : *Fear not, Mary, thou hast found* FAVOUR, χαριν, *with God.* Luke ii. 40 : *And the child grew—and the* GRACE *of God*, χαρις Θεου, the *favour of God was upon him.* Ib. ver. 52 : *And Jesus increased in* FAVOUR, χαριτι, GRACE, *with God and man.* Acts ii. 47 : *Having* FAVOUR, χαριν, GRACE, *with all the people.* Acts iv. 33 : *And great* GRACE, χαρις, FAVOUR, *was upon them all.* The apostles were at that time in universal *favour* with the multitude. In this sense the word occurs in a great variety of places, both in the Old and New Testaments.

2. Hence it is often used for the *blessing* which it *dispenses* ; for, if God be *favourably disposed* towards a person, his *beneficent* acts, in that person's behalf, will be a necessary consequence of such *favour.* John i. 14 : *Full of* GRACE *and truth* ; accomplished in all spiritual blessings. Ib. ver. 16 : *And* GRACE *upon* GRACE : he who is full of the most excellent blessings, confers them *liberally* on all believers. Acts xi. 23 : *When he had seen the* GRACE *of God*, i. e. had the fullest evidence that they were richly endowed with heavenly gifts. 1 Cor. i. 4 : *For the* GRACE *of God which is given you*—the *Divine blessings* conferred upon you. 2 Cor. ix. 8 : *God is able to make all* GRACE *abound toward you* ; i. e. to enrich you with every benediction. This is also a very common acceptation of the word ; and in this sense the word *grace* or *favour* is now generally understood among religious people. The *grace of God* meaning with them some *Divine* or *spiritual blessing communicated.*

3. It is sometimes taken for the whole of the *Christian religion*, as being the grandest possible display of God's *favour* to a lost, ruined world : and in this sense it appears to be used, John i. 17 : *For the* LAW *was given by Moses ; but* GRACE *and truth came by Jesus Christ :* where the term GRACE is evidently opposed to LAW ; the latter meaning the *Mosaic*, the other the *Christian*, dispensation. Acts xiii. 43 : *Barnabas persuaded them to continue in the* GRACE *of God* ; i. e. to hold fast their profession of the religion of Christ. Rom. vi. 14 : *Ye are not under the* LAW, *but under* GRACE—ye are no longer under obligation to fulfil the Mosaic precepts, but are under the *Christian dispensation.* See also ver. 15 of the same chapter ; and see 2 Cor. i. 12 ; vi. 1 ; Gal. i. 6 ; Col. i. 6 ; 2 Tim. ii. 1, Tit. ii. 11 : *The* GRACE *of God, that bringeth salvation unto all men, hath appeared.* The Jewish religion

2

| A. M. cir. 4062.
A. D. cir. 58.
An. Olymp.
cir. CCIX. 2.
A. U. C. cir.
811. | saints ^p Grace to you, and peace from God our Father, and the Lord Jesus Christ.
8 First, I ^q thank my God | through Jesus Christ for you all, that ^r your faith is spoken of throughout the whole world.
9 For ^s God is my witness, | A. M. cir. 4062.
A. D. cir. 58.
An. Olymp.
cir. CCIX. 2.
A. U. C. cir.
811. |

---

^p 1 Cor. i. 3; 2 Cor. i. 2; Gal. i. 3.——^q 1 Cor. i. 4; Phil. i. 3; Col. i. 3, 4; 1 Thess. i. 2; Phil. 4.

^r Chap xvi. 19; 1 Thess. i. 8.——^s Chap. ix. 1; 2 Cor. i. 23; Phil. i. 8; 1 Thess. ii. 5.

---

was restricted in its *benefits* to a *few;* but the *Christian religion* proposes the salvation of *all* men; and the author of it has become a sacrifice for the sins of the *whole world.* Heb. xii. 15: *Looking diligently lest any man fall from the* GRACE *of God*—lest any man apostatize from the Christian religion, and the blessings of pardon and holiness which he has received through it. 1 Pet. v. 12: *This is the true* GRACE *of God wherein ye stand*—the *Christian religion* which ye have received is the *genuine* religion of God.

4. It signifies all the *blessings* and *benefits* which Christ has *purchased,* and which he gives to true believers, both in *time* and *eternity.* See Rom. v. 15 and 17, where the *grace* of God is opposed to *death;* i. e. to all the wretchedness and misery brought into the world by Adam's transgression. 1 Cor. xvi. 23: *The* GRACE *of the Lord Jesus Christ be with you all*—May every blessing purchased by Christ's passion and death be the portion of you all. Gal. v. 4: *Ye are fallen from* GRACE—ye have lost the blessings of the Gospel by submitting to circumcision.

5. It signifies the *apostolic* and *ministerial office,* or the authority to propagate the Christian religion, and the unction or influence by which that office is executed; so in the 5th verse of this chapter, as has been already noted: *By whom we have received* GRACE *and apostleship,* or, *the apostolic office.* Rom. xiii. 3: *I say, through the* GRACE *given unto me;* i. e. I command you, by the *authority* of my *apostolic office,* &c. See also ver. 6.

6. It signifies a *gift,* salary, or money collected for the use of the poor. 1 Cor. xvi. 3: *Whomsoever ye shall approve*—*them will I send to bring your* LIBERALITY, την χαριν ὑμων, *your* GRACE; i. e. the collection made for the poor saints: see ver. 1. 2 Cor. viii. 4: *Praying us*—*that we would receive the* GIFT, την χαριν, the GRACE, the *contribution* made in the Churches of Macedonia, for the relief of the poor. In this sense it is used in Ecclus. xvii. 22: *He will keep the* GOOD DEEDS *of man,* χαριν, the same as ελεημοσυνη, *alms,* in the beginning of the verse; and it signifies a kind or *friendly* act, in the same author. Chap. xxix. 15: *Forget not the* FRIENDSHIP, χαριτας, *of thy surety.* GRACE, *or* χαρις, was a deity among the ancients; and the *three* GRACES, αἱ τρεις χαριτες, were called *Pitho, Aglaia,* and *Euphrosyne;* Πειθω, mild *persuasion;* Αγλαια, *dignity;* Ευφροσυνη, *liberality* and *joyfulness;* and these were always painted *naked,* to show that all *benefits* should be *gratuitous,* this being essential to the nature of a *gift.* See Suidas, in χαριτας.

7. It sometimes signifies merely *thanks* or *thanksgiving.* See Luke xvii. 9: *Doth he thank,* μη χαριν εχει, *that servant?* Rom. vi. 17: *But God be* THANKED, χαρις ὃε τῳ Θεῳ. 1 Cor. x. 30: *For if I by* GRACE, χαριτι, THANKSGIVING, as our *margin* has it, and properly.

8. It signifies *remuneration, wages,* or *reward* Luke vi. 32, 33, 34: *If ye love them that love you*—*do good to them which do good to you*—*lend to them of whom ye hope to receive, what* THANK *have ye?* ποια ὑμιν χαρις εστι; *what* REWARD *have ye?* This appears, from the parallel place, Matt. v. 46, to be most evidently the meaning: τινα μισθον εχετε; *what* REWARD *have ye?* The word is used in this sense by several Greek writers.

9. It signifies whatever is the *means* of *procuring* the *favour* or *kindness* of another. 1 Pet. ii. 19, 20: *For this is* THANKWORTHY, τουτο γαρ χαρις παρα τῳ Θεῳ, this is the *means* of PROCURING FAVOUR *from God.*

10. It signifies *joy, pleasure,* and *gratification,* which is the meaning of χαρα, and with which it is often confounded in the New Testament. Philemon 7: *For we have great* JOY, χαριν γαρ εχομεν πολλην. Tobit vii. 18: *The Lord give thee* JOY, χαριν, *for this thy sorrow.* In this sense the word is used by the best Greek writers; and in this sense it appears to be used, 2 Cor. i. 15.

11. It signifies the *performance* of an *act* which is *pleasing* or *grateful* to others. Acts xxiv 27 · *Felix, willing to show the Jews a* PLEASURE, χαριτας καταθεσθαι, to perform an act which he knew would be highly *gratifying* to them.

12. It signifies *whatever has the power or influence to procure favour, &c.* Suavity, kindness, benevolence, gentle demeanour. Luke iv. 22 · *All wondered at the* GRACIOUS WORDS, τοις λογοις της χαριτος, the *benevolent, kind,* and *tender expressions;* such as his text, ver. 18, would naturally lead him to speak · *He hath anointed me to preach the Gospel to the poor; he hath sent me to heal the broken-hearted, to preach deliverance to the captives,* &c. Eph. iv 29; Col. iv. 6: *Let your speech be always with* GRACE; i. e. gracious, kind, benevolent, savouring of the *doctrine* of Christ · it is thus used by several Greek writers. See *Schleusner.* As the word χαρις, GRACE, most frequently signifies some *blessing* or *benefit* calculated to promote human *happiness,* it is generally derived from χαιρω, I rejoice, because of the effect produced by the blessing.

And peace] Ειρηνη, the same as שלום *shalom* in Hebrew, generally signifying all *kinds of blessing,* but especially *harmony* and *unity,* and the *bond* of such *unity.* The most probable derivation of the word ειρηνη is from ειρω, I bind, and ἑν, one—because peace unites and binds those who were, by discord, before *disunited.* In the New Testament it signifies—1. *Peace,* public or private, in the general acceptation of the word, as implying *reconciliation* and *friendship;* and to the etymology of the word the apostle seems to allude in Eph. iv. 3: *Endeavouring to keep the* UNITY *of the Spirit in the* BOND *of* PEACE. Acts xii. 20: *They of Tyre and Sidon desired* PEACE—they sought *reconciliation,* with Herod, by means of Blastus, the king's chamberlain.

A. M. cir. 4062.
A. D. cir. 58.
An. Olymp.
cir. CCIX. 2.
A. U. C. cir.
811.

[t] whom I serve [u] with my spirit in the Gospel of his Son, that [v] without ceasing I make mention of you always in my prayers;

10 [w] Making request, if by any means now at length I might have a prosperous journey [x] by the will of God to come unto you.

11 For I long to see you, that [y] I may im-

A. M. cir. 4062.
A. D. cir. 58.
An. Olymp.
cir. CCIX. 2.
A. U. C. cir.
811.

part unto you some spiritual gift, to the end ye may be established;

12 That is, that I may be comforted together [z] with you by the [a] mutual faith both of you and me.

13 Now I would not have you ignorant, brethren, that [b] oftentimes I purposed to

---

[t] Acts xxvii. 23; 2 Tim. i. 3.——[u] Or, *in my spirit;* John iv. 23, 24; Phil. iii. 3.——[v] 1 Thess. iii. 10.

[w] Chap. xv. 23, 32; 1 Thess. iii. 10.——[x] James iv. 15.——[y] Ch. xv. 29.——[z] Or, *in you.*——[a] Tit. i. 4; 2 Pet. i. 1.——[b] Ch. xv. 23.

---

2. It signifies *regularity, good order.* 1 Cor. xiv. 33: *God is not the God of confusion, but* of PEACE.

3. It signifies the *labour* or *study* of preserving *peace* and *concord;* and this is supposed to be its meaning, Matt. x. 34; Luke xii. 51; and Acts vii. 26. Rom. xiv. 17: *For the kingdom of God is righteousness and* PEACE—the Christian dispensation admits of no contention, but inculcates *peace.* 1 Cor. vii. 15: *God hath called us to* PEACE—to *labour* to preserve *quietness* and *concord.* Heb. xii. 14: *Follow* PEACE—*labour* to preserve it.

4. It signifies the *author* or *procurer* of *peace* and *concord.* Eph. ii. 14: *He is our* PEACE—the *author* of concord betwixt Jews and Gentiles.

5. It signifies the *Gospel* and its *blessings.* Eph. ii. 17: *And came and preached* PEACE *to you which were afar off, and to them that were nigh.*

6. It signifies all kinds of *mental* and *corporeal happiness,* and especially the happiness of Christians. Luke i. 79: *To guide our feet into the way of* PEACE—to show us the way to obtain *true happiness.* Luke xix. 42: *The things* which belong *unto thy* PEACE—that by which thou mightest have been made truly *happy.* 1 Thess. v. 23: *The very God of* PEACE—God, the only source of true felicity. John xvi. 33: *These things have I spoken unto you, that in me ye might have* PEACE—that ye might have confidence and happiness in believing on me as your only Saviour.

7. It signifies *good wishes* and *affectionate prayers.* Matt. x. 13: *And if the house be worthy, let your* PEACE *come upon it.* Our Lord commands his disciples, ver. 12, to *salute* the house into which they entered; and this was done by saying, *Peace be unto this house!* that is, Let every blessing, *spiritual* and *temporal,* be the portion of this family! See Luke x. 6; John xiv. 27; Acts xv. 33: *They were let go in* PEACE—they had the most *fervent and affectionate prayers* of the Church.

8. It signifies *praise.* Luke xix. 38: PEACE *in heaven and glory in the highest!*—May all the heavenly host praise God, and give him the highest honour!

9. It signifies *benignity, benevolence, favour.* Rom. v. 1: *Being justified by faith, we have* PEACE *with God*—In consequence of having our sins forgiven, we have a clear sense of the Divine *favour.* Phil. iv. 7: *The* PEACE *of God which passeth all understanding*—the inexpressible blessedness of a *sense* of the Divine *favour.* See *Schleusner's* Lexicon.

From God our Father] The apostle wishes them all the blessings which can flow from GOD, as the *fountain of grace,* producing in them all the *happiness* which a heart filled with the *peace of God* can possess;

all of which are to be communicated to them through the Lord Jesus Christ. See the note on Acts xxviii. 31.

Verse 8. *First, I thank my God*] From this to the end of ver. 17 belongs to the *preface,* in which the apostle endeavours to conciliate the good opinion of the Christians at Rome, and to prepare their minds for his reproofs and exhortations.

Your faith is spoken] Καταγγελλεται, is *celebrated, throughout the whole world*—in every place where the Christian religion is professed, through all parts of the *Roman dominions;* for in this sense we should understand the words, the *whole world.*

Verse 9. *Whom I serve with my spirit*] Λατρευω, Whom *I worship* with the *profoundest religious reverence;* for so the original certainly means: I not only employ all the powers of my *body* in this service, but all those of my *soul;* being thoroughly convinced of the *absolute truth* of the religion I preach. Probably St. Paul opposes, in this place, the *spiritual* worship of the Gospel to the *external,* or what some call the *carnal,* worship of the Jews. Mine is not a religion of *ceremonies,* but one in which the *life* and *power* of the *eternal Spirit* are acknowledged and experienced.

Verse 10. *Making request, &c.*] By this we see how earnestly the apostle longed to see Rome. It had long been a subject of continual prayer to God, that he might have a prosperous journey to, or rather *meeting* with, them, for so we should understand the word ευοδωθησομαι: that he had a prosperous *meeting* with them we cannot doubt; that he had a disastrous journey to them the 27th of the Acts fully proves.

Verse 11. *Some spiritual gift*] This probably means some of the *extraordinary gifts* of the Holy Spirit, which, being given to them, might tend greatly to establish their faith in the Gospel of Christ; and it is very likely that such gifts were only conferred by means of *apostles;* and as the *apostle* had not yet been at Rome, consequently the Roman Christians had not yet received any of these miraculous gifts, and thus they differed widely from all the other Churches which had been raised by the apostle's ministry.

Verse 12. *That I may be comforted together with you*] He here, with great address, intimates that he longs for this opportunity, as well on his *own account* as on *theirs,* and to show them that he arrogates nothing to himself; for he intimates that it will require the conjoint action of *their faith* as well as *his own,* to be the means of receiving those blessings from God to which he refers.

Verse 13. *But was let hitherto*] The word *let,* from the Anglo-Saxon, lettan to *hinder,* signifies *impede*

2

A. M. cir. 4062.
A. D. cir. 58.
An. Olymp.
cir. CCIX. 2.
A. U. C. cir.
811.

come unto you, (but ^c was let hitherto,) that I might have some ^d fruit ^e among you also, even as among other Gentiles.

14 ^f I am debtor both to the Greeks, and to the barbarians ; both to the wise, and to the unwise.

15 So, as much as in me is, I am ready to

preach the Gospel to you that are at Rome also.

16 For ^g I am not ashamed of the Gospel of Christ : for ^h it is the power of God unto salvation to every one that believeth ; ⁱ to the Jew first, and also to the Greek.

17 For ^k therein is the righteousness of God

A. M. cir. 4062.
A. D. cir. 58.
An. Olymp.
cir. CCIX. 2.
A. U. C. cir.
811.

---

^c Acts xvi. 7 ; 2 Thess. i. 18.——^d Phil. iv. 17.——^e Or, *in you.*
^f 1 Cor. ix. 16.——^g Psa. xl. 9, 10 ; Mark viii. 38 ; 2 Tim. i. 8.

^h 1 Cor. i. 18 ; xv. 2.——ⁱ Luke ii. 30, 31, 32 ; xxiv. 47 ; Acts iii. 26 ; xiii. 26, 46 ; chap. ii. 9.——^k Chap. iii. 21.

---

ment or *hinderance* of any kind : but it is likely that the original word, εκωλυθην, *I was forbidden,* refers to a *Divine prohibition :*—he would have visited them long before, but God did not see right to *permit* him.

Verse 14. *I am a debtor both to the Greeks, and to the barbarians*] It has been remarked before that all the nations of the earth, themselves excepted, were termed *barbarians* by the *Greeks.* See the origin of the word *barbarous* in the note on Acts, chap. xxviii. 2. The apostle considers himself, by his apostolical office and call, under obligation to preach the Gospel to *all people,* as far as the providence of God might open his way ; for this is implied in the Divine commission :—*Go ye into all the world, and preach the Gospel to every creature—to the wise and the unwise ;* to the *learned* and *cultivated* as well as to the *unlearned* and *uncultivated.* This evidently appears to be the import of the terms.

Verse 15. *I am ready to preach*] Προθυμον ; I have a *ready* mind. I was only prevented by the providence of God from visiting you long *ago.* His time is best : in the mean time I write, by his direction, to comfort and instruct you.

Verse 16. *I am not ashamed of the Gospel of Christ*] This text is best illustrated by Isa. xxviii. 16 ; xlix. 23, quoted by the apostle, chap. x. 11 : For the Scripture saith, *Whosoever believeth on him, shall not be ashamed ;* i. e. they shall neither be *confounded,* nor *disappointed* of their hope. The *Jews,* by not believing on Jesus Christ, by not receiving him as the promised Messiah, but trusting in *others,* have been *disappointed, ashamed,* and *confounded,* from that time to the present day. Their expectation is cut off ; and, while rejecting Christ, and expecting *another* Messiah, they have continued under the displeasure of God, and are *ashamed* of their confidence. On the other hand, those who have believed on Christ have, in and through him, all the blessings of which the prophets spoke ; every promise of God being *yea* and *amen* through him. Paul, as a Jew, believed on Christ Jesus ; and in believing he had life through his name ; through him he enjoyed an abundance of grace ; so that, being filled with that happiness which an indwelling Christ produces, he could cheerfully say, *I am not ashamed of the Gospel of Christ.* And why ? Because he felt it to be *the power of God to the salvation* of his believing soul. This appears to be the true sense of this passage, and this interpretation acquires additional strength from the consideration that St. Paul is here most evidently addressing himself to the *Jews.*

It is the power of God unto salvation] Δυναμις γαρ

Θεου εστιν : The *almighty power* of God accompanies this preaching to the souls of them that believe ; and the consequence is, they are *saved ;* and what but the *power of God* can save a *fallen, sinful* soul !

To the Jew first] Not only the Jews have the *first* offer of this Gospel, but they have the *greatest* need of it ; being so *deeply fallen,* and having sinned against such *glorious privileges,* they are much more culpable than the Gentiles, who never had the light of a Divine revelation.

And also to the Greek] Though the salvation of God has hitherto been apparently *confined* to the Jewish people, yet it shall be so no longer, for the Gospel of Christ is sent to the *Gentiles* as well as the *Jews ;* God having put no difference between them ; and Jesus Christ having *tasted death for* EVERY *man.*

Verse 17. *For therein*] In the Gospel of Christ.

Is the righteousness of God] God's method of saving sinners.

Revealed from faith to faith] Shown to be by *faith,* and not by the works of *any* law ; for Abraham, the father and founder of the Jewish people, *was justified by faith,* before even the law was given ; and by believing, in reference to the spiritual object held forth in the various ordinances of the law, and now revealed under the Gospel, he and all his believing descendants have been justified. And thus the faith of the old covenant led on to the faith of the new covenant, which shows that salvation has been *by faith* from the call of Abraham to the present time. And, from the beginning, all that were *just* or *righteous* in the earth became such by *faith,* and by this principle alone they were enabled to persevere ; as it is written, *The just shall live by faith.* That δικαιοσυνη, which we translate *righteousness* in this verse, signifies *God's method of saving mankind by faith in Christ,* is fully evident from the use of the term in chap. ix. 30 : *The Gentiles which followed not after* RIGHTEOUSNESS—who had no knowledge by revelation, of *God's method of justifying* and saving sinners, *have attained to* RIGHTEOUSNESS—have had imparted to them God's method of salvation by faith in Christ. Verse 31 : *But Israel,* the Jews, *which followed after the law of righteousness* —that law, the *end* or object of which is CHRIST, and through him *justification* to all that believe (chap. x. 4,) *have not attained to the law of righteousness*—have not found out the genuine plan of salvation, even in that law which so strongly and generally proclaims justification by faith. And why have they not found it ? Verse 32 : *Because they sought it not by faith, but as it were by the works of the law*—they did not discern that even

A. M. cir. 4062.
A. D. cir. 58.
An. Olymp.
cir. CCIX. 2.
A. U. C. cir.
811.

revealed from faith to faith: as it is written, [1] The just shall live by faith.

18 [m] For the wrath of God is re-

vealed from heaven against all ungodliness and unrighteousness of men, who hold the truth in unrighteousness:

A. M. cir. 4062.
A. D. cir. 58.
An. Olymp.
cir. CCIX. 2.
A. U. C. cir.
811.

[1] Hab. ii. 4; John iii. 36; Gal. iii. 11; Phil. iii. 9; Heb. x. 38.

[m] Acts xvii. 30; Eph. v. 6; Col. iii. 6.

its works or prescribed religious observances were intended to lead to faith in that glorious Mediator of whom they were the *types* and *representatives;* but the Jews trusted in the observances themselves, hoping to acquire justification and final salvation by that means. *For they stumbled at the stumbling-stone*—at the doctrine of *Christ crucified* as the only sure ground on which the expectation of future salvation can be founded. Therefore, *being ignorant of God's righteousness*—God's method of saving sinners, *and going about to establish their own righteousness*—their own method of salvation, by the observance of those rites and ceremonies which should have led them by faith to Christ, *they did not submit themselves to the righteousness of God*—they would not submit to be saved in God's way, and therefore rejected, persecuted, and crucified the Lord Jesus; see chap. x. 3. This collation of passages most evidently shows that the word *righteousness* here means simply *God's method of saving sinners,* or God's way of salvation, in opposition to the ways and means invented by the fancies or prejudices of men.

There are few words in the sacred writings which are taken in a greater variety of acceptations than the word צדקה *tsedakah* in Hebrew, and δικαιοσυνη in Greek, both of which we generally translate *righteousness.* Our English word was originally *rightwiseness,* from the Anglo-Saxon, ריהτ, *justice, right,* and piτan, *to know;* and thus the *righteous* man was a person who was allowed to *understand* the claims of *justice* and *right,* and who, knowing them, acted according to their dictates. Such a man is *thoroughly wise;* he aims at the attainment of the *best end* by the use of the *best means.* This is a true definition of *wisdom,* and the righteous man is he that *knows* most and acts *best.* The Hebrew צדק *tsadak,* in its ideal meaning, contains the notion of a *beam* or *scales* in *equipoise,* what we call *even balance;* and it is well known that in all the personifications of justice, both ancient and modern, she is represented as a beautiful female with a bandage on her eyes, and a beam and scales in her hand, so perfectly poised that neither end preponderates.

The Greek word δικαιοσυνη has been derived from διχαζω, to *divide;* and hence δικη, *justice,* because it is the property of this virtue to *divide* to each his *due.* With other etymologies it is useless to trouble the reader. Both the noun δικαιοσυνη and the verb δικαιοω have a great variety of meaning in the New Testament; but they are all reducible to this original idea, *acting* according to the requisitions of *justice* or *right.* It may not be improper to notice some of the chief of these acceptations in this place.

1. The act of *distributing* to each man his *due* is the sense of the word, Acts xvii. 31: *He will judge the world in* RIGHTEOUSNESS, *i. e.* according to the principles of eternal justice and rectitude. See also Rev. xix. 2: *In* RIGHTEOUSNESS *doth he judge and make war.*

2. It signifies a *holy life,* as proceeding from *piety* towards God. Luke i. 75: *Might serve him in holiness and* RIGHTEOUSNESS *all the days of our life.*

3. It signifies *benignity, liberality,* and particularly *almsgiving,* as justice and righteousness require us, being only *stewards* of God's bounty, to share it with the necessitous. Matt. vi. 1: *Take heed that ye do not your* ALMS, δικαιοσυνην, *your* RIGHTEOUSNESS, *before men.* Rom. iii. 5: *But if our unrighteousness commend the* RIGHTEOUSNESS, *the benignity of God.* 2 Cor. ix. 10: *Increase the fruits of your* RIGHTEOUSNESS, *i. e. of your liberality.*

4. It signifies God's *method of saving sinners;* the way which is agreeable to his *righteousness* and *liberality.* See the former part of this note, and the scriptures there referred to.

5. It signifies the *reward* or *issue of liberality.* 2 Cor. ix. 9: *He hath scattered abroad; he hath given to the poor; his* RIGHTEOUSNESS—the reward of his bounty, *remaineth for ever.* See Psa. cxii. 9.

6. It signifies the whole collection of *graces,* which constitute the complete Christian character. Matt. v. 6: *Blessed are they that hunger and thirst after* RIGHTEOUSNESS—they who ardently long for the *full salvation* of God. Ib. v. 10, 20: *If your* RIGHTEOUSNESS *exceed not the righteousness,* &c. Ib. vi. 33 · *Seek the kingdom of God and his* RIGHTEOUSNESS.

7. It signifies the *result* of *faith in God* and *submission to his will,* exemplified in a holy and useful life. Heb. xi. 7: *By faith Noah prepared an ark, and became heir of the* RIGHTEOUSNESS *which is by faith*—he escaped the deluge and became the instrument of repeopling the world.

8. It signifies an *exact observance* of *religious ordinances* and *precepts.* Phil. iii. 6: *Touching the* RIGHTEOUSNESS *which is of the law, blameless*—having lived in an exact conformity to all the Mosaic precepts. In this sense it is to be understood, Matt. iii. 15: *Thus it becomes us to fulfil all* RIGHTEOUSNESS—to observe every precept of the law.

9. It signifies the *favour* or *pardoning mercy* of God. Rom. iv. 6: *The blessedness of the man unto whom God imputeth* RIGHTEOUSNESS—*without works*—the man is happy to whom God has granted the remission of sins, without respect to his observance of the law of Moses.

10. In 2 Cor. v. 21, δικαιοσυνη, *righteousness,* is put for δικαιος, *righteous: That we might become the righteousness of God*—that we might receive such a righteousness or holiness, such a salvation, as is worthy of God's grace to impart, and such as the necessities of mankind require.

A few of the leading acceptations of the verb δικαιοω, which we translate to *justify,* may be here properly subjoined, as this verb is so repeatedly used in this epistle.

1. It signifies to *declare* or *pronounce* one *just* or

A. M. cir. 4062.
A. D. cir. 58.
An. Olymp.
cir. CCIX. 2.
A. U. C. cir.
811.

19 Because ⁿ that which may be known of God is manifest ᵒ in them ; for ᵖ God hath showed *it* unto them.

20 For ᑫ the invisible things of him fron the creation of the world are clearly seen, being understood by the things that are

A. M. cir. 4062.
A. D. cir. 58.
An. Olymp.
cir. CCIX. 2.
A. U. C. cir.
811.

ⁿ Acts xiv. 17.——ᵒ Or, *to them.*

ᵖ John i. 9.——ᑫ Psa. xix. 1, &c. ; Acts xiv. 17 ; xvii. 27.

---

righteous; or, in other words, to declare him to be *what he really is.* 1 Tim. iii. 16 : *He was* JUSTIFIED *in the Spirit.*—By the almighty power of the Spirit he was *proved* to be the TRUE MESSIAH.

2. To *esteem* a thing *properly.* Matt. xi. 19 : *Wisdom is* JUSTIFIED *of her children.*—Wisdom, propriety of conduct, is properly *estimated* by wise men.

3. It signifies *to approve, praise,* and *commend.* The publicans JUSTIFIED God, Luke vii. 29 ; praised him for calling them to such a state of salvation. Ib. xvi. 15 : *Ye are they which* JUSTIFY *yourselves before men*—Ye are self-commended, self-applauded, and self-praised. In this sense it is often used in the Greek apocryphal books. Ecclus. vii. 5 : JUSTIFY *not thyself before the Lord*—Do not applaud thyself in the presence of thy Maker. Ib. x. 29 : *Who will* JUSTIFY *(praise or applaud) him that sinneth against his own soul.* Ib. xviii. 2 : *The Lord only is righteous,* δικαιωθησεται, *shall be* JUSTIFIED, i. e. *praised,* because *there is none other but he.*

4. The verb δικαιοομαι is used *to clear from all sin.* 1 Cor. iv. 4 : *For I know nothing by myself ; yet am I not hereby* JUSTIFIED—A man's own consciousness of integrity is not a *proof* that he is clear from all sin in the sight of God.

5. A judge is said to *justify* not only when he *condemns* and *punishes,* but also when he *defends* the cause of the innocent. See EURIP. *Heraclid.* ver. 190. THUCYD. iii. p. 200. POLYB. iii. 31, and SCHLEUSNER on δικαιοω. Hence δικαιουσθαι is taken in a *forensic* sense, and signifies to be *found* or *declared righteous, innocent,* &c. Matt. xii. 37 : *By thy words shalt thou be* JUSTIFIED—thou shalt be *declared* to be righteous. Rom. iii. 4 : *That thou mightest be* JUSTIFIED *in thy sayings*—that thou mightest be *proved* to be *true* in what thou hast said.

6. It signifies *to set free, to escape from.* Acts xiii. 39 : *And by him all that believe are* JUSTIFIED *from all things, from which ye could not be* JUSTIFIED *by the law*—by faith in Christ a man *escapes* those evils which, otherwise, the law of Moses would *inflict* upon him. Rom. vi. 7 : *For he that is dead,* δεδικαιωται, *is* JUSTIFIED, properly rendered by our translators, *is* FREED *from sin.*

7. It signifies also to *receive one into favour, to pardon sin.* Rom. viii. 30 : *Whom he called, them he also* JUSTIFIED—he received them into *favour* and *pardoned* their sins. Luke xviii. 14 : *This man went down to his house* JUSTIFIED—he humbled himself, repented of his iniquity, and God *forgave his sin.* Rom. iii. 20 : *By the deeds of the law there shall no flesh be* JUSTIFIED—no soul can have his sins forgiven through the observance of the Mosaic law. Ib. iv. 2 : *If Abraham were* JUSTIFIED (had his *sin pardoned*) *by works.* 1 Cor. vi. 11 : *Such were some of you, but ye are* JUSTIFIED—ye are received into the Divine *fa-*

vour, and have your *sins forgiven.* See James ii. 21–25 ; Rom. iii. 24, 28 ; v. 1, 9 ; Gal. ii. 16, 17 ; iii. 11, 24 ; v. 4 ; Tit. iii. 7. In all these texts the word *justify* is taken in the sense of *remission of sins* through faith in Christ Jesus ; and does not mean *making* the person *just* or *righteous,* but treating him as if he were so, having already *forgiven* him his sins.

The just shall live by faith.] This has been understood *two* ways : 1. That the just or righteous man cannot live a holy and useful life without exercising continual faith in our Lord Jesus : which is strictly true ; for He only who has brought him into that state of salvation can *preserve* him in it ; and he stands by faith. 2. It is contended by some able critics that the words of the original text should be pointed thus : Ὁ δε δικαιος εκ πιστεως, ζησεται. *The just by faith, shall live ;* that is, he alone that is justified by faith shall be *saved :* which is also true ; as it is impossible to get salvation in any other way. This last meaning is probably the true one, as the original text in Hab. ii. 4, speaks of those who *believed* the declarations of God when the Chaldeans besieged Jerusalem, and, having acted conformably to them, escaped with their *lives.*

Verse 18. *For the wrath of God is revealed*] The apostle has now finished his *preface,* and comes to the grand *subject* of the epistle ; namely, to show the *absolute need* of the Gospel of Christ, because of the *universal corruption* of mankind ; which was so great as to incense the justice of God, and call aloud for the *punishment* of the world. 1. He shows that all the heathen nations were utterly corrupt, and deserved this threatened punishment. And this is the subject of the first chapter, from verse 18 to the end. 2. He shows that the *Jews,* notwithstanding the greatness of their privileges, were no better than the *Gentiles ;* and therefore the wrath of God was revealed against *them* also. This subject he treats in chap. ii. and chap. iii. 1–19. 3. He returns, as it were, on both, chap. iii. 20–31, and proves that, as the Jews and Gentiles were equally corrupt, they could not be saved by the deeds of any law ; that they stood equally in *need* of that salvation which God had provided ; that both were equally entitled to that salvation, for God was the God of the *Gentiles* as well as of the *Jews.*

By οργη Θεου, *the wrath of God,* we are not to understand any *uneasy* passion in the Divine Being ; but the *displeasure* of his righteousness, which is expressed by the punishments inflicted on the *ungodly,* those who retain not God in their knowledge ; and the *unrighteous,* those whose lives are profligate.

As, in the Gospel, the *righteousness* of God is *revealed* for the *salvation of the ungodly,* so is the *wrath* of God *revealed* against the *workers of iniquity.* Those who refuse to be saved in the way revealed by his *mercy* must be consumed in the way revealed by his *justice.*

A. M. cir. 4062.
A. D. cir. 58.
An. Olymp.
cir. CCIX. 2.
A. U. C. cir.
811.

made, *even* his eternal power and Godhead ; ^r so that they are without excuse :

21 Because that, when they knew God, they glorified *him* not as God, neither were thankful; but ^s became vain in

their imaginations, and their foolish heart was darkened.

22 ^t Professing themselves to be wise, they became fools,

23 And changed the glory of the uncorruptible ^u God into an image made like to corrupt-

A. M. cir. 4062
A. D. cir. 58.
An. Olymp.
cir. CCIX. 2.
A. U. C. cir.
811.

---

^r Or, *that they may be.*——^s 2 Kings xvii. 15; Jer. ii. 5; Eph. iv. 17, 18.——^t Jer. x. 14.

^u Deut. iv. 16, &c.; Psa. cvi. 20; Isa. xl. 18, 26; Jer. ii. 11; Ezek. viii. 10; Acts xvii. 29.

Ungodliness] Ασεβειαν, from *a, negative,* and σεβω or σεβομαι, *I worship,* probably intended here to express *atheism, polytheism,* and *idolatry* of every kind.

Unrighteousness] Αδικιαν, from *a, negative,* and δικη, *justice;* every thing contrary to strict morality; all viciousness and profligacy of conduct.

Who hold the truth in unrighteousness] In what sense could it be said that the heathen *held the truth* in unrighteousness, when they really had not that truth? Some think this refers to the conduct of their best philosophers, such as *Socrates, Plato, Seneca,* &c., who knew much more of the Divine nature than they thought safe or prudent to discover ; and who acted in many things contrary to the light which they enjoyed. Others think this to be spoken of the *Gentiles* in general, who either *did know,* or *might* have known, much of God from the works of creation, as the apostle intimates in the following verses. But *Rosenmüller* and some others contend that the word κατεχειν here does not signify to *hold,* but to *hinder ;* and that the place should be translated, *who through maliciousness hinder the truth ;* i. e. prevent it from taking hold of their hearts, and from governing their conduct. This is certainly a very usual acceptation of the verb κατεχειν, which Hesychius interprets κρατειν, κωλυειν, συνεχειν, to *retain, hinder,* &c.; these men hindering, by their vicious conduct, the *truth* of God from being propagated in the earth.

Verse 19. *That which may be known of God*] Dr. Taylor paraphrases this and the following verse thus : " Although the Gentiles had no written revelation, yet what may be known of God is every where manifest among them, God having made a clear discovery of himself to them. For his being and perfections, invisible to our bodily eyes, have been, ever since the creation of the world, evidently to be seen, if attentively considered, in the visible beauty, order, and operations observable in the constitution and parts of the universe; especially his eternal power and universal dominion and providence : so that they cannot plead *ignorance* in excuse of their idolatry and wickedness."

Verse 20. *The invisible things of him*] His invisible perfections are manifested by his visible works, and may be apprehended by what he has made ; their *immensity* showing his *omnipotence;* their vast *variety* and *contrivance,* his *omniscience;* and their *adaptation* to the most *beneficent purposes,* his infinite *goodness* and *philanthropy*

His eternal power] Αϊδιος αυτου δυναμις, That all-powerful energy that *ever was,* and *ever will exist ;* so that, ever since there was a creation to be surveyed, there have been intelligent beings to make that survey.

And Godhead] Θειοτης, His *acting as God* in the

government and support of the universe. His *works* prove his *being ;* the *government* and *support* of these works prove it equally. *Creation* and *providence* form a *twofold* demonstration of God, 1st. in the *perfections* of his nature ; and, 2dly. in the *exercise* of those perfections.

Verse 21. *Because that when they knew God*] When they thus acquired a general knowledge of the unity and perfections of the Divine nature, *they glorified him not as God*—they did not *proclaim* him to the people, but shut up his *glory* (as Bishop Warburton expresses it) in their *mysteries,* and gave the people, in exchange for an *incorruptible God, an image made like to corruptible man.* Wherefore God, in punishment for their sins, thus *turning his truth into a lie,* suffered even their *mysteries,* which they had erected for a school of virtue, to degenerate into an odious sink of vice and immorality ; giving them up unto all uncleanness and vile affections.

They glorified him not] They did not give him that *worship* which his perfections required.

Neither were thankful] They manifested no *gratitude* for the blessings they received from his providence, but *became vain in their imaginations,* διαλογισμοις, *in their reasonings.* This certainly refers to the foolish manner in which even the wisest of their philosophers discoursed about the Divine nature, not excepting *Socrates, Plato,* or *Seneca.* Who can read their works without being struck with the vanity of their reasonings, as well as with the stupidity of their nonsense, when speaking about God? I might crowd my page with proofs of this ; but it is not necessary to those who are acquainted with their writings, and to others it would not be useful. In short, their foolish, darkened minds sought God no where but in the place in which he is never to be found ; viz. the vile, corrupted, and corrupting passions of their own hearts. As they did not discover him *there,* they scarcely sought him any where else.

Verse 22. *Professing themselves to be wise*] This is most strikingly true of all the ancient philosophers, whether Greeks or Romans, as their works, which remain, sufficiently testify. The word φασκοντες signifies not merely the *professing* but the *assumption* of the philosophic character. In this sense the word φασκειν is used by the best Greek writers. See *Kypke.* A dispassionate examination of the doctrine and lives of the most famed philosophers of antiquity, of every nation, will show that they were darkened in their mind and irregular in their conduct. It was from the Christion religion alone that true philosophy and genuine philosophers sprang.

Verse 23. *They changed the glory, &c.*] The finest

2

43

A. M. cir. 4062.
A. D. cir. 58.
An. Olymp.
cir. CCIX. 2.
A. U. C. cir.
811.

ible man, and to birds, and four-footed beasts, and creeping things.

24 ᵛ Wherefore God also gave them up to uncleanness, through the lusts of their own hearts, ʷ to dishonour their own bodies ˣ between themselves:

25 Who changed ʸ the truth of God ᶻ into a lie, and worshipped and served the creature ᵃ more than the Creator, who is blessed for ever. Amen.

26 For this cause God gave them up unto ᵇ vile affections: for even their women did change the natural use into that which is against nature:

27 And likewise also the men, leaving the natural use of the woman, burned in their lust one toward another; men with men working that which is unseemly, and receiving in themselves that recompense of their error which was meet.

28 ᶜ And even as they did not like ᵈ to retain God in *their* knowledge, God gave them over to ᵉ a reprobate mind, to do those things ᶠ which are not convenient;

29 Being filled with all unrighteousness, fornication, wickedness, covetousness, maliciousness; full of envy, murder, debate, deceit, malignity; whisperers,

A. M. cir. 4062.
A. D. cir. 58.
An. Olymp.
cir. CCIX. 2.
A. U. C. cir.
811.

ᵛ Psa. lxxxi. 12; Wisdom xii. 23; Acts vii. 42; Eph. iv. 18, 19; 2 Thess. ii. 11, 12.——ʷ 1 Cor. vi. 18; 1 Thess. iv. 4; 1 Peter iv. 3.——ˣ Lev. xviii. 22.——ʸ 1 Thess. i. 9; 1 John v. 20.

ᶻ Isa. xliv. 20; Jer. x. 14; xiii. 25; Amos ii. 4.——ᵃ Or, *rather*. ᵇ Lev. xviii. 22, 23; Eph. v. 12; Jude 10.——ᶜ Wisdom xiv. 22, 23, &c.——ᵈ Or, *to acknowledge*.——ᵉ Or, *a mind void of judgment*.——ᶠ Eph. v. 4.

---

representation of their deities was in the *human* figure; and on such representative figures the sculptors spent all their skill; hence the HERCULES of *Farnese*, the VENUS of *Medicis*, and the APOLLO of *Belvidere*. And when they had formed their gods according to the *human shape*, they endowed them with *human passions;* and as they clothed them with attributes of *extraordinary strength, beauty, wisdom, &c.*, not having the true principles of morality, they represented them as slaves to the most disorderly and disgraceful passions; excelling in irregularities the most profligate of men, as possessing unlimited powers of sensual gratification.

And to birds] As the *eagle* of Jupiter among the Romans, and the *ibis* and *hawk* among the Egyptians; which were all sacred animals.

Fourfooted beasts] As the *apis* or *white ox* among the Egyptians; from which the idolatrous Israelites took their *golden calf.* The *goat*, the *monkey*, and the *dog*, were also sacred animals among the same people.

Creeping things.] Such as the *crocodile* and *scarabeus*, or *beetle*, among the Egyptians.

Verse 24. *God—gave them up, &c.*] They had filled up the measure of their iniquities, and God, by permitting them to plunge into all manner of irregularities, thus, by one species of sin, inflicted punishment on another.

Dishonour their own bodies] Probably alluding here to what is more openly expressed, verses 26 and 27.

Between themselves] Εν ἑαυτοις, *Of themselves, of their own free accord*; none *inciting*, none *impelling*.

Verse 25. *Changed the truth of God into a lie*] In the place of the *true worship* of God, they established *idolatry.* In various places of Scripture *idols* are termed *lies.* Isa. xliv. 20; Jer. x. 14; and xiii. 25. The true God *was* known among the primitive inhabitants of the earth; those who first became *idolaters* literally changed the truth of God into a lie: they *did know* the true God, but they put *idols* in his place.

Verse 26. *For this cause God gave them up, &c.*] Their system of idolatry necessarily produced all kinds of *impurity.* How could it be otherwise, when the

highest objects of their worship were adulterers, fornicators, and prostitutes of the most infamous kind, such as *Jupiter, Apollo, Mars, Venus, &c.?* Of the abominable evils with which the apostle charges the Gentiles in this and the following verse I could produce a multitude of proofs from their own writings; but it is needless to make the subject *plainer* than the apostle has left it.

Verse 27. *Receiving in themselves that recompense, &c.*] Both the women and men, by their unnatural prostitutions, enervated their bodies, so that *barrenness* prevailed, and those disorders which are necessarily attendant on *prostitution* and *sodomitical* practices.

Verse 28. *They did not like to retain God*] It would, perhaps, be more literal to translate ουκ εδοκιμασαν, THEY DID NOT SEARCH *to retain God in* their *knowledge.* They did not *examine* the evidences before them (ver. 19 and 20) of his being and attributes; therefore *God gave them over to a* REPROBATE *mind*, εις αδοκιμον νουν, to an UNSEARCHING or *undiscerning* mind; for it is the same word in both places. They did not *reflect* on the proofs they had of the Divine nature, and God abandoned them to the operations of a mind incapable of *reflection.* How men of such powers and learning, as many of the Greek and Roman philosophers and poets really were, could reason so inconsecutively concerning things moral and Divine is truly astonishing. But here we see the hand of a just and avenging God; they abused their powers, and God deprived them of the *right use* of these powers.

Verse 29. *Being filled with all unrighteousness*] Αδικια, every vice contrary to *justice* and *righteousness.*

Fornication] Πορνεια, all commerce between the sexes out of the bounds of lawful marriage. Some of the best MSS. omit this reading; and others have ακαθαρσια, uncleanness.

Wickedness] Πονηρια, *malignity*, that which is oppressive to its possessor and to its object; from πονος, *labour, toil, &c.*

Covetousness] Πλεονεξια, from πλειον, *more*, and εξω *I will have;* the intense love or lust of gain; the de-

2

A. M. cir. 4062.
A. D. cir. 58.
An. Olymp.
cir. CCIX. 2.
A. U. C. cir.
811.

30 Backbiters, haters of God, despiteful, proud, boasters, inventors of evil things, disobedient to parents,

31 Without understanding, covenant-breakers, [g] without natural affection, implacable, unmerciful:

A. M. cir. 4062.
A. D. cir. 58
An. Olymp.
cir. CCIX. 2.
A. U. C. cir.
811.

32 Who, [h] knowing the judgment of God, that they which commit such things [i] are worthy of death, not only do the same, but [k] have [l] pleasure in them that do them.

[g] Or, *unsociable.*——[h] Chap. ii. 2.——[i] Chap. vi. 21.

[k] Or, *consent with them.*——[l] Hos. vii. 3; Psa. l. 18.

termination to be rich; the principle of a *dissatisfied* and *discontented* soul.

Maliciousness] Κακια, *malice, ill-will;* what is radically and essentially *vicious.*

Full of envy] Φθονον, from φθινω, *to wither, decay, consume, pine away, &c.;* "pain felt and malignity conceived at the sight of excellence or happiness in another." A fine personification of this vice is found in Ovid Metam. lib. ii. ver. 768—781, which I shall here insert, with Mr. Addison's elegant and nervous translation.

————————*Videt intus* edentem
Vipereas carnes, vitiorum alimenta suorum
Invidiam: *visaque oculos avertit. At illa
Surgit humo pigra: semesarumque relinquit
Corpora serpentum, passuque incedit inerti.
Utque deam vidit formaque armisque decoram,
Ingemuit: vultumque ima ad suspiria duxit.
Pallor in* ORE *sedet: macies in* CORPORE *toto:
Nusquam recta acies: livent rubigine dentes:
Pectora felle virent: lingua est suffusa veneno.
Risus abest, nisi quem visi movere dolores:
Nec fruitur somno, vigilacibus excita curis:
Sed videt ingratos, intabescitque videndo
Successus hominum; carpitque et carpitur una;
Suppliciumque suum est.*

————*A poisonous morsel* in her teeth she chewed,
And gorged the flesh of *vipers* for her food.
Minerva loathing, turned away her eye.
The hideous monster, rising heavily,
Came stalking forward with a sullen pace,
And left her mangled offals on the place.
Soon as she saw the goddess *gay* and *bright,*
She *fetched* a groan at such a *cheerful* sight.
Livid and *meagre* were her looks, her eye
In foul *distorted glances* turned *awry;*
A hoard of *gall* her *inward parts* possessed,
And spread a *greenness* o'er her *canker'd breast;*
Her teeth were *brown* with *rust,* and from her tongue
In dangling drops the *stringy poison* hung.
She never *smiles* but when the wretched *weep;*
Nor lulls her *malice* with a *moment's sleep;*
Restless in spite while *watchful to destroy,*
She *pines* and *sickens at another's joy;*
Foe *to herself, distressing* and *distressed,*
She bears her own tormentor in her breast.

Murder] Φονον, *taking away* the life of another by any means; *mortal hatred;* for he that hates his brother in his heart is a murderer.

Debate] Εριδος, *contention, discord, &c.* Of this vile passion the Greeks made a *goddess.*

Deceit] Δολον, *lying, falsity, prevarication, imposition, &c.;* from δελω, *to take with a bait.*

Malignity] Κακοηθειας, from κακος, *evil,* and ηθος,

a *custom;* bad customs, founded in *corrupt sentiment,* producing *evil habits,* supported by *general usage.* It is generally interpreted, a *malignity of mind,* which leads its possessor to put the worst construction on every action; ascribing to the *best deeds* the *worst motives.*

Whisperers] Ψιθυριστας, secret detractors; those who, under pretended secrecy, carry about accusations against their neighbours, whether true or false; blasting their reputation by clandestine tittle-tattle. This word should be joined to the succeeding verse. The *whispering* is well expressed by the Greek word ψιθυριστας, psithuristas.

Verse 30. *Backbiters*] Καταλαλους, from κατα, *against,* and λαλεω, *I speak;* those who speak against others; false accusers, slanderers.

Haters of God] Θεοστυγεις, atheists, *contemners of sacred things, maligners of providence, scorners, &c* All profligate deists are of this class; and it seems to be the finishing part of a diabolic character.

Despiteful] Υβριστας, from υβριζω, *to treat with injurious insolence;* stormy, boisterous; abusing both the characters and persons of those over whom they can have any power.

Proud] Υπερηφανους, from υπερ, *above* or *over,* and φαινω, *I show* or *shine.* They who are continually exalting themselves and depressing others; magnifying themselves at the expense of their neighbours; and wishing all men to receive their *sayings* as oracles.

Boasters] Αλαζονας, from λαζομαι, *to assume;* self-assuming, vain-glorious, and arrogant men.

Inventors of evil things] Εφευρετας κακων. Those who have *invented* destructive *customs, rites, fashions, &c.;* such as the different religious *ceremonies* among the *Greeks* and *Romans*—the *orgies* of *Bacchus,* the *mysteries* of *Ceres,* the *lupercalia,* feasts of the *Bona Dea, &c., &c.* Multitudes of which evil things, destructive and abominable ceremonies, are to be found in every part of the heathen worship.

Disobedient to parents] Though filial affection was certainly more recommended and cultivated than many other virtues, yet there are many instances on record of the grossest violation of this great branch of the law of nature.

Verse 31. *Without understanding*] Ασυνετους, from α, *negative,* and συνετος, *knowing;* persons incapable of comprehending what was spoken; destitute of capacity for spiritual things.

Covenant-breakers] Ασυνθετους, from α, *negative,* and συντιθημι, *to make an agreement;* persons who could be bound by no *oath,* because, properly speaking, they had *no God* to witness or avenge their misconduct. As every covenant, or agreement, is made as in the presence of God, so he that opposes the being and doctrine of God is incapable of being bound by any covenant; he can give no pledge for his conduct.

2

Without natural affection] Αστοργους; without that attachment which nature teaches the young of all animals to have to their mothers, and the mothers to have for their young. The heathens, in general, have made no scruple to *expose* the children they did not think proper to bring up, and to despatch their parents when they were grown old or past labour.

Implacable] Ασπονδους, from *α, negative;* and σπονδη, A LIBATION. It was customary among all nations to pour out *wine* as a libation to their gods, when making a treaty. This was done to appease the angry gods, and *reconcile* them to the contracting parties. The word here shows a *deadly enmity;* the highest pitch of an unforgiving spirit; in a word, persons who would not make *reconciliation* either to *God* or *man.*

Unmerciful] Ανελεημονας; those who were incapable, through the deep-rooted wickedness of their own nature, of showing mercy to an *enemy* when brought under their power, or doing any thing for the *necessitous,* from the principle of *benevolence* or *commiseration.*

Verse 32. *Who, knowing the judgment of God*] Δικαιωμα, the *grand rule of right* which God has revealed to every man, the knowledge of which he has, less or more, given to every nation of the world, relative to honouring parents, taking care of their own offspring, keeping their engagements, &c., &c. In the worst states of heathenism this great principle has been acknowledged; but, through the prevalence of corruption in the heart, this law, though acknowledged, was not obeyed; and the corruption increased so that those were highest in repute who had cast off all restraints of this kind; so that they even delighted in them; συνευδοκουσι, highly applauded, and gladly associated with those transgressors: which argues the very highest pitch of moral depravity.

1. THE preceding chapter gives us one of the finest views of the Gospel of Christ, to be met with any where. It is God's *method of saving a lost world,* in a way which that world could never have imagined: there is nothing *human* in it; it is all truly and gloriously *Divine;* essentially *necessary* to the salvation of man, and fully *adequate* to the purposes of its institution. Though it is an extension of the old covenant, yet it is almost wholly dissimilar; being as different from that as the *person* is from the *picture* which represents it, and as the *substance* is from the *shadow* projected by it. It is a scheme as *worthy* of God as it is *necessary* for *man;* hence there are no excluding clauses in it—it is for the *Jew* and for the *Greek;* for the *wise* and for the *unwise;* for all the *nations* of the universe, and for all the *individuals* of those nations. He blasphemes God who holds the contrary

2. As God never does any thing that is not *fitting, suitable,* and *necessary* to be done, he has not made an *unnecessary* display of his mercy and goodness in the incarnation and death of his Son—all this was *necessary,* else it had not been done. But how does the necessity appear? In the deep-rooted and widely extended corruption and profligacy of the nations of the earth. Of these the apostle gives a most affecting and distressing picture. 1. Almost every *trace* of original righteousness had been *obliterated.* 2 The proofs of God's eternal power and providence, so manifest in the creation and preservation of the universe, were wholly disregarded. 3. A vain philosophy, without right, *principle,* or *end,* was substituted for those Divine truths which had been discovered originally to man. 4. Their hearts were contaminated with every vice which could blind the understanding, pervert the judgment, corrupt the will, and debase the affections and passions. 5. This was proved in the most unequivocal manner, by a profligacy of conduct which had debased them far, far below the beasts that perish; and the apostle here gives a list of their crimes, every article of which can be incontrovertibly proved from their own history and their own writers: crimes which, even bad as the world is now, would shock common decency to describe. See the whole of the *second, third, sixth,* and *ninth* Satires of *Juvenal.*

3. So completely lost were the heathens to a knowledge of the influence of God on the soul, and the necessity of that influence, that they asserted, in the most positive manner, that man was the author of his own virtue and wisdom. Cicero, *Nat. Deor.,* lib. iii. c. 36, declares it a general opinion that, although mankind received from the gods the outward conveniencies of life—*virtutem autem nemo unquam acceptam Deo retulit*—"virtue none ever thought they received from the Deity." And again:—"This is the persuasion of all, that fortune is to be had from the gods; wisdom from ourselves." And again:—"Whoever thanked the gods for his being a good man? Men pray to Jupiter, not that he would make them *just, temperate,* and *wise;* but rich and prosperous."

JUVENAL, on this point, speaks thus:—

Monstro, quod ipse tibi possis dare : Semita certe
Tranquillæ per virtutem patet unica vitæ.

Sat. x. v. 363

The path to peace is *virtue;* which, I show,
Thyself may fully on *thyself* bestow.

In the same strain, HORACE, EPIST. lib. i. E. xviii. v penult.

Hæc satis est orare Jovem, qui donat et aufert:
Det vitam det opes : æquum mi animum ipse parabo.

To Jove for life and wealth I pray,
These Jove may give or take away;
But, for a *firm* and *tranquil mind,*
That *blessing for myself I find*

Thus, *they became vain in their imaginations, and their foolish heart was darkened; and professing themselves to be wise, they became fools.* See Madan's *Juvenal,* vol. ii. p. 53.

4. By all this we see what the world was, and what it would have continued to be had not God sent a *Divine* revelation of his will, and established a public ministry to proclaim and enforce it Were man left to the power and influence of his fallen nature he would be, in all places of his dispersion on the earth, what the apostle describes in the 29th, 30th, and 31st verses of this chapter

Reader, magnify God, who has called thee from such deep darkness, to the marvellous light of the glorious Gospel of his Son; and walk as a child of the light and of the day, in whom there shall be no cause of stumbling

CHAPTER II.

The apostle shows that the Jew, who condemns the Gentiles, and considers them utterly unworthy of the blessings of the Gospel, is inexcusable, because he is guilty of the same crimes; and therefore shall not escape the righteous judgment of God, 1—3. It is an awful thing to despise the goodness and long-suffering of God, which lead to repentance, 4, 5. God, the impartial judge, will render to every man according to his works, 6—11. The Jews and the Gentiles will be judged according to their respective advantages and disadvantages, 12, 13. In some cases, the Gentiles, who had no law, have shown a better disposition than the Jews, 14—16. The Jews, by their unfaithfulness, have been a stumbling-block to the Gentiles, 17—24. Jewish rites and ceremonies of no advantage, unless productive of change of heart and conduct, 25. The Gentiles, who attend to the small light which they have received from God, are in a better state than the unfaithful Jews, with all their superior religious privileges, 26, 27. What constitutes a real Jew in the sight of God, 28, 29.

A. M. cir. 4062.
A. D. cir. 58.
An. Olymp.
cir. CCIX. 2.
A. U. C. cir.
811.

THEREFORE thou art ᵃ inexcusable, O man, whosoever thou art that judgest; ᵇ for wherein thou judgest another, thou condemnest thyself; for thou that judgest doest the same things.

2 But we are sure that the judgment of God is according to truth

A. M. cir. 4062.
A. D. cir. 58.
An. Olymp.
cir. CCIX. 2.
A. U. C. cir.
811.

ᵃ Chap. i. 20.   ᵇ 2 Sam. xii. 5, 6, 7; Matt. vii. 1, 2; John viii. 9.

NOTES ON CHAP. II.

Dr. Taylor makes the following sensible observations at the commencement of this chapter.

"The representation of the moral state of the heathen world, in the foregoing chapter, is a demonstration of the *necessity of the Gospel* for the reformation and salvation of man. And how rich is the favour wherewith God has visited the world! To have destroyed a race of apostate rebels, who had abused their understandings and every gift of a bountiful Creator, would have been *justice*; to have spared them would have been *lenity* and *goodness*; but to send his only begotten Son from heaven to redeem us from all iniquity and ungodliness by his own blood; to grant us a free pardon for all our sins; to put us in a state of mercy and salvation; to take us into his kingdom and family; to give us an inheritance among his saints; to bless us with immortality and all spiritual blessings in heavenly places;—this is most wonderful and exuberant favour. Rightly is the doctrine which teaches it called the *Gospel*, or *glad tidings*. One would think it could not possibly have met with opposition from any part of mankind. But the JEW opposed it! He abhorred the *Gentile*, and contradicted the grace that honoured and saved him. The apostle pleads and defends our cause. His business is to confound the *Jew*, and to prove that *we* have as good a right as he to all the blessings of the Messiah's kingdom. And, y his description of the vicious state of the Gentiles, in the former chapter, he has wisely made his advantage of the prejudices of the *Jew*; for nothing could please him more than the preceding discourse, in which the Gentiles are reduced to so vile and abject a state. Thus the apostle gives him an opportunity to condemn the Gentiles; but he does this that he may the more effectually humble him in this chapter; in which he proves that the Jews, having in an aggravated manner despised the goodness and broken the law of God, were as obnoxious to his wrath as the Gentiles; and if so, how could they, with any conscience or modesty, arrogate all the Divine mercy to *themselves*, or pretend that others were unworthy of it, when *they* had done

as much or more to forfeit it! Must they not exclude themselves from being the people of God under the Gospel, by the same reason that they would have the Gentiles excluded! But this was an argument highly ungrateful to the Jew; and it would be very difficult to fix any conviction upon his mind. Therefore the apostle addresses him in a covert way :—*Thou art therefore inexcusable, O man, whosoever thou art that judgest;* not giving out expressly that he meant the *Jew*, that the Jew might more calmly attend to his reasoning, while he was not apprehensive that *he* was the man. This point secured, the apostle, very judiciously and with great force of reasoning, turns his thoughts from his present superior advantages to the awful day of judgment, ver. 5, 6, when God, in the most impartial equity, will render to all mankind, without exception, according to their works. Thus the apostle grounds his following argument, very methodically and solidly, in God's equal regards to all men, in all nations, who uprightly practise truth and godliness; and his disapproving, and at last condemning, all men, in any nation, however privileged, who live wickedly. This was a blow at the root, and demolished, in the most effectual manner, the *Jew's* prejudices in favour of his own nation, and the unkind thoughts he had entertained of the *Gentiles*. For, if a Jew could be convinced that a sober, upright heathen might be blessed with eternal salvation, he must be persuaded that it was no absurd matter that believing *Gentiles* should *now* be pardoned, and taken into the visible Church. Thus the apostle advances with great skill, insinuating himself, by degrees, into the Jew's conscience. This reasoning is well adapted to encourage the *Gentile*, humbled by the dismal representation in the preceding chapter; for he would here see that he was not utterly abandoned of God, but might, upon good grounds, hope for his mercy and kindness."

Verse 1. *That judgest*] Ὁ κρινων, *the judger*; thou *assumest* the character of a judge, and in that character condemnest others who are less guilty than thyself.

Verse 2. *We are sure that the judgment of God,*

A. M. cir. 4062.
A. D. cir. 58.
An. Olymp.
cir. CCIX. 2.
A. U. C. cir.
811.

against them which commit such things.

3 And thinkest thou this, O man, that judgest them which do such things, and doest the same, that thou shalt escape the judgment of God?

4 Or despisest thou [c] the riches of his goodness and [d] forbearance and [e] long-suffering; [f] not knowing that the goodness of God leadeth thee to repentance?

5 But after thy hardness and impenitent heart [g] treasurest up unto thyself wrath against the day of wrath and revelation of the righteous judgment of God;

6 [h] Who will render to every man according to his deeds:

A. M. cir. 4062.
A. D. cir. 58.
An. Olymp.
cir. CCIX. 2.
A. U. C. cir.
811.

7 To them who, by patient continuance in well doing, seek for glory and honour and immortality, eternal life:

8 But unto them that are contentious, and [i] do not obey the truth, but obey unrighteousness, indignation and wrath,

9 Tribulation and anguish, upon every soul of man that doeth evil, of the Jew [k] first, and also of the [l] Gentile;

10 [m] But glory, honour, and peace, to every man that worketh good, to the Jew first, and also to the [n] Gentile;

---

[c] Chap. ix. 23; Eph. i. 7; ii. 4, 7.——[d] Ch. iii. 25.——[e] Exod. xxxiv. 6.——[f] Isa. xxx. 18; 2 Pet. iii. 9, 15.——[g] Deut. xxxii. 34; James v. 3.——[h] Job xxxiv. 11; Psa. lxii. 12; Prov. xxiv. 12; Jer. xvii. 10; xxxii. 19; Matt. xvi. 27; chap. xiv. 12; 1 Cor.

iii. 8; 2 Cor. v. 10; Rev. ii. 23; xx. 12; xxii. 12.——[i] Job xxiv. 13; chap. i. 18; 2 Thess. i. 8.——[k] Amos iii. 2; Luke xii. 47, 48; 1 Peter iv. 17.——[l] Gr. *Greek.*——[m] 1 Peter i. 7.——[n] Gr. *Greek.*

&c.] God is impartial, and will punish sin wheresoever he finds it. *Transgression in a Jew* is not less criminal than *iniquity in a Gentile.*

Verse 4. *Or despisest thou the riches of his goodness*] Wilt thou render of none effect that marked benevolence of God towards thee which has given so many superior advantages, and that *forbearance* which has tolerated thy many miscarriages, and that *long-suffering* which, after repeated provocations, still continues to bear with thee?

Not knowing] Αγνοων, not *acknowledging* that this goodness of God, which has so long manifested itself in *forbearance* and *long-suffering, leadeth thee to repentance*—was designed to accomplish this blessed end; which thy want of *consideration* and *acknowledgment* has rendered, hitherto, ineffectual. This was a maxim among the Jews themselves; for, in *Synopsis Sohar*, it is said:—*The holy blessed God delays his anger against the wicked, to the end that they may repent and be converted.*

Verse 5. *But after thy hardness*] Occasioned by thy long course of iniquity. *And impenitent heart*—produced by thy hardness, through which thou art *callous* to the calls and expostulations of conscience. *Treasurest up*—continuest to *increase thy debt* to the Divine justice, which will infallibly inflict *wrath*—punishment in *the day of wrath*—the judgment day, in which he will render to every man according to his works. The word *treasure* the Hebrew uses to express any kind of *store* or *collection:*—*Treasure* or plenty of *rain.* Deut. xxviii. 12: *The Lord shall open unto thee his good* TREASURE, *to give the* RAIN *unto thy land.* Treasure of *punishment.* Deut. xxxii. 34, 35: *Is not this sealed up among my* TREASURES? *To me* belongeth VENGEANCE *and* RECOMPENSE. Treasures of *mines*, i. e. abundance of minerals. Deut. xxxiii. 19: *They shall suck of the* ABUNDANCE *of the seas, and of* TREASURES *hid in the sand.* So treasures of *gold, silver, corn, wine, oil,* &c., mean *collections* or an *abundance* of such things: the word is used by the Greek *writers* precisely in the same sense. By

wrath we are to understand *punishment*, as in chap. i. 18; and it is used so by the very best Greek writers. See *Kypke.*

The *treasure of wrath*, in this verse, is opposed to the *riches* of *goodness*, in the preceding. As surely as thou despisest, or neglectest to improve the RICHES *of God's* GOODNESS, so surely thou shalt share in the TREASURES of his WRATH. The *punishment* shall be proportioned to the *mercy* thou hast abused.

Verse 6. *Who will render*] Who, in the day of judgment, will reward and punish every man according as his life and conversation have been.

Verse 7. *To them, &c.*] In this manner will God, in the great day, dispense punishments and rewards: 1. He will give eternal life to them who, in all the *trials* and *difficulties* of the present state, have *persevered* in well doing—seeking for and expecting *glory, honour,* and *immortality.*

Verse 8. *But unto them, &c.*] 2. He will manifest his *indignation*, and inflict *wrath*—punishment, on all who are *contentious*—who obstinately dispute against the truth, and *obey unrighteousness*—who act under the influence of the principle of sin, and not under the influence of the Spirit of God.

Verse 9. *Tribulation and anguish*] Misery of all descriptions, without the possibility of escape, will this righteous Judge inflict upon every impenitent sinner. The *Jew first*, as possessing greater privileges, and having abused greater mercies; and also on the *Gentile*, who, though he had not the same advantages, had what God saw was sufficient for his state; and, having sinned against them, shall have punishment proportioned to his demerit.

Verse 10. *But glory, honour, and peace*] While the finally impenitent Jew and Gentile shall experience the fullest effects of the righteous indignation of the supreme Judge, every man that *worketh good*—that lives in a conscientious obedience to the *known will of God,* whether he be *Jew* or *Gentile,* shall have *glory, honour,* and *peace;* i. e. eternal blessedness.

A. M. cir. 4062.
A. D. cir. 58.
An. Olymp.
cir. CCIX. 2.
A. U. C. cir.
811.

11 For ° there is no respect of persons with God.

12 For as many as have sinned without law, shall also perish without law: and as many as have sinned in the law, shall be judged by the law;

13 (For ᵖ not the hearers of the law *are* just before God, but the doers of the law shall be justified.

14 For when the Gentiles, which have not

the law, do by nature the things contained in the law, these, having not the law, are a law unto themselves:

15 Which show the work of the law written in their hearts, � their conscience also bearing witness, and *their* thoughts, ʳ the mean while, accusing or else excusing one another;)

16 ˢ In the day when God shall judge the

A. M. cir. 4062.
A. D. cir. 58.
An. Olymp.
cir. CCIX. 2.
A. U. C. cir.
811.

° Deut. x. 17; 2 Chron. xix. 7; Job xxxiv. 19; Acts x. 34; Gal. ii. 6; Eph. vi. 9; Col. iii. 25; 1 Pet. i. 17.——ᵖ Matt. vii. 21; James i. 22, 23, 25; 1 John iii. 7.

� Or, *the conscience witnessing with them.*——ʳ Or, *between themselves.*——ˢ Eccles. xii. 14; Matt. xxv. 31; John xii. 48; chap. iii. 6; 1 Cor. iv. 5; Rev. xx. 12.

Verse 11. *For there is no respect of persons with God.*] The righteous Judge will not act according to any principle of *partiality*; the *character* and *conduct*, alone of the persons shall weigh with him. He will take no wicked man to glory, let his nation or advantages be what they may; and he will send no righteous man to perdition, though brought up in the very bosom of *Gentilism.* And as he will judge in that day according to *character* and *conduct*, so his judgment will proceed on the ground of the *graces*, *privileges*, and *blessings* which they had received, improved or abused. And as there is no respect of persons with God in judgment, so there can be none in the *previous* administration of his *saving* blessings. He that will be condemned for his unrighteousness, will be condemned on the ground that he had sufficient grace afforded him for the salvation of his soul; and his condemnation will rest on the simple principle, that he *abused the grace* which was sufficient to save him, by acting in opposition to its dictates and influence. No man, in that great day, shall be brought to heaven through any *partiality* of the Judge; and no man sent to hell because God did not afford him sufficient grace, or because he had made a *decree* which rendered even his use of it *ineffectual* to his salvation. In reference to the great design of God, in the salvation of man, it shall be said,—in time, at the day of judgment, and throughout eternity,—THERE IS NO RESPECT OF PERSONS WITH GOD.

Verse 12. *For as many as have sinned without law, &c.*] They, viz. the *Gentiles*, who shall be found to have transgressed against the mere *light of nature*, or rather, *that true light that lighteth every man that cometh into the world*, John i. 9, shall not come under the same rule with those, the *Jews*, who have in *addition* to this enjoyed an extraordinary *revelation*; but they shall be dealt with according to the inferior dispensation, under which they lived: while those, the *Jews*, who have *sinned against the law*—the positive Divine revelation granted to them, *shall be judged by that law*, and punished proportionably to the abuse of such an extraordinary advantage.

Verse 13. *For not the hearers of the law, &c.*] It does not follow, because one people are favoured with a Divine revelation, that therefore *they* shall be *saved*; while the others who have not had that revelation, shall finally perish: this is not God's procedure; where he has given a *law*—a *Divine revelation*, he requires *obedience* to that law; and only those who have been

doers of that law—who have lived according to the light and privileges granted in that revelation, *shall be justified*—shall be finally acknowledged to be such as are fit for the kingdom of God.

Verse 14. *For when the Gentiles, which have not the law, &c.*] Nor does it follow that the Gentiles, who have not had a Divine revelation, shall either perish, because they had it not; or their unrighteous conduct pass *unpunished*, because not having this revelation might be considered as an excuse for their sins.

Do by nature the things contained in the law] Do, without this Divine revelation, through that light which God imparts to every man, *the things contained in the law*—act according to justice, mercy, temperance and truth, the practice of which the revealed law so powerfully enjoins; *these are a law unto themselves*—they are not accountable to any other law, and are not to be judged by any dispensation different from that under which they live.

Rabbi Tanchum brings in the Supreme Being as saying: *When I decreed any thing against the Gentiles, to whom I have not given laws and statutes*, and they know what I have decreed, immediately they repent; but the Israelites do not so. *Tanchum*, fol. 43. 2.

Verse 15. *Which show the work of the law*] In acting according to justice, mercy, temperance, and truth, they show that the great object of the law, which was to bring men from *injustice*, *cruelty*, *intemperance*, and *falsity*, is accomplished so far in them: *their conscience also bearing witness*—that faculty of the soul, where that Divine light dwells and works, shows them that they are right; and thus they have a comfortable testimony in their own souls of their own integrity: *their thoughts, the mean while, accusing, or else excusing one another;* or rather, *their reasonings between one another accusing or answering for themselves.* As if the apostle had said:—And this point, that they have a law and act according to it, is farther proved from their conduct in *civil* affairs; and from that correct sense which they have of *natural justice* in their *debates*, either in their *courts of law*, or in their *treatises on morality.* All these are ample proofs that God has not left them without light; and that, seeing they have such correct notions of *right* and *wrong*, they are accountable to God for their conduct in reference to these notions and principles. This seems to be the true meaning of this difficult clause. See below.

Verse 16. *In the day when God shall judge*] And all this shall be farther exemplified and proved in the

| A. M. cir. 4062. |
| A. D. cir. 58. |
| An. Olymp. |
| cir. CCIX. 2. |
| A. U. C. cir. |
| 811. |

secrets of men [t] by Jesus Christ, [u] according to my Gospel.

17 Behold, [v] thou art called a Jew, and [w] restest in the law, [x] and makest thy boast of God,

18 And [y] knowest *his* will, and [z] approvest [a] the things that are

| A. M. cir. 4062. |
| A. D. cir. 58. |
| An. Olymp. |
| cir. CCIX. 2. |
| A. U. C. cir. |
| 811. |

---

[t] John v. 22; Acts x. 42; xvii. 31; 2 Tim. iv. 1, 8; 1 Pet. iv. 5.——[u] Chap. xvi. 25; 1 Tim. i. 11; 2 Tim. ii. 8.——[v] Matt. iii. 9; John viii. 33; chap. ix. 6, 7; 2 Cor. xi. 22.

[w] Mic. iii. 11; chap. ix. 4.——[x] Isa. xlv. 25; xlviii. 2; John viii. 41.——[y] Deut. iv. 8; Psa. cxlvii. 19, 20.——[z] Or, *triest the things that differ.*——[a] Phil. i. 10.

---

day when God shall judge the *secrets of men by Jesus Christ;* which judgment shall be according *to my Gospel*—according to what I am now laying down before you, relative to the *impartiality of God,* and his *righteous* procedure in judging men, not according to their opinions or prejudices, not according to revelations which they never possessed, but according to the various advantages or disadvantages of their political, religious, or domestic situation in life.

Much stress has been laid on the word, φυσει, *by nature,* in ver. 14, as if the apostle designed to intimate that *nature,* independently of the influence of Divine grace, possessed such principles as were sufficient to guide a man to glory. But certainly the term cannot be so understood here. I rather think that the sense given to it in *Suicer's* Thesaurus, vol ii. col. 1475, *reipsa, revera,* CERTAINLY, TRULY, is its sense here: *for when the Gentiles, which have not the law,* φυσει ποιη, TRULY, or in *effect,* DO *the things contained in the law, &c.* This seems to be its sense in Gal. iv. 8: *When ye knew not God, ye did service to them which* φυσει, CERTAINLY *are no gods;* i. e. are *false* gods. *Suicer* quotes *Cyril of Alexandria,* (sub Anathematismo iii. in Actis Ephesinis, p. 212,) speaking of the union of the two natures in Christ; he calls this *union* φυσικην, *natural;* that is, says he, αληθη, *true,* or *real.* He adds, that the word should be thus understood in Eph. ii. 3: *We were by nature,* φυσει, *children of wrath;* and says, φυσει αντι του αληθως· φυσει *is here used for* αληθως, TRULY; *We were* TRULY, INCONTESTABLY, *the children of wrath, even as others.* That is, like the rest of mankind, we have all sinned and come short of the glory of God, and, consequently are exposed to *punishment.* Some think that this text refers to the *natural corruption* of man; but, although it is true that man comes into the world corrupt, and that all men, since the *fall,* are very far gone from original righteousness, yet it is not *clear* that the text in Eph. ii. 3, speaks of any other thing than the *effects* of this degeneracy.

I prefer this sense, in the passage in question, to that which says the *light of nature,* or *natural instinct,* is here meant; for I know of no light in nature that is not kindled there by the *grace of God.* But I have no objection to this sense: "When the Gentiles, which have not the law, do, by the influence of God upon their hearts, the things contained in the law, they are a law unto themselves; that light and influence serving instead of a Divine revelation." That the Gentiles did *really* do the things contained in the law, in reference to what is termed *natural justice,* and made the wisest distinctions relative to the great principles of the doctrine of *civil* RIGHTS and WRONGS, every man conversant with their writings will admit. And in reference to this the word φυσει may be legitimately

understood thus—they *incontestably* did the things contained in the law, &c.

The passage in ver. 15, *Their thoughts—accusing or excusing one another,* certainly does not refer to any expostulations or operations of *conscience;* for this is referred to in the preceding clause. The words *accusing,* κατηγορουντων, and *excusing,* απολογουμενων, *answering* or *defending one another,* μεταξυ αλληλων, *among themselves,* are all forensic or *law* terms, and refer to the mode of conducting *suits of law* in courts of justice, where one is *plaintiff,* who produces his *accusation;* another is *defendant,* who *rebuts* the *charge* and defends himself; and then the business is argued before the judges. This process shows that they have a law of *their own,* and that to this law it belongs to adjust differences—to right those who have suffered wrong, and to punish the guilty.

As to the phrase *written in their hearts,* it is here opposed to the Jewish laws, which were *written* on *tables of stone.* The *Jews* drew the maxims by which their conduct was regulated from a *Divine revelation:* the GENTILES theirs from what God, in the course of his providence and gracious influence, had shown them to be right, useful, and necessary. And with them this law was *well known and affectionately regarded;* for this is one meaning of the phrase, *written in the heart.* It was from this true light, enlightening the Gentiles, that they had so many wise and wholesome laws; laws which had been among them from time immemorial, and of which they did not know the origin. Thus Sophocles, in the noble speech which he puts in the mouth of Antigone:—

Ου γαρ τι νυν γε καχθες, αλλ' αει ποτε
Ζη ταυτα, κουδεις οιδεν εξ οτου φανη·

" Not now, nor yesterday, but evermore
These laws have lived: nor know we whence they
came."   Antig. ver. 463–4.

These are the laws, νομινα, which the Spirit of God wrote originally on their hearts; and which, in different forms, they had committed to *writing.*

Verse 17. *Behold, thou art called a Jew*] What the apostle had said in the preceding verses being sufficient to enforce conviction on the conscience of the Jew, he now throws off the cover, and openly argues with him in the most plain and nervous manner; asserting that his superior knowledge, privileges, and profession, served only to aggravate his condemnation. And that, in fact, he who, under all his greater advantages, transgressed the law of God, stood condemned by the honest *Gentile,* who, to the best of his knowledge, obeyed it. Dr. *Taylor.*

And restest in the law] Thou trustest in it for thy endless salvation. The word επαναπαυη, implies the

50   (4**)

A. M. cir. 4062.
A. D. cir. 58.
An. Olymp.
cir. CCIX. 2.
A. U. C. cir.
811.

more excellent, being instructed out of the law ;

19 And ^b art confident that thou thyself art a guide of the blind, a light of them which are in darkness,

20 An instructer of the foolish, a teacher of babes, ^c which hast the form of knowledge and of the truth in the law.

21 ^d Thou therefore which teachest another, teachest thou not thyself ? thou that preachest a man should not steal, dost thou steal ?

A. M. cir. 4062.
A. D. cir. 58.
An. Olymp.
cir. CCIX. 2.
A. U. C. cir.
811.

---

^b Matt. xv. 14; xxiii. 16, 17, 19, 24; John ix. 34, 40, 41.——^c Ch. vi. 17; 2 Tim. i. 13; iii. 5.——^d Psa. l. 16, &c.; Matt. xxiii. 3, &c.

---

strongest confidence of safety and security. Thou *reposest* thy *whole trust and confidence* in this law.

And makest thy boast of God] That thou knowest his *nature* and *attributes*, which are not known to the Gentiles. The word, καυχασαι, implies the idea of *exulting* in any thing, as being a *proper object of hope* and *dependence :* and, when referred to GOD, it points out that HE is the sure cause of *hope, dependence, joy,* and *happiness ;* and that it is the highest *honour* to be called to know his name, and be employed in his service. As if the apostle had said : You rejoice in God as the object of your hope and dependence ; you praise and magnify him ; you account it your greatest *honour* that HE is your God, and that you worship him.

Verse 18. *Knowest his will*] Hast been favoured with a revelation of his own will, immediately from himself.

The things that are more excellent] Τα διαφεροντα, *The things that differ*—that revelation which God has given of himself makes the nicest *distinctions* between *right* and *wrong ;* between *vice* and *virtue ;* showing how you should walk so as to please God, and, consequently, acquire the *most excellent* portion that human spirits can have on this side heaven : for all these *blessings* ye acknowledge to receive from your *law,* being instructed, κατηχουμενος, being *catechized,* from your infancy, in the knowledge of Divine things.

Verse 19. *And art confident, &c.*] In consequence of all these religious advantages, ye believe that ye are able to teach others, and to be *guides* and *lights* to the *bewildered, darkened Gentiles,* who may become proselytes to your religion.

Verse 20. *An instructer of the foolish, &c.*] Ye believe the Gentiles to be *babes* and *fools* when compared with yourselves ; that ye alone possess the only *true knowledge ;* that ye are the only *favourites* of Heaven ; and that all nations must look up to you as possessing the only *form of knowledge,* μορφωσιν της γνωσεως, the grand *scheme* and *draught* of all true *science,* of every thing that is worthy to be learned : the system of eternal *truth,* derived *from the law.* If, therefore, ye act not as becomes those who have such eminent advantages, it must be to your endless disgrace and infamy.

Verse 21. *Thou therefore*] Dr. Taylor has paraphrased this and the three following verses thus : " What signify your pretensions to knowledge, and the office of teaching others, if you have no regard to your own doctrine ? What are you the better for preaching against *theft,* if you are a *thief* yourself ? Or for declaring *adultery* unlawful, if you live in the practice of it ? Or for representing *idolatry* abominable, if you are guilty of *sacrilege ?* What honours or singular favours do you deserve, if, while you glory in the law

and your religious privileges, you dishonour God, and discredit his religion, by transgressing his law, and living in open contradiction to your profession ? And this is more than supposition ; notorious instances might be produced of the forementioned crimes, whereby the Jews of the present age have brought a reproach upon religion among the *Gentiles ;* as well as those Jews of former times, of whom the Prophet Ezekiel speaks, chap. xxxvi. 23 : *And I will sanctify my great name, which was* PROFANED *among the* HEATHEN, *which ye have* PROFANED *in the midst of them.*"

That the Jewish *priesthood* was exceedingly corrupt in the time of the apostle, and that they were so long before, is fully evident from the sacred writings and from Josephus. The high-priesthood was a matter of *commerce,* and was *bought* and *sold* like other commodities. Of this Josephus gives many instances. The *rapine* of Eli's sons descended to several generations. Dr. Whitby well observes that of all these things mentioned by the apostle the Jewish doctors were notoriously guilty ; and of most of them they were accused by our Lord. 1. *They said and did not ;* and *laid heavy burdens upon others, which they would not touch with their own fingers,* Matt. xxiii. 3, 4. 2. They made the house of God a den of *thieves,* Matt. xxi. 13 ; John ii. 16. 3. They were guilty of *adultery* by unjust *divorces,* Matt. xix. 9. 4. Their *polygamy* was scandalous : even their rabbins, when they came to any place, would exclaim, *Who will be my wife for a day ?* As to *idolatry,* they were perfectly saved from it ever since the Babylonish captivity : but to this succeeded *sacrilege,* as is most evident in the profanation of the temple, by their commerce transacted even within its courts ; and their teaching the people that even their aged parents might be left to starve, provided the children made a *present to the temple* of that which should have gone for their support. According to Josephus, *Bell. Jud.* l. vi. c. 26, *They were guilty of theft, treachery, adultery, sacrilege, rapine, and murder.* And he adds, that *new ways of wickedness were invented by them ; and that of all their abominations the temple was the receptacle.* In his *Antiquities* of the Jews, lib. xx. c. 8, he says : *The servants of the high priests took away, by violence, the tithes of the priests, so that many of them perished for want of food.* Even their own writers acknowledge that there were great irregularities and abominations among the rabbins.

So *Bereshith rabba,* sect. 55, fol. 54 : " Rabbi Abun proposed a parable concerning a master who taught his disciples not to pervert justice, and yet did it himself ; not to show respect of persons, and yet did it himself ; not to receive bribes, and yet received them himself ; not to take usury, and yet took it himself.

A. M. cir. 4062.
A. D. cir. 58.
An. Olymp.
cir. CCIX. 2.
A. U. C. cir.
811.

22 Thou that sayest a man should not commit adultery, dost thou commit adultery ? thou that abhorrest idols, e dost thou commit sacrilege ?

23 Thou that f makest thy boast of the law, through breaking the law dishonourest thou God ?

24 For the name of God is blasphemed among the Gentiles through you, as it is g written.

25 h For circumcision verily profiteth, if thou keep the law : but if thou be a breaker of the law, thy circumcision is made uncircumcision.

26 Therefore i if the uncircumcision keep the righteousness of the law, shall not his uncircumcision be counted for circumcision ?

27 And shall not uncircumcision which is by nature, if it fulfil the law, k judge thee, who by the letter and circumcision dost transgress the law ?

28 For l he is not a Jew, which is one outwardly ; neither *is that* circumcision, which is outward in the flesh :

29 But he *is* a Jew, m which is one inwardly ; and n circumcision *is that* of the heart, d in the spirit, *and* not in the letter ; p whose praise *is* not of men, but of God.

A. M. cir. 4062.
A. D. cir. 58.
An. Olymp.
cir. CCIX. 2.
A. U. C. cir.
811.

---

e Mal. iii. 8.——f Ver. 17.——g 2 Sam. xii. 14 ; Isa. lii. 5 ; Ezek. xxxvi. 20, 23.——h Gal. v. 3.——i Acts x. 34, 35.——k Matt. xii. 41, 42.

l Matt. iii. 9 ; John viii. 39 ; chap. ix. 6, 7 ; Gal. vi. 15 ; Rev. ii. 9. m 1 Pet. iii. 4.——n Col. ii. 11 ; Phil. iii. 3.——o Chap. vii. 6. 2 Cor. iii. 6.——p 1 Cor. iv. 5 ; 2 Cor. x. 18 ; 1 Thess. ii. 4.

The disciple replied :—Rabbi, thou teachest me not to take usury, and yet thou takest it thyself ! Can that be lawful to *thee* which is forbidden to *me ?*"

Verse 24. *For the name of God is blasphemed, &c.*] In *Debarim rabba*, sect. 2, fol. 251, it is said :—"The rulers destroy the influence of their own words among the people ; and this is done when a rabbin, sitting and teaching in the academy, says, Do not take usury, and himself takes it ; do not commit rapine, and himself commits it ; do not steal, and himself steals." That they were exceedingly lax in their morals, the following fact proves :—"Rabbi Ilai said, If a man see that his evil propensities are likely to prevail against him, let him go to some place where he is not known, and let him put on black clothes, and cover his head with a black veil ; and then let him *do whatsoever he pleases*, lest the name of God should be *publicly* profaned." *Moed katon*, fol. 17 1. In *Sohar Levit.* fol. 31, col. 122, it is said :—"On *three* accounts the Jews are obliged to remain in captivity—1. Because they *openly reproach* the Shechinah—2. Because they *profane themselves* before the Shechinah—3. Because they *turn away their faces* from the Shechinah."

But it would be endless to collect from their history the proofs of the charges brought here against them by the apostle. See *Whitby, Schoettgen,* and others.

Verse 25. *For circumcision verily profiteth*] It is a blessing to belong to the Church of God and wear the sign of the covenant, provided the terms of the covenant are complied with.

But if thou be a breaker of the law] If thou do not observe the conditions of the covenant, the outward sign is both without meaning and without effect. This was a maxim of the rabbins themselves ; for they allowed that an apostate or ungodly Israelite must go to hell, notwithstanding his *circumcision.*

Verse 26. *Therefore if the uncircumcision, &c.*] If the *Gentile* be found to act according to the *spirit* and *design* of the *law*, his acting thus uprightly, according to the light which God has afforded him, will be reckoned to him as if he were circumcised and walked agreeably to the law.

Verse 27. *And shall not uncircumcision, which is by nature*] And shall not the Gentile, who is εκ φυσεως, according to the *custom of his country*—who is, *by birth*, not obliged to be circumcised.

If it fulfil the law] If such a person act according to the spirit and design of the law ; *judge* κρινει, *condemn thee,* who, whilst thou dost enjoy the *letter*, the written law, and bearest in thy body the proof of the *circumcision* which it requires, *dost transgress that law ?*

Verse 28. *For he is not a Jew*] A genuine *member of the Church* of God, who has only an *outward* profession.

Neither is that circumcision] Circumcision is a rite which represents a *spiritual* thing, viz. the change and purification of the heart, as may be seen, Jer. iv. 4, 6, 10 ; ix. 26 ; Ezek. xliv. 7, 9.

Verse 29. *But he is a Jew*] A true member of the Church of God.

Which is one inwardly] Who has his heart purified, according to what God has uniformly prescribed by his prophets ; see above : for *circumcision is of the heart, in the spirit,* εν πνευματι, *by the Spirit* of God, who is the author of all *spiritual affections* and *holy purposes :* or, every thing here is to be understood *spiritually*, and not *literally ;* for without holiness none can *please* God, and without holiness none can *see* him.

Whose praise is not of men] It has, with great probability, been conjectured that the apostle may here refer to the signification of the name *Jew,* or *Judah,* יהודה *Yehudah,* PRAISE, from ידה *Yadah,* he PRAISED. Such a one is a true Israelite, who walks in a conformity to the spirit of his religion : his *countrymen* may *praise* him because he is a steady professor of the Jewish faith ; but GOD *praises* him, because he has entered into the *spirit* and *design* of the covenant made with Abraham, and has got the end of his faith, the salvation of his soul. Sentiments like these, on the same subject, may be found in the ancient Jewish writers. *Rabbi Lipman* gives the opinion of their most ancient and pure writers in these words :—"A certain Christian mocked us, saying, 'Women, who cannot be circumcised, cannot be reckoned among

2

Jews.' Such persons are ignorant that *faith* does not consist in circumcision, but in the *heart*. He who has not genuine faith is not a partaker of the Jewish circumcision; but he who has genuine faith is a *Jew*, although *not circumcised.*" Nizzachon, Num. 21, p. 19. It is a curious maxim of the Talmudists, *That the Jews sit in the inmost recesses of the heart.* Nidda, fol. 20, 2. This is exactly the sentiment of St. Paul : *Circumcision is of the heart, in the spirit.* In short, common sense, as well as their law and their prophets, taught every considerate man among them that God could be pleased with their rites and external performances *no farther* than they led to *holiness of heart* and *righteousness of life.*

1. What the apostle says, in the preceding chapter, concerning the *Gentiles doing by nature the things contained in the law,* if properly considered, would lead certain persons from forming erroneous judgments concerning the Divine dispensations. We are not to suppose that God is not to be found where his *written word* does not appear ; nor that the salvation of the nations yet unblessed with the light of the Gospel is impossible. God has never confined himself to any *one particular way* of communicating his salvation, any more than he has confined his saving grace to one *people.* His word is an indescribable blessing ; but that word becomes effectual to salvation when accompanied by the power of the *Holy Spirit.* It was that *Spirit* which gave the *word originally ;* and that same Spirit can speak *without this word.* It is through *his* influence alone that the Gentiles do the things contained in his own law ; and it is not to be wondered at that the work is the same, both in the *law* and in the *heart,* when it has proceeded from the *same Spirit.*

2. God therefore will judge all nations according to the use and abuse they have made of this word, whether it was written in the *heart,* or written on tables of *stone.*

3. As he is no respecter of persons, all nations are equally dear to him ; and he *has* granted and *will* grant to them such discoveries of himself as have been and will be sufficient for their salvation.

4. His Word is an infinite blessing ; and he has given it to one people that they may be the means of conveying it to another. Europe, and especially Christian Europe, has got the Bible ; and God requires Europe to send the Bible throughout the earth. If this be not done, through their neglect, the Gentile nations will not be destroyed by a merciful God ; yet the Europeans will have a most solemn and awful account to render to their Judge, that they have hidden the heavenly light under their own bushel. Britain is shaking herself from the dust, and, by means of the British and Foreign Bible Society, is sending the holy Scriptures to every kingdom, and nation, and people, and tongue. The *Gentiles* are now learning from the *written* law more fully and savingly what the Spirit of God had before written on their *hearts ;* and it seems as if the *kingdom of God* were now about to *come,* with all-conquering *power.*

CHAPTER III.

The apostle points out the peculiar privileges of the Jews, 1—8. But shows that they, also, as well as the Gentiles, had sinned, and forfeited all right and title to God's especial favour, 9. The corrupt state of all mankind, 10—18. All the world is guilty before God, and none can be justified by the works of the law, 19, 20. God's mercy *in providing redemption for a lost world, by Jesus Christ, 21—26. This excludes boasting on the part both of Jew and Gentile ; provides salvation through faith for both ; and does not set aside, but establishes the law, 27—31.*

A. M. cir. 4062.
A. D. cir. 58.
An. Olymp.
cir. CCIX. 2.
A. U. C. cir.
811.

WHAT [a] advantage then hath the Jew ? or what profit *is there* of circumcision ?

2 Much every way: chiefly, because that [b] unto them were committed the oracles of God.

3 For what if [c] some did not

A. M. cir. 4062.
A. D. cir. 58.
An. Olymp.
cir. CCIX. 2.
A. U. C. cir.
811.

---

[a] Chap. ii. 25, 26, 28, 29 ; Psa. xxx. 9.——[b] Deut. iv. 7, 8 ; Psa. cxlvii. 19, 20 ; chap. ii. 18 ; ix. 4.——[c] Chap. x. 16 ; Heb. iv. 2.

NOTES ON CHAP. III.

Dr. Taylor observes:—" In the preceding chapter the apostle has carried his argument to the utmost length : what remains is to keep the Jew in temper, to fix his convictions, and to draw the grand *conclusion.*

" He has shown that the Jews were more wicked than the Gentiles ; that their possession of the law, circumcision, and outward profession of relation to God, were no ground of acceptance with him. This was in effect to say that the Jews had forfeited their right to the privileges of God's peculiar people, and that they were as unworthy to be *continued* in the Church as the Gentiles were to be taken into it ; and, consequently, in order to their enjoying the privileges of the Church under the Messiah, they stood in need of a fresh display of grace, which if they rejected, God would cast them out of the vineyard. The apostle was sensible that the Jew would understand what he said in this sense ; and that it must be very irritating to him to hear that his law, circumcision, and all his external advantages, were utterly insufficient to procure him the favour of God. This at once stripped him of all his peculiar honours and privileges ; and the apostle, who had often argued with his countrymen on these points, knew what they would be ready to say on this subject ; and, therefore, introduces a *dialogue* between himself and a Jew, in which he gives him leave to answer and defend himself. In this dialogue the apostle undoubtedly refers to the *rejection of the Jews,* which he considers at large in the ninth, tenth, and eleventh

A. M. cir. 4062.
A. D. cir. 58.
An. Olymp.
cir. CCIX. 2.
A. U. C. cir.
811.

believe ? ^d shall their unbelief make the faith of God without effect ?

4 ^e God forbid : yea, let ^f God be true, but ^g every man a liar ; as it is written, ^h That thou mightest be justified in thy sayings, and mightest overcome when thou art judged.

5 But if our unrighteousness commend the

righteousness of God, what shall we say ? *Is* God unrighteous who taketh vengeance ? (ⁱ I speak as a man.)

A. M. cir. 4062.
A. D. cir. 58.
An. Olymp.
cir. CCIX. 2.
A. U. C. cir.
811.

6 God forbid : for then ^k how shall God judge the world ?

7 For if the truth of God hath more abounded through my lie unto his glory, why yet am I also judged as a sinner ?

---

^d Num. xxiii. 19 ; chap. ix. 6 ; xi. 29 ; 2 Tim. ii. 13.——^e Job xl. 8.——^f John iii. 33.——^g Psa. lxii. 9 ; cxvi. 11.

^h Psa. li. 4.——ⁱ Chap. vi. 19 ; Gal. iii. 15.——^k Gen. xviii. 25 ; Job viii. 3 ; xxxiv. 17.

---

chapters. After the dialogue is finished, he resumes his argument, and proves, by their *own Scriptures*, that the Jews were guilty as well as other men ; and that no part of mankind could have any right to the blessings of God's kingdom by *any works* which they had performed, but merely through the propitiatory sacrifice offered by Christ ; and that this, far from destroying the law, was just the thing that the law required, and by which its claims were established.

"The sum and force of the apostle's argument is this : All sorts of men, *Jews* as well as *Gentiles*, have *sinned ;* therefore, none of them can lay claim to the blessings of his kingdom on the ground of *obedience*. The *Jew*, therefore, stands as much in need of God's *grace* to give him a title to those blessings as the *Gentile ;* and, consequently, the *Gentile* has as good a title as the *Jew*. And, when *all* are in the same circumstances, it is perfectly absurd for *any* to pretend to engross it to themselves, exclusively of others, who are only as bad as they.

"Thus the apostle solidly proves that we, *Gentiles*, through *faith alone*, have a good and firm title to all the blessings of the Gospel *covenant—election, adoption, pardon, privileges, ordinances*, the *Holy Spirit*, and the *hope of eternal life*."

As the nine first verses are a *dialogue* between the *apostle* and a *Jew*, I shall prefix the speakers to their respective questions and answers, to make the whole the more intelligible to the reader.

Verse 1. JEW. *What advantage then hath the Jew ? or what profit* is there *of circumcision ?*] As if he had said : You lately allowed, (chap. ii. 25,) that *circumcision verily profited ;* but if circumcision, or our being in covenant with God, raises us no higher in the Divine favour than the Gentiles ; if the virtuous among *them* are as acceptable as any of *us ;* nay, and condemn our nation too, as no longer deserving the Divine regards ; pray tell me, wherein lies the superior honour of the Jew ; and what benefit can arise to him from his *circumcision*, and being vested in the privileges of God's peculiar people ?

Verse 2. APOSTLE. *Much every way*] The *Jews*, in reference to the *means* and *motives* of obedience, enjoy many advantages beyond the *Gentiles ;* and, principally, because *to them were committed the oracles of God*—that revelation of his will to Moses and the prophets, containing a treasure of excellencies, with which no other part of the world has been favoured ; though they have most grievously abused these privileges

Verse 3. JEW. *For what*] Τι γαρ, *What then, if some did not believe, &c.* If some of the Jewish nation have abused their privileges, and acted contrary to their obligations, shall their wickedness *annul* the PROMISE which God made to Abraham, that he would, by an *everlasting* covenant, be a God to him and to his seed after him ? Gen. xvii. 7. Shall God, therefore, by stripping the Jews of their peculiar honour, as you intimate he will, falsify his promise to the *nation*, because some of the Jews are bad men ?

Verse 4. APOSTLE. *God forbid*] Μη γενοιτο, *Let it not be, far from it, by no means. Yea, let God be true, but every man a liar, &c.* We must ever maintain that God is true, and that if, in any case, his promise appear to fail, it is because the condition on which it was given has not been complied with ; which is the sense of what is written, Psa. li. 4 : I acknowledge my sin, and condemn *myself* that the truth of thy promise (2 Sam. vii. 15, 16) to *establish my house and throne for ever*, may be vindicated when thou shalt execute that dreadful threatening, (2 Sam. xii. 10,) that *the sword shall never depart from my house*, which I own I have brought upon myself by my own iniquity. Should any man say that the promise of God had failed toward him, let him examine his heart and his ways, and he will find that *he* has departed out of that way in which alone God could, consistently with his holiness and truth, fulfil the promise.

Verse 5. JEW. *But if our unrighteousness commend the righteousness of God*] May we not suppose that our unrighteousness may serve to commend and illustrate the mercy of God in keeping and fulfilling to us the promise which he made to our forefathers ? The *more wicked* we are, the *more* his *faithfulness* to his ancient promise is to be admired. And if so, would not God appear unjust in taking vengeance and casting us off?

I speak as a man] I feel for the situation both of myself and my countrymen, and it is natural for one to speak as I do.

Verse 6. APOSTLE. *God forbid*] Μη γενοιτο, by no means. God cannot be *unjust ;* were he unjust, he could not be qualified to judge the world, nor inflict that punishment on the unfaithful Jews, to which I refer.

Verse 7. JEW. *For if the truth of God, &c.*] But to resume my reasoning (see verse 5 :) If the faithfulness of God in keeping his promise made to our fathers is, through our unfaithfulness, made far more glorious than it otherwise would have been, why should we then

2

A. M. cir. 4062.
A. D. cir. 58.
An. Olymp.
cir. CCIX. 2.
A. U. C. cir.
811.

8 And not *rather,* (as we be slanderously reported, and as some affirm that we say,) [1] Let us do evil, that good may come? whose damnation is just.

9 What then? are we better *than they?* No, in no wise: for we have before [m] proved, both Jews and Gentiles, that [n] they are all under sin;

10 As it is written, [o] There is none righteous, no, not one:

11 There is none that understandeth, there is none that seeketh after God.

A. M. cir. 4062.
A. D. cir. 58.
An. Olymp.
cir. CCIX. 2.
A. U. C. cir.
811.

12 They are all gone out of the way, they are together become unprofitable; there is none that doeth good, no, not one.

13 [p] Their throat *is* an open sepulchre; with their tongues they have used deceit; [q] the poison of asps *is* under their lips:

14 [r] Whose mouth *is* full of cursing and bitterness:

15 [s] Their feet *are* swift to shed blood:

16 Destruction and misery *are* in their ways:

---

[l] Chap. v. 20; vi. 1, 15.——[m] Gr. *charged;* chap. i. 23, &c.; ii. 1, &c.——[n] Ver. 23; Gal. iii. 22.

[o] Psa. xiv. 1, 2, 3; liii. 1.——[p] Psa. v. 9; Jer. v. 16.——[q] Psa cxl. 3.——[r] Psa. x. 7.——[s] Prov. i. 16; Isa. lix. 7, 8.

---

be *blamed* for that which must redound so much to the honour of God?

Verse 8. APOSTLE. *And not* rather, &c.] *And why do you* not *say,* seeing you assume this ground, that in all cases we should do wickedly, because God, by freely pardoning, can so glorify his own grace? This is a most impious sentiment, but it follows from your reasoning; it has, indeed, been most injuriously laid to the charge of us apostles, who preach the *doctrine of free pardon, through faith, without the merit of works;* but this is so manifest a perversion of the truth that a just punishment may be expected to fall on the propagators of such a slander.

Verse 9. JEW. *What then?*] After all, have not we Jews a better claim to the privileges of the kingdom of God than the *Gentiles* have?

APOSTLE. *No, in no wise*] For I have already proved that both Jews and Gentiles are under the guilt of sin; that they are equally unworthy of the blessings of the Messiah's kingdom; and that they must both, equally, owe their salvation to the *mere mercy of God.* From this, to the end of the 26th verse, the apostle proceeds to prove his assertion, that *both Jews and Gentiles were all under sin;* and, that he might enforce the conviction upon the heart of the Jew, he quotes his own Scriptures, which he acknowledged had been given by the inspiration of GOD, and consequently *true.*

Verse 10. *As it is written*] See Psa. xiv. 1, 2, 3; from which this and the two following verses are taken.

There is none righteous] This is true, not only of the *Jews,* but of the Gentiles; of every soul of man, considered in his natural and practical state, previously to his receiving the mercy of our Lord Jesus Christ. There is no righteous principle in them, and, consequently, no righteous act can be expected from them; see on ver. 12. God himself is represented as looking down from heaven to see if there were any that feared and sought after him; and yet he, who cannot be deceived, could find *none!* And therefore we may safely conclude there was *none* to be found.

Verse 12. *They are all gone out of the way*] Παντες εξεκλιναν, they have all *diverged* from the right way, they have either *abandoned* or *corrupted* the *worship of God:* the *Jews,* in forsaking the *law* and the *prophets,* and the *Gentiles,* in acting contrary to the *law which God had written on their hearts.* And the de-

parture of both from the *truth* proves the evil propensity of human nature in general.

They are together become unprofitable] Ηχρειωθησαν. they are *useless,* good for nothing; or, as the Hebrew has it, נאלחו *neelachu, they are putrid:* he views the whole mass of mankind as *slain* and *thrown together,* to *putrefy* in heaps. This is what is termed the *corruption of human nature;* they are *infected* and *infectious.* What need of the *mercy* of God to save from such a state of degeneracy!

There is none that doeth good] In ver. 10 it is said, *There is none righteous;* here, *There is none that doeth good:* the first may refer to the want of a *righteous principle;* the second, to the necessary consequence of the absence of such a principle. If there be no *righteousness* within, there will be no *acts of goodness* without.

Verse 13. *Their throat is an open sepulchre*] This and all the following verses to the end of the 18th are found in the *Septuagint,* but not in the *Hebrew* text; and it is most evident that it was from this version that the apostle quoted, as the verses cannot be found in any other place with so near an approximation to the apostle's meaning and words. The verses in question, however, are not found in the *Alexandrian* MS. But they exist in the *Vulgate,* the *Æthiopic,* and the *Arabic.* As the most ancient copies of the Septuagint do not contain these verses, some contend that the apostle has quoted them from *different parts* of Scripture; and later transcribers of the Septuagint, finding that the 10th, 11th, and 12th verses were quoted from the xivth Psalm, imagined that the rest were found originally there too, and so incorporated them in their copies, from the apostle's text.

Their throat is an open sepulchre—By their malicious and wicked words they bury, as it were, the *reputation* of all men. The whole of this verse appears to belong to their habit of *lying, defamation, slandering, &c.,* by which they wounded, blasted, and poisoned the reputation of others.

Verse 14. *Whose mouth is full of cursing, &c.*] They never speak but in *profane oaths, blasphemies,* and malice

Verse 15. *Their feet are swift to shed blood*] They make use of every means in their power to destroy the reputation and lives of the innocent.

Verse 16. *Destruction and misery are in their ways*]

2

A. M. cir. 4062.
A. D. cir. 58.
An. Olymp.
cir. CCIX. 2.
A. U. C. cir.
811.

17 And the way of peace have they not known:

18 [t] There is no fear of God before their eyes.

19 Now we know that what things soever [u] the law saith, it saith to them who are under the law : that [v] every mouth may be stopped, and [w] all the world may become [x] guilty before God.

20 Therefore, [y] by the deeds of the law there

shall no flesh be justified in his sight : for [z] by the law *is* the knowledge of sin.

A. M. cir. 4062
A. D. cir. 58.
An. Olymp.
cir. CCIX. 2.
A. U. C. cir.
811.

21 But [a] now the righteousness of God without the law is manifested, [b] being witnessed by the law [c] and the prophets ;

22 Even the righteousness of God *which is* [d] by faith of Jesus Christ unto all and upon all them that believe : [e] for there is no difference :

---

[t] Psa. xxxvi. 1.——[u] John x. 34; xv. 25.——[v] Job v. 16; Psa. cvii. 42; Ezek. xvi. 63; chap. i. 20; ii. 1.——[w] Ver. 9, 23; ch. ii. 2.——[x] Or, *subject to the judgment of God.*——[y] Psa. cxliii. 2; Acts xiii. 39; Gal. ii. 16; iii. 11; Eph. ii. 8, 9; Tit. iii. 5.

[z] Chap. vii. 7.——[a] Acts xv. 11; chap. i. 17; Phil. iii. 9; Heb. xi. 4, &c.——[b] John v. 46; Acts xxvi. 22.——[c] Chap. i. 2; 1 Pet. i. 10.——[d] Chap. iv. throughout.——[e] Chap. x. 12; Gal. iii. 28; Col. iii. 11.

DESTRUCTION is their *work*, and MISERY to *themselves* and to the *objects* of their malice is the *consequence* of their impious and murderous conduct.

Verse 17. *And the way of peace have they not known*] They neither have peace in themselves, nor do they suffer others to live in quiet : they are brooders and fomenters of discord.

Verse 18. *There is no fear of God before their eyes.*] This completes their bad character ; they are downright atheists, at least practically such. They fear not God's judgments, although his eye is upon them in their evil ways. There is not one article of what is charged against the Jews and Gentiles here that may not be found justified by the histories of both, in the most ample manner. And what was true of *them* in those primitive times is true of them still. With very little variation, these are the evils in which the vast mass of mankind delight and live. Look especially at men in a state of *warfare ;* look at the nations of Europe, who enjoy most of the light of God ; see what has taken place among them from 1792 to 1814 ; see what *destruction* of millions, and what *misery* of hundreds of millions, have been the consequence of Satanic excitement in fallen, ferocious passions ! O SIN, what hast thou done ! How many myriads of souls hast thou *hurried, unprepared,* into the eternal world ! Who, among men or angels, can estimate the greatness of this calamity ! this butchery of souls ! What widows, what orphans, are left to deplore their sacrificed husbands and parents, and their own consequent wretchedness ! And whence sprang all this ? From that, whence come all *wars* and *fightings ;* the *evil desires* of men; the *lust* of *dominion ;* the insatiable thirst for money ; and the desire to be *sole* and independent. This is the sin that ruined our first parents, expelled them from paradise, and which has descended to all their posterity ; and proves fully, incontestably proves, that *we* are their legitimate offspring ; the fallen progeny of fallen parents ; children in whose ways are *destruction* and *misery;* in whose heart there is no faith ; and before whose eyes there is nothing of the fear of God.

Verse 19. *What things soever the law saith*] That the word *law,* here, does not mean the *pentateuch,* is evident from the preceding quotations, not one of which is taken from that work. Either the term *law* must here mean the *Jewish writings in general,* or that *rule of moral conduct* which God had given to both Jews

and Gentiles : to the former in their own *Scriptures ;* to the latter in that law written in their hearts by his own Spirit, and acknowledged in their written codes, and in their pleadings in every civil case. Now, according to this great law, *this rule of moral conduct,* whether given in a *written* revelation, as to the Jews, or by the secret inspiration of his Spirit, as in certain cases to the Gentiles, *every mouth must be stopped, and the whole world,* πας ὁ κοσμος, both Jews and Gentiles, *stand convicted before God :* for all mankind have sinned against this law.

Verse 20. *Therefore, by the deeds of the law*] On the score of *obedience* to this moral law, *there shall no flesh,* ου πασα σαρξ, *no human being,* be justified ; none can be accepted in the sight of God. And why ? Because *by the law is the knowledge of sin:* it is that which *ascertains* what sin is ; shows how men have deviated from its righteous demands ; and sentences them to death because they have broken it. Thus the law is properly considered as the *rule of right ;* and, unless God had given some such means of discovering *what* SIN *is,* the darkened heart of man could never have formed an adequate conception of it. For, as an acknowledged *straight edge* is the only way in which the *straightness* or *crookedness* of a *line* can be determined, so the moral obliquity of human actions can only be determined by the law of God ; that *rule of right* which proceeds from his *own* immaculate holiness.

Verse 21. *But now the righteousness of God*] God's *method of saving sinners* is now shown, by the Gospel, to be through his own mere mercy, by Christ Jesus ; *without the law*—without any right or claim which might result from obedience to the law ; and is evidently that which was intended by God from the beginning ; for *it is witnessed by the law and the prophets* —the *rites* and *ceremonies* of the one, and the *preachings* and *predictions* of the *others,* all bearing testimony to the great design of God, and to the absolute necessity there was for the sacrifice and salvation which God has provided.

Verse 22. *Even the righteousness of God*] That method of saving sinners which is not of *works,* but by faith in Christ Jesus ; and it is not restrained to any *particular people,* as the law and its privileges were ; but is unto *all* mankind in its *intention* and *offer,* and becomes effectual to them that believe ; for God hath now made *no difference* between the Jews and the Gentiles

A. M. cir. 4062.
A. D. cir. 58.
An. Olymp.
cir. CCIX. 2.
A. U. C. cir.
811.

23 For ^f all have sinned, and come short of the glory of God; 24 Being justified freely ^g by his grace, ^h through the redemption that is in Christ Jesus.

25 Whom God hath ⁱ set forth ^k *to be* a propitiation, through faith ^l in his blood, to declare his righteousness ^m for the ⁿ remission of ^o sins that are past, through the forbearance of God; 26 To declare, *I say,* at this time his righteousness: that he might be just, and the justifier of him which believeth in Jesus.

A. M. cir 4062.
A. D. cir 58.
An. Olymp.
cir. CCIX. 2.
A. U. C. cir.
811.

---

^f Ver. 9; chap. xi. 32; Gal. iii. 22.——^g Chap. iv. 16; Eph. ii. 8; Tit. iii. 5, 7.——^h Matthew xx. 28; Eph. i. 7; Col. i. 14; 1 Tim. ii. 6; Heb. ix. 12; 1 Pet. i. 18, 19.

ⁱ Or, *foreordained.*——^k Lev. xvi. 15; 1 John ii. 2; iv. 10. ^l Col. i. 20.——^m Acts xiii. 38, 39; 1 Tim. i. 15.——ⁿ Or, *passing over.*——^o Acts xvii. 30; Heb. ix. 15.

Verse 23. *For all have sinned*] And consequently are equally helpless and guilty; and, as God is no respecter of persons, all human creatures being equally his offspring, and there being *no reason* why *one* should be *preferred* before *another,* therefore his endless mercy has embraced ALL.

And come short of the glory of God] Και ὑστερουνται της δοξης του Θεου· These words have been variously translated. *Failed of* attaining *the glory of God: Have not been able to bring glory to God: Stand in need of the glory,* that is, *the mercy of God.* The simple heaning seems to be this: that all have *sinned,* and none can enjoy God's glory but they that are *holy;* consequently both Jews and Gentiles have failed in their endeavours to attain it, as, by the works of *any law,* no human being can be justified.

Verse 24. *Being justified freely by his grace*] So far from being able to attain the glory of God by their obedience, they are all guilty: and, to be saved, must be freely pardoned by God's grace; which is shown to them who believe, through the redemption, απολυτρωσεως, the *ransom price,* which *is in* the sacrifice of *Christ Jesus.* The original is compounded of *απο, from,* and *λυτροω, I redeem,* and properly means the *price* laid down for the *redemption of a captive.* Comprehendit hæc Christi απολυτρωσις, quicquid is docuit, fecit et passus est, eo consilio, ut homines malis liberati, præcipue peccato, malorum fonte immunes, veram felicitatem adipiscerentur.—*Rosenmuller.* This redemption of Christ comprehends whatsoever he *taught, did,* or *suffered,* in order to free men from evil; especially to free them from sin, the source of evils; that they might attain true felicity. And that it here means the *liberation* purchased by the blood-shedding of Christ, is evident from Eph. i. 7: *We have* REDEMPTION, *απολυτρωσιν δια του αιματος αυτου,* THROUGH HIS BLOOD, *the forgiveness of sins, according to the riches of his grace.* See also Coloss. i. 14, where the same words are found.

Λυτρα according to Suidas, is μισθος, η τα παρεχομενα ὑπερ ελευθεριας, επι τω λυτρωσασθαι βαρβαρων δουλειας· A reward; or *the price given to be redeemed from the slavery of the barbarians. Schleusner,* under the word απολυτρωσις, says, Negari quidem non potest, hanc vocem proprie notare redemptionem ejus, qui *captivus* detinetur, sive bello, sive alio captus sit modo, quæ fit per *pretii solutionem;* quo sensu verbum απολυτροω legitur haud raro in Scripp. Græcis. No man certainly can deny that this word properly means the *redemption of a captive,* (whether he may have been taken in war or in any other way,) which is procured by the *payment of a price.* That the word also means *any deliverance,* even where *no price* is paid down, nι hody will dispute; but that it means redemption by a *price laid down,* and the redemption of the soul by the *price of the death of Christ,* the above scriptures sufficiently prove.

Verse 25. *Whom God hath set forth*] Appointed and published to be a *propitiation,* ιλαστηριον, the *mercy-seat,* or *place* of atonement; because the blood of the sacrifice was sprinkled on and before *that,* in order to obtain remission of sin, punishment, &c. The *mercy-seat* was the *lid* or *cover* of the ark of the *covenant,* where God was manifest in the symbol of his presence, between the cherubim; therefore the atonement that was made in *this place* was properly made *to God* himself. See the note on Luke xviii. 13.

Through faith in his blood] This shows *what* we are to understand both by the *απολυτρωσις, redemption,* and the *ιλαστηριον, propitiation;* viz. that they refer to the *sacrificial death* of Jesus Christ, as the *atonement* made, and the *price* paid down, for the redemption of the souls of men.

To declare his righteousness] Εις ενδειξιν, for the manifestation of his righteousness; his *mercy* in saving sinners, by sending Jesus Christ to make an atonement for them; thereby declaring his readiness to remit all past transgressions committed both by Jews and Gentiles, during the time in which his merciful forbearance was exercised towards the world; and this applies to all who hear the Gospel now: to them is freely offered remission of all *past sins.*

Verse 26. *To declare, I say, at this time*] To manifest *now,* by the dispensation of the *Gospel,* his *righteousness,* his infinite mercy; and to manifest it in such a way, that he might still appear to be the *just* God, and yet *the justifier,* the pardoner, *of him who believeth in Jesus.* Here we learn that God designed to give the most *evident displays* both of his *justice* and *mercy.* Of his *justice,* in requiring a *sacrifice,* and absolutely refusing to give salvation to a lost world in any other way; and of his *mercy,* in *providing* THE *sacrifice* which his justice required. Thus, because Jesus was an *atonement,* a *ransom price,* for the sin of the world, therefore God can, consistently with his *justice,* pardon every soul that believeth in Jesus. This is the full discovery of God's righteousness, of his wonderful method of magnifying his law and making it honourable; of showing the infinite purity of his justice, and of saving a lost world.

Hitherto, from the ninth verse, the apostle had gone on without interruption, proving that Jew and Gentile

A. M. cir. 4062.
A. D. cir. 58.
An. Olymp.
cir. CCIX. 2.
A. U. C. cir.
811.

27 ᵖ Where *is* boasting then ? It is excluded. By what law ? of works ? Nay, but by the law of faith.

28 Therefore we conclude ᑫ that a man is justified by faith, without the deeds of the law.

29 *Is he* the God of the Jews only ? *is he* not

ᵖ Chap. ii. 17, 23 ; iv. 2 ; 1 Cor. i. 29, 31 ; Eph. ii. 9.——ᑫ Acts xiii. 38, 39 ; ver. 20, 21, 22 ; chap. viii. 3 ; Gal. ii. 16.

also of the Gentiles ? Yes, of the Gentiles also :

30 Seeing ʳ *it is* one God, which shall justify the circumcision by faith, and uncircumcision through faith.

31 Do we then ˢ make void the law through faith ? God forbid : yea, we establish the law.

A. M. cir. 4062.
A. D. cir. 58.
An. Olymp.
cir. CCIX. 2.
A. U. C. cir.
811.

ʳ Chap. x. 12, 13 ; Gal. iii. 8, 20, 28.——ˢ Matt. v. 17, 18 ; Gal. iii. 19, 23, 24.

were in a state of guilt and condemnation, and that they could be saved only by the redemption that is in Christ Jesus. The *Jew*, finding his boasted privileges all at stake, interrupts him, and asks :—

Verse 27. JEW. *Where is boasting then ?*] Ἡ καυχησις, *This glorying* of ours. Have we nothing in which we can *trust* for our acceptance with God ? No *merit* of our *own ?* Nothing accruing to us from our circumcision and being in covenant with God.

APOSTLE. *It is excluded*] Εξεκλεισθη, *It is shut out ;* the door of heaven is *shut* against every thing of this kind.

JEW. *By what law ?*] By what *rule, doctrine*, or *reason* is it shut out ? by the law *of works ?* The rule of obedience, which God gave to us, and by which obedience we are accepted by him ?

APOSTLE. *Nay*] Not by the law of works ; glorying is not cut off or *shut out* by that ; it stands in full force as the rule of life ; but you have *sinned* and need pardon. *The law of works* grants no *pardon*, it requires *obedience*, and threatens the disobedient with *death*. But all glorying in the expectation of salvation, through your *own obedience*, is excluded by the *law, the doctrine of faith :* faith alone, in the mercy of God, through the propitiation made by the blood of Jesus, (ver. 25,) is that by which you can be *justified*, pardoned, and taken into the Divine favour.

Verse 28. *Therefore we conclude, &c.*] Seeing these things cannot be denied, viz., that all have sinned ; that all are guilty , that all are helpless : that none can deliver his own soul . and that God, in his endless mercy, has opened *a new and living way to the holiest by the blood of Jesus*, Heb x. 19, 20, &c. ; therefore we, apostles and Christian teachers, conclude, λογιζομεθα, prove by fair, *rational consequence, that a man*—any man, *is justified*—has his sins blotted out, and is received into the Divine favour, *by faith* in *Christ's blood, without the deeds of the law*, which never could afford, either to *Jew* or *Gentile*, a *ground* for justification , because *both* have sinned against the law which God has given them , and, consequently, forfeited all right and title to the blessings which the *obedient* might claim.

Verse 29 *Is he the God of the Jews only ?*] Do not begin to suppose that because you cannot be justified by the works of the law and God has in his mercy found out a new method of saving you. that therefore this mercy shall apply to the *Jews* exclusively Is not God the maker, preserver. and redeemer. *also of the Gentiles ?* Yes, *of the Gentiles also*. as much as of the *Jews ;* for all have equally sinned and there is no reason, if God be disposed to show mercy at all. that

he should prefer the one to the other ; since they are all equally guilty, sinful, and necessitous.

Verse 30. *Seeing* it is *one God*] Επειπερ εἰς ὁ Θεος. This has been rendered, *Seeing God* is one. It however makes little difference in the sense : the apostle's meaning most evidently is, it is one and the same God who made both Jews and Gentiles, who shall *justify* —pardon, *the circumcision*—the believing *Jews*, by *faith ;* and the *uncircumcision*—the believing *Gentiles*, by the same faith ; as there is but one *Saviour* and one *atonement* provided for the whole.

It is fanciful to suppose that the apostle has one meaning when he says, εκ πιστεως, BY *faith*, and a different meaning when he says, δια της πιστεως, THROUGH *faith*. Both the prepositions are to be understood in precisely the same sense ; only the addition of the article της, in the last case, *extends* and more pointedly *ascertains* the meaning. It is one and the same God who shall justify the believing Jews by faith ; and the believing Gentiles δια της πιστεως, by THAT SAME *faith*.

Verse 31 *Do we then make void the law through faith ?*] 1 By *law* here we may understand the whole of the Mosaic law, in its *rites* and *ceremonies ;* of which Jesus Christ was the *subject* and the *end*. All that law had respect to *him ;* and the *doctrine* of faith in Christ Jesus, which the Christian religion proclaimed, established the very claims and demands of that law, by showing that all was accomplished in the passion and death of Christ ; for, *without shedding of blood*, the law would allow of *no remission ;* and Jesus was that Lamb of God which was slain from the foundation of the world, in whose blood we have redemption, even the remission of sins. 2. We may understand, also, the *moral law*, that which relates to the regulation of the *manners* or *conduct* of men. This law also was *established* by the doctrine of salvation by faith ; because this faith works by love, and love is the principle of obedience : and whosoever receives salvation through faith in Christ, receives power to live in holy obedience to every moral precept ; for such are God's workmanship, created anew in Christ Jesus, unto good works ; in which they find it their duty and their interest incessantly to live

1. ⸢IN the notes on the preceding chapter, I have, in general, followed the *plan* of Dr. Taylor, and especially in regard to its *dialogue* form , but I have often differed much from that very learned and judicious man, in the application of many words and doctrines. He cannot allow that the death of Christ should be considered as a *price paid down* for the salvation of men and, I confess, I cannot understand the apostle in *any*

other way. Nor can I see the weight of many of his observations, nor the force of his conclusions, on any other ground than this, that the passion and death of Christ were an atonement made to Divine justice in the behalf of man ; and that it is through the merit of that great sacrifice that God forgives sin. Nor can I see any reason why such great stress should be laid on *faith*, but as that lays hold on and takes up the sacrifice of Christ as a *ransom price* for the redemption of the soul from the thraldom and misery of sin and Satan.

2. This chapter contains a fine and striking synopsis of the whole Christian system. The wretched state of man is awfully exhibited, from the 10th to the 18th verse ; and the plan of salvation, in the 24th, 25th, and 26th verses. A pious writer calls these the Catechism of Christian Righteousness. The following points in this catechism are worthy of high consideration—viz. *How is God glorified in us, and we in him?*—By his GRACE. *What does his grace work in us?*—True holiness. *Upon what motive?*—Because it is *pleasing* to him. *By whom does he give us salvation?*—By Jesus Christ. *How has Christ obtained this for us?* —By *redeeming* us. *What price did he give?*—His BLOOD. *What does his blood effect?*—It *reconciles* us to God. *How is it applied?*—By FAITH. *Who has given this victim of reconciliation?*—God the Father. *Why did he choose these means?*—To confound the *false* righteousness of the Gentiles ; to abolish the FIGURATIVE righteousness of the Jews ; and to establish his *own*. *What does this grace of God perform?* —It pardons sin, and purifies the heart. *For whom is this designed?*—For *all mankind*, both Jews and Gentiles. *To whom are these blessings actually communicated?*—To all who *repent, turn from* their *sin*, and *believe* on the Lord Jesus. *Why did not God*

make known this grand method of salvation sooner?— 1. To make it the more valued : 2. To show his fidelity in the performance of his promises : and, 3. To make known the virtue and efficacy of the blood of Christ, which sanctifies the *present*, extends its influence to the *past*, and continues the availing sacrifice and way of salvation to all *future* ages.

3. On considering this glorious scheme of salvation, there is great danger, lest, while we stand amazed at what was done FOR us, we neglect what must be done IN us. Guilt in the conscience and sin in the heart ruin the man. Pardon in the conscience and Christ in the heart save the soul. Christ has done much to save us, and the way of salvation is made plain ; but, unless he *justify* our *conscience* from dead works, and *purify* our *hearts* from all sin, his passion and death will profit us nothing. While we *boast* in Christ Jesus, let us see that our *rejoicing, καυχησις,* our *boasting*, be this, *the testimony of our conscience, that in simplicity and godly sincerity, not with fleshly wisdom, but by the grace of God, we have our conversation in the world,* 2 Cor. i. 12.

4. We must beware of *Antinomianism* ; that is, of supposing that, because Christ has been *obedient* unto death, there is no necessity for our *obedience* to his righteous commandments. If this were so, the grace of Christ would tend to the *destruction* of the law, and not to its *establishment*. He only is saved from his sins who has the law of God written in his heart ; and he alone has the law written in his heart who lives an *innocent, holy,* and *useful* life. Wherever Christ *lives* he works : and his work of righteousness will *appear* to his servants, and its effect will be quietness and *assurance* for ever. The life of God in the soul of man is the principle which *saves* and *preserves* eternally

---

CHAPTER IV.

Abraham *was justified by faith, and not by the works of the law ; for his faith was imputed to him for righteousness,* 1–5. David *also bears testimony to the same doctrine,* 6–8. *Abraham, the father of the Jewish race, was justified by faith, even before he was circumcised ; therefore salvation must be of the Gentiles as well as the Jews,* 9–12. *And the promise that all the nations of the earth should be blessed in him, was made to him while he was in an uncircumcised state ; and, therefore, if salvation were of the Jews alone, the law, that was given after the promise, would make the promise of no effect,* 13–17. *Description of Abraham's faith, and its effects,* 18–22. *This account is left on record for our salvation, that we might believe on Christ, who was delivered for our offences, and raised again for our justification,* 23–25.

A. M. cir. 4062.
A. D. cir. 58.
An. Olymp.
cir. CCIX. 2.
A U. C. cir.
811.

WHAT shall we then say that [a] Abraham, our father as pertaining to the flesh, hath found ? 2 For if Abraham were [b] justi-

fied by works, he hath *whereof* to glory ; but not before God. 3 For, what saith the Scripture? [c] Abraham believed God, and it

A. M. cir. 4062.
A. D. cir 58.
An. Olymp.
cir. CCIX. 2.
A. U. C. cir.
811.

[a] Isa. li. 2 ; Matt. iii. 9 ; John viii. 33, 39 ; 2 Cor. xi. 22.   [b] Chap. iii. 20, 27, 28.——[c] Gen. xv. 6 ; Gal. iii. 6 ; James ii. 23.

NOTES ON CHAP. IV.

The apostle, having proved in the foregoing chapter that neither Jews nor Gentiles have a right to the blessing of God's peculiar kingdom, otherwise than by *grace*, which is as free for the one as the other, in this chapter advances a *new argument* to convince the *Jew*, and to show the believing Gentile, in a clear

light, the high value and strong security of the mercies freely bestowed on them in the Gospel ; and, at the same time, to display the scheme of Divine providence, as laid in the counsel and will of God. His argument is taken from Abraham's case : Abraham was the *father* and *head* of the Jewish nation ; he had been a *heathen*, but God pardoned him, and took him

2

59

A. M. cir. 4062.
A. D. cir. 58.
An. Olymp.
cir. CCIX. 2.
A. U. C. cir.
811.

was counted unto him for righteousness.

4 Now [d] to him that worketh is the reward not reckoned of grace, but of debt.

5 But to him that worketh not, but believeth on him that justifieth [e] the ungodly, his faith is counted for righteousness.

A. M. cir. 4062.
A. D. cir. 58.
An. Olymp.
cir. CCIX. 2.
A. U. C. cir.
811.

---

[d] Chap. xi. 6.   [e] Josh. xxiv. 2.

---

and his posterity into his special covenant, and bestowed upon them many extraordinary blessings above the rest of mankind; and it is evident that Abraham was not justified by any *obedience to law*, or *rule of right action*, but, in the only way in which a *sinner* can be justified, by *prerogative* or the *mercy* of the *lawgiver*. Now, this is the very same way in which the Gospel saves the believing Gentiles, and gives them a part in the blessings of God's covenant. Why then should the Jews oppose the Gentiles? especially as the Gentiles were actually included in the covenant made with Abraham; for the promise, Gen. xvii. 4, stated that he should be *the father of many nations*: consequently, the covenant being made with Abraham, as the *head* or *father of many nations*, all in any nation who stood on the same religious principle with him, were his *seed* and with him interested in the same covenant. But Abraham stood by faith in the mercy of God pardoning his idolatry; and upon this footing the believing Gentiles stand in the Gospel; and, therefore, they are the *seed of Abraham*, and included in the covenant and promise made to him.

To all this the apostle knew well it would be objected, that it was not *faith alone* that gave Abraham a right to the blessings of the covenant, but his *obedience to the law of circumcision*; and this, being *peculiar* to the *Jewish nation*, gave *them* an interest in the Abrahamic covenant; and that, consequently, whoever among the Gentiles would be interested in that covenant, ought to embrace *Judaism*, become *circumcised*, and thus come under obligation to the whole law. With this very objection the apostle very dexterously introduces his argument, ver. 1, 2; shows that, according to the Scripture account, Abraham was justified by faith, ver. 3–5; explains the nature of that justification, by a quotation out of the Psalms, ver. 6–9; proves that Abraham was justified long before he was circumcised, ver. 9–11; that the believing Gentiles are his seed to whom the promise belongs, as well as the believing Jews, ver. 12–17; and he describes Abraham's faith, in order to explain the faith of the Gospel, ver. 17–25. See Dr. *Taylor's* notes. We may still suppose that the *dialogue* is carried on between the apostle and the Jew, and it will make the subject still more clear to assign to each his respective part. The Jew asks a single question, which is contained in the first and part of the second verses. And the apostle's answer takes up the rest of the chapter.

Verse 1. JEW. *What shall we then say that Abraham, our father as pertaining to the flesh, hath found?*] The κατα σαρκα, *pertaining to the flesh*, must here refer to the sign in Abraham's flesh, viz. his *circumcision*; on which the Jew would found his right to peculiar blessings. That this is the meaning of κατα σαρκα, *according to the flesh*, Dr. Taylor has proved by a collation of several

parallel scriptures, which it is not necessary to produce here. We may, therefore, suppose the Jew arguing thus: But you set your argument on a wrong footing, viz. the *corrupt state* of our nation; whereas we hold our prerogative above the rest of mankind from Abraham, who is our father; and we have a right to the blessings of God's peculiar kingdom, in virtue of the promise made to *him*; his justification is the ground of ours. Now what shall we make of his case, on your principles? Of what use was his *obedience to the law of circumcision*, if it did not give him a *right* to the blessing of God? And if, by his *obedience to that law*, he obtained a grant of extraordinary blessings, then, according to your own concession, chap. iii. 27, he might ascribe his justification to something *in himself*; and, consequently, so may *we* too, in his right; and if so, this will exclude all those who are not *circumcised* as we are.

Verse 2. *For if Abraham were justified by works*] The JEW proceeds:—I conclude, therefore, that Abraham was *justified by works*, or by his *obedience to this law of circumcision*; and, consequently, he has cause for *glorying*, καυχημα, to *exult* in something which he has done to entitle him to these blessings. Now, it is evident that he has this *glorying*, and consequently that he was *justified* by *works*.

APOSTLE. *But not before God*] These seem to be the apostle's words, and contain the beginning of his answer to the arguments of the Jew, as if he had said:— Allowing that Abraham might *glory* in being called from heathenish darkness into such marvellous light, and *exult* in the privileges which God had granted to him; yet this *glorying* was not *before God* as a *reason* why those privileges should be granted; the *glorying* itself being a *consequence* of these very privileges.

Verse 3. *For, what saith the Scripture?*] The Scriptural account of this transaction, Gen. xv. 6, is decisive; for there it is said, *Abraham believed God, and it was counted*, ελογισθη, *it was reckoned to him for righteousness*, εις δικαιοσυνην, *for justification*.

Verse 4. *Now to him that worketh is the reward not reckoned of grace, but of debt.*] Therefore, if Abraham had been *justified by works*, the blessings he received would have been given to him as a *reward* for those works, and consequently his *believing* could have had no part in his *justification*, and his *faith* would have been useless.

Verse 5. *But to him that worketh not*] Which was the case with Abraham, for he was called when he was *ungodly*, i. e. an *idolater*; and, on his believing, was freely justified: and, as all men have *sinned*, none can be justified by *works*; and, therefore, justification, if it take place at all, must take place in behalf of the *ungodly*, forasmuch as all mankind are *such*. Now, as Abraham's *state* and *mode* in which he was

A. M. cir. 4062.
A. D. cir. 58.
An. Olymp.
cir. CCIX. 2.
A. U. C. cir.
811.

6 Even as David also describeth the blessedness of the man, unto whom God imputeth righteousness without works,

7 *Saying,* f Blessed *are* they whose iniquities are forgiven, and whose sins are covered.

8 Blessed *is* the man to whom the Lord will not impute sin.

9 *Cometh* this blessedness then upon the circision *only,* or upon the uncircumcision also?

for we say that faith was reckoned to Abraham for righteousness.

10 How was it then reckoned? when he was in circumcision, or in uncircumcision? Not in circumcision, but in uncircumcision.

11 And g he received the sign of circumcision, a seal of the righteousness of the faith which *he had yet* being uncircumcised: that h he might be the father of all them that be-

A. M. cir. 4062.
A. D. cir. 58.
An. Olymp.
cir. CCIX. 2.
A. U. C. cir.
811.

---

f Psa. xxxii. 1, 2.——g Gen. xvii. 10.

h Luke xix. 9; ver. 12, 16; Gal. iii. 7.

---

justified, are the plan and rule according to which God purposes to save men; and as his state was *ungodly,* and the *mode* of his justification was by *faith* in the goodness and mercy of God; and this is precisely the state of *Jews* and *Gentiles* at present; there can be no other mode of justification than by faith in that Christ who is Abraham's seed, and in whom, according to the promise, all the nations of the earth are to be blessed.

It is necessary to observe here, in order to prevent confusion and misapprehension, that although the verb δικαιοω has a variety of senses in the New Testament, yet here it is to be taken as implying the *pardon of sin; receiving a person into the favour of God.* See these different acceptations cited in the note on chap. i. ver. 17, and particularly under No. 7. It is also necessary to observe, that our translators render the verb λογιζομαι differently in different parts of *this* chapter. It is rendered *counted,* ver. 3, 5; *reckoned,* ver. 4, 9, 10; *imputed,* ver. 6, 8, 11, 22, 23, and 24. *Reckoned* is probably the best sense in all these places.

Verse 6. *Even as David also, &c.*] David, in Psa. xxxii. 1, 2, gives us also the true notion of this way of justification, i. e. by *faith,* without the merit of works, where he says—

Verse 7. *Blessed* are *they whose iniquities are forgiven*] That is, the man is truly *happy* whose iniquities αι ανομιαι, whose *transgressions of the law* are forgiven; for by these he was exposed to the most grievous punishment. *Whose sins, αι αμαρτιαι,* his innumerable *deviations* from the strict rule of truth and righteousness, *are covered*—entirely removed out of sight, and thrown into oblivion. See the meaning of the word *sin* in the note on Gen. xiii. 13.

Verse 8. *Blessed* is the man to whom the Lord will *not impute sin.*] That man is truly happy to whose *charge* God does not *reckon* sin; that is, they alone are happy who are redeemed from the curse of the law and the consequence of their ungodly life, by having their sins freely forgiven, through the mercy of God.

Verse 9. Cometh *this blessedness—upon the circumcision* only] The word μονον, *only,* is very properly supplied by our translators, and indeed is found in some excellent MSS., and is here quite necessary to complete the sense. The apostle's question is very nervous. If this pardon, granted in this way, be essential to *happiness*—and David says it is so—then is it the privilege of the *Jews* exclusively? This cannot be; for, as it is by the mere *mercy* of God, through *faith,*

the *circumcision* cannot even claim it. But if God offer it to the circumcision, not because they have been *obedient,* for they also have *sinned,* but because of his *mere mercy,* then of course the same blessedness may be offered to the *Gentiles* who believe in the Lord Jesus. And this is evident; *for we say,* following our own Scriptures, *that faith was reckoned to Abraham for righteousness;* he had no *merit,* he was an *idolater;* but he *believed in God,* and his *faith* was reckoned to him εις δικαιοσυνην, *in reference to his justification;* he brought *faith* when he could not bring *works;* and God accepted his *faith* in the place of *obedience;* and this became the *instrumental* cause of his justification.

Verse 10. *How was it then reckoned?*] In what *circumstances* was Abraham when this blessing was bestowed upon him? When he was *circumcised,* or *before?*

Not in circumcision, but in uncircumcision.] Faith was reckoned to Abraham for justification, as we read Gen. xv. 6, (where see the note;) but circumcision was not instituted till about fourteen or fifteen years after, Gen. xvii. 1, &c.; for faith was reckoned to Abraham for righteousness or justification at least *one year* before Ishmael was born; compare Gen. xv. and xvi. At Ishmael's birth he was eighty-six years of age, Gen. xvi. 16; and, at the institution of circumcision, Ishmael was thirteen, and Abraham ninety-nine years old. See Gen. xvii. 24, 25; and see Dr. *Taylor.*

Verse 11. *And he received the sign of circumcision, a seal, &c.*] So far was *obedience* to the law of *circumcision* from being the reason of his justification, that he not only received this justification *before* he was circumcised, but he received the *sign* of circumcision, as a *seal* of the pardon which he had *before* actually received. And thus he became the *father,* the great *head* and *representative,* of all them that believe; particularly the *Gentiles,* who are now in precisely the same state in which Abraham was when he received the mercy of God. Hence it appears, says Dr. Taylor, that the covenant established with Abraham, Gen. xvii. 2–15, is the *same* with that, Gen. xii. 2, 3, and xv. 5, &c.; for circumcision was not a seal of any *new grant,* but of the justification and promise which Abraham had received before he was circumcised; and that justification and promise included the Gospel covenant in which we are now interested. St. Paul refers to this, Gal. iii. 8: The Scripture foreseeing that God would justify *us,* heathens, through faith, preached before the Gospel *unto Abraham, say*

A. M. cir. 4062.
A. D. cir. 58:
An. Olymp.
cir. CCIX. 2.
A. U. C. cir.
811.

lieve, though they be not circumcised; that righteousness might be imputed unto them also:

12 And the father of circumcision to them who are not of the circumcision only, but who also walk in the steps of that faith of our father Abraham, which *he had* being *yet* uncircumcised.

13 For the promise, that he should be the [i] heir of the world, *was* not to Abraham, or to his seed, through the law; but through the righteousness of faith.

A. M. cir. 4062,
A. D. cir. 58.
An. Olymp.
cir. CCIX. 2.
A. U. C. cir.
811.

14 For, [k] if they which are of the law *be* heirs, faith is made void, and the promise made of none effect:

15 Because [l] the law worketh wrath: for where no law is, *there is* no transgression.

16 Therefore *it is* of faith, that *it might be* [m] by grace; [n] to the end the promise might be sure to all the seed; not to that only which is of the law, but to that also which is of the faith of Abraham, [o] who is the father of us all,

---

[i] Gen. xvii. 4, &c.; Gal. iii. 29.——[k] Gal. iii. 18.——[l] Chap. iii. 20; v. 13, 20; vii. 8, 10, 11; 1 Cor. xv. 56; 2 Cor. iii. 7, 9;

Gal. iii. 10, 19; 1 John iii. 4.——[m] Chap. iii. 24.——[n] Gal. iii. 22.
[o] Isa. li. 2; chap. ix. 8.

---

ing, In thee shall all nations be blessed. The whole of the apostle's argument, in this fourth chapter to the Romans, proves that we, believing Gentiles, are the seed of Abraham, to whom, as well as to himself, the promise was made; and that the promise made to him is the same in effect as that promise which is now made to *us;* consequently, it is the Abrahamic covenant in which we now stand; and any argument taken from the nature of that covenant, and applied to ourselves, must be good and valid. It is also undeniably evident, from this eleventh verse, as well as from Gen. xvii. 1–11, that *circumcision* was a *seal* or *sign* of the *Gospel* covenant in which we now stand. See *Taylor.*

There is nothing more common in the Jewish writers than the words אות *oth,* SIGN, and חותם *chotham,* SEAL, as signifying the *mark* in the flesh, by the rite of circumcision; see on Gen. iv. 15. SOHAR GENES., fol. 41, col. 161, has these words: And *God set a mark upon Cain;* this *mark* was the *sign* of the covenant of circumcision. TARGUM, Cant. iii. 8: The *seal* of circumcision is in your flesh; as Abraham was *sealed* in the flesh. YALCUT RUBENI, fol. 64: Joseph did not defile the *sign* of the holy covenant; i. e. he did not commit adultery with the wife of Potiphar. *Liber Cosri,* part i., c. 115, p. 70: Circumcision is a Divine *sign* which God has placed on the member of concupiscence, to the end that we may overcome evil desire. SHEMOTH RABBA, sec. 19, fol. 118: Ye shall not eat the passover unless the SEAL of Abraham be in your flesh. *Yalcut Rubeni,* fol. 36: God said to Abraham, I will seal thy flesh. *Sohar Levit.* fol. 6: Abraham was sealed with the holy seal. See *Schoettgen.*

Verse 12. *And the father of circumcision*] He is also the *head* and *representative* of all the circumcision of all the JEWS *who walk in the steps of that faith;* who seek for justification by *faith only,* and not by the *works of the law;* for this was the faith that Abraham had before he received circumcision. For, the covenant being made with Abraham while he was a *Gentile,* he became the representative of the *Gentiles,* and they *primarily* were included in that covenant, and the Jews were brought in only *consequentially;* but *salvation,* implying *justification by faith,* originally belonged to the *Gentiles;* and, when the Gospel came, they laid hold on *this* as their original right, having been granted to them by the free mercy of God in their father and

representative, Abraham. So that the Jews, to be saved, must come under that Abrahamic covenant, in which the *Gentiles* are included. This is an unanswerable conclusion, and must, on this point, for ever confound the Jews.

Verse 13. *For the promise, that he should be the heir of the world*] This promise intimated that he should be the medium through whom the mercy of God should be communicated to the *world,* to both *Jews* and *Gentiles;* and the *manner* in which *he* was justified, be the *rule* and *manner* according to which all men should expect this blessing. Abraham is here represented as having all the *world* given to him as his *inheritance;* because *in him* all nations of the earth are blessed: this must therefore relate to their being all interested in the *Abrahamic covenant;* and every person, now that the covenant is fully explained, has the privilege of claiming justification through faith, by the blood of the Lamb, in virtue of this original grant.

Verse 14. *For, if they which are of the law be heirs*] If the Jews only be heirs of the promise made to Abraham, and that on the ground of prior obedience to the law, *then faith is made void*—is entirely useless; *and the promise,* which was made to faith, is *made of none effect.*

Verse 15. *Because the law worketh wrath*] For *law,* νομος, any law, or *rule of duty.* No law makes provision for the exercise of *mercy,* for it *worketh wrath,* οργην, *punishment,* for the disobedient. *Law* necessarily subjects the transgressor to punishment; *for where no law is*—where no *rule of duty* is enacted and acknowledged, there is *no transgression;* and where there is no *transgression* there can be no *punishment,* for there is no *law* to enforce it. But the Jews have a law, which they have broken; and now they are exposed to the penal sanctions of that law; and, if the promises of *pardon without the works of the law,* do not extend to *them,* they must be finally miserable, because they have all broken the law, and the law exacts punishment. This was a home stroke, and the argument is unanswerable.

Verse 16. *Therefore* it is *of faith, that* it might be *by grace*] On this account the promise is mercifully grounded, not on *obedience* to a law, but on the infinite goodness of God: and thus the *promise is sure to all the seed*—to all, both *Jews* and *Gentiles,* who, *believing*

2

A. M. cir. 4062.
A. D. cir. 58.
An. Olymp.
cir. CCIX. 2.
A. U. C. cir.
811.

17 (As it is written, P I have made thee a father of many nations,) q before him whom he believed, *even* God, r who quickeneth the dead, and calleth those s things which be not as though they were.

18 Who against hope believed in hope, that he might become the father of many nations, according to that which was spoken, t So shall thy seed be.

19 And being not weak in faith, u he consid-

ered not his own body now dead, when he was about a hundred years old, neither yet the deadness of Sarah's womb :

A. M. cir. 4062.
A. D. cir. 58.
An. Olymp.
cir. CCIX. 2.
A. U. C. cir.
811.

20 He staggered not at the promise of God through unbelief; but was strong in faith, giving glory to God.

21 And being fully persuaded that, what he had promised, v he was able also to perform

22 And therefore it was imputed to him for righteousness.

P Gen. xvii. 5.——q Or, *like unto him.*——r Chap. viii. 11; Eph. ii. 1, 5.——s Chap. ix. 26; 1 Cor. i. 28; 1 Pet. ii. 10.

t Gen. xv. 5.——u Gen. xvii. 17; xviii. 11; Heb. xi. 11, 12. v Psa. cxv. 3; Luke i. 37, 45; Heb. xi. 19.

---

in Christ Jesus, have a right to all the blessings contained in the Abrahamic covenant. *All the seed* necessarily comprehends all mankind. Of the Gentiles there can be no doubt, for the promise was given to Abraham while he was a *Gentile;* and the salvation of the *Jews* may be inferred, because they all sprang from him *after* he became an heir of the righteousness or justification which is received by faith ; for *he is the father of us all,* both *Jews* and *Gentiles.* Dr. Taylor has an excellent note on this verse. " Here," says he, " it should be well observed that *faith* and *grace* do mutually and necessarily infer each other. For the *grace* and *favour* of God, in its own nature, requires faith in us ; and faith on our part, in its own nature, supposes the *grace* or *favour* of God. If any blessing is the gift of God, in order to influence our temper and behaviour, then, in the very nature of things, it is necessary that we be sensible of this blessing, and persuaded of the grace of God that bestows it ; otherwise it is not possible we should improve it. On the other hand, if *faith* in the goodness of God, with regard to any blessing, is the principle of our religious hopes and action, then it follows that the blessing is not due in strict justice, nor on the foot of law, but that it is the free gift of Divine goodness. If the promise to Abraham and his seed be of faith on their part, then it is of grace on the part of God. *And it is of faith, that it might be by grace :* grace, being the mere good will of the donor, is free and open to all whom he chooses to make the objects of it : and the Divine wisdom appointed *faith* to be the condition of the promise ; because *faith* is, on our part, the most *simple* principle, bearing an exact correspondence to *grace,* and reaching as far as that can extend ; that so the happy effects of the promise might extend far and wide, take in the largest compass, and be confined to no condition, but what is merely necessary in the nature of things."

Verse 17. *As it is written, I have made thee a father*] That Abraham's being a father of many nations has relation to the covenant of God made with him, may be seen, Gen. xvii. 4, 5 : *Behold my covenant is with thee, and thou shalt be a father of many nations: neither shall thy name any more be called* Abram ; *but thy name shall be* Abraham, *for a father of many nations have I made thee,* i. e. he was constituted the *head* of many nations, the Gentile world, by virtue of the covenant, which God made then with him.

God, who quickeneth the dead, &c.] God is the most proper object of trust and dependence ; for being *almighty, eternal,* and *unchangeable,* he can even raise the dead to life, and *call those things which be not as though they were.* He is the *Creator,* he gave *being* when there was *none ;* he can as infallibly assure the existence of those things which are not, as if they were already actually in being. And, on this account, he can never fail of accomplishing whatsoever he has promised.

Verse 18. *Who against hope believed in hope*] The faith of Abraham bore an exact correspondence to the power and never-failing faithfulness of God ; for though, in the ordinary course of things, he had not the best foundation of hope, yet he believed that he should be the *father of many nations, according to that which was spoken ;* namely, that his posterity should be *like the stars of heaven for multitude,* and *like the dust of the earth.*

Verse 19. *He considered not his own body now dead*] He showed at once the correctness and energy of his faith : God *cannot* lie ; Abraham *can* believe. It is true that, according to the course of nature, he and Sarah are so old that they cannot have children ; but God is almighty, and can do whatsoever he will, and will fulfil his promise. This was certainly a wonderful degree of faith ; as the promise stated that it was in *his posterity* that all the nations of the earth were to be blessed ; that he had, as yet, no child by Sarah ; that he was 100 years old ; that Sarah was 90 ; and that, added to the utter improbability of her bearing at that age, she had ever been barren before. All these were so many reasons why he should not credit the promise ; yet he believed ; therefore it might be well said, ver. 20, *that he staggered not at the promise,* though every thing was unnatural and improbable ; *but he was strong in faith,* and, by this almost inimitable confidence, *gave glory to God.* It was to God's honour that his servant put such unlimited confidence in him ; and he put this confidence in him on the rational ground that God was *fully able* to perform what he had promised.

Verse 21. *And being fully persuaded*] Πληροφορηθεις, his *measure :* his soul was *full of confidence,* that the *truth* of God bound him to fulfil his promise and his power enabled him to do it.

Verse 22. *And therefore it was imputed to him for*

2

A. M. cir. 4062.
A. D. cir. 58.
An. Olymp.
cir. CCIX. 2.
A. U. C. cir.
811.

23 Now ʷ it was not written for his sake alone, that it was imputed to him;

24 But for us also, to whom it shall be imputed, if we believe ˣ on him that

raised up Jesus our Lord from the dead;

25 ʸ Who was delivered for our offences, and ᶻ was raised again for our justification.

A. M. cir. 4062.
A. D. cir. 58.
An. Olymp.
cir. CCIX. 2.
A. U. C. cir.
811.

ʷ Chap. xv. 4; 1 Cor. x. 6, 11.——ˣ Acts ii. 24; xiii. 30. ʸ Isa. liii. 5, 6; chap. iii. 25; v. 6; viii. 32; 2 Cor. v. 21; Gal.

i. 4; 1 Peter ii. 24; iii. 18; Heb. ix. 28.——ᶻ 1 Cor. xv. 17; 1 Pet. i. 21.

---

righteousness] The verse is thus paraphrased by Dr. Taylor: " For which reason God was graciously pleased to *place* his faith *to his account;* and to allow his fiducial reliance upon the Divine goodness, power, and faithfulness, for a *title* to the Divine blessing, which, otherwise, having been an idolater, he had no right to."

Abraham's strong faith in the promise of the coming Saviour, for this was essential to his faith, was reckoned to him for justification : for it is not said that any *righteousness*, either *his own*, or *that of another*, was imputed or reckoned to him for justification ; but *it*, i. e. his *faith* in God. His faith was fully persuaded of the most merciful intentions of God's goodness ; and *this*, which, in effect, laid hold on Jesus Christ, the future Saviour, was the means of his justification ; being reckoned unto him in the *place* of personal righteousness, because it laid hold on the *merit* of Him who died to make an atonement for our offences, and rose again for our justification.

Verse 23. Now it was not written for his sake alone] The fact of Abraham's believing and receiving salvation through that faith is not recorded as a mere circumstance in the patriarch's life, intended to do *him* honour : see below.

Verse 24. But for us also] The mention of this circumstance has a much more extensive design than merely to honour Abraham. It is recorded as the *model*, according to which God will save both Jews and Gentiles : indeed there can be no other way of salvation ; as all have *sinned*, all must either be saved by faith through Christ Jesus, or finally perish. If God, therefore, will our salvation, it must be by *faith ;* and faith contemplates his *promise*, and his *promise* comprehends the *Son of his love.*

Verse 25. Who was delivered for our offences] Who was delivered up to death as a *sacrifice for our sins ;* for in what other way, or for what other purpose could He, who is *innocence* itself, be *delivered for our offences ?*

And was raised again for our justification.] He was raised that we might have the fullest assurance that the death of Christ had accomplished the end for which it took place ; viz. our reconciliation to God, and giving us a title to that eternal life, into which he has entered, and taken with him our *human nature*, as the first-fruits of the resurrection of *mankind*.

1. From a careful examination of the Divine oracles it appears that the *death of Christ* was an *atonement* or *expiation* for the *sin of the world :* For him hath God set forth to be a PROPITIATION *through* FAITH in HIS BLOOD, chap. iii. 25. *For when we were yet without strength, in due time Christ* DIED FOR *the* UNGODLY, chap. v. 6. *And when we were* ENEMIES, *we*

were RECONCILED *to God by the* DEATH *of his Son*, ver. 10. *In whom we have* REDEMPTION THROUGH HIS BLOOD, *the* FORGIVENESS *of* SINS, Eph. i. 7. *Christ hath loved us*, and GIVEN HIMSELF FOR US, *an* OFFERING *and a* SACRIFICE *to God for a sweet-smelling savour*, ibid. chap. v. 2. *In whom we have* REDEMPTION THROUGH HIS BLOOD, *the* FORGIVENESS *of* SINS, Col. i. 14. *And having made* PEACE THROUGH *the* BLOOD *of his* CROSS, *in the* BODY *of* HIS FLESH, *through* DEATH, ib. ver. 20, 22. *Who* GAVE HIMSELF *a* RANSOM *for all*, 1 Tim. ii. 6. *Who* GAVE HIMSELF FOR US, *that he might* REDEEM *us from all iniquity*, Tit. ii. 14. *By which will we are sanctified, through the* OFFERING *of the* BODY *of Jesus Christ*, Heb. x. 10. *So Christ was once* OFFERED TO BEAR THE SINS *of many*, Heb. ix. 28. See also Eph. ii. 13, 16 ; 1 Pet. i. 18, 19 ; Rev. v. 9. But it would be transcribing a very considerable part of the New Testament to set down all the texts that refer to this most important and glorious truth.

2. And as his *death* was an *atonement* for our sins, so his *resurrection* was the *proof* and *pledge* of our *eternal life.* See 1 Cor. xv. 17 ; 1 Pet. i. 3 ; Eph. i. 13, 14, &c. &c.

3. The doctrine of *justification by faith*, which i so nobly proved in the preceding chapter, is one of the grandest displays of the mercy of God to mankind. It is so very plain that *all* may *comprehend* it ; and so *free* that all may *attain* it. What more simple than this ? Thou art a sinner, in consequence condemned to perdition, and utterly unable to save thy own soul. All are in the same state with thyself, and no man can give a ransom for the soul of his neighbour. God, in his mercy, has provided a Saviour for thee. As thy life was forfeited to death because of thy transgressions, Jesus Christ has redeemed thy life by giving up his *own ;* he died in *thy stead*, and has made an atonement to God for thy *transgressions ;* and offers thee the pardon he has thus purchased, on the simple condition, that thou *believe that his death is a sufficient sacrifice, ransom, and oblation for thy sin ;* and that thou bring it as *such*, by confident faith, to the throne of God, and plead it in thy own behalf there. When thou dost so, thy *faith* in that sacrifice shall be imputed to thee for righteousness ; i. e. it shall be the means of receiving that salvation which Christ has bought by his blood.

4. The doctrine of the *imputed righteousness of Christ*, as held by many, will not be readily found in this chapter, where it has been supposed to exist in all its proofs. It is repeatedly said that FAITH *is imputed for righteousness ;* but in no place here, that *Christ's obedience to the moral law* is imputed to any man. The truth is, the *moral law* was *broken*, and did not now require *obedience ;* it required this *before* it was *broken ;* but, *after* it was broken, it required *death*.

2

Either the *sinner* must *die*, or some one in his *stead*: but there was none whose *death* could have been an equivalent for the transgressions of the *world* but JESUS CHRIST. Jesus therefore *died* for man; and it is through his *blood*, the merit of his *passion* and *death*, that we have redemption; and not by his *obedience to the moral law in our stead.* Our salvation was obtained at a *much higher price.* Jesus could not but be *righteous* and *obedient*; this is consequent on the immaculate purity of his nature: but his *death* was not a *necessary consequent.* As the law of God can claim only the *death* of a *transgressor*—for such only forfeit their right to life—it is the greatest miracle of all that Christ *could die*, whose *life* was never *forfeited.* Here we see the indescribable *demerit* of sin, that it *required such a death;* and here we see the stupendous mercy of God, in providing the *sacrifice* required. It is therefore by Jesus Christ's *death,* or *obedience unto death,* that we are saved, and not by his fulfilling any moral law. That he fulfilled the moral law we know; without which he could not have been qualified to be our mediator; but we must take heed lest we attribute that to *obedience* (which was the necessary consequence of his immaculate nature) which belongs to his *passion* and *death.* These were free-will offerings of eternal goodness, and not even a necessary consequence of his incarnation.

5. This doctrine of *the imputed righteousness of Christ* is capable of great abuse. To say that Christ's *personal righteousness* is imputed to every true believer, is not Scriptural: to say that he has fulfilled all righteousness for us, or in our stead, if by this is meant his fulfilment of all moral duties, is neither Scriptural nor true: that he has *died in our stead*, is a great, glorious, and Scriptural truth: that there is no redemption but through his blood is asserted beyond all contradiction in the oracles of God. But there are a multitude of duties which the moral law requires which Christ never fulfilled in our stead, and never could. We have various duties of a domestic kind which belong solely to ourselves, in the relation of *parents, husbands, wives, servants,* &c., in which relations Christ never stood. He has fulfilled none of these duties for us, but he furnishes grace to every true believer to fulfil them to God's glory, the edification of his neighbour, and his own eternal profit. The salvation which we receive from God's free mercy, through Christ, binds us to live in a strict conformity to the *moral law*; that law which prescribes our *manners*, and the spirit by which they should be regulated, and in which they should be performed. He who lives not in the due performance of every Christian duty, whatever faith he may profess, is either a vile hypocrite, or a scandalous *Antinomian.*

CHAPTER V.

The effects of justification by faith, peace with God, 1. *The joyous hope of eternal glory,* 2. *Glorying in tribulation,* 3. *And gaining thereby patience, experience, and hope,* 4. *And having the love of God shed abroad in the heart by the Holy Spirit,* 5. *The state of the world when Christ died for it,* 6–10. *Jesus Christ is an atonement,* 11. *Sin and death entered into the world by Adam's transgression, and all became guilty before God,* 12–14. *God's grace in sending Christ into the world to save fallen man,* 15– 19. *The law is brought in to show the exceeding sinfulness of sin,* 20. *The grace of Christ is to be as extensive in its influences and reign, as sin has been in its enslaving and destructive nature,* 21.

A. M. cir. 4062.
A. D. cir. 59.
An. Olymp.
cir. CCIX. 2.
A. U. C. cir.
811.

THEREFORE [a]being justified by faith, we have [b] peace with God through our Lord Jesus Christ:

2 [c] By whom also we have access by faith into this grace [d] wherein we stand, and [e] rejoice in hope of the glory of God.

A. M. cir. 4062.
A. D. cir. 58.
An. Olymp.
cir. CCIX. 2.
A. U. C. cir.
811.

[a] Isa. xxxii. 17; John xvi. 33; chap. iii. 28, 30.——[b] Eph. ii. 14; Col. i. 20.

[c] John x. 9; xiv. 6; Eph. ii. 18; iii. 12; Heb. x. 19.——[d] 1 Cor. xv. 1.——[e] Heb. iii. 6.

NOTES ON CHAP. V.

In the former chapter, the apostle, having proved that the believing Gentiles are justified in the same way with Abraham, and are, in fact, his seed, included with him in the promise and covenant; he judged this a proper place, as the Jews built all their *glorying* upon the *Abrahamic* covenant, to produce some of the chief of those privileges and blessings in which the Christian Gentile can glory, in consequence of his justification by faith. And he produces three particulars which, above all others, were adapted to this purpose. 1. The hope of eternal life, in which the law, wherein the Jew gloried, chap. ii. 17, was defective, ver. 2. 2. The persecutions and sufferings to which Christians were exposed, ver. 3, 4, and on account of which the Jews were greatly prejudiced against the Christian profession: but he shows that these had a happy

tendency to establish the heart in the hope of the Gospel. 3. An interest in God, as our GOD and FATHER —a privilege upon which the Jews valued themselves highly above all nations, ver. 11.

These three are the singular privileges belonging to the Gospel state, wherein true Christians may glory, as really belonging to *them*, and greatly redounding, if duly understood and improved, to their honour and benefit.

Verse 1. *Therefore being justified by faith*] The apostle takes it for granted that he has proved that justification *is* by *faith*, and that the Gentiles have an equal title with the Jews to *salvation by faith.* And now he proceeds to show the effects produced in the hearts of the believing Gentiles by this doctrine. *We are justified*—have all our sins pardoned *by faith*, as

A. M. cir. 4062.	

A. M. cir. 4062.
A. D. cir. 58.
An. Olymp.
cir. CCIX. 2.
A. U. C. cir.
811.

3 And not only *so*, but [f] we glory in tribulations also : [g] knowing that tribulation worketh patience ;

4 [h] And patience, experience ; and experience, hope :

5 [i] And hope maketh not ashamed ; [k] because the love of God is

A. M. cir. 4062
A. D. cir. 58.
An. Olymp.
cir. CCIX. 2.
A. U. C. cir.
811.

[f] Matt. v. 11, 12 ; Acts v. 41 ; 2 Cor. xii. 10 ; Phil. ii. 17 ; James i. 2, 12 ; 1 Pet. iii. 14.

[g] James i. 3.——[h] James i. 12.——[i] Phil. i. 20.——[k] 2 Cor. i. 22 ; Gal. iv. 6 ; Eph. i. 13, 14.

the instrumental cause ; for, being *sinners*, we have no works of righteousness that we can plead.

We have peace with God] Before, while sinners, we were in a state of *enmity* with God, which was sufficiently proved by our *rebellion* against his authority, and our transgression of his laws ; but now, being reconciled, we have peace with God. Before, while under a sense of the guilt of sin, we had nothing but terror and dismay in our own consciences ; now, having our sin forgiven, we have peace in our hearts, feeling that all our guilt is taken away. *Peace* is generally the first-fruits of our justification.

Through our Lord Jesus Christ] His passion and death being the sole cause of our reconciliation to God.

Verse 2. By whom also] We are not only indebted to our Lord Jesus Christ for the free and full pardon which we have received, but our *continuance* in a justified state depends upon his gracious influence in our hearts, and his intercession before the throne of God.

We have access] Προσαγωγην εσχηκαμεν, *We have received this access.* It was only through Christ that we could at first *approach God* ; and it is only through him that the privilege is continued to us. And this access to God, or *introduction* to the Divine presence, is to be considered as a lasting privilege. We are not brought to God for the purpose of an *interview*, but to *remain* with him ; to be his *household* ; and, by *faith*, to behold his face, and walk in the light of his countenance.

Into this grace] This *state* of favour and acceptance.

Wherein we stand] Having firm footing, and a just title through the blood of the Lamb to the full salvation of God.

And rejoice] Have solid happiness, from the *evidence* we have of our *acceptance* with Him.

In hope of the glory of God.] Having our sins *remitted*, and our souls *adopted* into the heavenly family, we are become *heirs* ; for if *children*, then *heirs*, Gal. iv. 7 ; and that glory of God is now become our endless inheritance. While the Jews boast of their external privileges—that they have the *temple of God* among them ; that their *priests* have an *entrance* to God as their representatives, carrying before the mercy-seat the *blood of their offered victims* ; we exult in being introduced by *Jesus Christ* to the Divine presence ; *his blood* having been shed and sprinkled for this purpose ; and thus we have, spiritually and essentially, all that these Jewish rites, &c., signified. We are in the peace of God, and we are happy in the enjoyment of that peace, and have a blessed foretaste of eternal glory. Thus we have heaven upon earth, and the ineffable glories of God in prospect.

Verse 3. And not only so] We are not only happy from being in this state of communion with our God, and the prospect of being eternally with him ;

But we glory in tribulations also] All the sufferings

we endure for the testimony of our Lord are so sanctified to us by his grace, that they become powerful instruments of increasing our happiness.

Tribulation worketh patience] Υπομονην, Endurance under trials, without sustaining loss or deterioration. It is a metaphor taken from refining metals. We do not speak thus from any sudden raptures, or extraordinary sensations we may have of spiritual joy : for we find that the tribulations through which we pass are the *means* of exercising and increasing our patience, our meek forbearance of injuries received, or persecutions experienced, on account of the Gospel.

Verse 4. And patience, experience] Δοκιμεν, *Full proof, by trial*, of the truth of our religion, the solidity of our Christian state, and the faithfulness of our God. In such cases we have the opportunity of putting our religion to the *test* ; and, by every such test, it receives the deeper *sterling stamp*. The apostle uses here also a metaphor taken from the *purifying, refining*, and *testing* of silver and gold.

Experience, hope] For we thus calculate, that he who has supported us in the *past* will support us in those which may *yet come* ; and as we have received so much spiritual profiting by means of the sufferings through which we have already passed, we may profit equally by those which are yet to come : and this *hope* prevents us from dreading coming trials ; we receive them as *means of grace*, and find that all things work together for good to them that love God.

Verse 5. And hope maketh not ashamed] A hope that is not *rationally* founded will have its expectation cut off ; and then *shame* and *confusion* will be the portion of its possessor. But our hope is of a different kind ; it is founded on the *goodness* and *truth* of God ; and our religious experience shows us that we have not misapplied it ; nor exercised it on wrong or improper objects.

Because the love of God is shed abroad in our hearts] We have the most solid and convincing *testimony* of God's love to us, by that measure of it which he has communicated to our hearts. There, εκκεχυται, it is *poured out*, and diffused abroad ; filling, quickening, and invigorating all our powers and faculties. This love is the *spring* of all our *actions* ; it is the *motive* of our *obedience* ; the *principle* through which we *love* God, we love him because he first loved us ; and we love him with a love worthy of himself, because it springs from him : it is his *own* ; and every *flame* that rises from this pure and vigorous *fire* must be pleasing in his sight : it *consumes* what is *unholy* ; *refines* every *passion* and *appetite* ; *sublimes* the whole, and *assimilates* all to itself. And we know that this is the *love of God* ; it differs widely from all that is *earthly* and *sensual*. The *Holy Ghost* comes with it ; by his energy it is diffused and pervades every part ; and by his *light* we discover *what* it is, and *know* the *state* of

(5**)

A. M. cir. 4062.
A. D. cir. 58.
An. Olymp.
cir. CCIX. 2.
A. U. C. cir.
811.

shed abroad in our hearts by the Holy Ghost which is given unto us.

6 For when we were yet with-

out strength, [1] in due time [m] Christ died for the ungodly.

7 For scarcely for a righteous man will one die : [n] yet perad-

A. M. cir. 4062.
A. D. cir. 5.\
An. Olymp
cir. CCIX. 2
A. U. C. cir.
811.

---

[1] Or, *according to the time ;* Gal. iv. 4.

[m] Ver. 8 ; chap. iv. 25.——[n] Luke vi. 33 ; Col. i. 13, 14.

---

grace in which we stand. Thus we are furnished to every good word and work ; have produced in us the mind that was in Christ ; are enabled to obey the pure law of our God in its *spiritual* sense, by *loving him with all our heart, soul, mind,* and *strength ;* and our *neighbour, any* and *every soul* of man, *as ourselves.* This *is,* or *ought* to be, the common experience of every genuine believer ; but, in addition to this, the primitive Christians had, *sometimes,* the *miraculous* gifts of the Holy Spirit. These were *then needful ;* and were they needful *now,* they would be again communicated.

Verse 6. *For when we were yet without strength*] The apostle, having pointed out the glorious state of the believing Gentiles, takes occasion to contrast this with their former state ; and the means by which they were redeemed from it. Their former state he points out in *four* particulars ; which may be applied to men in general.

I. They were ασθενεις, *without strength ;* in a *weak, dying* state : neither able to *resist sin,* nor *do any good :* utterly devoid of *power* to extricate themselves from the misery of their situation.

II. They were ασεβεις, *ungodly ;* without either the *worship* or *knowledge* of the true God ; they had not God *in them ;* and, consequently, were not partakers of the Divine nature : Satan lived in, ruled, and enslaved their hearts.

III. They were αμαρτωλοι, *sinners,* ver. 8, *aiming* at happiness, but constantly *missing the mark,* which is the ideal meaning of the Hebrew חטא *chata,* and the Greek αμαρτανω. See this explained, Gen. xiii. 13. And in *missing the mark,* they deviated from the right way ; walked in the wrong way ; *trespassed* in thus deviating ; and, by breaking the commandments of God, not only missed the mark of *felicity,* but exposed themselves to everlasting *misery.*

IV. They were εχθροι, *enemies,* ver. 10, from εχθος, *hatred, enmity,* persons who hated God and holiness ; and acted in continual *hostility* to both. What a gradation is here ! 1. In our fall from God, our first apparent state is, that we are *without strength ;* have lost our principle of spiritual *power,* by having lost the image of God, righteousness and true holiness, in which we were created. 2. We are *ungodly,* having lost our strength to do good ; we have also lost all power to *worship God* aright. The mind which was made for God is no longer his residence. 3. We are *sinners ;* feeling we have lost our centre of rest, and our happiness, we go about seeking rest, but find none : what we have lost in losing God, we seek in earthly things ; and thus are continually *missing the mark,* and multiplying transgressions against our Maker. 4. We are *enemies ;* sin, indulged, increases in strength ; evil *acts* engender fixed and rooted *habits ;* the mind, every where poisoned with sin, increases in averse-

ness from good ; and mere *aversion* produces *enmity ;* and *enmity, acts of hostility,* fell cruelty, &c. : so that the enemy of God hates his Maker and his service ; is cruel to his fellow creatures ; " a foe to God, was ne'er true friend to man ;" and even torments his own soul ! Though every man brings into the world the seeds of all these evils, yet it is only by *growing up* in him that they acquire their perfection—*nemo repente fuit turpissimus*—no man becomes a profligate at *once ;* he arrives at it by slow degrees ; and the speed he makes is proportioned to his circumstances, means of gratifying sinful passions, evil education, bad company, &c., &c. These make a great *diversity* in the moral states of men : all have the same seeds of evil—*nemo sine vitiis nascitur*—all come defiled into the world ; but all have not the same opportunities of *cultivating* these seeds. Besides, as God's *Spirit* is continually convincing the world of *sin, righteousness,* and *judgment,* and the *ministers* of God are seconding its influence with their pious exhortations, as the *Bible* is in almost every house, and is less or more heard or read by almost every person, these evil seeds are receiving continual *blasts* and *checks,* so that, in many cases, they have not a vigorous growth. These causes make the principal *moral differences* that we find among men ; though in evil *propensities* they are all radically the *same.*

That all the preceding characters are applied by some learned men to the *Gentiles,* exclusively as such, I am well aware ; and that they may be all applied to them in a *national* point of view, there can be little doubt. But there are too many correspondences between the state of the *modern Gentiles* and that of the *ancient Gentiles,* to justify the propriety of applying the whole as fully to the *former* as to the *latter.* Indeed, the *four* particulars already explained point out the *natural* and *practical* state of every human being, previously to his regeneration by the grace and Spirit of God.

In due time Christ died for the ungodly.] This due or proper time will appear in the following particulars :—1. Christ was manifested in the flesh when the world needed him most. 2. When the powers of the human mind had been cultivated to the utmost both in *Greece* and *Rome,* and had made every possible effort, but all in vain, to find out some efficient scheme of happiness. 3. When the Jews were in the lowest state of corruption, and had the greatest need of the promised deliverer. 4. When the fulness of the time came, foretold by the prophets. 5. When both Jews and Gentiles, the one from their *jealousy,* the other from their *learning,* were best qualified to detect imposture and to ascertain *fact.* 6. In a word, Christ came when his advent was most likely to promote its great object—glory to God in the highest, and peace and good will among men. And the *success* that at-

2

A. M. cir. 4062.
A. D. cir. 58.
An. Olymp.
cir. CCIX. 2.
A. U. C. cir.
811.

venture for a good man some would even dare to die.

8 But ° God commendeth his love toward us, in that, while we were yet sinners, Christ died for us.

9 Much more then, being now justified ᵖ by his blood, we shall be saved ᑫ from wrath through him.

10 For ʳ if, when we were enemies, ˢ we were reconciled to God by the death of his Son, much more, being reconciled, we shall be saved ᵗ by his life.

11 And not only *so*, but we also ᵘ joy in God through our Lord Jesus Christ, by whom we have now received the ᵛ atonement.

A. M. cir. 4062.
A. D. cir. 58.
An. Olymp.
cir. CCIX. 2.
A. U. C. cir.
811.

° John iii. 16; xv. 13; 1 Pet. iii. 18; 1 John iii. 16; iv. 9, 10.
ᵖ Chap. iii. 25; Eph. ii. 13; Heb. ix. 14; 1 John i. 7.——ᑫ Chap.
i. 18; 1 Thess. i. 10.——ʳ Chap. viii. 32.

ˢ 2 Cor. v. 18, 19; Eph. ii. 16; Col. i. 20, 21.——ᵗ John v. 26;
xiv. 19; 2 Cor. iv. 10, 11.——ᵘ Chap. ii. 17; iii. 29, 30; Gal. iv.
9.——ᵛ Or, *reconciliation*; ver. 10; 2 Cor. v. 18, 19.

---

tended the preaching of Christ and his apostles, together with the wide and rapid spread of the Gospel, all prove that it was the *due time*, κατα καιρον, the *proper season*; and that Divine wisdom was justified in fixing upon *that* time in preference to all others.

Died for the ungodly] Ὑπερ ασεβων απεθανε, He *died* INSTEAD *of the ungodly*, see also ver. 8; so Luke xxii. 19. *The body of Christ*, το ὑπερ ὑμων διδομενον, *which is given* FOR *you*; i. e. *the life that is laid down in your* STEAD. In this way the preposition ὑπερ, is used by the best *Greek* writers.

Verse 7. For scarcely for a righteous man will one die] The Jews divide men, as to their moral character, into *four* classes: 1. Those who say, "what is *mine*, is *my own*; and what is *thine*, is *thy own*." These may be considered the *just*, who render to every man his due; or rather, they who neither *give* nor *take*. The second class is made up of those who say, "what is *mine*, is *thine*; and what is *thine*, is *mine*." These are they who accommodate each other, who *borrow* and *lend*. The third class is composed of those who say, "What is *mine*, is *thine*; and what is *thine*, let it be *thine*." These are the *pious*, or *good*, who give up all for the benefit of their neighbour. The fourth class are those who say, "What is *thine*, is *mine*; and what is *thine*, shall be *mine*." These are the *impious*, who *take all*, and *give nothing*. Now, for one of the first class, who would die? There is nothing amiable in his life or conduct that would so endear him to any man, as to induce him to risk his life to save such a person.

Peradventure for a good man some would even dare to die.] This is for one of the third class, who gives all he has for the good of others. This is the truly *benevolent* man, whose life is devoted to the public good: for such a person, peradventure, some who have had their lives perhaps preserved by his bounty, would even dare to die: but such cases may be considered merely as *possible*: they exist, it is true, in *romance*; and we find a few rare instances of *friends* exposing themselves to death for their friends. See the case of Jonathan and David; Damon and Pythias, Val. Max. lib. iv. c, 7; Nisus and Euryalus, Virgil. And our Lord says, John xv. 13: *Greater love hath no man than this, that a man lay down his life for his friends.* This is the utmost we can expect among men.

Verse 8. *But God commendeth his love, &c.*] Συνιστησι: God *hath set* this act of infinite mercy in the most *conspicuous* light, so as to recommend it to the *notice* and *admiration* of all.

While we were yet sinners] We were neither *righteous* nor *good*; but *impious* and *wicked*. See the preceding verse, and see the note on ver. 6.

Verse 9. *Much more then, being now justified*] If Jesus Christ, in his endless compassion towards us, gave his *life* for ours, while we were yet enemies; being now justified *by his blood*—by his death on the cross, and thus reconciled to God, *we shall be saved from wrath*—from *punishment* for past transgression, *through him*—by what he has thus suffered for us.

Verse 10. *For if, when we were enemies*] See under ver. 6.

We were reconciled] The *enmity* existing before rendered the *reconciliation* necessary. In every human heart there is a measure of *enmity* to holiness, and, consequently to the author of it. Men seldom suspect this; for one property of sin is to *blind the understanding*, so that men do not know their own state.

We shall be saved by his life.] For, as he *died* for our sins, so he *rose* again for our justification; and his *resurrection* to *life*, is the grand proof that he has accomplished whatever he had purposed in reference to the salvation of man. 2. This may be also understood of his life of *intercession*: for it is written, He ever LIVETH to make INTERCESSION *for us*, Heb. vii. 25. Through this life of intercession at the right hand of God we are *spared* and blessed. 3. And it will not be amiss to consider that, as our salvation implies the *renovation* of our nature, and our being restored to the *image of God*, so, σωθησομεθα εν τη ζωη αυτου, may be rendered: *we shall be saved* IN *his life*; for, I suppose, it is pretty generally agreed, that *the life of God in the soul of man* is essential to its salvation. 4. The *example* also of the *life* of Christ is a means of salvation. He hath left us an example that we should follow his steps: and he that followeth him, *shall not walk in darkness, but shall have the light of* LIFE, John viii. 12.

Verse 11. *We also joy* (καυχωμενοι, *we exult*, or *glory*) *in God, &c.*] We now *feel* that God is reconciled to us, and we are reconciled to him: the *enmity* is removed from our souls; and He, for Christ's sake, *through whom we have received the atonement*, καταλλαγην, *the reconciliation*, has remitted the *wrath*, the *punishment* which we deserved: and now, through this *reconciliation*, we expect an eternal glory.

It was certainly improper to translate καταλλαγη here by *atonement*, instead of *reconciliation*; as καταλλασσω signifies to *reconcile*, and is so rendered by our translators in all the places where it occurs. It does not

　　　　　　　　　　　　　　　　　　　　　　　　　　　　　　2

A. M. cir. 4062.
A. D. cir. 58.
An. Olymp.
cir. CCIX. 2.
A. U. C. cir.
811.

12 Wherefore, as ^w by one man sin entered into the world, and ^x death by sin ; and so death passed upon all men, ^y for that all have sinned :

13 (For until the law sin was in the world : but ^z sin is not

A. M. cir. 4062.
A. D. cir. 58.
An. Olymp.
cir. CCIX. 2.
A. U. C. cir.
811.

---

^w Gen. iii. 6 ; 1 Cor. xv. 21.——^x Gen. ii. 17 ; chap. vi. 23 ;

1 Cor. xv. 21.——^y Or, *in whom.*——^z Chap. iv. 15 ; 1 John iii. 4 ;

---

mean the *atonement* here, as we generally understand that word, viz. the *sacrificial death of Christ;* but rather the *effect* of that atonement, the removal of the *enmity,* and by this, the *change* of our condition and state ; from κατα, intensive, and αλλασσω *to change ;* the *thorough change* of our state from enmity to friendship. God is reconciled to us, and *we are reconciled to him by the death of his Son ;* and thus there is a glorious *change* from *enmity* to *friendship ;* and we can exult in God through our Lord Jesus Christ, by whom we have received this *reconciliation.* Though *boasting* is forbidden to a Jew, because his is a *false* confidence, yet boasting is enjoined to a *Christian,* to one reconciled to God ; for, his boasting is *only* in that reconciliation, and *the endless mercy* by which it is procured. So he that glorieth (boasteth) must glory in the *Lord.*

Verse 12. *Wherefore, as by one man sin entered into the world*] From this verse, to the conclusion of the chapter, the apostle produces a strong argument to prove that, as all mankind stood in need of the grace of God in Christ to redeem them from their sins, so this grace has been afforded equally to all, both *Jews* and *Gentiles.*

Dr. Taylor has given the following analysis of the apostle's mode of argumentation. The argument stands thus :—" The consequences of Christ's *obedience* extend as far as the consequences of Adam's *disobedience.* The consequences of Adam's disobedience extend to all mankind ; and therefore, so do the consequences of Christ's obedience. Now, if the Jews will not allow the Gentiles any interest in Abraham, as not being naturally descended from him, yet they must own that the Gentiles are the descendants of *Adam,* as well as themselves ; and being all equally involved in the consequences of his sin, from which" (as far as the death of the body is concerned) " they shall all equally be released at the resurrection, through the *free gift* of God, therefore they could not deny the Gentiles a share in all the other blessings included in the same gift."

This argument, besides proving the main point, goes to show : 1. That the grace of God in the Gospel *abounds* beyond, or very far exceeds, the mere reversing of the sufferings brought upon mankind by Adam's one offence ; as it bestows a vast surplusage of blessings which have no relation to that offence, but to the *many offences* which mankind have committed, and to the exuberance of the Divine grace. 2. To show how justly the Divine grace is founded on the obedience of Christ, in correspondence to the dispensation Adam was under, and to the consequences of his disobedience : if this disobedience involved all mankind in death, it is proper that the obedience of Christ should be the cause not only of reversing that death to all mankind, but also of other blessings which God should see fit (through him) to bestow on the world. 3. It serves to explain,

and set in a clear view, the difference between the *law* and *grace.* It was the *law* which, for Adam's one transgression, subjected him and his posterity, as included in him when he transgressed, to death, without hopes of a revival. It is *grace* which restores all men to life at the resurrection ; and, over and above that, has provided a gracious dispensation for the pardon of their sins ; for reducing them to obedience ; for guarding them against temptations ; supplying them with strength and comfort ; and for advancing them to eternal life. This would give the attentive Jew a just notion of the *law* which himself was under, and under which he was desirous of bringing the Gentiles.

The order in which the apostle handles this argument is this :—1. He affirms that death passed upon all men by Adam's one transgression, ver. 12. 2. He proves this, ver. 13, 14 : 3. He affirms there is a *correspondence* between Adam and Christ ; or between the παραπτωμα, *offence,* and the χαρισμα, *free gift,* ver. 14. 4. This correspondence, so far as the two opposite parts answer to each other, is justly expressed, ver. 18 and 19 ; and there we have the main or fundamental position of the apostle's argument, in relation to the point which he has been arguing from the beginning of the epistle, namely, the *extensiveness of the grace of the Gospel,* that it actually reaches to ALL MEN, and is not confined to the *Jews.* 5. But, before he laid down this position, it was necessary that he should show that the correspondence between Adam and Christ, or between the *offence* and the *gift,* is not to be confined strictly to the bounds specified in the position, as if the *gift* reached no farther than the consequences of the *offence ;* when in reality it extends vastly beyond them, ver. 15, 16, 17. 6. Having settled these points, as previously necessary to clear his fundamental position, and fit to his argument, he then lays down that position in a diversified manner of speech, ver. 18, 19, just as in 1 Cor. xv. 20, 21, and leaves us to conclude, from the premises laid down, ver. 15, 16, 17, that the *gift* and the *grace* in its utmost extent, is as *free* to all mankind who are willing to accept of it, as this particular instance, the resurrection from the dead. They *shall* all be raised from the dead hereafter ; they *may* all be quickened by the Spirit here. 7. Having thus shown the extensiveness of the Divine *grace,* in opposition to the dire effects of the *law* under which Adam was ; that the Jews might not overlook what he intended they should particularly observe, he puts them in mind that the law given to Adam, *transgress and die,* was introduced into the Jewish constitution by the ministry of *Moses ;* and for this end, that *the offence,* with the penalty of *death* annexed to it, *might abound,* ver. 20. But, to illustrate the Divine grace by setting it in contrast to the law, he immediately adds : where *sin,* subjecting to death, *hath abounded, grace hath much more abound-*

A. M. cir. 4062.
A. D. cir. 58.
An. Olymp.
cir. CCIX. 2.
A. U. C. cir.
811.

imputed when there is no law.

14 Nevertheless, death reigned from ^a Adam to Moses, even over them that had not sinned after the simili-

tude of Adam's transgression, ^b who is the figure of him that was to come.

15 But not as the offence, so also *is* the free gift. ^c For if, through the

A. M. cir. 4062.
A. D. cir. 58.
An. Olymp.
cir. CCIX. 2.
A. U. C. cir.
811.

---

^a Chap. iv. 15 ; Hos. vi. 7 ; Wisd. i. 14.——^b 1 Cor. xv. 21, 22, 45 ; Col. ii. 17.——^c Isa. liii. 11 ; Dan. xii. 2 ; John i. 16.

---

ed ; that is, in blessings bestowed ; it has stretched far beyond both Adam's transgression, and the transgressions under the law of Moses, ver. 20, 21, and see the note on the first of these verses.

Upon this argument the learned doctor makes the following general remarks :—

"I. As to the order of time : the apostle carries his arguments *backwards* from the time when Christ came into the world (chap. i. 17 to chap. iv.) to the time when the *covenant* was made with Abraham, (chap. iv.,) to the time when the judgment to condemnation, pronounced upon Adam, came upon all men, chap. v. 12, to the end. And thus he gives us a view of the principal *dispensations* from the beginning of the world.

"II. In this last case, as well as in the two former, he uses *law* or forensic terms ; *judgment to condemnation, justification, justify, made sinners, made righteous.* And therefore, as he considers both Jews and Gentiles at the coming of Christ, and Abraham when the covenant was made with him, so he considers Adam, and all men, as *standing in the court before the tribunal of God.* And this was the clearest and concisest way of representing his arguments." Notes, p. 283.

[Sin entered into the world] There was neither *sin* nor *death* before the offence of Adam ; after that there were *both.* Adam's transgression was therefore the *cause* of both.

And death by sin] Natural evil is evidently the effect of *moral* evil ; if man had never sinned, he had never suffered. *Dust thou art, and unto dust shalt thou return,* was never spoken till *after* Adam had eaten the forbidden fruit.

Death passed upon all men] Hence we see that all human beings partook in the consequences of Adam's sin. He propagated *his like ;* and, with the rudiments of his own nature, propagated those of his *moral* likeness.

For that all have sinned] All are born with a sinful nature ; and the seeds of this evil soon vegetate, and bring forth corresponding fruits. There has never been one instance of an immaculate human soul since the fall of Adam. Every man sins, and sins too after the similitude of Adam's transgression. Adam endeavoured to be *independent* of God ; all his offspring act in the same way : hence *prayer* is little used, because prayer is the *language of dependence ;* and this is inconsistent with every emotion of *original* sin. When these degenerate children of degenerate parents are detected in their sins, they act just as their parents did ; each *excuses* himself, and lays the blame on *another.* What hast thou done ?—*The woman whom* THOU *gavest me, to be with me ;* SHE *gave me, and I did eat. What hast* THOU *done ?*—*The* SERPENT *beguiled me, and I did eat.* Thus, it is extremely difficult to find a person who ingenuously acknowledges his own transgressions.

See the notes on Gen. iii. 6, &c., where the doctrine of original sin is particularly considered.

Verse 13. *For until the law sin was in the world]* As *death* reigned from Adam to Moses, so also did *sin.* Now, as there was no *written law* from Adam to that given to Moses, the *death* that prevailed could not be the breach of that law ; for sin, so as to be punished with temporal death, *is not imputed where there is no law,* which shows the penalty of sin to be death. Therefore, men are not subjected to death for their *own personal transgressions,* but for the sin of Adam ; as, through his transgression, all come into the world with the seeds of death and corruption in their own nature, superadded to their moral depravity. All are *sinful*— all are *mortal*—and all *must die.*

Verse 14. *Nevertheless, death reigned from Adam to Moses]* This supposes, as Dr. Taylor very properly observes :—1. That *sin* was in the world from Adam to Moses. 2. That *law* was *not* in the world from Adam to Moses during the space of about 2500 years ; for, after Adam's transgression, that law was abrogated ; and, from that time, men were either under the general *covenant of grace* given to Adam or Noah, or under that which was specially made with *Abraham.* 3. That, therefore, the sins committed were not imputed unto them *to death,* for they did not sin *after the similitude of Adam's transgression ;* that is, they did not, like him, transgress a law, or rule of action, to which *death,* as the penalty, was annexed. And yet—4. Death reigned over mankind during the period between Adam and Moses ; therefore men did not die for their own transgressions, but in consequence of Adam's one transgression.

Who is the figure of him that was to come.] Adam was the *figure,* τυπος, the *type, pattern,* or *resemblance of him who was to come ;* i. e. of the *Messiah.* The correspondence between them appears in the following particulars :—1. Through him, as its spring and fountain, *sin* became diffused through the world, so that every man comes into the world with sinful propensities : for *by one man sin entered into the world, and death by sin ; and so death passed upon all men,* ver. 12. Through Christ, as its spring and fountain, *righteousness* becomes diffused through the earth ; so that every man is made partaker of a principle of grace and truth ; for *he is the true light that lighteth every man that cometh into the world,* John i. 9. 2. *As in Adam all die ; so in Christ shall all be made alive,* 1 Cor. xv. 22. *For, since by man came death, by man came also the resurrection of the dead,* ver. 21. 3. As in or through Adam *guilt* came upon all men, so, through Christ, the *free gift* comes upon all men unto *justification of life,* ver. 18. These alone seem to be the instances in which a similitude exists between Adam and Christ.

Verse 15. *But not as the offence, so also is the free*

A. M. cir. 4062.
A. D. cir. 58.
An. Olymp.
cir. CCIX. 2.
A. U. C. cir.
811.

offence of one, many be dead; much ^d more the grace of God, and the gift by grace, *which is* by one man, Jesus Christ, hath abounded ^e unto many.

16 And not as *it was* by one that sinned, *so*

---

^d Chap. viii. 29; John iii. 16.

---

is the gift : for the judgment *was* by one to condemnation; but the free gift *is* of many offences unto justification.

17 For, if ^f by one man's offence death reigned by one; much more they which receive

---

^e Isa. liii. 11; Matt. xx. 28; xxvi. 28.——^f Or, *by one offence.*

A. M. cir. 4062.
A. D. cir. 58.
An. Olymp.
cir. CCIX. 2.
A. U. C. cir.
811.

---

gift.] The same learned writer, quoted above, continues to observe :—" It is evident that the apostle, in this and the two following verses, is running a *parallel,* or making a *comparison* between the offence of Adam and its consequence; and the opposite *gift* of God and its consequences. And, in these three verses, he shows that the comparison will not hold good in all respects, because the *free gift, χαρισμα,* bestows blessings *far beyond* the consequences of the offence, and which, therefore, have no relation to it. And this was necessary, not only to prevent mistakes concerning the consequence of Adam's offence, and the extent of Gospel grace; but it was also necessary to the apostle's main design, which was not only to prove that the grace of the Gospel extends to all men, so far as it takes off the consequence of Adam's offence, [i. e. *death,* without the promise or probability of a *resurrection,*] but that it likewise extends to all men, with respect to the surplusage of blessings, in which it stretches far beyond the consequence of Adam's offence. For, the grace that takes off the consequence of Adam's offence, and the grace which *abounds* beyond it, are both included in the same *χαρισμα,* or *free gift,* which should be well observed; for in this, I conceive, lie the connection and sinews of the argument: the *free gift,* which stands opposed to Adam's offence, and which, I think, was bestowed immediately after the offence; Gen. iii. 15 : *The seed of the woman shall bruise the serpent's head.* This gift, I say, includes both the grace which exactly answers to the offence, and also that part of the grace which stretches far beyond it. And, if the one part of the gift be freely bestowed on all mankind, as the Jews allow, why not the other? especially, considering that the *whole gift* stands upon a reason and foundation in excellence and worth, vastly surpassing the malignity and demerit of the offence; and, consequently, capable of producing benefits vastly beyond the sufferings occasioned by the offence. This is the force of the apostle's argument; and therefore, supposing that in the 18th and 19th verses, literally understood, he compares the consequence of Adam's offence and Christ's obedience, only so far as the one is commensurate to the other, yet his reasoning, ver. 15, 16, 17, plainly shows that it is his meaning and intention that we should take into his conclusion the whole of the gift, so far as it can reach, to all mankind."

For, if, through the offence of one, many be dead] That the οι πολλοι, *the many* of the apostle here means *all mankind* needs no proof to any but that person who finds himself qualified to deny that all men are *mortal.* And if *the many,* that is, *all mankind,* have died through the offence of one; certainly, the *gift by grace,* which abounds unto τους πολλους, *the many,* by Christ Jesus, must have reference to *every human being.* If the

---

consequences of Christ's incarnation and death extend only to a *few,* or a *select number* of mankind—which, though they may be considered *many* in themselves, are *few* in comparison of the whole human race—then the consequences of Adam's sin have extended only to a *few,* or to the *same select number :* and if only *many,* and not *all* have fallen, only that *many* had need of a Redeemer. For it is most evident that the same persons are referred to in both clauses of the verse. If the apostle had believed that the benefits of the death of Christ had extended only to a select number of mankind, he never could have used the language he has done here : though, in the first clause, he might have said, without any qualification of the term, *Through the offence of one,* MANY *are dead ;* in the 2nd clause, to be consistent with the doctrine of particular redemption, he must have said, *The grace of God, and the gift by grace, hath abounded unto* SOME. *As by the offence of one judgment came upon* ALL *men to condemnation ; so, by the righteousness of one, the free gift came upon* SOME *to justification,* ver. 18. *As, by one man's disobedience,* MANY *were made sinners ; so, by the obedience of one, shall* SOME *be made righteous,* ver. 19. *As in Adam* ALL *die ; so, in Christ, shall* SOME *be made alive,* 1 Cor. xv. 22. But neither the doctrine nor the thing ever entered the soul of this divinely inspired man.

Hath abounded unto many.] That is, Christ Jesus died for every man; salvation is free for all; saving grace is tendered to every soul; and a measure of the Divine light is actually communicated to every heart, John i. 9. And, as the grace is *offered,* so it may be *received ;* and hence the apostle says, ver. 17 : *They which receive abundance of grace, and of the gift of righteousness, shall reign in life by Christ Jesus :* and by *receiving* is undoubtedly meant not only the act of *receiving,* but *retaining* and *improving* the grace which they *receive ;* and, as all may receive, so ALL *may* improve and retain the grace they do receive; and, consequently, ALL *may* be eternally saved. But of multitudes Christ still may say, *They* WILL *not come unto me, that they might have life.*

Verse 16. *And not as* it was *by one that sinned*] That is, the judicial act that followed Adam's sin (the sentence of death pronounced upon him, and his expulsion from paradise) took its rise from his *one offence* alone, and terminated in condemnation ; but the free gift of God in Christ takes its rise also from the *many offences* which men, in a long course of life, have personally committed; and the object of this grace is to justify them freely, and bring them to eternal life.

Verse 17. *Death reigned by one*] Death is here *personified,* and is represented as reigning over the human race ; and death, of course, reigns unto death ;

2

A. M. cir. 4062.
A. D. cir. 58.
An. Olymp.
cir. CCIX. 2.
A. U. C. cir.
811.

abundance of grace and of the gift of righteousness shall reign in life by one, Jesus Christ.)

18 Therefore, as ᵍ by the

offence of one, *judgment came* upon all men to condemnation; even so ʰ by the righteousness of one, *the free gift came*

A. M. cir. 4062.
A. D. cir. 58.
An. Olymp.
cir. CC.X. 2.
A. U. C. cir.
811.

ᵍ Or, *by one offence.*

ʰ Or, *by one righteousness.*

---

he is known as reigning, by the *destruction* of his subjects.

Shall reign in life] Those who *receive*, retain, and improve the abundant grace offered by Jesus Christ, shall be redeemed from the *empire* of death, and exalted to the *throne* of God, to live and *reign* with him ever, world without end. See Rev. i. 5, 6 ; ii. 7, 10, 11 ; iii. 21.

If we carefully compare ver. 15 with ver. 17, we shall find that there is a correspondence between περισσειαν, the *abounding*, ver. 17, and επερισσευσε *hath abounded*, ver. 15 ; between της δωρεας της δικαιοσυνης, the *gift of righteousness*, i. e. *justification*, ver. 17, and ἡ δωρεα εν χαριτι, the *gift by grace*, ver. 15 ; therefore, if we understand *the abounding of grace, and the gift of justification*, ver. 17, we shall understand *the grace of God, and the gift by grace which hath abounded unto the many*, ver. 15. But the *abounding of grace*, and the *gift of justification*, ver. 17, is that *grace* and *gift* which is RECEIVED by those who shall *reign in eternal life*. *Reigning* in *life* is the consequence of *receiving* the grace and gift. Therefore, receiving the grace is a necessary qualification on our part for reigning in life ; and this necessarily implies our believing in Christ Jesus, as having died for our offences, receiving the grace so freely offered us ; using the means in order to get *more* grace, and bringing forth the fruits of the Spirit. *Receive* must here have the same sense as in Matt. xiii. 20 : *He heareth the word, and anon with joy* RECEIVETH *it.* John i. 12 : *But as many as* RECEIVED *him, to them gave he power to become the sons of God.* John iii. 11 : *Ye* RECEIVE *not our witness.*—See also ver. 32, 33. John v. 43 : *I am come in my Father's name, and ye* RECEIVE *me not.* John xii. 48 : *He that* RECEIVETH *not my words.* John xiii. 20 : *He that receiveth whomsoever I send,* RECEIVETH *me.* John xiv. 17 : *The Spirit of truth; whom the world cannot* RECEIVE. John xvii. 8 : *I have given them the words which thou gavest me ; and they have* RECEIVED *them.* In all these passages it is evident that *receiving* and *not receiving* imply improving or not improving.

Verse 18. *Therefore, as by the offence of one, &c.*] The Greek text of this verse is as follows :—Αρα ουν, ως δι' ενος παραπτωματος, εις παντας ανθρωπους εις κατακριμα· ουτω και δι' ενος δικαιωματος, εις παντας ανθρωπους, εις δικαιωσιν ζωης ; which literally rendered stands thus :—*Therefore, as by one offence unto all men, unto condemnation ; so likewise, by one righteousness unto all men, to justification of life.* This is evidently an elliptical sentence, and its *full* meaning can be gathered only from the context. He who had no particular purpose to serve would, most probably, understand it, from the context, thus :—*Therefore, as by one sin all men* came *into condemnation ; so also by one righteous act all men* came *unto justification of life ;* which is

more fully expressed in the following verse. Now, leaving all particular *creeds* out of the question, and taking in the scope of the apostle's reasoning in this and the preceding chapter, is not the sense evidently this ?—Through the disobedience of Adam, a sentence of condemnation to death, without any promise or hope of a resurrection, passed upon all men ; so, by the obedience of Christ unto death, this one grand righteous act, the sentence was so far reversed, that death shall not *finally* triumph, for all shall again be restored to life. *Justice* must have its due ; and therefore all must *die.* The *mercy* of God, in Christ Jesus, shall have its due also ; and therefore all shall be put into a *salvable* state here, and the whole human race shall be raised to *life* at the great day. Thus both *justice* and *mercy* are magnified ; and neither is exalted at the expense of the other.

The apostle uses *three* remarkable words in these three verses :—1. Δικαιωμα, *justification*, verse 16. 2. Δικαιοσυνη, which we render *righteousness*, verse 17 ; but is best rendered *justification*, as expressing that *pardon* and *salvation* offered to us in the Gospel : see the note on chap. i. 16. 3. Δικαιωσις, which is also rendered *justification*, ver. 18.

The *first* word, δικαιωμα, is found in the following places : Luke i. 6 ; chap. i. 32 ; ii. 26 ; v. 16, 18 ; viii. 4 ; Heb. ix. 1, 10 ; Rev. xv. 4 ; and xix. 8 ; to which the reader may refer. Δικαιωμα signifies, among the Greek writers, *the sentence of a judge, acquitting the innocent, condemning and punishing the guilty ;* but in the New Testament it signifies whatever God has *appointed* or *sanctioned* as a *law ;* and appears to answer to the Hebrew משפט יהוה *mishpat Yehovah, the statute* or *judgment, of the Lord.* It has evidently this sense in Luke i. 6 : *Walking in all the commandments and* ORDINANCES, δικαιωμασι, *of the Lord blameless ;* and it has the like meaning in the principal places referred to above ; but in the verse in question it most evidently means *absolution*, or *liberation, from punishment*, as it is opposed to κατακριμα, *condemnation*, verse 18. See the note on chap. i. 16 ; and see *Schleusner* in voce.

The *second* word, δικαιοσυνη, I have explained at large in chap. i. 16, already referred to.

The *third* word δικαιωσις, is used by the Greek writers, almost universally, to denote the *punishment* inflicted on a *criminal*, or the *condemnatory sentence* itself ; but in the New Testament where it occurs only *twice*, (Rom. iv. 25, *he was raised for our justification*, δικαιωσιν ; and chap. v. 18, *unto justification of life*, δικαιωσιν ζωης,) it evidently signifies the *pardon* and *remission of sins ;* and seems to be nearly synonymous with δικαιωμα. Dr. Taylor thinks that " δικαιοσυνη is *Gospel pardon* and *salvation*, and has reference to *God's mercy.* Δικαιωμα is our being set *quite clear* and *right ;* or our being restored to *sanctity, delivered*

A. M. cir. 4062.
A. D. cir. 58.
An. Olymp.
cir. CCIX. 2.
A. U. C. cir.
811.

upon all men unto justification of life.

19 For, as by one man's ^k disobedience, many were made sinners; so, by the obedience of one, shall many be made righteous.

20 Moreover, ^l the law entered, that the of-

fence might abound. But where sin abounded, grace did much ^m more abound:

21 That as sin hath reigned unto death, even so ⁿ might grace reign through righteousness unto eternal life, by Jesus Christ our Lord.

A. M. cir. 4062.
A. D. cir. 58.
An. Olymp.
cir. CCIX. 2.
A. U. C. cir.
811.

ⁱ John xii. 32; Heb. ii. 9.——^k 1 Kings i. 21; Isa. liii. 4, 5, 6, 10; 2 Cor. v. 21.——^l John xv. 22; chap. iii. 20; iv. 15; vii.

8; Gal. iii. 19, 23.——^m Luke vii. 47; 1 Tim. i. 14.——ⁿ 1 Cor. xv. 56, 57; chap vi. 16, 21, 23.

---

from eternal death, and being *brought to eternal life;* and, has reference to the *power* and *guilt* of *sin.* And δικαιωσις he thinks may mean no more than our being *restored to life at the resurrection.*" Taking these in their order, there is: *First, pardon of sin. Secondly, purification of heart*, and preparation for glory. *Thirdly,* the *resurrection* of the *body*, and its being made like to his glorious body, so as to become a fit tabernacle for the soul in a glorified state for ever and ever.

The same writer observes that, when the apostle speaks of *forgiveness of sins* simply, he insists on *faith* as the *condition;* but *here*, where he speaks of *justification of life*, he mentions no *condition;* and therefore he supposes *justification of life*, the phrase being understood in a forensic sense, to mean no more than the *decree* or *judgment* that determines the *resurrection from the dead.* This is a favourite point with the doctor, and he argues largely for it: see his *notes.*

Verse 19. *For, as by one man's disobedience, &c.*] The explanation of this verse has been anticipated in the foregoing.

Verse 20. *The law entered that (ἱνα) the offence might abound.*] After considering various opinions concerning the true meaning of this verse, (see under verse 12,) I am induced to prefer my own, as being the most *simple.* By *law* I understand the Mosaic law. By *entering in*, παρεισηλθεν, or, rather, *coming in privily*, see Gal. ii. 4, (the only place where it occurs besides,) I understand the temporary or limited use of that law, which was, as far as its *rites* and *ceremonies* are considered, confined to the Jewish people, and to them only till the Messiah should come; but considered as the *moral law*, or *rule of conscience* and *life*, it has in its *spirit* and *power* been *slipped in* —*introduced* into every conscience, *that sin might abound*—that the true nature, deformity, and extent of sin might appear; for by the law is the knowledge of sin: for how can the finer deviations from a *straight line* be ascertained, without the application of a known *straight edge?* Without this *rule of right*, sin can only be known in a sort of *general* way; the innumerable *deviations* from *positive rectitude* can only be known by the application of the righteous statutes of which the law is composed. And it was necessary that this law should be given, that the true nature of *sin* might be seen, and that men might be the better prepared to receive the Gospel; finding that this law worketh only *wrath*, i. e. denounces *punishment*, forasmuch as all have sinned. Now, it is wisely ordered of God, that wherever the Gospel goes there the law goes also; *entering* every where, that *sin* may be seen *to abound*, and that men may be led to despair of sal-

vation in any other way or on any terms but those proposed in the Gospel of Christ. Thus the sinner becomes a *true penitent*, and is glad, seeing the curse of the *law* hanging over his soul, to flee for refuge to the hope set before him in the *Gospel.* On the meaning of *ἱνα*, in various places, see Chrisost. vol. iii. p. 241. See also Hammond on the word in his notes on the New Testament.

But where sin abounded] Whether in the *world*, or in the *heart* of the *individual*, being discovered by this most pure and righteous *law*, grace did much more *abound:* not only *pardon* for all that is past is offered by the Gospel, so that all the transgressions for which the soul is condemned to death by the law, are freely and fully forgiven; but also the Holy Spirit, in the abundance of his gifts and graces, is communicated, so as to prepare the receiver for an exceeding and eternal weight of glory. Thus the grace of the Gospel not only redeems from death, and restores to life, but brings the soul into such a relationship with God, and into such a participation of eternal glory, as we have no authority to believe ever would have been the portion even of *Adam* himself, had he even eternally retained his innocence. Thus, *where sin abounded, grace doth much more abound.*

Verse 21. *That as sin hath reigned unto death*] As extensively, as deeply, as universally, as *sin*, whether implying the *act of transgression* or the *impure principle* from which the act proceeds, or *both. Hath reigned*, subjected the whole earth and all its inhabitants; the whole soul, and all its powers and faculties, *unto death, temporal* of the *body*, *spiritual* of the *soul*, and *eternal* of *both; even so*, as extensively, deeply, and universally *might grace reign*— filling the whole earth, and pervading, purifying, and refining the whole soul: *through righteousness*— through this doctrine of *free salvation* by the blood of the Lamb, and by the principle of *holiness* transfused through the soul by the Holy Ghost: *unto eternal life* —the proper object of an immortal spirit's hope, the only sphere where the human intellect can rest, and be happy in the *place* and *state* where God is; where he is seen AS HE IS; and where he can be enjoyed without interruption in an eternal progression of knowledge and beatitude: *by Jesus Christ our Lord*—as the *cause* of our salvation, the *means* by which it is communicated, and the *source* whence it springs. Thus we find, that the salvation from sin here is as extensive and complete as the *guilt* and *contamination* of sin; death is conquered, hell disappointed, the devil confounded, and sin totally destroyed. Here is glorying: *To him that loved us, and washed us from our* sins in his own blood, and has made us kings and priests to God and his Father, be glory and dominion, for ever and ever. Amen. Hallelujah! The Lord God Omnipotent reigneth! Amen and Amen.

WHAT highly interesting and momentous truths does the preceding chapter bring to our view! No less than the doctrine of the *fall of man* from original righteousness; and the *redemption of the world* by the incarnation and death of Christ. On the subject of the FALL, though I have spoken much in the notes on Genesis, chap. iii., yet it may be necessary to make a few farther observations :—

1. That all mankind have *fallen under the empire of death*, through this original transgression, the apostle most positively asserts; and few men who profess to believe the Bible, pretend to dispute. This point is indeed ably stated, argued, and proved by Dr. Taylor, from whose observations the preceding notes are considerably enriched. But there is one point which I think not less evident, which he has not only not included in his argument, but, as far as it came in his way, has argued against it, viz. the degeneracy and moral corruption of the human soul. As no man can account for the death brought into the world but on the ground of this primitive transgression, so none can account for the moral evil that is in the world on any other ground. It is a fact, that every human being brings into the world with him the seeds of *dissolution* and *mortality*. Into this state we are fallen, according to Divine revelation, through the one offence of Adam. This fact is proved by the mortality of all men. It is not less a fact, that every man that is born into the world brings with him the seeds of *moral evil;* these he could not have derived from his Maker; for the most pure and holy God can make nothing impure, imperfect, or unholy. Into this state we are reduced, according to the Scripture, by the transgression of Adam; for by this one man *sin* entered into the world, as well as *death*.

2. The fact that all come into the world with sinful propensities is proved by another fact, that every man sins; that sin is his *first* work, and that no exception to this has ever been noticed, except in the human nature of Jesus Christ; and that exempt case is sufficiently accounted for from this circumstance, that *it* did not come in the common way of natural generation.

3. As *like produces its like*, if Adam became mortal and sinful, he could not communicate properties which he did not possess; and he must transmit those which constituted his natural and moral likeness : therefore all his posterity must resemble himself. Nothing less than a constant miraculous energy, presiding over the formation and developement of every human body and soul, could prevent the seeds of natural and moral evil from being propagated. That these seeds are not produced in men by their own *personal transgressions*, is most positively asserted by the apostle in the preceding chapter; and that they exist *before* the human being is capable of actual transgression, or of the exercise of *will* and *judgment*, so as to *prefer* and *determine*, is evident to the most superficial observer : 1st, from the most marked evil *propensities* of children, long before rea-

son can have any influence or control over passion; and, 2ndly, it is demonstrated by the *death* of millions in a state of infancy. It could not, therefore, be *personal* transgression that produced the evil *propensities* in the one case, nor *death* in the other.

4. While misery, death, and sin are in the world, we shall have incontrovertible proofs of the fall of man. Men may dispute against the doctrine of *original sin;* but such facts as the above will be a standing irrefragable argument against every thing that can be advanced against the doctrine itself.

5. The *justice* of permitting this general infection to become diffused has been strongly oppugned. " Why should the innocent suffer for the guilty ?" As God made man to propagate his like on the earth, his transmitting the same kind of nature with which he was formed must be a necessary consequence of that propagation. He might, it is true, have cut off for ever the offending pair; but this, most evidently, did not comport with his creative designs. " But he might have rendered Adam incapable of sin." This does not appear. If he had been incapable of sinning, he would have been incapable of holiness; that is, he could not have been a *free agent;* or in other words he could not have been an *intelligent* or intellectual being; he must have been a mass of inert and unconscious matter. " But God might have cut them off and created a new race." He certainly might; and what would have been gained by this? Why, just nothing. The *second* creation, if of *intelligent* beings at all, must have been precisely similar to the first; and the circumstances in which these last were to be placed, must be exactly such as infinite wisdom saw to be the most proper for their predecessors, and consequently, the most proper for *them*. They also must have been in a state of *probation;* they also must have been placed under a *law;* this law must be guarded by *penal sanctions;* the *possibility* of transgression must be the same in the second case as in the first; and the lapse as *probable*, because as *possible* to this second race of human beings as it was to their predecessors. It was better, therefore, to let the same pair continue to fulfil the great end of their creation, by propagating their like upon the earth; and to introduce an *antidote* to the *poison*, and by a dispensation as strongly expressive of *wisdom* as of *goodness*, to make the ills of life, which were the consequences of their transgression, the means of correcting the evil, and through the wondrous economy of grace, sanctifying even these to the eternal good of the soul.

6. Had not God provided a *Redeemer*, he, no doubt, would have terminated the whole mortal story, by cutting off the original transgressors; for it would have been unjust to permit them to propagate their like in such circumstances, that their offspring must be *unavoidably* and eternally wretched.

God has therefore provided such a Saviour, the *merit* of whose *passion* and *death* should apply to every human being, and should infinitely transcend the *demerit* of the original transgression, and put every soul that received that grace (and ALL *may*) into a state of greater excellence and glory than that was, or could have been, from which Adam, by transgressing, fell.

7. The state of *infants* dying before they are capa-

ble of hearing the Gospel, and the state of *heathens* who have no opportunity of knowing how to escape from their corruption and misery, have been urged as cases of peculiar hardship. But, first, there is no evidence in the whole book of God that any child dies eternally for Adam's sin. Nothing of this kind is intimated in the Bible; and, as Jesus took upon him *human nature*, and condescended to be born *of a woman* in a state of perfect helpless *infancy*, he has, consequently, sanctified this state, and has said, without limitation or exception, *Suffer little children to come unto me, and forbid them not, for of such is the kingdom of God.* We may justly infer, and all the *justice* as well as the *mercy* of the Godhead supports the inference, that all human beings, dying in an *infant* state, are regenerated by that *grace of God which bringeth salvation to all men*, Titus ii. 11, and go infallibly to the kingdom of heaven. As to the *Gentiles*, their case is exceedingly clear. The apostle has determined this; see chap. ii. 14, 15, and the notes there. He who, in the course of his providence, has withheld from them the *letter* of his *word*, has not denied them the *light* and *influence* of his Spirit; and will judge them in the great day only according to the grace and means of moral improvement with which they have been favoured. No man will be finally damned because he was a *Gentile*,

but because he has not made a proper use of the grace and advantages which God had given him. Thus we see that the Judge of all the earth has done right; and we may rest assured that he will eternally act in the same way.

8. The term FALL we use metaphorically, to signify *degradation*: literally, it signifies *stumbling*, so as to lose the *centre of gravity*, or the *proper poise* of our bodies, in consequence of which we are precipitated on the ground. The term seems to have been borrowed from the παραπτωμα of the apostle, chap. v. 15–18, which we translate *offence*, and which is more literally FALL, from παρα, intensive, and πιπτω, *I fall;* a grievous, dangerous, and ruinous fall, and is properly applied to *transgression* and *sin* in general; as every act is a *degradation* of the soul, accompanied with *hurt*, and *tending to destruction.* The term, in this sense, is still in common use; the degradation of a man in power we term his *fall;* the impoverishment of a *rich* man we express in the same way; and when a man of piety and probity is overcome by any act of sin, we say he is *fallen;* he has descended from his spiritual eminence, is degraded from his spiritual excellence, is impure in his soul, and becomes again exposed to the displeasure of his God.

CHAPTER VI.

We must not abuse the boundless goodness of God by continuing in sin, under the wicked persuasion that the more we sin the more the grace of God will abound, 1. For, having been baptized into Christ, we have professed thereby to be dead to sin, 2–4. And to be planted in the likeness of his resurrection, 5. For we profess to be crucified with him, to die and rise again from the dead, 6–11. We should not, therefore, let sin reign in our bodies, but live to the glory of God, 12–14. The Gospel makes no provision for living in sin, any more than the law did; and those who commit sin are the slaves of sin, 15–19. The degrading and afflictive service of sin, and its wages eternal death; the blessed effects of the grace of God in the heart, of which eternal life is the fruit, 20–23.

A. M. cir. 4062.
A. D. cir. 58.
An. Olymp.
cir. CCIX. 2.
A. U. C. cir.
811.

WHAT shall we say then? [a] Shall we continue in sin, that grace may abound?

2 God forbid. How shall we, that are [b] dead to sin, live any longer therein?

3 Know ye not, that [c] so many of us as [d] were baptized into

A. M. cir. 4062.
A. D. cir. 58.
An. Olymp.
cir. CCIX. 2.
A. U. C. cir.
811.

---

[a] Chap. iii. 8; ver. 15.——[b] Ver. 11; chap. vii. 4; Gal. ii. 19; vi. 14.——[c] Col. iii. 3; 1 Pet. ii. 24.——[d] Or, *are.*

NOTES ON CHAP. VI.

The apostle, having proved that salvation, both to Jew and Gentile, must come through the Messiah, and be received *by faith only*, proceeds in this chapter to show the obligations under which both were laid to live a holy life, and the means and advantages they enjoyed for that purpose. This he does, not only as a thing highly and indispensably necessary in itself—for without holiness none can see the Lord—but to confute a calumny which appears to have been gaining considerable ground even at that time, viz. that the doctrine of *justification by faith alone, through the grace of Christ Jesus*, rendered *obedience* to the moral law useless; and that the more evil a man did, the more the grace of God would abound to him, in his redemption from that evil. That this calumny was then propagated we learn from chap. iii. 8; and the apostle defends himself against it in the 31st verse of the same, by asserting, that his doctrine, far from making void the law, served to establish it. But in this and the two following chapters he takes up the subject in a regular, formal manner; and shows both Jews and Gentiles that the *principles* of the Christian religion absolutely require a *holy heart* and a *holy life*, and make the amplest provisions for both.

Verse 1. *Shall we continue in sin*] It is very likely that these were the words of a believing *Gentile*, who—having as yet received but little instruction, for he is but just brought out of his *heathen* state to believe in Christ Jesus—might imagine, from the manner in which God had magnified his mercy, in blotting out his sin on his simply believing on Christ, that, supposing he even gave way to the evil propensities of

A. M. cir. 4062.
A. D. cir. 58.
An. Olymp.
cir. CCIX. 2.
A. U. C. cir.
811.

Jesus Christ, e were baptized into his death?

4 Therefore, we are f buried with him by baptism into death: that g like as Christ was raised up from the dead by h the glory of the Father, i even so

we also should walk in newness of life.

5 k For, if we have been planted together in the likeness of his death, we shall be also *in the likeness* of *his* resurrection.

A. M. cir. 4062.
A. D. cir. 58.
An. Olymp.
cir. CCIX. 2.
A. U. C. cir.
811.

e 1 Cor. xv. 29.——f Col. ii. 12.——g Chap. viii. 11; 1 Cor. vi. 14; 2 Cor. xiii. 4.

h John ii. 11; xi. 40.——i Gal. vi. 15; Eph. iv. 22, 23, 24; Col. iii. 10.——k Phil. iii. 10, 11.

his own heart, his transgressions could do him no hurt now that he was in the favour of God. And we need not wonder that a *Gentile*, just emerging from the deepest darkness, might entertain such thoughts as these; when we find that eighteen centuries after this, persons have appeared in the most Christian countries of Europe, not merely asking such a question, but defending the doctrine with all their might; and asserting in the most unqualified manner, "that believers were under *no obligation* to keep the *moral law* of God; that Christ had kept it for them; that his keeping it was *imputed to them;* and that God, who had exacted it from *Him*, who was their surety and representative, would not exact it from *them;* forasmuch as it would be *injustice* to require *two payments* for *one debt.*" These are the *Antinomians* who once flourished in this land, and whose race is not yet utterly extinct.

Verse 2. God forbid.] Μη γενοιτο, *Let it not be; by no means; far from it; let not such a thing be mentioned!*—Any of these is the meaning of the Greek phrase, which is a strong expression of surprise and disapprobation: and is not properly rendered by our *God forbid!* for, though this may express the *same thing*, yet it is not proper to make the sacred NAME so familiar on such occasions.

How shall we, that are dead to sin] The phraseology of this verse is common among Hebrews, Greeks, and Latins. To DIE *to a thing* or person, is to *have nothing to do with it* or him; to be *totally separated* from them: and to *live to a thing* or *person* is to be *wholly given up to them;* to have the most *intimate connection* with them. So Plautus, Clitell. iii. 1, 16: *Nihil mecum tibi,* MORTUUS TIBI SUM. *I have nothing to do with thee; I am* DEAD *to thee.* Persa, i. 1, 20: *Mihi quidem tu jam* MORTUUS ERAS, *quia te non visitavi. Thou wast* DEAD *to me because I visited thee not.* So Ælian, Var. Hist. iii. 13: Ὁτι φιλοινοτατον εθνος το των Ταπυρων, τοσουτον, ὡστε ζην αυτους εν οινῳ, και το πλειστον του βιου εν τη προς αυτον ὁμιλια καταναλισκειν· "*The Tapyrians are such lovers of wine, that they* LIVE IN *wine; and the principal part of their* LIFE *is* DEVOTED *to it.*" *They live to wine;* they are insatiable drunkards. See more examples in *Wetstein* and *Rosenmuller.*

Verse 3. Know ye not, &c.] Every man who believes the Christian religion, and receives baptism as the proof that he believes it, and has taken up the profession of it, is bound thereby to a life of righteousness. *To be baptized into Christ*, is to receive the doctrine of Christ crucified, and to receive baptism as a proof of the genuineness of that faith, and the obligation to live according to its precepts.

Baptized into his death?] That, as Jesus Christ in his crucifixion died completely, so that no spark of the *natural* or *animal life* remained in his body, so those who profess his religion should be so completely *separated* and *saved from sin*, that they have no more *connection* with it, nor any more *influence* from it, than a *dead man* has with or from his *departed* spirit.

Verse 4. *We are buried with him by baptism into death*] It is *probable* that the apostle here alludes to the mode of administering baptism by *immersion*, the whole body being put *under the water*, which seemed to say, the man is *drowned*, is *dead;* and, when he came up out of the water, he seemed to have a *resurrection* to life; *the man is risen again; he is alive!* He was, therefore, supposed to throw off his old *Gentile* state as he threw off his clothes, and to assume a new character, as the baptized generally put on new or fresh garments. I say it is *probable* that the apostle alludes to this mode of immersion; but it is not absolutely *certain* that he does so, as some do imagine; for, in the next verse, our being incorporated into Christ by *baptism* is also denoted by our being *planted*, or rather, *grafted together in the likeness of his death;* and Noah's ark *floating* upon the water, and *sprinkled by the rain from heaven*, is a *figure* corresponding to *baptism*, 1 Pet. iii. 20, 21; but neither of these gives us the same idea of the outward form as *burying*. We must be careful, therefore, not to lay too much stress on such circumstances. Drowning among the ancients was considered the most noble kind of death; some think that the apostle may allude to this. The grand point is, that this baptism represents our *death to sin*, and our *obligation to walk in newness of life:* without which, of what use can *it* or any other *rite* be?

Raised up from the dead by the glory of the Father] From this we learn, that as it required the *glory of the Father*, that is, his *glorious energy*, to raise up from the grave the dead body of Christ, so it requires the same glorious energy to *quicken* the dead soul of a sinner, and enable him to walk in newness of life.

Verse 5. *For if we have been planted together*] Συμφυτοι γεγοναμεν. Dr. Taylor observes, that our translation does not completely express the apostle's meaning. Τα συμφυτα are such plants as grow, the one *upon* and *in the other*, deriving sap and nourishment from it, as the *misletoe* upon the *oak*, or the *scion* upon the *stock* in which it is grafted. He would therefore translate the words: *For if we have been* growers together *with Christ in the likeness of his death,* (or in that which is like his death,) *we shall be also* growers together *with him in the likeness of his resurrection;* or in that which is like *his resurrection.* He reckons it a beautiful metaphor, taken from *graft-*

A. M. cir. 4062.
A. D. cir. 58.
An. Olymp.
cir. CCIX. 2.
A. U. C. cir.
811.

6 Knowing this, that [1] our old man is crucified with *him*, that [m] the body of sin might be destroyed, that henceforth we should not serve sin.

A. M. cir. 4062.
A. D. cir. 58.
An. Olymp.
cir. CCIX. 2.
A. U. C. cir.
811.

7 For [n] he that is dead is [o] freed from sin.

8 Now [p] if we be dead with Christ, we believe that we shall also live with him:

---

[1] Gal. ii. 20; v. 24; vi. 14; Eph. iv. 22; Col. iii. 5, 9.

[m] Col. ii. 11.——[n] 1 Pet. iv. 1.——[o] Gr. *justified.*——[p] 2 Tim. ii. 11.

---

ing, or making the scion *grow together* with a new stock.

But if we take the word *planted* in its usual sense, we shall find it to be a metaphor as beautiful and as expressive as the former. When the seed or plant is inserted in the ground, it derives from that ground all its nourishment, and all those juices by which it becomes developed; by which it increases in size, grows firm, strong, and vigorous; and puts forth its leaves, blossoms, and fruit. The *death* of Jesus Christ is represented as the *cause* whence his *fruitfulness*, as the author of eternal salvation to mankind is derived; and genuine believers in him are represented as being *planted in his death*, and growing *out of it*; deriving their growth, vigour, firmness, beauty, and fruitfulness from it. In a word, it is by his *death* that Jesus Christ redeems a lost world; and it is from that vicarious death that believers derive that pardon and holiness which makes them so *happy* in *themselves*, and so *useful* to *others*. This sacrificial death is the *soil* in which they are *planted*; and from which they derive their *life, fruitfulness,* and their final *glory*.

Verse 6. *Our old man is crucified with* him] This seems to be a farther extension of the *same metaphor*. When a seed is planted in the earth, it appears as if the *whole body* of it *perished*. All *seeds*, as they are commonly termed, are composed of *two parts*; the *germ*, which contains the *rudiments* of the future plant; and the *lobes*, or *body* of the seed, which by their decomposition in the ground, become the first nourishment to the extremely fine and delicate roots of the embryo plant, and support it till it is capable of deriving grosser nourishment from the common soil. The *body* dies that the *germ* may live. Parables cannot go on all fours; and in metaphors or figures, there is always some *one* (or more) remarkable property by which the doctrine intended is illustrated. To apply this to the purpose in hand: how is the principle of *life* which Jesus Christ has *implanted* in us to be brought into full effect, vigour, and usefulness? By the destruction of the *body of sin*, our *old man*, our wicked, corrupt, and fleshly self, is to be crucified; to be as truly *slain* as Christ was crucified; that our souls may as truly be raised from a death of sin to a life of righteousness, as the body of Christ was raised from the grave, and afterwards ascended to the right hand of God. But how does this part of the metaphor apply to Jesus Christ? Plainly and forcibly. Jesus Christ took on him a body; a body *in the likeness of sinful flesh*, chap. viii. 3; and gave up that body to death; through which *death* alone an atonement was made for sin, and the way laid open for the vivifying Spirit, to have the fullest access to, and the most powerful operation in, the human heart. Here, the *body* of Christ *dies* that he may be a *quickening Spirit* to mankind. Our *body*

of sin is destroyed by this quickening Spirit, that henceforth we should live unto Him who died and rose again. Thus the metaphor, in all its leading senses, is complete, and applies most forcibly to the subject in question. We find that παλαιος ανθρωπος, *the old man*, used here, and in Eph. iv. 22, and Coloss. iii. 9, is the same as *the flesh with its affections and lusts*, Gal. v. 24; and *the body of the sins of the flesh*, Coloss. ii. 11; and the very same which the Jewish writers term אדם הקרמוני, *Adam hakkadmoni, the old Adam*; and which they interpret by יצר הרע *yetsar harâ*, "evil concupiscence," the same which we mean by *indwelling sin*, or the *infection of our nature*, in consequence of the *fall*. From all which we may learn that the design of God is to counterwork and destroy the very spirit and soul of sin, that we shall *no longer serve it*, δουλευειν, no longer be its *slaves*. Nor shall it any more be capable of performing its essential functions than a *dead body* can perform the functions of natural life.

Verse 7. *He that is dead is freed from sin.*] Δεδικαιωται, literally, is *justified* from sin; or, is *freed* or *delivered* from it. Does not this simply mean, that the man who has received Christ Jesus by faith, and has been, through believing, made a partaker of the Holy Spirit, has had his *old man*, all his *evil propensities* destroyed; so that he is not only justified freely from all sin, but wholly sanctified unto God? The context shows that this is the meaning. Every instance of violence is done to the whole scope and design of the apostle, by the opinion, that "this text is a proof that believers are *not* fully saved from sin *in this life*, because only he *that is dead is freed from sin*." Then *death* is his *justifier* and *deliverer!* Base and abominable insinuation, highly derogatory to the glory of Christ! Dr. Dodd, in his note on the preceding verse, after some inefficient criticism on the word καταργηθη, *destroyed*, which, he thinks, should be rendered *enervated*, has the following most unevangelical sentiment: "The body of sin in believers is, indeed, an enfeebled, conquered, and deposed tyrant, and the stroke of *death finishes its destruction*." So then, the death of Christ and the influences of the Holy Spirit were only sufficient to *depose* and *enfeeble* the tyrant sin; but OUR *death* must come in to effect his *total destruction!* Thus our death is, at least *partially*, our *Saviour*; and thus, that which was an *effect* of sin (for sin entered into the world, and death by sin) becomes the *means* of finally *destroying* it! That is, the *effect* of a *cause* can become so powerful, as to react upon that cause and produce its annihilation! The *divinity* and *philosophy* of this sentiment are equally absurd. It is the blood of Christ alone that cleanses from all unrighteousness; and the *sanctification* of a believer is no more dependent on *death* than his *justification*. If it be said,

2

77

A. M. cir. 4062.
A. D. cir. 58.
An. Olymp.
cir. CCIX. 2.
A. U. C. cir.
811.

9 Knowing that ^q Christ being raised from the dead dieth no more ; death hath no more dominion over him.

10 For, in that he died, ^r he died unto sin once : but in that he liveth, ^s he liveth unto God.

11 Likewise reckon ye also yourselves to be ^t dead indeed unto sin, but ^u alive unto God through Jesus Christ our Lord.

A. M. cir. 4062.
A. D. cir. 58.
An. Olymp.
cir. CCIX. 2.
A. U. C. cir.
811.

12 ^v Let not sin therefore reign in your mortal body, that ye should obey it in the lusts thereof.

13 Neither yield ye your ^w members *as* ^x instruments of unrighteousness unto sin : but ^y yield yourselves unto God, as those that are alive from the dead ; and your members *as* instruments of righteousness unto God.

---

q Rev. i. 18.——r Heb. ix. 27, 28.——s Luke xx. 38.——t Ver. 2.
u Gal. ii. 19.——v Psa. xix. 13 ; cxix. 133.

w Chap. vii. 5 ; Col. iii. 5 ; James iv. 1.——x Gr. *arms* or *weapons.*——y Chap. xii. 1 ; 1 Pet. ii. 24 ; iv. 2.

"that believers do not cease from sin till they die ;" I have only to say, they are such *believers* as do not make a proper use of their *faith ;* and what can be said more of the whole herd of transgressors and infidels? They *cease to sin,* when they *cease to breathe.* If the Christian religion bring no other privileges than this to its upright followers, well may we ask, wherein doth the *wise man* differ from the *fool,* for they have both one end? But the whole Gospel teaches a contrary doctrine.

Verse 8. *Now if we be dead with Christ*] According to what is stated in the preceding verses. See particularly on the 5th verse.

Verse 9. *Christ being raised from the dead dieth no more*] So we, believing in Christ Jesus, and having a death unto sin, and a life unto righteousness, should sin no more. If we be risen indeed with Christ, we should seek the things above, and set our affections on things above, and not on the earth. The man who walks in humble, loving obedience, to an indwelling Christ, sin has no more dominion over his soul than death has over the immortal and glorified body of his Redeemer.

Verse 10. *He died unto sin once*] On this clause Rosenmüller speaks thus : "Τη αμαρτια απεθανεν εφαπαξ· *propter peccatum mortuus est semel,* et quidem misera morte. Τη αμαρτια, i. e. υπερ της αμαρτιας, ad expianda peccata ; res ipsa docet aliter *homines* αποθνησκειν τη αμαρτια, aliter *Christum :* amat Paulus parallelismum, in quo interpretando multa cautione opus est."
" *He died unto sin once :* i. e. *he died on account of sin,* and truly a miserable death. Τη αμαρτια, is the same as υπερ της αμαρτιας, *for the expiation of sin.* Common sense teaches us that *men die to sin* in one sense ; *Christ in another :* St. Paul loves parallelisms, in the interpretation of which there is need of much caution." From the whole scope of the apostle's discourse it is plain that he considers the death of Christ as a death or sacrifice for sin ; a sin-offering : in this sense no *man* has ever died *for* sin, or ever can die.

Verse 11. *Reckon ye also yourselves to be dead*] Die as truly *unto* sin, as he died *for* sin. Live as truly *unto* God, as he lives *with* God. This seems to be the spirit of the apostle's meaning.

Verse 12. *Let not sin therefore reign*] This is a prosopopœia, or *personification.* Sin is represented as a *king, ruler,* or *tyrant,* who has the *desires of the mind* and the *members of the body* under his control ; so that by influencing the *passions* he governs the *body.*

Do not let sin reign, do not let him work ; that is, let him have no *place,* no *being* in your souls ; because, wherever he is he governs, less or more : and indeed *sin* is not *sin* without this. How is sin known? By evil *influences* in the mind, and *evil acts* in the *life.* But do not these *influences* and these *acts* prove his *dominion?* Certainly, the very existence of an evil thought to which *passion* or *appetite attaches itself,* is a proof that there sin has *dominion ;* for without dominion such passions could not be excited. Wherever sin is *felt,* there sin has *dominion ;* for sin is *sin* only as it *works* in *action* or *passion* against God. Sin cannot be a *quiescent* thing : if it do not *work* it does not *exist.*

That ye should obey it in the lusts thereof.] Αυτη εν ταις επιθυμιαις αυτου. This clause is *wanting* in the most ancient and reputable MSS. and in the principal versions. *Griesbach* has left it out of his text ; and Professor *White* says, *Certissime delenda :* " These words should certainly be expunged ;" they are not necessary to the apostle's argument ; it was enough to say, *Let not sin reign in your mortal bodies, that ye should obey it.* If it be *there* it will *reign* there ; and its reign supposes, necessarily, the *subjection* of that *in* which it reigns. A king reigns when his *laws* are enforced, and the *people obey them.* When there is no *executive* government there is no *reign.* There may be a *royal shadow* there, but there is no *king.*

Verse 13. *Neither yield ye your members*] Do not yield to temptation. It is no sin to be *tempted ;* the sin lies in *yielding.* While the sin exists only in Satan's solicitation, it is the *devil's sin,* not ours : when we yield, we make the devil's sin our *own :* then *we* ENTER INTO *temptation.* Resist the devil, and he will flee from you. Satan himself cannot *force* you to sin : till he *wins over* your *will,* he cannot bring you into *subjection.* You may be *tempted ;* but *yield* not to the temptation.

Yield yourselves unto God] Let God have your *wills ;* keep them ever on his side ; there they are *safe,* and there they will be *active.* Satan *cannot force* the will, and God will not. Indeed it would cease to be *will* were it *forced* by either : it is essential to its *being* that it be *free.*

And your members as instruments, &c.] Let soul and body be employed in the service of your Maker ; let him have your *hearts ;* and with them, your *heads,* your *hands,* your *feet.* Think and devise what is pure ; *speak* what is true, and to the use of edifying ;

A. M. cir. 4062.
A. D. cir. 58.
An. Olymp.
cir. CCIX. 2.
A. U. C. cir.
811.

14 For ᶻ sin shall not have dominion over you : for ye are not under the law, but under grace.

15 What then ? shall we sin, ᵃ because we are not under the law, but under grace ? God forbid.

16 Know ye not, that ᵇ to whom ye yield yourselves servants to obey, his servants ye are to whom ye obey ; whether of sin unto death, or of obedience unto righteousness ?

17 But God be thanked, that ye were the servants of sin, but ye have obeyed from the ᶜ heart that form of ᵈ doctrine which was delivered you.

A. M. cir. 4062.
A. D. cir. 58.
An. Olymp.
cir. CCIX. 2.
A. U. C. cir.
811.

18 Being then ᵉ made free from sin, ye became the servants of righteousness.

19 I speak after the manner of men, because of the infirmity of your flesh : for as ye have yielded your members servants to un-

---

ᶻ Chap. vii. 4, 6 ; viii. 2 ; Gal. v. 18.——ᵃ 1 Cor. ix. 21.——ᵇ Matt. vi. 24 ; John viii. 34 ; 2 Pet. ii. 19.

ᶜ 2 Tim. i. 13.——ᵈ Gr. *whereto ye were delivered.*——ᵉ John viii. 32 ; 1 Cor. vii. 22 ; Gal. v. 1 ; 1 Pet. ii. 16.

---

work that which is just and good ; and *walk* steadily in the *way* that leads to everlasting felicity. Be holy *within* and holy *without.*

Verse 14. *Sin shall not have dominion over you*] God delivers you from it ; and if you again become subject to it, it will be the effect of your own choice or negligence.

Ye are not under the law] That law which exacts obedience, without giving *power* to obey ; that condemns every transgression and every unholy thought without providing for the extirpation of evil or the pardon of sin.

But under grace.] Ye are under the merciful and beneficent dispensation of the *Gospel*, that, although it requires the strictest conformity to the will of God, affords sufficient power to be thus conformed ; and, in the death of Christ, has provided *pardon* for all that is past, and *grace* to help in every time of need.

Verse 15. *Shall we sin because we are not under the law*] Shall we abuse our high and holy calling because we are not under that *law* which makes no provision for *pardon*, but are under that *Gospel* which has opened the fountain to wash away all sin and defilement ? Shall we sin because grace abounds ! Shall we do evil that good may come of it ? This be far from us !

Verse 16. *To whom ye yield yourselves*] Can you suppose that you should continue to be the *servants* of Christ if ye give way to *sin* ? Is he not the *master* who exacts the *service*, and to whom the service is performed ? *Sin* is the service of *Satan* ; *righteousness* the service of *Christ.* If ye sin ye are the servants of Satan, and not the servants of God.

The word δουλος, which we translate *servant*, properly signifies *slave* ; and a slave among the Greeks and Romans was considered as his *master's property*, and he might dispose of him as he pleased. Under a *bad* master, the lot of the slave was most oppressive and dreadful ; his ease and comfort were never consulted ; he was treated worse than a beast ; and, in many cases, his life hung on the mere caprice of the master. This state is the state of every poor, miserable sinner ; he is the slave of Satan, and his own evil lusts and appetites are his most cruel task-masters. The same word is applied to the *servants of Christ*, the more forcibly to show that they are their *Master's property* ; and that, as he is infinitely *good* and *benevolent*, therefore his service must be perfect freedom. Indeed, he exacts no obedience from them which he does not turn

to their eternal advantage ; for this master has no self-interest to secure. See on chap. i. 1.

Verse 17. *But God be thanked, that ye were the servants of sin*] This verse should be read thus : *But thanks be to God that, although ye were the servants of sin, nevertheless ye have obeyed from the heart that form of doctrine that was delivered unto you ; or, that mould of teaching into which ye were cast.* The apostle does not thank God that they *were sinners ;* but that, *although* they were *such*, they had now received and obeyed the Gospel. The Hebrew phrase, Isa. xii. 1, is exactly the same as that of the apostle here : *In that day thou shalt say, I will praise thee, for thou wast angry with me :* that is, *although thou wast angry with me, thou hast turned away thy wrath, &c.*

That form of doctrine] Τυπον διδαχης ; here Christianity is represented under the notion of a *mould*, or *die*, into which they *were cast*, and from which they took the *impression* of its excellence. The *figure* upon this *die* is the image of God, *righteousness and true holiness*, which was *stamped* on their souls in believing the Gospel and receiving the Holy Ghost. The words εις ὁν παρεδοθητε τυπον refer to the *melting* of metal ; which, when it is liquified, is cast into the mould, that it may receive the impression that is *sunk* or *cut in* the mould ; and therefore the words may be literally translated, *into which mould of doctrine ye have been cast.* They were *melted* down under the preaching of the word, and then were capable of receiving the stamp of its purity.

Verse 18. *Being then made free from sin*] Ελευθερωθεντες is a term that refers to the *manumission of a slave.* They were *redeemed* from the slavery of sin, and became the servants of righteousness. Here is another *prosopopœia :* both *sin* and *righteousness* are *personified :* sin can enjoin no *good* and *profitable* work ; righteousness can require none that is *unjust* or *injurious.*

Verse 19. *I speak after the manner of men*] This phrase is often used by the Greek writers to signify what was *easy to be comprehended ;* what was *ad captum vulgi*, level with common understandings, delivered in a *popular style ;* what was different from the *high flights* of the *poets*, and the studied *sublime obscurity* of the *philosophers.*

Because of the infirmity of your flesh] As if he had said : I make use of metaphors and figures connected with well-known natural things ; with your *trades* and

A. M. cir. 4062.
A. D. cir. 58.
An. Olymp.
cir. CCIX. 2.
A. U. C. cir.
811.
cleanness, and to iniquity unto iniquity ; even so now yield your members servants to righteousness unto holiness.

20 For when ye were ^f the servants of sin, ye were free ^g from righteousness.

21 ^h What fruit had ye then in those things whereof ye are now ashamed ? for

ⁱ the end of those things *is* death.

22 But now ^k being made free from sin, and become servants to God, ye have your fruit unto holiness, and the end everlasting life.

23 For ^l the wages of sin *is* death ; but ^m the gift of God *is* eternal life through Jesus Christ our Lord.

A. M. cir. 4062.
A. D. cir. 58.
An. Olymp.
cir. CCIX. 2.
A. U. C. cir.
811.

---

^f John viii. 34.——^g Gr. *to righteousness.*——^h Chap. vii. 5.
ⁱ Chap. i. 32.——^k John viii. 32.

^l Gen. ii. 17; chap. v. 12; James i. 15.——^m Chap. ii. 7; v. 17, 21; 1 Pet. i. 4.

---

situation in life ; because of your inexperience in heavenly things, of which ye are only just beginning to know the *nature* and the *names.*

Servants to uncleanness, &c.] These different expressions show how deeply immersed in and enslaved by sin these Gentiles were before their conversion to Christianity. Several of the particulars are given in the first chapter of this epistle.

Verse 20. *Ye were free from righteousness.*] These two servitudes are incompatible ; if we cannot serve *God* and *Mammon,* surely we cannot serve *Christ* and *Satan.* We must be either *sinners* or *saints ;* God's *servants* or the devil's *slaves.* It cannot be as a good mistaken man has *endeavoured* to *sing :*—

　　" To good and evil equal bent,
　　　I'm both a devil and a saint."

I know not whether it be possible to paint the utter prevalence of sin in stronger colours than the apostle does here, by saying *they were* FREE *from righteousness.* It seems tantamount to that expression in Genesis, chap. vi. ver. 5, where, speaking of the total degeneracy of the human race, the writer says, *Every imagination of the thoughts of his heart was only evil continually.* They were all corrupt ; they were altogether abominable : there was none that did good ; no, not one.

Verse 21. *What fruit had ye then in those things*] God designs that every man shall reap *benefit* by *his* service. What *benefit* have ye derived from the *service of sin?*

Whereof ye are now ashamed?] Ye blush to remember your former life. It was *scandalous* to yourselves, *injurious* to others, and highly *provoking* to God.

The end of those things is death.] Whatever sin may promise of pleasure or advantage, the end to which it necessarily tends is the destruction of body and soul.

Verse 22. *But now being made free from sin*] As being *free from righteousness* is the finished character of a *sinner,* so being *made free* from *sin* is the finished character of a *genuine Christian.*

And become servants to God] They were transferred from the service of one master to that of another : they were freed from the slavery of sin, and engaged in the service of God.

Fruit unto holiness] Holiness of heart was the *principle ;* and *righteousness* of life the fruit.

Verse 23. *For the wages of sin is death*] The second *death,* everlasting *perdition.* Every sinner earns

this by long, sore, and painful service. O ! what pains do men take to get to hell ! Early and late they toil at sin ; and would not Divine justice be in their *debt,* if it did not pay them their due wages ?

But the gift of God is eternal life] A man may MERIT *hell,* but he cannot MERIT *heaven.* The apostle does not say that the *wages of righteousness is eternal life :* no, but that this eternal life, even to the righteous, is το χαριομα του Θεου, THE gracious GIFT of GOD. And even this gracious gift comes *through Jesus Christ our Lord.* He alone has procured it ; and it is given to all those who find redemption in his blood. A sinner goes to hell because he *deserves* it ; a righteous man goes to heaven because Christ *has died for him,* and communicated that grace by which his sin is pardoned and his soul made holy. The word οψωνια, which we here render *wages,* signified the *daily pay* of a Roman soldier. So every sinner has a *daily pay,* and this pay is *death ;* he has *misery* because he sins. Sin constitutes hell ; the sinner has a hell in his own bosom ; all is *confusion* and *disorder* where God does not reign : every indulgence of sinful passions increases the disorder, and consequently the misery of a sinner. If men were as much in earnest to get their souls saved as they are to prepare them for perdition, heaven would be highly peopled, and devils would be their own companions. And will not the *living* lay this to heart ?

1. IN the preceding chapter we see the *connection* that subsists between the doctrines of the Gospel and the practice of Christianity. A *doctrine* is a *teaching, instruction,* or *information* concerning some *truth* that is to be believed, as essential to our salvation. But all teaching that comes *from* God, necessarily leads *to* him. That Christ died for our sins and rose again for our justification, is a glorious doctrine of the Gospel. But this is of no use to him who does not die to sin, rise in the likeness of his resurrection, and walk in newness of life : this is the *use* that should be made of the *doctrine.* Every doctrine has its *use,* and the use of it consists in the *practice* founded on it. We hear there is a *free pardon*——we go to God and receive it ; we hear that we may be made *holy*——we apply for the sanctifying Spirit ; we hear there is a *heaven of glory,* into which the righteous alone shall enter——we watch and pray, believe, love, and obey, in order that, when he doth appear, we may be found of him in peace, without spot and blameless. *Those are* the *doctrines ;* these are the *uses* or *practice* founded on those doctrines.

2. It is strange that there should be found a person believing the whole Gospel system, and yet living in sin! SALVATION FROM SIN is the *long-continued sound,* as it is the spirit and design, of the Gospel. Our *Christian name,* our *baptismal covenant,* our *profession of faith* in Christ, and avowed belief in his word, all call us to this : can it be said that we have any louder calls than these ? Our *self-interest,* as it respects the happiness of a godly life, and the glories of eternal blessedness ; the pains and wretchedness of a life of sin, leading to the worm that never dies and the fire that is not quenched ; second most powerfully the above calls. Reader, lay these things to heart, and answer this question to God : *How shall I escape, if I neglect so* great *salvation ?* And then, as thy conscience shall answer, let thy mind and thy hand begin to act.

CHAPTER VII.

The law has power over a man as long as he lives, 1. *And a wife is bound to her husband only as long as he lives,* 2, 3. *Christian believers are delivered from the Mosaic law by Christ Jesus, and united to God,* 5–7. *By the law is the knowledge of sin,* 8. *But it gives no power over it,* 9–11. *Yet it is holy, just, and good,* 12. *How it convinces of sin, and brings into bondage,* 13–24. *No deliverance from its curse but by Jesus Christ,* 25.

A. M. cir. 4062.
A. D. cir. 58.
An. Olymp.
cir. CCIX. 2.
A. U. C. cir.
811.

KNOW ye not, brethren, (for I speak to them that know the law,) how [a] that the law hath dominion over a man as long as he liveth ?

2 For [b] the woman which hath a husband is bound by the law to *her* husband so long as he liveth ; but if the husband be dead, she is loosed from the law of *her* husband.

3 So then, [c] if, while *her* husband liveth, she be married to another man, she shall be call-

A. M. cir. 4062.
A. D. cir. 58.
An. Olymp.
cir. CCIX. 2.
A. U. C. cir.
811.

---

[a] Chap. vi. 14; Num. v. 11–31.

[b] 1 Cor. vii. 39.——[c] Matt. v. 32.

NOTES ON CHAP. VII.

The apostle having, in the preceding chapter, shown the *converted Gentiles* the obligations they were under to live a holy life, addresses himself here to the *Jews* who might hesitate to embrace the Gospel ; lest, by this means, they should renounce the *law,* which might appear to them as a renunciation of their allegiance to God. As they rested in the law, as sufficient for justification and sanctification, it was necessary to convince them of their mistake. That the law was insufficient for their *justification* the apostle had proved, in chapters iii., iv., and v. ; that it is insufficient for their *sanctification* he shows in this chapter ; and introduces his discourse by showing that a believing Jew is discharged from his obligations to the law, and is at liberty to come under another and much happier constitution, viz. that of the Gospel of Christ, 1–4. In the 5th verse he gives a general description of the state of a *Jew,* in servitude to sin, considered as under *mere law.* In the 6th verse he gives a summary account of the state of a *Christian,* or believing Jew, and the advantages he enjoys under the Gospel. Upon the 5th verse he comments, from verse 7 to the end of the chapter, and upon the 6th verse he comments, chap. viii. 1–11.

In explaining his position in the 5th verse he shows : 1. That the law reaches to all the branches and latent principles of sin, ver. 7. 2. That it subjected the sinner to death, ver. 8–12, without the expectation of pardon. 3. He shows the reason why the Jew was put under it, ver. 13. 4. He proves that the law, considered as a rule of action, though it was spiritual, just, holy, and good in itself, yet was insufficient for sanctification, or for freeing a man from the power of inbred sin. For, as the prevalency of sensual appetites cannot wholly extinguish the voice of *reason* and *conscience,* a man may acknowledge the law to be holy, just, and good, and yet his *passions* reign within him, keeping him in the most painful and degrading servitude, while the law supplied no power to deliver him from them, ver. 14–24, as that power can only be supplied by the grace of Jesus Christ, ver. 25. See Taylor.

Verse 1. *For I speak to them that know the law*] This is a proof that the apostle directs this part of his discourse to the *Jews.*

As long as he liveth ?] Or, *as long as IT liveth ;* law does not extend its influence to the dead, nor do *abrogated* laws *bind.* It is all the same whether we understand these words as speaking of a law *abrogated,* so that it cannot command ; or of its objects being dead, so that it has none to bind. In either case the *law* has no force.

Verse 2. *For the woman which hath a husband*] The apostle illustrates his meaning by a familiar instance. A married woman is bound to her husband while he lives ; but when her husband is dead she is discharged from the law by which she was bound to him *alone.*

Verse 3. *So then, if, while* her *husband liveth*] The object of the apostle's similitude is to show that each party is equally bound to the other ; but that the death of either dissolves the engagement.

So—she is no adulteress, though she be married to another] And do not imagine that this change would argue any disloyalty in you to your Maker ; for, as he has determined that this law of ordinances shall cease, you are no more bound to it than a woman is to a deceased husband, and are as free to receive the Gospel of Christ as a woman in such circumstances would be to remarry.

A. M. cir. 4062.
A. D. cir. 58.
An. Olymp.
cir. CCIX. 2.
A. U. C. cir.
811.

ed an adulteress : but, if her husband be dead, she is free from that law ; so that she is no adulteress, though she be married to another man.

4 Wherefore, my brethren, ye also are become ^d dead to the law by the body of Christ; that ye should be married to another, *even* to

him who is raised from the dead, that we should ^e bring forth fruit unto God.

A. M. cir. 4062.
A. D. cir. 58.
An. Olymp.
cir. CCIX. 2.
A. U. C. cir.
811.

5 For, when we were in the flesh, the ^f motions of sins, which were by the law, ^g did work in our members ^h to bring forth fruit unto death.

6 But now we are delivered from the law,

---

^d Chap. viii. 2; Gal. ii. 19; v. 18; Eph. ii. 15; Col. ii. 14.
^e Gal. v. 22.

^f Gr. *passions.*——^g Chap. vi. 13.——^h Chap. vi. 21; Gal. v. 19; James i. 15.

Verse 4. *Wherefore, my brethren*] This is a parallel case. You were once under the law of Moses, and were bound by its injunctions; but now ye are become dead to that law—a modest, inoffensive mode of speech, for, *The law, which was once your husband, is dead;* God has determined that it shall be no longer in force; so that now, as a woman whose husband is dead is freed from the law of that husband, or from her conjugal vow, and may legally be married to another, so God, who gave the law under which ye have hitherto lived, designed that it should be in force only till the advent of the Messiah; that advent *has* taken place, the *law* has consequently ceased, and now ye are called to take on you the yoke of the *Gospel,* and lay down the yoke of the law; and it is the design of God that you should do so.

That ye should be married to another—who is raised from the dead] As *Christ is the end of the law for righteousness to every one that believeth,* the object of God in giving the law was to unite you to Christ; and, as he has died, he has not only abolished that law which condemns every transgressor to *death,* without any hope of a *revival,* but he has also made that atonement for sin, by his own death, which is represented in the sacrifices prescribed by the law. And as Jesus Christ is *risen again from the dead,* he has thereby given the fullest proof that by his death he has procured the resurrection of mankind, and made that atonement required by the law. *That we should bring forth fruit unto God*—we, Jews, who believe in Christ, have, in consequence of our *union* with him, received the gifts and graces of the Holy Spirit; so that we bring forth that fruit of holiness unto God which, without this union, it would be impossible for us to produce. Here is a delicate allusion to the case of a promising and numerous progeny from a legitimate and happy marriage.

Verse 5. *For, when we were in the flesh*] When we were without the Gospel, in our carnal and unregenerated state, though believing in the law of Moses, and performing the *rites* and *offices* of our religion.

The motions of sins, which were by the law] Τα παθηματα των ἁμαρτιων, the *passions of sins,* the evil propensities to sins; to every particular sin there is a *propensity* : one propensity does not excite to all kinds of sinful acts; hence the apostle uses the *plural* number, the PASSIONS or *propensities of* SINS; sins being not more various than their *propensities* in the unregenerate heart, which excite to them. These παθηματα, *propensities,* constitute the *fallen nature* ; they are the

disease of the heart, the pollution and corruption of the soul.

Did work in our members] The evil propensity acts εν τοις μελεσιν, in the whole nervous and muscular system, applying that stimulus to every part which is necessary to excite them to action.

To bring forth fruit unto death.] To produce those acts of transgression which subject the sinner to death, temporal and eternal. When the apostle says, *the motions of sin which were by the law,* he points out a most striking and invariable characteristic of sin, viz. its *rebellious nature* ; it ever acts *against law,* and the most powerfully against *known* law. *Because* the law requires obedience, *therefore* it *will* transgress. The law is equally against *evil passions* and *evil actions,* and both these exert themselves against it. So, these motions which were by the law, became roused into the most powerful activity by the prohibitions of the law. They were comparatively dormant till the law said, *thou shalt* NOT *do this, thou shalt* DO *that* ; then the *rebellious* principle in the evil *propensity* became roused, and *acts* of *transgression* and *omissions* of *duty* were the immediate consequences.

Verse 6. *But now we are delivered from the law*] We, who have believed in Christ Jesus, are delivered from that yoke by which we were bound, which sentenced every transgressor to *perdition,* but provided no *pardon* even for the *penitent,* and no *sanctification* for those who are weary of their inbred corruptions.

That being dead wherein we were held] To us believers in Christ this commandment is abrogated; we are transferred to another constitution; that law which kills ceases to bind us; it is dead to us who have believed in Christ Jesus, who is the end of the law for justification and salvation to every one that believes.

That we should serve in newness of spirit] We are now brought under a more spiritual dispensation; now we know the *spiritual import* of all the Mosaic precepts. We see that the law referred to the Gospel, and can only be fulfilled by the Gospel.

The oldness of the letter.] The merely literal rites, ceremonies, and sacrifices are now done away; and the *newness of the spirit,* the true intent and meaning of all are now fully disclosed; so that we are got from an imperfect state into a state of perfection and excellence. We sought justification and sanctification, pardon and holiness, by the law, and have found that the law could not give them : we have sought these in the Gospel scheme, and have found them. We serve God now, not according to the old literal sense, but in the true spiritual meaning.

A. M. cir. 4062.
A. D. cir. 58.
An. Olymp.
cir. CCIX. 2.
A. U. C. cir.
811.

[i] that being dead wherein we were held; that we should serve [k] in newness of spirit, and not *in* the oldness of the letter.

7 What shall we say then? *Is* the law sin?

God forbid. Nay, [l] I had not known sin, but by the law: for I had not known [m] lust, except the law had said, [n] Thou shalt not covet.

A. M. cir. 4062.
A. D. cir. 58.
An. Olymp.
cir. CCIX. 2.
A. U. C. cir.
811.

---

[i] Or, *being dead to that;* chap. vi. 2; ver. 4.——[k] Chap. ii. 29; 2 Cor. iii. 6.——[l] Chap. iii. 20.

[m] Or, *concupiscence.*——[n] Exod. xx. 17; Deut. v. 21; Acts xx. 33 chap. xiii. 9.

Verse 7. Is *the law sin?*] The apostle had said, ver. 5: *The motions of sins, which were by the law, did bring forth fruit unto death;* and now he anticipates an objection, "Is therefore the law sin?" To which he answers, as usual, μη γενοιτο, by no means. Law is only the means of *disclosing* this sinful propensity, not of *producing* it; as a bright beam of the sun introduced into a room shows millions of motes which appear to be dancing in it in all directions; but these were not introduced by the light: they were there before, only there was not light enough to make them manifest; so the evil propensity was there before, but there was not light sufficient to discover it.

I had not known sin, but by the law] Mr. Locke and Dr. Taylor have properly remarked the skill used by St. Paul in dexterously avoiding, as much as possible, the giving offence to the Jews: and this is particularly evident in his use of the word *I* in this place. In the beginning of the chapter, where he mentions their knowledge of the law, he says YE; in the 4th verse he joins himself with them, and says *we;* but *here,* and so to the end of the chapter, where he represents the power of sin and the inability of the law to subdue it, he appears to leave *them* out, and speaks altogether in the *first* person, though it is plain he means all those who are under the law. So, chap. iii. 7, he uses the singular pronoun, *why am I judged a sinner?* when he evidently means the whole body of unbelieving Jews.

There is another circumstance in which his address is peculiarly evident; his demonstrating the insufficiency of the law under colour of vindicating it. He knew that the Jew would take fire at the least reflection on the law, which he held in the highest veneration; and therefore he very naturally introduces him catching at that expression, ver. 5, *the motions of sins, which were by the law,* or, notwithstanding the law. "What!" says this Jew, "do you vilify the law, by charging it with favouring sin?" By no means, says the apostle; I am very far from charging the law with favouring sin. *The law is holy, and the commandment is holy, just, and good,* ver. 12. Thus he writes in vindication of the law; and yet at the same time shows: 1. That the law requires the most extensive obedience, discovering and condemning sin in all its most secret and remote branches, ver. 7. 2. That it gives sin a deadly force, subjecting every transgression to the *penalty of death,* verse 8—14. And yet, 3. supplies neither help nor hope to the sinner, but leaves him under the power of sin, and the sentence of death, verse 14, &c. This, says Dr. Taylor, is the most ingenious turn of writing I ever met with. We have another instance of the same sort, chap. xiii. 1—7.

It is not likely that a *dark, corrupt* human heart can *discern* the will of God. His *law* is his *will.* It re-

commends what is just, and right, and good; and forbids what is improper, unjust, and injurious. If God had not revealed himself by this law, we should have done precisely what many nations of the earth have done, who have not had this revelation—put darkness for light, and sin for acts of holiness. While the human *heart* is its own *measure* it will rate its workings according to its own propensities; for *itself* is its highest *rule.* But when God gives a true insight of his own perfections, to be applied as a *rule* both of *passion* and *practice,* then sin is discovered, and discovered too to be *exceedingly sinful.* So strong propensities, because they appear to be inherent in our nature, would have passed for *natural* and *necessary operations;* and their *sinfulness* would not have been discovered, if the law had not said, *Thou shalt not covet;* and thus determined that the *propensity* itself, as well as its *outward operations,* is *sinful.* The law is the *straight edge* which determines the quantum of *obliquity* in the *crooked line* to which it is applied.

It is natural for man to do what is unlawful, and to desire especially to do that which is forbidden. The heathens have remarked this propensity in man.

Thus LIVY, xxxiv. 4:—

Luxuria—ipsis vinculis, sicut fera bestia, irritata.

"Luxury, like a wild beast, is *irritated* by its very *bonds.*"

   Audax omnia perpeti
   Gens humana ruit per vetitum nefas.

"The presumptuous human race obstinately rush into *prohibited* acts of wickedness."

      HOR. *Carm.* lib. i. Od. iii. ver. 25.

And OVID, *Amor.* lib. ii. Eleg. xix. ver. 3:—

Quod licet, ingratum est; quod non licet, acrius urit.

"What is *lawful* is *insipid;* the strongest propensity is excited towards that which is *prohibited.*"

And again, Ib. lib. iii. E. iv. ver. 17:—

   Nitimur in vetitum semper, cupimusque negata.

"Vice is provoked by every strong restraint, Sick men long most to *drink,* who know they *mayn't.*"

The same poet delivers the same sentiment in another place:—

Acrior admonitu est, irritaturque retenta
Et crescit rabies: remoraminaque ipsa nocebant.

      METAM. lib. iii. ver. 566.

"Being admonished, he becomes the more obstinate; and his fierceness is irritated by restraints. Prohibitions become incentives to greater acts of vice."

But it is needless to multiply examples; this most wicked principle of a sinful, fallen nature, has been felt and acknowledged by ALL *mankind.*

2

A. M. cir. 4062.
A. D. cir. 58.
An. Olymp.
cir. CCIX. 2.
A. U. C. cir.
811.

8 But ° sin, taking occasion by the commandment, wrought in me all manner of concupiscence. For ᵖ without the law, sin *was* dead.

9 For I was alive without the law once: but when the commandment came, sin revived, and I died.

A. M. cir. 4062.
A. D. cir. 58.
An. Olymp.
cir. CCIX. 2.
A. U. C. cir.
811.

° Chap. iv. 15; v. 20.

ᵖ 1 Cor. xv. 56.

Verse 8. *Sin, taking occasion by the commandment*] I think the pointing, both in this and in the 11th verse, to be wrong: the comma should be after *occasion*, and not after *commandment*. But sin taking occasion, *wrought in me by this commandment all manner of concupiscence.* There are different opinions concerning the meaning of the word αφορμη, which we here translate *occasion*. Dr. Waterland translates the clause, Sin, taking ADVANTAGE. Dr. Taylor contends that all commentators have mistaken the meaning of it, and that it should be rendered *having received* FORCE. For this acceptation of the word I can find no adequate authority except in its etymology—απο, *from*, and ὁρμη, *impetus*. The word appears to signify, in general, whatsoever is necessary for the completion or accomplishment of any particular purpose. Xenophon uses αφορμαι εις τον βιον to signify *whatever is necessary for the support of life.* There is a personification in the text: sin is represented as a *murderer* watching for *life*, and snatching at every means and embracing every opportunity to carry his fell purpose into effect. The miserable sinner has a murderer, sin, within him; this murderer can only destroy life in *certain circumstances;* finding that the law condemns the object of his cruelty to death, he takes occasion from this to work in the soul all manner of concupiscence, evil and irregular desires and appetites of every kind, and, by thus increasing the evil, exposes the soul to more condemnation; and thus it is represented as being *slain*, ver. 11. That is, the *law*, on the *evidence* of those sinful dispositions, and their corresponding *practices*, condemns the sinner to death: so that he is *dead in law.* Thus the very *prohibition*, as we have already seen in the preceding verse, becomes the instrument of exciting the evil propensity; for, although a sinner has the general propensity to do what is evil, yet he seems to feel most delight in transgressing *known* law: *stat pro ratione voluntas;* "I will do it, because I will."

For without the law, sin was *dead.*] Where there is no law there is no transgression; for sin is the transgression of the law; and no fault can be imputed on *death*, where there is no *statute* by which such a fault is made a *capital offence.*

Dr. Taylor thinks that χωρις νομου, *without the law,* means the *time* before the giving of the law from Mount Sinai, which took in the space of 430 years, during which time the people were under the Abrahamic covenant of grace; and *without the law* that was given on Mount Sinai, the sting of death, which is sin, had not power to slay the sinner; for, from the time that Adam sinned, the law was not *re-enacted* till it was given by Moses, chap. v. 13. The Jew was then *alive*, because he was not under the law subjecting him to death for his transgressions; *but when the commandment came*, with the penalty of death annexed, *sin revived, and the Jew died.* Then the sting of death acquired *life;* and

the Jew, upon the first transgression, was *dead in law.* Thus sin, the sting of death, received *force* or *advantage* to destroy by the commandment, ver. 8, 11.

All manner of concupiscence.] It *showed* what was *evil* and *forbade* it; and then the principle of *rebellion*, which seems essential to the very nature of sin, rose up against the prohibition · and he was the more strongly incited to *disobey* in proportion as *obedience* was enjoined. Thus the apostle shows that the law had authority to *prohibit, condemn,* and *destroy ;* but no *power* to *pardon* sin, *root out enmity,* or *save the soul.*

The word επιθυμια, which we render *concupiscence*, signifies simply *strong desire* of any kind; but in the New Testament, it is generally taken to signify *irregular* and *unholy desires*. Sin in the mind is the *desire* to *do*, or to *be*, what is *contrary* to the *holiness* and *authority* of GOD.

For without the law, sin was dead.] This means, according to Dr. Taylor's hypothesis, the *time* previous to the giving of the law. See before. But it seems also consistent with the apostle's meaning, to interpret the place as implying the time in which Paul, in his unconverted Jewish state, had not the proper knowledge of the law—while he was unacquainted with its *spirituality*. He felt *evil desire*, but he did not know the *evil* of it; he did not consider that the law tried the *heart* and its *workings*, as well as *outward actions*. This is farther explained in the next verse.

Verse 9. *I was alive without the law once*] Dr. Whitby paraphrases the text thus:—"*For* the seed of Abraham *was alive without the law once*, before the law was given, I being not obnoxious to death for that to which the law had not threatened death; *but when the commandment came*, forbidding it under that penalty, *sin revived, and I died;* i. e. it got strength to draw me to sin, and to condemn me to death. Sin is, in Scripture, represented as an enemy that seeks our ruin and destruction; and takes all occasions to effect it. It is here said *to war against the mind*, ver. 23; elsewhere, *to war against the soul*, 1 Pet. ii. 11; to *surround* and *beset us*, Heb. xii. 1; to *bring us into bondage* and subjection, and get the dominion over us, chap. vi. 12; to *entice us*, and so to work our death, James i. 14, 15, 16; and to do all that Satan, the grand enemy of mankind, doth, by tempting us to the commission of it. Whence *Chrysostom*, upon those words, Heb. xii. 4: *Ye have not yet resisted unto blood*, προς την ἁμαρτιαν ανταγωνιζομενοι, *striving against sin;* represents sin as an *armed* and *flagrant adversary*. When, therefore, it finds a law which threatens death to the violater of it, it takes occasion thence more earnestly *to* tempt and allure to the violation of it, that so it may more effectually subject us to death and condemnation on that account; for *the sting of death is sin, and the strength of sin is the law,* condemning us

2

A. M. cir. 4062.
A. D. cir. 58.
An. Olymp.
cir. CCIX. 2.
A. U. C. cir.
811.

10 And the commandment, ꟼ which *was ordained* to life, I found *to be* unto death.

11 For sin, ʳ taking occasion by the commandment, deceived me, and by it slew *me*.

12 Wherefore ˢ the law *is* holy, and the commandment holy, and just, and good.

13 Was then that ᵗ which is good made death unto me? God forbid. But ᵘ sin, that it might appear sin, working death

A. M. cir. 4062.
A. D. cir. 58.
An. Olymp.
cir. CCIX. 2.
A. U. C. cir.
811.

ꟼ Lev. xviii. 5; Ezek. xx. 11, 13, 21; 2 Cor. iii. 6.——ʳ Matt. v. 20; Heb. iii. 13; James i. 14.

ˢ Psa. xix. 8; cxix. 39, 137; 1 Tim. i. 8.——ᵗ Chap. i. 20; v. 20. ᵘ Chap. iii. 20; 2 Cor. xiii. 7; Gal. i. 13.

---

to death for transgressing it. Thus, when God had forbidden, on pain of death, the eating the fruit of the tree of knowledge, Satan thence took occasion to tempt our first parents to transgress, and so *slew* them, or made them subject to death; εξηπατησε, he *deceived* them, Gen. iii. 13; 1 Tim. ii. 14; which is the word used ver. 11. The phrase, *without the law*, sin was *dead*, means, that sin was then (before the law was given) comparatively dead, as to its power of condemning to death; and this sense the antithesis requires; *without the law*, ἁμαρτια νεκρα, εγω δε εζων, *sin was dead, but I was living; but when the commandment came*, (i. e. the law,) *sin revived, and I died.* How were men living *before* the law, but because then no law condemned them? Sin, therefore, must be then *dead*, as to its condemning power. How did they die when the law came, but by the law condemning them to death? Sin therefore *revived*, then, as to its power of condemning, which it received first from the *sin of Adam*, which brought death into the world; and next, from the *law of Moses*, which *entered that the offence might abound*, and reign more unto death, chap. v. 20, 21. For though sin was in the world from Adam to Moses, or until the law was given, yet it was not imputed unto *death, when there was no law that did threaten death;* so that death reigned from that interval by virtue of *Adam's sin* alone; even over them who had not sinned after the similitude of Adam's transgression, i. e. against a positive law, forbidding it under the penalty of death; which law being delivered by Moses, *sin revived;* i. e. it had again its *force* to condemn men as before to death, by virtue of a law which threatened death. And in this sense the apostle seems to say, Gal. iii. 19, *the law was added because of transgressions*, to convince us of the wrath and punishment due to them; and that *the law*, therefore, *worketh wrath*, because *where no law is there is no transgression*, chap. iv. 15, subjecting us to wrath; or no such sense of the Divine wrath as where a plain Divine law, threatening death and condemnation, is violated." See *Whitby*, in loco.

Verse 10. *And the commandment*] Meaning the *law* in general, *which* was ordained *to life;* the rule of righteousness teaching those statutes which if a man do he shall live in them, Lev. xviii. 5, I *found*, by transgressing it, *to be unto death;* for it only presented the *duty* and laid down the *penalty*, without affording any *strength* to resist sin or subdue evil propensities.

Verse 11. *Sin, taking occasion*] Sin, deriving strength from the law, threatening death to the transgressor, (see the note on verse 8,) *deceived me*, drew me aside to disobedience, promising me gratification, honour, independence, &c., as it promised to Eve; for

to her history the apostle evidently alludes, and uses the very same expression, *deceived me*, εξηπατησε με· See the preceding note; and see the Septuagint, Gen. iii. 13.

And by it slew me.] Subjected me to that death which the law denounced against transgressors; and rendered me *miserable* during the course of life itself. It is well known to scholars that the verb αποκτεινειν signifies not only *to slay* or *kill*, but also to *make wretched*. Every sinner is not only exposed to *death* because he has sinned, and must, sooner or later, die; but he is *miserable* in both body and mind by the influence and the effects of sin. He lives a *dying life*, or a *living death*.

Verse 12. *Wherefore the law* is *holy*] As if he had said, to soothe his countrymen, to whom he had been showing the absolute insufficiency of the law either to justify or save from sin: I do not intimate that there is any thing *improper* or *imperfect* in the law as a *rule of life:* it prescribes what is *holy, just*, and *good;* for it comes from a holy, just, and good God. The LAW, which is to regulate the whole of the *outward conduct*, is holy; and the COMMANDMENT, *Thou shalt not covet*, which is to regulate the *heart*, is not less so. All is excellent and pure; but it neither pardons sin nor purifies the heart; and it is because it is holy, just, and good, that it condemns transgressors to *death*.

Verse 13. *Was then that which is good made death unto me?*] This is the question of the *Jew*, with whom the apostle appears to be disputing. "Do you allow the law to be *good*, and yet say it is the *cause* of our *death?*" The apostle answers:—*God forbid!* μη γενοιτο, by no means: it is not the *law* that is the *cause* of your death, but *sin;* it was sin which subjected us to death by the law, justly threatening sin with death: which law was given that sin might appear—might be set forth in its own colours; when we saw it subjected us to death by a law perfectly holy, just, and good; that sin, by the law, might be represented what it really is:—καθ᾽ ὑπερβολην ἁμαρτωλος, an EXCEEDING GREAT and *deadly evil*.

Thus it appears that man cannot have a true notion of sin but by means of the law of God. For this I have already given sufficient reasons in the preceding notes. And it was one design of the law to show the abominable and destructive nature of sin, as well as to be a rule of life. It would be almost impossible for a man to have that just notion of the *demerit* of sin so as to produce repentance, or to see the nature and necessity of the death of Christ, if the law were not applied to his conscience by the light of the Holy Spirit; it is *then* alone that he sees himself to be carnal, and sold under sin; and that the law and the commandment are holy, just, and good. And let it be

2

A. M. cir. 4062.
A. D. cir. 58.
An. Olymp.
cir. CCIX. 2.
A. U. C. cir.
811.

in me by that which is good; that sin by the commandment might become exceeding sinful.

14 For, we know that the law

is spiritual: but I am carnal, ᵛ sold under sin.

15 For, that which I do, I ʷ allow not: for, ˣ what I would,

A. M. cir. 4062
A. D. cir. 58.
An. Olymp.
cir. CCIX. 2.
A. U. C. cir.
811.

ᵛ 1 Kings xxi. 20, 25; 2 Kings xvii. 17; 1 Mac. i. 15.

ʷ Gr. *know*, Psa. i. 6.——ˣ Gal. v. 17.

---

observed, that the law did not answer this end merely among the *Jews* in the *days of the apostle;* it is just as necessary to the *Gentiles* to the *present hour.* Nor do we find that true repentance takes place where the moral law is not preached and enforced. Those who preach only the *Gospel* to sinners, at best only heal the hurt of the daughter of my people *slightly.* The *law,* therefore, is the grand instrument in the hands of a faithful minister, to alarm and awaken sinners; and he may safely show that every sinner is *under* the law, and consequently under the curse, who has not fled for refuge to the hope held out by the Gospel: for, in this sense also, *Jesus Christ is the* END *of the* LAW *for justification to them that believe.*

Verse 14. *For, we know that the law is spiritual*] This is a general proposition, and probably, in the apostle's autograph, concluded the above sentence. The law is not to be considered as a system of *external rites* and *ceremonies;* nor even as a *rule of moral action:* it is a *spiritual system;* it reaches to the most hidden purposes, thoughts, dispositions, and desires of the heart and soul; and it reproves and condemns every thing, without hope of reprieve or pardon, that is contrary to eternal truth and rectitude.

But I am carnal, sold under sin.] This was probably, in the apostle's letter, the beginning of a new paragraph. I believe it is agreed, on all hands, that the apostle is here demonstrating the insufficiency of the law in opposition to the Gospel. That by the *former* is the *knowledge,* by the latter the *cure,* of sin. Therefore by *I* here he cannot mean *himself,* nor any *Christian believer:* if the contrary could be proved, the argument of the apostle would go to demonstrate the insufficiency of the *Gospel* as well as the *law.*

It is difficult to conceive how the opinion could have crept into the Church, or prevailed there, that " the apostle speaks here of his *regenerate state;* and that what was, in such a state, true of himself, must be true of all others in the same state." This opinion has, most pitifully and most shamefully, not only lowered the standard of Christianity, but destroyed its influence and disgraced its character. It requires but little knowledge of the spirit of the Gospel, and of the scope of this epistle, to see that the apostle is, here, either personating a Jew under the law and without the Gospel, or showing what his own state was when he was deeply convinced that by the deeds of the law no man could be justified, and had not as yet heard those blessed words: *Brother Saul, the Lord Jesus, that appeared unto thee in the way, hath sent me that thou mightest receive thy sight, and be filled with the Holy Ghost,* Acts ix. 17.

In this and the following verses he states the contrariety between *himself,* or any *Jew* while without Christ, and the *law* of God. Of the latter he says, *it is spiritual;* of the former *I am carnal, sold under*

sin. Of the *carnal man,* in opposition to the *spiritual,* never was a more complete or accurate description given. The expressions, *in the flesh,* and *after the flesh,* in ver. 5, and in chap. viii. 5, 8, 9, &c., are of the same import with the word *carnal* in this verse. To be *in the flesh,* or to be *carnally minded,* solely respects the *unregenerate.* While unregenerate, a man is in a state of death and enmity against God, chap. viii. 6–9. This is St. Paul's own account of a *carnal man.* The soul of such a man has no authority over the appetites of the body and the lusts of the flesh: *reason* has not the government of *passion.* The work of such *a person* is *to make provision for the flesh, to fulfil the lusts thereof,* chap. xiii. 14. *He minds the things of the flesh,* chap. viii. 5; he is at enmity with God. In all these things the *spiritual man* is the *reverse;* he lives in a state of *friendship* with God in Christ, and the Spirit of God dwells in him; his soul has dominion over the appetites of the body and the lusts of the flesh; his passions submit to the government of reason, and he, by the Spirit, mortifies the deeds of the flesh; *he mindeth the things of the Spirit,* chap. viii. 5. The Scriptures, therefore, place these two characters in direct opposition to each other. Now the apostle begins this passage by informing us that it is his *carnal state* that he is about to describe, in opposition to the spirituality of God's holy law, saying, *But I am carnal.*

Those who are of another opinion maintain that by the word *carnal* here the apostle meant that *corruption* which dwelt in him *after his conversion;* but this opinion is founded on a very great mistake; for, although there may be, after justification, the remains of the carnal mind, which will be less or more felt till the soul is completely sanctified, yet the man is never denominated from the *inferior* principle, which is under control, but from the superior principle which habitually prevails. Whatever epithets are given to *corruption* or *sin* in Scripture, opposite epithets are given to *grace* or *holiness.* By these different epithets are the *unregenerate* and *regenerate* denominated. From all this it follows that the epithet *carnal,* which is the characteristic designation of an unregenerate man, cannot be applied to St. Paul *after his conversion;* nor, indeed, to any *Christian* in that state.

But the word *carnal,* though used by the apostle to signify a state of death and enmity against God, is not sufficient to denote all the evil of the state which he is describing; hence he adds, *sold under sin.* This is one of the strongest expressions which the Spirit of God uses in Scripture, to describe the full depravity of fallen man. It implies a *willing slavery:* Ahab had *sold himself to work evil,* 1 Kings xxi. 20. And of the Jews it is said, in their utmost depravity, *Behold, for your iniquities have ye sold yourselves,* Isa. l. 1. *They forsook the holy covenant, and joined*

A. M. cir. 4062.
A. D. cir. 58.
An. Olymp.
cir. CCIX. 2.
A. U. C. cir.
811.

that do I not; but what I hate, that do I. •

16 If then I do that which I would not, I consent unto the law that *it is* good.

y Chap. viii. 9; Acts xxvi. 18.

17 Now then, it is no more I that do it, y but sin that dwelleth in me.

18 For I know that z in me (that is, in my flesh) dwelleth no good thing:

A. M. cir. 4062.
A. D. cir. 58.
An. Olymp.
cir. CCIX. 2.
A. U. C. cir.
811.

z Gen. vi. 5; viii. 21.

themselves to the heathen, and WERE SOLD *to do mischief,* 1 Maccab. i. 15. Now, if the word *carnal,* in its strongest sense, had been sufficiently significant of all he meant, why add to this charge another expression still stronger? We must therefore understand the phrase, *sold under sin,* as implying that the soul was *employed in the drudgery of sin;* that it was *sold over* to this service, and had no power to disobey this tyrant, until it was redeemed by another. And if a man be actually sold to another, and he acquiesce in the deed, then he becomes the *legal property* of that other person. This state of bondage was well known to the Romans. The sale of slaves they saw daily, and could not misunderstand the emphatical sense of this expression. Sin is here represented as a *person;* and the apostle compares the dominion which sin has over the man in question to that of a master over his legal slave. Universally through the Scriptures man is said to be in a state of bondage to sin until the Son of God make him free: but in no part of the sacred writings is it ever said that the *children of God* are *sold under sin.* Christ came to deliver the lawful captive, and take away the prey from the mighty. *Whom the Son maketh free, they are free indeed.* Then, they *yield not up their members as instruments of unrighteousness unto sin; for sin shall not have the dominion over them,* because *the law of the Spirit of life in Christ Jesus has made them free from the law of sin and death,* chap. vi. 13, 14, and viii. 2. Anciently, when regular *cartels* were not known, the captives became the slaves of their victors, and by them were *sold* to any purchaser; their slavery was as complete and perpetual as if the slave had resigned his own liberty, and sold himself: the laws of the land secured him to his master; he could not redeem himself, because he had nothing that was *his own,* and nothing could resue him from that state but a stipulated *redemption.* The apostle speaks here, not of the *manner* in which the person in question became a slave; he only asserts the fact, that sin had a full and permanent dominion over him.—*Smith,* on the carnal man's character.

I am carnal, sold under sin.] I have been the more particular in ascertaining the genuine sense of this verse, because it determines the general scope of the whole passage.

Verse 15. *For, that which I do, I allow not, &c.*] The first clause of this verse is a general assertion concerning the employment of the person in question in the state which the apostle calls *carnal, and sold under sin.* The Greek word κατεργαζομαι, which is here translated *I do,* means a *work* which the agent *continues* to *perform* till it is *finished,* and is used by the apostle, Phil. ii. 12, to denote the *continued employment* of God's saints in his service to the end of their

lives. WORK OUT *your own salvation;* the word here denotes an employment of a *different* kind; and therefore the man who now feels the galling dominion of sin says, What I am *continually labouring* at *I allow not,* ου γινωσκω, *I do not acknowledge* to be right, just, holy, or profitable.

But what I hate, that do I.] I am a *slave,* and under the absolute control of my tyrannical master: I hate his service, but am *obliged* to work his will. Who, without blaspheming, can assert that the apostle is here speaking this of a man in whom the *Spirit of the Lord dwells?* From ver. 7 to this one the apostle, says Dr. Taylor, denotes the *Jew in the flesh* by a single *I;* here, he divides that *I* into two *I's,* or figurative persons; representing two different and opposite principles which were in him. The one *I,* or principle, assents to the law that it is good, and wills and chooses what the other does not practise, ver. 16. This principle he expressly tells us, ver. 22, is the *inward man; the law of the mind,* ver. 23; the *mind,* or rational faculty, ver. 25; for he could find no other *inward man,* or *law of the mind,* but the rational faculty, in a person who was *carnal* and *sold under sin.* The other *I,* or principle, transgresses the law, ver. 23, and does those things which the former principle *allows not.* This principle he expressly tells us, ver. 18, is the *flesh,* the *law in the members,* or *sensual appetite,* ver. 23; and he concludes in the last verse, that these two principles were opposite to each other; therefore it is evident that those two principles, residing and counteracting each other in the same person, are *reason* and *lust,* or *sin that dwells in us.* And it is very easy to distinguish these two *I's,* or principles, in every part of this elegant description of iniquity, domineering over the light and remonstrances of reason. For instance, ver. 17: *Now then, it is no more I that do it, but* SIN *that dwelleth in me.* The *I* he speaks of here is opposed to indwelling or governing sin; and therefore plainly denotes the principle of reason, the *inward man,* or *law of the mind;* in which, I add, a measure of the light of the Spirit of God shines, in order to show the sinfulness of sin. These two different principles he calls, one *flesh,* and the other *spirit,* Gal. v. 17; where he speaks of their contrariety in the same manner that he does here.

And we may give a probable reason why the apostle dwells so long upon the struggle and opposition between these two principles; it appears intended to answer a tacit but very obvious objection. The Jew might allege: " But the law is holy and spiritual; and I assent to it as good, as a right rule of action, which ought to be observed; yea, I esteem it highly, I *glory* and *rest* in it, convinced of its truth and excellency. And is not this enough to constitute the law a sufficient principle of sanctification?" The apostle answers,

A. M. cir. 4062.
A. D. cir. 58.
An. Olymp.
cir. CCIX. 2.
A. U. C. cir.
811.

for to will is present with me; but *how* to perform that which is good, I find not.

19 For, the ª good that I

would, I do not: but the evil which I would not, that I do.

20 Now, if I do that I would not, ᵇ it is no more I that do

A. M. cir. 4062.
A. D. cir. 58.
An. Olymp.
cir. CCIX. 2.
A. U. C. cir.
811.

ª Verse 15.

ᵇ Verse 23.

"No; *wickedness* is consistent with a *sense* of *truth*. A man may assent to the best rule of action, and yet still be under the dominion of lust and sin; from which nothing can deliver him but a principle and power proceeding from the *fountain of life*."

The sentiment in this verse may be illustrated by quotations from the ancient heathens; many of whom felt themselves in precisely the same state, (and expressed it in nearly the same language,) which some most monstrously tell us was the state of this heavenly apostle, when vindicating the claims of the Gospel against those of the Jewish ritual! Thus OVID describes the conduct of a depraved man:—

Sed trahit invitam *nova vis; aliudque cupido,*
Mens aliud suadet. Video *meliora, proboque;*
Deteriora sequor. OVID, *Met.* lib. vii. ver. 19.

My *reason* this, my *passion* that persuades;
I see the *right*, and I approve it too;
Condemn the *wrong*, and yet the wrong *pursue.*

—— *indignum facinus! nunc ego et*
Illam scelestam esse, et me miserum sentio:
Et tædet: et amore ardeo: et prudens, sciens,
Vivus, vidensque pereo: nec quid agam scio.
TERENT. *Eun.* ver. 70.

An unworthy act! Now I perceive that she is wicked, and I am wretched. I burn with love, and am vexed at it. Although prudent, and intelligent, and active, and seeing, I perish; neither do I know what to do.

Sed quia mente minus validus, quam corpore toto,
Quæ nocuere, sequar; fugiam, quæ profore credam.
HOR. *Ep.* lib. i. E. 8, ver. 7.

More in my mind than body lie my pains:
Whate'er may *hurt* me, I with *joy* pursue;
Whate'er may do me *good*, with *horror* view.
Francis.

Επει γαρ ὁ ἁμαρτανων ου θελει ἁμαρτανειν, αλλα κατορθωσαι· δηλον ὁτι, ὁ μεν θελει, ου ποιει, και ὁμη θελει, ποιει. ARRIAN. *Epist.* ii. 26.

For, truly, he who sins does not will sin, but wishes to walk uprightly: yet it is manifest that what he *wills* he *doth* not; and what he *wills* not he *doth*.

——αλλα νικωμαι κακοις,
Και μανθανω μεν, οια τολμησω κακα·
Θυμος δε κρεισσων των εμων βουλευματων,
'Οσπερ μεγιστων αιτιος κακων βροτοις.
EURIP. *Med.* v. 1077.

—— But I am overcome by sin,
And I well understand the evil which I presume to commit.
Passion, however, is more powerful than my *reason*; Which is the *cause* of the *greatest evils* to mortal men.

Thus we find that enlightened heathens, both among the Greeks and Romans, had that same kind of religious experience which some suppose to be, not only the experience of St. Paul in his best state, but to be even the standard of Christian attainments! See more examples in *Wetstein.*

The whole spirit of the sentiment is well summed up and expressed by St. *Chrysostom:* ὁταν τινος επιθυμωμεν, ειτε κωλυωμεθα, αιρεται μαλλον της επιθυμιας ἡ φλοξ· If we lust after any thing which is afterwards prohibited, the flame of this desire burns the more *fiercely.*

Verse 16. *If then I do that which I would not, &c.*] Knowing that the law condemns it, and that therefore it must be *evil. I consent unto the law;* I show by this circumstance that I acknowledge the law to be good.

Verse 17. *Now then it is no more I*] It is not that *I* which constitutes *reason* and *conscience, but sin*—corrupt and sensual inclinations, *that dwelleth in me*—that has the entire domination over my reason, darkening my understanding, and perverting my judgment; for which there is *condemnation* in the law, but no *cure.* So we find here that there is a principle in the unregenerate man stronger than *reason* itself; a principle which is, properly speaking, not of the *essence of the soul*, but acts *in* it, as its *lord*, or as a *tyrant.* This is *inbred* and *indwelling sin*—the *seed of the serpent;* by which the whole soul is darkened, confused, perverted, and excited to rebellion against God.

Verse 18. *For I know that in me, &c.*] I have learned by experience that in an unregenerate man there is *no good.* There is no principle by which the soul can be brought into the light; no principle by which it can be *restored* to purity: fleshly appetites alone prevail; and the *brute* runs away with the *man.*

For to will is present with me] Though the whole soul has suffered indescribably by the FALL, yet there are some faculties that appear to have suffered less than others; or rather have received larger measures of the supernatural light, because their concurrence with the Divine principle is so necessary to the salvation of the soul. Even the most unconcerned about spiritual things have *understanding, judgment, reason*, and *will.* And by means of these we have seen even scoffers at Divine revelation become very eminent in arts and sciences; some of our best metaphysicians, physicians, mathematicians, astronomers, chemists, &c., have been known—to their reproach be it spoken and published—to be *without religion*; nay, some of them have blasphemed it, by leaving God out of his own work, and ascribing to an idol of their own, whom they call *nature*, the operations of the wisdom, power, and goodness of the Most High. It is true that many of the most eminent in all the above branches of knowledge have been conscientious believers in Divine revelation; but the case of the others proves that, *fallen* as man is, he yet possesses extra-

2

A. M. cir. 4062.
A. D. cir. 58.
An. Olymp.
cir. CCIX. 2.
A. U. C. cir.
811.

it, but sin that dwelleth in me.

21 I find then ᶜ a law, that, when I would do good, evil is present with me.

22 For I ᵈ delight in the law of God, after ᵉ the inward man.

23 But ᶠ I see another law in ᵍ my members, warring against the law of my

A. M. cir. 4062.
A. D. cir. 58.
An. Olymp.
cir. CCIX. 2.
A. U. C. cir.
811.

ᶜ Chap. viii. 2; Gal. v. 17.——ᵈ Psa. i. 2.——ᵉ 2 Cor. iv. 16;

Eph. iii. 16; Col. iii. 9, 10.——ᶠ Gal. v. 17.——ᵍ Chap. vi. 13, 19.

---

ordinary powers, which are capable of very high cultivation and improvement. In short, the soul seems capable of *any thing* but *knowing, fearing, loving,* and *serving God.* And it is not only incapable, *of itself,* for any truly religious acts; but what shows its fall in the most indisputable manner is its *enmity* to sacred things. Let an unregenerate man *pretend* what he pleases, his conscience knows that he *hates religion;* his *soul revolts against it;* his *carnal mind is not subject to the law of God, neither indeed can it be.* There is no reducing this fell principle to subjection; it is sin, and *sin is rebellion* against God; therefore sin must be *destroyed,* not *subjected;* if *subjected,* it would *cease to be sin,* because *sin* is in *opposition* to God: hence the apostle says, most conclusively, *it cannot be subjected,* i. e. it must be *destroyed,* or it will destroy the soul for ever. When the apostle says, *to will is present with me,* he shows that the *will* is on the side of God and truth, so far that it consents to the *propriety* and *necessity* of obedience. There has been a strange clamour raised up against this faculty of the soul, as if the very essence of evil dwelt in it; whereas the apostle shows, throughout this chapter, that the *will* was regularly on God's side, while every other faculty appears to have been in *hostility* to him. The truth is, men have confounded the *will* with the *passions,* and laid to the charge of the *former* what properly belongs to the *latter.* The *will* is *right,* but the *passions* are *wrong.* It *discerns* and *approves,* but is without *ability to perform:* it has no power over sensual appetites; in these the principle of *rebellion* dwells: it *nills* evil, it *wills* good, but can only *command* through the power of Divine grace: but this the person in question, the unregenerate man, has not received.

Verse 19. *For the good that I would I do not*] Here again is the most decisive proof that the *will* is on the side of God and truth.

But the evil which I would not] And here is equally decisive proof that the will is against, or opposed to evil. There is not a man in ten millions, who will carefully watch the operations of this faculty, that will find it opposed to good and obstinately attached to evil, as is generally supposed. Nay, it is found almost uniformly on God's side, while the whole sensual system is against him.—It is not the WILL that leads men astray; but the corrupt PASSIONS which oppose and oppress the *will.* It is truly astonishing into what endless mistakes men have fallen on this point, and what *systems of divinity* have been built on these mistakes. The *will,* this almost only *friend* to God in the human soul, has been slandered as God's *worst enemy,* and even by those who had the *seventh* chapter to the Romans before their eyes! Nay, it has been considered so fell a foe to God and goodness that

it is bound in the adamantine chains of a dire necessity to *do evil only;* and the doctrine of *will* (absurdly called *free will,* as if *will* did not essentially imply what is *free*) has been considered one of the most destructive heresies. Let such persons put themselves to school to their *Bibles* and to *common sense.*

The plain state of the case is this: the soul is so completely fallen, that it has no *power* to *do good* till it receive that power from on high. But it has power to *see* good, to *distinguish* between *that* and *evil;* to *acknowledge* the excellence of this good, and to *will* it, from a conviction of that excellence; but *farther* it cannot go. Yet, in various cases, it is solicited and *consents* to sin; and because it is *will,* that is, because it is a *free principle,* it must necessarily possess this power; and although it can do no good unless it receive grace from God, yet it is impossible to *force* it to sin. Even Satan himself cannot do this; and before he can get it to *sin,* he must gain its *consent.* Thus God in his endless mercy has endued this faculty with a power in which, humanly speaking, resides the *salvability* of the soul; and without this the soul must have eternally continued *under the power of sin,* or been saved as an inert, absolutely passive machine; which supposition would go as nearly to prove that it was as incapable of vice as it were of virtue.

"But does not this arguing destroy the doctrine of free grace?" No! it establishes that doctrine. 1. It is through the grace, the unmerited kindness, of God, that the soul has such a faculty, and that it has not been extinguished by sin. 2. This will, though a *free principle,* as it respects its *nilling* of evil and *choosing* good, yet, properly speaking, has *no power* by which it can *subjugate* the evil or *perform* the good. We know that the *eye* has a power to discern objects, but without *light* this power is perfectly useless, and no object can be discerned by it. So, of the person represented here by the apostle, it is said, *To will is present with me,* το γαρ θελειν παρακειται μοι. *To will is ever in readiness,* it is *ever at hand, it lies constantly before me;* but how to perform that which *is good, I find not;* that is, the man is unregenerate, and he is seeking justification and holiness from the *law.* The law was never designed to give these—it gives the *knowledge,* not the *cure of sin;* therefore, though he *nills* evil and *wills* good, yet he can neither *conquer* the one nor *perform* the other till he receives the grace of Christ, till he seeks and finds redemption in his blood. Here, then, the *free agency* of man is *preserved,* without which he could not be in a *salvable state;* and the *honour* of the *grace of Christ* is maintained, without which there can be no actual salvation. There is a good sentiment on this subject in the following words of an eminent poet:—

A. M. cir. 4062.
A. D. cir. 58.
An. Olymp.
cir. CCIX. 2.
A. U. C. cir.
811.

mind, and bringing me into ʰ captivity to the law of sin which is in my members.

24 O wretched man that I am! who shall deliver me from

ⁱ the body of this death? 25 ᵏ I thank God through Jesus Christ our Lord. So then with the mind I myself serve the law of God; but with the flesh the law of sin.

A. M. cir. 4062.
A. D. cir. 58.
An. Olymp.
cir. CCIX. 2.
A. U. C. cir.
811.

ʰ Chap. viii. 7; xii. 2; Eph. iv. 23; James iv. 1.

ⁱ Or, *this body of death.*——ᵏ 1 Cor. xv. 57.

Thou great first CAUSE, least understood;
Who all my sense confined
To know but this, that *thou art good;*
And that *myself am blind.*

Yet gave me in this *dark* estate
To *see* the *good* from *ill;*
And *binding nature* fast in *fate,*
Left *free* the human *will.*

POPE's *Universal Prayer.*

Verse 20. *It is no more I*] My *will* is against it; my *reason* and *conscience* condemn it. *But sin that dwelleth in me*—the *principle of sin,* which has possessed itself of all my *carnal appetites* and *passions,* and thus subjects my reason and domineers over my soul. Thus I am in perpetual contradiction to myself. Two principles are continually contending in me for the mastery: my *reason,* on which the light of God shines, to show what is evil; and my *passions,* in which the *principle of sin* works, to bring forth fruit unto death.

This strange self-contradictory propensity led some of the ancient philosophers to imagine that man has *two souls,* a *good* and a *bad* one; and it is on this principle that *Xenophon,* in his *life of Cyrus,* causes *Araspes,* a Persian nobleman, to account for some misconduct of his relative to *Panthea,* a beautiful female captive, whom *Cyrus* had entrusted to his care:—" O Cyrus, I am convinced that I have *two souls;* if I had but *one soul,* it could not at the same time pant after *vice* and *virtue;* wish and *abhor* the *same thing.* It is certain, therefore, that we have *two souls;* when the *good soul* rules, I undertake noble and virtuous actions; but when the *bad soul* predominates, I am constrained to do evil. All I can say at present is that I find my *good* soul, encouraged by thy presence, has got the better of my *bad* soul." See *Spectator,* vol. viii. No. 564. Thus, not only the *ancients,* but also many *moderns,* have trifled, and all will continue to do so who do not acknowledge the Scriptural account of the *fall of man,* and the lively comment upon that doctrine contained in the *seventh chapter of the Epistle to the Romans.*

Verse 21. *I find then a law*] I am in such a condition and state of soul, under the power of such habits and sinful propensities, *that when I would do good*—when my *will* and *reason* are strongly bent on obedience to the law of God and opposition to the principle of sin, *evil is present with me,* κακον παρακειται, *evil is at hand, it lies constantly before me.* That, as the *will* to do good is *constantly at hand,* ver. 18, so the principle of *rebellion* exciting me to sin is *equally present;* but, as the one is only *will,* wish, and *desire,* without *power* to *do* what is *willed,* to *obtain* what is *wished,* or to *perform* what is *desired,* sin continually prevails.

The word νομος, *law,* in this verse, must be taken as implying any *strong* or *confirmed habit,* συνηθεια, as *Hesychius* renders it, under the influence of which the man *generally acts;* and in this sense the apostle most evidently uses it in ver. 23.

Verse 22. *I delight in the law of God after the inward man*] Every *Jew,* and every *unregenerate man,* who receives the Old Testament as a revelation from God, must acknowledge the great purity, excellence and utility of its *maxims,* &c., though he will ever find that without the *grace of our Lord Jesus* he can never *act* according to those heavenly maxims; and without the *mercy* of God, can never be redeemed from the *curse* entailed upon him for his past transgressions. To say that the *inward man* means the *regenerate part* of the soul, is supportable by no argument. Ὁ εσω ανθρωπος, and ὁ εντος ανθρωπος, especially the *latter,* are expressions frequently in use among the purest Greek ethic writers, to signify the *soul* or *rational* part of man, in opposition to the *body* or *flesh.* See the quotations in Wetstein from *Plato* and *Plotinus.* The Jews have the same form of expression; so in *Yalcut Rubeni,* fol. 10, 3, it is said: *The flesh is the inward garment of the man;* but the SPIRIT *is the* INWARD *man, the garment of which is the body;* and St. Paul uses the phrase in precisely the *same sense* in 2 Cor. iv. 16, and in Eph. iii. 16. If it be said that it is impossible for an unregenerate man *to delight in the law of God,* the experience of millions contradicts the assertion. Every true *penitent* admires the moral law, longs most earnestly for a conformity to it, and feels that he can never be satisfied till he awakes up after this Divine likeness; and he hates himself, because he feels that he has *broken* it, and that his evil passions are still in a state of *hostility* to it.

The following observations of a pious and sensible writer on this subject cannot be unacceptable: " The *inward man* always signifies the *mind;* which either may, or may not, be the subject of grace. That which is asserted of either the *inward* or *outward man* is often performed by *one member* or *power,* and not with the *whole.* If any member of the body perform an *action,* we are said to do it with the *body,* although the other members be not employed. In like manner, if any *power* or *faculty* of the mind be employed about any action, the *soul* is said to act. This expression, therefore, *I delight in the law of God after the inward man,* can mean no more than this, that there are some *inward faculties* in the soul which delight in the law of God. This expression is particularly adapted to the principles of the *Pharisees,* of whom St. Paul was one before his conversion. They received the law as the oracles of God, and confessed that it deserved the most serious regard. Their veneration was inspired by a sense of its original, and a full conviction that it was true. To some parts of it they paid the most superstitious regard. They had it written upon their *phylacteries*, which they carried about with them at all times. It was often read and expounded in their synagogues : and they took delight in studying its precepts. On that account, both the prophets and our Lord agree in saying that *they delighted in the law of God*, though they regarded not its chief and most essential precepts." See farther observations on this point at the end of the chapter.

So far, then, is it from being true that *none but a* REGENERATE *man can delight in the law of God*, we find that even a *proud, unhumbled* PHARISEE can do it ; and much more a *poor sinner*, who is humbled under a sense of his sin, and sees, in the light of God, not only the *spirituality*, but the *excellence* of the Divine law.

Verse 23. *But I see another law in my members*] Though the person in question is less or more under the continual influence of *reason* and *conscience*, which offer constant testimony against sin, yet as long as help is sought only from the *law*, and the grace of Christ in the Gospel is not received, the remonstrances of reason and conscience are rendered of no effect by the prevalence of sinful passions ; which, from repeated gratifications, have acquired all the force of *habit*, and now *give law* to the whole carnal man.

Warring against the law of my mind] There is an allusion here to the case of a *city besieged*, at last *taken by storm*, and the inhabitants carried away into captivity ; αντιστρατευομενον, carrying on a *system of warfare ;* laying *continual siege* to the soul ; *repeating incessantly* its *attacks ; harassing, battering*, and *storming* the spirit ; and, by all these *assaults*, reducing the man to *extreme misery*. Never was a picture more impressively drawn and more effectually finished ; for the next sentence shows that this spiritual city was at last taken by storm, and the inhabitants who survived the sackage led into the most shameful, painful, and oppressive captivity.

Bringing me into captivity to the law of sin] He does not here speak of an *occasional advantage* gained by sin, it was a *complete* and final victory gained by corruption ; which, having stormed and reduced the city, carried away the inhabitants with irresistible force, into captivity. This is the consequence of being overcome ; he was now in the hands of the foe, as the victor's lawful captive ; and this is the import of the original word, αιχμαλωτιζοντα, and is the very term used by our Lord when speaking of the final ruin, dispersion, and captivity of the Jews. He says, αιχμαλωτισθησονται, *they shall be led away captives* into all the nations, Luke xxi. 24. When all this is considered, who, in his right mind, can apply it to the holy soul of the apostle of the Gentiles ? Is there any thing in it that can belong to his *gracious* state ? Surely nothing. The *basest slave of sin*, who has any remaining checks of conscience, cannot be brought into a *worse* state than that described here by the apostle. Sin and corruption have a *final triumph ;* and *conscience* and *reason* are taken *prisoners, laid in fetters*, and *sold for slaves*. Can this ever be said of a man in whom the Spirit of God dwells, and whom *the law of the Spirit of life in Christ Jesus has made free from the law of sin and death ?* See chap. viii. 2.

Verse 24. *O wretched man that I am, &c.*] This affecting account is finished more impressively by the *groans* of the *wounded* captive. Having long maintained a useless conflict against innumerable hosts and irresistible might, he is at last *wounded* and taken prisoner ; and to render his state more miserable, is not only encompassed by the slaughtered, but *chained to a dead body ;* for there seems to be here an allusion to an ancient custom of certain tyrants, who bound a *dead body* to a *living man*, and obliged him to carry it about, till the contagion from the putrid mass took away his life ! *Virgil* paints this in all its horrors, in the account he gives of the tyrant Mezentius. *Æneid*, lib. viii. ver. 485.

Quid memorem infandas cædes ? quid facta tyranni ?
MORTUA *quin etiam jungebat* corpora VIVIS,
Componens manibusque manus, *atque* oribus ora ;
Tormenti genus ! et sanie taboque *fluentes*
Complexu in misero, longa *sic morte necabat.*

What tongue can such barbarities record,
Or count the slaughters of his ruthless sword ?
'Twas not enough the good, the guiltless bled,
Still worse, he *bound* the *living* to the *dead :*
These, *limb to limb*, and *face to face*, he joined ;
O ! monstrous crime, of unexampled kind !
Till *choked* with *stench*, the *lingering wretches* lay,
And, in the *loathed embraces*, died away !   *Pitt.*

Servius remarks, in his comment on this passage, that *sanies*, mortui est ; *tabo*, viventis scilicet sanguis : " the *sanies*, or putrid *ichor*, from the dead body, produced the *tabes* in the blood of the living." Roasting, burning, racking, crucifying, &c., were nothing when compared to this diabolically invented punishment.

We may naturally suppose that the cry of such a person would be, *Wretched man that I am, who shall deliver me from this dead body ?* And how well does this apply to the case of the person to whom the apostle refers ! A *body*—a whole *mass of sin* and *corruption*, was *bound* to his *soul* with *chains* which he could not break ; and the mortal *contagion*, transfused through his whole nature, was pressing him down to the bitter pains of an eternal death. He now finds that the *law* can afford him no deliverance ; and he despairs of help from any *human being* ; but while he is emitting his *last*, or *almost expiring groan*, the *redemption* by Christ Jesus is proclaimed to him ; and, if the apostle refers to his *own case*, Ananias unexpectedly accosts him with—*Brother Saul ! the Lord Jesus, who appeared unto thee in the way, hath sent me unto thee, that thou mightest receive thy sight, and be filled with the Holy Ghost.* He sees then an open door of hope, and he immediately, though but in the *prospect* of this deliverance, returns God thanks for the well-grounded *hope* which he has of salvation, through Jesus Christ our Lord.

Verse 25. *I thank God through Jesus Christ*] Instead of ευχαριστω τω Θεω, I thank God, several excellent MSS., with the *Vulgate*, some copies of the *Itala*, and several of the *fathers*, read ἡ χαρις του Θεου, or του Κυριου, *the grace of God*, or *the grace of our Lord Jesus Christ ;* this is an *answer* to the almost despairing question in the preceding verse. The whole, therefore, may be read thus : *O wretched man that I am, who shall deliver me from the body of this death?* ANSWER—*The grace of God through our Lord Jesus Christ.* Thus we find that a case of the kind described by the apostle in the preceding verses, whether it were *his own*, before he was brought to the knowledge of Christ, particularly during the three days that he was at Damascus, without being able to eat or drink, in deep penitential sorrow ; or whether he personates a *pharisaic* yet *conscientious Jew*, deeply concerned for his salvation : I say, we find that such a case can be relieved by the Gospel of Christ only ; or, in other words, that no scheme of redemption can be effectual to the salvation of any soul, whether *Jew* or *Gentile*, but that laid down in the Gospel of Christ.

Let any or all means be used which human wisdom can devise, *guilt* will still continue *uncancelled ;* and *inbred sin* will laugh them all to scorn, prevail over them, and finally triumph. And this is the very conclusion to which the apostle brings his argument in the following clause, which, like the rest of the chapter, has been most awfully abused, to favour *anti-evangelical* purposes.

So then with the mind I myself serve the law of God] That this clause contains the *inference* from the preceding train of argumentation appears evident, from the αρα ουν, *therefore*, with which the apostle introduces it. As if he had said : "To conclude, the sum of what I have advanced, concerning the *power of sin* in the *carnal man*, and the utter *insufficiency* of all *human means* and *legal observances* to pardon sin and expel the corruption of the heart, is this : that the very same person, the αυτος εγω, *the same I*, while without the Gospel, under the killing power of the law, will find in himself *two opposite principles*, the one subscribing to and approving the law of God ; and the other, notwithstanding, bringing him *into captivity* to sin : his *inward man*—his *rational powers* and *conscience*, will assent to the *justice* and *propriety* of the requisitions of the law ; and yet, notwithstanding this, his *fleshly appetites*—the *law in his members*, will *war against the law of his mind*, and continue, till he receives the Gospel of Christ, to keep him in the galling captivity of sin and death."

1. THE strong expressions in this clause have led many to conclude that the *apostle* himself, in his *regenerated state*, is indisputably *the person* intended. That all that is said in this chapter of the *carnal man*, *sold under sin*, did apply to *Saul of Tarsus*, no man can doubt : that what is here said can ever be with propriety applied to *Paul the Apostle*, who can believe ? Of the former, all is natural ; of the latter, all here said would be monstrous and absurd, if not blasphemous.

2. But it is supposed that the words must be understood as implying a *regenerate man*, because the apostle says, ver. 22, *I delight in the law of God ;* and in this verse, *I myself with the mind serve the law of God.* These things, say the objectors, cannot be spoken of a wicked Jew, but of a *regenerate* man, such as the apostle then was. But when we find that the former verse speaks of a man who is *brought into captivity to the law of sin and death*, surely there is

no part of the regenerate state of the apostle to which the words can possibly apply. Had he been in captivity to the law of sin and death, *after* his conversion to Christianity, what did he gain by that conversion ? *Nothing* for his personal holiness. He had found no salvation under an inefficient law ; and he was left in thraldom under an equally inefficient Gospel. The very genius of Christianity demonstrates that nothing like this can, with any propriety, be spoken of a *genuine Christian.*

3. But it is farther supposed that these things cannot be spoken of a proud or wicked Jew ; yet we learn the contrary from the infallible testimony of the word of God. Of this people in their *fallen* and iniquitous state, God says, by his prophet, *They* SEEK *me* DAILY, *and* DELIGHT *to know my ways, as a nation that did* RIGHTEOUSNESS, *and* FORSOOK *not the* ORDINANCES *of their God : they ask of me the ordinances of* JUSTICE, *and* TAKE DELIGHT *in approaching to God,* Isa. lviii. 2. Can any thing be *stronger* than this ? And yet, at that time, they were *most dreadfully carnal*, and *sold under sin*, as the rest of that chapter proves. It is a most notorious fact, that how little soever the life of a Jew was conformed to the law of his God, he notwithstanding professed the highest *esteem* for it, and *gloried* in it : and the apostle says nothing stronger of them in this chapter than their *conduct* and *profession* verify to the *present day.* They are still *delighting in the law of God*, after the *inward man ; with their mind serving the law of God ;* asking for the ordinances of justice, seeking God daily, and taking delight in approaching to God ; they even glory, and greatly *exult* and *glory*, in the Divine *original* and *excellency* of their LAW ; and all this while they are most abominably *carnal*, *sold under sin*, and *brought into the most degrading captivity to the law of sin and death.* If then all that the apostle states of the person in question be true of the *Jews*, through the whole period of their history, even to the *present time ;* if they do in all their *professions* and their *religious services*, which they zealously maintain, confess, and conscientiously too, that the *law is holy*, and the *commandment holy*, *just*, and *good ;* and yet, with their *flesh*, serve the *law of sin ;* the same certainly may be said with equal propriety of a *Jewish penitent*, deeply convinced of his lost estate, and the total insufficiency of his legal observances to deliver him from his *body of sin and death.* And consequently, all this may be said of *Paul the* JEW, while *going about to establish his own righteousness*—his own plan of justification ; he had not as yet *submitted to the righteousness of God*—the Divine plan of redemption by Jesus Christ.

4. It must be allowed that, whatever was the *experience* of so eminent a man, Christian, and apostle, as St. Paul, it must be a very proper *standard of Christianity.* And if we are to take what is here said as *his experience* as a *Christian*, it would be presumption in *us* to expect to go higher ; for he certainly had pushed the principles of his religion to their utmost consequences. But his whole life, and the account which he immediately gives of himself in the succeeding chapter, prove that he, as a *Christian* and an *apostle*, had a *widely different experience ;* an experience which amply justifies that *superiority* which he attri-

butes to the *Christian* religion over the *Jewish ;* and demonstrates that it not only is well calculated to *perfect* all preceding dispensations, but that it affords *salvation to the uttermost* to all those who flee for refuge to the hope that it sets before them. Besides, there is nothing spoken here of the state of a *conscientious Jew,* or of St. *Paul* in his *Jewish state,* that is not true of every genuine *penitent ;* even *before,* and it may be, *long before,* he has believed in Christ to the saving of his soul. The assertion that " every Christian, howsoever advanced in the Divine life, will and must feel all this inward conflict," &c., is as *untrue* as it is *dangerous.* That many, called *Christians,* and probably *sincere,* do feel all this, may be readily granted ; and such we must consider to be in the same state with *Saul of Tarsus,* previously to his conversion ; but that they must *continue* thus is no where intimated in the Gospel of Christ. We must take heed how we make *our experience,* which is the result of our *unbelief* and *unfaithfulness,* the *standard* for the people of God, and lower down *Christianity* to OUR most reprehensible

and *dwarfish* state : at the same time, we should not be *discouraged* at what we thus feel, but apply to God, through Christ, as Paul did ; and then we shall soon be able, with him, to declare, to the eternal glory of *God's grace,* that *the law of the Spirit of life, in Christ Jesus, has made us free from the law of sin and death.* This is the inheritance of God's children ; and their salvation is of me, saith the Lord.

I cannot conclude these observations without recommending to the notice of my readers a learned and excellent discourse on the latter part of this chapter, preached by the Rev. *James Smith,* minister of the Gospel in *Dumfermline,* Scotland ; a work to which I am indebted for some useful observations, and from which I should have been glad to have copied much, had my limits permitted. Reader, do not plead for Baal ; try, fully try, the efficiency of the blood of the covenant ; and be not content with less salvation than God has provided for thee. Thou art not straitened in God, be not straitened in thy own bowels.

CHAPTER VIII.

The happy state of those who believe in Christ, and walk under the influence of his Spirit, 1, 2. *The design of God in sending his Son into the world was to redeem men from sin,* 3, 4. *The miserable state of the carnally minded,* 5—8. *How Christ lives and works in his followers ; their blessedness here, and their happiness hereafter,* 9—17. *Sufferings are the common lot of all men ; and from which Gentiles and Jews have the hope of being finally delivered,* 18—23. *The use and importance of hope,* 24, 25. *The Spirit makes intercession for the followers of Christ,* 26, 27. *All things work together for good to them that love God, and who act according to his gracious purpose in calling them,* 28. *The means used to bring men to eternal glory,* 29, 30. *The great blessedness, confidence, and security of all genuine Christians, whom, while they hold fast faith and a good conscience, nothing can separate from the love of God,* 31—39.

A. M. cir. 4062.
A. D. cir. 58.
An. Olymp.
cir. CCIX. 2.
A. U. C. cir.
811.

*T*HERE is, therefore, now no condemnation to them which are in Christ Jesus, who [a] walk not after the flesh, but after the Spirit.

2 For [b] the law of [c] the Spirit of life in Christ Jesus hath made me free from [d] the law of sin and death.

3 For, [e] what the law could not do, in that it

A. M. cir. 4062.
A. D. cir. 58.
An. Olymp.
cir. CCIX. 2.
A. U. C. cir.
811.

---

[a] Ver. 4 ; Gal. v. 16, 25.——[b] John viii. 36 ; chap. vi. 18, 22 ; Gal. ii. 19 ; v. 1.——[c] 1 Cor. xv. 45 ; 2 Cor. iii. 6.

[d] Chap. vii. 24, 25.——[e] Acts xiii. 39 ; chap. iii. 20 ; Heb. vii. 18, 19 ; x. 1, 2, 10, 14.

NOTES ON CHAP. VIII.

Verse 1. There is, *therefore, now no condemnation*] To do justice to St. Paul's reasoning, this chapter must be read in the closest connection with the preceding. There we have seen the unavailing struggles of an awakened Jew, who sought pardon and holiness from that law which he was conscious he had broken ; and in which he could find no provision for pardon, and no power to sanctify. This conviction having brought him to the very brink of despair, and, being on the point of giving up all hope, he hears of redemption by Jesus Christ, thanks God for the prospect he has of salvation, applies for and receives it ; and now magnifies God for the unspeakable gift of which he has been made a partaker.

Those who restrain the word *now,* so as to indicate by it the *Gospel dispensation* only, do not take in the whole of the apostle's meaning. The apostle has not

been dealing in general matters only, but also in those which are particular. He has not been pointing out merely the difference between the two dispensations, the Mosaic and the Christian ; but he marks out the state of a penitent under the former, and that of a believer under the latter. The last chapter closed with an account of the deep distress of the penitent ; this one opens with an account of his *salvation.* The *now,* therefore, in the text, must refer more to the happy transition from darkness to light, from condemnation to pardon, which this believer now enjoys, than to the Christian dispensation taking the place of the Jewish economy.

Who walk not after the flesh, &c.] In this one verse we find the power and virtue of the Gospel scheme ; it *pardons* and *sanctifies ;* the Jewish law could do neither. By faith in our Lord Jesus Christ the penitent, condemned by the law, is pardoned ; the *carnal man,* labouring under the overpowering influence of the

A. M. cir. 4062.
A. D. cir. 58.
An. Olymp.
cir. CCIX. 2.
A. U. C. cir.
811.

was weak through the flesh, [f] God sending his own Son in the likeness of sinful flesh, and [g] for sin, condemned sin in the flesh :

4 That the righteousness of the law might be fulfilled in us, [h] who walk not after the flesh, but after the Spirit.

5 For [i] they that are after the flesh do mind the things of the flesh ; but they that are after the Spirit [k] the things of the Spirit.

A. M. cir. 4062.
A. D. cir. 58.
An. Olymp.
cir. CCIX. 2.
A. U. C. cir.
811.

---

[f] Gal. iii. 13 ; 2 Cor. v. 21.——[g] Or, *by a sacrifice for sin.*

[h] Ver. 1.——[i] John iii. 6 ; 1 Cor. ii. 14.——[k] Gal. v. 22, 25.

---

sin of his nature, is sanctified. He is first freely justified ; he feels no condemnation ; he is fully sanctified ; *he walks not after the* FLESH, *but after the* SPIRIT.

This last clause is wanting in the principal MSS., *versions,* and *fathers.* Griesbach has excluded it from the text ; and Dr. *White* says, *Certissime delenda ;* it should most undoubtedly be expunged. Without it, the passage reads thus : *There is, therefore, no·condemnation to them that are in Christ Jesus ; for the law of the Spirit of life, &c.* It is a fairly assumed point, that those who are *in Christ Jesus,* who believe in his name, have redemption in his blood ; are made partakers of his Spirit, and have the mind in them that was in him ; will not walk after the flesh, but after the Spirit : therefore the thing itself is included in the *being in Christ,* whether it be *expressed* or not : and it was probably to make the thing more obvious, that this explanatory clause was added by some copyist, for it does not appear to have made an original part of the text ; and it is most likely that it was inserted here from the *fourth* verse.

Verse 2. For the law of the Spirit of life] The Gospel of the grace of Christ, which is not only a law or rule of life, but affords that sovereign *energy* by which guilt is removed from the conscience, the power of sin broken, and its polluting influence removed from the heart. The law was a *spirit of death,* by which those who were under it were bound down, because of their sin, to condemnation and death. The Gospel proclaims Jesus the Saviour ; and what the *law* bound unto death, IT looses unto life eternal. And thus the apostle says, whether of *himself* or the man whom he is still personating, *the law of the Spirit of life in Christ Jesus hath made me free from the law of sin and death.* Most people allow that St. Paul is here speaking of his *own state ;* and this state is so totally different from that described in the preceding chapter, that it is absolutely impossible that they should have been the state of the same being, at *one* and the *same time.* No creature could possibly be *carnal, sold under sin, brought into captivity to the law of sin and death ;* and at the same time be *made free from* that *law of sin and death, by the law of the Spirit of life in Christ Jesus !* Until the most palpable absurdities and contradictions can be reconciled, these two opposite states can never exist in the same person at the same time.

Verse 3. For what the law could not do] The law could not pardon ; the law could not sanctify ; the law could not dispense with its own requisitions ; it is the rule of righteousness, and therefore must condemn unrighteousness. This is its unalterable nature. Had there been perfect obedience to its dictates, instead of *condemning,* it would have *applauded* and *rewarded ;*

but as the *flesh,* the *carnal* and *rebellious principle,* had prevailed, and transgression had taken place, it was rendered *weak,* inefficient to undo this work of the *flesh,* and bring the sinner into a state of pardon and acceptance with God.

God sending his own Son in the likeness of sinful flesh] Did that which the law could not do ; i. e. purchased pardon for the sinner, and brought every believer into the favour of God. And this is effected by the incarnation of Christ : He, in whom dwelt the fulness of the Godhead bodily, took upon him the *likeness of sinful flesh,* that is, a *human body* like ours, but not *sinful* as ours ; and for sin, και περι αμαρτιας, *and as a* SACRIFICE FOR SIN, (this is the sense of the word in a multitude of places,) *condemned sin in the flesh*—condemned that to death and destruction which had condemned us to both.

Condemned sin in the flesh] The design and object of the incarnation and sacrifice of Christ was to condemn sin, to have it *executed* and *destroyed ;* not to *tolerate* it as some think, or to render it *subservient* to the purposes of his *grace,* as others ; but to annihilate its *power, guilt,* and *being* in the soul of a believer.

Verse 4. That the righteousness of the law might be fulfilled in us] That the guilt might be pardoned through the merit of that sacrifice ; and that we might be enabled, by the power of his own grace and Spirit, to walk in newness of life ; loving God with all our heart, soul, mind, and strength, and our neighbour as ourselves : and thus the righteousness, the spirit, design, and purpose of the law is fulfilled in us, through the *strength of the Spirit of Christ,* which is here put in opposition to *the weakness of the law through the flesh.*

It is very likely that the concluding clause of this verse, which is the very same as that found in the common text of the first verse, has been transferred to that verse from this place.

Verse 5. For they that are after the flesh] And here is the great distinction between *Jews* and *genuine Christians :* the former are *after the flesh*—are under the power of the carnal, rebellious principle ; and consequently mind, φρονουσιν, *relish, the things of the flesh*—the things which appertain merely to the *present life ;* having no relish for *spiritual* and *eternal things.*

But they that are after the Spirit] They who are regenerated, who are born of the Spirit, being redeemed from the influence and law of the carnal mind ; these relish *the things of the Spirit*—they are spiritually minded, and pass through things *temporal,* so as not to lose the things which are *eternal.* And this, which in these apostolic times distinguished between the carnal Jew and the spiritual believer in Christ, is the grand mark

A. M. cir. 4062.
A. D. cir. 58.
An. Olymp.
cir. CCIX. 2.
A. U. C. cir.
811.

6 For [l] to be [m] carnally minded *is* death ; but [n] to be spiritually minded *is* life and peace.

7 Because [o] the [p] carnal mind *is* enmity against God : for it is not subject to the law of God, [q] neither indeed can be.

8 So then, they that are in the flesh cannot please God.

9 But ye are not in the flesh, but in the Spirit, if so be that [r] the Spirit of God dwell in you.

Now, if any man have not [s] the Spirit of Christ, he is none of his.

10 And if Christ *be* in you, the body *is* dead because of sin ; but the Spirit *is* life because of righteousness.

11 But if the Spirit of [t] him that raised up Jesus from the dead dwell in you, [u] he that raised up Christ from the dead shall also quicken your mortal bodies [v] by his Spirit that dwelleth in you.

A. M. cir. 4062.
A. D. cir. 58.
An. Olymp.
cir. CCIX. 2.
A. U. C. cir.
811.

---

[l] Chap. vi. 21 ; ver. 13 ; Gal. vi. 8.——[m] Gr. *the minding of the flesh :* so ver. 7.——[n] Gr. *the minding of the Spirit.*——[o] Gr. *the minding of the flesh.*——[p] James iv. 4.——[q] 1 Cor. ii. 14.

[r] 1 Cor. iii. 16 ; vi. 19.——[s] John iii. 34 ; Gal. iv. 6 ; Phil. *i.* 19 ; 1 Pet. i. 11.——[t] Acts ii. 24.——[u] Chap. vi. 4, 5 ; 1 Cor. vi 14 ; 2 Cor. iv. 14 ; Eph. ii. 5.——[v] Or, *because of his Spirit.*

---

of distinction between the *nominal* and the *real* Christian now. The former is earthly minded, and lives for *this world* ; the latter is spiritually minded, and lives for the *world to come.*

Verse 6. *For to be carnally minded* is *death*] To live under the influence of the carnal mind is to live in the state of condemnation, and consequently liable to death eternal : whereas, on the contrary, he who is *spiritually minded* has the *life* and *peace* of God in his soul, and is in full prospect of life eternal.

Verse 7. *Because the carnal mind* is *enmity against God*] Because it is a *carnal mind*, and relishes earthly and sinful things, and lives in opposition to the pure and holy law of God : therefore, it *is enmity against God ;* it is irreconcilable and implacable hatred.

It is not subject to the law of God] It will come under no obedience ; for it is *sin*, and the very principle of rebellion ; and therefore it cannot be *subject*, nor *subjected ;* for it is essential to sin to show itself in *rebellion ;* and when it ceases to *rebel*, it ceases to be sin.

From this we learn that the design of God in the economy of the Gospel, is not to *weaken, curtail,* or *lay* the carnal principle *in bonds,* but to *destroy* it. As it is *not subject,* and cannot be subject, to the law of God, it must be *destroyed,* else it will continue to rebel against God. It cannot be *mended,* or rendered less offensive in its nature, even by the operations of God ; it is ever sin, and sin is ever enmity ; and enmity, wherever it has power, will invariably show itself in acts of hostility and rebellion.

Verse 8. *So then*] Because this carnal mind is enmity against God, *they that are in the flesh*—who are under the power of the workings of this carnal mind, (which every soul is that has not received redemption in the blood of the Lamb,)—

Cannot please God.] Because of the rebellious workings of this principle of *rebellion* and *hatred.* And, if they cannot *please* God, they must be *displeasing* to him ; and consequently in the broad road to final perdition.

Verse 9. *But ye are not in the flesh*] Ye Christians, who have believed in Christ Jesus as the sin offering which has condemned sin in the flesh ; and, having been justified by faith and made partakers of the Holy Spirit, are enabled to walk in newness of life.

If so be that the Spirit of God dwell in you.] Or

seeing that, ειπερ, the Spirit of God dwelleth in you The *flesh,* the *sinful principle,* dwelt in them before ; and its motions were the proofs of its indwelling ; but now the Spirit dwells in them ; and its testimony in their conscience, and its powerful operations in their hearts, are the proofs of its indwelling. God made man in union with himself, and his heart was his temple. Sin being committed, the temple was defiled, and God abandoned it. Jesus Christ is come by his sacrifice and Spirit to cleanse the temple, and make man again a habitation of God through the Spirit. And when this almighty Spirit again makes the heart his residence, then the soul is delivered from the moral effects of the fall. And that this is absolutely necessary to our present peace and final salvation is proved from this : that if any man have not the Spirit of Christ—the mind that was in *him,* produced there by the power of the Holy Ghost—*he is none of his ;* he does not belong to the kingdom, flock, or family of God. This is an awful conclusion ! Reader, lay it to heart.

Verse 10. *And if Christ* be *in you, &c.*] This is the criterion by which you may judge of the state of grace in which ye stand. If Christ dwell in your hearts by faith, *the body* is *dead because of sin,* δι' αμαρτιαν, in reference to sin ; the members of your body no more perform the work of sin than the body of a dead man does the functions of natural life. Or the apostle may mean, that although, *because of sin,* the *life* of man is forfeited ; and the sentence, *dust thou art, and unto dust thou shalt return,* must be fulfilled on every human being, until the judgment of the great day ; yet, their souls being quickened by the indwelling Spirit of Christ, which enables them to live a life of righteousness, they receive a full assurance that their bodies, which are now condemned to death because of sin, shall be raised again to a life of immortal glory.

Verse 11. *But if the Spirit, &c.*] This verse confirms the sense given to the preceding. He who here receives the grace and Spirit of Christ, and continues to live under its influence a life of obedience to the Divine will, shall have a resurrection to eternal life ; and the resurrection of Christ shall be the *pattern* after which they shall be raised.

By his Spirit that dwelleth in you.] Instead of δια του ενοικουντος αυτου πνευματος, *because of the Spirit of him who dwelleth in you,* DEFG, a great many

A. M. cir. 4062.
A. D. cir. 58.
An. Olymp.
cir. CCIX. 2.
A. U. C. cir.
811.

12 ᵂ Therefore, brethren, we are debtors, not to the flesh, to live after the flesh.

13 For ˣ if ye live after the flesh, ye shall die: but if ye through the Spirit do ʸ mortify the deeds of the body, ye shall live.

14 For ᶻ as many as are led by the Spirit of God, they are the sons of God.

15 For ᵃ ye have not received the spirit of bondage again ᵇ to fear; but ye have received the ᶜ Spirit of adoption, whereby we cry, ᵈ Abba, Father.

A. M. cir. 4062.
A. D. cir. 58.
An. Olymp.
cir. CCIX. 2.
A. U. C. cir.
811.

ᵂ Chap. vi. 7, 14.——ˣ Ver. 6; Gal. vi. 8.——ʸ Eph. iv. 22; Col. iii. 5.——ᶻ Gal. v. 18.

ᵃ 1 Cor. ii. 12; Heb. ii. 15.——ᵇ 2 Tim. i. 7; 1 John iv. 18. ᶜ Isa. lvi. 5; Gal. iv. 5, 6.——ᵈ Mark xiv. 36.

---

others, with the *Vulgate*, *Itala*, and several of the fathers, have δια το ενοικουν αυτου πνευμα, which gives almost no variety of meaning. The latter may be neater Greek, but it is not better sense than the preceding.

Verse 12. Therefore, brethren, &c.] Dr. Taylor is of opinion that the apostle having spoken *separately*, both to Jews and Gentiles, concerning holiness and the obligations to it, now addresses himself to *both* conjointly, and,

I. Draws the general conclusion from *all* his arguments upon this subject, ver. 12.

II. Proves the validity of their claims to eternal life, ver. 14—17.

III. And as the affair of *suffering persecution* was a great stumbling block to the *Jews*, and might very much discourage the *Gentiles*, he introduces it to the best advantage, ver. 17, and advances several arguments to fortify their minds under all trials: as— (1.) That they suffered with *Christ*; (2.) In order to be *glorified* with him in a manner which will infinitely compensate all sufferings, ver. 17, 18. (3.) All mankind are under *various pressures*, longing for a better state, ver. 19—22. (4.) Many of the most *eminent Christians* are in the same distressed condition, ver. 23. (5.) According to the plan of the Gospel, we are to be brought to glory after a course of patience exercised in a variety of trials, ver. 24, 25. (6.) The Spirit of God will supply patience to every upright soul under persecution and suffering, 26, 27. (7.) All things, even the severest trials, shall work together for their good, ver. 28. And this he proves, by giving us a view of the several steps which the wisdom and goodness of God have settled, in order to our complete salvation, ver. 29, 30. Thence he passes to the affair of our *perseverance*; concerning which he concludes, from the *whole* of his preceding arguments, that as we are brought into a state of *pardon* by the free grace of God, through the death of Christ, who is now our mediator in heaven; no possible cause, providing we continue to love and serve God, shall be able to pervert our minds, or separate us from his love in Christ Jesus, ver. 31–39. *Therefore*, αρα ουν, is the grand inference from all that he has been arguing in relation to sanctity of life, both to the *Gentiles*, chap. vi., and to the *Jews*, chap. vii. and viii. to this verse, where I suppose he begins to address himself to *both*, in a body, to the end of the chapter.—Taylor, page 317.

Verse 13. For if ye live after the flesh, ye shall die] Though μελλετε αποθνησκειν may mean, *ye shall afterwards die*, and this seems to indicate a *temporal*

death, yet not exclusively of an eternal death; for *both*, and especially the latter, are necessarily implied.

But if ye through the Spirit] If ye seek that grace and spiritual help which the Gospel of Christ furnishes, resist, and, by resisting, *mortify the deeds of the flesh*, against which the law gave you no assistance, *ye shall live* a life of *faith*, *love*, and *holy obedience* here, and a life of *glory* hereafter.

Verse 14. For as many as are led by the Spirit, &c.] No man who has not Divine assistance can either find the way to heaven, or walk in it when found. As Christ, by his sacrificial offering, has opened the kingdom of God to all believers; and, as a mediator, transacts the concerns of their kingdom before the throne; so the Spirit of God is the great agent here below, to enlighten, quicken, strengthen, and guide the true disciples of Christ; and all that are born of this Spirit are led and guided by it; and none can pretend to be the children of God who are not thus guided.

Verse 15. Ye have not received the spirit of bondage] All that were under the law were under bondage to its rites and ceremonies; and as, through the prevalence of that corrupt nature with which every human being is polluted, and to remove which the law gave no assistance, they were often *transgressing*, consequently they had forfeited their lives, and were continually, through *fear of death*, subject to *bondage*, Heb. ii. 15. The believers in Christ Jesus were brought from under *that* law, and from under its condemnation; and, consequently, were freed from its bondage. The Gentiles were also in a state of bondage as well as the Jews; they had also a multitude of burdensome rites and ceremonies, and a multitude of deities to worship; nor could they believe themselves secure of protection while one of their almost endless host of gods, celestial, terrestrial, or infernal, was left unpropitiated.

But ye have received the Spirit of adoption] Ye are brought into the family of God by adoption; and the agent that brought you into this family is the Holy Spirit; and this very Spirit continues to witness to you the grace in which ye stand, by enabling you to call God your Father, with the utmost filial confidence and affection.

The Spirit of adoption] Adoption was an act frequent among the ancient Hebrews, Greeks, and Romans: by which a person was taken out of one family and incorporated with another. Persons of property, who had no children of their own, adopted those of another family. The child thus adopted ceased to belong to his own family, and was in every respect

A. M. cir. 4062.
A. D. cir. 58.
An. Olymp.
cir. CCIX. 2.
A. U. C. cir.
811.

16 ^e The Spirit itself beareth witness with our spirit, that we are the children of God.

17 And if children, then heirs;

^f heirs of God, and joint heirs with Christ; ^g if so be that we suffer with *him*, that we may be also glorified together.

A. M. cir. 4062.
A. D. cir. 58.
An. Olymp.
cir. CCIX. 2.
A. U. C. cir.
811.

---

^e 2 Cor. i. 22; v. 5; Eph. i. 13; iv. 30.——^f Acts xxvi. 18;   Gal. iv. 7.——^g Acts xiv. 22; Phil. i. 29; 2 Tim. ii. 11, 12.

---

bound to the person who had adopted him, as if he were his own child ; and in consequence of the death of his adopting father he possessed his estates. If a person *after* he had adopted a child happened to have children of his own, then the estate was equally divided between the adopted and real children. The Romans had regular forms of law, by which all these matters were settled.——See in Aulus Gellius. Noctes Attic., vol. i. cap. xix. p. 331. Edit Beloe ; and the note there.

Whereby we cry, Abba, Father.] The reason why the Syriac and Greek words are here conjoined, may be seen in the note on Mark xiv. 36, to which the reader is referred. The introduction of the words here shows that the persons in question had the strongest evidence of the excellence of the state in which they stood ; they knew that they were thus adopted ; and they knew this by the Spirit of God which was given them on their adoption ; and let me say, they could know it by no other means. The Father who had adopted them could be seen by no mortal eye ; and the transaction being purely of a spiritual nature, and transacted in heaven, can be known only by God's supernatural testimony of it upon earth. It is a matter of such solemn importance to every Christian soul, that God in his mercy has been pleased not to leave it to *conjecture, assumption,* or *inductive reasoning ;* but attests it by his own Spirit in the soul of the person whom he adopts through Christ Jesus. It is the grand and most observable case in which the intercourse is kept up between heaven and earth ; and the genuine believer in Christ Jesus is not left to the *quibbles* or casuistry of polemic divines or critics, but receives the *thing,* and the *testimony* of it, immediately from God himself. And were not the testimony of the state thus given, no man could possibly have any assurance of his salvation which would beget confidence and love. If to any man his *acceptance with God* be *hypothetical,* then his *confidence* must be so too. His love to God must be hypothetical, his gratitude hypothetical, and his obedience also. IF God had forgiven me my sins, then I *should* love him, and I *should* be grateful, and I *should* testify this gratitude by *obedience.* But who does not see that these must necessarily depend on the IF in the first case. All this *uncertainty,* and the perplexities necessarily resulting from it, God has precluded by sending the Spirit of his Son into our hearts, by which we cry, Abba, Father : and thus our adoption into the heavenly family is testified and ascertained to us in the only way in which it can possibly be done, by the direct influence of the Spirit of God. Remove this from Christianity, and it is a *dead letter.*

It has been remarked that *slaves* were not permitted to use the term *Abba,* father, or *Imma,* mother, in accosting their *masters* and *mistresses.* The Hebrew

canon, relative to this, is extant in the tract *Bera-choth,* fol. 16. 2, הָעֲבָדִים וְהַשְּׁפָחוֹת אֵין קוֹרִין אוֹתָם לֹא אַבָּא פְּלוֹנִי וְלֹא אִמָּא פְּלוֹנִית haabadim vehashshe-phachoth ein korin otham, lo Abba N, velo Imma N. *Men-servants and maid-servants do not call to their master Abba, (father,) N. nor to their mistress Imma, (mother,) N.* And from this some suppose that the apostle intimates that being now brought from under the spirit of bondage, in which they durst not call God their *Father,* they are not only brought into a new state, but have got that language which is peculiar to that state. It is certain that no man who has not redemption in the blood of the cross has any right to call God *Father,* but merely as he may be considered the *Father of the spirits of all flesh.*

Some have supposed that the apostle, by using the *Syriac* and *Greek* words which express *Father,* shows the union of *Jewish* and *Gentile* believers in those devotions which were dictated by a filial spirit. Others have thought that these were the *first words* which those generally uttered who were made partakers of the Holy Spirit. It is enough to know that it was the *language* of their *sonship ;* and that it expressed the clear assurance they had of being received into the Divine favour, the affection and gratitude they felt for this extraordinary blessing, and their complete readiness to come under the laws and regulations of the family, and to live in the spirit of obedience.

Verse 16. *The Spirit itself beareth witness with our spirit*] Αυτο το πνευμα, that same Spirit, the Spirit of adoption ; that is, the Spirit who witnesses this adoption ; which can be no other than the Holy Ghost himself, and certainly cannot mean any *disposition* or *affection* of mind which the adopted person may feel ; for such a disposition must arise from a knowledge of this adoption, and the knowledge of this adoption cannot be given by any human or earthly means ; it must come from God himself : therefore the αυτο το πνευμα must have reference to that Spirit, by whom alone the knowledge of the adoption is witnessed to the soul of the believer.

With our spirit] In our *understanding,* the place or recipient of light and information ; and the place or faculty to which such information can properly be brought. This is done that we may have the highest possible evidence of the work which God has wrought. As the *window* is the proper *medium* to let the light of the sun into our apartments, so the *understanding* is the proper medium of conveying the *Spirit's influence* to the soul. We, therefore, have the utmost evidence of the fact of our adoption which we can possibly have ; we have the word and Spirit of God ; and the word sealed on our spirit by the Spirit of God. And this is not a momentary influx : if we take care to walk with God, and not grieve the Holy Spirit, we shall have an abiding testimony ; and while

A. M. cir. 4062.
A. D. cir. 58.
An. Olymp.
cir. CCIX. 2.
A. U. C. cir.
811.

18 For I reckon that [h] the sufferings of this present time *are* not worthy *to be compared* with the glory which shall be revealed in us.

A. M. cir. 4062.
A. D. cir. 58.
An. Olymp.
cir. CCIX. 2.
A. U. C. cir.
811.

19 For [i] the earnest expectation of the creature waiteth for the [k] manifestation of the sons of God. 20 For [l] the creature was made subject to vanity, not willingly, but by reason

---

[h] 2 Cor. iv. 17; 1 Pet. i. 6, 7; iv. 13.——[i] 2 Pet. iii. 13.

[k] 1 John iii. 2.——[l] Ver. 22; Gen. iii. 19.

---

we continue faithful to our adopting Father, the Spirit that witnesses that adoption will continue to witness it; and hereby we shall know that we are of God by the Spirit which he giveth us.

Verse 17. *And if children, then heirs*] For the *legitimate* children can alone inherit the estate. This is not an estate to which they succeed in consequence of the death of a former possessor; it is like the promised land, *given by God himself*, and divided among the children of the family.

Heirs of God] It is neither an *earthly* portion nor a *heavenly* portion; but GOD *himself*, who is to be their portion. It is not heaven they are to inherit; it is GOD, who is infinitely greater and more glorious than heaven itself. With such powers has God created the soul of man, that nothing less than *himself* can be a sufficient and satisfactory portion for the mind of this most astonishing creature.

Joint heirs with Christ] Partaking of the same eternal glory with the glorified human nature of Christ.

If so be that we suffer with him] Observe, says Dr. Taylor, how prudently the apostle advances to the harsh affair of *suffering*. He does not mention it till he had raised up their thoughts to the highest object of joy and pleasure—the happiness and glory of a joint inheritance with the ever-blessed Son of God.

We are *heirs, heirs of God, and joint heirs with Christ, if so be that we suffer with* him. This, with the additional consideration that we suffer *with Christ*, or, *as* he himself suffered, would greatly qualify the transitory afflictions of this world, and dispose them to attend to the other arguments he had to offer.

Verse 18. *For I reckon that the sufferings, &c.*] If the glory that is to be revealed be the enjoyment of God himself, (see above,) then the sufferings of this life, which, when compared with *eternity*, are but as for a *moment*, are not worthy to be put in competition with this glory which shall be revealed in us. This case is perfectly clear.

Verse 19. *For the earnest expectation of the creature*] There is considerable difficulty in this and the four following verses: and the difficulty lies chiefly in the meaning of the word ἡ κτισις, which we translate *the creature*, and *creation*. Some think that by it the *brute creation* is meant; others apply it to the *Jewish people*; others to the *godly*; others to the *Gentiles*; others to the *good angels*; and others to the *fallen spirits*, both *angelic* and *human*. Dissertations without end have been written on it; and it does not appear that the Christian world are come to any general agreement on the subject. Dr. Lightfoot's mode of explanation appears to me to be the best, on the whole. 'There is," says he, "a *twofold* key hanging at this place, which may unlock the whole, and make the sense plain and easy.

1. The *first* is the phrase, πασα ἡ κτισις, which we render *the whole creation*, ver. 22, and with which we meet twice elsewhere in the New Testament. Mark xvi. 15: *Preach the Gospel,* πασῃ τῃ κτισει, *to every creature*; and Col. i. 23: *The Gospel was preached,* εν πασῃ τῃ κτισει, *to every creature*. Now it is sufficiently apparent what is meant by πασα κτισις in both these places, viz. *all nations*, or the *heathen world*. For that which in St. Mark is, *preach the Gospel to every creature*, is, in St. Matthew, *go and teach*, παντα τα εθνη, *all nations*. And this very phrase in this place lays claim to that very interpretation. And the *Hebrew* כל הבריות *col habberioth*, which answers to the *Greek* πασα ἡ κτισις, *every creature*, is applied by the Jews to the *Gentiles*, and that by way of opposition to *Israel*.

2. The *second* key is the word ματαιοτητι, ver. 20, which is not unfitly rendered *vanity*; but then this vanity is improperly applied to the *vanishing*, dying, changing state of the creation. For ματαιοτης, *vanity*, does not so much denote the *vanishing condition* of the *outward state*, as it does the *inward* vanity or *emptiness* of the mind. So the apostle, speaking of the Gentiles concerning whom he speaks here, tells us εματαιωθησαν, *They became vain in their imaginations*, chap. i. 21; and again, *The Gentiles walk* εν ματαιοτητι, *in the vanity of their mind*, Eph. iv. 17; so also, *The Lord knoweth the thoughts of the wise,* ὁτι εισι ματαιοι, *that they are vain*, 1 Cor. iii. 20. To all which let me add this farther observation, that throughout this whole place the apostle seems to allude to the bondage of the Israelites in Egypt, and their deliverance from it; with a comparison made betwixt the *Jewish* and the *Gentile* Church. When God would deliver Israel from his bondage, he challenges him for *his Son*, and his *first-born*, Exod. iv. 22. And in like manner the *Gentiles* earnestly expect and wait for such a *kind of manifestation of the sons of God*, within and among themselves. The *Romans*, to whom the apostle writes, knew well how many predictions and promises it had pleased God to publish by his prophets, concerning gathering together and adopting *sons* to himself among the Gentiles; the *manifestation* of which *sons* the whole Gentile world with a *neck* as it were *stretched out*, as the word αποκαραδοκια implies, (απο, from, and καρα, the head, and δοκαω, to expect,) doth now wait for." See the observations at the end of this chapter.

Verse 20. *For the creature was made subject to vanity*] The Gentile world were subject to vanity of mind; but how? *not willingly*, but by reason of him who hath subjected the same. May we not say, *it became vain willingly*, but was made subject to vanity *unwillingly*? For, let us recur to the origin of Gentilism, the confusion of languages, by reason of the

A. M. cir. 4062.
A. D. cir. 58.
An. Olymp.
cir. CCIX. 2.
A. U. C. cir.
811.

of him who hath subjected *the same* in hope,

21 Because the creature itself also shall be delivered from the bondage of corruption into the glorious liberty of the children of God.

22 For, we know that ᵐ the whole creation ⁿ groaneth and travaileth in pain together until now.

ᵐ Or, *every creature,* Mark xvi. 15; Col. i. 23.——ⁿ Jer. xii. 11. ᵒ 2 Cor. v. 5; Eph. i. 14.

23 And not only *they,* but ourselves also, which have ᵒ the first fruits of the Spirit, ᵖ even we ourselves groan within ourselves, �q waiting for the adoption, *to wit,* the ʳ redemption of our body.

24 For we are saved by hope : but ˢ hope that is seen is not hope : for what a man seeth, why doth he yet hope for ?

A. M. cir. 4062.
A. D. cir. 58.
An. Olymp.
cir. CCIX. 2.
A. U. C. cir.
811.

ᵖ 2 Cor. v. 2, 4.——q Luke xx. 36.——ʳ Luke xxi. 28; Eph. iv. 30.——ˢ 2 Cor. v. 5, 7; Heb. xi. 1.

---

attempt to build the tower of Babel ; and though there are some passages in the gloss of the Targumists upon this matter that are sufficiently ridiculous, yet as to their *scope* and *design* they are worthy of notice. " *They said, Go to, let us build us a city and a tower, and let its head reach unto the top of heaven ; and let us make a house of worship in the top of it ; and let us put a sword in his hand that he may wage war for us against our enemies, before we be scattered abroad upon the face of the whole earth."* It is an ancient tradition among the Jews, that this tower was built on an *idolatrous* account. The confusion of tongues, by which true religion was lost in the world, is a proof that the builders of this tower sinned against God in the highest degree. They were inclined to *vanity,* i. e. idolatry, WILLINGLY ; but they were *subjected to vanity* UNWILLINGLY ; for this proceeded from the just indignation and vengeance of God. From this time the world lay under heathenism till the bringing in of the Gospel, upwards of 2000 years after. See *Lightfoot.*

Verse 21. *Because the creature*] This and the preceding verse should be thus connected: *in hope* THAT (ὅτι) *the creature itself also shall be delivered.* The word φθορά denotes, very frequently, *sinful corruption.* So, 2 Pet. i. 4 : *Corruption through lust,* τῆς ἐν ἐπιθυμίᾳ φθορᾶς. 2 Cor. xi. 3 : *Lest your minds should be corrupted.* 1 Cor. xv. 33 : *Evil communications corrupt good manners.* The sense, therefore, of the apostle in this place seems to be : the Gentile world shall, in time, be delivered from the bondage of their *sinful corruption,* i. e. the bondage of their lusts and vile affections ; and be brought into such a noble liberty as the sons of God enjoy.

Verse 22. *The whole creation groaneth and travaileth*] If it be inquired how the Gentile world groaned and travailed in pain ; let them who explain this of the fabric of the material world, tell us how *that* groans and travails ? They must needs own it to be a borrowed and allusive phrase : but in the sense above given, the very literal construction may be admitted.

Verse 23. *And not only* they, *but ourselves also*] Neither the *Gentiles* only, but we *Jews* also, (however we belong to a nation envious of the heathen,) to whom God hath granted the first fruits of the Spirit; we sigh among ourselves for their sakes, waiting for the adoption ; that is, the redemption of our mystical body, whereof the Gentiles make a very great part. *Lightfoot's* works, vol. ii. p. 359 and 707.

The scope and design of St. Paul in these verses may be thus summed up :—The apostle shows that the whole creation is in a suffering state, into which it has been brought by the disobedience of one man, Adam ; therefore, it was *made subject to vanity—* pain, sickness, and death ; not willingly, for mankind had no part in that transgression which " brought death into the world and all our wo ;" but God subjected the whole, purposing to afford them a deliverance and infusing into every heart a *hope* that a more auspicious era should take place ; and it is through the influence of this *hope,* which every man possesses, that the present ills are so patiently borne, because all are expecting better days. The great deliverer is the Messiah, and the Gospel days the auspicious era which God intended to bring forward. They who believe in Christ with a heart unto righteousness are freed from the bondage of their *sinful corruption,* and brought into the glorious liberty of the sons of God ; and they look forward with joyous expectation, waiting for the general resurrection, when their *bodies* also shall be redeemed from corruption, and the *whole man, body* and *soul,* be adopted into the *family of heaven* ABOVE, as their *souls* had been previously adopted into the *family of faith* BELOW. And although it may be said that the redemption provided by the Gospel can- not be an object of hope to those who have never heard of it ; yet, as every man has hope, and this hope is inspired by God for this very purpose, that it may be the means of supporting them in the ills of life, and God, in inspiring it, had respect to the glorious state of Christianity, therefore it is this state, in effect, that the whole creation are longing for. So Jesus Christ is said, by the Prophet Haggai, ii. 7, to be *the desire of all nations ;* and yet not one of the nations of the earth had, at that time, heard of him. And thus, as Dr. Whitby has very properly remarked, " desire and expectation are ascribed to creatures, in reference to things they *want,* and which tend to their advantage ; notwithstanding they explicitly know nothing of them."

Verse 24. *For we are saved by hope*] We are sup- ported and are comfortable in the expectation we have of receiving from the hand of our God all the good we need in the troubles and adversities of this life, and of having our bodies raised from corruption and death at the general resurrection.

Hope that is seen is not hope] As hope signifies *the expectation of future good,* so it necessarily sup- poses that the object of it is not *seen,* i. e. not *enjoyed ;* for to *see,* in Scripture language, sometimes signifies

A. M. cir. 4062.
A. D. cir. 58.
An. Olymp.
cir. CCIX. 2.
A. U. C. cir.
811.

25 But if we hope for that we see not, *then* do we with patience wait for *it*.

26 Likewise the Spirit also helpeth our infirmities: for [t] we know not what we should pray for as we ought: but [u] the Spirit itself maketh intercession for us

with groanings which cannot be uttered.

27 And [v] he that searcheth the hearts knoweth what *is* the mind of the Spirit, [w] because he maketh intercession for the saints [x] according to *the will of God.*

A. M. cir. 4062.
A D. cir. 58.
An. Olymp.
cir. CCIX. 2.
A. U. C. cir.
811.

---

[t] Matt. xx. 22; James iv. 3.——[u] Zech. xii. 13; Eph. vi. 18.
[v] 1 Chron. xxviii. 9; Psa. vii. 9; Prov. xvii. 3; Jer. xi. 20; xvii.   10; xx. 12; Acts i. 24; 1 Thess. ii. 4; Rev. ii. 23.——[w] Or, *that.*——[x] 1 John v. 14.

---

to *enjoy*, as in Job vii. 7 : *Mine eye shall no more* SEE (*margin,* ENJOY) *good.* Job ix. 25 : *My days flee away, and* SEE *no good ;* i. e. *enjoy* no prosperity. Psa. l. 23 : *I will* SHOW *the salvation of God :* I will give that man to *enjoy* my salvation who walks uprightly. Matt. v. 8 : *Blessed are the pure in heart, for they shall* SEE *God ;* that is, they shall *enjoy* his favour and blessing. See also John iii. 36 ; Heb. xii. 14, and 1 John iii. 2. *The hope that is seen*, that is, *enjoyed*, is no longer *hope*, it is *fruition :* and a man cannot *hope* for that which he has in his *possession.*

Verse 25. *But if we hope for that we see not*] If we have a well-grounded expectation of our resurrection and final glorification, knowing that such things are necessarily *future*, and must for a certain time be delayed ; then *do we patiently wait for them*, continue patiently to endure the common ills of life, and whatever tribulations we may be exposed to in consequence of our Christian profession ; for we know, FAITHFUL *is he who has promised. Hope* is a sort of universal blessing, and one of the greatest which God has granted to man. To mankind, in general, life would be intolerable without it ; and it is as necessary as *faith* is even to the followers of God.

The ancients have a very instructive and elegant fable concerning it. " *Prometheus* having made a human body, went up to heaven, and stole some celestial fire to animate it : *Jupiter*, incensed at the theft, sent down *Pandora*, with a box full of diseases and plagues of every kind, as an ensnaring present to *Prometheus* ; but he refused to accept it. *Epimetheus* took and opened it, and instantly all those diseases, &c., by which mankind have been made miserable, flew out, and spread themselves over the whole earth ; and only HOPE remained at the bottom of the box." This fable explains itself, as to its main design. Men find life, with its various and unavoidable ills, only supportable by the *hope* they have of not only getting safely through them, but of enjoying a state of blessedness in the end. Hope is still at the bottom ; and therefore man is encouraged to bear up in all the pressures of life. Take away *hope*, and then black *despair* and indescribable wretchedness would be the instant result. *Hope* stands justly among the highest mercies of God.

Verse 26. *The Spirit also helpeth our infirmities*] The *same Spirit*, το πνευμα, mentioned before as bearing witness with ours that we are the children of God ; and consequently it is not a *disposition* or *frame of mind*, for the disposition of our mind surely cannot help the infirmities of our minds.

The word συναντιλαμβανεται is very inadequately

expressed by *helpeth.* It is compounded of συν, *together*, αντι, *against*, and λαμβανομαι, *to support* or *help*, and signifies such assistance as is afforded by any two persons to each other, who mutually bear the same load or carry it between them. He who prays, receives help from the Spirit of God ; but he who prays not receives no such help. Whatever our strength may be, we must put it forth, even while most implicitly depending on the strength of God himself.

For we know not what we should pray for as we ought] And should therefore be liable to endless mistakes in our prayers, if suitable desires were not excited by the Holy Spirit and power received to bring these desires, by prayer, before the throne of grace.

But the Spirit itself] Αυτο το πνευμα, *The same Spirit*, viz. the Spirit that witnesses of our adoption and sonship, ver. 15, 16, *makes intercession for us.* Surely if the apostle had designed to teach us that he meant *our own sense* and *understanding* by the *Spirit*, he never could have spoken in a manner in which plain common sense was never likely to comprehend his meaning. Besides, how can it be said that our *own spirit*, our *filial disposition*, bears witness with our *own spirit* ; that our own spirit helps the infirmities of our own spirit ; that our own spirit teaches our own spirit that of which it is ignorant ; and that our own spirit maketh intercession for our own spirit, with groanings unutterable ? This would have been both incongruous and absurd. We must therefore understand these places of that help and influence which the followers of God receive from the Holy Ghost ; and consequently, of the fulfilment of the various promises relative to this point which our Lord made to his disciples, particularly in John xiv. 16, 17, and 26 ; xv. 26, 27 ; xvi. 7 ; and particularly ver. 13 and 14 : *Howbeit, when he, the Spirit of truth, is come, he will guide you into all truth ; and he will show you things to come. He shall glorify me : for he shall receive of mine, and shall show it unto you.*

Verse 27. *He maketh intercession for the saints*] The word εντυγχανω signifies to apply one's self to a person in behalf of another ; to *intercede* or *negotiate for.* Our Lord makes intercession for us, by *negotiating* and *managing*, as our friend and agent, all the affairs pertaining to our salvation. And the Spirit of God makes intercession for the saints, not by supplication to God on their behalf, but by *directing* and *qualifying* their supplications in a proper manner, by his agency and influence upon their hearts ; which, according to the Gospel scheme, is the peculiar work and office of the Holy Spirit, See *Taylor.*

According to the will of *God.*] Κατα Θεου· **Ac-**

A. M. cir. 4062.
A. D. cir. 58.
An. Olymp.
cir. CCIX. 2.
A. U. C. cir.
811.

28 And we know that all things work together for good to them that love God; to them ^y who are the called according to *his* purpose.

29 For whom ^z he did fore-know, ^a he also did predestinate ^b *to be* conformed to the image of his Son, ^c that he might be the first-born among many brethren.

A. M. cir. 4062.
A. D. cir. 58.
An. Olymp.
cir. CCIX. 2.
A. U. C. cir.
811.

y Chap. ix. 11, 23, 24; 2 Tim. i. 9.——z See Exod. xxxiii. 12, 17; Psa. i. 6; Jer. i. 5; Matt. vii. 23; chap. xi. 2; 2 Tim. ii. 19;

1 Pet. i. 2.——a Eph. i. 5, 11.——b John xvii. 22; 2 Cor. iii. 18; Phil. iii. 21; 1 John iii. 2.——c Col. i. 15, 18; Heb. i. 6; Rev. i. 5.

cording to the mind, intention, or design of God. And thus the prayers which we offer up, and the desires which subsist in the unutterable groanings, are all such as are pleasing in the sight of God. So that God, whose is the Spirit, and who is acquainted with the mind of the Spirit, knows what he means when he leads the saints to express themselves in words, desires, groans, sighs, or tears: in each God reads the language of the Holy Ghost, and prepares the answer according to the request.

From all this we learn that a *fluency in prayer* is not essential to *praying:* a man may pray most powerfully in the estimation of God, who is not able to utter even one word. The unutterable groan is big with meaning, and God understands it, because it contains the language of his own Spirit. Some desires are too mighty to be expressed; there is no language expressive enough to give them proper form and distinct vocal sound: such desires show that they came from God; and as they came from him, so they express what God is disposed to do, and what he has purposed to do. This is a matter of great encouragement to all those who are agonizing to enter in at the strait gate.

Verse 28. *And we know that all things work together for good to them that love God*] To understand this verse aright, let us observe: 1. That the persons in whose behalf all things work for good are they *who love God,* and, consequently, who live in the *spirit of obedience.* 2. It is not said that all things *shall* work for good, but that συνεργει, *they work now* in the behalf of him who *loveth now,* αγαπωσι; for both verbs are in the *present* tense. 3. All these things *work together;* while *they* are working, God's providence is working, his Spirit is working, and *they are working* TOGETHER *with him.* And whatever troubles, or afflictions, or persecutions may arise, God presses them into their service; and they make a part of the general working, and are caused to contribute to the general good of the person *who now loves God,* and who is working by faith and love under the influence and operation of the Holy Ghost. They who say sin *works* for good to them that love God speak blasphemous nonsense. A man who *now loves God* is not *now sinning* against God; and the promise belongs only to the *present* time: and as love is the true incentive to obedience, the man who is entitled to the promise can never, while thus entitled, (loving God,) be found in the commission of sin. But though this be a good general sense for these words, yet the *all things* mentioned here by the apostle seem more particularly to mean those things mentioned in the 28th, 29th, and 30th verses.

To them who are the called according to his *purpose.*] Dr. Taylor translates τοις κλητοις, the *invited;* and observes that it is a metaphor taken from *inviting*

guests, or making them welcome to a feast. As if he had said: Certainly all things work together for their good; for this reason, because they are called, invited, or made welcome to the blessings of the covenant, (which is ratified in eating of the covenant sacrifice,) according to God's original purpose first declared to Abraham, Gen. xvii. 4: *Thou shalt be a father of many nations—and all the nations of the earth shall be blessed in him,* xviii. 18. Thus this clause is to be understood; and thus it is an argument to prove that all things, how afflictive soever, shall work for our good while we continue to love God. Our being *called* or *invited,* according to God's *purpose,* proves that all things work for our good, on the supposition *that we love God,* and not otherwise. For our *loving God,* or making a due improvement of our calling, is evidently inserted by the apostle to make good his argument. He does not pretend to prove that all things shall concur to the everlasting happiness of *all* that are *called;* but only to those of the called *who love God.* Our calling, thus qualified is the ground of his argument, which he prosecutes and completes in the two next verses. Our *calling* he takes for granted, as a thing evident and unquestionable among all Christians. But you will say: How is it evident and unquestionable that we are *called?* I answer: From our being in the visible Church, and professing the faith of the Gospel. For always, in the apostolic writings, all that are in the visible Church, and profess the faith of the Gospel, are numbered among the *called* or *invited;* i. e. among the persons who are invited to feast on the covenant sacrifice, and who thus, in reference to themselves, confirm and ratify the covenant. As for what is termed *effectual calling,* as distinguished from the general invitations of the Gospel, it is a distinction which divines have invented without any warrant from the sacred writings. Our calling, therefore, is considered by the apostle in the nature of a self-evident proposition, which nobody doubts or denies; or which, indeed, no Christian ought to doubt, or can call in question. *Taylor's* notes.

Verse 29. *For whom he did foreknow, &c.*] "In this and the following verse the apostle shows *how* our *calling* is an argument that all things work together to advance our eternal happiness, by showing the several *steps* which the wisdom and goodness of God have settled, in order to complete our salvation. In order to this he first gives us, in this verse, the *foundation* and *finishing,* or the *beginning* and *end,* of the scheme of our redemption: *For whom God did foreknow, he also did predestinate to be conformed to the image of his Son.* To *foreknow,* here signifies to *design before,* or at the first forming of the scheme; to bestow the *favour* and *privilege* of being God's people upon any set of men, chap. xi. 2. This is the

A. M. cir. 4062.
A. D. cir. 58.
An. Olymp.
cir. CCIX. 2.
A. U. C. cir.
811.

30 Moreover whom he did predestinate, them he also ^d called: and whom he called, them he also ^e justified: and whom he justified, them he also ^f glorified.

31 What shall we then say to these things? ^g If God *be*

A. M. cir. 4062.
A. D. cir. 58.
An. Olymp.
cir. CCIX. 2.
A. U. C. cir.
811.

---

^d Chap. i. 6; ix. 24; Eph. iv. 4; Hebrews ix. 15; 1 Pet. ii. 9.
^e 1 Cor. vi. 11.

^f John xvii. 22; Ephesians ii. 6.——^g Numbers xiv. 9; Psalms cxviii. 6.

---

foundation or first step of our salvation; namely, the *purpose* and *grace of God,* which was given us in Christ Jesus, before the world began, 2 Tim. i. 9. Then, he *knew* or *favoured* us; for in this sense the word *to know* is taken in a great variety of places, both in the Old and New Testaments. And as he *knew* the GENTILES *then,* when the scheme was laid, and before any part of it was executed, consequently, in reference to the execution of this scheme, he *foreknew* us. This is the first step of our salvation, and the *end* .or *finishing* of it is our *conformity to the Son of God in eternal glory,* ver. 17, which includes and supposes our *moral* conformity to him. When God *knew* us, at the forming of the Gospel scheme; or, when he intended to bestow on us the privilege of being his people; he then *destinated* or designed us to be conformed to the image of his Son; and, as he *destinated* or *determined* us then to this very high honour and happiness, he *pre-destinated, fore-ordained,* or *pre-determined* us to it. Thus we are to understand the foundation and finishing of the scheme of our salvation. The *foundation* is the *foreknowledge,* or *gracious* purpose of God; the *finishing* is our being joint heirs with Christ. Now, our *calling* or *invitation* (see on ver. 28) stands in connection with both these. 1. It stands in connection with God's *foreknowledge;* and so it is a true and valid calling: for we are *called, invited,* or *chosen according to the foreknowledge of God the Father,* who may bestow his blessings upon any people, as may seem good in his sight, 1 Pet. i. 2; consequently, we have a good title to the blessings of the Gospel to which we are *called* or *invited.* And this was to be proved, that the Jew, to whom the apostle particularly wrote, might see that the Gentiles being now called into the Church of God was not an accidental thing, but a matter which God had determined when he conceived the Gospel scheme. Thus our calling is connected with God's *foreknowledge.* 2. It stands also in connection with our being *conformed to the image of his Son;* for we are *invited* by the Gospel to the obtaining of the glory of our Lord Jesus Christ, 2 Thess. ii. 14. And therefore, supposing, what the apostle supposes, that we *love God,* it is certain, from our being *called,* that we shall be *glorified* with the sons of God; and so our calling proves the point, that all things should work together for our good in our present state, because it proves that we are intended for eternal glory; as he shows in the next verse. For we must understand his *foreknowing, predestinating, calling,* and *justifying,* in relation to his *glorifying;* and that none are finally *glorified,* but those who, according .to his *purpose,* are *conformed to the image of his Son.*" *Taylor.*

The first-born among many brethren.] That he might be the chief or head of all the redeemed; for HIS *human nature* is the first fruits of the resurrection from the dead; and He is the first human being that, after having passed through death, was raised to eternal glory. See Dr. *Taylor.*

Verse 30. *Whom he did predestinate, &c.*] The *Gentiles,* whom He determined to call into his Church with the Jewish people, *He called*—He invited by the preaching of the Gospel, to believe on his Son Jesus Christ. It is worthy of note, that all that is spoken here refers to what *had already taken place;* for the *calling, justifying,* and *glorifying* are represented as having *already taken place,* as well as the *foreknowing* and the *predestinating.* It is therefore reasonable to suppose that the apostle refers to what God had *already done* among the Jews and Gentiles: though he may also speak of the things that *were not* as though they *were.*

He also justified] Pardoned the sins of all those who with hearty repentance and true faith turned unto him.

He also glorified.] He has *honoured* and *dignified* the Gentiles with the highest privileges, and he *has* already taken many of them to the kingdom of glory, and many more are on their way thither; and all who *love him,* and continue faithful unto death, shall inherit that glory eternally. Hence it is added, *them he also glorified;* for all the honours which he confers on them have respect to and are intended to promote their endless felicity; and though the terms are here used in a more general sense, yet, if we take them more restrictedly, we must consider that in the work of justification *sanctification* is implied; justification being the foundation and beginning of that work. From all this we learn that none will be *glorified* who have not been *sanctified* and *justified;* that the *justified* are those who have been *called* or *invited* by the Gospel of Christ; that those who have had this *calling* are they to whom God *determined* to grant this privilege—*they* did not choose this salvation first, but God sent it to them when they knew him not—and therefore the salvation of the Gentile world, as well as that of the Jews, comes through the gratuitous mercy of God himself, was the result of infinite designs, and stands on the same ground as the calling, &c., of the Jewish people. The word δοξα, which we render *glory,* and δοξαζω, to *glorify,* both mean to *render illustrious, eminent,* &c., &c., in various parts of the New Testament; and in this sense the verb is used John xi. 4; xii. 23, 28; xiii. 31, 32; xiv. 13; xv 8; xxi. 19; Acts iii. 13; and in chapter xi. 13; in none of which places *eternal beatification* can be intended. Here it seems to mean that those whom God had called into a state of justification he had rendered *illustrious* by innumerable gifts, graces, and privileges, in the same manner as he had done to the Israelites of old.

A. M. cir. 4062.
A. D. cir. 58.
An. Olymp.
cir. CCIX. 2.
A. U. C. cir.
811.

for us, who *can be* against us?

32 [h] He that spared not his own Son, but [i] delivered him up for us all, how shall he not with

him also freely give us all things?

33 Who shall lay any thing to the charge of God's elect? [k] *It is* God that justifieth.

A. M. cir. 4062.
A. D. cir. 58.
An. Olymp.
cir. CCIX. 2.
A. U. C. cir.
811.

[h] Chap. v. 6, 10.——[i] Chap. iv. 25.

[k] Isa. l. 8, 9; Rev. xii. 10, 11.

The whole of the preceding discourse will show that every thing here is *conditional*, as far as it relates to the ultimate salvation of any person professing the Gospel of Christ; for the promises are made to *character*, and not to *persons*, as some have most injudiciously affirmed. The apostle insists upon a *character* all along from the beginning of the chapter. Verse 1: *There is no condemnation to them that are in Christ Jesus, who walk not after the flesh, but after the Spirit.* Ver. 13: *If ye live after the flesh, ye shall die*, &c. The absolute necessity of *holiness* to salvation is the very *subject* of his discourse; this necessity he positively affirms, and establishes by the most solid arguments. At the very entrance of his argument here, he takes care to settle the connection between our *calling* and our love and obedience to God, on purpose to prevent that mistake into which so many have fallen, through their great inattention to the *scope* of his reasoning. Ver. 28: *All things work together for good*—To whom? *To* THEM *that* LOVE GOD: *to them that are the called according to his purpose.* To *them that love God*, because they are called according to his purpose; for those only who love God can reap any benefit by this *predestination*, vocation, or any other instance of God's favour. See the *observations* at the end of this chapter.

Verse 31. *What shall we then say to these things?*] What conclusion should we draw from the above premises? From all that was already laid down in the preceding chapters, but especially in the preceding verses, from verse 28 to 30 inclusive. As if he had said: What comfort may we derive from these doctrines? God has called us all to *holiness*, and to *love to him*, which is the principle of holiness. We are persecuted and despised, it is true, and we may be more so; but, as God has called us to love him, *and all things work together for good to them that love him;* and, as his covenant with Abraham, while he was in his *Gentile* state, shows his gracious *purpose* towards us *Gentiles*, whom he has foreknown, who have been objects of his *gracious foreknowledge*, as well as the *Jews*, and who have now the fullest proof that we were so, by his sending us the *Gospel*, and showing us, in it, that if the Israelites were to be a *holy priesthood*, a *royal nation*, we are no less favoured, as he has *predestinated*, from the *beginning determined*, that *we should be conformed to the image of his Son*, who is to be the *first-born among many brethren*, the head and *chief* of all *converted Jews* and *Gentiles*, and, in order to our final salvation, has *called*, invited us to believe on the Lord Jesus Christ, has *justified* those who do believe, and has *glorified*, highly *honoured*, and *adorned* them with *innumerable gifts and graces*, and, if they continue to possess that faith which worketh by love, will bring them, both *body* and *soul*,

to his *eternal glory*, their *bodies being made like unto his glorious body*:—seeing, therefore, all these things are so, what comfort in our tribulations shall we derive from them?—Why this: *If God be for us, who* can *be against us?* He who is infinitely *wise* has undertaken to *direct us:* He who is infinitely *powerful* has undertaken to *protect* us: He who is infinitely *good* has undertaken to *save* us. What *cunning, strength,* or *malice,* can prevail against his *wisdom, power,* and *goodness?* None. Therefore we are safe who love God; and not only shall sustain no essential damage by the persecutions of ungodly men, but even these things work together for our good.

Verse 32. *He that spared not his own Son*] And can we, his sincere followers, doubt of the safety of our state, or the certainty of his protection? No: for if he loved us, Gentiles and Jews, so intensely as to *deliver up* to death his own Son *for us all,* can he withhold from us any minor blessing? Nay, will he not, on the contrary, *freely give us all things?* For if he told Abraham, who is the father of the *faithful*, and representative of *us all*, and with whom the covenant was made, that, because he had not withheld from him *his* only son Isaac, but *delivered him up to that death* which he thought his God had required, in blessing, he would bless him; and in multiplying, he would multiply him; that his seed should possess the gate of his enemies; and that in it all the nations of the earth should be blessed, Gen. xxii. 16—19; will HE not give us all that was spiritually intended by these promises, whose only begotten Son was not sacrificed in a *figure*, but *really*, in order to purchase every blessing that the soul of man can need and that the hand of God can dispense.

Verse 33. This and the two following verses contain a string of questions, most appropriately introduced and most powerfully urged, tending to show the safety of the state of those who have believed the Gospel of the grace of God. I shall lay these verses down as they are pointed by the best Greek critics:—

"Who shall lay any thing to the charge of God's elect?—God who justifieth? Who is he that condemneth?—Christ who died? or, rather, who is risen again? He, who is at the right hand of God? He, who maketh intercession for us? Who shall separate us from the love of Christ?—Tribulation? or distress? or persecution? or famine? or nakedness? or peril? or sword?" In all these questions the apostle intimates that if neither GOD nor CHRIST *would* bring any charge against them who love him, none else *could*. And as God justifies through Christ who died, consequently no charge *can* lie against these persons, as God alone could produce any; and He, so far from doing this, has justified them—freely forgiven their trespasses.

2

A. M. cir. 4062.
A. D. cir. 58.
An. Olymp.
cir. CCIX. 2.
A. U. C. cir.
811.

34 ¹Who *is* he that condemn-eth? *It is* Christ that died, yea rather, that is risen again, ᵐ who is even at the right hand of God, ⁿ who also maketh intercession for us.

35 Who shall separate us from the love of Christ? *shall* tribulation, or distress, or perse-cution, or famine, or nakedness, or peril, or sword?

36 As it is written, ° For thy sake we are

killed all the day long; we are ac-counted as sheep for the slaughter.

37 ᵖ Nay, in all these things we are more than conquerors through him that loved us.

A. M. cir. 4062
A. D. cir. 58.
An. Olymp.
cir. CCIX. 2.
A. U. C. cir.
811.

38 For I am persuaded, that neither death, nor life, nor angels, nor �q principalities, nor pow-ers, nor things present, nor things to come,

39 Nor height, nor depth, nor any other crea-ture, shall be able to separate us from the love of God, which is in Christ Jesus our Lord.

¹ Job xxxiv. 29.——ᵐ Mark xvi. 19; Col. iii. 1; Heb. i. 3; viii. 1; xii. 1; 1 Pet. iii. 22.——ⁿ Heb. vii. 25; ix. 24; 1 John ii. 1.

° Psa. xliv. 22; 1 Cor. xv. 30, 31; 2 Cor. iv. 11.——ᵖ 1 Cor xv. 57; 2 Cor. ii. 14; 1 John iv. 4; v. 4, 5; Revelation xii. 11. q Eph. i. 21; vi. 12; Col. i. 16; ii. 15; 1 Pet. iii. 22.

For the proper meaning and sense of the terms *chosen, elect, called,* &c., &c., see the discourse pre-fixed to this epistle; and especially sect. vi. p. 19, &c., and sect. vii. p. 23, &c.

Verse 34. *Who is even at the right hand of God*] To which he has exalted our human nature, which he took in conjunction with his Divinity; and there he *maketh intercession for us*—manages all the concerns of his own kingdom in general, and of every member of his Church in particular.

Verse 35. *Who shall separate us from the love of Christ?*] I do think that this question has been gene-rally misunderstood. The apostle is referring to the persecutions and tribulations to which genuine Chris-tians were exposed through their attachment to Christ, and the gracious provision God had made for their support and final salvation. As in this provision God had shown his infinite love to them in providing Jesus Christ as their sin-offering, and Jesus Christ had shown his love in suffering death upon the cross for them; so, here, he speaks of the love of the *followers* of God to that Christ who had first loved *them*. There-fore the question is not, Who shall separate the love of Christ from us? or prevent Christ from loving us? but, Who shall separate *us* from the love of Christ? *Who* or *what* shall be able to remove *our affection* from him? And the questions that immediately follow show that this is the sense of the passage; for the *tribula-tion, distress, &c.,* which he enumerates, are things by which *they* might be affected, but by which *Christ* could not be affected; and, consequently, the question most evidently refers to *their love to him* who had first loved them, and, while it affords a strong *presumption* of their *perseverance,* furnishes a most powerful argument against *apostasy.*

Shall *tribulation?*] Θλιψις, grievous affliction, or distress of any kind . from θλιβω, to compress, oppress, straiten, &c.; any thing by which a man is rendered miserable.

Or distress?] Στενοχωρια, a word of nearly the same import with the former, but more *intense* in its signi-fication. It signifies *straitness,* being *hemmed in* on every side, without the possibility of getting out or escaping; from στενος, *strait* or *narrow,* and χωρος, a *place.*

Or persecution?] Διωγμος, from διωκω, to *pursue,*

press upon, prosecute, signifies such *pursuing* as an enemy uses in order to overtake the object of his malice, that he may destroy him.

Or famine?] Λιμος, from λειπω, to *fail;* the total want of bread, and all the necessaries of life.

Or nakedness?] Γυμνοτης, being absolutely without clothing; forcibly expressed by the derivation of the word γυια μονα εχων, *having one's limbs only,* being totally *unclothed.*

Or peril?] Κινδυνος, a state of extreme and continued danger, perplexing and distressing with grievous fore-bodings and alarms; derived from κινει τας οδυνας, *it excites anguish;* because much evil is *felt,* and much more *feared.*

Or sword?] Μαχαιρα, *slaughter;* the total destruc-tion of life, and especially *beheading,* and such like, done by the order of the civil magistrate; for the word is used in this epistle, chap. xiii. 4, to signify the *au-thority* and *power* which he has of judicially terminating life; i. e. of inflicting *capital punishment.*

Verse 36. *As it is written*] And these are no more than we may naturally expect from the present con-stitution of the world, and the positive predictions of the prophet, Psa. xliv. 22, who foresaw that a wicked world would always persecute and oppress the true followers of God.

Verse 37. *Nay*] as the prophet adds in the same place, *all this is come upon us, yet have we not for gotten thee, nor dealt falsely in thy covenant,* verses 17, 18, so all these things may happen unto us; but *in all these things we are more than conquerors;* WE abide faithful in the new covenant of our God; and HE is faithful who has promised to support and make us more than conquerors; i. e. to give us a complete *triumph* over sin, and death, and hell, not leaving one enemy unsubdued.

Verse 38. *For I am persuaded*] After the blessed experience we have had of support by the grace and Spirit of him that loved us, that neither fear of *death,* nor hope of *life,* nor evil *angels, nor principalities, nor powers,* persecuting us for Christ's sake; nor the *things* we endure at *present, nor* the *things to come,* whatever tribulation we may be called to suffer in future;

Verse 39. Nor *height*—of honour, nor *depth*—of ignominy, *nor any other creature,* ουτε τις κτισις ετερα, (nor any other thing whatever,) *shall be able to sepa-*

rate us, who love God, *from the love of God, which* he has vouchsafed to us *in Christ Jesus.* See *Whitby.* And for farther observations on the subject of the 29th and 30th verses, see at the end of the chapter.

1. THE confidence expressed by the apostle at the end of this chapter, is as *rational* as it is *bold.* On the *premises* laid down by him, in reference to which he has most logically conducted his whole argument, the *conclusion* to which he arrives is as natural and forcible as it is legitimate. The permanency of the Christian Church, in all the tribulations it has endured from pagans and papists, is a full proof of the correctness of the apostle's reasoning. The true followers of Christ can never be forsaken by him. And his Church, which is founded on the rock, can never be shaken down by the tempests of persecution. And what God does for his *Church* in general, (the collective body of those who believe in the Lord Jesus, love, and obey him,) he does for every *individual* in that body : no man that trusts in him can be confounded. While the *love of God* is in his *heart,* and the *work of God* in his *hand,* he may be as fully *persuaded* as he is of his own being, that *neither death, nor life, nor angels, nor principalities, nor powers, nor things present, nor things to come, nor height, nor depth, nor any other thing whatsoever, shall be able to separate him from the love of God which is in Christ Jesus.* The reader who has any knowledge of what is *great, commanding,* and *sublime* in composition, will not hesitate to add here, with Dr. Taylor : " The conclusion of this chapter is the most elegant and sublime piece of writing I remember ever to have read. It is founded on the grand and solid principles of the Gospel ; it breathes the true spirit of Christian magnanimity ; raises our minds far above all things created ; and shows, in a bright and heavenly view, the greatness of soul and the strong consolation which the Gospel inspires. God grant that it may stand clear before our understandings, and be transcribed into all our hearts ! They who despise the *Gospel* despise all that is *great,* and *happy,* and *glorious !"*

2. The doctrine of the necessity of personal holiness, so clearly and strongly laid down in the former part of this chapter, should be deeply considered by every person professing godliness ; and while from the seventh chapter they learn that they have an infected and morally diseased nature, they should learn from the eighth that to destroy the work of the devil was Jesus Christ manifested ; and that no soul can be said to be saved by Jesus Christ who is not saved from its sins. What a full proof is it of the fallen state of man, that there should be found persons professing Christianity more fervent in their pleadings for the *necessary* continuance of indwelling sin, than they are for the mind that was in Christ. The *seventh* chapter, because there are some expressions which, being misunderstood, seem to favour this doctrine, is read and incessantly quoted : the eighth chapter, though given by the same inspiration, yet because it so strongly shows the necessity of being saved from all sin, is seldom read and scarcely ever quoted !

3. The restoration of the brute creation to a state of happiness has been thought by several to be the doctrine of verses 19-25. In the notes on those verses I have given reasons against this opinion, and have proved that the *Gentiles,* and not the irrational part of the creation, are the persons of whom the apostle speaks ; nor can any consistent interpretation be given of the place, if it be applied to the brute creation. But, although this doctrine is not contained in the above verses, it does not follow that the doctrine itself is not true. Indeed, there are several reasons which render the supposition very probable. 1. The brute creation never sinned against God, nor are they capable of it, and consequently cannot be justly liable to punishment. 2. But the whole brute creation is in a state of suffering, and partake of the common infirmities and privations of life, as well as mankind : they suffer, but who can say that they suffer *justly ?* 3. As they appear to be necessarily involved in the sufferings of sinful man, and yet neither through their fault nor their folly, it is natural to suppose that the Judge of all the earth, who ever does right, will find some means by which these innocent creatures shall be compensated for their sufferings. 4. That they have no compensation *here,* their afflictions, labours, and death prove ; and if they are to have any compensation, they must have it in *another state.* 5. God, the fountain of all goodness, must have originally designed them for that measure of happiness which is suited to the powers with which he had endowed them ; but, since the fall of man, they never had that happiness ; and, in their present circumstances, never can. 6. In reference to *intelligent* beings, God has formed his purposes in reference to their happiness on the ground of their rational natures. He has decreed that they shall be happy *if they will,* all the means of it being placed within their power ; and, if they be ultimately miserable, it is the effect of their own unconstrained choice. Therefore his purpose is fulfilled, either in their happiness or misery ; because he has purposed that they shall be happy if they please, and that misery shall be the result of their refusal. 7. But it does not appear that the brute creation are capable of this choice ; and it is evident that they are not placed in their present misery through either their *choice* or their *sin ;* and if no purpose of God can be ultimately frustrated, these creatures must be restored to that state of happiness for which they have been made, and of which they have been deprived through the transgression of man. 8. To say that the enjoyments which they have in this life are a sufficient compensation, is most evidently false ; for, had not sin entered into the world, they would have had much greater enjoyments, without pain, excessive labour and toil, and without death, and all those sufferings which arise from its predisposing causes. Nor does it appear that they have much happiness from eating, drinking, and rest, as they have these only in the proportion in which they are necessary to their existence as the slaves of men. Therefore, allowing that they have even gratification and enjoyment in life, they have much less than they would have had had not sin entered into the world ; and consequently they have been deprived of the greater portion of the happiness designed for them by their bountiful Creator. 9. It is therefore obvious that the gracious purpose of

2

God has not been fulfilled in them ; and that, as they have not lost their happiness through their own fault, both the beneficence and justice of God are bound to make them a reparation. 10. Hence it is reasonable to conclude that, as from the present constitution of things they cannot have the happiness designed for them in *this state*, they must have it in *another*.

4. On the subject of the *foreknowledge* of God, some observations have been made at the conclusion of the notes on the second chapter of Acts. On the subject of the *prescience* and *predestination* mentioned here, verses 29 and 30, vast volumes have been written, and the Christian world greatly agitated and perplexed. These doctrines of men have very little place in the texts in question. After a long and serious investigation of this business, I am led to conclude that, whether the doctrine of the *decrees* be true or false, it does not exist in these verses:

No portion of the word of God has been more unhappily misunderstood than several parts of the Epistle to the Romans; because men have applied to *individuals* what belongs to *nations ;* and referred to *eternity* transactions which have taken place in *time*.

We have already seen that one grand aim of the apostle in writing this epistle was : 1. To prove, to both Jews and Gentiles, that they were all under sin, and that neither of them had any claim either on the justice or beneficence of God; yet he, of his own free mercy, had revealed himself to the Jews, and crowned them with innumerable privileges ; and, 2. That, as he was no respecter of persons, his mercy was as free to the *Gentiles* as to them, being equally their God as he was the God of the Jews, and therefore had, by the Gospel, called them to a state of salvation; and to this display of his mercy the two verses in question seem particularly to refer, and show us not what God *will* do for some selected individuals, but what he *has already done* for nations.

After having shown that the whole Gentile world was groaning and travailing in pain together, waiting for the manifestation of the sons of God, he shows that it was, according to the *affectionate purpose*, προθεσιν, of God, that' the Gentiles should be also *called* into the glorious liberty of the sons of God— into equal privileges with the Jews. He therefore represents them as objects of God's *gracious foreknowledge.* That the word προγινωσκω, which literally signifies to *know*, or *discern beforehand*, and *to know so as to determine*, signifies also to *approve*, or *love before*, *to be well affected to*, is not only evident from יֽרֽ *yada* in Hebrew, but also from the simple verb γινωσκω, in Greek, by which it is translated, and to which the compound verb repeatedly answers, without any *extension* of meaning by means of the *preposition*, as its use among the best Greek writers proves : and it is evident that the apostle uses the word in the sense of *loving, being graciously affected to*, in chap. xi. 1, 2. *I say then, hath God cast away his people, which he* FOREKNEW, *ὃν προεγνω ; to whom he has been so long graciously affected ? By no means.* As, therefore, he had been so long graciously affected towards the Jews, so has he towards the Gentiles. His call of Abraham, and the promises made to him, are the proofs of it. The Jews, thus *foreknown*, were

called into a glorious state of salvation, and endowed with privileges the most extraordinary ever bestowed on any people ; as their whole history testifies. But is God the God of the Jews only ? Is he not also the God of the Gentiles ? Yes, of the Gentiles also, chap. iii. 29 ; and to prove this is the main subject of the *ninth* chapter. Now, as he is the God of the Gentiles, he *foreknew*, had from the beginning a *gracious purpose* to them as well as to the Jews ; and, being thus graciously disposed towards them, he determined προωρισε, from προ, before, and ὁριζω, to *bound, define*, &c., he defined, circumscribed, and determined the boundaries of this important business from the beginning, that they also should be taken into his Church, and conformed to the image of his Son ; and, as Jesu Christ was to be their *pattern*, it must be by his *Gospel* that they should be brought into the·Church ; and consequently,· *that* bringing in could not take place *before* the revelation of Christ. Having therefore thus foreknown and thus predestinated *them* ALSO, he *called* them ALSO by the Gospel ; he *justified* them ALSO on their believing ; and he *glorified* them ALSO, dignified them also with the same privileges, blessings, honours, and Divine gifts : so that they were now what the Jews had been before, *the peculiar people of God*. The apostle, therefore, speaks here not of what they *should be*, or of what they *might be*, but of what they *then were*—the *called*, the *justified*, the highly *honoured* of God. See the note on ver. 30.

It is strange that so obvious a meaning of the passage should not have been noticed ; but the word δοξαζω, which we render *to glorify*, and by which we understand *eternal beatification*, which it is very seldom used to express, being taken in this sense in the passage in question, fixed the meaning of the preceding terms ; and thus the whole passage was applied to things *eternal*, which had reference only to things in time. This seems to me to be the true key of the passage, and the whole scope of the epistle, and especially of the context, which shows that this is the sense in which it should be understood. The passages understood in this way illustrate the infinite mercy and wisdom of God ; they show that whatever appearances his providential dealings may assume of partiality towards any particular people, yet he is equally the Father of the spirits of all flesh ; hateth nothing that he hath made ; is loving to all ; that his tender mercies are over all his works ; and that he is not willing that any should perish, but that all should come unto the knowledge of the truth and be saved. Hence, whatever he did for the Jews he purposed to do for the Gentiles : if he foreknew, predestinated, called, justified, and glorified the *former ;* he ALSO foreknew, predestinated, called, justified, and glorified the latter ; having brought them into the same state of salvation, with a vast extension of blessings and higher degrees of honour. As the Jews forfeited their privileges, and now, instead of being glorified, instead of being highly honoured, and rendered illustrious, they are degraded, brought down, and rendered contemptible; because they have not made a proper use of their election, they are now reprobated ; so a similar reverse awaits the Gentiles if they sin after the similitude of their transgression ; and it is against this that

2

the apostle so solemnly warns them, chap. xi. 20–22 : *Because of unbelief they* (the Jews) *were broken off— thou* (the Gentiles) *standest by faith. If God spared not the* NATURAL BRANCHES, *take heed lest he also spare not* THEE. *Behold the goodness and severity of God! on them which* FELL *severity ; but toward* THEE *goodness,* IF THOU CONTINUE *in his goodness ; otherwise* THOU ALSO *shalt be* CUT OFF.

5. This is also a lesson of solemn instruction to *Christians in general :* God has called them into a glorious state of salvation, and has furnished them with every requisite help to enable them to work out that salvation with fear and trembling. As it is an awful thing to receive the grace of God in vain, (whether that grace imply the common benefits of the Gospel, or those especial blessings received by believing souls,) so every person professing godliness should be jealous over himself lest he should trifle with matters of eternal moment ; for, should he even *neglect* so great a salvation, his escape would be impossible. Heb. ii. 3 ; and if so, to what severe punishment must they be exposed who *despise* and *reject* it ?

CHAPTER IX.

Paul expresses his great sorrow for the unbelief and obstinacy of the Jews, 1–3. Whose high privileges he enumerates, 4, 5. Points out the manner in which God has chosen to communicate the knowledge of his name to both Jews and Gentiles ; and how he deals, whether in judgment or mercy, with individuals ; and produces the cases of Abraham, Isaac, Jacob, Esau, and Pharaoh, 6–17. God shows mercy and judgment as he thinks proper, and none have a right to find fault with his proceedings, 18–20. He has the same power over the human race as the potter has over the clay, 21–23. The prophets predicted the calling of the Gentiles, and the rejection of the Jews, 24–29. The Gentiles have attained to the knowledge of God's method of saving sinners ; while the Jews have not attained this knowledge, 30, 31. The reason why the Jews have not attained the salvation provided for them in the Gospel, 32, 33.

A. M. cir. 4062.
A. D. cir. 58.
An. Olymp.
cir. CCIX. 2.
A. U. C. cir.
811.

I [a] SAY the truth in Christ, I lie not, my conscience also bearing me witness in the Holy Ghost,

2 [b] That I have great heaviness and continual sorrow in my heart.

3 For [c] I could wish that my-

A. M. cir. 4062.
A. D. cir. 58.
An. Olymp.
cir. CCIX. 2.
A. U. C. cir.
811.

---

[a] Chap. i. 9 ; 2 Cor. i. 23 ; xi. 31 ; xii. 19.

[b] Chap. x. 1.——[c] Exod xxxii. 32.

NOTES ON CHAP. IX.

To this and the tenth chapter, Dr. Taylor has prefixed the following judicious summary :—

The apostle has largely proved in the preceding chapters, that the *grace of God* extends to the *Gentiles* as well as to the *Jews* ; and that the dispensation of God's mercy was absolutely, and in itself, free to all who believe, whether Jews or Gentiles, in opposition to the merit of any works, or of conformity to any law whatever ; and that the Gentiles have, by *faith*, a good title to the blessings of God's covenant, to which blessings the Jews cannot have a title any other way. Hitherto the apostle has not considered the Jews as *rejected*, except in an indirect way, but that they had the possibility of continuing in the Church, from entering into which they should not attempt to prevent the Gentiles, but allow them to be sharers in the mercies of God ; and hence his language is in sum this : Why may not believing Gentiles be admitted, pardoned, and saved, as well as you ?

But in this chapter, and the two following, the apostle considers the reception of the Gentiles into the kingdom and covenant of God under the notion of *calling* or *invitation*, and of *election* or *choice :* which shows that he views the two parties in a light different to that in which he had before placed them. The *Gentiles* he considers as *invited* into the kingdom of God, and as *chosen* to be his people ; and the *Jews* he considers as *left out* and *rejected ;* for as the main body of them had now rejected the Gospel of Christ, he saw that God was about to unchurch them, over-

turn their polity, destroy their temple, and disperse them over the face of the earth. Thus he knew they would be accursed, or anathematized from Christ, and reduced to a level with the heathen nations of the world. And the event has proved that his declarations were dictated by the Spirit of truth.

It is observable that, agreeably to his delicate manner of writing, and his nice and tender treatment of his countrymen, he never mentions their *rejection*— a subject extremely painful to his thoughts—otherwise than in a *wish* that he *himself were accursed from Christ* for them, or to prevent them from being accursed from Christ, (ix. 3,) till he comes to chap. xi., where he has much to say in their favour, even considered, as at present, rejected. But it is very evident that his arguments in this chapter rest on the supposition that the main body of the Jewish nation would be cast out of the visible kingdom of God ; and it is for this reason that in this and the two following chapters he considers the reception of any people into the kingdom and covenant of God under the relative notion of *inviting* and *choosing,* or of *calling* and *election.* The Jews were *rejected* and *reprobated ;* the Gentiles were *chosen* and *called,* or *elected.* As this is most obviously the apostle's meaning, it is strange that any should apply his doctrine to the particular and unconditional reprobation and election of *individuals.*

It is upon this *rejection* of the *Jews* that the *calling* and *election* of the *Gentiles* rest. If the Jews be not rejected, but are still the visible Church and kingdom of God, then the *Gentiles,* according to the most proper

A. M. cir. 4062.
A. D. cir. 58.
An. Olymp.
cir. CCIX. 2.
A. U. C. cir.
811.

self were ^d accursed from Christ for my brethren, my kinsmen according to the flesh :

4 ^e Who are Israelites ; ^f to

whom *pertaineth* the adoption, and ^g the glory, and the ^h ⁱ covenants, and ^k the giving of the law, and ^l the service

A. M. cir. 4062
A. D. cir. 58.
An. Olymp.
cir. CCIX. 2.
A. U. C. cir.
811.

---

^d Or, *separated.*——^e Deut. vii. 6.——^f Exod. iv. 22 ; Deut. xiv. 1 ; Jer. xxxi. 9.——^g 1 Sam. iv. 21 ; 1 Kings iii. 11 ; Psa. lxiii. 2 ; lxxviii. 61.——^h Acts iii. 25 ; Heb. viii. 8, 9, 10.——ⁱ Or, *testaments.*——^k Psa. cxlvii. 19.——^l Heb. ix. 1.

---

inference from the apostle's doctrine, have no right to the blessings of the kingdom. Instead of being *invited* or *called*, they are intruders at the heavenly *feast ;* and this the unbelieving Jews laboured to prove, and thus unhinge the believing Gentiles by persuading them that they were not duly taken into the Church of God ; that the Jews were, and ever must continue to be, the *only* Church and kingdom of God, and that they could not be cast off so long as God was *faithful to his promise* to Abraham ; and that the Gentiles were most miserably deceived when they supposed they were brought into that kingdom by faith in Christ, whereas there was no way of entering it, or of being entitled to its privileges, but by *submitting to the law of Moses.* This being the fixed opinion of the Jews, and the ground on which they opposed the Gentiles and endeavoured to sap the foundation of their hope of salvation from the Gospel of Christ, it was therefore a matter of the utmost importance to be able to prove that the Jews, by rejecting Christ and his Gospel, were themselves cast out of the Church, and this in a way perfectly consistent with the truth of the promise made to Abraham. He had slightly touched on this subject at the beginning of the third chapter ; but it would have broken in too much on the thread of his discourse to have pursued the argument there, for which reason he appears to have reserved it to this place, where he (1) Solemnly declares his tenderest affection for his countrymen, and his real grief of heart for their infidelity and consequent rejection, ver. 1–5 ; (2) Answers objections against this rejection, ver. 6–23 ; (3) Proves the *calling of the Gentiles* from their own *Scriptures,* ver. 24–30 ; (4) Gives the true state and reasons of the *rejection* of the Jews and the *calling* of the Gentiles, ver. 30 to ver. 14 of chap. x. ; (5) Proves the necessity of the apostolic mission to the Gentiles in order to their salvation, chap. x. 14 to the end.

And all this was intended at once to vindicate the Divine dispensations ; to convince the infidel Jew ; to satisfy the believing Gentile that his *calling* or *invitation* into the Church of God was *valid ;* to arm him against the cavils and objections of the unbelieving Jews, and to dispose the Christian Jew to receive and own the believing Gentile as a member of the family and kingdom of God, by Divine right, equal to any to which he himself could pretend. See Taylor's notes, p. 321, &c.

Verse 1. *I say the truth in Christ, I lie not*] This is one of the most solemn oaths any man can possibly take. He appeals to Christ as the searcher of hearts that he tells the truth ; asserts that his conscience was free from all guile in this matter, and that the Holy Ghost bore him testimony that what he said was true. Hence we find that the *testimony* of a man's *own conscience,* and the *testimony* of the *Holy Ghost,* are two

distinct things, and that the apostle had *both* at the same time.

As the apostle had still remaining a very awful part of his commission to execute, namely, to declare to the Jews not only that God had *chosen the Gentiles,* but had *rejected them* because they had rejected Christ and his Gospel, it was necessary that he should assure them that however he had been persecuted by them because he had embraced the Gospel, yet it was so far from being a gratification to him that they had now fallen under the displeasure of God, that it was a subject of continual distress to his mind, and that it produced in him *great heaviness and continual sorrow.*

Verse 3. *For I could wish that myself were accursed from Christ*] This and the two preceding verses are thus paraphrased by Dr. Taylor : I am so far from insisting on the doctrine (of the rejection of the Jews) out of any ill-will to my countrymen, that I solemnly declare, in the sincerity of my heart, without the least fiction or dissimulation—and herein I have the testimony of my own conscience, enlightened and directed by the Spirit of God—that I am so far from taking pleasure in the rejection of the Jewish nation, that, contrariwise, it gives me continual pain and uneasiness, insomuch that, as Moses formerly (when God proposed to cut them off, and in their stead to make *him* a great nation, Exod. xxxii. 10) begged that he himself should rather die than that the children of Israel should be destroyed, ver. 32, so I could even wish that the exclusion from the visible Church, which will happen to the Jewish nation, might fall to my own share, if hereby *they* might be kept in it ; and to this I am inclined by natural affection, for the Jews are my dear brethren and kindred.

Very few passages in the New Testament have puzzled critics and commentators more than this. Every person saw the perfect absurdity of understanding it in a literal sense, as no man in his right mind could wish himself eternally damned in order to save another, or to save even the whole world. And the supposition that such an effect could be produced by such a sacrifice, was equally absurd and monstrous. Therefore various translations have been made of the place, and different solutions offered. Mr. Wakefield says : "I see no method of solving the difficulty in this verse, which has so exercised the learning and ingenuity of commentators, but by the ευχομαι ειναι of Homer, *I profess myself to be ;* and he translates the passage in a parenthesis, thus : (*for I also was once an alien from Christ*) *on account of my brethren,* &c. But how it does appear that Saul of Tarsus was ever an alien from Christ *on account of his kinsmen,* is to me perfectly indiscernible. Let us examine the Greek text. Ηυχομην γαρ αυτος εγω αναθεμα ειναι απο του Χριστου υπερτων αδελφων μου, ' For I did wish myself to be an anathema FROM Christ

2

A. M. cir. 4062.
A. D. cir. 58.
An. Olymp.
cir. CCIX. 2.
A. U. C. cir.
811.
of God, and ᵐ the pro-
mises ;

5 ⁿ Whose *are* the fathers,
and º of whom, as concerning
the flesh, Christ *came,* ᵖ who
is over all, God blessed for ever.
Amen.

6 �q Not as though the word of
A. M. cir. 4062.
A. D. cir. 58.
An. Olymp.
cir. CCIX. 2.
A. U. C. cir.
811.

ᵐ Acts xiii. 32 ; chap. iii. 2 ; Eph. ii. 12.——ⁿ Deut. x. 15 ; chap.
xi. 28.——º Luke iii. 23 ; chap. i. 3.

ᵖ Jer. xxiii. 6 ; John i. 1 ; Acts xx. 28 ; Heb. i. 8 ; 1 John v. 20.
q Num. xxiii. 19 ; chap. iii. 3.

(ὑπὸ, BY Christ, as some ancient MSS. read) for my
brethren.' As ηυχομην is the 1st per. sing. of the imperfect tense, some have been led to think that St.
Paul is here mentioning what *had* passed through his
own mind when, filled with the love of God, he learned
the rejection of the Jews ; and that he only mentions
it here as a thing which, in the effusions of his loving
zeal, had been felt by him inconsiderately, and without
any Divine afflatus leading him to it ; but that he does
not intimate that *now* he felt any such unreasonable
and preposterous wish." I am afraid this is but ill
calculated to solve the difficulty.

The Greek word αναθεμα, *anathema,* properly signifies any thing devoted to God, so as to be destroyed :
it answers to the *Hebrew* חרם *cherem,* which the Septuagint translate by it, and means either a *thing* or
person separated from its former state or *condition,*
and devoted to destruction. In this sense it is used,
Deut. vii. 25, 26 ; Josh. vi. 17, 18 ; vii. 12.

It is certain that the word, both among the Hebrews
and Greeks, was used to express a person *devoted to*
destruction for the public safety. In *Midrash hannee-*
lam, in *Sohar Chadash,* fol. 15, Rabbi Chaijah the
elder said : " There is no shepherd found like unto
Moses, who was willing to lay down his life for the
sheep ; for Moses said, Exod. xxxii. 32, If thou wilt
not pardon their sin, blot me, I pray thee, out of thy
book which thou hast written." Such anathemas, or
persons devoted to destruction for the public good, were
common among all ancient nations. See the case of
M. Curtius and *Decius* among the Romans. When a
plague took place, or any public calamity, it was customary to take one of the lowest or most execrable of
the people, and devote him to the *Dii Manes* or *infer-*
nal gods. See proofs in *Schleusner,* and see the observations at the end of the chapter. This one circumstance is sufficient to explain the word in this place.
Paul desired to be devoted to destruction, as the Jews
then were, in order to redeem his countrymen from this
most terrible excision. He was willing to become a
sacrifice for the public safety, and to give his life to
redeem theirs. And, as Christ may be considered as
devoting them to destruction, (see Matt. xxiv.,) Paul is
willing that in their place Christ should devote him :
for I could wish myself, αναθεμα ειναι απο (or, as some
excellent MSS. have it, ὑπο) του Χριστου, *to be devo-*
ted BY *Christ,* to that *temporal destruction* to which
he has adjudged the disobedient Jews, if by doing so I
might redeem them. This, and this alone, seems to
be the meaning of the apostle's wish.

Verse 4. *Who are Israelites*] Descendants of Jacob, a man so highly favoured of God, and from
whom he received his name *Israel—a prince of God,*
Gen. xxxii. 28 ; from which name his descendants
were called *Israelites,* and separated unto God for his
glory and praise. Their very name of *Israelites*
implied their very high dignity ; they were a *royal*
nation ; princes of the *most high God.*

The adoption] The Israelites were all taken into
the *family* of God, and were called his *sons* and *first-*
born, Exod. iv. 22 ; Deut. xiv. 1 ; Jer. xxxi. 9 ;
Hos. xi. 1 ; and this adoption took place when God
made the covenant with them at Horeb.

The glory] The manifestation of God among
them ; principally by the *cloud* and *pillar,* and the
Shekinah, or Divine presence, appearing between the
cherubim over the mercy-seat. These were peculiar
to the Jews ; no other nation was ever thus favoured.

The covenants] The covenants made with Abraham, both that which relates to the *spiritual seed,*
and that which was peculiar to his *natural descendants,*
Gal. iii. 16, 17 ; which covenants were afterwards
renewed by Moses, Deut. xxix. 1. Some suppose
that the *singular* is here put for the plural, and that
by *covenants* we are to understand the *decalogue,*
which is termed ברית *berith,* or *covenant,* Deut. iv.
13. But it is more likely that the apostle alludes to
the great *covenant* made with Abraham, and to its
various *renewals* and *extensions* at different times
afterwards, as well as to its twofold design—the
grant of the *land of Canaan,* and the *rest* that remains
for the people of God.

The giving of the law] The revelation of God by
God himself, containing a system of moral and political precepts. This was also peculiar to the Jews ;
for to no other nation had he ever given a revelation
of his will.

The service] Λατρεια. The particular ordinances,
rites, and ceremonies of their religious worship ; and
especially the sacrificial system, so expressive of the
sinfulness of sin and the holiness of God.

The promises] The land of Canaan, and the blessings of the Messiah and his kingdom ; which promises
had been made and often repeated to the patriarchs
and to the prophets.

Verse 5. *Whose* are *the fathers*] Abraham, Isaac,
Jacob, Joseph, the twelve patriarchs, Moses, Joshua,
Samuel, David, &c., &c., without controversy, the
greatest and most eminent men that ever flourished
under heaven. From these, in an uninterrupted and
unpolluted line, the *Jewish people* had descended ;
and it was no small glory to be able to reckon, in
their genealogy, persons of such incomparable merit
and excellency.

And of whom, as concerning the flesh Christ came]
These ancestors were the more renowned, as being
the *progenitors* of the *human nature* of the MESSIAH.
Christ, the Messiah, κατα σαρκα, *according to the flesh,*
sprang from *them.* But this Messiah was more than
man, he is *God over all ;* the very Being who gave
them being, though he appeared to receive a being
from *them.*

A. M. cir. 4062.
A. D. cir. 58.
An. Olymp.
cir. CCIX. 2.
A. U. C. cir.
811.

God hath taken none effect. For [r] they *are* not all Israel, which are of Israel:

7 [s] Neither, because they are the seed of Abraham, *are they* all children: but, In [t] Isaac shall thy seed be called.

8 That is, They which are the children of the flesh, these *are* not the children of God: but [u] the children of the promise are counted for the seed.

9 For this *is* the word of promise, [v] At this

A. M. cir. 4062
A. D. cir. 58
An. Olymp.
cir. CCIX. 2.
A. U. C. cir.
811.

---

[r] John viii. 39; chap. ii. 28, 29; iv. 12, 16; Galatians vi. 16.—[s] Gal. iv. 23.

[t] Gen. xxi. 12; Heb. xi. 18.——[u] Galatians iv. 28.——[v] Genesis xviii. 10, 14.

Here the apostle most distinctly points out the *twofold* nature of our Lord—his *eternal Godhead* and his *humanity*; and all the transpositions of *particles*, and alterations of *points* in the universe, will not explain away this doctrine. As this verse contains such an eminent proof of the deity of Christ, no wonder that the opposers of his divinity should strive with their utmost skill and cunning to destroy its force. And it must be truly painful to a mind that has nothing in view but *truth*, to see the mean and hypocritical methods used to elude the force of this text. Few have met it in that honest and manly way in which Dr. Taylor, who was a conscientious Arian, has considered the subject. "Christ," says he, " is *God over all*, as he is by the Father appointed *Lord, King*, and *Governor of all*. The *Father hath committed all judgment to the Son*, John v. 22; has given *all things into his hands*, Matt. xxviii. 18; he is *Lord of all*, Acts x. 36. *God has given him a name above every name*, Phil. ii. 9; above *every name that is named*, not only in this world, but also in *that which is to come*; and *has put all things* (himself excepted, 1 Cor. xv. 27) *under his feet* and given *him to be head over all things*, Eph. i. 21, 22. This is our Lord's supreme Godhead. And that he is ευλογητος, *blessed for ever*, or the object of *everlasting blessing*, is evident from Rev. v. 12, 13: *Worthy is the Lamb that was slain to receive power—and blessing and honour be unto him that sitteth upon the throne, and unto the Lamb for ever and ever.* Thus it appears the words may be justly applied to our blessed Lord." Notes, p. 329. Yes, and when we take *other scriptures* into the account, where his *essential Godhead* is particularly expressed, such as Colos. i. 16, 17: *For by him were all things created, that are in heaven, and that are in earth, visible and invisible, whether they be thrones, or dominions, or principalities, or powers: all things were created* BY *him, and* FOR *him: and he is* BEFORE *all things, and* BY *him do all things consist*; we shall find that he is not *God* by investiture or office, but properly and essentially such; for it is impossible to convey in human language, to human apprehension, a more complete and finished display of *what is essential* to *Godhead*, indivisible *from* it, and incommunicable to any created nature, than what is contained in the above verses. And while these words are allowed to make a part of Divine revelation, the *essential Godhead* of Jesus Christ will continue to be a doctrine of that revelation.

I pass by the groundless and endless conjectures about reversing some of the particles and placing points in different positions, as they have been all invented to get rid of the doctrine of Christ's divinity, which is so obviously acknowledged by the simple text; it is enough to state that there is no *omission* of these important words in any MS. or *version* yet discovered.

Verse 6. *Not as though the word of God hath taken none effect.*] A Jew might have objected, as in chap. iii. 3: " Is not God bound by his faithfulness to continue the Jews as his peculiar Church and people, notwithstanding the infidelity of the major part of them? If they are brought to a level with the Gentiles, will it not follow that God hath failed in the performance of his promise to Abraham? Gen. xvii. 7, 8: *I will establish my covenant between me and thee for an everlasting covenant, to be a God unto thee, and thy seed after thee.*" To which it may be answered: This awful dispensation of God towards the Jews is not inconsistent with the veracity of the Divine promise; for even the whole body of natural born Jews are not the whole of the Israelites comprehended in the promise. Abraham is the father of *many nations*; and his seed is not only that which is of the *law*, but that also which is of the *faith of Abraham*, chap. iv. 16, 17. The *Gentiles* were included in the Abrahamic covenant as well as the *Jews*; and therefore the Jews have no *exclusive* right to the blessings of God's kingdom.

Verse 7. *Neither because they are the seed of Abraham, &c.*] Nor can they conclude, because they are the natural descendants of Abraham, that therefore they are all of them, without exception, the *children* in whom the promise is to be fulfilled.

But, in Isaac shall thy seed be called.] The promise is not confined to immediate *natural descent*, but may be accomplished in any part of Abraham's posterity. For Abraham had several sons besides *Isaac*, Gen. xxv. 1, 2, particularly *Ishmael*, who was circumcised before *Isaac* was born, and in whom Abraham was desirous that the promise should be fulfilled, Gen. xvii. 18, and in him God might have fulfilled the promise, had he so pleased; and yet he said to Abraham, Gen. xxi. 12: *Not in Ishmael, but in Isaac, shall thy seed be called.*

Verse 8. *That is, They which are the children of the flesh*] Whence it appears that not the children who descend from Abraham's loins, nor those who were circumcised as he was, nor even those whom he might expect and desire, are *therefore* the Church and people of God; but those who are made children by the good pleasure and promise of God, as *Isaac* was, are alone to be accounted for the seed with whom the covenant was established.

Verse 9. *For this* is *the word of promise, &c.*]

A. M. cir. 4062.
A. D. cir. 58.
An. Olymp.
cir. CCIX. 2.
A. U. C. cir.
811.

time will I come, and Sarah shall have a son.

10 And not only *this;* but when ^w Rebecca also had conceived by one, *even* by our father Isaac;

11 (For *the children* being not yet born, nei-

ther having done any good or evil, that the purpose of God according to election, might stand, not of works, but of ^x him that calleth ;)

12 It was said unto her, ^y The ^z elder shall serve the ^a younger :

A. M. cir. 4062.
A. D. cir. 58.
An. Olymp.
cir. CCIX. 2.
A. U. C. cir.
811.

---

^w Gen. xxv. 21.——^x Chap. iv. 17; viii. 28.

^y Gen. xxv. 23.——^z Or, *greater.*——^a Or, *lesser.*

That is, this is evidently implied in the promise recorded Gen. xviii. 10 : *At this time I will come,* saith God, and exert my Divine power, and *Sarah,* though fourscore and ten years old, *shall have a son ;* which shows that it is the sovereign will and act of God alone, which singles out and constitutes the *peculiar seed* that was to inherit the promise made to Abraham.

It should be considered that the apostle, in this and the following quotations, does not give us the whole of the text which he intends should be taken into his argument, but only a *hint* or reference to the passages to which they belong ; directing us to recollect or peruse the whole passage, and there view and judge of the argument.

That he is so to be understood appears from the conclusion he draws, ver. 16 : *So then, it is not of him that willeth, nor of him that runneth, but of God that showeth mercy.* In his arguments, ver. 7 and 8, &c., he says not one word of Abraham's *willing* Ishmael to be the seed in whom the promise might be fulfilled ; nor of Isaac's *willing* Esau ; nor of Moses' *willing* and interceding that the Israelites might be spared ; nor of Esau's *running* for venison ; but by introducing these particulars into his *conclusion,* he gives us to understand that his quotations are to be taken in connection with the whole story, of which they are a part ; and without this the apostle's meaning cannot be apprehended.

The same may be said of his *conclusion,* ver. 18 : *Whom he will he hardeneth : hardeneth* is not in his argument, but it is in the *conclusion.* Therefore hardening is understood in the argument, and he evidently refers to the case of Pharaoh. The generality of the Jews were well acquainted with the Scripture, and a hint was sufficient to revive the memory of a whole passage.—*Taylor,* p. 330.

Verse 10. *And not only* this] A Jew might object : " Ishmael was rejected, not by the sovereign will of God, but because he was the son of the *handmaid,* or *bond-woman,* and therefore unworthy to be the peculiar seed ; but observe, this was not the only limitation of the seed of Abraham with regard to inheriting the promise, for when Rebecca was with child by that one person of Abraham's issue to whom the promise was made, namely, our father Isaac, she went to inquire of the Lord, Gen. xxv. 22, 23 : *And the Lord said unto her, Two nations are in thy womb, and two manner of* PEOPLE *shall be separated from thy bowels ; and the one* PEOPLE *shall be stronger than the other* PEOPLE ; *and the elder shall serve the younger.* That is, the posterity of the *younger* shall be a nation much more prosperous and happy than the posterity of the *elder.*

Verse 11. *For* the children *being not yet born*] As

the word *children* is not in the text, the word *nations* would be more proper ; for it is of *nations* that the apostle speaks, as the following verses show, as well as the history to which he refers.

Neither having done any good] To merit the distinction of being made the peculiar people of God ; *nor evil,* to deserve to be left out of this covenant, and the distinguishing national blessings which it conferred ; *that the purpose of God according to election might stand*—that such distinctions might appear to depend on nothing but God's free choice, not *of works,* or any desert in the *people* or *nations* thus chosen ; but of the mere purpose *of him who calleth* any people he pleases, to make them the depositories of his especial blessings, and thus to distinguish them from all others.

Verse 12. *The elder shall serve the younger*] These words, with those of Malachi, *Jacob have I loved, and Esau have I hated,* are cited by the apostle to prove, according to their typical signification, that the *purpose of God, according to election,* does and will stand, not of *works,* but of *him that calleth ;* that is, that the *purpose of God,* which is the ground of that *election* which he makes among men, unto the honour of being Abraham's seed, might appear to remain unchangeable in him ; and to be even the *same* which he had declared unto Abraham. That these words are used in a *national* and not in a *personal* sense, is evident from this : that, taken in the latter sense they are *not true,* for *Jacob* never did exercise any power over *Esau,* nor was Esau ever *subject* to him. Jacob, on the contrary, was rather subject to Esau, and was sorely afraid of him ; and, first, by his messengers, and afterwards personally, acknowledged his brother to be his *lord,* and himself to be his *servant ;* see Gen. xxxii. 4 ; xxxiii. 8, 13. And hence it appears that neither *Esau* nor *Jacob,* nor even *their posterities,* are brought here by the apostle as instances of any *personal* reprobation from eternity : for, it is very certain that very many, if not the far *greatest part,* of *Jacob's* posterity were *wicked,* and rejected by God ; and it is not less certain that some of *Esau's* posterity were partakers of the faith of their father Abraham.

From these premises the true sense of the words immediately following, *Jacob have I loved, and Esau have I hated,* Malachi i. 2, 3, fully appears ; that is, that what he had already cited from Moses concerning the two nations, styled by the names of their respective heads, *Jacob* and *Esau,* was but the same in substance with what was spoken many years after by the Prophet Malachi. The unthankful Jews had, in Malachi's time, either in words or in their heart, expostulated with God, and demanded of him wherein he had loved them ? *I have loved you,* saith the *Lord :* yet ye say, *Wherein hast thou loved us ?* Mal. i. 2, 3, 4, 5. To

2

A. M. cir. 4062.
A. D. cir. 58.
An. Olymp.
cir. CCIX. 2.
A. U. C. cir.
811.

13 As it is written, ^bJacob have I loved, but Esau have I hated.

14 What shall we say then?

^c*Is there* unrighteousness with God? God forbid.

15 For he saith to Moses, ^dI will have mercy on whom I will

A. M. cir. 4062.
A. D. cir. 58.
An. Olymp.
cir. CCIX. 2.
A. U. C. cir.
811.

^bMal. i. 2, 3; see Deut. xxi. 15; Prov. xiii. 24; Matt. x. 37; Luke xiv. 26; John xii. 25.

^cDeut. xxxii. 4; 2 Chron. xix. 7; Job viii. 3; xxxiv. 10; Psa. xcii. 15.——^dExod. xxxiii. 19.

this the Lord answers : *Was not Esau Jacob's brother? Yet I loved Jacob and hated Esau, and laid his mountains and his heritage waste for the dragons of the wilderness. Whereas Edom saith, We are impoverished, but we will return and build the desolate places; thus saith the Lord of hosts, They shall build, but I will throw down ; and they shall call them, The border of wickedness, and, The people against whom the Lord hath indignation for ever. And your eyes shall see, and ye shall say, The Lord will be magnified from the border of Israel.*

1. It incontestably appears from these passages that the prophet does not speak at all of the *person* of Jacob or Esau, but of their respective *posterities.* For it was not Esau in person that said, *We are impoverished,* neither were his *mountains* nor *heritage laid waste.* Now, if the *prophet* speaks neither of the *person* of the one nor of the person of the other, but of their *posterity* only, then it is evident that the *apostle* speaks of them in the *same way.*

2. If neither the *prophet* nor the *apostle* speaks of the *persons* of Jacob or Esau, but of their *posterity,* then it is evident that neither the *love of God to Jacob,* nor the *hatred of God to Esau,* were such, according to which the eternal states of men, either in happiness or misery, are to be determined; nor is there here any Scriptural or rational ground for the decree of unconditional personal election and reprobation, which, comparatively, modern times have endeavoured to build on these scriptures. For, 1. It is here proved that *Esau* is not mentioned under any *personal* consideration, but only as the *head* of his *posterity.* 2. The testimony of Scripture amply proves that all *Esau's posterity* were not, even in this sense, reprobated; nor all *Jacob's posterity* elected. 3. Neither does that *service,* or subjugation to Jacob, which the Divine oracle imposed on Esau, import any such *reprobation* as some contend for; as the *servant* may be *elected,* while the *master* himself is in a state of *reprobation.* 4. Were it even granted that *servitude* did import such a *reprobation,* yet it is certain that Esau, in person, never did *serve* Jacob. 5. Nor does the *hatred* of God against Esau import any such reprobation of the person of Esau, because it is demonstrable that it related, not to Esau *personally,* but to his *posterity.* 6. The scope of the apostle's reasoning is to show that God is the sovereign of his own ways, has a right to dispense his blessings as he chooses, and to give salvation to mankind, not in the ways of their devising, but in that way that is most suitable to his infinite wisdom and goodness.

Therefore, 1. He chose the Jewish people from all others, and revealed himself to them. Thus *they* were the *elect,* and all the *nations* of mankind *reprobate.* 2. When the fulness of the time came he revealed himself also to the *Gentiles,* who gladly received the Gospel ; and the *Jews,* rejecting it, were *cast off.* Thus

the *elect* became *reprobate,* and the *reprobate, elect.* 3. He published to all mankind that the pardon of sin could and should be obtained ONLY *by faith in his Son Jesus,* and not by *any obedience to any law.* And the Jews, the descendants of Jacob, who rejected this way of salvation, became precisely like the *Edomites,* the descendants of Esau ; *they builded, but God pulled down ; their mountains and heritage are* NOW *laid waste for the dragons of the wilderness ;* and *they* properly may now *be called the border of wickedness, a people against whom the Lord hath indignation for ever:* they have rejected the Lord that bought them, and so have brought upon themselves swift destruction. 7. That no *personal,* absolute, eternal reprobation of Esau can have been intended, we learn from this ; that he was most amply *reconciled* to his brother, who had so deeply wronged and offended him, by depriving him of his birthright and his blessing : and his having forgiven his brother his trespasses, was no mean proof that God had forgiven him. See our Lord's words, Matt. vi. 14. Therefore there can be assigned no competent ground of his damnation, much less of his *personal* reprobation from all eternity. 8. And were such a *personal* reprobation intended, is it not shocking to suppose that the God of endless mercy, in whose sight his pious parents had found favour, should inform *them, even before their child was born,* that he had *absolutely consigned him, by an irrevocable decree to eternal damnation?* A message of such horrid import coming immediately from the mouth of God, to a tender, weak, and delicate woman, whose hour of travail with two children was just at hand, could not have failed to produce abortion, and destroy her life. But the parents perfectly understood their God, and saw no decree of reprobation in his *message ; two manner of nations are in thy womb—and the elder shall serve the younger.* 9. There is no *reason,* worthy the most wise and gracious God, why he should make known to the world such a thing concerning *Esau,* who was yet unborn, that he had reprobated him from all eternity. Such a revelation could be of no spiritual advantage or edification to mankind, but rather of a malignant influence, as directly occasioning men to judge hardly of their Maker, and to conceive of him as no faithful Creator ; as having no care, no love, no bowels of compassion towards the workmanship of his own hands. See *Goodwin's* Exposition : and see my *notes* on Gen. xxvii.

Verse 14. *What shall we say then ?*] To what conclusion shall we come on the facts before us ? Shall we suggest that God's bestowing peculiar privileges in this unequal manner, on those who otherwise are in equal circumstances, is inconsistent with *justice* and *equity? By no means.* Whatever God does is *right,* and he may dispense his blessings to *whom* and on what *terms* he pleases.

A. M. cir. 4062.
A. D. cir. 58.
An. Olymp.
cir. CCIX. 2.
A. U. C. cir.
811.

have mercy, and I will have compassion on whom I will have compassion.

16 So then, *it is* not of him that willeth, nor of him that runneth, but of God that showeth mercy.

17 For [e] the scripture saith unto Pharaoh, [f] Even for this same purpose have I raised thee up, that I might show my power in thee, and

---

[e] See Gal. iii. 8, 22.——[f] Exod. ix. 16.——[g] 2 Chron. xx. 6; Job ix. 12; xxiii. 13; Dan. iv. 35.

---

that my name might be declared throughout all the earth.

18 Therefore hath he mercy on whom he will *have mercy,* and whom he will he hardeneth.

19 Thou wilt say then unto me, Why doth he yet find fault? For [g] who hath resisted his will?

20 Nay but, O man, who art thou that [h] repliest against God? [i] Shall the thing formed

A. M. cir. 4062.
A. D. cir. 58.
An. Olymp.
cir. CCIX. 2.
A. U. C. cir.
811.

---

[h] Or, *answerest again;* or, *disputest with God?* Job xxxiii. 13. [i] Isa. xxix. 16; xlv. 9; lxiv. 8.

Verse 15. *For he saith to Moses, I will have mercy, &c.*] The words of God to Moses, Exod. xxxiii. 19, show that God has a right to dispense his blessings as he pleases; for, after he had declared that he would spare the Jews of old, and continue them in the relation of his peculiar people, when they had deserved to have been cut off for their idolatry, he said: *I will make all my goodness pass before thee; and I will proclaim the name of the Lord before thee; and I will have mercy on whom I will have mercy; and I will have compassion on whom I will have compassion.* As if he had said: I will make such a display of my perfections as shall convince you that my nature is kind and beneficent; but know, that I am a debtor to none of my creatures. My benefits and blessings are merely from my own good will: nor can *any people,* much less a *rebellious* people, challenge them as their due in justice or equity. And therefore I now spare the Jews; not because either you, who intercede for them or they themselves have any *claim* upon my favour, but of my own free and sovereign grace I choose to show them mercy and compassion. I will give my salvation in my own way and on my own terms. He that believeth on my Son Jesus shall be saved; and he that believeth not shall be damned. This is God's ultimate design; this purpose he will never change; and this he has fully declared in the *everlasting Gospel.* This is the grand DECREE of *reprobation* and *election.*

Verse 16. *So then it is not of him that willeth, &c.*] I conclude, therefore, from these several instances, that the making or continuing any body of men the peculiar people of God, is righteously determined; not by the *judgment, hopes,* or *wishes* of men, but by the *will* and *wisdom* of God alone. For Abraham judged that the blessing ought, and he *willed,* desired, that it might be given to *Ishmael;* and Isaac also *willed,* designed, it for his first-born, *Esau:* and Esau, *wishing* and hoping that it might be his, *readily* went, *ran* a hunting for venison, that he might have the blessing regularly conveyed to him: but they were all disappointed—Abraham and Isaac, who *willed,* and Esau who *ran:* for God had originally intended that the blessing of being a great nation and distinguished people should, of his mere good pleasure, be given to Isaac and Jacob, and be confirmed in their posterity; and to them it was given. And when by their apostasy they had forfeited this privilege, it was not Moses' *willing,* nor any prior obligation God was under, but his own sovereign mercy, which *continued* it to them.

VOL. II.   (8)

Verse 17. *For the Scripture saith unto Pharaoh*] Instead of showing the Israelites mercy he might justly have suffered them to have gone on in sin, till he should have signalized his wisdom and justice in their destruction; as appears from what God in his word declares concerning his dealings with Pharaoh and the Egyptians, Exod. ix. 15, 16: *For now,* saith the Lord, *I had stretched forth my hand,* (in the plague of boils and blains,) *and I had smitten thee and thy people with the pestilence; and thou hadst* (by this plague) *been cut off from the earth;* (as thy cattle were by the murrain;) *but in very deed for this cause have I raised thee up*—I have restored thee to health by removing the boils and blains, and by respiting thy deserved destruction to a longer day, that I may, in thy instance, give such a demonstration of my power in thy final overthrow, that all mankind may learn that I am God, the righteous Judge of all the earth, the avenger of wickedness. See this translation of the original vindicated in my notes on Exod. ix. 15, 16; and, about the *hardening* of Pharaoh, see the notes on those places where the words occur in the same book.

Verse 18. *Therefore hath he mercy on whom he will*] This is the apostle's conclusion from the facts already laid down: that God, according to his own will and wisdom, in perfect righteousness, bestows *mercy;* that is to say, his blessings upon one part of mankind, (the Jews of old, and the Gentiles of the present time,) while he suffers another part (the *Egyptians* of old, and the *Jews* of the present day) to go on in the abuse of his goodness and forbearance, hardening themselves in sin, till he brings upon them a most just and exemplary punishment, unless this be prevented by their deep repentance and general return to God through Jesus the promised, the real *Messiah.*

Verse 19. *Why doth he yet find fault?*] The apostle here introduces the Jew making an objection similar to that in chap. iii. 7: *If the truth of God hath more abounded through my lie unto his glory,* that is, if God's faithfulness is glorified by my wickedness, *why yet am I also judged as a sinner?* Why am I condemned for that which brings so much glory to him? The question here is: If God's glory be so highly promoted and manifested by our obstinacy, and he suffers us to proceed in our hardness and infidelity, why does he find fault with us, or punish us for that which is according to his good pleasure?

Verse 20. *Nay but, O man, who art thou*] As if he had said: Weak, ignorant man, darest thou retort on the infinitely good and righteous GOD! Reflect on

113

A. M. cir. 4062.
A. D. cir. 58.
An. Olymp.
cir. CCIX. 2.
A. U. C. cir.
811.

say to him that formed *it*, Why hast thou made me thus?

21 Hath not the [k] potter power over the clay, of the same lump to make [l] one vessel unto honour, and another unto dishonour?

22 *What* if God, willing to show *his* wrath,

and to make his power known, endured with much long-suffering [m] the vessels of wrath [n] fitted [o] to destruction:

23 And that he might make known [p] the riches of his glory on the vessels of mercy, which he had [q] afore prepared unto glory,

A. M. cir. 4062.
A. D. cir. 58.
An. Olymp.
cir. CCIX. 2.
A. U. C. cir.
811.

---

[k] Prov. xvi. 4; Jer. xviii. 6; Wisdom xv. 7.——[l] 2 Tim. ii. 20.
[m] 1 Thess. v. 9.

[n] Or, *made up.*——[o] 1 Pet. ii. 8; Jude 4.——[p] Chap. ii. 4; Eph.
i. 7; Col. i. 27.——[q] Chap. viii. 28, 29, 30.

---

thyself; and tell me, after thou hast abused the grace of God, and transgressed his laws, wilt thou cavil at his dispensations? God hath *made, created, formed* the *Jewish* nation; and shall the thing *formed*, when it hath *corrupted* itself, pretend to correct the wise and gracious Author of its being, and say, *Why hast thou made me thus?* Why hast thou constituted me in this manner? Thou hast done me wrong in giving me my being under such and such conditions.

Old John Goodwin's note on this passage is at least curious: "I scarce (says he) know any passage of the Scripture more frequently abused than this. When men, in the great questions of predestination and reprobation, bring forth any text of Scripture which they conceive makes for their notion, though the sense which they put upon it be ever so uncouth and dissonant from the true meaning of the Holy Ghost, yet, if any man contradict, they frequently fall upon him with—*Nay but, O man, who art thou?* As if St. Paul had left them his heirs and successors in the infallibility of his spirit! But when men shall call a solid answer to their groundless conceits about the meaning of the Scriptures, *a replying against God*, it savours more of the spirit who was seen falling like lightning from heaven, than of His, who saw him in this his fall."

Verse 21. *Hath not the potter power over the clay*] The apostle continues his answer to the Jew. Hath not God shown, by the parable of the potter, Jerem. xviii. 1, &c., that he may justly dispose of nations, and of the Jews in particular, according as he in his infinite wisdom may judge most right and fitting; even as the potter has a right, out of the same lump of clay, to make one vessel to a more *honourable* and another to a *less honourable* use, as his own judgment and skill may direct; for no potter will take pains to make a vessel merely that he may show that he has power to dash it to pieces? *For the word came to Jeremiah from the Lord, saying, Arise, and go down to the potter's house, and there I will cause thee to hear my words. Then I went down to the potter's house, and, behold, he wrought a work upon the wheels. And the vessel that he made of clay was marred in the hands of the potter: so he made it again another vessel, as seemed good to the potter to make it.* It was not fit for the more honourable place in the mansion, and therefore he made it for a less honourable place, but as necessary for the master's use there, as it could have been in a more honourable situation. *Then the word of the Lord came to me, saying, O house of Israel, cannot I do with you as this potter? Behold, as the clay is in the potter's hand, so are ye*

in mine hand, O house of Israel. At what instant I shall speak concerning a nation, and concerning a kingdom, to pluck up, and to pull down, and to destroy it; if that nation, against whom I have pronounced, turn from their evil, I will repent of the evil that I thought to do unto them. And at what instant I shall speak concerning a nation—to build and to plant it; if it do evil in my sight, that it obey not my voice, then I will repent of the good wherewith I said I would benefit them. The reference to this parable shows most positively that the apostle is speaking of men, not *individually*, but *nationally;* and it is strange that men should have given his words any other application with this scripture before their eyes.

Verse 22. *What if God, willing to show his wrath*] The apostle refers here to the case of *Pharaoh* and the *Egyptians*, and to which he applies Jeremiah's parable of the potter, and, from them, to the then state of the Jews. Pharaoh and the Egyptians were *vessels of wrath*—persons deeply guilty before God; and by their obstinate refusal of his grace, and abuse of his goodness, they had fitted themselves for that destruction which the *wrath*, the vindictive justice of God, inflicted, after he had *endured* their obstinate rebellion *with much long-suffering;* which is a most absolute proof that the hardening of their hearts, and their ultimate punishment, were the consequences of their obstinate refusal of his grace and abuse of his goodness; as the history in Exodus sufficiently shows. As the Jews of the apostle's time had sinned after the similitude of the Egyptians, hardening their hearts and abusing his goodness, after every display of his long-suffering kindness, being now fitted for destruction, they were ripe for punishment; and that *power*, which God was *making known* for their salvation, having been so long and so much abused and provoked, was now about to show itself in their destruction as a nation. But even in this case there is not a word of their *final damnation;* much less that either *they* or any *others* were, by a sovereign decree, reprobated from all eternity; and that their very sins, the proximate cause of their punishment, were the necessary effect of that decree which had from all eternity doomed them to endless torments. As such a doctrine could never come from God, so it never can be found in the words of his apostle.

Verse 23. *And that he might make known*] God endured with much long-suffering the *vessels of wrath:* 1 To show *his wrath*, and to make his power known. And also, 2. That he might make known the riches of his glory on the vessels of mercy.

Which he had afore prepared unto glory] The Jews

A. M. cir. 4062.
A. D. cir. 58.
An. Olymp.
cir. CCIX. 2.
A. U. C. cir.
811.

24 Even us, whom he hath called, ʳ not of the Jews only, but also of the Gentiles?

25 As he saith also in Osee, ˢ I will call them my people, which were not my people; and her beloved, which was not beloved.

26 ᵗ And it shall come to pass, *that* in the place where it was said unto them, Ye *are* not my people; there shall they be called the children of the living God.

27 Esaias also crieth concerning Israel, ᵘ Though the number of the children of Israel be as the sand of the sea, ᵛ a remnant shall be saved:

28 For he will finish ʷ the work, and cut *it* short in righteousness: ˣ because a short work will the Lord make upon the earth.

29 And as Esaias said before, ʸ Except the

A. M. cir. 4062.
A. D. cir. 58.
An. Olymp.
cir. CCIX. 2
A. U. C. cir
811.

ʳ Chap. iii. 29.——ˢ Hos. ii. 23; 1 Pet. ii. 10.——ᵗ Hosea i. 10. ᵘ Isa. x. 22, 23.

ᵛ Chap. xi. 5.——ʷ Or, *the account.*——ˣ Isa. xxviii. 22.——ʸ Isa. i. 9; Lam. iii. 22.

---

were fitted for destruction long before; but the fittest time to destroy them was after he had prepared the believing Gentiles unto glory. For the rod of the Messiah's strength was to be sent out of Zion, Psa. cx. 2. The Jewish nation was to supply the first preachers of the Gospel, and from Jerusalem their sound was to go forth into all the earth. Therefore the Jewish state, notwithstanding its corruptions, was to be preserved till the Messiah came, and even till the Gospel preached by the apostles had taken deep root in the Gentile world. Another thing which rendered the time when the Jewish polity was overthrown the most proper, was this, because then the immediate occasion of it was the extensiveness of the Divine grace. They would not have the Gentiles admitted into the Church of God; but contradicted, and blasphemed, and rejected the Lord that bought them: thus, then, the extensiveness of the Divine grace occasioned their infidelity, ver. 33; chap. x. 3; xi. 11, 12, 15, 28, 30. Thus the Jews were *diminished by* that *abundance of grace* which has *enriched* the Gentiles. And so the grace of God was illustrated; or, so God *made known the riches of his glory on the vessels of mercy*—the apostles and primitive believers among the Jews, and the *Gentile world,* which received the Gospel by the preaching of the apostles and their successors.

Verse 24. *Even us, whom he hath called*] All the Jews and Gentiles who have been *invited* by the preaching of the Gospel to receive justification by faith in our Lord Jesus Christ, and have come to the *Gospel feast* on this invitation.

Verse 25. *As he saith also in Osee*] It is a cause of not a little confusion, that a uniformity in the orthography of the proper names of the Old and New Testaments has not been preserved. What *stranger* to our sacred books would suppose that the *Osee* above meant the Prophet *Hosea,* from whom, chap. ii. ver. 23, this quotation is taken: *I will have mercy on her that had not obtained mercy; and I will say to them which were not my people, Thou art my people* The apostle shows that this calling of the Gentiles was no *fortuitous* thing, but a *firm purpose* in the Divine mind, which he had largely revealed to the prophets; and by opposing the calling of the Gentiles, the Jews in effect renounced their *prophets,* and fought against God.

Verse 26. *And it shall come to pass, &c.*] These quotations are taken out of Hosea, chap. i. 10, where

(immediately after God had rejected the *ten tribes, or kingdom of Israel,* chap. i. 9, *then saith God, Call his name Lo-ammi; for ye are not my people, and I will not be your God,*) he adds, yet the number of the children of Israel shall be as the sand of the sea, which cannot be measured nor numbered: and it shall come to pass, that *in the place in which it was said unto them, Ye* are *not my people; there* it shall be said unto them, Ye are the sons of the living God. As if he had said: The *decrease* of numbers in the Church, by God's utterly taking away the *ten tribes,* (ver. 6,) shall be well supplied by what shall afterwards come to pass, by calling the *Gentiles* into it. They, the rejected Jews, which had been the people of God, should become a *Lo-ammi—not my people.* On the contrary, they, the *Gentiles,* who had been a *Lo-ammi—not my people,* should become *the children of the living God.* Again, chap. ii. 23: *I will sow her* (the Jewish Church) *unto me in the earth,* (alluding probably to the *dispersion* of the Jews over all the *Roman* empire, which proved a fruitful cause of preparing the Gentiles for the reception of the Gospel,) *and,* or *moreover, I will have mercy upon her,* the body of the believing Gentiles, *that had not obtained mercy.* See Taylor.

Verse 27. *Esaias also crieth*] The apostle pursues his argument, which had for its object the proof that God, for their infidelity, had rejected the great body of the Jews, and that but a few of them would embrace the Gospel, and be saved from that besom of destruction which was now coming to sweep them and their state away. Dr. Taylor paraphrases this and the following verses thus: And that but a small remnant of the Jews shall now be taken into the Church, is agreeable to former dispensations; for the Prophet Isaiah expressly declares concerning the Israelites, chap. x. 22, 23: *Though the number of the children of Israel be as the sand of the sea,* (for the promise to Abraham has been amply fulfilled,) *only a remnant shall be saved; the consumption decreed shall overflow in righteousness. For the Lord God of hosts shall make a consumption, even determined in the midst of all the land.*

Verse 28. *For he will finish the work, and cut it short, &c.*] These appear to be forensic terms, and refer to the *conclusion* of a *judicial proceeding;* the Lord has *tried* and *found them guilty,* and will *immediately execute* upon them the punishment due to their transgressions.

Verse 29. *And as Esaias said before*] What God

2

| A. M. cir. 4062. |
| A. D. cir. 58. |
| An. Olymp. |
| cir. CCIX. 2. |
| A. U. C. cir. |
| 811. |

Lord of Sabaoth had left us a seed, [z] we had been as Sodoma, and been made like unto Gomorrah.

30 What shall we say then? [a] That the Gentiles, which followed not after righteousness, have attained to righteousness, [b] even the righteousness which is of faith.

31 But Israel, [c] which followed after the law

of righteousness, [d] hath not attained to the law of righteousness.

32 Wherefore? Because *they sought it* not by faith, but as it were by the works of the law. For [e] they stumbled at that stumbling-stone;

33 As it is written, [f] Behold, I lay in Sion a stumbling-stone and rock of offence: and [g] whosoever believeth on him shall not be [h] ashamed.

| A. M. cir. 4062. |
| A. D. cir. 58. |
| An. Olymp. |
| cir. CCIX. 2. |
| A. U. C. cir. |
| 811. |

---

[z] Isa. xiii. 19; Jer. l. 40.——[a] Chap. iv. 11; x. 20.——[b] Chap. i. 17.——[c] Chap. x. 2; xi. 7.——[d] Gal. v. 4.——[e] Luke ii. 34;

1 Cor. i. 23.——[f] Psa. cxviii. 22; Isa. viii. 14; xxviii. 16; Matt. xxi. 42; 1 Pet. ii. 6, 7, 8.——[g] Chap. x. 11.——[h] Or, *confounded.*

---

designs to do with the Jews at present, because of their obstinacy and rebellion, is similar to what he has done before, to which the same prophet refers, chap. i. 9 : *Except the Lord of hosts had left unto us a very small remnant, we should have been as Sodom, and we should have been like unto Gomorrah:* i. e. had not God, who commands and overrules all the powers in heaven and earth, in mercy preserved a very small remnant, to keep up the name and being of the nation, it had been quite cut off and extinct, as Sodom and Gomorrah were. Thus we learn that it is no new thing with God to abandon the greatest part of the Jewish nation, when corrupt, and to confine his favour and blessing to a righteous, believing few.

Instead of *remnant,* שריד *sarid,* both the *Septuagint* and the *apostle* have σπερμα, a *seed,* intimating that there were left just enough of the righteous to be a *seed* for a future *harvest* of true believers. So the *godly* were not destroyed from the land; some remained, and the harvest was in the days of the apostles.

Verse 30. *What shall we say then?*] What is the final conclusion to be drawn from all these prophecies, facts, and reasonings? This: That *the Gentiles which followed not after righteousness,* &c. This, with the succeeding verses, together with what belongs to the same subject in the beginning of the following chapter, I have explained at large in the notes on chap. i. 17, to which I must refer the reader; and shall content myself in this place with Dr. Taylor's general paraphrase. We may suppose the apostle to express himself to the following effect. Thus I have vindicated the rejection of the Jews and the calling of the Gentiles, with regard to the Divine veracity and justice. Now let us turn our thoughts to the true reason and state of the affair considered in *itself.* And, in the first place, what just notion ought we to have of the calling of the Gentiles and the rejection of the Jews? I answer: The true notion of the calling or inviting of the Gentiles is this: whereas they had no apprehension of being reinstated in the privileges of God's peculiar kingdom, and consequently used no endeavours to obtain that blessing; yet, notwithstanding, they have attained to justification, to *the remission of sins,* and the privileges of God's people: not on account of their *prior worthiness* and *obedience,* but purely by the *grace and mercy of God,* received by *faith* on their part. And so, by embracing the scheme of life published by the Gospel, they are adopted into the family and Church of God. Thus the Gentiles are *called* or *invited.*

Verse 31. *But Israel, which followed after*] But the *Jews,* who have hitherto been the people of God, though they have been industrious in observing *a rule* by which they supposed they could secure the blessings of God's peculiar kingdom, yet have not come up to the *true* and *only rule* by which those blessings can be secured.

Verse 32. *Wherefore?*] And where lies their mistake? *Being ignorant of God's righteousness*—of his method of saving sinners by faith in Christ, *they went about to establish their own righteousness*—their own method of obtaining everlasting salvation. They attend not to the *Abrahamic covenant,* which stands on the extensive principles of *grace* and *faith;* but they turn all their regards to the *law of Moses.* They imagine that their obedience to that law gives them a right to the blessings of the Messiah's kingdom. But, finding that the Gospel sets our special interest in God and the privileges of his Church on a different footing, they are offended, and refuse to come into it.

Verse 33. *As it is written, Behold, I lay in Sion*] Christ, the Messiah, is become a stone of stumbling to them: and thus what is written in the prophecy of Isaiah is verified in their case, Isa. viii. 14; xxviii. 16 *Behold, I lay in Sion,* i. e. I shall bring in my Messiah; but he shall be a widely different person from him whom the Jews expect; for, whereas they expect the Messiah to be a *mighty secular prince,* and to set up a *secular kingdom,* he shall appear a *man of sorrows* and *acquainted with griefs;* and redeem mankind, not by his *sword* or *secular power,* but by his *humiliation, passion,* and *death.* Therefore they will be *offended* at him and reject him, and think it would be *reproachful* to trust in such a person for salvation.

And whosoever believeth on him] But so far shall any be from *confusion* or *disappointment* who believes in Christ; that on the contrary, every genuine believer shall find salvation—the remission of sins here, and eternal glory hereafter. See the notes on chap. i. 16 and 17, and Dr. *Taylor's* paraphrase and notes

1. On the subject of vicarious punishment, or rather the case of one becoming an *anathema* or sacrifice for the public good, in illustration of chap. ix. 3, I shall make no apology for the following extracts, taken from an author whose learning is vast, and whose piety is unblemished.

"When mankind lost sight of a beneficent Creator, the God of purity, and consecrated altars to the sun, the moon, the stars; to demons; and to hero gods,

2

under the names of Moloch, Ashtaroth and Baalim; these objects of their worship led them to the most horrid acts of cruelty, and to every species of obscenity; even their sons and their daughters they burnt in the fire to their gods, more especially in seasons of distress. Such was the conduct of the king of Moab; for, when he was besieged in his capital, and expected he should fall into the hands of his enemies, he took his eldest son, who should have reigned in his stead, and offered him for a burnt offering on the wall.

With these facts thus related from the Scriptures, all accounts, ancient and modern, exactly correspond. Homer, who it must be recollected wrote more than nine hundred years before the Christian era, although he describes chiefly the common sacrifices of quadrupeds, yet gives one account of human victims. But in succeeding generations, when it was conceived that one great and most malignant spirit was the proper object of their fear, or that subordinate provincial gods, equally malignant, *nesciaque humanis precibus mansuescere corda*, disposed of all things in our world, men bound their own species to the altar, and in circumstances of national distress presented such as they valued most, either their children or themselves. Herodotus informs us that, when the army of Xerxes came to the Strymon, the magi offered a sacrifice of white horses to that river. On his arrival at the Scamander, the king ascended the citadel of Priam; and having surveyed it, he ordered a thousand oxen to be sacrificed to the Trojan Minerva. But on other occasions he chose human victims; for we are informed that, when, having passed the Strymon, he reached the nine ways, he buried alive nine young men and as many virgins, natives of the country. In this he followed the example of his wife, for she commanded fourteen Persian children, of illustrious birth, to be offered in that manner to the deity who reigns beneath the earth. Thus, in the infancy of Rome we see Curtius, for the salvation of his country, devoting himself to the infernal gods, when, as it appears, an earthquake occasioned a deep and extensive chasm in the forum, and the augurs had declared that the portentous opening would never close until what contributed most to the strength and power of the Romans should be cast into it; but that by such a sacrifice they would obtain immortality for their republic. When all men were at a loss how to understand this oracle, M. Curtius, armed as for battle, presented himself in the forum, and explained it thus: 'What is more valuable to Rome than her courage and her arms?' So saying, he urged forward his impetuous steed, and buried himself in the abyss. His grateful countrymen admired his fortitude, and attributed the increasing splendour of their state to the sacrifice he made. Animated by this example, Decius, in the war between Rome and Latium, having solemnly offered himself as an expiatory sacrifice, rushed single into the thickest ranks of the astonished Latins, that by his death he might appease the anger of the gods, transfer their indignation to the enemy, and secure the victory to Rome. *Conspectus ab utroque acie aliquanto augustior humano visu, sicut Cœlo missus, piaculum omnis deorum iræ, qui pestem ab suis aversam in hostes ferret.*

Here we see distinctly marked the notion of vicarious suffering, and the opinion that the punishment of guilt may be transferred from the guilty to the innocent. The gods call for sacrifice—the victim bleeds—atonement is made—and the wrath of the infernal powers falls in its full force upon the enemy. Thus, while Themistocles at Salamine was offering sacrifice, three captives, the sons of Sandance, and nephews to Xerxes, all distinguished for their beauty, elegantly dressed and decked, as became their birth, with ornaments of gold, being brought on board his galley, the augur, Euphrantides, observing at the very instant a bright flame ascending from the altar, whilst one was sneezing on the right, which he regarded as a propitious omen, he seized the hand of Themistocles, and commanded that they should all be sacrificed to Bacchus, (ωμηστη Διονυσω—cruel and relentless Bacchus! Homer has the same expression,) predicting, on this occasion, safety and conquests to the Greeks. Immediately the multitude with united voices called on the god, and led the captive princes to the altar, and compelled Themistocles to sacrifice them.

So when Æneas was to perform the last kind office for his friend Pallas, he sacrificed (besides numerous oxen, sheep, and swine) eight captives to the infernal gods. In this he followed the example of Achilles, who had caused twelve Trojans of high birth to bleed by the sacerdotal knife, over the ashes of his friend Patroclus.

A hundred feet in length, a hundred wide,
The glowing structure spreads on every side,
High on the top the manly course they lay,
And well-fed sheep and sable oxen slay;
Achilles covered with their fat the dead,
And the piled victims round the body spread:
Then jars of honey and of fragrant oil
Suspends around, low bending o'er the pile.
Four sprightly coursers with a deadly groan
Pour forth their lives, and on the pyre are thrown
Of nine large dogs, domestic at his board,
Fell two, selected to attend their lord:
The last of all, and horrible to tell,
Sad sacrifice! twelve Trojan captives fell;
On these the rage of fire victorious preys,
Involves and joins them in one common blaze.
Smeared with the bloody rites, he stands on high,
And calls the spirit with a cheerful cry,
All hail, Patroclus! let thy vengeful ghost
Hear, and exult on Pluto's dreary coast.

POPE's *Homer*, IL. xxiii. ver. 203

How much was it to be lamented, that even civilized natures should forget the intention for which sacrifices were originally instituted! The bad effects, however, would not have been either so extensive or so great, had they not wholly lost the knowledge of Jehovah; and taken, as the object of their fear, that evil and apostate spirit whose name, with the utmost propriety is called Apollyon, or the destroyer, and whose worship has been universally diffused at different periods among all the nations of the earth.

The practice of shedding human blood before the altars of their gods was not peculiar to the *Trojans* and the *Greeks*; the Romans followed their example.

In the first ages of their republic they sacrificed children to the goddess Mania; in later periods, numerous gladiators bled at the tombs of the patricians, to appease the manes of the deceased. And it is particularly noticed of Augustus, that, after the taking of *Perusia,* he sacrificed on the ides of March, three hundred senators and knights to the divinity of Julius Cæsar.

The *Carthaginians,* as Diodorus Siculus informs us, bound themselves by a solemn vow to Chronus that they would sacrifice to him children selected from the offspring of their nobles; but in process of time they substituted for these the children of their slaves, which practice they continued, till, being defeated by Agathocles, tyrant of Sicily, and attributing their disgrace to the anger of the god, they offered two hundred children, taken from the most distinguished families in Carthage; besides which, three hundred citizens presented themselves, that by their voluntary death they might render the deity propitious to their country. The mode of sacrificing these children was horrid in the extreme, for they were cast into the arms of a brazen statue, and from thence dropped into a furnace, as was practised among the first inhabitants of Latium. It was probably in this manner the Ammonites offered up their children to Moloch. The *Pelasgi* at one time sacrificed a tenth part of all their children, in obedience to an oracle.

The *Egyptians,* in Heliopolis, sacrificed three men every day to Juno. The *Spartans* and *Arcadians* scourged to death young women; the latter to appease the wrath of Bacchus, the former to gratify Diana. The Sabian idolaters in *Persia* offered human victims to Mithras, the *Cretans* to Jupiter, the *Lacedemonians* and *Lusitanians* to Mars, the *Lesbians* to Bacchus, the *Phocians* to Diana, the *Thessalians* to Chiron.

The *Gauls,* equally cruel in their worship, sacrificed men, originally to Eso and Teutate, but latterly to Mercury, Apollo, Mars, Jupiter, and Minerva. Cæsar informs us that, whenever they thought themselves in danger, whether from sickness, or after any considerable defeat in war, being persuaded that unless life be given for life the anger of the gods can never be appeased, they constructed wicker images of enormous bulk, which they filled with men, who were first suffocated with smoke, and then consumed by fire. For this purpose they preferred criminals; but when a sufficient number of these could not be found, they supplied the deficiency from the community at large.

The *Germans* are said to have differed from the Gauls in having no druids, and in being little addicted to the service of the altar. Their only gods were the sun, Vulcan, and the moon; yet, among the objects of their worship was Tuisco their progenitor and Woden the hero of the north. It is true that neither Cæsar nor Tacitus say any thing of their shedding blood in sacrifice; yet the probability is, that, like the Saxons and other northern nations, they not only offered blood, but took their choicest victims from the human race.

In *Sweden* the altars of Woden smoked incessantly with blood: this flowed most abundantly at the solemn festivals celebrated every ninth year at Upsal. Then the king, attended by the senate and by all the great

officers about his court, entered the temple, which glittered on all sides with gold, and conducted to the altar nine slaves, or in time of war nine captives. These met the caresses of the multitude, as being about to avert from them the displeasure of the gods, and then submitted to their fate : but in times of distress more noble victims bled; and it stands upon record that when Aune their king was ill, he offered up to Woden his nine sons, to obtain the prolongation of his life.

The *Danes* had precisely the same abominable customs. Every ninth year, in the month of January, they sacrificed ninety-nine men, with as many horses, dogs, and cocks; and Hacon, king of Norway, offered his own son to obtain from Woden the victory over Harold, with whom he was at war.

In *Russia* the Slavi worshipped a multitude of gods, and erected to them innumerable altars. Of these deities *Peroun,* that is, the thunderer, was the supreme, and before his image many of their prisoners bled. Their god of physic, who also presided over the sacred fires, shared with him; and the great rivers, considered as gods, had their portion of human victims, whom they covered with their inexorable waves. But *Suetovid,* the god of war, was the god in whom they most delighted; to him they presented annually, as a burnt offering, three hundred prisoners, each on his horse; and when the whole was consumed by fire, the priests and people sat down to eat and drink till they were drunk. It is worthy of remark, that the residence of Suetovid was supposed to be in the sun.

To this luminary the *Peruvians,* before they were restrained by their Incas, sacrificed their children.

Among the sacred books of the Hindoos, the Ramayuna demands particular attention, because of its antiquity, the extent of country through which it is revered, and the view which it exhibits of the religion, doctrine, mythology, customs, and manners of their remote progenitors.

In this we have a golden age of short duration, succeeded by a state of universal wickedness and violence, which continued till the deity, incarnate, slew the oppressors of the human race, and thus restored the reign of piety and virtue.

This poem contains a description of the *Ushwamedha,* or most solemn sacrifice of the white horse, instituted by Swuymbhoo, that is, by the self-existent. At the celebration of this festival, the monarch, as the representative of the whole nation, acknowledged his transgressions; and when the offerings were consumed by the sacrificial fire, he was considered as perfectly absolved from his offences. Then follows a particular account of a human sacrifice, in which the victim, distinguished for filial piety, for resignation to his father's will, and for purity of heart, was bound by the king himself and delivered to the priest; but at the very instant when his blood was to have been shed, this illustrious youth was by miracle delivered; and the monarch, as the reward of his intended sacrifice, received virtue, prosperity, and fame.

It is well known that the Brahmins have in all ages had their human victims, and that even in our days thousands have voluntarily perished under the wheels of their god Jaghernaut."—*Townsend's character of Moses*, p. 76.

Though in the preceding notes I have endeavoured to make every point as clear and plain as possible; yet it may be necessary, in order to see the scope of the apostle's design more distinctly, to take a general survey of the whole. No man has written with more judgment on this epistle than Dr. Taylor, and from his notes I borrow the principal part of the following observations.

The principal thing that requires to be settled in this chapter is, what kind of *election* and *reprobation* the apostle is arguing about: whether *election*, by the *absolute decree* and purpose of God, to *eternal life*; and *reprobation*, by a like *absolute* decree, to *eternal misery*; or only *election* to the *present privileges and external advantages of the kingdom of God* in this world; and *reprobation*, or rejection, as it signifies the *not being favoured* with those *privileges* and *advantages*. I think it demonstrably clear that it is the latter election and rejection the apostle is discoursing on, and not the former; as the following considerations appear to me to demonstrate.

I. The subject of the apostle's argument is manifestly such privileges as are enumerated, verses 4, 5: *Who are Israelites, to whom pertains the adoption, &c.* From these privileges he supposes the Jews *had fallen*, or *would fall*; or, that for a *long time* they would be deprived of the benefit of them. For it is with regard to the *loss* of those privileges that he was so much concerned for his *brethren*, his *kinsmen according to the flesh*, ver. 2, 3. And it is with reference to their being stripped of these privileges that he vindicates the word and righteousness of God, ver. 24. *Not as though the word of God had taken no effect, or* failed, &c.; proving that God, according to his purpose of election, was free to confer them upon any branch of Abraham's family: consequently, those privileges were the singular blessings which by the *purpose of God according to election, not of works, but of him that calleth*, were conferred upon Jacob's posterity. But those privileges were only such as the *whole body of the Israelites* enjoyed in *this world*, while they were the Church and people of God, and such privileges as they might afterwards *lose*, or of which they might be *deprived*; therefore the election of Jacob's posterity to those privileges was not an absolute election to eternal life.

II. Agreeably to *the purpose of God according to election*, it was said unto Rebecca, *The elder shall serve the younger*, meaning the *posterity* of the elder and the younger; Gen. xxv. 23: *The Lord said unto her, two* NATIONS *are in thy womb, and two manner of* PEOPLE *shall be separated from thy bowels; and the one* PEOPLE *shall be stronger than the other* PEOPLE; *and the elder shall serve the younger.* These are the words which signify the *purpose of God according to election*: therefore the election refers to Jacob's *posterity*, or the *whole nation of Israel*. But all the nation of Israel were not absolutely elected to eternal life: therefore the purpose of God according to election referred to *temporal* and not to eternal blessings, and was a privilege of which they might be deprived.

III. Agreeably to *the purpose of God according to election*, it was said to Rebecca, *The elder shall serve*

the younger; but *to serve*, in Scripture, never meant to *be eternally damned in the world to come*: consequently the opposite blessing, bestowed upon the posterity of the younger, could not be *eternal salvation*, but certain privileges in *this life*; therefore the purpose according to election refers to those privileges, and the *servitude* does not imply everlasting perdition.

IV. The *election* the apostle speaks of is not of works, ver. 11, but of the *mere will of God*, who *calls* and *invites*, and refers to no *qualifications* in the persons thus *elected* and *called*. But in no part of the sacred writings is final salvation said to be given to any who are not *qualified* by *holiness* to receive and enjoy it; therefore election to *eternal glory* cannot be what the apostle speaks of in this epistle.

V. The *election* of which the apostle speaks took place, first in *Abraham* and his seed, before his seed was born; and then (secluding *Ishmael* and all his posterity) in *Isaac* and his seed before they were born. And then, secluding *Esau* and all his posterity, in *Jacob* and his seed before they were born. But the Scripture no where represents *eternal life* as bestowed upon any *family* or *race of men* in this manner; therefore this election mentioned by the apostle cannot be an election unto *eternal life*.

VI. *Vessels of mercy*, ver. 23, are manifestly opposed to *vessels of wrath*, ver. 22. *The vessels of mercy* are the *whole body* of the *Jews* and *Gentiles*, who were *called* or *invited* into the kingdom of God under the Gospel, ver. 24; consequently, the *vessels of wrath* are the *whole body of the unbelieving Jews*. So in ver. 30, 31, the *whole body of believing Gentiles*, who, according to God's purpose of election, had attained justification, are opposed to the *whole body of the Israelites*, who came short of it. But men shall not be received into eternal life or subjected to eternal damnation at the last day in *collective bodies*, but according as *particular persons* in those bodies have acted *well* or *ill*; therefore, this election is not of these *particular bodies* unto eternal life, &c.

VII. Whoever carefully peruses the ninth, tenth, and eleventh chapters, will find that those who *have not believed*, chap. xi. 31, are the present rejected *Jews*, or that *Israel* to whom *blindness hath happened in part*, ver. 25; the same who *fell*, and on whom God hath shown *severity*, ver. 22; the same with the *natural branches* whom *God spared not*, ver. 21; who were *broken off* from the olive tree, verses 20, 19, 17; who were *cast away*, ver. 15; who were *diminished* and *fallen*, ver. 12; who had *stumbled*, ver. 11; who were a *disobedient* and *gainsaying people*, chap. x. 21; who, *being ignorant of God's righteousness, went about to establish their own*, ver. 3; because they sought righteousness, not by faith, but as it were by the works of the law, chap. ix. 32, and therefore had not attained to the law of righteousness, ver. 31; the same people spoken of in all these places, are the *vessels of wrath fitted for destruction*, ver. 22, and the same for whom Paul had *great heaviness and continual sorrow of heart*, ver. 2, 3;—in short, they are the unbelieving nation, or people of Israel; and it is with regard to the reprobation or rejection of this people that he is arguing and vindicating the truth, justice, and wisdom of God in this *ninth* chapter.

Now, if we turn back and review those three chapters, we shall find that the apostle, chap. xi. 1, heartily desired and prayed that those same reprobated and rejected people of Israel *might be saved ;* he affirms that they had not *stumbled so as to fall* finally and irrecoverably, chap. xi. 11 ; that they should have again a *fulness,* ver. 12 ; that they should be *received* again into the Church, ver. 15 ; that a *holiness* still belonged to them, ver. 16 ; that if they did not *still abide in unbelief,* they should be *graffed into their own olive tree* again, ver. 23, 24 ; that *blindness* had *happened* unto them only for a time, *till the fulness of the Gentiles be come in,* ver. 25 ; and then he proves from Scripture, that *all Israel*—all those nations at present under *blindness,* shall be *saved,* ver. 26, 27 ; that, as touching the (original) *election, they were* still *beloved for the fathers',* the patriarchs', *sake,* ver. 28 ; that, in their case, *the gifts and calling of God were without repentance,* ver. 29 ; that *through our* (the believing Gentiles') *mercy, they shall* at length *obtain mercy,* ver. 31. All these several things are spoken of that *Israel,* or the body of people concerning whose rejection the apostle argues in the *ninth* chapter. And therefore the rejection which he there argues about cannot be *absolute reprobation* to *eternal damnation,* but to their being, as a nation, *stripped of those honours and privileges of God's peculiar Church and kingdom in this world,* to which, at a certain future period, they shall again be restored.

VIII. Once more : whoever carefully peruses those three chapters will find that the people who *in times past believed not God,* but *have* now *obtained mercy through the unbelief of the Jews,* chap. xi. 30, are the whole body of the believing Gentiles; the same who were *cut out of the olive tree which is wild by nature,* and *were graffed, contrary to nature, into the good olive tree,* ver. 24, 17 ; the same to whom God hath shown *goodness,* ver. 22 ; the world that was *reconciled,* ver. 15 ; the gentiles who were *enriched* by the *diminishing* of the Jews, ver. 12 ; to whom salvation came through *their fall,* ver. 11 ; the *Gentiles* who had *attained to righteousness,* (justification,) chap. ix. 30 ; who had *not been God's people,* nor *believed ;* but now were his *people, beloved,* and *children of the living God,* ver. 25, 26 ; even us *whom he hath called, not of the Jews only, but also of the Gentiles,* ver. 24, who are the *vessels of mercy, on whom God has made known the riches of his glory,* ver. 23 ; the *vessels made unto honour,* ver. 21. He speaks of the *same body of men* in all these places ; namely, of the *believing Gentiles* principally, but not excluding the *small remnant* of the *believing Jews,* who were incorporated with them. And it is this body of men, whose *calling* and *election* he is proving, in whose case the *purpose of God according to election stands* good, chap. ix. 11, and who are *the children of the promise that are counted for the seed,* ver. 8 :—these are the *election,* or the elect.

Now, concerning this *called* or *elect* body of people, or any particular person belonging to this body, the apostle writes thus, chap. xi. 20-22 : *Well, because of unbelief, they* (the Jews) *were broken off,* (reprobated, rejected,) *and thou standest* (in the Church among God's *called* and *elect) by faith ; be not high minded, but fear. For if God spared not the natural branches,* (the Jews,) *take heed, lest he also spare not thee,* (the Gentiles.) *Behold therefore the goodness and severity of God : on them* (the Jews) *which fell, severity ; but towards thee* (believing Gentiles) *goodness, if thou continue in his goodness ; otherwise thou also shalt be cut off,* rejected, reprobated. This proves that the *calling* and *election,* for which the apostle is arguing in the ninth chapter, is not *absolute election* unto *eternal life,* but to the *present privileges* of the Church—the *honours* and *advantages of God's peculiar people ;* which *election,* through unbelief and misimprovement, may be rendered void and come to nothing. See *Dr. Taylor,* p. 330, &c.

From thus carefully considering the apostle's discourse, and taking in his scope and design, and weighing the different expressions he uses, in connection with the Scripture facts and Scripture phrases employed in describing those facts, we must be fully convinced that the doctrines of eternal, absolute, unconditional election and reprobation have no place here, and that nothing but a pre-established creed, and a total inattention to the apostles scope and design, could ever have induced men to bend these scriptures to the above purpose, and thus to endeavour to establish as articles of faith, doctrines which, far from producing *glory to God in the highest, and peace and good will among men,* have filled the Church of God with contention, set every man's sword against his brother, and thus done the work of *Apollyon* in the name of *Christ.* If men will maintain these and such like for *Scriptural* doctrines, it is but reasonable to request that it be done in the *spirit* of the Gospel.

CHAPTER X.

The apostle expresses his earnest desire for the salvation of the Jews, 1.. *Having a zeal for God, but not according to knowledge, they sought salvation by works, and not by faith in Christ,* 2-4. *The righteousness which is of the law described,* 5. *That which is by faith described also,* 6-10. *He that believes and calls on the name of the Lord shall be saved,* 11-13. *What is necessary to salvation,—believing, hearing, preaching, a Divine mission, the Gospel, and obedience to its precepts,* 14-16. *Faith comes by hearing,* 17. *The universal spread of the Gospel predicted by the prophets,* 18-20. *The ingratitude and disobedience of the Israelites,* 21.

         2

A. M. cir. 4062.
A. D. cir. 58.
An. Olymp.
cir. CCIX. 2.
A. U. C. cir.
811.

BRETHREN, my heart's desire and prayer to God for Israel is, that they might be saved.

2 For I bear them record [a] that they have a zeal of God, but not according to knowledge.

3 For they being ignorant of [b] God's righteousness, and going about to establish their own [c] righteousness, have not submitted themselves unto the righteousness of God.

A. M. cir. 4062.
A. D. cir. 58.
An. Olymp.
cir. CCIX. 2.
A. U. C. cir.
811.

4 For [d] Christ *is* the end of the law for righteousness to every one that believeth.

5 For Moses describeth the righteousness which is of the law, [e] That the man which doeth those things shall live by them.

6 But the righteousness which is of faith speaketh on this wise, [f] Say not in thine heart, Who shall ascend into heaven? (that is, to bring Christ down *from above :*)

---

[a] Acts xxi. 20; xxii. 3; Gal. i. 14; iv. 17; see chap. ix. 31.
[b] Ch. i. 17; ix. 30.——[c] Phil. iii. 9.——[d] Matt. v. 17; Gal. iii. 24.

[e] Lev. xviii. 5; Neh. ix. 29; Ezek. xx. 11, 13, 21; Gal. iii. 12.
[f] Deut. xxx. 12, 13.

NOTES ON CHAP. X.

Verse 1. *My heart's desire, &c.*] Though the apostle knew that the Jews were now in a state of rejection, yet he knew also that they were in this state through their own obstinacy, and that God was still waiting to be gracious, and consequently, that they might still repent and turn to him. Of his concern for their salvation he had already given ample proof, when he was willing to become a sacrifice for their welfare, see chap. ix. 3.

Verse 2. *They have a zeal of God*] They believe their law to have come immediately from God himself, and are jealous of its glory and excellence; they conscientiously observe its rites and ceremonies, but they do not consider the *object* and *end* of those rites; they sin more through ignorance than malice; and this pleads in their excuse. By this fine apology for them, the apostle prepares them for the harsher truths which he was about to deliver.

Verse 3. *For—being ignorant of God's righteousness*] Not knowing God's method of saving sinners, which is the only proper and efficient method: *and going about to establish their own righteousness*—seeking to procure their salvation by means of their own contriving; *they have not submitted*—they have not bowed to the determinations of the Most High, relative to his mode of saving mankind, viz. through faith in Jesus Christ, as the only available sacrifice for sin—the end to which the law pointed.

Verse 4. *For Christ* is *the end of the law*] Where the law ends, Christ begins. The law ends with representative sacrifices; Christ begins with the *real* offering. The law is our schoolmaster to lead us to Christ; it cannot save, but it leaves us at his door, where alone salvation is to be found. Christ as an atoning sacrifice for sin, was the grand *object* of the whole sacrificial code of Moses; his passion and death were the fulfilment of its great object and design. Separate this sacrificial death of Christ from the law, and the law has no meaning, for it is impossible that the blood of bulls and goats should take away sins: wherefore the Messiah is represented as saying, *Sacrifice and offering thou didst not desire; burnt-offering and sin-offering thou hast not required; then said I, Lo, I come to do thy will; a body hast thou prepared me,* Psa. xl. 6, 7; Heb. x. 4–10; which proves that God never designed that the sacrifices of the law should be considered *the atonement* for sin, but

a type or representative of that atonement; and that THE atonement was the sacrifice offered by Christ. Thus he was the END *of the law,* in respect to its *sacrifices.* And, as sacrifices were offered merely to procure pardon of sin, righteousness, or justification, Christ is the end of the law for this justification *to every one that believeth* on him, as dying for their offences, and rising again for their justification, having made peace through the blood of his cross. Therefore every Jew who rejected Christ rejected salvation, and that very salvation which the law witnessed and required, and which could not be had but through Christ alone.

Verse 5. *For Moses describeth the righteousness which is of the law*] The place to which the apostle refers, seems to be Lev. xviii. 5: *Ye shall therefore keep my statutes and my judgments; which if a man do, he shall live in them.* These words seem to be spoken in answer to an objection which might be made by a Jew: " Did not Moses give us a law, the observance of which would secure our salvation?" Such a law Moses undoubtedly gave, and that law promises life to those who perform its precepts: but who can plead for life on this ground, who rejects that Christ who is the *end of the law?* No man ever did, nor ever can, fulfil that law, so as to *merit* salvation by the performance of it : for, as all have sinned and come short of the glory of God, they are all under the curse of the law, which says: *Cursed is every one who continueth not in all the things that are written in the book of the law to do them,* Deut. xxvii. 26; Gal. iii. 10; therefore by the deeds of this law none can be justified, because all are in a state of condemnation for transgressions already committed against it. If, therefore, there were not such a provision as is made by the death of Christ, no soul could be saved.

Verse 6. *But the righteousness which is of faith*] As it is most evident that there can be no justification by *works,* as all are *sinful* and all in a *guilty* state; if God will grant salvation at all, it must be by *faith :* but faith must have an *object* and a *reason* for its exercise; the *object* is Jesus Christ—the *reason* is the infinite merit of his passion and death.

Who shall ascend into heaven? &c.] As Christ is the end of the law for justification to every one that believes, no observance of the law can procure *him. Who,* by the practice of the law, can bring Christ down from heaven? or, when brought down, and cru-

A. M. cir. 4062.
A. D. cir. 58.
An. Olymp.
cir. CCIX. 2.
A. U. C. cir.
811.

7 Or, Who shall descend into the deep? (that is, to bring up Christ again from the dead.)

8 But what saith it? ᵍ The word is nigh thee, *even* in thy mouth, and in thy heart: that is, the word of faith, which we preach;

9 That ʰ if thou shalt confess with thy mouth the Lord Jesus, and shalt believe in thine heart that God hath raised him from the dead, thou shalt be saved.

10 For with the heart man believeth unto righteousness; and with the mouth confession is made unto salvation.

11 For the Scripture saith, ⁱ Whosoever believeth on him shall not be ashamed.

12 For ᵏ there is no difference between the Jew and the Greek: for ˡ the same Lord over all ᵐ is rich unto all that call upon him.

13 ⁿ For whosoever shall call ᵒ upon the name of the Lord shall be saved.

A. M. cir. 4062.
A. D. cir. 58.
An. Olymp.
cir. CCIX. 2.
A. U. C. cir.
811.

ᵍ Deut. xxx. 14.——ʰ Matthew x. 32; Luke xii. 8; Acts viii. 37.——ⁱ Isaiah xxviii. 16; xlix. 23; Jeremiah xvii. 7; chap. ix. 33.

ᵏ Chap. iii. 22; Acts xv. 9; Gal. iii. 28.——ˡ Acts x. 36; chap. iii. 29; 1 Tim. ii. 5.——ᵐ Eph. i. 7; ii. 4, 7.——ⁿ Joel ii. 32; Acts ii. 21.——ᵒ Acts ix. 14.

---

cified and buried, as a sacrifice for sin, who can bring him up again from the dead? And both his *death* and *resurrection* are essentially necessary for the salvation of a lost world. Or the sense of the apostle may be this: They who will not believe in Christ crucified must in effect be seeking another Messiah to come down from heaven with a different revelation; or they who will not credit the doctrine that we preach concerning his *resurrection* seem in effect to say, Christ yet remains to be raised from the dead, and reign over the Jews as a mighty secular sovereign, subjecting the Gentile world to the sway of his righteous sceptre.

Verse 8. *But what saith it? The word is nigh thee*] There is no occasion to seek *high* or *low* for the saving power; the word of reconciliation is nigh. The way of salvation is now both plain and easy. The law is magnified and made honourable by the death of Christ; and the doctrine of faith in his death and resurrection is fully proclaimed, and amply proved to be effectual to the purpose for which it was revealed. By the preaching of the Gospel the doctrine of salvation is *nigh* thee, and the saving influence is *at hand*: it is *in thy mouth*, easy to be understood, easy to be *professed*: and *in thy heart*, if thou art upright before God, sincerely desiring to be saved on his own terms, not striving to establish thy own method of justification by the law, which must for ever be ineffectual, but submitting to the method of justification which God has devised.

Verse 9. *That if thou shalt confess, &c.*] Acknowledge the Lord Jesus Christ as the only Saviour. *Believe in thy heart* that he who died for thy offences has been *raised* for thy justification; and depend solely on him for that justification, and *thou shalt be saved.*

Verse 10. *For with the heart man believeth, &c.*] And be sincere in this: *for with the heart*, duly affected with a sense of guilt, and of the sufficiency of the sacrifice which Christ has offered, *man believeth unto righteousness*, believeth to receive *justification*; for this is the proper meaning of the term here, and in many other parts of this epistle; *and with the mouth confession is made unto salvation.* He who believes aright in Christ Jesus will receive such a full conviction of the truth, and such an evidence of his redemption, that his mouth will boldly confess his

obligation to his Redeemer, and the blessed persuasion he has of the remission of all his sins through the blood of the cross. One grand object of the apostle is to show the simplicity of the Gospel scheme of salvation; and at the same time, its great efficacy. It is *simple*, and very unlike the law, which was full of rites, ordinances, ceremonies, &c., each of which required to be perfectly fulfilled: and yet, after all, even those who had the utmost zeal for God, and, as conscientiously as possible, observed all the precepts of the law, had not attained to justification nor peace of conscience. Whereas both Jews and Gentiles, who had believed on the Lord Jesus according to the simple declarations of the Gospel, were freely justified from all things from which they could not be justified by the law of Moses: and they had the witness in themselves that they were passed from death to life.

Verse 11. *For the Scripture saith*] And howsoever the Jews may despise this Gospel, because it comes not unto them with *pomp* and *ceremony*, it puts those who receive it into possession of every heavenly blessing: and this is according to the positive declarations of the prophets; for it is written, Isaiah xxviii. 16; xlix. 23.: *Whosoever believeth on him shall not be ashamed.* He shall neither be disappointed of his hope, nor ashamed of his confidence; because he has that *faith which is the evidence of things not seen, the subsistence of things hoped for,* Heb. xi. 1. See note on chap. i. 16.

Verse 12. *For there is no difference between the Jew and the Greek*] All are equally welcome to this salvation. Here the Jew has no exclusive privilege; and from this the Greek is not rejected. One simple way of being saved is proposed to all, viz. faith in the Lord Jesus Christ; because he is the same Lord who has made all and governs all, and is rich in mercy to all that call upon him.

Verse 13. *For whosoever shall call, &c.*] Nor shall any one who hears this doctrine of salvation, and credits it as he is commanded, be permitted to pray or supplicate the throne of grace in vain: for the Prophet Joel hath declared, chap. ii. 32: *Whosoever shall call upon,* invoke, *the name of the Lord* Jesus Christ, the Saviour of sinners, *shall be saved*—shall have his guilt pardoned, his heart purified; and if he abide in the faith, rooted and grounded in him, showing forth

A. M. cir. 4062.
A. D. cir. 58.
An. Olymp.
cir. CCIX. 2.
A. U. C. cir.
811.

14 How then shall they call on him in whom they have not believed? and how shall they believe in him of whom they have not heard? and how shall they hear [p] without a preacher?

15 And how shall they preach, except they be sent? as it is written, [q] How beautiful are the feet of them that preach the Gospel of peace, and bring glad tidings of good things!

16 But [r] they have not all obeyed the Gospel. For Esaias saith, [s] Lord, who hath believed [t] our [u] report?

A. M. cir. 4062.
A. D. cir. 58.
An. Olymp.
cir. CCIX. 2.
A. U. C. cir.
811.

---

[p] Titus i. 3.——[q] Isaiah lii. 7; Nahum i. 15.——[r] Chap. iii. 3; Heb. iv. 2.

[s] Isa. liii. 1; John xii. 38.——[t] Gr. *the hearing of us.*——[u] Or, *preaching.*

---

the virtues of him who has called him out of darkness into his marvellous light, *he shall be saved* with all the power of an *eternal* life.

" *Believing in Christ,* or God, ver. 11, and *calling upon God,* ver. 12, 13, 14, are in effect the same thing; as *calling upon God* necessarily connects and supposes faith in him : and he who duly believes in Christ has such a sense of his dependence upon Divine grace, that he looks unto God and trusts in his power and goodness alone for happiness : which is the true religion of the Gospel." Dr. *Taylor.*

It is evident that St. Paul understood the text of *Joel* as relating to our blessed Lord; and therefore his word Κυριος must answer to the prophet's word יהוה *Yehovah,* which is no mean proof of the Godhead of Jesus Christ. If the text be translated, *Whosoever shall invoke in the name of the Lord,* which translation יקרא בשם יהוה *yikra beshem Yehovah* will certainly bear, yet still the term *Yehovah,* the incommunicable name, is given to Christ; because *invoking in the name* signifies soliciting one in the name or on the account of another. He who is invoked is GOD; he, in whose name he is invoked, is JESUS CHRIST, who is here called *Yehovah.* He who asks mercy from GOD, in the *name* and for the *sake* of JESUS CHRIST, shall get his soul saved.

Verse 14. *How then shall they call on him*] As the apostle had laid so much stress on *believing* in order to salvation, and as this doctrine, without farther explanation, might be misunderstood, it was necessary to show how this faith was produced; and therefore he lays the whole doctrine down in a beautifully graduated order.

1. There can be no salvation without the *Gospel:* a dispensation of mercy and grace from God alone, here called, ver. 15, the *Gospel of peace; glad tidings of good things.*

2. This must be preached, proclaimed in the world for the obedience of faith.

3. None can effectually preach this unless he have a *Divine mission;* for *how shall they preach except they be* SENT, ver. 15. The *matter* must come from God; and the *person* who proclaims it must have both *authority* and *unction* from on high.

4. This Divinely-commissioned person must be *heard:* it is the duty of all, to whom this message of salvation is sent, to *hear* it with the deepest reverence and attention.

5. What is *heard* must be *credited;* for they who do not believe the Gospel as the record which God has given of his Son cannot be saved, ver. 14.

6. Those who believe must *invoke* God by Christ,

which they cannot do unless they *believe* in him; and in this way alone they are to expect salvation. *Professing* to believe in Christ, without earnest, importunate *prayer* for salvation, can save no man. All these things the apostle lays down as essentially necessary; and they all follow from his grand proposition, *Whosoever shall call upon the name of the Lord shall be saved.* But, says the apostle, *How shall they* CALL *upon him in whom they have not believed? And how shall they* BELIEVE *in him of whom they have not heard? And how shall they* HEAR *without a preacher? And how shall they* PREACH *except they be sent?* And with what message which can bring *salvation* can they be sent, but with the GOSPEL OF PEACE, the GLAD TIDINGS OF GOOD THINGS. When, therefore, there is : 1st, a proper MESSAGE; 2dly, a proper MESSENGER; 3dly, the message PREACHED, proclaimed, or properly delivered by him; 4thly, the proclamation properly HEARD and attentively considered by the people; 5thly, the message which they have *heard,* conscientiously BELIEVED; 6thly, the *name* of the Lord Jesus, by whom alone this salvation is provided, most fervently INVOKED; then, 7thly, salvation, or redemption from sin and misery, and the enjoyment of peace and happiness, will be the result of such *calling, believing, hearing, preaching, sending,* and *message* sent :—and thus the doctrine of salvation by grace through faith is guarded from abuse.

Verse 15. *How beautiful are the feet of them that preach*] Dr. Taylor remarks on this quotation, which is taken from Isa. lii. 7, that " *feet* are variously used in Scripture, and sometimes have respect to things *internal* and *spiritual.* For as the life of man and the practice of piety are compared to *walking,* Psa. i. 1, so his *feet* may signify the *principles* on which he acts, and the *dispositions* of his *mind.* Eccles. v. 1: *Keep thy foot when thou goest to the house of God.* Agreeably to this, the *feet* of the *messengers* in Isaiah, and of the *apostles* in this verse, may signify the *validity of their mission*—the authority upon which they acted, and any character or qualifications with which they were invested."

Verse 16. *But they have not all obeyed the Gospel.*] This seems to be the objection of a *Jew;* as if he had said : A Divine mission would be attended with success; whereas there are numbers who pay no attention to the glad tidings you preach. To this the apostle answers, that the Spirit of God, by Isaiah, chap. liii. 1, foretold it would be *so,* even in the *case of the Jews* themselves, when he said, *Lord, who hath believed our report?* For although God brings the message of salvation to men, he does not *oblige* them to embrace it

2

A. M. cir. 4062.
A. D. cir. 58.
An. Olymp.
cir. CCIX. 2.
A. U. C. cir.
811.

17 So then faith *cometh* by hearing, and hearing by the word of God.

18 But I say, Have they not heard? Yes, verily, [v] their sound went into all the earth, [w] and their words unto the ends of the world.

19 But I say, Did not Israel know? First Moses saith, [x] I will provoke you to jealousy by *them that are* no people, *and* by a

foolish nation I will anger you.

A. M. cir. 4062.
A. D. cir. 58.
An. Olymp.
cir. CCIX. 2.
A. U. C. cir.
811.

20 But Esaias is very bold, and saith, [z] I was found of them that sought me not; I was made manifest unto them that asked not after me.

21 But to Israel he saith, [a] All day long I have stretched forth my hands unto a disobedient and gainsaying people.

---

[v] Psa. xix. 4; Matt. xxiv. 14; xxviii. 19; Mark xvi. 15; Col. i. 6, 23.——[w] See 1 Kings xviii. 10; Matt. iv. 8.

[x] Deut. xxxii. 21; chap. xi. 11.——[y] Tit. iii. 3.——[z] Isa. lxv. 1; chap. ix. 30.——[a] Isa. lxv. 2.

It is *proposed* to their understanding and conscience; but it does not become the means of salvation unless it be *affectionately credited.*

Verse 17. *So then faith* cometh *by hearing*] Preaching the Gospel is the ordinary means of salvation; faith in Christ is the result of hearing the *word,* the *doctrine of God preached.* Preaching, God sends; if heard attentively, faith will be produced; and if they believe the report, the arm of the Lord will be revealed in their salvation.

Verse 18. *But I say, have they not heard?*] But to return to the objection: You say *they have not all* BELIEVED; I ask: *Have they not all* HEARD? Have not the means of salvation been placed within the reach of every Jew in Palestine, and within the reach of all those who sojourn in the different Gentile countries where we have preached the Gospel, as well to the Jews as to the Gentiles themselves? Yes: for we may say of the preaching of the Gospel what the psalmist has said (Psalm xix. 4) of the *heavenly bodies: Their sound went into all the earth, and their words unto the ends of the world.* As the celestial luminaries have given testimony of the eternal power and Godhead of the Deity to the habitable world, the Gospel of Christ has borne testimony to his eternal goodness and mercy to all the land of Palestine, and to the whole Roman empire. There is not a part of the promised land in which these glad tidings have not been preached; and there is scarcely a place in the Roman empire in which the doctrine of Christ crucified has not been heard: if, therefore, the Jews have not believed, the fault is entirely their own; as God has amply furnished them with the means of faith and of salvation.

In Psalm xix. 4, the psalmist has קום *kavvam,* their *line,* which the *Septuagint,* and the apostle who quotes from them, render φθογγος, *sound;* and hence some have thought that the word in the Psalm was originally קולם *kolam, voice.* But that קו *kav* is used for *word* or *speech* is sufficiently evident from Isaiah xxviii. 10, *line* upon *line,* precept upon precept, &c., where קו is analogous to *word* or *direction.* It is very remarkable that these words of David, quoted by St. Paul, are mentioned in *Sohar. Genes.* fol. 9, where it is said: עבדי משיחא אינון מלין *Abdey mashicha innun millin.* "These words are the servants of the Messiah, and measure out both the things above and the things beneath." To this notion of them the apostle may refer in his use of them in this place, and to a Jew the application would be legitimate.

Verse 19. *But I say, Did not Israel know?*] You object to this preaching among the *Gentiles;* but is not this according to the positive declaration of God? He, foreseeing your unbelief and rebellion, said by Moses, Deut. xxxii. 21, *I will provoke you to jealousy by them that are no people, and by a foolish nation I will anger you.* As you have provoked me to jealousy with worshipping those that are *no gods,* I will provoke you to jealousy by those which are *no people.* This most evidently refers to the *calling* or *inviting* of the Gentiles to partake of the benefits of the Gospel; and plainly predicts the envy and rage which would be excited in the Jews, in consequence of those offers of mercy made to the Gentiles.

Verse 20. *But Esaias* (the Greek orthography for *Isaiah*) *is very bold*] Speaks out in the fullest manner and plainest language, chap. lxv. 1, notwithstanding the danger to which such a declaration exposed him, among a crooked, perverse, and dangerous people: *I was found of them that sought me not;* I put my salvation *in the way* of those (the Gentiles) who were not seeking for it, and knew nothing of it: thus, the *Gentiles which followed not after righteousness have attained to the law of righteousness,* chap. ix. 30, and they have found that redemption which the Jews have rejected.

Verse 21. *But to Israel he saith*] In the very next verse, (Isa. chap. lxv. 2,) *All day long have I stretched forth my hands,* manifesting the utmost readiness and willingness to gather them all together under my protecting care; but *I stretched forth my hands* in vain, for they are *a disobedient and gainsaying people.* They not only disobey my command, but they gainsay and contradict my prophets. Thus the apostle proves, in answer to the objection made ver. 16, that the *infidelity* of the Jews was the effect of their own *obstinacy;* that the opposition which they are now making to the Gospel was foretold and deplored 700 years before; and that their opposition, far from being a proof of the insufficiency of the Gospel, proved that this was the grand means which God had provided for their salvation; and having rejected this, they could expect no other. And this gives the apostle opportunity to speak largely concerning their rejection in the following chapter.

I. IN the preceding chapter are several quotations from the *law,* the *prophets,* and the *Psalms;* and as the apostle seems to take them with considerable latitude of meaning, it has been thought that he only uses

2

their *words* as being well calculated to express his *sense*, without paying any attention to their *original import.* This principle is too lax to be introduced in such solemn circumstances. Dr. Taylor has made some judicious and useful distinctions here. After observing that, if we allow this principle, no argument can be built on any of the apostle's quotations; and that it must have been an indifferent thing with him whether he did or did not understand the Scripture—as, on this supposition, they would serve him as well *without* as with the *true meaning*—he adds: the apostle was a strict and close quoter of the Scripture; but he did not always quote them in the same manner, or for the same purpose.

1. *Sometimes* his intention goes no farther than using the *same strong expressions*, as being equally applicable to the point in hand. So, verses 6, 7, and 8, of this chapter, he uses the words of *Moses*, not to prove any thing, nor as if he thought Moses spoke of the same subject, but only as intimating that the strong and lively expressions which Moses used concerning the doctrine he taught, were equally applicable to the faith of the Gospel. So, in the same manner, verse 18, he quotes Psalm xix. 4, though it is likely (see the note in that place) that those expressions were used by the ancient Jews in application to the *Messiah* as the apostle applies them.

2. *Sometimes* the design of the quotation is only to show that the *cases* are *parallel:* or, that what happened in his times corresponded with what happened in former days. So chap. ii. 24; viii. 36; ix. 27, 28, 29; xi. 2, 3, 4, 5, 8, 9, 10; xv. 21.

3. *Sometimes* the quotation is only intended to *explain* a doctrinal point, as chap. i. 17; iv. 6, 7, 8, 18—21; ix. 20, 21; x. 15; xv. 3.

4. *Sometimes* the quotation is designed to *prove* a doctrinal point. Chap. iii. 4, 10—19; iv. 3—17; v. 12, 13, 14; ix. 7, 9, 12, 13, 15, 17; x. 5, 11, 13; xii. 19, 20; xiii. 9; xiv. 11.

5. *Sometimes* it is the intention of the quotation to prove that something was *predicted*, or *properly foretold* in the prophetic writings, as chap. ix. 25, 26, 33; x. 16, 19, 20, 21; xi. 26, 27; xv. 9—13.

These things duly considered, it will appear that the apostle has every where shown a just regard to the true sense of the Scripture he quotes, in the *view* in which he quotes it.

These rules may help to vindicate the quotations in all the apostolic writings. And it is evident that we cannot form a true judgment upon any quotation, unless we take in the *intention* of the writer, or the *view* in which he quotes.

II. The apostle here makes a just and proper distinction between the righteousness or justification that is of the law, and that which is by faith in Christ. And, in his view of the former, shows it to be absolutely impossible; for if no man is *to live thereby*—to have *spiritual* and *eternal life*, but he who *does* these things; then salvation on that ground must be impossible; for, 1. The law makes no *provision* for the *pardon of sin.* 2. It affords no *helps* for the performance of duty. 3. It makes no *allowances* for imperfections in duty, or for imperfections in our nature. 4. Its commandments, necessarily, suppose a *righteous soul*, and *a vigorous body;* and it does not lower its claims to the fallen state of man. 5. It requires *perfect obedience*, not only in all *things*, but in all *places* and *circumstances.* The man who comes up to this standard, has ever *been in it*, and has never swerved from it, shall, by the law, live for ever. But no man, since the fall, ever did so or ever can do so: therefore, salvation by the works of the law is absolutely impossible. But, 1. The righteousness or justification, which is by faith, receives Christ as an atoning sacrifice, by which all past sin is pardoned. 2. Receives continual supplies of grace from Christ by the eternal Spirit, through which the man is enabled to love God with all his heart, soul, mind, and strength, and his neighbour as himself. 3. This grace is afforded in sufficient degrees suited to all places, times, and circumstances, so that no trial can happen too great to be borne, as the grace of Christ is ever at hand to support and to save to the uttermost. The law is the letter that killeth; the Gospel is the spirit that giveth life. Reader, let thy whole soul say with the apostle, Thanks be unto God for his unspeakable gift!

CHAPTER XI.

God has not universally *nor* finally *rejected Israel; nor are they all at present rejecters of the Gospel, for there is a* remnant *of true believers now, as there was in the days of the Prophet Elijah, 1–5. These have embraced the Gospel, and are saved by* grace, *and not by the* works *of the law, 6. The body of the Israelites, having rejected this, are* blinded, *according to the prophetic declaration of David, 7–10. But they have not stumbled, so as to be finally* rejected; *but through their* fall, *salvation is come to the Gentiles, 11–14. There is hope of their restoration, and that the nation shall yet become a holy people, 15, 16. The converted Gentiles must not exult over the fallen Jews; the latter having fallen by unbelief, the former stand by faith, 17–20. The Jews, the natural branches, were broken off from the true olive, and the Gentiles having been grafted in, in their place, must walk uprightly, else they also shall be cut off, 21, 22. The Jews, if they abide not in unbelief, shall be again grafted in; and when the fulness of the Gentiles is come in, the great Deliverer shall turn away ungodliness from Jacob, according to the covenant of God, 23–27. For the sake of their* forefathers God loves them, and will again call them, and communicate His gifts to them, 28, 29. The Gospel shall be again sent to them, as it has now been sent to the Gentiles, 30–32. This procedure is according to the immensity of the wisdom, knowledge, and unsearchable judgments of God, who is the Creator, Preserver, and Governor of all things, and to whom all adoration is due, 33–36.*

A. M. cir. 4062.
A. D. cir. 58..
An. Olymp.
cir. CCIX. 2.
A. U. C. cir.
811.

I SAY then, ^a Hath God cast away his people? God forbid. For ^b I also am an Israelite, of the seed of Abraham, *of* the tribe of Benjamin.

2 God hath not cast away his people which ^c he foreknew. Wot ye not what the Scrip-

ture saith ^d of Elias? how he maketh intercession to God against Israel, saying,

A. M. cir. 4062.
A. D. cir. 58.
An. Olymp.
cir. CCIX. 2.
A. U. C. cir.
811.

3 ^e Lord, they have killed thy prophets, and digged down thine altars; and I am left alone, and they seek my life.

---

^a 1 Sam. xii. 22; Jer. xxxi. 37.——^b 2 Cor. xi. 22; Phil. iii. 5.

^c Chap. viii. 29.——^d Gr. *in Elias?*——^e 1 Kings xix. 10, 14.

NOTES ON CHAP. XI.

This chapter is of the *prophetic* kind. It was by the spirit of prophecy that the *apostle* foresaw the rejection of the Jews, which he supposes in the two preceding chapters; for when he wrote the epistle they were not, in *fact*, rejected, seeing their polity and Church were then standing. But the event has proved that he was a true prophet; for we know that in about *ten* or *eleven* years after the writing of this letter the temple was destroyed, the Jewish polity overthrown, and the Jews expelled out of the promised land, which they have never been able to recover to the present day.

This, 1. confirms the arguments which the apostle had advanced to establish the calling of the Gentiles. For the Jews are, in *fact*, rejected; consequently, our calling is, in fact, not invalidated by any thing they suggested, relative to the *perpetuity* of the *Mosaic dispensation*. But that dispensation being wholly subverted, our title to the privileges of God's Church and people stands clear and strong; the Jewish constitution only could furnish objections against our claim; and the event has silenced every objection from that quarter.

2. The actual rejection of the Jews proves Paul to be a *true apostle* of Jesus Christ, and that he spoke by the Spirit of God; otherwise, he could not have argued so fully upon a case which was yet to come, and of which there was no appearance in the state of things when he wrote this epistle. And this very circumstance should induce us to pay great attention to this chapter, in which he discourses concerning the *extent* and *duration* of the rejection of his countrymen, to prevent their being insulted and despised by the *Gentile Christians.* (1) As to the *extent* of this rejection, it is not absolutely *universal;* some of the Jews have embraced the Gospel, and are incorporated into the Christian Church with the believing Gentiles. Upon the case of these believing Jews he comments, ver. 1–7. (2) As to the *duration* of it, it is not *final* and *perpetual*, for *all* Israel, or the nation of the Jews, which is now *blinded*, shall one day be *saved* or brought again into the kingdom or covenant of God. Upon the state of these *blinded* Jews he comments, ver. 7 to the end of the chapter. His design, in discoursing upon this subject, was not only to make the thing itself known, but partly to engage the attention of the unbelieving Jew; to conciliate his favour, and, if possible, to induce him to come into the Gospel scheme; and partly to dispose the *Gentile Christians* not to treat the Jews with contempt; (considering that they derived all their present blessings from the *patriarchs*, the *ancestors* of the Jewish nation, and were engrafted into the good olive tree, whence the Jews had been broken;) and to admonish them to take warning by the fall of

the Jews; to make a good improvement of their religious privileges, lest, through unbelief, any of them should relapse into *heathenism*, or perish finally at the last day.

The thread of his discourse leads him into a general survey and comparison of the several dispensations of God towards the *Gentiles* and *Jews;* and he concludes this survey with adoration of the depths of the Divine knowledge and wisdom exercised in the various constitutions erected in the world, ver. 30–36.

Verse 1. *I say then, hath God cast away his people?*] Has he *utterly* and *finally* rejected them? for this is necessarily the apostle's meaning, and is the import of the Greek word απωσατο, which signifies to *thrust* or *drive away*, from απο, *from*, and ωθεω, to *thrust* or *drive;* has he thrust them off, and driven them eternally from him? *God forbid*—by no means. This rejection is neither *universal* nor *final. For I also am an Israelite*—I am a regular descendant from *Abraham*, through *Israel* or *Jacob*, and by his son *Benjamin.* And *I* stand in the Church of God, and in the peculiar covenant; for the rejection is only of the obstinate and disobedient; for those who believe on Christ, as I have done, are continued in the Church.

Verse 2. *God hath not cast away his people which he foreknew.*] God has not finally and irrecoverably rejected a people whom he has *loved* (or *approved*) *so long*, ὁν προεγνω, for this is evidently the meaning of the word in this place, as we have already seen, chap. viii. 29, and is a very general meaning of the original verb ידע *yada* in Hebrew and γινωσκω in Greek; as I have had often occasion to notice in different parts of this work, and what none will deny who consults the original. See *Schleusner, Parkhust, &c.*

Wot ye not what the Scripture saith] Ουκ οιδατε, *Do ye not know what the Scripture saith?* The reference is to 1 Kings xix. 10, 14. And the apostle's answer to the objecting Jew is to the following effect: God hath not universally thrust away his people, for whom in the promise to Abraham he intended, and to whom decreed, to grant his special favour and blessing; but the case is now much as it was in the days of Elijah: that prophet, in his addresses to God, made his complaint against Israel thus:—

Verse 3. *Lord, they have killed thy prophets*] They will not permit any person to speak unto them in thy name; and they murder those who are faithful to the commission which they have received from thee.

Digged down thine altars] They are profligate and profane beyond example, and retain not the slightest *form* of religion.

    2

A. M. cir. 4062.
A. D. cir. 58.
An. Olymp.
cir. CCIX. 2.
A. U. C. cir.
811.

4 But what saith the answer of God unto him? [f] I have reserved to myself seven thousand men, who have not bowed the knee to *the image of* Baal.

5 [g] Even so then at this present time also there is a remnant according to the election of grace.

6 And [h] if by grace, then *is it* no more of

works : otherwise grace is no more grace. But if *it be* of works, then is it no more grace : otherwise work is no more work.

A. M. cir. 4062.
A. D. cir. 58.
An. Olymp.
cir. CCIX. 2.
A. U. C. cir.
811.

7 What then ? [i] Israel hath not obtained that which he seeketh for ; but the election hath obtained it, and the rest were [k] blinded,

8 (According as it is written, [l] God hath

---

[f] 1 Kings xix. 18.——[g] Chap. ix. 27.——[h] Chap. iv. 4, 5; Gal. v. 4; see Deut. ix. 4, 5.

[i] Chap. ix. 31; x. 3.——[k] Or, *hardened;* 2 Cor. iii. 14.——[l] Isa. xxix. 10.

I am left alone] There is no prophet besides myself left, and they seek to destroy me.

Verse 4. *But what saith the answer of God*] The answer which God made assured him that there were *seven thousand*, that is, *several* or *many* thousands ; for so we must understand the word *seven*, a *certain* for an *uncertain* number. These had continued faithful to God ; but, because of Jezebel's persecution, they were obliged to *conceal* their attachment to the true religion ; and God, in his providence, preserved them from her sanguinary rage.

Who have not bowed the knee] Baal was the god of Jezebel ; or, in other words, his worship was then the worship of the *state ;* but there were several thousands of pious Israelites who had not acknowledged this idol, and did not partake in the idolatrous worship.

Verse 5. *Even so then at this present time*] As in the present day the irreligion of the Jews is very great ; yet there is a *remnant*, a considerable number, who have accepted of the grace of the Gospel.

According to the election of grace.] And these are saved just as God has saved all believers from the beginning ; they are chosen by his *grace*, not on account of any *worth* or *excellence* in themselves, but through his goodness are they chosen to have a place in his Church, and continue to be his people, entitled to all the privileges of the new covenant. The *election of grace* simply signifies God's gracious design in sending the Christian system into the world, and saving under it all those who believe in Christ Jesus, and none else. Thus the believers in Christ are *chosen* to inherit the blessings of the Gospel, while those who seek justification by the works of the law are *rejected*.

Verse 6. *And if by grace*] And let this very remnant of pious Jews, who have believed in Christ Jesus, know that *they* are brought in, precisely in the same way as God has brought in the *Gentiles ;* the one having no more *worthiness* to plead than the other ; *both* being brought in, and continued in by God's free grace, and not by any observance of the Mosaic law.

And this is done *according to the election of grace*, or the *rule* of choosing any persons to be the people of God upon the footing of grace ; which takes in all that *believe* in his Son Jesus Christ : some of the Jewish people did so believe ; therefore those believing Jews are a *remnant according to the election of grace*. They are saved in that way in which alone God will save mankind.

And if by grace] Then let these very persons remember, that their election and interest in the covenant of God has no connection with their *old Jewish*

works ; for were it of *works, grace* would lose its proper nature, and cease to be what it is—*a free undeserved gift.*

But if it be of works] On the other hand, could it be made to appear that they are invested in these privileges of the kingdom of Christ only by the *observance of the law of Moses*, then GRACE would be quite set aside ; and if it were not, *work*, or the *merit of obedience*, would lose its proper nature, which excludes *favour* and *free gift.* But it is not, and cannot be, of WORKS ; for those very Jews who now believe, and are happy in the *grace* of our Lord Jesus Christ, are so *according to the election of grace*, which does not mean a particular act of God's sovereignty, which has singled out some of the Jews who deserved to have been cast off as well as the rest ; but it is that general scheme of grace, according to which God purposed to take into his Church and kingdom any, among either Jews or Gentiles, who should believe on Christ. And the *remnant* here mentioned were not *selected* from their countrymen by such a *sovereign* act of God's grace as might have taken in the whole if it had so pleased ; but they were admitted into and received the privileges of the Messiah's kingdom, *because they believed on the Lord Jesus*, and received him as their *only Saviour ;* and thus came into that *scheme of election* which God had appointed. And we may observe, farther, that out of this election *they* as well as the *others* would have been excluded, had *they* like the *rest* remained in unbelief ; and into this *election of grace* all the Jews, to a man, notwithstanding they were all sinners, would have been taken, had they believed in Christ Jesus. This is the true notion of the *election of grace.* See *Taylor.*

Verse 7. *What then ?*] What is the real state of the case before us ? *Israel*—the body of the Jewish people, have not obtained that which they so earnestly desire, i. e. to be continued, as they have been hitherto, the peculiar people of God ; *but the election hath obtained it*—as many of them as have believed in Jesus Christ, and accepted salvation through him : this is the grand scheme of the *election by grace ;* God chooses to make those his peculiar people who believe in his Son, and none other shall enjoy the blessings of his kingdom. Those who would not receive him are *blinded ;* they have shut their eyes against the light, and are in the very circumstances of those mentioned by the Prophet Isaiah, chap. xxix. 10.

Verse 8. *God hath given them the spirit of slumber*] As they had *wilfully* closed their eyes against the light, so God has, in judgment, given them up to the *spirit*

2

A. M. cir. 4062.
A. D. cir. 58.
An. Olymp.
cir. CCIX. 2.
A. U. C. cir.
811.

given them the spirit of [m] slumber, [n] eyes that they should not see, and ears that they should not hear ;) unto this day.

9 And David saith, [o] Let their table be made a snare, and a trap, and a stumbling-block, and a recompense unto them :

10 [p] Let their eyes be darkened, that they may not see, and bow down their back alway.

11 I say then, Have they stumbled that they should fall ? God forbid : but *rather* [q] through their fall salvation *is come* unto the Gentiles, for to provoke them to jealousy.

12 Now if the fall of them *be* the riches of the world, and the [r] diminishing of them the riches of the Gentiles ; how much more their fulness ?

A. M. cir. 4062.
A. D. cir. 58.
An. Olymp.
cir. CCIX. 2.
A. U. C. cir.
811.

---

[m] Or, *remorse.*——[n] Deut. xxix. 4 ; Isa. vi. 9 ; Jer. v. 21 ; Ezek. xii. 2 ; Matt. xiii. 14 ; John xii. 40 ; Acts xxviii. 26, 27.

[o] Psa. lxix. 22.——[p] Psa. lxix. 23.——[q] Acts xiii. 46 ; xviii. 6 ; xxii. 18, 21 ; xxviii. 24, 28 ; chap. x. 19.——[r] Or, *decay, or, loss.*

---

of slumber. The very word and revelation of God, which should have awakened their consciences, and opened their eyes and ears, have had a very different effect ; and because *they did not receive the truth in the love thereof,* that which would otherwise have been the *savour of life unto life,* has become the *savour of death unto death ;* and this continues to the present day.

Verse 9. *And David saith, Let their table, &c.*] And from their present disposition it is reasonable to conclude that the same evils will fall upon them as fell upon the disobedient in former times, as predicted by David, Psalm lxix. 22, 23, that their very *blessings* should become *curses* to them, and their *temporal mercies* be their only recompense ; and yet even these earthly blessings, by not being enjoyed in the Lord, should be a stumbling block over which they should fall, and, instead of being a *blessing,* should be the means of their *punishment.* They *would* have a *worldly* Messiah, and therefore they rejected him whose kingdom was not of this world.

Verse 10. *Let their eyes be darkened*] All these words are *declarative,* and not *imprecatory.* God *declares* what will be the case of such obstinate unbelievers ; their *table,* their common providential blessings, will *become a snare,* a *trap,* a *stumbling block,* and the means of their punishment. Their eyes will be more and more darkened as they persist in their unbelief, and their *back shall be bowed down always ;* far from becoming a *great* and *powerful nation,* they shall continue ever in a state of *abject slavery* and oppression, till they acknowledge Jesus as the promised Messiah, and submit to receive redemption in his blood.

Verse 11. *Have they stumbled that they should fall ?*] Have the Jews, now for their disobedience and unbelief rejected, so sinned against God as to be for ever put out of the reach of his mercy ? *By no means.* Are they, as a nation, utterly irrecoverable ? This is the sense of the place, and here the prophecy of the restoration of the Jewish nation commences.

But rather *through their fall salvation* is come] The Church of God cannot fail ; if the Jews have *broken the everlasting covenant,* Isaiah xxiv. 5, the Gentiles shall be taken into it ; and this very circumstance shall be ultimately the means of exciting them to seek and claim a share in the blessings of the new covenant ; and this is what the apostle terms *provoking them to jealousy,* i. e. exciting them to emulation,

for so the word should be understood. We should observe here, that the *fall* of *the Jews* was not in *itself* the cause or reason of the *calling of the Gentiles ;* for whether the Jews had *stood* or *fallen,* whether they had *embraced* or *rejected* the Gospel, it was the original purpose of God to take the Gentiles into the Church ; for this was absolutely implied in the covenant made with Abraham : and it was in virtue of that covenant that the Gentiles were now called, and *not* BECAUSE of the *unbelief* of the *Jews.* And hence we see that their fall was not the necessary means of the salvation of the Gentiles ; for certainly the *unbelief* of the *Jews* could never produce *faith* in the *Gentiles.* The simple state of the case is : the Jews, in the most obstinate and unprincipled manner, rejected Jesus Christ and the salvation offered them in his name ; then the apostles *turned to the Gentiles,* and they heard and believed. The Jews themselves perceived that the Gentiles were to be put in possession of similar privileges to those which they, as the peculiar people of God, had enjoyed ; and this they could not bear, and put forth all their strength in opposition and persecution. The *calling of the Gentiles,* which existed in the original purpose of God, became in a certain way *accelerated* by the unbelief of the Jews, through which they forfeited all their privileges, and *fell* from that state of glory and dignity in which they had been long placed as the peculiar people of God. See Taylor.

Verse 12. *Now if the fall of them*] The English reader may imagine that, because *fall* is used in both these verses, the original word is the same. But *their fall,* and *the fall of them,* is παραπτωμα, the same word which we render *offence,* chap. v. 15, 17, 18, and might be rendered *lapse.* Whereas *that they should fall* (ver. 11) is, ινα πεσωσι. Now, πιπτω, *to fall,* is used in a sense so very emphatical as to signify *being slain.* So Homer, II. viii., ver. 475.

Ηματι τω, οτ' αν οι μεν επι πρυμνησι μαχωνται,
Στεινει εν αινοτατω, περι Πατροκλοιο πεσοντος·
Ὡς γαρ θεσφατον εστι.

And for Patroclus *slain,* the crowded hosts,
In narrow space, shall at the ships contend.
Such the divine decree.

And again, Il. xi., ver. 84.

Οφρα μεν ηως ην και αεξετο ιερον ημαρ,
Τοφρα μαλ' αμφοτερων βελε' ηπτετο, πιπτε δε λαος.

    2

A. M. cir. 4062.
A. D. cir. 58.
An. Olymp.
cir. CCIX. 2.
A. U. C. cir.
811.

13 For I speak to you Gentiles, inasmuch as I am [s] the apostle of the Gentiles, I magnify mine office :

14 If by any means I may provoke to emulation *them which are* my flesh, and [t] might save some of them.

[s] Acts ix. 15; xiii. 2; xxii. 21; chap. xv. 16; Gal. i. 16; ii. 2, 7, 8, 9; Eph. iii. 8; 1 Tim. ii. 7; 2 Tim. i. 11.

A. M. cir. 4062.
A. D. cir. 58.
An. Olymp.
cir. CCIX. 2.
A. U. C. cir.
811.

15 For if the casting away of them *be* the reconciling of the world, what *shall* the receiving *of them be*, but life from the dead ?

16 For if the [u] first fruit *be* holy, the lump *is* also *holy :* and if the root *be* holy, so *are* the branches.

[t] 1 Cor. vii. 16; ix. 22; 1 Tim. iv. 16; James v. 20.——[u] Lev. xxiii. 10; Num. xv. 18, 19, 20, 21.

While morning lasted, and the light of day
Increased, so long the weapons on both sides
Flew in thick vollies ; and the people *fell.*
COWPER.

It is well known, that to *fall* in battle means to be *killed.* It is in such a sense as this that St. Paul used the word *fall*, when he says, *Have they stumbled that they should* FALL ? He means a *fall* quite *destructive* and *ruinous ;* whereas by *their fall*, and *the fall of them*, he means no more than such a lapse as was *recoverable ;* as in the case of Adam's offence. See Dr. *Taylor.*

The riches of the world] If, in consequence of their unbelief, the *riches* of God's grace and goodness be poured out on the whole Gentile world, how much more shall that dispensation of grace and mercy enrich and aggrandize the Gentiles, which shall bring the whole body of the Jews to the faith of the Gospel ! Here the apostle supposes, or rather predicts, that such a dispensation shall take place ; and that, therefore, the Jews have not so *stumbled* as to be finally *irrecoverable.*

Verse 13. This and the following verse should be read in a parenthesis. St. Paul, as the apostle of the Gentiles, wished to show them the high pitch of glory and blessedness to which they had been called, that they might have a due sense of God's mercy in calling them to such a state of salvation ; and that they might be jealous over themselves, lest they should fall as the Jews had done before them : and he dwells particularly on the greatness of those privileges which the Gentiles had now received, that he might stir up the minds of his countrymen to emulation, and might be the means of *saving some of them*, as he states in the following verse.

I magnify mine office] This is a very improper translation of την διακονιαν μου δοξαζω, which is, literally, *I honour this my ministry.* Dr. Taylor has justly observed that *magnify*, except when applied to the Most High, carries with it, in our language, the idea of stretching beyond the bounds of truth; whereas the apostle simply means that he does justice to his ministry, by stating the glorious things which he was commissioned to preach among the Gentiles : blessings which the Jews by their obstinacy had forfeited.

Verse 14. *Might save some of them.*] And yet *all* these were among the *reprobate*, or *rejected*; however, the apostle supposed that *none* of them were *irrecoverably* shut out from the Divine favour ; and that *some* of them, by his preaching, might be disposed to receive salvation by Christ Jesus.

Verse 15. *But life from the dead*] If the rejection

of the Jews became the occasion of our receiving the Gospel, so that we can even glory in our tribulations, though they themselves became chief instruments of our sufferings ; yet so far must we feel from exulting over them that we should esteem their full conversion to God as great and choice a favour as we would the restoration of a most intimate friend to life, who had been at the gates of death.

The restoration of the Jews to a state of favour with God to which the apostle refers, and which is too plainly intimated by the spirit of prophecy to admit of a doubt, will be a most striking event. Their being preserved as a *distinct people* is certainly a strong collateral proof that they shall once more be brought into the Church of God : and their conversion to Christianity will be an incontestable proof of the truth of Divine revelation ; and doubtless will become the means of converting multitudes of deists, who will see the prophecies of God, which had been delivered so long before, so strikingly fulfilled in this great event. We need not wonder, if a whole nation should then be born as in a day.

Verse 16. *For if the first fruit* be *holy*] As the consecrating the first fruits to God was the means of drawing down his blessing upon the rest, so the conversion of Abraham to the true faith, and the several Jews who have now embraced Christianity, are pledges that God will, in process of time, admit the whole Jewish nation into his favour again, so that they shall constitute a part of the visible Church of Christ.

If the root be holy, so are the branches.] The word *holy* in this verse is to be taken in that sense which it has so frequently in the Old and New Testaments, viz. *consecrated, set apart to sacred uses.* It must not be forgotten that the first converts to Christ were from among the *Jews ;* these formed the *root* of the Christian Church : these were *holy*, αγιοι, *consecrated* to God, and those who among the Gentiles were converted by their means were also αγιοι, *consecrated ;* but the chief reference is to the ancestors of the Jewish people, Abraham, Isaac, and Jacob ; and, as these were *devoted to God* and received into his covenant, all their posterity, the *branches* which proceeded from this *root*, became entitled to the same privileges : and as the *root* still remains, and the *branches* also, the descendants from that root still remain : they still have a certain title to the blessings of the covenant ; though, because of their obstinate unbelief, these blessings are suspended, as they cannot, even on the ground of the *old covenant*, enjoy these blessings but through *faith :* for it was when Abraham *believed* God that it

129

A. M. cir. 4062.
A. D. cir. 58.
An. Olymp.
cir. CCIX. 2.
A. U. C. cir.
811.

17 And if some of the branch-es [v] be broken off, and [w] thou, being a wild olive tree, wert graffed in [x] among them, and with them partakest of the root and fatness of the olive tree ;

18 [y] Boast not against the branches. But if thou boast, thou bearest not the root, but the root thee.

19 Thou wilt say then, The branches were broken off, that I might be graffed in.

20 Well ; because of unbelief they were broken off, and thou standest by faith. [z] Be not high-minded, but [a] fear :

A. M. cir. 4062
A. D. cir. 58.
An. Olymp.
cir. CCIX. 2.
A. U. C. cir.
811.

21 For if God spared not the natural branches, *take heed* lest he also spare not thee.

22 Behold therefore the goodness and seve-rity of God : on them which fell, severity ; but toward thee, goodness, [b] if thou continue in *his* goodness : otherwise [c] thou also shalt be cut off.

[v] Jer. xi. 16.———[w] Acts ii. 39 ; Eph. ii. 12, 13.———[x] Or, *for them.* [y] 1 Cor. x. 12.———[z] Chap. xii. 16.

[a] Prov. xxviii. 14 ; Isa. lxvi. 2 ; Phi.. ii. 12.———[b] 1 Cor. xv. 2 ; Heb. iii. 6, 14.———[c] John xv. 2.

was accounted to him for righteousness ; and thus he became an heir of the righteousness which is by faith.

Verse 17. *And if some of the branches, &c.*] If the present nation of the Jews, because of their unbelief, are cut off from the blessings of the Church of God, and the high honour and dignity of being his peculiar people ; *and thou, being a wild olive*—ye *Gentiles,* being without the knowledge of the true God, and consequently bringing forth no fruits of righteousness, *wert grafted in among them*—are now inserted in the original stock, having been made partakers of the faith of Abraham, and consequently of his blessings ; and enjoy, as the people did who sprang from him, *the fatness of the olive tree*—the promises made to the patriarchs, and the spiritual privileges of the Jewish Church :—

Verse 18. *Boast not against the branches.*] While you are ready to acknowledge that you were inclu-ded in the covenant made with Abraham, and are now partakers of the same blessings with him, do not *exult over,* much less *insult, the branches,* his present descendants, whose room you now fill up, *according to the election of grace :* for remember, ye are not the *root,* nor do ye *bear the root, but the root bears you.* You have not been the *means* of deriving any blessing on the Jewish people ; but through that very people, which you may be tempted to despise, all the blessing and excellencies which you enjoy have been commu-nicated to you.

Verse 19. *Thou wilt say then, &c.*] You may think that you have reason to exult over them ; because it is a fact that God has been displeased with them, and therefore has *broken them off ;* has cast them out of the Church, and taken you into it in their place.

Verse 20. *Well ; because of unbelief, &c.*] This statement is all true ; but then, consider, *why* is it that they were *cast out ?* Was it not *because* of their un-*belief ?* And you stand by *faith ?* you were made par-takers of these blessings by faith ; *be not high-minded ;* let this humble, not exalt you in your own estimation ; for if the blessings were received by *faith,* consequently not by works ; and if not by works, you have no merit ; and what you have received is through the mere mercy of God. They once stood by *faith ;* they gave place to *unbelief,* and fell : you stand now by *faith ;* but it is as possible for you to be unfaithful as it was for them, and consequently *you* may fall under the Divine

displeasure, as *they* have done ; be not high-minded, but fear ; watch over yourselves with godly jealousy.

Verse 21. *For if God spared not the natural branches*] If He, in his infinite justice and holiness, could not tolerate sin in the *people whom he foreknew,* whom he had so *long loved,* cherished, miraculously preserved and blessed ; take heed *lest he also spare not thee.* Be convinced that the same righteous prin-ciple in him will cause him to act towards you as he has acted towards them, if you sin after the similitude of their transgression ; and to this, self-sufficiency and self-confidence will soon lead you. Remember, there-fore, the rock whence you were hewn, and the hole of the pit whence ye were digged. Depend incessantly on God's free grace, that ye may abide in his favour.

Verse 22. *Behold therefore the goodness*] The ex-clamation, *Behold the goodness of God !* is frequent among the Jewish writers, when they wish to call the attention of men to particular displays of God's mercy, especially towards those who are singularly unworthy. See several instances in *Schoettgen.*

And severity of God] As χρηστοτης, goodness, sig-nifies the essential quality of the Divine nature, the fountain of all good to men and angels, so αποτομια, *severity,* as it is here translated, signifies that particular exercise of his *goodness* and holiness which leads him to sever from his mystical body whatsoever would injure, corrupt, or destroy it. The apostle in these verses uses a metaphor taken from engrafting, εγκεντρι-σις, from the verb εγκεντριζω, from εν, *in,* and κεντριζω, *to puncture,* because engrafting was frequently done by making a *puncture* in the bark of a tree, and then *inserting* a bud taken from another. This was the practice in the Roman agriculture, as we learn from Virgil, Georg. ii, ver. 73 :—

Nam qua se medio trudunt de cortice gemmæ,
Et tenues rumpunt tunicas, angustus in ipso
Fit nodo sinus : huc aliena ex arbore germen
Includunt, udoque docent inolescere libro.

For where the tender rinds of trees disclose
Their shooting *gems,* a swelling knot there grows ;
Just in that space a *narrow slit* we make,
Then *other buds* from bearing trees we take ;
Inserted thus, the *wounded rind* we close,
In whose moist womb the admitted infant grows.

DRYDEN.

(9**)

A. M. cir. 4062.
A. D. cir. 58.
An. Olymp.
cir. CCIX. 2.
A. U. C. cir.
811.

23 And they also, [d] if they abide not in unbelief, shall be graffed in : for God is able to graff them in again.

24 For if thou wert cut out of the olive tree which is wild by nature, and wert graffed contrary to nature into a good olive

A. M. cir. 4062.
A. D. cir. 58.
An. Olymp.
cir. CCIX. 2.
A. U. C. cir.
811.

[d] 2 Corinthians, chap. iii. 16.

In all countries the *principle* is the same, though the *mode* is various.

The apostle, having adopted this metaphor as the best he could find to express that act of God's justice and mercy by which the Jews were rejected, and the Gentiles elected in their stead, and, in order to show that though the Jewish tree *was cut down,* or its *branches lopped off,* yet it was not *rooted up,* he informs the Gentile believers that, as it is *customary* to insert a *good scion* in a *bad* or *useless* stock, they who were bad, contrary to the custom in such cases, were grafted in a *good stock,* and their growth and fruitfulness proclaimed the excellence and vegetative life of the stock in which they were inserted. This was the *goodness* of the heavenly gardener to them ; but it was *severity,* απστομια, an act of *excision* to the Jews.

The reader will observe that this term belongs to engrafting : often, in this operation, a part of a *branch* is cut off ; in that part which remains in connection with the tree a little slit is made, and then a small twig or branch taken from another tree is, at its lower end, shaved thin, wedge-like, and then inserted in the cleft, after which the whole is tied together, clayed round, &c., and the bark unites to bark ; and the *stock* and the *scion* become thus one tree, the juices of the whole stock circulating through the tubes of the newly-inserted twig ; and thus both live, though the branch inserted bears a very different fruit from that which the parent stock bore. I have often performed this operation, and in this very way, with success : and I cannot conceive that the apostle could have chosen a more apt or more elegant metaphor. The *Jewish tree* does not bring forth proper fruit ; but it will answer well to ingraft a proper fruit-bearing tree on. The *Gentiles* are a *wild olive,* which is a tree that bears no fruit ; but it may be made to bear if grafted on the Jewish *stock. Some of the branches were cut off,* that the branches of this wild olive might be inserted : the act by which this insertion is made is termed χρηστοτης, *goodness, benignity :* the act by which the branches of the original stock are broken off is termed αποτομια, *excision ;* from απο, *from,* and τεμνω, *I cut,* still keeping the metaphor taken from *engrafting* in view. Now, let the apostle's mode of reasoning be observed : the tree is *cut down,* or its *branches lopped off ;* but the tree is not *rooted up.* The Jews have stumbled, but not so as to *fall* irrecoverably ; for *if they abide not still in unbelief,* they shall be grafted in, ver. 23. The Gentiles which are grafted in on these cut-off branches, like the scion inserted into another stock, *partake of the root,* which absorbs from the earth the nutritious juices, *and the fatness* of the Jewish tree, the blessings and privileges which that people have long enjoyed, in consequence of the Abrahamic covenant, ver. 17 ; *the root,* the Jewish covenant, *bears them ;* not they the *root,* ver. 18. As, therefore, the continuance of the Gentiles as the Church and people of God de-

pends upon their interest in the Abrahamic covenant, the blessings of which they derive through the medium of the Jews, they should be grateful to God, and tolerant to those through whom they have received such blessings. And as, in the case of grafting, the prosperity of the engrafted scion depends on the existence of the parent stock, so the continuance of the Gentiles in this state of favour, (following the metaphor,) in a certain way depends on the continuance of the Jewish people : and *they* are preserved, as so many *scions* which are in process of time to be engrafted on the *Gentiles ;* and thus the *Gentiles* shall become the *means* of salvation to the *Jews,* as the *Jews* have been the means of salvation to the *Gentiles.* Following, therefore, the metaphor a little farther, which seems to have been so well chosen in all its parts, the continued existence of the Jews as a distinct people, together with the acknowledgment of the Gentiles, that they have derived their salvation and state of blessedness through them—of which Jesus Christ, born of the stock of David, is the *author ;* and the Jewish *Scriptures,* which the Gentiles receive as inspired by God, are the *evidence*—then, the restoration of the Jews to the favour of God is a necessary consequence, and indeed seems to be the principal end in reference to which the apostle reasons. The Gentiles, however, are to take care that the restoration of the Jews be not at *their* expense ; as *their* calling and election were at the expense of the *Jews :* the *latter* being cut off, that the *former* might be grafted in, ver. 19. Of this there is no kind of necessity, for the original stock, the Abrahamic covenant, is sufficient to receive them all ; and so Jews and Gentiles become one eternal flock, under one Bishop and Shepherd of all their souls.

Verse 23. *If they abide not in unbelief*] So, we find that their rejection took place in consequence of their *wilful* obstinacy : and, that they *may* return into the fold, the door of which still stands open.

For God is able to graff them in again.] Fallen as they are and degraded, God can, in the course of his providence and mercy, restore them to all their forfeited privileges ; and this will take place if *they abide not in unbelief :* which intimates that God has furnished them with all the *power* and *means* necessary for *faith,* and that they *may believe* on the Lord Jesus whenever they will. The *veil* now continues on their heart ; but it is not a veil which God has spread there, but a veil occasioned by their own voluntary and obstinate unbelief : and, when they shall turn to the Lord, (Jesus,) the veil shall be taken away. See what the apostle has said, 2 Cor. iii. 6–18.

Verse 24. *The olive tree, which is wild by nature*] Which is κατα φυσιν, *naturally,* wild and barren ; for that the *wild olive* bore no fruit is sufficiently evident from the testimony of the authors who have written on the subject ; hence the proverb, Ακαρποτερος αγριππου· more unfruitful than the wild olive. Λακωνες γαρ

A. M. cir. 4062.
A. D. cir. 58.
An. Olymp.
cir. CCIX. 2.
A. U. C. cir.
811.

tree: how much more shall these, which be the natural *branches*, be graffed into their own olive tree?

25 For I would not, brethren, that ye should be ignorant of this mystery, lest ye should be

e wise in your own conceits; that f blindness g in part is happened to Israel, h until the fulness of the Gentiles be come in.

A. M. cir. 4062.
A. D. cir. 58.
An. Olymp.
cir. CCIX. 2.
A. U. C. cir.
811.

26 (And so all Israel shall be saved: as it is written, i There shall come out of Sion the

---

e Chap. xii. 16.——f Ver. 7; 2 Cor. iii. 14.——g Or, *hardness.*

h Luke xxi. 24; Rev. vii. 9.——i Isa. lix. 20; see Psa. xiv. 7.

αγριαν ελαιαν αγριππον καλουσι· for the Lacedemonians term the wild olive αγριππον. See SUIDAS. And hence HESYCHIUS interprets αγριελαιος, *the wild olive,* (the word used here by St. Paul,) by ακαρπος, *unfruitful:* and the reason given in DIOGEN. Proverb. Cent. ii. n. 63, is φυτον γαρ εστιν ὁ αγριππος ακαρπον· *for the wild olive is an unfruitful tree.* On this account the apostle very properly says: *Thou wert cut,* εκ της κατα φυσιν αγριελαιον, *out of that olive which is uncultivated,* because it is *barren:* the κατα φυσιν does not refer here to its being *naturally* barren; but to its being *commonly* or *customarily* permitted to remain so. And that this is the import of the phrase here is evident from the next clause of the verse.

And wert graffed contrary to nature] Παρα φυσιν, contrary to all *custom;* for a scion taken from a *barren* or *useless* tree is scarcely ever known to be graffed into a good stock; but here the *Gentiles,* a *fruitless* and *sinful* race, are grafted on the ancient *patriarchal stock.* Now, if it was possible to effect such a change in the *state* and *disposition* of the *Gentiles,* who were αθεοι εν τω κοσμω, Ephes. ii. 12, *without God,* ATHEISTS, *in the world;* how much more possible is it, speaking after the manner of men, to bring about a similar change in the *Jews,* who acknowledge the one, only, and true God, and receive the law and the prophets as a revelation from him. This seems to be the drift of the apostle's argument.

Verse 25. *I would not—that ye should be ignorant of this mystery*] Mystery, μυστηριον, signifies any thing that is *hidden* or *covered,* or not *fully made manifest.* The Greek word seems to have been borrowed from the Hebrew מסתר *mistar,* from the root סתר *sathar,* to *hide, conceal,* &c.; though some derive it from μυεισθαι, *to be initiated into sacred rites,* from μυειν, *to shut up.* In the New Testament it signifies, generally, *any thing or doctrine that has not, in former times, been fully known to men:* or, *something that has not been heard of, or which is so deep, profound, and difficult of comprehension, that it cannot be apprehended without special direction and instruction:* here it signifies the doctrine of the *future restoration of the Jews,* not fully known in *itself,* and not at all known as to the *time* in which it will take place. In chap. xvi. 25 it means the *Christian religion,* not known till the advent of Christ. The apostle wished the Romans not to be ignorant of this mystery, viz. that such a thing was intended; and, in order to give them as much instruction as possible on this subject, he gives them some characteristic or sign of the times when it was to take place.

Lest ye should be wise in your own conceits] It seems from this, and from other expressions in this epistle, that the converted Gentiles had not behaved to-

ward the Jews with that decorum and propriety which the relation they bore to them required. In this chapter the apostle strongly guards them against giving way to such a disposition.

Blindness in part is happened to Israel] Partial blindness, or blindness to a *part of them;* for they were not *all* unbelievers: several thousands of them had been converted to the Christian faith; though the *body* of the nation, and especially its *rulers,* civil and spiritual, continued opposed to Christ and his doctrine.

Until the fulness of the Gentiles be come in.] And this blindness will continue till the Church of the Gentiles be fully completed—till the Gospel be preached through all the nations of the earth, and multitudes of heathens every where embrace the faith. The words πληρωμα των εθνων may be borrowed from the מלא הגוים *melo haggoyim, a multitude of nations,* which the Septuagint translate by πληθος εθνων. By the πληρωμα, or *fulness, a great multitude* may be intended, which should be so dilated on every hand as to fill *various regions.* In this sense the words were understood by *Solomon ben Melec,* ארצות הגוים שימלאו מהם. *The nations of the Gentiles shall be filled with them:* the apostle, therefore, seems to give this sense of the mystery—that the Jews will continue in a state of blindness till such time as a *multitude of nations,* or *Gentiles,* shall be converted to the Christian faith; and the Jews, hearing of this, shall be excited, by a spirit of emulation, to examine and acknowledge the validity of the proofs of Christianity, and embrace the faith of our Lord Jesus Christ.

We should not restrict the meaning of these words too much, by imagining, 1. That the *fulness* must necessarily mean *all the nations of the universe,* and all the *individuals* of those nations: probably, no more than a *general* spread of Christianity over many nations which are now under the influence of *Pagan* or *Mohammedan* superstition may be what is intended. 2. We must not suppose that the *coming in* here mentioned necessarily means, what most religious persons understand by *conversion,* a thorough *change of the whole heart and the whole life:* the acknowledgment of the Divine mission of our Lord, and a cordial embracing of the Christian religion, will sufficiently fulfil the apostle's words. If we wait for the conversion of the *Jews* till such a time as *every Gentile and Mohammedan soul* shall be, in this *especial* sense, converted to God, then—we shall wait for ever.

Verse 26. *And so all Israel shall be saved*] Shall be brought *into the way of salvation,* by acknowledging the Messiah; for the word certainly does not mean eternal glory; for no man can conceive that a time will ever come in which every Jew then living, shall be taken to the *kingdom of glory.* The term *saved,* as

2

A. M. cir. 4062.
A. D. cir. 58.
An. Olymp.
cir. CCIX. 2.
A. U. C. cir.
811.

Deliverer, and shall turn away ungodliness from Jacob :

27 [k] For this *is* my covenant unto them, when I shall take away their sins.)

28 As concerning the Gospel, *they are* enemies for your sakes : but as touching the election, *they are* [l] beloved for the fathers' sakes.

29 For the gifts and calling of God *are* [m] without repentance.

30 For as ye [n] in times past have not [o] believed God, yet have now obtained mercy through their unbelief;

31 Even so have these also now not [p] believed, that through your mercy they also may obtain mercy.

A. M. cir. 4062.
A. D. cir. 58.
An. Olymp.
cir. CCIX. 2.
A. U. C. cir.
811.

---

[k] Isaiah xxvii. 9; Jeremiah xxxi. 31, &c.; Heb. viii. 8; x. 16.
[l] Deut. vii. 8; ix. 5; x. 15.

[m] Num. xxiii. 19.——[n] Eph. ii. 2; Col. iii. 7.——[o] Or, *obeyed.*
[p] Or, *obeyed.*

---

applied to the Israelites in different parts of the Scripture, signifies no more than *their being gathered out of the nations of the world, separated to God,* and *possessed of the high privilege of being his peculiar people.* And we know that this is the meaning of the term, by finding it applied to the body of the Israelites when this alone was the sum of their state. See the *Preface*, page viii, &c.

As it is written] The apostle supports what he advances on this head by a quotation from Scripture, which, in the main, is taken from Isa. lix. 20 : The Deliverer shall come out of Zion, and turn away ungodliness from Jacob. Now this cannot be understood of the manifestation of Christ among the Jews ; or of the multitudes which were converted *before, at,* and for some time *after,* the day of pentecost; for these times were all *past* when the apostle wrote this epistle, which was probably about the 57th or 58th year of our Lord ; and, as no remarkable conversion of that people has since taken place, therefore the fulfilment of this prophecy *is yet to take place.* In what manner Christ *is to come out of Zion,* and in what *way* or by what *means* he is to *turn away transgression from Jacob,* we cannot tell ; and to attempt to *conjecture,* when the time, occasion, means, &c., are all in *mystery,* would be more than reprehensible.

Verse 27. *For this is my covenant unto them, when I shall take away their sins.*] The reader on referring to Isa. lix. 20, 21, will find that the words of the original are here greatly abridged. They are the following :—

And the Redeemer shall come to Zion, and unto them that turn from transgression in Jacob, saith the Lord. As for me, this is my covenant with them, saith the Lord, My Spirit that is upon thee, and my words which I have put in thy mouth, shall not depart out of thy mouth, nor out of the mouth of thy seed, nor out of the mouth of thy seed's seed, saith the Lord, from henceforth and for ever.

For the manner in which St. Paul makes his quotation from Scripture, see the observations at the end of the preceding chapter. The whole of these two verses should be read in a parenthesis, as I have marked them in the text ; for it is evident that the 25th verse should be immediately connected with the 28th.

It may not be amiss to subjoin here a collection of those texts in the Old Testament that seem to point out a restoration of the Jewish commonwealth to a higher degree of excellence than it has yet attained. Isa. ii. 2–5 ; xix. 24, 25 ; xxv. 6, &c. ; xxx. 18, 19,

26 ; lx. *throughout*; lxv. 17, *to the end*; Jer. xxxi. 10, 11, 12 ; xlvi. 27, 28 ; Ezek. xx. 34, 40, &c. ; xxviii. 25, 26 ; xxxiv. 20, &c. ; xxxvi. 8–16 ; xxxvii. 21–28 ; xxxix. 25, &c. ; Joel iii. 1, 2, 17, 20, 21 ; Amos ix. 9, *to the end*; Obad. ver. 17, 21 ; Micah iv. 3–7 ; vii. 18, 19, 20 ; Zeph. iii. 19, 20.

Verse 28. *As concerning the Gospel*] The unbelieving Jews, with regard to the *Gospel* which they have rejected, are at present *enemies* to God, and aliens from his kingdom, under his Son Jesus Christ, on account of that extensive grace which has overturned their *peculiarity,* by admitting the Gentiles into his Church and family : but with regard to the original purpose of *election,* whereby they were chosen and separated from all the people of the earth to be the peculiar people of God, *they are beloved for the fathers' sake* ; he has still favour in store for them on account of their *forefathers the patriarchs.*

Verse 29. *For the gifts and calling of God, &c.*] The *gifts* which God had bestowed upon them, and *the calling*—the invitation, with which he has favoured them he will never revoke. In reference to this point there is no *change of mind* in him ; and therefore the *possibility* and *certainty* of their restoration to their original privileges, of being the people of God, of enjoying every spiritual blessing with the *fulness of the Gentiles,* may be both reasonably and safely inferred.

Repentance, when applied to God, signifies simply *change of purpose* relative to some declarations made subject to certain *conditions.* See this fully explained and illustrated by himself, Jer. xviii. 7, 8, 9.

Verse 30. *For as ye in times past*] The apostle pursues his argument in favour of the restoration of the Jews. *As ye,* Gentiles, *in times past*—for many ages back.

Have not believed] Were in a state of alienation from God, *yet* not so as to be totally and for ever excluded,

Have now obtained mercy] For ye are now taken into the kingdom of the Messiah ; through *their unbelief*—by that method which, in destroying the Jewish *peculiarity,* and fulfilling the Abrahamic covenant, has occasioned the unbelief and obstinate opposition of the Jews.

Verse 31. *Even so have these also*] In like manner the Jews are, through their infidelity, shut out of the kingdom of God :—

That through your mercy] But this exclusion will not be *everlasting* ; but this will serve to open a new scene

A. M. cir. 4062.
A. D. cir. 58.
An. Olymp.
cir. CCIX. 2.
A. U. C. cir.
811.

32 For q God hath r concluded them all in unbelief, that he might have mercy upon all.

33 O the depth of the riches both of the wisdom and knowledge of God ! s how unsearchable *are* his judgments, and t his ways past finding out !

34 u For who hath known the mind of the Lord ? or v who hath been his counsellor ?

35 Or w who hath first given to him, and it shall be recompensed unto him again ?

36 For x of him, and through him, and to him, *are* all things : y to z whom *be* glory for ever. Amen.

A. M. cir. 4062.
A. D. cir. 58.
An. Olymp.
cir. CCIX. 2.
A. U. C. cir.
811.

---

q Chap. iii. 9 ; Gal. iii. 22.——r Or, *shut them all up together.*
s Psa. xxxvi. 6.——t Job xi. 7 ; Psa. xcii. 5.——u Job xv. 8 ; Isa. xl.
13 ; Jer. xxiii. 18 ; Wisd. ix. 13 ; 1 Cor. ii. 16.——v Job xxxvi. 22.

w Job xxxv. 7 ; xli. 11.——x 1 Cor. viii. 6 ; Col. i. 16.——y Gal.
i. 5 ; 1 Tim. i. 17 ; 2 Tim. iv. 18 ; Heb. xiii. 21 ; 1 Peter v. 11 ;
2 Pet. iii. 18 ; Jude 25 ; Rev. i. 6.——z Gr. *him.*

---

when, through farther displays of mercy to you Gentiles, *they also may obtain mercy*—shall be received into the kingdom of God again ; and this shall take place whenever they shall consent to acknowledge the Lord Jesus, and see it their privilege to be fellow heirs with the Gentiles of the grace of life.

As sure, therefore, as the Jews were *once* in the kingdom, and the Gentiles were not ; as sure as the Gentiles *are now* in the kingdom, and the Jews are not ; so surely will the Jews be brought back into that kingdom.

Verse 32. *For God hath concluded them all in unbelief*] Συνεκλεισε γαρ ὁ Θεος, God hath *shut* or *locked* them all up under unbelief. This refers to the guilty state of both Jews and Gentiles. They had all broken God's law—the Jews, the written law ; the Gentiles, the law written in their hearts ; see chap. i. 19, 20, and ii. 14, 15. They are represented here as having been *accused* of their transgressions ; *tried* at God's bar ; *found guilty* on being tried ; *condemned* to the death they had merited ; *remanded* to prison, till the sovereign will, relative to their execution, should be announced ; *shut* or *locked up*, under the jailer, *unbelief* ; and there both continued in the same state, awaiting the execution of their sentence : but God, in his own compassion, moved by no merit in either party, caused a *general pardon* by the Gospel to be proclaimed to *all*. The *Jews* have refused to receive this pardon on the terms which God has proposed it, and therefore continue *locked up* under *unbelief*. The *Gentiles* have welcomed the offers of grace, and are delivered out of their prison. But, as the offers of mercy *continue* to be made to all indiscriminately, the time will come when the Jews, seeing the vast accession of the Gentile world to the kingdom of the Messiah, and the glorious privileges which they in consequence enjoy, shall also lay hold on the hope set before them, and thus become with the Gentiles one flock under one shepherd and bishop of all their souls. The same figure is used Gal. iii. 22, 23. *But the Scripture hath concluded* συνεκλεισεν, locked up *all under sin, that the promise, by faith of Christ Jesus, might be given to them that believe. But before faith came, we were kept*, εφρουρουμεθα, we were guarded as in a strong hold, *under the law* ; shut up, συγκεκλεισμενοι, locked up together *unto the faith which* should afterwards be revealed. It is a fine and well chosen metaphor in both places, and forcibly expresses the guilty, helpless, wretched state of both *Jews* and *Gentiles.*

Verse 33. *O the depth of the riches both of the*

wisdom and knowledge of God !] This is a very proper conclusion of the whole preceding discourse. *Wisdom* may here refer to the *designs* of God ; *knowledge*, to the *means* which he employs to accomplish these designs. The *designs* are the offspring of infinite wisdom, and therefore they are all right ; the *means* are the most proper, as being the choice of an infinite knowledge that cannot err ; we may safely credit the goodness of the *design*, founded in infinite *wisdom* ; we may rely on the due accomplishment of the *end*, because the *means* are chosen and applied by infinite knowledge and skill.

Verse 34. *For who hath known the mind of the Lord ?*] Who can pretend to penetrate the counsels of God, or fathom the reasons of his conduct ? His designs and his counsels are like himself, *infinite* ; and, consequently, inscrutable. It is strange that, with such a scripture as this before their eyes, men should sit down and coolly and positively write about counsels and decrees of God formed from all eternity, of which they speak with as much confidence and decision as if *they* had formed a part of the council of the Most High, and had been with him in the beginning of his ways ! A certain writer, (Mr. Perkins,) after having entered into all these counsels, and drawn out his *black-lined* scheme of absolute *and eternal reprobation*, with all its causes and effects ; and then his *light-lined* scheme of absolute and eternal ELECTION, with all its causes and effects, all deduced in the most regular and graduated order, link by link ; concludes with ver. 33 : *O the depth of the riches both of the wisdom and knowledge of God ! how* UNSEARCHABLE *are his judgments, and his ways* PAST FINDING OUT ! But this writer forgot that *he had searched out God's judgments* in the one case, and *found out his ways* in the other ; and that he had given, as a proof of the success of his researches, a complete exhibition of the *whole scheme !* This conduct is worthy of more than mere reprehension ; and yet he who differs from such opinions gives, in the apprehension of some, this proof of his being included in some of the links of the *black list !* We may rest with the conviction, that God is as *merciful* and *good* in all his ways, as he is *wise* and *just*. But as we cannot *comprehend* him, neither can we his operations, it is our place, who are the objects of his infinite mercy and kindness, to adore in silence, and to obey with alacrity and delight.

Verse 35. *Or, who hath first given to him*] Who can pretend to have any *demands* upon God ! To whom is he *indebted* ? Have either Jews or Gentiles

　　　　　　　　　　　　　　　　　　　　2

any *right* to his blessings? May not he bestow his favours *as* he pleases, and to *whom* he pleases? Does he do any injustice to the *Jews* in choosing the *Gentiles?* And was it because he was under *obligation* to the *Gentiles* that he has chosen them in the place of the *Jews?* Let him who has any *claim* on God prefer it, and he shall be *compensated.*

But how can the CREATOR be indebted to the *creature?* How can the CAUSE be dependent on the *effect?* How can the AUTHOR *of providence,* and the FATHER *of every good and perfect gift,* be under obligation to *them* for whom he provides, and who are wholly *dependent* on his bounty?

Verse 36. *For of him, &c.*] This is so far from being the case, *for εξ αυτου,* OF *him,* as the original designer and author; *and δι' αυτου,* BY *him,* as the prime and efficient cause; *and εις αυτον,* TO *him,* as the ultimate end for the manifestation of his eternal glory and goodness, *are all things* in *universal nature,* through the whole compass of *time* and *eternity.*

The Emperor *Marcus Antoninus* (εις εαυτον, lib. iv.) has a saying very much like this of St. Paul, which it is very probable he borrowed from this epistle to the Romans. Speaking of *nature,* whom he addresses as God, he says, Ω φυσις εκ σου παντα, εν σοι παντα, εις σε παντα; *O, Nature!* OF *thee are all things;* IN *thee are all things;* TO *thee are all things.* Several of the Gentile philosophers had expressions of the same import, as may be seen in *Wetstein's* quotations.

To whom be *glory*] And let him have the praise of all his works, from the hearts and mouths of all his intelligent creatures, *for ever*—throughout all the generations of men. *Amen*—so be it! Let this be established for ever!

I. THE apostle considers the designs of God inscrutable, and his mode of governing the world incomprehensible. His designs, schemes, and ends are all infinite, and consequently unfathomable. It is impossible to account for the dispensations either of his justice or mercy. He does things under both these characters which far surpass the comprehension of men. But though his dispensations are a great deep, yet they are never self-contradictory: though they far surpass our *reason,* yet they never *contradict* reason; nor are they ever *opposite* to those *ideas* which God has implanted in man, of goodness, justice, mercy, and truth. But it is worthy of remark, that we can more easily account for the dispensations of his *justice* than we can for the dispensations of his *mercy.* We can every where see ten thousand reasons why he should display his justice; but scarcely can we find *one* reason why he should display his mercy. And yet, these displays of mercy for which we can scarcely find a reason, are infinitely greater and more numerous than his displays of justice, for which the reasons are, in a vast variety of cases, as obvious as they are multiplied. The sacrifice of Christ is certainly an infinite reason why God should extend, as he does, his mercy to all men; but Jesus Christ is the *gift of God's love:* who can account for the *love* that gave him to redeem a fallen world? The Jews have fallen under the displeasure of Divine justice: why they should be objects of this displeasure is at once seen in their ingratitude, disobedience, unbelief, and rebellion. But a most especial providence has watched over them, and preserved them in all their dispersions for 1700 years: who can account for *this?* Again, these very persons have a most positive promise of a future deliverance, both great and glorious: *why* should this be? The Gentile world was long left without a Divine revelation, while the Jews enjoyed one: who can account for *this?* The Jews are now cast out of favour, in a certain sense, and the reasons of it are sufficiently obvious; and the Gentiles, without any apparent reason, are taken into favour. In all these things *his judgments are unsearchable, and his ways past finding out!*

II. Once more: Let it be remarked that, although God is every where promising and bestowing the greatest and most ennobling privileges, together with an eternal and ineffable glory, for which we can give no reason but his own endless goodness, through the death of his Son; yet, in no case does he remove those privileges, nor exclude from this glory, but where the reasons are most obvious to the meanest capacity.

III. This epistle has been thought by some to afford proofs that God, by an eternal decree, had predestinated to eternal perdition millions of millions of human souls before they had any existence, except in his own purpose, and for no other reason but his sovereign pleasure! But such a *decree* can be no more found in this *book,* than such a *disposition* in the *mind* of Him who is the *perfection,* as he is the *model,* of wisdom, goodness, justice, mercy, and truth. May God save the reader from profaning his name, by suppositions at once so monstrous and absurd!

CHAPTER XII.

Such displays of God's mercy as Jews and Gentiles have received should induce them to consecrate themselves to Him; and not be conformed to the world, 1, 2. Christians are exhorted to think meanly of themselves, 3. And each to behave himself properly in the office which he has received from God, 4—8. Various important moral duties recommended, 9—18. We must not avenge ourselves, but overcome evil with good, 19—21.

A. M. cir. 4062.
A. D. cir. 58.
An. Olymp.
cir. CCIX. 2.
A. U. C. cir.
811.

I [a] BESEECH you therefore, brethren, by the mercies of God, [b] that ye [c] present your bodies [d] a living sacrifice, holy,

acceptable unto God, *which is* your reasonable service.

2 And [e] be not conformed to this world; but [f] be ye trans-

A. M. cir. 4062.
A. D. cir. 58.
An. Olymp.
cir. CCIX. 2.
A. U. C. cir.
811.

---

[a] 2 Cor. x. 1.——[b] 1 Pet. ii. 5.——[c] Psa. l. 13, 14; chap. vi. 13, 16, 19; 1 Cor. vi. 13, 20.——[d] Heb. x. 20.

[e] 1 Pet. i. 14; 1 John ii. 15.——[f] Eph. i. 18; iv. 23; Col. i. 21, 22; iii. 10.

NOTES ON CHAP. XII.

The apostle having now finished the *doctrinal* part of this epistle, proceeds to the *practical :* and here it may be necessary to take a view of his arguments in the preceding chapters.

The *election, calling,* and *justification* of the believing Gentiles, and their being admitted into the kingdom and covenant of God, and having an interest in all the privileges and honours of his children. (1.) That they have a clear and substantial title to all these he has proved in chap. i., ii., and iii. (2.) That this right is set on the same footing with Abraham's title to the blessings of the covenant he proves chap. vi. (3.) That it gives us a title to privileges and blessings, as great as any the Jews could glory in, by virtue of that covenant, chap. v. 1–12. (4.) He goes still higher, and shows that our being interested in the gift and grace of God in Christ Jesus is perfectly agreeable to the grace which he has bestowed upon all mankind, in delivering them from that *death of the body* brought on them by Adam's transgression, chap. v. 12–21. (5.) He fully explains, both with regard to the Gentiles and Jews, the nature of the Gospel constitution in relation to its obligations to holiness, and the advantages it gives for encouragement, obedience, and support, under the severest trials and persecutions, chap. vi., vii., viii. (6.) As to the pretences of the Jews, that "God was bound by express promise to continue them as his only people for ever, and that this was directly inconsistent with the election and calling of the Gentiles, on the condition of *faith* alone ;" he demonstrates that the rejection of the Jews is consistent with the truth of God's word, and with his righteousness : he shows the true cause and reason of their rejection, and concludes with an admirable discourse upon the extent and duration of it ; which he closes with adoration of the Divine wisdom in its various dispensations, chap. ix., x., xi. Thus, having cleared this important subject with surprising judgment, and the nicest art and skill in writing, he now proceeds, after his usual manner in his epistles and the apostolic method of preaching, to inculcate various *Christian duties,* and to exhort to that *temper* of mind and conduct of life which are suitable to the profession of the Gospel, and the enjoyment of its privileges.—Dr. *Taylor.*

Verse 1. *I beseech you therefore, brethren*] This address is probably intended both for the *Jews* and the *Gentiles ;* though some suppose that the Jews are addressed in the first verse, the Gentiles in the second.

By the mercies of God] Δια των οικτιρμων του Θεου· By the *tender mercies* or *compassions* of God, such as a tender father shows to his refractory children ; who, on their humiliation, is easily persuaded to forgive their offences. The word οικτιρμος comes from οικτος, com-

passion ; and that from εικω, to *yield ;* because he that has *compassionate* feelings is easily prevailed on to do a kindness, or remit an injury.

That ye present your bodies] A metaphor taken from bringing sacrifices to the altar of God. The person offering picked out the *choicest* of his flock, brought it to the altar, and *presented* it there as an atonement for his sin. They are exhorted to give themselves up in the spirit of sacrifice ; to be as wholly the Lord's property as the *whole burnt-offering* was, no part being devoted to any other use.

A living sacrifice] In opposition to those *dead* sacrifices which were in the habit of offering while in their Jewish state ; and that they should have the lusts of the flesh *mortified,* that they might *live* to God.

Holy] Without *spot* or *blemish ;* referring still to the sacrifice required by the law.

Acceptable unto God] Ευαρεστον· The *sacrifice* being *perfect* in its *kind,* and the *intention* of the offerer being such that both can be *acceptable* and *well pleasing* to God, who searches the heart. All these phrases are *sacrificial,* and show that there must be a complete surrender of the person—the *body,* the whole man, mind and flesh, to be given to God ; and that he is to consider himself no more his own, but the entire property of his Maker.

Your reasonable service.] Nothing can be more consistent with reason than that the work of God should glorify its Author. We are not our *own,* we are the property of the Lord, by the right of creation and redemption ; and it would be as *unreasonable* as it would be *wicked* not to live to his glory, in strict obedience to his will. The *reasonable service,* λογικην λατρειαν, of the apostle, may refer to the difference between the *Jewish* and *Christian* worship. The former religious service consisted chiefly in its *sacrifices,* which were δι' αλογων, of *irrational* creatures, i. e. the lambs, rams, kids, bulls, goats, &c., which were offered under the law. The Christian service or worship is λογικη, *rational,* because performed according to the true intent and meaning of the law ; the heart and soul being engaged in the service. He alone lives the life of a *fool* and a *madman* who lives the life of a sinner against God ; for, in sinning against his Maker he wrongs his own soul, loves death, and rewards evil unto himself.

Reasonable service, λογικην λατρειαν, " a religious service according to reason," one *rationally performed.* The Romanists make this distinction between λατρεια, and δουλεια, latreia and douleia, (or dulia, as they corruptly write it,) *worship* and *service,* which they say signify *two kinds of religious worship ;* the *first* proper to God, the *other* communicated to the *creatures.* But δουλεια, douleia, services, is used by the Septuagint to express the *Divine worship.* See Deut. xiii. 4 ; Judg. ii. 7 ; 1 Sam, vii. 3, and xii. 10 : and in the New Tes-

A. M. cir. 4062.
A. D. cir. 58.
An. Olymp.
cir. CCIX. 2.
A. U. C. cir.
811.

formed by the renewing of your mind, that ye may *g* prove what *is* that good, and acceptable, and perfect will of God.

3 For I say, *h* through the grace given unto me, to every man that is among you, *i* not to think *of himself* more highly than

A. M. cir. 4062.
A. D. cir. 58.
An. Olymp.
cir. CCIX. 2.
A. U. C. cir.
811.

---

g Eph. v. 10, 17; 1 Thess. iv. 3.——*h* Chap. i. 5; xv. 15; 1 Cor. iii. 10; xv. 10; Gal. ii. 9; Eph. iii. 2, 7, 8.

i Proverbs xxv. 27; Ecclesiastes vii. 16; chapter xi. 20.

---

tament, Matt. vi. 24; Luke vi. 23; Rom. xvi. 18; Col. iii. 24. The angel refused δουλειαν, *douleia*, Rev. xxii. 7, because he was συνδουλος *sundoulos*, a *fellow servant*; and the Divine worship is more *frequently* expressed by this word δουλεια, *douleia*, *service*, than by λατρεια, *latreia*, *worship*. The first is thirty-nine times in the Old and New Testament ascribed unto God, the other about thirty times; and *latreia*, worship or service, is given unto the *creatures*, as in Lev. xxiii. 7, 8, 21; Num. xxviii. 18; yea, the word signifies *cruel* and *base* bondage, Deut. xxviii. 48: once in the New Testament it is taken for the *worship* of the *creatures*, Rom. i. 25. The worshipping of *idols* is forbidden under the word λατρεια, *latreia*, thirty-four times in the Old Testament, and once in the New, as above; and twenty-three times under the term δουλεια, *douleia*, in the Old Testament; and St. Paul uses δουλευειν Θεῳ, and λατρευειν Θεῳ indifferently, for the *worship we owe to God*. See Rom. i. 9, 25; xii. 1; Gal. iv. 8, 9; 1 Thess. i. 9; Matt. vi. 24. And *Ludovicus Vives*, a learned *Romanist*, has proved out of *Suidas, Xenophon,* and *Volla,* that these two words are usually taken the *one* for the *other,* therefore the popish distinction, that the first signifies " the religious worship due only to God," and the second, "that which is given to angels, saints, and men," is unlearned and false.—See *Leigh's Crit. Sacra.*

Verse 2. *And be not conformed to this world*] By *this world,* αιωνι τουτῳ, may be understood that *present state* of things both among the Jews and Gentiles; the customs and fashions of the people who then *lived,* the Gentiles particularly, who had neither the *power* nor the *form* of godliness; though some think that the Jewish economy, frequently termed עולם הזה *olam hazzeh,* this world, this peculiar state of things, is alone intended. And the apostle warns them against reviving usages that Christ had abolished: this exhortation still continues in full force. The world that now is— THIS *present state of things,* is as much opposed to the spirit of genuine Christianity as the world *then* was. Pride, luxury, vanity, extravagance in dress, and riotous living, prevail *now,* as they did *then,* and are as unworthy of a Christian's pursuit as they are injurious to his soul, and hateful in the sight of God.

Be ye transformed] Μεταμορφουσθε, *Be ye metamorphosed, transfigured,* appear as *new persons,* and with new *habits;* as God has given you a new form of worship, so that ye serve in the newness of the spirit, and not in the oldness of the letter. The word implies a *radical, thorough,* and *universal* change, both *outward* and *inward.* SENECA, *Epis.* vi., shows us the force of this word when used in a moral sense. *Sentio,* says he, *non* EMENDARI *me tantum, sed* TRANS- FIGURARI; "I perceive myself not to be amended merely, but to be transformed:" i. e. entirely renewed.

By the renewing of your mind] Let the inward

change produce the outward. Where the *spirit,* the temper, and disposition of *the mind,* Eph. iv. 23, are not *renewed,* an outward change is of but *little worth,* and but of *short standing.*

That ye may prove] Εις το δοκιμαζειν, That ye may have *practical proof* and *experimental knowledge of, the will of God*—of his purpose and determination, which is *good* in itself; infinitely so. *Acceptable,* ευαρεστον, *well pleasing* to and *well received* by every mind that is renewed and transformed.

And perfect] Τελειον, Finished and complete: when the mind is renewed, and the whole life changed, then the will of God is perfectly fulfilled; for this is its grand design in reference to *every human being.*

These words are supposed by *Schoettgen* to refer entirely to the *Jewish* law. The Christians were to renounce *this world*—the Jewish state of things; to be *transformed,* by having their minds enlightened in the pure and simple Christian worship, that they might prove the grand characteristic difference between the two covenants: the latter being *good* in opposition to the *statutes* which were *not good,* Ezek. xx. 25; *acceptable,* in opposition to those sacrifices and offerings which God *would not accept,* as it is written, Psalm xl. 6–8; and perfect, in opposition to that system which was *imperfect,* and which made nothing perfect, and was only the *shadow of good things to come.* There are both ingenuity and probability in this view of the subject.

Verse 3. *Through the grace given unto me*] By the grace given St. Paul most certainly means his apostolical *office,* by which he had the *authority,* not only to preach the Gospel, but also to *rule* the Church of Christ. This is the meaning of the word, ἡ χαρις, in Eph. iii. 8: *Unto me who am less than the least of all saints is this grace given*—is conceded this *office* or *employment* immediately by God himself; *that I should preach among the Gentiles the unsearchable riches of Christ.*

Not to think—more highly] Μη ὑπερφρονειν, Not to *act proudly;* to arrogate nothing to himself on account of any grace he had received, or of any office committed to him.

But to think soberly] Αλλα φρονειν εις το σωφρονειν. The reader will perceive here a sort of *paronomasia,* or play upon words: φρονειν, from φρην, the *mind,* signifies to *think, mind, relish, to be of opinion, &c.;* and σωφρονειν from σοος, *sound,* and φρην, the *mind,* signifies to be of a *sound mind;* to *think discreetly, modestly, humbly.* Let no man think himself more or greater than God has made him; and let him know that whatever he *is* or *has* of good or excellence, he has it *from* God; and that the glory belongs to the giver, and not to him who has received the gift.

Measure of faith.] Μετρον πιστεως. It is very likely, as Dr. Moore has conjectured, that the πιστις, *faith,*

2

A. M. cir. 4062.
A. D. cir. 58.
An. Olymp.
cir. CCIX. 2.
A. U. C. cir.
811.

he ought to think ; but to think [k] soberly, according as God hath dealt [l] to every man the measure of faith.

4 For [m] as we have many members in one body, and all members have not the same office :

A. M. cir. 4062.
A. D. cir. 58.
An. Olymp.
cir. CCIX. 2.
A. U. C. cir.
811.

5 So [n] we, *being* many, are one body in Christ, and every one members one of another.

6 [o] Having then gifts differing [p] according to the grace that is given to us, whether [q] prophecy, *let us prophesy* according to the proportion of faith ;

---

[k] Gr. *to sobriety.*——[l] 1 Cor. xii. 7, 11 ; Eph. iv. 7.——[m] 1 Cor. xii. 12 ; Eph. iv. 16.——[n] 1 Cor. x. 17 ; xii. 20, 27 ; Eph. i. 23 ; iv. 25.——[o] 1 Cor. xii. 4 ; 1 Pet. iv. 10, 11.——[p] Ver. 3.——[q] Acts xi. 27 ; 1 Cor. xii. 10, 28 ; xiii. 2 ; xiv. 1, 6, 29, 31.

---

here used, means the Christian religion ; and the *measure*, the degree of *knowledge* and *experience* which each had received in it, and the power this gave him of being useful in the Church of God. See ver. 6.

Verse 4. *For as we have many members*] As the human body consists of many parts, each having its respective office, and all contributing to the perfection and support of the whole ; each being indispensably necessary in the place which it occupies, and each equally useful though performing a different function ;

Verse 5. *So we, being many*] We who are members of the Church of Christ, which is considered the *body* of which he is the *head*, have various offices assigned to us, according to the measure of grace, faith, and religious knowledge which we possess ; and although each has a different office, and qualifications suitable to that office, yet all belong to the *same body ;* and each has as much need of the help of another as that other has of his ; therefore, let there be neither *pride* on the one hand, nor *envy* on the other. The same metaphor, in nearly the same words, is used in *Synopsis Sohar*, page 13. " As man is divided into various members and joints, united among themselves, and raised by gradations above each other, and collectively compose one body ; so all created things are members orderly disposed, and altogether constitute one body. In like manner the law, distributed into various articulations, constitutes but *one body*." See *Schoettgen.*

Verse 6. *Having then gifts differing, &c.*] As the goodness of God, with this view of our mutual subserviency and usefulness, has endowed us with different gifts and qualifications, let each apply himself to the diligent improvement of his particular office and talent, and modestly keep within the bounds of it, not exalting himself or despising others.

Whether prophecy] That *prophecy*, in the New Testament, often means the gift of *exhorting, preaching*, or of *expounding the Scriptures*, is evident from many places in the *Gospels, Acts*, and *St. Paul's Epistles*, see 1 Cor. xi. 4, 5 ; and especially 1 Cor. xiv. 3 : *He that prophesieth speaketh unto men to edification, and exhortation, and comfort.* This was the proper office of a preacher ; and it is to the exercise of this office that the apostle refers in the whole of the chapter from which the above quotations are made. See also Luke i. 76 ; vii. 28 ; Acts xv. 32 ; 1 Cor. xiv. 29. I think the apostle uses the term in the same sense here—Let every man who has the gift of preaching and interpreting the Scriptures do it in proportion to the grace and light he has received from God, and in no case *arrogate* to himself knowledge

which he has not received ; let him not esteem himself more highly on account of this gift, or affect to be wise above what is written, or indulge himself in fanciful interpretations of the word of God.

Dr. Taylor observes that the *measure of faith*, ver. 3, and the *proportion of faith*, ver. 6, seem not to relate to the degree of any gift considered in itself, but rather in the relation and proportion which it bore to the gifts of others ; for it is plain that he is here exhorting every man to keep soberly within his own sphere. It is natural to suppose that the new converts might be puffed up with the several gifts that were bestowed upon them ; and every one might be forward to magnify his own to the disparagement of others : therefore the apostle advises them to keep each within his proper sphere ; to know and observe the just measure and proportion of the gift *intrusted* to him, not to gratify his pride but to edify the Church.

The αναλογια της πιστεως, which we here translate the *proportion of faith*, and which some render the *analogy of faith*, signifies in grammar " the similar declension of similar words ;" but in Scriptural matters it has been understood to mean the *general and consistent plan or scheme of doctrines delivered in the Scriptures ;* where every thing bears its due relation and proportion to another. Thus the death of Christ is commensurate in its merits to the evils produced by the fall of Adam. The doctrine of justification by *faith* bears the strictest analogy or proportion to the grace of Christ and the helpless, guilty, condemned state of man : whereas the doctrine of *justification by* works is out of all analogy to the demerit of sin, the perfection of the law, the holiness of God, and the miserable, helpless state of man. This may be a good general view of the subject ; but when we come to inquire what those mean by the *analogy of faith* who are most frequent in the use of the term, we shall find that it means neither more nor less than *their own creed ;* and though they tell you that their doctrines are to be examined by the Scriptures, yet they give you roundly to know that you are to understand these Scriptures in precisely the same way as *they* have interpreted them. " *To the law and to the testimony*," says Dr. Campbell, " is the common cry ; only every one, the better to secure the decision on the side he has espoused, would have you previously resolve to put no sense whatever on the *law and the testimony* but what his favourite doctrine will admit. Thus they run on in a shuffling, circular sort of argument, which, though they studiously avoid exposing, is, when dragged into the open light, neither more nor less than this : ' you are to try our doctrine by the Scriptures only :

    2

A. M. cir. 4062.
A. D. cir. 58.
An. Olymp.
cir. CCIX. 2.
A. U. C. cir.
811.

7 Or ministry, *let us wait* on *our* ministering : or ^r he that teacheth, on teaching ;

8 Or ^s he that exhorteth, on exhortation : ^t he that ^u giveth, *let him do it* ^v with simplicity ; ^w he that ruleth, with diligence ; he that showeth mercy, ^x with cheerfulness.

^r Acts xiii. 1; Eph. iv. 11; Gal. vi. 6; 1 Tim. v. 17.——^s Acts xv. 32; 1 Cor. xiv. 3.——^t Matt. vi. 1, 2, 3.——^u Or, *imparteth.* ^v Or, *liberally ;* 2 Cor. viii. 2.——^w Acts xx. 28; 1 Tim. v. 17; Heb. xiii. 7, 24; 1 Pet. v. 2.

9 ^y *Let* love be without dissimulation. ^z Abhor that which is evil ; cleave to that which is good.

10 ^a *Be* kindly affectioned one to another ^b with brotherly love ; ^c in honour preferring one another ;

A. M. cir. 4062.
A. D. cir. 58.
An. Olymp.
cir. CCIX. 2.
A. U. C. cir.
811.

^x 2 Cor. ix. 7.——^y 1 Tim. i. 5; 1 Pet. i. 22.——^z Psa. xxxiv. 14; xxxvi. 4; xcvii. 10; Amos v. 15.——^a Heb. xiii. 1; 1 Pet. i. 22; ii. 17; iii. 8; 2 Pet. i. 7.——^b Or, *in the love of the brethren.* ^c Phil. ii. 3; 1 Pet. v. 5.

but then you are to be very careful that you explain the Scripture solely by our doctrine.' A wonderful plan of trial, which begins with giving judgment, and ends with examining the proof, wherein the whole skill and ingenuity of the judges are to be exerted in wresting the evidence so as to give it the appearance of supporting the sentence pronounced before hand." See Dr. Campbell's Dissertations on the Gospels, Diss. iv. sect. 14, vol. i, page 146, 8vo. edit., where several other sensible remarks may be found.

Verse 7. *Or ministry*] Διακονια simply means the *office* of a *deacon ;* and what this office was, see in the note on Acts vi. 4, where the subject is largely discussed.

Or he that teacheth] The teacher, διδασκαλος, was a person whose office it was to instruct others, whether by catechizing, or simply explaining the grand truths of Christianity.

Verse 8. *Or he that exhorteth*] Ὁ παρακαλων, The person who admonished and reprehended the unruly or disorderly ; and who supported the weak and comforted the penitents, and those who were under heaviness through manifold temptations.

He that giveth] He who distributeth the alms of the Church, *with simplicity*—being influenced by no *partiality,* but dividing to each according to the *necessity* of his case.

He that ruleth] Ὁ προϊσταμενος, He that presides over a particular business ; but as the verb προϊσταμαι also signifies to *defend* or *patronize,* it is probably used here to signify receiving and providing for *strangers,* and especially the persecuted who were obliged to leave their own homes, and were destitute, afflicted, and tormented. It might also imply the persons whose business it was to receive and entertain the apostolical teachers who travelled from place to place, establishing and confirming the Churches. In this sense the word προστατις is applied to *Phœbe,* chap. xvi. 2 : *She hath been a* succourer *of many, and of myself also.* The apostle directs that this office should be executed with diligence, that such destitute persons should have their necessities as promptly and as amply supplied as possible.

He that showeth mercy] Let the person who is called to perform any *act* of *compassion* or *mercy* to the *wretched* do it, not grudgingly nor of necessity, but from a spirit of pure benevolence and sympathy. The poor are often both wicked and worthless ; and, if those who are called to minister to them as stewards, overseers, &c., do not take care, they will get their hearts hardened with the frequent proofs they will

have of deception, lying, idleness, &c. And on this account it is that so many of those who have been called to minister to the poor in parishes, workhouses, and religious societies, when they come to relinquish their employment find that many of their moral feelings have been considerably blunted ; and perhaps the only reward they get for their services is the character of being *hard-hearted.* If whatever is done in this way be not done unto the *Lord,* it can never be done with *cheerfulness.*

Verse 9. *Let love be without dissimulation.*] Ἡ αγαπη ανυποκριτος· Have no *hypocritical* love ; let not your love wear a mask ; make no empty professions. Love God and your neighbour ; and, by obedience to the one and acts of benevolence to the other, show that your love is *sincere.*

Abhor that which is evil] Αποστυγουντες το πονηρον· Hate sin as you would hate that *hell* to which it leads. Στυγεω signifies to *hate* or *detest with horror ;* the preposition απο greatly strengthens the meaning. Στυξ, *Styx,* was a feigned river in hell by which the gods were wont to swear, and if any of them falsified this oath he was deprived of his nectar and ambrosia for a hundred years ; hence the river was reputed to be *hateful,* and στυγεω signified *to be as hateful as hell.* Two MSS. read μισουντες, which signifies *hating* in the lowest sense of the term. The word in the text is abundantly more expressive, and our translation is both nervous and appropriate.

Cleave to that which is good.] Κολλωμενοι τω αγαθω· Be cemented or glued *to that which is good ;* so the word literally signifies. Have an unalterable attachment to whatever leads to God, and contributes to the welfare of your fellow creatures.

Verse 10. *Be kindly affectioned one to another with brotherly love*] It is difficult to give a simple translation of the original : τη φιλαδελφια εις αλληλους φιλοστοργοι. The word φιλαδελφια signifies that affectionate regard which every Christian should feel for another, as being members of the same mystical body : hence it is emphatically termed the *love of the brethren.* When William Penn, of deservedly famous memory, made a treaty with the Indians in North America, and purchased from them a large *woody* tract, which, after its own *nature* and his *name,* he called *Pennsylvania,* he built a city on it, and peopled it with Christians of his own denomination, and called the city from the word in the text, φιλαδελφια, Philadelphia ; an appellation which it *then* bore with strict propriety : and still it bears the *name.*

The word φιλοστοργος, which we translate *kindly*

A. M. cir. 4062.
A. D. cir. 58.
An. Olymp.
cir. CCIX. 2.
A. U. C. cir.
811.

11 Not slothful in business; fervent in spirit; serving the Lord;

12 [d] Rejoicing in hope; [e] pa-tient in tribulation; [f] continuing instant in prayer;

13 [g] Distributing to the necessi-ty of saints; [h] given to hospitality.

A. M. cir. 4062.
A. D. cir. 58.
An. Olymp.
cir. CCIX. 2.
A. U. C. cir.
811.

---

[d] Luke x. 20; chap. v. 2; xv. 13; Phil. iii. 1; iv. 4; 1 Thess. v. 16; Hebrews iii. 6; 1 Peter iv. 13.——[e] Luke xxi. 19; 1 Tim. vi. 11; Hebrews x. 36; xii. 1; James i. 4; v. 7; 1 Pet. ii. 19, 20.

[f] Luke xviii. 1; Acts ii. 42; xii. 5; Col. iv. 2; Eph. vi. 18; 1 Thess. i. 17——[g] 1 Cor. xvi. 1; 2 Cor. ix. 1, 12; Heb. vi. 10; xiii. 16; 1 John iii. 17.——[h] 1 Tim. iii. 2; Tit. i. 8; Heb. xiii. 2; 1 Pet. iv. 9.

---

affectioned, from φιλος and στοργη, signifies that *tender* and *indescribable affection* which a *mother bears to her child*, and which almost all creatures manifest towards their young; and the word φιλος, or φιλεω, joined to it, signifies a delight in it. Feel the *tenderest* affection towards each other, and delight to feel it. "Love a brother Christian with the affection of a natural brother."

In honour preferring one another] The meaning appears to be this : Consider all your brethren as more worthy than yourself; and let neither grief nor envy affect your mind at seeing another *honoured* and yourself *neglected*. This is a hard lesson, and very few persons learn it thoroughly. If we wish to see our brethren honoured, still it is with the secret condition in our own minds that we be honoured *more* than they. We have no objection to the *elevation* of others, providing *we* may be at the *head*. But who can bear even to be what he calls *neglected*? I once heard the following conversation between two persons, which the reader will pardon my relating in this place, as it appears to be rather in point, and is worthy of regard. "I know not," said one, "that I neglect to do any thing in my power to promote the interest of true religion in this place, and yet I seem to be held in very little repute, scarcely any person even noticing me." To which the other replied : "My good friend, set yourself down for *nothing*, and if any person takes you for *something* it will be all *clear gain*." I thought this a queer saying: but how full of meaning and common sense! Whether the object of this good counsel was profited by it I cannot tell; but *I* looked on it and received instruction.

Verse 11. *Not slothful in business*] That God, who *forbade* working on the *seventh* day, has, by the same authority, *enjoined* it on the other *six days*. He who neglects to labour during the *week* is as culpable as he is who works on the *Sabbath*. An idle, slothful person can never be a Christian.

Fervent in spirit] Τω πνευματι ζεοντες· Do nothing at any time but what is to the glory of God, and do every thing as unto him; and in every thing let your *hearts* be engaged. Be always in *earnest*, and let your *heart* ever accompany your hand.

Serving the Lord] Ever considering that his eye is upon you, and that you are accountable to him for all that you do, and that you should do every thing so as to please him. In order to this there must be *simplicity* in the INTENTION, and *purity* in the AFFECTIONS.

Instead of τω Κυριω δουλευοντες, *serving the Lord*, several MSS., as DFG, and many editions, have τω καιρω δουλευοντες, *serving the time*—embracing the opportunity. This reading *Griesbach* has received

into the text, and most critics contend for its authenticity. Except the Codex *Claromontanus*, the Codex *Augiensis*, and the Codex *Boernerianus*, the first a MS. of the seventh or eighth century, the others of the ninth or tenth, marked in Griesbach by the letters DFG, all the other MSS. of this epistle have Κυριω, *the Lord*; a reading in which all the *versions* concur. Καιρω, *the time*, is not found in the two *original editions*; that of *Complutum*, in 1514, which is the *first* edition of the Greek Testament ever *printed*; and that of *Erasmus*, in 1516, which is the first edition *published*; the former having been suppressed for several years after it was finished at the press. As in the ancient MSS. the word Κυριω is written *contractedly*, ΚΩ, some appear to have read it καιρω instead of Κυριω; but I confess I do not see sufficient reason after all that the critics have said, to depart from the common reading.

Verse 12. *Rejoicing in hope*] Of that glory of God that to each faithful follower of Christ shall shortly be revealed.

Patient in tribulation] Remembering that what you suffer as Christians you suffer for Christ's sake ; and it is to his honour, and the honour of your Christian profession, that you suffer it with an even mind.

Continuing instant in prayer] Προσκαρτερουντες· Making the most fervent and intense application to the throne of grace for the light and power of the Holy Spirit; without which you can neither *abhor evil, do good, love the brethren*, entertain a comfortable *hope*, nor bear up patiently under the *tribulations* and ills of life.

Verse 13. *Distributing to the necessity of saints*] Relieve your poor brethren according to the power which God has given you. Do good unto all *men*, but especially to them which are of the household of faith. Instead of χρειαις, *necessities*, some ancient MSS. have μνειαις, *memorials*; distributing to the memorials of the saints, which some interpret as referring to saints that were *absent*; as if he had said : Do not *forget* those in other Churches who have a claim on your bounty. But I really cannot see any good sense which this various reading can make in the text; I therefore follow the common reading.

Given to hospitality.] Την φιλοξενιαν διωκοντες, *pursuing hospitality*, or the duty of *entertaining strangers*. A very necessary virtue in ancient times, when houses of public accommodation were exceedingly scarce. This exhortation might have for its object the apostles, who were all itinerants; and in many cases the Christians, flying before the face of persecution. This virtue is highly becoming in all Christians, and especially in all Christian *ministers*, who have the *means* of relieving a brother in distress, or of succour-

2

A. M. cir. 4062.
A. D. cir. 58.
An. Olymp.
cir. CCIX. 2.
A. U. C. cir.
811.

14 [i] Bless them which persecute you : bless, and curse not.
15 [k] Rejoice with them that do rejoice, and weep with them that weep.
16 [l] *Be* of the same mind one toward another.

[m] Mind not high things, but [n] condescend to men of low estate. [o] Be not wise in your own conceits.
17 [p] Recompense to no man evil for evil. [q] Provide things honest in the sight of all men.

A. M. cir. 4062.
A. D. cir. 58.
An. Olymp.
cir. CCIX. 2.
A. U. C. cir.
811.

---

[i] Matt. v. 44; Luke vi. 28; xxiii. 34; Acts vii. 60; 1 Cor. iv. 12; 1 Peter ii. 23; iii. 9.——[k] 1 Cor. xii. 26.——[l] Chap. xv. 5; 1 Cor. i. 10; Phil. ii. 2; iii. 16; 1 Pet. iii. 8.——[m] Psa. cxxxi. 1, 2; Jer. xlv. 5.

[n] Or, *be contented with mean things.*——[o] Proverbs iii. 7; xxvi. 12; Isaiah v. 21; chap. xi. 25.——[p] Proverbs xx. 22; Matthew v. 39; 1 Thess. v. 15; 1 Peter iii. 9.——[q] Chap. xiv. 16; 2 Cor. viii. 21.

---

ing the poor wherever he may find them. But providing for *strangers* in *distress* is the proper meaning of the term; and to be *forward* to do this is the *spirit* of the duty.

Verse 14. *Bless them which persecute you*] Ευλογειτε, Give *good words*, or *pray* for them that give you *bad words*, καταρασθε, who make *dire imprecations* against you. *Bless* them, pray for them, and on no account curse them, whatever the provocation may be. Have the loving, forgiving mind that was in your Lord.

Verse 15. *Rejoice with them that do rejoice*] Take a lively interest in the prosperity of others. Le it be a matter of rejoicing to you when you hear of he health, prosperity, or happiness of any brother.

Weep with them that weep.] Labour after a compassionate or sympathizing mind. Let your heart feel for the distressed; enter into their sorrows, and bear a part of their burdens. It is a fact, attested by universal experience, that by sympathy a man may receive into his own affectionate feelings a measure of the distress of his friend, and that his friend does find himself relieved in the same proportion as the other has entered into his griefs. "But how do you account for this?" I do not account for it at all; it depends upon certain laws of nature, the principles of which have not been as yet duly developed.

Verse 16. *Be of the same mind*] Live in a state of continual harmony and concord, and pray for the same good for all which you desire for yourselves.

Mind not high things] Be not ambitious; affect nothing above your station; do not court the rich nor the powerful; do not pass by the *poor man* to pay your court to the *great man;* do not affect *titles* or worldly *distinctions;* much less sacrifice your conscience for them. The attachment to *high things* and *high men* is the vice of *little, shallow minds.* However, it argues one important fact, that such persons are conscious that they are of *no worth* and of *no consequence* in THEMSELVES, and they seek to render themselves observable and to gain a little credit by their endeavours to *associate* themselves with men of *rank* and *fortune*, and if possible to get into honourable *employments;* and, if this cannot be attained, they affect honourable TITLES.

But condescend to men of low estate.] Be a companion of the humble, and pass through life with as little noise and *show* as possible. Let the poor, godly man be your chief companion; and learn from his humility and piety to be humble and godly. The term συναπαγομενοι, which we translate *condescend*, from συν, *together*, and απαγω, *to lead*, signifies *to be*

led, *carried*, or *dragged away to prison* with *another;* and points out the state in which the primitive Christians were despised and rejected of men, and often led forth to prison and death. False or man-pleasing professors would endeavour to escape all this disgrace and danger by getting into the favour of the great, the worldly, and the irreligious. There have not been wanting, in all ages of the Church, persons who, losing the savour of Divine things from their own souls by drinking into a worldly spirit, have endeavoured to shun the reproach of the cross by renouncing the company of the godly, speaking evil of the way of life, and perhaps sitting down in the chair of the scorner with apostates like themselves. And yet, strange to tell, these men will keep up a form of godliness! for a decent outside is often necessary to enable them to secure the ends of their ambition.

Be not wise in your own conceits.] Be not puffed up with an opinion of your own consequence; for this will prove that the consequence itself is *imaginary. Be not wise*, παρ' εαυτοις, *by yourselves*—do not suppose that wisdom and discernment dwell alone with *you.* Believe that you stand in need both of help and instruction from others.

Verse 17. *Recompense, &c.*] Do not take notice of every little injury you may sustain. Do not be *litigious.* Beware of too nice a sense of your own honour; intolerable pride is at the bottom of this. The motto of the royal arms of Scotland is in direct opposition to this Divine direction—*Nemo me impune lacesset*, of which "I render evil for evil to every man," is a pretty literal translation. This is both antichristian and abominable, whether in a *state* or in an *individual.*

Provide things honest] Be prudent, be cautious, neither *eat, drink*, nor *wear*, but as you pay for every thing. "Live not on *trust*, for that is the way to pay double;" and by this means the *poor* are still kept *poor.* He who *takes credit*, even for food or raiment, when he has no probable means of defraying the debt, is a *dishonest* man. It is no sin to die through lack of the necessaries of life when the providence of God has denied the means of support; but it is a *sin* to take up goods without the probability of being able to pay for them. Poor man! suffer poverty a little; perhaps God is only trying thee for a time; and who can tell if he will not turn again thy captivity. Labour hard to live honestly; if God still appear to withhold his providential blessing, do not despair; leave it all to him; do not make a sinful choice; so cannot err. He will bless *thy* poverty, while he curses the ungodly man's blessings.

2

A. M. cir. 4062.
A. D. cir. 58.
An. Olymp.
cir. CCIX. 2.
A. U. C. cir.
811.

18 If it be possible, as much as lieth in you, r live peaceably with all men.

19 Dearly beloved, s avenge not yourselves, but *rather* give place unto wrath: for it is written, t Vengeance *is* mine; I will repay, saith the Lord.

20 u Therefore, if thine enemy hunger, feed him; if he thirst, give him drink: for in so doing thou shalt heap coals of fire on his head.

21 v Be not overcome of evil, but overcome evil with good.

A. M. cir. 4062.
A. D. cir. 58.
An. Olymp.
cir. CCIX. 2,
A. U. C. cir.
811.

---

r Mark ix. 50; chap. xiv. 19; Heb. xii. 14.——s Lev. xix. 18; Prov. xxiv. 29; Ecclus. xxviii. 1, &c.; ver. 17.

t Deut. xxxii. 35; Heb. x. 30.——u Exod. xxiii. 4, 5; Prov. xxv 21, 22; Matt. v. 44.——v Gen. xlv. 4, 5; Luke xxiii. 34.

Verse 18. *If it be possible*] To live in a state of peace with one's neighbours, friends, and even family, is often very difficult. But the man who loves God must labour after this, for it is indispensably necessary even for his own sake. A man cannot have broils and misunderstandings with others, without having his own peace very materially disturbed: he must, to be happy, be at peace with all men, whether they will be at peace with him or not. The apostle knew that it would be difficult to get into and maintain such a state of peace, and this his own words amply prove: *And if it be possible, as much as lieth in you, live peaceably.* Though it be but barely *possible*, labour after it.

Verse 19. *Dearly beloved, avenge not yourselves*] Ye are the children of God, and he loves you; and because he loves you he will permit nothing to be done to you that he will not turn to your advantage. Never take the execution of the law into your own hands; rather suffer injuries. The Son of man is come, not to destroy men's lives, but to save: be of the same spirit. When he was reviled, he reviled not again. It is the part of a noble mind to bear up under *unmerited* disgrace; *little minds* are litigious and quarrelsome.

Give place unto wrath] Δοτε τοπον τη οργη· Leave room for the civil magistrate to do his duty; he holds the sword for this purpose; and if *he* be unfaithful to the trust reposed in him by the state, leave the matter to God, who is the righteous judge: for by avenging yourselves you take your cause both out of the hands of the civil magistrate and out of the hands of God. I believe this to be the meaning of *give place to wrath*, οργη, *punishment;* the penalty which the law, properly executed, will inflict. This is well expressed by the author of the book of *Ecclesiasticus*, chap. xix. 17: *Admonish thy neighbour before thou threaten him, and, not being angry,* GIVE PLACE TO THE LAW OF THE MOST HIGH.

Vengeance is mine] This fixes the meaning of the apostle, and at once shows that the exhortation, *Rather give place to wrath* or *punishment*, means, Leave the matter to the judgment of God; it is *his law* that in this case is broken; and to him the infliction of deserved punishment belongs. Some think it means, " Yield a little to a man when in a violent passion, for the sake of peace, until he grow cooler."

I will repay] In my own time and in my own way. But he gives the sinner space to repent, and this long-suffering leads to salvation. Dr. Taylor, after Dr. Benson, conjectures that the apostle in these directions had his eye upon the indignities which the *Jews*, and probably the *Christians* too, (for they were often con-

founded by the heathen,) suffered by the *edict of Claudius*, mentioned Acts xviii. 2, which " commanded all Jews to depart from Rome." Upon this occasion *Aquila* and *Priscilla* removed to Corinth, where Paul found them, and dwelt with them a considerable time. No doubt they gave him a full account of the state of the Christian Church at Rome, and of every thing relating to the late persecution under Claudius. That emperor's edict probably died with him, if it were not repealed before, and then the *Jews* and *Christians* (if the *Christians* were also expelled) returned again to Rome; for Aquila and Priscilla were there when Paul wrote this epistle, chap. xvi. 3, which was in the fourth year of *Nero*, successor to *Claudius*.

Verse 20. *If thine enemy hunger, feed him*] Do not withhold from any man the offices of mercy and kindness; *you* have been God's enemy, and yet God fed, clothed, and preserved you alive: do to your enemy as God has done to you. If your enemy be hungry, feed him; if he be thirsty, give him drink: so has God dealt with you. And has not a sense of his goodness and long-suffering towards you been a means of. melting down your heart into penitential compunction, gratitude, and love towards him? How know you that a similar conduct towards *your* enemy may not have the same gracious influence on him towards you? Your kindness may be the means of begetting in him a sense of his guilt; and, from being your *fell enemy*, he may become your *real friend*. This I believe to be the sense of this passage, which many have encumbered with difficulties of their own creating. The whole is a quotation from Prov. xxv. 21, 22, in the precise words of the *Septuagint;* and it is very likely that the latter clause of this verse, *Thou shalt heap coals of fire upon his head*, is a metaphor taken from *smelting metals.* The ore is put into the furnace, and fire put both *under* and *over*, that the metal may be liquefied, and, leaving the scoriæ and dross, may fall down pure to the bottom of the furnace. This is beautifully expressed by one of our own poets, in reference to this explanation of this passage:—

" So artists *melt* the *sullen* ore of *lead*,
  By *heaping coals of fire upon its head.*
In the *kind warmth* the metal learns to *glow*,
  And *pure from dross* the silver *runs below.*"

It is most evident, from the whole connection of the place and the apostle's use of it, that the *heaping of the coals of fire upon the head of the enemy* is intended to produce not an *evil*, but the most *beneficial effect;* and the following verse is an additional proof of this.

Verse 21. *Be not overcome of evil*] Do not, by

142

2

giving place to evil, become precisely the same character which thou condemnest in another. *Overcome evil with good*—however frequently he may grieve and injure thee, always repay him with kindness; thy *good*-will, in the end, may overcome his evil.

1. THOMAS AQUINAS has properly said: *Vincitur a malo qui vult peccare in alium, quia ille peccavit in ipsum.* "He is overcome of evil who sins against another, because he sins against him." A moral enemy is more easily overcome by *kindness* than by *hostility.* Against the latter he arms himself; and all the evil passions of his heart concentrate themselves in opposition to him who is striving to retaliate, by violence, the injurious acts which he has received from him. But where the injured man is labouring to do him *good* for his *evil*—to repay his *curses* with *blessings* and *prayers,* his evil passions have no longer any motive, any incentive; his mind relaxes; the turbulence of his passions is calmed; reason and conscience are permitted to speak; he is disarmed, or, in other words, he finds that he has no use for his weapons; he beholds in the injured man a magnanimous friend, whose mind is superior to all the insults and injuries which he has received, and who is determined never to permit the heavenly principle that influences his soul to bow itself before the miserable, mean, and wretched spirit of revenge. This amiable man views in his *enemy* a spirit which he beholds with horror, and he cannot consent to receive into his own bosom a disposition which he sees to be so destructive to another; and he knows that as soon as he begins to *avenge* himself, he places himself on a *par* with the unprincipled man whose *conduct* he has so much reason to blame, and whose *spirit* he has so much cause to abominate. He who avenges himself receives into his own heart all the evil and disgraceful passions by which his enemy is rendered both wretched and contemptible. There is the voice of *eternal reason* in "Avenge not yourselves:—overcome evil with good;" as well as the high authority and command of the living God.

2. The reader will, no doubt, have observed with pleasure the skill and address, as well as the Divine wisdom, with which the apostle has handled the important subjects which he has brought forth to view in the preceding chapters. Nothing can be more regular or judicious than his plan of proceeding. He *first* shows the *miserable, wretched, fallen, degraded state of man;* next, the *merciful provision* which God has made for his salvation, and *lastly,* the *use* which man should make of the mercies of his God. He shows us, in a most pointed manner, the *connection* that subsists between the *doctrines* of the Gospel and *practical piety.* From the beginning of the first to the end of the *eleventh* chapter he states and defends the grand truths of Christianity, and from the beginning of the twelfth to the end of the epistle he shows the practical use of these doctrines. This is a point which is rarely considered by professors; multitudes run to the Epistle to the Romans for texts to prop up their peculiar system of doctrine; but how few go to this sacred book for *rules* relative to *holy life!* They abound in quotations from the doctrinal parts, but seldom make that use of them which the apostle makes in this chapter "I beseech you, therefore, brethren, by the mercies of God, that ye present your bodies a living sacrifice, holy, acceptable unto God, which is your reasonable service; and be not conformed to this world, &c" Now we learn from the *use* which the apostle makes of his doctrines, that whatsoever teaching comes from God leads to a holy and useful life. And if we hold any doctrine that does not excite us to labour after the strictest conformity to the will of God in all our tempers, spirit, and actions, we may rest assured that either that doctrine is not of God, or we make an improper use of it. He that knows God best, loves and resembles him most.

CHAPTER XIII.

Subjection to civil governors inculcated, from the consideration that civil government is according to the ordinance of God; and that those who resist the lawfully constituted authorities shall receive condemnation 1, 2. And those who are obedient shall receive praise, 3. The character of a lawful civil governor, 4. The necessity of subjection, 5. The propriety of paying lawful tribute, 6, 7. Christians should love one another, 8—10 The necessity of immediate conversion to God proved from the shortness and uncertainty of time, 11, 12 How the Gentiles should walk so as to please God, and put on Christ Jesus in order to their salvation, 13, 14.

A. M. cir 4062.
A. D. cir 58
An. Olymp
cir. CCIX 2.
A. U. C. cir
811

LET every soul ª be subject unto the higher powers. For ᵇ there is no power but of God. the powers that be are ᶜ ordained of God.

2 Whosoever, therefore, resisteth ᵈ the power, resisteth the ordinance of God: ᵉ and they that resist shall receive to themselves damnation.

A M cir 4062.
A D cir 58
An. Olymp.
cir CCIX 2.
A. U. C cir
811

ª Tit. iii 1; 1 Pet. ii. 13.——ᵇ Prov viii 15, 16, Dan ii 21, iv. 32, Wisd. vi 3, John xix 11

ᶜ Or, *ordered.*——ᵈ Titus iii 1 ——ᵉ Deuteronomy xvii 12; xxi. 18.

NOTES ON CHAP XIII.

To see with what propriety the apostle introduces the important subjects which he handles in this chapter, it is necessary to make a few remarks on the circumstances in which the Church of God then was.

It is generally allowed that this epistle was written

A. M. cir. 4062.
A. D. cir. 58.
An. Olymp.
cir. CCIX. 2.
A. U. C. cir.
811.

3 For rulers are not a terror to good works, but to the evil. Wilt thou then not be afraid of the power? f do that which is

good, and thou shalt have praise of the same:

4 g For he is the minister of God to thee for good. But if

A. M. cir. 4062
A. D. cir. 58.
An. Olymp.
cir. CCIX. 2.
A. U. C. cir.
811.

---

f 1 Pet. ii. 14; iii. 13.

g Chap. ii. 8; xii. 19; 1 Kings x. 9; Jer. xxv. 9.

---

about the year of our Lord 58, four or five years after the edict of the Emperor Claudius, by which all the Jews were banished from Rome. And as in those early times the Christians were generally confounded with the Jews, it is likely that *both* were included in this decree.

For what reason this edict was issued does not satisfactorily appear. *Suetonius* tells us that it was because the Jews were making continual disturbances under their leader *Chrestus*. (See the note on Acts xviii. 2.) That the Jews were in general an uneasy and seditious people is clear enough from every part of their own history. They had the most rooted aversion to the heathen government; and it was a maxim with them that the *world was given to the Israelites;* that they should have supreme rule every where, and that the Gentiles should be their vassals. With such political notions, grounded on their native restlessness, it is no wonder if in several instances they gave cause of suspicion to the Roman government, who would be glad of an opportunity to expel from the city persons whom they considered dangerous to its peace and security; nor is it unreasonable on this account to suppose, with Dr. Taylor, that the Christians, under a notion of being the *peculiar people of God*, and the subjects of his kingdom alone, might be in danger of being infected with those unruly and rebellious sentiments: therefore the apostle shows them that they were, notwithstanding their honours and privileges as Christians, bound by the strongest obligations of conscience to be subject to the civil government. The judicious commentator adds: " I cannot forbear observing the admirable skill and dexterity with which the apostle has handled the subject. His views in writing are always comprehensive on every point; and he takes into his thoughts and instructions all parties that might probably reap any benefit by them. As Christianity was then growing, and the powers of the world began to take notice of it, it was not unlikely that this letter might fall into the hands of the Roman magistrates. And whenever that happened it was right, not only that *they* should see that Christianity was no favourer of sedition, but likewise that they should have an opportunity of reading their own duty and obligations. But as they were too proud and insolent to permit themselves to be instructed in a plain, direct way, therefore the apostle with a masterly hand, delineates and strongly inculcates the magistrate's duty; while he is pleading his cause with the subject, and establishing his duty on the most sure and solid ground, he dexterously sides with the magistrate, and vindicates his power against any subject who might have imbibed seditious principles, or might be inclined to give the government any disturbance; and under this advantage he reads the magistrate a fine and close lecture upon the nature and ends of civil government. A way of conveyance so ingenious and unexceptionable that even *Nero* himself, had this epistle fallen into his hands, could not fail of seeing

his duty clearly stated, without finding any thing servile or flattering on the one hand, or offensive or disgusting on the other.

"The attentive reader will be pleased to see with what dexterity, truth, and gravity the apostle, in a small compass, affirms and explains the foundation, nature, ends, and just limits of the magistrate's authority, while he is pleading his cause, and teaching the subject the duty and obedience he owes to the civil government."—*Dr. Taylor's Notes, page 352.*

Verse 1. *Let every soul be subject unto the higher powers.*] This is a very strong saying, and most solemnly introduced; and we must consider the apostle as speaking, not from his own private judgment, or teaching a doctrine of present *expediency*, but declaring the *mind of God* on a subject of the utmost importance to the peace of the world; a doctrine which does not exclusively belong to any *class* of people, *order* of the community, or *official* situations, but to *every soul;* and, on the principles which the apostle lays down, to every soul in all possible varieties of situation, and on all occasions. And what is this solemn doctrine? It is this: *Let every soul be subject to the higher powers.* Let every man be obedient to the civil government under which the providence of God has cast his lot.

For there is no power but of God] As God is the origin of power, and the supreme Governor of the universe, he delegates authority to whomsoever he will; and though in many cases the governor *himself* may not be *of God*, yet civil government is of him; for without this there could be no society, no security, no private property; all would be confusion and anarchy, and the habitable world would soon be depopulated. In ancient times, God, in an especial manner, on many occasions appointed the *individual* who was to govern; and he accordingly governed by a *Divine right*, as in the case of *Moses, Joshua*, the Hebrew *judges*, and several of the *Israelitish kings.* In after times, and to the present day, he does that by a general superintending providence which he did before by especial designation. In all nations of the earth there is what may be called a *constitution*—a plan by which a particular country or state is governed; and this constitution is less or more calculated to promote the interests of the community. The civil governor, whether he be *elective* or *hereditary*, agrees to govern according to that constitution. Thus we may consider that there is a *compact* and *consent* between the *governor* and the *governed*, and in such a case, the potentate may be considered as coming to the supreme authority in the direct way of God's providence; and as civil government is of God, who is the fountain of law, order, and regularity, the civil governor, who administers the laws of a state according to its *constitution*, is the *minister of God.* But it has been asked: If the

144

2

A. M. cir. 4062.
A. D. cir. 58.
An. Olymp.
cir. CCIX. 2.
A. U. C. cir.
811.
thou do that which is evil, be afraid; for he beareth not the sword in vain: for he is the minister of God, a revenger to

execute wrath upon him that doeth evil.

5 Wherefore [h] *ye* must needs be subject, not only for wrath,

A. M. cir. 4062,
A. D. cir. 58.
An. Olymp.
cir. CCIX. 2.
A. U. C. cir.
811.

[h] Ecclesiastes,   chap. viii. 2.

ruler be an immoral or profligate man, does he not prove himself thereby to be unworthy of his high office, and should he not be deposed? I answer, No: if he rule according to the *constitution*, nothing can justify rebellion against his authority. He may be *irregular* in his *own private life*; he may be an immoral man, and disgrace himself by an improper conduct: but if he rule *according to the law*; if he make no attempt to change the constitution, nor break the compact between him and the people; there is, therefore, no legal ground of opposition to his civil authority, and every act against him is not only *rebellion* in the worst sense of the word, but is unlawful and absolutely sinful.

Nothing can justify the opposition of the subjects to the ruler but *overt attempts* on his part to *change the constitution*, or to rule *contrary to law*. When the ruler acts thus he dissolves the compact between him and his people; his authority is no longer binding, because illegal; and it is illegal because he is acting *contrary to the laws* of that constitution, according to which, on being raised to the supreme power, he promised to govern. This conduct justifies opposition to his government; but I contend that no *personal misconduct* in the ruler, no immorality in his own life, while he *governs according to law*, can justify either rebellion against him or contempt of his authority. For his *political conduct* he is accountable to his *people*; for his *moral conduct* he is accountable to God, his conscience, and the *ministers of religion*. A king may be a *good moral man*, and yet a weak, and indeed a *bad and dangerous prince*. He may be a *bad man*, and stained with vice in his private life, and yet be a *good prince*. SAUL was a *good* moral *man*, but a *bad prince*, because he endeavoured to act contrary to the Israelitish constitution: he changed some essential parts of that constitution, as I have elsewhere shown; (see the note on Acts xiii. ver. 22;) he was therefore lawfully deposed. *James the Second* was a *good* moral *man*, as far as I can learn, but he was a *bad* and *dangerous prince;* he endeavoured to alter, and essentially change the British constitution, both in *Church* and *state;* therefore *he* was lawfully deposed. It would be easy, in running over the list of our own kings, to point out several who were deservedly reputed *good kings*, who in their private life were very *immoral*. Bad as they might be in private life, the *constitution* was in their hands ever considered a sacred deposit, and they faithfully preserved it, and transmitted it unimpaired to their successors; and took care while they held the reins of government to have it impartially and effectually administered.

It must be allowed, notwithstanding, that when a prince, howsoever heedful to the laws, is unrighteous in private life, his example is contagious; morality, banished from the throne, is discountenanced by the community; and happiness is diminished in proportion to the increase of vice. On the other hand, when a

king governs according to the constitution of his realms, and has his heart and life governed by the laws of his God, he is then a double blessing to his people; while he is ruling carefully according to the laws, his pious example is a great means of extending and confirming the reign of pure morality among his subjects. Vice is discredited from the throne, and the profligate dare not hope for a place of trust and confidence, (however in other respects he may be qualified for it,) because he is a *vicious* man.

As I have already mentioned some potentates by *name*, as apt examples of the doctrines I have been laying down, my readers will naturally expect that, on so fair an opportunity, I should introduce *another;* one in whom the double blessing meets; one who, through an unusually protracted reign, during every year of which he most conscientiously watched over the sacred constitution committed to his care, not only did not impair this constitution, but took care that its wholesome laws should be properly administered, and who in every respect acted as the father of his people, and added to all this the most exemplary *moral conduct* perhaps ever exhibited by a prince, whether in ancient or modern times; not only tacitly discountenancing vice by his truly religious conduct, but by his frequent *proclamations* most solemnly forbidding Sabbath-breaking, profane swearing, and immorality in general. More might be justly said, but when I have mentioned all these things, (and I mention them with exultation, and with gratitude to God,) I need scarcely add the venerable name of GEORGE *the Third, king of Great Britain;* as every reader will at once perceive that the description suits no potentate besides. I may just observe, that notwithstanding his long reign has been a reign of unparalleled troubles and commotions in the world, in which his empire has always been involved, yet, never did useful arts, ennobling sciences, and pure religion gain a more decided and general ascendancy: and much of this, under God, is owing to the manner in which this king has lived, and the encouragement he invariably gave to whatever had a tendency to promote the best interests of his people. Indeed it has been well observed, that, under the ruling providence of God, it was chiefly owing to the private and personal virtues of the sovereign that the house of Brunswick remained firmly seated on the throne amidst the storms arising from democratical agitations and revolutionary convulsions in Europe during the years 1792–1794. The stability of his throne amidst these dangers and distresses may prove a useful lesson to his successors, and show them the strength of a virtuous character, and that morality and religion form the best bulwark against those great evils to which all human governments are exposed. This small tribute of praise to the character and conduct of the British king, and gratitude to God for such a governor, will not be suspected of sinister motive; as the

A. M. cir. 4062.
A. D. cir. 58.
An. Olymp.
cir. CCIX. 2.
A. U. C. cir.
811.

i but also for conscience' sake.

6 For, for this cause pay ye tribute also: for they are God's

A. M. cir. 4062
A. D. cir. 58
An. Olymp.
cir. CCIX. 2
A. U. C. cir.
811.

ministers, attending continually upon this very thing.

7 k Render therefore to all their dues; tribute to whom tribute is

---

i 1 Pet. ii. 19.

k Matt. xxii. 21; Mark xii. 17; Luke xx. 25.

---

object of it is, by an inscrutable providence, placed in a situation to which neither *envy, flattery*, nor even just praise can approach, and where the majesty of the man is placed in the most awful yet respectable ruins. I have only one abatement to make : had this potentate been as *averse from* WAR as he was from public and private vices, he would have been the most immaculate sovereign that ever held a sceptre or wore a crown.

But to resume the subject, and conclude the argument : I wish particularly to show the utter unlawfulness of rebellion against a ruler, who, though he may be incorrect in his moral conduct, yet rules according to the laws ; and the additional blessing of having a prince, who, while his political conduct is regulated by the principles of the constitution, has his heart and life regulated by the dictates of eternal truth, as contained in that revelation which came from God.

Verse 2. *Whosoever resisteth the power*] 'Ο αντιτασσομενος, He who sets himself in *order* against this *order* of God ; τη του Θεου διαταγη, and *they who resist*, οι ανθεστηκοτες, they who obstinately, and for no right reason, oppose the ruler, and strive to unsettle the constitution, and to bring about illegal changes,

Shall receive to themselves damnation.] Κριμα, condemnation ; shall be *condemned* both by the spirit and letter of that constitution, which, under pretence of defending or improving, they are indirectly labouring to subvert.

Verse 3. *For rulers are not a terror to good works*] Here the apostle shows the civil magistrate what he should be : he is clothed with great power, but that power is entrusted to him, not for the terror and oppression of the upright man, but to overawe and punish the wicked. It is, in a word, for the *benefit of the community*, and not for the *aggrandizement of himself*, that God has entrusted the supreme civil power to any man. If he should use this to wrong, rob, spoil, oppress, and persecute his subjects, he is not only a *bad man*, but also a *bad prince*. He infringes on the essential principles of law and equity. Should he *persecute* his obedient, loyal subjects, on any religious account, this is contrary to all law and right ; and his doing so renders him unworthy of their confidence, and they must consider him not as a *blessing* but a *plague*. Yet, even in this case, though in our country it would be a breach of the constitution, which allows every man to worship God according to his conscience, the truly pious will not feel that even this would justify rebellion against the prince ; they are to suffer patiently, and commend themselves and their cause to him that judgeth righteously. It is an awful thing to rebel, and the cases are extremely rare that can justify rebellion against the constituted authorities. See the doctrine on ver. 1.

Wilt thou then not be afraid of the power?] If thou

wouldst not live in fear of the civil magistrate, live according to the laws ; and thou mayest expect that *he* will rule according to the laws ; and consequently instead of incurring *blame* thou wilt have *praise*. This is said on the supposition that the ruler is himself *a good man :* such the laws suppose him to be ; and the apostle, on the general question of obedience and protection, assumes the point that the magistrate *is* such.

Verse 4. *For he is the minister of God to thee for good*] Here the apostle puts the character of the ruler in the strongest possible light. *He is the minister of God*—the office is by Divine appointment : the man who is worthy of the office will act in conformity to the will of God : and as the eyes of the Lord are over the righteous, and his ears open to their cry, consequently the ruler will be the *minister of God to them for good.*

He beareth not the sword in vain] His power is delegated to him for the defence and encouragement of the good, and the punishment of the wicked ; and he has authority to punish *capitally*, when the law so requires : this the term *sword* leads us to infer.

For he is the minister of God, a revenger] Θεε διακονος εστιν εκδικος, For he is God's vindictive minister, to execute *wrath* ; εις οργην, to inflict *punishment* upon the transgressors of the law ; and this according to the statutes of that law ; for God's civil ministers are never allowed to pronounce or inflict punishment according to *their own minds* or *feelings*, but according to the express declarations of the law.

Verse 5. *Ye must needs be subject*] Αναγκη, There is a necessity that ye should be subject, not only for wrath, δια την οργην, on *account of the punishment* which will be inflicted on evil doers, *but also for conscience' sake* ; not only to avoid punishment, but also to preserve a clear conscience. For, as *civil government* is established in the order of God for the support, defence, and happiness of society, they who transgress its laws, not only expose themselves to the penalties assigned by the statutes, but also to guilt in their own consciences, because they sin against God. Here are *two* powerful motives to prevent the infraction of the laws and to enforce obedience. 1. The dread of punishment ; this weighs with the ungodly. 2. The keeping of a good conscience, which weighs powerfully with every person who fears God. These two motives should be frequently urged both among professors and profane.

Verse 6. *For this cause pay ye tribute also*] Because civil government is an order of God, and the ministers of state must be at considerable expense in providing for the safety and defence of the community, it is necessary that those in whose behalf these expenses are incurred should defray that expense ; and hence nothing can be more reasonable than an impartial and moderate *taxation*, by which the expenses of the state may be defrayed, and the various officers, whether

(10**)

A. M. cir. 4062.
A. D. cir. 58.
An. Olymp.
cir. CCIX. 2.
A. U. C. cir.
811.

due ; custom to whom custom ; fear to whom fear ; honour to whom honour.

8 Owe no man any thing, but to love one another : for [1] he that loveth another hath fulfilled the law.

9 For this, [m] Thou shalt not commit adultery, Thou shalt not kill, Thou shalt not steal, Thou shalt not bear false witness, Thou shalt

---

[1] Verse 10 ; Galatians v. 14 ; Colossians iii. 14 ; 1 Tim. i. 5 ; James ii. 8.——[m] Exodus xx. 13, &c. ; Deut. v. 17, &c. ; Matt. xix. 18.

---

not covet ; and if *there be* any other commandment, it is briefly comprehended in this saying, namely, [n] Thou shalt love thy neighbour as thyself.

10 Love worketh no ill to his neighbour : therefore [o] love *is* the fulfilling of the law.

11 And that, knowing the time, that now *it is* high time [p] to awake out of sleep : for now

A. M. cir. 4062.
A. D. cir. 58.
An. Olymp.
cir. CCIX. 2.
A. U. C. cir.
811.

---

[n] Lev. xix. 18 ; Matthew xxii. 39 ; Mark xii. 31 ; Gal. v. 14 ; James ii. 8.——[o] Matt. xxii. 40 ; verse 8.——[p] 1 Cor. xv. 34 ; Eph. v. 14 ; 1 Thess. v. 5, 6.

---

civil or military, who are employed for the service of the public, be adequately remunerated. All this is just and right, but there is no insinuation in the apostle's words in behalf of an *extravagant* and *oppressive taxation,* for the support of *unprincipled* and *unnecessary wars ;* or the *pensioning* of *corrupt* or *useless* men. The taxes are to be paid for the support of those who are *God's ministers*—the necessary civil officers, from the king downwards, *who are attending* CONTINUALLY *on this very thing.* And let the reader observe, that by *God's ministers* are not meant here the ministers of *religion,* but the *civil officers* in all departments of the state.

Verse 7. *Render therefore to all their dues*] This is an extensive command. Be rigidly just ; withhold neither from the *king* nor his *ministers,* nor his *officers* of *justice* and *revenue,* nor from even the lowest of the *community,* what the laws of God and your country require you to pay.

Tribute to whom tribute] Φορον· This word probably means such taxes as were levied on *persons* and *estates.*

Custom to whom custom] Τελος· This word probably means such duties as were laid upon *goods, merchandise,* &c., on *imports* and *exports ;* what we commonly call *custom.* Kypke on this place has quoted some good authorities for the above distinction and signification. Both the words occur in the following quotation from *Strabo :* Αναγκη γαρ μειουσθαι τα τελη, φορων επιβαλλομενων· *It is necessary to lessen the* CUSTOMS, *if* TAXES *be imposed. Strabo,* lib. ii., page **307.** See several other examples in *Kypke.*

Fear to whom fear] It is likely that the word φοβον, which we translate *fear,* signifies that *reverence* which produces *obedience.* Treat all *official* characters with respect, and be obedient to your superiors.

Honour to whom honour.] The word τιμην may here mean that *outward respect* which the principle *reverence,* from which it springs, will generally produce. Never behave rudely to any person ; but behave respectfully to men in office : if you cannot even respect the *man*—for an important office may be filled by an unworthy person—respect the *office,* and the man on account of his *office.* If a man habituate himself to disrespect *official characters,* he will soon find himself disposed to pay little respect or obedience to the *laws* themselves.

Verse 8. *Owe no man any thing, but to love one another*] In the preceding verses the apostle has been

showing the duty, reverence, and obedience, which all Christians, from the highest to the lowest, owe to the civil magistrate ; whether he be emperor, king, proconsul, or other state officer ; here he shows them their duty to *each other :* but this is widely different from that which they owe to the civil government : to the first they owe subjection, reverence, obedience, and tribute ; to the latter they owe nothing but *mutual love,* and those offices which necessarily spring from it. Therefore, the apostle says, *Owe no man ;* as if he had said : Ye owe to your fellow brethren nothing but mutual love, and this is what the law of God requires, and in this the law is fulfilled. Ye are not bound in obedience to them as to the civil magistrate ; for to him ye must needs be subject, *not merely for fear of punishment, but for conscience sake :* but to these ye are bound by *love ;* and by that love especially which utterly prevents you from doing any thing by which a brother may sustain any kind of injury.

Verse 9. *For this, Thou shalt not commit adultery*] He that loves another will not deprive him of his *wife,* of his *life,* of his *property,* of his *good name ;* and will not even permit a *desire* to enter into his heart which would lead him to wish to possess any thing that is the property of another : for the *law*—the sacred Scripture, has said : *Thou shalt love thy neighbour as thyself.*

It is remarkable that ου ψευδομαρτυρησεις, *thou shalt not bear false witness,* is wanting here in ABDEFG, and several other MSS. Griesbach has left it out of the text. It is wanting also in the Syriac, and in several of the primitive fathers. The generality of the best critics think it a spurious reading.

Verse 10. *Love worketh no ill*] As he that loves another will act towards that person as, on a reverse of circumstances, he would that his neighbour should act towards him ; therefore, this love can never work ill towards another : and, on this *head,* i. e. the duty we owe to our neighbour, *love is the fulfilling of the law.*

Verse 11. *And that, knowing the time*] Dr. Taylor has given a judicious paraphrase of this and the following verses : " And all the duties of a virtuous and holy life we should the more carefully and zealously perform, considering the nature and shortness of the present season of life ; which will convince us that it is now *high time* to *rouse* and shake off *sleep,* and apply with vigilance and vigour to the duties of our Christian life ; for that eternal *salvation,* which is

| A. M. cir. 4062. |
| A. D. cir. 58. |
| An. Olymp. |
| cir. CCIX. 2. |
| A. U. C. cir. |
| 811. |

is our salvation nearer than when we believed.

12 The night is far spent, the day is at hand: q let us therefore cast off the works of darkness, and r let us put on the armour of light.

13 s Let us walk t honestly, as in the day;

u not in rioting and drunkenness, v not in chambering and wantonness, w not in strife and envying.

14 But x put ye on the Lord Jesus Christ, and y make not provision for the flesh, to *fulfil* the lusts *thereof.*

| A. M. cir. 4062. |
| A. D. cir. 58. |
| An. Olymp. |
| cir. CCIX. 2. |
| A. U. C. cir. |
| 811. |

---

q Eph. v. 11; Col. iii. 8.——r Eph. vi. 13; 1 Thess. v. 8.
s Phil. iv. 8; 1 Thess. iv. 12; 1 Pet. ii. 12.——t Or, *decently.*
u Prov. xxiii. 20; Luke xxi. 34; 1 Pet. iv. 3.

v 1 Corinthians vi. 9; Ephesians v. 5.——w James iii. 14.
x Gal. iii. 27; Eph. iv. 24; Col. iii. 10.——y Galatians v. 16;
1 Pet. ii. 11.

---

the object of our Christian *faith* and hope, and the great motive of our religion, is every day *nearer* to us than when we first entered into the profession of Christianity."

Some think the passage should be understood thus: We have now many advantages which we did not formerly possess. *Salvation is nearer*—the whole Christian system is more fully explained, and the knowledge of it more easy to be acquired than formerly; on which account a greater progress in religious knowledge and in practical piety is required of us: and we have for a long time been too remiss in these respects. *Deliverance* from the *persecutions,* &c., with which they were then afflicted, is supposed by others to be the meaning of the apostle.

Verse 12. *The night is far spent*] If we understand this in reference to the *heathen* state of the Romans, it may be paraphrased thus: *The night is far spent*—heathenish darkness is nearly at an end. *The day is at hand*—the full manifestation of the Sun of righteousness, in the illumination of the whole Gentile world approaches rapidly. The manifestation of the Messiah is regularly termed by the ancient Jews יום yom, *day,* because previously to this all is *night,* Bereshith rabba sect. 91, fol. 89. *Cast off the works of darkness*—prepare to meet this rising light, and welcome its approach, by throwing aside superstition, impiety, and vice of every kind: *and put on the armour of light*—fully receive the heavenly teaching, by which your spirits will be as completely *armed* against the attacks of evil as your bodies could be by the best weapons and impenetrable armour. This sense seems most suitable to the following verses, where the *vices of the Gentiles* are particularly specified; and they are exhorted to abandon them, and to receive the Gospel of Christ. The common method of explanation is this: *The night is far spent*—our present imperfect life, full of afflictions, temptations, and trials, is almost run out; *the day* of eternal blessedness *is at hand*—is about to dawn on us in our glorious resurrection unto eternal life. Therefore, *let us cast off*—let us live as candidates for this eternal glory. But this sense cannot at all comport with what is said below, as the *Gentiles* are most evidently intended.

Verse 13. *Let us walk honestly, as in the day*] *Let us walk,* ευσχημονως, *decently,* from εν, *well,* and σχημα, *mien, habit,* or *dress.* Let our deportment be decent, orderly, and grave; such as we shall not be ashamed of in the eyes of the whole world.

Not in rioting and drunkenness] Μη κωμοις και με-

θαις· Κωμος, *rioting,* according to *Hesychius,* signifies ασελγη ασματα, πορνικα συμποσια, ωδαι, *unclean and dissolute songs,* banquets, and such like. Μεθαις signifies *drunken festivals,* such as were celebrated in honour of their gods, when *after* they had *sacrificed* (μετα το θυειν, SUIDAS) they drank to excess, accompanied with abominable acts of every kind. See *Suidas* and *Hesychius,* under this word.

Not in chambering] This is no legitimate word, and conveys no sense till, from its connection in this place, we force a meaning upon it. The original word, κοιταις, signifies *whoredoms* and *prostitution* of every kind.

And wantonness] Ασελγειαις, All manner of *uncleanness* and *sodomitical* practices.

Not in strife and envying.] Μη εριδι και ζηλω, Not in contentions and furious altercations, which must be the consequence of such practices as are mentioned above. Can any man suppose that this address is to the *Christians* at Rome? That they are charged with practices almost peculiar to the *heathens?* And practices of the most abandoned and dissolute sort? If those called Christians at Rome were guilty of such acts, there could be no difference except in *profession,* between them and the most *abominable* of the *heathens.* But it is impossible that such things should be spoken to the followers of Christ; for the very grace that brings *repentance* enables the penitent to cast aside and abominate all such vicious and abominable conduct.

The advices to the *Christians* may be found in the preceding chapter; those at the conclusion of this chapter belong *solely* to the *heathens.*

Verse 14. *Put ye on the Lord Jesus*] This is in reference to what is said ver. 13: *Let us put on decent garments*—let us make a different profession, unite with other company, and maintain that profession by a suitable conduct. *Putting on,* or *being clothed* with Jesus Christ, signifies *receiving* and *believing* the *Gospel;* and consequently taking its *maxims* for the government of life, having the mind that was in Christ. The ancient Jews frequently use the phrase putting on the shechinah, or Divine majesty, to signify the soul's being clothed with immortality, and rendered fit for glory.

To be clothed with a person is a Greek phrase, signifying to *assume the interests* of another—to *enter* into his *views,* to *imitate* him, and be *wholly on his side.* St. *Chrysostom* particularly mentions this as a common phrase, ὁ δεινα τον δεινα ενεδυσατο, *such a one hath put on such a one;* i. e. he closely *follows*

2

and *imitates* him. So *Dionysius Hal.*, Antiq., lib. xi., page 689, speaking of *Appius* and the rest of the *Decemviri*, says : ουκετι μετριαζοντες, αλλα τον Ταρκυνιον εκεινον ενδυομενοι, *They were no longer the servants of Tarquin, but they* CLOTHED THEMSELVES WITH HIM—they imitated and aped him in every thing. Eusebius, in his life of Constantine, says the same of his sons, *they put on their father*—they seemed to enter into his spirit and views, and to imitate him in all things. The mode of speech itself is taken from the custom of *stage players:* they assumed the *name* and *garments* of the person whose *character* they were to act, and endeavoured as closely as possible to imitate him in their spirit, words, and actions. See many pertinent examples in *Kypke.*

And make not provision for the flesh] By *flesh* we are here to understand, not only the *body*, but all the irregular appetites and passions which led to the abominations already recited. No *provision* should be made for the encouragement and gratification of such a principle as this.

To fulfil the lusts thereof.] Εις επιθυμιας, *in reference to its lusts;* such as the κωμοι, κοιται, μεθαι, and ασελγειαι, rioting, drunkenness, prostitutions, and uncleanness, mentioned ver. 13, to make provision for which the Gentiles *lived* and *laboured*, and *bought* and *sold*, and *schemed* and *planned;* for it was the whole business of their life to gratify the *sinful lusts of the flesh.* Their philosophers taught them little else ; and the whole circle of their deities, as well as the whole scheme of their religion, served only to excite and inflame such *passions*, and produce such *practices.*

I. IN these four last verses there is a fine metaphor, and it is continued and well sustained in every expression. 1. The apostle considers the state of the *Gentiles* under the notion of *night*, a time of darkness and a time of evil practices. 2. That this night is nearly at an *end*, the night is far spent. 3. He considers the Gospel as now visiting the Gentiles, and the *light* of a glorious *day* about to shine forth on them. 4. He calls those to *awake* who were in a *stupid, senseless* state concerning all spiritual and moral good ; and those who were employed in the vilest practices that could debase and degrade mankind. 5. He orders them to *cast off the works of darkness*, and *put on the armour* οπλα, the *habiliments of light*—of righteousness : to cease to do evil ; to learn to do well. Here is an allusion to laying aside their *night clothes*, and putting on their *day clothes.* 6. He exhorts them to this that they may *walk honestly, decently habited ;* and not spend their time, waste their substance, destroy their lives, and ruin their souls in such iniquitous practices as those which he immediately specifies. 7. That they might not mistake his meaning concerning the *decent* clothing which he exhorts them to walk in, he immediately explains himself by the use of a common form of speech, and says, still following his *metaphor, Put on the Lord Jesus Christ*—receive his doctrine, copy his example, and seek the things which belong to another

life ; for the Gentiles thought of little else than making provision for the *flesh* or *body*, to gratify its animal desires and propensities.

II. These last verses have been rendered famous in the Christian Church for more than 1400 years, as being the instrument of the conversion of St. Augustine. It is well known that this man was at first a *Manichean*, in which doctrine he continued till the 32d year of his age. He had frequent conferences and controversies on the Christian religion with several friends who were Christians ; and with his mother *Monica*, who was incessant in her prayers and tears for his conversion. She was greatly comforted by the assurance given her by St. Ambrose, bishop of Milan, where her son Augustine was then professor of rhetoric : that *a child of so many prayers and tears could not perish.* He frequently heard St. Ambrose preach, and was affected, not only by his eloquence, but by the important subjects which he discussed ; but still could not abandon his Manicheanism. Walking one day in a garden with his friend *Alypius*, who it appears had been reading a copy of St. Paul's epistle to the Romans, and had left it on a bank near which they then were, (though some say that Augustine was then alone,) he thought he heard a musical voice calling out distinctly, TOLLE *et* LEGE ! TOLLE *et* LEGE ! *take up and read ! take up and read !* He looked down, saw the book, took it up, and hastily opening it, the first words that met his eye were these—Μη κωμοις και μεθαις, &c., *Not in rioting and drunkenness, &c., but put ye on the Lord Jesus Christ.* He felt the import and power of the words, and immediately resolved to become a follower of Christ : he in consequence instantly embraced Christianity ; and afterwards boldly professed and wrote largely in its defence, and became one of the most eminent of all the *Latin* fathers. Such is the substance of the story handed down to us from antiquity concerning the conversion of St. Augustine. He was made bishop of Hippo in Africa, in the year 395, and died in that city, Aug. 28th, 430, at the very time that it was besieged by the Vandals.

III. After what I have said in the notes, I need add nothing on the great *political question* of *subordination* to the *civil powers ;* and of the *propriety* and *expediency* of submitting to every *ordinance of man for the Lord's sake.* I need only observe, that it is in things *civil* this obedience is enjoined ; in things *religious*, God alone is to be obeyed. Should the civil power attempt to usurp the place of the Almighty, and forge a new creed, or prescribe rites and ceremonies not authorized by the word of God, no Christian is bound to obey. Yet even in this case, as I have already noted, no Christian is authorized to rebel against the civil power ; he must bear the persecution, and, if needs be, seal the truth with his blood, and thus become a *martyr* of the Lord Jesus. This has been the invariable practice of the genuine Church of Christ. They committed their cause to him who judgeth righteously. See farther on this subject on Matt. xxii 20, &c.

CHAPTER XIV.

In things indifferent, Christians should not condemn each other, 1. Particularly with respect to different kinds of food, 2–4. And the observation of certain days, 5, 6. None of us should live unto himself, but unto Christ, who lived and died for us, 7–9. We must not judge each other; for all judgment belongs to God, 10–13. We should not do any thing by which a weak brother may be stumbled or grieved; lest we destroy him for whom Christ died, 14–16. The kingdom of God does not consist in outward things, 17, 18. Christians should endeavour to cultivate peace and brotherly affection, and rather deny themselves of certain privileges than be the means of stumbling a weak brother, 19–21. The necessity of doing all in the spirit of faith, 22, 23.

A. M. cir. 4062.
A. D. cir. 58.
An. Olymp.
cir. CCIX. 2.
A. U. C. cir.
811.

HIM that ᵃ is weak in the faith receive ye, *but* ᵇ not to doubtful disputations.

2 For one believeth that he ᶜ may eat all things : another, who is weak, eateth herbs.

3 Let not him that eateth despise him that eateth not ; and ᵈ let not him which eateth not judge him that eateth : for God hath received him.

4 ᵉ Who art thou that judgest another man's

A. M. cir. 4062.
A. D. cir. 58.
An. Olymp.
cir. CCIX. 2.
A. U. C. cir.
811.

ᵃ Chap. xv. 1, 7 ; 1 Cor. viii. 9, 11 ; ix. 22.——ᵇ Or, *not to judge his doubtful thoughts.*

ᶜ Ver. 14 ; 1 Cor. x. 25 ; 1 Tim. iv. 4 ; Tit. i. 15.——ᵈ Col. ii. 16.——ᵉ James iv. 12.

NOTES ON CHAP. XIV.

It seems very likely, from this and the following chapter, that there were considerable misunderstandings between the *Jewish* and *Gentile* Christians at Rome, relative to certain customs which were sacredly observed by the one and disregarded by the other. The principal subject of dispute was concerning *meats* and *days*. The converted Jew, retaining a veneration for the law of Moses, abstained from certain meats, and was observant of certain days ; while the converted Gentile, understanding that the Christian religion laid him under no obligations to such ceremonial points, had no regard to either. It appears, farther, that mutual censures and uncharitable judgments prevailed among them, and that brotherly love and mutual forbearance did not generally prevail. The apostle, in this part of his epistle, exhorts that in such things, not essential to religion, and in which both parties, in their different way of thinking, might have an *honest meaning*, and *serious regard to God*, difference of sentiments might not hinder Christian fellowship and love ; but that they would mutually forbear each other, make candid allowance, and especially not carry their Gospel liberty so far as to prejudice a weak brother, a Jewish Christian, against the Gospel itself, and tempt him to renounce Christianity. His rules and exhortations are still of great use, and happy would the Christian world be if they were more generally practised. See Dr. Taylor, who farther remarks, that it is probable St. Paul learned all these particulars from Aquila and Priscilla, who were lately come from Rome, Acts xviii. 2, 3, and with whom the apostle was familiar for a considerable time. This is very likely, as there is no evidence that he had any other intercourse with the Church at Rome.

Verse 1. *Him that is weak in the faith*] By this the apostle most evidently means the converted *Jew*, who must indeed be weak in the faith, if he considered this distinction of meats and days essential to his salvation. See on ver. 21.

Receive ye] Associate with him ; receive him into your religious fellowship ; but when there, let all religious altercations be avoided.

Not to doubtful disputations.] Μη εις διακρισεις δια λογισμων. These words have been variously translated and understood. Dr. *Whitby* thinks the sense of them to be this ; *Not discriminating them by their inward thoughts.* Do not reject any from your Christian communion because of their particular sentiments on things which are in themselves *indifferent*. Do not curiously inquire into their religious scruples, nor condemn them on that account. Entertain a brother of this kind rather with what may profit his soul, than with curious disquisitions on speculative points of doctrine. A good lesson for modern Christians in general.

Verse 2. *One believeth that he may eat all things*] He believes that whatsoever is *wholesome* and *nourishing*, whether *herbs* or *flesh*—whether enjoined or forbidden by the Mosaic law—may be safely and conscientiously used by every Christian.

Another, who is weak, eateth herbs.] Certain Jews, lately converted to the Christian faith, and having as yet little knowledge of its doctrines, believe the Mosaic law relative to clean and unclean meats to be still in force ; and therefore, when they are in a Gentile country, for fear of being defiled, avoid flesh entirely and live on vegetables. And a Jew when in a heathen country acts thus, because he cannot tell whether the flesh which is sold in the market may be of a *clean* or *unclean* beast ; whether it may not have been *offered* to an *idol* ; or whether the *blood* may have been taken properly from it.

Verse 3. *Let not him that eateth*] The *Gentile*, who eats flesh, *despise him*, the *Jew*, who *eateth not* flesh, but *herbs*. *And let not him*, the Jew, *that eateth not* indiscriminately, *judge*—condemn *him*, the Gentile, *that eateth* indiscriminately flesh or vegetables.

For God hath received him.] Both being *sincere* and upright, and acting in the fear of God, are *received as heirs* of *eternal life*, without any difference on account of these religious scruples or prejudices.

Verse 4. *Who art thou that judgest another man's servant ?*] Who has ever given thee the right to con-

2

A. M. cir. 4062
A. D. cir. 58.
An. Olymp.
cir. CCIX. 2.
A. U. C. cir.
811.

servant ? to his own master he standeth or falleth. Yea, he shall be holden up : for God is able to make him stand.

5 [f] One man esteemeth one day above another· another esteemeth every day *alike.* Let every man be [g] fully persuaded in his own mind.

6 He that [h] regardeth [i] the day, regardeth *it* unto the Lord ; and he that regardeth not the day, to the Lord he doth not regard *it.* He that eateth, eateth to the Lord, for [k] he giveth God thanks ; and he that eateth not, to the Lord he eateth not, and giveth God thanks.

7 For [1] none of us liveth to himself, and no man dieth to himself.

8 For whether we live, we live unto the Lord ; and whether we die, we die unto the Lord : whether we live therefore, or die, we are the Lord's.

9 For [m] to this end Christ both died, and rose, and revived, that he might be [n] Lord both of the dead and living.

A. M. cir. 4062.
A. D. cir. 58.
An. Olymp.
cir. CCIX. 2.
A. U. C. cir.
811.

---

[f] Gal. iv. 10 ; Col. ii. 16.——[g] Or, *fully assured.*——[h] Gal. iv. 10.
[i] Or, *observeth.*——[k] 1 Cor. x. 31 ; 1 Tim. iv. 3.

[1] Cor. vi. 19, 20 ; Gal. ii. 20 ; 1 Thess. v. 10 ; 1 Peter iv. 2.
[m] 2 Cor. v. 15.——[n] Acts x. 36.

---

demn the servant of another man, in things pertaining to his own master ? *To his own master he standeth or falleth.* He is to judge him, not thou ; thy intermeddling in this business is both rash and uncharitable.

Yea, he shall be holden up] He is sincere and upright, and *God, who is able to make him stand,* will uphold him ; and so teach him that he shall not essentially err. And it is the will of God that such upright though scrupulous persons should be continued members of his Church.

Verse 5. *One man esteemeth one day above another*] Perhaps the word ημεραν, day, is here taken for *time, festival,* and such like, in which sense it is frequently used. Reference is made here to the *Jewish institutions,* and especially their *festivals ;* such as the *passover, pentecost, feast* of *tabernacles, new moons, jubilee,* &c. The converted *Jew* still thought these of moral obligation ; the *Gentile* Christian not having been bred up in this way had no such prejudices. And as those who were the instruments of bringing him to the knowledge of God gave him no such injunctions, consequently he paid to these no religious regard.

Another] The converted *Gentile esteemeth every day*—considers that all *time* is the Lord's, and that each day should be devoted to the glory of God ; and that those festivals are not binding on him.

We add here *alike,* and make the text say what I am sure was never intended, viz. that there is no distinction of days, not even of the Sabbath : and that every Christian is at liberty to consider even this day to be holy or not holy, as he happens to be persuaded in his own mind.

That the *Sabbath* is of lasting obligation may be reasonably concluded from its *institution* (see the note on Gen. ii. 3) and from its *typical* reference. All allow that the Sabbath is a type of that *rest in glory* which *remains for the people of God.* Now, all types are intended to continue in full force till the antitype, or thing signified, take place ; consequently, the Sabbath will continue in force till the consummation of all things. The word *alike* should not be added ; nor is it acknowledged by any MS. or ancient *version.*

Let every man be fully persuaded] With respect to the propriety or non-propriety of keeping the above *festivals,* let every man act from the plenary convic-

tion of his own mind ; there is a sufficient latitude allowed : all may be fully satisfied.

Verse 6. *He that regardeth the day*] A beautiful apology for *mistaken sincerity* and *injudicious reformation.* Do not condemn the man for what is indifferent in itself: if he keep these *festivals,* his purpose is to honour God by the religious observance of them. On the other hand, he who finds that he cannot observe them in honour of God, not believing that God has enjoined them, he does not observe them at all. In like manner, he that eateth any creature of God, which is wholesome and proper food, *gives thanks to God* as the author of all good. And he who cannot eat of all indiscriminately, but is regulated by the precepts in the Mosaic law relative to *clean* and *unclean meats,* also *gives God thanks.* Both are sincere ; both upright ; both act according to their light ; God accepts both ; and *they* should bear with each other.

Verse 7. *None of us liveth to himself*] The Greek writers use the phrase, εαυτω ζην, to signify acting according to one's own judgment, following one's own opinion. Christians must act in all *things* according to the mind and will of God, and not follow their own *wills.* The apostle seems to intimate that in all the above cases each must endeavour to *please God,* for he is accountable to him alone for his conduct in these indifferent things. God is our master, we must *live to him,* as we live under his notice and by his bounty ; and when we cease to live among men, we are still in his hand. Therefore, what we do, or what we leave undone, should be in reference to that eternity which is ever at hand.

Verse 9. *Christ both died and rose*] That we are not our own, but are the Lord's both in life and death, is evident from this—that Christ lived, and died, and rose again, *that he might be the Lord of the dead and the living ;* for his power extends equally over both worlds : *separate,* as well as *embodied spirits,* are under his authority ; and he it is who is to raise even the dead to life : and thus all throughout eternity shall live under his dominion.

The clause και ανεστη, *and rose,* is wanting in several reputable MSS., and certainly is not necessary to the text. Griesbach omits the words, and reads απεθανε και εζησεν, *died and lived ;* of which Professor

A. M. cir. 4062.
A. D. cir. 58.
An. Olymp.
cir. CCIX. 2.
A. U. C. cir.
811.

10 But why dost thou judge thy brother? or why dost thou set at nought thy brother? for ᵒ we shall all stand before the judgment seat of Christ.

11 For it is written, ᵖ *As* I live, saith the Lord, every knee shall bow to me, and every tongue shall confess to God.

12 So then �q every one of us. shall give account of himself to God.

13 Let us not, therefore, judge one another any more: but judge this rather, that ʳ no man

put a stumbling-block or an occasion to fall in *his* brother's way.

14 I know, and am persuaded by the Lord Jesus, ˢ that *there is* nothing ᵗ unclean of itself: but ᵘ to him that esteemeth any thing to be ᵛ unclean, to him *it is* unclean.

15 But if thy brother be grieved with *thy* meat, now walkest thou not ʷ charitably. ˣ Destroy not him with thy meat, for whom Christ died.

A. M. cir. 4062.
A. D. cir. 58.
An. Olymp.
cir. CCIX. 2.
A. U. C. cir.
811.

ᵒ Matt. xxv. 31, 32; Acts x. 42; xvii. 31; 2 Cor. v. 10; Jude xiv. 15.——ᵖ Isa. xlv. 23; Phil. ii. 10.——q Matt. xii. 36; Gal. vi. 5; 1 Pet. iv. 5.——ʳ 1 Cor. viii. 9, 13; x. 32.

ˢ Acts x. 15; ver. 2, 20; 1 Cor. x. 25; 1 Tim. iv. 4; Tit. i. 15. ᵗ Gr. *common.*——ᵘ 1 Cor. viii. 7, 10.——ᵛ Gr. *common.*——ʷ Gr *according to charity.*——ˣ 1 Cor. viii. 11.

White says, *lectio indubie genuina:* "this reading is indisputably genuine."

Verse 10. *But why dost thou*] Christian Jew, observing the rites of the Mosaic law, *judge*—condemn *thy brother*—the Christian *Gentile*, who does not think himself bound by this law?

Or why dost thou] Christian *Gentile*, *set at nought* thy Christian Jewish brother, as if he were unworthy of thy regard, because he does not yet believe that the Gospel has set him free from the rites and ceremonies of the law?

It is a true saying of Mr. Heylin, on this verse: *The superstitious are prone* to judge, *and those who are* not superstitious *are prone* to despise.

We shall all stand before the judgment seat of Christ.] Why should we then judge and condemn each other? We are accountable to God for our conduct, and shall be judged at his bar; and let us consider that whatever measure we mete, the same shall be measured unto us again.

Verse 12. *Every one of us shall give account of himself*] We shall not, at the bar of God, be obliged to account for the conduct of *each other*—each shall give account of himself: and let him take heed that he be prepared to give up his accounts with joy.

Verse 13. *Let us not, therefore, judge one another any more*] Let us abandon such rash conduct; it is dangerous, it is uncharitable: judgment belongs to the Lord, and he will *condemn* those only who should *not* be *acquitted*.

That no man put a stumbling block] Let both the converted *Jew* and *Gentile* consider that they should labour to promote each other's spiritual interests, and not be a means of hindering each other in their Christian course; or of causing them to abandon the Gospel, on *which*, and not on questions of *rites* and *ceremonies*, the salvation of their soul depends.

Verse 14. *I know, and am persuaded by the Lord Jesus*] After reasoning so long and so much with these contending parties on the subject of their mutual misunderstandings, without attempting to give any opinion, but merely to show them the folly and uncharitableness of their conduct, he now expresses himself fully, and tells them that *nothing is unclean of itself*, and that he has the inspiration and authority of Jesus

Christ to say so; for to such an inspiration he must refer in such words as, *I know, and am persuaded by the Lord Jesus.* And yet, after having given them this decisive judgment, through respect to the tender, mistaken conscience of weak believers, he immediately adds: *But to him that esteemeth any thing to be unclean, to him* it is *unclean;* because if he act contrary to his conscience, he must necessarily contract guilt; for he who acts in opposition to his conscience in one case may do it in another, and thus even the *plain declarations* of the *word of God* may be set aside on things of the utmost importance, as well as the *erroneous* though well-intentioned dictates of his conscience, on matters which he makes of the *last consequence;* though others who are better taught know them to be *indifferent.*

It is dangerous to *trifle with conscience*, even when *erroneous;* it should be borne with and instructed; it must be won over, not *taken by storm.* Its feelings should be respected because they ever refer to God, and have their foundation in his fear. He who sins against his conscience in things which every one else knows to be indifferent, will soon do it in those things in which his salvation is most intimately concerned. It is a great blessing to have a *well-informed* conscience; it is a blessing to have a *tender* conscience; and even a *sore* conscience is infinitely better than none.

Verse 15. *If thy brother be grieved*] If he think that thou doest wrong, and he is in consequence stumbled at thy conduct.

Now walkest thou not charitably.] Κατα αγαπην, *According to love;* for *love worketh no ill to its neighbour;* but by thy eating some particular kind of meat, on which neither thy *life* nor *well-being* depends, thou *workest ill* to him by *grieving* and distressing his mind; and therefore thou breakest the *law of God* in reference to him, while pretending that *thy Christian liberty* raises thee above his *scruples.*

Destroy not him with thy meat, for whom Christ died.] This puts the uncharitable conduct of the person in question in the strongest light, because it supposes that the weak brother may be so *stumbled* as to *fall* and *perish finally;* even the man *for whom Christ died.* To injure a man in his *circumstances* is bad; to injure him in his *person* is worse; to injure him in

2

A. M. cir. 4062.
A. D. cir. 58.
An. Olymp.
cir. CCIX. 2.
A. U. C. cir.
811.

16 ʸ Let not then your good be evil spoken of:

17 ᶻ For the kingdom of God is not meat and drink ; but righteousness and peace, and joy in the Holy Ghost.

18 For he that in these things serveth Christ ᵃ *is* acceptable to God, and approved of men.

19 ᵇ Let us therefore follow after the things which make for peace, and things wherewith ᶜ one may edify another.

20 ᵈ For meat destroy not the work of God. ᵉ All things indeed *are* pure ; ᶠ but *it is* evil for that man who eateth with offence.

21 *It is* good neither to eat ᵍ flesh, nor to drink wine, nor *any thing* whereby thy brother

A. M. cir. 4062.
A. D. cir. 58.
An. Olymp.
cir. CIX. 2.
A. U. C. cir.
811.

ʸ Ch. xii. 17.—ᶻ 1 Cor. viii. 8.—ᵃ 2 Cor. viii. 21.—ᵇ Psa. xxxiv. 14 ; chap. xii. 18.——ᶜ Chap. xv. 2 ; 1 Cor. xiv. 12 ; 1 Thess. v. 11.

ᵈ Ver. 15.——ᵉ Matt. xv. 11 ; Acts x. 15 ; verse 14 ; Titus i. 15. ᶠ 1 Cor. viii. 9, 10, 11, 12.——ᵍ 1 Cor. viii. 13.

---

his *reputation* is still *worse ;* and to injure his *soul* is worst of all. No wickedness, no malice, can go farther than to injure and destroy the soul : thy uncharitable conduct may proceed thus far ; therefore thou art highly criminal before God.

From this verse we learn that a *man for whom Christ died* may *perish,* or have his soul *destroyed ;* and destroyed with such a *destruction* as implies *perdition ;* the original is very emphatic, μη—εκεινον απολλυε, ὑπερ οὑ Χριστος απεθανε. Christ died in his *stead ;* do not destroy his soul. The *sacrificial death* is as strongly expressed as it can be, and there is no word in the New Testament that more forcibly implies *eternal ruin* than the verb απολλυω, from which is derived that most significant name of the *Devil,* ὁ Απολλυων, the DESTROYER, the great universal murderer of souls.

Verse 16. *Let not then your good be evil spoken of*] Do not make such a use of your *Christian liberty* as to subject the *Gospel* itself to reproach. Whatsoever you do, do it in such a manner, spirit, and time, as to make it productive of the greatest possible good. There are many who have such an unhappy method of doing their good acts, as not only to do *little* or *no good* by them, but a great deal of *evil.* It requires much prudence and watchfulness to find out the proper time of performing even a good action.

Verse 17. *For the kingdom of God*] That holy religion which God has sent from heaven, and which he intends to make the instrument of establishing a counterpart of the kingdom of glory among men : see on Matt. iii. 2.

Is not meat and drink] It consists not in these outward and indifferent things. It neither particularly *enjoins* nor particularly *forbids* such.

But righteousness] Pardon of sin, and holiness of heart and life.

And peace] In the soul, from a sense of God's mercy ; peace regulating, ruling, and harmonizing the heart.

And joy in the Holy Ghost.] Solid spiritual *happiness ;* a *joy* which springs from a clear sense of God's mercy ; the love of God being shed abroad in the heart by the *Holy Ghost.* In a word, it is happiness brought into the soul by the Holy Spirit, and maintained there by the same influence. This is a genuine counterpart of heaven ; *righteousness* without sin, PEACE without inward *disturbance,* JOY without any kind of *mental agony* or distressing *fear.* See the note on Matt. iii. 2.

Verse 18. *For he that in these things*] The man,

whether *Jew* or *Gentile,* who *in these things*—righteousness, peace, and joy in the Holy Ghost, *serveth Christ*—acts according to his doctrine, is *acceptable to God ;* for he has not only the *form* of godliness in thus *serving Christ,* but he has the *power,* the very *spirit* and *essence* of it, in having righteousness, and peace, and joy in the Holy Ghost ; and therefore the whole *frame* of his *mind,* as well as his *acts,* must be acceptable to God.—*And approved of men ;* for although religion may be persecuted, yet the righteous man, who is continually labouring for the public good, will be generally esteemed. This was a very common form of speech among the Jews ; that *he who was a conscientious observer of the law, was pleasing to God and approved of men.* See several examples in *Schoettgen.*

Verse 19. *Let us therefore follow*] Far from contending about *meats, drinks,* and *festival times,* in which it is not likely that the *Jews* and *Gentiles* will *soon* agree, let us endeavour to the utmost of our power to promote *peace* and *unanimity,* that we may be instrumental in edifying each other, in promoting religious knowledge and piety instead of being *stumbling-blocks* in each other's way.

Verse 20. *For meat destroy not the work of God*] Do not hinder the *progress of the Gospel* either in your own souls or in those of others, by contending about lawful or unlawful meats. And do not destroy the soul of thy Christian brother, ver. 15, by offending him so as to induce him to *apostatize.*

All things indeed are pure] This is a repetition of the sentiment delivered, ver. 14, in different words. Nothing that is *proper* for *aliment* is *unlawful* to be eaten ; *but* it is *evil for that man who eateth with offence*—the man who either eats contrary to his own conscience, or so as to grieve and stumble another, does an *evil* act ; and however *lawful* the thing may be in *itself,* his conduct does not please God.

Verse 21. It is *good neither to eat flesh, &c.*] The spirit and self-denying principles of the Gospel teach us, that we should not only avoid every thing in eating or drinking which may be an occasion of offence or apostasy to our brethren, but even to lay down our lives for them should it be necessary.

Whereby thy brother stumbleth] Προσκοπτει, from προς, against, and κοπτω, to *strike,* to hit the foot against *a stone* in walking, so as to *halt,* and be *impeded* in one's *journey.* It here means, spiritually, any thing by which a man is so perplexed in his mind as to be prevented from making due *progress* in

2

A. M. cir. 4062.
A. D. cir. 58.
An. Olymp.
cir. CCIX. 2.
A. U. C. cir.
811.
stumbleth, or is offended, or is made weak.

22 Hast thou faith? have *it* to thyself before God.

h Happy *is* he that condemneth not him-

self in that thing which he al-loweth.

23 And he that i doubteth is damned if he eat, because *he eateth* not of faith : for k whatsoever *is* not of faith is sin.

A. M. cir. 4062.
A. D. cir. 58.
An. Olymp.
cir. CCIX. 2.
A. U. C. cir.
811.

---

h 1 John iii. 21.

i Or, *discerneth and putteth a difference between meats.*——k Tit. i. 15.

---

the Divine life. Any thing by which he is caused to *halt*, to be *undecisive*, and undetermined ; and under such an influence no man has ever yet *grown in grace* and in the *knowledge of Jesus Christ.*

Or is offended] Η σκανδαλιζεται, from σκανδαλον, a *stumbling-block* ; any thing by which a person is caus-ed to *fall*, especially into a *snare*, *trap*, or *gin*. Ori-ginally the word signified the *piece of wood* or *key* in a *trap*, which being trodden on caused the animal to fall into a pit, or the trap to close upon him. In the New Testament it generally refers to *total apostasy* from the Christian religion ; and this appears to be its meaning in this place.

Or is made weak.] Η ασθενει, from α, *negative*, and σθενος, *strength* ; without *mental vigour* ; without *power* sufficiently to distinguish between *right* and *wrong*, *good* and *evil*, *lawful* and *unlawful*. To get under the dominion of an *erroneous* conscience, so as to judge that to be *evil* or *unlawful* which is *not so.* The two last terms are omitted by two excellent MSS. (the *Codex Alexandrinus* and the *Codex Ephraim*,) by the *Syriac* of Erpen, the *Coptic* and the *Ethiopic*, and by some of the *primitive* fathers. It is very likely that they were *added* by some early hand by way of illustration. Griesbach has left them in the text with a note of *doubtfulness.*

Verse 22. *Hast thou faith ?*] The term *faith* seems to signify in this place a *full persuasion in a man's mind that he is right*, that what he does is *lawful*, and has the *approbation of God* and his *conscience.* Dr. Taylor has a judicious note on this passage. " There is no necessity," says he, " for reading the first clause *interrogatively* ; and it seems to be more agreeable to the structure of the Greek to render it, *Thou hast faith* ; as if he had said : ' I own thou hast a right persuasion.' Farther, there is an *anadi-plosis* in εχεις, and εχε, the first simply signifies *thou hast*, the latter, *hold fast.* Thou hast a right persua-sion concerning thy Christian liberty ; and I advise thee to hold that persuasion steadfastly, with respect to thyself in the sight of God. Εχω, *have*, has fre-quently this emphatical signification. See Matt. xxv. 29, &c."

Happy is he that condemneth not, &c.] That man only can enjoy *peace of conscience* who acts according to the full persuasion which God has given him of the lawfulness of his conduct : whereas he must be mis-erable who allows himself in the practice of any thing for which his conscience upbraids and accuses him. This is a most excellent maxim, and every genuine Christian should be careful to try every part of his conduct by it. If a man have not peace in his own bosom, he cannot be happy ; and no man can have peace who sins against his conscience. If a man's passions or appetite allow or instigate him to a par-

ticular thing, let him take good heed that his con-science *approve* what his passions *allow*, and that he live not the subject of continual self-condemnation and reproach. Even the man who has the too scrupulous conscience had better, in such matters as are in ques-tion, obey its *erroneous* dictates than violate this moral feeling, and live only to condemn the actions he is constantly performing.

Verse 23. *And he that doubteth*] This verse is a necessary part of the preceding, and should be read thus : *But he that doubteth is condemned if he eat*, *because* he eateth *not of faith.* The meaning is suffi-ciently plain. He that feeds on any kind of meats prohibited by the Mosaic law, with the persuasion in his mind that he may be wrong in so doing, is con-demned by his conscience for doing that which he has reason to think God has forbidden.

For whatsoever is *not of faith is sin.*] Whatever he does, without a *full persuasion* of its lawfulness, (see ver. 22,) is to him *sin* ; for he does it under a conviction that he may be wrong in so doing. There-fore, if he makes a distinction in his own conscience between different kinds of meats, and yet eats of all indifferently, he is a *sinner* before God ; because he eats either through *false shame*, *base compliance*, or an *unbridled appetite* ; and *any* of these is in itself a *sin* against the sincerity, ingenuousness, and self-de-nying principles of the Gospel of Christ.

Some think that these words have a more extensive signification, and that they apply to all who have not *true religion* and *faith in our Lord Jesus Christ* ; every work of such persons being sinful in the sight of a holy God, because it does not proceed from a pure motive. On this ground our Church says, *Art.* xiii, " Works done before the grace of Christ and the inspiration of his Spirit are not pleasant to God, for-asmuch as they are not of faith in Jesus Christ ; yea, for that they are not done as God hath willed and commanded them to be done, we doubt not but they have the nature of sin." To this we may add, that without faith it is impossible to please God ; every thing is wrong where this principle is wanting.

There are few readers who have not remarked that the last three verses of this epistle (chap. xvi. 25, 26, 27) appear to stand in their present place without any obvious *connection* ; and apparently *after* the epistle is concluded. And it is well known to critics, that two MSS. in *uncial* letters, the Cod. A and I, with upwards of 100 others, together with the *Slavonic*, the later *Syriac* and *Arabic*, add those verses at the end of the fourteenth chapter. The transposition is acknowledged by *Cyril*, *Chrysostom*, *Theodoret*, *Œcumenius*, *Theophylact*, *Theodulus*, *Damascenus*, and *Tertullian* ; see Wetstein. *Griesbach* inserts them at the end of this chapter as their proper place ;

2

and most learned men approve of this transposition. It may be necessary to repeat the words here that the reader may see with what propriety they connect with the subject which terminates the fourteenth chapter as it now stands. Chap. xiv. ver. 23 : *And he that doubteth is condemned if he eat, because* he eateth *not of faith : for whatsoever* is *not of faith is sin.* Chap. xvi. ver. 25. *Now, to him that is of power to stablish you according to my Gospel, and the preaching of Jesus Christ, (according to the revelation of the mystery which was kept secret since the world began,*

Verse 26. *But now is made manifest, and by the scriptures of the prophets, according to the commandment of the everlasting God, made known to all nations for the obedience of faith ;)*

Verse 27. *To God only wise* be *glory through Jesus Christ for ever. Amen.* Chap. xv. 1 : *We then that are strong ought to bear the infirmities of the weak, &c.*

These words certainly connect better with the close of the fourteenth chapter and the beginning of the fifteenth than they do with the conclusion of the sixteenth, where they are now generally found ; but I shall defer my observations upon them till I come to that place, with only this remark, that the *stablishing* mentioned chap. xvi. ver. 25, corresponds well with the *doubting*, chap. xiv. ver 23, and indeed the whole matter of these verses agrees so well with the subject so largely handled in the preceding chapter, that there can be very little doubt of their being in their proper place if joined to the end of this chapter, as they are in the preceding MSS: and versions.

CHAPTER XV.

The strong should bear the infirmities of the weak, and each strive to please, not himself, but his neighbour, after the example of Christ, 1–3. Whatsoever was written in old times was written for our learning, 4. We should be of one mind, that we might with one mouth glorify God, 5, 6. We should accept each other as Christ has accepted us, 7. Scripturls proofs that Jesus Christ was not only the minister of the circumcision, but came also for the salvation of the Gentiles, 8–12. The God of hope can fill us with all peace and joy in believing, 13. Character of the Church of Rome, 14. The reason why the apostle wrote so boldly to the Church in that city—what God had wrought by him, and what he purposed to do, 15–24. He tells them of his intended journey to Jerusalem, with a contribution to the poor saints—a sketch of this journey, 25–29. He commends himself to their prayers, 30–33.

A. M. cir. 4062.
A. D. cir. 58.
An. Olymp.
cir. CCIX. 2.
A. U. C. cir.
811.

WE [a] then that are strong ought to bear the [b] infirmities of the weak, and not to please ourselves.

2 [c] Let every one of us please *his* neighbour for *his* good to [d] edification.

3 [e] For even Christ pleased not himself; but, as it is written, [f] The reproaches of them that reproached thee fell on me.

4 For [g] whatsoever things were written aforetime were written for our learning ; that we,

A. M. cir. 4062.
A. D. cir. 58.
An. Olymp.
cir. CCIX. 2.
A. U. C. cir.
811.

---

[a] Gal. vi. 1.——[b] Chap. xiv. 1.——[c] 1 Cor. ix. 19, 22 ; x. 24, 33 ; xiii. 5 ; Phil. ii. 4, 5.——[d] Chap. xiv. 19.   [e] Matt. xxvi. 39 ; John v. 30 ; vi. 38.——[f] Psa. lxix. 9.——[g] Ch. iv. 23, 24 ; 1 Cor. ix. 9, 10 ; x. 11 ; 2 Tim. iii. 16, 17.

NOTES ON CHAP. XV.

Verse 1, *We then that are strong*] The sense of this verse is supposed to be the following : We, Gentile Christians, who perfectly understand the nature of our Gospel liberty, not only lawfully may, but are bound in duty to bear any inconveniences that may arise from the scruples of the weaker brethren, and to ease their consciences by prudently abstaining from such indifferent things as may offend and trouble them ; and not take advantage from our superior knowledge to make them submit to our judgment.

Verse 2. *Let every one of us please* his *neighbour*] For it should be a maxim with each of us to do all in our power to please our brethren ; and especially in those things in which their spiritual edification is concerned. Though we should not indulge men in mere whims and caprices, yet we should bear with their ignorance and their weakness, knowing that others had much to bear with from us before we came to our present advanced state of religious knowledge.

Verse 3. *For even Christ pleased not himself*] Christ never acted as one who sought his *own ease* or *profit* ; he not only bore with the weakness, but with the insults, of his creatures ; as it is written in Psalm lxix. 9 : *The reproaches of them that reproached thee fell on me*—I not only bore their insults, but bore the punishment due to them for their vicious and abominable conduct. That this Psalm refers to the Messiah and his sufferings for mankind is evident, not only from the quotation here, but also from John xix. 28, 29, when our Lord's receiving the vinegar during his expiatory suffering is said to be a fulfilling of the scripture, viz. of verse 21 of this very Psalm ; and his cleansing the temple, John ii. 15—17, is said to be a fulfilment of verse 9, *For the zeal of thy house hath eaten me up,* the former part of which verse the apostle quotes here.

Verse 4. *For whatsoever things were written aforetime*] This refers not only to the quotation from the 69th Psalm, but to all the *Old Testament* scriptures ; for it can be to no other scriptures that the apostle alludes. And, from what he says here of them, we learn that God had not intended them merely for those generations in which they were first delivered, but for the instruction of all the succeeding generations of

2

A. M. cir. 4062.
A. D. cir. 58.
An. Olymp.
cir. CCIX. 2.
A. U. C. cir.
811.

through patience and comfort of the scriptures, might have hope.

5 [h] Now the God of patience and consolation grant you to be like-minded one toward another [i] according to Christ Jesus :

6 That ye may [k] with one mind *and* one mouth glorify God, even the Father of our Lord Jesus Christ.

7 Wherefore [l] receive ye one another, [m] as

A. M. cir. 4062.
A. D. cir. 58.
An. Olymp.
cir. CCIX. 2.
A. U. C. cir.
811.

Christ also received us to the glory of God.

8 Now I say that [n] Jesus Christ was a minister of the circumcision for the truth of God, [o] to confirm the promises *made* unto the fathers :

9 And [p] that the Gentiles might glorify God for *his* mercy ; as it is written, [q] For this cause I will confess to thee among the Gentiles, and sing unto thy name.

---

[h] Chap. xii. 16 ; 1 Cor. i. 10 ; Phil. iii. 16.——[i] Or, *after the example of.*——[k] Acts iv. 24, 32.——[l] Ch. xiv. 1, 3.——[m] Ch. v. 2.

[n] Matt. xv. 24 ; John i. 11 ; Acts iii. 25, 26 ; xiii. 46.——[o] Ch. iii. 3 ; 2 Cor. i. 20.——[p] John x. 16 ; chap. ix. 23.——[q] Psa. xviii. 49.

---

mankind. *That we, through patience and comfort of the scriptures*—that we, through those remarkable examples of *patience* exhibited by the saints and followers of God, whose history is given in those scriptures, and the *comfort* which they derived from God in their patient endurance of sufferings brought upon them through their faithful attachment to truth and righteousness, *might have hope* that we shall be upheld and blessed as they were, and our sufferings become the means of our greater advances in faith and holiness, and consequently our *hope of eternal glory* be the more confirmed. Some think that the word παρακλησις, which we translate *comfort*, should be rendered *exhortation ;* but there is certainly no need here to leave the *usual* acceptation of the term, as the word *comfort* makes a regular and consistent sense with the rest of the verse.

Verse 5. *Now the God of patience and consolation*] May that God who endued them with *patience*, and gave them the *consolation* that supported them in all their trials and afflictions, *grant you to be like-minded* —give you the same mode of thinking, and the same power of acting towards each other, *according to* the example of *Christ.*

Verse 6. *That ye*—Jews and Gentiles—*may with one mind*] Thinking the same things, and bearing with each other, after the example of Christ ; and *one mouth*, in all your religious assemblies, without jarring or contentions, *glorify God* for calling you into such a state of salvation, and showing himself to be *your* loving compassionate *Father*, as he is *the Father of our Lord Jesus Christ.*

It is very likely that the apostle refers here to *religious acts* in *public worship*, which might have been greatly interrupted by the dissensions between the converted Jews and the converted Gentiles ; these differences he labours to compose ; and, after having done all that was necessary in the way of instruction and exhortation, he now pours out his soul to God, who alone could rule and manage the heart, that he would enable them to think the same things, to be of the same judgment, and that all, feeling their obligation to him, might join in the sweetest harmony in every act of religious worship.

Verse 7. *Wherefore receive ye one another*] Προσ-λαμβανεσθε· Have the most *affectionate regard* for each other, and acknowledge each other as the servants and children of God Almighty.

As Christ also received us] Καθως και ὁ Χριστος

προσελαβετο ἡμας· In the same manner, and with the same *cordial affection*, as *Christ has received* us into communion with himself, and has made us partakers of such inestimable blessings, condescending to be present in all our assemblies. And as Christ has *received us* thus to the glory of God, so should we, Jews and Gentiles, cordially *receive each other*, that God's glory may be promoted by our *harmony* and brotherly love.

Verse 8. *Jesus Christ was a minister of the circumcision*] To show the Gentiles the propriety of bearing with the scrupulous Jews, he shows them here that they were under the greatest obligations to this people ; to whom, in the days of his flesh, Jesus Christ confined his ministry ; giving the world to see that he allowed the claim of the Jews as having the *first* right to the blessings of the Gospel. And he confined his ministry thus to the Jews, to *confirm the truth of God*, contained in the *promises* made unto the *patriarchs ;* for God had declared that thus it should be ; and Jesus Christ, by coming according to the promise, has fulfilled this truth, by making good the promises : therefore, salvation is of the Jews, as a kind of *right* conveyed to them through the *promises* made to their *fathers*. But this salvation was not exclusively designed for the Jewish people ; as God by his prophets had repeatedly declared.

Verse 9. *And that the Gentiles might glorify God for* his *mercy*] As the Jews were to glorify God for his *truth*, so the Gentiles were to glorify God for his *mercy*. The Jews received the blessings of the Gospel by *right of promise*, which promise God had most punctually and circumstantially *fulfilled*. The Gentiles had received the same Gospel as an effect of God's mere *mercy*, having no *right* in consequence of any promise or engagement made with any of their ancestors, though they were originally included in the covenant made with Abraham ; and the *prophets* had repeatedly declared that they should be made *equal* partakers of those blessings with the Jews themselves ; as the apostle proceeds to prove.

I will confess to thee among the Gentiles] This quotation is taken from Psalm xviii. 49, and shows that the Gentiles had a right to glorify God for his mercy to them ; and we shall see the strength of this saying farther, when we consider a maxim of the Jews delivered in *Megillah*, fol. 14 : " From the time that the children of Israel entered into the promised land, no Gentile had any right to *sing a hymn of praise to*

A. M. cir. 4062.
A. D. cir. 58.
An. Olymp.
cir. CCIX. 2.
A. U. C. cir.
811.

10 And again he saith, [r] Rejoice, ye Gentiles, with his people.

11 And again, [s] Praise the Lord, all ye Gentiles; and laud him, all ye people.

12 And again Esaias saith, [t] There shall be a root of Jesse, and he that shall rise to reign over the Gentiles; in him shall the Gentiles trust.

13 Now the God of hope fill you with all [u] joy and peace in believing, that ye may

abound in hope, through the power of the Holy Ghost.

14 And [v] I myself also am persuaded of you, my brethren, that ye also are full of goodness, [w] filled with all knowledge, able also to admonish one another.

15 Nevertheless, brethren, I have written the more boldly unto you in some sort, as putting you in mind, [x] because of the grace that is given to me of God,

A. M. cir. 4062.
A. D. cir. 58.
An. Olymp.
cir. CCIX. 2.
A. U. C. cir.
811.

---

[r] Deut. xxxii. 43.——[s] Psa. cxvii. 1.——[t] Isa. xi. 1, 10; Rev. v. 5; xxii. 16.——[u] Chap. xii. 12; xiv. 17.

[v] 2 Pet. i. 12; 1 John ii. 21.——[w] 1 Cor. viii. 1, 7, 10.——[x] Chap. i. 5; xii. 3; Gal. i. 15; Eph. iii. 7, 8.

God. But after that the Israelites were led into captivity, then the Gentiles *began to have a right to glorify God."* Thus the Jews themselves confess that the Gentiles have a *right to glorify God;* and this on account of being made partakers of his grace and mercy. And if, says *Schoettgen,* we have a *right* to glorify God, then it follows that our worship must be *pleasing* to him; and if it be *pleasing* to him, then it follows that this worship must be *good,* otherwise God could not be pleased with it.

Dr. *Taylor* gives a good paraphrase of this and the three following verses: As you Jews glorify God for his *truth,* so the Gentiles have a right to join with you in glorifying God for his *mercy.* And you have Scripture authority for admitting them to such fellowship; for instance, *David* says, Psa. xviii. 49, *Therefore will I give thanks unto thee, O Lord, among the Gentiles, and sing praises unto thy name.* And again, *Moses* himself says, Deut. xxxii. 43, *Rejoice, O ye Gentiles, with his people.* And again, it is evident, from Psa. cxvii., that praise to God is not to be confined to the *Jews* only, but that *all* people, as they *all* share in his goodness, should also join in thanks to their common benefactor: *O praise the Lord, all ye nations,* (Gentiles,) *praise him all ye people; for his merciful kindness is great towards us; and the truth of the Lord endureth for ever.* Again the Prophet *Isaiah* expressly and clearly declares, chap. xi. ver. 10, *There shall be a root of Jesse,* (that is, the Messiah,) *and he shall rise to reign over the Gentiles,* and *in him shall the Gentiles hope:* ελπιουσιν· And thus the apostle proves, both to the Jews and to the Gentiles, who were probably unwilling to join with each other in religious fellowship, that they had both an equal right to glorify God, being equally interested in his mercy, goodness, and truth; and that, from the evidence of the above *scriptures,* the *Gentiles* had as much right *to hope in Christ,* for the full enjoyment of his kingdom, as the Jews had: and, taking occasion from the last word *hope,* ελπιουσιν, which we improperly translate *trust,* he pours out his heart in the following affectionate prayer.

Verse 13. *Now the God of hope, &c.*] 'Ο δε Θεος της ελπιδος, *May the God of this hope*—that God who caused both Jews and Gentiles to hope that the gracious promises which he made to them should be ful-

filled; and who, accordingly, has fulfilled them in the most punctual and circumstantial manner;

Fill you with all joy] Give you true spiritual *happiness; peace* in your own hearts, and *unity* among yourselves; *in believing* not only the promises which he has given you, but believing in Christ Jesus, in whom all the promises are *yea* and *amen.*

That ye may abound in hope] That ye may be excited to take more enlarged views of the salvation which God has provided for you, and have all your *expectations* fulfilled *by the power of the Holy Ghost,* enabling you to *hope* and *believe;* and then sealing the fulfilment of the promises upon your hearts.

Verse 14. *And I—am persuaded of you*] This is supposed to be an address to the Gentiles; and it is managed with great delicacy: he seems to apologize for the *freedom* he had used in writing to them; which he gives them to understand proceeded from the authority he had received by his apostolical office, the exercise of which office respected *them* particularly. So they could not be offended when they found themselves so particularly distinguished.

Ye—are full of goodness] Instead of αγαθωσυνης, *goodness,* some MSS. of good repute have αγαπης, *love.* In this connection both words seem to mean nearly the same thing. They were so full of *goodness* and *love* that they were disposed, of themselves, to follow any plan that might be devised, in order to bring about the most perfect understanding between them and their Jewish brethren.

Filled with all knowledge] So completely instructed in the mind and design of God, relative to their *calling,* and the *fruit* which they were to bring forth to the glory of God, that they were well qualified to give *one another* suitable exhortations on every important point.

Instead of αλληλους, *one another,* several MSS. have αλλους, *others;* which gives a clearer sense: for, if they were *all* filled with knowledge, there was little occasion for them to admonish *one another;* but by this they were well qualified to admonish *others*—to impart the wisdom they had to those who were less instructed.

Verse 15. *Nevertheless—I have written*] Notwithstanding I have this conviction of your extensive knowledge in the things of God, I have made bold to write to you *in some sort,* απο μερους, *to a party* among you, as some learned men translate the words,

2

A. M. cir. 4062.
A. D. cir. 58.
An. Olymp.
cir. CCIX. 2.
A. U. C. cir.
811.

16 That ^y I should be the minister of Jesus Christ to the Gentiles, ministering the Gospel of God, that the ^z offering ^a up of the Gentiles might be acceptable, being sanctified by the Holy Ghost.

17 I have therefore whereof I may glory through Jesus Christ ^b in those things which pertain to God.

18 For I will not dare to speak of any of those things ^c which Christ hath not wrought

by me, ^d to make the Gentiles obedient, by word and deed,

19 ^e Through mighty signs and wonders, by the power of the Spirit of God; so that from Jerusalem, and round about unto Illyricum, I have fully preached the Gospel of Christ.

20 Yea, so have I strived to preach the Gospel, not where Christ was named, ^f lest I should build upon another man's foundation:

A. M. cir. 4062.
A. D. cir. 58.
An. Olymp.
cir. CCIX. 2.
A. U. C. cir.
811.

---

^y Chap. xi. 13; Gal. ii. 7, 8, 9; 1 Tim. ii. 7; 2 Tim. i. 11; Phil. ii. 17.——^z Or, *sacrificing.*——^a Isa. lxvi. 20; Phil. ii. 17.

^b Heb. v. 1.——^c Acts xxi. 19; Gal. ii. 8.——^d Chap. i. 5; xvi. 26.——^e Acts xix. 11; 2 Cor. xii. 12.——^f 2 Cor. x. 13, 15, 16.

---

who stand more in need of such instructions than the others; and I do this, *because of the grace,* διὰ τὴν χάριν—because of the *office* which I have received from God, namely, to be the *apostle* of the Gentiles. This authority gave him full right to say, advise, or enjoin any thing which he judged to be of importance to their spiritual interests. This subject he pursues farther in the following verse.

Verse 16. *Ministering the Gospel of God*] Ἱερουργοῦντα, *Acting as a priest.* Here is a plain allusion, says Dr. Whitby, to the Jewish sacrifices offered by the priest, and *sanctified* or made acceptable by the *libamen* offered with them; for he compares himself, in preaching the Gospel, to the *priest performing his sacred functions*—preparing his sacrifice to be offered. The *Gentiles,* converted by him and dedicated to the service of God, are his sacrifices and oblation. The *Holy Spirit* is the *libamen* poured upon this sacrifice, by which it was sanctified and rendered *acceptable* to God. The words of *Isaiah,* lxvi. 20, *And they shall bring all your brethren for an* OFFERING *unto the Lord, out of all* NATIONS, might have suggested the above idea to the mind of the apostle.

Verse 17. *I have therefore whereof I may glory*] Being sent of God on this most honourable and important errand, I have matter of great exultation, not only in the *honour* which he has conferred upon me, but in the great *success* with which he has crowned my ministry.

Verse 18. *For I will not dare to speak*] If the thing were not as I have stated it, I would not dare to arrogate to myself honours which did not belong to me. But God has made me the apostle of the Gentiles; and the conversion of the Gentiles is the fruit of my ministry, Christ having *wrought by me* for this purpose.

By word and deed] Λόγῳ καὶ ἐργῳ· These words may refer to the *doctrines* which he taught and to the *miracles* which he wrought among them. So they became obedient to the *doctrines,* on the evidence of the *miracles* with which they were accompanied.

Verse 19. *Through mighty signs and wonders*] This more fully explains the preceding clause: through the power of the Holy Ghost he was enabled to work among the Gentiles *mighty signs and wonders;* so that they were fully convinced that both his doctrine

and mission were Divine; and therefore they cheerfully received the Gospel of the Lord Jesus.

Round about unto Illyricum] Among ancient writers this place has gone by a great variety of names, *Illyria, Illyrica, Illyricum, Illyris,* and *Illyrium.* It is a country of Europe, extending from the Adriatic gulf to Pannonia: according to Pliny, it extended from the river *Arsia* to the river *Drinius,* thus including Liburnia on the *west,* and Dalmatia on the *east.* Its precise limits have not been determined by either ancient or modern geographers. It seems, according to an inscription in *Gruter,* to have been divided by Augustus into *two* provinces, the *upper* and *lower.* It now forms part of Croatia, Bosnia, Istria, and Slavonia. When the apostle says that he preached the Gospel from Jerusalem *round about to Illyricum,* he intends his *land journeys* chiefly; and, by looking at the map annexed to the Acts of the Apostles, the reader will see that from Jerusalem the apostle went *round* the eastern coast of the Mediterranean Sea, and that he passed through *Syria, Phœnicia, Arabia, Cilicia, Pamphylia, Pisidia, Lycaonia, Galatia, Pontus, Paphlagonia, Phrygia, Troas, Asia, Caria, Lycia, Ionia, Lydia, Thrace, Macedonia, Thessaly,* and *Achaia;* besides the isles of *Cyprus* and *Crete.* And no doubt he visited many other places which are not mentioned in the New Testament.

I have fully preached the Gospel] Πεπληρωκέναι τὸ εὐαγγέλιον, I have *successfully preached*—I have not only *proclaimed* the word, but made *converts* and founded Churches. See the note on Matt. v. 17, where this sense of the word πληροῦν is noticed; for it signifies not only *fully* or *perfectly,* but also to *teach* with *prosperity* and *success.*

Verse 20. *So have I strived to preach the Gospel*] Οὕτω δε φιλοτιμούμενον· For I have considered it my *honour* to preach the Gospel where that Gospel was before unknown. This is the proper import of the word φιλοτιμεῖσθαι; from φίλος, a *friend,* and τιμή, *honour.* As I am *not ashamed of the Gospel of Christ,* so I esteem it an *honour* to preach it, and especially to proclaim it among the *heathen; not building on another man's foundation*—not watering what another apostle had planted; but cheerfully exposing myself to all kinds of dangers and hardships, in order to found new Churches.

2

A. M. cir. 4062.
A. D. cir. 58.
An. Olymp.
cir. CCIX.·2.
A. U. C. cir.
811.

21 But as it is written, g To whom he was not spoken of, they shall see: and they that have not heard, shall understand.

22 For which cause also h I have been i much hindered from coming to you.

23 But now having no more place in these parts, and k having a great desire these many years to come unto you;

24 Whensoever I take my journey into

A. M. cir. 4062.
A. D. cir. 58.
An. Olymp.
cir. CCIX. 2.
A. U. C. cir.
811.

Spain, I will come to you: for I trust to see you in my journey, l and to be brought on my way thitherward by you, if first I be somewhat filled m with your *company.*

25 But now n I go unto Jerusalem to minister unto the saints.

26 For o it hath pleased them of Macedonia and Achaia to make a certain contribution for the poor saints which are at Jerusalem.

g Isa. lii. 15.——h Chap. i. 13; 1 Thess. ii. 17, 18.——i Or, *many ways,* or *oftentimes.*——k Acts xix. 21; ver. 32; chap. i. 11.

l Acts xv. 3.——m Gr. *with you,* ver. 32.——n Acts xix. 21; xx. 22; xxiv. 17.——o 1 Cor. xvi. 1, 2; 2 Cor. viii. 1; ix. 2, 12.

Verse 21. *But as it is written*] These words, quoted from Isa. lii. 15, the apostle applies to his own conduct; not that the words themselves predicted what Paul had done, but that he endeavoured to fulfil such a declaration by his manner of preaching the Gospel to the heathen.

Verse 22. *For which cause, &c.*] My considering it *a point of honour to build on no other man's foundation;* and, finding that the Gospel has been long ago planted at Rome, I have been prevented from going thither, purposing rather to spend my time and strength in preaching where Christ has not, as yet, been proclaimed.

Verse 23. *But—having no more place in these parts*] Having nothing farther at present that I can do—for τοπον εχειν signifies not merely to *have a place of residence,* or the like, but *convenience, opportunity;* which is a frequent meaning of the phrase among the best Greek writers—having no large place or city, where Christianity has not yet been planted, in which I can introduce the Gospel. The apostle was then at *Corinth;* and having evangelized all those parts, he had no opportunity of breaking up any new ground.

Verse 24. *Whensoever I take my journey into Spain*] Where it is very likely the Gospel had not yet been planted; though *legendary tales* inform us that St. James had planted the Gospel there long before this time, and had founded many *bishoprics!* But this is as unfounded as it is ridiculous and absurd; for nothing like what is now termed a *bishopric,* nor even a *parish,* was founded for many years after this. An *itinerant preacher,* might, with more propriety, say *travelling circuits* were formed, rather than *bishoprics.* Whether the apostle ever fulfilled his design of going to Spain is unknown; but there is no evidence whatever that he did, and the presumption is that he did not undertake this voyage. Antiquity affords no proof that he fulfilled his intention.

I will come to you] Ελευσο μαιπρος υμας. These words are wanting in almost every MS. of note, and in the *Syriac* of *Erpen, Coptic, Vulgate, Ethiopic, Armenian,* and *Itala.* If the first clause of this verse be read in connection with the latter clause of the preceding, it will fully appear that this rejected clause is useless. *Having a great desire, these many years to come unto you whensoever I take my journey into Spain: for I trust to see you in my journey, &c.*

Somewhat filled with your company.] The word

εμπλησθω, which we translate *filled,* would be better rendered *gratified;* for εμπλησθηναι signifies to be *satisfied,* to *be gratified,* and to *enjoy.* ÆLIAN., *Hist. Anim.,* lib. v., c. 21, speaking of the *peacock* spreading out his beautiful plumage, says: εα γαρ εμπλησθηναι της θεας τον παριστωτα· " He readily permits the spectator to *gratify himself* by viewing him." And MAXIMUS TYRIUS, Dissert. 41, page 413: " That he may behold the heavens, και εμπλησθη, λαμπρου φωτος, and be *gratified* with the splendour of the light." HOMER uses the word in the same sense :—

Ἡ δ' εμη ουδε περ υιος ενιπλησθηναι ακοιτις
Οφθαλμοισιν εασε.   *Odyss.,* lib. xi., ver. 451.

" But my wife never suffered my eyes to be *delighted* with my son."

The apostle, though he had not the honour of having planted the Church at Rome, yet expected much *gratification* from the visit which he intended to pay them.

Verse 25. *Now I go unto Jerusalem*] From this and the two following verses we learn that the object of his journey to Jerusalem was, to carry a contribution made among the Gentile Christians of Macedonia and Achaia for the relief of the poor Jewish Christians at Jerusalem. About this affair he had taken great pains, as appears from 1 Cor. xvi. 1–4; 2 Cor. chapters viii. and ix. His design in this affair is very evident from 2 Cor. ix. 12, 13, where he says: *The administration of this service not only supplieth the want of the saints, but is abundant also by many thanksgivings unto God; whiles, by the experiment of this ministration, they glorify God for your professed subjection unto the Gospel of Christ, and for your liberal distribution unto them and unto all men.* The apostle was in hopes that this liberal contribution, sent by the *Gentile* Christians who had been converted by St. Paul's ministry, would engage the affections of the Jewish Christians, who had been much prejudiced against the reception of the Gentiles into the Church, without being previously obliged to submit to the *yoke of the law.* He wished to establish a coalition between the converted Jews and Gentiles, being sensible of its great importance to the spread of the Gospel; and his procuring this contribution was one laudable device to accomplish this good end. And this shows why he so earnestly requests the prayers of the Christians at Rome, that his service which he

2

A. M. cir. 4062.
A. D. cir. 58.
An. Olymp.
cir. CCIX. 2.
A. U. C. cir.
811.

27 It hath pleased them, *verily ;* and their debtors they are. For [p] if the Gentiles have been made partakers of their spiritual things, [q] their duty is also to minister unto them in carnal things.

28 When, therefore, I have performed this, and have sealed to them [t] this fruit, I will come by you into Spain.

29 [s] And I am sure that, when I come unto you, I shall come in the fulness of the blessing of the Gospel of Christ.

30 Now I beseech you, brethren, for the

Lord Jesus Christ's sake, and [t] for the love of the Spirit, [u] that ye strive together with me in *your* prayers to God for me ;

31 [v] That I may be delivered from them that [w] do not believe in Judea, and that [x] my service which *I have* for Jerusalem may be accepted of the saints ;

32 [y] That I may come unto you with joy [z] by the will of God, and may with you be [a] refreshed.

33 Now [b] the God of peace *be* with you all. Amen.

A. M. cir. 4062.
A. D. cir. 58.
An. Olymp.
cir. CCIX. 2.
A. U. C. cir.
811.

---

[p] Chap. xi. 17.——[q] 1 Cor. ix. 11 ; Gal. vi. 6.——[r] Phil. iv. 17. [s] Chap. i. 11.——[t] Phil. ii. 1.——[u] 2 Cor. i. 11 ; Col. iv. 12. [v] 2 Thess. iii. 2.——[w] Or, *are disobedient.*——[x] 2 Cor. viii. 4. [y] Chap. i. 10.

[z] Acts xviii. 21 ; 1 Cor. iv. 19 ; James iv. 15.——[a] 1 Cor. xvi. 18 ; 2 Cor. vii. 13 ; 2 Tim. i. 6 ; Philem. 7, 20.——[b] Chap. xvi. 20 ; 1 Cor. xiv. 33 ; 2 Cor. xiii. 11 ; Phil. iv. 9 ; 1 Thess. v. 23 ; 2 Thess. iii. 16 ; Heb. xiii. 20.

---

had for Jerusalem might be accepted of the saints. See *Dr. Taylor.*

Verse 27. *For if the Gentiles have been made partakers, &c.*] It was through and by means of the Jews that the Gentiles were brought to the knowledge of God and the Gospel of Christ. These were the *spiritual things* which they had received; and the pecuniary contribution was the *carnal things* which the Gentiles were now returning.

Verse 28. *When, therefore, I have performed this*] Service, *and have sealed*—faithfully delivered up, *to them this fruit,* of the success of my ministry and of your conversion to God, *I will come by you into Spain :* this was in his desire ; he had fully purposed it, if God should see meet to permit him ; but it does not appear that he ever went. See ver. 24.

Verse 29. *In the fulness of the blessing of the Gospel of Christ.*] The words του ευαγγελιου του, *of the Gospel,* are wanting in almost every MS. of importance. *Griesbach* has left them out of the text. There is no doubt they should be *omitted.* The *fulness of the blessing of Christ* is really *more* than the *fulness of the blessing of the Gospel of Christ.* He hoped to come to them not only with the *blessing of the Gospel,* but endued with the *gifts* and *graces* of the Lord Jesus himself ; which he was now a constant instrument, in the hand of God, to dispense among those who were converted to the Christian faith.

Verse 30. *For the love of the Spirit*] By that love of God which the *Holy Spirit* sheds abroad in your hearts.

That ye strive together] Συναγωνισασθαι, *That ye agonize with me.* He felt that much depended on the *success* of his present mission to the Christians at Jerusalem, and their acceptance of the charitable contribution which he was bringing with him, in order to conciliate them to the reception of the Gentiles into the Church of God without obliging them to submit to circumcision.

Verse 31 *That I may be delivered from them that do not believe*] He knew that his countrymen, who had not received the Gospel, lay in wait for his life ;

and, no doubt, they thought they should do God service by destroying him, not only as an apostate, in their apprehension, from the Jewish religion, but as one who was labouring to subvert and entirely destroy it.

And that my service] Διακονια. But several eminent MSS. read δωροφορια, *the gift which I bear.* This probably was a *gloss,* which in many MSS. subverted the word in the text ; for διακονια, *service,* in its connection here, could refer to nothing else but the *contribution* which he was carrying to the poor saints at Jerusalem.

Verse 32. *That I may come unto you with joy*] That his apprehensions of ill usage were not groundless, and the danger to which his life was exposed, real, we have already seen in the account given of this visit, Acts xxi., xxii., xxiii., and xxiv.; and that he had such intimations from the Holy Spirit himself appears from Acts xx. 23 ; xxi. 11 ; and xx. 38. Should his journey to Jerusalem be prosperous, and his service accepted, so that the converted Jews and Gentiles should come to a better understanding, he hoped to see them at Rome with *great joy :* and if he got his wishes gratified *through their prayers,* it would be the full proof that this whole business had been conducted according to *the will of God.*

Verse 33. *The God of peace be with you*] The whole object of the epistle is to establish peace between the believing Jews and Gentiles, and to show them their mutual obligations, and the infinite mercy of God to both ; and now he concludes with praying that the God of peace—he from whom it comes, and by whom it is preserved—may be for ever with them. The word *Amen,* at the end, does not appear to have been written by the apostle : it is wanting in some of the most ancient MSS.

1. In the preceding chapters the apostle enjoins a very hard, but a very important and necessary duty —that of bearing with each other, and endeavouring to think and let think, in those religious matters which are confessedly not *essential* to the salvation of the soul. Most of the disputes among Christians have

2

been concerning non-essential points. *Rites* and *ceremonies*, even in the *simple* religion of Christ, have contributed their part in promoting those animosities by· which Christians have been divided. *Forms* in worship and *sacerdotal garments* have not been without their influence in this general disturbance. Each side has been ready to take out of the 14th and 15th chapters of this epistle such *expressions* as seemed suitable to their own case ; but few have been found who have taken up the *whole*. You believe that a person who holds such and such opinions is *wrong* : pity him and set him right, *lovingly*, if possible. He believes you to be wrong because you *do not* hold those points ; he must bear with *you*. Both of you stand precisely on the same ground, and are mutually indebted to mutual forbearance.

2 Beware of contentions in religion , if you dis-

pute concerning any of its doctrines, let it be to find out *truth ;* not to support a preconceived and pre-established opinion. Avoid all polemical heat and rancour ; these prove the absence of the religion of Christ. Whatever does not lead you to love God and man more, is most assuredly from beneath. The *God of peace* is the author of Christianity ; and the *Prince of peace*, the priest and sacrifice of it : therefore love one another, and leave off contention before it be meddled with. On this subject the advice of the pious Mr. Herbert is good :—

Be *calm* in arguing ; for *fierceness* makes
Error a *fault*, and truth discourtesy.
Why should I *feel* another man's *mistake?*
More than his *sickness* or his *poverty ?*
In *love* I should ; but *anger* is not *love ;*
Nor *wisdom* neither :—therefore g-e-n-t-l-y m-o-v-a

CHAPTER XVI.

The apostle commends to the Christians at Rome Phœbe, a deaconess of the Church at Cenchrea, 1, 2. Sends greetings to Aquila and Priscilla, of whom he gives a high character ; and greets also the Church at their house, 3—5. Mentions several others by name, both men and women, who were members of the Church of Christ at Rome, 6—16. Warns them to beware of those who cause dissensions and divisions, of whom he gives an awful character, 17, 18. Extols the obedience of the Roman Christians, and promises them a complete victory over Satan, 19, 20. Several persons send their salutations, 21—23. To whose good wishes he subjoins the apostolic blessing ; commends them to God ; gives an abstract of the doctrines of the Gospel ; and concludes with ascribing glory to the only wise God, through Christ Jesus, 24—27.

A. M cir. 4062.
A. D. cir. 58.
An. Olymp.
cir. CCIX. 2.
A. U. C. cir.
811.

I COMMEND unto you Phœbe our sister, which is a servant of the Church which is at ᵃ Cenchrea :

2 ᵇ That ye receive her in the Lord, as be-

cometh saints ; and that ye assist her in whatsoever business she hath need of you : for she hath been a succourer of many, and of myself also.

A. M. cir. 4062
A. D. cir. 58,
An. Olymp.
cir. CCIX. 2,
A. U. C. cir.
811.

ᵃ Acts xviii. 18.

ᵇ Phil. ii. 29 ; 3 John 5, 6.

NOTES ON CHAP. XVI.

Verse 1. *I commend unto you Phœbe*] As the apostle had not been at Rome previously to his writing this epistle, he could not have had a personal acquaintance with those members of the Church there to whom he sends these friendly salutations. It is likely that many of them were his own converts, who, in different parts of Asia Minor and Greece, had heard him preach the Gospel, and afterwards became settlers at Rome.

Phœbe is here termed a *servant*, διακονον, *a deaconess of the Church at Cenchrea*. There were deaconesses in the primitive Church, whose business it was to attend the female converts at baptism ; to instruct the catechumens, or persons who were candidates for baptism ; to visit the sick, and those who were in prison , and, in short, perform those religious offices for the *female* part of the Church which could not with propriety be performed by *men*. They were chosen in general out of the most experienced of the Church, and were ordinarily *widows*, who had borne *children*. Some ancient constitutions required them to be forty, others fifty, and others sixty years of age. It is evident that they were *ordained* to their office by the *imposition of the hands of the bishop ;* and the

form of prayer used on the occasion is extant in the apostolical constitutions. In the tenth or eleventh century the order became extinct in the *Latin* Church, but continued in the *Greek* Church till the end of the twelfth century. See *Broughton's* Dictionary, article *deaconess.*

Cenchrea was a sea-port on the *east* side of the isthmus which joined the Morea to Greece, as the *Lechæum* was the sea-port on the *west* side of the same isthmus. These were the only two havens and towns of any note, next to *Corinth*, that belonged to this territory. As the *Lechæum* opened the road to the *Ionian* sea, so *Cenchrea* opened the road to the *Ægean ;* and both were so advantageously situated for commerce that they were very rich. These two places are now usually denominated the *Gulf* of *Lepanto*, and the *Gulf* of *Ingia* or *Egina.* It was on the isthmus, between these two *ports*, which was about six miles wide, that the Isthmian games were celebrated ; to which St. Paul makes such frequent allusions.

Verse 2. *Succourer of many*] One who probably entertained the apostles and preachers who came to minister at *Cenchrea*, and who was remarkable for entertaining strangers. See on chap. xii. 8.

A. M. cir. 4062.
A. D. cir. 58.
An. Olymp.
cir. CCIX. 2.
A. U. C. cir.
811.

3 Greet ᶜ Priscilla and Aquila, my helpers in Christ Jesus :

4 Who have for my life laid down their own necks : unto whom not only I give thanks, but also all the Churches of the Gentiles.

5 Likewise *greet* ᵈ the Church that is in their house. Salute my well-beloved Epenetus, who is ᵉ the first fruits of Achaia unto Christ.

6 Greet Mary, who bestowed much labour on us.

7 Saltue Andronicus and Junia, my kinsmen, and my fellow-prisoners, who are of note among the apostles, who also ᶠ were in Christ before me.

8 Greet Amplias, my beloved in the Lord.

9 Salute Urbane, our helper in Christ, and Stachys, my beloved.

10 Salute Apelles, approved in Christ. Salute them which are of Aristobulus' ᵍ *house hold.*

A. M. cir. 4062.
A. D. cir. 58.
An. Olymp.
cir. CCIX. 2.
A. U. C. cir.
811.

ᶜ Acts xviii. 2, 18, 26 ; 2 Tim. iv. 19.——ᵈ 1 Cor. xvi. 19 ; Col. iv. 15 ; Philem. 2.——ᵉ 1 Cor. xvi. 15.——ᶠ Gal. i. 22.——ᵍ Or, friends.

Verse 3. *Greet Priscilla and Aquila*] This pious couple had been obliged to leave Rome, on the edict of Claudius, see Acts xviii. 2, and take refuge in Greece. It is likely that they returned to Rome at the death of Claudius, or whenever the decree was annulled. It seems they had greatly contributed to assist the apostle in his important labours. Instead of *Priscilla*, the principal MSS. and versions have *Prisca*, which most critics suppose to be the genuine reading.

Verse 4. *Who have for my life laid down their own necks*] What transaction this refers to we know not ; but it appears that these persons had, on some occasion, hazarded their own lives to save that of the apostle ; and that the fact was known to all the Churches of God in that quarter, who felt themselves under the highest obligations to these pious persons, for the important service which they had thus rendered.

Verse 5. *The Church that is in their house.*] In these primitive times no such *places* existed as those which we now term *churches ;* the word always signifying the *congregation* or *assembly* of believers, and not the *place* they assembled in. See the term defined at the end of the notes on Matt. xvi.

Epenetus—the first fruits of Achaia] In 1 Cor. xvi. 15, the *house* or family of *Stephanas* is said to be the first fruits of Achaia : how then can it be said here, that *Epenetus* was the first fruits, or first person who had received the Gospel in that district ? *Ans.*—Epenetus might have been one of the family of Stephanas ; for it is not said that *Stephanas* was the first fruits, but his *house* or *family ;* and there can be no impropriety in supposing that one of that house or family was called *Epenetus ;* and that this person, being the only one of the family now at Rome, might be mentioned as the *first fruits* of Achaia ; that is, *one* of that *family* which *first* received the Gospel in that country. This would rationally account for the apparent difficulty, were we sure that Αχαιας, *of Achaia,* was the true reading : but this is more than doubtful, for Ασιας, *of Asia,* is the reading of ABCDEFG, some others ; the *Coptic, Æthiopic, Armenian, Vulgate,* and *Itala ;* and some of the chief of the *fathers.* On this evidence *Griesbach* has admitted it into the text. Yet the other reading is sufficiently natural, for the reasons already assigned.

Verse 6. *Greet Mary, who bestowed much labour on us.*] Who this *Mary* was, or what the *labour* was

which she bestowed upon the apostles, we know not. Her works, though hidden from man, are with God ; and her name is recorded with honour in this book of life.

Verse 7. *Andronicus and Junia, my kinsmen*] As the word συγγενεις signifies *relatives,* whether male or female, and as *Junia* may probably be the name of a *woman,* the wife of Andronicus, it would be better to say *relatives* than *kinsmen.* But probably St. Paul means no more than that they were *Jews ;* for, in chap. ix. 3, he calls all the Jews *his kinsmen according to the flesh.*

My fellow prisoners] As Paul was in prison often, it is likely that these persons shared this honour with him on some occasion, which is not distinctly marked.

Of note among the apostles] Whether this intimates that they were *noted apostles* or only highly reputed *by the apostles,* is not absolutely clear ; but the latter appears to me the most probable. They were not only well known to St. Paul, but also to the rest of the apostles.

In Christ before me.] That is, they were converted to Christianity before Paul was ; probably at the day of pentecost, or by the ministry of Christ himself, or by that of the seventy disciples.

Verse 8. *Amplias, my beloved in the Lord.*] One who is my *particular friend,* and also a genuine Christian.

Verse 9. *Urbane, our helper*] Who this Urbanus was we know not ; what is here stated is, that he had been a fellow labourer with the apostles.

Stachys, my beloved.] One of my *particular friends.*

Verse 10. *Apelles, approved in Christ*] A man who, on different occasions, had given the highest proofs of the sincerity and depth of his religion. Some suppose that *Apelles* was the same with *Apollos :* whoever he was, he had given every demonstration of being a genuine Christian.

Of Aristobulus' household.] It is doubted whether this person was converted, as the apostle does not salute *him,* but his *household ;* or as the margin reads, *his friends.* He might have been a Roman of considerable distinction, who, though not converted himself, had Christians among his *servants* or his *slaves.* But, whatever he was, it is likely that he was *dead* at this time, and therefore those of his household only are referred to by the apostle.

(11**)

A. M. cir. 4062.
A. D. cir. 58.
An. Olymp.
cir. CCIX. 2.
A. U. C. cir.
811.

11 Salute Herodion, my kinsman. Greet them that be of the [h] *household* of Narcissus, which are in the Lord.

12 Salute Tryphena and Tryphosa, who labour in the Lord. Salute the beloved Persis, which laboured much in the Lord.

13 Salute Rufus, [i] chosen in the Lord; and his mother and mine.

14 Salute Asyncritus, Phlegon, Hermas, Patrobas, Hermes, and the brethren which are with them.

15 Salute Philologus, and Julia, Nereus, and

A. M. cir. 4062
A. D. cir. 58.
An. Olymp.
cir. CCIX. 2.
A. U. C. cir.
811.

---

[h] Or, friends.

[i] 2 John 1.

Verse 11. *Herodion, my kinsman.*] Probably another converted *Jew.* See on ver. 7.

Of the household *of Narcissus*] Probably *dead* also, as we have supposed Aristobulus to have been at this time.

Which are in the Lord.] This might intimate that some of this family were not Christians; those only of that family that were converted to the Lord being saluted. There was a person of the name of *Narcissus*, who was a freed man of the Emperor Claudius, mentioned by *Suetonius* in his life of that prince, cap. 37; and by *Tacitus*, An., lib. xii. cap. 57: but there does not seem any reason to suppose that this was the person designed by St. Paul.

Verse 12. *Tryphena and Tryphosa*] Two holy women, who it seems were assistants to the apostle in his work, probably by *exhorting, visiting the sick, &c. Persis* was another woman, who it seems excelled the preceding; for, of her it is said, she *laboured much in the Lord.* We learn from this, that Christian *women,* as well as *men,* laboured in the ministry of the word. In those times of simplicity all persons, whether men or women, who had received the knowledge of the truth, believed it to be their duty to propagate it to the uttermost of their power. Many have spent much useless labour in endeavouring to prove that these women did not *preach.* That there were some *prophetesses,* as well as *prophets* in the Christian Church, we learn; and that a *woman* might *pray* or *prophesy,* provided she had her *head covered,* we know; and that whoever *prophesied* spoke unto others to *edification, exhortation, and comfort,* St. Paul declares, 1 Cor. xiv. 3. And that no preacher can do *more,* every person must acknowledge; because to *edify, exhort,* and *comfort,* are the prime ends of the Gospel ministry. If *women* thus *prophesied,* then women *preached.* There is, however, much more than this implied in the Christian ministry, of which men only, and men called of God, are capable.

Verse 13. *Rufus, chosen in the Lord*] Τον εκλεκτον, one of *great excellence* in Christianity; a *choice* man, as we would say. So the word εκλεκτος often signifies. Psa. lxxviii. 31 : *They smote* τους εκλεκτους, *the chosen men that were of Israel.* So εκλεκτα μνημεια are *choice sepulchres,* Gen. xxiii. 6 : εκλεκτα των δωρων *choice gifts,* Deut. xii. 11 ; and ανδρες εκλεκτοι, *choice men,* Judges xx. 16. By the same use of the word, the companions of Paul and Barnabas are termed *chosen men,* εκλεξαμενους ανδρας, persons in whom the Church of God could confide. See *Whitby.*

His mother and mine.] It is not likely that the mother of Rufus was the mother of Paul ; but while she was the natural mother of the former, she acted *as a mother* to the latter. We say of a person of this character, that she is a *motherly* woman. Among the ancients, he or she who acted a kind, instructing, and indulgent part to another, was styled the *father* or *mother* of such a one. So *Terence :*—

Natura tu illi pater es, consiliis ego.
Adelphi, Act. i. scen. 2, ver. 47.

Thou art his father by nature, I by instruction.

Verse 14. *Salute Asyncritus, &c.*] Who these were we know not. Hermas was probably the same to whom a work called the *Shepherd* is attributed ; a work with this title is still extant, and may be found among the writings of the *apostolical* fathers. But it is in vain to look for *identity* of *persons* in *similarity* of *names ;* for, among the Greeks and Romans at this time there were many persons who bore the same names mentioned in this chapter.

Verse 15. *Salute Philologus, &c.*] Of these several persons, though much has been conjectured, nothing certain is known. Even the names of some are so ambiguous that we know not whether they were *men* or *women.* They were persons well known to St. Paul, and undoubtedly were such as had gone from different places where the apostle had preached to sojourn or settle at Rome. One thing we may remark, that there is no mention of St. *Peter,* who, according to the Roman and papistical catalogue of bishops, must have been at Rome at this time ; if he were not now at Rome, the foundation stone of Rome's ascendancy, of Peter's supremacy, and of the uninterrupted succession, is taken away, and the whole fabric falls to the ground. But if Peter were at Rome at this time, Paul would have sent his salutations to *him* in the *first* place ; and if Peter were there, he must have been there, according to the papistical doctrine, as *bishop* and *vicar of Jesus Christ ;* but if he were there, is it likely that he should have been passed by, while *Andronicus* and *Junia* are mentioned as of *note among the apostles,* ver. 7, and that St. Paul should call on the *people* to remedy the *disorders* that had crept in among themselves ; should not these directions have been given to *Peter,* the *head of the Church?* And if there were a Church, in the papistical sense of the word, founded there, of which Peter was the *head,* is it likely that that Church should be in *the house of Priscilla and Aquila,* ver. 5. But it is a loss of time to refute such ridiculous and groundless pretensions. It is very likely that Peter, so far from being universal bishop at Rome, never saw the city in his life.

2

A. M. cir. 4062.
A. D. cir. 58.
An. Olymp.
cir. CCIX. 2.
A. U. C. cir.
811.

his sister, and Olympas, and all the saints which are with them.

16 ᵏ Salute one another with a holy kiss. The Churches of Christ salute you.

17 Now I beseech you, brethren, mark them ˡ which cause divisions and offences contrary to the doctrine which ye have learned; and ᵐ avoid them.

18 For they that are such serve not our Lord Jesus Christ, but ⁿ their own belly; and

ᵒ by good words and fair speeches deceive the hearts of the simple.

A. M. cir. 4062.
A. D. cir. 58.
An. Olymp.
cir. CCIX. 2.
A. U. C. cir.
811.

19 For ᵖ your obedience is come abroad unto all *men*. I am glad therefore on your behalf: but yet I would have you ᑫ wise unto that which is good, and ʳ simple concerning evil.

20 And ˢ the God of peace ᵗ shall ᵘ bruise Satan under your feet shortly. ᵛ The grace of our Lord Jesus Christ *be* with you. Amen.

ᵏ 1 Cor. xvi. 20; 2 Cor. xiii. 12; 1 Thess. v. 26; 1 Pet. v. 14. ˡ Acts xv. 1, 5, 24; 1 Tim. vi. 3.——ᵐ 1 Cor. v. 9, 11; 2 Thess. iii. 6, 14; 2 Tim. iii. 5; Tit. iii. 10; 2 John 10.——ⁿ Phil. iii. 19; 1 Tim. vi. 5.——ᵒ Col. ii. 4; 2 Tim. iii. 6; Titus i. 10;

2 Pet. ii. 3.——ᵖ Chap. i. 8.——ᑫ Matt. x. 16; 1 Cor. xiv. 20. ʳ Or, *harmless*.——ˢ Chap. xv. 33.——ᵗ Genesis iii. 15.——ᵘ Or, *tread*.——ᵛ Verse 24; 1 Cor. xvi. 23; 2 Cor. xiii. 14; Phil. iv. 23; 1 Thess. v. 28; 2 Thess. iii. 18; Rev. xxii. 21.

Verse 16. *Salute one another with a holy kiss.*] In those early times the *kiss*, as a token of *peace, friendship*, and *brotherly love*, was frequent among all people; and the Christians used it in their public assemblies, as well as in their occasional meetings. This was at last laid aside, not because it was abused, but because, the Church becoming very numerous, the thing was impossible. In some countries the kiss of friendship is still common; and in such countries it is scarcely ever abused, nor is it an incentive to evil, because it is *customary* and *common*. Shaking of hands is now substituted for it in almost all Christian congregations.

The Churches of Christ salute you.] The word πασαι, ALL, is added here by some of the most reputable MSS. and principal versions; and *Griesbach* has received it into his text. St. Paul must mean, here, that all the Churches in Greece and Asia, through which he had passed, in which the faith of the Christians at Rome was known, spoke of them affectionately and honourably; and probably knowing the apostle's design of visiting Rome, desired to be kindly remembered to the Church in that city.

Verse 17. *Mark them which cause divisions*] Several MSS. read ασφαλως σκοπειτε, *look sharply after them*; let *them* have no kiss of charity nor peace, because they strive to make *divisions*, and thus set the flock of Christ at variance among themselves; and from these *divisions, offences* (σκανδαλα, *scandals*) are produced; and this is contrary to that doctrine of *peace, unity*, and *brotherly love which you have* learned. *Look sharply* after such that they do you no evil, *and avoid them*—give them no countenance, and have no religious fellowship with them.

Verse 18. *They—serve not our Lord Jesus*] They profess to be apostles, but they are not apostles of CHRIST; they neither *do* his will, nor *preach* his *doctrine*; *they serve their own belly*—they have intruded themselves into the Church of Christ that they might get a secular support; it is for *worldly* gain alone that they take up the profession of the ministry: they have no Divine credentials; they convert not the *heathen* nor the *ungodly*, for they have no Divine unction; *but by good words and fair speeches* (for they have no

miraculous nor *saving* powers) *deceive the hearts of the simple, perverting* Christian *converts*, that they may get their property, and thus secure a maintenance for themselves. The Church of God has ever been troubled with such pretended *pastors*—men who FEED *themselves*, not the *flock*; men who are too proud to beg, and too lazy to work; who have neither grace nor gifts to plant the standard of the cross on the devil's territories, and by the power of Christ make inroads upon his kingdom, and spoil him of his subjects. On the contrary, by sowing the seeds of *dissension*, by means of *doubtful disputations*, and the propagation of *scandals*; by glaring and insinuating speeches, χρηστολογιας, for they affect *elegance* and *good breeding*, they rend Christian congregations, form a party for themselves, and thus live on the spoils of the Church of God.

Should it be asked, Whom do you intend by this description? I answer: No *soul*, nor *party*, but *such as the description suits*. *Irasceris?—De* TE *fabula narratur.* O, you are angry, are you? O, then, the cap fits you—put it on.

Verse 19. *For your obedience is come abroad*] The apostle gives this as a reason why they should continue to hear and heed those who had led them into the path of truth, and avoid those false teachers whose doctrines tended to the subversion of their souls.

Yet I would have you wise] I would wish you carefully to *discern* the good from the evil, and to show your *wisdom*, by carefully avoiding the one and cleaving to the other.

Verse 20. *The God of peace*] Who neither sends nor favours such disturbers of the tranquillity of his Church.

Shall bruise Satan] Shall give you the dominion over the great *adversary* of your souls, and over all his *agents* who, through his influence, endeavour to destroy your peace and subvert your minds.

Several critics suppose that the word *Satan* is a sort of collective term here, by which all *opposers* and *adversaries* are meant; and especially those false teachers to whom he refers above.

The grace of our Lord] That you may be truly wise, simple, obedient, and steady in the truth, may the

2

A. M. cir. 4062.
A. D. cir. 58.
An. Olymp.
cir. CCIX. 2.
A. U. C. cir.
811.

21 ʷ Timotheus my workfellow, and ˣ Lucius, and ʸ Jason, and ᶻ Sosipater, my kinsmen, salute you.

22 I Tertius, who wrote *this* epistle, salute you in the Lord.

23 ᵃ Gaius mine host, and of the whole Church, saluteth you. ᵇ Erastus the chamberlain of the city saluteth you, and Quartus a brother.

24 ᶜ The grace of our Lord Jesus Christ *be* with you all. Amen.

A. M. cir. 4062.
A. D. cir. 58.
An. Olymp.
cir. CCIX. 2.
A. U. C. cir.
811.

ʷ Acts xvi. 1; Col. i. 1; Phil. ii. 19; 1 Thess. iii. 2; 1 Tim. i. 2; Heb. xiii. 23.——ˣ Acts xiii. 1.——ʸ Acts xvii. 5.

ᶻ Acts xx. 4.——ᵃ 1 Cor. i. 14.——ᵇ Acts xix. 22; 2 Tim. iv. 20.
ᶜ Ver. 20; 1 Thess. v. 28.

---

favour or gracious influence of our Lord Jesus Christ be with you! without which you cannot be preserved from evil, nor do any thing that is good.

Here the apostle appears to have intended to conclude his epistle; but afterwards he added a *postscript*, if not *two*, as we shall see below. Several ancient MSS. omit the whole of this clause, probably thinking that it had been borrowed from ver. 24; but on the ground that the apostle might have added a postscript or two, not having immediate opportunity to send the epistle there is no need for this supposition.

Verse 21. *Timotheus my workfellow*] This is on all hands allowed to be the same *Timothy* to whom St. Paul directs the two epistles which are still extant. See some account of him in the notes on Acts xvi. 1, &c.

Lucius] This was probably Luke the *evangelist*, and writer of the book called *The Acts of the Apostles*. For a short account of him see the *Preface* to that book.

Jason] It is likely that this is the same person mentioned Acts xvii. 7, who at Thessalonica received the apostles into his house, and befriended them at the risk both of his property and life.

Sosipater] He was a Berean, the son of one *Pyrrhus*, a Jew, by birth, and accompanied St. Paul from Greece into Asia, and probably into Judea. See Acts xx. 4.

Verse 22. *I Tertius, who wrote* this *epistle*] Some eminent commentators suppose *Tertius* to be the same with *Silas*—the companion of St. Paul. If this were so, it is strange that the *name* which is generally given him elsewhere in Scripture should not be used in this place. I have already noticed (*Preface*, page v.) that some learned men have supposed that St. Paul wrote this epistle in *Syriac*, and that Tertius translated it into Greek; but this can never agree with the declaration here: I Tertius, who *wrote*, γραψας την επιστολην, this epistle; not *translated* or *interpreted* it. It appears that St. Paul dictated it to him, and he wrote it down from the apostle's mouth; and here introduces himself as joining with St. Paul in affectionate wishes for their welfare.

Salute you in the Lord.] I wish you well in the name of the Lord: or, I feel for you that affectionate respect which the grace of the Lord Jesus inspires. It is not clear whether the two following verses be the words of *Tertius* or St. Paul.

Verse 23. *Gaius mine host*] *Gaius* in Greek is the same as *Caius* in Latin, which was a very common name among the Romans. St. Luke (Acts xix. 29) mentions one *Gaius of Macedonia*, who was exposed to much violence at Ephesus in the tumult excited by

Demetrius the silversmith against St. Paul and his companions; and it is very possible that this was the same person. He is here called not only the *host*, ξενος, the *entertainer* of St. Paul, or Tertius, (if he wrote this and the following verse,) but also of the *whole Church*: that is, he received and lodged the apostles who came from different places, as well as the messengers of the Churches. All made his house their home; and he must have been a person of considerable property to be able to bear this expense; and of much piety and love to the cause of Christ, else he had not employed that property in this way.

Erastus the chamberlain of the city] Treasurer of the city of Corinth, from which St. Paul wrote this epistle. This is supposed to be the same person as is mentioned Acts xix. 22. He was one of St. Paul's companions, and, as appears from 2 Tim. iv. 20, was left about this time by the apostle at Corinth. He is called the *chamberlain* οικονομος, which signifies the same as *treasurer*; he to whom the *receipt* and *expenditure* of the public money were intrusted. He received the tolls, customs, &c., belonging to the city, and out of them paid the public expenses. Such persons were in very high credit; and if Erastus was at *this time* treasurer, it would appear that Christianity was then in considerable repute in Corinth. But if the Erastus of the Acts was the same with the Erastus mentioned here, it is not likely that he now held the office, for this could not at all comport with his travelling with St. Paul. Hence several, both ancients and moderns, who believe the identity of the persons, suppose that Erastus was not now treasurer, but that having formerly been so he still retained the *title*. *Chrysostom* thought that he still retained the employment.

Quartus a brother.] Whether the brother of *Erastus* or of *Tertius* we know not; probably nothing more is meant than that he was a *Christian*—one of the heavenly family, a *brother* in the Lord.

Verse 24. *The grace of our Lord*] This is the conclusion of *Tertius*, and is similar to what St. Paul used above. Hence it is possible that Tertius wrote the whole of the 22d, 23rd, and 24th verses, without receiving any particular instructions from St. Paul, except the bare permission to add his own salutations with those of his particular friends.

There is a great deal of disagreement among the MSS. and versions relative to this verse; some rejecting it entirely, and some of those which place the following verses at the end of chap. xiv., inserting it at the end of the 27th verse in that place. The reader who chooses may consult *Wetstein* and *Griesbach* on these discordances.

2

A. M. cir. 4062.
A. D. cir. 58.
An. Olymp.
cir. CCIX. 2.
A. U. C. cir.
811.

25 Now ^d to him that is of power to stablish you ^e according to my Gospel, and the preaching of Jesus Christ, ^f according to the revelation of the mystery, ^g which was kept secret since the world began,

26 But ^h now is made manifest, and by the scriptures of the prophets, according to the com-

mandment of the everlasting God, made known to all nations for ⁱ the obedience of faith.

27 To ^k God only wise, *be* glory through Jesus Christ for ever. ^l Amen.

¶ Written to the Romans from Corinthus, *and sent* by Phœbe, servant of the Church at Cenchrea.

A. M. cir. 4062.
A. D. cir. 58.
An. Olymp.
cir. CCIX. 2.
A. U. C. cir.
811.

---

^d Eph. iii. 20; 1 Thess. iii. 13; 2 Thess. ii. 17; iii. 3; Jude 24.——^e Chap. ii. 16.——^f Eph. i. 9; iii. 3, 4, 5; Col. i. 27. ^g 1 Cor. ii. 7; Eph. iii. 5, 9; Col. i. 26.

^h Eph. i. 9; 2 Tim. i. 10; Tit. i. 2, 3; 1 Pet. i. 20.——ⁱ Acts vi. 7; chap. i. 5; xv. 18.——^k Chap. ix. 5; Eph. iii. 20, 21; 1 Tim. i. 17; vi. 16; Jude 25.——^l 1 Cor. xiv. 16; Gal. i. 4, 5; Rev. iii. 14.

Verse 25. *Now to him*] In the note at the end of chap. xiv. I have shown that this and the following verses are by the most reputable MSS. and versions placed at the end of that chapter, which is supposed by most critics to be their proper place. Some of the arguments adduced in favour of this transposition may be found in the note above mentioned. I shall therefore refer to Griesbach, and proceed to make a few short remarks on the verses as they occur *here.*

Of power to stablish you] To that God, without whom nothing is *wise*, nothing *strong;* who is as willing to teach as he is *wise;* as ready to *help* as he is *strong.*

According to my Gospel] That Gospel which explains and publishes God's purpose of taking the Gentiles to be his people under the Messiah, without subjecting them to the law of Moses. This is what he here calls the preaching of Jesus Christ; for without this he did not think, as Mr. Locke observes, that Christ was preached to the Gentiles as he ought to be; and therefore in several places of his epistle to the *Galatians* he calls it *the truth,* and the *truth of the Gospel,* and uses the like expressions to the *Ephesians* and *Colossians.* This is that *mystery* which he is so much concerned that the *Ephesians* should understand and adhere to firmly, and which was revealed to him according to that Gospel whereof he was made a minister. And it is probable that this grand *mystery* of bringing the Gentiles into the kingdom of God, without passing through the *rites* of the Mosaic law, was revealed more particularly to St. Paul than to any other of the apostles, and that he preached it more *pointedly,* and certainly with *more success.* See *Taylor* and *Locke.*

Which was kept secret] This purpose of calling the Gentiles, and giving them equal privileges to the Jews, without obliging them to submit to *circumcision,* &c.

Verse 26. *But now is made manifest*] Now, under the New Testament dispensation, and by my preaching.

By the scriptures of the prophets] Hints relative to this important work being scattered up and down through all their works, but no clear revelation that the Gentiles, who should be admitted into the Church, should be admitted *without passing under the yoke of the Mosaic law.* This was the *point* which was kept secret: as to the *calling* of the Gentiles, this was declared in general terms by the prophets, and the apostle quotes and makes a most important use of their predictions; but the other was a point on which the

prophets gave no information, and it seems to have been peculiarly revealed to St. Paul, who received the *commandment of the everlasting God* to make it known ειϛ παντα τα εθνη, to all the Gentiles—all the people of the earth that were not of Jewish extraction. And it was to be made known for the *obedience of faith,* that they might *believe* its *doctrines* and *obey* its *precepts;* its universal voice requiring repentance towards God, faith in our Lord Jesus Christ, and circumcision of the heart, in the place of all Jewish rites and ceremonies.

Verse 27. *To God only wise*] This comes in with great propriety. He alone who is the fountain of *wisdom* and *knowledge,* had all this mystery in himself; and he alone who knew the *times, places, persons,* and *circumstances,* could reveal the whole; and he has revealed all in such a way as not only to manifest his unsearchable *wisdom,* but also his infinite goodness: therefore, *to him be glory* for his *wisdom* in devising this most admirable plan; and his *goodness* in sending *Christ Jesus* to execute it; to Him, through Christ Jesus, be glory *for ever!* Because this plan is to last for *ever;* and is to have no issue but in eternal glory.

Written to the Romans from Corinthus, &c.] That this epistle was written from Corinth is almost universally believed. That *Phœbe* was a deaconess of the Church at Cenchrea, we have seen in the first verse of this chapter; and that the epistle might have been sent by her to Rome is possible; but that she should have been the writer of the epistle, as this subscription states, εγραφη δια Φοιβης, is false, for the 22d verse shows that Tertius was the writer, though by inserting the words *and sent,* we represent her rather as the *carrier* than the writer. This subscription, however, stands on very questionable grounds. It is wanting in almost all the ancient MSS.; and even of those which are more modern, few have it *entirely,* as in our common editions. It has already been noted that the *subscriptions* to the sacred books are of little or no authority, all having been added in latter times, and frequently by injudicious hands. The most ancient have simply *To the Romans,* or the Epistle *to the Romans is finished.* The word *Amen* was seldom added by the inspired writers, and here it is wanting in almost all the ancient MSS. As this was a word in frequent use in religious services, pious people would naturally employ it in finishing the reading or copying of this epistle, as they would thereby express their conviction of the *truth* of its contents, and their desire that the promises contained in it might be fulfilled to them and to the Church at large ; and in this sense the word is not only harmless but useful. May the fulness of the Gentiles be brought in, and may all Israel be saved! This is treated of at large in this epistle ; and to this prayer let every pious reader say AMEN ! Often this word seems to be used as we use the word *finis,* i. e. the end. See the observations on this word at the end of the Gospel of John.

BEFORE I conclude this work, I shall beg leave to add several important observations, chiefly extracted from *Dr. Taylor.*

1. Paul, the apostle, writes to all the *Christians* at *Rome,* without distinction, as being called *of Jesus Christ,* beloved *of God,* called saints ; as justified *by faith and having* peace *with God ; as standing in the grace of* the Gospel, chap. v. 1, 2 ; *as alive from the dead,* chap. vi. 13, &c. He gives them various exhortations : *Walk in newness of life. Let not sin reign in your mortal body. Yield yourselves unto God.* Chap. xii. 1, &c. : *I beseech you, therefore, brethren, by the mercies of God, that ye present your bodies a living sacrifice, holy, acceptable unto God, which is your reasonable service.* Chap. xiv. 10, 12 : *We shall all stand before the judgment seat of Christ.* Every *one of us shall give account of himself to God.* xiii. 11, 12, 13, 14 : *It is high time to awake out of sleep; let us therefore cast off the works of darkness; let us not walk in rioting and drunkenness, in chambering and wantonness, in strife and envying ; make no provision for the flesh to fulfil the lusts thereof.* viii. 13 : *For if ye live after the flesh, ye shall die ;* Μελλετε αποθνησκειν, *ye shall hereafter die,* meaning, in the world to come. *But if ye, through the Spirit, do mortify the deeds of the body, ye shall live.*

2. The rites and ceremonies of the law of *Moses* were incorporated into the civil state of the *Jews,* and so might be considered as national and political usages. Now, as the Gospel did not interfere with or subvert any national polity upon earth, but left all men in all the several countries of the globe to live, in all things not sinful, according to the civil constitution under which it found them ; so it left the *Jews* also at liberty to observe all the rites and injunctions of the law of *Moses,* considered as a part of the civil and political usages of the nation. And in this respect they remained in force so long as the *Jews* were a nation, having the temple, the token of God's presence and residence among them. But when the temple was destroyed, and they were expelled the land of *Canaan,* their polity was dissolved, and the *Mosaic* rites were quite laid aside. And as the time in which this happened was near when the epistle to the *Hebrews* was written, therefore the apostle saith : *The first covenant, or Mosaical dispensation, was then decaying and waxing old, and ready to vanish away,* Heb. viii. 13.

3. But though the Gospel was not in itself intended to unchurch the *Jews,* yet the *Jews* every where warmly opposed the preaching of it, though not for the same reasons. Some *Jews* opposed it *totally,* and rejected the whole Gospel as unnecessary, judging the *Mosaical* constitution, and their conformity to the law

there delivered, completely sufficient for justification or salvation, without any farther provision made by the grace of God. These accounted *Christ* our Lord an impostor, and the Gospel a forgery ; and therefore persecuted the apostles with the utmost assiduity and outrage, as deceivers who had no Divine mission. Such were the *Jews* who put *Stephen* to death, Acts. chap. vi. and vii. Such were they at *Antioch,* in *Pisidia,* who were *filled with envy, and spake against the things that were spoken by Paul, contradicting and blaspheming,* Acts xiii. 45, 50. Such were the *Jews* at *Iconium,* Acts xiv. 2, 19 ; at *Thessalonica,* xvii. 5 ; at *Corinth,* xviii. 5, 6, and in other places. And such a *Jew* was *Paul* himself before his conversion. He consented to the death of *Stephen, made havoc of the Church,* (Acts viii. 3,) and breathed out threatenings and slaughter against the disciples of the Lord, ix. 1 ; xxii. 4 ; xxvi. 9, 10, 11.

4. What Paul's principles, and those of the unbelieving *Jews,* were, we may learn if we observe that the first persecution raised against the apostles at *Jerusalem* was *partly* on account of their *preaching through Jesus the resurrection from the dead,* Acts iv. 1, 2. This gave great offence to the Sadducees ; and *partly* because they openly affirmed that Jesus, whom the rulers of the *Jews* slew and hanged on a tree, was the *Messiah, whom God had exalted to be a prince and a Saviour.* This disgusted all the council and senate of the *Jews,* Acts v. 21, 28, 29, 30, 31. But with regard to these two particulars, the indignation of the *Jews* seems for some time abated, till the doctrine the apostles taught was better understood ; and *Stephen,* in his dispute with some learned *Jews,* had suggested that the Gospel was intended to abrogate the Mosaical constitution, Acts vi. 9—15. This irritated the *Jews* afresh, especially the Pharisees, the strictest and most numerous sect among them. And *Saul,* one of that sect, (Acts xxvi. 5 ; xxiii. 6,) being then a young man, just come out of *Gamaliel's* school, having finished his studies in the law, and being fully persuaded that the *Jewish* dispensation was instituted by God, never to be altered, but to abide for ever, he really believed that Jesus and his followers were deceivers, and that it was his duty to oppose them, and to stand up courageously for God and his truth.—Thus he honestly followed the dictates of his own conscience. How far other unbelieving Jews were or were not upright in their opposition to the Gospel, God only knows ; but their professed principles seem to be nearly the same. In short, they were for *seizing on the inheritance,* (Matt. xxi. 38,) and for engrossing all salvation and the favour of God to themselves. The *Jews* they judged were the only people of God, and the Jewish nation the only true Church, out of which there was no salvation. No man could be in a state of acceptance with God without observing the law of *Moses.* The works of the law, moral and ceremonial, must be performed in order to his being a member of God's Church and family, and having a right to future and eternal happiness. They expected the *Messiah* indeed and his kingdom ; but not as if either had a reference to another world. The law, and a punctual observance of it, were the ground of their expectations in a future world. And as for the *Messiah,* they supposed his

2

coming and kingdom related only to the temporal prosperity and grandeur of the *Jewish* nation, and the perpetual establishment of their law, by rescuing them out of the hands of the *Gentile* powers, who had greatly embarrassed and distressed their constitution. Thus they endeavoured to *establish their own righteousness,* (Rom. x. 3,) salvation, or interest in God; an interest which they imagined for themselves, and which excluded men of all other nations, who they thought were in fact utterly excluded from the Divine favour and eternal life, as quite lost and hopeless. Against us *Gentiles,* they had the strongest prejudices, accounting us as perfectly vile, as nothing, as abandoned of God, only because we were not included in their peculiarity; while they imagined themselves to be vastly superior to us, and the only people beloved of God, purely on account of their external privileges and relation to God as the seed of *Abraham;* being circumcised, enjoying the law, the promises, and ordinances of worship, &c.

5. And this was another ground of their opposition to the Gospel when it was preached to the *Gentiles.* Indeed the apostles themselves, and the first *Christians* among the *Jews,* had for some time no notion of the Gospel's being preached to the *Gentiles,* till God in a vision convinced *Peter* it was his will that it should, Acts x. But the unbelieving *Jews* regarded the preaching of the Gospel to the *Gentiles,* or the declaring that they were, upon their faith in *Christ,* pardoned and admitted into the Church of God, and to the hopes of eternal life, almost in the same manner as we should regard the preaching of the Gospel to brute creatures. They could not bear the thought that *the Gentiles*— any barbarous nations, should, only by faith, have an equal interest in God and the blessings of his covenant with themselves. They did not indeed deny the possibility of their being taken into the Church, and of obtaining salvation. But it must be only by their becoming *Jews;* they must first submit to the law, and yield obedience to its precepts and obligations, before they could be qualified objects of God's mercy. There was no grace, no part in the kingdom of God either here or hereafter, for a *Gentile,* unless he first became a *Jew,* and performed the works of the *Mosaical* law. By these sentiments they were led to do all they could to oppose the preaching of the Gospel to the *Gentiles,* and became very bitter enemies to Paul, who was the apostle particularly selected and commissioned for that purpose. They could not allow the *Gentiles* to have any access to the privileges of God's Church and people, but through the door of the law; and to introduce them any other way was, not only to overthrow their law and peculiarity, but to deceive the *Gentiles.* Therefore they did all in their power to withstand the apostle, and to persuade the *Gentiles* every where that he was an odious impostor; that his Gospel was a forgery, destitute of Divine authority; that he proposed admitting them into the Church and covenant of God in a way which had no foundation in the declared will of God. Their law was the only Divine establishment, and obedience to it the only means to introduce them into the kingdom of God; and *Paul* could have no commission from heaven to teach otherwise, whatever he might pretend, or what miracles soever he might

work. Of this sort of *Jews* the apostle speaks, 1 Thess. ii. 14, 15, 16.

Other *Jews* there were who believed the Gospel, and agreed that it ought to be preached to the *Gentiles;* but so that the *Gentiles,* at the same time they accepted the Gospel, were obliged to submit to the *law of Moses* in every part, otherwise they could not be *saved* or have any interest in the kingdom and covenant of God, Acts xv. 1. These taught that the *Gospel* was insufficient without the *law.* They differed from the forementioned *Jews* in that they embraced the faith of *Jesus Christ;* but agreed with them in this, that the law of *Moses* was to be in force for ever, and the observance of all its rituals absolutely necessary to a standing in the Church of God, and the hopes of eternal life. And for this reason they were upon pretty good terms with the unbelieving Jews, and avoided the persecution to which those who adhered to the pure and unmixed Gospel were exposed, Gal. vi. 12. These *Jews,* who were for joining *law* and *Gospel* together, were also great enemies to our apostle. He speaks of them, Phil. iii. 2, 3, &c.

6. Now against the mistakes of the infidel *Jews* the apostle thus argues in the epistle to the *Romans:* Jews, as well as *Gentiles,* have corrupted themselves, and are become obnoxious to the Divine wrath, and, if they repent not, will certainly fall under the wrath of God in the last day: consequently, as both are obnoxious to wrath, both must be indebted to grace and mercy for any favour shown them. The continuance of the *Jews* in the Church, as well as the admittance of the *Gentiles* into it, is wholly of *grace;* mere grace or favour. Upon which footing, the Gentiles must have as good a right to the blessings of God's covenant as the *Jews* themselves. And why not? Is not God the creator and governor of the *Gentiles,* as well as of the *Jews?* And if both *Jews* and *Gentiles* have corrupted themselves by wicked works, it is impossible that either should have a right to the privileges of God's Church and people on account of WORKS, or obedience to the law of God, whether natural or revealed. It must be pure *mercy,* accepted by faith through Christ, or a persuasion of that mercy on their part, which gives that right. All must be indebted to grace. The works of the law never gave the *Jews* themselves a right to the privileges and promises of the covenant. Even Abraham himself, (the head of the nation, who was first taken into God's covenant, and from whom the *Jews* derive all their peculiar blessings and advantages,) was not justified by works of the law. It was free grace, or favour, which at once admitted him and his posterity into the covenant and Church of God. And that the grace of the Gospel actually extends to all mankind, appears from the universality of the resurrection; which is the effect of God's grace or favour in a Redeemer, and is the first and fundamental part of the *new* dispensation with regard to the gift of eternal life. For, as all were involved in death in consequence of Adam's sin, so shall all be restored to life at the last day in consequence of Christ's obedience; and therefore it is certain that *all men* actually have a share in the mercy of God in *Christ Jesus.*—Thus the apostle argues.

7. And we ought particularly to observe how he

2

combats the engrossing temper of the *Jews* in his arguments. They could not engross all virtue to themselves, for they were as bad as other people ; they could not engross God and his favour to themselves, for he was the governor and creator of *Gentiles* as well as *Jews ;* they could not engross *Abraham* and the promise made to him to themselves, for he is the father of *many nations,* and the believing *Gentiles* are his seed as well as the *Jews ;* they could not engross the resurrection, the necessary introduction to eternal life, to themselves, because it is known and allowed to be common to all mankind.

8. And he had good reason to be so large and particular in confuting the mistakes of the infidel *Jews.* For had their principles prevailed, the Gospel could not have maintained its ground. For if we must have performed the works of the *law,* before we could have been interested in the blessings of the *covenant,* then the Gospel would have lost its nature and force ; for then it would not have been a *motive* to obedience, but the *result* of obedience ; and we could have had no hope towards God prior to obedience. Therefore the apostle has done a singular and eminent piece of service to the Church of God, in asserting and demonstrating the free grace and covenant of God as a foundation to stand upon, prior to any obedience of ours, and as the grand spring and motive of obedience. This sets our interest in the covenant, or promise of God, upon a foundation very clear and solid.

9. To understand rightly the epistle to the *Romans,* it is farther necessary to observe, that the apostle considers mankind as obnoxious to the Divine wrath, and as standing before God, the Judge of all. Hence it is that he uses forensic or law terms, usual in *Jewish* courts ; such as the LAW, RIGHTEOUSNESS or JUSTIFICATION, being JUSTIFIED, JUDGMENT to CONDEMNATION, JUSTIFICATION of LIFE, being made SINNERS, and being made RIGHTEOUS. These I take to be *forensic* or *court* terms ; and the apostle by using them naturally leads our thoughts to suppose a court held, a judgment seat to be erected by the most high God, in the several cases whence he draws his arguments. For instance, chap. v. 12–20, he supposes *Adam* standing in the court of God after he had committed the first transgression ; when the *judgment* passed upon him for his offence, *came upon all men to condemnation ;* and when he and his posterity, by the favour and in the purpose of God, were again *made righteous,* or obtained the *justification of life.* Again, chap. iv., he supposes *Abraham* standing before the bar of the supreme Judge ; when, as an idolater, he might have been condemned, but through the pure mercy of God he was justified, pardoned, and taken into God's covenant, on account of his faith. He also supposes, chap. iii. 19–29, all mankind standing before the universal Judge, when Christ came into the world. At that time neither *Jew* nor *Gentile* could pretend to justification upon the foot of their own works of righteousness, having both corrupted themselves, and come short of the glory of God. But at that time both had righteousness or salvation prepared for them in a Redeemer ; namely, the righteousness which results from the pure mercy or grace of God, the lawgiver and judge. And so both (instead of being

destroyed) had admittance into the Church and covenant of God, by faith, in order to their eternal salvation.

10. But besides these three instances, in which he supposes a court to be held by the supreme Judge, there is a fourth to which he points, chap. ii. 1–17, and that is the *final judgment,* or the court which will be held in the day when *God will judge the secrets of men by Jesus Christ.* And it is with regard to that future court of judicature that he argues chap. ii. 1–17. But in the other cases, whence he draws his arguments, he supposes the courts of judicature to be *already* held ; and, consequently, argues in relation to the economy, constitution, or dispensation of things to this present world. This is very evident with regard to the court which he supposes to be held when our Lord came into the world, or when the Gospel constitution was erected in its full glory ; for, speaking of the justification which mankind then obtained through the grace of God in *Christ,* he expressly confines that justification to the *present time,* chap. iii. 26, *To demonstrate, I say, his righteousness, εν τῳ* NYN *καιρῳ, at the* PRESENT TIME. This plainly distinguishes the righteousness or salvation, which God *then* exhibited, from that righteousness or justification which he will vouchsafe in the *day of judgment* to pious and faithful souls.

11. Before the coming of our Lord, the peculiar kingdom of God was confined to the *Jewish* nation, and to such only of the heathens as were incorporated among them by becoming *Jews,* and observing the whole law of *Moses.* And the Jews firmly believed it would always continue in the same state.

But when our Lord came, the mystery of God, which had been concealed both from *Jews* and *Gentiles,* was revealed ; namely, that the *Gentiles* also, even men of all nations, should be *freely* admitted into it. This was an act of great favour, considering the darkness, idolatry, and wickedness into which the heathen world was then sunk.

But God mercifully passed over their former sins ; and our Lord commissioned his apostles, and particularly St. *Paul,* to promulge a general pardon ; and to call or invite all who repented, and accepted of the grace, to all the blessings and privileges of his kingdom ; confirming their interests in those blessings by pouring out the Holy Ghost upon them, in various miraculous gifts, or endowments, above the ordinary capacity of men. This was a very evident seal to them (and to us too) of a title to the blessings of God's kingdom and covenant, Gal. iii. 2–5.

And it had such an effect upon the Christian *Jews* at *Jerusalem* that, though they were at first greatly disgusted at Peter for treating the first uncircumcised *Gentile* converts as members of the kingdom of God, (Acts xi. 2, 3,) yet, when they heard that the Holy Ghost was fallen upon those converts, they were much surprised *and glorified God,* saying, *Then hath God also to the Gentiles granted* (the benefit of) *repentance unto* (eternal) *life ;* which, before this, they verily believed could not have been granted unto them without obedience to the law of *Moses* by being circumcised.

But the unbelieving *Jews* paid no regard to this or any other argument in favour of the uncircumcised *Gentiles.* The notion of admitting them into the kingdom and congregation of God, only upon faith in

Christ, they opposed and persecuted every where with great zeal and bitterness. And it was not long before good impressions wore off, and old prejudices revived among even the believing *Jews*. Numbers of them very stiffly, and with much warmth and contention, endeavoured to persuade the *Gentile* converts that, *except they were circumcised after the manner of Moses, they could not be saved*, or admitted to the privileges of the kingdom of God and the hope of eternal life, Acts xv. 1, 2.

The *Gentiles*, even the most learned and wise amongst them, were wholly ignorant in the affair. They were perfect strangers to the Gospel scheme: they had no notion or expectation of being received into the kingdom and covenant of God, and could have no knowledge of it but what they received from some or other of the *Jews:* nor could they have any objection against it worth regarding but what came from that quarter. And the *Jews* had a considerable influence among them, having synagogues in most, if not all, the great towns in the empire, from the *Euphrates*, as far as *Rome* itself, which numbers of the *Gentiles* frequented, and so had received impressions in favour of the Jewish religion.

But had the Jewish notion prevailed, that no part of mankind could have any share in the blessings of God's covenant, the pardon of sin, and the hope of eternal life, but only such as were circumcised and brought themselves under obligations to the whole law of *Moses;* had this notion prevailed, the extensive scheme of the Gospel would have been ruined, and the gracious design of freeing the Church from the embarrassments of the law of *Moses* would have been defeated. The Gospel, or glad tidings of salvation, must not only have been confined to the narrow limits of the *Jewish* peculiarity, and clogged with all the ceremonial observances belonging to it, which to the greatest part of mankind would have been either impracticable, or excessively incommodious, but, which is still worse, must have sunk and fallen with that peculiarity. Had the Gospel been built upon the foundation of the *Jewish* polity, it must have been destroyed when that was demolished, and the *whole* kingdom of God in the world would have been overthrown and extinct at the same time; and so all the noble principles it was intended to inspire, to animate and comfort our hearts, would have been lost; and all the light it was calculated to diffuse throughout the world would have been quite extinguished.

It was therefore the apostle's duty to vindicate and assert the truth of the Gospel which he was commissioned to preach to the *Gentiles;* and of very great consequence to prove *that we Gentiles are called to be the children of God, and are interested in his covenant, and all the honours, blessings, and privileges of his family and kingdom here upon earth, only by faith in Christ, without coming under any obligations to the law of Moses, as such:* which is the main drift and subject of this epistle.

12. It is worth notice that there is this difference in one respect between the *gospels* and *epistles*, namely, that our Lord, in the *gospels*, represents the doctrines and principles of the Christian religion chiefly in an absolute sense, or as they are in themselves; but,

in the *epistles*, those doctrines and principles are chiefly considered in a relative view; as they respect, partly the foregoing *Jewish* dispensation, and partly the future corruption of the Christian Church; but principally, as they respect the different state of *Jews* and *heathens;* showing how just, true, and necessary they are with reference to both, and directing and exhorting both to value them and to make a right use of them. This was absolutely necessary to a full explication of the Gospel, to guard it against all objections, and to give it a solid establishment in the world.

And we must not forget that in the epistle to the *Romans*, the Gospel is presented in this relative view, as adapted to the circumstances of us *Gentiles*, and obliging us to all virtue and piety.

13. Farther, we can neither duly value this epistle, nor be sensible how much we are indebted to the author of it, unless we make this sentiment familiar to our thoughts; namely, *That St. Paul is the patron and defender of all that is by far the most valuable and important to us in the world, against the only opposition that could be made to our title and claim.* Give me leave to explain this by an easy comparison.—A person, to me unknown, leaves me at his death 1000*l.* a-year: I myself can have no objection against the noble donative; and the good pleasure of the donor, who had an undoubted right to dispose of his own, may silence any of the caviller's surmises. But a person claiming, as heir at law, gives me the greatest uneasiness. He alleges the estate was entailed, and that he has a prior title, which renders the donation to me invalid. Here I want an able advocate to prove that his pretensions are ill grounded, and that my title is perfectly good and firm. St. Paul is that advocate: he argues, and strongly proves, that we, believing *Gentiles*, have a just and solid title to all the blessings of God's covenant; and effectually establishes us in possession of all the noble principles, motives, comfort, hope and joy of the Gospel. The sum of what he demonstrates is comprehended in 1 Pet. ii. 8, 9, 10: *They*, the *Jews*, *stumble*, and lose their ancient honours and privileges; *but ye*, Gentiles, *are a chosen generation, a royal priesthood, a holy nation, a peculiar people; that ye should show forth the praises of him who has called you out of* heathenish *darkness into his marvellous light.* Thus, on the authority of God, we *Gentiles* have an indisputable right to all the blessings of the Gospel; and, if we receive by Christ Jesus that grace which pardons and cleanses the soul, we shall pass from the Church militant into the Church triumphant.

At the conclusion of my notes on this very important epistle I feel it necessary to make a few additional remarks. I have sincerely and conscientiously given that view of the apostle's work which I believe to be true and correct. I am well aware that many great and good men have understood this portion of Divine revelation differently, in many respects, from myself: they have the same right of private judgment which I claim, and to publish those opinions which they judge to accord best with their views of the Gospel. My business is to give what I think to be the mind of my author; and every where I have laboured to do this without even consulting any pre-established creed. I hope my readers will take in good part what is honestly intended. I wish to avoid controversy; I give my own views of Divine truth. The plan on which I have endeavoured to expound this epistle shows it a beautiful, highly important, and consistent whole; a work which casts the clearest light on the grand original designs of God relative to the diffusion of the Gospel and its blessings over the face of the earth; illustrating many apparently dark and unaccountable providences; fully proving that though clouds and darkness are often round the supreme Being, yet, righteousness and judgment are the habitation of his throne. Where this grand view of this epistle is not taken, the major part of its beauties are lost. God, who is not the God of the Jews only, but also of the Gentiles, shows by his apostle in this admirable epistle, that from the *beginning* he had purposed to call the whole Gentile world to that salvation which he appeared for a time to restrain to the Jews alone, and which they imagined should be exclusively theirs for ever. This prejudice the apostle overturns, and shows that the Gentiles also had an equal share in the election of grace. We should be careful how we make that *partial* and *exclusive* which shows the Fountain of goodness to be no *respecter of persons*, or even ultimately of *nations*, who like the sun, the faint though brightest image of his glory in this lower world, shines equally upon the just and the unjust. God, with the same benevolent design, orders his Gospel to be preached to every creature under heaven.

The peculiar phraseology of this epistle I have also endeavoured to explain, and where this could not be conveniently done in the notes, I have generally stated it at the end of the chapters. And, for the explanations of difficult points, or articles which may have been but slightly handled in the notes, I beg to refer to those concluding observations; and particularly to those at the end of chapters viii. and ix.——. But it is necessary to make some remarks on this epistle, as an *epistle* directed *to the Romans*; that is, to the Church of God founded at Rome. Though the Gospel was preached and established there long before either the apostle had visited this city, or written this epistle, yet we may rest assured that the doctrine contained here was the doctrine of the *Church of Rome*, and therefore that Church was *holy* and *apostolic*. If it do not continue to walk by the same rule, and mind the same thing, it is no longer so: in a time then when the Roman Church that *now is* invites the attention of the Christian world, by making great and bold pretensions—assuming to itself the titles of *holy*, *catholic*, and *apostolic*; representing Rome as the fountain whence pure truth and apostolical authority emanate—it may be useful to examine whether such pretensions are well founded, and not permit confident assumption, noise and parade, to carry away our understandings, and occupy the place of reason, argument, and truth. This however cannot be done to any extent in this place; only it may be necessary to state, that, as the doctrines, &c., of the Roman Church

profess to be *apostolic*, they must be found in the *epistle to the* ROMANS, this being the only apostolic work directed to that Church. If they are not to be met with *here*, it would be absurd to look for them any where else. But there is not one *distinguishing doctrine* or *practice* of the Romish Church found in this epistle. Here is no pope, no exclusive churchship, no Peter-pence, first fruits, legatine levies, dispensations, pardons, indulgences, reliques, Agnus Dei's, jubilees, pilgrimages, crusades, carnivals, canonizations, abbeys, monasteries, cells, shrines, privileged altars, auricular confessions, purgatories, masses, prayers for the dead, requiems, placebos, dirges, lamps, processions, holy water, chrisms, baptism of bells, justification by works, penances, transubstantiation, works of supererogation, extreme unction, invocation of saints and angels, worship of images, crossings of the body, rosaries, albs, stoles, &c.; nor the endless orders of priests, abbots, monks, friars, nuns, anchorets, hermits, capuchins, &c., &c. Here are no inquisitions, no writs of hæretico comburendo, no auto da fè's, no racks, gibbets, tortures, nor death in all variable and horrid forms, for those who may differ from this *mother* Church in any part of their religious creed. In vain will the reader look into this epistle for any thing that is not consistent with *sound sense*, inflexible *reason*, and the justice, purity, and endless benevolence of the great God, the equal Father of the spirits of all flesh. Here, indeed, he will see the total fall and degeneracy of all mankind strongly asserted and proved; the utter helplessness of the human race to rescue itself from this state of corruption; the endless mercy of God, in sending Christ Jesus into the world to die for sinners; the doctrine of justification by faith in the blood of the Lamb; regeneration by the energy of the Divine Spirit producing that holiness without which no man can see God. Here, the sacrificial death of Jesus Christ takes place of all Jewish sacrifices, and works or sufferings of man, in reference to justification. Here is nothing puerile, nugatory, or superstitious; no *dogma* degrading to the understanding; no religious *act* unworthy of the spirit and dignity of the Gospel; nothing that has not the most immediate tendency to enlighten the mind, and mend the heart of man; in a word, every thing is suitable to the state of man, and worthy of the majesty, justice, and benevolence of that God from whom this epistle came. Here, indeed, is the model of a pure Church. What a pity it is not more closely followed by all, whether Protestant or popish, that profess the faith of Christ crucified! Alas! that a Church which was once pure and apostolic, and still retains all the essential doctrines of the Gospel, should compound them with others which are not only the commandments and inventions of men, but which so counteract the influence of the truths still retained, as to destroy their efficacy; and no wonder, when this foreign admixture is an assemblage of rites and ceremonies borrowed partly from the *Jews* and partly from the ancient *heathens*; rendered palatable by a small proportion of *Christianity*.

2

A SHORT EXPLANATION

OF THE FOLLOWING

ANCIENT ROMAN CALENDAR,

WITH THE

FESTIVALS, &C., OF THE PRESENT ROMISH CHURCH.

INSTEAD of *Chronological Tables*, which the subject of this Epistle neither admits nor requires, for it was probably all written in the course of a few days, (and I have entered the supposed *year* at the top of every page,) I here insert the *ancient Roman Calendar*, regularly distinguished into all its *Calends*, *Nones*, and *Ides*, with the different *festivals* observed in honour of their gods, goddesses, &c., in each month, and their principal *astronomical* notes. The *modern Roman Calendar* I have also introduced, with as many of the *festivals, saints' days*, &c., as the margin would receive. The reader will no doubt be struck with the conformity that subsists between *ancient* and *modern* ROME on this subject; on which, in this place, I shall make no farther remarks.

This Calendar, which was made by Julius Cæsar in the year of Rome 708, and before Christ 45, is still exceedingly useful especially for understanding the writers of antiquity, particularly those of the *Latin Church*; as well as for ascertaining the precise dates of *bulls, diplomas*, and public *acts* in general.

The Roman month, the reader will observe, is divided into *Calends, Nones*, and *Ides*; all of which are reckoned *backward*. The *Calends* are the *first day* of the month; as *Calendis Januariis* is the first day of January; *Pridie Calendarum* or *Calendas*, is the 31st of *December; iii. Cal.* the 30th; *iv. Cal.* the 29th; *v. Cal.* the 28th, &c.

The *Nones*, which are *four*, follow the *Calends*; as *iv. Nonas Januarii* is January the 2nd; *iii. Nonas Januarii* is January the 3rd: *Pridie Nonas Jan.* is January the 4th; and *Nonis Januarii* is January the 5th. But in *March, May, July*, and *October*, there are six *Nones*.

After these the *Ides* in each month are *eight*; as *viii. Id. Jan.* (*Octavo Idus* or *Iduum Januarii*) is January the 6th; *vii. Id. Jan.* (*Septimo Idus* or *Iduum Januarii*) is January the 7th; *vi. Id. Jan.* (*Sexto Idus* or *Iduum Januarii*) is January the 8th; and so on, till you come to the *Ides* themselves, *Idibus Januarii* being January the 13th.

Observe—1. When the *accusative* case is used, as *Nonas, Idus, Calendas*, the preposition *ante*, before, which governs this case, is understood; as *tertio ante Calendas*, the third day *before* the Calends; *quarto ante Calendas*, the fourth day before the Calends, &c. Observe—2. That after the *Ides* which are on the 13th day of *January, February, April, June, August, September, November*, and *December;* and on the 15th of *March, May, July*, and *October*, which have six *Nones* a-piece, the *Calends* following are to be reckoned to the next month.

The *first column* in each month contains the regular days of that month; the next column, the Calends, Nones, and Ides; and the slightest inspection will show how the days of these denominations answer to the common days of the month in their regular order.

The *Nundinal Letters* I have not inserted, as they only refer to the custom of *administering law*, or trying causes, holding public assemblies, electing magistrates, &c., among the ancient Romans. I have thought it best to fill up that place with other matters belonging to this calendar, in which general readers might find more interest.

The last column, the reader will perceive, is the *modern* Roman Calendar, copiously filled with the days of *real* and *reputed* saints: these, however, are not the whole whose festivals are observed, and whose protection is implored in that Church; as, upon an average, there are not fewer than *five* of these real or imaginary beings to every day of the year!

The saints' days and festivals of the Romish Church are taken from Mr. Alban Butler's *Lives of the Saints*, (one of the best publications of this kind,) conferred with the *Connoissance des Temps*, edited by *La Lande.*

The ancient Roman Calendar has been taken chiefly from *Ainsworth;* the two copies, one English, the other Latin, in his second volume, being collated together, and mutually corrected.

JANUARY.—Under the protection of Juno.

Days of the Month.	Days of the ancient Roman Month.	Festivals, &c., of the ancient Romans.	Saints' Days, &c., of the Romish or Latin Church.
1	Cal. Januariis	Sacred to Janus, Juno, Jupiter, and Æsculapius.	St. Fulgentius, Odilo or Olon
2	IV Nonas	An unfortunate day, termed by the Romans dies atra.	Macarius, Adelard
3	III Nonas	Cancer sets. Birth-day of Cicero.	P. Balsam, Genevieve
4	Pridie Nonas	Prayer for the safety of the prince.	Titus, Rigobert, Rumon
5	Nonis Jan.	Lyra rises.	Simeon Stylites, Syncletica
6	VIII Idus		Melanius, Nilammon
7	VII Idus		Lucian, Cedd, Aldric
8	VI Idus	Sacrifice to Jupiter. [phin rises.	Apollinaris, Severinus, Pega
9	V Idus	Agonalia, or festivals in honour of Agonius. The Dol-	Julian, Marciana, Felan
10	IV Idus	Media hyems, or Mid-winter.	William, Agatho, Marcian
11	III Idus	Carmentalia, or festivals in honour of Carmenta. Temple dedicated to Juturna.	Theodosius, Hyginus
12	Pridie Idus	Compitalia, or festivals in honour of the Lares, or household gods.	Arcadius, Bennet, Aelred
13	Idibus Jan.	Sacred to Jupiter Stator. Octavius named Augustus.	
14	XIX Cal. Feb.		Veronica, Kentigern
15	XVIII Cal.	Sacred to Carmenta, Porrima and Postverta.	Hilary, Felix, Sabas
16	XVII Cal.	Temple of Concord raised by Camillus.	Paul the first hermit
17	XVI Cal.	Sun in Aquarius.	Honoratus, Pope Marcellus
18	XV Cal.		Antony patr. of the monks
19	XIV Cal.		Peter's chair at Rome
20	XIII Cal.		Canute, Henry, Wulstan
21	XII Cal.		Fabian, Sebastian, Fechin
22	XI Cal.		Agnes, Epiphanius, Publius
23	X Cal.	Lyra sets.	Vincent, Anastasius
24	IX Cal.		Raymund, Ildefensus
25	VIII Cal.	Sementinæ, Feriæ, or the feast of seed-time.	Timothy, Babylas, Cadoc
26	VII Cal.		Projectus, Apollo, Poppo
27	VI Cal.	Temple dedicated to Castor and Pollux.	Polycarp, Paula, Conon
28	V Cal.	[Martius.	J. Chrysostom, Marius
29	IV Cal.	Equiria, or horse-races in honour of Mars in the Campus	Charlemagne, Cyril
30	III Cal.	Sacred to Peace. Fidicula sets.	Francis, Gildas of Sales
31	Pridie Cal.	Sacred to the Dii Penates, or household gods.	Bathildes, Martina
			Cyrus, Maidoc, Galdus

FEBRUARY.—Under the protection of Neptune.

Days of the Month.	Days of the ancient Roman Month.	Festivals, &c., of the ancient Romans.	Saints' Days, &c., of the Romish or Latin Church.
1	Cal. Februariis	Lucaria, festivals at Rome celebrated in a large grove. The sacrificium bidens to Jupiter.	St. Ignatius, Sigebert, Kinnia
2	IV Nonas	Lyra and the middle of the Lion set.	Laurence abp. of Canterbury
3	III Nonas	Dolphin sets.	Blase, Wereburge
4	Pridie Nonas	[Country. Aquarius rises.	Gilbert, Isidore, Madan
5	Nonis Feb.	Augustus, surnamed Pater Patriæ, or Father of his	Martyrs of Japan, Vitus
6	VIII Idus		St. Dorothy, Vedast, Amandus
7	VII Idus		Romuald, Theodorus
8	VI Idus		Stephen, Cuthman, Paul
9	V Idus	Commencement of spring.	Theliau, Ansbert, Erhard
10	IV Idus		Scholastica, William
11	III Idus	Arctophylax, or Arcturus, rises. Genialic games.	Saturninus, Severinus
12	Pridie Idus		Benedict, Meletius, Eulalia
13	Idibus Feb.	Sacred to Faunus and Jupiter. Slaughter of the Fabii	Catharine, Modomnoc
14	XVI Cal. Mar.	The Crow, Crater, and Serpent rise.	Valentine, Maro, Conran
15	XV Cal.	Lupercalia, or festivals in honour of Pan.	Faustinus, Sigfrid, Jovita
16	XIV Cal.	Sun in Pisces.	Onesimus, Juliana, Tanco
17	XIII Cal.		Flavian, Silvin, Loman
18	XII Cal.	Quirinalia, or festivals in honour of Romulus. Fornacalia. Feralia.	Simeon, Leo, Paregorius
19	XI Cal.		Barbatus or Barbas
20	X Cal.	Muta, or goddess of silence. Charistia, or festivals at Rome for the distribution of mutual presents.	Tyrannio, Eucherin
21	IX Cal.		Severianus, Pepin, Verda
22	VIII Cal.	Terminalia, or festivals in honour of Terminus.	Margaret, Baradats
23	VII Cal.	[The place of the Bissextile.	Serenus, Dositheus, Boisil
24	VI Cal.	Regifugium, or banishment of the kings from Rome.	Matthias the apostle
25	V Cal.		Tarasius, Cæsarius [rius
26	IV Cal.		Alexander, Victor, Porphy-
27	III Cal.	Equiria, or horse-races in the Campus Martius.	Leander, Alnoth, Galmier
28	Pridie Cal.	The Tarquins overcome.	Proterius, Romanus

2

MARCH.—Under the protection of Minerva.

Day of the Month.	Days of the ancient Roman Month.	Festivals, &c., of the ancient Romans.	Saints' Days, &c., of the Romish or Latin Church.
1	*Cal.* Martiis	Matronalia, or festivals in honour of Mars. Ancilia in honour of the same god. Sacred to Lucina.	St. David, Monan, Albinus
2	VI Nonas	Birth of Jupiter.	Charles the Good, Joavan
3	V Nonas	The second Fish sets.	Cunegundes, Lamaliffe
4	IV Nonas	[Cancer rises.	Casimir pr.of Poland,Adrian
5	III Nonas	Arctophylax, or Arcturus sets. Vindemiator rises.	Kiaran, Breaca, Roger
6	Pridie Nonas	Feasts of Vesta. Augustus Cæsar created high priest.	Chrodegang, Fridolin
7	*Nonis* Mar.	Pegasus rises. Temple of Vejupiter.	Perpetua, Felicitas
8	VIII Idus	The Crown rises.	Duthak, Rosa, Senan
9	VII Idus	Orion rises. The northern Fish rises.	Pacian, Gregory of Nyssa
10	VI Idus		Forty martyrs of Sebaste
11	V Idus		St. Eulogius, Ængus
12	IV Idus		Pope Gregory the Great
13	III Idus	The opening of the sea. [the Tiber.	St. Nicephorus, Gerald
14	Pridie Idus	The second Equiria, or horse-races upon the banks of	Queen Mathildis, Lubin
15	*Idibus* Mar.	Sacred to Anna Perenna. The Parricide. Scorpio rises.	Pope Zachary, Mary
16	XVII Cal. Ap.	Middle of the Scorpion sets.	St. Julian, Finian the leper
17	XVI Cal.	Liberalia, or festivals in honour of Bacchus. Agonalia in honour of Agonius. Milvius rises.	Patrick,Joseph of Arimathea
18	XV Cal.	Sun in Aries. [tinued for five days.	King Edward, Anselm, Cyril
19	XIV Cal.	Quinquatria, or festivals in honour of Minerva. ..t con-	St. Joseph, Alcmund
20	XIII Cal.		Cuthbert, Wulfran
21	XII Cal.	The first day of the Century. Pegasus sets.	The three Serapions, Endeus
22	XI Cal.		St. Basil, Lea, Catherine
23	X Cal.	Tubilustrium, or solemn procession with trumpets.	Victorian, Edelwald [Simon
24	IX Cal.	[mother of the gods.	Irenæus bp. of Sirmium,
25	VIII Cal.	Vernal equinox. Hilaria, or festivals in honour of the	Annunciation B. V. M.
26	VII Cal.		St. Ludger, Braulio [Robert
27	VI Cal.	Cæsar made himself master of Alexandria.	John the hermit, Rupert or
28	V Cal.	Megalesia, or games in honour of Cybele.	Pope Sixtus III., K. Gontran
29	IV Cal.		St. Jonas, Armogastes, Mark
30	III Cal.	Sacred to Janus, Concord, Health, and Peace.	Zozimus, Rieul or Regulus
31	Pridie Cal.	Sacred to the Moon, or Diana, on the Aventine mount.	Benjamin, Guy, Achates.

APRIL.—Under the protection of Venus.

Day of the Month.	Days of the ancient Roman Month.	Festivals, &c., of the ancient Romans.	Saints' Days, &c., of the Romish or Latin Church.
1	*Cal.* April	Sacred to Venus, and Virile Fortune. Scorpion sets.	St. Hugh, Melito, Gibert
2	IV Nonas	The Pleiades set.	Apian, Ebba, Bronacha
3	III Nonas		Agape, Ulpian, Nicetas
4	Pridie Nonas		Isidore, Plato [Becan
5	*Nonis* Apr.	Megalesia, or games in honour of Cybele for eight days.	Vincent Ferrer, Tigernach,
6	VIII Idus	Sacred to Public Fortune. Birth-day of Diana.	Martyrs of Hadiab, William
7	VII Idus	Birth-day of Apollo, Socrates, and Plato.	St. Hegesippus, Finan, Aibert
8	VI Idus	Games for the victory of Cæsar. Libra and Orion set.	Dionysius, Walter, Albert
9	V Idus	Cerealia, or festivals in honour of Ceres. Ludi Circenses, or games in the Circus dedicated to Consus.	Waltrude, Dotto, Gaucher
10	IV Idus		Bademus, Mechtildes
11	III Idus		Pope Leo the Great, Antipas
12	Pridie Idus	The great mother brought to Rome.	St. Zeno, Sabas, Victor, Julius
13	*Idibus* Apr.	Sacred to Jupiter Victor, and Liberty.	Hermenegild, Caradoc
14	XVIII C. Mai.	[sacrificed.	Tiburtius, Carpus, Benezet
15	XVII Cal.	Fordicidia, or festivals wherein cows with calf were	Munde, Basilissa, Ruadhan
16	XVI Cal.	Augustus saluted emperor. Hyades set.	Martyrs of Saragossa, Druon
17	XV Cal.	[of the foxes.	Pope Anicetus, Simeon
18	XIV Cal.	Equiria, or horse-races in the Circus, and the burning	St. Galdin, Laferian [Bald
19	XIII Cal.	Sun in Taurus.	Pope Leo IX., Elphege the
20	XII Cal.	[tivals in honour of Agonius. Birth-day of Rome.	St. Agnes, Serf, James
21	XI Cal.	Palilia, or festivals in honour of Pales. Agonalia, or fes-	Anselm, Harluin, Bueno
22	X Cal.		Soter, Azades Leonides
23	IX Cal.	The first Vinalia, or festivals of Jupiter and Venus.	George the Martyr, Ibar
24	VIII Cal.	Destruction of Ilium.	Fidelis, Mellitus, Bona
25	VII Cal.	Robigalia, or festivals in honour of Robigo or Rubigo. Mid-spring. Aries sets. The Dog rises.	Mark the Evangelist, Ivia
26	VI Cal.	Feriæ Latinæ, or Latin festivals in honour of Jupiter	Cletus, Richarius, Radbert
27	V Cal.	Latialis. The Goat rises.	Anthimus, Zita, Anastasius
28	IV Cal.	Floralia, or games in honour of Flora for six days.	Vitalis, Cronan, Pollio
29	III Cal.		Fiachna, Robert, Hugh
30	Pridie Cal.	Sacred to Vesta Palatina. The first Larentalia.	Catherine, Sophia, Ajutte

MAY.—Under the protection of Apollo.

Days of the Month.	Days of the ancient Roman Month.	Festivals, &c., of the ancient Romans.	Saints' Days, &c., of the Romish or Latin Church.
1	Cal. Mai.	To the good goddess. Altar raised to the Lares. Games of Flora for three days. Capella rises.	St. Philip and James, apostles
2	VI Nonas	Hyades rise. The compitalia.	Athanasius
3	V Nonas	The Centaur and Hyades rise.	Invention of the Holy Cross
4	IV Nonas		St. Monica, Godard
5	III Nonas	Lyra rises.	Pope Pius V., Angelus, Hilary
6	Pridie Nonas	Middle of the Scorpion sets.	St. John before the Latin gate
7	Nonis Mai.	Virgiliæ rise.	Pope Benedict II., Stanislas
8	VIII Idus	The Goat rises.	St. Wiro, Odrian, Gybrian
9	VII Idus	Lemuria, or night festivals, to appease the manes of	Hermas, Brynoth
10	VI Idus	the dead.	Antoninus, Achard Isidore
11	V Idus	Orion sets. Unfortunate days to marry on.	Mammertus, Maieul [cras
12	IV Idus	Sacred to Mars, the avenger at the Circus.	Germanus, Rictrudes, Pan-
13	III Idus	Pleiades rise. Commencement of summer.	John the Silent, Servatius
14	Pridie Idus	Taurus rises. Sacred to Mercury.	Boniface, Pontius, Carthagh
15	Idibus Mai.	Birth-day of Mercury. Festival of the merchants.	Dympna, Genebern
16	XVII C, Jun.	Lyra rises. Sacred to Jupiter.	Hebedjesus, Abdas, Brendan
17	XVI Cal.		Possidius, Maw, Maden
18	XV Cal.		Eric, Potamon, Venantius
19	XIV Cal.	Sun in Gemini.	Dunstan, Pudentiana
20	XIII Cal.		Bernardin, Ethelbert
21	XII Cal.	Agonalia, or festivals in honour of Agonius. Sacred	Godric, Sospis, or Hospitius
22	XI Cal.	to Vejovis, or Vejupiter. The Dog rises.	Yvo, Bobo, Conall, Castus
23	X Cal.	Tubilustrium, or solemn procession with trumpets.	Julia, Desiderius
24	IX Cal.	The second Regifugium. The feriæ of Vulcan.]	Donatian, Rogatian, Vincent
25	VIII Cal.	Temple of Fortune. Aquila rises.	Pope Gregory VII., Urban
26	VII Cal.	Arctophylax, or Arcturus, sets.	St. Augustine, apos. of Eng.
27	VI Cal.	Hyades rise.	Bede, Pope John, Julius
28	V Cal.		Germanus, Caro
29	IV Cal.		Maximinus, Cyril, Conon
30	III Cal.		Pope Felix, Maguil, Walstan
31	Pridie Cal.		St. Petronilla, Cantius

JUNE.—Under the protection of Mercury.

Days of the Month.	Days of the ancient Roman Month.	Festivals, &c., of the ancient Romans.	Saints' Days, &c., of the Romish or Latin Church.
1	Cal. Jun.	Fabaria, or festivals in honour of Carna. Aquila rises.	St. Justin Martyr, Wistan
2	IV Nonas	Hyad. rise. [Sacred to Mars, Juno Moneta, & Tempest.	Erasmus, Pothinus
3	III Nonas	Sacred to Bellona.	Cecilius, Clotildis, Lifard
4	Pridie Nonas	Temple of Hercules in the Circus.	Quirinus, Nenooc, Petroc
5	Nonis Jun.	Sacred to Jupiter Sponsor. Temple of Faith.	Illidius, Dorotheus
6	VIII Idus	Temple of Vesta.	Philip the deacon, Gudwall
7	VII Idus	Piscatorian days in the Campus Martius.	Colman, Meriadec, Robert
8	VI Idus	Temple of the Mind. Arcturus sets.	Clou, William, abp. of York
9	V Idus	Altar of Jupiter Pistor. [Dolphin rises.	Richard, Pelagia, Vincent
10	IV Idus	Matralia, or festival in honour of Matuta, or Ino.	Margaret queen of Scotland
11	III Idus	Sacred to powerful Fortune. Temple of Concord.	Barnabas the apostle
12	Pridie Idus	Sacred to Mother Matuta.]	Eskill, Onuphrius, Ternan
13	Idibus Jun.	Invincible Jupiter. Quinquatria minuscula, or the minor festivals in honour of Minerva.	Antony of Padua, Damhnade
14	XVIII C. Jul.		Basil the Great, Nennus
15	XVII Cal.	Hyades rise. The carrying of the dung out of the	Vitus, Landelin, Vauge
16	XVI Cal.	Orion rises. temple of Vesta.]	Quiricus, Ferreolus, Aurelian
17	XV Cal.	Æqui and Volsci put to flight by Posthumus.	Nicander, Marcian, Avitus
18	XIV Cal.	[Cancer.	Marina, Amand, Marcus
19	XIII Cal.	Festival of Minerva on the Aventine Mount. Sun in	Gervasius, Die bp. of Nevers
20	XII Cal.	Summanalia, or festivals in honour of Pluto. Ophiu-	Gobain, Idaberga, Bain
21	XI Cal.	chus rises.	Aloysius, Eusebius, Meen
22	X Cal.		Alban, protomart. of Britain
23	IX Cal.	Flaminius conquered by the Carthaginians.	Etheldreda, Mary of Oignies
24	VIII Cal.	Sacred to powerful Fortune.	Nativity of John Baptist
25	VII Cal.	Crowned ships carried banquets along the Tiber	St. Prosper, Moloc, Adelbert
26	VI Cal.	Summer Solstice.	Vigilius Babolen, Anthelm
27	V Cal.	Sacred to Jupiter Stator and Lar.	Ladislas I. king of Hungary
28	IV Cal.	Temple of Quirinus.	Pope Leo II., Basilides
29	III Cal.		St. Peter prince of the apostles
30	Pridie Cal.	Sacred to Hercules and the Muses.	Paul the apostle

2

QUINTILIS, OR JULY.—UNDER THE PROTECTION OF JUPITER.

Days of the Month.	Days of the ancient Roman Month.	FESTIVALS, &c., of the ancient Romans.	Saints' Days, &c., of the Romish or Latin Church.
1	*Cal.* Jul.	Removing from one house to another.	St. Calais, Thierri, Leonorus
2	VI Nonas		Visitation of Blessed V. M.
3	V Nonas		St. Guthagon, Bertran, Phocas
4	IV Nonas	The crown sets. The Hyad. rise. [from their enemies.	Ulric, Odo, Finbar, Bertha
5	III Nonas	Populifugium, or day in which the people of Rome fled	Modwena, Edana, Peter
6	Pridie Nonas	Conflagration of the Capitol, in the time of Sylla.	Palladius apostle of the Scots
7	*Nonis* Jul.	[or wanton rejoicings.	Pope Benedict XI., Hedda
8	VIII Idus	Caprotinæ, or festivals in honour of Juno. Vitulatio,	St. Elizabeth Q. of Portugal
9	VII Idus	Cepheus rises. Festival of the Maids.	Ephrem doctor of the church
10	VI Idus	The Etesian winds begin to blow. [this time.	The seven brothers, Rufina
11	V Idus	Ludi Apollinares, or games in honour of Apollo, about	Pope Pius I., Drostan
12	IV Idus	Birth-day of Julius Cæsar. Festival of Female Fortune.	St. Nabor, Felix, J. Gualbert
13	III Idus		Anacletus, Turiaf, Eugenius
14	Pridie Idus	Sacred to Female Fortune.	Bonaventure, dr. of the ch.
15	*Idibus* Jul.	Festival of Castor and Pollux.	Henry II. emperor, Swithin
16	XVII Cal. Aug.	The Foremost Dog rises.	Eustathius, Elier the hermit
17	XVI Cal.	Alliensis dies atra, or anniversary of the unlucky bat-	Pope Leo IV., Marcellina
18	XV Cal.	tle of Allia.	St. Symphorosa, Bruno, Arnoul
19	XIV Cal.	Lucaria, games lasting four days.	Symmachus, Macrina
20	XIII Cal.	Plays for Cæsar's victory. Sun in Leo.	Joseph Barsabas, Ceslas
21	XII Cal.		Praxedes, Zoticus, Victor
22	XI Cal.		Mary Magdalene, Dabius
23	X Cal.	The games of Neptune.	Apollinaris, Liborius
24	IX Cal.	[censian games lasting six days.	Lupus, Kinga, Declan
25	VIII Cal.	Furinalia, or festivals in honour of Furina. The Cir-	James the greater, Thea
26	VII Cal	In this month dogs were sacrificed to the dog-star,	Anne mother of B.V. M.
27	VI Cal.	Aquila rises. according to Festus.]	Pantaleon, Congal, Luican
28	V Cal.		Pope Innocent I., Pope Victor
29	IV Cal.	Neptunalia, or festivals in honour of Neptune, were cele-brated some time in this month, according to Varro.	St. Martha, Olaus, Pope Felix
30	III Cal.	Aquila sets.	Abdon, Sennen, Julitta
31	Pridie Cal.		Ignatius of Loyola, Helen

SEXTILIS, OR AUGUST.—UNDER THE PROTECTION OF CERES.

Days of the Month.	Days of the ancient Roman Month.	FESTIVALS, &c., of the ancient Romans.	Saints' Days, &c., of the Romish or Latin Church.
1	*Cal.* Aug.	Temple of Mars consecrated. Sacred to Hope.	The seven Maccabees
2	IV Nonas	Feriæ upon account of Cæsar's subduing Spain.	St. Etheldritha, Pope Stephen
3	III Nonas		Invention of St. Stephen's relics
4	Pridie Nonas	The middle of Leo rises.	St. Dominic, Luanus
5	*Nonis* Aug.	Sacred to Health on the Quirinal mount.	Oswald, Memmius, Afra
6	VIII Idus	Sacred to Hope.	Transfiguration of our Lord
7	VII Idus	Middle of Aquarius sets.	St. Cajetan, Donatus
8	VI Idus	Sacred to Soli Indigeti on the Quirinal mount.	Cyriacus, Hormisdas, Largus
9	V Idus		Romanus, Nathy or David
10	IV Idus	Altars of Ops and Ceres in the Jugarian street.	Deusdedit, Blaan. Laurence
11	III Idus	Sacred to the great guardian Hercules in the Circus Fla-	Susannah, Equitius, Gery
12	Pridie Idus	Lignaposia. minius. The beginning of autumn.]	Clare, Euplius, Muredach
13	*Idibus* Aug.	Sacred to Diana in the Sylva Aricina, and Vertumnus.	Hippolytus, Wigbert, Cassian
14	XIX Cal. Sep.	The feast of slaves and servant maids.	Eusebius the priest
15	XVIII Cal.		Assumption of B.V.M.
16	XVII Cal.		St. Hyacinth, Roch [monks
17	XVI Cal.	Portumnalia, or festivals in honour of Portumnus.	Mamas, Liberatus and six
18	XV Cal.	Consualia, or festivals of Consus. Rape of the Sabines.	Helen, Agapetus, Clare
19	XIV Cal.	Death of Augustus. [Lyra sets.	Mochteus, Cumin, Lewis
20	XIII Cal.	Vinalia secunda, according to Pliny. Sun in Virgo.	Bernard, Oswin
21	XII Cal.	Vinalia rustica, according to Varro. The Grand Mys-teries.	Bonosus, Maximilian
22	XI Cal.		Symphorian, Philibert [mit
23	X Cal.	Vulcanalia, or festivals in honour of Vulcan.	Theonas, Justinian the her-
24	IX Cal.	The Feriæ of the Moon.	Bartholomew the apostle
25	VIII Cal.	Sacred to Ops Consiva in the Capitol.	Lewis IX. King of France
26	VII Cal.		Pope Zephyrinus, Genesius
27	VI Cal.	[the Etesian winds.	St. Pœmen, Hugh of Lincoln
28	V Cal.	Altars dedicated to Victory in the Court. The end of	Augustine Dr. of the church
29	IV Cal.	Vulcanalia, or festivals in honour of Vulcan, according	Decollation of John Baptist
30	III Cal.	Ornaments of Ceres exhibited. to Festus.]	St. Rose of Lima, Fiaker.
31	Pridie Cal.	Birth-day of Germanicus. Andromeda rises.	Raymond Nonnatus, Isabel

SEPTEMBER.—Under the protection of Vulcan.

Days of the Month.	Days of the ancient Roman Month.	Festivals, &c., of the ancient Romans.	Saints' Days, &c., of the Romish or Latin Church.
1	Cal. Sept.	Sacred to Jupiter Maimactes. Feasts to Neptune.	St. Giles, Firminus, Lupus
2	IV Nonas	Naval victory of Augustus over M. Antony and Cleo-	King Stephen, Justus
		patra.	[nisius
3	III Nonas	Dionysia, or festivals in honour of Bacchus.	St. Mansuet, Remaclus, Mac-
4	Pridie Nonas	Roman games for eight days.	Translation of St. Cuthbert, Ida
5	Nonis Sept.		St. Bertin, Alto of Ireland
6	VIII Idus	Sacred to Erebus.	Pambo of Nitria, Bega
7	VII Idus	The goat rises.	Cloud, Eunan, Regina
8	VI Idus	Jerusalem taken by Titus Vespasian.	Nativity and name of B. V. M.
9	V Idus		St. Omer, Kiaran, Osmanna
10	IV Idus	The head of Medusa rises.	Winin, Salvius, Pulcheria
11	III Idus	The middle of Virgo rises.	Protus, Patiens, Hyacinthus
12	Pridie Idus	[Capitol. Sacred to Jupiter.	Eanswide, Guy, Albeus
13	Idibus Sept.	The Prætor strikes the clavus. The dedication of the	Eulogius, Amatus, Maurilius
14	XVIII Cal. Oct.	The trial of horses.	Catherine, Exalt. Holy Cross
15	XVII Cal.	The Roman, or great games, which continued five days.	John the dwarf, Nicomedes
16	XVI Cal.	The departure of the swallows.	Lucia, Editha, Cyprian
17	XV Cal.		Lambert, Rouin, Columba
18	XIV Cal.	Virgin's spike rises in the morning.	Methodius, Ferreol, Joseph
19	XIII Cal.	Sun in Libra.	Januarius, Lucy, Sequanus
20	XII Cal.	Birthday of Romulus, according to Plutarch. The	Pope Agapetus, Eustachius
21	XI Cal.	Mercatus for the space of four days.	St. Matthew the apostle, Lo
22	X Cal.	Death of Virgil. Argo and Pisces set.	Maurice, Emmeran
23	IX Cal.	Birthday of Augustus, according to Suetonius. The	Pope Linus, Thecla, Adamnan
		Circensian games.	
24	VIII Cal.	The autumnal equinox.	St. Germer, Rusticus, Conald
25	VII Cal.	Sacred to Venus, Saturn, and Mania.	Barr or Finbarr, Aunaire
26	VI Cal.		Nilus the younger, Justina
27	V Cal.	Sacred to returning Fortune, and Venus the mother.	Cosmas, Elzear, Damian
28	IV Cal.	The end of Virgo's rising.	Lioba, Exuperius, Wenceslas
29	III Cal.	[of medicines. Birthday of Pompey the Great.	Feast of the holy angels
30	Pridie Cal.	Meditrinalia, or festivals in honour of Meditrina, goddess	Jerom Dr. of the Church

OCTOBER.—Under the protection of Mars.

Days of the Month.	Days of the ancient Roman Month.	Festivals, &c., of the ancient Romans.	Saints' Days, &c.
1	Cal. Oct.		Festival of the Rosary, Bavo
2	VI Nonas		Feast of the angel-guardians
3	V Nonas		St. Dionysius the Areopagite
4	IV Nonas	Boötes sets in the morning. The ornaments of Ceres	Ammon, King Edwin, Fran-
5	III Nonas	exhibited.	Placidus, Galla [cis
6	Pridie Nonas	Sacred to the gods Manes.	Bruno, Faith or Fides
7	Nonis Oct.		Pope Mark, Osith, Marcellus
8	VIII Idus	Pyanepsia, or festival in honour of Theseus and his	Thais, Bridget of Sweden
9	VII Idus	companions. The bright star in Corona rises.	Domninus, Guislain
10	VI Idus	Oschophoria, or festival to Minerva.	John of Bridlington, Paulinus
11	V Idus	Commence. of winter. [Rome, after establishing peace.	Tarachus, Probus, Gomer
12	IV Idus	Augustalia, or fest. in commem. of Augustus's return to	Wilfrid bishop of York
13	III Idus	Fontinalia, or festival wherein the Romans adorned	K. Edward the Confessor
14	Pridie Idus	their fountains and wells with chaplets.	Donatian, Burckard
15	Idibus Oct.	The merchants to Mercury.	Teresa, Tecla, Hospicius
16	XVII Cal. Nov.	Popular games. Arcturus sets.	Gall, Mummolin, Lullus
17	XVI Cal.		Andrew of Crete, Austrudis
18	XV Cal.	Sacred to Jupiter Liberator.	Luke the evangelist, Monon
19	XIV Cal.	Armilustrium, or festival at Rome, wherein the people	Peter of Alcantara, Egbin
20	XIII Cal.	Sun in Scorpio. [appeared under arms at the sacrifices.	Artemius, Aidan, Barsabias
21	XII Cal.		Ursula, Hilarion, Fintan
22	XI Cal.		Nunilo, Donatus, Mello
23	X Cal.	A day in this month was held sacred to Liber Pater.	Theodoret, Ignatius
24	IX Cal.		Proclus, Magloire, Felix
25	VIII Cal.	The feriæ of Vertumnus were celebrated in this month,	Crispin, Crispinian, Daria
26	VII Cal.	according to Varro.	Evaristus, Lucian, Marcian
27	VI Cal.	Games of Victory.	K. Elesbaan, Abban,
28	V Cal.	The less Mysteries.	St. Simon & Jude the apostles
29	IV Cal.		Narcissus, Chef [cellus
30	III Cal.	The feriæ of Vertumnus. Games consecrated.	Asterius, Germanus, Mar-
31	Pridie Cal.	Arcturus sets.	Quintin, Wolfgang, Foillan

NOVEMBER.—Under the protection of Diana.

Days of the Month.	Days of the ancient Roman Month.	Festivals &c., of the ancient Romans.	Saints' Days, &c., of the Romish or Latin Church.
1	*Cal.* Nov.	The banquet of Jupiter. The Circensian games. The head of Taurus sets.	All Saints, Benignus, Mary
2	IV Nonas	Arcturus sets at night.	All Souls, Vulgan [Rumwald
3	III Nonas	Fidicula rises in the morning.	Malachy, Winefride, Flour,
4	Pridie Nonas	Solemn feast of Jupiter in this month.	Vitalis, Clarus, Brinstan
5	*Nonis* Nov.	Neptunalia, or festivals in honour of Neptune.	Bertille abbess of Chelles
6	VIII Idus		Leonard the hermit, Winoc
7	VII Idus	An exhibition of ornaments.	Willibrord, Werenfrid
8	VI Idus	Scorpio rises with a clear light.	The four crowned brothers
9	V Idus		St. Mathurin, Vanne, Binen
10	IV Idus		Justus, Milles, Abrosimus
11	III Idus	The seas are shut up till the VI. Id. Mar. Virgiliæ	Martin, Mennas [Nilus
12	Pridie Idus	sets.	Pope Martin, Livin, Lebwin,
13	*Idibus* Nov.	Lectisternia, or a spreading of funeral banquets to the gods, in the ceremonies of heathen burials.	St. Didacus, Brice, Mitrius
14	XVIII Cal. Dec.	The trial of horses.	Laurence abp. of Dublin
15	XVII Cal	Plebeian games in the Circus, according to Suetonius, for three days.	Leopold, Maclou, Eugenius
16	XVI Cal.	The end of seed time for corn.	Edmund, Eucherius [nan
17	XV Cal.		Gregory Thaumaturgus, Ag-
18	XIV Cal.	The Mercatus for three days. Sun in Sagittarius.	Alphæus, Odo, Hilda
19	XIII Cal.	Supper of the pontiffs in honour of the Great Mother.	Pope Pontian, Barlaam
20	XII Cal.	The horns of the bull set.	King Edmund the martyr
21	XI Cal.	Sacred to Pluto and Proserpine. Liberalia. Lepus sets.	Presentation of B.V.M.
22	X Cal.		St. Cecily, Appia, Philemon
23	IX Cal.		Pope Clement the martyr
24	VIII Cal.	Brumalia, or festivals in honour of Bacchus for the	St. John of the cross, Flora
25	VII Cal.	space of thirty days.	Catharine, Erasmus [Peter
26	VI Cal.		Nicon, Conrad, Gazzolini,
27	V Cal.	In this month sacrifices were made to the infernal gods	Virgil of Ireland, Maximus
28	IV Cal.	for the Gauls and Greeks dug from under the	Stephen the younger
29	III Cal.	Boarian forum, according to Plutarch.	Saturninus, Radbod [Sapor
30	Pridie Cal.		Andrew the apostle, Narses

DECEMBER.—Under the protection of Vesta.

Days of the Month.	Days of the ancient Roman Month.	Festivals &c., of the ancient Romans.	Saints' Days, &c., of the Romish or Latin Church.
1	*Cal.* Dec.	Festival of female Fortune.	St. Eligius or Eloy
2	IV Nonas		Bibiana [Indies
3	III Nonas		Francis Xavier apos. of the
4	Pridie Nonas	Sacred to Neptune and Minerva.	Clement of Alexandria
5	*Nonis* Dec.	Faunalia, or festivals in honour of Faunus.	Sabas, Crispina, Nicetius
6	VIII Idus	Middle of Sagittarius sets.	Nicholas, Leontia, Dativa
7	VII Idus	Aquila rises in the morning.	Ambrose Dr. of the church,
8	VI Idus	Sacred to Juno Jugalis.	Conception of B.V.M. [Fara
9	V Idus		St. Leocadia, Wulfhilde
10	IV Idus	Agonalia, or festivals in honour of Agonius.	Pope Melchiades, Eulalia
11	III Idus	The fourteen Halcyonian days begin.	St. Damasus, Fuscian, Gentian
12	Pridie Idus	Equiria, or horse-races.	Epimachus, Valery, Corentin
13	*Idibus* Dec.		Jodoc, Aubert, Marinoni
14	XIX Cal. Jan.	Brumalia, or festivals in honour of Bacchus.	Spiridion, Nicasius
15	XVIII Cal.	Consualia. All Cancer rises in the morning.	Eusebius, Florence or Flann
16	XVII Cal		Ado, Adelaide, Beanus
17	XVI Cal.	Saturnalia, or festivals in honour of Saturn, for five days.	Olympias, Begga [Zozimus
18	XV Cal.	Sun in Capricorn. Cygnus rises.	Gatian, Winebald, Rufus,
19	XIV Cal.	Opalia, or festivals in honour of Ops.	Nemesion, Samthana
20	XIII Cal.	Sagillaria, lasting two days. [wine mixed with water.	Paul of Latrus, Philogonius
21	XII Cal.	Angeronalia. The Divalia. To Hercules and Venus with	Thomas the apos. Edburge
22	XI Cal.	Feriæ dedicated to the Lares. The Compitalia.	Ischyrion, Methodius, Cyril
23	X Cal.	The Feriæ of Jupiter. Laurentinalia, festivals in honour	Servulus, 10 martyrs of Crete
24	IX Cal.	The Ludi Juvenales. [of Laurentia. The Goat sets.	Gregory of Spoleto [tasia
25	VIII Cal.	The end of the Brumalia. Winter solstice.	*Christmas* day, Eugenia, Anas-
26	VII Cal.		St. Stephen the first martyr
27	VI Cal.	Dolphin rises.	John the apostle, T. Grapt
28	V Cal.	Sacred to Phœbus for three days.	The holy Innocents, Orsisius
29	IV Cal.	Aquila sets.	Thomas abp. of Canterbury
30	III Cal.	Canicula sets.	Sabinus, Anysia, Maximus
31	Pridie Cal.		Pope Sylvester, Columba

OBSERVATIONS ON THE

PROGRESSIVE IMPROVEMENT OF THE ROMAN CALENDAR,

FROM THE DAYS OF ROMULUS, ABOUT 730 YEARS BEFORE CHRIST, TO THE PRESENT TIME.

THE ROMAN CALENDAR before the time of Julius Cæsar was very defective : in the reign of Romulus, the first king of Rome, the science of astronomy was so little understood in Italy, that the calendar was made to consist of *ten* months, and the year only of 304 days. The names of the ten months were in order as follows :—March, April, May, June, Quintilis, Sextilis, September, October, November, and December. Besides the 304 days, Romulus is said to have intercalated days without name, to make up the number of 360 ; but whether this was the case, or in what way these days were intercalated, cannot be determined, as history, with reference to this point, is extremely obscure. The months, March, May, Quintilis, and October, contained 31 days each ; and the other six only 30 days each ; as may be seen in the following table which exhibits the state of the Roman calendar about 730 years previously to the incarnation.

March	April	May	June	Quintilis	Sextilis	September	October	November	December
Calend.	*Calend.*	*Calend.*	*Calend.*	*Calend.*	*Calend.*	*Calend.*	*Calend.*	*Calend.*	*Calend.*
VI	IV	VI	IV	VI	IV	IV	VI	IV	IV
V	III	V	III	V	III	III	V	III	III
IV	*Prid.*	IV	*Prid.*	IV	*Prid.*	*Prid.*	IV	*Prid.*	*Prid.*
III	*Non.*	III	*Non.*	III	*Non.*	*Non.*	III	*Non.*	*Non.*
Prid.	VIII	*Prid.*	VIII	*Prid.*	VIII	VIII	*Prid.*	VIII	VIII
Non.	VII	*Non.*	VII	*Non.*	VII	VII	*Non.*	VII	VII
VIII	VI	VIII	VI	VIII	VI	VI	VIII	VI	VI
VII	V	VII	V	VII	V	V	VII	V	V
VI	IV	VI	IV	VI	IV	IV	VI	IV	IV
V	III	V	III	V	III	III	V	III	III
IV	*Prid.*	IV	*Prid.*	IV	*Prid.*	*Prid.*	IV	*Prid.*	*Prid.*
III	*Id.*	III	*Id.*	III	*Id.*	*Id.*	III	*Id.*	*Id,*
Prid.	XVIII	*Prid.*	XVIII	*Prid.*	XVIII	XVIII	*Prid.*	XVIII	XVIII
Id.	XVII	*Id.*	XVII	*Id.*	XVII	XVII	*Id.*	XVII	XVII
XVII	XVI	XVII	XVI	XVII	XVI	XVI	XVII	XVI	XVI
XVI	XV	XVI	XV	XVI	XV	XV	XVI	XV	XV
XV	XIV	XV	XIV	XV	XIV	XIV	XV	XIV	XIV
XIV	XIII	XIV	XIII	XIV	XIII	XIII	XIV	XIII	XIII
XIII	XII	XIII	XII	XIII	XII	XII	XIII	XII	XII
XII	XI	XII	XI	XII	XI	XI	XII	XI	XI
XI	X	XI	X	XI	X	X	XI	X	X
X	IX	X	IX	X	IX	IX	X	IX	IX
IX	VIII	IX	VIII	IX	VIII	VIII	IX	VIII	VIII
VIII	VII	VIII	VII	VIII	VII	VII	VIII	VII	VII
VII	VI	VII	VI	VII	VI	VI	VII	VI	VI
VI	V	VI	V	VI	V	V	VI	V	V
V	IV	V	IV	V	IV	IV	V	IV	IV
IV	III	IV	III	IV	III	III	IV	III	III
III	*Prid.*	III	*Prid.*	III	*Prid.*	*Prid.*	III	*Prid.*	*Prid.*
Prid.		*Prid.*		*Prid.*			*Prid.*		

In the reign of Numa Pompilius, the second king of the Romans, the calendar was very much improved. This monarch, by means of the instructions he received from Pythagoras, the prince of the Italian philosophers, adopted very nearly the same kind of year which the Greeks then used ; with this principal exception, that he assigned to every one of his years 355 days, which is one day more than the Grecian and Rabbinical years usually contained. The reformation of the calendar of Romulus consisted in taking away one day from April, June, Sextilis, September, November, and December, (the day after the ides of these months being named the xviiith before the calends of the ensuing one,) and then adding these six days to the 51 which the year of Romulus wanted, to make up his own of 355 days : with these 57 days he made two new months, viz. January and February, the former of which was the first, and the other the last month of his year ; assigning to the former 29, and to the latter 28 days. In order to make his year equal to that which the Greeks used in their Olympiads, Numa is said to have intercalated 82 days in every eight years, in the following manner : At the end of the first two years, an intercalation of 22 days ; at the end of the next two, an intercalation of 23 days ; at the end of the third two, an intercalation of 22 days ; and at the end of the last two, an intercalation of the remaining 15 days.

The calendar of Numa Pompilius (with the slight variation in it at the time of the Decemviri, about 452, B. C., which consisted in constituting February the second instead of the last month) continued in use among

2   179

the Romans till the time of Julius Cæsar, who perceiving the great inconveniences that resulted from not making the *civil* year equal in length to the *solar revolution* through the twelve signs of the zodiac, employed Sosigenes of Alexandria, (esteemed the greatest astronomer of his time,) to reform the calendar in such a way that the seasons of the year might perpetually correspond to the same months. As, according to the calculations of Sosigenes, the solar ecliptical revolution took up about 365 days, six hours, it was found necessary to lengthen the civil year at least *ten* days, making it to consist of 365 days instead of 355 ; and to make a proper compensation for the six hours which the solar year exceeds 365 days, every fourth year was proposed to be an *intercalary* one, containing 366 days. Julius Cæsar, by public edict, accordingly ordered these corrections to be made ; and the calendar thus corrected, is the same as that already given in the preceding table, with the festivals, &c., of the ancient Romans.

In consequence of the ignorance of the priests, a considerable error was committed in the first 36 years after the Julian reformation of the calendar ; for the priests imagined that the fourth year in which the intercalation should be made, was to be computed from that in which the preceding intercalation took place, by which means they left only two common years instead of three between the two intercalary ones. Consequently, *twelve* days, instead of *nine*, were intercalated in 36 years, an error too considerable to escape the notice of the Augustan age ; and, accordingly the emperor directed that no intercalation should be made for the first twelve years, that the three superfluous days might be gradually dropped, and that the intercalations should be afterwards regulated in such a manner that *three* common years should continually intervene. This last alteration of the calendar continued without any interruption till the pontificate of *Gregory* XIII. in the latter part of the 16th century, when he gave orders that the Roman calendar should be again reformed.

The necessity for this reformation originated in Sosigenes, who assigned precisely 365 days, six hours, for the sun's passage through the twelve signs of the zodiac ; instead of 365 days, five hours, 48 minutes, and 48 seconds, as ascertained by the more perfect observations of modern astronomers. The error of Sosigenes, of about *eleven minutes* in the length of the solar year, amounts to *a whole day* in 134 years, insomuch that from the council of Nice, in A. D. 325, to the time of Gregory XIII., ten days too many had crept into the calendar, the vernal equinox which, in 325, was fixed on the 21st of March happening in 1582 on the 11th, though the calendar constantly placed it on the 21st.

To remedy this defect, Pope Gregory ordered that ten days should be suppressed in the almanac of 1582, the 5th of October being denominated the 15th, as in these days *fewer festivals* occurred than in any other *ten* consecutive days in the year ; and to prevent the recurrence of this error for the future, it was directed by a public bull, that every *three centurial years* out of four, after A. D. 1600, (which in the Julian calendar are leap-years,) should be only common years of 365 days each. Thus 1700, 1800, and 1900, are styled common years ; 2000, a bissextile ; 2100, 2200, and 2300, common years ; 2400, a bissextile ; &c., &c.

By this last correction of the calendar, the Gregorian year is so nearly commensurate with the revolution of the earth round the sun, that an error of a *day* cannot be made in less than 26,800 years. If the intercalations be made according to the calculations of the late M. de la Lande, and other eminent astronomers of the last and present centuries, an error of a day need not be committed in less than a *million* of years.

The papal bull, by which this alteration is made, is thus intituled :—" Constitutio Gregorii Papæ XIII. pro approbatione et introductione novi Kalendarii ad usum universæ Ecclesiæ Romanæ ; quâ, inter plura cætera præcipit et mandat, ut de mense Octobris hujus anni 1582, decem dies inclusive a III Nonarum usque ad Pridie Idus eximantur, et dies qui festum S. Francisci IV. Nonas celebrari solitum sequitur, dicatur Idus Octobris. Datum Tusculi, Anno Incarnationis Dom. 1582, sexto Kal. Martii, Pontif. sui anno X."

" The constitution of Pope Gregory XIII. for the approval and introduction of the new calendar for the use of the Romish Church universally ; in which, among many other things, he decrees and commands, that ten days be struck off from the month of October of this present year 1582 ; namely, from the third of the Nones, (Oct. 5,) to the day before the Ides, (Oct. 14,) both inclusive ; and that the day which follows the festival of St. *Francis*, usually celebrated as *the IVth of the Nones*, should be called the *Ides of October.* Given at Tusculum, in the year of the Incarnation of our Lord, 1582, on the sixth of the Calends of March, (Feb. 24,) and in the tenth year of his pontificate." See Suppl. au Corps Diplomatique, tome II., part I., pp. 187, 188.

This alteration of the calendar was not adopted by the British till 1752, in which year, the day after the second of September was called Sept. 14. All the nations of Europe have adopted this mode of reckoning except the Russians, who follow the *Julian* account, introduced among them by Peter the Great, instead of the Constantinopolitan era by which their chronology had been previously regulated. This is not the only point in which that barbarous nation is behind in reformation and improvement.

The commentator should make an apology to his readers for the introduction of the preceding tables and calculations, as having apparently but little relation to the subject of the *Epistle to the Romans :* but the very obvious *utility* of what is here inserted, will more than plead his excuse.

Finished correcting for a new edition November 8th, 1831.—A. C.

2

INTRODUCTION TO THE FIRST EPISTLE

TO THE

CORINTHIANS.

IN my preface to the Epistle to the Romans I have made several extracts from Dr. Paley's *Horæ Paulinæ*, in which, from internal evidence, he demonstrates the *authenticity* of that epistle. His observations on the first Epistle to the Corinthians are distinguished by the same profound learning and depth of thought: and as, in an age in which *skepticism* has had an unbridled range, it may be of great consequence to a sincere inquirer after truth to have all his doubts removed relative to the *authenticity* of the epistle in question; and as Dr. Paley's observations cast considerable light on several passages in the work, I take the liberty to introduce them, as something should be said on the subject; and I do not pretend to have any thing equal to what is here prepared to my hands. I have scarcely made any other change than to introduce the word *section* for *number*.

SECTION I.

§ Before we proceed to compare this *epistle* with the *history*, says Dr. Paley, or with any other *epistle*, we will employ one section in stating certain remarks applicable to our argument, which arise from a perusal of the epistle itself.

By an expression in the first verse of the seventh chapter, " Now, concerning the things whereof *ye wrote unto me*," it appears that this letter to the Corinthians was written by St. Paul in *answer* to one which he had received from them; and that the *seventh* and some of the following chapters are taken up in resolving certain doubts, and regulating certain points of order, concerning which the Corinthians had in their letter consulted him. This alone is a circumstance considerably in favour of the *authenticity* of the epistle; for it must have been a far-fetched contrivance in a forgery, first to have feigned the receipt of a letter from the Church of Corinth, which letter does not appear, and then to have drawn up a fictitious answer to it, relative to a great variety of doubts and inquiries, purely economical and domestic; and which, though likely enough to have occurred to an infant society, in a situation and under an institution so novel as that of a Christian Church then was, it must have very much exercised the author's invention, and could have answered no imaginable purpose of forgery, to introduce the mention of it at all. Particulars of the kind we refer to are such as the following: the rule of duty and prudence relative to entering into marriage, as applicable to *virgins* and to *widows*; the case of *husbands* married to *unconverted wives*, of wives having *unconverted husbands*; that case where the *unconverted party* chooses to *separate*, or where he chooses to *continue* the union; the effect which their conversion produced upon their prior state; of *circumcision*; of *slavery*; the *eating of things offered to idols*, as it was in *itself*, or as *others* were affected by it; the *joining in idolatrous sacrifices*; the *decorum* to be observed in their *religious assemblies*, the *order of speaking*, the *silence of women*, the *covering* or *uncovering* of the *head*, as it became *men*, as it became *women*. These subjects, with their several subdivisions, are so particular, minute, and numerous, that though they be exactly agreeable to the circumstances of the persons to whom the letter was written, nothing I believe but the existence and the reality of those circumstances could have suggested them to the writer's thoughts.

But this is not the *only* nor the *principal* observation upon the correspondence between the Church of Corinth and their apostle which I wish to point out. It appears, I think, in this correspondence, that although the Corinthians *had written* to St. Paul, requesting his *answer* and his directions in the several points above enumerated; yet that they had not said one syllable about the enormities and disorders which had crept in amongst them, and in the blame of which they all shared; but that St. Paul's information concerning the irregularities then prevailing at Corinth had come round to him from other quarters. The quarrels and disputes excited by their contentious adherence to their different teachers, and by their placing of them in competition with one another, were not mentioned in their *letter*, but communicated to St. Paul by more private intelligence: " It hath been declared unto me, my brethren, *by them which are of the house of Chloe*, that there are contentions among you. Now this I say, that every one of you saith, I am of Paul, and I of Apollos, and I of Cephas, and I of Christ." (i. 11, 12.) The incestuous marriage " of a man with his father's wife," which St. Paul reprehends with so much severity in the fifth chapter of this epistle, and which was not the crime of an individual only, but a crime in which the whole Church, by tolerating and conniving at it, had rendered themselves partakers, did not come to St. Paul's knowledge by the *letter*, but by a rumour which had reached his ears : " *It is reported commonly* that there is fornication among you, and such fornication as is not so much as named among the Gentiles, that one should have his father's wife ; and ye are puffed up and have not rather mourned, that he that hath done this deed might be taken away from among you." (v. 1, 2.) Their *going to law before* the *judicature of the country* rather than arbitrate and adjust their disputes *among themselves*, which St. Paul animadverts upon with his usual plainness, was not intimated to him in the *letter*, because he tells them his opinion of this conduct before he comes to the contents of the letter. Their *litigiousness* is censured by St. Paul in the *sixth* chapter of his epistle : and it is only at the beginning of the seventh chapter that he proceeds upon the articles which he found in their letter ; and he proceeds upon them with this preface : " Now concerning the things whereof ye wrote unto me ; " (vii. 1 ;) which introduction he would not have used if he had been already discussing any of the subjects concerning which they had written. Their *irregularities* in celebrating the *Lord's Supper*, and the utter perversion of the institution which ensued, were not in the letter, as is evident from the terms in which St. Paul mentions the notice he had received of it : " Now in this that I declare unto you I praise you not, that ye come together not for the better, but for the worse ; for first of all, when ye come together in the Church, *I hear* that there be divisions among you, and *I partly believe it*." Now that the Corinthians should, in their own letter, exhibit the fair side of their conduct to the apostle, and conceal from him the faults of their behaviour, was extremely natural and extremely probable : but it was a distinction which would not, I think, have easily occurred to the author of a forgery ; and much less likely is it, that it should have entered into his thoughts to make the distinction *appear* in the way in which it does appear, viz. not by the original letter, not by any express observation upon it in the answer, but distantly by marks perceivable in the manner, or in the order in which St. Paul takes notice of their faults.

Section II.

§ This epistle purports to have been written after St. Paul had already been at Corinth : " I, brethren, *when I came unto you*, came not with excellency of speech or of wisdom," (ii. 1 :) and in many other places to the same effect. It purports also to have been written upon the *eve of another visit* to that Church : " I will come to you shortly, if the Lord will," (iv. 19 ;) and again : " I will come to you when I shall pass through Macedonia," (xvi. 5.) Now the history relates that St. Paul did in fact visit Corinth *twice ;* once as recorded at length in the *eighteenth*, and a *second* time as mentioned briefly in the *twentieth* chapter of the Acts. The same history also informs us (Acts xx. 1) that it was from Ephesus St. Paul proceeded upon his second journey into Greece. Therefore, as the epistle purports to have been written a short time preceding that journey ; and as St. Paul, the history tells us, had resided more than two years at Ephesus before he set out upon it, it follows that it must have been from Ephesus, to be consistent with the history, that the epistle was written ; and every note of *place* in the epistle agrees with this supposition. " If, after the manner of men, I have fought with beasts at *Ephesus*, what advantageth it me, if the dead rise not ?" (xv. 32.) I allow that the apostle might say this wherever he was ; but it was more natural and more to the purpose to say it if he was at Ephesus at the time, and in the midst of those conflicts to which the expression relates. " The Churches of Asia salute you," (xvi. 19.) Asia, throughout the Acts of the Apostles and the epistles of St. Paul, does not mean the whole of Asia Minor or Anatolia, nor even the whole of the proconsular Asia, but a district in the anterior part of that country called Lydian Asia, divided from the rest much as Portugal is from Spain, and of which district *Ephesus* was the capital. " Aquila and Priscilla salute you," (xvi. 19.) Aquila and Priscilla were at *Ephesus* during the period within which this epistle was written. (Acts xviii. 18, 26.) " I will tarry at *Ephesus* until Pentecost," (xvi. 8.) This, I apprehend, is in terms almost asserting that he was at Ephesus at the time of writing the epistle.——" A great and effectual door is opened unto me," (xvi. 9.) How well this declaration corresponded with the state of things at Ephesus and the progress of the Gospel in these parts, we learn from the reflection with which the historian concludes the account of certain transactions which passed there : " So mightily grew the word of God and prevailed ;" (Acts xix. 20 ;) as well as from the complaint of Demetrius, " that not only at Ephesus, but also throughout all Asia, this Paul hath persuaded and turned away much people." (xix. 26.) " And there are many adversaries," says the epistle. (xvi. 9.) Look into the history of this period : " When divers were hardened and believed not, but spake evil of that way before the multitude, he departed from them and separated the disciples." The conformity therefore upon this head of comparison is circumstantial and perfect. If any one think that this is a conformity so obvious, that any forger of tolerable caution and sagacity would have taken care to preserve it, I must desire such a one to read the epistle for himself ; and when he has done so, to declare whether he has discovered one mark of art or design ; whether the notes of *time* and *place* appear to him to be inserted with any reference to each other, with any view of their being compared with each other, or for the purpose of establishing a visible agreement with the history in respect of them.

Section III.

§ Chap. iv. 17–19 : " For this cause I have sent unto you Timotheus, who is my beloved son, and faithful in the Lord ; who shall bring you into remembrance of my ways which be in Christ, as I teach every where in every Church. Now some are puffed up, as though I would not come unto you; but I will come unto you shortly, if the Lord will."

With this I compare Acts xix. 21, 22 : "After these things were ended, Paul purposed in the spirit, when he had passed through Macedonia and *Achaia*, to go to Jerusalem ; saying, After I have been there, I must also see Rome ; so he sent into Macedonia two of them that ministered unto him, *Timotheus* and Erastus."

Though it be not said, it appears I think with sufficient certainty, I mean from the history, independently of the epistle, that Timothy was sent upon this occasion into *Achaia*, of which Corinth was the capital city, as well as into Macedonia : for the sending of Timothy and Erastus is, in the passage where it is mentioned, plainly connected with St. Paul's own journey : *he sent them before him.* As he therefore purposed to go into *Achaia* himself, it is highly probable that they were to go thither also. Nevertheless, they are said only to have been sent into Macedonia, because Macedonia was in truth the country to which they went immediately from Ephesus ; being directed, as we suppose, to proceed afterwards from thence into Achaia. If this be so, the *narrative* agrees with the *epistle* ; and the agreement is attended with very little appearance of design. One thing at least concerning it is certain ; that if this passage of St. Paul's history had been taken from his letter, it would have sent Timothy to Corinth by name, or expressly however into Achaia.

But there is another circumstance in these two passages much less obvious, in which an agreement holds without any room for suspicion that it was produced by design. We have observed that the sending of Timothy into the peninsula of Greece was connected in the narrative with St. Paul's own journey thither ; it is stated as the effect of the same resolution. Paul purposed to go into Macedonia ; " so he sent two of them that ministered unto him, Timotheus and Erastus." Now in the epistle also you remark, that when the apostle mentions his having sent Timothy unto them, in the very next sentence he speaks of his own visit : " For this cause have I sent unto you Timotheus, who is my beloved son, &c. Now some are puffed up, as though I would not come to you ; but I will come to you shortly, if God will." Timothy's journey, we see, is mentioned, in the *history* and in the *epistle*, in close connection with St. Paul's own. Here is the same order of thought and intention ; yet conveyed under such diversity of circumstances and expression, and the mention of them in the epistle so allied to the occasion which introduces it, viz. the insinuation of his adversaries that he would come to Corinth no more, that I am persuaded no attentive reader will believe that these passages were written in concert with one another, or will doubt that the agreement is unsought and uncontrived.

But in the Acts, Erastus accompanied Timothy in this journey, of whom no mention is made in the epistle. From what has been said in our observations upon the Epistle to the Romans, it appears probable that Erastus was a Corinthian. If so, though he accompanied Timothy to Corinth, he was only returning home, and Timothy was the messenger charged with St. Paul's orders. At any rate, this discrepancy shows that the passages were not taken from one another.

SECTION IV.

§ Chap. xvi. 10, 11 : " Now if Timotheus come, see that he may be with you without fear ; for he worketh the work of the Lord, as I also do : let no man therefore despise him, but conduct him forth in peace, that he may come unto me, for I look for him with the brethren."

From the passage considered in the preceding section, it appears that Timothy was sent to Corinth, either with the epistle, or before it : " For this cause have I sent unto you Timotheus." From the passage now quoted we infer that Timothy was not sent *with* the epistle ; for had he been the bearer of the letter, or accompanied it, would St. Paul in that letter have said, " *If* Timothy come ?" Nor is the sequel consistent with the supposition of his carrying the letter ; for if Timothy was with the apostle when he wrote the letter, could he say as he does, " I look for him with the brethren ?" I conclude therefore that Timothy had left St. Paul to proceed upon his journey before the letter was written. Farther, the passage before us seems to imply that Timothy was not expected by St. Paul to arrive at Corinth till after they had received the letter. He gives them directions in the letter how to treat him when he should arrive : " If he come," act towards him so and so. Lastly, the whole form of expression is most naturally applicable to the supposition of Timothy's coming to Corinth, not directly from St. Paul, but from some other quarter ; and that his instructions had been, when he should reach Corinth, to return. Now how stands this matter in the history ? Turn to the *nineteenth chapter* and *twenty-first verse* of the Acts, and you will find that Timothy did not, when sent from Ephesus, where he left St. Paul, and where the present epistle was written, proceed by straight course to Corinth, but that he went *round through Macedonia.* This clears up every thing ; for although Timothy was sent forth upon his journey before the letter was written, yet he might not reach Corinth till after the letter arrived there ; and he would come to Corinth when he did come, not *directly* from St. Paul at Ephesus, but from some part of Macedonia. Here therefore is a circumstantial and critical agreement, and unquestionably without design ; for neither of the two passages in the epistle mentions Timothy's journey into Macedonia at all, though nothing but a circuit of that kind can explain and reconcile the expression which the writer uses.

SECTION V.

§ Chap. i. 12 : " Now this I say, that every one of you saith, I am of Paul, and I of Apollos, and I of Cephas, and I of Christ."

Also iii. 6 : " I have planted, Apollos watered, but God gave the increase."

This expression, " I have planted, Apollos watered," imports two things ; first, that Paul had been at Corinth before Apollos; secondly, that Apollos had been at Corinth after Paul, but before the writing of this epistle. This implied account of the several events and of the order in which they took place, corresponds exactly with the history, St. Paul, after his first visit into Greece, returned from Corinth into Syria, by the way of Ephesus; and dropping his companions Aquila and Priscilla at Ephesus, he proceeded forwards to Jerusalem; from Jerusalem he descended to Antioch, and from thence made a progress through some of the upper or northern provinces of the Lesser Asia, Acts xviii. 19, 23; during which progress, and consequently in the interval between St. Paul's first and second visit to Corinth, and consequently also before the writing of this epistle, which was at Ephesus, two years at least after the apostle's return from his progress, we hear of Apollos, and we hear of him at Corinth. While St. Paul was engaged, as hath been said, in Phrygia and Galatia, Apollos came down to Ephesus; and being, in St. Paul's absence, instructed by Aquila and Priscilla, and having obtained letters of recommendation from the Church at Ephesus, he passed over to Achaia; and when he was there we read that he "helped them much which had believed through grace, for he mightily convinced the Jews, and that publicly;" Acts xviii. 27, 28. To have brought Apollos into Achaia, of which Corinth was the capital city, as well as the principal Christian Church, and to have shown that he preached the Gospel in that country, would have been sufficient for our purpose. But the history happens also to mention Corinth by name as the place in which Apollos, after his arrival in Achaia, fixed his residence; for, proceeding with the account of St. Paul's travels, it tells us that while Apollos was at Corinth, Paul, having passed through the upper coasts, came down to Ephesus, xix. 1. What is said, therefore, of Apollos in the *epistle*, coincides exactly and especially in the point of *chronology* with what is delivered concerning him in the *history*. The only question now is, whether the allusions were made with a regard to this coincidence? Now the occasions and purposes for which the name of Apollos is introduced in the Acts and in the epistles are so independent and so remote, that it is impossible to discover the smallest reference from one to the other. Apollos is mentioned in the Acts in immediate connection with the history of Aquila and Priscilla, and for the very singular circumstance of his "knowing only the baptism of John." In the epistle, where none of these circumstances are taken notice of, his name first occurs, for the purpose of reproving the contentious spirit of the Corinthians; and it occurs only in conjunction with that of some others: "Every one of you saith, I am of Paul, and I of Apollos, and I of Cephas, and I of Christ." The second passage in which Apollos appears, "I have planted, Apollos watered," fixes, as we have observed, the order of *time* amongst three distinct events; but it fixes this, I will venture to pronounce, without the writer perceiving that he was doing any such thing. The sentence fixes this order in exact conformity with the *history*; but it is itself introduced solely for the sake of the reflection which follows: "Neither is he that planteth any thing, neither he that watereth, but God that giveth the increase."

Section VI.

◊ Chap. iv. 11, 12: "Even unto this present hour we both hunger and thirst, and are naked, and are buffeted, and have no certain dwelling place; and labour, working with our own hands."

We are expressly told in the *history*, that at Corinth St. Paul laboured with his own hands: "He found Aquila and Priscilla; and, because he was of the same craft, he abode with them and wrought; for by their occupation they were tent-makers." But in the text before us he is made to say, that "he laboured *even unto this present hour*," that is, to the time of writing the epistle at Ephesus. Now, in the narration of St. Paul's transactions at Ephesus, delivered in the *nineteenth* chapter of the Acts, nothing is said of his *working with his own hands*; but in the *twentieth* chapter we read, that upon his return from Greece he sent for the elders of the Church of Ephesus to meet him at Miletus; and in the discourse which he there addressed to them, amidst some other reflections which he calls to their remembrance, we find the following: "I have coveted no man's silver, or gold, or apparel; yea, you yourselves also know, that *these hands have ministered unto my necessities*, and to them that were with me." The reader will not forget to remark, that though St. Paul be now at Miletus, it is to the elders of the Church of Ephesus he is speaking, when he says, "Ye yourselves know that these hands have ministered to my necessities;" and that the whole discourse relates to his conduct during his last preceding residence at Ephesus. That manual labour, therefore, which he had exercised at Corinth, he continued at Ephesus; and not only so, but continued it during that particular residence at Ephesus, near the conclusion of which this epistle was written; so that he might with the strictest truth say, at the time of writing the epistle, "Even *unto this present hour* we labour, working with our own hands." The correspondency is sufficient, then, as to the undesignedness of it. It is manifest to my judgment, that if the *history* in this article had been taken from the *epistle*, this circumstance, if it appeared at all, would have appeared in its *place*, that is in the direct account of St. Paul's transactions at Ephesus. The correspondency would not have been effected, as it is, by a kind of reflected stroke, that is, by a reference in a subsequent speech to what in the narrative was omitted. Nor is it likely, on the other hand, that a circumstance which is not extant in the history of St. Paul at Ephesus, should have been made the subject of a factitious allusion, in an epistle purporting to be written by him from that place; not to mention that the allusion itself, especially as to time, is too oblique and general to answer any purpose of forgery whatever.

Section VII.

◊ Chap. ix. 20: "And unto the Jews I became as a Jew, that I might gain the Jews; to them that are under the law, as under the law."

2

We have the disposition here described exemplified in two instances which the *history* records ; one, Acts xvi. 3 : " Him (Timothy) would Paul have to go forth with him, and took and circumcised him, *because of the Jews in those quarters* ; for they knew all that his father was a Greek." This was before the writing of the epistle. The other, Acts xxi. 23, 26, and after the writing of the epistle : " Do this that we say to thee ; we have four men which have a vow on them ; them take, and purify thyself with them, that they may shave their heads ; and all may know that those things whereof they were informed concerning thee are nothing ; but that thou thyself also walkest orderly, and keepest the law. Then Paul took the men, and the next day, *purifying himself with them, entered into the temple.*" Nor does this concurrence between the *character* and the *instances* look like the result of contrivance. St. Paul, in the *epistle*, describes, or is made to describe, his own accommodating conduct towards Jews and towards Gentiles, towards the weak and over-scrupulous, towards men indeed of every variety of character : " To them that are without law as without law, being not without law to God, but under the law to Christ, that I might gain them that are without law ; to the weak became I as weak, that I might gain the weak ; I am made all things to all men that I might gain some." This is the sequel of the text which stands at the head of the present section. Taking therefore the whole passage together, the apostle's condescension to the Jews is mentioned only as a part of his general disposition towards all. It is not probable that this character should have been made up from the instances in the Acts, which relate solely to his dealings with the Jews. It is not probable that a sophist should take his hint from those instances, and then extend it so much beyond them ; and it is still more incredible that the two instances in the Acts, circumstantially related and interwoven with the history, should have been fabricated, in order to suit the character which St. Paul gives of himself in the epistle.

SECTION VIII.

§ Chap. i. 14–17 : " I thank God that I baptized none of you but Crispus and Gaius, lest any should say that I baptized in my own name ; and I baptized also the household of Stephanas : besides, I know not whether I baptized any other ; for Christ sent me not to baptize, but to preach the Gospel."

It may be expected that those whom the apostle baptized with his own hands were converts distinguished from the rest by some circumstance, either of eminence or of connection with him. Accordingly, of the three names here mentioned, *Crispus*, we find from Acts xviii. 8, was a " chief ruler of the Jewish synagogue at Corinth, who believed in the Lord with all his house." *Gaius*, it appears from Romans xvi. 23, was St. Paul's host at Corinth, and the host, he tells us, " of the whole Church." The household of *Stephanas*, we read in the sixteenth chapter of this epistle, " were the first fruits of Achaia." Here therefore is the propriety we expected ; and it is a proof of reality not to be contemned ; for their names appearing in the several places in which they occur, with a mark of distinction belonging to each, could hardly be the effect of chance, without any truth to direct it : and on the other hand, to suppose that they were picked out from these passages, and brought together in the text before us in order to display a conformity of names, is both improbable in itself, and is rendered more so by the purpose for which they are introduced. They come in to assist St. Paul's exculpation of himself against the possible charge of having assumed the character of the founder of a separate religion, and with no other visible or, as I think, imaginable design.*

SECTION IX.

§ Chap. xvi. 10, 11 : " Now if Timotheus come, let no man despise him."—Why *despise* him ? This charge is not given concerning any other messenger whom St. Paul sent : and, in the different epistles, many such messengers are mentioned. Turn to 1st of Timothy, chap. iv. 12, and you will find that Timothy was

---

* Chap. i. 1 : " Paul, called to be an apostle of Jesus Christ through the will of God, and Sosthenes, our brother, unto the Church of God, which is at Corinth." The only account we have of any person who bore the name of Sosthenes is found in the eighteenth chapter of the Acts. When the Jews at Corinth had brought Paul before Gallio, and Gallio had dismissed their complaint as unworthy of his interference, and had driven them from the judgment seat ; " then all the Greeks," says the historian, " took Sosthenes, the chief ruler of the synagogue, and beat him before the judgment seat." The *Sosthenes* here spoken of was a Corinthian ; and, if he was a Christian, and *with* St Paul when he wrote this epistle, was likely enough to be joined with him in the salutation of the Corinthian Church. But here occurs a difficulty : If Sosthenes was a *Christian* at the time of this uproar, why should the *Greeks* beat him ? The assault upon the Christians was made by the *Jews*. It was the *Jews* who had brought Paul before the magistrate. If it had been the Jews also who had beaten Sosthenes, I should not have doubted that he had been a favourer of St. Paul, and the same person who is joined with him in the epistle. Let us see, therefore, whether there be not some error in our present text. The Alexandrian manuscript gives παντες alone, without οἱ Ἑλληνες, and is followed in this reading by the Coptic version, by the Arabic version published by Erpenius, by the Vulgate, and by Bede's Latin version. Three Greek manuscripts again, as well as Chrysostom, give οἱ Ιουδαιοι, in the place of οἱ Ἑλληνες. A great plurality of manuscripts authorize the reading which is retained in our copies. In this variety it appears to me extremely probable that the historian originally wrote παντες alone, and that οἱ Ἑλληνες, and οἱ Ιουδαιοι, have been respectively added as explanatory of what the word παντες was supposed to mean. The sentence without the addition of either name would run very perspicuously, thus : " Και απηλασεν αυτους απο του βηματος. Επιλαβομενοι δε παντες Σωσθενην τον αρχισυναγωγον, ετυπτον εμπροσθεν του βηματος· and he drove them away from the judgment seat ; and they all," viz. the crowd of Jews whom the judge had bid begone, " took Sosthenes, and beat him before the judgment seat." It is certain that, as the whole body of the people were Greeks, the application of *all* to them was unusual and hard. If I were describing an insurrection at Paris, I might say *all* the Jews, *all* the Protestants, or *all* the English, acted so and so ; but I should scarcely say *all* the French, when the whole mass of the community were of that description.—See the note on Acts xviii. 17, where the subject mentioned here by the learned archdeacon is particularly considered.

2

INTRODUCTION TO THE FIRST EPISTLE TO THE CORINTHIANS.

a *young man*, younger probably than those who were usually employed in the Christian mission; and that St. Paul, apprehending lest he should on that account be exposed to contempt, urges upon him the caution which is there inserted: " Let no man despise thy youth."

SECTION X.

§ Chap. xvi. 1 : " Now concerning the collection for the saints, as I have given order to the Churches of Galatia, even so do ye."

The Churches of Galatia and Phrygia were the last Churches which St. Paul had visited before the writing of this epistle. He was now at Ephesus, and he came thither immediately from visiting these Churches: " He went over all the country of Galatia and Phrygia in order, strengthening all the disciples. And it came to pass that Paul, having passed through the upper coasts, (viz. the above-named countries, called the upper coasts, as being the northern part of Asia Minor,) came to Ephesus;" Acts xviii. 23 ; xix. 1. These, therefore, probably, were the last Churches at which he left directions for their public conduct during his absence. Although two years intervened between his journey to Ephesus and his writing this epistle, yet it does not appear that during that time he visited any other Church. That he had not been silent when he was in Galatia upon this subject of contribution for the poor, is farther made out from a hint which he lets fall in his epistle to that Church: " Only they (viz. the other apostles) would that we should remember the poor; the same which I also was forward to do."

SECTION XI.

§ Chap. iv. 18 : " Now some are puffed up, as though I would not come to you."

Why should they suppose that he would not come? Turn to the first chapter of the *second epistle* to the Corinthians, and you will find that he had already *disappointed* them : " I was minded to come unto you before, that you might have a second benefit ; and to pass by you into Macedonia, and to come again out of Macedonia unto you, and of you to be brought on my way toward Judea. When I therefore was thus minded, did I use lightness ? Or the things that I purpose, do I purpose according to the flesh, that with me there should be yea, yea, and nay, nay ? But, as God is true, our word toward you was not yea and nay." It appears from this quotation that he had not only *intended*, but that he had *promised* them a visit before ; for, otherwise, why should he apologize for the change of his purpose, or express so much anxiety lest this change should be imputed to any culpable fickleness in his temper ; and lest he should thereby seem to them as one whose word was not in any sort to be depended upon ? Besides which, the terms made use of plainly refer to a promise : " Our *word toward you* was not yea and nay." St. Paul, therefore, had signified an intention which he had not been able to execute ; and this seeming breach of his word, and the delay of his visit, had, with some who were evil affected towards him, given birth to a suggestion that he would come no more to Corinth.

SECTION XII.

§ Chap. v. 7, 8 : " For even Christ, our passover, is sacrificed for us : therefore let us keep the feast, not with old leaven, neither with the leaven of malice and wickedness, but with the unleavened bread of sincerity and truth."

Dr. Benson tells us, that from this passage, compared with chapter xvi. 8, it has been conjectured that this epistle was written about the time of the Jewish passover ; and to me the conjecture appears to be very well founded. The passage to which Dr. Benson refers us is this: " I will tarry at Ephesus until Pentecost." With this passage he ought to have joined another in the same context : " And it may be that I will abide, yea, and winter with you ;" for, from the two passages laid together, it follows that the epistle was written before Pentecost, yet after winter ; which necessarily determines the date to the part of the year within which the passover falls. It was written before Pentecost, because he says, " I will tarry at Ephesus until Pentecost." It was written after winter, because he tells them, " It may be that I may abide, yea, and winter with you." The winter which the apostle purposed to pass at Corinth was undoubtedly the winter next ensuing to the date of the epistle ; yet it was a winter subsequent to the ensuing Pentecost, because he did not intend to set forwards upon his journey till after that feast. The words, " Let us keep the feast, not with old leaven, neither with the leaven of malice and wickedness, but with the unleavened bread of sincerity and truth," look very like words suggested by the season ; at least they have, upon that supposition, a force and significancy which do not belong to them upon any other ; and it is not a little remarkable that the hints casually dropped in the epistle concerning particular parts of the year should coincide with this supposition.

London, Oct. 1, 1814.

2

PREFACE TO THE FIRST EPISTLE

TO THE

CORINTHIANS.

CORINTH, to which this and the following epistle were sent, was one of the most celebrated cities of Greece. It was situated on a gulf of the same name, and was the capital of the Peloponnesus or Achaia, and was united to the continent by an isthmus or neck of land that had the port of *Lecheum* on the *west* and that of *Cenchrea* on the *east*, the former in the gulf of Lepanto, the latter in the gulf of Egina, by which it commanded the navigation and commerce both of the *Ionian* and *Ægean* seas, consequently of Italy on the one hand and of all the Greek islands on the other : in a word, it embraced the commerce of the whole *Mediterranean* Sea, from the *straits* of *Gibraltar* on the *west* to the port of *Alexandria* on the *east*, with the coasts of *Egypt, Palestine, Syria,* and *Asia Minor*. It is supposed, by some, to have been founded by Sisyphus, the son of Eolus, and grandfather of Ulysses, about the year of the world 2490 or 2500, and before the Christian era 1504 years. Others report that it had both its origin and name from *Corinthus,* the son of Pelops. It was at first but a very inconsiderable town ; but at last, through its extensive commerce, became the most opulent city of Greece, and the capital of a powerful state. It was destroyed by the Romans under Mummius, about 146 years before Christ, but was afterwards rebuilt by Julius Cæsar.

Corinth exceeded all the cities of the world, for the splendour and magnificence of its public buildings, such as temples, palaces, theatres, porticos, cenotaphs, baths, and other edifices ; all enriched with a beautiful kind of columns, capitals, and bases, from which the Corinthian order in architecture took its rise. Corinth is also celebrated for its statues ; those, especially, of Venus, the Sun, Neptune and Amphitrite, Diana, Apollo, Jupiter, Minerva, &c. The temple of Venus was not only very splendid, but also very rich, and maintained, according to Strabo, not less than 1000 courtesans, who were the means of bringing an immense concourse of strangers to the place. Thus riches produced luxury, and luxury a total corruption of manners ; though arts, sciences, and literature continued to flourish long in it, and a measure of the martial spirit of its ancient inhabitants was kept alive in it by means of those public games which, being celebrated on the isthmus which connects the Peloponnesus to the main land, were called the *Isthmian* games, and were exhibited once every *five* years. The exercises in these games were, *leaping, running,* throwing the *quoit* or *dart, boxing,* and *wrestling.* It appears that, besides these, there were contentions for *poetry* and *music ;* and the conquerors in any of these exercises were ordinarily crowned either with *pine leaves* or with *parsley.* It is well known that the apostle alludes to these games in different parts of his epistles, which shall all be particularly noticed as they occur.

Corinth, like all other opulent and well-situated places, has often been a subject of contention between rival states, has frequently changed masters, and undergone all forms of government. The Venetians held it till 1715, when the Turks took it from them ; under whose dominion it has till lately remained. Under this deteriorating government it was greatly reduced, its whole population amounting only to between 13 and 14,000 souls. It has now got into the hands of the Greeks, its natural owners. It lies about 46 miles to the east of Athens, and 342 south-west of Constantinople. A few vestiges of its ancient splendour still remain, which are objects of curiosity and gratification to all intelligent travellers.

As we have seen that Corinth was well situated for *trade,* and consequently very *rich,* it is no wonder that, in its heathen state, it was exceedingly corrupt and profligate. Notwithstanding this, every part of the Grecian learning was highly cultivated here ; so that, before its destruction by the Romans, Cicero (Pro lege Manl. cap. v.) scrupled not to call it *totius Græciæ lumen*—the eye of all Greece. Yet the inhabitants of it were as *lascivious* as they were *learned.* Public prostitution formed a considerable part of their religion ; and they were accustomed in their public prayers, to request the gods to multiply their prostitutes ! and in order to express their gratitude to their deities for the favours they received, they bound themselves, by *vows,* to increase the number of such women ; for commerce with them was neither esteemed sinful nor disgraceful. *Lais,* so famous in history, was a Corinthian prostitute, and whose price was not less than 10,000 drachmas. Demosthenes, from whom this price was required by her for one night's lodging, said, "I will not buy repentance at so dear a rate." So notorious was this city for such conduct, that the verb κορινθιαζεσθαι, to

2

Corinthize, signified to act the prostitute ; and Κορινθια κόρη, *a Corinthian damsel*, meant a harlot or common woman.   I mention these things the more particularly because they account for several things mentioned by the apostle in his letters to this city, and things which, without this knowledge of their previous Gentile state and customs, we could not comprehend.   It is true, as the apostle states, that they carried these things to an extent that was not practised in any other Gentile country.   And yet, even in Corinth—the Gospel of Jesus Christ prevailing over universal corruption—there was founded a Christian Church!

Analysis of the First Epistle to the Corinthians.

This epistle, as to its subject matter, has been variously divided: into *three* parts by some; into *four, seven, eleven*, &c., parts, by others.   Most of these divisions are merely artificial, and were never intended by the apostle.   The following seven particulars comprise the whole :—

I.—The *Introduction*, chap. i. 1–9.

II.—Exhortations relative to their *dissensions*, chap. i. 9 to chap. iv., inclusive.

III.—What concerns the *person who had married his step-mother*, commonly called the *incestuous person*, chap. v., vi., and vii.

IV.—The question concerning the lawfulness of *eating things* which had been *offered to idols*, chap. viii., ix., and x., inclusive.

V.—Various *ecclesiastical regulations*, chap. xi.–xiv., inclusive.

VI.—The important question concerning the *resurrection of the dead*, chap. xv.

VII.—*Miscellaneous* matters; containing exhortations, salutations, commendations, &c., &c., chap. xvi.

THE FIRST
EPISTLE OF PAUL THE APOSTLE
TO THE
CORINTHIANS.

Chronological Notes relative to this Epistle.

Year of the Constantinopolitan era of the world, as used by the emperors of the east in their diplomata, &c., and thence also called the " civil era of the Greeks," 5564.—Year of the Alexandrian era of the world, or Greek ecclesiastical epocha, 5558.—Year of the Antiochian era of the world, 5548.—Year of the Eusebian epocha of the creation, or that used in the Chronicon of Eusebius, and the Roman Martyrology, 4284.—Year of the Julian period, 4764.—Year of the Usherian era of the world, or that used in the English Bibles, 4060.—Year of the minor Jewish era of the world, 3816.—Year of the greater Rabbinical era of the world, 4415.—Year since the Deluge, according to Archbishop Usher and the English Bible, 2404. —Year of the Cali Yuga, or Indian era of the Deluge, 3158.—Year of the Iphitus, or since the first commencement of the Olympic games, 996.—Year of the two hundred and eighth Olympiad, 4.—Year from the building of Rome, according to Fabius Pictor, who flourished in the time of the first Punic war, and who is styled by Dionysius of Halicarnassus an accurate writer, 803. (This epoch is used by Diodorus Siculus.) —Year from the building of Rome, according to Polybius, 807.—Year from the building of Rome, according to Cato and the Fasti Consulares ; and adopted by Solinus, Eusebius, Dionysius of Halicarnassus, &c., 808.—Year from the building of Rome according to Varro, which was that adopted by the Roman emperors in their proclamations, by Plutarch, Tacitus, Dio Cassius, Gellius, Censorinus, Onuphrius, Baronius, and by most modern chronologers, 809. N. B. Livy, Cicero, Pliny, and Velleius Paterculus, fluctuate between the Varronian and Catonian computations.—Year of the epocha of Nabonassar, king of Babylon, or that used by Hipparchus, by Ptolemy in his astronomical observations, by Censorinus and others, 803. (The years of this era constantly contained 365 days, so that 1460 Julian were equal to 1461 Nabonassarean years. This epoch began on Feb. 26th, B. C. 747 ; and consequently, the commencement of the 803d year of the era of Nabonassar corresponded to the IVth of the Ides of August, A. D. 55.)—Year of the era of the Seleucidæ, or since Seleucus, one of the generals of Alexander's army, took Babylon, and ascended the Asiatic throne ; sometimes called the Grecian era, and the era of Principalities, in reference to the division of Alexander's empire, 368.—Year of the Cæsarean era of Antioch, 104.—Year of the Julian era, or since the calendar of Numa Pompilius was reformed by Julius Cæsar, 101.—Year of the Spanish era, or since the second division of the Roman provinces among the Triumviri, 94. (This epoch continued in use among the Spaniards till A. D. 1383, and among the Portuguese till about A. D. 1422.)—Year since the defeat of Pompey, by Julius Cæsar, at Pharsalia in Thessaly, called by Catrou and Rouillé, the commencement of the Roman empire, 104.—Year of the Actiac, or Actian era, or proper epocha of the Roman empire, commencing with the defeat of Antony by Augustus at Actium, 86.—Year from the birth of Jesus Christ, 60.—Year of the vulgar era of Christ's nativity, 56.—Year of the Dionysian period, or Easter Cycle, 57.—Common Golden Number, or year of the Grecian or Metonic Cycle of 19 years, 19, or the seventh Embolismic.—Jewish Golden Number, or year of the Rabbinical Cycle of 19 years, 16, or the second after the fifth Embolismic.—Year of the Solar Cycle, 9.—Dominical Letters, it being Bissextile or Leap-year, DC ; D standing till the 24th of February, or the sixth of the Calends of March, (the two following days after Feb. 23rd, or the seventh of the Calends of March, being named the sixth of the same month,) and the other letter for the remainder of the year.—Jewish passover, (15th of Nisan,) Saturday, April 17th, or the XVth of the Calends of May.—Number of Direction, or number of days on which Easter Sunday happens after the 21st of March, 28.—Mean time of the Paschal Full Moon at Corinth, (its longitude being twenty-three degrees to the east of London,) according to Ferguson's Tables, April 19th, or the XIIIth of the Calends of May, at fifteen minutes and fifty-eight seconds past eleven at night. (The reason of the discrepance of the fifteenth of Nisan, with the day of the mean Paschal Full Moon arises from the inaccuracy of the Metonic Cycle, which reckoned 235 mean lunations to be precisely equal to nineteen solar years, these lunations being actually performed in one hour and a half less time. The correspondence of the Passover with the mean Full Moon, according to the Julian account, was in A. D. 325.)—True time of the Paschal Full Moon at Corinth, according to Ferguson's Tables, the XIIth of the Calends of May, (April 20th,) at fifty-seven minutes and forty-one seconds past five in the morning.—Easter Sunday, April 18th, or the XIVth of the Calends of May.—Epact, or moon's age on the twenty-second of March, or the XIth of the Calends of April, 18.—Year of the reign of Nero Cæsar, the Roman emperor, and fifth Cæsar, 3.—Year of Claudius Felix, the Jewish Governor, 4.—Year of the reign of Vologesus, king of the Parthians, of the family of the Arsacidæ, 7.—Year of Caius Numidius Quadratus, governor of Syria, 6.—Year of Ishmael, high priest of the Jews, 2.—Year of the reign of Corbred I., king of the Scots, brother to the celebrated Caractacus, who was carried prisoner to Rome, but afterwards released by the emperor, 2.—According to Struyk's catalogue of eclipses, which he collected from the Chinese chronology, the sun was eclipsed at Canton in China, on the 25th of December of this year, or on the VIIIth of the Calends of January, A. D. 57. The middle of the eclipse was at twenty-eight minutes past twelve at noon; the quantity eclipsed at this time being nine digits and twenty minutes. The day of this eclipse was the 19th of Tybi, in the 804th year of the Nabonassarean era, and on the 24th of Cisleu, of the minor Rabbinical or Jewish era of the world, 3817, or 4416 of their greater era.—Roman Consuls, Q. Volusius Saturninus, and P. Cornelius Scipio.

CHAPTER I.

The salutation of Paul and Sosthenes, 1, 2. The apostolical benediction, 3. Thanksgiving for the prosperity of the Church at Corinth, 4. In what that prosperity consisted, 5–9. The apostle reproves their dissensions, and vindicates himself from being any cause of them, 10–17. States the simple means which God uses to convert sinners and confound the wisdom of the wise, &c., 18–21. Why the Jews and Greeks did not believe, 22. The matter of the apostle's preaching, and the reasons why that preaching was effectual to the salvation of men, 23–29. All should glory in God, because all blessings are dispensed by Him through Christ Jesus, 30, 31.

Written a little before the passover of A. D. 56.

PAUL, [a] called *to be* an apostle of Jesus Christ [b] through the will of God, and [c] Sosthenes our brother,

2 Unto the Church of God which is at Corinth, [d] to them that [e] are sanctified in Christ Jesus, [f] called *to be* saints, with all that in every place [g] call upon the name of Jesus Christ [h] our Lord, [i] both theirs and ours :

Written a little before the passover of A. D. 56.

3 [k] Grace *be* unto you, and peace, from God our Father, and *from* the Lord Jesus Christ.

---

[a] Rom. i. 1.——[b] 2 Cor. i. 1; Eph. i. 1; Col. i. 1.——[c] Acts xviii. 17. [d] Jude 1.——[e] John xvii. 19; Acts xv. 9.——[f] Rom. i. 7; 2 Tim. i. 9.

[g] Acts ix. 14, 21; xxii. 16; 2 Tim. ii. 22.——[h] Ch. viii. 6.——[i] Rom. iii. 22; x. 12.——[k] Rom. i. 7; 2 Cor. i. 2; Eph. i. 2; 1 Pet. i. 2.

NOTES ON CHAP. I.

Verse 1. *Paul, called* to be *an apostle*] Bishop Pearce contends that a *comma* should be placed after κλητος, *called*, which should not be joined to αποστολος, *apostle:* the first signifies being *called to*, the other *sent from*. He reads it, therefore, *Paul the called; the apostle of Jesus Christ.* The word κλητος, *called*, may be here used, as in some other places, for *constituted*. For this, and the meaning of the word *apostle*, see the note on Rom. i. 1.

As the apostle had many irregularities to reprehend in the Corinthian Church, it was necessary that he should be explicit in stating his *authority*. He was *called*—invited to the *Gospel feast*; had partaken of it, and, by the grace he received, was qualified to proclaim salvation to others : Jesus Christ therefore made him an *apostle*, that is, gave him a Divine commission to preach the Gospel to the Gentiles.

Through the will of God] By a particular appointment from God alone; for, being an *extraordinary* messenger, he derived no part of his authority from man.

Sosthenes our brother] Probably the same person mentioned Acts xviii. 17, where see the note.

Verse 2. *The Church of God which is at Corinth*] This Church was planted by the apostle himself about A. D. 52, as we learn from Acts xviii. 1, &c., where see the notes.

Sanctified in Christ Jesus] Ἡγιασμενοις, *Separated* from the corruptions of their place and age.

Called to be *saints*] Κλητοις ἁγιοις, *Constituted saints*, or *invited* to become such ; this was the design of the Gospel, for Jesus Christ came to save men from their sins.

With all that in every place, &c.] All who profess Christianity, both in *Corinth*, *Ephesus*, and other parts of *Greece* or *Asia Minor;* and by this we see that the apostle intended that this epistle should be a general property of the universal Church of Christ ; though there are several matters in it that are suited to the state of the Corinthians only.

Both theirs and ours] That is, Jesus Christ is the *common Lord* and Saviour of *all*. He is the *exclusive* property of no one Church, or people, or nation. *Calling on* or *invoking* the name of the Lord Jesus, was the proper distinguishing mark of a *Christian*. In those times of apostolic light and purity no man attempted to invoke God but in the name of Jesus Christ ; this is what genuine Christians still mean when they ask any thing from God *for Christ's* SAKE.

Verse 3. *Grace be unto you*] For a full explanation of all these terms, see the notes on Rom. i. 7

     2

A. M. 4060.
A. D. 56.
A. U. C. 809.
Anno Imp.
Neronis Cæs. 3.

4 [1] I thank my God always on your behalf, for the grace of God which is given you by Jesus Christ;

5 That in every thing ye are enriched by him, [m] in all utterance, and *in* all knowledge;

6 Even as [n] the testimony of Christ was confirmed in you:

7 So that ye come behind in no gift; [o] waiting for the [p] coming of our Lord Jesus Christ:

8 [q] Who shall also confirm you unto the end, [r] *that ye may be* blameless in the day of our Lord Jesus Christ.

9 [s] God *is* faithful, by whom ye were called unto [t] the fellowship of his Son Jesus Christ our Lord.

10 Now I beseech you, brethren, by the name of our Lord Jesus Christ, [u] that ye all speak the same thing, and *that* there be no

A. M. 4060.
A. D. 56.
A. U. C. 809.
Anno Imp.
Neronis Cæs. 3.

---

[1] Rom. i. 8.——[m] Chap. xii. 8; 2 Cor. viii. 7.——[n] Chap. ii. 1; 2 Tim. i. 8; Rev. i. 2.——[o] Phil. iii. 20; Titus ii. 13; 2 Peter iii. 12.——[p] Gr. *revelation;* Col. iii. 4.——[q] 1 Thess. iii. 13. [r] Col. i. 22; 1 Thess. v. 23.

[s] Isaiah xlix. 7; chap. x. 13; 1 Thess. v. 24; 2 Thess. iii. 3; Hebrews x. 23.——[t] John xv. 4; xvii. 21; 1 John i. 3; iv. 13. [u] Rom. xii. 16; xv. 5; 2 Cor. xiii. 11; Philemon ii. 2; iii. 16; 1 Pet. iii. 8.

Verse 4. *For the grace—which is given you*] Not only their calling to be saints, and to be sanctified in Christ Jesus; but for the various spiritual gifts which they had received, as specified in the succeeding verses.

Verse 5. *Ye are enriched—ye abound—in all utterance*] Εν παντι λογῳ, *In all doctrine;* for so the word should certainly be translated and understood. All the truths of God relative to their salvation had been explicitly declared to them; and they had *all knowledge;* so that they perfectly *comprehended* the doctrines which they had heard.

Verse 6. *As the testimony of Christ, &c.*] The testimony of Christ is the *Gospel* which the apostle had preached, and which had been *confirmed* by various gifts of the Holy Spirit, and miracles wrought by the apostle.

Verse 7. *So that ye come behind in no gift*] Every gift and grace of God's Spirit was possessed by the members of that Church, some having their gifts after this manner, others after that.

Waiting for the coming of our Lord] It is difficult to say whether the apostle means the *final judgment,* or our Lord's *coming to destroy Jerusalem,* and make an end of the Jewish polity.—See 1 Thess. iii. 13. As he does not explain himself particularly, he must refer to a subject with which they were well acquainted. As the Jews in general continued to contradict and blaspheme, it is no wonder if the apostle should be directed to point out to the believing Gentiles that the judgments of God were speedily to fall upon this rebellious people, and scatter them over the face of the earth; which shortly afterwards took place.

Verse 8. *Who shall—confirm you*] As the testimony of Christ was *confirmed* among you, so, in conscientiously believing and obeying, God will *confirm* you through that testimony.—See ver. 6.

In the day of our Lord Jesus] In the day that he comes to judge the world, according to some; but, in the day in which he comes to destroy the Jewish polity, according to others. While God destroys them who are disobedient, he can save you who believe.

Verse 9. *God is faithful*] The *faithfulness of God* is a favourite expression among the ancient Jews; and by it they properly understand the integrity of God in preserving whatever is entrusted to him. And they suppose that in this sense the *fidelity of man* may illustrate the *fidelity of God,* in reference to which they

tell the two following stories. " Rabbi *Phineas,* the son of *Jair,* dwelt in a certain city, whither some men came who had two measures of barley, which they desired him to preserve for them. They afterwards forgot their barley and went away. Rabbi *Phineas* each year sowed the barley, reaped, thrashed, and laid it up in his granary. When seven years had elapsed the men returned, and desired to have the barley with which they had entrusted him. Rabbi *Phineas* recollected them, and said, ' Come and take your treasure,' i. e. the barley they had left, with all that it had produced for seven years. Thus, from the faithfulness of man ye may know the faithfulness of God."

" Rabbi *Simeon,* the son of *Shetach,* bought an ass from some Edomites, at whose neck his disciples saw a *diamond* hanging; they said unto him, Rabbi, *the blessing of the Lord maketh rich,* Prov. x. 22. But he answered: The *ass* I have bought, but the *diamond* I have not bought; therefore he returned the diamond to the Edomites. Thus, from the fidelity of man ye may know the fidelity of God." This was an instance of rare honesty, not to be paralleled among the *Jews* of the present day, and probably among few *Gentiles.* Whatever is committed to the keeping of God he will most carefully preserve; for he is *faithful.*

Unto the fellowship, &c.] Εις κοινωνιαν, Into the communion or participation of Christ, in the graces of his Spirit and the glories of his future kingdom. God will continue to uphold and save you, if you entrust your bodies and souls to him. But can it be said that God will keep what is either *not* entrusted to him; or, after being entrusted, is *taken away?*

Verse 10. *Now I beseech you, brethren*] The apostle having finished his *introduction* comes to his *second* point, exhorting them to abstain from dissensions, that they might be of the same heart and mind, striving together for the hope of the Gospel.

By the name of our Lord Jesus] By his *authority,* and in his place; and on account of your infinite obligations to his mercy in calling you into such a state of salvation.

That ye all speak the same thing] If they did not agree exactly in *opinion* on every subject, they might, notwithstanding, agree in the words which they used to express their religious faith. The members of the Church of God should labour to be of the *same mind,* and to speak the *same thing,* in order to prevent divi-

2

A. M. 4060.
A. D. 56.
A. U. C.
809.
Anno Imp.
Neronis Cæs. 3.

ᵛ divisions among you; but *that* ye be perfectly joined together in the same mind, and in the same judgment.

11 For it hath been declared unto me of you, my brethren, by them *which are of the house* of Chloe, that there are contentions among you.

12 Now this I say, ʷ that every one of you saith, I am of Paul; and I of ˣ Apollos; and I of ʸ Cephas; and I of Christ.

13 ᶻ Is Christ divided? was Paul crucified for you? or were ye baptized in the name of Paul?

14 I thank God that I baptized none of you, but ᵃ Crispus and ᵇ Gaius;

A. M. 4060.
A. D. 56.
A. U. C.
809.
Anno Imp.
Neronis Cæs. 3.

ᵛ Gr. *schisms*, chap. xi. 18.——ʷ Chap. iii. 4.——ˣ Acts xviii. 24; xix. 1; chap. xvi. 12.

ʸ John i. 42.——ᶻ 2 Cor. xi. 4; Eph. iv. 5.——ᵃ Acts xviii. 8 ᵇ Rom. xvi. 23.

---

sions, which always hinder the work of God. On every essential doctrine of the Gospel all genuine Christians agree: why then need religious communion be interrupted? This *general* agreement is all that the apostle can have in view; for it cannot be expected that any number of men should in *every respect* perfectly coincide in their views of all the minor points, on which an exact conformity in sentiment is impossible to minds so variously constituted as those of the human race. *Angels* may thus agree, who see nothing through an *imperfect* or *false* medium; but to man this is impossible. Therefore men should bear with each other, and not be so ready to imagine that none have the truth of God but they and their party.

Verse 11. *By them* which are of the house *of Chloe*] This was doubtless some very religious matron at Corinth, whose family were converted to the Lord; some of whom were probably sent to the apostle to inform him of the dissensions which then prevailed in the Church at that place. *Stephanas, Fortunatus,* and *Achaicus*, mentioned chap. xvi. 17, were probably the sons of this *Chloe*.

Contentions] Εριδες, *Altercations;* produced by the σχισματα, *divisions*, mentioned above. When once they had *divided*, they must necessarily *have contended*, in order to support their respective parties.

Verse 12. *Every one of you saith*] It seems from this expression that the whole Church at Corinth was in a state of *dissension:* they were all *divided* into the following sects: 1. *Paulians*, or followers of St. Paul; 2. *Apollonians*, or followers of Apollos; 3. *Kephians*, or followers of Kephas; 4. *Christians*, or followers of Christ. See the introduction, sec. v.

The converts at Corinth were partly *Jews*, and partly *Greeks*. The *Gentile* part, as Dr. Lightfoot conjectures, might boast the names of *Paul* and *Apollos;* the *Jewish*, those of *Kephas* and *Christ*. But these again might be subdivided; some probably considered themselves disciples of *Paul*, he being the immediate instrument of their conversion, while others might prefer *Apollos* for his extraordinary eloquence.

If by *Kephas* the apostle *Peter* be meant, some of the *circumcision* who believed might prefer him to all the rest; and they might consider him more immediately sent to *them;* and therefore have him in higher esteem than they had *Paul*, who was the minister or apostle of the *uncircumcision:* and on this very account the converted Gentiles would prize him more highly than they did Peter.

Instead of *Christ*, Χριστου, some have conjectured that we should read Κρισπου, of *Crispus;* who is

mentioned ver. 14. And some think that Χριστου, *of Christ*, is an interpolation, as it is not likely that Christ in any sense of the word could be said to be the *head of a sect*, or *party*, in his own Church; as *all* those parties held that *Gospel*, of which himself was both the *author* and the *subject*. But it is very easy to conceive that, in a Church so divided, a party might be found, who, dividing Christ from his ministers, might be led to say, "We will have nothing to do with your *parties*, nor with your *party spirit;* we are the *disciples of Christ*, and will have nothing to do with *Paulians, Apollonians*, or *Kephians*, as contradistinguished from Christ." The reading Κρισπου for Χριστου is not acknowledged by any MS. or version.

Verse 13. *Is Christ divided?*] Can he be split into different sects and parties? Has he different and opposing systems? Or, is the Messiah to appear under different persons?

Was Paul crucified for you?] As the Gospel proclaims salvation through the *crucified* only, has Paul poured out his blood as an atonement for you? This is impossible, and therefore your being called by my name is absurd; for his disciples you should be, alone, who has bought you by his blood.

Were ye baptized in the name of Paul?] To be *baptized in*, or *into* the *name* of one, implied that the *baptized* was to be the *disciple* of him into whose name, religion, &c., he was baptized. As if he said: Did I ever attempt to set up a *new* religion, one founded on *my own authority*, and coming from myself? On the contrary, have I not preached Christ crucified for the sin of the world; and called upon all mankind, both Jews and Gentiles, to believe on Him?

Verse 14. *I thank God that I baptized none of you*] None of those who now live in Corinth, except *Crispus*, the ruler of the synagogue, Acts xviii. 8. *And Gaius*, the same person probably with whom Paul lodged, Rom. xvi. 23, where see the notes. Dr. Lightfoot observes: "If this be Gaius, or Caius, to whom the third epistle of John was written, which is very probable when the first verse of that epistle is compared with Rom. xvi. 23, then it will appear probable that John wrote his first epistle to the *Corinthians*. *I wrote*, says he, *unto the Church*—What Church? Certainly it must have been some *particular* Church which the apostle has in view, and the Church *where* Gaius himself resided. And if this be true, we may look for *Diotrephes* (3 John ver. 9) in the Corinthian Church; and the author of the *schism* of which the apostle complains. See the *Introduction*, sect. viii.

A. M. 4060.
A. D. 56.
A. U. C.
809.
Anno Imp. Nero-
nis Cæs. 3.

15 Lest any should say that I had baptized in mine own name.

16 And I baptized also the household of ᶜ Stephanas : besides, I know not whether I baptized any other.

17 For Christ sent me not to baptize, but

to preach the Gospel : ᵈ not with wisdom of ᵉ words, lest the cross of Christ should be made of none effect.

18 For the preaching of the cross is to ᶠ them that perish ᵍ foolishness ; but unto us

A. M. 4060.
A D. 56.
A. U. C.
809.
Anno Imp. Nero-
nis Cæs. 3.

ᶜ Ch. xvi. 15, 17.——ᵈ Ch. ii. 1, 4, 13 ; 2 Pet. i. 16.——ᵉ Or, *speech.*

ᶠ 2 Cor. ii. 15.——ᵍ Acts xvii. 18 ; chap. ii. 14.

Verse 15. *Lest any should say, &c.*] He was careful not to baptize, lest it should be supposed that he wished to make a party for himself ; because superficial observers might imagine that he baptized them *into his own name*—to be his *followers,* though he baptized them into the name of Christ only.

Instead of εβαπτισα, *I have baptized,* the Codex *Alexandrinus,* the Codex *Ephraim,* and several others, with the *Coptic, Sahidic,* later *Syriac* in the margin, *Armenian Vulgate,* some copies of the *Itala,* and several of the *fathers,* read εβαπτισθητε, *ye were baptized.* And if we read ινα, *so that,* instead of *lest,* the sentence will stand thus : *So that no one can say that ye were baptized into my name.* This appears to be the true reading, and for it Bp. Pearce offers several strong arguments.

Verse 16. *The household of Stephanas*] From chap. xvi. 15, we learn that the family of *Stephanas* were the *first converts* in Achaia, probably converted and baptized by the apostle himself. *Epenetus* is supposed to be one of this family. See the note on Rom. chap. xvi. 5.

I know not whether I baptized any other.] I do not recollect that there is any person now residing in *Corinth,* or *Achaia.* besides the above mentioned, whom I have baptized. It is strange that the *doubt* here expressed by the apostle should be construed so as to affect his *inspiration !* What, does the inspiration of prophet or apostle necessarily imply that he must understand the geography of the universe, and have an intuitive knowledge of all the inhabitants of the earth, and how *often,* and *where* they may have changed their residence ! Nor was that *inspiration* ever given so to work on a man's memory that he could not forget any of the *acts* which he had performed during life. Inspiration was given to the holy men of old that they might be able to write and proclaim the *mind of God* in the things which concern the *salvation* of men.

Verse 17. *For Christ sent me not to baptize*] Bp. Pearce translates thus : *For Christ sent me, not so much to baptize as to preach the Gospel :* and he supports his version thus—" The writers of the Old and New Testaments do, almost every where (agreeably to the Hebrew idiom) express a preference given to one thing beyond another by an *affirmation* of *that* which is *preferred,* and a *negation* of *that* which is *contrary* to it : and so it must be understood here, for if St. Paul was not sent *at all* to baptize, he baptized *without a commission ;* but if he was sent, not only to baptize but to preach *also,* or to preach *rather* than baptize, he did in fact discharge his duty aright." It appears sufficiently evident that *baptizing* was considered to be an *inferior* office ; and though every minister of Christ might administer it, yet apostles had

more *important* work. Preparing these adult heathens for baptism by the continual preaching of the word was of much greater consequence than baptizing them when thus prepared to receive and profit by it.

Not with wisdom of words] Ουκ εν σοφια λογου. In several places in the New Testament the term λογος is taken not only to express a *word,* a *speech,* a *saying,* &c., but *doctrine,* or the *matter of teaching* Here, and in 1 Thess. i. 5, and in several other places, it seems to signify *reason,* or that mode of *rhetorical argumentation* so highly prized among the Greeks. The apostle was sent not to pursue this mode of conduct, but simply to announce the truth ; to proclaim Christ crucified for the sin of the world ; and to do this in the *plainest* and *simplest* manner possible, lest the numerous conversions which followed might be attributed to the *power* of the apostle's *eloquence,* and not to the *demonstration* of the *Spirit of God.* It is worthy of remark that, in all the revivals of religion with which we are acquainted, God appears to have made very little use of human *eloquence,* even when possessed by pious men. His own nervous truths, announced by plain common sense, though in homely phrase, have been the general means of the conviction and conversion of sinners. Human *eloquence* and *learning* have often been successfully employed in defending the *outworks* of Christianity ; but *simplicity* and *truth* have preserved the *citadel.*

It is farther worthy of remark, that when God was about to promulgate his laws he chose *Moses* as the instrument, who appears to have laboured under some natural *impediment in his speech,* so that *Aaron* his brother was obliged to be his spokesman to Pharaoh ; and that, when God had purposed to publish the Gospel to the Gentile world—to Athens, Ephesus, Corinth, and Rome, he was pleased to use *Saul* of *Tarsus* as the principal instrument ; a man *whose bodily presence was weak, and his speech contemptible,* 2 Cor. x. 1, 10. And thus it was proved that *God sent him to preach, not with human eloquence, lest the cross of Christ should be made of none effect* but with the *demonstration and power of his own Spirit ;* and thus *the excellence of the power* appeared *to be of God, and not of man.*

Verse 18. *For the preaching of the cross*] Ὁ λογος γαρ ὁ του σταυρου, *The doctrine of the cross ;* or the *doctrine* that is *of* or *concerning the cross ;* that is, the doctrine that proclaims salvation to a lost world through the *crucifixion* of Christ.

Is to them that perish foolishness] There are, properly speaking, but two classes of men known where the Gospel is preached : απολλυμενοι, the *unbelievers* and *gainsayers,* who are *perishing ;* and σοζομενοι, the *obedient believers,* who are in a state of *salvation.* To those who *will* continue in the first state, the preaching

Vol. II.   (13)

A. M. 4060.
A. D. 56.
A. U. C.
809.
Anno Imp. Nero-
nis Cæs. 3.

[h] which are saved it is the [i] power of God.

19 For it is written, [k] I will destroy the wisdom of the wise, and will bring to nothing the understanding of the prudent.

20 [l] Where *is* the wise? where *is* the scribe?

where *is* the disputer of this world? [m] hath not God made foolish the wisdom of this world?

21 [n] For after that in the wisdom of God the world by wisdom knew not God, it pleased God by the foolishness of preaching to save them that believe.

A. M. 4060
A. D. 56.
A. U. C.
809.
Anno Imp. Nero-
nis Cæs. 3.

[h] Chap. xv. 2.——[i] Rom. i. 16; ver. 24.——[k] Job v. 12, 13; Isa. xxix. 14; Jer. viii. 9.——[l] Isa. xxxiii. 18.

[m] Job xii. 17, 20, 24; Isa. xliv. 25; Rom. 1. 22.——[n] Rom. 1. 20, 21, 28; see Matt. xi. 25; Luke x. 21.

---

of salvation through the merit of a crucified Saviour is *folly*. To those who believe this doctrine of Christ crucified is the power of God to their salvation; it is divinely efficacious to deliver them from all the power, guilt, and pollution of sin.

Verse 19. *For it is written*] The place referred to is Isa. xxix. 14.

I will destroy the wisdom of the wise] Των σοφων, Of *wise men*—of the *philosophers* who in their investigations seek nothing less than God, and whose highest discoveries amount to nothing in comparison of the grand truths relative to God, the invisible world, and the true end of man, which the Gospel has brought to light. Let me add, that the very discoveries which are really useful have been made by men who feared God, and conscientiously credited Divine revelation: witness *Newton, Boyle, Pascal*, and many others. But all the skeptics and deists, by their schemes of natural religion and morality, have not been able to save one soul! No sinner has ever been converted from the error of his ways by their preaching or writings.

Verse 20. *Where is the wise—the scribe—the disputer of this world?*] These words most manifestly refer to the Jews; as the places (Isa. xxix. 14; xxxiii. 18; and xliv. 25) to which he refers cannot be understood of any but the *Jews*.

The *wise man* σοφος, of the apostle, is the הכם *chakam* of the prophet, whose office it was to teach others.

The *scribe*, γραμματευς, of the apostle, is the ספר *sopher* of the prophet; this signifies any man of learning, as distinguished from the common people, especially any master of the traditions.

The *disputer*, συζητητης, answers to the דרש *derosh*, or דרשן *darshan*, the *propounder of questions;* the *seeker* of allegorical, mystical, and cabalistical senses from the Holy Scriptures. Now as all these are characters well known among the Jews, and as the words αιωνος τουτου, *of this world*, are a simple translation of עולם הזה *olam hazzeh*, which is repeatedly used to designate the Jewish republic, there is no doubt that the apostle has the Jews immediately in view. This wisdom of theirs induced them to seek out of the sacred oracles any sense but the true one; and they made the word of God of none effect by their traditions. After them, and precisely on their model, the *schoolmen* arose; and they rendered the doctrine of the Gospel of no effect by their *hypercritical questions*, and endless *distinctions* without *differences*. By the preaching of Christ crucified God made foolish the wisdom of the *Jewish wise men*; and, after that the pure religion of Christ had been corrupted by a Church that

was of this world, God rendered the wisdom and *disputing* of the schoolmen foolishness, by the revival of pure Christianity at the *Reformation*. The Jews themselves allow that nothing is *wise*, nothing *strong*, nothing *rich*, without God.

"Our rabbins teach that there were two *wise men* in this world; one was an Israelite, *Achitophel*, the other was a Gentile, *Balaam;* but both were miserable in this world."

"There were also two *strong men* in the world, one an Israelite, *Samson*, the other a Gentile, *Goliah;* but they were both miserable in this world."

"There were two *rich men* in the world; one an Israelite, *Korah*, the other a Gentile, *Haman;* but both these were miserable in this world. And why? Because their gifts came not from God." See *Schoettgen*.

In truth the world has derived very little, if any, moral good, either from the Jewish rabbins or the Gentile philosophers.

Verse 21. *For after that in the wisdom of God*] Dr. Lightfoot observes, "That σοφια του Θεου, *the wisdom of God*, is not to be understood of that wisdom which had God for its *author*, but that wisdom which had God for its *object*. There was, among the heathen, σοφια της φυσεως, *wisdom about natural things*, that is, *philosophy;* and σοφια του Θεου, *wisdom about God;* that is, *divinity*. But the world in its *divinity* could not, by *wisdom*, know God." The plain meaning of this verse is, that the wise men of the world, especially the Greek philosophers, who possessed every advantage that human nature could have, independently of a Divine revelation, and who had cultivated their minds to the uttermost, could never, by their learning, wisdom, and industry, find out God; nor had the most refined philosophers among them just and correct views of the Divine nature, nor of that in which human happiness consists. The work of LUCRETIUS, *De Natura Rerum*, and the work of CICERO, *De Natura Deorum*, are incontestable proofs of this. Even the writings of *Plato* and *Aristotle* have contributed little to remove the veil which clouded the understanding of men. No wisdom but that which came from God could ever penetrate and illuminate the human mind.

By the foolishness of preaching] By the preaching of Christ crucified, which the Gentiles termed μωρια, *foolishness*, in opposition to their own doctrines, which they termed σοφια, *wisdom*. It was not by the foolishness of preaching, literally, nor by the foolish preaching, that God saved the world; but by that Gospel which they called μωρια, *foolishness;* which was, in fact, the wisdom of God, and also the **power** of God to the salvation of them that believed.

A. M. 4060. A. D. 56. A. U. C. 809. Anno Imp. Neronis Cæs. 3.

22 For the [o] Jews require a
sign, and the Greeks seek after
wisdom :
23 But we preach Christ cru-
cified, [p] unto the Jews a stumbling block, and
unto the Greeks [q] foolishness ;
24 But unto them which are called, both
Jews and Greeks, Christ [r] the
power of God, and [s] the wisdom
of God.
25 Because the foolishness of
God is wiser than men ; and the weakness of
God is stronger than men.
26 For ye see your calling, brethren, how

A. M. 4060. A. D. 56. A. U. C. 809. Anno Imp. Neronis Cæs. 3.

[o] Matt. xii. 38 ; xvi. 1 ; Mark viii. 11 ; Luke xi. 16 ; John iv. 48.——[p] Isa. viii. 14 ; Matt xi. 6 ; xiii. 57 ; Luke ii. 34 ; John vi. 60, 66 ; Rom ix. 32 ; Gal. v. 11 ; 1 Peter ii. 8.——[q] Ver. 18 ; chap. ii. 14.——[r] Rom. i. 4, 16 ; ver. 18.——[s] Col. ii. 3.

Verse 22. *For the Jews require a sign*] Instead of *σημειον*, *a sign*, ABCDEFG, several others, both the *Syriac*, *Coptic*, *Vulgate*, and *Itala*, with many of the *fathers*, have *σημεια*, *signs;* which reading, as undoubtedly genuine, Griesbach has admitted into the text. There never was a people in the universe more difficult to be persuaded of the truth than the Jews : and had not their religion been incontestably proved by the most striking and indubitable miracles, they never would have received it. This slowness of heart to believe, added to their fear of being deceived, induced them to require *miracles* to attest every thing that professed to come from God. They were a wicked and adulterous generation, continually seeking signs, and never saying, It is enough. But the *sign* which seems particularly referred to here is the assumption of *secular power*, which they expected in the Messiah ; and because this sign did not appear in Christ, therefore they rejected him.

And the Greeks seek after wisdom.] Such wisdom, or *philosophy*, as they found in the writings of *Cicero*, *Seneca*, *Plato*, &c., which was called *philosophy*, and which came recommended to them in all the beauties and graces of the Latin and Greek languages.

Verse 23. *But we*] Apostles, differing widely from these Gentile philosophers—

Preach Christ crucified] Call on men, both Jews and Gentiles, to believe in Christ, as having purchased their salvation by shedding his blood for them.

Unto the Jews a stumbling block] Because Jesus came meek, lowly, and impoverished ; not seeking worldly glory, nor affecting worldly pomp ; whereas *they* expected the Messiah to come as a mighty prince and conqueror; because Christ did not come so, they were offended at him. Out of their own mouths we may condemn the gainsaying Jews. In *Sohar Chadash*, fol. 26, the following saying is attributed to Moses, relative to the brazen serpent : "Moses said, This serpent is a stumbling block to the world. The holy blessed God answered : Not at all ; it shall be for punishment to sinners, and life to upright men." This is a proper illustration of the apostle's words.

Unto the Greeks foolishness] Because they could not believe that proclaiming supreme happiness through a man that was crucified at Judea as a malefactor could ever comport with reason and common sense ; for both the *matter* and *manner* of the preaching were opposite to every notion they had formed of what was dignified and philosophic. In *Justin Martyr's* dialogue with *Trypho* the Jew we have these remarkable words, which serve to throw light on the above. "Your Jesus," says Trypho, "having fallen under the extreme curse of God, we cannot sufficiently admire how you can expect any good from God, who place your hopes *επ' ανθρωπον σταυρωθεντα*, upon a man that was CRUCIFIED." The same writer adds : "They count us mad, that after the eternal God, the Father of all things, we give the second place, *ανθρωπῳ σταυρωθεντι*, *to a man that was crucified.*" "Where is your *understanding*," said the Gentiles, "who worship for a god him who was crucified ?" Thus Christ crucified was to the Jews a stumbling block, and to the Greeks foolishness. See *Whitby* on this verse.

Verse 24. *But unto them which are called*] *Τοις κλητοις.* Those, both of Jews and Greeks, who were by the preaching of the Gospel *called* or *invited* to the *marriage feast*, and have accordingly believed in Christ Jesus ; they prove this doctrine to be divinely powerful, to enlighten and convert the soul, and to be a proof of God's infinite wisdom, which has found out such an effectual way to glorify both his justice and mercy, and save, to the uttermost, all that come to him through Christ Jesus. The *called*, or *invited*, *κλητοι*, is a title of genuine *Christians*, and is frequently used in the New Testament. *Ἁγιοι*, *saints*, is used in the same sense.

Verse 25. *The foolishness of God is wiser, &c.*] The meaning of these strong expressions is, that the things of God's appointment, which seem to men *foolishness*, are infinitely beyond the highest degree of human wisdom ; and those works of God, which appear to superficial observers weak and contemptible, surpass all the efforts of human power. The *means* which God has appointed for the salvation of men are so *wisely* imagined and so *energetically powerful*, that all who properly use them shall be infallibly brought to the *end*—final blessedness, which he has promised to them who *believe* and *obey*.

Verse 26. *Ye see your calling*] *Την κλησιν.* The *state* of grace and blessedness to which ye are *invited.* I think *βλεπετε την κλησιν*, &c., should be read in the imperative : *Take heed to*, or *consider your calling*, *brethren ; that* (*ὁτι*) *not many* of you *are wise after the flesh*, *not many mighty*, *not many noble : men* is not in the original, and Paul seems to allude to the Corinthian believers in particular. This seems to have been said in opposition to the high and worldly notions of the Jews, who assert that the Divine Spirit never rests upon any man, unless he be *wise*, *powerful*, and *rich.* Now this Divine Spirit did rest upon the Christians at Corinth, and yet these were, in the sense of the *world*, neither *wise*, *rich*, nor *noble.* We spoil, if

A. M. 4060.
A. D. 56.
A. U. C. 809.
Anno Imp. Neronis Cæs. 3.

that [t] not many wise *men* after the flesh, not many mighty, not many noble, *are called ;*

27 But [u] God hath chosen the foolish things of the world to confound the wise ; and God hath chosen the weak things of the world to confound the things which are mighty ;

28 And base things of the world, and things which are despised, hath God chosen, *yea,*

and [v] things which are not, [w] to bring to nought things that are :

29 [x] That no flesh should glory in his presence.

30 But of him are ye in Christ Jesus, who of God is made unto us [y] wisdom, and [z] righteousness, and [a] sanctification, and [b] redemption.

31 That, according as it is written, [c] He that glorieth, let him glory in the Lord.

A. M. 4060.
A. D. 56.
A. U. C. 809.
Anno Imp. Nero nis Cæs. 3.

---

[t] John vii. 48.——[u] Matt. xi. 25 ; James ii. 5 ; see Psa. viii. 2.
[v] Rom. iv. 17.——[w] Chap. ii. 6.——[x] Rom. iii. 27 ; Eph. ii. 9.
[y] Ver. 24.

[z] Jer. xxiii. 5, 6 ; Rom. iv. 25 ; 2 Cor. v. 21 ; Phil. iii. 9.
[a] John xvii. 19.——[b] Eph. i. 7.——[c] Jer. ix. 23, 24 ; 2 Cor. x. 17.

---

not corrupt the apostle's meaning, by adding *are called,* as if God did not send his Gospel to the *wise,* the *powerful,* and the *noble,* or did not *will* their salvation. The truth is, the Gospel has an equal call to all classes of men ; but the *wise,* the *mighty,* and the *noble,* are too busy, or too sensual, to pay any attention to an invitation so *spiritual* and so *Divine ;* and therefore there are few of these in the Church of Christ in general.

Verse 27. *But God hath chosen the foolish things*] God has chosen by means of men who are esteemed *rude* and *illiterate* to confound the greatest of the Greek *philosophers,* and overturn their *systems ;* and, by means of men *weak,* without secular *power* or *authority,* to confound the *scribes* and *Pharisees,* and in spite of the exertions of the Jewish *sanhedrin,* to spread the doctrine of Christ crucified all over the land of Judea, and by such instruments as these to convert thousands of souls to the faith of the Gospel, who are ready to lay down their lives for the truth. The Jews have proverbs that express the same sense as these words of the apostle. In *Shemoth Rabba,* sec. 17, fol. 117, it is said : " There are certain matters which appear *little* to men, yet by them God points out *important precepts.* Thus hyssop in the sight of man is *worth nothing,* but in the sight of God its *power* is great ; sometimes he equals it to the *cedar,* particularly in the ordinance concerning the *lepers,* and in the burning of the *red heifer.* Thus God commanded them in Egypt, Exod. xii. 22 : *And ye shall take a bunch of hyssop,* &c. And concerning Solomon it is said, 1 Kings iv. 33 : *And he discoursed of trees, from the cedar on Lebanon to the hyssop that grows out of the wall.* Whence we may learn that *great* and *small things* are *equal* in the eyes of the Lord, and that even by *small things* He can work *great miracles.*"

Verse 28. *And base things—and things which are despised*] It is very likely that the apostle refers here to the *Gentiles* and to the Gentile converts, who were considered base and despicable in the eyes of the Jews, who counted them no better than *dogs,* and who are repeatedly called *the things that are not.* By these very people, converted to Christianity, God has *brought to nought* all the Jewish pretensions ; and by means of the Gentiles themselves, he has annihilated the whole Jewish polity ; so that even Jerusalem itself was, soon after this, trodden under foot of the Gentiles.

Verse 29. *That no flesh should glory*] God does his mighty works in such a way as proves that though he may condescend to employ *men* as instruments, yet they have no part either in the *contrivance* or *energy* by which such works are performed.

Verse 30. *But of him are ye in Christ Jesus*] Even the good which you possess is granted by God, for it is by and through him that Christ Jesus comes, and all the blessings of the Gospel dispensation.

Who of God is made unto us wisdom] As being the author of that *evangelical wisdom* which far excels the wisdom of the philosopher and the scribe, and even that *legal constitution* which is called the *wisdom* of the Jews, Deut. iv. 6.

And righteousness] Δικαιοσυνη, *Justification,* as procuring for us that remission of sins which the law could not give, Gal. ii. 21 ; iii. 21.

And sanctification] As procuring for and working in us, not. only an external and relative *holiness,* as was that of the Jews, but ὁσιοτητα της αληθειας, *true* and eternal *holiness,* Eph. iv. 24, wrought in us by the Holy Spirit.

And redemption] He is the author of *redemption,* not from the Egyptian *bondage,* or Babylonish *captivity,* but from the *servitude of Satan,* the *dominion of sin* and *death,* and from the *bondage of corruption into the glorious liberty of the sons of God,* or the *redemption of the body,* Rom. viii. 21, 23. See *Whitby.*

The object of the apostle is to show that man of himself possesses no good, that whatever he has comes from God, and from God only through Christ. For the different acceptations of the word *righteousness* the reader may consult the note on Rom. i. 17, where the subject is considered in every point of view.

Verse 31. *According as it is written*] In Jer. ix. 23, 24 : *Thus saith the Lord, Let not the wise* man *glory in his wisdom, neither let the mighty* man *glory in his might ; let not the rich* man *glory in his riches ; but let him that glorieth glory in this—That he understandeth and knoweth me, that I am the Lord, which exercise loving-kindness, judgment, and righteousness, in the earth.* So then, as all good is of and from God, let him that has either *wisdom, strength, riches, pardon, holiness,* or any other blessing, whether *temporal* or *spiritual,* acknowledge that he has nothing but what he has received ; and that, as he has cause of *glorying* (*boasting* or *exultation*) in being made a partaker of

2

these benefits and mercies of his Creator and Redeemer, let him *boast* in God alone, by whom, through Christ Jesus, he has received the whole.

1. THIS is an admirable chapter, and drawn up with great skill and address. The *divided* state of the Corinthian Church we have already noticed, and it appears that in these factions the apostle's authority had been set at nought by some, and questioned by many. St. Paul begins his letter with showing his authority; he had it immediately through Christ Jesus himself, by the *will of God.* And indeed the *success* of his preaching was a sufficient proof of the Divinity of his call. Had not God been with him he never could have successfully opposed the whole system of the national religion of the Corinthians, supported as it was by the prejudice of the people, the authority of the laws, and the eloquence and learning of their most eminent philosophers. It was necessary, therefore, that he should call the attention of this people to the Divine origin of his mission, that they might acknowledge that the excellency of the power was of God, and not of man.

2. It was necessary also that he should conciliate their esteem, and therefore speak as favourably concerning them as truth would allow; hence he shows them that they were a *Church of God, sanctified in Christ Jesus,* and *called to be saints;* that they abounded and even *excelled* in many extraordinary *gifts* and graces; and that they were not *inferior* to any Church of God in any gift. And he shows them that they received all these through God's *confirmation* of that *testimony* which he had delivered among them, ver. 4–7.

3. When he had thus prepared their minds to receive and profit by his admonitions he proceeds to their schisms, which he mentions and reprehends in the most delicate manner, so that the most obstinate and prejudiced could take no offence.

4. Having gained this point, he gently leads them to consider that, as God is the fountain of all good, so their good had all come from him; and that none of them should *rest* in the *gift,* but in the *giver;* nor should they consider themselves as of particular consequence on account of possessing such gifts, because all earthly good is transitory, and those who trust in power, wisdom, or wealth, are confounded and brought to nought; and that they alone are *safe* who receive every thing as from the hand of God, and, in the strength of his gifts, *glorify* him who is the *donor* of all good. He who can read this chapter without getting much profit has very little spirituality in his soul, and must be utterly unacquainted with the work of God in the heart.

CHAPTER II.

The apostle makes an apology for his manner of preaching, 1. And gives the reason why he adopted that manner, 2–5. He shows that this preaching, notwithstanding it was not with excellence of human speech or wisdom, yet was the mysterious wisdom of God, which the princes of this world did not know, and which the Spirit of God alone could reveal, 6–10. It is the Spirit of God only that can reveal the things of God, 11. The apostles of Christ know the things of God by the Spirit of God, and teach them, not in the words of man's wisdom, but in the words of that Spirit, 12, 13. The natural man cannot discern the things of the Spirit, 14. But the spiritual man can discern and teach them, because he has the mind of Christ, 15, 16.

A. M. 4060.
A. D. 56.
A. U. C.
809.
Anno Imp. Neronis Cæs. 3.

AND I, brethren, when I came to you, [a] came not with excellency of speech or of wisdom, declaring unto you [b] the testimony of God:

2 For I determined not to know any thing among you, [c] save Jesus Christ, and him crucified.

3 And [d] I was with you [e] in weakness, and in fear, and in much trembling.

A. M. 4060.
A. D. 56.
A. U. C.
809.
Anno Imp. Neronis Cæs. 3.

---

[a] Chap. i. 17; ver. 4, 13; 2 Cor. x. 10; xi. 6.——[b] Chap. i. 6.
[c] Gal. vi. 14; Phil. iii. 8.

[d] Acts xviii. 1, 6, 12.——[e] 2 Cor. iv. 7; x. 1, 10; xi. 30; xii. 5, 9; Gal. iv. 13.

NOTES ON CHAP. II.

Verse 1. *When I came to you*] Acting suitably to my mission, which was to preach the Gospel, but not with human eloquence, chap. i. 17. I declared to you the *testimony,* the Gospel, of *God, not with excellency of speech,* not with arts of rhetoric, used by your own philosophers, where the excellence of the speech recommends the matter, and compensates for the want of solidity and truth: on the contrary, the testimony concerning Christ and his salvation is so supremely excellent, as to dignify any kind of language by which it may be conveyed.—See the *Introduction,* sect. ii.

Verse 2. *I determined not to know any thing among you*] Satisfied that the Gospel of God could alone make you wise unto salvation, I determined to cultivate no other knowledge, and to teach nothing but Jesus Christ, and him crucified, as the foundation of all true wisdom, piety, and happiness. No other doctrine shall I *proclaim* among you.

Verse 3. *I was with you in weakness*] It is very likely that St. Paul had not only something in his *speech* very unfavourable to a ready and powerful elocution, but also some infirmity of *body* that was still more disadvantageous to him. A fine *appearance* and a fine *voice* cover many weaknesses and defects, and strongly and forcibly recommend what is spoken, though not remarkable for depth of thought or solidity

2

A. M. 4060.
A. D. 56.
A. U. C.
809.
Anno Imp. Nero-
nis Cæs. 3.

4 And my speech and my preaching ᶠ *was* not with ᵍ enticing words of man's wisdom, ʰ but in demonstration of the Spirit and of power:

5 That your faith should not ⁱ stand in the wisdom of men, but ᵏ in the power of God.

6 Howbeit, we speak wisdom among them ˡ that are perfect: yet not ᵐ the

A. M. 4060.
A. D. 56.
A. U. C.
809.
Anno Imp. Nero-
nis Cæs. 3.

ᶠ Ver. 1; chap. i. 17; 2 Peter i. 16.——ᵍ Or, *persuasible.* ʰ Rom. xv. 19; 1 Thess. i. 5.——ⁱ Gr. *be.*——ᵏ 2 Cor. iv. 7; vi. 7.

ˡ Chap. xiv. 20; Eph. iv. 13; Phil. iii. 15; Heb. v. 14. ᵐ Chap. i. 20; iii. 19; ver. 1, 13; 2 Cor. i. 12; James iii. 15.

---

of reasoning. Many popular orators have little besides their *persons* and their *voice* to recommend them. Louis XIV. styled Peter du Bosc *le plus beau parleur de son royaume,* the finest speaker in his kingdom; and among his own people he was styled *l'orateur parfait,* the *perfect orator.* Look at the works of this French protestant divine, and you find it difficult to subscribe to the above sayings. The difficulty is solved by the information that the *person* of M. du Bosc was noble and princely, and his *voice* full, harmonious, and majestic. Paul had none of these advantages, and yet idolatry and superstition fell before him. Thus GOD was seen in the work, and the *man* was forgotten.

In fear, and in much trembling.] This was often the state of his mind; dreading lest he should at any time be unfaithful, and so grieve the Spirit of God; or that, after having preached to others, himself should be a castaway. See chap. ix. 27.

An eminent divine has said that it requires three things to make a good preacher; *study, temptation,* and *prayer.* The latter, no man that lives near to God can neglect; the former, no man who endeavours rightly to divide the word of truth will neglect; and with the *second* every man will be more or less exercised whose whole aim is to save souls. Those of a different cast the devil permits to pass quietly on in their own indolent and prayerless way.

Verse 4. *And my speech*] 'Ο λογος μου, My *doctrine;* the *matter* of my preaching.

And my preaching] Το κηρυγμα μου, My proclamation, my *manner* of recommending the grand but simple truths of the Gospel.

Was not with enticing words of man's wisdom] Ενπειθοις ανθρωπινης σοφιας λογοις, *With persuasive doctrines of human wisdom:* in every case I left *man* out, that God might become the more evident. I used none of the means of which great orators avail themselves in order to become *popular,* and thereby to gain *fame.*

But in demonstration of the Spirit] Αποδειξει, In the *manifestation;* or, as two ancient MSS. have it, αποκαλυψει, in the *revelation* of the Spirit. The doctrine that he preached was *revealed* by the Spirit: that it was a *revelation* of the Spirit, the holiness, purity, and usefulness of the doctrine rendered *manifest:* and the overthrow of idolatry, and the conversion of souls, by the *power* and energy of the preaching, were the *demonstration* that all was Divine. The greater part of the best MSS., *versions,* and *fathers,* leave out the adjective ανθρωπινης, *man's,* before σοφιας, *wisdom:* it is possible that the word may be a *gloss,* but it is necessarily implied in the clause. *Not with the persuasive discourses,* or *doctrines of wisdom;* i. e. of *human* philosophy.

Verse 5. *That your faith should not stand*] That the illumination of your souls and your conversion to God might appear to have nothing *human* in it: your belief, therefore, of the truths which have been proposed to you is founded, not in *human wisdom,* but in *Divine power:* human *wisdom* was not employed; and human *power,* if it had been employed, could not have produced the change.

Verse 6. *We speak wisdom among them that are perfect*] By the εν τοις τελειοις, *among those that are perfect,* we are to understand *Christians* of the highest knowledge and attainments—those who were *fully instructed* in the knowledge of God through Christ Jesus. Nothing, in the judgment of St. Paul, deserved the name of *wisdom* but this. And though he apologizes for his not coming to them with excellency of speech or wisdom, yet he means what was reputed wisdom among the Greeks, and which, in the sight of God, was mere *folly* when compared with that wisdom that came from above. Dr. Lightfoot thinks that the apostle mentions a *fourfold* wisdom. 1. *Heathen wisdom,* or that of the Gentile philosophers, chap. i. 22, which was termed by the Jews חכמה יונית *chokmah yevanith, Grecian* wisdom; and which was so undervalued by them, that they joined these two under the same curse: *Cursed is he that breeds hogs; and cursed is he who teaches his son Grecian wisdom.*— Bava Kama, fol. 82.

2. *Jewish wisdom;* that of the scribes and Pharisees, who crucified our Lord, ver. 8.

3. The *Gospel,* which is called *the wisdom of God in a mystery,* ver. 7.

4. The *wisdom,* του αιωνος τουτου, of *this world;* that system of knowledge which the *Jews* made up out of the writings of their scribes and doctors. This state is called העולם הזה *haolam hazzeh,* this or the present world; to distinguish it from העולם הבא *haolam habba,* the world to come; i. e. the days of the Messiah. Whether we understand the term, *this world,* as relating to the state of the Gentiles, cultivated to the uttermost in philosophical learning, or the then state of the Jews, who had made the word of God of no effect by their traditions, which contained a sort of learning of which they were very fond and very proud; yet, by this Grecian and Jewish wisdom, no soul could have arrived at any such knowledge or wisdom as that communicated by the revelation of Christ. This was *perfect wisdom;* and they who were thoroughly instructed in it, and had received the grace of the Gospel, were termed τελειοι, *the perfect.* This, says the apostle, is not *the wisdom of this world,* for that has not the *manifested Messiah* in it; nor *the wisdom of the rulers of this world*—the *chief* men, whether *philosophers* among the Greeks, or *rabbins*

2

A. M. 4060.
A. D. 56.
A. U. C.
809.
Anno Imp. Nero-
nis Cæs. 3.

wisdom of this world, nor of the princes of this world ⁿ that come to nought :

7 But we speak the wisdom of God in a mystery, *even* the hidden *wisdom,* ° which God ordained before the world unto our glory :

8 ᵖ Which none of the princes of this world knew : for ᵠ had they known *it,* they would not have crucified the Lord of glory.

ⁿ Chap. i. 28.——° Rom. xvi. 25, 26; Eph. iii. 5, 9; Col. i. 26. 2 Tim. i. 9.——ᵖ Matt. xi. 25; John vii. 48; Acts xiii. 27; 2 Cor. iii. 14.

9 But, as it is written, ʳ Eye hath not seen, nor ear heard, neither have entered into the heart of man, the things which God hath prepared for them that love him.

10 But ˢ God hath revealed *them* unto us by his Spirit : for the Spirit searcheth all things, yea, the deep things of God.

11 For what man knoweth the things of a man, ᵗ save the spirit of man which is in him ?

A. M. 4060.
A. D. 56.
A. U. C.
809.
Anno Imp. Nero-
nis Cæs. 3.

ᵠ Luke xxiii. 34; Acts iii. 17; see John xvi. 3.——ʳ Isa. lxiv. 4.——ˢ Matt. xiii. 11; xvi. 17; John xiv. 26; xvi. 13; 1 John ii. 27.——ᵗ Prov. xx. 27; xxvii. 19; Jer. xvii. 9.

among the *Jews* (for those we are to understand as implied in the term *rulers,* used here by the apostle)— these rulers *came to nought ;* for they, their wisdom, and their government, were shortly afterwards over- turned in the destruction of Jerusalem. This declara- tion of the apostle is *prophetic.* The ruin of the Grecian superstition soon followed.

Verse 7. *The wisdom of God in a mystery*] The GOSPEL of Jesus Christ, which had been comparatively *hidden* from the *foundation of the world,* (the settling of the Jewish economy, as this phrase often means,) though appointed from the beginning to be *revealed* in the fulness of time. For, though this Gospel was, in a certain sense, announced by the prophets, and pre- figured by the law, yet it is certain that even the most intelligent of the Jewish *rulers,* their *doctors, scribes,* and *Pharisees,* had no adequate knowledge of it ; there- fore it was still a mystery to them and others, till it was so gloriously revealed by the preaching of the apostles.

Verse 8. *Which none of the princes of this world knew*] Here it is evident that *this world* refers to the Jewish state, and to the degree of knowledge in that state : and the *rulers,* the *priests, rabbins,* &c., who were principally concerned in the crucifixion of our Lord.

The Lord of glory.] Or the *glorious Lord,* infi- nitely transcending all the *rulers* of the universe ; whose is *eternal glory ;* who gave that *glorious* Gos- pel in which his followers may glory, as it affords them such cause of triumph as the heathens had not, who gloried in their *philosophers.* Here is a teacher who is come from God ; who has taught the most *glorious* truths which it is possible for the soul of man to con- ceive ; and has promised to lead all the followers of his crucified Master to that state of *glory* which is ineffable and eternal.

Verse 9. *But, as it is written*] The quotation is taken from Isa. lxiv. 4. The sense is continued here from verse the seventh, and λαλουμεν, *we speak,* is un- derstood—We do not *speak* or preach the wisdom of this world ; but that mysterious wisdom of God, of which the prophet said : *Eye hath not seen, nor ear heard, neither have entered into the heart of man the things which God has prepared for them that love him.* These words have been applied to the state of glory in a *future* world ; but they certainly belong to the

present state, and express merely the wondrous light, life, and liberty which the Gospel communicates to them that believe in the Lord Jesus Christ in that way which the Gospel itself requires. To this the prophet himself refers ; and it is evident, from the following verse, that the apostle also refers to the same thing. Such a scheme of salvation, in which God's glory and man's felicity should be equally secured, had never been seen, never heard of, nor could any mind but that of God have conceived the idea of so vast a project ; nor could any power but his own have brought it to effect.

Verse 10. *But God hath revealed* them *unto us*] A manifest proof that the apostle speaks here of the glories of the *Gospel,* and not of the glories of the *future* world.

For the Spirit searcheth all things] This is the Spirit of God, which spoke by the prophets, and has now given to the apostles the *fulness* of that heavenly truth, of which He gave to the former only the out- lines.

Yea, the deep things of God.] It is only the Spirit of God which can reveal the counsels of God : these are the purposes which have existed in His infinite wisdom and goodness from eternity ; and particularly what refers to creation, providence, redemption, and eternal glory, as far as men and angels are concerned in these purposes. The apostles were so fully con- vinced that the scheme of redemption proclaimed by the Gospel was Divine, that they boldly asserted that these things infinitely surpassed the wisdom and com prehension of man. God was now in a certain way become *manifest ;* many attributes of his, which to the heathen world would have for ever lain in obscurity, (for the world by wisdom knew not God,) were now not only brought to light as existing in him, but illus- trated by the gracious displays which He had made of himself. It was the Spirit of God alone that could reveal these things ; and it was the energy of that Spirit alone that could bring them all into effect—stamp and seal them as attributes and works of God for ever. The apostles were as truly conscious of their *own in- spiration* as they were that they had consciousness at all ; and what they spoke, they spoke as they were moved by the Holy Ghost.

Verse 11. *For what man knoweth the things of a man*] The word ανθρωπων in the first clause is omitted

2

A. M. 4060.
A. D. 56.
A. U. C.
809.
Anno Imp. Nero-
nis Cæs. 3.

[u] even so the things of God knoweth no man, but the Spirit of God.

12 Now we have received, not the spirit of the world, but [v] the Spirit which is of God ; that we might know the things that are freely given to us of God.

13 [w] Which things also we speak, not in the words which man's wisdom teacheth, but which the Holy Ghost teacheth ; comparing spiritual things with spiritual.

14 [x] But the natural man receiveth not the things of the Spirit of God : [y] for they are

A. M. 4060.
A. D. 56.
A. U. C.
809.
Anno Imp. Nero-
nis Cæs. 3.

---

[u] Rom. xi. 33, 34.——[v] Rom. viii. 15.——[w] 2 Pet. i. 16; see chap. i. 17; ver. 4.——[x] Matt. xvi. 23.——[y] Chap. i. 18, 23

---

by the *Codex Alexandrinus*, and one other; and by *Athanasius, Cyril,* and *Vigil* of Tapsus. Bishop *Pearce* contends strongly against the authenticity of the word, and reads the passage thus : " For what· is there that knoweth the things of a man, except the spirit of a man that is in him ?" " I leave out," says the learned bishop, " ανθρωπων, with the Alexandrian MS., and read τι̣ γαρ οιδεν τα του ανθρωπου ; because I conceive that the common reading is wide of St. Paul's meaning ; for to say, *What man except the spirit of a man,* is I think) to speak improperly, and to suppose that the spirit of a man is a man : but it is very proper to say, *What except the spirit of a man :* τις is feminine as well as masculine, and therefore may be supplied with ουσια, or some such word, as well as with ανθρωπος." Though the authority for omitting this word is comparatively slender, yet it must be owned that its omission renders the text much more intelligible. But even *one* MS. may preserve the true reading.

The spirit of a man knows the things of a man : that is, a man is conscious of all the schemes, plans, and purposes, that pass in his own mind ; and no man can know these things but himself. So, the Spirit of God, He whom we call the *Third Person* of the glorious Trinity, knows all the counsels. and determinations of the Supreme Being. As the Spirit is here represented to live in God as the soul lives in the body of a man, and as this Spirit knows all the things of God, and had revealed those to the apostles which concern the salvation of the world, therefore what they spoke and preached was true, and men may implicitly depend upon it. The miracles which they did, in the name of Christ, were the proof that they had that Spirit, and spoke the truth of God.

Verse 12. *Now we have received, not the spirit of the world*] We, who are the genuine apostles of Christ, have received this Spirit of God, by which we know the deep things of God ; and, through the teaching of that Spirit, we preach Christ crucified. We have not therefore *received the spirit of the world*—of the *Jewish* teachers, who are all looking for a *worldly kingdom* and a *worldly Messiah,* and interpret all the scriptures of the Old Testament which relate to Him in a *carnal* and *worldly* sense.

That we might know the things] We receive this teaching that we may know what those supereminently excellent things are which God has purposed *freely* to *give* to mankind. It is evident that, as the apostle means by *princes of the world* the rulers of the Jews, ver. 6-8, so by *spirit of the world* he here means **Jewish** wisdom, or their carnal mode of interpreting

the sacred oracles, and their carnal expectation of a worldly kingdom under the Messiah.

Verse 13. *Which things also we speak*] We dare no more use the *language* of the Jews and the Gentiles in speaking of those glorious things, than we can indulge their *spirit.* The Greek orators affected a high and florid language, full of tropes and figures, which dazzled more than it enlightened. The rabbins affected *obscurity,*.and were studious to find out *cabalistical* meanings, which had no tendency to make the people wise unto salvation. The apostles could not follow. any of these ; they spoke the *things* of God in the *words* of God ; every thing was plain and intelligible ; every word well placed, clear, and nervous. He who has a spiritual mind will easily comprehend an apostle's preaching.

Comparing spiritual things with spiritual.] This is commonly understood to mean, comparing the spiritual things under the Old Testament with the spiritual things under the New : but this does not appear to be the apostle's meaning. The word συγκρινοντες, which we translate *comparing,* rather signifies *conferring, discussing,* or *explaining ;* and the word πνευματικοις should be rendered *to spiritual men,* and not be referred to *spiritual things.* The passage therefore should be thus translated : *Explaining spiritual things to spiritual persons.* And this sense the following verse absolutely requires.

Verse 14. *But the natural man*] Ψυχικος, The *animal* man—the man who is in a mere state of nature, and lives under the influence of his animal passions ; for the word ψυχη, which we often translate *soul,* means the lower and sensitive part of man, in opposition to νους, the *understanding* or *rational* part. The Latins use *anima* to signify these lower passions ; and *animus* to signify the higher. The person in question is not only one who either has had no spiritual teaching, or has not profited by it ; but one who lives for the present world, having no respect to spiritual or eternal things. This ψυχικος, or *animal man,* is opposed to the πνευματικος, or *spiritual man :* and, as this latter is one who is under the influence of the Spirit of God, so the former is one who is without that influence.

The apostle did *speak* of those high and sublime spiritual things to these *animal men ;* but he *explained* them to those which were spiritual. He uses this word in this sense, chap. iii. 1 ; ix. 11 ; and particularly in verse 15 of the present chapter : *He that is spiritual judgeth all things.*

But .the natural man—The apostle appears to give this as a reason why he explained those deep spiritual things to spiritual men ; because the *animal man*—the

200   2

A. M. 4060.
A. D. 56.
A. U. C.
809.
Anno Imp. Nero-
nis Cæs. 3.

foolishness unto him : ᶻ neither can he know *them*, because they are spiritually discerned.

15 ᵃ But he that is spiritual ᵇ judgeth all things, yet he himself is ᶜ judged of no man.

16 ᵈ For who hath known the mind of the Lord, that he ᵉ may in-struct him ? ᶠ But we have the mind of Christ.

A. M. 4060.
A. D. 56.
A. U. C.
809.
Anno Imp. Nero-
nis Cæs. 3.

ᶻ Rom. viii. 5, 6, 7; Jude 19.——ᵃ Prov. xxviii. 5; 1 Thess. v. 21; 1 John iv. 1.——ᵇ Or, *discerneth.*——ᶜ Or, *discerned.*

ᵈ Job xv. 8; Isa. xl. 13; Jer. xxiii. 18; Wisd. ix. 13; Rom. xi. 34.——ᵉ Gr. *shall.*——ᶠ John xv. 15.

---

man who is in a state of nature, without the regene-rating grace of the Spirit of God, *receiveth not the things of the Spirit*—neither apprehends nor compre-hends them : he has no relish for them ; he considers it the highest *wisdom* to live for *this world.* There-fore these spiritual things *are foolishness to him;* for while he is in his *animal* state he cannot see their excellency, *because they are spiritually discerned,* and he has no spiritual mind.

Verse 15. *But he that is spiritual judgeth all things*] He who has the mind of Christ discerns and judges of all things spiritual : yet he himself is not discerned by the mere animal man. Some suppose that the word ανακρινεται should be understood thus : *He examines, scrutinizes, convinces, reproves,* which it appears to mean in chap. xiv. 24 ; and they read the verse thus : *The spiritual man*—the well-taught Christian, con-vinces, i. e. can easily convict, all men, (παντα, accus. sing.,) every animal man, of error and vice ; yet he himself is convicted of no man ; his mind is enlighten-ed, and his life is holy ; and therefore the animal man cannot convict him of sin. This is a good sense, but the first appears the most natural. See *Pearce* and *Rosenmüller.*

Verse 16. *For who hath known the mind of the Lord*] Who that is still an animal man can know the mind of God ? so as to instruct him, viz. the spiritual man, the same that is spoken of, ver. 15. But the words may be better understood thus : How can the animal man know the mind of the Lord ? and how can any man communicate that knowledge which he has never acquired, and which is foolishness to him, because it is spiritual, and he is animal ? This quotation is made from Isa. xl. 13.

But we have the mind of Christ.] He has endowed us with the same disposition, being born again by his Spirit ; therefore we are capable of knowing his mind and receiving the teachings of his Spirit. These teachings we do receive, and therefore are well quali-fied to convey them to others.

The words, *that he may instruct him,* ὁς συμβιβασει αυτον, should be translated *that he may teach* IT : that is, the mind of God ; not instruct God, but teach his mind to others. And this interpretation the Hebrew will also bear.

Bishop Pearce observes : " The principal questions here are, what συμβιβασει signifies, and what αυτον is relative to. The Hebrew word which the Septuagint translate by these two is וֹדִיעֶנֹּו *yodiennu* : now, since יְדִיַע *yodia* signifies as well to *make known* as to *know,* (and indeed this is the most frequent sense of it in the Old Testament,) the suffix (postfix) נו *nu,* may relate to a *thing,* as well as to a *person ;* and therefore it may be rendered not by *him,* but by *it,* i. e. the *mind* of the Lord. And in this sense the apostle seems to have used the words of the Seventy ; for, if we understand αυτον here to be the relative to Κυριου, Lord, this verse contains no reason for what went before ; whereas, if it be a relative to νουν, mind, it affords a reason for what had been said before, ver. 14." The true trans-lation of the passage, as used by the apostle, appears to be this : *For who hath known the mind of the Lord, that he should* TEACH IT ? And this translation agrees with every part of the context, and particularly with what follows.

1. THIS chapter might be considered a good model for a Christian minister to regulate his conduct by, or his public ministry ; because it points out the mode of preaching used by St. Paul and the apostles in general. This great apostle *came not* to the people *with excel-lency of speech and of wisdom, when he declared unto them the counsel of God.* They know little either of the spirit of St. Paul or the design of the Gospel, who make the chief excellence of their preaching to consist in the eloquence of language, or depth of human rea-soning. That may be *their* testimony, but it is not *God's.* The *enticing words of man's wisdom* are seldom accompanied by the *demonstration and power of the Holy Spirit.*

2. One justly remarks, that " the foolishness of preaching has its wisdom, loftiness, and eloquence ; but this consists in the sublimity of its truths, the depth of its mysteries, and the ardour of the Spirit of God." In this respect Paul may be said to have *preached wisdom among those which were perfect.* The wisest and most learned men in the world, who have seriously read the Bible, have acknowledged that there is a depth and height of wisdom and knowledge in that book of God which are sought in vain any where else : and indeed it would not be a revelation from God were it not so. The men who can despise and ridicule this sacred book are those who are too *blind* to discover the objects presented to them by this brilliant light, and are too *sensual* to feel and relish spiritual things. They, above all others, are incapable of judging, and should be no more regarded when employed in talking against the sacred writings than an ignorant peasant should be, who, not knowing his alphabet, pretends to decry mathematical learning.

3. A new mode of preaching has been diligently recommended,—" Scriptural phraseology should be generally avoided where it is antiquated, or conveys ideas inconsistent with modern delicacy." St. Paul did not preach in the words which man's wisdom teacheth—such words are too mean and too low for a religion so Divine. That which the Holy Spirit alone can discover, he alone can explain. Let no man dare.

2

to speak of God in any other way than he speaks of himself in his word. Let us take care not to profane his truths and mysteries, either by such *low* and *abject* ideas as are merely *human*, or by *new* and *worldly* expressions altogether unworthy of the Spirit of God.

4. It is the glory of God, and ought to be ours, not to be acceptable to carnal men. The *natural man* always finds some pretence to excuse himself from believing, by looking on the mysteries of religion as being either too much above man or too much below God; the spiritual man judges them to be so much the more credible, the less credible they are to the natural man.

The opposition, contempt, and blindness of the world, with regard to the things of God, render all its judgments concerning them liable to exception : this blindness in spiritual things is the just punishment of a carnal life. The principal part of the above is extracted from the reflections of the pious *Quesnel*

CHAPTER III.

Because of the carnal, divided state of the people at Corinth, the apostle was obliged to treat them as children in the knowledge of sacred things, 1–3. Some were for setting up Paul, others Apollos, as their sole teachers, 4. The apostle shows that himself and fellow apostles were only instruments which God used to bring them to the knowledge of the truth; and even their sowing and watering the seed was of no use unless God gave the increase, 5–8. The Church represented as God's husbandry, and as God's building, the foundation of which is Christ Jesus, 9–11. Ministers must beware how and what they build on this foundation, 12–15. The Church of God is his temple, and he that defiles it shall be destroyed, 16, 17. No man should depend on his own wisdom; for the wisdom of the world is foolishness with God, 18–20. None should glory in man as his teacher; God gives his followers every good, both for time and eternity, 21–23.

A. M. 4060.
A. D. 56.
A. U. C. 809.
Anno Imp. Neronis Cæs. 3.

AND I, brethren, could not speak unto you as unto [a] spiritual, but as unto [b] carnal, *even* as unto [c] babes in Christ.

2 I have fed you with [d] milk, and not with meat : [e] for hitherto ye were not able *to bear it,* neither yet now are ye able.

3 For ye are yet carnal : for [f] whereas *there is* among you envying, and strife, and [g] divisions, are ye not carnal, and walk as [h] men ?

4 For while one saith, [i] I am of Paul ; and another, I *am* of Apollos ; are ye not carnal ?

A. M. 4060.
A. D. 56.
A. U. C. 809.
Anno Imp. Neronis Cæs. 3.

[a] Chap. ii. 15.——[b] Chap. ii. 14.——[c] Heb. v. 13.——[d] Heb. v. 12, 13 ; 1 Pet. ii. 2.——[e] John xvi. 12.

[f] Chap. i. 11 ; xi. 18 ; Gal. v. 20, 21 ; James iii. 16.——[g] Or, *factions.*——[h] Gr. *according to man.*——[i] Chap. i. 12.

NOTES ON CHAP. III.

Verse 1. *I, brethren, could not speak unto you as unto spiritual*] This is a continuation of the preceding discourse. See the notes there.

But as unto carnal] Σαρκικοις, Persons under the influence of fleshly appetites ; coveting and living for the things of this life.

Babes in Christ.] Just beginning to acquire some notion of the Christian religion, but as yet very incapable of judging what is most suitable to yourselves, and consequently utterly unqualified to discern between one teacher and another ; so that your making the distinctions which you do make, so far from being a proof of mature judgment, is on the contrary a proof that you have no right judgment at all ; and this springs from your want of knowledge in Divine things.

Verse 2. *I have fed you with milk*] I have instructed you in the *elements* of Christianity—in its *simplest* and *easiest* truths ; because from the low state of your minds in religious knowledge, you were incapable of comprehending the higher truths of the Gospel : and in this state you will still continue. The apostle thus exposes to them the absurdity of their conduct in pretending to judge between preacher and preacher, while they had but a very partial acquaintance even with the *first principles* of Christianity.

Verse 3. There is *among you envying, and strife, and divisions*] Ζηλος και ερις και διχοσταοιαι. There are *three* things here worthy of note : these people were wrong in *thought, word,* and *deed.* Ζηλος, *envying,* refers to the state of their souls ; they had inward grudgings and disaffection towards each other. Ερις, *strife* or *contention,* refers to their *words ;* they were continually *disputing* and *contending* whose party was the best, each endeavouring to prove that he and his party were alone in the right. Διχοσταοιαι, *divisions,* refers to their *conduct ;* as they could not agree, they contended till they separated from each other, and thus rent the Church of Christ. Thus the *envying* and grudging led to *strife* and evil SPEAKING, and this led to *divisions* and fixed parties. In this state well might the apostle say, *Are ye not carnal, and walk as men ?* Ye act just as the *people of the world,* and have no more of the *spirit* of religion than they.

Verse 4. *For while one saith, I am of Paul, &c.*] It was notorious that both Paul and Apollos held the *same creed ;* between *them* there was not the slightest difference : when, therefore, the dissentients began to prefer the one to the other, it was the fullest proof of their *carnality ;* because in the *doctrines* of these apostles there was no difference : so that what the people were captivated by must be something in their *outward manner,* Apollos being probably more *eloquent* than Paul. Their preferring one to another on such an account proved that they were *carnal*—led by their senses and mere outward appearances, without being

2

A. M. 4060.
A. D. 56.
A. U. C.
809.
Anno Imp. Neronis Cæs. 3.

5 Who then is Paul, and who is Apollos, but [k] ministers by whom ye believed, [l] even as the Lord gave to every man?

6 [m] I have planted, [n] Apollos watered; [o] but God gave the increase.

7 So then, [p] neither is he that planteth any thing, neither he that watereth; but God that giveth the increase.

8 Now he that planteth and he that watereth are one; [q] and every man shall receive his own reward, according to his own labour.

9 For [r] we are labourers together with God: ye are God's [s] husbandry, *ye are* [t] God's building.

10 [u] According to the grace of God which is given unto me, as a wise master-builder, I

A. M. 4060.
A. D. 56.
A. U. C.
809.
Anno Imp. Neronis Cæs. 3.

---

[k] Chap. iv. 1; 2 Cor. iii. 3.——[l] Rom. xii. 3, 6; 1 Pet. iv. 11. [m] Acts xviii. 4, 8, 11; chap. iv. 15; ix. 1; xv. 1; 2 Cor. x. 14, 15. [n] Acts xviii 24, 27; xix. 1.——[o] Chap. i. 30; xv. 10; 2 Cor. iii. 5.——[p] 2 Cor. xii. 11; Gal. vi. 3.

[q] Psa. lxii. 12; Rom. ii. 6; chap. iv. 5; Gal. vi. 4, 5; Rev. ii. 23; xxii. 12.——[r] Acts xv. 4; 2 Cor. vi. 1.——[s] Or, *tillage*. [t] Eph. ii. 20; Col. ii. 7; Heb. iii. 3, 4; 1 Pet. ii. 5.——[u] Rom. i. 5; xii. 3.

---

under the guidance either of reason or grace. There are thousands of such people in the Christian Church to the present day. See the notes on chap. i. 10, &c.

Verse 5. Ministers by whom ye believed] The different apostles who have preached unto you the word of life are the *means* which God has used to bring you to the knowledge of Christ. No one of those has either preached or recommended *himself*; they all preach and recommend Christ Jesus the Lord.

Even as the Lord gave to every man?] Whatever difference there may be in our talents, it is of God's making; and he who knows best what is best for his Church, has distributed both *gifts* and *graces* according to his own mind; and, as his judgment is infallible, all these dispensations must be right. Paul, therefore, is as necessary to the perfecting of the Church of Christ as Apollos; and Apollos, as Paul. Both, but with various gifts, point out the same Christ, building on one and the same foundation.

Verse 6. I have planted] I first sowed the seed of the Gospel at Corinth, and in the region of Achaia.

Apollos watered] Apollos came after me, and, by his preachings and exhortations, watered the seed which I had sowed; *but God gave the increase.* The seed has taken root, has sprung up, and borne much fruit; but this was by the especial blessing of God. As in the *natural* so in the *spiritual* world; it is by the especial blessing of God that the grain which is sown in the ground brings forth thirty, sixty, or a hundred fold : it is neither the sower nor the waterer that produces this strange and inexplicable *multiplication;* it is God alone. So it is by the particular agency of the Spirit of God that even good seed, sown in good ground, the purest doctrine conveyed to the honestest heart, produces the salvation of the soul.

Verse 7. So then, neither is he that planteth any thing] God alone should have all the glory, as the *seed* is his, the *ground* is his, the *labourers* are his, and the *produce* all comes from himself.

Verse 8. He that planteth and he that watereth are one] Both Paul and Apollos have received the same doctrine, preach the same doctrine, and labour to promote the glory of God in the salvation of your souls. Why should you be divided with respect to Paul and Apollos, while these apostles are intimately ONE in *spirit, design,* and *operation?*

According to his own labour.] God does not reward his servants according to the *success* of their labour,

because that depends on himself; but he rewards them according to the *quantum* of faithful *labour* which they bestow on his work. In this sense none can say, I have laboured in vain, and spent my strength for nought.

Verse 9. For we are labourers together with God] We do nothing of ourselves, nor in reference to ourselves; we labour together in that work which God has given us to do, expect all our success from him, and refer the whole to his glory. It would perhaps be more correct to translate Θεου γαρ εσμεν συνεργοι, *we are fellow labourers of God;* for, as the preposition συν may express the joint labour of the teachers one *with* another, and not with God, I had rather, with Bishop Pearce, translate as above : i. e. we labour together in the work of God. Far from being divided among ourselves, we *jointly* labour, as oxen in the same yoke, to promote the honour of our Master.

Ye are God's husbandry, ye are God's building.] Θεου γεωργιον, Θεου οικοδομη εστε· The word γεωργιον, which we translate *husbandry,* signifies properly an *arable field ;* so Prov. xxiv. 30 : *I went by the* FIELD, γεωργιον, *of the slothful ;* and chap. xxxi. 16 : *The wise woman considereth a* FIELD, γεωργιον, *and buyeth it.* It would be more literal to translate it, *Ye are God's farm :* γεωργιον in Greek answers to שדה *sadeh* in Hebrew, which signifies properly a *sown field.*

Ye are God's building.——Ye are not only the *field* which God cultivates, but ye are the *house* which God builds, and in which he intends to dwell. As no man in viewing a fine building extols the *quarryman* that dug up the stones, the *hewer* that cut and squared them, the *mason* that placed them in the wall, the *woodman* that hewed down the timber, the *carpenter* that squared and jointed it, &c., but the *architect* who planned it, and under whose direction the whole work was accomplished ; so no man should consider *Paul,* or *Apollos,* or *Kephas,* any thing, but as persons employed by the great Architect to form a building which is to become a habitation of himself through the Spirit, and the *design* of which is entirely his own.

Verse 10. As a wise master builder] Ὡς σοφος αρχιτεκτων. The *design* or *plan* of the building is from God ; all things must be done according to the *pattern* which he has exhibited ; but the *execution* of this plan was entrusted chiefly to St. Paul ; he was the *wise* or *experienced* architect which God used in order to lay the foundation ; to ascertain the essential and immu-

A. M. 4060
A. D. 56.
A. U. C.
809.
Anno Imp. Nero-
nis Cæs. 3.

have laid ^v the foundation, and another buildeth thereon. But ^w let every man take heed how he buildeth thereupon.

11 For other foundation can no man lay than ^x that is laid, ^y which is Jesus Christ.

12 Now if any man build upon this foundation gold, silver, precious stones, wood, hay, stubble;

13 ^z Every man's work shall be made manifest : for the day ^a shall declare it, because ^b it ^c shall be revealed by fire : and the fire shall try every man's work of what sort it is.

14 If any man's work abide which he hath built thereupon, ^d he shall receive a reward.

15 If any man's work shall be burned, he

A. M. 4060.
A. D. 56.
A. U. C.
809.
Anno Imp. Nero-
nis Cæs. 3.

---

^v Rom. xv. 20 ; ver. 6 ; chap. iv. 15 ; Rev. xxi. 14.——^w 1 Pet. iv. 11.——^x Isa. xxviii. 16 ; Matt. xvi. 18 ; 2 Cor. xi. 4 ; Gal. i. 7.

^y Eph. ii. 20.——^z Chap. iv. 5.——^a 1 Pet. i. 7 ; iv. 12.——^b Luke ii. 35.——^c Gr. *is revealed.*——^d Chap. iv. 5.

---

table doctrines of the Gospel—those alone which came from God, and which alone he would bless to the salvation of mankind.

Let every man take heed how he buildeth thereupon.] Let him take care that the doctrines which he preaches be answerable to those which I have preached; let him also take heed that he enjoin no other practice than that which is suitable to the doctrine, and in every sense accords with it.

Verse 11. *Other foundation can no man lay*]. I do not speak particularly concerning the *foundation* of this spiritual building; it can have no other foundation than Jesus Christ : there cannot be two opinions on this subject among the true apostles of our Lord. The only fear is, lest an improper use should be made of this heavenly doctrine ; lest a bad superstructure should be raised on this foundation.

Verse 12. *If any man build—gold, silver, &c.*] Without entering into curious criticisms relative to these different expressions, it may be quite enough for the purpose of edification to say, that, by *gold, silver,* and *precious stones,* the apostle certainly means pure and wholesome doctrines : by *wood, hay,* and *stubble,* false doctrines ; such as at that time prevailed in the Corinthian Church ; for instance, that there should be no resurrection of the body ; that a man may, on his father's death, lawfully marry his step-mother ; that it was necessary to incorporate much of the Mosaic law with the Gospel ; and, perhaps, other matters, equally exceptionable, relative to marriage, concubinage, fornication, frequenting heathen festivals, and partaking of the flesh which had been offered in sacrifice to an idol ; with many other things, which, with the above, are more or less hinted at by the apostle in these two letters.

Verse 13. *The day shall declare it, because it shall be revealed by fire*] There is much difference of opinion relative to the meaning of the terms in this and the two following verses. That the apostle refers to the approaching destruction of Jerusalem I think very probable ; and when this is considered, all the terms and metaphors will appear clear and consistent.

The *day* is the time of punishment coming on this disobedient and rebellious people. And this day being *revealed by fire,* points out the extreme rigour, and totally destructive nature, of that judgment.

And the fire shall try every man's work] If the apostle refers to the Judaizing teachers and their insinuations that the law, especially circumcision, was of

eternal obligation ; then the *day of fire*—the time of vengeance, which was at hand, would sufficiently disprove such assertions ; as, in the judgment of God, the whole temple service should be destroyed ; and the people, who fondly presumed on their permanence and stability, should be dispossessed of their land and scattered over the face of the whole earth. The difference of the Christian and Jewish systems should *then* be seen : the latter should be destroyed in that *fiery day,* and the former prevail more than ever.

Verse 14. *If any man's work abide*] Perhaps there is here an allusion to the purifying of different sorts of vessels under the law. All that could stand the fire were to be purified by the fire ; and those which could not resist the action of the *fire* were to be purified by *water,* Num. xxxi. 23. The *gold, silver, and precious stones,* could stand the fire ; but the *wood, hay,* and *stubble,* must be necessarily consumed. So, in that great and terrible day of the Lord, all *false doctrine,* as well as the *system* that was to *pass away,* should be made sufficiently manifest ; and God would then show that the *Gospel,* and that alone, was that system of doctrine which he should bless and protect, and none other.

He shall receive a reward.] He has not only preached the *truth,* but he has *laboured* in the word and doctrine. And the *reward* is to be *according* to the *labour.* See on ver. 8.

Verse 15. *If any man's work shall be burned, he shall suffer loss*] If he have preached the necessity of incorporating the *law* with the *Gospel,* or proclaimed as a doctrine of God any thing which did not proceed from heaven, *he shall suffer loss*—all his time and labour will be found to be uselessly employed and spent. Some refer the *loss* to the *work,* not to the *man ;* and understand the passage thus : *If any man's work be burned,* IT *shall suffer loss*—much shall be taken away from it ; nothing shall be left but the measure of truth and uprightness which it may have contained.

But he himself shall be saved] If he have sincerely and conscientiously believed what he preached, and yet preached what was wrong, not through *malice* or *opposition* to the Gospel, but through mere *ignorance,* he *shall be saved ;* God in his mercy will pass by his errors ; and he shall not suffer punishment because he was *mistaken.* Yet, as in most erroneous teachings there is generally a portion of *wilful* and *obstinate* ignorance, the salvation of such erroneous teachers is very

A. M. 4060.
A. D. 56.
A. U. C.
809.
Anno Imp. Nero-
nis Cæs. 3.

shall suffer loss: but he himself shall be saved; [e] yet so as by fire.

16 [f] Know ye not that ye are the temple of God, and *that* the Spirit of God dwelleth in you?

17 If any man [g] defile the temple of God, him shall God destroy; for the temple of

God is holy, which *temple* ye are.

18 [h] Let no man deceive himself. If any man among you seemeth to be wise in this world, let him become a fool, that he may be wise.

19 For [i] the wisdom of this world is foolishness with God: for it is written, [k] He taketh

A. M. 4060.
A. D. 56.
A. U. C.
809.
Anno Imp. Nero-
nis Cæs. 3.

---

[e] Jude 23.——[f] Chap. vi. 19; 2 Cor. vi. 16; Eph. ii. 21, 22; Heb. iii. 6; 1 Pet. ii. 5.

[g] Or, *destroy.*——[h] Prov. v. 7; Isa. v. 21.——[i] Chap. i. 20; ii. 6. [k] Job v. 13.

---

rare; and is expressed here, *yet so as by fire,* i. e. with great difficulty; a *mere escape;* a *hair's breadth deliverance;* he shall be like a *brand plucked out of the fire.*

The apostle obviously refers to the case of a man, who, having builded a house, and begun to dwell in it, the house happens to be set on fire, and he has warning of it just in time to escape with his life, losing at the same time his house, his goods, his labour, and *almost* his own life. So he who, while he holds the doctrine of Christ crucified as the only foundation on which a soul can rest its hopes of salvation, builds at the same time, on that foundation, *Antinomianism,* or any other erroneous or destructive doctrine, he shall lose all his labour, and his own soul scarcely escape everlasting perdition; nor even this unless sheer ignorance and inveterate prejudice, connected with much sincerity, be found in his case.

The popish writers have applied what is here spoken to the *fire* of *purgatory;* and they might with equal propriety have applied it to the discovery of the *longitude,* the *perpetual motion,* or the *philospher's stone;* because it speaks just as much of the former as it does of any of the latter. The *fire* mentioned here is to try the man's *work,* not to purify his *soul;* but the dream of *purgatory* refers to the *purging* in another state what left this *impure;* not the *work* of the man, but the *man himself;* but here the *fire* is said to *try the work:* ergo, purgatory is not meant even if such a place as purgatory could be proved to exist; which remains yet to be demonstrated.

Verse 16. *Ye are the temple of God*] The apostle resumes here what he had asserted in ver. 9: *Ye are God's building.* As the whole congregation of Israel were formerly considered as the *temple* and *habitation* of God, because God *dwelt among them,* so here the whole Church of Corinth is called the *temple of God,* because all genuine believers have the *Spirit* of God to dwell in them; and Christ has promised to be always in the midst even of two or three who are gathered together in his name. Therefore where God is, *there* is his temple.

Verse 17. *If any man defile the temple*] This clause is not consistently translated. Ει τις τον ναον του Θεου φθειρει, φθερει τουτον ὁ Θεος *If any man destroy the temple of God, him will God destroy.* The verb is the same in both clauses. If any man injure, corrupt, or destroy the Church of God by false doctrine, God will destroy him—will take away his part out of the book of life. This refers to him who wilfully opposes the truth; the erring, mistaken man shall

barely *escape;* but the obstinate opposer shall be destroyed. The former shall be treated *leniently;* the latter shall have judgment without *mercy.*

Verse 18. *If any man among you seemeth to be wise*] Ει τις δοκει σοφος ειναι· *If any pretend or affect to be wise.* This seems to refer to some *individual* in the Church of Corinth, who had been very troublesome to its peace and unity: probably *Diotrephes* (see on chap. i. 14) or some one of a similar spirit, who wished to have the *pre-eminence,* and thought himself wiser than seven men that could render a reason. Every Christian Church has less or more of these.

Let him become a fool] Let him divest himself of his worldly wisdom, and be contented to be *called* a *fool,* and *esteemed* one, that he may become wise unto salvation, by renouncing his own wisdom, and seeking that which comes from God. But probably the apostle refers to him who, *pretending* to great wisdom and information, taught doctrines contrary to the Gospel; endeavouring to show reasons for them, and to support his own opinions with arguments which he thought unanswerable. This man brought his worldly wisdom to bear against the doctrines of Christ; and probably through such teaching many of the scandalous things which the apostle reprehends among the Corinthians originated.

Verse 19. *The wisdom of this world*] Whether it be the pretended deep and occult wisdom of the rabbins, or the wire-drawn speculations of the Grecian philosophers, *is foolishness with God;* for as folly consists in spending time, strength, and pains to no purpose, so these may be fitly termed *fools* who acquire no saving knowledge by their speculations. And is not this the case with the major part of all that is called *philosophy,* even in the present day? Has one soul been made wise unto salvation through it? Are our most eminent philosophers either pious or useful men? Who of them is meek, gentle, and humble! Who of them directs his researches so as to meliorate the moral condition of his fellow creatures? Pride, insolence, self-conceit, and complacency, with a general forgetfulness of God, contempt for his word, and despite for the poor, are their general characteristics.

He taketh the wise in their own craftiness.] This is a quotation from Job v. 13, and powerfully shows what the wisdom of this world is: it is a sort of *craft,* a *subtle trade,* which they carry on to wrong others and benefit themselves; and they have generally too much *cunning* to be caught by *men;* but God often overthrows them with their own devisings. *Paganism* raised up *persecution* against the Church of Christ, in

2

A. M. 4060.
A. D. 56.
A. U. C.
809.
Anno Imp. Nero-
nis Cæs. 3.

the wise in their own craftiness.

20 And again, ¹ The Lord
knoweth the thoughts of the
wise, that they are vain.

21 Therefore ᵐ let no man glory in men:
for ⁿ all things are yours;

A. M. 4060.
A. D. 56.
A. U. C.
809.
Anno Imp. Nero
nis Cæs. 3.

22 Whether Paul, or Apollos,
or Cephas, or the world, or life,
or death, or things present, or
things to come; ° all are
yours;

23 And ᵖ ye are Christ's; and Christ *is*
God's.

---

¹ Psa. xciv. 11.——ᵐ Chap. i. 12; iv. 6; ver. 4, 5, 6.——ⁿ 2 Cor. iv. 5, 15.

° Ch. vi. 2; Rom. viii. 28; 2 Cor. iv. 15; 1 Tim. iv. 8.——ᵖ Rom. xiv. 8; chap. xi. 3; 2 Cor. x. 7; Gal. iii. 29.

---

order to destroy it: this became the very means of quickly spreading it over the earth, and of destroying the whole pagan system. Thus the wise were taken in their own craftiness.

Verse 20. The Lord knoweth the thoughts of the wise] They are always full of schemes and plans for earthly good; and God knows that all this is *vain*, *empty*, and unsatisfactory; and will stand them in no stead when he comes to take away their souls. This is a quotation from Psalm xciv. 11. What is here said of the vanity of human knowledge is true of every kind of wisdom that leads not immediately to God himself.

Verse 21. Let no man glory in men] Let none suppose that he has any cause of *exultation* in any thing but God. *All are yours*; he that has God for his portion has every thing that can make him happy and glorious: *all are his.*

Verse 22. Whether Paul, or Apollos] As if he had said: God designs to help you by all *things* and *persons*; every teacher sent from him will become a blessing to you, if you abide faithful to your calling. God will press every thing into the service of his followers. The *ministers* of the Church of Christ are appointed for the *hearers*, not the *hearers* for the *ministers*. In like manner, all the ordinances of grace and mercy are appointed for them, not they for the ordinances.

Or the world] The word κοσμος, here, means rather the *inhabitants* of the world than what we commonly understand by the world itself; and this is its meaning in John iii. 16, 17; vi. 33; xiv. 31; xvii. 21. See particularly John xii. 19: Ὁ κοσμος οπισω αυτου απηλθεν, *the* world *is gone after him*—the great mass of the people believe on him. The Greek word has the same meaning, in a variety of places, both in the *sacred* and the *profane writers*, as *le monde*, the world, literally has in *French*, where it signifies, not only the *system* of *created things*, but, by metonymy, the people—*every body*, the *mass*, the *populace*. In the same sense it is often found in English. The apostle's meaning evidently is: Not only Paul, Apollos, and Kephas, are yours—appointed for and employed in your service; but *every person* besides with whom you may have any intercourse or connection, whether Jew or Greek, whether enemy or friend. God will cause every person, as well as every thing to work for your good, while you love, cleave to, and obey Him.

Or life] With all its trials and advantages; every *hour* of it, every tribulation in it, the *whole course* of it, as the grand state of your probation, is a general blessing to you: and you have *life*, and that life preserved in order to prepare you for an eternity of blessedness.

Or death] That solemn hour, so dreadful to the

wicked; and so hateful to those who live without God: *that* is *yours*. *Death* is your *servant*; he comes a special messenger from God for you; he comes to undo a knot that now connects body and soul, which it would be unlawful for yourselves to untie; he comes to take your souls to glory: and he cannot come *before* his due time to those who are waiting for the salvation of God. A saint wishes to live only to glorify God; and he who wishes to live longer than he can *get* and *do* good, is not worthy of life.

Or things present] Every occurrence in *providence* in the *present life*; for God rules in *providence* as well as in *grace.*

Or things to come] The whole order and economy of the *eternal world*; all in *heaven* and all in *earth* are even now working together for your good.

Verse 23. And ye are Christ's] You are called by his name; you have embraced his doctrine; you depend on him for your salvation; he is your foundation stone; he has gathered you out of the world, and acknowledges you as his people and followers. Ὑμεις δε Χριστου, *ye are of Christ*; all the light and life which ye enjoy ye have received *through* and *from* him, and he has bought you with his blood.

And Christ is God's.] Χριστος δε Θεου, *And Christ is of God*. Christ, the *Messiah*, is the gift of God's eternal love and mercy to mankind; *for God so loved the world that he gave his only begotten Son, that they who believe in him should not perish, but have everlasting life.* Christ in his *human nature* is as much the property of God as any other human being. And as *mediator* between God and man, he must be considered, in a certain way, *inferior* to God; but in his own *essential*, *eternal nature*, there is no inequality —he is God over all. Ye, therefore, do not belong to *men*. Why then take *Paul, Apollos, Kephas*, or any other man for your *head*? All these are your *servants*; ye are not their property, ye are Christ's property: and as he has taken the human nature into heaven, so will he take yours; because he that sanctifieth, and they that are sanctified are all of one · ye are his brethren; and as his *human nature* is eternally safe at the throne of God, so shall your bodies and souls be, if ye cleave to him and be faithful unto death.

1. A FINER and more conclusive argument, to correct what was wrong among this people, could not have been used than that with which the apostle closes this chapter. It appears to stand thus: "If you continue in these *divisions*, and arrange yourselves under *different teachers*, you will meet with nothing but disappointment, and lose much good. If ye *will* have Paul,

Apollos, &c., on your present plan, you will have *them* and nothing else; nor can they do you any good, for they are only *instruments* in God's hand, at best, to communicate good, and he will not use them to help you while you act in this unchristian way. On the contrary, if you take GOD as your portion, you shall get *these* and every good besides. Act as you *now* do, and you get *nothing* and lose *all!* Act as I advise you to do, and you shall not only lose nothing of the good which you now possess, but shall have every possible advantage: the *men* whom you now wish to make your *heads*, and who, *in that* capacity, cannot profit you, shall become God's *instruments* of doing you endless good. Leave your dissensions, by which you offend God, and grieve his Christ; and then God, and Christ, and all will be yours." How agitated, convinced, and humbled must they have been when they read the masterly conclusion of this chapter!

2. A want of *spirituality* seems to have been the grand fault of the Corinthians. They regarded *outward things* chiefly, and were carried away with *sound* and *show.* They lost the *treasure* while they eagerly held fast the *earthen vessel* that contained it. It is a true saying, that he who lends only the *ear* of his *body* to the word of God, will follow that man most who pleases the *ear;* and these are the persons who generally profit the soul least.

3. All the ministers of God should consider themselves as *jointly* employed by Christ for the salvation of mankind. It is their interest to serve God and be faithful to his calling; but shall they dare to make *his* Church *their* interest? This is generally the origin of religious disputes and schisms. Men will have the Church of Christ for their own property, and Jesus Christ will not trust it with any man.

4. Every man employed in the work of God should take that part only upon himself that God has assigned him. The *Church* and the *soul*, says pious *Quesnel*, are a *building*, of which GOD is the *master* and chief *architect;* JESUS CHRIST the main *foundation;* the APOSTLES the subordinate *architects;* the BISHOPS the *workmen;* the PRIESTS their *helpers;* GOOD WORKS the main *body* of the building; FAITH a sort of *second foundation;* and CHARITY the *top* and *perfection.* Happy is that man who is a *living stone* in this building.

5. He who expects any good *out of God* is confounded and disappointed in all things. God alone can *content*, as he alone can *satisfy* the soul. All our restlessness and uneasiness are only proofs that we are endeavouring to live without God in the world. A contented mind is a continual feast; but none can have such a mind who has not taken God for his portion. How is it that Christians are continually forgetting this most plain and obvious truth, and yet wonder how it is that they cannot attain true peace of mind?

CHAPTER IV.

Ministers should be esteemed by their flocks as the stewards of God, whose duty and interest it is to be faithful, 1, 2. Precipitate and premature judgments condemned, 3–5. The apostle's caution to give the Corinthians no offence, 6. We have no good but what we receive from God, 7. The worldly mindedness of the Corinthians, 8. The enumeration of the hardships, trials, and sufferings of the apostles, 9–13. For what purpose St. Paul mentions these things, 14–16. He promises to send Timothy to them, 17. And to come himself shortly, to examine and correct the abuses that had crept in among them, 18–21.

A. M. 4060.
A. D. 56.
A. U. C. 809.
Anno Imp. Neronis Cæs. 3.

LET a man so account of us, as of [a] the ministers of Christ, [b] and stewards of the mysteries of God.

2 Moreover, it is required in stewards, that a man be found faithful.

3 But with me it is a very

A. M. 4060.
A. D. 56.
A. U. C. 809.
Anno Imp. Neronis Cæs. 3.

[a] Matt. xxiv. 45; chap. iii. 5; ix. 17; 2 Cor. vi. 4; Col. i. 25.

[b] Luke xii. 42; Tit. i. 7; 1 Pet. iv. 10.

NOTES ON CHAP. IV.

Verse 1. *Let a man so account of us*] This is a continuation of the subject in the preceding chapter; and should not have been divided from it. The *fourth* chapter would have begun better at ver. 6, and the *third* should have ended with the fifth verse.

As of the ministers of Christ] Ὡς ὑπηρετας Χριστου. The word ὑπηρετης means an *under-rower*, or one, who, in the *trireme, quadrireme*, or *quinquereme* galleys, rowed in one of the *undermost* benches; but it means also, as used by the Greek writers, any inferior officer or assistant. By the term here the apostle shows the Corinthians that, far from being *heads* and *chiefs*, he and his fellow apostles considered themselves only as inferior officers, employed under Christ; from whom alone they received their appointment, their work, and their recompense.

Stewards of the mysteries of God.] Και οικονομους μυστηριων Θεον, *Economists* of the Divine mysteries. See the explanation of the word *steward* in the note on Matt. xxiv. 45; Luke viii. 3; and xii. 42.

The *steward*, or *oikonomos*, was the master's deputy in regulating the concerns of the family, providing food for the household, seeing it served out at the proper times and seasons, and in proper quantities. He received all the cash, expended what was necessary for the support of the family, and kept exact accounts, which he was obliged at certain times to lay before the master. The *mysteries*, the *doctrines of God*, relative to the salvation of the world by the passion and death of Christ; and the inspiration, illumination, and purification of the soul by the Spirit of Christ, constituted a principal part of the Divine treasure intrusted to the hands of the stewards by their heavenly Master;

2

A. M. 4060.
A. D. 56.
A. U. C. 809.
Anno Imp. Nero-
nis Cæs. 3.

small thing that I should be judged of you, or of man's ᶜ judgment; yea, I judge not mine own self:

4 For I know nothing by myself, ᵈ yet am I not hereby justified: but he that judgeth me is the Lord.

5 ᵉ Therefore judge nothing before the time, until the Lord come, ᶠ who both will bring to light the hidden things of darkness, and will

make manifest the counsels of the hearts: and ᵍ then shall every man have praise of God.

6 And these things, brethren, ʰ I have in a figure transferred to myself and *to* Apollos for your sakes; ⁱ that ye might learn in us not to think *of men* above that which is written; that no one of you ᵏ be puffed up for one against another.

7 For who ˡ maketh thee to differ *from an-*

A. M. 4060.
A. D. 56.
A. U. C. 809.
Anno Imp. Nero
nis Cæs. 3.

ᶜ Gr. *day*; chap. iii. 13.——ᵈ Job ix. 2; Psa. cxxx. 3; cxliii. 2; Prov. xxi. 2; Rom. iii. 20; iv. 2.——ᵉ Matt. vii. 1; Rom. ii. 1, 16; xiv. 4, 10, 13; Rev. xx. 12.

ᶠ Chap. iii. 13.——ᵍ Rom. ii. 29; 2 Cor. v. 10.——ʰ Chap. i. 12; iii. 4.——ⁱ Rom. xii. 3.——ᵏ Chap. iii. 21; v. 2, 6.——ˡ Gr. *distinguisheth thee.*

---

as the *food* that was to be dispensed at proper times, seasons, and in proper proportions to the children and domestics of the *Church*, which is the *house of God.*

Verse 3. *It is a very small thing that I should be judged of you*] Those who preferred *Apollos* or *Kephas* before St. Paul, would of course give their reasons for this preference; and these might, in many instances, be very unfavourable to his character as a man, a Christian, or an apostle; of this he was regardless, as he sought not his own glory, but the glory of God in the salvation of their souls.

Or of man's judgment] Η ύπο ανθρωπινης ήμερας, literally, *or of man's day*: but ανθρωπινη ήμερα signifies any day set apart by a judge or magistrate to try a man on. This is the meaning of ήμερα, Psa. xxxvii. 13: *The Lord shall laugh at him: for he seeth that his* DAY, ή ήμερα αυτου, *his judgment is coming.* Mal. iii. 17: *And they shall be mine in the* DAY, εις ήμεραν, *in the judgment, when I make up my jewels.* It has the same meaning in 2 Pet. iii. 10: *But the* DAY *the* JUDGMENT, *of the Lord will come.* The word ανθρωπινος, *man's,* signifies *miserable, wretched, woful;* so Jerem. xvii. 16: *Neither have I desired,* שונא םוי *yom enosh, the day of man;* but very properly translated in our version, the *woful day.* God's DAYS, Job xxiv. 1, certainly signify *God's* JUDGMENTS. And the DAY of our *Lord Jesus,* in this epistle, chap. i. 8, and v. 5, signifies the *day* in which Christ will *judge* the world; or rather the *judgment* itself.

I judge not mine own self.] I leave myself entirely to God, whose I am, and whom I serve.

Verse 4. *For I know nothing by myself*] Ουδεν γαρ εμαυτω συνοιδα· I am not *conscious* that I am *guilty* of any evil, or have neglected to fulfil faithfully the duty of a steward of Jesus Christ. The import of the verb συνειδειν is *to be conscious of guilt;* and *conscire* has the same meaning: so, in Horace, *Nil* CONSCIRE *sibi, to know nothing to one's self,* is the same as *nulla pallescere culpa, not to grow pale at being charged with a crime,* through a *consciousness* of guilt.

Yet am I not hereby justified] I do not pretend to say that though I am not *conscious* of any offence towards God I must therefore be pronounced innocent; no: I leave those things to God; he shall pronounce in my favour, not I myself. By these words the apostle, in a very gentle yet effectual manner, censures

those rash and precipitate judgments which the Corinthians were in the habit of pronouncing on both men and things—a conduct than which nothing is more reprehensible and dangerous.

Verse 5. *Judge nothing before the time*] God, the righteous Judge, will determine every thing shortly: it is his province alone to search the heart, and *bring to light the hidden things of darkness.* If you be so pure and upright in your conduct, if what you have been doing in these divisions, &c., be right in his sight, then shall you have praise for the same; if otherwise, yourselves are most concerned. Some refer the praise to St. Paul and his companions: *Then shall every one of us* apostles *have praise of God.*

Verse 6. *These things*] Which I have written, chap. iii. 5, &c.

I have in a figure transferred to myself and to Apollos] I have written as if myself and Apollos were the authors of the sects which now prevail among you; although *others,* without either our consent or knowledge, have proclaimed us *heads* of parties. Bishop Pearce paraphrases the verse thus: "I have made use of my own and Apollos' name in my arguments against your divisions, because I would spare to name those teachers among you who are guilty of making and heading parties; and because I would have you, by our example, not to value them above what I have said of teachers in general in this epistle; so that none of you ought to be puffed up for one against another." Doubtless there were persons at Corinth who, taking advantage of this spirit of innovation among that people, set themselves up also for teachers, and endeavoured to draw disciples after them. And perhaps some even of these were more valued by the fickle multitude than the very *apostles* by whom they had been brought out of heathenish darkness into the marvellous light of the Gospel. I have already supposed it possible that *Diotrephes* was one of the ringleaders in these schisms at Corinth. See on chap. i. 14.

Verse 7. *For who maketh thee to differ*] It is likely that the apostle is here addressing himself to some *one of those puffed up teachers,* who was glorying in his *gifts,* and in the knowledge he had of the Gospel, &c. As if he had said: If thou hast all that knowledge which thou professest to have, didst thou not receive it from *myself* or some other of my *fellow helpers* who first preached the Gospel at Corinth? God never

　　2

A. M. 4060.
A. D. 56.
A. U. C.
809.
Anno Imp. Nero-
nis Cæs. 3.

other? and ^m what hast thou that thou didst not receive? now, if thou didst receive *it*, why dost thou glory, as if thou hadst not received *it*?

8 Now ye are full, ⁿ now ye are rich, ye have reigned as kings without us : and I would to God ye did reign, that we also might reign with you.

9 For I think that God hath set forth ^o us the apostles last, ^p as it were appointed to death : for ^q we are made a ^r spectacle unto the world, and to angels, and to men.

A. M. 4060.
A. D. 56.
A. U. C.
809.
Anno Imp. Nero-
nis Cæs. 3.

10 ^s We *are* ^t fools for Christ's sake, but ye *are* wise in Christ; ^u we *are* weak, but ye *are* strong; ye *are* honourable, but we *are* despised.

---

^m John iii. 27; James i. 17; 1 Pet. iv. 10.——ⁿ Rev. iii. 17. ^o Or, *us the last apostles, as.*——^p Psa. xliv. 22; Rom. viii. 36; chap. xv. 30, 31 ; 2 Cor. iv. 11; vi. 9

^q Heb. x. 33.——^r Gr. *theatre.*——^s Chap. ii. 3.——^t Acts xvii. 18; xxvi. 24; chap. i. 18, &c.; ii. 14; iii. 18; see 2 Kings ix. 11.——^u 2 Cor. xiii. 9.

---

spoke to *thee* to make thee an *apostle*. Hast thou a particle of light that thou hast not received from our preaching? Why then dost thou glory, boast, and exult, as if God had *first* spoken by *thee*, and not by us!

This is the most likely meaning of this verse; and a meaning that is suitable to the whole of the context. It has been applied in a more general sense by religious people, and the doctrine they build on it is true in *itself*, though it does not appear to me to be any part of the apostle's meaning in this place. The doctrine I refer to is this : God is the foundation of all good ; no man possesses any good but what he has derived from God. If any man possess that grace which saves him from scandalous enormities, let him consider that he has received it as a mere free gift from God's mercy. Let him not despise his neighbour who has it not ; there was a time when he himself did not possess it ; and a time may come when the man whom he now affects to despise, and on whose conduct he is unmerciful and severe, may receive it, and probably may make a more evangelical use of it than he is now doing. This caution is necessary to many religious people, who imagine that they have been eternal objects of God's favour, and that others have been eternal objects of his hate, for no reason that they can show for either the one or the other. He can have little acquaintance with his own heart, who is not aware of the possibility of *pride* lurking under the exclamation, *Why me!* when comparing his own gracious state with the unregenerate state of another.

Verse 8. *Now ye*] Corinthians *are full* of secular wisdom ; *now ye are rich*, both in wealth and spiritual gifts; (chap. xiv. 26 :) *ye have reigned as kings*, flourishing in the enjoyment of these things, in all tranquillity and honour ; *without* any want of *us : and I would to God ye did reign*, in *deed*, and not in *conceit* only, *that we also*, poor, persecuted, and despised apostles, *might reign with you*.—Whitby.

Though this paraphrase appears natural, yet I am of opinion that the apostle here intends a strong *irony;* and one which, when taken in conjunction with what he had said before, must have stung them to the heart. It is not an unusual thing for many people to *forget*, if not *despise*, the men by whom they were brought to the knowledge of the truth ; and take up with *others* to whom, in the things of God, they owe nothing. Reader, is this *thy* case?

Verse 9. *God hath set forth us the apostles last*] This whole passage is well explained by Dr. Whitby.

" Here the apostle seems to allude to the Roman spectacles, της των θηριομαχων, και μονομαχιας ανδροφονου, that of the *Bestiarii* and the *gladiators;* where in the *morning* men were brought upon the theatres to fight with *wild beasts*, and to them was allowed armour to defend themselves and smite the beasts that assailed them ; but in the *meridian* or noon-day spectacles the gladiators were brought forth *naked*, and without any thing to defend themselves from the sword of the assailant ; and he that then escaped was only kept for slaughter to another day, so that these men might well be called επιθανατιοι, *men appointed for death;* and this being the *last* appearance on the theatre for that day, they are said here to be set forth εσχατοι, *the last*." Of these two spectacles *Seneca* speaks thus, Epist. vii. : " In the *morning* men are exposed to lions and bears : at *mid-day* to their spectators ; those that kill are exposed to one another ; the victor is detained for another slaughter ; the conclusion of the fight is *death*. The *former* fighting compared to this was mercy ; now it is mere *butchery :* they have nothing to cover them ; their whole body is exposed to every blow, and every stroke produces a wound," &c.

We are made a spectacle] 'Οτι θεατρον εγενηθημεν, We are exhibited on the *theatre* to the *world ;* we are lawful booty to all mankind, and particularly to the *men of the world*, who have their portion in this life. *Angels* are astonished at our treatment, and so are the more considerate part of *men*. Who at that time would have coveted the apostolate?

Verse 10. *We are fools for Christ's sake*] Here he still carries on the allusion to the public spectacles among the Romans, where they were accustomed to hiss, hoot, mock, and variously insult the poor victims. To this *Philo* alludes, in his embassy to *Caius*, speaking of the treatment which the Jews received at Rome : ωσπερ γαρ εν θεατρω κλωσμοσυριττοντων, καταμωκωμενων, αμετρα χλευαζοντων· " For, as if exhibited upon a theatre, we are hissed, most outrageously hooted, and insulted beyond all bounds." Thus, says the apostle, we are fools on Christ's account ; we walk in a conformity to his will, and we bear his cross : and did we walk according to the course of this world, or according to the *man-pleasing* conduct of some among you, we should have no such cross to bear.

Ye are wise in Christ] Surely all these expressions are meant *ironically ;* the *apostles* were neither *fools*, nor *weak*, nor *contemptible ;* nor were the *Corinthians*, morally speaking, *wise*, and *strong*, and *honourable.*

A. M. 4060.
A. D. 56.
A. U. C.
809.
Anno Imp. Nero-
nis Cæs. 3.

11 [v] Even unto this present hour we both hunger and thirst, and [w] are naked, and [x] are buffeted, and have no certain dwelling place;

12 [y] And labour, working with our own hands: [z] being reviled, we bless; being persecuted, we suffer it;

13 Being defamed, we entreat: [a] we are made as the filth of the earth, *and are* the offscouring of all things unto this day.

14 I write not these things to shame you, but [b] as my beloved sons I warn *you.*

15 For though ye have ten thousand instructers in Christ, yet *have ye* not many fathers: for, [c] in Christ Jesus I have begotten you through the Gospel.

A. M. 4060
A. D. 56.
A. U. C.
809.
Anno Imp. Nero
nis Cæs. 3.

---

[v] 2 Cor. iv. 8; xi. 23–27; Phil. iv. 12.——[w] Job xxii. 6; Rom. viii. 35.——[x] Acts xxiii. 2.——[y] Acts xviii. 3; xx. 34; 1 Thess. ii. 9; 2 Thess. iii. 8; 1 Tim. iv. 10.——[z] Matt. v. 44; Luke vi. 28;

xxiii. 34; Acts vii. 60; Rom. xii. 14, 20; 1 Pet. ii. 23; iii. 9. [a] Lam. iii. 45.——[b] 1 Thess. ii. 11.——[c] Acts xviii. 11; Rom. xv. 20; chap. iii. 6; Gal. iv. 19; Phil. 10; James i. 18.

Change tne *versons,* ana then the *epithets* will perfectly apply.

Verse 11. *We both hunger and thirst, &c.*] Who would then have been an apostle of Christ, even with all its spiritual honours and glories, who had not a soul filled with love both to God and man, and the fullest *conviction* of the reality of the doctrine he preached, and of that spiritual world in which alone he could expect rest? See the *Introduction,* sect. vi.

Have no certain dwelling place] We are mere itinerant preachers, and when we set out in the morning know not *where,* or whether we shall or not, get a night's lodging.

Verse 12. *Working with our own hands*] They were obliged to labour in order to supply themselves with the necessaries of life while preaching the Gospel to others. This, no doubt, was the case in every place where no Church had been as yet formed: afterwards, the people of God supplied their ministers, according to their power, with food and raiment.

Being reviled, we bless, &c.] What a most amiable picture does this exhibit of the power of the grace of Christ! Man is naturally a *proud* creature, and his pride prompts him always to *avenge* himself in whatever manner he can, and repay insult with insult. It is only the grace of Christ that can make a man patient in bearing injuries, and render blessing for cursing, beneficence for malevolence, &c. The apostles suffered all indignities for Christ's sake; for it was on *his* account that they were exposed to persecutions, &c.

Verse 13. *Being defamed*] Βλασφημουμενοι, Being *blasphemed.* I have already remarked that βλασφημειν signifies to *speak injuriously,* and may have reference either to God or to man. God is *blasphemed* when his attributes, doctrines, providence, or grace, are treated contemptuously, or any thing said of him that is contrary to his holiness, justice, goodness, or truth. *Man* is blasphemed when any thing injurious is spoken of his person, character, conduct, &c. *Blaspheming* against men is any thing by which they are *injured* in their *persons, characters,* or *property.*

We are made as the filth of the earth—the offscouring of all things] The Greek word which we render *filth,* is περικαθαρματα, a *purgation,* or *lustrative sacrifice*; that which we translate *offscouring* is περιψημα, a *redemption sacrifice.* To understand the full force of these words, as applied by the apostle in this place, we must observe that he alludes to certain customs

among the heathens, who, in the time of some public calamity, chose out some unhappy men of the most abject and despicable character to be a public *expiation* for them; these they maintained a whole year at the public expense; and then they led them out, crowned with flowers, as was customary in sacrifices; and, having heaped all the curses of the country upon their heads, and whipped them seven times, they burned them alive, and afterwards their ashes were thrown into the sea, while the people said these words: περιψημαῆμων γινου, *be thou our propitiation.* Sometimes the person thus chosen was thrown into the sea as a sacrifice to *Neptune,* the people saying the words as before. Hence *Origen* says that our Lord, in giving up himself as a propitiation for our sins, was much more than his apostles—περικαθαρματα του κοσμου, παντων περιψημα, *the lustration of the world, and the peculiar sacrifice for all men.* The apostle, therefore, means that he and his fellows were treated like those wretched beings who were judged to be fit for nothing but to be expiatory victims to the infernal gods, for the safety and redemption of others. Our words *filth* and *offscouring,* convey no legitimate sense of the original. See several useful remarks upon these terms in *Pearce, Whitby,* and *Parkhurst.*

Verse 14. *I write not these things to shame you*] It is not by way of *finding fault* with you for not providing me with the necessaries of life that I write thus; but I do it to warn you to act differently for the time to come; and be not so ready to be drawn aside by every pretender to apostleship, to the neglect of those to whom, under God, you owe your salvation.

Verse 15. *For though ye have ten thousand instructers*] Μυριους παιδαγωγους, *Myriads of leaders,* that is, an indefinite multitude; for so the word is often used. The παιδαγωγος, from which we have our word *pedagogue,* which we improperly apply to a *school master,* was, among the Greeks, the person or *servant* who attended a child, had the general care of him, and who *led him to school* for the purpose of being instructed by the διδασκαλος, or teacher. It seems there were many at Corinth who offered their services to instruct this people, and who were not well affected towards the apostle.

Not many fathers] Many offer to instruct you who have no *parental* feeling for you; and how can they? you are not their spiritual children, you stand in this relation to *me* alone; for *in Christ Jesus*—by the power

A. M. 4060.
A. D. 56.
A. U. C.
809.
Anno Imp. Nero-
nis Cæs. 3.

16 Wherefore, J beseech you, [d] be ye followers of me.

17 For this cause have I sent unto you [e] Timotheus, [f] who is my beloved son, and faithful in the Lord, who shall bring you [g] into remembrance of my ways which be in Christ, as I [h] teach every where [i] in every Church.

18 [k] Now some are puffed up, as though I would not come to you.

19 [l] But I will come to you shortly, [m] if the Lord will; and will know, not the speech of them which are puffed up, but the power.

20 For [n] the kingdom of God *is* not in word, but in power.

21 What will ye? [o] shall I come unto you with a rod, or in love, and *in* the spirit of meekness?

A. M. 4060.
A. D. 56.
A. U. C.
809.
Anno Imp. Nero-
nis Cæs. 3.

---

[d] Chap. xi. 1; Phil. iii. 17; 1 Thess. i. 6; 2 Thess. iii. 9. [e] Acts xix. 22; chap. xvi. 10; Phil. ii. 19; 1 Thess. iii. 2. [f] 1 Tim. i. 2; 2 Tim. i. 2.——[g] Chap. xi. 2.——[h] Chap. vii. 17.

[i] Chap. xiv. 33.——[k] Ch. v. 2.——[l] Acts xix. 21; chap. xvi. 5; 2 Cor. i. 15, 23.——[m] Acts xviii. 21; Rom. xv. 32; Heb. vi. 3; James iv. 15.——[n] Ch. ii. 4; 1 Thess. i. 5.——[o] 2 Cor. x. 2; xiii. 10.

---

and unction of his Spirit, *I have begotten you*—I was the means of bringing you into a state of salvation, so that you have been born again : ye are my children alone in the Gospel. *Schoettgen* produces a good illustration of this from *Shemoth Rabba*, sect. 46, fol. 140. "A girl who had lost her parents was educated by a guardian, who was a good and faithful man, and took great care of her; when she was grown up, he purposed to bestow her in marriage; the scribe came, and beginning to write the contract, said, What is thy name? The maid answered, N. The scribe proceeded, What is the name of thy father? The maid was silent. Her guardian said, Why art thou silent? The maid replied, Because I know *no other father but thee;* for he who educates a child well, is more properly the father than he who begot it." This is the same kind of sentiment which I have already quoted from *Terence*, Rom. xvi. 13.

> *Natura tu illi pater es, consiliis ego.*
> *Adelphi*, Act i., scene 2, ver. 47.

Thou art his father by *nature*, I by *instruction*.

Verse 16. *Wherefore, I beseech you, be ye followers of me.*] It should rather be translated, Be ye imitators of me; μιμηται, from which we have our word *mimic*, which, though now used only in a *bad* or *ludicrous* sense, simply signifies an *imitator* of another person, whether in *speech, manner, habit,* or otherwise. As children should imitate their *parents* in preference to all others, he calls on them to *imitate* him, as he claims them for his *children.* He lived for God and eternity, seeking not his own glory, emolument, or ease : those sowers of sedition among them were actuated by different motives. Here then the apostle compares himself with them : follow and imitate me, as I follow and imitate Christ : do not imitate them who, from their worldly pursuits, show themselves to be actuated with a worldly spirit.

Verse 17. *For this cause*] That you imitate me, and know in what this consists :

I sent unto you Timotheus] The same person to whom he wrote the two epistles that are still extant under his name, and whom he calls here his *beloved son,* one of his most *intimate disciples;* and whom he had been the means of *bringing to God* through Christ.

My ways which be in Christ] This person will also

inform you of the *manner* in which I regulate all the Churches; and show to you. that what I require of you is no other than what I require of all the Churches of Christ which I have formed, as I follow the same plan of discipline in every place. See the *Introduction,* sect. iii.

Verse 18. *Some are puffed up*] Some of your teachers act with great haughtiness, imagining themselves to be safe, because they suppose that I shall not revisit Corinth.

Verse 19. *But I will come to you shortly*] God being my helper, I fully purpose to visit you; and then I shall put those proud men to the proof, not of their *speech*—eloquence, or pretensions to great knowledge and influence, but of their *power*—the authority they profess to have from God, and the evidences of that authority in the works they have performed. See the *Introduction,* sect. xi.

Verse 20. *For the kingdom of God*] The religion of the Lord Jesus is *not in word*—in human eloquence, excellence of speech, or even in *doctrines; but in power,* εν δυναμει, in the mighty energy of the Holy Spirit; enlightening, quickening, converting, and sanctifying believers; and all his genuine apostles are enabled, on all necessary occasions, to demonstrate the truth of their calling by *miracles;* for this the original word often means.

Verse 21. *Shall I come unto you with a rod, or in love*] Here he alludes to the case of the *teacher* and *father,* mentioned in ver. 15. Shall I come to you with the *authority* of a *teacher,* and use the *rod* of *discipline?* or shall I come in the *tenderness* of a *father,* and entreat you to do what I have authority to enforce? Among the Jews, those who did not amend, after being faithfully admonished, were *whipped,* either publicly or privately, in the synagogue. If on this they did not amend, they were liable to be stoned. We see, from the cases of Ananias and Sapphira, Elymas the sorcerer, Hymenæus and Alexander, &c., that the apostles had sometimes the power to inflict the most awful punishments on transgressors. The Corinthians must have known this, and consequently have dreaded a visit from him in his *apostolical authority.* That there were many irregularities in this Church, which required both the presence and authority of the apostle, we shall see in the subsequent chapters.

2

1. In the preceding chapter we find the ministers of God compared to STEWARDS, of whom the strictest *fidelity* is required. (1.) *Fidelity* to GOD, in publishing his truth with *zeal*, defending it with *courage*, and recommending it with *prudence*. (2.) *Fidelity* to CHRIST, whose representatives they are, in honestly and fully recommending his grace and salvation on the ground of his *passion* and *death*, and preaching his *maxims* in all their *force* and *purity*. (3.) *Fidelity* to the CHURCH, in taking heed to keep up a godly discipline, admitting none into it but those who have abandoned their sins ; and permitting none to continue in it that do not continue to adorn the doctrine of God their Saviour. (4.) *Fidelity* to their own MINISTRY, walking so as to bring no blame on the Gospel ; avoiding the extremes of *indolent tenderness* on one hand, and *austere severity* on the other. Considering the flock, not as *their* flock, but the flock of Jesus Christ ; watching, ruling, and feeding it according to the order of their Divine Master.

2. A minister of God should act with great caution : every man, properly speaking, is placed between the secret judgment of God and the public censure of men. He should do nothing rashly, that he may not *justly* incur the censure of men ; and he should do nothing but in the loving fear of God, that he may not incur the censure of his Maker. The man who scarcely ever allows himself to be *wrong*, is one of whom it may be safely said, he is seldom *right*. It is possible for a man to mistake his own will for the will of God, and his own obstinacy for inflexible adherence to his duty. With such persons it is dangerous to have any commerce. Reader, pray to God to save thee from an inflated and self-sufficient mind.

3. *Zeal* for God's truth is essentially necessary for every minister; and *prudence* is not less so. They should be wisely tempered together, but this is not always the case. *Zeal* without *prudence* is like a flambeau in the hands of a blind man ; it may *enlighten* and *warm*, but it may also destroy the spiritual building. *Human prudence* should be avoided as well as *intemperate zeal* ; this kind of prudence consists in a man's being careful not to bring himself into trouble, and not to hazard his reputation, credit, interest, or fortune, in the performance of his duty. *Evangelical wisdom* consists in our suffering and losing all things, rather than be wanting in the discharge of our obligations.

4. From St. Paul's account of himself we find him often suffering the severest hardships in the prosecution of his duty. He had for his patrimony, hunger, thirst, nakedness, stripes, &c.; and wandered about testifying the Gospel of the grace of God, without even a *cottage* that he could claim as his own. Let those who dwell in their elegant houses, who profess to be *apostolic* in their *order*, and *evangelic* in their *doctrines*, think of this. In their state of affluence they should have extraordinary degrees of *zeal*, humility, meekness, and charity, to recommend them to our notice as *apostolical men*. If God, in the course of his providence, has saved them from an apostle's hardships, let them devote their lives to the service of that Church in which they have their emoluments ; and labour incessantly to build it up on its most holy faith. Let them not be *masters* to govern with rigour and imperiousness ; but tender *fathers*, who feel every member in the Church as their own child, and labour to feed the heavenly family with the mysteries of God, of which they are stewards.

5. And while the people require much of their spiritual pastors, these pastors have equal right to require much of their people. The obligation is not all on one side ; those who watch for our souls have a right not only to their own support, but to our reverence and confidence. Those who despise their ecclesiastical rulers, will soon despise the Church of Christ itself, neglect its ordinances, lose sight of its doctrines, and at last neglect their own salvation.

CHAPTER V.

Account of the incestuous person, or of him who had married his father's wife, 1. The apostle reproves the Corinthians for their carelessness in this matter, and orders them to excommunicate the transgressor, 2–5. They are reprehended for their glorying, while such scandals were among them, 6. They must purge out the old leaven, that they may properly celebrate the Christian passover, 7–9. They must not associate with any who, professing the Christian religion, were guilty of any scandalous vice, and must put away from them every evil person, 10–13.

A. M. 4060.
A. D. 56.
A. U. C. 809.
Anno Imp. Neronis Cæs. 3.

IT is reported commonly *that there is* fornication among you, and such fornication as is not so much as [a] named among the Gentiles, [b] that one should have his [c] father's wife.

2 [d] And ye are puffed up, and have not rather [e] mourned, that

A. M. 4060.
A. D. 56.
A. U. C. 809.
Anno Imp. Neronis Cæs. 3.

---

[a] Eph. v. 3.——[b] Lev. xviii. 8 ; Deut. xxii. 30 ; xxvii. 20.   [c] 2 Cor. vii. 12.——[d] Chap. iv. 18.——[e] 2 Cor. vii. 7, 10.

NOTES ON CHAP. V.

Verse 1. There is *fornication among you*] The word πορνεια, which we translate *fornication* in this place, must be understood in its utmost latitude of meaning, as implying all kinds of impurity ; for, that the Corinthians were notoriously guilty of every species of irregularity and debauch, we have already seen ; and it is not likely that in speaking on this subject, in reference to a people so very notorious, he would refer to only one species of impurity, and that not the most flagitious.

That one should have his father's wife.] Commen-

2

A. M. 4060.
A. D. 56.
A. U. C.
809.
Anno Imp. Nero-
nis Cæs. 3.

he that hath done this deed might be taken away from among you.

3 [f] For I verily, as absent in body, but present in spirit, have [g] judged already, as though I were present, *concerning* him that hath so done this deed;

4 In the name of our Lord Jesus Christ, when ye are gathered together, and my spirit,

[h] with the power of our Lord Jesus Christ,

A. M. 4060.
A. D. 56.
A. U. C.
809.
Anno Imp. Nero-
nis Cæs. 3.

5 [i] To deliver such a one unto [k] Satan for the destruction of the flesh, that the spirit may be saved in the day of the Lord Jesus.

6 [l] Your glorying *is* not good. Know ye not that [m] a little leaven leaveneth the whole lump?

---

[f] Col. ii. 5.——[g] Or, *determined*.——[h] Matt. xvi. 19; xviii. 18; John xx. 23; 2 Cor. ii. 10; xiii. 3, 10.——[i] Job ii. 6; Psa. cix.

6; 1 Tim. i. 20.——[k] Acts xxvi. 18.——[l] Ver. 2; ch. iii. 21; iv. 19; James iv. 16.——[m] Chap. xv. 33; Gal. v. 9; 2 Tim. ii. 17.

---

tators and critics have found great difficulties in this statement. One part of the case is sufficiently clear, that a man who professed Christianity had illegal connections with his father's wife; but the principal question is, was his father *alive* or *dead*? Most think that the father was *alive*, and imagine that to this the apostle refers, 2 Cor. vii. 12, where, speaking of the person who *did* the wrong, he introduces also him who had *suffered* the wrong; which must mean the father, and the father then *alive*. After all that has been said on this subject, I think it most natural to conclude that the person in question had married the wife of his *deceased* father, not his *own* mother, but *stepmother*, then a *widow*.

This was a crime which the text says *was not so much as named among the Gentiles*; the apostle must only mean that it was not *accredited* by them, for it certainly did often occur: but by their best writers who notice it, it was branded as superlatively infamous. Cicero styles it, *scelus incredibile et inauditum*, an incredible and unheard-of wickedness; but it was *heard* of and *practised*; and there are several stories of this kind in heathen authors, but they *reprobate* not *commend* it. The word ονομαζεται, *named*, is wanting in almost every MS. and version of importance, and certainly makes no part of the text. The words should be read, *and such fornication as is not amongst the Gentiles*, i. e., not *allowed*. Some think that this woman might have been a proselyte to the Jewish religion from heathenism; and the rabbins taught that proselytism annulled all former relationship, and that a woman was at liberty in such a case to depart from an unbelieving husband, and to marry even with a believing *son*, i. e., of her husband by some former wife.

Verse 2. Ye are puffed up] Ye are full of strife and contention relative to your parties and favourite teachers, and neglect the discipline of the Church. Had you considered the greatness of this crime, ye would have rather *mourned*, and have put away this flagrant transgressor from among you.

Taken away from among you.] Ἱνα εξαρθη εκ μεσου ὑμων. This is supposed by some to refer to the punishment of *death*, by others to excommunication. The Christian Church was at this time too young to have those *forms of excommunication* which were practised in succeeding centuries. Probably no more is meant than a simple *disowning* of the person, accompanied with the refusal to admit him to the sacred ordinances, or to have any intercourse or connection with him.

Verse 3. Absent in body, but present in spirit]

Perhaps St. Paul refers to the gift of the discernment of spirits, which it is very likely the apostles in general possessed on extraordinary occasions. He had already seen this matter so clearly, that he had determined on that sort of punishment which should be inflicted for this crime.

Verse 4. In the name of our Lord Jesus] Who is the *head* of the Church; and under whose authority every act is to be performed.

And my spirit] My apostolical authority derived from him; *with the power*, συν δυναμει, with the *miraculous energy of the Lord Jesus*, which is to inflict the punishment that you pronounce:—

Verse 5. To deliver such a one unto Satan] There is no evidence that delivering to Satan was any *form* of excommunication known either among the Jews or the Christians. *Lightfoot, Selden*, and *Schoettgen*, who have searched all the Jewish records, have found nothing that answers to this: it was a species of punishment administered in extraordinary cases, in which the body and the mind of an incorrigible transgressor were delivered by the authority of God into the power of Satan, to be tortured with diseases and terrors as a warning to all; but while the body and mind were thus tormented, the immortal spirit was under the influence of the Divine mercy; and the affliction, in all probability, was in general only for a season; though sometimes it was evidently unto *death*, as the *destruction of the flesh* seems to imply. But the soul found mercy at the hand of God; for such a most extraordinary interference of God's power and justice, and of Satan's influence, could not fail to bring the person to a state of the deepest humiliation and contrition; and thus, while the *flesh* was *destroyed*, the *spirit was saved in the day of the Lord Jesus*. No such power as this remains in the Church of God; none such should be assumed; the pretensions to it are as *wicked* as they are *vain*. It was the same power by which *Ananias* and *Sapphira* were struck dead, and *Elymas* the sorcerer struck blind. *Apostles* alone were intrusted with it.

Verse 6. Your glorying is not good.] You are triumphing in your superior knowledge, and busily employed in setting up and supporting your respective teachers, while the Church is left under the most scandalous corruptions—corruptions which threaten its very existence if not purged away.

Know ye not] With all your boasted wisdom, do you not know and acknowledge the truth of a common maxim, *a little leaven leaveneth the whole lump?* If

2

A. M. 4060.
A. D. 56.
A. U. C.
809.
Anno Imp. Nero-
nis Cæs. 3.

7 Purge out therefore the old leaven, that ye may be a new lump, as ye are unleavened. For even [n] Christ our [o] passover [p] is sacrificed for us:

8 Therefore [q] let us keep [r] the feast, [s] not with old leaven, neither [t] with the leaven of malice and wickedness; but with the unleavened *bread* of sincerity and truth.

9 I wrote unto you in an epistle [u] not to company with fornicators:

10 [v] Yet not altogether with the fornicators [w] of this world, or with the covetous, or extortioners, or with idolaters; for then must ye needs go [x] out of the world.

11 But now I have written unto you not to keep company, [y] if any man that is called a

A. M. 4060.
A. D. 56.
A. U. C.
809.
Anno Imp. Nero
nis Cæs. 3.

---

[n] Isa. liii. 7; John i. 29; chap. xv. 3; 1 Pet. i. 19; Rev. v. 6, 12.——[o] John xix. 14.——[p] Or, *is slain.*——[q] Exod. xii. 15; xiii. 6.——[r] Or, *holiday.*——[s] Deut. xvi. 3.——[t] Matt. xvi. 6, 12; Mark viii. 15; Luke xii. 1.

[u] See ver. 2, 7; 2 Cor. vi. 14; Eph. v. 11; 2 Thess. iii. 14. [v] Chap. x. 27.——[w] Chap. i. 20.——[x] John xvii. 15; 1 John v. 19.——[y] Matt. xviii. 17; Rom. xvi. 17; 2 Thess. iii. 6, 14; 2 John 10.

---

this *leaven*—the incestuous person, be permitted to remain among you; if his conduct be not exposed by the most formidable censure; the flood-gates of impurity will be opened on the Church, and the whole state of Christianity ruined in Corinth.

Verse 7. Purge out therefore the old leaven] As it is the custom of the Jews previously to the *passover* to search their houses in the most diligent manner for the old leaven, and throw it out, sweeping every part clean; so act with this incestuous person. I have already shown with what care the Jews purged their houses from all leaven previously to the *passover;* see the note on Exod. xii. 8–19, and on the term *passover,* and Christ as represented by this ancient Jewish sacrifice; see on Exod. xii. 27, and my *Discourse on the Nature and Design of the Eucharist.*

Verse 8. Therefore let us keep the feast] It is very likely that the time of the passover was now approaching, when the Church of Christ would be called to extraordinary acts of devotion, in commemorating the passion, death, and resurrection of Christ; and of this circumstance the apostle takes advantage in his exhortation to the Corinthians. See the *Introduction,* sect. xii.

Not with old leaven] Under the Christian dispensation we must be saved equally from *Judaism, heathenism,* and from sin of every kind; *malice* and *wickedness* must be destroyed; and *sincerity* and *truth,* inward purity and outward holiness, take their place.

The apostle refers here not more to wicked *principles* than to wicked *men;* let us keep the feast, not with the old leaven—the impure principles which actuated you while in your heathen state; neither with the leaven of malice and wickedness, κακιας και πονηριας, wickedness, radical depravity, producing unrighteousness in the life; nor with the *persons* who are thus influenced, and thus act; *but with the unleavened* bread, αλλ' εν αζυμοις, but with *upright* and *godly men,* who have *sincerity,* ειλικρινεια, such purity of affections and conduct, that even the light of God shining upon them discovers no flaw, and *truth*—who have received the testimony of God, and who are inwardly as well as outwardly what they profess to be.

The word πονηριας, which we translate *wickedness,* is so very like to πορνειας, *fornication,* that some very ancient MSS. have the latter reading instead of the former; which, indeed, seems most natural in this place; as κακιας, which we translate *malice,* includes

every thing that is implied in πονηριας, *wickedness;* whereas πορνειας, as being the subject in question, see ver. 1, would come more pointedly in here: *Not with wickedness and fornication,* or rather, *not with wicked men and fornicators:* but I do not contend for this reading.

Verse 9. I wrote unto you in an epistle] The wisest and best skilled in Biblical criticism agree that the apostle does not refer to any other epistle than *this;* and that he speaks here of some general directions which he had given in the foregoing part of it; but which he had now in some measure changed and greatly strengthened, as we see from ver. 11. The words εγραψα εν τη επιστολη may be translated, I HAD *written to you in* THIS EPISTLE; for there are many instances in the New Testament where the *aorist,* which is here used, and which is a sort of indefinite tense, is used for the *perfect* and the *plusquam-perfect.* Dr. Whitby produces several proofs of this, and contends that the conclusion drawn by some, viz. that it refers to some epistle that is lost, is not legitimately drawn from any premises which either this text or antiquity affords. The principal evidence against this is 2 Cor. vii. 8, where εν τη επιστολη, the same words as above, appear to refer to this *first* epistle. Possibly the apostle may refer to an epistle which he had written though not sent; for, on receiving farther information from *Stephanas, Fortunatus,* and *Achaicus,* relative to the state of the Corinthian Church, he suppressed that, and wrote this, in which he considers the subject much more at large. See Dr. *Lightfoot.*

Not to company with fornicators] With which, as we have already seen, Corinth abounded. It was not only the *grand* sin, but *staple,* of the place.

Verse 10. For then must ye needs go out of the world.] What an awful picture of the general corruption of manners does this exhibit! The Christians at Corinth could not transact the ordinary affairs of life with any others than with fornicators, covetous persons, extortioners, railers, drunkards, and idolaters, *because* there were none others in the place! How necessary was Christianity in that city!

Verse 11. But now I have written] I not only write this, but I add more: if any one *who is called a brother,* i. e. professes the Christian religion, be a *fornicator, covetous, idolater, railer, drunkard,* or *extortioner,* not even to eat with such—have no communion with such a one, in things either *sacred* or *civil.* You

A. M. 4060.
A. D. 56.
A. U. C.
809.
Anno Imp. Nero-
nis Cæs. 3.
brother be a fornicator, or covetous, or an idolater, or a railer, or
a drunkard, or an extortioner;
with such a one, ᶻ no not to eat.

12 For what have I to do to judge ᵃ them
also that are without? do not ye
judge ᵇ them that are within?

13 But them that are without
God judgeth. Therefore ᶜ put
away from among yourselves that wicked person.
A. M. 4060.
A. D. 56.
A. U. C.
809.
Anno Imp. Nero-
nis Cæs. 3.

ᶻ Gal. ii. 12.——ᵃ Mark iv. 11; Col. iv. 5; 1 Thess. iv. 12;
1 Tim. iii. 7.

ᵇ Chap. vi. 1, 2, 3, 4.——ᶜ Deut. xiii. 5; xvii. 7; xxi. 21; xxii.
21, 22, 24.

may transact your worldly concerns with a person that
knows not God, and makes no profession of Christianity, whatever his moral character may be; but ye
must not even thus far acknowledge a man *professing
Christianity*, who is scandalous in his conduct. Let
him have this extra mark of your abhorrence of all
sin; and let the world see that the Church of God
does not tolerate iniquity.

Verse 12. *For what have I to do to judge them
also that are without?*] The term *without*, τους εξω,
signifies those who were not members of the Church,
and in this sense its correspondent term החיצונים *hach-
itsonim*, those that *are without*, is generally understood
in the Jewish writers, where it frequently occurs. The
word και, *also*, which greatly disturbs the sense here,
is wanting in ABCFG, and several others, with the
Syriac, Coptic, Slavonic, Vulgate, and the *Itala*; together with several of the *fathers*. The sentence, I
think, with the omission of και, *also*, should stand
thus: *Does it belong to me to pass sentence on those
which are without*—which are *not* members of the
Church? *By no means* (ουχι.) *Pass ye sentence on
them which are within*—which are members of the
Church: *those which are without*—which are not members of the Church, *God will pass sentence on*, in that
way in which he generally deals with the heathen
world. *But put ye away the evil from among yourselves.* This is most evidently the apostle's meaning,
and renders all comments unnecessary. In the last
clause there appears to be an allusion to Deut. xvii.
7, where the like directions are given to the congregation of Israel, relative to a person found guilty of
idolatry: *Thou shalt put away the evil from among
you*—where the version of the Septuagint is almost
the same as that of the apostle: *και εξαρεις τον πονη-
ρον εξ υμων αυτων.*

THERE are several important subjects in this chapter which intimately concern the Christian Church in
general.

1. If evil be tolerated in religious societies, the
work of God cannot prosper there. If one scandal
appear, it should be the cause of general humiliation
and mourning to the followers of God where it occurs;
because the soul of a brother is on the road to perdition, the cause of God so far betrayed and injured,
and Christ recrucified in the house of his friends.
Pity should fill every heart towards the transgressor,
and prayer for the backslider occupy all the members
of the Church.

2. *Discipline* must be exercised in the Christian
Church; without this it will soon differ but little from
the *wilderness of this world.* But what judgment,
prudence, piety, and caution, are requisite in the execution of this most important branch of a minister's
duty! He may be too *easy* and *tender*, and permit
the gangrene to remain till the flock be infected with
it. Or he may be *rigid* and *severe*, and destroy parts
that are vital while only professing to take away what
is vitiated. A backslider is one who once knew less
or more of the salvation of God. Hear what God
says concerning such: *Turn, ye backsliders, for I am
married unto you.* See how unwilling *He* is to give
them up! He suffers long, and is kind: do thou
likewise; and when thou art obliged to cut off the
offender from the Church of Christ, follow him still
with thy best advice and heartiest prayers.

3. A soul cut off from the flock of God is in an
awful state! his outward defence is departed from him;
and being no longer accountable to any for his conduct,
he generally plunges into unprecedented depths of iniquity; and the last state of that man becomes worse
than the first. Reader, art thou *without the pale of
God's Church?* remember it is here written, *them that
are* WITHOUT *God judgeth*, verse 13.

4. Christians who wish to retain the spirituality of
their religion should be very careful how they mingle
with the world. He who is *pleased* with the company
of ungodly men, no matter howsoever witty or learned,
is either himself one with them, or is drinking into
their spirit. It is impossible to associate with such
by choice without receiving a portion of their contagion.
A man may be amused or delighted with such people,
but he will return even from the *festival of wit* with
a lean soul. Howsoever contiguous they may be, yet
the Church and the world are separated by an impassa-
ble gulf.

5. If all the fornicators, adulterers, drunkards, extortioners, and covetous persons which bear the Christian name, were to be publicly excommunicated from
the Christian Church, how many, and how awful would
the examples be! If however the discipline of the
visible Church be so lax that such characters are
tolerated in it, they should consider that this is no passport to heaven. In the sight of God they are not
members of his Church; their citizenship is not in
heaven, and therefore they have no right to expect
the heavenly inheritance. It is not under *names,
creeds*, or *professions*, that men shall be saved at the
last day; those alone who were holy, who were here
conformed to the image of Christ, shall inherit the
kingdom of God. Those who expect it in any
other way, or on any other account, will be sadly
deceived.

2

CHAPTER VI.

*The Corinthians are reproved for their litigious disposition ; brother going to law with brother, and that be-
fore the heathen, 1–6. They should suffer wrong rather than do any, 7, 8. No unrighteous person can
enter into the glory of God, 9, 10. Some of the Corinthians had been grievous sinners, but God had
saved them, 11. Many things may be lawful which are not at all times expedient, 12. Meats are for
the belly, and the belly for meats ; but the body is not for uncleanness, 13. Christ's resurrection a pledge
of ours, 14. The bodies of Christians are members of Christ, and must not be defiled, 15–17. He that
commits fornication sins against his own body, 18. Strong dissuasives from it, 19, 20.*

A. M. 4060.
A. D. 56.
A. U. C. 809.
Anno Imp. Nero-
nis Cæs. 3.

DARE any of you, having a
matter against another, go to
law before the unjust, and not
before the saints ?

2 Do ye not know that [a] the saints shall

judge the world ? and if the world
shall be judged by you, are ye
unworthy to judge the smallest
matters ?

3 Know ye not that we shall [b] judge angels ?

A. M. 4060.
A. D. 56.
A. U. C. 809.
Anno Imp. Nero-
nis Cæs. 3.

[a] Psa. xlix: 14 ; Dan. vii. 22 ; Matt. xix. 28 ; Luke xxii. 30 ; Rev. ii. 26 ; iii. 21 ; xx. 4.——[b] 2 Pet. ii. 4 ; Jude 6.

NOTES ON CHAP. VI.

Verse 1. Dare any of you, &c.] From the many
things that are here reprehended by the apostle, we
learn that the Christian Church at Corinth was in a
state of great imperfection, notwithstanding there were
very many eminent characters among them. Divided
as they were among themselves, there was no one
person who possessed any public authority to settle
differences between man and man ; therefore, as one
party would not submit to the decisions of another,
they were obliged to carry their contentions before
heathen magistrates ; and probably these very subjects
of litigations arose out of their ecclesiastical *divisions*.
The thing, and this issue of it, the apostle strongly
reprehends.

Before the unjust, and not before the saints ?] The
heathen judges were termed δικασται from their presumed *righteousness* in the administration of *justice ;*
here the apostle, by a paronomasia, calls them αδικοι,
unrighteous persons ; and it is very likely that at
Corinth, where such corruption of manners reigned,
there was a great *perversion* of public *justice ;* and it
is not to be supposed that matters relative to the Christians were fairly decided. The Christians the apostle
terms ἁγιοι, *saints,* which they were all by *profession ;*
and doubtless many were so in *spirit* and in *truth.*

Verse 2. The saints shall judge the world ?] Nothing can be more evident than that the writers of the New
Testament often use ὁ κοσμος, *the world,* to signify the
Jewish people ; and sometimes the *Roman empire,* and
the *Jewish state ;* and in the former sense it is often
used by our Lord. *When,* says he, *the Son of man
shall sit on the throne of his glory, then shall ye sit
on twelve thrones, judging the twelve tribes of Israel,*
Matt. xix. 28. It is supposed that he refers to the
same subject as that mentioned here—the saints judging the world ; and that St. Paul has *his* words in
view in what he says here to the Corinthians. By
judging the twelve tribes of Israel, some have imagined
that *having authority in the Church* is merely intended ;
but Dr. Lightfoot contends that the words referred to
the coming of our Lord to execute judgment on the
Jews, and to destroy their state ; and that the *doctrine*
of the apostles, not *themselves,* was to judge and condemn that most disobedient people. The place before
us is generally understood to imply, that the redeemed
of the Lord shall be, on the great day, *assessors* with
him in judgment ; and shall give their award in the
determinations of his justice. On reviewing this subject, I am fully of opinion that this cannot be the
meaning of the words, and that no such *assessorship*
as is contended for ever will take place ; and that the
interpretation is clogged with a multitude of absurdities.

1. The *saints* themselves are to appear before the
judgment seat of Christ, and shall be judged by him,
after which they shall *reign with him ;* but it is never
said in Scripture that they shall *judge with him.*

2. It would be absurd to suppose that *thrones*
should be erected for the purpose of saints sitting on
them to give their *approbation* in the condemnation of
the wicked ; of what use can such an approbation be ?
is it necessary to the validity of Christ's decision ?
and will not even the damned themselves, without this,
acknowledge the justice of their doom ? I therefore
think with Dr. Lightfoot, that these words of the
apostle refer to the prediction of Daniel, chap. vii. 18,
27, and such like prophecies, where the *kingdoms of
the earth* are promised to *the saints of the Most High ;*
that is, that a time shall come when Christianity shall
so far prevail that the civil government of the world
shall be administered by *Christians,* which, at that
time, was administered by *heathens.* And this is even
now true of all those parts of the earth which may be
considered of the greatest political consequence. They
profess Christianity, and the kings and other governors
are *Christians* in this general sense of the term.

Verse 3. Know ye not that we shall judge angels ?]
Dr. Lightfoot observes that " the apostle does not say
here, as he said before, the *saints* shall judge the
angels, but WE shall judge them. By *angels,* all confess that *demons* are intended ; but certainly all *saints,*
according to the *latitude* with which that word is understood, i. e. all who profess Christianity, shall not
judge angels. Nor is this judging of angels to be
understood of the *last day ;* but the apostle speaks of
the ministers of the Gospel, himself and others, who, by
the preaching of the Gospel, through the power of Christ,
should spoil the devils of their oracles and their idols,
should deprive them of their worship, should drive them
out of their seats, and strip them of their dominion.

A. M. 4060.
A. D. 56.
A. U. C.
809.
Anno Imp. Nero-
nis Cæs. 3.

how much more things that pertain to this life?

4 ^c If then ye have judgments of things pertaining to this life, set them to judge who are least esteemed in the Church.

5 I speak to your shame. Is it so, that there is not a wise man among you? no, not one that shall be able to judge between his brethren?

6 But brother goeth to law with brother, and that before the unbelievers.

7 Now, therefore, there is utterly a fault among you, because ye go to law one with another. ^d Why do ye not rather take wrong?

why do ye not rather *suffer your-selves to* be defrauded?

8 Nay, ye do wrong, and defraud, ^e and that *your* brethren?

9 Know ye not that the unrighteous shall not inherit the kingdom of God? Be not deceived; ^f neither fornicators, nor idolaters, nor adulterers, nor effeminate, nor abusers of themselves with mankind,

10 Nor thieves, nor covetous, nor drunkards, nor revilers, nor extortioners, shall inherit the kingdom of God.

11 And such were ^g some of you: ^h but ye are washed, but ye are sanctified, but ye are

A. M. 4060.
A. D. 56.
A. U. C.
809.
Anno Imp. Nero-
nis Cæs. 3.

---

^c Chap. v. 12.——^d Prov. xx. 22; Matt. v. 39, 40; Luke vi. 29; Rom. xii. 17, 19; 1 Thess. v. 15.——^e 1 Thess. iv. 6.

^f Ch. xv. 50; Gal. v. 21; Eph. v. 5; 1 Tim. i. 9; Heb. xii. 14; xiii. 4; Rev. xxii. 15.——^g Chap. xii. 2; Eph. ii. 2; iv. 22; v. 8; Col. iii. 7; Tit. iii. 3.——^h Chap. i. 30; Heb. x. 22.

Thus would God subdue the whole world under the Christian power, so that Christian *magistrates* should judge *men*, and Christian *ministers* judge *devils*."

Verse 4. *Things pertaining to this life*] They could examine all civil cases among themselves, which they were permitted to determine without any hinderance from the heathen governments under which they lived.

Who are least esteemed in the Church.] Τους εξουθενημενους, Those who were in the *lowest order of judges*; for the apostle may refer here to the *order* in the Jewish benches, as Dr. Lightfoot conjectures, of which there were *five*, viz :—

1. The great *Sanhedrin*, consisting of seventy-two elders, which presided in Jerusalem.

2. The little *Sanhedrin* of twenty-five, in large cities, out of Jerusalem.

3. The Bench of *Three* in every synagogue.

4. The *Authorized*, or *Authentic* Bench.

5. The Bench *not authorized*, εξουθενημενος. This latter bench was so called because it received not its authority *immediately* from the *Sanhedrin*, but was chosen by the parties between whom the controversy depended. The apostle certainly does not mean persons of *no repute*, but such as these *arbitrators*, who were chosen for the purpose of settling private differences, and preventing them from going before the regular magistrates. The following verse makes it pretty evident that the apostle refers to this *lower kind of tribunal*; and hence he says,

Verse 5. *Is it so, that there is not a wise man among you?*] Have you none among yourselves that can be arbitrators of the differences which arise, that you go to the heathen tribunals?

Verse 6. *Brother goeth to law with brother*] One Christian sues another at law! This is almost as great a scandal as can exist in a Christian society. Those in a religious community who *will* not submit to a proper arbitration, made by persons among themselves, should be expelled from the Church of God.

Verse 7. *There is utterly a fault among you*]

2

There is a most manifest *defect* among you, 1. Of *peaceableness*; 2. Of *brotherly love*; 3. Of *mutual confidence*; and 4. Of *reverence* for *God*, and concern for the *honour* of his cause.

Why do ye not rather take wrong?] Better suffer an injury than take a method of redressing yourselves which must injure your own peace, and greatly dishonour the cause of God.

Verse 8. *Nay, ye do wrong*] Far from suffering, ye are the aggressors; and defraud your pious, long-suffering brethren, who submit to this wrong rather than take those methods of redressing their grievances which the spirit of Christianity forbids. Probably the apostle refers to him who had taken his father's wife.

Verse 9. *The unrighteous shall not inherit the kingdom*] The unrighteous, ᾿αδικοι, those who act *contrary* to *right*, cannot *inherit*, for the inheritance is by *right*. He who is not a *child of God* has no *right* to the family inheritance, for that inheritance is for the *children*. If children, then heirs; heirs of God, and joint heirs with Christ, Rom. viii. 17. There are here *ten* classes of transgressors which the apostle excludes from the kingdom of God; and any man who is guilty of any one of the evils mentioned above is thereby excluded from this kingdom, whether it imply the *Church of Christ* here below, or the *state of glory* hereafter.

Several of the evils here enumerated will not bear to be particularly explained; they are, however, sufficiently plain of themselves, and show us what abominations were commonly practised among the Corinthians.

Verse 11. *And such were some of you*] It was not with the prospect of collecting *saints* that the apostles went about preaching the Gospel of the kingdom. None but *sinners* were to be found over the face of the earth; they preached that sinners might be converted unto God, made saints, and constituted into a Church; and this was the *effect* as well as the *object* of their preaching.

But ye are washed] Several suppose that the *order*

A. M. 4060.
A. D. 56.
A. U. C.
809.
Anno Imp. Nero-
nis Cæs. 3.

justified in the name of the Lord Jesus, and by the Spirit of our God.

12. *j* All things are lawful unto me, but all things are not *k* expedient: all

things are lawful for me, but I will not be brought under the power of any.

13 *l* Meats for the belly, and the belly for meats; but God shall destroy

A. M. 4060.
A. D. 56.
A. U. C.
809.
Anno Imp. Nero-
nis Cæs. 3.

---

j Chap. x. 23.——*k* Or, *profitable*.

l Matt. xv. 17; Rom. xiv. 17; Col. ii. 22, 23.

---

in which the operations of the grace of God take place in the soul is here inverted; but I am of a very different mind. Every thing will appear here in its order, when we understand the *terms* used by the apostle.

Ye are washed, απελουσασθε; ye have been *baptized* into the Christian faith, and ye have promised in this baptism to put off all filthiness of the flesh and spirit; and the *washing* of your bodies is emblematical of the purification of your souls.

Ye are sanctified] Ἡγιασθητε; from *a, privative,* and *γη, the earth;* ye are *separated* from *earthly* things to be *connected* with *spiritual*. Ye are *separated* from *time* to be *connected* with *eternity*. Ye are *separated* from *idols* to be *joined* to the *living God*. *Separation* from common, earthly, or sinful uses, to be wholly employed in the service of the true God, is the *ideal* meaning of this word, both in the Old and New Testaments. It was in consequence of their being separated from the world that they became a Church of God. Ye were formerly workers of iniquity, and *associated* with workers of iniquity; but now ye are separated from them, and united together to work out your salvation with fear and trembling before God.

Ye are justified] Εδικαιωθητε· Ye have been brought into a state of favour with God; your sins having been blotted out through Christ Jesus, the *Spirit of God* witnessing the same to your conscience, and carrying on by his energy the great work of regeneration in your hearts. The process here is plain and simple :—
1. Paul and his brother apostles preached the Gospel at Corinth, and besought the people to turn from darkness to light—from idol vanities to the living God, and to believe in the Lord Jesus for the remission of sins.
2. The people who heard were convinced of the Divine truths delivered by the apostle, and flocked to baptism.
3. They were baptized *in the name of the Lord Jesus,* and thus took upon them the public profession of the Gospel. 4. Being now baptized into the Christian faith, they were separated from idols and idolaters, and became incorporated with the Church of God. 5. As penitents, they were led to the Lord Jesus for *justification,* which they received through faith in his blood.
6. Being *justified* freely—having their *sins forgiven* through the redemption that is in Jesus, they received the *Spirit of God* to attest this glorious work of grace to their consciences; and thus became possessed of that principle of righteousness, that true leaven which was to leaven the whole lump, producing that universal holiness without which none can see the Lord.

Verse 12. All things are lawful unto me] It is likely that some of the Corinthians had pleaded that the offence of the man who had his father's wife, as well as the eating the things offered to idols, was not contrary to the law, as it then stood. To this the

apostle answers: Though such a thing be lawful, yet the case of fornication, mentioned chap. v. 1, is not expedient, ου συμφερει—it is not agreeable to propriety, decency, order, and purity. It is contrary to the established usages of the best and most enlightened nations, and should not be tolerated in the Church of Christ.

They might also be led to argue in favour of their eating things offered to idols, and attending idol feasts, thus :—that an idol was nothing in the world; and as food was provided by the bounty of God, a man might partake of it any where without defiling his conscience, or committing sin against the Creator. This excuse also the apostle refers to : All these things are lawful, taken up merely in the light that none of your laws is against the *first;* and that, on the ground that an idol is nothing in the world, there can be no reason against the *last;*

But I will not be brought under the power of any.] Allowing that they are all lawful, or at least that there is no law against them, yet they are not expedient; there is no necessity for them; and some of them are abominable, and forbidden by the law of God and nature, whether forbidden by yours or not; while others, such as eating meats offered to idols, will almost necessarily lead to bad moral consequences : and who, that is a Christian, would obey his appetite so far as to do these things for the sake of gratification? A man is *brought under the power of any thing* which he cannot give up. He is the *slave* of that thing, whatsoever it be, which he cannot relinquish; and then, to him, it is sin.

Verse 13. Meats for the belly] I suppose that κοιλια means the animal *appetite,* or *propensity* to food, &c., and we may conceive the apostle to reason thus : I acknowledge that God has provided different kinds of aliments for the appetite of man, and among others those which are generally offered to idols; and he has adapted the *appetite* to these *aliments,* and the *aliments* to the *appetite: but God shall destroy both it and them;* none of these is eternal; all these *lower appetites* and *sensations* will be destroyed by death, and have no existence in the resurrection body; and the earth and its productions shall be burnt up.

Now the body is not for fornication] Though God made an appetite for food, and provided food for that appetite, yet he has not made the *body* for any *uncleanness,* nor *indulgence* in sensuality; but he has made it for Christ; and Christ was provided to be a sacrifice for this body as well as for the soul, by taking our nature upon him; so that now, as *human* beings, we have an intimate relationship to the Lord; and our bodies are made not only for his *service,* but to be his *temples.*

   2

A. M. 4060.
A. D. 56.
A. U. C.
809.
Anno Imp. Nero-
nis Cæs. 3.

both it and them. Now the body *is* not for fornication, but [m] for the Lord; [n] and the Lord for the body.

14 And [o] God hath both raised up the Lord, and will also raise up us [p] by his own power.

15 Know ye not that [q] your bodies are the members of Christ? shall I then take the members of Christ, and make *them* the members of a harlot? God forbid.

16 What! know ye not that he which is joined to a harlot is one body? for [r] two, saith he, shall be one flesh.

17 [s] But he that is joined unto the Lord is one spirit.

18 [t] Flee fornication. Every sin that a man doeth is without the body; but he that committeth fornication sinneth [u] against his own body.

19 What! [v] know ye not that your body is the temple of the Holy Ghost *which is* in you, which ye have of God, [w] and ye are not your own?

20 For [x] ye are bought with a price: therefore glorify God in your body, and in your spirit, which are God's.

A. M. 4060.
A. D. 56.
A. U. C.
809.
Anno Imp. Nero-
nis Cæs. 3.

---

[m] Ver. 15, 19, 20; 1 Thess. iv. 3, 7.——[n] Eph. v. 23.——[o] Rom. vi. 5, 8; viii. 11; 2 Cor. iv. 14.——[p] Eph. i. 19, 20.——[q] Rom. xii. 5; chap. xii. 27; Eph. iv. 12, 15, 16; v. 30.——[r] Gen. ii. 24; Matt. xix. 5; Eph. v. 31.——[s] John xvii. 21, 22, 23; Eph. iv. 4; v. 30.——[t] Rom. vi. 12, 13; Heb. xiii. 4.——[u] Rom. i. 24; 1 Thess iv. 4.——[v] Chap. iii. 16; 2 Cor. vi. 16.——[w] Rom. xiv. 7, 8. [x] Acts xx. 28; chap. vii. 23; Gal. iii. 13; Heb. ix. 12; 1 Pet. i. 18, 19; 2 Peter ii. 1; Rev. v. 9.

Verse 14. *And God hath both raised up the Lord*] He has raised up the human nature of Christ from the grave, as a pledge of our resurrection; and will also raise us up by his own power, that we may dwell with him in glory for ever.

Verse 15. *Know ye not that your bodies are the members of Christ?*] Because he has taken your nature upon him, and thus, as believers in him, ye are the members of Christ.

Shall I then take, &c.] Shall we, who profess to be members of his body, of his flesh, and of his bones, connect ourselves with *harlots*, and thus dishonour and pollute the bodies which are members of Christ? *God forbid!* These passages admit of a more *literal* interpretation. This, if given at all, I must give in a strange language.

Membra humana, ad generationem pertinentia, vocantur Membra Christi, quia mysterium conjunctionis Christi et Ecclesiæ per conjunctionem maris et fœminæ indigitatur, Ephes. v. 32. *In Vet. Test. idem valebat de membro masculino, quippe quod circumcisione, tanquam signo fœderis, honoratum est.* Vide Schoettgen, Hor. Hebr.

Verse 16. *He that is joined to a harlot is one body*] In *Sohar Genes.*, fol. 19, we have these remarkable words: *Whosoever connects himself with another man's wife, does in effect renounce the holy blessed God, and the Church of the Israelites.*

Verse 17. *Is one spirit.*] He who is united to God, by faith in Christ Jesus, receives his Spirit, and becomes a partaker of the Divine nature. Who can change such a relationship for communion with a harlot; or for any kind of sensual gratification? He who can must be far and deeply fallen!

Verse 18. *Flee fornication.*] Abominate, detest, and escape from every kind of uncleanness. Some sins, or solicitations to sin, may be *reasoned* with; in the above cases, if you *parley* you are undone; *reason not, but* FLY!

Sinneth against his own body.] Though sin of every species has a tendency to destroy life, yet none are so mortal as those to which the apostle refers; they strike immediately at the basis of the constitution. By the

just judgment of God, all these irregular and sinful connections are married to death. Neither prostitutes, whoremongers, nor unclean persons of any description, can live out half their days. It would be easy to show, and *prove* also, how the end of these things, even with respect to the *body*, is death; but I forbear, and shall finish the subject with the words of the prophet: *The show of their countenance doth witness against them, and they declare their sin as Sodom, they hide it not; wo unto their soul, for they have rewarded evil unto themselves.*

Verse 19. *Your body is the temple of the Holy Ghost*] What an astonishing saying is this! As truly as the living God dwelt in the Mosaic tabernacle, and in the temple of Solomon, so truly does the Holy Ghost dwell in the souls of genuine Christians; and as the *temple* and all its *utensils* were holy, *separated* from all common and profane uses, and dedicated alone to the service of God, so the bodies of genuine Christians are holy, and all their members should be employed in the service of God alone.

And ye are not your own?] Ye have no right over yourselves, to dispose either of your body, or any of its members, as *you* may think proper or lawful; you are bound to God, and to him you are accountable.

Verse 20. *Ye are bought with a price*] As the *slave* who is purchased by his master for a sum of money is the sole property of that master, so ye, being bought with the price of the blood of Christ, are not *your own*, you are his *property*. As the slave is bound to use all his skill and diligence for the emolument of his master, so you should employ body, soul, and spirit in the service of your Lord; promoting, by every means in your power, the honour and glory of your God, whom you must also consider as your *Lord* and *Master*.

There are strange discordances in MSS., *versions*, and *fathers*, on the conclusion of this verse; and the clause, καὶ ἐν τῷ πνεύματι ὑμῶν, ἅτινα ἐστι τοῦ Θεοῦ, *and in your spirit, which is God's*, is wanting in ABC* D*EFG, some others, Coptic, Æthiopic, Vulgate, and *Itala*, and in several of the primitive *fathers*. Almost every critic of note considers them to be spurious Whether retained or expunged the sense is the same.

Instead of *price* simply, the Vulgate and some of the Latin fathers, read, *pretio magno*, with a *great* price; and instead of *glorify*, simply, they read *glorificate et portate*, glorify and *carry* God in your bodies. These readings appear to be glosses intended to explain the text. Litigious Christians, who will have recourse to law for every little difference, as well as the impure, may read this chapter either to their conviction or confusion

---

CHAPTER VII.

A solution of several difficult cases concerning marriage and married persons, 1–6. God has given every man his proper gift, 7. Directions to the unmarried and widows, 8, 9. Directions to the married, 10, 11. Directions to men married to heathen women, and to women married to heathen men, 12–16. Every man should abide in his vocation, 17–24. Directions concerning virgins, and single persons in general, 25–28. How all should behave themselves in the things of this life, in reference to eternity, 29–31. The trials of the married state, 32–35. Directions concerning the state of virginity or celibacy, 36–38. How the wife is bound to her husband during his life, and her liberty to marry another after his death, 39, 40.

A. M. 4060.
A. D. 56.
A. U. C. 809.
Anno Imp. Neronis Cæs. 3.

NOW, concerning the things whereof ye wrote unto me: a *It is* good for a man not to touch a woman.

2 Nevertheless, b *to avoid* fornication, let every man have his own wife, and let every woman have her own husband.

3 c Let the husband render unto the wife due benevolence: and like-

A. M. 4060.
A. D. 56.
A. U. C. 809.
Anno Imp. Neronis Cæs. 3.

a Ver. 8, 26; Matt. xix. 10; Prov. vi. 29.——b Ch. vi. 18; Matt. xiv. 4; xv. 19; Heb. xiii. 4.——c Exod. xxi. 10; 1 Pet. iii. 7.

NOTES ON CHAP. VII.

Verse 1. *The things whereof ye wrote unto me*] It is sufficiently evident that the principal part of this epistle was written in answer to some questions which had been sent to the apostle in a letter from the Corinthian Church; and the first question seems to be this: *"Is it proper for a man to marry in the present circumstances of the Church?"*

The question concerning the expediency or inexpediency of marriage was often agitated among the ancient philosophers; and many, though inclined to decide *against* it, because of the troubles and cares connected with it, tolerated it in their opinions; because, though an *evil*, it was judged to be a *necessary* evil. The words of *Menander* are full to this effect: Γαμειν, εαν τις την αληθειαν σκοπη, κακον μεν εστιν, αλλ' αναγκαιον κακον· "If a man consider marriage in a proper point of view, it is an evil; but then it is a necessary evil." *Metellus Numidicus* spoke of it nearly in the same way. *Si sine uxore possemus, Quirites, esse, omnes ea molestia careremus; sed quoniam ita natura tradidit, ut nec* CUM ILLIS *satis commode, nec* SINE ILLIS *ullo modo vivi possit, saluti perpetuæ potius quam brevi voluptati consulendum.* "If, O ye Romans, we could live unmarried, we should be saved from a great deal of trouble; but, seeing that nature has so ordered it that we cannot live very comfortably with wives, and without them cannot live at all, marriage should be adopted, not for the sake of the short-lived pleasure, but rather for perpetual safety." But this was not the common opinion; the Jews absolutely required that every man should marry, and reputed those as murderers who did *not.*—See on ver. 6. By the laws of *Lycurgus* unmarried persons were prohibited from seeing the public games. By the laws of the *Spartans* bachelors were punished. And *Plato* declares all such unworthy of any honour. And to this the commentator says, Amen.

Not to touch a woman] Γυναικος μη ἁπτεσθαι· The learned reader need not be informed in what sense ἁπτομαι is used among the Greeks, and *tangere* among the Latins. For examples *Wetstein* may be consulted.

Verse 2. To avoid *fornication*] Δια τας πορνειας· verto, *propter exercendam libidinem*, vel *ut libidinem licite exercere liceat*. Probo hanc notionem ex Hebræo, ibi זנה *zanah*, est *libidinem exercere*, Hos. iv. 10: *For they shall eat and not have enough; they shall commit whoredom*, חזנו, *libidinem exercebunt, and shall not increase.* Here the prophet certainly does not speak of *whoredom* in our sense of the word; for the persons he mentions expected to *have children*, which cannot be said of those who are addicted to improper connections: the prophet speaks concerning *married* persons, whom he threatens with a privation of children, notwithstanding *libidinem exercebant* in order to have numerous families. See *Schoettgen*. The following verse shows that this is the apostle's meaning.

Let every man have his own wife] Let every man have *one* woman, *his own*; and every woman *one* man, *her own*. Here, *plurality* of wives and husbands is most strictly forbidden; and they are commanded to marry for the purpose of procreating children.

In the Jewish constitutions there are some things not only curious, but useful, respecting marriage. "There are *four* causes which induce men to marry: 1. *Impure desire*; 2. To get *riches*; 3. To become *honourable*; 4. For the *glory of God*. Those who marry through the first motive beget *wicked* and *rebellious* children. Those who marry for the sake of riches have the *curse* of *leaving them to others*. Those who marry for the sake of *aggrandizing* their family, their families shall be *diminished*. Those who marry to promote the *glory of God*, their children shall be *holy*, and by them shall the true Church be increased."

Verse 3. *Let the husband render unto the wife due benevolence*] Την οφειλομενην εννοιαν· Though our version is no translation of the original, yet few persons are at a loss for the meaning, and the context is

2

A. M. 4060.
A. D. 56.
A. U. C.
809.
Anno Imp. Nero-
nis Cæs. 3.

wise also the wife unto the husband.

4 The wife hath not power of
her own body, but the husband :
and likewise also the husband hath not power
of his own body, but the wife.

5 ^d Defraud ye not one the other, except *it
be* with consent for a time, that ye may give
yourselves to fasting and prayer ; and come

together again, that ^e Satan
tempt you not for your incontinency.

6 But I speak this by permis-
sion, ^f *and* not of commandment.

7 For ^g I would that all men were ^h even as
I myself. But ⁱ every man hath his proper
gift of God, one after this manner, and another
after that.

A. M. 4060.
A. D. 56.
A. U. C
809.
Anno Imp. Nero-
nis Cæs. 3.

---

^d Joel ii. 16 ; Zech. vii. 3 ; Exod. xix. 15 ; 1 Sam. xxi. 4, 5.   ^g Acts xxvi. 29.——^h Chapter ix. 5.——ⁱ Matthew xix. 12 ; chap.
^e 1 Thess. iii. 5.——^f Ver. 12, 25 ; 2 Cor. viii. 8 ; xi. 17.   xii. 11.

---

sufficiently plain. Some have rendered the words, not
unaptly, the *matrimonial debt*, or *conjugal duty*—that
which a wife owes to her husband, and the husband to
his wife ; and which they must take care *mutually* to
render, else alienation of affection will be the infallible
consequence, and this in numberless instances has
led to adulterous connections. In such cases the
wife has to blame herself for the infidelity of her husband, and the *husband* for that of his wife. What
miserable work has been made in the peace of families
by a wife or a husband pretending to be wiser than the
apostle, and too holy and spiritual to keep the commandments of God !

Verse 4. *The wife hath not power, &c.*] Her person
belongs to her husband ; her husband's person belongs
to her : neither of them has any authority to refuse
what the other has a matrimonial right to demand.
The woman that would act so is either a knave or a
fool. It would be trifling to attribute her conduct to
any other cause than *weakness* or *folly*. She does not
love her husband ; or she loves some one else better
than her husband ; or she makes pretensions to a fancied
sanctity unsupported by Scripture or common sense.

Verse 5. *Defraud ye not one the other*] What ye
owe thus to each other never refuse paying, unless by
mutual consent ; and let that be only for a certain *time*,
when prudence dictates the temporary separation, or
when some extraordinary spiritual occasion may render
it mutually agreeable, in order that ye may *fast* and
pray, and derive the greatest possible benefit from
these duties by being enabled to wait on the Lord without distraction.

That Satan tempt you not for your incontinency.]
It is most evident that the separations *permitted* by the
Apostle, for he *enjoins* none, are only for a *season*, on
extraordinary occasions ; and that the persons may
come together again, lest Satan, taking advantage of
their matrimonial abstinence, might tempt either party
to illicit commerce.

There are a multitude of rules prescribed in such
cases by the *rabbins*, and indeed even by *heathen*
writers ; for this was a matter in which common sense
could always judge ; and under the direction of experience, *heathens*, as well as those favoured with Divine
revelation, could see what was proper in all such cases.

Incontinence, ειкρασια, *want of strength* to regulate
one's desires or appetites ; from *a, negative*, and κρατος,
strength. It is remarkable that the apostle supposes
that even this *temporary continence* might produce

incontinence ; and universal observation confirms the
supposition.

Verse 6. *I speak this by permission, &c.*] It was
a constant custom of the more conscientious rabbins,
to make a difference between the things which they
enjoined on their *own judgment*, and those which they
built on the authority of the *law*. Thus Rabbi *Tancum:*
" The washing of hands *before* meat is *in our own
power* ; washing *after* meat is *commanded.*" In relation to this point Dr. Lightfoot produces some examples from the Jewish writers : " The man is commanded
concerning begetting and multiplying, but not the
woman. And when does the man come under this
command ? From the age of *sixteen* or *seventeen* years ;
but, if he exceeds *twenty* years without marrying, behold he violates and renders an affirmative precept
vain. The *Gemara* says : It is forbidden a man to be
without a wife ; because it is written, *It is not good
for man to be alone*. And whosoever gives not himself to generation and multiplying is all one with a
murderer : he is as though he diminished from the
image of God, &c." We may understand the apostle
here as saying that the directions already given were
from his *own judgment*, and not from any Divine
inspiration ; and we may take it for granted that where
he does not make this observation he is writing under
the immediate afflatus of the Holy Spirit.

Verse 7. *For I would that all men, &c.*] He wished
that all that were then in the Church were, like himself, *unmarried* ; but this was in reference to the *necessities* of the Church, or what he calls, ver. 26, the
present distress : for it never could be his wish that
marriage should cease among men, and that human
beings should no longer be propagated upon earth ;
nor could he wish that the Church of Christ should
always be composed of *single persons* ; this would have
been equally absurd ; but as the Church was *then* in
straits and *difficulties*, it was much better for its single
members not to encumber themselves with domestic
embarrassments.

Every man hath his proper gift of God] Continence
is a *state* that cannot be acquired by human art or industry ; a man has it from God, or not at all : and if
he have it from God, he has it from him as the author
of his nature ; for where it does not exist *naturally*, it
never can exist, but either by *miraculous* interference,
which should never be expected, or by *chirurgical operation*, which is a shocking abomination in the sight of
God. See the note on Matt. xix. 12.

2

A. M. 4060.
A. D. 56.
A. U. C.
809.
Anno Imp. Nero-
nis Cæs. 3.

8 I say, therefore, to the un-married and widows, ᵏ It is good for them if they abide even as I:

9 But ¹ if they cannot contain, let them marry; for it is better to marry than to burn.

10 And unto the married I command, ᵐ yet

not I, but the Lord, ⁿ Let not the wife depart from *her* husband:

11 But, and if she depart, let her remain unmarried, or be re-conciled to *her* husband: and let not the husband put away *his* wife.

12 But to the rest speak I, ° not the Lord:

A. M. 4060
A. D. 56
A. U. C.
809.
Anno Imp. Nero
nis Cæs. 3.

ᵏ Verse 1, 26.——¹ 1 Timothy v. 14.——ᵐ See verse 12, 25, 40.

ⁿ Mal. ii. 14, 16; Matt. v. 32; xix. 6, 9; Mark x. 11, 12; Luke xvi. 18.——° Ver. 6.

Verse 8. *The unmarried and widows*] It is sup-posed that the apostle speaks here of men who *had been married*, in the word αγαμοι, but were now *widow-ers;* as he does of women who had been married, in the word χηραι, but were now *widows*. And when he says ὡς κᾳγω, *even as I*, he means that he himself was a *widower;* for several of the ancients rank Paul among the *married* apostles.

Verse 9. *But if they cannot contain*] If they find it inconvenient and uncomfortable to continue as wid-owers and widows, let them remarry.

It is better to marry than to burn.] Bishop Pearce translates the original thus: *For it is better to marry than to be made uneasy.* Πυρουσθαι, says he, " signi-fies primarily *to burn;* but in a metaphorical sense, to be *troubled, vexed,* or *made uneasy.* So in 2 Cor. xi. 29: *Who is offended and I burn not,* και ουκ εγω πυρου-μαι, *and I am not troubled.* So in Terence, Uro ho-minem, is *I vex him.*" It would be well to *soften* the sense of this word in reference to the subject of which the apostle speaks. He cannot mean *burning with lust,* no more than Virgil means so when he says, Æn. iv. ver. 68: *Uritur infelix Dido,* the unfortunate Dido is *tormented;* and in Eccl. ii. 68: *Me tamen urit amor, love torments me.* All this may be said with the strictest truth in such cases where the *impure fire* referred to above has no existence.

A curious story, which certainly casts light on the *phraseology* of this place, is related by Dr. Lightfoot, from the tract *Kiddushin,* fol. 81. " Some captive women were brought to Nehardea, and disposed in the house and the upper room of Rabbi Amram. They took away the ladder [that the women might not get down, but stay there till they were ransomed.] As one of these captives passed by the window, the light of her great beauty shined into the house. Amram [cap-tivated] set up the ladder; and when he was got to the middle of the steps [checked by his conscience] he stopped short, and with a loud voice cried out FIRE! FIRE! *in the house of Amram!* [This he did that, the neighbours flocking in, he might be *obliged* to desist from the evil affection which now prevailed in him.] The rabbins ran to him, and [seeing no fire] they said, *Thou hast disgraced us.* To which he replied: *It is better that ye be disgraced in the house of Amram in this world, than that ye be disgraced by me in the world to come.* He then adjured that evil affection to go out of him, and it went out as a *pillar* of FIRE. Amram said: *Thou art* FIRE, *and I am* FLESH; *yet for all that I have prevailed against thee.*" From this story much instruction may be derived.

Verse 10. *I command, yet not I, but the Lord*] I

do not give my own private opinion or judgment in this case; for the Lord Jesus commands that man shall not put asunder them whom God hath joined, Matt. v. 32; xix. 6. And God has said the same, Gen. ii. 24. The following extracts will prove that the law among the Jews was very loose relative to the firmness of the marriage bond:—

A woman might put away or depart from her hus-band by giving this simple reason to the elders, who would give the following certificate. " In —— day of —— week, of —— year, A., daughter of B., put away before us and said: My mother, or my brethren, deceived me, and wedded me or betrothed me, when I was a very young maid, to C., son of D.; but I now reveal my mind before you, that I will not have him."

Sometimes they parted with mutual consent, and this also was considered legal, as was also the marriage of the separated parties to others. Witness the following story: " A good man had a good wife; but because they had no children, they mutually put away each other. The good man married a bad (a heathen) wife, and she made him bad (a heathen;) the good woman married a bad (a heathen) husband, and she made him good."

Divorces were easily obtained among them, and they considered them the dissolving of the marriage bond; and, in consequence of these, the parties might remarry with others. This was contrary to the original institution of marriage, and is opposed both by our Lord and the apostle.

Verse 11. *But, and if she depart*] He puts the case as probable, because it was frequent, but lays it under restrictions.

Let her remain unmarried] She *departs* at her own peril; but she must not marry another: she must either continue unmarried, or be reconciled to her husband.

And let not the husband put away his *wife.*] Divorces cannot be allowed but in the case of *fornication:* an act of this kind dissolves the marriage *vow;* but no-thing else can. It is a fact that, among the Jews, the wife had just as much right to put away her husband as the husband had to put away his wife. As divorces were granted, it was right that each should have an equal power; for this served as a mutual check.

Verse 12. *But to the rest speak I, not the Lord*] As if he had said: For what I have already spoken I have the testimony of the Lord by Moses, and of my own Lord and Master, Christ; but for the directions which I am now about to give there is no *written tes-timony,* and I deliver them now for the first time. These words do not intimate that the apostle was not

2

A. M. 4060. A. D. 56. A. U. C. 809. Anno Imp. Neronis Cæs. 3.

If any brother hath a wife that
believeth not, and she be pleased
to dwell with him, let him not
put her away.
13 And the woman which hath a husband
that believeth not, and if he be pleased to dwell
with her, [p] let her not leave him.
14 For the unbelieving husband is sanctified
by the wife, and the unbelieving
wife is sanctified by the husband: else [q] were your children
unclean; but now are they holy.
15 But if the unbelieving depart, let him
depart. A brother or a sister is not under
bondage in such *cases:* but God hath called
us [r] to [s] peace.

A. M. 4060. A. D. 56. A. U. C. 809. Anno Imp. Neronis Cæs. 3.

[p] 1 Pet. iii. 1, 2.——[q] Mal. ii. 15.——[r] Rom. xii. 18; xiv. 19; chap. xiv. 33; Heb. xii. 14.——[s] Gr. *in peace.*

now under the influences of the Divine Spirit; but, that there was nothing in the sacred writings which bore directly on this point.

If any brother] A Christian man, *have a wife that believeth not*, i. e. who is a heathen, not yet converted to the Christian *faith, and she be pleased to dwell with him*, notwithstanding his turning Christian *since* their marriage, *let him not put her away* because she still continues in her heathen superstition.

Verse 13. *And the woman*] Converted from heathenism to the Christian faith; *which hath a husband*, who still abides in heathenism; *if he be pleased to dwell with her*, notwithstanding she has become a Christian *since* their marriage; *let her not leave him* because he still continues a heathen.

Verse 14. *The unbelieving husband is sanctified by the wife*] Or rather, is to be *reputed* as sanctified on account of his wife; she being a *Christian* woman, and he, though a *heathen*, being by marriage *one flesh* with her: her sanctity, as far as it refers to outward things, may be considered as imputed to him so as to render their connection not *unlawful*. The case is the same when the wife is a *heathen* and the husband a *Christian*. The word sanctification here is to be applied much more to the *Christian* state than to any moral change in the persons; for ἁγιοι, *saints*, is a common term for Christians—those who were baptized into the faith of Christ; and as its corresponding term קרושים *kedoshim* signified all the Jews who were in the covenant of God by circumcision, the *heathens* in question were considered to be in this holy state by means of their connection with those who were by their Christian profession *saints*.

Else were your children unclean] If this kind of relative sanctification were not allowed, the children of these persons could not be received into the Christian Church, nor enjoy any rights, or privileges as *Christians;* but the Church of God never scrupled to admit such children as members, just as well as she did those who had sprung from parents both of whom were Christians.

The Jews considered a child as born *out of holiness* whose parents were not proselytes at the time of the birth, though afterwards they became proselytes. On the other hand, they considered the children of heathens born *in holiness*, provided the parents became proselytes *before* the birth. All the children of the heathens were reputed *unclean* by the Jews; and all their own children *holy*.—See Dr. Lightfoot. This shows clearly what the apostle's meaning is.

If we consider the apostle as speaking of the children of *heathens*, we shall get a remarkable comment on this passage from *Tertullian*, who, in his treatise *De Carne Christi*, chaps. 37, 39, gives us a melancholy account of the height to which superstition and idolatry had arrived in his time among the Romans. "A child," says he, "from its very conception, was dedicated to the idols and demons they worshipped. While pregnant, the mother had her body swathed round with bandages, prepared with *idolatrous rites*. The embryo they conceived to be under the inspection of the goddess *Alemona*, who nourished it in the womb. *Nona* and *Decima* took care that it should be born in the *ninth* or *tenth* month. *Partula* adjusted every thing relative to the *labour;* and *Lucina* ushered it into the *light*. During the week preceding the birth a table was spread for *Juno;* and on the last day certain persons were called together to mark the *moment* on which the *Parcæ*, or *Fates*, had fixed its *destiny*. The first step the child set on the earth was consecrated to the goddess *Statina;* and, finally, some of the hair was cut off, or the whole head shaven, and the hair offered to some god or goddess through some public or private motive of devotion." He adds that "no child among the heathens was born in a state of purity; and it is not to be wondered at," says he, "that demons possess them from their youth, seeing they were thus early dedicated to their service." In reference to this, he thinks, St. Paul speaks in the verse before us: *The unbelieving husband is sanctified by the wife—else were your children unclean; but now are they holy;* i. e. "As the parents were converted to the Christian faith, the child comes into the world without these impure and unhallowed rites; and is from its infancy consecrated to the true God."

Verse 15. *But if the unbelieving depart*] Whether husband or wife: if such *obstinately* depart and utterly refuse all cohabitation, *a brother or a sister*—a Christian man or woman, *is not under bondage* to any particular laws, so as to be prevented from *remarrying*. Such, probably, the law stood *then;* but it is not so *now;* for the marriage can only be dissolved by *death*, or by the *ecclesiastical court*. Even *fornication* or *adultery* does not dissolve the marriage contract; nor will the obstinate *separation* of any of the parties, however long continued, give the party abandoned authority to remarry. If the person have been beyond sea, and not heard of for seven years, it is presumed he may be dead; and marriage has been connived at in such cases. If there be no person to *complain*, it may be presumed that there is none *injured*. But I have known instances where even a marriage after *seven*

A. M. 4060.
A. D. 56.
A. U. C.
809.
Anno Imp. Nero-
nis Cæs. 3.

16 For what knowest thou, O wife, whether thou shalt [t] save *thy* husband? or [u] how knowest thou, O man, whether thou shalt save *thy* wife?

17 But as God hath distributed to every man, as the Lord hath called every one, so let him walk. And [v] so ordain I in all Churches.

18 Is any man called being circumcised? let him [w] not become uncircumcised. Is any called in uncircumcision? [x] let him not be circumcised.

19 [y] Circumcision is nothing, and uncircumcision is nothing, [z] but the keeping of the commandments of God.

20 Let every man abide in the same calling wherein he was called.

21 Art thou called *being* a servant? care not for it: but if thou mayest be made free, use *it* rather.

22 For he that is called in the Lord, *being* a servant, is [a] the Lord's [b] freeman: likewise also he that is called, *being* free, is [c] Christ's servant.

A. M. 4060.
A. D. 56
A. U. C.
809.
Anno Imp. Nero-
nis Cæs. 3

---

[t] 1 Pet. iii. 1,——[u] Gr. *what.*——[v] Chap. iv. 17; 2 Cor. xi. 28.
[w] 1 Mac. i. 15.——[x] Acts xv. 1, 5, 19,.24, 28; Gal. v. 2.——[y] Gal.
v. 6; vi. 15.

[z] John xv. 14; 1 John ii 3; iii. 24.——[a] John viii. 36, Rom.
vi. 18, 22; Philem. 16.——[b] Gr. *made free.*——[c] Chap. ix. 21; Gal.
v. 13; Eph. vi. 6; 1 Pet. ii. 16.

---

years' absence has been very unfortunate; the husband returning at the end of ten or twelve years, and to his utter distress finding his wife married to another man, and with issue of that marriage! There can be. no safety in this case, unless there be absolute certainty of the *death* of the party in question.

God hath called us to peace.] The refractory and disagreeing party should not be *compelled* to fulfil such matrimonial engagements as would produce continual *jarring* and *discord.* At the same time each should take care that he give no cause for disagreements and separations, for the author of the Christian religion is the author of *peace,* and has *called* us to it.

Verse 16. *For what knowest thou, O wife*] You that are *Christians,* and who have *heathen* partners, do not give them up because they are such, for you may become the means of saving them unto eternal life. Bear your cross, and look up to God, and he may give your unbelieving husband or wife to your prayers.

Verse 17. *But as God hath distributed to every man, &c.*] Let every man fulfil the duties of the state to which God in the course of his providence has called him.

So ordain I in all Churches.] I do not lay on *you* a burden which others are not called to bear: this is the general rule which, by the authority of God, I impose on every Christian society.

Verse 18. *Is any man called being circumcised?*] Is any man who was formerly a *Jew* converted to Christianity?

Let him not become uncircumcised.] Let him not endeavour to abolish the sign of the old covenant, which he bears in his flesh. The Greek words μη επισπασθω, let him not *draw over,* are evidently an elliptical expression: the word την ακροβυστιαν, *the fore-skin,* being understood; which, indeed, is added by the *Armenian* and the *Itala,* and several of the Latin *fathers.* It is a fact that it was possible by the assistance of *art* to do this; and *Celsus* himself prescribes the mode, *De Medic.* vii. 25. By frequent stretching, the circumcised skin could be again *so drawn over,* as to prevent the ancient sign of circumcision from appearing. Some in their zeal against Judaism endeavoured to abolish this sign of it in their

flesh: it is most evidently against this that the apostle speaks. Many false Jews made use of this practice, that they might pass through heathen countries unobserved; otherwise, in frequenting the baths they would have been detected.

Let him not be circumcised.] Let no man who, being a Gentile, has been converted to the Christian faith, submit to circumcision as something necessary to his salvation.

Verse 19. *Circumcision is nothing*] Circumcision itself, though commanded of God, is nothing *of itself,* it being only a sign of the justification which should be afterwards received by faith. At present, neither *it* nor its opposite either *hinders* or *furthers* the work of grace; and *keeping the commandments of God,* from his love shed abroad in a believing heart, is the sum and substance of religion.

Verse 20. *Let every man abide in the same calling*] As both the circumcised and uncircumcised, in Christ, have the same advantages, and to their believing the same facilities; so any situation of life is equally friendly to the salvation of the soul, if a man be faithful to the grace he has received. Therefore, in all situations a Christian should be content, for all things work together for good to him who loves God.

Verse 21. *Art thou called being a servant?*] Δουλος εκληθης, Art thou converted to Christ while thou art a *slave*—the property of another person, and bought with his money? care not for it—this will not injure thy Christian condition but if thou canst obtain thy liberty—*use it rather*—prefer this state for the sake of *freedom,* and the temporal advantages connected with it.

Verse 22. *For he that is called*] The man who, being a *slave,* is converted to the Christian faith, is the Lord's freeman; his condition as a slave does not vitiate any of the privileges to which he is entitled as a *Christian:* on the other hand, all free men, who receive the grace of Christ, must consider themselves the *slaves of the Lord,* i. e. his real property, to be employed and disposed of according to his godly wisdom, who, notwithstanding their state of subjection, will find the service of their Master to be perfect freedom.

A. M. 4060.
A. D. 56.
A. U. C. 809.
Anno Imp Nero-
nis Cæs. 3.

23 ^dYe are bought with a price; be not ye the servants of men.

24 Brethren, ^e let every man, wherein he is called, therein abide with God.

25 Now concerning virgins, ^f I have no commandment of the Lord; yet I give my judgment, as one ^g that hath obtained mercy of the Lord ^h to be faithful.

26 I suppose, therefore, that this is good for

the present ⁱ distress; *I say,* ^k that *it is* good for a man so to be.

27 Art thou bound unto a wife? seek not to be loosed. Art thou loosed from a wife? seek not a wife.

28 But, and if thou marry, thou hast not sinned; and if a virgin marry, she hath not sinned. Nevertheless such shall have trouble in the flesh: but I spare you.

A. M. 4060.
A. D. 56.
A. U. C. 809.
Anno Imp. Nero-
nis Cæs. 3.

---

^dChap. vi. 20; 1 Pet. i. 18, 19; see Lev. xxv. 42.——^e Ver. 20.——^f Ver. 6, 10, 40; 2 Cor. viii. 8, 10.

^g1 Tim. i. 16.——^h Chap. iv. 2; 1 Tim. i. 12.——ⁱ Or, *necessity.* ^k Ver. 1, 8.

Verse 23. *Ye are bought with a price*] As truly as your bodies have become the property of your masters, in consequence of his paying down a price for you; so sure you are now the Lord's property, in consequence of your being purchased by the blood of Christ.

Some render this verse interrogatively: *Are ye bought with a price* from your slavery? *Do not* again *become slaves of men.* Never *sell yourselves;* prefer and retain your liberty now that ye have acquired it.

In these verses the apostle shows that the Christian religion does not abolish our *civil* connections; in reference to *them*, where it finds us there it leaves us. In whatever relation we stood before our embracing Christianity, there we stand still; our secular condition being no farther changed than as it may be affected by the amelioration of our moral character. But *slavery*, and all buying and selling of the bodies and souls of men, no matter what colour or complexion, is a high offence against the holy and just God, and a gross and unprincipled attack on the liberty and rights of our fellow creatures.

Verse 24. *Let every man—abide with God.*] Let him live to God in whatsoever station he is placed by Providence. If he be a slave, God will be with him even in his *slavery*, if he be faithful to the grace which he has received. It is very likely that some of the slaves at Corinth, who had been converted to Christianity, had been led to think that their Christian privileges absolved them from the necessity of continuing slaves; or, at least, brought them on a level with their Christian masters. A spirit of this kind might have soon led to confusion and insubordination, and brought scandals into the Church. It was therefore a very proper subject for the apostle to interfere in; and to his authority, the persons concerned would doubtless respectfully bow.

Verse 25. *Now concerning virgins*] This was another subject on which the Church at Corinth had asked the advice of the apostle. The word παρθενος, *virgin*, we take to signify a *pure, unmarried young woman;* but it is evident that the word in this place means young unmarried persons of either sex, as appears from verses 26, 27, 32–34, and from Rev. xiv. 4. The word παρθενος, *virgin*, is frequently applied to *men* as well as to *women*. See *Suidas*, under the word Αβελ· ουτος παρθενος και δι καιος υπηρχε, *He* (Abel) *was a virgin, and a righteous man.* In ver. 36 the word is supposed to mean the *state* of vir-

ginity or *celibacy*, and very probable reasons are assigned for it; and it is evident that persons of either sex in a state of celibacy are the persons intended.

I have no commandment of the Lord] There is nothing in the sacred writings that directly touches this point.

Yet I give my judgment] As every way equal to such commandments had there been any, seeing I have received the teaching of his own Spirit, and have obtained *mercy of the Lord to be faithful* to this heavenly gift, so that it abides with me to lead me into all truth. In this way I think the apostle's words may be safely understood.

Verse 26. *This is good for the present distress*] There was no period in the heathen times when the Church was not under persecutions and afflictions; on some occasions these were more oppressive than at others.

The word αναγκη signifies, *necessity, distress, tribulation,* and *calamity;* as it does in Luke xxi. 23; 2 Cor. vi. 4; and xii. 10. In such times, when the people of God had no certain dwelling-place, when they were lying at the mercy of their enemies without any protection from the state—the *state* itself often among the *persecutors*—he who had a *family* to care for, would find himself in very embarrassed circumstances, as it would be much more easy to provide for his *personal* safety than to have the care of a wife and children. On this account it was much better for unmarried persons to continue for the *present* in their celibacy.

Verse 27. *Art thou bound unto a wife?*] i. e. Married; for the marriage contract was considered in the light of a *bond*.

Seek not to be loosed.] Neither regret your circumstances, notwithstanding the present distress, nor seek on this account for a dissolution of the marriage contract. But if thou art under no matrimonial engagements, do not for the present enter into any.

Verse 28. *But, and if thou marry*] As there is no law against this, even in the *present distress*, thou hast not sinned, because there is no law against this; and it is only on account of prudential reasons that I give this advice.

And if a virgin marry] Both the man and the woman have equal privileges in this case; either of them may marry without sin. It is probable, as there were many sects and parties in Corinth, that there were among them those who *forbade to marry*, 1 Tim

A. M. 4060.
A. D. 56.
A. U. C. 809.
Anno Imp. Neronis Cæs. 3.

29 But [1] this I say, brethren, the time *is* short: it remaineth, that both they that have wives be as though they had none;

30 And they that weep, as though they wept not; and they that rejoice, as though they rejoiced not; and they that buy, as though they possessed not;

31 And they that use this world, as not

[m] abusing *it*: for [n] the fashion of this world passeth away.

32 But I would have you without carefulness. [o] He that is unmarried careth for the things [p] that belong to the Lord, how he may please the Lord:

33 But he that is married careth for the things that are of the world, how he may please *his* wife.

A. M. 4060.
A. D. 56.
A. U. C. 809.
Anno Imp. Neronis Cæs. 3.

---

[1] Romans xiii. 11; 1 Peter iv. 7; 2 Peter iii. 8, 9. [m] Chap. ix. 18.

[n] Psa. xxxix. 6; James i. 10; iv. 14; 1 Pet. i. 24; iv. 7; 1 John ii. 17.——[o] 1 Tim. v. 5.——[p] Gr. *of the Lord,* as ver. 34.

---

iv. 3, and who might have maintained other *doctrines of devils* besides. These persons, or such doctrines, the apostle has in view when he says, *They may marry and yet not sin.*

Trouble in the flesh] From the simple circumstance of the incumbrance of a family while under persecution; because of the difficulty of providing for its comfort and safety while flying before the face of persecution.

But I spare you.] The evil is coming; but I will not press upon you the observance of a prudential caution, which you might deem too heavy a cross.

Verse 29. The time is short] These persecutions and distresses are at the door, and life itself will soon be run out. Even *then* Nero was plotting those grievous persecutions with which he not only afflicted, but devastated the Church of Christ.

They that have wives] Let none begin to think of any comfortable settlement for his family; let him sit loose to all earthly concerns, and stand ready prepared to escape for his life, or meet death, as the providence of God may permit. The husband will be dragged from the side of his wife to appear before the magistrates, and be required either to abjure Christ or die.

Linquenda tellus, et domus, et placens
Uxor; neque harum, quas colis, arborum
Te, præter invisas cupressos,
Ulla brevem dominum sequetur.
    Hor. Odar. lib. ii., *Od.* xiv., v. 22.

Your pleasing consort must be left;
And you, of house and lands bereft,
  Must to the shades descend:
The cypress only, hated tree!
Of all thy much-loved groves, shall thee,
  Its short-lived lord, attend.   Francis.

Poor *heathenism!* thou couldst give but cold comfort in such circumstances as these: and *infidelity,* thy younger brother, is no better provided than thou.

Verse 30. They that weep, &c.] There will shortly be such a complete system of distress and confusion that private sorrows and private joys will be absorbed in the weightier and more oppressive public evils: yet, let every man still continue in his calling, let him buy, and sell, and traffic, as usual; though in a short time, either by the coming persecution or the levelling hand of death, he that had earthly property will be brought into the same circumstances with him who had none.

Verse 31. And they that use this world] Let them who have earthly property or employments discharge conscientiously their duties, from a conviction of the

instability of earthly things. Make a *right use* of every thing, and *pervert* nothing from its *use.* To *use* a thing is to employ it properly in order to accomplish the end to which it refers. To *abuse* a thing signifies to *pervert* it *from* that *use.* Pass through things *temporal,* so as not to lose those which are eternal.

For the fashion of this world] Το σχημα του κοσμου τουτου signifies properly the *present state* or constitution of things; the *frame of the world,* that is, the *world* itself. But often the term κοσμος, *world,* is taken to signify the *Jewish state* and *polity;* the destruction of this was then at hand, and this the Holy Spirit might then signify to the apostle.

Verse 32. Without carefulness.] Though all these things will shortly come to pass, yet do not be anxious about them. Every occurrence is under the direction and management of God. The wrath of man shall praise him, and the remainder of it he shall restrain, and none can harm you if ye be followers of that which is good. We should all take the advice of the poet:—

  "With patient mind thy course of duty run;
    God *nothing does,* nor *suffers to be done,*
  But *thou* wouldst *do thyself,* couldst thou but *see*
    The *end* of all *events* as well as He."—Byrom.

He that is unmarried careth for the things that belong to the Lord] He has nothing to do with a family, and therefore can give his whole time to the service of his Maker, having him alone to please.

Verse 33. But he that is married] He has a *family* to provide for, and his wife to please, as well as to fulfil his duty to God, and attend to the concerns of his own soul. The *single* man has nothing to attend to but what concerns his own salvation: the *married* man has all this to attend to, and besides to provide for his wife and family, and take care of their eternal interests also. The *single* man has very little trouble comparatively; the *married man* has a great deal. The *single man* is an *atom* in society; the *married man* is a *small community* in himself. The *former* is the *centre* of his *own existence,* and lives for *himself* alone; the *latter* is *diffused abroad,* makes a much more important part of the body social, and provides both for its support and continuance. The *single man* lives for and does good to *himself* only; the *married* man lives both for *himself* and the *public.* Both the *state* and the *Church* of Christ are dependent on the *married* man, as from him under God the one has *subjects,* the other *members;* while the *single man* is but an indi-

A. M. 4060.
A. D. 56.
A. U. C.
809.
Anno Imp. Nero-
nis Cæs. 3.

34 There is difference *also* between a wife and a virgin. The unmarried woman ᑫ careth for the things of the Lord, that she may be holy both in body and in spirit: but she that is married careth for the things of the world, how she may please *her* husband.

35 And this I speak for your own profit; not that I may cast a snare upon you, but for

---

q Luke x. 40, &c.

---

that which is comely, and that ye may attend upon the Lord without distraction.

36 But if any man think that he behaveth himself uncomely toward his virgin, if she pass the flower of *her* age, and need so require, let him do what he will, he sinneth not: ʳ let them marry.

37 Nevertheless he that standeth steadfast in

A. M. 4060.
A. D. 56
A. U. C.
809.
Anno Imp. Nero-
nis Cæs. 3.

---

r Deut. vii. 3.

---

vidual in either, and by and by will cease from both, and having no *posterity* is *lost to the public for ever*. The *married man*, therefore, far from being in a state of *inferiority* to the *single man*, is *beyond* him out of the limits of comparison. He can do all the good the other can do, though perhaps sometimes in a *different* way; and he can do ten thousand goods that the other cannot possibly do. And therefore both himself and his *state* are to be preferred infinitely before those of the other. Nor could the apostle have meant any thing less; only for the *present distress* he gave his opinion that it was best for those who were *single* to continue *so*. And who does not see the propriety of the advice?

Verse 34. *There is a difference* also *between a wife and a virgin.*] That is: There is this difference between a *married* and an *unmarried* woman. *The unmarried careth* (only) *for the things of the Lord*, having no domestic duties to perform. *That she may be holy*—separated to Divine employments, both *in body and spirit*. Whereas *she that is married careth* (also) *for the things of the world, how she may please her husband*, having many domestic duties to fulfil, her husband being obliged to leave to her the care of the family, and all other domestic concerns.

On this verse there is a profusion of various readings in *MSS.*, *versions*, and *fathers*, for which I must refer to *Griesbach*, as it would be impossible to introduce them here so as to make them look like sense.

Verse 35. *This I speak for your own profit*] The advices belong to yourselves *alone*, because of the peculiar circumstances in which you are placed. Nothing spoken here was ever designed to be of *general* application; it concerned the Church at Corinth alone, or Churches in similar circumstances.

Not that I may cast a snare upon you] Ουχ ινα βροχον ὑμιν επιβαλω—Here is a manifest allusion to the *Retiarius* among the *Romans*, who carried a small *casting net*, which he endeavoured to throw over the head of his adversary and thus entangle him. Or to a similar custom among the *Persians*, who made use of a noose called the كَمَنْد *camand*, which they employed in the same way. One of these lies before me; it is a strong silken cord, one end of which is a loop to be held in the hand, and the rest is in the form of a *common snare* or *noose*, which, catching hold of any thing, *tightens* in proportion as it is pulled by the hand that holds the loop.

The apostle, therefore, intimates that what he says was not intended absolutely to *bind* them, but to show them the propriety of following an advice which in

the present case would be helpful to them in their religious connections, that they might *attend upon the Lord without distraction*, which they could not do in times of persecution, when, in addition to their own personal safety, they had a wife and children to care for.

For that which is comely, and that ye may attend upon the Lord without distraction.] The original αλλα προς το ευσχημον και ευπροσεδρον τῳ Κυριῳ απερισπαστως, of which our version is only a *paraphrase*, is thus translated by Bishop Pearson: *But for the sake of decency, and of attending more easily upon the Lord without distraction*. This is much more literal than ours.

Verse 36. *Uncomely towards his virgin*] Different meanings have been assigned to this verse. I shall mention *three* of the principal. 1. "In those early times, both among the Hebrews and Christians, the *daughters* were wholly in the power of the *father*, so that he might give or not give them in marriage as he chose; and might bind them to perpetual celibacy if he thought proper; and to this case the apostle alludes: If the father had devoted his daughter to perpetual virginity, and he afterwards found that she had fixed her affections upon a person whom she was strongly inclined to marry, and was now *getting past the prime of life*; he, seeing from his daughter's circumstances that it would be *wrong* to *force* her to continue in her state of celibacy, though he had determined before to keep her single, yet he might in this case alter his purpose without sin, and let her and her suitor marry."

2. "The whole verse and its context speaks of young women dedicated to the service of God, who were called παρθενοι, virgins, in the primitive Church. And a case is put here, 'that circumstances might occur to render the breach of even a *vow* of this kind *necessary*, and so no sin be committed.'"

3. "The apostle by παρθενος does not mean a *virgin*, but the *state* of virginity or *celibacy*, whether in *man* or *woman*." Both Mr. Locke and Dr. Whitby are of this opinion, and the *latter* reasons on it thus:—

It is generally supposed that these three verses relate to virgins under the power of parents and guardians; and the usual inference is, that children are to be disposed of in marriage by the parents, guardians, &c. Now this may be true, but it has no foundation in the text, for τηρειν την ἑαυτου παρθενον is not to keep his *daughter's*, but his own *virginity*, or rather his *purpose* of *virginity*; for, as *Phavorinus* says, *He is called a virgin who freely gives himself up to the Lord, renouncing matrimony, and preferring a life spent in continency.* And that this must be the true

2

A. M. 4060.
A. D. 56.
A. U. C. 809.
Anno Imp. Neronis Cæs. 3.

his heart, having no necessity, but hath power over his own will, and hath so decreed in his heart that he will keep his virgin, doeth well.

38 ª So then, he that giveth *her* in marriage doeth well; but he that giveth *her* not in marriage doeth better.

39 ᵗ The wife is bound by the law as long as her husband liveth; but if her husband be dead, she is at liberty to be married to whom she will; ᵘ only in the Lord.

40 But she is happier if she so abide, ᵛ after my judgment: and ʷ I think also that I have the Spirit of God.

A. M. 4060.
A. D. 56.
A. U. C. 809.
Anno Imp. Neronis Cæs. 3.

ª Heb. xiii. 4.——ᵗ Rom. vii. 2.——ᵘ 2 Cor. vi. 14.

ᵛ Ver. 25.——ʷ 1 Thess. iv. 8.

---

import of these words appears from this consideration, that this depends upon the purpose of his own heart, and the power he has over his *own will*, and the *no necessity* arising from himself to change this purpose. Whereas the keeping a daughter unmarried depends not on these *conditions* on her *father's* part but on her *own; for*, let her have *a necessity*, and surely the apostle would not advise the father to keep her a virgin, *because he had determined so to do;* nor could there be any doubt whether the father *had power over his own will* or not, when *no necessity* lay upon *him* to betroth his virgin. The Greek runs to this sense: *if he had stood already firm in his heart, finding no necessity,* viz. to change his purpose; and hath *power over his own will,* not to marry; finding himself able to persist in the resolution he had made to *keep his virginity,* he *does well* to continue a vîrgin: and then the phrase, *if any man think he behaves himself unseemly towards his virgin, if it be over-aged,* and thinks he ought rather to join in marriage, refers to the opinions both of *Jews* and *Gentiles* that *all ought to marry.* The Jews say that the time of marriage is from 16 or 17 to 20; while some of the Gentiles specify from 30 to 35. *If any think thus,* says the apostle, *let them do what they will, they sin not: let them marry.* And then he concludes with those words applied to both cases: *so then, both he that marries doeth well, and he that marries not, doeth better.*

This last opinion seems to be the true sense of the apostle.

It may be necessary to make a few general observations on these verses, summing up what has been said.

1. Παρθενος here should be considered as implying not a *virgin*, but the *state* of *virginity* or *celibacy.*

2. Ὑπερακμος, *over-aged*, must refer to the passing of that time in which both the laws and customs of Jews and Gentiles required men to marry. See above, and see the note on ver. 6.

3. Και οὑτως οφειλει γινεσθαι, *And need so require;* or, if *there appear to be a necessity;* is to be understood of any particular change in his circumstances or in his feelings; or, that he finds, from the *law* and *custom* in the case, that it is a *scandal* for him not to marry; then let him *do what he wills* or *purposes.*

4. Instead of γαμειτωσαν, *let* THEM *marry,* I think γαμειτω, *let* HIM *marry,* is the true reading, and agrees best with the context. This reading is supported by D*EFG, *Syriac,* all the *Arabic, Slavonic,* one of the *Itala,* and St. *Augustine.* Si nubat, *if he marry,* is the reading of the *Vulgate,* several copies of the *Itala, Ambrose, Jerome, Ambrosiaster, Sedulius,* and *Bede.*

This reading is nearly of the same import with the other : *Let him do what he willeth, he sinneth not, let him marry ;* or, *he sinneth not if he marry.*

5. The whole of the 37th verse relates to the *purpose* that the man has formed ; and the *strength* that he has to keep his purpose of perpetual celibacy, being under no *necessity* to change that purpose.

6. Instead of ὁ εκγαμιζων, *he who giveth* her in marriage, I purpose to read ὁ γαμιζων, *he who marrieth,* which is the reading of the *Codex Alexandrinus,* the *Codex Vaticanus,* No. 1209, and of some others : with *Clement, Methodius,* and *Basil.* Την ἑαυτου παρθενον, *his own virgin,* is added after the above, by several very ancient and reputable MSS., as also by the *Syriac, Armenian, Vulgate, Æthiopic, Clement, Basil, Optatus,* and others ; but it seems so much like a *gloss,* that Griesbach has not made it even a candidate for a place in the text. *He then who marrieth,* though previously intending *perpetual virginity, doeth well ;* as this is agreeable to laws both Divine and human : and *he who marrieth not, doeth better,* because of the *present distress.* See ver. 26.

Verse 39. *The wife is bound by the law*] This seems to be spoken in answer to some other question of the Corinthians to this effect : "May a woman *remarry* whose husband is dead, or who has abandoned her ?" To which he replies, in general, That as long as her husband is living the law binds her to *him* alone ; but, if the husband die, she is free to remarry, *but only in the Lord ;* that is, she must not marry a *heathen* nor an *irreligious* man ; and she should not only marry a genuine Christian, but one of her own religious sentiments ; for, in reference to *domestic peace,* much depends on this.

Verse 40. *But she is happier if she so abide*] If she continue in her *widowhood* because of the *present distress;* for this must always be taken in, that consistency in the apostle's reasoning may be preserved. If this were not understood, how could St. Paul tell the widow that it would be *more happy* for her to continue in her *widowhood* than to *remarry?* She who had *tried* both the state of *celibacy* and the state of *marriage* could certainly *best tell which* was most for her comfort ; and he could not tell any thing but by an express revelation from heaven, relative to the future state of any widow : it is certain that he can never be understood as speaking in *general,* as there are multitudes of persons abundantly more happy in their married than in their single state ; and there are many widows also much more happy in their second marriage than they have been in their first.

2

After my judgment] According to the view I have of the subject, which view I take by the light of the Divine Spirit, who shows me the tribulations which are *coming on the Church.* But, says he, ver. 28 : *I spare you*—I will not be more explicit concerning coming evils, as I wish to save you from all *forebodings* which bring *torment.*

I think—I have the Spirit of God.] Δοκω δε κᾳγω Πνευμα Θεον εχειν might be translated, *I am* CERTAIN *that I have the Spirit of God.* This sense of δοκειν (which we translate to *seem*, to *think*, to *appear, &c.*) I have noticed in another part of this work. *Ulpian*, on *Demosthen. Olynth.* 1, says, Το δοκειν ου παντως επι αμφιβολου ταττουσιν οι παλαιοι αλλα πολλακις και επι του αληθευειν· *The word* δοκειν *is used by the ancients, not always to express what is* DOUBTFUL, *but often to express what is* TRUE *and* CERTAIN.—See Bp. *Pearce.* The apostle cannot be understood as expressing any doubt of his being under the inspiration of the Divine Spirit, as this would have defeated his object in giving the above advices ; for if they were not dictated by the *Spirit of God*, can it be supposed that, in the face of apparent self-interest, and the prevalence of strong passions, they could have been expected to have become *rules* of conduct to this people ? They must have understood him as *asserting* that he had the direction of the Spirit of God in giving those opinions, else they could not be expected to obey.

1. IN the preceding chapter we have met with subjects both of *difficulty* and *importance.* As to the *difficulties*, it is hoped that they have been so generally considered in the notes that few or none of them remain ; and on the subjects of peculiar *importance* much time has been spent, in order to impress them on the mind of the reader. The *delicacy* of some of them would not admit of greater plainness ; and in a few instances I have been obliged to wrap the meaning in a foreign language.

2. On the important subject of *marriage* I have said what I believe to be true, and scruple not to say that it is the most *useful* state in which the human being can be placed ; and consequently that in which most *honour* may be brought to God. I have listened with much attention for the better part of half a century to the arguments *against* marriage and in favour of *celibacy ;* and I have had the opportunity of being acquainted with many who endeavoured to *exemplify* their own doctrine. But I have seen an end of all their perfection : neither the world nor the Church are under any obligations to them : they either married when they could do it to their mind and convenience ; or, continuing in their celibacy, they lived a comparatively useless life ; and died as they should, *unregretted.* The doctrine is not only dangerous but anti-scriptural : and I hope I have sufficiently vindicated Paul from being its patron or supporter.

3. While I contend for the superior excellence of the *marriage state*, I hope I shall not be understood to be the apologist of *indiscriminate marriages*—no, many of them are blamable in a very high degree. Instead of consulting *common sense* and *propriety*, childish affections, brutish passions, or the love of money are the motives on which many of them have

been contracted. Such marriages are miserable ; must be so, and should not be otherwise ; and superficial people looking at *these* form an estimate of the *state* itself, and then indulge themselves in exclaiming against an ordinance of God, either perverted by *themselves* or the equally *foolish persons* who are the subjects of their animadversion. That genuine Christians can never be so useful in any state as that of marriage I am fully convinced ; but to be happy, the marriage must be *in the Lord.* When *believers* match with *unbelievers*, generally *pars sincera trahitur ;* the good becomes perverted ; and Satan has his triumph when he has got an immortal soul out of the Church of Christ into his own synagogue. But who among young people will lay this to heart ? And how few among young men and young women will not sell their *Saviour* and his *people* for a *husband* or a *wife !*

4. The doctrine of *second marriages* has been long a subject of controversy in the Church. The Scriptures, properly understood, have not only nothing against them, but much for them. And in this chapter St. Paul, in the most pointed manner, admits of them. A *widow* may marry again, *only let it be in the Lord ;* and a *widower* has certainly the same privilege.

5. The *conversion* which the Scripture requires, though it makes a most essential change in our *souls* in reference to God, and in our *works* in reference both to God and man, makes none in our *civil* state : even if a man is *called*, i. e. converted in a state of slavery, he does not gain his manumission in consequence of his conversion ; he stands in the same relation both to the *state* and to his fellows that he stood in *before ;* and is not to assume any *civil* rights or privileges in consequence of the conversion of his soul to God. The apostle decides the matter in this chapter, and orders that every man should abide in the calling wherein he is called.

6. From the 20th to the 23d verse the apostle refers to the state of *slavery* among the Greeks ; and from what he says we find that even among the *slaves* there were *Christian converts*, to whom, though he recommends *submission* and *contentment*, yet he intimates that if they could get their *freedom* they should prefer it ; and he strongly charges those that were *free* not to become again the slaves of men, ver. 23 ; from which we learn that a man might dispose of his own liberty, which, in a *Christian*, would be a disgrace to his redemption by Christ. The word ελευθερος, which we translate *freeman*, means properly *freed-man*, one who had been a *slave* but had regained his liberty. It is the same as *libertus* among the Romans, one who was *manumitted.* The manumission was performed *three* several ways : 1. The *consent* of the master that the slave should have his name entered in the census, or public register of the citizens. 2. The slave was led before the prætor, and the magistrate laid his wand, called *vindicta*, on his head, and declared him free. 3. By *testament* or *will*, the master bequeathing to the slave his freedom.

The manner in which the second mode of manumission was performed is curious. The prætor having laid the rod *vindicta* upon the slave's head, pronounced these words, *Dico eum liberum esse more Quiritum*, " I pronounce him free according to the custom of the Romans." This done he gave the rod to the *lictor*, or serjeant, who struck the slave with it upon the head, and afterwards with the hand upon the face and back. The head also of the slave was shaven, and a cup given him by his master as a token of freedom, and the notary entered the name of the new *freed-man* in the public register, with the reasons of his manumission: it was customary also to give him another surname.

7. Among our *Saxon ancestors*, and also *after* the conquest, there was a species of slavery: all the *villani* were slaves to their respective lords, and each was bound to serve him in a great variety of ways. There is a profusion of curious examples of this in the ancient record preserved in the bishop's auditor's office in the cathedral of Durham, commonly known by the name of the Bolden Book. This record has been lately printed under the direction of his majesty's commissioners on the public records of the kingdom, in the supplement to Domesday Book.

8. Among our Saxon ancestors *manumissions* were granted on various accounts: 1. A person might, if able, purchase his own freedom. 2. One man might purchase the freedom of another. 3. Manumissions were granted to procure by their merit the salvation of departed souls. 4. Persons were manumitted also in order to be consecrated to the service of God. These manumissions were usually recorded in some *holy book*, especially in copies of the *four Evangelists*, which, being preserved in the libraries of abbeys, &c., were a continual record, and might at all convenient times be consulted. Several entries of these manumissions exist in a MS. of the four Evangelists, s. 4, 14, in the library of *Corpus Christi* or *Bennet* college, Cambridge.

I shall produce a specimen of one of the several kinds mentioned above, giving the original only of the first; and of the others, verbal translations.

1. *The certificate of a man's having purchased his own freedom.*

ꝼen ꞃpuꞇelað on ðiꞃꞃeꝼe Cꞃiꞃꞇeꞃ bec ðac Ælꝼꝥiꞡ ꞃe ꝡeð hæꝥð ꞡebohꞇ hine ꝼelꝼne uꞇ æꞇ Ælꝼꝥiꞡe abb. ꞡ eallon hineðe   miſ anon punðe ðaꞃ iꞃ ꞇa ꞡepiꞇneꞃ eall ꞃe hineð on ꝥaðan.

Cꞃiꞃꞇ hine ablenðe.
ðe ðiꞃ ꞡeꝼꞃiꞇ apenðe.

"Here is witnessed, in this book of Christ, that *Ælfwig the Red* hath redeemed himself from Abbot *Ælfsig*, and the whole convent, with one pound. And this is witnessed by the whole convent at *Bath*,

May Christ strike him blind
Who this writing perverts."

This is a usual execration at the end of these forms, and is in rhyme in the original.

2. *Certificate of one having purchased the liberty of another.*

"Here is witnessed, in this book of Christ, that *Ædric Atford* has redeemed *Sægyfa*, his daughter, from the Abbot *Ælfsig*, and from the convent of Bath, to be for ever free, and all her posterity."

3. *Certificate of redemption in behalf of one* departed.

"Here is witnessed, in this book of Christ, that *Ælfric Scot* and *Ægelric Scot* are manumitted for the soul of Abbot *Ælfsig*, to perpetual liberty. This was done with the testimony of the whole convent."

4. *Certificate of* persons *manumitted to be* devoted *to the* service of God.

"Here is witnessed, in this book of Christ, that *John* bought *Gunnilda* the daughter of *Thurkill*, from *Goda*, widow of *Leafenath*, with half a pound. With the testimony of the whole convent.

May Christ strike him blind
Who this writing perverts.

And he has dedicated her to *Christ* and *St. Peter*, in behalf of his mother's soul."

9. When a man was made free, it was either in the church or at some public meeting: the sheriff of the county took him by the right hand and proclaimed him a freeman, and showed him the open door and the public highway, intimating that he was free to go whithersoever he pleased, and then gave him the arms of a freeman, viz. a *spear* and a *sword*. In some cases the man was to pay thirty pence to his master of *hide money*, intimating that he was no longer under *restraint, chastisement*, or *correction*. From which it appears that our ancestors were in the habit of *flogging* their slaves. See the laws of *Ina*, c. 24, 39; of *Wm.* the *Conqueror*, c. 65; and of *Hen.* I. c. 78.

10. Among the *Gentoos* the manumission of a slave was as follows: The slave took a pitcher, filled it with water, and put therein *berenge-àrook* (rice that had been cleansed without boiling) and flowers of *doob*, (a kind of small *salad*,) and taking the pitcher on his shoulder he stands near his master; the master then puts the pitcher on the slave's head, breaks it so that the water, rice, flowers, and doob that were in the pitcher may fall on the slave's body: when this is done the master thrice pronounces, *I have made thee free;* then the slave steps forward a few paces towards the east, and then the manumission is complete. See *Code of Gentoo* laws, chap. viii. sec. 2, page 160. It is evident that the whole of this ceremony is emblematical: 1. The pitcher represents the confined, servile state of the slave. 2. The articles contained in it, his *exclusion* while in a state of slavery from the grand *benefits* and *comforts of life.* 3. The *water* contained in the *pitcher*, his exclusion from the refreshing influences of heaven; for slaves were not permitted to take part in the ordinances of religion. 4. The *clean, unboiled rice*, his incapacity to have secular possessions; for slaves were not permitted to *possess lands* either by inheritance or purchase: a slave could sow no seed for himself, and consequently have no legal claim on support from this staff of life. 5. The *doob* or *salad shut up*, his being without *relish* for that state of being which was rendered insupportable to him by his thraldom. 6. The *breaking* of the *pitcher*, his manumission and enjoyment of liberty: being as free to go whithersoever he would as the water was to run, being now disengaged from the pitcher. 7. The *shedding of the water, rice, flower, &c.*, over his body, his privilege of enjoying and possessing every heavenly and earthly good. 8. His *stepping towards the east*, his acknowledgment to the supreme Being, the fountain of light and life, (of whom the sun was the emblem,) for his enlargement; and his *eagerness* to possess the light and comfort of that *new state* of happiness into

which he was now brought in consequence of his manumission.

11. The description that Dr. *John Taylor* gives, in his *Elements of Civil Law*, of the state of *slaves* among the ancients, will nearly suit with their state among our ancestors, though scarcely as bad as their state in the West Indies. "They were held among the Romans, *pro nullis; pro mortuis; pro quadrupedibus:* —for *no men;* for *dead men;* for *beasts:* nay, were in a much worse state than any *cattle* whatever. They had no *head* in the state, no *name,* no *tribe* or *register.* They were not *capable* of being *injured,* nor could they take by purchase or descent: had no *heirs,* and could make no *will.* Exclusive of what was called their *peculium,* whatever they acquired was their master's they could neither *plead* nor be *im-pleaded;* but were entirely excluded from all *civil concerns;* were not entitled to the *rights of matrimony,* and therefore had no relief in case of *adultery;* nor were they proper objects of *cognation* or *affinity.* They might be *sold, transferred,* or *pawned,* like other *goods* or personal estate; for *goods* they were, and such were they esteemed. They might be *tortured* for evidence, *punished* at the *discretion* of their *lord,* and even *put to death,* by his authority. They were laid under several other civil incapacities, too tedious to mention."

When all this is considered, we may at once see the horrible evil of *slavery,* and wonder at the grace which could render them happy and contented in this situation: see the preceding chapter, verses 20, 21, and 22 And yet we need not be surprised that the apostle should say to those who were *free* or *freed,* Ye *are bought with a price; do not become slaves of men.*

12. I have entered the more particularly into this subject, because *it,* or *allusions* to it, are frequently occurring in the New Testament; and I speak of it here once for all. And, to conclude, I here register my testimony against the unprincipled, inhuman, anti-Christian, and diabolical *slave-trade,* with all its *authors, promoters, abettors,* and *sacrilegious gains;* as well as against the great devil, the father of it and them.

CHAPTER VIII.

The question of the Corinthians concerning meats offered to idols, and the apostle's preface to his instructions on that head, 1–3. The nature of idolatry, 4, 5. Of genuine worship, 6. Some ate of the animals that had been offered to idols knowingly, and so defiled their conscience, 7. Neither eating nor abstinence in themselves recommend us to God, 8 But no man should use his Christian liberty so as to put a stumbling block before a brother, 9, 10 If he act otherwise, he may be the means of a brother's destruction, 11. Those who act so as to wound the tender conscience of a brother, sin against Christ, 12. The apostle's resolution on this head, 13.

A. M. 4060.
A. D. 56.
A. U. C. 809.
Anno Imp. Neronis Cæs. 3.

NOW, [a] as touching things offered unto idols, we know that we all have [b] knowledge.

[c] Knowledge puffeth up, but charity edifieth.

2 And [d] if any man think that

A M 4060.
A. D. 56.
A. U C. 809.
Anno Imp. Neronis Cæs. 3

---

[a] Acts xv 20, 29; chap. x. 19 —— [b] Rom. xiv 14, 22.—— [c] Rom. xiv 3, 10.—— [d] Chap. xiii. 8, 9, 12, Gal. vi. 3, 1 Tim. vi 4.

NOTES ON CHAP VIII

Verse 1 *As touching things offered unto idols*] This was another subject on which the Corinthians had asked the apostle's advice, and we shall understand the whole of this chapter the better when we consider one fact, viz. That there had long subsisted a controversy between the *Karaïtes* and the *Traditionists,* how far it was lawful to derive any benefit or advantage from things used by the Gentiles. The *Karaïtes* were a sect of the Jews who scrupulously held to the *letter* of the sacred writings, taking this alone for their directory. The *Traditionists* were those who followed the voice of the *elders,* interpreting the Divine testimonies by their decisions. From a work of the *Karaïtes,* entitled *Addereth Eliyahu,* Triglandus has extracted the following decisions, which will throw light upon this subject. " It is unlawful to receive any benefit from any kind of heathen worship, or from any thing that has been offered to an idol."—" It is unlawful to buy or sell an idol, and if, by accident, any such thing shall come into thy power, thou shalt derive no emolument from it."—" The animals that are destined and prepared for the worship of idols are universally prohibited; and particularly those which bear the mark of the idol. This should be maintained against the opinion of the *Traditionists,* who think they may lawfully use these kinds of animals, provided they be not marked with the sign of the idol." Thus far the *Karaïtes;* and here we see one strong point of difference between these two sects. The *Karaïtes totally* objected to every thing used in idolatrous services, the *Traditionists,* as the Talmud shows, did *generally* the same; but it appears that they scrupled not to use any animal employed in idolatrous worship, provided they did not see the *sign* of the idol on it. Now the sign of the idol must be that placed on the animal previously to its being sacrificed, such as *gilded horns* and *hoofs, consecrated fillets, garlands,* &c. And as, after it had been sacrificed, and its flesh exposed for sale in the shambles, it could bear none of these *signs,* we may take it for granted that the Jews might think it lawful to buy and eat this flesh, this the *Karaïte* would most solemnly scruple It may be just necessary to state here, that it was customary, after the blood and life of an animal had been offered in sacrifice to an idol, to sell the flesh in the market indiscriminately with that of other animals which had not been *sacrificed,* but merely *killed for common use.* Even the

2

A. M. 4060.
A. D. 56.
A. U. C.
809.
Anno Imp. Nero-
nis Cæs. 3.

he knoweth any thing, he knoweth nothing yet as he ought to
know.

3 But if any man love God,
e the same is known of him.

4 As concerning, therefore, the eating of those
things that are offered in sacrifice unto idols,

we know that f an idol *is* nothing
in the world, g and that *there is*
none other God but one.

5 For though there be that are
h called gods, whether in heaven or in earth,
(as there be gods many, and lords many,)

6 But i to us *there is but* one God, the Fa-

A. M. 4060.
A. D. 56.
A. U. C.
809.
Anno Imp. **Nero**
nis Cæs. 3.

---

e Exod. xxxiii. 12, 17; Nah. i. 7; Matt. vii. 23; Gal. iv. 9;
2 Tim. ii. 19.——f Isa. xli. 24; chap. x. 19.——g Deut. iv. 39;
vi. 4; Isa. xliv. 8; Mark xii. 29; ver. 6; Eph. iv. 6; 1 Tim. ii.
5.——h John x. 34.——i Mal. ii. 10; Eph. iv. 6.

---

less scrupulous Jews, *knowing* that any particular flesh
had been thus offered, would abhor the use of it; and
as those who lived among the Gentiles, as the Jews
at Corinth, must know that this was a common case,
hence they would be generally scrupulous; and those
of them that were converted to Christianity would have
their scruples increased, and be as rigid on this point
as the *Karaïtes* themselves. On the other hand, those
of the *Gentiles* who had received the faith of Christ,
knowing that an *idol was nothing in the world*, nor was
even a representation of any thing, (for the beings represented by idol images were purely *imaginary*,) made
no scruple to buy and eat the flesh as they used to do,
though not with the same *intention*; for when, in their
heathen state, they ate the flesh offered to idols, they
ate it as a *feast with the idol*, and were thus supposed
to have *communion* with the idol; which was the
grossest idolatry.

From these observations it will at once appear that
much misunderstanding and offence must have existed
in the Corinthian Church; the converted Jews abominating every thing that they knew had been used in
the heathen worship, while the converted Gentiles, for
the reasons above assigned, would feel no scruple on
the account.

We know that we all have knowledge.] I am inclined
to think that these are not St. Paul's words, but a
quotation from the letter of the Corinthians to him, and
a proof of what the apostle says below, *knowledge
puffeth up;* but however the words may be understood
as to their origin, they contain a general truth, as they
relate to Christians of those times, and may be thus paraphrased: " All we who are converted to God by Christ
have sufficient knowledge concerning idols and idol
worship; and we know also the *liberty* which we have
through the Gospel, not being bound by Jewish laws,
rites, ceremonies, &c.; but many carry their knowledge
in this liberty too far, and do what is neither seemly
nor convenient, and thus give offence to others."

Knowledge puffeth up, but charity edifieth.] This
knowledge is very nearly allied to pride; it *puffeth up*
the mind with vain conceit, makes those who have it
bold and rash, and renders them careless of the consciences of others. And this knowledge, boasted of
by the Corinthians, led them to *contemn* others; for so
the word φυσιοι is understood by some eminent critics.

Verse 2. *He knoweth nothing yet, &c.*] The person
who acts in this rash, unfeeling way, from the general
knowledge which he has of the vanity of idolatry and
the liberty which the Gospel affords from Jewish rites,
with all his knowledge does not know this, that though
the *first* and greatest commandment says, *Thou shalt*

love the Lord thy God with all thy heart, &c., yet the
second is like unto it: *Thou shalt love thy neighbour
as thyself.* He, then, that can torment his neighbour's
weak or tender conscience with his food or his conduct,
does not love him as himself, and therefore knows
nothing as he ought to know.

Verse 3. *But if any man love God*] In that way
which the commandment requires, which will necessarily beget love to his neighbour, *the same is known
of him*—is approved of God, and acknowledged as his
genuine follower.

Verse 4. *Things that are offered in sacrifice*] See
on the first verse.

An idol is nothing in the world] Dr. Lightfoot
translates this, *We know that there is no idol in the
world;* which he explains thus : Ειδωλον, idol, is ὁμο-
ιωμα, εικων, σημειον, χαρακτηριον, σκιοειδες, a *likeness*,
an *image*, a *sign*, a *character*, a *shadow*: now ουδεν
ειδωλον signifies *there is no idol*, no *representation* of
GOD, in the world. *Images* there are of stone, wood,
and metal; but none of these is any representation of
the infinite Spirit. But I prefer the meaning given in
the note on verse 1; as the expression, *an idol is
nothing in the world*, was common in the Old Testament, and among the Jews; and was understood by
them in this way: they are not אלהים *Elohim*, the
true GOD; but they are אלילים, *nothings*, and הבלים
habalim, VANITY.

Verse 5. *There be that are called gods*] There are
many *images* that are supposed to be *representations*
of divinities : but these divinities are nothing, the figments of mere fancy; and these images have no corresponding *realities*.

Whether in heaven or in earth] As the sun, *moon*,
planets, *stars*, the *ocean*, *rivers*, *trees*, &c. And thus
there are, nominally, *gods many*, and *lords many*.

Verse 6. *But to us* there is but *one God*, *the Father*]
Who produced all things, himself uncreated and unoriginated. *And we in him*, και ἡμεις εις αυτον, *and
we* FOR *him;* all intelligent beings having been created
for the purpose of manifesting his glory, by receiving
and reflecting his *wisdom*, *goodness*, and *truth*.

And one Lord Jesus] Only one visible *Governor* of
the world and the Church, *by whom* are *all things:*
who was the *Creator*, as he is the *Upholder* of the
universe. *And we by him*, being brought to the
knowledge of the true God, by the revelation of Jesus
Christ; for it is the only begotten Son alone that can
reveal the Father. The *gods* of whom the apostle
speaks were their *divinities*, or objects of religious
worship; the *lords* were the *rulers* of the world, such
as *emperors*, who were considered next to gods, and

2

A. M. 4060.
A. D. 56.
A. U. C.
809.
Anno Imp. Nero-
nis Cæs. 3.

ther, [k] of whom *are* all things, and we [l] in him; and [m] one Lord Jesus Christ, [n] by whom *are* all things, and we by him.

7 Howbeit, *there is* not in every man that knowledge : for some, [o] with conscience of the idol unto this hour, eat *it* as a thing offered unto an idol ; and their conscience being weak is [p] defiled.

8 But [q] meat commendeth us not to God : for, neither, if we eat, [r] are we the better ; neither, if we eat not, [s] are we the worse.

9 But [t] take heed, lest by any means this [u] liberty of yours become [v] a stumbling-block to them that are weak.

10 For if any man see thee which hast knowledge sit at meat in [w] the idol's temple, shall not [x] the conscience of him which is weak be [y] emboldened to eat those things which are offered to idols ;

11 And [z] though thy knowledge shall the weak brother perish, for whom Christ died ?

A. M. 4060.
A. D. 56.
A. U. C.
809.
Anno Imp. Nero-
nis Cæs. 3.

---

[k] Acts xvii. 28 ; Rom. xi. 36.——[l] Or, *for him*.——[m] John xiii. 13 ; Acts ii. 36 ; chap. xii. 3 ; Eph. iv. 5 ; Phil. ii. 11.——[n] John i. 3 ; Col. i. 6 ; Heb. i. 2.——[o] Chap. x. 28, 29.——[p] Rom. xiv. 14, 23.

[q] Rom. xiv. 17.——[r] Or, *have we the more*.——[s] Or, *have we the less*.——[t] Gal. v. 13.——[u] Or, *power*.——[v] Rom. xiv. 13, 20. [w] 1 Mac. i. 47.——[x] Chap. x. 28, 32.——[y] Or, *edified*.——[z] Rom. xiv. 15, 20.

---

some of them were deified. In opposition to those *gods* he places GOD *the Father*, the fountain of plenitude and being ; and in opposition to the *lords* he places *Jesus Christ*, who made and who governs all things. We, as *creatures*, live in *reference*, εἰς αυτον, *to him*, God the Father, who is the fountain of our being : and, as *Christians*, we live δι' αυτου, *by or through him*, Jesus Christ ; by whom we are bought, enlightened, pardoned, and saved.

Verse 7. There is *not in every man that knowledge*] This is spoken in reference to what is said, ver. 4 : *We know that an idol is nothing in the world ; for some with a conscience of the idol*, viz. that it is *something*, *eat it*—the flesh that was offered to the idol, as a thing thus offered, considering the feast as a *sacred banquet*, by which they *have fellowship with the idol*. *And their conscience being weak*—not properly instructed in Divine things, *is defiled*—he performs what he does as an act of religious worship, and thus his conscience contracts guilt through this idolatry.

As in the commencement of Christianity, among the *Jews* that were converted, there were many found who incorporated the rites of the law with the principles of the Gospel ; so, doubtless, among the *Gentiles*, there were several who did not at once throw aside all their idolatry or idolatrous notions, but preserved some of its more spiritual and imposing parts, and might think it necessary to mingle idolatrous feasts with the rites of Christianity ; as the sacrament of the Lord's supper was certainly considered as a feast upon a sacrifice, as I have proved in my *Discourse on the Nature and Design of the Eucharist*. As the minds of many of these young Gentile converts could not, as yet, have been deeply endued with spiritual knowledge, they might incorporate these feasts, and confound their nature and properties.

Verse 8. Meat commendeth us not to God] No such feasts as these can be a recommendation of our souls or persons to the Supreme Being. As to the *thing*, considered in *itself*, the *eating* gives us no spiritual advantage ; and the *eating not* is no spiritual loss.

Verse 9. But take heed] Lest by frequenting such feasts and eating things offered to idols, under the conviction that *an idol is nothing*, and that you may eat

those things innocently, this liberty of yours should become a means of grievously offending a weak brother who has not your knowledge, or inducing one who respects you for your superior knowledge to partake of these things with the conscience, the persuasion and belief, that an idol is *something*, and to conclude, that as you partake of such things, so he may also, and with safety. He is not possessed of your superior information on this point, and he eats *to the idol* what you take as a *common meal*.

Verse 10. If any man see thee which hast knowledge] Of the true God, and who art reputed for thy skill in Divine things.

Sit at meat in the idol's temple] Is it not strange that any professing the knowledge of the true God should even enter one of those temples ? And is it not more surprising that any *Christian* should be found to feast there ? But by all this we may see that the boasted knowledge of the Corinthians had very little *depth* in things purely *spiritual*.

There are many curious thin-spun theories in the rabbinical writings concerning *entering idol temples*, and *eating* there, and even *worshipping* there, providing the mind be towards the true God. Dr. Lightfoot produces several quotations to prove this. Perhaps the *man of knowledge* mentioned by the apostle was one of those who, possessing a *convenient conscience*, could accommodate himself to all circumstances ; be a *heathen* without and a *Christian* within, and *vice versá*, as circumstances might require.

Be emboldened to eat] Οικοδομηθησεται, Be *built up*—be *confirmed* and *established* in that opinion which before he doubtingly held, that on seeing you eat he may be led to think there is no harm in feasting in an idol temple, nor in eating things offered to idols.

Verse 11. Shall the weak brother perish] Being first taught by thy conduct that there was no harm in thus eating, he grieves the Spirit of God ; becomes again darkened and hardened ; and, sliding back into idolatry, dies in it, and so finally perishes.

For whom Christ died ?] So we learn that a man may *perish* for whom Christ died : this admits of no quibble. If a man *for whom Christ died*, apostatizing from Christianity, (for he is called a *brother* though

A. M. 4060.
A. D. 56.
A. U. C.
809.
Anno Imp. Neronis Cæs. 3.

12 But ^a when ye sin so against the brethren, and wound their weak conscience, ye sin against Christ.

13 Wherefore, ^b if meat make my brother to offend, I will eat no flesh while the world standeth, lest I make my brother to offend.

A. M. 4060.
A. D. 56.
A. U. C.
809.
Anno Imp. Neronis Cæs. 3.

^a Matt. xxv. 40, 45.

^b Rom. xiv. 21 ; 2 Cor. xi. 29.

weak,) return again to and die in idolatry, cannot go to heaven ; then a man for whom Christ died may perish everlastingly. And if it were possible for a believer, whether strong or weak, to retrace his steps back to idolatry and die in it, surely it is possible for a man, who had escaped the pollutions that are in the world, to return to it, live and die in its spirit, and perish everlastingly also. Let him that readeth understand.

Verse 12. But when ye sin so against the brethren] Against *Christians*, who are called by the Gospel to abhor and detest all such abominations.

Ye sin against Christ.] By sending to perdition, through your bad example, a soul for whom he shed his blood ; and so far defeating the gracious intentions of his sacrificial death. This is a farther intimation, that a person for whom Christ died may perish ; and this is the drift of the apostle's argument.

Verse 13. Wherefore, &c.] Rather than give any occasion to a Christian to sin against and so to harden his conscience that he should return to idolatry and perish, I would not only abstain from all *meats offered to idols,* but I would eat *no flesh,* should I exist through the *whole course of time,* but live on the herbs of the field, rather than cause my brother to stumble, and thus fall into idolatry and final ruin.

The following words of Origen contain a very solemn lesson and warning : " If we did more diligently attend to these things, we should avoid sinning against our brethren and wounding their weak conscience, that we might not *sin against Christ ;* our brethren that are among us, for whom Christ died, often perishing, not only by our *knowledge,* but by many other *ways* and *things,* in which things we, *sinning against Christ,* shall suffer punishment ; the souls of them that perish by us being required of and avenged upon us."—See *Whitby* on this place.

1. THE greater our reputation for knowledge and sanctity, the greater mischief we shall do by our influence and example if we turn aside from the holy commandment delivered unto us. Every man should walk so as either to *light* or *lead* his brother to heaven.

2. It is the duty of every Christian to watch against *apostasy* in his own case, and to prevent it as much as possible in that of others. That a person for whom Christ died may *finally perish* is strongly argued, says Dr. Whitby, from this place, and Rom. xiv. 15 ; for here the apostle dissuades the Corinthians from scandalizing their weak brethren, by an argument taken from the irreparable mischiefs they may do them, the *eternal ruin* they may bring upon them by this scandal ; whereas if it be, as some assert, that *all things, even the sins of the elect, shall work together for their good, and that they shall never perish ;* if the apostle knew and taught this doctrine to them, why does he endeavour to affright them from this scandal, by telling them

that it might have that effect which he had before told them was impossible ? If you interpret his words thus : *So shall he perish, for whom in charity ye ought to judge Christ died ;* it is certain, from this doctrine, that they must be assured that this judgment of *charity* must be *false,* or that their brother could *not* perish. In the *first* place, they could not be obliged to act by it ; and in the *second,* they could not rationally be moved by it to abstain from giving scandal on that impossible supposition.

If you interpret the apostle thus : *So shalt thou do that which, in its nature, tends to make thy brother perish ; and might have that effect, had not God determined to preserve all from perishing, for whom Christ died ;* since this determination renders it sure to me, who know it, that they cannot actually perish, it must assure me that there can be no cause of abstinency from this scandal, lest they should perish by it.

Moreover, by thus offending, saith the apostle, *ye sin against Christ ;* viz. by sinning against him whom he has purchased by his blood ; and destroying them for whose salvation he has suffered. If this intent of Christ's death be denied, how can we show in what Christ has demonstrated his great love to them that perish ? Is it possible that they can sin against redeeming love ? and how, by thus offending them who neither *do* nor *can* belong to him as members of his mystical body, are we injurious to Christ ?—See *Whitby* on this place.

3. It is natural for man to *wish* and *affect* to be *wise ;* and when this desire is cultivated in reference to *lawful* objects, it will be an indescribable good ; but when, like *Eve,* we see, in a *prohibition, something to be desired to make one wise,* we are then, like *her,* on the verge of our *fall.* Though extensive knowledge is not given *to* all, yet it is given *for* all ; and is the public property of the Church. He who does not use it for general edification robs the public of its right. For the misuse and misapplication of this talent we shall give account to God, as well as of other gifts and graces.

4. Persons of an *over tender* and *scrupulous* conscience may be very troublesome in a Christian society ; but as this excessive scrupulosity comes from want of more *light,* more *experience,* or more *judgment,* we should bear with them. Though such should often run into ridiculous extremes, yet we must take care that we do not attempt to cure them either with *ridicule* or *wrath.* Extremes generally beget extremes ; and such persons require the most judicious treatment, else they will soon be stumbled and turned out of the way. We should be very careful lest in using what is called *Christian liberty* we occasion their fall ; and for our own sake we must take heed that we do not denominate *sinful indulgences, Christian* liberties.

5. Though we are bound to take heed that we put

2

not a stumbling block in the way of a weak brother, yet if such a brother be stumbled at any part of our conduct which is not blamable in itself, but of which he may have taken a wrong view, we are not answerable for the consequences. We are called to walk by the testimony of God; not according to the measure of any man's conscience, how sincere soever he may be.

6. Many persons cover a spirit of envy and uncharitableness with the name of godly zeal and tender concern for the salvation of others; they find fault with all; their spirit is a spirit of universal censoriousness; none can please them; and every one suffers by them. These destroy more souls by tithing mint and cummin, than others do by neglecting the weightier matters of the law. Such persons have what is termed, and very properly too, *sour godliness.* Both are extremes, and he who would avoid perdition must avoid *them.*

CHAPTER IX.

St. Paul vindicates his apostleship, and shows that he has equal rights and privileges with Peter and the brethren of our Lord; and that he is not bound, while doing the work of an apostle, to labour with his hands for his own support, 1–6. He who labours should live by the fruit of his own industry, 7. For the law will not allow even the ox to be muzzled which treads out the corn, 8–10. Those who minister in spiritual things have a right to a secular support for their work, 11–14. He shows the disinterested manner in which he has preached the Gospel, 15–18. How he accommodated himself to the prejudices of men, in order to bring about their salvation, 19–23. The way to heaven compared to a race, 24. The qualifications of those who may expect success in the games celebrated at Corinth, and what that success implies, 25. The apostle applies these things spiritually to himself; and states the necessity of keeping his body in subjection, lest, after having proclaimed salvation to others, he should become a castaway, 26, 27.

A. M. 4060.
A. D. 56.
A. U. C. 809.
Anno Imp. Neronis Cæs. 3.

AM [a]I not an apostle? am I not free? [b]have I not seen Jesus Christ our Lord? [c]are not ye my work in the Lord?

2 If I be not an apostle unto others, yet doubtless I am to you: for [d]the seal of mine apostleship are ye in the Lord.

3 Mine answer to them that do examine me is this.

A. M. 4060.
A. D. 56.
A. U. C. 809.
Anno Imp. Neronis Cæs. 3.

---

[a] Acts ix. 15; xiii. 2; xxvi. 17; 2 Cor. xii. 12; Gal. ii. 7, 8; 1 Tim. ii. 7; 2 Tim. i. 11.

[b] Acts ix. 3, 17; xviii. 9; xxii. 14, 18; xxiii. 11; chap. xv. 8. [c] Chap. iii. 6; iv. 15.——[d] 2 Cor. iii. 2; xii. 12.

NOTES ON CHAP. IX.

Verse 1. *Am I not an apostle?*] It is sufficiently evident that there were persons at Corinth who questioned the apostleship of St. Paul; and he was obliged to walk very circumspectly that they might not find any occasion against him. It appears also that he had given them all his apostolical labours gratis; and even this, which was the highest proof of his disinterested benevolence, was produced by his opposers as an argument against him. " Prophets, and all divinely commissioned men, have a right to their secular support; you take nothing:—is not this from a conviction that you have no apostolical *right?*" On this point the apostle immediately enters on his own defence.

Am I not an apostle? Am I not free?] These questions are all designed as assertions of the affirmative: *I am an apostle*; and *I am free*—possessed of all the rights and privileges of an apostle.

Have I not seen Jesus Christ? From whom in his *personal appearance* to me, I have received my apostolic commission. This was judged essentially necessary to constitute an apostle.—See Acts xxii. 14, 15; xxvi. 16.

Are not ye my work] Your conversion from heathenism is the proof that I have preached with the Divine unction and authority.

Several good MSS. and versions transpose the two first questions in this verse, thus: *Am I not free?* *am I not an apostle?* But I cannot see that either perspicuity or sense gains any thing by this arrangement. On the contrary, it appears to me that his being an *apostle* gave him the *freedom* or *rights* to which he refers, and therefore the common arrangement I judge to be the best.

Verse 2. *If I be not an apostle unto others*] If there be other Churches which have been founded by other apostles; yet it is not so with you.

The seal of mine apostleship are ye] Your conversion to Christianity is God's *seal* to my apostleship. Had not God sent me, I could not have profited your souls.

The σφραγις, or seal, was a figure cut in a *stone,* and that set in a *ring,* by which letters of credence and authority were stamped. The ancients, particularly the Greeks, excelled in this kind of engraving. The cabinets of the curious give ample proof of this; and the moderns contend in vain to rival the perfection of those ancient *masters.*

In the Lord.] The apostle shows that it was by the grace and influence of God alone that he was an apostle, and that *they* were converted to Christianity.

Verse 3. *Mine answer to them*] Ἡ εμη απολογια τοις εμε ανακρινουσιν· This is my *defence* against those who examine me. The words are *forensic;* and the apostle considers himself as brought before a legal tribunal, and questioned so as to be obliged to

A. M. 4060.
A. D. 56.
A. U. C.
809.
Anno Imp. Nero-
nis Cæs. 3.

4 [e] Have we not power to eat and to drink?

5 Have we not power to lead about a sister, a [f] wife, as well as other apostles, and *as* [g] the brethren of the Lord, and [h] Cephas?

6 Or I only and Barnabas, [i] have not we power to forbear working?

7 Who [k] goeth a warfare any time at his own charges? who [l] planteth a vineyard, and eateth not of the fruit thereof? or who [m] feedeth a flock, and eateth not of the milk of the flock?

8 Say I these things as a man? or saith not the law the same also?

9 For it is written in the law of Moses,

A. M. 4060.
A. D. 56.
A. U. C.
809.
Anno Imp. Nero-
nis Cæs. 3.

---

[e] Ver. 14; 1 Thess. ii. 6; 2 Thess. iii. 9.——[f] Or, *woman.*
[g] Matt. xiii. 55; Mark vi. 3; Luke vi. 15; Gal. i. 19.——[h] Matt. viii. 14.

[i] 2 Thess. iii. 8, 9.——[k] 2 Cor. x. 4; 1 Tim. i. 18; vi. 12 2 Tim. ii. 3; iv. 7.——[l] Deut. xx. 6; Prov. xxvii. 18; chap. iii. 6, 7, 8.——[m] John xxi. 15.

---

answer as upon oath. His defence therefore was this, that they were converted to God by his means. This verse belongs to the two preceding verses.

Verse 4. Have we not power to eat and to drink?] Have we not *authority*, or *right*, εξουσιαν, to expect sustenance, while we are labouring for your salvation? Meat and drink, the *necessaries*, not the superfluities, of life, were what those primitive messengers of Christ required; it was just that they who *laboured* in the Gospel should *live* by the Gospel; they did not wish to make a fortune, or accumulate wealth; a *living* was all they desired. It was probably in reference to the same moderate and reasonable desire that the provision made for the clergy in this country was called a *living;* and their *work* for which they got this *living* was called the *cure of souls.* Whether we derive the word *cure* from *cura*, care, as signifying that the *care* of all the souls in a particular parish or place devolves on the minister, who is to instruct them in the things of salvation, and lead them to heaven; or whether we consider the term as implying that the souls in that district are in a state of spiritual *disease*, and the minister is a spiritual *physician*, to whom the cure of these souls is intrusted; still we must consider that such a labourer is worthy of his hire; and he that preaches the Gospel should live by the Gospel.

Verse 5. Have we not power to lead about a sister, a wife] The word εξουσιαν is to be understood here, as above in ver. 4, as implying authority or right; and authority, not merely derived from their office, but from Him who gave them that office; from the constitution of nature; and from universal propriety or the fitness of things.

When the apostle speaks of leading about a sister, a wife, he means *first*, that he and all other apostles, and consequently all ministers of the Gospel, had a *right* to marry. For it appears that our Lord's brethren *James* and *Jude* were married; and we have infallible evidence that Peter was a married man, not only from this verse, but from Matt. viii. 14, where his *mother-in-law* is mentioned as being cured by our Lord of a fever.

And *secondly*, we find that their wives were persons of the *same faith;* for less can never be implied in the word *sister.* This is a decisive proof against the papistical celibacy of the clergy: and as to their attempts to evade the force of this text by saying that the apostles had holy women who attended them, and ministered to them in their peregrinations, there is no proof of it; nor could they have suffered either young

women or other men's wives to have accompanied them in this way without giving the most palpable occasion of scandal. And *Clemens Alexandrinus* has particularly remarked that the apostles carried their *wives* about with them, " not as wives, but as *sisters*, that they might minister to those who were mistresses of families; that so the doctrine of the Lord might without reprehension or evil suspicion enter into the apartments of the women." And in giving his finished picture of his *Gnostic*, or perfect Christian, he says: εσθιει, και πινει, και γαμει—εικονας εχει τους Αποστολους, *He eats, and drinks, and marries—having the apostles for his example.* Vid. *Clem. Alex.* Strom., lib. vii., c. 12.

On the propriety and excellence of *marriage*, and its *superiority* to *celibacy*, see the notes on chap. vii.

Verse 6. Or I only and Barnabas] Have we alone of all the apostles no right to be supported by our converts? It appears from this, 1. That the apostles did not generally support themselves by their own labour. 2. That Paul and Barnabas did thus support themselves. Some of the others probably had not a business at which they could conveniently work; but Paul and Barnabas had a trade at which they could conveniently labour wherever they came.

Verse 7. Who goeth a warfare—at his own charges?] These questions, which are all supposed from the necessity and propriety of the cases to be answered in the *affirmative*, tend more forcibly to point out that the common sense of man joins with the providence of God in showing the propriety of every man living by the fruits of his labour. The first question applies particularly to the case of the apostle, τις στρατευεται ιδιοις οψωνιοις· Does a soldier provide his own *victuals?* Οψωνιον is used to express the military pay or wages, by the Greek writers; for the Roman soldiers were paid not only in *money* but in *victuals;* and hence *corn* was usually distributed among them. See on Luke iii. 14.

Verse 8. Say I these things as a man?] Is this only human reasoning? or does not God say in effect the same things? See note on Rom. vi. 19.

Verse 9. Thou shalt not muzzle the mouth of the ox] See this largely explained in the note on Deut. xxv. 4.

Doth God take care for oxen?] This question is to be understood thus: Is it likely that God should be solicitous for the comfort of *oxen*, and be regardless of the welfare of *man?* In this Divine precept the kindness and providential care of God are very forcibly pointed

A. M. 4060. A. D. 56. A. U. C. 809. Anno Imp. Neronis Cæs. 3.

[n] Thou shalt not muzzle the mouth of the ox that treadeth out the corn. Doth God take care for oxen?

10 Or saith he *it* altogether for our sakes? For our sakes, no doubt, *this* is written: that [o] he that ploweth should plow in hope; and that he that thresheth in hope should be partaker of his hope.

11 [p] If we have sown unto you spiritual things, *is it* a great thing if we shall reap your carnal things?

12 If others be partakers of *this* power over you, *are* not we rather? [q] Nevertheless we have not used this power; but suffer all things, [r] lest we should hinder the Gospel of Christ.

13 [s] Do ye not know that they which minister about holy things, [t] live *of the things* of the temple? and they which wait at the altar, are partakers with the altar?

A. M. 4060. A. D. 56. A. U. C. 809. Anno Imp. Neronis Cæs. 3.

14 Even so [u] hath the Lord ordained, [v] that they which preach the Gospel should live of the Gospel.

15 But [w] I have used none of these things: neither have I written these things, that it should be so done unto me: for [x] *it were* better for me to die, than that any man should make my glorying void.

16 For though I preach the Gospel, I have nothing to glory of: for [y] necessity is laid upon me: yea, wo is unto me if I preach not the Gospel.

[n] Deut. xxv. 4; 1 Tim. v. 18.——[o] 2 Tim. ii. 6.——[p] Rom. xv. 27; Gal. vi. 6.——[q] Acts xx. 33; ver. 15, 18; 2 Cor. xi. 7, 9; xii. 13; 1 Thess. ii. 6.——[r] 2 Cor. xi. 12.——[s] Lev. vi. 16, 26; vii. 6, &c.; Num. v. 9, 10; xviii. 8–20; Deut x. 9; xviii. 1.

[t] Or, *feed.*——[u] Matt. x. 10; Luke x. 7.——[v] Gal. vi. 6; 1 Tim. v. 17.——[w] Ver. 12; Acts xviii. 3; xx. 34; chap. iv. 12; 1 Thess. ii. 9; 2 Thess. iii. 8.——[x] 2 Cor. xi. 10. [y] Rom. i. 14.

out. He takes care of oxen; he *wills* them all that happiness of which their nature is susceptible; and can we suppose that he is *unwilling* that the human soul shall have that happiness which is suited to its spiritual and eternal nature? He could not reprobate an ox, because *the Lord careth for oxen;* and surely he cannot reprobate a *man.* It may be said the *man* has *sinned* but the *ox* cannot. I answer: The decree of reprobation is supposed to be from all *eternity;* and certainly a man can no more sin *before* he *exists,* than an ox can *when* he *exists.*

Verse 10. *And he that thresheth in hope should be partaker of his hope.*] Instead of ὁ αλοων της ελπιδος αυτου μετεχειν, επ' ελπιδι, many of the best MSS. and versions read the passage thus: ὁ αλοων επ' ελπιδι του μετεχειν· *And he who thresheth in hope of partaking.* "The words της ελπιδος, which are omitted by the above, are," says Bp. Pearce, "superfluous, if not wrong; for men do not live *in hope* to partake of *their hope,* but to partake of what was the *object* and *end* of their *hope.* When these words are left out, the former and latter sentence will be both of a piece, and more resembling each other: for μετεχειν may be understood after the first επ' ελπιδι, as well as after the last." Griesbach has left the words in question out of the text.

Verse 11. *If we have sown unto you spiritual things*] If we have been the means of bringing you into a state of salvation by the Divine doctrines which we have preached unto you, is it too much for us to expect a temporal support when we give ourselves up entirely to this work? Every man who preaches the Gospel has a right to his own support and that of his family while thus employed.

Verse 12. *If others be partakers of* this *power*] If those who in any matter serve you have a *right* to a recompense for that service, surely we who have served you in the most essential matters have a right to our support while thus employed in your service.

We have not used this power] Though we had this *right,* we have not availed ourselves of it, but have worked with our hands to bear our own charges, lest any of you should think that we preached the Gospel merely to procure a temporal support, and so be prejudiced against us, and thus prevent our success in the salvation of your souls.

Verse 13. *They which minister about holy things*] All the officers about the temple, whether priests, Levites, Nethinim, &c., had a right to their support while employed in its service. The priests partook of the sacrifices; the others had their maintenance from tithes, first fruits, and offerings made to the temple; for it was not lawful for them to live on the sacrifices. Hence the apostle makes the distinction between those who *minister about holy things* and those who *wait at the altar.*

Verse 14. *Even so hath the Lord ordained*] This is evidently a reference to our Lord's ordination, Matt. x. 10: *The workman is worthy of his meat.* And Luke x. 7: *For the labourer is worthy of his hire.* And in both places it is the *preacher* of the *Gospel* of whom he is speaking. It was a maxim among the Jews, "that the inhabitants of a town where a wise man had made his abode should support him, because he had forsaken the world and its pleasures to study those things by which he might please God and be useful to men." See an ordinance to this effect in the tract *Shabbath,* fol. 114.

Verse 15. *Neither have I written, &c.*] Though I might plead the authority of God in the law, of Christ in the Gospel, the common consent of our own doctors, and the usages of civil society, yet I have not availed myself of my privileges; nor do I now write with the intention to lay in my claims.

Verse 16. *For though I preach the Gospel*] I have cause of glorying that I preach the Gospel free of all charges to you; but I cannot *glory* in being a preacher

A. M. 4060.
A. D. 56.
A. U. C.
809.
Anno Imp. Nero-
nis Cæs. 3.

17 For if I do this thing willing-ly, z I have a reward; but if against my will, a a dispensation *of the Gospel* is committed unto me.

18 What is my reward then? *Verily* that, b when I preach the Gospel, I may make the Gospel of Christ without charge, that I c abuse not my power in the Gospel.

19 For though I be d free from all *men*, yet

have e I made myself servant unto all, f that I might gain the more.

20 And g unto the Jews I be-came as a Jew, that I might gain the Jews; to them that are under the law, as under the law, that I might gain them that are under the law:

21 h To i them that are without law, as with-out law, (k being not without law to God, but

A. M. 4060.
A. D. 56.
A. U. C.
809.
Anno Imp. Nero
nis Cæs. 3.

z Chap. iii. 8, 14.——a Chap. iv. 1; Gal. ii. 7; Phil. i. 17; Col. i. 25.——b Chap. x. 33; 2 Cor. iv. 5; xi. 7.——c Chap. vii. 31.——d Ver. 1.

e Gal. v. 13.——f Matt. xviii. 15; 1 Pet. iii. 1.——g Acts xvi. 3; xviii. 18; xxi. 23, &c.——h Gal. iii. 2.——i Rom. ii. 12, 14.——k Chap. vii. 22.

of the Gospel, because I am not such either by my own skill or power. I have received both the *office*, and the grace by which I execute the office, from God. I have not only his authority to preach, but that au-thority *obliges* me to preach; and if I did not, I should endanger my salvation: *yea, wo is unto me, if I preach not the Gospel.* As every genuine preacher receives his commission from God alone, it is God alone who can take it away. Wo to that man who runs when God has not sent him; and wo to him who *refuses* to run, or who *ceases* to run, when God has sent him.

Verse 17. *For if I do this thing willingly*] If I be a cordial co-operator with God, *I have a reward*, an incorruptible crown, ver. 25. Or, if I freely preach this Gospel without being burthensome to any, I have a special reward; but if I do not, I have simply an office to fulfil, into which God has put me, and may fulfil it conscientiously, and claim my privileges at the same time; but then I lose that special reward which I have in view by preaching the Gospel without charge to any.

This and the 18th verse have been variously trans-lated: Sir *Norton Knatchbull* and, after him, Mr. *Wakefield* translate the two passages thus: *For if I do this willingly, I have a reward; but if I am in-trusted with an office without my consent, what is my reward then? to make the Gospel of Christ, whilst I preach it, without charge, in not using to the utmost my privileges in the Gospel.*

Others render the passage thus: *But if I do it merely because I am obliged to it, I only discharge an office that is committed to me*, ver. 18. *For what then shall I be rewarded? It is for this, that, preaching the Gospel of Christ, I preach it freely, and do not insist on a claim which the Gospel itself gives me.*

Verse 18. *That I abuse not my power*] I am in-clined to think that καταχρησασθαι is to be understood here, not in the sense of *abusing*, but of *using to the uttermost*—exacting every thing that a man can claim by law. How many proofs have we of this in preachers of different denominations, who insist so strongly and so frequently on their *privileges*, as they term them, that the people are tempted to believe they seek not their *souls*' interests, but their secular *goods*. Such preachers can do the people no good. But the people who are most liable to think thus of their mi-nisters, are those who are unwilling to grant the com-

mon necessaries of life to those who watch over them in the Lord. For there are such people even in the Christian Church! If the preachers of the Gospel were as parsimonious of the bread of life as some congregations and Christian societies are of the bread that perisheth, and if the preacher gave them a spirit-ual nourishment as base, as mean, and as scanty as the temporal support which they afford him, their souls must without doubt have nearly a famine of the bread of life.

Verse 19. *For though I be free*] Although I am under no obligation to any man, yet I act as if every individual had a particular property in me, and as if I were the *slave* of the public.

Verse 20. *Unto the Jews I became as a Jew*] In Acts xvi. 3, we find that for the sake of the uncon-verted Jews he circumcised Timothy. See the note there.

To them that are under the law] To those who con-sidered themselves still under obligation to observe its rites and ceremonies, though they had in the main em-braced the Gospel, he became as if under the same obligations; and therefore purified himself in the tem-ple, as we find related, Acts xxi. 26, where also see the notes.

After the first clause, *to them that are under the law as under the law*, the following words, μη ων αυτος υπο νομον, *not being myself under the law*, are added by ABCDEFG, several others; the later *Syriac*, *Sahidic*, *Armenian*, *Vulgate*, and all the *Itala*; *Cyril*, *Chrysostom*, *Damascenus*, and others; and on this evi-dence *Griesbach* has received them into the text.

Verse 21. *To them that are without law*] The *Gen-tiles*, who had no written law, though they had the *law written in their hearts*; see on Rom. ii. 15.

Being not without law to God] Instead of Θεω, το *God*, and Χριστω, το *Christ*, the most important MSS. and versions have Θεου, or *God*, and Χριστου, of *Christ*; being not without the law of God, but under the law of Christ.

Them that are without law.] Dr. Lightfoot thinks the *Sadducees* may be meant, and that in certain cases, as far as the *rites* and *ceremonies* of the Jewish reli-gion were concerned, he might conform himself to *them*, not observing such rites and ceremonies, as it is well known that *they* disregarded them; for the doc-tor cannot see how the apostle could conform himself in any thing to them that were *without law*, i. e. the

2

A. M. 4060.
A. D. 56.
A. U. C.
809.
Anno Imp. Nero-
nis Cæs. 3.

under the law to Christ,) that I might gain them that are without law.

22 [1] To the weak became I as weak, that I might gain the weak : [m] I am made all things to all *men,* [n] that I might by all means save some.

23 And this I do for the Gospel's sake, that

I might be partaker thereof with *you.*

A. M. 4060.
A. D. 56.
A. U. C.
809.
Anno Imp. Nero-
nis Cæs. 3.

24 Know ye not that they which run in a race run all, but one receiveth the prize ? [o] So run, that ye may obtain.

25 And every man that [p] striveth for the mastery is temperate in all things. Now they *do*

---

[1] Rom. xv. 1 ; 2 Cor. xi. 29.——[m] Chap. x. 33.——[n] Rom. xi. 14 ; chap. vii. 16.

[o] Gal. ii. 2 ; v. 7 ; Phil. ii. 16 ; iii. 14 ; 2 Tim. iv. 7 ; Heb. xii. 1. [p] Eph. vi. 12 ; 1 Tim. vi. 12 ; 2 Tim. ii. 5 ; iv. 7.

---

heathen. But, 1. It is not likely that the apostle could conform himself to the *Sadducees ;* for what success could he expect among a people who denied the *resurrection,* and consequently a *future world,* a *day of judgment,* and all *rewards* and *punishments ?* 2. He might among the heathen appear as if he were not a Jew, and discourse with them on the great principles of that eternal law, the outlines of which had been written in their hearts, in order to show them the necessity of embracing that Gospel which was the power of God unto salvation to every one that believed.

Verse 22. To the weak became I as weak] Those who were conscientiously *scrupulous,* even in respect to lawful things.

I am made all things to all men] I assumed every shape and form consistent with innocency and perfect integrity ; giving up my own will, my own way, my own ease, my own pleasure, and my own profit, that I might save the souls of all. Let those who plead for the system of *accommodation* on the example of St. Paul, attend to the *end* he had in view, and the *manner* in which he pursued that *end.* It was not to *get money, influence,* or *honour,* but to *save* souls ! It was not to get *ease* but to increase his *labours.* It was not to *save his life,* but rather that it should be a *sacrifice* for the good of *immortal souls !* A parallel saying to this of St. Paul has been quoted from Achilles Tatius, lib. v., cap. xix., where Clitophon says, on having received a letter from Leucippe : Τουτοις εντυχων π α ν τ α ε γ ι ν ο μ η ν ὁμου, ανεφλεγομην, ωχριων, εθαυμαζον, ηπιστουν, εχαιρον, ηχθομην· "When I read the contents, I *became all things at once* ; I was inflamed, I grew pale, I was struck with wonder; I doubted, I rejoiced, became sad." The same form of speech is frequent among Greek writers. I think this casts some light on the apostle's meaning.

That I might by all means save some.] On this clause there are some very important readings found in the MSS. and versions. Instead of παντως τινας σωσω, *that I might by all means save some ;* παντας σωσω, *that I might save all,* is the reading of DEFG, *Syriac, Vulgate, Æthiopic,* all the *Itala,* and several of the *fathers.* This reading Bishop *Pearce* prefers, because it is more agreeable to St. Paul's meaning here, and exactly agrees with what he says, chap. x. 33, and makes his design more extensive and noble. *Wakefield* also prefers this reading.

Verse 23. And this I do for the Gospel's sake] Instead of τουτο, *this,* παντα, *all things,* (I do all things for the Gospel's sake,) is the reading of ABCDEFG,

several others, the *Coptic, Æthiopic, Vulgate, Itala, Armenian,* and *Sahidic ;* the two latter reading ταυτα παντα, *all these things.*

Several of the fathers have the same reading, and there is much reason to believe it to be *genuine.*

That I might be partaker thereof with you.] That I might attain to the *reward* of eternal life which it sets before me ; and this is in all probability the meaning of το ευαγγελιον, which we translate *the Gospel,* and which should be rendered here *prize* or *reward ;* this is a frequent meaning of the original word, as may be seen in my preface to St. Matthew : *I do all this for the sake of the prize, that I may partake of it* with you.

Verse 24. They which run in a race run all] It is sufficiently evident that the apostle alludes to the athletic exercises in the games which were celebrated every fifth year on the isthmus, or narrow neck of land, which joins the Peloponnesus, or Morea, to the main land ; and were thence termed the *Isthmian games.* The exercises were *running, wrestling, boxing, throwing* the *discus* or *quoit, &c. ;* to the three first of these the apostle especially alludes.

But one receiveth the prize ?] The apostle places the Christian race in contrast to the Isthmian games ; in them, only one received the prize, though all ran ; in this, if all run, all will receive the prize ; therefore he says, *So run that ye may obtain.* Be as much in earnest to get to heaven as others are to gain their prize ; and, although only one of *them* can win, *all* of *you* may obtain.

Verse 25. Is temperate in all things] All those who contended in these exercises went through a long state and series of painful preparations. To this exact discipline *Epictetus* refers, cap. 35 : Θελεις Ολυμπια νικησαι ; Δει σ' ευτακτειν, αναγκοτροφειν, απεχεσθαι πεμματων, γυμναζεσθαι προς αναγκην εν ὡρᾳ τεταγμενῃ, εν καυματι, εν ψυχει, μη ψυχρον πινειν, μη οινον ὡς ετυχεν· ἁπλως, ὡς ιατρῳ, παραδεδωκεναι σεαυτον τῳ επιστατῃ· ειτα εις τον αγωνα παρερχεσθαι κ. τ. λ. "Do you wish to gain the prize at the Olympic games ?—Consider the requisite preparations and the consequences : you must observe a strict regimen ; must live on food which you dislike ; you must abstain from all delicacies ; must exercise yourself at the necessary and prescribed times both in heat and in cold ; you must drink nothing cooling ; take no wine as formerly ; in a word, you must put yourself under the directions of a *pugilist,* as you would under those of a *physician,* and afterwards enter the lists. Here you may get your arm broken,

2

A. M. 4060.
A. D. 56.
A. U. C.
809.
Anno Imp. Nero-
nis Cæs. 3.

it to obtain a corruptible crown; but we ᑫ an incorruptible.

26 I therefore so run, ʳ not as uncertainly; so fight I, not as one that beateth the air:

27 ˢ But I keep under my body, and ᵗ bring *it* into subjection; lest that by any means, when I have preached to others, I myself should be ᵘ a castaway.

A. M. 4060.
A. D. 56.
A. U. C.
809.
Anno Imp. Nero
nis Cæs. 3.

ᑫ 2 Tim. iv. 8; James i. 12; 1 Peter i. 4; v. 4; Revelations ii. 10; iii. 11.——ʳ 2 Tim. ii. 5.

ˢ Rom. viii. 13; Col. iii. 5.——ᵗ Rom. vi. 18, 19.——ᵘ Jer. vi. 30; 2 Cor. xiii. 5, 6.

your foot put out of joint, be obliged to swallow mouthfuls of dust, to receive many stripes, and after all be conquered." Thus we find that these suffered much hardships in order to conquer, and yet were *uncertain* of the *victory.*

Horace speaks of it in nearly the same way—

Qui studet optatam cursu contingere metam,
Multa tulit fecitque *puer:* sudavit *et* alsit:
Abstinuit Venere *et* Baccho.
        De Arte Poet., ver. 412.

A youth who hopes the Olympic prize to gain,
All arts must try, and every toil sustain;
Th' extremes of heat and cold must often prove;
And shun the weakening joys of wine and love.
        Francis.

These quotations show the propriety of the apostle's words: *Every man that striveth for the mastery,* παντα εγκρατευεται, *is temperate,* or *continent, in all things.*

They do it *to obtain a corruptible crown*] The *crown* won by the victor in the *Olympian* games was made of the *wild olive*; in the *Pythian* games of *laurel*; in the *Nemean* games of *parsley*; and in the *Isthmian* games of the *pine.* These were all *corruptible,* for they began to *wither* as soon as they were separated from the trees, or plucked out of the earth. In opposition to these, the apostle says, he contended for an incorruptible crown, the heavenly inheritance. He sought not *worldly* honour; but that honour which comes from God.

Verse 26. *I therefore so run, not as uncertainly*] In the foot-course in those games, how many soever ran, only *one* could have the prize, however strenuously they might exert themselves; therefore, *all* ran uncertainly; but it was widely different in the Christian course, if every one ran as he ought, *each* would receive the prize.

The word αδηλως, which we translate *uncertainly,* has other meanings. 1. It signifies *ignorantly*; I do not run like one *ignorant* of what he is about, or of the *laws* of the *course*; I know that there is an eternal life; I *know* the *way* that leads to it; and I *know* and feel the *power* of it. 2. It signifies *without observation*; the eyes of all the spectators were fixed on those who ran in these races; and to gain the applause of the multitude, they stretched every nerve; the apostle knew that the eyes of all were fixed upon him. 1. His false brethren waited for his halting: 2. The persecuting Jews and Gentiles longed for his downfall: 3. The Church of Christ *looked* on him with anxiety: 4. And he acted in all things as under the immediate *eye* of God.

Not as one that beateth the air] Kypke observes, that there are *three* ways in which persons were said,

αερα δερειν, *to beat the air.* 1. When in practising for the combat they threw their arms and legs about in different ways, thus practising the attitudes of offence and defence. This was termed σκιαμαχια, *fighting with a shadow.* To this Virgil alludes when representing *Dares* swinging his arms about, when he rose to challenge a competitor in the *boxing* match:—

Talis prima Dares caput altum in prælia tollit,
Ostenditque humeros latos, alternaque jactat
Brachia *protendens, et* verberat ictibus auras.
        Æn. v., ver. 375.

Thus, glorying in his strength, in open view
His arms around the towering Dares threw;
Stalked high, and laid his brawny shoulders bare,
And dealt his *whistling blows* in *empty air.* *Pitt.*

2. Sometimes boxers were to aim blows at their adversaries which they did not intend to take place, and which the others were obliged to exert themselves to prevent as much as if they had been really *intended*, and by these means some dexterous pugilists vanquished their adversaries by mere fatigue, without giving them a single blow. 3. Pugilists were said to *beat the air* when they had to contend with a nimble adversary, who, by running from side to side, stooping, and various contortions of the body, eluded the blows of his antagonist; who spent his strength on the *air,* frequently *missing* his *aim,* and sometimes *overturning himself* in attempting to hit his adversary, when this, by his agility, had been able to elude the blow. We have an example of this in Virgil's account of the boxing match between *Entellus* and *Dares,* so well told Æneid. v., ver. 426, &c., and which will give us a proper view of the subject to which the apostle alludes: viz. boxing at the Isthmian games.

Constitit in digitos extemplo arrectus uterque,
Brachiaque ad superas interritus extulit auras.
Abduxere retro longe capita ardua ab ictu;
Immiscentque manus manibus, pugnamque lacessunt.
Ille [*Dares*] pedum melior motu, fretusque juventa;
Hic [*Entellus*] membris et mole valens; sed tarda
        trementi
Genua labant, vastos quatit æger anhelitus artus.
Multa viri nequicquam inter se vulnera jactant,
Multa cavo lateri ingeminant, et pectore vasto
Dant sonitus; errataque aures et tempora circum
Crebra manus; duro crepitant sub vulnere malæ.
Stat gravis Entellus, nisuque immotus eodem,
Corpore tela modo atque oculis vigilantibus exit.
Ille, velut celsam oppugnat qui molibus urbem,
Aut montana sedet circum castella sub armis;
Nunc hos, nunc illos aditus, omnemque pererrat
Arte locum, et variis assultibus irritus urget.

2

Ostendit dextram insurgens Entellus, et alte
Extulit : ille ictum venientem a vertice velox
Prævidit, celerique elapsus corpore cessit.
Entellus VIRES IN VENTUM EFFUDIT ; et ultro
Ipse gravis, graviterque ad terram pondere vasto
Concidit : ut quondam cava concidit, aut Erymantho,
Aut Ida in magna, radicibus eruta pinus.——
Consurgunt studiis Teucri et Trinacria pubes ;
It clamor cœlo : primusque accurrit Acestes,
Æquævumque ab humo miserans attollit amicum.
At non tardatus casu, neque territus heros,
Acrior ad pugnam redit, ac vim suscitat ira :
Tum pudor incendit vires, et conscia virtus ;
Præcipitemque Daren ardens agit æquore toto ;
Nunc dextra ingeminans ictus, nunc ille sinistra.
Nec mora, nec requies : quam multa grandine nimbi
Culminibus crepitant ; sic densis ictibus heros
Creber utraque manu pulsat versatque Dareta.

Both on the tiptoe stand, at full extent ;
Their arms aloft, their bodies inly bent ;
Their heads from aiming blows they bear afar,
With clashing gauntlets then provoke the war.
One [*Dares*] on his youth and pliant limbs relies ;
One [*Entellus*] on his sinews, and his giant size.
The last is stiff with age, his motions slow ;
He heaves for breath, he staggers to and fro.——
Yet equal in success, they ward, they strike ;
Their ways are different, but their art alike.
Before, behind, the blows are dealt ; around
Their hollow sides the rattling thumps resound.
A storm of strokes, well meant, with fury flies,
And errs about their temples, ears, and eyes :
Nor always errs ; for oft the gauntlet draws
A sweeping stroke along the crackling jaws.
  Hoary with age, Entellus stands his ground ;
But with his warping body wards the wound ;
His head and watchful eye keep even pace,
While Dares traverses and shifts his place ;
And, like a captain who beleaguers round
Some strong-built castle, on a rising ground,
Views all the approaches with observing eyes ; }
This, and that other part, in vain he tries, }
And more on industry than force relies. }
With hands on high, Entellus threats the foe ; }
But Dares watched the motion from below, }
And slipped aside, and shunned the long descend- }
   ing blow. }
Entellus *wastes his forces on the wind* ;
And thus deluded of the stroke designed,
Headlong and heavy fell : his ample breast,
And weighty limbs, his ancient mother pressed.
So falls a hollow pine, that long had stood
On Ida's height or Erymanthus' wood.——
Dauntless he rose, and to the fight returned ;
With shame his cheeks, his eyes with fury burned :
Disdain and conscious virtue fired his breast,
And, with redoubled force, his foe he pressed ;
He lays on loads with either hand amain,
And headlong drives the Trojan o'er the plain,
Nor stops, nor stays ; nor rest, nor breath allows ; }
But storms of strokes descend about his brows ; }
A rattling tempest, and a hail of blows. }
                         Dryden.

To such a combat as this the apostle most manifestly alludes : and in the above description the reader will see the full force and meaning of the words, *So fight I, not as one that beateth the air*—I have a *real* and a *deadly* foe ; and as I fight not only for my *honour* but for my *life*, I aim every blow well, and do execution with each.

No man, who had not *seen* such a fight, could have given such a description as that above ; and we may fairly presume that when Virgil was in Greece he saw such a contest at the Isthmian games, and therefore was enabled to paint from *nature*.

Homer has the same image of missing the foe and *beating the air*, when describing Achilles attempting to kill Hector, who, by his *agility* and *skill*, (Poetice by *Apollo*,) eluded the blow :——

Τρις μεν επειτ᾽ επορουσε ποδαρκης διος Αχιλλευς
Εγχεϊ χαλκειῳ, τρις δ᾽ ηερα τυψε βαθειαν.
            ILIAD, lib. xx., ver. 445

Thrice struck Pelides with indignant heart,
Thrice, in *impressive air*, he plunged the dart.—*Pope.*

Verse 27. *But I keep under my body, &c.*] This is an allusion, not only to *boxers*, but also to *wrestlers* in the same games, as we learn from the word ὑπωπιαζω, which signifies to *hit in the eyes* ; and δουλαγωγω, which signifies to trip, and give the antagonist a fall, and then *keep him down* when he was down, and having obliged him to acknowledge himself conquered, make him a *slave*. The apostle considers his body as an enemy with which he must contend ; he must mortify it by self-denial, abstinence, and severe labour ; it must be the *slave* of his soul, and not the soul the *slave* of the body, which in all unregenerate men is the case.

Lest—having preached to others] The word κηρυξας, which we translate *having preached*, refers to the *office* of the κηρυξ, or *herald*, at these games, whose business it was to proclaim the conditions of the games, display the prizes, exhort the combatants, excite the emulation of those who were to contend, declare the terms of each contest, pronounce the name of the victors, and put the crown on their heads. See my observations on this *office* in the notes at the end of Matt. iii.

Should be a castaway.] The word αδοκιμος signifies such a person as the βραβευται, or *judges of the games*, reject as not having deserved the prize. So Paul himself might be rejected by the great Judge ; and to *prevent* this, he ran, he contended, he denied himself, and *brought his body into subjection* to his spirit, and had his spirit governed by the Spirit of God. Had this heavenly man lived in our days, he would by a certain class of people have been deemed a *legalist* ; a people who widely differ from the practice of the apostle, for they are conformed to the world, and they feed themselves without fear.

ON the various important subjects in this chapter I have already spoken in great detail ; not, indeed, *all* that might be said, but as much as is necessary. A few general observations will serve to recapitulate and impress what has been already said.

1. St. Paul contends that a preacher of the Gospel has a right to his support ; and he has proved this from the *law*, from the *Gospel*, and from the *common*

sense and consent of men. If a man who does not labour takes his maintenance from the Church of God, it is not only a domestic theft but a sacrilege. He that gives up his time to this labour has a *right* to the support of himself and family: he who takes more than is sufficient for this purpose is a covetous hireling. He who does nothing for the cause of God and religion, and yet obliges the Church to support him, and minister to his idleness, irregularities, luxury, avarice, and ambition, is a *monster* for whom human language has not yet got a *name.*

2. Those who refuse the labourer his hire are condemned by God and by good men. How liberal are many to public places of amusement, or to some *popular charity,* where their *names* are sure to be *published* abroad; while the man who watches over their souls is fed with the most parsimonious hand! Will not God abate this *pride* and reprove this *hard-heartedness?*

3. As the husbandman plows and sows in *hope,* and the God of providence makes him a partaker of his *hope,* let the upright preachers of God's word take example and encouragement by him. Let them labour in *hope;* God will not permit them to spend their strength for nought. Though much of their seed, through the fault of the bad ground, may be unfruitful, yet some will spring up unto eternal life.

4. St. Paul *became all things to all men, that he might gain all.* This was not the effect of a fickle or man-pleasing disposition; no man was ever of a more *firm* or *decided* character than St. Paul; but whenever he could with a good conscience yield so as to please his neighbour for his good to edification, he did so; and his yielding disposition was a proof of the *greatness of his soul.* The unyielding and *obstinate* mind is always a *little* mind: a want of true *greatness* always produces *obstinacy* and *peevishness.* Such a person as St. Paul is a blessing wherever he goes: on the contrary, the obstinate, *hoggish* man, is either a general curse, or a general cross; and if a preacher of the Gospel, his is a burthensome ministry. Reader, let me ask thee a question: If there be no *gentleness* in thy *manners,* is there any in thy *heart?* If there be little of Christ *without,* can there be much of Christ *within?*

5. A few general observations on the Grecian games may serve to recapitulate the subject in the four last verses.

1. The Isthmian games were celebrated among the Corinthians; and therefore the apostle addresses them, ver. 24: Know *ye not, &c.*

2. Of the *five* games there used, the apostle speaks only of *three.* Running, ver. 24: *They which run in a race;* and ver. 26: *I therefore so run, not as uncertainly.* Wrestling, ver. 25: *Every man that striveth;* ὁ ἀγωνιζομενος, *he who wrestleth.* Boxing, ver. 26, 27: *So fight I, not as one that beateth the air;* οὑτω πυκτευω, *so fist I, so I hit;* but *I keep my body under;* ὑπωπιαζω, *I hit in the eye, I make the face black and blue.*

3. He who won the race by *running* was to observe the *laws* of racing—keeping within the *white line* which marked out the path or compass in which they ran; and he was also to outrun the rest, and to come

first to the goal; otherwise he ran *uncertainly,* ver. 24, 26, and was ἀδοκιμος, one to whom the prize could not be judged by the judges of the games.

4. The *athletic* combatants, or wrestlers, observed a *set diet.* See the quotation from *Epictetus,* under ver. 25. And this was a *regimen* both for *quantity* and *quality;* and they carefully abstained from all things that might render them less able for the combat; whence the apostle says they *were temperate in all things,* ver. 25.

5. No person who was not of respectable family and connections was permitted to be a competitor at the Olympic games. St. *Chrysostom,* in whose time these games were still celebrated, assures us that no man was suffered to enter the lists who was either a *servant* or a *slave,* ουδεις αγωνιζεται δ ο υ λ ο ς, ουδεις στρατευεται ο ι κ ε τ η ς· and if any such was found who had got himself inserted on the military list, his name was erased, and he was expelled and punished. Αλλ' εαν ἁλῳ δουλος ων, μετα τιμωριας εκβαλλεται του των στρατιωτων καταολγου. To prevent any person of bad character from entering the list at the Olympic games, the kerux, or *herald,* was accustomed to proclaim aloud in the theatre when the combatant was brought forth: Μη τις τουτον κατηγορει; ὡστε αυτον αποσκευασαμενον της δουλειας την ὑποψιαν ουτως εις τους αγωνας εμβηναι: *Who can accuse this man?* For which he gives this reason: "that being free from all suspicion of being in a state of slavery, (and elsewhere he says of being a thief, or of corrupt morals,) he might enter the lists with credit." *Chrysost.* Homil. in Inscript. Altaris, &c., vol. iii. page 59, Edit. Benedict.

6. The *boxers* used to prepare themselves by a sort of σκιαμαχια, or going through all their *postures of defence* and *attack* when no adversary was before them. This was termed *beating the air,* verse 26; but when such came to the combat, they endeavoured to *blind* their adversaries by hitting them in the eye, which is the meaning of ὑπωπιαζειν, as we have seen under ver. 27.

7. The *rewards* of all these exercises were only a *crown* made of the *leaves* of some *plant,* or the *bough* of some *tree;* the *olive, bay, laurel, parsley, &c.,* called here by the apostle φθαρτον στεφανον, a *corruptible, withering,* and *fading crown;* while he and his fellow Christians expected a crown *incorruptible* and immortal, and that could not fade away.

8. On the subject of the *possibility* of St. Paul *becoming a castaway,* much has been said in contradiction to his own words. He most absolutely states the *possibility* of the case: and who has a right to call this in question? The ancient Greek commentators, as *Whitby* has remarked, have made a good use of the apostle's saying, Ει δε Παυλος τουτο δεδοικεν ὁ τοσουτους διδαξας, τι αν ειποιμεν ἡμεις; "If Paul, so great a man, one who had preached and laboured so much, dreaded this, what cause have we to fear lest this should befall us!"

9. On the necessity of being workers together with God, in order to avoid apostasy, *Clemens Alexandrinus* has some useful observations in his *Stromata,* lib. vii., page 448, Edit. Oberthur: Ὡς δε, says he, ὁ ιατρος ὑγειαν παρεχεται τοις συνεργουσι προς ὑγειαν, ουτως και ὁ Θεος την αιδιον σωτηριαν τοις συνεργουσι προς γνωσιν τε και ευπρα-

γιαν· " As a physician gives health to those who co-operate with him in their cure ; so God also gives eternal salvation to them who are workers together with him in knowledge and a godly life." " Therefore," says he, " it is well said among the Greeks, that when a certain wrestler, who had long inured his body to manly exercises, was going to the Olympic games, as he was passing by the statue of Jupiter he offered up this prayer : Ει παντα, ω Ζευ, δεοντως μοι τα προς τον αγωνα ταοεσκευασται, αποδος φερων δικαιως την νικην εμοι· 'Ο

Jupiter, if I have performed every thing as I ought in reference to this contest, grant me the victory !' " May we not feel something of this spirit in seeking the kingdom of God ? And can any thing of this kind be supposed to derogate from the glory of Christ ? St. Paul himself says, if a man contend for the mastery, yet is he not crowned except he strive lawfully. Shall we pretend to be wiser than the apostle ; and say, that we may gain the *crown*, though we neither *fight the good fight* nor *finish the course ?*

CHAPTER X.

Peculiar circumstances in the Jewish history were typical of the greatest mysteries of the Gospel ; particularly their passing through the Red Sea, and being overshadowed with the miraculous cloud, 1, 2. The manna with which they were fed, 3. And rock out of which they drank, 4. The punishments inflicted on them for their disobedience are warnings to us, 5. We should not lust as they did, 6.. Nor commit idolatry, 7. Nor fornication as they did ; in consequence of which twenty-three thousand of them were destroyed, 8. Nor tempt Christ as they did, 9. Nor murmur, 10. All these transgressions and their punishments are recorded as warnings to us, that we may not fall away from the grace of God, 11, 12. God never suffers any to be tempted above their strength, 13. Idolatry must be detested, 14. And the sacrament of the Lord's Supper properly considered and taken, that God may not be provoked to punish us, 15—22. There are some things which may be legally done which are not expedient ; and we should endeavour so to act as to edify each other, 23, 24. The question concerning eating things offered to idols considered, and finally settled, 25—30. . We should do all things to the glory of God, avoid whatsoever might be the means of stumbling another, and seek the profit of others in spiritual matters rather than our own gratification 31—33.

A. M. 4060.
A. D. 56.
A. U. C. 809.
Anno Imp Neronis Cæs. 3.

MOREOVER, brethren, I would not that ye should be ignorant, how that all our fathers were under ᵃ the cloud, and all passed through ᵇ the sea ;

2 And were all baptized unto Moses in the cloud and in the sea ;

3 And did all eat the same ᶜ spiritual meat ;

A. M. 4060.
A. D. 56.
A. U. C. 809.
Anno Imp. Neronis Cæs. 3.

ᵃ Exod. xiii. 21 ; xl. 34 ; Num. ix. 18 ; xiv. 14 ; Deut. i. 33 ; Neh. ix. 12, 19 ; Psa. lxxviii. 14 ; cv. 39.

ᵇ Exod. xiv. 22 ; Num. xxxiii. 8 ; Josh. iv. 23 ; Psa. lxxviii. 13. ᶜ Exod. xvi. 15, 35 ; Neh. ix. 15, 20 ; Psa. lxxviii. 24.

NOTES ON CHAP. X.

Verse 1. *I would not that ye should be ignorant*] It seems as if the Corinthians had supposed that their being made partakers of the ordinances of the Gospel, such as *baptism* and the *Lord's Supper*, would secure their salvation, notwithstanding they might be found partaking of idolatrous feasts ; as long, at least, as they considered an *idol to be nothing in the world.* To remove this destructive supposition, which would have led them to endless errors both in principle and practice, the apostle shows that the Jews had sacramental ordinances in the wilderness, similar to those of the Christians ; and that, notwithstanding they had the typical baptism from the cloud, and the typical eucharist from the paschal lamb, and the manna that came down from heaven, yet, when they joined with idolaters and partook of idolatrous feasts, God was not only *displeased* with them, but signified this displeasure by pouring out his judgments upon them, so that in one day 23,000 of them were destroyed.

Under the cloud] It is manifest from Scripture that the miraculous cloud in the wilderness performed a three fold office to the Israelites. 1. It was a cloud in the form of a *pillar* to direct their journeyings by

day. 2. It was a pillar of *fire* to give light to the camp by *night.* 3. It was a covering for them during the day, and preserved them from the scorching rays of the sun ; and supplied them with a sufficiency of *aqueous particles*, not only to cool that burning atmosphere, but to give refreshment to themselves and their cattle ; and its *humidity* was so abundant that the apostle here represents the people as thoroughly sprinkled and enveloped in its aqueous vapour. See the note on Exod. xiii. 21.

Verse 2. *And were all baptized unto Moses*] Rather INTO Moses—into the *covenant* of which Moses was the mediator ; and by this typical baptism they were brought under the obligation of acting according to the Mosaic precepts, as Christians receiving Christian baptism are said to be baptized INTO *Christ*, and are thereby brought under obligation to keep the precepts of the *Gospel.*

Verse 3. *Spiritual meat*] The manna which is here called *spiritual.* 1. Because it was provided supernaturally ; and, 2. Because it was a type of Christ Jesus, who speaking of it, John vi. 31, &c., tells us that it was a type of that *true bread which came down from heaven*, which *gives life to the world,*

A. M. 4060.
A. D. 56.
A. U. C.
809.
Anno Imp. Nero-
nis Cæs. 3.

4 And did all drink the same ^d spiritual drink; (for they drank of that spiritual rock that ^e followed them: and that rock was Christ.)

5 But with many of them God was not well pleased; for they ^f were overthrown in the wilderness.

A. M. 4060.
A. D. 56.
A. U. C.
809.
Anno Imp. Nero-
nis Cæs. 3.

6 Now these things were ^g our examples, to the intent we should not lust after evil things, as ^h they also lusted.

7 ⁱ Neither be ye idolaters, as *were* some of them; as it is written, ^k The people sat down to eat and drink, and rose up to play.

---

^d Exod. xvii. 6; Num. xx. 11; Psalm lxxviii. 15.——^e Or, *went with them;* Deut. ix. 21; Psa. cv. 41.——^f Num. xiv. 29, 32, 35; xxvi. 64, 65; Psa. cvi. 26; Heb. iii. 17; Jude 5.

^g Gr. *our figures.*——^h Num. xi. 4, 33, 34; Psalm cvi. 14. ⁱ Ver. 14.——^k Exod. xxxii. 6.

---

ver. 33, and that himself was the *bread of life,* ver. 48.

Verse 4. Spiritual drink] By the βρωμα πνευμα-τικον, *spiritual meat,* and πομα 'πνευματικον, *spiritual drink,* the apostle certainly means both *meat* and *drink,* which were furnished to the Israelitish assembly *miraculously,* as well as *typically :* and he appears to borrow his expression from the Jews themselves, who expressly say הלחם הלז רוחני *hallechem hallaz ruchani,* that bread was spiritual, and מים רוחניים היו *meyim ruchainiyim haiu,* the waters were spiritual. *Alschech* in legem. fol. 238, to which opinion the apostle seems particularly to refer.—See *Schoettgen.*

The spiritual rock that followed them] There is some difficulty in this verse. How could the rock *follow* them? It does not appear that the rock ever moved from the place where Moses struck it. But to solve this difficulty, it is said that *rock* here is put, by *metonymy,* for the *water* of the rock; and that this water did follow them through the wilderness. This is more likely; but we have not direct proof of it. The ancient Jews, however, were of this opinion, and state that the streams followed them in all their journeyings, up the mountains, down the valleys, &c., &c.; and that when they came to encamp, the waters formed themselves into *cisterns* and *pools;* and that the rulers of the people guided them, by their staves, in rivulets to the different tribes and families. And this is the sense they give to Num. xxi. 17 : *Spring up, O well, &c.*—See the places in *Schoettgen.*

Others contend, that by the *rock following them* we are to understand their having *carried of its waters* with them on their journeyings. This we know is a common custom in these deserts to the present day; and that the Greek verb ακολουθεω, *to follow,* has this sense, Bishop Pearce has amply proved in his note on this place. The Jews suppose that the *rock* itself went with the Israelites, and was present with them in their thirty-eight stations, for only so many are mentioned. See *Alschech* in legem. fol. 236. And see *Schoettgen.*

Now, though of all the senses already given that of Bishop Pearce is the best, yet it does appear that the apostle does not speak about the *rock* itself, but of *Him* whom it represented; namely, Christ : this was the Rock that followed them, and ministered to them; and this view of the subject is rendered more probable by what is said ver. 9, that they tempted *Christ,* and were destroyed by serpents. The same rock is in the *vale of Rephidim* to the present day; and it bears

aboriginal marks of the water that flowed from it in the *fissures* that appear on its sides. It is one block of fine *granite,* about seven yards long, five broad, and — high. A fragment of this typical rock now lies before me, brought by a relative of my own, who broke it off, and did not let it pass into any hand till he placed it in mine. See the note on Exod. xvii. 6.

Verse 5. They were overthrown in the wilderness.] And yet ALL these persons *were* under the cloud—ALL passed through the sea—ALL were baptized into Moses in the cloud and in the sea—ALL ate the same spiritual meat—ALL drank the same spiritual drink, for they were made partakers of the spiritual Rock, CHRIST. Nothing can be a more decisive proof than this that people, who have every outward ordinance, and are made partakers of the grace of our Lord Jesus, may so abuse their privileges and grieve the Spirit of God as to fall from their state of grace, and perish everlastingly. Let those who are continually asserting that this is impossible, beware lest they themselves, *if* in a state of grace, become, through their overmuch security, proofs in point of the possibility of ending in the *flesh,* though they began in the *Spirit.* Reader, remember who said, *Ye shall not surely die;* and remember the mischiefs produced by a belief of his doctrine.

Verse 6. These things were our examples] The punishments which God inflicted on *them* furnish us with evidences of what God will inflict upon *us,* if we sin after the similitude of those transgressors.

We should not lust after evil things] It is most evident that the apostle refers here to the history in Num. xi. 4, &c.: *And the mixed multitude fell a lusting, and said, Who shall give us flesh to eat ?* Into the same spirit the Corinthians had most evidently fallen; they *lusted* after the *flesh* in the idol feasts, and therefore frequented them to the great scandal of Christianity. The apostle shows them that their sin was of the same nature as that of the murmuring rebellious Israelites whom God so severely punished; and if he did not spare the *natural branches,* there was no likelihood that he should spare *them.*

Verse 7. Neither be ye idolaters] The apostle considers partaking of the idolatrous feasts as being real acts of *idolatry ;* because those who offered the flesh to their gods considered them as feeding invisibly with them on the flesh thus offered, and that every one that partook of the feast was a real participator with the god to whom the flesh or animal had been offered in sacrifice. See ver. 21.

Rose up to play.] See the note on Exod. xxxii. 6

2

A. M. 4060.
A. D. 56.
A. U. C.
809.
Anno Imp. Nero-
nis Cæs. 3.

8 ¹ Neither let us commit fornication, as some of them committed, and ᵐ fell in one day three
and twenty thousand.

9 Neither let us tempt Christ, as ⁿ some of them
also tempted, and ᵒ were destroyed of serpents.

10 Neither murmur ye, as ᵖ some of them

also murmured, and ᑫ were destroyed of ʳ the destroyer.

11 Now all these things
happened unto them for ˢ ensamples : and ᵗ they are written for our
admonition, ᵘ upon whom the ends of the world
are come.

A. M. 4060.
A. D. 56.
A. U. C.
809.
Anno Imp. Nero-
nis Cæs. 3.

---

¹ Chap. vi. 18 ; Rev. ii. 14.——ᵐ Num. xxv. 1, 9 ; Psa. cvi. 29.
ⁿ Exod. xvii. 2, 7 ; Num. xxi. 5 ; Deut. vi. 16 ; Psa. lxxviii. 18,
56 ; xcv. 9 ; cvi. 14.——ᵒ Num. xxi. 6.——ᵖ Exod. xvi. 2 ; xvii.
2 ; Num. xiv. 2, 29 ; xvi. 41:

ᑫ Num. xiv. 37 ; xvi. 49.——ʳ Exod. xii. 23 ; 2 Sam. xxiv. 16 ;
1 Chron. xxi. 15.——ˢ Or, *types.*——ᵗ Rom. xv. 4 ; chap. ix. 10.
ᵘ Chapter vii. 29 ; Phil. iv. 5 ; Hebrews x. 25, 37 ; 1 John
ii. 18.

The Jews generally explain this word as implying
idolatrous acts only : I have considered it as implying
acts of *impurity*, with which idolatrous acts were often
accompanied. It also means those *dances* which were
practised in honour of their gods. That this is one
meaning of the verb παιζειν, *Kypke* has largely proved.
The whole idolatrous process was as follows : 1. The
proper victim was prepared and set apart. 2. It was
slain, and its blood poured out at the altar of the deity.
3. The flesh was dressed, and the priests and offerers
feasted on it, and thus endeavoured to establish a *communion* between *themselves* and the *object* of their
worship. 4. After eating, they had idolatrous dances
in honour of their god ; and, 5. as might be expected,
impure mixtures, in consequence of those *dances. The
people sat down to eat and to drink, and rose up to
play* ; and it is in reference to this issue of idolatrous
feasts and dancings that the apostle immediately subjoins : *Neither let us commit* FORNICATION, &c.

Verse 8. *Fell in one day three and twenty thousand.*]
In Num. xxv. 9, the number is 24,000 ; and, allowing this to be the genuine reading, (and none of the
Hebrew MSS. exhibit any various reading in the
place,) Moses and the apostle may be thus reconciled :
in Num. xxv. 4, God commands Moses to *take all
the heads* (the rulers) *of the people, and hang them
up before the Lord against the sun* ; these possibly
amounted to 1000, and those who fell by the *plague*
were 23,000, so that the whole amounted to 24,000.
Instead of εικοσιτρεις χιλιαδες, 23,000, two MSS., with
the later *Syriac* and the *Armenian*, have εικοσιτεσσαρες
χιλιαδες, 24,000 ; but this authority is too slender to
establish a various reading, which recedes so much
from the received text. I think the discordance may
be best accounted for by supposing, as above, that
Phineas and his *companions* might have slain 1000
men, who were heads of the people, and chief in this
idolatry ; and that the plague sent from the Lord destroyed 23,000 more ; so an equal number to the whole
tribe of Levi perished in one day, who were just
23,000. See Num. xxvi. 62 ; and see Lightfoot.

Verse 9. *Neither let us tempt Christ*] I have already supposed, in the note on ver. 4, that Christ is
intended by the spiritual rock that followed them : and
that it was *he*, not the rock, that did *follow* or *accompany* the Israelites in the wilderness. This was the
angel of God's presence who *was with the Church in
the wilderness, to whom our fathers would not obey,*
as St. Stephen says, Acts vii. 38 and 39. Instead of
Χριστον, *Christ*, several MSS. and a few versions have

Κυριον, *the Lord*, and some few Θεον, *God.* But though
some respectable MSS. have *the Lord* instead of
Christ, yet this latter has the greatest proportion of
authority on its side. And this affords no mean proof
that the person who is called יהוה *Yehovah* in the Old
Testament, is called *Christ* in the New. By *tempting
Christ* is meant disbelieving the providence and goodness of God ; and presuming to prescribe to him how
he should send them the necessary supplies, and of
what kind they should be, &c.

Verse 10. *Neither murmur ye*] How the Israelites
murmured because of the manna, which their souls
despised as a *light bread*—something incapable of affording them nourishment, &c., and because they had
been brought out of Egypt into the wilderness, and
pretended that the promises of God had failed ; and
how they were destroyed by serpents, and by the destroyer or plague ; may be seen at large in the texts
referred to in the *margin* on this and the preceding
verses. It appears from what the apostle says here,
that the Corinthians were murmuring against God and
his apostle for prohibiting them from partaking of the
idolatrous feasts, just as the Israelites did in the wilderness in reference to a similar subject. See the
history of Phineas, with Zimri and Cosbi, and the
rebellion of Corah and his company, &c., &c.

Destroyed of the destroyer.] The Jews suppose
that God employed *destroying angels* to punish those
rebellious Israelites ; they were *five* in number, and
one of them they call משחית *Meshachith*, the *destroyer ;*
which appears to be another name for *Samael*, the
angel of death, to whose influence they attribute all
deaths which are not *uncommon* or *violent*. Those who
die violent deaths, or deaths that are not in the *common
manner* of men, are considered as perishing by immediate judgments from God.

Verse 11. *Upon whom the ends of the world are
come.*] Τα τελη των αιωνων· The end of the times included within the whole duration of the Mosaic economy. For although the word αιων means, in its
primary sense, *endless being*, or *duration* ; yet, in its
accommodated sense, it is applied to any round or
duration that is *complete in itself* : and here it evidently means the whole duration of the Mosaic economy.
"Thus, therefore," says Dr. Lightfoot, "the apostle
speaks in this place that those things, which were
transacted in the beginning of the Jewish ages, are
written for an example to you upon whom the ends of
those ages are come ; and the beginning is like to the
end, and the end to the beginning. Both were forty

2

A. M. 4060.
A. D. 56.
A. U. C.
809.
Anno Imp. Nero-
nis Cæs. 3.

12 Wherefore ᵛ let him that thinketh he standeth take heed lest he fall.

13 There hath no temptation taken you but ʷ such as is common to man : but ˣ God *is* faithful, ʸ who will not suffer you to be. tempted above that ye are able ; but will, with the temptation, also ᶻ make a way to escape, that ye may be able to bear *it.*

14 Wherefore, my dearly beloved, ᵃ flee from idolatry.

15 I speak as to wise ᵇ men ; judge ye what I say.

16 ᶜ The cup of blessing which we bless, is it not the communion of the blood of Christ ? ᵈ the bread which we break, is it not the communion of the body of Christ ?

17 For ᵉ we, *being* many, are one bread, *and*

A. M. 4060.
A. D. 56.
A. U. C.
809.
Anno Imp. Nero-
nis Cæs. 3.

ᵛ Rom. xi. 20.——ʷ Or, *moderate.*——ˣ Chap. i. 9.——ʸ Psa. cxxv. 3 ; 2 Pet. ii. 9.——ᶻ Jer. xxix. 11.——ᵃ Ver. 7 ; 2 Cor. vi.

17 ; 1 John v. 21.——ᵇ Chap. viii. 1.——ᶜ Matt.· xxvi. 26, 27, 28 ᵈ Acts ii. 42, 46 ; chap. xi. 23, 24.——ᵉ Rom. xii. 5 ; chap. xii. 27

---

years ; both consisted of temptation and unbelief ; and both ended in the destruction of the unbelievers—*that,* in the destruction of those who perished in the wilderness ; *this,* in the destruction of those that believed not : viz. the destruction of their city and nation." The phrase כוף יומיא *soph yomaiya,* the end of days, says the Targum of Jerusalem, Gen. iii. 15, means ביומוי דמלכא משיחא *beyomoi demalca Meshicha,* in the days of the King Messiah. We are to consider the apostle's words as referring to the end of the Jewish dispensation and the commencement of the Christian, which is the last dispensation which God will vouchsafe to man in the state of probation.

Verse 12. Let him that thinketh he standeth] Ὁ δοκων ἑσταναι· *Let him who most confidently standeth*—him who has the *fullest conviction* in his own conscience that his heart is right with God, and that his mind is right in the truth, take heed lest he fall from his faith, and from the state of holiness in which the grace of God has placed him. I have already shown that the verb δοκειν, which we render to *seem,* to *think,* to *suppose,* is used by the best Greek writers, not to *lessen* or *weaken* the sense, but to render it *stronger* and more *emphatic.* See the note on Luke viii. 18.

In a state of probation every thing may change ; while we are in this life we may *stand* or *fall* : our standing in the faith depends on our union with God ; and that depends on our watching unto prayer, and continuing to possess that faith that worketh by love. The highest saint under heaven can stand no longer than he depends upon God and continues in the obedience of faith. He that ceases to do so will fall into sin, and get a darkened understanding and a hardened heart : and he may *continue* in this state till God come to take away his soul. Therefore, *let him who most assuredly standeth, take heed lest he fall ;* not only *partially,* but *finally.*

Verse 13. But such as is common to man] Ανθρωπινος· Chrysostom has properly translated this word ανθρωπινος, τουτεστι μικρος, βραχυς, συμμετρος ; that is, *small, short, moderate.* Your temptations or trials have been but trifling in comparison of those endured by the Israelites ; they might have been easily resisted and overcome. Besides, God will not suffer you to be tried above the strength he gives you ; but as the trial comes, he will provide you with sufficient strength to resist it ; as the trial *comes in,* he will make your *way out.* The words are very remarkable, ποιησει συν τῳ πειρασμῳ και την εκβασιν, " He will, with the

temptation, make the deliverance, or way out." Satan is never permitted to *block* up our way, without the providence of God making a *way through the wall.* God ever makes a *breach* in his otherwise impregnable fortification. Should an upright soul get into difficulties and straits, he may rest assured that there is *a way out,* as there was a *way in ;* and that the trial shall never be above the strength that God shall give him to bear it.

Verse 14. Wherefore—flee from idolatry.] This is a trial of no great magnitude ; to escape from so *gross* a temptation requires but a moderate portion of grace and circumspection.

Verse 15. I speak as to wise men] The Corinthians valued themselves not a little on their *wisdom* and various gifts ; the apostle admits this, and draws an argument from it against themselves. As ye are *so wise,* surely ye can see the propriety of abominating idolatry of every kind : for an idol is nothing in the world, and can do nothing *for* you and nothing *against* you.

Verse 16. The cup of blessing] The apostle speaks here of the Eucharist, which he illustrates by the כוס הברכה *cos habberacah,* cup of blessing, over which thanks were expressed at the. conclusion of the passover. See this largely explained at the conclusion of the notes on Matt. xxvi., and in my *Discourse upon the Eucharist,* 8vo. 2d edit. 1814.

The communion of the blood of Christ ?] We who partake of this sacred cup, in commemoration of the death of Christ, are *made partakers of his body and blood,* and thus have *fellowship* with him ; as those who partake of an *idol feast,* thereby, as much as they can, participate with the idol, to whom the sacrifice was offered. This I have proved at large in the above tract, to which I must refer the reader, as the subject is too voluminous to be inserted here.

Verse 17. For we, being many, are one bread] The original would be better translated thus : *Because there is one bread,* or *loaf, we, who are many, are one body.* As only one loaf was used at the passover, and those who partook of it were considered to be *one religious body ;* so we who partake of the *eucharistical bread* and *wine,* in commemoration of the sacrificial death of Christ, are one spiritual society, because we are all made partakers of that *one Christ* whose blood was shed for us to make an atonement for our sins ; as the blood of the paschal lamb was shed and sprinkled in reference to this of which it was the type.

2

A. M. 4060.
A. D. 56.
A. U. C.
809.
Anno Imp. Nero-
nis Cæs. 3.

one body; for we are all partakers of that one bread.

18 Behold f Israel g after the
flesh: h are not they which eat
of the sacrifices partakers of the altar?

19 What say I then? i that the idol is any
thing? or that which is offered in sacrifice to
idols is any thing?

20 But *I say*, that the things which the Gentiles k sacrifice, they sacrifice to devils, and not
to God: and I would not that ye should have
fellowship with devils.

21 ¹ Ye cannot drink the cup of
the Lord, and m the cup of devils:
ye cannot be partakers of the Lord's
table, and of the table of devils.

22 Do we n provoke the Lord to jealousy?
o are we stronger than he?

23 p All things are lawful for me, but all things
are not expedient: all things are lawful for me,
but all things edify not.

24 q Let no man seek his own, but every
man another's *wealth*.

25 r Whatsoever is sold in the shambles, *that*

A. M. 4060.
A. D. 56.
A. U. C.
809.
Anno Imp. Nero-
nis Cæs. 3.

---

f Rom. iv. 12; Gal. vi. 16.——g Rom. iv. 1; ix. 3, 5; 2 Cor. xi.
18.——h Lev. iii. 3; vii. 15.——i Chap. viii. 4.——k Lev. xvii. 7;
Deut. xxxii. 17; Psa. cvi. 37; Rev. ix. 20.——l 2 Cor. vi. 15, 16.

m Deut. xxxii. 38.——n Deut. xxxii. 21.——o Ezek. xxii. 14.
p Chap. vi. 12.——q Rom. xv. 1, 2; ver. 33; chap. xiii. 5; Phil.
ii. 4, 21.——r Baruch vi. 28; 1 Tim. iv. 4.

Verse 18. *Behold Israel after the flesh*] The Jews
not yet *converted* to Christianity: the latter being
Israel after the Spirit. As the design of the apostle
was to withdraw his converts at Corinth from all
temptations to idolatry, he produces *two* examples to
show the propriety of his endeavours. 1. All who
join together in celebrating the Lord's Supper, and are
partakers of that one bread, give proof by this that
they are Christians, and have fellowship with Christ.
2. All the Israelites who offer sacrifice, and partake
of those sacrifices, give proof thereby that they are
Jews, and are in fellowship with the object of their
worship: so they who join in idol festivals, and eat
things which have been offered to idols, give proof
that they are in *communion with those idolaters*, and
that they have *fellowship with the demons* they worship.

Verse 19. *What say I then?*] A Jewish phrase for,
I conclude; and this is his conclusion: that although
an idol is nothing, has neither power nor influence, nor
are things offered to idols any thing the worse for
being thus offered; yet, as the things sacrificed by the
Gentiles are sacrificed to demons and not to God, those
who partake of them have fellowship with demons:
those who profess Christianity cannot have fellowship
both with Christ and the devil.

Verse 21. *Ye cannot drink the cup of the Lord*] It
is in vain that you who frequent these idol festivals
profess the religion of Christ, and commemorate his
death and passion in the holy eucharist; for you cannot have that fellowship with Christ which this ordinance implies, while you are partakers of the table of
demons. That the Gentiles, in their sacrifices, fed
on the slain beasts, and ate bread and drank wine in
honour of their gods, is sufficiently clear from various
accounts. *See my Discourse on the Holy Eucharist,*
where many examples are produced. The following
from Virgil, Æn. viii. verse 179–273, is proof in
point:—

Tum lecti juvenes certatim aræque sacerdos
Viscera tosta ferunt taurorum, onerantque canistris
Dona laboratæ Cereris, Bacchumque ministrant.
Vescitur Æneas simul et Trojana juventus
Perpetui tergo bovis et lustralibus extis.——
Quare agite, O juvenes, tantarum in munere laudum,

Cingite fronde comas, et pocula porgite dextris,
Communemque vocate Deum, et date vina *volentes.*

The *loaves* were served in canisters; the *wine*
In bowls; the priests renewed the rites divine:
Broiled entrails are their food, and beef's continued
    chine
Ye warlike youths, your heads with garlands crown,
Fill high the *goblets* with a sparkling flood,
And with *deep draughts invoke our common god.*

Verse 22. *Do we provoke the Lord to jealousy?*]
All idolatry is represented as a sort of spiritual *adultery;* it is giving that heart to Satan that should be
devoted to God; and he is represented as being *jealous,*
because of the infidelity of those who have *covenanted*
to give their hearts to him.

Are we stronger than he?] As he has threatened to
punish such transgressors, and will infallibly do it, can
we resist his omnipotence? A sinner should consider,
while he is in rebellion against God, whether he be
able to resist that power whereby God will inflict vengeance.

Verse 23. *All things are lawful for me*] I may
lawfully eat all kinds of food, *but all are not expedient;*
ου παντα συμφερει· It would not be *becoming* in me
to eat of all, because I should by this offend and grieve
many weak minds. See the notes on chap. vi. 12, &c.

Verse 24. *Let no man seek his own, &c.*] Let none,
for his private gratification or emolument, disturb the
peace or injure the soul of another. Let every man
live, not for *himself,* but for every part of the great
human family with which he is surrounded.

Verse 25. *Whatsoever is sold in the shambles, that
eat*] The case to which the apostle refers is simply
this; it was customary to bring the flesh of the animal
to market, the blood of which had been poured out in
sacrifice to an idol; or, taken more *particularly,* the
case was this; *one* part of the sacrifice was *consumed*
on the altar of the idol: a *second* part was *dressed* and
eaten by the *sacrificer;* and a *third* belonged to the
priest, and was often sold in the shambles. To partake of the *second share,* or to *feast upon the sacrifice,* St. Paul absolutely forbids, because this was one
part of the *religious worship* which was paid to the
idol; it was sitting down as guests at his table, in

2

A. M. 4060.
A. D. 56.
A. U. C.
809.
Anno Imp. Nero-
nis Cæs. 3.

eat, asking no question for conscience' sake :

26 For [s] the earth *is* the Lord's, and the fulness thereof.

27 If any of them that believe not bid you *to a feast*, and ye be disposed to go, [t] whatsoever is set before you, eat, asking no question for conscience' sake.

28 But if any man say unto you, This is offered in sacrifice unto idols, eat not, [u] for his sake that showed it, and for conscience sake :

for [v] the earth *is* the Lord's, and the fulness thereof :

29 Conscience, I say, not thine own, but of the other : for [w] why is my liberty judged of another *man's* conscience ?

30 For if I by [x] grace be a partaker, why am I evil spoken of for that [y] for which I give thanks ?

31 [z] Whether therefore ye eat, or drink, or whatsoever ye do, do all to the glory of God.

A. M. 4060.
A. D. 56.
A. U. C.
809.
Anno Imp. Nero-
nis Cæs. 3.

---

[s] Exod. xix. 5; Deut. x. 14; Psa. xxiv. 1; I. 12; ver. 28.
[t] Luke x. 7.——[u] Chap. viii. 10, 12.——[v] Deut. x. 14; Psa. xxiv. 1; ver. 26.——[w] Rom. xiv. 16.——[x] Or, *thanksgiving.*——[y] Rom. xiv. 6; 1 Tim. iv. 3, 4.——[z] Col. iii. 17; 1 Pet. iv. 11.

---

token that they were in *fellowship* with him. This was utterly incompatible with receiving the sacrament of the Lord's Supper, which was the *communion of the body and blood of Christ.* But as to the *third* share, the apostle leaves them at liberty either to eat of it or forbear; except that, by eating, their weak brethren should be offended; in that case, though the thing was *lawful*, it was their duty to abstain. See the notes on chap. viii. 1, &c. *Hindoos* eagerly embrace whatever has been offered to an idol : hence it is common to see the *flowers* that have been thus *offered* placed in the hair of a Hindoo. *Water* that has been thus made sacred is preserved in Hindoo houses, and with it they rub their bodies, and occasionally *sip a drop,* regarding it as the water *of life.*—See *Ward.*

Asking no questions for conscience' sake] Dr. Lightfoot observes, that " the Jews were vexed with innumerable scruples in their *feasts*, as to the *eating* of the *thing*, as well as to the *company* with which they ate ; and even the *manner* of their eating. Of *fruits* and *herbs* brought to the table, they were to inquire whether they were *tithed* according to custom; whether they were consecrated by the *Truma*, or whether they were profane ; whether they were clean, or touched with some pollution, &c. And concerning *flesh* set on the table, they were to inquire whether it was of that which had been offered to idols ; whether it were the flesh of an *animal* that had been *torn* by wild beasts ; or of that which had been *strangled*, or not *killed* according to the *canons* ; &c., &c. All which doubts the liberty of the Gospel abolished as to one's own conscience, with this *proviso*, that no scandal or offence be cast before another man's weak or scrupulous conscience."

From this it is evident that the apostle had the case of the *Jewish converts* in view, and not the Gentiles. The latter were not troubled with such extraordinary scrupulousness.

Verse 26. *For the earth* is *the Lord's*] And because God made the earth and its *fulness*, all animals, plants, and vegetables, there can be nothing in it or them impure or unholy ; because all are the creatures of God.

Verse 27. *If any—bid you* to a feast] The apostle means any *common meal*, not an idol festival; for to such no Christian could lawfully go.

Whatsoever is set before you, eat] Do not act as the

Jews generally do, torturing both *themselves* and *others* with questions, such as those mentioned on ver. 25.

Verse 28. *This is offered in sacrifice unto idols*] While they were not apprized of this circumstance they might lawfully eat ; but when told that the flesh set before them had been offered to an idol, then they were not to eat, for the sake of his weak conscience who pointed out the circumstance. For the apostle still takes it for granted that even the flesh offered in sacrifice to an idol might be eaten innocently at any *private* table, as in that case they were no longer in danger of being *partakers with devils*, as this was no idol festival.

For the earth is *the Lord's, and the fulness thereof*] This whole clause, which appears also in ver. 26, is wanting here in ABCDEFGH, several others, the *Syriac, Erpen, Coptic, Sahidic, Æthiopic, Armenian, Vulgate, Itala*; and in several of the *fathers.* Griesbach has left it out of the text : and Professor *White* says, " *Certissime delendum ;*" it should most undoubtedly be erased. It has scarcely any authority to support it.

Verses 29, 30. *For why is my liberty judged of another* man's *conscience ? &c.*] Though in the case of flesh offered to idols, and other matters connected with idolatry, (on which it appears there was much of a tender conscience among some of the Corinthians,) it was necessary to sacrifice something to an over-scrupulous conscience, yet the Gospel of Christ did not lay any man under this general burthen, that he must do nothing at which *any weak brother* might *feel hurt* or be *stumbled ;* for the liberty of the Gospel must not take for its *rule* the scrupulosity of any conscience ; for if a man, by *grace*—by the allowance or authority of the Gospel, partake of any thing that God's bounty has sent, and which the Gospel has not forbidden, and give thanks to God for the blessing, no man has right or authority to condemn such a person. This seems to be the meaning of these two verses ; and they read a lesson of caution to rash judges, and to those who are apt to take offence.

Verse 31. *Whether therefore ye eat, or drink*] As no general rule can be laid down in reference to the above particulars, there is one maxim of which no Christian must lose sight—that *whether he eats or drinks* of this or the other kind of aliments, or *whatever else he may do*, he must do it so as to bring *glory to*

A. M. 4060.
A. D. 56.
A. U. C.
809.
Anno Imp. Nero-
nis Cæs. 3.

32 [a] Give none offence, neither to the Jews, nor to the [b] Gentiles, nor to [c] the Church of God:

33 Even as [d] I please all *men* in all *things*, [e] not seeking mine own profit, but the *profit* of many, that they may be saved.

A. M. 4060.
A. D. 56.
A. U. C.
809.
Anno Imp. Nero-
nis Cæs. 3.

---

[a] Romans xiv. 13; chapter viii. 13; 2 Cor. vi. 3.——[b] Gr. *Greeks.*

[c] Acts xx. 28; chap. xi. 22; 1 Tim. iii. 5.——[d] Rom. xv. 2; chap. ix. 19, 22.——[e] Ver. 24.

God. This is a sufficient rule to regulate every man's conscience and practice in all *indifferent* things, where there are no express commands or prohibitions.

Verse 32. *Give none offence, &c.*] Scrupulously avoid giving any cause of offence either to the unconverted *Jews* or the unconverted *Gentiles*, so as to prejudice them against Christianity : *nor to the Church of God,* made up of converts from the above parties.

Verse 33. *Even as I please all* men] Act as *I* do: forgetting myself, my own interests, convenience, ease, and comfort, I labour for the welfare of others ; and particularly that they may be *saved.* How blessed and amiable was the spirit and conduct of this holy man !

This chapter has already presented the serious reader with a variety of maxims for his regulation.— 1. As to his own *private walk ;* 2. His *domestic duties ;* and 3. His connection with the *Church* of God. Let us review some of the principal parts.

1. We should be on our guard against what are called *little sins,* and all *occasions* and *excitements* to sin. Take heed what *company* you frequent. One thing, apparently *harmless,* may lead by almost imperceptible links to sins of the *deepest dye.* See the example in this chapter : 1. The people sat down to *eat* and to *drink.* 2. They rose up to *play, dance,* and *sing :* and 3. They committed *fornication,* and brought upon themselves *swift destruction.*

2. However conscious we may be of our own sincerity and uprightness, we should ever distrust ourselves. God has made nothing *independent* of himself ; the soul has no principle of self-dependence either in itself or its attainments : it is wise, powerful, and happy, only while it is depending on infinite wisdom, unlimited power, and endless mercy.

3. The Gentiles were in communion with demons by their idolatrous services. In what communion are those who feed themselves without fear, who eat with the glutton and drink with the drunkard ? Do they partake of the Lord Jesus who are under the influence of pride, self-will, hatred, censoriousness, &c., and who carry their self-importance and worldly spirit even into the house and worship of God ?

4. A spirit of *curiosity* too much indulged may, in an irreligious man, lead to *covetousness* and *theft :* in a godly man, to a *troublesome* and *unscriptural scrupulosity* of conscience, productive of nothing but uneasiness to itself, and disturbance to others. *Simplicity* of heart saves from this, and is an excellent *gift.*

5. In many actions we have a *twofold* rule—the *testimony* of God and *charity :* and in many things *charity* is the best interpreter of the *testimony.* The testimony often *permits* what *charity forbids,* because circumstances in time, place, &c., may render a thing improper on one occasion that might be proper on another.

6. Pious Quesnel has well said : Every thing *honours* God when it is done for his *sake :* every thing *dishonours* him when any ultimate end is proposed beside his *glory.* It is an unchangeable principle of the Christian morality that all comes from God by his *love,* and all should be returned to him by ours. This rule we should keep inviolate.

7. Though many of the advices given in this chapter appear to respect the Corinthians alone, yet there is none of them that is not applicable to Christians in general in certain circumstances. God has given no portion of his word to any people or age exclusively ; the *whole* is given to the Church universal in all ages of the world. In reading this epistle let us seriously consider what parts of it apply to ourselves ; and if we are disposed to appropriate its *promises,* let us act conscientiously, and inquire how many of its *reprehensions* we may fairly appropriate also.

CHAPTER XI.

The apostle reprehends the Corinthians for several irregularities in their manner of conducting public worship ; the men praying or prophesying with their heads covered, and the women with their heads uncovered, contrary to custom, propriety, and decency, 1–6. Reasons why they should act differently, 7–16. They are also reproved for their divisions and heresies, 17–19. And for the irregular manner in which they celebrated the Lord's Supper, 20–22. The proper manner of celebrating this holy rite laid down by the apostle, 23–26. Directions for a profitable receiving of the Lord's Supper, and avoiding the dangerous consequences of communicating unworthily, 27–34.

2

A. M. 4060.
A. D. 56.
A. U. C.
809.
Anno Imp. Nero-
nis Cæs. 3.

BE [a] ye followers of me, even as I also *am* of Christ.

2 Now I praise you, brethren, [b] that ye remember me in all things, and [c] keep the [d] ordinances, as I delivered *them* to you.

3 But I would have you know, that [e] the head of every man is Christ; and [f] the head of the woman *is* the man; and [g] the head of Christ *is* God.

4 Every man praying or [h] prophesying, having *his* head covered, dishonoureth his head.

5 But [i] every woman that prayeth or prophesieth with *her* head uncovered, dishonoureth her head: for that is even all one as if she were [k] shaven.

A. M. 4060.
A. D. 56.
A. U. C.
809.
Anno Imp. Nero-
nis Cæs. 3.

---

[a] Chap. iv. 16; Eph. v. 1; Phil. iii. 17; 1 Thess. i. 6; 2 Thess. iii. 9.——[b] Chap. iv. 17.——[c] Chap. vii. 17.——[d] Or, *traditions.* 2 Thess. ii. 15; iii. 6.——[e] Eph. v. 23.

[f] Gen. iii. 16; 1 Tim. ii. 11, 12; 1 Pet. iii. 1, 5, 6.——[g] John xiv. 28; chap. iii. 23; xv. 27, 28; Phil. ii. 7, 8, 9.——[h] Chap. xii. 10, 28; xiv. 1, &c.——[i] Acts xxi. 9.——[k] Deut. xxi. 12.

NOTES ON CHAP. XI.

Verse 1. *Be ye followers of me*] This verse certainly belongs to the preceding chapter, and is here out of all proper place and connection.

Verse 2. *That ye remember me in all things*] It appears that the apostle had previously given them a variety of directions relative to the matters mentioned here; that some had paid strict attention to them, and that others had not; and that contentions and divisions were the consequences, which he here reproves and endeavours to rectify. While Paul and Apollos had preached among them, they had undoubtedly prescribed every thing that was necessary to be observed in the Christian worship: but it is likely that those who joined in idol festivals wished also to introduce something relative to the mode of conducting the idol worship into the Christian assembly, which they might think was an improvement on the apostle's plan.

Verse 3. *The head of every man is Christ*] The apostle is speaking particularly of Christianity and its ordinances: *Christ is the Head* or Author of this religion; and is the creator, preserver, and *Lord* of every man. The *man* also *is the lord* or *head of the woman*; and the *Head* or Lord *of Christ*, as Mediator between *God* and man, *is God* the Father. Here is the *order*—God sends his Son Jesus Christ to redeem man; Christ comes and lays down his life for the world; every man who receives Christianity confesses that Jesus Christ is Lord, to the glory of God the Father; and every believing woman will acknowledge, according to Genesis iii. 16, that God has placed her in a dependence on and subjection to the man. So far there is no difficulty in this passage.

Verse 4. *Praying or prophesying*] Any person who engages in public acts in the worship of God, whether prayer, singing, or exhortation: for we learn, from the apostle himself, that προφητευειν, *to prophesy*, signifies to *speak unto men to edification, exhortation, and comfort*, chap. xiv. 3. And this comprehends all that we understand by *exhortation*, or even *preaching*.

Having his *head covered*] With his cap or turban on, *dishonoureth his head*; because the head being covered was a sign of subjection; and while he was employed in the public ministration of the word, he was to be considered as a *representative* of Christ, and on this account his being veiled or covered would be improper. This decision of the apostle was in point blank hostility to the canons of the Jews; for they would not suffer a man to pray unless he was *veiled*, for which they gave this reason: " He should veil himself to show that he is *ashamed* before God, and unworthy with open face to behold him." See much in *Lightfoot* on this point.

Verse 5. *But every woman that prayeth, &c.*] Whatever may be the meaning of *praying* and *prophesying*, in respect to the *man*, they have precisely the same meaning in respect to the *woman*. So that some women at least, as well as some men, might speak to others to *edification*, and *exhortation*, and *comfort*. And this kind of prophesying or teaching was predicted by Joel, ii. 28, and referred to by Peter, Acts ii. 17. And had there not been such gifts bestowed on *women*, the prophecy could not have had its fulfilment. The only difference marked by the apostle was, the man had his head *uncovered*, because he was the *representative* of Christ; the woman had hers *covered*, because she was placed by the order of God in a state of subjection to the man, and because it was a *custom*, both among the Greeks and Romans, and among the Jews an express *law*, that no woman should be seen abroad without a *veil*. This was, and is, a common custom through all the east, and none but public prostitutes go without veils. And if a woman should appear in public without a veil, she would *dishonour her head*—her *husband*. And she must appear like to those women who had their hair shorn off as the punishment of whoredom, or adultery.

Tacitus informs us, *Germ.* 19, that, considering the greatness of the population, adulteries were very rare among the Germans; and when any woman was found guilty she was punished in the following way: *accisis crinibus, nudatam coram propinquis expellit domo maritus:* " having cut off her hair, and stripped her before her relatives, her husband turned her out of doors." And we know that the woman suspected of adultery was ordered by the law of Moses to be stripped of her veil, Num. v. 18. Women reduced to a state of servitude, or slavery, had their hair cut off: so we learn from *Achilles Tatius.* Clitophon says, concerning Leucippe, who was reduced to a state of slavery: πεπραται, δεδουλευκεν, γην εσκαψεν, σεσυληται της κεφαλης το καλλος, την κουραν ορᾳς· lib. viii. cap. 5, " she was sold for a slave, she dug in the ground, and her hair being shorn off, her head was deprived of its ornament," &c. It was also the custom among the Greeks to cut off their hair in time of mourning. See Euripides in *Alcest.*, ver. 426. Admetus, ordering a common mourning for his wife Alcestis, says: πενθος γυναικος της δε κοινουσθαι λεγω, κουρᾳ ξυρηκει και μελαμπεπλῳ στολῃ· " I order a general mourning for this

     2

A. M. 4060.
A. D. 56.
A. U. C.
809.
Anno Imp. Nero-
nis Cæs. 3.

6 For if the woman be not covered, let her also be shorn: but if it be [1] a shame for a woman to be shorn or shaven, let her be covered.

7 For a man indeed ought not to cover *his* head, forasmuch as [m] he is the image and glory

of God: but the woman is the glory of the man.

8 For [n] the man is not of the woman; but the woman of the man.

9 [o] Neither was the man created for the woman: but the woman for the man.

10 For this cause ought the woman [p] to have

A. M. 4060.
A. D. 56.
A. U. C.
809.
Anno Imp. Nero-
nis Cæs. 3.

---

[1] Num. v. 18; Deut. xxii. 5.——[m] Gen. i. 26, 27; v. 1; ix. 6.   [n] Gen. ii. 21, 22.——[o] Gen. ii. 18, 21, 23.——[p] Gen. xxiv. 65.

---

woman! let the hair be shorn off, and a black garment put on." Propriety and decency of conduct are the points which the apostle seems to have more especially in view. As a woman who dresses *loosely* or *fantastically*, even in the present day, is considered a disgrace to her husband, *because* suspected to be not very sound in her morals; so in those ancient times, a woman appearing without a veil would be considered in the same light.

Verse 6. *For if the woman be not covered*] If she will not wear a veil in the public assemblies, *let her be shorn*—let her carry a public badge of infamy: *but if it be a shame*—if to be shorn or shaven would appear, as it must, a badge of infamy, *then let her be covered*—let her by all means wear a veil. Even in mourning it was considered disgraceful to be obliged to shear off the hair; and lest they should lose this ornament of their heads, the women contrived to evade the custom, by cutting off the *ends* of it only. *Euripides*, in *Orest.*, ver. 128, speaking of Helen, who should have shaved her head on account of the death of her sister Clytemnestra, says: ειδετε παρ' ακρας ως απεθρισεν τριχας, σωζουσα καλλος, εστι δε ἡ παλαι γυνη: " see how she cuts off only the very points of her hair, that she may preserve her beauty, and is just the same woman as before." See the note on the preceding verse.

In *Hindostan* a woman cuts off her *hair* at the death of her husband, as a token of *widowhood*; but this is never performed by a *married* woman, whose hair is considered an *essential ornament*. The *veil* of the Hindoo women is nothing more than the *garment* brought over the face, which is always very carefully done by the higher classes of women when they appear in the streets.—*Ward's Customs.*

Verse 7. *A man indeed ought not to cover* his *head*] He should not wear his *cap* or *turban* in the public congregation, for this was a badge of servitude, or an indication that he had a conscience overwhelmed with guilt; and besides, it was contrary to the custom that prevailed, both among the Greeks and Romans.

He is the image and glory of God] He is God's vicegerent in this lower world; and, by the *authority* which he has received from his Maker, he is his *representative* among the creatures, and exhibits, more than any other part of the creation, the *glory* and perfections of the *Creator*.

But the woman is the glory of the man.] As the man is, among the creatures, the representative of the glory and perfections of God, so that the fear of him and the dread of him are on every beast of the field, &c.; so the woman is, in the house and family, the representative of the power and authority of the man.

I believe this to be the meaning of the apostle; and that he is speaking here principally concerning *power* and *authority*, and skill to use them. It is certainly not the *moral image* of God, nor his *celestial glory*, of which he speaks in this verse.

Verse 8. *For the man is not of the woman*] Bishop Pearce translates ου γαρ εστιν ανηρ εκ γυναικος, αλλα γυνη εξ ανδρος, thus: " For the man doth not BELONG to the woman, but the woman to the man." And vindicates this sense of εκ, by its use in chap. xii. 15. If the foot shall say, ουκ ειμι εκ του σωματος, I am not of the body, i. e. I do not belong to the body. He observes that as the verb εστιν is in the *present* tense, and will not allow that we should understand this verse of something that is *past*, γαρ, *for*, in the following verse, which is unnoticed by our translators, will have its full propriety and meaning, because it introduces a reason *why* the woman belongs to the man and not the man to the woman. His meaning is, that the man does not belong to the woman, as if she was the *principal*; but the woman belongs to the man in that view.

Verse 9 *Neither was the man created, &c.*] Και γαρ ουκ εκτισθη· for the man was not created upon the woman's account. The reason is plain from what is mentioned above; and from the original creation of woman she was made *for* the man, to be his proper or suitable helper.

Verse 10. *For this cause ought the woman to have* power on her *head because of the angels.*] There are few portions in the sacred writings that have given rise to such a variety of conjectures and explanations, and are less understood, than this verse, and ver. 29 of chap. xv. Our translators were puzzled with it; and have inserted here one of the largest marginal readings found any where in their work; but this is only on the words *power on her head*, which they interpret thus: that is, *a covering, in sign that she is under the power of her husband.* But, admitting this marginal reading to be a satisfactory solution so far as it goes, it by no means removes all the difficulty. Mr. Locke ingenuously acknowledged that he did not understand the meaning of the words; and almost every critic and learned man has a different explanation. Some have endeavoured to *force* out a meaning by *altering* the text. The emendation of Mr. Toup, of Cornwall, is the most remarkable: he reads εξιουσα, *going out*, instead of εξουσιαν, *power*; wherefore the woman, *when she goes out*, should *have a veil on her head.* Whatever ingenuity there may appear in this emendation, the consideration that it is not acknowledged by any MS., or *version*, or primitive writer, is sufficient proof against it. Dr. Lightfoot, Schoettgen, and Bishop Pearce, have written best on the subject,

A. M. 4060.
A. D. 56.
A. U. C.
809.
Anno Imp. Nero-
nis Cæs. 3.

^q power on *her* head ^r because of the angels.

11 Nevertheless ^s neither *is* the man without the woman,

neither the woman without the man, in the Lord.

12 For as the woman *is* of the man, even so *is* the man

A. M. 4060.
A. D. 56.
A. U. C.
809.
Anno Imp. Nero
nis Cæs. 3.

---

^q That is, *a covering, in sign that she is under the power of her husband.*——^r Eccles. v. 6.——^s Gal. iii. 28.

---

in which they allow that there are many difficulties. The latter contends, 1. That the original should be read, *Wherefore the woman ought to have* A *power upon her head,* that is, the power of the husband over the wife; the word *power* standing for the *sign* or *token* of that power which was a *covering* or *veil.* *Theophylact* explains the word, το του εξουσιαζεσθαι συμβολον, τουτεστι, το καλυμμα, "the symbol of being under power, that is, a *veil,* or *covering.*" And *Photius* explains it thus: της υποταγης συμβολον το επι της κεφαλης καλυμμα φερειν; *to wear a veil on the head is a symbol of subjection.* It is no unusual thing, in the Old and New Testament, for the *signs* and *tokens* of things to be called by the names of the *things themselves,* for thus *circumcision* is called the *covenant,* in Gen. xvii. 10, 13, though it was only the *sign* of it.

2. The word *angels* presents another difficulty. Some suppose that by these the apostle means the *fallen angels,* or devils; others, the *governors of the Church;* and others, those who were *deputed* among the Jews *to espouse a virgin in the name of a lover.* All these senses the learned bishop rejects, and believes that the apostle uses the word *angels,* in its most obvious sense, for the heavenly angels; and that he speaks according to the notion which then prevailed among Jews, that the holy angels interested themselves in the affairs of men, and particularly were present in their religious assemblies, as the cherubim, their representation, were present in their temple. Thus we read in Eccles. v. 6: *Neither say thou before the* ANGEL, *it was an error;* and in 1 Tim. v. 21: *I charge thee before God and the Lord Jesus Christ, and the elect* ANGELS, *&c.* Parallel to these is what Agrippa says in his oration to the Jews, Josephus, War, b. ii. chap. 16: *I protest before God, your holy temple, and all the* ANGELS *of heaven, &c.* All which passages *suppose,* or were spoken to *those who supposed,* that the angels know what passes here upon earth. The notion, whether just or not, prevailed among the Jews; and if so, St. Paul might speak according to the common opinion.

3. Another difficulty lies in the phrase δια τουτο, *wherefore,* which shows that this verse is a *conclusion* from what the apostle was arguing before; which we may understand thus: that his conclusion, from the foregoing argument, ought to have the more weight, upon account of the presence, real or supposed, of the holy angels, at their religious meetings. See Bishop *Pearce,* in loc.

The learned bishop is not very willing to allow that the doctrine of the presence of angelic beings in religious assemblies is legitimate; but what difficulty can there be in this, if we take the words of the apostle in another place: *Are they not all ministering spirits, sent forth to minister for them who shall be heirs of salvation?* Heb. i. 14. And perhaps there is no time

in which they can render more essential services to the followers of God than when they are engaged in Divine ordinances. On the whole, the bishop's sense of the passage and paraphrase stands thus: "And because of this superiority in the man, I conclude that the woman should have on her head a veil, the mark of her husband's power over her, especially in the religious assemblies, where the angels are supposed to be invisibly present."

The ancient versions make little alteration in the common reading, and the MSS. leave the verse nearly as it stands in the common printed editions. The Armenian has a word that answers to *umbram,* a shade or *covering.* The Æthiopic, *her head should be veiled.* The common editions of the Vulgate have *potestatem,* power; but in an ancient edition of the Vulgate, perhaps one of the first, if not the first, ever printed, 2 vols. fol., *sine ulla nota anni, &c.:* the verse stands thus: *Ideo debet mulier* velamen *habere super caput suum: et propter angelos.* My old MS. translation seems to have been taken from a MS. which had the same reading: Wherefore the woman schal haue a veyl on her heuyd; and for aungels. Some copies of the *Itala* have also *velamen,* a veil.

In his view of this text, *Kypke* differs from all others; and nothing that so judicious a critic advances should be lightly regarded. 1. He contends that εξουσιαν occurs nowhere in the sense of *veil,* and yet he supposes that the word καλυμμα, *veil* is understood, and must in the translation of the passage be supplied. 2. He directs that a comma be placed after εξουσιαν, and that it be construed with οφειλει, *ought;* after which he translates the verse thus: *Propterea mulier potestati obnoxia est, ita ut velamen in capite habeat propter angelos;* On this account the woman is subject to power, so that she should have a veil on her head, because of the angels. 3. He contends that both the Latins and Greeks use *debere* and οφειλειν elegantly to express that to which one is *obnoxious* or *liable.* So *Horace:*—

—— Tu, nisi ventis
Debes ludibrium, cave.
Carm. lib. i. Od. xiv. ver. 15.

Take heed lest thou owe *a laughing stock to the winds; i. e. lest thou* become *the sport of the winds;* for to these thou art now *exposing* thyself.

So *Dionys. Hal.* Ant. lib. iii., page 205: Και πολλην οφειλοντες αισχυνην απηλθον εκ της αγορας· They departed from the market, *exposed* to great dishonour. So *Euripides,* Οφειλω σοι βλαβην· *I am exposed to thy injury.*

4. He contends that the words taken in this sense agree perfectly with the context, and with δια τουτο, *wherefore,* in this verse, "Because the man was not created for the woman, but the woman for the man,

2

A. M. 4060.
A. D. 56.
A. U. C.
809.
Anno Imp. Nero-
nis Cæs. 3.

also by the woman; [t] but all things of God.

13 Judge in yourselves : is it comely that a woman pray unto God uncovered ?

14 Doth not even nature itself teach you, that, if a man have long hair, it is a shame unto him ?

15 But if a woman have long hair, it is a glory to her : for *her* hair is given her for a [u] covering.

16 But [v] if any man seem to be contentious, we have no such custom, [w] neither the Churches of God.

17 Now in this that I declare *unto you*

A. M. 4060.
A. D. 56.
A. U. C.
809.
Anno Imp. Nero-
nis Cæs. 3.

---

[t] Rom. xi. 36.——[u] Or, *veil.*

[v] 1 Tim. vi. 4.——[w] Chap. vii. 17 ; xiv. 33.

---

therefore she is subject to his authority, and should have a veil on her head as a token of that subjection; and particularly before the holy angels, who are present in the congregations of the saints."

For Dr. Lightfoot's opinion, that by *angels* we are to understand the *paranymphs,* or messengers who came on the part of others, to look out for proper spouses for their friends, I must refer to his works, vol. ii. fol., p. 772. The reader has now before him every thing that is likely to cast light on this difficult subject, and he must either adopt what he judges to be best, or else *think for himself.*

After all, the custom of the *Nazarite* may cast some light upon this place. As *Nazarite* means one who has *separated* himself by vow to some religious austerity, wearing his *own* hair, &c.; so a married woman was considered a *Nazarite* for life, i. e. separated from all others, and *joined* to *one husband,* who is her lord : and hence the apostle, alluding to this circumstance, says, *The woman ought to have power on her head,* i. e. wear *her* hair and *veil,* for her *hair* is a proof of her being a *Nazarite,* and of her subjection to *her husband,* as the Nazarite was under subjection to the Lord, according to the rule or law of his order. See notes on Num. vi. 5–7.

Verse 11. *Neither is the man without the woman*] The apostle seems to say : I do not intimate any *disparagement* of the female sex, by insisting on the necessity of her being under the power or authority of the man; for they are both equally dependent on each other, *in the Lord,* εν Κυριω : but instead of this reading, Theodoret has εν τω κοσμω, *in the world.* Probably the apostle means that the human race is continued by an especial providence of God. Others think that he means that men and women equally make a Christian society, and in it have equal rights and privileges.

Verse 12. *For as the woman is of the man*] For as the woman was first formed out of the side of man, man has ever since been formed out of the womb of the woman; but they, as all other created things, are of God.

Verse 13. *Judge in yourselves*] Consider the subject *in your own common sense,* and then say whether it be decent for a woman to pray in public without a veil on her head ? The heathen priestesses prayed or delivered their oracles bare-headed or with dishevelled hair, *non comptæ mansere comæ,* as in the case of the Cumæan Sibyl, Æn. vi., ver. 48, and otherwise in great disorder : to be conformed to *them* would be very disgraceful to Christian women. And in reference to such things as these, the apostle appeals to their sense of honour and decency.

Verse 14. *Doth not—nature—teach you, that, if a man have long hair*] Nature certainly teaches us, by bestowing it, that it is proper for women to have long hair ; and it is not so with men. The hair of the male rarely grows like that of a female, unless *art* is used, and even then it bears but a scanty proportion to the former. Hence it is truly *womanish* to have long hair, and it is a shame to the man who affects it. In ancient times the people of Achaia, the province in which Corinth stood, and the Greeks in general, were noted for their *long hair* ; and hence called by *Homer,* in a great variety of places, καρηκομοωντες Αχαιοι, *the long-haired Greeks,* or *Achæans.* Soldiers, in different countries, have been distinguished for *their long hair* ; but whether this can be said to their praise or blame, or whether *Homer* uses it always as a term of *respect,* when he applies it to the Greeks, I shall not wait here to inquire. *Long hair* was certainly not in repute among the Jews. The Nazarites let their hair grow, but it was as a token of *humiliation* ; and it is possible that St. Paul had this in view. There were consequently two reasons why the apostle should condemn this practice :—1. Because it was a sign of *humiliation* ; 2. Because it was *womanish.* After all it is possible that St. Paul may refer to *dressed, frizzled* and *curled* hair, which shallow and effeminate men might have affected in *that* time, as they do in *this.* Perhaps there is not a sight more ridiculous in the eye of common sense than a high-dressed, curled, cued, and powdered head, with which the *operator* must have taken considerable pains, and the silly *patient* lost much time and comfort in submitting to what all but senseless custom must call an indignity and degradation. Hear *nature,* common sense, and reason, and they will inform you, *that if a man have long hair, it is a shame unto him.*

Verse 15. *But if a woman have long hair*] The Author of their being has given a larger proportion of hair to the head of women than to that of men ; and to them it is an especial ornament, and may in various cases serve as a *veil.*

It is a certain fact that a man's long hair renders him contemptible, and a woman's long hair renders her more amiable. *Nature* and the *apostle* speak the same language ; we may account for it as we please.

Verse 16. *But if any man seem to be contentious*] Ει δε τις δοκει φιλονεικος ειναι· If any person *sets himself up* as a wrangler—*puts himself forward* as a defender of such points, that a *woman may pray or teach with her head uncovered,* and that *a man may,* without reproach, *have long hair* ; let him know that we have no such custom as either, nor are they sanc-

2

253

A. M. 4060.
A. D. 56.
A. U. C.
809.
Anno Imp. Nero-
nis Cæs. 3.

I praise *you* not, that ye come together not for the better, but for the worse.

18 For first of all, when ye come together in the church, ˣ I hear that there be ʸ divisions among you; and I partly believe it.

19 For ᶻ there must be also ᵃ heresies among you, ᵇ that they which are approved may be made manifest among you.

20 When ye come together therefore into one

place, ᶜ *this* is not to eat the Lord's Supper.

A. M. 4060.
A. D. 56.
A. U. C.
809.
Anno Imp. Nero-
nis Cæs. 3.

21 For in eating, every one taketh before *other* his own supper: and one is hungry, and ᵈ another is drunken.

22 What! have ye not houses to eat and to drink in? or despise ye ᵉ the church of God, and ᶠ shame ᵍ them that have not? What shall I say to you? shall I praise you in this? I praise *you* not.

23 For ʰ I have received of the Lord that

ˣ Chap. i. 10, 11, 12; iii. 3.——ʸ Or, *schisms.*——ᶻ Matt. xviii. 7; Luke xvii. 1; Acts xx. 30; 1 Tim. iv. 1; 2 Pet. ii. 1, 2. ᵃ Or, *sects.*——ᵇ Luke ii. 35; 1 John ii. 19; see Deut. xiii. 3.

ᶜ Or, *ye cannot eat.*——ᵈ 2 Pet. ii. 13; Jude 12.——ᵉ Chap. x. 32.——ᶠ James ii. 6.——ᵍ Or, *them that are poor.*——ʰ Chap. xv. 3; Gal. i. 1, 11, 12.

---

tioned by any of the Churches of God, whether among the *Jews* or the *Gentiles*. We have already seen that the verb δοκειν, which we translate to *seem*, generally *strengthens* and increases the sense. From the attention that the apostle has paid to the subject of *veils* and *hair*, it is evident that it must have occasioned considerable disturbance in the Church of Corinth. They have produced evil effects in much later times.

Verse 17. *Now in this—I praise* you *not*] In the beginning of this epistle the apostle did *praise* them for their attention in general to the rules he had laid down, see ver. 2; but here he is obliged to *condemn* certain irregularities which had crept in among them, particularly relative to the celebration of the Lord's Supper. Through some false teaching which they had received, in the absence of the apostle, they appear to have celebrated it precisely in the same way the Jews did their *passover*. That, we know, was a regular meal, only accompanied with certain peculiar circumstances and ceremonies: two of these ceremonies were, eating bread, solemnly broken, and drinking a cup of wine called the cup of blessing. Now, it is certain that our Lord has taken these two things, and made them expressive of the *crucifixion* of his *body*, and the *shedding* of his *blood*, as an atonement for the sins of mankind. The teachers which had crept into the Corinthian Church appear to have perverted the whole of this Divine institution; for the celebration of the Lord's Supper appears to have been made among them a part of an *ordinary* meal. The people came together, and it appears brought their provisions with them; some had much, others had less; some ate to excess, others had scarcely enough to suffice nature. *One was hungry*, and the *other was drunken*, μεθυει, was *filled to the full;* this is the sense of the word in many places of Scripture. At the conclusion of this irregular meal they appear to have done something in reference to our Lord's institution, but more resembling the Jewish passover. These irregularities, connected with so many indecencies, the apostle reproves; for, instead of being *benefited* by the Divine ordinance, they were *injured;* they *came together not for the better, but for the worse.*

Verse 18. *There be divisions among you*] They had σχισματα, schisms, among them: the old parties were kept up, even in the place where they assembled

to eat the *Lord's Supper.* The Paulians, the Kephites, and the Apollonians, continued to be distinct parties; and ate their meals separately, even in the same house.

Verse 19. *There must be also heresies*] Αἱρεσεις· Not a common *consent* of the members of the Church, either in the *doctrines* of the Gospel, or in the *ceremonies* of the Christian religion. Their difference in religious *opinion* led to a difference in their religious *practice*, and thus the Church of God, that should have been one body, was split into sects and parties. The *divisions* and the *heresies* sprung out of each other. I have spoken largely on the word *heresy* in Acts v. 17, to which place I beg leave to refer the reader.

Verse 20. This *is not to eat the Lord's Supper.*] They did not come together to eat the Lord's Supper *exclusively*, which they should have done, and not have made it a *part* of an ordinary meal.

Verse 21. *Every one taketh before—his own supper*] They had a grand feast, though the different sects kept in parties by themselves; but all took as ample a supper as they could provide, (each bringing his own provisions with him,) before they took what was called the *Lord's Supper.* See on ver. 17.

Verse 22. *Have ye not houses to eat and to drink in?*] They should have taken their ordinary meal at *home*, and have come together in the church to celebrate the Lord's Supper.

Despise ye the church of God] Ye render the sacred assembly and the place contemptible by your conduct, and ye show yourselves destitute of that respect which ye owe to the place set apart for Divine worship.

And shame them that have not?] Τους μη εχοντας, *Them that are poor;* not them who *had not victuals* at that time, but those who are *so poor* as to be incapable of furnishing themselves as others had done. See the note on Matt. xiii. 12.

Verse 23. *I have received of the Lord*] It is possible that several of the people at Corinth did receive the bread and wine of the eucharist as they did the paschal bread and wine, as a mere commemoration of an event. And as our Lord had by this institution consecrated that bread and wine, not to be the means of commemorating the deliverance from Egypt, and their joy on the account, but their deliverance from sin

A. M. 4060.
A. D. 56.
A. U. C.
809.
Anno Imp. Nero-
nis Cæs. 3.

which also I delivered unto you, [i] That the Lord Jesus, the *same* night in which he was betrayed, took bread :

24 And when he had given thanks, he brake *it*, and said, Take, eat : this is my body, which is broken for you : this do [k] in remembrance of me.

25 After the same manner also *he took* the cup, when he had supped, saying, This cup is the New Testament in my blood : this do ye, as oft as ye drink *it*, in remembrance of me.

26 For as often as ye eat this bread, and

drink this cup, [l] ye do show the Lord's death [m] till he come.

27 [n] Wherefore, whosoever shall eat this bread, and drink *this* cup of the Lord, unworthily, shall be guilty of the body and blood of the Lord.

28 But [o] let a man examine himself, and so let him eat of *that* bread, and drink of *that* cup.

29 For he that eateth and drinketh unworthily, eateth and drinketh [p] damnation to himself, not discerning the Lord's body.

30 For this cause many *are* weak and sickly among you, and many sleep.

A. M. 4060.
A. D. 56.
A. U. C.
809.
Anno Imp. Nero-
nis Cæs. 3.

---

[i] Matt. xxvi. 26; Mark xiv. 22; Luke xxii. 19.——[k] Or, *for a remembrance.*——[l] Or, *show ye.*——[m] John xiv. 3; xxi. 22; Acts i. 11; chap. iv. 5; xv. 23; 1 Thess. iv. 16; 2 Thess. i. 10; Jude 14; Rev. i. 7.——[n] Num. ix. 10, 13; John vi. 51, 63, 64; xiii. 27; chap. x. 21.——[o] 2 Cor. xiii. 5; Gal. vi. 4.——[p] Or, *judgment;* Rom. xiii. 2.

---

and death by his passion and cross ; therefore the apostle states that he had received from the Lord what he delivered ; *viz.* that the eucharistic bread and wine were to be understood of the accomplishment of that of which the paschal lamb was the type—the body broken for them, the blood shed for them.

The Lord Jesus—took bread] See the whole of this account, collated with the parallel passages in the four Gospels, amply explained in my *Discourse on the Eucharist,* and in the notes on Matt. xxvi.

Verse 24. *This do in remembrance of me.*] The papists believe the apostles were not ordained priests before these words. Si quis dixerit, illis verbis, hoc facite in meam commemorationem, Christum non instituisse apostolos sacerdotes, anathema sit : " If any one shall say that in these words, ' This do in remembrance of me,' Christ did not ordain his apostles priests, let him be accursed." Conc. Trid. Sess. 22. Conc. 2. And he that does believe such an absurdity, on such a ground, is contemptible.

Verse 26. *Ye do show the Lord's death*] As in the passover they showed forth the bondage they had been in, and the redemption they had received from it ; so in the eucharist they showed forth the sacrificial death of Christ, and the redemption from sin derived from it.

Verse 27. *Whosoever shall eat—and drink—unworthily*] To put a final end to controversies and perplexities relative to these words and the context, let the reader observe, that to *eat* and *drink* the *bread* and *wine* in the Lord's Supper *unworthily,* is to eat and drink as the Corinthians did, who ate it not in reference to Jesus Christ's sacrificial death; but rather in such a way as the Israelites did the passover, which they celebrated in remembrance of their deliverance from Egyptian bondage. Likewise, these mongrel Christians at Corinth used it as a kind of historical commemoration of the death of Christ ; and did not, in the whole institution, discern the Lord's body and blood as a sacrificial offering for sin : and besides, in their celebration of it they acted in a way utterly unbecoming the gravity of a sacred ordinance. Those who acknowledge it as a sacrificial offering, and receive it in remembrance of God's love to them in sending his

Son into the world, can neither bring *damnation* upon themselves by so doing, nor eat nor drink *unworthily.* See our translation of this verse vindicated at the end of the chapter.

Shall be guilty of the body and blood of the Lord.] If he use it irreverently, if he deny that Christ suffered unjustly, (for of some such persons the apostle must be understood to speak,) then he in effect joins issue with the Jews in their condemnation and crucifixion of the Lord Jesus, and renders himself guilty of the death of our blessed Lord. Some, however, understand the passage thus : is guilty, *i. e.* eats and drinks unworthily, and brings on himself that punishment mentioned ver. 30.

Verse 28. *Let a man examine himself*] Let him try whether he has proper faith in the Lord Jesus ; and whether he discerns the Lord's body ; and whether he duly considers that the *bread* and *wine* point out the crucified body and spilt blood of Christ.

Verse 29. *Eateth and drinketh damnation*] Κριμα, *Judgment, punishment ;* and yet this is not unto *damnation,* for the judgment or punishment inflicted upon the disorderly and the profane was intended for their *emendation ;* for in ver. 32 it is said, when we are *judged,* κρινομενοι, we are chastened, παιδευομεθα, corrected as a father does his children, *that we should not be condemned with the world.*

Verse 30. *For this cause*] That they partook of this sacred ordinance without discerning the Lord's body ; *many* are *weak* and *sickly :* it is hard to say whether these words refer to the consequences of their own intemperance or to some extraordinary disorders inflicted immediately by God himself. That there were disorders of the most reprehensible kind among these people at this sacred supper, the preceding verses sufficiently point out ; and after such excesses, many might be *weak* and *sickly* among them, and *many* might *sleep,* i. e. *die ;* for continual experience shows us that many fall *victims* to their own intemperance. However, acting as they did in this solemn and awful sacrament, they might have " provoked God to plague them with divers diseases and sundry kinds of death." *Communion service.*

2

A. M. 4060. A. D. 56. A. U. C. 809. Anno Imp. Neronis Cæs. 3.

31 For [q] if we would judge ourselves, we should not be judged.
32 But when we are judged, [r] we are chastened of the Lord, that we should not be condemned with the world.
33 Wherefore, my brethren, when ye come together to eat, tarry one for another.
34 And if any man [s] hunger, let him eat at [t] home; that ye come not together unto [u] condemnation. And the rest [v] will I set in order when [w] I come.

[q] Psa. xxxii. 5; 1 John i. 9.——[r] Psa. xciv. 12, 13; Heb. xii. 5–11.——[s] Ver. 21.——[t] Verse 22.——[u] Or, *judgment*.——[v] Chap. vii. 17; Tit. i. 5.——[w] Chap. iv. 19.

Verse 31. *If we would judge ourselves*] If, having acted improperly, we condemn our conduct and humble ourselves, we shall not be *judged*, i. e. *punished* for the sin we have committed.

Verse 32. *But when we are judged*] See on ver. 29.

Verse 33. *When ye come together to eat*] The Lord's Supper, *tarry one for another*—do not eat and drink in *parties* as ye have done heretofore; and do not connect it with any other meal.

Verse 34. *And if any man hunger*] Let him not come to the house of God to eat an ordinary meal, *let him eat at home*—take that in his own house which is necessary for the support of his body before he comes to that sacred repast, where he should have the feeding of his soul alone in view.

That ye come not together unto condemnation] That ye may avoid the *curse* that must fall on such worthless communicants as those above mentioned; and that ye may get that especial *blessing* which every one that discerns the Lord's body in the eucharist must receive.

The rest will I set in order, &c.] All the other matters relative to this business, to which you have referred in your letter, I will regulate when I come to visit you; as, God permitting, I fully design. The apostle did visit them about one year after this, as is generally believed.

I HAVE already been so very particular in this long and difficult chapter, that I have left neither room nor necessity for many supplementary observations. A few remarks are all that is requisite.

1. The apostle inculcates the necessity of *order* and *subjection*, especially in the Church. Those who are *impatient of rule*, are generally those who wish to *tyrannize*. And those who are loudest in their complaints against authority, whether civil or ecclesiastical, are those who wish to have the power in their own hands, and would infallibly abuse it if they had. They alone who are *willing to obey*, are capable of *rule;* and he who can rule well, is as willing to *obey* as to *govern*. Let all be submissive and orderly; let the woman know that the man is head and protector; let the man know that Christ is his head and redeemer, and the gift of God's endless mercy for the salvation of a lost world.

2. The apostle insisted on the woman having her *head covered* in the Church or Christian assembly. If he saw the manner in which Christian women *now* dress, and appear in the ordinances of religion, what would he think? What would he say? How could he even distinguish the *Christian* from the *infidel?* And if they who are in Christ are *new creatures*, and the persons who ordinarily appear in religious assemblies are really *new creatures* (as they profess in general to be) in Christ, he might reasonably inquire: If these are *new* creatures, what must have been their appearance when they were *old* creatures. Do we dress to be *seen?* And do we go to the house of God to exhibit ourselves? Wretched is that man or woman who goes to the house of God to be seen by any but God himself.

3. The Lord's Supper may be well termed the *feast of charity;* how unbecoming this sacred ordinance to be the subject of dispute, party spirit, and division! Those who make it such must answer for it to God. Every man who believes in Christ as his atoning sacrifice should, as frequently as he can, receive the sacrament of the Lord's Supper. And every minister of Christ is bound to administer it to every man who is seeking the salvation of his soul, as well as to all *believers*. Let no man dare to oppose this ordinance; and let every man receive it according to the institution of Christ.

4. Against the fidelity of our translation of ver. 27 of this chapter, *Whosoever shall eat this bread* AND *drink this cup unworthily*, several popish writers have made heavy complaints, and accused the Protestants of wilful corruption; as both the *Greek* and *Vulgate* texts, instead of *και* and *et*, AND, have *η* and *vel*, OR: *Whosoever shall eat this bread*, OR *drink this cup*. As this criticism is made to countenance their unscriptural communion in *one kind*, it may be well to examine the ground of the complaint. Supposing even this objection to be valid, their cause can gain nothing by it while the 26th and 28th verses stand, both in the Greek text and Vulgate, as they now do: *For as often as ye eat this bread*, AND *drink this cup, &c. Let him eat of that bread*, AND *drink of that cup*. But although *η*, OR, be the reading of the *common* printed text, *και* AND, is the reading of the *Codex Alexandrinus*, and the *Codex Claromontanus*, two of the best MSS. in the world: as also of the *Codex Lincolniensis*, 2, and the *Codex Petavianus*, 3, both MSS. of the first character: it is also the reading of the ancient *Syriac*, all the *Arabic*, the *Coptic*, the margin of the *later Syriac*, the *Æthiopic*, different MSS. of the *Vulgate*, and of one in my own possession; and of *Clemens Chromatius*, and *Cassiodorus*. Though the present text of the Vulgate has *vel*, OR, yet this is a *departure* from the *original editions*, which were all professedly taken from the *best* MSS. In the famous Bible without *date, place*, or *printer's name*, 2 vols. fol., two columns, and forty-five lines in each, supposed by many to be the *first Bible* ever *printed*, the text stands thus: *Itaque quicunque manducaverit panem*, ET *biberit calicem, &c.; Wherefore whosoever shall eat this bread*

AND *drink this cup, &c.* : here is no *vel*, OR. The Bible printed by Fust, 1462, the *first* Bible with a *date*, has the same reading. Did the *Protestants corrupt* these texts ? In the *editio princeps* of the Greek Testament, printed by the authority of Cardinal *Ximenes* at Complutum, and published by the authority of *Pope Leo X.*, though η, OR, stands in the Greek text ; yet, in the opposite column, which contains the *Vulgate*, and in the opposite line, ET, *and*, is found, and not VEL, *or* ; though the Greek text would have authorized the editor to have made this change : but he conscientiously preserved the text of his *Vulgate*. Did the *Protestants* corrupt this *Catholic text* also ? Indeed, so little design had any of those who differed from the Romish Church to make any alteration here, that even Wiclif, having a faulty MS. of the Vulgate by him, which read *vel* instead of *et*, followed that faulty MS. and translated, 𝔄𝔫𝔡 𝔰𝔬 𝔴𝔥𝔬 𝔢𝔟𝔢𝔯 𝔰𝔠𝔥𝔞𝔩 𝔢𝔱𝔢 𝔱𝔥𝔢 𝔟𝔯𝔢𝔢𝔡 𝔬𝔯 𝔡𝔯𝔦𝔫𝔨𝔢 𝔱𝔥𝔢 𝔠𝔲𝔭.

That και, AND, is the *true reading*, and not η, *or*, both MSS. and *versions* sufficiently prove : also that *et*, not *vel*, is the proper reading in the *Vulgate*, those original editions formed by Roman Catholics, and one of them by the highest authority in the papal Church, fully establish : likewise those MSS., versions, fathers, and original editions, must be allowed to be, not only competent, but also unsuspected and incontrovertible witnesses.

But as this objection to our translation is brought forward to vindicate the withholding the *cup* from the laity in the Lord's Supper, it may be necessary to show that without the *cup* there can be no eucharist. With respect to the *bread*, our Lord had simply said, *Take; eat, this is my body* ; but concerning the *cup*, he says, *Drink ye all of this* ; for as this pointed out the very essence of the institution, *viz.* the *blood of atonement,* it was necessary that each should have a particular application of it, therefore he says, Drink ye ALL of THIS. By this we are taught that the *cup* is essential to the sacrament of the Lord's Supper ; so that they who deny the *cup* to the *people*, sin against God's institution ; and they who receive not the cup, are not partakers of the body and blood of Christ. If either could without mortal prejudice be omitted, it might be the *bread* ; but the *cup*, as pointing out the blood poured out, i. e. the *life*, by which alone the great sacrificial act is performed, and remission of sins procured, is absolutely indispensable. On this ground it is demonstrable, that there is not a popish priest under heaven, who denies the cup to the people, (and they all do this,) that can be said to celebrate the Lord's Supper at all ; nor is there one of their votaries that ever received the holy sacrament. All pretension to this is an absolute farce so long as the *cup*, the emblem of the atoning blood, is denied. How strange is it that the very men who plead so much for the bare *literal* meaning of *this is my body*, in the preceding verse, should deny all meaning to *drink ye all of this cup*, in this verse ! And though Christ has, in the most positive manner, enjoined it, they will not permit one of the laity to taste it ! See the whole of this argument, at large, in my *Discourse on the Nature and Design of the Eucharist.*

CHAPTER XII.

The apostle proceeds to the question of the Corinthians concerning spiritual gifts, 1. *He calls to their remembrance their former state, and how they were brought out of it,* 2, 3. *Shows that there are diversities of gifts which proceed from the Spirit,* 4. *Diversities of administrations which proceed from the Lord Jesus,* 5. *And diversities of* operations *which proceed from God,* 6. *What these gifts are, and how they are dispensed,* 7–11. *Christ is the Head, and the Church his members ; and this is pointed out under the similitude of the human body,* 12, 13. *The relation which the members of the body have to each other ; and how necessary their mutual support,* 14–26. *The members in the Church, or spiritual body, and their respective offices,* 27–30. *We should earnestly covet the best gifts,* 31.

A. M. 4060.
A. D. 56.
A. U. C. 809.
Anno Imp. Neronis Cæs. 3.

NOW [a] concerning spiritual gifts, brethren, I would not have you ignorant.

2 Ye know [b] that ye were Gentiles, carried away unto these [c] dumb idols, even as ye were led.

3 Wherefore I give you to un-

A. M. 4060.
A. D. 56.
A. U. C. 809.
Anno Imp. Nero nis Cæs. 3.

---

[a] Chap. xiv. 1, 37.——[b] Chap. vi. 11 ; Eph. ii. 11, 12; 1 Thess. i. 9 ; Tit. iii. 3 ; 1 Pet. iv. 3.——[c] Psa. cxv. 5.

NOTES ON CHAP. XII.

Verse 1. *Now concerning spiritual* gifts] This was a subject about which they appear to have written to the apostle, and concerning which there were probably some contentions among them. The words περι των πνευματικων may as well be translated *concerning spiritual persons*, as *spiritual gifts* ; and indeed the former agrees much better with the context.

I would not have you ignorant.] I wish you fully to know whence all such gifts come, and for what end they are given, that each person may serve the Church in the capacity in which God has placed him ; that there may be no misunderstandings and no schism in the body.

Verse 2. *Ye were Gentiles*] Previously to your conversion to the Christian faith ; ye were *heathens, carried away*, not guided by *reason* or *truth*, but *hurried* by your passions into a senseless worship, the chief part of which was calculated only to excite and gratify animal propensities.

Dumb idols] Though often supplicated, could never return an answer ; so that not only the *image* could

A. M. 4060.
A. D. 56.
A. U. C
809.
Anno Imp. Nero-
nis Cæs. 3.

derstand, d that no man speaking by the Spirit of God calleth Jesus e accursed ; and f *that* no man can say that Jesus is the Lord, but by the Holy Ghost.

4 Now g there are diversities of gifts, but h the same Spirit.

5 i And there are differences of k administrations, but the same Lord.

A. M. 4060.
A. D. 56.
A. U. C.
809.
Anno Imp. Nero-
nis Cæs. 3.

6 And there are diversities of operations, but it is the same God l which worketh all in all.

7 m But the manifestation of the Spirit is given to every man to profit withal.

8 For to one is given, by the Spirit, n the word of wisdom ; to another o the word of knowledge, by the same Spirit ;

---

d Mark ix. 39 ; 1 John iv. 2, 3.——e Or, *anathema.*——f Matt. xvi. 17 ; John xv. 26 ; 2 Cor. iii. 5.——g Rom. xii. 4, &c. ; Heb. ii. 4 ; 1 Pet. iv. 10.——h Eph. iv. 4

i Rom. xii. 6, 7, 8 ; Eph. iv. 11.——k Or, *ministeries.*——l Eph. i. 23.——m Rom. xii. 6, 7, 8 ; chap. xiv. 26 ; Eph. iv. 7 ; 1 Pet. iv. 10, 11.——n Ch. ii. 6, 7.——o Chap. i. 5 ; xiii. 2 ; 2 Cor. viii. 7.

---

not speak, but the *god* or *demon* pretended to be represented by it could not speak : a full proof that an *idol was nothing in the world.*

Verse 3. *No man speaking by the Spirit of God*] It was granted on all hands that there could be no religion without *Divine inspiration*, because God alone, could make his will known to men : hence heathenism *pretended* to this inspiration ; Judaism *had* it in the law and the prophets ; and it was the very *essence* of the *Christian* religion. The heathen priests and priestesses pretended to receive, by inspiration from their god, the *answers* which they gave to their votaries. And as far as the people believed their pretensions, so far they were *led* by their teaching.

Both *Judaism* and *heathenism* were full of expectations of a *future teacher* and *deliverer ;* and to this person, especially among the Jews, the Spirit in all the prophets gave witness. This was the *Anointed One*, the *Messiah* who was manifested in the person of Jesus of Nazareth ; and him the Jews rejected, though he proved his Divine mission both by his *doctrines* and his *miracles.* But as he did not come as they fancied he would—as a mighty secular conqueror, they not only rejected but blasphemed him ; and persons among them professing to be *spiritual* men, and under the *influence* of the *Spirit* of God, did so. But as the Holy Spirit, through all the law and the prophets gave testimony to the Messiah, and as Jesus proved himself to be the *Christ* both by his *miracles* and doctrines, no man under the *inspiration* of the Divine Spirit could say to him *anathema*—thou art a deceiver, and a person worthy of *death*, &c., as the Jews did : therefore the Jews were no longer under the inspiration of the Spirit of God. This appears to be the meaning of the apostle in this place . *No man speaking by the Spirit, &c.*

And that no man can say that Jesus is the Lord] Nor can we demonstrate this person to be the Messiah and the Saviour of men, but by the *Holy Ghost*, enabling us to speak with *divers tongues*, to *work miracles ;* heattesting the truth of our doctrines to them that hear, by *enlightening* their *minds, changing* their *hearts*, and *filling* them with the *peace* and *love* of God.

Verse 4. *There are diversities of gifts*] Χαρισματων· *Gracious endowments*, leading to *miraculous* results ; such as the gift of prophecy, speaking different tongues, &c. And these all came by the extraordinary influences of the Holy Spirit.

Verse 5. *Differences of administrations*] Διακονιων· Various offices in the Church, such as *apostle, prophet*, and *teacher ;* under which were probably included *bishop* or *presbyter, pastor, deacon, &c. ;* the *qualifications* for such offices, as well as the *appointments* themselves, coming immediately from the one Lord Jesus Christ.

Verse 6. *Diversities of operations*] Ενεργηματων· Miraculous influences exerted on others ; such as the expulsion of demons, inflicting extraordinary punishments, as in the case of Ananias and Sapphira, Elymas the sorcerer, &c., the healing of different diseases, raising the dead, &c. : all these proceeded from God the Father, as the *fountain* of all *goodness* and *power*, and the immediate dispenser of every good and perfect gift.

In the three preceding verses we find more than an indirect reference to the doctrine of the sacred Trinity Gifts are attributed to the Holy Spirit, ver. 4. Administrations to the Lord Jesus, ver. 5. Operations to God the Father, ver. 6. He who may think this *fanciful* must account for the very evident *distinctions* here in some more satisfactory way.

Verse 7. *The manifestation of the Spirit*] Φανερωσις του Πνευματος. This is variably understood by the fathers ; some of them rendering φανερωσις by *illumination*, others *demonstration*, and others *operation*. The apostle's meaning seems to be this : Whatever gifts God has bestowed, or in what various ways soever the Spirit of God may have manifested himself, it is all for the *common benefit* of the Church. God has given no gift to any man for his *own private* advantage, or exclusive profit. He has it for the benefit of others as well as for his own salvation.

Verse 8. *Word of wisdom*] In all these places I consider that the proper translation of λογος is *doctrine*, as in many other places of the New Testament. It is very difficult to say what is intended here by the different kinds of gifts mentioned by the apostle : they were probably all *supernatural*, and were necessary at that time only for the benefit of the Church. On the 8th, 9th, and 10th verses, much may be seen in *Lightfoot*, *Whitby*, *Pearce*, and others.

By *doctrine of wisdom* we may understand, as Bp. Pearce and Dr. Whitby observe, the mystery of our *redemption*, in which the *wisdom* of God was most eminently conspicuous : see chap. ii. 7, 10 ; and which is called the *manifold wisdom of God*, Eph iii

A. M. 4060.
A. D. 56.
A. U. C.
809.
Anno Imp. Nero-
nis Cæs. 3.

9 To another ᵖ faith, by the same Spirit ; to another �q the gifts of healing, by the same Spirit ;

10 To another ʳ the working of miracles ; to another ˢ prophecy ; to another ᵗ discerning of spirits; to another ᵘ *divers* kinds of tongues ; to another the interpretation of tongues :

11 But all these worketh that one and the self-same Spirit, ᵛ dividing to every man severally ʷ as he will.

12 For ˣ as the body is one, and hath many members, and all the members of that one body, being many, are one body ; ʸ so also *is* Christ.

13 Fòr ᶻ by one Spirit are we all baptized into one body, ᵃ whether *we be* Jews, or ᵇ Gentiles, whether *we be* bond or free ; and ᶜ have

A. M. 4060.
A. D. 56.
A. U. C.
809.
Anno Imp. Nero-
nis Cæs. 3.

ᵖ Matt. xvii. 19, 20 ; chap. xiii. 2 ; 2 Cor. iv. 13.——�q Mark xvi. 18 ; James v. 14.——ʳ Ver. 28, 29 ; Mark xvi. 17 ; Gal. iii. 5. ˢ Rom. xii. 6 ; chap. xiii. 2 ; xiv. 1, &c.——ᵗ Ch. xiv. 29 ; 1 John iv. 1.——ᵘ Acts ii. 4 ; x. 46 ; chap. xiii. 1.——ᵛ Rom. xii. 6 ; ch.

vii. 7 ; 2 Cor. x. 13 ; Eph. iv. 7.——ʷ John iii. 8 ; Heb. ii. 4. ˣ Rom. xii. 4, 5 ; Eph. iv. 4, 16.——ʸ Ver. 27 ; Gal. iii. 16. ᶻ Rom. vi. 5.——ᵃ Gal. iii. 28 ; Eph. ii. 13, 14, 16 ; Col. iii. 11. ᵇ Gr. *Greeks.*——ᶜ John vi. 63 ; vii. 37, 38, 39.

---

10. Christ, the great teacher of it, is called the *wisdom of God*, chap. i. 24 ; and in him are said to be contained *all the treasures of wisdom and knowledge*, Col. ii. 3. The apostles to whom this doctrine was committed are called σοφοι, *wise men* ; (Matt. xxiii. 34 ;) and they are said to teach this Gospel according to the *wisdom given them*, 2 Pet. iii. 15.

2. By *the doctrine of knowledge* we may understand either a knowledge of the *types*, &c., in the *Old Testament* ; or what are termed *mysteries* ; the *calling of the Gentiles*, the *recalling* of the *Jews*, the *mystery* of *iniquity*, of the *beast*, &c., and especially the *mystical sense* or *meaning* of the Old Testament, with all its types, rites, ceremonies, &c., &c.

3. By *faith*, ver. 9, we are to understand that miraculous faith by which they could remove mountains, chap. xiii. 2 ; or a peculiar impulse, as Dr. Whitby calls it, that came upon the apostles when any difficult matter was to be performed, which inwardly assured them that God's power would assist them in the performance of it. Others think that justifying faith, received by means of Gospel *teaching*, is what is intended.

4. *Gifts of healing* simply refers to the power which at particular times the apostles received from the Holy Spirit to cure diseases ; a power which was not always resident in them ; for Paul could not cure Timothy, nor remove his own thorn in the flesh ; because it was given only on extraordinary occasions, though perhaps more *generally* than many others.

5. *The working of miracles*, ενεργηματα δυναμεων, verse 10. This seems to refer to the same class as the *operations*, ενεργηματων, ver. 6, as the words are the same ; and to signify those powers by which they were enabled at particular times to work miraculously on others ; ejecting demons, inflicting punishments or judgments, as in the cases mentioned under ver. 6. It is a hendyadis for mighty operations.

6. *Prophecy.* This seems to import two things : 1st, the *predicting future events*, such as then particularly concerned the state of the Church and the apostles ; as the *dearth* foretold by *Agabus*, Acts xi. 28 ; and the *binding of* St. Paul, and *delivering him to the Romans*, Acts xxi. 10, &c. ; and St. Paul's *foretelling* his *own shipwreck on Malta*, Acts xxvii. 25, &c. And 2dly, as implying the faculty of *teaching* or *expounding* the Scriptures, which is also a common acceptation of the word.

7. *Discerning of spirits.* A gift by which the person so privileged could discern a *false miracle* from a *true one* ; or a *pretender* to *inspiration* from him who was made *really* partaker of the Holy Ghost. It probably extended also to the discernment of *false professors* from *true ones*, as appears in Peter in the case of Ananias and his wife.

8. *Divers kinds of tongues.* Γενη γλωσσων, *Different languages*, which they had never learned, and which God gave them for the immediate instruction of people of different countries who attended their ministry.

9. *Interpretation of tongues.* It was necessary that while one was speaking the deep things of God in a company where several were present who did not *understand*, though the *majority* did, there should be a person who could immediately interpret what was said to that part of the congregation that did not understand the language. This power to interpret was also an immediate gift of God's Spirit, and is classed here among the miracles.

Verse 11. *But all these worketh that one and the self-same Spirit*] All these gifts are miraculously bestowed ; they cannot be acquired by human art or industry, the different *languages* excepted ; but *they* were *given* in such a way, and in such circumstances, as sufficiently proved that *they* also were miraculous gifts.

Verse 12. *For as the body is one*] Though the human body have many *members*, and though it be composed of a great variety of *parts*, yet it is but one *entire system* ; every part and member being necessary to the integrity or completeness of the whole.

So also is Christ.] That is, So is the Church the body of Christ, being composed of the different officers already mentioned, and especially those enumerated, ver. 28, *apostles, prophets, teachers, &c.* It cannot be supposed that Christ is *composed of many members, &c.*, and therefore the term *Church* must be understood, unless we suppose, which is not improbable, that the term Ὁ Χριστος, *Christ*, is used to express the *Church*, or whole body of Christian believers.

Verse 13. *For by one Spirit are we all baptized, &c.*] As the body of man, though composed of many members, is informed and influenced by one soul ; so the Church of Christ, which is his body, though composed of many members, is informed and influenced by one Spirit, the Holy Ghost ; actuating and working by his spiritual body, as the human soul does in the body of man.

A. M. 4060.
A. D. 56.
A. U. C. 809.
Anno Imp. Neronis Cæs. 3.

been all made to drink into one Spirit.

14 For the body is not one member, but many.

15 If the foot shall say, Because I am not the hand, I am not of the body; is it therefore not of the body?

16 And if the ear shall say, Because I am not the eye, I am not of the body; is it therefore not of the body?

17 If the whole body *were* an eye, where

were the hearing? If the whole *were* hearing, where *were* the smelling?

18 But now hath ᵈ God set the members every one of them in the body, ᵉ as it hath pleased him.

19 And if they were all one member, where *were* the body?

20 But now *are they* many members, yet but one body.

21 And the eye cannot say unto the hand, I

A. M. 4060.
A. D. 56.
A. U. C. 809.
Anno Imp. Neronis Cæs. 3.

ᵈ Verse 28.

ᵉ Rom. xii. 3; chap. iii. 5; ver. 11.

To drink into one Spirit.] We are to understand being made partakers of the gifts and graces of the Holy Ghost agreeably to the words of our Lord, John vii. 37, &c.: *If any man thirst, let him come unto me and drink: this he spake of the Spirit which they that believed on him should receive.*

On this verse there is a great profusion of various readings, which may be found in *Griesbach,* but cannot be conveniently noticed here.

Verse 14. *For the body is not one member*] The *mystical* body, the Church, as well as the *natural* body, is composed of many members.

Verse 15. *If the foot shall say, &c.*] As all the members of the body are necessarily dependent on each other, and minister to the general support of the system, so is it in the Church. All the private members are intimately connected among themselves, and also with their pastors; without which union no Church can subsist.

Verse 21. *And the eye cannot say unto the hand, I have no need of thee*] The apostle goes on, with his principal object in view, to show that the gifts and graces with which their different teachers were endowed were all necessary for their salvation, and should be *collectively* used; for not one of them was unnecessary, nor could they dispense with the least of them; the body of Christ needed the whole for its nourishment and support. The famous apologue of *Menenius Agrippa,* related by Livy, will serve to illustrate the apostle's reasoning: the Roman *people,* getting into a state of insurrection and rebellion against the *nobility,* under pretext that the *great men* not only had all the *honours* but all the *emoluments* of the nation, while *they* were obliged to bear all the burdens, and suffer all the privations; they then in riotous assemblage left their homes and went to Mount Aventine. Matters were at last brought to such an issue, that the *senators* and *great men* were obliged to fly from the city, and the public peace was on the point of being utterly ruined: it was then thought expedient to send *Menenius Agrippa* to them, who was high in their esteem, having vanquished the *Sabines* and *Samnites,* and had the first triumph at Rome. This great general, who was as eloquent as he was valiant, went to the *Mons Sacer,* to which the insurgents had retired, and thus addressed them: *Tempore, quo in homine non, ut nunc omnia in unum consentiebant, sed singulis membris suum cuique consilium, suus sermo fuerat, indignatas*

reliquas partes, sua cura, suo labore ac ministerio ventri omnia quæri; ventrem, in medio quietum, nihil aliud, quam datis voluptatibus frui. Conspirasse inde, ne manus ad os cibum ferrent, nec os acciperet datum, nec dentes conficerent. Hac ira, dum ventrem fame domare vellent, ipsa una membra totumque corpus ad extremam tabem venisse. Inde apparuisse, ventris quoque haud segne ministerium esse: nec magis ali, quam alere eum, reddentem in omnes corporis partes hunc, quo vivimus vigemusque, divisum pariter in venas maturum, confecto cibo, sanguinem. T. Livii, Histor. lib. ii. cap. 32. "In that time in which the different *parts* of the human body were not in a state of *unity* as they now are, but each *member* had its *separate* office and *distinct language,* they all became discontented, because whatever was procured by their care, labour, and industry, was spent on the *belly;* while this, lying at ease in the midst of the body, did nothing but enjoy whatever was provided for it. They therefore conspired among themselves, and agreed that the hands should not convey food to the mouth, that the mouth should not receive what was offered to it, and that the teeth should not masticate whatever was brought to the mouth. Acting on this principle of revenge, and hoping to reduce the belly by famine, all the members, and the whole body itself, were at length brought into the last stage of a consumption. It then plainly appeared that the *belly* itself did no small service; that it contributed not less to *their* nourishment than they did to *its* support, distributing to every part that from which they derived life and vigour; for by properly concocting the food, the pure blood derived from it was conveyed by the arteries to every member."

This sensible comparison produced the desired effect: the *people* were persuaded that the *senators* were as necessary to *their* existence as they were to that of the senators, and that it required the strictest *union* and mutual support of *high* and *low* to preserve the body politic. This transaction took place about 500 years before the Christian era, and was handed down by unbroken tradition to the time of *Titus Livius,* from whom I have taken it, who died in the year of our Lord 17, about forty years before St. Paul wrote this epistle. As his works were well known and universally read among the Romans in the time of the apostle, it is very probable that St. Paul had this famous apologue in view when he wrote from the 14th verse to the end of the chapter.

2

A. M. 4060.
A. D. 56.
A. U. C.
809.
Anno Imp. Nero-
nis Cæs. 3.

have no need of thee ; nor again, the head to the feet, I have no need of you.

22 Nay, much more those members of the body, which seem to be more feeble, are necessary :

23 And those *members* of the body, which we think to be less honourable, upon these we *f* bestow more abundant honour ; and our uncomely *parts* have more abundant comeliness.

24 For our comely *parts* have no need : but

God hath tempered the body together, having given more abundant honour to that *part* which lacked :

A. M. 4060.
A. D. 56.
A. U. C.
809.
Anno Imp. Nero-
nis Cæs. 3.

25 That there should be no *g* schism in the body ; but *that* the member should have the same care one for another.

26 And whether one member suffers, all the members suffer with it ; or one member be honoured, all the members rejoice with it.

27 Now *h* ye are the body of Christ, and *i* members in particular.

---

f Or, *put on.*——*g* Or, *division.*——*h* Rom. xii. 5 ; Eph. i. 23 ; iv. 12 ; v. 23, 30 ; Col. i. 24.——*i* Eph. v. 30.

Verse 22. *Those members—which seem to be more feeble*] These, and the *less honourable* and *uncomely*, mentioned in the next verses, seem to mean the principal *viscera*, such as the *heart, lungs, stomach*, and *intestinal canal*. These, when compared with the *arms* and *limbs*, are comparatively *weak*; and some of them, considered in *themselves, uncomely* and less honourable ; yet these are more essential to life than any of the others. A man may lose an *eye* by accident, and an *arm* or a *leg* may be amputated, and yet the *body* live and be vigorous ; but let the *stomach, heart, lungs*, or any of the *viscera* be removed, and life becomes necessarily extinct. Hence these parts are not only *covered*, but the parts in which they are lodged are surrounded, ornamented, and fortified for their preservation and defence, on the proper performance of whose functions life so immediately depends.

Verse 24. *For our comely* parts *have no need*] It would be easy to go into great detail in giving an *anatomical* description of the different members and parts to which the apostle refers, but it would not probably answer the end of general edification ; and to explain every *allusion* made by the apostle, would require a minuteness of description which would not be tolerated except in a treatise on the anatomy of the human body. My readers will therefore excuse my entering into this detail.

Verse 25. *That there should be no schism in the body*] That there should be no unnecessary and independent part in the whole human machine, and that every part should contribute something to the general proportion, symmetry, and beauty of the body. So completely has God tempered the whole together, that not the smallest visible part can be removed from the body without not only injuring its proportions, but producing deformity. Hence the members have the same care one for another. The *eyes* and *ears* watch for the general safety of the whole ; and they are placed in the *head*, like sentinels in a tower, that they may perceive the first approach of a foe, and give warning. The *hands* immediately on an attack exert themselves to defend the *head* and the *body ;* and the *limbs* are swift to carry off the body from *dangers* against which *resistance* would be *vain*. Even the *heart* takes alarm from both the *eyes* and the *ears ;* and when an attack is made on the body, every external muscle becomes inflated and contracts itself, that, by thus *collecting*

and *concentrating* its force, it may the more effectually resist the assailants, and contribute to the defence of the system.

Verse 26. *And whether one member suffer*] As there is a mutual exertion for the general defence, so there is a mutual sympathy. If the *eye*, the *hand*, the *foot*, &c., be injured, the *whole man* grieves ; and if by *clothing*, or *any* thing else, any particular member or part is *adorned, strengthened*, or *better secured*, it gives a general pleasure to the whole man.

Verse 27. *Now ye are the body of Christ*] The apostle, having finished his *apologue*, comes to his application.

As the members in the human body, so the different members of the mystical body of Christ. All are intended by him to have the same relation to each other ; to be mutually subservient to each other ; to mourn for and rejoice with each other. He has also made each necessary to the *beauty, proportion, strength*, and *perfection* of the whole. Not one is *useless ;* not one *unnecessary*. Paul, Apollos, Kephas, &c., with all their variety of gifts and graces, are *for the perfecting of the saints, for the work of the ministry, for the edifying of the body of Christ*, Eph. iv. 12. Hence no teacher should be *exalted* above or *opposed* to another. As the *eye* cannot say to the *hand*, I have no need of thee, so *luminous* Apollos cannot say to *laborious* Paul, I can build up and preserve the Church without thee. The *foot* planted on the ground to support the whole fabric, and the *hands* that swing at liberty, and the *eye* that is continually taking in near and distant prospects, are all equally serviceable to the whole, and mutually helpful to and dependent on each other. So also are the different ministers and members of the Church of Christ.

From a general acquaintance with various ministers of Christ, and a knowledge of their different *talents* and endowments manifested either by their *preaching* or *writings*, and with the aid of a little *fancy*, we could here make out a sort of correspondency between *their services* and the *uses* of the different *members* of the human body. We could call one *eye*, because of his *acute observation* of men and things, and *penetration* into cases of conscience and Divine *mysteries*. Another *hand*, from his *laborious* exertions in the Church. Another *foot*, from his industrious *travels* to spread abroad the knowledge of Christ crucified : and so of

2

A. M. 4060.
A. D. 56.
A. U. C.
809.
Anno Imp. Nero-
nis Cæs. 3.

28 And ᵏ God hath set some in the Church, first, ˡ apostles; secondarily, ᵐ prophets; thirdly, teachers; after that ⁿ miracles; then ᵒ gifts of healings, ᵖ helps, �q governments, ʳ diversities of tongues.

29 *Are* all apostles? *are* all prophets? *are* all teachers? *are* all ˢ workers of miracles?

30 Have all the gifts of healing? do all speak with tongues? do all interpret?

31 But ᵗ covet earnestly the best gifts: and yet show I unto you a more excellent way.

A. M. 4060.
A. D. 56.
A. U. C.
809.
Anno Imp. Nero-
nis Cæs. 3.

ᵏ Eph. iv. 11.——ˡ Eph. ii. 20; iii. 5.——ᵐ Acts xiii. 1; Rom. xii. 6.——ⁿ Ver. 10.——ᵒ Ver. 9.——ᵖ Num. xi. 17. ——q Rom. xii. 8; 1 Tim. v. 17; Heb. xiii. 17, 24.——ʳ Or, *kinds*; ver. 10.——ˢ Or, *powers:*——ᵗ Chap. xiv. 1, 39.

---

others. But this does not appear to be any part of the apostle's plan.

Verse 28. God hath set some in the Church] As God has made evident distinctions among the members of the human body, so that some occupy a more eminent place than others, so has he in the Church. And to prove this, the apostle numerates the principal offices, and in the order in which they should stand.

First, apostles] Αποστολους, from απο, *from*, and στελλω, *I send*; to *send* from one *person* to *another*, and from one *place* to *another*. Persons immediately designated by Christ, and *sent* by him to preach the Gospel to all mankind.

Secondarily, prophets] Προφητας, from προ, *before*, and φημι, *I speak*; a person who, under Divine inspiration, predicts future events; but the word is often applied to those who preach the Gospel. See on ver. 10.

Thirdly, teachers] Διδασκαλους, from διδασκω, *I teach*; persons whose chief business it was to instruct the people in the elements of the Christian religion, and their duty to each other. See on Rom. viii. 8.

Miracles] Δυναμεις· Persons endued with miraculous gifts, such as those mentioned Mark xvi. 17, 18; casting out devils, speaking with new tongues, &c. See on ver. 10, and at the end of the chapter.

Gifts of healings] Χαρισματα ιαματων· Such as laying hands upon the sick, and healing them, Mark xvi. 18; which, as being one of the most *beneficent* miraculous powers, was most frequently conceded. See on ver. 8.

Helps] Αντιληψεις. Dr. Lightfoot conjectures that these were the apostles' helpers; persons who accompanied them, baptized those who were converted by them, and were sent by them to such places as they could not attend to, being otherwise employed. The *Levites* are termed by the Talmudists *helps of the priests.* The word occurs Luke i. 54; Rom. viii. 26.

Governments] Κυβερνησεις. Dr. Lightfoot contends that this word does not refer to the *power of ruling*, but to the case of a person endued with a *deep and comprehensive mind*, who is *profoundly wise* and *prudent*; and he thinks that it implies the same as *discernment of spirits*, ver. 10, where see the note. He has given several proofs of this use of the word in the *Septuagint.*

Diversities of tongues.] Γενη γλωσσων· *Kinds of tongues*; that is, *different kinds*. The power to speak, on all necessary occasions, languages which they had not learned. See on ver. 10.

Verse 29. Are all apostles, &c.] That is: All are *not* apostles, all are not *prophets*, &c.; God has dis-
tributed his various gifts among various persons, each of whom is necessary for the complete edification of the body of Christ. On these subjects see the notes on verses 7, 8, 9, 10.

Verse 31. But covet earnestly] To *covet* signifies to *desire earnestly*. This disposition towards *heavenly* things is *highly laudable*; towards *earthly* things, is *deeply criminal*. A man may possess the best of all these gifts, and yet be deficient in what is essentially necessary to his salvation, for he may be without that love or charity which the apostle here calls the *more excellent way*, and which he proceeds in the next chapter to describe.

Some think that this verse should be read *affirmatively, Ye earnestly contend about the best gifts; but I show unto you a more excellent way;* i. e. get your hearts filled with *love to God* and *man*—love, which is the *principle of obedience,* which *works no ill to its neighbour,* and which is the *fulfilling of the law.* This is a likely reading, for there were certainly more contentions in the Church of Corinth about the *gifts* than about the *graces* of the Spirit.

1. AFTER all that has been said on the different offices mentioned by the apostle in the preceding chapter, there are some of them which perhaps are not understood. I confess I scarcely know what to make of those which we translate *helps* and *governments.* Bishop Pearce, who could neither see *Church government* nor *state government* in these words, expresses himself thus: " These two words, after all that the commentators say about them, I do not understand; and in no other part of the New Testament is either of them, in any sense, mentioned as the *gift of the Spirit*; especially it is observable that in ver. 29, 30, where the gifts of the Spirit are again enumerated, no notice is taken of any thing like them, while all the other several parts are exactly enumerated. Perhaps these words were put in the margin to explain δυναμεις, *miracles* or *powers*; some taking the meaning to be *helps, assistances,* as in 2 Cor. xii. 9; others to be κυβερνησεις, *governments,* as in Rom. viii. 38; and from being marginal explanations, they might have been at last incorporated with the text." It must, however, be acknowledged that the omission of these words is not countenanced by any MS. or *version.* One thing we may fully know, that there are some men who are peculiarly qualified for *governing* by either providence or grace; and that there are others who can neither *govern* nor *direct*, but are good *helpers.* These characters I have often seen in different places in the Church of God.

2. In three several places in this chapter the apostle sums up the gifts of the Spirit. Dr. Lightfoot thinks they answer to each other in the following order, which the reader will take on *his* authority.

Verses 8, 9, and 10.

Is given
The word of Wisdom ;
The word of Knowledge.

Ver. 9.   *Faith ;*
         Gifts of Healing.

Ver. 10.   *Working of Miracles ;*
         Prophecy ;
         Discerning of Spirits ;
         Divers kinds of Tongues ;
         Interpretation of Tongues.

Verse 28.

God hath set some
First, Apostles ;
Secondly, Prophets ;
Thirdly, Teachers ;
After that, Miracles ;
The gifts of Healings ;
Helps ;
Governments ;
Divers kinds of Tongues.

Verses 29, and 30.

Are all
Apostles ;
Prophets ;
Teachers ;
Miracles ;

Ver. 30.   *Gifts of Healing.*
         Speak with Tongues ;
         Interpret.

If the reader think that this is the best way of explaining these different gifts and offices, he will adopt it ; and he will in that case consider, 1. That the *word* or doctrine of *wisdom* comes from the apostles. 2. The *doctrine* of *knowledge*, from the *prophets.* 3. *Faith*, by means of the *teachers.* 4. That *working of miracles* includes the *gifts of healing.* 5. That to *prophecy*, signifying *preaching*, which it frequently does, *helps* is a parallel. 6. That *discernment of spirits* is the same with *governments*, which Dr. Lightfoot supposes to imply a deeply comprehensive, wise, and prudent mind. 7. As to the *gift of tongues*, there is no variation in either of the *three* places.

3. It is strange that in this enumeration only *three* distinct officers in the Church should be mentioned ; viz. *apostles*, *prophets*, and *teachers*. We do not know that *miracles*, *gifts of healing*, *helps*, *governments*, and *diversity* of *tongues*, were *exclusive* offices ; for it is probable that *apostles*, *prophets*, and *teachers* wrought miracles occasionally, and spoke with divers tongues. However, in all this enumeration, where the *apostle* gives us *all the officers* and *gifts* necessary for the *constitution* of a *Church*, we find not one word of *bishops*, *presbyters*, or *deacons* ; much less of the various officers and offices which the Christian Church at present exhibits. Perhaps the *bishops* are included under the *apostles*, the *presbyters* under the *prophets*, and the *deacons* under the *teachers*. As to the other ecclesiastical officers with which the *Romish* Church teems, they may seek them who are determined to find them, any where *out* of the New Testament.

4. Mr. *Quesnel* observes on these passages that there are *three* sorts of *gifts* necessary to the forming Christ's mystical body. 1. Gifts of *power*, for the working of miracles, in reference to the *Father*. 2. Gifts of *labour* and *ministry*, for the exercise of *government* and other *offices*, with respect to the *Son*. 3. Gifts of *knowledge*, for the *instruction* of the people, with relation to the *Holy Ghost*.

The Father is the *principle* and *end* of all created power ; let us then ultimately *refer* all things to *him*.

The Son is the *Institutor* and *Head* of all the hierarchical ministries ; let us *depend* upon *him*.

The Holy Ghost is the *fountain* and *fulness* of all spiritual graces ; let us *desire* and *use* them only *in* and *by* him.

There is nothing good, nothing profitable to salvation, unless it be done in the *power* of God *communicated* by Christ Jesus, and in that *holiness* of heart which is produced by his Spirit. Pastors are only the *instruments* of God, the *depositaries* of the *authority* of *Christ*, and the *channels* by whom the love and graces of the *Spirit* are conveyed. Let these act as receiving all from God by Christ, through the Holy Ghost ; and let the Church receive them as the ambassadors of the *Almighty.*

CHAPTER XIII.

Charity, or love to God and man, the sum and substance of all true religion ; so that without it, the most splendid eloquence, the gift of prophecy, the most profound knowledge, faith by which the most stupendous miracles might be wrought, benevolence the most unbounded, and zeal for the truth, even to martyrdom, would all be unavailing to salvation, 1–3. The description and praise of this grace, 4–7. Its durableness ; though tongues, prophecies, and knowledge shall cease, yet this shall never fail, 8–10. Description of the present imperfect state of man, 11, 12. Of all the graces of God in man, charity, or love, is the greatest, 13.

A. M. 4060.
A. D. 56.
A. U. C.
809.
Anno Imp. Nero-
nis Cæs. 3.

THOUGH I speak with the tongues of men and of angels, and have not [a] charity, I am become *as* sound-ing brass, or a tinkling cymbal,

2 And though I have *the gift* of [b] prophecy, and understand

A. M. 4060.
A. D. 56.
A. U. C.
809.
Anno Imp. Nero-
nis Cæs. 3.

---

[a] Lev. xix. 18 ; Deut. vi. 5 ; x. 12 ; xxx. 6 ; Matt. xxi. 37, 38, 39, 40 ; Mark xii. 31 ; Luke x. 27 ; xx. 41.

[b] Chapter xii. 8, 9, 10, 28 ; xiv. 1. &c. ; see Matthew vii. 22.

NOTES ON CHAP. XIII.

Verse 1. *Though I speak, &c.*] At the conclusion of the preceding chapter the apostle promised to show the Corinthians a *more excellent way* than that in which they were now proceeding. They were so distracted with contentions, divided by parties, and envious of each other's gifts, that *unity* was nearly destroyed. This was a full proof that *love to God* and *man* was wanting ; and that without this, their numerous *gifts* and other *graces* were nothing in the eyes of God ; for it was evident that they did not love one another, which is a proof that they did not love God ; and consequently, that they had not true religion. Having, by his advices and directions, corrected many abuses, and having shown them how in outward things they should walk so as to please God, he now shows them the *spirit, temper,* and *disposition* in which this should be done, and without which all the rest must be ineffectual.

Before I proceed to the consideration of the different parts of this chapter, it may be necessary to examine whether the word *αγαπη* be best translated by *charity* or *love*. Wiclif, translating from the *Vulgate*, has the word *charity* ; and him our authorized version follows. But *Coverdale, Matthews, Cranmer,* and the *Geneva Bible,* have *love ;* which is adopted by recent translators and commentators in general ; among whom the chief are Dodd, Pearce, Purver, Wakefield, and Wesley ; all these strenuously contend that the word *charity,* which is now confined to *almsgiving,* is utterly improper ; and that the word *love,* alone expresses the apostle's sense. As the word *charity* seems now to express little else than almsgiving, which, performed even to the uttermost of a man's power, is *nothing* if he lack what the apostle terms *αγαπη,* and which we here translate *charity ;* it is best to omit the use of a word in this place which, taken in its ordinary signification, makes the apostle contradict himself ; see ver. 3 : *Though I give all my goods to feed the poor, and have not charity, it profiteth me nothing.* That is : " Though I have the utmost charity, and act in every respect according to its dictates, yet, if I have *not* charity, my utmost *charity* is unprofitable." Therefore, to shun this contradiction, and the probable misapplication of the term, LOVE had better be substituted for CHARITY.

The word *αγαπη, love,* I have already considered at large in the note on Matt. xxii. 37 ; and to that place I beg leave to refer the reader for its derivation and import. Our English word *love* we have from the Teutonic leben to *live,* because love is the means, dis-penser, and preserver of *life ;* and without it life would have nothing *desirable,* nor indeed any thing even *supportable :* or it may be taken immediately from the Anglo-Saxon lofa and lufa, *love,* from lufian and lufian, to *desire,* to *love,* to *favour.* It would be ridiculous to look to the Greek verb *φιλειν* for its derivation.

Having said so much about the word *love,* we should say something of the word *charity,* which is supposed to be improper in this place. *Charity* comes to us immediately from the French *charite,* who borrowed it from the Latin *charitas,* which is probably borrowed from the Greek *χαρις,* signifying *grace* or *favour,* or *χαρα, joy,* as a benefit bestowed is a *favour* that inspires him who receives it with *joy ;* and so far contributes to his *happiness.* The proper meaning of the word CHARUS, is *dear, costly ;* and CHARITAS, is *dearth, scarcity, a high price,* or *dearness.* Hence, as in times of dearth or scarcity, many, especially the poor, must be in want, and the benevolent will be excited to relieve them ; the term which expressed the *cause* of this *want* was applied to the *disposition* which was excited in behalf of the sufferer. Now, as he who relieves a person in distress, and preserves his life by communicating a portion of his property to him, will feel a sort of *interest* in the person thus preserved ; hence he is said to be *dear* to him : i. e. he has *cost* him something ; and he *values* him in proportion to the trouble or *expense* he has *cost* him. Thus *charity* properly expresses that *affectionate attachment* we may feel to a person whose *wants* we have been enabled to relieve ; but originally it signified that *want* of the necessaries of life which produced *dearth* or *dearness* of those necessaries ; and brought the poor man into that state in which he stood so much in need of the active benevolence of his richer neighbour. If the word be applied to God's benevolence towards man, it comes in with all propriety and force : we are *dear* to God, for we have not been purchased with *silver* or *gold,* but with the *precious* (*τιμιω αιματι, costly*) blood of Christ, who so loved us as to give his life a ransom for ours.

As Christians in general acknowledge that this chapter is the most important in the whole New Testament, I shall give here the *first translation* of it into the *English* language which is known to exist, extracted from an ancient and noble MS. in my own possession, which seems to exhibit both a *text* and *language,* if not prior to the time of Wiclif, yet certainly not posterior to his days. The reader will please to observe that there are no *divisions* of *verses* in the MS.

The XIII. Chapter of I. Corinthians, from an ancient MS.

Ʒef I speke with tungis of men and aungels sotheli I haue not charitee : I am maad as brasse sounynge, or a symbale tynking. And gif I schal haue prophecie and haue knowen alle mysteries and alle kunynge or science. and gif I schal haue al feith so that I ouer bere hillis fro oo place to an other. forsothe gif I schal not haue cha-

2

A. M. 4060.
A. D. 56.
A. U. C. 809.
Anno Imp. Neronis. Cæs. 3.

all mysteries,, and all knowledge; and though I have all faith, [c] so that I could remove mountains, and have not charity, I am nothing.

3 And [d] though I bestow all my goods to feed *the poor,*

A. M. 4060.
A. D. 56.
A. U. C. 809.
Anno Imp. Nero nis Cæs. 3.

---

[c] Matt. xvii. 20; Mark xi. 23; Luke xvii. 6. | [d] Matt. vi. 1, 2.

---

rite: I am nougt. And gif I schal deperte al my goodis into metis of pore men And gif I schal bitake my body so that I brenne forsothe gif I schal not have charite it profitith to me no thing. Charite is pacient or suffringe. It is benyngne or of good wille Charite enuyeth not. It doth not gyle· it is not inblowen with pride it is not ambycfouse or couetouse of wirschippis. It seekyth not the thingis that ben her owne. It is not stirid to wrath it thinkith not yuel. It ioyeth not on wickidnesse· forsothe it ioyeth to gydre to treuthe. It suffreth alle thingis. It bileeveth alle thingis. it hopith alle thingis· it susteeneth alle thingis. Charite fallith not doun. Whether prophecies schuln be bolde eyther langagis schuln ceese: eyther science schal be distruyed. Forsothe of party we han knowen: and of partye prophecien. Forsothe whenne that schal cum to that is perfit: that thing that is of partye schal be avoydid. Whenne I was a litil childe: I spake as a litil childe. I understode as a litil childe: I thougte as a litil childe. Forsothe whenn I was maad a man: I avoydid tho thingis that weren of a litil childe. Forsothe we seen now bi a miror in derenesse: thanne forsothe face to face. Nowe I knowe of partye: thanne forsothe I schal knowe and as I am knowen. Nowe forsothe dwellen feith hoope charite. These three: forsothe the more of hem is charite.

This is the whole of the chapter as it exists in the MS., with all its peculiar *orthography*, *points*, and *lines*. The words with lines under may be considered the translator's marginal readings; for, though incorporated with the text, they are distinguished from it by those lines.

I had thought once of giving a literal translation of the whole chapter from all the ancient versions. This would be both curious and useful; but the reader might think it would take up too much of *his* time, and the writer has none to spare.

The tongues of men] All human languages, with all the eloquence of the most accomplished orator.

And of angels] i. e. Though a man knew the language of the eternal world so well that he could hold conversation with its inhabitants, and find out the secrets of their kingdom. Or, probably, the apostle refers to a notion that was common among the Jews, that there was a language by which angels might be invoked, adjured, collected, and dispersed; and by the means of which many secrets might be found out, and curious arts and sciences known.

There is much of this kind to be found in their cabalistical books, and in the books of many called Christians. *Cornelius Agrippa's* occult philosophy abounds in this; and it was the main object of Dr. *Dee's* actions with spirits to get a complete vocabulary of this language. See what has been published of his work by Dr. Casaubon; and the remaining manuscript parts in the *Sloane library*, in the British museum.

In *Bava Bathra*, fol. 134, mention is made of a famous rabbin, *Jochanan ben Zaccai*, who understood the language of *devils*, *trees*, and *angels*.

Some think that the apostle means only the most splendid eloquence; as we sometimes apply the word *angelic* to signify any thing *sublime, grand, beautiful,* &c.; but it is more likely that he speaks here after the manner of his countrymen, who imagined that there was an angelic language which was the key to many mysteries; a language which might be acquired, and which, they say, had been learned by several.

Sounding brass] Χαλκος ηχων· That is, like a trumpet made of *brass;* for although χαλκος signifies *brass,* and *æs* signifies the same, yet we know the latter is often employed to signify the *trumpet,* because generally made of this metal. Thus Virgil, when he represents Misenus endeavouring to fright away the *harpies* with the sound of his trumpet :—

Ergo, ubi delapsæ sonitum per curva dedere
Littora, dat signum specula Misenus ab alta
Ære cavo: invadunt socii, et nova prælia tentant,
Obscænas pelagi ferro fædare volucres.
    Æneid, lib. iii. ver. 238.

Then as the harpies from the hills once more
Poured shrieking down, and crowded round the shore,
On his high stand Misenus *sounds* from far
The *brazen trump,* the signal of the war.
With unaccustomed fight, we flew to slay
The forms obscene, dread monsters of the sea.—*Pitt.*

The *metal* of which the instrument was made is used again for the *instrument* itself, in that fine passage of the same poet, Æneid, lib. ix. ver. 503, where he represents the Trojans rushing to battle against the Volscians :—

At tuba terribilem sonitum procul *ære canoro*
Increpuit: sequitur clamor, cælumque remugit.

And now the *trumpets,* terrible from far,
With rattling clangour rouse the sleepy war.
The soldiers' shouts succeed the *brazen sounds*
And heaven from pole to pole their noise rebounds.
    Dryden.

And again, in his *Battle of the Bees,* Geor., lib. iv. ver. 70 :—

————*namque morantes*
Martius ille æris rauci *cænor increpat, et vox*
Auditur fractos sonitus imitata tubarum.

With shouts the cowards' courage they excite,
And martial *clangours* call them out to fight;
With hoarse alarms the hollow camp rebounds,
That imitate the *trumpet's* angry sounds.
    Dryden

2

and though I give my body to be burned, and have not charity, it profiteth me nothing.

4 [e] Charity suffereth long, *and*

is kind; charity envieth not; charity [f] vaunteth not itself, is not puffed up,

5 Doth not behave itself un-

---

[e] Prov. x. 12 ; 1 Pet. iv. 8.

[f] Or, *is not rash.*

Examples of the same figure might be multiplied ; but these are sufficient.

Tinkling cymbal.] " The cymbal was a concavo-convex plate of brass, the concave side of which being struck against another plate of the same kind produced a tinkling, inharmonious sound." We may understand the apostle thus : "Though I possessed the knowledge of all languages, and could deliver even the *truth of God* in them in the most eloquent manner, and had not a heart full of love to God and man, producing *piety* and *obedience* to the ONE, and *benevolence* and *beneficence* to the *other*, doing unto all as I would wish them to do to me were our situations reversed, my religion is no more to my salvation than the sounds emitted by the brazen trumpet, or the jingling of the *cymbals* could contribute intellectual pleasure to the instruments which produce them ; and, in the sight of God, I am of no more moral worth than those *sounds* are. I have, it is true, a profession ; but, destitute of a heart filled with love to God and man, producing meekness, gentleness, long-suffering, &c., I am without the soul and essence of religion."

I have quoted several passages from heathens of the most cultivated minds in *Greece* and *Rome* to illustrate passages of the sacred writers. I shall now quote one from an *illiterate collier* of *Paulton*, in *Somerset ;* and, as I have named *Homer, Horace, Virgil,* and others, I will quote *Josiah Gregory,* whose mind might be compared to a diamond of the first water, whose native splendour broke in various places through its incrustations, but whose brilliancy was not *brought out* for want of the hand of the lapidary. Among various energetic sayings of this great, unlettered man, I remember to have heard the following : " People of *little religion* are always *noisy ;* he who has not the love of God and man filling his heart is like an *empty wagon* coming *violently* down a *hill :* it makes a *great noise,* because there is *nothing in it.*"

Verse 2. *And though I have* the gift of *prophecy*] Though I should have received from God the knowledge of future events, so that I could correctly foretell what is coming to pass in the world and in the Church ;—

And understand all mysteries] The meaning of all the types and figures in the Old Testament, and all the unexplored secrets of nature ; *and all knowledge*— every human art and science ; and *though I have all faith*—such miraculous faith as would enable me even to remove mountains ; or had such powerful discernment in sacred things that I could solve the greatest difficulties, see the note on Matt. xxi. 21, *and have not charity*—this love to God and man, as the principle and motive of all my conduct, the characteristics of which are given in the following verses ; *I am nothing* —nothing in *myself*, nothing in the sight of *God*, nothing in the *Church*, and good for nothing to *mankind*. Balaam, and several others not under the influence of this love of God, *prophesied ;* and we daily see many

men, who are profound *scholars*, and well skilled in *arts* and *sciences*, and yet not only careless about religion but downright infidels ! It does not require the tongue of the *inspired* to say that these men, in the sight of God, are *nothing ;* nor can their literary or scientific acquisitions give them a passport to glory.

Verse 3. *And though I bestow all my goods to feed the poor*] This is a proof that *charity*, in *our sense of the word*, is not what the apostle means ; for surely almsgiving can go no farther than to give up *all* that a man possesses in order to relieve the wants of others. The word ψωμιζω, which we translate *to feed the poor,* signifies to *divide into morsels, and put into the mouth ;* which implies *carefulness* and *tenderness* in applying the bounty thus freely given.

And though I give my body to be burned] Ἱνα καυθησομαι· Mr. Wakefield renders this clause thus : *And though I give up my body so as to have cause of boasting :* in vindication of which he, first, refers to Dan. iii. 28 ; Acts xv. 26 ; Rom. viii. 32 ; Phil. i. 20. 2. He says that there is no such word as καυθησωμαι. 3. That καυχησωμαι, *that I may boast,* is the reading of the Æthiopic and Coptic, and he might have added of the *Codex Alexandrinus ;* several *Greek* and *Latin* MSS. referred to by St. *Jerome ;* of *Ephraim ;* and of St. *Jerome* himself, who translates the passage thus : *Si tradidero corpus meum ut glorier :* i. e. " If I deliver up my body that I may *glory,* or have cause of *boasting.*" 4. He adds that *burning,* though a common punishment in after times, was not prevalent when this *epistle* was written.

Some of the foreign critics, particularly *Schulzius,* translate it thus : *Si traderem corpus, ut mihi stigma inureretur :* " If I should deliver up my body to receive a stigma with a hot iron ;" which may mean, If I should, in order to redeem another, willingly give up myself to *slavery,* and receive the *mark* of my owner, by having my flesh stamped with a hot iron, and have not *love,* as before specified, it profits me nothing. This gives a good sense ; but will the passage bear it ? In the MSS. there are several various readings, which plainly show the original copyists scarcely knew what to make of the word καυθησωμαι, which they found in the text generally. The various readings are, καυθησομαι, which Griesbach seems to prefer ; καυθησεται ; and καυθη ; all of which give little variation of meaning. Which should be preferred I can scarcely venture to say. If we take the commonly received word, it states a possible case ; a man may be so obstinately wedded to a particular opinion, demonstrably false in itself, as to give up his body to be burned in its defence, as was literally the case with *Vanini,* who, for his obstinate atheism, was burnt alive at Paris, February 19th, A. D. 1619. In such a cause, his *giving his body to be burned* certainly *profited him nothing.*

"We may observe," says Dr. Lightfoot, " in those

A. M. 4060.
A. D. 56.
A. U. C.
809.
Anno Imp. Nero-
nis Cæs. 3.

seemly, ^g seeketh not her own,
is not easily provoked, thinketh
no evil;

6 ^h Rejoiceth not in iniquity,
but ⁱ rejoiceth ^k in the truth;

7 ^l Beareth all things, believeth all things, hopeth all things,
endureth all things.

8 Charity never ^m faileth: but
whether *there be* prophecies, they shall fail;

A. M. 4060.
A. D. 56.
A. U. C.
809.
Anno Imp. Nero-
nis Cæs. 3.

---

^g Chapter x. 24; Phil. ii. 4.——^h Psa. x. 3; Romans i. 32.
ⁱ 2 John 4.——^k Or, *with the truth.*

^l Rom. xv. 1; Gal. vi. 2; 2 Tim. ii. 24.——^m Chap. xii. 31;
Phil. i. 9–11; 2 Pet. i. 19; Rev. xxii. 4, 5.

---

instances which are compared with *charity,* and are as good as nothing if charity be absent, that the apostle mentions those which were of the noblest esteem in the Jewish nation; and also that the most precious things that could be named by them were compared with this more precious, and were of no account in comparison of it.

" 1. To *speak with the tongues of men,* among the Jewish interpreters, means, to speak the languages of the *seventy* nations. To the praise of *Mordecai,* they say that he understood all those languages; and they require that the fathers of the Sanhedrin should be skilled in many languages that they may not be obliged to hear any thing by an interpreter. Maim. in Sanh., c. 2.

" 2. To *speak with the tongues of angels* they thought to be not only an excellent gift, but to be possible; and highly extol *Jochanan ben Zaccai* because he understood them: see the note on ver. 1.

" 3. To *know all mysteries and all knowledge* was not only prized but affected by them. Of Hillel, the elder, they say he had *eighty* disciples: *thirty* who were worthy to have the Holy Spirit dwell upon them, as it did upon Moses; *thirty* who were worthy that the sun should stop his course for them, as it did for Joshua; and there were *twenty* between both. The greatest of all was *Jonathan ben Uzziel;* the least was *Jochanan ben Zaccai.* He omitted not (i. e. perfectly understood) the Scripture, the Mishna, the Gemara, the idiotisms of the law, and the scribes, traditions, illustrations, comparisons, equalities, gematries, parables, &c.

" 4. The *moving* or *rooting up of mountains,* which among them signified the removing of the *greatest difficulties,* especially from the sacred text, they considered also a high and glorious attainment: see the note on Matt. xxi. 21. And of his salvation, who had it, they could not have formed the slightest doubt. But the apostle says, a man might have and enjoy all those gifts, &c., and be nothing in himself, and be nothing profited by them."

The reader will consider that the *charity* or *love,* concerning which the apostle speaks, is that which is described from ver. 4 to 7, inclusive: it is not left to the conjectures of men to find it out. What the apostle means is generally allowed to be *true religion;* but if he had not described it, this true religion would have been as *various* as the parties are who suppose they have it. Let the reader also observe that, not only the things which are in the highest repute among the Jews, but the things which are in the highest repute among Christians and Gentiles are those which the apostle shows to be of no use, if the *love* hereafter described be wanting. And yet, who can suppose that the man already described can be destitute of true

religion, as he must be under an especial influence of God; else, how, 1st, could he speak all the *languages of men?* for this was allowed to be one of the extraordinary gifts of God's Spirit. 2. He must have Divine teaching to know the *language of angels,* and thus to get acquainted with the economy of the invisible world. 3. Without immediate influence from God he could not be a *prophet,* and predict future events. 4. Without this he could not *understand* all the *mysteries* of the Divine word, nor those of Providence. 5. All *knowledge,* suppose this to be confined to human arts and sciences, could not be acquired without especial assistance. 6. And without the most powerful and extraordinary assistance, he could not have a faith that could remove mountains, or miraculous faith of any kind: and the apostle supposes that a man might have all these *six* things, and not possess that religion which could save his soul! And may we not say that, if all these could not avail for salvation, a thousand times less surely cannot. How blindly, therefore, are multitudes of persons trusting in that which is almost infinitely less than that which the apostle says *would profit them nothing!*

The charity or love which God recommends, the apostle describes in sixteen particulars, which are the following:—

Verse 4. (1.) *Charity suffereth long*] Μακροθυμει, *Has a long mind;* to the *end* of which neither trials, adversities, persecutions, nor provocations, can reach. The love of God, and of our *neighbour* for God's sake, is patient towards all men: it suffers all the weakness, ignorance, errors, and infirmities of the children of God; and all the malice and wickedness of the children of this world; and all this, not merely for a *time,* but *long,* without end; for it is still a *mind* or *disposition,* to the *end* of which trials, difficulties, &c., can never reach. It also waits God's time of accomplishing his gracious or providential purposes, without murmuring or repining; and bears its own infirmities, as well as those of others, with humble submission to the will of God.

(2.) *Is kind*] Χρηστευεται· It is tender and compassionate in itself, and *kind* and *obliging* to others; it is mild, gentle, and benign; and, if called to suffer, inspires the sufferer with the most amiable sweetness, and the most tender affection. It is also submissive to all the dispensations of God; and creates trouble to no one.

(3.) *Charity envieth not*] Ου ζηλοι· Is not grieved because another possesses a greater portion of earthly, intellectual, or spiritual blessings. Those who have this pure love rejoice as much at the happiness, the honour, and comfort of others, as they can do in their own. They are ever willing that *others* should be preferred before *them.*

2

A. M. 4060.
A. D. 56.
A. U. C.
809.
Anno Imp. Nero-
nis Cæs. 3.

whether *there be* tongues, they shall cease ; whether *there be* knowledge, it shall vanish away.

9 [n] For we know in part, and we prophesy in part ;

10 But when that which is [o]perfect is come, then that

A. M. 4060.
A. D. 56.
A. U. C.
809.
Anno Imp. Nero-
nis Cæs. 3.

---

[n] Chap. viii. 2 ; John xvi. 13.   [o] Heb. vii. 28 ; Rev. xxi. 1.

(4.) *Charity vaunteth not itself*] Ου περπερευεται· This word is variously translated ; *acteth not rashly, insolently ;* is not *inconstant, &c.* It is not agreed by learned men whether it be *Greek, Latin,* or *Arabic.* Bishop Pearce derived it from the latter language ; and translates it, *is not inconstant.* There is a phrase in our own language that expresses what I think to be the meaning of the original, does not *set itself forward* —does not desire to be noticed or applauded ; but wishes that God may be all in all.

(5.) *Is not puffed up*] Ου φυσιουται· Is not *in-flated* with a sense of its own importance ; for it knows it has nothing but what it has received ; and that it deserves nothing that it has got. Every man, whose heart is full of the love of God, is full of humility ; for there is no man so humble as he whose heart is cleansed from all sin. It has been said that indwelling sin humbles us ; never was there a greater *falsity :* PRIDE is the very essence of *sin ;* he who has sin has *pride,* and pride too in proportion to his sin : this is a mere popish doctrine ; and, strange to tell, the doctrine in which their doctrine of *merit* is founded ! They say God leaves concupiscence in the heart of every Christian, that, in striving with and overcoming it from time to time, he may have an accumulation of meritorious acts. Certain Protestants say, it is a true sign of a very gracious state when a man *feels* and deplores his inbred corruptions. How near do these come to the Papists, whose doctrine they profess to detest and abhor ! The truth is, it is no sign of grace whatever ; it only argues, as they use it, that the man has got *light* to show him his corruptions ; but he has not yet got *grace* to destroy them. He is convinced that he should have the mind of Christ, but he feels that he has the mind of Satan ; he deplores it, and, if his bad doctrine do not prevent him, he will not rest till he feels the blood of Christ cleansing him from all sin.

True humility arises from a sense of the fulness of God in the soul ; abasement from a sense of corruption is a widely different thing ; but this has been put in the place of humility, and even called grace : many, very many, verify the saying of the poet :—

" Proud I am my wants to see ;
Proud of my humility."

Verse 5. (6.) *Doth not behave itself unseemly*] Ουκ ασχημονει, from α, *negative,* and σχημα, *figure, mein ;* love never acts out of its place or character ; observes due decorum and good manners ; is never *rude, bearish,* or *brutish ;* and is ever willing to become all things to all men, that it may please them for their good to edification. No ill-bred man, or what is termed *rude* or *unmannerly,* is a Christian. A man may have a natural bluntness, or be a clown, and yet there be nothing *boorish* or *hoggish* in his manner. I must apologize for using such words ; they best express the evil against which I wish both powerfully

and successfully to declaim. I never wish to meet with those who *affect* to be called " blunt, honest men ;" who feel themselves above all the forms of respect and civility, and care not how many they put to pain, or how many they displease. But let me not be misunderstood ; I do not contend for *ridiculous ceremonies,* and *hollow compliments ;* there is surely a *medium :* and a sensible Christian man will not be long at a loss to find it out. Even *that people* who profess to be above all worldly forms, and are generally *stiff* enough, yet are rarely found to be *rude, uncivil,* or *ill-bred.*

(7.) *Seeketh not her own*] Ου ζητει τα ἑαυτης· Is not desirous of her own spiritual welfare only, but of her neighbour's also : for the writers of the Old and New Testament do, almost every where, agreeably to their Hebrew idiom, express a *preference* given to one thing before another by an *affirmation* of that which is *preferred,* and a *negative* of that which is *contrary* to it. See Bishop Pearce, and see the notes on chap. i. 17, and chap. x. 24, 33. Love is never satisfied but in the welfare, comfort, and salvation of *all.* That man is no Christian who is solicitous for his own happiness alone ; and cares not how the world goes, so that himself be comfortable.

(8.) *Is not easily provoked*] Ου παροξυνεται· Is not *provoked, is not irritated, is not made sour* or *bitter.* How the word *easily* got into our translation it is hard to say ; but, however it got in, it is utterly improper, and has nothing in the original to countenance it. By the transcript from my old MS., which certainly contains the *first translation* ever made in English, we find that the word did not exist there the conscientious translator rendering it thus :— It is not stirid to wrath.

The New Testament, printed in 1547, 4to., the first year of Edward VI., in English and Latin, has simply, is not provoked to angre. The edition published in English in the following year, 1548, has the same rendering, but the orthography better : is not provoked to anger. The Bible in folio, with notes, published the next year, 1549, by *Edmund Becke,* preserves nearly the same reading, is not provoketh to anger. The large folio printed by *Richard Cardmarden,* at Rouen, 1566, has the same reading. The translation made and printed by the command of King James I., fol., 1611, &c. departs from all these, and improperly inserts the word *easily,* which might have been his majesty's own ; and yet this translation was not followed by some subsequent editions ; for the 4to. Bible printed at London four years after, 1615, not only retains this original and correct reading, *it is not provoked to anger,* but has the word *love* every where in this chapter instead of *charity,* in which all the preceding versions and editions agree. In short, this is the reading of *Coverdale, Matthews, Cranmer,* the *Geneva,* and others ; and our own authorized version

A. M. 4060.
A. D. 56.
A. U. C.
809.
Annc Imp Nero-
nis Cæs. 3.

which is in part shall be done away.

11 When I was a child, I spake as a child, I understood

as a child, I [p] thought as a child; but when I became a man, I put away childish things.

12 For [q] now we see through

A. M. 4060.
A. D. 56.
A. U. C.
809.
Anno Imp. Nero
nis Cæs. 3.

[p] Or, *reasoned.*

[q] 2 Cor. iii. 18; v. 7; Phil. iii. 12

is the only one which I have seen. where this *false* reading appears.

As to the ancient versions, they all, Vulgate, Syriac, Arabic, Æthiopic, Coptic, and Itala, strictly follow the Greek text; and supply no word that tends to abate the signification of the apostle's ου παροξυνεται, is not provoked; nor is there a *various reading* here in all the numerous MSS. It is of importance to make these observations, because the common version of this place destroys the meaning of the apostle, and makes him speak very improperly. If love IS *provoked* at all, it then ceases to be *love;* and if it be not *easily* provoked, this grants, as almost all the commentators say, that in special cases it *may* be *provoked;* and this they instance in the case of Paul and Barnabas, Acts xv. 39; but I have sufficiently vindicated this passage in my note on that place, and given at large the meaning of the word παροξυνω; and to that place I beg leave to refer the reader. The apostle's own words in ver. 7 are a sufficient proof that the love of which he speaks can *never* be *provoked.* When the man who possesses this love gives way to provocation, he *loses* the balance of his soul, and grieves the Spirit of God. In that instant he ceases from loving God with all his soul, mind, and strength; and surely if he get *embittered* against his neighbour, he does not *love* him as himself. It is generally said that, though a man may feel himself highly *irritated* against the *sin,* he may feel tender concern for the *sinner. Irritation* of any kind is inconsistent with self-government, and consequently with internal peace and communion with God. However favourably we may think of our own state, and however industrious we may be to find out excuses for sallies of passion, &c., still the testimony of God is, *Love is not provoked;* and if I have not such a love, whatever else I may possess, *it profiteth me nothing.*

(9.) *Thinketh no evil*] Ουλογιζεται το κακον· " Believes no evil where no evil seems." Never supposes that a good action may have a bad motive; gives every man credit for his profession of religion, uprightness, godly zeal, &c., while nothing is seen in his *conduct* or in his *spirit* inconsistent with this profession. His heart is so governed and influenced by the love of God, that he cannot think of evil but where it appears. The original implies that he does not *invent* or *devise* any evil; or, does not *reason* on any particular act or word so as to *infer* evil from it; for this would destroy his love to his brother; it would be ruinous to *charity* and benevolence.

Verse 6. (10.) *Rejoiceth not in iniquity*] Ου χαιρει επι τη αδικια· *Rejoiceth not in falsehood,* but on the contrary, *rejoiceth in the truth:* this meaning αδικια has in different parts of the Scriptures. At first view, this character of love seems to say but little in its favour; for who can rejoice in unrighteousness or falsity? But is it not a frequent case that persons,

who have received any kind of injury, and have forborne to avenge themselves, but perhaps have left it to God; when evil falls upon the sinner do console themselves with what appears to them an evidence that God has *avenged their quarrels;* and do at least secretly rejoice that the man is suffering for his misdeeds? Is not this, in some sort, rejoicing in iniquity? Again: is it not common for interested persons to rejoice in the successes of an unjust and sanguinary war, in the sackage and burning of cities and towns; and is not the joy always in proportion to the slaughter that has been made of the enemy? And do these call themselves *Christians?* Then we may expect that Moloch and his sub-devils are not so far behind this description of Christians as to render their case utterly desperate. If such Christians can be saved, demons need not despair!

(11.) *But rejoiceth in the truth*] Αληθεια· Every thing that is opposite to falsehood and irreligion. Those who are filled with the love of God and man rejoice in the propagation and extension of Divine truth—in the spread of true religion, by which alone peace and good will can be diffused throughout the earth. And because they rejoice in the truth, therefore they do not persecute nor hinder true religion, but help it forward with all their might and power.

Verse 7. (12.) *Beareth all things*] Παντα στεγει. This word is also variously interpreted; to *endure, bear, sustain, cover, conceal, contain.* Bishop Pearce contends that it should be translated *covereth all things,* and produces several plausible reasons for this translation; the most forcible of which is, that the common translation confounds it with *endureth all things,* in the same verse. We well know that it is a grand and distinguishing property of *love* to *cover* and *conceal* the *fault* of another; and it is certainly better to consider the passage in this light than in that which our common version holds out; and this perfectly agrees with what St. Peter says of charity, 1 Pet. iv. 8: *It shall cover the multitude of sins;* but there is not sufficient evidence that the original will fully bear this sense; and perhaps it would be better to take it in the sense of *contain, keep in,* as a vessel does liquor; thus Plato compared the souls of foolish men to a seive, and *not able,* στεγειν δια απιστιαν τε και ληθην, *to contain any thing through unfaithfulness and forgetfulness.* See *Parkhurst* and *Wetstein.* Some of the versions have στεργει, *loveth,* or is *warmly affectioned* to all things or persons. But the true import must be found either in *cover* or *contain. Love conceals* every thing that should be concealed; betrays no secret; *retains* the grace given; and goes on to continual increase. A person under the influence of this love never makes the sins, follies, faults, or imperfections of any man, the subject either of censure or conversation. He *covers* them as far as he *can;* and if

A. M. 4060.
A. D. 56.
A. U. C.
809.
Anno Imp. Nero-
nis Cæs. 3.

a glass, ʳ darkly; but then ˢ face to face: now I know in part; but then shall I know even as also I am known.

13 And now abideth faith, hope, charity, these three; but the ᵗ greatest of these *is* charity.

A. M. 4060.
A. D. 56.
A. U. C.
809.
Anno Imp. Nero-
nis Cæs. 3.

ʳ Gr. *in a riddle.*——ˢ Matt. xviii. 10; 1 John iii. 2.

ᵗ Chap. xv. 19; Rom. xiii. 8–10.

---

alone privy to them, he *retains* the knowledge of them in his own bosom as far as he *ought.*

(13.) *Believeth all things*] Παντα πιστευει· Is ever ready to believe the *best* of every person, and will credit no evil of any but on the most positive evidence; gladly receives whatever may tend to the *advantage* of any person whose character may have suffered from obloquy and detraction; or even *justly,* because of his *misconduct.*

(14.) *Hopeth all things*] Παντα ελπιζει· When there is no place left for *believing good* of a person, then love comes in with its *hope,* where it could not *work* by its *faith;* and begins immediately to make allowances and excuses, as far as a good conscience can permit; and farther, anticipates the *repentance* of the transgressor, and his restoration to the good opinion of society and his place in the Church of God, from which he had fallen.

(15.) *Endureth all things.*] Παντα ὑπομενει· Bears up under all persecutions and mal-treatment from open enemies and professed friends; bears adversities with an even mind, as it submits with perfect resignation to every dispensation of the providence of God; and never says of any trial, affliction, or insult, *this cannot be endured.*

Verse 8. (16.) *Charity never faileth*] Ἡ αγαπη ουδεποτε εκπιπτει· *This love never falleth off,* because it *bears, believes, hopes,* and *endures* all things; and while it does so it cannot *fail;* it is the means of *preserving* all other graces; indeed, properly speaking, it includes them all; and all receive their perfection from it. Love to God and man can never be dispensed with. It is essential to social and religious life; without it no communion can be kept up with God; nor can any man have a preparation for eternal glory whose heart and soul are not deeply imbued with it. Without it there never was true religion, nor ever can be; and it not only is necessary through life, but will exist throughout eternity. What were a state of blessedness if it did not comprehend love to God and human spirits in the most exquisite, refined, and perfect degrees?

Prophecies—shall fail] Whether the word imply *predicting* future events, or *teaching* the truths of religion to men, all such shall soon be rendered useless. Though the accurate prophet and the eloquent, persuasive preacher be useful in their day, they shall not be always so; nor shall their gifts fit them for glory; nothing short of the love above described can fit a soul for the kingdom of God.

Tongues—shall cease] The miraculous gift of different languages, that also shall cease, as being unnecessary.

Knowledge—shall vanish away.] All human arts and sciences, as being utterly useless in the eternal world, though so highly extolled and useful here.

Verse 9. *For we know in part*] We have here but little knowledge even of *earthly,* and much less of *heavenly,* things. He that knows most knows little in comparison of what is known by angels, and the spirits of just men made perfect. And as we *know* so very little, how deficient must we be if we have not much *love!* Angels may wonder at the imperfection of our knowledge; and separate spirits may wonder at the perfection of their own, having obtained so much more in consequence of being separated from the body, than they could conceive to be possible while in that body. When Sir Isaac Newton had made such astonishing discoveries in the laws of nature, far surpassing any thing that had been done by all his predecessors in science from the days of Solomon; one of our poets, considering the scantiness of human knowledge when compared with that which is possessed by the inhabitants of heaven, reduced his meditations on the subject to the following nervous and expressive epigram :—

Superior beings, when of late they saw
A mortal man explain all nature's law,
Admired such wisdom in an *earthly* shape,
And show'd our Newton as *we* show an *ape.*

These fine lines are a paraphrase from a saying of Plato, from whom our poet borrows without acknowledging the debt. The words are these : ανθρωπων ὁ σοφωτατος προς θεον πιθηκος φανειται· "The wisest of mortals will appear but an ape in the estimation of God." Vid. Hipp. Maj. vol. xi. p. 21. Edit. Bipont.

We prophesy in part] Even the sublimest *prophets* have been able to say but little of the heavenly state; and the best *preachers* have left the *Spirit* of God very much to supply. And had we no more religious knowledge than we can derive from men and books, and had we no farther instruction in the knowledge of God and ourselves than we derive from preaching, our religious experience would be low indeed. Yet it is our duty to acquire all the knowledge we possibly can; and as preaching is the *ordinary means* by which God is pleased to instruct and convert the soul, we should diligently and thankfully use it. For we have neither reason nor Scripture to suppose that God will give us that immediately from himself which he has promised to convey only by the use of *means.* Even this his blessing makes effectual; and, after all, his *Spirit* supplies much that *man* cannot teach. Every preacher should take care to inculcate this on the hearts of his hearers. When you have learned all you can from your ministers, remember you have much to learn from God; and for this you should diligently wait on him by the reading of his word, and by incessant prayer.

Verse 10. *But when that which is perfect*] The state of eternal blessedness; *then that which is in part—*that which is *imperfect,* shall be done away;

2

the *imperfect* as well as the *probationary* state shall cease for ever.

Verse 11. *When I was a child*] This future state of blessedness is as far beyond the utmost perfection that can be attained in this world, as our adult state of Christianity is above our state of natural infancy, in which we understand only as children understand; speak only a few broken articulate words, and reason only as children reason; having few ideas, little knowledge but what may be called mere instinct, and that much less perfect than the instinct of the brute creation; and having no experience. But when we became *men*—adults, having gained much knowledge of men and things, we spoke and reasoned more correctly, having left off all the manners and habits of our childhood.

Verse 12. *Now we see through a glass, darkly*] Δι' εσοπτρου εν αινιγματι. Of these words some *literal* explanation is necessary. The word εσοπτρον, which we translate *a glass*, literally signifies a mirror or reflector, from εις, *into*, and οπτομαι, *I look*; and among the ancients mirrors were certainly made of fine polished *metal* The word here may signify any thing by which the image of a person is reflected, as in our *looking*, or *look in glass*. The word is not used for a glass to *look through*; nor would such an image have suited with the apostle's design.

The εσοπτρον, or *mirror*, is mentioned by some of the most ancient Greek writers; so *Anacreon*, Ode xi. ver. 1:—

Λεγουσιν αι γυναικες,
Ανακρεων, γερων ει·
Λαβων ΕΣΟΠΤΡΟΝ αθρει
Κομας μεν ουκετ' ουσας.

The women tell me,
Anacreon, thou art grown old;
Take thy *mirror*, and view
How few of thy hairs remain.

And again, in Ode xx. ver. 5:—

Εγω δ' εσοπτρον ειην,
Ὁπως αει βλεπης με.

I wish I were a *mirror*
That thou mightst always look into me.

In Exod. xxxviii. 8, we meet with the term *looking glasses*; but the original is מראת *maroth*, and should be translated *mirrors*; as out of those very articles, which we absurdly translate *looking* GLASSES, the *brazen* laver was made!

In the Greek version the word εσοπτρον is not found but twice, and that in the apocryphal books. In the book of the Wisdom of Solomon, chap. vii. 26, speaking of *wisdom* the author says: "She is the brightness of the everlasting light, και εσοπτρον ακηλιδωτον, and the *unspotted mirror* of the power of God, and the image of his goodness."

In Ecclus. xii. 11, exhorting to put no trust in an *enemy*, he says: "Though he humble himself, and go crouching, yet take good heed and beware of him, and thou shalt be unto him, ὡς εκμεμαχως εσοπτρον, as if thou hadst wiped a *looking glass*, (mirror,) and thou shalt know that his *rust* hath not altogether been wiped

away." All these passages must be understood of *polished metal*, not of *glass*, which, though it existed among the Romans and others, yet was brought to very little perfection; and as to *grinding* and *silvering* of glass, they are modern inventions.

Some have thought that the apostle refers to something of the *telescopic* kind, by which *distant* and *small* objects become visible, although their surfaces become *dim* in proportion to the quantum of the *magnifying* power; but this is too refined; he appears simply to refer to a *mirror* by which images were *reflected*, and not to any *diaphanous* and *magnifying* powers, *through* which objects were perceived.

Possibly the true meaning of the words δι' εσοπτρου εν αινιγματι, *through a glass darkly*, may be found among the Jewish writers, who use a similar term to express nearly the same thing to which the apostle refers. A revelation of the will of God, in *clear* and *express* terms, is called by them אספקלריא מאירה *aspecularia maira*, a *clear* or *lucid glass*, or *specular* in reference, *specularibus lapidibus*, to the *diaphanous polished stones*, used by the ancients for *windows* instead of *glass*. An *obscure* prophecy they termed אספקלריא דלא נהריא *aspecularia dela naharia*, "a specular which is not clear."

Num. xii. 6: *If there be a prophet—I the Lord will make myself known unto him in a vision, and I will speak unto him in a dream*; Rab. Tanchum thus explains: "My Shechinah shall not be revealed to him, באספקלריא מאירה *beaspecularia maira*, in a *lucid specular*, but only in a dream and a vision."

On Ezek. i. 4, 5: *And I looked, and behold a whirlwind—a great cloud, and a fire unfolding itself, &c.*; Sohar Chadash, fol. 33, says: "This is a vision באספקלריא דלא נהרא *beaspecularia dela nahara*, by an obscure or dark specular."

From a great variety of examples produced by Schoettgen it appears that the rabbins make a great deal of difference between seeing through the *lucid glass* or *specular*, and seeing through the *obscure one*. The first is attributed only to Moses, who conversed with God *face to face*, i. e. through the *lucid specular*; and between the other prophets, who saw him in *dreams* and *visions*, i. e. through the *obscure specular*. In these distinctions and sayings of the ancient Jews we must seek for that to which the apostle alludes. See Schoettgen.

The word αινιγματι, which we render *darkly*, will help us to the true meaning of the place. The following is Mr. *Parkhurst's* definition of the *term* and of the *thing*: "Αινιγμα, from ηνιγμαι, the *perfect passive* of ιανιττω, to *hint*, *intimate*, *signify* with some degree of obscurity; an enigma, in which one thing *answers* or stands in correspondence to, or as the *representative* of, another, which is in *some respects similar* to it; occurs chap. xiii. 12: *Now*—in this life, *we see by means of a mirror* reflecting the images of heavenly and spiritual things, εν αινιγματι, in an enigmatical manner, invisible things being represented by visible, spiritual by natural, eternal by temporal; *but then*—in the eternal world, *face to face*, every thing being seen in itself, and not by means of a representative or similitude."

Now I know in part] Though I have an immediate revelation from God concerning his **great design** in the dispensation of the Gospel, yet there are lengths, breadths, depths, and heights of this design, which even that revelation has not discovered ; nor can they be known and apprehended in the present imperfect state. Eternity alone can unfold the whole scheme of the Gospel.

As—I am known.] In the same manner in which disembodied spirits know and understand.

Verse 13. *And now* [in this present life] *abideth faith, hope, charity*] These three supply the place of that *direct vision* which no human *embodied* spirit can have ; these *abide* or *remain* for the present state. *Faith*, by which we apprehend spiritual blessings, and walk with God. *Hope*, by which we view and expect eternal blessedness, and pass through things temporal so as not to lose those which are eternal. *Charity* or *love*, by which we show forth the virtues of the grace which we receive by faith in living a life of obedience to God, and of good will and usefulness to man.

But the greatest of these is charity.] Without *faith* it is impossible to please God ; and without it, we cannot partake of the grace of our Lord Jesus : without *hope* we could not *endure*, as seeing him who is invisible ; nor have any adequate notion of the eternal world ; nor *bear up* under the afflictions and difficulties of life : but great and useful and indispensably necessary as these are, yet *charity* or *love* is *greater :* LOVE is the *fulfilling of the law ;* but this is never said of *faith* or *hope*.

It may be necessary to enter more particularly into a consideration of the *conclusion* of this very important chapter.

1. *Love* is properly the *image of God* in the soul ; for *God is* LOVE. By *faith* we *receive* from our Maker ; by *hope* we *expect* a future and eternal good ; but by *love* we *resemble God ;* and by it alone are we *qualified* to *enjoy* heaven, and be one with him throughout eternity. *Faith*, says one, is the *foundation* of the Christian life, and of good works ; *hope* rears the *superstructure ;* but love *finishes, completes, and crowns* it in a blessed eternity. *Faith* and *hope* respect *ourselves* alone ; *love* takes in both GOD and MAN. *Faith* helps, and *hope* sustains us ; but love to God and man makes us *obedient* and *useful*. This one consideration is sufficient to show that *love* is *greater* than either *faith* or *hope*.

2. Some say *love* is the *greatest* because it *remains* throughout eternity, whereas *faith* and *hope* proceed only through *life ;* hence we say that *there faith* is lost in *sight*, and hope in *fruition*. But does the apostle say so ? Or does any man *inspired* by God say so ? I believe not. *Faith* and *hope* will as necessarily enter into eternal glory as *love* will. The perfections of God are absolute in their nature, infinite in number, and eternal in their duration. However high, glorious, or sublime the soul may be in that eternal state, it will ever, in respect to God, be *limited* in its powers, and must be *improved* and *expanded* by the *communications* of the supreme Being. Hence it will have infinite glories in the nature of God to *apprehend* by *faith*, to *anticipate* by *hope*, and *enjoy* by *love*.

3. From the nature of the Divine perfections there must be infinite glories in them which must be objects

of *faith* to disembodied spirits ; because it is impossible that they should be *experimentally* or *possessively known* by any creature. Even in the heaven of heavens we shall, in reference to the infinite and eternal excellences of God, *walk by faith*, and *not by sight*. We shall *credit* the existence of infinite and illimitable glories in him, which, from their *absolute* and *infinite* nature, must be incommunicable. And as the very nature of the soul shows it to be capable of eternal *growth* and *improvement ;* so the communications from the Deity, which are to produce this growth, and effect this improvement, must be objects of *faith* to the pure spirit ; and, if objects of *faith*, consequently *objects* of *hope ;* for as *hope* is " the expectation of future good," it is inseparable from the nature of the soul, to *know* of the existence of any attainable good without making it immediately the object of *desire* or *hope*. And is it not this that shall constitute the eternal and progressive happiness of the immortal spirit ; viz. knowing, from what it has received, that there is infinitely more to be received ; and desiring to be put in possession of every communicable good which it knows to exist ?

4. As *faith* goes forward to *view*, so *hope* goes forward to *desire ;* and God continues to *communicate ;* every communication making way for another, by preparing the soul for greater enjoyment, and this enjoyment must produce *love*. To say that the soul can have neither *faith* nor *hope* in a future state is to say that, as soon as it enters heaven, it is as happy as it can possibly be ; and this goes to exclude all *growth* in the eternal state, and all *progressive manifestations* and *communications* of God ; and consequently to fix a spirit, which is a composition of infinite desires, in a state of eternal *sameness*, in which it must be greatly changed in its constitution to find endless gratification.

5. To sum up the reasoning on this subject I think it necessary to observe, 1. That the term *faith* is here to be taken in the general sense of the word, for that belief which a soul has of the infinite sufficiency and goodness of God, in consequence of the discoveries he has made of himself and his designs, either by *revelation*, or immediately by his *Spirit*. Now we know that God has revealed himself not only in reference to *this world*, but in reference to *eternity ;* and much of our *faith* is employed in things pertaining to the *eternal world*, and the *enjoyments* in that state. 2. That *hope* is to be taken in its common acceptation, *the expectation of future good ;* which expectation is necessarily founded on *faith*, as faith is founded on knowledge. God gives a revelation which concerns both worlds, containing exceeding great and precious promises relative to *both*. We *believe* what he has said on his own *veracity ;* and we *hope* to enjoy the promised blessings in both worlds, because he is *faithful* who has promised. 3. As the promises stand in reference to both worlds, so also must the *faith* and *hope* to which these promises stand as objects. 4. The enjoyments in the eternal world are all spiritual, and must proceed immediately from God himself. 5. God, in the plenitude of his excellences, is as incomprehensible to a glorified spirit, as he is to a spirit resident in flesh and blood. 6. Every created, intellectual nature is capable of eternal improvement. 7. If

seeing God as he is be essential to the eternal happiness of beatified spirits, then the discoveries which he makes of himself must be *gradual;* forasmuch as it is impossible that an infinite, eternal nature can be manifested to a created and limited nature in any other way. 8. As the perfections of God are infinite, they are capable of being eternally *manifested,* and, after all manifestations, there must be an infinitude of perfections still to be brought to view. 9. As every soul that has any just notion of God must know that he is possessed of all possible perfections, so these perfections, being objects of *knowledge,* must be objects of *faith.* 10. Every holy spirit feels itself possessed of *unlimited desires* for the enjoyment of spiritual good, and *faith* in the infinite goodness of God necessarily implies that he will satisfy every desire he has excited. 11. The *power to gratify,* in the Divine Being, and the *capacity* to be *gratified,* in the immortal spirit, will necessarily excite continual *desires,* which desires, on the evidence of *faith,* will as necessarily produce *hope,* which is the *expectation of future good.* 12. All possible perfections in God are the objects of *faith ;* and the communication of all possible blessedness, the object of *hope.* 13. Faith goes forward to *apprehend,* and hope to *anticipate,* as God continues to *discover* his unbounded glories and perfections. 14. Thus discovered and desired, their influences become communicated, love *possesses* them, and is *excited* and *increased* by the communication. 15. With respect to those which are communicated, *faith* and *hope* cease, and go forward to *new appre-*

hensions and *anticipations,* while *love* continues to *retain* and *enjoy the whole.* 16. Thus an eternal interest is kept up, and infinite blessings, in endless succession, *apprehended, anticipated* and *enjoyed.*

6. My opinion that *faith* and *hope,* as well as *love,* will continue in a future state, will no doubt appear singular to many who have generally considered the two former as necessarily terminating in this lower world ; but this arises from an improper notion of the beatified state, and from inattention to the state and capacity of the soul. If it have the same faculties *there* which it has *here,* howsoever improved they may be, it must acquire its happiness from the supreme Being in the way of *communication,* and this communication must necessarily be *gradual* for the reasons already alleged ; and if gradual, then there must be (if in that state we have any *knowledge* at all of the Divine nature) *faith* that such things exist, and may be communicated ; *desire* to possess them because they are good ; and *hope* that these good things shall be communicated.

7. I conclude, therefore, from these and a multitude of other reasonings which might be brought to bear on this subject, that *faith* and *hope* will exist in the eternal world as well as *love ;* and that *there,* as well as *here,* it may endlessly be said, the greatest of these is love. With great propriety therefore does the apostle exhort, *Follow after love,* it being so essential to our comfort and happiness here, and to our beatification in the eternal world ; and how necessary faith and hope are to the same end we have already seen.

CHAPTER XIV.

We should earnestly desire spiritual gifts ; but prophesying is to be preferred, because it is superior to the gift of tongues, 1, 2. Prophesying defined, 3. How to regulate this supernatural gift of tongues, in teaching for the edification of the Church, 4—13. In praying and giving thanks, 14—17. Those who speak with tongues should interpret that others may be edified, 18—22. What benefit may accrue from this in the public assemblies, 23—28. How the prophets or teachers should act in the Church, 29—33. Women should keep silence in the church, 34, 35. All should be humble, and every thing should be done in love, 36—40.

A. M. 4060.
A. D. 56.
A. U. C. 809.
Anno Imp. Neronis Cæs. 3.

FOLLOW after charity, and [a] desire spiritual *gifts ;* but [b] rather that ye may prophesy.

2 For he that [c] speaketh in an *unknown* tongue speaketh not unto men, but unto God : for no man [d] understandeth *him;* howbeit in the spirit he speaketh mysteries.

A. M. 4060.
A. D. 56.
A. U. C. 809.
Anno Imp. Nero nis Cæs. 3.

---

[a] Chap. xii. 31.——[b] Num. xi. 25, 29.

[c] Acts ii. 4 ; x. 46.——[d] Gr. *heareth ;* Acts xxii. 9.

NOTES ON CHAP. XIV.

Verse 1. *Follow after charity*] Most earnestly labour to be put in possession of that love which beareth, believeth, hopeth, and endureth all things. It may be difficult to acquire, and difficult to retain this blessed state, but it is essential to your present peace and eternal happiness. This clause belongs to the preceding chapter.

Desire spiritual gifts] Ye are very intent on getting those *splendid* gifts which may add to your worldly consequence, and please your carnal minds ; but labour rather to get the gifts of God's Spirit, by which ye may grow in grace, and be useful to others ; and particularly desire that *ye may prophesy*——that ye may be

able to *teach* and *instruct* others in the things of their salvation.

Verse 2. *For he that speaketh in an* unknown *tongue*] This chapter is crowded with difficulties. It is not likely that the Holy Spirit should, in the church, suddenly inspire a man with the knowledge of some foreign language, which none in the church understood but himself ; and lead him to treat the mysteries of Christianity in *that* language, though none in the place could profit by his teaching.

Dr. Lightfoot's mode of reconciling these difficulties is the most likely I have met with. He supposes that by the unknown *tongue* the *Hebrew* is meant, and that God restored the true knowledge of this language when

A. M. 4060.
A. D. 56.
A. U. C.
809.
Anno Imp. Nero-
nis Cæs. 3.

3 But he that prophesieth speaketh unto men to edification, and exhortation, and comfort.

4 He that speaketh in an *unknown* tongue edifieth himself; but he that prophesieth edifieth the Church.

5 I would that ye all spake with tongues, but rather that ye prophesied; for greater *is* he that prophesieth than he that speaketh with tongues, except he interpret, that the Church may receive edifying.

6 Now, brethren, if I come unto you speaking with tongues, what shall I profit you, except I shall speak to you either by ᵉ revelation, or by knowledge, or by prophesying, or by doctrine?

7 And even things without life giving sound, whether pipe or harp, except they give a distinction in the ᶠ sounds, how shall it be known what is piped or harped?

8 For if the trumpet give an uncertain sound,

A. M. 4060.
A. D. 56.
A. U. C.
809.
Anno Imp. Nero-
nis Cæs. 3.

ᵉ Verse 26.

ᶠ Or, *tunes.*

he gave the apostles the gift of tongues. As the Scriptures of the Old Testament were contained in this language, and it has beauties, energies, and depths in it which no verbal translation can reach, it was necessary, for the proper elucidation of the prophecies concerning the Messiah, and the establishment of the Christian religion, that the full meaning of the words of this sacred language should be properly understood. And it is possible that the Hebrew Scriptures were sometimes read in the Christian congregations as they were in the Jewish synagogues; and if the person who read and understood them had not the power and faculty of explaining them to others, in vain did he read and understand them himself. And we know that it is possible for a man to understand a language, the force, phraseology, and idioms of which he is incapable of explaining even in his mother tongue. We shall see, in the course of these notes, how this view of the subject will apply to the illustration of the apostle's words throughout the chapter.

Speaketh not unto men, but unto God] None present understanding the language, God alone knowing the truth and import of what he says :—

In the spirit he speaketh mysteries.] Though his *own mind* (for so πνευματι is understood here by many eminent critics) apprehends the mysteries contained in the words which he reads or utters; but if, by the *spirit*, we understand the Spirit of God, it only shows that it is by that Spirit that he is enabled to speak and apprehend these mysteries. See the note on ver. 19.

Verse 3. *But he that prophesieth*] The person who has the gift of *teaching* is much more useful to the Church than he is who has only the gift of *tongues*, because he speaks to the profit of men : viz. to their *edification*, by the Scriptures he expounds; to their *exhortation*, by what he teaches; and to their *comfort*, by his revelation.—*Whitby.* I must here refer to my sermon on this text, intituled, "The Christian Prophet and his Work," in which I have endeavoured to consider the whole of this subject at large.

Verse 4. *He that speaketh in an* unknown *tongue*] In the *Hebrew* for instance, the knowledge of the depth and power of which he has got by a Divine revelation, *edifieth himself* by that knowledge.

But he that prophesieth] Has the gift of preaching.

Edifieth the Church.] Speaketh unto men to *edification, exhortation,* and *comfort,* ver. 3.

Verse 5. *I would that ye all spake with tongues*]

The word θελω does not so much imply a *wish or desire,* as a *command* or *permission.* As if he had said : I do not restrain you to *prophesying* or *teaching,* though I prefer that; but I give you full permission to speak in *Hebrew* whenever it is proper, and when one is present who can interpret for the edification of the Church, provided yourselves have not that gift, though you understand the language. The apostle said *tongue,* in the singular number, ver. 2, 4, because he spoke of a *single man;* now he says *tongues,* in the plural number, because he speaks of *many* speaking; but he has the same meaning in both places.—*Lightfoot.*

Greater is *he that prophesieth*] A useful, zealous preacher, though unskilled in learned languages, is much *greater* in the sight of God, and in the eye of sound common sense, than he who has the gift of those learned tongues; *except he interpret* : and we seldom find *great scholars good preachers.* This should humble the scholar, who is too apt to be proud of his attainments, and despise his less learned but more useful brother. This judgment of St. Paul is too little regarded.

Verse 6. *Speaking with tongues*] Without interpreting.

What shall I profit you?] i. e. I shall not profit you;

Except I shall speak to you either by revelation] Of some secret thing; *or by knowledge,* of some mystery; *or by prophesying,* foretelling some future event ; *or by doctrine,* instructing you what to believe and practise.—See *Whitby.* These *four* words are taken in different acceptations by learned men. The general sense of the terms is that given above : but the peculiar meaning of the apostle is perhaps not easily discerned.

Verse 7. *And even things without life*] I may, as if he had said, illustrate this farther by referring to a *pipe or harp;* if these were to utter mere *sounds* without order, harmony, or melody, though every tone of music might be in the sounds, surely no person could discern a tune in such sounds, nor receive pleasure from such discords : even so is the person who speaks in an unknown tongue, but does not interpret. His speech tends no more to edification than those discordant and unmeaning sounds do to pleasure and delight.

Verse 8. *If the trumpet give an uncertain sound*] If, when the soldier should prepare himself for the battle, the trumpet should give a different sound to

     (18**)

A. M. 4060.
A. D. 56.
A. U. C.
809.
Anno Imp. Nero-
nis Cæs. 3.

who shall prepare himself to the battle?

9 So likewise ye, except ye utter by the tongue words ^g easy to be understood, how shall it be known what is spoken? for ye shall speak into the air.

10 There are, it may be, so many kinds of voices in the world, and none of them *is* without signification.

11 Therefore if I know not the meaning of the voice, I shall be unto him that speaketh a barbarian, and he that speaketh *shall be* a barbarian unto me.

12 Even so ye, forasmuch as ye are zealous ^h of spiritual *gifts*, seek that ye may excel to the edifying of the Church.

13 Wherefore let him that speaketh in an *unknown* tongue, pray that he may interpret.

14 For if I pray in an *unknown* tongue, my spirit prayeth, but my understanding is unfruitful.

15 What is it then? I will pray with the spirit; and I will pray with the understanding also: ⁱ I will sing with the spirit, and I will sing ^k with the understanding also.

A. M. 4060.
A. D. 56.
A. U. C.
809.
Anno Imp. Nero
nis Cæs. 3.

---

^g Gr. *significant.*——^h Gr. *of spirits.*

ⁱ Eph. v. 19; Col. iii. 16.——^k Psa. xlvii. 7.

---

that which is ordinarily used on such occasions, the soldier is not informed of what he should do, and therefore does not arm himself; consequently, that vague, unintelligible sound of the trumpet, is of no use.

Verse 9. *Likewise ye*] If ye do not speak in the Church so as to be understood, your labour is useless; *ye shall speak into the air*—your speech will be lost and dissipated in the air, without conveying any meaning to any person: there will be a noise or sound, but nothing else. Gifts of that kind, thus used, are good for nothing.

Verse 10. *There are, it may be*] Ει τυχοι, For example.

So many kinds of voices] So many different languages, each of which has its distinct articulation, pronunciation, emphasis, and meaning; or there may be so many different nations, each possessing a different language, &c.

Verse 11. *If I know not the meaning of the voice*] Την δυναμιν της φωνης, The power and signification of the language.

I shall be unto him that speaketh a barbarian] I shall appear to him, and he to me, as a person who had no distinct and articulate sounds which can convey any kind of meaning. This observation is very natural: when we hear persons speaking in a language of which we know nothing, we wonder how they can understand each other, as, in their speech, there appears to us no regular distinction of sounds or words. For the meaning and origin of the word *barbarian*, see the note on Acts xxviii. 2.

Verse 12. *Forasmuch as ye are zealous*] Seeing ye affect so much to have spiritual gifts, seek that ye may get those by which ye may excel in edifying the Church.

Verse 13. *Pray that he may interpret.*] Let him who speaks or reads the prophetic declarations in the Old Testament, in that tongue in which they were originally spoken and written, pray to God that he may so understand them himself, and receive the gift of interpretation, that he may be able to explain them in all their depth and latitude to others.

Verse 14. *For if I pray in an* unknown *tongue*] If my prayers are composed of sentences and sayings taken out of the prophets, &c., and in their own lan-

guage—*my spirit prayeth*, my heart is engaged in the work, and my prayers answer all the purpose of prayers to *myself; but my understanding is unfruitful* to all others, because they do not understand my prayers, and I either do not or cannot interpret them. See the note on ver. 19.

Verse 15. *I will pray with the spirit*] I will endeavour to have all my prayers influenced and guided by the Spirit of God; and to have my own heart deeply affected in and by the work.

And I will pray with the understanding also] I will endeavour so to pray that others may understand me, and thus be edified and improved by my prayers. And therefore I will pray in a language in the public congregation that may be understood by all present, so that all may join, not only in the *act*, but in the spirit of devotion.

I will sing with the spirit] It does appear that *singing psalms* or *spiritual hymns* was one thing that was implied in what is termed *prophesying* in the Old Testament, as is evident from 1 Sam. x. 5, 6, 10, &c. And when this came through an immediate afflatus or inspiration of God, there is no doubt that it was exceedingly edifying; and must have served greatly to improve and excite the devotional spirit of all that were present. But I rather suppose that their singing consisted in solemn, well measured *recitative*, than in the jingling and often foolish sounds which we use when a single monosyllable is sometimes shivered into a multitude of semiquavers!

Here it may not be improper to remark that the *spirit* and the *understanding* are seldom united in our congregational singing. Those whose hearts are right with God have generally no *skill* in music, and those who are well skilled in music have seldom a devotional spirit, but are generally proud, self-willed, contentious, and arrogant. Do not these persons entirely overrate themselves? Of all the liberal arts surely *music* is the least useful, however ornamental it may be. And should any thing be esteemed in the Church of God but in proportion to its *utility*? A good singer, among the people of God, who has not the life of God in his soul, is *vox et præterea nihil*, as Heliogabalus said of the nightingale's brains on which he desired to sup, *he is nothing but a sound*. Some of those persons, I

A. M. 4060.
A. D. 56.
A. U. C.
809.
Anno Imp. Nero-
nis Cæs. 3.

16 Else, when thou shalt bless with the spirit, how shall he that occupieth the room of the unlearned say Amen [1] at thy giving of thanks, seeing he understandeth not what thou sayest?

17 For thou verily givest thanks well, but the other is not edified.

18 I thank my God, I speak with tongues more than ye all:

19 Yet in the church I had rather speak five words with my understanding, that *by my voice* I might teach others also, than ten thousand words in an *unknown* tongue.

20 Brethren, [m] be not children in understanding: howbeit in malice [n] be ye children but in understanding be [o] men.

21 [p] In the law it is [q] written, With *men of other tongues and other lips* will I speak unto

A. M. 4060.
A. D. 56.
A. U. C.
809
Anno Imp. Nero-
nis Cæs. 3.

---

[1] Chap. xi. 24.——[m] Psa. cxxxi. 2; Matt. xi. 25; xviii. 3; xix. 14; Rom. xvi. 19; chap. iii. 1; Eph. iv. 14; Heb. v. 12, 13.

[n] Matt. xviii. 3; 1 Pet. ii. 2.——[o] Gr. *perfect,* or, *of a ripe age;* chap. ii. 6.——[p] John x. 34.——[q] Isa. xxviii. 11, 12.

---

mean they who sing with the *understanding* without the *spirit*, suppose themselves of great consequence in the Church of Christ; and they find foolish superficial people whom they persuade to be of their own mind, and soon raise parties and contentions if they have not every thing their *own* way; and that way is generally as *absurd* as it is unscriptural and contrary to the spirit and simplicity of the Gospel.

Verse 16. He that occupieth the room of the unlearned] One who is not acquainted with the language in which you speak, sing, or pray.

Say Amen] Give his assent and ratification to what he does not understand. It was very frequent in primitive times to express their approbation in the public assemblies by *Amen.* This practice, soberly and piously conducted, might still be of great use in the Church of Christ.

This response was of the highest authority and merit among the Jews; they even promised the remission of all sins, the annihilation of the sentence of damnation, and the opening of the gates of paradise, to those who fervently say *Amen.* And it is one of their maxims that " *greater* is he who says *Amen* than he who *prays.*" See many testimonies of this kind in *Schoettgen.* Now, allowing that this was of so much consequence in the time of St. Paul, it was a very serious matter for a person to be in a congregation where prayer was offered, who could not say *Amen,* because the prayers were in a language which he did not understand.

Verse 17. Thou verily givest thanks well] Because he felt *gratitude,* and, from a sense of his obligation, gave praise to God; but because this was in an unknown tongue, those who heard him received no edification.

Verse 18. I speak with tongues more than ye all] He understood more languages than any of them did: and this was indispensably necessary, as he was the apostle of the Gentiles in general, and had to preach to different provinces where different dialects, if not languages, were used. In the *Hebrew, Syriac, Greek,* and *Latin,* he was undoubtedly well skilled from his education; and how many he might understand by miraculous gift we cannot tell. But, even literally understood, it is very probable that he knew more languages than any man in the Church of Corinth.

Verse 19. Yet in the church] As the grand object of public worship is the edification of those who

attend, *five words* spoken so as to convey edification, were of much more consequence than *ten thousand* which, not being understood, could convey none. By the word γλωσση, *tongue,* to which we add *unknown,* I suppose the apostle always means the *Hebrew,* for the reasons offered in the note on ver. 1.

One of the greatest difficulties, says Bishop Pearce, in this epistle is contained in the words πνευμα and νους, *spirit* and *understanding,* which are frequently used in this chapter; and fixing the true meaning of these words will solve the difficulty. In this verse the apostle explains λαλειν τω νοι, *to speak with the understanding,* by ἱνα αλλους κατηχησω, *that I might teach others;* so that the sense of νους, *understanding,* seems to be, *that understanding which the hearer has of what is said;* and this sense will agree well with, *I will sing with the spirit,* and *with the understanding,* ver. 15.

He observes also that πνευμα, *spirit,* and νους, *understanding,* have a sense opposite to each other; so that if νους is rightly rendered, the *understanding which another has of what is said;* then πνευμα will signify a *man's own mind,* i. e. *his own understanding of what he himself speaks;* and this sense agrees well with ver. 2: *In the spirit he speaketh mysteries.*

Verse 20. Be not children in understanding] There are *three* words here to which we must endeavour to affix the proper sense. 1. παιδια signifies *children* in general, but particularly such as are grown up, so as to be fit to send to *school* in order to receive instruction; 2. νηπιος, from νη, not, and ειπω, I speak, signifies an *infant;* one that *cannot yet speak,* and is in the lowest stage of infancy; 3. τελειοι, from τελεω, I complete or perfect, signifies those who are arrived at perfect maturity, both of *growth* and *understanding.* We shall now see the apostle's meaning: *Brethren, be not,* παιδια, as *little children,* just beginning to go to *school,* in order to learn the first elements of their mother tongue, and with an understanding only sufficient to apprehend those elements.

In malice] Κακια, *In wickedness,* νηπιαζετε, *be ye as infants,* who neither *speak, do,* nor *purpose* evil.

But in understanding] Τελειοι γινεσθε, *Be ye perfect men,* whose *vigour* of *body,* and *energy* of *mind* show a complete growth, and a well cultivated understanding.

Verse 21. In the law it is written] But the passage quoted is in Isa. xxviii. 11. Here is no contradiction,

A. M. 4060.
A. D. 56.
A. U. C.
809.
Anno Imp. Nero-
nis Cæs. 3.

this people; and yet for all that will they not hear me, saith the Lord.

22 Wherefore tongues are for a sign, not to them that believe, but to them that believe not: but prophesying *serveth* not for them that believe not, but for them which believe.

23 If therefore the whole Church be come together into one place, and all speak with tongues, and there come in *those that are* unlearned or unbelievers, ʳ will they not say that ye are mad?

24 But if all prophesy, and there come in one that believeth not, or *one* unlearned, he is

convinced of all, he is judged of all:

25 And thus are the secrets of his heart made manifest; and so, falling down on *his* face, he will worship God, and report ˢ that God is in you of a truth.

A. M. 4060.
A. D. 56.
A. U. C.
809.
Anno Imp. Nero-
nis Cæs. 3.

26 How is it then, brethren? when ye come together, every one of you hath a psalm, ᵗ hath a doctrine, hath a tongue, hath a revelation, hath an interpretation. ᵘ Let all things be done unto edifying.

27 If any man speak in an *unknown* tongue, *let it be* by two, or at the most *by* three, and *that* by course; and let one interpret.

ʳ Acts ii. 13.——ˢ Isa. xlv. 14; Zech. viii. 23.——ᵗ Ver. 6; chap. xii. 8, 9, 10.——ᵘ Chap. xii. 7; 2 Cor. xii. 19; Eph. iv. 12.

---

for the term תורה *torah*, LAW, was frequently used by the Jews to express the whole *Scriptures*, law, prophets, and hagiographia; and they used it to distinguish these sacred writings from the words of the *scribes*.

With men of *other tongues*] Bishop Pearce paraphrases this verse as follows: "With the tongues of foreigners and with the lips of foreigners will I speak to this people; and yet, for all that, will they not hear me, saith the Lord." To enter into the *apostle's* meaning we must enter into that of the *prophet*. The Jewish people were under the *teaching* of the prophets who were sent from God; these *instructed, reproved, and corrected* them by this Divine authority. They however became so refractory and disobedient that God purposed to cast them off, and abandon them to the Babylonians: then, they had a people to *teach, correct,* and *reprove* them, whose language they did not understand. The *discipline* that they received in this way was widely different from that which they received while under the teaching of the prophets and the government of God; and yet for all this they did not humble themselves before their Maker that this affliction might be removed from them.

Verse 22. *Wherefore tongues are for a sign*] The miraculous gift of tongues was never designed for the benefit of those who have already *believed*, but for the instruction of *unbelievers*, that they might see from such a miracle that this is the *work of God;* and so embrace the Gospel. But as, in the times of the prophet, the strange Babylonish tongues came in the way of *punishment*, and not in the way of *mercy;* take heed that it be not the case *now:* that, by dwelling on the gift, ye forget the Giver; and what was designed for you as a blessing, may prove to you to be a curse. For if, because ye have the gift of tongues, ye will choose for your own aggrandizement to use them in the public congregation where none understands them, God may curse your blessings.

Prophesying] Teaching the things of God in a known language is of infinitely more consequence than speaking in all the foreign tongues in the universe.

Verse 23. *Will they not say that ye are mad?*] So they well might, finding a whole assembly of people

talking languages which those who had most need of instruction could not understand.

Verse 24. *But if all prophesy*] If all those who teach do it in the tongue which all understand; if an unbeliever, or one who knows nothing of the sacred language, come in and hear things just suited to his own state, he is convicted by all, and he is judged by all.

Verse 25. *And thus are the secrets of his heart*] As these, who were the *prophets* or *teachers*, had often the discernment of spirits, they were able in certain cases, and probably very frequently, to tell a man the *secrets* of his own heart; and, where this was not *directly* the case, God often led his ministers to speak those things that were suitable to the case before them, though they themselves had no particular design. The sinner, therefore, convinced that God alone could uncover the secrets of his heart, would be often obliged to *fall down on his face*, abashed and confounded, and acknowledge that God was truly among them. This seems to be the plain meaning of the passages before us.

Verse 26. *How is it—every one of you hath a psalm, &c.*] Dr. Lightfoot understands this in the following manner: When the congregation came together, some were for spending the time in *psalmody;* others in *explaining* particular *doctrines;* others in reading, praying, or speaking in the *Hebrew* tongue; others were curious to hear of farther *revelations;* and others wished to spend the time in the *interpretation* of what had already been spoken. This may be specious, but to me it is not satisfactory. It seems more likely that, when the whole Church came together, among whom there were many persons with extraordinary gifts, each of them wished to put himself forward, and occupy the time and attention of the congregation: hence confusion must necessarily take place, and perhaps not a little contention. This was contrary to that edifying which was the intention of these gifts.

Verse 27. *Speak in an* unknown *tongue*] The *Hebrew*, as has already been conjectured.

Let it be by two, *or at the most* by three, *and that* by course] Let only two or three in one assembly act in this way, that too much time may not be taken up

A. M. 4060.
·A. D. 56.
A. U. C.
809.
Anno Imp. Nero-
nis Cæs. 3.

28 But if there be no interpreter, let him keep silence in the church; and let him speak to himself, and to God.

29 Let the prophets speak two or three, and ᵛ let the other judge.

30 If *any thing* be revealed to another that sitteth by, ʷ let the first hold his peace.

31 For ye may all prophesy one by one, that all may learn, and all may be comforted.

32 And ˣ the spirits of the prophets are subject to the prophets.

33 For God is not *the author* of ʸ confusion, but of peace, ᶻ as in all churches of the saints.

34 ª Let your women keep silence in the churches : for it is not permitted unto them to speak ; but ᵇ *they are commanded* to be under obedience, as also saith the ᶜ law.

A. M. 4060.
A. D. 56.
A. U. C.
809.
Anno Imp. Nero
nis Cæs. 3.

ᵛ Chap. xii. 10.——ʷ 1 Thess. v. 19, 20.——ˣ 1 John iv. 1.——ʸ Gr. *tumult,* or, *unquietness.*——ᶻ Chap. xi. 16.

ª 1 Tim. ii. 11, 12.——ᵇ Chap. xi. 3 ; Eph. v. 22 ; Col. iii. 18, Tit. ii. 5 ; 1 Pet. iii. 1.——ᶜ Gen. iii. 16.

---

with one exercise ; and let this be done *by course,* the one after the other, that two may not be speaking at the same time : *and let one interpret* for all that shall thus speak.

Verse 28.- *But if there be no interpreter*] If there be none present who can give the proper sense of this Hebrew reading and speaking, then let him keep silence, and not occupy the time of the Church, by speaking in a language which only himself can understand.

Verse 29. *Let the prophets*] Those who have the gift of speaking to men to edification, and exhortation, and comfort; ver. 3.

Two or three] As *prophesying* implied psalmody, teaching, and exhortation, Dr. Lightfoot thinks that the meaning of the place is this: Let one *sing* who has a *psalm ;* let another *teach* who has a *doctrine ;* and let a third *exhort,* or *comfort,* who has a gift of that kind.

And let the other judge.] The other prophets, or qualified persons, judge of the propriety of what had been spoken ; or let them *discern,* διακρινετωσαν, how the revelation under the new covenant confirmed and illustrated the revelation granted under the Old Testament. It appears to have been taken for granted, that a man might *pretend* to this spirit of prophecy who was not sent of God; and therefore it was the duty of the accredited teachers to examine whether what he spoke was according to *truth,* and the *analogy of faith.* For *the spirits of the prophets are subject to the prophets ;* every man's gift was to be judged of by those whose age, experience, and wisdom, gave them a right to decide. Besides, though the person who did speak might do it from an impulse of God, yet, if he was not *sufficiently known,* his testimony ought to be received with caution; and therefore the aged prophets should judge of his gift, lest false doctrines should slide into the Church.

But all these provisions, as *Schoettgen* justly observes, were in imitation of the practice in the Jewish synagogues; for there it was customary for them to *object, interrogate, judge, refute, &c.*

Verse 30. *Be revealed to another that sitteth by*] Probably those who were teachers sat on a particular seat, or place, from which they might most readily address the people ; and this may be the meaning of *sitting by.* If such a person could say, I have just received a particular revelation from God, then let

him have the liberty immediately to speak it; as it might possibly relate to the circumstances of that time and place.

Verse 31. *For ye may all prophesy one by one*] The gifts which God grants are given for the purpose of edification ; but there can be no edification where there is confusion ; therefore let them speak one by one.

Verse 32. *And the spirits of the prophets, &c.*] Let no one interrupt another ; and let all be ready to prefer others before themselves ; and let each feel a spirit of subjection to his brethren. God grants no ungovernable gifts.

Verse 33 *For God is not* the author *of confusion*] Let not the persons who act in the congregation in this disorderly manner, say, that they are under the influence of God; for he is not the author of confusion ; but two, three, or more, praying or teaching in the same place, at the same time, is *confusion ;* and God is not the author of such work ; and let men beware how they attribute such disorder to the God of order and peace. The apostle calls such conduct ακαταστασια, *tumult, sedition ;* and such it is in the sight of God, and in the sight of all good men. How often is a work of God marred and discredited by the folly of men ! for *nature* will always, and *Satan* too, mingle themselves as far as they can in the genuine work of the Spirit, in order to discredit and destroy it. Nevertheless, in great revivals of religion it is almost impossible to prevent wild-fire from getting in amongst the true fire ; but it is the duty of the ministers of God to watch against and prudently check this ; but if themselves encourage it, then there will be confusion and every evil work.

Verse 34. *Let your women keep silence in the churches*] This was a Jewish ordinance ; women were not permitted to *teach* in the assemblies, or even to *ask questions.* The rabbins taught that " a woman should know nothing but the use of her distaff." And the sayings of Rabbi Eliezer, as delivered, *Bammidbar Rabba,* sec. 9, fol. 204, are both worthy of remark and of execration ; they are these : ימסרו לנשים ישרפו דברי תורה ואל *yisrephu dibrey torah veal yimsaru lenashim,* " Let the words of the law be burned, rather than that they should be delivered to women."

This was their condition till the time of the Gospel, when, according to the prediction of Joel, the Spirit of God was to be poured out on the *women* as well as the *men,* that they might *prophesy,* i. e. *teach.*

A. M. 4060.
A. D. 56.
A. U. C.
809.
Anno Imp. Nero-
nis Cæs. 3.

35 And if they will learn any thing, let them ask their husbands at home; for it is a shame for women to speak in the church.

36 What! came the word of God out from you? or came it unto you only?

37 ^d If any man think himself to be a prophet, or spiritual, let him acknowledge that the

things that I write unto you are the commandments of the Lord.

38 But if any man be ignorant, let him be ignorant.

39 Wherefore, brethren, ^e covet to prophesy, and forbid not to speak with tongues.

40 ^f Let all things be done decently and in order.

A. M. 4060.
A. D. 56.
A. U. C.
809.
Anno Imp. Nero-
nis Cæs. 3.

---

^d 2 Cor. x. 7; 1 John iv. 6.

^e Chap. xii. 31; 1 Thess. v. 20.——^f Ver. 33.

And that they did *prophesy* or *teach* is evident from what the apostle says, chap. xi. 5, where he lays down rules to regulate this part of their conduct while ministering in the church.

But does not what the apostle says here contradict that statement, and show that the words in chap. xi. should be understood in another sense? For, here it is expressly said that they should *keep silence in the church;* for it *was not permitted to a woman to speak.* Both places seem perfectly consistent. It is evident from the context that the apostle refers here to *asking questions,* and what we call *dictating* in the assemblies. It was permitted to any *man* to *ask questions,* to *object, altercate, attempt* to *refute,* &c., in the synagogue; but this liberty was not allowed to any woman. St. Paul confirms this in reference also to the Christian Church; he orders them to *keep silence;* and, if they wished to *learn any thing, let them inquire of their husbands at home;* because it was perfectly indecorous for *women* to be contending with *men* in public assemblies, on points of doctrine, cases of conscience, &c. But this by no means intimated that when a woman received any particular *influence from God* to enable her to teach, that she was not to obey that influence; on the contrary, she was to obey it, and the apostle lays down directions in chap. xi. for regulating her *personal appearance* when thus employed. All that the apostle opposes here is their *questioning, finding fault, disputing, &c.,* in the Christian Church, as the Jewish men were permitted to do in their synagogues; together with the attempts to usurp any authority over the man, by setting up their judgment in *opposition* to them; for the apostle has in view, especially, acts of *disobedience, arrogance, &c.,* of which no woman would be guilty who was under the influence of the Spirit of God.

But—to be under obedience, as also saith the law.] This is a reference to Gen. iii. 16: *Thy desire shall be to thy husband, and he shall rule over thee.* From this it is evident that it was the *disorderly* and *disobedient* that the apostle had in view; and not any of those on whom God had poured out his Spirit.

Verse 35. *For it is a shame for women to speak in the church.*] The Jews would not suffer a woman to *read* in the synagogue; though a *servant* or even a *child,* had this permission; but the apostle refers to irregular conduct, such conduct as proved that they were not under obedience, ver. 34.

Verse 36. *Came the word of God out from you?*] Was it from you that other Churches received the Gospel? Are you the *mother Church?* that you should have rules, and orders, and customs, different

from all others; and set yourselves up for a model to be copied by all the Churches of Christ?

Or came it unto you only?] Are you the only Church of God? Are there not many others founded before you that have no such customs, and permit no such disorders?

Verse 37. *If any man think himself to be a prophet, &c.*] He who is really a *spiritual* man, under the influence of the Spirit of God, and capable of *teaching* the Divine will, he will acknowledge that what I now say is from the same Spirit; and that the things which I now write are the *commandments* of God, and must be obeyed on pain of his displeasure.

Verse 38. *But if any man be ignorant*] If he affect to be so, or pretend that he is ignorant; *let him be ignorant*—let him be so at his peril.

Verse 39. *Covet to prophesy*] Let it be your endeavour and prayer to be able to *teach the way of God* to the ignorant; this is the most *valuable,* because the most *useful* gift of the Spirit.

And forbid not to speak with tongues.] Let every gift have its own *place* and *operation;* let none envy another; nor prevent him from doing that part of the work to which God, by giving the *qualification,* has evidently called him.

Verse 40. *Let all things be done decently*] Ενσχημονως· In their *proper forms;* with becoming reverence; according to their dignity and importance. Every thing in the Church of God should be conducted with gravity and composure, suitable to the importance of the things, the infinite dignity of the object of worship, and the necessity of the souls in behalf of which those religious ordinances are instituted.

And in order.] Κατα ταξιν· Every thing in its *place,* every thing in its *time,* and every thing *suitably.*

Let all things be done decently and in order, is a direction of infinite moment in all the concerns of religion, and of no small consequence in all the concerns of life. How much pain, confusion, and loss would be prevented, were this rule followed! There is scarcely an embarrassment in *civil* or *domestic* life that does not originate in a neglect of this precept. No *business, trade, art,* or *science,* can be carried on to any advantage or comfort, unless peculiar attention be paid to it. And as to *religion,* there can be absolutely none without it. Where *decency* and *order* are not observed in every part of the worship of God, no spiritual worship can be performed. The *manner* of doing a thing is always of as much consequence as the *act* itself. And often the *act* derives all its consequence and utility from the manner in which it is performed.

2

CHAPTER XV.

The Gospel which the apostle preached to the Corinthians; viz. that Christ died for our sins, and rose again the third day, 1–4. The witnesses of his resurrection, Peter, James, and more than five hundred brethren, 5–7. Lastly, Paul himself saw him, and was called by him to the apostleship, 8–11. Objections against the resurrection of the dead answered, 12–34. The manner in which this great work shall be performed, 35–49. The astonishing events that shall take place in the last day, 50–57. The use we should make of this doctrine, 58.

A. M. 4060.
A. D. 56.
A. U. C. 809.
Anno Imp. Nero-
nis Cæs. 3.

MOREOVER, brethren, I declare unto you the Gospel ᵃ which I preached unto you, which also ye have received, and ᵇ wherein ye stand :

2 ᶜ By which also ye are saved, if ye ᵈ keep in memory ᵉ what I preached unto you, unless ᶠ ye have believed in vain.

3 For ᵍ I delivered unto you first of all that ʰ which I also received, how that Christ died for our sins, ⁱ according to the Scriptures :

4 And that he was buried, and that he rose again the third day ᵏ according to the Scriptures.

5 ˡ And that he was seen of Cephas, then ᵐ of the twelve :

A. M. 4060.
A. D. 56.
A. U. C. 809.
Anno Imp. Nero-
nis Cæs. 3.

ᵃ Gal. i. 11.——ᵇ Rom. v. 2.——ᶜ Rom. i. 16; chap. i. 21. ᵈ Or, *hold fast.*——ᵉ Gr. *by what speech.*——ᶠ Gal. iii. 4.——ᵍ Chap. xi. 2, 23,——ʰ Gal. i. 12.——ⁱ Psa. xxii. 15, &c.; Isa. liii. 5, 6, &c.; Dan. ix. 26; Zech. xiii. 7; Luke xxiv. 26, 46; Acts iii. 18; xxvi. 23; 1 Pet. i. 11; ii. 24.

ᵏ Psa. ii. 7; xvi. 10; Isa. liii. 10; Hos. vi. 2; Luke xxiv. 26, 46; Acts ii. 25–31; xiii. 33, 34, 35; xxvi. 22, 23; 1 Pet. i. 11.——ˡ Luke xxiv. 34.——ᵐ Matthew xxviii. 17; Mark xvi. 14; Luke xxiv. 36; John xx. 19, 26; Acts x. 41.

NOTES ON CHAP. XV.

It appears from this chapter that there were some false apostles at Corinth, who denied the *resurrection,* see verse 12 ; in consequence of which St. Paul discusses *three* questions in this chapter :—

1. Whether there be a resurrection of the dead ? ver. 1–35.
2. What will be the nature of the resurrection bodies ? 35–51.
3. What should become of those who should be found alive in the day of judgment ? 51–57.

I. The resurrection he proves,—

1. From *Scripture,* ver. 1–4.
2. From *eye witnesses,* 5–12.

II. He proves the resurrection by showing the *absurdity* of the contrary doctrine :—

1. If the dead rise not, Christ is not risen, ver. 13.
2. It would be absurd to have faith in Him, according to the preaching of the Gospel, if he be not risen, ver. 14.
3. The apostles must be false witnesses who attest this resurrection, ver. 15.
4. The faith of the Corinthians must be vain who believe it, ver. 16, 17.
5. All the believers who have died in the faith of Christ have perished, if Christ be not risen, ver. 18.
6. Believers in Christ are in a more miserable state than any others, if there be no resurrection, ver. 19.
7. Those who were baptized in the faith that Christ died for them and *rose again,* are deceived, ver. 29.
8. The apostles, and Christians in general, who suffer persecution on the ground that, after suffering awhile here, they shall have a glorious resurrection, are acting a foolish and unprofitable part, ver. 30–32.

Verse 1. *The Gospel which I preached unto you*] This Gospel is contained in *Christ dying for our sins, being buried,* and *rising again the third day.* See the following verses.

Verse 2. *By which also ye are saved*] That is, ye are now in a salvable state ; and are saved from your Gentilism, and from your former sins.

If ye keep in memory] Your future salvation, or being brought finally to glory, will now depend on your *faithfulness* to the grace that ye have received.

Verse 3. *For I delivered unto you first of all*] Εν πρωτοις· As the *chief things,* or matters of the greatest importance ; fundamental truths.

That which I—received] By revelations from God himself, and not from man.

That Christ died for our sins] The death of Jesus Christ, as a vicarious sacrifice for sin, is εν πρωτοις ; among the *things* that are of *chief importance,* and is essential to the Gospel scheme of salvation.

According to the Scriptures] It is not said any where in the Scriptures, in express terms, that Christ should rise on the *third* day ; but it is fully implied in his *types,* as in the case of *Jonah,* who came out of the belly of the fish on the *third day ;* but particularly in the case of *Isaac,* who was a very expressive *type* of Christ ; for, as his being brought to the Mount Moriah, bound and laid on the wood, in order to be *sacrificed,* pointed out the *death* of Christ ; so his being brought *alive* on the *third day* from the mount was a figure of Christ's resurrection. Bishop *Pearce* and others refer to Matt. xii. 40 ; xvi. 21 ; and Luke ix. 22 ; " which two Gospels, having been written at the time when Paul wrote this epistle, were properly called by the name of the Sacred *Scriptures.*" It might be so ; but I do not know of one proof in the New Testament where its *writings,* or any *part of them,* are called the *Scriptures.*

Verse 5. *That he was seen of Cephas, then of the twelve*] This refers to the journey to Emmaus, Luke

A. M. 4060.
A. D. 56.
A. U. C.
809.
Anno Imp. Nero-
nis Cæs. 3.

6 After that, he was seen of above five hundred brethren at once; of whom the greater part remain unto this present, but some are fallen asleep.

7 After that, he was seen of James, then ⁿ of all the apostles.

8 ° And last of all he was seen of me also, as of ᵖ one born out of due time.

9 For I am ۹ the least of the apostles, that

am not meet to be called an apostle, because ʳ I persecuted the Church of God.

10 But, ˢ by the grace of God I am what I am: and his grace which *was be* stowed upon me was not in vain; but ᵗ I labour ed more abundantly than they all: ᵘ yet not I, but the grace of God which was with me.

11 Therefore whether *it were* I or they, so we preach, and so ye believed.

A. M. 4060.
A. D. 56.
A. U. C.
809.
Anno Imp. Nero-
nis Cæs. 3.

ⁿ Luke xxiv. 50; Acts i. 3, 4.——° Acts ix. 4, 17; xxii. 14, 18; chap. ix. 1.——ᵖ Or, *an abortive.*——۹ Eph. iii. 8.——ʳ Acts viii. 3; ix. 1; Gal. i. 13; Phil. iii. 6; 1 Tim. i. 13.

ˢ Eph. ii. 7, 8.——ᵗ 2 Cor. xi. 23; xii. 11.——ᵘ Matt. x. 20; Rom. xv. 18, 19; 2 Corinthians iii. 5; Gal. ii. 8; Eph. iii. 7; Phil. ii. 13.

---

xxiv. 13 and 34; and to what is related Mark xvi. 14.

Then of the twelve] Instead of δωδεκα, *twelve,* ενδεκα, *eleven,* is the reading of D*EFG, *Syriac* in the margin, some of the *Slavonic, Armenian, Vulgate, Itala,* and several of the *fathers;* and this reading is supported by Mark xvi. 14. Perhaps the term *twelve* is used here *merely* to point out the *society of the apostles,* who, though at this time they were only *eleven,* were still called the *twelve,* because this was their *original* number, and a number which was afterward *filled* up. See John xx. 24.

Verse 6. Above five hundred brethren at once] This was probably in *Galilee,* where our Lord had many disciples. See Matt. xxviii. 16. What a remarkable testimony is this to the truth of our Lord's resurrection! *Five hundred* persons saw him at one time; the greater part of whom were *alive* when the apostle wrote, and he might have been confronted by many if he had dared to assert a falsity.

Verse 7. After that, he was seen of James] But *where,* and on what *occasion,* we are not told; nor indeed do we know which *James* is intended; *James* the son of *Zebedee,* or *James* the son of *Alpheus.* But one thing is sufficiently evident, from what is here said, that this James, of whom the apostle speaks, was still *alive;* for the apostle's manner of speaking justifies this conclusion.

Then of all the apostles.] Including, not only the *eleven,* but, as some suppose, the *seventy-two* disciples.

Verse 8. And last of all—of me also] It seems that it was essential to the character of a primitive *apostle* that he had *seen* and *conversed* with Christ; and it is evident, from the history of Saul's conversion, Acts ix. 4–7, where see the notes, that Jesus Christ did *appear* to him; and he pleaded this ever after as a *proof of his call to the apostleship.* And it does not appear that, after this time, Jesus ever did make any *personal discovery* of himself to any one.

As of one born out of due time.] The apostle considers himself as coming *after* the time in which Jesus Christ personally conversed with his disciples; and that, therefore, to see him at all, he must see him in this *extraordinary* way. Some have entered into a very disgusting detail on the *figure* used here by the apostle. The words, ωσπερει τῳ εκτρωματι, signify not merely one *born out of due time,* but one born *before*

his time; and consequently, not bidding fair for vigour, usefulness, or long life. But it is likely that the apostle had a different meaning; and that he refers to the original institution of the *twelve* apostles, in the *rank* of whom he never stood, being appointed not to *fill up a place* among the *twelve,* but as an *extra* and *additional* apostle. *Rosenmüller* says that those who were beyond the number of *twelve* senators were termed *abortivi,* abortives; and refers to *Suetonius* in *Octavio,* cap. 35. I have examined the place, but find no such epithet. According to *Suetonius,* in that place, they were called *orcini*—persons who had assumed the senatorial dignity *after the death* of Julius Cæsar, pretending that they had derived that honour from *him.*

Verse 9. I am the least of the apostles] This was literally *true* in reference to his being chosen *last,* and chosen not in the *number* of the twelve, but as an *extra* apostle. How much pains do some men take to make the apostle *contradict* himself, by attempting to show that he was the very *greatest* of the apostles, though he calls himself the *least!* Taken as a *man* and a *minister of Christ,* he was greater than any of the *twelve;* taken as an *apostle* he was less than any of the *twelve,* because not originally in that body.

Am not meet to be called an apostle] None of the *twelve* had ever *persecuted* Christ, nor withstood his doctrine: Saul of Tarsus had been, before his conversion, a *grievous persecutor;* and therefore he says, ουκ ειμι ικανος, *I am not proper to be called an apostle, because I persecuted the Church of God,* i. e. of Christ, which none of the *apostles* ever did.

Verse 10. But, by the grace of God I am what I am] God, by his mere grace and good will, has called me to be an apostle, and has denominated me such.

And his grace, &c.] Nor have I been unfaithful to the Divine call; I used the grace which he gave me; and when my labours, travels, and sufferings are considered, it will be evident that *I have laboured more abundantly than the whole twelve.* This was most literally true.

Yet not I, but the grace of God] It was not through my own power or wisdom that I performed these things, but through the Divine influence which accompanied me.

Verse 11. Whether it were I or they] All the apostles of Christ agree in the same doctrines; we all preach *one* and the *same thing;* and, as we preached, so ye believed; having received from us the true apos

A. M. 4060.
A. D. 56.
A. U. C.
809.
Anno Imp. Nero-
nis Cæs. 3.

12 Now if Christ be preached that he rose from the dead, how say some among you that there is no resurrection of the dead?

13 But if there be no resurrection of the dead, [v] then is Christ not risen:

14 And if Christ be not risen, then *is* our preaching vain, and your faith *is* also vain.

15 Yea, and we are found false witnesses of God; because [w] we have testified of God that he raised up Christ: whom he raised not

up, if so be that the dead rise not.

16 For if the dead rise not, then is not Christ raised:

17 And if Christ be not raised, your faith *is* vain; [x] ye are yet in your sins.

18 Then they also which are fallen asleep in Christ are perished.

19 [y] If in this life only we have hope in Christ we are of all men most miserable.

20 But now [z] is Christ risen from the dead,

A. M. 4060.
A. D. 56.
A. U. C.
809.
Anno Imp. Nero
nis Cæs. 3.

---

[v] 1 Thess. iv. 14.——[w] Acts ii. 24, 32; iv. 10, 33; xiii. 30.

[x] Rom. iv. 25.——[y] 2 Tim. iii. 12.——[z] 1 Pet. i. 3.

---

tolical faith, that Jesus died for our sins, and rose again for our justification; and that *his resurrection* is the *pledge* and *proof* of *ours*. Whoever teaches contrary to this does not preach the true apostolic doctrine.

Paul was the last of the *primitive* apostles. The *primitive* apostles were those who had *seen* Christ, and got their call to the apostolate immediately from *himself*. There were many apostles after this time, but they were all *secondary*; they had a Divine call, but it was *internal*, and never accompanied by any *vision* or *external* demonstration of that Christ who had been manifested in the flesh.

Verse 12. *Now if Christ be preached, &c.*] Seeing it is true that we have thus preached Christ, and ye have credited this preaching, *how say some among you*, who have professed to receive this doctrine from us, *that there is no resurrection of the dead*, though we have shown that *his* resurrection is the *proof* and *pledge* of *ours?* That there was some *false teacher*, or *teachers*, among them, who was endeavouring to incorporate *Mosaic rites* and ceremonies with the Christian doctrines, and even to blend *Sadduceeism* with the whole, appears pretty evident. To confute this mongrel Christian, and overturn his bad doctrine, the apostle writes this chapter.

Verse 13. *If there be no resurrection of the dead*] As Christ was partaker of the same *flesh* and *blood* with us, and he promised to raise mankind from the dead through his resurrection, *if the dead rise not* then Christ has had no resurrection. There seem to have been some at Corinth who, though they denied the resurrection of the dead, admitted that Christ had risen again: the apostle's argument goes therefore to state that, if *Christ* was raised from the dead, *mankind* may be raised; if *mankind* cannot be raised from the dead, then the body of Christ was never raised.

Verse 14. *Then is our preaching vain*] Our whole doctrine is useless, nugatory, and false.

And your faith is also vain.] Your belief of a false doctrine must necessarily be to you unprofitable.

Verse 15. *False witnesses*] As having testified the fact of Christ's resurrection, as a matter which ourselves had witnessed, when we knew that we bore testimony to a falsehood. But could five hundred persons agree in this imposition? And if they did, is it possible that some one would not *discover* the cheat, when he could have *no interest* in keeping the secret, and might greatly promote his secular interest by mak-

ing the discovery? Such a case never occurred, and never can occur. The testimony, therefore, concerning the resurrection of Christ, is incontrovertibly true.

If so be that the dead rise not.] This clause is wanting in DE, *Syriac*, some of the *Slavonian*, and *Itala;* several also of the primitive *fathers* omit it. Its great *similarity* to the following words might be the cause of its omission by some copyists.

Verse 17. *Ye are yet in your sins.*] If Christ has not risen from the dead, there is no proof that he has not been *justly* put to death. If *he* were a *malefactor*, God would not work a miracle to raise him from the dead. If he has not been raised from the dead, there is a presumption that he has been put to death *justly;* and, if so, consequently he has made no *atonement;* and *ye are yet in your sins*—under the power, guilt, and condemnation of them. All this reasoning of the apostle goes to prove that at Corinth, even among those false teachers, the *innocency* of our Lord was allowed, and the *reality* of his resurrection not questioned.

Verse 18. *They also which are fallen asleep*] All those who, either by *martyrdom* or *natural death*, have departed in the faith of our Lord Jesus Christ, *are perished;* their hope was without *foundation*, and their faith had not *reason* and *truth* for its object. Their bodies are dissolved in the earth, finally decomposed and destroyed, notwithstanding the promise of Christ to such, that he would raise them up at the last day. See John v. 25, 28, 29; xi. 25, 26, &c.

Verse 19. *If in this life only we have hope*] It would be better to translate and *point* this verse as follows:—

And, if in this life we have hoped in Christ only, we are more to be pitied than all men. If, in this life, we have no other hope and confidence but in Christ, (and if he be still *dead*, and not yet risen,) we are more to be pitied than any other men; we are sadly deceived; we have denied ourselves, and been denied by others; have mortified ourselves, and been persecuted by our fellow creatures on account of our belief and hope in One who is not existing, and therefore can neither succour us here, nor reward us hereafter Bishop *Pearce.*

Verse 20. *But now is Christ risen*] On the contrary, Christ is raised from the dead, and is become the *first fruits of them that slept.* His resurrection has been *demonstrated*, and our resurrection necessarily follows; as sure as the *first fruits* are the proof

2

A. M. 4060.
A. D. 56.
A. U. C.
809.
Anno Imp. Nero-
nis Cæs. 3.

and become ª the first fruits of them that slept.

21 For ᵇ since by man *came* death, ᶜ by man *came* also the resurrection of the dead.

22 For as in Adam all die, even so in Christ shall all be made alive.

23 But ᵈ every man in his own order : Christ

the first fruits ; afterward they that are Christ's, at his coming.

24 Then *cometh* the end, when he shall have delivered up ᵉ the kingdom to God, even the Father ; when he shall have put down all rule, and all authority and power.

25 For he must reign ᶠ till he hath

A. M. 4060.
A. D. 56.
A. U. C.
809.
Anno Imp. Nero-
nis Cæs. 3.

Acts xxvi. 23 ; ver. 23 ; Col. i. 18 ; Rev. i. 5.——ᵇ Rom. v. 12, 17.——ᶜ John xi. 25 ; Rom. vi. 23.

ᵈ Ver. 20 ; 1 Thess. iv. 15, 16, 17.——ᵉ Dan. vii. 14, 27.——ᶠ Psa. cx. 1 ; Acts ii. 34, 35 ; Eph. i. 22 ; Heb. i. 13 ; x. 13.

---

that there is a *harvest*, so surely the resurrection of Christ is a *proof* of *ours*. The *Judaizing* teacher at Corinth would feel the force of this observation much sooner than we can, who are not much acquainted with Jewish customs. "Although," says Dr. Lightfoot, " the resurrection of Christ, compared with some *first fruits*, has very good harmony with them ; yet especially it agrees with the offering of the *sheaf*, commonly called עומר *omer*, not only as the *thing* itself, but also as to the circumstances of the *time*. For first there was the *passover*, and the day following was a *Sabbatic* day, and on the day *following* that the first fruits were offered. So Christ, our *passover*, was crucified : the day following his crucifixion was the *Sabbath*, and the day following *that*, He, the *first fruits of them that slept*, rose again. All who died before Christ, and were raised again to life, died afterwards ; but Christ is the first fruits of all who shall be raised from the dead to die no more."

Verse 21. *For since by man* came *death*] *Mortality* came by Adam, *immortality* by Christ ; so sure as all have been subjected to natural death by Adam, so sure shall all be raised again by Christ Jesus. Mortality and immortality, on a general ground, are the subject of the apostle's reasoning here ; and for the explanation of the transgression of Adam, and the redemption by Christ, see the notes on Rom. v. 10, &c.

Verse 23. *But every man in his own order*] The apostle mentions *three* orders here : 1. Christ, who rose from the dead by his own power. 2. Them that are Christ's ; all his apostles, martyrs, confessors, and faithful followers. 3. Then cometh the *end*, when the whole mass shall be raised. Whether this *order* be exactly what the apostle intends, I shall not assert. Of the *first*, Christ's own resurrection, there can be no question. The *second*, the resurrection of his followers, *before* that of the common dead, is thought by some very reasonable. " They had here a resurrection from a *death of sin* to a *life of righteousness*, which the others had not, because they *would* not be saved in Christ's way. That they should have the privilege of being raised *first*, to behold the astonishing *changes* and *revolutions* which shall then take place, has nothing in it contrary to propriety and fitness ;" but it seems contrary to ver. 52, in which *all the dead* are said to rise in a moment, in the twinkling of an eye. " And, *thirdly*, that all the other mass of mankind should be raised last, just to come forward and receive their doom, is equally reasonable :" but it is apparently inconsistent with the manner in which God chooses to act ; see ver. 53. Some think that by *them that are*

Christ's at his coming, " we are to understand Christ's coming to *reign on earth a thousand years with his saints*, previously to the general judgment ;" but I must confess I find nothing in the sacred writings distinctly enough marked to support this opinion of the *millennium*, or *thousand years'* reign ; nor can I conceive any important end that can be answered by this procedure.

We should be very cautious how we make a *figurative* expression, used in the most *figurative book* in the Bible, the foundation of a very important *literal system* that is to occupy a measure of the *faith*, and no small portion of the *hope*, of Christians. The strange conjectures formed on this very uncertain basis have not been very creditable either to reason or religion.

Verse 24. *When he shall have delivered up the kingdom*] The *mediatorial* kingdom, which comprehends all the displays of his grace in saving sinners, and all his spiritual influence in governing the Church.

All rule, and all authority and power.] Αρχην— εξουσιαν και δυναμιν. As the apostle is here speaking of the *end* of the present system of the world, the rule, authority, and power, may refer to all earthly governments, emperors, kings, princes, &c. ; though angels, principalities, and powers, and the rulers of the darkness of this world, and all spiritual wickedness in high places, may be also intended. Our Lord Jesus is represented here as administering the concerns of the kingdom of grace in this lower world during the time that this Divine economy lasts ; and when the *end*— the time determined by the wisdom of God, comes, then, as there is no longer any need of this administration, the kingdom is delivered up unto the Father : an allusion to the case of *Roman viceroys* or *governors* of provinces, who, when their administration was ended, delivered up their *kingdom* or *government* into the hands of the emperor.

The apostle may refer, also, to an opinion of the ancient Jews, that there should be *ten kings* who should have the supreme government of the whole world : the *first* and *last* of which should be God himself ; but the *ninth* should be the *Messiah* ; after whose empire the kingdom should be delivered up into the hands of God for ever. See the place in *Schoettgen* on this verse, and on Luke i. 33.

Verse 25. *For he must reign, &c.*] This is according to the promise, Psa. cx. 1 : " The Lord said unto my Lord, Sit thou at my right hand, until I make thine enemies thy footstool." Therefore the kingdom cannot be given up till all rule and government be cast down. So that while the world lasts, Jesus, as the

2

A. M. 4060.
A. D. 56.
A. U. C.
809.
Anno Imp. Nero-
nis Cæs. 3.

put all enemies under his feet.

26 g The last enemy *that* shall be destroyed *is* death.

27 (For he h hath put all things under his feet. But when he saith, all things are put under *him*, it is manifest that he is excepted, which did put all things under him.)

A. M. 4060.
A. D. 56.
A. U. C.
809.
Anno Imp. Nero-
nis Cæs. 3.

28 i And when all things shall be subdued unto him, then k shall the Son also himself be subject unto him that put all things under him, that God may be all in all.

29 Else what shall they do which are baptized for the dead, if the dead rise not at all? why are they then baptized for the dead?

---

g 2 Tim. i. 10; Rev. xx. 14.——h Psa. viii. 6; Matt. xxviii. 18; Heb. ii. 8; 1 Pet. iii. 22.——i Phil. iii. 21.——k Chap. iii. 23; xi. 3.

Messiah and *Mediator*, must reign; and all human beings are properly his subjects, are under his government, and are accountable to *him*.

Verse 26. *The last enemy*] Death, shall be destroyed; καταργειται, shall be *counter-worked, subverted,* and finally *overturned.* But death cannot be *destroyed* by there being simply no farther death; death can only be destroyed and annihilated by a *general resurrection;* if there be no general resurrection, it is most evident that death will still retain his empire. Therefore, the fact that *death shall be destroyed* assures the fact that there shall be a *general resurrection;* and this is a proof, also, that after the resurrection there shall be *no more death.*

Verse 27. *For he hath put all things under his feet*] The Father hath put all things under the feet of Christ according to the prophecy, Psa. cx.

He is excepted] i. e. The *Father,* who hath put all things under him, the *Son.* This observation seems to be introduced by the apostle to show that he does not mean that the Divine nature shall be subjected to the human nature. Christ, as Messiah, and Mediator between God and man, must ever be considered inferior to the Father: and his human nature, however dignified in consequence of its union with the Divine nature, must ever be inferior to God. The whole of this verse should be read in a *parenthesis.*

Verse 28. *The Son also himself be subject*] When the administration of the *kingdom of grace* is finally closed; when there shall be no longer any state of *probation,* and consequently no longer need of a distinction between the *kingdom of grace* and the *kingdom of glory;* then the Son, as being *man* and Messiah, shall cease to exercise any distinct dominion; and *God be all in all:* there remaining no longer any distinction in the persons of the glorious Trinity, as acting any *distinct* or *separate* parts in either the kingdom of grace, or the kingdom of glory; and so the one infinite essence shall appear undivided and eternal. And yet, as there appears to be a *personality* essentially in the infinite Godhead, that personality must exist eternally; but *how* this shall be we can neither tell nor know till that time comes in which *we shall* SEE HIM AS HE IS. 1 John iii. 2.

Verse 29. *Else what shall they do which are baptized for the dead*] This is certainly the most difficult verse in the New Testament; for, notwithstanding the greatest and wisest men have laboured to explain it, there are to this day nearly as many different interpretations of it as there are interpreters. I shall not employ my time, nor that of my reader, with a vast

number of discordant and conflicting opinions; I shall make a few remarks: 1. The doctrine of the resurrection of our Lord was a grand doctrine among the apostles; they considered and preached this as the *demonstration* of the *truth* of the *Gospel.* 2. The multitudes who embraced Christianity became converts on the *evidence* of this resurrection. 3. This resurrection was considered the *pledge* and *proof* of the resurrection of all believers in Christ to the possession of the same glory into which he had entered. 4. The baptism which they received they considered as an emblem of their *natural death* and resurrection. This doctrine St. Paul most pointedly preaches, Rom. vi. 3, 4, 5: *Know ye not that so many of us as were baptized into Jesus Christ, were baptized into his death? Therefore we are buried with him by baptism into death; that like as Christ was raised up from the dead, even so we also should walk in newness of life: for, if we have been planted together in the likeness of his death, we shall be also in his resurrection.* 5. It is evident from this that all who died in the faith of Christ died in the faith of the *resurrection;* and therefore cheerfully gave up their lives to death, as they *took joyfully the spoiling of their goods, knowing in themselves that they had in heaven a better and an enduring substance,* Heb. x. 34. 6. As is the *body,* so are the *members;* those who were properly instructed, and embraced Christianity, believed that as all who had died in the faith of Christ should *rise again,* so they were baptized in the same faith. 7. As so many of the primitive followers of Christ sealed the truth with their *blood,* and Satan and his followers continued unchanged, every man who took on him the profession of Christianity, which was done by receiving *baptism,* considered himself as *exposing his life* to the most imminent hazard, and offering his life with those who had already offered and laid down theirs. 8. He was therefore *baptized* in reference to this *martyrdom;* and, having a regard to those dead, he cheerfully received baptism, that, whether he were taken off by a *natural* or *violent death,* he might be raised in the likeness of Jesus Christ's resurrection, and that of his illustrious martyrs. 9. As *martyrdom* and *baptism* were thus so closely and intimately connected, βαπτιζεσθαι, to be baptized, was used to express *being put to a violent death* by the hands of persecutors. So Matt. xx. 22, 23: "But Jesus answered and said, Are ye able to drink of the *cup* that I shall drink of? &c." (Can ye go through my *sufferings?*) "They say unto him, We are able. He saith unto them, Ye shall indeed drink of my *cup,*" (ye shall bear your part

30 And [1] why stand we in jeopardy every hour?

31 I protest by [m] your [n] rejoicing which I have in Christ Jesus our Lord, [o] I die daily.

32 If, [p] after the manner of men, [q] I have fought with beasts at Ephesus, what advantageth it me, if the dead rise not? [r] let us eat and drink; for to-morrow we die.

A. M. 4060.
A. D. 56.
A. U. C.
809.
Anno Imp. Nero
nis Cæs. 3.

[1] 2 Cor. xi. 26; Gal. v. 11.——[m] Some read *our*.——[n] 1 Thess. ii. 19.——[o] Rom. viii. 36; chap. iv. 9; 2 Cor. iv. 10, 11; xi. 23.

[p] Or, to speak *after the manner of men*.——[q] 2 Cor. i. 8.——[r] Isa. xxii. 13, lvi. 12; Eccles. ii. 24; Wisd. ii. 6; Luke xii. 19.

of the *afflictions* of the Gospel,) "and be *baptized* with the *baptism* that I am *baptized* with (that is, ye shall suffer *martyrdom*.) See also Mark x. 38. So Luke xii. 50: "I have a *baptism* to be *baptized* with; and how am I straitened till it be accomplished!" That is, I must *die a violent death* for the salvation of men. 10. The sum of the apostle's meaning appears to be this: If there be no resurrection of the dead, those who, in becoming Christians, expose themselves to all manner of privations, crosses, severe sufferings, and a violent death, can have no compensation, nor any motive sufficient to induce them to expose themselves to such miseries. But as they receive baptism as an emblem of *death* in voluntarily going under the water, so they receive it as an emblem of the *resurrection* unto eternal *life*, in coming up out of the water; thus they are *baptized for the dead*, in perfect faith of the resurrection. The three following verses seem to confirm this sense.

Verse 30. And why stand we in jeopardy every hour?] Is there any reason why we should voluntarily *submit* to so many *sufferings*, and every hour be in danger of losing our lives, if the dead rise not? On the conviction of the possibility and certainty of the resurrection, we are thus baptized for the dead. We have counted the cost, despise sufferings, and exult at the prospect of death, because we know we shall have a resurrection unto eternal life.

Verse 31. I protest by your rejoicing] Νη την ὑμετεραν καυχησιν· *By your exultation or boasting.* Dr. Lightfoot understands this of "the *boasting* of the Corinthians *against* the apostle; that he considered himself continually trampled on by them; rejected and exposed to infamy and contempt; but that he took this as a part of the reproach of Christ; and was happy in the prospect of death and a glorious resurrection, when all those troubles and wrongs would terminate for ever." Instead of ὑμετεραν, YOUR *exultation or boasting*, ἡμετεραν, OUR *exultation*, is the reading of the *Codex Alexandrinus*, and several others; with the *Æthiopic, Origen*, and *Theophylact*. This will lead to an easier sense: I declare by the exultation which I have in Christ Jesus, as having died for my offences, and risen again for my justification, that I neither fear sufferings nor death; and am daily ready to be offered up, and feel myself continually exposed to death. But the common reading is probably to be preferred; for *your glorying* is the same as *glorying on your account*: I profess by the glorying or exultation which I have on *account of your salvation*, that I anticipate with pleasure the end of my earthly race.

I die daily.] A form of speech for, I am continually exposed to death. The following passages will illustrate this. So *Philo*, p. 990. *Flaccus*, who was

in continual fear of death, says: καθ᾽ ἑκαστην ἡμεραν, μαλλον δε ὡραν, προαποθνησκω, πολλους θανατους ὑπομενων ανθ᾽ ἑνος του τελευταιου· "Every day, rather every hour, I anticipate death; enduring many deaths before that last one comes." So *Libanius*, speaking of his own miseries and those of the people of Antioch, epist. 1320, page 615, says: ετι ζωντες τεθνηκαμεν· "Though living, we are dead." *Livy* has a similar form of expression to signify *continual danger*, xxix. 17: *Quotidie capitur urbs nostra, quotidie diripitur.* "Daily is our city taken, daily is it pillaged."

Verse 32. If, after the manner of men, &c.] Much learned criticism has been employed on this verse, to ascertain whether it is to be understood *literally* or *metaphorically*. Does the apostle mean to say that he had *literally* fought with wild beasts at Ephesus? or, that he had met with brutish, savage men, from whom he was in danger of his life? That St. Paul *did not* fight with wild beasts at Ephesus, may be argued, 1. From his *own silence* on this subject, when enumerating his various sufferings, 2 Cor. xi. 23, &c. 2. From the silence of his *historian*, Luke, who, in the acts of this apostle, gives no intimation of this kind; and it certainly was too *remarkable* a *circumstance* to be passed over, either by Paul in the catalogue of his own sufferings, or by Luke in his history. 3. From similar modes of speech, which are employed metaphorically, and are so understood. 4. From the improbability that a Roman citizen, as Paul was, should be condemned to such a punishment, when in other cases, by pleading his privilege, he was exempted from being scourged, &c. And, 5. From the positive testimony of Tertullian and Chrysostom, who deny the *literal* interpretation.

On the other hand, it is strongly argued that the apostle is to be *literally* understood; and that he *did*, at some particular time, contend with wild beasts at Ephesus, from which he was miraculously delivered. 1. That the phrase κατα ανθρωπον signifies *as men used to do*, and never means *according to the manner of men*, as implying their *purpose*, or, *to use their forms of speech*, &c. 2. From the circumstances of the *case* in Ephesus usually referred to, viz. the insurrection by Demetrius and his fellow craftsmen; where, though Paul would have been in danger had he gone into the theatre, he was in little or none, as he did not adventure himself. 3 From his having endured much greater conflicts at *Lystra* and at *Philippi* than at Ephesus, at the former of which he was *stoned to death*, and again miraculously raised to life: see the notes on Acts xiv. 19, &c. And yet he calls not those greater dangers by this name. 4. That it cannot refer to the insurrection of Demetrius and his fellows, for St. Paul had no contention with them, and was

A. M. 4060.
A. D. 56.
A. U. C.
809.
Anno Imp. Nero-
nis Cæs. 3.

33 Be not deceived: ^s evil communications corrupt good manners.

34 ^t Awake to righteousness,

and sin not; ^u for some have not the knowledge of God: ^v I speak *this* to your shame.

35 But some *man* will say,

A. M. 4060.
A. D. 56.
A. U. C
809.
Anno Imp. Nero-
nis Cæs. 3.

---

^s Chap. v. 6.——^t Rom. xiii. 11 ; Eph. v. 14.   ^u 1 Thess. iv. 5.——^v Chap. vi. 5.

---

scarcely in any danger, though *Gaius* and *Aristarchus* were : see the whole of Acts xix. And, 5. As we do not read of any other imminent danger to which he was exposed at Ephesus, and that already mentioned is not sufficient to justify the expression, *I have fought with beasts at Ephesus,* therefore we must conclude that he was at some time, not directly mentioned by his historian or himself, actually exposed to wild beasts at Ephesus. 6. That this is the case he refers to, 2 Cor i. 8, 9, 10 : *For we would not, brethren, have you ignorant of our trouble which came to us in Asia, that we were pressed out of measure, above strength,* καθ' ὑπερβολην εβαρηθημεν ὑπερ δυναμιν, *insomuch that we despaired even of life. But we had the sentence of death in ourselves, that we should not trust in ourselves, but in God which raiseth the dead ; who delivered us from so great a death :* for these expressions refer to some excessive and unprecedented danger, from which nothing less than a miraculous interference could have saved him ; and that it might have been an actual exposure to wild beasts, or any other danger equally great, or even greater.

What advantageth it me, if the dead rise not ?] I believe the common method of pointing this verse is erroneous ; I propose to read it thus : *If, after the manner of men, I have fought with beasts at Ephesus, what doth it advantage me ? If the dead rise not, let us eat and drink, for to-morrow we die.*

What the apostle says here is a regular and legitimate conclusion from the doctrine, that *there is no resurrection :* For if there be no *resurrection,* then there can be no *judgment*—no *future state* of *rewards* and *punishments* ; why, therefore, should we bear crosses, and keep ourselves under continual discipline ? Let us eat and drink, take all the pleasure we can, for to-morrow we die ; and there is an *end* of us for ever. The words, *Let us eat and drink, for to-morrow we die,* are taken from Isa. xxii. 13, as they stand now in the *Septuagint* ; and are a pretty smooth proverbial saying, which might be paralleled from the writings of several epicurean heathens, φαγωμεν και πιωμεν· αυριον γαρ αποθνησκομεν. The words of Isaiah are אכל ושתו כי מחר נמות *akol reshatho, ki machar namuth :* "In eating and drinking, for to-morrow we die ;" i. e. Let us spend our time in eating and drinking, &c. See a similar speech by *Trimalchio* in *Petronius Arbiter,* Satiric. cap. xxxvii :—

Heu, heu nos miseros ! quam totus homuncio nil est !
Sic erimus cuncti, postquam nos auferet orcus.

Ergo vivamus, dum licet esse bene.

Alas ! alas ! what wretches we are ! all mankind are a worthless pack : thus shall we all be, after death hath taken us away. Therefore, while we may, let us enjoy life.

Verse 33. *Be not deceived*] Do not impose on yourselves, and permit not others to do it.

Evil communications corrupt good manners.] There are many sayings like this among the Greek poets ; but this of the apostle, and which according to the best MSS. makes an Iambic verse, is generally supposed to have been taken from *Menander's lost* comedy of *Thaïs.*

Φθειρουσιν ηθη χρησθ' ὁμιλιαι κακαι·
Bad company good morals doth corrupt.

There is a proverb much like this among the rabbins :

תרי אודי יבישי וחד רטיבא אוקדן יבישי לרטיבא

" There were two *dry logs* of wood, and one *green log* ; but the *dry logs* burnt up the *green log.*"

There is no difficulty in this saying ; he who frequents the company of bad or corrupt men will soon be as they are. He may be sound in the faith, and have the life and power of godliness, and at first frequent their company only for the sake of their pleasing conversation, or their literary accomplishments : and he may think his *faith* proof against their *infidelity* ; but he will soon find, by means of their glozing speeches, his faith weakened ; and when once he gets under the empire of *doubt,* unbelief will soon prevail ; his bad company will corrupt his morals ; and the two dry logs will soon burn up the green one.

The same sentiment in nearly the same words is found in several of the Greek writers ; Æschylus, Sept. Theb. ver. 605 : Εν παντι πραγει δ' εσθ' ὁμιλιας κακης κακιον ουδεν· "In every matter there is nothing more deleterious than evil communication."——Diodorus Siculus, lib. xvi. cap. 54 : Ταις πονηραις ὁμιλιαις διεφθειρε τα ηθη των ανθρωπων· "With these evil communications he corrupted the morals of men."

Ταυτα μεν οὑτως ισθι· κακοισι δε μη προσομιλ**ᴅ**
Ανδρασιν, αλλ' αιει των αγαθων εχεο·
Και μετα τοισιν πινε και εσθιε, και μετα τοισιν
Ἱζε, και ἁνδανε τοις, ὡν μεγαλη δυναμις.
Εσθλων μεν γαρ απ' εσθλα μαθησεαι· ην δε κακοισι
Συμμιχθης, απολεις και τον εοντα νοον.

Theogn. Sent., ver. 31–36.

Know this : Thou must not keep company with the wicked, but converse always with good men. With such eat, drink, and associate. Please those who have the greatest virtue. From good men thou mayest learn good things ; but if thou keep company with the wicked, thou wilt lose even the intelligence which thou now possessest.

Verse 34. *Awake to righteousness*] Shake off your slumber ; awake fully, thoroughly, δικαιως, as ye *ought to do :* so the word should be rendered ; not *awake to righteousness.* Be in earnest : do not trifle with God, your souls, and eternity.

Sin not] For this will lead to the destruction both of body and soul. Life is but a *moment ;* improve it. Heaven has blessings without end.

A. M. 4060.
A. D. 56.
A. U. C.
809.
Anno Imp. Nero-
nis Cæs. 3.

ʷ How are the dead raised up? and with what body do they come?

36 *Thou* fool, ˣ that which thou sowest is not quickened, except it die:

37 And that which thou sowest, thou sowest not that body that shall be, but bare grain; it may chance of wheat, or of some other *grain* :

38 But God giveth it a body as it hath pleased him, and to every seed his own body.

39 All flesh *is* not the same flesh: but *there is* one *kind of* flesh of men, another flesh of beasts, another of fishes, *and* another of birds.

40 *There are* ʸ also celestial bodies, and bodies terrestrial: but the glory of the celestial

A. M. 4060.
A. D. 56.
A U. C.
809.
Anno Imp. Nero-
nis Cæs. 3.

ʷ Ezek. xxxvii. 3.——ˣ John xii. 24.

ʸ Matt. xxviii. 3; Luke ix. 29.

Some have not the knowledge of God] The original is very emphatic : αγνωσιαν γαρ Θεου τινες εχουσι, *some have an ignorance of God*; they do not acknowledge God. They have what is their *bane*; and they have not what would be their *happiness* and glory. To have an *ignorance* of God—a sort of substantial darkness, that prevents the light of God from penetrating the soul, is a worse state than to be simply in the dark, or without the Divine knowledge. The apostle probably speaks of those who were once enlightened, had once good morals, but were corrupted by bad company. It was to their *shame* or reproach that they had left the good way, and were now posting down to the chambers of death.

Verse 35. *But some* man *will say*] Αλλα ερει τις. It is very likely that the apostle, by τις, *some, some one, some man*, means particularly the *false apostle*, or teacher at Corinth, who was chief in the opposition to the pure doctrine of the Gospel, and to whom, in this covert way, he often refers.

The *second* part of the apostle's discourse begins at this verse. What shall be the nature of the resurrection body? 1. The question is *stated*, ver. 35. 2. It is *answered*: first, by a *similitude*, ver. 36—38; secondly, by an *application*, ver. 39—41; and thirdly, by *explication*, ver. 42—50.

Verse 36. Thou *fool*] Αφρον. If this be addressed, as it probably is, to the *false apostle*, there is a peculiar propriety in it; as this man seems to have magnified his own wisdom, and set it up against both God and man; and none but a *fool* could act so. At the same time, it is folly in *any* to assert the impossibility of a thing because *he* cannot comprehend it.

That which thou sowest is not quickened, except it die] I have shown the propriety of this simile of the apostle in the note on John xii. 24, to which I must refer the reader. A grain of wheat, &c., is composed of the *body* or *lobes*, and the *germ*. The latter forms an inconsiderable part of the mass of the grain; the *body*, *lobes*, or *farinaceous* part, forms nearly the whole This body dies—becomes decomposed, and forms a fine earth, from which the germ derives its first nourishment; by the nourishment thus derived the germ is *quickened*, receives its first vegetable life, and through this means is rendered capable of deriving the rest of its nourishment and support from the grosser earth in which the grain was deposited. Whether the apostle would intimate here that there is a certain *germ* in the present body, which shall become the *seed* of the resurrection body, this is not the place to inquire; and

on this point I can with pleasure refer to Mr. Drew's work on the " Resurrection of the Human Body;" where this subject, as well as every other subject connected with this momentous question, is considered in a very luminous and cogently argumentative point of view.

Verse 37. *Thou sowest not that body that shall be*] This is decomposed, and becomes the means of nourishing the whole plant, *roots, stalk, leaves, ear*, and *full corn* in the ear.

Verse 38. *But God giveth it a body*] And is there any other way of accounting for it but by the miraculous working of God's power? For out of that one bare grain is produced a system of *roots*, a tall and vigorous *stalk*, with all its appendages of *leaves*, &c., besides the full corn in the ear; the whole making several hundred times the quantum of what was originally deposited. There are no proofs that what some call *nature* can effect this : it will ever be a philosophical as well as a Scriptural truth, that *God giveth it a body as it pleaseth him*; and so doth he manage the whole of the work, that every seed shall have its *own body* : that the *wheat* germ shall never produce *barley*; nor the *rye*, oats. See the note on Gen. i. 12.

Verse 39. *All flesh* is *not the same flesh*] Though the organization of all animals is, in its general principles, the same, yet there are no *two* different kinds of *animals* that have flesh of the same flavour, whether the animal be *beast*, *fowl*, or *fish*. And this is precisely the same with *vegetables*.

In opposition to this general assertion of St. Paul, there are certain people who tell us that *fish* is not *flesh*; and while their religion prohibits, at one time of the year, the flesh of *quadrupeds* and *fowls*, it allows them to eat *fish*, fondly supposing that *fish* is not *flesh* : they might as well tell us that a *lily* is not a *vegetable*, because it is not a *cabbage*. There is a Jewish canon pronounced by *Schoettgen* which my readers may not be displeased to find inserted here : *Nedarim*, fol. 40 : הנודר מן הבשר יהא אסור בבשר דגים והגבים *He who is bound by a vow to abstain from flesh, is bound to abstain from the flesh of fish and of locusts.* From this it appears that they acknowledged that there was one flesh of beasts and another of fishes, and that he was religiously bound to abstain from the one, who was bound to abstain from the other.

Verse 40. There are *also celestial bodies, and bodies terrestrial*] The apostle certainly does not speak of *celestial* and *terrestrial bodies* in the sense in which we use those terms : we invariably mean by the for-

A. M. 4060.
A. D. 56.
A. U. C.
809.
Anno Imp. Nero-
nis Cæs. 3.
is one, and the *glory* of the ter-restrial *is* another.

41 *There is* one glory of the sun, and another glory of the moon, and another glory of the stars : for *one* star differeth from *another* star in glory.

42 ᶻ So also *is* the resurrection of the dead.

z Dan. xii. 3 ; Matt. xiii. 43.

It is sown in corruption ; it is raised in incorruption :

A. M. 4060.
A. D. 56.
A. U. C.
809.
Anno Imp. Nero-
nis Cæs. 3.

43 ᵃ It is sown in dishonour ; it is raised in glory : it is sown in weakness ; it is raised in power :

44 It is sown a ᵇ natural body ; it is raised a spiritual body. There is a natural

a Phil. iii. 21.——b Gal. vi. 8.

mer the *sun, moon, planets,* and *stars ;* by the latter, masses of *inanimate matter.* But the apostle speaks of *human beings,* some of which were clothed with *celestial,* others with *terrestrial* bodies. It is very likely, therefore, that he means by the *celestial bodies* such as those refined human bodies with which *Enoch, Elijah,* and *Christ* himself, appear in the realms of glory : to which we may add the bodies of those *saints* which arose after our Lord's resurrection ; and, after having *appeared to many,* doubtless were taken up to paradise. By *terrestrial* bodies we may understand those in which the saints now live.

But the glory of the celestial is one] The *glory*—the excellence, beauty, and perfection. Even the present *frail human body* possesses an indescribable degree of *contrivance, art, economy, order, beauty,* and excellence ; but the *celestial body,* that in which Christ now appears, and according to which ours shall be raised, (Phil. iii. 21,) will exceed the excellence of this beyond all comparison. A *glory* or *splendour* will belong to that which does not belong to this : *here* there is a *glory* of excellence ; there, there will be a *glory* of *light* and effulgence ; for the bodies of the saints shall shine like the *sun* in the kingdom of their Father. See Matt. xiii. 43.

Verse 41. *There is one glory of the sun*] As if he had said : This may be illustrated by the present *appearance* of the celestial bodies which belong to our system. The *sun* has a greater degree of splendour than the *moon ;* the moon than the *planets ;* and the planets than the *stars.* And even in the fixed stars, one has a *greater degree* of *splendour* than another, which may proceed either from their different *magnitudes,* or from the comparative *proximity* of some of them to our earth ; but from which of these causes, or from what other cause unknown, we cannot tell, as it is impossible to ascertain the distance of any of the fixed stars ; even the nearest of them being too remote to afford any sensible *parallax,* without which their distances cannot be measured. See the concluding observations.

Verse 42. *So also is the resurrection of the dead.*] That is, the bodies of the dead, though all immortal, shall possess different degrees of *splendour* and *glory,* according to the state of holiness in which their respective souls were found. The rabbins have some crude notions concerning different *degrees* of glory, which the righteous shall possess in the kingdom of heaven. They make out *seven* degrees :—

" The *first* of which is possessed by צדיקים *tsaddikim,* the just, who observe the covenant of the holy, blessed God, and subjugate all evil affections."

" The *second* is possessed by those who are ישרים

yesharim, the upright ; whose delight it is to walk in the ways of God and please him."

" The *third* is for תמימים *temimim,* the perfect ; those who, with integrity, walk in the ways of God, and do not *curiously pry* into his dispensations."

" The *fourth* is for קדושים *kedoshim,* the holy ones ; those who are the excellent of the earth, in whom is all God's delight." Psa. xvi. 3.

" The *fifth* is for בעלי תשובה *baaley teshubah,* the chief of the penitents ; who have broken through the brazen doors, and returned to the Lord."

" The *sixth* is for תינוקות של בית רבן *tinukoth shel beith raban,* the scholars and tender ones ; who have not transgressed."

" The *seventh* is for חסידים *chasidim,* the godly ; and this is the innermost of all the departments." These seven degrees require a comment by themselves.

There is a saying among the rabbins very like that of the apostle in this and the preceding verse. *Siphri,* in *Yalcut Simeoni,* page 2, fol. 10 : " The faces of the righteous shall be, in the world to come, like suns, moons, the heaven, stars, lightnings : and like the lilies and candlesticks of the temple."

It is sown in corruption] The body is *buried* in a state of degradation, decay, and corruption. The apostle uses the word *sown* to intimate that the body shall rise again, as a seed springs up that has been sown in the earth.

It is raised in incorruption] Being no more subject to corruption, dissolution, and death.

Verse 43. *It is sown in dishonour*] Being now stripped of all the glory it had as a machine, fearfully and wonderfully made by the hands of God ; and also consigned to death and destruction *because* of *sin.* This is the most *dishonourable* circumstance.

It is raised in glory] It is raised a glorious body, because immortal, and for ever redeemed from the empire of death.

It is sown in weakness] The principles of dissolution, corruption, and decay, have prevailed over it : disease undermined it ; and death made it his prey.

It is raised in power] To be no more liable to weakness, through labour ; decay, by age ; wasting, by disease ; and dissolution, by death.

Verse 44. *It is sown a natural body*] Σωμα ψυχικον· An *animal body,* having a multiplicity of *solids* and *fluids* of different kinds, with different functions ; composed of muscles, fibres, tendons, cartilages, bones, arteries, veins, nerves, blood, and various juices, requiring continual support from aliment ; and hence the necessity of *labour* to provide food, and *skill* to prepare it ; which food must be masticated, digested, and refined ; what is proper for

2

A. M. 4060.
A. D. 56.
A. U. C. 809.
Anno Imp. Neronis Cæs. 3.

body, and there is a spiritual body.

45 And so it is written, The first man Adam [c] was made a living soul; [d] the last Adam *was made* [e] a quickening spirit.

46 Howbeit, that *was* not first which is spiritual, but that which

A. M. 4060.
A. D. 56.
A. U. C. 809.
Anno Imp. Nero nis Cæs. 3.

---

[c] Gen. ii. 7.——[d] Rom. v. 14.

[e] John v. 21; vi. 33, 39, 40, 54, 57; Phil. iii. 21; Col. iii. 4.

---

nourishment secreted, brought into the circulation, farther elaborated, and prepared to enter into the composition of every part; hence *growth* and *nutrition;* without which no organized body can possibly exist.

It is raised a spiritual body.] One perfect in all its parts; no longer dependent on natural productions for its support; being built up on indestructible principles, and existing in a region where there shall be no more *death;* no more causes of *decay* leading to dissolution; and consequently, no more necessity for food, *nutrition,* &c. The body is spiritual, and has a spiritual existence and spiritual support.

What the apostle says here is quite consistent with the views his countrymen had on this subject.

In *Sohar Chadash,* fol. 43, it is said: "So shall it be in the resurrection of the dead; only, the old uncleanness shall not be found."

R. Bechai, on the law, fol. 14, says: "When the godly shall arise, their bodies shall be pure and innocent; obedient to the instinct of the soul: there shall be no adversary, nor any evil disease."

Rab. Pinchas says: "The holy blessed God shall make the bodies of the righteous as beautiful as the body of Adam was when he entered into paradise."

Rab. Levi says: "When the soul is in heaven, it is clothed with celestial light; when it returns to the body, it shall have the same light; and then the body shall shine like the splendour of the firmament of heaven. Then shall men gain the knowledge of what is perfect." *Sohar. Gen.,* fol. 69.

The Jews have an opinion that the *os coxendicis,* the lower joint of the backbone, *survives* the corruption of the body; and that it is out of this bone that the resurrection body is formed. In the place last quoted, fol. 70, we have the following teachings on this subject: "Let us borrow an example from what relates to the purifying of silver. First, the ore is cast into the burning furnace, that it may be separated from its earthly impurities; it is then *silver,* but not *perfect silver.* They put it into the furnace a *second* time, and then all its scoriæ are separated from it, and it becomes *perfect silver,* without any adulteration. Thus does the holy blessed God: he *first* buries our bodies under the earth, where they putrefy and corrupt, that nothing remains but that *one bone:* from this a new body is produced, which is indeed a *body,* but not a *perfect body.* But in that great day, when all bodies are hidden in the earth, and the soul departs, then even that bone decays, and the body which was formed out of it remains, and is as the *light of the sun,* and the *splendour of heaven.* Thus, as the silver was purified, so is the body: and no imperfect mixture remains." See *Schoettgen.*

These things must not be treated as rabbinical dotages; the different *similes* used by the apostle

have the same spirit and design: as the seed which is sown in the earth rots, and out of the germ contained in it God in his providence produces a root, stalk, leaves, ear, and a great numerical increase of grains; is it not likely that God, out of some *essential* parts of the body that now is, will produce the resurrection body; and will then give the soul a body as it pleaseth him; and so completely preserve the *individuality* of every human being, as he does of every grain; giving to each its *own* body? ver. 38. So that as surely as the *grain* of *wheat* shall produce *wheat* after it is cast in the earth, corrupts, and dies; so surely shall our *bodies* produce the *same bodies* as to their *essential* individuality. As the germination of seeds is produced by his *wisdom* and *power,* so shall the pure and perfect human body be in the resurrection. Hence he does not say the body is *buried;* but the body is *sown;* it is *sown* in weakness, it is *sown* in dishonour, &c., &c.

There is a natural body, and there is a spiritual body.] This very saying is found in so many words, in *Yalcut Rubeni,* fol. 126: "There are different kinds of men." אית אדם דאיהו אדם דנשמתא ואית אדם רגופא "There is a spiritual Adam, and there is also a corporeal Adam."

Verse 45. *The first man Adam was made a living soul*] These forms of expression are also common among the Jews: hence we find אדם הראשון *Adam harishon,* "Adam the first;" and אדם קדמאי *Adam kadmai,* "Adam the last." They assert that there are two Adams: 1. The *mystical* heavenly Adam; and 2. The mystical earthly Adam. See *Sohar Exod.,* fol. 29; and the several examples in *Schoettgen.* The apostle says this is written: *The first man Adam was made a living soul:* this is found Gen. ii. 7, in the words נשמת חיים *nishmath chaiyim,* the *breath* of *lives;* which the apostle translates ψυχην ζωσαν, a living soul.

The last Adam—a quickening spirit.] This is also said to be *written;* but *where,* says Dr. Lightfoot, is this *written* in the whole sacred book? *Schoettgen* replies, In the very same verse, and in these words: ויהי האדם לנפש חיה *vayehi ha-Adam le-nephesh chaiyah,* and Adam became a living soul; which the apostle translates πνευμα ζωοποιουν, a quickening, or life-giving *spirit.* Among the cabalistic Jews נפש *nephesh* is considered as implying greater *dignity* than נשמה *nishma.* The former may be considered as pointing out the *rational,* the latter the *sensitive* soul. All these references to Jewish opinions and forms of speech the apostle uses to convince them that the thing was possible; and that the resurrection of the body was generally credited by all their wise and learned men. The Jews, as Dr. Lightfoot observes, speak frequently of the *Spirit of the Messiah;* and they allow that it was this Spirit that *moved on the*

A. M. 4060.
A. D. 56.
A. U. C.
809.
Anno Imp. Nero-
nis Cæs. 3.

is natural; and afterward that which is spiritual.

47 [f] The first man *is* of the earth, [g] earthy: the second man *is* the Lord [h] from heaven.

48 As *is* the earthy, such *are* they also that

are earthy: [i] and **as** *is* the heavenly, such *are* they also that are heavenly.

49 And [k] as we have borne the image of the earthy, [l] we shall also bear the image of the heavenly.

A. M. 4060.
A. D. 56.
A. U. C.
809.
Anno Imp. Nero-
nis Cæs. 3.

---

[f] John iii. 31.——[g] Gen. ii. 7; iii. 19.——[h] John iii. 13, 31. [i] Phil. iii. 20, 21.

[k] Gen. v. 3.——[l] Rom. viii. 29; 2 Cor. iii. 18; iv. 11; Phil. iii. 21; 1 John iii. 2.

---

face of the waters, Gen. i. 2. And they assert that *the Messiah shall quicken those who dwell in the dust.* "It ought not to be passed by," says the same author, "that Adam, receiving from God the promise of Christ—*The seed of the woman shall bruise the head of the serpent,* and believing it, named his wife חוה *Chavvah,* that is, *life;* so the *Septuagint,* και εκαλεσεν Αδαμ το ονονα της γυναικος αυτου Ζωη· *And Adam called the name* of *his wife, Life.* What! Is she called *Life* that brought *death* into the world? But Adam perceived τον εσχατον Αδαμ, the last Adam exhibited to him in the promise, to be πνευμα ζωο, ποιουν, a *quickening* or *life-giving spirit;* and had brought in a *better life* of the *soul;* and should at last bring in a *better life* of the *body.* Hence is that saying, John i. 4: Εν αυτω ζωη ην, In HIM was LIFE."

Some contend that the *first Adam* and the *last Adam* mean the same person in *two* different states: the first man with the body of his *creation;* the same person with the body of his *resurrection.* See on ver. 49.

Verse 46. *That* was *not first which is spiritual*] The *natural* or *animal* body, described ver. 44, was the *first;* it was the body with which Adam was created. The *spiritual* body is the *last,* and is that with which the *soul* is to be clothed in the *resurrection.*

Verse 47. *The first man* is *of the earth*] That is: Adam's body was made out of the *dust of the earth;* and hence the apostle says he was χοϊκος, *of the dust;* for the body was made עפר מן האדמה *aphar min ha-adamah, dust from the ground;* Gen. ii. 7.

The second man is—*from heaven.*] Heavenly, ουρανιος, as several good MSS. and versions read. The resurrection body shall be of a *heavenly* nature, and not subject to decay or death. What is formed of *earth* must live after an *earthly manner;* must be *nourished* and supported by the earth: what is from *heaven* is of a *spiritual* nature; and shall have no farther connection with, nor dependence upon, earth. I conceive both these clauses to relate to *man;* and to point out the difference between the *animal* body and the *spiritual* body, or between the bodies which we *now* have and the bodies which we shall have in the *resurrection.* But can this be the meaning of the clause, *the second man is the Lord from heaven?* In the quotation I have omitted ὁ Κυριος, the Lord, on the following authorities: MANUSCRIPTS—BCD*EFG, and two others. VERSIONS—*Coptic, Æthiopic, Armenian* in the margin, *Vulgate,* and *Itala.* FATHERS—*Origen,* who quotes it once and omits it once; *Athanasius, Basil,* the two *Gregories, Nyssen* and *Nazianzen; Isidore, Cyril, Tertullian, Cyprian, Hilary,*

Zeno, Ambrose, Augustine, Jerome, Ambrosiaster, Philaster, Leo, Pacianus, Primasius, Sedulius, Bede, and *others.* See these authorities more at large in *Wetstein.* Some of the most eminent of modern critics leave out the word, and Tertullian says that it was put in by the heretic Marcion. I do think that the word is not legitimate in this place. The verse is read by the MSS., versions, and fathers referred to, thus: *The first man is of the earth, earthy; the second man is of heaven, heavenly;* Κυριος being *omitted,* and ουρανιος added. The *first man* and the *second man* of this verse are the same as the *first Adam* and the *second Adam* of ver. 45, and it is not clear that *Christ* is meant in either place. Some suppose that there is a reference here to what *Eve* said when she brought forth Cain: *I have gotten a man from the Lord,* קניתי איש את יהוה *kanithi ish eth Yehovah, I have possessed* or *obtained* a *man, the Lord;* that is, as Dr. Lightfoot explains it, that the Lord himself should become man: and he thinks that Eve had respect to the promise of Christ when she named her *son;* as Adam had when he named his *wife.* If Eve had this in view, we can only say she was sadly mistaken: indeed the conjecture is too refined.

The terms *first man of the earth,* and *second man from heaven,* are frequent among the Jews: ארם לעילא the *superior* Adam; and ארם תתאה Adam the *inferior;* that is, the *earthly* and the *heavenly* Adam: Adam *before* the resurrection, and Adam *after* it.

Verse 48. *As is the earthy, &c.*] As Adam was, who was formed from the earth, so are all his descendants; frail, decaying, and subject to death.

As is the heavenly] As is the heavenly state of Adam and all glorified beings, so shall be the state of all those who, at the resurrection, are found fit for glory.

Verse 49. *And as we have borne the image of the earthy*] As being descendants from Adam we have all been born in his likeness, and subject to the same kind of corruption, disgrace, and death; we shall also be raised to a life immortal, such as he now enjoys in the kingdom of God. This interpretation proceeds on the ground that what is here spoken belongs to *Adam* in his *twofold* state: viz. of *mortality* and *immortality;* of disgrace and honour; of earth and heaven.

But by many commentators the words are understood to refer to *Adam* and *Christ,* in ver. 45, 47, 48, and 49. By *these,* Christ is called the *second Adam,* the *quickening Spirit,* the *second man,* and the *heavenly;* whose *image* of righteousness and true holiness we are *to bear.*

But when I consider, 1st. How all these terms are used and applied in the *Jewish writings,* it appears to

A. M. 4060.
A. D. 56.
A. U. C.
809.
Anno Imp. Nero-
nis Cæs. 3.

50 Now this I say, brethren, that ^m flesh and blood cannot inherit the kingdom of God ; neither doth corruption inherit incorruption.

51 Behold, I show you a mystery : ⁿ We

shall not all sleep, ^o but we shall all be changed,

52 In a moment, in the twinkling of an eye, at the last trump : ^p for the trumpet shall sound, and the dead shall be raised incorruptible, and we shall be changed.

A. M. 4060.
A. D. 56.
A. U. C.
809.
Anno Imp. Nero
nis Cæs. 3.

---

^m Matt. xvi. 17; John iii. 3, 5.——ⁿ 1 Thess. iv. 15, 16, 17.
^o Phil. iii. 21.

^p Zech. ix. 14; Matthew xxiv. 31; John v. 25; 1 Thess.
iv. 16.

---

me that as this was not their import among *them,* so it was not the design of Paul ; and it would be very difficult to find any place where Jesus Christ is called the *second Adam* in either Old or New Testament. The discourse of the apostle, Rom. v. 14–19, will not prove it, though in those verses there is a *comparison* drawn between Adam and Christ ; but that comparison refers to the extent of the *sin* and *condemnation* brought upon all men by the transgression of the *first ;* and the *redemption* purchased for all men by the sacrifice of the *last ;* and the superabundant grace procured by that sacrifice. But here, the comparison most evidently is between the state of man in *this mortal* life, and his state after the resurrection. *Here,* all men are corrupt and mortal, and *here,* all men die. *There,* all men shall be incorrupt and immortal, and, whether holy or unholy, shall be eternally immortal.

Of the *image of Adam,* in his *heavenly* or paradisaical *state,* the rabbins talk largely : they say that " God created Adam with a double image, earthly and heavenly ; that he was the most perfect of all beings ; that his *splendour* shone from one extremity of the earth to the other ; that all feared before him ; that he knew all wisdom, both *earthly* and *heavenly* ; but when he sinned, his glory was diminished, and his wisdom departed from him." *Yalcut Rubeni,* fol. 10.

They add farther, that " in the time in which Adam received בדיוקנה עילאה the *heavenly image,* all creatures came to him, and acknowledged him king of the earth." Ibid., fol. 21.

2. From all this, and much more might be produced on the subject, (see *Schoettgen,*) it appears that the apostle follows, as far as it could comport with his design, the sentiments of his countrymen, and that he adopts their very *phraseology ;* and that it is through the medium of these sentiments and this phraseology that he is to be understood and interpreted. Others may understand all these passages differently ; and still consider them as a parallel between *Adam* and *Christ,* which is the general view of interpreters. The view which I have taken of them appears to me to be much more consistent with the nature of the discourse, and the scope and design of the apostle. The common opinion is *orthodox :* what I here propose is no *heresy.* There are many difficulties in the chapter, and not a few in the verses immediately under consideration.

Verse 50. *Flesh and blood cannot inherit the kingdom*] This is a *Hebrew* periphrasis for *man,* and *man* in his present state of *infirmity* and *decay.* Man, in his present state, cannot inherit the kingdom of God ; his nature is not suited to that place ; he could not, in his present *weak state,* endure an *exceeding great and*

eternal weight of glory. Therefore, it is necessary that he should *die,* or be *changed ;* that he should have a *celestial body* suited to the celestial *state.* The apostle is certainly not speaking of *flesh and blood* in a *moral* sense, to signify corruption of mind and heart ; but in a *natural* sense : as such, *flesh* and *blood* cannot inherit glory, for the reasons already assigned.

Verse 51. *I show you a mystery*] That is, a thing which you have never known before. But what is this *mystery ?* Why, that *we shall not all sleep* ; we shall not all *die ;* but we shall all be *changed :* of this the Jews had not *distinct* notions. For, as flesh and blood cannot inherit glory, and all shall not be found *dead* at the day of judgment, then all must be *changed* —undergo such a change that their bodies may become *spiritual,* like the bodies of those who shall be raised from the dead.

Verse 52. *In a moment*] Εν ατομω· *In an atom ;* that is, an *indivisible* point of time. *In the twinkling of an eye ;* as soon as a man can *wink ;* which expressions show that this mighty work is to be done by the almighty power of God, as he does all his works : He *calls,* and it *is done.* The resurrection of *all* the *dead,* from the foundation of the world to that time, and the change of all the *living* then upon earth, shall be the work of a *single moment.*

At the last trump] This, as well as all the rest of the peculiar phraseology of this chapter, is merely *Jewish,* and we must go to the Jewish writers to know what is intended. On this subject, the *rabbins* use the very same expression. Thus *Rabbi Akiba :* " How shall the holy blessed God raise the dead ? We are taught that God has a *trumpet* a thousand ells long, according to the ell of God : this *trumpet* he shall *blow,* so that the sound of it shall extend from one extremity of the earth to the other. At the *first* blast the *earth* shall be shaken ; at the *second,* the *dust* shall be separated ; at the *third,* the *bones* shall be gathered together ; at the *fourth,* the *members* shall *wax warm ;* at the *fifth,* the *heads* shall be covered with *skin ;* at the *sixth,* the *souls* shall be *rejoined* to their *bodies ;* at the *seventh,* all shall *revive* and stand *clothed.*" See *Wetstein.* This tradition shows us what we are to understand by the *last trump* of the apostle ; it is the *seventh* of Rab. *Akiba,* when the dead shall be all raised, and, being *clothed upon* with their eternal vehicles, they shall be ready to appear before the judgment seat of God.

For the trumpet shall sound] By this the apostle confirms the *substance* of the tradition, there shall be the *sound of a trumpet* on this great day ; and this other scriptures teach : see Zech. ix. 14 ; Matt. xxiv. 31 ; John v. 25 ; 1 Thess. iv. 16, in which latter place,

2

A. M. 4060.
A. D. 56.
A. U. C.
809.
Anno Imp. Nero-
nis Cæs. 3.

53 For this corruptible must put on incorruption, and ^q this mortal *must* put on immortality.

54 So, when this corruptible shall have put on incorruption, and this mortal shall have put on immortality, then shall be brought to pass

the saying that is written, ^r Death is swallowed up in victory.

55 ^s O death, where *is* thy sting? O ^t grave, where *is* thy victory?

56 The sting of death *is* sin; and ^u the strength of sin *is* the law.

A. M. 4060.
A. D. 56.
A. U. C.
809.
Anno Imp. Nero-
nis Cæs. 3.

---

q 2 Cor. v. 4.——r Isa. xxv. 8; Heb. ii. 14, 15; Rev. xx. 14.

s Hos. xiii. 14.——t Or, *hell.*——u Rom. iv. 15; v. 13; vii. 5, 13.

---

the apostle treats this subject among the Thessalonians, as he does here among the Corinthians. See the notes there.

Shall be raised incorruptible] Fully clothed with a new body, to die no more.

We shall be changed.] That is, those who shall then be found *alive.*

Verse 53. *For this corruptible, &c.*] Because flesh and blood cannot inherit glory; therefore, there must be a refinement by *death,* or a *change* without it.

Verse 54. *Death is swallowed up in victory.*] Κατεποθη ὁ θανατος εις νικος. These words are a quotation from Isa. xxv. 8, where the Hebrew is בלע המות לנצח *billá hammaveth lanetsach:* He (God) *hath swallowed up death in victory;* or, *for ever.* These words in the *Septuagint* are thus translated: κατεπιεν ὁ θανατος ισχυσας· Death *having prevailed,* or *conquered, hath swallowed up.* But in the verson of *Theodotion,* the words are the same with those of the apostle. The Hebrew לנצח *lanetsach* the *Septuagint* sometimes translate εις νικος, *in victory,* but most commonly εις τελος, *for ever;* both, as Bishop Pearce observes, in such kind of phrases, signifying the same thing, because eternity conquers all things; and accordingly, in 2 Sam. ii. 26, where the Septuagint have μη εις νικος καταφαγεται ἡ ρομφαια, our English version has, *Shall the sword devour* FOR EVER? And the same may be seen in Job xxxvi. 7; Lam. v. 20; Amos i. 11; and viii. 7; from which authority the bishop translates the clause here, *Death is swallowed up* FOR EVER.

Death is here personified and represented as a devouring being, swallowing up all the generations of men; and by the resurrection of the body and the destruction of the empire of death, God is represented as swallowing him up; or that *eternity* gulps him down; so that he is endlessly lost and absorbed in its illimitable waste. How glorious a time to the righteous, when the inhabitant shall no more say, I am sick; when God shall have wiped away all tears from off all faces, and when there shall be no more death. This time must come. Hallelujah! The Lord God Omnipotent reigneth.

Verse 55. *O death, where is thy sting? O grave, where is thy victory?*] Που σου, Θανατε, το κεντρον· που σου, ᾁδη, το νικος· These words are generally supposed to be taken from Hos. xiii. 14, where the Hebrew text stands thus: אהי דבריך מות אהי קטבך שאול *ehi debareyca maveth; ehikatabca sheol:* which we translate, *O death! I will be thy plagues; O grave! I will be thy destruction;* and which the *Septuagint* translate very nearly as the apostle, που ἡ δικη σου, Θανατε; που το κεντρον σου, ᾁδη; O death, where is thy revenge, or *judicial process?* O grave, where is thy sting! And it may

be remarked that almost all the MSS., *versions,* and many of the *fathers,* interchange the two members of this sentence as they appear in the Septuagint, attributing *victory* to *death;* and the *sting,* to *hades* or the *grave;* only the Septuagint, probably by mistake or corruption of copyists, have δικη, dike, *revenge* or a *judicial process,* for νικος, nikos, *victory:* a mistake which the similarity of the words, both in *letters* and *sound,* might readily produce. We may observe, also, that the אהי *ehi* (I will be) of the Hebrew text the Septuagint, and the apostle following them, have translated που, *where,* as if the word had been written איה *where,* the two last letters interchanged; but אהי *ehi* is rendered *where* in other places; and our translators, in the 10th verse of this same chapter (Hos. xiii.) render אהי כלך *ehi malca,* "I will be thy king," but have this note in the margin, "Rather, *where is thy king?*" King Hoshea being then in prison." The apostle, therefore, and the Septuagint, are sufficiently vindicated by the use of the word elsewhere: and the best Jewish commentators allow this use of the word. The *Targum, Syriac, Arabic, Vulgate,* and some MSS. of Kennicott and De Rossi, confirm this reading.

Having vindicated the translation, it is necessary to inquire into the meaning of the apostle's expressions. Both *Death* and *Hades* are here personified. *Death* is represented as having a *sting, dagger,* or *goad,* by which, like the driver of oxen, he is continually irritating and urging on; (these irritations are the *diseases* by which men are urged on till they fall into *Hades,* the empire of Death;) to *Hades, victory* is attributed, having overcome and conquered all human life, and subdued all to its own empire. By the transposition of these two members of the sentence, the *victory* is given to *Death,* who has extinguished all human life; and the *sting* is given to *Hades,* as in his empire the *evil* of death is fully displayed by the extinction of all animal life, and the destruction of all human bodies. We have often seen a personification of death in ancient paintings—a skeleton crowned, with a dart in his hand; probably taken from the apostle's description. The Jews represent the angel of death as having a sword, from which deadly drops of gall fall into the mouths of all men.

Hades, which we here translate *grave,* is generally understood to be the *place of separate spirits.* See the note on Matt. xi. 23.

Verse 56. *The sting of death is sin*] The apostle explains himself particularly here: death could not have entered into the world if sin had not entered *first;* it was *sin* that not only introduced *death,* but has armed him with all his *destroying* force; the *goad* or *dagger* of death is *sin;* by this both body and soul are slain

2

A. M. 4060.
A. D. 56.
A. U. C.
809.
Anno Imp. Nero-
nis Cæs. 3.

57 ᵛ But thanks *be* to God, which giveth us ʷ the victory through our Lord Jesus Christ. 58 ˣ Therefore, my beloved bre-

thren, be ye steadfast, unmovable, always abounding in the work of the Lord; forasmuch as ye know ʸ that your labour is not in vain in the Lord.

A. M. 4060.
A. D. 56.
A. U. C.
809.
Anno Imp. Nero-
nis. Cæs. 3.

ᵛ Rom. vii. 25.——ʷ 1 John v. 4, 5.

ˣ 2 Pet. iii. 14.——ʸ Chap. iii. 8.

The strength of sin is *the law.*] The law of God forbids all transgression, and sentences those who commit it to temporal and eternal death. Sin has its controlling and *binding* power from the law. The law *curses* the transgressor, and provides no help for him; and if nothing else intervene, he must, through it, continue ever under the empire of death.

Verse 57. *But thanks* be *to God*] What the law could not do, because it is *law*, (and law cannot provide *pardon*,) is done by the *Gospel* of our Lord Jesus Christ: he has *died* to slay death; he has *risen* again to bring mankind from under the empire of *hades*. All this he has done through his mere unmerited *mercy*; and eternal *thanks* are due to God for this *unspeakable gift*. He has given us the *victory* over sin, Satan, death, the grave, and hell.

Verse 58. *Be ye steadfast*] Ἑδραιοι, from ἑδρα, a *seat*; be *settled*; confide in the truth of this doctrine of the resurrection, and every thing that pertains to it, as confidently as a man *sits* down on a SEAT, which he knows to be solid, firm, and safe; and on which he has often *sat.*

Unmovable] Αμετακινητοι, from *a*, *negative*, and μετακινεω, *to move away*; let nothing *shake* your faith; let nothing *move you away* from this hope of the Gospel which is given unto you. What I tell you I receive from God; your false teachers cannot say so: in a declaration of God you may unshakingly confide.

Always abounding in the work of the Lord] The *work of the Lord* is *obedience* to his holy word; every believer in Christ is a *workman* of God. He that *works* not, to bring glory to God and good to man, is not acknowledged as a *servant of Christ*; and if he be not a servant, he is not a *son*; and if not a son, then not an *heir*. And he must not only *work*, but *abound* in that work; ever exceeding his former self; and this, not for a *time*, but *always*; beginning, continuing, and ending every act of life to God's glory and the good of his fellows.

Your labour is not in vain] *Your labour in the Lord is not in vain*; you must not only *work*, but you must *labour*—put forth all your strength; and you must work and labour *in the Lord*—under his *direction*, and by his *influence*; for without him ye can do nothing. And this labour cannot be *in vain*; you shall have a resurrection unto eternal life: not because you have *laboured*, but because Christ died and gave you grace to be faithful.

1. THE chapter through which the reader has passed is a chapter of great importance and difficulty; and on its difficulties much has been written in the preceding notes. Though I have used all the helps in my power to guide me in explaining it, I have, upon the whole, been obliged to think for myself, and claim only the praise of severe labour, ever directed by honest intention and an earnest desire to find out the truth.

2. There are many questions connected with the doctrine of the resurrection which I could not introduce here without writing a *book* instead of *short notes* on a very long chapter. On such subjects, I again beg leave to direct the reader to Mr. *Samuel Drew's* Essay on that subject.

3. One remark I cannot help making; the doctrine of the *resurrection* appears to have been thought of much more consequence among the primitive Christians than it is *now!* How is this? The apostles were continually insisting on it, and exciting the followers of God to diligence, obedience, and cheerfulness through it. And their successors in the present day seldom mention it! So apostles preached, and so primitive Christians believed; so we preach, and so our hearers believe. There is not a doctrine in the Gospel on which more stress is laid; and there is not a doctrine in the present system of preaching which is treated with more neglect!

4. Though all men shall rise again, yet it will be in widely different circumstances: some will rise to glory and honour; others to shame and everlasting contempt. Those alone who here received the salvation of God, and continued faithful unto death, shall have a resurrection to everlasting glory; not every *believer*, but every loving obedient believer, shall enter into the paradise of God, and have a body fashioned like unto his Lord's glorious body.

5. All glorified spirits will not have the same *degree* of glory. *Two* things will necessarily cause great difference: 1. The quantum of *mind*; and 2. The quantum of *grace.*

(1.) It is idle to suppose that God has made all human souls with the *same capacities*: he has not. There is an infinite diversity; he who has the greatest mind can *know* most, *do* most, *suffer* most, and *enjoy* most.

(2.) The quantum of *grace* will be another great cause of diversity and glory. He who received most of Christ here, and was most devoted to his service, shall have the nearest *approach* to him in his own kingdom. But all equally holy and equally faithful souls shall not have equal degrees of glory; for the glory will be according to the *capacity* of the *mind*, as well as the degree of *grace* and *improvement*. The greater the capacity, provided it be properly influenced by the grace of Christ, the greater will be the enjoyment.

6. That there will be great diversity in the states of glorified saints is the apostle's doctrine; and he illustrates it by the different degrees of *splendour* between the *sun, moon, planets,* and *stars*. This needs little application. There are some of the heavenly bodies that give *heat, light,* and *splendour,* as the sun; and are of the utmost service to the world: some that give *light*, and comparative *splendour*, without *heat*, as the MOON; and yet are of very great use to mankind: others, again, which give a *steady* but not a *splendid light,* as the PLANETS; and are serviceable

in their particular spheres: and lastly, others which *twinkle* in their respective systems, as the stars of different magnitudes.

7. *One star*, says the apostle, *differs from another in glory*, i. e. in *splendour*, according to what is called their different *magnitudes*. I will state a remarkable fact: The northern and southern hemispheres of the heavens have been divided into 102 *constellations*, and in these constellations Professor *Bode* has set down the places of 17,240 stars; *simple, nebulous, conglobate,* and *double*. The stars have been distinguished by their *apparent magnitudes*, or rather *splen-* *dour*, into stars of the first, second, third, fourth, fifth, sixth, seventh, eighth, &c., magnitudes: of these 17,240, only *sixteen* are, by astronomers in general, agreed to be of the *first* magnitude, all of which are set down in the following catalogue, with some of those that are remarkable in the second, third, fourth, fifth, and sixth magnitudes. The reader will observe that the name of the *constellation* or *star* is first mentioned; the Greek letters, &c., are those by which they are distinguished on maps and globes; and they are, by astronomers, referred to by these letters and numbers. My inferences shall follow the *table*.

A TABLE of the most remarkable FIXED STARS, from the FIRST to the SIXTH MAGNITUDE.

First Magnitude.	Second Magnitude.	Third Magnitude.	Fourth Magnitude.	Fifth Magnitude.	Sixth Magnitude.
α In the mouth of Canis Major, or the Greater Dog, (Sirius, or the Dog-star)	γ In the wing of Pegasus, (Algenib)	η Brightest of the Pleiades	In Libra, η θ	In Pisces, d 19 29 30 33	In Cancer, 37
α Bright star in Lyra, or the Harp, (Wega or Vega)	β In the head of the Phœnix	γ In Taurus	In Scorpio,	In Cetus, 20	In the Sextant, 38 56 *79
α Bright star in Boötes, (Arcturus)	α In the tail of Cetus	ε In Gemini	In Ophiuchus,	In Aries,	In Leo,
α In the heart of Leo Major, or the Great Lion, (Regulus)	β In the girdle of Andromeda	In Virgo,	In Sagittarius,	In Taurus, 105	In Sagittarius,
α In the left shoulder of Auriga, or the Charioteer, (Capella)	β In the Ram's following horn	*γ 1 ι In Libra,	In Capricorn,	In Orion,	In Aquarius, 1h
β In the right foot of Orion, (Rigel)	In the neck of Cetus,	In Scorpio,	In Aquarius,	In Auriga,	In Orion, 4
α In the southern, or left eye of the Bull, (Aldebaran)	α In the jaw of Cetus	In Ophiuchus,	In Pisces,	In Gemini,	In Ursa Minor,
α In Eridanus, (Alnahar or Acharnar)	β In the head of Medusa, (Algol)	In Sagittarius,	In Aries,	In Cancer,	In Cepheus,
α In the shoulder of Orion, (Betelgeuse)	In Perseus' girdle,	In Capricorn,	In Taurus,	In Leo,	In the Dragon,
α In the poop of the ship Argo, (Canopus)	β In the northern horn of the Bull	2 α In Ursa Minor,	In Gemini,	In Virgo,	In Cassiopeia,
α In the loins of Canis Minor, or the little Dog, (Procyon)	*α In Gemini, (Castor)	γ In Cassiopeia,	In Cancer,	In Libra,	In Perseus,
α Bright star in the foot of the Cross	*β In Gemini, (Pollux)	β In Perseus,	In Leo,	In Scorpio,	In Auriga, 10
α In the spike of the Virgin	γ In Orion's shoulder	In Ursa Major,	In Virgo,	In Ophiuchus,	
α In the foot of the Centaur	δ In the belt of Orion	β In the Dragon,		In Sagittarius,	
α In the Scorpion's heart, (Antares)	α In the Dove	δ In the Swan,		In Capricorn,	
α In the mouth of the south Fish, (Fomalhaut)	α In the female Hydra			In Aquarius,	
	*α In Ursa Major, (Upper Pointer)				
	β In Ursa Major, (Lower Pointer)				
	β The Lion's tail, (Deneb)				
	β In the Cross				
	β In the Dragon's tail				
	β In the Balance				
	α In the Swan's tail				
	α In Pegasus, (Markab)				
	α In Andromeda's head				
	α In the shoulder of Pegasus				
	β In the Crane's wing				
	*α In the Eagle, (Atteer)				
	*β In the ship Argo				

2

Observations on the preceding Table.

The *five* stars of the *second* magnitude in the above list, marked with an asterisk, are by some writers denominated of the *first* magnitude; and those named of the *third, fourth, fifth,* and *sixth* magnitudes, (the stars of the last-mentioned order being barely visible to the naked eye,) are such as the moon can occult, or make a near appulse to; except the last sixteen, in the column of stars of the *third* magnitude, and the last twenty-nine in that of the *sixth* magnitude, which never set in the latitude of London. The stars *Algol* and *o Ceti* are set down according to their *brightest* appearance; the former varying from the second to the fourth magnitude every two days, 20 hours, 48 minutes, 58 seconds, 18 thirds, and 25 fourths; and the latter, from the second to the seventh, and sometimes to the tenth, every 331 days, 10 hours, and 19 minutes. The stars of the first magnitude, Capella and Lyra, never set in the latitude of London; Acharnar, Canopus, β in Argo, and α in the Cross and Centaur, never rise. Of the stars of the second magnitude in the preceding list, β in Medusa's head, or Algol, α in Perseus, the two Pointers, the Dragon's tail, and the Swan's tail, never set; the head of the Phœnix and the bright star in the Crane never rise. The stars marked with an asterisk in the third column are between the third and fourth magnitudes; and those in the last column with the same mark are between the fifth and sixth magnitudes. Stars fainter than those of the sixth magnitude cannot be discerned without the help of a glass, and are therefore called *telescopic.* The 2 h, and 3 h, in Aquarius, are of this last description, both of the *seventh* magnitude, and such as the moon can occult.

8. This subject, as far as it concerns the present place, admits of few remarks or reflections. It has already been observed, that, of all the stars which our best astronomers have been able to describe and lay down in tables and maps, only *sixteen* are of the *first* magnitude; *i. e.* appear more *luminous* than any other stars in the firmament: some, indeed, increase the number to twenty-one, by taking in *Castor* and *Pollux,* the *upper Pointer, Atteer,* or *Atair,* in the *Eagle,* and β in the ship Argo, which I have placed among those of the second magnitude, because astronomers are not agreed on the subject, some ranking them with stars of the *first* magnitude, others, with stars of the *second.*

The reader is probably amazed at the *paucity* of large stars in the whole firmament of heaven! Will he permit me to carry his mind a little farther, and either stand *astonished* at or *deplore* with me the fact, that, out of the *millions* of Christians in the vicinity and splendour of the *eternal Sun of righteousness,* how very few are found of the *first order!* How very few can stand examination by the *test* laid down in the 13th chapter of this epistle! How very few love God with all their heart, soul, mind, and strength; and their neighbour as themselves! How few *mature* Christians are found in the Church! How few are, in all things, living for eternity! How little *light,* how little *heat,* and how little *influence* and *activity* are to be found among them that bear the name of Christ! How few *stars* of the FIRST *magnitude* will the Son of God have to deck the crown of his glory! Few are striving to *excel* in righteousness; and it seems to be a principal concern with many to find out *how little grace they may have, and yet escape hell;* how little *conformity to the will of God* they may have, and yet get to heaven! In the fear of God I register this testimony, that I have perceived it to be the labour of many *to lower the standard of Christianity,* and to soften down, or explain away, those *promises* of God that himself has *linked with duties;* and because they know that they cannot be saved *by* their *good works,* they are contented to have *no good works at all:* and thus the necessity of Christian *obedience,* and Christian *holiness,* makes no prominent part of some modern creeds. Let all those who retain the *apostolic doctrine,* that *the blood of Christ cleanseth from all sin in this life,* press every believer to go on to *perfection,* and expect to be saved, *while here below,* into the fulness of the blessing of the Gospel of Jesus. To all such my soul says, Labour to show yourselves approved unto God; workmen that need not be ashamed, rightly dividing the word of truth; and may the pleasure of the Lord prosper in your hands!—Amen.

CHAPTER XVI.

The apostle exhorts the Corinthians to make a contribution for the relief of the poor Christians at Jerusalem - and directs to the best mode of doing it, 1–4. Promises to pay them a visit after pentecost, 5–9. Gives directions about the treatment of Timothy and Apollos, 10–12. And concerning watchfulness, &c., 13, 14. Commends the house of Stephanas, and expresses his satisfaction at the visit paid him by Stephanas, Fortunatus and Achaicus, 15–18. Sends the salutations of different persons, 19, 21. Shows the awful state of those who were enemies to Christ, 22. And concludes the epistle with the apostolical benediction, 23, 24.

A. M. 4060.
A. D. 56.
A. U. C. 809.
Anno Imp. Neronis Cæs. 3.

NOW concerning [a] the collection for the saints, as I have given order to the Churches of Galatia, even so do ye.

2 [b] Upon the first *day* of the week let every one of you lay by him in store, as *God* hath prospered him, that

A. M. 4060.
A. D. 56.
A. U. C. 809.
Anno Imp. Neronis Cæs. 3.

[a] Acts xi. 29; xxiv. 17; Rom. xv. 26; 2 Cor. viii. 4; ix. 1, 12; Gal. ii. 10.——[b] Acts xx. 7; Rev. i. 10.

NOTES ON CHAP. XVI.

Verse 1. *The collection for the saints*] Περι——της λογιας, from λεγω, to *gather,* or *collect*; translated by the *Vulgate, de collectis,* a contribution made by the rich for the relief of the poor. The *Christians* living at Jerusalem, we may naturally suppose, were greatly

2

A. M. 4060.
A. D. 56.
A. U. C.
809.
Anno Imp. Nero-
nis Cæs. 3.

there be no gatherings when I come.

3 And when I come, ᶜ whomsoever ye shall approve by *your*

letters, them will I send to bring your ᵈ liberality unto Jerusalem.

4 ᵉ And if it be meet that I go also, they shall go with me.

A. M. 4060.
A. D. 56.
A. U. C.
809.
Anno Imp. Nero-
nis Cæs. 3.

ᶜ 2 Cor. viii. 19.——ᵈ Gr. *gift;* 2 Cor. viii. 4, 6, 19.

ᵉ 2 Cor. viii. 4, 19.

---

straitened; as the enmity of their countrymen to the Gospel of Christ led them to treat those who professed it with cruelty, and spoil them of their goods; (see Heb. x. 34; and Rom. xv. 26; and see the note on the 27th verse of that chapter;) and the apostle hereby teaches that it was the duty of one Christian congregation to help another when in distress.

Verse 2. *Upon the first* day *of the week*] The apostle prescribes the most convenient and proper method of making this contribution. 1. Every man was to feel it his duty to succour his brethren in distress. 2. He was to do this according to the ability which God gave him. 3. He was to do this at the conclusion of the week, when he had cast up his weekly earnings, and had seen how much God had prospered his labour. 4. He was then to bring it on the *first day* of the week, as is most likely, to the church or assembly, that it might be put in the common treasury. 5. We learn from this that the weekly contribution could not be always the *same,* as each man was to lay by *as God had prospered him:* now, some weeks he would gain more; others, less. 6. It appears from the whole that the *first day* of *the week,* which is the Christian Sabbath, was the day on which their principal religious meetings were held in *Corinth* and the Churches of *Galatia;* and, consequently, in all other places where Christianity had prevailed. This is a strong argument for the keeping of the Christian Sabbath. 7. We may observe that the apostle follows here the *rule of the synagogue;* it was a regular custom among the Jews to make their collections for the poor on the *Sabbath day,* that they might not be without the necessaries of life, and might not be prevented from coming to the synagogue. 8. For the purpose of making this provision, they had a *purse,* which was called צדקה של ארנקי *Arneki shel tsedakah,* "The purse of the alms," or what we would term, *the poor's box.* This is what the apostle seems to mean when he says, *Let him lay by him in store*—let him put it in the *alms' purse,* or in the *poor's box.* 9. It was a maxim also with them that, if they *found* any money, they were not to put it in their *private* purse, but in that which belonged to the *poor.* 10. The pious Jews believed that as *salt* seasoned food, so did *alms,* riches; and that he who did not give alms of what he had, his riches should be dispersed. The *moth* would *corrupt* the *bags,* and the *canker corrode* the *money,* unless the mass was sanctified by giving a part to the poor.

Verse 3. *Whomsoever ye shall approve by* your *letters*] Why should Paul require *letters* of approbation in behalf of certain persons, when he himself should be *among them,* and could have their characters *viva voce?* It is probable that he refers here to letters of recommendation which they *had* sent to him while he was away; and he now promises that when he should come to Corinth, he would appoint these persons, whom they *had recommended,* to carry the alms to Jerusalem. If

δοκιμασητε be read *ye shall have approved,* as Bishop Pearce does, the difficulty will vanish.

Some MSS. and several *versions* join δι' επιστολων, *by letters,* to the following words, and read the verse thus: *When I come, those whom ye shall approve I will send with letters to bring your liberality to Jerusalem.* This seems most natural.

Verse 4. *And if it be meet, &c.*] If it be a business that requires my attendance, and it be judged proper for me to go to Jerusalem, I will take those persons for my companions. On the delicacy with which St. Paul managed the business of a collection for the poor, Archdeacon Paley makes the following appropriate remarks:—

"The following observations will satisfy us concerning the purity of our apostle's conduct in the suspicious business of a pecuniary contribution.

"1st, He disclaims the having received any inspired authority for the directions which he is giving: 'I speak not by commandment, but by occasion of the forwardness of others, and to prove the sincerity of your love.' (2 Corinthians, chap. viii. 8.) Who, that had a sinister purpose to answer by the recommending of subscriptions, would thus distinguish, and thus lower the credit of his own recommendation?

"2d, Although he asserts the general right of Christian ministers to a maintenance from their ministry, yet he protests against the making use of this right in his own person: 'Even so hath the Lord ordained, that they who preach the Gospel should live of the Gospel; but I have used none of these things; neither have I written these things that it should be so done unto me; for it were better for me to die, than that any man should make my glorying, i. e. my professions of disinterestedness, void.' (1 Corinthians, chap. ix. 14, 15.)

"3d, He repeatedly proposes that there should be associates with himself in the management of the public bounty; not colleagues of his own appointment, but persons elected for that purpose by the contributors themselves. 'And when I come, whomsoever ye shall approve by your letters, them will I send to bring your liberality unto Jerusalem; and if it be meet that I go also, they shall go with me.' (1 Cor., chap. xvi. 3, 4.) And in the second epistle, what is here proposed we find actually done, and done for the very purpose of guarding his character against any imputation that might be brought upon it in the discharge of a pecuniary trust: 'And we have sent with him the brother, whose praise is in the Gospel throughout all the Churches; and not that only, but who was also chosen of the Churches to travel with us with this grace, (gift,) which is administered by us to the glory of the same Lord, and the declaration of your ready mind: avoiding this, that no man should blame us in this abundance which is administered by us; providing for things honest, not only in the sight of the Lord, but also in

A. M. 4060.
A. D. 56
A. U. C.
809.
Anno Imp. Nero-
nis Cæs. 3.

5 Now I will come unto you, [f] when I shall pass through Macedonia: for I do pass through Macedonia.

6 And it may be that I will abide, yea, and winter with you, that ye may [g] bring me on journey whithersoever I go.

7 For I will not see you now by the way; but I trust to tarry awhile with you, [h] if the Lord permit.

8 But I will tarry at Ephesus until pentecost.

9 For [i] a great door and effectual is opened

unto me, and [k] *there are* many adversaries.

A. M. 4060.
A. D. 56.
A. U. C.
809.
Anno Imp. Nero-
nis Cæs. 3.

10 Now, [l] if Timotheus come, see that he may be with you without fear; for [m] he worketh the work of the Lord, as I also *do*.

11 [n] Let no man therefore despise him: but conduct him forth [o] in peace, that he may come unto me: for I look for him with the brethren.

12 As touching *our* brother [p] Apollos, I greatly desired him to come unto you with the brethren: but his will was not at all to come at this

---

[f] Acts xix. 21; 2 Cor. i. 16.——[g] Acts xv. 3; xvii. 15; xxi. 5; Rom. xv. 24; 2 Cor. i. 16.——[h] Acts xviii. 21; chap. iv. 19; James iv. 15.——[i] Acts xiv. 27; 2 Cor. ii. 12; Col. iv. 3; Rev.

iii. 8.——[k] Acts xix. 9.——[l] Acts xix. 22; chap. iv. 17.——[m] Rom. xvi. 21; Phil. ii. 20, 22; 1 Thess. iii. 2.——[n] 1 Tim. iv. 12. [o] Acts xv. 33.——[p] Chap. i. 12; iii. 5.

---

the sight of men:' i. e. not resting in the consciousness of our own integrity, but, in such a subject, careful also to approve our integrity to the public judgment. (2 Cor., chap. viii. 18–21.") *Horæ Paulinæ,* page 95.

Verse 5. *I will come unto you, when I shall pass through Macedonia*] St. Paul was now at *Ephesus;* for almost all allow, in opposition to the *subscription* at the end of this epistle that states it to have been written from *Philippi,* that it was written from *Ephesus:* and this is supported by many strong arguments; and the 8th verse here seems to put it past all question: *I will tarry at Ephesus;* i. e. I am in Ephesus, and here I purpose to remain until *pentecost.* Though Macedonia was not in the direct way from Ephesus to Corinth, yet the apostle intended to make it in his way. And it was because it was not in the direct road, but lay at the upper end of the Ægean Sea, and very far out of his direct line, that he says, *I do pass through Macedonia*—I have purposed to go thither before I go to Corinth.

Verse 6. *Yea, and winter with you*] He purposed to stay till *pentecost* at Ephesus; after that to go to Macedonia, and probably to spend the *summer* there; and come in the *autumn* to Corinth, and there spend the *winter.*

That ye may bring me on my journey] That ye may furnish me with the means of travelling. It appears that, in most cases, the different Churches paid his expenses to other Churches; where this was not done, then he laboured at his business to acquire the means of travelling.

Verse 7. *I will not see you now by the way*] From Ephesus to Corinth was merely across the Ægean Sea, and comparatively a short passage.

Verse 8 *I will tarry at Ephesus*] And it is very probable that he did so; and that all these journeys were taken as he himself had projected. See on ver. 5.

Verse 9. *A great door and effectual is opened*] Θυρα γαρ μοι ανεωγε μεγαλη και ενεργης· *A great and energetic door is opened to me;* that is, God has made a grand opening to me in those parts, which I perceive will require *much labour;* and besides, I shall have *many adversaries* to oppose me. So Bp. Pearce understands the words ενεργης, not as signifying *effectual,* but

as implying *full of labour.* *Door* often signifies *occasion* or *opportunity;* but here, the apostle may allude to the throwing open of the great doors of the *Circus Maximus* before the chariot races began; and the *many adversaries* may refer to the numerous *competitors* in those races.

God gave him a grand *opportunity* to preach the Gospel; but he was not to expect that either Satan or wicked men would leave him unmolested.

Verse 10. *Now, if Timotheus come*] Of Timothy we have heard before, chap. iv. 17. And we learn, from Acts xix. 22, that Paul sent him with *Erastus* from Ephesus to Macedonia. It is evident, therefore, in opposition to the very exceptionable *subscription* at the end of this epistle, that the epistle itself was *not* sent by Timothy, as there stated.

That he may be with you without fear] That he may be treated well, and not perplexed and harassed with your divisions and jealousies; for *he worketh the work of the Lord*—he is Divinely appointed, as I also am.

Verse 11. *Let no man—despise him*] Let none pretend to say that he has not full authority from God to do the work of an evangelist.

But conduct him forth in peace] I believe, with Bp. Pearce, that this clause should be translated and pointed thus: *accompany him upon his journey, that he may come unto me in peace,* (εν ειρηνη, *in safety,*) as the word is used in Mark v 34; and Luke vii. 50.

For I look for him with the brethren.] Εκδεχομαι —αυτον μετα των αδελφων. This clause should not be understood as if Paul was expecting *certain brethren with* Timothy; but it was the *brethren* that were *with Paul* that were looking for him; I, *with the brethren, am looking for him.*

Verse 12. *As touching* our *brother Apollos*] It appears from this that the *brethren,* of whom the apostle speaks in the preceding verse, were then *with him* at Ephesus; I, *with the brethren, greatly desired to come.*

But his will was not at all to come] As there had been a faction set up in the name of Apollos at Corinth, he probably thought it not prudent to go thither at this time, lest his presence might be the means of giving it either strength or countenance

A. M. 4060.
A. D. 56.
A. U. C.
809.
Anno Imp. Nero-
nis Cæs. 3.

time ; but he will come when he shall have convenient time.

13 ^q Watch ye, ^r stand fast in the faith, quit you like men, ^s be strong.

14 ^t Let all your things be done with charity.

15 I beseech you, brethren, (ye know ^u the house of Stephanas, that it is ^v the first fruits of Achaia, and *that* they have addicted themselves to ^w the ministry of the saints,)

16 ^x That ye submit your-selves unto such, and to every one that helpeth with *us,* and ^y laboureth.

17 I am glad of the coming of Stephanas and Fortunatus and Achaicus : ^z for that which was lacking on your part they have supplied.

18 ^a For they have refreshed my spirit and yours : therefore ^b acknowledge ye them that are such.

A. M. 4060.
A. D. 56.
A. U. C.
809.
Anno Imp. Nero-
nis Cæs. 3.

---

q Matt. xxiv. 42 ; xxv. 13 ; 1 Thess. v. 6 ; 1 Pet. v. 8.——r Chap. xv. 1 ; Phil. i. 27 ; iv. 1 ; 1 Thess. iii. 8 ; 2 Thess. ii. 15.——s Eph. vi. 10 ; Col. i. 11.——t Chap. xiv. 1 ; 1 Pet. iv. 8.

u Chap. i. 16.——v Rom. xvi. 5.——w 2 Cor. viii. 4 ; ix. 1 ; Heb. vi. 10.——x Heb. xiii. 17.——y Heb. vi. 10.——z 2 Cor. xi. 9 ; Phil. ii. 30 ; Phil. 13.——a Col. iv. 8.——b 1 Thess. v. 12 ; Phil. ii. 29.

Verse 13. *Watch ye*] You have many enemies ; be continually on your *guard ;* be always *circum-spect :*—1. Watch against evil ; 2. Watch for oppor-tunities to *receive* good ; 3. Watch for opportunities to *do* good ; 4. Watch over each other in love ; 5. Watch, that none may draw you aside from the belief and unity of the Gospel.

Stand fast in the faith] Hold in conscientious credence what you have already received as the truth of God ; for it is the Gospel by which ye shall be saved, and by which ye are now put into a state of salvation : see chap. xv. 1, 2.

Quit you like men] Be not like *children tossed to and fro with every wind of doctrine ;* let your *under-standing* receive the truth ; let your *judgment* deter-mine on the absolute necessity of retaining it ; and give up life rather than give up the testimony of God.

Be strong.] Put forth all the *vigour* and *energy* which God has given you in maintaining and propa-gating the truth, and your spiritual strength will in-crease· by usage. The terms in this verse are all *military :* Watch ye, γρηγορειτε, watch, and be con-tinually on your guard, lest you be surprised by your enemies ; keep your *scouts* out, and all your *sentinels* at their posts, lest your enemies *steal a march* upon you. See that the place you are in be properly de-fended ; and that each be alert to perform his duty.

Stand fast in the faith—Στηκετε εν τη πιστει· Keep in your *ranks ;* do not be *disorderly ;* be determined to keep your ranks *unbroken ;* keep *close together.* On your *unity* your preservation depends ; if the enemy succeed in breaking your ranks, and dividing one part of this sacred army from another, your rout will be inevitable.

Quit yourselves like men—Ανδριζεσθε· When you are attacked, do not *flinch ;* maintain your *ground ;* resist ; press forward ; strike home ; keep compact ; conquer.

Be strong—Κραταιουσθε. If one company or divi-sion be opposed by too great a force of the enemy, strengthen that division, and maintain your position ; if an attack is to be made on any part or intrenchment of the foe, summon up all your courage, sustain each other ; fear not, for fear will enervate you. Your cause is good ; it is *the faith,* the religion of Jesus ; he is your *Captain* in the field ; and, should you even die in the contest, the victory is yours.

Verse 14. *Let all your things be done with charity.*] Let *love* to God, to man, and to one another, be the motive of all your conduct.

Verse 15. *Ye know the house of Stephanas*] Ye know that Stephanas and his *family* have addicted them to the help of the followers of Christ ; they have been the chief instruments of supporting the work of God in Achaia, of which work they themselves have been the *first fruits.* See the note on Rom. xvi. 5.

Verse 16. *That ye submit yourselves unto such*] That ye have *due regard* to them, and consider them as especial instruments in the hand of God for coun-tenancing and carrying on his great work. The *sub-mission* here recommended does not imply *obedience,* but *kind* and *courteous demeanour.* Kypke vindicates this sense of the word from Eph. v. 21 ; 1 Pet. v. 5.

Verse 17. *I am glad of the coming of Stephanas, &c.*] It was by these that the Corinthians had sent that letter to the apostle, to answer which was a main part of the design of St. Paul in this epistle.

Fortunatus] This man is supposed to have sur-vived St. Paul ; and to be the same mentioned by Clement in his epistle to the Corinthians, sec. 59, as the bearer of that epistle from Clement at Rome to the Christians at Corinth.

For that which was lacking on your part] This may either refer to additional *communications* besides those contained in the letter which the Corinthians sent to the apostle—which additional circumstances were furnished by the persons above ; and from them St. Paul had a fuller account of their spiritual state than was contained in the letter—or to some *contri-butions* on their part for the support of the apostle in his peregrinations and labours.

Verse 18. *They have refreshed my spirit and yours*] They have been a means of contributing greatly to my comfort ; and what contributes to *my* comfort must increase *yours.* This is probably the meaning of the apostle.

Therefore acknowledge ye them] Pay them parti-cular respect, and let all be held in esteem in propor-tion to their work and usefulness. When this is made the *rule* of *respect* and *esteem,* then *foolish and capri-cious attachments* will have no place. A man will then be *honoured* in proportion to his *merit ;* and his merit will be estimated by his *usefulness* among men,

2

A. M. 4060.
A. D. 56.
A. U. C.
809.
Anno Imp. Nero-
nis Cæs. 3.

19 The Churches of Asia salute you. Aquila and Priscilla salute you much in the Lord, ᶜ with the Church that is in their house.

20 All the brethren greet you. ᵈ Greet ye one another with a holy kiss.

21 ᵉ The salutation of *me* Paul with mine own hand.

22 If any man ᶠ love not the Lord Jesus Christ, ᵍ let him be anathema, ʰ maran-atha

A. M. 4060.
A. D. 56.
A. U. C
809.
Anno Imp. Nero
nis Cæs. 3.

ᶜ Rom. xvi. 5, 15; Phil. 2.——ᵈ Rom. xvi. 16.——ᵉ Col. iv. 18;   2 Thess. iii. 17.——ᶠ Eph. vi. 24.——ᵍ Gal. i. 8, 9.——ʰ Jude 14, 15.

Verse 19. *The Churches of Asia salute you.*] i. e. The Churches in *Asia Minor.* Ephesus was in this Asia, and it is clear from this that the apostle was not at *Philippi*; had he been at Philippi, as the subscription states, he would have said, The *Churches of* MACEDONIA, not *the Churches of* ASIA, *salute you.* How these places lay, in reference to each other, the reader will at once ᴅerceive by consulting the *map* in Acts.

Aquila and Priscilla] Of these eminent persons we have heard before: see Acts xviii. 2, 18, 26; and Rom. xvi. 3.

With the Church that is in their house.] That is, the *company of believers* who generally worshipped there. There were no *churches* or *chapels* at that time built; and the assemblies of Christians were necessarily held in private houses. It appears that *Aquila* and *Priscilla* devoted *their house* to this purpose. The house of *Philemon* was of the same kind; Philem. ver. 2. So was likewise the house of *Nymphas*, Col. iv. 15. See the note on Rom. xvi. 5.

Verse 20. *With a holy kiss.*] The ancient patriarchs, and the Jews in general, were accustomed to *kiss each other* whenever they met; and this was a token of *friendship* and *peace* with them, as *shaking of hands* is with us. The primitive Christians naturally followed this example of the Jews. See the note on Rom. xvi. 16.

Verse 21. *The salutation of* me *Paul with mine own hand.*] This should be rendered: "The salutation is written by the hand of me Paul;" γεγραπται, *is written*, being understood. It is very likely that the apostle wrote this and the following verses with his own hand. The rest, though *dictated* by him, was *written* by an amanuensis.

Verse 22. *If any man love not the Lord Jesus*] This is directed immediately against the *Jews.* From chap. xii. 3, we find that the Jews, who pretended to be under the *Spirit* and *teaching of God*, called Jesus αναθεμα, or *accursed*; i. e. a person who should be 'devoted to destruction: see the note there. In this place the apostle *retorts* the whole upon *themselves*, and says: *If any man love not the Lord Jesus Christ, let* HIM be αναθεμα, *accursed*, and *devoted to destruction.* This is not said in the way of a *wish* or *imprecation*, but as a *prediction* of what would certainly come upon them if they did not repent, and of what *did* come on them because they did not repent; but continued to *hate* and *execrate* the Lord Jesus; and of what *still lies upon them*, because they continue to *hate* and *execrate* the Redeemer of the world.

It is generally allowed that the apostle refers here to some of the modes of *excommunication* among the Jews, of which there were *three*, viz.--

1. *Niddui* נדוי, which signifies a simple *separation* or exclusion of a man from the synagogue, and from his wife and family, for THIRTY days.

2. *Cherem* חרם, which was inflicted on him who had borne the *niddui*, and who had not, in the thirty days, made proper compensation, in order to be reconciled to the synagogue. This was inflicted with dire execrations, which he was informed must all come upon him if he did not *repent*; but the *cherem* always supposed *place for repentance.*

Shammatha שמתא: this was the *direst* of all, and cut off all *hope* of reconciliation and repentance; after which the man was neither reconcilable to the *synagogue*, nor acknowledged as belonging even to the *Jewish nation.* See these different forms in *Buxtorf's* Rabbinical and Talmudical *Lexicon*, under their respective words.

In the Lexicon just now quoted, Buxtorf gives a form of the *cherem*, which he says he copied from an ancient Hebrew MS. Of this awful piece I shall lay a translation before the reader.

" By the sentence of the Lord of lords, let P. the son of P. be anathematized in both houses of judgment; the superior and inferior. Let him be anathematized among the highest saints; let him be anathematized among the *seraphim* and *ophanim*; and finally, let him be anathematized by all the congregations of the great and the small! Let great and continued plagues rest upon him; with great and horrible diseases! Let his house be the habitation of dragons! and let his constellation be darkened in the clouds! Let him be for indignation, and wrath, and burning! Let his carcass be thrown to the wild beasts and serpents! Let his enemies and his adversaries triumph over him! Let his silver and gold be given to others! And let all his children be exposed at the doors of their enemies! And let posterity be astonished at his day! Let him be accursed by the mouth of *Addiriron* and *Achtariel*; by the mouth of *Sandalphon* and *Hadraniel*; by the mouth of *Ansisiel* and *Patchiel*; by the mouth of *Seraphiel* and *Sagansael*; by the mouth of *Michael* and *Gabriel*; by the mouth of *Raphael* and *Mesharetiel*! Let him be anathematized by the mouth of *Zaafzavif*, and by the mouth of *Hafhavif*, who is the great God; and by the mouth of the *seventy names* of the supreme King; and lastly, by the mouth of *Tsortak* the great chancellor.

" Let him be swallowed up like Korah and his companions! Let his soul depart with fear and terror! Let the chiding of the Lord slay him! Let him be confounded as Achitophel was in his counsel! Let the leprosy of Gehazi be his leprosy! and let there be no resurrection of his ruins! In the sepulchres of the children of Israel let him not be buried! Let his wife

A. M. 4060.
A. D. 56.
A. U. C. 809.
Anno Imp. Neronis Cæs. 3.

23 [i] The grace of our Lord Jesus Christ *be* with you.

24 My love *be* with you all in Christ Jesus. Amen.

¶ The first *epistle* to the Corinthians was written from Philippi by Stephanas, and Fortunatus, and Achaicus, and Timotheus.

A.M. 4060.
A. D. 56.
A. U. C. 809.
Anno Imp. Nero nis Cæs. 3.

[i] Romans,   chap. xvi. 20.

be given to another, and let others bow themselves upon her in his death! In this anathema, let P. the son of P. be; and let this be his inheritance! But vpon me and upon all Israel may God extend his peace and blessing, Amen." To this is added the 18th, 19th, and 20th verses of Deut. xxix., which the reader may read at his leisure. There are many things in this *cherem* which require a *comment*, but this is not the place.

Anathema, maran-atha.] "Let him be accursed; our Lord cometh." I cannot see the reason why these words were left *untranslated*. The former is Greek, and has been already explained; the latter is Syriac ܡܪܢ ܐܬܐ *maran-atha, our Lord is coming:* i. e. to execute the judgment denounced. Does not the apostle refer to the last verse in the Bible? *Lest I come and smite the land* (חרם *cherem*) *with a curse?* And does he not intimate that the Lord was coming to smite the *Jewish land* with that curse? Which took place a very few years after, and continues on that gainsaying and rebellious people to the present day. What the apostle has said was *prophetic*, and *indicative* of what was about to happen to that people. God was then *coming* to inflict punishment upon them: he came, and they were broken and dispersed.

Verse 23. The grace of our Lord Jesus] May the favour, influence, mercy, and salvation procured by Jesus Christ, be *with you*—prevail among you, rule in you, and be exhibited by you, in your life and conversation! Amen.

Verse 24. My love be *with you all in Christ Jesus.*] It appears exceedingly strange that the apostle should say, *My love* be *with you;* as he said, *The grace of our Lord Jesus Christ* be *with you.* We can easily conceive what the latter means: the *grace* of Christ is an *active, powerful, saving principle;* it is essential to the existence of the Christian Church that this grace should be ever with it: and without this grace no individual can be saved. But what could the *love* of the apostle do *with them?* Has it any meaning? I confess I can see none, unless it be intended to say, *I love you;* or, I continue to *love* you. The pronoun μου, *my*, is wanting in the *Codex Alexandrinus*, and in 73, an excellent MS. in the Vatican, written about the eleventh century. This will help us to a better sense, for it either says, *May love prevail among you!* or supplying the word Θεου, GOD, as in 2 Cor. xiii. 14, *The love of God be with you!* This gives a sound sense; for the *love of God* is as much a *principle* of *light, life,* and *salvation,* as the *grace* of Christ. And probably ΜΟΥ, *my*, is a corruption for ΘΕΟΥ, of GOD. And this is the more likely, because he uses this very form in the conclusion of his second epistle to this Church, as we have seen above. I conclude, therefore, that the reading of the two MSS. above is the

true reading; or else that μου is a corruption for Θεου, and that the verse should be read thus: *The love of* GOD *be with you all,* in (or *by*) *Christ Jesus.*

Amen.] So be it: but this word is wanting in most MSS. of repute, and certainly was not written by the apostle.

1. THE *subscription* to this epistle in our common English Bibles, and in the common *editions* of the *Greek* text, is palpably absurd. That it was not written from *Philippi*, but from *Ephesus*, see the notes on ver. 5, 8, 10, and 19; and that it could not be "written by Silvanus, and Fortunatus, and Achaicus, and Timotheus," needs no proof. But this subscription is wanting in all the best MSS. and versions, either in *whole* or in *part*. In some it is simply said, *The first to the Corinthians;* in others, *The first to the Corinthians is finished; written from Ephesus—from Asia—from Ephesus of Asia—from Philippi of Macedonia—from Philippi of Macedonia, and sent by the hands of Timothy;* so the SYRIAC. *Written from Ephesus, by Stephanas* and *Fortunatus;* COPTIC. *Written from Philippi by Stephanas,* and *Fortunatus,* and *Achaicus;* SLAVONIC. *Written, &c., by Paul and Sosthenes. Written from the city of Philippi, and sent by Stephanas,* and *Fortunatus,* and *Achaicus,* and *Timotheus;* ARABIC. There are other variations, which need not be set down. Those only appear to be correct that state the epistle to have been sent from *Ephesus*, of which there can be no reasonable doubt.

2. In closing my observations on this epistle, I feel it necessary once more to call the reader's attention to the many *difficulties* contained in it as an excuse for any thing he may find handled in an unsatisfactory manner. Perhaps it will be of little consequence for him to know that this epistle has cost me more labour and difficulty than any portion of the same quantity which I have yet passed over either in the Old or New Testament.

3. It has been already noticed that the Church at Corinth *had written to the apostle* for advice, direction, and information on a variety of points; and that this epistle is, in the main, an answer to the epistle from Corinth. Had we *that epistle*, all difficulty would vanish in this; but, as the apostle only refers to *their* questions by mere *catch words* from their letter, it is impossible to know, in *all cases*, what the questions contained. To them the answers would be clear, because they knew on what they had consulted him; to *us* the answers must be, as they really are in some cases, necessarily obscure, because we know not the whole bearing and circumstances of the questions. Indeed the epistle contains more *local* matter, and more matter of *private* application, than any other in the New Testament; and there is in it, on the whole, less

matter for general use than in most other parts of the sacred writings. Yet it is both very curious and useful; it gives insight into several *customs*, and not a few *forms of speech*, and matters relative to the *discipline* of the primitive Church, which we can find nowhere else : and it reads a very awful lesson to those who disturb the peace of society, make schisms in the Church of Christ, and endeavour to set up one preacher at the expense of another.

4. It shows us also how many *improper* things may, in a state of *ignorance* or Christian infancy, be consistent with a *sincere belief* in the Gospel of Christ, and a conscientious and *zealous* attachment to it.

5. In different parts of the epistle we find the apostle speaking very highly of the *knowledge* of this Church; and its *various gifts* and *endowments*. How then can we say that its blemishes arose from *ignorance?* I answer, that certainly only a few of the people at Corinth could possess those eminent *spiritual* qualifications; because the things that are attributed to this Church in other places are utterly inconsistent with that state of grace for which the apostle, in other places, appears to give them credit. The solution of the difficulty is this : There were in the Church at Corinth many *highly gifted* and very *gracious* people; there were also there many more, who, though they might have been partakers of some *extraordinary* gifts, had very little of that *religion* which the apostle describes in the *thirteenth* chapter of this epistle.

6. Besides, we must not suppose that eminent *endowments* necessarily imply *gracious dispositions.* A man may have *much* light and *little* love; he may be very *wise* in secular matters, and know but little of *himself*, and less of his *God.* There is as truly a *learned ignorance*, as there is a *refined* and *useful learning.* One of our old writers said, " Knowledge that is not *applying*, is only like a candle which a man holds to light himself to hell." The Corinthians abounded in *knowledge*, and *science*, and *eloquence*, and various *extraordinary gifts*; but in many cases, distinctly enough marked in this epistle, they were grossly *ignorant* of the *genius* and *design* of the Gospel. Many, since their time, have put *words* and *observances* in place of the *weightier matters* of the LAW, and the *spirit* of the GOSPEL. The apostle has taken great pains to correct these abuses among the Corinthians, and to insist on that great, unchangeable, and eternal truth, that *love to God and man*, filling the heart, hallowing the passions, regulating the affections, and producing universal benevolence and beneficence, is the fulfilling of all law; and that all *professions, knowledge, gifts, &c.*, without this, are absolutely useless. And did this epistle contain no more than what is found in the 13th chapter, yet that would be an unparalleled monument of the apostle's deep acquaintance with God; and an invaluable record of the sum and substance of the Gospel, left by God's mercy to the Church, as a *touchstone* for the *trial* of creeds, confessions of faith, and ritual observances, to the end of the world.

7. I have often had occasion to note that the whole *epistle* refers so much to *Jewish* affairs, customs, forms of speech, ceremonies, &c., that it necessarily supposes the people to have been well acquainted with them : from this I infer that a great majority of the Christian Church at *Corinth* was composed of *converted* JEWS; and it is likely that this was the case in all the Churches of *Asia Minor* and *Greece*. Many *Gentiles* were undoubtedly brought to the knowledge of the truth; but the chief converts were from among the *Hellenistic Jews*. In many respects Jewish phraseology prevails more in this epistle than even in that to the *Romans*. Without attention to this it would be impossible to make any consistent sense out of the 15th chapter, where the apostle treats so largely on the doctrine of the *resurrection*, as almost every *form* and *turn of expression* is JEWISH; and we must know what ideas they attached to such *words* and *forms* of speech, in order to enter into the spirit of the apostle's meaning. His ignorance of this caused a late eminent writer and philosopher to charge the apostle with " inconsistent reasoning." Had he understood the apostle's language, he would not have said so; and as he did not understand it, he should have said nothing. A man may be qualified to make great and useful discoveries in the doctrine of *gases* or *factitious airs*, who may be ill qualified to elucidate the meaning of the *Holy Spirit*.

8. Before I finish my concluding observations on this epistle, I must beg leave to call the reader's attention once more to the concluding words of the apostle : *If any man love not the Lord Jesus Christ, let him be anathema, maran-atha.* These words have been as often *misunderstood*, and perhaps as dangerously *applied*, as another passage in this epistle, *He that eateth and drinketh unworthily, eateth and drinketh damnation to himself, &c.* Though I am ready to grant that the *bad Christian*, i. e. the man who professes Christianity, and yet lives under the power of sin, is in a very dangerous state; and that he who, while he credits Christianity, is undecided as to the public part he should take in its profession and practice, is putting his eternal interests to the most awful hazard; yet I must also grant that the meaning generally put on the words in question is *not* correct. The words apply to the *gainsaying* and *blasphemous* Jews; to those who were calling Christ *anathema*, or *accursed*; and cannot be applied to any person who *respects his name*, or *confides* in him for his salvation; much less do they apply to *him* who finds through the *yet* prevalence of evil in his heart, and the power of *temptation*, that he has *little*, and, to his own apprehension, *no love* to the Lord Jesus. The *anathema* of the apostle is denounced against him *only* who gives the *anathema* to *Christ :* of this, not one of my readers is capable. It is the duty of all to love him with an undivided heart : if any be not yet able to do it, let him not be discouraged : if the *Lord cometh* to execute judgment *on* him who calleth Jesus *accursed*, he *cometh* also to fulfil the desire of them who fear him; to make them partake of the Divine nature, and so cleanse their hearts by the inspiration of his Holy Spirit, that they shall *perfectly love him, and worthily magnify his name.*

INTRODUCTION TO THE SECOND EPISTLE

TO THE

CORINTHIANS.

FOR an account of *Corinth*, the reader is referred to the *preface* to the first epistle, where every thing relative to the geographical, political, and religious situation of that celebrated city, as far as such subjects are proper for a work of this kind is amply detailed.

As I have borrowed from the learned and accurate Archdeacon *Paley* several arguments to prove the *authenticity* of the *first* epistle, and the same able writer having bestowed equal pains on the *second*, I shall make those extracts which bear particularly on the subject; referring my reader to the work itself for ampler information.

Section I.

I will not say that it is impossible, having seen the First Epistle to the Corinthians, to construct a second with ostensible allusions to the first; or that it is impossible that both should be fabricated, so as to carry on an order and continuation of story, by successive references to the same events. But I say that this, in either case, must be the effect of craft and design: whereas, whoever examines the allusions to the former epistle which he finds in this, whilst he will acknowledge them to be such as would rise spontaneously to the hand of the writer, from the very subject of the correspondence, and the situation of the corresponding parties, supposing these to be real, will see no particle of reason to suspect, either that the clauses containing these allusions were *insertions* for the purpose, or that the several transactions of the Corinthian Church were feigned, in order to form a train of narrative, or to support the appearance of connection between the two epistles.

1. In the first epistle, St. Paul announces his intention of passing through Macedonia in his way to Corinth: "I will come to you when I shall pass through Macedonia." In the second epistle we find him arrived in Macedonia, and about to pursue his journey to Corinth. But observe the manner in which this is made to appear: "I know the forwardness of your mind, for which I boast of you to them of Macedonia, that Achaia was ready a year ago, and your zeal hath provoked very many: yet have I sent the brethren, lest our boasting of you should be in vain in this behalf; that, as I said, ye may be ready; lest, haply, if they of Macedonia come with me, and find you unprepared, we (that we say not you) be ashamed in this same confident boasting." (Chap. ix. 2, 3, 4.) St. Paul's being in Macedonia at the time of writing the epistle is, in this passage, inferred only from his saying that he had boasted to the Macedonians of the alacrity of his Achaian converts; and the fear which he expresses, lest, if any of the Macedonian Christians should come with him unto Achaia, they should find his boasting unwarranted by the event. The business of the contribution is the sole cause of mentioning Macedonia at all. Will it be insinuated that this passage was framed merely to state that St. Paul was now in Macedonia; and by that statement to produce an apparent agreement with the purpose of visiting Macedonia, notified in the first epistle? Or will it be thought probable that, if a sophist had meant to place St. Paul in Macedonia, for the sake of giving countenance to his forgery, he would have done it in so oblique a manner as through the medium of a contribution? The same thing may be observed of another text in the epistle, in which the name of Macedonia occurs: "Farthermore, when I came to Troas to preach the Gospel, and a door was opened unto me of the Lord, I had no rest in my spirit, because I found not Titus, my brother; but taking my leave of them, I went from thence into Macedonia." I mean, that it may be observed of this passage also, that there is a reason for mentioning Macedonia, entirely distinct from the purpose of showing St. Paul to be *there*. The text, however, in which it is most strongly implied that St. Paul wrote the present epistle from Macedonia, is found in the fourth, fifth, and sixth verses of the seventh chapter. Yet, even here, I think no one will contend that St. Paul's coming to Macedonia, or being in Macedonia, was the principal thing intended to be told; or that the telling of it, indeed, was any part of the intention with which the text was written; or that the mention even of the name of Macedonia was not purely incidental, in the description of those tumultuous sorrows with which the writer's mind had been lately agitated, and from which he was relieved by the coming of Titus. The first five verses of the eighth chapter, which commend the liberality of the Macedonian Churches, do not, in my opinion, by themselves, prove St. Paul to have been at Macedonia at the time of writing the epistle.

2. In the first epistle, St. Paul denounces a severe censure against an incestuous marriage, which had taken place amongst the Corinthian converts, with the connivance, not to say with the approbation, of the Church; and enjoins the Church to purge itself of this scandal, by expelling the offender from its society,

2

(chap. v. 1–5.) In the second epistle we find this sentence executed, and the offender to be so affected with the punishment, that St. Paul now intercedes for his restoration: "Sufficient to such a man is this punishment, which was inflicted of many; so that, contrariwise, ye ought rather to forgive him and comfort him, lest perhaps such a one should be swallowed up with overmuch sorrow; wherefore I beseech you, that ye would confirm your love towards him." (2 Cor., chap. ii. 7, 8.) Is this whole business feigned for the sake of carrying on a continuation of story through the two epistles? The Church also, no less than the offender, was brought by St. Paul's reproof to a deep sense of the impropriety of their conduct. Their penitence and their respect to his authority were, as might be expected, exceedingly grateful to St. Paul: "We were comforted not by Titus's coming only, but by the consolation wherewith he was comforted in you, when he told us your earnest desire, your mourning, your fervent mind towards me, so that I rejoiced the more; for though I made you sorry with a letter, I do not repent, though I did repent; for I perceive that the same epistle made you sorry, though it were but for a season. Now I rejoice, not that ye were made sorry, but that ye sorrowed to repentance; for ye were made sorry after a godly manner, that ye might receive damage by us in nothing." (Chap. vii. 7–9.) That this passage is to be referred to the incestuous marriage is proved by the twelfth verse of the same chapter: "Though I wrote unto you, I did it not for his cause that had done the wrong, nor for his cause that had suffered wrong; but that our care for you, in the sight of God, might appear unto you." There were, it is true, various topics of blame noticed in the first epistle; but there was none, except this of the incestuous marriage, which could be called a transaction between private parties, or of which it could be said that one particular person had "done the wrong," and another particular person "had suffered it." Could all this be without foundation?

3. In the sixteenth chapter of the first epistle, a collection for the saints is recommended to be set forwards at Corinth, (chap. xvi. 1.) In the ninth chapter of the second epistle, such a collection is spoken of, as in readiness to be received: "As touching the ministering to the saints, it is superfluous for me to write to you, for I know the forwardness of your mind, for which I boast of you to them of Macedonia, that Achaia was ready a year ago, and your zeal hath provoked very many." (Chap. ix. 1, 2.) This is such a continuation of the transaction as might be expected, or, possibly it will be said, as might easily be counterfeited; but there is a circumstance of nicety in the agreement between the two epistles, which I am convinced the author of a forgery would not have hit upon, or which, if he had hit upon it, he would have set forth with more clearness. The second epistle speaks of the Corinthians as having begun this eleemosynary business a year before: "This is expedient for you, who have begun before, not only to do, but also to be forward a year ago." (Chap. viii. 10.) "I boast of you to them of Macedonia, that Achaia was ready a year ago." (Chap. ix. 2.) From these texts it is evident that something had been done in the business a year before. It appears, however, from other texts in the epistle, that the contribution was not yet collected or paid; for brethren were sent from St. Paul to Corinth, "to make up their bounty." (Chap. ix. 5.) They are urged to "perform the doing of it." (Chap. viii. 11.) "And every man was exhorted to give as he purposed in his heart." (Chap. ix. 7.) The contribution, therefore, as represented in our present epistle, was in readiness, yet not received from the contributors; was begun, was forward long before, yet not hitherto collected. Now this representation agrees with one, and only with one, supposition, namely, that every man had laid by in store—had already provided the fund, from which he was afterwards to contribute—the very case which the first epistle authorizes us to suppose to have existed; for in that epistle St. Paul had charged the Corinthians, "upon the first day of the week, every one of them, to lay by in store as God had prospered him" (1 Cor., chap. xvi. 2.)

Section II.

In comparing the Second Epistle to the Corinthians with the Acts of the Apostles, we are soon brought to observe, not only that there exists no vestige either of the epistle having been taken from the history or the history from the epistle, but also that there appears in the contents of the epistle positive evidence that neither was borrowed from the other. Titus, who bears a conspicuous part in the epistle, is not mentioned in the Acts of the Apostles at all. St. Paul's sufferings, enumerated chap. xi. 24, "Of the Jews five times received I forty stripes save one; thrice was I beaten with rods; once was I stoned; thrice I suffered shipwreck; a night and a day I have been in the deep," cannot be made out from his history as delivered in the Acts; nor would this account have been given by a writer, who either drew his knowledge of St. Paul from that history, or who was careful to preserve a conformity with it. The account in the epistle, of St. Paul's escape from Damascus, though agreeing in the main fact with the account of the same transaction in the Acts, is related with such difference of circumstance as renders it utterly improbable that one should be derived from the other. The two accounts, placed by the side of each other, stand as follows:—

2 Cor., chap. xi. 32, 33. In Damascus, the governor, under Aretas the king, kept the city of the Damascenes with a garrison, desirous to apprehend *me*; and through a window in a basket was I let down by the wall, and escaped his hands.	Acts, chap. ix. 23–25. And after many days were fulfilled, the Jews took counsel to kill him; but their laying in wait was known of Saul, and they watched the gates day and night to kill him: then the disciples took him by night, and let him down by the wall in a basket.

Now, if we be satisfied in general concerning these two ancient writings, that the one was not known to the writer of the other, or not consulted by him, then the accordances which may be pointed out between them will admit of no solution so probable as the attributing of them to truth and reality, as to their common foundation.

Section III.

The opening of this epistle exhibits a connection with the history, which alone would satisfy my mind that the epistle was written by St. Paul, and by St. Paul in the situation in which the history places him. Let it be remembered, that in the *nineteenth* chapter of the Acts, St. Paul is represented as driven away from Ephesus; or as leaving, however, Ephesus, in consequence of an uproar in that city, excited by some interested adversaries of the new religion. " Great is Diana of the Ephesians—And after the uproar was ceased, Paul called unto him the disciples, and embraced them, and departed for to go into Macedonia." When he was arrived in Macedonia, he wrote the *Second* Epistle to the Corinthians, which is now before us ; and he begins his epistle in this wise : " Blessed be God, even the Father of our Lord Jesus Christ, the Father of mercies, and the God of all comfort, who comforteth us in all our tribulation, that we may be able to comfort them which are in any trouble, by the comfort wherewith we ourselves are comforted of God, &c. For we would not, brethren, have you ignorant of our trouble *which came to us in Asia*, that we were pressed out of measure, above strength, insomuch that we despaired even of life ; but we had the sentence of death in ourselves, that we should not trust in ourselves, but in God, which raiseth the dead, who delivered us from so great a death, and doth deliver ; in whom we trust that He will yet deliver us." Nothing could be more expressive of the circumstances in which the history describes St. Paul to have been, at the time when the epistle purports to be written ; or rather, nothing could be more expressive of the sensations arising from these circumstances, than this passage. It is the calm recollection of a mind emerged from the confusion of instant danger. It is that devotion and solemnity of thought which follows a recent deliverance. There is just enough of particularity in the passage to show that it is to be referred to the tumult at Ephesus : " We would not, brethren, have you ignorant of our trouble which came to us in Asia." And there is nothing more ; no mention of Demetrius, of the seizure of St. Paul's friends, of the interference of the town-clerk, of the occasion or nature of the danger which St. Paul had escaped, or even of the city where it happened ; in a word, no recital upon which a suspicion could be conceived, either that the author of the epistle had made use of the narrative in the Acts ; or, on the other hand, that he had sketched the outline, which the narrative in the Acts only filled up. That the forger of an epistle, under the name of St. Paul, should borrow circumstances from a history of St. Paul, then extant ; or, that the author of a history of St. Paul should gather materials from letters bearing St. Paul's name, may be credited : but I cannot believe that any forger whatever should fall upon an expedient so refined, as to exhibit sentiments adapted to a situation, and to leave his readers to seek out that situation from the history ; still less that the author of a history should go about to frame facts and circumstances, fitted to supply the sentiments which he found in the letter.

Section IV.

It has already been remarked, that St. Paul's original intention was to have visited Corinth in his way to Macedonia : " I was minded to come unto you before, and to pass by you into Macedonia." (2 Cor., chap. i. 15, 16.) It has also been remarked, that he changed his intention, and ultimately resolved upon going through Macedonia *first*. Now upon this head there exists a circumstance of correspondency between our epistle and the history, which is not very obvious to the reader's observation ; but which, when observed, will be found, I think, close and exact. Which circumstance is this : that though the change of St. Paul's intention be expressly mentioned only in the second epistle, yet it appears, both from the history and from this second epistle, that the change had taken place before the writing of the first epistle ; that it appears however from neither, otherwise than by an inference, unnoticed perhaps by almost every one who does not sit down professedly to the examination.

First, then, how does this point appear from the history ? In the nineteenth chapter of the Acts, and the twenty-first verse, we are told that " Paul purposed in the spirit, when he had passed through Macedonia and Achaia, to go to Jerusalem. So he sent into Macedonia two of them that ministered unto him, Timotheus and Erastus : but he himself stayed in Asia for a season." A short time after this, and evidently in pursuance of the same intention, we find (chap. xx. 1, 2) that " Paul departed from Ephesus for to go into Macedonia ; and that, when he had gone over those parts, he came into Greece." The resolution, therefore, of passing first through Macedonia, and from thence into Greece, was formed by St. Paul previous to the sending away of Timothy. The order in which the two countries are mentioned shows the direction of his intended route " when he passed through Macedonia and Achaia." Timothy and Erastus, who were to precede him in his progress, were sent by him from Ephesus into Macedonia. He himself, a short time afterwards, and, as hath been observed, evidently in continuation and pursuance of the same design, " departed for to go into Macedonia." If he had ever, therefore, entertained a different plan of his journey, which is not hinted in the history, he must have changed that plan before this time. But from the seventeenth verse of the fourth chapter of the First Epistle to the Corinthians, we discover that Timothy had been sent away from Ephesus before that epistle was written : " For this cause have I sent unto you Timotheus, who is my beloved son.". The change, therefore, of St. Paul's resolution, which was prior to the sending away of Timothy, was necessarily prior to the writing of the First Epistle to the Corinthians.

3

Thus stands the order of dates as collected from the history, compared with the first epistle. Now let us inquire, secondly, how this manner is represented in the epistle before us. In the *sixteenth* verse of the first chapter of this epistle, St. Paul speaks of the intention which he had once entertained of visiting Achaia, in his way to Macedonia : "In this confidence I was minded to come unto you before, that ye might have a second benefit ; and to pass by you into Macedonia." After protesting in the *seventeenth* verse against any evil construction that might be put upon his laying aside of this intention, in the *twenty-third* verse he discloses the cause of it : "Moreover I call God for a record upon my soul, that to spare you I came not as yet unto Corinth." And then he proceeds as follows : "But I determined this with myself, that I would not come again to you in heaviness ; for, if I make you sorry, who is he then that maketh me glad, but the same which is made sorry by me ? *And I wrote this same unto you,* lest when I came I should have sorrow from them of whom I ought to rejoice ; having confidence in you all, that my joy is the joy of you all, for out of much affliction and anguish of heart *I wrote unto you with many tears ;* not that ye should be grieved, but that ye might know the love which I have more abundantly unto you ; but if any have caused grief, he hath not grieved me but in part, that I may not overcharge you all. Sufficient to such a man is this punishment, which was inflicted of many." In this quotation let the reader first direct his attention to the clause marked by Italics, "and I wrote this same unto you," and let him consider, whether from the context, and from the structure of the whole passage, it be not evident that this writing was after St. Paul had "determined with himself that he would not come again to them in heaviness ?" whether, indeed, it was not in consequence of this determination, or at least with this determination upon his mind ? And in the next place, let him consider whether the sentence, "I determined this with myself, that I would not come again to you in heaviness," do not plainly refer to that postponing of his visit to which he had alluded in the verse but one before, when he said, "I call God for a record upon my soul, that to spare you I came not as yet unto Corinth :" and whether this be not the visit of which he speaks in the sixteenth verse, wherein he informs the Corinthians, "that he had been minded to pass by them into Macedonia ;" but that, for reasons which argued no levity or fickleness in his disposition, he had been compelled to change his purpose. If this be so, then it follows that the writing here mentioned was posterior to the change of his intention. The only question, therefore, that remains, will be, whether this writing relate to the letter which we now have under the title of the First Epistle to the Corinthians, or to some other letter not extant. And upon this question I think Mr. Locke's observation decisive ; namely, that the second clause marked in the quotation by Italics, "I wrote unto you with many tears," and the first clause so marked, "I wrote this same unto you," belong to one writing, whatever that was ; and that the second clause goes on to advert to a circumstance which is found in our present First Epistle to the Corinthians ; namely, the case and punishment of the incestuous person. Upon the whole, then, we see that it is capable of being inferred from St. Paul's own words, in the long extract which we have quoted, that the First Epistle to the Corinthians was written after St. Paul had determined to postpone his journey to Corinth ; in other words, that the change of his purpose with respect to the course of his journey, though expressly mentioned only in the second epistle, had taken place before the writing of the first ; the point which we made out to be implied in the history, by the order of the events there recorded, and the allusions to those events in the first epistle. Now this is a species of congruity of all others the most to be relied upon. It is not an agreement between two accounts of the same transaction, or between different statements of the same fact, for the fact is not stated ; nothing that can be called an account is given ; but it is the junction of two conclusions deduced from independent sources, and deducible only by investigation and comparison.

SECTION V.

But if St. Paul had changed his purpose before the writing of the first epistle, why did he defer explaining himself to the Corinthians concerning the reason of that change until he wrote the second ? This is a very fair question ; and we are able, I think, to return to it a satisfactory answer. The real cause, and the cause at length assigned by St. Paul for postponing his visit to Corinth, and not travelling by the route which he had at first designed, was the disorderly state of the Corinthian Church at the time, and the painful severities which he should have found himself obliged to exercise if he had come amongst them during the existence of these irregularities. He was willing therefore to try, before he came in person, what a letter of authoritative objurgation would do amongst them, and to leave time for the operation of the experiment. That was his scheme in writing the first epistle. But it was not for him to acquaint them with the scheme. After the epistle had produced its effect ; (and to the utmost extent, as it should seem, of the apostle's hopes ;) when he had wrought in them a deep sense of their fault, and an almost passionate solicitude to restore themselves to the approbation of their teacher ; when Titus (chap. vii. 6, 7, 11) had brought him intelligence " of their earnest desire, their mourning, their fervent mind towards him, of their sorrow and their penitence ; what carefulness, what clearing of themselves, what indignation, what fear, what vehement desire, what zeal, what revenge," his letter, and the general concern occasioned by it, had excited amongst them ; he then opens himself fully upon the subject. The affectionate mind of the apostle is touched by this return of zeal and duty. He tells them that he did not visit them at the time proposed, lest their meeting should have been attended with mutual grief ; and with grief to him embittered by the reflection that he was giving pain to those from whom alone he could receive comfort : "I determined this with myself, that I would not come again to you in heaviness ; for, if I make you sorry, who is he that maketh me glad but the same which is made sorry by me ?"

(Chap. ii. 1, 2 ;) that he had written his former epistle to warn them beforehand of their fault, "lest when he came he should have sorrow of them of whom he ought to rejoice :" (chap. ii. 3 :) that he had the farther view, though perhaps unperceived by them, of making an experiment of their fidelity, to know the proof of them, whether they are obedient in all things." (Chap. ii. 9.) This full discovery of his motive came very naturally from the apostle after he had seen the success of his measures, but would not have been a seasonable communication before. The whole composes a train of sentiment and of conduct resulting from real situation, and from real circumstance ; and as remote as possible from fiction or imposture.

SECTION VI.

Chap. xi. 9 : " When I was present with you and wanted, I was chargeable to no man; for that which was lacking to me, the brethren which came from Macedonia supplied." The principal fact set forth in this passage, the arrival at Corinth of brethren from Macedonia during St. Paul's first residence in that city, is explicitly recorded, Acts, chap. xviii. 1, 5. " After these things Paul departed from Athens, and came to Corinth. And when Silas and Timotheus were come from Macedonia, Paul was pressed in spirit, and testified to the Jews that Jesus was Christ."

SECTION VII.

The above quotation from the Acts proves that Silas and Timotheus were assisting St. Paul in preaching the Gospel at Corinth ; with which correspond the words of the epistle, (chap. i. 19 :) " For the Son of God, Jesus Christ, who was preached among you by us, even by me, and Silvanus and Timotheus, was not yea and nay, but in him was yea." I do admit that the correspondency, considered by itself, is too direct and obvious ; and that an impostor, with the history before him, might, and probably would, produce agreements of the same kind. But let it be remembered that this reference is found in a writing which, from many discrepancies, and especially from those noted sec. ii., we may conclude, was not composed by any one who had consulted, and who pursued the history. Some observation also arises upon the variation of the name. We read Silas in the Acts, Silvanus in the epistle. The similitude of these two names, if they were the names of different persons, is greater than could easily have proceeded from accident ; I mean, that it is not probable that two persons placed in situations so much alike should bear names so nearly resembling each other. On the other hand, the difference of the name in the two passages negatives the supposition of either the passages, or the account contained in them, being transcribed from the other. That they were the same person is farther confirmed by 1 Thess., chap. i. 1, compared with Acts, chap. xvii. 10.

SECTION VIII.

Chap. ii. 12, 13 : " When I came to Troas to preach Christ's Gospel, and a door was opened unto me of the Lord, I had no rest in my spirit because I found not Titus my brother ; but taking my leave of them, I went from thence into Macedonia."

To establish a conformity between this passage and the history, nothing more is necessary to be presumed than that St. Paul proceeded from Ephesus to Macedonia upon the same course by which he came back from Macedonia to Ephesus, or rather to Miletus, in the neighbourhood of Ephesus ; in other words, that in his journey to the peninsula of Greece he went and returned the same way. St. Paul is now in Macedonia, where he had lately arrived from Ephesus. Our quotation imports that in his journey he had stopped at Troas. Of this the history says nothing, leaving us only the short account, that " Paul departed from Ephesus for to go into Macedonia." But the history says that, in his *return* from Macedonia to Ephesus, " Paul sailed from Philippi to *Troas !* and that when the disciples came together on the first day of the week to break bread, Paul preached unto them all night ; that from Troas he went by land to Assos ; from Assos, taking ship, and coasting along the front of Asia Minor, he came by Mitylene to Miletus." Which account proves, first, that Troas lay in the way by which St. Paul passed between Ephesus to Macedonia ; secondly, that he had disciples there. In one journey between these two places the epistle, and in another journey between the same places the history, makes him stop at this city. Of the first journey he is made to say, " that a door was in that city opened unto me of the Lord ;" in the second, we find disciples there collected around him, and the apostle exercising his ministry with what was even in him more than ordinary zeal and labour. The epistle, therefore, is in this instance confirmed, if not by the terms, at least by the probability, of the history ; a species of confirmation by no means to be despised, because, as far as it reaches, it is evidently uncontrived.

SECTION IX.

Chap. xi. 24, 25 : " Of the Jews five times received I forty stripes save one ; thrice was I beaten with rods ; once was I stoned ; thrice I suffered shipwreck ; a night and a day I have been in the deep."

These particulars cannot be extracted out of the Acts of the Apostles ; which proves, as hath been already observed, that the *epistle* was not framed from the *history :* yet they are consistent with it, which, considering how numerically circumstantial the account is, is more than could happen to arbitrary and independent fictions. When I say that these particulars are *consistent* with the history, I mean, first, that there is no article in the

(20**)

enumeration which is contradicted by the history; secondly, that the history, though silent with respect to many of the facts here enumerated, has left space for the existence of these facts, consistent with the fidelity of its own narration.

First, no contradiction is discoverable between the epistle and the history. When St. Paul says, *thrice* was I beaten with rods, although the history record only *one* beating with rods, viz. at Philippi, Acts xvi. 22, yet is there no contradiction. It is only the omission in one book of what is related in another. But had the history contained accounts of *four* beatings with rods, at the time of writing this epistle, in which St. Paul says that he had only suffered *three*, there would have been a contradiction properly so called. The same observation applies generally to the other parts of the enumeration, concerning which the history is silent: but there is one clause in the quotation particularly deserving of remark; because, when confronted with the history, it furnishes the nearest approach to a contradiction, without a contradiction being actually incurred, of any I remember to have met with. "Once," saith St. Paul, "was I stoned." Does the history relate that St. Paul, prior to the writing of this epistle, had been stoned more than once? The history mentions distinctly one occasion upon which St. Paul was stoned, viz. at Lystra in Lycaonia. "Then came thither certain Jews from Antioch and Iconium, who persuaded the people; and, having stoned Paul, drew him out of the city, supposing he had been dead." (Chap. xiv. 19.) And it mentions also another occasion, in which "an assault was made, both of the Gentiles, and also of the Jews with their rulers, to use them despitefully, and to stone them; but they were aware of it," the history proceeds to tell us, "and fled into Lystra and Derbe." This happened at Iconium, prior to the date of the epistle. Now, had the assault been completed; had the history related that a stone was thrown, as it relates that preparations were made both by Jews and Gentiles to stone Paul and his companions; or even had the account of this transaction stopped, without going on to inform us that Paul and his companions were "aware of their danger and fled," a contradiction between the history and the epistle would have ensued. Truth is necessarily consistent; but it is scarcely possible that independent accounts, not having truth to guide them, should thus advance to the *very brink of contradiction* without falling into it.

Secondly, I say, that if the Acts of the Apostles be silent concerning many of the instances enumerated in the epistle, this silence may be accounted for, from the plan and fabric of the history. The date of the epistle synchronizes with the beginning of the twentieth chapter of the Acts. The part, therefore, of the history which precedes the twentieth chapter, is the only part in which can be found any notice of the persecutions to which St. Paul refers. Now it does not appear that the author of the history was with St. Paul until his departure from Troas, on his way to Macedonia, as related chap. xvi. 10; or rather indeed the contrary appears. It is in this point of the history that the language changes. In the seventh and eighth verses of this chapter the *third* person is used. "After *they* were come to Mysia, *they* assayed to go into Bithynia, but the Spirit suffered *them* not; and *they* passing by Mysia, came to Troas:" and the third person is in like manner constantly used throughout the foregoing part of the history. In the tenth verse of this chapter the *first* person comes in: "After Paul had seen the vision, immediately *we* endeavoured to go into Macedonia; assuredly gathering that the Lord had called *us* to preach the Gospel unto them." Now, from this time to the writing of the epistle, the history occupies four chapters; yet it is in these, if in any, that a regular or continued account of the apostle's life is to be expected: for how succinctly his history is delivered in the preceding part of the book, that is to say, from the time of his conversion to the time when the historian joined him at Troas, except the particulars of his conversion itself, which are related circumstantially, may be understood from the following observations:—

The history of a period of sixteen years is comprised in less than three chapters; and of these a material part is taken up with discourses. After his conversion he continued in the neighbourhood of Damascus, according to the history, for a certain considerable though indefinite length of time, according to his own words (Gal. i. 18) for three years; of which no other account is given than this short one, that "straightway he preached Christ in the synagogues, that he is the Son of God; that all that heard him were amazed, and said, Is not this he that destroyed them which called on this name in Jerusalem? that he increased the more in strength, and confounded the Jews which dwelt at Damascus; and that, after many days were fulfilled, the Jews took counsel to kill him." From Damascus he proceeded to Jerusalem: and of his residence there nothing more particular is recorded, than that "he was with the apostles, coming in and going out; that he spake boldly in the name of the Lord Jesus, and disputed against the Grecians, who went about to kill him." From Jerusalem, the history sends him to his native city of Tarsus, (Acts, chap. ix. 30.) It seems probable, from the order and disposition of the history, that St. Paul's stay at Tarsus was of some continuance; for we hear nothing of him until, after a long apparent interval and much interjacent narrative, Barnabas, desirous of Paul's assistance upon the enlargement of the Christian mission, "went to Tarsus for to seek him," (chap. xi. 25.) We cannot doubt that the new apostle had been busied in his ministry; yet of what he did or what he suffered during this period, which may include three or four years, the history professes not to deliver any information. As Tarsus was situated upon the seacoast, and as, though Tarsus was his home, it is probable he visited from thence many other places, for the purpose of preaching the Gospel, it is not unlikely that in the course of three or four years he might undertake many short voyages to neighbouring countries, in the navigating of which we may be allowed to suppose that some of those disasters and shipwrecks befell him to which he refers in the quotation before us, "Thrice I suffered shipwreck, a night and a day I have been in the deep." This last clause I am inclined to interpret of his being obliged to take to an open boat upon the loss of the ship, and his continuing out at sea in that dangerous situation a night and a day. St. Paul is here recounting his sufferings, not relating miracles. From Tarsus, Barnabas brought Paul to Antioch, and there he remained a year : but of the transactions of that year no other description is given than what is contained in the *last four verses* of the *eleventh chapter.* After a more solemn dedication to the ministry, Barnabas and Paul proceeded from Antioch to Cilicia, and from thence they sailed to Cyprus, of which voyage no particulars are mentioned. Upon their return from Cyprus they made a progress together through the Lesser Asia ; and though two remarkable speeches be preserved, and a few incidents in the course of their travels circumstantially related, yet is the account of this progress, upon the whole, given professedly with conciseness ; for instance, at Iconium it is said that they abode a long time, (chap. xiv. 3,) yet of this long abode, except concerning the manner in which they were driven away, no memoir is inserted in the history. The whole is wrapped up in one short summary : " They spake boldly in the Lord, which gave testimony unto the word of his grace, and granted signs and wonders to be done by their hands." Having completed their progress, the two apostles returned to Antioch, " and there they abode long time with the disciples." Here we have another large portion of time passed over in silence. To this succeeded a journey to Jerusalem, upon a dispute which then much agitated the Christian Church, concerning the obligation of the law of Moses. When the object of that journey was completed, Paul proposed to Barnabas to go again and visit their brethren in every city where they had preached the word of the Lord. The execution of this plan carried our apostle through Syria, Cilicia, and many provinces of the Lesser Asia ; yet is the account of the whole journey despatched in *four verses* of the *sixteenth* chapter.

Section X.

Chap. iii. 1 : " Do we begin again to commend ourselves ? or need we, as some others, epistles of commendation to you ?"

" As some others." Turn to Acts xviii. 27, and you will find that, a short time before the writing of this epistle, Apollos had gone to Corinth with letters of commendation from the Ephesian Christians : " And when Apollos was disposed to pass into Achaia, the brethren wrote, exhorting the disciples to receive him." Here the words of the epistle bear the appearance of alluding to some specific instance, and the history supplies that instance ; it supplies at least an instance as apposite as possible to the terms which the apostle uses, and to the date and direction of the epistle in which they are found. The letter which Apollos carried from Ephesus, was precisely the letter of commendation which St. Paul meant ; and it was to Achaia, of which Corinth was the capital, and indeed to Corinth itself, (Acts xix. 1,) that Apollos carried it ; and it was about two years before the writing of this epistle. If St. Paul's words be rather thought to refer to some general usage which then obtained among Christian Churches, the case of Apollos exemplifies that usage, and affords that species of confirmation to the epistle, which arises from seeing the manners of the age, in which it purports to be written, faithfully preserved.

Section XI.

Chap. xiii. 1 : " This is the third time I am coming to you ;" τριτον τουτο ερχομαι.

Do not these words import that the writer had been at Corinth *twice* before ? Yet, if they import this, they overset every congruity we have been endeavouring to establish. The Acts of the Apostles record only *two journeys* of St. Paul to Corinth. We have all along supposed, what every mark of time except this expression indicates, that the epistle was written between the first and second of these journeys. If St. Paul had been already *twice* at Corinth, this supposition must be given up ; and every argument or observation which depends upon it, falls to the ground. Again, the Acts of the Apostles not only record no more than *two journeys* of St. Paul to Corinth, but do not allow us to suppose that more than *two* such journeys could be made or intended by him within the period which the history comprises ; for, from his first journey into Greece to his first imprisonment at Rome, with which the history concludes, the apostle's time is accounted for. If, therefore, the epistle was written after the second journey to Corinth, and upon the view and expectation of a third, it must have been written after his first imprisonment at Rome, i. e. after the time to which the history extends. When I first read over this epistle with the particular view of comparing it with the history, which I chose to do without consulting any commentary whatever, I own that I felt myself confounded by the text. It appeared to contradict the opinion which I had been led by a great variety of circumstances to form, concerning the date and occasion of the epistle. At length, however, it occurred to my thoughts to inquire whether the passage did necessarily imply that St. Paul had been at Corinth twice ; or, whether, when he says, " This is the third time I am coming to you," he might mean only that this was the third time that he was *ready*, that he was *prepared*, that he *intended* to set out upon his journey to Corinth. I recollected that he had once before this purposed to visit Corinth, and had been disappointed in this purpose, which disappointment forms the subject of much apology and protestation in the first and second chapters of the epistle. Now, if the journey in which he had been disappointed was reckoned by him one of the times in which " he was coming to them," then the present would be the *third* time, i. e. of his being *ready* and *prepared* to come, although he had been actually at Corinth only *once* before. This conjecture being taken up, a farther examination of the passage and the epistle produced proofs which placed it beyond doubt. " This is the third time I am coming to you :" in the verse following these words, he adds, " I told

2

you before, and foretell you, as if I were present the *second time*; and being absent, now I write to them which heretofore have sinned, and to all other, that, if I come again, I will not spare." In this verse the apostle is declaring beforehand what he would do in his intended visit; his expression therefore, " as if I were present the second time," relates to that visit. But, if his future visit would only make him present among them a second time, it follows that he had been already there but *once*. Again, in the *fifteenth* verse of the first chapter, he tells them, " In this confidence I was minded to come unto you before, that ye might have a *second* benefit." Why a second, and not a third benefit? why δευτεραν, and not τριτην χαριν, if the τριτον ερχομαι in the thirteenth chapter meant a *third* visit? for though the visit in the first chapter be that visit in which he was disappointed, yet, as it is evident from the epistle that he had never been at Corinth from the time of the disappointment to the time of writing the epistle, it follows that, if it were only a second visit in which he was disappointed *then*, it could only be a second visit which he proposed *now*. But the text which I think is decisive of the question, if any question remain upon the subject, is the *fourteenth* verse of the *twelfth* chapter: " Behold, the third time I am ready to come to you:" Ιδου τριτον ετοιμως εχω ελθειν. It is very clear that the τριτον ετοιμως εχω ελθειν of the *twelfth* chapter, and the τριτον τουτο ερχομαι of the *thirteenth* chapter, are equivalent expressions, were intended to convey the same meaning, and to relate to the same journey. The comparison of these phrases gives us St. Paul's own explanation of his own words; and it is that very explanation which we are contending for, viz. that τριτον τουτο ερχομαι does not mean that he *was coming a third time*, but that this *was the third time* he was in *readiness* to come, τριτον ετοιμως εχω. Upon the whole, the matter is sufficiently certain; nor do I propose it as a new interpretation of the text which contains the difficulty, for the same was given by Grotius long ago; but I thought it the clearest way of explaining the subject, to describe the manner in which the difficulty, the solution, and the proofs of that solution successively presented themselves to my inquiries. Now, in historical researches, a reconciled inconsistency becomes a positive argument: First, because an impostor generally guards against the appearance of inconsistency; and, secondly, because, when apparent inconsistencies are found, it is seldom that any thing but truth renders them capable of reconciliation. The existence of the difficulty proves the want or absence of that caution which usually accompanies the consciousness of fraud; and the solution proves that it is not the collusion of fortuitous propositions which we have to deal with, but that a thread of truth winds through the whole, which preserves every circumstance in its place.

Section XII.

Chap. x. 14–16: " We are come as far as to you also in preaching the Gospel of Christ; not boasting of things without our measure, that is, of other men's labours; but having hope, when your faith is increased that we shall be enlarged by you according to our rule abundantly, to preach the Gospel in the regions beyond you."

This quotation affords an indirect, and therefore unsuspicious, but at the same time a distinct and indubitable recognition of the truth and exactness of the history. I consider it to be implied, by the words of the quotation, that Corinth was the extremity of St. Paul's travels *hitherto*. He expresses to the Corinthians his hope that in some future visit he might " preach the Gospel to the regions beyond them;" which imports that he had not hitherto proceeded " beyond them," but that Corinth was as yet the farthest point or boundary of his travels. Now, how is St. Paul's first journey into Europe, which was the only one he had taken before the writing of the epistle, traced out in the history? Sailing from Asia, he landed at Philippi; from Philippi, traversing the eastern coast of the peninsula, he passed through Amphipolis and Apollonia to Thessalonica; from thence through Berea to Athens, and from Athens to Corinth, *where he stopped*; and from whence, after a residence of a year and a half, he sailed back into Syria. So that Corinth was the last place which he visited in the peninsula; was the place from which he returned into Asia; and was, as such, the boundary and limit of his progress. He could not have said the same thing, viz. " I hope hereafter to visit the regions beyond you," in an epistle to the Philippians, or in an epistle to the Thessalonians, inasmuch as he must be deemed to have already visited the regions beyond *them*, having proceeded from those cities to other parts of Greece. But from Corinth he returned home; every part therefore beyond that city might properly be said, as it is said in the passage before us, to be unvisited. Yet is this propriety the spontaneous effect of truth, and produced without meditation or design.

For St. Paul's journeys, the reader is referred to the *map* which accompanies the Acts of the Apostles.

Dr. *Lightfoot*, in his *Chronology of the New Testament*, has made some good observations on the *date* of this epistle, and the *circumstances* by which that date is ascertained; collating, as Dr. *Paley* has done, the *epistle* with those parts of the *history* in the Acts, which refer to it.

The following is the substance of what he says on this subject:—

A new year being now entered, and Paul intending for *Syria*, as soon as the spring was a little up, he sends *Titus* beforehand to *Corinth*, to hasten their collections for the saints in *Judea*, that they might be ready against Paul should come thither. And with *Titus* he sends two other brethren; and by them all, he sends the Second Epistle to the Corinthians. The proof that it was written and sent at this time, and in this manner, is plain, by these places and passages in it:—Chap. ix. 2, 3, 4: " I know the forwardness of your mind, for which I boast of you to them of Macedonia: yet have I sent the brethren, lest our boasting of you should be in vain; lest haply they of Macedonia come with me," &c. Chap. xii. 14: "Behold, the third time I am coming to you." Chap. xiii. 1: "This is the third time I am coming to you." And, chap. viii. 16: "But thanks be unto God, who put the same earnest care into the heart of Titus for you." Ver. 17: "Being more forward, of his own accord he went unto you." Ver. 18: "And with him we have sent the brother, whose praise is in the Gospel." Ver. 22: "And we have sent with them our brother, whom we have often times proved diligent in many things," &c.

The apostle, in this second epistle to *Corinth*, first excuses his not coming to them, according as he had promised in his first epistle, 1 Cor. xvi. 5, clearing himself from all lightness in making, and from all unfaithfulness in breaking, that promise; and fixing the principal reason upon themselves and their present condition; because he had not yet intelligence, when he went first into *Macedonia*, of any reformation among them of those enormities that he had reproved in his first epistle; therefore he was unwilling to come to them in heaviness, and with a scourge. This, his failing to come according to his promise, had opened the mouths of several in his disgrace, and false teachers took any other occasion to vilify him, which he copiously satisfies, and vindicates himself all along in the epistle. His exceeding zealous plainness with them, and dealing so home and thoroughly against their misdemeanors as he did, was one advantage that his enemies took to open their mouths against him, and to withdraw the *hearts* of the Corinthians from him; and chiefly because he was so urgent against the works of the law as to justification, and those rites which the Jews, even the most of those that were converted to the Gospel, too much doated on.

After he had sent away this epistle by *Titus, Erastus,* and *Mark,* if our conjecture fail not, and had given notice to the *Corinthians* of his speedy coming to them, and warning them to get their collections ready against he came, he provided for his journey into *Syria,* which he had intended so long: partly to visit the Churches in these parts, and partly to bring up the collections he had got for the poor of *Judea;* of which he had promised to the three ministers of the circumcision, *Peter, James,* and *John,* that he would be careful, Gal. ii. 10.

Acts xx. 4: "And there accompanied him into Asia, Sopater of Berea; and of the Thessalonians, Aristarchus and Secundus; and Gaius of Derbe, and Timotheus; and of Asia, Tychicus and Trophimus." Ver. 5: "These going before tarried for us at Troas." Ver. 6: "And we sailed away from Philippi, after the days of unleavened bread."

But when Paul, and this his company, are all going for Asia together, why should they not set out together; but these go before, and tarry at *Troas,* and *Paul* and some other of his company come after? Nay, they were all to meet at *Troas,* as it appeareth, ver. 6. Why might they not then have gone altogether to *Troas?*

The reason of this was, because *Paul* himself was to go by *Corinth;* and not minding to stay there but very little, because he hastened to Jerusalem, he would not take his whole train thither, but send them off the next way they could go to Troas, himself promising and resolving to be speedily with them there. He had promised a long time to the Church of *Corinth* to come unto them, and he had newly sent word in that epistle that he had lately sent, that now his coming would be speedy, 2 Cor. xii. 14 "Behold, the third time I am ready to come to you;" and chap. xiii. 1: "This is the third time that I am coming to you." Not that he had been there *twice* before, for since his first departing thence, (when he had stayed a long time together, at his first planting of the Gospel in that place,) there is neither mention nor probability of his being there again; but this was the third time *that he was coming,* having promised and intended a journey thither once before, but was prevented, 2 Cor. i. 15, 16, 17. But now he not only promises by the epistle that he will come, but staketh the three brethren that he had sent thither for witnesses and sureties of that promise, 2 Cor. xiii. 1, 2, that in the mouth of these witnesses his promise might be established and assured. See the *Introduction,* section xi.

Now the time is come that he makes good his promise; and whilst the rest of his company go directly the next cut to *Troas,* he himself and Luke, and whom else he thought good to retain with him, go about by *Corinth.*

And now, to look a little farther into the reason of their thus parting company, and of Paul's short stay at *Corinth* when he came there, we may take into our thoughts, (besides how much he hastened to *Jerusalem,*) the jealousy that he had, lest he should not find all things at *Corinth* so comfortable to himself, and so creditable to them, before those that should come with him, as he desired. He has many passages in the second epistle that he wrote to them that glance that way; for though, as to the general, there was reformation wrought among them, upon the receiving his first epistle, and thereupon he speaks very excellent things of them; yet were there not a few that thought basely of him, 2 Cor. x. 12, and traduced him and his doctrine, chap. xi. and xii., and gave him cause to suspect that his boasting of that Church to the Churches of *Macedonia* might come off but indifferently, if the *Macedonians* should come with him to see how all things were there, 2 Cor. ix. 4. And therefore it was but the good policy of just fear, grief, and prudence to send them by another way, and he had very just cause to stay but a little while when he came there.—*Lightfoot's Works,* vol. i. p. 310, &c,

PREFACE TO THE SECOND EPISTLE

CORINTHIANS.

IT is a general opinion among learned men that this epistle was written *about a year after the former ;* and this seems to be supported by the words, chap. ix. 2 : *Achaia was ready a year ago ;* for the apostle having given instructions for that collection, to which he refers in these words at the close of the preceding epistle, they would not have had the *forwardness* there mentioned till a year had elapsed. As the apostle had purposed to stay at Ephesus till *pentecost,* 1 Cor. xvi. 8 ; and he stayed some time in Asia after his purpose to leave Ephesus and go to Macedonia, Acts ix. 21, 22 ; and yet making here his apology for not *wintering* in Corinth, as he thought to do, 1 Cor. xvi. 6 ; this epistle must have been written *after* the winter, and consequently when a *new year* was begun. It therefore, says *Dr. Whitby,* seems to have been written after his *second* coming to *Macedonia,* mentioned Acts xx. 3. For, (1.) It was written after he had been at *Troas,* and had left that place to return to *Macedonia :* now that was at his *second* going thither; see chap. ii. 12. (2.) It was written when Timothy was *with* him : now, when he left *Ephesus* to go into *Macedonia,* Timothy went not *with* him, but was sent *before* him, Acts xix. 22 ; but at his *second* going through *Macedonia,* Timothy *was with him,* Acts xx. 4. (3.) He speaks of some *Macedonians* who were likely to accompany him, chap. ix. 4. Now, at his *second* going from *Macedonia,* there accompanied him *Aristarchus, Secundus,* and *Gaius* of *Thessalonica,* the metropolis of Macedonia, Acts xx. 4. (4.) The postscript says that this epistle was written from *Philippi,* where Paul was till the days of unleavened bread, Acts xx. 6 ; it therefore seems to have been sent thence to them by *Titus,* and some *other person,* not long before St. Paul's coming to them ; which he speaks of as *instant,* chap. xiii. 1 ; and that which he was *now ready to do,* chap. xii. 14 ; and *did,* according to Dr. *Lightfoot,* in his journey from *Philippi* to *Troas ;* he sailing *about* from *Philippi* to Corinth, to make good his promise ; whilst the rest that were with him, Acts xx. 4, went *directly the next cut* to Troas, and there waited for him. See *Whitby.*

That the first epistle had produced powerful effects among the Corinthians is evident from what the apostle mentions in this. Titus had met him in Macedonia, and told him of the reformation produced by this epistle, see chap. vii. 5 ; that the Church had excommunicated the incestuous man ; that the epistle had overwhelmed them with great distress ; had led them to a close examination of their conduct and state ; and had filled them with respect and affection for their apostle, &c. Hearing this, St. Paul wrote this second epistle, to comfort, to commend them, and to complete the work which he had begun, by causing them to finish the contribution for the poor saints at Jerusalem ; and also to vindicate his own apostolic character, and to unmask the *pretended apostle,* who had led them so long astray. See the preceding *Introduction.*

Its principal divisions are—

I.—The PREFACE, chap. i. ver. 1–7.

II.—The NARRATION, comprehending an account of what had happened to himself ; his answer to their questions concerning the incestuous person, with different other matters ; among which, the following are the chief :—

    (1.) The *persecution* which he had suffered in Asia, and from which he had been miraculously rescued, chap. i. 8–14.

    (2.) His *purpose* to pay them a visit, chap. i. 15–24.

    (3.) Concerning the *sorrow* which they had suffered on account of the *excommunication* of the incestuous person, chaps. ii. and vii.

    (4.) His own vindication against the false apostle ; in which he gives an account of his *doctrine,* chap. iii. 6–18. His *conduct,* chap. iv. 1–6. His bodily infirmities, chap. iv. 7 ; and chap. v.

    (5.) Strongly exhorts them to a *holy life,* chap. vi. and vii.

III.—Of the ALMS that had been collected, and were yet to be collected, chaps. viii. and ix.

IV. His DEFENCE against the false apostle and his calumniators in general, chaps. x.–xii.

V.—MISCELLANEOUS matters, chap. xiii.

It may be remarked, once for all, that none of these or such *artificial divisions* are made by the apostle himself, no more than the divisions into *chapters* and *verses.* All these are the work of *man,* and certainly contribute nothing to a proper understanding of the epistle itself. The apostle appears to have sat down, and, under the influence of the Divine Spirit, he wrote on the different subjects treated of in the epistle just in the order that these things occurred to his mind, without intending particular *heads, divisions* or *subdivisions.* And, as he probably wrote the whole with very little intermission of time, his sense will be best apprehended by those who carefully read over the whole at *one sitting.*

2

THE

SECOND EPISTLE OF PAUL THE APOSTLE

TO THE

CORINTHIANS.

Chronological Notes relative to this Epistle.

ear of the Constantinopolitan era of the world, or that used by the emperors of the east in their diplomata, &c., and thence also called the "civil era of the Greeks," εφξέ (5565.)—Year of the Alexandrian era of the world, or ecclesiastical epoch of the Greeks, εφνθ' (5559.)—Year of the Antiochian era of the world, εφμθ' (5549).—Year of the Eusebian epoch of the creation, or that used in the Chronicon of Eusebius, and the Roman martyrology, δςπέ (4285.)—Year of the Julian period, 4767.—Year of the world, according to Bedford and Kennedy, in their Scripture Chronology, 4065.—Year of the Usherian era of the world, or that used in the English Bibles, 4061.—Year of the world according to Scaliger, 4001. The difference of sixty years in the era of the world, as fixed by Scaliger and Usher, arises from the former chronologer placing the birth of Abraham in the 70th, and the latter in the 130th year of the life of his father Terah.   For Scaliger's computation, see on Gen. xi. 26 ; and for Usher's computation, see on Gen. xi. 26, and xi. 32, conferred with Acts vii. 4.—Year of the minor Jewish era of the world, 3817. Year of the greater Rabbinical era of the world, 4416.—Year since the Deluge, according to Archbishop Usher and the English Bible, 2405.—Year of the Cali Yuga, or Indian era of the Deluge, 3159.—Year of the era of Iphitus, who re-established the Olympic Games 338 years after their institution by Hercules, or about 884 years before the commencement of the Christian era, 997.—Year of the two hundred and ninth Olympiad, 1.   This epoch commenced, according to the most accurate calculations of some of the moderns, precisely 776 years before the Christian era, and 23 years before the building of Rome ; and computations of time by it ceased about A. D. 440.—Year from the building of Rome, according to Fabius Pictor, who flourished about 225 years before Christ, and who is styled by Dionysius of Halicarnassus an accurate writer, 804.   (This epoch is used by Diodorus Siculus.)—Year from the building of Rome, according to Polybius the historian, 808.—Year from the building of Rome, according to Cato and the Fasti Consulares, and adopted by Solinus, Eusebius, Dionysius of Halicarnassus, &c., 809.—Year from the building of Rome, according to Varro, which was that adopted by the Roman emperors in their proclamations, by Plutarch, Tacitus, Dio Cassius, Gellius Censorinus, Onuphrius, Baronius, and by most modern chronologers, 810.   N. B. Livy, Cicero, Pliny, and Velleius Paterculus, fluctuate between the Varronian and Catonian computations.—Year of the epoch of Nabonassar, king of Babylon, after the division of the Assyrian monarchy, or that used by Hipparchus, by Ptolemy in his astronomical observations, by Censorinus and others, 805.   (The years of this era constantly contained 365 days, so that 1460 Julian were equal to 1461 Nabonassarean years.   This epoch commenced on the IVth of the calends of March, (Feb. 26,) B. C. 747 ; and, consequently, the beginning of the 805th year of the era of Nabonassar coincided with the Vth of the Ides of August, (Aug. 9,) A. D. 57.—Year of the era of the Seleucidæ, or since Seleucus, one of the generals of Alexander the Great, took Babylon and ascended the Asiatic throne, sometimes called the Grecian era, and the era of principalities, in reference to the division of Alexander's empire, 369.—Year of the Cæsarean era of Antioch, 105.—Year of the Julian era, or year since the Calendar of Numa Pompilius, the second Roman king, was reformed by Julius Cæsar, 102.—Year of the Spanish era, or since the second division of the Roman provinces among the Triumviri, 95.—Year since the defeat of Pompey, by Julius Cæsar, at Pharsalia, called by Catrou and Rouille the commencement of the Roman empire, 105.— Year of the Actiac, or Actian era, or proper epoch of the Roman empire, commencing with the defeat of Antony by Augustus at Actium, 87.—Year from the birth of Jesus Christ, 61.—Year of the vulgar era of Christ's nativity, 57.—Year of the Dionysian period or Easter Cycle, 58.—Common Golden Number, or year of the Grecian or Metonic Cycle of nineteen years, 1, or the first common year.—Jewish Golden Number, or year of the Rabbinical Cycle of nineteen years, 17, or the sixth Embolismic.—Year of the Solar Cycle, 10.—Dominical Letter B; or, which is the same thing, the Calends of January, (Jan. 1,) happened on the Jewish Sabbath, or our Saturday.—Jewish Passover, (15th of Nisan, or Abib,) Tuesday, April 5, or on the Nones of April.—Number of Direction, or number of days that Easter Sunday happens after the 21st of March, 21; or the XIIth of the Calends of April.—Mean time of the Paschal Full Moon at Corinth, (its longitude being twenty-three degrees to the east of London,) according to Ferguson's Tables, which are sufficiently exact for this purpose, April 7, or the VIIth of the Ides of April, at forty-eight minutes and thirty-eight seconds past eight in the evening. True time of the Paschal Full Moon at Corinth, according to Ferguson's Tables, April 8, or the VIth of the Ides of April, at thirty-seven minutes and one second past five in the morning; the true time of the Paschal Full Moon being eight hours, forty-eight minutes, and twenty-three seconds after the mean.—Easter Sunday, April 10, or the IVth of the Ides of April.—Epact, or moon's age on the twenty-second of March, or the XIth of the Calends of April, (the day on which the earliest Easter happens) 29.—Year of the reign of Nero Cæsar, the Roman emperor, and fifth Cæsar, 4.—Year of Claudius Felix, the Jewish governor, 5.—Year of the reign of Vologesus, king of the Parthians, or the family of the Arsacidæ, 8.—Year of Caius Numidius Quadratus, governor of Syria, 7.—Year of Ishmael, high priest of the Jews, 3.—Year of the reign of Corbred I., king of the Scots, brother to the celebrated Caractacus, who was carried prisoner to Rome, but afterwards released by the emperor, 3.—Roman consuls; Nero Cæsar Augustus, (the second time,) and L. Calpurnius Piso

Eminent men, contemporaries with St. Paul.

L. *Annæas Seneca*, the Stoic philosopher and poet, son of M. Annæus Seneca, the rhetorician; born about the commencement of the Christian era, and put to death about A. D. 65.—*Annæus Cornutus*, the Stoic philosopher, and preceptor to Persius the satirist; flourished under Nero.—*Lucan*, nephew to Seneca the philosopher; born about A. D. 29, put to death about A. D. 65.—*Andromachus* of Crete, a poet, and Nero's physician.—*T. Petronius Arbiter*, of Massila, died A. D. 66.—*Aulus Persius Flaccus*, the Latin poet, of Volaterræ in Italy; died in the ninth year of the reign of Nero, aged 28.—*Dioscorides*, the physician; the age in which this physician lived is very uncertain.—*Justus*, of Tiberias, in Palestine.—*Flavius Josephus*, the Jewish historian; born A. D. 37, died A. D. 93.—*Silius Italicus*, the poet who was several times consul; born about A. D. 23, died in the beginning of the reign of Trajan, aged 75.—*Valerius Flaccus*, the Latin poet; flourished under Vespasian.—*C. Plinius Secundus*, of Verona, born under Tiberius, flourished under Vespasian, and died under Titus, A. D. 79, aged 56.—*Thraseus Pætus*, the Stoic philosopher, famous for his independence and generous sentiments; slain by order of Nero, A. D. 65.—*Quintius Curtius Rufus*, the historian; the time when he flourished is uncertain, some placing him under Claudius, others under Vespasian, and others under Trajan.—*Asconius Pedianus*, the historian and annotator, died A. D. 76, aged 85.—*Marcus Valerius Martialis*, the epigrammatist; born about A. D. 29, died A. D. 104, aged 75.—*Philo-Byblius*, born about A. D. 53, died A. D. 133, aged 80.—*Acusilaus*, the rhetorician; flourished under Galba.—*Afer*, an orator and preceptor of Quintilian, died A. D. 59.—*Afranius*, the satirist, put to death by Nero, in the Pisonian conspiracy.—*Marcus Aper*, a Latin orator of Gaul, died A. D. 85.—*Babilus*, the astrologer, who caused the Emperor Nero to put all the leading men of Rome to death.—*C. Balbillus*, the historian of Egypt; flourished under Nero.—*P. Clodius Quirinalis*, the rhetorician, flourished under Nero.—*Fabricus*, the satirist; flourished under Nero.—*Decius Junius Juvenalis*, the satirist; born about A. D. 29, died A. D. 128, aged about 100 years.—*Longinus*, the lawyer, put to death by Nero.—*Plutarch*, the biographer and moralist; born about A. D. 50, died about A. D. 120, or A. D. 140, according to others.—*Polemon*, the rhetorician, and master of Persius the celebrated satirist, died in the reign of Nero.—*Seleucus*, the mathematician, intimate with the Emperor Vespasian.—*Servilius Nonianus*, the Latin historian; flourished under Nero.—*Caius Cornelius Tacitus*, the celebrated Roman historian; born in the reign of Nero, and died at an advanced age in the former part of the second century

---

CHAPTER I.

St. Paul encourages them to trust in God in all adversities, from a consideration of the support which he had granted them already in times of afflictions: and expresses his strong confidence of their fidelity, 1–7. Mentions the heavy tribulation which he had passed through in Asia; as also his deliverance, 8–11. Shows in what the exultation of a genuine Christian consists, 12. Appeals to their own knowledge of the truth of the things which he wrote to them, 13, 14. Mentions his purpose of visiting them; and how sincere he was in forming it; and the reason why he did not come, as he had purposed, 15–24

313

A. M. 4061.
A. D. 57.
A. U. C.
810.
Anno Imp. Nero-
nis Cæs. 4.

PAUL, ª an apostle of Jesus Christ by the will of God, and Timothy *our* brother, unto the Church of God which is at Corinth ; ᵇ with all the saints which are in all Achaia :

2 ᶜ Grace *be* to you and peace from God our Father, and *from* the Lord Jesus Christ.

3 ᵈ Blessed *be* God, even the Father of our Lord Jesus Christ, the Father of mercies, and the God of all comfort ;

4 Who comforteth us in all our tribulation, that we may be able to comfort them which are in any trouble, by the comfort wherewith we ourselves are comforted of God.

5 For as ᵉ the sufferings of Christ abound in us, so our consolation also aboundeth by Christ.

A. M. 4061.
A. D. 57.
A. U. C.
810.
Anno Imp. Nero-
nis Cæs. 4.

6 And whether we be afflicted, ᶠ *it is* for your consolation and salvation, which ᵍ is effectual in the enduring of the same sufferings which we also suffer : or whether we be comforted, *it is* for your consolation and salvation.

7 And our hope of you *is* steadfast, knowing, that ʰ as ye are partakers of the sufferings, so *shall ye be* also of the consolation.

8 For we would not, brethren, have you ignorant of ⁱ our trouble which came to us in Asia, that we were pressed out of measure,

---

ª 1 Cor. i. 1 ; Eph. i. 1 ; Col. i. 1 ; 1 Tim. i. 1 ; 2 Tim. i. 1. ᵇ Phil. i. 1 ; Col. i. 2.——ᶜ Rom. i. 7 ; 1 Cor. i. 3 ; Gal. i. 3 ; Phil. i. 2 ; Col. i. 2 ; 1 Thess. i. 1 ; 2 Thess. i. 2 ; Philem. 3.——ᵈ Eph. i. 3 ; 1 Pet. i. 3.——ᵉ Acts ix. 4 ; chap. iv. 10 ; Col. i. 24. ᶠ Chap. iv. 15.——ᵍ Or, *is wrought.*——ʰ Rom. viii. 17 ; 2 Tim. ii. 12.——ⁱ Acts xix. 23 ; 1 Cor. xv. 32 ; xvi. 9.

NOTES ON CHAP. I.

Verse 1. Paul, an apostle] Paul, commissioned immediately by Jesus Christ himself, *according to the will of God*, to preach the Gospel to the Gentiles. See on 1 Cor. i. 1.

In all Achaia] The whole of the *Peloponnesus*, or that country separated from the main land by the *Isthmus of Corinth*. From this we may learn that this epistle was not only sent to the Church at *Corinth*, but to all the Churches in that country.

Verse 2. Grace be to you and peace] See Rom. i. 7.

Verse 3. Blessed be God] Let God have universal and eternal praise : 1. Because he is the *Father of our Lord Jesus Christ*, who is the gift of his endless love to man, John i. 16. 2. Because he is *the Father of mercies*, ὁ Πατηρ των οικτιρμων, the source whence *all* mercy flows, whether it respect the body or the soul, time or eternity ; the *source of tender mercy ;* for so the word implies. See on Rom. xii. 1. And, 3. Because he is *the God of all comfort*—the Fountain whence all consolation, happiness, and bliss flow to angels and to men.

Verse 4. Who comforteth us] Who shows himself to be the God of tender mercy, by condescending to notice us, who have never deserved any good at his hand ; and also the God of all consolation, by *comforting us in all our tribulation*—never leaving us a prey to anxiety, carking care, persecution, or temptation ; but, by the comforts of his Spirit, bearing us up *in, through,* and *above,* all our trials and difficulties.

That we may be able to comfort them] Even *spiritual* comforts are not given us for our use alone ; they, like all the gifts of God, are given that they may be distributed, or become the instruments of help to others. A minister's trials and comforts are permitted and sent for the benefit of the Church. What a miserable preacher must he be who has all his divinity by study and learning, and nothing by experience ! If his soul have not gone through all the travail of regeneration, if his heart have not felt the love of God shed abroad in it by the Holy Ghost, he can neither instruct the ignorant nor comfort the distressed. See ver. 6.

Verse 5. The sufferings of Christ] Suffering endured for the cause of Christ : such as persecutions, hardships, and privations of different kinds.

Our consolation also aboundeth] We stood as well, as firmly, and as easily, in the heaviest trial, as in the lightest ; because the consolation was always proportioned to the trial and difficulty. Hence we learn, that he who is upheld in a slight trial need not fear a great one ; for if he be faithful, his consolation shall *abound,* as his sufferings *abound.* Is it not as easy for a *man* to lift one hundred pounds' weight, as it is for an *infant* to lift a few *ounces ?* The proportion of strength destroys the comparative difficulty.

Verse 6. And whether we be afflicted] See on ver. 4.

Which is effectual] There is a strange and unusual variation in the MSS. and versions in this passage. Perhaps the whole should be read thus : *For if we be afflicted, it is for your encouragement and salvation ; and if we be comforted, it is also for your encouragement, which exerted itself by enduring the same sufferings which we also suffer.*

This transposition of the *middle* and *last* clauses is authorized by the best MSS. and versions. The meaning seems to be this : While ye abide faithful to God, no suffering can be prejudicial to you ; on the contrary, it will be advantageous ; God having your comfort and salvation continually in view, by all the dispensations of his providence : and while you patiently endure, your salvation is advanced ; sufferings and consolations all becoming energetic means of accomplishing the great design, for all things work together for good to them that love God. See the variations in *Griesbach.*

Verse 7. And our hope of you is steadfast] We have no doubt of your continuing in the truth ; because we see that you have such a full, experimental knowledge of it, that no sufferings or persecutions can turn you aside. And we are sure that, as ye suffer, so shall ye *rejoice.*

Verse 8. Our trouble which came to us in Asia] To what part of his history the apostle refers we know not : some think it is to the *Jews lying in wait to kill him,* Acts xx. 3 ; others, to the *insurrection raised*

   2

A. M. 4061.
A. D. 57.
A. U. C.
810.
Anno Imp. Nero-
nis Cæs. 4.

above strength, insomuch that we despaired even of life:

9 But we' had the [k] sentence of death in ourselves, that we should [l] not trust in ourselves, but in God which raiseth the dead:

10 [m] Who delivered us from so great a death, and doth deliver: in whom we trust that he will yet deliver *us*;

11 Ye also [n] helping together by prayer for us, that [o] for the gift *bestowed* upon us by the means of many persons, thanks may be given by many on our behalf.

12 For our rejoicing is this, the testimony of our conscience, that in simplicity and [p] godly sincerity, [q] not with fleshly wisdom, but by the grace of God, we have had our conversa-

A. M. 4061.
A. D. 57.
A. U. C.
810.
Anno Imp. Nero-
nis Cæs. 4.

': Or, *answer.*——[l] Jer. xvii. 5, 7.——[m] 2 Pet. ii. 9.——[n] Rom. xv. 30 ; Phil. i. 19 ; Philem. 22.

[o] Chapter iv. 15.——[p] Chapter ii. 17 ; iv. 2.——[q] 1 Cor. ii. 4, 13.

---

against him by Demetrius and his fellow craftsmen, Acts xix. 23 ; others, to his *fighting with beasts at Ephesus,* 1 Cor. xv. 32, which they understand *literally ;* and others think that there is a reference here to some persecution which is not recorded in any part of the apostle's history.

We were pressed out of measure, above strength] The original is exceedingly emphatic : καθ' ὑπερβολην εβαρηθημεν ὑπερ δυναμιν· we were weighed down beyond what is credible, even beyond what any natural strength could support. There is no part of St. Paul's history known to us which can justify these strong expressions, except his being *stoned* at Lystra ; which if not what is here intended, the facts to which he refers are not on record. As Lystra was properly in Asia, unless he mean Asia Minor, and his stoning at Lystra did most evidently destroy his life, so that his being raised was an effect of the miraculous power of God ; he might be supposed to refer to this. See the notes on Acts xiv. 19, &c. But it is very likely that the reference is to some terrible persecution which he had endured some short time before his writing this epistle ; and with the outlines of which the Corinthians had been acquainted.

Verse 9. *We had the sentence of death in ourselves*] The tribulation was so violent and overwhelming, that he had no hope of escaping death.

That we should not trust in ourselves] The tribulation was of such a nature as to take away all expectation of help but from GOD alone.

But in God which raiseth the dead] This is very like the business at Lystra ; and would be sufficient to fix the apostle's reference to that fact could the *time* and other circumstances serve.

Verse 10. *Who delivered us from so great a death*] For the circumstances were such that no human power could avail.

Will yet deliver us]. Having had such a signal evidence of His interposition already, we will confide in him with an unshaken confidence that he will continue to support and deliver.

Verse 11. *Ye also helping together by prayer*] Even an *apostle* felt the prayers of the Church of God necessary for his comfort and support. What innumerable blessings do the prayers of the followers of God draw down on those who are the objects of them !

The gift bestowed—by the means of many persons] The blessings communicated by means of their prayers.

Thanks may be given by many] When they who have prayed hear that their prayers are so particularly answered, then all that have prayed will feel themselves led to *praise God* for his gracious answers. Thus, the *prayers of many* obtain the *gift ;* and the *thanksgivings of many* acknowledge the *mercy.*

The *gift*, or χαρισμα, which the apostle mentions, was his deliverance from the dangers and deaths to which he was exposed.

Verse 12. *For our rejoicing is this*] Ἡ καυχησις Our *boasting, exultation, subject* of *glorying.*

The testimony of our conscience] Μαρτυριον τη συνειδησεως· That testimony or witness which conscience, under the light and influence of the Spirit of God, renders to the soul of its state, sincerity, safety, &c.

In simplicity] Ἁπλοτητι· from *a,* denoting *unity* or *together,* and πελω, *to be ;* or from *a, negative,* and πολυς, *many ;* not *compounded,* having *one end* in view, having no *sinister* purpose, no *by end* to answer. Instead of ἁπλοτητι, many MSS. and versions have ἁγιοτητι, *holiness.*

In godly sincerity] Ειλικρινεια Θεου· *The sincerity of God :* that is, such a sincerity as comes from his work in the soul. Ειλικρινεια, sincerity, and ειλικρινης, sincere, come from ειλη, the *splendour,* or *bright shining of the sun ;* and here signifies such *simplicity of intention,* and *purity of affection,* as can stand the test of the light of God shining upon it, without the discovery being made of a single blemish or flaw.

Not with fleshly wisdom] The cunning and duplicity of man, who is uninfluenced by the Spirit of God, and has his secular interest, ease, profit, pleasure, and worldly honour in view.

But by the grace of God] Which alone can produce the simplicity and godly sincerity before mentioned, and inspire the wisdom that comes from above.

We have had our conversation] Ανεστραφημεν· We have conducted ourselves. The word properly refers to the whole tenor of a man's life—all that he does says, and intends ; and the object or end he has in view, and in reference to which he speaks, acts, and thinks ; and is so used by the best Greek writers. The verb αναστρεφω is compounded of *ava, again,* and στρεφω, *to turn ;* a continual coming back again to the point from which he set out ; a circulation ; beginning, continuing, and ending every thing to the glory of God ; setting out with Divine views, and still maintaining them ; beginning in the Spirit, and ending in the Spirit ; acting in reference to *God,* as the *planets* do in refer-

2

A. M. 4061.
A. D. 57.
A. U. C.
810.
Anno Imp. Nero-
nis Cæs. 4.

tion in the world, and more abundantly to you-ward.

13 For we write none other things unto you than what ye read or acknowledge ; and I trust ye shall acknowledge even to the end ;

14 As also ye have acknowledged us in part, ʳ that we are your rejoicing, even as ˢ ye also *are* ours in the day of the Lord Jesus.

15 And in this confidence ᵗ I was minded to come unto you before, that ye might have a ᵘ second ᵛ benefit ;

16 And to pass by you into Macedonia,

and ʷ to come again out of Macedonia unto you, and of you to be brought on my way toward Judea.

A. M. 4061.
A. D. 57.
A. U. C.
810.
Anno Imp. Nero-
nis Cæs. 4.

17 When I therefore was thus minded, did I use lightness ? or the things that I purpose, do I purpose ˣ according to the flesh, that with me there should be yea, yea and nay, nay ?

18 But *as* God *is* true, our ʸ word toward you was not yea and nay.

19 For ᶻ the son of God, Jesus Christ, who was preached among you by us, *even by me*

ʳ Chap. v. 12.——ˢ Phil. ii. 16 ; iv. 1 ; 1 Thess. ii. 19, 20. ᵗ 1 Cor. iv. 19.——ᵘ Rom. i. 11.

ᵛ Or, *grace.*——ʷ 1 Cor. xvi. 5, 6.——ˣ Chap. x. 2.——ʸ Or, *preaching.*——ᶻ Mark i. 1 ; Luke i. 35 ; Acts ix. 20.

---

ence to the *sun,* deriving all their light, heat, and motion from him ; and incessantly and regularly revolving round him. Thus acted Paul ; thus acted the primitive Christians ; and thus must every Christian act who expects to see God in his glory. The word *conversation* is not an unapt Latinism for the Greek term, as *conversatio* comes from *con,* together, and *verto,* I turn ; and is used by the *Latins* precisely the same sense as the other is by the *Greeks,* signifying the whole of a man's conduct, the tenor and practice of his life : and *conversio astrorum,* and *conversiones cœlestes,* is by Cicero used for the *course of the stars* and *heavenly bodies.*— De Leg. c. 8 : *Cœlum una* conversione *atque eadem, ipse circum se torquetur et vertitur.*—Cic. de Univers., c. 8 : "The heaven itself is, with one and the same revolution, whirled about, and revolves round itself."

In the world] Both among Jews and Gentiles have we always acted as seeing Him who is invisible.

More abundantly to you-ward.] That is, We have given the fullest proof of this in our *conduct* towards *you;* you have witnessed the holy manner in which we have always acted ; and God is witness of the purity of the motives by which we have been actuated ; and our conscience tells us that we have lived in uprightness before him.

Verse 13. *Than what ye read*] Viz. In the first epistle which he had sent them.

Or acknowledge] To be the truth of God ; and which he hoped they would continue to acknowledge, and not permit themselves to be turned aside from the hope of the Gospel.

Verse 14. *Have acknowledged us in part*] Απο μερους may signify here not *in part,* but *some of you;* and it is evident, from the distracted state of the Corinthians, and the opposition raised there against the apostle, that it was only *a part of them* that did acknowledge him, and receive and profit by his epistles and advice.

We are your rejoicing, &c.] You boast of *us* as the ministers of Christ through whom ye have believed ; as we boast of *you* as genuine converts to the Christian faith, and worthy members of the Church of God.

Verse 15. *And in this confidence*] Under the con-

viction or persuasion that this is the case ; that ye exult in us, as we do in you ;

I was minded] I had purposed *to come to you before,* as he had intimated, 1 Cor. xvi. 5 ; for he had intended to call on them in his way from Macedonia, but this purpose he did not fulfil ; and he gives the reason, ver. 23.

A second benefit] He had been with them *once,* and they had received an especial blessing in having the *seed* of life *sown* among them by the preaching of the Gospel ; and he had purposed to visit them again that they might have a *second* blessing, in having that seed *watered.* Instead of χαριν, grace or *benefit,* several MSS. read χαραν, *joy, pleasure ;* but the word *grace* or *benefit,* seems to express the apostle's meaning best.

Verse 16. *To pass by you into Macedonia*] He had purposed to go to Macedonia first, and then from Macedonia return to them, and probably winter in Corinth. Therefore we must understand the δι' ὑμων, *by you,* as implying that he would sail up the Ægean Sea, leaving Corinth to the west ; though he might have taken in his way, and have gone by land through Greece up to Macedonia. Some think that the meaning is, that he purposed to take Achaia in his way to Macedonia, without calling at Corinth ; but Achaia was out of his way considerably, and he could scarcely go through Achaia without passing close by Corinth. I consider the words, therefore, as implying that he purposed not to call at Corinth at that time, but to pass by it, as before stated.

Verse 17. *Did I use lightness ?*] When I formed this purpose, was it without due consideration ? and did I abandon it through fickleness of mind ?

That with me there should be yea, &c.] That I should act as *carnal* men, who change their purposes, and falsify their engagements, according as may seem best to their secular interest ?

Verse 18. *But as God is true*] Setting the God of truth before my eyes, I could not act in this way : and as sure as he is true, so surely were my purposes sincere ; and it was only my uncertainty about your state that induced me to postpone my visit. See ver. 23.

Verse 19. *For the Son of God, &c.*] If I could have changed my purpose through *carnal* or *secular* interest, then I must have had the same interest in

    2

A. M. 4061.
A. D. 57.
A. U. C. 810.
Anno Imp. Nero-
nis Cæs. 4.

and Silvanus, and Timotheus, was not yea and nay, ᵃ but in him was yea.

20 ᵇ For all the promises of God in him *are* yea, and in him amen, unto the glory of God by us.

21 Now he which stablisheth us with you in Christ, and ᶜ hath anointed us, *is* God;

22 Who ᵈ hath also sealed us, and ᵉ given

the earnest of the Spirit in our hearts.

23 Moreover ᶠ I call God for a record upon my soul, ᵍ that to spare you I came not as yet unto Corinth.

24 Not for ʰ that we have dominion over your faith, but are helpers of your joy: for ⁱ by faith ye stand.

A. M. 4061.
A. D. 57.
A. U. C. 810.
Anno Imp. Nero-
nis Cæs. 4.

ᵃ Heb. xiii. 8.——ᵇ Rom. xv. 8, 9.——ᶜ 1 John ii. 20, 27. ᵈ Eph. i. 13; iv. 30; 2 Tim. ii. 19; Rev. ii. 17.——ᵉ Chap. v. 5; Eph. i. 14.

ᶠ Rom. i. 9; chap. xi. 31; Gal. i. 20; Phil. i. 8.——ᵍ 1 Cor. iv. 21; chap. ii. 3; xii. 2; xiii. 2, 10.——ʰ 1 Cor. iii. 5; 1 Pet. v. 3.——ⁱ Rom. xi. 20; 1 Cor. xv. 1.

view when I first preached the Gospel to you, with Silvanus and Timotheus. But did not the whole of our conduct prove that we neither *had*, nor could *have* such interest in view?

Verse 20. *For all the promises of God*] Had we been light, fickle, worldly-minded persons; persons who could only be bound by our engagements as far as comported with our secular interest; would God have confirmed our testimony among you? Did we not lay before you the promises of God? And did not God fulfil those promises *by us*—by our instrumentality, to your salvation and his own glory? God is true; therefore every promise of God is true; and consequently each must have its due fulfilment. God will not make use of *trifling*, *worldly* men, as the instruments by which he will fulfil his promises; but he has fulfilled them by *us*; therefore we are just and spiritual men, else God would not have used us.

In him are *yea, and in him amen*] All the promises which God has made to mankind are *yea*—true in themselves, and *amen*—faithfully fulfilled to them who believe in Christ Jesus. The *promises* are all made in reference to Christ; for it is only on the *Gospel system* that we can have *promises of grace*; for it is only on that system that we can have *mercy*. Therefore, the promise comes originally *by* Christ, and is *yea*; and it has its fulfilment *through* Christ, and is *amen*; and this is to the glory of God, by the preaching of the *apostles*.

From what the apostle says here, and the serious and solemn manner in which he vindicates himself, it appears that his enemies at Corinth had made a handle of his not coming to Corinth, according to his proposal, to defame his character, and to depreciate his ministry; but he makes use of it as a means of exalting the *truth* and *mercy* of God through Christ Jesus; and of showing that the promises of God not only come by *him*, but are fulfilled *through* him.

Verse 21. *Now he which stablisheth us with you*] It is God that has brought both us and you to this sure state of salvation through Christ; and he has *anointed us*, giving us the extraordinary influences of the Holy Ghost, that we might be able effectually to administer this Gospel to your salvation. Through this unction we know and preach the truth, and are preserved by it from dissimulation and falsity of every kind.

Verse 22. *Who hath also sealed us*] Not only deeply *impressed* His *truth* and *image* upon our *hearts*; but, by the miraculous gifts of the Holy Spirit, attested

the truth of our extraordinary *unction* or calling to the ministry.

And given the earnest of the Spirit] Τον αρραβωνα του Πνευματος. From this *unction* and sealing we have a *clear testimony* in our souls, the Divine Spirit dwelling constantly in us, of our acceptance with God, and that our ways please him. The αρραβων of the apostle is the same as the ערבן *erabon* of Moses, Gen. xxxviii. 17, 18, and 20, which we there translate *pledge*. The word properly signifies an *earnest* of something promised; *a part of the price* agreed for between a *buyer* and *seller*, by giving and receiving of which the bargain was ratified; or a *deposit*, which was to be restored when the thing promised was given. From the use of the term in *Genesis*, which the apostle puts here in Greek letters, we may at once see his meaning above, and in Eph. i. 14; the Holy Spirit being an *earnest* in the *heart*, and an *earnest of the promised inheritance* means a security given in hand for the fulfilment of all God's promises relative to grace and eternal life. We may learn from this, that eternal life will be given in the great day to all who can *produce* the *arrhabon*, or *pledge*. He who is found *then* with the earnest of God's Spirit in his heart, shall not only be saved from death, but have that eternal life of which it is the *pledge*, the *earnest*, and the *evidence*. Without this *arrhabon* there can be no glory. See the whole case of Judah and Tamar, Gen. xxxviii. 13, &c., and the notes there.

Verse 23. *I call God for a record upon my soul*] The apostle here resumes the subject which he left ver. 16, and in the most solemn manner calls God to *witness*, and consequently to punish, if he asserted any thing *false*, that it was through tenderness to them that he did not visit Corinth at the time proposed. As there were so many scandals among them, the apostle had reason to believe that he should be obliged to use the *severe* and authoritative part of his function in the *excommunication* of those who had sinned, and delivering them over to Satan for the destruction of the flesh, &c.; but to give them space to amend, and to see what effect his epistle might produce, (not having heard as yet from them,) he proposed to delay his coming. It is plain, as several commentators have observed, 1. That St. Paul's *doctrine* had been opposed by some of Corinth, 1 Cor. xv. 12. His *apostleship* questioned, 1 Cor. ix. 1, 2, and 2 Cor. xii. 13. 2. Himself *despised*, and treated as a person who, because of the consciousness he had of his own *worth-*

lessness, dared not to come, 1 Cor. iv. 18. *His let-ters, say they, are weighty and powerful*—full of boastings of what he *can* and what he *will* do ; *but his bodily presence is weak, and his speech contempti-ble,* 2 Cor. x. 10. 3. This being the state in which his reputation was then at Corinth, and he having pro-mised to come to them, 1 Cor. xvi. 5, he could not but think it necessary to vindicate his failing them by reasons which should be both convincing and kind, such as those contained in the preceding verses. See *Dodd* and others.

Verse 24. *Not for that we have dominion over your faith*] I will not come to exercise my aposto-lical authority in punishing them who have acted sin-fully and disorderly ; for this would be to several of you a cause of distress, the delinquents being friends and relatives ; but I hope to come to promote your *joy,* to increase your spiritual happiness, by watering the seed which I have already sowed. This I think to be the meaning of the apostle. It is certain that the *faith* which they had already received was preach-ed by the apostles ; and, therefore, in a certain sense, according to our meaning of the term, they had a right to propound to them the *articles* which they ought to believe ; and to forbid them, in the most solemn man-ner, to believe any thing else as *Christianity* which was opposed to those articles. In that sense *they had dominion over their faith ;* and this dominion was essential to them as *apostles.* But shall any others— persons who are not *apostles,* who are not under the *unerring* and *infallible* influence of the *Holy Ghost,* arrogate to themselves this *dominion over the faith of mankind ;* not only by insisting on them to receive *new* doctrines, taught nowhere by apostles or aposto-lic men ; but also threatening them with perdition if they do not credit doctrines which are *opposed* to the very spirit and letter of the *word of God ?* These things men, not only not *apostles,* but *wicked, profli-gate,* and *ignorant,* have insisted on as their *right.* Did they succeed ? Yes, for a time ; and that time was a time of thick darkness ; a darkness that might be felt ; a darkness producing nothing but misery, and lengthening out and deepening the *shadow of death.* But the light of God shone ; the *Scriptures* were read ; those vain and wicked pretensions were brought to the eternal *touchstone :* and what was the consequence ? The splendour of truth pierced, dissipated, and annihi-lated them for ever !

British *Protestants* have learned, and *Europe* is learning that the SACRED WRITINGS, and they *alone,* contain what is necessary to faith and practice ; and that no man, number of men, society, church, council, presbytery, consistory, or conclave, has *dominion over any man's faith.* The word of God alone is his rule, and to its Author he is to give account of the use he has made of it.

For by faith ye stand.] You believe not in *us,* but in GOD. We have prescribed to you on *his au-thority,* what you are to believe ; you received the Gospel as coming from *Him,* and *ye stand in* and *by* that faith.

THE subjects in this chapter which are of the most importance have been carefully considered in the pre-

ceding notes. That alone of the *apostle's oath* has been passed by with general observations only. But, that it is an *oath* has been questioned by some. An *oath,* properly speaking, is an appeal to God, as the Searcher of the heart, for the truth of what is spoken ; and an appeal to Him, as the *Judge* of *right* and *wrong,* to punish the falsity and perjury. All this ap-pears to be implied in the awful words above : *I call God for a record upon my soul ;* and this is not the only place in which the apostle uses words of the same import. See Rom. i. 9, and ix. 1, and the note on this latter passage.

On this subject I have spoken pretty much at large at the end of the sixth chapter of Deuteronomy ; but as it appears that there I have made a mistake in saying that the people called *Quakers hold up their hand* in a court of justice, when called upon to make *affirma-tion,* I take this opportunity to correct that expression, and to give the *form of the oath,* for so the *law* con-siders it, which the statute (7 and 8 of William III., cap. 34, sec. 1) required of this sect of Christians : " *I, A. B., do declare in the presence of almighty God, the witness of the truth of what I say.*" Though this act was only intended at first to continue in force for *seven* years, yet it was afterwards made *perpetual.* See *Burn,* vol. iii., page 654.

A more solemn and more awful form of an oath was never *presented* nor *taken* by man than this ; no *kissing* of the book, holding up of the hand, nor laying hand on the Bible, can add either *solemnity* or *weight* to such an *oath !* It is as awful and as binding as any thing can be ; and him, who would break this, no obligation can bind.

But the religious people in question found their con-sciences aggrieved by this form, and made application to have another substituted for it ; in consequence of this the form has undergone a little alteration, and the solemn affirmation which is to stand instead of an oath taken in the usual manner, as finally settled by the 8th Geo., cap. 6, is the following : " *I, A. B., do solemn-ly, sincerely, and truly declare and affirm.*" *Burn,* vol. iii., page 656.

It may be well to examine this *solemn affirmation,* and see whether it does not contain the *essential prin-ciples* of an *oath ;* and whether it should not be reput-ed by all people, as being equal to any oath taken in the common form, and sufficiently binding on every conscience that entertains the belief of a God, and the doctrine of a future state. The word *solemnly* refers to the *presence* and *omniscience* of GOD, before whom the *affirmation* is made ; and the word *sincerely* to the *consciousness* that the person has of the *uprightness* of his own *soul,* and the total *absence* of *guile* and *de-ceit ;* and the word *truly* refers to the *state* of his *un-derstanding* as to his *knowledge* of the fact in question. The word *declare* refers to the *authority requiring,* and the *persons before whom* this declaration is made ; and the term *affirm* refers back to the words *solemnly, sincerely,* and *truly,* on which the *declaration* and *af-firmation* are founded. This also contains all that is vital to the spirit and essence of an oath ; and the honest man, who *takes* or *makes* it, feels that there is no *form* used among men by which his conscience can be more solemnly bound. As to the *particular* form, as long as it is not absurd or superstitious, it is a matter of perfect indifference as to the thing itself as long as the *declaration* or *affirmation* contains the spirit and essence of an *oath;* and that the law considers this as an *oath* is evident from the following clause : " That if any one be convicted of having wilfully or falsely made this declaration or affirmation, such offender shall incur the same penalties and forfeitures as are enacted against persons convicted of wilful and

corrupt perjury." I believe it may be said wit. strict truth, that few instances can be produced where this *affirmation*, which I must consider as a most solemn oath, was corruptly made by any accredited member of that religious society for whose peace and comfort it was enacted. And when this most solemn affirmation is properly considered, no man of reason will say that the persons who take it are not bound by a sufficient and available *oath*.

CHAPTER II.

The apostle farther explains the reasons why he did not pay his intended visit to the Corinthians, 1.　And why he wrote to them in the manner he did, 2–5.　He exhorts them also to forgive the incestuous person, who had become a true penitent; and therefore he had forgiven him in the name of Christ, 6–11.　He mentions the disappointment he felt when he came to Troas in not meeting with Titus, from whom he expected to have heard an account of the state of the Corinthian Church, 12, 13.　Gives thanks to God for the great success he had in preaching the Gospel, so that the influence of the name of Christ was felt in every place, 14.　Shows that the Gospel is a savour of life to them that believe, and of death to them that believe not, 15, 16.　And that he and his brethren preached the pure, unadulterated doctrine of God among the people, 17.

A. M. 4061.
A. D. 57.
A. U. C.
810.
Anno Imp. Neronis Cæs. 4.

BUT I determined this with myself, [a] that I would not come again to you in heaviness.

2 For if I make you sorry, who is he then that maketh me glad, but the same which is made sorry by me ?

3 And I wrote this same unto you, lest, when I came, [b] I should have sorrow from them of whom I ought to rejoice ; [c] having confidence in you all, that my joy is *the joy* of you all.

4 For out of much affliction and anguish of heart I wrote unto you with many tears ; [d] not that ye should be grieved, but that ye might know the love which I have more abundantly unto you.

5 But, [e] if any have caused grief, he hath not [f] grieved me, but in part : that I may not overcharge you all.

6 Sufficient to such a man *is* this [g] punish-

A. M. 4061.
A. D. 57.
A. U. C.
810.
Anno Imp. Neronis Cæs. 4.

---

[a] Chap. i. 23 ; xii. 20, 21 ; xiii. 10.——[b] Chap. xii. 21.——[c] Chap. vii. 16 ; viii. 22 ; Gal. v. 10.

[d] Chap. vii. 8, 9, 12.——[e] 1 Cor. v. 1.——[f] Gal. iv. 12.——[g] Or, *censure.*

NOTES ON CHAP. II.

Verse 1. *But I determined this*] The apostle continues to give farther reasons why he did not visit them at the proposed time. Because of the scandals that were among them he could not see them comfortably ; and therefore he determined not to see them at all till he had reason to believe that those evils were put away.

Verse 2. *For if I make you sorry*] Should he have come and used his *apostolical authority*, in inflicting punishment upon the transgressors, this would have been a common cause of distress. And though he might expect that the *sound part* of the Church would be a cause of consolation to him, yet as all would be overwhelmed with trouble at the punishment of the transgressors, he could not rejoice to see those whom he loved in distress.

Verse 3. *And I wrote this same unto you*] This I particularly marked in my first epistle to you ; earnestly desiring your reformation, lest, if I came before this had taken place, I must have come with a *rod*, and have inflicted punishment on the transgressors. See 1 Cor. v.

My joy is the joy *of you all.*] I know that ye wish my comfort as much as I wish yours.

Verse 4. *For out of much affliction, &c.*] It is very likely that the apostle's enemies had represented him as a *harsh, austere, authoritative* man ; who was better pleased with inflicting wounds than in healing them.　But he vindicates himself from this charge by solemnly asserting that this was the most painful part of his office ; and that the writing of his first epistle to them cost him much affliction and anguish of heart, and *many tears.*

Verse 5. *But, if any have caused grief*] Here he seems to refer particularly to the cause of the incestuous person.

Grieved me, but in part] I cannot help thinking that the εκ μερους and απο μερους, which we render *in part*, and which the apostle uses so frequently in these epistles, are to be referred to the *people*.　A part of them had acknowledged the apostle, chap. i. 14 ; and here, *a part of them* had given him cause of grief ; and therefore he immediately adds, *that I may not overcharge you all* ; as only a part of you has put me to pain, (viz. the transgressor, and those who had taken his part,) it would be unreasonable that I should *load you all*, επιβαρω παντας ὑμας, with the blame which attaches to that party alone.

Verse 6. *Sufficient to such a man* is *this punish*

A. M. 4061.
A. D. 57.
A. U. C.
810.
Anno Imp. Nero-
nis Cæs. 4.

ment, which *was inflicted* [h] of many.

7 [i] So that contrariwise ye *ought* rather to forgive *him,* and comfort *him,* lest perhaps such a one should be swallowed up with over-much sorrow.

8 Wherefore I beseech you that ye would confirm *your* love toward him.

9 For to this end also did I write, that I might know the proof of you, whether ye be [k] obedient in all things.

10 To whom ye forgive any thing, I *forgive* also : for if I forgave any thing, to whom I forgave *it,* for your sakes *forgave I it* [l] in the person of Christ ;

A. M. 4061.
A. D. 57.
A. U. C.
810.
Anno Imp. Nero
nis Cæs. 4.

11 Lest Satan should get an advantage of us : for we are not ignorant of his devices.

12 Furthermore, [m] when I came to Troas to *preach* Christ's Gospel, and [n] a door was opened unto me of the Lord,

13 [o] I had no rest in my spirit, because I found not Titus my brother : but taking my leave of them, I went from thence into Macedonia.

14 Now, thanks *be* unto God, which always causeth us to triumph in Christ ; and maketh manifest [p] the savour of his knowledge by us in every place.

---

[h] 1 Cor. v. 4, 5 ; 1 Tim. v. 20.——[i] Gal. vi. 1.——[k] Chap. vii. 15 ; x. 6.

[l] Or, *in the sight.*——[m] Acts xvi. 8 ; xx. 6.——[n] 1 Cor. xvi. 9. [o] Chap. viii. 5, 6.——[p] Cant. i. 3.

---

ment] That is, the man has already suffered sufficiently. Here he gives a proof of his parental tenderness towards this great transgressor. He had been disowned by the Church ; he had deeply repented ; and now the apostle pleads for him.

Verse 7. Ye ought rather to forgive him] He had now suffered enough ; for the punishment inflicted had answered the end for which it was inflicted ; and there was some danger that, if this poor culprit were not restored to the bosom of the Church, his distress and anguish would destroy his life, or drive him to despair.

Verse 8. That ye would confirm your *love toward him.*] You do love him, notwithstanding the reproach he has brought on the Gospel ; and notwithstanding your love to him, ye were obliged to cut him off for the credit of the Gospel. Now that he has repented, *I beseech you to confirm,* κυρωσαι, *to ratify,* by a public act of the Church, your love to him ; give him the *fullest proof* that you do love him, by forgiving him and restoring him to his place in the Church.

Verse 9. For to this end also did I write] Εγραψα, *I have written* this also, the advices and commands which I now give you, *that I might know whether ye be obedient in all things.*

Verse 10. To whom ye forgive any thing] Here he farther shows them that his sole object in the punishment inflicted on the transgressor, was his amendment and therefore promises to *ratify,* in the *name* and *authority* of *Christ,* the free pardon which he exhorts them to dispense.

In the person of Christ] As I believe Christ acts towards his penitent soul, so do I. Christ forgives his sin, and takes him to his favour ; let us forgive him his offence against the Church, and restore him to its communion.

Verse 11. Lest Satan should get an advantage] If the man who has given sufficient proof of the sincerity of his repentance be not restored, he may be overwhelmed with sorrow, and sink into despair ; and then the discipline of the Church will be represented, not as *emendatory,* but as leading to *destruction.* Of this our enemies would most gladly avail themselves, as

they wish to discredit this ministry ; and there is always at hand a devil to suggest evil, and prompt men to do it ; for in this respect we have thorough acquaintance with *his devices.* Let us therefore be careful to remove, both from Satan and his partisans, all those occasions which might turn to the disadvantage or disparagement of the Gospel of Christ.

Verse 12. When I came to Troas] After having written the former epistle, and not having heard what effect it had produced on your minds ; though the Lord had opened me a particular door to preach the Gospel, in which I so especially rejoice and glory ;

Verse 13. I had no rest in my spirit] I was so concerned for you, through the love I bear you, that I was greatly distressed because I did not find Titus returned to give me an account of your state.

But taking my leave of them] I went thence into Macedonia, expecting to find him there ; and thither he did come, and gave me a joyous account of your state. See chap. viii. 6, 7.

Verse 14. Now, thanks be *unto God*] His coming dispelled all my fears, and was the cause of the highest satisfaction to my mind ; and filled my heart with gratitude to God, who is the Author of all good, and who *always causes us to triumph in Christ ;* not only gives us the *victory,* but such a victory as involves the *total ruin* of our enemies ; and gives us cause of *triumphing* in him, through whom we have obtained this victory.

A triumph, among the Romans, to which the apostle here alludes, was a public and solemn honour conferred by them on a victorious general, by allowing him a magnificent procession through the city.

This was not granted by the senate unless the general had gained a *very signal* and *decisive victory ;* conquered a *province,* &c. On such occasions the general was usually clad in a rich purple robe, interwoven with figures of gold, setting forth the grandeur of his achievements ; his buskins were beset with pearls, and he wore a crown, which at first was of *laurel,* but was afterwards of pure *gold.* In one hand he had a branch of *laurel,* the emblem of *victory ;* and in the other, his truncheon. He was carried in a

A. M. 4061.
A. D. 57.
A. U. C.
810.
Anno Imp. Nero-
nis Cæs. 4.

15 For we are unto God a sweet savour of Christ, q in them that are saved, and r in them that perish :

16 s To the one *we are* the savour of death unto death ; and to the other the savour of

life unto life. And t who *is* suffi-cient for these things ?

17 For we are not as many, which u corrupt v the word of God ; but as w of sincerity, but as of God, in the sight of God speak we x in Christ.

A. M. 4061.
A. D. 57.
A. U. C.
810.
Anno Imp. Nero
nis Cæs. 4.

---

q 1 Cor. i. 18.——r Chap. iv. 3.——s Luke ii. 34 ; John ix. 39 ;
1 Pet. ii. 7, 8.——t 1 Cor. xv. 10 ; chap. iii. 5, 6.

u Or, *deal deceitfully with.*——v Chap. iv. 2 ; xi. 13 ; 2 Pet. ii. 3.
w Chap. i. 12 ; iv. 2.——x Or, *of.*

---

magnificent chariot, adorned with ivory and plates of gold, and usually drawn by two *white horses.* (Other *animals* were also used : when *Pompey triumphed* over Africa, his chariot was drawn by *elephants ;* that of *Mark Antony,* by *lions ;* that of *Heliogabalus,* by *tigers ;* and that of *Aurelius,* by *deer.*) His children either sat at his feet in the chariot, or rode on the chariot horses. To keep him humble amidst these great honours a slave stood at his back, casting out incessant railings, and reproaches ; and carefully enu-merating all his vices, &c. *Musicians* led up the pro-cession, and played triumphal pieces in praise of the general ; and these were followed by young men, who led the *victims* which were to be sacrificed on the oc-casion, with their horns gilded, and their heads and necks adorned with ribbons and garlands. Next fol-lowed *carts* loaded with the spoils taken from the enemy, with their horses, chariots, &c. These were followed by the *kings, princes,* or *generals* taken in the war, loaded with chains. Immediately after these came the *triumphal chariot,* before which, as it passed, the people strewed flowers, and shouted *Io, triumphe !*

The triumphal chariot was followed by the *senate ;* and the procession was closed by the priests and their attendants, with the different sacrificial utensils, and a *white ox,* which was to be the *chief victim.* They then passed through the *triumphal arch,* along the *via sacra* to the *capitol,* where the victims were slain.

During this time all the temples were opened, and every altar *smoked* with offerings and *incense.*

The people at Corinth were sufficiently acquainted with the nature of a *triumph :* about two hundred years before this, *Lucius Mummius,* the Roman con-sul, had conquered all *Achaia,* destroyed *Corinth, Thebes,* and *Chalcis ;* and, by order of the senate, had a grand triumph, and was surnamed *Achaicus.* St. Paul had now a *triumph* (but of a widely different kind) over the same people ; his *triumph* was in Christ, and to Christ he gives all the glory ; his *sacrifice* was that of *thanksgiving* to his Lord ; and the *incense* offered on the occasion caused the *savour* of the knowledge of Christ to be manifested in every place. As the *smoke* of the victims and *incense* offered on such an occasion would fill the whole city with their *perfume,* so the *odour* of the *name* and *doctrine* of Christ filled the whole of Corinth and the neighbouring regions ; and the apostles appeared as triumphing in and through Christ, over devils, idols, superstition, ignorance, and vice, wherever they came.

Verse 15. *For we are unto God a sweet savour of Christ*] The apostle still alludes to the case of a *tri-umph ;* the conqueror always represented the person of *Jupiter ;* as even the heathens supposed that God

alone could give the victory : and as the punishment of death was inflicted on *some* of the *captives,* who had often rebelled and broken leagues and covenants ; so others were spared, made *tributaries,* and often be-came *allies.* Alluding to this, the apostle says : We are a *sweet savour to God*—we have fulfilled his will in faithfully proclaiming the Gospel, and fighting against sin. And as he has determined that those who *believe* shall be *saved,* and those who *believe not* shall *perish,* we are equally acceptable to him though we unsuccessfully preach the Gospel to some who obstinately reject it, and so *perish,* as we are in preaching to others who believe, and are *saved.*

Verse 16. *To the one* we are *the savour of death unto death*] There are several sayings among the ancient Jewish writers similar to this. In *Debarim Rabba,* sec. i. fol. 248, it is said : " As the bee brings home honey to its owner, but stings others ; so it is with the words of the law ;" סם חיים לישראל *sam chaiyim leyisrael,* " They are a savour of lives to the Israelites :" וסם המות לאומות העולם *vesam hamma-veth leomoth haólam,* " And a savour of death to the people of this world." The learned reader may see much more to this effect in *Schoettgen.* The apostle's meaning is plain : those who believe and receive the Gospel are saved ; those who reject it, perish. The meaning of the rabbins is not less plain : the *Israelites* received the law and the prophets as from God, and thus possessed the *means of salvation ;* the *Gentiles* ridiculed and despised them, and thus continued in the path of death. The same happens to the present day to those who receive and to those who reject the Gos pel : it is the *means* of *salvation* to the former, it is the means of *destruction* to the latter ; for they are not only *not saved* because they do not believe the Gospel, but they are *condemned* because they *reject* it For how can they escape who neglect so great a sal-vation ? The *sun* which nourishes the *tree* that is planted *in a good soil,* decomposes and destroys it if plucked up and laid on the surface.

That the *saved,* σωζομενοι, and *they* that *perish,* απολλυμενοι, mean those who receive and obey the Gospel, and those who reject it and live and die in sin, needs no proof. No other kinds of *reprobate* and *elect,* in reference to the *eternal world,* are known in the Book of God, though they abound in the *books of men.* The Jews were possessed with such an exalted opinion of their own excellence that they imagined that all the *love* and *mercy* of God were *concentrated among themselves,* and that God never would extend his *grace* to the Gentiles.

Such sentiments may *become* Jews : but when we find some *Gentiles* arrogating to themselves all the sal-

VOL. II.   (21)

vation of God, and endeavouring to prove that he has excluded the major part even of *their own world*—the *Gentiles*, from the *possibility* of obtaining mercy ; and that God has made an *eternal purpose*, that the death of Christ shall never avail them, and that no *saving grace* shall ever be granted to them, and that they shall infallibly and eternally perish ; what shall we say to such things ? It is *Judaism* in its worst shape : Judaism with innumerable *deteriorations*. The propagators of such systems must answer for them to God.

Who is sufficient for these things?] Is it the *false apostle* that has been labouring to *pervert* you ? Or, is it the *men* to whom God has given an extraordinary commission, and sealed it by the miraculous gifts of the Holy Ghost ? That this is the apostle's meaning is evident from the following verse.

Verse 17. *For we are not as many, which corrupt the word of God*] God has made us *sufficient for these things* by giving us his own pure *doctrine*, the *ministry of reconciliation*, which we conscientiously preserve and preach ; and we act, not like *many* among you, who, having received that doctrine, *corrupt* it ; *mingling* with it their own inventions, and explaining away its force and influence, so as to accommodate it to men of carnal minds.

The word καπηλευοντες, from καπηλος, a *tavern-keeper*, signifies acting like an unprincipled vintner ; for this class of men have ever been *notorious* for *adulterating* their wines, mixing them with liquors of no worth, that thereby they might increase their quantity ; and thus the *mixture* was sold for the same price as the *pure wine*. Isa. i. 22, *Thy wine* is *mixed with water*, the Septuagint thus translate : οι καπηλοι σου μισγουσι τον οινον υδατι· " *Thy vintners* mix thy wine with water ;" that is, thy *false prophets* and *corrupt priests adulterate* the *word of God*, and render it of none effect, by their explanations and traditions.

The word has been used, both among the Greeks and Latins, to signify a prostitution of what was *right* and *just*, for the sake of *gain*. So *Herodian*, lib. vi. cap. 11 : Ειρηνην χρυσιον καπηλευοντες, " Making peace for money." So *cauponari bellum* is, " To make war for money." In short, the word is used to signify any *artifice* employed to get *gain* by making a thing look *more* or *better* than it is ; or *mingling* that which is *excellent* with what is not so to promote the gain of the adulterater.

It is used by *Aristophanes*, Plut. Act. iv., scene 5, ver. 1064, to express an old woman who was *patched* and *painted* to hide her deformity.

Ου δητ', επει μεν νυν καπηλικως εχει·
Ει δ' εκπλυνειται τουτο το ψιμυθιον,
Οψει καταδηλα του προσωπου γε τα ρακη.

Not at all ; the old woman is painted :
If the paint were washed off, then you
Would plainly see her wrinkled face.

Where see the note of the *Scholiast*, who observes that the term is applied to those who deal in *clothes*,

patching, mending, &c., as well as to those who *mix bad wine* with *good*. Καπηλικως εχει· Πανουργικως· επει οι καπηλοι χριειν και αναποιειν τα ιματια ειωθασι, και τον οινον δε νωθυλευουσι, συμμιγνυντες αυτω σαπρον. Vid. *Kusteri* Aristoph., page 45.

But as of sincerity] Εξ ειλικρινειας. See the note on chap. i. ver. 12. We *receive* the doctrine *pure* from God ; we *keep* it *pure*, and *deliver* it in its purity to mankind. For *we speak in Christ*—in the things of his Gospel, as being *in the sight of God*—our whole souls and all their motives being known to him. As the unprincipled vintner *knows* that he *adulterates* the *wine*, his conscience testifying this ; so we know that we deliver the sincere truth of God, our conscience witnessing that we deliver it to you, as we receive it, by the inspiration of the Spirit of truth.

1. THAT St. Paul was a man of a very *tender* and *loving spirit* is evident from all his epistles ; but especially from this, and particularly from the chapter before us. It was not an *easy* thing with him to give a *reproof ;* and nothing but a sense of his duty to God and his Church could have led him to use his *apostolical power*, to inflict spiritual punishment on transgressors. He felt like a loving and tender father, who, being obliged to correct his froward and disobedient child, feels in his own heart the pain of a *hundred blows* for that occasioned by *one* laid on the body of his son. There are some ministers who think nothing of cutting off members from the Church of Christ ; they seem to do it, if not cheerfully, yet with indifference and unconcern ! How can this be ? Nothing but absolute duty to God should induce any man to separate any person from the visible Church ; and then it must be on the conviction that the *case is totally hopeless*. And who, even in those circumstances, that knows the worth of a soul, can do it without *torture* of heart ?

2. We must not only love the *doctrines*, but also the *morality* of the Gospel. He who loves this will not corrupt it ; but, as *Quesnel* says truly, in order to love the truth a man must practise it ; as in order to practise it he must love it. That a minister, says he, may preach the word of God in such a manner as is worthy of him, he must, with St. Paul, be always mindful of these *three* things : 1. That he be sent by God, and that he speak directly from him, and as his ambassador. 2. That he speak as in his *presence*, and under his *immediate inspection*. 3. That he consider himself as being in the place of Christ, and endeavour to minister to the souls of men, as he has reason to believe Christ would do, were he in the place ; and as he knows Christ *did*, when he sojourned among men. The minister of the Gospel is Christ's ambassador ; and he prays men in Christ's stead to be reconciled to God. See chap. v. 20. The *people* should consider the nature of this *embassage*, and receive it as coming immediately from God, that it may accomplish the *end* for which he has sent it.

(21**)

CHAPTER III.

The apostle shows, in opposition to his detractors, that the faith and salvation of the Corinthians were a sufficient testimony of his Divine mission; that he needed no letters of recommendation, the Christian converts at Corinth being a manifest proof that he was an apostle of Christ, 1–3. He extols the Christian ministry, as being infinitely more excellent than that of Moses, 4–12. Compares the different modes of announcing the truth under the law and under the Gospel: in the former it was obscurely delivered; and the veil of darkness, typified by the veil which Moses wore, is still on the hearts of the Jews; but when they turn to Christ this veil shall be taken away, 13–16. On the contrary, the Gospel dispensation is spiritual; leads to the nearest views of heavenly things; and those who receive it are changed into the glorious likeness of God by the agency of his Spirit, 17, 18.

A. M. 4061.
A. D. 57.
A. U. C.
810.
Anno Imp. Neronis Cæs. 4.

DO [a] we begin again to commend ourselves? or need we, as some *others,* [b] epistles of commendation to you, or *letters* of commendation from you?

2 [c] Ye are our epistle written in our hearts, known and read of all men:

3 *Forasmuch as ye are* manifestly declared to be the epistle of Christ [d] ministered by us; written not with ink, but with the Spirit of the living God, not [e] in tables of stone, but [f] in fleshly tables of the heart.

A. M. 4061.
A. D. 57.
A. U. C.
810.
Anno Imp. Neronis Cæs. 4.

4 And such trust have we through Christ to God-ward:

5 [g] Not that we are sufficient of ourselves to

---
[a] Chap. v. 12; x. 8, 12; xii. 11.——[b] Acts xviii. 27.——[c] 1 Cor. ix. 2.——[d] 1 Cor. iii. 5.——[e] Exod. xxiv. 12; xxxiv. 1.

[f] Psa. xl. 8; Jer. xxxi. 33; Ezek. xi. 19; xxxvi. 26; Heb. viii. 10.——[g] John xv. 5; chap. ii. 16.

NOTES ON CHAP. III.

Verse 1. *Do we begin again to commend ourselves*] By speaking thus of our sincerity, Divine mission, &c., is it with a design to conciliate your esteem, or ingratiate ourselves in your affections? By no means.

Or need we—epistles of commendation] Are we so destitute of ministerial abilities and Divine influence that we need, in order to be received in different Churches, to have letters of recommendation? Certainly not. God causes us to triumph through Christ in *every place;* and your conversion is such an evident *seal* to our ministry as leaves no doubt that God is with us.

Letters of commendation] Were frequent in the *primitive* Church; and were also in use in the *apostolic* Church, as we learn from this place. But these were, in all probability, not used by the *apostles;* their helpers, successors, and those who had not the miraculous gifts of the Spirit, needed such letters; and they were necessary to prevent the Churches from being imposed on by false teachers. But when *apostles* came, they brought their own testimonials, the miraculous gifts of the Holy Spirit.

Verse 2. *Ye are our epistle*] I bear the most ardent love to you. I have no need to be put in remembrance of you by any epistles or other means; *ye are written in my heart*—I have the most affectionate remembrance of you.

Known and read of all men] For wherever I go I mention you; speak of your various gifts and graces; and praise your knowledge in the Gospel.

Verse 3. *Manifestly declared to be the epistle of Christ*] Ye are in our hearts, and Christ has written you there; but yourselves are the *epistle of Christ;* the change produced in your hearts and lives, and the salvation which you have received, are as truly the work of Christ as a letter dictated and written by a man in his work.

Ministered by us] Ye are the writing, but Christ used me as the *pen;* Christ *dictated,* and I wrote; and the Divine characters are not made with *ink, but by the Spirit of the living God;* for the gifts and graces that constitute the mind that was in Christ are produced in you by the Holy Ghost.

Not in tables of stone] Where men engrave contracts, or record events; *but in fleshly tables of the heart*—the work of salvation taking place in all your affections, appetites, and desires; working that change *within* that is so signally manifested *without.* See the parts of this figurative speech: 1. Jesus Christ *dictates.* 2. The apostle *writes.* 3. The *hearts* of the Corinthians are the substance on which the writing is made. And, 4. The Holy Spirit produces that *influence* by which the *traces* are made, and the mark becomes evident. Here is not only an allusion to making inscriptions on stones, where one *dictates* the matter, and another *cuts* the letters; (and probably there were certain cases where some *colouring matter* was used to make the inscription the more *legible;* and when the stone was engraved, it was set up in some public place, as monuments, inscriptions, and contracts were, that they might be *seen, known,* and *read of all men;*) but the apostle may here refer to the *ten commandments,* written by the finger of God upon *two tables of stone;* which writing was an evidence of the Divine mission of Moses, as the conversion of the Corinthians was an evidence of the mission of St. Paul. But it may be as well to take the words in a general sense, as the expression is not unfrequent either in the Old Testament, or in the rabbinical writers. See *Schoettgen.*

Verse 4. *Such trust have we*] We have the fullest conviction that God has thus accredited our ministry; and that ye are thus converted unto him, and are monuments of his mercy, and proofs of the truth of our ministry.

Verse 5. *Not that we are sufficient of ourselves*] We do not arrogate to ourselves any power to en-

2

A. M. 4061.
A. D. 57.
A. U. C.
810.
Anno Imp. Nero-
nis Cæs. 4.

think any thing as of ourselves ; but [h] our sufficiency *is* of God ;

6 Who also hath made us able [i] ministers of [k] the new testament ; not [l] of the letter, but of the spirit :

for [m] the letter killeth, [n] but the spirit [o] giveth life.

7 But if [p] the ministration of death, [q] written *and* engraven in stones, was glorious, [r] so that the children of

A. M. 4061.
A. D. 57.
A. U. C.
810.
Anno Imp. Nero-
nis Cæs. 4.

---

[h] 1 Cor. xv. 10 ; Phil. ii. 13.——[i] 1 Cor. iii. 5 ; xv. 10 ; chap. v. 18 ; Eph. iii. 7 ; Col. i. 25, 29 ; 1 Tim. i. 11, 12 ; 2 Tim. i. 11. [k] Jer. xxxi. 31 ; Matt. xxvi. 28 ; Heb. viii. 6, 8.——[l] Rom. ii. 27, 29 ; vii. 6.

[m] Rom. iii. 20 ; iv. 15 ; vii. 9, 10, 11 ; Gal. iii. 10.——[n] John vi. 63 ; Rom. viii. 2.——[o] Or, *quickeneth.*——[p] Rom. vii. 10. [q] Exod. xxxiv. 1, 28 ; Deut. x. 1, &c.——[r] Exod. xxxiv. 29, 30, 35.

---

lighten the mind or change the heart, we are only *instruments* in the hand of God. Nor was it possible for us apostles to *think*, to *invent*, such a scheme of salvation as is the Gospel ; and if we even had been equal to the *invention*, how could we have *fulfilled* such *promises* as this scheme of salvation abounds with? God alone could fulfil these promises, and he fulfils only those which he makes himself. All these promises have been *amen*—ratified and fulfilled to you who have believed on Christ Jesus according to our preaching ; therefore, ye are God's workmanship ; and it is only by God's *sufficiency* that we have been able to do any thing. This I believe to be the apostle's meaning in this place, and that he speaks here merely of the Gospel scheme, and the inability of human wisdom to invent it ; and the words λογισασθαι τι, which we translate *to think any thing*, signify, properly, to *find any thing out by reasoning* ; and as the Gospel scheme of salvation is the subject in hand, to that subject the words are to be referred and limited. The words, however, contain also a *general truth* ; we can neither *think, act*, nor *be*, without God. From him we have received all *our powers*, whether of *body* or of *mind*, and without him we can do nothing. But we may abuse both our power of *thinking* and *acting* ; for the power to *think*, and the power to *act*, are widely different from the *act of thinking*, and the *act of doing*. God gives us the power or capacity to *think* and *act*, but he neither *thinks* nor *acts* for us. It is on this ground that we may abuse our powers, and think evil, and act wickedly ; and it is on *this ground* that we are accountable for our thoughts, words, and deeds.

Verse 6. Who—hath made us able ministers] This is a more formal answer to the question, *Who is sufficient for these things ?* προς ταυτα τις ικανος ; chap. ii. 16. God, says the apostle, has made us *able ministers* ; ικανωσεν ημας διακονους. *he has made us sufficient for these things* ; for the reader will observe that he uses the same word in both places. We apostles execute, under the Divine influence, what God himself has devised. We are ministers of the new covenant ; of this new dispensation of truth, light, and life, by Christ Jesus ; a system which not only proves itself to have come from God, but necessarily implies that God himself by his own Spirit is a continual agent in it, ever bringing its mighty purposes to pass. On the words καινη διαθηκη, new covenant, see the PREFACE to the gospel of St. Matthew.

Not of the letter, but of the Spirit] The apostle does not mean here, as some have imagined, that he states himself to be a minister of the New Testament, in opposition to the Old ; and that it is the *Old Testament* that kills, and the *New* that gives life ; but that the New Testament gives the proper meaning of the Old ; for the old covenant had its *letter* and its *spirit*, its *literal* and its *spiritual* meaning. The *law* was founded on the very supposition of the *Gospel* ; and all its sacrifices, types, and ceremonies refer to the Gospel. The Jews *rested* in the *letter*, which not only afforded no *means of life*, but *killed*, by condemning every transgressor to death. They did not look at the *spirit* ; did not endeavour to find out the spiritual meaning ; and therefore they rejected Christ, who was the *end of the law for justification* ; and so for redemption from death to every one that believes. The *new covenant* set all these spiritual things at once before their eyes, and showed them the *end, object*, and *design* of the *law* ; and thus the apostles who preached it were ministers of that *Spirit* which gives life.

Every institution has its *letter* as well as its *spirit*, as every *word* must refer to *something* of which it is the *sign* or *significator*. The *Gospel* has both its *letter* and its *spirit* ; and multitudes of professing Christians, by *resting in the* LETTER, receive not the *life* which it is calculated to impart. *Water*, in baptism, is the *letter* that points out the *purification of the soul* ; they who rest in this letter are without this purification ; and dying in that state they die eternally. *Bread* and *wine* in the sacrament of the Lord's Supper, are the *letter* ; the *atoning efficacy of the death* of Jesus, and the *grace* communicated by this to the soul of a believer, are the *spirit*. Multitudes rest in this *letter*, simply receiving these symbols, without reference to the *atonement*, or to their guilt ; and thus lose the benefit of the atonement and the salvation of their souls. The whole Christian life is comprehended by our Lord under the letter, *Follow me.* Does not any one see that a man, taking up this *letter* only, and following Christ through *Judea, Galilee, Samaria,* &c., to the *city, temple, villages, seacoast, mountains,* &c., fulfilled no part of the *spirit* ; and might, with all this *following*, lose his soul ! Whereas the SPIRIT, viz. *receive* my *doctrine*, believe my *sayings*, look by *faith* for the fulfilment of my *promises*, imitate my *example*, would necessarily lead him to life eternal. It may be safely asserted that the *Jews*, in no period of their history, ever rested more in the *letter* of their *law* than the vast majority of Christians are doing in the *letter* of the *Gospel*. Unto multitudes of Christians Christ may truly say : *Ye will not come unto me that ye may* have *life*.

Verse 7. The ministration of death] Here the apostle evidently intends the *law*. It was a ministration, διακονια, or *service* of *death* It was the province

    2

A. M. 4061.
A. D. 57.
A. U. C.
810.
Anno Imp. Nero-
nis Cæs. 4.

Israel could' not steadfastly behold the face of Moses for the glory of his countenance ; which *glory* was to be done away ;

8 How shall not ˢ the ministration of the Spirit be rather glorious ?

9 For if the ministration of condemnation *be* glory, much more doth the ministration ᵗ of righteousness exceed in glory.

10 For even that which was made glorious had no glory in this respect, by reason of the glory that excelleth.

11 For if that which is done away *was* glorious, much more that which remaineth *is* glorious.

12 Seeing then that we have such hope, ᵘ **we** use great ᵛ plainness of speech :

13 And not as Moses, ʷ *which* put a veil over

A. M. 4061.
A. D. 57.
A. U. C.
810.
Anno Imp. Nero-
nis Cæs. 4.

ˢ Gal. iii. 5.——ᵗ Rom. i. 17 ; iii. 21.——ᵘ Chap. vii. 4 ;

Eph. vi. 19.——ᵛ Or, *boldness.*——ʷ Exod. xxxiv. 33, 35.

---

of the law to ascertain the *duty* of man ; to *assign* his *duties ;* to fix *penalties* for transgressions, &c.; and by it is the knowledge of sin. As man is prone to sin, and is continually committing it, this law was to him a continual *ministration of death.* Its *letter* killed ; and it was only the *Gospel* to which it referred that could *give life,* because that Gospel held out the only available *atonement.*

Yet this ministration of death (the ten commandments, written on stones ; a part of the Mosaic institutions being put for the whole) was *glorious*—was full of *splendour ;* for the apostle refers to the *thunderings,* and *lightnings,* and *luminous appearances,* which took place in the giving of the law ; so that the very *body* of Moses partook of the *effulgence* in such a manner that the children of Israel could not look upon his face ; and he, to hide it, was obliged to use a *veil.* All this was intended to show the excellency of that law, as an institution coming immediately from God : and the apostle gives it all its heightenings, that he may compare it to the Gospel, and thereby prove that, *glorious* as it was, it had no glory that could be compared with that of the *Gospel ;* and that even the glory it had was a glory that was to be *done away*—to be absorbed, as the light of the stars, planets, and moon, is absorbed in the splendour of the sun. See the notes on the viith chapter of Romans ; and see those on Exod. xix., xx., and xxxiv. 29, &c., where this subject is treated in all its details.

Verse 8. *The ministration of the Spirit*] The Gospel dispensation, which gives the true spiritual sense of the law.

Be rather glorious ?] Forasmuch as the thing signified is of infinitely more consequence than that *by which* it is signified. The THING *bread* will preserve a man *alive ;* the WORD *bread* can give life to nothing.

Verse 9. *The ministration of condemnation*] The *law,* which ascertained sin, and condemned it to just punishment.

The ministration of righteousness] The Gospel, the grand business of which was to proclaim the doctrine δικαιοσυνης, *of justification ;* and to show how *God* could *be just* and *yet the justifier of him who believeth in Jesus.*

Exceed in glory.] For great, glorious, and awful as the law may be, in its opposition to sin, which is a reproach to man, and a dishonour to God ; and in its punishment of sin ; yet it must be vastly exceeded by that system which, evidencing an *equal* abhorrence of sin, finds out a method to *forgive* it ; to take away its

guilt from the conscience, and remove all its infection from the soul. That this *could* be done the law pointed out by its *blood of bulls and of goats :* but every considerate mind must see that it was impossible for these to take away sin ; it is the *Gospel* that does what the law signified ; and forasmuch as the *performance* of a promise is greater than the *promise* itself, and the *substance* of a man is greater than the *shadow* projected by that substance ; so is the Gospel of Jesus Christ greater than the law, with all its promises, types, ceremonies, and shadows.

Verse 10. *For even that which was made glorious*] The *law,* which was exhibited for a time in great glory and splendour, partly when it was given, and partly by the splendour of God in the tabernacle and first temple ; but all this *ceased* and *was done away ;* was intended to give place to the *Gospel ;* and has actually given place to that system ; so that *now,* in no part of the world is that law performed, even by the people who are attached to it and reject the Gospel.

The glory that excelleth.] The Gospel dispensation, giving supereminent displays of the justice, holiness, goodness, mercy, and majesty of God.

Verse 11. *For if that which is ᵇdone away, &c.*] Here is another striking difference between the *law* and the *Gospel.* The former is termed το καταργουμενον, that *which* is *counterworked* and *abolished ;* the latter το μενον, *that* which *continues,* which is not for a particular *time, place,* and *people,* as the law was ; but for ALL times, all places, and all *people.* As a *great, universal,* and *permanent* GOOD vastly excels a *good* that is *small, partial,* and *transitory ;* so does the Gospel dispensation, that of the law.

Verse 12. *Seeing—we have such hope*] Such glorious prospects as those blessings which the Gospel sets before us, producing such *confidence,* as the fulfilment of so many promises has already done, that God will still continue to work for us and by us ;

We use great plainness of speech] Πολλη παρρησια χρωμεθα· We speak not only with all *confidence,* but with all imaginable *plainness ;* keeping back nothing ; disguising nothing ; concealing nothing : and here we differ greatly from the Jewish doctors, and from the Gentile philosophers, who affect *obscurity,* and endeavour, by figures, metaphors, and allegories, to hide every thing from the vulgar. But we wish that all may *hear ;* and we speak so that all may *understand.*

Verse 13. *And not as Moses*] The splendour of Moses' countenance was so great that the Israelites could not bear to look upon his face, and therefore he

A. M. 4061.
A. D 57.
A. U. C.
810.
Anno Imp. Nero-
nis Cæs. 4.

his face, that the children of Israel could not steadfastly look to ˣ the end of that which is abolished:

14 But ʸ their minds were blinded : for until this day remaineth the same veil untaken away in the reading of the old testament ; which *veil* is done away in Christ.

15 But even unto this day, when Moses is read, the veil is upon their heart.

16 Nevertheless, ᶻ when it shall turn to the Lord, ᵃ the veil shall be taken away.

17 Now ᵇ the Lord is that Spirit : and where the Spirit of the Lord *is*, there *is* liberty.

18 But we all, with open face beholding ᶜ as in a glass ᵈ the glory of the Lord, ᵉ are changed into the same image from glory to glory, *even as* ᶠ by the Spirit of the Lord.

A. M. 4061.
A. D. 57.
A. U. C.
810.
Anno Imp. Nero-
nis Cæs. 4.

ˣ Rom. x. 4 ; Gal. iii. 23.——ʸ Isa. vi. 10 ; Matt. xiii. 11, 14 ; John xii. 40 ; Acts xxviii. 26 ; Rom. xi. 7, 8, 25 ; chap. iv. 4. ᶻ Exod. xxxiv. 34 ; Rom. xi. 23, 26.

ᵃ Isa. xxv. 7.——ᵇ Ver. 6 ; 1 Cor. xv. 45.——ᶜ 1 Cor. xiii. 12. ᵈ Chap. iv. 4, 6 ; 1 Tim. i. 11.——ᵉ Rom. viii. 29 ; 1 Cor. xv. 49 ; Col. iii. 10.——ᶠ Or, *of the Lord the Spirit.*

---

was obliged to veil his face : this, it appears, he did *typically*, to represent the types and shadows by which the whole dispensation of which he was the minister was covered. So that the Israelites could not *steadfastly look*—could not then have the *full view* or *discernment* of *that* in which the Mosaic dispensation should *issue* and *terminate*.

Verse 14. But their minds were blinded] By resting in the letter, shutting their eyes against the light that was granted to them, they contracted a *hardness* or *stupidity* of heart. And the veil that was on the face of Moses, which prevented the glory of his face from shining *out*, may be considered as emblematical of the veil of darkness and ignorance that is on their hearts, and which hinders the glory of the Gospel from shining *in*.

Until this day remaineth the same veil] They are still ignorant of the spiritual meaning and intention of their own law, called here παλαια διαθηκη, the old covenant. See the word explained in the *preface* to St. Matthew.

In the reading of the Old Testament] Here is an evident allusion to the conduct of the Jews in their synagogues : when they read the law they cover their whole head with a veil, which they term the תלית *tallith, veil*, from כלל *talal, to cover* ; and this voluntary usage of theirs, the apostle tells us, is an emblem of the darkness of their hearts while they are employed even in sacred duties.

Which veil is done away in Christ.] It is only by acknowledging *Christ* that the darkness is removed, and the *end* and *spiritual meaning* of the law discerned.

Verse 16. When it shall turn to the Lord] When the Israelitish *nation* shall turn to the Lᴏʀᴅ *Jesus*, the veil shall be taken away ; the true light shall shine ; and they shall see all things clearly.

There is an evident allusion here to the case of Moses, mentioned Exod. xxxiv. 34. When he *came from* the Lord, and spoke to the Israelites, he put the veil over his face ; but when he *returned* to speak with the Lord, then he *took off the veil*. So, when the Israelitish nation shall *return* to speak with and *pray* to the *Lord Jesus*, the veil of darkness and ignorance shall be taken away from their hearts ; but *never before* that time. The words seem to imply : 1. That there will be a *conversion* of the Jews to Christianity ; and, 2. That this conversion will be *en masse*; that

a time will come when the *whole nation* of the Jews, in every place, shall turn to Christ ; and then the Gentiles and Jews make one fold, under one Shepherd and Bishop of all souls.

Verse 17. Now the Lord is that Spirit] In verses 6 and 8, the word το πνευμα, spirit, evidently signifies the Gospel ; so called because it points out the *spiritual nature* and *meaning* of the *law* ; because it produces spiritual effects ; and because it is especially the dispensation of the Spirit of God. Here Jesus Christ is represented as that *Spirit*, because he is the *end* of the *law* for justification to every one *that believes* ; and because the residue of the Spirit is with him, and he is the dispenser of all its gifts, graces, and influences.

And where the Spirit of the Lord is] Wherever this Gospel is received, there the Spirit of the Lord is given ; and wherever that Spirit lives and works, there is *liberty*, not only from Jewish bondage, but from the *slavery* of sin—from its *power*, its *guilt*, and its *pollution.* See John viii. 33–36, and the notes there.

Verse 18. But we all, with open face] The Jews were not able to look on the face of Moses, the *mediator* of the *old covenant*, and therefore he was obliged to *veil* it ; but *all we* Christians, with *face uncovered, behold*, as clearly as we can see our own natural face in a *mirror*, the glorious promises and privileges of the Gospel of Christ ; and while we contemplate, we anticipate them by *desire* and *hope*, and apprehend them by *faith*, and *are changed from the glory* there represented to the *enjoyment* of the *thing* which is represented, even the glorious image—righteousness and true holiness—of the God of glory.

As by the Spirit of the Lord.] By the energy of that Spirit of Christ which gives life and being to all the promises of the Gospel ; and thus we are made partakers of the Divine nature and escape all the corruptions that are in the world. This appears to me to be the general sense of this verse : its peculiar terms may be more particularly explained.

The word κατοπτριζομενοι, catoptrizomenoi, acting on the doctrine of *catoptrics*, which we translate *beholding in a glass*, comes from κατα, *against*, and οπτομαι, *I look* ; and properly conveys the sense of looking *into* a mirror, or discerning by *reflected* light. Now as *mirrors*, among the Jews, Greeks, and Romans, were made of highly polished *metal*, (see the

     2

note on 1 Cor. xiii. 12,) it would often happen, especially in strong light, that the face would be greatly *illuminated* by this strongly *reflected* light ; and to this circumstance the apostle seems here to allude. So, by earnestly contemplating the Gospel of Jesus, and believing on him who is its Author, the soul becomes illuminated with his Divine splendour, for this sacred mirror reflects back on the believing soul the *image* of Him whose perfections it exhibits ; and thus we see the glorious *form* after which our minds are to be fashioned ; and by believing and receiving the influence of his Spirit, μεταμορφουμεθα, our form *is changed*, την αυτην εικονα, *into the same image*, which we behold there ; and this is the image of God, lost by our *fall*, and now recovered and restored by Jesus Christ : for the *shining* of the face of God upon us, i. e. approbation, through Christ, is the cause of our transformation into the Divine image.

Dr. Whitby, in his notes on this chapter, produces six instances in which the apostle shows the Gospel to be superior to the law ; I shall transcribe them without farther illustration :—

1. The glory appearing on mount *Sinai* made the people *afraid of death*, saying : *Let not God speak to us any more, lest we die;* Exod. xx. 19 ; Deut. xviii. 16 ; and thus *they received the spirit of bondage to fear*, Rom. viii. 15. Whilst *we* have given to us the *spirit of power*, and *love*, and *of a sound mind*, 2 Tim. i. 7 ; and *the spirit of adoption, whereby we cry, Abba, Father !* and to this difference the Epistle to the Hebrews alludes, chap. xii. 18–24.

2. Moses, with all his glory, was only the minister of the law, written on *tables of stone;* the apostles are ministers of the Gospel, written on the *hearts of believers.* Moses gave the Jews only the *letter that killeth;* the apostles gave the *Gospel*, which is accompanied with the *spirit* that gives *life.*

3. The glory which Moses received at the giving of the law did more and more *diminish*, because his law was to *vanish away;* but the glory which is received from Christ is an *increasing* glory ; the *doctrine* and the *Divine influence* remaining for ever.

4. The *law* was *veiled* under *types* and *shadows;* but the *Gospel* has scarcely any ceremonies ; *baptism* and the *Lord's Supper* being all that can be properly called such : and BELIEVE, LOVE, OBEY, the great precepts of the Gospel, are delivered with the utmost perspicuity. And indeed the whole doctrine of *Christ crucified* is made as plain as human language can make it.

5. The *Jews* only saw the *shining* of the face of Moses *through a veil;* but *we* behold the glory of the Gospel of Christ, in the person of Christ our Lawgiver, *with open face.*

6. *They* saw it through a veil, which prevented the reflection or shining of it *upon them;* and so this glory shone only on the *face of Moses*, but not at all upon the people. Whereas the *glory of God*, in *the face of Jesus Christ*, shines as in a mirror which reflects the image upon Christian believers, so that they are *transformed into the same image*, deriving the glorious gifts and graces of the Spirit, with the Gospel, from Christ the Lord and Distributor of them, 1 Cor. xii. 5 ; and so, the glory which he had from the Father he has given to his genuine followers, John xvii. 22. It is, therefore, rather with true Christians as it was with Moses himself, concerning whom God speaks thus : *With him will I speak mouth to mouth, even apparently, and not in dark speeches; and the similitude of the Lord* (την δοξαν Κυριου, *the glory of the Lord*) *shall he behold;* Num. xii. 8. For as he saw the glory of God *apparently*, so we *with open face* behold the glory of the Lord : as he, by seeing of this glory, was *changed into the same likeness*, and his *face shone*, or was δεδοξασμενη, *made glorious;* so *we*, beholding the glory of the Lord in the face of Jesus Christ, chap. iv. 6, are changed into the same glory.

Thus we find that in every thing the *Gospel* has a decided superiority over the *law* and its *institutions,*

CHAPTER IV.

St. Paul shows the integrity with which he had preached the Gospel of Christ, 1, 2. And that, if it was unprofitable to any who had heard it, it was because their unbelieving hearts were blinded, 3, 4. How he preached, and how he was qualified for the work, 5–7. The troubles and difficulties he met with in his labours, and the hope and consolations by which he was supported, 8–15. And the prospect he had of eternal blessedness, 16–18.

A. M. 4061. A. D. 57. A. U. C. 810. Anno Imp. Neronis Cæs. 4.	THEREFORE, seeing we have ª this ministry, ᵇ as we have received mercy, we faint not;

ª Chap. iii. 6.——ᵇ 1 Cor. vii. 25 ; 1 Tim. i. 13.

2 But have renounced the hidden things of ᶜ dishonesty, not walking in craftiness, ᵈ nor handling the word of God deceitfully ;	A. M. 4061. A. D. 57. A. U. C. 810. Anno Imp. Neronis Cæs. 4.

ᶜ Gr. *shame*, Rom. i. 16 ; vi. 21.——ᵈ Chap. ii. 17 ; 1 Thess. ii. 3, 5.

NOTES ON CHAP. IV.

Verse 1. *Seeing we have this ministry*] The Gospel, of which he gave that noble account which we read in the preceding chapter.

We faint not] We meet with many tribulations, but are supported in and through all by the grace of the Gospel. Instead of ουκ εκκακουμεν, *we faint not*, ουκ εγκακουμεν, *we act not wickedly*, is the reading of ADFG, and some, others. Wakefield thinks it the genuine reading ; it certainly makes a very good sense with what goes before and what follows. If we follow this reading the whole verse may be read thus : *Where-*

A. M. 4061.
A. D. 57.
A. U. C.
810.
Anno Imp. Nero-
nis Cæs. 4.

but ^e by manifestation of the truth ^f commending ourselves to every man's conscience in the sight of God.

3 But if our Gospel be hid, ^g it is hid to them that are lost;

4 In whom ^h the god of this world ⁱ hath blinded the minds of them which believe not, lest ^k the light of the glorious Gospel of Christ, ^l who is the image of God, should shine unto them.

A. M. 4061.
A. D. 57.
A. U. C.
810.
Anno Imp. Nero·
nis Cæs. 4.

---

^e Chap. vi. 4, 7; vii. 14.——^f Chap. v. 11.——^g 1 Cor. i. 18; chap. ii. 15; 2 Thess. ii. 10.——^h John xii. 31; xiv. 30; xvi. 11; Eph. vi. 12.

ⁱ Isa. vi. 10; John xii. 40; chap. iii. 14.——^k Chap. iii. 8, 9, 11, 18; ver. 6.——^l John i. 18; xii. 45; xiv. 9; Phil. ii. 6; Col. i. 15; Heb. i. 3.

---

fore, as we have obtained mercy, or *been graciously intrusted,* ηλεηθημην, *with this ministry, we do not act wickedly, but have renounced the hidden things of dishonesty,* &c.

Verse 2. *But have renounced*] Απειπαμεθα· We have disclaimed *the hidden things of dishonesty;* τα κρυπτα της αισχυνης, *the hidden things of shame;* those things which wicked men do; and which they are ashamed to have known, and ashamed to own. Dr. *Whitby* thinks that the apostle refers to carnal abomi-nations, of which the Jews and their rabbins were notoriously guilty. And it does appear from the first epistle that there were persons in Corinth who taught that *fornication* wás no sin; and it appears also that several had taken the part of the *incestuous* person.

Not walking in craftiness] Πανουργια· In *subtilety* and *clever cunning,* as the false teachers did, who were accomplished fellows, and *capable* of *any thing.* The word is compounded of παν, *all,* and εργον, *work.*

Nor handling the word of God deceitfully] Not using the doctrines of the Gospel to serve any *secular* or *carnal* purpose; not explaining away their force so as to palliate or excuse sin; not generalizing its pre-cepts so as to excuse many in particular circumstances from obedience, especially in that which most crossed their inclinations. There were deceitful handlers of this kind in Corinth, and there are many of them still in the garb of Christian ministers; persons who disguise that part of their creed which, though they believe it is of God, would make them *unpopular,* affecting *moderation* in order to procure a larger audience and more extensive support; not attacking prevalent and popular vices; calling *dissipation of mind, relaxation;* and worldly and carnal *pleasures,* innocent amusements, &c. In a word, turning with the tide, and shifting with the wind of popular opinion, prejudice, fashion, &c.

But by manifestation of the truth] An open, ex-plicit acknowledgment of what we know to be the *truth*—what we are assured is the Gospel of Jesus; concealing nothing; blunting the edge of no truth; explaining spiritual things, not in the words of man's wisdom, but in those taught by the Spirit of God.

Commending ourselves to every man's conscience] Speaking so that every man's conscience shall bear its testimony that we proclaim the truth of God. This is one characteristic of Divine truth: even every man's *conscience* will acknowledge it, though it speak de-cidedly against his own practices.

In the sight of God.] Whose eye is ever on the heart and conscience of man, and who always bears testimony to his own word.

Verse 3. *But if our Gospel be hid*] Κεκαλυμμενον·

Veiled; he refers to the subject that he had treated so particularly in the conclusion of the preceding chapter. If there be a *veil on the Gospel,* it is only to the wilfully blind; and if any man's heart be *veiled* that hears this Gospel, it is a proof that he is among the *lost,* απολλυμενοι, those who are fully under the power of sin; who have given up themselves to work wickedness; persons who are mere *heathens,* or live like such, and yet such as Jesus Christ came to *seek* and *save;* for the word does not necessarily imply those that will *perish eternally,* but is a common epi-thet to point out a man without the Gospel and without God in the world. Christ commands his disciples in preaching the Gospel *to go to* προβατα τα απολωλοτα, *the* LOST *sheep of the house of Israel;* Matt. x. 6; for himself says, Matt. xviii. 11, and Luke xix. 10: *The Son of man is come* ζητησαι και σωσαι το απολωλος, *to seek and to* SAVE *that which is* LOST. And such persons he represents under the parable of the *lost sheep;* for *to find* το απολωλος, *that which is* LOST, the good shepherd *leaves the ninety-and-nine in the wil-derness,* and goes in search of *it;* Matt. xviii. 12; Luke xv. 4. The word more properly signifies, in all those connections, and in the parallel passages, not those who ARE LOST, but those who *are perishing;* and will perish, if not sought and saved.

Verse 4. *In whom the god of this world,* &c.] We see here that those whose minds are blinded, are they who believe not; and because they believe not, their minds continue in darkness, and are proper subjects for *Satan* to work on; and he *deepens the darkness,* and *increases the hardness.* But who is meant by the *god of this world?* It is generally answered, the same who is called the *prince of this world,* John xvi. 11. But the question recurs, who *is the prince of this world?* and the answer to both is, SATAN. The reader will do well to consult the notes on John xii. 31, and the concluding observations on John xiv. I must own I feel considerable reluctance to assign the epithet ὁ Θεος, THE *God,* to *Satan;* and were there not a rooted prejudice in favour of the common opinion, the contrary might be well vindicated, viz. that by *the god of this world* the supreme *Being* is meant, who in his judgment gave over the minds of the *unbelieving Jews* to spiritual darkness, so that *destruction* came upon them to the uttermost. Satan, it is true, has said that the kingdoms of the world and their glory are his, and that he gives them to whomsoever he will; Matt. iv. 8, 9. But has God ever said *so?* and are we to take this assertion of the *boasting* devil and father of lies for *truth?* Certainly not. We are not willing to attribute the blinding of men's minds to

328

2.

A. M. 4061.
A. D. 57.
A. U. C.
810.
Anno Imp. Nero-
nis Cæs. 4.

5 ^m For we preach not ourselves, but Christ Jesus the Lord;
and ⁿ ourselves your servants for
Jesus' sake.

6 For God, ° who commanded the light to

shine out of darkness, ^p hath
^q shined in our hearts, to *give*
^r the light of the knowledge of
the glory of God in the face of
Jesus Christ.

A. M. 4061.
A. D. 57.
A. U. C.
810.
Anno Imp. Nero-
nis Cæs. 4.

---

^m1 Cor. i. 13, 23 ; x. 33.——ⁿ 1 Cor. ix. 19 ; chap. i. 24.——° Gen. i. 3.

^p Or, *is he who hath.*——^q 2 Peter i. 19.——^r Ver. 4 ; 1 Peter ii. 9.

God, because we sometimes forget that he is the God of *justice*, and may in *judgment* remove mercies from those that *abuse* them ; but this is repeatedly attributed to him in the Bible, and the expression before us is quite a parallel to the following, Isa. vi. 9 : *Go and tell this people, Hear ye indeed, but understand not ; and see ye indeed, but perceive not.* MAKE *the* HEART *of this* PEOPLE FAT, *and* MAKE *their* EARS HEAVY, *and* SHUT *their* EYES ; LEST *they see with their eyes, and hear with their ears, and understand with their heart, &c.* And see the parallel places, Matt. xiii. 14, 15 ; Mark iv. 12 ; John xii. 40 ; and particularly Rom. xi. 8–10 : *God* HATH GIVEN THEM THE SPIRIT *of* SLUMBER, EYES *that they* SHOULD *not* SEE, *and* EARS *that they* SHOULD *not* HEAR ; *let their* EYES *be* DARK-ENED, &c. Now all this is spoken of the same people, in the same circumstances of *wilful rebellion* and *obstinate unbelief* ; and the great God of heaven and earth is he who judicially *blinds their eyes* ; *makes their hearts fat,* i. e. *stupid* ; *gives them the spirit of slumber* ; and *bows down their back,* &c. On these very grounds it is exceedingly likely that the apostle means the *true God* by the words *the god of this world.*

And as to the expression *this world,* αιωνος τουτου, we are not to imagine that it necessarily means *wicked men,* or a *wicked age* ; for it is frequently used to express the *whole mundane system,* and all that is called *time* : *Whosoever speaketh against the Holy Ghost, it shall not be forgiven him, neither* εν τουτῳ τῳ αιωνι, *in* THIS WORLD, *nor in the world to come* ; Matt. xii. 32. In Luke xx. 34, *the children,* υιοι του αιωνος τουτου, *of* THIS WORLD, mean simply *mankind at large* in their state of *probation* in this lower world, in opposition to their state in the *world to come.* The same meaning the word has in several other places, to which I need not refer ; it simply implying the *present state of things,* governed by the *Divine providence,* in contradistinction from the *eternal state* : and it is very remarkable that, in 1 Tim. i. 17, God himself is called Βασιλευς των αιωνων, the *King of the* WORLD ; what we call *King eternal* ; but here *it* evidently means him who governs *both worlds,* and rules in *time and eternity.* This character among the Asiatics is considered essential to God ; and therefore in the very first surat of the *Koran* he is called رب العلمين *Rubbi Alálameen,* "the Lord of both worlds," an expression perfectly similar to that above. But it is needless to multiply examples ; they exist in abundance. Some, and particularly the ancient fathers, have connected του αιωνος τουτου with των απιστων, and have read the verse : *But God hath blinded the minds of the unbelievers of this world,* &c. Irenæus, Tertullian, Chrysostom, Theodoret, Photius, Theophylact, and Augustine, all plead for the above meaning ;

and St. Augustine says that it was the opinion of *almost all the ancients.*

Lest the light of the glorious Gospel] They have resisted the grace which God gave them, and have refused to yield to the evidences which amply prove the *Messiahship* of Jesus ; and therefore their eyes were judicially darkened, as it is said in the prophet : *He hath closed their eyes, and hath given them the spirit of slumber.* That is, they have shut their eyes against the light, and their blindness and stupor are the consequence.

By *glorious Gospel* we are to understand the *luminous Gospel* ; that which comes with so much *light* and *evidence* to every candid mind.

Who is the image of God] Christ is called, Heb. i. 3, *the brightness of God's glory, and the express image of his person.* See the note there.

Verse 5. *For we preach not ourselves*] We neither proclaim our own *wisdom* nor *power* ; we have nothing but what we have received ; we do not wish to establish our own *authority,* nor to procure our own *emolument.*

But Christ Jesus the Lord] We proclaim the author of this glorious Gospel as CHRIST, ὁ Χριστος, the same as המשיח *hammashiach,* the MESSIAH, the *Anointed One* ; him of whom the prophets wrote ; and who is the expectation, as he is the glory, of Israel. We proclaim him as JESUS יהושע *Yehoshua,* the *Saviour* and *Deliverer,* who saves men from their sins, See Matt. i. 21. And we proclaim *Jesus of Nazareth* to be the long-expected *Messiah* ; and that there will be none other. And farther we proclaim this Jesus the Messiah to be the LORD, ὁ Κυριος, the great *Ruler* who has all power in heaven and earth ; who made and governs the world ; and who can save to the uttermost all that come to God through him. Such was the *Redeemer* preached by St. Paul.

And ourselves your servants] Labouring as fervently and as faithfully for your *eternal* interests as your most trusty *slaves* can do for your *secular* welfare. And we do this for *Christ's sake* ; for although we by our labour show ourselves to be your *servants,* yea, your *slaves,* δουλους, yet it is a *voluntary* service ; and we are neither employed by you nor receive our wages from you. We belong to Jesus ; and are your servants on his account, and by his order.

Verse 6. *For God, who commanded the light to shine out of darkness*] The apostle refers here to Gen. i. 3. For when God created the heavens and the earth DARKNESS *was on the face of the deep ; and God said,* Let THERE BE LIGHT ; *and there was light.* Thus he caused the light to shine out of darkness.

Hath shined in our hearts] He has given our hearts the glorious light of the *Gospel,* as he has given

2

A. M. 4061.
A. D. 57.
A. U. C.
810.
Anno Imp. Nero-
nis Cæs. 4.

7 But we have this treasure in ^s earthen vessels, ^t that the excellency of the power may be of God, and not of us.

8 *We are* ^u troubled on every side, yet not distressed; *we are* perplexed, but ^v not in despair;

A. M. 4061.
A. D. 57.
A. U. C.
810.
Anno Imp. Nero-
nis Cæs. 4.

---

^s Chap. v. 1.——^t 1 Cor. ii. 5; chap. xii. 9.——^u Chap. vii. 5.

^v Or, *not altogether without help,* or *means.*

---

the *world* the glorious light of the *sun.* As sure, therefore, as God is the author of the *light* and the creator of the universe, so sure is he the author of the Gospel; it is no human invention; and is as far beyond the power of man's wisdom and might, as the creation of the world is beyond all created power, energy, and skill.

The light of the knowledge] To give us that light, that we might *enlighten others;* this appears to me to be the design of the apostle's προς φωτισμον της γνωσεως της δοξης του Θεου, or, as Dr. *Whitby* paraphrases it, *to give us, and enable us to give to others, the light of the knowledge of God through Christ.*

In the face of Jesus Christ.] It is *in* and *through* Jesus that we can receive the Divine light, and it is *in* and *by* him that we can be made partakers of the Divine glory. The light mercy, holiness, and glory of God, are reflected upon and communicated to us through Jesus the Christ; and it is εν προσωπω, in the *appearance* and *person* of Jesus Christ that these blessings are communicated to us.

Verse 7. *But we have this treasure in earthen vessels*] The original, οστρακινοις σκευεσιν, signifies, more literally, *vessels* made of *shells,* which are very *brittle;* and as the *shell* is the outward part of a fish, it is very fit, as Dr. Hammond observes, to resemble our bodies in which our souls dwell. The Platonists make *two bodies* of a man: the one they call οχημα ψυχης, the *chariot of the soul;* the other, that which we see and touch; and this they call οστρακινον, which is the same to us as the shell is to the *fish.* The word οστρακον not only signifies a *shell,* or vessel made of shell, but also πηλος ωπτημενος, an *earthen vessel* which has been *burnt in the kiln,* and earthen vessels or *pottery* in general; the difference between σκευη οστρακινα, *earthen ware,* and σκευη κεραμεως, the *potter's vessel,* is this: the latter implies the *vessel as it comes out of the hands of the potter* BEFORE *it is burnt;* and the other is the vessel AFTER it has *passed through the kiln.* St. Chrysostom, speaking of this difference, observes that the vessels once baked in the kiln, if broken, are incapable of being *restored,* δια την εκ τουπυρος εγγινομενην αυτοις απαξ αντιτυπιαν, *because of the hardness once gotten by fire;* whereas the others are of *clay unbaken,* if they be spoiled ραδιωςπρος το δευτερον επανελθη σχημα, *they may easily, by the skill of the potter, be restored to some second form.* See *Hammond.* This comports excellently with the idea of St. Paul: our bodies are in a *recoverable* form: they are very frail, and easily *marred;* but by the skill of the workman they may be easily built up anew, and made like unto his glorious body. The light and salvation of God in the soul of man is a heavenly treasure in a very mean casket.

The rabbins have a mode of speech very similar to this. "The daughter of the emperor thus addressed Rabbi Joshua, the son of Chananiah: O! how great is thy skill in the law, and yet how deformed thou

art! what a great deal of wisdom is laid up in a *sordid vessel!* The rabbi answered, Tell me, I pray thee, of what are those vessels in which you keep your wines? She answered, They are *earthen vessels.* He replied, How is it, seeing ye are *rich,* that ye do not lay up your wine in *silver* vessels, for the common people lay up their wine in *earthen vessels?* She returned to her father, and persuaded him to have all the wine put into *silver* vessels; but the wine turned acid; and when the emperor heard it he inquired of his daughter who it was that had given her that advice? She told him that it was Rabbi Joshua. The rabbi told the whole story to the emperor, and added this sentence: *The wisdom and study of the law cannot dwell in a comely man.* Cæsar objected, and said, There are comely persons who have made great progress in the study of the law. The rabbi answered, Had they not been so comely they would have made greater progress; for a man who is comely has not an *humble mind,* and therefore he soon forgets the whole law." See *Schoettgen.* There is a great deal of good sense in this allegory; and the most superficial reader may find it out.

That the excellency of the power may be of God, and not of us.] God keeps us continually dependent upon himself; we have nothing but what we have received, and we receive every necessary supply just *when* it is necessary; and have nothing at our own command. The good therefore that is done is so evidently from the power of God, that none can pretend to share the glory with him.

Verse 8. We are *troubled on every side*] We have already seen, in the notes on the ninth chapter of the preceding epistle, that St. Paul has made several allusions to those *public games* which were celebrated every *fifth* year at the *Isthmus of Corinth;* and those games have been in that place particularly described. In this and the three following verses the apostle makes allusion to the contests at those games: and the terms which he employs in these verses cannot be understood but in reference to those *agonistical* exercises to which he alludes. Dr. Hammond has explained the whole on this ground; and I shall here borrow his help. There are *four pairs* of expressions taken from the customs of the *agones.* 1. *Troubled on every side, yet not distressed.* 2. *Perplexed, but not in despair.* 3. *Persecuted, but not forsaken.* 4. *Cast down, but not destroyed.* *Three* of these pairs belong to the customs of *wrestling;* the fourth, to that of *running* in the race.

Troubled on every side, &c.] Εν παντι θλιβομενοι. The word θλιβεσθαι belongs clearly to παλη, *wrestling.* So says Aristotle, Rhet. lib. i. cap. 5, (and the Scholiast on that place,) ο γαρ δυναμενος——θλιβειν και κατεχειν, παλαιστικος· "He that can gripe his adversary, and take him up, is a good wrestler;" there being two dexterities in that exercise: 1. to *gripe,* and, 2. to

A. M. 4061.
A. D. 57.
A. U. C.
810.
Anno Imp. Nero-
nis Cæs. 4.

9 Persecuted, but not forsaken; ʷ cast down, but not destroyed.

10 ˣ Always bearing about in the body the dying of the Lord Jesus, ʸ that the life also of Jesus might be made manifest in our body.

11 For we which live ᶻ are always delivered unto death for Jesus' sake, that the life also of Jesus might be made manifest in our mortal flesh.

12 So then ᵃ death worketh in us, but life in you.

13 We having ᵇ the same spirit of faith, according as it is written, ᶜ I believed, and therefore have I spoken; we also believe, and therefore speak;

14 Knowing that ᵈ he which raised up the Lord Jesus shall raise up us also by Jesus, and shall present *us* with you.

15 For ᵉ all things *are* for your sakes, that ᶠ the abundant grace might, through the thanksgiving of many, redound to the glory of God.

16 For which cause we faint not; but though

A. M. 4061.
A. D. 57.
A. U. C.
810.
Anno Imp. Nero-
nis Cæs. 4.

ʷ Psa. xxxvii. 24.——ˣ 1 Cor. xv. 31; chap. i. 5, 9; Gal. vi. 17; Phil. iii. 10.——ʸ Rom. viii. 17; 2 Tim. ii. 11, 12; 1 Pet. iv. 13.——ᶻ Rom. viii. 36; 1 Cor. xv. 31, 49.

ᵃ Chap. xiii. 9.——ᵇ Rom. i. 12; 2 Pet. i. 1.——ᶜ Psa. cxvi. 10. ᵈ Rom. viii. 11; 1 Cor. iii. 21; chap. i. 6; Col. i. 24; 2 Tim. ii. 10.——ᶠ Chap. i. 11; viii. 19; ix. 11, 12.

---

throw down, which *Hesychius* calls ωθειν and κρατειν; the first of these is here mentioned, and expressed by θλιβεσθαι, *to be pressed down;* to which is here opposed, as in a higher degree, στενοχωρεισθαι, *to be brought to distress*, as when one cannot get out of his antagonist's hands, nor make any resistance against him. So in Isaiah : στενοχωρουμενοι ου δυναμεθα μαχεσθαι, *we are brought to such extremities that we can fight no longer.*

Perplexed, but not in despair] Απορουμενοι, αλλ' ουκ εξαπορουμενοι. The word απορεισθαι, *to be in perplexity*, is fit for the *wrestler*, who being puzzled by his antagonist's skill knows not what to do : so in *Hesychius*, απορουντες, αμηχανουντες, *they that are not able to do* or *attempt any thing*, yet are not εξαπορουμενοι, they miscarry not finally, ορθοι ισταμενοι, *stand after all upright;* ουκ απογινωσκοντες και ἡττωμενοι, *despair not, nor are they overcome*, but find a happy issue out of all, being at last *conquerors.*

Verse 9. Persecuted, but not forsaken] Διωκομενοι, αλλ' ουκ εγκαταλειπομενοι. The διωκομενοι, *pursued,* is peculiar to the δρομος, or *race,* when one being foremost others pursue, and get up close after him, endeavouring to *outstrip* him, but cannot succeed : this is the meaning of ουκ εγκαταλειπομενοι, not *outstripped,* or *outgone,* as the word implies. So in PLUTARCH : τους απολειφθεντας ου στεφανουσι, *they do not crown them that are distanced* or *left behind.* So says the apostle, 1 Cor. ix. 24 : *All run, but only* ONE *receiveth the* PRIZE.

Cast down, but not destroyed.] Καταβαλλομενοι αλλ' ουκ απολλυμενοι. This also belongs to *wrestlers,* where he that *throws* the other first is *conqueror.* And so Hesychius : καταβαλει, νικησει, ριψει, to cast down is to overcome, to throw. And then, the being not *destroyed* signifies that, although they were *thrown down*—cast into troubles and difficulties, yet they *rose again,* and surmounted them all.

Verse 10. Always bearing about in the body. &c.] Being every moment in danger of losing our lives in the cause of truth, as Jesus Christ was. We, in a word, bear his cross, and are ready to offer up our lives for him. There is probably an allusion here to the marks, wounds, and bruises which the contenders in those games got, and continued to carry throughout life.

That the life also of Jesus might be made manifest] That in our preservation, the success of our ministry, and the miracles we work, we might be able to give the fullest demonstration that Jesus *is risen again* from the dead; and that we are strengthened by him to do all these mighty works.

Verse 11. For we which live] And yet, although we are preserved alive, we are in such continual dangers that we carry our life in our hands, and are constantly in the spirit of sacrifice. But the *life*—the preserving power, of Christ is manifest in our continual support.

Verse 12. Death worketh in us, &c.] We apostles are in continual danger, and live a dying life; while you who have received this Gospel from us are in no danger.

Verse 13. We having the same spirit of faith] As David had when he wrote Psa. cxvi. 10 : *I believed, therefore have I spoken: we also believe* that we shall receive the fulfilment of all God's promises; and being fully convinced of the truth of the Christian religion, we *speak* and testify that our deliverance is from God; and that he does not fail those who trust in him; and that he saves to the uttermost them who come unto him through Christ Jesus.

Verse 14. Knowing that he which raised up the Lord, &c.] And though we shall at last seal this truth with our blood, we fear not, being persuaded that as the body of Christ was raised from the dead by the power of the Father, so shall our bodies be raised, and that we shall have an eternal life with him in glory.

Verse 15. For all things are *for your sakes*] We proclaim all these truths and bear all these sufferings for your sakes, thinking all our sufferings nothing if we can gain converts to Christ, and build believers up on their most holy faith.

That the abundant grace] Ἡ χαρις πλεονασασα· The *abounding benefit*—the copious outpouring of the gifts and graces of the Holy Spirit, by which you have been favoured and enriched, *may,* through *the thanksgiving of many, redound to the glory of God :* i. e. that the *gratitude* of the multitudes which have been converted may keep pace with the blessings which they have received, and περισσευσῃ, *abound,* as these blessings have *abounded.*

Verse 16. For which cause we faint not] Ουκ εκκα

A. M. 4061.
A. D. 57.
A. U. C.
810.
Anno Imp. Nero-
nis Cæs. 4.

our outward man perish, yet [g] the inward *man* is renewed day by day.

17 For [h] our light affliction, which is but for a moment, work-eth for us a far more exceeding *and* eternal weight of glory;

18 [i] While we look not at the things which are seen, but at the things which are not seen : for the things which are seen *are* temporal ; but the things which are not seen *are* eternal.

A. M. 4061.
A. D. 57.
A. U. C.
810.
Anno Imp. Nero-
nis Cæs. 4.

[g] Rom. vii. 22 ; Eph. iii. 16 ; Col. iii. 10 ; 1 Pet. iii. 4.——[h] Matt. v. 12 ; Rom. viii. 18 ; 1 Pet. i. 6 ; v. 10.

[i] Rom. i. 17 ; viii. 24 ; chap. v. 7 ; Gal. iii. 11 ; Hebrews x. 38 ; xi. 1.

κουμεν. See on verse 1. Here we have the same various reading ; εγκακουμέν, *we do no wickedness ;* and it is supported by BDEFG, and some others : but it is remarkable that Mr. Wakefield follows the common reading *here,* though the various reading is at least as well supported in this verse as in verse first. The common reading, *faint not,* appears to agree best with the apostle's meaning.

But though our outward man] That is, our *body*—that part of us that can be *seen, heard,* and *felt, perish* —be slowly consumed by continual trials and afflictions, and be martyred at last ;

Yet the inward man] Our *soul*—that which cannot be felt or seen by others, is *renewed*—is *revived,* and receives a daily increase of light and life from God, so that we grow more holy, more happy, and more meet for glory every day.

It was an opinion among the Jews that even *spirits* stood in need of continual *renovation.* They say that " God renews the angels daily, by putting them into the fiery river from which they proceeded, and then gives them the same name they had before." And they add, that in like manner he renews the hearts of the Israelites every year, when they turn to him by repentance. It is a good antidote against the fear of death to find, as the body *grows old and decays,* the soul *grows young and is invigorated.* By the *outward* man and the *inward man* St. Paul shows that he was no *materialist :* he believed that we have both a *body* and a *soul ;* and so far was he from supposing that when the *body* dies the *whole man* is decomposed, and continues so to the resurrection, that he asserts that the decays of the one lead to the invigorating of the other ; and that the very decomposition of the body itself leaves the soul in the state of renewed youth. The vile doctrine of *materialism* is not *apostolic.*

Verse 17. *For our light affliction, &c.*] Mr. Black-wall, in his sacred classics, has well illustrated this passage. I shall here produce his paraphrase as quoted by Dr. *Dodd :* " This is one of the most emphatic passages in all St. Paul's writings, in which he speaks as much like an *orator* as he does as an *apostle.* The *lightness* of the trial is expressed by το ελαφρον της θλιψεως, *the lightness of our affliction ;* as if he had said, it is even levity itself in such a comparison. On the other hand, the καθ' ὑπερβολην εις ὑπερβολην, which we render *far more exceeding,* is infinitely emphatical, and cannot be fully expressed by any translation. It signifies that all hyperboles fall short of describing that weight—eternal glory, so solid and lasting, that you may pass from hyperbole to hyperbole, and yet, when you have gained the last, are infinitely below it. It is every where visible what influence St. Paul's Hebrew

had on his Greek : כבד *cabad,* signifies to be *heavy,* and to be *glorious ;* the apostle in his Greek unites these two significations, and says, WEIGHT *of* GLORY."

St. *Chrysostom's* observations on these words are in his very best manner, and are both judicious and beautiful : ΤΙΟΗΣΙ παραλληλα τα παροντα τοις μελλουσι· το παραυτικα προς το αιωνιον· το ελαφρον .προς το βαρυ· την θλιψιν προς την δοξαν· και ουδε τουτοις αρκειται, αλλ' ετεραν τιθησι λεξιν, διπλασιαζων αυτην, και λεγων, καθ' ὑπερβολην εις ὑπερβολην—τουτεστι, μεγεθος ὑπερβολικως ὑπερβολικον.

" The apostle opposes things *present* to things *future ;* a *moment* to *eternity ; lightness* to *weight ; affliction* to *glory.* Nor is he satisfied with this, but he adds another word, and *doubles* it, saying, καθ' ὑπερβολην εις ὑπερβολην. This is a magnitude excessively exceeding." See *Parkhurst,* sub voce ὑπερβολην.

Verse 18. *While we look not at the things which are seen*] Μη σκοπουντων. While we *aim not* at the things which are seen ; do not make them our *object ;* are not striving to obtain them ; for they are not worthy the pursuit of an immortal spirit, because they are *seen ;* they are objects to which the natural eye can reach ; and they are προσκαιρα, *temporary ;* they are to have a short duration, and must have an *end.* But the things which we make our *scope* and *aim* are *not seen ;* they are *spiritual,* and therefore *invisible* to the eye of the body ; and besides, they are αιωνια, *eternal* —things that are permanent ; that can have no end ; they are things which belong to God ; holiness, happiness, and the endless communication and fruition of himself.

But we must remark that the light afflictions work out this far more exceeding and eternal weight of glory only to those who *do not look* at the *things which are seen.* A man may be grievously afflicted, and yet have his eye bent on temporal good ; from his afflictions he can derive no benefit ; though many think that their glorification must be a necessary consequence of their afflictions, and hence we do not unfrequently hear among the afflicted poor, " Well, we shall not suffer both here and in the other world too." Afflictions may be *means* of preparing us for glory, if, during them, we receive grace to save the soul ; but afflictions of *themselves* have no *spiritual* nor *saving* tendency ; on the contrary, they *sour* the unregenerated mind, and cause murmurings against the dispensations of Divine Providence. Let us, therefore, look to God, that they may be sanctified ; and when they are, then we may say exultingly, These light afflictions, which are but for a moment,· work for us a far more exceeding and eternal weight of glory. O world to come, in exchange for the present! O eternity, for a moment! O eternal communion in the holy, blessed, and eternal life of God, for the sacrifice of a poor, miserable, and corrupted life here on earth! Whoever sets no value on this seed of a blessed eternity knows

not what it comprehends. That which the eyes of the flesh are capable of perceiving is not worthy of a soul capable of possessing God. Nothing which is of a perishable nature can be the chief good of a being that was made for eternity!—*Quesnel.*

CHAPTER V.

The apostle's strong hope of eternal glory, and earnest longings after that state of blessedness, 1–4. The assurance that he had of it from the Holy Spirit, and his carefulness to be always found pleasing to the Lord, 5–9. All must appear before the judgment seat of Christ, 10. Knowing that this awful event must take place, he laboured to convince men of the necessity of being prepared to meet the Lord, being influenced to this work by his love of Christ, 11–13. Jesus Christ having died for all, is a proof that all were dead, 14. Those for whom he died should live to him, 15. We should know no man after the flesh, 16. They who are in Christ are new creatures, 17. The glorious ministry of reconciliation, 18–21.

A. M. 4061.
A. D. 57.
A. U. C. 810.
Anno Imp. Neronis Cæs. 4.

FOR we know that if ª our earthly house of *this* tabernacle were dissolved, we have a building of God, a house not

made with hands, eternal in the heavens.

2 For in this ᵇ we groan, earnestly desiring to be clothed

A. M. 4061.
A. D. 57.
A. U. C. 810.
Anno Imp. Neronis Cæs. 4.

ª Job iv. 19; chap. iv. 7; 2 Pet. i. 13, 14.

ᵇ Rom. viii. 23.

NOTES ON CHAP. V.

Verse 1. *If our earthly house of* this *tabernacle*] By earthly house, the apostle most evidently means the *body* in which the *soul* is represented as dwelling or sojourning for a time, and from which it is to be liberated at death; for as death *dissolves the tabernacle,* it can then be no habitation for the soul. The apostle also alludes here to the ancient *Jewish tabernacle,* which, on all removals of the congregation, was *dissolved* and *taken in pieces;* and the ark of the covenant, covered with its own curtains, was carried by itself; and when they came to the place of rest, then the dissolved parts of the tabernacle were *put together* as before. When we consider this simile in connection with the doctrine of the resurrection, which the apostle has treated so much at large in these epistles, and which he keeps constantly in view, then we shall see that he intends to convey the following meaning: that as the tabernacle was *taken down* in order to be *again put together,* so the body is to be *dissolved,* in order to be *re-edified;* that as the ark of the covenant subsisted *by itself,* while the *tabernacle* was *down,* so can the soul when separated from the body; that as the ark had then its own veil for its covering, Exod. xl. 21, so the soul is to have some vehicle in which it shall subsist till it receives its body at the resurrection.

A building of God] Some think this refers to a certain *celestial vehicle* with which God invests holy souls on their dismissal from the body; others suppose it relates to the *resurrection body;* and some imagine that it relates merely to the *state* of blessedness which the saints shall possess in the kingdom of glory. See the following note.

Verse 2. *For in this we groan*] While in this *state,* and in this *body,* we are encompassed with many infirmities, and exposed to many trials, so that life is a state of discipline and affliction, and every thing within and around us says, "Arise and depart, for this is not your rest!" Those who apply these words to

what they call the *apostle's sense of indwelling sin,* abuse the passage. There is nothing of the kind either mentioned or intended.

Desiring to be clothed upon with our house] This and the following verses are, in themselves, exceedingly obscure, and can be only interpreted by considering that the expressions used by the apostle are all *Jewish,* and should be interpreted according to *their* use of them. *Schoettgen* has entered largely into the argument here employed by the apostle, and brought forth much useful information.

He observes, 1. That the Hebrew word לבש *labash,* which answers to the apostle's ενδυσασθαι, *to be clothed,* signifies to be *surrounded, covered,* or *invested with any thing.* So, to be *clothed* with the *uncircumcision,* signifies to be *uncircumcised.* *Yalcut Rubeni,* fol. 163.

On the words, Exod. xxiv. 18, *Moses went into the midst of the cloud, and gat him up into the mount,* Sohar Exod., fol. 77, has these words, *He went into the midst of the cloud, as if one put on a garment; so he was* CLOTHED *with the* CLOUD. Sohar Levit., fol. 29: "The righteous are in the terrestrial paradise, where their souls are *clothed with the lucid crown;*" i. e. they are *surrounded, encompassed* with light, &c.

2. The word בית *beith,* HOUSE, in Hebrew often denotes a *cover, case,* or *clothing.* So, in the *Targum* of Onkelos, בית אפי *beith appei,* the HOUSE of the FACE, is a *veil;* and so בית אצבעים *beith etsbaim,* the HOUSE of the FINGERS, and בית יד *beith yad,* the HOUSE of the HAND, signify *gloves;* בית רגלים *beith regalim,* the HOUSE of the FEET, *shoes.* Therefore, οικητηριον—επενδυσασθαι, *to be clothed on with a house,* may signify any particular *qualities of the soul;* what we, following the very same form of speech, call a *habit,* i. e. a *coat* or *vestment.* So we say the man has got a *habit of vice, a habit of virtue, a habit of swearing, of humility, &c., &c.*

3. The Jews attribute *garments* to the soul, both in

A. M. 4061.
A. D. 57.
A. U. C.
810.
Anno Imp. Nero-
nis Cæs. 4.

upon with our house which is from heaven:

3 If so be that *c* being clothed we shall not be found naked.

4 For we that are in *this* tabernacle do groan, being burdened: not for that we would be unclothed, but *d* clothed upon, that mortal-

ity might be swallowed up of life.

5 Now *e* he that hath wrought us for the self-same thing *is* God, who also *f* hath given unto us the earnest of the Spirit.

6 Therefore *we are* always confident, know-

A. M. 4061.
A. D. 57.
A. U. C.
810.
Anno Imp. Nero
nis Cæs. 4.

---

c Rev. iii. 18 ; xvi. 15.——*d* 1 Cor. xv. 53, 54.——*e* Isa. xxix. 23 ; Eph. ii. 10.——*f* Rom. viii. 23 ; chap. i. 22 ; Eph. i. 14 ; iv. 30.

---

this and the other world; and as they hold that all human souls pre-exist, they say that, previously to their being appointed to bodies, they have a *covering* which answers the same end to them before they come into *life* as their bodies do *afterwards*. And they state that the design of God in sending souls into the world is, that they may get themselves a *garment* by the study of the law and good works. See several proofs in *Schoettgen*.

4. It is plain, also, that by this *garment* or *covering* of the soul they mean simply what we understand by acquiring the *image of God*—being made holy. This image they assert "Adam lost by his fall, and they represent man in a sinful state as being *naked*." So they represent the Israelites before their making the molten calf, as having received *holy garments* from Mount Sinai; but afterwards, having worshipped the calf, they were stripped of these, and left *naked*.

5. But notwithstanding they speak of this clothing as implying *righteous* and *holy* dispositions, and *hea-venly qualities*, yet they all agree in assigning certain *vehicles* to separate spirits, in which they act; but of these *vehicles* they have strange notions; yet they acknowledge that without them, whether they be of *light, fire, &c.*, or whatever else, they cannot see and contemplate the Supreme Wisdom. In *Synopsis Sohar*, page 137, we have these words: "When the time draws near in which a man is to depart from this world, the angel of death takes off his *mortal garment* and *clothes* him with one from paradise, in which he may see and contemplate the Supreme Wisdom; and therefore the angel of death is said to be very kind to man, because he takes off from him the *garment* of this world, and *clothes* him with a much more precious one prepared in paradise."

When the apostle says that they earnestly desired *to be clothed upon with our house which is from hea-ven*, he certainly means that the great concern of all the genuine followers of God was to be fully *prepared* to enjoy the beatific vision of their Maker and Redeemer.

Verse 3. *If so be that being clothed*] That is, *fully prepared* in this life for the glory of God;

We shall not be found naked.] Destitute in that future state of that Divine image which shall render us capable of enjoying an endless glory.

Verse 4. *For we that are in* this *tabernacle*] We who are in this *state* of trial and difficulty *do groan, being burdened*; as if he had said: The whole of human life is a state of suffering, and especially *our lot*; who are *troubled on every side, perplexed, persecuted, cast down, bearing about in the body the dying of our Lord Jesus*, and *being always delivered unto death on*

the account of Jesus, chap. iv. 8–11. These were sufficient *burdens*, and sufficient causes of *groaning*.

Not for that we would be unclothed] We do not desire *death*; nor to die, even with the full prospect of eternal glory before our eyes, an hour before that time which God in his wisdom has assigned.

But clothed upon] To have the fullest preparation for eternal glory. We wish not to die, whatever tribulation we may be called to pass through, till the whole will of God is accomplished *in* us and *by* us.

That mortality might be swallowed up of life.] Being fully prepared for the eternal state we shall scarcely be said to die, all that is mortal being absorbed and annihilated by immortality and glory. See the notes on 1 Cor. xv. 51–56. From the use of these expressions among the Jews, this seems to be the general meaning of the apostle.

Verse 5. *Now he that hath wrought us for the self-same thing*] God has given us our *being* and our *body* for this very purpose, that both might be made immortal, and both be glorified together. Or, God himself has given us this *insatiable hungering* and *thirsting* after *righteousness* and immortality. Mr. Addison has made a beautiful paraphrase of the sense of the apostle, whether he had his words in view or not :—

"——Whence this pleasing hope, this fond desire,
This *longing* after *immortality?*
Or whence this *secret dread* and *inward horror*
Of falling into nought? Why shrinks the soul
Back on herself, and startles at *destruction?*
'Tis the *Divinity* that *stirs within us;*
'Tis *Heaven* itself that points out an *hereafter,*
And intimates *eternity* to man.——
The soul, secured in her existence, smiles
At the drawn dagger, and defies its point.
The stars shall fade away, the sun himself
Grow dim with age, and nature sink in years;
But thou shalt flourish in *immortal youth,*
Unhurt amidst the war of elements,
The wreck of matter, and the crush of worlds."

The earnest of the Spirit.] See the note on chap. i. 22.

Verse 6. We are *always confident*] Θαρρουντες ουν παντοτε· We are always *full of courage*; we never despond; we know where our help lies; and, having the *earnest of the Spirit*, we have the full assurance of hope.

Whilst we are at home in the body, &c.] The original words in this sentence are very emphatic: ενδη-μειν signifies to *dwell among one's own people*; εκδη-μειν, to be a *sojourner among a strange people*. Heaven

334   2

A. M. 4061.
A. D. 57.
A. U. C.
810.
Anno Imp. Nero-
nis Cæs. 4.

ing that, whilst we are at home in the body, we are absent from the Lord:

7 (For ᵍ we walk by faith, not by sight :)

8 We are confident, *I say*, and ʰ willing rather to be absent from the body, and to be present with the Lord.

9 Wherefore we ⁱ labour, that, whether present or absent, we may be accepted of him.

10 ᵏ For we must all appear before the judgment seat of Christ; ˡ that every one may receive the things *done* in *his* body, according to that he hath done, whether *it be* good or bad.

11 Knowing therefore ᵐ the terror of the Lord, we persuade men; but ⁿ we are made manifest unto God, and I trust also are made manifest in your consciences.

A. M. 4061.
A. D. 57.
A. U. C.
810.
Anno Imp. Nero-
nis Cæs. 4.

ᵍ Rom. viii. 24, 25; chap. iv. 18; 1 Cor. xiii. 12; Heb. xi. 1.
ʰ Phil. i. 23.——ⁱ Or, *endeavour.*——ᵏ Matt. xxv. 31, 32; Rom. xiv. 10.

ˡ Rom. ii. 6; Gal. vi. 7; Eph. vi. 8; Col. iii. 24, 25; Rev. xxii. 12.——ᵐ Job xxxi. 23; Heb. x. 31; Jude 23.——ⁿ Chap. iv. 2.

---

is the *home* of every genuine Christian, and is claimed by them as such; see Phil. i. 23. Yet, while here below, the *body* is the proper *home of the soul;* but as the soul is made for *eternal glory,* that glory is its *country;* and therefore it is considered as being from its *proper home* while below in the body. As all human souls are made for this glory, therefore all are considered, while here, to be absent from their own country. And it is not merely heaven that they have in view, but the *Lord;* without whom, to an immortal spirit possessed of infinite desires, *heaven* would neither be a *home* nor a *place of rest.* We see plainly that the apostle gives no intimation of an intermediate state between *being at home* in the *body* and being *present* with the *Lord.* There is not the slightest intimation here that the *soul sleeps,* or rather, that there is no soul; and, when the body is decomposed, that there is no more of the man till the resurrection: I mean, according to the sentiments of those who do condescend to allow us a *resurrection,* though they deny us a *soul.* But this is a philosophy in which St. Paul got no lessons, either from Gamaliel, Jesus Christ, the Holy Ghost, or in the third heaven, where he heard even unutterable things.

Verse 7. *For we walk by faith*] While we are in the present state *faith* supplies the place of *direct vision.* In the future world we shall have *sight*—the utmost *evidence* of spiritual and eternal things; as we shall be *present with them,* and live in them. *Here* we have the testimony of *God,* and believe in their reality, because we cannot doubt his word. And to make this more convincing he gives us the *earnest of his Spirit,* which is a foretaste of glory.

Verse 8. *We are confident*] We are of *good courage,* notwithstanding our many difficulties; because we have this earnest of the Spirit, and the unfailing testimony of God. And notwithstanding this, *we are willing rather to be absent from the body*—we certainly prefer a state of glory to a state of suffering, and the enjoyment of the beatific vision to even the anticipation of it by faith and hope; but, as Christians, we cannot desire to die before our time.

Verse 9. *Wherefore we labour*] Φιλοτιμουμεθα· from φιλος, *loving,* and τιμη, *honour;* we act at all times on the *principles of honour;* we are, in the proper sense of the word, ambitious to do and say every thing consistently with our high vocation; and,

as we claim kindred to the inhabitants of heaven, to act as they do.

We may be accepted of him.] Ευαρεστοι αυτω ειναι *To be pleasing to him.* Through the love we have to God, we study and labour to please him. This *is* and *will be* our heaven, to study to love, please, and serve him from whom we have received both our *being* and its *blessings.*

Verse 10. *For we must all appear before the judgment seat*] We labour to walk so as to please him, because we know that we shall have to give a solemn account of ourselves before the judgment seat of Christ; where he, whose religion we profess, will judge us according to its precepts, and according to the light and grace which it affords.

That every one may receive the things] Κομισηται εκαστος· That *each may receive to himself, into his own hand,* his own reward and his own wages.

The things done *in his body*] That is, while he was in this lower *state;* for in this sense the term *body* is taken often in this epistle. We may observe also that the soul is the grand *agent,* the body is but its *instrument.* And it shall receive according to what it has done in *the body.*

Verse 11. *Knowing therefore the terror of the Lord*] This, I think, is too harsh a translation of ειδοτες ουν τον φοβον του Κυριου, which should be rendered, *knowing therefore the fear of the Lord;* which, strange as it may at first appear, often signifies the *worship* of the Lord, or that religious reverence which we owe to him; Acts ix. 31; Rom. iii. 18; xiii. 7; 1 Pet. i. 17; ii. 18; iii. 2. As *we know therefore* what God requires of man, because we are favoured with his own *revelation,* we *persuade men* to become Christians, and *to labour to be acceptable to him,* because they *must all stand before the judgment seat;* and if they receive not the grace of the Gospel *here,* they must *there* give up their accounts with *sorrow* and not with *joy.* In short, a man who is not saved from his sin in *this life,* will be separated from God and the glory of his power in the *world to come.* This is a powerful *motive* to *persuade men* to accept the salvation provided for them by Christ Jesus. The *fear of God* is the *beginning of wisdom;* the *terror* of God confounds and overpowers the soul. We lead men to God through his *fear* and *love,* and with the *fear* of God the *love* of God is ever consistent; but

2

A. M. 4061.
A. D. 57.
A. U. C.
810.
Anno Imp. Nero-
nis Cæs. 4.

12 For ° we commend not ourselves again unto you, but give you occasion ᴾ to glory on our behalf, that ye may have somewhat to *answer* them which glory �q in appearance, and not in heart.

13 For ʳ whether we be beside ourselves, *it is* to God: or whether we be sober, *it is* for your cause.

A. M. 4061.
A. D. 57.
A. U. C.
810.
Anno Imp. Nero-
nis Cæs. 4.

14 For the love of Christ constraineth us; because we thus judge, that ˢ if one died for all, then were all dead:

15 And *that* he died for all, ᵗ that they which live should not henceforth live unto themselves, but unto him which died for them, and rose again.

16 ᵘ Wherefore, henceforth know we no man

° Chap. iii. 1.——ᴾ Chap. i. 14.——q Gr. *in the face.*——ʳ Chap. xi. 1, 16, 17; xii. 6, 11.——ˢ Rom. v. 15.——ᵗ Rom. vi. 11, 12; xiv.

7, 8; 1 Cor. vi. 19; Gal. ii. 20; 1 Thess. v. 10; 1 Pet. iv. 2.
ᵘ Matt. xii. 50; John xv. 14; Gal. v. 6; Phil. iii. 7, 8; Col. iii. 11.

---

where the *terror* of the Lord reigns there can neither be *fear*, *faith*, nor *love*; nay, nor *hope* either. Men who vindicate their *constant* declamations on hell and perdition by quoting this text, know little of its meaning; and, what is worse, seem to know but little of the nature of man, and perhaps less of the spirit of the Gospel of Christ. Let them go and learn a lesson from Christ, weeping over Jerusalem: "O Jerusalem, Jerusalem, how oft would I have gathered you together, as a hen would her brood under her wings!" And another from his last words on the cross, "Father, forgive them, for they know not what they do!"

But we are made manifest unto God] God, who searches the heart, knows that we are upright in our endeavours to please him; and because we are fully persuaded of the *reality of eternal things*, therefore we are fully in earnest to get sinners converted to him.

Manifest in your consciences.] We have reason to believe that you have had such proof of our integrity and disinterestedness, that your consciences must acquit us of every unworthy motive, and of every sinister view.

Verse 12. For we commend not ourselves] I do not say these things to bespeak your good opinion, to procure your praise; but *to give you an occasion to glory*—to exult on our behalf; and to furnish you with an answer to all those who either malign us or our ministry, and who only *glory in appearance*—have no *solid ground* of exultation, and whose heart is dishonest and impure. St. Paul probably speaks here concerning the false apostle, who had been dividing the Church and endeavouring to raise a party to himself, by vilifying both the apostle and his doctrine.

Verse 13. Beside ourselves] Probably he was reputed by some to be *deranged*. Festus thought so: *Paul, thou art beside thyself; too much learning hath made thee mad.* And his enemies at Corinth might insinuate not only that he was *deranged*, but attribute his derangement to a less worthy cause than intense study and deep learning.

It is to God] If we do appear, in speaking of the glories of the eternal world, to be transported beyond ourselves, it is through the good hand of our God upon us, and we do it to promote his honour.

Whether we be sober] Speak of Divine things in a more *cool* and *dispassionate* manner, it is that we may the better instruct and encourage *you*.

Verse 14. For the love of Christ constraineth us]

We have the love of God shed abroad in our hearts, and this causes us to love God intensely, and to love and labour for the salvation of men. And it is the effect produced by this love which συνεχει ημας, *bears us away with itself*, which causes us to love after the similitude of that love by which we are influenced; and as God so loved the world as to give his Son for it, and as Christ so loved the world as to pour out his life for it, so we, influenced by the very same love, desire to spend and be spent for the glory of God, and the salvation of immortal souls. By *the fear of God* the apostles endeavoured to persuade and convince men, and the love of Christ *constrained* them so to act.

If one died for all, then were all dead] The *first* position the apostle takes for granted; *viz.* that Jesus Christ *died for* ALL *mankind*. This no apostolic man nor primitive Christian ever did doubt or could doubt.

The *second* position he infers from the *first*, and justly too; for if *all had not been guilty*, and *consigned to eternal death* because of their sin, there could have been no need of his death. Therefore, as he most certainly died for ALL, then all were dead, and needed his sacrifice, and the quickening power of his Spirit.

Verse 15. And that he died for all, that they which live, &c.] This *third* position he draws from the preceding: If *all were dead*, and in danger of endless perdition; and if *he died for all*, to save them from that perdition; then it justly follows that they *are not their own*, that they are bought by his blood; and *should not live unto themselves*, for this is the way to final ruin; *but unto him who died for them*, and thus made an atonement for their sins, and *rose again* for their justification.

Verse 16. Know we no man after the flesh] As we know that all have sinned and come short of the glory of God; and as we know that all are alienated from God, and are dead in trespasses and sins; therefore we esteem no man on account of *his family relations*, or the *stock* whence he proceeded, because we see all are shut up in unbelief, and all are children of wrath.

Yea, though we have known Christ after the flesh] We cannot esteem a man who is a *sinner*, were he even allied to the blood royal of David, and were he of the same *family* with the *man Christ* himself; nor can we prize a man because he has seen Christ in the

A. M. 4061.
A. D. 57.
A. U. C.
810.
Anno Imp. Nero-
nis Cæs. 4.

after the flesh: yea, though we have known Christ after the flesh, ᵛ yet now henceforth know we *him* no more.

17 Therefore if any man ʷ *be* in Christ, ˣ *he is* ʸ a new creature: ᶻ old things are passed away; behold, all things are become new.

18 And all things *are* of God, ᵃ who hath re-

A. M. 4061.
A. D. 57.
A. U. C.
810.
Anno Imp. Nero-
nis Cæs. 4.

conciled us to himself by Jesus Christ, and hath given to us the ministry of reconciliation;

19 To wit, that ᵇ God was in Christ, reconciling the world unto himself, not imputing their trespasses unto them; and hath ᶜ committed unto us the word of reconciliation.

ᵛ John vi. 63.——ʷ Rom. viii. 9; xvi. 7; Gal. vi. 15.——ˣ Or, let him be.——ʸ Gal. v. 6; vi. 15.——ᶻ Isa. xliii. 18, 19; lxv. 17;

Eph. ii. 15; Rev. xxi. 5.——ᵃ Rom. v. 10; Eph. ii. 16; Col. i. 20; 1 John ii. 2; iv. 10.——ᵇ Rom. iii. 24, 25.——ᶜ Gr. *put in us*

---

flesh; for many have seen him in the flesh to whom he will say: *Depart from me, for I never knew you.* So we: nothing weighs with us, nor in the sight of God, but redemption from this death, and *living to him* who died for them.

We know that the Jews valued themselves much in having Abraham for their father; and some of the Judaizing teachers at Corinth might value themselves in having *seen Christ in the flesh,* which certainly St. Paul did not; hence he takes occasion to say here that this kind of privilege availed nothing; for the *old creature,* however *noble,* or *well descended* in the sight of men, is under the *curse;* and the *new creature* only is such as God can approve.

Verse 17. *If any man be in Christ, he is a new creature*] It is vain for a man to profess affinity to Christ according to the *flesh,* while he is unchanged in his heart and life, and dead in trespasses and sins; for he that is *in Christ,* that is, a genuine Christian, having Christ dwelling in his heart by faith, is a *new creature;* his *old state* is changed: he was a *child of Satan,* he is now a *child of God;* he was a *slave of* sin, and his works were death; he is now made *free* from sin, and has his fruit unto holiness, and the end everlasting life. He was before full of *pride* and *wrath;* he is now *meek* and *humble.* He formerly had his *portion* in *this life,* and lived for this world alone; he now has GOD for his *portion,* and he looks not at the things which are seen, but at the things which are eternal. Therefore, *old things are passed away.*

Behold, all things are become new.] The man is not only *mended,* but he is *new made;* he is *a new creature,* καινη κτισις, a *new creation,* a *little world* in himself; formerly, all was in *chaotic* disorder; now, there is a *new creation,* which God himself owns as his workmanship, and which he can look on and pronounce *very good.* The conversion of a man from idolatry and wickedness was among the Jews denominated a *new creation. He who converts a man to the true religion is the same,* says R⁰ Eliezer, *as if he had created him.*

Verse 18. *And all things are of God*] As the thorough conversion of the soul is compared to a new *creation,* and *creation* is the proper work of an *all-wise, almighty Being;* then this total change of heart, soul, and life, which takes place under the preaching of the Gospel, is effected by the *power* and *grace* of God: this is *salvation,* and salvation must ever be of the Lord; and therefore men should apply to him, who alone can work this wondrous change.

Who hath reconciled us to himself by Jesus Christ] Having given Jesus Christ to die for sinners, they have through him access unto God; for his sake and on his account God can receive them; and it is only by the *grace* and *Spirit* of Christ that the proud, fierce, and diabolic nature of men can be changed and reconciled to God; and *by* and *through* this sacrifice God can be propitious to them. There is an *enmity* in the heart of man against sacred things; the grace of Christ alone can remove this enmity.

The ministry of reconciliation] Διακονιαν της κα-ταλλαγης· The OFFICE or *function of this reconciliation;* called, ver. 19, *the word;* τον λογον της καταλλαγης· the DOCTRINE *of this reconciliation.* Καταλλαγη, *recon-ciliation,* comes from καταλλασσω, *to change thoroughly;* and the grand object of the Gospel is to make a complete change in men's *minds* and *manners;* but the first object is the removal of enmity from the heart of man, that he may be disposed to accept of the salvation God has provided for him, on the terms which God has promised. The *enmity* in the heart of man is the grand hinderance to his salvation.

Verse 19. *That God was in Christ*] This is the doctrine which this ministry of reconciliation holds out, and the doctrine which it uses to bring about the reconciliation itself.

God was in Christ: 1. *Christ* is the same as *Mes-siah,* the *Anointed* One, who was to be *prophet, priest,* and *king,* to the human race; not to the *Jews* only, but also to the *Gentiles.* There had been prophets, priests, and kings, among the Jews and their ancestors; and some who had been *priest* and *prophet, king* and *priest,* and *king* and *prophet;* but none have ever sustained in his *own person* the *threefold* office except Christ; for none have ever ministered in reference to the *whole world* but he. The functions of all the others were *restrained* to the *ancient people* of God alone. 2. Now all the others were appointed of God in reference to this Christ; and as his types, or representatives, till the fulness of the time should come. 3. And that this Christ might be adequate to the great work of reconciling the whole human race to God, by making atonement for their sins, *God was in him.* The man Jesus was the *temple* and *shrine* of the *eternal Divinity;* for *in him dwelt all the fulness of the Godhead bodily,* Col. ii. 9; and *he made peace by the blood of his cross.* 4. Christ, by his offering upon the cross, made ·atonement for the sins of the world; and therefore one important· branch of the doctrine of this reconciliation was to show that God

A. M. 4061.
A. D. 57.
A. U. C.
810.
Anno Imp. Nero-
nis Cæs. 4.

20 Now then we are ᵈ ambassadors for Christ, as ᵉ though God did beseech *you* by us : we pray *you* in Christ's stead, be ye reconciled to God.

21 For ᶠ he hath made him *to be* sin for us, who knew no sin ; that we might be made ᵍ the righteousness of God in him.

A. M. 4061.
A. D. 57.
A. U. C.
810.
Anno Imp. Nero-
nis Cæs. 4.

ᵈ Job xxxiii. 23 ; Mal. ii. 7 ; chap. iii. 6 ; Eph. vi. 20.——ᵉ Chap. vi. 1.

ᶠ Isa. liii. 6, 9, 12 ; Gal. iii. 13 ; 1 Pet. ii. 22, 24 ; 1 John iii. 5.   ᵍ Rom. i. 17 ; v. 19 ; x. 3.

---

would not *impute* or account *their trespasses to them*, so as to exact the *penalty*, because this Jesus had died in their stead.

The whole of this important doctrine was *short*, *simple*, and *plain*. Let us consider it in all its connections : 1. You believe there is a God. 2. You know he has made you. 3. He requires you to love and serve him. 4. To show you how to do this he has given a revelation of himself, which is contained in his law, &c. 5. You have broken this law, and incurred the penalty, which is death. 6. Far from being able to undo your offences, or make reparation to the offended majesty of God, your hearts, through the deceitfulness and influence of sin, are blinded, hardened, and filled with *enmity*, against your Father and your Judge. 7. To redeem you out of this most wretched and accursed state, God, in his endless love, has given his Son for you ; who has assumed your nature, and died in your stead. 8. In consequence of this he has commanded repentance towards God, and remission of sins, to be published in his name in all the earth. 9. All who repent, and believe in Christ as having died for them as a *sin-offering*, (ver. 21,) shall receive remission of sins. 10. And if they abide in him they shall have an eternal inheritance among them that are sanctified.

Verse 20. *We are ambassadors for Christ*] Ὑπερ Χριστου—πρεσβευομεν. We execute the function of ambassadors in Christ's stead. He came from the Father to mankind on this important embassy. He has left the world, and appointed us in his place.

Ambassador is a person sent from one sovereign power to another ; and is supposed to represent the person of the sovereign by whom he is deputed. Christ while on earth represented the person of the Sovereign of the world ; his *apostles* and their successors represent the person of Christ. Christ declared the will of the Father to mankind ; apostles, &c., declare the will of Christ to the world. *We are ambassadors for Christ.*

As though God did beseech you *by us*] What we say to you we say on the authority of God ; our entreaties are his entreaties ; our warm love to you, a faint reflection of his infinite love ; we pray you to return to God, it is his will that you should do so ; we promise you remission of sins, we are authorized to do so by God himself. In Christ's stead we pray you to lay aside your enmity and *be reconciled to God* ; i. e. accept pardon, peace, holiness, and heaven ; which are all procured for you by his blood, and offered to you on his own authority.

"What unparalleled condescension and divinely tender mercies are displayed in this verse ! Did the *judge* ever *beseech* a condemned criminal to accept

of pardon ? Does the creditor ever beseech a ruined debtor to receive an acquittance in full ? Yet our almighty Lord, and our eternal Judge, not only vouchsafes to offer these blessings, but invites us, entreats us, and with the most tender importunity solicits us not to reject them." The Rev. J. Wesley's notes in loc.

This sentiment is farther expressed in the following beautiful poetic version of this place, by the Rev. *Charles Wesley :*—

" God, the offended God most high,
   Ambassadors to rebels sends ;
  His *messengers his place* supply,
  And *Jesus* begs us to *be friends.*
      Us, *in the stead of Christ*, they pray,
      Us, *in the stead of Christ*, entreat,
      To cast our arms, our sins, away,
      And find forgiveness at his feet.
  Our God, in Christ, thine *embassy*
  And proffer'd mercy we embrace ;
  And, gladly *reconciled* to thee,
  Thy condescending mercy praise.
      Poor *debtors*, by our Lord's request
      A full *acquittance* we receive ;
      And *criminals*, with pardon blest,
      We, at our Judge's instance, live."

Verse 21. *For he hath made him* to be *sin for us*] Τον μη γνοντα ἁμαρτιαν, ὑπερ ἡμων ἁμαρτιαν εποιησεν· *He made him who knew no sin*, (who was innocent,) *a sin-offering for us.* The word ἁμαρτια occurs here *twice :* in the *first place* it means *sin*, i. e. transgression and guilt ; and of Christ it is said, *He knew no sin*, i. e. was *innocent ;* for not to *know* sin is the same as to be *conscious of innocence ;* so, *nil conscire sibi*, to be conscious of nothing against one's self, is the same as *nulla pallescere culpa*, to be unimpeachable.

In the second place, it signifies a *sin-offering*, or *sacrifice for sin*, and answers to the חטאה *chattaah* and חטאת *chattath* of the Hebrew text ; which signifies both *sin* and *sin-offering* in a great variety of places in the Pentateuch. The *Septuagint* translate the Hebrew word by ἁμαρτια in ninety-four places in *Exodus*, *Leviticus*, and *Numbers*, where a *sin-offering* is meant ; and where our version translates the word not *sin*, but an *offering for sin.* Had our translators attended to their own method of translating the word in other places where it means the *same* as here, they would not have given this false view of a passage which has been made the foundation of a most blasphemous doctrine ; viz. that *our sins were imputed to Christ*, and that he was a *proper object* of the *indignation of Divine justice*, because he was *blackened with imputed sin ;* and some have proceeded so far in this blasphemous career as to say, that *Christ may be considered as*

(22**)

the greatest of sinners, *because all the sins of mankind,* or of the *elect,* as they say, *were imputed to him, and reckoned as his own.* One of these writers translates the passage thus: *Deus Christum pro maximo peccatore habuit, ut nos essemus maxime justi,* God accounted Christ the greatest of sinners, that we might be supremely righteous. Thus they have confounded *sin* with the *punishment due to sin.* Christ *suffered in our stead ; died for us ; bore our sins,* (the *punishment* due to them,) *in his own body upon the tree,* for *the Lord laid upon him the iniquities of us all ;* that is, the *punishment* due to them ; explained by *making his soul*—his life, *an offering for sin ;* and *healing us by his stripes.*

But that it may be plainly seen that *sin-offering,* not *sin,* is the meaning of the word in this verse, I shall set down the places from the *Septuagint* where the word occurs ; and where it answers to the Hebrew words already quoted ; and where our translators have rendered correctly what they render here incorrectly.

In Exodus, chap. xxix. 14, 36 : Leviticus, chap. iv. 3, 8, 20, 21, 24, 25, and 29 twice, 32, 33, and 34 ; chap. v. 6, 7, 8, 9 twice, 11 twice, 12 ; chap. vi. 17, 25 twice, 30 ; chap. vii. 7, 37 ; chap. viii. 2, 14 twice ; chap. ix. 2, 3, 7, 8, 10, 15, 22 ; chap. x. 16, 17, 19 twice ; chap. xii. 6, 8 ; chap. xiv. 13 twice, 19, 22, 31 ; chap. xv. 30 ; chap. xvi. 3, 5, 6, 9, 11 twice, 15, 25, 27 twice ; chap. xxiii. 19 : Numbers, chap. vi. 11, 14, 16 ; chap. vii. 16, 22, 28, 34, 40, 46, 52, 58, 70, 76, 82, 87 ; chap. viii. 8, 12 ; chap. xv. 24, 25, 27 ; chap. xviii. 9 ; chap. xxviii. 15, 22 ; chap. xxix. 5, 11, 16, 22, 25, 28, 31, 34, 38.

Besides the above places, it occurs in the same signification, and is properly translated in our version, in the following places :—

2 Chronicles, chap. xxix. 21, 23, 24 : Ezra, chap. vi. 17 ; chap. viii. 35 : Nehemiah, chap. x. 33 : Job, chap. i. 5 : Ezekiel, chap. xliii. 19, 22, 25 ; chap. xliv. 27, 29 ; chap. xlv. 17, 19, 22, 23, 25. In all, one hundred and eight places, which, in the course of my own reading in the Septuagint, I have marked.

That we might be made the righteousness of God in him.] *The righteousness of God* signifies here the *salvation* of God, as comprehending *justification* through the blood of Christ, and *sanctification* through his Spirit ; or, as the *mountains of God,* the *hail of God,* the *wind of God,* mean *exceeding high mountains, extraordinary hail,* and *most tempestuous wind ;* so, here, the righteousness of God may mean a *thorough righteousness, complete justification, complete sanctification ;* such as none but *God* can give, such as the *sinful nature* and *guilty conscience* of man require, and such as is *worthy* of God to impart. And all this *righteousness, justification,* and *holiness,* we receive *in, by, for,* and *through* him, as the grand, sacrificial, procuring, and meritorious cause of these, and every other blessing. Some render the passage : *We are justified through him, before God ;* or, *We are justified, according to God's plan of justification, through him.*

In many respects, this is a most important and instructive chapter.

1. The terms *house, building, tabernacle,* and others connected with them, have already been explained from the Jewish writings. But it has been thought by some that the apostle mentions these as readily offering themselves to him from his own avocation, that of a *tentmaker ;* and it is supposed that he borrows these terms from his own *trade* in order to illustrate his doctrine. This supposition would be natural enough if we had not full evidence that these terms were used in the *Jewish theology* precisely in the sense in which the apostle uses them here. Therefore, it is more likely that he borrowed them from that theology, than from his own *trade.*

2. In the terms *tabernacle, building of God, &c.,* he may refer also to the tabernacle in the wilderness, which was a *building of God,* and a *house of God ;* and as God dwelt in that building, so he will dwell in the souls of those who *believe* in, *love,* and *obey* him. And this will be his *transitory temple* till mortality is swallowed up of life, and we have a glorified body and soul to be his eternal residence.

3. The doctrines of the resurrection of the same body ; the witness of the Spirit ; the immateriality of the soul ; the fall and miserable condition of all mankind ; the death of Jesus, as an atonement for the sins of the whole world ; the necessity of obedience to the Divine will, and of the total change of the human heart, are all introduced here : and although only a few words are spoken on *each,* yet these are so *plain* and so *forcible* as to set those important doctrines in the most clear and striking point of view.

4. The chapter concludes with such a view of the mercy and goodness of God in the *ministry of reconciliation,* as is no where else to be found. He has here set forth the Divine mercy in all its heightenings ; and who can take this view of it without having his heart melted down with love and gratitude to God, who has called him to such a state of salvation.

5. It is exceedingly remarkable that, through the whole of this chapter, the apostle speaks of himself in the first person *plural ;* and though he may intend other apostles, and the Christians in general, yet it is very evident that he uses this form when only himself can be meant, as in verses 12 and 13, as well as in several places of the following chapter. This may be esteemed rather more curious than important.

CHAPTER VI.

We should not receive the grace of God in vain, having such promises of support from him, 1, 2. *We should act so as to bring no disgrace on the Gospel,* 3. *How the apostles behaved themselves, preached, suffered, and rejoiced,* 4–10. *St. Paul's affectionate concern for the Corinthians,* 11–13. *He counsels them not to be yoked with unbelievers, and advances several arguments why they should avoid them,* 14–16. *Exhorts them to avoid evil companions and evil practices, on the promise that God will be their Father, and that they shall be his sons and his daughters,* 17, 18.

A. M. 4061.
A. D. 57.
A. U. C.
810.
Anno Imp. Nero-
nis Cæs. 4.

WE then, *as* ª workers together *with him,* ᵇ beseech *you* also ᶜ that ye receive not the grace of God in vain.

2 (For he saith, ᵈ I have heard thee in a time accepted, and in the day of salvation have

I succoured thee : behold, now *is* the accepted time ; behold, now *is* the day of salvation.)

3 ᵉ Giving no offence in any thing, that the ministry be not blamed :

4 But in all *things* ᶠ approving ourselves ᵍ as

A. M. 4061.
A. D. 57.
A. U. C.
810.
Anno Imp. Nero-
nis Cæs. 4.

ª 1 Cor. iii. 9.——ᵇ Chap. v. 20.——ᶜ Heb. xii. 15.——ᵈ Isa. xlix. 8.

ᵉ Rom. xiv. 13 ; 1 Cor. ix. 12 ; x. 32.——ᶠ Gr. *commending* ; chap. iv. 2.——ᵍ 1 Cor. iv. 1.

NOTES ON CHAP. VI.

Verse 1. *We then, as workers together* with him] Συνεργουντες δε και παρακαλουμεν. The two last words, *with him,* are not in the text, and some supply the place thus : *we then, as workers together* WITH YOU, and the *Armenian* version seems to have read it so ; but no MS. has this reading, and no other version. For my own part I see nothing wanting in the text if we only suppose the term *apostles* ; *we,* (i. e. apostles,) *being fellow workers, also entreat you not to receive the grace of God in vain.*

By the *grace of God,* την χαριν του Θεου, this grace or *benefit of God,* the apostle certainly means the *grand sacrificial offering* of Christ for the sin of the world, which he had just before mentioned in speaking of the *ministry of reconciliation.* We learn, therefore, that it was possible to *receive the grace of God* and not ultimately benefit by it ; or, in other words, to begin in the Spirit and end in the flesh. Should any one say that it is the *ministry of reconciliation,* that is, the *benefit of apostolic* preaching, that they might receive in vain ; I answer, that the apostolic preaching, and the whole ministry of reconciliation, could be no *benefit* to any man farther than it might have been a means of conveying to him the salvation of God. And it is most evident that the apostle has in view that grace or benefit that reconciles us to God, and makes us Divinely righteous. And this, and all other benefits of the death of Christ, may be received in vain.

Verse 2. *For he saith*] That is, God hath said it, by the prophet Isaiah, chap. xlix. 8 ; which place the apostle quotes *verbatim et literatim* from the *Septuagint.* And from this we may at once see what is the *accepted time,* and what *the day of salvation.* The *advent* of the *Messiah* was the עֵת רָצוֹן *eth'ratson,* the time of God's pleasure or benevolence, of which all the faithful were in expectation ; and the *day of salvation,* יוֹם שׁוּעָה *yom yeshuah,* was the time in which this salvation should be manifested and applied. The apostle therefore informs them that *this* is the *time* predicted by the prophet ; and the *ministry of reconciliation* being exercised in full force is a proof that the prophecy is fulfilled ; and therefore the apostle confidently asserts, *Behold,* NOW *is this accepted time,* NOW the Messiah reigns, NOW is the Gospel dispensation, and therefore NOW *is the day of salvation;* that is, the very time in which the power of God is present to heal, and in which every sinner believing on the Lord Jesus may be saved.

I rather think that this *second verse* should be read immediately after the last verse of the preceding chapter ; as where it now stands it greatly disturbs the connection between the *first* and the *third* verses. I will set down the whole in the order in which I think

they should stand. Chap. v. 20 : *Now then we are ambassadors for Christ ; as though God did beseech you by us, we pray you in Christ's stead, to be reconciled to God. For he hath made him a sin-offering for us, who knew no sin, that we might be made the righteousness of God in him : for he saith,* "I have heard thee in a time accepted, and in the day of salvation have I succoured thee." *Behold, now is the accepted time ; behold, now is the day of salvation.* Immediately after this, the sixth chapter will very properly commence, and we shall see that the connection will be then undisturbed :—

We then, *as fellow workers, beseech you also, that ye receive not this grace of God in vain, giving no offence in any thing, that this ministry be not blamed.* This change of the place of the second verse, which every one allows must, if it stand here, be read in a parenthesis, preserves the whole connection of the apostle's discourse, and certainly sets his argument before us in a stronger light. Let us review the whole : 1. God was in Christ, reconciling the world to himself, chap. v. 18. 2. He appointed the apostles to proclaim to mankind the doctrine of reconciliation, chap. v. 19. 3. The apostles, in consequence, proclaim this doctrine ; and show that Christ was a sacrifice for sin, and that through him we may be perfectly saved, chap. v. 20, 21. ɩ 4. They show also that all this was agreeable to the declaration of God by the prophet Isaiah, chap. xlix. 8, where he predicts the days of the Messiah, and the *grace* then to be communicated, chap. vi. 2. 5. The apostle then, speaking in the person of all his fellow labourers, who had this ministry of reconciliation intrusted to them, exhorts them not to receive such a benefit of God in vain, chap vi. 1. 6. He exhorts those who had embraced the Gospel not to put a stumbling block in the way of others, by acting irreligiously, lest this ministry of reconciliation should be reproached on their account, chap. vi. 3. 7. He shows what conscientious and scrupulous care he and his fellow apostles took to preach and walk so that this ministry might have its full effect, ch. vi. 4, &c.

This view of the subject, if I mistake not, shows a beautiful consistency throughout the whole.

Verse 3. *Giving no offence*] The word προσκοπη, read προσκομμα, Rom. xiv. 13, signifies a *stumbling-block* in general, or any thing over which a man stumbles or falls ; and here means any *transgression* or *scandal* that might take place among the ministers, or the Christians themselves, whereby either Jews or Gentiles might take occasion of offence, and vilify the Gospel of Christ.

Verse 4 *But in all things approving ourselves*] The apostle now proceeds to show how conscientiously

A. M. 4061.
A. D. 57.
A. U. C.
810.
Anno Imp. Nero-
nis Cæs. 4.

the ministers of God, in much patience, in afflictions, in necessities, in distresses,

5 [h] In stripes, in imprisonments, [i] in tumults, in labours, in watchings, in fastings ;

6 By pureness, by knowledge, by long-suffering, by kindness, by the Holy Ghost, by love unfeigned,

7 [k] By the word of truth, by [l] the power of God, by [m] the armour of righteousness

A. M. 4061.
A. D. 57.
A. U. C.
810.
Anno Imp. Nero-
nis Cæs. 4.

[h] Chap. xi. 23, &c.——[i] Or, *in tossings to and fro.*——[k] Chap. iv. 2, vii. 14.

[l] 1 Cor. ii. 4.——[m] Chapter x. 4 ; Eph. vi. 11, 13 ; 2 Timothy iv. 7.

himself and his fellow labourers acted, in order to render the ministry of reconciliation effectual to the salvation of men. They not only gave no offence in any thing, but they laboured to manifest themselves to be the genuine ministers of God, *in much patience*—bearing calmly up under the most painful and oppressive afflictions.

In afflictions] Εν θλιψεσιν. This may signify the *series* of persecutions and distresses in general ; the *state* of cruel suffering in which the Church of God and the apostles then existed.

In necessities] Εν αναγκαις· *Straits* and *difficulties* ; including all that *want* and affliction which arose from the *impoverished* state of the Church.

In distresses] Εν στενοχωριαις. Such straits and difficulties as were absolutely *unavoidable* and *insurmountable*. The word implies, *being reduced to a narrow place, driven to a corner, hemmed in on every side,* as the Israelites were at the Red Sea ; the sea before them, Pharaoh and his host behind them, and Egyptian fortresses on either hand. God alone could bring them out of such difficulties, when their enemies themselves saw that *the wilderness had shut them in.* So was it often with the apostles ; all human help failed, and their deliverance came from God alone.

Verse 5. *In stripes, in imprisonments*] Of these the history of the Acts of the Apostles gives ample testimony ; and there were doubtless many instances of persecution in various forms which are not on record.

In tumults] Ακαταστασιαις· *Insurrections* raised against them because of the Gospel It is more natural to understand the word thus, than of *agitations,* or *tossings to and fro* in consequence of their unsettled state of life ; or because of persecution, which obliged them to flee from place to place.

In labours] Both with our own *hands* to provide for ourselves the necessaries of life, that we might not be chargeable to others, and *in labours* to *spread the Gospel* of God through all countries where his providence opened our way.

In watchings] Passing many nights without sleep or rest

In fastings] Partly *constrained* through want of food, and partly *voluntary,* as a means of obtaining an increase of grace both for ourselves and for the Churches.

Verse 6. *By pureness*] Εν αγνοτητι· In *simplicity* of intention, and *purity* of *affection* ; together with that *chastity* and *holiness* of life which the Gospel enjoins.

By knowledge] Of the Divine mysteries.

By long-suffering] Under all provocations.

By kindness] To our most virulent persecutors, and to all men.

By the Holy Ghost] There are doubts among learned men whether the apostle here means that SPIRIT who is called the *third person* of the *holy* TRINITY ; or some *grace, disposition,* or *quality* of the soul, which was thus denominated, as implying a *spirit* wholly *purified,* and fitted to be a *habitation* of God.

Schoettgen quotes a passage from *Rabbi Bechai,* in which it appears to him to have this latter meaning : " Rabbi Pinchas, the son of Jair, said : *Reflection* leads to sedulity ; *sedulity* to innocence ; *innocence* to abstinence ; *abstinence* to cleanness ; *cleanness* to sanctity ; *sanctity* to the fear of sin ; *fear* of *sin* to humility ; *humility* to piety ; and *piety* to the *Holy Spirit.* Of these *ten* virtues *five* are external, or belong to the body ; and *five* internal, or belonging to the soul ; but all men prefer the *tenth,* which is רוח הקדש *ruach hakkodesh,* the *Holy Spirit.*" Even allowing Rabbi Pinchas to be a person on whose judgment we could rely, and whose authority was decisive, there does not appear to me any reason why we should depart from the usual meaning of the term from any thing that is said here. It appears to me plain enough that the rabbi means the constant indwelling of the Holy Spirit ; and St. Paul, in this place, may have the same thing in view, and with it the various *gifts* of the Holy Spirit by which he was enabled to work *miracles.*

By love unfeigned] Εν αγαπη ανυποκριτω· *Love without hypocrisy* ; such as disposed us at all times to lay down our life for the brethren, and to spend and be spent for the glory of God and the good of mankind.

Verse 7. *By the word of truth*] The doctrine of truth received immediately from God, and faithfully and affectionately preached to men.

By the power of God] Confirming this doctrine, not only by the miracles which we were enabled to work, but also by the application of that truth to the souls of the people by the energy of God.

By the armour of righteousness] Such as that described by the apostle, Eph. vi. 13–17, which he calls there *the whole armour of God,* consisting of the following pieces. the *girdle* of *truth,* the *breastplate* of *righteousness,* the *shoes* of the Gospel of *peace,* the *shield* of *faith,* the *helmet* of *salvation,* and the *sword* of the Spirit.

On the right hand and on the left] Particularly, the *shield* and the *sword* ; the former on the *left arm,* the latter in the *right hand.* We have the doctrine of truth, and the power of God, as an armour to protect us on *all sides, every where,* and *on all occasions.*

It seems far-fetched to understand the *right hand* as signifying *prosperity,* and the *left* as signifying *adversity* ; as if the apostle had said : We have this

2

A. M. 4061.
A. D. 57.
A. U. C.
810.
Anno Imp. Nero-
nis Cæs. 4.

on the right hand and on the left,

8 By honour and dishonour, by evil report and good report: as deceivers, and *yet* true ;

9 As unknown, and ⁿ *yet* well known ; ° as dying, and, behold, we live : ᵖ as chastened, and not killed ;

10 As sorrowful, yet alway rejoicing ; as poor, yet making many rich ; as having no-

---

ᵖ Chap. iv. 2 ; v. 11 ; xi. 6.——° 1 Cor. iv. 9 ; chap. i. 9 ; iv. 10, 11.——ᵖ Psa. cxviii. 18.

---

thing, and *yet* possessing all things.

11 O *ye* Corinthians, our mouth is open unto you, �q our heart is enlarged.

12 Ye are not straitened in us, but ʳ ye are straitened in your own bowels.

13 Now for a recompense in the same, (ˢ I speak as unto *my* children,) be ye also enlarged.

14 ᵗ Be ye not unequally yoked together with

A. M. 4061.
A. D. 57.
A. U. C.
810.
Anno Imp. Nero-
nis Cæs. 4.

---

q Chap. vii. 3.——ʳ Chap. xii. 15.——ˢ 1 Cor. iv. 14.——ᵗ Deut. vii. 2, 3 ; 1 Cor. v. 9 ; vii. 39.

---

armour to defend us both in prosperity and adversity. By the doctrine of the Gospel, and by the power of God, the apostles were furnished with *offensive* and *defensive* weapons ; they could ever *defend themselves,* and *discomfit* their *foes.*

Verse 8. *By honour and dishonour*] By going through both ; sometimes respected, sometimes despised.

By evil report and good report] Sometimes praised, at other times calumniated.

As deceivers] Said to carry about a false doctrine for our secular emolument.

And yet true] Demonstrated by the nature of the doctrine, as well as by our life and conversation, that we are true men ; having nothing in view but God's glory and the salvation of the world.

Verse 9. *As unknown*] Persons who are to be suspected as harbouring dark designs ; persons of neither birth, parentage, nor respectable connections in life ;

And yet well known] *Proved* by our whole conduct to have no such designs, and demonstrated to be holy, upright, and useful, by the whole train of our peregrinations, through which we can be readily traced from place to place ; having preached openly, and done nothing in a corner.

As dying] Through continual dangers, fatigues, and persecutions ;

And, behold, we live] We are preserved by the mighty power of God in the greatest dangers and deaths.

As chastened] As though we were disobedient children ;

And not killed] Though we continue in the very same line of conduct that is supposed to bring on us those chastisements, and which, if it were criminal, would justly expose us to death for incorrigible obstinacy ; but our preservation is a proof that we please God.

Verse 10. *As sorrowful*] Considerate men supposing, from our persecuted state and laborious occupation, (often destitute of the necessaries of life ; seldom enjoying its conveniences ; and scarcely ever, its comforts,) that we must be the most miserable of all men.

Yet alway rejoicing] Having the consolation of God's Spirit at all times, and a glorious prospect of a blessed immortality.

As poor] Destitute of all worldly good and secular interest,

Yet making many rich] By dispensing to them the *treasures of salvation* ; making them *rich* in *faith,* and *heirs of the kingdom.*

The Gospel, when faithfully preached, and fully received, *betters the condition of the poor.* It makes them *sober* ; so they *save* what before they *profusely* and *riotously* spent. It makes them *diligent* ; and thus they *employ time* to useful purposes which they before squandered away. They therefore both *save* and *gain* by religion ; and these must lead to an increase of property. Therefore they are *made rich* ; at least in comparison with that sinful, profligate state in which they were before they received the truth of the Gospel.

As having nothing] Being the most abject of the poor,

And yet possessing all things.] That are really necessary to the preservation of our lives. For the wants under which we labour for a time are supplied again by a bountiful Providence. The man who possesses a *contented spirit* possesses *all things* ; for he is satisfied with every dispensation of the providence of God ; and " a contented mind is a continual feast.'

Verse 11. *O ye Corinthians, our mouth is open unto you*] I speak to you with the utmost *freedom* and *fluency,* because of my affection for you.

Our heart is enlarged.] It is expanded to take you and all your interests in ; and to keep you in the most affectionate remembrance.

The preceding verses contain a very fine specimen of a very powerful and commanding *eloquence.*

Verse 12. *Ye are not straitened in us*] That is, Ye have not a *narrow place* in our affections : the metaphor here is taken from the case of a person pent up in a small or narrow place, where there is scarcely room to breathe.

Ye are straitened in your own bowels.] I have not the same place in your affections which you have in mine. The *bowels* are used in Scripture to denote the most *tender affections.* See the note on Matt. ix. 36.

Verse 13. *Now for a recompense in the same*] That you may, in some sort, *repay me* for my affection towards you, *I speak to you as unto* my *children,* whom I have a right to command, *be ye also enlarged* —love me as I love you.

Verse 14. *Be ye not unequally yoked together with unbelievers*] This is a military term : keep in your own *ranks* ; do not leave the *Christian* community to join in that of the *heathens.* The verb ἑτεροζυγειν

2

A. M. 4061.
A. D. 57.
A. U. C.
810.
Anno Imp. Nero-
nis Cæs. 4.

unbelievers : for ᵘ what fellow-ship hath righteousness with un-righteousness ? and what com-munion hath light with darkness ?

15 And what concord hath Christ with Be-lial ? or what part hath he that believeth with an infidel ?

16 And what agreement hath the temple of God with idols ? for ᵛ ye are the temple of the living God ; as God hath said, ʷ I will dwell in

them, and walk in *them ;* and I will be their God, and they shall be my people.

17 ˣ Wherefore come out from among them, and be ye separate, saith the Lord, and touch not the unclean *thing ;* and I will receive you,

18 ʸ And will be a Father unto you, and ye shall be my sons and daughters, saith the Lord Almighty.

A. M. 4061.
A. D. 57.
A. U. C.
810.
Anno Imp. Nero-
nis Cæs. 4.

ᵘ 1 Sam. v. 2, 3 ; 1 Kings xviii. 21 ; Ecclus. xiii. 17 ; 1 Cor. x. 21 ; Eph. v. 7, 11.——ᵛ 1 Cor. iii. 16 ; vi. 19 ; Eph. ii. 21, 22 ; Heb. iii. 6.——ʷ Exod. xxix. 45 ; Lev. xxvi. 12 ; Jer. xxxi. 33 ;

xxxii. 38 ; Ezek. xi. 20 ; xxxvi. 28 ; xxxvii. 26. &c. ; Zech. viii. 8 ; xiii. 9.——ˣ Isa. lii. 11 ; chap. vii. 1 ; Rev. xviii. 4.——ʸ Jer. xxxi. 1, 9 ; Rev. xxi. 7.

---

signifies to leave one's own rank, place, or order, and go into another ; and here it must signify not only that they should not *associate* with the Gentiles in their idolatrous feasts, but that they should not *apos-tatize* from Christianity ; and the questions which fol-low show that there was a sort of fellowship that some of the Christians had formed with the heathens which was both wicked and absurd, and if not speedily check-ed would infallibly lead to final apostasy.

Some apply this exhortation to pious persons *mar-rying* with those who are not *decidedly religious,* and *converted to God.* That the exhortation may be *thus* applied I grant ; but it is certainly not the meaning of the apostle in this place. Nevertheless, common sense and true piety show the absurdity of two such persons pretending to walk together in a way in which they are not agreed. A very wise and very holy man has given his judgment on this point : " A man who is truly pious, marrying with an unconverted woman, will either draw back to perdition, or have a cross during life." The same may be said of a *pious woman* marrying an *unconverted man.* Such persons cannot say this petition of the Lord's prayer, *Lead us not into temptation.* They *plunge* into it of their own accord.

For what fellowship, &c.] As *righteousness* cannot have communion with *unrighteousness,* and *light* can-not dwell with *darkness ;* so *Christ* can have no con-cord with *Belial,* nor can he that *believeth* have any with an *infidel.* All these points were self-evident ; how then could they keep up the *profession* of Chris-tianity, or pretend to be under its influence, while they *associated* with the *unrighteous,* had *communion* with *darkness,* concord with *Belial,* and partook with *infidels?*

Verse 16. *What agreement hath the temple of God with idols*] Nothing could appear more abominable to a Jew than an idol in the temple of God : here, then, could be no agreement ; the worship of the two is wholly incompatible. An *idolater* never worships the true God ; a *Christian* never worships an idol. If ye join in idolatrous rites, it is impossible that ye should be *Christians.*

Ye are the temple of the living God] God intends to make the heart of every believer his own house.

I will dwell in them, and walk in them] The words are very emphatic : ενοικησω εν αυτοις· *I will inhabit in them.* I will not be as a *wayfaring* man, who turns aside to tarry as for a *night,* but I will take up

my *constant residence* with them ; I will dwell *in* and *among* them.

I will be their God] They shall have no other God, they shall have none besides me ; and if they take me for their God, I will be to them all that an infinite, eternal, and self-sufficient Being can be to his intel-ligent offspring.

They shall be my people.] If they take me for their GOD, their supreme and eternal GOOD, I will take them for my *people ;* and instruct, enlighten, defend, provide for, support, and bless them, as if I had none else to care for in the creation.

Verse 17. *Wherefore come out from among them*] Is it not plain from this and the following verse that God would be their God only on the ground of *their taking him for such,* and that this depended on their being *separated* from the works and workers of ini-quity ? for God could not *inhabit in them* if they had concord with Belial, a portion with infidels, &c. Those who will have the promises of God fulfilled to them must come under the *conditions* of these pro-mises : if they are not *separate*—if they *touch the unclean thing,* God will not receive them ; and there-fore will not be their God, nor shall they be his people.

Verse 18. *Will be a Father unto you*] I will act towards you as the most affectionate father can act towards his most tender and best beloved child.

And ye shall be my sons and daughters] Ye shall all be of the *household* of God, the *family* of heaven ; ye shall be *holy, happy,* and *continually safe.*

Saith the Lord Almighty.] Κυριος παντοκρατωρ· The *Lord,* the *Governor of all things.*

Earthly fathers, however loving and affectionate, may fail to provide for their children, because every thing is not at *their disposal ;* they may frequently lack both the *power* and the *means,* though to *will* may be present with them ; but the Lord who *made* and who *governs all things* can never lack *will, power,* nor *means.* The promise is sure to the *children ;* and the *children* are those who *take the Almighty for their God.* For the promise belongs to no soul that is not *separate* from sinful ways, works, and men ; those who *touch the unclean thing,* i. e. who *do* what God *forbids,* and hold communion with unrighteousness, can never stand in the endearing relation of *children* to God Almighty : and this is most forcibly stated by God himself in these verses, and in the beginning

2

of the following chapter, the first verse of which should conclude this.

To the *Jews* the promises were originally made; they would not have God for their God, but *would* work iniquity. What was the consequence? God cast them off; and those who were *joined to iniquity* were *separated* from *him.* " Then said God, Call his name *Lo-ammi; for ye are not my people*, and *I will not be your God.*" Hos. i. 9. The *Jews* were therefore cast off, and the *Gentiles* taken in their place; but even these, under the new covenant, are taken in expressly under the *same conditions* as the apostle here most fully states. Those who apply these words in any other way pervert their meaning, and sin against their souls.

CHAPTER VII.

The apostle's inference from the preceding exhortation, 1. *He presses them to receive him with affection, because of his great love towards them,* 2–4. *He tells them what distress he felt on their account in Macedonia, till he had met with Titus, and heard of their prosperity,* 5–7. *He rejoices that his first epistle was made the means of their reformation,* 8, 9. *States how they were affected by his letter, and the process of their reformation,* 10, 11. *Shows why he had written to them,* 12. *Rejoices that his boasting of them to Titus is found to be a truth; and takes occasion to mention the great affection of Titus for them, and his own confidence in them,* 13–16.

A. M. 4061.
A. D. 57.
A. U. C.
810.
Anno Imp. Neronis Cæs. 4.

HAVING [a] therefore these promises, dearly beloved, let us cleanse ourselves from all filthiness of the flesh and spirit, perfecting holiness in the fear of God.

2 Receive us; we have wronged no man, we have corrupted

A. M. 4061.
A. D. 57.
A. U. C.
810.
Anno Imp. Neronis Cæs. 4.

---

[a] Chap. vi. 17, 18; 1 John iii. 3; Isa. i. 16; viii, 13; xxix. 23; 1 Thess, v. 23; 1 Tim. iv. 8.

NOTES ON CHAP. VII,

Verse 1. *Having therefore these promises*] The promises mentioned in the three last verses of the preceding chapter, to which this verse should certainly be joined.

Let us cleanse ourselves] Let us apply to him for the requisite grace of purification; and avoid every thing in spirit and practice which is opposite to the doctrine of God, and which has a tendency to pollute the soul.

Filthiness of the flesh] The apostle undoubtedly means, *drunkenness, fornication, adultery,* and all such sins as are done immediately *against the body;* and by *filthiness of the spirit*, all impure desires, unholy thoughts, and polluting imaginations. If we avoid and abhor evil inclinations, and turn away our eyes from beholding vanity, incentives to evil being thus lessened, (for the eye affects the heart,) there will be the less danger of our falling into outward sin. And if we avoid all *outward* occasions of sinning, evil propensities will certainly be lessened. All this is *our* work under the common aids of the grace of God. We may turn away our eyes and ears from evil, or we may indulge both in what will infallibly beget evil desires and tempers in the soul; and under the same influence we may avoid every *act* of iniquity; for even Satan himself cannot, by any power he has, *constrain* us to commit uncleanness, robbery, drunkenness, murder, &c. These are things in which both *body* and *soul* must consent. But still withholding the eye, the ear, the hand, and the body in general, from *sights, reports,* and *acts* of evil, will not purify a fallen spirit; it is the grace and Spirit of Christ alone, powerfully applied for this very purpose, that can purify the conscience and the heart from all dead works. But if we do not withhold the food by which the man of sin is nourished and supported, we cannot expect God to purify our hearts. While we are *striving against sin*, we may expect the Spirit of God to purify us by his inspiration from all unrighteousness, that we may perfectly love and magnify our Maker. How can those expect God to purify their hearts who are continually indulging their *eyes, ears,* and *hands* in what is forbidden, and in what tends to increase and bring into action all the evil propensities of the soul?

Perfecting holiness] Getting the whole mind of Christ brought into the soul. This is the grand object of a genuine Christian's pursuit. The means of accomplishing this are, 1. Resisting and avoiding sin, in all its inviting and seducing forms. 2. Setting the *fear of God* before our eyes, that we may dread his displeasure, and abhor whatever might excite it, and whatever might provoke him to withhold his manna from our mouth. We see, therefore, that there is a strong and orthodox sense in which we may *cleanse ourselves from all filthiness of the flesh and of the spirit*, and thus *perfect holiness in the fear of God.*

Verse 2. *Receive us*] Χωρησατε ημας. This address is variously understood. *Receive us* into your *affections*—love us as we love you. *Receive us* as your *apostles* and *teachers*; we have given you full proof that God hath both sent and owned us. *Receive, comprehend,* what we now say to you, and carefully mark it.

We have wronged no man] We have never acted contrary to the strictest justice.

We have corrupted no man] With any false doctrine or pernicious opinion.

We have defrauded no man.] Of any part of his property. But what have your false teachers done?

2

A. M. 4061.
A. D. 57.
A. U. C.
810.
Anno Imp. Nero-
nis Cæs. 4.

no man, [b] we have defrauded no man.

3 I speak not *this* to condemn *you:* for [c] I have said before, that ye are in our hearts to die and live with *you.*

4 [d] Great *is* my boldness of speech toward you, [e] great *is* my glorying of you : [f] I am filled with comfort, I am exceeding joyful in all our tribulation.

5 For, [g] when we were come into Macedonia, our flesh had no rest, but [h] we were troubled on every side ; [i] without *were* fightings, within *were* fears.

6 Nevertheless [k] God, that comforteth those that are cast down, comforted us by [l] the coming of Titus ;

7 And not by his coming only, but by the consolation wherewith he was comforted in you, when he told us your earnest desire, your mourning, your fervent mind toward me ; so that I rejoiced the more.

8 For though I made you sorry with a letter, I do not repent, [m] though I did repent : for I perceive that the same epistle hath made you sorry, though *it were* but for a season.

A. M. 4061.
A. D. 57.
A. U. C.
810.
Anno Imp. Nero-
nis Cæs. 4.

---

[b] Acts xx. 33 ; chap. xii. 17.——[c] Chap. vi. 11, 12.——[d] Chap. iii. 12.
[e] 1 Cor. i. 4 ; chap. i. 14.——[f] Chap. i. 4 ; Phil. ii. 17 ; Col. i. 24.
[g] Chap. ii. 13.——[h] Chap. iv. 8.——[i] Deut. xxxii. 25.——[k] Chap. i. 4.——[l] See chap. ii. 13.——[m] Chap. ii. 4.

They *have beguiled you from the simplicity of the truth*, and thus *corrupted your minds.* Chap. xi. 3. They have *brought you into bondage ;* they have *taken of you ; devoured you ; axalted themselves against you,* and ye have patiently *suffered* all this. Chap. xi. 20. It is plain that he refers here to the false apostle or teacher which they had among them.

Verse 3. I speak not this *to condemn* you] I do not speak to reproach but to correct you. I wish you to open your eyes and see how you are corrupted, spoiled, and impoverished by those whom ye have incautiously preferred to the true apostles of Jesus Christ.

I have said before, that ye are in our hearts] He has in effect and substance said this, chap. i. 6–8 ; ii. 4, 12 ; iii. 2 ; and ver. 13 ; where see the passages at length, and the notes.

To die and live with you.] An expression which points out the strongest affection, as in cases where love blinds us to the faults of those whom we love, and causes us to prefer them to all others ; like that in *Horace :*—

Quanquam sidere pulchrior
    Ille est, tu levior cortice, et improbo
Iracundior Adria.

    Tecum vivere amem, tecum obeam libens.
                ODAR. lib. iii. Od. ix. ver. 21.

" Though he exceed in beauty far
    The rising lustre of a star ;
Though light as cork thy fancy strays,
Thy passions wild as angry seas
When vex'd with storms ; *yet gladly I*
With thee would live, with thee would die."
                FRANCIS.

From all appearance there never was a Church less worthy of an apostle's affections than this Church was at this time ; and yet no one ever more beloved. The above quotation applies to this case in full force.

Verse 4. Great is *my boldness of speech*] He seems to refer to the manner in which he spoke of them to *others.*

Great is *my glorying of you*] They had probably been very loving and affectionate previously to the time in which they were perverted by their false apostle. He therefore *had* boasted of them in all the Churches.

I am filled with comfort] My affection for you has still the most powerful ascendancy in my soul. Here we may see the affection of the most tender father to his children.

I am exceeding joyful] Ὑπερπερισσευομαι· I superabound in joy ; I have a joy beyond expression.— Ὑπερπερισσευω is an extremely rare verb. I have not met with it in any Greek author ; and it occurs no where in the New Testament but here and in Rom. v. 20.

In all our tribulation.] Perhaps επι here should be rendered *under* instead of *in,* as it signifies, Mark ii. 26 ; Luke iii. 2 ; Acts xi. 28. *Under* all our *tribulations, I feel inexpressible joy on your account.*

Verse 5. When we were come into Macedonia] St. Paul, having left Ephesus, came to Troas, where he stopped some time ; afterwards he came to Macedonia, whence he wrote this epistle,

Our flesh had no rest] So exceedingly anxious was he to know the success of his first epistle to them.

Without were *fightings*] The oppositions of pagans, Jews, and false brethren.

Within were *fears.*] Uncertain conjectures relative to the success of his epistle ; fears lest the severity of it should alienate their affections utterly from him ; fears lest the party of the incestuous person should have prevailed ; fears lest the teaching of the false apostle should have perverted their minds from the simplicity of the truth ; all was uncertainty, all apprehension ; and the Spirit of God did not think proper to remove the causes of these apprehensions in any extraordinary way.

Verse 6. Comforted us by the coming of Titus] Who brought him a most satisfactory account of the success of his epistle, and the good state of the Corinthian Church.

Verse 7. He told us your earnest desire] To see me, and correct what was amiss among yourselves.

Your mourning] Because you had sinned.

Your fervent mind] The zeal you felt to testify your affectionate regard for me.

Verse 8. I do not repent, though I did repent] Though I had many doubts in my mind concerning the

A. M. 4061.
A. D. 57.
A. U. C.
810.
Anno Imp. Nero-
nis Cæs. 4.

9 Now I rejoice, not that ye were made sorry, but that ye sorrowed to repentance : for ye were made sorry [n] after a godly manner, that ye might receive damage by us in nothing.

10 For [o] godly sorrow worketh repentance to salvation, not to be repented of : [p] but the sorrow of the world worketh death.

11 For behold this self-same thing, that ye sorrowed after a godly sort, what carefulness it wrought in you ; yea, *what* clearing of yourselves ; yea, *what* indignation ; yea, *what* fear ; yea, *what* vehement desire ; yea, *what*

zeal ; yea, *what* revenge ! In all *things* ye have approved yourselves to be clear in this matter.

A. M. 4061.
A. D. 57.
A. U. C.
810.
Anno Imp. Nero-
nis Cæs. 4.

12 Wherefore, though I wrote unto you, *I did it* not for his cause that had done the wrong, nor for his cause that suffered wrong, [q] but that our care for you in the sight of God might appear unto you.

13 Therefore we were comforted in your comfort : yea, and exceedingly the more joyed we for the joy of Titus, because his spirit [r] was refreshed by you all.

14 For if I have boasted any thing to him of you, I am not ashamed ; but as we spake

---

[n] Or, *according to God.*——[o] 2 Sam. xii. 13 ; Matt. xxvi. 75.

[p] Prov. xvii. 22.——[q] Chap. ii. 4.——[r] Rom. xv. 32.

---

success of my letter ; and though I grieved that I was obliged to write with so much severity, the case absolutely requiring it ; yet now I am not sorry that I have written that letter, because I find it has completely answered the end for which it was sent.

Verse 9. Ye sorrowed to repentance] Ye had such a sorrow as produced a complete change of mind and conduct. We see that a man may *sorrow,* and yet not *repent.*

Made sorry after a godly manner] It was not a sorrow because ye were found out, and thus solemnly reprehended, but a sorrow because ye had sinned against God, and which consideration caused you to grieve more than the apprehension of any punishment.

Damage by us in nothing.] Your repentance prevented that exercise of my apostolic duty, which would have consigned your bodies to destruction, that your souls might be saved in the day of the Lord Jesus.

Verse 10. For godly sorrow] That which has the breach of God's holy law for its object.

Worketh repentance] A thorough *change of mind unto salvation,* because the person who feels it cannot rest till he finds *pardon* through the mercy of God.

But the sorrow of the world worketh death.] Sorrow for lost goods, lost friends, death of relatives, &c., when it is poignant and deep, produces diseases, increases those that already exist, and often leads men to lay desperate hands on themselves. This sorrow leads to destruction, the other leads to salvation ; the one leads to *heaven,* the other to *hell.*

Verse 11. What carefulness it wrought in you] Carefulness of obeying my directions, ver. 15 ; *yea, what clearing of yourselves* from guilt by inflicting censures on the guilty person, and putting away evil from among you, 1 Cor. xv. 18 ; *yea, what indignation* against him who had dishonoured his profession, and defiled the Church ; *yea, what fear* of my displeasure, and the *rod* which I threatened, 1 Cor. iv. 21 ; *yea, what vehement desire* to rectify what was amiss in this matter, ver. 7 ; *yea, what zeal* for me ; *yea, what revenge* in punishing the delinquent. See *Whitby.*

In all things, *&c.*] In the whole of your conduct in this affair since ye have received my letter, *ye have*

approved yourselves to be clear, ἁγνους ; not only to be clear of contumacy and obstinate persistance in your former conduct, but to have done all in the compass of your power to rectify the abuses which had crept in among you. The Corinthians were not *clear,* i. e. innocent or void of blame in the fact, but they were *clear* of all blame in their endeavours to remove the evil.

Verse 12. Not for his cause that had done the wrong] Viz. the incestuous person.

Nor for his cause that suffered wrong] Some think the apostle means *himself* ; others, that he means the *Church* at Corinth, the *singular* being put for the *plural* ; others, the *family* of the incestuous person ; and others, the *father* of the incestuous person. If this latter opinion be adopted, it would seem to intimate that the father of this person was yet *alive,* which would make the transgression more flagrant ; but these words might be spoken in reference to the father, if *dead,* whose cause should be vindicated ; as his injured honour might be considered, like Abel's blood, to be crying from the earth.

But that our care for you—might appear] It was not to get the delinquent punished, nor merely to do justice to those who had suffered in this business, that the apostle wrote his epistle to them, but that they might have the fullest proof of his fatherly affection for them, and his concern for the honour of God ; and that they might thereby see how unnatural their opposition to him was, and what cause they had to prefer him, who was ready to give up his life in their service, to that false apostle or teacher who was corrupting their minds, leading them from the simplicity of the truth, and making a gain of them.

Verse 13. For the joy of Titus] Titus, who had now met St. Paul in Macedonia, gave him the most flattering accounts of the improved state of the Corinthian Church ; and indeed their kind usage of Titus was a full proof of their affection for St. Paul.

Verse 14. For if I have boasted] The apostle had given Titus a very high character of this Church, and of their attachment to himself ; and doubtless this was the case previously to the evil teacher getting among them, who had succeeded in changing their conduct, and changing in a great measure their character also ;

2

A. M. 4061.
A. D. 57.
A. U. C.
810.
Anno Imp. Nero-
nis Cæs. 4.

all things to you in truth, even so our boasting, which *I made* before Titus, is found a truth.

15 And his *ˢ inward affection* is more abundant toward you, whilst he re-

membereth ᵗ the obedience of you all, how with fear and trembling ye received him.

16 I rejoice, therefore, that ᵘ I have confidence in you in all *things.*

A. M. 4061.
A. D. 57.
A. U. C.
810.
Anno Imp. Nero-
nis Cæs. 4.

ˢ Gr. *bowels;* chap. vi. 12.——ᵗ Chap. ii. 9; Phil. ii. 12.

ᵘ 2 Thess. iii. 4; Philem. 8, 21.

---

but now they return to themselves, resume their lost ground, so that the good character which the apostle gave them before, and which they had for a time forfeited, is now as applicable to them as ever. Therefore his *boasting of them is still found a truth.*

Verse 15. *And his inward affection*] Τα σπλαγχνα αυτου· *Those bowels of his*—his most tender affection. For the meaning of this word see the note on Matt. ix. 36.

Whilst he remembereth the obedience of you all] This is a very natural picture; he represents Titus as overjoyed even while he is delivering his account of the Corinthian Church. He expatiated on it with extreme delight, and thereby showed at once both his love for St. Paul and his love for them. He loved them because they so loved the apostle; and he loved them because they had shown such kindness to himself; and he loved them because he found so many excellent and rare gifts, joined to so much humility, producing such an exemplary and holy life.

With fear and trembling ye received him.] Ye *reverenced* his authority; ye were *obedient* to his directions; and ye *dreaded* lest any thing should be undone or ill done which he had delivered to you in the name of God.

Verse 16. *I have confidence in you, in all things.*] It appears that the apostle was now fully persuaded, from the accounts given by Titus, that every scandal had been put away from this Church; that the faction which had long distracted and divided them was nearly broken; that all was on the eve of being restored to its primitive purity and excellence; and that their character was now so firmly fixed, that there was no reason to apprehend that they should be again tossed to and fro with every wind of doctrine.

1. Thus a happy termination was put to an affair that seemed likely to ruin the Christian Church, not only t Corinth, but through all Greece; for, if this bad

man, who had been chief in opposing the apostle's authority, bringing in licentious doctrines, and denying the resurrection of the dead, had ultimately succeeded at Corinth, his doctrine and influence might soon have extended over Greece and Asia Minor, and the great work of God which had been wrought in those parts would have been totally destroyed. This one consideration is sufficient to account for the apostle's great anxiety and distress on account of the divisions and heresies at Corinth. He knew it was a most pernicious leaven; and, unless destroyed, must destroy the work of God. The loss of the affections of the Church at Corinth, however much it might affect the tender, fatherly heart of the apostle, cannot account for the awful apprehensions, poignant distress, and deep anguish, which he, in different parts of these epistles, so feelingly describes; and which he describes as having been invariably his portion from the time that he heard of their perversion, till he was assured of their restoration by the account brought by Titus.

2. A scandal or heresy in the Church of God is ruinous at all times, but particularly so when the cause is in its infancy; and therefore the messengers of God cannot be too careful to lay the foundation well in *doctrine*, to establish the strictest *discipline*, and to be very cautious whom they admit and accredit as members of the Church of Christ. It is certain that the *door* should be *opened wide* to admit penitent sinners; but the *watchman* should ever stand by, to see that no improper person enter in. Christian prudence should ever be connected with Christian zeal. It is a great work to bring sinners to Christ; it is a greater work to preserve them in the faith; and it requires much grace and much wisdom to keep the Church of Christ pure, not only by not permitting the unholy to enter, but by casting out those who apostatize or work iniquity. *Slackness* in *discipline* generally precedes *corruption* of *doctrine;* the *former* generating the *latter.*

CHAPTER VIII.

The apostle stirs them up to make a collection for the poor Christians at Jerusalem, by the very liberal contributions of the people of Macedonia for the same purpose, who were comparatively a poor people, 1–5. He tells them that he had desired Titus to finish this good work among them which he had begun; hoping that as they abounded in many excellent gifts and graces, they would abound in this also, 6–8. He exhorts them to this by the example of Jesus Christ, who, though rich, subjected himself to voluntary poverty, that they might be enriched, 9. He shows them that this contribution, which had been long ago begun, should have been long since finished, 10. And that they should do every thing with a ready and willing mind, according to the ability which God had given them; that abundance should not prevail on one hand, while pinching poverty ruled on the other; but that there should be an equality, 11–14. He shows from the distribution of the manna in the wilderness, that the design of God was, that every member of his spiritual household should have the necessaries of life, 15. He tells them that he had now sent Titus, and another with him, to Corinth, to complete this great work, 16–22. The character which he gives of Titus and the others employed in this business, 23, 24.

2

A. M. 4061
A. D. 57.
A. U. C.
810.
Anno Imp. Nero-
nis Cæs. 4.

MOREOVER, brethren, we do you to wit of the grace of God bestowed on the Churches of Macedonia;

2 How that, in a great trial of affliction, the abundance of their joy and ^a their deep poverty abounded unto the riches of their ^b liberality.

3 For to *their* power, I bear record, yea, and beyond *their* power, *they were* willing of themselves;

4 Praying us with much entreaty that we would receive the gift, and *take upon us* ^c the

fellowship of the ministering to the saints.

A. M. 4061
A. D. 57
A. U. C.
810.
Anno Imp. Nero
nis Cæs. 4.

5 And *this did they*, not as we hoped, but first gave their own selves to the Lord, and unto us by the will of God;

6 Insomuch that ^d we desired Titus, that as he had begun, so he would also finish in you the same ^e grace also.

7 Therefore, as ^f ye abound in every *thing*, *in* faith, and utterance, and knowledge, and *in* all diligence, and *in* your love to us, see ^g that ye abound in this grace also.

---

^a Mark xii. 44.——^b Gr. *simplicity*; chap. ix. 11.——^c Acts xi. 29; xxiv. 17; Rom. xv. 25, 26; 1 Cor. xvi. 1, 3, 4; chap. ix. 1.

^d Ver. 17; chap. xii. 18.——^e Or, *gift*; ver. 4, 19.——^f 1 Cor. i. 5; xii. 13.——^g Chap. ix. 8.

NOTES ON CHAP. VIII.

Verse 1. *Moreover, brethren, we do you to wit*] In all our dignified version very few ill-constructed sentences can be found; however here is one, and the worst in the book. *We do you to wit* is in the original γνωριζομεν δε υμιν, *we make known unto you*. This is plain and intelligible, the other is not so; and the form is now obsolete.

The grace of God bestowed] Dr. Whitby has made it fully evident that the χαρις Θεου signifies the charitable ·contribution made by the Churches in Macedonia, to which they were excited by the grace or influence of God upon their hearts; and that δεδομε-νην εν cannot signify *bestowed on*, but *given in*. That χαρις means *liberality*, appears from ver. 6 : *We desired Titus that as he had begun, so he would finish* την χαριν ταυτην, *this charitable contribution*. And ver. 7 : That ye abound εν ταυτη τη χαριτι, *in this liberal contribution*. And ver. 19 : Who was chosen of the Church to travel with us συν τη χαριτι ταυτη, *with this charitable contribution, which is administered*—which is to be *dispensed, by us*. So chap. ix. 8 : *God is able to make* πασαν χαριν, *all liberality, to abound towards you*. And 1 Cor. xvi. 3 : *To bring* την χαριν, *your liberality*, to the poor saints. Hence χαρις is by *Hesychius* and *Phavorinus* interpreted a *gift*, as it is here by the apostle : *Thanks be to God for his unspeakable gift*, chap. ix. 15. This charity is styled the *grace of God*, either from its *exceeding greatness*, (as the *cedars of God* and *mountains of God* signify *great cedars* and *great mountains*, Psalm xxxvi. 6 ; lxxx. 10 ;) or rather, it is called so as proceeding from God, who is the dispenser of all good, and the giver of this disposition; for the motive of charity must come from him. So, in other places, *the zeal of God*, Rom. x. 2 ; *the love of God*, 2 Cor. v. 14 ; *the grace of God*, Tit. ii. 11.

The Churches of Macedonia] These were *Philippi, Thessalonica, Berea, &c.*

Verse 2. *In a great trial of affliction*] The sense of this verse is the following : The Macedonians, though both poor and persecuted, rejoiced exceedingly that an opportunity was afforded them of doing good to their *more impoverished* and *more persecuted* brethren. We can scarcely ever speak of *poverty* and

affliction in an *absolute* sense ; they are only *comparative*. Even the *poor* are called to *relieve* those who are *poorer* than themselves ; and the *afflicted*, to *comfort* those who are *more afflicted* than they are. The poor and afflicted Churches of Macedonia felt this duty, and therefore came forward to the uttermost of their power to relieve their *more* impoverished and afflicted brethren in Judea.

Verse 3. *For to their power, &c.*] In their liberality they had no *rule* but their ability ; they believed they were bound to contribute all they could ; and even this *rule* they transgressed, for they went *beyond their power*—they deprived themselves for a time of the *necessaries of life*, in order to give to others who were destitute even of *necessaries*.

Verse 4. *Praying us with much entreaty*] We had not to *solicit them* to this great act of kindness ; they even *entreated us* to accept their bounty, and to take on ourselves the administration or application of it to the wants of the poor in Judea.

Verse 5. *Not as we hoped*] They far exceeded our expectations, for they consecrated themselves entirely to the work of God ; *giving* themselves and all they possessed *first* unto the *Lord* ; and then, as they saw that it was the *will of God* that they should come especially forward in this charitable work, *they gave themselves to us*, to assist to the uttermost in providing relief for the suffering Christians in Judea.

Verse 6. *That we desired Titus*] Titus had probably laid the plan of this contribution when he was before at Corinth, according to the direction given by the apostle, 1 Cor. xvi. 1, &c.

The same grace] Liberality. See the note on ver. 1.

Verse 7. *As ye abound in every* thing] See the note on 1 Cor. i. 5. *In faith*, crediting the whole testimony of God ; *in utterance*, λογῳ, *in doctrine*, knowing what to teach ; *knowledge* of God's will, and prudence to direct you in teaching and doing it ; *in diligence*, to amend all that is wrong among you, and to do what is right ; *and in love to us*, whom *now* ye prize as the apostles of the Lord, and your pastors in him.

Abound in this grace also.] Be as eminent for your *charitable disposition* as ye are for your *faith*, doctrine, knowledge, diligence, and *love*

A. M. 4061.
A. D. 57.
A. U. C.
810.
Anno Imp. Nero-
nis Cæs. 4.

8 ʰ I speak not by commandment, but by occasion of the
forwardness of others, and to
prove the sincerity of your love.

9 For ye know the grace of our Lord Jesus Christ, ⁱ that, though he was rich, yet for
your sakes he became poor, that ye through
his poverty might be rich.

10 And herein ᵏ I give *my* advice : for ˡ this
is expedient for you, who have begun before,
not only to do, but also to be ᵐ forward ⁿ a
year ago.

11 Now therefore perform the doing *of it* ;

that as *there was* a readiness to
will, so *there may be* a performance also out of that which ye
have.

A. M. 4061.
A. D. 57.
A. U. C.
810.
Anno Imp. Nero-
nis Cæs. 4.

12 For ᵒ if there be first a willing mind, *it
is* accepted according to that a man hath, *and*
not according to that he hath not.

13 For *I* mean not that other men be eased,
and ye burdened :

14 But by an equality, *that* now at this time
your abundance *may be a supply* for their
want ; that their abundance also may be *a supply* for your want, that there may be equality :

ʰ 1 Cor. vii. 6.——ⁱ Matt. viii. 20 ; Luke ix. 58 ; Phil. ii. 6, 7.
ᵏ 1 Cor. vii. 25.——ˡ Prov. xix. 17 ; Matt. x. 42 ; 1 Tim. vi. 18,

19 ; Heb. xiii. 16.——ᵐ Gr. *willing.*——ⁿ Chap. ix. 2.——ᵒ Mark
xii. 43, 44 ; Luke xxi. 3.

Verse 8. *I speak not by commandment*] I do not
positively order this ; I assume no right or authority
over your *property* ; what you devote of your substance
to charitable purposes must be your own work, and a
free-will offering.

The forwardness of others] Viz. the Churches of
Macedonia, which had already exerted themselves so
very much in this good work. And the apostle here
intimates that he takes this opportunity to apprise
them of the zeal of the Macedonians, lest those at
Corinth, who excelled in every other gift, should be
outdone in this. Their own *honour*, if better motives
were absent, would induce them to exert themselves,
that they might not be outdone by others. And then,
as they had professed great love for the apostle, and
this was a service that lay near his heart, they would
prove the *sincerity* of that professed love by a liberal contribution for the afflicted and destitute Jewish
Christians.

Verse 9. *For ye know the grace of our Lord Jesus
Christ*] This was the strongest argument of all ; and
it is urged home by the apostle with admirable address.

Ye know] Ye are acquainted with God's ineffable
love in sending Jesus Christ into the world ; and ye
know the *grace*—the infinite benevolence of Christ
himself.

That, though he was rich] The possessor, as he
was the creator, of the heavens and the earth ; *for
your sakes he became poor*—he emptied himself, and
made himself of no reputation, and took upon himself
the form of a servant, and humbled himself unto death,
even the death of the cross ; *that ye, through his
poverty*—through his humiliation and death, *might be
rich*—might regain your forfeited inheritance, and be
enriched with every grace of his Holy Spirit, and
brought at last to his eternal glory.

If Jesus Christ, as some contend, were only a *mere
man*, in what sense could he be said to be *rich* ? His
family was *poor* in Bethlehem ; his *parents* were very
poor also ; he *himself* never possessed any *property*
among men from the *stable* to the *cross* ; nor had he
any thing to *bequeath* at his death but his *peace.* And
in what way could the *poverty* of one man make a
multitude *rich* ? These are questions which, on the

Socinian scheme, can never be satisfactorily answered.

Verse 10. *Herein I give* my *advice*] For I speak
not by way of *commandment*, ver. 8.

For this is expedient for you] It is necessary you
should do this to preserve a *consistency of conduct* ;
for ye began this work a *year ago*, and it is necessary
that ye should complete it as soon as possible.

Not only (to do, but also to be forward] Το ποιησαι
—και το θελειν, literally, *to do and to will* ; but as the
will must be *before* the *deed*, θελειν must be taken here
in the sense of *delight*, as it frequently means in the Old
and New Testaments. See several examples in *Whitby.*
Some MSS. transpose the words · allowing this,
there is no difficulty.

A year ago.] Απο περυσι. It was about a year
before this that the apostle, in his first epistle, chap.
xvi. 2, had exhorted them to make this contribution ;
and there is no doubt that they, in obedience to his
directions, had begun to lay up in store for this charitable purpose ; he therefore wishes them to complete
this good work, and thus show that they were not led
to it by the example of the Macedonians, seeing they
themselves had been *first movers* in this business.

Verse 11. *A readiness to will, so there may be a
performance*] Ye have *willed* and *purposed* this :
now *perform* it.

Out of that which ye have.] Give as God has
enabled you ; and give as God has *disposed* you. He
requires each man to do as he *can* ; and accepts the
will where the *means* are wanting to perform the *deed.*

Verse 12. *According to that a man hath*] According
to his *real property* ; not taking that which belongs to
his own *family*, and is indispensably necessary for
their support ; and not taking that which belongs to
others ; viz. what he *owes* to any man.

Verse 13. *That other men be eased*] I do not de
sign that you should impoverish yourselves in order
that others may live affluently.

Verse 14. *But by an equality*] That you may do to
those who are distressed now, as, on a change of circumstances, you would wish them to do to you. And
I only wish that of your *abundance* you would now
minister to their wants ; and it may be that *then*

A. M. 4061.
A. D. 57.
A. U. C. 810.
Anno Imp. Neronis Cæs. 4.

15 As it is written, ᑫ He that *had gathered* much had nothing over ; and he that *had gathered* little had no lack.

16 But thanks *be* to God, which put the same earnest care into the heart of Titus for you.

17 For indeed he accepted ᑫ the exhortation ; but being more forward, of his own accord he went unto you.

18 And we have sent with him ʳ the brother, whose praise *is* in the Gospel throughout all the Churches ;

19 And not *that* only, but who was also ˢ chosen of the Churches to travel with us with

this ᵗ grace, which is administered by us ᵘ to the glory of the same Lord, and *declaration of* your ready mind :

A. M. 4061.
A. D. 57.
A. U. C. 810.
Anno Imp. Neronis Cæs. 4.

20 Avoiding this, that no man should blame us in this abundance which is administered by us :

21 ᵛ Providing for honest things, not only in the sight of the Lord, but also in the sight of men.

22 And we have sent with them our brother, whom we have oftentimes proved diligent in many things ; but now much more diligent, upon the great confidence which ʷ *I have* in you.

23 Whether *any do inquire* of Titus, he is

ᵖ Exod. xvi. 18.——ᑫ Ver. 6.——ʳ Chap. xii. 18.——ˢ 1 Cor. xvi. 3, 4.——ᵗ Or, *gift* ; ver. 4, 6, 7 ; chap. ix. 8.

ᵘ Chapter iv. 15.——ᵛ Romans xii. 17 ; Phil. iv. 8 ; 1 Peter ii. 12.——ʷ Or, he hath.

---

abundance may yet *supply your wants ;* for so liable are all human affairs to *change*, that it is as possible that you rich Corinthians should need the charitable help of others as it is that those Jews, who once had need of nothing, should now be dependent on your bounty.

That there may be equality] That ye may exert yourselves so in behalf of those poor people that there may be between you an *equality* in the *necessaries* of life ; your abundance supplying them with that of which they are utterly destitute.

Verse 15. *He that* had gathered *much, had nothing over*] On the passage to which the apostle alludes, Exod. xvi. 18, I have stated that, probably, every man gathered as much manna as he could, and when he brought it home and measured it by the *omer*, (for this was the measure for each man's eating,) if he had a surplus it went to the supply of some other family that had not been able to collect enough ; the family being *large*, and the *time* in which the manna might be gathered, before the heat of the day, not being sufficient to collect a supply for so numerous a household ; several of whom might be so confined as not to be able to collect for themselves. Thus there was an *equality* among the Israelites in reference to this thing ; and in this light these words of St. Paul lead us to view the passage. To apply this to the present case : the Corinthians, in the course of God's providence, had *gathered more* than was absolutely necessary for their own support ; by giving the surplus to the persecuted and impoverished Christian Jews there would be an *equality* ; both would then possess the *necessaries* of life, though still the one might have more *property* than the other.

Verse 16. *But thanks* be to God] He thanks God who had already disposed the heart of Titus to attend to this business ; and, with his usual address, considers all this as done in the behalf of the *Corinthian* Church ; and that though the poor Christians in *Judea* are to have the *immediate benefit*, yet God put *honour* upon them in making them his instruments in supplying the wants of others. He who is an almoner to God Almighty is highly honoured indeed.

Verse 17. *He accepted the exhortation*] I advised him to visit you and excite you to this good work, and I found that he was already disposed in his heart to do it ; God put this earnest care in the heart of Titus for you, ver. 16.

Verse 18. *The brother, whose praise* is *in the Gospel*] Who this *brother* was we cannot tell ; some suppose it was St. Luke, who wrote a gospel, and who was the companion of St. Paul in several of his travels ; others think it was *Silas* ; others, *Barnabas* ; others, *Mark* ; and others, *Apollos*. Neither ancients nor moderns agree in either ; but *Luke, John,* and *Mark*, seem to have the most probable opinions in their favour. Whoever the person was he was sufficiently known to the Corinthians, as we learn by what the apostle says of him in this place.

Verse 19. *Chosen of the Churches to travel with us*] Χειροτονηθεις· Appointed by a *show of hands ;* from χειρ the *hand*, and τεινω, to *extend*. This appointment, by the suffrage of the Churches, seems to refer more to St. *Luke* than any one else ; unless we suppose he refers to the transaction, Acts xv. 40, 41, and then it would appear that *Silas* is the person intended.

With this grace] Liberal contribution. See on ver. 1.

Your ready mind.] Your willingness to relieve them. But, instead of ὑμων, *your*, ἡμων, *our*, is the reading of almost all the best MSS. and all the versions. This is, doubtless, the true reading.

Verse 20. *Avoiding this, that no man should blame us*] Taking this prudent caution to have witnesses of our conduct, and such as were chosen by the Churches themselves, that we might not be suspected of having either embezzled or misapplied their bounty. See the note on 1 Cor. xvi. 4.

Verse 21. *Providing for honest things*] Taking care to act so as not only to be clear in the sight of God, but also to be clear in the sight of all men ; avoiding even the appearance of evil. I wish the reader to refer to the excellent note on 1 Cor. xvi. 4, which I have extracted from Dr. *Paley*.

Verse 22. *We have sent with them*] Titus and, probably, *Luke, our brother*, probably *Apollos*.

A. M. 4061.
A. D. 57.
A. U. C.
810.
Anno Imp. Neronis Cæs. 4.

my partner ⸳and fellow helper concerning you : or our brethren *be inquired of, they are* ˣ the messengers of the Churches, *and* the glory of Christ.

ˣ Phil. ii. 25.

Now much more diligent] Finding that I have the fullest confidence in your complete reformation and love to me, he engages in this business with alacrity, and exceeds even his former diligence.

Verse 23. *Whether any do inquire of Titus*] Should it be asked, *Who is this* Titus? I answer, he is my companion, and my fellow labourer in reference to you; chap. ii. 13 ; vii. 6, 7. Should any inquire, Who are these *brethren*, Luke and Apollos? I answer, *They are* Αποστολοι, *apostles of the Churches*, and intensely bent on promoting the *glory of Christ.*

Verse 24. *Wherefore show ye to them, and before the Churches, &c.*] Seeing they are persons every way *worthy* in themselves, and coming to you on such an *important* occasion, and so highly recommended, receive them affectionately ; and let them thus see that the very high character I have given of you is not exaggerated, and that you are as ready in every work of charity as I have stated you to be. Act in this for your honour.

1. THE whole of this chapter and the following is occupied in exciting the *richer* followers of Christ to be liberal to the *poorer ;* the *obligation* of each to be so, the *reasons* on which that obligation is founded, the *arguments* to enforce the obligation from those

24 Wherefore show ye to them, and before the Churches, the proof of your love, and of our ʸ boasting on your behalf.

A. M. 4061.
A. D. 57.
A. U. C.
810.
Anno Imp. Neronis Cæs. 4.

Chap. vii. 14 ; ix. 2.

reasons, are all clearly stated, and most dexterously and forcibly managed. These two chapters afford a perfect model for a Christian minister who is pleading the cause of the poor.

2. In the management of charities a man ought carefully to avoid the least suspicion of avarice, self-interest, and unfaithfulness. How few persons are entirely free from the upbraidings of their own consciences in the matter of alms! But who will be able to hear the upbraidings of Christ at the time of death and judgment? No man can waste without injustice, or neglect without sin, those things of which he is only the dispenser and steward.

3. God has not settled an *equality* among men by their *birth* to the end that this equality might be the work of his grace. He has put the *temporal portion* of the *poor* into the hands of the *rich*, and the *spiritual portion* of the rich into the hands of the poor, on purpose to keep up a good understanding betwixt the members of the same body by a mutual dependence on one another. He who withholds the part belonging to the poor steals more from himself than from them. Let every one answer this admirable design of God, and labour to re-establish *equality :* the *poor*, in *praying* much for the *rich ;* and the *rich*, in *giving* much to the *poor.*—See *Quesnel.*

CHAPTER IX.

St. Paul intimates that so ready were the Corinthians to make this charitable contribution, that it was scarcely necessary for him to write, 1, 2. But lest they should not be ready when he came, he had sent the brethren, Titus, &c., beforehand ; lest, if any of the Macedonians should come with him, they should find them not prepared, though he had boasted so much of their ready mind, 3–5. He gives them directions how they shall contribute ; and the advantage to be gained by it, in the fulfilment of the promises of God, 6–11. He shows them that by this means the poor shall be relieved, God glorified, their Christian temper manifested, and the prayers of many engaged in their behalf, 12–14. And concludes with giving thanks to God for his unspeakable gift, 15.

A. M. 4061.
A. D. 57.
A. U. C.
810.
Anno Imp. Neronis Cæs. 4.

FOR as touching ᵃ the ministering to the saints, it is superfluous for me to write to you :

2 For I know ᵇ the forwardness of your mind, ᶜ for which I boast of you to them of Macedonia, that ᵈ Achaia was ready a year

A. M. 4061.
A. D. 57.
A. U. C.
810.
Anno Imp. Neronis Cæs. 4.

ᵃ Acts xi. 29 ; Rom. xv. 26 ; 1 Cor. xvi. 1 ; chap. viii. 4 ; Gal.

ii. 10.——ᵇ Chap. viii. 19.——ᶜ Chap. viii. 24.——ᵈ Chap. viii. 10.

NOTES ON CHAP. IX.

Verse 1. *It is superfluous for me to write to you*] I need not *enlarge*, having already said enough. See the preceding chapter.

Verse 2. *I know the forwardness of your mind*] You have already *firmly purposed* to contribute to the support of the poor and suffering saints.

That Achaia was ready a year ago] The whole of the *Morea* was anciently called *Achaia*, the capital

of which was *Corinth.* The apostle means, not only *Corinth*, but other Churches in different parts about Corinth ; we know there was a Church at *Cenchrea*, one of the ports on the Corinthian Isthmus.

Your zeal hath provoked very many.] Hearing that the Corinthians were so intent on the relief of the sufferers in Palestine, other Churches, and especially they of *Macedonia*, came forward the more promptly and liberally.

A. M. 4061.
A. D. 57.
A. U. C.
810.
Anno Imp. Nero-
nis Cæs. 4.

ago; and your zeal hath provoked very many.

3 ^e Yet have I sent the brethren, lest our boasting of you should be in vain in this behalf; that, as I said, ye may be ready:

4 Lest haply if they of Macedonia come with me, and find you unprepared, we (that we say not, ye) should be ashamed in this same confident boasting.

5 Therefore I thought it necessary to exhort the brethren, that they would go before unto you, and make up beforehand your ^f bounty, ^g whereof ye had notice before, that the same might be ready, as a *matter of* bounty, and not as *of* covetousness.

6 ^h But this *I say*, He which soweth sparingly shall reap also sparingly; and he which soweth bountifully shall reap also bountifully.

7 Every man according as he purposeth in his heart, *so let him give;* ⁱ not grudgingly, or of necessity: for ^k God loveth a cheerful giver.

8 ^l And God *is* able to make all grace abound toward you; that ye, always having all sufficiency in all *things,* may abound to every good work:

9 (As it is written, ^m He hath dispersed abroad; he hath given to the poor: his righteousness remaineth for ever.

10 Now he that ⁿ ministereth seed to the

A. M. 4061.
A. D. 57.
A. U. C.
810.
Anno Imp. Nero-
nis Cæs. 4.

---

^e Chap. viii. 6, 17, 18, 22.——^f Gr. *blessing;* Gen. xxxiii. 11; 1 Sam. xxv. 27; 2 Kings v. 15.——^g Or, *which hath been so much spoken of before.*——^h Prov. xi. 24; xix. 17; xxii. 9; Gal. vi. 7, 9.

ⁱ Deut. xv. 7.——^k Exod. xxv. 2; xxxv. 5; Prov. xi. 25; Ecclus. xxxv. 9, 10; Rom. xii. 8; chap. viii. 12.——^l Prov. xi. 24, 25; xxviii. 27; Phil. iv. 19.——^m Psa. cxii. 9.——ⁿ Isa. lv. 10.

Verse 3. *Yet have I sent the brethren*] Titus and his companions, mentioned in the preceding chapter.

That, as I said, ye may be ready] And he wished them to be ready, that they might preserve the good character he had given them: this was for their *honour;* and if they did not take care to do so, he might be reputed a *liar;* and thus both they and himself be *ashamed* before the Macedonians, should any of them at this time accompany him to Corinth.

Verse 5. *Whereof ye had notice before*] Instead of προκατηγγελμενην, *spoken of before,* BCDEFG, several others, with the *Coptic, Vulgate, Itala,* and several of the *fathers,* have προεπηγγελμενην, *what was promised before.* The sense is not very different; probably the latter reading was intended to explain the former.—See the margin.

Bounty, and not as of covetousness.] Had they been *backward,* strangers might have attributed this to a *covetous* principle; as it would appear that they were loth to give up their money, and that they parted with it only when they could not for shame keep it any longer. This is the property of a *covetous* heart; whereas *readiness* to give is the characteristic of a *liberal* mind. This makes a sufficiently plain sense; and we need not look, as some have done, for any new sense of πλεονεξια, *covetousness,* as if it were here to be understood as implying a *small gift.*

Verse 6. *He which soweth sparingly*] This is a plain maxim: no man can expect to reap but in proportion as he has sowed. And here *almsgiving* is represented as a *seed sown,* which shall bring forth a *crop.* If the sowing be liberal, and the seed good, the crop shall be so too.

Sowing is used among the Jews to express *almsgiving:* so they understand Isa. xxxii. 20: *Blessed are ye who sow beside all waters;* i. e. who are ready to help every one that is in need. And Hos. x. 12, they interpret: *Sow to yourselves almsgiving, and ye shall reap in mercy*—if you show mercy to the poor, God will show mercy to you.

Verse 7. *Not grudgingly, or of necessity*] The Jews had in the temple *two chests* for alms; the one was של חובה of what was *necessary,* i. e. what the law required, the other was של נרבה of the *free-will offerings.* To escape perdition some would *grudgingly* give what *necessity* obliged them; others would give *cheerfully,* for the love of God, and through pity to the poor. Of the *first,* nothing is said; they simply did what the law required. Of the *second,* much is said; *God loves them.* The benefit of almsgiving is lost to the giver when he does it with a *grumbling heart.* And, as he does not do the *duty* in the *spirit* of the duty, even the performance of the *letter* of the law is an abomination in the sight of God.

To these two sorts of alms in the temple the apostle most evidently alludes. See *Schoettgen.*

Verse 8. *God is able to make all grace abound*] We have already seen, chap. viii. 1, that the word χαρις, in the connection in which the apostle uses it in these chapters, signifies a *charitable gift;* here it certainly has the same meaning: God is able to give you, in his mercy, abundance of temporal good; that, having a sufficiency, ye may abound in every good work. This refers to the *sowing plenteously:* those who do so shall *reap plenteously*—they shall have an abundance of God's blessings.

Verse 9. *He hath dispersed abroad*] Here is still the allusion to the *sower.* He *sows much;* not at *home* merely, or among those with whom he is acquainted, but *abroad*—among the *strangers,* whether of his own or of another nation. The quotation is taken from Psa. cxii. 9.

He hath given to the poor] This is the interpretation of *he hath scattered abroad;* and therefore it is said, *his righteousness remaineth for ever*—his good work is had in remembrance before God. By *righteousness* we have already seen that the Jews understand *almsgiving.* See the note on Matt. vi. 1.

Verse 10. *Now he that ministereth seed to the sower*] The *sower,* as we have already seen, is he that *gives*

2

A. M. 4061.
A. D. 57.
A. U. C.
810.
Anno Imp. Neronis Cæs. 4.

sower, both minister bread for *your* food, and multiply your seed sown, and increase the fruits of your ° righteousness ;)

11 Being enriched in every thing to all ᵖ bountifulness,�q ʳ which causeth through us thanksgiving to God.

12 For the administration of this service not only ˢ supplieth the want of the saints, but is abundant also by many thanksgivings unto God ;

13 Whiles by the experiment of this ministration they ᵗ glorify God for your professed subjection unto the Gospel of Christ, and for *your* liberal ᵘ distribution unto them, and unto all *men ;*

14 And by their prayer for you, which long after you for the exceeding ᵛ grace of God in you.

15 Thanks *be* unto God ʷ for his unspeakable gift.

A. M. 4061.
A. D. 57.
A. U. C.
810.
Anno Imp. Nero nis Cæs. 4.

ˢ Hos. x. 12 ; Matt. vi. 1.——ᵖ Or, *liberality.*——q Gr. *simplicity ;* chap. viii. 2.——ʳ Chap. i. 11 ; iv. 15.

ˢ Chap. viii. 14.——ᵗ Matt. v. 16.——ᵘ Heb. xiii. 16.——ᵛ Chap. viii. 1.——ʷ James i. 17.

---

alms of what he hath ; and God, who requires him to give these alms, is here represented as *providing* him with the *means.* As in the creation, if God had not created the earth *with every tree and plant with its seed in itself,* so that a *harvest* came, without a *previous ploughing and sowing,* there could have been no seed to deposit in the earth ; so, if God had not, in the course of his providence, given them the *property* they had, it would be impossible for them to give *alms.* And as even the well cultivated and sowed field would be unfruitful if God did not, by his unseen energy and blessing, cause it to bring forth, and bring to maturity ; so would it have been with their property : it could not have *increased;* for without his blessing riches take wings and flee away, as an eagle towards heaven. Therefore, in every sense, it is God who *ministers seed to the sower, and multiplies the seed sown.* And as all this properly comes from God, and cannot exist without him, he has a right to require that it be dispensed in that way which he judges best.

The word ὁ—επιχορηγων, *he that ministereth,* is very emphatic ; it signifies *he who leads up the chorus,* from επι, to, and χορηγω, to *lead the chorus ;* it means also to *join to, associate, to supply* or *furnish one thing after another* so that there be no *want* or *chasm.* Thus God is represented, in the course of his providence, *associating* and *connecting causes* and *effects ; keeping every thing* in its *proper place* and *state* of *dependence* on another, and all upon himself ; so that summer and winter, heat and cold, seed time and harvest, regularly succeed each other. Thus God *leads up this grand chorus of causes and effects:* provides the *seed* to the hand of the sower ; gives him *skill* to discern the times when the earth should be prepared for the grain, and when the grain should be sowed ; blesses the earth, and causes it to bring forth and bud, so that it may again minister seed to the sower and bread to the eater ; and, by a watchful providence, preserves every thing. The figure is beautiful, and shows us the grand system of causes and effects, all directed by and under the immediate guidance and government of God himself.

There is a fine exemplification of this in the same figure thus produced by the prophet. Hos. ii. 21, 22 : I will hear, saith the Lord, I will hear the *heavens ;* and they shall hear the *earth ;* and the *earth* shall hear

the *corn,* and the *wine* and the *oil ;* and they shall hear *Jezreel.* See the note there.

The fruits of your righteousness] Your beneficence ; for so δικαιοσυνη is here to be understood. See the note on Matt. vi. 1, already referred to.

Verse 11. *Being enriched in every thing*] Observe, Why does God give riches ? That they may be applied to his glory, and the good of men. Why does he *increase* riches ? That those who have them may *exercise all bountifulness.* And if they be *enriched in every thing,* what will be the consequence if they do not exercise *all bountifulness?* Why, God will curse their blessings ; the rust shall canker them, and the moth shall consume their garments. But if, on the other hand, they do thus apply them, then *they cause thanksgiving to God.* The 9th and 10th verses should be read in a parenthesis, for this verse connects with the *eighth.*

Verse 12. *For the administration of this service*] The poor are relieved, see the hand of God in this relief, and give God the glory of his grace.

Verse 13. *By the experiment of this ministration*] In this, and in the preceding and following verses, the apostle enumerates the good *effects* that would be produced by their *liberal almsgiving* to the poor saints at Jerusalem. 1. The wants of the saints would be supplied. 2. Many thanksgivings would thereby be rendered unto God. 3. The Corinthians would thereby give proof of their subjection to the Gospel. And, 4. The prayers of those relieved will ascend up to God in the behalf of their benefactors.

Verse 14. *The exceeding grace of God in you.*] By the ὑπερβαλλουσαν χαριν, superabounding or transcending grace, of God, which was in them, the apostle most evidently means the *merciful* and *charitable disposition* which they had towards the suffering saints. The whole connection, indeed the whole *chapter,* proves this ; and the apostle attributes this to its right source, the grace or goodness of God. They had the *means* of charity, but God had given these means ; they had a *feeling* and *charitable heart,* but God was the author of it. Their charity was *superabundant,* and God had furnished both the *disposition,* the *occasion,* and the *means* by which that disposition was to be made manifest.

Verse 15. *Thanks be unto God for his unspeak-*

able gift.] Some contend that Christ only is here intended; others, that the almsgiving is meant.

After all the difference of commentators and preachers, it is most evident that the ανεκδιηγητος δωρεα, *unspeakable gift*, is precisely the *same* with the ὑπερβαλλουσῃ χαρις, *superabounding grace* or *benefit*, of the preceding verse. If therefore *Jesus Christ*, the gift of God's unbounded love to man, be the meaning of the *unspeakable gift* in this verse, he is also intended by the *superabounding grace* in the preceding. But it is most evident that it is the *work of Christ in them*, and not Christ *himself*, which is intended in the 14th verse; and consequently, that it is the same *work*, not the *operator*, which is referred to in this last verse.

A FEW farther observations may be necessary on the conclusion of this chapter.

1. JESUS CHRIST, *the gift of God's love* to mankind, is an *unspeakable blessing;* no man can *conceive*, much less *declare*, how great this gift is; for these things the angels desire to look into. Therefore he may be well called the unspeakable gift, as he is the highest God ever gave or can give to man; though this is not the meaning of the last verse.

2. The *conversion* of a soul from darkness to light, from sin to holiness, from Satan to God, is not less *inconceivable*. It is called a *new creation*, and *creative energy* cannot be *comprehended*. To have the grace of God to rule the heart, subduing all things to itself and filling the soul with the Divine nature, is an *unspeakable blessing;* and the energy that produced it is an *unspeakable gift*. I conclude, therefore, that it is

the *work of Christ* in the soul, and not Christ *himself*, that the apostle terms the *superabounding* or *exceeding great grace*, and the *unspeakable gift;* and Dr. Whitby's paraphrase may be safely admitted as giving the *true sense* of the passage. " *Thanks be unto God for his unspeakable gift:* i. e. this admirable charity (proceeding from the work of Christ in the soul) by which God is so much glorified, the Gospel receives such credit, others are so much benefited, and you will be by God so plentifully rewarded." This is the sober sense of the passage; and no other meaning can comport with it. The passage itself is a grand proof that every *good disposition* in the soul of man comes from God; and it explodes the notion of *natural good*, i. e. good which God *does not work*, which is absurd; for no *effect* can exist without a *cause;* and God being the *fountain* of *good*, all that can be called good must come immediately from himself. See James, chap. i. 17.

3. Most men can see the hand of God in the dispensations of his justice, and yet these very seldom appear. How is it that they cannot equally see his hand in the dispensations of his mercy, which are great, striking, and unremitting! Our afflictions we scarcely ever forget; our mercies we scarcely ever remember! Our hearts are alive to *complaint*, but dead to *gratitude*. We have had ten thousand mercies for one judgment, and yet our complaints to our thanksgivings have been ten thousand to one! How is it that God endures this, and bears with us! Ask his own eternal clemency; and ask the Mediator before the throne. The mystery of our preservation and salvation can be *there alone* explained

---

CHAPTER X.

The apostle vindicates himself against the aspersions cast on his person by the false apostle; and takes occasion to mention his spiritual might and authority, 1—6. He shows them the impropriety of judging after the outward appearance, 7. Again refers to his apostolical authority, and informs them that when he again comes among them he will show himself in his deeds as powerful as his letters intimated, 8—11. He shows that these false teachers sat down in other men's labours, having neither authority nor influence from God to break up new ground, while he and the apostles in general had the regions assigned to them through which they were to sow the seed of life; and that he never entered into any place where the work was made ready to his hand by others, 12—16. He concludes with intimating that the glorying of those false apostles was bad; that they had nothing but self-commendation; and that they who glory should glory in the Lord, 17, 18.

A. M. 4061.
A. D. 57.
A. U. C.
810.
Anno Imp. Neronis Cæs. 4.

NOW [a] I Paul myself beseech you by the meekness and gentleness of Christ, [b] who [c] in presence *am* base among you,

but being absent am bold toward you:

2 But I beseech *you*, [d] that I may not be bold when I am

A. M. 4061.
A. D. 57.
A. U. C.
810.
Anno Imp. Neronis Cæs. 4.

---

[a] Rom. xii. 1.——[b] Ver. 10; chap. xii. 5, 7, 9.

[c] Or, *in outward appearance.*——[d] 1 Cor. iv. 21; chap. xiii. 2, 10.

NOTES ON CHAP. X.

Verse 1. *I Paul myself beseech you by the meekness*] Having now finished his directions and advices relative to the *collection for the poor*, he resumes his argument relative to the false apostle, who had gained considerable influence by representing St. Paul as despicable in his person, his ministry, and his influence. Under this obloquy the apostle was supported by

the meekness and gentleness of Christ; and through the same heavenly disposition he delayed inflicting that punishment which, in virtue of his apostolical authority, he might have inflicted on him who had disturbed and laboured to corrupt the Christian Church.

Who in presence am *base among you, but being absent am bold toward you*] He seems to quote *these* as the *words* of his *calumniator*, as if he had said:

A. M. 4061.
A. D. 57.
A. U. C.
810.
Anno Imp. Neronis Cæs. 4.

present with that confidence, wherewith I think to be bold against some, which [e] think of us as if we walked according to the flesh.

3 For though we walk in the flesh, we do not war after the flesh:

4 ([f] For the weapons [g] of our warfare *are* not

carnal, but [h] mighty [i] through God to the pulling down of strong holds;)

5 [k] Casting down [l] imaginations, and every high thing that exalteth itself against the knowledge of God, and bringing into captivity every thought to the obedience of Christ;

A. M. 4061.
A. D. 57.
A. U. C.
810.
Anno Imp. Neronis Cæs. 4.

---

[e] Or, *reckon.*——[f] Eph. vi. 13; 1 Thess. v. 8.——[g] 1 Tim. i. 18; 2 Tim. ii. 3.

[h] Acts vii. 22; 1 Cor. ii. 5; chap. vi. 7; xiii. 3, 4.——[i] Or, *to God.*——[k] 1 Cor. i. 19; iii. 19.——[l] Or, *reasonings.*

" This apostle of yours is a mere braggadocio; when he is among you, you know how *base* and *contemptible* he is; when absent, see how he *brags* and *boasts.*" The word ταπεινος, which we render *base,* signifies *lowly,* and, as some think, *short of stature.* The insinuation is, that when there was danger or opposition at hand, St. Paul acted with great obsequiousness, fearing for his person and authority, lest he should lose his secular influence. See the following verse.

Verse 2. *Some, which think of us as if we walked according to the flesh.*] As it is customary for *cowards* and *overbearing men* to *threaten* the *weak* and the *timid* when *present;* to *bluster* when *absent;* and to be very *obsequious* in the presence of the *strong* and *courageous.* This conduct they appear to have charged against the apostle, which he calls here *walking after the flesh*—acting as a man who had worldly *ends* in view, and would use any *means* in order to accomplish them.

Verse 3. *Though we walk in the flesh*] That is: Although I am in the common condition of human nature, and must live as a human being, yet I do *not war after the flesh*—I do not act the coward or the poltroon, as they insinuate. I have a good cause, a good captain, strength at will, and courage at hand. I neither fear *them* nor their *master.*

Verse 4. *The weapons of our warfare*] The apostle often uses the metaphor of a *warfare* to represent the life and trials of a Christian minister See Eph. vi. 10–17; 1 Tim. i. 18; 2 Tim. ii. 3 4, 5.

Are not carnal] Here he refers to the means used by the false apostle in order to secure his party; he calumniated St. Paul, traduced the truth, preached false and licentious doctrines, and supported these with sophistical reasonings.

But mighty through God] Our doctrines are true and pure, they come from God and lead to him, and he accompanies them with his mighty power to the hearts of those who hear them; and the *strong holds* —the apparently solid and cogent reasoning of the philosophers, we, by these doctrines, *pull down;* and thus the fortifications of heathenism are destroyed, and the cause of Christ triumphs wherever we come; and we put to flight the armies of the aliens.

Verse 5. *Casting down imaginations*] Λογισμους· *Reasonings* or *opinions.* The Greek philosophers valued themselves especially on their *ethic systems,* in which their reasonings appeared to be very *profound* and *conclusive;* but they were obliged to *assume principles* which were either such as did not exist, or

were false in themselves, as the whole of their *mythologic* system most evidently was: truly, from what remains of them we see that their *metaphysics* were generally bombast; and as to their *philosophy,* it was in general good for nothing. When the apostles came against their *gods many* and their *lords many* with the ONE SUPREME and ETERNAL BEING, they were confounded, scattered, annihilated: when they came against their various *modes* of *purifying the mind*—their *sacrificial* and *mediatorial* system, with the LORD JESUS CHRIST, his *agony* and *bloody sweat,* his *cross* and *passion,* his *death* and *burial,* and his *glorious resurrection* and *ascension,* they sunk before them, and appeared to be what they really were, as dust upon the balance, and lighter than vanity.

Every high thing] Even the pretendedly *sublime* doctrines, for instance, of *Plato, Aristotle,* and the *Stoics* in general, fell before the simple preaching of Christ crucified.

The knowledge of God] The doctrine of the *unity* and *eternity* of the *Divine nature,* which was opposed by the *plurality* of their idols, and the *generation* of their gods, and their *men-made* deities. It is amazing how feeble a resistance heathenism made, by *argument* or *reasoning,* against the doctrine of the Gospel! It instantly shrunk from the Divine light, and called on the *secular* power to contend for it! *Popery* sunk before *Protestantism* in the same way, and defended itself by the same *means.* The *apostles* destroyed *heathenism* wherever they came; the *Protestants* confuted *popery* wherever their voice was permitted to be heard.

Bringing into captivity every thought] HEATHENISM could not recover itself; in vain did its thousands of altars smoke with reiterated hecatombs, their demons were silent, and their idols were proved to be *nothing in the world.* POPERY could never, by any power of self-reviviscence, restore itself after its defeat by the Reformation: it had no *Scripture,* consecutively understood; no *reason,* no *argument;* in vain were its *bells* rung, its *candles* lighted, its *auto da fe's* exhibited; in vain did its *fires blaze;* and in vain were innumerable human victims immolated on *its* altars! The light of God penetrated its hidden works of darkness, and dragged its *three-headed* Cerberus into open day; the monster sickened, vomited his *henbane,* and fled for refuge to his native *shades.*

The obedience of Christ] Subjection to idols was annihilated by the progress of the Gospel among the heathens; and they soon had but *one* Lord, and his

2

A. M. 4061.
A. D. 57.
A. U. C.
810.
Anno Imp. Nero-
nis Cæs. 4.

6 [m] And having in a readiness to revenge all disobedience, when [n] your obedience is fulfilled.

7 [o] Do ye look on things after the outward appearance? [p] If any man trust to himself that he is Christ's, let him of himself think this again, that, as he *is* Christ's, even so *are* [q] we Christ's.

8 For though I should boast somewhat more

[r] of our authority, which the Lord hath given us for edification, and not for your destruction, [s] I should not be ashamed:

9 That I may not seem as if I would terrify you by letters.

10 For *his* letters, [t] say they, *are* weighty and powerful; but [u] *his* bodily presence *is* weak, and *his* [v] speech contemptible.

A. M. 4061.
A. D. 57.
A. U. C.
810.
Anno Imp. Nero
nis Cæs. 4.

---

[m] Chap. xiii. 2, 10.——[n] Chap. ii. 9; vii. 15.——[o] John vii. 24; chap. v. 12; xi. 18.——[p] 1 Cor. xiv. 37; 1 John iv. 6.——[q] 1 Cor. iii. 23; ix. 1; chap. xi. 23.

[r] Chap. xiii. 10.——[s] Chap. vii. 14; xii. 6.——[t] Gr. *saith he.* [u] 1 Cor. ii. 3, 4; ver. 1; chap. xii. 5, 7, 9; Gal. iv. 13.——[v] 1 Cor. i. 17; ii. 1, 4; chap. xi. 6.

---

name *one.* In like manner the doctrines of the *reformation,* mighty through God, *pulled down*—demolished and *brought into captivity,* the whole papal system; and instead of *obedience to the pope,* the pretended vicar of God upon earth, *obedience to Christ,* as the sole almighty Head of the Church, was established, particularly in Great Britain, where it continues to prevail. Hallelujah! the Lord God Omnipotent reigneth!

Verse 6. *And having in a readiness to revenge all disobedience*] I am ready, through this mighty armour of God, to punish those opposers of the doctrine of Christ, and the disobedience which has been produced by them.

When your obedience is fulfilled.] When you have in the fullest manner, discountenanced those men, and separated yourselves from their communion. The apostle was not in haste to pull up the *tares,* lest he should pull up the *wheat* also.

All the terms in these two verses are *military.* Allusion is made to a *strongly fortified city,* where the enemy had made his *last stand;* entrenching himself about the *walls;* strengthening all his *redoubts* and *ramparts;* raising *castles, towers,* and *various engines* of defence and offence upon the walls; and neglecting nothing that might tend to render his *strong hold* impregnable. The army of God comes against the place and attacks it; the *strong holds* οχυρωματα, all the *fortified places,* are carried. The *imaginations,* λογισμοι, engines, and whatever the *imagination* or *skill* of man could raise, are speedily taken and destroyed. Every *high thing,* παν υψωμα, *all the castles* and *towers* are sapped, *thrown down* and *demolished;* the *walls* are *battered* into *breaches;* and the besieging army, carrying every thing at the point of the sword, enter the city, storm and take the citadel. Every where defeated, the conquered submit, and are brought *into captivity,* αιχμαλωτιζοντες, *are led away captives;* and thus the whole government is destroyed.

It is easy to apply these things, as far as may be consistent with the apostle's design. The general *sense* I have given in the preceding notes.

Verse 7. *Do ye look on things after the outward appearance?*] Do not be carried away with *appearances;* do not be satisfied with *show* and *parade.*

If any man trust to himself that he is Christ's] Here, as in several other places of this and the preceding epistle, the τις, *any* or *certain, person,* most evidently refers to the *false apostle* who made so

much disturbance in the Church. And this man *trusted to himself*—assumed to himself that he was *Christ's* messenger: it would not do to attempt to *subvert* Christianity at once; it had got too strong a hold of Corinth to be easily dislodged; he therefore pretended to be on Christ's side, and to derive his authority from him.

Let him of himself] Without any authority, certainly, from God; but, as he arrogates to himself the character of a minister of Christ, let him acknowledge that even so we are Christ's ministers; and that *I* have, by my preaching, and the miracles which I have wrought, given the fullest proof that *I* am especially commissioned by him.

Verse 8. *For, though I should boast, &c.*] I have a greater authority and spiritual power than I have yet shown, both to *edify* and to *punish;* but I employ this for your *edification in righteousness,* and not for the *destruction* of any delinquent. "This," says Calmet, "is the rule which the pastors of the Church ever propose to themselves in the exercise of their authority; whether to enjoin or forbid, to dispense or to oblige, to bind or to loose. They should use this power only as Jesus Christ used it—for the salvation, and not for the destruction, of souls."

Verse 9. *That I may not seem, &c.*] This is an elliptical sentence, and may be supplied thus: "I have not used this authority; nor will I add any more concerning this part of the subject, lest I should seem, as my adversary has insinuated, to wish to terrify you by my letters.

Verse 10. *For his letters, say they, are weighty and powerful*] He boasts of high powers, and that he can do great things. See on ver. 1, 2.

But his bodily presence is weak] When you behold the *man,* you find him a feeble, contemptible mortal; and when ye hear him *speak,* his speech, ὁ λογος, probably, his *doctrine,* εξουθενημενος, is good for nothing; his *person, matter,* and *manner,* are altogether uninteresting, unimpressive, and too contemptible to be valued by the wise and the learned. This seems to be the spirit and design of this slander.

Many, both among the ancients and moderns, have endeavoured to find out the *ground* there was for any part of this calumny; as to the *moral conduct* of the apostle, that was invulnerable; his *motives,* it is true, were suspected and denounced by this false apostle and his partisans; but they could never find any thing in his *conduct* which could support their insinuations.

A. M. 4061.
A. D. 57.
A. U. C.
810.
Anno Imp. Nero-
nis Cæs. 4.

11 Let such a one think this, that, such as we are in word by letters when we are absent, such *will we be* also in deed when we are present.

12 ^w For we dare not make ourselves of the number, or compare ourselves with some that commend themselves : but they, measuring

---

^w Chap. iii. 1 ; v. 12.——^x Or, *understand it not.*

---

themselves by themselves, and comparing themselves among themselves, ^x are not wise.

13 ^y But we will not boast of things without *our* measure, but according to the measure of the ^z rule which God hath distributed to us, a measure to reach even unto you.

14 For we stretch not ourselves beyond *our*

---

^y Ver. 15.——^z Or, *line.*

A. M. 4061.
A. D. 57.
A. U. C.
810.
Anno Imp. Nero
nis Cæs. 4.

What they could not attach to his *character*, they disingenuously attached to his *person* and his *elocution*.

If we can credit some ancient writers, such as *Nicephorus*, we shall find the apostle thus described : Παυλος μικρος ην και συνεσταλμενος το του σωματος μεγεθος· και ὡσπερ αγκυλον αυτο κεκτημενος· σμικρον δε, και κεκυφος· την οψιν λευκος, και το προσωπον προφερης, ψιλος. την κεφαλην, κ. τ. λ.—Nicephor., lib. ii., cap. 17. " Paul was a little man, crooked, and almost bent like a bow ; with a pale countenance, long and wrinkled ; a bald head ; his eyes full of fire and benevolence ; his beard long, thick, and interspersed with grey hairs, as was his head, &c." I quote from *Calmet*, not having *Nicephorus* at hand.

An old Greek writer, says the same author, whose works are found among those of *Chrysostom*, tom. vi. hom. 30, page 265, represents him thus :—Παυλος ὁ τριπηχυς ανθρωπος, και των ουρανων ἁπτομενος· " Paul was a man of about three cubits in height, (four feet six,) and yet, nevertheless, touched the heavens." Others say that " he was a little man, had a bald head, and a large nose." See the above, and several other authorities in *Calmet*. Perhaps there is not one of these statements correct : as to *Nicephorus*, he is a writer of the fourteenth century, weak and credulous, and worthy of no regard. And the writer found in the works of *Chrysostom*, in making the apostle little more than a *pigmy*, has rendered his account incredible.

That St. Paul could be no such diminutive person we may fairly presume from the office he filled under the high priest, in the persecution of the Church of Christ ; and that he had not an *impediment* in his speech, but was a *graceful orator*, we may learn from his whole history, and especially from the account we have, Acts xiv. 12, where the Lycaonians took him for *Mercury*, the god of eloquence, induced thereto by his powerful and persuasive elocution. In short, there does not appear to be any substantial evidence of the apostle's *deformity, pigmy stature, bald head, pale and wrinkled face, large nose, stammering speech, &c., &c.* These are probably all figments of an unbridled fancy, and foolish surmisings.

Verse 11. *Such as we are in word*] A threatening of this kind would doubtless alarm the false apostle ; and it is very likely that he did not await the apostle's coming, as he would not be willing to try the fate of *Elymas*.

Verse 12. *We dare not make ourselves, &c.*] As if he had said : I dare neither associate with, nor compare myself to, those who are full of self-commendation. Some think this to be an *ironical* speech.

But they, measuring themselves by themselves] They are not sent of God ; they are not inspired by his Spirit ; therefore they have no *rule* to think or act by. They are also full of pride and self-conceit ; they look within themselves for accomplishments which their self-love will soon find out ; for to it *real* and *fictitious* are the same. As they dare not compare themselves with the true apostles of Christ, they compare themselves with each other ; and, as they have no *perfect standard*, they can have no *excellence ;* nor can they ever attain true *wisdom*, which is not to be had from looking at what we *are* but to what we *should* be ; and if without a directory, *what we should be* will never appear, and consequently our *ignorance* must continue. This was the case with these self-conceited false apostles ; but ου συνιουσιν, *are not wise*, Mr. Wakefield contends, is an elegant *Græcism* signifying they are *not aware* that they are measuring themselves by themselves, &c.

Verse 13. *Things without* our *measure*] There is a great deal of difficulty in this and the three following verses, and there is a great diversity among the MSS. ; and *which* is the *true reading* can scarcely be determined. Our version is perhaps the plainest that can be made of the text. By the *measure* mentioned here, it seems as if the apostle meant the commission he received from God to preach the Gospel to the Gentiles ; *a measure* or *district* that extended through all Asia Minor and Greece, down to Achaia, where Corinth was situated, *a measure to reach even unto you*. But the expressions in these verses are all agonistical, and taken from the stadium or race course in the Olympic and Isthmian games. ' The μετρον, or *measure*, was the length of the δρομος, or *course ;* and the κανων, *rule* or *line*, ver 15 and 16, was probably the same with the γραμμα, or *white line*, which marked out the boundaries of the stadium ; and the verbs *reach unto, stretch out, &c.*, are all references to the *exertions* made to win the *race*. As this subject is so frequently alluded to in these epistles, I have thought it of importance to consider it particularly in the different places where it occurs.

Verse 14. *For we stretch not ourselves beyond*] We have not proceeded straight from Macedonia through Thessaly, and across the Adriatic Gulf into Italy, which would have led us *beyond* you *westward ;* but knowing the mind of our God we left this direct path, and came *southward* through *Greece*, down into *Achaia*, and there we planted the Gospel. The false apostle has therefore got into our *province*, and entered into our labours, and there boasts as if the conversion of the heathen Achaians had been his own

A. M. 4061.
A. D. 57.
A. U. C. 810.
Anno Imp. Neronis Cæs. 4.

measure, as though we reached not unto you : ^a for we are come as far as to you also in *preaching* the Gospel of Christ :

15 Not boasting of things without *our* measure, *that is*, ^h of other men's labours ; but having hope, when your faith is increased, that we shall be ^c enlarged by you according to our rule abundantly,

16 To preach the Gospel in the *regions* beyond you, *and* not to boast in another man's ^d line of things made ready to our hand.

17 ^e But he that glorieth, let him glory in the Lord.

18 For ^f not he that commendeth himself is approved, but ^g whom the Lord commendeth.

A. M. 4061.
A. D. 57.
A. U. C. 810.
Anno Imp. Nero nis Cæs. 4.

a 1 Cor. iii. 5, 10 ; iv. 15 ; ix. 1.——b Rom. xv. 20.——c Or, *magnified in you.*——d Or, *rule.*

e Isa. lxv. 16 ; Jer. ix. 24 ; 1 Cor. i. 31.——f Prov. xxvii. 2.
g Rom. ii. 29 ; 1 Cor. iv. 5.

work. As there is an allusion here to the *stadium*, and to the Olympic games in general, we may consider the apostle as laying to the charge of the disturber at Corinth that he had got his name surreptitiously inserted on the military list ; that he was not striving lawfully ; had no right to the *stadium*, and none to the *crown.* See the observations at the end of 1 Cor., chap. ix. ; and the note on ver. 13 of this chapter.

Verse 15. *Not boasting of things without* our *measure*] We speak only of the work which God has done by us ; for we have never attempted to enter into other men's labours, and we study to convert those regions assigned to us by the Holy Spirit. We enter the course lawfully, and *run* according to *rule.* See above.

When your faith is increased] When you receive more of the life and power of godliness, and when you can better spare me to go to other places.

We shall be enlarged by you] Μεγαλυνθηναι probably signifies here to be *praised* or *commended ;* and the sense would be this : We hope that shortly, on your gaining an increase of true religion, after your long distractions and divisions, you will plainly see that we are the true messengers of God to you ; and that in all your intercourse with your neighbours, or foreign parts, you will speak of this Gospel preached by us as a glorious system of saving truth ; and that, in consequence, the heathen countries around you will be the better prepared to receive our message ; and thus our *rule* or *district* will be abundantly *extended.* This interpretation agrees well with the following verse.

Verse 16. *To preach the Gospel in the* regions *beyond you*] He probably refers to those parts of the *Morea*, such as *Sparta, &c.*, that lay *southward* of them ; and to *Italy*, which lay on the *west ;* for it does not appear that he considered his *measure* or *province* to extend to *Libya*, or any part of *Africa.* See the Introduction, sec. xii.

Not to boast in another man's line] So very scrupulous was the apostle not to build on another man's foundation, that he would not even go to those places where other apostles were labouring. He appears to think that every apostle had a particular *district* or *province* of the heathen world allotted to him, and which God commissioned him to convert to the Christian faith. No doubt every apostle was influenced in the same way ; and this was a wise order of God ; for by these means the Gospel was

more *quickly* spread through the heathen provinces than it otherwise would have been. The apostles had *deacons* or *ministers* with them whose business it was to *water* the seed sown ; but the *apostles* alone, under Christ, *sowed* and *planted.*

Verse 17. *He that glorieth, let him glory in the Lord.*] Instead of boasting or exulting even in your own success in preaching the Gospel, as none can be successful without the especial blessing of God, let God who gave the blessing have the glory. Even the genuine apostle, who has his commission immediately from God himself, takes no praise to himself from the prosperity of his work, but gives it all to God. How little cause then have your *uncommissioned men* to boast, to whom God has assigned no province, and who only *boast in another man's line of things made ready to their hand !*

Verse 18. *Not he that commendeth himself*] Not the person who makes a parade of his own *attainments ;* who preaches *himself*, and not *Christ Jesus the Lord ;* and, far from being your *servant* for Christ's sake, affects to be your *ruler ;* not such a one shall be *approved of God*, by an especial blessing on his labours ; *but he whom the Lord commendeth*, by giving him the *extraordinary gifts* of the Holy Spirit, and *converting* the *heathen* by his ministry. These were qualifications to which the false apostle at Corinth could not pretend. He had *language* and *eloquence*, and *show* and *parade ;* but he had neither the *gifts* of an apostle nor an apostle's *success.*

1. Dr. Whitby observes that the apostle, in the 13th, 14th, 15th, and 16th verses, endeavours to advance himself above the false apostles in the three following particulars :—

(1.) That whereas *they* could show no commission to preach to the Corinthians, no *measure* by which God had distributed the Corinthians to them as their province, *he* could do so. *We have a measure to reach even to you*, ver. 13.

(2.) That whereas they went out of *their line*, leaping from one Church to another, he went on *orderly*, in the conversion of the heathens, from *Judea* through all the *interjacent provinces*, till he came to *Corinth.*

(3.) Whereas they only came in and perverted the Churches where the faith had already been preached, and so could only boast of things made ready to their hands, ver. 16, he had laboured to preach the Gospel where Christ had not been *named*, lest he

2

should build on another man's foundation, Rom. xv. 20.

2. We find that from the beginning God appointed to every man his *promise*, and to every man his *labour ;* and would not suffer even one apostle to interfere with another. This was a very wise appointment ; for by this the Gospel was not only more speedily diffused over the heathen nations, as we have already remarked, but the Churches were better attended to, the Christian doctrine preserved in its purity, and the Christian discipline properly enforced. What is *any man's work* is *no man's* in particular ; and thus the work is neglected. In every Church of God there should be some *one* who for the time being has the care of it, who may be properly called its *pastor ;* and who is accountable for its purity in the faith, and its godly discipline.

3. Every man who ministers in holy things should be well assured of his *call* to the work ; without this he can labour neither with *confidence* nor *comfort.* And he should be careful to watch over the flock, that no *destroying wolf* be permitted to enter the sacred fold, and that the *fences* of a *holy discipline* be kept in proper repair.

4. It is base, abominable, and deeply sinful, for a man to thrust himself into other men's labours, and, by sowing doubtful disputations among a Christian people, distract and divide them, that he may get a party to himself. Such persons generally act as the false apostle at Corinth ; preach a *relaxed morality ;* place great stress upon *certain doctrines* which flatter and soothe self-love ; calumniate the person, *system of doctrines,* and *mode of discipline,* of the *pastor* who perhaps *planted* that Church, or who in the order of God's providence has the oversight of it. This is an evil that has prevailed much in all ages of the Church ; there is at *present* much of it in the Christian world, and Christianity is disgraced by it.

CHAPTER XI.

The apostle apologizes for expressing his jealousy relative to the true state of the Corinthians, still fearing lest their minds should have been drawn aside from the simplicity of the Gospel, 1–3: From this he takes occasion to extol his own ministry, which had been without charge to them, having been supported by the Churches of Macedonia while he preached the Gospel at Corinth, 4–11. Gives the character of the false apostles, 12–15. Shows what reasons he has to boast of secular advantages of birth, education, Divine call to the ministry, labours in that ministry, grievous persecutions, great sufferings, and extraordinary hazards, 16–33.

A. M. 4061.
A. D. 57.
A. U. C. 810.
Anno Imp. Neronis Cæs. 4.

WOULD to God ye could bear with me a little in [a] my folly : and indeed [b] bear with me.

2 For I am [c] jealous over you with godly jealousy : for [d] I have espoused you to one husband, [e] that I may present *you* [f] as a chaste virgin to Christ.

3 But I fear, lest by any means, as [g] the serpent beguiled Eve through his

A. M. 4061.
A. D. 57.
A. U. C. 810.
Anno Imp. Neronis Cæs. 4.

---

[a] Ver. 16 ; chap. v. 13.——[b] Or, *ye do bear with me.*——[c] Gal. iv. 17, 18.

[d] Hos. ii. 19, 20 ; 1 Cor. iv. 15.——[e] Col. i. 28.——[f] Lev. xxi. 13.   [g] Gen. iii. 4 ; John viii. 44.

NOTES ON CHAP. XI.

Verse 1. Would to God ye could bear with me] Οφελον ηνειχεσθε μου μικρον. As the word *God* is not mentioned here, it would have been much better to have translated the passage literally thus : *I wish ye could bear a little with me.* The too frequent use of this sacred name produces a *familiarity* with it that is not at all conducive to *reverence* and *godly fear.*

In my *folly*] In my *seeming* folly ; for, being obliged to vindicate his ministry, it was necessary that he should speak much of himself, his sufferings, and his success. And as this would appear like *boasting ;* and boasting is always the effect of an *empty, foolish mind ;* those who were not acquainted with the *necessity* that lay upon him to make this defence, might be led to impute it to *vanity.* As if he had said : Suppose you allow this to be *folly,* have the goodness to bear with me ; *for though I glory, I should not be a fool,* chap. xii. 6. *And let no man think me a fool for my boasting,* chap. xi. 16.

Verse 2. I am jealous over you, &c.] The apostle evidently alludes either to the שושבינים *shoshabinim*

or *paranymphs* among the Hebrews, whose office is largely explained in the notes on John iii. 29, and the observations at the end of that chapter ; or to the *harmosyni,* a sort of magistrates among the Lacedemonians who had the care of virgins, and whose business it was to see them well *educated,* kept *pure,* and properly *prepared* for married life.

That I may present you as *a chaste virgin*] The allusion is still kept up ; and there seems to be a reference to Lev. xxi. 14, that the high priest must no marry any one that was not a *pure virgin.* Here, then, *Christ* is the high priest, the *spouse* or *husband ;* the *Corinthian Church* the *pure virgin* to be espoused ; the *apostle* and his helpers the *shoshabinim,* or *harmosyni,* who had *educated* and *prepared* this virgin for her husband, and espoused her to him. See the observations already referred to at the end of the *third chapter of John.*

Verse 3. As the serpent beguiled Eve through his subtilty] This is a strong reflection on the false apostle and his teaching : he was *subtle,* πανουργος, and by his subtlety (πανουργια, from παν, *all,* and εργον, *work ;* his

2

A. M. 4061.
A. D. 57.
A. U. C.
810.
Anno Imp. Nero-
nis Cæs. 4.

subtilty, so your minds [h] should be corrupted from the simplicity that is in Christ.

4 For if he that cometh preacheth another Jesus, whom we have not preached ; or *if* ye receive another spirit, which ye have not received ; or [i] another Gospel, which ye have not accepted ; ye might well bear [k] with *him*.

5 For I suppose [l] I was not a whit behind the very chiefest apostles.

6 But though [m] *I be* rude in speech, yet not [n] in knowledge ; but [o] we have been throughly made manifest among you in all things.

7 Have I committed an offence [p] in abasing myself that ye might be exalted, because I have preached to you the Gospel of God freely ?

8 I robbed other Churches, taking wages *of them*, to do you service.

A. M. 4061.
A. D. 57.
A. U. C
810.
Anno Imp. Nero-
nis Cæs. 4.

---

[h] Eph. vi. 24 ; Col. ii. 4, 8, 18 ; 1 Tim. i. 3 ; iv. 1 ; Heb. xiii. 9 ; 2 Pet. iii. 17.——[i] Gal. i. 7, 8.——[k] Or, *with me*.——[l] 1 Cor. xv. 10 ; chap. xii. 11 ; Gal. ii. 6.

[m] 1 Cor. i. 17 ; ii. 1, 13 ; chap. x. 10.——[n] Eph. iii. 4.——[o] Ch. iv. 2 ; v. 11 ; xii. 12.——[p] Acts xviii. 3 ; 1 Cor. ix. 6, 12 ; chap. x. 1.

---

versatility of character and conduct, his *capability of do-ing all work,* and accommodating himself to the caprices, prejudices, and evil propensities of those to whom he mi-nistered) he was enabled to corrupt the minds of the peo-ple from the simplicity of the Gospel of Christ ; or, to follow the *metaphor*, he had *seduced* the *pure, chaste, well educated virgin*, from her duty, affection, and al-legiance to her one only true husband, the high priest, Jesus Christ. And here he seems to intimate that the serpent had seduced the mind of Eve from her affec-tions and allegiance to Adam, her true husband ; and certainly from God, her creator and governor. See at the end of the chapter.

Verse 4. For if he that cometh] The false apos-tle, who came *after* St. Paul had left Corinth.

Preacheth another Jesus] Who can save more fully and more powerfully than that Jesus *whom I have preached.*

Or if ye receive another spirit] And if in conse-quence of believing in this new saviour ye receive another *spirit*, the gifts, graces, and consolations of which are greater than those which ye have received from the *Holy Ghost*, which has been given to you on your believing on the Christ whom we preached.

Or another Gospel] Containing more privileges, spiritual advantages, and stronger excitements to holi-ness, than that which we have preached and which ye have accepted, *ye might well bear with him*. This would be a sufficient reason why you should not only *bear with him*, but prefer him to me.

Others think that the last clause should be rendered, *Ye might well bear with* ME—notwithstanding he brought you another Jesus, spirit, and gospel, ye might bear with me, who have already ministered so long to and done so much for you. But the former sense seems best.

Verse 5. I was not—behind the very chiefest apos-tles.] That is : The most eminent of the apostles have not preached Christ, ministered the Spirit, ex-plained and enforced the doctrines of the Gospel in a more powerful and effectual manner than I have done.

Verse 6. But though I be rude in speech] Ιδιωτης τω λογω Though I speak like a *common unlettered man*, in plain unadorned phrase, studying none of the graces of eloquence ; yet I am not unskilled in the most profound *knowledge* of God, of spiritual and eter-nal things, of the nature of the human soul, and the

sound truths of the Gospel system : ye yourselves are witnesses of this, as in all these things *I have been thoroughly manifested among you.*

Inspired men received all their doctrines immediately from God, and often the very *words* in which those doctrines should be delivered to the world ; but in ge-neral the Holy Spirit appears to have left them to their own language, preventing them from using any expression that might be equivocal, or convey a con-trary sense to that which God intended.

That St. Paul wrote a strong, nervous, and suffi-ciently pure language, his own writings sufficiently testify ; but the *graces* of the Greek tongue he appears not to have *studied*, or at least he did not think it pro-per to use them ; for perhaps there is no tongue in the world that is so apt to *seduce the understanding* by its *sounds* and *harmony*, as the Greek. It is not an unusual thing for Greek scholars to the present day to be in raptures with the *harmony* of a *Greek verse*, the sense of which is but little regarded, and perhaps is little worth ! I should suppose that God would *pre-vent* the inspired writers from either speaking or writ-ing thus, that *sound* might not carry the hearer away from *sense;* and that the persuasive force of truth might alone prevail, and the excellence of the power appear to be of God and not of man. Taking up the subject in this point of view, I see no reason to have recourse to the supposition, or *fable* rather, that the apostle had an *impediment in his speech*, and that he alludes to this infirmity in the above passage.

Verse 7. Have I committed an offence in abasing myself] Have I transgressed in *labouring with my hands* that I might *not be chargeable to you ?* and get-ting my deficiencies supplied by contributions from other Churches, while I was employed in labouring for your salvation ? Does your false apostle insinuate that I have disgraced the apostolic office by thus descend-ing to servile labour for my support ? Well ; I have done this *that you might be exalted*—that you might receive the pure doctrines of the Gospel, and be ex-alted to the highest pitch of intellectual *light* and *bless-edness.* And will you complain that I preached the Gospel *gratis* to you ? Surely not. The whole passage is truly ironical.

Verse 8. I robbed other Churches] This part of the sentence is explained by the latter, *taking wages to do you service.* The word οψωνιον signifies the *pay*

A. M. 4061.
A. D. 57.
A. U. C.
810.
Anno Imp. Neronis Cæs. 4.

9 And when I was present with you, and wanted, q I was chargeable to no man: for that which was lacking to me r the brethren which came from Macedonia supplied: and in all *things* I have kept myself s from being burdensome unto you, and *so* will I keep *myself*.

10 t As the truth of Christ is in me, u no man shall stop me of this boasting v in the regions of Achaia.

11 Wherefore? w because I love you not? God knoweth.

12 But what I do, that I will do, x that I may cut off occasion from them which desire occasion; that wherein they glory, they may be found even as we.

13 For such y *are* false apostles, z deceitful workers, transforming themselves into the apostles of Christ.

14 And no marvel; for Satan himself is transformed into a an angel of light.

A. M. 4061.
A. D. 57.
A. U. C.
810.
Anno Imp. Neronis Cæs. 4.

q Acts xx. 33; chap. xii. 13; 1 Thess. ii. 9; 2 Thess. iii. 8, 9.——r Phil. iv. 10, 15, 16.——s Chap. xii. 14, 16.——t Rom. ix. 1.——u Gr. *this boasting shall not be stopped in me.*——v 1 Cor. ix. 15.

w Chap. vi. 11; vii. 3; xii. 15.——x 1 Cor. ix. 12.——y Acts xv. 24; Rom. xvi. 18; Gal. i. 7; vi. 12; Phil. i. 15; 2 Pet. ii. 1; 1 John iv. 1; Rev. ii. 2.——z Chap. ii. 17; Phil. iii. 2; Tit. i. 10, 11.——a Gal. i. 8.

of money and provisions given daily to a *Roman soldier.* As if he had said: I received food and raiment, the bare necessaries of life, from other Churches while labouring for *your* salvation. Will *you* esteem this a crime?

Verse 9. *And when I was present with you*] The particle καὶ, which we translate *and*, should be rendered *for* in this place: *For when I was with you, and was in want, I was chargeable to no man.* I preferred to be, for a time, even without the *necessaries* of life, rather than be a burden to you. To *whom* was this a reproach, to *me* or to *you?*

The brethren which came from Macedonia] He probably refers to the supplies which he received from the Church at Philippi, which was in Macedonia; of which he says, that *in the beginning of the Gospel no Church communicated with me, as concerning giving and receiving, but you only; for even at Thessalonica ye sent once and again to my necessity*, Phil. iv. 15, 16. See the *Introduction*, sec. vi.

Verse 10. *As the truth of Christ is in me*] Εστιν αληθεια Χριστου εν εμοι· *The truth of Christ is in me.* That is: I speak as becomes a Christian man, and as influenced by the Gospel of Christ. It is a *solemn form* of asseveration, if not to be considered in the sense of an *oath.*

In the regions of Achaia.] The whole of the *Peloponnesus*, or *Morea*, in which the city of Corinth stood. From this it appears that he had received no help from any of the other Churches in the whole of that district.

Verse 11. *Wherefore*] Why have I acted thus? and why do I propose to *continue* to act thus? is it *because I love you not*, and will not permit you to contribute to my support? *God knoweth* the contrary; I do most affectionately love you.

Verse 12. *But what I do, &c.*] I act thus that I *may cut off occasion* of glorying, boasting, or calumniating *from them*——the false prophets and his partisans, *who seek occasion*——who would be glad that I should become *chargeable* to you, that it might in some sort vindicate them who exact much from you; for they *bring you into bondage*, and *devour you*, ver. 20.

Nothing could mortify these persons more than to find that the apostle did take nothing, and was resolved

to take nothing; while *they* were fleecing the people. It is certain that the passage is not to be understood as though the false apostles took nothing from the people, to whatever disinterestedness they might pretend, for the apostle is positive on the contrary; and he was determined to act so that his example should not authorize these deceivers, who had nothing but their *self-interest* in view, to exact contribution from the people; so that if they continued to boast, they must be *bound even as the apostle*, taking *nothing for their labours;* which could never comport with *their* views of gain and secular profit.

Verse 13. *For such* are *false apostles*] Persons who *pretend* to be apostles, but have no mission from Christ.

Deceitful workers] They *do* preach and labour, but they have nothing but their *own emolument* in view.

Transforming themselves] Assuming as far as they possibly can, *consistently with their sinister views*, the habit, manner, and doctrine of the apostles of Christ.

Verse 14. *And no marvel*] Και ου θαυμαστον· And no wonder; it need not surprise you what the *disciples* do, when you consider the character of the *master.*

Satan himself is transformed into an angel of light.] As in ver. 3 the apostle had the history of the *temptation* and *fall of man* particularly in view, it is very likely that Here he refers to the same thing. In whatever *form* Satan appeared to our first mother, his pretensions and professions gave him the appearance of a *good* angel; and by pretending that Eve should get a great increase of *light*, that is, *wisdom* and *understanding*, he *deceived* her, and led her to transgress. It is generally said that Satan has *three forms* under which he tempts men: 1. The *subtle serpent.* 2. The *roaring lion.* 3 The *angel of light.* He often, as the *angel of light*, persuades men to do things under the *name of religion*, which are subversive of it. Hence all the *persecutions, faggots*, and *fires* of a certain Church, under pretence of keeping *heresy* out of the Church; and hence all the *horrors* and *infernalities* of the *inquisition.* In the form of heathen persecution, like a *lion* he has ravaged the heritage of the Lord. And by means of our *senses* and *passions*, as the *subtle serpent*, he is frequently deceiving us, so that often the *workings* of *corrupt nature* are mistaken for the *operations* of the *Spirit* of God.

2

A. M. 4061.
A. D. 57.
A. U. C.
810.
Anno Imp. Neronis Cæs. 4.

15 Therefore *it is* no great thing if his ministers also be transformed as the [b] ministers of righteousness; [c] whose end shall be according to their works.

16 [d] I say again, Let no man think me a fool; if otherwise, yet as a fool [e] receive me, that I may boast myself a little.

17 That which I speak, [f] I speak *it* not after the Lord, but as it were foolishly, [g] in this confidence of boasting.

18 [h] Seeing that many glory after the flesh, I will glory also.

19 For ye suffer fools gladly, [i] seeing ye *yourselves* are wise.

A. M. 4061.
A. D. 57.
A. U. C.
810.
Anno Imp. Neronis Cæs. 4.

20 For ye suffer, [k] if a man bring you into bondage, if a man devour *you*, if a man take *of you*, if a man exalt himself, if a man smite you on the face.

21 I speak as concerning reproach, [l] as though we had been weak. Howbeit [m] whereinsoever any is bold, (I speak foolishly,) I am bold also.

22 Are they Hebrews? [n] so *am* I. Are they Israelites? so *am* I. Are they the seed of Abraham? so *am* I.

23 Are they ministers of Christ? (I speak as a fool) I *am* more; [o] in labours more abundant, [p] in stripes above measure, in

---

[b] Chap. iii. 9.——[c] Phil. iii. 19.——[d] Ver. 1; chap. xii. 6, 11.
[e] Or, *suffer.*——[f] 1 Cor. vii. 6, 12.——[g] Chap. ix. 4.——[h] Phil.
iii. 3, 4.——[i] 1 Cor. iv. 10.——[k] Gal. ii. 4; iv. 9.

[l] Chap. x. 10.——[m] Phil. iii. 4.——[n] Acts xxii. 3; Rom. xi. 1;
Phil. iii. 5.——[o] 1 Cor. xv. 10.——[p] Acts ix. 16; xx. 23; xxi. 11;
chap. vi. 4, 5.

Verse 15. *Whose end shall be according to their works.*] A bad *way* leads to a bad *end.* The way of *sin* is the way to *hell.*

Verse 16. *Let no man think me a fool*] See the note on ver. 1. As the apostle was now going to enter into a particular detail of his qualifications, natural, acquired, and spiritual; and particularly of his *labours* and *sufferings;* he thinks it necessary to introduce the discourse *once more* as he did ver. 1.

Verse 17. *I speak it not after the Lord*] Were it not for the *necessity* under which I am laid to vindicate my apostleship, my present glorying would be inconsistent with my Christian profession of *humility,* and knowing no one *after the flesh.*

Verse 18. *Seeing that many glory after the flesh*] Boast of *external* and *secular* things.

Verse 19. *Ye suffer fools gladly, seeing ye yourselves are wise.*] A very fine irony. Ye are so profoundly *wise* as to be able to discern that I am a *fool.* Well, it would be dishonourable to you as *wise men* to fall out with a *fool;* you will therefore gladly bear with his impertinence and foolishness because of your own profound wisdom.

Verse 20. *For ye suffer*] As you are so *meek* and *gentle* as to submit to be brought into *bondage,* to have your property *devoured,* your goods *taken* away, yourselves laid in the dust, so that others may *exalt* themselves over you, yea, and will bear from those the most degrading *indignity;* then of course, you will bear with *one* who has never *insulted, defrauded, devoured, taken* of you, *exalted* himself against you, or offered you any kind of indignity; and who only wishes you to bear his confident boasting, concerning matters which he can substantiate.

The expressions in this verse are some evidence that the false apostle was a *Judaizing* teacher. *You suffer,* says the apostle, *if a man,* καταδουλοι, *bring you into bondage,* probably meaning to the Jewish *rites* and *ceremonies,* Gal. iv. 9; ver. 1. *If he devour you;* as the Pharisees did the patrimony of the widows, and for a pretence made long prayers; *if a*

man take of you, exact different contributions, pretendedly for the temple at Jerusalem, &c. *If he exalt himself,* pretending to be of the seed of Abraham, infinitely higher in honour and dignity than all the families of the Gentiles; *if he smite you on the face*—treat you with indignity, as the Jews did the Gentiles, considering them only as *dogs,* and not fit to be ranked with any of the descendants of Jacob.

Verse 21. *I speak as concerning reproach*] Dr. Whitby thus paraphrases this verse: "That which I said of *smiting you upon the face, I speak as concerning* the *reproach* they cast upon you as profane and uncircumcised, whereas *they* all profess to be a holy nation; *as though we had been weak*—inferior to them in these things, not able to ascribe to ourselves those advantages as well as they. *Howbeit, whereinsoever any is bold,* and can justly value himself on these advantages, *I am bold also,* and can claim the same distinctions, though *I speak foolishly* in setting any value on those things; but it is necessary that I should show that such men have not even one *natural good* that they can boast of beyond *me.*"

Verse 22. *Are they Hebrews*] Speaking the *sacred language,* and *reading* in the congregation from the Hebrew Scriptures? the same is my own language.

Are they Israelites] Regularly descended from *Jacob,* and not from *Esau?* I am also one.

Are they the seed of Abraham] Circumcised, and in the bond of the covenant? *So am I.* I am no *proselyte,* but I am a *Hebrew of the Hebrews* both by father and mother; and can trace my genealogy, through the tribe of *Benjamin,* up to the father of the faithful.

Verse 23. *Are they ministers of Christ*] So we find that these were professors of Christianity; and that they were genuine *Jews,* and such as endeavoured to incorporate *both* systems, and, no doubt, to oblige those who had believed to be circumcised; and this appears to have been the *bondage* into which they had brought many of the believing Corinthians.

I am more] More of a minister of Christ than they

2

A. M. 4061.
A. D. 57.
A. U. C. 810.
Anno Imp. Neronis Cæs. 4.

prisons more frequent, q in deaths oft.

24 Of the Jews five times received I r forty *stripes* save one.
25 Thrice was I s beaten with rods, t once was I stoned, thrice I u suffered shipwreck, a night and a day I have been in the deep ;

26 *In* journeyings often, *in* perils of waters, *in* perils of robbers, v *in* perils by *mine own* countrymen, w *in* perils by the heathen, *in* perils in the city, *in* perils in the wilderness, *in* perils in the sea, *in* perils among false brethren ;

A. M. 4061.
A. D. 57.
A. U. C. 810.
Anno Imp. Neronis Cæs. 4.

---

q 1 Cor. xv. 30, 31, 32 ; chap. i. 9, 10 ; iv. 11 ; vi. 9.——r Deut. xxv. 3.——s Acts xvi. 22.——t Acts xiv. 19.

u Acts xxvii. 41.——v Acts ix. 23 ; xiii. 50 ; xiv. 5 ; xvii. 5 ; xx. 3 ; xxi. 31 ; xxiii. 10, 11 ; xxv. 3.——w Acts xiv. 5 ; xix. 23.

---

are, and have given fuller proofs of it. I have suffered persecution for the cross of Christ, and of the *Jews* too ; and had I preached up the necessity of *circumcision*, I should have been as free from opposition as these are.

In labours more abundant] Far from sitting down to take my ease in a Church already gathered into Christ ; I travel incessantly, preach every where, and at all risks, in order to get the heathen brought from the empire of darkness into the kingdom of God's beloved Son.

In stripes above measure] Being beaten by the *heathen*, who had no particular *rule* according to which they scourged criminals ; and we find, from Acts xvi. 22, 23, that they beat Paul *unmercifully* with *many stripes*. See the note on the above passage.

In prisons more frequent] See Acts xxi. 11, and the whole of the apostle's history ; and his long imprisonment of at least *two years* at Rome, Acts xxviii. It does not appear that there is any one instance of a false apostle having been imprisoned for the testimony of Christ ; this was a badge of the true apostles.

In deaths oft.] That is, in the most imminent dangers. See 1 Cor. xv. 31 ; 2 Cor. iv. 11. And see the apostle's history in the Acts.

Verse 24. *Of the Jews five times received I forty stripes save one.*] That is, he was five times scourged by the Jews, whose law (Deut. xxv. 3) allowed forty stripes ; but they, pretending to be lenient, and to act *within the letter* of the law, inflicted but thirty-nine.

To except *one* stripe from the *forty* was a very ancient canon among the Jews, as we learn from *Josephus*, Antiq. lib. iv. ch. viii. sec. 21, who mentions the same thing : πληγας μιας λειπουσης τεσσαρακοντα· *forty stripes, excepting one.*

The *Mishna* gives this as a rule, Mish., *Maccoth*, fol. 22, 10 : " How often shall he, the culprit, be smitten ? Ans. ארבעים חסר אחד forty stripes, wanting one ; i. e. with the number which is nighest to forty." Frequently a man was scourged according to his *ability* to bear the punishment ; and it is a canon in the *Mishna*, " That he who cannot bear *forty* stripes should receive only *eighteen*, and yet be considered as having suffered the whole punishment."

They also thought it right to stop under *forty*, lest the person who counted should make a mistake, and the criminal get more than *forty* stripes, which would be injustice, as the law required only *forty*.

The manner in which this punishment was inflicted is described in the *Mishna*, fol. 22, 2 : " The two hands of the criminal are bound to a post, and then the

servant of the synagogue either pulls or tears off his clothes till he leaves his breast and shoulders bare. A stone or block is placed behind him on which the servant stands ; he holds in his hands a scourge made of leather, divided into four tails. He who scourges lays one third on the criminal's *breast*, another third on his *right shoulder*, and another on his *left*. The man who receives the punishment is neither *sitting* nor *standing*, but all the while *stooping ;* and the man smites with all his strength, with one hand." The severity of this punishment depends on the nature of the *scourge*, and the *strength* of the executioner.

It is also observed that the Jews did not *repeat* scourgings except for enormous offences. But they had scourged the apostle *five* times ; for with those murderers no quarter would be given to the *disciples*, as none was given to the *Master*. See *Schoettgen*.

Verse 25. *Thrice was I beaten with rods*] This was under the *Roman* government, as their *lictors* beat criminals in this way. We hear of the apostle's being treated thus *once*, namely at Philippi, Acts xvi. 22. See sec. 9 of the introduction.

Once was I stoned] Namely, at *Lystra*, Acts xiv. 19, &c.

A night and a day I have been in the deep] To what this refers we cannot tell ; it is generally supposed that in some shipwreck not on record the apostle had saved himself on a plank, and was a whole day and night on the sea, tossed about at the mercy of the waves. Others think that βυθος, the deep, signifies a *dungeon* of a terrible nature at *Cyzicum*, in the *Propontis*, into which Paul was cast as he passed from Troas. But this is not likely.

Verse 26. *In journeyings often*] He means the particular journeys which he took to different places, for the purpose of propagating the Gospel.

In perils of waters] Exposed to great dangers in crossing *rivers ;* for of *rivers* the original, ποταμων, must be understood.

Of robbers] Judea itself, and perhaps every other country, was grievously infested by banditti of this kind ; and no doubt the apostle in his frequent peregrinations was often attacked, but, being *poor* and having nothing to lose, he passed unhurt, though not without great danger.

In perils by mine own countrymen] The Jews had the most rooted antipathy to him, because they considered him an *apostate* from the true faith, and also the means of perverting many others. There are several instances of this in the Acts ; and a remarkable conspiracy against his life is related, Acts xxiii. 12, &c.

A. M. 4061.
A. D. 57.
A. U. C.
810.
Anno Imp. Nero-
nis Cæs. 4.

27 In weariness and painfulness, ˣ in watchings often, ʸ in
hunger and thirst, in fastings
often, in cold and nakedness.

28 Beside those things that are without, that
which cometh upon me daily, ᶻ the care of all
the Churches.

29 ᵃ Who is weak, and I am
not weak ? who is offended, and
I burn not ?

30 If I must needs glory, ᵇ I
will glory of the things which concern mine
infirmities.

31 ᶜ The God and Father of our Lord Jesus

A. M. 4061.
A. D. 57.
A. U. C.
810.
Anno Imp. Nero
nis Cæs. 4.

ˣ Acts xx. 31 ; chap. vi. 5.——ʸ 1 Cor. iv. 11.——ᶻ See Acts xx.
18, &c. ; Rom. i. 14.

ᵃ 1 Cor. viii. 13 ; ix. 22.——ᵇ Chap. xii. 5, 9, 10.——ᶜ Rom. i. 9 ;
ix. 1 ; chap. i. 23 ; Gal. i. 2 ; 1 Thess. ii. 5.

In *perils by the heathen*] In the heathen provinces
whither he went to preach the Gospel. Several instances of these perils occur also in the *Acts.*

In *perils in the city*] The different seditions raised
against him ; particularly in *Jerusalem,* to which *Ephesus* and *Damascus* may be added.

Perils in the wilderness] Uninhabited countries
through which he was obliged to pass in order to reach
from city to city. In such places it is easy to imagine many dangers from banditti, wild beasts, cold,
starvation, &c.

Perils in the sea] The different voyages he took
in narrow seas, such as the Mediterranean, about dangerous coasts, and without *compass.*

False brethren] Persons who joined themselves
to the Church, pretending faith in Christ, but intending to act as *spies,* hoping to get some matter of accusation against him. He no doubt suffered much also
from *apostates.*

Verse 27. *In weariness and painfulness*] Tribulations of this kind were his constant companions. Lord
Lyttleton and others have made useful reflections on
this verse : " How hard was it for a man of a genteel
and liberal education, as St. Paul was, to bear such
rigours, and to wander about like a vagabond, hungry
and almost naked, yet coming into the presence of
persons of high life, and speaking in large and various
assemblies on matters of the utmost importance !"
Had not St. Paul been deeply convinced of the truth
and absolute certainty of the Christian religion, he could
not have continued to expose himself to such hardships.

Verse 28. *Beside those things that are without*]
Independently of all these outward things, I have innumerable troubles and mental oppressions.

Which cometh upon me] Ἡ ἐπισυστασις· This continual *press* of business ; this *insurrection* of cases to
be heard, solved, and determined, relative to the doctrine, discipline, state, persecution, and supply of all
the Churches.

All his perils were little in comparison of what he
felt relative to the peace, government, and establishment of all the Churches among the Gentiles ; for as
he was the apostle of the Gentiles, the government of
all the Churches among them fell in some sort on him,
whether they were of his own planting or of the planting of others. See Col. ii. 1. None but a conscientious minister, who has at heart the salvation of souls,
can enter into the apostle's feelings in this place.

Verse 29. *Who is weak*] What Church is there
under persecution, with which I do not immediately
sympathize ? or who, from his *weakness* in the *faith,*
and *scrupulousness* of conscience, is likely to be stum-

bled, or turned out of the way, to whom I do not condescend, and whose burden I do not bear ?

Who is offended] Or likely to be turned out of
the way, *and I burn not* with zeal to restore and confirm him ? This seems to be the sense of these different questions.

Verse 30. *I will glory—which concern mine infirmities.*] I will not boast of my *natural* or *acquired
powers;* neither in what *God* has done by me ; but
rather in what I have *suffered* for *him.*

Many persons have understood by *infirmities* what
they call *the indwelling sin* of the apostle, and say
that " he gloried in this, because the grace of Christ
was the more magnified in his being preserved from
ruin, notwithstanding this indwelling adversary." And
to support this most unholy interpretation, they quote
those other words of the apostle, chap. xii. 9 : *Most
gladly therefore will I rather glory in my infirmities,
my indwelling corruptions, that the power of Christ,*
in chaining the fierce lion, *may rest upon me.* But it
would be difficult to produce a single passage in the
whole New Testament where the word ασθενεια, which
we translate *infirmity,* has the sense of *sin* or *moral
corruption.* The verb ασθενεω signifies to be *weak,
infirm, sick, poor, despicable* through *poverty,* &c.
And in a few places it is applied to *weakness in the
faith,* to *young converts,* who are poor in religious
knowledge, not yet fully instructed in the nature of
the Gospel ; Rom. iv. 19 ; xiv. 1, 2. And it is applied to the works of the law, to point out their *inability to justify* a sinner, Rom. viii. 3. But to *inward
sin,* and *inward corruption* it is never applied. I am
afraid that what these persons call their *infirmities*
may rather be called their *strengths;* the *prevailing*
and *frequently ruling* power of pride, anger, ill-will,
&c. ; for how few think *evil tempers* to be *sins !* The
gentle term *infirmity* softens down the iniquity ; and
as St. Paul, so great and so holy a man, say they,
had his infirmities, how can they expect to be without
theirs ? These should know that they are in a dangerous error ; that St. Paul means nothing of the kind ;
for he speaks of his *sufferings,* and of these alone.
One word more : would not the *grace* and *power* of
Christ appear more conspicuous in *slaying the lion*
than in keeping him *chained ?* in *destroying sin, root*
and branch ; and filling the soul with his own *holiness,*
with *love to God and man,* with the *mind*—all the
holy heavenly tempers, that were in *himself ;* than in
leaving these impure and unholy tempers, ever to *live*
and *often* to *reign* in the heart ? The doctrine is dis-
creditable to the Gospel, and wholly antichristian.

Verse 31. *The God and Father of our Lord*]

2

A. M. 4061
A. D. 57.
A. U. C. 810.
Anno Imp. Neronis Cæs. 4.

Christ, [d] which is blessed for evermore, knoweth that I lie not. 32 [e] In Damascus the governor under Aretas, the king, kept the [f] city of the Damascenes with a garri-

son, desirous to apprehend me:

33 And [g] through a window in a basket was I let down by the wall, and escaped his hands.

A. M. 4061.
A. D. 57.
A. U. C. 810.
Anno Imp. Neronis Cæs. 4.

[d] Rom. ix. 5.——[e] Acts ix. 24, 25.

[f] John vii. 30, 44 ; Acts ix. 3.——[g] Josh. ii. 15 ; Psa. xxxiv. 19.

Here is a very solemn *asseveration;* an *appeal* to the *ever blessed God* for the truth of what he asserts. It is something similar to his *asseveration* or *oath* in ver. 10 of this chapter; see also Rom. ix. 5, and Gal. i. 20. And from these and several other places we learn that the apostle thought it right thus to *confirm* his assertions on these particular occasions. But here is nothing to countenance profane swearing, or taking the name of God in vain, as many do in *exclamations,* when surprised, or on hearing something unexpected, &c.; and as others do who, conscious of their own *falsity,* endeavour to gain credit by appeals to God for the truth of what they say. St. Paul's *appeal to God* is in the same spirit as his most earnest *prayer.* This solemn appeal the apostle makes in reference to what he mentions in the following verses. This was a fact not yet generally known.

Verse 32. *In Damascus the governor under Aretas*] For a description of Damascus see the note on Acts ix. 2. And for the transaction to which the apostle refers see Acts ix. 23. As to King *Aretas,* there were three of this name. The *first* is mentioned 2 *Maccab.* v. 8. The *second* by *Josephus,* Antiq. l. xiii. c. 15, sec. 2; and l. xvi. c. 1, sec. 4. The *third,* who is the person supposed to be referred to here, was the father-in-law of Herod Antipas, of whom see the notes, Acts ix. 23, &c.

But it is a question of some importance, How could Damascus, a city of *Syria,* be under the government of an Arabian king? It may be accounted for thus: Herod Antipas, who married the daughter of Aretas, divorced her, in order to marry Herodias, his brother Philip's wife. Aretas, on this indignity offered to his family, made war upon Herod. Herod applied to *Tiberius* for help, and the emperor sent *Vitellius* to reduce Aretas, and to bring him alive or dead to Rome. By some means or other Vitellius delayed his operations, and in the meantime Tiberius died; and thus Aretas was snatched from ruin, Joseph., Antiq. lib. xviii. c. 5. What Aretas did in the interim is not known; but it is conjectured that he availed himself of the then favourable state of things, made an irruption into Syria, and seized on Damascus. See *Rosenmuller;* and see the introduction to this epistle, sec. ii.

The governor] Εθναρχης· Who this ethnarch was we cannot tell. The word *ethnarch* signifies the governor of a province, under a king or emperor.

Desirous to apprehend me] The enemies of the apostle might have represented him to the governor as a dangerous spy, employed by the *Romans.*

Verse 33. *Through a window in a basket*] Pro-

bably the house was situated on the wall of the city. See the notes on this history, Acts ix. 23–25.

In ver. 2 of this chapter the apostle most evidently alludes to the history of the *temptation* and *fall* of Adam and Eve, as related in Gen. iii. 1, &c.; and which fall is there attributed to the agency of a being called נחש *nachash,* here, and in other places, translated οφις, *serpent.* In my notes on Genesis I have given many, and, as I judge, solid reasons, why the word cannot be understood *literally* of a *serpent* of any kind; and that most probably a creature of the *simia* or *ape* genus was employed by the devil on this occasion. The arguments on this subject appeared to me to be corroborated by innumerable probabilities; but I left the *conjecture* afloat, (for I did not give it a more decisive name,) and placed it in the hands of my readers to adopt, reject, or amend, as their judgments might direct them. To several this sentiment appeared a monstrous *heresy!* and speedily the *old serpent* had a host of *defenders.* The very modest opinion, or *conjecture,* was controverted by some who were both *gentlemen* and *scholars,* and by several who were *neither;* by some who could not affect *candour* because they had not even the *appearance* of it, but would affect *learning* because they wished to be reputed *wise.* What *reason* and *argument* failed to produce they would supply with *ridicule;* and as *monkey* was a convenient term for this purpose, they attributed it to him who had never used it. What is the result? They no doubt believe that they have established their system; and their arguments are to *them* conclusive. They have my full consent; but I think it right to state that I have neither seen nor heard of any thing that has the *least tendency to weaken my conjecture,* or produce the *slightest* wavering in my opinion. Indeed their arguments, and mode of managing them, have produced a very different effect on my mind to what they designed. I am now more firmly persuaded of the probability of my *hypothesis* than ever. I shall, however, leave the subject as it is: I never proposed it as an *article of faith;* I press it on no man. I could fortify it with many additional arguments if I judged it proper; for its *probability* appears to me as strong as the utter *improbability* of the common opinion, to defend which its abettors have descended to insupportable conjectures, of which infidels have availed themselves, to the discredit of the sacred writings. To those who choose to be *wise* and *witty,* and wish to provoke a controversy, this is my answer: *I am doing a great work, so that I cannot come down. Why should the work cease, while I leave it* and *come* DOWN *to* YOU? Neh. vi. 3.

2

CHAPTER XII.

St. Paul mentions some wonderful revelations which he had received from the Lord, 1–5. He speaks of his sufferings in connection with these extraordinary revelations, that his character might be duly estimated, 6. That he might not be too much exalted, a messenger of Satan is sent to buffet him; his prayer for deliverance, and the Divine answer, 7–9. He exults in sufferings and reproaches, and vindicates his apostleship, 10–13. Promises to come and visit them, 14, 15. Answers some objections, 16–18. And expresses his apprehensions that when he visits them he shall find many evils and disorders among them, 19–21.

A. M. 4061.
A. D. 57.
A. U. C.
810.
Anno Imp. Neronis Cæs. 4.

IT is not expedient for me doubtless to glory. ᵃ I will come to visions and revelations of the Lord.

2 I knew a man ᵇ in Christ about fourteen years ago, (whether in the body, I cannot tell; or whether out of the body, I cannot tell; God knoweth :) such a one ᶜ caught up to the third heaven.

A. M. 4061.
A. D. 57.
A. U. C.
810.
Anno Imp. Neronis Cæs. 4.

ᵃ Gr. *For I will come.*——ᵇ Rom. xvi. 7 ; chap. v. 17 ; Gal. i. 22.   ᶜ Acts xxii. 17 ; A. D. 46, at *Lystra* ; Acts xiv. 6.

NOTES ON CHAP. XII.

Verse 1. *It is not expedient for me*] There are several various readings on this verse which are too minute to be noticed here; they seem in effect to represent the verse thus: " If it be expedient to glory, (which does not become me,) I will proceed to visions," &c. The plain meaning of the apostle, in this and the preceding chapter, in reference to *glorying* is, that though to boast in any attainments, or in what God did by him, was in all possible cases to be avoided, as being contrary to the *humility* and *simplicity* of the Gospel; yet the circumstances in which he was found, in reference to the Corinthian Church, and his detractors there, rendered it absolutely necessary; not for his personal vindication, but for the honour of the Gospel, the credit of which was certainly at stake.

I will come to visions] Οπτασιας· Symbolical representations of spiritual and celestial things, in which matters of the deepest importance are exhibited to the eye of the mind by a variety of emblems, the nature and properties of which serve to illustrate those spiritual things.

Revelations] Αποκαλυψεις· A manifestation of things not before known, and such as God alone can make known, because they are a part of his own inscrutable counsels.

Verse 2. *I knew a man in Christ*] I knew a Christian, or a Christian man; for to such alone God now revealed himself, for vision and prophecy had been shut up from the Jews.

Fourteen years ago] On what occasion or in what place this transaction took place we cannot tell; there are many conjectures among learned men concerning it, but of what utility can they be when every thing is so palpably uncertain ? Allowing this epistle to have been written *some time* in the year 57, *fourteen* years counted backward will lead this transaction to the year 42 or 43, which was *about* the time that Barnabas brought Paul from Tarsus to Antioch, Acts xi. 25, 26, and when he and Paul were sent by the Church of Antioch with alms to the poor Christians at Jerusalem. It is very possible that, on this journey, or while in Jerusalem, he had this vision, which was intended to be the means of establishing him in the faith, and supporting him in the many trials and difficulties through which he was to pass. This vision the apostle had kept secret for *fourteen years*.

Whether in the body I cannot tell] That the apostle was in an *ecstasy* or *trance*, something like that of Peter, Acts x. 9, &c., there is reason to believe; but we know that being carried literally into heaven was possible to the Almighty. But as he could not decide himself, it would be ridiculous in us to attempt it.

Caught up to the third heaven.] He appeared to have been carried up to this place; but whether *bodily* he could not tell, or whether the spirit were not separated for the time, and taken up to the third heaven, he could not tell.

The third heaven—The Jews talk of *seven* heavens, and Mohammed has received the same from them ; but these are not only *fabulous* but *absurd*. I shall enumerate those of the Jews.

1. The VELUM, or *curtain*, וילון—" Which in the morning is folded up, and in the evening stretched out." Isa. xl. 22 : *He stretcheth out the heavens as a* CURTAIN, *and* spreadeth *them out as a tent to dwell in.*

2. The *firmament*, or EXPANSE, רקיע—" In which the sun, moon, stars, and constellations are fixed." Gen. i. 17 : *And God placed them in the* FIRMAMENT *of heaven.*

3. The CLOUDS, or ÆTHER, שקים—" Where the mill-stones are which grind the manna for the righteous." Psa. lxxviii. 23, &c. : *Though he had commanded the* CLOUDS *from above, and opened the doors of heaven, and had rained down manna, &c.*

4. The HABITATION, זבול—" Where Jerusalem, and the temple, and the altar, were constructed ; and where Michael the great prince stands and offers sacrifices." 1 Kings viii. 13 : *I have surely built thee a* HOUSE TO DWELL IN, *a settled place for thee to abide in for ever.* " But where is heaven so called ?" Ans. In Isa. lxiii. 15 : *Look down from* HEAVEN, *and behold from the* HABITATION, מזבול, *of thy holiness.*

5. The DWELLING-PLACE, מעון—" Where the troops of angels sing throughout the night, but are silent in the day time, because of the glory of the Israelites." Psa. xlii. 8 : *The Lord will* command his *loving-kind-*

2

A. M. 4061.
A. D. 57.
A. U. C.
810
Anno Imp. Neronis Cæs. 4.

3 And I knew such a man, (whether in the body, or out of the body, I cannot tell, God knoweth:) 4 How that he was caught up into ^d paradise, and heard unspeakable words, which it is not ^e lawful for a man to utter.

5 Of such a one will I glory: ^f yet of myself I will not glory, but in mine infirmities. 6 For ^g though I would desire to glory, I shall not be a fool; for I will say the truth: but *now* I forbear, lest any man

A. M. 4061.
A. D. 57.
A. U. C.
810.
Anno Imp. Neronis Cæs. 4.

---

^d Luke xxiii. 43.——^e Or, *possible*

^f Chap. xi. 30.——^g Chap. x. 8; xi. 16.

---

ness in the day time, and *in the night his song shall be with me*. " But how is it proved that this means heaven ?" Ans. From Deut. xxvi. 15 . *Look down from thy holy habitation*, ממעון, *the* DWELLING-PLACE *of thy holiness; and from heaven*, השמים, *and bless thy people Israel*.

6. The FIXED RESIDENCE, מכון—" Where are the treasures of snow and hail, the repository of noxious dews, of drops, and whirlwinds; the grotto of exhalations," &c. " But where are the heavens thus denominated ?" Ans. In 1 Kings viii. 39, 49, &c. : *Then hear thou in* HEAVEN *thy* DWELLING-PLACE, מכון שבת, *thy* FIXED RESIDENCE.

7. The ARABOTH, ערבות—" Where are justice, judgment, mercy, the treasures of life; peace and blessedness; the souls of the righteous, the souls and spirits which are reserved for the bodies yet to be formed, and the dew by which God is to vivify the dead." Psa. lxxxix. 14, Isa. lix. 17; Psa. xxxvi. 9, Judges vi. 24; Psa. xxiv. 4; 1 Sam. xxv. 29; Isa. lvii. 20; Psa. lxvii. 9 : All of which are termed *Araboth*, Psa. lxviii. 4 . *Extol him who rideth on the heavens*, בערבות *ba* ARABOTH, *by his name Jah*.

All this is sufficiently unphilosophical, and in several cases ridiculous.

In the sacred writings *three* heavens only are mentioned. The *first* is the *atmosphere*, what appears to be intended by רקיע *rekia*, the firmament or expansion, Gen. i. 6. The *second*, the starry heaven; where are the sun, moon, planets, and stars; but these two are often expressed under the one term שמים *shamayim*, the *two heavens*, or expansions, and in Gen. i. 17, they appear to be both expressed by רקיע השמים *rekia hashshamayim*, the *firmament of heaven*. And, *thirdly*, the *place of the blessed*, or the *throne of the Divine glory*, probably expressed by the words שמי השמים *shemei hashshamayim*, the *heavens of heavens*. But on these subjects the Scripture affords us but little light; and on this distinction the reader is not desired to rely.

Much more may be seen in *Schoettgen*, who has exhausted the subject; and who has shown that *ascending to heaven*, or being *caught up to heaven*, is a form of speech among the Jewish writers to express the *highest degrees of inspiration*. They often say of Moses that he *ascended on high, ascended on the firmament, ascended to heaven;* where it is evident they mean only by it that he was favoured with the nearest intimacy with God, and the highest revelations relative to his will, &c. If we may understand St. Paul thus, it will remove much of the difficulty from this place; and perhaps the *unspeakable words*, ver. 4, are thus to be understood. He had the most sublime communications from God, such as would be

improper to mention, though it is very likely that we have the substance of these in his epistles. Indeed, the two epistles before us seem, in many places, to be the effect of most extraordinary revelations.

Verse 4. *Caught up into paradise*] The Jewish writers have no less than *four paradises*, as they have *seven* heavens; but it is needless to wade through their fables. On the word *paradise* see the note on Gen. ii. 8. The Mohammedans call it جنّت الفردوس *jennet alferdoos*, the garden of paradise, and say that God created it out of *light*, and that it is the habitation of the prophets and wise men.

Among Christian writers it generally means the *place of the blessed*, or the state of separate spirits. Whether the third heaven and paradise be the same place we cannot absolutely say; they probably are not; and it is likely that St. Paul, at the time referred to, had at least *two* of these *raptures*.

Which it is not lawful for a man to utter.] The Jews thought that the Divine name, the Tetragrammaton יהוה *Yehovah*, should not be uttered, and that it is absolutely *unlawful* to pronounce it; indeed they say that the true pronunciation is utterly lost, and cannot be recovered without an express revelation. Not one of them, to the present day, ever attempts to utter it; and, when they meet with it in their reading, always supply its place with אדני *Adonai*, Lord. It is probable that the apostle refers to some communication concerning the Divine nature and the Divine economy, of which he was only to make a *general* use in his *preaching* and *writing*. No doubt that what he learned at this time formed the *basis* of all his doctrines.

Cicero terms God *illud inexprimibile*, that inexpressible Being. And *Hermes* calls him ανεκλαλητος. αρρητος, σιωπη φωνουμενος : The *ineffable, the unspeakable, and that which is to be pronounced in silence*. We cannot have views too exalted of the majesty of God; and the less frequently we pronounce his *name*, the more reverence shall we feel for his *nature*. It is said of Mr. *Boyle* that he never pronounced the name of God without either *taking off his hat* or *making a bow*. Leaving out profane swearers, blasphemers, and such like open-faced servants of Satan, it is distressing to hear many well intentioned people making unscripturally free with this sacred name.

Verse 5. *Of such a one will I glory*] Through modesty he does not mention *himself*, though the account can be understood of no other person; for, did he mean any other, the whole account would be completely irrelevant.

Verse 6. *I shall not be a fool*] Who that had got

2

A. M. 4061.
A. D. 57.
A. U. C.
810.
Anno Imp. Nero-
nis Cæs. 4.

should think of me above that which he seeth me *to be*, or *that* he heareth of me.

7 And lest I should be exalted above measure through the abundance of the revelations, there was given to me a [h] thorn in the flesh, [i] the messenger of Satan, to buffet me, lest I should be exalted above measure.

A. M. 4061.
A. D. 57.
A. U. C.
810.
Anno Imp. Nero
nis Cæs. 4.

8 [k] For this thing I besought the Lord thrice, that it might depart from me.

9 And he said unto me, My grace is sufficient for thee: for my strength is made perfect in weakness. Most gladly, therefore, [l] will I rather glory in my infirmities, [m] that the power of Christ may rest upon me.

---

[h] See Ezek. xxviii. 24; Gal. iv. 13, 14.——[i] Job ii. 7; Luke xiii. 16.

[k] See Deut. iii. 23–27; Matthew xxvi. 44.——[l] Chapter xi. 30. [m] 1 Pet. iv. 14.

---

such honour from God would have been fourteen years silent on the subject?

I will say the truth] I speak nothing but truth; and the apostle seems to have intended to proceed with something else of the same kind, but, finding some reason probably occurring suddenly, says, *I forbear*—I will say no more on this subject.

Lest any man should think of me above] The apostle spoke of these revelations for *two* purposes: *first*, lest his *enemies* might suppose they had cause to think *meanly* of him; and, *secondly*, having said thus much, he forbears to speak any farther of them, lest his *friends* should think *too highly* of him. It is a rare gift to discern *when to speak*, and *when* to be *silent*; and to know when enough is said on a subject, neither *too little* nor *too much*.

Verse 7. *And lest I should be exalted*] There were three evils to be guarded against: 1. The *contempt* of his gifts and call by his *enemies*. 2. The *overweening fondness* of his *friends*. And, 3. *Self-exultation*.

A thorn in the flesh] The word σκολοψ signifies a *stake*, and ανασκολοπιζεσθαι, to be *tied to a stake* by way of punishment; and it is used, says *Schoettgen*, to signify the *most oppressive afflictions*. Whatever it was, it was τη σαρκι, *in the flesh*, i. e. of an *outward* kind. It was neither *sin* nor *sinfulness*, for this could not be *given him* to prevent his being *exalted* above measure; for *sin* never had and never can have this tendency. What this *thorn in the flesh* might be has given birth to a multitude of conjectures: *Tertullian* thought it *dolor auriculæ*, the *ear ache*; *Chrysostom*, κεφαλαλγια, the *head ache*; *Cyprian*, *carnis et corporis multa ac gravia tormenta*, many and grievous bodily torments. I believe the apostle to refer simply to the distresses he had endured through the opposition he met with at Corinth; which were as painful and grievous to him as *a thorn in his flesh*, or his being *bound to a stake*; for, if he could have devoted himself to destruction, Rom. ix. 3, for his rebellious and unbelieving countrymen, what must he have suffered on account of an eminent *Church* being perverted and torn to pieces by a false teacher? God permitted this to keep the apostle humble, and at last completely delivered the Church out of the hands and influence of this deceiver; none, not even the incestuous person, having been turned finally out of the way by the false doctrines there preached.

The messenger of Satan] Another mode of expressing what he calls the *thorn in the flesh*; and he seems most plainly to refer to the *false apostle* at

Corinth. The apostle himself was, as he styles himself to this Church, αποστολος Ιησου Χριστου, chap. i. 1, *the apostle of Jesus Christ*. The person in question is styled here αγγελος Σαταν, *the apostle* or *angel of Satan*. It is almost impossible to mistake the apostle's meaning and reference. JESUS CHRIST *sent* Paul to proclaim his truth, and found a Church at Corinth. SATAN, the *adversary* of God's truth, *sent* a man to preach lies at the same place, and turn the Church of God into his own *synagogue*; and by his teaching lies and calumnies the apostle was severely *buffeted*. We need seek no other sense for these expressions. Many, however, think that the apostle had really some *bodily infirmity* that rendered him contemptible, and was the means of obstructing the success of his ministry; and that the false apostle availed himself of this to set St. Paul at nought, and to hold him out to ridicule. I have shown this, elsewhere, to be very unlikely.

The best arguments in favour of this opinion may be found in *Whitby*; but I forbear to transcribe them because I think the meaning given above is more correct. No infirmity of body nor corporeal sufferings can affect and distress a minister of the Gospel, equally to the perversion or scattering of a flock, which were the fruit of innumerable labours, watchings, fastings, prayers, and tears.

Verse 8. *I besought the Lord*] That is, *Christ*, as the next verse absolutely proves, and the Socinians themselves confess. And if Christ be an object of prayer in such a case as this, or indeed in any case, it is a sure proof of his *divinity*; for only an omniscient Being can be made an object of prayer.

Thrice] Several suppose this to be a *certain number* for an *uncertain*; as if he had said, I *often* besought Christ to deliver me from this tormentor; or, which is perhaps more likely, the apostle may refer to *three* solemn, fixed, and fervent applications made to Christ at *different* times; at the last of which he received the answer which he immediately subjoins. It is worthy of remark, that our Lord in his agony acted in the same way: at three different times he applied to God that the cup might depart from him; and in each application he spoke the same words, Matt. xxvi. 39–44. There is, therefore, a manifest allusion to our Lord's conduct in these words of the apostle.

Verse 9. *My grace is sufficient for thee*] Thou shalt not be permitted to sink under these afflictions. Thy enemies shall not be able to prevail against thee.

My strength is made perfect in weakness.] The more, and the more *violently*, thou art afflicted and

A. M. 4061.
A. D. 57.
A. U. C.
810.
Anno Imp. Neronis Cæs. 4.

10 Therefore [n] I take pleasure in infirmities, in reproaches, in necessities, in persecutions, in distresses for Christ's sake : [o] for when I am weak, then am I strong.

11 I am become [p] a fool in glorying; ye have compelled me : for I ought to have been commended of you : for [q] in nothing am I behind the very chiefest apostles, though [r] I be nothing.

12 [s] Truly the signs of an apostle were wrought among you in all patience, in signs, and wonders, and mighty deeds.

13 [t] For what is it wherein you were inferior to other Churches, except *it be* that [u] I myself was not burdensome to you ? forgive me [v] this wrong.

14 [w] Behold, the third time I am ready to

A. M. 4061.
A. D. 57.
A. U. C.
810.
Anno Imp. Neronis Cæs. 4.

---

[n] Rom. v. 3 ; chap. vii. 4.——[o] Chap. xiii. 4.——[p] Chap. xi. 1, 16, 17.——[q] Chap. xi. 5; Gal. ii. 6, 7, 8.——[r] 1 Cor. iii. 7 · xv. 8, 9 ; Eph. iii. 8.

[s] Rom. xv. 18, 19 ; 1 Cor. ix. 2 ; chap. iv. 2 ; vi. 4 ; xi. 6. [t] 1 Cor. i. 7.——[u] 1 Cor. ix. 12 ; chap. xi. 9.——[v] Chap. xi. 7. [w] Chap. xiii. 1.

---

tried, being upheld by my power, and prospered in all thy labours, the more eminently will my power be seen and acknowledged. For the weaker the instrument I use, the more the power of my grace shall be manifested. See at the end of this chapter.

Will I rather glory in my infirmities] Therefore, his *infirmities* do not mean his *corruptions,* or *sins,* or *sinfulness* of any kind ; for it would be blasphemous for any man to say, I will rather glory that God leaves my corruptions in me, than that he should take them away.

That the power of Christ may rest upon me.] Επισκηνωση επ' εμε· That it may *overshadow* me as a *tent,* or *tabernacle ;* affording me *shelter, protection, safety,* and *rest.* This expression is like that, John i. 14 : *And the word was made flesh,* και εσκηνωσεν εν ημιν *and made his tabernacle among us—full of grace and truth.* The same *eternal* WORD promised to make his *tabernacle* with the apostle, and gives him a proof that he was still the same—*full of grace and truth,* by assuring him that his *grace should be sufficient for him.* Paul, knowing that the promise of *grace* could not fail, because of the Divine *truth,* says : *Most gladly, therefore, will I rather glory in my afflictions, that such a* power of Christ *may overshadow* and defend me.

The words are also similar to those of the Prophet Isaiah, chap. iv. 5 : *On all the glory shall be a defence.* God gives the *glory,* and God gives the *defence* of that glory. The apostle had much *glory* or *honour ;* both Satan and his apostles were very envious ; in himself the apostle, as well as all human beings, was *weak,* and therefore needed the *power of God* to defend such glory. Grace alone can preserve grace. When we get a particular blessing we need *another* to *preserve* it ; and without this we shall soon be shorn of our strength, and become as other men. Hence the necessity of continual *watchfulness* and *prayer,* and *depending* on the *all-sufficient grace of Christ.* See on chap. xi. 30.

Verse 10. Therefore I take pleasure] I not only *endure* them *patiently,* but am *pleased* when they occur ; for I do it *for Christ's sake*—on his account ; for on his account I suffer. *For when I am weak*—most oppressed with trials and afflictions, *then am I strong ;* God supporting my mind with his most powerful influences, causing me to rejoice with joy unspeakable and full of glory.

Verse 11. I am become a fool in glorying] It is not the part of a *wise* or *gracious* man to *boast ;* but

ye have compelled me—I have been obliged to do it, in order to vindicate the cause of God.

I ought to have been commended of you] You should have vindicated both myself and my ministry against the detractors that are among you.

The very chiefest apostles] See chap. xi. 1.

Though I be nothing.] Though I have been thus *set at nought* by your false apostle ; and though, in consequence of what he has said, some of you have been ready to consider me *as nothing*—what we call *good for nothing.* This must be the meaning of the apostle, as the following verses prove.

A kind of *technical* meaning has been *imposed* on these words, of which many good people seem very fond. *I am nothing*—I am all sin, defilement, and unworthiness in myself ; but *Jesus Christ is all in all.* This latter clause is an eternal truth ; the former may be very true also ; the person who uses it may be all *sin, defilement,* &c., but let him not say that the *apostle of the Gentiles* was so too, because this is not true ; it is false, and it is injurious to the character of the apostle and to the grace of Christ ; besides, it is not the meaning of the text, and the use commonly made of it is abominable, if not wicked.

Verse 12. The signs of an apostle were wrought among you] Though I have been reputed as *nothing,* I have given the fullest proof of my *Divine mission* by various signs, wonders, and miracles, and by that *patience* which I have manifested towards you : though I had power from God to inflict punishment on the transgressors, I have in every case forborne to do it. Is the man *nothing* who wrought such *miracles* among you ?

Verse 13. For what is it wherein you were inferior] This is a fine, forcible, yet delicate *stroke.* It was *your* duty and your interest to have supported your apostle ; other Churches have done so : I did not require this from you ; in this respect all other Churches are *superior* to *you.* I am the cause of your *inferiority,* by not giving you an opportunity of *ministering* to my necessities · *forgive me the wrong* I have done you. It is the *privilege* of the Churches of Christ to support the ministry of his Gospel among them. Those who do not contribute their part to the support of the Gospel ministry either care nothing for it, or derive no good from it.

Verse 14. The third time I am ready] That is, this is the third time that *I am ready*—have formed the *resolution,* to visit you. He had formed this

A. M. 4061.
A. D. 57.
A. U. C.
810.
Anno Imp. Nero-
nis Cæs. 4.

come to you; and I will not be burdensome to you: for ˣ I seek not yours, but you: ʸ for the children ought not to lay up for the parents, but the parents for the children.

15 And ᶻ I will very gladly spend and be spent ᵃ for ᵇ you; though ᶜ the more abundantly I love you, the less I be loved.

16 But be it so, ᵈ I did not burden you; nevertheless, being crafty, I caught you with guile.

17 ᵉ Did I make a gain of you by any of them whom I sent unto you?

18 ᶠ I desired Titus, and with him I sent a ᵍ brother. Did Titus make a gain of you? walked we not in the same spirit? walked we not in the same steps?

A. M. 4061.
A. D. 57.
A. U. C.
810.
Anno Imp. Nero
nis Cæs. 4.

19 ʰ Again, think ye that we excuse ourselves unto you? ⁱ we speak before God in Christ: but ᵏ we do all things, dearly beloved, for your edifying.

20 For I fear, lest, when I come, I shall not find you such as I would; and that ˡ I shall be found unto you such as ye would not: lest

---

ˣ Acts xx. 33; 1 Cor. x. 33.——ʸ 1Cor. iv. 14, 15.——ᶻ 1 Thess. ii. 8; Phil. ii. 17.——ᵃ John x. 11; chap. i. 6; Col i. 24; 2 Tim. ii. 10.——ᵇ Gr. *your souls.*——ᶜ Chap. vi. 12, 13.

ᵈ Chap. xi. 9.——ᵉ Chap. vii. 2.——ᶠ Chap. viii. 6, 16, 22. ᵍ Chap. viii. 18.——ʰ Chap. v. 12.——ⁱ Rom. ix. 1; chap. xi. 31. ᵏ 1 Cor. x. 33.——ˡ 1 Cor. iv. 21; chap. x. 2; xiii. 2, 10.

---

solution *twice* before, but was disappointed. See 1 Cor. xvi. 5, and 2 Cor. i. 15, 16. He now formed it a *third time*, having more probability of seeing them now than he had before. See chap. xiii. 2.

I seek not yours, but you] I seek your *salvation*, I desire not your *property;* others have sought your *property*, but not your *salvation.* See chap. xi. 20.

For the children ought not to lay up for the parents] You may have *many teachers*, but you have but one FATHER; *for in Christ Jesus I have begotten you through the Gospel;* see 1 Cor. iv. 15. Ye are my *children*, and I am your father. You have not contributed to *my* support, but I have been labouring for your life. I will act towards you as the loving father who works hard, and lays up what is necessary to enable his children to get their bread.

Verse 15. *And I will very gladly spend and be spent for you*] I will continue to act as a loving father, who spends all he has upon his children, and expends his own strength and life in providing for them the things necessary for their preservation and comfort.

Though the more abundantly I love you] I will even act towards you with the most affectionate tenderness, though it happen to me, as it often does to loving fathers, that their disobedient children love them less, in proportion as their love to them is increased. Does it not frequently happen that the most disobedient child in the family is that one on which the parents' tenderness is more especially placed? See the parable of the prodigal son. It is in the order of God that it should be so, else the case of every prodigal would be utterly deplorable. The shepherd feels more for the lost sheep than for the ninety-nine that have not gone astray.

If I be asked, " Should Christian parents lay up money for their children?" I answer: It is the duty of every parent who can, to lay up what is necessary to put every child in a condition to earn its bread. If he neglect this, he undoubtedly sins against God and nature. " But should not a man lay up, besides this, a *fortune* for his children, if he can honestly?" I answer: Yes, if there be no poor within his reach; no good work which he can assist; no heathen region on the earth to which he can contribute to send the Gospel of Jesus; but not otherwise. God shows, in

the course of his providence, that this laying up of fortunes for children is not right; for there is scarcely ever a case where money has been saved up to make the children *independent* and *gentlemen*, in which God has not cursed the blessing. It was saved from the *poor*, from the *ignorant*, from the *cause of God;* and the canker of his displeasure consumed this *ill-saved* property.

Verse 16. *But be it so, I did not burden you*] That is: You grant that I did not burden you, that I took nothing from you, but preached to you the Gospel freely; but you say that, BEING CRAFTY, *I caught you with guile;* i. e. getting from you, by means of *others*, what I pretended to be unwilling to receive immediately from yourselves.

Many persons suppose that the words, *being crafty, I caught you with guile*, are the words of the apostle, and not of his slanderers; and therefore have concluded that it is lawful to use guile, deceit, &c., in order to serve a good and a religious purpose. This doctrine is abominable; and the words are most evidently those of the apostle's detractors, against which he defends his conduct in the two following verses.

Verse 17. *Did I make a gain of you*] Did any person I ever sent to preach the Gospel to you, or help you in your Christian course, ever get any thing from you for me? Produce the proof if you can.

Verse 18. *I desired Titus*] I never sent any to you but *Titus* and *another brother;* chap. viii. 6, 18. And did *Titus make a gain of you?* Did he get any thing from you, either for *himself* or for *me?* You know he did not. He was actuated by the *same spirit*, and he *walked* in the *same steps.*

Verse 19. *Think ye that we excuse ourselves*] Απολογουμεθα; That we make an apology for our conduct; or, that I have sent Titus and that brother to you because I was ashamed or afraid to come myself?

We speak before God in Christ] I have not done so; I speak the truth before God; he is judge whether I was actuated in this way by any sinister or unworthy motive.

For your edifying.] Whatever I have done in this or any other way, I have done for your *edifying;* not for any *emolument* to myself or friends.

Verse 20. *I fear, lest, when I come*] I think the

A. M. 4061.
A. D. 57.
A. U. C.
810.
Anno Imp. Nero-
nis Cæs. 4.

there be debates, envyings, wraths, strifes, backbitings, whisperings, swellings, tumults :

21 *And* lest, when I come again, my God ᵐ will humble me among you,

and *that* I shall bewail many ⁿ which have sinned already, and have not repented of the uncleanness and ᵒ fornication and lasciviousness which they have committed.

A. M. 4061.
A. D. 57.
A. U. C.
810.
Anno Imp. Nero
nis Cæs. 4.

ᵐ Chap. ii. 1, 4.——ⁿ Chap. xiii. 2.

ᵒ 1 Cor. v. 1.

---

present time is used here for the *past ;* the apostle seems most evidently to be giving them the *reason* why he *had not come* to them according to his former purposes, and why he sent Titus and his companion. He was afraid to come at that time lest he should have found them perverted from the right way, and he be obliged to make use of his apostolical *rod*, and punish the offenders ; but, feeling towards them the heart of a tender *father*, he was unwilling to use the *rod ;* and sent the first epistle to them, and the messengers above mentioned, being reluctant to go himself till he had satisfactory evidence that their divisions were ended, and that they had repented for and put away the evils that they had committed ; and that he should not be obliged to bewail them who had sinned so abominably, and had not repented for their crimes. If this verse be understood in this way, all difficulty will vanish ; otherwise, what is here said does seem to contradict what is said, chap. vii. 6, 16, &c. ; as well as many things both in the *eighth* and *ninth* chapters.

Debates, envyings] From these different expressions, which are too *plain* to need interpretation, we see what a *distracted* and *divided* state the Church at Corinth must have been in. *Brotherly love* and *charity* seem to have been driven out of this once heavenly assembly. These *debates*, &c., are precisely the opposites to that *love* which the apostle recommends and explains by its different *properties* in the 13th chapter of his first epistle.

Mr. Wakefield translates the original thus : *strifes, rivalries, passions, provocations, slanders, whisperings, swellings, quarrels.*

Verse 21. *Lest, when I come again*] And even after all that has been done for you, I fear that when I *do come*—when I pay you my *second* visit, *my God will humble me*—will permit me to be *affected* with deep sorrow through what I may see among you ; as I have been by the *buffetings* of the *apostle of Satan*, who has perverted you. Humiliation is repeatedly used for *affliction*, and here ταπεινωση has certainly that meaning.

Have sinned already] Προημαρτηκοτων· *Who have sinned before ;* who were some of the *first* offenders, and have not yet repented.

Of the uncleanness, &c.] There must have been a total relaxation of discipline, else such abominations could not have been tolerated in the Christian Church. And although what is here spoken could only be the case of a *few ;* yet the *many* were ill disciplined, else these must have been cast out. On the whole, this Church seems to have been a composition of excellences and defects, of vices and virtues ; and should not be quoted as a *model* for a Christian Church.

1. From St. Paul we receive *two remarkable sayings* of our Lord, which are of infinite value to the welfare and salvation of man ; which are properly parts of the Gospel, but are not mentioned by any evangelist. The *first* is in Acts xx. 35 : *I have showed you the words of the Lord Jesus, how he said*, IT IS MORE BLESSED TO GIVE THAN TO RECEIVE. Every liberal heart feels this in bestowing its bounty ; and every poor man, who is obliged to receive help, and whose independency of spirit is still whole in him, feels this too. To the *genuine* poor, it is more *burdensome* to *receive* a kindness, than it is to the *generous* man who gives it. The *second* is recorded in the *ninth* verse of this chapter : *He said unto me*, MY GRACE IS SUFFICIENT FOR THEE ; FOR MY STRENGTH IS MADE PERFECT IN WEAKNESS. Of these two most blessed sayings, St. Paul is the only *evangelist*. This last is of *general* application. In all *states* and *conditions* of life God's grace is sufficient for us. If in any case we *miscarry*, it is because we have not *sought God earnestly*. Let no man say that he is overcome by sin through want of grace ; God's grace was sufficient for him, but he did not apply for it *as did* St. Paul, and therefore he did not receive it. Men often lay the issue of their own infidelity to the charge of God, they excuse their commission of sin through their scantiness of grace ; whereas the whole is owing to their *carelessness*, and *refusal to be saved in God's own way ;* and in *this way* alone will God save any man, because it is the only effectual way.

2. The apostle must have been brought into a blessed state of subjection to God, when he could say, *I take pleasure in infirmities ;* that is, in *afflictions* and *sufferings* of different kinds. Though this language was spoken on *earth*, we may justly allow, with one, that he learned it in HEAVEN.

3. St. Paul preached the Gospel without being *burdensome*. In every case the *labourer is worthy of his hire*. He who labours for the cause of God should be supported by the cause of God ; but wo to that man who aggrandizes himself and grows *rich* by the *spoils of the faithful !* And to him especially who has made a fortune out of the *pence* of the poor ! In such a man's heart the *love of money* must have its *throne*. As to his professed *spirituality*, it is *nothing ;* he is a *whited sepulchre*, and an abomination in the sight of the Lord. If a man will love the world, (and he does love it who makes a fortune by the offerings of the poor,) the love of the Father is not in him

CHAPTER XIII.

The apostle again says that this is the third time he has purposed to come and see them; and threatens that he will, by the power of Christ, punish every incorrigible sinner, 1–4. Exhorts them to examine themselves, whether they be in the faith, 5, 6. Prays that they may do no evil, 7. And shows how ardently he wished their complete restoration to unity and purity, 8, 9. Tells them for what reason he writes to them, 10. Bids them farewell, 11. Gives them some directions, and concludes with his apostolical benediction, 12–14.

A. M. 4061.
A. D. 57.
A. U. C.
810.
Anno Imp. Neronis Cæs. 4.

THIS *is* ᵃ the third *time* I am coming to you. ᵇ In the mouth of two or three witnesses shall every word be established.

2 ᶜ I told you before, and foretell you, as if I were present, the second time; and being absent now I write to them ᵈ which heretofore

have sinned, and to all other, that, if I come again, ᵉ I will not spare;

3 Since ye seek a proof of Christ ᶠ speaking in me, which to you-ward is not weak, but is mighty ᵍ in you.

4 ʰ For though he was crucified through

A. M. 4061.
A. D. 57.
A. U. C.
810.
Anno Imp. Neronis Cæs. 4.

ᵃ Chap. xii. 14.——ᵇ Num. xxxv. 30; Deut. xvii. 6; xix. 15; Matt. xviii. 16; John viii. 17; Heb. x. 28.——ᶜ Chap. x. 2. ᵈ Chap. xii. 21.——ᵉ Chap. i. 23.——ᶠ Matt. x. 20; 1 Cor. v. 4; chap. ii. 10.——ᵍ 1 Cor. ix. 2.——ʰ Phil. ii. 7, 8; 1 Pet. iii. 18.

NOTES ON CHAP. XIII.

Verse 1. *This is the third* time *I am coming to you.*] These words are nearly the same with those chap. xii. 14; and probably refer to the purpose which he had *twice* before formed of seeing them. But the latter clause seems to attach a different meaning to the passage; at least so it has been understood by some learned men.

Schoettgen thus interprets the whole: the *first* coming of the apostle to Corinth was when he *personally* visited them, and there founded the Christian Church. By his *second* coming we are to understand his first epistle to them; and, by his being now ready to come to them the *third* time, we are to understand this *second* epistle, which he was then going to send them. These were the *two* witnesses, and the apostle the *third*, which he gave to the Corinthians concerning the truth of his own ministry, or the falsity of the ministry of the pretended apostle.

Calmet contends that the apostle had been *twice* before at Corinth, and that he now purposed to go a *third* time; and that these visits were the *two* or *three witnesses* to which the apostle appeals.

Dr. *Lightfoot* thinks that the two or three witnesses were *Stephanas*, *Fortunatus*, and *Achaicus*, sent to assure them of his coming. But this opinion cannot be supported.

With respect to the *two* or *three witnesses* establishing the subject, Dr. *Whitby* says: "Though these words seem to be cited from Deut. xix. 15, rather than from Matt. xviii. 16, it being rare to find this apostle citing any thing from the New Testament, without calling it *an ordinance of the Lord*, yet it is probable that he here alludes to the practice there prescribed for the reclaiming of offenders. And then his *first* epistle being written with this introduction: *Paul an apostle, and Sosthenes*; his *second* thus: *Paul and Timotheus*; may pass for *two or three witnesses*; and his *presence* the *third* time in *person*, to exercise his censures on those offenders, before the body of the Church, may bear a fair resemblance to our Lord's prescription in the above case: *If thy bro-*

ther offend," &c.—So far *Whitby*. See my notes on Matt. xviii. 16.

Verse 2. *I told you before, &c.*] As *Calmet* maintains that Paul had already been *twice* at Corinth, it is well to hear his reasons: "St. Paul came to Corinth the latter end of the year of our Lord 52, and remained there eighteen months, Acts xviii. 1, &c. He came there a *second* time in the year 55, but stayed only a short time, as he had to return speedily to Ephesus, 1 Cor. xvi. 7; hence it is that St. Luke makes no mention of this *second* journey in the Acts. Finally he determined to visit them a *third* time; as in effect he did about the year 57. Of his *second* voyage to Corinth, which is not mentioned in the Acts, he speaks expressly in this verse."

I do not see sufficient evidence to induce me to subscribe to this opinion of Calmet. I believe the apostle had been but *once* before at Corinth; and this matter is set in a clear point of view by Dr. *Paley*.—See the Introduction, sec. xi.

I will not spare] I will inflict the proper punishment on every incorrigible offender. It *does* appear, from all the apostle's threatenings, that he was possessed of a miraculous power, by which he could inflict punishment on offenders; that he *could deliver the body to Satan for the destruction of the flesh, that the spirit might be saved in the day of the Lord Jesus*, 1 Cor. iv. 21; v. 5. What he says he told them before probably relates to 1 Cor. iv. 21: *Shall I come with a rod, &c.*

Verse 3. *Since ye seek a proof of Christ*] The conversion of the Corinthians was to themselves a solid proof that Christ spoke by the apostle; and therefore he could, with great propriety, say that this *power of Christ*, far from being *weak*, was *mighty among them*.

Verse 4. *For though he was crucified through weakness*] It is true Christ was crucified, and his crucifixion appeared to be the effect of his *weakness*; yet even this was not so; he gave up his life, none could take it away from him; and in his last struggle, had he even been deficient in power, he could have had more than twelve legions of angels to support him against the

A. M. 4061.
A. D. 57.
A. U. C.
810.
Anno Imp. Neronis Cæs. 4.

weakness, yet [i] he liveth by the power of God. For [k] we also are weak [l] in him, but we shall live with him by the power of God toward you.

5 [m] Examine yourselves, whether ye be in the faith; prove your own selves. Know ye not your own selves, [n] how that Jesus Christ is in you, except ye be [o] reprobates?

A. M. 4061.
A. D. 57.
A. U. C.
810.
Anna Imp. Neronis Cæs. 4.

6 But I trust that ye shall know that we are not reprobates.

7 Now I pray to God that ye do no evil; not that we should appear approved, but that ye should do that which is honest, though [p] we be as reprobates.

8 For we can do nothing against the truth, but for the truth.

9 For we are glad, [q] when we are weak, and

---

[i] Rom. vi. 4.——[k] See chap. x. 3, 4.——[l] Or, *with him.*——[m] 1 Cor. xi. 28.

[n] Rom. viii. 10; Gal. iv. 19.——[o] 1 Cor. ix. 27.——[p] Chap. vi. 9. [q] 1 Cor. iv. 10; chap. xi. 30; xii. 5, 9, 10.

---

high priest's mob, Matt. xxvi. 53; but how then could the Scripture be fulfilled? And had he *not died*, how could the human race have been *saved?*

Yet he liveth by the power of God.] Though he appeared to be crucified through his own weakness, yet he now liveth by the power of God; exerting an almighty energy by which all things are subject to him.

We also are weak in him] Because we are on Christ's side we appear to *you* as *weak* as he did to the *Jews;* but it is not so, for *we live with him*—under the same influence, and partaking of the same life; manifesting by our preaching and miracles the *power of God towards you.* While I do not use the *rod,* I appear to you *weak;* I will use it, and then you shall find me to be *strong.*

Verse 5. *Examine yourselves, whether ye be in the faith*] Ἑαυτους πειραζετε· *Try yourselves;* pierce your hearts; *bore yourselves throughout;* try yourselves by what I have written, and see whether ye retain the true faith of the Gospel.

Prove your own selves.] Ἑαυτους δοκιμαζετε· Put *yourselves to the test,* as you would try *gold* or *silver* suspected of *adulteration.* No more take that for *Gospel* which is not so, than you would take *adulterated money* for *sterling* coin. This is a metaphor taken from *testing* or *assaying* adulterated metals.

Know ye not your own selves] Are ye not full of wisdom and understanding? And is it not as easy to find out a *spurious* faith as it is to detect a *base coin?* There is an *assay* and *touchstone* for both. If *base* metal be mixed with the *pure* you can readily detect it; and as easily may you know that you are *in the faith* as you can know that *base metal* is mixed with the *pure.* Does Jesus Christ dwell in you? You have his *Spirit,* his power, his mind, if ye be Christians; and the Spirit of Christ bears witness with your spirit that ye are the children of God. And this is the case except ye *be reprobates;* αδοκιμοι, base *counterfeit coin;* mongrel Christians. This metaphor holds excellently here. They had a *Judaizing* Christian among them; such, presumptively, was the *false apostle:* they had received his *Judaico-Christian* doctrine, and were what the prophet said of some of the Israelites in his time *Reprobate silver,* adulterated coin, *shall men call them,* Jer. vi. 30. And thus, when they were brought to the *test,* they were found reprobate; that is, adulterated with this mixture of bad doctrine. There is no other kind of reprobation mentioned here than that which refers to the trial and rejection of

adulterated coin; and, by way of metaphor, to the detection of false Christianity. This reprobation came of the people themselves: they, not God, adulterated the pure metal. Man pollutes himself; then God reprobates the polluted.

Verse 6. *Ye shall know that we are not reprobates.*] Ye have had, and ye shall have, the fullest proof that I have preached the true faith among you; and that God has confirmed it by his testimony; and thus that I am *proved* and manifested to be what I ought to be, and shown to be *approved* of God.

Verse 7. *I pray to God that ye do no evil*] That ye do not persist in that course which will oblige me to use the power of Christ, with which I am endued, to punish you. Some apply this prayer to the apostle himself: *Now I pray to God that I may do* you *no evil*—that I may not be obliged to use my apostolic *rod,* and inflict evil upon you.

Not that we should appear approved] We do not wish to give this proof that we are approved of God, by inflicting this punishment on the transgressors.

But that ye should do that which is honest] That ye may do that which is *right* and *seemly,* το καλον, *though we should be,* in consequence of that, *as reprobates*—as persons *not approved* of God; because your reformation will *prevent* the exercise of this power, which would otherwise have given an *awful proof* that we are *approved* of God.

Verse 8. *For we can do nothing against the truth, but for the truth.*] As we are the apostles of God, we cannot bring to you any *false* doctrine; and, as we profess to be under the influence of God's Spirit, we cannot do any thing that is opposed to that truth, or which might be prejudicial to it. On the contrary, what we say and do is *for* that *truth,* to propagate and establish it. The Gospel of Jesus is truth; and my testimony concerning it is truth also. In my coming, and in my *rod,* you have nothing to fear, if you retain and abide in this truth.

Verse 9. *For we are glad, when we are weak*] It will give me indescribable pleasure that I should still appear to be *poor, despicable,* and *destitute of this extraordinary power* with which God has clothed me, so that you *be strong* in all the gifts and graces of the Holy Spirit.

And this also we wish, even *your perfection.*] We cannot be satisfied that persons, with such eminent endowments, and who have once received the truth as it is in Jesus, should be deficient in any of the graces

2

A. M. 4061.
A. D. 57.
A. U. C.
810.
Anno Imp. Nero-
nis Cæs. 4.

ye are strong: and this also we wish, ʳ *even* your perfection.

10 ˢ Therefore I write these things being absent, lest being present ᵗ I should use sharpness, ᵘ according to the power which the Lord hath given me to edification, and not to destruction.

11 Finally, brethren, farewell. Be perfect, be of good comfort, ᵛ be of one mind, live in peace ; and the God of love ʷ and peace shall be with you.

A. M. 4061.
A. D. 57.
A. U. C.
810.
Anno Imp. Nero
nis Cæs. 4.

12 ˣ Greet one another with a holy kiss.

13 All the saints salute you.

14 ʸ The grace of the Lord Jesus Christ, and the love of God, and ᶻ the communion of the Holy Ghost, *be* with you all. Amen.

¶ The Second *Epistle* to the Corinthians was written from Philippi, *a city* of Macedonia, by Titus and Lucas.

ʳ 1 Thess. iii. 10.——ˢ 1 Cor. iv. 21 ; chap. ii. 3 ; x. 2 ; xii. 20, 21.——ᵗ Tit. i. 13.——ᵘ Chap. x. 8.——ᵛ Rom. xii. 16, 18 ; xv. 5 ; 1 Cor. i. 10 ; Phil. ii. 2 ; iii. 16 ; 1 Pet. iii. 8.

ʷ Romans xv. 33.——ˣ Rom. xvi. 16 ; 1 Corinthians xvi. 20 ; 1 Thess. v. 26 ; 1 Peter v. 14.——ʸ Romans xvi. 24.——ᶻ Phil. ii. 1.

---

that constitute the mind of Christ ; such as brotherly love, charity, harmony, unity, and order. I have given the above paraphrase to this verse, because of the last term καταρτισιν, which we render *perfection*. Καταρ-τισις, from κατα, *intensive*, and αρτιζω, to *fit* or *adapt*, signifies the reducing of a *dislocated* limb to its proper place ; and hence, as *Beza* says on this passage : " The apostle's meaning is, that whereas the *members* of the Church were all, as it were, *dislocated* and *out of joint*, they should be *joined together* in love ; and they should endeavour to make *perfect* what was amiss among them, either in faith or morals."

It is a metaphor, also, taken from a *building ;* the several *stones* and *timbers* being all put in their proper places and situations, so that the whole building might be *complete*, and be a *proper habitation* for the owner. The same *figure*, though not in the same *terms*, the apostle uses, Eph. ii. 20—22.

The *perfection* or *rejointing* which the apostle wishes is that which refers to the *state of the Church* in its *fellowship, unity, order,* &c. And *perfection* in the *soul* is the same, in reference to it, as perfection in the *Church* is to its order and unity. The perfection or rejointing of the soul implies its purification, and placing every *faculty, passion,* and *appetite* in its proper place ; so that the original order, harmony, unity, and purity of the soul may be restored ; and the whole builded up to be a habitation of God through the Spirit, Eph. ii. 22.

Verse 10. *Therefore I write these things*] I only threaten you now, by this epistle, to put you on your guard, and lead you to reformation before I visit you ; that I may not then have to use *sharpness*, αποτομια, *a cutting off,* employing thus my apostolical authority to inflict punishment ; a *power* which God has *given* me, rather to be employed in your *edification* than in your *destruction*.

Verse 11. *Finally*] Λοιπον· All that *remains* for me now to write is, to wish you all manner of happiness, and so to take my leave.

Farewell.] A good wish, from our old mother tongue, compounded of ꝼaꞃan, *to go,* and ꝑel, *fairly, properly,* or ꝑela, with *felicity ; go on prosperously !* This is the spirit of this good wish.

The Greek χαιρετε signifies nearly the same thing. Χαιρω means to be *very joyous ;* χαιρετε, *be joyous and*

happy, be ever prosperous ; this was among the last words which Cyrus, when dying, spoke to his friends.

Be perfect] Καταρτιζεσθε· *Be compact ; get into joint again ;* let *unity* and *harmony* be restored. See the note on ver. 9.

Be of good comfort] Παρακαλεισθε· *Receive admonition ;* for παρακαλεω signifies to *admonish, beg, entreat,* and also *to comfort. Receive admonition,* that ye may *receive comfort.* If ye take my *advice,* ye shall have *consolation ;* if ye do *not,* ye will have nothing but *misery* and *wo.*

Be of one mind] Το αυτο φρονειτε· *Think the same ;* let there be no dissensions among you. Be of the same creed, and let disputes about that religion which should be the *bond* of *peace* for ever subside.

Live in peace] Ειρηνευετε· *Cultivate peace ;* or, as he says elsewhere, *Follow peace, and pursue it,* Heb. xii. 14. Cultivate a *peaceable disposition,* and neither say nor do any thing which has a tendency to irritate each other.

And the God of love and peace shall be with you.] While ye are full of contentions, dissensions, and discord, *peace* can have no place among you ; and as to *love,* the fulfilling of the law, that worketh no ill to its neighbour, it has necessarily taken its flight. *Love* cannot live, neither exist, where there are brawls, contentions, and divisions. And where neither *peace* nor *love* is to be found, there God cannot be. And if ʜᴇ be not there, *yourselves* and the *devil* make the whole assembly.

Verse 12. *Greet one another with a holy kiss.*] Use every means by which a *good understanding* may be brought about. Let the *spirit of friendship* live among you, and encourage its continuance by every *friendly act.* See the note on Rom. xvi. 16.

Verse 13. *All the saints*] The *Christians* of *Macedonia* or *Philippi,* from which he wrote this epistle. In the primitive Church a *saint* and a *Christian* were the same thing ; for the Christian religion calls every man to be *holy.*

Verse 14. *The grace of the Lord Jesus Christ*] All the *favour* and *beneficence* that come *from* and *through* the Redeemer of the world ; as the Lᴏʀᴅ, the *ruler* and *governor* of all things ; as Jᴇsᴜs, the *Saviour* of all men by his passion and death ; as *Christ,* the distributer of all that Divine *unction* which enlightens, comforts, harmonizes, and purifies the mind. May this most exalted, glorious, and all-sufficient Saviour, be ever with you!

And the love of God] God, your *Maker*, in that infinite love which induced him to create the world, and form man in his own image and in his own likeness, that he might be capable of knowing, loving, and enjoying him for ever; and God in the fullest manifestations of that love which caused him to give his only begotten Son, to the end that they who believe on him should not perish, but have everlasting life. May this *God of love*, and this *love of God*, be ever with you!

And the communion of the Holy Ghost] May that Holy Spirit, that Divine and eternal energy which proceeds from the Father and the Son; that heavenly *fire* that gives *light* and *life*, that purifies and refines, sublimes and exalts, comforts and invigorates, make you all *partakers* with himself!

Κοινωνια, which we translate *fellowship* and *communion*, signifies properly *participation*; having things *in common*; *partaking with each other*. This points out the astonishing privileges of true believers: they have *communion* with God's Spirit; share in all its *gifts* and *graces*; *walk* in its *light*; through him they have the fullest *confidence* that they are of God, that he is their father and friend, and has blotted out all their iniquities: this they know by the Spirit which he has given them. And is it possible that a man shall be a *partaker* with the *Holy Ghost*, and *not know it*! that he shall be *full of light* and *love*, and *not know* it! that he shall have the *spirit* of *adoption*, by which he can cry, Abba! Father! and yet *know nothing* of his *relationship* to God, but by *inference* from indirect proofs! In a word, that he shall have the *grace of our Lord Jesus Christ, the love of God, and the communion of the Holy Ghost with him*, and all the while *know* nothing *certain* of the *grace*, as to his *portion* in it; *feel* nothing *warming* from the *love*, as to its part *in him*; and nothing *energetic* from the *communion*, as to his *participation* in the gifts and graces of this Divine energy! This is all as absurd as it is impossible. Every genuine Christian, who maintains a close walk with God, may have as *full an evidence of his acceptance with God* as he has of his *own existence*. And the doctrine that explains away this privilege, or softens it down to nothing, by making the most gracious and safe state consistent with innumerable *doubts* and *fears* and *general uncertainty*, is not of God. It is a *spurious gospel*, which, under the show of a *voluntary humility*, not only *lowers*, but almost *annihilates*, the *standard* of *Christianity*.

This text, as well as that, Matt. iii. 16, 17, and that other, Matt. xxviii. 19, *strongly* marks the doctrine of the *holy* TRINITY. See the note on this latter text. And had not the apostle been convinced that there was a *personality* in this *ever-blessed* and *undivided Trinity*, he could not have expressed himself thus. And had not our Lord intended to be understood in *this way*, he would not have given such a commission to his apostles, to baptize the nations in the name of the *Father*, and of the *Son*, and of the *Holy Ghost*. The doctrine is the teaching of God, let men make of it what they please. And the genuine Church of God have ever received and understood it in this way.

Amen.] This word is wanting, as usual, in almost every MS. of authority. *Amen* seems to have been anciently added at the conclusion of books, exactly as we add the word *finis*, both merely signifying the end.

As to the *inscription*, it is wanting, either in whole or in part, in almost all the ancient MSS. The principal forms in which it exists are the following:—

To the Corinthians, the second.—The second to the Corinthians is completed.—The second to the Corinthians is finished.—To the Corinthians, the second, written from Philippi.—Written from Philippi by Titus.—Written from Philippi by Titus and Luke.—By Titus, Barnabas, and Luke.—The Second Epistle to the Corinthians was written from Philippi of Macedonia, and sent by Titus, SYRIAC.—*The End of the Epistle. It was written from the city of Philippi by Titus and Luke. Praise be to God for ever,* ARABIC. —In the VULGATE *there is no subscription; nor in the* ETHIOPIC.—*Written in Philippi of Macedonia, and sent by Titus and Luke,* COPTIC.—*The Second Epistle to the Corinthians is ended; which was written from Philippi of Macedonia, by Titus and Luke,* SYR. PHILOX.

It has been often remarked that no dependence can be placed on many of the subscriptions to the sacred books, which are found in MSS. and versions, because those subscriptions were not written by the *authors* of those books, but were afterwards added by the *transcribers* or *copiers*, who followed either tradition or their own judgment. It is generally allowed that this second epistle was written from *Macedonia*; and probably from the city of *Philippi*, in that province. See the *introduction* and *preface* to this epistle.

Finished the correction for a new edition, Dec. 13th, 1831.—A. C.

INTRODUCTION

TO THE

EPISTLE OF PAUL THE APOSTLE

TO THE

GALATIANS.

THE authenticity of this epistle is ably vindicated by Dr. Paley : the principal part of his arguments I shall here introduce, and doubt not that they will be considered demonstrative evidence by every candid and unprejudiced reader.

SECTION I.

The argument of this epistle in some measure proves its antiquity. It will hardly be doubted that it was written whilst the dispute concerning the circumcision of Gentile converts was fresh in men's minds ; for, even supposing it to have been a forgery, the only credible motive that can be assigned for the forgery was, to bring the name and authority of the apostle into this controversy. No design could be so insipid, or so unlikely to enter into the thoughts of any man, as to produce an epistle written earnestly and pointedly upon one side of a controversy, when the controversy itself was dead, and the question no longer interesting to any description of readers whatever. Now the controversy concerning the circumcision of the Gentile Christians was of such a nature that, if it arose at all, it must have arisen in the beginning of Christianity. As Judea was the scene of the Christian history ; as the author and preachers of Christianity were Jews ; as the religion itself acknowledged and was founded upon the Jewish religion, in contradistinction to every other religion then professed amongst mankind ; it was not to be wondered at that some of its teachers should carry it out in the world rather as a *sect* and modification of Judaism, than as a separate original revelation ; or that they should invite their proselytes to those observances in which they lived themselves. This was likely to happen ; but if it did not happen *at first*, if, whilst the religion was in the hands of Jewish teachers, no such claim was advanced, no such condition was attempted to be imposed, it is not probable that the doctrine would be started, much less that it should prevail, in any future period. I likewise think that those pretensions of Judaism were much more likely to be insisted upon whilst the Jews continued a nation, than after their fall and dispersion ; whilst Jerusalem and the temple stood, than after the destruction brought upon them by the Roman arms, the fatal cessation of the sacrifice and the priesthood, the humiliating loss of their country, and, with it, of the great rites and symbols of their institution. It should seem, therefore, from the nature of the subject, and the situation of the parties, that this controversy was carried on in the interval between the preaching of Christianity to the Gentiles and the invasion of Titus ; and that our present epistle, which was undoubtedly intended to bear a part in this controversy, must be referred to the same period.

But again : the epistle supposes that certain designing adherents of the Jewish law had crept into the Churches of Galatia, and had been endeavouring, and but too successfully, to persuade the Galatic converts that they had been taught the new religion imperfectly, and at second hand ; that the founder of their Church himself possessed only an inferior and deputed commission, the seat of truth and authority being in the apostles and elders of Jerusalem ; moreover, that, whatever he might profess amongst them, he had himself, at other times and in other places, given way to the doctrine of circumcision. The epistle is unintelligible without supposing all this. Referring therefore to this, as to what had actually passed, we find St. Paul treating so unjust an attempt to undermine his credit, and to introduce amongst his converts a doctrine which he had uniformly reprobated, in terms of great asperity and indignation. And, in order to refute the suspicions which had been raised concerning the fidelity of his teaching, as well as to assert the independency and Divine original of his mission, we find him appealing to the history of his conversion, to his conduct under it, to the manner in which he had conferred with the apostles when he met with them at Jerusalem ; alleging that, so far was his doctrine from being derived from them, or they from exercising any superiority over him, that they had simply assented to what he had already preached amongst the Gentiles, and which preaching was communicated not by them to him, but by himself to them ; that he had maintained the liberty of the Gentile

2

Church, by opposing upon one occasion an apostle to the face, when the timidity of his behaviour seemed to endanger it; that from the first, that all along, that to that hour, he had constantly resisted the claims of Judaism; and that the persecutions which he daily underwent, at the hands or by the instigation of the Jews, and of which he bore in his person the marks and scars, might have been avoided by him, if he had consented to employ his labours in bringing, through the medium of Christianity, converts over to the Jewish institution; for then " would the offence of the cross have ceased." Now an impostor, who had forged the epistle for the purpose of producing St. Paul's authority in the dispute, which, as hath been observed, is the only credible motive that can be assigned for the forgery, might have made the apostle deliver his opinion upon the subject in strong and decisive terms, or might have put his name to a train of reasoning and argumentation upon that side of the question which the imposture was intended to recommend. I can allow the possibility of such a scheme as that. But for a writer, with this purpose in view, to feign a series of transactions supposed to have passed amongst the Christians of Galatia, and then to counterfeit expressions of anger and resentment excited by these transactions; to make the apostle travel back into his own history, and into a recital of various passages of his life, some indeed directly, but others obliquely, and others even obscurely bearing upon the point in question; in a word, to substitute narrative for argument, expostulation and complaint for dogmatic positions and controversial reasoning, in a writing properly controversial, and of which the aim and design was to support one side of a much agitated question, is a method so intricate, and so unlike the methods pursued by all other impostors, as to require the very flagrant proofs of imposition to induce us to believe it to be one.

SECTION II.

In this section I shall endeavour to prove,—

1. That the Epistle to the Galatians and the Acts of the Apostles were written without any communication with each other.

2. That the epistle, though written without any communication with the history, by recital, implication, or reference, bears testimony to many of the facts contained in it.

1. The epistle and the Acts of the Apostles were written without any communication with each other.

To judge of this point we must examine those passages in each which describe the same transaction; for, if the author of either writing derived his information from the account which he had seen in the other, when he came to speak of the same transaction he would follow that account. The history of St. Paul at Damascus, as read in the Acts, and as referred to by the epistle, forms an instance of this sort. According to the Acts, Paul (after his conversion) was certain days with the " disciples which were at Damascus. And straightway he preached Christ in the synagogues, that he is the Son of God. But all that heard him were amazed, and said: Is not this he which destroyed them which called on this name in Jerusalem, and came hither for that intent, that he might bring them bound unto the chief priests? But Saul increased the more in strength, confounding the Jews which were at Damascus, proving that this is very Christ. And after that many days were fulfilled, the Jews took counsel to kill him. But their laying wait was known to Saul; and they watched the gates day and night to kill him. Then the disciples took him by night, and let him down by the wall in a basket. And when Saul was come to Jerusalem, he assayed to join himself to the disciples." Acts ix. 19–26.

According to the epistle, "When it pleased God, who separated me from my mother's womb, and called me by his grace, to reveal his own Son in me, that I might preach him among the heathen; immediately I conferred not with flesh and blood; neither went I up to Jerusalem to them which were apostles before me; but I went into Arabia, and returned again to Damascus; then, after three years, I went up to Jerusalem."

Besides the difference observable in the terms and general complexion of these two accounts, " the journey into Arabia," mentioned in the epistle, and omitted in the history, affords full proof that there existed no correspondence between these writers. If the narrative in the Acts had been made up from the epistle, it is impossible that this journey should have been passed over in silence; if the epistle had been composed out of what the author had read of St. Paul's history in the Acts, it is unaccountable that it should have been inserted.*

The journey to Jerusalem related in the second chapter of the epistle (" then, fourteen years after, I went up again to Jerusalem") supplies another example of the same kind. Either this was the journey described in the fifteenth chapter of the Acts, when Paul and Barnabas were sent from Antioch to Jerusalem, to consult the apostles and elders upon the question of the Gentile converts, or it was some journey of which the history does not take notice. If the first opinion be followed, the discrepancy in the two accounts is so considerable, that it is not without difficulty they can be adapted to the same transaction, so that upon this supposition there is no place for suspecting that the writers were guided or assisted by each other. If the latter opinion be preferred, we have then a journey to Jerusalem, and a conference with the principal members of the Church there, circumstantially related in the epistle, and entirely omitted in the Acts; and we are at liberty to repeat the observation, which we before made, that the omission of so material a fact in the

---

* N. B. The Acts of the Apostles simply inform us that St. Paul left Damascus in order to go to Jerusalem, " after many days were fulfilled." If any one doubt whether the words " many days" could be intended to express a period which included a term of three years, he will find a complete instance of the same phrase, used with the same latitude, in the first book of Kings, chap. ii. 38, 39: " And Shimei dwelt at Jerusalem *many days;* and it came to pass at the end of *three years*, that two of the servants of Shimei ran away."

history is inexplicable if the historian had read the epistle, and that the insertion of it in the epistle, if the writer derived his information from the history, is not less so.

St. Peter's visit to Antioch, during which the dispute arose between him and St. Paul, is not mentioned in the Acts.

If we connect with these instances the general observation, that no scrutiny can discover the smallest trace of transcription or imitation, either in things or words, we shall be fully satisfied in this part of our case, namely, that the two records, be the facts contained in them true or false, come to our hands from independent sources.

Secondly, I say that the epistle, thus proved to have been written without any communication with the history, bears testimony to a great variety of particulars contained in the history.

1. St. Paul in the early part of his life had addicted himself to the study of the Jewish religion, and was distinguished by his zeal for the institution and for the traditions which had been incorporated with it. Upon this part of his character the history makes St. Paul speak thus : " I am verily a man which am a Jew, born in Tarsus, a city of Cilicia, yet brought up in this city at the feet of Gamaliel, and taught according to the perfect manner of the law of the fathers, and was zealous towards God, as ye all are this day." Acts xxii. 3. The epistle is as follows : " I profited in the Jews' religion above many my equals in mine own nation, being more exceedingly zealous of the traditions of my fathers." Chap. i. 14.

2. St. Paul before his conversion had been a fierce persecutor of the new sect. " As for Saul, he made havoc of the Church ; entering into every house, and haling men and women, committed them to prison." Acts viii. 3.

This is the history of St. Paul, as delivered in the Acts ; in the recital of his own history in the epistle, " Ye have heard," says he, " of my conversation in times past in the Jews' religion, how that beyond measure I persecuted the Church of God." Chap. i. 13.

3. St. Paul was miraculously converted on his way to Damascus. " And as he journeyed he came near to Damascus : and suddenly there shined round about him a light from heaven : and he fell to the earth, and heard a voice saying unto him, Saul, Saul, why persecutest thou me ! And he said, Who art thou, Lord ? And the Lord said, I am Jesus, whom thou persecutest : it is hard for thee to kick against the pricks. And he, trembling and astonished, said, Lord, what wilt thou have me to do ? Acts ix. 3—6. With these compare the epistle, chap. i. 15—17 : " When it pleased God, who separated me from my mother's womb, and called me by his grace, to reveal his Son in me, that I might preach him among the heathen ; immediately I conferred not with flesh and blood, neither went I up to Jerusalem, to them that were apostles before me ; but I went into Arabia, and returned again unto Damascus."

In this quotation from the epistle, I desire it to be remarked how incidentally it appears that the affair passed at *Damascus*. In what be may called the direct part of the account no mention is made of the place of his conversion at all ; a casual expression at the end, and an expression brought in for a different purpose, alone fixes it to have been at Damascus : " I returned again to Damascus." Nothing can be more like simplicity and undesignedness than this is. It also draws the agreement between the two quotations somewhat closer, to observe that they both state St. Paul to have preached the Gospel immediately upon his call : " And straightway he preached Christ in the synagogues, that he is the Son of God ;" Acts ix. 20. " When it pleased God to reveal his Son in me, that I might preach him among the heathen ; immediately I conferred not with flesh and blood." Gal. i 15.

4. The course of the apostle's travels after his conversion was this : He went from Damascus to Jerusalem, and from Jerusalem into Syria and Cilicia. " At Damascus the disciples took him by night, and let him down by the wall in a basket ; and when Saul was come to Jerusalem, he assayed to join himself to the disciples ; Acts ix. 25. Afterwards, " when the brethren knew the conspiracy formed against him at Jerusalem, they brought him down to Cæsarea, and sent him forth to Tarsus, a city in Cilicia ;" chap. ix. 30. In the epistle St. Paul gives the following brief account of his proceedings within the same period : " After three years I went up to Jerusalem to see Peter, and abode with him fifteen days ; afterwards I came into the regions of Syria and Cilicia." The history told us that Paul passed from Cæsarea to Tarsus : if he took this journey by land, it would carry him through Syria into Cilicia ; and he would come, after his visit at Jerusalem, " into the regions of Syria and Cilicia," in the very order in which he mentions them in the epistle. This supposition of his going from Cæsarea to Tarsus *by land* clears up also another point. It accounts for what St. Paul says in the same place concerning the Churches of Judea : " Afterwards I came into the regions of Syria and Cilicia, and was unknown by face unto the Churches of Judea which were in Christ ; but they had heard only that he which persecuted us in times past, now preacheth the faith which once he destroyed ; and they glorified God in me." Upon which passage I observe, first, that what is here said of the Churches of Judea is spoken in connection with his journey into the regions of Syria and Cilicia. Secondly, that the passage itself has little significancy, and that the *connection* is inexplicable, unless St. Paul went through Judea* (though probably by a hasty journey) at the time that he came into the regions of Syria and Cilicia. Suppose him to have passed by land from Cæsarea to Tarsus, all this, as hath been observed, would be precisely true.

* Dr. Doddridge thought that the Cæsarea here mentioned was not the celebrated city of that name upon the Mediterranean Sea, but Cæsarea Philippi, near the borders of Syria, which lies in a much more direct line from Jerusalem to Tarsus than the other. The objection to this, Dr. Benson remarks, is, that Cæsarea, without any addition, usually denotes Cæsarea Palestinæ.

INTRODUCTION TO THE EPISTLE TO THE GALATIANS.

5. Barnabas was with St. Paul at Antioch. "Then departed Barnabas to Tarsus, for to seek Saul; and when he had found him, he brought him unto Antioch. And it came to pass that a whole year they assembled themselves with the Church;" Acts xi. 25, 26. Again, and upon another occasion, "They (Paul and Barnabas) sailed to Antioch; and there they continued a long time with the disciples;" chap. xiv. 26.

Now what says the epistle? "When Peter was come to Antioch, I withstood him to the face, because he was to be blamed; and the other Jews dissembled likewise with him; insomuch that Barnabas also was carried away with their dissimulation;" chap. ii. 11, 13.

6. The stated residence of the apostle was at Jerusalem. "At that time there was a great persecution against the Church which was at Jerusalem, and they were all scattered abroad throughout the regions of Judea and Samaria, except the apostles;" Acts viii. 1. "They (the Christians at Antioch) determined that Paul and Barnabas should go up to Jerusalem, unto the apostles and elders, about this question;" Acts xv. 2. With these accounts agrees the declaration in the epistle: "Neither went I up to Jerusalem to them which were apostles before me;" chap. i. 17; for this declaration implies, or rather assumes it to be known, that Jerusalem was the place were the apostles were to be met with.

7. There were at Jerusalem two apostles, or at least two eminent members of the Church, of the name of James. This is directly inferred from the Acts of the Apostles, which in the second verse of the twelfth chapter relates the death of James, the brother of John; and yet in the fifteenth chapter, and in a subsequent part of the history, records a speech delivered by James in the assembly of the apostles and elders. It is also strongly implied by the form of expression used in the epistle: "Other apostles saw I none, save James, the *Lord's brother;*" i. e. to distinguish him from James, the brother of John.

To us, who have been long conversant in the Christian history as contained in the Acts of the Apostles, these points are obvious and familiar; nor do we readily apprehend any greater difficulty in making them appear in a letter purporting to have been written by St. Paul, than there is in introducing them into a modern sermon. But to judge correctly of the argument before us, we must discharge this knowledge from our thoughts. We must propose to ourselves the situation of an author who sat down to the writing of the epistle without having seen the history; and then the concurrences we have deduced will be deemed of importance. They will, at least, be taken for separate confirmations of the several facts, and not only of these particular facts, but of the general truth of the history.

For what is the rule with respect to corroborative testimony which prevails in courts of justice, and which prevails only because experience has proved that it is a useful guide to truth? A principal witness in a cause delivers his account; his narrative, in certain parts of it, is confirmed by witnesses who are called afterwards. The credit derived from their testimony belongs not only to the particular circumstances in which the auxiliary witnesses agree with the principal witness, but in some measure to the whole of his evidence; because it is improbable that accident or fiction should draw a line which touched upon truth in so many points.

In like manner, if two records be produced, manifestly independent, that is, manifestly written without any participation of intelligence, an agreement between them, even in few and slight circumstances, (especially if from the different nature and design of the writings few points only of agreement, and those incidental, could be expected to occur,) would add a sensible weight to the authority of both, in every part of their contents. The same rule is applicable to history, with at least as much reason as any other species of evidence.

Section III.

But although the references to various particulars in the epistle, compared with the direct account of the same particulars in the history, afford a considerable proof of the truth not only of these particulars but of the narrative which contains them; yet they do not show, it will be said, that the epistle was written by St. Paul; for, admitting (what seems to have been proved) that the writer, whoever he was, had no recourse to the Acts of the Apostles; yet many of the facts referred to, such as St. Paul's miraculous conversion, his change from a virulent persecutor to an indefatigable preacher, his labours among the Gentiles, and his zeal for the liberties of the Gentile Church, were so notorious as to occur readily to the mind of any Christian, who should choose to personate his character and counterfeit his name; it was only to write what every body knew. Now I think that this supposition, viz. that the epistle was composed upon general information, and the general publicity of the facts alluded to, and that the author did no more than weave into his work what the common fame of the Christian Church had reported to his ears, is repelled by the particularity of the recitals and references. This particularity is observable in the following instances, in perusing which I desire the reader to reflect whether they exhibit the language of a man who had nothing but general reputation to proceed upon, or of a man actually speaking of himself and of his own history, and consequently of things concerning which he possessed a clear, intimate, and circumstantial knowledge.

1. The history, in giving an account of St. Paul after his conversion, relates, "that, after many days," effecting, by the assistance of the disciples, his escape from Damascus, "he proceeded to Jerusalem;" Acts ix. 25. The epistle, speaking of the same period, makes St. Paul say that he "went into Arabia," that he returned again to Damascus, that after three years he went up to Jerusalem; chap. i. 17, 18.

2. The history relates that when Saul was come from Damascus, "he was with the disciples coming in and going out;" Acts ix. 28. The epistle, describing the same journey, tells us, "that he went up to Jerusalem to see Peter, and abode with him fifteen days;" chap. i. 18.

2

3. The history relates that, when Paul was come to Jerusalem, "Barnabas took him and brought him to the apostles;" Acts ix. 27. The epistle, "that he saw Peter; but other of the apostles saw he none, save James the Lord's brother;" chap. i. 19.

Now this is as it should be. The historian delivers his account in general terms, as of facts to which he was not present. The person who is the subject of that account, when he comes to speak of these facts himself, particularizes time, names, and circumstances.

4. The like notation of places, persons, and dates, is met with in the account of St. Paul's journey to Jerusalem, given in the second chapter of the epistle. It was fourteen years after his conversion; it was in company with Barnabas and Titus; it was then that he met with James, Cephas, and John; it was then also that it was agreed amongst them that they should go to the circumcision, and he unto the Gentiles.

5. The dispute with Peter, which occupies the sequel of the second chapter, is marked with the same particularity. It was at Antioch; it was after certain came from James; it was whilst Barnabas was there, who was carried away by their dissimulation. These examples negative the insinuation that the epistle presents nothing but indefinite allusions to public facts.

Section IV.

Chap. iv. 11–16: "I am afraid of you, lest I have bestowed upon you labour in vain. Brethren, I beseech you, be as I am, for I am as ye are. Ye have not injured me at all. Ye know how through infirmity of the flesh I preached the Gospel unto you at first; and *my temptation which was in the flesh* ye despised not, nor rejected; but received me as an angel of God, even as Christ Jesus. Where is then the blessedness YOU SPAKE OF? for I bear you record, that, if it had been possible, ye would have plucked out your own eyes, and have given them unto me. Am I therefore become your enemy, because I tell you the truth?"

With this passage compare 2 Cor. xii. 1–9: "It is not expedient for me, doubtless, to glory; I will come to visions and revelations of the Lord. I knew a man in Christ above fourteen years ago, (whether in the body, I cannot tell, or whether out of the body, I cannot tell, God knoweth;) such a one was caught up to the third heaven; and I knew such a man, (whether in the body, or out of the body, I cannot tell, God knoweth,) how that he was caught up into paradise, and heard unspeakable words, which it is not lawful for a man to utter. Of such a one will I glory, yet of myself will I not glory, but in mine infirmities; for, though I would desire to glory, I shall not be a fool; for I will say the truth. But now I forbear, lest any man should think of me above that which he seeth me to be, or that he heareth of me. And lest I should be exalted above measure, through the abundance of the revelations, there was given to me *a thorn in the flesh, the messenger of Satan to buffet me,* lest I should be exalted above measure. For this thing I besought the Lord thrice, that it might depart from me. And he said unto me, My grace is sufficient for thee; for my strength is made perfect in weakness. Most gladly therefore will I rather glory in my infirmities, that the power of Christ may rest upon me."

There can be no doubt that "the temptation which was in the flesh," mentioned in the Epistle to the Galatians, and "the thorn in the flesh, the messenger of Satan to buffet him," mentioned in the epistle to the Corinthians, were intended to denote the same thing. Either, therefore, it was, what we pretend it to have been, the same person in both—that is, we are reading the letters of a real apostle; or it was that a sophist, who had seen the circumstance in one epistle, contrived, for the sake of correspondency, to bring it into another; or, lastly, it was a circumstance in St. Paul's personal condition supposed to be well known to those into whose hands the epistle was likely to fall, and for that reason introduced into a writing designed to bear his name. I have extracted the quotations at length, in order to enable the reader to judge accurately of the manner in which the mention of this particular occurs in each; because that judgment, I think, will acquit the author of the epistle of the charge of having studiously inserted it, either with a view of producing an apparent agreement between them, or for any other purpose whatever.

The context, by which the circumstance before us is introduced, is in the two places totally different, and without any mark of imitation; yet in both places does the circumstance rise aptly and naturally out of the context, and that context from the train of thought carried on in the epistle.

The Epistle to the Galatians, from the beginning to the end, runs in a strain of angry complaint of their defection from the apostle, and from the principles which he had taught them. It was very natural to contrast with this conduct the zeal with which they had once received him; and it was not less so to mention, as a proof of their former disposition towards him, the indulgence which, whilst he was amongst them, they had shown to his infirmity: "My temptation which was in the flesh ye despised not, nor rejected; but received me as an angel of God, even as Christ Jesus. Where is then the blessedness *you spake of,* i. e. the benedictions which you bestowed upon me? for I bear you record, that, if it had been possible, ye would have plucked out your own eyes, and have given them to me."

In the two epistles to the Corinthians, especially in the *second,* we have the apostle contending with certain teachers in Corinth, who had formed a party in that Church against him. To vindicate his personal authority, as well as the dignity and credit of his ministry amongst them, he takes occasion (but not without apologizing repeatedly for the folly, that is, for the indecorum of pronouncing his own panegyric) to meet his adversaries in their boastings: "Whereinsoever any is bold, (I speak foolishly,) I am bold also. Are they

Hebrews? so am I. Are they Israelites? so am I. Are they the seed of Abraham? so am I. Are they the ministers of Christ? (I speak as a fool). I am more; in labours more abundant, in stripes above measure, in prisons more frequent, in deaths oft." Being led to the subject, he goes on, as was natural, to recount his trials and dangers, his incessant cares and labours in the Christian mission. From the proofs which he had given of his zeal and activity in the service of Christ, he passes (and that with the same view of establishing his claim to be considered as "not a whit behind the very chiefest of the apostles") to the visions and revelations which from time to time had been vouchsafed to him. And then, by a close and easy connection, comes in the mention of his infirmity: "Lest I should be exalted," says he, "above measure, through the abundance of the revelations, there was given to me a thorn in the flesh, the messenger of Satan to buffet me."

Thus, then, in both epistles the notice of his infirmity is suited to the place in which it is found. In the epistle to the Corinthians the train of thought draws up the circumstance by a regular approximation; in this epistle it is suggested by the subject and occasion of the epistle itself. Which observation we offer as an argument to prove that it is not, in either epistle, a circumstance industriously brought forward for the sake of procuring credit to an imposture.

A reader will be taught to perceive the force of this argument, who shall attempt to introduce a *given* circumstance into the body of a writing. To do this without abruptness, or without betraying marks of design in the transition, requires, he will find, more art than he expected to be necessary; certainly more than any one can believe to have been exercised in the composition of these epistles.

SECTION V.

Chap. iv. 29: "But as then he that was born after the flesh persecuted him that was born after the Spirit, even so it is now."

Chap. v. 11: "And I, brethren, if I yet preach circumcision, why do I yet suffer persecution? Then is the offence of the cross ceased."

Chap. vi. 17: "From henceforth let no man trouble me, for I bear in my body the marks of the Lord Jesus."

From these several texts it is apparent that the persecutions which our apostle had undergone were from the hands or by the instigation of the Jews; that it was not for preaching Christianity in opposition to heathen ism, but it was for preaching it as distinct from Judaism, that he had brought upon himself the sufferings which had attended his ministry. And this representation perfectly coincides with that which results from the detail of St. Paul's history as delivered in the Acts. At Antioch, in Pisidia, the "word of the Lord was published throughout all the region; but the *Jews stirred up* the devout and honourable women and the chief men of the city, and raised persecution against Paul and Barnabas, and expelled them out of their coasts." (Acts, chap. xiii. 50.) Not long after, at Iconium, "a great multitude of the Jews and also of the Greeks believed; but the *unbelieving Jews* stirred up the Gentiles, and made their minds evil affected against the brethren." (Chap. xiv. 1, 2.) "At Lystra there came certain Jews from Antioch and Iconium, who persuaded the people; and having stoned Paul, drew him out of the city, supposing he had been dead." (Chap. xiv. 19.) The same enmity, and from the same quarter, our apostle experienced in Greece: "At Thessalonica, some of them (the Jews) believed, and consorted with Paul and Silas; and of the devout Greeks a great multitude, and of the chief women not a few: but *the Jews which believed not*, moved with envy, took unto them certain lewd fellows of the baser sort, and gathered a company, and set all the city in an uproar, and assaulted the house of Jason, and sought to bring them out to the people." (Acts, chap. xvii. 4, 5.) Their persecutors follow them to Berea: "When the *Jews* of Thessalonica had knowledge that the word of God was preached of Paul at Berea, they came hither also, and stirred up the people." (Chap. xvii. 13.) And, lastly, at Corinth, when Gallio was deputy of Achaia, "*the Jews* made insurrection with one accord against Paul, and brought him to the judgment seat." I think it does not appear that our apostle was ever set upon by the Gentiles, unless they were first stirred up by the Jews, except in two instances; in both which the persons who began the assault were immediately interested in his expulsion from the place. *Once* this happened at Philippi, after the cure of the Pythoness: "When the masters saw the hope of their gains was gone, they caught Paul and Silas, and drew them into the market-place unto the rulers." (Chap. xvi. 19.) And a *second* time at Ephesus, at the instance of Demetrius, a silversmith, who made silver shrines for Diana, "who called together workmen of like occupation, and said, Sirs, ye know that by this craft we have our wealth; moreover ye see and hear that not only at Ephesus, but almost throughout all Asia, this Paul hath persuaded away much people, saying, that they be no gods which are made with hands; so that not only this our craft is in danger to be set at nought, but also that the temple of the great goddess Diana should be despised, and her magnificence should be destroyed, whom all Asia and the world worshippeth."

SECTION VI.

I observe an agreement in a somewhat peculiar rule of Christian conduct as laid down in this epistle, and as exemplified in the Second Epistle to the Corinthians. It is not the repetition of the same general precept, which would have been a coincidence of little value; but it is the general precept in one place, and the application of that precept to an actual occurrence in the other. In the sixth chapter and first verse of this epistle, our apostle gives the following direction: "Brethren, if a man be overtaken in a fault, ye which are spiritual, restore such a one in the spirit of meekness." In 2 Cor. ii. 6–8, he writes thus: "Sufficient to such a man (the

2

INTRODUCTION TO THE EPISTLE TO THE GALATIANS.

incestuous person mentioned in the first epistle) is this punishment, which was inflicted of many; so that, contrariwise, ye ought rather to forgive him, and comfort him, lest perhaps such a one should be swallowed up with over-much sorrow."

SECTION VII.

This epistle goes farther than any of St. Paul's epistles, for it avows in direct terms the supersession of the Jewish law, as an instrument of salvation, even to the Jews themselves. Not only were the Gentiles exempt from its authority, but even the Jews were no longer either to place any dependence upon it, or consider themselves as subject to it on a religious account. " Before faith came, we were kept under the law, shut up unto the faith which should afterwards be revealed : wherefore the law was our schoolmaster to bring us unto Christ, that we might be justified by faith ; but, after that faith is come, *we are no longer under a schoolmaster ;* chap. iii. 23–25. This was undoubtedly spoken of Jews, and to Jews. In like manner, chap. iv. 1–5 : " Now I say that the heir, as long as he is a child, differeth nothing from a servant, though he be lord of all ; but is under tutors and governors, until the time appointed of the father : even so we, when we were children, were in bondage under the elements of the world ; but when the fulness of time was come, God sent forth his Son, made of a woman, made under the law, to *redeem them that were under the law,* that we might receive the adoption of sons." These passages are nothing short of a declaration, that the obligation of the Jewish law, considered as a religious dispensation, the effects of which were to take place in another life, had ceased, with respect even to the Jews themselves. What then should be the conduct of a Jew (for such St. Paul was) who preached this doctrine ? To be consistent with himself, either he would no longer comply, in his own person, with the directions of the law ; or, if he did comply, it would be for some other reason than any confidence which he placed in its efficacy, as a religious institution. Now so it happens, that, whenever St. Paul's compliance with the Jewish law is mentioned in the history, it is mentioned in connection with circumstances which point out the motive from which it proceeded ; and this motive appears to have been always exoteric, namely, a love of order and tranquillity, or an unwillingness to give unnecessary offence. Thus, Acts xvi. 3 : " Him (Timothy) would Paul have to go forth with him, and took and circumcised him, *because of the Jews which were in those quarters.*" Again, Acts xxi. 26, when Paul consented to exhibit an example of public compliance with a Jewish rite, by purifying himself in the temple, it is plainly intimated that he did this to satisfy " many thousands of Jews, who believed, and who were all zealous of the law." So far the instances related in one book correspond with the doctrine delivered in another.

SECTION VIII.

Chap. i. 18 : " Then, after three years, I went up to Jerusalem to see Peter, and abode with him fifteen days."

The *shortness* of St. Paul's stay at Jerusalem is what I desire the reader to remark. The direct account of the same journey in the Acts, chap. ix. 28, determines nothing concerning the time of his continuance there : " And he was with them (the apostles) coming in and going out, at Jerusalem ; and he spake boldly in the name of the Lord Jesus, and disputed against the Grecians : but they went about to slay him ; which when the brethren knew, they brought him down to Cæsarea." Or rather, this account, taken by itself, would lead a reader to suppose that St. Paul's abode at Jerusalem had been longer than fifteen days. But turn to the twenty-second chapter of the Acts, and you will find a reference to this visit to Jerusalem, which plainly indicates that Paul's continuance in that city had been of short duration : " And it came to pass, that when I was come again to Jerusalem, even while I prayed in the temple, I was in a trance, and saw him saying unto me, Make haste, get thee *quickly* out of Jerusalem, for they will not receive thy testimony concerning me." Here we have the general terms of one text so explained by a distinct text in the same book, as to bring an indeterminate expression into a close conformity with a specification delivered in another book—a species of consistency not, I think, usually found in fabulous relations.

SECTION IX.

Chap. vi. 11 : " Ye see how large a letter I have written unto you with mine own hand."

These words imply that he did not always write with his own hand ; which is consonant to what we find intimated in some other of the epistles. The Epistle to the Romans was written by Tertius : " I, Tertius, who wrote this epistle, salute you in the Lord ;" chap. xvi. 22. The First Epistle to the Corinthians, the Epistle to the Colossians, and the second to the Thessalonians, have all, near the conclusion, this clause : " The salutation of me, Paul, with mine own hand ; which must be understood, and is universally understood, to import that the rest of the epistle was written by another hand. I do not think it improbable that an impostor, who had marked this subscription in some other epistle, should invent the same in a forgery ; but that is not done here. The author of this epistle does not imitate the manner of giving St. Paul's signature ; he only bids the Galatians observe how large a letter he had written to them with his own hand. He does not say this was different from his ordinary usage ; that is left to implication. Now, to suppose that this was an artifice to procure credit to an imposture, is to suppose that the author of the forgery, because he knew that others of St. Paul's were *not* written by himself, therefore made the apostle say that this was ; which seems

382   2

an odd turn to give to the circumstance, and to be given for a purpose which would more naturally and more directly have been answered, by subjoining the salutation or signature in the form in which it is found in other epistles.

SECTION X.

An exact conformity appears in the manner in which a certain apostle or eminent Christian, whose name was James, is spoken of in the epistle and in the history. Both writings refer to a situation of his at Jerusalem, somewhat different from that of the other apostles—a kind of *eminence* or *presidency* in the Church there, or, at least, a more fixed and stationary residence. Chap. ii. 12 : " When Peter was at Antioch, before that certain came from James, he did eat with the Gentiles." This text plainly attributes a kind of *pre-eminence* to James ; and as we hear of him twice in the same epistle dwelling at Jerusalem, chap. i. 19 and ii. 9, we must apply it to the situation which he held in that Church. In the Acts of the Apostles divers intimations occur, conveying the same idea of James's situation. When Peter was miraculously delivered from prison, and had surprised his friends by his appearance among them, after declaring unto them how the Lord had brought him out of prison, " Go, show," says he, " these things unto James, and to the brethren ;" Acts xii. 17. Here James is manifestly spoken of in terms of *distinction*. He appears again with like distinction in the twenty-first chapter and the seventeenth and eighteenth verses : " And when we (Paul and his company) were come to Jerusalem, the day following Paul went in with us unto James, and all the elders were present." In the debate which took place upon the business of the Gentile converts, in the council at Jerusalem, this same person seems to have taken the *lead*. It was he who closed the debate, and proposed the resolution in which the council ultimately concurred : " Wherefore *my sentence is, &c.*"

Upon the whole, that there exists a conformity in the expressions used concerning James, throughout the history and in the epistle, is unquestionable. This proves that the circumstance itself is founded in truth ; viz. that James was a real person, who held a situation of eminence in a real society of Christians at Jerusalem. It confirms also those parts of the narrative which are connected with this circumstance. Suppose, for instance, the truth of the account of Peter's escape from prison was to be tried upon the testimony of a witness who, among other things, made Peter, after his deliverance, say, " Go, show these things to James and to the brethren ;" would it not be material, in such a trial, to make out by other independent proofs, or by a comparison of proofs, drawn from independent sources, that there was actually at that time, living at Jerusalem, such a person as James ; that this person held such a situation in the society amongst whom these things were transacted as to render the words which Peter is said to have used concerning him proper and natural ! If this would be pertinent in the discussion of oral testimony, it is still more so in appreciating the credit of remote history.

2   383

PREFACE

TO THE

EPISTLE OF PAUL THE APOSTLE

TO THE

GALATIANS.

GALATIA was anciently a part of *Phrygia* and the neighbouring countries. It had its name from the *Gauls*, who, having in several bodies invaded *Asia Minor*, as *Pausanius* (Attic., cap. iv.) relates, conquered this country and settled in it. As these were mixed with various *Grecian* families, the country was also salled *Gallogræcia*, see *Justin*, lib. xxiv. 4; xxv. 2; xxvii. 3; xxviii. 3; and *Strabo*, xiv. Under the reign of *Augustus Cæsar*, about the year of Rome 727, and 26 years before our Lord, it was reduced into the form of a Roman *colony*, and was governed by a *proprætor*, appointed by the emperor.

This country is bounded on the *east* by *Cappadocia*; on the *west* by *Bithynia*; on the *south* by *Pamphylia*; and on the *north* by the *Euxine Sea*. These are its limits according to *Strabo*, which some think too extensive; but the different provinces of Asia Minor being the subjects of continual contentions and inroads, very frequently changed their *boundaries* as well as their *masters*, and were seldom at one stay.

The *Galatæ* were divided into three tribes, the *Tectosages*, the *Trocmi*, and the *Tolistobogi*. According to *Pliny* their country was divided into 195 *tetrarchies*, and, according to *Strabo*, each of the *three* divisions above mentioned was subdivided into four *cantons*, each of which had a *tetrarch*; and besides these twelve tetrarchs, there was a general council of the nation, consisting of 300 *senators*. These tetrarchs were at last reduced in number to *three*, then to *two*, and lastly to *one*; the last tetrarch and king of Galatia was *Amyntas*, who, from being secretary to *Dejotarus*, the first person that possessed the whole tetrarchy, was made king of Pisidia in the year of Rome 714. And in the year 718, *Mark Antony* made him tetrarch of Galatia. After the death of Amyntas, Galatia was ranked by Augustus among the Roman *provinces*, and governed as aforesaid. The administration of the proprætors continued till the reign of *Theodosius* the *Great*, or *Valens*; and, under the Christian emperors, it was divided into *two* provinces, *Galatia prima* being subject to a *consul*; *Galatia secunda*, or *salutaris*, governed by a *president*.

The *religion* of the ancient *Galatæ* was extremely corrupt and superstitious; and they are said to have worshipped the *mother of the gods* under the name of *Agdistis*, and to have offered human sacrifices of the prisoners they took in war.

They are mentioned by historians as a *tall* and valiant people, who went nearly naked; and used for arms only a sword and buckler. The impetuosity of their attack is stated to have been *irresistible*; and this generally made them victorious.

It appears, from the *Acts of the Apostles*, that St. Paul visited this country more than once. Two visits to this region are particularly marked in the Acts, viz. the first about A. D. 53, Acts xvi. 6: " Now when they had gone through Phrygia and the region of Galatia," &c.; the second about A. D. 56, Acts xviii. 23: " He went over all the country of Galatia and Phrygia in order, strengthening all the disciples."

St. Paul was probably the *first* who had preached the Gospel in this region, as appears pretty evident from Gal. i. 6: " I marvel that ye are so soon removed from him that CALLED YOU INTO THE GRACE OF CHRIST ;" and from chap. iv. 13: " Ye know how, through infirmity of the flesh, I preached the Gospel unto you at the first." Others suppose that it is not unlikely that St. Peter had preached the Gospel there to the *Jews* or *Helenists* only, as his first epistle is directed " to the strangers who were scattered abroad throughout Pontus, GALATIA, Cappadocia, Asia, and Bithynia;" and it is supposed, also, that the persons converted by St. Peter probably occasioned those differences among the Galatian converts, which induced St. Paul to write this epistle, in which he takes pains to establish his own character as an apostle, which had been disputed by some, with a view of placing him below Peter, who preached generally to the Jews only, and observed the law. See *Calmet* and the *New Encyclopedia*, article GALATIA. That St. Peter thought *at first* that the Gospel should be confined to the Jews is sufficiently evident from the Acts of the Apostles; but *after* his Divine vision, which happened about A. D. 41, related Acts x., he saw that God had also called the Gentiles into the Church; and his first epistle, which was written in A. D. 64, was probably *twelve* years *posterior* to *that* written by St. Paul to the Galatians.

2

PREFACE TO THE EPISTLE TO THE GALATIANS.

As to the precise *time* in which this epistle was written, there have been various opinions among learned men. Some of the ancients believed it to be the very first written of all St. Paul's epistles. See *Epiphanius,* tom. i., Hæres. 42. Others have supposed that it was written after his second journey to Galatia, Acts xviii. 23, which in the chronology I have placed in A. D. 54; and others, with more probability, after his *first* journey, see Acts xvi. 6, which in the chronology I have placed in A. D. 53. That it was written soon after *one* of the apostle's visits to that region seems evident from the following complaint: "I marvel that ye are so soon removed from him that hath called you," chap. i. 6; it has been therefore conjectured that only one or two years had elapsed from that time, and that the epistle must have been written about A. D. 52 or 53. Beausobre and L'Enfant speak very judiciously on this subject: "We do not find in the Epistle to the Galatians any mark that can enable us to determine with certainty at what *time* or in what *place* it was written. It is dated at *Rome* in some *printed* copies and MSS., but there is nothing in the epistle itself to confirm this date. Paul does not here make any mention of his *bonds,* as he does in all his epistles written from *Rome.* He says, indeed, chap. vi. 17: 'I bear about in my body the marks of the Lord Jesus;' but he had often *suffered* before he came to Rome. Some learned chronologers think that it was written between the third and fourth journey of St. Paul to Jerusalem, and between his *first* and *second* into Galatia; which opinion appears very probable; for, since the apostle says, he wonders that they were so soon turned to another gospel, this epistle must have been written a short time after he had preached in Galatia.

"Nor can we discern in the epistle any notice of the *second* journey which St. Paul made into this country. For this reason it is thought that the Epistle to the Galatians was written at *Corinth,* where the apostle made a long stay, or else in some city of Asia, particularly *Ephesus,* where he stayed some days on his way to Jerusalem, Acts xviii. 19–21; therefore, in all probability the epistle was written from *Corinth,* or from *Ephesus,* in the year 52 or 53."

Dr. Lardner confirms this opinion by the following considerations:—

1. St. Paul says to the Corinthians, 1st Epis. xvi. 1: "Now, concerning the collection for the saints, as I have given orders to the Churches of Galatia, so do ye;" which shows that at the writing of that epistle to the Corinthians, in 56, he had a good opinion of his converts in Galatia; and that he had no doubt of their respect to his directions, which probably had been sent to them from Ephesus during his long abode there.

2. And now we shall be better able to account for what appears very remarkable: when Paul left Corinth, after his long stay there, he went to Jerusalem, having a vow; in his way he came to Ephesus, Acts xviii. 19–21: "And when they desired him to tarry longer with them, he consented not, but bade them farewell; saying, I must by all means keep this feast that cometh at Jerusalem; but I will return unto you again, if God will." When we read this, we might be apt to think that Paul should hasten back to Ephesus and return thither presently, after he had been at Jerusalem; but instead of doing so, after he had been at Jerusalem, he went down to Antioch; "And after he had spent some time there he departed, and went over all the country of Galatia and Phrygia in order, strengthening the disciples," ver. 22, 23. We now seem to see the reason of this course. At Corinth he heard of the defection of many in Galatia, whereupon he sent a sharp letter to them; but, considering the nature of the case, he judged it best to take the first opportunity to go to Galatia, and support the instructions of his letter; and both together had a good effect. Gal. iv. 19, 20: "My little children, of whom I travail in birth again—I desire to be present with you, and to change my voice; for I stand in doubt of you;" or, I am perplexed for you. Now, then, we see the reason of the apostle's not coming directly from Jerusalem to Ephesus. However, he was not unmindful of his promise, and came thither *after* he had been in Galatia.

3. Upon the whole, the Epistle to the Galatians is an *early* epistle, and, as seems to me most probable, was written at Corinth near the *end* of A. D. 52, or the very *beginning* of 53, before St. Paul set out to go to Jerusalem by the way of Ephesus.

But if any should rather think that it was written at *Ephesus,* during the apostle's short stay there, on his way from Corinth to Jerusalem, that will make but very little difference; for still, according to our computation, the epistle was written at the *beginning* of the year 53. See *Lardner's* Works, vol. vi., page 309.

Every thing considered, I feel no hesitation to place this epistle in the 52d or 53d year of our Lord; either the *end* of the former or the *beginning* of the latter.

From the complexion of this epistle it appears to have been written to the *Jews* who were dispersed in Galatia; see Acts ii. 9. And although in chap. iv. 8, it is said that the persons to whom the apostle writes *did not know God, and did service to them which by nature were no gods;* this must be understood of those who had been *proselytes* to the Jewish religion, as the 9th verse sufficiently shows; for, after they had been converted to Christianity, they turned AGAIN *to the weak and beggarly elements.*

These Galatians were doubtless converted by St. Paul; see Acts xvi. 6; xviii. 23; but, after his departure from them, some teachers had got in among them who endeavoured to persuade them, and successfully too, that they should be circumcised and keep the Mosaic law. See chap. i. 6; iv. 9, 10, 21; v. 1, 2; vi. 12. And the apostle labours to bring them back from the errors of these false teachers.

The *arguments* which the apostle uses to prove the *truth of the Christian religion,* as well as the *nullity of the Mosaic institutions,* are the following:—

1. That himself, immediately after his conversion, without having any conference with any of the apostles, preached the *pure doctrines of Christianity* doctrines strictly conformable to those preached by the genuine

disciples of the Lord; and this was a proof that he had received them by immediate inspiration, as he could have known them no other way.

2. That he was led to oppose *Peter* because he had withdrawn himself from communion with the converted Gentiles, and thereby gave occasion to some to suppose that he considered the law as still binding on those who believed; and that the Gentiles were not to be admitted to an equality of religious privileges with the Jews.

3. That no *rites* or *ceremonies* of the Jewish law could avail any thing in the justification of a sinner; and that faith in Christ was the only means of justification.

4. That their *own works* could avail nothing towards their justification: (1.) For the Spirit of God was given them in consequence of receiving the *Christian* doctrine, chap. iii. ver. 2–5. (2.) That the works of the law cannot justify, because *Abraham was justified by faith* long before the law of Moses was given, chap. iii. 6, 7. (3.) That the curse of the law, under which every sinner lives, is not removed but by the *sacrifice of Christ*, chap. iii. 8, 9.

5. That it is absurd for the *sons of God* to become *slaves to Mosaic rites* and *ceremonies*.

The rest of the epistle is of a practical nature. Although subjects of this kind may be *gathered* out of the epistle, yet it is very evident that the apostle himself has observed no *technical division* or *arrangement* of his matter; his chief design being, 1. To vindicate his own apostleship, and to show that he was not inferior to Peter himself, whom their false teachers appear to have set up in opposition to St. Paul. 2. To assert and maintain *justification by faith* in opposition to all *Judaizing teachers*. 3. To call them back to the liberty of the Gospel, from which, and its privileges, they had shamelessly apostatized. And, 4. To admonish and exhort them to walk worthy of their vocation, by devoting themselves to the glory of God and the benefit of their brethren. *Lastly*, he asserts his own determination to be faithful, and concludes with his apostolical benediction.

THE

EPISTLE OF PAUL THE APOSTLE

TO THE

GALATIANS.

Chronological Notes relative to this Epistle.

Usherian year of the world, 4056.—Alexandrian era of the world, 5554.—Antiochian era of the world, 5544.—Constantinopolitan era of the world, 5560.—Year of the Eusebian epocha of the Creation, 4280. —Year of the Julian period, 4762.—Year of the minor Jewish era of the world, 3812.—Year of the greater Rabbinical era of the world, 4411.—Year from the Flood, according to Archbishop Usher, and the English Bible, 2400.—Year of the Cali yuga, or Indian era of the Deluge, 3154.—Year of the era of Iphitus, or since the first commencement of the Olympic games, 992.—Year of the Nabonassarean era, 799.—Year of the era of the Seleucidæ, 364.—Year of the Spanish era, 90.—Year of the Actiac or Actian era, 83.—Year of the vulgar era of Christ's nativity, 52.—Year from the building of Rome, according to Varro, 805.—Year of the CCVIIth Olympiad, 4.—Year of Ananias, high priest of the Jews, 8.— Common Golden Number, 15.—Jewish Golden Number, 12.—Year of the Solar Cycle, 5.—Dominical Letters; it being Bissextile or Leap year, BA.—Jewish Passover, April 1st.—Easter Sunday, April 2d.— Epact, or the moon's age on the 22d of March, or the Xth of the Calends of April, 4.—Year of the reign of Claudius Cæsar, the fifth emperor of the Romans, 12.—In the last year of Ventidius Cumanus, governor of the Jews.—Year of Vologesus, king of the Parthians, 2.—Year of Caius Numidius Quadratus, governor of Syria, 1.—Roman Consuls; Publius Cornelius Sylla Faustus, and Lucius Salvius Otho Titianus; and for the following year, viz. A. D. 53, (which is supposed by some to be the date of the epistle,) Decimus Junius Silanus, and Quintus Haterius Antoninus.

CHAPTER I.

St. Paul shows that he was especially called of God to be an apostle, 1. Directs his epistle to the Churches through the regions of Galatia, 2. Commends them to the grace of Christ, who gave himself for their sins, 3—5. Marvels that they had so soon turned away from the grace of the Gospel of Christ, to what falsely pretended to be another gospel, 6, 7. Pronounces him accursed who shall preach any other doctrine than that which he had delivered to them, 8, 9. Shows his own uprightness, and that he received his doctrine from God, 10—12. Gives an account of his conversion and call to the apostleship, 13—17. How three years after his conversion he went up to Jerusalem, and afterwards went through the regions of Syria and Cilicia, preaching the faith of Christ to the great joy of the Christian Churches in Judea, 18—24.

A. M. cir. 4056.
A. D. cir. 52.
A. U. C.
805.
An. Imp. Claudii
Cæsaris 12.

PAUL, an apostle, (ᵃ not of men, neither by man, but ᵇ by Jesus Christ, and God the Father, ᶜ who raised him from the dead;)

2 And all the brethren ᵈ which are with me, ᵉ unto the Churches of Galatia :

3 ᶠ Grace be to you and peace

A. M. cir. 4056.
A. D. cir. 52.
A. U. C.
805.
An. Imp. Claudii
Cæsaris 12.

ᵃ Ver. 11, 12.——ᵇ Acts ix. 6; xxii. 10, 15, 21; xxvi. 16; Tit. i. 3.——ᶜ Acts ii. 24.——ᵈ Phil. ii. 22; iv. 21.——ᵉ 1 Cor. xvi. 1.

ᶠ Rom. i 7; 1 Cor. i. 3; 2 Cor. i. 2; Eph. i. 2; Phil. i. 2; Col. i. 2; 1 Thess. i. 1; 2 Thess. i. 2; 2 John 3.

NOTES ON CHAP. I.

Verse 1. *Paul, an apostle, not of men*] Not commissioned by any *assembly* or *council* of the *apostles.*

Neither by man] Nor by any *one* of the *apostles*; neither by *James*, who seems to have been *president* of the apostolic council at Jerusalem; nor by *Peter*,

to whom, in a particular manner, the keys of the kingdom were intrusted.

But by Jesus Christ] Having his mission immediately from Christ himself, and *God the Father who raised him from the dead*, see Acts xxii. 14, 15, and commanded him to go both to the Jews and to the

2

387

A. M. cir. 4056.
A. D. cir. 52.
A. U. C.
805.
An. Imp. Claudii
Cæsaris 12.

from God the Father, and *from* our Lord Jesus Christ,

4 ᵍ Who gave himself for our sins, that he might deliver us ʰ from this present evil world, according to the will of God and our Father:

5 To whom *be* glory for ever and ever. Amen.

6 I marvel that ye are so soon removed

ⁱ from him that called you into the grace of Christ unto another gospel:

7 ᵏ Which is not another; but there be some ˡ that trouble you, and would pervert the Gospel of Christ.

8 But though ᵐ we, or an angel from heaven, preach any other Gospel unto you than that

A. M. cir. 4056.
A. D. cir. 52.
A. U. C.
805.
An. Imp. Claudii
Cæsaris 12.

ᵍ Matt. xx. 28; Rom. iv. 25; chap. ii. 20; Tit. ii. 14.——ʰ See Isa. lxv. 17; John xv. 19; xvii. 14; Heb. ii. 5; vi. 5; 1 John v. 19.

ⁱ Chap. v. 8.——ᵏ 2 Cor. xi. 4.——ˡ Acts xv. 1, 24; 2 Cor. ii. 17; xi. 13; chap. v. 10, 12.——ᵐ 1 Cor. xvi. 22.

Gentiles, to open their eyes, to turn them from darkness to light, and from the power of Satan unto God, that they might obtain remission of sins, and an inheritance among them that are sanctified. See Acts ix. 1, &c., and the notes there.

Verse 2. And all the brethren which are with me] It is very likely that this refers to those who were his *assistants* in preaching the Gospel, and not to any *private members* of the Church.

Churches of Galatia] Galatia was a *region* or *province* of Asia Minor; there was neither *city* nor *town* of this name. See the *preface*. But as, in this province, St. Paul had planted several Churches, he directs the epistle to the whole of them; for it seems they were all pretty nearly in the same state, and needed the same instructions.

Verse 3. Grace be *to you, &c.*] See on Rom i. 7.

Verse 4. Who gave himself for our sins] Who became a *sin-offering* to God in behalf of mankind, that they might be saved from their sins.

Deliver us from this present evil world] These words cannot mean *created nature*, or the *earth and its productions*, nor even *wicked men*. The former we shall need while we live, the *latter* we cannot *avoid;* indeed they are those who, when converted, form the Church of God; and, by the successive conversion of sinners is the Church of Christ maintained; and the followers of God must live and labour *among them*, in order to their conversion. The apostle, therefore, must mean the *Jews*, and their *system of carnal ordinances; statutes which were not good, and judgments by which they could not live;* Ezek. xx. 25; and the whole of their ecclesiastical economy, which was a burden neither they nor their fathers were able to bear, Acts xv. 10. *Schoettgen* contends that the word πονηρος, which we translate *evil*, should be translated *laborious* or *oppressive*, as it comes from πονος, *labour, trouble,* &c. The apostle takes occasion, in the very commencement of the epistle, to inform the Galatians that it was according to the *will* and counsel of God that *circumcision* should cease, and all the other *ritual parts* of the Mosaic economy; and that it was for this express purpose that Jesus Christ *gave himself* a sacrifice for *our sins*, because *the law could not make the comers thereunto perfect.* It had pointed out the *sinfulness* of sin, in its various *ordinances, washings, &c.;* and it had showed forth the *guilt* of sin in its numerous *sacrifices;* but the common sense, even of its own votaries, told them that it *was impossible that the blood of bulls and goats should take away sin.* A

higher atonement was necessary; and when God provided *that*, all its shadows and representations necessarily ceased. See the note on chap. iv. ver. 3.

Verse 5. To whom be *glory for ever*] Let him have the glory to whom alone it is due, for having *delivered us from the present evil world*, and from all bondage to Mosaic rites and ceremonies.

Verse 6. I marvel that ye are so soon removed] It was a matter of *wonder* to the apostle that a people, so soundly converted to God, should have so soon made shipwreck of their faith. But *mutability* itself has not a more apt subject to work upon than the *human heart;* the alternate workings of different passions are continually either *changing the character*, or giving it a *different colouring. Reason*, not *passion*, the *word* of God, not the *sayings* of men, should alone be consulted in the concerns of our salvation.

From him that called you] The apostle seems here to mean *himself*. Hᴇ called them *into the grace of Christ;* and they not only abandoned that grace, but their hearts became greatly *estranged* from him; so that, though at first they would have *plucked out their eyes* for him, they at last counted him their *enemy*, chap. iv. 14—16.

Another gospel] It is certain that in the very earliest ages of the Christian Church there were several *spurious gospels* in circulation, and it was the multitude of these *false* or *inaccurate relations* that induced St. Luke to write his own. See Luke i. 1. We have the names of more than *seventy* of these *spurious narratives* still on record, and in ancient writers many fragments of them remain; these have been collected and published by *Fabricius*, in his account of the *apocryphal books* of the *New Testament*, 3 vols. 8vo. In some of these gospels, the necessity of circumcision, and subjection to the Mosaic law in unity with the Gospel, were strongly inculcated. And to one of these the apostle seems to refer.

Verse 7. Which is not another] It is called a *gospel*, but it differs most essentially from the *authentic narratives* published by the *evangelists*. It is not *gospel*, i. e. *good tidings*, for it loads you again with the *burdens* from which the *genuine Gospel* has disencumbered you. Instead of giving you *peace*, it *troubles you;* instead of being a useful *supplement* to the Gospel of Christ, it *perverts* that Gospel. You have gained nothing but loss and damage by the change.

Verse 8. But though we, or an angel] That Gospel which I have already preached to you is the only true Gospel; were I to preach *any other*, I should

2

A. M. cir. 4056.
A. D. cir. 52.
A. U. C
805.
An. Imp. Claudii
Cæsaris 12.

which we have preached unto you, let him be accursed.

9 As we said before, so say I now again, If any *man* preach any other Gospel unto you [n] than that ye have received, let him be accursed.

10 For, [o] do I now [p] persuade men, or God? or [q] do I seek to please men? for if I yet pleased men, I should not be the servant of Christ.

11 [r] But I certify you, brethren, that the Gospel which was preached of me is not after man.

12 For [s] I neither received it of man, nei-

ther was I taught *it*, but [t] by the revelation of Jesus Christ.

13 For ye have heard of my conversation in time past in the Jews' religion, how that [u] beyond measure I persecuted the Church of God, and [v] wasted it;

14 And profited in the Jews' religion above many my [w] equals in mine own nation, [x] being more exceedingly zealous [y] of the traditions of my fathers.

15 * But when it pleased God, [z] who separated me from my mother's womb, and called *me* by his grace,

16 [a] To reveal his Son in me, that [b] I might

A. M. cir. 4056.
A. D. cir. 52.
A. U. C.
805.
An. Imp. Claudii
Cæsaris 12.

---

[n] Deut. iv. 2; xii. 32; Prov. xxx. 6; Rev. xxii. 18.——[o] 1 Thess. ii. 4.——[p] 1 Sam. xxiv. 7; Matt. xxviii. 14; 1 John iii. 9. [q] 1 Thess. ii. 4; James iv. 4.——[r] 1 Cor. xv. 1.——[s] 1 Cor. xv. 1, 3; ver. 1.——[t] Eph. iii. 3.——[u] Acts ix. 1; xxii. 4; xxvi. 11; 1 Tim. i. 13.——[v] Acts viii. 3.

[w] Gr. *equals in years.*——[x] Acts xxii. 3; xxvi. 9; Phil. iii. 6. [y] Jer. ix. 14; Matt. xv. 2; Mark vii. 5.——* A. D. 35.——[z] Isa. xlix. 1, 5; Jer. i. 5; Acts ix. 15; xiii. 2; xxii. 14, 15; Rom. i. 1.——[a] 2 Cor. iv. 6.——[b] Acts ix. 15; xxii. 21; xxvi. 17, 18; Rom. xi. 13; Eph. iii. 8.

---

incur the curse of God. If your false teachers pretend, as many in early times did, that they received their accounts by the *ministry of an angel*, let them be accursed; *separate them* from your company, and have no *religious communion* with them. Leave them to that God who will show his displeasure against all who *corrupt*, all who *add to*, and all who *take from* the word of his revelation.

Let all those who, from the fickleness of their own minds, are ready to favour the *reveries* of every pretended *prophet* and *prophetess* who starts up, consider the awful words of the apostle. As, in the law, the *receiver* of stolen goods is as bad as the *thief*; so the *encouragers* of such *pretended* revelations are as bad, in the sight of God, as those impostors themselves. What says the word of God to them? *Let them be accursed.* Reader, lay these things to heart.

Verse. 9. *Let him be accursed.*] Perhaps this is not designed as an *imprecation*, but a simple direction; for the word here may be understood as implying that such a person should have no countenance in his bad work, but let him, as Theodoret expresses it, Αλλοτριος εστω του κοινου σωματος της εκκλησιας, *be separated* from the communion of the Church. This, however, would also imply that unless the person repented the Divine judgments would soon follow.

Verse 10. *Do I now persuade men, or God?*] The words πειθειν τον Θεον may be rendered *to court or solicit the favour of God* as the after clause sufficiently proves. This acceptation of πειθειν is very common in Greek authors. While the apostle was a persecutor of the Christians, he was the *servant of men*, and *pleased men*. When he embraced the Christian doctrine, he became the *servant* of GOD, and *pleased* HIM. He therefore intimates that he was a widely different person now from what he had been while a Jew.

Verse 11. *But I certify you, brethren, &c.*] I wish you fully to comprehend that the Gospel which I preached to you is not after man; there is not a

spark of human invention in it, nor the slightest touch of human cunning.

Verse 12. *I neither received it of man*] By means of any *apostle*, as was remarked on ver. 1. No man taught me what I have preached to you.

But by the revelation of Jesus Christ.] Being commissioned by himself alone; receiving the knowledge of it from Christ crucified.

Verse 13. *Ye have heard of my conversation*] Την εμην αναστροφην· My *manner of life*; the *mode* in which I *conducted myself.*

Beyond measure I persecuted the Church] For proofs of this the reader is referred to Acts ix. 1, 2; xxii. 4, and the notes there. The apostle tells them that *they had heard this*, because, being *Jews*, they were acquainted with what had taken place in Judea, relative to these important transactions.

Verse 14. *And profited in the Jews' religion*] The apostle does not mean that he became more exemplary in the *love* and *practice* of the *pure law* of God than any of his countrymen, but that he was more profoundly skilled in the *traditions* of the *fathers* than most of his *fellow students* were, or, as the word συνη-λικιωτας may mean his *contemporaries.*

Verse 15. *Who separated me from my mother's womb*] Him whom I acknowledge as the GOD of *nature* and the GOD of *grace;* who *preserved* me by his *providence* when I was a *helpless infant*, and *saved* me by his *grace* when I was an *adult persecutor.* For some useful remarks on these passages see the *introduction*, sec. ii.

Verse 16. *To reveal his Son in me*] To make me know Jesus Christ, and the power of his resurrection.

That I might preach him among the heathen] For it was to the *Gentiles*, and the *dispersed Jews among the Gentiles*, that St. Paul was especially sent. Peter was sent more particularly to the *Jews* in the *land of Judea;* Paul to those in the different Greek provinces.

I conferred not with flesh and blood] I did not take counsel with *men*; σαρξ και αιμα, which is a lite-

2

A. M. cir. 4056.
A. D. cir. 52.
A. U. C.
805.
An. Imp. Claudii
Cæsaris 12.
preach him among the heathen; immediately I conferred not with c flesh and blood:

17 Neither went I up to Jerusalem to them which were apostles before me; but I went into Arabia, and returned again unto Damascus.

18 * Then after three years d I e went up to Jerusalem to see Peter, and abode with him fifteen days.

19 But f other of the apostles saw I none, save g James the Lord's brother.

20 Now the things which I write unto you, h behold, before God, I lie not.

21 i Afterwards I came into the regions of Syria and Cilicia;

22 And was unknown by face k unto the Churches of Judea which l were in Christ:

23 But they had heard only, That he which persecuted us in times past, now preacheth the faith which once he destroyed.

24 And they glorified God in me.

A. M. cir. 4056.
A. D. cir. 52.
A. U. C.
805.
An. Imp. Claudii
Cæsaris 12.

---

c Matt. xvi. 17; 1 Cor. xv. 50; Eph. vi. 12.——* A. D. 38.
d Acts ix. 26.——e Or, *returned.*——f 1 Cor. ix. 5.

g Matt. xiii. 55; Mark vi. 3.——h Rom. ix. 1.——i Acts ix. 30.
k 1 Thess. ii. 14.——l Rom. xvi. 7.

---

ral translation of the Hebrew בשר ורם *basar vedam,* flesh and blood, is a periphrasis for *man, any man,* a *human being,* or *beings* of *any kind.* Many suppose that the apostle means he did not dally, or take counsel, with the erroneous suggestions and *unrenewed propensities* of *his own heart,* or those of others; but no such thing is intended by the text. St. Paul was satisfied that his *call* was of God; he had therefore no occasion to consult *man.*

Verse 17. *Neither went I up to Jerusalem*] The aim of the apostle is to show that he had his call so immediately and pointedly from God himself, that he had no need of the concurrence even of the apostles, being appointed by the same authority, and fitted to the work by the same grace and Spirit, as they were.

But I went into Arabia.] That part of *Arabia* which was contiguous to *Damascus,* over which *Aretas* was then king. Of this journey into Arabia we have no other account. As St. Luke was not then with him, it is not inserted in the Acts of the Apostles. See *introduction* to this epistle. Jerusalem was the stated residence of the apostles; and, when all the other believers were scattered throughout the regions of Judea and Samaria, we find the apostles still remaining, unmolested, at Jerusalem! Acts viii. 1.

Verse 18. *After three years I went up to Jerusalem to see Peter*] These three years may be reckoned either from the departure of Paul from Jerusalem, or from his return from Arabia to Damascus.

To see Peter—Ἱστορησαι Πετρον, to become *personally acquainted* with Peter; for this is the proper import of the verb ἱστορειν, from which we have the word ἱστορια, *history,* which signifies a *relation of things from personal knowledge* and *actual acquaintance.* How far this is, *now,* from the sense in which we must take the word, *ninety-nine* of every *hundred* of our *histories* sufficiently show. They are *any thing* but *true* relations of *facts* and *persons.*

And abode with him fifteen days.] It was not, therefore, to get religious knowledge from him that he paid him this visit. He knew as much of the *Jewish religion* as Peter did, if not more; and as to the *Gospel,* he received that from the same source, and had preached it *three years* before this.

Verse 19. *James the Lord's brother.*] Dr. Paley observes: There were at Jerusalem *two apostles,* or at least *two* eminent members of the Church, of the name of *James.* This is distinctly inferred from the Acts of the Apostles, chap. xii. 2, where the historian relates the death of *James,* the *brother of John;* and yet, in chap. xv., and in chap xxi. 18, he records a speech delivered by *James* in the assembly of the apostles and elders. In this place JAMES, the *Lord's brother,* is mentioned thus to distinguish him from JAMES the *brother of John.* Some think there were *three* of this name:—1. JAMES, our *Lord's brother,* or *cousin,* as some will have it; 2. JAMES, the son of *Alphæus;* and 3. JAMES, the son of *Zebedee.* But the two former names belong to the same person.

Verse 20. *Before God I lie not.*] This he speaks in reference to having seen only *Peter* and *James* at Jerusalem; and consequently to prove that he had not learned the Gospel from the assembly of the apostles at Jerusalem, nor consequently received his commission from them.

Verse 21. *Afterwards I came into the regions of Syria, &c.*] The course of the apostle's travels, after his conversion, was this: He went from Damascus to Jerusalem, and from Jerusalem into Syria and Cilicia. " At Damascus the disciples took him by night, and let him down by the wall in a basket; and when Saul was come to Jerusalem, he assayed to join himself to the disciples;" Acts ix. 25, 26. Afterwards, when the brethren knew the conspiracy formed against him at Jerusalem, they brought him down to *Cæsarea,* and sent him forth to *Tarsus,* a city of *Cilicia,* Acts ix. 30. This account in the *Acts* agrees with that in this *epistle.*

Verse 22. *And was unknown by face*] I was not personally acquainted with any of the Churches of Judea; I was converted in another place, and had not preached the Gospel in any Christian congregation in that country; I knew only those at Jerusalem.

Verse 23. *They had heard only*] As a *persecutor* of the Church of Christ, I was well known; and as a *convert to Christ* I was not less so. The fame of both was great, even where I was personally unknown.

Verse 24. *They glorified God in me.*] Hearing now that I preached that faith which before I had persecuted and endeavoured to destroy, they glorified God for the grace which had wrought my conversion. I owe nothing to them; I owe all to God; and they

2

themselves acknowledge this. I received all from God, and God has all the glory.

1. IT appeared of great importance to St. Paul to defend and vindicate his Divine mission. As he had *none* from *man*, it was the more necessary that he should be able to show plainly that he had *one from God.* Paul was not brought into the Christian ministry by any *rite* ever used in the Christian Church. Neither *bishop* nor *presbyter* ever *laid hands* on him; and he is more anxious to prove *this*, because his chief honour arose from being sent immediately by God himself: his conversion and the purity of his doctrine showed whence he came. Many since his time, and in the present day, are *far more anxious to* show that they are legitimately appointed by MAN than by GOD; and are fond of displaying their *human credentials.* *These* are easily shown; those that come from God are out of their reach. How idle and vain is a boasted *succession from the apostles*, while ignorance, intolerance, pride, and vain-glory prove that those very persons have no commission from heaven! Endless cases may occur where *man sends* and yet *God* will not *sanction.* And *that man* has no right to preach, nor administer the sacraments of the Church of Christ, whom God *has not sent;* though the whole assembly of *apostles* had *laid their hands* on him. God never sent, and never will send, to convert others, a man who is not converted himself. He will never send him to teach *meekness, gentleness,* and *long suffering,* who is *proud, overbearing, intolerant,* and *impatient.* He, in whom the Spirit of Christ does not dwell, never had a commission to preach the Gospel; he may boast of his human authority, but God will laugh him to scorn. On the other hand, let none run before he is sent; and when he has got the authority of *God,* let him be careful to take that of the *Church* with him also.

2. The apostle was particularly anxious that the Gospel should not be corrupted, that the Church might not be perverted. Whatever *corrupts the* GOSPEL, subverts the CHURCH. The Church is a spiritual building, and stands on a spiritual foundation. Its members are compared to *stones in a building,* but they are *living stones*—each instinct with the spirit of a Divine life; Jesus is not only the *foundation* and the *head-stone,* but the *spirit* that *quickens* and *animates* all. A Church, where the *members* are not *alive to God,* and where the *minister* is not *filled with the meekness and gentleness of Jesus,* differs as much from a *genuine* Church as a *corpse* does from an *active human being.* False teachers in Galatia corrupted the Church, by introducing those Jewish ceremonies which God had abolished; and the doctrine of *justification* by the *use of those ceremonies* which God had shown by the death of his Son to be of none effect. "If those," says Quesnel, "are justly said to pervert the gospel of Christ, who were for joining with it human ceremonies which God himself instituted, what do those do, who would fondly reconcile and blend it with the *pomps of the devil?* The purity of the Gospel cannot admit of any mixture. Those who do not love it, are so far from building up that they *trouble* and *overturn* all. There is no ground of trust and confidence for such workmen."

3. If he be a dangerous man in the Church who introduces *Jewish* or human *ceremonies* which God has not appointed, how much more is he to be dreaded who introduces any *false doctrine*, or who *labours* to *undermine* or *lessen* the *influence* of that which is *true?* And even he who does not faithfully and earnestly preach and inculcate the true doctrine is not a true pastor. It is not sufficient that a man preach *no error;* he must preach the *truth,* the whole *truth,* and *nothing but the truth.*

4. How is it that we have so many Churches like those in *Galatia?* Is it not because, on one hand, we *disturb* the *simplicity* of the Christian worship by Jewish, heathenish, or improper rites and ceremonies; and on the other, *corrupt* the *purity* of its doctrines by the inventions of men? How does the apostle speak of such corrupters? *Let them be accursed.* How awful is this! Let every man who officiates as a Christian minister look well to this. His own soul is at stake; and, if any of the flock perish through his ignorance or neglect, their blood will God require at the watchman's hand.

5. St. Paul well knew that, if he endeavoured to *please man,* he could *not be the servant of Christ.* Can any minor minister hope to succeed, were even an apostle, had he followed that line, could not? The interests of *Christ* and those of the *world* are so opposite, that it is impossible to reconcile them; and he who attempts it shows thereby that he knows neither *Christ* nor the *world,* though so deeply immersed in the spirit of the latter.

6. God generally confounds the expectations of men-pleasing ministers; they never ultimately succeed even with men. God abhors them, and those whom they have flattered find them to be dishonest, and cease to trust them. He who is unfaithful to his God should not be trusted by man.

CHAPTER II.

The apostle mentions his journey to Jerusalem with Barnabas and Titus, 1. Shows that he went thither by revelation; and what he did while there, and the persons with whom he had intercourse, 2–8. How the apostles gave him the right hand of fellowship, 9, 10. How he opposed Peter at Antioch, and the reason why, 11–14. Shows that the Jews as well as the Gentiles must be justified by faith, 15, 16. They who seek this justification should act with consistency, 17, 18. Gives his own religious experience, and shows, that through the law he was dead to the law, and crucified with Christ, 19, 20. Justification is not of the law, but by the faith of Christ, 21.

2

A. M. cir. 4056.
A. D. cir. 52.
A. U. C.
805.
An. Imp. Claudii
Cæsaris 12.

THEN, fourteen years after, [a] I went up again to Jerusalem with Barnabas, and took Titus with *me* also.

2 And I went up by revelation, [b] and communicated unto them that Gospel which I preach among the Gentiles, but [c] privately to them which were of reputation, lest by any means [d] I should run, or had run, in vain.

3 But neither Titus, who was with me, being a Greek, was compelled to be circumcised :

A. M. cir. 4056.
A. D. cir. 52.
A. U. C.
805.
An. Imp. Claudii
Cæsaris 12.

4 And that because of false [e] brethren unawares brought in, who came in privily to spy out our [f] liberty which we have in Christ Jesus, [g] that they might bring us into bondage :

5 To whom we gave place by subjection, no, not for an hour ; that [h] the truth of the Gospel might continue with you.

---

[a] Acts xv. 12.——[b] Acts xv. 12.——[c] Or, *severally.*——[d] Phil. ii. 16 ; 1 Thess. iii. 5.——[e] Acts xv. 1, 24 ; 2 Cor. xi. 26.

[f] Chap. iii. 25 ; chap. v. 1, 13.——[g] 2 Cor. xi. 20 ; chap. iv. 3, 9. [h] Ver. 14 ; chap. iii. 1 ; iv. 16.

NOTES ON CHAP. II.

Verse 1. *Then fourteen years after*] There is a considerable difference among critics concerning the time specified in this verse ; the apostle is however generally supposed to refer to the journey he took to Jerusalem, about the question of circumcision, mentioned in Acts xv. 4, &c. These years, says Dr. Whitby, must be reckoned from the time of his conversion, mentioned here chap. i. 18, which took place A. D. 35 (33;) his journey to Peter was A. D. 38 (36,) and then between that and the council of Jerusalem, assembled A. D. 49 (52,) will be *fourteen* intervening years. The dates in brackets are according to the chronology which I follow in the *Acts* of the Apostles. Dr. Whitby has some objections against this chronology, which may be seen in his notes.

Others contend that the journey of which the apostle speaks is that mentioned Acts xi. 27, &c., when Barnabas and Saul were sent by the Church of Antioch with relief to the poor Christians in Judea ; there being at that time a great *dearth* in that land. St. Luke's not mentioning *Titus* in that journey is no valid objection against it ; for he does not mention him in any part of his history, this being the first place in which his name occurs. And it does seem as if St. Paul did intend purposely to supply that defect, by his saying, *I went up with Barnabas,* and *took Titus with me also.* The former St. Luke relates, Acts xi. 30 ; the latter St. Paul supplies.

Verse 2. *I went up by revelation*] This either means, that he went up at that time by an *express revelation* from God that it was his duty to do so, made either to the Church of Antioch to send these persons to Jerusalem, or to these persons to go according to the directions of that Church ; or the apostle here wishes to say, that, having received the Gospel *by revelation* from God, to preach Christ among the Gentiles, he went up *according* to that revelation, and told what God had done by him among the Gentiles : or it may refer to the revelation made to *certain prophets* who came to Antioch, and particularly *Agabus,* who signified by the Spirit that there would be a dearth ; in consequence of which the disciples purposed to send relief to their poor brethren at Jerusalem. See Acts xi. 27–30.

But privately to them which were of reputation] Τοις δοκουσι· To the *chief men;* those who were *highest* in *reputation* among the apostles. Δοκουντες,

according to *Hesychius,* is οι ενδοξοι, *the honourable.* With these the apostle intimates that he had some private conferences.

Lest by any means] And he held these private conferences with those more eminent men, to give them information how, in consequence of his Divine call, he had preached the Gospel to the Gentiles, and the great good which God had wrought by his ministry ; but they, not knowing the nature and end of his call, might be led to suppose he had acted wrong, and thus *laboured in vain;* and that, if he still continued to act thus, he *should labour in vain.* It was necessary, therefore, that he should give the apostolic council the fullest information that he had acted according to the Divine mind in every respect, and had been blessed in his deed.

Verse 3. *But neither Titus, who was with me*] The apostle proceeds to state that his account was so satisfactory to the apostles, that they not only did not require him to insist on the necessity of circumcision among the Gentiles, but did not even require him to have Titus, who was a *Greek,* circumcised ; though that might have appeared expedient, especially at Jerusalem, to have prevented false brethren from making a handle of his uncircumcision, and turning it to the prejudice of the Gospel in Judea.

To spy out our liberty] The Judaizing brethren got introduced into the assembly of the apostles, in order to find out what was implied in the *liberty of the Gospel,* that they might know the better how to oppose St. Paul and his fellows in their preaching Christ to the Gentiles, and admitting them into the Church without obliging them to observe circumcision and keep the law. The apostle saw that while such men were in the assembly it was better not to mention his mission among the Gentiles, lest, by means of those false brethren, occasion should be given to altercations and disputes; therefore he took the opportunity, by *private conferences,* to set the whole matter, relative to his work among the Gentiles, before the chief of the apostles.

Verse 5. *To whom we gave place by subjection*] So fully satisfied was he with his Divine call, and that he had in preaching among the Gentiles acted in strict conformity to it, that he did not submit in the least to the opinion of those Judaizing teachers ; and therefore he continued to insist on the *exemption* of the Gentiles from the necessity of submitting to Jewish

A. M. cir. 4056.
A. D. cir. 52.
A. U. C. 805.
An. Imp. Claudii Cæsaris 12.

6 But of those [i] who seemed to be somewhat, whatsoever they were, it maketh no matter to me: [k] God accepteth no man's person: for they who seemed *to be somewhat* [l] in conference added nothing to me:

7 But contrariwise, [m] when they saw that the Gospel of the uncircumcision [n] was committed unto me, as *the Gospel* of the circumcision *was* unto Peter;

8 (For he that wrought effectually in Peter to the apostleship of the circumcision, [o] the same was [p] mighty in me toward the Gentiles:)

A. M. cir. 4056.
A. D. cir. 5t.
A. U. C. 805.
An. Imp. Claudii Cæsaris 12.

9 And when James, Cephas, and John, who seemed to be [q] pillars, perceived [r] the grace that was given unto me, they gave to me and Barnabas the right hands of fellowship; that we *should go* unto the heathen, and they unto the circumcision.

10 Only *they would* that we should remember the poor; [s] the same which I also was forward to do.

11 [t] But when Peter was come to Antioch, I withstood him to the face, because he was to be blamed.

---

[i] Chap. vi. 3.——[k] Acts x. 34; Rom. ii. 11.——[l] 2 Cor. xii. 11. [m] Acts xiii. 46; Rom. i. 5; xi. 13; 1 Tim. ii. 7; 2 Tim. i. 11. [n] 1 Thess. ii. 4.——[o] Acts ix. 15; xiii. 2; xxii. 21; xxvi. 17, 18; 1 Cor. xv. 10; chap. i. 16; Col. i. 29.

[p] Chap. iii. 5.——[q] Matt. xvi. 18; Eph. ii. 20; Rev. xxi. 14. [r] Rom. i. 5; xii. 3, 6; xv. 15; 1 Cor. xv. 10; Eph. iii. 8. [s] Acts xi. 30; xxiv. 17; Rom. xv. 25; 1 Cor. xvi. 1; 2 Cor. viii. and ix.——[t] Acts xv. 35.

---

rites; that the *truth of the Gospel*—this grand doctrine, that the Gentiles are admitted by the Gospel of Christ to be fellow-heirs with the Jews, *might continue;* and thus the same doctrine is *continued with you* Gentiles.

Verse 6. *Those who seemed to be somewhat*] Των δοκουντων ειναι τι· *Those who were of acknowledged reputation;* so the words should be understood, see ver. 2. The verb δοκειν, *to seem,* is repeatedly used by the best Greek writers, not to call the sense in question, or to lessen it, but to *deepen* and *extend* it. See the note on Luke viii. 18. Perhaps this verse had best be translated thus, connecting διαφερει with απο των δοκουντων : *But there is no difference between those who were of acknowledged reputation and myself; God accepts no man's person; but, in the conferences which I held with them, they added nothing to me*—gave me no *new light;* did not attempt to *impose* on me any obligation, because they saw that God had appointed me my work, and that his counsel was with me.

Verse 7. *But contrariwise*] They were so far from wishing me to alter my plan, or to introduce any thing *new* in my doctrine to the Gentiles, that they saw plainly that my doctrine was the *same* as their own, coming immediately from the same source; and therefore gave to me and to Barnabas the right hand of fellowship.

The Gospel of the uncircumcision] They saw, to their utmost satisfaction, that I was as expressly sent by God to preach the Gospel to the Gentiles, as Peter was to preach it to the Jews.

Verse 8. *For he that wrought effectually*] Ὁ ενεργησας Πετρῳ, ενηργησε και εμοι· *He who wrought powerfully with Peter, wrought powerfully also with me.* He gave us both those talents which were suited to our work, and equal success in our different departments.

Verse 9. *James, Cephas, and John, who seemed to be pillars*] Οι δοκουντες στυλοι ειναι· *Who were known to be very eminent,* and *acknowledged as chief men* among the apostles. See the note on Luke viii. 18, for the meaning of the verb δοκειν, and see before on ver. 6.

Among the Jews, persons of great eminence and importance are represented as *pillars* and *foundations* of the world. So Abraham is said to be עמוד העולם *ammud haolam,* "the *pillar* of the universe; for by him to this day are the earth and heavens supported." *Yalcut Rubeni,* fol. 29. "Rabbi Simeon said, Behold, we are the *pillars* of the world." *Idra Rabba,* s. 23:

"When Rabbi Jochanan ben Zachai was near death, he wept with a loud voice. His disciples said unto him, O Rabbi, thou *high pillar,* thou light of the world, thou strong hammer, why dost thou weep?" *Aboth R. Nathan,* chap. 24.

So, in *Sohar Genes,* fol. 5, it is said: "And he saw that Rab. Eleazar went up, and stood there, and with him שאר עמודין *shear ammudin,* the rest of the pillars (eminent men) who sat there."

Ibid., fol. 13: "These are the seven righteous men who cleave to the holy blessed God with a pure heart, and they are the seven *pillars* of the world."

Ibid., fol. 21, on the words *bearing fruit,* Gen. i. 11, it is said: "By this we are to understand the just one, who is the *pillar* of the world." See Schoettgen, who adds: "These *pillars* must be distinguished from the *foundation.* The *foundation* of the Church is Jesus Christ alone; the *pillars* are the more *eminent teachers,* which, without the *foundation,* are of no value."

The right hands of fellowship] Giving the *right hand* to another was the mark of confidence, friendship, and fellowship. See Lev. vi. 2: *If a soul—lie unto his neighbor in that which was delivered him to keep, or in fellowship,* יד בתשומת *bithsumeth yad,* "in giving the hand."

Verse 10. *Only they would that we should remember the poor*] They saw plainly that God had as expressly called Barnabas and me to go to the *Gentiles* as he had called them to preach to the *Jews;* and they did not attempt to give us any new injunctions, only wished us to remember the poor in Judea; but this was a thing to which we were previously disposed.

Verse 11. *When Peter was come to Antioch*] There has been a controversy whether Πετρος, *Peter,* here should not be read Κηφας, *Kephas;* and whether this

A. M. cir. 4056.	14 But when I saw that they
A. D. cir. 52.	walked not uprightly, according to
A. U. C.	ᵛ the truth of the Gospel, I said unto
805.	Peter ʷ before *them* all, ˣ If thou,
An. Imp. Claudii	being a Jew, livest after the manner of Gen
Cæsaris 12.	tiles, and not as do the Jews, why compellest

A. M. cir. 4056.
A. D. cir. 52.
A. U. C.
805.
An. Imp. Claudii
Cæsaris 12.

12 For, before that certain came from James, ᵘ he did eat with the Gentiles: but when they were come, he withdrew and separated himself, fearing them which were of the circumcision.

13 And the other Jews dissembled likewise with him; insomuch that Barnabas also was carried away with their dissimulation.

thou the Gentiles to live as do the Jews?

15 ʸ We *who are* Jews by nature, and not ᶻ sinners of the Gentiles,

---

ᵘ Acts x. 28; xi. 3.——ᵛ Ver. 5.——ʷ 1 Tim. v. 20.——ˣ Acts x. 28; xi. 3.——ʸ Acts xv. 10, 11.——ᶻ Matt. ix. 11; Eph. ii. 3, 12

Kephas was not a *different person* from *Peter* the apostle. This controversy has lasted more than 1500 years, and is not yet settled. Instead of Πετρος, *Peter*, ABCH, several others of good note, with the *Syriac, Erpenian, Coptic, Sahidic, Æthiopic, Armenian,* later *Syriac* in the margin, *Vulgate*, and several of the Greek *fathers*, read Κηφας. But whichsoever of these readings we adopt, the controversy is the same; for the great question is, whether this *Peter* or *Kephas*, no matter which name we adopt, be the same with *Peter the apostle?*

I shall not introduce the arguments *pro* and *con*, which may be all seen in Calmet's dissertation on the subject, but just mention the side where the strength of the evidence appears to lie.

That *Peter* the *apostle* is meant, the most sober and correct writers of antiquity maintain; and though some of the *Catholic* writers have fixed the whole hat is here *reprehensible* on one *Kephas*, one of the seventy disciples, yet the most learned of their writers and of their popes, believe that *St. Peter* is meant. Some apparently plausible arguments support the contrary opinion, but they are of no weight when compared with those on the opposite side.

Verse 12. *Before that certain came from James, he did eat with the Gentiles*] Here was Peter's fault. He was convinced that God had pulled down the middle wall of partition that had so long separated the Jews and Gentiles, and he acted on this conviction, associating with the latter and eating with them; but when certain Jews came from James, who it appears considered the law still to be in force, lest he should place a *stumbling-block* before them he withdrew from all commerce with the *converted Gentiles*, and acted as if he himself believed the law to be still in force, and that the distinction between the *Jews* and the *Gentiles* should still be kept up.

Verse 13. *And the other Jews dissembled likewise*] That is: Those who were converted to Christianity from among the *Jews*, and who had also been convinced that the obligation of the Jewish ritual had ceased, seeing Peter act this part, and also *fearing them that were of the circumcision*, they separated themselves from the converted Gentiles, and acted so as to convince the Jews that *they* still believed the law to be of moral obligation; and so powerful was the torrent of their example, that the gentle, loving-hearted *Barnabas was carried away by their dissimulation*, αυτων τη υποκρισει, with their hypocrisy—feigning to be what they really were not.

Verse 14. *That they walked not uprightly*] Ουκ ορθοποδουσι· They did not walk with a *straight step*—they did not maintain a firm footing.

According to the truth of the Gospel] According to that *true* doctrine, which states that *Christ is the end of the law for justification to every one that believes;* and that such are under no obligation to observe circumcision and the other peculiar *rites* and ceremonies of the law.

If thou, being a Jew, livest] This was a cutting reproof. He was a Jew, and had been circumstantially scrupulous in every thing relative to the law, and it required a miracle to convince him that the Gentiles were admitted, on their believing in Christ, to become members of the same Church, and fellow heirs of the hope of eternal life; and in consequence of this, he went in with the Gentiles and ate with them; i. e. associated with them as he would with Jews. But now, *fearing them of the circumcision*, he withdrew from this fellowship.

Why compellest thou the Gentiles] Thou didst *once* consider that *they* were not under such an obligation, and *now* thou actest as if thou didst consider the law in full force; but thou art convinced that the contrary is the case, yet actest differently! This is *hypocrisy.*

Verse 15. *We who are Jews by nature*] We who belong to the Jewish *nation*—who have been *born, bred,* and *educated* Jews.

And not sinners of the Gentiles] 'Αμαρτωλοι· Not *without the knowledge of God*, as they have been. 'Αμαρτωλος often signifies a *heathen*, merely one who had no knowledge of the true God. But among the *nations* or *Gentiles* many Jews sojourned; who in Scripture are known by the name of *Hellenists*, and these were distinguished from those who were termed εξ εθνων αμαρτωλοι, sinners of the Gentiles—*heathens*, in our common sense of the word; while the others, though living among them, were worshippers of the true God, and addicted to no species of idolatry. Some have translated this passage thus: *We Jews, and not Gentiles, by nature sinners;* for it is supposed that φυσει here refers to that *natural corruption* which every man brings into the world. Now, though the *doctrine* be true, (and the state of man, and universal experience confirm it,) yet it can neither be supported from this place, nor even from Eph. ii. 3. See the note on Rom. ii. 16. It appears, from the use of this word by some of the best Greek authors, that φυσει did not signify *by nature*, as we use the word, but

A. M. cir. 4056.
A. D. cir. 52.
A. U. C.
805.
An. Imp. Claud..
Cæsaris 12.

16 ^a Knowing that a man is not justified by the works of the law, but ^b by the faith of Jesus Christ, even we have believed in Jesus Christ, that we might be justified by the faith of Christ, and not by the works of the law: for ^c by the works of the law shall no flesh be justified.

17 But if, while we seek to be justified by Christ, we ourselves also are found ^d sinners,

is therefore Christ the minister of sin? God forbid.

18 For if I build again the things which I destroyed, I make myself a transgressor.

19 For I ^e through the law ^f am dead to the law, that I might ^g live unto God.

20 I am ^h crucified with Christ : nevertheless I live ; yet not I, but Christ liveth in me :

A M. cir. 4056.
A. D. cir. 52.
A. U. C.
805.
An. Imp. Claudii
Cæsaris 12.

---

^a Acts xiii. 38, 39.——^b Rom. i. 17, iii. 22, 28 ; viii 3 ; chap iii. 24, Heb. vii. 18, 19.——^c Psa. cxliii. 2, Rom. iii 20, chap. iii. 11.——^d 1 John iii. 8, 9

^e Rom. viii 2.——^f Rom. vi. 14 ; vii. 4, 6.——^g Rom. vi. 11 ; 2 Cor. v 15 ; 1 Thess. v. 10 ; Heb. ix. 14 ; 1 Pet. iv. 2.——^h Rom. vi. 6 ; chap v. 24 ; vi. 14.

---

expressed the *natural birth, family,* or *nation* of a man ; to distinguish him from any *other family* or *nation.* I can give a few instances of this, which are brought to my hand in a small elegant pamphlet, written by Dr. *Münter,* the present bishop of Zealand, entitled *Observationum ex marmoribus Græcis Sacrarum Specimen,* and which has been lent to me by the right honourable Lord Teignmouth, to whose condescension, kindness, and learning, many of my studies have been laid under particular obligation.

The word in question is the xxviiith example in the above pamphlet, the substance of which is as follows : In an inscription on a Greek marble, given by Dr. *Chandler,* page 27, we find these words : Ὁ γαμβρος μου Λεων Αρτεμεισιον, ὁ επικαλουμενος Ιασων, οικονει μεν Μειλησιος, φυσει δε Ιασευς· "My son-in-law, Leo, the son of Artemisius, who is called a Jasian, is of the house of Milesius, though *by nature* he is from Jaso." That is : Jaso being a town of Caria, this Leo is said to be φυσει Ιασευς, by nature a Jasian, although he sprang from the *Milesian* family. The following examples will place this in a clearer light. *Josephus,* Ant. Jud., lib. xi. cap. vi. sec. 5, speaking of *Amanes,* the Amalekite, says : Και γαρ φυσει τοις Ιουδαιοις απηχθανετο, ὁτι και το γενος των Αμαλεκιτων, εξ ὡν ην αυτος, ὑπ' αυτων διεφθαρτο· "For he was *by nature* incensed against the Jews, because the nation of the Amalekites, from whom he sprang, had been destroyed by them ;" that is, he had a *national* prejudice or hatred to the Jewish people on the above account. The following example from *Dio Chrysostom,* Orat. xxxi., is also to the point : Οἱγε (Αθηναιοι) τον δεινα μεν Ολυμπιον κεκληκασι, ουδε φυσει πολιτην ἑαυτων· "For they (the Athenians) called this person an Olympian, though *by nature* he was not their citizen ;" that is, he was called an Olympian, though he was not *naturally* of that city, or, in other words, he was not *born* there. From these examples, and the scope of the place, we may argue that the words, *we* who are *Jews by nature,* mean, we who were *born* in the *land of Judea,* and of *Jewish parents.* And hence the passage in Eph. ii. 3, which speaks most evidently of the *heathens,* " *and were by nature the children of wrath, even as others,*" may be thus understood . Being *Gentiles,* and brought up in gross darkness, without any knowledge of God, abandoned to all sensual living, we were, from our very *condition,* and practical state, exposed to punishment. This sense is at least equally good with that given of the words

in Rom. ii. 16, where it is proved that φυσει, in several connections, means *truly, certainly, incontestably* ; " we were, *beyond all controversy,* exposed to punishment, because we had been *born* among idolaters, and have *lived* as they did. Here both senses of the word apply.

Verse 16. *Knowing that a man is not justified*] See the notes on Rom. i. 17 ; iii. 24, 27 ; and viii. 3. And see on Acts xiii. 38, 39, in which places the subject of this verse is largely discussed. Neither the works of the Jewish law, nor of *any other* law, could justify any man ; and if justification or pardon could not have been attained in some other way, the world must have perished. Justification by faith, in the boundless mercy of God, is as reasonable as it is Scriptural and necessary.

Verse 17. *But if, while we seek to be justified*] If, while we acknowledge that we must be justified by faith in Christ, *we ourselves are found sinners,* enjoining the necessity of observing the rites and ceremonies of the law, which never could and never can justify, and yet, by submitting to circumcision, we lay ourselves under the necessity of *fulfilling the law,* which is impossible, we thus constitute ourselves *sinners* ; is, *therefore, Christ the minister of sin ?*—— Christ, who has taught us to renounce the law, and expect justification through his death ? *God forbid !* that we should either act so, or think so.

Verse 18. *For if I build again the things which I destroyed*] If I act like a Jew, and enjoin the observance of the law on the Gentiles, which I have repeatedly asserted and proved to be *abolished* by the death of Christ, then I *build up what I destroyed,* and thus *make myself a transgressor,* by not observing the law in that way in which I appear to enjoin the observance of it upon others.

Verse 19. *For I through the law am dead to the law*] In consequence of properly considering the *nature* and *requisitions* of the law, *I am dead* to all hope and expectation of help or salvation from *the law,* and have been obliged to take refuge in the Gospel of Christ. Or, probably the word νομος, LAW, is here put for a *system of doctrine* ; as if he had said, *I through the Gospel am dead to the law.* The law itself is consigned to death ; and another, the Gospel of Christ, is substituted in its stead. The *law* condemns to death , and I have embraced the *Gospel* that I might be saved from *death,* and *live unto God.*

Verse 20. *I am crucified with Christ*] The death

2

A. M. cir. 4056.
A. D. cir. 52.
A. U. C.
805.
An. Imp. Claudii
Cæsaris 12.

and the life which I now live in the flesh, i I live by the faith of the Son of God, k who loved me, and gave himself for me.

21 I do not frustrate the grace of God : for ¹ if righteousness *come* by the law, then Christ is dead in vain.

A. M. cir. 4056.
A D. cir. 52.
A. U. C.
805.
An. Imp. Claudii
Cæsaris 12.

---

i 2 Cor. v. 15; 1 Thess. v. 10; 1 Pet. iv. 2.——k Chap. i. 4; Eph. v. 2; Tit. ii. 14.

¹ Chapter iii. 21; Hebrews vii. 11; see Romans xi. 6; chapter v. 4.

---

of Christ on the cross has showed me that there is no hope of salvation by the law; I am therefore as truly *dead* to all expectation of justification by the law, as Christ was *dead* when he gave up the ghost upon the cross. Through him alone *I live*—enjoy a present life, and have a prospect of future glory.

Yet not I] It is not of my *natural life* I speak, nor of any *spiritual things* which I myself have procured ; *but Christ liveth in me.* God made man to be a *habitation of his own Spirit :* the law cannot *live* in me so as to give me a *Divine life;* it does not *animate,* but *kill;* but Christ *lives* in me ; he is the *soul* of my *soul;* so that I now live to God. But this *life* I have *by the faith of the Son of God*—by believing on Christ as a sacrifice for sin ; for he *loved me,* and because he did so *he gave himself for me*—made himself a sacrifice unto death, that I might be saved from the bitter pains of death eternal.

Verse 21. *I do not frustrate*] Ουκ αθετω· I do not *contemn, despise,* or *render useless, the grace of God*—the doctrine of Christ crucified ; which I must do if I preach the necessity of observing the *law.*

For if righteousness] If *justification* and salvation *come by* an observance of *the law,* then *Christ is dead in vain;* his death is *useless* if an observance of the law can save us ; but no observance of the law can save us, and therefore there was an *absolute necessity* for the *death* of *Christ.*

1. THE account of the *prevarication* of Peter in the preceding chapter teaches us a most useful lesson. Let him who assuredly standeth take heed lest he fall. No person in a state of *probation* is infallible ; a man may fall into sin every moment ; and he will, if he do not walk with God. Worldly prudence and fleshly wisdom would have concealed this account of the prevarication of Peter ; but God tells truth. HE is the fountain of it ; and from him we are to expect not only *nothing but the truth,* but also the *whole truth.* If the Gospel were not of God we had never heard of the *denial* and *prevarication* of Peter, nor of the *contention* between Paul and Barnabas. And these accounts are recorded, not that men may *justify* or *excuse* their own delinquencies by them, but that they may avoid them ; for he must be inexcusable who, with these histories before his eyes, ever *denies his Master,* or *acts the part of a hypocrite.* Had the apostles acted in concert to impose a *forgery* on the world as a Divine revelation, the imposture would have now come out. The falling out of the parties would have led to a discovery of the cheat. This relation, therefore, is an additional evidence of the truth of the Gospel.

2. On, *I through the law am dead to the law, &c.,* pious *Quesnel* makes the following useful reflections : " The *ceremonial law,* which is no more than a *type* and *shadow* of him, destroys itself by showing us *Jesus Christ,* who is the *truth* and the *substance.* The *moral law,* by leaving us under our own inability under sin and the curse, makes us perceive the necessity of the *law of the heart,* and of a *Saviour* to give it. The *law* is for the *old man,* as to its terrible and servile part ; and it was *crucified* and *died* with Christ upon the cross as well as the *old man.* The *new man,* and the *new law,* require a *new sacrifice.* What need has he of other sacrifices who has *Jesus Christ?* They *in* whom this sacrifice *lives,* do themselves live to God alone ; but none can live to him except by *faith ;* and this *life of faith* consists in *dying with Christ* to the things of the present world, and in expecting, as co-heirs with him, the blessings of the eternal world. And who can work all this in us but only he who lives in us ? That man has arrived to a high degree of *mortification,* who can say *Christ liveth in me, and I am crucified to the world.* Such a one must have renounced not only *earthly things,* but *his own self* also."

3. Is there, or can there be, one well grounded hope of eternal life but what comes through the *Gospel ?* In vain has the ingenuity of man tortured itself for more than 5000 years, to find out some method of *mending* the human heart : none has been discovered that even *promised* any thing likely to be effectual. The *Gospel of Christ* not only *mends* but completely *cures* and *new makes* infected nature. Who is duly apprised of the infinite excellency and importance of the Gospel! What was the world before its appearance ? What would it be were this light extinguished ? Blessed Lord ! let neither *infidelity* nor *false doctrine* rise up to obscure this heavenly *splendour !*

CHAPTER III.

The apostle inquires how they could be so foolish as to renounce the Gospel of Christ and turn back to the law, after having heard, received, and suffered so much for the Gospel, 1–5. *Asserts the doctrine of justification by faith, on the example of Abraham,* 6–9. *Shows that all who are under the law are under the curse, from which Christ alone redeems us ; and the promise made to Abraham comes to the Gentiles who believe,* 10–14. *For the covenant is not by the works of the law, but by promise,* 15–18. *The law was given to show the sinfulness of sin, and to act as a schoolmaster till Christ should come,* 19–25. *It is*

2

---

by faith only that any become children of God, 26. And under the Gospel, all those distinctions which subsisted under the law are done away; and genuine believers, whether Jews or Gentiles, bond or free, are one in Christ Jesus, and accounted the genuine children of Abraham, 27–29.

A. M. cir. 4056.
A. D. cir. 52.
A. U. C.
805.
An. Imp. Claudii
Cæsaris 12.

O FOOLISH Galatians, [a] who hath bewitched you, that ye should not obey [b] the truth, before whose eyes Jesus Christ hath been evidently set forth, crucified among you?

2 This only would I learn of you, Received ye [c] the Spirit by the works of the law, [d] or by the hearing of faith?

3 Are ye so foolish? [e] having begun in the Spirit, are ye now made perfect by the [f] flesh?

4 [g] Have ye suffered [h] so many things in vain? if *it be* yet in vain.

5 He therefore that [i] ministereth to you the Spirit, and worketh miracles among you, *doeth he it* by the works of the law, or by the hearing of faith?

6 Even as [k] Abraham believed God, and it

A. M. cir. 4056.
A. D. cir. 52.
A. U. C.
805.
An. Imp. Claudii
Cæsaris 12.

---

[a] Chap. v. 7.——[b] Chap. ii. 14; v. 7.——[c] Acts ii. 38; viii. 15; x. 47; xv. 8; ver. 14; Eph. i. 13; Heb. vi. 4.——[d] Rom. x. 16, 17.——[e] Chap. iv. 9.——[f] Heb. vii. 16; ix. 10.

[g] Heb. x. 35, 36; 2 John 8.——[h] Or, *so great.*——[i] 2 Cor. iii. 8.——[k] Genesis xv. 6; Romans iv. 3, 9, 21, 22; James ii. 23.

NOTES ON CHAP. III.

Verse 1. *O foolish Galatians*] O infatuated people; you make as little use of *reason* as those who have *none;* you have acted in this business as those do who are *fascinated*—they are led blindly and unresistingly on to their own destruction.

That ye should not obey the truth] This clause is wanting in ABD*FG, some others, the *Syriac, Erpenian, Coptic, Sahidic, Itala, Vulgate* MS., and in the most important of the Greek and Latin *fathers.* Of the clause Professor *White* says, *Certissime* delenda, "It should *certainly* be expunged."

There are several various readings on this verse, from which it appears that the verse in the best ancient MSS. and versions was read thus: *O foolish Galatians, who hath bewitched you? Before whose eyes Jesus Christ crucified hath been plainly set forth.*

Among you?] Εν υμιν is wanting in ABC, several others, the *Syriac, Erpenian, Coptic, Sahidic, Æthiopic, Armenian, Vulgate* MS., one copy of the *Itala,* and in several of the *fathers.* The words appear to disturb the sense, and have obliged commentators to have recourse to a sort of technical meaning; viz. "The doctrine of the Gospel had been so fully preached among these people that it might be said Jesus Christ had been crucified among them; so fully had his sufferings been detailed, and the design of them pointed out."

Verse 2. *Received ye the Spirit by the works of the law*] This may refer to the *miraculous gifts* of the Spirit, which were very common in the apostolic Church. Did ye receive these extraordinary gifts in consequence of your circumcision, and observing the Mosaic precepts? or was it by the *hearing* of the Gospel, prescribing *faith* in Christ crucified? It may also refer to the *spirit of adoption,* and consequently to their *sonship.*

Verse 3. *Having begun in the Spirit*] Having received a spiritual religion, which refined and purified your hearts; and having received the Holy Spirit of God, by which ye were endued with various miraculous influences; and the spirit of adoption, by which he were assured of the remission of sins, and incorporation with the family of God:

Are ye now made perfect by the flesh?] Are ye

seeking to complete that spiritual religion, and to perfect these spiritual gifts, by the *carnal* rite of circumcision? It appears that by the *Spirit,* here, not only the Holy Spirit, but his gifts, are to be understood; and by the *flesh, illud membrum in quo circumcisio peragitur;* and, by a metonymy, *circumcision* itself.

Verse 4. *Have ye suffered so many things in vain?*] Have ye received and lost so much good? The verb πασχων, as compounded with εν, *well,* or κακως, *ill,* and often without either, signifies to *suffer pain* or *loss,* or to *possess* and *enjoy.* In such a case the man is considered as the *patient,* and the good or ill *acts* upon him. Though it is possible that the Galatians had *suffered* some persecution for the truth of Christ, yet it is as likely that the apostle refers to the *benefits* which they had received. Ye have received faith, the pardon of your sins, the gift of the Holy Spirit, and with it many extraordinary gifts and graces; and have ye *suffered the loss* of all these things? Have ye *received* all these *in vain? if yet in vain*—if it be credible that ye have sacrificed so many excellent benefits for an imaginary good.

Verse 5. *He therefore that ministereth to you the Spirit*] The apostle means himself: he had been the means of conveying the Holy Spirit to them, and by that *Spirit* he wrought miracles among them; and he did all this, not as a *Jew,* (for as *such* he had no *power,*) but he did all as a *believer in Christ.* The word επιχορηγων, which we translate *ministereth,* is very emphatic, and signifies *leading up the chorus,* bringing up one *after another, adding grace to grace, benefit to benefit;* so that it appears that they had not only some, but *many* benefits; God, by means of his apostle, having greatly enriched them with various spiritual blessings.

Verse 6. *Abraham believed God*] This is quoted from Gen. xv. 6, where see the note; and St. Paul produces it, Rom. iv. 3–5, where also see the notes. Abraham, while even uncircumcised, believed in God, and his faith was reckoned to him for justification; and Abraham is called the *father of the faithful,* or, *of believers.* If, then, he was justified without the deeds of the law, he was justified by *faith;* and if he was justified by faith, long before the law was given then the law is not necessary to salvation.

It is remarkable that the Jews themselves main-

2

A. M. cir. 4056.
A. D. cir. 52.
A. U. C.
805.
An. Imp. Claudii
Cæsaris 12.

was [1] accounted to him for right-eousness.

7 Know ye therefore that [m] they which are of faith, the same are the children of Abraham.

8 And [n] the Scripture, foreseeing that God would justify the heathen through faith, preach-ed before the Gospel unto Abraham, *saying*, [o] In thee shall all nations be blessed.

9 So then they which be of faith are bless-ed with faithful Abraham.

10 For as many as are of the works of the law are under the curse: for it is written, [p] Cursed *is* every one that continueth not in

all things which are written in the book of the law to do them.

11 But [q] that no man is jus-tified by the law in the sight of God, *it is* evident: for, [r] The just shall live by faith;

12 And [s] the law is not of faith: but, [t] The man that doeth them shall live in them.

13 [u] Christ hath redeemed us from the curse of the law, being made a curse for us: for it is written, [v] Cursed *is* every one that hangeth on a tree:

14 [w] That the blessing of Abraham might come on the Gentiles through Jesus Christ; that we

A. M. cir. 4056.
A. D. cir. 52.
A. U. C.
805.
An. Imp. Claudii
Cæsaris 12.

---

[1] Or, *imputed*.——[m] John viii. 39; Rom. iv. 11, 12, 16.——[n] See Rom. ix. 17; ver. 22.——[o] Gen. xii. 3; xviii. 18; xxii. 18; Ecclus. xliv. 21; Acts iii. 35.——[p] Deut. xxvii. 26; Jer. xi. 3.——[q] Ch. ii. 16.

[r] Hab. ii. 4; Rom. i. 17; Heb. x. 38.——[s] Rom. iv. 4, 5; x. 5, 6; xi. 6.——[t] Lev. xviii. 5; Neh. ix. 29; Ezek. xx. 11; Rom. x. 5.——[u] Rom. viii. 3; 2 Cor. x. 21; chap. iv. 5.——[v] Deut. xxi. 23.——[w] Rom. iv. 9, 16.

---

tained that Abraham was saved by faith. *Mehilta, in Yalcut Simeoni*, page 1, fol. 69, makes this assertion: " It is evident that Abraham could not obtain an in-heritance either in this world or in the world to come, but by faith."

Verse 8. *The Scripture, foreseeing*] See the notes on Rom. iv. 3—16. As God intended to justify the heathen through faith, he preached the Gospel that contains the grand display of the doctrine of salvation by faith, *before*, to Abraham, while he was in his hea-then state; and thus he is called *the father of be-lievers*: therefore it must refer to *them* who shall believe the same Gospel among the Gentiles; and, as the door of faith was open to all the Gentiles, con-sequently the promise was fulfilled: *In thee shall all the nations of the earth be blessed.*

Verse 9. *They which be of faith*] All who believe, as Abraham has believed, are made partakers of Abraham's blessings.

Verse 10. *As many as are of the works of the law*] All that seek salvation by the performance of the works of the law are under the curse, because it is impossible for them to come up to the spiritual meaning and in-tent of the law; and the law pronounces them *cursed* that *continue not in all things which are written in the book of the law to do them.* Hence, every *Jew* is necessarily under the curse of God's broken law; and every *sinner* is under the same curse, though he be not a *Jew*, who does not take refuge in the salvation provided for him by the Gospel. It is worthy of re-mark that no *printed* copy of the Hebrew Bible pre-serves the word כל *col*, ALL, in Deut. xxvii. 26, which answers to the apostle's word πασι, *all*, here. St. Je-rome says that the Jews suppressed it, lest it should appear that they were bound to perform *all* things that are written in the book of the law. Of the genuine-ness of the reading there is no cause to doubt: it ex-ists in *six* MSS. of *Kennicott* and *De Rossi*, in the *Samaritan* text, in several copies of the *Targum*, in the *Septuagint*, and in the quotation made here by the apostle, in which there is no variation either in the MSS. or in the *versions*.

Verse 11. *But that no man is justified by the law*] By the *observance* of the law, suppose he had even continued in all things that are written in it to do them, *is evident*; for the Prophet *Habakkuk*, chap. ii. 4, has declared, under the direct influence of the Spirit of God, *The just shall live by faith*; or, he who is just by faith shall live: therefore this justification comes not by *works*, or the observance of the law, but by *faith*.

Verse 12. *And the law is not of faith*] It pro-mises no forgiveness to believing, but requires obedi-ence. It is not, What do you *believe?* but, What have you *done?* *The man that doeth them* perfectly, at all times, and in all places, *he shall live in them*; but if in any case he fails, he forfeits his life. See the notes on Rom. i. 17, &c.

Verse 13. *Christ hath redeemed us*] Εξηγορασεν· Hath bought us with a price; viz. his *blood*, or life.

Being made a curse for us] Being made an *atone-ment* for our sins; for whatever was offered as an atonement for sin was considered as *bearing the pu-nishment due to sin*, and the person who suffered for transgression was considered as bearing the *curse* in his body; therefore, in the same day in which a cri-minal was executed it was ordered that his body should be buried, that the land might not be polluted, because *he that was hanged*, which was the case with every heinous culprit, was considered *accursed of God*, Deut. xxi. 22, 23; hence the necessity of *removing* the ac-cursed THING *out of sight*.

Verse 14. *That the blessing of Abraham*] That is, justification or the pardon of sin, with all other blessings consequent on it, such as *peace with God, spiritual life*, and *eternal glory*.

Might come on the Gentiles through Jesus Christ] So we find that he was made a *curse for us*, that the *blessings* promised to Abraham might be given to them who believe on him, as having been made a *curse*; i. e. an *expiatory victim* for them.

The promise of the Spirit] The spirit of adoption, *sonship* with God; and the *Spirit* of God to attest that *sonship*. And all this was *through faith*. Hence,

A. M. cir. 4056.
A. D. cir. 52.
A. U. C.
805.
An Imp. Claudii
Cæsaris 12.
might receive [x] the promise of the Spirit through faith.

15 Brethren, I speak after the manner of men ; [y] Though *it be* but a man's [z] covenant, yet *if it be* confirmed, no man disannulleth, or addeth thereto.

16 Now [a] to Abraham and his seed were the promises made. He saith not, And to seeds,

as of many ; but as of one, And to thy seed, which is [b] Christ.

17 And this I say, *that* the covenant, that. was confirmed before of God in Christ, the law, [c] which was four hundred and thirty years after, cannot disannul, [d] that it should make the promise of none effect.

A. M. cir. 4056.
A. D. cir. 52.
A. U. C.
805.
An. Imp. Claudii
Cæsaris 12.

---

[x] Isa. xxxii. 15 ; xliv. 3 ; Jer. xxxi. 33 ; xxxii. 40 ; Ezek. xi. 19 ; xxxvi. 27 ; Joel ii. 28, 29 ; Zech. xii. 10 ; John vii. 39 ; Acts ii. 33.

[y] Heb. ix. 17.——[z] Or, *testament*.——[a] Gen. xii. 3, 7 ; xvii. 7 ; ver. 8.——[b] 1 Cor. xii. 12.——[c] Exod. xii. 40, 41.——[d] Rom. iv. 13, 14 ; ver. 21.

---

from the beginning God had purposed that salvation should be *through faith*, and never expected that any soul of man should be justified by the works of the law ; and only gave that law that the exceeding sinfulness of sin might appear, and that man might be prepared to welcome the *Gospel*, which proclaimed salvation to a lost world through the atoning passion and death of Christ.

Verse 15. *I speak after the manner of men*] I am about to produce an example taken from civil transactions. *If it be confirmed*—if an agreement or bond be signed, sealed, and witnessed, and, in this country, *being first duly stamped ;*

No man disannulleth] It stands under the protection of the civil law, and nothing can be legally erased or added.

Verse 16. *Now to Abraham and his seed*] The promise of salvation by faith was made to Abraham and his posterity.

He saith not, And to seeds] It was one particular kind of posterity which was intended : *but as of one— which is Christ ;* i. e. to the spiritual head, and all believers in him, who are children of Abraham, because they are *believers*, ver. 7. But why does the apostle say, *not of seeds, as of many ?* To this it is answered, that Abraham possessed in his family *two seeds*, one *natural*, viz. the members of his own household ; and the other *spiritual*, those who were like himself because of their faith. The promises were not of a *temporal* nature ; had they been so, they would have belonged to his *natural* seed ; but they did not, therefore they must have belonged to the *spiritual* posterity. And as we know that promises of justification, &c., could not properly be made to *Christ* in himself, hence we must conclude his *members* to be here intended. and the word *Christ* is put here for *Christians*. It is from Christ that the grace flows which constitutes Christians. Christians are those who believe after the example of Abraham ; they therefore are the spiritual seed. Christ, working in and by these, makes them the *light* and *salt* of the *world ;* and through them, *under* and *by* Christ, are all the nations of the earth blessed. This appears to be the most consistent interpretation, though every thing must be understood of *Christ* in the first instance, and then of *Christians* only through him.

Verse 17. *Confirmed before of God in Christ*] i. e. The promise of justification, &c., made to believers in Christ Jesus, who are the spiritual seed of Christ, as they are children of Abraham, from the similitude

of their faith. Abraham believed in God, and it was reckoned to him for justification ; the Gentiles believed in Christ, and received justification. Probably the word *Christ* is to be taken, both here and in the preceding verse, for *Christians*, as has already been hinted. However it be taken, the sense is plainly the same ; the promise of salvation must necessarily be to them who believe in Christ, for he is the *promised seed*, Gen. iii. 15, through whom every blessing is derived on mankind ; and through his *spiritual seed*—the true *Christians*, the conquests of the cross are daily spreading over the face of the earth. The present unparalleled dispersion of the sacred writings, in all the regular languages of the universe, is a full proof that all the nations of the earth are likely to be blessed through them ; but they have nothing but what *they* have received from and through Christ.

Four hundred and thirty years after] God made a covenant with Abraham that the Messiah should spring from his posterity. This covenant stated that justification should be obtained by faith in the Messiah. The Messiah did not come till 1911 years after the making of this covenant, and the law was given 430 years after the covenant with Abraham, therefore the law, which was given 1481 years before the promise to Abram *could be fulfilled*, (for so much time elapsed between the giving of the law and the advent of Christ,) could not possibly annul the Abrahamic covenant. This argument is absolute and conclusive. Let us review it. The promise to Abraham respects the Messiah, and cannot be fulfilled but in him. Christians say the Messiah *is come*, but the advent of him whom they acknowledge as the Messiah did not take place till 1911 years after the covenant was made, therefore no *intermediate* transaction can affect that covenant. But the law was an *intermediate* transaction, taking place 430 years after the covenant with Abraham, and could neither annul nor affect that which was not to have its fulfilment till 1481 years after. Justification by faith is promised in the Abrahamic covenant, and attributed to that alone, therefore it is not to be expected from the law, nor can its works justify any, for the law in this respect cannot annul or affect the Abrahamic covenant. But suppose ye say that the law, which was given 430 years after the covenant with Abraham, has superseded this covenant, and limited and confined its blessings to the Jews ; I answer : This is impossible, for the covenant most specifically refers to the *Messiah*, and takes in, not the Jewish people only, but *all nations ;* for it is writ-

2

A. M. cir. 4056.
A. D. cir. 52.
A. U. C.
805.
An. Imp. Claudii
Cæsaris 12.

18 For, if ^e the inheritance *be* of the law, ^f *it is* no more of promise: but God gave *it* to Abraham by promise.

19 Wherefore then *serveth* the law? ^g It was added because of transgressions, till ^h the

seed should come to whom the promise was made; *and it was* ⁱ ordained by angels in the hand ^k of a mediator.

20 Now a mediator is not a *mediator* of one, ^l but God is one.

A. M. cir. 4056.
A. D. cir. 52.
A. U. C.
805.
An. Imp. Claudii
Cæsaris 12.

---

^e Rom. viii. 17.——^f Rom. iv. 14.——^g John xv. 22 ; Rom. iv. 15 ; v. 20 ; vii. 8, 13 ; 1 Tim. i. 9.——^h Ver. 16.——ⁱ Acts vii.

53 ; Heb. ii. 2.——^k Exod. xx. 19, 21, 22 ; Deut. v. 5, 22, 23, 27, 31 ; John i. 17 ; Acts vii. 38 ; 1 Tim. ii 5.——^l Rom. iii. 29, 30.

---

ten, *In thy seed—the Messiah* and his spiritual progeny, *shall all the nations of the earth be blessed.* This universal blessedness can never be confined, by any figure of speech, or by any legal act, to the *Jewish* people exclusively ; and, as the covenant was legally made and confirmed, it cannot be annulled, it must therefore remain in reference to its object.

In opposition to us, the Jews assert that the Messiah is *not yet come ;* then we assert, on that ground, that the promise is not yet fulfilled ; for the giving of the law to *one people* cannot imply the fulfilment of the Abrahamic covenant, because that extends to *all nations.* However, therefore, the case be argued, the Jewish cause derives no benefit from it ; and the conclusion still recurs, salvation cannot be attained by the works of the law, forasmuch as the covenant is of *faith ;* and he only, as your prophets declare, who is *justified by faith, shall live,* or be *saved.* Therefore we still conclude that those who are only *under the law* are under the *curse ;* and, as it says, *he that doeth these things shall live in them,* and *he that sinneth shall die,* there is no hope of salvation for any man from the law of Moses. And the Gospel of Jesus Christ, proclaiming salvation by faith to a sinful and ruined world, is absolutely necessary, nor can it be superseded by any other institution, whether human or Divine.

How we arrive at the sum of 430 years may be seen in the note on Exod. xii. 40. Dr. Whitby also gives a satisfactory view of the matter. " The apostle refers to the promise made, Gen. xii. 3, since from that only are the 430 years to be computed, for then Abraham was 75 *years old,* Gen. xii. 4 ; from thence to the birth of Isaac, which happened when Abraham was 100 *years old,* (Gen. xxi. 5,) 25 *years ;* from his birth to the birth of Jacob, 60 *years,* for *Isaac was* 60 *years old when Rebecca bare him,* Gen. xxv. 26. From Jacob's birth to the descent into Egypt, 130 *years,* as he said to Pharaoh, Gen. xlvii. 9. The abode of him and his posterity in Egypt was 215 *years ;* so *that,* with their sojourning in Canaan, was 430 *years ;*" the sum given here, and in Exod. xii. 40, where see the notes.

Verse 18. *For if the inheritance* be *of the law*] See the preceding arguments, in which this is proved.

Verse 19. *Wherefore then serveth the law ?*] If the law does not annul the Abrahamic covenant, and cannot confer salvation on its votaries, why did God give it ? This was a very natural objection, and must arise in the mind of any Jew who had paid attention to the apostle's reasoning.

It was added because of transgressions] It was given that we might know our sinfulness, and the need

we stood in of the mercy of God. The law is the *right line,* the *straight edge,* that determines the *obliquity* of our conduct. See the notes on Rom. iv. 15 ; and especially on Rom. v. 20, where this subject is largely discussed, and the figure explained.

Till the seed should come] The law was to be in force till the advent of the Messiah. After that it was to cease.

It was ordained by angels] The ministry of angels was certainly used in giving the law ; see Psa. lxviii. 17 ; Acts vii. 53 ; and Heb. ii. 2 ; but they were only *instruments* for *transmitting ;* Moses was the *mediator* between God and the people, Deut. v. 5.

Verse 20. *A mediator is not a mediator of one*] As a mediator, μεσιτης, signifies a *middle* person, there must necessarily be *two* parties, between whom he stands, and acts in reference to both, as he is supposed to have the interests of both equally at heart.

This verse is allowed to be both *obscure* and *difficult ;* and it is certain that there is little consent among learned men and critics in their opinions concerning it. *Rosenmuller* thinks that the opinion of *Nosselt* is to be preferred to all others.

He first translates the words ὁ δε μεσιτης ἑνος ουκ εστιν thus : *But he* (viz. Moses) *is not the mediator of that one race* of Abraham, viz. the *Christians ;* for ἑνος relates to the σπερμα ᾧ επηγγελται, *the seed that should come,* ver. 19, of which he said, ὡς εφ᾽ ἑνος, *as of one,* ver. 16. If Paul had written ὁ δε μεσιτης του ἑνος εκεινου ουκ εστι, *he is not the mediator of one,* no person would have had any doubt that σπερματος, *seed,* ought to be supplied after ἑνος, *of one,* ver. 19. The same mode of speaking Paul uses, Rom. v. 17 ; ὁ δε, *but he,* ὁ for αυτος, Matt. xii. 3, 11, 39, ὁ δε ειπεν, *but he said.* Though Moses was the Mediator between God and the Israelites, yet he was not the mediator between God and *that one seed which was to come ;* viz. the Gentiles who should believe in Christ.

But God is one.] He is the *one* God, who is the Father of the spirits of all flesh ; the God of the Gentiles as well as the God of the Jews. That this is St. Paul's meaning is evident from his use of the same words in other places, 1 Tim. ii. 5 : εἱς γαρ Θεος, &c. *for there is one God,* and *one mediator between God and man,* that is, there is *only* one God and one mediator for the whole human race ; Eph. iv. 5, 6 : *One Lord, one faith, one baptism,* εἱς Θεος και πατηρ παντων, ONE GOD *and Father of* ALL. The sense of the whole is : Moses was the mediator of *one part* of Abraham's seed, viz. the *Israelites :* but of the other seed, the *Gentiles,* he was certainly not the mediator ; for the mediator of that seed, according to the promise of God, and covenant made with Abraham, is Christ

2

A. M. cir. 4056.
A. D. cir. 52.
A. U. C. 805.
An. Imp. Claudii Cæsaris 12.

21 *Is* the law then against the
promises of God? God forbid:
[m] for if there had been a law given
which could have given life, verily righteousness should have been by the law.
22 But [n] the Scripture hath concluded [o] all
under sin, [p] that the promise by faith of Jesus
Christ might be given to them that believe.
23 But before faith came, we were kept
under the law, shut up unto the faith which
should afterwards be revealed.
24 Wherefore [q] the law was
our schoolmaster *to bring us*
unto Christ, [r] that we might be
justified by faith.
25 But, after that faith is come, we are no
longer under a schoolmaster.
26 For [s] ye are all the children of God by
faith in Christ Jesus.
27 For [t] as many of you as have been
baptized into Christ, [u] have put on
Christ.

A. M. cir. 4056.
A. D. cir. 52.
A. U. C. 805.
An. Imp. Claudii Cæsaris 12.

[m] Chap. ii. 21.——[n] Ver. 8.——[o] Rom. iii. 9, 19, 23; xi. 32.——[p] Rom. iv. 11, 12, 16.——[q] Matt. v. 17; Rom. x. 4; Col. ii. 17; Heb. ix. 9, 10.——[r] Acts xiii. 39; chap. ii. 16.——[s] John i. 12; Rom. viii. 14, 15, 16; chap. iv. 5; 1 John iii. 1, 2.——[t] Rom. vi. 3.——[u] Rom. xiii. 14.

Though *Nosselt* has got great credit for this interpretation, it was given in substance long before him by Dr. Whitby, as may be seen in the following words: "But this mediator (Moses) was only the mediator of the *Jews*, and so was only the mediator of *one party*, to whom belonged the blessings of Abraham, ver. 8, 14. But God, who made the promise that in one should all the families of the earth be blessed, is one; the God of the *other party*, the *Gentiles*, as well as of the *Jews*, *επειπερ εἱς ὁ Θεος, seeing he is* one God, *who will justify the circumcision by faith, and the uncircumcision through faith*, Rom. iii. 30." This exposition is so plain, and so well supported by the different scriptures already quoted, that there can be but small, if any, doubt of its propriety. The clause has been translated thus: "*Now a mediator supposes two parties, of which God is but one.*"

Verse 21. Is *the law then against the promises of God?*] Is it possible that the intervention of the law, in reference to one part of the Abrahamic seed, should annul the promise made to the other? It is impossible.

For if there had been a law, &c.] If any *law* or *rule* of life could have been found out that would *have given life*—saved sinners from death, and made them truly happy, then *righteousness*—justification, *should have been by that law.*

Verse 22. *But the Scripture hath concluded*] All the writings of the *prophets* have uniformly declared that men are all *sinners*, and the *law* declares the same by the continual *sacrifices* which it prescribes. All, therefore have sinned, and come short of the glory of God; and, being tried and found guilty, *συνεκλεισεν ἡ γραφη, the Scripture hath shut them up*—put them in *prison*, and *locked* them up, till the time should come in which the sentence of the law should be executed upon them: (See Rom. iii. 9–20, and the notes there; and particularly Rom. xi. 32, where the apostle uses the same metaphor, and which in the note is particularly explained.)

That the promise of justification, *by faith of Jesus Christ, might be given to them that believe.*

Verse 23. *But before faith came*] Before the *Gospel* was published.

We were kept under the law, shut up] Εφρουρουμεθα· *We were kept as in a strong hold*, *συγκεκλεισμενοι, locked up, unto the faith*—the *religion* of the Lord Jesus, *which should afterwards be revealed.* Here the same metaphor is used as above, and for its explanation I must refer the reader to the same place, Rom. xi. 32.

Verse 24. *The law was our schoolmaster*] Ὁ νομος παιδαγωγος ἡμων γεγονεν εις Χριστον· *The law was our pedagogue unto Christ.* The *παιδαγωγος*, pedagogue, is not the *schoolmaster*, but the *servant* who had the *care of the children* to *lead them* to and *bring them back* from school, and had the care of them out of school hours. Thus the law did not *teach* us the *living, saving* knowledge; but, by its *rites* and *ceremonies*, and especially by its *sacrifices*, it directed us to *Christ*, that *we might be justified by faith.* This is a beautiful metaphor, and highly illustrative of the apostle's doctrine. See the note on Rom. x. 4, where this figure is farther explained.

Verse 25. *But, after that faith is come*] When Christ was manifested in the flesh, and the *Gospel* was preached, we were no longer under the pedagogue; we came to Christ, learned of him, became wise unto salvation, had our fruit unto holiness, and the end eternal life.

It is worthy of remark that, as *ὁ νομος*, the law, is used by St. Paul to signify, not only the *law*, properly so called, but the *whole of the Mosaic economy*, so *ἡ πιστις*, the faith, is used by him to express, not merely the *act of believing* in Christ, but the *whole* of the *Gospel.*

Verse 26. *For ye*, who have believed the Gospel, *are all the children of God by faith in Christ Jesus.*] But no man is a child of God by *circumcision*, nor by any observance of the Mosaic law.

Verse 27. *As many of you as have been baptized into Christ*] All of you who have believed in Christ as the promised Messiah, and received *baptism* as a public proof that ye had received Christ as your *Lord* and *Saviour, have put on Christ*—have received his Spirit, and entered into his interests, and copied his manners. To *put on*, or to be *clothed with one*, is to assume the *person* and *character* of that one; and they who do so are bound to act *his* part, and to *sustain* the *character* which they have *assumed.* The *profession* of *Christianity* is an assumption of the *character of Christ;* he has left us an example that we should follow his steps, and we should, as Christians, have that

A. M. cir. 4056.
A. D. cir. 52.
A. U. C.
805.
An. Imp. Claudii
Cæsaris 12.

28 ᵛ There is neither Jew nor Greek, there is neither bond nor free, there is neither male nor female : for ye are all ʷ one in Christ Jesus.

29 And ˣ if ye *be* Christ's, then are ye Abraham's seed, and ʸ heirs according to the promise.

A. M. cir. 4056.
A. D. cir. 52.
A. U. C.
805.
An. Imp. Claudii
Cæsaris 12.

ᵛ Rom. x. 12 ; 1 Cor. xii. 13 ; chap. v. 6 ; Col. iii. 11.——ʷ John x. 16 ; xvii. 20, 21 ; Eph. ii. 14, 15, 16 ; iv. 4, 15.

ˣ Gen. xxi. 10, 12 ; Rom. ix. 7 ; Heb. xi. 18.——ʸ Rom. viii. 17 ; chap. iv. 7, 28 ; Eph. iii. 6.

---

mind in us which was in him. See the notes on Rom. vi. 3, 4 ; and especially those on Rom. xiii. 14, where this phrase is farther explained.

Verse 28. There is neither Jew nor Greek] Ἑλλην, *Greek*, is put here for εθνικος, *heathen.* Under the Gospel all distinctions are done away, as either *helping* or *hindering ;* all are equally welcome to Christ, and all have an equal need of him ; all persons of all *sects*, and *conditions*, and *sexes*, who believe in him, become one family through him ; they are *one body*, of which he is the *head.*

Neither male nor female] With great reason the apostle introduces this. Between the privileges of *men* and *women* there was a great disparity among the Jews. A *man* might shave his head, and rend his clothes in the time of mourning ; à *woman* was not permitted to do so. A *man* might impose the vow of *nasirate* upon his son ; a *woman* could not do this on her daughter. A *man* might be shorn on account of the *nasirate* of his father ; a *woman* could not. A *man* might betroth his daughter ; a *woman* had no such power. A *man* might sell his daughter ; a *woman* could not. In many cases they were treated more like *children* than *adults ;* and to this day are not permitted to assemble with the men in the synagogues, but are put up in galleries, where they can scarcely see, nor can they be seen. Under the blessed spirit of Christianity, they have equal *rights*, equal *privileges*, and equal *blessings ;* and, let me add, they are equally *useful.*

Verse 29. And if ye be Christ's] Or, as several good MSS. read, *If ye be one in Christ.* If ye have all received justification through his blood, and the mind that was in him, then are ye Abraham's seed ; ye are that real, spiritual posterity of Abraham, that *other seed*, to whom the promises were made ; and then heirs, according to that promise, being fitted for the rest that remains for the people of God, that heavenly inheritance which was typified by the earthly Canaan, even to the Jews.

1. THE Galatians, it appears, had *begun well*, and for a time *run well*, but they permitted Satan to *hinder*, and they stopped short of the prize. Let us beware of those *teachers* who would draw us away from trusting in Christ crucified. By listening to such the Galatians lost their religion.

2. The temptation that leads us astray may be as *sudden* as it is *successful.* We may lose in one moment the fruit of a *whole life !* How frequently is this the case, and how few lay it-to heart ! A man may fall by the means of his *understanding*, as well as by means of his *passions.*

3. How strange is it that there should be found any *backslider !* that one who once felt the power of Christ should ever turn aside ! But it is still stranger that any one who has felt it, and given in his life and conversation full-proof that he has felt it, should not only *let it slip*, but at last *deny* that he ever had it, and even ridicule a work of grace in the heart ! Such instances have appeared among men.

4. The Jewish covenant, the sign of which was *circumcision*, is annulled, though the *people* with whom it was made are still preserved, and they preserve the *rite* or *sign.* Why then should the covenant be annulled ? This question admits a twofold answer. 1. This covenant was designed to last only *for a time*, and when that time came, having waxed old, it vanished away. 2. It was long before that void, through want of the performance of the *conditions.* The covenant did not state merely, ye shall be *circumcised*, and observe all the *rites* and *ceremonies* of the law ; but, *ye shall love the Lord your God with all your heart, soul, mind, and strength, and your neighbour as yourself.* This condition, which was the very soul of the covenant, was universally broken by that people. Need they wonder, therefore, that God has cast them off ? Jesus alone can restore them, and him they continue to reject. To *us* the *new covenant* says the same things : *Ye shall love the Lord, &c. ;* if we do not so, we also shall be cut off. *Take heed, lest he who did not spare the natural branches, spare not thee ;* therefore, make a profitable use of the *goodness* and *severity* of God.

CHAPTER IV.

The apostle shows that, as an heir in nonage is under tutors and guardians, so were the Galatians while under the law ; and, as the heir when he comes of age is no longer under guardians, so they, when the Gospel came, arrived at full maturity, and were redeemed from the law, 1–3. He shows, farther, that when the fulness of the time came God sent forth his Son, that we might obtain the adoption of sons, and have the strongest evidence of that adoption, 4–6. Those who are children of God are heirs of heaven, 7. He compares their former and latter state, and shows the reason he had to fear that his labour on their behalf was in vain, 8–11. He mentions his trials among them, and their kindness to him, 12–16. Shows his tender affection for them, and exhorts them to return to the Gospel, 17–20. Shows the excellence of the Gospel beyond that of the law, by the allegory of Mount Sinai and Jerusalem, 21–27. Shows also that the believing Gentiles are children of the promise, as Isaac was; and have been elected in the place of the Jews, who have been cast out according to the Scriptures, 28–31.

A. M. cir. 4056.
A. D. cir. 52.
A. U. C.
805.
An. Imp. Claudii
Cæsaris 12.

NOW I say, *That* the heir, as long as he is a child, differeth nothing from a servant, though he be lord of all;

2 But is under tutors and governors until the time appointed of the father.

3 Even so we, when we were children, [a] were in bondage under the [b] elements of the world:

4 But [c] when the fulness of the time was come, God sent forth his Son, [d] made [e] of a woman, [f] made under the law,

5 [g] To redeem them that were under the law, [h] that we might receive the adoption of sons.

A. M. cir. 4056.
A. D. cir. 52.
A. U. C.
805.
An. Imp. Claudii
Cæsaris 12.

6 And because ye are sons, God hath sent forth [i] the Spirit of his Son into your hearts, crying, Abba, Father.

7 Wherefore thou art no more a servant, but a son; [k] and if a son, then an heir of God through Christ.

8 Howbeit then, [l] when ye knew not God,

---

[a] Ver. 9; chap. ii. 23; v. 1; Col. ii. 8, 20; Heb. ix. 10.
[b] Or *rudiments.*——[c] Gen. xlix. 10; Dan. ix. 24; Mark i. 15; Eph. i. 10.——[d] John i. 14; Rom. i. 3; Phil. ii. 7; Heb. ii. 14.
[e] Gen. iii. 15; Isa. vii. 14; Mic. v. 3; Matt. i. 23; Luke i. 31; ii. 7.

[f] Matt. v. 17; Luke ii. 27.——[g] Matt. xx. 28; chap. iii. 13; Tit. ii. 14; Heb. ix. 12; Eph. i. 7; 1 Pet. i. 18, 19.——[h] John i. 12; chap. iii. 26; Eph. i. 5.——[i] Rom. v. 5; viii. 15.——[k] Rom. viii. 16, 17; chapter iii. 29.——[l] Eph. ii. 12; 1 Thessalonians iv. 5.

NOTES ON CHAP. IV.

Verse 1. *The heir, as long as he is a child*] Though he be appointed by his father's *will* heir of all his possessions, yet till he arrive at the legal age he is master of nothing, and does not differ from one of the common domestics.

Verse 2. *But is under tutors*] Επιτροπους· *Guardians* and *governors;* οικονομους· those who have the *charge* of the *family.* These words are nearly similar; but we may consider the first as *executor,* the last as the person who *superintends the concerns of the family and estate* till the heir become of age; such as we call trustee.

Until the time appointed of the father.] The time mentioned in the father's will or testament.

Verse 3. *Even so we*] The whole Jewish people were in a state of nonage while under the law.

The elements of the world] A mere Jewish phrase, יסודי עולם הזה *yesodey olam hazzeh,* "the principles of this world;" that is, the *rudiments* or *principles* of the *Jewish religion.* The apostle intimates that the law was not the science of salvation, it was only the *elements* or *alphabet* of it; and in the *Gospel* this alphabet is composed into a most glorious system of Divine knowledge: but as the alphabet is nothing of itself, unless compounded into syllables, words, sentences, and discourses; so the *law,* taken by itself, gives no salvation; it contains indeed the *outlines* of the Gospel, but it is the Gospel alone that *fills up* these outlines.

Verse 4. *When the fulness of the time was come*] The time which God in his infinite wisdom counted best; in which all his counsels were *filled up;* and the time which his Spirit, by the prophets, had specified; and the time to which he intended the Mosaic institutions should extend, and beyond which they should be of no avail.

God sent forth his Son] Him who came immediately from God himself, *made of a woman,* according to the promise, Gen. iii. 15; produced by the power of God in the womb of the Virgin Mary without any

intervention of man; hence he was called *the Son of God.* See Luke, chap. i. 35, and the note there.

Made under the law] In subjection to it, that in him all its designs might be fulfilled, and by his *death* the whole might be abolished; the law *dying* when the Son of God expired upon the cross.

Verse 5. *To redeem them*] Εξαγορασῃ· To *pay down a price* for them, and thus *buy them off* from the necessity of observing *circumcision,* offering *brute sacrifices,* performing different *ablutions,* &c., &c.

That we might receive the adoption of sons.] Which adoption we could not obtain by the law; for it is the Gospel only that puts us among the children, and gives us a place in the heavenly family. On the nature of *adoption* see the notes on Rom. viii. 15.

Verse 6. *And because ye are sons*] By faith in Christ Jesus, being redeemed both from the *bondage* and *curse* of the law; GOD—the *Father,* called generally the *first* person of the glorious TRINITY, hath sent forth the SPIRIT—the *Holy Ghost,* the *second* person of that *Trinity,* of his SON—*Jesus Christ,* the *third* person of the *Trinity*—crying, *Abba, Father!* from the fullest and most satisfactory evidence that God, the Father, Son, and Spirit, had become their portion. For the explanation of the phrase, and why the *Greek* and *Syriac* terms are joined together here, see the notes on Mark xiv. 36, and on Rom. viii. 15.

Verse 7. *Thou art no more a servant*] Thou who hast believed in Christ art no longer a *slave,* either under the *dominion of sin* or under *obligation* to the Mosaic ritual; *but a son* of God, adopted into the heavenly family.

And if a son, then an heir] Having a right to the inheritance, because *one of the family,* for none can *inherit* but the *children;* but this heirship is the most extraordinary of all: it is not an heirship of any *tangible possession,* either in *heaven* or *earth;* it is not to possess a *part* or ever the *whole* of *either,* it is to possess *Him* who made all things; not God's *works,* but God *himself:* heirs of GOD through Christ.

Verse 8. *When ye knew not God*] Though it is

A. M. cir. 4056.
A. D. cir. 52.
A. U. C.
805.
An. Imp. Claudii
Cæsaris 12.

^m ye did service unto them which by nature are no gods.

9 But now, ⁿ after that ye have known God, or rather are known of God, ^o how turn ye ^p again to ^q the weak and beggarly ^r elements, whereunto ye desire again to be in bondage?

10 ^s Ye observe days, and months, and times, and years.

11 I am afraid of you, ^t lest I have bestowed upon you labour in vain.

12 Brethren, I beseech you, be as I *am;* for I *am* as ye *are:* ^u ye have not injured me at all.

13 Ye know how ^v through infirmity of the flesh I preached the Gospel unto you ^w at the first.

14 And my temptation which was in my flesh ye despised not, nor rejected; but received me ^x as an angel of God, ^y *even* as Christ Jesus.

A. M. cir. 4056.
A. D. cir. 52.
A. U. C.
805.
An. Imp. Claudii
Cæsaris 12.

---

^m Rom. i. 25; 1 Cor. xii. 2; Eph. ii. 11, 12; 1 Thess. i. 9. ⁿ 1 Cor. viii. 3; xiii. 12; 2 Tim. ii. 19.——^o Chap. iii. 3; Col. ii. 20.——^p Or, *back.*——^q Rom. viii. 3; Heb. vii. 18.——^r Or, *rudiments;* ver. 3.——^s Rom. xiv. 5; Col. ii. 16.

^t Chap. ii. 2; v. 2, 4; 1 Thess. iii. 5.——^u 2 Cor. ii. 5.——^v 1 Cor. ii. 3; 2 Cor. xi. 30; xii. 7, 9.——^w Chap. i. 6.——^x 2 Sam. xix. 27; Mal. ii. 7; see Zech. xii. 8.——^y Matt. x. 40; Luke x. 16; John xiii. 20; 1 Thess. ii. 13.

---

evident, from the complexion of the whole of this epistle, that the great body of the Christians in the Churches of Galatia were converts from among the *Jews* or *proselytes* to Judaism; yet from this verse it appears that there were some who had been converted from *heathenism;* unless we suppose that the apostle here particularly addresses those who had been proselytes to Judaism and thence converted to Christianity; which appears to be most likely from the following verses.

Verse 9. *Now, after that ye have known God*] After having been brought to the knowledge of God as your Saviour.

Or rather are known of God] Are *approved* of him, having received the adoption of sons.

To the weak and beggarly elements] After receiving all this, *will ye turn again* to the ineffectual rites and ceremonies of the Mosaic law—*rites* too *weak* to counteract your sinful habits, and too *poor* to *purchase pardon* and *eternal life* for you? If the Galatians were *turning again* to them, it is evident that they had been *once* addicted to them. And this they might have been, allowing that they had become *converts* from *heathenism* to *Judaism,* and from Judaism to Christianity. This makes the sense consistent between the 8th and 9th verses.

Verse 10. *Ye observe days*] Ye superstitiously regard the Sabbaths and particular days of your own appointment;

And months] New moons; *times*—festivals, such as those of tabernacles, dedication, passover, &c.

Years.] Annual atonements, sabbatical years, and jubilees.

Verse 11. *I am afraid of you*] I begin now to be seriously alarmed for you, and think you are so thoroughly perverted from the Gospel of Christ, that all my pains and labour in your conversion have been thrown away.

Verse 12. *Be as I* am] Thoroughly addicted to the Christian faith and worship, from the deepest conviction of its truth.

For I am as ye are] I was formerly a Jew, and as zealously addicted to the rites and ceremonies of Judaism as ye are, but I am saved from that mean and unprofitable dependence: " Be therefore as I am now;

who was once as you now are." Others think the sense to be this: " Be as affectionate to me as I am to you; for ye were once as loving to me as I am now to you."

Ye have not injured me at all.] I do not thus earnestly entreat you to return to your Christian profession because your perversion has been any loss to me, nor because your conversion can be to me any gain: ye have not injured me at all, ye only injure yourselves; and I entreat you, through the intense love I bear to you, as my once beloved brethren in Christ Jesus, to return to him from whom ye have revolted.

Verse 13. *Ye know how through infirmity*] The apostle seems to say that he was much afflicted in body when he first preached the Gospel to them. And is this any strange thing, that a minister, so laborious as St. Paul was, should be sometimes overdone and overcome by the severity of his labours? Surely not. This might have been only an occasional affliction, while labouring in that part of Asia Minor; and not a continual and incurable infirmity, as some have too hastily conjectured.

Verse 14. *And my temptation which was in my flesh*] On this verse there are a great many various readings, as there are various opinions.

Instead of μου, MY *temptation,* ABC*D*FG, some others, with the *Coptic, Vulgate, Itala,* and several of the primitive *fathers,* have ὑμῶν, YOUR temptation.

The word πειρασμον, which we translate *temptation,* signifies *trial* of any kind. The verse therefore may be read, " Ye despised not the trial which was in my flesh;" or, " Ye despised not your trial, which was in my flesh:" i. e. what my flesh suffered on your account, the afflictions I passed through in consequence of my severe labours on your account. You did not consider me less an apostle of God on account of my sinking for a time under the weight of my work. Had they been disaffected towards him at that time, they would have used this to the prejudice of his apostolic mission. " What! do you pretend to be an extraordinary messenger from God, and yet are suffered to fall into sickness under the severity of your labour? If God *sent* you, would he not *sustain* you?" This would have been quite natural, had they not been well affected toward him. But, on the contrary, notwithstanding these afflictions, they *received him as an*

    2

A. M. cir. 4056.
A. D. cir. 52.
A. U. C.
805.
An. Imp. Claudii
Cæsaris 12.

15 ^z Where is then the blessedness ye spake of? for I bear you record, that, if *it had been* possible, ye would have plucked out your own eyes, and have given them to me.

16 Am I therefore become your enemy, ^a because I tell you the truth?

17 They ^b zealously affect you, *but* not well;

yea, they would exclude ^c you, that ye might affect them.

18 But *it is* good to be zealously affected always in *a* good *thing*, and not only when I am present with you.

19 ^d My little children, of whom I travail in birth again until Christ be formed in you,

A. M. cir. 4056.
A. D. cir. 52.
A. U. C.
805.
An. Imp. Claudii
Cæsaris 12.

---

^z Or, *What was then?*——^a Chap. ii. 5, 14.——^b Rom. x. 2 ; 1 Cor. xi. 2.——^c Or, *us.*——^d 1 Cor. iv. 15 ; Philem. 10 ; James i. 18.

---

angel of God—as a messenger from heaven, and *as Jesus Christ* himself. This appears to me to be the simple meaning of the apostle, and that he neither alludes to a *bodily* nor *mental* infirmity, which *generally* or *periodically* afflicted him, as some have imagined. Nor does he appear at all to speak of the *same case* as that mentioned 2 Cor. xii. 7, where I wish the reader to consult the notes. That St. Paul had frequent and severe afflictions, in consequence of his constant and severe exertions in the Gospel ministry, we may readily believe, and of this his own words bear sufficient testimony.

See his affecting account, 2 Cor. xi. 23–29, and the notes there.

Verse 15. *Where is then the blessedness ye spake of?*] *Ye spake of* should be in italics, there being no corresponding word in the Greek text. Perhaps there is not a sentence in the New Testament more variously translated than this. I shall give the original : τις ουν ην ὁ μακαρισμος ὑμων· *What was then your blessedness!* Or, *How great was your happiness at that time!* Or, *What blessings did ye then pour on me!* It is worthy of remark, that, instead of τις, *what,* ABCFG, several others, the older *Syriac,* the later *Syriac* in the *margin,* the *Armenian, Vulgate,* one copy of the *Itala,* and some of the *fathers,* have πον, *where* ; and ην, *was,* is omitted by ACD, several others, also the *Vulgate, Itala,* and the *Latin fathers.* According to these authorities the text should be read thus : *Where then is your blessedness?* Having renounced the Gospel, you have lost your *happiness.* What have your false teachers given you to compensate the loss of communion with God, or that *Spirit of adoption,* that *Spirit of Christ,* by which you cried *Abba, Father !* If, however, we understand the words as implying the *benedictions* they then heaped on the *apostle,* the sense will be sufficiently natural, and agree well with the concluding part of the verse ; *for I bear you record, that, if possible, ye would have plucked out your own eyes, and have given them to me.* You had then the strongest affection for me ; you loved God, and you loved me for God's sake, and were ready to give me the most unequivocal proof of your love.

Dearer than one's eyes, or to profess to *give one's eyes* for the sake of a person, appears to have been a proverbial expression, intimating the highest tokens of the strongest affection. We find a similar form of speech in *Terence,* Adelphi, act iv., scene 5, ver. 67.

————————*Di me pater*

Omnes oderint, ni magis te quam oculos *nunc ego* amo meos.

" O father, may all the gods hate me, if I do not love you now more than my own eyes "

Verse 16. *Am I therefore become your enemy*] How is it that you are so much altered towards me, that you now treat me as an enemy, who formerly loved me with the most fervent affection? Is it *because I tell you the truth* ; that very *truth* for which you at first so ardently loved me ?

Verse 17. *They zealouly affect you,* but *not well*] It is difficult for common readers to understand the meaning of these words : perhaps it would be better to translate Ζηλουσιν ὑμας ου καλως, these false teachers *endeavour to conciliate your esteem, but not in honest* or true *principles* ; they work themselves into your good graces ; they wish you to place all your affection upon themselves.

They would exclude you] They wish to *shut you* out from the affection of your apostle, *that you might affect them,* ἱνα αυτους ζηλουτε, that you might love them alone, hear them alone, abide by their directions only, and totally abandon him who called you into the grace of the Gospel of Christ. Some MSS. read ἡμας, *us,* instead of ὑμας, *you* ; they wish to shut *us* entirely out from among you, that you may receive and believe *them* alone. The sense is nearly the same but the former appears to be the more authentic reading.

Verse 18. *It is good to be zealously affected*] It is well to have a *determined mind* and an *ardent heart* in reference to things which are laudable and good.

Not only when I am present] You were thus attached to me when I was among you, but now ye have lost both your reverence and affection for me. Your false teachers pretended great concern for you, that you might put all your confidence in *them* ; they have gained their end ; they have estranged you from me, and got you to renounce the Gospel, and have brought you again into your former bondage.

Verse 19. *My little children*] Τεκνια μου· My beloved children. As their conversion to God had been the fruit of much labour, prayers, and tears, so he felt them as his children, and peculiarly dear to him, because he had been the means of bringing them to the knowledge of the truth ; therefore he represents himself as suffering the same anxiety and distress which he endured at first when he preached the Gospel to them, when their conversion to Christianity was a matter of great doubt and uncertainty. The metaphor which he uses needs no explanation.

Until Christ be formed in you] Till you once more receive the Spirit and unction of Christ in your hearts,

2

A. M. cir. 4056.
A. D. cir. 52.
A. U. C.
805.
An. Imp. Claudii
Cæsaris 12.

20 I desire to be present with you now, and to change my voice; for [e] I stand in doubt of you.

21 Tell me, ye that desire to be under the law, do ye not hear the law?

22 For it is written, that Abraham had two sons; [f] the one by a bond maid, [g] the other by a free woman.

A. M. cir. 4056.
A. D. cir. 52.
A. U. C.
805.
An. Imp. Claudii
Cæsaris 12.

23 But he *who was* of the bond woman [h] was born after the flesh; [i] but he of the free woman *was* by promise.

24 Which things are an allegory: for these are the two [k] covenants; the one from the mount [l] Sinai, [m] which gendereth to bondage, which is Agar.

25 For this Agar is mount Sinai in Arabia,

---

[e] Or, *I am perplexed for you.*——[f] Gen. xvi. 15.——[g] Gen. xxi. 2.
[h] Rom. ix. 7, 8.

[i] Gen. xviii. 10, 14; xxi. 1, 2; Heb. xi. 11.——[k] Or, *testament.*
[l] Gr. *Sina.*——[m] Deut. xxxiii. 2.

---

from which you are fallen, by your rejection of the spirit of the Gospel.

Verse 20. *I desire to be present with you*] I wish to accommodate my doctrine to your state; I know not whether you need stronger reprehension, or to be dealt with more leniently.

I stand in doubt of you.] I have doubts concerning your state; the progress of error and conviction among you, which I cannot fully know without being among you. This appears to be the apostle's meaning, and tends much to soften and render palatable the severity of his reproofs.

Verse 21. *Ye that desire to be under the law*] Ye who desire to incorporate the Mosaic institutions with Christianity, and thus bring yourselves into bondage to circumcision, and a great variety of oppressive rites.

Do ye not hear the law?] Do ye not understand what is written in the *Pentateuch* relative to Abraham and his children. It is evident that the word *law* is used in *two senses* in this verse. It first means the *Mosaic institutions*; secondly, the *Pentateuch,* where the history is recorded to which the apostle refers.

Verse 22. *For it is written*] Viz. in Gen. xvi. 15, and xxii. 1, &c., that *Abraham had two sons,* Ishmael and Isaac, *the one,* Ishmael, *by a bond maid,* Hagar; *the other,* Isaac, *by a free woman,* Sarah.

Verse 23. *Was born after the flesh*] *Ishmael* was born *according to the course of nature,* his parents being both of a proper age, so that there was nothing uncommon or supernatural in his birth: this is the proper meaning of the apostle's κατα σαρκα, *after* or *according to the flesh,* and answers to the Hebrew phrase, בשר דרך עַל *al derec basar,* according to the manner of the flesh, i. e. *naturally, according to the common process of nature.*

By promise.] Both Abraham and Sarah had passed that age in which the procreation of children was possible on *natural principles.* The birth, therefore, of Isaac was *supernatural;* it was the effect of an especial promise of God; and it was only on the ground of that promise that it was either credible or possible.

Verse 24. *Which things are an allegory*] They are to be understood *spiritually;* more being intended in the account than meets the eye.

Allegory, from αλλος, *another,* and αγορεω, or αγορευω, *to speak,* signifies a *thing that is a representative of another,* where the *literal sense* is the representative of a *spiritual meaning;* or, as the glossary expresses it, ἑτερως κατα μεταφρασιν νοουμενα, και ου κατα την αναγνωσιν· "where the thing is to be understood

differently in the interpretation than it appears in the reading."

Allegories are frequent in all countries, and are used by all writers. In the life of *Homer,* the author, speaking of the marriage of *Jupiter* and *Juno,* related by that poet, says: δοκει ταυτα αλληγορεισθαι, ὁτι Ἡρα μεν νοειται ὁ αηρ—Ζευς δε, ὁ αιθηρ· "It appears that these things are to be understood *allegorically;* for Juno means the *air,* Jupiter the *æther.*" *Plutarch,* in his treatise *De Iside et Osir.,* says: ὡσπερ Ἑλληνες Κρονον αλληγορουσι τον χρονον· "As the Greeks allegorize *Cronos* (Saturn) into *Chronos* (Time.)" It is well known how fond the Jews were of *allegorizing.* Every thing in the *law* was with them an *allegory.* Their *Talmud* is full of these; and one of their most sober and best educated writers, *Philo,* abounds with them. Speaking (De *Migrat. Abrah.,* page 420) of the five daughters of Zelophehad, he says: ὡς αλληγορουντες αισθησεις ειναι φαμεν· "which, *allegorizing,* we assert to be the *five senses!*"

It is very likely, therefore, that the allegory produced here St. Paul had borrowed from the Jewish writings; and he brings it in to convict the *Judaizing* Galatians on their own principles; and neither he nor we have any thing farther to do with this allegory than as it applies to the subject for which it is quoted; nor does it give any license to those men of vain and superficial minds who endeavour to find out *allegories* in every portion of the sacred writings, and, by what they term *spiritualizing,* which is more properly *carnalizing,* have brought the testimonies of God into disgrace. May the *spirit of silence* be poured out upon all such *corrupters* of the word of God!

For these are the two covenants] These *signify* two different systems of religion; the one by *Moses,* the other by the *Messiah.*

The one from the Mount Sinai] On which the law was published; which was typified by *Hagar,* Abraham's bond maid.

Which gendereth to bondage] For as the *bond maid* or *slave* could only gender—bring forth her children, in a *state of slavery,* and subject also to become *slaves,* so all that are born and live under those Mosaic institutions are *born* and *live* in a state of bondage—a bondage to various *rites* and *ceremonies;* under the *obligation* to keep the *whole law,* yet, from its severity and their frailness, obliged to live in the habitual breach of it, and in consequence exposed to the *curse* which it pronounces.

Verse 25. *For this Agar is Mount Sinai in Arabia*]

2

A. M. cir. 4056.
A. D. cir. 52.
A. U. C.
805.
An. Imp. Claudii
Cæsaris 12.

and ⁿ answereth to Jerusalem which now is, and is in bondage with her children.

26 But ° Jerusalem which is above is free, which is the mother of us all.

27 For it is written, ᵖ Rejoice, *thou* barren that bearest not; break forth and cry, thou that travailest not: for the desolate hath many more children than she which hath a husband.

A. M. cir. 4056.
A. D. cir. 52.
A. U. C.
805.
An. Imp. Claudii
Cæsaris 12

28 Now we, brethren, as Isaac was, are �q the children of promise.

29 But as then ʳ he that was born after the flesh, persecuted him *that was born* after the Spirit, ˢ even so *it is* now.

30 Nevertheless what saith ᵗ the Scripture ?

ⁿ Or, *is in the same rank with.*——° Isa. ii. 2; Heb. xii. 22; Rev. iii. 12; xxi. 2, 10.——ᵖ Isa. liv. 1.

q Acts iii. 25; Rom. ix. 8; chap. iii. 29.——ʳ Gen. xxi. 9——ˢ Ch. v. 11; vi. 12.——ᵗ Chap. iii. 8, 22.

Το γαρ Αγαρ Σινα ορος εστιν εν τη Αραβια. This is the common reading; but it is read differently in some of the most respectable MSS., *versions,* and *fathers;* thus: το γαρ Σινα ορος εστιν εν τη Αραβια, *for this Sinai is a mountain of Arabia;* the word Αγαρ, *Agar,* being omitted. This reading is supported by CFG, some others, the Æthiopic, Armenian, Vulgate, and one copy of the *Itala;* by *Epiphanius, Damascenus, Ambrosiaster, Jerome, Augustine, Hilary, Sedulius,* and *Bede;* and the word is sometimes, though not always, omitted by *Cyril* and *Origen,* which proves that in their time there were doubts concerning the common reading.

Of the word *Agar* in this verse, which renders the passage very obscure and difficult, Professor *White* says, *forsitan* delendum, "probably it should be expunged." *Griesbach* has left it in the text with a note of *doubtfulness.*

Answereth to Jerusalem] Hagar, the bond maid, bringing forth children in a state of slavery, *answereth to Jerusalem that now is,* συστοιχει, points out, or, *bears a similitude* to, Jerusalem in her present state of subjection; which, with *her children*—her citizens, is not only in *bondage to the Romans,* but in a worse bondage to the *law,* to its oppressive *ordinances,* and to the heavy curse which it has pronounced against all those who do not keep them.

Verse 26. But Jerusalem which is above] The apostle still follows the Jewish *allegory,* showing not only how the story of *Hagar* and *Sarah, Ishmael* and *Isaac,* was allegorized, but pointing out also that even *Jerusalem* was the subject of allegory; for it was a maxim among the rabbins, that "whatsoever was in the earth, the same was also found in heaven; for there is no matter, howsoever small, in this world, that has not something similar to it in the spiritual world." On this maxim, the Jews imagine that every earthly thing has its *representative* in heaven; and especially whatever concerns *Jerusalem,* the *law,* and its *ordinances.* Rab. *Kimchi,* speaking of Melchizedec, king of Salem, says: זו ירושלם של מעלה *zu Yerushalem shel malah,* "This is the Jerusalem that is from above." This phrase frequently occurs among these writers, as may be seen in *Schoettgen,* who has written an express dissertation upon the subject. *Hor. Hebr.,* vol. i. page 1205.

Is free, which is the mother of us all.] There is a spiritual Jerusalem, of which this is the type; and this Jerusalem, in which the souls of all the righteous are, is free from all bondage and sin: or by this, probably, the kingdom of the Messiah was intended; and

this certainly answers best to the apostle's meaning, as the subsequent verse shows. There is an *earthly* Jerusalem, but this earthly Jerusalem typifies a *heavenly Jerusalem:* the former, with all her *citizens,* is in *bondage;* the latter is a *free city,* and all her *inhabitants* are *free* also. And this Jerusalem is *our mother;* it signifies the Church of Christ, the metropolis of Christianity, or rather the *state* of *liberty* into which all true believers are brought. The word παντων, *of all,* is omitted by almost every MS. and *version* of antiquity and importance, and by the most eminent of the *fathers* who quote this place; it is undoubtedly spurious, and the text should be read thus: *But Jerusalem, which is above, is free, which is our mother.*

Verse 27. Rejoice, thou barren that bearest not] This quotation is taken from Isa. liv. 1, and is certainly a promise which relates to the *conversion of the Gentiles,* as the following clause proves; for *the desolate*—the Gentile world, *hath many more children*—is a much larger and more numerous Church, than *she*—Jerusalem, the Jewish state, *which hath a husband*—has been so long in *covenant with God,* living under his continual protection, and in possession of a great variety of spiritual advantages; and especially those offered to her by the Gospel, which she has rejected, and which the Gentiles have accepted.

Verse 28. Now we] Who believe in the Lord Jesus, *are the children of promise*—are the spiritual offspring of the Messiah, the seed of Abraham, in whom the promise stated that *all the nations of the earth should be blessed.*

Verse 29. But as then he] Ishmael, *who was born after the flesh*—whose birth had nothing *supernatural* in it, but was according to the ordinary course of nature,

Persecuted him] Isaac, *who was born after the Spirit*—who had a supernatural birth, according to the *promise,* and through the efficacy, of the *Holy Spirit,* giving effect to that promise—*Sarah shall have a son,* Gen. xvii. 16–21; xxi. 1, &c.

Persecuted him; the persecution here referred to is that mentioned Gen. xxi. 9. It consisted in mocking his brother Isaac.

Even so it is now.] So the Jews, in every place, persecute the Christians; and show thereby that they are rather of the posterity of *Hagar* than of *Sarah.*

Verse 30. What saith the Scripture ?] (In Gen xxi. 10:) *Cast out the bond woman and her son:* and what does this imply in the present case ? Why, that the present Jerusalem and her children shall be *cast*

A. M. cir. 4056.
A. D. cir. 52.
A. U. C.
805.
An Imp. Claudii
Cæsaris 12.

ᵘ Cast out the bond woman and her son: for ᵛ the son of the bond woman shall not be heir with the son of the free woman.

31 So then, brethren, we are not children of the bond woman, ʷ but of the free.

A. M. cir. 4056.
A. D. cir. 52.
A. U. C.
805.
An. Imp. Claudii
Cæsaris 12.

ᵘ Gen. xxi. 10, 12.——ᵛ John viii. 35.

ʷ John viii. 36; chap. v. 1, 13.

---

out of the favour of God, and *shall not be heirs with the son of the free woman*—shall not inherit the blessings promised to Abraham, because they believe not in the promised seed.

Verse 31. *So then*] *We*—Jews and Gentiles, who believe on the Lord Jesus, *are not children of the bond woman*—are not in subjection to the Jewish law, *but of the free ;* and, consequently, are delivered from all its bondage, obligation, and curse.

Thus the apostle, from their own Scripture, explained by their own allegory, proves that it is only by Jesus Christ that they can have redemption ; and because they have not believed in him, therefore *they continue to be in bondage ;* and that shortly God will deliver them up into a long and grievous captivity : for we may naturally suppose that the apostle has reference to what had been so often foretold by the prophets, and confirmed by Jesus Christ himself ; and this was the strongest argument he could use, to show the Galatians their folly and their danger in submitting again to the bondage from which they had escaped, and exposing themselves to the most dreadful calamities of an earthly kind, as well as to the final ruin of their souls. *They desired to be under the law ;* then they must take all the consequences; and these the apostle sets fairly before them.

1. WE sometimes pity the *Jews*, who continue to reject the Gospel. Many who do so have no pity for themselves ; for is not the state of a Jew, who systematically rejects Christ, because he does not believe him to be the promised Messiah, infinitely better than his, who, believing every thing that the Scripture teaches concerning Christ, lives under the power and guilt of sin ? If the Jews be in a state of *nonage*, because they believe not the doctrines of Christianity, he is in a worse state than that of *infancy* who is not *born again* by the power of the Holy Ghost. Reader, whosoever thou art, lay this to heart.

2. The 4th, 5th, 6th, and 7th verses of this chapter contain the sum and marrow of Christian divinity. (1.) The determination of God to redeem the world by the incarnation of his Son. (2.) The manifestation of this Son in the fulness of time. (3.) The circumstances in which this Son appeared : *sent forth ; made of a woman ; made under the law ;* to be *a sufferer ;* and to *die as a sacrifice.* (4.) The redemption of the world, by the death of Christ : he came to redeem them that were under the law, who were condemned and cursed by it. (5.) By the redemption price he purchases *sonship* or *adoption* for mankind. (6.) He, God the *Father*, sends the *Spirit*, God the *Holy Ghost*, of God the *Son*, into the hearts of believers, by which they, through the full confidence of their adoption, call him their Father. (7.) Being made *children*, they become *heirs*, and God is their portion

throughout eternity. Thus, in a few words, the whole doctrine of grace is contained, and an astonishing display made of the unutterable mercy of God. See the notes on these verses.

3. While the Jews were rejecting the *easy yoke* of Christ, they were *painfully* observing *days*, and *months*, and *times* and *years*. *Superstition* has far more labour to perform than true religion has; and at last profits nothing ! Most men, either from *false views* of religion, or through the *power* and *prevalency* of their own evil *passions* and *habits*, have ten thousand times more trouble to get to *hell*, than the followers of God have to get to *heaven*.

4. Even in the perverted Galatians the apostle finds some good ; and he mentions with great feeling those amiable qualities which they once possessed. The only way to encourage men to seek farther good is to show them what they have got, and to make this a reason why they should seek more. He who wishes to do good to men, and is constantly dwelling on their *bad qualities* and *graceless state*, either irritates or drives them to *despair*. There is, perhaps, no sinner on this side perdition who has not something good in him. Mention the good—it is God's work ; and show what a pity it is that he should not have more, and how ready God is to supply all his wants through Christ Jesus. This plan should especially be used in addressing *Christian societies*, and particularly those which are in a declining state.

5. The Galatians were once the *firm friends* of the apostle, and loved him so well that they would have even *plucked out their eyes for him ;* and yet these very people cast him off, and counted and treated him as an *enemy !* O sad *fickleness* of human nature ! O uncertainty of *human friendships !* An *undesigned* word, or look, or action, becomes the reason to a fickle heart why it should divest itself of the spirit of friendship ; and he who was as dear to them as their own souls, is neglected and forgotten ! Blessed God ! hast thou not said that there is a *friend that sticketh closer than a brother ? Where* is he ? Can such a one be trusted long on this unkindly earth ? He is fit for the society of angels and the spirits of just men made perfect ; and thou takest him in mercy lest he should lose his friendly heart, or lest his own heart should be broken in losing that of his friend. Hasten, Lord, a more perfect state, where the spirit of thy own love in thy followers shall expand, without controul or hinderance, throughout eternity ! Amen.

6. On *allegorizing*, in explaining the word of God, something has already been said, under ver. 24 ; but on the subject of *allegory* in general much might be said. The very learned and accurate critic, Dr. *Lowth*, in his work, *De Sacra Poesi Hebræorum*, has entered at large into the subject of *allegory*, as existing in the sacred writings, in which he has discovered *three*

species of this rhetorical figure. 1. That which rhetoricians term a *continued metaphor.* See Solomon's portraiture of old age, Eccles. xii. 2–6. A *second* kind of allegory is that which, in a more proper and restricted sense, may be called *parable.* See Matt. xiii., and the note on ver. 3 of that chapter. The *third* species of allegory is that in which a *double meaning* is couched under the same words. These are called *mystical* allegories, and the two meanings are termed the *literal* and *mystical* senses. For examples of all these kinds I must refer to the learned prelate above named.

CHAPTER V.

The apostle exhorts the Galatians to stand fast in the liberty of the Gospel, and not by receiving circumcision bring themselves into a yoke of bondage, 1–4. Shows the superior excellence of Christianity, 5, 6. Mentions their former steadiness, and warns them against the bad doctrine which was then preached among them, 7–9. Expresses his confidence that they will yet return; and shows that he who perverted them shall bear his own punishment, 10–12. States that they are called to liberty, and that love is the fulfilling of the law, 13, 14. Warns them against dissensions, and enumerates the fruits of the flesh, which exclude those who bear them from the kingdom of God, 15–21. Enumerates also the fruits of the Spirit, which characterize the disciples of Christ, 22–24. Exhorts them to live in the Spirit, and not provoke each other, 25, 26.

A. M. cir. 4056.
A. D. cir. 52.
A. U. C.
805.
An. Imp. Claudii
Cæsaris 12.

STAND fast therefore in [a] the liberty wherewith Christ hath made us free, and be not entangled again [b] with the yoke of bondage.

2 Behold, I Paul say unto you, that [c] if ye be circumcised, Christ shall profit you nothing.

3 For I testify again to every man that is circumcised, [d] that he is a debtor to do the whole law.

A. M. cir. 4056.
A. D. cir. 52.
A. U. C.
805.
An. Imp. Claudii
Cæsaris 12.

4 [e] Christ is become of no effect unto you, whosoever of you are justified by the law; [f] ye are fallen from grace.

5 For we through the Spirit [g] wait for the hope of righteousness by faith.

---

[a] John viii. 32; Rom. vi. 18; 1 Pet. ii. 16.——[b] Acts xv. 10; chap. ii. 4; iv. 9.——[c] Acts xv. 1; see Acts xvi. 3.——[d] Chap. iii. 10.——[e] Rom. ix. 31, 32; chap. ii. 21.——[f] Heb. xii. 15.——[g] Rom. viii. 24, 25; 2 Tim. iv. 8.

NOTES ON CHAP. V.

Verse 1. *Stand fast therefore in the liberty*] This is intimately connected with the preceding chapter: the apostle having said, just before, *So then, brethren, we are not children of the bond woman, but of the free,* immediately adds, *Stand fast therefore in the liberty wherewith Christ hath made us free.* Hold fast your Christian profession; it brings spiritual liberty: on the contrary, Judaism brings spiritual bondage. Among the Jews, the Messiah's reign was to be a reign of liberty, and hence the Targum, on Lament. ii. 22, says: "Liberty shall be publicly proclaimed to thy people of the house of Israel, על יד משיחא *al yad Mashicha,* by the hand of the Messiah, such as was granted to them by Moses and Aaron at the time of the passover."

The liberty mentioned by the apostle is freedom from Jewish rites and ceremonies, called properly here the *yoke of bondage*; and also liberty from the power and guilt of sin, which nothing but the grace of Christ can take away.

Verse 2. *If ye be circumcised*] By circumcision you take on you the whole obligation of the Jewish law, and consequently profess to seek salvation by means of its observances; and therefore Christ can profit you nothing; for, by seeking justification by the *works of the law,* you renounce justification by *faith in Christ.*

Verse 3. *He is a debtor to do the whole law.*] Lays himself, by receiving circumcision, under the obligation to fulfil all its precepts, ordinances, &c.

Verse 4. *Christ is become of no effect unto you*]. It is vain for you to attempt to unite the two systems. You must have the law and no Christ, or Christ and no law, for your *justification.*

Ye are fallen from grace.] From the *Gospel.* They had been brought into the grace of the Gospel; and now, by readopting the Mosaic ordinances, they had apostatized from the *Gospel* as a system of religion, and had lost the *grace* communicated to their souls, by which they were preserved in a state of salvation. The peace and love of God, received by Jesus Christ, could not remain in the hearts of those who had rejected Christ. They had, therefore, in every sense of the word, *fallen from grace*; and whether some of them ever rose again is more than we can tell.

Verse 5. *For we,* Christians, *through the Spirit*] Through the operation of the Holy Ghost, under this spiritual dispensation of the Gospel, *wait for the hope of righteousness*—expect that which is the object of our hope, on our being *justified* by faith in Christ. *Righteousness,* δικαιοσυνη, may here, as in many other places of St. Paul's epistles, mean *justification,* and the hope of justification, or the hope excited and inspired by it, is the *possession of eternal glory*; for, says the apostle, Rom. v. 1, 2, *Being justified by faith we have peace with God—and rejoice in* HOPE *of the* GLORY *of* GOD. But, as this glory is necessarily future, it is to be *waited for*; but this waiting, in a thorough Christian, is not only a blessed expectation,

2

A. M. cir. 4056.
A. D. cir. 52.
A. U. C.
805.
An. Imp. Claudii
Cæsaris 12.

6 For [h] in Jesus Christ neither circumcision availeth any thing, nor uncircumcision; but [i] faith which worketh by love.

7 Ye [k] did run well; [l] who [m] did hinder you, that ye should not obey the truth?

8 This persuasion *cometh* not of him [n] that calleth you.

9 [o] A little leaven leaveneth the whole lump.

10 [p] I have confidence in you, through the Lord, that ye will be none otherwise minded: but [q] he that troubleth you [r] shall bear his judgment, whosoever he be.

11 [s] And I, brethren, if I yet preach circum-

A. M. cir. 4056.
A. D. cir. 52.
A. U. C.
805.
An. Imp. Claudii
Cæsaris 12.

[h] 1 Cor. vii. 19; chap. iii. 28; vi. 15; Col. iii. 11.——[i] 1 Thess. i. 3; James ii. 18, 20, 22.——[k] 1 Cor. ix. 24.——[l] Chapter iii. 1.

[m] Or, *who did drive you back?*——[n] Chap. i. 6.——[o] 1 Cor. v. 6; xv. 33.——[p] 2 Cor. ii. 3; viii. 22.——[q] Chap. i. 7.——[r] 2 Cor. x. 6.——[s] Chap. vi. 12.

but also a continual *anticipation* of it; and therefore the apostle says, απεκδεχομεθα, we *receive out of it*, from απο, *from* εκ, *out of*, and δεχομαι, *I receive*. This is no fanciful derivation; it exists in the experience of every genuine Christian; he is continually *anticipating* or *receiving foretastes* of that glory, the fulness of which he expects after death. Thus they are *receiving the end of their faith, the salvation of their souls.* 1 Pet. i. 9.

That they could not have the Holy Spirit without *faith*, was a doctrine also of the Jews; hence it is said, *Mechilta*, fol. 52: "*That* faith was of great consequence with which the Israelites believed in Him who, with one word, created the universe; and because the Israelites believed in God, the Holy Spirit dwelt in them; so that, being filled with God, they sang praises to him." Cicero, De *Nat. Deor.*, lib. ii., has said: *Nemo vir magnus sine aliquo afflatu divino unquam fuit:* "There never was a great man who had not some measure of the Divine influence." However true this may be with respect to the *great men* of the Roman orator, we may safely assert there never was a true *Christian* who had not the inspiration of God's Holy Spirit.

Verse 6. *For in Jesus Christ*] By the dispensation of the Gospel all legal observances, as essential to salvation, are done away; and uncircumcision, or the *Gentile state*, contributes as much to salvation as *circumcision*, or the *Jewish state*; they are both equally ineffectual; and nothing now avails in the sight of God but that faith δι' αγαπης ενεργουμενη, *which is made active*, or *energetic, by love.* God acknowledges no faith, as of the operation of his Spirit, that is not *active* or *obedient;* but the principle of all obedience to God, and beneficence to man, is *love;* therefore faith cannot work unless it be associated with love. Love to God produces obedience to his will: love to man *worketh no ill;* but, on the contrary, every act of kindness. Faith which does not work by love is either *circumcision* or *uncircumcision*, or whatever its possessor may please to call it; it is, however, nothing that will stand him in stead when God comes to take away his soul. *It availeth nothing.* This humble, holy, operative, obedient LOVE, is the grand touchstone of all *human creeds* and *confessions of faith. Faith* without this has neither soul nor operation; in the language of the Apostle James, it is *dead*, and can perform no function of the spiritual life, no more than a dead man can perform the duties of animal or civil life.

Verse 7. *Ye did run well*] Ye once had the faith

that worked by love—ye were genuine, active, useful Christians.

Who did hinder] Who prevented you from continuing to obey the truth? Ye could only be turned aside by your own consent. St. Paul here, as in 1 Cor. ix. 24, compares Christianity to a *race.* See the notes on the above text.

Verse 8. *This persuasion*] Of the necessity of your being circumcised and obeying the law of Moses, is *not of him that calleth you.* I never preached such a doctrine to you; I called you out of *bondage to liberty*, from a *galling yoke* to a *cheerful service.* Some translate πεισμονη, *obedience* or *subjection.* This *subjection* of yours to the Mosaic law is opposed to the will of God, and never was preached by me.

Verse 9. *A little leaven leaveneth the whole lump.*] A proverbial expression, see 1 Cor. v. 6, very aptly applied to those who receive the smallest tincture of false doctrine, relative to the things essential to salvation, which soon influences the whole conduct, so that the man becomes totally perverted. They might have argued, "It is a *small thing*, and should not be made a subject of serious controversy, whether we be circumcised or not." Granted, that in *itself* it is a small matter; but, as every man who is circumcised is a debtor to do the whole law, ver. 3, then your circumcision leads necessarily to your total perversion; as the *little* portion of *leaven*, mixed with the batch, soon leavens the whole lump.

Verse 10. *I have confidence in you*] I now feel a persuasion from the Lord that I shall not be permitted to expostulate with you in vain; *that ye will be none otherwise minded*—that ye will be aware of the danger to which ye are exposed, that ye will retreat in time, and recover the grace which ye have lost.

But he that troubleth you] The false teacher, who sowed doubtful disputations among you, and thus has troubled the repose of the whole Church, *shall bear his judgment*—shall meet with the punishment he deserves, for having sown *his* tares among *God's wheat.*

Verse 11. *If I yet preach circumcision*] It is very likely that some of the false apostles, hearing of Paul's having circumcised Timothy, Acts xvi. 3, which must have been done *about this time*, reported him as being an advocate for circumcision, and by this means endeavoured to sanction their own doctrine. To this the apostle replies: Were it so, that I am a friend to this measure, is it likely that I should suffer persecution from the Jews? But I am every where persecuted by them, and I am persecuted *because I am*

    2

A. M. cir. 4056.
A. D. cir. 52.
A. U. C.
805.
An. Imp. Claudii
Cæsaris 12.

cision, [t] why do I yet suffer persecution? then is [u] the offence of the cross ceased.

12 [v] I would they were even cut off [w] which trouble you.

13 For, brethren, ye have been called unto liberty; only [x] use not liberty for an occasion to the flesh, but [y] by love serve one another.

14 For [z] all the law is fulfilled in one word,

even in this, [a] Thou shalt love thy neighbour as thyself.

15 But, if ye bite and devour one another, take heed that ye be not consumed one of another.

16 *This* I say then, [b] Walk in the Spirit, and [c] ye shall not fulfil the lust of the flesh.

17 For [d] the flesh lusteth against the Spirit, and the Spirit against the flesh; and these are

A. M. cir. 4056.
A. D. cir. 52.
A. U. C.
805.
An. Imp Claudii
Cæsaris 12.

---

[t] 1 Cor. xv. 30; chapter iv. 29; vi. 17.——[u] 1 Cor. i. 23. [v] Josh. vii. 25; 1 Cor. v. 13; chap. i. 8, 9.——[w] Acts xv. 1, 2, 24. [x] 1 Cor. viii. 9; 1 Pet. ii. 16; 2 Pet. ii. 19; Jude 4.——[y] 1 Cor. ix. 19; chap. vi. 2.

[z] Matt. vii. 12; xxii. 40; James ii. 8.——[a] Lev. xix. 18; Matt. xxii. 39; Rom. xiii. 8, 9.——[b] Rom. vi. 12; viii. 1, 4, 12; xiii. 14; ver. 25; 1 Pet. ii. 11.——[c] Or, *fulfil not.*——[d] Rom. vii. 23; viii. 6, 7.

---

known to be an enemy to circumcision; were I a friend to this doctrine, the *offence of the cross*—preaching salvation only through the sacrifice of Christ, would soon cease; because, to be consistent with myself, if I preached the necessity of circumcision I must soon cease to preach Christ crucified, and then the Jews would be no longer my enemies.

Verse 12. *I would they were even cut off which trouble you.*] This saying has puzzled many, and different interpretations of the place have been proposed by learned men.

At first sight it seems as if the apostle was praying for the *destruction* of the false teachers who had perverted the Churches of Galatia. Mr. Wakefield thought οφελον αποκοφονται might be translated, *I wish that they were made to weep;* and· in his translation of the New Testament the passage stands thus: "I wish that they who are unsettling you may lament it." I believe the apostle never meant any such thing. As the persons who were breeding all this confusion in the Churches of Galatia were *members of that Church,* the apostle appears to me to be simply expressing his desire that they might be *cut off* or *excommunicated* from the Church. *Kypke* has given an abundance of examples where the word is used to signify *amputating; cutting off from society, office, &c.; excluding.* In opposition to the notion of excommunication, it might be asked: "Why should the apostle wish these to be excommunicated when it was his own office to do it?" To this it may be answered: The apostle's authority was greatly weakened among that people by the influence of the false teachers, so that in all probability he could exercise no ecclesiastical function; he could therefore only *express his wish.* And the whole passage is so parallel to that, 1 Cor. v. 6, 7, that I think there can be no reasonable doubt of the apostle's meaning: "Let those who are unsettling the Church of Christ in your district be excommunicated; this is my wish, that they should no longer have any place among you."

Verse 13. *Ye have been called unto liberty*] A total freedom from all the burthensome rites and ceremonies of the Mosaic law. *Only use not that liberty for an occasion to the flesh.* By *flesh,* here, we may understand all the unrenewed desires and propensities of the mind; whatsoever is not under the influence and guidance of the Holy Spirit of God. Your liberty is from that which would *oppress the spirit;* not from that

which would lay *restraints* on the *flesh.* The Gospel proclaims liberty from the *ceremonial* law: but binds you still faster under the *moral* law. To be freed from the *ceremonial* law is the *Gospel liberty;* to pretend freedom from the *moral* law is *Antinomianism.*

By love serve one another.] Having that faith which worketh by love, serve each other to the uttermost of your power: δουλευετε, serve each other, when necessary, as *slaves* serve their masters. Several excellent MSS. and *versions,* instead of δια της αγαπης, *by love,* have τη αγαπη του Πνευματος, *in the love of the Spirit serve one another.*

Verse 14. *For all the law*] Which respects our duty to our fellows, is *fulfilled*—is comprehended, *in* one word: *Thou shalt love thy neighbour as thyself.* See the notes on Matt. xix. 19, and Rom. xiii. 9.

Verse 15. *If ye bite and devour one another*] These Churches seem to have been in a state of great distraction; there were continual altercations among them. They had fallen from the grace of the Gospel; and, as Christ no longer dwelt in their hearts by faith, pride, anger, ill-will, and all unkind and uncharitable tempers, took possession of their souls, and they were in consequence alternately destroying each other. Nothing is so destructive to the peace of man, and to the peace of the soul, as religious disputes; where they prevail, religion in general has little place.

Verse 16. *Walk in the Spirit*] Get back that Spirit of God which you have grieved and lost; take up that *spiritual* religion which you have abandoned.

Ye shall not fulfil the lust of the flesh.] If the Spirit of God dwell in and rule your heart, the whole *carnal mind* will be destroyed; and then, not only carnal ordinances will be abandoned, but also the works and propensities of the flesh.

Verse 17. *For the flesh lusteth against the Spirit*] God still continues to strive with you, notwithstanding your apostasy, showing you whence you have fallen, and exciting you to return to him; but your own obstinacy renders all ineffectual; and through the influence of these different principles, you are kept in a state of self-opposition and self-distraction, *so that you cannot do the things that ye would.* You are convinced of what is *right,* and ye wish to do it; but, having abandoned the Gospel and the grace of Christ, the law and its ordinances which ye have chosen in their place afford you no *power* to conquer your evil propensities. It was on this ground that the apostle exhorted them,

2

A. M. cir. 40.6.
A. D. cir. 52.
A. U. C.
805.
An. Imp. Claudii
Cæsaris 12.

contrary the one to the other ; **e** so that ye cannot do the things that ye would.

18 But, **f** if ye be led of the Spirit, ye are not under the law.

19 Now **g** the works of the flesh are manifest, which are *these :* Adultery, fornication, uncleanness, lasciviousness,

A. M. cir. 4056.
A. D. cir. 52.
A. U. C.
805.
An. Imp. Claudii
Cæsaris 12.

20 Idolatry, witchcraft, hatred, variance, emulations, wrath, strife, seditions, heresies,

21 Envyings, murders, drunkenness, revellings, and such like : of the which I tell you before, as I have also told *you* in time past, that **h** they which do such things shall not inherit the kingdom of God.

---

e Rom. vii. 15, 19.——**f** Rom. vi. 14 ; viii. 2.——**g** 1 Cor. iii. 3 ; Eph. v. 3 ; Col. iii. 5 ; James iii. 14, 15.

h 1 Corinthians vi. 9 ; Eph. v. 5 ; Col. iii. 6 ; Revelation xxii. 15.

---

ver. 16, to *walk in the Spirit, that they might not fulfil the lust of the flesh ;* as without the grace of God they could do nothing. Who can suppose that he speaks this of *adult Christians ?*

Verse 18. *But, if ye be led of the Spirit*] If ye receive again the Gospel and the grace of Christ, and permit yourselves to be influenced by the Holy Spirit whom you are now grieving, *ye are not under the law* —ye will not feel those evil propensities which now disgrace and torment you ; but they must prevail while you are not under the influence of the grace and Spirit of Christ.

Verse 19. *Now the works of the flesh are manifest*] By *flesh* we are to understand the evil and fallen state of the soul, no longer under the guidance of God's Spirit and right reason, but under the animal passions ; and they are even rendered more irregular and turbulent by the influence of *sin ;* so that man is in a worse state than the brute : and so all-commanding is this evil nature that it leads men into all kinds of crimes ; and among them the following, which *are manifest*— known to all, and most prevalent ; and, though these are most solemnly forbidden by your *law,* the observance of its ordinances gives no power to overcome them, and provides no pardon for the guilt and condemnation produced by them.

Adultery] Μοιχεια· Illicit connection with a *married* person. This word is wanting in this place in the best MSS., versions, and fathers ; the next term often comprehending both.

Fornication] Πορνεια· Illicit connection between *single* or *unmarried* persons ; yet often signifying *adultery* also.

Uncleanness] Ακαθαρσια· Whatever is opposite to *purity ;* probably meaning here, as in Rom. i. 24 ; 2 Cor. xii. 21, *unnatural* practices ; sodomy, bestiality.

Lasciviousness] Ασελγεια· Whatever is contrary to *chastity ;* all *lewdness.*

Verse 20. *Idolatry*] Worshipping of idols ; frequenting idol festivals ; all the rites of Bacchus, Venus, Priapus, &c., which were common among the Gentiles.

Witchcraft] Φαρμακεια, from φαρμακον, *a drug* or *poison ;* because in all spells and enchantments, whether true or false, *drugs* were employed. As *a drug,* φαρμακον, might either be the means of *removing* an evil, or *inflicting* one, etymologists have derived it from φερον ακος, *bringing ease,* or *φερον αχος, bringing pain.* So spells and incantations were used sometimes for the *restoration* of the health ; at others, for the *destruction* of an enemy. Sometimes, these *φαρμακα* were used to procure *love ;* at other times, to produce *hatred.*

Hatred] Εχθραι· *Aversions* and *antipathies*, when opposed to *brotherly love* and *kindness.*

Variance] Ερεις· *Contentions*, where the principle of *hatred* proceeds to *open acts ;* hence contests, altercations, lawsuits, and disputes in general.

Emulations] Ζηλοι· *Envies* or *emulations ;* that is strife to excel at the expense of another ; lowering others to set up one's self ; unholy zeal, fervently adopting a bad cause, or supporting a good one by cruel means. *Inquisitions,* pretending to support true religion by torturing and burning alive those who both profess and practise it.

Wrath] Θυμοι· Turbulent passions, disturbing the harmony of the mind, and producing *domestic* and *civil* broils and disquietudes.

Strife] Εριθειαι· Disputations, janglings, logomachics, or *strife* about *words.*

Seditions] Διχοστασιαι· Divisions into separate factions ; parties, whether in the *Church* or *state.*

Heresies] Αιρεσεις· *Factions ;* parties in the *Church* separating from communion with each other, and setting up *altar* against *altar.* The word, which is harmless in itself, is here used in a bad sense. In stead of αιρεσεις the Slavonic has σκανδαλα, *scandals* offences or stumbling-blocks.

Verse 21. *Envyings*] Φθονοι· " Pain felt, and malignity conceived, at the sight of excellence or happiness." A passion the most base and the least curable of all that disgrace or degrade the fallen soul. See on Rom. xiii. 13.

Murders] Φονοι· Similarity of *sound* to the preceding seems to have suggested the word in this association ; it is wanting in several MSS. *Murder* signifies the destruction of human life ; and as he who *hates his brother in his heart* is ready to take away his life, so he is called a *murderer.* After all the casuistry of man, it does not appear that the *right* of taking away a human life on any pretence, except for the crime of *murder* belongs to any but the Maker and Judge of all men.

Drunkenness] Μεθαι· Taking more wine or any kind of inebriating liquor than is necessary for health ; whatever unfits for *public, domestic,* or *spiritual* duties ; even the *cares of the world*, when they intoxicate the mind. See on Rom. xiii. 13.

Revellings] Κωμοι· Lascivious feastings, with obscene songs, music, &c. See on Rom. xiii. 13.

And such like] Και τα ὁμοια τουτοις· All that proceeds from the evil passions of a fallen spirit, besides those above specified ; and all that the law of God specifies and condemns.

3

A. M. cir. 4056.
A. D. cir. 52.
A. U. C.
805.
An. Imp. Claudii
Cæsaris 12.

22 But ⁱ the fruit of the Spirit is love, joy, peace, long-suffering, ^k gentleness, ^l goodness, ^m faith,

23 Meekness, temperance : ⁿ against such there is no law.

24 And they that are Christ's ^o have cruci-

fied the flesh with the ^p affections and lusts.

25 ^q If we live in the Spirit, let us also walk in the Spirit.

26 ^r Let us not be desirous of vain glory, provoking one another, envying one another.

A. M. cir. 4056
A. D. cir. 52.
A. U. C.
805.
An. Imp. Claudii
Cæsaris 12.

ⁱ John xv. 2 ; Eph. v. 9.——^k Col. iii. 12 ; James iii. 17.——^l Rom. xv. 14.——^m 1 Cor. xiii. 7.——ⁿ 1 Tim. i. 9.

^o Rom. vi. 6 ; xiii. 14 ; chap. ii. 20 ; 1 Pet. ii. 11.——^p Or, *passions.*
^q Rom. viii. 4, 5 ; ver. 16.——^r Phil. ii. 3.

Of the which I tell you before] When I *first* preached the Gospel to you.

As I have also told you in time past] When I paid my *second* visit to you ; for the apostle did visit them *twice.* See Acts xvi. 6, and xviii. 23 ; and see *preface,* p. 385.

Shall not inherit] They are not *children* of God, and therefore cannot *inherit* the kingdom which belongs only to the *children* of the Divine *family.*

Verse 22. *But the fruit of the Spirit*] Both *flesh* —the sinful dispositions of the human heart and *spirit*— the changed or purified state of the soul, by the grace and Spirit of God, are represented by the apostle as *trees,* one yielding *good* the other *bad fruit* ; the productions of each being according to the nature of the *tree,* as the *tree* is according to the nature of the *seed* from which it sprung. The *bad seed* produced a *bad tree,* yielding all manner of *bad fruit* ; the *good seed* produced a *good tree,* bringing forth *fruits* of the most *excellent* kind. The *tree* of the *flesh,* with all its bad fruits, we have already seen ; the *tree* of the *Spirit,* with its good fruits, we shall now see.

Love] Αγαπη· An intense desire to please God, and to do good to mankind ; the very soul and spirit of all true religion ; the fulfilling of the law, and what gives energy to faith itself. See ver. 6.

Joy] Χαρα· The exultation that arises from a sense of God's mercy communicated to the soul in the pardon of its iniquities, and the prospect of that eternal glory of which it has the foretaste in the pardon of sin. See Rom. v. 2.

Peace] Ειρηνη· The calm, quiet, and order, which take place in the justified soul, instead of the doubts, fears, alarms, and dreadful forebodings, which every true penitent less or more feels, and must feel till the assurance of pardon brings peace and satisfaction to the mind. Peace is the first sensible fruit of the pardon of *sin.* See Rom. v. 1, and the notes there.

Long-suffering] Μακροθυμια· Long-mindedness, bearing with the frailties and provocations of others, from the consideration that God has borne long with ours ; and that, if he had not, we should have been speedily consumed : bearing up also through all the troubles and difficulties of life without murmuring or repining ; submitting cheerfully to every dispensation of God's providence, and thus deriving benefit from every occurrence.

Gentleness] Χρηστοτης· Benignity, affability ; a very rare grace, often wanting in many who have a considerable share of Christian excellence. A good education and polished manners, when brought under the influence of the grace of God, will bring out this grace with great effect.

Goodness] Αγαθωσυνη· The perpetual desire and sincere study, not only to abstain from every appearance of evil, but to do good to the bodies and souls of men to the utmost of our ability. But all this must spring from a *good heart*—a heart purified by the Spirit of God ; and then, the *tree* being made *good,* the *fruit* must be good also.

Faith] Πιστις, here used for *fidelity*—punctuality in performing promises, conscientious carefulness in preserving what is committed to our trust, in restoring it to its proper owner, in transacting the business confided to us, neither betraying the secret of our friend, nor disappointing the confidence of our employer.

Verse 23. *Meekness*] Πραοτης· Mildness, indulgence toward the weak and erring, patient suffering of injuries without feeling a spirit of revenge, an even balance of all tempers and passions, the entire opposite to *anger.*

Temperance] Εγκρατεια· Continence, self-government, or *moderation,* principally with regard to *sensual* or *animal appetites. Moderation* in *eating, drinking, sleeping, &c.*

Several very respectable MSS., as D*EFG, with the *Vulgate,* most copies of the *Itala* and several of the *fathers,* add αγνεια, *chastity.* This we are sure cannot be separated from the genuine Christian character, though it may be included in the word εγκρατεια, *continence* or *moderation,* immediately preceding.

Against such there is no law.] Those, whose lives are adorned by the above virtues, cannot be *condemned* by any law, for the whole purpose and design of the moral law of God is fulfilled in those who have the Spirit of God, producing in their hearts and lives the preceding fruits.

Verse 24. *And they that are Christ's*] All genuine Christians *have crucified the flesh*—are so far from obeying its dictates and acting under its influence, that they have crucified their sensual appetites ; they have nailed them to the cross of Christ, where they have expired with him ; hence, says St. Paul, Rom. vi. 6, *our old man*—the flesh, with its affections and lusts, *is crucified with him, that the body of sin might be destroyed, that henceforth we should not serve sin.* By which we see that God has fully designed to save all who believe in Christ from *all sin,* whether outward or inward, with all the *affections,* παθημασι, irregular *passions,* and *lusts,* επιθυμιαις, disorderly *wishes* and *desires.* All that a man may *feel* contrary to love and purity ; and all that he may *desire* contrary to *moderation* and that *self-denial* peculiar to the Christian character.

Verse 25. *If we live in the Spirit*] If we profess to believe a spiritual religion, *let us walk in the Spirit*

2

—let us show in our lives and conversation that the Spirit of God dwells in us.

Verse 26. *Let us not be desirous of vain glory*] Κενοδοξοι· *Let us not be vain glorious*—boasting of our attainments; vaunting ourselves to be superior to others; or seeking honour from those things which do not possess moral good ; in birth, riches, eloquence, &c., &c.

Provoking one another] What this may refer to we cannot tell ; whether to the Judaizing teachers, endeavouring to set themselves up beyond the apostle, and their attempts to lessen *him* in the people's eyes, that they might secure to themselves the public confidence, and thus destroy St. Paul's influence in the Galatian Churches ; or whether to some other matter in the internal economy of the Church, we know not. But the exhortation is necessary for every Christian, and for every Christian Church. He who professes to seek the honour that comes from God, should not ɒe desirous of *vain glory*. He who desires to keep the *unity of the Spirit* in the bond of peace, should not ʋrovoke another. He who knows that he never deserved any gift or blessing from God should not *envy* another those blessings which the Divine goodness may have thought proper to bestow upon him. May not God do what he will with his own ? If Christians in general would be *content* with the *honour that comes from God,* if they would take heed to give no *provocations* to their fellow Christians, if they would cease from *envying* those on whom either God or man bestows honours or advantages, we should soon have a happier and more perfect state of the Christian Church than we now see. Christianity requires us to esteem each other better than ourselves, or in honour to prefer one another. Had not such a disposition been necessary to the Christian character, and to the peace and perfection of the Church of Christ, it would not have been so strongly recommended. But who lays this to heart, or even thinks that this is indispensably necessary to his salvation ? Where this disposition lives not, there are both the *seed* and *fruit* of the *flesh.* *Evil tempers* are the bane of religion and totally contrary to Christianity.

CHAPTER VI.

The apostle teaches them to be tender and affectionate towards any who, through surprise and the violence of temptation, had fallen into sin ; and to bear each other's burdens, 1, 2. To think humbly of themselves, and to conclude concerning their own character rather from the evidence of their works than from any thing else, 3–5. To minister to the support of those who instruct them in righteousness, 6. He warns them against self-deception, because whatever a man soweth that he shall reap, 7, 8. Exhorts them not to be weary in well doing, and to embrace every opportunity to do good, 9, 10. Intimates that his love to them led him to write this whole epistle with his own hand, 11. Points out the object that those had in view who wished them to be circumcised, 12, 13. He exults in the cross of Christ, and asserts that a new creation of the soul is essential to its salvation ; and wishes peace to them who act on this plan, 14–16. States that he bears in his body the marks of the Lord Jesus, 17. And concludes with his apostolical benediction, 18.

A. M. cir. 4056.
A. D. cir. 52.
A. U. C.
805.
An. Imp. Claudii
Cæsaris 12.

BRETHREN, [a] if [b] a man be overtaken in a fault, ye [c] which are spiritual restore such a one [d] in the spirit of meekness ; considering thyself, [e] lest thou also be tempted.

2 [f] Bear ye one another's burdens, and so fulfil [g] the law of Christ.

A. M. cir. 4056.
A. D. cir. 52.
A. U. C.
805.
An. Imp. Claudii
Cæsaris 12.

[a] Rom. xiv. 1 ; xv. 1 ; Heb. xii. 13 ; James v. 19.——[b] Or, *although.*——[c] 1 Cor. ii. 15 ; iii. 1.——[d] 1 Cor. iv. 21 ; 2 Thess. iii. 15 ; 2 Tim. ii. 25.

[e] 1 Cor. vii. 5 ; x. 12.——[f] Rom. xv. 1 ; chap. v. 13 ; 1 Thess. v. 14.——[g] John xiii. 14, 15, 34 ; xv. 12 ; James ii. 8 ; 1 John iv. 21.

NOTES ON CHAP. VI.

Verse 1. *Brethren, if a man be overtaken*] Εαν προληφθη· If he be *surprised, seized on* without warning, *suddenly involved, taken before he is aware:* all these meanings the word has in connections similar to this. *Strabo,* lib xvi., page 1120, applies it to the *rhinoceros,* in its contests with the elephant : he suddenly rips up the belly of the elephant, αν μη προληφθη τη προβοσκιδι, *that he may not be surprised with his trunk.* For, should the elephant seize him with his trunk first, all resistance would be afterwards in vain ; therefore he endeavours to rip up the elephant's belly with the horn which is on his nose, in order to prevent this. It is used also by *Arrian,* in *Peripl. Mar. Eryth.,* page 164, and page 168, to signify a vessel being *suddenly agitated* and *whirled* by the waves, and then *dashed on the rocks.* See *Kypke.*

Ye which are spiritual] Ye who still retain the grace of the Gospel, and have wisdom and experience in Divine things ;

Restore such a one] Καταρτιζετε τον τοιουτον· Bring the man *back into his place.* It is a metaphor taken from a *dislocated limb,* brought back by the hand of a skilful and tender surgeon into its place.

In the spirit of meekness] Use no *severity* nor *haughty carriage* towards him ; as the man was *suddenly* overtaken, he is already deeply humbled and distressed, and needs much encouragement and lenient usage. There is a great difference between a man who being *suddenly assailed* falls into sin, and the man who transgressed in consequence of having WALKED in *the counsel of the* UNGODLY, *or* STOOD *in the way of* SINNERS.

Considering thyself] Σκοπων σεαυτον· Looking to

2

A. M. cir. 4056.
A. D. cir. 52.
A. U. C.
805.
An. Imp. Claudii
Cæsaris 12.

3 For [h] if a man think himself to be something, when [i] he is nothing, he deceiveth himself.

4 But [k] let every man prove his own work, and then shall he have rejoicing in himself alone, and [l] not in another.

5 [m] For every man shall bear his own burden.

6 [n] Let him that is taught in the word communicate unto him that teacheth in all good things.

7 [o] Be not deceived ; [p] God is not mocked : for [q] whatsoever a man soweth, that shall he also reap.

8 [r] For he that soweth to his flesh, shall of the flesh reap corruption ; but he that soweth

A. M. cir. 4056.
A. D. cir. 52.
A. U. C.
805.
An. Imp. Claudii
Cæsaris 12.

---

[h] Rom. xii. 3 ; 1 Cor. viii. 2 ; chap. ii. 6.——[i] 2 Cor. iii. 5 ; xii. 11.——[k] 1 Cor. xi. 28 ; 2 Cor. xiii. 5.——[l] See Luke xviii. 11. [m] Rom. ii. 6 ; 1 Cor. iii. 8.——[n] Rom. xv. 27 ; 1 Cor. ix. 11, 14.

[o] 1 Cor. vi. 9 ; xv. 33.——[p] Job xiii. 9.——[q] Luke xvi. 25 ; Rom. ii. 6 ; 2 Cor. ix. 6.——[r] Job iv. 8 ; Prov. xi. 18 ; xxii. 8 ; Hosea viii. 7 ; x. 12 ; Rom. viii. 13 ; James iii. 18.

---

thyself ; as *he* fell through a moment of *unwatchfulness, look about,* that *thou* be not surprised ; as *he* fell, so mayest *thou :* thou art now warned at his expense ; therefore *keep a good look out.*

Lest thou also be tempted.] And having had this warning, thou wilt have less to plead in extenuation of thy offence. It is no wonder if a *harsh* and *cruel censurer* of a *weak, backsliding* brother, should be taught moderation and mercy by an awful proof of his own frailty. Such a one may justly dread the most violent attacks from the arch enemy ; he will disgrace him if he can, and if he can *overtake him* he will have no small triumph. Consider the possibility of such a case, and show the *mercy* and *feeling* which thou wouldst then wish to receive from another. From the consideration of what we *are,* what we *have been,* or what we *may be,* we should learn to be compassionate. The poet *Mantuanus* has set this in a fine light in his Eclogue, *De honesto Amore :*—

Id commune malum ; semel insanivimus omnes :
Aut sumus, aut fuimus, aut possemus omne quod hic est.

" This is a common evil ; at one time or other we have all done wrong. Either we *are,* or *have been,* or *may be,* as bad as he whom we condemn."

Verse 2. Bear ye one another's burdens] Have *sympathy ;* feel for each other ; and consider the case of a distressed brother as your own.

And so fulfil the law of Christ.] That law or commandment, *Ye shall love one another ;* or that, *Do unto all men as ye would they should do unto you.* We should be as indulgent to the infirmities of others, as we can be consistently with truth and righteousness : our brother's *infirmity* may be his *burden ;* and if we do not choose to help him to bear it, let us not reproach him because he is obliged to carry the load.

Verse 3. If a man think himself to be something] i. e. To be a proper Christian man ; *when he is nothing ;* being destitute of that *charity* which *beareth, hopeth,* and *endureth* all things. See 1 Cor. xiii. 1, &c. Those who suppose themselves to excel all others in piety, understanding, &c., while they are *harsh, censorious,* and *overbearing,* prove that they have not the *charity* that *thinketh no evil ;* and in the sight of God are only as sounding brass and a tinkling cymbal. There are no people more censorious or uncharitable than those among some religious people who pretend to more light and a deeper communion with God. They are generally carried away with a sort of sublime, high sounding phraseology, which seems to

argue a wonderfully deep acquaintance with Divine things ; stripped of this, many of them are like Samson without his hair.

Verse 4. Prove his own work] Let him examine himself and his conduct by the words and example of Christ ; and if he find that they bear this *touchstone,* then he shall have *rejoicing in himself alone,* feeling that he resembles his Lord and Master, *and not in another*—not derive his consolation from comparing himself with another who may be *weaker,* or less instructed than himself. The only *rule* for a Christian is the word of Christ ; the only *pattern* for his imitation is the *example* of Christ. He should not compare himself with *others ;* they are not his *standard.* Christ hath left us an example that we should follow *his* steps.

Verse 5. Every man shall bear his own burden.] All must answer for *themselves,* not for their *neighbours.* And every man must expect to be dealt with by the Divine Judge, as his character and conduct have been. The greater offences of another will not excuse thy smaller crimes. Every man must give account of himself to God.

Verse 6. Let him that is taught in the word] He who receives instructions in Christianity by the public preaching of the word ;

Communicate unto him that teacheth] Contribute to the support of the man who has dedicated himself to the work of the ministry, and who gives up his time and his life to preach the Gospel. It appears that some of the believers in Galatia could receive the Christian ministry without contributing to its support. This is both ungrateful and base. We do not expect that a common schoolmaster will give up his time to teach our children their *alphabet* without being paid for it ; and can we suppose that it is *just* for any person to sit under the preaching of the Gospel in order to grow wise unto salvation by it, and not contribute to the support of the spiritual teacher ? It is *unjust.*

Verse 7. Be not deceived] Neither deceive yourselves, nor permit yourselves to be deceived by others. He seems to refer to the Judaizing teachers.

God is not mocked] Ye cannot deceive him, and he will not permit you to mock him with *pretended* instead of *real* services.

Whatsoever a man soweth] Whatsoever kind of grain a man sows in his field, of that shall he reap ; for no *other species* of grain can proceed from that which is sown. *Darnel* will not produce *wheat,* nor *wheat, darnel.*

Verse 8. He that soweth to his flesh] In like

2

A. M. cir. 4056.
A. D. cir. 52.
A. U. C.
805.
An. Imp. Claudii
Cæsaris 12.

to the Spirit, shall of the Spirit reap life everlasting.

9 And ˢ let us not be weary in well-doing ; for in due season we shall reap, ᵗ if we faint not.

10 ᵘ As we have therefore opportunity, ᵛ let us do good unto all *men*, especially unto them who are of ʷ the household of faith.

11 Ye see how large a letter I have written unto you with mine own hand.

12 As many as desire to make a fair show in the flesh, ˣ they constrain you to be circumcised, ʸ only lest they should ᶻ suffer persecution for the cross of Christ.

13 For neither they themselves who are

A. M. cir. 4056.
A. D. cir. 52.
A. U. C.
805.
An. Imp. Claudii
Cæsaris 12.

ˢ 2 Thess. iii. 13 ; 1 Cor. xv. 58.——ᵗ Matt. xxiv. 13 ; Heb. iii. 6, 14 ; x. 36 ; xii. 3, 5 ; Rev. ii. 10.——ᵘ John ix. 4 ; xii. 35.

ᵛ 1 Thess. v. 15 ; 1 Tim. vi. 18 ; Tit. iii. 8.——ʷ Eph. ii. 19 ; Heb. iii. 6.——ˣ Ch. ii. 3, 14.——ʸ Phil. iii. 18.——ᶻ Ch. v. 11.

---

manner, he that *sows to the flesh*—who indulges his sensual and animal appetites, shall have *corruption* as the *crop:* you cannot expect to lead a bad life and go to heaven at last. According as your present life is, so will be your eternal life ; whether your *sowing* be to the *flesh* or to the *Spirit*, so will your eternal *reaping* be. To *sow*, here, means transacting the concerns of a man's *natural life*. To *reap*, signifies his *enjoyment* or *punishment* in *another* world. Probably by *flesh* and *Spirit* the apostle means *Judaism* and *Christianity*. Circumcision of the *flesh* was the principal *rite* of the former ; circumcision in the *heart*, by the *Spirit*, the chief rite of the latter ; hence the one may have been called *flesh*, the other, *Spirit*. He who rejects the Gospel, and trusts only in the rites and ceremonies of the law for salvation, will reap endless disappointment and misery. He who trusts in Christ, and receives the gifts and graces of the Holy Spirit, shall reap life everlasting.

Verse 9. *Let us not be weary*] *Well-doing* is easier in itself than *ill-doing ;* and the danger of *growing weary* in the former arises only from the *opposition* to good in our *own nature*, or the *outward hinderances* we may meet with from a gainsaying and persecuting world.

In due season we shall reap] As the husbandman, in ploughing, sowing, and variously labouring in his fields, is supported by the hope of a plentiful harvest, which he cannot expect before the right and appointed time ; so every follower of God may be persuaded that he shall not be permitted to pray, weep, deny himself, and live in a conformity to his Maker's will, without reaping the fruit of it in eternal glory. And although no man obtains glory *because* he has prayed, &c., yet none can expect glory who do not seek it in this way. This is *sowing to the Spirit ;* and the *Spirit* and the *grace* are furnished by Christ Jesus, and by him the kingdom of heaven is *opened* to all believers ; but only those who *believe, love*, and *obey*, shall enter into it.

Verse 10. *As we have—opportunity*] While it is the *time* of *sowing* let us sow the good seed ; and let our love be, as the love of Christ is, *free, manifested to all*. Let us help all who need help according to the uttermost of our power : but let the first objects of our regards be those who are of the household of faith—the members of the Church of Christ, who form one *family*, of which Jesus Christ is the *head*. Those have the first claims on our attention ; but *all others* have their claims also, and therefore we should do good unto *all*.

Verse 11. *Ye see how large a letter*] There is a strange diversity of opinions concerning the apostle's meaning in this place. Some think he refers to the *length* of the epistle, others to the *largeness* of the *letters* in which this epistle is written, others to the *inadequacy* of the apostle's *writing*. It appears plain that most of his epistles were written by an *amanuensis*, and simply *subscribed* by himself ; but the *whole* of the Epistle to the Galatians was written by his *own hand*. To say that the apostle was *unskilled in Greek*, and especially in the *Greek characters*, is in my opinion absurd. He was born in *Tarsus*, a city which, according to *Strabo*, rivalled both *Athens* and *Alexandria* in philosophy, and in arts and sciences ; and therefore he could not be ignorant of a *tongue* which must have been the very *means* of conveying all this instruction. As to *writing it*, there was in his time nothing difficult, because the *uncial* character was that which was alone in use in those days, and this character is as easily made as the *capitals* in the *Roman* alphabet, which have been taken from it. I conclude, therefore, that what the apostle says must be understood of the *length of the epistle*, in all probability the largest he had ever written with *his own hand ;* though several, much larger, have been dictated by him, but they were written by his *scribe* or *amanuensis*.

Verse 12. *A fair show in the flesh.*] The Jewish religion was general in the region of Galatia, and it was respectable, as it appears that the principal inhabitants were either *Jews* or *proselytes*. As it was then professed and practised among the Jews, this religion had nothing very grievous to the old man ; an unrenewed nature might go through all its observances with little pain or cross-bearing. On the other hand, Christianity could not be very popular ; it was too strict. A Jew made a *fair show* there, according to his *carnal system*, and it was a temptation to a weak Christian to swerve into *Judaism*, that he might be *exempted from persecution*, and be creditable among his countrymen. This is what the apostle intimates : " They constrain you to be circumcised, lest they should suffer persecution for the cross of Christ."

Verse 13. *Neither they themselves who are circumcised*] They receive circumcision and profess Judaism, not from a desire to be conformed to the *will of God ;* but *Judaism* was popular, and the more converts the false teachers could make ; the more occasion of glorying they had ; and they wished to get those Christian converts, who had been before *proselytes of the gate*,

A. M. cir. 4056.
A. D. cir. 52.
A. U. C.
805.
An. Imp. Claudii
Cæsaris 12.

circumcised keep the law; but desire to have you circumcised, that they may glory in your flesh.

14 [a] But God forbid that I should glory, save in the cross of our Lord Jesus Christ, [b] by whom the world is [c] crucified unto me, and I unto the world.

15 For [d] in Christ Jesus neither circumcision availeth any thing, nor uncircumcision, but [e] a new creature.

16 [f] And as many as walk [g] according to this rule, peace *be* on them, and mercy, and upon [h] the Israel of God.

A. M. cir. 4056.
A. D. cir. 52.
A. U. C.
805.
An. Imp. Claudii
Cæsaris 12.

17 From henceforth let no man trouble me for [i] I bear in my body the marks of the Lord Jesus.

18 Brethren, [k] the grace of our Lord Jesus Christ *be* with your spirit. Amen.

¶ Unto the Galatians, written from Rome.

---

[a] Phil. iii. 3, 7, 8.——[b] Or, *whereby.*——[c] Rom. vi. 6; chap. ii. 20.——[d] 1 Cor. vii. 19; chap v. 6; Col. iii. 11.——[e] 2 Cor. v. 17.——[f] Psa. cxxv. 5.——[g] Phil iii. 16

[h] Rom. ii. 29; iv. 12; ix. 6, 7, 8; chap. iii. 7, 9, 29; Phil. iii. 3.——[i] 1 Cor. i. 5; iv. 10; xi. 23; chap. v. 11; Col. i. 24. [k] 2 Tim. iv. 22; Philem. 25.

---

to receive circumcision, that they might glory in their *flesh.* Behold my converts! Thus they gloried, or *boasted*, not that the people were *converted to God*, but that they were *circumcised.*

Verse 14. *But God forbid that I should glory*] Whatever others may do, or whatever they may exult or glory in, God forbid that I should *exult*, except in the cross of our Lord Jesus Christ; in the grand *doctrine*, that justification and salvation are only through Christ crucified, he having made an atonement for the sin of the world by his passion and death. And I glory, also, in the *disgrace* and *persecution* which I experience through my attachment to this crucified Christ.

By whom the world is crucified unto me] Jewish rites and Gentile vanities are equally insipid to me; I know them to be empty and worthless. If Jews and Gentiles despise me, I despise that in which they trust; through Jesus, all are *crucified to me*—their objects of dependence are as vile and execrable to me, as I am to them, in whose sight these things are of great account.

Verse 15. *In Christ Jesus*] Under the dispensation of the Gospel, of which he is head and supreme, *neither circumcision*—nothing that the *Jew* can boast of, nothing that the *Gentile* can call excellent, *availeth any thing*— can in the least contribute to the salvation of the soul.

But a new creature.] Αλλα καινη κτισις· *But a new creation;* not a *new creature* merely, (for this might be restrained to any *new power* or *faculty*,) but a total renewal of the whole man, of all the powers and passions of the soul; and as *creation* could not be effected but by the power of the Almighty, so this change cannot be effected but by the same energy; no circumcision can do this; only the power that made the man at first can *new make him.* See the note on 1 Cor. vii. 19, and on 2 Cor. v. 17.

Verse 16. *As many as walk according to this rule*] Τῳ κανονι τουτῳ· *This canon;* viz. what is laid down in the preceding verses, that redemption is through the sacrifice of Christ; that circumcision and uncircumcision are equally unavailable; and that none can be saved without being *created anew.* This is the *grand canon* or *rule* in Christianity.

Peace be *on them*] Those who act from this con-

viction will have the *peace* and *mercy* of God; for it is in this way that *mercy* is communicated and *peace* obtained.

The Israel of God.] The *true Christians*, called here the *Israel of God*, to distinguish them from *Israel according to the flesh.* See the notes on Rom. ii. 29, and iv. 12.

Verse 17. *From henceforth let no man trouble me*] Put an end to your contentions among yourselves; return to the pure doctrine of the Gospel; abandon those who are leading you astray; separate from the Church those who corrupt and disturb it; and let me be grieved no longer with your defections from the truth.

I bear in my body the marks of the Lord Jesus.] The στιγματα, *stigmata*, of which the apostle speaks here, may be understood as implying the *scars* of the *wounds* which he had *received in the work of the ministry*; and that he had such scars, we may well conceive, when we know that he had been *scourged, stoned*, and maltreated in a variety of ways. The writer could show such *scars* himself, received in the same way. Or, the apostle may allude to the *stigmata* or *marks* with which servants and slaves were often impressed, in order to ascertain whose property they were. A *Burman* servant often has *indelible marks* on his *thighs* and *elsewhere*, which ascertain to whose service he belongs. "Do not trouble me; I bear the marks of my Lord and Master, *Jesus*; I am his, and will remain so. You glory in your *mark of circumcision*; I glory in the *marks which I bear in* my body for the testimony of the Lord; I am an open, professed Christian, and have given full proof of my attachment to the cause of Christianity."

The first sense appears to be the best: "I have suffered already sufficiently; I am suffering still; do not add any more to my afflictions."

Verse 18. *The grace*] Favour, benevolence, and continual influence of the Lord Jesus, *be with your spirit*—may it live in your heart, enlighten and change your souls, and be conspicuous in your life!

Amen.] So let it be; and the prayer which I offer up for you on earth, may it be registered in heaven!

Unto the Galatians, written from Rome.] This, or the major part of it, is wanting in the best and most ancient MSS. *Written from Rome* is wanting in

ACDEFG, and others. *Claudius Antissiodor*, has εγραφη απ' Εφεσου· *Written from Ephesus.* Some add, *by the hands of Paul*, others, *by Titus*. The SYRIAC has, *The end of the Epistle to the Galatians, which was written from the city of Rome.* The ÆTHIOPIC, *To the Galatians.* The COPTIC, *Written from Rome.* The VULGATE, *nothing.* The ARABIC, *Written from the city of Rome by Titus and Luke.*

Little respect is to be paid to these subscriptions. The epistle was written by *Paul himself*, not *Titus, Luke* nor *Tychicus*; and there is no evidence that it was written from *Rome*, but rather from *Corinth* or *Ephesus.* See the *preface,* page 385.

THE great similarity between the Epistle to the Romans and that to the Galatians has been remarked by many; and indeed it is so obvious, that the same mode of interpretation may be safely pursued in the elucidation of both; as not only the great subject, but the phraseology, in many respects, is the same. The design of the apostle is to show that God has called the Gentiles to equal privileges with the Jews, pulling down the partition wall that had separated them and the Gentiles, calling all to believe in Christ Jesus, and forming out of the believers of both people one holy and pure Church, of which, equally, himself was the head; none of either people having any preference to another, except what he might derive from his personal sanctity and superior usefulness. The calling of the Gentiles to this state of salvation was the mystery which had been hidden from all ages, and concerning which the apostle has entered into such a laborious discussion in the Epistle to the Romans; justifying the reprobation as well as the election of the Jews, and vindicating both the justice and mercy of God in the election of the Gentiles. The same subjects are referred to in this epistle, but not in that *detail* of argumentation as in the former. In both, the *national* privileges of the Jews are a frequent subject of consideration; and, as these *national privileges* were intended to point out *spiritual advantages*, the terms which express them are used frequently in both these senses with no change; and it requires an attentive mind, and a proper knowledge of the analogy of faith, to discern when and where they are to be restricted exclusively to one or the other meaning, as well as where the one is intended to shadow forth the other; and where it is used as expressing *what they ought to be*, according to the spirit and tenor of their original calling.

Multitudes of interpreters of different sects and parties have strangely mistaken both epistles, by not attending to these most necessary, and to the unprejudiced, most obvious, distinctions and principles. Expressions which point out national privileges have been used by them to point out those which were spiritual; and merely *temporal* advantages or disadvantages have been used in the sense of *eternal* blessings or miseries. Hence, what has been spoken of the Jews in their *national* capacity has been applied to the Church of God in respect to its future destiny; and thus, out of the temporal election and reprobation of the Jews, the doctrine of the irrespective and eternal election of a small part of mankind, and the unconditional and eternal reprobation of the far greater part of the human race,

has been formed. The contentions produced by these misapprehensions among Christians have been uncharitable and destructive. In snatching at the shadow of religion in a great variety of metaphors and figures, the substance of Christianity has been lost: and the man who endeavours to draw the contending parties to a consistent and rational interpretation of those expressions, by showing the grand nature and design of these epistles, becomes a prey to the zealots of both parties! Where is *truth* in the mean time? It is fallen in the streets, and *equity* is gone backwards; for the most sinister designs and most heterodox opinions have been attributed to those who, regarding the words of God only, have refused to swim with either torrent; and, without even consulting their own peculiar creed, have sought to find out the meaning of the inspired writers, and with simplicity of heart, and purity of conscience, to lay that meaning before mankind.

The *Israelites* were denominated *a peculiar treasure unto God, above all people; a kingdom of priests, and a holy nation*, Exod. xix. 5, 6. *A holy people whom he had chosen to be a special people unto himself, above all the people who were upon the face of the earth*, Deut. vii. 6. This was their *calling*, this was their *profession*, and this was their *denomination*; but how far they fell practically short of this character their history most painfully proves. Yet still they were called a holy people, because called to holiness, (Levit. xi. 44; xix. 2; xx. 7,) and separated from the impure and degrading idolatries of the neighbouring nations.

Under the *New Testament*, all those who believe in Christ Jesus *are called to holiness—to have their fruit unto holiness, that their end may be eternal life;* and hence they are called *saints* or *holy persons.* And the same epithets are applied to *them* as to the *Israelites* of old; they are *lively stones, built up a spiritual house, a holy priesthood, to offer up spiritual sacrifices acceptable to God through Christ*; they are also called a *chosen generation, a royal priesthood, a holy nation, a peculiar people, that should show forth the praises of him who had called them from darkness into his marvellous light*, 1 Pet. ii. 5, 9. All this they were *called to*, all this was their *profession*, and to have all these excellences was their indisputable *privilege.*

As they professed *to be* what God had called them to be, they are often *denominated* by their *profession*; and this denomination is given frequently to those who, in *experience* and *practice*, fall far short of the blessings and privileges of the Gospel. The Church of *Corinth*, which was in many respects the most imperfect, as well as the most impure, of all the apostolic Churches, is nevertheless denominated *the Church of God, sanctified in Christ Jesus, and called to be saints*, 1 Cor. i. 2. That there were many *saints* in the Corinthian Church, and many *sanctified in Christ Jesus* both in *it* and in the Churches of *Galatia*, the slightest perusal of the epistles to those Churches will prove: but that there were many, and in the Galatian Churches the majority, of a *different character*, none can doubt; yet they are all indiscriminately called the *Churches of God, saints, &c.* And, even in those early times, *saint* appears to have been as general an appellative for a person professing faith in Christ Jesus, as the term *Christian* is at the present day, which is given to all who profess the Christian religion; and yet these terms, taken in their *strict* and *proper* sense, signify, a *holy person*, and one who has *the Spirit and mind of Christ*.

In my notes on the *Epistle to the Romans* I have entered at large into a discussion of the subjects to which I have referred in these observations; and, to set the subject in a clear point of view, I have made a copious extract from *Dr. Taylor's Key to that epistle*; and I have stated, that a consistent exposition of that epistle cannot be given but upon that plan. *I am still of the same opinion.* It is by attending to the above *distinctions*, which are most obvious to all unprejudiced persons, that we plainly see that the doctrines of *eternal, unconditional reprobation and election*, and the *impossibility of falling finally from the grace of God*, have no foundation in the Epistle to the Romans. Dr. Taylor has shown that the phrases and expressions on which these doctrines are founded refer to national privileges, and those exclusive advantages which the Jews, as God's peculiar people, enjoyed during the time in which that *peculiarity* was designed to last; and that it is doing violence to the sense in which those expressions are generally used, to apply them to the support of such doctrines. In reference to *this*, I have quoted Dr. Taylor; and those illustrations of his which I have adopted, I have adopted *on this ground*, taking care never to pledge myself to any peculiar or heterodox opinions, by whomsoever held; and, where I thought an expression might be misunderstood, I took care to guard it by a *note* or *observation*.

Now I say that it is *in this sense* I understand the quotations I have made, and in *this sense alone* these quotations *ought* to be understood; and my whole work sufficiently shows that neither Dr. Taylor's nor any person's *peculiar* theological system makes any part of mine; that, on the doctrine of the *fall of man* or *original sin*, the doctrine of the *eternal deity of Jesus Christ*, the doctrine of *justification by faith in the atoning blood*, and the doctrine of the *inspiration and regenerating influence of the Holy Ghost*, I stand on the pure orthodox creed, diametrically opposite to that of the Arians and Socinians. Yet this most distinguishing difference cannot blind me against the excellences I find in any of their works, nor can I meanly borrow from Dr. Taylor, or any other author, without acknowledging my obligation; nor could I suppress a *name*, however obnoxious that might be, as associated with any heterodox system, when I could mention it with *deference* and *respect*. Let this be my apology for quoting Dr. Taylor, and for the frequent use I have made of his industry and learning in my exposition of the Epistle to the Romans. If I have quoted, to illustrate the sacred writings, passages almost innumerable from *Greek* and *Roman heathens*; from *Jewish Talmudists* and *rabbinical* expositors; from the *Koran*; from *Mohammedan* writers, both *Arabic* and *Persian*; and from *Brahminical polytheists*; and these illustrations have been well received by the Christian public; surely I may have liberty to use, in the same way, the works of a very learned man, and a most conscientious believer in the books of Divine revelation, how-

ever erroneous he may appear to be in certain doctrines which I myself deem of vital importance to the creed of an experimental Christian. Let it not be said that, by thus largely quoting from his work, I tacitly recommend an Arian creed, or any part of that system of theology peculiar to him and his party; I no more do so than the Indian matron who, while she gives the *nourishing* farina of the *cassava* to her household, recommends them to drink the *poisonous* juice which she has previously expressed from it.

After this declaration, it will be as *disingenuous* as *unchristian* for either *friends* or *foes* to attribute to me opinions which I never held, or an indifference to those doctrines which (*I speak as a fool*) stand in no work of the kind, in any language, so fully explained, fortified, and demonstrated, as they do in that before the reader. On such a mode of judgment and condemnation as that to which some resort in matters of this kind, I might have long ago been reputed a *Pagan* or a *Mohammedan*, because I have quoted *heathen* writers and the *Koran*. And, by the same mode of argumentation, St. Paul might be convicted of having abandoned his *Jewish creed* and *Christian faith*, because he had quoted the heathen poets *Aratus* and *Cleanthes*. The man is entitled to my pity who refuses to take advantage of useful discoveries in the philosophical researches of Dr. Priestley, because Dr. Priestley, as a theologian, was not sound in the faith.

I have made that use of Dr. Taylor which I have done of others; and have reason to thank God that his *Key*, passing through several wards of a *lock* which appeared to me inextricable, has enabled me to bring forth and exhibit, in a fair and luminous point of view, objects and meanings in the Epistle to the Romans which, without this assistance, I had perhaps been unable to discover.

I may add, farther, that I have made that use of Dr. Taylor which himself has recommended to his readers: some of his censors will perhaps scarcely believe that the *four* following articles constitute the charge with which this learned man commences his theological lectures:—

I. "I do *solemnly charge you*, in the name of the God of truth, and of our Lord Jesus Christ, who is the way, the truth, and the life, and before whose judgment seat you must in no long time appear, that, in all your studies and inquiries of a religious nature, present or future, you do constantly, carefully, impartially, and conscientiously attend to evidence, as it lies in the Holy Scriptures, or in the nature of things and the dictates of reason, cautiously guarding against the sallies of imagination, and the fallacy of ill-grounded *conjecture*.

II. "That you admit, embrace, or assent to no principle or sentiment, by me taught or advanced, *but only so far as it shall appear to you to be justified by proper evidence from revelation*, or the reason of things.

III. "That if at any time hereafter any principle or sentiment by me taught or advanced, or by you admitted or embraced, shall, upon impartial and faithful examination, appear to you to be *dubious*

2

or *false*, you either suspect or totally reject such principle or sentiment.

IV. " That you keep your mind always *open to evidence*; that you labour to banish from your breast all *prejudice, prepossession,* and *party zeal*; that you study to live in peace and love with all your fellow Christians; and that you *steadily assert for yourself,* and *freely allow to others,* the *unalienable rights* of *judgment* and *conscience.*"—Taylor's Scheme of Scripture Divinity, preface, page vi.

Thus I have done with Dr. Taylor's works; and thus I desire every intelligent reader to do with my own.

When I was a *child* I had for a lesson the following words: *Despise not advice, even from the meanest; the cackling of geese once preserved the Roman state.* And since I became a *man,* I have learned wisdom from that saying: *Blessed are ye who sow beside* ALL WATERS; *that send forth* thither *the feet of the* ox *and the* ASS. May He, who is the way, the truth, and the life, lead the reader into all truth, and bring him to life everlasting! Amen.

Finished the correction for a new edition, Dec. 14th, 1831.—A. C.

INTRODUCTION

TO THE

EPISTLE OF PAUL THE APOSTLE

TO THE

EPHESIANS.

IN many points of view the *Epistle to the Ephesians* presents a variety of *difficulties*. A learned man calls it "the most inartificial piece of composition in the universe:" this is not correct if it be intended to convey a censure on the composition itself; for the subject (which is a vindication of the providence and mercy of God, in admitting the Gentiles into his Church, and forming one flock of *them* and the converted Jews, giving them the same privileges which his peculiar people had enjoyed almost exclusively for 2000 years) has led the apostle to make such a variety of references to the *Mosaic economy* and its *peculiarities*, as, without this consideration, will make many parts of the epistle seem obscure to most readers; and this obscurity may be very improperly laid to the charge of inartificial composition: good judges, however, have allowed it to be one of the most sublime compositions of the kind that ever came from the pen of man. This was the opinion of *Grotius*.

The subject in this and the Epistle to the Colossians is certainly the same; and as it is supposed that they were written *about the same time*, it is natural to expect a similarity of expression. This subject, and others connected with these epistles, Dr. Paley has discussed with his usual sagacity; the substance of whose reasonings I beg leave to present to the reader.

SECTION I.

This epistle and the Epistle to the Colossians appear to have been transmitted to their respective Churches by the same messenger: "But that ye also may know my affairs, and how I do, Tychicus, a beloved brother and faithful minister in the Lord, shall make known to you all things; whom I have sent unto you for the same purpose, that ye might know our affairs, and that he might comfort your hearts;" Eph. vi. 21, 22. This text, if it do not expressly declare, clearly (I think) intimates, that the letter was sent by Tychicus. The words made use of in the Epistle to the Colossians are very similar to these, and afford the same implication that Tychicus, in conjunction with Onesimus, was the bearer of the letter to that Church: "All my state shall Tychicus declare unto you, who is a beloved brother, and a faithful minister and fellow servant in the Lord; whom I have sent unto you for the same purpose, that he might know your estate, and comfort your hearts; with Onesimus, a faithful and beloved brother, who is one of you. They shall make known unto you all things which are done here;" Col. iv. 7–9. Both epistles represent the writer as under imprisonment for the Gospel, and both treat of the same general subject. The Epistle therefore to the Ephesians and the Epistle to the Colossians import to be two letters written by the same person, at or nearly at the same time, and upon the same subject, and to have been sent by the same messenger. Now, every thing in the sentiments, order, and diction of the two writings, corresponds with what might be expected from this circumstance of identity or cognation in their original. The leading doctrine of both epistles is the union of Jews and Gentiles under the Christian dispensation; and that doctrine in both is established by the same arguments, or, more properly speaking, illustrated by the same similitudes: "one head," "one body," "one new man," "one temple," are in both epistles the figures under which the society of believers in Christ, and their common relation to him as such, is represented. The ancient, and, as had been thought, the indelible distinction between Jew and Gentile, in both epistles, is declared to be "now abolished by his cross." Beside this consent in the general tenor of the two epistles, and in the run also and warmth of thought with which they are composed, we may naturally expect, in letters produced under the circumstances in which these appear to have been written, a closer resemblance of style and diction than between other letters of the same person but of distant dates, or between letters adapted to different occasions. In particular, we may look for many of the same expressions, and sometimes for whole sentences being alike; since such expressions and sentences would be repeated in the second letter (whichever that was) as yet fresh in the author's mind, from the writing of the first. This repetition occurs in the following examples :—

Eph. i. 7 : " In whom we have redemption through his blood, the forgiveness of sins."

Col. i. 14 : " In whom we have redemption through his blood, the forgiveness of sins."

Besides the sameness of the words, it is farther remarkable that the sentence is, in both places, preceded by the same introductory idea. In the Epistle to the Ephesians it is the " Beloved," (ηγαπημενῳ,) in that to the Colossians it is " his dear Son," (Υιου της αγαπης αυτου, the Son of his love,) " in whom we have redemption." The sentence appears to have been suggested to the mind of the writer, by the idea which had accompanied it before.

Eph. i. 10 : " All things, both which are in heaven and which are on earth, even in him."

Col. i. 20 : " All things by him, whether they be things in earth, or things in heaven."

This quotation is the more observable, because the connecting of things in earth with things in heaven is a very singular sentiment, and found no where else but in these two epistles. The words also are introduced and followed by a train of thought nearly alike. They are introduced by describing the union which Christ had effected ; and they are followed by telling the Gentile Churches that they were incorporated into it.

Eph. iii. 2 : " The dispensation of the grace of God, which is given me to you-ward."

Col. i. 25 : " The dispensation of God, which is given to me for you."

Of these sentences it may likewise be observed, that the accompanying ideas are similar. In both places they are immediately preceded by the mention of his present sufferings ; in both places they are immediately followed by the mention of the mystery which was the great subject of his preaching.

Eph. v. 19 : " In psalms, and hymns, and spiritual songs, singing and making melody in your heart to the Lord."

Col. iii. 16 : " In psalms, and hymns, and spiritual songs, singing with grace in your hearts to the Lord."

Eph. vi. 22 : " Whom I have sent unto you for the same purpose, that ye might know our affairs, and that he might comfort your hearts."

Col. iv. 8 : " Whom I have sent unto you for the same purpose, that he might know your estate, and comfort your hearts."

In these examples we do not perceive a cento of phrases gathered from one composition and strung together in the other ; but the occasional occurrence of the same expression to a mind a second time revolving the same ideas.

2. Whoever writes two letters, or two discourses, nearly upon the same subject, and at no great distance of time, but without any express recollection of what he had written before, will find himself repeating some sentences in the very order of the words in which he had already used them ; but he will more frequently find himself employing some principal terms, with the order inadvertently changed, or with the order disturbed by the intermixture of other words and phrases expressive of ideas rising up at the time ; or in many instances repeating not single words, nor yet whole sentences, but parts and fragments of sentences. Of all these varieties, the examination of these two epistles will furnish plain examples ; and I should rely upon this class of instances more than upon the last ; because, although an impostor might transcribe into a forgery entire sentences and phrases, yet the dislocation of words, the partial recollection of phrases and sentences, the intermixture of new terms and new ideas with terms and ideas before used, which will appear in the examples that follow, and which are the natural properties of writings produced under the circumstances in which these epistles are represented to have been composed, would not, I think, have occurred to the invention of a forger ; nor, if they had occurred, would they have been so easily executed. This studied variation was a refinement in forgery which I believe did not exist ; or if we can suppose it to have been practised in the instances adduced below, why, it may be asked, was not the same art exercised upon those which we have collected in the preceding class ?

Eph. i. 19–ii. 5 : " Towards us who believe according to the working of his mighty power, which he wrought in Christ when he raised him from the dead ; (and set him at his own right hand in the heavenly places, far above all principality, and power, and might, and dominion, and every name that is named, not only in this world, but in that which is to come. And hath put all things under his feet ; and gave him to be the head over all things to the Church, which is his body, the fulness of him that filleth all in all ;) and you hath he quickened, who were dead in trespasses and sins, (wherein in time past ye walked according to the course of this world, according to the prince of the power of the air, the spirit that now worketh in the children of disobedience ; among whom also we all had our conversation in times past, in the lusts of our flesh, fulfilling the desires of the flesh and of the mind, and were by nature the children of wrath, even as others. But God, who is rich in mercy, for his great love wherewith he loved us,) even when we were dead in sins, hath quickened us together with Christ."

Col. ii. 12, 13 : " Through the faith of the operation of God, who hath raised him from the dead : and you being dead in your sins and the uncircumcision of the flesh, hath he quickened together with him."

Out of the long quotation from the Ephesians, take away the parentheses, and you have left a sentence almost in terms the same as the short quotation from the Colossians. The resemblance is more visible in the original than in our translation ; for what is rendered in one place " the working," and in another " the operation," is the same Greek term, ενεργεια : in one place it is τους πιστευοντας κατα την ενεργειαν ; in the other δια της πιστεως της ενεργειας. Here, therefore, we have the same sentiment, and nearly in the same words ;

2

but, in the Ephesians, twice broken or interrupted by incidental thoughts, which St. Paul, as his manner was enlarges upon by the way, and then returns to the thread of his discourse. It is interrupted the first time by a view which breaks in upon his mind of the exaltation of Christ, and the second time by a description of heathen depravity. I have only to remark, that Griesbach, in his very accurate edition, gives the parentheses very nearly in the same manner in which they are here placed; and that without any respect to the comparison which we are proposing.

Eph. iv. 2–4 : " With all lowliness and meekness, with long-suffering, forbearing one another in love ; endeavouring to keep the unity of the Spirit in the bond of peace. There is one body and one Spirit, even as ye are called in one hope of your calling."

Col. iii. 12–15 : " Put on therefore, as the elect of God, holy and beloved, bowels of mercies, kindness, humbleness of mind, meekness, long-suffering, forbearing one another and forgiving one another, if any man have a quarrel against any : even as Christ forgave you, so also do ye : and, above all these things, put on charity, which is the bond of perfectness ; and let the peace of God rule in your hearts, to the which also ye are called in one body."

In these two quotations the words ταπεινοφροσυνη, πρᾳοτης, μακροθυμια, ανεχομενοι αλληλων, lowliness, meekness, long-suffering, forbearing one another, occur in exactly the same order : αγαπη, love, is also found in both, but in a different connection ; συνδεσμος της ειρηνης, the bond of peace, answers to συνδεσμος της τελειοτητος, the bond of perfectness ; εκληθητε εν ενι σωματι, called into one spirit, to εν σωμα καθως και εκληθητε εν μια ελπιδι, one body, even as ye are called into one hope ; yet is this similitude found in the midst of sentences otherwise very different.

Eph. iv. 16 : " From whom the whole body fitly joined together and compacted by that which every joint supplieth, according to the effectual working in the measure of every part, maketh increase of the body."

Col. ii. 19 : " From which all the body by joints and bands having nourishment ministered and knit together, increaseth with the increase of God."

In these quotations are read εξ ου παν το σωμα συμβιβαζομενον, from whom the whole body fitly joined together, in both places ; επιχορηγουμενον answering to επιχορηγιας : δια των αφων to δια πασης αφης : αυξει την αυξησιν to ποιειται την αυξησιν : and yet the sentences are considerably diversified in other parts.

Eph. iv. 32 : " And be kind one to another, tender-hearted, forgiving one another ; even as God, for Christ's sake, hath forgiven you."

Col. iii. 13 : " Forbearing one another, and forgiving one another, if any man have a quarrel against any : even as Christ forgave you, so also do ye."

Here we have " forgiving one another, even as God, for Christ's sake (εν Χριστω) hath forgiven you," in the first quotation, substantially repeated in the second. But in the second the sentence is broken by the interposition of a new clause, " If any man have a quarrel against any ;" and the latter part is a little varied ; instead of " God in Christ," it is " Christ hath forgiven you."

Eph. iv. 22–24 : " That ye put off, concerning the former conversation, the old man, which is corrupt according to the deceitful lusts, and be renewed in the spirit of your mind ; and that ye put on the new man, which after God is created in righteousness and true holiness."

Col. iii. 9, 10 : " Seeing that ye have put off the old man with his deeds, and have put on the new man, which is renewed in knowledge, after the image of him that created him."

In these quotations, " putting off the old man, and putting on the new," appears in both. The idea is farther explained by calling it a renewal ; in the one, " renewed in the spirit of your mind," in the other, " renewed in knowledge." In both, the new man is said to be formed according to the same model ; in the one, he is " after God created in righteousness and true holiness ;" in the other, " he is renewed after the image of him who created him." In a word, it is the same person writing upon a kindred subject, with the terms and ideas which he had before employed still floating in his memory.

In these comparisons we often perceive the reason why the writer, though expressing the same idea, uses a different term ; namely, because the term before used is employed in the sentence under a different form : thus, in the quotations under our eye, the new man is καινος ανθρωπος in the Ephesians, and τον νεον in the Colossians ; but then it is because τον καινον is used in the next word, ανακαινουμενον, being renewed.

Eph. v. 6–8 : " *Because of these things cometh the wrath of God upon the children of disobedience·:* be not ye therefore partakers with them ; for ye were sometimes darkness, but now are ye light in the Lord : walk as children of light."

Col. iii. 6–8 : " *For which things' sake the wrath of God cometh on the children of disobedience ;* in the which ye also walked some time, when ye lived in them. But now ye also put off all these."

These verses afford a specimen of that *partial* resemblance which is only to be met with when no imitation is designed, when no studied recollection is employed ; but when the mind, exercised upon the same subject, is left to the spontaneous return of such terms and phrases as, having been used before, may happen to present themselves again. The sentiment of both passages is throughout alike ; half of that sentiment, the denunciation of God's wrath, is expressed in identical words ; the other half, viz. the admonition to quit their former conversation, in words entirely different.

Eph. v. 15, 16 : " See then that ye walk circumspectly ; not as fools, but as wise, redeeming the time."

Col. iv. 5 · " Walk in wisdom towards them that are without, redeeming the time."

This is another example of that mixture which we remarked of sameness and variety in the language of one writer. "Redeeming the time," (εξαγοραζομενοι τον καιρον,) is a literal repetition. "Walk not as fools, but as wise," (περιπατειτε μη ως ασοφοι, αλλ᾽ ως σοφοι,) answers exactly in sense, and nearly in terms, to "walk in wisdom," (εν σοφια περιπατειτε.) Περιπατειτε ακριβως is a very different phrase, but is intended to convey precisely the same idea as περιπατειτε προς τους εξω. Ακριβως is not well rendered "circumspectly." It means what in modern speech we should call "correctly ;" and when we advise a person to behave "correctly," our advice is always given with a reference "to the opinion of others," προς τους εξω. "Walk correctly, redeeming the time," i. e. suiting yourselves to the difficulty and ticklishness of the times in which we live, "because the days are evil."

Eph. vi. 19, 20 : "And (praying) for me, that utterance may be given unto me, that I may open my mouth boldly, to make known the mystery of the Gospel, for which I am an ambassador in bonds, that therein I may speak boldly, as I ought to speak."

Col. iv. 3, 4 : "Withal praying also for us, that God would open unto us a door of utterance to speak the mystery of Christ, for which I am also in bonds, that I may make it manifest as I ought to speak."

In these quotations the phrase, "as I ought to speak," (ως δει με λαλησαι,) the words "utterance," (λογος,) "a mystery," (μυστηριον,) "open," (ανοιξη and εν ανοιξει,) are the same. "To make known the mystery of the Gospel," (γνωρισαι το μυστηριον,) answers to "make it manifest ;" (ινα φανερωσω αυτο ;) "for which I am an ambassador in bonds," (υπερ ου πρεσβευω εν αλυσει,) to "for which I am also in bonds," (δι᾽ ὁ και δεδεμαι.)

Eph. v. 22 : "*Wives, submit yourselves to your own husbands, as unto the Lord;* for the husband is the head of the wife, even as Christ is the head of the Church ; and he is the Saviour of the body. Therefore, as the Church is subject unto Christ, so let the wives be to their own husbands in every thing. *Husbands, love your wives,* even as Christ also loved the Church, and gave himself for it, that he might sanctify and cleanse it with the washing of water by the word ; that he might present it to himself a glorious Church, not having spot, or wrinkle, or any such thing ; but that it should be holy and without blemish. So ought men to love their wives as their own bodies. He that loveth his wife, loveth himself ; for no man ever yet hated his own flesh, but nourisheth and cherisheth it, even as the Lord the Church ; for we are members of his body, of his flesh and of his bones. For this cause shall a man leave his father and his mother, and be joined unto his wife, and they two shall be one flesh. This is a great mystery ; but I speak concerning Christ and the Church. Nevertheless, let every one of you in particular so love his wife even as himself ; and the wife see that she reverence her husband. *Children, obey your parents in the Lord, for this is right.* Honour thy father and thy mother, (which is the first commandment with promise,) that it may be well with thee, and that thou mayest live long on the earth. *And ye fathers, provoke not your children to wrath*, but bring them up in the nurture and admonition of the Lord. *Servants, be obedient to them that are your masters according to the flesh, with fear and trembling, in singleness of your heart, as unto Christ ; not with eye-service, as men-pleasers, but as the servants of Christ, doing the will of God from the heart ; with good will doing service, as to the Lord, and not to men; knowing that whatsoever good thing any man doeth, the same shall he receive of the Lord, whether he be bond or free.* And, ye masters, do the same things unto them, forbearing threatening ; *knowing that your Master also is in heaven*, neither is there respect of persons with him."

Col. iii. 18 : "Wives, submit yourselves unto your own husbands, as it is fit in the Lord. Husbands, love your wives, and be not bitter against them. Children, obey your parents in all things, for this is well pleasing unto the Lord. Fathers, provoke not your children to anger, lest they be discouraged. Servants, obey in all things your masters according to the flesh ; not with eye-service, as men-pleasers, but in singleness of heart, fearing God : and whatever ye do, do it heartily, as to the Lord, and not unto men, knowing that of the Lord ye shall receive the reward of the inheritance ; for ye serve the Lord Christ. But he that doeth wrong shall receive for the wrong which he hath done ; and there is no respect of persons. Masters, give unto your servants that which is just and equal, knowing that ye also have a Master in heaven."

The passages marked by Italics in the quotation from the Ephesians bear a strict resemblance, not only in signification but in terms, to the quotation from the Colossians. Both the words and the order of the words are in many clauses a duplicate of one another. In the Epistle to the Colossians these passages are laid together ; in that to the Ephesians, they are divided by intermediate matter, especially by a long digressive allusion to the mysterious union between Christ and his Church ; which possessing, as Mr. Locke hath well observed, the mind of the apostle, from being an incidental thought grows up into the principal subject. The affinity between these two passages, in signification, in terms, and in the order of the words, is closer than can be pointed out between any parts of any two epistles in the volume.

If the reader would see how the same subject is treated by a different hand, and how distinguishable it is from the production of the same pen, let him turn to the second and third chapters of the First Epistle of St. Peter. The duties of servants, of wives, and of husbands, are enlarged upon in that epistle, as they are in the Epistle to the Ephesians ; but the subjects both occur in a different order, and the train of sentiment subjoined to each is totally unlike.

3. In two letters issuing from the same person, nearly at the same time, and upon the same general occasion, we may expect to trace the influence of association in the order in which the topics follow one another. Certain ideas universally or usually suggest others. Here the order is what we call natural, and from such an order nothing can be concluded. But when the order is arbitrary, yet alike, the concurrence indicates the effect of that principle, by which ideas, which have been once joined, commonly revisit the thoughts together. The epistles under consideration furnish the two following remarkable instances of this species of agreement.

2

Eph. iv. 24 : "And that ye put on the new man, which after God is created in righteousness and true holiness : wherefore putting away lying, speak every man truth with his neighbour, for we are members one of another."

Col. iii. 9 : "Lie not one to another; seeing that ye have put off the old man with his deeds; and have put on the new man, which is renewed in knowledge."

The vice of "lying," or a correction of that vice, does not seem to bear any nearer relation to the "putting on the new man," than a reformation in any other article of morals. Yet these two ideas we see stand in both epistles in immediate connection.

Eph. v. 20, 21, 22 : "Giving thanks always for all things unto God and the Father, in the name of our Lord Jesus Christ ; submitting yourselves one to another in the fear of God. Wives, submit yourselves unto your own husbands, as unto the Lord."

Col. iii. 17 : "Whatsoever ye do, in word or deed, do all in the name of the Lord Jesus, giving thanks to God and the Father by him. Wives, submit yourselves unto your own husbands, as it is fit in the Lord."

In both these passages submission follows giving of thanks, without any similitude in the ideas which should account for the transition.

It is not necessary to pursue the comparison between the two epistles farther. The argument which results from it stands thus : No two other epistles contain a circumstance which indicates that they were written at the same, or nearly at the same, time. No two other epistles exhibit so many marks of correspondency and resemblance. If the original which we ascribe to these two epistles be the true one, that is, if they were both really written by St. Paul, and both sent to their respective destination by the same messenger, the similitude is, in all points, what should be expected to take place. If they were forgeries, then the mention of Tychicus in both epistles, and in a manner which shows that he either carried or accompanied both epistles, was inserted for the purpose of accounting for their similitude : or else, the structure of the epistles was designedly adapted to the circumstance : or lastly, the conformity between the contents of the forgeries, and what is thus directly intimated concerning their date, was only a happy accident. Not one of these three suppositions will gain credit with a reader who peruses the epistles with attention, and who reviews the several examples we have pointed out, and the observations with which they were accompanied.

SECTION II.

There is such a thing as a peculiar word or phrase cleaving, as it were, to the memory of a writer or speaker, and presenting itself to his utterance at every turn. When we observe this we call it a *cant* word, or a *cant* phrase. It is a natural effect of habit, and would appear more frequently than it does, had not the rules of good writing taught the ear to be offended with the iteration of the same sound, and oftentimes caused us to reject, on that account, the word which offered itself first to our recollection. With a writer who, like St. Paul, either knew not these rules, or disregarded them, such words will not be avoided. The truth is, an example of this kind runs through several of his epistles, and in the epistle before us *abounds*; and that is in the word *riches*, ($\pi\lambda o \upsilon \tau o \varsigma$,) used metaphorically as an augmentative of the idea to which it happens to be subjoined. Thus " the *riches* of his glory," " his *riches* in glory," " *riches* of the glory of his inheritance," " *riches* of the glory of this mystery," Rom. ix. 23 ; Eph. iii. 16 ; Eph. i. 18 ; Col. i. 27 ; " *riches* of his grace," twice in the Ephesians, chap. i. 7, and ii. 7 ; " *riches* of the full assurance of understanding," Col. ii. 2 ; " *riches* of his goodness," Rom. ii. 4 ; " *riches* of the wisdom of God," Rom. xi. 33 ; " *riches* of Christ," Eph. iii. 8. In a like sense the adjective, Rom. x. 12, " *Rich* unto all that call upon him," Eph. ii. 4, " *Rich* in mercy;" 1 Tim. vi. 18, " *Rich* in good works." Also the adverb Col. iii. 16 : " Let the word of Christ dwell in you *richly*." This figurative use of the word, though so familiar to St. Paul, does not occur in any part of the New Testament, except once in the Epistle of St. James, ii. 5 : " Hath not God chosen the *poor* of this world *rich* in faith?" where it is manifestly suggested by the antithesis. I propose the frequent, yet seemingly unaffected, use of this phrase in the epistle before us, as one internal mark of its genuineness.

SECTION III.

There is another singularity in St. Paul's style which, wherever it is found, may be deemed a badge of authenticity ; because, if it were noticed, it would not, I think, be imitated, inasmuch as it almost always produces embarrassment and interruption in the reasoning. This singularity is a species of digression which may probably, I think, be denominated *going off at a word*. It is turning aside from the subject upon the occurrence of some particular word, forsaking the train of thought then in hand, and entering upon a parenthetic sentence in which that word is the prevailing term. I shall lay before the reader some examples of this, collected from the other epistles, and then propose two examples of it which are found in the Epistle to the Ephesians. 2 Cor. ii. 14, at the word *savour* : " Now thanks be unto God, which always causeth us to triumph in Christ, and maketh manifest the *savour* of his knowledge by us in every place. (For we are unto God a sweet *savour* of Christ, in them that are saved, and in them that perish ; to the one we are the *savour* of death unto death, and to the other the *savour* of life unto life ; and who is sufficient for these things ?) For we are not as many, which corrupt the word of God : but as of sincerity, but as of God, in the sight of God speak we in Christ." Again, 2 Cor. iii. 1, at the word *epistle* : " Need we, as some others,

2   425

epistles of commendation to you, or of commendation from you ? (Ye are our *epistle*, written in our hearts known and read of all men ; forasmuch as ye are manifestly declared to be the *epistle* of Christ, ministered by us, written not with ink, but with the Spirit of the living God ; not in tables of stone, but in fleshly tables of the heart.") The position of the words in the original shows, more strongly than in the translation, that it was the occurrence of the word επιστολη which gave birth to the sentence as follows, 2 Cor. iii. 1 : Ει μη χρηζομεν, ως τινες, συστατικων επιστολων προς υμας, η εξ υμων συστατικων ; η επιστολη ημων υμεις εστε, εγγεγραμμενη εν ταις καρδιαις ημων, γινωσκομενη και αναγινωσκομενη υπο παντων ανθρωπων· φανερουμενοι ότι εστε επιστολη Χριστου διακονηθεισα ύφ' ημων, εγγεγραμενη ου μελανι, αλλα πνευματι Θεου ζωντος, ουκ εν πλαξι λιθιναις, αλλ' εν πλαξι καρδιας σαρκιναις.

Again, 2 Cor. iii. 12, &c., at the word *veil:* " Seeing then that we have such hope, we use great plainness of speech : and not as Moses, which put a *veil* over his face, that the children of Israel could not steadfastly look to the end of that which is abolished. But their minds were blinded ; for until this day remaineth the same *veil* untaken away in the reading of the Old Testament, which *veil* is done away in Christ ; but even unto this day, when Moses is read, the *veil* is upon their heart ; nevertheless, when it shall turn to the Lord, the *veil* shall be taken away, (now the Lord is that Spirit ; and where the Spirit of the Lord is, there is liberty.) But we all, with open face beholding as in a glass the glory of the Lord, are changed into the same image, from glory to glory, even as by the Spirit of the Lord. Therefore, seeing we have this ministry, as we have received mercy, we faint not."

Who sees not that this whole allegory of the *veil* arises entirely out of the occurrence of the word, in telling us that " Moses put a *veil* over his face," and that it drew the apostle away from the proper subject of his discourse, the dignity of the office in which he was engaged ? which subject he fetches up again almost in the words with which he had left it : " Therefore, seeing we have this ministry, as we have received mercy, we faint not." The sentence which he had before been going on with, and in which he had been interrupted by the *veil*, was, " Seeing then that we nave such hope, we use great plainness of speech."

In the Epistle to the Ephesians the reader will remark two instances in which the same habit of composition obtains ; he will recognize the same pen. One he will find, chap. iv. 8–11, at the word *ascended:* " Wherefore he saith, When he *ascended* up on high, he led captivity captive, and gave gifts unto men. (Now that he *ascended*, what is it but that he also descended first into the lower parts of the earth ? He that descended is the same also that *ascended* up far above all heavens, that he might fill all things.) And he gave some, apostles," &c.

The other appears, chap. v. 12–15, at the word *light:* " For it is a shame even to speak of those things which are done of them in secret : but all things that are reproved are made manifest by the *light;* (for whatsoever doth make manifest, is *light;* wherefore he saith, Awake, thou that sleepest, and arise from the dead, and Christ shall give thee *light;)* see then that ye walk circumspectly:"

Section IV.

As our epistle purports to have been written during St. Paul's imprisonment at Rome, which lies beyond the period to which the Acts of the Apostles brings up his history, and as we have seen and acknowledged that the epistle contains no reference to any transaction at Ephesus during the apostle's residence in that city, we cannot expect that it should supply many marks of agreement with the narrative. One coincidence, however, occurs, and a coincidence of that minute and less obvious kind, which, as hath been repeatedly observed, is of all others the most to be relied upon.

Chap. vi. 19, 20, we read, " Praying for me, that I may open my mouth boldly, to make known the mystery of the Gospel, for which I am an ambassador in bonds." " *In bonds,*" εν άλυσει, in a chain. In the twenty-eighth chapter of the Acts we are informed that Paul, after his arrival at Rome, was suffered to dwell by himself with a soldier that kept him. Dr. Lardner has shown that this mode of custody was in use amongst the Romans, and that whenever it was adopted, the prisoner was bound to the soldier by a single chain : in reference to which St. Paul, in the twentieth verse of this chapter, tells the Jews, whom he had assembled, " For this cause, therefore, have I called for you, to see you and to speak with you, because that for the hope of Israel I am bound *with this chain,*" την άλυσιν ταυτην περικειμαι. It is in exact conformity, therefore, with the truth of St. Paul's situation at the time, that he declares of himself in the epistle, πρεσβευω εν άλυσει. And the exactness is the more remarkable, as άλυσις (a chain) is no where used in the singular number to express any other kind of custody. When the prisoner's hands or feet were bound together, the word was δεσμοι, (bonds ;) Acts xxvi. 29. When the prisoner was confined between two soldiers, as in the case of Peter, Acts xii. 6, two chains were employed ; and it is said, upon his miraculous deliverance, that the " chains (άλυσεις, in the plural) fell from his hands."

If it can be suspected that the writer of the present epistle, who in no other particular appears to have availed himself of the information concerning St. Paul delivered in the Acts, had, in this verse, borrowed the word which he read in that book, and had adapted his expression to what he found there recorded of St. Paul's treatment at Rome ; in short, that the coincidence here noted was effected by craft and design, I think it a strong reply, to remark that in the parallel passage of the Epistle to the Colossians the same allusion is not preserved ; the words there are, " praying also for us, that God would open unto us a door of utterance to speak the mystery of Christ, for which *I am also in bonds,*" δι' ό και δεδεμαι. After what has been shown in a preceding section, there can be little doubt that these two epistles were written by the same person.

2

E P H E S I A N S.

EPHESUS was a city of *Ionia*, in *Asia Minor*, and once the metropolis of that part of the world. The ancient city was situated at the mouth of the river *Cayster*, on the shore of the *Ægean Sea*, about 50 miles south of *Smyrna*. The Ephesus in which St. Paul founded a Church, and which for a time flourished gloriously, was not the ancient Ephesus; for that was destroyed, and a new city of the same name was built by Lysimachus.

This most famous of all the Asiatic cities is now a miserable *village*, composed of mean huts formed out of the ruins of its once magnificent structures; and these huts are now the residence of about forty or fifty Turkish families, without a single *Christian* among them! For other particulars see the note on Acts xviii. 19.

It is, however, a doubt with many learned men, whether *this* epistle was sent to the Church at *Ephesus*. They think that the proper direction is, The Epistle of St. Paul to the *Laodiceans;* and suppose it to be the same which the apostle mentions, Col. iv. 16: "When this epistle is read among you, cause that it be read also in the Church of the Laodiceans; and that ye likewise read the epistle from Laodicea." Dr. Paley's arguments in the affirmative are entitled to much regard.

"Although it does not appear to have ever been disputed that the epistle before us was written by St. Paul, yet it is well known that a doubt has long been entertained concerning the persons to whom it was addressed. The question is founded partly in some ambiguity in the external evidence. Marcion, a heretic of the second century, as quoted by Tertullian, a father in the beginning of the third, calls it, The Epistle to the Laodiceans. From what we know of Marcion, his judgment is little to be relied upon; nor is it perfectly clear that Marcion was rightly understood by Tertullian. If, however, Marcion be brought to prove that some copies in his time gave εν Λαοδικεια in the superscription, his testimony, if it be truly interpreted, is not diminished by his heresy; for, as Grotius observes, '*cur in ea re mentiretur nihil erat causæ.*' The name εν Εφεσω, *in Ephesus,* in the first verse, upon which word singly depends the proof that the epistle was written to the Ephesians, is not read in all the manuscripts now extant. I admit, however, that the external evidence preponderates with a manifest excess on the side of the received reading. The objection therefore principally arises from the contents of the epistle itself, which, in many respects militate with the supposition that it was written to the Church of Ephesus. According to the history, St. Paul had passed two whole years at Ephesus, Acts xix. 10. And in this point, viz. of St. Paul having preached for a considerable length of time at Ephesus, the history is confirmed by the two epistles to the Corinthians, and by the two epistles to Timothy : 'I will tarry at *Ephesus* until pentecost;' 1 Cor. xvi. 8. 'We would not have you ignorant of our trouble which came to us in *Asia;*' 2 Cor. i. 8. 'As I besought thee to abide still at *Ephesus,* when I went into Macedonia;' 1 Tim. i. 3. 'And in how many things he ministered to me at *Ephesus* thou knowest well;' 2 Tim. i. 18. I adduce these testimonies because, had it been a competition of credit between the history and the epistle, I should have thought myself bound to have preferred the epistle. Now, every epistle which St. Paul wrote to Churches which he himself had founded, or which he had visited, abounds with references and appeals to what had passed during the time that he was present amongst them; whereas there is not a text in the Epistle to the Ephesians from which we can collect that he had ever been at Ephesus at all. The two epistles to the Corinthians, the Epistle to the Galatians, the Epistle to the Philippians, and the two Epistles to the Thessalonians, are of this class; and they are full of allusions to the apostle's history, his reception, and his conduct whilst amongst them; the total want of which in the epistle before us is very difficult to account for, if it was in truth written to the Church of Ephesus, in which city he had resided for so long a time. This is the first and strongest objection. But farther, the Epistle to the Colossians was addressed to a Church in which St. Paul had never been. This we infer from

2

the first verse of the second chapter : 'For I would that ye knew what great conflict I have for you and for them at Laodicea, and for as many as have not seen my face in the flesh.' There could be no propriety in thus joining the Colossians and Laodiceans with those 'who had not seen his face in the flesh,' if they did not also belong to the same description. Now, his address to the Colossians, whom he had not visited, is precisely the same as his address to the Christians to whom he wrote in the epistle which we are now considering : 'We give thanks to God and the Father of our Lord Jesus Christ, praying always for you, *since we heard of your faith* in Christ Jesus, and of the love which ye have to all the saints ;' Col. i. 3. Thus he speaks to the Christians, in the epistle before us, as follows : 'Wherefore I also, *after I heard of your faith* in the Lord Jesus, and love unto all the saints, cease not to give thanks for you in my prayers ;' chap. i. 15. The terms of this address are observable. The words, 'having *heard* of your faith and love,' are the very words, we see, which he uses towards strangers ; and it is not probable that he should employ the same in accosting a Church in which he had long exercised his ministry, and whose 'faith and love' he must have personally known. The Epistle to the Romans was written before St. Paul had been at Rome ; and his address to them runs in the same strain with that just now quoted : 'I thank my God, through Jesus Christ, for you all, that your faith is *spoken* of throughout the whole world ;' Rom. i. 8. Let us now see what was the form in which our apostle was accustomed to introduce his epistles, when he wrote to those with whom he was already acquainted. To the Corinthians it was this : 'I thank my God always on your behalf, for the grace of God which is given you by Christ Jesus ;' 1 Cor. i. 4. To the Philippians : 'I thank my God upon every remembrance of you ;' Phil. i. 3. To the Thessalonians : 'We give thanks to God always for you all, making mention of you in our prayers, remembering without ceasing your work of faith and labour of love ;' 1 Thess. i. 3. To Timothy : 'I thank God, whom I serve from my forefathers with a pure conscience, that without ceasing I have remembrance of thee in my prayers night and day ;' 2 Tim. i. 3. In these quotations it is usually his *remembrance*, and never his *hearing* of them, which he makes the subject of his thankfulness to God.

" As great difficulties stand in the way, supposing the epistle before us to have been written to the Church of Ephesus ; so I think it probable that it is actually the epistle to the Laodiceans, referred to in the fourth chapter of the Epistle to the Colossians. The text which contains that reference is this : 'When this epistle is read among you, cause that it be read also in the Church of the Laodiceans, and that ye likewise read the epistle from Laodicea ;' chap. iv. 16. The 'epistle *from* Laodicea' was an epistle sent by St. Paul to that Church, and by them transmitted to Colosse. The two Churches were mutually to communicate the epistles they had received. This is the way in which the direction is explained by the greater part of commentators, and is the most probable sense that can be given to it. It is also probable that the epistle alluded to was an epistle which had been received by the Church of Laodicea *lately*. It appears, then, with a considerable degree of evidence, that there existed an epistle of St. Paul nearly of the same date with the Epistle to the Colossians, and an epistle directed to a Church (for such the Church of Laodicea was) in which St. Paul had never been. What has been observed concerning the epistle before us, shows that it answers perfectly to that character.

" Nor does the mistake seem very difficult to account for. Whoever inspects the map of Asia Minor will see, that a person proceeding from Rome to Laodicea would probably land at Ephesus, as the nearest frequented seaport in that direction. Might not Tychicus, then, in passing through Ephesus, communicate to the Christians of that place the letter with which he was charged ? And might not copies of that letter be multiplied and preserved at Ephesus ? Might not some of the copies drop the words of designation εν τη Λαοδικεια, which it was of no consequence to an Ephesian to retain ? Might not copies of the letter come out into the Christian Church at large from Ephesus ; and might not this give occasion to a belief that the letter was written to that Church ? And, lastly, might not this belief produce the error which we suppose to have crept into the inscription ?

" And it is remarkable that there seem to have been some ancient copies without the words of designation, either the words *in Ephesus*, or the words *in Laodicea*. St. Basil, a writer of the fourth century, speaking of the present epistle, has this very singular passage : 'And writing to the Ephesians, as truly united to him who is through knowledge, he (Paul) calleth them in a peculiar sense *such who are* ; saying, *to the saints who are and* (or *even*) *the faithful in Christ Jesus ;* for so those before us have transmitted it, and we have found it in ancient copies.' Dr. Mill interprets (and, notwithstanding some objections that have been made to him, in my opinion, rightly interprets) these words of Basil, as declaring that this father had seen certain copies of the epistle in which the words 'in Ephesus' were wanting. And the passage, I think, must be considered as Basil's fanciful way of explaining what was really a corrupt and defective reading ; for I do not believe it possible for the author of the epistle could have originally written αγιοις τοις ουσιν, without any name of place to follow it."

It must be allowed that the arguments of Dr. Paley, the sum of which may be found in *Wetstein*, that this is the epistle to the *Laodiceans*, are both plausible and strong ; and yet almost the whole of antiquity, with the exceptions which those learned men mention, is in favour of the epistle being sent originally to the Church at *Ephesus*. Puzzled with these two considerations, some critics have pointed out a *middle* way. They suppose that several copies of this epistle were directed to no particular Church, but were intended for all the Churches in Asia Minor ; and that different copies might have different directions, from this circumstance, that St. Paul, in writing the first verse Παυλος αποστολος Ιησου Χριστου—τοις ἁγιοις τοις ουσιν, *Paul, an apostle of*

2

Jesus Christ, to the saints which are, left a blank after ουσιν, *are,* which was in some cases filled up with εν Εφεσω, *in Ephesus;* in others, with εν Λαοδικεια, *in Laodicea;* though there might be one copy expressly sent by him to the Church of the Laodiceans, while he wished that others should be directed to the different Churches through Asia Minor. That there were copies which had no *place* specified, we learn from St. Basil; and the arguments in favour of *Laodicea* are certainly the strongest; the circumstance, that the apostle salutes no person, agrees well with *Laodicea,* where *he had never been,* Col. ii. 1; but cannot agree with *Ephesus,* where he was well known, and where, in preaching the Gospel, he had spent *three years.* See Acts xx. 31.

As this point is very dubious, and men of great abilities and learning have espoused different sides of the question, I judge myself incompetent to determine any thing; but I felt it my duty to bring the arguments for *Laodicea* fairly before the reader; those in favour of *Ephesus* may be met with every where. The passages in the body of the epistle, alleged by critics who espouse opposite sides of this subject, I have seldom noticed in a controversial way; and the notes on those passages are constructed as though no controversy existed.

Many expositors, and particularly Drs. *Chandler* and *Macknight,* have thought that they have perceived a great number of references to the *temple of Diana* at Ephesus; to the *sacred mysteries* among the Greeks; to the *Hierophants, Mystagogues, Neocoroi, &c.,* in the temple of the celebrated goddess. It may appear strange that, with these opinions before me, I have not referred to the same things; nor adduced them by way of illustration; the truth is, I have not been able to discover them, nor do I believe that any such allusions exist. I see many allusions to the *temple of God* at Jerusalem, but none to the *temple of Diana* at Ephesus. I find also many references to the sacred service and sacerdotal officers in the Jewish temple; but none to Mystagogues, &c., among the heathens. I find much said about, what is to be understood most literally, the *mystery* which had been hidden from all ages, viz. of uniting Jews and Gentiles in one Church, but no reference to the *Eleusinian, Bacchic,* or other mysteries in the abominable worship of the Greeks, as suggesting to the mind of the apostle any parallel between *their mysteries* and those of the Almighty. My reasons for my dissent from these respectable authorities I have given in the notes.

June 20th, 1815.

2

THE
EPISTLE OF PAUL THE APOSTLE
TO THE
EPHESIANS.

Chronological Notes relative to this Epistle.

Usherian year of the world, 4065.—Alexandrian era of the world, 5563.—Antiochian era of the world, 5553.—Constantinopolitan era of the world, 5569.—Year of the Eusebian epocha of the Creation, 4289. —Year of the Julian period, 4771.—Year of the minor Jewish era of the world, 3821.—Year of the Greater Rabbinical era of the world, 4420.—Year from the Flood, according to Archbishop Usher, and the English Bible, 2409.—Year of the Cali yuga, or Indian era of the Deluge, 3163.—Year of the era of Iphitus, or since the first commencement of the Olympic games, 1001.—Year of the Nabonassarean era, 808. Year of the era of the Seleucidæ, 373.—Year of the Spanish era, 99.—Year of the Actiac or Actian era, 92.—Year from the birth of Christ, 65.—Year of the vulgar era of Christ's nativity, 61.—Year from the building of Rome, according to Varro, 813.—Year of the CCXth Olympiad, 1.—Jesus, high priest of the Jews.—Common Golden Number, 5.—Jewish Golden Number, 2.—Year of the Solar Cycle, 14.— Dominical Letter, D.—Jewish Passover, March 22d.—Easter Sunday, March 29th.—Epact, or the moon's age on the 22d of March, or the Xth of the Calends of April, 14.—Year of the reign of Nero Cæsar, the sixth emperor of the Romans, 8.—In the first year of Porcius Festus, governor of the Jews.— Year of Vologesus, king of the Parthians, 11.—Year of Domitius Corbulo, governor of Syria, 2.—Roman Consuls; C. Cæsonius Pætus, and C. Petronius Turpilianus.

CHAPTER I.

The apostle's salutation to the Church, 1, 2. He blesses God for calling the Gentiles to the adoption of children by Jesus Christ, by whose sacrificial death both they and the Jews find redemption, 3–7. He shows that it was through the great abundance of God's wisdom and goodness that the Gentiles were called into a state of salvation, and that they should receive the Holy Spirit as the earnest of their inheritance, 8–15. He praises God for their conversion, and prays that they may be farther enlightened, that they may see the glory of Christ, and partake of the blessings procured by his passion and exaltation, 16–23.

| A. M. cir. 4065. |
| A. D. cir. 61. |
| A. U. C. 813. |
| An. Imp. Neronis Cæs. |
| Aug. 8. |

PAUL, an apostle of Jesus Christ [a] by the will of God, [b] to the saints which are at Ephesus, [c] and to the faithful in Christ Jesus:

2 [d] Grace *be* to you, and peace, from God our Father, and *from* the Lord Jesus Christ.

| A. M. cir. 4065. |
| A. D. cir. 61. |
| A. U. C. 813. |
| An. Imp. Neronis Cæs. |
| Aug. 8. |

3 [e] Blessed *be* the God and Father of our Lord Jesus Christ, who hath

---

[a] 2 Cor. i. 1.——[b] Rom. i. 7; 2 Cor. i. 1.——[c] 1 Cor. iv. 17; ch. vi. 21; Col. i. 2.——[d] Gal. i. 3; Tit. i. 4.——[e] 2 Cor. i. 3; 1 Pet. i. 3.

NOTES ON CHAP. I.

Verse 1. *To the saints which are at Ephesus*] As some learned men think that this epistle was written to the Church of the *Laodiceans*, and that the words εν Εφεσω, *in Ephesus*, were not originally in this epistle, the consideration of the subject has appeared to be more proper for the *preface;* and to that the reader is referred for a particular discussion of this opinion By the term *saints* we are to understand

those who in that place *professed* Christianity, and were members of the Christian Church. *Saint* properly signifies a *holy person*, and such the Gospel of Christ requires every man to be, and such every true believer *is*, both in heart and life; but *saint* appears to have been as ordinary a denomination of a believer in Christ in those primitive times, as the term *Christian* is now. Yet many had the *name* who had not the *thing.*

A. M. cir. 4065.
A. D. cir. 61.
A. U. C. 813.
An. Imp. Ne-
ronis Cæs.
Aug. 8.

blessed us with all spiritual bless-ings in heavenly f *places* in Christ :

4 According as g he hath chosen us in him h before the foundation of the world, that we should i be holy, and

without blame before him in love :

5 k Having predestinated us unto l the adoption of children by Jesus Christ to himself, m according to the good pleasure of his will,

A. M. cir. 4065.
A. D. cir. 61.
A. U. C. 813.
An. Imp. Ne-
ronis Cæs.
Aug. 8.

---

f Or, things; chap. vi. 12.——g Rom. viii. 28; 2 Thess. ii. 13; 2 Tim. i. 9; James ii. 5; 1 Pet. i. 2; ii. 9.——h 1 Pet. i. 20.——i Luke i. 75; chap. ii. 10; v. 27; Col. i. 22; 1 Thess. iv. 7; Tit. ii. 12.

k Rom. viii. 29, 30; ver. 11.——l John i. 12; Rom. viii. 15 2 Cor. vi. 18; Gal. iv. 5; 1 John iii. 1.——m Matt. i. 26; Luke xii. 32; 1 Cor. i. 21; ver. 9.

The faithful in Christ Jesus] Πιστοις· the *believ-ers*—the persons who received Christ as the promised Messiah, and the Saviour of the world, and continued in the grace which they had received.

Verse 2. *Grace be to you*] See the note on Rom. i. 7.

Verse 3. *Blessed be the God*] See the note on 2 Cor. i. 3, where the same form is used.

With all spiritual blessings] With the pure *doc-trines* of the Gospel, and the *abundant gifts* and *graces* of the Holy Ghost, justifying, sanctifying, and build-ing us up on our most holy faith.

In heavenly places] Εν τοις επουρανιοις· *In hea-venly things*, such as those mentioned above; they were not. yet in *heavenly places*, but they had abun-dance of *heavenly things* to prepare them for heavenly *places*. Some think the word should be understood as signifying *blessings* of the most *exalted* or *excellent kind*, such as are *spiritual* in opposition to those that are *earthly*, such as are *eternal* in opposition to those that are *temporal*; and all these *in*, *through* and *by* Christ. We have already seen, on Gal. iv. 26, that the *heavenly Jerusalem*, or *Jerusalem which is from above*, is used by the Jews to signify the days of the Messiah, and that state of grace and glory which should follow the Levitical worship and ceremonies; and it is possible that St. Paul may use the word επουρανια, *heavenly things*, in this sense : *God hath blessed us with all spiritual blessings in heavenly things*, or *in this heavenly state*, in which life and immortality are brought to light by the Gospel. This is apparently the preferable sense.

Verse 4. *According as he hath chosen us in him*] As he has decreed from the beginning of the world, and has kept in view from the commencement of the *religious system of the Jews*, (which the phrase some-times means,) to bring us Gentiles to the knowledge of this glorious state of salvation by Christ Jesus. The Jews considered themselves an *elect* or *chosen* people, and wished to monopolize the whole of the Divine love and beneficence. The apostle here shows that God had the Gentiles as much in the contempla-tion of his mercy and goodness as he had the Jews; and the blessings of the Gospel, now so freely dis-pensed to them, were the proof that God had *thus* chosen them, and that his end in giving them the Gos-pel was the same which he had in view by giving the law to the Jews, viz. that they might be holy and without blame before him. And as his object was the same in respect to them *both*, they should consider that, as he loved *them*, so they should love *one ano-ther* : God having provided for each the same bless-

ings, they should therefore be αγιους, *holy*—fully *sepa-rated* from *earth* and *sin*, and consecrated to God and αμωμους, *without blame*—having no *spot* nor im-perfection, their inward *holiness* agreeing with their outward *consecration*. The words are a metaphor taken from the *perfect* and *immaculate* sacrifices which the law required the people to bring to the altar of God. But as *love* is the *fulfilling of the law*, and *love* the *fountain* whence their salvation flowed, there-fore *love* must fill their hearts towards God and each other, and *love* must be the *motive* and *end* of all their *words* and *works*.

Verse 5. *Having predestinated us*] Προορισας. As the doctrine of eternal *predestination* has produced much controversy in the Christian world, it may be necessary to examine the meaning of the term, that those who do use it may employ it according to the sense it has in the oracles of God. The verb προορι-ζω, from προ, *before*, and οριζω, I *define*, *finish*, *bound*, or *terminate*, whence ὁρος, a *boundary* or *limit*, sig-nifies to *define beforehand*, and *circumscribe by cer-tain bounds* or *limits*; and is originally a geographi-cal term, but applied also to any thing concluded, or determined, or demonstrated. Here the word is used to point out God's fixed purpose or predetermination to bestow on the *Gentiles* the blessing of *the adoption of sons* by Jesus Christ, which adoption had been be-fore granted to the *Jewish* people; and without *cir-cumcision*, or any other Mosaic rite, to admit the Gentiles to all the privileges of his Church and people. And the apostle marks that all this was *foredetermined* by God, as he had foredetermined the bounds and precincts of the land which he gave them according to the promise made to their fathers; that the Jews had no reason to complain, for God had formed this pur-pose *before* he had given the *law*, or called them out of Egypt; (for it was *before* the *foundation of the world*, ver. 2;) and that, therefore, the conduct of God in calling the Gentiles *now*—bringing them into his Church, and conferring on them the gifts and graces of the Holy Spirit, was in pursuance of his *origina. design*; and, if he did not do so, his eternal purposes could not be fulfilled; and that, as the Jews were taken to be his *peculiar* people, not because they had any *goodness* or *merit* in themselves; so the Gentiles were *called*, not for any merit they had, but *according to the good pleasure of his will*; that is, according to his *eternal benevolence*, showing mercy and conferring privileges in this new creation, as he had done in the original creation; for, as, in creating man, he drew every consideration from his own innate eternal bene-volence, so now, in redeeming man, and sending the

2

A. M. cir. 4065.	
A. D cir. 61.	
A. U. C. 813.	
An. Imp. Ne-	
ronis Cæs.	
Aug. 8.	

6 To the praise of the glory of his grace, [n] wherein he hath made us accepted in [o] the Beloved:

7 [p] In whom we have redemption through his blood, the forgiveness of sins, according to [q] the riches of his grace;

8 Wherein he hath abounded toward us in all wisdom and prudence;

A. M. cir. 4065.	
A. D. cir. 61.	
A. U. C. 813.	
An. Imp. Ne-	
ronis Cæs.	
Aug. 8.	

---

[n] Rom. iii. 24; v. 15.——[o] Matt. iii. 17; xvii. 5; John iii. 35; x. 17.——[p] Acts xx. 28; Rom. iii. 24; Col. i. 14; Heb. ix. 12; 1 Pet. i. 18, 19; Rev. v. 9.——[q] Rom. ii. 4; iii. 24; ix. 23; chap. ii. 7; iii. 8, 16; Phil. iv. 19.

---

glad tidings of salvation both to the Jews and the Gentiles, he acted on the same principles, deriving all the reasons of his conduct from his own infinite *goodness.*

This argument was exceedingly conclusive, and must silence the Jews on the ground of their *original, primitive,* and *exclusive* rights, which they were ever ready to plead against all pretensions of the Gentiles. If therefore God, *before the foundation of the Jewish economy,* had determined that the Gentiles, in the *fulness of time,* should be called to and admitted into all the privileges of the Messiah's kingdom, then the *exclusive* salvation of the Jews was chimerical; and what God was doing now, by the preaching of the apostles in the Gentile world, was in pursuance of his original design. This same argument St. Paul repeatedly produces in his Epistle to the Romans; and a proper consideration of it *unlocks* many difficulties in that epistle. See the notes on Rom. viii. 29, 30; and elsewhere, in the course of that epistle, where this subject is handled. But why is the word πρooρι-σας, foredetermined, *limited,* or *circumscribed,* used here? Merely in reference to the settlement of the Israelites in the promised land. God *assigned* to them the *portions* which they were to *inherit;* and these portions were *described,* and their *bearings, boundaries, vicinities* to other *portions, extent* and *length,* as *exactly ascertained* as they could be by the most correct *geographical* map. As God, therefore, had dealt with the Jews in making them his peculiar people, and when he divided the earth among the sons of Noah reserved to himself the *twelve portions* which he afterwards gave to the twelve tribes; (see on Deut. xxxii. 8;) and as his dealings with *them* were typical of what he intended to do in the calling and salvation of the Gentiles; so he uses the terms by which their allotment and settlement were pointed out to show that, what he had thus designed and typified, he had now fulfilled according to the original predetermination; the Gentiles having now the spiritual inheritance which God had pointed out by the grant *made* of the promised land to the children of Israel. This is the grand key by which this predestination business is unlocked. See on ver. 11.

Verse 6. *To the praise of the glory of his grace*] Δοξης της χαριτος αυτου· *The glory of his grace,* for χαρις ενδοξος, *his glorious* or *illustrious grace,* according to the Hebrew idiom. But the grace or mercy of God is peculiarly illustrated and glorified in the plan of redemption by Christ Jesus. By the giving of the LAW, God's *justice* and *holiness* were rendered most glorious; by the giving of the GOSPEL, his *grace* and *mercy* are made equally conspicuous.

Wherein he hath made us accepted in the Beloved]

This translation of εν ἡ εχαριτωσεν ἡμας εν τῳ Ηγα-πημενῳ is not clear; *with which he has graciously favoured us through the Beloved,* is at once more literal and more intelligible. *Whitby, Macknight,* and *Wakefield* translate the passage in nearly the same way.

In the Beloved must certainly mean *in Christ,* who is termed God's *beloved Son,* Matt. iii. 17; but several excellent MSS., such as D*EFG, the later *Syriac,* the *Æthiopic, Vulgate, Itala,* with several of the *fathers,* add, υιῳ αυτου, *his beloved Son.* This is the *meaning,* whether the *reading* be received or rejected.

Verse 7. *In whom we have redemption*] God has glorified his grace by giving us redemption by the blood of his Son, and this redemption consists in forgiving and delivering us from our sins; so then Christ's blood was the *redemption price* paid down for our salvation: and this was according to the riches of his grace; as his grace is *rich* or *abundant* in *benevolence,* so it was manifested in *beneficence* to mankind, in their redemption by the sacrifice of Christ, the *measure* of redeeming grace being the measure of God's own eternal goodness.

It may not be useless to remark that, instead of της χαριτος αυτου, *his grace,* the Codex Alexandrinus and the *Coptic* version have της χρηστοτητος, *his goodness.*

Verse 8. *Wherein he hath abounded*] That is, in the dispensation of mercy and goodness by Christ Jesus.

In all wisdom and prudence] Giving us apostles the most complete instructions in heavenly things by the inspiration of his Spirit; and at the same time *prudence,* that we might know *when* and *where* to preach the Gospel so that it might be effectual to the salvation of those who heard it. Nothing less than the *Spirit* of *God* could teach the apostles that *wisdom* by which they were to instruct a dark and sinful world; and nothing less than the same Spirit could inspire them with that *prudence* which was necessary to be exercised in every step of their life and ministry. Every wise man is not a prudent man, and every prudent man is not a wise man. *Wisdom* and *prudence* may be expected in an apostle who is constantly living under the inspiration of the Holy Ghost. " *Wisdom,*" according to *Sir William Temple,* " is that which makes men judge what are the best ends, and what the best means to attain them; and gives a man advantage of counsel and direction." " *Prudence* is wisdom applied to practice; or that discreet, apt suiting as well of actions as words, in their due place, time, and manner." Every minister of Christ needs these still; and if he abide not under the influence of both, not only his *prayers* but his *ministerial* labours will be all hindered.

432　　　　　　　　　　　　　　　　　　　2

A. M. cir. 4065.
A. D. cir. 61.
A. U. C. 813.
An. Imp. Ne-
ronis Cæs.
Aug. 8.

9 ʳ Having made known unto us the mystery of his will, according to his good pleasure ˢ which he hath purposed in himself:

10 That in the dispensation of ᵗ the fulness of times, ᵘ he might gather together in one ᵛ all

things in Christ, both which are in ʷ heaven, and which are on earth; *even* in him:

11 ˣ In whom also we have obtained an inheritance, ʸ being predestinated according to ᶻ the purpose of him who worketh all things after the counsel of his own will:

A. M. cir. 4065.
A. D. cir. 61.
A. U. C. 813.
An. Imp. Ne-
ronis Cæs.
Aug. 8.

ʳ Rom. xvi. 25; chap. iii. 4, 9; Col. i. 26.——ˢ Chap. iii. 11; 2 Tim. i. 9.——ᵗ Gal. iv. 4; Heb. i. 2; ix. 10; 1 Pet. i. 20. ᵘ 1 Cor. iii. 22, 23; xi. 3; chap. ii. 15; iii. 15.

ᵛ Phil. ii. 9, 10; Col. i. 20.——ʷ Gr. *the heavens.*——ˣ Acts xx. 32; xxvi. 18; Rom. viii. 17; Col. i. 12; iii. 24; Tit. iii. 7; James ii. 5; 1 Pet. i. 4.——ʸ Ver. 5.——ᶻ Isa. xlvi. 10, 11.

Verse 9. *Having made known unto us the mystery*] That the Gentiles should ever be received into the Church of God, and have all the privileges of the Jews, without being obliged to submit to circumcision, and perform the rites and ceremonies of the Jewish law was a *mystery*—a *hidden thing* which had never been published before; and *now* revealed only to the apostles. It was *God's will* that it should be so, but that will he kept *hidden* to the present time. A *mystery* signifies something *hidden,* but it ceases to be a *mystery* as soon as it is *revealed.* See the note on Matt. xiii. 11; and particularly that on Rom xi. 25.

Good pleasure] Την ευδοκιαν· *That benevolent design which he had purposed in himself,* not being induced by any consideration from *without.*

Verse 10. *In the dispensation of the fulness of times*] Εις οικονομιαν του πληρωματος των καιρων. The word οικονομια, which is the same as our word *economy,* signifies, as Dr. Macknight has well observed, " the plan which the master of a family, or his steward, has established for the management of the family;" it signifies, also, a plan for the management of any sort of business: and here it means the dispensation of the Gospel, that *plan* by which God has provided salvation for a lost world; and according to which he intends to gather all believers, both Jews and Gentiles, into one Church under Jesus Christ, their head and governor. See the note on Matt. xxiv. 45, where the *word* and the *office* are particularly explained.

The fulness of times—By this phrase we are to understand either the *Gospel dispensation,* which is the consummation of all preceding dispensations, and the last that shall be afforded to man; or that *advanced state* of the world which God saw to be the most proper for the full manifestation of those benevolent purposes which he had formed in himself relative to the salvation of the world by Jesus Christ.

That he might gather together in one] Ανακεφαλαιωσασθαι, from ανα, *again,* and κεφαλαιω, *to reduce to one sum; to add up; to bring different sums together,* and fractions of sums, so as to reduce them under *one denomination; to recapitulate* the *principal matters* contained in a *discourse.* Here it means the *gathering together* both Jews and Gentiles, who have believed in Christ, into one Church and flock. See the preceding note.

All things—which are in heaven, and which are on earth] This clause is variously understood: some think, by *things in heaven* the *Jewish state* is meant; and by *things on earth* the *Christian.* The Jews had been long considered a *Divine* or *heavenly people;*

their doctrine, their government, their constitution, both civil and ecclesiastical, were all Divine or heavenly: as *the powers of the heavens,* Matt. xxiv. 29, Luke xxi. 26, mean the *Jewish rulers* in *Church and state,* it is very possible that *the things which are in heaven* mean this same state; and as the Gentiles were considered to have nothing *Divine* or *heavenly* among them, they may be here intended by the *earth,* out of the corruption of which they are to be gathered by the preaching of the Gospel. But there are others who imagine that the *things in heaven* mean the *angelical hosts;* and *the things on earth* believers of *all nations,* who shall all be joined together at last in one assembly to worship God throughout eternity. And some think that the *things in heaven* mean the *saints* who *died before Christ's advent,* and who are not to be made perfect till the resurrection, when the full power and efficacy of Christ shall be seen in raising the bodies of believers and uniting them with their holy souls, to reign in his presence for ever. And some think that, as the Hebrew phrase שמים והארץ *shamayim vehaarets,* the *heavens and the earth,* signifies *all creatures,* the words in the text are to be understood as signifying *all mankind,* without discrimination of peoples, kindreds, or tongues; Jews, Greeks, or barbarians. All that are saved of all nations, (being saved in the *same way,* viz. by *faith* in Christ Jesus, without any distinction of nation or previous condition,) and all gathered into *one Church* or *assembly.*

I believe that the forming one Church out of both Jews and Gentiles is that to which the apostle refers. This agrees with what is said, chap. ii. 14–17.

Verse 11. *In whom*] Christ Jesus, *also we* believing *Jews have obtained an inheritance*—what was promised to Abraham and his spiritual seed, viz. the *adoption of sons,* and the *kingdom of heaven,* signified by the privileges under the Mosaic dispensation, and the possession of the promised land; but all these privileges being forfeited by the rebellion and unbelief of the Jews, they are now about to be finally cut off, and the believing part to be re-elected, and put in possession of the blessings promised to Abraham and his spiritual seed, by faith; for without a re-election, they cannot get possession of these spiritual privileges.

Being predestinated] God having determined to bring both Jews and Gentiles to salvation, not by *works,* nor by any human *means* or *schemes,* but by Jesus Christ; that salvation being *defined* and *determined before* in the Divine mind, and the means by which it should be brought about all being according to his purpose, who consults not his creatures, but

A. M. cir. 4065.
A. D. cir. 61.
A. U. C. 813.
An. Imp. Ne-
ronis Cæs.
Aug. 8.

12 ᵃ That we should be to the praise of his glory, ᵇ who first ᶜ trusted in Christ.

13 In whom ye also *trusted*, after that ye heard ᵈ the word of truth, the Gospel of your salvation : in whom also, after

that ye believed, ᵉ ye were sealed with that holy Spirit of promise,

14 ᶠ Which is the earnest of our inheritance, ᵍ until the redemption of ʰ the purchased possession, ⁱ unto the praise of his glory.

A. M. cir. 4065.
A. D. C. 61.
A. U. C 813.
An. Imp. Ne-
ronis Cæs.
Aug. 8.

ᵃ Ver. 6, 14, 2 Thess. ii. 13.——ᵇ James 1. 18.——ᶜ Or, *hoped*. ᵈ John 1. 17 ; 2 Cor. vi. 7.——ᵉ 2 Cor i. 22 ; chap. iv. 30.

ᶠ 2 Cor. i. 22 ; v. 5.——ᵍ Luke xxi. 28 ; Rom. viii. 23 ; chap. iv 30.——ʰ Acts xx. 28.——ⁱ Ver. 6, 12 ; 1 Pet. ii. 9.

---

operates according to the *counsel of his own will*, that being ever wise, gracious, and good.

The original reference is still kept up here in the word προορισθεντες, *being predestinated*, as in the word προορισας, ver. 5. And as the apostle speaks of *obtaining the inheritance*, he most evidently refers to that of which the *promised land* was the *type* and *pledge*. And as that land was *assigned* to the Israelites by *limit* and *lot*, both of which were *appointed* by God ; so the salvation now sent to the Gentiles was as expressly *their lot* or *portion*, as the *promised land* was *that* of the people of Israel. All this shows that the Israelites were a *typical people* ; their *land*, the *manner* of possessing it, their *civil and religious code*, &c., &c., all typical, and that *in*, *by*, and *through* them, God had *foredetermined*, *foredescribed*, and *fore-ascertained* a greater and more glorious people, among whom the deepest counsels of his wisdom should be manifested, and the most powerful works of his eternal mercy, grace, holiness, goodness, and truth, be fully exhibited. Thus there was nothing *fortuitous* in the Christian scheme , all was the result of infinite counsel and design. See on ver. 5

Verse 12 *That we*] Jews, now apostles and messengers of God, to whom the first offers of salvation were made, and who were the *first* that *believed in Christ* ;

Should be to the praise of his glory] By being the means of preaching Christ crucified to the *Gentiles*, and spreading the Gospel throughout the world

Verse 13 *In whom ye also* trusted] Ye Gentiles, having heard from us the *word*, τον λογον, the doctrine, *of the truth*, which is the *Gospel*, or glad tidings, *of your salvation*, have believed, as we Jews have done, and received similar blessings to those with which God has favoured us.

In whom also, εν ῳ, *through whom*, Christ Jesus, *after that ye had believed*, viz. that he was the only Saviour, and that through his blood redemption might be obtained, *ye were sealed with that holy Spirit of promise* ; that is The Holy Spirit, which is promised to them who believe on Christ Jesus, was given to you, and thus you were *ascertained* to be the children of God , for God has no child who is not a partaker of the Holy Ghost, and he who has this Spirit has God's *seal* that he belongs to the heavenly family It was customary among all nations, when a person purchased goods of any kind, to mark with his *seal* that which he had bought, in order that he might know it, and be able to claim it if mixed with the goods of others ; to this custom the apostle may here allude but it was also customary to set a *seal* upon what was

dedicated to God, or what was to be *offered to him in sacrifice*. See this proved in the note on John vi. 27. The Jews themselves speak of the *seal of God*, which they term אמת *emeth*, truth, and which they consider as a representation of the unoriginated and endless perfections of God. As the apostle is here speaking of the *doctrine of truth*, which came by the Holy Spirit, and is *sealed* on the souls of believers by this Spirit, he may have in view the Jewish notion, which is at once both correct and elevated. This *Spirit of truth*, John xiv. 17, *who leads into all truth*, chap. xvi. 13, and *teaches all things*, chap. xiv. 26, makes the impression of his own eternal purity and truth in the souls of them who believe, and thus they bear the *seal* of God Almighty. And they who in the day of judgment are found to bear this *seal*—TRUTH ; *truth* in the inward parts, having *truly* repented, *truly* believed, and having been in consequence *truly* justified, and *truly* sanctified , and having walked in *truth* and *sincerity* towards God and man ; these are *sealed* to the day of redemption , for, having this *seal*, they are seen to have a right to eternal life.

Verse 14 *Which is the earnest of our inheritance*] This Holy Spirit, sealing the soul with truth and righteousness, is the *earnest*, *foretaste*, and *pledge* of the heavenly inheritance. And he who can produce this *earnest*—this *witness of the Spirit*, in the day of judgment, shall have an abundant entrance into the holiest On the αρραβων, or *earnest*, see the notes on Gen xxxviii. 13, &c., and on 2 Cor. 1. 22

The redemption of the purchased possession] That is, till the time when body and soul are redeemed from all their miseries, and glorified in the kingdom on heaven

The redemption of the purchased possession—Απολυτρωσις της περιποιησεως is variously understood ; and indeed the original is variously translated Dr *Whitby* has observed that the verb πεειποιειν signifies to *save alive* ; and he refers the περιποιησις, here, to the redemption of the body from corruption, and to its final glorification with the soul.

All those who believe in Christ Jesus are considered as his peculiar people and property, and to them eternal glory is promised. The Spirit of promise, which is given them, is a pledge that they shall have a resurrection from the dead, and eternal blessedness ; the *redemption*, or bringing to life of the body, cannot take place till the day of judgment, but the Holy Spirit promises this redemption, and is now in their hearts an *earnest* or *pledge* of this complete restoration at the great day, which will then be, in an especial manner, *to the praise of his glory*, viz. of Christ, who has bought them by his blood.

           (28**)

A. M. cir. 4065.
A. D. cir. 61.
A. U. C. 813.
An. Imp. Ne-
ronis Cæs.
Aug. 8.

15 Wherefore I also, ^k after I heard of your faith in the Lord Jesus, and love unto all the saints,

16 ^l Cease not to give thanks for you, making mention of you in my prayers;

17 That ^m the God of our Lord Jesus Christ, the Father of glory, ⁿ may give unto you the Spirit of wisdom and revelation, ^o in the knowledge of him:

18 ^p The eyes of your understanding being enlightened; that ye may know what is ^q the hope of his calling, and what the riches of the glory of his ^r inheritance in the saints,

19 And what *is* the exceeding greatness of

A. M. cir. 4065.
A. D. cir. 61.
A. U. C. 813.
An. Imp. Ne-
ronis Cæs.
Aug. 8.

^k Col. i. 4; Philem. 5.——^l Rom. i. 9; Phil. i. 3, 4; Col. i. 3; 1 Thess. i. 2; 2 Thess. i. 3.——^m John xx. 17.

ⁿ Col. i 9.——^o Or, *for the acknowledgment;* Col. ii. 2.——^p Acts xxvi. 18.——^q Chap. ii. 12; iv. 4.——^r Ver. 11.

Verse 15. *Faith in the Lord Jesus*] Cordial reception of the Christian religion, amply proved by their *love to all the saints*—to all the *Christians.* Perhaps *love* here implies, not only the kind affection so called, but also all the fruits of love—benevolence, and kind offices of every description.

Verse 16. *Cease not to give thanks*] The apostle intimates, so fully satisfied was he of the genuineness of their conversion, and of their steadiness since their conversion, that it was to him a continual cause of *thanksgiving* to God, who had brought them into that state of salvation; and of *prayer*, that they might be preserved blameless to the end.

Making mention of you] While praying for the prosperity of the Christian cause generally, he was led, from his particular affection for them, to *mention them by name* before God.

Verse 17. *That the God of our Lord Jesus*] Jesus Christ, as *man* and *mediator*, has the *Father* for his God and Father: and it is in reference to this that he himself says: *I ascend unto my Father and your Father, and to my God and your God;* John xx. 17.

The Father of glory] The *author* and giver of that glory which you expect at the end of your Christian race. This may be a Hebraism for *glorious Father,* but the former appears to be the best sense.

The Spirit of wisdom and revelation] I pray that God may give you his Holy Spirit, by whom his will is *revealed* to men, that he may *teach* and make you *wise* unto salvation, that you may continue to *acknowledge* him, Christ Jesus, as your only Lord and Saviour.

Verse 18. *The eyes of your understanding being enlightened*] The *understanding* is that *power* or *faculty* in the soul by which *knowledge* or *information* is *received*, and the recipient power is here termed the EYES of the understanding; and we learn from this that ὅπερ ὁ ὀφθαλμος εν τῳ σωματι, τουτο ὁ νους εν τῃ ψυχῃ, as *Philo* expresses it: *What the eye* is to the *body*, the *understanding* is to the *soul;* and that as the eye is not light in itself, and can discern nothing but by the means of *light* shining, not only on the objects to be viewed, but into the eye itself; so the understanding of man can discern no sacred thing of or by itself, but sees by the influence of the Spirit of wisdom and revelation; for without the influence of God's *Holy Spirit* no man ever became wise unto salvation, no more than a man ever discerned an *object*, (no matter how perfect soever his eye might have been,) without the instrumentality of *light.*

Instead of τῆς διανοιας, *of* your *understanding*, τῆς καρδιας, *of* your *heart*, is the reading of ABDEFG, and several others; also both the *Syriac*, all the *Arabic*, the *Coptic*, the *Æthiopic*, Armenian, Sahidic, Slavonian, *Vulgate*, and *Itala*, besides several of the *fathers.* *The eyes of your* HEART is undoubtedly the true reading.

The hope of his calling] That you may clearly discern the glorious and important *objects* of your *hope*, to the enjoyment of which God has *called* or *invited* you.

The riches of the glory of his inheritance] That you may understand what is the *glorious abundance* of the spiritual things to which you are entitled, in consequence of being made children of God; for if *children*, then *heirs*, heirs of that glorious inheritance which God has provided for the *saints*—for all genuine Christians, whether formerly *Jews* or *Gentiles.* On the chief subject of this verse, see the notes on Gal. iv. 6, 7.

Verse 19. *The exceeding greatness of his power*] As the apostle is here speaking of the glorious state of believers after death, *the exceeding greatness of his power*, or that power which surpasses all difficulties, being itself omnipotent, is to be understood of that *might* which is to be exerted in raising the body at the last day; as it will require the same power or energy which he wrought in Christ, when he raised *his* body from the grave, to raise up the bodies of all mankind; the resurrection of the human nature of Christ being a proof of the resurrection of mankind in general.

According to the working of his mighty power] Κατα την ενεργειαν του κρατους της ισχυος αυτου· *According to the energy of the power of his might.* We may understand these words thus: MIGHT, ισχυς, is the *state* or simple *efficiency* of this attribute in God; POWER, κρατος, is this might or *efficiency in action;* ENERGY, ενεργεια, is the quantum of *force, momentum,* or *velocity*, with which the power is *applied.* Though they appear to be synonymous terms they may be thus understood: *passive power* is widely different from *power* in *action;* and power in action will be in its results according to the *energy* or *momentum* with which it is applied. The resurrection of the dead is a stupendous work of God; it requires his *might* in sovereign action; and when we consider that all mankind are to be raised and changed in a *moment*, in the *twinkling of an eye*, then the *momentum*, or *velocity*, with which the power is to be applied must be incon-

A. M. cir. 4065.
A. D. cir. 61.
A. U. C. 813.
An. Imp. Ne-
ronis Cæs.
Aug. 8.

his power to us-ward who believe, ⁸ according to the working
ᵗ of his mighty power,

20 Which he wrought in Christ,
when ᵘ he raised him from the dead, and ᵛ set
him at his own right hand in the heavenly *places,*

21 ʷ Far above all ˣ principality, and power,
and might, and dominion, and every name that

is named, not only in this world,
but also in that which is to
come ;

A. M. cir. 4065.
A. D. cir. 61.
A. U. C. 813.
An. Imp. Ne-
ronis Cæs.
Aug. 8.

22 And ʸ hath put all *things*
under his feet, and gave him ᶻ *to be* the head
over all *things* to the Church,

23 ᵃ Which is his body, ᵇ the fulness of him
ᶜ that filleth all in all.

ˢ Chap. iii. 7 ; Col. i. 29 ; ii. 12.——ᵗ Gr. *of the might of his power.*——ᵘ Acts ii. 24, 33.——ᵛ Psa. cx. 1 ; Acts vii. 55, 56 ; Col. iii. 1 ; Heb. i. 3 ; x. 12.——ʷ Phil. ii. 9, 10 ; Col. ii. 10 ; Heb. i. 4.——ˣ Rom. viii. 38 ; Col. i. 16 ; ii. 15.

ʸ Psa. viii. 6 ; Matt. xxviii. 18 ; 1 Cor. xv. 27 ; Heb. ii. 8. ᶻ Chap. iv. 15, 16 ; Col. i. 18 ; Heb. ii. 7.——ᵃ Rom. xii. 5 ; 1 Cor. xii. 12, 27 ; chap. iv. 12 ; v. 23, 30 ; Col. i. 18, 24.——ᵇ Col. ii. 10.——ᶜ 1 Cor. xii. 6 ; chap. iv. 10 ; Col. iii. 11.

ceivably great. All motion is in proportion to the *quantity of matter* in the *mover,* and the *velocity* with which it is applied. The *effect* here is in proportion to the *cause* and the *energy* he puts forth in order to produce it. But such is the nature of God's power in action, that it is perfectly inconceivable to us ; and even these astonishingly *strong* words of the apostle are to be understood as used in condescension to human *weakness.*

Verse 20. *Set* him *at his own right hand in the heavenly* places] Gave him, as mediator between God and man, the highest honours and dignities, Phil. ii. 9 ; in which state of exaltation he transacts all the affairs of his Church, and rules the universe. The *right hand* is the place of friendship, honour, confidence, and authority.

Verse 21. *Far above all principality*] The difficulty in this verse does not arise from the *words* themselves, the meaning of each being easily understood, but from the *sense* in which the apostle uses them. Some think he has reference here to the different orders among good and evil angels ; he is superior to all the *former,* and rules all the *latter.* Others think he refers to *earthly governments ;* and as αρχη, *principality,* the first word, signifies the most sovereign and extensive kind of dominion ; and κυριοτης, *lordship,* the last word, signifies the *lowest degree* of authority ; hence we are to understand that to our Lord, in his human nature, are subjected the *highest,* the *intermediate,* and the *lowest* orders of beings in the universe.— *Chandler.* Others imagine that the apostle has in view, by whatsoever *is named in this world,* all the dignitaries of the *Jewish Church ;* and by what is named *in the world to come,* all the dignities that should be found in the Christian Church.

Schoettgen supposes that the "apostle's αρχη (for αρχοντες, the abstract for the concrete) means the same as the נשיאים *Nesiim* among the Jews, whose chief business it was to clear and decide all contentions which arose concerning traditions and legal controversies.

"That εξουσια, *power,* is the same as צורבא *tsorba,* he who possesses *authority* to propound, expound, persuade, convince, and refute.

"That δυναμις, *might,* answers to רבנות *rabbanoth,* signifying all the class of rabbins, whose office it was to expound the law, and teach the people generally

"And that κυριοτης, *dominion,* answers to כר *mar,*

which signifies a person above the lower orders of men. And he observes that Jesus Christ, after his resurrection, called fishermen, publicans, and men from the lowest orders of the people, to the work of the ministry ; and made them instruments of confounding and overturning all the Jewish rulers, rabbins, and doctors. And that in *the world which is to come—* the successive ages of Christianity, he should ever be exalted above all those powers and authorities which Antichrist might bring into the Christian Church ; such as popes, cardinals, wicked archbishops, bishops, deans, and canons ; and all those who among the schoolmen were termed seraphic doctors, angelic doctors, most illuminated, most perfect, and irrefragable doctors. And although *Wiclif, Huss, Luther, Melancthon,* and the rest of the *reformers,* were men of little or no note when compared with the rulers of the popish Church, so eminently did the power of Christ work in and by them, that the pope and all his adjutants were every where confounded, and their power and authority annihilated in several entire regions."

It is certain that the apostle means that all created power, glory, and influence, are under Christ ; and hence it is added :

Verse 22. *And hath put all* things *under his feet*] All beings and things are subject to him, whether they be *thrones, dominions, principalities,* or *powers,* Col. i. 16–18, and ii. 10 ; for he, God the Father, has *given him to be head*—chief, and supreme, over all, *to the Church,* the Church having no ruler but Jesus Christ ; others may be *officers* in his Church, but he alone is *head* and *supreme.*

Verse 23. *Which is his body*] As he is *head over all* things, he is *head* to the *Church ;* and this Church is considered as the *body* of which he is *especially* the head ; and from him, as the head, the Church receives light, life, and intelligence.

And is the fulness of him] That in which he especially manifests his power, goodness, and truth ; for though he *fills* all the world with his presence, yet he fills all the members of his mystical body with wisdom, goodness, truth, and holiness, in an especial manner. Some understand the *fulness* or πληρωμα, here, as signifying the *thing to be filled ;* so the Christian Church is to be filled by him, whose fulness fills all his members, with all spiritual gifts and graces. And this corresponds with what St. John says, chap. i. 16 : *And of his fulness have all we received, and grace for grace.* And with what is said, Col. ii. 9, 10 : *Ye are complete in him ;* και εστε εν αυτω πεπληρωμενοι· *And ye are in him filled full ;* i. e. with *gifts* and *grace.*

How, in any other sense, the Church can be said to be *the fulness of him who fills all in all,* is difficult to say. However, as Jesus Christ is represented to be the *head,* and the Church, the *body* under that head, the *individuals* being so many *members* in that *body ;*

and as it requires a *body* and *members* to make a *head* complete ; so it requires a Church, or *general assembly* of believers, to make up the *body* of Christ. When, therefore, the *Jews* and *Gentiles* are brought into this Church, the *body* may be said to be complete ; and thus Christ has his visible *fulness* upon earth, and the Church may be said to be the *fulness of him,* &c. See ver. 10.

CHAPTER II.

The character of the Ephesians previously to their conversion to Christianity, 1–3. By what virtue they were changed, and for what purpose, 4–7. They were saved by faith, 8, 9. And created unto good works, 10. The apostle enters into the particulars of their former miserable state, 11, 12. And those of their present happy state, 13. Christ has broken down the middle wall of partition between the Jews and Gentiles, and proclaims reconciliation to both, 14–17. The glorious privileges of genuine believers, 18–22.

A. M. cir. 4065.
A. D. cir. 61.
A. U. C. 813.
An. Imp. Neronis Cæs.
Aug. 8.

A ND [a] you *hath he quickened,* [b] who were dead in trespasses and sins ;

2 [c] Wherein in time past ye

walked according to the course of this world, according to [d] the prince of the power of the air, the spirit that now worketh in

A. M. cir. 4065.
A. D. cir. 61.
A. U. C. 813.
An. Imp. Neronis Cæs.
Aug. 8.

---

[a] John v. 24 ; Col. ii. 13.——[b] Ver. 5 ; chap. iv. 18.——[c] 1 Cor.

[continued] vi. 11 ; chap. iv. 22 ; Col. i. 21 ; iii. 7 ; 1 John v. 19.——[d] Ch. vi. 12.

NOTES ON CHAP. II.

Verse 1. *And you* hath he quickened] This chapter should not have been separated from the preceding, with which it is most intimately connected. As Christ fills the whole body of Christian believers with his fulness, (chap. i. 23,) so had he dealt with the converted Ephesians, who before were *dead in trespasses, and dead in sins.* DEATH is often used by all writers, and in all nations, to express a state of extreme misery. The Ephesians, by trespassing and sinning, had brought themselves into a state of deplorable wretchedness, as had all the heathen nations ; and having thus sinned against God, they were condemned by him, and might be considered as *dead in law*—incapable of performing any legal act, and always liable to the punishment of death, which they had deserved, and which was ready to be inflicted upon them.

Trespasses, παραπτωμασι, may signify the *slightest deviation* from the line and rule of moral equity, as well as any *flagrant* offence ; for these are equally *transgressions,* as long as the *sacred line* that separates between vice and virtue is *passed over.*

Sins, ἁμαρτιαις, may probably mean here habitual transgression ; sinning *knowingly* and *daringly.*

Verse 2. *Wherein in time past ye walked*] There is much *force* in these expressions ; the Ephesians had not sinned *casually,* or *now* and *then,* but *continually ;* it was their continual employment ; they *walked in trespasses and sins :* and this was not a *solitary* case, all the nations of the earth acted in the same way ; it was the *course of this world,* κατα τον αιωνα του κοσμου τουτου, *according to the life,* mode of living, or *successive ages of this world.* The word αιων, the literal meaning of which is *constant duration,* is often applied to things which have a *complete course,* as the Jewish dispensation, a particular government, and the *term of human life ;* so, here, the *whole of*

life is a tissue of sin, from the cradle to the grave ; every human soul, unsaved by Jesus Christ, continues to transgress. And the *nominally* Christian world is in the same state to the present day. Age after age passes on in this way and the living lay it not to heart !

The prince of the power of the air] As the former clause may have particular respect to the *Jewish* people, who are frequently denominated עולם הזה *olam hazzeh, this world,* this latter clause may especially refer to the *Gentiles,* who were most manifestly under the power of the devil, as almost every object of their worship was a *demon,* to whom the worst of passions and practices were attributed, and whose conduct his votaries took care to copy.

Satan is termed *prince of the power of the air,* because the *air* is supposed to be a region in which malicious spirits dwell, all of whom are under the direction and influence of Satan, their chief.

The spirit that now worketh] Του νυν ενεργουντος The operations of the prince of the aerial powers are not confined to *that region ;* he has *another* sphere of action, viz. the wicked heart of man, and *in* this he *works* with energy. He seldom inspires *indifference* to religion ; the subjects *in* whom he works are either *determinate* opposers of true religion, or they are systematic and energetic transgressors of God's laws.

Children of disobedience] Perhaps a Hebraism for *disobedient children ;* but, taken as it stands here, it is a strong expression, in which disobedience, ἡ απειθεια, appears to be *personified ;* and wicked men exhibited as her children ; the *prince of the power of the air* being their *father,* whil *disobedience* is their *mother.* Thus they are emphatically, what our Lord calls them, Matt. xiii. 38, *children of the wicked* one ; for they show themselves to be of their *father the devil,* because they *will* do his *works,* John viii. 44. Some think that by *children of disobedience* the apostle

2

A. M. cir. 4065.
A. D. cir. 61.
A. U. C. 813.
An. Imp. Ne-
ronis Cæs.
Aug. 8.

e the children of disobedience :

3 Among whom also we all
had our conversation in times
past i in g the lusts of our flesh, fulfilling h the
desires of the flesh and of the mind; and
i were by nature the children of wrath, even
as others.

4 But God, k who is rich in mercy, for his
great love wherewith he loved us,

5 l Even when we were dead
in sins, hath m quickened us together with Christ, (n by grace
ye are saved ;)

6 And hath raised *us* up together, and made
us sit together o in heavenly *places* in Christ
Jesus ;

7 That in the ages to come he might show
the exceeding riches of his grace, in p *his* kind
ness toward us through Christ Jesus.

A. M. cir. 4065.
A. D. cir. 61.
A. U. C. 813.
An. Imp. Ne-
ronis Cæs.
Aug. 8.

---

e Chap. v. 6 ; Col. iii. 6.——f Tit. iii. 3 ; 1 Pet. iv. 3.——g Gal.
v. 16.——h Gr. *the wills.*——i Psa. li. 5 ; Rom. v. 12, 14.
k Rom. x. 12 ; chap. i, 7 ; ver, 7.

l Rom. v. 6, 8, 10 ; ver. 1.——m Rom. vi. 4, 5 ; Col. ii. 12, 13 ;
iii. 1, 3.——n Or, *by whose grace;* see Acts xv. 11 ; ver. 8 ; Tit.
iii. 5.——o Chap. i. 20.——p Tit. iii. 4.

---

means particularly the disobedient, unbelieving, refractory, and persecuting *Jews ;* but I rather think
he speaks this *generally*, and refers to the Jews in the
following verse.

Verse 3. *Among whom also we all had our conversation*] We JEWS, as well as you *Gentiles*, have
lived in transgressions and sins ; ανεστραφημεν, this
was the *course* of our *life ;* we lived in sin, walked in
sin, it was woven through our whole constitution, it
tinged every temper, polluted every faculty, and perverted every transaction of life. The *lusts*—the evil,
irregular, and corrupt affections of the *heart*, showed
themselves in the perversion of the *mind* as well as
in our general conduct. The *mind* was *darkened* by
the *lusts* of the *flesh*, and both conjoined to produce
acts of unrighteousness. It was not the *will of God*
that was done by us, but the *will of the flesh and of
the mind.*

And were by nature the children of wrath] For
the import of the phrase, *by nature,* φυσει, see the note
on Gal. ii. 15, and Rom. ii. 14. To what is said on
those passages, I may add, from Dr. *Macknight :*—
" *Nature* often signifies one's *birth* and *education,* Gal.
ii. 15 : *We, who are Jews* BY NATURE. Also, men's
natural *reason* and *conscience,* Rom. ii. 14 : *The Gentiles who have not the law, do* BY NATURE *the things
contained in the law,* &c. Also, the *general sense*
and *practice* of mankind, 1 Cor. xi. 14 : *Doth not even*
NATURE *itself teach you, that if a man have long hair,*
&c. Also, the *original constitution* of any thing, Gal.
iv. 8 : *Who are not gods* BY NATURE. Also, a *disposition* formed by *custom* and *habit ;* thus Demetrius
Phalereus said of the Lacedemonians : φυσει εβραχυ-
λογουν Λακωνες' 'The Lacedemonians had *naturally*
a concise mode of speaking.' Hence our word *laco-
nic ;* a short speech, or much sense conveyed in a few
words." The words in the text have often been quoted
to prove the doctrine of *original sin ;* but, though that
doctrine be an *awful truth,* it is not, in my opinion,
intended here ; it is rather found in the *preceding*
words, *the lusts of the flesh,* and *the desires of the
flesh and of the mind.* The apostle appears to speak
of sinful *habits ;* and as we say HABIT is a *second nature,* and as these persons acted from their *originally
corrupt nature*—from the *lusts of the flesh* and *of the
mind,* they thus became, by their vicious habits, or
second nature, children of wrath—persons exposed to

perdition, because of the impurity of their hearts and
the wickedness of their lives. Here we see that the
fallen, apostate nature produces the fruits of unrighteousness. The *bad tree* produces *bad fruit.*

Children of wrath is the same as *son of perdition,
son of death,* &c. ; i. e. persons exposed to God's displeasure, because of their sins.

Verse 4. *But God, who is rich in mercy*] As they
were *corrupt* in their *nature*, and *sinful* in their *practice*, they could possess no *merit*, nor have any *claim*
upon God ; and it required much *mercy* to remove so
much *misery,* and to pardon such transgressions.

His great love] God's infinite love is the ground-
work of our salvation ; in reference to *us* that love
assumes the form of *mercy,* and that mercy provides
the Saviour, the Lord Jesus Christ. And therefore
the apostle adds, ver. 5 : *By grace ye are saved*—it
is by God's free mercy in Christ that ye are brought
into this state of salvation. See on ver. 8.

Verse 5. *Even when we were dead in sins*] Dead
in our souls ; dead towards God ; dead in law ; and
exposed to death eternal.

Hath quickened us together with Christ] God has
given us as complete a *resurrection* from the *death of
sin* to a *life of righteousness,* as the body of Christ has
had from the grave. And as this *quickening,* or *making
alive,* was most gratuitous on God's part, the apostle,
with great propriety, says : *By grace ye are saved.*

Verse 6. *And hath raised us up together—in Christ*]
Or rather, *by Christ ;* his resurrection being the proof
that he had made the full atonement, and that we might
be justified by his blood. Believing, therefore, the
record which God gave of his Son, we received this
atonement, and were raised from a death of sin to a
life of righteousness ; and now we *sit in heavenly*
places—we have a *right* to the kingdom of God, anticipate this glory, and are indescribably happy in the
possession of this salvation, and in our fellowship with
Christ Jesus.

Verse 7. *That in the ages to come*] God has produced us an *example,* and one which shall be on record through all generations, that he quickens dead
souls ; that he forgives the sins of the most sinful,
when they repent and believe in Christ Jesus. So that
what God has done for the sinners at *Ephesus* will
serve as an encouragement to all ages of the world ;
and on this *evidence* every preacher of the Gospel

438

2

A. M. cir. 4065.
A. D. cir. 61.
A. U. C. 813.
An. Imp. Ne-
ronis Cæs.
Aug. 8.

8 q For by grace are ye saved, r through faith; and that not of yourselves: s *it is* the gift of God:

9 t Not of works, lest any man should boast.

10 For we are his u workmanship, created in Christ Jesus unto good works, v which God

hath before w ordained that we should walk in them.

11 Wherefore x remember, that ye *being* in time past Gentiles in the flesh, who are called Uncircumcision by that which is called y the Circumcision in the flesh made by hands;

12 z That at that time ye were without Christ,

A. M. cir. 4065.
A. D. cir. 61.
A. U. C. 813.
An. Imp. Ne-
ronis Cæs.
Aug. 8.

---

q Ver. 5; Romans iii. 24; 2 Tim. i. 9.——r Rom. iv. 16.
s Matt. xvi. 17; John vi. 44, 65; Rom. x. 14, 15, 17; chapter i. 19; Phil. i. 29.——t Romans iii. 20, 27, 28; iv. 2; ix. 11; xi. 6; 1 Corinthians i. 29, 30, 31; 2 Timothy i. 9; Titus iii. 5.

u Deut. xxxii. 6; Psa. c. 3; Isa. xix. 25; xxix. 23; xliv. 21; John iii. 3, 5; 1 Cor. iii. 9; 2 Cor. v. 5, 17; chap. iv. 24; Tit. ii. 14.——v Chap. i. 4.——w Or, *prepared.*——x 1 Cor. xii. 2; chap. v. 8; Col. i. 21; ii. 13.——y Rom. ii. 28, 29; Col. ii. 11.——z Ch. iv. 18; Col. i. 21.

---

may boldly proclaim that Christ saves unto the uttermost all that come unto God through him. And thus the *exceeding riches of his grace* will appear in the provision he has made for the salvation of both Jews and Gentiles.

This observation of the apostle is of great use and importance; because we are authorized to state, in all the successive ages of the world, that he who saved the sinners at Ephesus is ever ready to save all who, like them, repent of their sins, and believe in Christ Jesus.

Verse 8. *For by grace are ye saved, through faith*] As ye are now brought into a state of salvation, your sins being all blotted out, and you made partakers of the Holy Spirit; and, having a hope full of immortality, you must not attribute this to any *works* or *merit* of yours; for when this Gospel reached you, you were all found *dead in trespasses and dead in sins;* therefore it was God's free mercy to you, manifested through Christ, in whom ye were commanded to believe; and, having believed by the power of the Holy Spirit, ye received, and were sealed by, the Holy Spirit of promise; so that this salvation is in no sense *of yourselves,* but is the *free gift of God;* and not of any kind of *works;* so that no man can *boast* as having *wrought out his own salvation,* or even contributed any thing towards it. *By grace are ye saved, through faith* in Christ. This is a true doctrine, and continues to be essential to the salvation of man to the end of the world.

But whether are we to understand, *faith* or *salvation* as being the *gift of God?* This question is answered by the Greek text: τη γαρ χαριτι εστε σεσωσμενοι δια της πιστεως· και τουτο ουκ εξ ὑμων· Θεου το δωρον, ουκ εξ εργων· ἱνα μη τις καυχησηται· "By this grace ye are saved through faith; and THIS (τουτο, *this salvation*) not of you; it is the gift of God, not of works: so that no one can boast." "The relative τουτο, *this,* which is in the *neuter gender,* cannot stand for πιστις, *faith,* which is the *feminine;* but it has the whole sentence that goes before for its antecedent." But it may be asked: Is not *faith* the *gift of God?* Yes, as to the *grace* by which it is produced; but the *grace* or *power* to believe, and the *act of believing,* are two different things. Without the *grace* or *power* to believe no man ever did or can believe; but with that *power* the act of *faith* is a man's own. God never believes *for* any man, no more than he *repents* for him;

the penitent, through this grace enabling him, believes for himself: nor does he believe *necessarily,* or *impulsively* when he has that power; the power to believe may be present long before it is exercised, else, why the solemn warnings with which we meet every where in the word of God, and threatenings against those who do not believe? Is not this a proof that such persons have the *power* but do not *use* it? *They believe not,* and therefore *are not established.* This, therefore, is the true state of the case: God gives the power, man uses the power thus given, and brings glory to God: without the power no man can believe; with it, any man may.

Verse 10. *For we are his workmanship*] So far is this salvation from being *our own work,* or granted for our own *works' sake,* that we are ourselves not only the *creatures* of God, but our *new creation* was produced by his power; for we are *created in Christ Jesus unto good works.* He has saved us that we may show forth the virtues of Him who called us from darkness into his marvellous light. For though we are not saved *for* our good works, yet we are saved that we *may perform good works,* to the glory of God and the benefit of man.

Which God hath before ordained] Οἱς προητοιμασεν· *For which God before prepared us, that we might walk in them.* For being saved from sin we are made partakers of the Spirit of holiness; and it is natural to that Spirit to lead to the *practice* of holiness; and he who is not holy in his life is not saved by the grace of Christ. The *before ordaining,* or rather *preparing,* must refer to the time when God began the new creation in their hearts; for from the first inspiration of God upon the soul it begins to love holiness; and obedience to the will of God is the very *element* in which a holy or regenerated soul lives.

Verse 11. *Wherefore remember*] That ye may ever see and feel your obligations to live a pure and holy life, and be unfeignedly *thankful* to God for your salvation, remember that ye *were once heathens in the flesh*—without the pure doctrine, and under the influence of your corrupt nature; such as by the Jews (who gloried, in consequence of their *circumcision,* and their being in covenant with God) were called *uncircumcision;* i. e. persons out of the Divine covenant, and having no right or title to any blessing of God.

Verse 12. *That at that time ye were without Christ*] Not only were not *Christians,* but had no knowledge

A. M. cir. 4065.
A. D. cir. 61.
A. U. C. 813.
An. Imp. Ne-
ronis Cæs.
Aug. 8.

ᵃ being aliens from the commonwealth of Israel, and strangers
from ᵇ the covenants of promise,
ᶜ having no hope, ᵈ and without
God in the world :

13 ᵉ But now, in Christ Jesus, ye who some-

times were ᶠ far off, are made
nigh by the blood of Christ.

14 For ᵍ he is our peace, ʰ who
hath made both one, and hath bro-
ken down the middle wall of partition *between us;*

15 ⁱ Having abolished ᵏ in his flesh the en-

A. M. cir. 4065.
A. D. cir. 61.
A. U. C. 813.
An. Imp. Ne-
ronis Cæs.
Aug. 8.

ᵃ See Ezek. xiii. 9 ; John x. 16.——ᵇ Rom. ix. 4, 8.——ᶜ 1 Thess.
iv. 13.——ᵈ Gal. iv. 8 · 1 Thess. iv. 5.——ᵉ Gal. iii. 28.——ᶠ Acts
ii. 39 ; ver. 17.

ᵍ Mic. v. 5 ; John xvi. 33 ; Acts x. 36 ; Rom. v. 1 ; Col. i. 20.
ʰ John x. 16 ; Galatians iii. 28.——ⁱ Col. ii. 14, 20.——ᵏ Col.
i. 22.

---

of the *Christ* or *Messiah*, and no title to the blessings
which were to proceed from him.

Aliens from the commonwealth of Israel] Ye were
by your birth, idolatry, &c., *alienated* from the commonwealth of Israel—from the *civil* and *religious privileges* of the Jewish people.

Strangers from the covenants of promise] Having
no part in the *promise* of the covenant made with Abraham, whether considered as relating to his *natural* or
spiritual seed ; and no part in that of the covenant
made at Horeb with the Israelites, when a holy law
was given them, and God condescended to dwell among
them, and to lead them to the promised land.

Having no hope] Either of the *pardon* of sin or of
the *resurrection* of the *body*, nor indeed of the *immortality* of the *soul*. Of all these things the Gentiles
had no rational or well-grounded hope.

Without God in the world] They had gods many,
and lords many ; but in no Gentile nation was the true
God known : nor indeed had they any correct notion
of the Divine nature. Their idols were by *nature no
gods*—they could neither do evil nor good, and therefore they were properly *without God*, having no true
object of worship, and no source of comfort. He who
has neither *God* nor *Christ* is in a most deplorable
state ; he has neither a God to worship, nor a Christ
to justify him. And this is the state of every man
who is living without the *grace* and *Spirit of Christ.*
All such, whatever they may profess, are no better than
practical atheists.

Verse 13. Ye who sometimes were far off] To be
far off, and to be *near*, are sayings much in use among
the Jews ; and among them, to be *near* signifies, 1. To
be in the *approbation* or *favour* of God ; and to be *far
off* signifies to be under his *displeasure.* So a *wicked*
Jew might be said to be *far off* from God when he was
exposed to his *displeasure ;* and a *holy man*, or a genuine *penitent*, might be said to be *nigh to God*, because such persons are in his *favour.* 2. Every person who offered a *sacrifice* to God was considered as
having *access* to him by the *blood* of that *sacrifice :*
hence the priests, whose office it was to offer sacrifices,
were considered as being *nigh to God ;* and all who
brought gifts to the altar were considered as *approaching* the Almighty. 3. Being *far off*, signified the state
of the *Gentiles* as contradistinguished from the *Jews*,
who were *nigh.* And these expressions were used in
reference to the tabernacle, God's dwelling-place among
the Israelites, and the sacrifices there offered. All
those who had *access* to this *tabernacle*, or were *nigh
to it* or encamped about it, were said to be *nigh to God ;*
those who had *no access* to it were said to be *far off.*

Hence the latter phrase is used to distinguish the *Gentiles* from the *Jewish* people ; and this appears to be
the meaning of the prophet, Isa. lvii. 19 : *I create the
fruit of the lips ; Peace* to him that is *far off*,
and to him that is *near, saith the Lord ;* i. e. I give
cause of *praise* and *rejoicing* to the *Gentile* as well as
to the *Jew.* And to this scripture, and to this thing,
the apostle seems here to allude. You Gentiles, who
were *unacquainted* with God, and were even *without
God in the world*, are brought to an *acquaintance* with
him ; and are now, through Christ Jesus, brought into
the favour and fellowship of God. And as the Jews
of old *approached* God by the *blood* of their *sacrifices,*
so *you* approach him *by the blood of Christ.*

Verse 14. For he is our peace] Jesus Christ has
died for both Jews and Gentiles, and has become a
peace-offering, שלום *shalom*, to reconcile both to God
and to each other.

Who hath made both one] Formed one Church out
of the believers of both people.

The middle wall of partition] By abolishing the law
of Jewish ordinances, he has removed that which kept
the two parties, not only in a state of *separation*, but
also at *variance.*

This expression, the *middle wall*, can refer only to
that most marked *distinction* which the Jewish laws
and customs made between them and all other nations
whatsoever.

Some think it refers to their ancient manner of living among the Gentiles, as they always endeavoured to
live in some place *by themselves*, and to have a *river*
or a *wall* between them and their heathen neighbours.
Indeed, wherever they went, their own rites, ordinances, and customs were a sufficient separation between
them and others ; and as Jesus Christ abolished those
customs, admitting all into his Church, both Jews and
Gentiles, by *repentance* and *faith*, he may be said to
have *broken down the middle wall of partition.* When,
at the death of Christ, the *veil* of the temple was *rent*
from the top to the bottom, it was an emblem that *the
way to the holiest was laid open*, and that the people
at large, both Jews and Gentiles, were to have *access*
to the *holiest* by the *blood of Jesus.*

Some think there is an allusion here to the wall
called *chel*, which separated the *court of Israel* from
the *court of the Gentiles ;* but this was not broken down
till the temple itself was destroyed : and to this transaction the apostle cannot be supposed to allude, as it did
not take place till long after the writing of this epistle.

Verse 15. Having abolished in his flesh] By his
incarnation and *death* he not only made an atonement
for sin, but he appointed the *doctrine of reconciliation*

3

A. M. cir. 4065.
A. D. cir. 61.
A. U. C. 813.
An. Imp. Ne-
ronis Cæs.
Aug. 8.

mity, *even* the law of command-ments *contained* in ordinances; for to make in himself of twain one [1] new man, *so* making peace;

16 And that he might [m] reconcile both unto God in one body by the cross, [n] having slain the enmity [o] thereby:

17 And came [p] and preached peace to you

which were afar off, and to [q] them that were nigh.

18 For [r] through him we both have access [s] by one spirit unto the Father.

19 Now therefore, ye are no more strangers and foreigners, but [t] fellow citizens with the saints, and of [u] the household of God;

A. M. cir. 4065.
A. D. cir. 61.
A. U. C. 813.
An. Imp. Ne-
ronis Cæs.
Aug. 8.

---

[1] 2 Cor. v. 17; Gal. vi. 15; chap. iv. 24.——[m] Col. i. 20, 21, 22. [n] Rom. vi. 6; viii. 3; Col. ii. 14.——[o] Or, *in himself.*——[p] Isa. lvii. 19; Zech. ix. 10; Acts ii. 39; x. 36; Romans v. 1; verse 13, 14.

[q] Psa. cxlviii. 14.——[r] John x. 9; xiv. 6; Rom. v. 2; chap. iii. 12; Heb. iv. 19; x. 19, 20; 1 Pet. iii. 18.——[s] 1 Cor. xii. 13; chap. iv. 4.——[t] Phil. iii. 20; Heb. xii. 22, 23.——[u] Gal. vi. 10; chap. iii. 15.

---

to God, and of *love to each other*, to be preached in all nations; and thus glory was brought to God in the highest, and on earth, peace and good will were diffused among men.

The *enmity* of which the apostle speaks was reciprocal among the *Jews* and *Gentiles*. The *former* detested the *Gentiles*, and could hardly allow them the denomination of *men*; the *latter* had the *Jews* in the most sovereign contempt, because of the peculiarity of their religious rites and ceremonies, which were different from those of all the other nations of the earth.

The law of commandments] Contained in, or rather *concerning, ordinances*; which law was made merely for the purpose of keeping the Jews a *distinct* people, and pointing out the Son of God till he should come. When, therefore, the *end* of its institution was answered, it was no longer *necessary*; and Christ by his death abolished it.

To make in himself] To make one Church out of both people, which should be considered the *body* of which Jesus Christ is the *head*. Thus he makes *one new man*—one new Church; and thus he *makes* and establishes *peace*. I think the apostle still alludes to the *peace-offering*, שלום *shalom*, among the Jews. They have a saying, *Sephra*, fol. 121: *Whosoever offers a peace-offering sacrifice, brings peace to the world*. Such a peace-offering was the death of Christ, and by it *peace* is restored to the earth.

Verse 16. *That he might reconcile both—in one body*] That the Jews and Gentiles, believing on the Lord Jesus, might lay aside all their causes of contention, and become one spiritual *body*, or *society* of men, influenced by the *Spirit*, and acting according to the *precepts* of the *Gospel*.

Having slain the enmity thereby] Having, by his death upon the cross, made reconciliation between God and man, and by his Spirit in their hearts removed the *enmity* of their fallen, sinful nature. Dr. Macknight thinks that *abolishing the enmity* is spoken of the removal of the *hatred* which the Jews and Gentiles mutually bore to each other, because of the *difference* of their *respective religious worship*; and that *slaying* the *enmity* refers to the *removal* of evil *lusts* and *affections* from the heart of man, by the power of Divine grace. This is nearly the sense given above.

Verse 17. *And came and preached peace*] Proclaimed the readiness of God to forgive and save both Jews and Gentiles. See the note on ver. 13.

Verse 18. *For through him*] Christ Jesus, *we both*—Jews and Gentiles, *have access by one Spirit*—through the influence of the Holy Ghost, *unto the Father*—God Almighty. This text is a plain proof of the *holy Trinity*. Jews and Gentiles are to be presented unto God *the* FATHER; the SPIRIT of God works in their hearts, and prepares them for this presentation; and JESUS CHRIST himself *introduces* them. No soul can have access to God but by Jesus Christ, and he introduces none but such as receive his *Holy Spirit*. All who receive that Spirit are equally dear to him; and, whatever their names be among men, they are known in heaven as *children of God*, and *heirs of eternal glory*.

Verse 19. *Ye are no more strangers*] In this chapter the *Church* of God is compared to a *city*, which has a variety of privileges, rights, &c., founded on regular *charters* and *grants*. The *Gentiles*, having believed in Christ, are all incorporated with the believing *Jews* in this holy city. Formerly, when any of them came to Jerusalem, being ξένοι, *strangers*, they had no kind of rights whatever; nor could they, as *mere heathens*, settle among them. Again, if any of them, convinced of the errors of the Gentiles, acknowledged the God of Israel, but did not receive *circumcision*, he might dwell in the land, but he had no right to the blessings of the covenant; such might be called πάροικοι, *sojourners*—persons who have no property in the land, and may only rent a house for the time being.

Fellow citizens with the saints] Called to the enjoyment of *equal privileges* with the *Jews* themselves, who, by profession, were a *holy* people; who were bound to be *holy*, and therefore are often called *saints*, or *holy persons*, when both their hearts and conduct were far from being right in the sight of God. But the *saints* spoken of here are the *converted* or *Christianized* Jews.

Of the household of God] The *house of God* is the *temple*; the temple was a *type* of the Christian Church; this is now become God's house; all genuine believers are considered as being οἰκεῖοι, *domestics*, of this house, the *children* and *servants* of God Almighty, having all equal rights, privileges, and advantages; as all, through one Spirit, by the sacred head of the family, had equal access to God, and each might receive as much grace and as much glory as his soul could possibly contain.

2

A. M. cir. 4065.
A. D. cir. 61.
A. U. C. 813.
An. Imp. Ne-
ronis Cæs.
Aug. 8.

20 And are ᵛ built ʷ upon the foundation of the ˣ apostles and prophets, Jesus Christ himself being ʸ the chief corner *stone;*

21 ᶻ In whom all the building, fitly framed together, groweth unto ᵃ a holy temple in the Lord:

22 ᵇ In whom ye also are builded together for a habitation of God through the Spirit.

A. M. cir. 4065.
A. D. cir. 61.
A. U. C. 813.
An. Imp. Ne-
ronis Cæs.
Aug. 8.

ᵛ 1 Cor. iii. 9, 10; chap. iv. 12; 1 Pet. ii. 4, 5.——ʷ Matt. xvi. 18; Gal. ii. 9; Rev. xxi. 14.——ˣ 1 Cor. xii. 28; chap. iv. 11.

ʸ Psa. cxviii. 22; Isa. xxviii. 16; Matt. xxi. 42.——ᶻ Ch. iv. 15, 16.——ᵃ 1 Cor. iii. 17; vi. 19; 2 Cor. vi. 16.——ᵇ 1 Pet. ii. 5.

Verse 20. *And are built upon the foundation*] Following the same metaphor, comparing the Church of Christ to a *city*, and to the *temple*, the believing Ephesians are represented as *parts of that building;* the *living stones* out of which it is principally formed, 1 Pet. ii. 4, 5, having for *foundation*—the ground plan, specification, and principle on which it was builded, the *doctrine* taught by the *prophets* in the Old Testament, and the *apostles* in the New. Jesus Christ being that *corner stone*, or ακρογωνιαιος, the chief angle or foundation corner stone, the *connecting* medium by which both Jews and Gentiles were united in the same building. Elsewhere Jesus Christ is termed the *foundation stone: Behold I lay in Zion a foundation stone, a tried stone, a precious corner stone*, Isa. xxviii. 16; but the meaning is the *same* in all the places where these terms, *foundation* and *corner stone*, occur; for in laying the foundation of a building, a large stone is generally placed at one of the *angles* or *corners*, which serves to form a part of the two walls which meet in that angle. When, therefore, the apostle says that Jesus Christ is the *chief corner stone*, it means such a foundation stone as that above mentioned.

Verse 21. *In whom*] By which foundation corner stone, Christ Jesus, *all the building*, composed of converted Jews and Gentiles, *fitly framed together*, συναρμολογουμενη, *properly jointed and connected together, groweth unto a holy temple*—is continually increasing, as new converts from Judaism or heathenism flock into it. It is not a *finished* building, but will continue to *increase*, and be *more* and *more perfect*, till the day of judgment.

Verse 22. *In whom ye also are builded*] The apostle now applies the *metaphor to the purpose for which he produced it*, retaining however some of the figurative expressions. As the stones in a temple are all properly placed so as to form a complete house, and be a habitation for the *Deity* that is worshipped there, so ye are all, both believing Jews and Gentiles, prepared by the doctrine of the prophets and apostles, under the influence of the Spirit of Christ, to become a habitation of God, a Church in which God shall be worthily worshipped, and in which he can continually dwell.

1. MANY suppose that the apostle in the preceding chapter alludes to the splendour of the *temple of Diana* at *Ephesus*, which was reputed one of the *wonders of the world.* But to me this opinion does not seem sufficiently founded. I believe he has the *Jewish temple* continually in view; for that temple, above all in the universe, could alone be said to be *a habitation of God.* Both in the tabernacle and temple *God dwelt* between the cherubim; *there* was the *symbol* of his presence, and *there* was the *worship* performed which himself had prescribed. After the *model* of this was the spiritual temple, the Christian Church, constructed; and God was to *dwell* in the one, as he had dwelt in the *other.* This simile, drawn from the temple at Jerusalem, was alone worthy of the apostle's design; to have alluded to the temple of *Diana* would have disgraced his subject. And as many at Ephesus were *Jews*, and well acquainted with the temple at Jerusalem, they would both feel and venerate the apostle's simile, and be led to look for the *indwelling of God;* that which distinguished the Jewish temple from all others on the face of the earth.

2. The Church of God is very properly said to be a most noble and wonderful work, and truly worthy of GOD himself.

There is nothing, says one, so *august* as this Church, seeing it is the *temple* of GOD.

Nothing so worthy of *reverence*, seeing God *dwells* in it.

Nothing so *ancient*, since the *patriarchs* and *prophets* laboured in building it.

Nothing so *solid*, since *Jesus Christ* is the *foundation* of it.

Nothing more *closely united* and *indivisible*, since he is the *corner stone.*

Nothing so *lofty*, since it reaches as high as *heaven*, and to the *bosom of God* himself.

Nothing so *regular* and *well proportioned*, since the *Holy Spirit* is the *architect.*

Nothing more *beautiful*, or *adorned* with greater variety, since it consists of *Jews* and *Gentiles*, of every *age, country, sex*, and *condition:* the mightiest *potentates*, the most renowned *lawgivers*, the most profound *philosophers*, the most eminent *scholars*, besides all those of *whom the world was not worthy*, have formed a part of this building.

Nothing more *spacious*, since it is spread over the whole earth, and takes in all who have washed their robes, and made them white in the blood of the Lamb.

Nothing so *inviolable*, since it is consecrated to Jehovah.

Nothing so *Divine*, since it is a *living* building, animated and *inhabited* by the *Holy Ghost.*

Nothing so *beneficent*, seeing it gives *shelter* to the poor, the *wretched*, and *distressed*, of every nation, and kindred, and tongue.

It is the *place* in which God does his marvellous works; the *theatre* of his justice, mercy, goodness, and truth; where he is to be sought, where he is to be *found*, and in which alone he is to be *retained.*

As we have *one* only GOD, and *one* only *Saviour* and *Mediator* between God and man, and *one* only inspiring *Spirit;* so there is but *one Church*, in which

    2

this ineffable Jehovah performs his work of salvation. That Church, however scattered and divided throughout the world, is but *one building*, founded on the *Old* and *New Testaments*; having but one *sacrifice*, the Lord Jesus, the Lamb of God that takes away the sin of the world.

3. Of this glorious Church every Christian soul is an *epitome*; for as God dwells in the Church at large, so he dwells in every believer in particular: each is a *habitation of God through the Spirit.* In vain are all pretensions among sects and parties to the privileges of the Church of Christ, if they have not the *doctrine* ánd *life* of Christ. *Traditions* and *legends* are not

apostolic *doctrines*, and *showy ceremonies* are not the *life of God* in the soul of man.

4. *Religion* has no need of human ornaments or trappings; it shines by its own light, and is refulgent with its own glory. Where it is not in life and power, men have endeavoured to produce a *specious image*, dressed and ornamented with their own hands. Into this God never breathed, therefore it can do no good to man, and only imposes on the ignorant and credulous by a vain show of lifeless pomp and splendour. This phantom, called *true religion* and *the Church* by its votaries, is in heaven denominated *vain superstition;* the speechless symbol of departed piety.

CHAPTER III.

Paul, a prisoner for the testimony of Jesus, declares his knowledge of what had been a mystery from all ages, that the Gentiles should be fellow heirs and of the same body with the Jews, 1–6. Of which doctrine he was made a minister, that he might declare the unsearchable riches of Christ, and make known to principalities and powers this eternal purpose of God, 7–12. He desires them not to be discouraged on account of his tribulations, 13. His prayer that they might be filled with all the fulness of God, 14–19. His doxology, 20, 21.

A. M. cir. 4065.
A. D. cir. 61.
A. U. C. 813.
An. Imp. Neronis Cæs.
Aug. 8.

FOR this cause I Paul, [a] the prisoner of Jesus Christ [b] for you Gentiles,

2 (If ye have heard of [c] the dispensation of the grace of God, [d] which is given me to you-ward:

3 [e] How that [f] by revelation [g] he made known unto me the mystery; [h] as I wrote [i] afore in few words;

4 Whereby, when ye read, ye may understand my knowledge [k] in the mystery of Christ,

A. M. cir. 4065.
A. D. cir. 61.
A. U. C. 813.
An. Imp. Neronis Cæs.
Aug. 8.

---

[a] Acts xxi. 33; xxviii. 17, 20; chap. iv. 1, vi. 20; Phil. i. 7, 13, 14, 16; Col. iv. 3, 18; 2 Tim. i. 8; ii. 9; Phil. i. 9.——[b] Gal. v. 11; Col. i. 24; 2 Tim. ii. 10.——[c] Rom. i. 5; xi. 13; 1 Cor. iv. 1; chap. iv. 7; Col. i. 25.

[d] Acts ix. 15; xiii. 2; Rom. xii. 3; Gal. i. 16; ver. 8. [e] Acts xxii. 17, 21; xxvi. 17, 18.——[f] Gal. i. 12.——[g] Rom. xvi. 25; Col. i. 26, 27.——[h] Chap. i. 9, 10.——[i] Or, *a little before.* [k] 1 Cor. iv. 1; chap. vi. 19.

NOTES ON CHAP. III.

Verse 1. *For this cause*] Because he maintained that the Gentiles were admitted to all the privileges of the Jews, and all the blessings of the new covenant, without being obliged to submit to circumcision, the Jews persecuted him, and caused him to be imprisoned, first at *Cæsarea*, where he was obliged to appeal to the Roman emperor, in consequence of which he was sent prisoner to Rome. See Acts xxi. 21–28, &c.

The prisoner of Jesus Christ for you Gentiles] For preaching the Gospel to the Gentiles, and showing that they were not bound by the law of Moses, and yet were called to be fellow citizens with the saints; for this very cause the Jews persecuted him unto bonds, and conspired his death.

Verse 2. *If ye have heard of the dispensation*] The compound particle ειγè, which is commonly translated *if indeed*, in several places means *since indeed, seeing that*, and should be translated so in this verse, and in several other places of the New Testament. *Seeing ye have heard of the dispensation of God, which is given me to you-ward:* this they had amply learned from the apostle during his stay at Ephesus, for *he had not shunned to declare unto them the whole counsel of God*, Acts xx. 27, and *kept nothing back that was profitable to them*, ver. 20. And this was

certainly among those things that were *most profitable*, and most necessary to be known.

By the *dispensation of the grace of God* we may understand, either the *apostolic office* and *gifts* granted to St. Paul, for the purpose of preaching the Gospel among the Gentiles, see Rom. i. 5; or the *knowledge* which God gave him of that gracious and Divine *plan* which he had formed for the conversion of the Gentiles. For the meaning of the word *economy* see the note on chap. i. 10.

Verse 3. *By revelation he made known unto me*] Instead of εγνωρισε, *he made known*, εγνωρισθη, *was made known*, is the reading of ABCD*FG, several others, both the *Syriac, Coptic, Slavonic, Vulgate*, and *Itala*, with *Clemens, Cyril, Chrysostom, Theodoret, Damascenus*, and others: it is doubtless the *true* reading.

The apostle wishes the Ephesians to understand that it was not an opinion of his own, or a doctrine which he was taught by others, or which he had gathered from the ancient prophets; but one that came to him by immediate revelation from God, as he had informed them before *in a few words*, referring to what he had said chap. i. 9–12.

Verse 4. *Whereby, when ye read*] When ye refer back to them.

2

A. M. cir. 4065.
A. D. cir. 61.
A. U. C. 813.
An. Imp. Ne-
ronis Cæs.
Aug. 8.

5 [1] Which in other ages was not made known unto the sons of men, [m] as it is now revealed unto the holy apostles and prophets by the Spirit ;

6 That the Gentiles [n] should be fellow heirs, and [o] of the same body, and [p] partakers of his promise in Christ by the Gospel :

7 [q] Whereof I was made a minister, [r] according to the gift of the grace of God given unto me by [s] the effectual working of his power.

8 Unto me, [t] who am less than the least of all saints, is this grace given, that [u] I should preach among the Gentiles [v] the unsearchable riches of Christ ;

A. M. cir. 4065.
A. D. cir. 61.
A. U. C. 813.
An. Imp. Ne-
ronis Cæs.
Aug. 8.

---

[l] Acts x. 28 ; Rom. xvi. 25 ; ver. 9.——[m] Chap. ii. 20.——[n] Gal. iii. 28, 29 ; chap. ii. 14.——[o] Chap. ii. 15, 16.——[p] Gal. iii. 14. [q] Rom. xv. 16 ; Col. i. 23, 25.——[r] Rom. i. 5.

[s] Rom. xv. 18 ; chap. i. 19 ; Col. i. 29.——[t] 1 Cor. xv. 9 ; 1 Tim. i. 13, 15.——[u] Gal. i. 16 ; ii. 8 ; 1 Tim. ii. 7 ; 2 Tim. i. 11. [v] Chap. i. 7 ; Col. i. 27.

Ye may understand my knowledge] Ye may see what God has given me to know concerning what has been hitherto a *mystery*—the calling of the Gentiles, and the breaking down the *middle wall* between them and the Jews, so as to make *both one spiritual body*, and on the same conditions.

Verse 5. *Which in other ages was not made known*] That the calling of the Gentiles was made known by the prophets in different ages of the Jewish Church is exceedingly clear ; but it certainly was not made known in that *clear and precise manner* in which it was now revealed by the Spirit unto the ministers of the New Testament : nor was it made known unto them at all, that the Gentiles should find salvation *without coming under the yoke of the Mosaic law*, and that the *Jews* themselves should be *freed from that yoke of bondage ;* these were *discoveries* totally *new*, and now revealed for the first time by the Spirit of God.

Verse 6. *That the Gentiles should be fellow heirs*] This is the *substance* of that mystery which had been hidden from all ages, and which was now made known to the New Testament apostles and prophets, and more particularly to St. Paul.

His promise in Christ] That the promise made to Abraham extended to the *Gentiles*, the apostle has largely proved in his Epistle to the Romans ; and that it was to be fulfilled to them *by* and *through Christ*, he proves there also ; and particularly in his Epistle to the Galatians, see Gal. iii. 14. And that these blessings were to be announced in the preaching of the Gospel, and received on believing it, he every where declares, but more especially in *this* epistle.

Verse 7. *Whereof I was made a minister*] Διακονος· A *deacon*, a *servant* acting *under* and by the *direction* of the *great Master*, Jesus Christ ; from whom, by an especial call and revelation, I received the apostolic gifts and office, and by την ενεργειαν της δυναμεως αυτου, the *energy*, the *in-working of his power*, this Gospel which I preached was made effectual to the salvation of vast multitudes of Jews and Gentiles.

Verse 8. *Less than the least of all saints*] Ελαχιστοτερω παντων ἁγιων. As the design of the apostle was to *magnify* the grace of Christ in the salvation of the world, he uses every precaution to prevent the eyes of the people from being turned to *any thing but Christ crucified ;* and although he was obliged to speak of *himself* as the particular instrument which God had chosen to bring the Gentile world to the knowledge of the truth, yet he does it in such a manner as to show that the excellency of the power was of God, and not

of him ; and that, highly as he and his fellow apostles were honoured they had the *heavenly treasure* in *earthen vessels*. To lay himself as *low* as possible, consistently with his being in the number of Divinely commissioned men, he calls himself *less than the least ;* and is obliged to make a *new word*, by strangely forming a *comparative* degree, not from the *positive*, which would have been a regular grammatical procedure, but from the *superlative*. The adjective ελαχυς signifies *little*, ελασσων or ελαττων, *less*, and ελαχιστος, *least*. On this latter, which is the *superlative* of ελαχυς, *little*, St. Paul forms his *comparative*, ελαχιστοτερος, *less than the least*, a word of which it would be vain to attempt a better translation than that given in our own version. It most strongly marks the unparalleled *humility* of the apostle ; and the amazing condescension of God, in favouring him, who had been before a persecutor and blasphemer, with the knowledge of this glorious scheme of human redemption, and the power to preach it so successfully among the Gentiles.

The unsearchable riches of Christ] The word ανεξιχνιαστος, from *a*, *privative*, and εξιχνιαζω, *to trace out*, from ιχνος, a *step*, is exceedingly well chosen here : it refers to the *footsteps* of God, the *plans* he had formed, the *dispensations* which he had published, and the innumerable *providences* which he had combined, to prepare, mature, and bring to full effect and view his gracious designs in the salvation of a ruined world, by the incarnation, passion, death, and resurrection of his Son. There were in these schemes and providences such *riches*—such an abundance, such a variety, as could not be comprehended even by the naturally vast, and, through the Divine inspiration, unparalledly capacious mind of the apostle.

Yet he was to proclaim among the Gentiles these astonishing wonders and mysteries of grace ; and as he proceeds in this great and glorious work, the Holy Spirit that dwelt in him opens to his mind more and more of those *riches*—leads him into those *footsteps* of the Almighty which could not be *investigated* by man nor angel, so that his preaching and epistles, taken all in their chronological order, will prove that his views brighten, and his discoveries become more numerous and more distinct in proportion as he advances. And had he lived, preached, and written to the present day, he had not *exhausted* the subject, nor fully declared to the Gentiles the *unsearchable riches of Christ*—the endless depths of wisdom and knowledge treasured up in him, and the infinity of saving acts and saving power displayed by him.

A. M. cir. 4065.
A. D. cir. 61.
A. U. C. 813.
An. Imp. Ne-
ronis Cæs.
Aug. 8.

9 And to make all *men* see what *is* the fellowship of ʷ the mystery, ˣ which from the beginning of the world hath been hid in God, ʸ who created all things by Jesus Christ : 10 ᶻ To the intent that now ᵃ unto the principalities and powers in heavenly *places* ᵇ might be known by the Church, the manifold wisdom of God,

11 ᶜ According to the eternal purpose which he purposed in Christ Jesus our Lord :

A. M. cir. 4065
A. D. cir. 61.
A. U. C. 813.
An. Imp. Ne-
ronis Cæs.
Aug. 8.

ʷ Ver. 3; chap. i. 9.——ˣ Rom. xvi. 25; ver. 5; 1 Cor. ii. 7; Col. i 26.——ʸ Psa. xxxiii. 6; John i. 3; Col. i. 16; Heb. i. 2.   ᶻ 1 Pet. i. 12.——ᵃ Rom. viii. 38; chap. i. 21; Col. i. 16; 1 Pet. iii. 22.——ᵇ 1 Cor. ii. 7; 1 Tim. iii. 16.——ᶜ Chap. i. 9.

Verse 9. *And to make all* men *see*] Και φωτισαι παντας· *And to illuminate all ;* to give *information* both to Jews and Gentiles ; to afford them a *sufficiency of light,* so that they might be able distinctly to discern the great objects exhibited in this Gospel.

What is *the fellowship of the mystery*] The word κοινωνια, which we properly translate *fellowship,* was used among the Greeks to signify their *religious communities ;* here it may intimate the *association* of Jews and Gentiles in *one Church* or *body,* and their *agreement* in that glorious mystery which was now so fully opened relative to the salvation of both. But instead of κοινωνια, fellowship, οικονομια, *dispensation* or *economy,* is the reading of ABCDEFG, and more than fifty others ; both the *Syriac, Coptic, Æthiopic, Armenian, Slavonian, Vulgate* and *Itala,* with the chief of the *Greek fathers.* Some of the best *printed editions* of the Greek text have the same reading, and that in our common text has very little authority to support it. *Dispensation* or *economy* is far more congenial to the scope of the apostle's declaration in this place; he wished to show them the *economy* of that *mystery* of bringing Jews and Gentiles to salvation by faith in Christ Jesus, which God from the beginning of the world had kept hidden in his own infinite mind, and did not think proper to reveal even when he projected the creation of the world, which had respect to the economy of human redemption. And although the *world was made by Jesus Christ,* the great Redeemer, yet at that period this revelation of the *power* of God, the design of saving men, whose fall infinite wisdom had foreseen, was not then revealed. This reading *Griesbach* has received into the text.

Who created all things by Jesus Christ] Some very judicious critics are of opinion that this does not refer to the *material creation ;* and that we should understand the whole as referring to the *formation of all God's dispensations of grace, mercy,* and *truth,* which have been *planned, managed,* and *executed* by Christ, from the foundation of the world to the present time. But the words δια Ιησου Χριστου, *by Jesus Christ,* are wanting in ABCD*FG, and several others; also in the *Syriac, Arabic* of Erpen, *Coptic, Æthiopic, Vulgate,* and *Itala ;* as also in several of the *fathers.* Griesbach has thrown the words out of the text ; and *Professor White* says, " certissime delenda," *they are indisputably spurious.* The text, therefore, should be read : *which from the beginning of the world had been hidden in God who created all things.* No *inferiority* of Christ can be argued from a clause of whose spuriousness there is the strongest evidence.

Verse 10. *That now unto the principalities and powers in heavenly* places] Who are these principalities and powers ? Some think *evil angels* are intended, because they are thus denominated, chap. vi. 12. Others think *good angels* are meant ; for as these heavenly beings are curious to investigate the wondrous economy of the Gospel, though they are not its *immediate objects,* see 1 Pet. i. 12, it is quite consistent with the goodness of God to give them that satisfaction which they require. And in this discovery of the Gospel plan of salvation, which *reconciles things in heaven and things on earth*—both men and angels, these pure spirits are greatly interested, and their praises to the Divine Being rendered much more abundant. Others imagine the *Jewish rulers* and *rabbins* are intended, particularly those of them who were converted to Christianity, and who had now learned from the preaching of the Gospel what, as *Jews,* they could never have known. I have had several opportunities of showing that this sort of phraseology is frequent among the Jews, and indeed not seldom used in the New Testament. Dr. Macknight, whose mode of arguing against this opinion is not well chosen, supposes that " the different orders of angels in heaven are intended, whose knowledge of God's dispensations must be as gradual as the dispensations themselves; consequently their knowledge of the manifold wisdom of God must have been greatly increased by the constitution of the Christian Church." Of this there can be no doubt, whether the terms in the text refer to them or not.

By the Church] That is, by the *Christians* and by the wonderful things done in the Church ; and by the apostles, who were its pastors.

The manifold wisdom of God] Ἡ πολυποικιλος σοφια· *That multifarious* and *greatly diversified wisdom of God ;* laying great and infinite plans, and accomplishing them by endless means, through the whole lapse of ages; making every occurrence subservient to the purposes of his infinite mercy and goodness. God's gracious design to save a lost world by Jesus Christ, could not be defeated by any cunning skill or malice of man or devils : whatever hinderances are thrown in the way, his wisdom and power can remove ; and his infinite wisdom can never want *ways* or *means* to effect its gracious designs.

Verse 11. *According to the eternal purpose*] Κατα προθεσιν των αιωνων· *According to the purpose concerning the periods.* This seems to refer to the complete round of the *Jewish system,* and to that of the Gospel. I have often observed, that though the proper grammatical meaning of the word is *ever-during,* or *endless duration,* yet it is often applied to those *systems, periods, governments,* &c., which have a complete *duration,* taking in the whole of them, from their

A. M. cir. 4065.
A. D. cir. 61.
A. U. C. 813.
An. Imp. Ne-
ronis Cæs.
Aug. 8.

12 In whom we have boldness and ^d access ^e with confidence by the faith of him.

13 ^f Wherefore I desire that ye faint not at my tribulations ^g for you, ^h which is your glory.

14 For this cause I bow my knees unto the Father of our Lord Jesus Christ,

15 Of whom ⁱ the whole family in heaven and earth is named,

16 That he would grant you, ^k according to the riches of his glory, ^l to be strengthened with might by his Spirit in ^m the inner man;

A. M. cir. 4065
A. D. cir. 61.
A. U. C. 813.
An. Imp. Ne-
ronis Cæs.
Aug. 8.

---

^d Chap. ii. 18.——^e Heb. iv. 16.——^f Acts xiv. 22 ; Phil. i. 14 ; 1 Thess. iii. 3.——^g Ver. 1.——^h 2 Cor. i. 6.——ⁱ Chap. i. 10 ; Phil. ii. 9, 10, 11.——^k Rom. ix. 23 ; chap. i. 7 ; Phil. iv. 19 ; Col. i. 27. ^l Chap. vi. 10 ; Col. i. 11.——^m Romans vii. 22 ; 2 Cor. iv. 16

---

commencement to their *termination*, leaving nothing of their duration unembraced. So, here, God purposed that the Jewish dispensation should commence at such a time, and terminate at such a time ; that the Gospel dispensation should commence when the Jewish ended, and terminate only with life itself; and that the *results* of both should be *endless*. This is probably what is meant by the above phrase.

Which he purposed in Christ Jesus] Ἣν εποιησεν· *Which he made* or *constituted in* or *for Christ Jesus.* The manifestation of Christ, and the glory which should follow, were the grand objects which God kept in view in all his dispensations.

Verse 12. In whom we have boldness] By whom *we*, Gentiles, ƙave την παρῥησιαν, *this liberty of speech;* so that we may *say* any thing by *prayer* and supplication, and την προσαγωγην, *this introduction*, into the Divine presence by faith in Christ. It is only *in his name* we can *pray* to God, and it is only *by him* that we can *come* to God ; none can give us an *introduction* but Christ Jesus, and it is only for his sake that God will either *hear* or *save* us. It is on the ground of such scriptures as these that we conclude all our prayers *in the name, and for the sake, of Jesus Christ our Lord.*

Verse 13. I desire that ye faint not] In those primitive times, when there was much persecution, people were in continual danger of falling away from the faith who were not well grounded in it. This the apostle deprecates, and advances a strong reason why they should be *firm :* " I suffer my present imprisonment on account of demonstrating your privileges, of which the Jews are envious : I bear my afflictions patiently, knowing that what I have advanced is of God, and thus I give ample proof of the sincerity of my own conviction. The sufferings, therefore, of your apostles are *honourable* to you and to your cause ; and far from being any cause why you should *faint*, or *draw back* like *cowards*, in the day of distress, they should be an additional argument to induce you to persevere."

Verse 14. For this cause I bow my knees] That you may not faint, but persevere, I frequently pray to God, who is our God and the Father of our Lord Jesus. Some very ancient and excellent MSS. and versions omit the words του Κυριου ἡμων Ιησου Χριστου, *of our Lord Jesus Christ.* And in them the passage reads : *I bow my knees unto the Father.* The apostle prays to God the Father, that they may not *faint ;* and he bows his knees in this praying. What can any man think of himself, who, in his addresses to God, can either *sit* on his seat or *stand* in the presence

of the *Maker* and *Judge* of all men ? Would they *sit* while addressing any person of ordinary respectability ? If they did so they would be reckoned very *rude* indeed. Would they *sit* in the presence of the *king* of their own land ? They would not be permitted so to do. Is God then to be treated with less respect than a *fellow mortal ? Paul* kneeled in praying, Acts xx. 36 ; xxi. 5. *Stephen* kneeled when he was stoned, Acts vii. 60. And *Peter* kneeled when he raised Tabitha, Acts ix. 40.

Many parts of this prayer bear a strict resemblance to that offered up by Solomon, 2 Chron. vi. 1, &c., when dedicating the temple : *He kneeled down upon his knees before all the congregation of Israel, and spread forth his hands towards heaven;* 2 Chron. vi. 13. The apostle was now dedicating the Christian Church, that then was and that ever should be, to God ; and praying for those blessings which should ever rest on and distinguish it ; and he kneels down after the example of Solomon, and invokes him to whom the first temple was dedicated, and who had made it a type of the Gospel Church.

Verse 15. Of whom the whole family] *Believers* in the Lord Jesus Christ on *earth*, the *spirits of just men made perfect* in a *separate state*, and all the holy *angels* in heaven, make but *one family*, of which **God** is the Father and Head. St. Paul does not say, of whom the *families*, as if each order formed a *distinct household ;* but he says *family*, because they are all *one*, and of *one*. And all this family is *named*—derives its *origin* and *being*, from God, as children derive their name from him who is the father of the family : holy persons in heaven and earth derive their being and their holiness from God, and therefore his name is called upon them. *Christ* gives the name of *Christians* to all the real members of his Church upon earth ; and to all the spirits of just men (saved since his advent, and through his blood) in heaven. They are all the *sons and daughters of God Almighty.*

Verse 16. That he would grant you] This prayer of the apostle is one of the most grand and sublime in the whole oracles of God. The riches of the grace of the Gospel, and the extent to which the soul of man may be saved here below, are most emphatically pointed out here. Every word seems to have come immediately from heaven ; labouring to convey ideas of infinite importance to mankind. No paraphrase can do it justice, and few commentators seem to have entered into its spirit ; perhaps deterred by its unparalleled sublimity. I shall only attempt a few observations upon the *terms*, to show their force and meaning ; and leave all the rest to that Spirit by which these

2

A. M. cir. 4065.
A. D. cir. 61.
A. U. C. 813.
An. Imp. Ne-
ronis Cæs.
Aug. 8.

17 [n] That Christ may dwell in your hearts by faith; that ye, [o] being rooted and grounded in love,

18 [p] May be able to comprehend with all saints, [q] what *is* the breadth, and length, and depth, and height;

A. M. cir. 4065.
A. D. cir. 61.
A. U. C. 813.
An. Imp. Ne-
ronis Cæs.
Aug. 8.

[n] John xiv. 23; chap. ii. 22.——[o] Col. i. 23; ii. 7.

[p] Chap. i. 18.——[q] Rom. x. 3, 11, 12.

most important words were dictated. In the mean time referring the reader to the discourse lately published on this prayer of the apostle, entitled, *The Family of God and its Privileges.*

That he would grant you—You can expect nothing from him but as a *free gift* through Christ Jesus; let this be a ruling sentiment of your hearts when you pray to God.

According to the riches of his glory] According to the measure of his own eternal *fulness;* God's infinite mercy and goodness being the *measure* according to which we are to be saved. In giving alms it is a maxim that every one should act according to his *ability.* It would be a disgrace to a *king* or a *nobleman* to give no more than a *tradesman* or a *peasant.* God acts up to the dignity of his infinite perfections; he gives *according* to the *riches* of his *glory.*

To be strengthened with might] Ye have *many enemies,* cunning and *strong; many trials,* too great for your *natural strength; many temptations,* which no *human power* is able successfully to *resist; many duties* to *perform,* which cannot be accomplished by the *strength* of *man;* therefore you need *Divine strength;* ye must have might; and ye must be *strengthened every where,* and *every way fortified* by that might; *mightily* and most *effectually strengthened.*

By his Spirit] By the sovereign energy of the Holy Ghost. This fountain of spiritual *energy* can alone supply the *spiritual strength* which is necessary for this *spiritual work* and *conflict.*

In the inner man] In the soul. Every man is a *compound* being; he has a *body* and a soul. The *outward man* is that alone which is *seen* and *considered* by men; the *inward man* is that which stands particularly in reference to God and eternity. The outward man is strengthened by *earthly food,* &c.; the inward man, by *spiritual* and *heavenly influences.* Knowledge, love, peace, and holiness, are the food of the inward man; or rather Jesus Christ, that bread of life which came down from heaven: he that eateth this bread shall live and be strengthened by it. The soul must be as truly fed and nourished by Divine food as the body by natural food.

Verse 17. *That Christ may dwell in your hearts by faith*] In this as well as in many other passages, and particularly that in chap. ii. 21, (where see the note,) the apostle compares the *body* or *Church* of true believers to a *temple,* which, like that of Solomon, is built up to be a *habitation of God* through the Spirit. Here, as Solomon did at the dedication of the temple at Jerusalem, 2 Chron. vi. 1, &c., Paul, having considered the Church at Ephesus *completely formed,* as to every external thing, prays that God may come down and *dwell in it.* And as there could be no indwelling of God but by *Christ,* and no indwelling of Christ but by *faith,* he prays that they may have such

faith in Christ, as shall keep them in constant possession of his love and presence. God, at the beginning, formed man to be his *temple,* and while in a state of purity he inhabited this temple; when the temple became defiled, God left it. In the order of his eternal mercy, Christ, the repairer of the breach, comes to purify the temple, that it may again become a fit habitation for the blessed God. This is what the apostle points out to the believing Ephesians, in praying that Christ κατοικησαι, might *intensely* and *constantly dwell in their hearts by faith:* for the man's heart, which is not God's house, must be a hold of every foul and unclean spirit; as Satan and his angels will endeavour to *fill* what God does not.

That ye, being rooted and grounded in love] Here is a *double* metaphor; one taken from *agriculture,* the other, from *architecture.* As *trees,* they are to be *rooted in love*—this is the *soil* in which their souls are to *grow;* into the infinite love of God their souls by faith are to strike their *roots,* and from this love derive all that nourishment which is essential for their full growth, till they have the mind in them that was in Jesus, or, as it is afterwards said, till they are *filled with all the fulness of God.* As a *building,* their *foundation* is to be laid in this *love.* *God so loved the world, that he gave his only begotten Son,* &c. Here is the *ground* on which alone the soul, and all its hopes and expectations, can be safely *founded.* This is a *foundation* that cannot be shaken; and it is from this alone that the doctrine of redemption flows to man, and from this alone has the soul its form and comeliness. In this, as its proper *soil,* it *grows.* On this, as its only *foundation,* it *rests.*

Verse 18. *May be able to comprehend with all saints*] Ἱνα εξισχυσητε καταλαβεσθαι. These words are so exceedingly nervous and full of meaning, that it is almost impossible to translate them. The first word, εξισχυσητε, from εξ, *intensive,* and ισχυω, *to be strong,* signifies that they might be *thoroughly able,* by having been *strengthened with might,* by God's *power.* The second word καταλαβεσθαι, from κατα, *intensive,* and λαμβανω, *to take, catch,* or *seize on,* may be translated, *that ye may fully catch, take in,* and *comprehend this wonderful mystery of God.* The mind must be rendered apt, and the soul invigorated, to take in and *comprehend* these mysteries.

What is the breadth, and length, and depth, and height] Here the apostle still keeps up the metaphor, comparing the Church of God to a building; and as, in order to rear a proper building, formed on scientific principles, a *ground plan* and *specification* must be previously made, according to which the building is to be constructed, the apostle refers to this; for this must be thoroughly understood, without which the building could not be formed. They were to be builded up a *heavenly house,* a *habitation of God through the*

A. M. cir. 4065.
A. D. cir. 61.
A. U. C. 813.
An. Imp. Ne-
ronis Cæs.
Aug. 8.

19 And to know the love of Christ, which passeth knowledge, that ye might be filled ^rwith all the fulness of God.

20 Now ^s unto him that is able to do exceeding abundantly ^t above all that we ask or think,

^u according to the power that worketh in us,

21 ^v Unto him *be* glory in the Church by Christ Jesus, throughout all ages, world without end. Amen.

A. M. cir. 4065
A. D. cir. 61.
A. U. C. 813.
An. Imp. Ne
ronis Cæs.
Aug. 8.

^rJohn i. 16; chapter i. 23; Col. ii. 9, 10.——^s Romans xvi. 25; Jude 24.   ^t1 Cor. ii. 9.——^u Ver. 7; Col. i. 29.——^v Rom. xi. 36; xvi. 27; Heb. xiii. 21.

Spirit; and this must have its *latitude* or *breadth,* its *longitude* or *length,* its *altitude* or *height,* and its *profundity* or *depth.*

It is supposed by some that the apostle is nere alluding to the famous *temple of Diana* at Ephesus, which, as I have already had occasion to remark, was reputed one of the *wonders of the world,* being in length 425 feet, in breadth 220; it was supported by 127 pillars, each 60 feet high; was builded at the expense of all Asia; and was 220 years in being completed. I cannot, however, allow of this allusion while the apostle had a *nobler model* at hand, and one every way more worthy of being brought into the comparison. The temple at Jerusalem was that alone which he had in view; that alone could be fitly compared here; for that was built to be a habitation of God; that was his house, and that the place of his rest: so the Christian temple, and the believing heart, are to be the constant, the endless residence of God; and how august must that edifice be in which the eternal Trinity dwells!

But what can the apostle mean by the *breadth, length, depth,* and *height,* of *the love of God?* Imagination can scarcely frame any satisfactory answer to this question. It takes in the *eternity* of God. God is LOVE; and in that, an infinity of *breadth, length, depth,* and *height,* is included; or rather all *breadth, length, depth,* and *height,* are lost in this *immensity.* It comprehends all that is *above,* all that is *below,* all that is *past,* and all that is *to come.* In reference to human beings, the love of God, in its BREADTH, is a girdle that encompasses the globe; its LENGTH reaches from the *eternal* purpose of the mission of Christ, to the *eternity* of blessedness which is to be spent in his ineffable glories; its DEPTH reaches to the *lowest fallen* of the sons of Adam, and to the *deepest* depravity of the human heart; and its HEIGHT to the infinite dignities of the throne of Christ. *He that overcometh will I give to sit down with me upon my throne, as I have overcome and sat down with the Father upon his throne.* Thus we see that the *Father,* the *Son,* and all true believers in him, are to be seated on the *same throne!* This is the *height* of the love of God, and the *height* to which that love raises the souls that believe in Christ Jesus!

Verse 19. *To know the love of Christ, which passeth knowledge*] It is only by the *love of Christ* that we can know the *love of God:* the love of God to man induced him to give Christ for his redemption; Christ's love to man induced him to give his life's blood for his salvation. The gift of Christ *to* man is the *measure* of God's love; the *death* of Christ *for* man is the *measure* of Christ's love. *God so loved the*

world, &c. Christ loved us, and *gave himself for us.*

But how can the love of Christ, *which passeth knowledge,* be *known?* Many have laboured to *reconcile* this seeming *contradiction.* If we take the verb γνωναι in a sense in which it is frequently used in the New Testament, *to approve, acknowledge,* or *acknowledge with approbation,* and γνωσις to signify *comprehension,* then the difficulty will be partly removed: "That ye may *acknowledge, approve,* and *publicly acknowledge,* that love of God which surpasseth knowledge." We can *acknowledge* and *approve* of that which *surpasses* our comprehension. We cannot comprehend GOD; yet we can *know* that he is; *approve* of, *love, adore,* and *serve* him. In like manner, though we cannot *comprehend* the immensity of the *love of Christ,* yet we *know* that he has loved us, and washed us from our sins in his own blood; and we approve of, and acknowledge, him as our only Lord and Saviour. In this sense we may be said to *know* the love of Christ that passeth *knowledge.*

But it is more likely that the word γνωσις, which we translate *knowledge,* signifies here *science* in general, and particularly that *science* of which the *rabbins* boasted, and that in which the Greeks greatly exulted. The former professed to have the *key of knowledge.* the *secret* of all Divine mysteries; the latter considered their *philosophers,* and their *systems of philosophy,* superior to every thing that had ever been known among men, and reputed on this account all other nations as *barbarians.* When the apostle prays that they *may know the love of Christ which passeth knowledge,* he may refer to all the boasted knowledge of the Jewish doctors, and to all the greatly extolled science of the Greek philosophers. To know the love of Christ, infinitely surpasseth all other science. This gives a clear and satisfactory sense.

That ye might be filled with all the fulness of God.] Among all the great sayings in this prayer, this is the greatest. To be FILLED *with God* is a great thing; to be *filled with* the FULNESS *of God* is still greater; but to be *filled with* ALL *the fulness of God,* παν το πληρωμα του Θεου, utterly bewilders the sense and confounds the understanding.

Most people, in quoting these words, endeavour to *correct* or *explain* the apostle, by adding the word *communicable;* but this is as idle as it is useless and impertinent. The apostle *means what he says,* and would be *understood in his own meaning.* By the *fulness of God,* we are to understand all those gifts and graces which he has promised to bestow on man, and which he dispenses to the Church. To be *filled with all the fulness of God,* is to have the whole soul filled with meekness, gentleness, goodness, love, justice, holiness, mercy, and truth. And as what God *fills*, neither sin nor Satan can fill: consequently, it implies that the soul shall be emptied of sin, that sin shall neither have dominion *over* it, nor a being *in* it. It is impossible for us to understand these words in a *lower* sense than this. But *how much more* they imply, (for more they do imply,) I cannot tell. As there is no end to the merits of *Christ*, no bounds to the mercy and love of God, no limits to the improvability of the human soul, so there can be no bounds set to the saving influence which God will dispense to the heart of every believer. We may *ask*, and we shall *receive*, and our joy shall be *full*.

Verse 20. *Now unto him*] Having finished his short, but most wonderfully comprehensive and energetic *prayer*, the apostle brings in his *doxology*, giving praise to Him from whom all blessings come, and to whom all thanks are due.

That is able to do exceeding abundantly] It is impossible to express the full meaning of these words, God is *omnipotent*, therefore he is able to do all things, and able to do ὑπερ εκ περισσου, *superabundantly above the greatest abundance*. And who can doubt this, who has any rational or Scriptural views of his power or his love ?

All that we ask or think] We can *ask* every good of which we have heard, every good which God has promised in his word; and we can *think* of, or *imagine*, goods and blessings beyond all that we have either *read* of or *seen* : yea, we can *imagine* good things to which it is impossible for us to give a *name ;* we can go beyond the limits of all human descriptions; we can imagine more than even God has specified in his word ; and can feel no *bounds* to our imagination of good, but *impossibility* and *eternity :* and after all, *God is able to do more for us than we can ask or think ;* and his *ability* here is so necessarily connected with his *willingness*, that the one indisputably implies the other ; for, of what consequence would it be to tell the Church of God that he had *power to do* so and so, if there were not implied an assurance that he *will do* what his power *can*, and what the soul of man needs to have done ?

According to the power that worketh in us] All that he can do, and all that he has promised to do, will be done *according* to what he has done, by that *power* of the Holy Ghost την ενεργουμενην, *which worketh strongly in us*—acts with *energy* in our hearts, expelling evil, purifying and refining the affections and desires, and implanting good.

Verse 21. *Unto him*] Thus possessed of power and goodness, *be glory in the Church*—be unceasing praises ascribed in all the *assemblies* of the people of God, wherever these glad tidings are preached, and wherever this glorious doctrine shall be credited.

By Christ Jesus] Through whom, and *for* whom, all these miracles of mercy and power are wrought.

Throughout all ages] Εις πασας τας γενεας· Through *all succeeding generations*—while the race of human beings continues to exist on the face of the earth.

World without end.] Του αιωνος των αιωνων· *Throughout eternity*—in the *coming world* as well as in *this*. The song of praise, begun upon *earth*, and

protracted through all the generations of men, shall be continued in *heaven*, by all that are redeemed from the earth, where eras, limits, and periods are no more for ever.

Amen.] So be it ! So let it be ! and so it will be ; for all the counsels of God are faithfulness and truth ; and not one jot or tittle of his promise has failed, from the foundation of the world to the present day ; nor can fail, till mortality is swallowed up of life :

Therefore, to the Father, Son, and Holy Ghost, be glory, dominion, power, and thanksgiving, now, henceforth, and for ever.—Amen and Amen.

1. For the great importance of the *matter* contained in this chapter, and the sublimity of the *language* and *conceptions*, there is no portion of the New Testament equal to this. The apostle was now shut up in prison, but the word of the Lord was not bound ; and the kingdom of God seems to have been opened to him in a most astonishing manner. There seems to have been exhibited to him a *plan of the Divine counsels and conduct* relative to the salvation of man, before and from the foundation of the world to the end of time ; and while, with the eye of his mind, he contemplates this plan, he describes it in language at once the most elevated that can be conceived, and every where dignified and appropriate to the subject ; so that he may with safety be compared with the finest of the Grecian writers. In the notes I have already observed how hard it is to give any literal translation of the many *compound epithets* which the apostle uses. Indeed his own nervous language seems to bend and tremble under the weight of the Divine ideas which it endeavours to express. This is most observable in the *prayer* and *doxology* which are contained in verses 14–21. A passage in Thucydides, lib. vii. cap. lxxxvii, *in fine*, where he gives an account of the total overthrow of the Athenian general, Nicias, and his whole army, by the Sicilians, has been compared with this of the apostle ; it is truly a grand piece, and no reader can be displeased with its introduction here : ξυνεβη τε εργον τουτο Ἑλληνικον των κατα τον πολεμον τονδε μεγιστον γενεσθαι—και τοις τε κρατησασι λαμπροτατον, και τοις διαφθαρεισι δυστυχεστατον· κατα παντα γαρ παντως νικηθεντες, και ουδεν ολιγον ες ουδεν κακοπαθησαντες, πανωλεθρια δη, το λεγομενον, και πεζος και νηες, και ουδεν ὁ, τι ουκ απωλετο· και ολιγοι απο πολλων επ᾽ οικου απενοστησαν· "This was the greatest discomfiture which the Greeks sustained during the whole war, and was as brilliant to the conquerors as it was calamitous to the vanquished. In *every respect* they were *totally defeated ;* and they *suffered no small evil* in *every particular :* the *destruction was universal,* both of army and navy ; there was *nothing that did not perish ;* and scarcely any, out of vast multitudes, returned to their own homes."

The learned may compare the two passages ; and while due credit is given to the splendid Greek historian, no critic will deny the palm to the inspired writer.

2. With such portions of the word of God before us, how is it that we can be said conscientiously to credit the doctrines of Christianity, and live satisfied with such *slender attainments* in the divine life ? Can any man that pleads for the *necessary* and *degrading*

continuance of *indwelling sin*, believe what the apostle has written? Can we, who profess to believe it, be excusable, and live under the influence of any temper or passion that does not belong to the mind of Christ? Will it be said in answer, that " this is only a *prayer* of the apostle, and contains his *wish* from the over-flowings of his heart for the spiritual prosperity of the Ephesians?" Was the apostle *inspired* or *not* when he penned this prayer? If he were *not* inspired, the prayer makes no part of Divine *revelation*; if he *were* inspired, every *petition* is tantamount to a positive *promise*; for what God inspires the heart to pray for, that God purposes to bestow. Then it is his *will* that all these blessings should be enjoyed by his true followers, that Christ should inhabit their hearts, and that

they should be filled with all the fulness of God; yea, and that God should do for them more abundantly than they can ask or think. This necessarily implies that they should be *saved from all sin, inward and outward*, in *this life*; that the thoughts of their hearts should be cleansed by the inspiration of God's Holy Spirit, that they might perfectly love him, and worthily magnify his holy name.

As *sin* is the cause of the ruin of mankind, the Gospel system, which is its *cure*, is called *good news*, or *glad tidings*; and it is *good news* because it proclaims *him* who saves his people from their sins. It would be dishonourable to the *grace* of Christ to suppose that sin had made *wounds* which that could not heal.

CHAPTER IV.

The apostle exhorts them to walk worthy of their vocation, and to live in peace and unity, 1–6. Shows that God has distributed a variety of gifts, and instituted a variety of offices in his Church, for the building up and perfecting of the body of Christ, 7–13. Teaches them the necessity of being well instructed and steady in Divine things, 14. Teaches how the body or Church of Christ is constituted, 15, 16. Warns them against acting like the Gentiles, of whose conduct he gives a lamentable description, 17–19. Points out how they had been changed, in consequence of their conversion to Christianity, 20, 21. Gives various exhortations relative to the purification of their minds, their conduct to each other, and to the poor, 22–28. Shows them that their conversation should be chaste and holy, that they might not grieve the Spirit of God; that they should avoid all bad tempers, be kindly affectioned one to another, and be of a forgiving spirit, 29–32.

A. M. cir. 4065.
A. D. cir. 61.
A. U. C. 813.
An. Imp. Neronis Cæs.
Aug. 8.

I THEREFORE, [a] the prisoner [b] of the Lord, beseech you that ye [c] walk worthy of the vocation wherewith ye are called,

2 [d] With all lowliness and meekness, with long-suffering, forbearing one another in love;

A. M. cir. 4065.
A. D. cir. 61.
A. U. C. 813.
An. Imp. Neronis Cæs.
Aug. 8.

[a] Ch. iii. 1; Philem. 9.——[b] Or, *in the Lord*.——[c] Phil. i. 27; Col. i. 10; 1 Thess. ii. 12.——[d] Acts xx. 19; Gal. v. 22, 23; Col. iii. 12, 13.

NOTES ON CHAP. IV.

Verse 1. *I therefore*] Therefore, because God has provided for you such an abundant salvation, and ye have his testimonies among you, and have full liberty to use all the means of grace;

The prisoner of the Lord] Who am deprived of my liberty for the Lord's sake,

Beseech you that ye walk] Ye have your liberty, and may *walk*; I am deprived of mine, and *cannot*. This is a fine stroke, and wrought up into a strong argument. You who are at *large* can show forth the virtues of him who called you into his marvellous *light*; I am in *bondage*, and can only exhort others by my writing, and show my submission to God by my *patient suffering*.

The vocation wherewith ye are called] The *calling*, κλησις, is the free invitation they have had from God to receive the privileges of the Gospel, and become his sons and daughters, without being obliged to observe Jewish rites and ceremonies. Their vocation, or calling, took in their Christian profession, with all the doctrines, precepts, privileges, duties, &c., of the Christian religion.

Among us, a man's *calling* signifies his *trade*, or

occupation in life; that at which he *works*, and by which he *gets his bread*; and it is termed his *calling*, because it is supposed that God, in the course of his providence, calls the person to be thus employed, and thus to acquire his livelihood. Now, as it is a very poor *calling* by which a man *cannot live*, so it is a poor *religion* by which a man cannot get his soul *saved*. If, however, a man have an honest and useful trade, and employ himself diligently in labouring at it, he will surely be able to maintain himself by it; but without care, attention, and industry, he is not likely to get, even by this *providential calling*, the necessaries of life. In like manner, if a man do not walk worthy of his heavenly calling, i. e. suitable to its prescriptions, spirit, and design, he is not likely to get his soul saved unto eternal life. The best *trade*, unpractised, will not support any man; the most pure and holy religion of the Lord Jesus, unapplied, will save no soul. Many suppose, because they have a *sound faith*, that all is safe and well: as well might the mechanic, who knows he has a *good trade*, and that he understands the principles of it well, suppose it will maintain him, though he brings none of its principles into action by honest, assiduous, and well-directed labour.

A. M. cir. 4065.
A. D. cir. 61.
A. U. C. 813.
An. Imp. Ne-
ronis Cæs.
Aug. 8.

3 Endeavouring to keep the unity of the Spirit *e* in the bond of peace.

4 *f There is* one body, and *g* one Spirit, even as ye are called in one *h* hope of your calling,

5 *i* One Lord, *k* one faith, *l* one baptism,

6 *m* One God and Father of all, who *is* above all, and *n* through all, and in you all.

7 But *o* unto every one of us is given grace according to the measure of the gift of Christ.

8 Wherefore he saith, *p* When he ascended up on high, *q* he led *r* captivity captive, and gave gifts unto men.

A. M. cir. 4065.
A. D. cir. 61.
A. U. C. 813.
An. Imp. Ne-
ronis Cæs.
Aug. 8.

---

e Col. iii. 14.——*f* Rom. xii. 5; 1 Cor. xii. 12, 13; chap. ii. 16. *g* 1 Cor. xii. 4, 11.——*h* Chap. i. 18.——*i* 1 Cor. i. 13; viii. 6; xii. 5; 2 Cor. xi. 4.——*k* Jude 3; ver. 13.——*l* Gal. iii. 27, 28;

m Mal. ii. 10; 1 Cor. viii. 6; xii. 6.——*n* Rom. xi. 36.——*o* Rom. xii. 3, 6; 1 Cor. xii. 11.——*p* Psa. lxviii. 18; *q* Judges v. 12; Col. ii. 15.——*r* Or, *a multitude of captives.*

Some suppose that the *calling* refers to the epithets usually given to the Christians; such as *children of Abraham, children of God, true Israel of God, heirs of God, saints, fellow citizens with the saints,* &c., &c.; and that these honourable appellations must be a strong excitement to the Ephesians to walk worthy of these exalted characters. But I do not find that the word κλησις, *calling,* is taken in this sense any where in the New Testament; but that it has the meaning which I have given it above is evident from 1 Cor. vii. 20: Ἑκαστος εν τη κλησει ᾗ εκληθη, εν ταυτη μενετω· *Let every man abide in the calling to which he hath been called.* The context shows that *condition, employment,* or *business of life,* is that to which the apostle refers.

Verse 2. With all lowliness] It is by acting as the apostle here directs that a man walks worthy of this high vocation; ταπεινοφροσυνη signifies *subjection* or *humility of mind.*

Meekness] The opposite to anger and irritability of disposition.

Long-suffering] Μακροθυμια· *Long-mindedness*—never permitting a trial or provocation to get to the *end* of your patience.

Forbearing one another] Ανεχομενοι αλληλων· *Sustaining one another*—helping to *support* each other in all the miseries and trials of life: or, if the word be taken in the sense of *bearing with each other,* it may mean that, through the love of God working in our hearts, we should bear with each other's infirmities, ignorance, &c., knowing how much others have been or are still obliged to bear with us.

Verse 3. Endeavouring to keep the unity of the Spirit in the bond of peace.] There can be no doubt that the Church at Ephesus was composed partly of converted *Jews,* as well as *Gentiles.* Now, from the different manner in which they had been brought up, there might be frequent causes of *altercation.* Indeed, the Jews, though converted, might be envious that the Gentiles were admitted to the same glorious privileges with themselves, without being initiated into them by bearing the *yoke* and *burden* of the Mosaic law. The apostle guards them against this, and shows them that they should *intensely labour* (for so the word σπουδαζειν implies) to promote and preserve *peace* and *unity.* By the *unity of the Spirit* we are to understand, not only a *spiritual* unity, but also a unity of sentiments, desires, and affections, such as is worthy of and springs from the Spirit of God. By the *bond of peace* we are to understand a peace or union, where the interests of all parties are concentrated, cemented, and sealed; the Spirit of God being the seal upon this knot.

Verse 4. There is one body] Viz. of Christ, which is his Church.

One Spirit] The Holy Ghost, who animates this body.

One hope] Of everlasting glory, to which glory ye have been called by the preaching of the Gospel; through which ye have become the body of Christ, instinct with the energy of the Holy Ghost.

Verse 5. One Lord] Jesus Christ, who is the governor of this Church.

One faith] One system of religion, proposing the same objects to the faith of all.

One baptism] Administered in the name of the holy Trinity; indicative of the influences, privileges, and effects of the Christian religion.

Verse 6. One God] The fountain of all being, self-existent and eternal; and *Father of all,* both Jews and Gentiles, because he is the Father of the spirits of all flesh.

Who is above all] Ὁ επι παντων· *Who is over all;* as the King of kings, and Lord of lords.

And through all] Pervading every thing; being present with every thing; providing for all creatures; and by his energy supporting all things.

And in you all.] By the energy of his Spirit, enlightening, quickening, purifying, and comforting; in a word, making your hearts the temples of the Holy Ghost. Some think the mystery of the blessed Trinity is contained in this verse: God is over all, as *Father; through all,* by the *Logos* or *Word;* and *in all,* by the *Holy Spirit.*

Verse 7. Unto every one of us is given grace] *Grace* may here signify a particular *office;* as if the apostle had said: Though we are all *equal* in the respects already mentioned, yet we have all different offices and situations to fill up in the Church and in the world; and we receive a *free gift* from Christ, according to the nature of the *office,* that we may be able to discharge it according to his own mind. So the *free gift,* which we receive from Christ, is according to the office or function which he has given us to fulfil; and the *office* is according to that *free gift,* each suited to the other.

Verse 8. Wherefore he saith] The reference seems to be to Psa. lxviii. 18, which, however it may speak of the removal of the tabernacle, appears to have been intended to point out the glorious ascension of Christ after his resurrection from the dead. The expositions

A. M. cir. 4065.
A. D. cir. 61.
A. U. C. 813.
An. Imp. Ne-
ronis Cæs.
Aug. 8.

9 ^s (Now that he ascended, what is it but that he also descended first into the lower parts of the earth?

10 He that descended is .the same also ^t that ascended up far above all heavens, ^u that he might ^v fill all things.)

11 ^w And he gave some, apostles; and some,

prophets; and some, ^x evangelists · and some, ^y pastors and ^z teachers;

12 ^a For the perfecting of the saints, for the work of the ministry, ^b for the edifying of ^c the body of Christ:

13 Till we all come ^d in the unity of the faith, ^e and of the knowledge of the Son of God,

A. M. cir. 4065.
A. D. cir. 61.
A. U. C. 813.
An. Imp. Ne-
ronis Cæs.
Aug. 8.

---

^s John iii. 13; vi. 33, 62.——^t Acts i. 9, 11; 1 Tim. iii. 16; Heb. iv. 14; vii. 26; viii. 1; ix. 24.——^u Acts ii. 33.——^v Or, *fulfil.*——^w 1 Cor. xii. 28; chap. ii. 20.

^x Acts xxi. 8; 2 Tim. iv. 5.——^y Acts xx. 28.——^z Rom. xii. 7.——^a 1 Cor. xii. 7.——^b 1 Cor. xiv. 26.——^c Chap. i. 23; Col. i. 24.——^d Or, *into the unity.*——^e Col. ii. 2.

---

of various commentators have made the place extremely difficult. I shall not trouble my reader with them; they may be seen in *Rosenmüller.*

When he ascended up on high] The whole of this verse, as it stands in the psalm, seems to refer to a military triumph. Take the following paraphrase: *Thou hast ascended on high:* the conqueror was placed in a very *elevated* chariot. *Thou hast led captivity captive:* the conquered kings and generals were usually bound behind the chariot of the conqueror, to grace the triumph. *Thou hast received gifts for* (Paul, *given gifts unto) men:* at such times the conqueror was wont to throw *money* among the crowd. *Even to the rebellious:* those who had fought against him now submit unto him, and share his munificence; for it is the property of a hero to be generous. *That the Lord God might dwell among them:* the conqueror being now come to fix his abode in the conquered provinces, and subdue the people to his laws.

All this the apostle applies to the resurrection, ascension, and glory of Christ; though it has been doubted by some learned men whether the psalmist had this in view. I shall not dispute about this; it is enough for me that the apostle, under the inspiration of God, applied the verse in this way; and whatever David might intend, and of whatever event he might have written, we see plainly that the sense in which the apostle uses it was the sense of the Spirit of God; for the Spirit in the Old and New Testaments is the same. I may venture a short criticism on a few words in the original: *Thou hast received gifts for men,* לקחת כהנות באדם *lakachta mattanoth baadam,* thou hast taken gifts in man, in Adam. The gifts which Jesus Christ distributes *to man* he has received *in man,* in and by virtue of his *incarnation;* and it is in consequence of his being made man that it may be said, *The Lord God dwells among them;* for Jesus was called *Immanuel,* God with us, in consequence of his incarnation. This view of the subject is consistent with the whole economy of grace, and suits well with the apostle's application of the words of the psalmist in this place.

Verse 9. *But that he also descended*] The meaning of the apostle appears to be this: The person who *ascended* is the Messiah, and his *ascension* plainly intimates his *descension;* that is, his incarnation, humiliation, death, and resurrection.

Verse 10. *He that descended*] And he who descended *so low* is the same who has ascended *so high.* He came to the *lower parts of the earth*—the very deepest abasement; having emptied himself, taken

upon him the form of a servant, and humbled himself unto death, even the death of the cross; now he is ascended *far above all heavens*—higher than all height; he has a name above every name. Here his descending into the *lower parts of the earth* is put in opposition to his ascending *far above all heavens.* His abasement was unparalleled; so also is his exaltation.

That he might fill all things.] That he might be the fountain whence all blessings might flow; dispensing all good things to all his creatures, according to their several capacities and necessities; and, particularly, fill both converted Jews and Gentiles with all the gifts and graces of his Holy Spirit. Hence it follows:

Verse 11. *He gave some, apostles*] He established several *offices* in his Church; furnished these with the proper *officers;* and, to qualify them for their work, gave them the proper *gifts.* For a full illustration of this verse, the reader is requested to refer to the notes on 1 Cor., chap. xii. 6–10, and 28–30; and to the concluding observations at the end of that chapter.

Verse 12. *For the perfecting of the saints*] For the complete instruction, purification, and union of all who have believed in Christ Jesus, both Jews and Gentiles. For the meaning of καταρτισμος, *perfecting,* see the note on 2 Cor. xiii. 9.

For the work of the ministry] All these various officers, and the gifts and graces conferred upon them, were judged necessary, by the great Head of the Church, for its full instruction in the important doctrines of Christianity. The same officers and gifts are still necessary, and God gives them; but they do not know their *places.* In most Christian Churches there appears to be but one office, that of *preacher;* and one gift, that by which he professes to preach. The apostles, prophets, evangelists, pastors, and teachers, are all compounded in the class *preachers;* and many, to whom God has given nothing but the *gift of exhortation,* take texts to explain them; and thus lose their time, and mar their ministry.

Edifying of the body] The body of Christ is his Church, see chap. ii. 20, &c.; and its edification consists in its thorough instruction in Divine things, and its being filled with faith and holiness.

Verse 13. *In the unity of the faith*] Jews and Gentiles being all converted according to the doctrines laid down in the *faith*—the Christian system.

The knowledge of the Son of God] A true understanding of the mystery of the incarnation; why God was manifest in the flesh, and why this was necessary in order to human salvation.

A. M. cir. 4065.
A. D. cir. 61.
A. U. C. 813.
An. Imp. Ne-
ronis Cæs.
Aug. 8.

unto ^f a perfect man, unto the measure of the ^g stature of the fulness of Christ :

14 That we *henceforth* be no more ^h children, ⁱ tossed to and fro, and carried about with every ^k wind of doctrine, by the sleight of men, *and* cunning craftiness, ^l whereby they lie in wait to deceive ;

15 But ^m speaking ⁿ the truth in love, ^o may

grow up into him in all things, ^p which is the head, *even* Christ :

16 ^q From whom the whole body fitly joined together and compacted by that which every joint supplieth, according to the effectual working in the measure of every part, maketh increase of the body unto the edifying of itself in love.

A. M. cir. 4065.
A. D. cir. 61.
A. U. C. 813.
An. Imp. Ne-
ronis Cæs.
Aug. 8.

---

^f 1 Cor. xiv. 20; Col. i. 28.——^g Or, *age.*——^h Isa. xxviii. 9;
1 Cor. xiv. 20.——ⁱ Heb. xiii. 9.——^k Matt. xi. 7.——^l Rom. xvi.
18 ; 2 Cor. ii. 17.

^m Zech. viii. 16; 2 Cor. iv. 2 ; ver. 25 ; John iii. 18.——ⁿ Or,
being sincere.——^o Chap. i. 22 ; ii. 21.——^p Col. i. 18.——^q Col.
ii. 19.

Unto a perfect man] Εις ανδρα τελειον· One thoroughly instructed ; the whole body of the Church being fully taught, justified, sanctified, and sealed.

Measure of the stature] The full measure of knowledge, love, and holiness, which the Gospel of Christ requires. Many preachers, and multitudes of professing people, are studious to find out how many imperfections and infidelities, and how much inward sinfulness, is consistent with a *safe state* in religion : but how few, very few, are bringing out the fair Gospel standard to try the height of the members of the Church ; whether they be fit for the heavenly army ; whether their stature be such as qualifies them for the ranks of the Church militant ! The *measure of the stature of the fulness* is seldom seen ; the *measure of the stature of littleness, dwarfishness,* and *emptiness,* is often exhibited.

Verse 14. Be no more children] *Children,* here, are opposed to the *perfect man* in the preceding verse ; and the state of both is well explained by the apostle's allusions. The man is grown up strong and healthy, and has attained such a measure or height as qualifies him for the most respectable place in the ranks of his country.

The child is ignorant, weak, and unsteady, tossed about in the nurse's arms, or whirled round in the giddy sports or mazes of youth ; this seems to be the apostle's allusion. Being tossed to and fro, and carried about with every wind of doctrine, refers to some kind of ancient play, but *what* I cannot absolutely determine ; probably to something similar to a *top,* or to our paper *kite.*

By the sleight of men] The words εν τη κυβεια refer to the arts used by gamesters, who employ false *dice* that will always throw up one kind of number, which is that by which those who play with them cannot win.

Cunning craftiness] It is difficult to give a literal translation of the original words : εν πανουργια προς την μεθοδειαν της πλανης· "By cunning, for the purpose of using the various means of deception." Πανουργια signifies *craft* and *subtlety* in general, *cheating* and *imposition :* μεθοδεια, from which we have our term *method,* signifies a *wile,* a *particular sleight, mode of tricking* and *deceiving* ; it is applied to the *arts* which the devil uses to deceive and destroy souls ; see chap. vi. 11, called there the WILES *of the devil.* From this it seems that various arts were used, both

by the Greek sophists and the Judaizing teachers, to render the Gospel of none effect, or to adulterate and corrupt it.

Verse 15. But, speaking the truth in love] The *truth* recommended by the apostle is the whole system of Gospel doctrine ; this they are to teach and preach, and this is opposed to the *deceit* mentioned above. This truth, as it is the doctrine of God's eternal love to mankind, must be preached in *love.* Scolding and abuse from the pulpit or press, in matters of religion, are truly *monstrous.* He who has the truth of God has no need of any means to defend or propagate it, but those which love to God and man provides.

Grow up into him] This is a continuance of the metaphor taken from the members of a human body receiving nourishment equally and growing up, each in its due proportion to other parts, and to the body in general. The truth of God should be so preached to all the members of the Church of God, that they may all receive an increase of grace and life ; so that each, in whatever state he may be, may get forward in the way of truth and holiness. In the Church of Christ there are persons in various states : the *careless,* the *penitent,* the *lukewarm,* the *tempted,* the *diffident,* the *little child,* the *young man,* and the *father.* He who has got a talent for the edification of only one of those classes should not stay long in a place, else the whole body cannot grow up in all things under *his* ministry.

Verse 16. From whom the whole body] Dr. Macknight has a just view of this passage, and I cannot express my own in more suitable terms : " The apostle's meaning is, that, as the human body is formed by the union of all the members to each other, under the head, and by the fitness of each member for its own office and place in the body, so the Church is formed by the union of its members under Christ, the head. Farther, as the human body increases till it arrives at maturity by the energy of every part in performing its proper function, and by the sympathy of every part with the whole, so the body or Church of Christ grows to maturity by the proper exercise of the gifts and graces of individuals for the benefit of the whole."

This verse is another proof of the wisdom and learning of the apostle. Not only the general ideas here are anatomical, but the whole phraseology is the same. The *articulation* of the *bones,* the *composition* and *action* of the *muscles,* the *circulation* of the *fluids,* car-

17 This I say therefore, and testify in the Lord, that ʳ ye henceforth walk not as other Gentiles walk, ˢ in the vanity of their mind,

18 ᵗ Having the understanding darkened, ᵘ being alienated from the life of God through the ignorance that is in them, because of the ᵛ blindness ʷ of their heart:

19 ˣ Who being past feeling, ʸ have given themselves over unto lasciviousness, to work all uncleanness with greediness.

A. M. cir. 4065. A. D. cir. 61. A. U. C. 813. An. Imp. Neronis Cæs. Aug. 8.

rying nourishment to every part, and depositing some in every place, the *energy* of the *system* in keeping up all the functions, being particularly introduced, and the whole terminating in the general process of *nutrition*, increasing the body, and supplying all the *waste* that had taken place in consequence of labour, &c. Let any medical man, who understands the apostle's language, take up this verse, and he will be convinced that the apostle had all these things in view. I am surprised that some of those who have looked for the discoveries of the *moderns* among the *ancients*, have not brought in the apostle's word επιχορηγια, *supply*, from επιχορηγεω, to *lead up, lead along, minister, supply*, &c., as some proof that the *circulation of the blood* was not unknown to St. Paul.

Verse 17. *Walk not as other Gentiles walk*] Ye are called to holiness by the Gospel, the other Gentiles have no such calling; walk not as *they* walk. In this and the two following verses the apostle gives a most awful account of the conduct of the heathens who were without the knowledge of the true God. I shall note the particulars.

1. They walked *in the vanity of their mind*, εν ματαιοτητι του νοος αυτων· *In the foolishness of their mind*; want of *genuine wisdom* is that to which the apostle refers, and it was through this that the Gentiles became addicted to every species of *idolatry*; and they fondly imagined that they could obtain help from gods which were the work of their own hands! Here their foolishness was manifested.

2. Verse 18. *Having the understanding darkened*] This is the *second* instance alleged by the apostle of the degradation of the Gentiles. Having no means of knowledge, the heart, naturally dark, became more and more so by means of habitual transgression; every thing in the Gentile system having an immediate tendency to blind the eyes and darken the whole soul.

3. *Being alienated from the life of God*] The original design of God was to *live in man*; and the life of God in the soul of man was that by which God intended to make man happy, and without which true happiness was never found by any human spirit: from this *through the ignorance that was in them*, δια την αγνοιαν την ουσαν, through the *substantial* or continually existing ignorance, which there was nothing to instruct, nothing to enlighten; for the most accurate writings of their best philosophers left them entirely ignorant of the real nature of God. And if they had no correct knowledge of the true God they could have no *religion*; and if no religion, no *morality*. Their moral state became so wretched that they are repre-

sented as *abhorring* every thing spiritual and pure, for this is the import of the word απηλλοτριωμενοι (which we translate *alienated*) in some of the best Greek writers. They *abhorred* every thing that had a tendency to lay any restraint on their vicious passions and inclinations.

4. *Blindness of their heart*] Δια την πωρωσιν· Because of the *callousness* of their hearts. *Callous* signifies a thickening of the outward skin of any particular part, especially on the hands and feet, by repeated exercise or use, through which such parts are rendered *insensible*. This may be metaphorically applied to the conscience of a sinner, which is rendered stupid and insensible by repeated acts of iniquity.

5. Verse 19. *Who being past feeling*] Οιτινες απηλγηκοτες. The verb απαλγειν signifies, 1. To throw off all *sense of shame*, and to be utterly *devoid of pain*, for committing unrighteous acts. 2. To be *desperate*, having neither *hope* nor *desire* of reformation; in a word, to be *without remorse*, and to be utterly regardless of conduct, character, or final blessedness. Instead of απηλγηκοτες, several excellent MSS. and versions have απηλπικοτες, *being without hope*; that is, persons who, from their manner of life in this world, could not possibly hope for blessedness in the world to come, and who might feel it their interest to deny the *resurrection* of the body, and even the *immortality* of the soul.

6. *Have given themselves over unto lasciviousness*] Lasciviousness, ασελγεια, is here personified; and the Gentiles in question are represented as having delivered themselves over to her jurisdiction. This is a true picture of the Gentile world: uncleanness, lechery, and debauchery of every kind, flourished among them without limit or restraint. Almost all their gods and goddesses were of this character.

7. *To work all uncleanness with greediness.*] This is a complete finish of the most abandoned character; to *do* an unclean act is *bad*, to *labour* in it is *worse*, to *labour in all uncleanness* is worse still; but to do all this in *every case* to the *utmost extent*, εν πλεονεξια, *with a desire exceeding* time, place, opportunity, and strength, is *worst of all*, and leaves nothing more profligate or more abandoned to be described or imagined; just as *Ovid* paints the drunken Silenus, whose wantonness survives his strength and keeps alive his desires, though old age has destroyed the power of gratification:—

Te quoque, inextinctæ Silene libidinis, urunt:
Nequitia est, quæ te non sinit esse senem.

Fast., lib. i. v. 413.

A. M. cir. 4065.
A. D. cir. 61.
A. U. C. 813.
An. Imp. Neronis Cæs.
Aug. 8.

20 But ye have not so learned Christ;

21 [z] If so be that ye have heard him, and have been taught by him, as the truth is in Jesus:

22 That ye [a] put off, concerning [b] the former conversation, [c] the old man, which is corrupt according to the deceitful lusts;

23 And [d] be renewed in the spirit of your mind;

24 And that ye [e] put on the new man, which after God [f] is created in righteousness and [g] true holiness.

25 Wherefore putting away lying, [h] speak every man truth with his neighbour: for [i] we are members one of another.

A. M. cir. 4065.
A. D. cir. 61.
A. U. C. 813.
An. Imp. Neronis Cæs.
Aug. 8.

---

[z] Chap. i. 13.——[a] Col. ii. 11; iii. 8, 9; Heb. xii. 1; 1 Pet. ii. 1.——[b] Chapter ii. 2, 3; verse 17; Col. iii. 7; 1 Peter iv. 3. [c] Rom. vi. 6.

[d] Rom. xii. 2; Col. iii. 10——[e] Rom. vi. 4; 2 Cor. v. 17; Gal. vi. 15; chap. vi. 11; Col. iii. 10—[f] Chap. ii. 10.——[g] Or, *holiness of truth.*——[h] Zech. viii. 16; ver. 15; Col. iii. 9.——[i] Rom. xii. 5.

Thee also, O Silenus, of inextinguishable lust, they inflame;
Thou art old in every thing except in lust.

Such was the state of the Gentiles before they were blessed with the light of the Gospel; and such is the state of those nations who have not yet received the Gospel; and such is the state of multitudes of those in *Christian countries* who refuse to receive the Gospel, endeavour to decry it, and to take refuge in the *falsities* of infidelity against the testimony of eternal *truth.*

Verse 20. *But ye have not so learned Christ*] Ye have received the doctrines of Christianity, and therefore are taught differently; ye have received the Spirit of Christ, and therefore are saved from such dispositions. Some would point and translate the original thus: Ὑμεις δε ουχ οὑτως εμαθετε τον Χριστον· *But ye are not thus; ye have learned Christ.*

Verse 21. *If so be that ye have heard him*] Ειγε, *Seeing that, since indeed,* ye have heard us proclaim his eternal truth; we have delivered it to you as we received it from Jesus.

Verse 22. *That ye put off*] And this has been one especial part of our teaching, that ye should abandon all these, and live a life totally opposite to what it was before.

The old man] See the note on Rom. vi. 6, and especially the notes on Rom. xiii. 13, 14.

Which is corrupt] The whole of your former life was corrupt and abominable; ye lived in the pursuit of *pleasure* and *happiness*; ye sought this in the *gratification* of the *lusts* of the *flesh*; and were ever *deceived* by these lusts, and *disappointed* in your expectations.

Verse 23. *And be renewed in the spirit of your mind*] Their *old mode* of living was to be abandoned; a *new* one to be assumed. The *mind* is to be renovated; and not only its *general* complexion, but the very *spirit* of it; all its faculties and powers must be thoroughly, completely, and universally renewed. Plautus uses a similar expression describing deep distress, and answerable to our phrase *innermost soul*:—

Paupertas, pavor territat mentem animi.

Poverty and dread alarm my innermost soul.

Epid., l. 519.

Verse 24. *Put on the new man*] Get a new nature; for in Christ Jesus—under the Christian dispensation, neither circumcision avails any thing, nor uncircumcision, but a new *creation.* Therefore ye must be renewed in the spirit of your mind.

Which after God is created in righteousness] Here is certainly an allusion to the creation of man. Moses tells us, Gen. i. 27, that *God created man in his own image*; that is, God was the *model* according to which he was *formed* in the spirit of his mind. St. Paul says here that they *should put on the new man, which after God is created in righteousness and true holiness,* or, ὁσιοτητι της αληθειας, in the holiness of truth. Both certainly refer to the same thing, and the one illustrates the other. From the apostle we learn what Moses meant by the *image of God*; it was *righteousness and the truth of holiness.* See the note on Gen. i. 26. It is not this or the other *degree* of moral good which the soul is to receive by Jesus Christ, it is the *whole image* of God; it is to be formed κατα Θεον, *according to God*; the likeness of the Divine Being is to be traced upon his soul, and he is to bear that as fully as his first father Adam bore it in the beginning.

Verse 25. *Wherefore putting away lying*] All *falsity*, all *prevarication*, because this is opposite to the *truth* as it is in Jesus, ver. 21, and to the *holiness of truth*, ver. 24.

Speak every man truth with his neighbour] Truth was but of small account among many of even the best heathens, for they taught that on many occasions a *lie* was to be *preferred* to the *truth* itself. Dr. *Whitby* collects some of their maxims on this head.

Κρειττον δε ἑλεσθαι ψευδος, η αληθες κακον· "A lie is better than a hurtful truth."—*Menander.*

Το γαρ αγαθον κρειττον εστι της αληθειας· "Good is better than *truth.*"—*Proclus.*

Ενθα γαρ τι δει και ψευδος λεγεσθαι, λεγεσθω. "When telling a lie will be profitable, let it be told."—*Darius* in *Herodotus*, lib. iii. p. 191.

"He may lie who knows how to do it εν δεοντι καιρῳ, in a suitable time."—*Plato* apud *Stob.*, ser. 12.

"There is nothing decorous in truth but when it is profitable; yea, sometimes και ψευδος ωνησεν ανθρωπους, και τ' αληθες εβλαψεν, truth is hurtful, and lying is profitable to men."—*Maximus Tyrius*, Diss. 3, p. 29.

Having been brought up in such a loose system of morality, these converted Gentiles had need of these apostolic directions; *Put away lying; speak the truth:* Let lying never come near you; let truth be ever present with you.

We are members one of another.] Consider yourselves as *one body*, of which Jesus Christ is the *head*; and as a man's right hand would not deceive or wrong his left hand, so deal honestly with each other; *for ye are members one of another.*

2

A. M. cir. 4065.
A. D. cir. 61.
A. U. C. 813.
An. Imp. Ne-
ronis Cæs.
Aug. 8.

26 [k] Be ye angry, and sin not : let not the sun go down upon your wrath :

27 [l] Neither give place to the devil.

28 Let him that stole steal no more : but rather [m] let him labour, working with *his* hands the thing which is good, that he may have [n] to give [o] to him that needeth.

29 [r] Let no corrupt communication proceed out of your mouth, but [q] that which is good [r] to the use of edifying, [s] that it may minister grace unto the hearers.

30 And [t] grieve not the Holy Spirit of God, [u] whereby ye are sealed unto the day of [v] redemption.

A. M. cir. 4065.
A. D. cir. 61.
A. U. C. 813.
An. Imp. Ne-
ronis Cæs.
Aug. 8.

---

[k] Psa. iv. 4 ; xxxvii. 8.——[l] 2 Cor. ii. 10, 11 ; James iv. 7 ; 1 Pet. v. 9.——[m] Acts xx. 35 ; 1 Thess. iv. 11 ; 2 Thess. iii. 8, 11, 12.——[n] Or, *to distribute.*——[o] Luke iii. 11.——[p] Matt. xii. 36 ; chap. v. 4 ; Col. iii. 8.

[q] Col. iv. 6 ; 1 Thess. v. 11.——[r] Or, *to edify profitably.*——[s] Col. iii. 16.——[t] Isa. vii. 13 ; lxiii. 10 ; Ezek. xvi. 43 ; 1 Thess. v. 19. [u] Chapter i. 13.——[v] Luke xxi. 28 ; Romans viii. 23 ; chapter i. 14.

Verse 26. *Be ye angry, and sin not*] Οργιζεσθε, here, is the same as ει μεν οργιζεσθε, IF YE *be angry, do not sin.* We can never suppose that the apostle delivers this as a *precept,* if we take the words as they stand in our version. Perhaps the sense is, *Take heed that ye be not angry, lest ye sin ;* for it would be very difficult, even for an apostle himself, to be angry and *not sin.* If we consider anger as implying *displeasure* simply, then there are a multitude of cases in which a man may be *innocently,* yea, *laudably angry ;* for he should be displeased with every thing which is not for the glory of God, and the good of mankind. But, in any other sense, I do not see how the words can be safely taken.

Let not the sun go down upon your wrath] That is : If you do get angry with any one, see that the fire be cast with the utmost speed out of your bosom. Do not go to sleep with any unkind or unbrotherly feeling ; anger, continued in, may produce *malice* and *revenge.* No temper of this kind can consist with *peace of conscience,* and the *approbation* of God's Spirit in the soul.

Verse 27. *Neither give place to the devil.*] Your adversary will strive to influence your mind, and irritate your spirit ; watch and pray that he may not get any place *in* you, or ascendancy *over* you.

As the word διαβολος is sometimes used to signify a *calumniator, tale-bearer, whisperer,* or *backbiter ;* (see in the original, 1 Tim. iii. 11 ; 2 Tim. iii. 3, and Tit. ii. 3 ;) here it may have the same signification : Do not open your ear to the *tale-bearer,* to the *slanderer,* who comes to you with accusations against your brethren, or with surmisings and evil speakings. These are human devils ; they may be the means of making you angry, even without any solid pretence ; therefore give them no place, that you may not be angry at any time ; but if, unhappily, you should be overtaken in this fault, let not the sun go down upon your wrath ; go to your brother, against whom you have found your spirit irritated ; tell him what you have heard, and what you fear ; let your ears be open to receive his own account ; carefully listen to his own explanation ; and, if possible, let the matter be finally settled, that Satan may not gain advantage over either.

Verse 28. *Let him that stole steal no more*] It is supposed that, among the rabbins, stealing was not entirely discountenanced, provided a portion was given to the poor : The apostle here teaches them a different doctrine : as they should speak truth every man with his neighbour, so they should in every respect act ho-

nestly, for nothing contrary to *truth* and *righteousness* could be tolerated under the Christian system. Let no man, under pretence of helping the poor, defraud another ; but let him *labour, working with his hands* to provide that which is *good,* that he may have to give to him who is in necessity. *Stealing, overreaching defrauding, purloining, &c.,* are consistent with no kind of religion that acknowledges the *true God.* If Christianity does not make men honest, it does nothing for them. Those who are not saved from dishonesty *fear* not *God,* though they may *dread man.*

Verse 29. *Let no corrupt communication*] Πας λογος σαπρος. *Kypke* observes that λογος σαπρος signifies a *useless, putrid, unsavoury,* and *obscene word* or *conversation.* 1. *Useless,* particularly that which has been rendered so by old age and corruption. 2. *Putrid, impure ;* so Aristophanes in Lysistrat., p. 859, calls a *bad woman* σαπρα : εμοι συ λουτρον, ω σαπρα· *Tune, Spurca! balneum mihi parabis ?* 3. *Calumnious,* or *reproachful ;* whatever has a tendency to *injure* the *name, fame,* or *interest* of another. In short, it appears to mean any word or thing *obscene,* any thing that *injures virtue, countenances vice,* or *scoffs at religion.* In the parallel place, Col. iv. 6, the apostle exhorts that our speech may be *seasoned with salt,* to preserve it from *putrefaction.* See *Kypke* and *Macknight.*

But that which is good to the use of edifying] To be *good for a thing* is a *Græcism,* as well as an *Anglicism,* for, to be *fit, proper, suitable, &c. ;* so *Achilles Tatius,* lib. iv. p. 231 : Αγαθον εις φιλιαν οιδα σε· *I know thee to be good* (formed) *for friendship.* And *Appian,* de *Bell. Hisp.,* p. 439, terms both the Scipios, Ανδρας ες παντα αγαθους γενομενους, *men who were good* (suitable) *for all things.* And also *Lucian,* in *Toxari,* p. 53 : Ου μονον αρα τοξευειν αγαθοι ησαν Σκυθαι· *The Scythians were not good* (expert) *in archery* only. See *Kypke,* from whom I quote.

That it may minister grace] Ἱνα δῳ χαριν. This may be understood thus : 1. Let your conversation be pure, wise, and holy, that it may be the means of conveying grace, or Divine influences, to them that hear. 2. Let it be such as to be *grateful* or *acceptable to the hearers.* This is the meaning of Ἱνα δῳ χαριν in some of the most correct Greek writers. Never wound modesty, truth, or religion with your discourse ; endeavour to *edify* those with whom you converse ; and if possible, speak so as to *please* them.

Verse 30. *Grieve not the Holy Spirit of God*] By

2

A. M. cir. 4065.
A. D. cir. 61.
A. U. C. 813.
An. Imp. Neronis Cæs.
Aug. 8.

31 ^w Let all bitterness, and wrath, and anger, and clamour, and ^x evil speaking, be put away from you, ^y with all malice:

32 And ^z be ye kind one to another, tenderhearted, ^a forgiving one another, even as God for Christ's sake hath forgiven you.

A. M. cir. 4065.
A. D. cir. 61.
A. U. C. 813.
An. Imp. Neronis Cæs.
Aug. 8.

^w Col. iii. 8, 19.——^x Tit. iii. 2; James iv. 11; 1 Pet. ii. 1. ^y Tit. iii. 3.

^z 2 Cor. ii. 10; Col. iii. 12, 13.——^a Matthew vi. 14; Mark xi. 25.

giving way to any wrong temper, unholy word, or unrighteous action. Even those who have already a measure of the light and life of God, both of which are not only brought in by the Holy Spirit, but maintained by his constant indwelling, may give way to sin, and so grieve this Holy Spirit that it shall *withdraw* both its *light* and *presence;* and, in proportion as it withdraws, then *hardness* and *darkness* take place; and, what is still worse, a state of *insensibility* is the consequence; for the *darkness* prevents the fallen state from being *seen,* and the *hardness* prevents it from being *felt.*

Whereby ye are sealed] The Holy Spirit in the soul of a believer is *God's seal,* set on his heart to testify that he is God's property, and that he should be wholly *employed* in God's *service.* It is very likely that the apostle had in view the words of the prophet, Isa. lxiii. 10: *But they rebelled,* and VEXED *his* HOLY SPIRIT; *therefore he was turned to be their enemy, and fought against them.* The psalmist refers to the same fact in nearly the same words, Psa. lxxviii. 40: *How oft did they* PROVOKE *him in the wilderness, and* GRIEVE *him in the desert!* Let every man, therefore, take heed that he grieve not the Spirit of God, lest God *turn to be his enemy,* and *fight against him.*

Verse 31. *Let all bitterness*] Πασα πικρια. It is astonishing that any who profess the Christian name should indulge *bitterness* of spirit. Those who are *censorious,* who are *unmerciful* to the *failings* of others, who have fixed a *certain standard* by which they measure all persons in all circumstances, and unchristian every one that does not come up to this standard, these have the *bitterness* against which the apostle speaks. In the last century there was a compound medicine, made up from a variety of drastic acrid drugs and ardent spirits, which was called *Hiera Picra,* ιερα πικρα, the *holy bitter;* this medicine was administered in a multitude of cases, where it did immense evil, and perhaps in scarcely any case did it do good. It has ever appeared to me to furnish a proper epithet for the disposition mentioned above, the *holy bitter;* for the religiously censorious act under the pretence of superior *sanctity.* I have known such persons do much evil in a Christian society, but never knew an instance of their doing any good.

And wrath] Θυμος is more properly *anger,* which may be considered the *commencement* of the passion.

Anger] Οργη is more properly *wrath*—the passion carried to its *highest pitch,* accompanied with *injurious words* and *outrageous acts,* some of which are immediately specified.

And clamour] Κραυγη Loud and obstreperous speaking, brawling, railing, *boisterous* talk, often the offspring of *wrath;* all of which are highly unbecoming the *meek, loving, quiet, sedate* mind of Christ and his followers.

And evil speaking] Βλασφημια· Blasphemy; that is, *injurious speaking*—words which tend to hurt those *of* whom or *against* whom they are spoken.

With all malice] Κακια· All malignity; as *anger* produces *wrath,* and wrath *clamour,* so all together produce *malice;* that is, settled, sullen, fell wrath, which is always looking out for opportunities to revenge itself by the destruction of the object of its indignation. No state of society can be even *tolerable* where these prevail; and, if *eternity* were out of the question, it is of the utmost consequence to have these banished from *time.*

Verse 32. *Be ye kind one to another*] Γινεσθε — χρηστοι· Be *kind* and *obliging* to each other; study *good breeding* and *gentleness of manners.* A Christian *cannot* be a *savage,* and he *need not* be a *boor.* Never put any person to needless pain.

Tender-hearted] Ευσπλαγχνοι· Compassionate; having the *bowels easily moved* (as the word implies) to commiserate the state of the wretched and distressed.

Forgiving one another] Should you receive any injury from a brother, or from any man, be as ready to forgive *him,* on his *repentance* and *acknowledgment,* as God was, for Christ's sake, to forgive you when you repented of your sins, and took refuge in his mercy,

1. THE *exhortations* given in this chapter, if properly attended to, have the most direct tendency to secure the *peace* of the *individual,* the *comfort* of every *family,* and the *welfare* and *unity* of every *Christian society.* That God never *prohibits* any thing that is useful to us, is an unshaken truth. And that he never *commands* what has not the most pointed relation to our present and eternal welfare, is not less so. How is it, then, that we do not *glory* in his *commandments* and *rejoice* in his *prohibitions?* If the gratification of our fleshly propensities could do us good, that gratification had never been forbidden. God plants *thorns* in the way that would lead us to death and perdition.

2. From the provision which God has made for the soul's salvation, we may see the *nature,* and in some sense the *extent,* of the salvation provided. Much on this subject has been said in the preceding chapter, and the same subject is continued here. God requires that the Church shall be holy, so that it may be a proper habitation for himself; and he requires that *each* believer should be holy, and that he should, under the influences of his grace, arrive at the measure of the stature of the fulness of Christ ' ver. 13. This is astonishing; but God is able to make all grace abound towards us.

3. It is the will of God that Christians should be *well instructed;* that they should become *wise* and *intelligent;* and have their understandings well cultivated and improved. *Sound learning* is of great worth, even in religion; the wisest and best instructed Christians

are the most *steady*, and may be the most *useful*. If a man be a *child* in *knowledge*, he is likely to be *tossed to and fro*, and *carried about with every wind of doctrine*; and often lies at the mercy of interested, designing men: the more knowledge he has, the more *safe* is his state. If our circumstances be such that we have few means of improvement, we should turn them to the best account. " Partial knowledge is better than total ignorance; he who cannot get all he may wish, must take heed to acquire all that he can." If total ignorance be a bad and dangerous thing, every degree of knowledge lessens both the *evil* and the *danger*. It must never be forgotten that the Holy Scriptures themselves are capable of making men wise unto salvation, if read and studied with *faith* in Christ.

4. *Union* among the followers of Christ is strongly recommended. How can spiritual brethren fall out by the way? Have they not all *one Father*, all *one Head?* Do they not form *one body*, and are they not all *members* of *each other?* Would it not be *monstrous* to see the *nails* pulling out the *eyes*, the *hands* tearing off the *flesh* from the body, the *teeth* biting out the *tongue*, &c., &c.? And is it less so to see the members of a Christian society bite and devour each other, till they are consumed one of another? Every member of the mystical body of Christ should labour for the comfort and edification of the *whole*, and the honour of the *Head*. He that would live a quiet life, and keep the unity of the Spirit in the bond of peace, must be as backward to *take* offence as to *give* it. Would all act on this plan (and surely it is as *rational* as it is *Christian*) we should soon have glory to God in the highest, and on earth peace and good will among men.

5. A *roughness of manners* is to some unavoidable; it is partly owing to the peculiar texture of their mind, and partly to their education. But there are others who glory in, and endeavour to cultivate, this ungentle disposition; under this is often concealed a great degree of spiritual pride, and perhaps some malignity; for they think that this *roughness* gives them a *right* to say grating, harsh, and severe things. They should be taught another lesson; and if they will not demean themselves as they ought, they should be left to themselves, and no man should associate with them. They are not *Christians*, and they act beneath the character of *men*.

CHAPTER V.

Christians should imitate their heavenly Father, and walk in love, after the example of Christ, 1, 2. They should avoid all uncleanness, impurity, covetousness, and foolish jesting, and idolatry, because these things exclude from the kingdom of God, 3–7. The Ephesians were once in darkness, but being now light in the Lord, they are exhorted to walk in that light, and bring forth the fruits of the Spirit; and to have no fellowship with the workers of iniquity, whose evil deeds are manifested by the light, 8–13. All are exhorted to awake; to walk circumspectly; to redeem the time; and to learn what the will of the Lord is, 14–17. The apostle gives particular directions relative to avoiding excess of wine, 18. To singing and giving thanks, 19, 20. Submission to each other, 21. To husbands that they should love their wives, as Christ loved the Church; for by the marriage union, the union between Christ and the Church is pointed out; and wives are exhorted to reverence their husbands, 22–33.

A. M. cir. 4065.
A. D. cir. 61.
A. U. C. 813.
An. Imp. Neronis Cæs.
Aug. 8.

BE [a] ye therefore followers of God, as dear children;

2 And [b] walk in love, [c] as Christ also hath loved us, and hath given himself for us an offering and a sacrifice to God [d] for a sweet-smelling savour.

A. M. cir. 4065.
A. D. cir. 61.
A. U. C. 813.
An. Imp. Neronis Cæs.
Aug. 8.

---

[a] Matt. v. 45, 48; Luke vi. 36; chap. iv. 32.——[b] John xiii. 34; xv. 12; 1 Thess. iv. 9; 1 John iii. 11, 23; iv. 21.

[c] Gal. i. 4; ii. 20; Heb. vii. 27; ix. 14, 26; x. 10, 12; 1 John iii. 16.——[d] Gen. viii. 21; Lev. i, 9; 2 Cor. ii. 15.

NOTES ON CHAP. V.

Verse 1. *Be ye therefore followers of God*] The beginning of this chapter is properly a continuation of the preceding, which should have ended with the second verse of this. The word μιμηται, which we translate *followers*, signifies such as *personate others*, assuming their gait, mode of speech, accent, carriage, &c.; and it is from this Greek word that we have the word *mimic*. Though this term is often used in a ludicrous sense, yet here it is to be understood in a very solemn and proper sense. Let your whole conduct be like that of your Lord; *imitate* him in all your actions, words, spirit, and inclinations; imitate him as children do their beloved parents, and remember that you stand in the relation of *beloved children* to him. It is natural for children to imitate their parents; it is their constant aim to learn of them, and to copy them in all things; whatever they see the parent do, whatever they hear him speak, that they endeavour to copy and imitate; yea, they go farther, they insensibly copy the very *tempers* of their parents. If ye therefore be children of God, show this love to your heavenly Father, and imitate all his moral perfections, and acquire the mind that was in Jesus.

Verse 2. *And walk in love*] Let every act of life be dictated by love to God and man.

As Christ—hath loved us] Laying down your lives for your brethren if necessary; counting nothing too difficult to be done in order to promote their eternal salvation.

Hath given himself for us] Christ hath died in our stead, and become thereby a sacrifice for our sins.

2

A. M. cir. 4065.
A. D. cir. 61.
A. U. C. 813.
An. Imp. Ne-
ronis Cæs.
Aug. 8.

3 But ^e fornication, and all uncleanness, or covetousness, ^f let it not be once named among you, as becometh saints;

4 ^g Neither filthiness, nor foolish talking, nor jesting, ^h which are not convenient: but rather giving of thanks.

5 For this ye know, that ⁱ no whoremonger, nor unclean person, nor covetous man, ^k who is an idolater, ^l hath any inheritance in the kingdom of Christ and of God.

6 ^m Let no man deceive you with vain words: for because of these things ⁿ cometh the wrath

A. M. cir. 4065.
A. D. cir. 61.
A. U. C. 813.
An. Imp. Ne-
ronis Cæs.
Aug. 8.

---

^e Rom. vi. 13; 1 Cor. vi. 18; 2 Cor. xii. 21; chap. iv. 19, 20; Col. iii. 5; 1 Thess. iv. 3, &c.——^f 1 Cor. v. 1.——^g Matt. xii. 35; chap. iv. 29.——^h Rom. i. 28.

ⁱ 1 Cor. vi. 9; Gal. v. 19, 21.——^k Col. iii. 5; 1 Tim. vi. 17. ^l Gal. v. 21; Rev. xxii. 15.——^m Jer. xxix. 8; Matt. xxiv. 4; Col. ii. 4, 8, 18; 2 Thess. ii. 3.——ⁿ Rom. i. 18.

An offering] Προσφορα· An oblation, an eucharistic offering; the same as מנחה *minchah*, Lev. ii. 1, &c., which is explained to be *an offering made unto the Lord, of fine flour, with oil and frankincense.* It means, any offering by which *gratitude* was expressed for temporal blessings received from the *bounty* of God.

A sacrifice] Θυσια· A sin-offering, a victim for sin; the same as זבח *zebach*, which almost universally means that sacrificial act in which the blood of an *animal* was poured out as an atonement for sin. These terms may be justly considered as including every kind of *sacrifice, offering,* and *oblation* made to God on any account; and both these terms are with propriety used here, because the apostle's design was to represent the *sufficiency* of the offering made by Christ for the sin of the world. And the passage strongly intimates, that as man is bound to be *grateful* to God for the good things of *this life*, so he should testify that gratitude by *suitable offerings*; but having *sinned* against God, he has forfeited all *earthly* blessings as well as those that come from *heaven*; and that Jesus Christ gave himself ὑπερ ἡμων, in our stead and on our account, as the gratitude-offering, προσφορα, which we owed to our MAKER, and without which a continuance of *temporal* blessings could not be expected; and also as a *sacrifice for sin*, θυσια, without which we could never approach God, and without which we must be punished with an everlasting destruction from the presence of God and the glory of his power. Thus we find that even our *temporal* blessings come *from* and *by* Jesus Christ, as well as all our spiritual and eternal mercies.

For a sweet-smelling savour.] Εις οσμην ευωδιας· The same as is expressed in Gen. viii. 21; Lev. i. 9; iii. 16: ריח ניחוח ליהוה *reiach nichoach laihovah*, "a sweet savour unto the Lord:" i. e. an offering of his own prescription, and one with which he was well pleased; and by accepting of which he showed that he accepted the person who offered it. The *sweet-smelling savour* refers to the burnt-offerings, the fumes of which ascended from the fire in the act of *burning*; and as such odors are grateful to man, God represents himself as pleased with them, when offered by an upright worshipper according to his own appointment.

Verse 3. But fornication] It is probable that the *three* terms used here by the apostle refer to different species of the same thing. The word *fornication*, πορνεια, may imply not only *fornication* but *adultery* also, as it frequently does; *uncleanness*, ακαθαρσια may refer to all abominable and unnatural lusts—sodomy, bestiality, &c.; and *covetousness*, πλεονεξια, to exces-

sive indulgence in that which, moderately used, is lawful. As the covetous man never has enough of wealth, so the pleasure-taker and the libertine never have enough of the gratifications of sense, the appetite increasing in proportion to its indulgence. If, however, simple *covetousness*, i. e. the *love of gain*, be here intended, it shows from the connection in which it stands, (for it is linked with *fornication, adultery,* and *all uncleanness*,) how degrading it is to the soul of man, and how abominable it is in the eye of God. In other places it is ranked with *idolatry*, for the man who has an inordinate love of gain makes *money* his god.

Let it not be once named] Let no such things ever exist among you, for ye are called to be saints.

Verse 4. Neither filthiness] Αισχροτης· Any thing *base* or *vile* in words or acts.

Foolish talking] Μωρολογια· Scurrility, buffoonery, ridicule, or what tends to expose another to contempt.

Nor jesting] Ευτραπελια· Artfully turned discourses or words, from ευ, *well* or *easily*, and τρεπω, *I turn*; words that can be easily turned to other meanings; *double entendres*; chaste words which, from their connection, and the manner in which they are used, convey an obscene or offensive meaning. It also means jests, puns, *witty sayings*, and *mountebank repartees* of all kinds.

Which are not convenient] Ουκ ανηκοντα· *They do not come up* to the proper standard; they are utterly improper in themselves, and highly unbecoming in those who profess Christianity.

But rather giving of thanks.] Ευχαριστια· Decent and *edifying discourse* or thanksgiving to God. *Prayer* or *praise* is the most suitable language for man; and he who is of a trifling, light disposition, is ill fitted for either. How can a man, who has been talking foolishly or jestingly in company, go in private to magnify God for the use of his tongue which he has abused, or his rational faculties which he has degraded?

Verse 5. For this ye know] Ye must be convinced of the dangerous and ruinous tendency of such a spirit and conduct, when ye know that persons of this character can never inherit the kingdom of God. See on ver. 3; and see the observations on the *Greek article* at the end of this epistle.

Verse 6. Let no man deceive you] Suffer no man to persuade you that any of these things are innocent, or that they are unavoidable frailties of human nature; they are all *sins* and *abominations* in the sight of God; those who practise them are *children of disobedience*; and on account of such practices the *wrath of God*—Divine punishment, must come upon them.

A. M. cir. 4065
A. D. cir. 61.
A. U. C. 813.
An. Imp. Ne-
ronis Cæs.
Aug. 8.

of God ° upon the children of ᴾ disobedience.

7 Be not ye therefore partakers with them.

8 ᑫ For ye were sometimes darkness, but now ʳ *are ye* light in the Lord : walk as ˢ children of light ;

9 (For ᵗ the fruit of the Spirit *is* in all good-

ness, and righteousness, and truth ;)

10 ᵘ Proving what is acceptable unto the Lord.

11 And ᵛ have no fellowship with ʷ the unfruitful works of darkness, but rather ˣ reprove *them.*

12 ʸ For it is a shame even to speak of

A. M. cir. 4065.
A. D. cir. 61.
A. U. C. 813.
An. Imp. Ne-
ronis Cæs.
Aug. 8.

ᵛ Chap. ii. 2.——ᴾ Or, *unbelief* ; Col. iii. 6.——ᑫ Isa. ix. 2 ; Matt. iv. 16 ; Acts xxvi. 18 ; Rom. i. 21 ; ch. ii. 11, 12 ; iv. 18 ; Tit. iii. 3 ; 1 Pet. ii. 9.——ʳ John viii. 12 ; xii. 46 ; 2 Cor. iii. 18 ; iv. 6 ; 1 Thess. v. 5 ; 1 John ii. 9.——ˢ Luke xvi. 8 ; John xii. 36.

ᵗ Gal. v. 22.——ᵘ Rom. xii. 2 ; Phil. i. 10 ; 1 Thess. v. 21 ; 1 Tim. ii. 3.——ᵛ 1 Cor. v. 9, 11 ; x. 20 ; 2 Cor. vi. 14 , 2 Thess. iii. 6, 14.——ʷ Rom. vi. 21 ; xiii. 12 ; Gal. vi. 8.——ˣ Lev. xix. 17 ; 1 Tim. v. 20.——ʸ Rom. i. 24, 26 ; ver. 3.

Verse 7. *Be not ye therefore partakers with them*] Do not act as your fellow citizens do ; nor suffer their philosophy, *with vain words,* κενοις λογοις, with *empty* and *illusive doctrines,* to lead you astray from the path of truth.

That there was much need for such directions and cautions to the people of Ephesus has been often remarked. It appears, from Athenæus, that these people were addicted to *luxury, effeminacy,* &c. He tells us that the famous *Aspasia,* who was herself of the *Socratic sect,* brought a vast number of beautiful women into Greece, and *by their means filled the country with prostitutes,* και επληθυνεν απο των ταυτης εταιριδων ἡ Ελλας, lib. xiii. cap. 25. Ibid. cap. 31, he observes that the Ephesians had dedicated temples εταιρᾳ Αφροδιτῃ, to the prostitute Venus ; and again, cap. 32, he quotes from Demosthenes, in *Orat. contra Neæram :* τας μεν εταιρας ἡδονης ενεκα εχομεν, τας δε παλλακας της καθ' ἡμεραν παλλακειας, τας δε γυναικας ᵹου παιδοποιεισθαι γνησιως, και των ενδον φυλακα πιστην εχειν· "We have *whores* for our pleasure, *harlots* for daily use, and *wives* for the procreation of legitimate children, and for the faithful preservation of our property." Through the whole of this 13th book of Athenæus the reader will see the most melancholy proofs of the most abominable practices among the *Greeks,* and the high estimation in which public prostitutes were held ; the greatest *lawgivers* and the wisest *philosophers* among the Greeks supported this system both by their authority and example. Is it not in reference to their *teaching* and *laws* that the apostle says : *Let no man deceive you with vain words ?*

Verse 8. *For ye were sometimes* (ποτε, *formerly*) *darkness*] While ye lived in darkness, ye lived in these crimes.

But now are ye *light in the Lord*] When ye were in heathenish *darkness* ye served divers lusts and pleasures, but now ye have the *light*—the wisdom and teaching which come from God ; therefore *walk as children of the light*—let the world see that ye are not slaves to the flesh, but free, willing, rational servants of the Most High ; not brutish followers of devil gods.

Verse 9. *For the fruit of the Spirit*] Instead of *Spirit,* Πνευματος, ABD*EFG, the *Syriac, Coptic, Sahidic, Æthiopic, Armenian, Vulgate,* and *Itala,* together with several of the *fathers,* read φωτος, *light,* which is supposed by most critics to be the *true* reading, because there is no mention made of the *Spirit*

in any part of the context. As light, ver. 8, not only means the Divine influence upon the soul, but also the *Gospel,* with great propriety it may be said : *The fruit of the light,* i. e. of the *Gospel, is in all goodness, and righteousness, and truth.* Goodness, αγαθωσυνη, in the *principle* and *disposition* ; righteousness, δικαιοσυνη, the *exercise* of that *goodness* in the whole conduct of life ; *truth,* αληθεια, the *director* of that *principle,* and its *exercise,* to the glorification of God and the good of mankind.

Verse 10. *Proving what is acceptable*] By walking in the light—under the influence of the Divine Spirit, according to the dictates of the Gospel, ye shall be able to *try,* and bring to *full proof,* that by which God is best pleased. Ye shall be able to please him well in all things.

Verse 11. *Have no fellowship*] Have no religious connection whatever with heathens or their worship.

Unfruitful works of darkness] Probably alluding to the *mysteries* among the heathens, and the different lustrations and rites through which the *initiated* went in the caves and dark recesses where these mysteries were celebrated ; all which he denominates *works of darkness,* because they were destitute of true *wisdom* ; and *unfruitful works,* because they were of no use to mankind ; the initiated being obliged, on pain of death, to keep secret what they had *seen, heard,* and *done :* hence they were called απορρητα μυστηρια, unspeakable *mysteries*—things that were *not to be divulged.* That the apostle may refer to magic and incantations is also probable, for to these the Ephesians were greatly addicted. See the proofs in the notes on Acts xix. 19.

Rather reprove them.] Bear a *testimony* against them ; *convince* them that they are wrong ; *confute* them in their ᵛain reasons ; *reprove* them for their vices, which are flagrant, while pretending to superior illumination. All these meanings has the Greek word ελεγχω, which we generally render *to convince* or *reprove.*

Verse 12. *For it is a shame even to speak*] This no doubt refers to the *Eleusinian* and *Bacchanalian* mysteries, which were performed in the night and darkness, and were known to be so impure and abominable, especially the *latter,* that the Roman senate banished them both from Rome and Italy. How the discovery of these depths of Satan was made, and the whole proceedings in that case, may be seen in Livy, Hist. lib. xxxix. cap. 8—19, where the reader will see the force of what the apostle says here : *It is a shame*

2

A. M. cir. 4065.
A. D. cir 61.
A. U. C. 813.
An. Imp. Ne-
ronis Cæs.
Aug. 8.

those things which are done of them in secret.

13 But ^z all things that are ^a reproved are made manifest by the light: for whatsoever doth make manifest is light.

14 Wherefore ^b he saith, ^c Awake, thou that

sleepest, and ^d arise from the dead, and Christ shall give thee light.

15 ^e See then that ye walk circumspectly, not as fools, but as wise,

16 ^f Redeeming the time, ^g because the days are evil.

A. M. cir. 4065.
A. D. cir. 61.
A. U. C. 813.
An. Imp. Ne-
ronis Cæs
Aug. 8.

---

^z John iii. 20, 21; Heb. iv. 13.——^a Or, *discovered.*——^b Or, *it.*
^c Isa. lx. 1; Romans xiii. 11, 12; 1 Cor. xv. 34; 1 Thess. v. 6.

^d John v. 25; Rom. vi. 4, 5; chap. ii. 5; Col. iii. 1.——^e Col iv. 5.——^f Col. iv. 5; Gal. vi. 10.——^g Eccles. xi. 2; xii. 1; John xii. 35; chap. vi. 15.

---

even to speak of those things which are done of them in secret; the abominations being of the most stupendous kind, and of the deepest dye.

Verse 13. *But all things that are reproved*] Dr. Macknight paraphrases this verse as follows : " *Now all these reprovable actions,* ελεγχομενα, which are practised in celebrating these mysteries, *are made manifest as sinful by the Gospel ;* and, seeing *every thing which discovers the true nature of actions is light,* the Gospel, which discovers the evil nature of the actions performed in these mysteries, is light."

The apostle speaks against these mysteries as he speaks against fornication, uncleanness, and covetousness; but by no means either borrows expression or similitude from them to illustrate Divine truths; for, as it would be a *shame* even *to speak of those things,* surely it would be an *abomination* to allude to them in the illustration of the doctrines of the Gospel.

Verse 14. *Wherefore he saith*] It is a matter of doubt and controversy whence this saying is derived. Some think it taken from Isa. xxvi. 19 : *Thy dead men shall live ; with my dead body shall they arise ; Awake and sing, ye that dwell in the dust,* &c. Others think that it is taken from Isa. lx. 1–3 : *Arise, shine ; for thy light is come,* &c. But these passages neither give the words nor the meaning of the apostle. *Epiphanius* supposed them to be taken from an ancient prophecy of *Elijah,* long since lost: *Syncellus* and *Euthalius* think they were taken from an apocryphal work attributed to *Jeremiah* the prophet : others, that they made part of a *hymn* then used in the Christian Church ; for that there were, in the apostle's time, hymns and spiritual songs, as well as psalms, we learn from himself, in ver. 19, and from Col. iii. 16. The hymn is supposed to have begun thus :——

Εγειραι ὁ καθευδων,
Και αναστα εκ των νεκρων,
Επιφανσει σοι ὁ Χριστος.

Awake, O thou who sleepest,
And from the dead arise thou,
And Christ shall shine upon thee.

See *Rosenmüller, Wolf,* and others. But it seems more natural to understand the words *he saith* as referring to the *light,* i. e. the *Gospel,* mentioned ver. 13. And the δ̀ιο λεγει should be translated, *Wherefore* IT *saith, Awake thou,* &c. ; that is : This is the general, the strong, commanding voice of the Gospel in every part—Receive instruction ; leave thy sins, which are leading thee to perdition : believe on the Lord Jesus Christ, and he will enlighten and save thee.

As a man *asleep* neither knows nor does any thing that can be called good or useful, so the Gentiles and all others, while without the knowledge of Christianity, had not only no proper knowledge of vice and virtue, but they had no correct notion of the true God.

As the *dead* can perform no function of life, so the Gentiles and the unconverted were incapable of performing any thing worthy either of *life* or *being.* But though they were asleep—in a state of complete spiritual torpor, yet they might be awoke by the voice of the Gospel ; and though *dead* to all goodness, and to every function of the spiritual life, yet, as their *animal life* was whole in them, and *perception* and *reason* were still left, they were capable of hearing the Gospel, and under that influence which always accompanies it when faithfully preached, they could discern its excellency, and find it to be the power of God to their salvation. And they are addressed by the apostle as possessing this capacity ; and, on their using it properly, have the promise that Christ shall enlighten them.

Verse 15. *Walk circumspectly*] Our word *circumspect,* from the Latin *circumspicio,* signifies to look round about on all hands ; to be every way watchful, wary, and cautious, in order to avoid danger, discern enemies before they come too nigh, and secure a man's interest by every possible and lawful means. But the original word ακριβως signifies *correctly, accurately, consistently,* or *perfectly.* Be ye, who have received the truth, careful of your conduct ; walk by the rule which God has given you ; do this as well in little as in great matters ; exemplify your principles, which are holy and good, by a corresponding conduct ; do not only profess, but *live* the Gospel. As you embrace all its *promises,* be careful also to embrace all its *precepts ;* and behave yourselves so, that your enemies may never be able to say that ye are *holy* in your *doctrines* and *profession,* but *irregular* in your *lives.*

Not as fools, but as wise] Μη ὡς ασοφοι, αλλ' ὡς σοφοι. The heathens affected to be called σοφοι, or *wise men.* Pythagoras was perhaps the first who corrected this vanity, by assuming the title of φιλοσοφος, *a lover of wisdom ;* hence our term *philosopher,* used now in a much *prouder* sense than that in which the great Pythagoras wished it to be applied. The apostle here takes the term σοφος, and applies it to the *Christian ;* and, instead of it, gives the empty Gentile philosopher the title of ασοφος, *without wisdom, fool.*

Verse 16. *Redeeming the time*] Εξαγοραζομενοι τον καιρον· Buying up those moments which others seem to throw away ; steadily improving every present moment, that ye may, in some measure, *regain*

A. M. cir. 4065.
A. D. cir. 61.
A. U. C. 813.
An. Imp. Ne-
ronis Cæs.
Aug. 8.

17 [h] Wherefore be ye not un-wise, but [i] understanding [k] what the will of the Lord *is*.

18 And [l] be not drunk with wine, wherein is excess; but be filled with the Spirit;

19 Speaking to yourselves [m] in psalms and hymns, and spiritual songs, singing and mak-

ing melody in your heart to the Lord;

20 [n] Giving thanks always for all things unto God and the Father, [o] in the name of our Lord Jesus Christ;

21 [p] Submitting yourselves one to another in the fear of God.

A. M. cir. 4065.
A. D. cir. 61.
A. U. C. 813.
An. Imp. Ne-
ronis Cæs.
Aug. 8.

---

[h] Col. iv. 5.——[i] Rom. xii. 2.——[k] 1 Thess. iv. 3; v. 18.——[l] Prov. xx. 1; xxiii. 29, 30; Isa. v. 11, 22; Luke xxi. 34.——[m] Acts xvi. 25; 1 Cor. xiv. 26; Col. iii. 16; James v. 13.

[n] Psa. xxxiv. 1; Isa. lxiii. 7; Col. iii. 17; 1 Thess. v. 18; 2 Thess. i. 3.——[o] Heb. xiii. 15; 1 Peter ii. 5; iv. 11. [p] Phil. ii. 3; 1 Pet. v. 5.

---

the time ye have *lost*. Let *time* be your chief commodity; deal in that alone; buy it all up, and use every portion of it yourselves. *Time* is that on which *eternity* depends; in *time* ye are to get a preparation for the kingdom of God; if you get not this *in* time, your ruin is inevitable; therefore, buy up the time.

Some think there is an allusion here to the case of *debtors*, who, by giving some valuable consideration to their creditors, obtain farther time for paying their debts. And this appears to be the sense in which it is used by the Septuagint, Dan. ii. 8 : Επ' αληθειας οιδα εγω, οτι καιρον ὑμεις εξαγοραζετε· *I know certainly that ye would gain* or *buy time*—ye wish to have the time *prolonged*, that ye may seek out for some plausible explanation of the dream. Perhaps the apostle means in general, *embrace* every *opportunity* to glorify God, save your own souls, and do good to men.

Because the days are evil.] The present times are dangerous, they are full of trouble and temptations, and only the watchful and diligent have any reason to expect that they shall keep their garments unspotted.

Verse 17. *Wherefore be ye not unwise*] Μη γινεσθε αφρονες· *Do not become madmen.* Here is a most evident allusion to the *orgies of Bacchus*, in which his votaries acted like madmen; running about, tossing their heads from shoulder to shoulder, appearing to be in every sense completely frantic. See the whole of the passage in *Livy,* to which I have referred on ver. 12.

But understanding what the will of the Lord is.] It is the will of God that ye should be *sober, chaste, holy,* and *pure.* Get a thorough understanding of this; acquaint yourselves with God's will, that ye may know how to glorify him.

Verse 18. *Be not drunk with wine, wherein is excess*] This is a farther allusion to the *Bacchanalian mysteries ;* in them his votaries got drunk, and ran into all manner of excesses. *Plato,* though he forbade *drunkenness* in general, yet allowed that the people should get drunk in the solemnities of that god who invented wine. And indeed this was their common custom; when they had offered their sacrifices they indulged themselves in drunkenness, and *ran* into all kinds of extravagance. Hence it is probable that μεθυω, *to get drunk,* is derived from μετα, *after,* and θυω, *to sacrifice ;* for, having *completed* their *sacrifices,* they indulged themselves in *wine.* The word ασωτια, which we translate *excess,* means profligacy and debauchery of every kind; such as are the general concomitants of drunkenness, and especially among the votaries of Bacchus in Greece and Italy.

But be filled with the Spirit] The heathen priests pretended to be filled with the influence of the god they worshipped; and it was in these circumstances that they gave out their oracles. See a remarkable instance of this quoted in the note on Luke ix. 39, where the case of a *Bacchanalian* is described. The apostle exhorts the Ephesians not to resemble these, but, instead of being filled with wine, to be filled with the Spirit of God; in consequence of which, instead of those *discoveries* of the Divine will to which in their drunken worship the votaries of Bacchus pretended, they should be wise indeed, and should understand what the will of the Lord is.

Verse 19. *Speaking to yourselves in psalms*] We can scarcely say what is the exact difference between these three expressions. *Psalms,* ψαλμοι, may probably mean those of David.

Hymns] 'Υμνοις· Extemporaneous effusions in praise of God, uttered under the influence of the Divine Spirit, or a sense of his especial goodness. See Acts xvi. 25.

Songs] Ωιδαις· Odes; premeditated and regular poetic compositions; but, in whatever form they were composed, we learn that they were all πνευματικα, *spiritual*—tending to magnify God and edify men.

Singing and making melody in your heart] The *heart* always going with the *lips.* It is a shocking profanation of Divine worship to draw nigh to God with the *lips,* while the *heart* is far from him. It is too often the case that, in public worship, men are carried off from the *sense* of the words by the *sounds* that are put to them. And how few choirs of singers are there in the universe whose *hearts* ever accompany them in what *they* call *singing the praises of God!*

Verse 20. *Giving thanks always*] God is continually loading you with his benefits; you *deserve* nothing of his kindness; therefore give him thanks for his unmerited bounties.

God and the Father] That is: God, who is your Father, and the Father of mercies. See the observations on the *Greek article* at the end of this epistle.

In the name of our Lord Jesus] He is the only *mediator ;* and through him alone can ye approach to God; and it is for his sake only that God will hear your *prayers* or receive your *praises.*

Verse 21. *Submitting—one to another*] Let no man be so tenacious of his own will or his opinion in matters indifferent, as to disturb the peace of the Church; in all such matters *give way* to each other, and let *love* rule

A. M. cir. 4065.
A. D. cir. 61.
A. U. C. 813.
An. Imp. Ne-
ronis Cæs.
Aug. 8.

22 ^q Wives, submit yourselves unto your own husbands, ^r as unto the Lord.

23 For ^s the husband is the head of the wife, even as ^t Christ is the head of the Church; and he is the Saviour of ^u the body.

24 Therefore, as the Church is subject unto Christ, so *let* the wives *be* to their own husbands ^v in every thing.

A. M. cir. 4065.
A. D. cir. 61.
A. U. C. 813.
An. Imp. Ne-
ronis Cæs.
Aug. 8.

25 ^w Husbands, love your wives, even as Christ also loved the Church, and ^x gave himself for it;

26 That he might sanctify and cleanse it ^y with the washing of water ^z by the word;

27 ^a That he might present it to himself a glorious Church, ^b not having spot, or wrinkle, or any such thing; ^c but that it should be holy and without blemish.

---

^q Gen. iii. 16; 1 Cor. xiv. 34; Col. iii. 18; Tit. ii. 5; 1 Pet. iii. 1.——^r Ch. vi. 5.——^s 1 Cor. xi. 3.——^t Chap. i. 22; iv. 15; Col. i. 18.——^u Ch. i. 23.——^v Col. iii. 20, 22; Tit. ii. 9.——^w Col.
iii. 19; 1 Pet. iii. 7.——^x Acts xx. 28; Gal. i. 4; ii. 20; ver. 2. ^y John iii. 5; Tit. iii. 5; Heb. x. 22; 1 John v. 6.——^z John xv. 3; xvii. 17.——^a 2 Cor. xi. 2; Col. i. 22.——^b Cant. iv. 7.——^c Ch. i. 4.

In the fear of God.] Setting him always before your eyes, and considering that he has commanded you to *love one another*, and *to bear each other's burdens;* and that what you do in this or any other commanded case, you do as unto the Lord. Instead of εν φοβω Θεου, *in the fear of* God, εν φοβω Χριστου, *in the fear of* Christ, is the reading of ABDEFG, with all others of most value; besides the *Syriac, Coptic, Sahidic, Æthiopic, Armenian, Vulgate,* and *Itala; Basil* the Great, and *Chrysostom.* Neither reading makes any difference in the *sense.*

Verse 22. *Wives, submit yourselves unto your own husbands*] As the *Lord,* viz. *Christ,* is the *head* or *governor* of the *Church,* and the head of the man, so is the man the *head* or *governor* of the *woman.* This is God's ordinance, and should not be transgressed. The husband should not be a *tyrant,* and the wife should not be the *governor.* Old *Francis Quarles,* in his homely rhymes, alluding to the superstitious notion, that the *crowing* of a *hen bodes ill luck* to the family, has said:—

" Ill thrives the hapless family that shows
    A *cock* that's *silent,* and a *hen* that *crows:*
    I know not which live most *unnatural* lives,
    Obeying husbands or *commanding* wives."

As unto the Lord.] The word *Church* seems to be necessarily understood here; that is: Act under the authority of your husbands, as the *Church* acts under the authority of Christ. As the *Church* submits to the Lord, so let wives submit to their husbands.

Verse 23. *For the husband is the head of the wife*] This is the reason which the apostle gives for his injunctions. See above.

He is the Saviour of the body.] As Christ exercises authority over the Church so as to *save* and *protect* it, so let the husband exercise authority over his wife by *protecting, comforting,* and *providing* her with every *necessary* and *comfort* of life, according to his power.

Verse 24. *In every thing.*] That is, every *lawful thing;* for it is not intimated that they should obey their husbands in any thing *criminal,* or in any thing detrimental to the *interests of their souls.* The husband may be profligate, and may wish his wife to become such also; he may be an enemy to true religion, and use his authority to prevent his wife from those means

of grace which she finds salutary to her soul; in *none* of *these things* should she obey him.

Verse 25. *Husbands, love your wives*] Here is a grand rule, according to which every husband is called to act: *Love your wife as Christ loved the Church.* But *how* did Christ love the Church? *He gave himself for it*—he laid down his life for it. So then husbands should, if necessary, lay down their lives for their wives: and there is more implied in the words than mere protection and support; for, as Christ gave himself for the Church to *save* it, so husbands should, by all means in their power, labour to promote the salvation of their wives, and their constant edification in righteousness. Thus we find that the authority of the man over the woman is founded on his *love* to her, and this love must be such as to lead him to risk his life for her. As the care of the family devolves on the wife, and the children must owe the chief direction of their minds and formation of their manners to the mother, she has need of all the assistance and support which her husband can give her; and, if she performs her duty well, she deserves the utmost of his love and affection.

Verse 26. *That he might sanctify and cleanse it*] The Church is represented as the *spouse of Christ,* as the woman is the *spouse* of the man; and, to prepare this Church for himself, he *washes, cleanses,* and *sanctifies* it. There is certainly an allusion here to the ancient method of *purifying women,* who were appointed to be consorts to kings; *twelve months,* it appears, were in some instances spent in this purification: *Six months with oil of myrrh, and six months with sweet odours and with other things, for the purifying of women.* See the case of Esther, chap. ii. 12; see also Psa. xlv. 13, 14; Ezek. xvi. 7–14.

With the washing of water] Baptism, accompanied by the purifying influences of the Holy Spirit.

By the word] The *doctrine* of Christ crucified, through which baptism is administered, sin cancelled, and the soul purified from all unrighteousness; the *death of Christ* giving efficacy to all.

Verse 27. *That he might present it to himself*] It was usual to bring the royal bride to the king in the most *sumptuous apparel;* and is there not here an allusion to Psa. xlv. 13, 14: *The king's daughter* (Pharaoh's) *is all glorious within, her clothing is of wrought gold; she shall be brought unto the king*

A. M. cir. 4065.
A. D. cir. 61.
A. U. C. 813.
An. Imp. Ne-
ronis Cæs.
Aug. 8.

28 So ought men to love their wives as their own bodies. He that loveth his wife loveth himself.

29 For no man ever yet hated his own flesh; but nourisheth and cherisheth it, even as the Lord the Church:

30 For d we are members of his body, of his flesh, and of his bones.

31 e For this cause shall a man leave his father and mother, and shall be joined unto his wife, and they f two shall be one flesh.

32 This is a great mystery: but I speak concerning Christ and the Church.

33 Nevertheless, g let every one of you in particular so love his wife even as himself; and the wife *see* that she h reverence *her* husband.

A. M. cir. 4065
A. D. cir. 61
A. U. C. 813
An. Imp. Ne
ronis Cæs.
Aug. 8.

---

d Gen. ii. 23; Rom. xii. 5; 1 Cor. vi. 15; xii. 27.——e Gen. ii. 24; Matt. xix. 5; Mark x. 7, 8.

f 1 Corinthians vi. 16.——g Verse 25; Col. iii. 19.——h 1 Peter iii. 6.

(Solomon) *in raiment of needlework?* This *presentation* here spoken of by the apostle will take place on the last day. See the note on 2 Cor. xi. 2.

A glorious Church] Every way splendid and honourable, because pure and holy.

Not having spot] Σπιλον· No blemish on the *face*; no spots upon the *garment*; the *heart* and *life* both holy.

Wrinkle] 'Ρυτιδα· No mark of *superannuation* or *decay*. The word is commonly applied to *wrinkles on the face*, indicative of *sickness* or *decrepitude*.

Holy and without blemish.] In every sense holy, pure, and perfect. Now it was for this purpose that *Christ gave himself for the Church*; and for this purpose he continues the different ordinances which he has appointed ; and, particularly, the preaching of the *word*—the doctrine of reconciliation through faith in his blood. And it is in *this life* that all this purification is to take place; for none shall be *presented* at the day of judgment to him who has not here been *sanctified, cleansed, washed,* made *glorious,* having neither *spot, wrinkle, blemish,* nor *any such thing.* How vain is the pretension of multitudes to be members of the true Church while full of *spots, wrinkles, blemishes,* and MANY *such things;* fondly supposing that their holiness is in their surety, because not in themselves ! Reader, lay thy hand on thy conscience and say, Dost thou believe that this is St. Paul's meaning? See the notes on chap. iii. 14, &c.

Verse 28. *As their own bodies*] For the woman is, properly speaking, a *part* of the man; for God made man *male and female,* and the woman was taken out of his side : therefore is she *flesh of his flesh, and bone of his bone ;* and therefore, he that loveth his wife loveth himself, for they two are one flesh. The apostle, in all these verses, refers to the creation and original *state* of the first human pair.

Verse 29. *No man ever yet hated his own flesh*] And this is a natural reason why he should love his wife, and nourish and cherish her.

Verse 30. *We are members of his body*] He has partaken of *our* nature, as we have partaken of the nature of *Adam.* And as he is the head of the Church and the Saviour of this *body ;* so we, being members of the Church, are members of his mystical body. That is, we are united to him by one Spirit in the closest intimacy, even similar to that which the members have with the body.

Verse 31. *Shall be joined unto his wife*] Προσκολλη- θησεται· He shall be *glued* or *cemented* to her ; and,

as a *well-glued* board will sooner *break* in the *whole wood* than in the *glued* joint, so death alone can *part* the husband and wife ; and nothing but *death* should dissolve their *affection.* See the notes on Gen. ii 21—24.

Verse 32. *This is a great mystery*] Το μυστηριον τουτο μεγα εστιν· *This mystery is great. Sacramentum hoc magnum est ; this sacrament is great.* VULGATE. And on the evidence of this version the Church of Rome has made matrimony a sacrament, which, as they use it, is no meaning of the original. By *mystery,* here, we may understand a natural thing by which some *spiritual* matter is signified, which signification the Spirit of God alone can give. So, here, the creation and union of Adam and Eve, were intended, in the design of God, to point out the union of Christ and the Church: a union the most important that can be conceived; and therefore the apostle calls it *a great mystery.* See the observations at the end of this chapter.

Verse 33. *Nevertheless*] Πλην· *Moreover,* or *therefore,* on the consideration of God's design in the institution of marriage, let every one of you love his wife as himself, because she is both *naturally* and by a *Divine ordinance* a part of himself.

That she reverence her *husband.*] Let the wife ever consider the husband as her head , and this he is, not only by nature, but also by the ordinance of God. These are very important matters, and on them the apostle lays great stress. See the following *observations.*

THERE is one subject in the preceding verse on which I could not enlarge sufficiently in the notes, and which I have reserved for this place; viz. what the apostle says concerning the *mystery of marriage,* which certainly has a deeper meaning than what is generally apprehended. Dr. Macknight has some good observations on this part of the subject, which I shall beg leave to lay before my readers.

1. "The apostle calls the formation of Eve from Adam's body, his marriage with her ; and the intimate union established between them by that marriage, *a great mystery,* because it contained an important emblematical meaning concerning the regeneration of believers, and their union with Christ, which hitherto had been kept secret, but which he had discovered in the 30th verse. For there, in allusion to what Adam said concerning Eve, 'This now is bone of my bones, and flesh of my flesh,' the apostle says, concerning Christ

464   2

and believers : 'We are bone of his bones, and flesh of his flesh :' that is, we are parts of his body, the Church. And by this application of Adam's words concerning Eve to Christ and to his Church, he intimates, First, That the formation of Eve of a rib taken out of Adam's body was a figure of the regeneration of believers by the breaking of Christ's body, mentioned ver. 25. Secondly, That Adam's love to Eve, on account of her being formed of his body, was a figure of Christ's love to believers because they are become his body, ver. 30. Thirdly, That Adam's marriage with Eve was a figure of the eternal union of Christ with believers in heaven, mentioned verse 27. For he left his Father to be united to his Church.

2. "In giving this emblematical representation of these ancient facts, the apostle has not exceeded the bounds of probability. In the first age, neither the art of writing, nor any permanent method of conveying instruction, being invented, it was necessary to make such striking actions and events as could not easily be forgotten emblems of the instruction meant to be perpetuated. On this supposition, Adam, in whom the human race began, was a natural image of Christ, in whom the human race was to be restored ; and his deep sleep, the opening of his side, and the formation of Eve of a rib taken out of his side, were fit emblems of Christ's death, of the opening of his side on the cross, and of the regeneration of believers by his death. The love which Adam expressed towards Eve, and his union with her by marriage, were lively images of Christ's love to believers, and of his eternal union with them in one society after their resurrection ; and Eve herself, who was formed of a rib taken from Adam's side, was a natural image of believers, who are regenerated, both in their body and in their mind, by the breaking of Christ's side on the cross. Thus, the circumstances which accompanied the formation of Eve being fit emblems of the formation of the Church, we may suppose they were brought to pass to prefigure that great event ; and, by prefiguring it, to show that it was decreed of God from the very beginning.

3. "The aptness, however, of these images is not the only reason for supposing that the formation of Eve, and her marriage with Adam in paradise, were emblems of the regeneration of believers by the death of Christ, and of their eternal union with him in hea-ven. The singular manner in which Eve was formed, and the declaration at her marriage with Adam, 'Therefore shall a man leave his father and his mother, and cleave unto his wife, and they shall be one flesh,' strongly lead to that conclusion. Eve was not formed of the dust of the earth, as all other living things were made, (not excepting Adam himself,) but of a rib taken from Adam's side while he was in a deep sleep. Now, for this diversity, what reason can be assigned, if that which the apostle hath suggested is not admitted ! Farther : unless some deep instruction were couched under the formation of Eve, what occasion was there for Adam, at his marriage with her, to declare, ' This is now bone of my bones, and flesh of my flesh ; she shall be called woman, because she was taken out of man : therefore shall a man leave,' &c. ? For although the taking of Eve out of Adam might be a reason for Adam's affection towards her, it was no reason for the affection of his posterity towards their wives, who were not so formed. The reason of their love to their wives is their being creatures of the same species with themselves. This Eve might have been, though, like Adam, she had been formed of the dust of the earth. Wherefore Adam's declaration concerning Eve being taken out of his body, and concerning his love to her on that account, was intended for some purpose peculiar to himself ; namely, as he was a type of Him who was to restore the human race by the breaking of his body on the cross, and who on that account loves them, and will unite them to himself for ever. Upon the whole, the formation of Eve and her marriage with Adam, and his love to and union with her because she was taken out of his side, and the declaration that, on that account, all his posterity should love their wives, and continue united to them through life, (a union which does not subsist among other animals,) are events so singular, that I do not see what account can be given of them, unless, with the Apostle Paul, we suppose that, agreeably to the most ancient method of instruction, God intended these things as figurative representations of the regeneration of believers by the death of Christ, and of his eternal union with them in heaven ; and that Adam and Eve were taught by God himself to consider them as such.

4. "It is no small confirmation of the apostle's emblematical interpretation of the formation and marriage of Eve, that in Scripture we find a variety of images and expressions founded on that interpretation. For example, Rom. v. 14, Adam is expressly called *a type of him who was to come,* on which account, 1 Cor. xv. 45, Christ is called *the last Adam.* Next, the catholic Church, consisting of believers of all nations, is called *the body of Christ,* and the members thereof are said to be *members of his body, of his flesh, and of his bones ;* in allusion to the formation of Eve, the emblem of the Church. For, as Eve was formed of a rib taken out of Adam's body during his deep sleep, so believers are regenerated both in mind and body, and formed into one great society, and united to Christ as their head and governor, by the breaking of his body on the cross. Thirdly, to this emblematical meaning of the formation of Eve, our Lord, I think, alluded when he instituted his supper. For, instead of appointing one symbol only of his death, he appointed two ; and, in explaining the first of them, he expressed himself in such a manner as to show that he had his eye on what happened to Adam when Eve was formed : *This is my body which is broken for you*—for your regeneration. Fourthly, the eternal union of the regenerated with Christ after the resurrection is called a marriage, Rev. xix. 7 ; and the *new Jerusalem,* that is, the *inhabitants* of the new Jerusalem, the society of the redeemed, is termed *the bride, the Lamb's wife ;* and the preparing of men for that happy union, by introducing them into the Church upon earth through faith, and by sanctifying them through the word, is called, 2 Cor. xi. 2, A *fitting them for one husband, that* at the resurrection *they may be presented a chaste virgin to Christ ;* in allusion, I suppose, to the presenting of Eve to Adam, in order to her marriage with him ; and to show that, in this expression, the apostle had the figurative meaning

of Eve's marriage in his mind, he mentions, ver. 3, the subtlety of the devil in deceiving Eve. Finally, the union of the Jewish Church with God, as the figure of the catholic Church, consisting of the regenerated of all nations, is by God himself termed *a marriage*, Jer. iii. 14 ; Ezek. xvi. 8–32 ; and God is called the *husband* of that people, Isa. liv. 5 ; and their union to him by the law of Moses is termed, *The day of their espousals*, Jer. ii. 2." 1. A truly Christian marriage has an excellence, holiness, and unity in it, that cannot be easily described ; and let it be observed that, while it prefigures the union of Christ with his Church, it is one means of giving children to the Church, and members to the mystical body of Christ. It is an ordinance of God, and cannot be too highly honoured ; endless volumes might be written on its utility to man : without marriage, by which every man is assigned *his own wife*, and every woman *her own husband*, even the multitude of spurious births which would take place would fail to keep up the population of the earth; and natural, moral, and political wretchedness would be the consequence of promiscuous, fortuitous, and transitory connections. For without that ascertainment of peculiar property which marriage gives to every man in his wife, and to every woman in her husband, the human progeny would be unnoticed, unclaimed, uneducated, and totally neglected. This would continually increase the wretchedness, and in process of time bring about the total depopulation of the world.

2. The husband is to love his wife, the wife to obey and venerate her husband ; love and protection on the one hand, affectionate subjection and fidelity on the other. The husband should provide for his wife without encouraging profuseness ; watch over her conduct without giving her vexation ; keep her in subjection without making her a slave ; love her without jealousy ; oblige her without flattery ; honour her without making her proud ; and be hers entirely, without becoming either her footman or her slave. In short, they have equal rights and equal claims ; but superior strength gives the man dominion, affection and subjection entitle the woman to love and protection. Without the woman, man is but half a human being ; in union with the man, the woman finds her safety and perfection.

In the above remarks there are many things *solid* and *useful ;* there are others which rest more on *fancy* than *judgment.*

3. Of marriage the Church of Rome has made a *sacrament*, and it is one of the *seven* which that Church acknowledges. That it is an *ordinance* of *God* is sufficiently evident ; that *he* has *not* made it a *sacrament* is not less so. Though the *minister* of *religion* celebrates it, yet the regulation of it, in reference to inheritance, &c., is assumed by the *state*. This is of great moment, as by it many evils are prevented, and many political and domestic advantages secured. If a man enter hastily into this state it is at his own risk ; after he has once entered it the seal of the legislature is imposed upon it, and with his engagements he cannot trifle. A consideration of this has prevented many hasty and disproportionate alliances. Though they might hope to trifle with the *Church*, they dare not do it with the *state*.

CHAPTER VI.

Children should obey their parents, that they may live long and be happy, 1–3. Parents should be tender towards their children, 4. Servants should show all obedience and fidelity to their masters, 5–8. And masters should treat their servants with humanity, 9. All should be strong in the Lord, and be armed with his armour, because of their wily, powerful, and numerous foes, 10–13. The different parts of the Christian armour enumerated, 14–17. The necessity of all kinds of prayer and watchfulness, 18–20. Tychicus is commissioned to inform the Ephesians of the apostle's affairs, 21, 22. The apostolic benediction and farewell, 23, 24.

A. M. cir. 4065.
A. D. cir. 61.
A. U. C. 813.
An. Imp. Neronis Cæs.
Aug. 8.

CHILDREN, [a] obey your parents in the Lord : for this is right.

2 [b] Honour thy father and mother, (which is the first commandment with promise,)

3 That it may be well with thee, and thou mayest live long on the earth.

4 And [c] ye fathers, provoke not your children to wrath : but [d] bring them

A. M. cir. 4065.
A. D. cir. 61.
A. U. C 813.
An. Imp. Neronis Cæs.
Aug. 8.

---

[a] Prov. xxiii. 22 ; Col. iii. 20.——[b] Ex. xx. 12 ; Deut. v. 16 ; xxvii. 16 ; Jer. xxxv. 18 ; Ezek. xxii. 7 ; Mal. i. 6 ; Eccles. iii. 8 ; Matt. xv.

4 ; Mark vii. 10.——[c] Col. iii. 21.——[d] Gen. xviii. 19 ; Deut. iv 9 ; vi. 7, 20 ; xi. 19 ; Psa. lxxviii. 4 ; Prov. xix. 18 ; xxii. 6 , xxix. 17.

NOTES ON CHAP VI.

Verse 1. *Children, obey your parents*] This is a duty with which God will never dispense ; he commands it, and one might think that gratitude, from a sense of the highest obligations, would most strongly enforce the command.

In the Lord] This clause is wanting in several reputable MSS., and in some *versions*. *In the Lord* may mean, on account of the commandment of the Lord ; or, as far as the parents' commands are accord-

ing to the will and word of God. For surely no child is called to obey any parent if he give unreasonable or unscriptural commands.

Verse 2. *Honour thy father*] See the notes on Exod. xx. 12, &c., where this subject, together with the *promises* and *threatenings* connected with it, is particularly considered, and the *reasons* of the duty laid down at large.

Verse 4. *Fathers, provoke not your children to wrath*] Avoid all *severity* ; this will hurt your own

(30**)

A. M. cir. 4065.
A. D. cir. 61.
A. U. C. 813.
An. Imp. Ne-
ronis Cæs.
Aug. 8.

up in the nurture and admonition of the Lord.

5 e Servants, be obedient to them that are *your* masters according to the flesh, f with fear and trembling, g in singleness of your heart, as unto Christ ;

6 h Not with eye-service, as men-pleasers ; but as the servants of Christ, doing the will of God from the heart ;

7 With good will doing service, as to the Lord, and not to men ;

8 i Knowing that whatsoever good thing any man doeth, the same shall he receive of the Lord, k whether *he be* bond or free.

9 And, ye l masters, do the same things unto them, m forbearing n threatening : knowing that o your p Master also is in heaven ; q neither is there respect of persons with him.

10 Finally, my brethren, be strong in the Lord, and r in the power of his might.

A. M. cir. 4065.
A. D. cir. 61.
A. U. C. 813.
An. Imp. Ne-
ronis Cæs.
Aug. 8.

---

e Col. iii. 22 ; 1 Tim. vi. 1 ; Tit. ii. 9 ; 1 Pet. ii. 18.——f 2 Cor. vii. 15 ; Phil. ii. 12.——g 1 Chron. xxix. 17 ; Col. iii. 22.——h Col. iii. 22, 23.——i Rom. ii. 6 ; 2 Cor. v. 10 ; Col. iii. 24.——k Gal. iii. 28 ; Col. iii. 11.——l Col. iv. 1.

m Or, *moderating.*——n Lev. xxv. 43.——o Some read, *both your and their master.*——p John xiii. 13 ; 1 Cor. vii. 22.——q Wisd. vi. 7 ; Eccles. xxxv. 12 ; Rom. ii. 11 ; Col. iii. 25.——r Chap i 19 ; iii. 16 ; Col. i. 11.

---

souls, and do them no good ; on the contrary, if punished with *severity* or *cruelty*, they will be only hardened and made desperate in their sins. *Cruel parents* generally have *bad children.* He who corrects his children according to God and reason will feel every blow on his own heart more sensibly than his child feels it on his body. Parents are called to *correct*, not to *punish*, their children. Those who *punish* them do it from a principle of *revenge* ; those who *correct* them do it from a principle of *affectionate concern.*

Bring them up, &c.] Εκτρεφετε αυτα εν παιδεια και νουθεσια Κυριου· literally, *Nourish them in the discipline and instruction of the Lord.* The *mind* is to be nourished with wholesome discipline and instruction, as the *body* is with proper food. Παιδεια, *discipline*, may refer to all that knowledge which is proper for children, including elementary principles and rules for behaviour, &c. Νουθεσια, *instruction*, may imply whatever is necessary to form the mind ; to touch, regulate, and purify the passions ; and necessarily includes the whole of religion. Both these should be administered *in the Lord*—according to his will and word, and in reference to his eternal glory. All the important lessons and doctrines being derived from his revelation, therefore they are called *the discipline and instruction of the Lord.*

Verse 5. *Servants, be obedient*] Though δουλος frequently signifies a *slave* or *bondman*, yet it often implies a *servant* in general, or any one bound to another, either for a limited time, or for life. Even a *slave*, if a Christian, was bound to serve him faithfully by whose money he was bought, howsoever illegal that traffic may be considered. In heathen countries slavery was in some sort excusable ; among Christians it is an enormity and a crime for which perdition has scarcely an adequate state of punishment.

According to the flesh] Your masters in secular things ; for they have no authority over your religion, nor over your souls.

With fear and trembling] Because the law gives them a power to punish you for every act of disobedience.

In singleness of your heart] Not merely through fear of punishment, but from a principle of uprightness, serving them as you would serve Christ.

Verse 6. *Not with eye-service*] Not merely in their presence, when their eye is upon you, as unfaith ful and hypocritical servants do, without consulting conscience in any part of their work.

Doing the will of God] Seeing that you are in the state of servitude, it is the will of God that you should act conscientiously in it.

Verse 7. *With good will*] Μετ' εννοιας· With *cheerfulness* ; do not take up your service as a cross, or bear it as a burden ; but take it as coming in the order of God's providence, and a thing that is pleasing to him.

Verse 8. *Whatsover good thing any man doeth*] Though your masters should fail to give you the due reward of your fidelity and labour, yet, as ye have done your work as unto the Lord, he will take care to give you the proper recompense.

Whether he be bond] A *slave*, bought with money ;

Or free.] A person who has *hired* himself of his own free accord.

Verse 9. *Ye masters, do the same things unto them*] Act in the same affectionate, conscientious manner towards your slaves and servants, as they do towards you.

Forbearing threatening] If they should transgress at any time, lean more to the side of *mercy* than *justice* ; and when ye are obliged to punish, let it be as light and as moderate as possible ; and let *revenge* have no part in the chastisement, for that is of the devil, and not of God.

The words, *forbearing threatening*, ανιεντες την απειλην, signify to mitigate, relax, or not exact threatening ; that is, the *threatened punishment.* The sense is given above.

In *Shemoth Rabba*, sect. 21, fol. 120, there is a good saying concerning *respect of persons* : " If a poor man comes to a rich man to converse with him, he will not regard him ; but if a rich man comes he will hear and rehear him. The holy and blessed God acts not thus ; for all are alike before him, women, slaves, the poor, and the rich."

Knowing that your Master also is in heaven] You are *their* masters, God is *yours.* As *you* deal with *them*, so God will deal with *you* ; for do not suppose, because their condition on earth is inferior to yours, that God considers them to be less worthy of his regard than you are ; this is not so, for *there is no respect of persons with Him.*

Verse 10. *Finally*] Having laid before you your

2

A. M. cir. 4065.
A. D. cir. 61.
A. U. C. 813.
An. Imp. Ne-
ronis Cæs.
Aug. 8.

11 ˢ Put on the whole armour of God, that ye may be able to stand against the wiles of the devil.

12 For we wrestle not against ᵗ flesh ᵘ and blood, but against ᵛ principalities, against pow-

ers, against ʷ the rulers of the darkness of this world, against ˣ spiritual wickedness in ʸ high places.

13 ᶻ Wherefore take unto you the whole armour of God, that ye may be able to withstand

A. M. cir. 4065.
A. D. cir. 61.
A. U. C. 813.
An. Imp. Ne-
ronis Cæs.
Aug. 8.

ˢ Rom. xiii. 12; 2 Cor. vi. 7; ver. 13; 1 Thess. v. 8.——ᵗ Gr. *blood and flesh.*——ᵘ Matt. xvi. 17; 1 Cor. xv. 50.——ᵛ Rom. viii. 38; chap. i. 24; Col. ii. 15.

ʷ Luke xxii. 53; John xii. 31; xiv. 30; chap. ii. 2; Col. i. 13. ˣ Or, *wicked spirits.*——ʸ Or, *heavenly,* as chap. i. 3.——ᶻ 2 Cor. x. 4; ver. 11.

---

great and high calling, and all the doctrines and precepts of the Gospel, it is necessary that I should show you the enemies that will oppose you, and the strength which is requisite to enable you to repel them.

Be strong in the Lord] You must have strength, and strength of a *spiritual* kind, and such strength too as the *Lord* himself can furnish; and you must have this strength through an *indwelling God, the power of his might* working in you.

Verse 11. *Put on the whole armour of God*] Ενδυσασθε την πανοπλιαν του Θεου. The apostle considers every Christian as having a warfare to maintain against numerous, powerful, and subtle foes; and that therefore they would need much strength, much courage, complete armour, and skill to use it. The *panoply* which is mentioned here refers to the armour of the *heavy troops* among the Greeks; those who were to sustain the rudest attacks, who were to sap the foundations of walls, storm cities, &c. Their ordinary armour was the *shield,* the *helmet,* the *sword,* and the *greaves* or *brazen boots.* To all these the apostle refers below. See on ver. 13.

The wiles of the devil.] Τας μεθοδειας του διαβολου· *The methods of the devil;* the different *means, plans, schemes,* and *machinations* which he uses to deceive, entrap, enslave, and ruin the souls of men. A *man's method* of sinning is *Satan's method* of ruining his soul. See on chap. iv. 14.

Verse 12. *For we wrestle not against flesh and blood*] Ουκ εστιν ημιν η παλη προς αιμα και σαρκα· Our *wrestling* or *contention is not with men* like ourselves: *flesh and blood* is a Hebraism for *men,* or *human beings.* See the note on Gal. i. 16.

The word παλη implies the athletic exercises in the Olympic and other national games; and παλαιστρα was the *place* in which the contenders exercised. Here it signifies warfare in general.

Against principalities] Αρχας· *Chief rulers;* beings of the first rank and order in their own kingdom.

Powers] Εξουσιας, *Authorities,* derived from, and constituted by the above.

The rulers of the darkness of this world] Τους κοσμοκρατορας του σκοτους του αιωνος τουτου· The *rulers of the world;* the *emperors of the darkness of this state of things.*

Spiritual wickedness] Τα πνευματικα της πονηριας· *The spiritual things of wickedness;* or, *the spiritualities of wickedness;* highly refined and sublimed evil; disguised *falsehood* in the garb of *truth;* Antinomianism in the guise of *religion.*

In high places.] Εν τοις επουρανιοις· *In the most sublime stations.* But who are *these* of whom the

apostle speaks? *Schoettgen* contends that the *rabbins* and *Jewish* rulers are intended. This he thinks proved by the words του αιωνος τουτου, *of this world,* which are often used to designate the *Old Testament,* and the *Jewish system;* and the words εν τοις επουρανιοις, *in heavenly places,* which are not unfrequently used to signify the time of the NEW TESTAMENT, and the *Gospel system.*

By the spiritual wickedness in heavenly places, he thinks false teachers, who endeavoured to corrupt Christianity, are meant; such as those mentioned by St. John, 1st Epist. ii. 19: *They went out from us, but they were not of us,* &c. And he thinks the meaning may be extended to all corrupters of Christianity in all succeeding ages. He shows also that the Jews called their own city שר של עולם *sar shel olam,* κοσμοκρατωρ, *the ruler of the world;* and proves that David's words, Psa. ii. 2, *The kings of the earth set themselves, and the rulers take counsel together,* are applied by the apostles, Acts iv. 26, to the Jewish *rulers,* αρχοντες, who persecuted Peter and John for preaching Christ crucified. But commentators in general are not of this mind, but think that by *principalities,* &c., we are to understand different orders of evil spirits, who are all employed under the devil, their great head, to prevent the spread of the Gospel in the world, and to destroy the souls of mankind.

The *spiritual wickedness* are supposed to be the *angels* which kept not their first estate; who fell from the *heavenly places* but are ever longing after and striving to regain them; and which have their station in the *regions of the air.* " Perhaps," says Mr. Wesley, " the *principalities and powers* remain mostly in the citadel of their kingdom of *darkness;* but there are other spirits which range abroad, to whom the provinces of the *world* are committed; *the darkness* is chiefly *spiritual* darkness which prevails during the present state of things, and the *wicked spirits* are those which continually oppose faith, love, and holiness, either by force or fraud; and labour to infuse unbelief, pride, idolatry, malice, envy, anger, and hatred." Some translate the words εν τοις επουρανιοις, *about heavenly things;* that is: We contend with these fallen spirits for the heavenly things which are promised to us; and we strive against them, that we may not be deprived of those we have.

Verse 13. *Wherefore*] Because ye have such enemies to contend with, *take unto you*—assume, as provided and prepared for you, *the whole armour of God;* which armour if you put on and use, you shall be both invulnerable and immortal. The ancient heroes are fabled to have had armour sent to them by the *gods;*

A. M. cir. 4065.
A. D. cir. 61.
A. U. C. 813.
An. Imp. Ne-
ronis Cæs.
Aug. 8.

[a] in the evil day, and, [b] having done all, to stand.

14 Stand therefore, [c] having your loins girt about with truth,

and [d] having on the breast-plate of righteousness ;

15 [e] And your feet shod with the preparation of the Gospel of peace ;

A. M. cir. 4065.
A. D. cir. 61.
A. U. C. 813.
An. Imp. Ne-
ronis Cæs.
Aug. 8.

---

[a] Chap. v. 16.——[b] Or, *having overcome all.*——[c] Isa. xi. 5 ; Luke xii. 35 ; 1 Pet. i. 13.

[d] Isa. lix. 17 ; 2 Cor. vi. 7 ; 1 Thess. v. 8.——[e] Isa. lii. 7 ; Rom. x. 15.

---

and even the great armour-maker, *Vulcan*, was reputed to be a *god* himself. This was *fable* : what Paul speaks of is *reality*. See before on ver. 11.

That ye may be able to withstand] That ye may not only stand fast in the liberty wherewith Christ hath made you free, but also discomfit all your spiritual foes ; and continuing in your ranks, maintain your ground against them, never putting off your armour, but standing always ready prepared to repel any new attack.

And having done all, to stand.] Και απαντα κατεργασαμενοι στηναι· rather, *And having conquered all, stand :* this is a military phrase, and is repeatedly used in this sense by the best Greek writers. So *Dionys. Hal.* Ant., lib. vi., page 400 : Και παντα πολεμια εν ολιγῳ κατεργασαμενοι χρονῳ· "Having in a short time discomfited all our enemies, we returned with numerous captives and much spoil." See many examples in *Kypke*. By *evil day* we may understand any time of trouble, affliction, and sore temptation.

As there is here allusion to some of the most important parts of the Grecian armour, I shall give a short account of the whole. It consisted properly of two sorts : 1. Defensive armour, or that which protected themselves. 2. Offensive armour, or that by which they injured their enemies. The apostle refers to both.

I. *Defensive armour :*

Περικεφαλαια, the HELMET ; this was the armour for the head, and was of various forms, and embossed with a great variety of figures. Connected with the helmet was the *crest* or *ridge* on the top of the helmet, adorned with several emblematic figures ; some for *ornament*, some to strike *terror*. For crests on ancient helmets we often see the winged lion, the griffin, chimera, &c. St. Paul seems to refer to one which had an emblematical representation of *hope*.

Ζωμα, the GIRDLE ; this went about the loins, and served to brace the armour tight to the body, and to support daggers, short swords, and such like weapons, which were frequently stuck in it. This kind of girdle is in general use among the Asiatic nations to the present day.

Θωραξ, the BREAST-PLATE ; this consisted of two parts, called πτερυγες or *wings :* one covered the whole region of the thorax or *breast*, in which the principal viscera of life are contained ; and the other covered the back, as far down as the front part extended.

Κνημιδες, GREAVES or *brazen boots*, which covered the shin or front of the leg ; a kind of *solea* was often used, which covered the sole, and laced about the instep, and prevented the foot from being wounded by rugged ways, thorns, stones, &c.

Χειριδες, GAUNTLETS ; a kind of *gloves* that served to defend the hands, and the arm up to the elbow.

Ασπις, the *clypeus* or SHIELD ; it was perfectly round, and sometimes made of *wood*, covered with bullocks' hides ; but often made of *metal*. The *aspis* or *shield* of Achilles, made by Vulcan, was composed of *five* plates, two of *brass*, two of *tin*, and one of *gold* ; so Homer, Il. Υ. v. 270 : ——

――― επει πεντε πτυχας ηλασε Κυλλοποδιων,
Τας δυο χαλκειας, δυο δ' ενδοθι κασσιτεροιο,
Την δε μιαν χρυσην.

Five plates of various metal, various mould,
Composed the shield ; of brass each outward fold,
Of tin each inward, and the middle gold.

Of *shields* there were several sorts :

Γερρων or γερρα, the *gerron ;* a small *square* shield, used first by the *Persians.*

Λαισηιον, LAISEÏON ; a sort of *oblong* shield, covered with rough hides, or skins with the hair on.

Πελτη, the PELTA ; a small *light shield*, nearly in the form of a demicrescent, with a small ornament, similar to the recurved leaves of a flower *de luce*, on the centre of a diagonal edge or straight line ; this was the *Amazonian* shield.

Θυρεος, the *scutum* or OBLONG SHIELD ; this was always made of *wood*, and covered with hides. It was exactly in the shape of the *laiseïon*, but differed in *size*, being much larger, and being covered with hides from which the hair had been taken off. It was called θυρεος from θυρα, a *door*, which it resembled in its oblong shape ; but it was made curved, so as to embrace the whole foreparts of the body. The *aspis* and the *thureos* were the shields principally in use ; the former for light, the latter for *heavy* armed troops.

II. *Offensive armour*, or weapons ; the following were chief :

Εγχος, *enchos*, the SPEAR ; which was generally a head of brass or iron, with a long shaft of *ash*.

Δορυ, the LANCE ; differing perhaps little from the former, but in its size and lightness ; being a missile used, both by infantry and cavalry, for the purpose of annoying the enemy at a *distance*.

Ξιφος, the SWORD ; these were of various sizes, and in the beginning all of *brass*. The swords of Homer's heroes are all of this metal.

Μαχαιρα, called also a *sword*, sometimes a *knife ;* it was a *short sword*, used more frequently by gladiators, or in single combat. What other difference it had from the *xiphos* I cannot tell.

Αξινη, from which our word AXE ; the common *battle-axe.*

Πελεκυς, the BIPEN ; a sort of *battle-axe*, with double face, one opposite to the other.

2

A. M. cir. 4065.
A. D. cir. 61.
A. U. C. 813.
An. Imp. Ne-
ronis Cæs.
Aug. 8.

16 Above all, taking ^f the shield of faith, wherewith ye shall be able to quench all the fiery darts of the wicked.

17 And ^g take the helmet of salvation, and ^h the sword of the Spirit, which is the word of God :

A. M. cir. 4065.
A. D. cir. 61.
A. U. C. 813.
An. Imp. Ne-
ronis Cæs.
Aug. 8.

f 1 John v. 4.——g Isa. lix. 17; 1 Thess. v. 8.

h Heb. iv. 12; Rev. i. 16; ii. 16; xix. 15.

Κορυνη, an *iron club* or *mace*, much used both among the ancient Greeks and Persians.

Τοξον, the BOW; with its *pharetra* or *quiver*, and its stock or sheaf of *arrows*.

Σφενδονη, the SLING; an instrument in the use of which most ancient nations were very expert, particularly the Hebrews and ancient Greeks.

The arms and armour mentioned above were not always in use; they were found out and improved by degrees. The account given by *Lucretius* of the arms of the first inhabitants of the earth is doubtless as correct as it is natural.

Arma antiqua manus, ungues, dentesque fuere,
Et lapides, et item silvarum fragmina rami,
Et flammæ, atque ignes postquam sunt cognita primum :
Posterius ferri vis est, ærisque reperta ;
Sed prius æris erat quam ferri cognitus usus :
Quo facilis magis est natura, et copia major.

De Rerum Nat., lib. v. ver. 1282.

Whilst *cruelty* was not improved by *art*,
And *rage* not furnished yet with *sword* or *dart* ;
With *fists*, or *boughs*, or *stones*, the warriors fought ;
These were the only weapons *Nature* taught :
But when *flames* burnt the trees and scorched the ground,
Then *brass* appeared, and *iron* fit to wound.
Brass first was used, because the softer ore,
And earth's cold veins contained a greater store.

CREECH.

I have only to observe farther on this head, 1. That the ancient Greeks and Romans went *constantly armed* ; 2. That before they engaged they always *ate together* ; and 3. That they commenced every attack with prayer to the gods for success.

Verse 14. *Stand therefore*] Prepare yourselves for combat, *having your loins girt about with truth.* He had told them before *to take the whole armour of God*, ver. 13, and to *put on* this *whole armour.* Having got all the pieces of it *together*, and the defensive parts *put on*, they were then to gird them close to their bodies with the ζωμα or *girdle* ; and instead of a fine ornamented *belt*, such as the ancient warriors used, they were to have *truth.* The Gospel of Jesus Christ is the *truth of God* ; unless this be *known* and *conscientiously believed* no man can enter the spiritual warfare with any advantage or prospect of success. By this alone we discover who our enemies are, and how they come on to attack us ; and by this we know where our strength lies ; and, as the truth is great, and must prevail, we are to gird ourselves with this against all false religion, and the various winds of doctrine by which cunning men and insidious devils lie in wait to deceive. *Truth* may be taken here for *sincerity* ; for if a man be not conscious to himself that his *heart is right* before God, and that he makes no

false pretences to religion, in vain does he enter the spiritual lists. This alone can give him confidence :

———— *Hic murus aheneus esto,*
Nil conscire sibi, nulla pallescere culpa.

Let this be my brazen wall ; that no man can reproach me with a crime, and that I am conscious of my own integrity.

The breast-plate of righteousness] What the θωραξ or *breast-plate* was, see before. The word *righteousness*, δικαιοσυνη, we have often had occasion to note, is a word of very extensive import : it signifies the *principle* of *righteousness* ; it signifies the *practice* of *righteousness*, or living a *holy* life ; it signifies *God's method* of *justifying sinners* ; and it signifies *justification* itself. Here it may imply a consciousness of justification through the blood of the cross ; the principle of righteousness or true holiness implanted in the heart ; and a holy life, a life regulated according to the testimonies of God. As the *breast-plate* defends the heart and lungs, and all those vital functionaries that are contained in what is called the *region of the thorax* ; so this righteousness, this life of God in the soul of man, defends every thing on which the man's spiritual existence depends. While he possesses this principle, and acts from it, his spiritual and eternal life is secure.

Verse 15. *Your feet shod*] The κνημιδες, or *greaves*, have been already described ; they were deemed of essential importance in the ancient armour ; if the feet or legs are materially wounded, a man can neither stand to resist his foe, pursue him if vanquished, nor flee from him should he have the worst of the fight.

That the apostle has *obedience to the Gospel* in general in view, there can be no doubt ; but he appears to have more than this, a *readiness to publish* the Gospel : for, *How beautiful upon the mountains are the feet of him that bringeth good tidings, that publisheth* PEACE ; *that bringeth good tidings of good, that publisheth salvation ; that saith unto Zion, Thy God reigneth !* Isa. lii. 7 ; Rom. x. 15.

The Israelites were commanded to eat the passover with their *feet shod*, to show that they were *ready* for their journey. And our Lord commands his disciples to be *shod with sandals*, that they might be ready to go and publish the Gospel, as the Israelites were to go to possess the promised land. Every Christian should consider himself on his journey from a strange land to his own country, and not only stand every moment prepared to proceed, but be every moment in actual progress towards his home.

The preparation of the Gospel] The word ετοιμασια which we translate *preparation*, is variously understood. some think it means an *habitual readiness* in walking in the way prescribed by the Gospel ; others that *firmness and solidity* which the Gospel gives to

2

A. M. cir. 4065.
A. D. cir. 61.
A. U. C. 813.
An. Imp. Ne-
ronis Cæs.
Aug. 8.

18 [i] Praying always with all prayer and supplication in the Spirit, and [k] watching thereunto with all perseverance and [l] supplication for all saints;

19 [m] And for me, that utterance may be given unto me,

A. M. cir. 4065.
A. D. cir. 61.
A. U. C. 813.
An. Imp. Ne-
ronis Cæs.
Aug. 8.

---

[i] Luke xviii. 1; Rom. xii. 12; Col. iv. 2; 1 Thess. v. 17.
[k] Matt. xxvi. 41; Mark xiii. 33.

[l] Chap. i. 16; Phil. i. 4; 1 Tim. ii. 1.——[m] Acts iv. 29; Col. iv. 3; 2 Thess. iii. 1.

---

them who conscientiously believe its doctrines; others, those *virtues* and *graces* which in the *first planting* of Christianity were indispensably necessary to those who published it.

Should we take the word *preparation* in its common acceptation, it may imply that, by a conscientious belief of the Gospel, receiving the salvation provided by its author, and walking in the way of obedience which is pointed out by it, the soul is *prepared* for the kingdom of heaven.

The Gospel is termed the *Gospel of peace*, because it establishes peace between God and man, and proclaims peace and good will to the universe. Contentions, strife, quarrels, and all wars, being as alien from its nature and design, as they are opposed to the nature of Him who is love and compassion to man.

Verse 16. *Above all*, (Επι πασιν, over all the rest of the armour,) *taking the shield of faith*] In the word θυρεος, *thureos*, the apostle alludes to the great *oblong shield*, or *scutum*, which covers the whole body. See its description before. And as *faith* is the grace by which all others are preserved and rendered active, so it is properly represented here under the notion of a *shield*, by which the whole body is covered and protected. Faith, in this place, must mean that evidence of things unseen which every genuine believer has, that God, for Christ's sake, has blotted out his sins, and by which he is enabled to call God his Father, and feel him to be his portion. It is such an *appropriating* faith as this which can quench any dart of the devil.

The fiery darts of the wicked.] Βελος, a dart, signifies any kind of *missile weapon*; every thing that is projected to a distance by the hand, as a *javelin*, or short spear; or by a *bow*, as an *arrow*; or a stone by a *sling*.

The fiery darts—Τα βελη τα πεπυρωμενα. It is probable that the apostle alludes to the darts called *falarica*, which were headed with lead, in or about which some combustible stuff was placed that took fire in the passage of the arrow through the air, and often burnt up the enemy's engines, ships, &c.; they were calculated also to stick in the shields and set them on fire. Some think that *poisoned arrows* may be intended, which are called *fiery* from the burning heat produced in the bodies of those who were wounded by them. To quench or extinguish such fiery darts the shields were ordinarily covered with metal on the outside, and thus the fire was prevented from catching hold of the shield. When they stuck on a shield of another kind and set it on fire, the soldier was obliged to cast it away, and thus became defenceless.

The fiery darts of the *wicked*, του πονηρου, or *devil*, are evil thoughts, and strong *injections*, as they are termed, which in the unregenerate inflame the passions, and excite the soul to acts of transgression. While

the *faith* is strong in Christ it acts as a shield to quench these. He who walks so as to feel the witness of God's Spirit that he is his child, has all evil thoughts in abhorrence; and, though they pass through his mind, they never fix in his passions. They are caught on this shield, blunted, and extinguished.

Verse 17. *Take the helmet of salvation*] Or, as it is expressed, 1 Thess. v. 8, *And for a helmet, the hope of salvation.* It has already been observed, in the description of the Grecian armour, that on the crest and other parts of the helmet were a great variety of emblematical figures, and that it is very likely the apostle refers to helmets which had on them an emblematical representation of *hope;* viz. that the person should be *safe* who wore it, that he should be prosperous in all his engagements, and ever escape safe from battle. So the *hope* of conquering every adversary and surmounting every difficulty, through the blood of the Lamb, is as a helmet that protects the head; an impenetrable one, that the blow of the battle-axe cannot cleave. The *hope* of continual safety and protection, built on the promises of God, to which the upright follower of Christ feels he has a Divine right, protects the *understanding* from being darkened, and the judgment from being confused by any temptations of Satan, or subtle arguments of the sophistical ungodly. He who carries Christ in his heart cannot be cheated out of the hope of his heaven.

The sword of the Spirit] See what is said before on ξιφος and μαχαιρα, in the account of the Greek armour. The *sword* of which St. Paul speaks is, as he explains it, *the word of God;* that is, the revelation which God has given of himself, or what we call the *Holy Scriptures.* This is called *the sword of the Spirit*, because it comes from the Holy Spirit, and receives its fulfilment in the soul through the operation of the Holy Spirit. An ability to quote this on proper occasions, and especially in times of temptation and trial, has a wonderful tendency to cut in pieces the snares of the adversary. In God's word a genuine Christian may have unlimited confidence, and to every purpose to which it is applicable it may be brought with the greatest effect. The *shield, faith,* and the *sword*—the *word of God,* or faith in God's unchangeable word, are the principal armour of the soul. He in whom the word of God dwells richly, and who has that faith by which he knows that he has redemption, even the forgiveness of sins, need not fear the power of any adversary. He stands fast in the liberty wherewith Christ hath made him free. Some suppose that του Πνευματος, *of the Spirit,* should be understood of our *own spirit* or *soul;* the word of God being the proper sword of the soul, or that offensive weapon the only one which the soul uses. But though it is true that every Christian soul has this for its sword, yet the first meaning is the most likely.

A. M. cir. 4065.
A. D. cir. 61.
A. U. C. 813.
An. Imp. Neronis Cæs.
Aug. 8.

that I may open my mouth ⁿ boldly, to make known the mystery of the Gospel,

20 For which ^o I am an ambassador ^p in ^q bonds ; that ^r therein ^s I may

speak boldly, as I ought to speak.

21 But ^t that ye also may know my affairs, *and* how I do, ^u Tychicus, a beloved brother and faithful

A. M. cir. 4065.
A. D. cir. 61.
A. U. C. 813.
An. Imp. Neronis Cæs.
Aug. 8.

ⁿ 2 Cor. iii. 12.——^o 2 Cor. v. 20.——^p Acts xxvi. 29 ; xxviii. 20 ; chapter iii. 1 ; Phil. 1. 7, 13, 14 ; 2 Timothy i. 16 ; ii. 9 ; Philem. 10.

^q Or, *in a chain.*——^r Or, *thereof.*——^s Acts xxviii. 31 ; Phil. i. 20 ; 1 Thess. ii. 2.——^t Col. iv. 7.——^u Acts xx. 4 ; 2 Tim. iv. 12 ; Tit. iii. 12.

Verse 18. *Praying always*] The apostle does not put praying among the armour ; had he done so he would have referred it, as he has done all the rest, to some of the Grecian armour ; but as he does not do this, therefore we conclude that his account of the armour is ended, and that now, having equipped his spiritual soldier, he shows him the necessity of *praying*, that he may successfully resist those principalities, powers, the rulers of the darkness of this world, and the spiritual wickednesses in heavenly places, with whom he has to contend. The *panoply*, or *whole armour* of God, consists in, 1. the *girdle*; 2. the *breast-plate*; 3 the *greaves*; 4. the *shield*; 5. the *helmet*; and 6. the *sword*. He who had these was completely armed. And as it was the custom of the Grecian armies, before they engaged, to *offer prayers* to the gods for their success, the apostle shows that these spiritual warriors must depend on the Captain of their salvation, and pray with all prayer, i. e. incessantly, being always in the spirit of prayer, so that they should be ever ready for public, private, mental, or ejaculatory prayer, always depending on HIM who can alone *save*, and who alone can *destroy*.

When the apostle exhorts Christians to *pray with all prayer*, we may at once see that he neither means *spiritual* nor *formal* prayer, in exclusion of the other. *Praying*, προσευχομενοι, refers to the *state* of the *spirit* as well as to the *act*.

With all prayer] Refers to the different *kinds* of prayer that is performed in *public*, in the *family*, in the *closet*, in *business*, on the *way*, in the *heart* without a *voice*, and *with* the *voice* from the heart. All these are necessary to the genuine Christian ; and he whose heart is right with God will be frequent in the whole. "Some there are," says a very pious and learned writer, "who use only *mental* prayer or ejaculations, and think they are in a state of grace, and use a way of worship far superior to any other ; but such only fancy themselves to be *above* what is really above *them* ; it requiring far more grace to be enabled to pour out a fervent and continued prayer, than to offer up mental aspirations." Rev. *J. Wesley*.

And supplication] There is a difference between προσευχη, *prayer*, and δεησις, *supplication*. Some think the former means prayer *for the attainment of good* ; the latter, prayer for *averting evil*. Supplication however seems to mean *prayer continued in*, strong and incessant pleadings, till the *evil* is *averted*, or the *good communicated*. There are two things that must be attended to in prayer . 1. That it be εν παντι καιρω, in every *time*, *season*, or *opportunity* ; 2. That it should be εν Πνευματι, *in* or *through the Spirit*—that the *heart* should be engaged in it, and that its infirmities should be helped by the Holy Ghost,

Watching thereunto] Being always on your *guard* lest your enemies should surprise you. Watch, not only against evil, but also for opportunities to do good, and for opportunities to receive good. Without watchfulness, prayer and all the spiritual armour will be ineffectual.

With all perseverance] Being always intent on your object, and never losing sight of your *danger*, or of your *interest*. The word implies *stretching out the neck*, and *looking about*, in order to discern an enemy at a distance.

For all saints] For all *Christians* ; for this was the character by which they were generally distinguished.

Verse 19. *And for me, that utterance may be given unto me*] Ἱνα μοι δοθειη λογος. Kypke has proved by many examples that λογον διδοναι signifies permission and power to defend one's self in a court of justice ; and this sense of the phrase is perfectly applicable to the case of St. Paul, who was an ambassador in bonds, (ver. 20,) and expected to be called to a public hearing, in which he was not only to *defend himself*, but to prove the *truth* and *excellency* of the *Christian religion*. And we learn, from Phil. i. 12–14, that he had his desire in this respect ; for *the things which happened to him fell out to the furtherance of the Gospel, so that his bonds in Christ were manifest in all the palace, and in all other places*. Thus God had enabled him to make a most noble defence, by which the Gospel acquired great credit.

The mystery of the Gospel] The whole *doctrine* of Christ, not fully revealed previously to that time.

Verse 20. *An ambassador in bonds*] An ambassador being the representative of his king, his person was in all civilized countries held sacred. Contrary to the rights of nations, this ambassador of the King of heaven was put in chains ! He had however the opportunity of defending himself, and of vindicating the honour of his Master. See above,

As I ought to speak.] As *becomes* the dignity and the importance of the subject.

Verse 21. *That ye also*] As well as other Churches to whom I have communicated the dealings both of God and man to me.

May know my affairs] May be acquainted with my situation and circumstances.

And how I do] How I employ my time, and what fruit there is of my apostolical labours.

Tychicus, a beloved brother] We learn, from Acts xx. 4, that Tychicus was of Asia, and that he was a useful companion of St. Paul. See the note on the above place.

This same person, and with the same character and commendation, is mentioned in the Epistle to the Colossians, chap. iv. 7. He is mentioned also in Tit

A. M. cir. 4065.
A. D. cir. 61.
A. U. C. 813.
An. Imp. Ne-
ronis Cæs.
Aug. 8.

minister in the Lord, shall make known to you all things:

22 Whom I have sent unto you for the same purpose, that ye might know our affairs, and *that* he might comfort your hearts.

23 ᵛ Peace *be* to the brethren, and love with faith, from God the Father, and the Lord Jesus Christ.

24 Grace *be* with all them that love our Lord Jesus Christ ʷ in ˣ sincerity. Amen.

¶ Written from Rome unto the Ephesians by Tychicus.

A. M. cir. 4065.
A. D. cir. 61.
A. U. C. 813.
An. Imp. Ne-
ronis Cæs.
Aug. 8.

ᵛ 1 Pet. v. 14.——ʷ Tit. ii. 7.

ˣ Or, *with incorruption.*

---

iii. 12, and in 2 Tim. iv. 12; from all these places it is evident that he was a person in whom the apostle had the highest confidence, and that he was a very eminent minister of Christ.

Verse 22. Whom I have sent—for the same purpose] Namely, that the Ephesians might know his affairs, and those of the Church at Rome: messengers of this kind frequently passed between the Churches in those ancient times.

Comfort your hearts.] By showing you how powerfully he was upheld in all his tribulations, and how God turned his bonds to the furtherance of the Gospel. This must have been great consolation to all the followers of God; and particularly to those in *Ephesus* or *Laodicea*, or to whomsoever the epistle was directed. The question, To whom was it sent? is divided between the *Ephesians* and the *Laodiceans.* Dr. Lardner has argued strongly in favour of the *former;* Dr. Paley not less so in favour of the *latter.*

Verse 23. Peace be to the brethren] If the epistle were really sent to the *Ephesians*, a people with whom the apostle was so intimately acquainted, it is strange that he mentions no person by name. This objection, on which Dr. Paley lays great stress, (see the preface to this epistle,) has not been successfully answered.

Peace] All *prosperity*, and continual union with God and among yourselves; *and love* to God and man, the principle of all obedience and union; *with faith*, continually increasing, and growing stronger and stronger, *from God the Father*, as the fountain of all our mercies, *and the Lord Jesus Christ*, through whose sacrifice and mediation they all come.

Verse 24. Grace be with all them] May the Divine *favour*, and all the benedictions flowing from it, be with all them who love our Lord Jesus Christ, who has so loved us as to give his life to redeem ours, and to save us unto life eternal.

In sincerity.] Εν αφθαρσια· In *incorruptibility.* Those who show the genuineness of their love, by walking before him in holiness of life. Many profess to love our Lord Jesus who are corrupt in all their ways; on these the *grace* or *favour* of God cannot rest; they profess to know him, but in works deny him. Such can neither expect favour *here*, nor hereafter.

Amen.] This is wanting in ABFG, and some others. It is, however, more likely to be a *genuine subscription* here than most others of its kind. The apostle might have sealed his most earnest wish by this *word*, which means not so much, *so be it!* or *may it be so!* but rather implies the *faithfulness* of him who had given the promises, and whose prerogative it

was to give effect to the prayers which his own Spirit had inspired.

The principal *subscriptions* to this epistle are the following: *To the Ephesians. The Epistle to the Ephesians is finished. To the Ephesians, written from Rome. To the Ephesians, written from Rome by Tychicus.* (This is the subscription which we have followed; and it is that of the larger number of modern MSS. and *editions.*) *The Epistle to the Ephesians, written from Rome, and sent by Tychicus* —Syriac. *To the Ephesians.*—Æthiopic. Vulgate, no subscription. *The end of this epistle, which was written from Rome by Tychicus.* Praise be to God for ever. Amen.—Arabic. *Written at Rome, and sent by Tychicus.*—Coptic. The Sahidic is defective. *The Epistle to the Ephesians is ended, which was written at Rome by Tychicus.*—Philoxenian Syriac.

We have had already occasion to observe that the *subscriptions* to the sacred books were not written by the authors themselves, but were added in a much later age, and generally by unskilful hands. They are consequently not much to be depended on, and never should be quoted as a part of the Divine oracles.

1. It may be supposed that on the principal subject of this concluding chapter, *the armour of God*, I should have been much more diffuse. I answer, my constant aim is just to say *enough*, and no more, on any point. Whether I attain this, in general, or not, I can still say it is what I have desired. As to the *Christian armour*, it does not appear to me that the apostle has couched such a profusion of mystical meaning in it as to require a huge volume to explain. I believe the Ephesians did not understand it so; nor did the primitive Church of God. Men of rich imaginations may write large volumes on such subjects; but when they come to be fairly examined, they will be found not to be explanations of the text, on which they professedly treat, but immense *bodies of divinity*, in which the peculiar creed of the writer, both with respect to doctrine and discipline, is amply set forth. *Mr. Gurnal's Christian Armour* contains a great many excellences; but surely it does not require such a volume to explain the *five* verses of this chapter, in which the apostle speaks of the spiritual armour. The grand design of the apostle was to show that *truth, righteousness, obedience to the Gospel, faith in our Lord Jesus Christ*, a *well-grounded hope* of *salvation*, a thorough *knowledge* of *the word of God*, and a continual *dependence on* and *application* to him *by prayer*, were essentially necessary to every soul who desired to walk uprightly in this life, and finally to attain everlasting blessedness   This is

the obvious meaning of the apostle; in this sense it was understood by the Ephesians, and by the primitive Church; *we* may amplify it as we please.

2. In two or three places, in the preceding notes, I have referred to a piece on a very remarkable rule relative to the *Greek article,* to be introduced at the end. From the labours of several learned men this subject has acquired considerable importance, and has excited no small interest among Biblical critics. The late benevolent, learned, and excellent Mr. *Granville Sharp* was, I believe, the first who brought this subject fairly before the public; he was followed by the Rev. Dr. *Wordsworth,* a learned and intelligent clergyman of the Established Church.

The Rev. Dr. Middleton, late bishop of *Calcutta,* has presented the subject in all its force and excellence, fortified by innumerable proofs, and a great variety of critical disquisition. The principal design of these writers was to exhibit a new and substantial mode of proving the *Divinity of our Lord* and *Saviour.* Their works are before the public, and within the reach of all who are capable of judging of this mode of proof.

The piece which I now subjoin is the result of the researches of one of my literary friends, H. S. Boyd, Esq., author of *Translations from Chrysostom,* &c., who has read the Greek writers, both sacred and profane, with peculiar attention; and has collected a vast number of additional examples, both from prose and poetic writers, for the confirmation and illustration of the rule in question, and in support of the great doctrine of the *Godhead of Christ.*

The critical reader, who has entered into this subject, will be glad to see such a number of pointed examples brought within his reach, which at once serve the purpose both of *philology* and *divinity.* The learned author has transmitted them to me for the purpose of insertion in this place; but want of room has obliged me to omit several of his quotations.[*]

I would not wish the reader to suppose that these are the only proofs of the grand doctrine of the Godhead of Christ; they are not: the Holy Scripture, in its plain, obvious meaning, independently of such criticism, affords the most luminous and convincing proofs of the doctrine in question; but this is no sufficient reason that we should reject any additional light which may come to us in the way of Divine Providence.

---

[*] Since Dr. Clarke wrote this paragraph, the Essay on the Greek Article has undergone a careful revision by the author, and several additions have been made to it, which will, it is hoped, be valuable to the critical reader. It is now introduced in a separate form from the Commentary —THE PUBLISHERS,

Finished the correction for a new edition, Dec. 15th, 1831.

AN ESSAY ON THE GREEK ARTICLE.

BY HUGH STUART BOYD.

It has now been completely proved, and irrefragably established by the labours of learned men, that, independently of the common laws of syntax, the Greek prepositive article is governed by a very remarkable rule, to which it is universally subjected. The rule is this:—When two or more personal nouns (of the same gender, number, and case) are coupled together by the conjunction και, and the article is prefixed to the *first*, but not to the *second, third*, &c., those two or more nouns, whether they be substantives or adjectives, denote *one* and the *same person*. This also is the case when two *participles* are thus coupled together.

I have given the rule nearly as it is laid down by Mr. Sharp: it is, however, subject to certain limitations. Whenever we meet, in a Greek writer, with a sentence constructed according to the rule, if the substantives, adjectives, or participles, be indicatory of qualities and properties which are inconsistent and contradictory; in that case two different persons may be intended, although the article be not prefixed to the latter. The reason of this is obvious. When a Greek writer was speaking of two persons, whom he designated by terms which were opposite and irreconcilable to one another, it was not necessary that he should prefix the article to the second, although he had placed it before the first. Every reader would see at once that the same person could not be both sober and drunken, both virtuous and wicked, both handsome and ugly, &c. It is manifest that all proper names must, for the same reason, be excepted. Every body knows that Paul and Peter cannot be the same person; therefore the article may be placed before Paul, but omitted before Peter. But if a Greek writer was speaking of two different persons, and the substantives, &c., which he employed, were indicatory of qualities and attributes which might harmonize and coalesce in one person, it then became necessary that the article, if prefixed to the first, should be placed before the second also; for otherwise the reader might be misled. It follows from hence that, whenever we meet with a passage constructed according to our rule, if the substantives, &c., indicate qualities and properties which are not contradictory, but may be united in one person, we may then be absolutely certain that one person only is intended.

Corollary. It follows, that when two personal nouns are united by the conjunction και, and those nouns are descriptive of two different persons, but imply qualities which might meet in the same person, the article must be prefixed to both, or prefixed to the last only, or prefixed to neither.

Let us apply this doctrine to the criticism of the New Testament, and see if we can arrive at any conclusion of importance.

I shall first select some passages, where different persons are plainly and obviously meant.

Οἱ τελωναι και οἱ ἁμαρτωλοι.—"The publicans and the sinners."

Οἱ Φαρισαιοι και οἱ γραμματεις.—"The Pharisees and the scribes." Luke xv. 1, 2.

Οἱ αρχιερεις και οἱ γραμματεις.—"The high priests and the scribes." Luke xx. 1.

Οἱ αποστολοι και οἱ αδελφοι.—"The apostles and the brethren." Acts xi. 1.

Ὁ βασιλευς και ὁ ἡγεμων.—"The king and the governor (viz. Agrippa and Festus.") Acts xxvi. 30.

Οἱ φαρμακοι και οἱ πορνοι.—"The enchanters and the fornicators." Rev. xxii. 15.

Απο Θεου Πατρος ἡμων, και Κυριου Ιησου Χριστου.—"From God our Father, and the Lord Jesus Christ." 2 Thess. i. 2.

Ιακωβος, Θεου και Ιησου Χριστου δουλος.—"James, a servant of God, and of Jesus Christ." James i. 1.

We see that in the above instances the article is either used *twice*, or is wholly *omitted*.

Let us now examine some passages, wherein it is evident, from the context, that two nouns, coupled together by the conjunction, refer to one and the *same person*. And here I would observe, that the examples which I have just adduced, and am about to adduce, are not all which the New Testament contains. The catalogue might be easily increased; but my object is to be as brief and as plain as possible.

Ὁ Θεος και Πατηρ του Κυριου ἡμων.—"The God and Father of our Lord." 2 Cor. i. 3; 2 Cor. xi. 31; Eph. i. 3.

Του Θεου και Πατρος ἡμων.—"Of our God and Father." 1 Thess. i. 3.

Τῳ Θεῳ και Πατρι του Κυριου ἡμων.—"To the God and Father of our Lord." Col. i. 3.

Τῳ Θεῳ και Πατρι αυτου.—"To his God and Father." Rev. i. 6.

Επεστραφητε νυν επι τον Ποιμενα και Επισκοπον των ψυχων ὑμων.—"Ye are now returned to the Shepherd and Bishop of your souls." 1 Peter ii. 25.

Τυχικος, ὁ αγαπητος αδελφος και πιστος διακονος.—"Tychicus, a beloved brother and faithful deacon." Eph. vi. 21.

Ὁ Βασιλευς των βασιλευοντων και Κυριος των κυριευοντων.—"The King of kings and Lord of lords." 1 Tim. vi. 15.

Τον αποστολον και αρχιερεα της ὁμολογιας ἡμων, Χριστον Ιησουν.—"The apostle and high priest of our confession, Christ Jesus." Heb. iii. 1.

Τον της πιστεως αρχηγον και τελειωτην, Ιησουν.—"Jesus, the author and perfecter of our faith." Heb. xii. 2.

Του Κυριου και Σωτηρος, Ιησου Χριστου.—"Of the Lord and Saviour Jesus Christ." 2 Peter ii. 20; iii. 18.

In all the above cases the nouns are *substantives*; in the following they are *adjectives*.

Ὥστε τον τυφλον και κωφον και λαλειν και βλεπειν.—
" So that the man who was blind and dumb both saw
and spake." Matt. xii. 22.

Ὁ μακαριος και μονος Δυναστης.—" The blessed and
only Potentate." 1 Tim. vi. 15.

Ὁ πιστος δουλος και φρονιμος.—" The faithful and
wise servant." Matt. xxiv. 45.

Ουκ οιδας ὁτι συ ει ὁ ταλαιπωρος, και ελεεινος, και
πτωχος, και τυφλος, και γυμνος.—" Thou knowest not
that thou art wretched, and miserable, and poor, and
blind, and naked." Rev. iii. 17.

Φιλημονι τω αγαπητω και συνεργω ἡμων.—" To Philemon, our beloved and coadjutor." Philem. 1.

In the following instances the connected words are
participles.

Ὁ δε φιλος του Νυμφιου, ὁ ἑστηκως και ακουων αυτου.
—" But the friend of the Bridegroom, who standeth
and heareth him." John iii. 29.

Τῳ αγαπησαντι και λουσαντι ἡμας.—" To Him who
loved and washed us." Rev. i. 5.

Εγω Ιωαννης, ὁ βλεπων ταυτα και ακουων.—" I John,
the man seeing and hearing these things." Rev.
xxii. 8.

Πας ὁ φιλων και ποιων ψευδος.—" Every person who
loveth and maketh a lie." Rev. xxii. 15.

Ὁ τρωγων μου την σαρκα, και πινων μου το αἱμα.—
" He that eateth my flesh, and drinketh my blood."
John vi. 54.

I have now laid before the reader examples of the
phraseology employed in the Greek Testament, when
two *different persons* are manifestly and obviously
spoken of in the same member of a sentence ; and
when *one person* is as obviously depicted under *two
different appellations*. We see that in the one case
the article is prefixed to *both* words, or to *neither* : we
see that in the other case the article is *prefixed to the
first word*, but *wanting before the second*, whether
they be *substantives*, or *adjectives*, or *participles*. Let
us then apply the rule in question, as we do the other
rules of syntax, to the explication of a passage in
Ephesians, chap. v., verse 5 :—

Εν τῃ βασιλειᾳ του Χριστου και Θεου.

" In the kingdom of the Christ and God."

This passage speaks for itself ; and to make any
comment upon it would be utterly superfluous. I shall
only observe, that, as far as certainty can be attained
in this present life, as far as we can be assured of the
meaning and import of human language, so far may
we be certain that the writer of the Epistle to the
Ephesians here pronounces Christ to be God.

But what will the Arian say to this ? He will tell
us that in this passage, the apostle pronounces Jesus
Christ to be a god ; (mark, *a* GOD ;) that is, a being of
a high and exalted nature. There are one or two
passages in the Old Testament where *angels* are called
gods on account of their transcendent dignity ; and
Christ, whom we allow, in dignity and power, to be
equal or superior to the highest of the angels, may
therefore be called a god. This, I believe, is the sum
and substance of the Arian doctrine.

In the second chapter of the Epistle to Titus, and
the thirteenth verse, we have the following overwhelming testimony :—

Επιφανειαν της δοξης του μεγαλου Θεου και Σωτηρος
ἡμων, Ιησου Χριστου.

" The glorious manifestation of the great God and
Saviour of us, Jesus Christ."

In the last passage that I quoted Christ is styled
God ; but here he is called the great God. If angels
have a right to be denominated gods, we must confess
that there are in heaven myriads of gods ; but by the
words, the great God, one Being only can be designated. Angels may be termed θεοι, but ὁ μεγας Θεος
is the incommunicable appellation of the Lord God
Jehovah ! Every one who is at all acquainted with
the subject, knows that some hundred MSS. of the
Greek Testament, or at least of different parts of it,
have now been collated, and that many, many thousands of various readings have been accumulated.
Surely it is remarkable that, in the case of these two
texts, viz. that in Ephesians, and that in Titus, *not one
various reading* has ever been discovered. Does it
not appear that these texts have been providentially
guarded, yea, miraculously shielded ? Two or three
more passages of the Greek Testament might be adduced, which, through the application of this sacred
rule, (surely I may call it sacred,) most powerfully confirm the divinity of Christ. I forbear, however, to
cite them, restricting myself to those expressions only,
which, as they have no various reading, cannot possibly
be exposed to cavil.

Although I have already proved, to the satisfaction
of the unprejudiced, that the rule I have laid down is
inherent in the language, and that certain passages of
Scripture can admit of no other interpretation than
that which I have given, an objection may be started,
and a question may be proposed, which claim our most
serious attention. The question I mean is this : In
what sense were these passages understood by the
fathers of the Greek Church ? As they lived nearer
to the primitive times of Christianity than we do, we
must allow that they were at least as competent as
ourselves to pass judgment in any subject of theological discussion ; but in the case now before us, their
authority must be considerably greater. In addition
to the circumstance of the Greek being their native
tongue, some of them were men of very extensive
learning, and of distinguished skill in philological researches ; they must, therefore, have had a more accurate perception than the most learned amongst us
can pretend to, of the precise application of every rule
in syntax, the exact meaning of the minutest particle,
and the determinate effect of the slightest inflection in
the language. They are therefore the properest persons to decide, if such expressions as του Χριστου και
Θεου, and του μεγαλου Θεου και Σωτηρος, have, according
to the laws of grammar, the meaning which we affix
to them. If they perceived in them the force and
evidence that we do, they would of course have appealed to them in their controversies with the Arians ;
and happy would they have been in bringing forward
such resistless testimonies to the divinity of our Lord.
And they did appeal to them ! yes the most illustrious

of the fathers, St. *Chrysostom* himself, appealed to them! In his fifth discourse on the incomprehensible nature of Deity, he sums up those texts of Scripture wherein Christ is called God; and he reckons among them the 5th verse of the 5th chapter of Ephesians, and the 13th verse of the second of Titus. For the satisfaction of the reader I shall translate the passage; and that he may have the clearest view of the subject, I shall translate a considerable portion of the context.

An extract from St. Chrysostom's Fifth Homily, Περι Ακαταληπτου, *tom.* vi., *pages* 417, 418. *Edit. Savil.*

" Of the titles which are attributed to the Deity, some are *common* and some *particular;* the common denote the *indivisibility* of the Divine essence; the *particular* characterize the personality of the hypostases. Thus, the names of *Father* and of *Son* appertain each to its peculiar hypostasis; but the names of *God* and of *Lord* are common to both. Since the Scripture has applied the appellation of God to all the persons of the Trinity, it was needful also to make use of a distinguishing appellation, that we might know of which person it was speaking, and not run into the error of *Sabellius.* For that the name *God* is not greater than that of *Lord,* nor the name *Lord* inferior to that of *God,* is manifest from hence: in every part of the Old Testament the *Father* is styled *Lord,* The Lord *thy God.* Again: There is *one* Lord. And again: *Thou shalt worship the* Lord *thy God, and Him only shalt thou serve.* And again: *Great is our* Lord, *and mighty is his power.* And again: *Let them know that thy name is* Lord; *Thou only art the highest over all the earth.* Now, if the name Lord be inferior to that of God, and consequently unworthy of the Divine essence, it should not have been said, *Let them know that thy name is* Lord. Again: if the name of God be greater and more venerable than that of *Lord,* the Son, who according to them is an inferior being, should not have been addressed by a name appropriated to the *Father,* and which was his own peculiar title; but far otherwise is the case, for neither is the Son of a lower nature than the Father, nor is the name of Lord inferior to that of God. Wherefore, with regard to the Father and the Son, the Scripture uses, indiscriminately, the self-same appellations.

" Having laid before you the passages wherein the *Father* is called Lord, it is necessary to adduce those passages wherein the Son is styled God. *Behold, a virgin shall conceive, and shall bear a son, and they shall call his name* Emanuel; *which signifies,* God *is with us.* We now perceive that the name of *Lord* is given to the *Father,* and that of *God* unto the *Son;* for, as in the other place it is said: *Let them know that thy name is Lord;* so here it saith, *They shall call his name* Emanuel. And again: *A child is born to us, and a son is given to us, and his name is called The Angel of high counsels, The great and mighty* God. And here observe the cautious prudence and spiritual wisdom of the prophetic writers; for when they are speaking of the great and mighty God, lest they should seem to be speaking of the Father, they make the most particular mention of the miraculous conception. It is evident, at once, that the *Father* was

not born of a virgin, and did not become a little child. Again, another of the prophets somewhere saith, *This is our* God. But concerning whom doth he say it? Is it of the *Father?* By no means; for he also alludes to the miraculous economy. Having said, *This is our* God, he adds, *He explored the way of knowledge, and gave it to Jacob his child, and to Israel his well beloved. After this he was seen upon the earth, and he dwelt among men.* Paul also writes: *Of whom, as to the flesh, is Christ, who is over all,* God *blessed for evermore.* Again: *No fornicator or covetous man hath any inheritance in the kingdom of the Christ and* God. And again: *The glorious appearance of the* great God *and Saviour of us, Jesus Christ.* John likewise calls him by the same name, for he says, *In the beginning was the Word, and the Word was with* God, *and the Word was* God.

" But perhaps an adversary will say, Can you show me any passage where the Scripture, ranking him with the Father, calls the Father *Lord?* I will not only show this, but I will produce passages where the Scripture calls both the *Father* Lord, and the *Son* Lord; and where it calls both the *Father* God, and the *Son* God. Christ, one day discoursing with the Jews, said, *What think ye concerning Christ? Whose son is he? They say unto him, He is the son of David. He saith to them, How then doth David, in Spirit, call him* Lord; *saying, The* Lord *said unto my* Lord, *Sit thou on my right hand?* Mark, here are *two* Lords. I will now show you where the Scripture, speaking at once of the *Father* and the *Son,* calls both the one and the other God. Hear then the words of the Prophet *David,* and of the Apostle *Paul,* commenting upon that prophet: *Thy throne, O God, is for ever and ever; a sceptre of righteousness is the sceptre of thy kingdom. Thou hast loved righteousness and abhorred iniquity; therefore, O* God, *thy* God *hath anointed thee with the oil of gladness above thy fellows.* And *Paul,* bringing forward this testimony concerning Christ, writes thus: *Of His angels he saith, Who maketh his* angels *spirits. But of the* Son *He saith, Thy throne, O* God, *is for ever and ever!*"

In his 5th Hom. on the Epistle to Titus, he thus comments on chap. ii., ver 13.

Που εισιν οἱ του Πατρος ελαττονα τον Ὑιον λεγοντες; του μεγαλου, φησι, Θεου και Σωτηρος.

" Where are they who assert that the Son is inferior to the Father? Mark, he saith, ' of the great God and Saviour!' "—Tom. iv., page 401. Edit. Sav.

There is, however, another passage in the writings of this eminent father, more absolute and conclusive than those which are already given. The original may be found in the 4th vol. of Sir Henry Savile's edition, page 32. It is in English as follows:—

" He that is small cannot be God; for every where in the Scripture God is denominated great. Great is the Lord, says David, and greatly to be praised. (Mark, he also speaks of the Son, for every where he calls him *Lord.*) And again: Great art thou, and doing wonders: thou art God alone. And again: Great is our Lord, and mighty is his power. But these things, you will say, are spoken of the Father; but the Son is small. *You* say this, but the *Scripture* asserts the contrary; for as it speaks of the Father, so likewise does it of the Son. Listen unto Paul, who says, *Expecting the blessed hope and glorious appearance of the* GREAT GOD. Surely he could not apply the word *appearance* to the Father. And that he may refute you more completely, he adds, *of the* GREAT GOD. Well, then, must not this have been spoken of the Father? Certainly not; for the words which follow will not admit it: *The appearance of the great God* AND *Saviour of us,* JESUS CHRIST. You perceive that the Son also is denominated great. Away, then, with your idle talk about *small* and *great!* Listen to the prophet also, who calls him *The* ANGEL *of* GREAT COUNSEL. The Angel of great counsel, is he not great? The mighty God, is he not great, but small? How, then, can these obstinate and shameless wretches assert that he is a less God? I often repeat their words, that ye may the more eschew them."

If a reader wholly impartial could be found, I think he would pronounce that, as far as we can attain to certainty in any thing, we may be certified from the above extract, that the canon laid down by Mr. Sharp is correct and genuine. Chrysostom supposes an adversary to address him thus:—

" I see that in this sentence God is spoken of, and not merely spoken of, but likewise styled *The* GREAT *God.* Surely such an expression as this must refer to the Father." " No, replies our saint, that is impossible, for the phrase και Σωτηρος, which follows, shows at once that Θεος and Σωτηρ mean the same person; and Σωτηρ, in this place, is spoken of Jesus Christ."

Such is the testimony of *Chrysostom,* the most eloquent, if not the most learned, of the fathers. *Basil,* archbishop of Cæsarea, though inferior to Chrysostom in richness of imagination and brilliancy of rhetoric, far surpassed him and almost all the fathers, in the universality of his learning, and in his profound knowledge of the sacred writings. No authority can be higher or more unquestionable than his. Let me, however, just observe that, although somewhat inferior on the whole to Chrysostom, he was still a most accomplished orator, and a very polished writer. In his fourth book against *Eunomius,* speaking of the Divinity of Christ, he cites the latter of these texts; but having done so, he is fearful lest some of his hearers should be misled by it. The expression του μεγαλου Θεου, appears to him so strong, that he is apprehensive lest it should be thence inferred that the Son is *greater* than the Father!

This passage will be found in the first volume of the Benedictine edition, and at page 294—tom. ii. p. 107. Edit. Par., 1618.

As I have proved that the best and purest of the Greek fathers were well acquainted with the full force of the article, it may be asked, Do their own writings abound with examples to confirm it? I answer, that they every where abound with them. Let a few examples suffice.

From Chrysostom.

'Ο άγιαζων αυτα και μετασκευαζων, Αυτος εστι.—" It is He who sanctifies and transforms them; namely, the bread and wine." Homil. 82, in Matt.

Εγκαλοιη τω Σωτηρι και Ευεργετη.—" He would accuse the Saviour and Benefactor." De Sacerd. lib. iv.

Ή σφοδρα εναγης και ακαθαρτος, (πορνη)—" The very criminal and impure." Orat. in Eutrop.

Συν τω ζωοποιω και παναγιω Πνευματι.—" With the life-bestowing and all-holy Spirit." De Incompreh. Hom. 2.

Που δε οι σοβουντες και μυρια εγκωμια λεγοντες.— " And where are they who walk insolently, and utter ten thousand panegyrics?" Orat. in Eutrop.

Και τι λεγω τον προφητην; αυτον αγω σοι, τον του προφητου δεσποτην, τον κοινον ημων Θεον και Κυριον, τον Χριστον. Αυτος γαρ φησιν, ότι πεινωντα με ειδετε, και εθρεψατε.—" But why do I mention the prophet? I will bring against you Him who is the Master of the prophet, our common God and Lord, the Christ. For he says, ' Ye saw me hungering, and ye fed me.' " Orat. in Eliam, et in viduam.

Mark, either Chrysostom speaks of one single person, or the sentence is ungrammatical. Now the passage in the 13th of the 2d chapter of Titus, του μεγαλου Θεου και Σωτηρος, must be construed in the same manner as τον κοινον Θεον και Κυριον.

From Gregory Nazianzen.

'Ο Ζευς, ό των Θεων μηστωρ και ύπατος.—" Jove, the counsellor and highest of the gods." Orat. 2, adv. Julian.

Οι την πενιαν ήμιν ονειδιζοντες, και τον πλουτον κομπαζοντες.—" Reproaching my poverty, and boasting of their own wealth." Orat. in Arianos.

Των ώραιων ετι και τω ζην επιτηδειων.—" Who were yet in the bloom of youth, and fitted to enjoy life." Orat. Funebr. in Patrem.

Των έστωτων και ου ρεοντων.—" Beings, permanent and imperishable." Ibid.

Τον σον ίερον και όμωνυμον.—" Thy priest and namesake." Ibid.

From Basil.

Οι αηττητοι και γενναιοι του Χριστου στρατιωται. " The unconquered and noble soldiers of Christ." Orat. in quadragint. Martyr.

Τον λυοντα και επαναγοντα.—" Him who liberates and brings us back." Orat. in Martyr. Julitt.

But what say the heathen authors? Is this doctrine of the Greek article founded upon the phraseology of *ecclesiastical* writers only, or does it exist in the works of those who wrote in the utmost purity and perfection of the language? It reigns triumphant in them all. Examine whatever authority you please, whether in prose or verse: consult the *poets,* the *philosophers,* and the *historians;* peruse the writings of *Homer* and of *Sophocles,* of *Aristotle* and of *Plato,* of *Thucydides* and *Xenophon,* of *Isocrates* or *Demosthenes:* in them you will meet with the most decisive testimonies to the truth of the doctrine already laid down. If you appeal to *Lucian,* you will find that Ulysses is called του ξενου και φιλον, " the host and friend." You may, perchance, have heard that the great Porson pronounced *Lucian* to be a writer of small authority; and you may wish to be convinced from the example of a pure Attic writer. Was ever writer more pure than *Xenophon?* And he will tell you, that *Cyrus* was at once, ό βασιλευς και ήγεμων, ." The king and general."

Was ever writer more pure than Plato ? This sublime and wondrous man declares in his Phædo, that God is τον αγαθον και φρονιμον, " The good and sapient." He elsewhere styles him, τον των παντων Θεον του τε ηγεμονος και αιτιου πατερα : " The God of all things, and Father of the ruler and efficient cause." In the following passage he is speaking of two different classes of persons. Having connected them by και, and prefixed the article to the first, he places it before the second also, τοις καταψηφισαμενοις μου, και τοις κατηγοροις : " Those who condemned me, and mine accusers."

In the Agamemnon of Æschylus (and indeed in almost every tragedy of that poet) we are presented with confirmations of our rule.

'Ο χρυσαμοιβος δ' Αρης σωματων,
Και ταλαντουχος εν μαχη δορος.
V. 426, edit. Blomfield.

" Mars, the exchanger of bodies, and holder of the balance in the conflict of the spear."

Πατερα Θυεστην τον εμον,——
Αύτου τ' αδελφον. V. 1574.

" Thyestes, my father and his brother."

This last is a happy instance. Ægisthus is speaking of his father, who was brother to Atreus.

Του θυτηρος και σε τιμωντος.

" Of the sacrificer and him honouring thee."
Æschyli Choephoræ, v. 253.

Orestes, in a prayer to Jupiter, is speaking of Agamemnon. We have here an instance of a substantive and a participle being connected.

One of the passages which I have cited from the New Testament may be thought by some to be liable to an objection. I mean the 5th verse of the 5th chapter of Ephesians. It may be said that the word Χριστος is not a substantive, but an adjective, ανηρ, or ανθρωπος, being understood ; and it may be asked, Does this rule apply when an *adjective* and a *substantive* are united by the conjunction, the article being prefixed to the first and not to the second ? I answer, by referring the objector to an example which I have given from St. Gregory Nazianzen ; there, μηστωρ is a substantive, and ύπατος an adjective ; and it is manifest that Jupiter, and Jupiter only, is intended.

Lest it should appear to any that I have been too concise, and have not furnished a sufficient number of corroborating examples, I shall subjoin the following ; two from the New Testament, some from the fathers, and some from heathen poets.

Αναβαινω προς τον Πατερα μου και Πατερα ύμων, και Θεον μου και Θεον ύμων.——" I ascend to my Father and your Father, and my God and your God." John xx. 17. This is an excellent example, where the supreme Being is considered in the four distinct relations of God and Father of Christ, and God and Father of men ; the article being placed before the first only.

Αναγκαιον δε ηγησαμην Επαφροδιτον τον αδελφον και συνεργον και συστρατιωτην μου, ύμων δε αποστολον, και λειτουργον της χρειας μου, πεμψαι προς ύμας.——" Yet I supposed it necessary to send to you Epaphroditus, my brother and companion in labour, and fellow soldier, but your messenger, and him who ministered to my wants." Phil. ii. 25. This is a very remarkable example, where the article is placed before αδελφον, and wanting before συνεργον, συστρατιωτην, αποστολον, and λειτουργον, because they all refer to Επαφροδιτον.

Εις Δια, τον ξενιον και ίκεσιον.——" Unto Jove, the friend of strangers, and guardian of suppliants." *Heliod.* p. 82. edit. Coray.

Πειθομενος παρ' 'Ερμου, τον καλλιστου και αγαθωτατου των θεων.——" Being persuaded by Mercury, the fairest and best of the gods." Ibid.

Αμφι τον αναρχον και ανωλεθρον Βασιλεα.——" Around the King without beginning and imperishable." *Methodius,* Sympos. Virg.

Τον κορυφαιοτατον παρ' ύμων και πρωτον των ποιητων, 'Ομηρου.——" Of Homer, whom ye consider the first and most eminent of the poets." Justin Martyr, Cohortatio ad Græcos.

'Ο δυστυχης δαιμων, ὁ σος καμος.
".Mine and thine evil genius."
Sophocles Electra.

'Ο Αρχιστρατηγος και Ποιμην των κατ' ουρανον, ῷ παντα πειθονται.——" The supreme Ruler and Shepherd of them in heaven, whom all things obey." *Methodius.*

'Ινα τον Βασιλεα γεραιρη παντων και Ποιητην.——" That he may venerate the King and Maker of all." Ibid.

'Ο στρατηγος ήμων και ποιμην Ιησους, και αρχων, και νυμφιος.——" Jesus, our leader, and shepherd, and governor, and bridegroom." Ibid.

The three following instances are from the poems of Gregory Nazianzen. It will be seen that even in poetry he cannot deviate from the established rule ; and yet we here find one false quantity and three violations of the laws of Iambic trimeter.

'Ο μανιωδης και κακιστος ζωγραφος.
Adv. Iram, tom. 2, p. 284. Edit. Paris, 1609.
" The insane and most execrable painter."

Τι λοιπον ; ὁρκιζω σε των κακων φιλοι,
Τον δυσμενη συνηγορον και προστατην.
Ib. p. 237.

" What remains ? I adjure thee, the friend of the wicked, the malevolent advocate and patron."

'Ο λυσσωδης και βασκανος οια τιν Ιωβ
Ες δηριν καλεει Ib. p. 77.

" Doth the infuriate and invidious demon call me, like another Job, unto the combat ?"

Most of the above writers, and most of those I am about to cite, have not yet been quoted on this subject. The examples from *Methodius* appear to me to be the most valuable. It must now be clearly seen that any Greek writer whatever will furnish sufficient examples to illustrate and establish this important rule.

Τον Θεον μονον αρνεισθε, τον δεσποτην και δημιουργον του παντος.——" Ye deny the only God, the Lord and Creator of all." *Chrysostomi* Orat. De non anathem, vivis aut defunctis.

Τον μακαριον και αοιδιμον τουτον.——" This blessed and celebrated man." *Georg. Archiep. Alexand.* De Vita Chrysostomi.

Οἱ ταχεις τα παντα και ουκ ασφαλεις, οἱ ῥᾳδιως οικοδομουντες και καταλυοντες.—" They who are swift in every thing, and not firm ; who readily rear superstructures, and destroy them." *Gregor. Nazianz.* Orat. Apol. de Fuga.

Αρης—ὁ της χρυσης Αφροδιτης αφνης εραστης και μοιχος απερισκεπτος.—" Mars, the unskilful lover of the golden Venus, and uncircumspect adulterer." Ibid. Orat. 1. adv. Julianum.

Μωυσης—ὁ μεν θεος Φαραω, και του Ισραηλ προστατης και νομοθετης.—" Moses, the god of Pharaoh, and president and lawgiver of Israel." Ibid. Orat. 2. adv. Julian.

Ὁ μεν αρχων αρχοντων, και ἱερευς ἱερεων (speaking of Moses.)—"The ruler of rulers, and priest of priests." Ibid.

Συ τε, ὁ της εμης φιλοσοφιας βασανιστης και κριτης.—" And thou, the investigator and judge of my philosophy." Ibid.

Εν ἡμερᾳ επιφανειας και αποκαλυψεως του μεγαλου Θεου και Αρχιποιμενος ἡμων, Ιησου Χριστου.—" In the day of the appearance and revelation of Jesus Christ, the great God and chief Shepherd of us." Ibid.

Τον των γεννητων ἁπαντων Κυριον και Θεον και Βασιλεα.—" The Lord, and God, and King of all mortals." (De Christo loquitur.) Eusebii Pamph. Eccles. Hist., lib. i. c. 2.

Περσων,
Των μεγαλαυχων και πολυανδρων.

" Of the proud and numerous Persians."
Æschyli Persæ, v. 538. Edit. Blomfield.

Ταν δοριγαμβρον αμφινεικη θ'
Ἑλεναν.
" Helen, the spear wedded and much contended for."
Æschyli Agam. v. 669.

Ἡ τ' αιχμαλωτος ἡδε και τερασκοπος,
Και κοινολεκτρος τουδε.

" And this woman, the captive, and observer of prodigies, and sharer of his bed."
Æschyli Agam. v. 1415.

Οπα τας Τηρειας
Μητιδος οικτρας αλοχου,
Κιρκηλατου τ' αηδονος.

" The voice of the wretched wife of Tereus, and the nightingale, pursued by the falcon."
Æschyli Supplices, v. 60. Edit. Porson.

This is an excellent example. It may be necessary to inform the unlearned that, according to Æschylus, the wife, and not the sister-in-law of Tereus, was changed into the nightingale. See the Agamemnon, v. 1146. Edit. Porson.

Ὁ μακαριος Ειρηναιος, ὁ μαρτυρ και επισκοπος Λουγδουνου.—" The blessed Irenæus, the martyr and bishop of Lugdunum." *Justinus,* in Responsione ad Quæstionem 115, ad Orthodoxos.

Ιουστινον του φιλοσοφου και μαρτυρος.—" Of Justin, the philosopher and martyr." *Theodoretus,* in Præfactione Hæreticarum Fabularum.

Ἱνα Χριστῳ Ιησου τῳ Κυριῳ ἡμων, και Θεῳ, και Σωτηρι, και Βασιλει, κατα την ευδοκιαν του Πατρος του αορατου, παν

γονυ καμψῃ.—" That to Christ Jesus, our Lord, and God, and Saviour, and King, according to the good pleasure of the invisible Father, every knee may bow." *Irenæus,* adversus Hæreses, lib. i. c. 2. p. 45. Edit. Oxon. 1702.

Τον Κτιστην και Δημιουργον.—" The Creator and Maker." Ibid. c. 4, p. 48.

Ὁ Πατηρ —— ὁ ανεννοητος και ανουσιος.—" The Father that cannot be fathomed by the understanding, and who is immaterial." Ibid. c. 10, p. 63.

Ἁ εστι κατα πιστιν και αγαπην Ιησου Χριστου, του Θεου και Σωτηρος ἡμων.—" Which are according to the faith and love of Jesus Christ, our God and Saviour." *Ignatii* Epist. ad Romanos.

Μονον, ινα τον Χριστον ιδω τον Σωτηρα μου και Θεον.—" So that I may but behold Christ, my Saviour and God." Epistola ad Tarsenses, *Ignatio* adscripta.

Οἱ παντα προς χαριν ποιουντες και λεγοντες.—" They who do and say every thing to gain favour." *Chrysostom.* Orat. in Eutrop.

Ὁ αλαζων και βαρβαρος.
" The insolent and barbarous."
Basilii Homil. in quadragint martyres.

Ἡ καλη και σοφη Χαρικλεια.
" The fair and sapient Chariclea."
Heliod. lib. 3.

Της θηλυπαιδος και τριανορος κορης.
" Of the girl who bore a female child, and had three husbands." Lycophron.

Τοις σοισι καμοις παισι.
" To thine and my children."
Euripid. Alcest.

Ὁ εμος γενετας και σος.—(Creusa loquitur de Ion.)
" My son and thine." *Euripid.* Ion.

Τον ψευδορκον και ξειναπατα.
" The false swearer and deceiver of thine host."
Euripidis Medea. v. 1389.

—Οἱα τε πασχομεν εκ της μυσαρας
Και παιδοφονου τησδε λεαινης.

" What things we suffer from this execrable and child-slaying lioness !" Ibid. v. 1405.

These two passages of the Medea I have given from the *corrected text* of the learned Professor Porson.

Ἡ του μεγαλου Διος αδελφη και ὁμοζυγος, [sc. Ἡρα]— " The sister and wife of the great Jove." *Gregor. Nazianz.* Orat. adv. Julian.

Οικεται του σταυρουμενου και λεγοντος, Αφες αυτοις. —" The servants of Him who was crucified, and said, ' Forgive them.' " *Chrysostom.* Orat. in Eutrop.

Τῳ αθλητῃ και μαρτυρι Χριστου.—" To the champion and martyr of Christ." Martyrium S. *Ignatii.*

Τον ιδιον Βασιλεα και Διδασκαλον.—" His own king and teacher." Epist. De Polycarpi Martyrio.

Τον μακαριον και ενδοξον Παυλον.—" Of the blessed and glorious Paul." *Polycarpi* Epistola ad Philipp.

Ιησου Χριστῳ, τῳ Υἱῳ ανθρωπου, και Υἱῳ Θεου.

2

"To Jesus Christ, the Son of man, and Son of God."
Ignat. ad Ephes.

Ὁ καθαρσιος και σωτηριος και μειλιχος.

"The purificatory and preservative and propitiatory."
Clemens Alexand. Προτρεπτ.

Τον των παντων Δημιουργον και Πατερα.

"The Creator and Father of all."
Clemens Alexand. ibid.

The learned reader will perceive, from the numerous examples which I have given, and the unlearned may perceive through the subjoined translations, that all the Greek authors, whether of an ancient or a more modern date, whether writing in prose or in verse, whether Christian or heathen, unite in one general chorus of attestation to the Divinity of Christ, and that Parnassian flowers, blent with the roses of Carmel and Sharon, encircle the brow of the Redeemer. Such is the cheering, the beneficial influence of learning. Such are the glorious effects resulting from the study of antiquity. Who shall contemn hereafter our classical acquirements; acquirements which can boast they have illustrated the glory of the Gospel? Who shall hereafter despise philology, when philology is become a handmaid of the Lord? The learning of the Gentiles is indeed the bulwark of Christianity, the outpost which secures the citadel, the foliage which protects the fruit. The star of Athens never beams with such resplendence as when it illuminates the path to Palestine; and never does Castalia's fountain so sweetly murmur, as when, emulous of Siloa's brook, it flows by the mount of Zion, and laves the oracle of God. Thus may it flow eternally! and, as its increasing current rolls over the instructed nations, may it cleanse them, as it has cleansed us, from the pollution of those who have dishonoured it!

POSTSCRIPT

TO THE

ESSAY ON THE GREEK ARTICLE.

As they who disbelieve the Divinity of Christ are naturally ready to assail whatever tends to confirm and to establish it; and as the lovers of disputation are often prone to the same conduct, without having the same excuse, I deem it necessary to answer the objections which have been brought against me in conversation and by letter. The most ingenious objection which I have yet heard, I shall notice first. It was made by a Unitarian of considerable acuteness. "You allow," said he, "that when two nouns of an opposite and contradictory meaning are coupled by the conjunction, two different persons are intended, although the article be prefixed to the first, but not to the second. Do you not perceive that you hereby furnish us with a reply? We have only to say that Χριστος and Θεος are opposite and irreconcilable terms. The passage in Ephesians is therefore an exception." This is the most subtle objection I have met with, but it is not unanswerable. The fallacy consists in this—my opponent takes for granted the very thing which it is his business to prove. Whether Χριστος and Θεος be opposite and irreconcilable terms, is the point at issue. Instead of making assertions, I will demonstrate that Χριστος and Θεος are not irreconcilable, but consistent, and capable of application to the same person. In the opening of St. John's gospel we read that *the Word was God.* A little after we are informed that *the Word was made flesh and dwelt among us.* From hence it is evident, to the humblest capacity, that the *Word* means Christ. But the *Word was God;* therefore Χριστος and Θεος are not inconsistent, but compatible. If, however, the gospel of St. John were not in existence, I should still be able to answer this objection by an appeal to the passage in Titus. We there find that Θεου and Σωτηρος are most providentially united by the conjunction. Now Θεος and Σωτηρ are unquestionably compatible. God may be a Saviour if he please, and we know that in the Scripture he is sometimes styled a Saviour. The expression, του μεγαλου Θεου και Σωτηρος is therefore subject to the influence of the rule, and one person only is intended. But Σωτηρ is spoken of Christ; therefore Christ is here styled *the great God;* consequently Χριστος and Θεος are perfectly consistent, perfectly compatible.

I shall next take notice of an objection which has less strength and force than the preceding. "You admit," said the objector, "because the very numerous instances oblige you to admit it, that proper names are excepted from the influence of the rule. Do you not see that by this confession your whole system is completely overthrown? A Unitarian will immediately observe, that Χριστος and Θεος are proper names, and consequently exceptions." In answer to this objection, I beg leave to state, first, with respect to Θεος, it is simply an appellation. Jehovah is the proper name of God; but the word *God* is a term by which we designate the incomprehensible Being, the Great First Cause. Secondly, with regard to Χριστος, it is evident, from the various places where it occurs, that it is simply a title of office given unto that Divine person whose name is Jesus. That the word *Christ* has become a proper name amongst us, I readily admit; but we must not confound English with Greek idioms. As I have no right, however, to expect that my unsupported assertion should be admitted as an authority, I shall cite the learned Professor Michaelis.

"In the time of the apostles," says he, "the word Christ was never used as the proper name of a person, but as an epithet expressive of the ministry of Jesus." Introduct., vol. i. p. 337. See also Dr. A. Clarke's notes on Matthew, chap. i. ver. 16.

I have now to offer my observations on an argument which at first sight appears plausible. It was urged against me by the same man who made the above objection, but it had already passed through my own mind, and I had already answered it to my own satisfaction. Whether it be answered to the satisfaction of my reader, he will now determine. "In St. John, chap. xx., ver. 28, we find the following expression: Ὁ Κυριος μου και ὁ Θεος μου. All the orthodox are agreed that Jesus is here styled both Lord and God. If, then, the rule you contend for, was real and genuine, the article ought not to have been repeated before the second noun, inasmuch as one person only is intended. The same argument may be deduced from a passage in Revelation, chap. xxii., ver 13." I answer: It is well known to every mathematician that the converse of a proposition does not necessarily hold. Now it is the same in philology as in science. I have maintained, and do still maintain, that when two substantives, &c., are coupled by the conjunction, the article being prefixed to the first, but not to the second, one person only is intended. It does not follow from hence, that when one person only is intended, the article must be prefixed to the first, but not to the second. It may be affixed to neither, or it may be affixed to both, as in the example above quoted, for the purpose of giving greater force and energy.

I have now to answer another objection, which I should have passed unregarded if it had not been made by persons of considerable consequence, and of opposite creeds. "We cannot admit," say they, "that a doctrine of such importance should rest upon a mere form of speech, a mere rule of syntax." Now I should be glad to know, what truth is there, however sacred, what doctrine, however important, which does not rest upon some form of speech, upon some rule of syntax. A single example will suffice. How can we be certain whether, in John iii. 16, Christ meant to inform us that God so loved the world, that he gave his only begotten Son; or that the world so loved God, that he gave his only begotten Son? What other answer, than the following, can be given? It is a universal law of syntax that a verb in the indicative mood must be preceded by a nominative; and if there be an accusative case in the sentence, that accusative must be governed either by a verb, or by a preposition. We are therefore certain that the passage admits of one meaning only. All Divine knowledge, as well as all human knowledge, is communicated through the medium of language; and where would be the certainty of language, if it were not governed by fixed unalterable rules?

If my memory be correct, it has been asserted by a Unitarian writer, that the passage in Titus ii. 13, may be understood thus: "The appearance of the glory of the great God, and the appearance of our Saviour Jesus Christ;" and a reference has been made to the passage wherein it is said, that Christ will come in the glory of his Father. I reply: It is also said that he will come in his own glory; and it is at least as probable that the apostle refers to the latter as to the former. But if the probabilities be equal, then neither interpretation can be admitted. I have said, it is at least as probable that the apostle refers to the latter; but the fact is, that it is much

more probable. If he had alluded to the former, it is most likely that he would have written *the glory of the Father,* or *the glory of God;* but not of *the great God.* There is no reason however to believe that he referred to either. Bishop Burgess has clearly shown, by references to other passages, that επιφανειαν της δοξης is a Hebrew idiom, and that *the glorious appearance* is its proper translation.

I have now gone through the principal objections which have been urged against our system. If it should appear to the enlightened reader that I have not sufficiently refuted them, I hope, I entreat, that he will attribute this to the inability of the advocate, and not to the imperfection of the cause. When the admirable Porson was alive, he might have lulled the question into an everlasting rest. With one effort of his mind, with one glance of his eye, with one stroke of his pen, he could have poured upon the subject a flood of light which Satan could never have extinguished, and our opponents could never have withstood. But, alas! except in one instance, his studies were not directed to subjects of sacred criticism.

I shall conclude this postscript with a few general observations on the subject.

When the Monthly Reviewers sat down to criticise Dr. Middleton's work upon the Greek article, the subject was but in its infancy. It had not attained the matured vigour and perfect bloom which it now displays. These gentlemen imagined that they had given a death blow to the system, by bringing forward such examples as the following: τον σωφρονα, και ακολαστον· *the temperate, and intemperate.* We now see that their arguments are most successfully turned against themselves. It is evident, from what has been said at the beginning of my Essay, that this instance is no exception to the rule. A temperate, and an intemperate person, are characters essentially different, and therefore it was unnecessary to repeat the article. Thus Æschylus, in his Agamemnon, speaking of the Trojans and the Greeks, says,

Και των ἁλοντων και κρατησαντων·

"And of the captured, and those who gained the victory;"

in which place it is manifest that the repetition of the article would have been needless.

I have also stated that proper names are exempted from the jurisdiction of the rule. It is clear that Peter and John are distinct persons: therefore, St. Luke, chap. ix. 28, writes: παραλαβων τον Πετρον, και Ιωαννην, και Ιακωβον· *Having taken Peter, and John, and James.*

In Acts xxvi. 30, St. Luke informs us that the king and the governor arose. If we examine the original we shall find that the article is prefixed to both these nouns, ανεστη ὁ βασιλευς, και ὁ ἡγεμων. Why was the article here repeated? Was it to give force and energy to the expression? No: it was for a reason more important; the evangelist intended us to understand that, when Paul had ceased to speak, the king, Agrippa, and the governor, Festus, arose. Now, the offices of a king and a governor are perfectly compatible. If, then, he had written ὁ βασιλευς και ἡγεμων, he would have conveyed a very different idea to that which was intended. The reader would have supposed that Agrippa united in his own person the offices of king and governor; that he and Bernice rose up, and that Festus was left by himself, unless indeed he was included among those, οἱ συγκαθημενοι αυτοις, *who sat together with them.* But St. Luke knew, and felt the force, the influence, and the universality, of the rule which I contend for, and wrote accordingly.

In the course of my essay, I quoted those passages of Chrysostom wherein he proves the godhead of Christ from Titus ii. 13. I then brought forward the testimony of Basil, and appealed to his fourth book against Eunomius. It may, however, be objected that some critics have doubted whether that book was genuine. If we even allow that it is spurious, and admit as a fact what is merely a matter of opinion, we shall not be thereby deprived of the testimony of St. Basil. His Homilies on the Psalms are unquestionably genuine; and in the very first of these he quotes Titus i. 13, and applies the whole of it to Christ. The homily is in the first volume both of the Benedictine edition, and the Paris edition of 1618. This important verse is cited by Athanasius, by Gregory of Nyssa, and by Cyril of Alexandria.

When I look attentively at the two passages of Holy Writ, which have been the especial objects of this discussion, I think that, leaving the doctrine of the Greek article out of the question, I perceive sufficient evidence to warrant our belief that one person only is intended. In the passage from Ephesians, two circumstances claim our notice: Θεου is placed last in the sentence, and the article is not prefixed to it, although it had been prefixed to Χριστου:—but this is abhorrent from the phraseology of St. Paul. When he speaks of God the Father, and of Jesus Christ, and connects them by the conjunction, it is his custom to mention the Father first, and to omit the article altogether. In the following texts the reader may see a few examples: Rom. i. 7; 1 Cor. i. 3; 2 Cor. i. 2; Gal. i. 3; Eph. i. 2; Phil. i. 2. The article, however, is sometimes prefixed to both; see, for instance, Col. ii. 2. This passage, by the way, is a most powerful confirmation of Mr. Sharp's rule; but with that rule we have nothing to do at present. St. John expresses himself in the same manner in the Apocalypse, xi. 15. We see then what is the prevailing diction of St. Paul; and we may defy any man to produce a single passage, either from him or from any other inspired writer, where God the Father and Christ are manifestly spoken of, the Father placed last in the sentence, and yet unhonoured by the article, while on Christ that distinction is conferred. We may conclude, that if, in Eph. v. 5, St. Paul had spoken both of the Father and of the Son, he would have said Τον Θεου και του Χριστου, or at least του Χριστου και του Θεου.

On Titus ii. 13, I have an observation to offer, which also is unconnected with Mr. Sharp's rule. If God the Father be meant in the first clause, then the Son is simply called σωτηρος ἡμων. But this expression, as applied to Christ, hath no parallel in the whole book of God. I wish the intelligent reader to mark this distinctly. The following are, I believe, all the passages of the New Testament where Christ is styled *our Saviour,* without any conjoined appellation; and

in every one of these the article is affixed. 2 Tim. i. 10; Tit. i. 4; Tit. iii. 6. We have reason then to believe that, if St. Paul had here meant the glorious appearance of God the Father, he would have added, και του σωτηρος ἡμων. I may add, that, as the three passages where Christ is styled our Saviour, all occur in the writings of this apostle, the reason of our belief is greatly strengthened.

I have reasoned boldly and confidently on the doctrine of the prepositive article, because I am persuaded that my reasoning can never be overturned. If, however, an example in the singular number, such as ὁ βασιλευς και ἡγεμων, should be brought against me; if the two nouns be perfectly compatible; and if, notwithstanding this, it be manifest that two different persons are intended; I must acknowledge that my labours have ended in uncertainty.*

It is my unalterable opinion that, at all times and on all occasions, truth should be explored; and, when discovered, exhibited to view, whatever be the consequences. I think it will be impossible for the opposers of this doctrine to produce such an example as I have been supposing; but should any be inclined to look for such an example, I think it necessary to mention, that two things are indispensable. In the first place, the citation must be made from an unexceptionable Greek writer; in the second place, there must be no various reading to the passage in any extant manuscript. First, it must be from an unexceptionable Greek writer; it must be from an author whose native language was Greek, and who flourished not later than the first century after Christ. When I have established a fact,

---

* Although I have made numerous corrections, both in my essay and postscript, I have republished this part of the postscript as it stood in the first edition. The intelligent reader, however, will perceive that I have made too large and liberal a concession; and he will see that I must consider my cause indeed a strong one, when I am not afraid of granting so much to my opponent. The concession is too liberal, for this reason: When a rule of grammar is established by the concurrent practice of all writers, the discovery of an exception cannot be considered as invalidating it. For instance: it is an invariable rule that the article must agree with the substantive to which it is prefixed, in gender, number, and case. If a student were to meet with a passage in some Greek author, wherein an article masculine was affixed to a noun feminine, an article plural to a noun singular, or an article in the genitive to a noun in the accusative; what, in such a case, would be his conclusion? Not that the laws of grammar were dubious, but that the passage in question was most unquestionably corrupted. Surely the same inference should be drawn in the case before us. He who labours to overthrow our doctrine, should come armed with at least five or six legitimate exceptions. Let not any one imagine that I have any fear or doubt on this subject. I repeat my conviction, that not one genuine exception could be produced, even if I were to extend the prescribed period to the termination of the fourth century. If however such an exception should be found, but found in a writer of whose works all the extant manuscripts are notoriously corrupt, it would be uncandid in the discoverer to bring it forward.

2

by instances taken from the best and purest of the Greek authors, I may then call to my assistance whatever writers I please, for the purpose of farther corroboration ; but the opponent who comes forward to dispute and to destroy, must deduce the streams of his criticisms from the fountain head. His weapons must be taken from the armoury of Homer or Plato, of Sophocles or Pindar, of Xenophon or Demosthenes. Secondly, there must be no various reading in any MS. which is extant. If there be but one various reading, the passage will be inadmissible ; in rejecting it, I shall be acting with impartial justice ; for I have passed over a very important passage in my favour, because there is a various reading. By the application of Mr. Sharp's rule to 2 Pet. i. 1, it might have been shown that Jesus is there styled *our God*. There is no doubt that τον Θεον ημων και σωτηρος is the genuine reading. If not quite as precious as the instance in Tit. ii. 13, it is more valuable than that in Eph. v. 5, and yet I passed it over, being determined to make use of nothing to which the slightest objection might be made.

If, at some future period, an exception, in itself unexceptionable, shall be brought against the rule, I will acknowledge, though painful the confession, that my sweetest, because my best directed, labours have been unavailing. I shall retire from the field discomfited, but not disheartened ; disappointed, but not dispirited ; sorrowful, and yet rejoicing. Yea, I shall still rejoice ; because I am assured there are other proofs of the Divinity of Jesus ; proofs, which neither the subtlety of philologists, nor the sophistry of Unitarians, nor the rage of demons can overthrow.

Supplement to the Postscript.

In the conclusion of the postscript to my essay, I observed that there were other proofs of the Divinity of Jesus, besides that which I had laboured to establish. One of these I brought forward in the commencement of the postscript ; and I now desire, through the blessing of God, to set forth and elucidate another. It occurs in Romans ix. 5. I select this, because the Godhead of Christ is here established on the soundest principles of criticism ; and because we see to what a desperate state the Unitarians must be reduced, when, in order to evade it, they fly in the very face of philology, and set at defiance her decisions. I choose it for this reason also : that as far as my knowledge extends, it has not been sufficiently investigated by previous writers. Και εξ ων ὁ Χριστος, το κατα σαρκα, ὁ ων επι παντων Θεος ευλογητος εις τους αιωνας. " And from whom sprang the Christ, the part according to the flesh, (or, the human nature,) who is over all, God blessed for ever." It is known to all persons acquainted with the subject, that in the oldest Greek manuscripts every letter is a capital, that there is no division of words, and that there are no stops. We must therefore divide the words, and arrange the stops, according to our own judgment. The enemies of our Lord's Divinity of course oppose every thing that supports it. At one time some of them admitted a conjectural emendation into the text ; but the most judicious among them have rejected an expedient so desperate, and so unjustifiable. At present they would

evade the force of this passage, by introducing a different mode of punctuation ; some of them placing a full stop after παντων, and some placing it after σαρκα. They thus form a new sentence, which they consider as exclamatory. When the stop is placed after παντων, they construe the remainder thus : " God be blessed for ever." Now, any man who is a sound scholar and critic, will immediately propose the following question : Does St. Paul ever make such exclamations ? And if he make them, does he express them in this strange manner ? The fact is, that he twice utters this ejaculation ; but his phraseology is different from what we find above. The exclamation, " Blessed be God," occurs twice in his epistles ; but *in both places* he writes thus : ευλογητος ὁ Θεος. It occurs in 2 Cor. i. 3 ; Eph. i. 3. St. Peter makes use of the same ejaculation ; and his phraseology is precisely the same. See 1st Epist. i. 3. In St. Luke, i. 68, we find the following exclamation : " Blessed be the Lord God of Israel." The phrase is exactly the same, excepting the introduction of Κυριος after ευλογητος. In the Septuagint, ευλογητος ὁ Θεος occurs twice ; ευλογητος Κυριος, ten times ; and ευλογητος Κυριος ὁ Θεος, twelve times. Thus, in twenty-eight cases there is not a single one wherein ευλογητος is placed last ; and in eighteen cases there is not one wherein the article is wanting before Θεος. A sentence occurs in Psalm lxvii. 19, wherein the exclamation occurs twice, without any intervening words : Κυριος ὁ Θεος ευλογητος· ευλογητος Κυριος. The reader will observe that in one of the clauses, ευλογητος is placed last ; but as this is evidently done to vary the expression, and as the article is affixed to Θεος, it cannot be brought forward as an exception. We see, then, that throughout the Old and New Testament, one mode of speech prevails. The truth is,* that any Greek writer would have so expressed himself. Of this the eloquent Chrysostom is an example. Among his works there are twenty-one orations to the people of Antioch ; in the course of these he uses the exclamation, " Blessed be God," no less than *seven times*, and in every case we find ευλογητος ὁ Θεος. Surely every intelligent reader must be now convinced that, if St. Paul had here meant to exclaim, " Blessed be God," he would have written ευλογητος ὁ Θεος.

Let us now examine the other method of construing the passage. If the full stop be placed after σαρκα, the following sentence will be formed : Ὁ ων επι παν-των Θεος ευλογητος εις τους αιωνας. The Unitarians understand it thus : " May God, who is over all, be blessed for ever." Now, we may feel assured that neither St. Paul, nor any other Greek author, would have thus expressed himself, for the collocation of the

---

* The fact is certain ; the reason may perhaps be found in the following canon, which prevails generally in the Greek language. If a person be spoken of, and something be predicated of him, the predicate is put first, and the article precedes the subject. The reader will find several examples in a paper of mine published by Dr. A. Clarke, in his Commentary on the first chapter of Hebrews. Now, when a Greek writer exclaims, " Blessed be God," the phraseology seems to be determined by the rule.

Words is still more opposed to the genius and idiom of the Greek language, as well as to the established usage, both of St. Paul, and of the other sacred writers ; and the article is wanting before ,Θεος, though yet more needed. If he had meant this sentence to be an exclamation, he would undoubtedly have written either ευλογητος ὁ Θεος ὁ ων επι παντων, or ειη ὁ Θεος ὁ ων επι παντων ευλογητος, (or, ηυλογημενος) εις κ. τ. λ. This method of punctuation therefore is untenable.

As I have shown that our opponents cannot justify by any parallel expressions the perversion of Rom., chap. ix., ver. 5, I may perhaps be asked whether the orthodox mode of punctuation, and of construction, can be supported by any parallel passages. I shall feel happy in replying that it can. In Rom. i. 25, we find και ελατρευσαν τη κτισει παρα τον κτισαντα, ὁς εστιν ευλονητος εις τους αιωνας. Every person at all acquainted with Greek, knows that the phrase ὁ ων is equivalent to ὁς εστι, and every one will agree as to the mode of construing the above words. But I can adduce a passage, wherein the phraseology is not *equivalent*, but *exactly the same.* It is in 2 Cor. xi. 31 : Ὁ Θεος και πατηρ του Κυριου ἡμων Ιησου Χριστου οιδεν, ὁ ων ευλογητος εις τους αιωνας. This is an invaluable example, for it most powerfully confirms the sense in which we understand the passage in Romans. I might offer some remarks on the clause το κατα σαρκα, for this is of great importance ; but I fear there would not be room for their insertion.* I have surely said enough to convince any competent judge that the Unitarian devices are directly opposed to sound criticism ; and that, leaving religion out of the question, no man can lay claim to the character of a scholar and a critic, who rejects the orthodox interpretation. From the decisions of stern Philology there is no appeal. She is the mighty arbitress of truth. As soon as she ascends her august tribunal, error begins to tremble. When she raises her imperious voice, and pronounces the irrevocable judgment, Popery is annihilated, Unitarianism is extirpated, Arianism is effaced, and nothing remains but the unadulterated gold, the unpolluted gem, the cloudless sunshine, of the Gospel.

As the hallowed doctrine of the atonement is so closely connected with the Divinity of Christ, I cannot refrain from observing that it is remarkably confirmed

---

* It has been asserted by a Unitarian writer, that the latter clause of Rom. ix. 5, was never applied to Christ by the early Christian writers ! In *every instance* wherein they quote it, it is applied to Christ. All the passages are given by the learned Burton in his invaluable work on the Ante-Nicene fathers. It has been said that the word Θεος appears to have been wanting in Chrysostom's copy of the New Testament ! Chrysostom has the word Θεος in his Commentary on Romans, and he has it when he quotes the verse in another place. See my Select Passages of St. Chrysostom, St. Gregory Nazianzen, and St. Basil, p. 283, 3d edition. See also the foregoing Essay. The Unitarians still maintain that the Ante-Nicene fathers were all of their creed ! The supreme Divinity of Christ was held by *all the fathers, from the very apostolic age.* It has been stated that Θεος did not appear in 1 Tim. iii. 16, until the sixth century. Chrysostom has Θεος in 1 Tim. iii. 16, and he wrote at the end of the fourth.

by philological investigation. Though various opinions be entertained respecting the nature of Christ and the object of his sufferings, every scholar in every country will concur as to the meaning of the Alcestis of Euripides. It will be allowed at once that the following is the subject of this pathetic tragedy. Admetus is about to die. Apollo intercedes with the Fates, and they consent to spare him on condition of one of his friends devoting himself and dying in his stead. Alcestis offers herself as a substitute, and dies in the place of her husband. Let us examine the principal passages which relate to the event.

———Πως δ' αν μαλλον ενδειξαιτο τις
Ποσιν προτιμωσ', η θελουσ' ὑπερθανειν.

Alcestis, v. 155, edit. Monk.

" How could any one more clearly demonstrate how much she preferred her husband than by being willing to die for him ?"

Εγω σε πρεσβευουσα, καντι της εμης
Ψυχης καταστησασα φως τοδ' εισοραν,
Θνησκω, παρον μοι μη θανειν, ὑπερ σεθεν.

Ib. v. 293.

" Honouring thee, and resolving that in exchange for my life thou shouldst behold this light ; when it is at my option not to die, I die for thee."

Συ δ', αντιδουσα της εμης τα φιλτατα
Ψυχης, εσωσας.   Ib. v. 350.

" But thou, giving what was most dear to thee in exchange for my life, hast saved me."

Συ τον αυτας
Ετλας ποσιν αντι σας αμειψαι
Ψυχας εξ Αιδα.   Ib. v. 473.

" Thou at least hast dared to rescue tny husband from the grave, given in exchange for thine own life."

——— αντι σου γε κατθανειν.   Ib. v. 540.

" To die instead of thee."

Καθρεψ', οφειλων ουχ' ὑπερθνησκειν σεθεν.

Ib. v. 698.

" And I reared thee up, owing thee thus much, but not to die for thee."

Μη θνησχ' ὑπερ τουδ' ανδρος, ουδ' εγω προ σου.

Ib. v. 706.

" Die not thou for this man, (meaning himself,) nor I for thee."

Ει την παρουσαν κατθανειν πεισειας αν
Γυναιχ' ὑπερ σου.   Alcestis, v. 716.

" If thou couldst persuade thy present wife to die for thee."

Αλλ' ου συ νεκρον αντι, σου τουδ' εκφερεις.

Ib. v. 732.

" But thou shalt not bear out this person (meaning himself) dead in the place of thee."

The English reader will be enabled, by the translations which I have subjoined, to appreciate the force of the argument. The learned will observe, that αντι and ὑπερ are promiscuously employed ; but ὑπερ in these passages unquestionably signifies *in the place of* and not *for the sake of.* Some other passages occur which bear upon the subject; but, as προ is used instead of αντι and ὑπερ, I have not cited them. In one instance we find δια.

As I am afraid of extending my remarks to too great a length, I shall content myself with referring the reader to the following, among many other passages of the New Testament. I particularly request that he will compare the first extract which I have given from the heathen poet, with the first of the texts to which I shall refer him. John xv. 13; 1 Peter iv. 1; 1 Tim. ii. 6; Matt. xx. 28; Mark x. 45; Rom. v. 6, 7, 8; 2 Cor. v. 15–21; 1.Thess. v. 10; 1 Peter iii. 18; 1 Cor. viii. 11; 2 Cor. v. 20. In this text ὑπερ occurs twice; and St. Chrysostom in his Commentary on this verse, thus writes: τουτεστιν, αντι Χριστου, " That is, in the place of Christ."

If we attentively compare the texts just referred to, with the passages which have been given from Euripides, we shall especially observe two things: 1st. The phraseology in both cases is the same; ὑπερ and αντι being promiscuously used. 2d. Some strong and remarkable expressions are applied to Christ which are not applied to Alcestis. He is declared to be the oblation; (προσφορα;) the sacrifice; (θυσια;) the redemption; (ἀπολυτρωσις;) the propitiation; (ἱλασμος;) the propitiatory; (ἱλαστηριος;) the redemption price, or ransom; (λυτρον;) the redemption price paid for the life of a captive (αντιλυτρον.) Now it is at once *admitted by all* that Alcestis offered up herself as a vicarious sacrifice for her husband, that she redeemed his life with her own; yet this admission is made on evidence *less strong* and *less decisive* than the evidence for the vicarious sacrifice of Christ. It is surely unnecessary to point out the obvious deduction. Can any man be so blind as not to perceive it, or so uncandid as not to acknowledge it ?*

* At the end of my " Brief Refutation of Popery, from the Writings of the Fathers," I stated my ideas of the ar-

After this supplement had been sent to press, I met with a translation of Romans ix. 5, given by Mr. Jones in his futile work on the Greek Article. It is inadmissible for several philological reasons; and it is so very forced and unnatural that I should think no sensible man would defend it for an instant. Some persons have acknowledged that Christ is here called God, but have thought that he is called so in an inferior sense, because the article is omitted before Θεος. A little more knowledge of Greek would have shown them the reason of this omission. It is wanting because Θεος in this place is a predicate. For the same reason it is omitted before Θεος in John i. 1.

Let me, in conclusion, address a few words to the Unitarian, respecting the passage on which I have so largely dwelt. I have shown that both your attempts to evade its force are ineffectual; that the words cannot have the meaning you still attach to them, because they would not be good Greek, and because they would be at variance with the established diction, both of the Greek Testament, and of the Septuagint. In the present state of critical learning, is it not degrading to uphold and to perpetuate a mode of translation which is subversive of all sound criticism? Were you influenced by no higher motive, I should have thought you would have had more decent pride, than to pursue a system which must sink you so low, so very low, in the estimation of the learned. But I would that you were actuated by better motives. I exhort, I conjure you, to bend before that cross which you have so long despised; to read the Scripture with humility; to seek the grace of repentance; to implore the gift of faith, and to pray for the illumination of the Spirit.

Sidmouth, July 30th, 1833.

gument which I have pursued above; but being weary of writing, at the time of my publishing that work, I expressed a wish that some Christian scholar would pursue the inquiry. I have not however heard that any person has taken up the subject.

ΕΙΣ ΤΟΝ ΕΜΟΝ ΛΟΓΟΝ ΤΟΝ ΠΕΡΙ ΤΟΥ ΑΡΘΡΟΥ.

Χθιζος εμοισι τρυφων λειμωσι νεηθαλεεσσιν,
Ηρεμα συριζων, και ποιμνια λευκα νομευων·
Ομματα δ' αρ λαμπρα, πτερυγεσσι τε πορφυρεησι
Καλλιμος, ἡ Κλειω κραδιην παλλουσαν ἱκανε,
Χαιρε δ' εφη, μεγα χαιρε· σε Τιτυρος αυτος επαινει·
Ανθεμα σοι θαλλειν νυν Τιτυρος αυτος εδωκεν·
Ερνεα νυν κεινου σοις ανθεσιν εστεφανωται.
Ὡς εφαθ'· ἡ σοφιη δ' ιερη ψιθυριζεν ανωθεν,
Μη τιμαις χθονιησιν ὑπερφρονει, αλλα ταπεινου·
Πνευμα καθαιρε τεον, σαις δ' ελπισιν ουρανον ἱκε.

Υ. Σ. Β.

EPISTLE OF PAUL THE APOSTLE

PHILIPPIANS.

WE have already seen, Acts xvi. 12, that *Philippi* was a town of *Macedonia*, in the territory of the *Edones*, on the confines of *Thrace*, and very near the northern extremity of the *Ægean Sea*. It was a little eastward of Mount *Pangæus*, and about midway between *Nicopolis* on the east, and *Thessalonica* on the west. It was at first called *Crenides*, and afterwards *Datus*; but *Philip*, king of Macedonia and father of Alexander, having taken possession of it and fortified it, called it *Philippi*, after his own name. *Julius Cæsar* planted a colony here, which was afterwards enlarged by *Augustus*; and hence the inhabitants were considered as *freemen* of Rome. Near this town, it is thought, the famous battle was fought between *Brutus* and *Cassius* on the one side, and *Augustus* and *Mark Antony* on the other, in which the former were defeated, and the fate of the empire decided. Others think that this battle was fought at *Philippi*, a town of Thebes in Thessaly.

The Gospel was preached first here by St. Paul. About the year of our Lord 53, St. Paul had a vision in the night; a man of Macedonia appeared to him and said, Come over to Macedonia and help us. He was then at *Troas* in *Mysia*; from thence he immediately sailed to *Samothracia*, came the next day to *Neapolis*, and thence to *Philippi*. There he continued for some time, and converted *Lydia*, a seller of purple, from *Thyatira*; and afterwards cast a demon out of a *Pythoness*, for which he and *Silas* were persecuted, cast into prison, scourged, and put into the stocks: but the magistrates afterwards finding that they were Romans, took them out of prison and treated them civilly. See the account, Acts xvi. 9, &c.

.The Philippians were greatly attached to their apostle, and testified their affection by sending him supplies, even when he was labouring for other Churches; and they appear to have been the only Church that did so. See chap. iv. 15, 16.

There is not much controversy concerning the date of this epistle; it was probably written in the end of A. D. 62, and about a year after that to the *Ephesians*. Dr. Paley conjectures the date by various intimations in the epistle itself. "It purports," says he, "to have been written near the conclusion of St. Paul's imprisonment at Rome, and after a residence in that city of considerable duration. These circumstances are made out by different *intimations*; and the intimations upon the subject preserve among themselves a just consistency, and a consistency certainly unmeditated. *First*, the apostle had already been a prisoner at Rome so long, as that the reputation of his bonds, and of his constancy under them, had contributed to advance the success of the Gospel. See chap. i. 12–14. *Secondly*, the account given of *Epaphroditus* imports that St. Paul, when he wrote the epistle, had been in Rome a considerable time. ' He longed after you all, and was full of heaviness because ye had heard that he had been sick;' chap. ii. 26. Epaphroditus had been with Paul at Rome; he had been sick; the Philippians had heard of his sickness; and he again had received an account how much they had been affected by the intelligence. The passing and repassing of these advices must necessarily have occupied a large portion of time, and must have all taken place during St. Paul's residence at Rome. *Thirdly*, after a residence at Rome, thus proved to have been of considerable duration, he now regards the decision of his fate as nigh at hand: he contemplates either alternative; that of his *deliverance*, chap. ii. 23, 24: ' Him, therefore, (Timothy,) I hope to send presently, so soon as I shall see how it will go with me; but I trust in the Lord that I also myself shall come shortly;' that of his *condemnation*, ver. 17: *Yea, and if I be offered upon the sacrifice and service of your faith, I joy and rejoice.with you all.* This consistency is material, if the consideration of it be confined to the epistle. It is farther material, as it agrees, with respect to the duration of St. Paul's first imprisonment at Rome, with the account delivered in the Acts, which, having brought the apostle to Rome, closes the history, by telling us that he dwelt there *two whole years in his own hired house.*" Hor. Paul., page 242.

2

PREFACE TO THE EPISTLE TO THE PHILIPPIANS.

On the agreement between the epistle and the history, as given in the Acts, Dr. Paley makes many judicious remarks, which I cannot insert here, but must refer to the work itself; and I wish all my readers to get and peruse the whole work as an inestimable treasure of sacred criticism on the authenticity of Paul's epistles.

The Epistle to the Philippians is written in a very pleasing and easy style; every where bearing evidence of that contented state of mind in which the apostle then was, and of his great affection for the people. It appears that there were false apostles, or Judaizing teachers, at Philippi, who had disturbed the peace of the Church; against these he warns them, exhorts them to concord, comforts them in their afflictions for the Gospel, returns them thanks for their kindness to him, tells them of his state, and shows a great willingness to be a sacrifice for the faith he had preached to them. There is a Divine unction in this epistle which every serious reader will perceive.

488   2

THE
EPISTLE OF PAUL THE APOSTLE

TO THE

PHILIPPIANS.

Chronological Notes relative to this Epistle.

Usherian year of the world, 4066.—Alexandrian era of the world, 5564.—Antiochian era of the world, 5554.—Constantinopolitan era of the world, 5570.—Year of the Eusebian epocha of the Creation, 4290. —Year of the Julian period, 4772.—Year of the minor Jewish era of the world, 3822.—Year of the Greater Rabbinical era of the world, 4421.—Year from the Flood, according to Archbishop Usher, and the English Bible, 2410.—Year of the Cali yuga, or Indian era of the Deluge, 3164.—Year of the era of Iphitus, or since the first commencement of the Olympic games, 1002.—Year of the Nabonassarean era, 809.—Year of the era of the Seleucidæ, 374.—Year of the Spanish era, 100.—Year of the Actiac or Actian era, 93.—Year from the birth of Christ, 66.—Year of the vulgar era of Christ's nativity, 62.— Year from the building of Rome, according to Varro, 814.—Year of the CCXth Olympiad, 2.—Jesus, high priest of the Jews.—Common Golden Number, 6.—Jewish Golden Number, 3.—Year of the Solar Cycle, 15.—Dominical Letter C.—Jewish Passover, April 10th.—Easter Sunday, April 11th.—Epact, or the moon's age on the 22d of March, or the Xth of the Calends of April, 25.—Year of the reign of Nero Cæsar, the sixth emperor of the Romans, 9.—In the first year of Albinus, governor of the Jews.—Year of Vologesus, king of the Parthians, 12.—Year of Domitius Corbulo, governor of Syria, 3.—Roman Consuls ; P. Marius Celsus, and L. Asinius Gallus, from Jan. 1st to July 1st; and L. Annæus Seneca the philosopher, and Trebellius Maximus, for the remainder of the year.

CHAPTER I.

Paul, in conjunction with Timothy, addresses himself to the saints at Philippi, and gives them his apostolical benediction, 1, 2. Thanks God for their conversion and union, and expresses his persuasion that God will continue his work among them, 3–6. Tells them of his strong affection for them, and prays that they may be filled with the salvation of God, 7–11. Shows them how much his persecution had contributed to the success of the Gospel, 12–14. Informs that there were some at Rome who preached the Gospel from unworthy motives; yet he was convinced that this, which was designed to injure him, should turn to his advantage, 15–19. Mentions his uncertainty whether he should be liberated or martyred, and his perfect readiness to meet either; yet, on the whole, expresses a hope that he should again visit them, 20–26. Exhorts them to a holy life, and comforts them under their tribulations, 27–30.

A. M. cir. 4066.
A. D. cir. 62.
A. U. C. 814.
An. Imp. Neronis Cæs.
Aug. 9.

PAUL and Timotheus, the servants of Jesus Christ, to all the saints a in Christ Jesus which are at Philippi, with the bishops and deacons :

2 b Grace *be* unto you, and peace, from God our Father,

A. M. cir. 4066.
A. D. cir. 62.
A. U. C. 814.
An. Imp. Neronis Cæs.
Aug. 9.

---

a 1 Cor. i. 2.

b Rom. i. 7; 2 Cor. i. 2 ; 1 Pet. i. 2.

NOTES ON CHAP. I.

Verse 1. *Paul and Timotheus*] That Timothy was at this time with the apostle in Rome we learn from chap. ii. 19, and also that he was very high in the apostle's estimation. He had also accompanied the apostle on his two voyages to *Philippi*, see Acts xvi. and xx., and was therefore deservedly dear to the Church in that city. It was on these accounts that St. Paul joined his name to his own, not because he was in any part the author of this epistle, but he might have been the apostle's amanuensis, though the *subscription* to the epistle gives this office to *Epaphroditus*. Neither in this epistle, nor in those to the *Thessalonians* and to *Philemon* does St. Paul call himself

2

489

A. M. cir. 4066.
A. D. cir. 62.
A. U. C. 814.
An. Imp. Ne-
ronis Cæs.
Aug. 9.

and *from* the Lord Jesus Christ.

3 ^c I thank my God upon every ^d remembrance of you,

4 Always in every prayer of mine for you all making request with joy,

5 ^e For your fellowship in the Gospel from the first day until now ;

6 Being confident of this very thing, that he which hath begun ^f a good work in you ^g will perform *it* ^h until the day of Jesus Christ :

7 Even as it is meet for me to think this of you all, because ⁱ I have you ^k in my heart ; inasmuch as both in ^l my bonds, and in ^m the defence and confirmation of the Gospel, ⁿ ye all are ^o partakers of my grace.

8 For ^p God is my record, ^q how greatly I long after you all in the bowels of Jesus Christ.

9 And this I pray, ^r that your love may abound yet more and more in knowledge and *in* all ^s judgment ;

10 That ^t ye may ^u approve things that ^v are

A. M. cir. 4066.
A. D. cir. 62.
A. U. C. 814.
An. Imp. Ne-
ronis Cæs.
Aug. 9.

---

^c Romans i. 8, 9 ; 1 Cor. i. 4 ; Eph. i. 15, 16 ; Col. i. 3 ; 1 Thess. i. 2 ; 2 Thess. i. 3.——^d Or, *mention.*——^e Rom. xii. 13 ; xv. 26 ; 2 Cor. viii. 1 ; chap. iv. 14, 15.——^f John vi. 29 ; 1 Thess. i. 3.——^g Or, *will finish it.*——^h Verse 10.——ⁱ Or, *ye have me in your heart.*——^k 2 Cor. iii. 2 ; vii. 3.

^l Eph. iii. 1 ; vi. 20 ; Col. iv. 3, 18 ; 2 Tim. i. 8.——^m Ver. 17. ⁿ Chap. iv. 14.——^o Or, *partakers with me of grace.*——^p Rom. i. 9 ; ix. 1 ; Gal. i. 20 ; 1 Thess. ii. 5.——^q Chap. ii. 26 ; iv. 1. ^r 1 Thess. iii. 12 ; Philem. 6.——^s Or, *sense.*——^t Rom. ii. 18 ; xii. 2 ; Eph. v. 10.——^u Or, *try.*——^v Or, *differ.*

---

an apostle ; the reason of which appears to be, that in none of these places was his apostolical authority called in question.

Bishops and deacons] Επισκοποις· The *overseers* of the Church of God, and those who ministered to the poor, and preached occasionally. There has been a great deal of paper wasted on the inquiry, " Who is meant by *bishops* here, as no place could have more than one bishop ?" To which it has been answered : " Philippi was a metropolitan see, and might have several bishops." This is the extravagance of trifling. I believe no such officer is meant as we now term *bishop.*

Verse 2. *Grace* be *unto you*] See on Rom. i. 7.

Verse 3. *Upon every remembrance*] As often as you recur to my mind, so often do I thank God for the great work wrought among you. Some think that the words should be translated, *for all your kind remembrance ;* referring to their kind attention to the apostle, in supplying his wants, &c.

Verse 4. *Always in every prayer*] I pray often for you, and have great pleasure in doing it, seeing what God has already wrought among you.

Verse 5. *For your fellowship in the Gospel*] If we consider κοινωνια as implying spiritual *fellowship* or *communion,* then it signifies, not only their attention to the Gospel, their readiness to continue it, and perseverance in it, but also their *unity* and affection among themselves. Some understand the word as expressing their *liberality* to the apostle, and to the Gospel in general ; for the term may not only be applied to communion among themselves, but to *communications* to others. This sense, though followed by *Chrysostom* and *Theophylact,* does not appear to be the best ; though we know it to be a fact that they were liberal in supplying the apostle's necessities, and, no doubt, in ministering to the support of others.

Verse 6. *Being confident*] There shall be nothing lacking on God's part to support you ; and to make you wise, holy and happy ; and bring you at last to his kingdom and glory.

Verse 7. *It is meet for me to think this*] Εστι δικαιον· It is *just* that I should think so, because I have you in my heart—you live in my warmest love and most affectionate remembrance.

Inasmuch as both in my bonds] Because you have set your hearts upon me in my bonds, sending Epaphroditus to minister to me in my necessities, chap. ii. 25, and contributing of your own substance to me, chap. iv. 14, sending once and again to me while I was in bonds for the defence of the faith, ver. 15, 16 ; those things which being *a sweet savour, a sacrifice well pleasing and acceptable to God,* ver. 18, confirm my hope concerning you ; especially when I find you yet standing firm under the like afflictions, *having the same conflict which ye saw in me,* when I was among you, Acts xvi. 12, &c., and *now hear to be in me,* chap. i. 30. *Whitby.*

Verse 8. *For God is my record*] I call God to witness that I have the strongest affection for you, and that I love you with that same kind of tender concern with which Christ loved the world when he gave himself for it ; for I am even ready *to be offered on the sacrifice and service of your faith,* chap. ii. 17.

Verse 9. *This I pray*] This is the substance of all my prayers for you, *that your love* to God, to one another, and to all mankind, *may abound yet more and more,* ετι μαλλον και μαλλον περισσευη, that it may be like a river, perpetually fed with rain and fresh streams so that it continues to swell and increase till it fills all its banks, and floods the adjacent plains.

In knowledge] Of God's nature, perfections, your own duty and interest, his work upon your souls, and his great designs in the Gospel.

And in all judgment] Και παση αισθησει· In all *spiritual* or *moral feeling ;* that you may at once have the clearest perception and the fullest enjoyment of those things which concern your salvation ; that ye may not only know but *feel* that you are of God, by the Spirit which he has given you ; and that your feeling may become more exercised in Divine things, so that it may be increasingly *sensible* and *refined.*

Verse 10. *That ye may approve things that are excellent*] Εις το δοκιμαζειν υμας τα διαφεροντα· *To the end that ye may put to proof the things that differ,* or the things that are *more profitable.* By the pure and abundant love which they received from God they would be able to *try* whatever *differed* from the

2

A. M. cir. 4066.
A. D. cir. 62.
A. U. C. 814.
An. Imp. Ne-
ronis Cæs.
Aug. 9.
excellent; ᵂ that ye may be sincere and without offence ˣ till the day of Christ;

11 Being filled with the fruits of righteousness, ʸ which are by Jesus Christ, ᶻ unto the glory and praise of God.

12 But I would ye should understand, brethren, that the things *which happened* unto me have fallen out rather unto the furtherance of the Gospel;

13 So that my bonds ᵃ in Christ are manifest ᵇ in all ᶜ the palace, and ᵈ in all other *places;*

A. M. cir. 4066.
A. D. cir. 62.
A. U. C. 814.
An. Imp. Ne-
ronis Cæs.
Aug. 9.

14 And many of the brethren in the Lord, waxing confident by my bonds, are much more bold to speak the word without fear.

15 Some indeed preach Christ even of envy and ᵉ strife, and some also of good will:

ᵂ Acts xxiv. 16; 1 Thess. iii. 13; v. 23.——ˣ 1 Cor. i. 8.
ʸ John xv. 4, 5; Eph. ii. 10; Col. i. 6.

ᶻ John xv. 8; Eph. i. 12, 14.——ᵃ Or, *for Christ.*——ᵇ Chap. iv. 22.
ᶜ Or, *Cæsar's court.*——ᵈ Or, *to all others.*——ᵉ Chap. ii. 3.

---

teaching they had received, and from the *experience* they had in spiritual things.

That ye may be sincere] Ἵνα ἦτε ειλικρινεις. The word ειλικρινεια, which we translate *sincerity*, is compounded of ειλη, the *splendour of the sun*, and κρινω, I *judge;* a thing which may be examined in the clearest and strongest light, without the possibility of detecting a single flaw or imperfection. " A metaphor," says Mr. *Leigh*, " taken from the usual practice of chapmen, in the view and choice of their wares, that bring them forth into the light and hold up the cloth against the sun, to see if they can espy any default in them. *Pure* as the *sun.*" Be so purified and refined in your souls, by the indwelling Spirit, that even the *light* of God shining into your hearts, shall not be able to discover a fault that the *love* of God has not purged away.

Our word *sincerity* is from the Latin *sinceritas*, which is compounded of *sine*, without, and *cera*, wax, and is a metaphor taken from clarified honey; for the *mel sincerum*, pure or clarified honey, is that which is *sine cera*, without wax, no part of the *comb* being left in it. *Sincerity*, taken in its full meaning, is a word of the most extensive import; and, when applied in reference to the state of the soul, is as strong as the word *perfection* itself. The soul that is sincere is the soul that is *without sin*.

Without offence] Απροσκοποι· Neither offending God nor your neighbour; neither being stumbled yourselves, nor the cause of stumbling to others.

Till the day of Christ] Till he comes to judge the world, or, till the day in which you are called into the eternal world. According to this prayer, a man, under the power and influence of the grace of God, may so love as never to offend his Maker, to the latest period of his life. Those who deny this, must believe that the Spirit of God either cannot or will not do it; or, that the blood of Christ cannot cleanse from all unrighteousness. And this would be not only *antiscriptural*, but also *blasphemous*.

Verse 11. *Being filled with the fruits of righteousness*] By *righteousness* we may understand, here, the whole work of the Spirit of God, in the soul of a believer; and by the *fruits* of righteousness, all holy *tempers*, holy *words*, and right *actions*. And with these they are to be *filled*, πεπληρωμενοι, filled up, filled full; the whole soul and life occupied with them, ever doing something by which glory is brought to God, or good done to man.

By Jesus Christ] That is, according to his *doctrine*, through the power of his *grace*, and by the agency of his *Spirit*.

Unto the glory and praise of God.] God being honoured when the work of his grace thus appears to men in the fruits of righteousness; and God is praised by all the faithful when his work thus appears. Every genuine follower of God has his glory in view by all that he does, says, or intends. He loves to glorify God, and he glorifies him by showing forth in his conversion the glorious working of the glorious power of the Lord.

Verse 12. *That the things* which happened *unto me*] St. Paul was at this time a prisoner at Rome, and it appears probable that he had already been called to make a defence for himself, and to vindicate the doctrines of the Gospel; and this he had been enabled to do in such a manner that the honour of the Gospel had been greatly promoted by it. As the Philippians loved him greatly, he felt it right to give them this information relative to his state, and how God had turned his bonds to the advantage of that cause on account of which he was bound.

Verse 13. *My bonds—are manifest in all the palace*] In consequence of the public *defence* which he was obliged to make, his doctrines must be fully known in the court, and throughout the whole city, as on his trial he would necessarily explain the whole. The *prætorium*, πραιτωριον, which we here translate *palace*, signifies the court where causes were heard and judged by the *prætor* or civil magistrate; it sometimes signifies the *general's tent*, and at others, the *emperor's palace*. It is supposed that it is used in this latter sense here. There were, no doubt, persons belonging to the emperor's household who would bring the news of so remarkable a case to the palace; for we find that there were *Christians* even in Cæsar's household; chap. iv. 22.

Verse 14. *Waxing confident*] Finding the effect produced by the public defence which the apostle made, they were greatly encouraged, and the more boldly and openly proclaimed the doctrine of Christ crucified.

The word] The doctrine of Christ; several excellent MSS. and *versions* add, some Θεου, others Κυριου, the *word of God*, or *the word of the Lord*. This is a respectable reading, and is probably genuine.

Verse 15. *Some—preach Christ even of envy and strife*] These must have been the Judaizing teachers,

A. M. cir. 4066.
A. D. cir. 62.
A. U. C. 814.
An. Imp. Ne-
ronis Cæs.
Aug. 9.

16 The one preach Christ of contention, not sincerely, supposing to add affliction to my bonds :

17 But the other of love, knowing that I am set for [f] the defence of the Gospel.

18 What then ? notwithstanding, every way, whether in pretence, or in truth, Christ is preached ; and I therein do rejoice, yea, and will rejoice.

19 For I know that this shall turn to my salvation [g] through your prayer, and the

supply of [h] the Spirit of Jesus Christ,

A. M. cir. 4066.
A. D. cir. 62.
A. U. C. 814.
An. Imp. Ne-
ronis Cæs.
Aug. 9.

20 According to my [i] earnest expectation and *my* hope, that [k] in nothing I shall be ashamed ; but *that* [l] with all boldness, as always, *so* now also, Christ shall be magnified in my body, whether *it be* by life or by death.

21 For to me to live *is* Christ, and to die *is* gain.

22 But if I live in the flesh, this *is* the fruit of my labour : yet what I shall choose I wot not.

---

[f] Ver. 7.——[g] 2 Cor. i. 11.——[h] Rom. viii. 9.

[i] Rom. viii. 19.——[k] Rom. v. 5.——[l] Eph. vi. 19, 20.

---

who insisted on the necessity of connecting the Mosaic rites with the Christian institutions ; and, probably, denounced Paul to the Jews dwelling at Rome as not only an enemy to the law and the prophets, but also as a very imperfect Christian, because he declared strongly against the doctrine of circumcision, &c. ; and no doubt endeavoured to prejudice him with the heathen Romans.

The word *preach* is not to be taken here as implying that the different persons mentioned were what we call *preachers of the Gospel :* all that we can understand from St. Paul's use of the word is, that they *proclaimed* Christ as the promised *Messiah,* espoused the Christian cause, and contended, whether in public or private, that this Jesus was the Christ ; but nothing of this kind appears to have been intended in reference to the *conversion of sinners.*

Some also of good will.] Some, through mere benevolence to the apostle, both espoused his doctrine and vindicated his cause.

Verse 16. *Preach Christ of contention*] The Judaizing teachers, they also preach Christ ; they acknowledge that Jesus is the Christ or promised *Messiah,* and preach him as such.

Not sincerely] Ουχ αγνως· *Not chastely,* garbling the Gospel ; not speaking the whole truth, but just what served their purpose ; and at the same time they denounced the apostle as an enemy to the Divine institutions, because he spoke against circumcision.

Verse 17. *The other of love*] Through a sincere desire, not only to make known the way of salvation to the people, but also to vindicate and help the apostle, because they considered him as appointed by God to preach and defend the Gospel. The 16th and 17th verses are *transposed* by ABDEFG, and several others ; the *Syriac, Arabic* of Erpen, *Coptic, Sahidic, Æthiopic, Armenian, Vulgate, Itala,* and several of the *fathers.* On this evidence Griesbach transposed them in his edition.

Verse 18. *What then ?*] It is a matter of little importance to me *how* Christ is preached, provided he be preached. I rejoice that any thing is known of him ; and am truly glad that the Gospel is even made partially known, for this will lead to farther inquiries, and in the end be of service to the truth.

Verse 19. *This shall turn to my salvation*] That is : It will be the means of my *temporal safety ;* of

my *deliverance ;* for so the word σωτηρια is here to be understood. The Jews had denounced the apostle as an enemy to Cæsar ; but he knew that, when the nature of the Gospel should be fully known, the Romans would see that *he* could be no enemy to Cæsar who proclaimed a prince whose kingdom was not of this world ; and who had taught, in the most unequivocal manner, that all Christians were to give tribute to whom tribute was due, and while they feared God to honour also the king, though that king was *Nero.*

Through your prayer] Knowing them to be genuine followers of Christ, he was satisfied that their prayers would be very available in his behalf ; and under God he places much dependence upon them.

The supply of the Spirit of Jesus Christ] The word επιχορηγια, which we translate *supply,* signifies also *furnishing whatever is necessary.* The Spirit of God he expected to help all his infirmities, and to furnish him with all the wisdom, prudence, strength of reason, and argument, which might be necessary for him in the different trials he had to pass through with his persecutors, and the civil powers, at whose judgment-seat he stood.

Verse 20. *Earnest expectation*] He had the most confident expectation that God would stand by him, so that he should be enabled, with the *utmost liberty of speech,* εν παση παρρησια, to testify the Gospel of the grace of God ; and, should he have the liberty of doing so, he was utterly regardless what the issue might be relative to himself. Whether life or death, was to him perfectly equal, and perfectly indifferent, providing Christ were magnified—his person, nature, doctrine, &c., shown to be, what they really are, most noble, most excellent, most necessary, and most glorious.

Verse 21. *For to me to live* is *Christ*] Whether I live or die, Christ is gain to me. While I live I am Christ's property and servant, and Christ is my portion ; if I die—if I be called to witness the truth at the expense of my life, this will be gain ; I shall be saved from the remaining troubles and difficulties in life, and be put immediately in possession of my heavenly inheritance. As, therefore, it respects myself, it is a matter of perfect indifference to me whether I be taken off by a violent death, or whether I be permitted to continue here longer ; in either case I can lose nothing.

Verse 22. *But if I live in the flesh*] Should I be

A. M. cir. 4066.
A. D. cir. 62.
A. U. C. 814.
An. Imp. Ne-
ronis Cæs.
Aug. 9.

23 For ^m I am in a strait betwixt two, having a desire to ⁿ depart, and to be with Christ; which is far better:

24 Nevertheless, to abide in the flesh *is* more needful for you.

25 And ^o having this confidence, I know that I shall abide and continue with you all, for your furtherance and joy of faith;

26 That ^p your rejoicing may be more abundant in Jesus Christ for me, by my coming to you again.

27 Only ^q let your conversation be as it becometh the Gospel of Christ; that, whether I come and see you, or else be absent, I may hear of your affairs, ^r that ye stand fast in one spirit, ^s with one mind ^t striving together for the faith of the Gospel;

28 And in nothing terrified by your adversaries: ^u which is to them an evident token of perdition, ^v but to you of salvation, and that of God.

A. M. cir. 4066.
A. D. cir. 62.
A. U. C. 814.
An. Imp. Ne-
ronis Cæs.
Aug. 9.

---

^m 2 Cor. v. 8.——ⁿ 2 Tim. iv. 6.——^o Chap. ii. 24.——^p 2 Cor. i. 14; v. 12.——^q Eph. iv. 1; Col. i. 10; 1 Thess. ii. 12; iv. 1.

^r Chap. iv. 1.——^s 1 Cor. i. 10;——^t Jude 3.——^u 2 Thess. i. 5 ^v Rom. viii. 17; 2 Tim. ii. 11.

---

spared longer, I shall labour for Christ as I have done; and *this is the fruit of my labour*, that Christ shall be magnified by my longer life, ver. 20.

Yet what I shall choose I wot not.] Had I the two conditions left to my own choice, whether to die now and go to glory, or whether to live longer in persecutions and affliction, (glorifying Christ by spreading the Gospel,) I could not tell which to prefer.

Verse 23. *For I am in a strait betwixt two*] Viz. the dying now, and being immediately with God; or living longer to preach and spread the Gospel, and thus glorify Christ among men.

Having a desire to depart, and to be with Christ] Τὴν ἐπιθυμίαν ἔχων εἰς τὸ ἀναλῦσαι. It appears to be a metaphor taken from the commander of a vessel, in a foreign port, who feels a strong desire ἀναλῦσαι, to set sail, and get to his own country and family; but this desire is counterbalanced by a conviction that the general interests of the voyage may be best answered by his longer stay in the port where his vessel now rides; for he is not in dock, he is not aground, but rides at anchor in the port, and may any hour *weigh* and be gone. Such was the condition of the apostle: he was not at *home*, but although he was abroad it was on his employer's business; he wishes to return, and is cleared out and ready to set sail, but he has not received his last orders from his owner, and whatever desire he may feel to be at *home* he will faithfully wait till his final orders arrive.

Which is far better] Πολλῷ—μᾶλλον κρεῖσσον· *Multo magis melior*, VULGATE; *much more better.* The reader will at once see that the words are very emphatic.

Verse 24. *To abide in the flesh*] It would certainly be gain to *myself* to die, but it will be a gain to *you* if I live. If I die I shall go immediately to glory; if I live I shall continue to minister to you, and strengthen you in the faith.

Verse 25. *Having this confidence, I know that I shall abide*] Convinced that it is necessary that I should live longer, for the spreading and defence of the Gospel, I am persuaded that I shall now be liberated. This was in fact the case, for, after having been two years in bonds at Rome, he was released.

For your furtherance] In the way of righteousness.

And joy of faith] And happiness in that way.

The farther a man proceeds in the way of truth, the stronger his faith will be; and the stronger his faith, the greater his *joy* or *happiness.*

Verse 26. *That your rejoicing may be more abundant*] Men rejoice more in recovering a thing that was lost, than they do in a continual possession of what is of much greater value.

Verse 27. *Let your conversation be as it becometh the Gospel*] The apostle considers the Church at Philippi as a *free* or *imperial city*, which possesses great honours, dignities, and privileges; and he exhorts them to act, αξιως, *worthy of* or *suitably to* those honours and privileges. This is the idea that is expressed by the word πολιτευεσθε, act according to the nature of your political situation, the citizenship and privileges which you possess in consequence of your being free inhabitants of Christ's imperial city, the Church. The apostle resumes the same metaphor, chap. iii. 20: ἡμῶν—το πολιτευμα εν ουρανοις ὑπαρχει· *For our citizenship is in heaven;* but in this last verse he puts *heaven* in the place of the *Church*, and this is all right; for he, who is not a member of the Church of Christ on earth, can have no right to the kingdom of heaven, and he who does not walk *worthy* of the Gospel of Christ cannot be counted worthy to enter through the gates into the city of the eternal King.

Whether I come and see you] Leaving the matter still in doubt as to them, whether he should again visit them.

In one spirit] Being all of *one mind* under the influence of the Holy Ghost.

Striving together] Συναθλουντες· *Wrestling together*, not in contention with each other, but in union against the enemies of the *Gospel faith*—the doctrine of Christ crucified, and freedom from all Mosaic rites and ceremonies, as well as from sin and perdition, through his passion and sacrifice.

Verse 28. *In nothing terrified by your adversaries*] So it appears that the Church at Philippi was then under persecution.

Which is to them] Ἥτις αυτοις εστιν. Some very judicious critics consider ἥτις as referring to πιστις, the faith of the Gospel, which they, the heathen, considered to be a token of perdition to all them who embraced it; but, as the apostle says, it was to them the Philippians, on the contrary, the most evident

2

A. M. cir. 4066.
A. D. cir. 62.
A. U. C. 814.
An. Imp. Ne-
ronis Cæs.
Aug. 9.

29 For unto you ^w it is given in the behalf of Christ, ^x not only to believe on him, but also to suffer for his sake;

30 ^y Having the same conflict ^z which ye saw in me, *and* now hear *to be* in me.

A. M. cir. 4066.
A. D. cir. 62.
A. U. C. 814.
An. Imp. Ne-
ronis Cæs.
Aug. 9.

---

^w Acts v. 41; Rom. v. 3.——^x Eph. ii. 8.——^y Col. ii. 1

^z Acts xvi. 19, &c.; 1 Thess. ii. 2.

---

token of salvation; for, having embraced the faith of our Lord Jesus Christ, they were incontestably in the way to eternal blessedness.

Verse 29. *Unto you it is given in the behalf of Christ*] Ὑμιν εχαρισθη· *To you it is graciously given;* it is no small *privilege* that God has so far honoured you as to permit you to suffer on Christ's account. It is only his most faithful servants that he thus honours. Be not therefore terrified by your enemies; they can do nothing to you which God will not turn to your eternal advantage. We learn from this that it is as great a privilege to *suffer* for Christ as to *believe* on him; and the *former* in certain cases (as far as the *latter* in all cases) becomes the means of salvation to them who are thus exercised.

Verse 30. *Having the same conflict*] When Paul preached the Gospel at Philippi he was grievously persecuted, as we learn from Acts xvi. 19—40, being stripped, scourged, thrown into prison, even into the dungeon, and his feet made fast in the stocks. This

was the *conflict* they had seen in him; and now *they heard* that he had been sent prisoner to Rome as an evil doer, and that he was at present in bonds, and shortly to be tried for his life before the Roman emperor, to whom he had been obliged to appeal.

1. It was no small encouragement to these persons, (1.) That whatever sufferings they met with they were supported under them. (2.) That they suffered in the same cause in which their illustrious apostle was suffering. (3.) That they suffered, not because they had done any evil, or could be accused of any, but because they believed in the Son of God, who died for them and for all mankind. (4.) That all these sufferings were sanctified to their eternal good.

2. And God is able to make the same grace abound towards *us* in like circumstances; it is for this purpose that such consolatory portions are left on record. He who is persecuted or afflicted for Christ's sake, is most eminently honoured by his Creator.

CHAPTER II.

The apostle beseeches them by various considerations, to live in unity and in the spirit of the Gospel, loving each other; and each to prefer his brother to himself, 1—4. He exhorts them to be like-minded with Christ, who, though in the form of God, and equal with God, made himself of no reputation, and humbled himself to the death of the cross for the salvation of man; in consequence of which he was highly exalted, and had a name above every name; to whose authority every knee should bow, and whose glory every tongue should acknowledge, 5—11. They are exhorted to work out their own salvation through his power who works in them, that they may be blameless, and that the apostle's labour may not be in vain, 12—16. He expresses his readiness to offer his life for the Gospel, 17, 18. Intends to send Timothy to them, of whom he gives a very high character; yet hopes to see them himself shortly, 19—24. In the meantime sends Epaphroditus, who had been near death, and whom he begs them to receive with especial tenderness, 25—30.

A. M. cir. 4066.
A. D. cir. 62.
A. U. C. 814.
An. Imp. Ne-
ronis Cæs.
Aug. 9.

IF *there be* therefore any consolation in Christ, if any comfort of love, ^a if any fellowship of the Spirit, if any ^b bowels and mercies,

2 ^c Fulfil ye my joy, ^d that ye be like-minded, having the same love, *being* of one accord, of one mind.

A. M. cir. 4066.
A. D. cir. 62.
A. U. C. 814.
An. Imp. Ne-
ronis Cæs.
Aug. 9.

---

^a 2 Corinthians xiii. 14.——^b Colossians iii. 12.——^c John iii. 29.

^d Rom. xii. 16; xv. 5; 1 Cor. i. 10; 2 Cor. xiii. 11; chap. i 27, iii. 16; iv. 2; 1 Pet. iii. 8.

NOTES ON CHAP. II.

Verse 1. *If there be therefore any consolation*] The ει, *if*, does not express any *doubt* here, but on the contrary is to be considered as a *strong affirmation;* as *there is* consolation in Christ, as there is comfort of love, &c.

The word παρακλησις, translated here *consolation*, is in other places rendered *exhortation*, and is by several critics understood so here; as if he had said: If *exhorting* you in the name of Christ have any influence with you, &c. It is extremely difficult to give the force of these expressions; they contain a torrent of most affecting eloquence, the apostle pouring out

his whole heart to a people whom with all his heart he loved, and who were worthy of the love even of an apostle.

If any comfort of love] If the followers of Christ, by giving proofs of their ardent love to each other in cases of distress, alleviate the sufferings of the persecuted;

If any fellowship of the Spirit] If there be an intimate relation established among all Christians, by their being made mutual partakers of the Holy Ghost;

If any bowels and mercies] If you, as persons whom I have brought to God at the hazard of my life, feel sympathetic tenderness for me now, in a farther state of suffering;

    2

A. M. cir. 4066.
A. D. cir. 62.
A. U. C. 814.
An. Imp. Ne-
ronis Cæs.
Aug. 9.

3 ᵉ *Let* nothing *be done* through strife or vain glory; but ᶠ in lowliness of mind let each esteem other better than themselves.

4 ᵍ Look not every man on his own things, but every man also on the things of others.

A. M. cir. 4066.
A. D. cir. 62.
A. U. C. 814.
An. Imp. Ne-
ronis Cæs.
Aug. 9.

5 ʰ Let this mind be in you, which was also in Christ Jesus;

6 Who, ⁱ being in the form of God, ᵏ thought it not robbery to be equal with God;

ᵉ Gal. v. 26; ch. i. 15, 16; James iii. 14.——ᶠ Rom. xii. 10; Eph. v. 21; 1 Pet. v. 5.——ᵍ 1 Cor. x. 24, 33; xiii. 5.——ʰ Matt. xi. 29;

John xiii. 15; 1 Pet. ii. 21; 1 John ii. 6.——ⁱ John i. 1, 2; xvii. 5; 2 Cor. iv. 4; Col. i. 15; Heb. i. 3.——ᵏ John v. 18; x. 33.

Verse 2. *Fulfil ye my joy*] Ye ought to complete my joy, who have suffered so much to bring you into the possession of these blessings, by being *like-minded* with myself, *having the same love* to God, his cause, and me, as I have to him, his cause, and you.

Being of one accord] Being perfectly agreed in labouring to promote the honour of your Master; and *of one mind*, being constantly *intent* upon this great subject; keeping your eye fixed upon it in all you say, do, or intend.

Verse 3. *Let nothing be done through strife*] Never be opposed to each other; never act from *separate interests;* ye are all *brethren*, and of one *body;* therefore let every member feel and labour for the welfare of the whole. And, in the exercise of your different functions, and in the use of your various gifts, do nothing so as to promote your own reputation, separately considered from the comfort, honour, and advantage of all.

But in lowliness of mind] Have always an humbling view of yourselves, and this will lead you to prefer others to yourselves; for, as you know your own secret defects, charity will lead you to suppose that your brethren are more holy, and more devoted to God than you are; and *they* will think the same of *you*, their secret defects also being known only to themselves.

Verse 4. *Look not every man on his own things*] Do nothing through self-interest in the things of God; nor arrogate to yourselves *gifts*, *graces*, and *fruits*, which belong to *others;* ye are all called to promote God's glory and the salvation of men. Labour for this, and every one shall receive the honour that comes from God; and let each rejoice to see another, whom God may be pleased to use in a *special* way, acquiring much reputation by the successful application of his talents to the great work.

Verse 5. *Let this mind be in you, which was also in Christ Jesus*] Christ laboured to promote no separate interest; as man he studied to promote the glory of God, and the welfare and salvation of the human race. See then that ye have the same *disposition* that was in Jesus: he was ever *humble, loving, patient,* and *laborious;* his meat and drink was to do the will of his Father, and to finish his work.

Verse 6. *Who, being in the form of God*] This verse has been the subject of much criticism, and some controversy. Dr. *Whitby* has, perhaps, on the whole, spoken best on this point; but his arguments are too diffuse to be admitted here. Dr. *Macknight* has abridged the words of Dr. *Whitby*, and properly observes that, " As the apostle is speaking of what Christ *was before he took the form of a servant*, the *form of*

God, of which he divested himself when he became man, cannot be any thing which he *possessed* during his *incarnation* or in his divested state; consequently neither the opinion of *Erasmus*, that the *form of God* consisted in those *sparks of divinity* by which Christ, during his incarnation, manifested his Godhead, nor the opinion of the *Socinians*, that it consisted in the *power of working miracles*, is well founded; for Christ did not divest himself either of one or the other, but possessed both all the time of his public ministry. In like manner, the opinion of those who, by the *form of God* understand the *Divine nature* and the government of the world, cannot be admitted; since Christ, when he became *man*, could not divest himself of the nature of God; and with respect to the government of the world, we are led, by what the apostle tells, Heb. i. 3, to believe that he did not part with even that; but, in his divested state, still continued *to uphold all things by the word of his power*. By the *form of God* we are rather to understand that *visible, glorious light* in which the Deity is said to dwell, 1 Tim. vi. 16, and by which he manifested himself to the patriarchs of old, Deut. v. 22, 24; which was commonly accompanied with a *numerous retinue of angels*, Psa. lxviii. 17, and which in Scripture is called The *Similitude*, Num. xii. 8; The *Face*, Psa. xxxi. 16; The *Presence*, Exod. xxxiii. 15; and The *Shape* of God, John v. 37. This interpretation is supported by the term μορφη, *form*, here used, which signifies a person's external *shape* or *appearance*, and not his *nature* or *essence*. Thus we are told, Mark xvi. 12, that Jesus appeared to his disciples in another μορφη, *shape*, or *form*. And, Matt. xvii. 2, μετεμορφωθη, *he was transfigured before them*—his outward *appearance* or *form* was changed. Farther, this interpretation agrees with the fact: the *form of God*, that is, his *visible glory*, and the *attendance of angels*, as above described, the Son of God enjoyed with his Father before the world was, John xvii. 5; and on that as on other accounts he is the *brightness of the Father's glory*, Heb. i. 3. Of this he divested himself when he became flesh; but, having resumed it after his ascension, he will come with it in the human nature to judge the world; so he told his disciples, Matt. xvi. 27: *The Son of man will come in the glory of his Father, with his angels, &c.* Lastly, this sense of μορφη Θεου is confirmed by the meaning of μορφη δουλου, ver. 7; which evidently denotes the *appearance* and *behaviour* of a *servant* or *bondman*, and not the *essence* of such a person." See *Whitby* and *Macknight*.

Thought it not robbery to be equal with God] If we take these words as they stand here, their meaning is, that, as he was from the *beginning* in the same in-

A. M. cir. 4066.
A. D. cir. 62.
A. U. C. 814.
An. Imp. Ne-
ronis Cæs.
Aug. 9.

7 [1] But made himself of no reputation, and took upon him the form [m] of a servant, and [n] was made in the [o] likeness of men :

8 And being found in fashion as a man, he humbled himself, and [p] became obedient unto

death, even the death of the cross.

A. M. cir. 4066.
A. D. cir. 62.
A. U. C. 814.
An. Imp. Ne-
ronis Cæs.
Aug. 9.

9 Wherefore God also [q] hath highly exalted him, and [r] given him a name which is above every name :

10 [s] That at the name of Jesus every knee

---

[1] Psa. xxii. 6; Isa. liii. 3; Dan. ix. 26; Mark ix. 12; Rom. xv. 3.——[m] Isa. xlii. 1; xlix. 3, 6; lii. 13; liii. 11; Ezek. xxxiv. 23, 24; Zech. iii. 8; Matt. xx. 28; Luke xxii. 27.——[n] John i. 14; Rom. i. 3; viii. 3; Gal. iv. 4; Heb. ii. 14, 17.

[o] Or, *habit.*——[p] Matt. xxvi. 39, 42; John x. 18; Heb. v. 8; xii. 2.——[q] John xvii. 1, 2, 5; Acts ii. 33; Heb. ii. 9.——[r] Eph. i. 20, 21; Heb. i. 4.——[s] Isa. xlv. 23; Matt. xxviii. 18; Rom. xiv. 11; Rev. v. 13.

---

finite glory with the Father, to appear in *time*—during his humiliation, as God and equal with the Father, was no encroachment on the Divine prerogative; for, as he had an *equality* of *nature*, he had an *equality* of *rights.*

But the word ἁρπαγμον, which we translate *robbery,* has been supposed to imply *a thing eagerly to be seized, coveted, or desired ;* and on this interpretation the passage has been translated : *Who, being in the form of God, did not think it a matter to be earnestly desired to appear equal to God ; but made himself of no reputation,* &c. However the word be translated, it does not affect the eternal Deity of our Lord. Though he was from eternity in the form of God—possessed of the same glory, yet he thought it right to *veil* this glory, and not to *appear with it* among the children of men; and therefore he was made in the *likeness of men,* and took upon him the *form* or *appearance* of a *servant :* and, had he retained the appearance of this ineffable glory, it would, in many respects, have prevented him from accomplishing the work which God gave him to do ; and his *humiliation,* as necessary to the salvation of men, could not have been complete. On this account I prefer this sense of the word ἁρπαγμον before that given in our text, which does not agree so well with the other expressions in the context. In this sense the word is used by *Heliodorus,* in his *Æthiopics,* lib. vii. cap. 19, &c., which passage *Whitby* has produced, and on which he has given a considerable paraphrase. The reader who wishes to examine this subject more particularly, may have recourse to *Heliodorus* as above, or to the notes of Dr. *Whitby* on the passage.

Verse 7. *But made himself of no reputation*] Ἑαυτον εκενωσε· *He emptied himself*—did not appear in his glory, for he assumed the form of a servant, being made in the likeness of man. And his being made in the likeness of man, and assuming the form of a servant, was a *proof* that he had *emptied* himself—laid aside the effulgence of his glory.

Verse 8. *And being found in fashion as a man*] Και σχηματι ευρεθεις ως ανθρωπος. This clause should be joined to the preceding, and thus translated : *Being made in the likeness of man, and was found in fashion as a man.*

He humbled himself] Laid himself as low as possible : 1. In *emptying himself*—*laying aside the effulgence* of his *glory.* 2. In being *incarnate*—taking upon him the *human form.* 3. In becoming a *servant* —assuming the *lowest* innocent character, that of being the servant of all. 4. In condescending to *die,* to which he was not naturally liable, as having never

sinned, and therefore had a right in his human nature to immortality, without passing under the empire of death. 5. In condescending, not only to death, but to the *lowest* and most *ignominious kind of death,* the *death of the cross ;* the punishment of the meanest of slaves and worst of felons. What must sin have been in the sight of God, when it required such abasement in Jesus Christ to make an atonement for it, and *undo* its influence and malignity !

Verse 9. *Wherefore God also hath highly exalted him*] If by his *humiliation* he has merited pardon and final salvation for the whole world, is it to be wondered that the human body, in which this fulness of the Godhead dwelt, and in which the punishment due to our sins was borne upon the tree, should be exalted above all human and all created beings ? And this is the fact; for *he hath given him a name,* το ονομα, the *name, which is above every name :* το is prefixed to ονομα here by ABC, 17, *Origen, Dionysius Alexandrinus, Eusebius, Cyril,* and *Procopius.* This makes it much more emphatic. According to Eph. i. 20, 21, the man Christ Jesus *is exalted to the right hand of God, far above all principality, and power, and might, and dominion, and every name that is named, not only in this world, but also in that which is to come.* From which it appears that no creature of God is so far exalted and so glorious as the *man* Christ Jesus, *human nature* being in him dignified infinitely beyond the *angelic nature ;* and that this nature has an authority and pre-eminence which no being, either in heaven or earth, enjoys. In a word, as man was in the beginning at the head of all the creatures of God, Jesus Christ, by assuming human nature, suffering and dying in it, has raised it to its *pristine state.* And this is probably what is here meant by this high exaltation of Christ, and giving him a name which is above every name. But if we refer to any particular *epithet,* then the name JESUS or *Saviour* must be that which is intended ; as no being either in heaven or earth can possess this name as he who is the *Redeemer* of the world does, for he is the only *Saviour ;* none has or could *redeem* us to God but he ; and throughout eternity he will ever appear as the sole *Saviour* of the human race. Hence, before his birth, Gabriel stated that *his name should be called* Jesus ; giving for reason, *he shall* SAVE *his people from their sins.* The *qualifications* of the Saviour of the world were so extraordinary, the *redeeming acts* so stupendous, and the *result* of all so glorious both to God and man, that it is impossible to conceive a higher *name* or *title* than that of JESUS, or *Saviour of the world.*

Verse 10. *That at the name of Jesus every knee should bow*] That all human beings should consider

A. M. cir. 4066.
A. D. cir. 62.
A. U. C. 814.
An. Imp. Ne-
ronis Cæs.
Aug. 9.

should bow, of *things* in heaven, and *things* in earth, and *things* under the earth;

11 And ^t *that* every tongue should confess that Jesus Christ *is* Lord, to the glory of God the Father.

12 Wherefore, my beloved, ^u as ye have al-

ways obeyed, not as in my presence only, but now much more in my absence, work out your own salvation with ^v fear and trembling;

13 For ^w it is God which worketh in you both to will and to do of *his* good pleasure.

A. M. cir. 4066.
A. D. cir. 62.
A. U. C. 814.
An. Imp. Ne-
ronis Cæs.
Aug. 9.

---

^t John xiii. 13; Acts ii. 36; Rom. xiv. 9; 1 Cor. viii. 6; xii. 3.

^u Chap. i. 5.——^v Eph. vi. 5.——^w 2 Cor. iii. 5; Heb. xiii. 21.

---

themselves redeemed unto God by his blood, and look for an application of this redemption price; and that all who are saved from their sin should acknowledge him the author of their salvation. In a word, that παν επουρανιων, all the *spirits of just men made perfect,* now in a state of *blessedness;* και επιγειων, all human beings still in their state of *probation on earth;* και καταχθονιων, and all that are in the *shades below,* who have, through their own fault, died without having received his salvation; should acknowledge him.

Verse 11. And that every *tongue should confess*] That all those before mentioned should acknowledge that Jesus Christ is Lord, or *absolute governor,* and thus glorify God the Father, who has exalted this human nature to this state of ineffable glory, in virtue of its passion, death, resurrection, and the atonement which it has made, by which so many attributes of the Divine nature have become illustrated, the Divine law magnified and made honourable, and an eternal glory provided for man.

Others by *things in heaven* understand the *holy angels;* by *things on earth,* human beings generally; and by *things under the earth, fallen spirits* of every description. Perhaps the *three* expressions are designed to comprehend all beings of all kinds, all creatures; as it is usual with the Hebrews, and indeed with all ancient nations, to express, by things in heaven, things on earth, and things under the earth, all beings of all kinds; universal nature. See similar forms of speech, Exod. xx. 4; Deut. iv. 17, 18; Psa. xcvi. 11; and Ezek. xxxviii. 20. But *intelligent beings* seem to be those which are chiefly intended by the words of the apostle; for it appears that nothing less than absolute rule over *angels, men,* and *devils,* can be designed in these extraordinary words, and by *confessing him to be Lord* we may understand that worship which all intelligent creatures are called to pay to God manifested in the flesh; for all should *honour the Son even as they honour the Father.* And the worship thus offered is to the glory of God; so that far from being idolatrous, as some have rashly asserted, it is to the honour of the Divine Being. We may add, that the *tongue which does not confess* thus, is a tongue that dishonours the Almighty.

Verse 12. As ye have always obeyed] Continue to act on the same *principles* and from the same *motives;* having the *same disposition* which was in Christ; labouring so as to promote his glory.

Work out your own salvation] Go on, walking by the same rule, and minding the same thing, till your salvation be completed: till, filled with love to God and man, ye walk unblamably in all his testimonies, having your fruit unto holiness, and your end everlasting life.

With fear and trembling] Considering the *difficulty* of the *work,* and the *danger* of *miscarriage.* If you do not watch, pray and continually depend on God, your enemies will surprise you, and your light and life will become extinct; and then consider what an awful account you must give to Him whose Spirit ye have grieved, and of whose glory ye have come short.

Verse 13. For it is God which worketh in you] Every holy purpose, pious resolution, good word, and good work, must come from him; ye must be *workers together with him.* that ye receive not his grace in vain; *because he worketh in you,* therefore work with him, and work out your own salvation.

To will and to do] Το θελειν και το ενεργειν. The *power* to *will* and the *power* to *act* must necessarily come from God, who is the author both of the *soul* and *body,* and of all their powers and energies, but the *act* of *volition* and the *act* of *working* come from the *man.* God gives *power* to will, man wills through that power; God gives *power* to act, and *man* acts through that power. Without the *power* to *will,* man can *will nothing;* without the *power* to *work,* man can *do nothing.* God neither wills *for* man, nor *works* in man's *stead,* but he furnishes him with power to do both; he is therefore accountable to God for these powers.

Because God works in them the power to will and the power to do, therefore the apostle exhorts them *to work out their own salvation;* most manifestly showing that the *use* of the powers of *volition* and *action* belongs to *themselves.* They cannot do God's work, they cannot produce in themselves a power *to will and to do;* and God will not do their work, *he* will not work out *their* salvation *with fear and trembling.*

Though men have grievously puzzled themselves with questions relative to the *will* and *power* of the human being; yet no case can be plainer than that which the apostle lays down here: the *power* to *will* and *do* comes from GOD; the *use* of that power belongs to *man.* He that has not got this power can neither will nor work; he that has this power can do both. But it does not necessarily follow that he who has these powers will use them; the *possession* of the powers does not necessarily imply the *use* of those powers, because a man might have them, and not use or abuse them; therefore the apostle exhorts: *Work out your own salvation.*

This is a general exhortation, it may be applied to all men, for to all it is applicable, there not being a rational being on the face of the earth, who has not from God both *power* to *will* and *act* in the things which concern his salvation. Hence the *accountableness of man.*

Of his good pleasure.] Every good is freely given

A. M. cir. 4066.
A. D. cir. 62.
A. U. C. 814.
An. Imp. Ne-
ronis Cæs.
Aug. 9.

14 Do all things ˣ without mur- murings and ʸ disputings ;

15 That ye may be blameless, and ᶻ harmless, ᵃ the sons of God, without rebuke, ᵇ in the midst of ᶜ a crooked and perverse nation, among whom ᵈ ye ᵉ shine as lights in the world :

16 Holding forth the word of life ; that ᶠ I may rejoice in the day of Christ, that ᵍ I have not run in vain, neither laboured in vain.

17 Yea, and if ʰ I be ⁱ offered upon the sa-

crifice ᵏ and service of your faith, ˡ I joy, and rejoice with you all.

18 For the same cause also do ye joy, and rejoice with me.

19 ᵐ But I trust in the Lord Jesus to send ⁿ Timotheus shortly unto you, that I also may be of good comfort, when I know your state.

20 For I have no man ᵒ like-minded, ᵖ who will naturally care for your state.

21 For all ᑫ seek their own, not the things which are Jesus Christ's.

A. M. cir. 4066
A. D. cir. 62.
A. U. C. 814.
An. Imp. Ne-
ronis Cæs.
Aug. 9.

ˣ 1 Cor. x. 10 ; 1 Pet. iv. 9.——ʸ Rom. xiv. 1.——ᶻ Or, *sincere.*
ᵃ Matt. v. 45 ; Eph. v. 1.——ᵇ 1 Pet. ii. 12.——ᶜ Deut. xxxii.
5.——ᵈ Or, *shine ye.*——ᵉ Matt. v. 14, 16 ; Eph. v. 8.——ᶠ 2 Cor.
i. 14 ; 1 Thess. ii. 9.——ᵍ Gal. ii. 2 ; 1 Thess. iii. 5.

ʰ 2 Tim. iv. 6.——ⁱ Greek, *poured forth.*——ᵏ Romans xv. 16.
ˡ 2 Cor. vii. 4 ; Col. i. 24.——ᵐ Or, *moreover.*——ⁿ Rom. xvi. 21 ;
1 Thess. iii. 2.——ᵒ Psa. lv. 13.——ᵖ Or, *so dear unto me.*
ᑫ 1 Cor. x. 24, 33 ; xiii. 5 ; 2 Tim. iv. 10, 16.

---

of God ; no man *deserves* any thing from him ; and as it *pleaseth* him, so he deals out to men those *measures* of *mental* and *corporeal* energy which he sees to be necessary ; giving to some *more,* to others *less,* but to all what is sufficient for their salvation.

Verse 14. *Do all things without murmurings*] Γογγυσμων, και διαλογισμων· *Without grumblings and altercations.* Be *patient* in, and *contented* with, your work ; and see that ye *fall not out by the way.*

Verse 15. *That ye may be blameless*] In your-selves, and *harmless* to others.

The sons of God] Showing by your holy conduct that ye are partakers of the *Divine nature.*

Without rebuke] Persons against whom no charge of transgression can justly be laid.

A crooked and perverse] Probably referring to the *Jews,* who were the chief opponents and the most viru-lent enemies which the Christian Church had.

Among whom ye shine] Be like the *sun* and *moon* ; bless even the *perverse* and *disobedient* by your light and splendour. Let your light shine before men ; some will walk in that light, and by its shining God will be glorified. It is evident that the apostle, by φωστηρες εν κοσμω, *lights in the world,* refers to the *sun* and *moon* particularly, and perhaps to the *heavenly bodies* in general.

Verse 16. *Holding forth the word of life*] An al-lusion, some think, to those *towers* which were built at the entrance of harbours, on which *fires* were kept during the night to direct ships into the port. Genuine Christians, by their holy lives and conversation, are the means of *directing* others, not only how to escape those *dangers* to which they are exposed on the tem-pestuous ocean of human life, but also of leading them into the *haven* of *eternal safety* and *rest.*

That I have not run in vain] This appears to be a part of the same metaphor ; and alludes to the case of a *weather-beaten* mariner who has been *long tossed* on a tempestuous sea, in *hazy weather* and *dark nights,* who has been obliged to *run* on different *tacks,* and *labour* intensely to keep his ship from *foundering,* but is at last, by the assistance of the *luminous fire* on the top of the *tower,* directed safely into port. Live so to glorify God and do good to men, that it shall ap-pear that I have not run and laboured in vain for your salvation.

Verse 17. *Yea, and if I be offered upon the sacri-fice and service*] The metaphor appears to be still carried on. As it was customary for the weather-beaten mariner, when he had gained his port, to offer a sacrifice, θυσια, to God, of some particular animal which he had vowed while in his state of danger, and this was considered to be a *religious service,* λειτουργια· the apostle, pursuing the idea, states himself to be willing to become the *libation,* (for so much the word σπενδομαι imports,) that was to be *poured upon the sacrifice.* Parkhurst observes that the apostle com-pares the faith of the Philippians to the sacrificial victim, and *his own blood shed in martyrdom* to the *libation,* i. e. *the wine poured out* on occasion of the sacrifice. *Raphelius* observes that *Arrian* uses the phrase σπενδειν επι τη θυσια for *pouring out the liba-tion after the sacrifice.* The apostle *had* guided them safely into port ; their faith in the atoning death of Christ was their sacrifice ; and he was willing that his blood in martyrdom should be poured out as a libation on that sacrificial offering.

Verse 18. *For the same cause also do ye joy*] Should I be thus offered, as I shall rejoice in it, do ye also rejoice that I am counted worthy of this high honour.

Verse 19. *But I trust in the Lord Jesus*] He is governor and disposer of all events, being above all principality and power ; and I humbly confide in his power and goodness that I shall be a little longer spared to visit you again, ver. 24, and to be able to send Timothy shortly to you.

When I know your state.] By the correct informa-tion which I shall receive from Timothy.

Verse 20. *For I have no man like-minded*] None of all my fellow helpers in the Gospel have the same zeal and affectionate concern for your prosperity in every respect as he has. He is ισοψυχος· *of the same soul ;* a man after my own heart.

Verse 21. *For all seek their own*] This must relate to the persons who *preached Christ even of envy and strife,* chap. i. 15 ; these must be very careless whether souls were saved or not by such preaching ; and even those who preached the Gospel *out of good will* might not be fit for such an embassy as this, which required many sacrifices, and consequently much love and zeal to be able to make them.

A. M. cir. 4066.
A. D. cir. 62.
A. U. C. 814.
An. Imp. Neronis Cæs.
Aug. 9.

22 But ye know the proof of him, ˣ that, as a son with the father, he hath served with me in the Gospel.

23 Him therefore I hope to send presently, so soon as I shall see how it will go with me.

24 But ˢ I trust in the Lord that I also myself shall come shortly.

25 Yet I supposed it necessary to send to you ᵗ Epaphroditus, my brother, and companion in labour, and ᵘ fellow soldier, ᵛ but your messenger, and ʷ he that ministered to my wants.

26 ˣ For he longed after you all, and was full of heaviness, because that ye had heard that he had been sick.

A. M. cir. 4066.
A. D. cir. 62.
A. U. C. 814.
An. Imp. Neronis Cæs.
Aug. 9.

27 For indeed he was sick nigh unto death: but God had mercy on him; and not on him only, but on me also, lest I should have sorrow upon sorrow.

28 I sent him therefore the more carefully, that, when ye see him again, ye may rejoice, and that I may be the less sorrowful.

29 Receive him therefore in the Lord with all gladness; and ʸ hold ᶻ such in reputation:

30 Because for the work of Christ he was nigh unto death, not regarding his life, ᵃ to supply your lack of service toward me.

ʳ 1 Cor. iv. 17; 1 Tim. i. 2; 2 Tim. i. 2.——ˢ Chap. i. 25; Philem. 22.——ᵗ Chapter iv. 18.——ᵘ Philem. 2.——ᵛ 2 Corinthians viii. 23.

ʷ 2 Cor. xi. 9; chap. iv. 18.——ˣ Chap. i. 3.——ʸ Or, *honour such.*——ᶻ 1 Cor. xvi. 18; 1 Thess. v. 12; 1 Tim. v. 7.——ᵃ 1 Cor xvi. 17; chap. iv. 10.

Verse 22. *Ye know the proof of him, that, as a son with the father, he hath served with me*] The Philippians had *full proof* of the affectionate attachment of Timothy to Paul, for he had laboured with him there, as we learn from Acts xvi. 1–3, and xvii. 14; and we find from what is said here that Timothy was not a servant *to* the apostle, but that he had served *with* him. They both laboured together in the word and doctrine; for *apostles* and Christian *bishops,* in those times, laboured as hard as their *deacons.* There were no *sinecures;* every one was a *labourer,* every labourer had his *work,* and every *workman* had his *wages.*

Verse 23. *How it will go with me.*] The apostle was now in *captivity;* his *trial* appears to have been approaching, and of its *issue* he was doubtful; though he seems to have had a general persuasion that he should be spared, see ver. 19 and ver. 24.

Verse 25. *Epaphroditus, my brother, &c.*] Here is a very high character of this minister of Christ; he was, 1. A *brother*—one of the *Christian family;* a thorough convert to God, without which he could not have been a preacher of the Gospel. 2. He was a *companion in labour;* he laboured, and laboured in union with the apostle in this great work. 3. He was a *fellow soldier;* the work was a work of difficulty and danger, they were obliged to maintain a continual warfare, fighting against the world, the devil, and the flesh. 4. He was *their apostle*—a man whom God had honoured with apostolical gifts, apostolical graces, and apostolical fruits; and, 5. He was an *affectionate friend* to the apostle; knew his soul in adversity, acknowledged him in prison, and contributed to his comfort and support.

Verse 26. *Ye had heard that he had been sick.*] "In this passage," says Dr. Paley, "no intimation is given that the recovery of Epaphroditus was *miraculous,* it is plainly spoken of as a *natural event.* This instance, together with that in the Second Epistle to Timothy, *Trophimus have I left at Miletum sick,* affords a proof that the power of performing cures, and, by parity of reason, of working other miracles, was a power which only visited the apostles occasionally, and did not at all depend upon their own will. Paul undoubtedly would have healed Epaphroditus if he could; nor would he have left Trophimus at Miletum sick, had the power of working cures awaited his disposal. Had this epistle been a forgery, forgery on this occasion would not have spared a *miracle;* much less would it have introduced St. Paul professing the utmost anxiety for the safety of his friend, yet acknowledging himself unable to help him, which he does almost expressly in the case of Trophimus, *Him have I left sick;* and virtually in the passage before us, in which he felicitates himself on the recovery of Epaphroditus in terms which almost exclude the supposition of any supernatural means being used to effect it. This is a reverse which nothing but *truth* would have imposed." *Horæ Paulinæ,* page 234.

Verse 27. *Lest I should have sorrow upon sorrow.*] The sorrows of his *death,* added to the sorrow he endured on account of his *sickness;* or he may refer to his own state of *affliction,* being *imprisoned* and *maltreated.*

Verse 28. *The more carefully*] Σπουδαιοτερως· With the *more haste* or *despatch;* because, having suffered so much on account of his apprehended death, they could not be too soon comforted by seeing him alive and restored.

Verse 29. *Receive him therefore in the Lord*] For the Lord's sake receive him, and as the Lord's servant; *and hold such* zealous, disinterested, and holy preachers *in reputation*—honour those whom ye perceive God hath honoured.

Verse 30. *For the work of Christ*] Preaching the Gospel, and ministering to the distressed.

He was nigh unto death] Having laboured far beyond his strength.

Not regarding his life] Instead of παραβουλευσαμενος τῃ ψυχῃ, not regarding his life, παραβολευσαμενος, risking his life, is the reading of ABDEFG, and is received by Griesbach into the text. His frequent and intense preaching, and labouring to supply the apostle's wants, appear to have brought him nigh to the gates of death.

THE *humiliation* and *exaltation* of Christ are subjects which we cannot contemplate too frequently, and in which we cannot be too deeply instructed.

1. God destroys opposites by opposites : through *pride* and self-*confidence* man fell , and it required the *humiliation* of Christ to destroy that pride and self-*confidence*, and to raise him from his *fall.* There must be an indescribable malignity in sin, when it required the deepest abasement of the highest Being to remove and destroy it. The humiliation and passion of Christ were not accidental, they were absolutely necessary; and had they not been necessary, they had not taken place. Sinner, behold what it cost the Son of God to save *thee !* And wilt thou, after considering this, imagine that *sin* is a small thing ? Without the humiliation and sacrifice of Christ, even *thy soul* could not be saved. Slight not, therefore, the *mercies* of thy God, by underrating the *guilt* of thy transgressions and the malignity of thy sin !

2. As we cannot contemplate the humiliation and death of Christ without considering it a sufficient sacrifice, oblation, and atonement for sin, and for the sin of the whole world ; so we cannot contemplate his unlimited power and glory, in his state of exaltation, without being convinced that he is able to save them to the uttermost that come unto God through him. What can *withstand* the *merit* of his *blood ?* What can *resist* the *energy* of his *omnipotence ?* Can the power of sin ?—its infection ?—its malignity ? No ! He can as easily say to an impure heart, Be thou clean, and it shall be clean ; as he could to the leper, Be thou clean, and immediately his leprosy was cleansed. Reader, have faith in Him ; for all things are possible to him that believeth.

3. There are many ungodly men in the world who deny the inspiration of God's Holy Spirit, and affect to ridicule those who profess to have received what they know Christ, has purchased and God has promised, and which, in virtue of this, they have claimed by *faith*; because, say these mockers, "If you had the Spirit of God, you could work miracles : show us a miracle, and we will believe you to be inspired." Will these persons assert that St. Paul had not God's Spirit when he could neither heal himself, nor restore his friends and fellow helpers from apparent death ? What then doth *their* arguing prove ? Silly men, of shallow minds !

CHAPTER III.

The apostle exhorts the Philippians to rejoice in the Lord, 1. *And to beware of false teachers,* 2. *Shows that Christians are the true circumcision, who worship God in the Spirit,* 3. *And that himself had more reason to trust in the flesh than any of the Jews,* 4–6. *But that he counted all things loss for Christ,* 7–11. *He longs after a conformity to Christ in his death, and presses onward to the attainment of his high calling,* 12–14. *Exhorts them to be like-minded,* 15–17. *Warns them against certain persons who were enemies to the cross of Christ,* 18, 19. *Shows the nature of their heavenly privileges, and the resurrection and glorification of the human body,* 20, 21.

A. M. cir. 4066.
A. D. cir. 62.
A. U. C. 814.
An. Imp. Neronis Cæs.
Aug. 9.

FINALLY, my brethren, [a] rejoice in the Lord. To write the same things to you, to me indeed *is* not grievous, but for you *it is* safe.

2 [b] Beware of dogs, beware of [c] evil workers, [d] beware of the concision.

3 For we are [e] the circumcision, [f] which worship God in the spirit, and

A. M. cir. 4066.
A. D. cir. 62.
A. U. C. 814.
An. Imp. Neronis Cæs.
Aug. 9.

---

[a] 2 Cor xiii. 11 ; chap. iv. 4 ; 1 Thess. v. 16.——[b] Isa. lvi. 10 ; Gal. v. 15.——[c] 2 Cor. xi. 13.——[d] Rom. ii. 28 ; Gal. v. 2.

[e] Deut. x. 16 ; xxx. 6 ; Jer. iv. 4 ; Rom. ii. 29 ; iv. 11,12 ; Col. ii. 11.——[f] John iv. 23, 24 ; Rom. vii. 6.

NOTES ON CHAP. III.

Verse 1. *Rejoice in the Lord.*] Be always *happy*; but let that happiness be such as you derive from *the Lord.*

To write the same things] He means those which he had formerly preached to them or to other Churches, for he had but one Gospel ; and we may rest assured that the doctrine of this epistle was the same with his preaching.

For you it is *safe.*] It is much better to have these Divine things committed to *writing* than confided to *memory.* By the *latter* they may be either lost or corrupted, by the *former* they will be preserved.

Verse 2. *Beware of dogs*] The *Jews,* who have here the same appellative which they formerly gave to the *Gentiles :* because the Gentiles were not included in the covenant, they called *them* DOGS ; and themselves, the *children of the Most High.* Now, *they* are cast out of the covenant and the Gentiles taken in ; therefore *they* are the *dogs,* and the *Gentiles* the *children.*

Evil workers] Judaizing teachers, who endeavoured to pervert the Gospel.

The concision.] Κατατομην· The *cutting* or *excision*; not περιτομην, the *circumcision :* the word is used by the apostle to degrade the pretensions which the Jews made to sanctity by the *cutting* in their flesh. *Circumcision* was an honourable thing, for it was a *sign* of the *covenant*; but as they now had rejected the *new covenant,* their circumcision was rendered uncircumcision, and is termed a *cutting,* by way of degradation.

Verse 3. *We are the circumcision*] WE, who have embraced the faith of Christ crucified, are now entered

2

A. M. cir. 4066.
A. D. cir. 62.
A. U. C. 814.
An. Imp. Ne-
ronis Cæs.
Aug. 9.

g rejoice in Christ Jesus, and have no confidence in the flesh:

4 Though h I might also have confidence in the flesh. If any other man thinketh that he hath whereof he might trust in the flesh, I more :

5 i Circumcised the eighth day, k of the stock of Israel, l *of* the tribe of Benjamin, m a Hebrew of the Hebrews ; as touching the law, n a Pharisee ;

6 o Concerning zeal, p persecuting the Church;

q touching the righteousness which is in the law, r blameless.

7 But s what things were gain to me, those I counted loss for Christ.

8 Yea doubtless, and I count all things *but* loss t for the excellency of the knowledge of Christ Jesus my Lord : for whom I have suffered the loss of all things, and do count them *but* dung, that I may win Christ,

9 And be found in him, not having u mine

A. M. cir. 4066.
A. D. cir. 62.
A. U. C. 814
An. Imp. No
ronis Cæs
Aug. 9.

---

g Gal. vi. 14.——h 2 Cor. xi. 18, 21.——i Genesis xvii. 12. k 2 Cor. xi. 22.——l Rom. xi. 1.——m 2 Cor. xi. 22.——n Acts xxiii. 6; xxvi. 4, 5.——o Acts xxii. 3 ; Gal. i. 13, 14.

p Acts viii. 3; ix. 1.——q Rom. x. 5.——r Luke i. 6.——s Matt xiii. 44.——t Isa. liii. 11 ; Jer. ix. 23, 24 ; John xvii. 3 ; 1 Cor ii. 2 ; Col. ii. 2.——u Rom. x. 3, 5.

---

into the new covenant, and according to that new covenant, *worship God in the Spirit, exulting, καυχωμενοι, making our boast of Christ Jesus,* as our only Saviour, *having no confidence in the flesh*—in any *outward rite* or *ceremony* prescribed by the Jewish institutions.

Verse 4. *Though I might also have confidence*] If any of them have any cause to boast in outward rites and privileges, I have as much ; yea, *more.*

Verse 5. *Circumcised the eighth day*] This was the time that the law required the males to be circumcised ; and we find, from Gen. xvii. 14, both in the *Samaritan* Pentateuch and in the *Septuagint*, though the clause is now lost out of the common Hebrew text, that *the male child, which is not circumcised the eighth day, shall be cut off from among his people :* this precept was literally observed in the case of St. Paul.

Of the stock of Israel] Regularly descended from the patriarch Jacob.

Of *the tribe of Benjamin*] The most favourite son of that patriarch ; and a tribe that did not revolt with Jeroboam, 1 Kings xii. 21, nor pollute the worship of God by idolatry.

A Hebrew of the Hebrews] Though born in a heathen country, Tarsus, yet both my parents were Hebrews ; nor has there ever been any strange blood mixed with that of our family.

Touching the law; a Pharisee] One that not only received the law and the prophets as coming from God ; but belonged to that *sect* which, of all others, was most scrupulously attached to it.

Verse 6. *Concerning zeal*] As to my zeal for Pharisaism, I gave the fullest proof of it by persecuting the Church of Christ; and this is known to all my countrymen.

Touching the righteousness] And as to that *plan of justification,* which justification the Jews say is to be obtained by an observance of the law, I have done every thing so conscientiously from my youth up, that in this respect I am *blameless ;* and may, with more confidence than most of *them,* expect that justification which the law appears to promise.

Verse 7. *But what things were gain*] The *credit* and *respect* which I had, as being zealously attached to the law, and to the traditions of the elders, *I counted loss for Christ*—I saw that this could stand me in no stead ; that all my acts of righteousness were nothing

on which I could depend for salvation ; and that *Christ crucified* could alone profit me ; for I found that it is impossible that the blood of bulls and goats could take away sin.

Verse 8. *I count all things* but *loss*] Not only my Jewish privileges, but all others of every kind ; with every thing that men count valuable or gainful, or on which they usually depend for salvation.

The excellency of the knowledge of Christ] That superior light, information, and blessedness, which come through the Gospel of Jesus Christ ; justification through his blood, sanctification by his Spirit, and eternal glory through his merits and intercession. These are the blessings held out to us by the Gospel, of which, and the law, Jesus Christ is the sum and substance.

I have suffered the loss of all things] Some translate δι' ὁν τα παντα εζημιωθην, *for whom I have thrown away all things*—I have made a voluntary choice of Christ, his cross, his poverty, and his reproach ; and for these I have freely sacrificed all I had from the world, and all I could expect from it.

And do count them but *dung*] The word σκυβαλα means the vilest dross or *refuse* of any thing ; the worst excrement. The word shows how utterly insignificant and unavailing, in point of salvation, the apostle esteemed every thing but the Gospel of Jesus. With his best things he freely parted, judging them all *loss* while put in the place of Christ crucified ; and Christ crucified he esteemed infinite *gain,* when compared with all the rest. Of the utter unavailableness of any thing but *Christ* to save the soul the Apostle Paul stands as an incontrovertible proof. Could the law have done any thing, the apostle must have known it. He tried, and found it vanity ; he tried the Gospel system, and found it the power of God to his salvation. By *losing all* that the world calls excellent, he *gained* Christ, and endless salvation through him. Of the glorious influence of the Gospel he is an unimpeachable witness. See the concluding observations on the 9th chapter of the Acts, on the character of St. Paul.

Verse 9. *And be found in him*] Be found a believer in Christ, *not having mine own righteousness*— not trusting in any thing I have done or could do, in order to my salvation ; relying on no scheme of justification, set up either formerly by myself or by others,

A. M. cir. 4066.
A. D. cir. 62.
A. U. C. 814.
An. Imp. Ne-
ronis Cæs.
Aug. 9.

own righteousness, which is of the law, but [v] that which is through the faith of Christ, the righteousness which is of God by faith:

10 That I may know him, and the power of his resurrection, and [w] the fellowship of his

sufferings, being made conformable unto his death;

11 If by any means I might [x] attain unto the resurrection of the dead.

A. M. cir. 4066.
A. D. cir. 62.
A. U. C. 814.
An. Imp. Ne-
ronis Cæs.
Aug. 9.

12 Not as though I had already [y] attained, either were already [z] perfect: but I follow after,

---

[v] Rom. i. 17; iii. 21, 22; ix. 30; x. 3, 6; Gal. ii. 16.——[w] Rom. vi. 3, 4, 5; viii. 17; 2 Cor. iv. 10, 11; 2 Tim. ii. 11, 12; 1 Pet. iv. 13.——[x] Acts xxvi. 7.——[y] 1 Timothy vi. 12.——[z] Hebrews xii. 23.

But that which is through the faith of Christ] That justification which is received by faith through the atonement made by Christ.

The righteousness which is of God] God's method of justifying sinners through faith in his Son. See the notes on Rom. iii. 21, 23, and 25, where this subject is treated at large.

Verse 10. That I may know him] To be the true and promised Messiah, and *experience* all that salvation which he has bought by his blood.

The power of his resurrection] In having this *body of my humiliation* raised from death, and *made like unto his glorious body.* This seems to be the sole meaning of the apostle; for it is in virtue of Christ's resurrection that we are to be raised incorruptible and immortal.

And the fellowship of his sufferings] Christ died, not only as a *victim* for sin, but as a *martyr* to the truth. No creature can have *fellowship* with him in his *vicarious* sufferings; as a *martyr* to the truth, St. Paul wished to imitate him. Not only in the apostle, but in the primitive Christians generally, there seems to have been a strong desire after martyrdom.

Verse 11. The resurrection of the dead.] That is, the resurrection of those who, having died in the Lord, rise to glory and honour; and hence St. Paul uses a peculiar word which occurs no where else in the New Testament, εξαναστασις. The words, as they stand in the best MSS., are as follow: εις την εξαναστασιν την εκ νεκρων, *to that resurrection which is of the dead.* This glorious resurrection, and perhaps peculiarly glorious in the case of *martyrs*, is that to which St. Paul aspired. The word αναστασις signifies the *resurrection* in general, both of the just and unjust; εξαναστασις may signify that of the *blessed* only.

Verse 12. Not as though I had already attained] Ουχ οτι ηδη ελαβον· For I have not yet received the prize; I am not glorified, for I have not finished my course; and I have a *conflict* still to maintain, and the issue will prove whether I should be crowned. From the beginning of the 11th to the end of the 17th verse there is one continued allusion to the contests at the Olympic games; exercises with which, and their laws, the Philippians were well acquainted.

Either were already perfect] Η ηδη τετελειωμαι· *Nor am I yet perfect*; I am not yet crowned, in consequence of having suffered martyrdom. I am quite satisfied that the apostle here alludes to the Olympic games, and the word τετελειωμαι is the proof; for τελειωθηναι is spoken of those who have *completed their race, reached the goal*, and are *honoured* with the

prize. Thus it is used by *Philo*, Allegoriar. lib. iii. page 101, edit. Mangey: Ποτε ουν, ω ψυχη, μαλιστα νεκροφορειν (νικοφορειν) σεαυτην υποληψη· αραγε ουχ οταν τελειωθης και βραβειων και στεφανων αξιωθης "When is it, O soul, that thou shalt appear to have the victory? Is it not when thou *shalt be perfected*, (have completed thy course by death,) and be honoured with prizes and crowns?"

That τελειωσις signified *martyrdom*, we learn most expressly from *Clemens Alexand.*, Stromata, lib. iii. page 480, where he has these remarkable words:— τελειωσιν μαρτυριον καλουμεν, ουχ οτι τελος του βιου ο ανθρωπος ελαβεν, ως οι λοιποι, αλλ᾽ οτι τελειον εργον αγαπης ενεδειξατο· "We call *martyrdom* τελειωσις, or *perfection*, not because man receives it as the end, τελος, or completion of life; but because it is the consummation τελειον, of the work of charity."

So *Basil* the great, Hom. in Psa. cxvi., ver. 13: Ποτηριον σωτηριον ληψομαι· τουτεστι, διψων επι την δια του μαρτυριου τελειωσιν ερχομαι· "I will receive the cup of salvation; that is, thirsting and earnestly desiring to come, by martyrdom, to the consummation."

So *Œcumenius*, on Acts xxviii.: Παντα ετη απο της κλησεως του Παυλου, μεχρι της τελειωσεως αυτου, τριακοντα και πεντε· "All the years of Paul, from his calling to his *martyrdom*, were thirty and five."

And in *Balsamon*, Can. i. Ancyran., page 764: Τον της τελειωσεως στεφανον αναδησασθαι is, "To be crowned with the crown of *martyrdom*."

Eusebius, Hist. Eccles., lib. vii. cap. 13, uses the word τελειουσθαι to express *to suffer martyrdom.* I have been the more particular here, because some critics have denied that the word has any such signification. See *Suicer, Rosenmüller, Macknight, &c.*

St. Paul, therefore, is not speaking here of any *deficiency* in his own grace, or spiritual state; he does not mean by not being yet *perfect*, that he had a *body of sin and death* cleaving to him, and was still polluted with *indwelling sin*, as some have most falsely and dangerously imagined; he speaks of his not having terminated his course by martyrdom, which he knew would sooner or later be the case. This he considered as the τελειωσις, or *perfection*, of his whole career, and was led to view every thing as *imperfect* or *unfinished* till this had taken place.

But I follow after] Διωκω δε· *But I pursue*; several are gone before me in this glorious way, and have obtained the crown of martyrdom; I am hurrying after them.

That I may apprehend] That I may receive those blessings to which I am called by Christ Jesus. **There**

2

A. M. cir. 4066.
A. D. cir. 62.
A. U. C. 814.
An. Imp. Ne-
ronis Cæs.
Aug. 9.

if that I may apprehend that for which also I am apprehended of Christ Jesus.

13 Brethren, I count not myself to have apprehended ; but *this* one thing *I do,* [a] forgetting those things which are behind, and [b] reaching forth unto those things which are before,

14 [c] I press toward the mark for the prize

of [d] the high calling of God in Christ Jesus.

A. M. cir. 4066.
A. D. cir. 62.
A. U. C. 814.
An. Imp. Ne-
ronis Cæs.
Aug. 9.

15 Let us therefore, as many as be [e] perfect, [f] be thus minded : and if in any thing ye be otherwise minded, God shall reveal even this unto you.

16 Nevertheless, whereto we have already attained, [g] let us walk [h] by the same rule, [i] let us mind the same thing.

---

[a] Psa. xlv. 10 ; Luke ix. 62 ; 2 Cor. v. 16.——[b] 1 Cor. ix. 24, 26 ; Heb. vi. 1.——[c] 2 Tim. iv. 7, 8 ; Heb. xii. 1.

[d] Heb. iii. 1.——[e] 1 Cor. ii. 6 ; xiv. 20.——[f] Gal. v. 10.——[g] Rom. xii. 16 ; xv. 5.——[h] Gal. vi. 16.——[i] Chap. ii. 2.

---

is still an allusion here to the *stadium,* and *exercises* there : the apostle considers Christ as the *brabeus,* or judge in the games, who proclaimed the victor, and distributed the prizes ; and he represents himself as being introduced by this very *brabeus,* or judge, into the contest ; and this *brabeus* brought him in with the design to crown him, if he contended faithfully. To complete this faithful contention is what he has in view ; that he may *apprehend,* or *lay hold* on that for which he had been *apprehended,* or *taken by the hand* by Christ, who had converted, strengthened, and endowed him with apostolical powers, that he might fight the good fight of faith, and *lay hold* on eternal life.

Verse 13. *I count not myself to have apprehended*] Whatever gifts, graces, or honours I may have received from Jesus Christ, I consider every thing as incomplete till I have finished my course, got this crown, and have my body raised and fashioned after his glorious body.

This one thing I do] This is the concern, as it is the sole business, of my life.

Forgetting those things which are behind] My conduct is not regulated nor influenced by that of others ; I consider my *calling,* my *Master,* my *work,* and my *end.* If others think they have time to loiter or trifle, I have none : *time is flying ; eternity* is at hand ; and my. all is at *stake.*

Reaching forth] The Greek word επεκτεινομενος points out the strong exertions made in the *race* ; every muscle and nerve is exerted, and he puts forth every particle of his strength in *running.* He was running for life, and running for his life.

Verse 14. *I press toward the mark*] Κατα σκοπον διωκω· *I pursue along the line* ; this is a reference to the *white line* that marked the ground in the stadium, from the *starting* place to the *goal,* on which the *runners* were obliged to keep their eye fixed ; for they who transgressed or *went beyond* this line did not *run awfully,* and were not *crowned,* even though they got *first* to the goal. See the concluding observations on 1 Cor. chap. ix.

What is called σκοπος, *mark* or *scope,* here, is called κανων, the *line,* i. e. the *marked line,* ver. 16. When it was said to *Diogenes,* the cynic, "Thou art now an old man, rest from thy labours ;" to this he answered : Ει δολιχον εδραμον, προς τῳ τελει εδει με ανειναι, και μη μαλλον επιτειναι; "If I have run long in the race, will it become me to *slacken* my pace when come near the end ; should I not rather *stretch forward ?*" *Diog. Laert.,* lib. vi. cap. 2, sec. 6.

For the prize of the high calling of God] The reward which God from above calls me, by Christ Jesus, to receive. The apostle still keeps in view his crown of martyrdom and his glorious resurrection.

Verse 15. *As many as be perfect*] As many as are *thoroughly instructed* in Divine things, who have cast off all dependence on the law and on every other system for salvation, and who discern God calling them from *above* by Christ Jesus ; *be thus minded* ; be intensely in earnest for eternal life, nor ever halt till the race is finished.

The word τελειοι, *perfect,* is taken here in the same sense in which it is taken 1 Cor. xiv. 20 : *Be not* CHILDREN *in understanding—but in understanding be* ye MEN, τελειοι γινεσθε, *be ye perfect—*thoroughly instructed, deeply experienced. 1 Cor. ii. 6 : *We speak wisdom among the perfect,* εν τοις τελειοις, among those who are *fully instructed, adults* in Christian knowledge. Eph. iv. 13 : *Till we all come—unto a perfect man,* εις ανδρα τελειον, to the state of *adults* in Christianity. Heb. v. 14 : *But strong meat belongeth to them that are of full age,* τελειων, *the perfect—*those who are thoroughly instructed and experienced in Divine things. *Let us therefore,* says the apostle, *as many as be perfect—*as have entered fully into the spirit and design of the Gospel, *be thus minded,* viz. Forget the things which are behind, and stretch forward along the mark for the prize.

If in any thing ye be otherwise minded] If ye have not yet entered into the full spirit and design of this Gospel, if any of you have yet remaining any doubts relative to Jewish ordinances, or their expediency in Christianity, *God shall reveal even this unto you* ; for while you are sincere and upright, God will take care that ye shall have full instruction in these Divine things.

Verse 16. *Whereto we have already attained*] Let us not lose that part of the race which we have already run, *let us walk by the same rule—*let us keep the *white line* continually in view, *let us mind the same thing,* always considering the glorious prize which is held out by God through Christ Jesus to animate and encourage us.

The MSS., versions and fathers of the Alexandrian *recension* or *edition,* and which are supposed by *Griesbach* and others to contain the purest text, omit the words κανονι, το αυτο φρονειν, and read the verse thus : *Whereunto we have already attained let us walk* ; or, *according to what we have already attained, let us regulate our life.* There is so much disagreement

A. M. cir. 4066.
A. D. cir. 62.
A. U. C. 814.
An. Imp. Ne-
ronis Cæs.
Aug. 9.

17 Brethren, [k] be followers together of me, and mark them which walk so, as [l] ye have us for an ensample.

18 (For many walk, of whom I have told you often, and now tell you even weeping, *that they are* [m] the enemies of the cross of Christ:

19 [n] Whose end *is* destruction, [o] whose god *is their* belly, and [p] *whose* glory *is* in their shame, [q] who mind earthly things.)

20 For [r] our conversation is in heaven; [s] from whence also we [t] look for the Saviour, the Lord Jesus Christ:

21 [u] Who shall change our vile body, that it may be fashioned like unto his glorious body, [v] according to the working whereby he is able [w] even to subdue all things unto himself.

A. M. cir. 4066.
A. D. cir. 62.
A. U. C. 814.
An. Imp. Ne-
ronis Cæs.
Aug. 9.

Lord Jesus

---

[k] 1 Cor. iv. 16; xi. 1; chap. iv. 9; 1 Thess. i. 6.——[l] 1 Pet. v. 3.——[m] Gal. i. 7; ii. 21; vi. 12; chap. i. 15, 16.——[n] 2 Cor. xi. 15; 2 Peter ii. 1.——[o] Rom. xvi. 18; 1 Tim. vi. 5; Tit. i. 11. [p] Hos. iv. 7; 2 Cor. xi. 12; Gal. vi. 13.

[q] Rom. viii. 5.——[r] Eph. ii. 6, 19; Col. iii. 1, 3.——[s] Acts i. 11.——[t] 1 Cor. i. 7; 1 Thess. i. 10; Tit. ii. 13.——[u] 1 Cor. xv. 43, 48, 49; Col. iii. 4; 1 John. iii. 2.——[v] Eph. i. 19.——[w] 1 Cor. xv. 26, 27.

---

about the above words in the MSS., &c., that most critics consider them as a sort of gloss, which never made an original part of the text. Dr. *White* says, *Certissime* delenda; "Most certainly they should be obliterated."

Verse 17. *Brethren, be followers—of me*] In the things of Christ let me be your *line*; and my writing, preaching, and conduct, your *rule*.

And mark them] Σκοπειτε. Still alluding to the *line* in the stadium; keep your eye steadily fixed on those *who walk*—live, *as ye have us*—myself, Timothy, and Epaphroditus, *for an ensample*.

Verse 18. *For many walk, &c.*] The Judaizing teachers continue to preach, who wish to incorporate *circumcision*, and other ordinances of the law, with the Gospel.

They are *the enemies of the cross of Christ*] They rather attribute justification to the *Levitical sacrifices*, than to the *sacrificial death* of Christ; and thus they are enemies to that cross, and will not suffer persecution for its sake. They please the world, and are in no danger of reproach.

Verse 19. *Whose end is destruction*] This is the *issue* of their doctrine, and of their conduct. They are here described by *three* characters: 1. *Their god* is their *belly*—they live not in any reference to *eternity*; their religion is for *time*; they make a gain of godliness; and live only to *eat, drink,* and be *merry*. 2. *Their glory* is *in their shame*—they lay it down as a proof of their address, that they can fare sumptuously every day, in consequence of preaching a doctrine which flatters the passions of their hearers. 3. They *mind earthly things*—their whole study and attention are taken up with earthly matters; they are given to the *flesh* and its *lusts*; they have no spirituality, nor do they believe that there is or can be any intercourse between God and the souls of men. But their *lasciviousness* and *uncleanness* seem to be principally intended. See *Kypke*. Despicable as these men were, the apostle's heart was deeply pained on their account: 1. Because they held and taught a false creed; 2. Because they perverted many by that teaching; and, 3. Because they themselves were perishing through it.

Verse 20. *Our conversation is in heaven*] Ἡμων—το πολιτευμα· Our city, or citizenship, or civil rights. The word properly signifies the administration, government, or form of a republic or state; and is thus used by *Demosthenes*, page 107, 25, and 262, 27. Edit. *Reiske*. It signifies also a *republic*, a *city*, or the inhabitants of any city or place; or a *society* of persons living in the *same place*, and under the *same rules* and *laws*. See more in *Schleusner*.

While those gross and Jewish teachers have no *city* but what is on *earth*; no *rights* but what are derived from their *secular* connections; no society but what is made up of men *like themselves*, who *mind earthly things*, and whose *belly is their god*; we have a *heavenly* city, the New Jerusalem; we have *rights* and *privileges* which are *heavenly* and *eternal*; and our *society* or *fellowship* is with God the Father, Son, and Spirit, the spirits of just men made perfect, and the whole Church of the first-born. We have crucified the flesh with its affections and lusts; and regard not the body, which we know must perish, but which we confidently expect shall be raised from death and corruption into a state of immortal glory.

Verse 21. *Who shall change our vile body*] Ὁς μετασχηματισει το σωμα της ταπεινωσεως ἡμων· Who will *refashion*, or *alter the fashion* and condition of, *the body of our humiliation*; this body that *is dead*—adjudged to death because of sin, and must be putrefied, dissolved, and decomposed.

That it may be fashioned like unto his glorious body] Εις το γενεσθαι αυτο συμμορφον τῳ σωματι της δοξης αυτου· *That it may bear a similar form to the body of his glory*. That is: the bodies of true believers shall be raised up at the great day in the same likeness, immortality, and glory, of the glorified humanity of Jesus Christ; and be so thoroughly changed, as to be not only capable through their *immortality* of eternally existing, but also of the infinite spiritual enjoyments at the right hand of God.

According to the working] Κατα την ενεργειαν· *According to that energy, by which he can bring all things under subjection to himself*. Thus we find that the resurrection of the body is attributed to that power which governs and subdues all things; for nothing less than the energy that produced the human body at the beginning, can restore it from its lapsed and degraded state into that state of glory which it had at its creation, and render it capable of enjoying God throughout eternity. The thought of this glorious consummation was a subject of the highest joy and confidence amongst the primitive Christians. This earth was not their

2

home ; and they passed through things temporal so as not to lose those which were eternal.

1. THE preceding chapter, to which the first verse of the succeeding should be joined, contains a fund of matter the most interesting that can well be conceived. The apostle seems to stand on the *verge of eternity,* and to have *both worlds* opened to his view. The one he sees to be the place in which a *preparation* for the other is to be attained. In the one he sees the *starting place,* where the Christian is to commence his race ; in the other the *goal* at which his course terminates, and the prize which he is there to obtain. One is the place *from* and *over* which the Christian is to run ; the other is that *to* which he is to direct his course, and in which he is to receive infinite blessedness. In the one he sees all manner of temptations and hinderances, and dangers standing thick through all the ground ; in the other he sees the forerunner, the Lord Jesus, who has entered into the heaven of heavens for him, through whom God calls him from above, της ανω κλησεως του Θεου, ver. 14 : for what

he hears in the Gospel, and what he sees by faith, is *the calling of God from above* ; and therefore he departs from this, for this is not his rest.

2. The nearer a faithful soul comes to the verge of eternity, the more the light and influence of heaven are poured out upon it : *time* and *life* are fast sinking away into the shades of death and darkness ; and the effulgence of the dawning glory of the eternal world is beginning to illustrate the blessed state of the genuine Christian, and to render clear and intelligible those counsels of God, partly displayed in various inextricable providences, and partly revealed and seen as through a glass darkly in his own sacred word. Unutterable glories now begin to burst forth ; pains, afflictions, persecutions, wants, distresses, sickness, and death, in any or all of its forms, are exhibited as the way to the kingdom, and as having in the order of God an ineffable glory for their result. Here are the wisdom, power, and mercy of God ! Here, the patience, perseverance, and glory of the saints ! Reader, is not earth and its concerns lost in the effulgence of this glory ? Arise and depart, for this is not thy *rest*

CHAPTER IV.

The apostle exhorts them to stand fast in the Lord, 1. *And beseeches* Euodias *and* Syntyche *to be of one mind in Divine things,* 2. *And requests his true yokefellow to help them to a good understanding,* 3. *Gives them directions concerning their temper and frame of mind,* 4—7. *And how to act in all respects as becomes the purity and excellence of the Gospel, as they had heard from and seen in him,* 8, 9. *Thanks them for their attention to him in his captivity, in sending him what was necessary for his support, though he had learned to be contented in all situations in life,* 10—14. *Mentions particular cases in which they had ministered to him ; promises them, through the riches of glory in Christ, a supply of all their spiritual wants ; and renders thanks to God,* 15—20. *Salutes all the saints, and those particularly of the emperor's household,* 21, 22. *And concludes with his usual apostolical benediction,* 23.

A. M. cir. 4066.
A. D. cir. 62.
A. U. C. 814.
An. Imp. Neronis Cæs.
Aug. 9.

THEREFORE, my brethren, dearly beloved and [a] longed for, [b] my joy and crown, so [c] stand fast in the Lord, *my dearly beloved.*

2 I beseech Euodias, and beseech Syntyche,

[d] that they be of the same mind in the Lord.

3 And I entreat thee also, true yokefellow, help those women which [e] laboured with me in the Gospel, with Clement also, and *with* other my fellow labour-

A. M. cir. 4066.
A. D. cir. 62.
A. U. C. 814.
An. Imp. Neronis Cæs.
Aug. 9.

---

[a] Chap. i. 8.——[b] 2 Cor. i. 14 ; chap. ii. 16 ; 1 Thess. ii. 19, 20.

[c] Chap. i. 27.——[d] Chap. ii. 2 ; iii. 16.——[e] Rom. xvi. 3 ; chap. i. 27.

NOTES ON CHAP. IV.

Verse 1. *Therefore, my—beloved*] Because ye have this armour, and those enemies, and God for your support, see that ye stand fast in him. This verse most unquestionably belongs to the preceding chapter.

Verse 2. *I beseech Euodias, and beseech Syntyche*] These were two pious women, as it is generally supposed, who were deaconesses in the Church at Philippi, and who in some points of doctrine and discipline had disagreed. He exhorts them to be of the same mind, that is, to compose their differences ; and, if they could not perfectly agree, to think and let think, and to avoid all public opposition, as their dissension would strengthen the hands of the common enemy, and stumble those who were weak. But it is more likely that *Euodias* was a woman, and *Syntyche* a man, and probably the

husband of *Euodias ;* and that it is *Syntyche* whom the apostle calls *true yokefellow* in the next verse.

Verse 3. *Help those women which laboured with me*] Both in the Grecian and Asiatic countries women were kept much secluded, and it was not likely that even the apostles had much opportunity of conversing with them ; it was therefore necessary that they should have some experienced Christian *women* with them, who could have access to families, and preach Jesus to the female part of them. The apostle tells us that certain women *laboured with him in the Gospel,* and were assistants to others also who had assisted him.

Some think the women here were *Euodias* and *Syntyche ;* but I rather incline to the opinion that Syntyche was a male, and Euodias his wife. EUODIAS signifies

2

A. M. cir. 4066.
A. D. cir. 62.
A. U. C. 814.
An. Imp. Ne-
ronis Cæs.
Aug. 9.
ers, whose names *are* in ᶠ the book of life.

4 ᵍ Rejoice in the Lord alway : *and* again I say, Rejoice.

5 Let your moderation be known unto all men. ʰ The Lord *is* at hand.

6 ⁱ Be careful for nothing ; but in every thing by prayer and supplication, with thanksgiving,

let your requests be made known unto God.

7 And ᵏthe peace of God, which passeth all understanding, shall keep your hearts and minds through Christ Jesus.

8 Finally, brethren, whatsoever things are true, whatsoever things *are* ˡ honest, whatsoever

A. M. cir. 4066.
A. D. cir. 62.
A. U. C. 814.
An. Imp. Ne-
ronis Cæs.
Aug. 9.

ᶠ Exod. xxxii. 32 ; Psa. lxix. 28 ; Dan. xii. 1 ; Luke x. 20 ; Rev. iii. 5 ; xiii. 8 ; xx. 12 ; xxi. 27.——ᵍ Rom. xii. 12 ; chap. iii. 1 ; 1 Thess. v. 16 ; 1 Peter iv. 13.——ʰ Heb. x. 25 ; James v. 8, 9 ;

1 Pet. iv. 7 ; 2 Pet. iii. 8, 9 ; see 2 Thess. ii. 2.——ⁱ Psa. lv. 22 ; Prov. xvi. 3 ; Matt. vi. 25 ; Luke xii. 22 ; 1 Pet. v. 7.——ᵏ John xiv. 27 ; Rom. v. 1 ; Col. iii. 15.——ˡ Or, *venerable.*

---

a *pleasant scent* ; Syntyche, *fortunate.* There have been a number of conjectures who these persons were, and who is meant by the *true yokefellow* ; but as there is nothing certain known on the subject, it is useless to propagate conjecture.

With Clement also] Supposed to be the same who was afterwards bishop of Rome, and who wrote an epistle to the *Corinthians*, which is still extant.

Whose names are *in the book of life.*] Who are genuine Christians ; who are *enlisted* or *enrolled* in the armies of the Lord, and have received a title to eternal glory. The reader is requested to refer to the note on Exod. xxxii. 32, 33, and the concluding observations at the end of that chapter, where the *writing in* and *blotting out* of the book of life are particularly considered, and the difficulties on the subject removed. See also on Luke x. 20.

Verse 4. *Rejoice in the Lord alway*] Be continually happy ; but this happiness you can find only *in the Lord.* Genuine happiness is *spiritual* ; as it can only come from God, so it infallibly tends to him. The apostle repeats the exhortation, to show, not only his earnestness, but also that it was God's will that it should be so, and that it was their *duty* as well as *interest.*

Verse 5. *Let your moderation be known*] The word επιεικες is of very extensive signification ; it means the same as επιεικεια, mildness, patience, yieldingness, gentleness, clemency, *moderation*, unwillingness to litigate or contend ; but *moderation* is expressive enough as a general term. " Moderation," says Dr. Macknight, " means meekness under provocation, readiness to forgive injuries, equity in the management of business, candour in judging of the characters and actions of others, sweetness of disposition, and the entire government of the passions."

The Lord is at hand.] A phrase something similar to the *Maranatha* of 1 Cor. xvi. 22 : The Lord is Judge, and is at hand to punish. *Schoettgen* supposes, from this verse, taken in connection with the preceding, that Euodias and Syntyche were of a *quarrelsome* disposition ; and hence the exhortation and threatening in the third and fifth verses.

Verse 6. *Be careful for nothing*] Μηδεν μεριμνατε· Be not anxiously solicitous ; do not give place to carking care, let what will occur ; for anxiety cannot change the state or condition of any thing from bad to good, but will infallibly injure your own souls.

By prayer and supplication] God alone can help you ; he is disposed to do it, but you must ask by

prayer and supplication ; without this he has not promised to help you.

By prayer—solemn application to God from a sense of want. *Supplication*—continuance in earnest prayer. *With thanksgiving*, for innumerable favours already received ; and for dangers, evils, and deaths turned aside. And let your souls be found in this exercise, or in the *disposition* in which this exercise can be performed, at all *times*, on all *occasions*, and in all *places.*

Verse 7. *And the peace of God*] That harmonizing of all passions and appetites which is produced by the Holy Spirit, and arises from a sense of pardon and the favour of God ;

Shall keep your hearts] Φρουρησει· Shall keep them as in a strong place or castle. *Your hearts*—the seat of all your affections and passions, *and minds* —your understanding, judgment, and conscience *through Christ Jesus* ; by whom ye were brought into this state of favour, *through* whom ye are preserved in it, and *in* whom ye possess it ; for Christ keeps that heart in peace in which he dwells and rules. This peace passeth all understanding ; it is of a very different nature from all that can arise from human occurrences ; it is a peace which Christ has purchased, and which God dispenses ; it is felt by all the truly godly, but can be explained by none ; it is communion with the Father, and his Son Jesus Christ, by the power and influence of the Holy Ghost.

Verse 8. *Finally, brethren*] The object of the apostle is to recommend holiness and righteousness to them in every point of view ; and to show that the Gospel of Christ requires all its professors to have the *mind* that was in Christ, and to *walk* as he himself also walked. That they were not to attend to one branch of righteousness or virtue only, but to every thing by which they might bring honour to God, good to their fellow creatures, and credit to themselves.

Whatsoever things are true] 'Οσα—αληθη· All that is agreeable to unchangeable and eternal *truth.* Whether that which is to be learned from the *nature* and *state* of created things, or that which comes immediately from God by *revelation.*

Whatsoever things are *honest*] 'Οσα σεμνα· Whatever is *grave, decent*, and *venerable.* Whatever becomes you as men, as citizens, and as Christians.

Whatsover things are *just*] 'Οσα δικαια· Whatsoever is agreeable to justice and righteousness. All that ye owe to God, to your neighbour, and to yourselves.

Whatsoever things are *pure*] 'Οσα αγνα· What-

2

A. M. cir. 4066.
A. D. cir. 62.
A. U. C. 814.
An. Imp. Ne-
ronis Cæs
Aug. 9

things *are* just, whatsoever things *are* pure, whatsoever things *are* lovely, ^m whatsoever things *are* of good report ; if *there be* any virtue, and if *there be* any praise, think on these things.

9 ⁿ Those things, which ye have both learned, and received, and heard, and seen in me, do : and ^o the God of peace shall be with you.

10 But I rejoiced in the Lord greatly, that now at the last ^p your care of me ^q hath flourished again ; wherein ye were also

careful, but ye lacked oppor-tunity.

11 Not that I speak in respect of want : for I have learned, in what-soever state I am, ^r *therewith* to be content.

12 ^s I know both how to be abased, and I know how to abound : every where and in all things I am instructed, both to be full and to be hungry, both to abound and to suffer need.

13 I can do all things ^t through Christ which strengtheneth me.

14 Notwithstanding ye have well done that

A. M. cir. 4066.
A. D. cir. 62.
A. U. C. 814.
An. Imp. Ne-
ronis Cæs.
Aug. 9.

---

^m 1 Thess. v. 22.——ⁿ Ch. iii. 17.——^o Rom. xv. 33 ; xvi. 20 ; 1 Cor. xiv. 33 ; 2 Cor. xiii. 11 ; 1 Thess. v. 23 ; Heb. xiii. 20.

^p 2 Cor. xi. 9.——^q Or, *is revived.*——^r 1 Tim. vi. 6, 8.——^s 1 Cor. iv. 11 ; 2 Cor. vi. 10 ; xi. 27.——^t John xv. 5 ; 2 Cor. xii. 9.

---

soever is *chaste.* In reference to the *state* of the *mind,* and to the *acts* of the *body.*

Whatsoever things are *lovely*] 'Οσα προσφιλη· What-soever is *amiable* on its own account and on account of its usefulness to others, whether in *your* conduct or conversation.

Whatsoever things are *of good report*] 'Οσα ευφημα· Whatsoever things the *public* agree to acknowledge as *useful* and *profitable* to men ; such as *charitable institutions* of every kind, in which genuine Christians should ever take the lead.

If there be *any virtue*] If they be calculated to promote the general good of mankind, and are thus *praiseworthy.*

Think on these things.] Esteem them highly, re-commend them heartily, and practise them fervently.

Instead of ει τις επαινος, *if there be any praise,* several eminent MSS., as D*EFG, add επιστημης, *of knowledge ;* and the *Vulgate* and the *Itala* have *disci-plinæ,* of *discipline ;* but none of these appear to be an original reading.

Verse 9. *Those things, which ye have—learned*] From my preaching and writing ;

And received] By faith, as a revelation from God ;

And heard] From my preaching, and that of those who laboured with me ; *and heard from* me, in my private communications with you ; and heard *of* me from other Churches ;

And seen in me] While living and labouring among you ;

Do] Take them for the *rule* of your *faith* and *practice.*

And the God of peace] He who is the author of peace, the lover of peace, and the maintainer of peace ; he who has made peace between heaven and earth, by the mission and sacrifice of his Son, shall be ever with you while you believe and act as here recom-mended.

Verse 10. *But I rejoiced in the Lord*] Every good comes from God, either. immediately from his provi-dence or from his grace ; therefore the apostle thanks God for the kindness of the Philippians towards him ; for it was God that gave them the power, and directed their hearts to use it.

Hath flourished again] They had helped him be-

fore, chap. ii. 25 ; they had ceased for a time, and now they began again. This is evidently designed by the apostle, as the word ανεθαλετε implies, which is a me-taphor taken from the *reviviscence* of flowers in *spring* which seemed dead in *winter.* For the time in which they were apparently remiss he makes a delicate apo-logy : *Ye were careful, but ye lacked opportunity ;* or rather ηκαιρεισθε, ye *had not ability,* ye *wanted the means ;* as the word sometimes implies.

Verse 11. *Not that I speak in respect of want*] I am quite unconcerned in this respect ; leaving the whole of my support, while bound for the testimony of Jesus, to the providence of God.

For I have learned] I am so satisfied with the wise providence and goodness of God, that I know whatever he determines is the best ; and therefore I am perfectly contented that he should govern the world in that way which seems best to his godly wisdom. How true is the proverb, *A contented mind is a con-tinual feast !* What do we get by murmuring and complaining ?

Verse 12. *I know—how to be abased*] I have passed through all these states ; I know how to con-duct myself in each, and how to extract good from all. And he had passed through these things, especially the hardships, so that he had learned the lesson *per-fectly,* as the word μεμνημαι implies ; he was tho-roughly instructed ; fully *initiated* into all the myste-ries of poverty and want, and of the supporting hand of God in the whole. See here the state to which God permitted his chief apostle to be reduced ! And see how powerfully the grace of Christ supported him under the whole ! How few of those who are called Christian ministers or Christian men have learned this important lesson ! When want or affliction comes, their complaints are loud and frequent ; and they are soon at the end of their patience.

Verse 13. *I can do all things*] It was not a *habit* which he had acquired by *frequent exercise,* it was a disposition which he had by *grace ;* and he was enabled to do all by the power of an indwelling Christ. *Through Him who strengtheneth me* is the reading of some of the best MSS., versions, and fathers ; the word Χριστω, *Christ,* being omitted.

Verse 14. *Ye have well done*] Though I have

2

A. M. cir. 4066.
A. D. cir. 62.
A. U. C. 814.
An. Imp. Ne-
ronis Cæs.
Aug. 9.

[u] ye did communicate with my affliction.

15 Now, ye Philippians, know also, that in the beginning of the Gospel, when I departed from Macedonia, [v] no Church communicated with me, as concerning giving and receiving, but ye only.

16 For even in Thessalonica ye sent once and again unto my necessity.

17 Not because I desire a gift; but I desire [w] fruit that may abound to your account.

18 But [x] I have all, and abound: I am full, having received [y] of Epaphroditus the things *which were sent* from you, [z] an odour of a sweet smell, [a] a sacrifice acceptable, well pleasing to God.

19 But my God [b] shall supply all your need, [c] according to his riches in glory by Christ Jesus.

A. M. cir. 4066.
A. D. cir. 62.
A. U. C. 814.
An. Imp. Ne-
ronis Cæs.
Aug. 9.

20 [d] Now unto God and our Father *be* glory for ever and ever. Amen.

21 Salute every saint in Christ Jesus. The [e] brethren which are with me greet you.

22 All the saints salute you, [f] chiefly they that are of Cæsar's household.

23 [g] The grace of our Lord Jesus Christ *be* with you all. Amen.

¶ It was written to the Philippians from Rome by Epaphroditus.

---

[u] Chap. i. 7.——[v] 2 Cor. xi. 8, 9.——[w] Rom. xv. 28; Tit. iii. 14.——[x] Or, *I have received all.*——[y] Chap. ii. 25.——[z] Heb. xiii. 16.——[a] 2 Cor. ix. 12.

[b] Psa. xxiii. 1; 2 Cor. ix. 8.——[c] Eph. i. 7; iii. 16.——[d] Rom. xvi. 27; Gal. i. 5.——[e] Gal. i. 2.——[f] Chap. i. 13.——[g] Romans xvi. 24.

---

learned all these important lessons, and am never miserable in *want*, yet ye have done well in sending me relief in the time of affliction.

Verse 15. *In the beginning of the Gospel*] When, having preached to you, I went forth into Macedonia, I received help from none of the Churches which I had founded, but from you alone. I *received* nothing from any others, and nothing was *offered* me.

Verse 16. *For even in Thessalonica*] While labouring to plant the Church there, he was supported partly by working with his hands, 1 Thess. ii. 9; 2 Thess. iii. 7—9; and partly by the contributions sent him from Philippi. Even the Thessalonians had contributed little to his maintenance: this is not spoken to their credit.

Verse 17. *Not because I desire a gift*] I do not speak thus to incite you to send me a farther gift; I speak this on the general subject, because I wish you to bear such fruit as shall abound to your account in the day of the Lord.

Verse 18. *I have all*] Ye have now sent me so much by Epaphroditus, that I abound in all the necessaries of life.

Having received—the things] Probably a supply of *clothes* and such like *necessaries*, as well as of *money*.

An odour of a sweet smell] Alluding to the sacrifices offered up under the law. With what ye have done to me, his servant, God is well pleased. See Eph. v. 2, and the note there.

Verse 19. *My God shall supply all your need*] As you have given to me in my distress, God will never suffer you to want without raising up help to you, as he raised you up for help to me.

According to his riches] His fulness is infinite; and through Christ, whose followers we are, he will dispense every requisite blessing of *providence, grace,* and *glory,* to you.

Verse 20. *Now unto God and our Father*] God is our *Father* in Christ Jesus; and such pity as a father hath for his children, such has the Lord for them that fear him; as a father is concerned for the support and

life of his children, so is God concerned for you. A father may be poor, and unable to help his most beloved children; God, your Father, is infinite in the riches of his grace and glory, and out of his abundance we have all received, and grace for grace. Therefore, *to God our Father, be glory for ever and ever!*

Verse 21. *Salute every saint*] Remember to present my affectionate wishes to every Christian at Philippi.

The brethren which are with me] Those who were fellow labourers with him, generally supposed to be Aristarchus, Mark, Justus, Epaphras, Luke, and Demas. See the end of the epistles to the *Colossians,* and to *Philemon.*

Verse 22. *All the saints*] All the Christians now at Rome.

They that are of Cæsar's household.] Nero was at this time emperor of Rome: a more worthless, cruel, and diabolic wretch never disgraced the name or form of man; yet in *his family* there were Christians: but whether this relates to the members of the *imperial family,* or to *guards,* or *courtiers,* or to *servants,* we cannot tell. If even some of his *slaves* were converted to Christianity, it would be sufficiently marvellous. Converts to Christianity in this family there certainly were; and this shows how powerfully the Divine word had been preached and spread. That the Empress *Poppæa* may have been favourably inclined to Christianity is possible; for Josephus relates of her, Antiq., lib. xx. cap. 7: Θεοσεβης γαρ ην· *She was a worshipper of the true God;* it is not likely, therefore, that she threw any hinderances in the way of her servants who might wish to embrace the Christian faith. St. *Jerome,* in Philem., states that St. Paul had converted many in Cæsar's family; *A Cæsare missus in carcerem, notior familiæ ejus factus, persecutoris Christi domum fecit ecclesiam.* "Being by the emperor cast into prison, he became the more known to his family, and he turned the house of Christ's persecutor into a church." Some imagine that *Seneca,* the preceptor of Nero, and the poet

Lucan, were converted by St. Paul; and there are still extant, and in a MS. now before me, letters which profess to have passed between Paul and *Seneca;* but they are worthy of neither. They have been printed in some editions of *Seneca's* works. See the remarks below.

Verse 23. *The grace of our Lord*] The usual apostolical benediction, which has often occurred, and been more than once explained. See on Rom. i. 7, and Gal. vi. 18. The word ἡμων, *our,* is omitted by many MSS. and several versions, which simply read, *The grace of the Lord Jesus Christ.*

Be *with you all.*] Instead of παντων, *all,* Πνευματος, *Spirit,* is the reading of ADEFG, several others, with the *Coptic, Sahidic, Æthiopic, Armenian, Vulgate,* and *Itala;* besides several of the Fathers.

There are various subscriptions to this epistle in the different MSS. and versions. In the common GREEK text it stands thus : *It was written to the Philippians from Rome by Epaphroditus. The Epistle to the Philippians was written from Rome, and sent by Epaphroditus.*—SYRIAC. *To the Philippians.*—ÆTHIOPIC. *The end of the Epistle; it was written at Rome, and sent by Epaphroditus.*—ARABIC. *To the Philippians by Timothy and Epaphroditus.*—COPTIC.

1. THE MSS. generally agree with the versions, and all unite in stating that this epistle was written and sent from *Rome,* so that the common subscription may well stand. Yet there have been some strong objections made against this, as far as the *place* is concerned. Some foreign critics have maintained, that were it to be granted that the apostle was now a *prisoner* for the testimony of Christ, yet it does not follow that he was a prisoner at *Rome,* for he himself tells us, 2 Cor. xi. 23, that he was *in prisons more abundant ;* and, consequently, he might be in prison somewhere else : but they have gone farther, and denied that this epistle was written while Paul was a *prisoner ;* affirming that he had been already liberated, and that of this there are several evidences in the epistle itself. *J. Christopher Wolf,* in his *Curæ,* has considered all these objections in detail, and appears to have answered them in a very satisfactory manner. That St. Paul was *now* in prison, these words seem clearly to prove, chap. i. 16 : *The one preach Christ* *of contention, not sincerely, supposing to add affliction to my bonds.* This strongly argues that he was then suffering imprisonment, and that certain persons of perverse minds preached the Gospel in such a way as was calculated to make his bonds still more grievous. And, as he sends the salutations of saints which were of Cæsar's household, it seems most evident that he was then at *Rome ;* as, had he been a prisoner in any of the *provinces,* it is not likely that he would send to *Philippi* the greetings of those who lived at *Rome.*

2. The *cause* of this imprisonment has been variously understood. *Theodorus Metochita* says it was in consequence of his having converted Nero's *baker,* and one of his *concubines ;* at which the emperor, being enraged, ordered him to be cast into prison : but the authority on which this rests is scarcely sufficient to render it credible.

3. Paul is generally allowed to have been twice imprisoned at Rome : this was, without doubt, the *first* time of his being there in *bonds,* as there is every appearance that he was delivered after this ; but his *second* imprisonment issued in his *martyrdom.* Every apostle of God is immortal till his work is done. Paul became a martyr when God saw that there was no farther need either for his preaching or his writing ; he had kept and defended the faith, and had finished his course ; God took him then from the evil to come, and crowned him with the glory which his Redeemer had provided for him, in reference to which he lived, and after which he had continually aspired.

4. Reader, be thankful to God, who, in pity to thy weakness, has called thee to *believe* and *enjoy,* and not to *suffer* for his sake. It is not for us to *covet* seasons of *martyrdom ;* we find it difficult to be faithful even in ordinary trials : yet, as offences may come, and times of sore trial and proof may occur, we should be prepared for them ; and we should know that nothing less than Christ in us, the hope of glory, will enable us to stand in the cloudy and dark day. Let us, therefore, put on the whole armour of God ; and, fighting under the Captain of our salvation, expect the speedy destruction of every inward foe ; and triumph in the assurance that *death,* the last enemy, will, in his destructions, shortly be brought to a perpetual end. Hallelujah ! The Lord God Omnipotent reigneth. Amen and Amen.

Finished correction for the press, Dec. 16th, 1831.—A. C.

PREFACE

TO THE

EPISTLE OF PAUL THE APOSTLE

TO THE

COLOSSIANS.

COLOSSE, or rather *Colassa*, (see on chap. i. 1,) was a city of Phrygia Pacatiana, now a part of *Natolia*, in Asia Minor, seated on an eminence on the south side of the river Mæander, now *Meinder*, near to the place where the river *Lycas* enters the earth, and begins to run under ground, which course it continues for about three-quarters of a mile, before it emerges and falls into the Mæander. Of this ancient city not much is known: it was situated between Laodicea and Hierapolis, and at an equal distance from either; and to this place Xerxes came in his expedition against Greece.

The government of this city is said to have been *democratic*, and its first magistrate bore the title of *archon* and *prætor*. The Macedonians transferred Colosse to the Persians; and it afterwards passed under the government of the Seleucidæ. After the defeat of Antiochus III., at the battle of Magnesia, it became subject to Eumenes, king of Pergamus: and when Attalus, the last of his successors, bequeathed his dominions to the Romans, this city, with the whole of Phrygia, formed a part of the proconsular province of Asia; which division subsisted till the time of Constantine the Great. After the time of this emperor, Phrygia was divided into Phrygia Pacatiana, and Phrygia Salutaris: and Colosse was the sixth city of the first division.

The ancient city of Colosse has been extinct for nearly eighteen hundred years; for about the tenth year of the Emperor Nero, about a year after the writing of this epistle, not only Colosse, but Laodicea and Hierapolis, were destroyed by an earthquake, according to Eusebius; and the city which was raised in the place of the former was called *Chonos* or *Konos*, which name it now bears. See New Encyclopædia. On modern maps Konos is situated about twenty miles NE. of *Degnizlu*, in lat. about 38° north, and in long. 29° 40′ east of London.

The epistle to this city appears to have been written about the same time with that to the Philippians, viz. towards the end of the year 62, and in the ninth of the Emperor Nero.

That the two epistles were written about the same time is rendered probable by the following circumstance: In the Epistle to the Philippians, chap. ii. 19, St. Paul purposes to send Timothy to Philippi, who was then with him at Rome, that he might know their state. As Timothy joins with the apostle in the salutation at the beginning of *this* epistle, it is evident that he was still at Rome, and had not yet been sent to Philippi; and as St. Paul wrote the former epistle nearly at the close of his first imprisonment at Rome, the two epistles must have been written within a short space of each other. See the *preface* to the Epistle to the Philippians.

When, or by *whom*, Christianity was first preached at Colosse, and a Church founded there, we cannot tell; but it is most likely that it was by St. Paul himself, and during the three years in which he dwelt at Ephesus; for he had then employed himself with such zeal and diligence that we are told, Acts xix. 10: "That all they that dwelt in Asia heard the word of the Lord Jesus, both Jews and Greeks." And that Paul preached in *Phrygia*, the district in which this city was situated, we learn from Acts xvi. 6: "Now when they had gone through *Phrygia* and the region of Galatia;" and at another time we find that "he went over all the country of Galatia and *Phrygia* in order, strengthening all the disciples;" Acts xviii. 23. It has, however, been argued, from chap. ii. ver. 1, of this epistle, that Paul had never been at Colosse; for he there says: *I would that ye knew what great conflict I have for you, and for them at Laodicea, and* for *as many as have not seen my face in the flesh.* But the consequence drawn from these words does not absolutely follow. Dr. Lardner alleges a variety of considerations which induced him to believe that the Churches of Colosse and Laodicea were founded by St. Paul, viz.

1. That the apostle was twice in Phrygia, in which were Colosse, Laodicea, and Hierapolis. See the places above quoted from the *Acts* of the Apostles.

2. That he does in effect, or even expressly, say that he had dispensed the Gospel to the Colossians, chap. i. 21–25. See particularly the 23d, 24th, and 25th verses.

2

3. From several passages in the epistle it appears that the apostle does not speak as to *strangers*, but to acquaintances, disciples, and converts. Some think that Epaphras, who is called their *apostle*, chap. i. 7, was the first who planted Christianity among the Colossians.

But the arguments drawn from Acts xvi. and xviii., referred to above, are quite invalidated, if we allow the opinion of some learned men, among whom are *Suidas, Calepine, Munster*, and others, that the *Colossus*, a gigantic statue at Rhodes, gave its own name to the *people* among whom it stood; for the ancient poets call the inhabitants of the island of Rhodes, *Colossians*; and hence they thought that the *Colossians*, to whom St. Paul directs this epistle, were the *inhabitants* of *Rhodes*. This opinion, however, is not generally adopted. From a great similarity in the doctrine and phraseology of this epistle to that written to the Ephesians, this to the Colossians has been considered an epitome of the former, as the Epistle to the Galatians has been considered an abstract of that to the Romans. See the concluding observations on the Epistle to the Galatians; and the notes on chap. i. 4, of this epistle, and elsewhere.

Whether the *Colossians* to whom the apostle addresses this epistle were Jews or Gentiles, cannot be absolutely determined. It is most probable that they were a *mixture* of both; but that the principal part were converted Jews is most likely. This, indeed, appears to have been the case in most of the Asiatic and Grecian Churches; for there were Jews, at this time, sojourning in almost every part of the Roman empire, which then comprehended the greatest portion of the known world.

The *language* of this epistle is bold and energetic, the *sentiments* are grand, and the *conceptions* vigorous and majestic. The *phraseology* is in many places *Jewish*; and the reason is obvious: the apostle had to explain subjects which never had a name in any other language. The mythology of the Gentiles could not furnish terms to explain the theology of the Jews; much less, the more refined and spiritual system of Christianity

2

THE

EPISTLE OF PAUL THE APOSTLE

TO THE

COLOSSIANS.

Chronological Notes relative to this Epistle

Usherian year of the world, 4066.—Alexandrian era of the world, 5564.—Antiochian era of the world 5554.—Constantinopolitan era of the world, 5570.—Year of the Eusebian epocha of the Creation, 4290. —Year of the Julian period, 4772.—Year of the minor Jewish era of the world, 3822.—Year of the Greater Rabbinical era of the world, 4421.—Year from the Flood, according to Archbishop Usher, and the English Bible, 2410.—Year of the Cali yuga, or Indian era of the Deluge, 3164.—Year of the era of Iphitus, or since the first commencement of the Olympic games, 1002.—Year of the Nabonassarean era. 809. Year of the era of the Seleucidæ, 374.—Year of the Spanish era, 100.—Year of the Actiac or Actian era, 93.—Year from the birth of Christ, 66.—Year of the vulgar era of Christ's nativity, 62.—Year from the building of Rome, according to Varro, 814.—Year of the CCXth Olympiad, 2.—Jesus, high priest of the Jews.—Common Golden Number, 6.—Jewish Golden Number, 3.—Year of the Solar Cycle, 15.— Dominical Letter, C.—Jewish Passover, April 10th.—Easter Sunday, April 11th.—Epact, or the moon's age on the 22d of March, or the Xth of the Calends of April, 25.—Year of the reign of Nero Cæsar, the sixth emperor of the Romans, 9.—In the first year of Albinus, governor of the Jews.—Year of Vologesus, king of the Parthians, 12.—Year of Domitius Corbulo, governor of Syria, 3.—Roman Consuls , P. Marius Celsus, and L. Asinius Gallus, from Jan. 1st to July 1st; and L. Annæus Seneca, the philoso pher, and Trebellius Maximus, for the remainder of the year.

CHAPTER I.

The salutation of Paul and Timothy to the Church at Colosse, 1, 2. They give thanks to God for the good estate of that Church, and the wonderful progress of the Gospel in every place, 3–6 ; having received particulars of their state from Epaphroditus, which not only excited their gratitude, but led them to pray to God that they might walk worthy of the Gospel ; and they give thanks to Him who had made them meet for an inheritance among the saints in light, 7–12. This state is described as a deliverance from the power of darkness, and being brought into the kingdom of God's dear Son, 13, 14. The glorious character of Jesus Christ, and what He has done for mankind, 15–20. The salvation which the Colossians had received, and of which the apostle had been the minister and dispenser, 21–26. The sum and substance of the apostle's preaching, and the manner in which he executed his ministry, 27–29.

A. M. cir. 4066.
A. D. cir. 62.
A. U. C. 814.
An. Imp. Neronis Cæs.
Aug. 9.

PAUL, [a] an apostle of Jesus Christ by the will of God, and Timotheus *our* brother,

2 To the saints [b] and faithful brethren in Christ which are at Colosse : [c] Grace *be* unto you, and peace, from God our Father, and the Lord Jesus Christ.

A. M. cir. 4066.
A D cir. 62.
A. U C 814.
An. Imp. Neronis Cæs.
Aug 9.

[a] Eph. i. 1.——[b] 1 Cor. iv. 17; Eph. vi. 21.   [c] Gal. i. 3.

NOTES ON CHAP. I.

Verse 1. *Paul, an apostle—by the will of God*] As the word αποστολος, *apostle*, signifies *one sent*, an envoy or messenger, any person or persons may be the *senders :* but the word is particularly restrained to the messengers of the everlasting Gospel, sent immediately from God himself; and this is what St. Paul particularly remarks here when he calls himself an *apostle by the will of God ;* signifying that he had derived his commission from an express volition or purpose of the Almighty.

And Timotheus] Though Timothy is here joined

2

A. M. cir. 4066.
A. D. cir. 62.
A. U. C. 814.
An. Imp. Ne-
ronis Cæs.
Aug. 9.

3 [d] We give thanks to God and the Father of our Lord Jesus Christ, praying always for you,

4 [e] Since we heard of your faith in Christ Jesus, and of [f] the love *which ye have* to all the saints ;

5 For the hope [g] which is laid up for you in heaven, whereof ye heard before in the word of the truth of the Gospel ;

6 Which is come unto you, [h] as *it is* in all the world ; and [i] bringeth forth fruit, as *it doth* also in you, since the day ye heard *of it*, and knew [k] the grace of God in truth

A. M. cir. 4066.
A. D. cir. 62.
A. U. C. 814.
An. Imp. Ne-
ronis Cæs.
Aug. 9.

---

[d] 1 Cor. i. 4; Ephesians i. 16; Phil. i. 3; iv. 6.——[e] Ver. 9; Eph. i. 15; Philemon 5.——[f] Heb. vi. 10.——[g] 2 Tim. iv. 8; 1 Pet. i. 4.

[h] Matthew xxiv. 14; Mark xvi. 15; Rom. x. 18; ver. 23. [i] Mark iv. 8; John xv. 16; Phil. i. 11.——[k] 2 Cor. vi. 1; Eph. iii. 2; Tit. ii. 11 ; 1 Pet. v. 12.

---

in the salutation, yet he has never been understood as having any part in composing this epistle. He has been considered as the amanuensis or scribe of the apostle.

Verse 2. To the saints] Those who professed Christianity. See the note on Eph. i. 1.

Which are at Colosse] Instead of εν Κολοσσαις, at Colosse, or among the Colossians, ABC, and many other excellent MSS., with both the *Syriac, Coptic, Slavonic, Origen,* Gregory Nyssen, Amphilochus, Theodoret, Damascenus, Theophylact, and others, read εν Κολασσαις, in *Colassa,* or among the *Colassians;* and this is most probably the true reading. That this city perished by an earthquake, a short time after the date of this epistle, we have the testimony of Eusebius. That which at present is supposed to occupy the site of this ancient city is called *Konos.* For other particulars see the *preface* to this epistle.

Grace be unto you] See on Rom. i. 7.

And the Lord Jesus Christ.] This clause is omitted by many MSS., several *versions,* and some of the *fathers.* Griesbach has left it out of the text, not, in my opinion, on sufficient evidence.

Verse 3. We give thanks to God] Who is the author of all good ; and from whom the *grace,* which has produced your conversion, has sprung by his mission of Christ Jesus. See the note on Eph. i. 15, 16.

Verse 4. Since we heard of your faith] This is very similar to Eph. i. 15. And it is certain that the apostle seems to have considered the Church at Ephesus, and that at Colassa to have been nearly in the same state, as the two epistles are very similar in their doctrine and phraseology.

Verse 5. For the hope which is laid up for you in heaven] That eternal life, both of body and soul, which the apostle mentions, Titus i. 2 : *In hope of eternal life, which God, that cannot lie, promised before the world began.* The *hope* is here used for the *object* of hope ; as every person that is born of God hopes for the resurrection of his body, and the glorification of both it and his soul in the realms of eternal blessedness.

In the word of the truth of the Gospel] In the *doctrine* of that Gospel of your salvation which is the *truth* of God. Of this hope, by this doctrine, *they had heard before,* probably by persons who had heard and received the Gospel either at Ephesus or some other place, either in Asia Minor or Greece, where the apostles had preached. Some critics suppose that the word προηκουσατε, *heard before,* refers to their heathen state previously to their having heard the Gospel ; as they could have no rational hope either of eternal life or the resurrection of the body, till they had heard the *doctrine of the truth of the Gospel.* Heathenism knew nothing of the *resurrection* of the *body,* and had very indistinct and uncertain notions of the *immortality* of the soul.

Verse 6. Which is come unto you] The doctrine of the Gospel is represented as a *traveller,* whose object it is to visit the whole habitable earth ; and, having commenced his journey in Judea, had proceeded through Syria and through different parts of Asia Minor, and had lately arrived at their city, every where proclaiming glad tidings of great joy to all people.

As it is in all the world] So rapid is this *traveller* in his course, that he had already gone nearly through the whole of the countries under the Roman dominion ; and will travel on till he has proclaimed his message to every people, and kindred, and nation, and tongue.

In the beginning of the apostolic age the word of the Lord had certainly *free course,* did *run* and was *glorified.* Since that time the population of the earth has increased greatly ; and, to follow the metaphor, the *traveller* still continues in his great journey. It is the glory of the present day that, by means of the *British and Foreign Bible Society,* Bibles are multiplied in all the languages of Europe ; and by means of the Christian missionaries, *Carey, Marshman,* and *Ward,* whose zeal, constancy, and ability, have been rarely equalled, and perhaps never surpassed, the sacred writings have been, in the compass of a few years, translated into most of the written languages of India, in which they were not previously extant. In this labour they have been ably seconded by the Rev. Henry Martyn, one of the East India Company's chaplains, who was taken to his great reward just when he had *completed* a pure and accurate version of the New Testament into *Persian.* The Rev. R. Morrison, at Canton, has had the honour to present the whole of the New Testament, in Chinese, to the immense population of that greatest empire of the earth. May that dark people receive it, and walk in the light of the Lord ! And, by means of the *Wesleyan missionaries,* the sacred writings have been printed and widely circulated in the Singhalese and Indo-Portuguese, through the whole of the island of Ceylon, and the pure word of the Gospel has been preached there, and also on the whole continent of India, to the conversion of multitudes. Let every reader pray that all these noble attempts may be crowned with unlimited success, till the earth is filled both with the

A. M. cir. 4066.
A. D. cir. 62.
A. U. C. 814.
An. Imp. Ne-
ronis Cæs.
Aug. 9.

7 As ye also learned of [1] Epaphras, our dear fellow servant, who is for you [m] a faithful minister of Christ;

8 Who also declared unto us your [n] love in the Spirit.

9 [o] For this cause we also, since the day we heard *it*, do not cease to pray for you, and to desire [p] that ye might be filled with [q] the know-

---

[1] Ch. iv. 12; Phil. 23.——[m] 2 Cor. xi. 23; 1 Tim. iv. 6.——[n] Rom.
xv. 30.——[o] Eph. i. 15, 16; ver. 3, 4.——[p] 1 Cor. i. 5.——[q] Rom.
xii. 2; Eph. v. 10, 17.——[r] Eph. i. 8.——[s] Eph. iv. 1; Phil. i. 27;

---

ledge of his will, [r] in all wisdom and spiritual understanding;

10 [s] That ye might walk worthy of the Lord [t] unto all pleasing, [u] being fruitful in every good work, and increasing in the knowledge of God;

11 [v] Strengthened with all might, according to his glorious power, [w] unto all patience and long-suffering [x] with joyfulness;

A. M. cir. 4066.
A. D. cir. 62.
A. U. C. 814.
An. Imp. Ne-
ronis Cæs.
Aug. 9.

---

[1] Thess. ii. 12.——[t] 1 Thess. iv. 1.——[u] John xv. 16; 2 Cor. ix.
8; Phil. i. 11; Tit. iii. 1; Heb. xiii. 21.——[v] Eph. iii. 16; vi. 10
[w] Eph. iv. 2.——[x] Acts v. 41; Rom. v. 3.

---

knowledge and glory of the Lord. *Talia secla currite!* Amen.

And bringeth forth fruit] Wherever the pure Gospel of Christ is preached, it is the *seed of the kingdom*, and must be fruitful in all those who receive it by faith, in simplicity of heart.

After καρποφορουμενον, *bringeth forth fruit*, ABCD* EFG, many others, both the *Syriac*, Erpen's *Arabic*, the *Coptic*, *Sahidic*, *Æthiopic*, *Armenian*, *Slavonic*, *Vulgate*, and *Itala*, together with many of the *fathers*, add και αυξανομενον, *and increaseth*. It had not only *brought forth fruit*, but was *multiplying* its own kind; every fruit containing *seed*, and every seed producing thirty, sixty, or a hundredfold. This reading is very important, and is undoubtedly *genuine*.

The grace of God in truth] Ye were *fruitful*, and went on *increasing* in the salvation of God, from the time that ye heard and acknowledged this doctrine to be of God, to spring from the *grace* or *benevolence* of God; and received it in truth, sincerely and uprightly, as his greatest gift to man.

Verse 7. As ye also learned of Epaphras—who is for you] Who this Epaphras was we cannot tell; only it is likely that he was a Colossian, and became, by the call and grace of Christ, a deacon of this Church, faithfully labouring with the apostle, to promote its best interests. Some think that he is the same with *Epaphroditus*, *Epaphras* being a contraction of that name, as *Demas* is of *Demetrius*; and it is remarkable that one of the *Slavonic* versions has *Epaphroditus* in this place. That he was a Colossian is evident from chap. iv. 12: *Epaphras, who is one of you*, ὁ εξ ὑμων· and some think that he was the first who preached the Gospel among this people, and hence called an *apostle*. He was raised up among themselves to be their minister in the absence of the apostle, and he showed himself to be worthy of this calling by a faithful discharge of his ministry, and by *labouring fervently for them all*, and pressing them forward, that *they might stand perfect and complete in all the will of God.*

Verse 8. Your love in the Spirit.] So we preached, *and so ye believed.* The heavenly flame in the heart of this minister communicated itself to those who heard him; it was *like priest like people.* They enjoyed a spiritual, energetic ministry, and they were a *spiritual* people; they had a *loving spirit*, and *love* through the *Spirit* of God which dwelt in them. And of this love of theirs in the Spirit, and particularly towards the apostle, Epaphras gave full proof, not only

by describing to the apostle the affection they felt for him, but in presenting to him those *supplies* which their love to him caused them to furnish.

Verse 9. For this cause] See on Eph. i. 15, 16, where the same sentiment occurs.

That ye might be filled] Nothing could satisfy the apostle, either for himself or his hearers, but the fulness of the blessing of the Gospel of peace. The Colossians had knowledge, but they must have *more*; it is their privilege to be filled with it. As the bright shining of the *sun* in the firmament of heaven fills the whole world with light and heat, so the light of the Sun of righteousness is to illuminate their whole souls, and fill them with Divine splendour, so that they might know *the will of God, in all wisdom and spiritual understanding*; in a word, that they might have such a knowledge of Divine things as the Spirit of truth can teach to the soul of man.

Verse 10. That ye might walk worthy of the Lord] Suitably to your Christian profession, exemplifying its holy doctrines by a holy and useful life. See the notes on Eph. iv. 1, and on Phil. i. 27.

Unto all pleasing] Doing every thing in the best *manner*, in the most proper *time*, and in a becoming *spirit*. Even a good work may be marred and rendered fruitless by being done *improperly*, out of *season*, or in a *temper* of mind that grieves the Holy Spirit.

Being fruitful in every good work] See on ver. 6. St. Paul exhorts the Christians at Colosse, 1. To *walk*—to be active in their Christian calling. 2. To *walk worthily*—suitably to the dignity of that calling, and to the purity of that God who had called them into this state of salvation. 3. To do every thing *unto all pleasing*; that God might be pleased with the *manner*, the *time*, the *motive*, *disposition*, *design*, and *object* of every act. 4. That they should be *fruitful*; mere *harmlessness* would not be sufficient; as God had sown good seed, he expected good fruit. 5. That *every work* should be *good*; they must not be fruitful in some works and fruitless in others. 6. That they should increase in religious knowledge as time rolled on, knowing, by genuine Christian *experience*, more of God, of his love, and of his peace, day by day.

Verse 11. Strengthened with all might] That they might be able to walk worthy of the Lord, bring forth fruit, &c. See the notes on Eph. iii. 13, &c.

According to his glorious power] According to that sufficiency of strength which may be expected from him who has all power both in the heavens and in the earth.

A. M. cir. 4066.
A. D. cir. 62.
A. U C. 814.
An. Imp. Neronis Cæs.
Aug. 9.

12 ʸ Giving thanks unto the Father, which hath made us meet to be partakers of ᶻ the inheritance of the saints in light :

13 Who hath delivered us from ᵃ the power of darkness, ᵇ and hath translated *us* into the kingdom of ᶜ his dear Son ;

14 ᵈ In whom we have redemption through his blood, *even* the forgiveness of sins :

15 Who is ᵉ the image of the invisible

A. M. cir. 4066.
A. D. cir. 62.
A. U. C. 814.
An. Imp. Neronis Cæs.
Aug. 9.

ʸ Eph. v 20; chap. iii. 15.——ᶻ Acts xxvi. 18; Ephesians i. 11. ᵃ Eph. vi 12; Heb. ii. 14; 1 Pet. ii 9.

ᵇ 1 Thess. ii. 12; 2 Peter i. 11.——ᶜ Gr. *the Son of his love* ᵈ Eph. i. 7.——ᵉ 2 Cor iv. 4; Heb. i. 3.

Unto all patience] Believing, hoping, and enduring all things.

With joyfulness] Feeling the continual testimony that ye please God, which will be a spring of perpetual comfort. See the notes on Eph. iv. 2.

Verse 12. *Giving thanks unto the Father*] Knowing that ye have nothing but what ye have received from his mere mercy, and that in point of *merit* ye can never *claim* any thing from him.

Which hath made us meet] Ικανωσαντι· Who has qualified us to be partakers, &c. Instead of ικανωσαντι, some MSS. and versions have καλεσαντι, called; and B (the Codex Vaticanus) has both readings . *Giving thanks unto the Father, who hath called and qualified us to be partakers*

Of the inheritance] Εις την μεριδα του κληρου. A plain allusion to the division of the promised land by *lot* among the different families of the twelve Israelitish tribes. The κληρος was the *lot* or *inheritance* belonging to the *tribe;* the μερις was the *portion* in that *lot* which belonged to each *family* of that tribe. This was a type of the kingdom of God, in which *portions* of eternal blessedness are dispensed to the genuine Israelites; to them who have the circumcision of the heart by the Spirit, whose praise is of God, and not of man.

Of the saints in light] *Light,* in the sacred writings, is used to express knowledge, *felicity,* purity, comfort, and joy of the most substantial kind ; here it is put to point out the state of glory at the right hand of God. As in Egypt, while the judgments of God were upon the land, there was a *darkness* which might be felt, yet all the Israelites had *light* in their dwellings; so in this world, while the *darkness* and wretchedness occasioned by sin remain, the disciples of Christ are light in the Lord, walk as children of the *light* and of the *day,* have in them no occasion of *stumbling,* and are on their way to the *ineffable light* at the right hand of God. Some think there is an allusion here to the *Eleusinian mysteries,* celebrated in deep caves and *darkness* in honour of Ceres; but I have already, in the notes to the Epistle to the Ephesians, expressed my doubts that the apostle has ever condescended to use such a simile The phraseology of the text is frequent through various parts of the sacred writings, where it is most obvious that no such allusion could possibly be intended.

Verse 13 *Delivered us from the power of darkness*] Darkness is here *personified,* and is represented as having εξουσια, *power, authority,* and *sway ;* all Jews and Gentiles, which had not embraced the Gospel, being under this authority and power. And the apostle intimates here that nothing less than the power of

God can redeem a man from this darkness, or prince of darkness, who, by means of sin and unbelief, keeps men in ignorance, vice, and misery.

Translated us into the kingdom, &c.] He has thoroughly changed our state, brought us out of the dark region of vice and impiety, and placed us in the kingdom under the government of *his dear Son,* Υιου της αγαπης αυτου, *the Son of his love;* the person whom, in his infinite love, he has given to make an atonement for the sin of the world.

Verse 14. *In whom we have redemption*] Who has paid down the redemption price, even his own blood, that our sins might be cancelled, and we made fit to be partakers of the inheritance among the saints in light.

The clause, δια του αιματος αυτου, *Through his blood,* is omitted by ABCDEFG, and by most others of weight and importance ; by the *Syriac, Arabic* of Erpen, *Coptic, Æthiopic, Sahidic,* some copies of the *Vulgate* and by the *Itala ;* and by most of the *Greek fathers.* Griesbach has left it out of the text. It is likely that the reading here is *not genuine ;* yet that we have redemption any other way than through the sacrifice of Christ, the Scriptures declare not. The same phrase is used Eph. i. 7, where there is no *various* reading in any of the MSS., *versions,* or *fathers.*

The forgiveness of sins] Αφεσιν των αμαρτιων· The *taking away* of sins ; all the *power, guilt,* and *infection* of sin. All sin of every kind, with all its influence and consequences.

Verse 15. *Who is the image of the invisible God*] The counterpart of God Almighty, and if the *image* of the *invisible* God, consequently nothing that *appeared* in him could be that *image ;* for if it could be *visible* in the *Son,* it could also be *visible* in the *Father ;* but if the Father be *invisible,* consequently his *image* in the Son must be *invisible* also. This is that *form of God* of which he divested himself; the ineffable glory in which he not only did not appear, as to its *splendour* and *accompaniments,* but concealed also its essential nature ; that inaccessible light which no man, no created being, can possibly see. This was that Divine nature, the *fulness of the Godhead bodily,* which dwelt in him.

The first-born of every creature] I suppose this phrase to mean the same as that, Phil. ii. 9 : *God hath given him a name which is above every name ;* he is as *man* at the *head* of all the creation of God ; nor can he with any propriety be considered as a *creature,* having himself created all things, and existed before any thing was made. If it be said that God created *him* first, and that he, by a delegated power from God, created all things, this is most flatly contradicted by the apostle's reasoning in the 16th and 17th verses

2

A. M. cir. 4066.
A. D. cir. 62.
A. U. C. 814.
An. Imp. Ne-
ronis Cæs.
Aug. 9.

God, [f] the first-born of every creature :

16 For [g] by him were all things created, that are in heaven, and that are in earth, visible and invisible, whether *they be* thrones, or [h] dominions, or principali-

ties, or powers : all things were created [i] by him, and for him :

17 [k] And he is before all things, and by him all things consist :

18 And [l] he is the head of the body, the Church ; who is the beginning, [m] the first-born

A. M. cir. 4066.
A. D. cir. 62.
A. U. C. 814.
An. Imp. Ne-
ronis Cæs.
Aug. 9.

---

[f] Rev. iii. 14.——[g] John. i. 3 ; 1 Cor. viii. 6 ; Eph. iii. 9 ; Heb. i. 2.——[h] Rom. viii. 38 ; Eph. i. 21 ; chap. ii. 10, 15 ; 1 Pet. iii. 22.——[i] Rom. xi. 36 ; Heb. ii. 10.

[k] John i. 1, 3 ; xvii. 5 ; 1 Cor. viii. 6.——[l] Eph. i. 10, 22 ; iv. 15 ; v. 23 ; 1 Cor. xi. 3.——[m] Acts xxvi. 23 ; 1 Cor. xv. 20, 23 ; Rev. i. 5.

As the Jews term Jehovah בכורו של עולם *becoro shel olam, the first-born of all the world,* or *of all the creation,* to signify his having created or produced all things ; (see Wolfius in loc.) so Christ is here termed, and the words which follow in the 16th and 17th verses are the proof of this. The phraseology is Jewish ; and as they apply it to the supreme Being merely to denote his eternal *pre-existence,* and to point him out as the *cause* of all things ; it is most evident that St. Paul uses it in the same way, and illustrates his meaning in the following words, which would be absolutely absurd if we could suppose that by the former he intended to convey any idea of the *inferiority* of Jesus Christ.

Verses 16, 17. *For by him were all things created, &c.*] These two verses contain parts of the same subject. I shall endeavour to distinguish the statements of the apostle, and reason from them in such a way as the premises shall appear to justify, without appealing to any other scripture in proof of the doctrine which I suppose these verses to vindicate.

Four things are here asserted : 1. That Jesus Christ is the *Creator of the universe* ; of *all things visible and invisible* ; of all things that had a *beginning,* whether they exist in *time* or in *eternity.* 2. That whatsoever was created was created FOR *himself* ; that he was the *sole end* of his own work. 3. That he was *prior* to all *creation,* to all *beings,* whether in the *visible* or *invisible* world. 4. That he is the *preserver* and *governor* of all things ; for *by him all things consist.*

Now, allowing St. Paul to have understood the terms which he used, he must have considered Jesus Christ as being truly and properly *God.* I. Creation is the proper work of an infinite, unlimited, and unoriginated Being ; possessed of all perfections in their highest degrees ; capable of knowing, willing, and working infinitely, unlimitedly, and without control : and as creation signifies the production of *being* where all was *absolute nonentity,* so it necessarily implies that the Creator acted *of* and *from himself* ; for as, previously to this creation, there was no being, consequently he could not be actuated by any *motive, reason,* or *impulse, without himself* ; which would argue there was some being to produce the *motive* or *impulse,* or to *give* the *reason.* Creation, therefore, is the work of him who is *unoriginated,* infinite, unlimited, and eternal. But *Jesus Christ is the Creator of all things,* therefore Jesus Christ must be, according to the plain construction of the apostle's words, truly and properly GOD.

II. As, previously to creation, there was no *being* but God, consequently the great *First Cause* must, in

the exertion of his creative energy, have respect to himself alone ; for he could no more have respect to that which had *no existence,* than he could be *moved* by *nonexistence,* to produce existence or creation. the Creator, therefore, must make every thing FOR *himself.*

Should it be objected that Christ created *officially* or by *delegation,* I answer : This is impossible ; for, as creation requires absolute and unlimited power, or omnipotence, there can be but *one* Creator ; because it is impossible that there can be *two* or *more* Omnipotents, Infinites, or Eternals. It is therefore evident that creation cannot be effected *officially,* or by *delegation,* for this would imply a *Being conferring the office,* and *delegating* such *power* ; and that the Being *to* whom it was delegated was a *dependent Being* ; consequently not *unoriginated* and *eternal* ; but this the nature of creation proves to be absurd. 1. The thing being impossible in itself, because no limited being could produce a work that necessarily requires omnipotence. 2. It is impossible, because, if omnipotence be *delegated,* he to whom it is delegated *had it not before,* and he who delegates it *ceases to have it,* and consequently *ceases to be* GOD ; and the other to whom it was delegated *becomes* God, because such attributes as those with which he is supposed to be invested are *essential* to the nature of God. On this supposition *God ceases to exist,* though infinite and eternal, and another not naturally *infinite* and *eternal* becomes such ; and thus an *infinite* and *eternal* Being ceases to exist, and another infinite and eternal Being is produced in *time,* and has a *beginning,* which is absurd. Therefore, as *Christ* is the *Creator,* he did not create by *delegation,* or in any *official way.*

Again, if he had created by *delegation* or *officially,* it would have been *for* that *Being who gave him that office,* and delegated to him the requisite power ; but the text says that *all things were made* BY *him and* FOR *him,* which is a demonstration that the apostle understood Jesus Christ to be truly and essentially God.

III. As all *creation* necessarily exists in *time,* and had a *commencement,* and there was an *infinite duration* in which it *did not exist,* whatever was *before* or *prior* to that must be *no part of creation* ; and the Being who existed prior to creation, *and before all things*—all existence of every kind, must be the unoriginated and eternal God : but St. Paul says, *Jesus Christ was before all things* ; ergo, the apostle conceived Jesus Christ to be truly and essentially God.

IV. As every *effect* depends upon its *cause,* and cannot exist without it ; so *creation,* which is an *effect* of the *power* and *skill* of the Creator, can only exist and be preserved by a continuance of that energy that

A. M. cir. 4066.
A. D. cir. 62.
A. U. C. 814.
An. Imp. Ne-
ronis Cæs.
Aug. 9.

from the dead; that ⁿ in all *things* he might have the pre-eminence :

19 For it pleased *the Father* that ᵒ in him should all fulness dwell ;

20 And, ᵖ having ᑫ made peace through the blood of his cross, ʳ by him to reconcile ˢ all things unto himself ; by him, *I say,* whether *they be* things in earth, or things in heaven.

A. M. cir. 4066.
A. D. cir. 62.
A. U. C. 814.
An. Imp. Ne-
ronis Cæs.
Aug. 9.

ⁿ Or, *among all.*——ᵒ John i. 16; iii. 34; chapter ii. 9; iii. 11.

ᵖ Or, *making peace.*——ᑫ Eph. ii. 14, 15, 16.——ʳ 2 Cor. v. 18 ˢ Eph. i 10.

---

first gave it being. Hence, God, as the *Preserver*, is as necessary to the continuance of all things, as God the *Creator* was to their original production. But this *preserving* or *continuing* power is here ascribed to *Christ,* for the apostle says, And *by him do all things consist ;* for as all being was derived from him as its *cause,* so all being must *subsist by him,* as the *effect* subsists *by* and *through* its *cause.* This is another proof that the apostle considered Jesus Christ to be truly and properly God, as he attributes to him the *preservation* of all created things, which property of preservation belongs to God alone ; ergo, Jesus Christ is, according to the plain obvious meaning of every expression in this text, truly, properly, independently, and essentially God.

Such are the reasonings to which the simple letter of these two verses necessarily leads me. I own it is possible that I may have misapprehended this awful subject, for *humanum est errare et nescire;* but I am not conscious of the slightest intentional flaw in the argument. Taking, therefore, the apostle as an *uninspired* man, giving *his own view* of the Author of the Christian religion, it appears, beyond all controversy, that himself believed Christ Jesus to be God ; but considering him as writing under the *inspiration of the Holy Ghost,* then we have, from the plain grammatical meaning of the words which he has used, the fullest *demonstration* (for the Spirit of God cannot lie) that he who died for our sins and rose again for our justification, and in whose blood we have redemption, was God *over all.* And as *God* alone can give salvation to men, and God only can remit sin ; hence with the strictest propriety we are commanded to believe on the *Lord Jesus,* with the assurance that we shall be saved. Glory be to God for this unspeakable gift ! See my discourse on this subject.

Verse 18. *He is the head of the body*] What the apostle has said in the two preceding verses refers to the *Divine* nature of Jesus Christ ; he now proceeds to speak of his *human* nature, and to show how highly that is exalted beyond all created things, and how, in that, he is *head* of the *Church*—the author and dispenser of light, life, and salvation, to the Christian world ; or, in other words, that from him, as the *man* in whom the fulness of the Godhead bodily dwelt, all the mercy and salvation of the Gospel system is to be received.

The beginning, the first-born from the dead] In 1 Cor. xv. 20, Christ is called *the first-fruits of them that slept ;* and here, the *chief and first-born from the dead ;* he being the first that ever resumed the natural life, with the employment of all its functions, never more to enter the empire of death, after having died a natural death, and in such circumstances as precluded

the possibility of deception. The αρχη, *chief, head,* or *first,* answers in this verse to the απαρχη, or *first-fruits,* 1 Cor. xv. 20. Jesus Christ is not only the first who rose from the dead to die no more, but he is the first-fruits of human beings ; for as surely as the *first-fruits* were an indication and pledge of the *harvest,* so surely was the *resurrection* of Christ the proof that all mankind should have a resurrection from the dead.

That in all—he might have the pre-eminence] That he might be considered, in consequence of his mediatorial office, as possessing the *first* place in and being *chief* over all the creation of God ; for is it to be wondered at that the human nature, with which the great Creator condescended to unite himself, should be set over all the works of his hands ?

Verse 19. *For it pleased* the Father *that in him should all fulness dwell*] As the words, *the Father* are not in the text, some have translated the verse thus : *For in him it seemed right that all fulness should dwell ;* that is, that the majesty, power, and goodness of God should be manifested in and by Christ Jesus, and thus by him the Father reconciles all things to himself. The πληρωμα, or *fulness,* must refer here to the Divine nature dwelling in the *man* Christ Jesus.

Verse 20. *And, having made peace through the blood of his cross*] Peace between God and man for man being in a sinful state, and there being no peace to the wicked, it required a reconciliation to be made to restore peace between heaven and earth ; but peace could not be made without an atonement for sin, and the consequence shows that the blood of Christ shed on the cross was necessary to make this atonement.

To reconcile all things unto himself] The enmity was on the part of the *creature ;* though God is angry with the wicked every day, yet he is never *unwilling* to be reconciled. But man, whose carnal mind is *enmity* to God, is naturally *averse* from this reconciliation ; it requires, therefore, the *blood of the cross* to atone for the sin, and the influence of the Spirit to reconcile the transgressor to him against whom he has offended ! See the notes on 2 Cor. v. 19, &c.

Things in earth, or things in heaven.] Much has been said on this very obscure clause ; but, as it is my object not to write *dissertations* but *notes,* I shall not introduce the opinions of learned men, which have as much ingenuity as variety to recommend them. If the phrase be not a kind of collective phrase to signify *all the world,* or *all mankind,* as Dr. Hammond supposed *the things in heaven* may refer, according to some, to those persons who died under the Old Testament dispensation, and who could not have a title to glory but through the sacrificial death of Christ : and the apostle may have intended these merely to show

2

A. M. cir. 4066.
A. D. cir. 62.
A. U. C. 814.
An. Imp. Ne-
ronis Cæs.
Aug. 9.

21 And you, [t] that were some-time alienated and enemies [u] in *your* mind [v] by wicked works, yet now hath he reconciled.

22 [w] In the body of his flesh through death, [x] to present you holy, and unblamable, and unreprovable in his sight;

23 If ye continue in the faith [y] grounded and settled, and *be* [z] not moved away from the hope of the Gospel, which ye have heard, [a] *and* which was preached [b] to every creature which is under heaven; [c] whereof I Paul am made a minister:

A. M. cir. 4066
A. D. cir. 62.
A. U. C. 814.
An. Imp. Ne-
ronis Cæs.
Aug. 9.

24 [d] Who now rejoice in my sufferings [e] for you, and fill up [f] that which is behind of the afflictions of Christ in my flesh for [g] his body's sake, which is the Church;

---

[t] Eph. ii. 1, 2, 12, 19; iv. 18; [u] Or, *by your mind in wicked works.*——[v] Tit. i. 15, 16.——[w] Eph. ii. 15, 16.——[x] Luke i. 75; Eph. i. 4; v. 27; 1 Thess. iv. 7; Tit. ii. 14; Jude 24.——[y] Eph. iii. 17; chap. ii. 7.——[z] John xv. 6.

[a] Rom. x. 18.——[b] Ver. 6.——[c] Acts i. 17; 2 Cor. iii. 6; iv. 1; v. 18; Eph. iii. 7; ver. 25; 1 Tim. ii. 7.——[d] Rom. v. 3; 2 Cor. vii. 4.——[e] Eph. iii. 1, 13.——[f] 2 Cor. i. 5, 6; Phil. iii. 10; 2 Tim. i. 8; ii. 10.——[g] Eph. i. 23.

---

that without this sacrifice no human beings could be saved, not only those who were then on the earth, and to whom in their successive generations the Gospel should be preached, but even those who had died before the incarnation; and, as those of them that were faithful were now in a state of blessedness, they could not have arrived there but through the *blood of the cross*, for the blood of calves and goats could not take away sin. After all, the apostle probably means the *Jews* and the *Gentiles*; the state of the former being always considered a sort of *Divine* or *celestial* state, while that of the latter was reputed to be merely *earthly*, without any mixture of *spiritual* or *heavenly* good. It is certain that a grand part of our Lord's design, in his incarnation and death, was to reconcile the Jews and the Gentiles, and make them *one fold* under himself, the great Shepherd and Bishop of souls. That the enmity of the Jews was great against the Gentiles is well known, and that the Gentiles held them in supreme contempt is not less so. It was therefore an object worthy of the mercy of God to form a scheme that might reconcile these two grand divisions of mankind; and, as it was his purpose to reconcile and make them one, we learn from this circumstance, as well as from many others, that his design was to save the whole human race.

Verse 21. *And you, that were sometime alienated*] All men are *alienated* from God, and all are *enemies in their minds* to him, and show it by their *wicked works*; but this is spoken particularly of the *Gentiles*. The word απαλλοτριοω, which we render to *alienate*, to *give to another*, to *estrange*, expresses the state of the Gentiles: while the Jews were, at least by profession, *dedicated to God*, the Gentiles were *alienated*, that is, *given up to others*; they worshipped not the true God, but had gods many and lords many, to whom they dedicated themselves, their religious service, and their property. The verb αλλοτριοω, to *alienate*, being compounded here with the preposition απο, *from*, signifies to abalienate, to *estrange utterly*, to be *wholly the property of another.* Thus the Gentiles had alienated themselves from God, and were alienated or rejected by him, because of their wickedness and idolatry.

Enemies in your *mind*] They had the *carnal mind*, which is enmity against God; and this was expressed in their outward conduct by *wicked works*. See the note on Rom. v. 10. The *mind* is taken here for all the *soul, heart, affections, passions,* &c.

Verse 22. *In the body of his flesh*] By Christ's assumption of a human body, and dying for man, he has made an atonement for sin, through which men become reconciled to God and to each other.

To present you holy] Having saved you from your sins.

Unblamable] Having filled you with his Spirit, and written his law in your *hearts*, so that his love, shed abroad in your hearts, becomes the principle and motive to every action. The *tree* therefore being good, the *fruit* is also good.

And unreprovable] For, being filled with love, joy, peace, meekness, gentleness, and goodness, against these there is no law; and as they were called to love God with all their heart, soul, mind, and strength, and their neighbour as themselves, the whole *spirit* and *design* of the law was fulfilled in them, for *love is the fulfilling of the law.*

In his sight] At the day of judgment. None can enjoy heaven who have not been *reconciled* to God here, and shown forth the fruits of that reconciliation in being made *holy* and *unblamable*, that, when they come to be judged, they may be found *unreprovable.*

Verse 23. *If ye continue in the faith*] This will be the case if you, who have already believed in Christ Jesus, continue in that faith, *grounded* in the knowledge and love of God, and *settled*—made *firm* and perseveringly *steadfast*, in that state of salvation.

And be not moved away] Not permitting yourselves to be seduced by false teachers.

The hope of the Gospel] The resurrection of the body, and the glorification of it and the soul together, in the realms of blessedness. This is properly the Gospel HOPE.

To every creature which is under heaven] A Hebraism for the whole human race, and particularly referring to the two grand divisions of mankind, the Jews and Gentiles; to both of these the Gospel had been preached, and to each, salvation by Christ had been *equally* offered. And as none had been excluded from the offers of mercy, and Jesus Christ had tasted death for every man, and the Jews and Gentiles, in their great corporate capacity, had all been invited to believe the Gospel; therefore, the apostle concludes that the Gospel was preached to every creature under heaven, as being offered without restrictions or limitations to these two grand divisions of mankind, including the whole human race.

Verse 24. *Rejoice in my sufferings for you*] St.

2

A. M. cir. 4066.
A. D. cir. 62.
A. U. C. 814.
An. Imp. Ne-
ronis Cæs.
Aug. 9.

25 Whereof I am made a minister, according to ^h the dispensation of God which is given to me for you, ⁱ to fulfil the word of God;

26 *Even* ^k the mystery which hath been hid from ages and from generations, ^l but now is made manifest to his saints :

A. M. cir. 4066
A. D. cir. 62.
A. U. C. 814.
An. Imp. Ne-
ronis Cæs.
Aug. 9.

27 ^m To whom God would make known what *is* ⁿ the riches of the glory of this mystery among the Gentiles; which is Christ ^o in you, ^p the hope of glory :

28 Whom we preach, ^q warning every man,

---

^h 1 Cor. ix. 17; Gal. ii. 7; Eph. iii. 2; ver. 23.——ⁱ Or, *fully to preach the word of God;* Rom. xv. 19.——^k Rom. xvi. 25; 1 Cor. ii. 7; Eph. iii. 9.

^l Matt. xiii. 11; 2 Tim. i. 10.——^m 2 Cor. ii. 14.——ⁿ Rom. ix. 23; Eph. i. 7; iii. 8.——^o Or, *among you.*——^p 1 Tim. i. 1 ^q Acts xx. 20, 27, 31.

Paul always considers his persecutions, as far as the Jews were concerned in them, as arising from this simple circumstance—his asserting that God had chosen the Gentiles, and called them to enjoy the *very same privileges* with the Jews, and to constitute one Church with them.

It was on this account that the Jews attempted his life at Jerusalem, when, in order to save it, he was obliged to appeal to Cæsar; the consequences of which persecution he was now suffering in his imprisonment in Rome. See on chap. iv. 2.

That which is behind of the afflictions of Christ] I have still some afflictions to pass through before my race of glory be finished; afflictions which fall on me on account of the Gospel; such as Christ bore from the same persecuting people.

It is worthy of remark that the apostle does not say παθηματα, the *passion* of Christ, but simply θλιψεις, the *afflictions;* such as are common to all good men who bear a testimony against the ways and fashions of a wicked world. In these the apostle had his share, in the *passion* of Christ he could have none. He trod the wine press *alone*, of the people there were none with him.

His body's sake] Believers, both of Jews and Gentiles, who form that one *body,* of which Christ is the *head.*

Verse 25. *Whereof I am made a minister*] Having received especial commission from God to preach salvation to the Gentiles.

According to the dispensation] Κατα την οικονομιαν· According to the Gospel *economy* or *institution;* the *scheme* or *plan* of salvation by Christ crucified.

To fulfil the word of God] The Greek πληρωσαι τον λογον του Θεου may be translated, *fully to preach the doctrine of God.* See Rom. xv. 19, and the note there. Were we to take the word in its common meaning, it might signify to accomplish the purpose of God, as predicted by the prophets.

Verse 26. *The mystery which hath been hid*] The mystery is this : that God had designed to grant the Gentiles the same privileges with the Jews, and make them his people who were not his people. That this is what St. Paul means by the *mystery,* see Eph. iii. 3, &c.

Made manifest to his saints] It is fully known to all who have embraced the doctrine of Christ crucified; to all Christians.

Verse 27. *The riches of the glory*] God manifests to these how abundantly glorious this Gospel is among the Gentiles; and how effectual is this doctrine of Christ crucified to the salvation of multitudes.

Which is Christ in you, the hope of glory] In this and the following verse there are several remarkable particulars :—

I. We find here the *sum* and *substance* of the apostle's preaching.

1. He preached *Christ,* as the only Saviour of sinners.

2. He proclaimed this Christ as being *in* them; for the design of the Gospel is to put men in possession of the Spirit and power of Christ, to make them partakers of the Divine nature, and thus prepare them for an eternal union with himself. Should it be said that the preposition εν should be translated· *among,* it amounts to the same; for Christ was *among* them, to enlighten, quicken, purify, and refine them, and this he could not do without dwelling *in* them.

3. He preached this *present* and *indwelling* Christ as the *hope of glory;* for no man could rationally hope for glory who had not the *pardon* of his sins, and whose nature was not sanctified; and none could have pardon but through the blood of his cross; and none could have glorification but through the indwelling, sanctifying Spirit of Christ.

II. We see the *manner* in which the apostles preached.

1. *They warned every one*—they showed every man his danger; they proved that both Jews and Gentiles were under sin; and that the wrath of God was revealed against all ungodliness and unrighteousness of men; that time and life were uncertain; and that now was the day of salvation.

2. *They taught every man in all wisdom*—they considered the world in a state of ignorance and darkness, every man being through sin ignorant of himself and God; and the apostles taught them to know themselves, viz., that they were sinners, wretched, helpless, and perishing; and they taught them to know God, in his purity, justice, and truth, and in his mercy through Christ Jesus. Thus they instructed men in all wisdom; for the knowledge of a man's self and his God constitutes all that is essentially necessary to be known for present and eternal happiness.

III. The *end* which the apostles had in view in thus preaching Christ : to *present every man perfect in Christ Jesus.* The words τελειον εν Χριστῳ, perfect in or through Christ, signify two things : 1. That they should be *thoroughly instructed* in the doctrines of Christianity, so that they should know the truth as

A. M. cir. 4066.	and teaching every man in all	29 ˢ Whereunto I also labour,	A. M. cir. 4066.
A. D. cir 62.	wisdom; ʳ that we may present	ᵗ striving ᵘ according to his	A. D. cir. 62.
A. U. C. 814.	every man perfect in Christ	working, which worketh in me	A. U. C. 814.
An. Imp. Neronis Cæs.	Jesus:	mightily.	An. Imp. Neronis Cæs.
Aug. 9.			Aug. 9.

ʳ 2 Cor. xi. 2; Eph. v. 27; ver. 22.   ˢ 1 Cor. xv. 10.——ᵗ Chap. ii. 1.——ᵘ Eph. i. 19; iii. 7, 20.

it is in Jesus. 2. That they should be made partakers of the grace of the Gospel, so that they might be saved from all their sins, and be filled with His fulness. The succeeding chapter amply proves that nothing less than this entered into the apostle's design. Men may dispute as they please about *Christian perfection,* but without it no soul shall ever see God. He who is not saved from *all sin* here, cannot, to his joy, see God hereafter. This perfection of which the apostle speaks, and to which he laboured to bring all men, was something to be attained *in* and *through Christ.* The apostles preached Christ *in* the people; and they preached him as crucified for mankind. He who *died for* them was to *live in* them, and fill their whole souls with his own purity. No *indwelling sin* can be tolerated by an *indwelling Christ;* for he came into the world to save his people from their sins.

IV. We see who were the objects of the apostle's ministry: the Jews and Gentiles; παντα ανθρωπον, every man, the *whole human race.* Every man had sinned; and for every sinner Christ had died; and he died for them that they might be saved from all their sins. The apostles never restrained the offers of salvation; they made them frankly to all, believing that it was the will of God that all should believe and be saved: hence they warned and taught every man that they might, at the day of judgment, present every man perfect in Christ Jesus; for, although their own personal ministry could not reach all the inhabitants of the earth, yet it is by the doctrines which they preached, and by the writings which they have left on record, that the earth is to be filled with the knowledge and glory of God, and the souls of men brought to the enjoyment of the fulness of the blessing of the Gospel of peace.

Verse 29. *Whereunto I also labour*] In order to

accomplish this end, I labour with the utmost zeal and earnestness; and with all that strength with which God has most powerfully furnished me. Whoever considers the original words, αγωνιζομενος κατα την ενεργειαν αυτου την ενεργουμενην—εν δυναμει, will find that no verbal translation can convey their sense. God worked *energetically* in St. Paul, and he *wrought energetically* with God; and all this was in reference to the salvation of mankind.

1. THE preceding chapter contains the highest truths in the Christian religion, conveyed in language peculiar to this apostle; a language never taught by man, clothing ideas as vast as the human mind can grasp, and both coming immediately from that inspiration of the Almighty which giveth understanding.

2. What the apostle says on the Godhead of Christ has already been distinctly noted; and from this we must conclude that, unless there be some secret way of understanding the 16th and 17th verses, which God has nowhere revealed, taken in their sober and rational sense and meaning they must for ever settle this very important point. Let any man of common sense and reason hear these words, whose mind had not been previously warped by any sentiment on the subject, and who only knew, in religious matters, this one great truth, that there is a God, and that he made and governs all things; and then let him be asked, Of whom doth the apostle speak this? Would he not immediately answer, *He speaketh of God?* As to the difficulties on this subject, we must consider them difficulties rather to our limited intellect, than as belonging to the subject. We can know but little of an infinite and eternal Being; nothing, properly speaking, but what himself is pleased to reveal. Let us receive *this* with gratitude and reverence. See my discourse on the sum and substance of apostolic preaching.

CHAPTER II.

The apostle shows his great concern for the Church at Colosse and at Laodicea; and exhorts them to steadfastness in the faith, and to beware of being seduced by specious and enticing words, 1–5. And to walk in Christ, as they had been taught, and to abound in faith and holiness, 6, 7. To beware of false teachers, who strove to pervert the Gospel, and to lead their minds from him in whom the fulness of the Godhead dwells; with whom they were filled; by whom they had received spiritual circumcision; and into whom they were baptized and were quickened, and raised from a death of sin to a life of righteousness, 8–12. He points out their former state, and the great things which Christ had done for them, 13–15. Warns them against particular tenets of the Judaizing teachers relative to meats, drinks, holydays, festivals, and the specious pretences of deceivers, 16–19. And shows that all the things taught by these, though they had a show of wisdom, yet perished in the using, and were the commandments and doctrines of men, 20–23.

A. M. cir. 4066.
A. D. cir. 62.
A. U. C. 814.
An. Imp. Ne-
ronis Cæs.
Aug. 9.

FOR I would that ye knew what great ᵃ conflict ᵇ I have for you, and *for* them at Laodicea, and *for* as many as have not seen my face in the flesh;

2 ᶜ That their hearts might be comforted, ᵈ being knit together in love, and unto all riches of the full assurance of understanding, ᵉ to the acknowledgment of the mystery of God, and of the Father, and of Christ;

3 ᶠ In ᵍ whom are hid all the treasures of wisdom and knowledge.

4 And this I say, ʰ lest any man should beguile you with enticing words.

5 For ⁱ though I be absent in the flesh, yet

A. M. cir. 4066.
A. D. cir. 62.
A. U. C. 814.
An. Imp. Ne-
ronis Cæs.
Aug. 9.

ᵃ Or, *fear*; or, *care.*——ᵇ Chap. i. 29; Phil. i. 30; 1 Thess. ii. 2.——ᶜ 2 Cor i. 6.——ᵈ Chap. iii. 14.——ᵉ Phil. iii. 8; chap. i. 9. ᶠ Or, *wherein.*
ᵍ 1 Cor. i. 24; ii. 6, 7; Eph. i. 8; chap. i. 9.——ʰ Rom. xvi. 18; 2 Cor. xi. 13; Eph. iv. 14; v. 6; ver. 8, 18.——ⁱ 1 Cor. v. 3; 1 Thess. ii. 17.

NOTES ON CHAP II.

Verse 1. *What great conflict*] The word αγων, which we here render *conflict*, is to be understood as implying *earnest care* and *solicitude*, accompanied, undoubtedly, with the most fervent application to the throne of grace in their behalf. The αγωνιζομενος of the preceding verse gave the apostle occasion to use the word αγων here. He *agonized* with God, and his *agony* was for them.

Laodicea] A city of Asia Minor, on the borders of *Caria*, *Phrygia*, and *Lydia*. It was originally called *Diospolis*, or the city of Jupiter, and afterwards *Rhoas*; but obtained the name of *Laodicea* from *Laodice*, the wife of Antiochus. It is now called *Ladik*. It was formerly celebrated for its commerce, and the fine black wool of its sheep. Colosse, or the city of the Colossians, lay between it and Hierapolis. This *Hierapolis* was also a town of Phrygia, famous for its hot baths: it is now called *Bambukholasi*.

As many as have not seen my face in the flesh] From this it has been conjectured that St. Paul had never been at either Colosse or Laodicea, and this, from the letter of the text, appears probable; and yet, his having passed more than once through this country, preaching and strengthening the Churches, renders it very improbable. It is, therefore, most likely that we should understand the apostle as speaking collectively; that he had the most earnest concern, not only for the welfare of those Churches with which he was acquainted, such as Colosse and Laodicea, but also for those to whom he was not personally known.

Verse 2. *That their hearts might be comforted*] That they might have continual happiness in God, having constant affiance in him.

Being knit together in love] The word συμβιβασθεντων, or συμβιβασθεντες, which is the true reading, but both of equal import here, signifies being united, as the beams or the timbers of a building, by mortices and pins. The visible Church of Christ cannot be in *union* with God unless it have *unity* in itself, and without *love* this unity is impossible.

Unto all riches of the full assurance of understanding] That is, that they might have the most indubitable certainty of the truth of Christianity, of their own salvation, and of the general design of God to admit the Gentiles into his Church. This is the grand mystery of God, which was now laid open by the preaching of the Gospel.

And of the Father, and of Christ] These words are variously written in different MSS., *versions*, and *fathers*: The *mystery of God—of God in Christ— of God who is in Christ—of God concerning Christ— of God who is Christ—of the God Christ—of God and Christ—of God the Father of Christ—of God the Father, and our Lord Christ—of God and the Father of Christ—of God the Father, in Christ—of the God Christ Jesus, Father and Lord, &c., &c., &c.*

This great variety of versions leaves the strongest presumption that the words in question are glosses which have crept into the text, and are of no authority *Griesbach* has left them out of the text.

Verse 3. *In whom are hid*] Or rather *in which*; referring to the *mystery* mentioned above. In this glorious scheme of Christianity all the treasures—the abundance and excellency, of wisdom and knowledge are contained. No scheme of salvation, or Divine knowledge, ever equalled in its depth and excellency the Gospel plan. A scheme which the wisdom of God alone could devise, and which his power and infinite mercy alone could accomplish.

Verse 4. *Lest any man should beguile you*] The word παραλογιζηται means to deceive by sophistry or subtle reasoning, in which all the *conclusions* appear to be fairly drawn from the *premises*, but the premises are either *assumed* without evidence, or *false* in themselves; but this not being easily discovered, the unthinking or unwary are carried away by the conclusions which are drawn from these premises. And this result is clearly intimated by the term πιθανολογια, *enticing words*, *plausible conclusions* or *deductions* from this mode of reasoning. The apostle seems to allude to the Gentile philosophers, who were notorious for this kind of argumentation. Plato and Socrates are not free from it.

Verse 5. *For though I be absent in the flesh*] It is hardly possible that such words as these in this verse could have been used to perfect *strangers*; they argue a considerable knowledge of the people, and a knowledge founded on personal acquaintance. The original is exceedingly soft and musical:—

Ει γαρ και τη σαρκι απειμι,
Αλλα τω πνευματι συν ὑμιν ειμι,
Χαιρων και βλεπων ὑμων την ταξιν, κ. τ. λ

The whole verse shows that this Church was *sound* in *doctrine*, and *strict* in *discipline*. They had *steadfast faith* in Christ, and regular *order* or discipline among themselves.

2

A. M. cir. 4066.
A. D. cir. 62.
A. U. C. 814.
An. Imp. Ne-
ronis Cæs.
Aug. 9.

am I with you in the spirit, joying and beholding ^k your order, and the ^l steadfastness of your faith in Christ.

6 ^m As ye have therefore received Christ Jesus the Lord, *so* walk ye in him ;

7 ⁿ Rooted and built up in him, and stablished in the faith, as ye have been taught, abound-

ing therein with thanksgiving.

8 ^o Beware lest any man spoil you through philosophy and vain deceit, after ^p the tradition of men, after the ^q rudiments ^r of the world, and not after Christ :

9 For ^s in him dwelleth all the fulness of the Godhead bodily.

A. M. cir. 4066
A. D. cir. 62.
A. U. C. 814.
An. Imp. Ne-
ronis Cæs.
Aug. 9.

---

^k 1 Cor. xiv. 40.——^l 1 Pet. v. 9.——^m 1 Thess. iv. 1 ; Jude 3. ⁿ Eph. ii. 21, 22 ; iii. 17 ; ch. i. 23.——^o Jer. xxix. 8 ; Rom. xvi. 17 ;

Eph. v. 6 ; ver. 18 ; Heb. xiii. 9.——^p Matt. xv. 2 ; Gal. i. 14 ; ver. 22 ^q Or, *elements.*——^r Gal. iv. 3, 9 ; ver. 20.——^s John i. 14 ; chap. i. 19.

Verse 6. *As ye have therefore received Christ Jesus*] Many persons lay a certain stress on the words *as* and *so*, and make various fine heads of discourses from them ; viz. *As* ye received Christ in a spirit of *humility, so* walk in him ; *as* ye received him in a spirit of *faith, so* walk in him, &c., &c. This may be all proper in itself ; but nothing of the kind was intended by the apostle. His meaning is simply this . Seeing ye have embraced the doctrine of Christ, continue to hold it fast, and not permit yourselves to be turned aside by sophistical or Judaizing teachers.

Verse 7. *Rooted and built up in him*] It is not usual with the apostle to employ this double metaphor, taken partly from the *growth of a tree* and the *increase of a building*. They are to be *rooted ;* as the good *seed* had been already *sown,* it is to take root, and the roots are to spread far, wide, and deep. They are to be *grounded ;* as the *foundation* has already been *laid,* they are to *build* thereon. In the one case, they are to bear much fruit ; in the other, they are to grow up to be a habitation of God through the Spirit. See the notes on Eph. ii. 21, 22, and iii. 17.

Abounding therein with thanksgiving.] No limitation is ever set to the operations of God on the soul, or to the growth of the soul in the knowledge, love, and image of God. Those who are brought into such a state of salvation should abound in gratitude and loving obedience, as they grow in grace.

Verse 8. *Beware lest any man spoil you*] The word συλαγωγων, from συλη, *prey,* and αγειν, *to lead* or *carry away,* signifies to *rob,* or *spoil* of their goods, as if by *violence* or *rapine.* Their goods were the salvation they had received from Christ ; and both the Gentile and Jewish teachers endeavoured to deprive them of these, by perverting their minds, and leading them off from the truths of Christianity.

Philosophy and vain deceit] Or, *the vain* or *empty deceit of philosophy ;* such philosophizing as the Jewish and Gentile teachers used. As the term *philosophy* stood in high repute among the Gentiles, the Jews of this time affected it ; and both *Philo* and *Josephus* use the word to express the whole of the Mosaic institutions. So the former : Οἱ κατα Μωσην φιλοσοφουντες· "Those who embraced the philosophy of Moses ;" PHIL., *De Nomin. Mutand.* And the latter : Τρια παρα Ιουδαιοις ειδη φιλοσοφειται· "There are three systems of philosophy among the Jews," (Bell. Jud., lib. ii. cap 8, sec. 2,) meaning the *Pharisees, Sadducees.* and *Essenes,* as immediately follows. The Jewish philosophy, such as is found in the

Cabala, Midrashim, and other works, deserves the character of *vain deceit,* in the fullest sense and meaning of the words. The inspired writers excepted, the Jews have ever been the most puerile, absurd, and ridiculous reasoners in the world. Even *Rabbi Maymon,* or *Maimonides,* the most intelligent of them all, is often in his master piece (the *Moreh Nevochim,* the *Teacher of the Perplexed*) most deplorably empty and vain.

After the rudiments of the world] According to the doctrine of the *Jewish teachers ;* or, according to the *Mosaic institutions,* as explained and glossed by the scribes, Pharisees, and rabbins in general. We have often seen that העולם הזה *haolam hazzeh, this world,* of which του κοσμου τουτου is a literal translation, is frequently used to express the Jewish system of rites, ceremonies, and institutions in general ; what the apostle calls the *tradition of men,* namely, what men, unauthorized by God, have taught as doctrines received from him. Our Lord frequently refers to and condemns these traditions.

Not after Christ.] Not according to the simple doctrine of Christ, viz. : HE died for our offences ; believe on the Lord Jesus, and thou shalt be saved.

Verse 9. *For in him dwelleth all the fulness*] This is opposed to the *vain* or *empty* doctrine of the Gentile and Jewish philosophers : there is a *fulness* in Christ suited to the *empty, destitute* state of the human soul, but in the philosophy of the Jews and Gentiles nothing like this was found ; nor indeed in the more refined and correct philosophy of the present day. No substitute has ever been found for the grace of the Lord Jesus, and those who have sought for one have disquieted themselves in vain.

By the *Godhead* or *Deity,* Θεοτης, we are to understand the *state or being of the Divine nature ;* and by the *fulness* of that *Deity,* the infinite attributes essential to such a nature.

Bodily.] Σωματικως signifies *truly, really ;* in opposition to *typically, figuratively.* There was a *symbol* of the Divine presence in the Hebrew *tabernacle,* and in the Jewish *temple ;* but in the *body* of CHRIST the *Deity,* with all its plenitude of attributes, dwelt *really* and *substantially :* for so the word σωματικως means ; and so it was understood by the ancient Greek fathers, as is fully shown by SUICER, in his *Thesaurus,* under the word.

"The *fulness of the Godhead* dwelt in Christ '*bodily,*' as opposed to the Jewish *tabernacle,* or *temple ; truly* and *really,* in opposition to *types* and *figures ;*

    2

A. M. cir. 4066.
A. D. cir. 62.
A. U. C. 814.
An. Imp. Ne-
ronis Cæs.
Aug. 9.

10 [t] And ye are complete in him, [u] which is the head of all [v] principality and power;

11 In whom also ye are [w] circumcised with the circumcision made without hands, in [x] putting off the body of the sins of the flesh by the circumcision of Christ;

12 [y] Buried with him in baptism, wherein also [z] ye are risen with *him* through [a] the faith of the operation of God, [b] who hath raised him from the dead.

A. M. cir. 4066.
A. D. cir. 62.
A. U. C. 814.
An. Imp. Ne-
ronis Cæs.
Aug. 9.

13 [c] And you, being dead in your sins and the uncircumcision of your flesh, hath he quickened together with him, having forgiven you all trespasses;

14 [d] Blotting out the hand-writing of ordinances that was against us, which was contrary to us, and took it out of the way, nailing it to his cross;

15 *And* [e] having spoiled [f] principalities and powers, he made a show of them openly, triumphing over them [g] in it.

---

[t] John i. 16.——[u] Eph. i. 20, 21; 1 Peter iii. 22.——[v] Chap. i. 16.——[w] Deut. x. 16; xxx. 6; Jer. iv. 4; Rom. ii. 29; Phil. iii. 3.——[x] Rom. vi. 6; Eph. iv. 22; chap. iii. 8. 9.——[y] Rom. vi. 4. [z] Chap. iii. 1.——[a] Eph. i. 19; iii. 7.

[b] Acts ii. 24.——[c] Eph. ii. 1, 5, 6, 11.——[d] Eph. ii. 15, 16. [e] Gen. iii. 15; Psa. lxviii. 18; Isa. liii. 12; Matt. xii. 29; Luke x. 18; xi. 22; John xii. 31; xvi. 11; Eph. iv. 8; Heb. ii. 14. [f] Eph. vi. 12.——[g] Or, *in himself.*

---

not only effectively, as God dwells in good men, but *substantially* or *personally*, by the strictest union, as the soul dwells in the body; so that God and man are one Christ." See *Parkhurst.*

Verse 10. And ye are complete in him] Και εστε εν αυτω πεπληρωμενοι *And ye are filled with him.* Our word *complete* quite destroys the connection subsisting in the apostle's ideas. The philosophy of the world was *empty*, κενη, but there was a πληρωμα, or *fulness*, in Christ; the Colossians were *empty*—spoiled and deprived of every good, while following the *empty* philosophy and groundless traditions of Jewish and Gentile teachers; but since they had received Christ Jesus they were πεπληρωμενοι, *filled* with him. This is the true meaning of the word, and by this the connection and assemblage of ideas in the apostle's mind are preserved. No fanciful *completeness in Christ*, of a believer, while incomplete in himself, is either expressed or intended by St. Paul. It is too bad a doctrine to exist in the oracles of God.

The head of all principality] See the notes on chap. i. 16. 17.

Verse 11. In whom also ye are circumcised] All that was designed by circumcision, literally performed, is accomplished in them that believe through the Spirit and power of Christ. It is not a cutting off of a *part* of the *flesh*, but a *putting off* the *body* of the *sins* of the flesh, through the circumcision of Christ; he having undergone and performed this, and all other rites necessary to qualify him to be a mediator between God and man; for, being made under the *law*, he was subject to all its ordinances, and every act of his contributed to the salvation of men. But by the circumcision of Christ, the operation of his grace and Spirit may be intended; the law required the circumcision of the flesh, the Gospel of Christ required the circumcision of the heart. The words των αμαρτιων, *of the sins*, are omitted by ABCD*EFG, several others, by the *Coptic, Æthiopic, Armenian, Vulgate,* and *Itala*; and by *Clement, Athanasius, Basil, Cyril,* and several others. Griesbach has omitted them.

Verse 12. Buried with him in baptism] Alluding to the *immersions* practised in the case of *adults*, wherein the person appeared to be buried under the water, as Christ was buried in the heart of the earth.

His rising again the third day, and their emerging from the water, was an emblem of the resurrection of the body; and, in them, of a total change of life.

The faith of the operation of God] They were quickened, changed, and saved, by means of faith in Christ Jesus; which faith was produced by the operation or energy of God. *Believing* is the act of the soul; but the *grace* or *power* to *believe* comes from God himself.

Verse 13. And you, being dead in your sins] See the notes on Eph. ii. 1, &c.

The uncircumcision of your flesh] This must refer to that part of the Colossian Church which was made up of converted *heathens*, for the *heathens* alone were *uncircumcised.*

Verse 14. Blotting out the hand-writing of ordinances] By the hand-writing of ordinances the apostle most evidently means the *ceremonial law*: this was *against* them, for they were bound to fulfil it; and it was *contrary* to them, as condemning them for their neglect and transgression of it. This law God himself has blotted out.

Blotting out the hand-writing is probably an allusion to Num. v. 23, where the curses written in the book, in the case of the woman suspected of adultery, are directed to be blotted out with the bitter waters. And there can be little doubt of a farther allusion, viz., to the custom of discharging the writing from parchment by the application of such a fluid as the *muriatic acid*, which immediately dissolves those ferruginous calces which constitute the *blackening* principle of most inks. But the East India inks, being formed only of simple *black*, such as burnt *ivory*, or *cork*, and gum water, may be wiped clean off from the surface of the paper or parchment by the application of a *wet sponge*, so as to leave not one legible vestige remaining: this I have often proved.

Nailing it to his cross] When Christ was nailed to the cross, our obligation to fulfil these ordinances was done away. There may be another reference here to some ancient mode of *annulling* legal obligations, by *nailing them to a post*; but I do not recollect at present an instance or example. Antiquated *laws* are said to have been thus abrogated.

Verse 15. And *having spoiled principalities and*

A. M. cir. 4066.
A. D. cir. 62.
A. U. C. 814.
An. Imp. Ne-
ronis Cæs.
Aug. 9.

16 Let no man, therefore, [h] judge you [i] in [k] meat, or in drink, or [l] in respect [m] of a holy-day, or of the new moon, or of the sabbath *days;*

17 [n] Which are a shadow of things to come; but the body *is* of Christ. .

18 [o] Let no man [p] beguile you of your reward [q] in a voluntary humility and

A. M. cir. 4066.
A. D. cir. 62.
A. U. C. 814.
An. Imp. Ne-
ronis Cæs.
Aug. 9.

[h] Rom. xiv. 3, 10, 13.——[i] Or, *for eating and drinking.*——[k] Rom. xiv. 2, 17; 1 Cor. viii. 8.——[l] Or, *in part.*——[m] Rom. xiv. 5; Gal. iv. 10.——[n] Heb. viii. 5; ix. 9; x. 1.——[o] Ver. 4.——[p] Or, *judge against you.*——[q] Gr. *being a voluntary in humility;* ver. 23.

powers] Here is an allusion to the treatment of enemies when conquered : they are *spoiled of their armour,* so much the word απεκδυειν implies; and they are *exhibited* with contumely and reproach to the populace, especially when the victor has the honour of a *triumph;* to the former of which there is an allusion in the words εδειγματισεν εν παρρησια, *making a public exhibition of them;* and to the latter in the words Θριαμβευσας αυτους, *triumphing over them.* And the *principalities* and *powers* refer to the emperors, kings, and generals taken in battle, and reserved to grace the victor's triumph. It is very likely that by the αρχας και εξουσιας, *principalities* and *powers,* over whom Christ triumphed, the apostle means the נשיאות *nesioth* and ראשות *roshoth,* who were the *rulers* and *chiefs* in the *Sanhedrin* and *synagogues,* and who had great authority among the people, both in making constitutions and explaining traditions. The propagation of *Christianity* in Judea quite destroyed their spiritual power and domination ; just as the propagation of *Protestantism,* which was Christianity revived, destroyed, wherever it appeared, the false doctrine and domination of the pope of Rome.

In it.] The words εν αυτω refer rather to *Christ* than to the *cross,* if indeed they be genuine ; of which there is much reason to doubt, as the *versions* and *fathers* differ so greatly in quoting them. Griesbach has left them out of the text.

Verse 16. *Let no man—judge you in meat, or in drink*] The apostle speaks here in reference to some particulars of the *hand-writing of ordinances,* which had been *taken away,* viz., the distinction of *meats* and *drinks,* what was *clean* and what *unclean,* according to the law ; and the necessity of observing certain *holydays* or *festivals,* such as the *new moons* and particular *sabbaths,* or those which should be observed with more than ordinary solemnity ; all these had been taken out of the way and nailed to the cross, and were no longer of moral obligation. There is no intimation here that the *Sabbath* was done away, or that its moral use was superseded, by the introduction of Christianity. I have shown elsewhere that, *Remember the Sabbath day, to keep it holy,* is a command of *perpetual obligation,* and can never be superseded but by the final termination of time. As it is a *type* of that rest which remains for the people of God, of an eternity of bliss, it must continue in full force till that eternity arrives ; for no *type* ever ceases till the *antitype* be come. Besides, it is not clear that the apostle refers at all to the *Sabbath* in this place, whether Jewish or Christian ; his σαββατων, *of sabbaths* or *weeks,* most probably refers to their *feasts of weeks,* of which much has been said in the notes on the Pentateuch.

Verse 17. *Which are a shadow*] All these things

were *types,* and must continue in force till the Christ, whom they represented, came ; the apostle therefore says that the *body*—the *substance* or *design* of them was *of Christ*—pointed him out, and the excellent blessings which he has procured. The word σκια, *shadow,* is often used to express any thing *imperfect* or *unsubstantial;* while the term σωμα, *body,* was used in the opposite sense, and expressed any thing *substantial, solid,* and *firm.* The law was but the *shadow* or *representation* of good things to come ; none should rest in it ; all that it pointed out is to be sought and obtained in Christ.

Verse 18. *Let no man beguile you*] Μηδεις υμας καταβραβευετω· Let no man take the *prize* from you which the βραβευς, *brabeus,* or judge in the contests, has assigned you, in consequence of your having obtained the victory. This, any reader will see, is an allusion to the Olympic and Isthmian games, and to the prizes assigned to those who had obtained the victory in one or more of the contests which there took place. The Colossians had fought and conquered under the direction of Christ, and he, as the sole judge in this contest, had assigned to them the prize ; the false teachers, affecting great modesty, humility, and sanctity, endeavoured to turn them aside from the Gospel, and to induce them to end in the *flesh* who had begun in the *Spirit.* Against these the apostle warns them.

In a voluntary humility and worshipping of angels] This is a difficult passage, and in order to explain it I shall examine the meaning of some of the principal terms of the original. The word θελειν, *to will,* signifies also *to delight;* and ταπεινοφροσυνη signifies not only *lowliness* or *humility of mind,* but also *affliction of mind;* and ταπεινουν την ψυχην, Lev. xvi. 29, 31, and in many other places, signifies to *afflict the soul by fasting,* and *self-abnegation;* and θρησκεια signifies *reverence* and *modesty.* Hence the whole passage has been paraphrased thus : Let no man spoil you of the prize adjudged to you, who delights in mortifying his body ; and walking with the apparent *modesty of an angel,* affecting superior sanctity in order to gain disciples ; *intruding into things which he has not seen ;* and, notwithstanding his apparent humility, his mind is *carnal,* and he is *puffed up* with a sense of his superior knowledge and piety. It is very likely that the apostle here alludes to the *Essenes,* who were remarkably strict and devout, spent a principal part of their time in the contemplation of the Divine Being, abstained from all sensual gratifications, and affected to live the *life of angels* upon earth. With their pretensions all the apostle says here perfectly agrees, and on this one supposition the whole of the passage is plain and easy. Many have understood the passage

524

2

A. M. cir. 4066.
A. D. cir. 62.
A. U. C. 814.
An. Imp. Ne-
ronis Cæs.
Aug. 9.

worshipping of angels, intruding into those things [r] which he hath not seen, vainly puffed up by his fleshly mind ;

19 And not holding [s] the Head, from which all the body by joints and bands having nourishment ministered, and knit together, increaseth with the increase of God.

20 Wherefore, if ye be [t] dead with Christ from [u] the [v] rudiments of the world, [w] why, as though living in the world, are ye subject to ordinances,

A. M. cir. 4066
A. D. cir. 62.
A. U. C. 814.
An. Imp. Ne-
ronis Cæs.
Aug. 9.

21 ([x] Touch not ; taste not ; handle not ;

22 Which all are to perish with the using ;) [y] after the commandments and doctrines of men ?

23 [z] Which things have indeed a show of wisdom in [a] will-worship, and humility, and [b] neglecting of the body ; not in any honour to the satisfying of the flesh.

---

[r] Ezek. xiii. 3 ; 1 Tim. i. 7.——[s] Eph. iv. 15, 16.——[t] Rom. vi. 3, 5 ; vii. 4, 6 ; Gal. ii. 19 ; Eph. ii. 15.——[u] Ver. 8.——[v] Or, *elements.*

[w] Gal. iv. 3, 9.——[x] 1 Tim. iv. 3.——[y] Isa. xxix. 13 ; Matt. xv. 9 ; Titus i. 14.——[z] 1 Tim. iv. 8.——[a] Ver. 8.——[b] Or, *punishing,* or, *not sparing.*

---

as referring to the *adoration of angels*, which seems to have been practised among the Jews, who appear (from *Tobit*, xii. 15 ; *Philo*, in lib. de Somn. ; *Josephus*, War. lib. ii. cap. 8, sec. 7) to have considered them as a sort of *mediators* between God and man ; presenting the prayers of men before the throne ; and being, as Philo says, μεγαλου Βασιλεως οφθαλμοι και ωτα, *the eyes and ears of the great King*. But this interpretation is not so likely as the foregoing.

Verse 19. *And not holding the Head*] Not acknowledging Jesus Christ as the only Saviour of mankind, and the only *Head* or *chief* of the Christian Church, on whom every member of it depends, and *from* whom each derives both light and life. For a farther explanation of these words see the notes on Eph. iv. 16, where the figures and phraseology are the same.

Verse 20. *If ye be dead with Christ*] See the notes on Rom. vi. 3, 5.

From the rudiments of the world] Ye have renounced all hope of salvation from the observance of Jewish rites and ceremonies, which were only *rudiments, first elements*, or the *alphabet*, out of which the whole science of Christianity was composed. We have often seen that *the world* and *this world* signify the Jewish dispensation, or the rites, ceremonies, and services performed under it.

Why, as though living in the world] Why, as if ye were still under the same dispensation from which you have been already freed, are ye subject to its ordinances, performing them as if expecting salvation from this performance ?

Verse 21. *Touch not ; taste not ; handle not*] These are forms of expression very frequent among the Jews. In *Maccoth*, fol. xxi. 1 : "If they say to a Nazarite, *Don't drink, don't drink* ; and he, notwithstanding, drinks ; he is guilty. If they say, *Don't shave, don't shave* ; and he shaves, notwithstanding ; he is guilty. If they say, *Don't put on these clothes, don't put on these clothes* ; and he, notwithstanding, puts on heterogeneous garments ; he is guilty." See more in *Schoettgen*.

Verse 22. *Which all are to perish with the using*] These are not matters of eternal moment ; the different kinds of meats were made for the body, and go with it into corruption : in like manner, all the rites and ceremonies of the Jewish religion now perish, having accomplished the *end* of their institution ; namely, to lead us to Christ, that we might be justified by faith.

After the commandments and doctrines of men ?] These words should follow the 20th verse, of which they form a part ; and it appears from them that the apostle is here speaking of the traditions of the elders, and the load of cumbrous ceremonies which they added to the significant rites prescribed by Moses.

Verse 23. *Which things have indeed a show of wisdom*] All these prescriptions and rites have indeed the appearance of wisdom, and are recommended by plausible reasons ; but they form a worship which God has not commanded, and enjoin macerations of the body, accompanied with a humiliation of spirit, that are neither profitable to the soul, nor of any advantage to the body ; so that the whole of their religion is nothing worth.

WHAT is here termed *will-worship*, εθελοθρησκεια, signifies simply a mode of worship which a man chooses for himself, independently of the *revelation* which God has given. The whole system of *Deism* is an εθελοθρησκεια, a worship founded in the will or caprices of man, and not in the wisdom or *will* of God ; and it is just as profitable to body and soul as that of which the apostle speaks. God will be served in his own way ; it is right that he should prescribe to man the truths which he is to believe, and the ordinances which he is to use. To refuse to receive his teaching in order to prefer our own fancies, is to light a farthing candle as a substitute for the noonday sun. From the beginning of the world God has prescribed the worship which was best pleasing to himself, and never left a matter of such moment to man. The nations which have either not had a revelation, or refused to receive that which God has given, show, by their diversity of worship, superstition, absurdity, and in many cases *cruelty*, what the state of the whole would have been, had not God, in his infinite mercy, blessed it with a revelation of his will. God has given directions concerning his worship ; and he has appointed the *seventh day* for the peculiar exercises of spiritual duties : other times he has left to man's convenience ; and they abuse the text

2

who say that the appointment of particular times and places for religious service is *will-worship*. God prescribes the *thing*, and leaves it to man, except in the case of the Sabbath, to appoint the *time* and the *place*; nor is it possible to be too *frequent* in God's worship, any more than to be too *fervent*.

CHAPTER III.

The apostle exhorts the Colossians to heavenly-mindedness after the example of Christ, that they may be prepared to appear with him in glory, 1–4. Exhorts them also to mortify their members, and calls to their remembrance their former state, 5–7. Shows how completely they were changed from that state, and gives them various directions relative to truth, compassion, meekness, long-suffering, forgiveness, charity, 8–14. Shows that they are called to unity and holiness; and commands them to have the doctrine of Christ dwelling richly in them; and how they should teach and admonish each other, and do every thing in the name of the Lord Jesus, 15–17. The relative duties of wives, 18. Of husbands, 19. Of children, 20. Of fathers, 21. Of servants, 22. He concludes by showing that he that does wrong shall be treated accordingly, for God is no respecter of persons, 23–25.

A. M. cir. 4066.
A. D. cir. 62.
A. U. C. 814.
An. Imp. Neronis Cæs.
Aug. 9.

IF ye then [a] be risen with Christ, seek those things which are above, where [b] Christ sitteth on the right hand of God.

2 Set your [c] affection on things above, not on things on the earth.

3 [d] For ye are dead, [e] and your life is hid with Christ in God.

4 [f] When Christ, *who is* [g] our life, shall appear, then shall ye also appear with him [h] in glory.

A. M. cir. 4066.
A. D. cir. 62.
A. U. C. 814.
An. Imp. Neronis Cæs.
Aug. 9.

5 [i] Mortify, therefore, [k] your members which are upon the earth; [l] fornication, uncleanness, inordinate affection, [m] evil concupiscence, and covetousness, [n] which is idolatry:

---

[a] Rom. vi. 5; Eph. ii. 6; chap. ii. 12.——[b] Rom. viii. 34; Eph. i. 20.——[c] Or, *mind*.——[d] Rom. vi. 2; Gal. ii. 20; chap. ii. 20.——[e] 2 Cor. v. 7; chap. i. 5.

[f] 1 John iii. 2.——[g] John xi. 25; xiv. 6.——[h] 1 Cor. xv. 43; Phil. iii. 21.——[i] Rom. viii. 13; Gal. v. 24.——[k] Rom. vi. 13 [l] Eph. v. 3.——[m] 1 Thess. iv. 5.——[n] Eph. v. 5.

NOTES ON CHAP. III.

Verse 1. *If ye then*] Eι ουν· *Seeing then that ye are risen with Christ*; this refers to what he had said, chap. ii. 12 : *Buried with him in baptism, wherein also ye are risen with him.* As, therefore, ye have most cordially received the doctrine of Christ; and profess to be partakers of a spiritual religion, that promises spiritual and eternal things, seek those things, and look to be prepared for the enjoyment of them.

Verse 2. *Set your affection on things above*] Ta ανω φρονειτε· Love *heavenly things*; *study* them; let your hearts be entirely *engrossed* by them. Now, that ye are converted to God, act in reference to heavenly things as ye did formerly in reference to those of earth; and *vice versa.* This is a very good general rule: "Be as much in earnest for heavenly and eternal things, as ye formerly were for those that are earthly and perishing."

Verse 3. *For ye are dead*] To all hopes of happiness from the present world; and, according to your profession, should feel no more appetite for the things of this life, than he does whose soul is departed into the invisible state.

Your life is hid with Christ in God.] Christ is your *treasure*; and where your treasure is, there is your heart. Christ lives in the bosom of the Father; as your heart is in him, ye also sit in heavenly places with Christ Jesus. Christ is the *life* of your souls; and as *he* is hidden in the bosom of the Father, so are ye, who live through and in him.

Verse 4. *When Christ, who is our life*] When Christ comes to judge the world, ye shall appear with him in his glory, and in an eternal state of blessedness.

Verse 5. *Mortify, therefore, your members*] Νεκρωσατε· *Put them to death*: the verb is used metaphorically to signify, to *deprive a thing of its power*, to *destroy its strength*. Use no member of your body to sin against God; keep all under dominion; and never permit the *beast* to run away with the *man*. To *gratify* any sensual appetite is to give it the very food and nourishment by which it lives, thrives, and is active. However the body may suffer by excessive sensual indulgences, the *appetite* increases with the indulgence. Deny yourselves, and let reason rule; and the *animal* will not get the ascendency over the *rational man*. See the notes on Rom. vi. 11, &c.

Inordinate affection] Παθος· *Unnatural* and degrading *passion*; bestial lusts. See Rom. i. 26, 27; and the notes there.

Evil concupiscence] Επιθυμιαν κακην. As επιθυμια signifies *strong* and *vehement desire* of any kind, it is here joined with κακη, *evil*, to show the sense more particularly in which the apostle uses it.

Covetousness, which is idolatry] For the covetous man makes his money his god. Now, it is the prerogative of God to confer happiness; every godly man seeks his happiness in God; the covetous man seeks that in his money which God alone can give; therefore his covetousness is properly *idolatry.* It is true his idol is of *gold* and *silver*, but his idolatry is not the less criminal on that account.

2

A. M. cir. 4066.
A. D. cir. 62.
A. U. C. 814.
An. Imp. Ne-
ronis Cæs.
Aug. 9.

6 ° For which things' sake the wrath of God cometh on ᴾ the children of disobedience :

7 �q In the which ye also walked sometime, when ye lived in them.

8 ʳ But now ye also put off all these ; anger, wrath, malice, blasphemy, ˢ filthy communication out of your mouth.

9 ᵗ Lie not one to another, ᵘ seeing that ye have put off the old man with his deeds ;

10 And have put on the new man, which ᵛ is renewed in knowledge ʷ after the image of him that ˣ created him :

11 Where there is neither ʸ Greek nor Jew, circumcision nor uncircumcision, barbarian, Scythian, bond *nor* free : ᶻ but Christ *is* all, and in all.

A. M. cir. 4066.
A. D. cir. 62.
A. U. C. 814.
An. Imp. Ne-
ronis Cæs.
Aug. 9.

° Rom. i. 18; Eph. v. 6; Rev. xxii. 15.——ᴾ Eph. ii. 2.——q Rom. vi. 19, 20; vii. 5; 1 Cor. vi. 11; Eph. ii. 2; Tit. iii. 3.——ʳ Eph. iv. 22; 1 Pet. ii. 1; Heb. xii. 1; James i. 21.—— ˢ Eph. iv. 29;

v. 4.——ᵗ Lev. xix. 11; Ephes. iv. 25.——ᵘ Ephes. iv. 22, 24. ᵛ Rom. xii. 2.——ʷ Eph. iv. 23, 24.——ˣ Eph. ii. 10.——ʸ Rom. x. 12; 1 Cor. xii. 13; Gal. iii. 28; v. 6; Eph. vi. 8.——ᶻ Eph. i. 23.

Verse 6. *The wrath of God cometh*] God is angry with such persons, and he inflicts on them the punishment which they deserve.

Verse 7. *In the which ye also walked sometime*] When ye were in your unconverted state, ye served divers lusts and pleasures. See on Rom. vii. 5, and Eph. ii. 2.

Verse 8. *But now ye also put off all these*] See on Eph. iv. 22. Being now converted, sin had no more dominion over them.

Anger, wrath, &c.] They had not only lived in the evils mentioned ver. 5, but also in those enumerated here ; and they had not only laid aside the former, but they had laid aside the latter also. They retained no bosom, no easily besetting, sin. They were risen with Christ, and they sought the things which were above.

Blasphemy] The word seems here to mean *injurious* and *calumnious speaking*.

Verse 9. *Lie not one to another*] Do not deceive each other ; speak the truth in all your dealings ; do not say, "My goods are so and so," when you know them to be otherwise ; do not undervalue the goods of your neighbour, when your conscience tells you that you are not speaking the truth. *It is naught, it is naught, saith the buyer ; but afterwards he boasteth ;* i. e. he underrates his neighbour's property till he gets him persuaded to part with it for less than its worth ; and when he has thus got it he boasts what a good bargain he has made. Such a knave speaks not truth with his neighbour.

Ye have put off the old man] See the notes on Rom. vi. 6 ; and particularly on Rom. xiii. 11–14. Ye have received a religion widely different from that ye had before ; act according to its principles.

Verse 10. *And have put on the new man*] See on Rom. xii. 1, 2.

Is renewed in knowledge] IGNORANCE was the grand characteristic of the heathen state ; KNOWLEDGE, of the Christian. The utmost to which heathenism could pretend was a certain knowledge of nature. How far this went, and how much it fell short of the truth, may be seen in the writings of *Aristotle* and *Pliny*. Christianity reveals God himself, the author of nature ; or, rather, God has revealed himself, in the Christian system with which he has blessed mankind. Christianity teaches a man the true knowledge both of himself and of God, but it is impossible to know

one's self but in the light of God ; the famous γνωθι σεαυτον, *know thyself,* was practicable only under the Christian religion.

After the image of him that created him] We have already seen that God made man in his own image ; and we have seen in *what* that *image* consisted. See the notes on Gen. i. 26, and on Eph. iv. 23, 24. Does not the apostle refer here to the case of an artist, who wishes to make a perfect resemblance of some exquisite form or person ? God in this case is the artist, man is the copy, and God himself the *original* from which this copy is to be taken. Thus, then, man is made by his *Creator,* not according to the image or likeness of any *other being,* but according to *his own ;* the image του Κτισαντος, of the Creator. And as the Divine nature cannot exist in *forms* or *fashions,* moral qualities alone are those which must be produced. Hence the apostle, interpreting the words of Moses, says that the image in which man was made, and in which he must be *remade,* ανακαινουμενον, *made anew,* consists in *knowledge, righteousness,* and *true holiness.*

Verse 11. *Where there is neither Greek nor Jew*] In which new creation no inquiry is made what *nation* the persons belonged to, or from what *ancestry* they had sprung, whether in *Judea* or *Greece.*

Circumcision nor uncircumcision] Nor is their peculiar form of religion of any consideration, whether *circumcised* like the *Jews,* or *uncircumcised* like the *heathens.*

Barbarian, Scythian] Nor whether of the more or less tractable of the nations of the world ; for although *knowledge,* and the most refined and sublime knowledge, is the object to be attained, yet, under the teaching and influence of the blessed Spirit, the most dull and least informed are perfectly capable of comprehending this Divine science, and becoming wise unto salvation.

Bond nor free] Nor does the particular *state* or *circumstances* in which a man may be found, either help him to or exclude him from the benefit of this religion ; the *slave* having as good a title to *salvation by grace* as the *freeman.*

But Christ is all, and in all.] All *mankind* are his creatures, all *conditions* are disposed and regulated by his providence, and all *human beings* are equally purchased by his blood. He alone is the source whence all have proceeded, and to him alone all must return.

2

A. M. cir. 4066.
A. D. cir. 62.
A. U. C. 814.
An. Imp. Neronis Cæs.
Aug. 9.

12 [a] Put on therefore, [b] as the elect of God, holy and beloved, [c] bowels of mercies, kindness, humbleness of mind, meekness, long-suffering ;

13 [d] Forbearing one another, and forgiving one another, if any man have a [e] quarrel against

any ; even as Christ forgave you, so also *do* ye.

14 [f] And above all these things [g] *put on* charity, which is the [h] bond of perfectness.

15 And let [i] the peace of God rule in your hearts, [k] to the which also ye are called [l] in

A. M. cir. 4066.
A. D. cir. 62.
A. U. C. 814.
An. Imp. Neronis Cæs.
Aug. 9.

---

[a] Eph. iv. 24.——[b] 1 Thess. i. 4 ; 1 Pet. i. 2 ; 2 Pet. i. 10. [c] Gal. v. 22 ; Phil. ii. 1 ; Eph. iv. 2, 32.——[d] Mark xi. 25 ; Eph. iv. 2, 32.——[e] Or, *complaint.*——[f] 1 Pet. iv. 8.——[g] John xiii. 34 ;

Rom. xiii. 8 ; 1 Cor. xiii. ; Eph. v. 2 ; chap. ii. 2 ; 1 Thess. iv. 9. 1 Tim. i. 5 ; 1 John iii. 23 ; iv. 21.——[h] Eph. iv. 3.——[i] Rom. xiv 17 ; Phil. iv. 7.——[k] 1 Cor. vii. 15.——[l] Eph. ii. 16, 17 ; iv. 4.

He is the Maker, Preserver, Saviour, and Judge of all men.

Verse 12. *Put on—as the elect of God*] As the principal design of the apostle was to show that God had *chosen the Gentiles,* and *called* them to the same privileges as the Jews, and intended to make them as truly his people as the Jews ever were, he calls them the *elect* or *chosen* of God ; and as the Jews, who were formerly the *elect,* were still *beloved,* and called to be *holy,* so he calls the Colossians *beloved,* and shows them that *they* are called with the same *holy calling.*

Bowels of mercies, &c.] Be merciful, not in *act* merely, but in *spirit* and *affection.* In all cases of this kind let your *heart* dictate to your *hand ;* be *clothed* with *bowels of mercy*—let your tenderest feelings come in contact with the miseries of the distressed as soon as ever they present themselves. Though I know that to *put on,* and to be *clothed with,* are figurative expressions, and mean to *assume* such and such characters and *qualities ;* yet there may be a higher meaning here. The apostle would have them to *feel* the *slightest touch* of another's misery ; and, as their clothes are put over their body, so their tenderest feeling should be always within the reach of the miserable. Let your feelings be at hand, and feel and commiserate as soon as touched. See on Eph. iv. 2. Instead of οικτιρμον, *mercies,* in the *plural,* almost every MS. of importance, with many of the fathers, read οικτιρμον, bowels of *mercy,* in the *singular.* This various reading makes scarcely any alteration in the sense.

Verse 13. *Forbearing one another*] Avoid all occasions of irritating or provoking each other.

Forgiving one another] If ye receive offence, be instantly ready to forgive on the first acknowledgment of the fault.

Even as Christ forgave you] Who required no satisfaction, and sought for nothing in you but the broken, contrite heart, and freely forgave you as soon as you returned to Him. No man should for a moment harbour ill will in his heart to any ; but the offended party is not called actually to forgive, till the offender, with sorrow, acknowledges his fault. He should be *ready* to forgive, and while he is so, he can neither feel hatred nor malice towards the offender ; but, as Christ does not forgive us till with penitent hearts we return unto him, acknowledging our offences, so those who have trespassed against their neighbour are not to expect any act of forgiveness from the person they have injured, till they acknowledge their of-

fence. *Forgive,* says the apostle, καθως και ὁ Χριστος even as Christ forgave you—show the same disposition and the same readiness to forgive your offending brethren, as Christ showed towards you.

Verse 14. *And above all these things*] Επι πασι δε τουτοις· Upon all, over all ; as the *outer garment* envelopes all the clothing, so let *charity* or *love* invest and encompass all the rest. Even *bowels of mercy* are to be set in motion by *love ;* from love they derive all their *feeling,* and all their *power* and *promptitude* to action. Let this, therefore, be as the *upper garment ;* the *surtout* that invests the whole man.

Which is the bond of perfectness.] Love to God and man is not only to *cover* all, but also to *unite* and *consolidate* the whole. It is therefore represented here under the notion of a *girdle,* by which all the rest of the clothing is *bound* close about the body. To love God with all the heart, soul, mind, and strength, and one's neighbour as one's self, is the *perfection* which the new covenant requires, and which the grace and Spirit of Christ work in every sincerely obedient, humble believer ; and that very love, which is the fulfilling of the law and the *perfection* itself which the Gospel requires, is also the *bond* of that *perfection.* It is by love to God and man that love is to be preserved. *Love begets love ;* and the more a man loves God and his neighbour, the more he is enabled to do so. Love, while properly exercised, is ever *increasing* and *reproducing* itself.

Instead of τελειοτητος, *perfection,* several reputable MSS., with the *Itala,* read ἑνοτητος, *unity ;* but the former is doubtless the genuine reading.

Verse 15. *And let the peace of God*] Instead of Θεου, *God,* Χριστου, *Christ,* is the reading of ABC* D*FG, several others, both the *Syriac,* the *Arabic* of Erpen, *Coptic, Æthiopic, Armenian, Vulgate,* and *Itala,* with several of the *fathers ;* on this evidence *Griesbach* has inserted it in the text.

Rule in your hearts] Βραβευετω· Let the peace of Christ *judge, decide,* and *govern* in your hearts, as the *brabeus,* or judge, does in the Olympic contests. No heart is right with God where the *peace of Christ* does not rule ; and the continual prevalence of the peace of Christ is the decisive proof that the heart *is* right with God. When a man loses his *peace,* it is an awful proof that he has lost something else ; that he has given way to evil, and grieved the Spirit of God. While peace rules, all is safe.

In one body] Ye cannot have peace with God, in yourselves, nor among each other, unless ye continue

5

A. M. cir. 4066.
A. D. cir. 62.
A. U. C. 814.
An. Imp. Ne-
ronis Cæs.
Aug. 9.

one body; [m] and be ye thankful.

16 Let the word of Christ dwell in you richly in all wisdom; teaching and admonishing one another [n] in psalms and hymns and spiritual songs, singing [o] with grace in your hearts to the Lord.

17 And [p] whatsoever ye do in word or deed, *do* all in the name of the Lord Jesus, [q] giving thanks to God and the Father by him.

18 [r] Wives, submit yourselves unto your own husbands, [s] as it is fit in the Lord.

A. M. cir. 4066
A. D. cir. 62.
A. U. C. 814.
An. Imp. Ne-
ronis Cæs.
Aug. 9.

---

[m] Chap. ii. 7; ver. 17.——[n] 1 Cor. xiv. 26; Eph. v. 19.——[o] Ch. iv. 6.——[p] 1 Cor. x. 31.——[q] Rom. i. 8; Eph. v. 20; chap. i. 12;

ii. 7; 1 Thess. v. 18; Heb. xiii. 15.——[r] Eph. v. 22; Tit. ii. 5; 1 Pet. iii. 1.——[s] Eph. v. 3.

---

in *unity;* and, as *one body,* continue in *connection* and *dependence* on him who is your only *head:* to this *ye are called;* it is a glorious state of salvation, and ye should be for ever *thankful* that ye are thus privileged.

Verse 16. *Let the word of Christ dwell in you richly*] I believe the apostle means that the Colossians should be *well instructed in the doctrine of Christ;* that it should be their constant study; that it should be frequently preached, explained, and enforced among them; and that *all* the *wisdom* comprised in it should be well understood. Thus the doctrine of God would dwell richly, that is, abundantly, among them. But there appears to be here an allusion to the *Shechinah,* or symbol of the Divine presence, which *dwelt* in the *tabernacle* and first *temple;* and to an opinion common among the Jews, which is thus expressed in *Melchita,* fol. 38, 4 : כל מקום שהתורה שם שכינה שם עמה; *In whatever place the* LAW *is, there the* SHECHINAH *is present with it.* Nor is this a vain supposition; wherever God's word is seriously read, heard, or preached, *there* is God himself; and in that Church or religious society where the truth of God is proclaimed and conscientiously believed, there is the *constant dwelling of God.* Through bad *pointing* this verse is not very intelligible; the several members of it should be distinguished thus : *Let the doctrine of Christ dwell richly among you; teaching and admonishing each other in all wisdom; singing with grace in your hearts unto the Lord, in psalms, hymns, and spiritual songs.* This arrangement the original will not only bear, but it absolutely requires it, and is not sense without it. See the note on Eph. v. 19.

The *singing* which is here recommended is widely different from what is commonly used in most Christian congregations; a congeries of *unmeaning* sounds, associated to bundles of nonsensical, and often ridiculous, *repetitions,* which at once both deprave and disgrace the Church of Christ. *Melody,* which is allowed to be the most proper for devotional music, is now sacrificed to an exuberant *harmony,* which requires, not only many *different kinds* of *voices,* but *different musical instruments* to support it. And by these preposterous means the *simplicity* of the Christian worship is destroyed, and all *edification* totally prevented. And this kind of singing is amply proved to be very injurious to the personal piety of those employed in it; even of those who enter with a considerable share of humility and Christian meekness, how few continue *to sing with* GRACE *in their hearts unto the Lord?*

Verse 17. *Whatsoever ye do in word or deed*] Let your words be right, and your actions upright.

Do all in the name of the Lord Jesus] Begin with him, and end with him; invoke his name, and pray for his direction and support, in all that ye do; and thus every work will be crowned with all requisite success. Doing every thing in the name of God, and referring every thing to his glory, is as rational as it is pious. Could it be ever supposed that any person would begin a *bad* work in God's name? However, it is so. No people in the universe more strictly adhere to the *letter* of this advice than the *Mohammedans;* for they never undertake a work, eat meat, nor write a book, without prefacing all with——

بسم الله الرحمن الرحيم

Bismillahi, Arrahmani, Arraheemi;

"In the name of the most merciful and compassionate God."

Not only books of *devotion,* but books on all *arts* and *sciences,* books of *tales* and *romances,* books of *poetry,* and those on the *elements* of reading, &c., begin thus; nay, it is prefixed to the لذت ال نسا *Lizit un Nissa,* one of the most abominable productions that ever came from the pen of man; and is precisely the same among the Mohammedans, as the infamous work of *Nicholas Chorier,* called *Elegantiæ Latini Sermonis,* falsely attributed to *John Meursius,* has been among some called Christians. Of both, with a trifling hyberbole, it may be said : "Surely these books were written in hell, and the author of them must certainly be the devil."

Giving thanks to God] Even *praises,* as well as *prayers,* must ascend to God through this *Mediator.* We have no authority to say that God will accept even our *thanksgiving,* unless it ascend to him through Christ Jesus.

Verse 18. *Wives, submit yourselves*] Having done with *general* directions, the apostle comes to *particular* duties, which are commonly called *relative;* because they only belong to persons in certain *situations;* and are not incumbent on all. No *woman* has the duty of a *wife* to perform but she who is one, and no *man* has the duty of a *husband* to perform but he who is married.

The directions here to wives, husbands, children, parents, servants, and masters, are so exactly the same in substance with those in Eph. v. 22–33, and vi. 1–9, that there is no need to repeat what has been said on those passages; and to the notes there the reader is requested to refer.

A. M. cir. 4066.
A. D. cir. 62.
A. U. C. 814.
An. Imp. Ne-
ronis Cæs.
Aug. 9.

19 [t] Husbands, love *your* wives, and be not [u] bitter against them.

20 [v] Children, obey *your* parents [w] in all things : for this is well pleasing unto the Lord.

21 [x] Fathers, provoke not your children *to anger,* lest they be discouraged.

22 [y] Servants, obey [z] in all things *your* masters [a] according to the flesh ; not with eye-service, as men-pleasers ; but in

singleness of heart, fearing God :

A. M. cir. 4066.
A. D. cir. 62.
A. U. C. 814.
An. Imp. Ne-
ronis Cæs.
Aug. 9.

23 [b] And whatsoever ye do, do *it* heartily, as to the Lord, and not unto men ;

24 [c] Knowing that of the Lord ye shall receive the reward of the inheritance ; [d] for ye serve the Lord Christ.

25 But he that doeth wrong shall receive for the wrong which he hath done : and [e] there is no respect of persons.

---

[t] Eph. v. 25, 28, 33 ; 1 Pet. iii. 7.——[u] Eph. iv. 31.——[v] Eph. vi. 1.——[w] Eph. v. 24 ; Titus ii. 9.——[x] Eph. vi. 4.——[y] Eph. vi. 5, &c. ; 1 Tim. vi. 1 ; Tit. ii. 9 ; 1 Pet. ii. 18.

[z] Ver. 20.——[a] Philem. 16.——[b] Eph. vi. 6, 7.——[c] Eph. vi. 8. [d] 1 Cor. vii. 22.——[e] Rom. ii. 11 ; Eph. vi. 9 ; 1 Pet. i. 17 ; see Deut. x. 17.

As it is fit in the Lord.] God commands it ; and it is both *proper* and *decent.*

Verse 19. *Be not bitter against them.*] Wherever *bitterness* is, there *love* is wanting. And where love is wanting in the married life, there is hell upon earth.

Verse 20. *Children, obey—in all things*] That is, *in the Lord*—in every thing that your parents command you, which is not contrary to the will or word of God.

Verse 21. *Fathers, provoke not*] See the notes on Eph. vi. 4.

Verse 22. *Servants, obey*] See on Eph. vi. 5—8.

Verse 24. *The reward of the inheritance*] Here, ye have neither *lands* nor *property* ; ye are *servants* or *slaves* ; be not discouraged, ye have an inheritance in store ; be faithful unto God and to your employers, and Christ will give you a heavenly inheritance.

Verse 25. *But he that doeth wrong*] It is possible for an unfaithful servant to wrong and defraud his master in a great variety of ways without being detected ; but let all such remember what is here said : He that doeth wrong shall receive for the wrong which he has done ; God sees him, and will punish him for his breach of honesty and trust. Wasting, or not taking proper care of the goods of your master, is such a *wrong* as God will resent. He that is unfaithful in that which is *little,* will be unfaithful in *much,* if he have opportunity ; and God alone is the defence against an unfaithful servant.

There is no respect] God neither *esteems* nor *despises* any man because of his *outward condition* and *circumstances* ; for there is no respect of persons with him. Every man is, in the eye of God, what he is in his soul : if *holy,* loved ; if *wicked,* despised and rejected.

CHAPTER IV.

The duty of masters to their servants, 1.   *Continuance in prayer recommended, to which watchfulness and thanksgiving should be joined,* 2.   *And to pray particularly for the success of the Gospel,* 3, 4.   *Directions concerning walking wisely, redeeming of time, and godly conversation,* 5, 6.   *He refers them to Tychicus and Onesimus, whom he sends to them, for particulars relative to his present circumstances,* 7–9.   *Mentions the salutations of several then at Rome, of whom he gives some interesting particulars,* 10–14.   *Sends his own salutations to the brethren in Laodicea, and to Nymphas and the Church at his house,* 15.   *Directs this epistle to be read in the Church of the Laodiceans, and that to them to be read at Colosse,* 16.   *Directions to Archippus relative to his ministry,* 17.   *Concludes with salutations to the people at Colosse, to whom he sends his apostolical benediction,* 18.

A. M. cir. 4066.
A. D. cir. 62.
A. U. C. 814.
An. Imp. Ne-
ronis Cæs.
Aug. 9.

MASTERS, [a] give unto *your* servants that which is just and equal ; knowing that ye also have a Master in heaven.

2 [b] Continue in prayer, and watch in the same [c] with thanksgiving ;

3 [d] Withal, praying also for

A. M. cir. 4066.
A. D. cir. 62.
A. U. C. 814.
An. Imp. Ne-
ronis Cæs.
Aug. 9.

---

[a] Eph. vi. 9.——[b] Luke xviii. 1 ; Rom. xii. 12 ; Eph. vi. 18 ; 1 Thess.

v. 17, 18.——[c] Chap. ii. 7 ; iii. 15.——[d] Eph. vi. 19 ; 2 Thess. iii. 1.

NOTES ON CHAP. IV.

Verse 1. *Masters, give unto* your *servants*] This verse should have been added to the preceding, to which it properly belongs ; and this chapter should have begun with ver. 2.

That which is just and equal] As they are *bondmen* or *slaves* of whom the apostle speaks, we may at once see with what propriety this exhortation is given. The condition of *slaves* among the Greeks and Romans was wretched in the extreme : they could appeal

    (34**)

A. M. cir. 4066.
A. D. cir. 62.
A. U. C. 814.
An. Imp. Ne-
ronis Cæs.
Aug. 9.

us, that God would ^e open unto us a door of utterance, to speak ^f the mystery of Christ, ^g for which I am also in bonds :

4 That I may make it manifest, as I ought to speak.

5 ^h Walk in wisdom toward them that are without, ⁱ redeeming the time.

A. M. cir. 4066.
A. D. cir. 62.
A. U. C. 814
An. Imp. Ne-
ronis Cæs.
Aug. 9.

---

^e 1 Cor. xvi. 9 ; 2 Cor. ii. 12.——^f Matt. xiii. 11 ; 1 Cor. iv. 1 ; Eph. vi. 19 ; chap. i. 26 ; ii. 2.

^g Eph. vi. 20 ; Phil. i. 7.——^h Eph. v. 15 ; 1 Thess. iv. 12. ⁱ Eph. v. 16.

---

to no law ; and they could neither expect justice nor equity. The apostle, therefore, informs the proprietors of these slaves that they should act towards them both according to *justice* and *equity* ; for God, their Master, required this of them, and would at last call them to account for their conduct in this respect. Justice and equity required that they should have proper food, proper raiment, due rest, and no more than moderate work. This is a lesson that all masters throughout the universe should carefully learn. Do not treat your servants as if God had made them of an inferior blood to yours.

Verse 2. *Continue in prayer*] This was the apostle's general advice to all ; without this, neither wives, husbands, children, parents, servants, nor masters, could fulfil the duties which God, in their respective stations, required of them.

All light, power, and life come from God ; his creatures are continually dependent upon him for all these : to earnest, persevering prayer, he has promised every supply ; but he who prays not has no promise. How few *wives* feel it their duty to pray to God to give them grace to behave *as wives !* How few husbands pray for the grace suited to their situation, that they may be able to fulfil its duties ! The like may be said of *children, parents, servants,* and *masters.* As every situation in life has its peculiar duties, trials, &c. ; so to every situation there is peculiar grace appointed. No man can fulfil the duties of any station without the grace suited to that station. The grace suited to him, as a *member of society in general,* will not be sufficient for him as a husband, father, or master. Many proper marriages become unhappy in the end, because the parties have not earnestly besought God for the grace necessary for them as husbands and wives. This is the origin of family broils in general ; and a proper attention to the apostle's advice would prevent them all.

Watch in the same] Be always on your guard ; and when you have got the requisite grace by praying, take care of it, and bring it into its proper action by watchfulness ; by which you will know *when,* and *where,* and *how* to apply it.

With thanksgiving] Being always grateful to God, who has called you into such a state of salvation, and affords you such abundant means and opportunities to glorify him.

Verse 3. *Praying also for us*] Let the success and spread of the Gospel be ever dear to you ; and neglect not to pray fervently to God that it may have free course, run, and be glorified.

A door of utterance] Θυραν του λογου· The word Θυρα, which commonly signifies a *door,* or such like entrance into a house or passage through a wall, is often used metaphorically for an *entrance* to any business, *occasion* or *opportunity* to commence or perform

any particular work. So in Acts xiv. 27 : *The* DOOR *of faith is opened to the Gentiles ;* i. e. there is now an *opportunity* of preaching the Gospel to the nations of the earth. 1 Cor. xvi. 9 : *A great and effectual* DOOR *is opened unto me ;* i. e. I have now a glorious *opportunity* of preaching the truth to the people of Ephesus. 2 Cor. ii. 12 : *When I came to Troas—a* DOOR *was opened unto me ;* I had a fine *opportunity* of preaching Christ crucified at that place. So, here, the θυρατου λογου, which we translate *door of utterance,* signifies an *occasion, opportunity,* or *entrance,* for the *doctrine* of the Gospel. The same metaphor is used by the best Latin writers. Cicero, xiii. Ep. 10 : *Amicitiæ fores aperiuntur ; the* DOORS *of friendship are opened—* there is now an *opportunity* of reconciliation. And Ovid, Amor. lib. iii., Eleg. xii. ver. 12 :—

JANUA per nostras est adaperta manus.

" The gate is opened by our hands."

Of this use of the word among the Greek writers, *Schleusner* gives several examples. See also Rev. iii. 8, where the word is used in the same sense. To multiply examples would be needless ; the apostle excites them to pray, not that a *door of utterance,* i. e. a *readiness* and *fluency of speech,* may be given to him and his fellow labourers, but that they may have an *opportunity* of *preaching the doctrine* of Christ ; and so the term *λογος* is to be understood here, as well as in many other places of the New Testament, in most of which we have either lost or obscured its meaning by translating it *word* instead of *doctrine.*

The mystery of Christ] The Gospel, which had been *hidden* from all former, times, and which revealed that purpose long hidden in the Divine councils, that the Gentiles should be called to enjoy the same privileges with the Jews.

For which I am also in bonds] He was suffering under Jewish malice, and for preaching this very mystery ; for they could not bear to hear announced, as from heaven, that the *Gentiles,* whom they considered eternally shut out from any participation of the Divine favour, should be made fellow heirs with them of the grace of life ; much less could they bear to hear that *they* were about to be *reprobated,* and the Gentiles *elected* in their place. It was for asserting these things that they persecuted Paul at Jerusalem, so that to save his life he was obliged to appeal to Cæsar ; and being taken to Rome, he was detained a prisoner till his case was fully heard ; and he was a prisoner at Rome on this very account when he wrote this Epistle to the Colossians. See the note on chap. i. 24.

Verse 4. *That I may make it manifest*] It was a *mystery,* and he wished to make it *manifest*—to lay it *open,* and make all men *see* it.

Verse 5. *Walk in wisdom*] Act wisely and pru-

A. M. cir. 4066.
A. D. cir. 62.
A. U. C. 814.
An. Imp. Ne-
ronis Cæs.
Aug. 9.

6 Let your speech *be* alway [k] with grace, [l] seasoned with salt, [m] that ye may know how ye ought to answer every man.

7 [n] All my state shall Tychicus declare unto you, *who is* a beloved brother, and a faithful minister and fellow servant in the Lord:

8 [o] Whom I have sent unto you for the same purpose, that he might know your estate, and comfort your hearts;

9 With [p] Onesimus, a faithful and beloved brother, who is *one* of you. They shall make known unto you all things which *are done* here.

A. M. cir. 4066.
A. D. cir. 62.
A. U. C. 814.
An. Imp. Ne-
ronis Cæs.
Aug. 9.

---

[k] Eccles. x. 12; chap. iii. 16.——[l] Mark ix. 50.——[m] 1 Pet. iii. 15.

[n] Eph. vi. 21.——[o] Eph. vi. 22.——[p] Philem. 10.

---

dently in reference to them who are *without*—who yet continue unbelieving Gentiles or persecuting Jews.

The Church of Christ was considered an *enclosure;* a *field,* or *vineyard,* well hedged or walled. Those who were not members of it, were considered *without;* i. e. not under that especial protection and defence which the true followers of Christ had. This has been since called "The pale of the Church," from *palus,* a *stake;* or, as Dr. Johnson defines it, " A narrow piece of wood, joined above and below to a rail, to enclose grounds." As to be a Christian was essential to the salvation of the soul, so to be in the Church of Christ was essential to the being a Christian; therefore it was concluded that "there was no salvation out of the pale of the Church." Now this is true in all places where the doctrines of Christianity are preached; but when *one description* of people professing Christianity, with their own peculiar mode of worship and creed, arrogate to themselves, *exclusive of all others,* the title of THE Church; and then, on the ground of a maxim which is true in itself, but falsely understood and applied by them, assert that, as they are THE *Church,* and there is no Church besides, then you must be one of them, believe as they believe, and worship as they worship, or you will be infallibly damned; I say, when this is asserted, every man who feels he has an immortal spirit is called on to examine the pretensions of such spiritual monopolists. Now, as the Church of Christ is formed on the foundation of the *prophets* and *apostles,* Jesus Christ being the chief corner stone, the doctrines of this Christian Church must be sought for in the *sacred Scriptures.* As to *fathers, councils,* and human authorities of all kinds, they are, in this question, lighter than vanity; the *book of God* alone must decide. The Church, which has been so hasty to condemn all others, and, by its own *soi disant* or self-constituted authority, to make itself the determiner of the fates of men, dealing out the mansions of glory to its partisans, and the abodes of endless misery to all those who are out of its antichristian and inhuman *pale;* this Church, I say, has been brought to this standard, and proved by the Scriptures to be fallen from the faith of God's elect, and to be most awfully and dangerously corrupt; and to be *within its pale,* of all others professing Christianity, would be the most likely means of endangering the final salvation of the soul. Yet even in it many sincere and upright persons may be found, who, in spirit and practice, belong to the true Church of Christ. Such persons are to be found of all religious persuasions, and in all sorts of Christian societies.

Redeeming the time.] See on Eph. v. 16.

Verse 6. *Let your speech* be *alway with grace, sea-*

soned with salt] Let it be such as has a tendency to oppose and preserve from the corruption of sin. The rabbins say: " He who, in prayer, omits any word, should begin again at the beginning; for he who does not is like boiled pottage, in which there is no salt." *Berachoth,* fol. 34, 1. Let all your conversation be such as may tend to exemplify and recommend Christianity; let it not only be *holy,* but wise, gracious, and intelligent. A *harsh method* of *proposing* or *defending* the doctrines of Christianity only serves to repel men from those doctrines, and from the way of salvation. *Salt,* from its use in preserving food from corruption, and rendering it both savoury and wholesome, has always been made the emblem of *wisdom.* The word has been also used to express in composition or conversation what is terse, comprehensive, useful, elegant, and impressive. The term *Attic salt* has been used to express some of the principal beauties of the Greek tongue; of such beauties the Gospel of Christ has an endless store. See on Matt. v. 13, and Mark ix. 50.

How ye ought to answer every man.] That your discourse may be so judiciously managed, that ye may discern how to treat the prejudices and meet the objections both of *Jews* and *Gentiles.*

Verse 7. *All my state shall Tychicus*] See the note on Eph. vi. 21. Tychicus well knew the apostle's zeal and perseverance in preaching the Gospel, his sufferings on that account, his success in converting both Jews and Gentiles, and the converts which were made in Cæsar's household; he could give these to the Colossians in ample detail, and some of them it would not have been prudent to commit to writing.

Verse 8. *That he might know your estate*] Instead of ἱνα γνῳ τα περι ὑμων, *that* HE *may know* YOUR *affairs,* ABD*FG, many others, with the Æthiopic, Itala, Theodoret, and Damascenus, read ἱνα γνωτε τα περι ἡμων, *that* YE *may know* OUR *affairs;* which is probably the true reading. Tychicus was sent to them, not to know their affairs, but with Onesimus, to carry this epistle and make the apostle's state known to them, and comfort their hearts by the good news which he brought. The next verse confirms this meaning.

Verse 9. *With Onesimus—who is one of you.*] Onesimus was a native of some part of Phrygia, if not of Colosse itself; and being lately converted to the Christian faith by the instrumentality of the apostle, he would be able, on this account, to give them satisfactory information concerning the apostle's state, which would be doubly acceptable to them as he was their countryman. See the *Epistle* to Philemon.

All things which are done *here.*] FG, the *Vulgate, Itala, Jerome,* and *Bede,* add here πραττομενα, *what is*

532

2

A. M. cir. 4066.
A. D. cir. 62.
A. U. C. 814.
An. Imp. Neronis Cæs. Aug. 9.

10 [q] Aristarchus my fellow prisoner saluteth you, and [r] Marcus, sister's son to Barnabas; (touching whom ye received commandments; if he come unto you, receive him;)

11 And Jesus, which is called Justus, who are of the circumcision. These only *are my* fellow workers unto the kingdom of God, which have been a comfort unto me.

12 [s] Epaphras, who is *one* of you, a servant of Christ, saluteth you, always [t] labouring [u] fervently for you in prayers, that ye may stand [v] perfect and [w] complete in all the will of God.

A. M. cir. 4066.
A. D. cir. 62.
A. U. C. 814.
An. Imp. Neronis Cæs. Aug. 9.

13 For I bear him record, that he hath a great zeal for you, and them *that are* in Laodicea, and them in Hierapolis.

[q] Acts xix. 29; xx. 4; xxvii. 2; Philem. 24.——[r] Acts xv. 37; 2 Tim. iv. 11.——[s] Chap. i. 7; Philem. 23.

[t] Or, *striving*.——[u] Rom. xv. 30.——[v] Matt. v. 48; 1 Cor. ii. 6; xiv. 20; Phil. iii. 15; Heb. v. 14.——[w] Or, *filled*.

done, which we have supplied in *Italics* in our translation. These brethren could give an account of the transactions at Rome, relative to the apostle and Christianity, which it might not be prudent for him to commit to writing. See on ver. 7. The reign of Nero was not only cruel, but suspicious, jealous, and dangerous.

Verse 10. *Aristarchus my fellow prisoner*] Concerning Aristarchus, see Acts xix. 29; xx. 4; and xxvii. 2; and see the note on this latter place. Aristarchus and Epaphras are mentioned as saluters in this epistle, and in that to Philemon written at the same time; but here he is said to be a *prisoner*, and Epaphras not. In that to Philemon, Epaphras is called a *prisoner*, and Aristarchus not. One of them is wrong, though it is uncertain which; unless both were prisoners. See *Wall's* Crit. Notes. As Aristarchus had been a zealous and affectionate adherent to St. Paul, and followed him in all his journeys, ministering to him in prison, and assisting him in preaching the Gospel in Rome, he might have been imprisoned on this account. We need not suppose that both he and Epaphras were imprisoned *at* the same time; *about* the same time they might be imprisoned, but it might be so ordered by the providence of God that when Aristarchus was imprisoned Epaphras was at liberty, and while Epaphras was in prison Aristarchus was at liberty. This is a very possible and easily to be conceived case.

Marcus] See the account of this person, Acts xv. 39. Though there had been some difference between the apostle and this *Mark*, yet from this, and 2 Tim. iv. 11, we find that they were fully reconciled, and that Mark was very useful to St. Paul in the work of the ministry.

Touching whom ye received commandments] What these were we cannot tell; it was some private communication which had been previously sent to the Colossian Church.

Verse 11. *Jesus, which is called Justus*] Jesus, Joshua, or Jehoshua, was his name among his countrymen the Jews; *Justus* was the name which he bore among the Greeks and Romans.

These only] That is, only Aristarchus, Marcus, and Jesus Justus, who were formerly Jews or proselytes; for *οἱ οντες εκ περιτομης, they were of the circumcision*, and assisted the apostle in preaching the Gospel. There were others who did preach Christianity; but they did it from envy and strife, in order to add affliction to the apostle's bonds. It is evident, therefore, that St. Peter was not now at Rome, else he certainly would have been mentioned in this list; for we cannot suppose that he was in the list of those who preached Christ in an exceptionable way, and from impure and unholy motives: indeed, there is no evidence that St. Peter ever saw Rome. And as it cannot be *proved* that he ever was bishop or pope of that city, the *key-stone* of the triumphal arch of the pope of Rome is pulled out; this building, therefore, of his *supremacy*, cannot stand.

Verse 12. *Epaphras, who is* one *of you*] A native of some part of Phrygia, and probably of Colosse itself.

A servant of Christ] A minister of the Gospel.

Labouring fervently for you] Αγωνιζομενος· *Agonizing*; very properly expressed by our translators, *labouring fervently*.

That ye may stand perfect and complete] Ἱνα στητε τελειοι και πεπληρωμενοι That ye may stand firm, perfectly instructed, and fully persuaded of the truth of those doctrines which have been taught you as the revealed will of God: this I believe to be the meaning of the apostle.

Instead of πεπληρωμενοι, *complete* or *filled up*, almost all the MSS. of the Alexandrian rescension, which are considered the most authentic and correct, have πεπληροφορημενοι, *that ye may be fully persuaded*. The word πληροφορια signifies such a complete persuasion of the certainty of a thing, as leaves the mind which has it neither room nor inclination to doubt; and πληροφορεω, the verb, has the same meaning, viz., to be thus persuaded, or to persuade thus, by demonstrative argumentation and exhibition of unquestionable facts.

This is such a persuasion as the Spirit of God, by means of the Gospel, gives to every sincere and faithful man; and from which arises the solid happiness of the genuine Christian. They who argue against it, prove, at least, that they have not got it.

Verse 13. *He hath a great zeal for you*] Instead of ζηλον πολυν, *much zeal*, ABCD**, several others, with *versions* and *fathers*, read πολυν πονον, *much labour*; they are here nearly of the same meaning, though the latter appears to be the better and genuine reading.

Laodicea, and—Hierapolis] These were both cities of Phrygia, between which Colosse, or the city of *Colassa*, was situated. See on chap. ii. 1. The latter was called *Hierapolis*, or the *holy city*, from the multitude of its temples. Apollo, Diana, Æsculapius, and Hygeia, were all worshipped here, as appears by the coins of this city still extant.

A. M. cir. 4066.
A. D. cir. 62.
A. U. C. 814.
An. Imp. Ne-
ronis Cæs.
Aug. 9.

14 *ˣ* Luke, the beloved physician, and *ʸ* Demas, greet you.

15 Salute the brethren which are in Laodicea, and Nymphas, and *ᶻ* the Church which is in his house.

16 And when *ᵃ* this epistle is read among you, cause that it be read also in the Church of the Laodiceans; and that ye likewise read the *epistle* from Laodicea.

17 And say to *ᵇ* Archippus, Take heed to *ᶜ* the ministry which thou hast received in the Lord, that thou fulfil it.

18 *ᵈ* The salutation by the hand of me Paul. *ᵉ* Remember my bonds. *ᶠ* Grace *be* with you. Amen.

¶ Written from Rome to the Colossians, by Tychicus and Onesimus.

A. M. cir. 4066.
A. D. cir. 62.
A. U. C. 814.
An. Imp. Ne-
ronis Cæs.
Aug. 9.

ˣ 2 Tim. iv. 11.——ʸ 2 Tim. iv. 10; Philem. 24.——ᶻ Rom. xvi. 5; 1 Cor. xvi. 19.——ᵃ 1 Thess. v. 27.

ᵇ Philem. 2.——ᶜ 1 Tim. iv. 6.——ᵈ 1 Cor. xvi. 21; 2 Thess. iii. 17.——ᵉ Heb. xiii. 3.——ᶠ Heb. xiii. 25.

Verse 14. *Luke, the beloved physician*] This is generally supposed to be the same with Luke the evangelist. See the preface to the notes on this gospel. Some, however, suppose them to be different persons; because, where it is evident that Luke the evangelist is meant, he never has more than his simple name Luke; and because the apostle is supposed to intend a different person here, he adds, ὁ ιατρος ὁ αγαπητος, the beloved physician. The word ιατρος signifies a *healer*, and must not be restricted to *physician*, in the sense in which we use that word; he was surgeon, physician, and dispenser of medicines, &c., for all these were frequently combined in the same person.

Verse 15. *Salute—Nymphas, and the Church—in his house.*] This person, and his whole family, which probably was very numerous, appear to have received the Gospel; and it seems that, for their benefit and that of his neighbours, he had opened his house for the worship of God. In those primitive times there were no *consecrated* places, for it was supposed that the simple setting apart of any place for the worship of God was a sufficient consecration. See of those domestic churches, Rom. xvi. 5; 1 Cor. xvi. 19.

Verse 16. *Cause that it be read also in the Church of the Laodiceans*] That is: Let a copy be taken, and sent to them, that it may be read there also. This appears to have been a regular custom in the apostolic Church.

That ye likewise read the epistle *from Laodicea.*] Some suppose that this was an epistle sent from Laodicea to the apostle, which he now sent by Aristarchus to the Colossians, that they might peruse it; that thereby they might see the propriety of sending a copy of his epistle to them, to the Laodicean Church. Many eminent critics are of this opinion, which appears to me to be both forced and far fetched. Others think that the Epistle to the Ephesians is the epistle in question, and that it was originally directed to them, and not to the Ephesians. See the notes on Eph. i. 1, &c. But others, equally learned, think that there was an epistle, different from that to the Ephesians, sent by St. Paul to the Laodiceans, which is now lost. There was an epistle under this direction in the times of Theodoret and Jerome, for both of them mention it; but the latter mentions it as apocryphal, *Legunt quidam et ad Laodicenses Epistolam, sed ab omnibus exploditur*; "Some read an Epistle to the Laodiceans, but it is exploded by all." The seventh Œcumenic council, held in 787, states that the ancients allowed that there was an epistle with this direction, but that all the orthodox rejected it as supposititious.

An epistle *ad Laodicenses* is still extant in the Latin language, a very ancient copy of which is in the library *Sancti Albani Andegavensis*, St. Alban's of Anjou. Hutter has translated it into Greek, but his translation is of no authority. Calmet has published this epistle, with various readings from the above MS. I shall subjoin it at the end of this epistle, and give my opinion relative to its use and authenticity. A copy of this epistle stands in this place as a portion of Divine revelation in one of my own MSS. of the Vulgate.

Verse 17. *Say to Archippus*] Who this person was we cannot tell; there have been various conjectures concerning him; some think he was bishop, or overseer of the Church at Colosse, in the absence of Epaphras. Whatever he was, it has been supposed that he had been remiss in discharging the duties of his office; and hence this direction of the apostle, which appears here in the light of a *reprehension*. But if the same person be meant as in the Epistle to Philemon, ver. 2, whom St. Paul calls his *fellow labourer* and *fellow soldier*, it cannot be supposed that any reproof is here intended; for, as the Epistle to the Colossians, and that to Philemon, were evidently written about the end of the year 62, Archippus could not be a fellow labourer and fellow soldier of the apostle at Rome, and yet a delinquent at Colosse at the same time. It is more likely, therefore, that the words of the apostle convey no censure, but are rather intended to stir him up to farther diligence, and to encourage him in the work, seeing he had so much false doctrine and so many false teachers to contend with.

Verse 18. *The salutation by the hand of me Paul.*] The preceding part of the epistle was written by a scribe, from the mouth of the apostle: this, and what follows, was written by the hand of St. Paul himself. A similar distinction we find, 1 Cor. xvi. 21, and in 2 Thess. iii. 17; and this, it seems, was the means by which the apostle authenticated every epistle which he sent to the different Churches. *The salutation of Paul with mine own hand, which is the token in every epistle, so I write.*

Remember my bonds] See what proof ye have of the truth of the Gospel; I am in bonds on this account; I suffer patiently, yea, exult in the Lord Jesus, so perfectly am I upheld by the grace of the Gospel.

2

Remember my bonds, and take courage. How eloquent were these concluding words! That such a man should be in bonds for the Gospel, was the fullest proof of the truth of the Gospel. A cunningly devised fable could not have imposed on Saul of Tarsus; he was fully satisfied of the truth of the doctrines of Christianity; he proclaimed them as truths from heaven; and for their sake cheerfully suffered the loss of all things. The bonds of such a man are a plenary proof of the truth of the doctrines for which he was bound.

Grace be with you.] May you still possess the favour and blessing of our Lord Jesus Christ: the apostle ends, as he began, this epistle. Without the grace of Christ they could not have *become* a Church; without this grace they could not *continue* to be one.

Amen] This is omitted by the most ancient and correct MSS.

The subscriptions, as usual, are various and uncertain:—

The common GREEK *text* has, *To the Colossians, written from Rome by Tychicus and Onesimus.*

The Epistle to the Colossians; written at Rome, and sent by the hand of Tychicus. SYRIAC.

To the Colossians. ÆTHIOPIC.

In the *Vulgate* there is no subscription.

The end of the epistle; and it was written from Rome, and sent by the hand of Tychicus and Onesimus. Praise be to God for ever and ever; and may his mercy be upon us. Amen. ARABIC.

Written from Athens by Tychicus, and Onesimus, and Mark, his disciples. COPTIC.

The MSS. are not less various than the *versions:*
To the Colossians.—That to the Colossians is completed; that to the Philippians begins.—That to the Colossians is finished; the First Epistle to the Thessalonians begins.—To the Colossians, from Rome.—Written to the Colossians from Rome.—Written from Rome by Tychicus, and Timotheus, and Onesimus.—Written by Paul and Timothy, and sent by Tychicus, and Onesimus.

That the epistle was written from *Rome* there is little cause to doubt: that Timothy might be the *scribe* is very probable, because it appears he was at Rome with the apostle in the same year in which this epistle was written. See Phil. ii. 19. And that it was sent by *Tychicus* and *Onesimus,* seems evident from the 8th and 9th verses of this chapter.

The common subscription has the consent of the greater number of the most recent and comparatively recent MSS., but this is not, in general, a proof of authenticity.

In the note on ver. 16 I promised to subjoin what is called the *Epistle to the Laodiceans:* I give it here from the best copies, and add a literal translation, that the curious, whether learned or unlearned, may have what some have believed to be authentic, and what has doubtless existed, in one form or other, from a very remote antiquity.

EPISTOLA PAULI APOSTOLI AD LAODICENSES.

1. Paulus, Apostolus, non ab hominibus, neque per hominem, sed per Jesum Christum. Fratribus qui estis (sunt) Laodiceæ.
2. Gratia vobis et pax a Deo Patre nostro, et Domino Jesu Christo.
3. Gratias ago Christo per omnem orationem meam, quod permanentes estis, et perseverantes in operibus bonis, promissionem expectantes in die judicii.
4. Neque disturbent (deficiunt) vos quorumdam vaniloquia insimulantium veritatem (insanientium) ut vos avertant a veritate evangelii, quod a me prædicatur.
5. Et nunc faciet Deus, ut qui sunt ex me ad perfectionem veritatis evangelii sint deservientes, et benignitatem operum facientes quæ sunt salutis vitæ æternæ.
6. Et nunc palam sunt vincula mea, quæ patior in Christo; in quibus lætor et gaudeo.
7. Et hoc mihi est ad salutem perpetuam, quod (ipsum) factum est in orationibus vestris, et administrante Spiritu Sancto, sive per vitam, sive per mortem.
8. Est enim mihi vivere vita in Christo, et mori gaudium (et lucrum.)
9. Et ipse Dominus noster in vobis faciet misericordiam suam, ut eandem dilectionem habeatis; et sitis unanimes.

THE EPISTLE OF PAUL THE APOSTLE TO THE LAODICEANS.

1. Paul, an apostle, not from men, nor by man, but by Jesus Christ, to the brethren which are in Laodicea.
2. Grace be to you, and peace from God our Father, and from the Lord Jesus Christ.
3. I give thanks to Christ in all my prayers, that ye continue and persevere in good works; waiting for the promise in the day of judgment.
4. Be not troubled with the vain speeches of certain who pretend to the truth, that they may draw away your hearts from the truth of the Gospel which was preached by me.
5. And may God grant that those who are of me, may be led forward to the perfection of the truth of the Gospel, and perform the benignity of works which *become* the salvation of eternal life.
6. And now my bonds are manifest, which I suffer in Christ, and in them I rejoice and am glad.
7. And this shall turn to my perpetual salvation, by means of your prayers and the assistance of the Holy Spirit, whether they be for life or for death.
8. For my life is to live in Christ; and to die will be joyous.
9. And may our Lord himself grant you his mercy, that ye may have the same love, and be of one mind.

10. ¶ Ergo, dilectissimi, ut audistis præsentiam Domini, ita sentite (retinete) et facite in timore; (Domini;) et erit vobis vita in æternum :

11. Est enim Dominus qui operatur in vobis :

12. Et facite sine peccato quæcunque facitis, (sine reatu,) et quod est optimum.

13. Dilectissimi, gaudete in Domino Jesu Christo, et cavete omnes sordes (sordidos) in omni lucro.

14. Omnes petitiones vestræ sint palam apud Deum.

15. Estote firmi in sensu Christi et quæ integra, et vera, et pudica, et casta, et justa, et amabilia sunt, facite.

16. Et quæ audistis, et accepistis, in corde retinete; et erit vobis pax.

17. Salutant vos omnes sancti.

18. Salutate omnes fratres in osculo sancto.

19. Gratia Domini nostri Jesu Christi cum spiritu vestro. Amen.

20. Et hanc facite legi Colossensibus; et eam quæ est Colossensium vobis.

    Ad Laodisenses scripta fuit e Roma, per Tychicum et Onesimum.

10. Therefore, my beloved, as ye have heard of the coming of the Lord, so think and act in the fear of the Lord, and it shall be to you eternal life.

11. For it is the Lord that worketh in you.

12. Whatsoever you do, do it without sin, and do what is best.

13. Beloved, rejoice in the Lord Jesus Christ, and beware of filthy lucre.

14. Let all your prayers be manifest before God :

15. And be firm in the sentiments you have of Christ. And whatsoever is perfect, and true, and modest, and chaste, and just, and amiable, that do.

16. And whatsoever ye have heard and received retain in your hearts, and it shall tend to your peace.

17. All the saints salute you.

18. Salute all the brethren with a holy kiss.

19. The grace of our Lord Jesus Christ *be* with your spirit. Amen.

20. And cause this epistle to be read to the Colossians; and that to the Colossians to be read to you

    To the Laodiceans, written from Rome, by Tychicus and Onesimus.

Such is the composition which pretends to be the *Epistle of Paul the Apostle to the Laodiceans,* and of which I have endeavoured to give a literal version; though even with the assistance of the various readings of the Anjou MS., which I have included in brackets, I found this difficult, so as to preserve any sense. Elias Hutter has published it after the Epistle to the Colossians, as if it were the genuine production of the apostle to whom it was attributed; and has taken the pains to exhibit it in twelve languages, viz. : Syriac, Hebrew, Greek, Latin, German, Bohemian, Italian, Spanish, French, English, Danish, and Polish. All, the *Latin* excepted, appear to be of his own composing. To criticise them would be lost labour; the *Greek* is too bald to be the production of any remote age, and as to the *English,* no Englishman can understand it. The editor deserves the strongest reprehension, because he has associated it with the genuine epistles of St. Paul, without a single note of its spuriousness.

As to its being a work of St. Paul, little or nothing need be said; its barrenness of meaning, poverty of style, incoherency of manner, and total want of design and object, are a sufficient refutation of its pretensions. It is said to be the work of some *heretics* of ancient times : this is very unlikely, as there is no heresy, ever broached in the Christian Church, that could derive any support from any thing found in this epistle. It is a congéries of *scraps,* very injudiciously culled, here and there, from St. Paul's epistles; without arrangement, without connection, and, as they stand here, almost without sense. It is a poor, wretched tale, in no danger of ever being denominated even a *cunningly devised fable.* It should keep no company but that of the pretended *Epistles of Paul to Seneca,* to which I have in other cases referred, and of which I have given my opinion.

Should it be asked : " Why I have introduced it here !" I answer : To satisfy the curious reader, and to show how little ground there is for the opinion of some, that this epistle is of any importance; and to prove how miserably forgery itself succeeds when it endeavours to *add* to or *corrupt* the word of God. The sacred writings are of such a *peculiar character* that it is utterly impossible to *imitate* them with any kind of success. They bear, deeply impressed, the seal of infinite wisdom—a seal which no human art can counterfeit. This is the criterion by which the spurious gospels and apocryphal writings in general have been judged and detected; and this *heavenly stamp,* under the care of Divine Providence, will continue to be their chief preservative, as long as the sun and moon shall endure.

Finished correcting for a new edition, Dec. 16*th,* 1831.—A. C.

THESSALONICA, now called by the Turks *Salonichi*, a mere corruption of its ancient name, is a seaport town of Turkey in Europe, situated on what was called the *Thermaic* Gulf, and was anciently the capital of *Macedonia*. According to *Stephanus Byzantinus*, it was embellished and enlarged by *Philip*, king of Macedon, father of Alexander the Great, who called it *Thessalonica*, or the *Victory of Thessalia*, on account of the *victory* he obtained there over the *Thessalians*; prior to which it was called *Thermæ*. *Strabo, Tzetzes,* and *Zonaras* say that it obtained the name of *Thessalonica* from *Thessalonica*, wife of *Cassander*, and daughter of *Philip*.

In 1431, it was taken from the Venetians by the Turks, in whose possession it still continues. It is still a large, rich, and populous city, being ten miles in circumference, and carrying on an extensive trade in *silk*, the principal merchants being Greek Christians and Jews.

Christianity has never been extinct in Thessalonica since the year 51 or 52, in which it was planted there by the Apostle Paul; see Acts xvii., &c. It contains at present thirty *churches* belonging to the Greek Christians, and as many Jewish *synagogues*, besides some Mohammedan *mosques*. Thessalonica is the see of an archbishop; and is well fortified, being surrounded with walls flanked with towers, and defended on the land side by a citadel; and near the harbour, with three forts.

St. Paul, in company with Silas, first preached the Gospel in this city and the adjacent country, about A. D. 52 or 53. Though the Jews, who were sojourners in this city, rejected the Gospel in general, yet a great multitude of the *devout Greeks*, i. e., such as were proselytes to Judaism, or the descendants of Jewish parents, born and naturalized in Greece, *believed and associated with Paul and Silas*, and *not a few of the chief women* of the city embraced the Christian faith. Acts xvii. 4.

As the Jews found that, according to the doctrine of the Gospel, the *Gentiles* were called to enjoy the same privileges with themselves, without being obliged to submit to circumcision and other ordinances of the law, they persecuted that Gospel, and those who proclaimed it; for, *moved with indignation*, they employed *certain lewd fellows of the baser sort*—the beasts of the people, *set the city on an uproar, assaulted the house of Jason*, where the apostles lodged, dragged *him* and *certain brethren before the rulers*, and charged them with seditious designs and treason against the Roman emperor! The apostles escaped, and got to *Berea*, where they began anew their important evangelical labours: thither the Jews of Thessalonica, pursuing them, raised a fresh tumult; so that the apostle, being counselled by the brethren, made his escape to *Athens*; Acts xvii. 5—15. Thus he followed the command of his Master: *Being persecuted in one city, he fled to another;* not to hide himself, but to proclaim, in every place, the saving truths of the Gospel of Christ.

It does not appear that St. Paul stayed long at *Athens;* he soon went thence to *Corinth*, where Timothy and Silas were, but probably not before Timothy met him, for whom he had sent, Acts xvii. 15, to come to him speedily; and whom, it appears, he sent immediately back to Thessalonica, to establish the believers there, and comfort them concerning the faith; 1 Thess. iii. 2. While Paul abode at Corinth, Timothy and Silas came to him from Thessalonica, and hearing by them of the steadfastness of the Thessalonian converts in the faith of Christ, he wrote this epistle, and shortly after the second, to comfort and encourage them; to give them farther instructions in the doctrines of Christianity, and to rectify some mistaken views, relative to the day of judgment, which had been propagated amongst them. See the preface to the second epistle.

Who the persons were who formed the apostolic Church at Thessalonica is not easy to determine. They were not *Jews*, for these in general persecuted the apostle and the Gospel in this place. We are therefore left to infer that the Church was formed, 1st, of *Jewish proselytes*, called, Acts xvii. 4, *devout Greeks*. And 2dly, of converts from *heathenism*; for, on the preaching of the Gospel to them, it is said, chap. i. 9, that *they turned to God from idols, to serve the living and true God.* Though *some* of the Jews believed on the preaching of Paul and Silas, Acts xvii. 3, 4, yet it is evident that the great bulk of the Church was composed of Grecian proselytes and converts from heathenism. Hence we find in this epistle but few allusions to the Jews, and but few references to the peculiarities of their religious or civil institutions.

There is a remarkable reading in the text of Acts xvii. 4, which I neglected to quote in the note on that place: instead of των σεβομενων, Ελληνων πολυ πληθος, of devout Greeks a great multitude; the *Codex Alexandrinus, Codex Bezæ*, both in the *Greek* and *Latin*, *two* others, with the *Vulgate*, read των σεβομενων και 'Ελληνων, *of the devout*, i. e., those who worshipped the true God; AND *of the Greeks*, i. e., those who were previously *heathens, a great multitude;* so that, 1. Some few *Jews;* 2. A great number of those who *acknowledged the true God;* and 3. A great multitude of *heathens*, besides *many* of *the chief women*, received the doctrine preached by the apostle, and became members of the Church at Thessalonica. See Dr. Paley's remarks on this various reading.

The First Epistle to the Thessalonians is allowed on all hands to be the *first* epistle that St. Paul wrote to any of the Churches of God; and from it *two* things may be particularly noted: 1. That the apostle was full of the Spirit of love; 2. That the Church at Thessalonica was pure, upright, and faithful, as we scarcely find any reprehension in the whole epistle: the Thessalonian converts had FAITH that *worked*, a LOVE that *laboured*, and a HOPE which induced them to bear afflictions *patiently* and *wait* for the coming of the Lord Jesus Christ.

This epistle has been *divided* into *different parts* by commentators; but these are arbitrary, the apostle having made no division of this kind; for, although he treats of several subjects, yet he has not so distinguished them from each other as to show that he had any formal division in his mind. In the divisions imposed on this epistle by commentators we do not find *two* of them alike; a full proof that the apostle has made no divisions, else some of these learned men would have certainly found them out. *Technical distinctions* of this nature are of little use to a proper understanding of the contents of this epistle.

538   2

THE
FIRST EPISTLE OF PAUL THE APOSTLE

TO THE

THESSALONIANS.

Chronological Notes relative to this Epistle.

Year of the Constantinopolitan era of the world, or that used by the Byzantine historians, 5560.—Year of the Alexandrian era of the world, 5554.—Year of the Antiochian era of the world, 5544.—Year of the Julian period, 4762.—Year of the world, according to Archbishop Usher, 4056.—Year of the world, according to Eusebius, in his Chronicon, 4280.—Year of the minor Jewish era of the world, or that in common use, 3812.—Year of the Greater Rabbinical era of the world, 4411.—Year from the Flood, according to Archbishop Usher, and the English Bible, 2400.—Year of the Cali yuga, or Indian era of the Deluge, 3154. —Year of the era of Iphitus, or since the first commencement of the Olympic games, 992.—Year of the era of Nabonassar, king of Babylon, 799.—Year of the CCVIIth Olympiad, 4.—Year from the building of Rome, according to Fabius Pictor, 799.—Year from the building of Rome, according to Frontinus, 803.—Year from the building of Rome, according to the Fasti Capitolini, 804.—Year from the building of Rome, according to Varro, which was that most generally used, 805.—Year of the era of the Seleucidæ, 364.—Year of the Cæsarean era of Antioch, 100.—Year of the Julian era, 97.—Year of the Spanish era, 90.—Year from the birth of Jesus Christ according to Archbishop Usher, 52.—Year of the vulgar era of Christ's nativity, 52.—Year of Ventidius Cumanus, governor of the Jews, 4.—Year of Vologesus, king of the Parthians, 3. —Year of Caius Numidius Quadratus, governor of Syria, 2.—Year of Ananias, high priest of the Jews, 8. Year of the Dionysian period, or Easter Cycle, 53.—Year of the Grecian Cycle of nineteen years, or Common Golden Number, 15 ; or the first after the fifth embolismic.—Year of the Jewish Cycle of nineteen years, 12, or the first after the fourth embolismic.—Year of the Solar Cycle, 5.—Dominical Letters, it being Bissextile, or Leap Year, BA.—Day of the Jewish Passover, according to the Roman computation of time, the Calends of April, i. e. April 1st, which happened in this year on the Jewish Sabbath.—Easter Sunday, April 2.—Epact, or the moon's age on the 22d of March, or the Xth of the Calends of April, 4. —Epact, according to the present mode of computation, or the moon's age on New Year's day, or the Calends of January, 11.—Monthly Epacts, or the moon's age on the Calends of each month respectively, (beginning with January,) 11, 13, 12, 14, 15, 16, 17, 18, 18, 20, 20.—Number of Direction, or the number of days from the twenty-first of March (or the XIth of the Calends of April) to the Jewish Passover, 10. —Year of Claudius Cæsar, the fifth emperor of the Romans, 12.—Roman Consuls, Publius Cornelius Sylla Faustus, and Lucius Salvius, Otho Titianus ; and for the following year, (which is by some supposed to be the date of this epistle,) Decimus Junius Silanus, and Quintus Haterius Antoninus.

CHAPTER I.

The inscription by Paul, Silvanus, and Timotheus, to the Church of the Thessalonians, 1. St. Paul gives thanks to God for their good estate, and prays for their continuance in the faith, 2–4. Shows how the Gospel came to them, and the blessed effects it produced in their life and conversation, 5–7. How it became published from them through Macedonia and Achaia, and how their faith was everywhere celebrated, 8. He shows farther, that the Thessalonians had turned from idolatry, become worshippers of the true God, and were waiting for the revelation of Christ, 9, 10.

A. M. cir. 4056.
A. D. cir. 52.
A. U. C. 805.
Anno Claudii Cæs.
Aug. 12.

PAUL, and [a] Silvanus, and Timotheus, unto the Church of the Thessalonians *which is* in God the Father, and *in* the Lord Jesus Christ : [b] Grace *be* unto you, and peace, from God our Father, and the Lord Jesus Christ.

A. M. cir. 4056.
A. D. cir. 52.
A. U. C. 805.
Anno Clau
dii Cæs.
Aug. 12.

---

[a] 2 Cor. i. 19 ; 2 Thess. i. 1 ; 1 Pet. v. 12.——[b] Eph. i. 2.

NOTES ON CHAP. I.

Verse 1. *Paul, and Silvanus, and Timotheus*] Though St. Paul *himself* dictated this letter, yet he joins the names of Silas and Timothy, because they had been with him at Thessalonica, and were well known there. See Acts xvii. 4, 14.

2

A. M. cir. 4056.
A. D. cir. 52.
A. U. C. 805.
Anno Clau-
dii Cæs.
Aug. 12.

2 ^c We give thanks to God always for you all, making mention of you in our prayers;

3 ^d Remembering without ceasing ^e your work of faith, ^f and labour of love, and patience of hope, in our Lord Jesus Christ, in the sight of God and our Father;

4 Knowing, brethren ^g beloved, ^h your election of God.

5 For ⁱ our Gospel came not unto you in word only, but also in power, and ^k in the Holy Ghost, ^l and in much assurance; as ^m ye know what manner of men we were among you for your sake.

A. M. cir. 4056.
A. D. cir. 52.
A. U. C. 805.
Anno Clau-
dii Cæs.
Aug. 12.

---

^c Rom. i. 8; Eph. i. 16; Philem. 4.——^d Chap. ii. 13.——^e John vi. 29; Gal. v. 6; chap. iii. 6; 2 Thess. i. 3, 11; James ii. 17. ^f Rom. xvi. 6; Heb. vi. 10.——^g Or, *beloved of God, your election.*

^h Col. iii. 12; 2 Thess. ii. 13.——ⁱ Mark xvi. 20; 1 Cor. ii. 4; iv. 20.——^k 2 Cor. vi. 6.——^l Col. ii. 2; Heb. ii. 3.——^m Chap. ii. 1, 5, 10, 11; 2 Thess. iii. 7.

And Silvanus] This was certainly the same as *Silas*, who was St. Paul's companion in all his journeys through Asia Minor and Greece; see Acts xv. 22; xvi. 19; xvii. 4, 10. Him and Timothy the apostle took with him into Macedonia, and they continued at Berea when the apostle went from thence to Athens; from this place St. Paul sent for them to come to him speedily, and, though it is not said that they came while he was at Athens, yet it is most probable that they did; after which, having sent them to Thessalonica, he proceeded to Corinth, where they afterwards rejoined him, and from whence he wrote this epistle. See the *preface.*

Verse 2. *We give thanks*] See Phil. i. 3, 4, and Col. i. 3; where the same forms of speech are used.

Verse 3. *Your work of faith*] This verse contains a very high character of the believers at Thessalonica. They had FAITH, not *speculative* and *indolent*, but *true, sound,* and *operative;* their *faith worked.* They had LOVE, not that *gazed* at and became enamoured of the perfections of God, but such a love as *laboured* with faith to fulfil the whole will of God. Faith worked; but love, because it can do more, did more, and therefore *laboured*—worked energetically, to promote the glory of God and the salvation of men. They had HOPE; not an idle, cold, heartless expectation of future good, from which they felt no excitement, and for which they could give no reason, but such a hope as produced a satisfying expectation of a future life and state of blessedness, the reality of which faith had descried, and love anticipated; a *hope,* not hasty and impatient to get out of the trials of life and possess the heavenly inheritance, but one that was as willing to *endure hardships* as to *enjoy glory* itself, when God might be most honoured by this patient endurance. FAITH *worked,* LOVE *laboured,* and HOPE *endured patiently.*

It is not a mark of much grace to be longing to get to heaven because of the troubles and difficulties of the present life; they who love Christ are ever willing to suffer with him; and he may be as much glorified by *patient suffering,* as by the most *active faith* or *laborious love.* There are times in which, through affliction or other hinderances, we cannot *do* the will of God, but we can *suffer* it; and in such cases he seeks a heart that bears submissively, suffers patiently, and endures, as seeing him who is invisible, without repining or murmuring. This is as full a proof of Christian perfection as the most intense and ardent love. Meekness, gentleness, and long-suffering, are in our present state of more use to ourselves and others,

and of more consequence in the sight of God, than all the ecstasies of the spirits of just men made perfect, and than all the raptures of an archangel. That Church or Christian society, the members of which manifest the *work* of *faith, labour* of *love,* and *patience* of *hope,* is most nearly allied to heaven, and is on the suburbs of glory.

Verse 4. *Knowing—your election of God.*] Being assured, from the doctrine which I have delivered to you, and which God has confirmed by various miracles, and gifts of the Holy Spirit, that he has *chosen* and *called* the Gentiles to the same privileges to which he *chose* and *called* the Jews; and that, as they have rejected the offers of the Gospel, God has now *elected* the Gentiles in their stead. This is the *election* which the Thessalonians *knew;* and of which the apostle treats at large in his Epistle to the *Romans,* and also in his Epistles to the *Galatians* and *Ephesians.* No irrespective, unconditional, eternal, and personal election to everlasting glory, is meant by the apostle. *As* God had chosen the Jews, whom, because of *their* obstinate unbelief, he had now rejected; *so* he had now chosen or elected the Gentiles. And in neither case was there any thing absolute; all was most specifically conditional, as far as their *final salvation* was concerned; without any merit on their side, they were *chosen* and *called* to those blessings which, if *rightly used,* would lead them to eternal glory. That these blessings could be *abused*—become finally useless and forfeited, they had an ample proof in the case of the Jews, who, after having been the *elect* of God for more than 2000 years, were now become *reprobates.*

Verse 5. *For our Gospel*] That is, the glad tidings of salvation by Jesus Christ, and of your being elected to enjoy all the privileges to which the Jews were called, without being obliged to submit to circumcision, or fulfil the rites and ceremonies of the Mosaic law.

Came not unto you in word only] It was not by *simple teaching* or mere *reasoning* that the doctrines which we preached recommended themselves ·to you, we did not insist on your using this or the other religious institution; we insisted on a change of heart and life, and we held out the energy which was able to effect it.

But also in power] Εν δυναμει· With *miraculous* manifestations, to your eyes and to your hearts, which induced you to acknowledge that this Gospel was the *power of God unto salvation.*

And in the Holy Ghost] By his influence upon your hearts, in changing and renewing them; and by the testimony which ye received from him, that you

A. M. cir. 4056.
A. D. cir. 52.
A. U. C. 805.
Anno Clau-
dii Cæs.
Aug. 12.

6 And [n] ye became followers of us, and of the Lord, having received the word in much affliction, [o] with joy of the Holy Ghost;

7 So that ye were ensamples to all that believe in Macedonia and Achaia.

8 For from you [p] sounded out the word of the Lord, not only in Macedonia and Achaia, but also [q] in every place your faith to Godward

is spread abroad; so that we need not to speak any thing.

9 For they themselves show of us [r] what manner of entering in we had unto you, [s] and how ye turned to God from idols, to serve the living and true God;

10 And [t] to wait for his Son [u] from heaven, [v] whom he raised from the dead, *even* Jesus, which delivered us [w] from the wrath to come.

A. M. cir. 4056.
A. D. cir. 52.
A. U. C. 805.
Anno Clau-
dii Cæs.
Aug. 12.

[n] 1 Cor. iv. 16; xi. 1; Phil. iii. 17; chap. ii. 14; 2 Thess. iii. 9.——[o] Acts v. 41; Heb. x. 34.——[p] Rom. x. 18.——[q] Rom. i. 8; 2 Thess. i. 4.——[r] Chap. ii. 1.——[s] 1 Cor. xii. 2; Gal. iv. 8.

[t] Rom. ii. 7; Phil. iii. 20; Tit. ii. 13; 2 Pet. iii. 12; Rev. i. 7. [u] Acts i. 11; chapter iv. 16; 2 Thess. i. 7.——[v] Acts ii. 24. [w] Matt. iii. 7; Rom. v. 9; chap. v. 9.

were accepted through the Beloved, and become the adopted children of God.

And in much assurance] Εν πληροφορια πολλη. The Holy Spirit which was given you *left no doubt* on your mind, either with respect to the *general truth* of the doctrine, or the safety of your own state. Ye had the fullest assurance that the Gospel was true, and the fullest assurance that ye had received the remission of sins through that Gospel; the Spirit himself bearing witness with your spirit, that you are the sons and daughters of God Almighty.

What manner of men we were] How we *preached*, and how we *lived; our doctrines* and our *practices* ever corresponding. And *for your sakes* we sustained difficulties, endured hardships, and were incessant in our labours.

Verse 6. *Ye became followers of us*] Ye became *imitators*, μιμηται, of us—ye believed the same truths, walked in the same way, and minded the same thing; knowing that our doctrine was of the Lord, and that the way in which we walked was prescribed by himself, and that he also suffered the contradictions of ungodly men.

Having received the word in much affliction] That they received the doctrine of the Gospel in the midst of much persecution we may learn from the history in general, and from Acts xvii. 5, 6.

With joy of the Holy Ghost] The consolations which they received, in consequence of believing in Christ, more than counterbalanced all the afflictions which they suffered from their persecutors.

Verse 7. *Ye were ensamples*] Τυπους· *Types, models,* or *patterns;* according to which all the Churches in Macedonia and Achaia formed both their *creed* and their *conduct.*

Verse 8. *From you sounded out*] As Thessalonica was very conveniently situated for traffic, many merchants from thence traded through Macedonia, Achaia, and different parts of Greece. By these, the fame of the Thessalonians having received the doctrine of the Gospel was doubtless carried far and wide. And it appears that they had walked so conscientiously before God and man, that their friends could speak of them without a blush, and their adversaries could say nothing to their disgrace.

Verse 9. *How ye turned to God from idols*] This could not be spoken either of the *Jews* or of the

devout persons, but of the *heathen Greeks;* and of such it appears that the majority of the Church was formed. See what is said on this subject in the *preface* to this epistle.

To serve the living and true God] The living God; in opposition to the idols, which were either *inanimate* stocks or stones, or the representations of *dead* men.

The true God—In opposition to the whole system of idolatry, which was *false* in the *objects* of its *adoration, false* in its *pretensions, false* in its *promises,* and false in all its *prospects.*

Verse 10. *And to wait for his Son from heaven*] To *expect a future state* of *glory,* and *resurrection* of the body, according to the Gospel doctrine, after the example of Jesus Christ, who was raised from the dead, and ascended unto heaven, ever to appear in the presence of God for us.

Delivered us from the wrath to come.] From all the punishment due to us for our sins, and from the destruction which is about to come on the unbelieving and impenitent Jews.

This was the *news,* the *sounding out,* that went abroad concerning the converted Thessalonians. Every where it was said: They have believed the Gospel; they have renounced idolatry; they worship the living and true God; they have received the gifts and graces of the Holy Spirit; they are happy in their souls, unspotted in their lives, and full of joy; expecting an eternal glory through that Christ who had died for and purged their sins, and who shall fashion their degraded bodies and make them like to his glorious body, and give them an eternal residence with himself in a state of blessedness.

These were glorious news; and, wherever they were told, prepared the way of the Gospel among the heathen. The mere *preaching* of the Gospel has done much to convince and convert sinners, but the *lives* of the sincere followers of Christ, as *illustrative* of the truth of these doctrines, have done much more: Truth represented in *action* seems to assume a *body,* and thus renders itself *palpable.* In heathen countries, which are under the dominion of Christian powers, the Gospel, though established there, does little good, because of the profane and irreligious lives of those who profess it. Why has not the whole peninsula of India been long since evangelized? The Gospel has been preached there ; but the lives of the Europeans professing Christianity there have been, in general, profligate, sordid, and base. From them sounded out no good report of the Gospel ; and therefore the *Mohammedans* continue to prefer their *Koran*, and the *Hindoos* their *Vedas* and *Shasters*, to the *Bible*. It should however be acknowledged, to the glory of God, that of late years a few apostolic men in that country are turning the tide in favour of the Gospel ; and several eminent Europeans have warmly espoused the doctrine of Christ, and are labouring to circulate the *word of God* through the whole of British India.

CHAPTER II.

The apostle sets forth how the Gospel was brought and preached to the Thessalonians, in consequence of his being persecuted at Philippi, 1, 2. The manner in which the apostles preached, the matter of their doctrine, and the tenor of their lives, 3–11. He exhorts them to walk worthy of God, 12. And commends them for the manner in which they received the Gospel, 13. How they suffered from their own countrymen, as the first believers did from the Jews, who endeavoured to prevent the apostles from preaching the Gospel to the Gentiles, 14–16. St. Paul's apology for his absence from them ; and his earnest desire to see them, founded on his great affection for them, 17–20.

A. M. cir. 4056.
A. D. cir. 52.
A. U. C. 805.
Anno Claudii Cæs.
Aug. 12.

FOR [a] yourselves, brethren, know our entrance in unto you, that it was not in vain :

2 But even after that we had suffered before, and were shamefully entreated, as ye know, at [b] Philippi, [c] we were bold in our God [d] to speak unto you the Gospel of God [e] with much contention.

3 [f] For our exhortation *was* not of deceit, nor of uncleanness, nor in guile :

4 But as [g] we were allowed of God [h] to be put in trust with the Gospel, even so we speak ; [i] not as pleasing men, but God, [k] which trieth our hearts.

5 For [l] neither at any time used we flatter-

A. M. cir. 4056.
A. D. cir. 52.
A. U. C. 805.
Anno Claudii Cæs.
Aug. 12.

---

[a] Chap. i. 5, 9.——[b] Acts xvi. 22.——[c] Chap. i. 5.——[d] Acts xvii. 2.——[e] Phil. i. 30 ; Col. ii. 1.——[f] 2 Cor. vii. 2 ; ver. 5 ; 2 Pet. i. 16.——[g] 1 Cor. vii. 25 ; 1 Tim. i. 11, 12.

[h] 1 Cor. ix. 17 ; Gal. ii. 7 ; Tit. i. 3.——[i] Gal. i. 10.——[k] Prov. xvii. 3 ; Rom. viii. 27.——[l] Acts xx. 33 ; 2 Cor. ii. 17 ; iv. 2 ; vii. 2 ; xii. 17.

NOTES ON CHAP. II.

Verse 1. *Our entrance in unto you*] His first coming to preach the Gospel was particularly owned of the Lord, many of them having been converted under his ministry. This consideration gave him a *right* to deliver all the following exhortations.

Verse 2. *Shamefully entreated—at Philippi*] There Paul and Silas had been beaten with many stripes, shut up in the inner prison, and their feet made fast in the stocks. See Acts xvi. 23, &c. ; and the notes there.

With much contention.] The words εν πολλω αγωνι not only signify, *with intense labour and earnestness*, but may here mean, *exposed to the greatest danger ; at the peril of our lives.* The Greek phrase quoted by *Rosenmüller* is to the point, αγων προφασιν ουκ αναμενει, *in danger we must not delay*—activity and despatch are then indispensably necessary.

Verse 3. *Our exhortation*] The word παρακλησις has a very extensive meaning ; it signifies not only *exhortation* and *teaching* in general, but also *encouragement, consolation,* and the like. When the apostles exhorted or admonished men, it was that they should turn from *evil* to *good*, from *misery* to *happiness*, from *Satan* to *God*, and from *hell* to *heaven*. Their exhortations having this object, every word was *consolatory* ; and as the truth which they delivered was unquestionable, therefore their ministry was a subject of the highest encouragement and joy.

Not of deceit] We did not endeavour to allure you with false pretences ; we did not deceive you, nor were we deceived ourselves.

Nor of uncleanness] Such as the teachings of the Gentile philosophers were ; their supreme gods were celebrated for their adulteries, fornications, uncleannesses, thefts, barbarities, and profligacies of the most odious kind. Our Gospel was pure ; came from the pure and holy God ; was accompanied with the influences of the Holy Spirit, and produced purity both in the hearts and lives of all that received it.

Nor in guile] We had no false pretences, and were influenced by no sinister motives.

Verse 4. *But as we were allowed of God*] Καθως δεδοκιμασμεθα· *As we were accounted worthy* to be put in trust—as God put confidence in us, and sent us on his most especial message to mankind, *even so we speak*, keeping the dignity of our high calling continually in view ; and, acting as in the *sight of God*, we speak *not to please* or flatter men, though our doctrine is the most *consolatory* that can be conceived, but to *please* that *God who searcheth the heart*, and before whom all our motives are constantly without a veil.

Verse 5. *Flattering words*] Though we proclaimed the *Gospel* or glad tidings, yet we showed that without holiness none should see the Lord.

Ye know] That while we preached the whole Gospel we never gave any countenance to sin.

Nor a cloak of covetousness] We did not seek temporal emolument ; nor did we preach the Gospel for a cloak to our covetousness : *God is witness* that

A. M. cir. 4056.
A. D. cir. 52.
A. U. C. 805.
Anno Clau-
dii Cæs.
Aug. 12.

ing words, as ve know, nor a cloak of covetousness ; [m] God *is* witness :

6 [n] Nor of men sought we glory, neither of you, nor *yet* of others, when [o] we might have [p] been [q] burdensome, [r] as the apostles of Christ.

7 But [s] we were gentle among you, even as a nurse cherisheth her children :

8 So, being affectionately desirous of you, we were willing [t] to have imparted unto you, not the Gospel of God only, but also [u] our

own souls, because ye were dear unto us.

9 For ye remember, brethren, our labour and travail : for [v] labouring night and day, [w] because we would not be chargeable unto any of you, we preached unto you the Gospel of God.

10 [x] Ye *are* witnesses, and God *also*, [y] how holily and justly and unblamably we behaved ourselves among you that believe :

11 As ye know how we exhorted and comforted and charged every one of you,

A. M. cir. 4056.
A. D. cir. 52.
A. U. C. 805.
Anno Clau-
dii Cæs.
Aug. 12.

---

[m] Rom. i. 9.——[n] John v. 41, 44; xii. 43; 1 Tim. v. 17.
[o] 1 Cor. ix. 4, 6, 12, 18; 2 Cor. x. 1, 2, 10, 11 ; xiii. 10 ; 2 Thess.
iii. 9 ; Philem. 8, 9.——[p] Or, *used authority.*——[q] 2 Cor. xi. 9 ;
xii. 13, 14 ; 2 Thess. iii. 8.——[r] 1 Cor. ix. 1, 2, 5.

[s] 1 Cor. ii. 3 ; ix. 22; 2 Cor. xiii. 4 ; 2 Tim. ii. 24.——[t] Rom.
i. 11 ; xv. 29.——[u] 2 Cor. xii. 15.——[v] Acts xx. 34 ; 1 Cor. iv.
12 ; 2 Cor. xi. 9 ; 2 Thess. iii. 8.——[w] 2 Cor. xii. 13, 14.——[x] Ch.
i. 5.——[y] 2 Cor. vii. 2 ; 2 Thess. iii. 7.

---

we did not ; we sought *you*, not *yours.* Hear this, ye that preach the Gospel ! Can ye call God to witness that in preaching it ye have no end in view by your ministry but his glory in the salvation of souls ? Or do ye enter into the priesthood for a morsel of bread, or for what is ominously and impiously called a *living*, a *benefice?* In better days your place and office were called *a cure of souls ;* what *care* have *you* for the *souls* of them by whose labours you are in general more than sufficiently supported ? Is it your study, your earnest labour, to bring sinners to God ; to preach among your heathen parishioners the unsearchable riches of Christ ?

But I should speak to the *thousands* who have no *parishes*, but who have their *chapels*, their *congregations, pew* and *seat rents*, &c., &c Is it for the sake of *these* that ye have *entered* or continue in the Gospel ministry ? Is God witness that, in all these things, ye have no cloak of covetousness ? Happy is the man who can say so, whether he has the provision which the *law* of the land allows him, or whether he lives on the free-will offerings of the people.

The faithful labourer is worthy of his hire ; for the **ox** that treads out the corn should not be muzzled ; and they that preach the Gospel should *live*, not *riot*, by the Gospel. But wo to that man who enters into the *labour* for the sake of the *hire !* he knows not Christ ; and how can he preach him !

Verse 6. *Nor of men sought we glory*] As we preached not for worldly gain, so we preached not for popular applause ; we had what we sought for—the approbation of God, and the testimony of a good conscience.

When we might have been burdensome] They had a right to their maintenance while they devoted themselves wholly to the work of the Gospel for the sake of the people's souls. Others understand the words εν βαρει ειναι, *to be honourable ;* we sought no *glory* of you nor of others, though we were *honourable* as the apostles of Christ. כבד *cabod*, in Hebrew, to which the Greek βαρος answers, signifies not only *weight* but *glory ;* and in both these senses the apostle uses it, 2 Cor. iv. 17.

Verse 7. *But we were gentle among you*] Far from assuming the authority which we had, we acted towards you as a tender nurse or parent does to a delicate child. We fed, counselled, cherished, and bore with you ; we taught you to walk, preserved you from stumbling, and led you in a right path.

Instead of ηπιοι, *gentle*, many MSS., and several versions and fathers, have νηπιοι, *young children.* But this never can be considered the original reading, the scope of the place being totally opposed to it. It is the Thessalonians whom the apostle considers as *young children*, and *himself* and fellow labourers as the *nurse ;* he could with no propriety say that he was among them as a *little child*, while himself professed to be *their nurse.*

Verse 8. *Being affectionately desirous of you*] We had such intense love for you that we were not only willing and forward to preach the unsearchable riches of Christ to you, but also to give our *own lives* for your sake, *because ye were dear*, διοτι αγαπητοι ημιν, *because ye were beloved by us.* The words used here by the apostle are expressive of the strongest affection and attachment.

Verse 9. *Ye remember—our labour and travail*] From this it appears that St. Paul spent much more time at Thessalonica than is generally supposed ; for the expressions in this verse denote a long continuance of a constantly exercised ministry, interrupted only by manual labour for their own support ; *labouring night and day, because we would not be chargeable to you.* Probably Paul and his companions worked with their hands by *day*, and spent a considerable part of the *night*, or *evenings*, in preaching Christ to the people.

Verse 10. *Ye are witnesses, and God also, how holily*] i. e., in reference to GOD ; how *justly* in reference to *men ;* and *unblamably* in reference to our *spirit* and *conduct*, as ministers of Christ, *we behaved ourselves among you.* What a consciousness of his own integrity must St. Paul have had to use the expressions that are here ! No hypocrite, and none who did the work of the Lord carelessly, could make such an appeal both to God and man.

Verse 11. *How we exhorted*] What pastoral care

2

A. M. cir. 4056.
A. D. cir. 52.
A. U. C. 805.
Anno Clau-
dii Cæs.
Aug. 12.

as a father *doth* his children,

12 [z] That ye would walk
worthy of God, [a] who hath called
you unto his kingdom and glory.

13 For this cause also thank we God [b] without ceasing, because, when ye received the
word of God which ye heard of us, ye received
it [c] not *as* the word of men, but, as it is in truth,
the word of God, which effectually worketh also
in you that believe.

14 For ye, brethren, became
followers [d] of the Churches of
God which in Judea are in Christ
Jesus: for [e] ye also have suffered
like things of your own countrymen, [f] even as
they *have* of the Jews;

15 [g] Who both killed the Lord Jesus and
[h] their own prophets, and have [i] persecuted us;
and they please not God, [k] and are contrary to
all men;

16 [l] Forbidding us to speak to the Gentiles

A. M. cir. 4056.
A. D. cir. 52.
A. U. C. 805.
Anno Clau-
dii Cæs.
Aug. 12.

---

[z] Eph. iv. 1; Phil. i. 27; Col. i. 10; chap. iv. 1.——[a] 1 Cor. i.
9; chap. v. 24; 2 Thess. i. 14; 2 Tim. ii. 9.——[b] Chap. i. 3.
[c] Matt. x. 40; Gal. iv. 14; 2 Pet. iii. 2.——[d] Gal. i. 22.——[e] Acts
xvii. 5, 13.——[f] Heb. x. 33, 34.

[g] Acts ii. 23; iii. 15; v. 30; vii. 52.——[h] Matt. v. 12; xxiii.
34, 37; Luke xiii. 33, 34; Acts vii. 52.——[i] Or, *chased us out.*
[k] Esther iii. 8.——[l] Luke xi. 52; Acts xiii. 50; xiv. 5, 19; xvii.
5, 13; xviii. 12; xix. 9; xxii. 21, 22.

---

is marked here! They *exhorted*—were continually
teaching and instructing, the objects of their charge;
this was their *general* work.

And comforted] They found many under trials and
temptations, and those they encouraged.

And charged] Μαρτυρούμενοι· Continued to *witness*
to the people that all the threatenings and promises of
God were true; that he required faith, love, and obedience; that he could not behold sin with allowance;
that Jesus died to save them from their sins; and that,
without holiness, none should see God. And all these
things they did, not in a general way only, but they
spoke to *every man;* none was left unnoticed, unad-
monished, uncomforted. The spirit in which they
performed all these branches of the pastoral care was
that which was most likely to insure success; as a
father treats his children, so they treated every member of the Church.

Verse 12. *That ye would walk worthy of God*]
That they should, in every respect, act up to their high
calling, that it would not be a reproach to the God of
holiness to acknowledge them as his sons and daughters. See the notes on Eph. iv. 1; Phil. i. 27; and
Col. i. 10.

His kingdom and glory.] His *Church* here, for that
is the *kingdom of God* among men; and his *glory*
hereafter, for that is the state to which the dispensations of grace in his Church lead. The words, however, may be a *hendiadys*, and signify his *glorious
kingdom.*

Verse 13. *Ye received the word of God*] Ye received the *doctrine* of God, not as any thing fabricated
by *man*, but as coming immediately from God himself,
we being only his *messengers* to declare what he had
previously revealed to us. And ye have had the fullest proof that ye have not believed in vain; for that
doctrine, under the power and influence of the Holy
Ghost, has *worked most powerfully* in you, filling you
with light, life, and holiness.

Verse 14. *Ye—became followers of the Churches
of God*] There is not a word here of the *Church of
Rome* being the *model* after which the other Churches
were to be formed; it had no such pre-eminence: this
honour belonged to the *Churches of Judea*; it was
according to *them*, not the Church at *Rome*, that the

Asiatic Churches were modelled. The purest of all
the apostolic Churches was that of the *Thessalonians*,
and this was formed after the Christian Churches in
Judea.

Had any pre-eminence or authority belonged to the
Church of Rome, the apostle would have proposed this
as a model to all those which he formed either in Judea, Asia Minor, Greece, or Italy.

Ye also have suffered—of your own countrymen]
It is worthy of remark that, in almost every case, the
Jews were the leaders of all persecutions against the
apostles and the infant Church. And what they could
not do *themselves*, they instigated others to do; and,
by gathering together lewd fellows of the baser sort
from among the Gentiles, they made frequent uproars,
and especially at Thessalonica, where the opposition
to the Gospel was very high, and the persecution of
the Christians very hot.

Verses 15, 16. *Who both killed the Lord Jesus, &c.*]
What a finished but just character is this of the *Jews!*
1. *They slew the Lord Jesus*, through the most unprincipled and fell malice. 2. They *killed their own
prophets*; there was no time in which the seed of the
serpent did not hate and oppose spiritual things, they
slew even their own prophets who declared to them
the will of God. 3. They *persecuted the apostles;*
showing the same spirit of enmity to the Gospel which
they had shown to the *law.* 4. *They did not please
God*, nor seek to please him; though they pretended
that their opposition to the Gospel was through their
zeal for God's glory, they were *hypocrites* of the
worst kind. 5. They *were contrary to all men*; they
hated the whole human race, and judged and wished
them to perdition. 6. They *forbade the apostles to
preach to the Gentiles, lest they should be saved;* this
was an inveteracy of malice completely superhuman;
they persecuted the body to death, and the soul to
damnation! They were afraid that the Gentiles should
get their souls saved if the Gospel was preached to
them! 7. They *filled up their sins always*; they had
no mere *purposes* or *outlines* of iniquity, all were filled
up; every *evil purpose* was followed, as far as possible,
with a *wicked act!* Is it any wonder, therefore, that
wrath should *come upon them to the uttermost?* It is
to be reckoned among the highest mercies of God that

2

A. M. cir. 4056.
A. D. cir. 52.
A. U. C. 805.
Anno Clau-
dii Cæs.
Aug. 12.

that they might be saved, [m] to fill up their sins alway: [n] for the wrath is come upon them to the uttermost.

17 But we, brethren, being taken from you for a short time [o] in presence, not in heart, endeavoured the more abundantly [p] to see your face with great desire.

18 Wherefore we would have come unto you (even I Paul) once and again; but [q] Satan hindered us.

19 For [r] what *is* our hope, or joy, or [s] crown of [t] rejoicing? *Are* not even ye in the presence of our Lord Jesus Christ [u] at his coming?

20 For ye are our glory and joy.

A. M. cir. 4056.
A. D. cir. 42.
A. U. C. 805.
Anno Clau-
dii Cæs.
Aug. 12.

---

[m] Gen. xv. 16; Matt. xxiii. 32.——[n] Matt. xxiv. 6, 14.——[o] 1 Cor. v. 3; Col. ii. 5.——[p] Chap. iii. 10.——[q] Rom. i. 13; xv. 22.

[r] 2 Cor. i. 14; Phil. ii. 16; iv. 1.——[s] Prov. xvi. 31.——[t] Or, *glorying.*——[u] 1 Cor. xv. 23; chap. iii. 13; Rev. i. 7; xxii. 12.

---

the whole nation was not pursued by the Divine justice to utter and final extinction.

Verse 17. *Being taken from you for a short time*] Through the persecution raised by the Jews, see Acts xvii., he was obliged to leave Thessalonica, and yield to a storm that it would have been useless for him to have withstood.

Being taken from you—in presence, not in heart] The apostle had compared himself to a *parent* or *nurse*, ver. 7 and 11; and the people he considered as his most beloved children; here he represents himself as feeling what an affectionate father must feel when *torn from his children;* for this is the import of the word απορφανισθεντες, *bereft of children,* which we tamely translate *being taken from you.*

Endeavoured the more abundantly] His separation from them did not destroy his parental feelings, and the manner in which he was obliged to leave them increased his desire to visit them as soon as possible.

Verse 18. *Even I Paul*] He had already sent Timothy and Silas to them; but he himself was anxious to see them, and had purposed this *once and again, but Satan hindered;* i. e., some *adversary,* as the word means, whether the *devil* himself, or some of his children. There was, however, such a storm of persecution raised up against him, that his friends did not think it prudent to permit him to go till the storm had been somewhat allayed.

Verse 19. *For what is our hope*] I can have no prospects from earth; I have forsaken all for the Gospel; and esteem every thing it can afford as dross and dung, that I may gain Christ. Why then should I continually labour at the risk of my life, preaching the Gospel? Is it not to get your souls saved, that ye may be *my crown of rejoicing in the day of Christ?* For this I labour; and, having *planted* the Gospel among you, I wish to take every opportunity of *watering* it, that it may grow up unto eternal life.

Verse 20. *For ye are our glory and joy.*] Ye are the seal of our apostleship; your conversion and steadiness are a full proof that God hath sent us. Converts to Christ are our ornaments; persevering believers, our joy in the day of judgment.

1. In the preceding chapter we have the *character* and *marks* of a genuine pastor laid down in such a manner as not to be misunderstood. Every man who preaches the Gospel should carefully read *this* chapter and examine himself by it. Most preachers, on reading it conscientiously, will either give up their place to others, or purpose to do the work of the Lord more fervently for the future. He who expects nothing but the approbation of Christ, will labour for Christ; and he, who has the glory of his Master only in view, will ever have his Master's presence and blessing. Those who enter into this work for human applause or secular emolument, may have their reward; but in that, one smile of approbation from Christ is not included.

2. God, for reasons best known to himself, often permits the most pious and benevolent purposes of his servants to be frustrated for a time. It is well that the good purpose was in the heart; but God knows the *fittest time* and *place* to bring it to effect. Satan is ever opposing all that is pure, good, and benevolent, and he *appears* frequently to succeed; but this is not *really* the case: if at any time he prevents the followers of God from bringing a pious purpose into effect, that was the time in which it could not have been done to secure its full effect. Let the purpose be retained, and the best *time* and *place* will be duly provided. As Satan *constantly* endeavours to oppose every good work, no wonder he is found opposing a good purpose, even *at the very time* that God sees it improper to bring it to the intended effect. *Man proposes, but God disposes.*

3. The apostle speaks of the *wrath* coming upon the Jews: it was about twenty years after this that their city was destroyed, their temple burnt, more than a million of them destroyed, their civil polity utterly subverted, and what remained of this wretched nation scattered to all the winds of heaven; and in this state, without a nation, without a temple, without worship, and apparently without any religion, they continue, to this day, a monument of God's displeasure, and a proof of the Divine inspiration both of the prophets and apostles, who, in the most explicit manner, had predicted all the evils which have since befallen them. Their crimes were great; to these their punishment is proportioned. For what end God has preserved them distinct from all the people of the earth among whom they sojourn, we cannot pretend to say; but it must unquestionably be for an object of the very highest importance. In the meantime, let the Christian world treat them with humanity and mercy.

CHAPTER III.

St. Paul informs them how, being hindered himself from visiting them, he had sent Timothy to comfort them, of whom he gives a high character, 1, 2. Shows that trials and difficulties are unavoidable in the present state, 3, 4. Mentions the joy he had on hearing by Timothy of their steadiness in the faith, for which he returns thanks to God; and prays earnestly for their increase, 5—10. Prays also that God may afford him an opportunity of seeing them, 11. And that they may abound in love to God and one another, and be unblamable in holiness at the coming of Christ, 12, 13.

A. M. cir. 4056.
A. D. cir. 52.
A. U. C. 805.
Anno Claudii Cæs.
Aug. 12.

WHEREFORE, [a] when we could no longer forbear, [b] we thought it good to be left at Athens alone;

2 And sent [c] Timotheus, our brother, and minister of God, and our fellow labourer in the Gospel of Christ, to establish you, and to comfort you, concerning your faith;

3 [d] That no man should be moved by these afflictions: for yourselves know that [e] we are appointed thereunto.

4 [f] For verily, when we were with you, we told you before that we should suffer tribula-

tion; even as it came to pass, and ye know.

A. M. cir. 4056.
A. D. cir. 52.
A. U. C. 805.
Anno Claudii Cæs.
Aug. 12.

5 For this cause, [g] when I could no longer forbear, I sent to know your faith, [h] lest by some means the tempter have tempted you, and [i] our labour be in vain.

6 [k] But now, when Timotheus came from you unto us, and brought us good tidings of your faith and charity, and that ye have good remembrance of us always, desiring greatly to see us, [l] as we also *to see* you;

7 Therefore, brethren, [m] we were comforted

---

[a] Ver. 5.——[b] Acts xvii. 15.——[c] Rom. xvi. 21; 1 Cor. xvi. 10; 2 Cor. i. 19.——[d] Eph. iii. 13.——[e] Acts ix. 16; xiv. 22; xx. 23; xxi. 11; 1 Cor. iv. 9; 2 Tim. iii. 12; 1 Pet. ii. 21.

[f] Acts xx. 24.——[g] Ver. 1.——[h] 1 Cor. vii. 5; 2 Cor. xi. 3. [i] Gal. ii. 2; iv. 11; Phil. ii. 16.——[k] Acts xviii. 1, 5.——[l] Phil. i. 8.——[m] 2 Cor. i. 4; vii. 6, 7, 13.

NOTES ON CHAP. III.

Verse 1. *Wherefore, when we could no longer, &c.*] The apostle was anxious to hear of their state, and as he could obtain no information without sending a messenger express, he therefore sent Timothy from Athens; choosing rather to be left alone, than to continue any longer in uncertainty relative to their state.

Verse 2. *Timotheus, our brother*] It appears that Timothy was but a youth when converted to God; he had now however been some years in the work of God; Paul therefore calls him his *brother*, being one of the same Christian *family*, a *son of God by adoption:* elsewhere he calls him *his own son*, 1 Tim. i. 2; and his *dearly beloved son*, 2 Tim. i. 2; because he was brought to the knowledge of the true God, and to salvation by Christ, through the apostle's instrumentality. See the *preface* to the First Epistle to Timothy.

Minister of God] Employed by God to preach the Gospel; this was God's work, and he had appointed Timothy to do it, and to do it at this time in conjunction with St. Paul; and therefore he calls him his *fellow labourer*. There were no *sinecures* then; preaching the Gospel was God's *work;* the primitive preachers were his *workmen*, and *laboured* in this calling. It is the same still, but who *works?*

Verse 3. *That no man should be moved*] That is, caused to apostatize from Christianity.

We are appointed thereunto.] Εις τουτο κειμεθα· *We are exposed to this, we lie open to such, they are unavoidable* in the present state of things; as the Latins say, *sic est sors nostra,* "this is our lot." God *appoints* nothing of this kind, but he *permits* it; for he has made man a *free agent.*

Verse 4. *That we should suffer tribulation*] I pre-

pared you for it, because I knew that it was according to their nature for wicked men to persecute the followers of God.

Verse 5. *For this cause*] Knowing that you would be persecuted, and knowing that your apostasy was possible, *I sent to know your faith*—whether you continued steadfast in the truth, lest you might have been tempted by Satan to consult your present ease, and abandon the Gospel, for which you suffered persecution.

Verse 6. *When Timotheus came*] We have already seen that he and Silas stayed behind at Thessalonica, when Paul was obliged to leave it; for the persecution seems to have been principally directed against him. When Paul came to Athens, he sent pressingly to him and Silas to come to him with all speed to that city. We are not informed that they did come, but it is most likely that they did, and that Paul sent Timothy back to Thessalonica to comfort and build up these new converts. After Paul had sent away Timothy, it is likely he went himself straight to Corinth, and there Timothy soon after met him, with the good news of the steadiness of the Thessalonian Church.

Your faith and charity] The *good tidings* which Timothy brought from Thessalonica consisted of *three* particulars: 1. Their *faith;* they continued steadfast in their belief of the Gospel. 2. Their *charity;* they loved one another, and lived in unity and harmony. 3. They were *affectionately attached* to the apostle; they had *good remembrance* of him, and *desired earnestly* to see him.

Verse 7. *Therefore—we were comforted*] My afflictions and persecutions seemed trifles when I heard of your perseverance in the faith.

A. M. cir. 4056.
A. D. cir. 52.
A. U C. 805.
Anno Clau-
dii Cæs.
Aug. 12.
over you in all our affliction and distress, by your faith :

8 For now we live, if ye [n] stand fast in the Lord.

9 [o] For what thanks can we render to God again for you, for all the joy wherewith we joy for your sakes before our God ;

10 [p] Night and day [q] praying exceedingly [r] that we might see your face, [s] and might perfect that which is lacking in your faith ?

11 Now God himself and our Father, and our Lord Jesus Christ, [t] direct [u] our way unto you. A. M. cir. 4056.
A. D. cir. 52.
A. U. C. 805.
Anno Clau-
dii Cæs.
Aug. 12.

12 And the Lord [v] make you to increase and abound in love [w] one toward another, and toward all *men*, even as we *do* toward you :

13 To the end he may [x] establish your hearts unblamable in holiness before God, even our Father, at the coming of our Lord Jesus Christ [y] with all his saints.

---

[n] Phil. iv. 1.——[o] Chap. i. 2.——[p] Acts xxvi. 7; 2 Tim. i. 3. [q] Rom. i. 10, 11 ; xv 32.——[r] Chap. ii. 17.——[s] 2 Cor. xiii. 9, 11 ; Col. iv. 12.——[t] Or, *guide*.

[u] Mark i. 3.——[v] Chap. iv. 10.——[w] Chap. iv. 9 ; v. 15 ; 2 Pet. i. 7.——[x] 1 Cor. i. 8 ; Phil. i. 10; chap. v. 23; 2 Thess. ii. 17; 1 John iii. 20, 21.——[y] Zech. xiv. 5 ; Jude 14.

Verse 8. *For now we live*] Your steadfastness in the faith gives me new life and comfort ; I now feel that I live to some purpose, as my labour in the Lord is not in vain.

Verse 9. *What thanks can we render to God*] The high satisfaction and uncommon joy which the apostle felt are strongly depicted in the language he uses. How near his heart did the success of his ministry lie ! It was not enough for him that he preached so often, laboured so hard, suffered so much ; what were all these if souls were not converted ? And what were all conversions, if those who embraced the Gospel did not walk steadily in the way to heaven, and persevere ?

Verse 10. *Night and day praying exceedingly*] Supplicating God at *all times ;* mingling this with all my prayers ; ὑπερεκπερισσου δεομενοι, abounding and superabounding in my entreaties to God to permit me to revisit you. How strong was his affection for this Church !

Might perfect that which is lacking] That I might have the opportunity of giving you the fullest instructions in the doctrine of Christ, that ye might have every thing in the most ample *detail ;* so that the great *outlines* of truth which you already know may be *filled up*, that ye may be perfectly fitted to every good word and work.

Verse 11. *Now God himself and our Father*] That is : God who is our Father, who has *adopted* us into the *heavenly family*, and called us his *sons* and *daughters.*

Direct our way] As he was employed in God's work he dared not consult his own inclinations, he looked for continual directions from God, *where, when,* and *how* to do his Master's work.

Verse 12. *Make you to increase and abound in love*] They had already love to each other, so as to unite them in one Christian body ; and he prays that they may have an *increase* and an *abundance* of it ; that they might feel the same love to each other which he felt for them all.

Verse 13. *To the end he may establish your hearts*] Without *love* to God and man, there can be no establishment in the religion of Christ. It is *love* that produces both *solidity* and *continuance.* And, as *love is the fulfilling of the law,* he who is filled with love is *unblamable in holiness :* for he who has the love of God in him is a partaker of the Divine nature, for *God is love.*

At the coming of our Lord] God is coming to judge the world ; every hour that passes on in the general lapse of time is advancing his approach ; whatsoever he does is in reference to this great event : and whatsoever *we* do should be in reference to the same. But who in that great day shall give up his accounts with joy ? That person only whose heart is established in holiness *before God ;* i. e., so as to bear the eye and strict scrutiny of his Judge. Reader, lay this to heart, for thou knowest not what a moment may bring forth. When thy soul departs from thy body it will be the *coming of the Lord* to thee.

CHAPTER IV.

The apostle exhorts them to attend to the directions which he had already given them, that they might know how to walk and please God, 1, 2. Gives them exhortations concerning continence, chastity, and matrimonial fidelity, 3—8. Speaks concerning their love to each other, and love to the Churches of Christ ; and exhorts them to continue and increase in it, 9, 10. Counsels them to observe an inoffensive conduct, to mind their own affairs, to do their own business, and to live honestly, 11, 12. Not to sorrow for the dead, as persons who have no hope of a resurrection ; because to Christians the resurrection of Christ is a proof of the resurrection of his followers, 13, 14. Gives a short but awful description of the appearing of Christ to judge the world, 15.

2

A. M. cir. 4056.
A. D. cir. 52.
A. U. C. 805.
Anno Claudii Cæs.
Aug. 12.

FURTHERMORE then we [a] beseech you, brethren, and [b] exhort *you* by the Lord Jesus, [c] that as ye have received of us [d] how ye ought to walk [e] and to please God, *so* ye would abound more and more.

2 For ye know what commandments we gave you by the Lord Jesus.

3 For this is [f] the will of God, *even* [g] your sanctification, [h] that ye should abstain from fornication :

4 [i] That every one of you should know how to possess his vessel in sanctification and honour ;

5 [k] Not in the lust of concupiscence, [l] even as the Gentiles [m] which know not God :

6 [n] That no *man* go beyond and [o] defraud his brother [p] in *any* matter : because that the Lord [q] *is* the avenger of all such, as we also have forewarned you and testified.

A. M. cir. 4056.
A. D. cir. 52.
A. U. C. 805.
Anno Claudii Cæs.
Aug. 12.

---

[a] Or, *request.*——[b] Or, *beseech.*——[c] Phil. i. 27 ; Col. ii. 6.——[d] Ch. ii. 12.——[e] Col. i. 10.——[f] Rom. xii. 2 ; Eph. v. 17.——[g] Eph. v. 27.——[h] 1 Cor. vi. 15, 18 ; Eph. v. 3 ; Col. iii. 5.——[i] Rom. vi. 19 ; 1 Cor. vi. 15, 18.

[k] Col. iii. 5 ; Rom. i. 24, 26.——[l] Eph. iv. 17, 18.——[m] 1 Cor. xv. 34 ; Gal. iv. 8 ; Eph. ii. 12 ; iv. 18 ; 2 Thess. i. 8.——[n] Lev. xix. 11, 13 ; 1 Cor. vi. 8.——[o] Or, *oppress;* or *overreach.*——[p] Or, *in the matter*——[q] 2 Thess. i. 8.

NOTES ON CHAP. IV.

Verse 1. *We beseech you, brethren, and exhort*] We give you proper *instructions* in heavenly things, and *request* you to attend to our advice. The apostle used the most pressing entreaties ; for he had a strong and affectionate desire that this Church should excel in all righteousness and true holiness.

Please God—more and more.] God sets no *bounds* to the communications of his grace and Spirit to them that are faithful. And as there are no bounds to the *graces*, so there should be none to the *exercise* of those graces. No man can ever *feel* that he loves God too much, or that he loves man too much for God's sake.

Verse 2. *Ye know what commandments we gave you*] This refers to his instructions while he was among them ; and to instructions on particular subjects, which he does not *recapitulate*, but only *hints* at.

Verse 3. *This is the will of God*, even *your sanctification*] God has called you to holiness ; he requires that you should be holy ; for without holiness none can see the Lord. This is the *general* calling, but in it many particulars are included. Some of these he proceeds to mention ; and it is very likely that these had been points on which he gave them particular instructions while among them.

That ye should abstain from fornication] The word πορνεια, as we have seen in other places, includes *all sorts of uncleanness;* and it was probably this consideration that induced several MSS., some *versions* and *fathers*, to add here πασης, *all*. Directions of this kind were peculiarly necessary among the Greeks, and indeed heathens in general, who were strongly addicted to such vices.

Verse 4. *How to possess his vessel*] Let every man use his *wife* for the purpose alone for which God created her, and instituted *marriage*. The word σκευος answers to the Hebrew כלי *keli*, which, though it signifies *vessel* in general, has several other meanings. That the rabbins frequently express *wife* by it, *Schoettgen* largely proves ; and to me it appears very probable that the apostle uses it in that sense here. St. Peter calls the wife the *weaker* VESSEL, 1 Pet. iii. 7. Others think that the *body* is meant, which is the *vessel* in which the *soul* dwells. In this sense St. Paul uses it, 2 Cor. iv. 7 : *We have this treasure in earthen*

VESSELS ; and in this sense it is used by both Greek and Roman authors. There is a *third* sense which interpreters have put on the word, which I forbear to name. The general sense is plain ; *purity* and *continency* are most obviously intended, whether the word be understood as referring to the *wife* or the *husband*, as the following verse sufficiently proves.

Verse 5. *Not in the lust of concupiscence*] Having no rational object, aim, nor end. Some say, " not like *beasts ;*" but this does not apply as they who use it wish ; for the males and females of the brute creation are regular and consistent in their intercourse, and scarcely ever exceed such bounds as reason itself would prescribe to those most capable of observing and obeying its dictates.

The Gentiles which know not God] These are the *beasts ;* their own *brutes* are *rational creatures* when compared with them. Enough has been said on this subject on Rom. i. and ii. They who wish to see more may consult *Juvenal*, and particularly his 6th and 9th Satires ; and indeed all the writers on Greek and Roman morals.

Verse 6. *That no* man *go beyond and defraud his brother*] That no man should by any means endeavour to corrupt the wife of another, or to alienate her affections or fidelity from her husband ; this I believe to be the apostle's meaning, though some understand it of *covetousness, overreaching, tricking, cheating,* and *cozenage* in general.

The Lord is *the avenger of all such*] He takes up the cause of the injured husband wherever the case has not been detected by man, and *all such vices* he will signally punish. Every species of uncleanness was practised among the heathens, nor were they reputed as *vices*. Their *gods*, their *emperors*, their *philosophers*, and their *great* men in general, gave them examples of every species of impurity ; and they had no system of ethics which forbade these abominations. The Christian religion not only discountenances these things, but forbids them on the most awful penalties ; therefore wherever Christianity prevails, these vices, if practised at all, are obliged to seek the deepest gloom of midnight to cover them from the eyes of men. On this account they are comparatively rare, even among the mere professors of Christianity ; they *exist*, but do not *flourish*.

                2

A. M. cir. 4056.
A. D. cir. 52.
A. U. C. 805.
Anno Clau-
dii Cæs.
Aug. 12.

7 For God hath not called us unto uncleanness, ʳ but unto holiness.

8 ˢ He therefore that ᵗ despiseth, despiseth not man, but God, ᵘ who hath also given unto us his Holy Spirit.

9 But as touching brotherly love ᵛ ye need not that I write unto you; for ʷ ye yourselves are taught of God ˣ to love one another.

10 ʸ And indeed ye do it toward all the

brethren which are in all Macedonia: but we beseech you, brethren, ᶻ that ye increase more and more;

11 And that ye study to be quiet, and ᵃ to do your own business, and ᵇ to work with your own hands, as we commanded you;

12 ᶜ That ye may walk honestly toward them that are without, and *that* ye may have lack ᵈ of nothing.

A. M. cir. 4056.
A. D. cir. 52.
A. U. C. 805.
Anno Clau-
dii Cæs.
Aug. 12.

ʳ Lev. xi. 44; xix. 2; 1 Cor. i. 2; Heb. xii. 14; 1 Pet. i. 14, 15. ˢ Luke x. 16.——ᵗ Or, *rejecteth.*——ᵘ 1 Cor. ii. 10; vii. 40; 1 John iii. 24.——ᵛ Chap. v. 1.——ʷ Jer. xxxi. 34; John vi. 45; xiv. 26; Heb. viii. 11; 1 John ii. 20, 27.——ˣ Matt. xxii. 39; John xiii. 34; xv. 12; Eph. v. 2; 1 Pet. iv. 8; 1 John iii. 11, 23; iv. 21. ʸ Ch. i. 7.——ᶻ Ch. iii. 12.——ᵃ 2 Thess. iii. 11; 1 Pet. iv. 15. ᵇ Acts xx. 35; Eph. iv. 28; 2 Thess. iii. 7, 8, 12.——ᶜ Rom. xiii. 13; 2 Cor. viii. 21; Col. iv. 5; 1 Pet. ii. 12.——ᵈ Or, *of no man.*

Verse 7. *God hath not called us unto uncleanness*] He is the creator of male and female, and the institutor of marriage, and he has called men and women to this state; but the *end* of this and all the other callings of God to man is *holiness,* not *uncleanness.* And they who use the marriage state as he directs, will find it conducive to their holiness and perfection.

Verse 8. *He therefore that despiseth*] He who will not receive these teachings, and is led either to undervalue or despise them, despises not us but God, from whom we have received our commission, and by whose Spirit we give these directions. See on ver. 15.

Hath also given unto us his Holy Spirit.] Instead of εις ἡμας, *unto us,* εις ὑμας, *unto* you, is the reading of BDEFG, a great many others, the *Syriac,* all the *Arabic, Armenian,* later *Syriac* in the margin, some of the *Itala, Clement, Didymus,* and *Ambrosiaster;* this seems to be the better reading. God has taught *us* that we may teach *you;* and he has also given *you* his Holy Spirit that ye might understand and be enabled to practise these things. It is one thing to *receive* a *revelation* from the Spirit of God; it is another thing to *receive* that *Spirit* to enable a man to live according to that revelation. In the first sense the apostles alone received this Holy Spirit; in the latter sense all true Christians, as well as the Thessalonians, receive it. I think ὑμας, *you,* is the true reading, and that it is confirmed by the following verse: *For ye yourselves are* TAUGHT OF GOD *to love one another.* Griesbach has inserted it in the margin, but has not admitted it into the text, because it has not what he deemed full support from those MSS. which are of the *Alexandrian recension;* but he thought its genuineness very probable.

Verse 9. *Touching brotherly love*] They were remarkable for this; and though the apostle appears to have had this as a topic on which he intended to write to them, yet, from the account which he received of their prosperous state by Timothy, he finds that it is unnecessary to spend any time in inculcating a doctrine which they fully understood and practised. See chap. iii. 6.

Verse 10. *Ye do it toward all the brethren*] Ye not only love one another at Thessalonica, but ye love all the brethren in Macedonia; ye consider them all as children of the same Father; and that all the

Churches which are in Christ make one great and glorious *body,* of which he is the *head.*

Verse 11. *That ye study to be quiet*] Though in general the Church at Thessalonica was pure and exemplary, yet there seem to have been some *idle, tattling* people among them, who disturbed the peace of others; persons who, under the pretence of religion, *gadded about from house to house;* did not *work,* but were burdensome to others; and were continually *meddling* with other people's business, *making parties,* and procuring their bread by religious gossipping. To these the apostle gives those directions which the whole Church of God should enforce wherever such troublesome and dangerous people are found; viz: That they should *study to be quiet,* ἡσυχαζειν, *to hold their peace,* as their religious cant will never promote true religion; that they should *do their own business,* and let that of others alone; and that they should *work with their own hands,* and not be a burden to the Church of God, or to those well meaning but weak and inconsiderate people who entertain them, being imposed on by their apparent sanctity and glozing conversation. An *idle* person, though able to discourse like an angel, or pray like an apostle, cannot be a Christian; all such are hypocrites and deceivers; the true members of the Church of Christ *walk, work,* and *labour.*

Verse 12. *That ye may walk honestly*] Ευσχημονως· *Becomingly, decently, respectably;* us is *consistent* with the *purity, holiness, gravity,* and *usefulness* of your Christian calling.

Them that are without] The unconverted *Gentiles* and *Jews.* See this expression explained at large on Col. iv. 5.

That ye may have lack of nothing.] That ye may be able to get your bread by honest labour, which God will ever bless; and be chargeable to no man. He that is dependent on another is necessarily in bondage; and he who is able to get his own bread by the sweat of his brow, should not be under obligation even to a king.

I do not recollect whether, in any other part of this work, I have given the following story from the *Hatem Taï Nameh.* Hatem Taï was an Arabian nobleman, who flourished some time before the Mahommedan era; he was reputed the most *generous* and *liberal* man in all the east. One day he slew one hundred

2

A. M. cir. 4056.
A. D. cir. 52.
A. U. C. 805.
Anno Clau-
dii Cæs.
Aug. 12.

13 But I would not have you to be ignorant, brethren, concerning them which are asleep, that ye sorrow not, ^e even as others ^f which have no hope.

14 For ^g if we believe that Jesus died and rose again, even so ^h them also which sleep in Jesus will God bring with him.

A. M. cir. 4056.
A. D. cir. 52.
A. U. C. 805.
Anno Clau-
dii Cæs.
Aug. 12.

15 For this we say unto you ⁱ by the word of the Lord, that ^k we which are alive, *and* remain unto the coming of the Lord, shall not prevent them which are asleep.

---

^e See Lev. xix. 28; Deut. xiv. 1, 2; 2 Sam. xii. 20.——^f Eph. ii. 12.——^g 1 Cor. xv. 13.

^h 1 Cor. xv. 18, 23; chap. iii. 13.——ⁱ 1 Kings xiii. 17, 18; xx. 35. ^k 1 Cor. xv. 51.

---

camels, and made a feast, to which all the Arabian lords and all the peasantry in the district were invited. About the time of the feast he took a walk towards a neighbouring wood, to see if he could find any person whom he might invite to partake of the entertainment which he had then provided. Walking along the skirt of the wood, he espied an old man coming out of it, laden with a burden of faggots; he accosted him and asked if he had not heard of the entertainment made that day by *Hatem Taï.* The old man answered in the affirmative. He asked him why he did not attend and partake with the rest. The old man answered: " He that is able to gain his bread even by collecting faggots in the wood, should not be beholden even *to Hatem Taï.*" This is a noble saying, and has long been a rule of conduct to the writer of this note.

Verse 13. *I would not have you to be ignorant*] Instead of εχομεν, *have*, θελομεν, *wish*, is the reading of ADEFG, many others, besides the *Arabic, Æthiopic, Armenian*, some of the *Slavonian*, the *Vulgate*, and *Itala*, with many of the Greek *fathers.* This is undoubtedly the true reading: *Brethren, I would not wish you to be ignorant;* or, *I would not that you should be ignorant.*

This was probably one of the points which were *lacking in their faith*, that he wished to go to Thessalonica to instruct them in.

Them which are asleep] That is, those who are *dead.* It is supposed that the apostle had heard that the Thessalonians continued to lament over their dead, as the heathens did in general who had *no hope* of the resurrection of the body; and that they had been puzzled concerning the doctrine of the resurrection. To set them right on this important subject, he delivers three important truths: 1. He asserts, as he had done before, that they who died in the Lord should have, in virtue of Christ's resurrection, a resurrection unto eternal life and blessedness. 2. He makes a new discovery, that the *last generation* should not die at all, but be in a moment changed to immortals. 3. He adds another new discovery, that, though the living should not die, but be transformed, yet the dead should first be raised, and be made glorious and immortal; and so, in some measure, have the preference and advantage of such as shall then be found alive. See *Dodd.*

Verse 14. *For if we believe that Jesus died and rose again*] Ει γαρ· *Seeing that we believe;* knowing that the *resurrection* of Christ is as fully authenticated as his death.

Even so them] It necessarily follows that them who *sleep*—die, *in him*—in the faith of the Gospel, *will*

God bring with him—he will raise them up as Jesus was raised from the dead, in the same manner, i. e. by his own eternal power and energy; and he will bring them *with him*—with Christ, for he is the *head* of the Church, which is his *body.*

Verse 15. *This we say unto you by the word of the Lord*] This I have, by *express revelation*, from the Lord: what he now delivers he gives as coming immediately from the Spirit of God. Indeed, human reason could not have found out the points which he immediately subjoins; no *conjectures* could lead to them. Allowing even the general doctrine of the resurrection to be believed, yet what follows does not flow from the premises; they are doctrines of pure revelation, and such as never could have been found out by human ingenuity. In no place does the apostle speak more confidently and positively of his *inspiration* than here; and we should prepare ourselves to receive some momentous and interesting truth.

We which are alive, and remain] By the pronoun *we* the apostle does not intend *himself*, and the Thessalonians to whom he was then writing; he is speaking of the genuine Christians which shall be found on earth when Christ comes to judgment. From not considering the manner in which the apostle uses this word, some have been led to suppose that he imagined that the day of judgment would take place in *that generation*, and while he and the then believers at Thessalonica *were in life.* But it is impossible that a man, under so direct an influence of the Holy Spirit, should be permitted to make such a mistake : nay, no man in the exercise of his sober reason could have formed such an opinion; there was nothing to warrant the supposition; no premises from which it could be fairly deduced; nor indeed any thing in the *circumstances* of the *Church*, nor in the *constitution* of the *world*, that could have suggested a hint of the kind. The apostle is speaking of the thing *indefinitely* as to the *time* when it shall happen, but *positively* as to the ORDER that shall be then observed.

Shall not prevent them which are asleep.] Those who shall be found living in that day, though they shall not pass through death, but be suddenly changed, shall not go to glory *before* them that are dead, *for the dead in Christ shall rise first*—they shall be raised, their bodies made glorious, and be caught up to meet the Lord, *before* the others shall be changed. And this appears to be the meaning of the apostle's words, μη φθασωμεν, which we translate *shall not prevent;* for, although this word *prevent*, from *præ* and *venio*, literally signifies to *go before*, yet we use it now in the sense of *to hinder* or *obstruct.* Φθανειν τινα sig-

2

A. M. cir. 4056.
A. D. cir. 52.
A. U. C. 805.
Anno Clau-
dii Cæs.
Aug. 12.

16 For [1] the Lord himself shall descend from heaven with a shout, with the voice of the archangel, and with [m] the trump of God; [n] and the dead in Christ shall rise first:

17 [o] Then we which are alive *and* remain

shall be caught up together with them [p] in the clouds, to meet the Lord in the air: and so [q] shall we ever be with the Lord.

18 [r] Wherefore [s] comfort one another with these words.

A. M. cir. 4056.
A. D. cir. 52.
A. U. C. 805.
Anno Clau-
dii Cæs.
Aug. 12.

---

[1] Matt. xxiv. 30, 31 ; Acts i. 11 ; 2 Thess. i. 7.——[m] 1 Cor. xv. 52.——[n] 1 Cor. xv. 23, 52.

[o] 1 Cor. xv. 51.——[p] Acts i. 9 ; Rev. xi. 12.——[q] John xii. 26 ; xiv. 3 ; xvii. 24.——[r] Chap. v. 11.——[s] Or, *exhort.*

---

nifies the same, according to *Hesychius,* as προηκειν, *to go before,* προλαμβανειν, *to anticipate, be before.* Those who shall be found alive on that day shall not anticipate glory before the dead in Christ; for they shall rise *first,* and begin the enjoyment of it before the others shall be changed. This appears to be the apostle's meaning.

Verse 16. *The Lord himself*] That is: Jesus Christ *shall descend from heaven;* shall descend in like manner as he was seen by his disciples to ascend, i. e. in his human form, but now infinitely more glorious ; for *thousands of thousands shall minister unto him,* and *ten thousand times ten thousand shall stand before him ;* for *the Son of man shall come on the throne of his glory :* but who may abide the day of his coming, or stand when he appeareth ?

With a shout] Or order, εν κελευσματι· and probably in these words *Arise, ye dead, and come to judgment ;* which order shall be repeated by the archangel, who shall accompany it with the sound of the trump of God, whose great and terrible blasts, like those on mount Sinai, *sounding louder and louder,* shall shake both the heavens and the earth !

Observe the order of this terribly glorious day : 1. Jesus, in all the dignity and splendour of his eternal majesty, *shall descend from heaven* to the mid region, what the apostle calls the *air,* somewhere within the earth's *atmosphere.* 2. Then the κελευσμα, *shout* or *order,* shall be given for the dead to arise. 3. Next the archangel, as the *herald* of Christ, shall repeat the order, *Arise, ye dead, and come to judgment !* 4. When all the dead in Christ are raised, then the *trumpet shall sound,* as the signal for them all to flock together to the throne of Christ. It was by the *sound of the trumpet* that the solemn assemblies, under the

law, were convoked ; and to such convocations there appears to be here an allusion. 5. When the dead in Christ are raised, their vile bodies being made like unto his glorious body, then, 6. Those who *are alive* shall be *changed,* and made immortal. 7. These shall be *caught up together with them to meet the Lord in the air.* 8. We may suppose that the judgment will now be set, and the books opened, and the dead judged out of the things written in those books. 9. The eternal states of quick and dead being thus determined, then all who shall be found to *have made a covenant with him by sacrifice,* and to have *washed their robes, and made them white in the blood of the Lamb,* shall be taken to his eternal glory, and *be for ever with the Lord.* What an inexpressibly terrific glory will then be exhibited ! I forbear to call in here the descriptions which men of a poetic turn have made of this terrible scene, because I cannot trust to their correctness ; and it is a subject which we should speak of and contemplate as nearly as possible in the words of Scripture.

Verse 18. *Comfort one another with these words.*] Strange saying ! comfort a man with the information that he is going to appear before the judgment-seat of God ! Who can feel comfort from these words ? That man alone with whose spirit the Spirit of God bears witness that his sins are blotted out, and the thoughts of whose heart are purified by the inspiration of God's Holy Spirit, so that he can perfectly love him, and worthily magnify his name. Reader, thou art not in a safe state unless it be thus with thee, or thou art hungering and thirsting after righteousness. If so, thou shalt be filled ; for it is impossible that thou shouldst be taken away in thy sins, while mourning after the salvation of God. They that seek *shall* find,

---

CHAPTER V.

The apostle continues to speak of Christ's coming to judgment, and the uncertainty of the time in which it shall take place, and the careless state of sinners, 1–3. *Shows the Thessalonians that they are children of the light ; that they should watch and pray, and put on the armour of God, being called to obtain salvation by Christ, who died for them ; that whether dead or alive, when the day of judgment comes, they may live for ever with him ; and that they should comfort and edify each other with these considerations,* 4–11. *He exhorts them to remember those who labour among them, and are over them in the Lord ; and to esteem such highly for their work's sake,* 12, 13. *He charges them to warn, comfort, and support those who stood in need of such assistance, and to be patient and beneficent towards all,* 14, 15. *He points out their high spiritual privileges ; warns them against neglecting or misimproving the gifts of the Spirit, and the means of grace,* 16–20. *They are also exhorted to prove all things ; to abstain from all evil ; and to expect to be sanctified, through spirit, soul, and body, by him who has promised this, and who is faithful to his promises,* 21–24. *Recommends himself and brethren to their prayers ; shows them how they are to greet each other ; charges them to read this epistle to all the brethren ; and concludes with the usual apostolical benediction,* 25–28.

2

A. M. cir. 4056.
A. D. cir. 52.
A. U. C. 805.
Anno Claudii Cæs.
Aug. 12.

BUT of [a] the times and the seasons, brethren, [b] ye have no need that I write unto you.

2 For yourselves know perfectly, that [c] the day of the Lord so cometh as a thief in the night.

3 For when they shall say, Peace and safety; then [d] sudden destruction cometh upon them, [e] as travail upon a woman with child; and they shall not escape.

4 [f] But ye, brethren, are not in darkness, that that day should overtake you as a thief.

5 Ye are all [g] the children of light, and the children of the day: we are not of the night, nor of darkness.

6 [h] Therefore let us not sleep, as *do*

A. M. cir. 4056
A. D. cir. 52.
A. U. C. 805
Anno Claudii Cæs.
Aug. 12.

---

[a] Matt. xxiv. 3, 36; Acts i. 7.——[b] Chap. iv. 9.——[c] Matt. xxiv. 43, 44; xxv. 13; Luke xii. 39, 40; 2 Pet. iii. 10; Rev. iii. 3; xvi. 15.

[d] Isa. xiii. 6-9; Luke xvii. 27, 28, 29; xxi. 34, 35; 2 Thess. i. 9.——[e] Jer. xiii. 21; Hos. xiii. 13.——[f] Rom. xiii. 12, 13; 1 John ii. 8.——[g] Eph. v. 8.——[h] Matt. xxv. 5.

NOTES ON CHAP. V.

Verse 1. *But of the times and the seasons*] It is natural to suppose, after what he had said in the conclusion of the preceding chapter concerning the coming of Christ, the raising of the dead, and rendering those immortal who should then be found alive, without obliging them to pass through the empire of death, that the Thessalonians would feel an innocent curiosity to know, as the disciples did concerning the destruction of Jerusalem, *when those things should take place, and what should be the signs of those times, and of the coming of the Son of man.* And it is remarkable that the apostle answers, here, to these anticipated questions as our Lord did, in the above case, to the direct question of his disciples; and he seems to refer in these words, *Of the times and the seasons ye have no need that I write unto you, for yourselves know that the day of the Lord cometh as a thief in the night,* to what our Lord said, Matt. xxiv. 44; xxv. 13; and the apostle takes it for granted that they were acquainted with our Lord's prediction on the subject: *For you yourselves know perfectly that the day of the Lord so cometh as a thief in the night.* It is very likely therefore, that the apostle, like our Lord, couples these two grand events—the destruction of Jerusalem and the final judgment. And it appears most probable that it is of the *former event chiefly* that he speaks here, as it was certainly of the *latter* that he treated in the conclusion of the preceding chapter. In the notes on Acts i. 6, 7, it has already been shown that the χρονους η καιρους, *times or seasons,* (the very same terms which are used here,) refer to the *destruction of the Jewish commonwealth;* and we may fairly presume that they have the same meaning in this place.

Verse 3. *For when they shall say, Peace and safety*] This points out, very particularly, the state of the Jewish people when the Romans came against them; and so fully persuaded were they that God would not deliver the city and temple to their enemies, that they refused every overture that was made to them.

Sudden destruction] In the storming of their city and the burning of their temple, and the massacre of several hundreds of thousands of themselves; the rest being sold for slaves, and the whole of them dispersed over the face of the earth.

As travail upon a woman] This figure is perfectly consistent with what the apostle had said before, viz.: that *the times and seasons* were not known; though

the *thing* itself was expected, our Lord having predicted it in the most positive manner. So, a woman with child knows that, if she be spared, she will have a bearing time; but the *week,* the *day,* the *hour,* she cannot tell. In a great majority of cases the time is accelerated or retarded much *before* or *beyond* the time that the woman expected; so, with respect to the Jews, neither the *day, week, month,* nor *year* was known. All that was specifically known was this: their destruction was *coming,* and it should be *sudden,* and *they should not escape.*

Verse 4. *But ye, brethren, are not in darkness*] Probably St. Paul refers to a notion that was very prevalent among the Jews, viz.: that God would judge the *Gentiles* in the *night time,* when utterly secure and careless; but he would judge the *Jews* in the *day time,* when employed in reading and performing the words of the law. The words in *Midrash Tehillim,* on Psalm ix. 8, are the following: *When the holy blessed God shall judge the Gentiles, it shall be in the night season, in which they shall be asleep in their transgressions; but when he shall judge the Israelites, it shall be in the day time, when they are occupied in the study of the law.* This maxim the apostle appears to have in view in the 4th, 5th, 6th, 7th, and 8th verses.

Verse 5. *Ye are all the children of light*] Ye are children of God, and enjoy both his *light* and *life.* Ye are *Christians*—ye belong to him who has brought life and immortality *to light* by his Gospel. This dispensation, under which ye are, has *illustrated* all the preceding dispensations; in its *light* all is become *luminous;* and ye, who walked formerly in heathen *ignorance,* or in the *darkness* of Jewish prejudices, are now *light* in the Lord, because ye have believed in him who is the *light* to lighten the *Gentiles,* and the *glory* and *splendour* of his people *Israel.*

We are not of the night, nor of darkness.] Our actions are such as we are not afraid to expose to the fullest and clearest light. Sinners hate the *light;* they are enemies to *knowledge;* they love *darkness;* they will not receive *instruction;* and their deeds are such as cannot bear the *light.*

Verse 6. *Let us not sleep, as do others*] Let *us* who are of the *day*—who believe the Gospel and belong to Christ, not give way to a careless, unconcerned state of mind, like to the Gentiles and sinners in general, who are stupified and blinded by sin, so that

A. M. cir. 4056.
A. D. cir. 52.
A. U. C. 805.
Anno Claudii Cæs.
Aug. 12.

others; but ⁱ let us watch and be sober.

7 For ^k they that sleep, sleep in the night; and they that be drunken, ^l are drunken in the night.

8 But let us, who are of the day, be sober, ^m putting on the breastplate of faith and love;

---

and for a helmet, the hope of salvation.

9 For ⁿ God hath not appointed us to wrath, ^o but to obtain salvation by our Lord Jesus Christ,

10 ^p Who died for us, that, whether we wake or sleep, we should live together with him.

A. M. cir. 4056.
A. D. cir. 52.
A. U. C. 805.
Anno Claudii Cæs.
Aug. 12.

ⁱ Matt. xxiv. 42; xxv. 13; Rom. xiii. 11, 12, 13; 1 Pet. v. 8. ^k Luke xxi. 34, 36; Rom. xiii. 13; 1 Cor. xv. 34; Eph. v. 14. ^l Acts ii. 15.

^m Isa. lix. 17; Eph. vi. 14, 16, 17.——ⁿ Rom. ix. 22; chap. i. 10; 1 Pet. ii. 8; Jude 4.——^o 2 Thess. ii. 13, 14.——^p Rom. xiv. 8, 9; 2 Cor. v. 15.

---

they neither *think* nor *feel;* but live in time as if it were eternity; or rather, live as if there were no eternity, no future state of existence, rewards, or punishments.

Let us watch] Be always on the alert; *and be sober,* making a *moderate* use of all things.

Verse 7. For they that sleep] Sleepers and drunkards seek the night season; so the careless and the profligate persons indulge their evil propensities, and avoid all means of instruction; they prefer their ignorance to the word of God's grace, and to the light of life. There seems to be here an allusion to the opinion mentioned under ver. 4, to which the reader is requested to refer. It may be remarked, also, that it was accounted doubly scandalous, even among the heathen, to be drunk in the day time. They who were drunken *were drunken in the night.*

Verse 8. Putting on the breastplate] We are not only called to WORK, but we are called also to *fight;* and that we may not be surprised, we must *watch;* and that we may be in a condition to defend ourselves, we must be sober; and that we may be enabled to conquer, we must be *armed :* and what the *breastplate* and *helmet* are to a *soldier's heart* and *head,* such are *faith, love,* and *hope* to us. *Faith* enables us to *endure,* as seeing him who is invisible; *love* excites us to *diligence* and *activity,* and makes us bear our troubles and difficulties pleasantly; *hope* helps us to *anticipate* the great *end,* the glory that shall be revealed, and which we know we shall in due time obtain, if we faint not. For an explanation of the different parts of the Grecian armour, as illustrating that of the Christian, see the notes on Eph. vi., where the subject is largely explained.

Verse 9. For God hath not appointed us to wrath] So then it appears that *some* were *appointed to wrath,* εις οργην, *to punishment;* on this subject there can be no dispute. But *who* are they? *When* did this appointment take place? And for what *cause?* These are supposed to be "very difficult questions, and such as cannot receive a satisfactory answer; and the whole must be referred to the *sovereignty* of God." If we look carefully at the apostle's words, we shall find all these difficulties vanish. It is very obvious that, in the preceding verses, the apostle refers simply to the destruction of the Jewish polity, and to the terrible judgments which were about to fall on the Jews as a *nation ;* therefore, they are the *people* who were appointed *to wrath;* and they were thus appointed, not from *eternity,* nor from any indefinite or remote time, but from that time in which they utterly rejected the

offers of salvation made to them by Jesus Christ and his apostles; the privileges of their *election* were still continued to them, even after they had crucified the Lord of glory; for, when he gave commandment to his disciples *to go into all the world, and preach the Gospel to every creature,* he bade them *begin at Jerusalem.* They did so, and continued to offer salvation to them, till at last, being everywhere persecuted, and the whole nation appearing with one consent to reject the Gospel, the kingdom of God was wholly taken away from them, and the apostles turned to the *Gentiles. Then* God appointed them to wrath; and the *cause* of that appointment was their final and determined rejection of Christ and his Gospel. But even this *appointment to wrath* does not signify *eternal damnation ;* nothing of the kind is intended in the word. Though we are sure that those who die in their sins can never see God, yet it is possible that many of those wretched Jews, during their calamities, and especially during the siege of their city, did turn unto the Lord who smote them, and found that *salvation* which he never denies to the sincere penitent.

When the Jews were *rejected,* and *appointed to wrath,* then the *Gentiles* were *elected,* and appointed to *obtain salvation* by our Lord Jesus Christ, whose Gospel they gladly received, and continue to prize; while the remnant of the Jews continue, in all places of their dispersion, the same irreconcilable and blasphemous opponents of the Gospel of Christ. On *these accounts* the *election* of the *Gentiles* and the *reprobation* of the *Jews* still continue.

Verse 10. Who died for us] His death was an atoning sacrifice for the Gentiles as well as for the Jews.

Whether we wake or sleep] Whether we *live* or *die,* whether we are in this state or in the other world, we shall live together with him—shall enjoy his life, and the consolations of his Spirit, while *here ;* and shall be glorified together with him in the eternal world. The words show that *every where* and in *all circumstances* genuine believers, who walk after God, have life and communion with him, and are continually happy, and constantly safe. The apostle, however, may refer to the doctrine he has delivered, chap. iv. 15, concerning the *dead in Christ rising first;* and the *last generation* of men not *dying,* but undergoing such a change as shall render them *immortal.* On that great day, all the followers of God, both those who had long *slept* in the dust of the earth, and all those who shall be found *living,* shall be acknowledged by Christ as his own, and *live together* for ever *with him.*

A. M. cir. 4056.
A. D. cir. 52.
A. U. C. 805.
Anno Claudii Cæs.
Aug. 12.

11 �q Wherefore ʳ comfort yourselves together, and edify one another, even as also ye do.

12 And we beseech you, brethren, ˢto know them which labour among you, and are over you in the Lord, and admonish you;

13 And to esteem them very highly in love for their work's sake. ᵗ*And* be at peace among yourselves.

14 Now we ᵘexhort you, brethren, ᵛ warn them that are ʷ unruly, ˣ comfort the feebleminded, ʸsupport the weak, ᶻ be patient toward all *men.*

15 ª See that none render evil for evil unto any *man;* but ever ᵇ follow that which is good, both among yourselves, and to all *men*

16 ᶜ Rejoice evermore.

17 ᵈ Pray without ceasing.

A. M. cir. 4056.
A. D. cir. 52
A. U. C. 805.
Anno Clau dii Cæs.
Aug. 12.

 q Chap. iv. 18.——ʳ Or, *exhort.*——ˢ 1 Cor. xvi. 18; Phil. ii. 29; 1 Tim. v. 17; Heb. xiii. 7, 17.——ᵗ Mark ix. 50.——ᵘ Or, *beseech.*——ᵛ 2 Thess. iii. 11, 12.——ʷ Or, *disorderly.*——ˣ Heb. xii. 12.——ʸ Rom. xiv. 1; xv. 1; Gal. vi. 1, 2.——ᶻ Gal. v. 22; Eph. iv. 2; Col. iii. 12; 2 Tim. iv. 2.

ª Lev. xix. 18; Prov. xx. 22; xxiv. 29; Matt. v. 39, 44; Rom. xii. 17; 1 Cor. vi. 7; 1 Pet. iii. 9.——ᵇ Gal. vi. 10; chapter iii. 12.——ᶜ 2 Cor. vi. 10; Phil. iv. 4.——ᵈ Luke xviii. 1; xxi. 36; Romans xii. 12; Ephesians vi. 18; Colossians iv. 2; 1 Peter iv. 7.

Verse 11. *Comfort—one another*] Rest assured that, in all times and circumstances, it shall be well with the righteous; let every man lay this to heart; and with this consideration *comfort* and *edify each other* in all trials and difficulties.

Verse 12. *Know them*] Act *kindly* towards them; *acknowledge* them as the messengers of Christ; and treat them with *tenderness* and *respect.* This is a frequent meaning of the word γινωσκω. See on John i. 10.

Them which labour among you] The words τους κοπιωντας have appeared to some as expressing those who *had* laboured among them; but as it is the *participle* of the *present* tense, there is no need to consider it in this light. Both it and the word προϊσταμενους, the *superintendents,* refer to persons then actually employed in the work of God. These were all *admonishers, teachers,* and *instructers* of the people, devoting their time and talents to this important work.

Verse 13. *Esteem them very highly in love*] Christian ministers, who preach the *whole truth,* and *labour* in the word and doctrine, are entitled to more than *respect;* the apostle commands them to be esteemed, ὑπερεκπερισσου, *abundantly,* and *superabundantly;* and this is to be done *in love;* and as men delight to serve those whom they love, it necessarily follows that they should provide for them, and see that they want neither the *necessaries* nor *conveniences* of life; I do not say *comforts,* though these also should be furnished; but of these the genuine messengers of Christ are frequently destitute. However, they should have *food, raiment,* and *lodging* for themselves and their household. This they ought to have *for their work's sake;* those who do not *work* should not *eat.* As *ministers of Christ,* such as labour not are unworthy either of respect or support.

Verse 14. *Warn them that are unruly*] The whole phraseology of this verse is *military;* I shall consider the import of each term. Ατακτους· Those who are *out of their ranks,* and are neither in a *disposition* nor *situation* to perform the work and duty of a soldier; those who will not do the work prescribed, and who will meddle with what is not commanded. There are many such in every Church that is of considerable magnitude.

Comfort the feeble-minded] Τους ολιγοψυχους· Those

of *little souls;* the *faint-hearted;* those who, on the eve of a battle, are *dispirited,* because of the number of the enemy, and their own feeble and unprovided state. Let them know that the battle is not theirs, but the Lord's; and that those who trust in him shall conquer.

Support the weak] Αντεχεσθε των ασθενων· *Shore up, prop* them that are weak; strengthen those wings and companies that are likely to be most exposed, that they be not overpowered and broken in the day of battle.

Be patient toward all] Μακροθυμειτε προς παντας· The *disorderly,* the *feeble-minded,* and the *weak,* will exercise your patience, and try your temper. If the troops be irregular, and cannot in every respect be reduced to proper order and discipline, let not the *officers* lose their temper nor courage; let them do the best they can; God will be with them, and a victory will give confidence to *their* troops. We have often seen that the Christian life is compared to a warfare, and that the directions given to *soldiers* are, *mutatis mutandis;* allowing for the different systems, suitable to Christians. This subject has been largely treated on, Eph. vi. The ministers of Christ, being considered as *officers,* should acquaint themselves with the officers' duty. He who has the direction and management of a Church of God will need all the skill and prudence he can acquire.

Verse 15. *See that none render evil for evil*] Every temper contrary to *love* is contrary to *Christianity.* A peevish, fretful, vindictive man may be a child of Satan; he certainly is not a child of God.

Follow that which is good] That by which ye may profit your brethren and your neighbours of every description, whether *Jews* or *Gentiles.*

Verse 16. *Rejoice evermore.*] Be always happy; the religion of Christ was intended to remove misery. He that has God for his portion may constantly exult. Four MSS. of good note add εν τω Κυριω, *in the Lord: Rejoice in the Lord evermore.*

Verse 17. *Pray without ceasing.*] Ye are *dependent* on God for every good; without him ye can do nothing; *feel* that dependence at all times, and ye will always be in the spirit of prayer; and those who feel this spirit will, as frequently as possible, be found in the exercise of prayer.

2

A. M. cir. 4056.
A. D. cir. 52.
A. U. C. 805.
Anno Clau-
dii Cæs.
Aug. 12.

18 ^e In every thing give thanks: for this is the will of God in Christ Jesus concerning you.

19 ^f Quench not the Spirit.

20 ^g Despise not prophesyings.

21 ^h Prove all things, ⁱ hold fast that which is good.

22 ^k Abstain from all appearance of evil.

23 And ^l the very God of peace ^m sanctify you wholly: and *I pray God* your whole spirit and soul and body ⁿ be preserved blameless unto the coming of our Lord Jesus Christ.

A. M. cir. 4056.
A. D. cir. 52.
A. U. C. 805.
Anno Clau-
dii Cæs.
Aug. 12.

^e Eph. v. 20; Col. iii. 17.——^f Eph. iv. 30; 1 Tim. iv. 14; 2 Tim. i. 6; see 1 Cor. xiv. 30.——^g 1 Cor. xiv. 1, 39.

^h 1 Cor. ii. 11, 15; 1 John iv. 1.——ⁱ Phil. iv. 8.——^k Chap. 1. 12.——^l Phil. iv. 9.——^m Chap. iii. 13.——ⁿ 1 Cor. i. 8.

Verse 18. *In every thing give thanks*] For this reason, that all things work together for good to them that love God; therefore, every occurrence may be a subject of gratitude and thankfulness. While ye live to God, prosperity and adversity will be equally helpful to you.

For this is the will of God] That ye should be always happy; that ye should ever be in the spirit of prayer; and that ye should profit by every occurrence in life, and be continually grateful and obedient; for *gratitude* and *obedience* are inseparably connected.

Verse 19. *Quench not the Spirit.*] The Holy Spirit is represented as a *fire*, because it is his province to *enlighten* and quicken the soul; and to purge, purify, and refine it. This Spirit is represented as being *quenched* when any *act* is done, *word* spoken, or *temper* indulged, contrary to its dictates. It is the Spirit of *love*, and therefore anger, malice, revenge, or any unkind or unholy temper, will quench it so that it will withdraw its influences; and then the heart is left in a state of *hardness* and *darkness*. It has been observed that fire may be quenched as well by heaping *earth* on it as by throwing water on it; and the *love of the world* will as effectually grieve and quench the Spirit as any ordinary act of transgression.

Every genuine Christian is made a partaker of the Spirit of God; and he who has not the spirit of Christ is none of his. It cannot be the *miraculous gifts* of the Spirit which the apostle means, for these were given to *few*, and not *always*; for even apostles could not work miracles when they pleased; but the direction in the text is *general*, and refers to a gift of which they were generally partakers.

Verse 20. *Despise not prophesyings.*] Do not suppose that ye have no need of continual instruction; without it ye cannot preserve the Christian life, nor go on to perfection. God will ever send a message of salvation by each of his ministers to every faithful, attentive hearer. Do not suppose that ye are already wise enough; you are no more wise enough than you are holy enough. They who slight or neglect the means of grace, and especially the preaching of God's holy word, are generally vain, empty, self-conceited people, and exceedingly superficial both in knowledge and piety.

Verse 21. *Prove all things*] Whatever ye hear in these *prophesyings* or preachings, examine by the words of Christ, and by the doctrines which, from time to time, we have delivered unto you in our preaching and writings. *Try the spirits*—the different teachers, by the word of God.

Hold fast that which is good.] Whatever in these

prophesyings has a tendency to increase your *faith, love, holiness,* and *usefulness,* that receive and hold fast. There were *prophets* or *teachers* even at that time who professed to be of God, and yet were not.

Verse 22. *Abstain from all appearance of evil.*] Sin not, and avoid even the *appearance* of it. Do not drive your morality so near the bounds of evil as to lead even weak persons to believe that ye actually touch, taste, or handle it. Let not the *form* of it, ειδος, appear with or among you, much less the *substance.* Ye are called to holiness; *be ye holy, for God is holy.*

Verse 23. *And the very God of peace*] That same God who is the author of peace, the giver of peace; and who has sent, for the redemption of the world, the *Prince of peace*; may that very God *sanctify you wholly*; leave no more evil in your hearts than his precepts tolerate evil in your conduct. The word *wholly,* ὁλοτελεις, means precisely the same as our phrase, *to all intents and purposes.* May he sanctify you to the end and to the uttermost, that, *as sin hath reigned unto death, even so may grace reign through righteousness unto eternal life, by Jesus Christ our Lord.*

Your whole spirit and soul and body] Some think that the apostle alludes to the Pythagorean and Platonic doctrine, which was acknowledged among the Thessalonians. I should rather believe that he refers simply to the *fact,* that the creature called *man* is a compound being, consisting, 1. Of a *body,* σωμα, an organized system, formed by the creative energy of God out of the dust of the earth; composed of bones, muscles, and nerves; of arteries, veins, and a variety of other vessels, in which the blood and other fluids circulate. 2. Of a *soul,* ψυχη, which is the seat of the different *affections* and *passions,* such as love, hatred, anger, &c., with sensations, appetites, and propensities of different kinds. 3. Of *spirit,* πνευμα, the immortal principle, the source of life to the body and soul, without which the animal functions cannot be performed, how perfect soever the bodily organs may be; and which alone possesses the faculty of intelligence, understanding, thinking, and reasoning, and produces the faculty of speech wherever it resides, if accident have not impaired the organs of speech.

The apostle prays that this compound being, in all its parts, powers, and faculties, which he terms ὁλο-κληρον, *their whole,* comprehending all parts, every thing that constitutes *man* and *manhood,* may be *sanctified and preserved blameless till the coming of Christ;* hence we learn, 1. That body, soul, and spirit are debased and polluted by sin. 2. That each is capable

| A. M. cir. 4056. |
| A. D. cir. 52. |
| A. U. C. 805. |
| Anno Clau- |
| dii Cæs. |
| Aug. 12. |

24 ° Faithful *is* he that calleth you, who also will do *it*.

25 Brethren, P pray for us.

26 q Greet all the brethren with a holy kiss.

27 I ʳ charge you by the Lord, that ˢ this

epistle be read unto all the holy brethren.

28 ᵗ The grace of our Lord Jesus Christ *be* with you. Amen.

¶ The First *Epistle* unto the Thessalonians was written from Athens.

| A. M. cir. 4056 |
| A. D. cir. 52. |
| A. U. C. 805. |
| Anno Clau- |
| dii Cæs. |
| Aug. 12. |

° 1 Cor. i. 9; x. 13; 2 Thess. iii. 3.——P Col. iv. 3; 2 Thess. iii. 1.——q Rom. xvi. 16.

ʳ Or, *adjure*.——ˢ Col. iv. 16; 2 Thess. iii. 14.——ᵗ Rom. xvi. 20, 24; 2 Thess. iii. 18.

---

of being sanctified, consecrated in all its powers to God, and made holy. 3. That the whole man is to be preserved to the coming of Christ, that body, soul, and spirit may be then glorified for ever with him. 4. That in *this* state the whole man may be so sanctified as to be preserved *blameless* till the coming of Christ. And thus we learn that the sanctification is not to take place *in*, *at*, or *after* death. On the pollution and sanctification of *flesh* and *spirit*, see the note on 2 Cor. vii. 1.

Verse 24. *Faithful is he that calleth you*] In a great variety of places in his word God has promised to *sanctify* his followers, and his faithfulness binds him to fulfil his promises; therefore *he will do it*. He who can believe will find this thing also possible to him.

Verse 25. *Pray for us*.] Even apostles, while acting under an extraordinary mission, and enjoying the inspiration of the Holy Ghost, felt the necessity of the prayers of the faithful. God requires that his people should pray for his ministers; and it is not to be wondered at, if they who pray not for their preachers should receive no benefit from their teaching. How can they expect God to send a message by him, for whom they, who are the most interested, have not prayed? If the grace and Spirit of Christ be not worth the most earnest prayers which a man can offer, they, and the heaven to which they lead, are not worth having.

Verse 26. *Greet all the brethren*] See the note on Rom. xvi. 16. Instead of *all the brethren*, the *Coptic* has, *greet one another*; a reading not noticed by either Griesbach or Wetstein.

Verse 27. *I charge you by the Lord, that this epistle be read*] There must have been some particular reason for this solemn charge; he certainly had some cause to suspect that the epistle would be suppressed in some way or other, and that the *whole* Church would not be permitted to hear it. or he may refer to the smaller Churches contiguous to Thessalonica, or the Churches in Macedonia in general, whom he wished to hear it, as well as those to whom it was more immediately directed. There is no doubt that the apostles designed that their epistles should be copied, and sent to all the Churches in the vicinity of that to which they were directed. Had this not been the case, a great number of Churches would have known scarcely any thing of the New Testament. As every Jewish synagogue had a copy of the law and the prophets, so every Christian Church had a copy of the gospels and the epistles, which were daily, or at least every Sabbath, read for the instruction of the people. This the apostle deemed so necessary, that he adjured them by

the Lord to read this epistle to all the brethren; i. e. to all the Christians in that district. Other Churches might get copies of it; and thus, no doubt, it soon became general. In this way other parts of the sacred writings were disseminated through all the Churches of the Gentiles; and the errors of the different scribes, employed to take copies, constituted what are now called the *various readings*.

Verse 28. *The grace of our Lord Jesus*] As the epistle *began* so it ends; for the *grace of Christ* must be at the *beginning* and *end* of every work, in order to complete it, and bring it to good effect.

Amen.] This is wanting in BD*FG and some others. It was probably not written by St. Paul.

The *subscriptions* are, as in other cases, various and contradictory. The chief MSS. conclude as follows: *The first to the Thessalonians is completed; the second to the Thessalonians begins.*—DFG. The first to the Thessalonians written from Athens.—AB, and others. From *Laodicea*.—Cod. *Claromont*. The first to the Thessalonians, *written from Athens*.—Common Greek text.

The VERSIONS conclude thus:——*The First Epistle to the Thessalonians was written at Athens, and sent by the hands of Timotheus.*—SYRIAC. *To the Thessalonians.*—ÆTHIOPIC. Nothing in the VULGATE. *The end of the epistle: it was written from a city of the Athenians, and sent by the hand of Timotheus. And to the Lord be praise for ever and ever. Amen.*—ARABIC. *Written from Athens, and sent by Silvanus and Timotheus.*—COPTIC.

That it was not sent by either *Silvanus* or *Timothy* is evident enough from the *inscription*, for St. Paul associates these two with himself, in directing it to the Thessalonian Church. Others say that it was sent by *Tychicus* and *Onesimus*, but this also is absurd; for Onesimus was not converted till a considerable time after the writing of this epistle. That it was written by St. *Paul*, there is no doubt; and that it was written at *Corinth*, and not at *Athens*, has been shown in the *preface*.

1. THE two preceding chapters are certainly among the most important and the most sublime in the New Testament. The *general judgment*, the resurrection *of the body*, and the *states* of the *quick* and *dead*, the *unrighteous* and the *just*, are described, concisely indeed, but they are exhibited in the most striking and affecting points of view. I have attempted little else than verbal illustrations; the subject is too vast for my comprehension; I cannot order my speech by reason of darkness. Though there are some topics handled here which do not appear in other parts of the sacred

2

writings, yet the main of what we learn is this. "Our God will come, and will not keep silence ; a fire shall burn before him, and it shall be very tempestuous round about him ; he shall call to the heavens above, and to the earth beneath, that he may judge his people." The *day* of *judgment!* what an awful word is this! what a truly terrific time! when the heavens shall be shrivelled as a scroll, and the elements melt with fervent heat; when the earth and its appendages shall be burnt up, and the fury of that conflagration be such that *there shall be no more sea!* A time when the noble and ignoble dead, the *small* and the *great*, shall stand before God, and all be judged according to the deeds done in the body ; yea, a time when the thoughts of the heart and every *secret thing* shall be brought to light; when the innumerable millions of transgressions, and embryo and abortive sins, shall be exhibited in all their *purposes and intents;* a time when Justice, eternal Justice, shall sit alone upon the throne, and pronounce a sentence as impartial as irrevocable, and as awful as eternal! There is a *term* of human life; and every human being is rapidly gliding to it as fast as the wings of time, in their *onward* motion, incomprehensibly swift, can carry him! And shall not the living lay this to heart? Should we not live in order to die? Should we not die in order to be judged? And should we not live and die so as to live again to all eternity, not with Satan and his angels, but with God and his saints? O thou man of God! thou Christian! thou immortal spirit! think of these things.

2. The subject in verse 27 of the last chapter I have but slightly noticed · *I charge you, by the Lord, that this epistle be read unto all the holy brethren.* This is exceedingly strange ; the Epistles to the *Romans*, the *Corinthians, Galatians, Ephesians, Philippians, Colossians,* and *Thessalonians,* were directed to the *whole Church* in each of those places ; why, then, after directing this, as he did all the rest, to the *whole Church*, should he at the conclusion *adjure them, by the Lord, that it should be read to all the holy brethren;* that is, to the very persons to whom it was addressed? Is there not some *mystery* here? Has it not been the endeavour of Satan, from the beginning, to keep men from consulting the oracles of God ; and has he not used even the authority of the Church to accomplish this his purpose? Was not the prohibiting the use of the Scriptures to the people at large the *mystery of iniquity* which *then began to work*, and against which the adjuration of the apostle is directed? see second epistle, chap. ii. ; this *mystery*, which was the grand agent in the hands of *Mystery, Babylon the Great,* to keep the people in darkness, that the unauthorized and wicked pretensions of this *mother of the abominations of the earth* might not be brought to the test; but that she might continue to wear her crown, sit on her scarlet beast, and subject the Christian world to her empire. Was it not the Christian world's total ignorance of God's book which the Romish Church took care to keep from the people at large, that induced them patiently, yet with *terror*, to bow down to all her usurpations, and to swallow down monstrous doctrines which she imposed upon them as Christian *verities?* Was it not this deplorable ignorance which induced kings and emperors to put their necks, literally, under the feet of this usurped and antichristian power? This *mystery of iniquity* continues *still to work;* and with all the pretensions of the Romish Church, the Scriptures are in general withheld from the *people*, or suffered to be read under such *restrictions* and with such *notes* as totally subvert the sense of those passages on which this Church endeavours to build her unscriptural pretensions. It is generally allowed that the *Vulgate* version is the most favourable to these pretensions, and yet even that version the rulers of the Church dare not trust in the hands of any of their people, even under their general ecclesiastical restrictions, without their counteracting notes and comments. How strange is this! and yet in this Church there have been, and still are, many enlightened and eminent men; surely *truth* has nothing to fear from the *Bible*. When the Romish Church permits the free use of this book, she may be stripped, indeed, of some of her appendages, but she will lose nothing but her dross and tin, and become what the original Church at Rome was, *beloved of God, called to be saints;* and *have her faith*, once more, *spoken of throughout all the world*, Rom. i. 7, 8. She has in her own hands the means of her own *regeneration;* and a genuine *Protestant* will wish, not her *destruction*, but her *reformation ;* and if she consent not to be *reformed*, her total destruction is inevitable.

Finished correcting for a new edition, on the shortest day of 1831.—A. C.

FOR an account of Thessalonica, and St. Paul's labours there, the reader is requested to consult the preface to the preceding epistle. That this second epistle was written shortly after the first, and from the same place too, is very probable, from this circumstance, that the same persons, *Paul, Silvanus,* and *Timotheus,* who addressed the Church at Thessalonica in the former epistle, address the same Church in this; and as three such apostolic men were rarely long together in the same place, it is very likely that the two epistles were written not only in the *same year,* but also within a very short time of each other. It appears that the person who carried the first epistle returned speedily to Corinth, and gave the apostle a particular account of the state of the Thessalonian Church; and, among other things, informed him that many were in expectation of the speedy arrival of the day of judgment; and that they inferred from his epistle already sent, chap. iv. 15, 17, and v. 4, 6, that it was to take place while the apostle and themselves should be yet alive. And it appears probable, from some parts of *this* epistle, that he was informed also that some, expecting this sudden appearance of the Lord Jesus, had given up all their secular concerns as inconsistent with a due preparation for such an important and awful event; see chap. iii. 6–13. To correct such a misapprehension, and redeem them from an error, which, if appearing to rest on the authority of an apostle, must in its issue be ruinous to the cause of Christianity, St. Paul would feel himself constrained to write *immediately;* and this is a sufficient reason why these epistles should appear to have been written at so short a distance from each other. What rendered this speedy intervention of the apostle's authority and direction the more necessary, was, that there appear to have been some in that Church who professed to have a *revelation* concerning this thing, and to have endeavoured to confirm it by a *pretended report* from the apostle himself, and from the *words* already referred to in the *former epistle;* see here on chap. ii. 1, 2: "We beseech you, brethren, be not soon shaken in mind, or be troubled, neither by SPIRIT, nor by WORD, nor by LETTER as from us, as that the day of Christ is at hand." As the apostle, in this epistle, chap. iii. 2, entreats the Thessalonians to pray the Lord that he and his companions *might be delivered from unreasonable and wicked men,* Dr. Macknight supposes that the epistle was written soon after the insurrection of the Jews at Corinth, in which they dragged Paul before Gallio, the proconsul of Achaia, and accused him of persuading men to worship God contrary to the law; Acts xviii. 13. This argument places it also in the year 52, or 53, in the *twelfth* or *thirteenth* of Claudius, the successor of Caius.

As there have been some eminent Christian writers who have entertained the same opinion with those at Thessalonica, that not only St. Paul, but other apostles of Christ, did believe that the day of general judgment should take place in their time, which opinion is shown by the event to be absolutely false; it appears to be a matter of the utmost consequence to the credit of Divine revelation, to rescue the character of the apostles from such an imputation. Dr. Macknight has written well on this subject, as the following extract from his preface to this epistle will prove:—

"Grotius, Locke, and others," says he, "have affirmed that the apostles believed that the end of the world was to happen in their time; and that they have declared this to be their belief in various passages of their epistles. But these learned men, and all who join them in that opinion, have fallen into a most pernicious error; for thereby they destroy the authority of the Gospel revelation, at least so far as it is contained in the discourses and writings of the apostles; because, if they have erred in a matter of such importance, and which they affirm was revealed to them by Christ, they may have been mistaken in other matters also, where their inspiration is not more strongly asserted by them than in this instance. It is therefore necessary to clear them from so injurious an imputation.

"And first, with respect to Paul, who was an apostle of Christ, and Silvanus, who was a prophet, and a chief man among the brethren, and Timothy, who was eminent for his spiritual gifts, I observe that the epistle under our consideration affords the clearest proof that these men knew the truth concerning the coming of

Christ to judge the world; for in it they expressly assured the Thessalonians that the persons who made them believe the day of judgment was at hand were deceiving them; that, before the day of judgment, there was to be a great apostasy in religion, occasioned by the man of sin, who at that time was restrained from showing himself, but who was to be revealed in his season; that, when revealed, he will *sit*, that is, remain a long time in the Church of God, as God, and showing himself that he is God; and that, afterwards, he is to be destroyed. Now, as these events could not be accomplished in the course of a few years, the persons who foretold they were to happen before the coming of Christ certainly did not think the day of judgment would be in their lifetime. Besides, St. Paul, Rom. xi. 23–36, by a long chain of reasoning, having showed that, after the genera. conversion of the Gentiles, the Jews, in a body, are to be brought into the Christian Church, can any person be so absurd as to persevere in maintaining that this apostle believed the end of the world would happen in his lifetime?

" Next, with respect to the Apostle Peter, I think it plain, from the manner in which he has spoken of the coming of Christ, that he knew it was at a great distance; 2 Pet. iii. 3, 4, 8, 9: 'Knowing this first, that scoffers will come in the last days, walking after their own lusts, and saying, Where' is the promise of his coming? For, from the time the fathers fell asleep, all things continue as at the beginning of the creation. But this one thing, let it not escape you, beloved, that one day is with the Lord as a thousand years, and a thousand years as one day. The Lord, who hath promised, doth not delay, in the manner some account delaying.' Now, seeing Peter has here foretold that, in the last age, the wicked will mock at the promise of Christ's coming, on account of its being long delayed; and, from the stability and regularity of the course of nature during so many ages, will argue that there is no probability that the world will ever come to an end; it is evident that he also knew the coming of Christ to judgment was at a very great distance at the time he wrote that epistle.

" The same may be said of James; for, in the hearing of the apostles, elders, and brethren assembled in the council of Jerusalem, he quoted passages from the Jewish prophets, to show that all the Gentiles were, at some future period, to seek after the Lord; Acts xv. 17. But, if James looked for the general conversion of the Gentiles, he certainly could not imagine the end of the world would happen in his time.

" Lastly, the Apostle John, in his book of the Revelation, having foretold a great variety of important events respecting the political and religious state of the world, which could not be accomplished in a few years, but required a series of ages to give them birth; there cannot be the least doubt that he likewise knew the truth concerning his Master's second coming; and therefore, to suppose that he imagined the day of judgment was to happen in his own lifetime, is a palpable mistake.

" Upon the whole, seeing the apostles and other inspired teachers of our religion certainly knew that the coming of Christ to judgment was at a great distance, every impartial person must be sensible they have been much injured, not by the enemies of revelation alone, but by some of its friends; who, upon the strength of certain expressions, the meaning of which they evidently misunderstood, have endeavoured to persuade the world that the apostle ignorantly believed the day of judgment was at hand. These expressions may all be applied to other events, as shall be showed in the next section, and therefore they ought to be so applied; because candour requires that sense to be put on an author's words which renders him most consistent with himself."

As the term *coming of Christ* has several acceptations in the sacred writings, and the applying any one of these to the subject to which in a given place it does not belong, may lead to very erroneous if not dangerous conclusions, as it appears to have done at Thessalonica; it is necessary to consider the different senses in which this phrase is used, that we may know its specific meaning in the different places where it occurs. Dr. Macknight, in the fourth section of his preface, intituled, *Different Comings of Christ are spoken of in the New Testament*, has treated this subject also with considerable judgment, as the reader will at once perceive.

. " In this article I propose to show that there are other *comings* of Christ spoken of in Scripture besides his *coming to judgment*; and that there are other things besides this mundane system whose end is there foretold; and that it is of these other matters the apostles speak, when they represent the *day of their Master* and the *end of all things* as at hand.

" First, then, in the prophetic writings of the Jews (2 Sam. xxii. 10, 12; Psalm xcvii. 2–5; Isa. xix. 1) great exertions of the Divine power, whether for the salvation or destruction of nations, are called *the coming, the appearance, the presence of God*. Hence it was natural for the apostles, who were Jews, to call any signal and evident interposition of Christ, as Governor of the world, for the accomplishment of his purposes, *his coming* and *his day*; accordingly, those exertions of his power and providence, whereby he destroyed Jerusalem and the temple, abrogated the Mosaic institutions, and established the Gospel, are called by the apostles *his coming* and *day*; not only in allusion to the ancient prophetic language, but because Christ himself, in his prophecy concerning these events, recorded Matt. xxiv., has termed them *the coming of the Son of man*, in allusion to the following prophecy of Daniel, of which his own prophecy is an explication; Dan. vii. 13, 14: 'I saw in the night visions, and, behold, one like the Son of man came with the clouds of heaven, and came to the Ancient of days. And they brought him near before him. And there was given him dominion, and glory, and a kingdom; that all people, nations, and languages, should serve him. His dominion is an everlasting dominion, which shall not pass away; and his kingdom that which shall not be destroyed.' This prophecy the Jewish doctors, with one consent, attribute to the Messiah, and of that

2

temporal kingdom which they expected was to be given him. Farther, they supposed he would erect that temporal kingdom by great and visible exertions of his power for the destruction of his enemies; but they little suspected that themselves were of the number of those enemies whom he was to destroy; and that his kingdom was to be established upon the ruin of their state. Yet that was the true meaning of *the coming of the Son of man in the clouds of heaven.* For, while the Jewish nation continued in Judea, and observed the institutions of Moses, they violently opposed the preaching of the Gospel, by which the Messiah was to reign over all people, nations, and languages. Wherefore, that the everlasting kingdom might be established effectually, it was necessary that Jerusalem and the Jewish state should be destroyed by the Roman armies. Now, since our Lord foretold this sad catastrophe in the words of the Prophet Daniel, Matt. xxiv. 30, 'And they shall see the Son of man coming in the clouds of heaven with power and great glory;' and after describing every particular of it with the greatest exactness, seeing he told his disciples, ver. 34, 'This generation shall not pass till all these things be fulfilled;' can there be any doubt that the apostles, (who, when they wrote their epistles, certainly understood the true import of this prophecy,) by *their Master's coming* and by *the end of all things,* which they represent as at hand, mean his coming to destroy Jerusalem, and to put an end to the institutions of Moses? It is no objection to this, that, when the apostles heard Christ declare, 'There shall not be left here one stone upon another that shall not be thrown down,' they connected the end of the world or age with that event; Matt. xxiv. 3: 'Tell us, when shall these things be? and what shall be the sign of thy coming, και συντελειας του αιωνος, and of the end of the age?' For as the Jewish doctors divided the duration of the world into three ages; the age before the law, the age under the law, and the age under the Messiah; the apostle knew that the age under the law was to end when the age under the Messiah began; and therefore by the *end of the age* they meant, even at that time, not the end of the world, but the end of the age under the law, in which the Jews had been greatly oppressed by the heathens. And although they did not then understand the purpose for which their Master was to come, nor the true nature of his kingdom; nor suspect that he was to make any change in the institutions of Moses; yet when they wrote their epistles, being illuminated by the Holy Ghost, they certainly knew that the institutions of Moses were to be abolished; and that their Master's kingdom was not a temporal but a spiritual dominion, in which all people, nations, and languages were to be governed, not by external force, but by the operation of truth upon their minds through the preaching of the Gospel.

" Farther, that the apostles, by *the coming* of Christ, which they represented as at hand when they wrote their epistles, meant his coming to establish his spiritual kingdom over all people, nations, and languages, and not his coming to put an end to this mundane system, is evident from what Christ himself told them, Matt. xvi. 28: 'There be some standing here who shall not taste of death till they see the Son of man coming in his kingdom.' And, agreeably to this account of the coming of Christ and of the end of all things, I observe that every passage of their epistles, in which the apostles have spoken of these things *as at hand,* may with the greatest propriety be interpreted of Christ's coming to establish his everlasting kingdom over all people, nations, and languages, by destroying Jerusalem, putting an end to the law of Moses, and spreading the Gospel through the world. Thus, 1 Cor. x. 11: 'These things—are written for our admonition, upon whom τα τελη των αιωνων, the ends of the ages are come,' means the end of the age under the law, and the beginning of the age under the Messiah. Phil. iv. 5: 'Let your moderation be known to all men: the Lord is nigh;' namely, to destroy the Jews, your greatest adversaries. Heb. ix. 26: 'But now once επι συντελεια των αιωνων, at the conclusion of the ages, (the Jewish jubilees,) hath he been manifested to abolish sin-offering by the sacrifice of himself.' Heb. x. 25: 'Exhorting one another daily; and so much the more, as ye see the day approaching,' the day of Christ's coming to destroy Jerusalem and the Jewish state. Verse 37: 'For yet a little while, and he who is coming will come, and will not tarry.' James v. 7: 'Wherefore, be patient, brethren, unto the coming of the Lord.' Verse 8: 'Be ye also patient, strengthen your hearts, for the coming of the Lord (to destroy the Jews, your persecutors) draweth nigh.' Verse 9: 'Behold the Judge standeth before the door.' 1 Pet. iv. 7: 'The end of all things (the end of Jerusalem, and of the temple, and of all the Mosaic institutions) hath approached. Be ye therefore sober, and watch unto prayer.' 1 John ii. 18: 'Young children, it is the last hour of the Jewish state; and as ye have heard (from Christ, in his prophecy of the destruction of Jerusalem) that antichrist cometh, so now there are many antichrists, whence we know that it is the last hour of the Jewish state.'

2. "There is another coming of Christ spoken of by the apostles, different likewise from his coming to judge the world, and to put an end to the present state of things; viz. his coming to destroy the *man of sin.* Chap. ii. 8: 'Him the Lord will consume by the breath of his mouth, and will render ineffectual by the bright shining of his coming.' This singular event, which will contribute greatly to the honour of God and the good of his Church, being accomplished by a visible and extraordinary interposition of the power of Christ in the government of the world, is, agreeably to the Scripture style, fitly called *the coming of the Lord,* and *the bright shining of his coming;* but this coming is nowhere in the Scriptures said to be at hand.

3. "There is likewise *a day* or *coming of Christ,* spoken of by Paul, different from his coming to judgment, and from both the former comings; I mean his releasing his people from their present trial by death. 1 Cor i. 8: 'He also will confirm you unto the end, without accusation, in the day of our Lord Jesus Christ.' Phil. i. 6: 'He who hath begun in you a good work, will be completing it until the day of our Lord Jesus Christ.' It is true, the release of Christ's servants from their present trial by death is

2

accomplished, for the most part, by no extraordinary display of his power; yet it is fitly enough called his *day* and *coming*, because by his appointment all men die, and by his power each is carried to his own place after death. Besides, his servants in particular being put on their duty, like soldiers, must remain at their several posts till released by their commander: and when he releases them, he is fitly said to come for that purpose.

4. "Besides all these, there is a day or *coming of the Lord* to judge the world, and to put an end to the present state of things. This coming Christ himself has promised. Matt. xvi. 27: 'The Son of man shall come in the glory of his Father with his holy angels; and then shall he reward every man according to his work.' Now this, being a real, personal appearing of Christ in the body, is, more properly than any other of his comings, called *the day* and *coming of Christ*. And the purposes of it being more important than those of his other comings, the exertions of his power for accomplishing them will be most signal and glorious. Hence this coming is, with great propriety, termed *the revelation of Jesus Christ*, and *the day* of his revelation, *when he shall be glorified in his saints, and admired of all them who believe.*

"Thus it appears that, when the apostles wrote, there were *four* comings of Christ to happen, three of them figurative, but the fourth a real appearance; that these different comings are frequently spoken of in Scripture; and that, although the coming of Christ to destroy Jerusalem, and to establish his everlasting kingdom, be represented by the apostles as then at hand, no passage from their writings can be produced in which his personal appearance to judge the world is said, or even insinuated, to be at hand The truth is, if the different comings of Christ are distinguished as they ought to be, we shall find that the apostles have spoken of each of them according to truth; and that the opinion which some Christians have unadvisedly espoused, to the great discredit of the inspiration of the apostles, has not the least foundation in Scripture."

The epistle naturally divides itself into three parts, and each is contained in a separate chapter.

PART 1. CHAP. I.—Contains the address, and motives of consolation in their afflicted and persecuted state.

PART 2. CHAP. II.—Is partly prophetical, and partly didactic. It contains the doctrine concerning Christ's coming to judgment, and a prophecy concerning some future but great apostasy from the Christian faith.

PART 3. CHAP. III.—Is wholly hortatory; and contains a number of important advices relative to Christian virtues, and a proper behaviour in those situations in life in which it had pleased God to call them.

This is the *shortest* of all St. Paul's espistles to the Churches, but is of very great importance, and in many places very sublime, especially in the second part; and in this there are several very great difficulties, and some things hard to be understood. After all the pains and labour of learned men, it would be hazardous to say, *the meaning of every part is now clearly made out.* What increases the difficulty is, that the apostle refers to some *private communication* with themselves, no part of which is on record, and without which it would require St. Paul's inspiration to be able to fix the sense and meaning of all we find here. May the Father of lights give the reader a wise understanding in all things! Amen.

THE

SECOND EPISTLE OF PAUL THE APOSTLE

TO THE

THESSALONIANS

Chronological Notes relative to this Epistle.

Year of the Constantinopolitan era of the world, or that used by the Byzantine historians, 5560.—Year of the Alexandrian era of the world, 5554.—Year of the Antiochian era of the world, 5544.—Year of the Julian period, 4762.—Year of the world, according to Archbishop Usher, 4056.—Year of the world, according to Eusebius, in his Chronicon, 4280.—Year of the minor Jewish era of the world, or that in common use, 3812.—Year of the Greater Rabbinical era of the world, 4411.—Year from the Flood, according to Archbishop Usher, and the English Bible, 2400.—Year of the Cali yuga, or Indian era of the Deluge, 3154. —Year of the era of Iphitus, or since the first commencement of the Olympic games, 992.—Year of the era of Nabonassar, king of Babylon, 799.—Year of the CCVIIth Olympiad, 4.—Year from the building of Rome, according to Fabius Pictor, 799.—Year from the building of Rome, according to Frontinus, 803.—Year from the building of Rome, according to the Fasti Capitolini, 804.—Year from the building of Rome, according to Varro, which was that most generally used, 805.—Year of the era of the Seleucidæ, 364.—Year of the Cæsarean era of Antioch, 100.—Year of the Julian era, 97.—Year of the Spanish era, 90.—Year from the birth of Jesus Christ according to Archbishop Usher, 56.—Year of the vulgar era of Christ's nativity, 52.—Year of Ventidius Cumanus, governor of the Jews, 4.—Year of Vologesus, king of the Parthians, 3. —Year of Caius Numidius Quadratus, governor of Syria, 2.—Year of Ananias, high priest of the Jews, 8. Year of the Dionysian period, or Easter Cycle, 53.—Year of the Grecian Cycle of nineteen years, or Common Golden Number, 15 ; or the second year after the fifth embolismic.—Year of the Jewish Cycle of nineteen years, 12, or the first after the fourth embolismic.—Year of the Solar Cycle, 5.—Dominical Letters, it being Bissextile, or Leap Year, BA.—Day of the Jewish Passover, according to the Roman computation of time, the Calends of April, i. e. April 1st, which happened in this year on the Jewish Sabbath.—Easter Sunday, April 2.—Epact, or the moon's age on the 22d of March, or the XIth of the Calends of April, 4. —Epact, according to the present mode of computation, or the moon's age on New Year's day, or the Calends of January, 11.—Monthly Epacts, or the moon's age on the Calends of each month respectively, (beginning with January,) 11, 13, 12, 13, 14, 15, 16, 17, 18, 18, 20, 20.—Number of Direction, or the number of days from the twenty-first of March (or the XIIth of the Calends of April) to the Jewish Passover, 10. —Year of Claudius Cæsar, the fifth emperor of the Romans, 12.—Roman Consuls, Publius Cornelius Sylla Faustus, and Lucius Salvius Otho Titianus ; and for the following year, (which is by some supposed to be the date of this epistle,) Decimus Junius Silanus, and Quintus Haterius Antoninus.

CHAPTER I.

The salutation of St. Paul and his companions, 1, 2. The apostle gives thanks to God for their faith, love, and union ; and for their patience under persecutions, 3, 4. Speaks of the coming of our Lord Jesus Christ, the punishment of the ungodly, and the glorification of the righteous, 5–10. Prays that God may count them worthy of their calling, that the name of Jesus may be glorified in them, 11, 12.

A. M. cir. 4056.
A. D. cir. 52.
A. U. C. 805.
Anno Claudii Cæs.
Aug. 12.

PAUL, and ᵃ Silvanus, and Timotheus, unto the Church of the Thessalonians ᵇ in God our Father and the Lord Jesus Christ :

2 ᶜ Grace unto you, and peace, from God our Father and the Lord Jesus Christ.

3 ᵈ We are bound to thank

A. M. cir. 4056.
A. D. cir. 52.
A. U. C. 805.
Anno Claudii Cæs.
Aug. 12.

ᵃ 2 Cor. i. 19.——ᵇ 1 Thess. i. 1.——ᶜ 1 Cor. i. 3.

ᵈ 1 Thess. i. 2, 3 ; iii. 6, 9 ; chap. ii. 13.

NOTES ON CHAP. I.

Verse 1. *Paul, and Silvanus, &c.*] See the notes on 1 Thess. i. 1. This epistle was written a short time after the former ; and as Silas and Timothy were

still at Corinth, the apostle joins their names with his own, as in the former case.

Verse 3. *Your faith groweth exceedingly*] The word ὑπεραυξανει signifies *to grow luxuriantly*, as a good

(36**)

A. M. cir. 4056.
A. D. cir. 52.
A. U. C. 805.
Anno Clau-
dii Cæs.
Aug. 12.

God always for you, brethren, as it is meet, because that your faith groweth exceedingly, and the charity of every one of you all toward each other aboundeth;

4 So that ᶜ we ourselves glory in you in the Churches of God ᶠ for your patience and faith ᵍ in all your persecutions and tribulations that ye endure :

5 *Which is* ʰ a manifest token of the righteous judgment of God, that ye may be counted worthy of the kingdom of God, ⁱ for which ye also suffer :

6 ᵏ Seeing *it is* a righteous thing with God to recompense tribulation to them that trouble you ;

7 And to you who are troubled, ˡ rest with us ; when ᵐ the Lord Jesus shall be revealed from heaven with, ⁿ his mighty angels,

8 ᵒ In flaming fire, ᵖ taking vengeance on them �q that know not God, and ʳ that obey not the Gospel of our Lord Jesus Christ:

9 ˢ Who shall be punished with everlasting destruction from the presence of the Lord, and ᵗ from the glory of his power ;

A. M. cir. 4056.
A. D. cir. 52.
A. U. C. 805.
Anno Clau-
dii Cæs.
Aug. 12.

ᶜ 2 Cor. vii. 14; ix. 2; 1 Thess. ii. 19, 20.——ᶠ 1 Thess. i. 3. ᵍ 1 Thess. ii. 14.——ʰ Phil. i. 28.——ⁱ 1 Thess. ii. 14.——ᵏ Rev. vi. 10.——ˡ Rev. xiv. 13.——ᵐ 1 Thess. iv. 16; Jude 14.——ⁿ Gr. *the angels of his power.*

ᵒ Heb. x. 27; xii. 29; 2 Pet. iii. 7; Rev. xxi. 8.——ᵖ Or, *yielding.*——q Psa. lxxix. 6; 1 Thess. iv. 5.——ʳ Rom. ii. 8.——ˢ Phil. iii. 19; 2 Pet. iii. 7.——ᵗ Deut. xxxiii. 2; Isa. ii. 19; chapter ii. 8.

---

and healthy tree planted in a good soil ; and if a *fruit tree,* bearing an abundance of fruit to compensate the labour of the husbandman. Faith is one of the *seeds* of the kingdom ; this the apostle had *sowed* and *watered,* and God gave an abundant increase. Their faith was *multiplied,* and their love *abounded ;* and this was not the case with some distinguished characters only, it was the case with *every one of them.*

Verse 4. *We ourselves glory in you in the Churches of God*] We hold you up as an example of what the grace of God can produce when communicated to honest and faithful hearts.

For your patience and faith] From Acts xvii. 5, 13, and from 1 Thess. ii. 14, we learn, that the people of Thessalonica had suffered much persecution, both from the *Jews* and *their own countrymen ;* but being thoroughly convinced of the truth of the Gospel, and feeling it to be the power of God unto salvation, no persecution could turn them aside from it. And having suffered for the truth, it was precious to them. Persecution never essentially injured the genuine Church of God.

Verse 5. *A manifest token of the righteous judgment of God*] The persecutions and tribulations which you endure, are a manifest proof that God has judged righteously in calling you Gentiles into his Church ; and these sufferings are also a proof that ye are *called in ;* for they who enter into the kingdom of God go through great tribulation ; your going through that tribulation is a proof that ye are entering in, and God sees it *right* and *just* that ye should be permitted to *suffer* before ye enjoy that endless felicity.

The words, however, may be understood in another sense, and will form this maxim : " The sufferings of the just, and the triumphs of the wicked, in this life, are a sure proof that there will be a future judgment, in which the wicked shall be punished and the righteous rewarded." This maxim is not only true in itself, but it is most likely that this is the apostle's meaning.

That ye may be counted worthy] Your patient endurance of these sufferings is a proof that ye are *rendered meet* for that glory on account of which ye suffer, and, in a true Gospel sense of the word, *worthy*

of that glory ; for he who is a *child of God,* and a *partaker of the Divine nature,* is worthy of God's kingdom, not because he has done any thing to merit it, but because he bears the *image of God ;* and the *image* is that which gives the *title.*

Verse 6. *Seeing* it is *a righteous thing*] Though God neither rewards nor punishes in this life in a general way, yet he often gives proofs of his displeasure, especially against those who persecute his followers. They, therefore, who have given you tribulation, shall have tribulation in recompense.

Verse 7. *And to you who are troubled, rest with us*] And while they have *tribulation,* you shall have that eternal *rest* which remains for the people of God.

When the Lord Jesus shall be revealed] But this fulness of *tribulation* to them, and *rest* to you, shall not take place till the Lord Jesus come to judge the world.

With his mighty angels] The coming of God to judge the world is scarcely ever spoken of in the sacred writings without mentioning the holy angels, who are to accompany him, and to form his court or retinue. See Deut. xxxiii. 2 ; Matt. xxv. 31 ; xvi. 27 ; xxvi. 64 ; Mark viii. 38.

Verse 8. *In flaming fire*] Εν φλογι πυρος· In *thunder and lighting, taking vengeance*—inflicting just punishment *on them that know not God*—the heathen who do not worship the true God, and will not *acknowledge* him, but worship idols ; and on them *that obey not the Gospel*—the Jews, particularly who have rejected the Gospel, and persecuted Christ and his messengers ; and all nominal Christians who, though they believe the Gospel as a revelation from God, yet do not *obey* it as a rule of life.

Verse 9. *Who shall be punished*] What this *everlasting destruction* consists in we cannot tell. It is not *annihilation,* for their *being* continues ; and as the destruction is *everlasting,* it is an eternal *continuance* and *presence* of *substantial evil,* and *absence* of all *good ;* for a part of this punishment consists in being banished from the *presence of the Lord*—excluded from his *approbation,* for ever ; so that the light of his countenance can be no more enjoyed, as there will be

2

A. M. cir. 4056.
A. D. cir. 52.
A. U. C. 805.
Anno Clau-
dii Cæs.
Aug. 12.

10 ^u When he shall come to be glorified in his saints, ^v and to be admired in all them that believe (because our testimony among you was believed) in that day.

11 Wherefore also we pray always for you, that our God would ^w count ^x you worthy of

this calling, and fulfil all the good pleasure of *his* goodness, and ^y the work of faith with power :

A. M. cir. 4056
A. D. cir. 52.
A. U. C. 805.
Anno Clau-
dii Cæs.
Aug. 12.

12 ^z That the name of our Lord Jesus Christ may be glorified in you and ye in him, according to the grace of our God and the Lord Jesus Christ.

---

^u Psa. lxxxix. 7.——^v Psa. lxviii. 35.——^w Or, *vouchsafe.*

^x Ver. 5.——^y 1 Thess. i. 3.——^z 1 Pet. i. 7; iv. 14.

---

an eternal impossibility of ever being reconciled to him.

The glory of his power] Never to see the face of God throughout eternity is a heart-rending, soul-appalling thought ; and to be *banished* from the *glory of his power*, that power the *glory* of which is peculiarly manifested in *saving the lost* and *glorifying the faithful*, is what cannot be reflected on without confusion and dismay. But this must be the lot of all *who acknowledge not God, and obey not the Gospel of our Lord Jesus Christ.*

Verse 10. *When he shall come to be glorified in his saints*] As the grace of God is peculiarly glorified in saving sinners and making them into *saints*, this gracious *power* will be particularly manifested in the great day, when countless millions will appear before that throne who have come out of great tribulation, and have washed their robes and made them white in the blood of the Lamb.

And to be admired] Θαυμασθηναι· *To be wondered at among* and on the account of *all them that believe.* Much as true believers *admire* the perfections of the Redeemer of mankind, and much as they *wonder* at his amazing condescension in becoming man, and dying for the sins of the world ; all their present amazement and wonder will be as nothing when compared with what they shall feel when they come to see him *in all his glory*, the glory that he had with the Father before the world was. In reference to this we may apply those words of St. John : " Beloved, now are we the sons of God ; and it doth not yet appear what we shall be : but we know that when he shall appear we shall be like him ; for we shall see him as he is." 1 John, chap. iii. 2.

Instead of τοις πιστινουσιν, *them that believe*, τοις πιστευσασιν, *them that have believed*, is the reading of ABCDEF, many others, the later *Syriac, Slavonic, Vulgate,* and *Itala*, with most of the *Greek fathers.* This reading is undoubtedly genuine.

Because our testimony—was believed in that day.] The members of this sentence seem to have been strangely transposed. I believe it should be read thus : " In that day, when he shall come to be glorified in his saints, and admired among all them that have believed ; for our testimony was believed among you." The Thessalonians had credited what the apostles had said and written, not only concerning Jesus Christ in general, but concerning the day of judgment in particular.

Verse 11. *We pray—that our God would count you worthy*] It is our earnest prayer that God would *make you worthy*, αξιωση, afford those continual supplies of grace by his Holy Spirit, without which you

cannot adorn your holy vocation ; you are called into the Christian Church, and, to be proper members of this Church, you must be members of the mystical *body* of Christ ; and this implies that you should be holy, as he who has called you is holy.

Fulfil all the good pleasure of his goodness] 1. The goodness of God—his own innate eternal kindness, has led him to call you into this state of salvation. 2. It is the *pleasure* of that goodness to save you unto eternal life. 3. It is the *good pleasure ;* nothing can please God more than your receiving and retaining his utmost salvation. 4. It is *all* the good pleasure of his goodness thus to save you ; this he has amply proved by sending his Son to die for you, *beyond* which gift he has none greater. In this, all the good pleasure of his goodness is astonishingly manifested. 5. And if you be faithful to his grace, he will *fulfil*—completely accomplish, all the good pleasure of his goodness in you ; which goodness is to be apprehended and is to work by *faith*, the *power* of which must come from him, though the *act* or exercise of that power must be of yourselves ; but the very *power* to believe affords *excitement* to the exercise of faith.

Verse 12. *That the name of our Lord*] This is the great *end* of your Christian calling, that Jesus who hath died for you may have his *passion* and *death* magnified in your *life* and *happiness ;* that ye may show forth the virtues of him who called you from darkness into his marvellous light.

And ye in him] That his glorious excellence may be seen *upon you ;* that ye may be *adorned* with the graces of his Spirit, as he is glorified by your salvation from all sin.

According to the grace] That your salvation may be such as God requires, and such as is worthy of his grace to communicate. God saves as becomes God to save ; and thus the dignity of his nature is seen in the excellence and glory of his work.

1. IT is an awful consideration to the people of the world, that persecutions and afflictions should be the lot of the true Church, and should be the proof of its being such ; because this shows more than any thing else the *desperate state* of mankind, their total enmity to God ; they persecute, not because the followers of God have done or can do them hurt, but they persecute because they have not the Spirit of Christ in them ! Men may amuse themselves by arguing against the doctrine of *original sin*, or the *total depravity* of the soul of man ; but while there is religious persecution in the world, there is the most absolute disproof of all their arguments. Nothing but a

2

heart *wholly alienated from God* could ever devise the persecution or maltreatment of a man, for no other cause but that he has given himself up to glorify God with his body and spirit, which are his.

2. The *everlasting destruction* of the ungodly is a subject that should be continually placed before the eyes of men by the preachers of the Gospel. How shall a man be induced to take measures to escape a danger of the existence of which he is not convinced? Show him the *hell* which the justice of God has lighted up for the devil and his angels, and in which all Satan's children and followers must have their eternal portion. All the perfections of God require that he should *render to every man his due.* And what is the *due* of a sinner or a persecutor, of one who is a *determinate enemy to God,* goodness, and *good men?* Why, *everlasting destruction* from the presence of the Lord and the glory of his power. And if God did not award this to such persons, he could not be the *God of justice.*

3. The grand object of God in giving his Gospel to mankind is *to save them from their sins,* make them like himself, and take them to his eternal glory. He saves *according* to the *measure* of his eternal good-

ness; the scanty salvation contended for and expected by the generality of Christians, it would be dishonourable to God to administer. He saves *according to his grace.* His own eternal goodness and holiness is the *measure* of his salvation to man; not the *creeds* and *expectations* of any class of Christians. To be saved at all, we must not only be saved in God's *way,* and upon his own *terms,* but also *according* to his own *measure.* He who is not filled with the *fulness* of God cannot expect the *glory* of God.

4. Another proof of the fall and degeneracy of men is, their general enmity to the *doctrine* of *holiness;* they cannot bear the thought of being sanctified through body, soul, and spirit, so as to perfect holiness in the fear of God. A spurious kind of Christianity is gaining ground in the world. Weakness, doubtfulness, littleness of faith, consciousness of inward corruptions, and sinful infirmities of different kinds, are by some considered the highest proofs of a *gracious state;* whereas in the primitive Church they would have been considered as evidences that the persons in question had received just light enough to show them their wretchedness and danger, but not the healing virtue of the blood of Christ.

CHAPTER II.

He exhorts the Thessalonians to stand fast in the faith, and not to be alarmed at the rumours they heard concerning the sudden coming of Christ, 1, 2. Because, previously to this coming, there would be a great apostasy from the true faith, and a manifestation of a son of perdition, of whose unparalleled presumption he gives an awful description; as well as of his pernicious success among men, and the means which he would use to deceive and pervert the world; and particularly those who do not receive the love of the truth, but have pleasure in unrighteousness, 3-12. He thanks God for their steadfastness; shows the great privileges to which they were called; and prays that they may be comforted and established in every good word and work, 13-17.

A. M. cir. 4056.
A. D. cir. 52.
A. U. C. 805.
Anno Claudii Cæs.
Aug. 12.

NOW we beseech you, brethren, [a] by the coming of our Lord Jesus Christ, [b] and *by* our gathering together unto him,

2 [c] That ye be not soon shaken in mind, or be troubled, neither by spirit, nor by word, nor by letter as from us, as

A. M. cir. 4056.
A. D. cir. 52.
A. U. C. 805.
Anno Claudii Cæs.
Aug. 12.

[a] 1 Thess. iv. 16.——[b] Matt. xxiv. 31; Mark xiii. 27; 1 Thess. iv. 17.——[c] Matthew xxiv. 4; Ephesians v. 6; 1 John iv. 1.

NOTES ON CHAP. II.

Verse 1. *We beseech you—by the coming of our Lord*] It is evident that the Thessalonians, incited by deceived or false teachers, had taken a wrong meaning out of the words of the first epistle, chap. iv. 15, &c., concerning the *day of judgment;* and were led then to conclude that that day was *at hand;* and this had produced great confusion in the Church: to correct this mistake, the apostle sent them this second letter, in which he shows that this day must be necessarily *distant,* because a great work is to be done previously to its appearing.

Of the day of general judgment he had spoken before, and said that it should *come as a thief in the night,* i. e. when not expected; but he did not attempt to fix the time, nor did he insinuate that it was either *near at hand,* or *far off.* Now, however, he shows that it must necessarily be far off, because of the great transactions which must take place before it can come.

Verse 2. *Be not soon shaken in mind*] Απο του νοος· *From the mind;* i. e. that they should retain the persuasion they had of the truths which he had before delivered to them; that they should still hold the same opinions, and hold fast the doctrines which they had been taught.

Neither by spirit] Any pretended *revelation.*

Nor by word] Any thing which any person may profess to have heard the apostle speak.

Nor by letter] Either the former one which he had sent, some passages of which have been misconceived and misconstrued; or by any other letter, *as from us* —pretending to have been written by us, the apostles, containing predictions of this kind. There is a diversity of opinion among critics concerning this last clause, some supposing that it refers simply to the *first epistle;* others supposing that a *forged epistle* is intended. I have joined the two senses.

The word σαλευθναι, *to be shaken,* signifies to be

A. M. cir. 4056. A. D. cir. 52. A. U. C. 805. Anno Claudii Cæs. Aug. 12.	that the day of Christ is at hand. 3 ^d Let no man deceive you by any means : for *that day shall not come*, ^e except there come a falling away first, and ^f that man of sin be revealed, ^g the son of perdition ; 4 Who opposeth and ^h exalteth himself

ⁱ above all that is called God, or that is worshipped ; so that he, as God, sitteth in the temple of God, showing himself that he is God. 5 Remember ye not, that, when I was yet with you, I told you these things ? 6 And now ye know what ^k withholdeth, that he might be revealed in his time.	A. M. cir. 4056. A. D. cir. 52. A. U. C. 805. Anno Claudii Cæs. Aug. 12.

^d Matt. xxiv. 4 ; Eph. v. 6.——^e 1 Tim. iv. 1.——^f Dan. vii. 25 ; 1 John ii. 18 ; Revelation xiii. 11, &c. ; see 1 Mac. ii. 48, 62.

^g John xvii. 12.——^h Isa. xiv. 13 ; Ezek. xxviii. 2, 6, 9 ; Dan. vii. 25 ; xi. 36 ; Revelations xiii. 6.——ⁱ 1 Cor. viii. 5.——^k Or, holdeth.

agitated as a ship at sea in a storm, and strongly marks the confusion and distress which the Thessalonians had felt in their false apprehension of this coming of Christ.

As that the day of Christ is at hand.] In the preface to this epistle I have given a general view of the meaning of the phrase *the coming of Christ*. Now the question is : Whether does the apostle mean, the coming of Christ to execute judgment upon the *Jews*, and destroy their *polity*, or his coming, at the end of time, to *judge the world?* There are certainly many expressions in the following verses that may be applied indifferently to *either*, and some seem to apply to the *one*, and not to the *other;* and yet the whole can scarcely be so interpreted as to suit *any one* of these *comings* exclusively. This is precisely the case with the predictions of our Lord relative to these great events; one is used to point out and illustrate the other. On this ground I am led to think that the apostle, in the following confessedly obscure words, has both these in view, speaking of none of them exclusively; for it is the custom of the inspired penmen, or rather of that Spirit by which they spoke, to point out as *many* certain events by one prediction as it was possible to do, and to choose the figures, metaphors, and similes accordingly ; and thus, from the beginning, God has pointed out the things that *were not* by the things that *then existed*, making the one the types or significations of the other. As the apostle spoke by the same Spirit, he most probably followed the same plan ; and thus the following prophecy is to be interpreted and understood,

Verse 3. *Except there come a falling away first*] We have the original word αποστασια in our word *apostasy;* and by this term we understand a *dereliction of the essential principles of religious truth—* either a *total abandonment* of Christianity itself, or such a *corruption* of its doctrines as renders the whole system completely inefficient to salvation. But what *this* apostasy means is a question which has not yet, and perhaps never will be, answered to general satisfaction. At present I shall content myself with making a few literal remarks on this obscure prophecy, and afterwards give the opinions of learned men on its principal parts.

That man of sin] Ὁ ανθρωπος της ἁμαρτιας· The same as the Hebrew expresses by און איש *ish aven*, and בליעל איש *ish beliyaal;* the perverse, obstinate, and iniquitous man. It is worthy of remark that,

among the rabbins, *Samael*, or the devil, is called בליעל ואיש און איש *ish beliyaal veish aven*, the man of Belial, and the man of iniquity ; and that these titles are given to *Adam* after his fall.

The son of perdition] Ὁ υἱος της απωλειας· *The son of destruction;* the same epithet that is given to Judas Iscariot, John xvii. 12, where see the note. *The son of perdition*, and the *man of sin*, or, as some excellent MSS. aud versions, with several of the fathers, read, ανθρωπος της ανομιας, *the lawless man*, see ver. 8, must mean the same person or thing. It is also remarkable that the wicked Jews are styled by Isaiah, chap. i. 4, משחיתם בנים *benim mashchithim*, "children of perdition ;" persons who *destroy themselves* and *destroy others*.

Verse 4. *Who opposeth and exalteth*] He *stands against* and *exalts* himself *above* all Divine authority, and above every *object of adoration*, and every *institution* relative to Divine worship, σεβασμα, himself being the *source*, whence must originate all the *doctrines* of religion, and all its *rites* and *ceremonies;* so that *sitting in the temple of God*—having the *highest place* and *authority* in the *Christian Church*, he acts *as God*—taking upon himself God's titles and attributes, and arrogating to himself the authority that belongs to the Most High.

The words ως Θεον, *as God*, are wanting in ABD, many others, Erpen's *Arabic*, the *Coptic, Sahidic, Æthiopic, Armenian*, the *Vulgate*, some copies of the *Itala*, and the chief of the Greek *fathers*. *Griesbach* has left them out of the text, and *Professor White* says, *Certissime delenda;* "They should most certainly be erased," There is indeed no evidence of their being authentic, and the text reads much better without them : *So that he sitteth in the temple of God*, &c.

Verse 5. *I told you these things*] In several parts of this description of the *man of sin*, the apostle alludes to a conversation which had taken place between him and the members of this Church when he was at Thessalonica ; and this one circumstance will account for much of the *obscurity* that is in these verses. Besides, the apostle appears to speak with great *caution*, and does not at all wish to *publish* what he had communicated to them ; the *hints* which he drops were sufficient to call the whole to their remembrance.

Verse 6. *And now ye know what withholdeth*] I told you this among other things ; I informed you what it was that *prevented* this man of sin, this son of perdition, from revealing himself fully,

2

A. M. cir. 4056.
A. D. cir. 52.
A. U. C. 805.
Anno Claudii Cæs.
Aug. 12.

7 For [1] the mystery of iniquity doth already work : only he who now letteth *will let*, until he be taken out of the way.

8 And then shall that Wicked be revealed, [m] whom the Lord shall consume [n] with the spirit of his mouth, and shall destroy [o] with the brightness of his coming :

9 *Even him*, whose coming is [p] after the working of Satan, with all power and [q] signs and lying wonders,

10 And with all deceivableness of unrighteousness in [r] them that perish ; because they

received not the love of the truth, that they might be saved.

11 And [s] for this cause God shall send them strong delusion, [t] that they should believe a lie :

12 That they all might be damned who believed not the truth, but [u] had pleasure in unrighteousness.

13 But [v] we are bound to give thanks alway to God for you, brethren, beloved of the Lord, because God [w] hath [x] from the beginning chosen you to salvation [y] through sanctification of the Spirit and belief of the truth ;

A. M. cir. 4056.
A. D. cir. 52.
A. U. C. 805.
Anno Claudii Cæs.
Aug. 12.

---

[1] 1 John ii. 18 ; iv. 3.——[m] Dan. vii. 10, 11.——[n] Job iv. 9 ; Isa. xi. 4 ; Hos. vi. 5 ; Rev. ii. 16 ; xix. 15, 20, 21.——[o] Chap. i. 8, 9 ; Hebrews x. 27.——[p] John viii. 41 ; Eph. ii. 2 ; Rev. xviii. 23. [q] See Deut. xiii. 1 ; Matt. xxiv. 24 ; Rev. xiii. 13 ; xix. 21.

[r] 2 Cor. ii. 15 ; iv. 3.——[s] Rom. i. 24, &c. ; see 1 Kings xxii. 22 ; Ezek. xiv. 9.——[t] Matt. xxiv, 5, 11.; 1 Tim. iv. 1.——[u] Rom. i. 32.——[v] Chap. i. 3.——[w] 1 Thess. i. 4.——[x] Eph. i. 4.——[y] Luke i. 75 ; 1 Pet. i. 2.

Verse 7. *For the mystery of iniquity doth already work*] There is a system of corrupt doctrine, which will lead to the general apostasy, already in existence, but it is a *mystery*; it is as yet *hidden*; it dare not show itself, because of that which *hindereth* or *withholdeth*. But when that which now *restraineth* shall be taken out of the way, then shall that wicked one be revealed—it will then be manifest who he is, and what he is. See the observations at the end of this chapter.

Verse 8. *Whom the Lord shall consume*] He shall *blast* him so, that he shall *wither* and *die away*; and this shall be done by the *spirit of his mouth*—the *words of eternal life*, the *true doctrine of the Gospel of Jesus*; this shall be the instrument used to destroy this man of sin : therefore it is evident his death will not be a *sudden* but a *gradual* one ; because it is by the *preaching of the truth* that he is to be exposed, overthrown, and finally destroyed.

The brightness of his coming] This may refer to that full manifestation of the truth which had been obscured and kept under by the *exaltation of this man of sin.*

Verse 9. *Whose coming is after the working of Satan*] The operation of God's Spirit sends his messengers ; the operation of Satan's spirit sends his emissaries. The one comes κατ᾽ ενεργειαν του θεου, *after* or *according to the energy* or inward powerful *working of God* ; the other comes κατ᾽ ενεργειαν του Σατανα, according to the energy or inward working of Satan.

With all power] Πασῃ δυναμει· All kinds of miracles, like the Egyptian magicians ; *and signs and lying wonders :* the word *lying* may be applied to the whole of these ; they were *lying* miracles, *lying* signs, and *lying* wonders ; only *appearances* of what was *real*, and done to give credit to his presumption and imposture. Whereas God sent his messengers with *real* miracles, *real* signs, and *real* wonders ; such Satan cannot produce.

Verse 10. *And with all deceivableness of unrighteousness*] With every art that cunning can invent and unrighteousness suggest, in order to delude and deceive.

In them that perish] Εν τοις απολλυμενοις· Among

them that are destroyed ; and they are destroyed and perish because they *would not receive the love of the truth, that they might be saved.* So they perish because they obstinately refuse to be saved, and receive a *lie* in preference to the *truth.* This has been true of all the Jews from the days of the apostle until *now.*

Verse 11. *God shall send them strong delusion*] For this very cause, that they *would not receive the love of the truth*, but *had pleasure in unrighteousness*, therefore God permits *strong delusion* to occupy their minds ; so that they believe a *lie* rather than the truth, prefer false apostles and their erroneous doctrines to the pure truths of the Gospel, brought to them by the well-accredited messengers of God ; being ever ready to receive any false Messiah, while they systematically and virulently reject the true one.

Verse 12. *That they all might be damned*] Ἵνα κριθωσι· So that they may all be condemned who believed *not the truth* when it was proclaimed to them ; *but took pleasure in unrighteousness*, preferring that to the way of holiness. Their condemnation was the effect of their refusal to believe the truth ; and they refused to believe it because they loved their sins. For a farther and more pointed illustration of the preceding verses, see the conclusion of this chapter.

Verses 13 and 14. *God hath from the beginning chosen you to salvation, &c.*] In your *calling* God has shown the *purpose* that he had formed from the *beginning*, to call the Gentiles to the same privileges with the Jews, not through *circumcision*, and the observance of the Mosaic law, but by *faith* in Christ Jesus ; but this simple way of salvation referred to the same *end* —holiness, without which no man, whether Jew or Gentile, can see the Lord.

Let us observe the order of Divine grace in this business : 1. They were to hear the *truth*—the doctrines of the Gospel. 2. They were to *believe* this *truth* when they heard it preached. 3. They were to receive the *Spirit* of God in believing the truth. 4. That Spirit was to *sanctify* their souls—produce an inward holiness, which was to lead to all outward conformity to God. 5. All this constituted their *salvation*—their being fitted for the inheritance among

2

A. M. cir. 4056.
A. D. cir. 52.
A. U. C. 805.
Anno Clau-
dii Cæs.
Aug. 12.

14 Whereunto he called you by our Gospel, to ᶻ the obtaining of the glory of our Lord Jesus Christ.

15 Therefore, brethren, ᵃ stand fast, and hold ᵇ the traditions which ye have been taught, whether by word or our epistle.

16 ᶜ Now our Lord Jesus Christ himself, and God, even our Father, ᵈ which hath loved us, and hath given *us* everlasting consolation and ᵉ good hope through grace,

17 Comfort your hearts, ᶠ and stablish you in every good word and work.

A. M. cir. 4056.
A. D. cir. 52.
A. U. C. 805.
Anno Clau-
dii Cæs.
Aug. 12.

ᶻ John xvii. 22; 1 Thess. ii. 12; 1 Pet. v. 10.——ᵃ 1 Cor. xvi. 13; Phil. iv. 1.——ᵇ 1 Cor. xi. 2; chap. iii. 6.

ᶜ Chap. i. 1, 2.——ᵈ 1 John iv 10; Rev. i. 5.——ᵉ 1 Pet. i. 3. ᶠ 1 Cor. i. 8; 1 Thess. iii. 13; 1 Pet. v. 10.

---

the saints in light. 6. They were to *obtain the glory of our Lord Jesus Christ*—that state of felicity for which they were fitted, by being saved here from their sins, and by being sanctified by the Spirit of God.

Verse 15. *Therefore, brethren, stand fast*] Their obtaining eternal glory depended on their *faithfulness* to the grace of God; for this *calling* did not necessarily and irresistibly lead to faith; nor their faith to the sanctification of the spirit; nor their sanctification of the spirit to the glory of our Lord Jesus. Had they not *attended* to the *calling*, they could not have *believed*; had they not *believed*, they could not have been *sanctified*; had they not been *sanctified* they could not have been *glorified*. All these things depended on each other; they were *stages* of the great journey; and at any of these stages they might have halted, and never finished their Christian race.

Hold the traditions which ye have been taught] The word παραδοσις, which we render *tradition*, signifies any thing *delivered* in the way of *teaching*; and here most obviously means the *doctrines* delivered by the apostle to the Thessalonians; whether in his *preaching, private conversation*, or by these *epistles*; and particularly the *first epistle*, as the apostle here states. Whatever these traditions were, as to their matter, they were a *revelation from God*; for they came by men who *spake* and *acted* under the *inspiration of the Holy Spirit*; and on this ground the passage here can never with any propriety be brought to support the unapostolical and anti-apostolical traditions of the Romish Church; those being matters which are, confessedly, not taken from either Testament, nor were spoken either by a *prophet* or an *apostle*.

Verse 16. *Now our Lord Jesus*] As all your *grace* came from God through Christ, so the *power* that is necessary to strengthen and confirm you unto the end must come in the same way.

Everlasting consolation] Παρακλησιν αιωνιαν· The glad tidings of the Gospel, and the *comfort* which ye have received through believing; a gift which God had in his *original* purpose, in reference to the Gentiles; a purpose which has respected *all times* and *places*, and which shall continue to the *conclusion* of time; for the Gospel is *everlasting*, and shall not be superseded by any other dispensation. It is the *last* and *best* which God has provided for man; and it is *good tidings, everlasting consolation*—a complete system of complete peace and happiness. The words may also refer to the happiness which the believing Thessalonians then possessed.

And good hope through grace] The *hope* of the Gospel was the *resurrection of the body*, and the final

glorification of it and the soul throughout eternity. This was the good hope which the Thessalonians had; not a hope that they *should be pardoned* or *sanctified*, &c. Pardon and holiness they *enjoyed*, therefore they were no objects of *hope*; but the resurrection of the body and eternal glory were necessarily *future*; these they had in expectation; these they hoped for; and, through the *grace* which they had already received they had a *good hope*—a well-grounded expectation, of this glorious state.

Verse 17. *Comfort your hearts*] Keep your souls ever under the influence of his Holy Spirit: *and stablish you*—confirm and strengthen you in your *belief* of every *good word* or doctrine, which we have delivered unto you; and in the *practice* of every *good work*, recommended and enjoined by the doctrines of the Gospel.

It is not enough that we *believe* the truth; we must *love* the truth. Antinomianism says: " Believe the doctrines, and ye are safe." The testimony borne by the Gospel is: *Believe, love, obey:* none of these can subsist without the other. The faith of a devil may exist without loving obedience; but the faith of a true believer *worketh by love*; and this faith and love have not respect to some *one* commandment, but to all; for God writes his *whole law* on the heart of every genuine Christian, and gives him that *love* which is the *fulfilling of the law*.

THE reader will have observed that, in going through this chapter, while examining the import of every leading word, I have avoided *fixing* any *specific meaning* to terms: the *apostasy* or *falling away*; the *man of sin; son of perdition; him who letteth* or *withholdeth*, &c. The reason is, I have found it extremely difficult to fix any sense to my own satisfaction; and it was natural for me to think that, if I could not satisfy myself, it was not likely I could satisfy my readers. But, as something should be said relative to the *per sons* and *things* intended by the apostle, I choose to give rather what others have said, than attempt any new mode of interpretation. The great *variety* of explanations given by wise and learned men only prove the difficulty of the place.

1. The general run of *Protestant* writers understand the whole as referring to the *popes* and *Church* of *Rome*, or the whole system of the *papacy*. 2. *Others* think that the defection of the *Jewish nation*, from their allegiance to the Roman emperor, is what is to be understood by the *apostasy* or *falling off*; and that all the other terms refer to the *destruction of Jerusalem*. 3. The *fathers* understood the *Antichrist* to be

2

intended, but of this person they seem to have formed no specific idea. 4. Dr. *Hammond* refers the *apostasy* to the defection of the primitive Christians to the *Gnostic heresy ;* and supposes that, by the *man of sin* and *son of perdition, Simon Magus* is meant. 5. *Grotius* applies the whole to *Caius Cæsar.* 6. *Wetstein* applies the *apostasy* to the rebellion and slaughter of the three princes that were proclaimed by the Roman armies, previously to the reign of *Vespasian ;* and supposes *Titus* and the *Flavian family* to be intended by the *man of sin* and *son of perdition.* 7. *Schoettgen* contends strongly that the whole refers to the case of the Jews, incited to rebellion by the scribes and Pharisees, and to the utter and final destruction of the *rabbinic* and *Pharisaic system ;* and thinks he finds something in their spirit and conduct, and in what has happened to them, to illustrate every word in this prophecy. Dr. *Whitby* is nearly of the same sentiments. 8. *Calmet* follows, in the main, the interpretation given by the ancient *fathers ;* and wonders at the want of candour in the Protestant writers, who have gleaned up every abusive tale against the bishops and Church of Rome ; and asks them, would they be willing that the Catholics should credit all the aspersions cast on Protestantism by its enemies ? 9. Bishop *Newton* has examined the whole prophecy with his usual skill and judgment. The sum of what he says, as abridged by Dr. Dodd, I think it right to subjoin. The principal part of modern commentators follow his steps. He applies the whole to the *Romish Church :* the *apostasy,* its defection from the pure doctrines of Christianity ; and the *man of sin, &c.,* the general succession of the popes of Rome. But we must hear him for himself, as he takes up the subject in the order of the verses.

Verses 3, 4. *For that day shall not come, except, &c.*—"The day of Christ shall not come except there come the apostasy first." The apostasy here described is plainly not of a civil but of a religious nature ; not a revolt from the government, but a defection from the true religion and worship. In the original, it is *the apostasy,* with an article to give it an emphasis ; the article being added signifies, " that famous and beforementioned prophecy." So likewise is the *man of sin* with the like article, and the like emphasis. If, then, the notion of the *man of sin* be derived from any ancient prophet, it must be derived from Dan. vii. 25, and xi. 36. Any man may be satisfied that St. Paul alluded to Daniel's description, because he has not only borrowed the same ideas, but has even adopted some of the phrases and expressions. *The man of sin* may signify either a single man, or a succession of men ; a succession of men being meant in Daniel, it is probable that the same was intended here also. It is the more probable, because a single man appears hardly sufficient for the work here assigned ; and it is agreeable to the phraseology of Scripture, and especially to that of the prophets, to speak of a body or number of men, under the character of one : thus, *a king,* Dan. vii. 8 ; Rev. xvii., is used for a succession of kings. The man of sin being to be expressed from Dan. vii. 24, according to the Greek translation, *He shall exceed in evil all that went before him ;* and he may fulfil the character either by promoting wicked-

ness in general, or by advancing *idolatry* in particular, as the word sin signifies frequently in Scripture. The *son of perdition* is also the denomination of the traitor Judas, John xvii. 12, which implies that the *man of sin* should be, like Judas, a false apostle ; like him, betray Christ ; and, like him, be devoted to destruction. *Who opposeth, &c.,* is manifestly copied from Daniel, *He shall exalt himself, &c.* The features exactly resemble each other : *He opposeth and exalteth himself above all ;* or, according to the Greek, *above every one that is called God,* or *that is worshipped.* The Greek word for *worshipped* is σεβασμα, alluding to the Greek title of the Roman emperors, σεβαστος, which signifies *august* or *venerable. He shall oppose ;* for the prophets speak of things future as present ; he shall oppose and exalt himself, not only above inferior magistrates, (who are sometimes called *gods* in holy writ,) but even above the greatest emperors ; and shall arrogate to himself Divine honours. *So that he, as God, sitteth in the temple, &c.* By the temple of God the apostle could not well mean the temple of Jerusalem ; because that, he knew, would be destroyed within a few years. After the death of Christ the temple of Jerusalem is never called by the apostles the *temple of God ;* and if at any time they make mention of *the house* or *temple of God,* they mean the Church in general, or every particular believer. Whoever will consult 1 Cor. iii. 16, 17 ; 2 Cor. vi. 16 ; 1 Tim. iii. 15 ; Rev. iii. 12 ; will want no examples to prove that, under the Gospel dispensation, the *temple of God* is the Church of Christ ; and the *man of sin sitting* implies his ruling and presiding there ; and *sitting there as God* implies his claiming Divine authority in things spiritual as well as temporal ; and *showing himself that he is God,* implies his doing it with ostentation.

Verses 5, 6, 7. *Remember ye not, &c.*—The apostle thought it part of his duty, as he made it a part of his preaching and doctrine, to forewarn his new converts of the grand apostasy that would infect the Church, even while he was at Thessalonica. From these verses it appears that *the man of sin* was not then revealed ; *his time* was not yet come, or the season of his manifestation. *The mystery of iniquity was indeed already working ;* the seeds of corruption were sown, but they were not grown up to maturity ; the *man of sin* was yet hardly conceived in the womb ; it must be some time before he could be brought forth ; there was some obstacle that hindered his appearing. What this was we cannot determine with absolute certainty at so great a distance of time ; but if we may rely upon the concurrent testimony of the fathers, it was the Roman empire. Most probably it was somewhat relating to the higher powers, because the apostle observes such caution ; he mentioned it in discourse, but would not commit it to writing.

Verse 8. *Then shall that Wicked be revealed.*— When the obstacle, mentioned in the preceding verse, should be removed, *then shall that wicked, &c.* Nothing can be plainer than that the lawless, (ὁ ανομος,) as the Greek signifies, *the wicked one,* here mentioned, and the *man of sin,* must be one and the same person. The apostle was speaking before of what *hindered* that he should *be revealed,* and would continue to hinder it till it was taken away; *and then the wicked one, &c.* Not that he should be consumed immediately after he was revealed. But the apostle, to comfort the Thessalonians, no sooner mentions his revelation than he foretells also his destruction, even before he describes his other qualifications. His other qualifications should have been described first, in order of time; but the apostle hastens to what was first and warmest in his thoughts and wishes: *Whom the Lord shall consume, &c.* If these two clauses refer to two distinct and different events, the meaning manifestly is, that the Lord Jesus shall gradually consume him with the free preaching and publication of his word; and shall utterly destroy him at his second coming, in the glory of his Father, with all the holy angels. If these two clauses relate to one and the same event, it is a pleonasm very usual in the sacred, as well as other oriental writings; and the purport plainly is, that the Lord Jesus shall destroy him with the greatest facility, *when he shall be revealed from heaven*, as the apostle has expressed it in the preceding chapter.

Verses 9–12. *Whose coming is after, &c.*—The apostle was eager to foretell the destruction of the man of sin; and for this purpose having broken in upon his subject, he now returns to it again, and describes the other qualifications by which this wicked one should advance and establish himself in the world. He should rise to credit and authority by the most diabolical methods; should pretend to supernatural powers; and boast of revelations, visions, and miracles, false in themselves, and applied to promote false doctrines. Verse 9. He should likewise practise all other wicked acts of deceit; should be guilty of the most impious frauds and impositions upon mankind; but should prevail only among those who are destitute of a sincere affection for the truth; whereby they might attain eternal salvation. Verse 10. And indeed it is a just and righteous judgment of God, to give *them* over to vanities and lies in this world, and to condemnation in the next, who have no regard to truth and virtue, but delight in falsehood and wickedness; ver. 11, 12.

Upon this survey there appears little room to doubt of the genuine sense and meaning of the passage. The Thessalonians, as we have seen from some expressions in the former epistle, were alarmed as if the end of the world was at hand. The apostle, to correct their mistake and dissipate their fears, assures them that a great apostasy, or defection of the Christians from the true faith and worship, must happen before the coming of Christ. This apostasy all the concurrent marks and characters will justify us in charging upon the Church of Rome. The true Christian worship is the worship of *the one only God, through the one only Mediator, the man Christ Jesus*; and from this worship the Church of Rome has most notoriously departed, by substituting other mediators, and invocating and adoring saints and angels, nothing is apostasy, if idolatry be not. And are not the members of the Church of Rome guilty of idolatry in the worship of images, in the adoration of the host, in the invocation of angels and saints, and in the oblation of prayers and praises to the Virgin Mary, as much or more than to God blessed for ever! This is the grand corruption of the Christian Church; this is the *apostasy*, as it is emphatically

called, and deserves to be called; which was not only predicted by St. Paul, but by the Prophet Daniel likewise. If the apostasy be rightly charged upon the Church of Rome, it follows of consequence that the *man of sin* is the pope; not meaning any pope in particular, but *the pope* in general, as the chief head and supporter of this apostasy. He is properly *the man of sin*, not only on account of the scandalous lives of many popes, but by reason of their most scandalous doctrines and principles; dispensing with the most necessary duties; and granting, or rather selling, pardons and indulgences to the most abominable crimes. Or, if by sin be meant *idolatry* in particular, as in the Old Testament, it is evident how he has perverted the worship of God to superstition and idolatry of the grossest kind. He also, like the false apostle, Judas, is *the son of perdition*; whether actively, as being the cause of destruction to others; or passively, as being devoted to destruction himself. *He opposeth*—he is the great adversary of God and man; persecuting and destroying, by *croisades*, inquisitions, and massacres, those Christians who prefer the word of God to the authority of men. The *heathen emperor* of Rome may have slain his thousands of innocent Christians; but the *Christian bishop* of Rome has slain his ten thousands. *He exalteth himself above all that is called God, or is worshipped*—not only above inferior magistrates, but likewise above bishops and primates; not only above bishops and primates, but likewise above kings and emperors; deposing some, obliging them to kiss his toe, to hold his stirrup, treading even upon the neck of a king, and kicking off the imperial crown with his foot; nay, not only kings and emperors, but likewise above Christ and God himself; *making even the word of God of none effect by his traditions*—forbidding what God has commanded; as marriage, the use of the Scriptures, &c.; and also commanding or allowing what God has forbidden, as idolatry, persecution, &c. *So that he, as God, sitteth in the temple of God, &c.*; he is therefore in profession a Christian, and a Christian bishop. *His sitting in the temple of God* implies plainly his having a seat or *cathedra* in the Christian Church; and he sitteth there *as God*, especially at his inauguration, when he sits upon the high altar in St. Peter's church, and makes the table of the Lord his footstool, and in that position receives adoration. At all times he exercises Divine authority in the Church, *showing himself that he is God*—affecting Divine titles, and asserting that his decrees are of the same or greater authority than the word of God. So that the pope is evidently, according to the titles given him in the public decretals, *The God upon earth*; at least there is no one, like him, *who exalteth himself above every god*; no one, like him, *who sitteth as God in the temple of God, showing himself that he is God*. The foundations of popery were laid in the apostle's days, but of *which* the superstructure was raised by degrees; and several ages passed before the building was completed, and *the man of sin revealed* in full perfection. The tradition that generally prevailed was, that *that which hindered* was the Roman empire: this tradition might have been derived even from the apostle himself; and therefore the primitive Christians, in the public offices of the Church, prayed for its peace and welfare, as knowing that, when the Roman empire should be dissolved and broken in pieces, the empire of *the man of sin* would be raised upon its ruins. In the same proportion as the power of the empire decreased, the authority of the Church increased, and the latter at the expense and ruin of the former; till at length the pope grew up above all, and the *wicked*, or *lawless one*, was fully manifested and revealed. His coming is *after the energy of Satan, &c;* and does it require any particular proof that the pretensions of the pope, and the corruption of the Church of Rome, are all supported and authorized by feigned visions and miracles, by pious frauds and impositions of every kind? But how much soever the *man of sin* may be exalted, and how long soever he may reign, yet at last *the Lord shall consume him, &c.* This is partly taken from Isa. xi. 4, *And with the breath of his lips shall he slay the wicked one;* where the Jews put an emphasis upon the words *the wicked one;* as appears from the Chaldee, which renders it, " He shall destroy the *wicked Roman.*" If the two clauses, as said in the note on ver. 8, relate to two different events, the meaning is, " that the Lord Jesus shall gradually consume him with the free preaching of the Gospel; and shall utterly destroy him at his second coming in the glory of the Father." The former began to take effect at the Reformation; and the latter will be accomplished in God's appointed time. The *man of sin* is now upon the decline, and he will be totally abolished when Christ shall come in judgment. *Justin Martyr, Tertullian, Origen, Lactantius, Cyril* of Jerusalem, *Ambrose, Hilary, Jerome, Augustine,* and *Chrysostom,* give much the same interpretation that has here been given of the whole passage. And it must be owned that this is the genuine meaning of the apostle; that this only is consistent with the context; that every other interpretation is forced and unnatural; that this is liable to no material objection; that it coincides perfectly with Daniel; that it is agreeable to the tradition of the primitive Church; and that it has been exactly fulfilled in all its particulars; which cannot be said of any other interpretation whatever. Such a prophecy as this is an illustrious proof of Divine revelation, and an excellent antidote to the poison of popery.

See the *Dissertations on the Prophecies ;* and *Dodd,* as above.

10. Dr. *Macknight* proceeds, in general, on the plan of Bishop Newton; but, as he thinks that the apostle had the prophecy of Daniel, in chap. vii. and viii., particularly in view, he collates his words with those of the prophet in the following way:—

Verse 3. *That man of sin be revealed, the son of perdition.*—Ὁ ανθρωπος της ἁμαρτιας, ὁ·υἱος της απωλειας. " The *article,*" says he, " joined to these appellations, is emphatical, as in the former clause, importing that the ancient prophets had spoken of these persons, though under different names; particularly the Prophet Daniel, whose description of *the little horn* and *blasphemous king* agrees so exactly in meaning with Paul's descriptions of the *man of sin,* and *son of perdition,* and *lawless one,* that there can be little doubt of their being the same persons; but this will best appear by a comparison of the passages :—

---

2 Thess. ii. 3.—And that man of sin be revealed, *the son of perdition.*

Dan. vii. 21.—And the same horn *made war with the saints, and prevailed against them.*

Verse 25.—And he shall speak great words against the Most High; and shall *wear out the saints of the Most High.*

2 Thess. ii. 4.—Who opposeth and *exalteth himself above all that is called God, or that is worshipped;* so that he, as God, sitteth in the temple of God, showing himself that he is God.

Dan. xi. 36.—And the king shall do according to his will; and *he shall exalt himself above every god,* and shall speak marvellous things against the God of gods.

Dan. viii. 25.—He shall also stand up against the Prince of princes.

2 Thess. ii. 7.—Only he who now letteth *will let,* until he be taken out of the way.

Dan. vii. 8.—I considered the horns, and, behold, there came up among them another little horn, before whom there were three of the first horns plucked up by the roots.

Dan. vii. 25.—And he shall think to change times and laws, and they shall be given into his hand, See Dan. viii. 24.

2 Thess. ii. 8.—And then shall that *wicked one* be revealed.

Dan. xi. 38.—In his estate he shall *honour the god of forces (Mahuzzim, gods who are protectors,* that is, *tutelary angels and saints.*)

1 Tim. iv. 1.—Giving heed to seducing spirits, and *doctrines of devils.*

Dan. xi. 37.—Neither shall he regard the God of his fathers, nor the *desire of women.*

Verse 3.—*Forbidding to marry.*

Dan. vii. 11.—I beheld then, because of the voice of the great words which the horn spake; I beheld, even till *the beast was slain,* and his body destroyed, and given to the *burning flame.*

2 Thess. ii. 8.—Whom the Lord shall consume *with the Spirit of his mouth,* and shall destroy with the brightness of his coming.

Verse 26.—And they shall take away his dominion, *to consume and destroy it* unto the end.

Dan. viii. 25.—He shall be broken without hand.

After entering into great detail in his notes, he sums up in the following manner:—

" Now as, in the prophecies of Daniel, empires governed by a succession of kings are denoted by a single emblem; such as, by a part of an image, a single beast, a horn, &c., of a beast; so in Paul's prophecy, *the man of sin*, and *son of perdition*, and the *lawless one*, may denote an impious tyranny, exercised by a succession of men who cause great misery and ruin to others; and who, at length, shall be destroyed themselves. It is true, the papists contend that one person only is meant by these appellations, because they are in the singular number, and have the Greek article prefixed to them. But in Scripture we find other words in the singular number, with the article, used to denote a multitude of persons; for example, Rom. i. 17; *ὁ δίκαιος, the just one, by faith, shall live;* that is, all just persons whatever: Tit. i. 7; *ὁ ἐπίσκοπος, the bishop must be blameless;* that is, all bishops must be so: 2 John, ver. 7; *ὁ πλάνος, the deceiver*, signifies many deceivers, as is plain from the preceding clause, where *many deceivers* are said *to have gone out.* In like manner the false teachers, who deceived Christ's servants to commit fornication and idolatry, are called *that woman Jezebel*, Rev. ii. 20, and the *whore of Babylon*, Rev. xvii. 5; and in this prophecy, ver. 7, the Roman emperors, and magistrates under them, are called *ὁ κατέχων, he who restraineth.* Farther, a succession of persons, arising one after another, is denoted by appellations in the singular number with the article; for example: the succession of the Jewish high priests is thus denoted in the laws concerning them, Lev. xxi. 10, 15; Num. xxxv. 25–28. As also the succession of the Jewish kings, Deut. xvii. 14; 1 Sam. viii. 11. From these examples, therefore, it is plain that the names, *man of sin, son of perdition, lawless one*, although in the singular number, and with the article prefixed, may, according to the Scripture idiom, denote a multitude, and even a succession of persons arising one after another.

" The facts and circumstances mentioned in these prophecies are, for the most part, so peculiarly marked, that they will not easily apply, except to the persons and events intended by the Spirit of God. And therefore, in every case where different interpretations have been given of any prophecy, the proper method of ascertaining its meaning is to compare the various events to which it is thought to relate with the words of the prophecy, and to adopt that as the event intended which most exactly agrees in all its parts to the prophetic description.

" According to this rule, though many different interpretations have been given of the prophecy under consideration, that, in my opinion, will appear the best founded which makes it a prediction of the corruptions of Christianity, which began to be introduced into the Church in the apostle's days, and wrought secretly all the time the heathen magistrates persecuted the Christians, but which showed themselves more openly after the empire received the faith of Christ, A. D. 312, and, by a gradual progress, ended in the monstrous errors and usurpations of the bishops of Rome, when the restraining power of the emperors was taken out of the way by the incursions of the barbarous nations, and the breaking of the empire into the ten kingdoms prefigured by the ten horns of Daniel's fourth beast. Now, to be convinced of this, we need only compare the rise and progress of the papal tyranny with the descriptions of *the man of sin*, and of *the mystery of iniquity*, given in the writings of Daniel and Paul.

" And first, we have shown in note 1, on verse 7, that the mystery of iniquity, or the corrupt doctrines which ended in the errors and usurpations of the see of Rome, was working secretly in the apostle's days, as he affirms, ver. 7; and that the power of the Roman emperors, and of the magistrates under them, was that which then, and during the succeeding ages, restrained the *mystery of iniquity* in its working, and the *man of sin* from revealing himself. For, while the power of the state continued in the hands of the heathen rulers, and while they employed that power in persecuting the Christians, the corrupt doctrines and practices introduced by the false teachers did not spread so fast as otherwise they would have done. At least they were not produced to public view as the decisions of Heaven, to which all men were bound to pay implicit obedience. But, after the heathen magistrates were taken out of the way by the conversion of Constantine, and after he and his successors called the Christian bishops to meet in general councils, and enforced their assumption of Divine authority by the civil power; then did they in these councils arrogate to themselves the right of establishing what articles of faith and discipline they thought proper, and of anathematizing all who rejected their decrees; a claim which, in after times, the bishops of Rome transferred from general councils to themselves. It was in this period that the worship of saints and angels was introduced; celibacy was praised as the highest piety; meats of certain kinds were prohibited; and a variety of superstitious mortifications of the body were enjoined by the decrees of councils, in opposition to the express laws of God. In this period, likewise, idolatry and superstition were recommended to the people by false miracles, and every deceit which wickedness could suggest; such as the miraculous cures pretended to be performed by the bones and other relics of the martyrs, in order to induce the ignorant vulgar to worship them as mediators; the feigned visions of angels, who they said had appeared to this or that hermit, to recommend celibacy, fastings, mortifications of the body, and living in solitude; the apparitions of souls from purgatory, who begged that certain superstitions might be practised, for delivering them from that confinement: by all which, those assemblies of ecclesiastics, who by their decrees enjoined these practices, showed themselves to be the *man of sin*, and *lawless one*, in his first form, whose coming was to be with all power, and signs, and miracles of falsehood; and who opposed every one that is called god, or that is worshipped. For these general councils, by introducing the worship of saints and angels, robbed God of the worship due to him; and, by substituting saints and angels as mediators, in the place of Christ, they degraded him from his office as mediator, or rendered it altogether useless. However, though they thus opposed God and Christ by their unrighteous decrees, they did not yet *exalt themselves* above every one who is called God, or an object of worship; neither did they sit yet in the temple of God, as God, and openly show themselves to be God. These blasphemous extravagances were to be acted in after times by a number of particular persons in succession, I mean by the bishops of Rome, after the power of the Christian Roman emperors and of the magistrates under them, was taken out of the way. For the bishops of that see, having very early obtained from the Christian emperors decrees in their own favour, soon raised themselves above all other bishops; and, by a variety of artifices, made the authority and influence of the whole body of the clergy centre in themselves; and claimed that infallible authority which was formerly exercised by general councils, of making articles of faith; and of establishing rules of discipline for the whole Christian community; and of determining, in the last resort, all differences among the clergy; and of anathematizing every one who did not submit to their unrighteous decisions. In this manner did the bishops of Rome establish in their own persons a spiritual dominion over the whole Christian world. But not content with this height of power, by dexterously employing the credit and influence which the ecclesiastics, now devoted to their will, had over the laity in all the countries where they lived, they interfered in many civil matters also; till at length they reared that intolerable fabric of spiritual and civil tyranny conjoined, whereby the understandings, the persons, and the properties, not of the laity only, but also of the clergy themselves, have for a long time been most grievously enthralled, in all the countries where Christianity was professed.

"This height, however, of spiritual and civil tyranny united, the bishops of Rome did not attain till, as the apostle foretold, *that which restrained* was taken out of the way; or, till an end was put to the authority of the Roman emperors in the west, by the inroads of the barbarous nations; and, more especially, till the western empire was broken into the ten kingdoms, prefigured in Daniel's vision by the ten horns of the fourth beast; for then it was that the bishops of Rome made themselves the sovereigns of Rome and of its territory, and so became the little horn which Daniel beheld coming up among the ten horns, and which had *the eyes of a man, and a mouth speaking great things;* to show that its dominion was founded on the deepest policy, and that its strength consisted in the bulls, excommunications, and anathemas, which, with intolerable audacity, it uttered against all who opposed its usurpations. And in process of time, the bishops of Rome having got possession of three of the kingdoms into which the western empire was broken, signified by three of the horns of Daniel's fourth beast being plucked up by the roots before the little horn, they call themselves the *vicars of Christ,* on pretence that Christ had transferred his whole authority to them. They also thought to change times and laws, as Daniel foretold; for, as the vicars of Christ, they assumed the power of saving and damning men at their own pleasure; and altered the terms of salvation, making it depend, not on faith and holiness, but on the superstitious practices which they had established; and sold the pardon of sins past, and even the liberty of sinning for the future, for money. Moreover, they openly

made war with the saints who resisted their corrupt doctrines and practices, and prevailed against them, and wore out the saints of the Most High; for, by the cruel and bloody persecutions which they obliged the princes who acknowledged their authority to carry on against those who adhered to the pure doctrines and worship of Christ, they destroyed incredible numbers of them. Nay, by the terror of their excommunications and interdicts, they forced even the most powerful sovereigns to bend to their yoke: thus *with their mouth did they speak very great things.* At length they assumed the right of conferring kingdoms and of deposing princes, and actually deposed some, with the help of the potentates of their communion, who put their mandates in execution. Lastly, to render this exercise of their tyranny the more effectual, they arrogated the power of loosing subjects from their oaths of allegiance; whereby they made void the most sacred of all moral obligations, the obligation of allegiance. But this impious scheme of false doctrine, and the spiritual tyranny built upon it, agreeably to the predictions of the Prophet Daniel and of the Apostle Paul, began at the Reformation to be consumed by the breath of the Lord's mouth; that is, by the Scriptures put into the hands of the laity, and by the preaching of true doctrine out of the Scriptures.

"Upon the whole, I think every impartial person who attentively considers the foregoing sketch must be sensible that, in the bishops of Rome, all the characters and actions ascribed by Daniel to the *little horn,* and by Paul to *the man of sin* and *the lawless one,* are clearly united. For, according to the strong workings of Satan, with all power, and signs, and miracles of falsehood, they have opposed Christ, and exalted themselves above all that is called god, or an object of worship; and have long sat in the temple of God, as God, showing themselves that they are God: that is, they exercise the power and prerogatives of God. And seeing, in the acquisition and exercise of their spiritual tyranny, they have trampled upon all laws, human and Divine; and have encouraged their votaries in the most enormous acts of wickedness; the Spirit of God has, with the greatest propriety, given them the appellations of *the man of sin,* *the son of perdition,* and *the lawless one.* Farther, as it is said the man of sin was to *be revealed in his season,* there can be little doubt that the dark ages, in which all learning was overturned by the irruption of the northern barbarians, were the season allotted to *the man of sin* for revealing himself. Accordingly, we know that in these ages the corruptions of Christianity and the usurpations of the clergy were carried to the greatest height. In short, the annals of the world cannot produce persons and events to which the things written in this passage can be applied with so much fitness as to the bishops of Rome. Why then should we be in any doubt concerning the interpretation and application of this famous prophecy?

"At the conclusion of our explication of the prophecy concerning *the man of sin,* it may be proper to observe, that the events foretold in it being such as never took place in the world before, and, in all probability, never will take place in it again; the foreknowledge of them was certainly a matter out of the reach of human conjecture or foresight. It is evident, therefore, that this prophecy, which from the beginning has stood on record, taken in conjunction with the accomplishment of it verified by the concurrent testimony of history, affords an illustrious proof of the Divine original of that revelation of which it makes a part, and of the inspiration of the person from whose mouth it proceeded." See Dr. *Macknight's* Commentary and Notes, vol. iii., p. 100, &c.

With all this evidence before him, the intelligent reader will now be enabled to judge for himself, and to adopt for his own that opinion which appears to be the best supported by circumstances and facts. The labours of the above learned men have certainly *narrowed* the principal subjects of inquiry; and we may now safely state that, in this very obscure prophecy, the Spirit of God had in view either the *Jewish* or an *apostate Christian Church*, possessing great *spiritual* and *secular influence* and *jurisdiction*. That the words appear to apply best to the conduct of many of the *popes*, and the *corruptions of the Romish Church*, needs no proof; but to which of these Churches, or to what other Church or system, we should apply them, some men, as eminent for their piety as for their learning, hesitate to declare: yet I must acknowledge, that the most pointed part of the evidence here adduced tends to fix the whole on the *Romish* Church, and on none other.

Whatever may be intended here by the words *mystery of iniquity*, we may safely assert that it is a *mystery* of *iniquity* to *deny the use of the sacred Scriptures to the common people;* and that the Church that does so is afraid to come to the light. Nothing can be more preposterous and monstrous than to call people to embrace the doctrines of Christianity, and refuse them the opportunity of consulting the book in which they are contained. Persons who are denied the use of the sacred writings may be *manufactured* into different forms and modes; and be *mechanically* led to believe certain dogmas, and perform certain religious acts; but without the use of the Scriptures, they never can be intelligent Christians; they do not search the Scriptures, and therefore they cannot know Him of whom these Scriptures testify. The *mystery of iniquity* contained in this prohibition *works now*, and has worked *long;* but did it work in the apostles' times? Did it work in the Church at Thessalonica? Is it possible that the present *crop* should have been produced from so *remote* a seed? What does that most solemn adjuration of the apostle, 1 Thess. v. 27, mean? *I charge you by the Lord, that this epistle be* READ *unto* ALL *the holy brethren.* Why was such a charge necessary? Why should it be given in so awful a manner? Does it not absolutely imply that there would be attempts made to keep *all* the holy brethren from seeing this epistle? And can we conceive that *less* was referred to in the delivery of this very awful adjuration? This *mystery of iniquity* did work *then* in the Christian Church; even *then* attempts were made to *hide* the Scriptures from the common people. And does not this one consideration serve more to identify the prophecy than any thing else? Let him that readeth understand. See the notes on 1 Thess. v. 27, and at the end of that chapter.

CHAPTER III.

The apostle recommends himself and his brethren to the prayers of the Church, that their preaching might be successful, and that they might be delivered from wicked men, 1, 2. Expresses his confidence in God and them, and prays that they may patiently wait for the coming of Christ, 3–5. Gives them directions concerning strict discipline in the Church; and shows how he and his fellow labourers had behaved among them, not availing themselves of their own power and authority, 6–9. Shows them how to treat disorderly and idle people, and not to get weary in well doing, 10–13. Directs them not to associate with those who obey not the orders contained in this epistle, 14, 15. Prays that they may have increasing peace, 16. And concludes with his salutation and benediction, 17, 18.

A. M. cir. 4056.
A. D. cir. 52.
A. U. C. 805.
Anno Claudii Cæs.
Aug. 12.

FINALLY, brethren, [a] pray for us, that the word of the Lord [b] may have *free* course, and be glorified, even as *it is* with you:

2 And [c] that we may be delivered from [d] unreasonable and wicked men; [e] for all *men* have not faith.

A. M. cir. 4056.
A. D. cir. 52.
A. U. C. 805.
Anno Claudii Cæs.
Aug. 12.

[a] Eph. vi. 19; Col. iv. 3, 1 Thess. v. 25.——[b] Gr. *may run.*
[c] Rom. xv. 31.——[d] Gr. *absurd.*——[e] Acts xxviii. 24; Rom. x. 16.

NOTES ON CHAP. III.

Verse 1. *Finally, brethren*] The words τo λοιπoν do not mean *finally*, but, *furthermore—to come to a conclusion—what remains is this—I shall only add—* any of these phrases expresses the sense of the original.

Pray for us] God, in the order of his grace and providence, has made even the success of his Gospel dependent, in a certain measure, on the prayers of his followers. *Why* he should do so we cannot tell, but that he has done so we know; and they are not a little criminal who neglect to make fervent supplications for the prosperity of the cause of God.

May have free *course*] They were to pray that the doctrine of the Lord, ὁ λογος του Κυριου, might *run*, τρεχη, an allusion to the races in the Olympic games: that, as it had already got into the stadium or race course, and had started fairly, so it might *run on*, get to the goal, and *be glorified;* i. e., gain the crown, appointed for him that should get first to the end of the course.

2

A. M. cir. 4056.
A. D. cir. 52.
A. U. C. 805.
Anno Claudii Cæs.
Aug. 12.

3 But ᶠ the Lord is faithful, who shall stablish you, and ᵍ keep *you* from evil.

4 And ʰ we have confidence in the Lord touching you, that ye both do and will do the things which we command you.

5 And ⁱ the Lord direct your hearts into the love of God, and ᵏ into the patient waiting for Christ.

6 Now we command you, brethren, in the name of our Lord Jesus Christ, ˡ that ye with-

draw yourselves ᵐ from every brother that walketh ⁿ disorderly, and not after º the tradition which he received of us.

A. M. cir. 4056.
A. D. cir. 52.
A. U. C. 805.
Anno Claudii Cæs.
Aug. 12.

7 For yourselves know ᵖ how ye ought to follow us : for ᑫ we behaved not ourselves disorderly among you ;

8 Neither did we eat any man's bread for naught ; but ʳ wrought with labour and travail night and day, that we might not be chargeable to any of you :

9 ˢ Not because we have not power, but to

ᶠ 1 Cor. i. 6 ; 1 Thess. v. 24.——ᵍ John xvii. 15 ; 2 Pet. ii. 9. ʰ 2 Cor. vii. 16 ; Gal. v. 10——ⁱ 1 Chron. xxix. 18.——ᵏ Or, *the patience of Christ ;* 1 Thess. i. 3.——ˡ Rom. xvi. 17; ver. 14 ; 1 Tim. vi. 5 ; 2 John 10.

ᵐ 1 Cor. v. 11, 13.——ⁿ 1 Thess. iv. 11 ; v. 14 ; ver. 11, 12, 14.——º Chap. ii. 15.——ᵖ 1 Cor. iv. 16 ; xi. 1 ; 1 Thess. i. 6, 7. ᑫ 1 Thess. ii. 10.——ʳ Acts xviii. 3 ; xx. 34 ; 2 Cor. xi. 9 ; 1 Thess. ii. 9.——ˢ 1 Cor. ix. 6 ; 1 Thess. ii. 6.

Verse 2. *Unreasonable and wicked men*] The word ατοπων, which we translate *unreasonable*, signifies rather *disorderly, unmanageable ;* persons *out of their place*—under no discipline, regardless of law and restraint, and ever acting agreeably to the disorderly and unreasonable impulse of their own minds.

For all men *have not faith.*] The word πιστις is, without doubt, to be taken here for *fidelity* or *trustworthiness*, and not for *faith ;* and this is agreeable to the meaning given to it in the very next verse : *But the Lord is faithful,* πιστος δε εστιν ο Κυριος.

There are many, even of those who have received a measure of the Divine light, in whom we cannot *confide ;* they are irregular, disorderly, and cannot be brought under regular discipline : to these we cannot trust either ourselves or any thing that concerns the cause of God. But the Lord is worthy of your whole *confidence ;* doubt him not ; he will establish you, and keep you from any evil to which you may be exposed by these or such like persons.

Verse 3. *From evil.*] Απο του πονηρου may be translated, *from the devil* or *from the evil one.* They had disorderly men, wicked men, and the evil one or the devil, to contend with ; God alone could support and give them the victory ; he had *promised* to do it, and he might ever be *confided* in as being invariably *faithful.*

Verse 4. *And we have confidence*] We have no doubt of *God's* kindness towards you ; he loves you, and will support you : and we can confide in *you,* that ye are now acting as we have desired you, and will continue so to do.

Verse 5. *The Lord direct your hearts into the love of God*] The love of God is the grand motive and principle of obedience ; this must occupy your hearts : the heart is irregular in all its workings ; God alone, by his Spirit, can *direct* it into his love, and *keep it right ;* κατευθυναι, give a *proper direction* to all its passions, and keep them in order, regularity and purity.

The patience of Christ.] Such patience, under all your sufferings and persecutions, as Christ manifested under his. He bore meekly the contradiction of sinners against himself ; and when he was reviled, he reviled not again.

Verse 6. *That ye withdraw yourselves*] Have no fellowship with those who will not submit to proper discipline ; who do not keep their place ; ατακτως, such as are out of their *rank,* and act according to their own wills and caprices ; and particularly such as are *idle* and *busybodies.* These he had ordered, 1 Thess. iv. 11, 12, that they should *study to be quiet, mind their own business, and work with their hands ;* but it appears that they had paid no attention to this order, and now he desires the Church to exclude such from their communion.

And not after the tradition] This evidently refers to the orders contained in the *first epistle ;* and that first epistle was the *tradition* which they had received from him. It was, therefore, no *unwritten word,* no *uncertain saying,* handed about from one to another ; but a part of the *revelation* which God had given, and which they found in the body of his epistle. These are the only *traditions* which the Church of God is called to regard.

Verse 7. *We behaved not ourselves disorderly*] Ουκ ητακτησαμεν· We did not go out of our rank—we kept our *place,* and discharged all its duties.

Verse 8. *Neither did we eat any man's bread for naught*] We paid for what we bought, and worked with our hands that we might have money to buy what was necessary.

Labour and travail night and day] We were incessantly employed, either in preaching the Gospel, visiting from house to house, or working at our calling. As it is very evident that the Church at Thessalonica was very pious, and most affectionately attached to the apostle, they must have been *very poor,* seeing he was obliged to work hard to gain himself the necessaries of life. Had they been able to support him he would not have worked *with labour and travail night and day,* that he might not be burdensome to them ; and, as we may presume that they were very poor, he could not have got his support among them without adding to their burdens. To this his generous mind could not submit ; it is no wonder, therefore, that he is so severe against those who would not labour, but were a burden to the poor followers of God.

Verse 9. *Not because we have not power*] We

2

A. M. cir. 4056.
A. D. cir. 52.
A. U. C. 805.
Anno Claudii Cæs.
Aug. 12.

make [t] ourselves an ensample unto you to follow us.

10 For even when we were with you, this we commanded you, [u] that if any would not work, neither should he eat.

11 For we hear that there are some [v] which walk among you disorderly, [w] working not at all, but are busybodies.

12 [x] Now them that are such we command and exhort by our Lord Jesus Christ, [y] that

A. M. cir. 4056
A. D. cir. 52.
A. U. C. 805.
Anno Claudii Cæs.
Aug. 12.

with quietness they work, and eat their own bread.

13 But ye, brethren, [z] be [a] not weary in well-doing.

14 And if any man obey not our word [b] by this epistle, note that man, and [c] have no company with him, that he may be ashamed.

15 [d] Yet count *him* not as an enemy, [e] but admonish *him* as a brother.

16 Now [f] the Lord of peace himself give

---

[t] Verse 7.——[u] Genesis iii. 19; 1 Thess. iv. 11.——[v] Verse 6.
[w] 1 Thess. iv. 11; 1 Tim. v. 13; 1 Pet. iv. 15.——[x] 1 Thess.
iv. 11.——[y] Ephesians iv. 28.——[z] Galatians vi. 9.——[a] Or,
faint not.

[b] Or, *signify that man by an epistle.*——[c] Matt. xviii 17; 1 Cor.
v. 9, 11; ver. 6.——[d] Lev. xix. 17; 1 Thess. v. 14.——[e] Tit. iii.
10——[f] Rom. xv. 33; xvi 20; 1 Cor. xiv. 33; 2 Cor. xiii. 11;
1 Thess. v. 23.

---

have the power, εξουσιαν, the *right*, to be maintained by those in whose behalf we labour. *The labourer is worthy of his hire*, is a maxim universally acknowledged and respected; and *they who preach the Gospel should live by the Gospel:* the apostle did not claim his privilege, but laboured for his own support, that he might be an *example* to those whom he found otherwise disposed, and that he might spare the poor. See 1 Cor. ix. 1, &c.

Verse 10. If any would not work, neither should he eat.] This is a just maxim, and universal nature inculcates it to man. If man *will work*, he *may eat*; if he do *not work*, he *neither can eat*, nor *should he eat*. The maxim is founded on these words of the Lord: *In the sweat of thy brow thou shalt eat bread.* Industry is crowned with God's blessing; idleness is loaded with his curse. This maxim was a proverb among the Jews. Men who can work, and will rather support themselves by begging, should not get one morsel of bread. It is a sin to minister to necessities that are merely artificial.

Verse 11. For we hear that there are some] It is very likely that St. Paul kept up some sort of correspondence with the Thessalonian Church; for he had *heard* every thing that concerned their state, and it was from this information that he wrote his second epistle.

Disorderly] Ατακτως· *Out of their rank*—not keeping their *own place.*

Working not at all] Either lounging at home, or becoming religious gossips; μηδεν εργαζομενους, *doing nothing.*

Busybodies.] Περιεργαζομενους· *Doing every thing they should not do*—impertinent meddlers with other people's business; prying into other people's circumstances and domestic affairs; magnifying or minifying, mistaking or underrating, every thing; newsmongers and telltales; an abominable race, the curse of every neighbourhood where they live, and a pest to religious society. There is a fine *paronomasia* in the above words, and evidently intended by the apostle.

Verse 12. With quietness they work] Μετα ἡσυχιας· *With silence;* leaving their tale-bearing and officious intermeddling. *Less noise and more work!*

That—they work, and eat their own bread.] Their

own bread, because earned by their own honest industry. What a degrading thing to live on the *bounty* or *mercy* of another, while a man is able to acquire his own livelihood! He who can submit to this has lost the spirit of *independence;* and has in him a beggar's heart, and is capable of nothing but base and beggarly actions. Witness the great mass of the people of England, who by their dependence on the *poor rates* are, from being laborious, independent, and respectable, become idle, profligate, and knavish; the propagators and perpetrators of crime; a discredit to the nation, and a curse to society. The apostle's command is a cure for such; and the Church of God should discountenance such, and disown them.

Verse 13. Be not weary in well-doing.] While ye stretch out no hand of relief to the *indolent* and *lazy*, do not forget the *real poor*—the genuine representatives of an impoverished Christ; and rather relieve a hundred undeserving objects, than pass by one who is a real object of charity.

Verse 14. If any man obey not] They had disobeyed his word in the *first epistle*, and the Church still continued to bear with them; now he tells the Church, if they still continue to disregard what is said to them, and particularly his word by this *second epistle*, they are to *mark them* as being totally incorrigible, and have no fellowship with them.

Some construe the words δια της επιστολης with τουτον σημειουσθε· *Give me information of that man by a letter*—let me hear of his continued obstinacy, and send me his name. This was probably in order to excommunicate him, and deliver him over to Satan for the destruction of the body, that the spirit might be saved in the day of the Lord Jesus. The words of the original will bear either construction, that in the *text*, or that given above.

Verse 15. Count him not as an enemy] Consider him still more an enemy to himself than to you; and *admonish him as a brother*, though you have ceased to hold religious communion with him. His soul is still of infinite value; labour to get it saved.

Verse 16. The Lord of peace] Jesus Christ, who is called *our peace*, Eph. ii. 14; and *The Prince of peace*, Isa. ix. 6. May he give you peace, for he is the *Fountain* and *Dispenser* of it.

2

A. M. cir. 4056.
A. D. cir. 52.
A. U. C. 805.
Anno Clau-
dii Cæs.
Aug. 12.

you peace always by all means. The Lord *be* with you all.

17 [g] The salutation of Paul with mine own hand, which is the token in every epistle : so I write.

---

[g] 1 Cor. xvi. 21 ; Col. iv. 18.

Always] Both in your own consciences, and among yourselves.

By all means.] Παντι τροπῳ· By all means, methods, occasions, instruments, and occurrences ; peace or *prosperity* in every form and shape.

Instead of εν παντι τροπῳ, *in every way, &c.,* εν παντι τοπῳ, *in every place,* is the reading of A*D*FG, some others ; with the *Vulgate* and *Itala. Chrysostom, Ambrosiaster, Augustine,* and others, have the same reading : *May God grant you prosperity always, and everywhere.*

The Lord be with you all.] This is agreeable to the promise of our Lord : *Lo, I am with you alway, even unto the end of the world ;* Matt. xxviii. 20. May the Lord, who has promised to be always with his true disciples, be with you! Christians are the temple of God, and the temple of God has the Divine presence in it. May you ever continue to be his Church, that the Lord God may dwell among you!

Verse 17. *The salutation of Paul with mine own hand*] It is very likely that Paul employed an *amanuensis* generally, either to *write* what he *dictated,* or to make a *fair copy* of what he wrote. In either case the apostle always subscribed it, and wrote the salutation and benediction with his own hand ; and this was what *authenticated* all his epistles. A measure of this kind would be very necessary if forged epistles were carried about in those times. See the note on 1 Cor. xvi. 21, and see Col. iv. 18.

Verse 18. *The grace*] The favour, blessing, and influence of our Lord Jesus Christ, *be with you all*— be your constant companion. May you ever feel his presence, and enjoy his benediction!

Amen.] So let be! God grant it! This word in this place, has more evidence in favour of its genuine-

18 [h] The grace of our Lord Jesus Christ *be* with you all. Amen.

¶ The Second *Epistle* to the Thessalonians was written from Athens.

A. M. cir. 4056.
A. D. cir. 52.
A. U. C. 805.
Anno Clau-
dii Cæs.
Aug. 12.

---

[h] Rom. xvi. 24.

---

ness than it has in most other places ; and was probably added here by the apostle himself, or by the Church of the Thessalonians.

The *subscriptions* to this epistle are various in the MSS. and VERSIONS. The latter are as follows :—

The Second Epistle to the Thessalonians was written from Athens.—*Common Greek text.*

The Second Epistle to the Thessalonians, which was written at Laodicea in Pisidia, was sent by the hands of Tychicus.—SYRIAC.

The end of the Epistle ; and it was written at Athens.—ARABIC.

To the Thessalonians.—ÆTHIOPIC.

Written from Athens, and sent by Silvanus and Timotheus.—COPTIC.

No subscription in the VULGATE.

Written at Corinth.—Author of the SYNOPSIS.

———— sent by Titus and Onesimus.—*Latin Prologue.*

The Second Epistle to the Thessalonians, written from *Rome.*—No. 71, a MS. of the *Vatican* library, written about the eleventh century.

The chief of the MSS. either have no subscription, or agree with some of the above *versions.*

That the epistle was neither written at *Athens, Laodicea,* nor *Rome,* has been sufficiently proved ; and that it was written, as well as the first, at *Corinth,* is extremely probable. See the preface, and what has been said on the preceding epistle.

I have often had occasion to observe that the *subscriptions* at the end of the sacred books are not of Divine origin : they are generally false ; and yet some have quoted them as making a part of the sacred text, and have adduced them in support of some favourite opinions.

Finished correcting this epistle for a new edition, the shortest day in 1831.—A. C.

IN order to find out who this person was, it will be necessary to consult the Acts of the Apostles, where the first mention is made of him; and by collating what is there said with certain passages in the epistle, we shall find who he was, and the probable time in which the epistle was addressed to him.

Paul and Barnabas, in the course of their first apostolic journey among the Gentiles, came to *Lystra*, a city of Lycaonia, where they preached the Gospel for some time, and, though persecuted, with considerable success. See Acts xiv. 5, 6. It is very likely that here they converted to the Christian faith a Jewess named Lois, with her daughter Eunice, who had married a Gentile, by whom she had Timothy, and whose father was probably at this time dead; the grandmother, daughter, and son living together. Compare Acts xvi. 1–3 with 2 Tim. i. 5. It is likely that Timothy was the only child; and it appears that he had been brought up in the fear of God, and carefully instructed in the Jewish religion by means of the Holy Scriptures. Compare 2 Tim. i. 5 with 2 Tim. iii. 15. It appears, also, that this young man drank into the apostle's spirit, became a thorough convert to the Christian faith, and that a very tender intimacy subsisted between St. Paul and him.

When the apostle came from Antioch, in Syria, the second time to *Lystra*, he found Timothy a member of the Church, and so highly reputed and warmly recommended by the Church in that place, that St. Paul took him to be his companion in his travels. Acts xvi. 1–3. From this place we learn that, although Timothy had been educated in the Jewish faith, he had not been circumcised, because his father, who was a Gentile, would not permit it. When the apostle had determined to take him with him, he found it necessary to have him circumcised, not from any supposition that circumcision was necessary to salvation, but because of the Jews, who would neither have heard him nor the apostle had not this been done : the Gospel testimony they would not have received from Timothy, because a heathen; and they would have considered the apostle in the same light, because he associated with such. See the notes on Acts xvi. 3.

It is pretty evident that Timothy had a special call of God to the work of an evangelist, which the elders of the Church at Lystra knowing, set him solemnly apart to the work by the imposition of hands; 1 Tim. iv. 14. And they were particularly led to this by several prophetic declarations relative to him, by which his Divine call was most clearly ascertained. See 1 Tim. i. 18, and iii. 14. Some think that, after this appointment by the *elders*, the apostle himself laid his hands on him, not for the purpose of his evangelical designation, but that he might receive those extraordinary gifts of the Holy Spirit so necessary in those primitive times to demonstrate the truth of the Gospel. See 2 Tim. i. 6, 7. Yet, it is likely that Timothy had not *two ordinations*; one by the *elders* of Lystra, and another by the apostle; as it is most probable that St. Paul acted with that πρεσβυτεριον or *eldership* mentioned 1 Tim. iv. 14, among whom, in the imposition of hands, he would undoubtedly act as chief.

Timothy, thus prepared to be the apostle's fellow labourer in the Gospel, accompanied him and Silas when they visited the Churches of Phrygia, and delivered to them the decrees of the apostles and elders at Jerusalem, freeing the Gentiles from the law of Moses, as a term of salvation. Having gone through these countries, they at length came to Troas, where Luke joined them; as appears from the phraseology of his history, Acts xvi. 10, 11, &c. In Troas a vision appeared to Paul, directing them to go into Macedonia. Loosing therefore from Troas, they all passed over to Neapolis; and from thence went to Philippi, where they converted many, and planted a Christian Church. From Philippi they went to Thessalonica, leaving Luke at Philippi; as appears from his changing the phraseology of his history at verse 40. We may therefore suppose, that at their departing they committed the converted at Philippi to Luke's care. In Thessalonica they were opposed by the unbelieving Jews, and obliged to flee to Beræa, whither the Jews from Thessalonica followed them. To elude their rage, Paul, who was most obnoxious to them, departed from

Beræa by night to go to Athens, leaving Silas and Timothy at Beræa. At Athens, Timothy came to the apostle and gave him such an account of the afflicted state of the Thessalonian brethren, as induced him to send Timothy back to comfort them. After that Paul preached at Athens, but with so little success that he judged it proper to leave Athens and go forward to Corinth, where Silas and Timothy came to him, and assisted in converting the Corinthians. And when he left Corinth they accompanied him, first to Ephesus, then to Jerusalem, and after that to Antioch, in Syria. Having spent some time in Antioch, Paul set out with Timothy on his third apostolical journey; in which, after visiting all the Churches of Galatia and Phrygia, in the order in which they had been planted, they came to Ephesus the second time, and there abode for a considerable time. In short, from the time Timothy first joined the apostle, as his assistant, he never left him except when sent by him on some special errand. And by his affection, fidelity, and zeal, he so recommended himself to all the disciples, and acquired such authority over them, that Paul inserted his name in the inscription of several of the letters which he wrote to the Churches, to show that their doctrine was one and the same. His esteem and affection for Timothy the apostle expressed still more conspicuously, by writing to him those excellent letters in the canon which bear his name; and which have been of the greatest use to the ministers of the Gospel ever since their publication, by directing them to discharge all the duties of their function in a proper manner.

The date of this epistle has been a subject of much controversy, some assigning it to the year 56, which is the common opinion; and others to 64 or 65. A great balance of probability appears to be in favour of this later date; and it appears to me that the arguments of Drs. Macknight and Paley are decisive in favour of the later date. The former, in his preface, gives a very clear view of the question.

In the third verse of the first chapter of this epistle the apostle says: "As I entreated thee to abide in Ephesus, when going into Macedonia, so do; that thou mayest charge some not to teach differently." From this it is plain, 1. That Timothy was in Ephesus when the apostle wrote his first letter to him; 2. That he had been left there by the apostle, who at parting with him entreated him to abide at Ephesus; 3. That this happened when Paul was going from Ephesus to Macedonia; and, 4. That he had entreated Timothy to abide in Ephesus, for the purpose of charging some teachers in that Church not to teach differently from the apostles. In the history of the Acts of the Apostles there is no mention of Paul's going from Ephesus to Macedonia but once; viz. after the riot of Demetrius, Acts xx. 1, for which reason Theodoret, among the ancients, and among the moderns, Estius, Baronius, Capellus, Grotius, Lightfoot, Salmasius, Hammond, Witsius, Lardner, Pearson, and others, have given it as their opinion, that the apostle speaks of that journey in his First Epistle to Timothy. Yet, if I am not mistaken, the following circumstance will show their opinion to be ill founded :—

1. When the apostle went from Ephesus to Macedonia, as related Acts xx..1, Timothy was not in Ephesus, having gone from that city into Macedonia with Erastus by the apostle's direction; Acts xix. 22. And in the First Epistle to the Corinthians, which was written after Timothy's departure from Ephesus, we are informed that he was to go from Macedonia to Corinth. 1 Cor. iv. 17: "I have sent to you Timothy." 1 Cor. xvi. 10, 11: "If Timothy be come, take care that he be among you without fear. Send him forward in peace, that he may come to me, for I expect him with the brethren." But before Timothy returned from Corinth, the apostle left Ephesus and went into Macedonia, where the brethren above mentioned met him, 2 Cor. ii. 12, 13, having Timothy in their company; as is plain from his joining the apostle in his Second Epistle to the Corinthians, which all agree was written from Macedonia, immediately after the brethren from Corinth gave the apostle an account of the success of his first letter. Wherefore, since Timothy was not in Ephesus when the apostle left the city after the riot, it could not be the occasion on which the apostle said to him: "As I entreated thee to abide in Ephesus, when going into Macedonia, so do." But the journey into Macedonia, of which he speaks, must have been some other journey not mentioned in the Acts. To remove this difficulty we are told that Timothy returned from Corinth to the apostle before his departure from Ephesus, and that he was left there after the riot; but that something happened which occasioned him to follow the apostle into Macedonia; that there he joined him in writing his Second Epistle to the Corinthians; and, having finished his business in Macedonia, he returned to Ephesus and abode there, agreeably to the apostle's request. But as these suppositions are not warranted by the history of the Acts, Timothy's joining the apostle in his Second Epistle to the Corinthians may still be urged as a proof that he came with the brethren directly from Corinth to Macedonia. Farther, that Timothy did not go from Macedonia to Ephesus after joining the apostle in his Second Epistle to the Corinthians, but returned with him to Corinth to receive the collections, is, I think, plain from Acts xx. 4, where he is mentioned as one of those who accompanied Paul from Corinth to Jerusalem with the collections.

2. When the apostle wrote his First Epistle to Timothy, "he hoped to come to him soon," chap. iii. 14; but from the history of the Acts it is certain that in no letter written to Timothy after the riot, till his first confinement in Rome, could the apostle say *that he hoped to come to him soon.* He could not say so in any letter written from Troas, the first place he stopped at after leaving Ephesus; for at that time he was going into Macedonia and Achaia to receive the collections for the poor from the Churches in these provinces. Neither could he say so after writing his Second Epistle to the Corinthians from Macedonia; for in that epistle he told the Corinthians he was coming to them with the Macedonian brethren, who were commissioned to attend him in his voyage to Jerusalem, with the collections, 2 Cor. ix. 4, and that he meant to sail directly from Corinth to Judea, 2 Cor. i. 16. As little could he write to Timothy that *he hoped to come to him soon,*

when he altered his resolution on the occasion of the lying in wait of the Jews, and returned into Macedonia, Acts xx. 3. For he was then in such haste to be in Jerusalem on the day of pentecost, that when he came to Miletus, instead of going to Ephesus, he sent for the elders of that Church to come to him, Acts xx. 16, 17. When he arrived in Judea, he could not write that *he hoped to come to Ephesus soon*, for he was imprisoned a few days after he went up to Jerusalem; and having continued two years in prison at Cæsarea, he was sent bound to Rome, where likewise being confined, he could not, till towards the conclusion of that confinement, write to Timothy that *he hoped to come to him soon*. And even then he did not write his First Epistle to Timothy, for Timothy was with him at the conclusion of his confinement, Phil. ii. 19, 23.

3. From the first epistle we learn that the following were the errors Timothy was left in Ephesus to oppose: 1. Fables invented by the Jewish doctors to recommend the observance of the law of Moses as necessary to salvation. 2. Uncertain genealogies, by which individuals endeavoured to trace their descent from Abraham, in the persuasion that they would be saved, merely because they had Abraham for their father. 3. Intricate questions and strifes about some words in the law; perverse disputings of men of corrupt minds, who reckoned that which produced most gain to be the best kind of godliness. 4. Oppositions of knowledge, falsely so named. But these errors had not taken place in the Ephesian Church before the apostle's departure; for in his charge to the Ephesian elders at Miletus, he foretold that the false teachers were to enter in among them *after* his departing. Acts xx. 29, 30: "I know that after my departing, shall grievous wolves enter in among you, not sparing the flock. Also of your own selves shall men arise, speaking perverse things to draw away disciples after them." The same thing appears from the two epistles which the apostle wrote to the Corinthians; the one from Ephesus before the riot of Demetrius, the other from Macedonia after that event; and from the epistle which he wrote to the Ephesians themselves from Rome, during his confinement there. For in none of these letters is there any notice taken of the above mentioned errors, as subsisting among the Ephesians at the time they were written; which cannot be accounted for on supposition that they were prevalent in Ephesus when the apostle went into Macedonia after the riot. I am therefore of opinion that the first to Timothy, in which the apostle desired him to abide in Ephesus for the purpose of opposing the Judaizers and their errors, could not be written either from Troas or from Macedonia after the riot, as those who contend for the early date of the epistle suppose; but it must have been written some time after the apostle's release from confinement in Rome, when no doubt he visited the Church at Ephesus, and found the Judaizing teachers there busily employed in spreading their pernicious errors.

4. In the first Epistle to Timothy the same sort of persons, doctrines, and practices, are reprobated, which are condemned in the second. Compare 1 Tim. iv. 1–6 with 2 Tim. iii. 1–5; and 1 Tim. vi. 20 with 2 Tim. ii. 14; and 1 Tim. vi. 4 with 2 Tim. ii. 16. The same commands, instructions, and encouragements are given to Timothy in the first epistle as in the second. Compare 1 Tim. vi. 13, 14, with 2 Tim. iv. 1–5. The same remedies for the corruptions which had taken place among the Ephesians are prescribed in the first epistle as in the second. Compare 1 Tim. iv. 14 with 2 Tim. i. 6, 7; and as in the second epistle, so in the first, every thing is addressed to Timothy as superintendent both of the teachers and of the laity in the Church at Ephesus; all which, I think, imply that the state of things among the Ephesians was the same when the two epistles were written; consequently that the first epistle was written only a few months before the second, and not long before the apostle's death.

These arguments appeared so convincing to Pearson, Le Clerc, L'Enfant, Cave, Fabricius, Mill, Whitby, and others, that they were unanimously of opinion Timothy was left by the apostle in Ephesus as he went into Macedonia, not after the riot of Demetrius, but after he was released from his first confinement at Rome. And from that circumstance they infer that he did not write his first epistle till some time in the end of the year 64, or in the beginning of 65. I think it was written from Nicopolis.

To the late date of this first epistle, there are three plausible objections which must not be overlooked:—

1. It is thought that, if the First Epistle to Timothy was written after the apostle's release, he could not with any propriety have said to Timothy, chap. iv. 12: "Let no man despise thy youth;" but it is replied: That Servius Tullius, in classing the Roman people, as Aulus Gellius relates, *lib.* x. *c.* 28, divided their age into three periods: *Childhood* he limited to the age of seventeen; *youth*, from that to forty-six; and *old age*, from that to the end of life. Now, supposing Timothy to have been eighteen years old, A. D. 50, when he became Paul's assistant, he would be no more than 32, A. D. 64, two years after the apostle's release, when it is supposed this epistle was written. Wherefore, being then in the period of life which, by the Greeks as well as the Romans, was considered as *youth*, the apostle with propriety might say to him, *Let no man despise thy youth*.

2. When the apostle touched at Miletus, in his voyage to Jerusalem with the collections, the Church at Ephesus had a number of *elders*, that is, of *bishops* and *deacons*, who came to him at Miletus, Acts xx. 17. It is therefore asked: What occasion was there in an epistle written after the apostle's release, to give Timothy directions concerning the ordination of *bishops* and *deacons*, in a Church where there were so many elders already? The answer is: The elders who came to the apostle at Miletus in the year 58 may have been too few for the Church at Ephesus, in her increased state, in the year 65. Besides, false teachers had then entered, to oppose whom more bishops and deacons might be needed than were necessary in the year 58; not to mention that some of the first elders having died, others were wanted to supply their places.

3. Because the apostle wrote to Timothy that "he hoped to come to him soon," 1 Tim. iii. 14, it is argued that the letter in which this is said must have been written before the apostle said to the Ephesian elders,

PREFACE TO THE FIRST EPISTLE TO TIMOTHY.

Acts xx. 25 : " I know that ye all, among whom I have gone preaching the kingdom of God, shall see my face no more." But if, by this, the First Epistle to Timothy is proved to have been written before the apostle's interview with the elders at Miletus, his Epistles to the Philippians, to the Hebrews, and to Philemon, in which he promised to visit *them*, must likewise have been written before the interview ; in regard, his declaration respected the Philippians, the Hebrews, and Philemon, as well as the Ephesians ; for they certainly were persons among whom the apostle had gone preaching the kingdom of God. Yet no commentator ever thought the epistles above mentioned were written to them before the apostle's interview with the Ephesian elders ; on the contrary, it is universally acknowledged that these epistles were written four years after the interview ; namely, during the apostle's first imprisonment at Rome. Wherefore, when he told the Ephesian elders that they, and his other converts, among whom he had gone preaching the kingdom of God, should see his face no more, as it was no point either of faith or practice which he spake, he may well be supposed to have declared nothing but his own opinion, resulting from his fears. He had lately escaped the rage of the Jews, who laid wait for him in Cenchrea to kill him, Acts xx. 3. This, with their fury on former occasions, filled him with such anxiety that, in writing to the Romans from Corinth; he requested them " to strive together with him in their prayers that he might be delivered from the unbelieving in Judea ;" Rom. xv. 30, 31. Farther, that in his own speech to the Ephesian elders the apostle only declared his own persuasion, dictated by his fears, and not any suggestion of the Spirit, I think plain from what he had said immediately before, Acts xx. 22, 23 : " Behold, I go bound in the spirit to Jerusalem, not knowing the things that shall befall me there : save that the Holy Ghost witnesseth in every city, saying that bonds and afflictions abide me." Wherefore, although his fears were happily disappointed, and he actually visited the Ephesians after his release; his character as an inspired apostle is not hurt in the least, if, in saying *he knew they should see his face no more*, he declared, as I have said, his own persuasion only, and no dictate of the Holy Ghost.

Dr. Paley's arguments are the same in substance ; but he does not mention Dr. Macknight, who wrote before him, and whose work he must have seen.

The principal difficulty in this opinion is, that it necessarily implies that St. Paul visited Ephesus after his liberation at Rome ; which appears so contrary to what he said to the Ephesian Church, *that they should see his face no more*. Dr. Paley, however, finds some farther presumptive evidences that the apostle must have visited Ephesus. The Epistles to the Philippians and to Philemon were written while the apostle was a prisoner at Rome ; to the former he says : " I trust in the Lord, that I also myself shall come shortly ;" and to the latter, who was a Colossian, he gives this direction : " But withal, prepare me also a lodging, for I trust that through your prayers I shall be given unto you." An inspection of the *map* will show us that Colosse was a city of Asia Minor, lying eastward, and at no great distance from Ephesus ; Philippi was on the other, i. e. the western, side of the Ægean Sea. Now if the apostle executed his purpose, and came to Philemon at Colosse soon after his liberation, it cannot be supposed that he would omit to visit Ephesus, which lay so near it, and where he had spent three years of his ministry. As he was also under a promise to visit the Church at Philippi *shortly*, if he passed from Colosse to Philippi he could hardly avoid taking Ephesus in his way. See Paley's Horæ Paulinæ, page 293. This, taken in connection with the preceding arguments, can leave little doubt that the date of this epistle must be referred to a time subsequent to St. Paul's liberation from Rome, and consequently to the end of the year 64, or the beginning of the year 65.

2

THE

FIRST EPISTLE OF PAUL THE APOSTLE

TO

TIMOTHY.

Chronological Notes relative to this Epistle.

Year of the Constantinopolitan era of the world, or that used by the Byzantine historians, 5573.—Year of the Alexandrian era of the world, 5567.—Year of the Antiochian era of the world, 5557.—Year of the Julian period, 4775.—Year of the world, according to Archbishop Usher, 4069.—Year of the world, according to Eusebius, in his Chronicon, 4293.—Year of the minor Jewish era of the world, or that in common use, 3825.—Year of the Greater Rabbinical era of the world, 4424.—Year from the Flood, according to Archbishop Usher, and the English Bible, 2413.—Year of the Cali yuga, or Indian era of the Deluge, 3167. —Year of the era of Iphitus, or since the first commencement of the Olympic games, 1005.—Year of the era of Nabonassar, king of Babylon, 812.—Year of the CCXIth Olympiad, 1.—Year from the building of Rome, according to Fabius Pictor, 812.—Year from the building of Rome, according to Frontinus, 816.—Year from the building of Rome, according to the Fasti Capitolini, 817.—Year from the building of Rome, according to Varro, which was that most generally used, 818.—Year of the era of the Seleucidæ, 377.—Year of the Cæsarean era of Antioch, 113.—Year of the Julian era, 110.—Year of the Spanish era, 103.—Year from the birth of Jesus Christ according to Archbishop Usher, 69.—Year of the vulgar era of Christ's nativity, 65.—Year of Gessius Florus, governor of the Jews, 1.—Year of Vologesus, king of the Parthians, 16.— Year of L. C. Gallus, governor of Syria, 1.—Year of Matthias, high priest of the Jews, 3.—Year of the Dionysian period, or Easter Cycle, 66.—Year of the Grecian Cycle of nineteen years, or Common Golden Number, 9; or the first year after the third embolismic.—Year of the Jewish Cycle of nineteen years, 6, or the second embolismic.—Year of the Solar Cycle, 18.—Dominical Letter, it being the first after Bissextile, or Leap Year, F.—Day of the Jewish Passover, according to the Roman computation of time, the VIIth of the ides of April, or in our common mode of reckoning, the seventh of April, which happened in this year on the day after the Jewish Sabbath.—Easter Sunday, the day after the ides of April, or the XVIIIth of the Calends of May, named by the Jews the 22d of Nisan or Abib; and by Europeans in general, the 14th of April.—Epact, or the age of the moon on the 22d of March, (the day of the earliest Easter Sunday possible,) 28.—Epact, according to the present mode of computation, or the moon's age on New Year's day, or the Calends of January, 5.—Monthly Epacts, or the moon's age on the Calends of each month respectively, (beginning with January,) 5, 7, 6, 7, 8, 9, 10, 11, 12, 12, 14, 14.—Number of Direction, or the number of days from the twenty-first of March to the Jewish Passover, 17.—Year of the reign of Caius Tiberius Claudius Nero Cæsar, the fifth Roman emperor computing from Augustus Cæsar, 12.—Roman Consuls, A. Licinius Nerva Silanus, and M. Vestinius Atticus; the latter of whom was succeeded by Anicius Cerealis, on July 1st. Dr. Lardner and others suppose this epistle to have been written in A. D. 56, *i. e.* nine years earlier than is stated above. See the preceding preface, where this point is largely considered, and also the general observations prefixed to the Acts of the Apostles.

2

CHAPTER I.

Paul's salutation to Timothy, 1, 2. For what purpose he had left him at Ephesus, 3. What the false apostles taught in opposition to the truth, 4–7. The true use of the law, 8–11. He thanks God for his own conversion, and describes his former state, 12–17. Exhorts Timothy to hold fast faith and a good conscience, and speaks of Hymeneus and Alexander who had made shipwreck of their faith, 18–20.

A. M. cir. 4069.
A. D. 64 or 65.
A. U. C. 818.
An. Imp. Ne-
ronis Cæs.
Aug. 12.

PAUL, an apostle of Jesus Christ, [a] by the commandment [b] of God our Saviour, and Lord Jesus Christ, [c] *which is* our hope;

2 Unto [d] Timothy, [e] *my* own son in the faith : [f] Grace, mercy, *and* peace, from God our Father and Jesus Christ our Lord.

3 As I besought thee to abide still at Ephesus, [g] when I went into Macedonia, that thou mightest charge some [h] that they teach no other doctrine,

4 [i] Neither give heed to fables and endless genealogies, [k] which minister questions, rather than godly edifying, which is in faith : *so do.*

A. M. cir. 4069.
A. D. 64 or 65.
A. U. C. 818.
An. Imp. Ne-
ronis Cæs.
Aug. 12.

---

[a] Acts ix. 15; Gal. i. 1, 11.——[b] Chap. ii. 3; iv. 10; Tit. i. 3; ii. 10; iii. 4; Jude 25.——[c] Col. i. 27.——[d] Acts xvi. 1; 1 Cor. iv. 17; Phil. ii. 19; 1 Thess. iii. 2.——[e] Tit. i. 4.

[f] Gal. i. 3; 2 Tim. i. 2; 1 Pet. i. 2.——[g] Acts xx. 1, 3; Phil. ii. 24.——[h] Gal. i. 6, 7; chap. vi. 3, 10.——[i] Chap. iv. 7; vi. 4, 20; 2 Tim ii. 14, 16, 23; Tit. i. 14; iii. 9.——[k] Chap. vi. 4.

NOTES ON CHAP. I.

Verse 1. *Paul an apostle—by the commandment of God*] We have already seen that the term απoστoλoς, *apostle,* literally signifies a *person sent* from one to another, without implying any particular *dignity* in the person, or *importance* in the message. But it is differently used in the New Testament, being applied to those who were *sent expressly from God Almighty,* with the message of salvation to mankind. It is, therefore, the highest character any human being can have ; and the message is the most important which even God himself can send to his intelligent creatures. It was by the express command of God that St. Paul went to the Gentiles preaching the doctrine of salvation by faith in Christ Jesus.

Jesus Christ—our hope] Without Jesus, the world was *hopeless ;* the *expectation* of being saved can only come to mankind by his Gospel. He is called our *hope,* as he is called our *life,* our *peace,* our *righteousness,* &c., because from him hope, life, peace, righteousness, and all other blessings proceed.

Verse 2. *My own son in the faith*] Brought to salvation through Christ by my ministry alone. Probably the apostle speaks here according to this Jewish maxim : כל המלמד בן חבירו תורה מעלה עליו הכתוב כאלו ילדו *He who teaches the law to his neighbour's son is considered by the Scripture as if he had begotten him ;* Sanhedrin, fol. xix. 2. And they quote Num. iii. 1, as proving it : *These are the generations of Aaron and Moses—and these are the names of the sons of Aaron.* "Aaron," say they, " *begot* them, but Moses *instructed* them ; therefore they are called by his name." See *Schoettgen.*

But γνησιω τεκνω may mean *my beloved son;* for in this sense το γνησιον is not unfrequently used.

In the faith] The word πιστις, *faith,* is taken here for the whole of the Christian religion, *faith in Christ* being its essential characteristic.

Grace, mercy, and peace] GRACE, the favour and approbation of God. MERCY, springing from that grace, pardoning, purifying, and supporting. PEACE, the consequence of this manifested mercy, peace of conscience, and peace with God ; producing internal happiness, quietness, and assurance.

Verse 3. *I besought thee*] The apostle had seen that a bad seed had been sown in the Church ; and, as he was obliged to go then into Macedonia, he wished Timothy, on whose prudence, piety, and soundness in the faith he could depend, to stay behind and prevent the spreading of a doctrine that would have been pernicious to the people's souls. I have already supposed that this epistle was written *after* Paul had been delivered from his first imprisonment at Rome, about the end of the year 64, or the beginning of 65. See the *preface.* When, therefore, the apostle came from Rome into Asia, he no doubt visited Ephesus, where, ten years before, he had planted a Christian Church , and, as he had not time to tarry then, he left Timothy to correct abuses.

That thou mightest charge some] He does not name any persons ; the *Judaizing teachers* are generally supposed to be those intended ; and the term τισι, *some, certain persons,* which he uses, is expressive of high disapprobation, and at the same time of delicacy : they were not *apostles,* nor *apostolic men ;* but they were undoubtedly *members* of the Church at Ephesus, and might yet be reclaimed.

Verse 4. *Neither give heed to fables*] Idle fancies ; things of no moment ; doctrines and opinions unauthenticated ; silly legends, of which no people ever possessed a greater stock than the Jews. Their *Talmud* abounds with them ; and the English reader may find them in abundance in *Stehlin's* Jewish Traditions, 2 vols. 8vo.

Endless genealogies] I suppose the apostle to mean those genealogies which were *uncertain*—that never could be *made out,* either in the *ascending* or *descending* line ; and, principally, such as referred to the great promise of the *Messiah,* and to the *priesthood.* The Jews had scrupulously preserved their genealogical tables till the advent of Christ ; and the evangelists had recourse to them, and appealed to them in reference to our Lord's descent from the house of David ; Matthew taking this genealogy in the *descend-*

2

A. M. cir. 4069.
A. D. 64 or 65.
A. U. C. 818.
An. Imp. Ne-
ronis Cæs.
Aug. 12.

5 Now ¹ the end of the commandment is charity ᵐ out of a
pure heart, and *of* a good conscience, and *of* faith unfeigned ;

6 From which some ⁿ having
swerved have turned aside unto
° vain jangling ;
7 Desiring to be teachers of

A. M. cir 4069
A. D. 64 or 65.
A. U. C. 818.
An. Imp. Ne-
ronis Cæs.
Aug. 12.

---

¹ Rom. xiii. 8, 10; Gal. v. 14.——ᵐ 2 Tim. ii. 22.

ⁿ Or, *not aiming at.*——° Chap. vi. 4, 20.

---

ing, Luke in the *ascending*, line. And whatever difficulties we may now find in these genealogies, they
were certainly clear to the Jews ; nor did the most
determined enemies of the Gospel attempt to raise one
objection to it from the appeal which the evangelists
had made to their own public and accredited tables.
All was then *certain ;* but we are told that Herod destroyed the public registers : he, being an Idumean,
was jealous of the noble origin of the Jews ; and, that
none might be able to reproach him with his descent,
he ordered the genealogical tables, which were kept
among the archives in the temple, to be burnt. See
Euseb. H. E., lib. i. cap. 8. From this time the
Jews could refer to their genealogies only from *memory*, or from those imperfect tables which had been
preserved in private hands ; and to make out any regular *line* from these must have been *endless* and uncertain. It is probably to this that the apostle refers;
I mean the endless and useless labour which the attempts to make out these genealogies must produce,
the authentic tables being destroyed. This, were all
other proofs wanting, would be an irresistible argument
against the Jews that the Messiah is come ; for their
own prophets had distinctly marked out the line by
which he was to come ; the genealogies are now all
lost ; nor is there a Jew in the universe that can show
from what tribe he is descended. There can, therefore, be no Messiah to come, as none could show, let
him have what other pretensions he might, that he
sprang from the house of David. The Jews do not,
at present, pretend to have any such tables ; and, far
from being able to prove the Messiah from his descent,
they are now obliged to say that, when the Messiah
comes, he will restore the genealogies by the Holy
Spirit that shall rest upon him. " For," says *Maimonides,* " in the days of the Messiah, when his kingdom
shall be established, all the Israelites shall be gathered
together unto him ; and all shall be classed in their
genealogies by his mouth, through the Holy Spirit that
shall rest upon him ; as it is written, Mal. iii. 3 : *He
shall sit as a refiner and purifier of silver, and he shall
purify the sons of Levi.* First he will purify the *Levites*, and shall say : ' This man is a descendant from
the *priests ;* and this, of the stock of the *Levites ;*'
and he shall cast out those who are not of the stock
of Israel ; for behold it is said, Ezra ii. 63 : *And the
Tirshatha said—they should not eat of the most holy
things, till there stood up a priest with Urim and
Thummim.* Thus, by the Holy Spirit, the genealogies
are to be revised." See *Schoettgen.*
   Some learned men suppose that the apostle alludes
here to the *Æons*, among the *Gnostics* and *Valenti-
nians*, of whom there were endless numbers to make
up what was called their *pleroma ;* or to the *sephiroth*,
or splendours of the *Cabalists*. But it is certain that
these heresies had not arrived to any formidable head

in the apostle's time ; and it has long been a doubt
with me whether they even existed at that time : and
I think it the most simple way, and most likely to be
the intention of the apostle, to refer all to the Jewish
genealogies, which he calls *Jewish fables*, Tit. i. 14,
to which we know they were strongly and even conscientiously attached ; and which, at this time, it must
have been extremely difficult to make out.
   Instead of γενεαλογιαις, *genealogies*, some learned
men have conjectured that the original word was κενο-
λογιαις, *empty words, vain speeches ;* but this conjecture is not supported by any MS. or *version*.
   Which minister questions] They are the foundation of endless altercations and disputes ; for, being
uncertain and not *consecutive*, every person had a right
to call them in question ; as we may naturally suppose,
from the state in which the genealogical tables of the
Jews then were, that many *chasms* must be supplied
in different *lines*, and consequently much must be done
by *conjecture.*
   Rather than godly edifying] Such discussions as
these had no tendency to promote *piety*. Many, no
doubt, employed much of that time in inquiring *who*
were their *ancestors*, which they should have spent in
obtaining that grace by which, being *born from above*,
they might have become the *sons and daughters of
God Almighty.*
   Instead of οικοδομιαν Θεου, *godly edifying*, or *the
edification of God*, οικονομιαν Θεου, the economy or dispensation of God, is the reading of almost every MS.
in which this part of the epistle is extant, (for some
MSS. are here mutilated,) and of almost all the *versions*, and the chief of the Greek *fathers*. Of the
genuineness of this reading scarcely a doubt can be
formed ; and though the old reading, which is supported by the *Latin* fathers and the *Vulgate*, gives a good
sense, yet the connection and spirit of the place show
that the latter must be the true reading. *Griesbach*
has received this reading into the text.
   What had Jewish *genealogies* to do with the Gospel ? Men were not to be saved by virtue of the *privileges* or *piety* of their ancestors. The Jews depended much on this. *We have Abraham to our father* imposed silence on every check of conscience,
and every godly reproof which they received for their
profligacy and unbelief. In the *dispensation of God*,
FAITH in Christ Jesus was the only means and way of
salvation. These *endless* and *uncertain genealogies*
produced no faith ; indeed they were intended as a
substitute for it ; for those who were intent on making
out their *genealogical descent* paid little attention to
faith in Christ. They *ministered questions rather
than that economy of God which is by faith.* This
dispensation, says the apostle, *is by faith*, οικονομιαν
Θεου την εν πιστει· It was not by *natural descent*, nor
by *works*, but by *faith* in Christ ; therefore it was

584

2

A. M. cir. 4069.
A. D. 64 or 65.
A. U. C. 818.
An. Imp. Ne-
ronis Cæs.
Aug. 12.

the law ; ᵖ understanding neither what they say, nor whereof they affirm.

8 But we know that ᑫ the law *is* good, if a man use it lawfully ;

9 ʳ Knowing this, that the law is not made

for a righteous man, but for the lawless and disobedient, for the ungodly and for sinners, for unholy and profane, for murderers of fathers and murderers of mothers, for man-slayers,

A. M. cir. 4069.
A. D. 64 or 65.
A. U. C. 818.
An. Imp. Ne-
ronis Cæs.
Aug. 12.

ᵖ Chap. vi. 4.——ᑫ Rom. vii. 12.

ʳ Gal. iii. 19 ; v. 23.

necessary that the people who were seeking salvation in any other way should be strictly informed that all their toil and labour would be vain.

Verse 5. Now the end of the commandment is charity] These genealogical questions lead to *strife* and *debate ;* and the *dispensation of God* leads to *love* both to God and man, through faith in Christ. These genealogical questions leave the *heart* under the influence of all its *vile tempers* and *evil propensities ;* FAITH in Jesus *purifies* the heart. No inquiry of this kind can add to any thing by which the *guilt of sin* can be taken away ; but the Gospel proclaims *pardon,* through the blood of the Lamb, to every believing penitent. The *end,* aim, and design of God in giving this dispensation to the world is, that men may have an *unfeigned faith,* such as lays hold on Christ crucified, and produces a *good conscience* from a sense of the pardon received, and leads on to *purity of heart ;* LOVE to God and man being the grand issue of the grace of Christ here below, and this fully preparing the soul for eternal glory. He whose soul is filled with love to God and man has a *pure heart,* a *good conscience,* and *unfeigned faith.* But these blessings no soul can ever acquire, but according to *God's dispensation of faith.*

The paraphrase and note of Dr. *Macknight* on this verse are very proper : "*Now the scope of the charge* to be given by thee to these teachers *is,* that, instead of inculcating fables and genealogies, they inculcate *love* to God and man, proceeding from *a pure heart,* and directed by *a good conscience, and* nourished by *unfeigned faith* in the Gospel doctrine. The word παραγγελια denotes a *message* or *order,* brought to one from another, and delivered by word of mouth. The *charge* here meant is that which the apostle ordered Timothy to deliver to the teachers in Ephesus ; for he had said,' ver. 3 : I had besought thee *to abide still at Ephesus,* ινα παραγγειλης, *that thou mightest charge some :* here he tells him what the scope of this charge was to be."

Of *faith unfeigned*] Πιστεως ανυποκριτου· A *faith not hypocritical.* The apostle appears to allude to the Judaizing teachers, who *pretended faith* in the Gospel, merely that they might have the greater opportunity to bring back to the Mosaic system those who had embraced the doctrine of Christ crucified. This is evident from the following verse.

Verse 6. From which some having swerved] *From which some,* though they have pretended to aim at the τελος, *scope,* or *mark,* have *missed that mark.* This is the import of the original word αστοχησαντες.

Turned aside unto vain jangling] The original term, ματαιολογιαν, signifies *empty* or *vain talking ;* discourses that turn to no profit ; a great many words

and little sense ; and that sense not worth the pains of hearing. Such, indeed, is all preaching where Jesus Christ is not held forth.

Verse 7. Teachers of the law] To be esteemed or celebrated as *rabbins ;* to be reputed cunning in solving knotty questions and enigmas, which answered no end to true religion. Of such the rabbinical teaching was full.

Understanding neither what they say] This is evident from almost all the Jewish comments which yet remain. Things are *asserted* which are either *false* or *dubious ;* words, the import of which they did not understand, were brought to illustrate them : so that it may be said, They *understand not what they say, nor whereof they affirm.* I will give one instance from the *Jerusalem Targum,* on Gen. i. 15 : *And God made two great lights, and they were equal in splendour twenty-one years, the six hundred and seventy-second part of an hour excepted : and afterwards the moon brought a false accusation against the sun, and therefore she was lessened ; and God made the sun the greater light to superintend the day, &c.* I could produce a thousand of a similar complexion.

Verse 8. But we know that the law is good] The law as given by God, is both *good in itself,* and has a good *tendency.* This is similar to what the apostle had asserted, Rom. vii. 12—16 : *The law is holy ; and the commandment is holy, just, and good ;* where see the note.

If a man use it lawfully] That is, interpret it according to its own spirit and design, and use it for the purpose for which God has given it ; for the *ceremonial law* was a schoolmaster to lead us unto Christ, and Christ is the end of that law for justification to every one that believes. Now those who did not use the law in reference to these ends, did not use it *lawfully*—they did not construe it according to its original design and meaning.

Verse 9. The law is not made for a righteous man] There is a *moral law* as well as a *ceremonial law :* as the object of the *latter* is to *lead us to Christ,* the object of the *former* is to *restrain crimes,* and inflict punishment on those that commit them. It was, therefore, not made for the *righteous* as a restrainer of crimes, and an inflicter of punishments ; for the righteous avoid sin, and by living to the glory of God expose not themselves to its censures. This seems to be the mind of the apostle ; he does not say *that the law was not* MADE *for a righteous man,* but ου κειται, *it does not* LIE *against a righteous man ;* because *he* does not transgress it : but it *lies against the wicked ;* for such as the apostle mentions have broken it, and grievously too, and are condemned by it. The word κειται, lies, refers to the custom of writing laws on boards, and hanging them up in public places within

A. M. cir. 4069.
A. D. 64 or 65.
A. U. C. 818.
An. Imp. Neronis Cæs.
Aug. 12.

10 For whoremongers, for them that defile themselves with mankind, for men-stealers, for liars, for perjured persons, and if there be any other thing that is contrary ^s to sound doctrine ;

11 According to the glorious Gospel of ^t the blessed God, ^u which was committed to my trust.

A. M. cir. 4069.
A. D. 64 or 65.
A. U. C. 818.
An. Imp. Neronis Cæs.
Aug. 12.

12 And I thank Christ Jesus our Lord, ^v who hath enabled me, ^w for that he counted

---

^s Chap. vi. 3 ; 2 Tim. iv. 3 ; Tit. i. 9 ; ii. 1.——^t Chap. vi. 15.
^u1 Cor. ix. 17 ; Gal. ii. 7 ; Col. i. 25 ; 1 Thess. ii. 4 ; chapter ii.

7 ; 2 Timothy i. 11 ; Tit. i. 3.——^v 2 Cor. xii. 9.——^w 1 Cor. vii. 25.

---

reach of every man, that they might be read by all ; thus all would see against whom the law *lay*.

The lawless] Ανομοις· Those who will not be *bound by a law*, and acknowledge none, therefore have no rule of moral conduct.

Disobedient] Ανυποτακτοις· Those who acknowledge no *authority* ; from *a*, *negative*, and ὑποτασσω, *to subject* ; they neither acknowledge *law*, nor *executive authority*, and consequently endeavour to live as they list ; and from such dispositions all the crimes in the following catalogue may naturally spring.

For the ungodly] Ασεβεσι· The *irreligious*—those who do *not worship God*, or have no *true worship* ; from *a*, *negative*, and σεβω, to *worship*. For *sinners*, ἁμαρτωλοις, those who *transgress* the laws ; from *a*, *negative*, and μαρπτω, *to hit the mark*. This has been elsewhere explained.

For unholy] Ανοσιοις· Persons *totally polluted*—unclean *within*, and unclean *without* ; from *a*, *negative*, and ὁσιος, *holy*.

And profane] Βεβηλοις· Such who are so unholy and abominable as not to be fit to attend any public worship ; from βε, denoting *privation* or *separation*, and βηλος, a *threshold* or *pavement*, particularly of a temple. Our word *profane* comes from *procul a fano*, "*far from the temple*." When the ancients, even heathens, were about to perform some very sacred rites, they were accustomed to command the irreligious to keep at a distance ; hence that saying in a fragment of *Orpheus* :—

Φθεγξομαι οἱς θεμις εστι· θυρας δ' επιθεσθε βεβηλοις Πασιν ὁμως.

" I will speak to whom it is lawful ; but these doors, O, shut against the profane."

And that of *Virgil*, Æn. vi. ver. 258.

Procul ! O procul ! este profani.

Far ! ye *profane* ! get hence.

Murderers of fathers] Πατραλωαις. The murderer of a father or a mother, notwithstanding the deep fall of man, and the general profligacy of the world, has been so rare, and is a crime so totally opposite to nature, that few civilized nations have found it necessary to make laws against it. Yet, such monsters, like the most awful and infrequent *portents*, have .sometimes terrified the world with their appearance. But I think the original does not necessarily imply the *murder* of a father or of a mother ; πατραλωας comes from πατερα, a *father*, and αλοιαω, *to strike*, and may mean simply *beating* or *striking* a *father* or *mother* : this is horrible enough ; but to murder a parent *out-herods* Herod.

Manslayers] Ανδροφονοις· *Murderers* simply ; all

who take away the life of a human being contrary to law. For no *crime*, unless it be *murder*, should any man lose his life. If the law did not speak differently, I should not scruple to say that he whose life is taken away, except for murder, is murdered.

Verse 10. *For whoremongers*] Πορνοις· Adulterers, fornicators, and prostitutes of all sorts.

Them that defile themselves with mankind] Αρσενοκοιταις· From αρσην, a *male*, and κοιτη, a *bed* ; a word too bad to be explained. A *sodomite*.

Men-stealers] Ανδραποδισταις· *Slave-dealers* ; whether those who *carry on the traffic* in human *flesh and blood* ; or those who *steal* a person in order to sell him into bondage ; or those who *buy* such stolen men or women, no matter of what *colour* or what *country* ; or those who *sow dissensions* among barbarous tribes in order that they who are taken in war may be sold into slavery ; or the *nations* who *legalize* or *connive* at such traffic : all these are *men-stealers*, and God classes them with the most flagitious of mortals.

For liars] Ψευσταις· They who speak for *truth* what they know to be *false* ; and even they who tell *the truth* in such a way as to lead others to draw a contrary meaning from it.

For perjured persons] Επιορκοις· From επι, *against*, and ὁρκος, *an oath* ; such as *do* or leave *undone* any thing *contrary* to an oath or moral engagement, whether that engagement be made by what is called *swearing*, or by an *affirmation* or *promise* of any kind.

And if there be any other thing] Every species of vice and immorality, all must be necessarily included, that is contrary to *sound doctrine*—to the immutable moral law of God, as well as to the pure precepts of Christianity where that law is incorporated, explained, and rendered, if possible, more and more binding.

Verse 11. *According to the glorious Gospel*] The *sound doctrine* mentioned above, which is here called εναγγελιον της δοξης του μακαριου Θεου, the *Gospel of the glory of the blessed* or *happy God*—a dispensation which exhibits the *glory* of all his *attributes* ; and, by saving man in such a way as is consistent with the *glory* of all the Divine perfections, while it brings peace and good will among men, brings *glory* to God in the highest. Sin has dishonoured God, and robbed him of his *glory* ; the Gospel provides for the total destruction of sin, even in this world, and thus brings back to God his glory.

Verse 12. *I thank Christ*] I feel myself under infinite obligation to Christ who hath *strengthened me*, ενδυναμωσαντι, who hath *endued me with various miraculous gifts* of his Holy Spirit, and put me into the *ministry*, διακονιαν, the *deaconship*, the *service of mankind*, by preaching the Gospel, for that he *counted me*

2

A. M. cir. 4069.
A. D. 64 or 65.
A. U. C. 818.
An. Imp. Ne-
ronis Cæs.
Aug. 12.

me faithful, ˣ putting me into the ministry;

13 ʸ Who was before a blasphemer, and a persecutor, and injurious: but I obtained mercy, because ᶻ I did it ignorantly in unbelief.

14 ᵃ And the grace of our Lord was exceeding abundant ᵇ with faith ᶜ and love which is in Christ Jesus.

---

x 2 Cor. iii. 5, 6; iv. 1; Col. i. 25.——y Acts viii. 3; ix. 1; 1 Cor. xv. 9; Phil. iii. 6.——z Luke xxiii. 34; John ix. 39, 41; Acts iii. 17; xxvi. 9.——a Rom. v. 20; 1 Cor. xv. 10.

---

15 ᵈ This *is* a faithful saying, and worthy of all acceptation, that ᵉ Christ Jesus came into the world to save sinners; of whom I am chief.

16 Howbeit for this cause ᶠ I obtained mercy, that in me first Jesus Christ might show forth all long-suffering, ᵍ for a pattern to them which should hereafter believe on him to life everlasting.

A. M. cir. 4069.
A. D. 64 or 65.
A. U. C. 818.
An. Imp. Ne-
ronis Cæs.
Aug. 12.

---

b 2 Tim. i. 13.——c Luke vii. 47.——d Chap. iii. 1; iv. 9; 2 Tim. ii. 11; Tit. iii. 8.——e Matt. ix. 13; Mark ii. 17; Luke v. 32; xix. 10; Rom. v. 8; 1 John iii. 5.——f 2 Cor. iv. 1.——g Acts xiii. 39.

—he knew that I would be, *faithful* to the charge that was delivered to me.

Verse 13. *A blasphemer*] Speaking impiously and unjustly of Jesus, his doctrine, his ways, and his followers.

And—persecutor] Endeavouring, to the uttermost of his power, to *exterminate* all who called on the name of the Lord Jesus.

And injurious] Και ὑβριστην· As full of insolence as I was of malevolence; and yet, all the while, thinking I did God service, while sacrificing men and women to my own prejudices and intolerance.

I did it ignorantly in unbelief.] Not *having considered* the nature and evidences of Christianity, and not having *believed* that Jesus was the promised *Messiah*, I acted wholly under the prejudices that influenced my countrymen in general. God therefore showed me mercy, because I acted under this influence, not knowing better. This extension of mercy, does not, however, excuse the infuriated conduct of Saul of Tarsus, for he says himself that he was *exceedingly mad against them.* Let us beware, lest we lose the man's former crimes in his after character.

Verse 14. *The grace of our Lord was exceeding abundant*] The original is very emphatic, *that grace of our Lord,* ὑπερεπλεονασε, *hath superabounded*—it manifested itself in a way of *extraordinary* mercy.

With faith and love] Not only pardoning such offences, but leading me to the full experimental knowledge of Christianity; of that *faith* and *love* which are essential to it; and giving me authority to proclaim it to mankind.

Verse 15. *Christ Jesus came into the world to save sinners*] This is one of the most glorious truths in the book of God; the most important that ever reached the human ear, or can be entertained by the heart of man. *All men* are sinners; and as such condemned, justly condemned, to eternal death. Christ Jesus became incarnate, suffered, and died to redeem them; and, by his grace and Spirit, *saves* them from their sins. This *saying* or *doctrine* he calls, *first,* a *faithful* or *true* saying; πιστος ὁ λογος, it is a doctrine that may be *credited,* without the slightest doubt or hesitation; God himself has spoken it; and the death of Christ and the mission of the Holy Ghost, sealing pardon on the souls of all who believe, have confirmed and established the truth.

Secondly, it is *worthy of all acceptation;* as all

need it, it is worthy of being received by *all*. It is designed for the whole human race, for all that are *sinners* is applicable to *all,* because all are *sinners;* and may be received by *all,* being put within every man's reach, and brought to every man's ear and bosom, either by the letter of the word, or, where that revelation is not yet come, by the power of the Divine Spirit, the true light from Christ that lightens every man that cometh into the world. From this also it is evident that the death of Christ, and all its eternally saving effects, were designed for *every man.*

Of whom I am chief.] Ὡν πρωτος ειμι εγω. Confounding *Paul* the *apostle,* in the fulness of his faith and love, with *Saul* of *Tarsus,* in his ignorance, unbelief, and persecuting rage, we are in the habit of saying: "This is a *hyperbolical* expression, arguing the height of the apostle's modesty and humility; and must not be taken according to the letter." I see it not in this light; I take it not with abatement; it is strictly and literally true: take the whole of the apostle's conduct, previously to his conversion, into consideration, and was there a greater sinner converted to God from the incarnation to his own time? Not one; he was the *chief;* and, keeping his *blasphemy, persecution,* and *contumely* in view, he asserts: Of all that the Lord Jesus came into the world to save, and of all that he *had saved* to that time, *I am chief.* And who, however humble now, and however flagitious before, could have contested the points with him? He *was what* he has said, and *as* he has said it. And it is very probable that the apostle refers to those in whom the grace and mercy of God were, at the *first* promulgation of the Gospel, manifested: and comparing himself with all these he could with propriety say, ὡν πρωτος ειμι, *of whom I am the first;* the *first* who, from a blasphemer, persecutor (and might we not add *murderer?* see the part he took in the martyrdom of Stephen,) became a preacher of that Gospel which I had persecuted. And hence, keeping this idea strictly in view, he immediately adds: *Howbeit, for this cause I obtained mercy; that in me* FIRST, πρωτῳ, *Jesus Christ might show forth all long-suffering, for a pattern* TO THEM *which should* HEREAFTER, των μελλοντων *believe on him to life everlasting.* And this great display of the pardoning mercy of God, granted in so singular a manner, at the very *first* promulgation of the Gospel, was most proper to be produced as a *pattern* for the encouragement of all

2

A. M. cir. 4069.
A. D. 64 or 65.
A. U. C. 818.
An. Imp. Ne-
ronis Cæs.
Aug. 12.

17 Now unto ʰ the King eternal, ⁱ immortal, ᵏ invisible, ˡ the only wise God, ᵐ *be* honour and glory for ever and ever. Amen.

18 This charge ⁿ I commit unto thee, son Timothy, ᵒ according to the prophecies which went before on thee, that thou by them mightest ᵖ war a good warfare;

19 ۹ Holding faith, and a good conscience; which some having put away, concerning faith, ʳ have made shipwreck:

20 Of whom is ˢ Hymeneus and ᵗ Alexander; whom I have ᵘ delivered unto Satan, that they may learn not to ᵛ blaspheme.

A. M. cir. 4069.
A. D. 64 or 65
A. U. C. 818.
An. Imp. Ne
ronis Cæs.
Aug. 12.

ʰ Psa. x. 16; cxlv. 13; Dan. vii. 14; chap. vi. 15, 16.——ⁱ Rom. i. 23.——ᵏ John i. 18; Heb. xi. 27; 1 John iv. 12.——ˡ Rom. xvi. 27; Jude 25.——ᵐ 1 Chron. xxix. 11.——ⁿ Chap. vi. 13, 14, 20;

2 Tim. ii. 2.——ᵒ Eccles. xvi. 1; chap. iv. 14.——ᵖ Chap. vi. 12; 2 Tim. ii. 3; iv. 7.——۹ Chap. iii. 9.——ʳ Chap. vi. 9. ˢ 2 Tim. ii. 17.——ᵗ 2 Tim. ii. 14.——ᵘ 1 Cor. v. 5.——ᵛ Acts xiii. 45.

penitent sinners to the end of time. If Jesus Christ, with whom there can be no *respect of persons*, saved Saul of Tarsus, no sinner need despair.

Verse 17. Now unto the King eternal] This burst of thanksgiving and gratitude to God, naturally arose from the subject then under his pen and eye. God has most wondrously manifested his mercy, in this *beginning* of the Gospel, by saving me, and making me a *pattern* to all them that shall *hereafter believe* on Christ. He is βασιλευς των αιωνων, *the king of eternities*; the eternity *a parte ante*, and the eternity *a parte post*; the eternity that *was* before *time* was, and the *eternity* that *shall* be when *time* is *no more*. Therefore, *ever living* to justify and save sinners, to the end of the world.

Immortal] Αφθαρτω· *Incorruptible*—not liable to decay or corruption; a simple uncompounded essence, incapable, therefore, of decomposition, and consequently permanent and eternal. One MS., the later *Syriac* in the margin, the *Vulgate*, one copy of the *Itala*, and some of the *Latin fathers*, read αθανατω, *immortal*, which our translation follows; but it is not the original reading.

Invisible] Αορατω· One who fills all things, works everywhere, and yet is *invisible* to angels and men; the perfect reverse of false gods and idols, who are *confined* to *one spot*, *work nowhere*, and, being stocks and stones, *are seen* by every body.

The only wise God] The word σοφω, *wise*, is omitted by AD*FG, *Syriac, Erpen's Arabic, Coptic, Sahidic, Æthiopic, Armenian, Vulgate*, and *Itala* Some of the Greek fathers quote it sometimes, and omit it at others; which shows that it was an unsettled reading, probably borrowed from Rom. xvi. 27. See the note there. *Griesbach* leaves it out of the text. Without it the reading is very strong and appropriate: *To the only God*; nothing visible or invisible being worthy of adoration but himself

Be honour] All the *respect* and *reverence* that can be paid by intelligent beings, ascribing to him at the same time all the *glory*—excellences, and perfections, which can be possessed by an intelligent, unoriginated, independent, and eternal Being; and this for ever and ever—through *eternity*.

Verse 18. This charge] See the note on ver. 5. It was a *charge* that the Judaizing teachers should not teach differently from that doctrine which the apostle had delivered to him. See ver. 3

According to the prophecies] This may refer to some predictions by inspired men, relative to what Timothy should be and he wishes him to act in all

things conformably to those predictions. It was predicted that he should have this high and noble calling; but his behaviour in that calling was a matter of *con tingency*, as it respected the *use* he might make of the grace of his calling. The apostle therefore exhorts him to *war a good warfare, &c.* He was now called to that estate to which the prophecies referred; and now he is to act *worthily* or *unworthily* of that calling, according as he *fought* or *did not fight* the good warfare, and according as he *held* or did *not hold* faith and a good conscience.

Some think that the προαγουσας προφητειας, *the foregoing prophecies*, refer to *revelations* which the apostle himself had received concerning Timothy; while others think that the word is to be understood of *advices, directions,* and *exhortations*, which the apostle had previously delivered to him; we know that προφητευω signifies to *speak to men to edification, to exhortation,* and *to comfort.* See 1 Cor. xiv. 3. This is a very sober and good sense of the passage.

War a good warfare] The trials and afflictions of the followers of God are often represented as a *warfare* or *campaign.* See Isa. xl. 2; 1 Cor. ix. 7; 2 Cor. x. 4; and see the reasons of this metaphorical form of speech, in the notes on Eph. vi. 13.

Verse 19. Holding faith] All the *truths* of the *Christian religion*, firmly believing them, and fervently proclaiming them to others.

And a good conscience] So holding the *truth* as to *live* according to its dictates, that a *good conscience* may be ever preserved. As the apostle had just spoken of the Christian's *warfare*, so he here refers to the Christian *armour*, especially to the *shield* and *breastplate*; the shield of *faith*, and the *breastplate* of *righteousness* See on Eph vi. 13, &c., and 1 Thess v 8·

Which some having put away] Απωσαμενοι· Having thrust away; as a fool-hardy soldier might his *shield* and his *breastplate*, or a mad sailor his pilot, helm, and compass.

Concerning faith] The great *truths* of the Christian religion.

Have made shipwreck] Being without *the faith*, that only infallible system of truth; *and a good conscience*, that skilful *pilot*, that steady and commanding helm, that faithful and invariable loadstone; *have been driven to and fro by every wind of doctrine*, and, getting among *shoals, quicksands*, and *rocks*, have been shipwrecked and ingulfed.

Verse 20. Of whom is Hymeneus and Alexander]

Who *had* the *faith* but *thrust it away;* who *had a good conscience* through believing, but made *shipwreck* of it. Hence we find that all this was not only *possible,* but did *actually* take place, though some have endeavoured to maintain the contrary ; who, confounding eternity with a state of probation, have supposed that if a man once enter into the grace of God in this life, he must necessarily continue in it to all eternity. Thousands of texts and thousands of facts refute this doctrine.

Delivered unto Satan] For the destruction of the flesh, that the spirit might be saved in the day of the Lord Jesus. See what is noted on 1 Cor. v. 5 ; what this sort of punishment was no man now living knows. There is nothing of the kind referred to in the Jewish writings. It seems to have been something done by mere apostolical authority, under the direction of the Spirit of God.

Hymeneus, it appears, denied the resurrection, see 2 Tim. ii. 17, 18 ; but whether this *Alexander* be the same with *Alexander the coppersmith,* 2 Tim. iv. 14, or the *Alexander,* Acts xix. 33, cannot be determined. Probably, he was the same with the *coppersmith.* Whether they were brought back to the acknowledgment of the truth does not appear. From what is said in the second epistle the case seems extremely doubtful. Let him who most assuredly standeth, take heed lest he fall.

He that is *self-confident* is already half fallen. He who professes to believe that God will *absolutely* keep him from falling finally, and neglects watching unto prayer, is not in a safer state. He who lives by the moment, walks in the light, and maintains his communion with God, is in no danger of apostasy.

CHAPTER II.

Prayer, supplication, and thanksgiving, must be made for all men ; because God wills that all should be saved,
    1–4. There is but one God and one Mediator, 5–7. How men should pray, 8. How women should adorn themselves, 9, 10. They are not suffered to teach, nor to usurp authority over men, 11–14. How they may expect to be saved in child-bearing, 15.

A. M. cir. 4069.
A. D. 64 or 65.
A. U. C. 818.
An. Imp. Neronis Cæs.
Aug. 12.

I [a] EXHORT therefore, that, first of all, supplications, prayers, intercessions, *and* giving of thanks, be made for all men ;

2 [b] For kings, and [c] *for* all that are in [d] authority ; that we may lead a quiet and peaceable life in all godliness and honesty.

A. M. cir. 4069.
A. D. 64 or 65.
A. U. C. 818.
An. Imp. Neronis Cæs.
Aug. 12.

---

[a] Or, *desire.*——[b] Ezra vi. 10 ; Jer. xxix. 7.

[c] Rom. xiii. 1.——[d] Or, *eminent place.*

NOTES ON CHAP. II.

Verse 1. *I exhort—that, first of all*] *Prayer* for the pardon of sin, and for obtaining necessary supplies of grace, and continual protection from God, with gratitude and thanksgiving for mercies already received, are duties which our sinful and dependent state renders absolutely necessary ; and which should be chief in our view, *first of all* performed. It is difficult to know the precise difference between the four words used here by the apostle. They are sometimes distinguished thus :—

Supplications] Δεησεις· Prayers for *averting evils* of every kind.

Prayers] Προσευχας· Prayers *for obtaining the good things,* spiritual and temporal, which ourselves need.

Intercessions] Εντευξεις· Prayers *in behalf of others.*

Giving of thanks] Ευχαριστιας· Praises to God, as the parent of all good, for all the blessings which we and others have received. It is probable that the apostle gives directions here for public worship ; and that the words may be thus paraphrased : " *Now, I exhort first of all* that, in the public assemblies, *deprecations* of evils, and *supplications* for such good things as are necessary, and *intercessions* for their conversion, and *thanksgiving* for mercies, *be offered in behalf of all men*—for heathens as well as for Christians, and for enemies as well as for friends." See *Macknight.*

Verse 2. *For kings*] As it is a positive maxim of Christianity to pray for all secular governors, so it

has ever been the practice of Christians. When *St. Cyprian* defended himself before the Roman proconsul, he said : *Hunc* (*Deum*) *deprecamur—pro nobis et pro omnibus hominibus ; et pro incolumitate ipsorum Imperatorum.* " We pray to God, not only for ourselves, but for all mankind ; and particularly for the emperors."

Tertullian, in his Apology, is more particular : *Oramus pro omnibus Imperatoribus, vitam illis prolixam, imperium securum, domum tutam, exercitus fortes, senatum fidelem, populum probum, orbem quietum, et quæcunque hominis et Cæsaris vota sunt.* Apol., cap. 30. " We pray for all the emperors, that God may grant them long life, a secure government, a prosperous family, vigorous troops, a faithful senate, an obedient people ; that the whole world may be in peace ; and that God may grant, both to Cæsar and to every man, the accomplishment of their just desires."

So *Origen :* Ευχομεθα τους βασιλεις και αρχοντας μετα της βασιλικης δυναμεως και σωφρονα τον λογισμον εχοντας ευρεθηναι. Cont. Cels., lib. viii. " We pray for kings and rulers, that with their royal authority they may be found possessing a wise and prudent mind." Indeed they prayed even for those by whom they were persecuted. If the state be not in safety, the individual cannot be secure ; self-preservation, therefore, should lead men to pray for the government under which they live. Rebellions and insurrections seldom terminate even in political good ; and even where the government

A. M. cir. 4069.
A. D. 64 or 65.
A. U. C. 818.
An. Imp. Neronis Cæs
Aug 12

3 For this *is* e good and acceptable in the sight f of God our Saviour;

4 g Who will have all men to be saved, h and to come unto the knowledge of the truth.

5 i For *there is* one God, and k one mediator between God and men, the man Christ Jesus;

6 l Who gave himself a ransom for all, m to n be testified o in due time.

A. M. cir 4069.
A. D. 64 or 65.
A. U. C. 818.
An. Imp. Ne ronis Cæs.
Aug. 12.

---

e Romans xii. 2; chapter v. 4.——f Chapter i. 1; 2 Tim i. 9. g Ezekiel xviii. 23; John iii. 16, 17; Titus ii. 11; 2 Pet. iii. 9. h John xvii. 3; 2 Tim. ii. 25.——i Rom. iii. 29, 30; x. 12; Gal. iii. 20.

k Heb. viii. 6; ix. 15.——l Matt. xx. 28; Mark x. 45; Eph. i. 7; Tit. ii. 14.——m 1 Cor. i. 6 r 2 Thess. i. 10; 2 Timothy i. 8. n Or, *a testimony*.——o Rom. v. 6, Gal. iv. 4, Eph. i. 9; iii * 5; Tit. i. 3.

---

is radically bad, *revolutions* themselves are most precarious and hazardous. They who wish such commotions would not be quiet under the most mild and benevolent government.

That we may lead a quiet and peaceable life] We thus pray for the government that the public peace may be preserved. *Good rulers* have power to do much good; we pray that their authority may be ever preserved and well directed. *Bad rulers* have power to do much evil; we pray that they may be prevented from thus using their power. So that, whether the rulers be *good* or *bad*, prayer for them is the positive duty of all Christians; and the answer to their prayers, in either case, will be the means of their being enabled to *lead a quiet and peaceable life in all godliness and honesty.*

Verse 3. *This is good and acceptable*] Prayer for all legally constituted authorities is *good* in itself, because useful to ourselves and to the public at large, and it is *acceptable in the sight of God our Saviour;* and this is its highest sanction and its highest character: it is *good;* it is *well pleasing to God.*

Verse 4. *Who will have all men to be saved*] Because he wills the salvation of all men; therefore, he wills that all men should be prayed for. In the face of such a declaration, how can any Christian soul suppose that God ever unconditionally and eternally reprobated any man? Those who can believe so, one would suppose, can have little acquaintance either with the *nature* of GOD, or the *bowels* of *Christ.*

And to come unto the knowledge of the truth] The *truth*—the Gospel of Christ, should be *proclaimed* to them; and it is the duty of all who know it, to diffuse it far and wide, and when it is made known, then it is the duty of those who hear it to acknowledge and receive it. This is the proper import of the original word, that they may come, εις επιγνωσιν αληθειας, *to the acknowledgment of the truth*—that they may receive it as the truth, and make it the rule of their faith, the model and director of their life and actions.

Verse 5. There is *one God*] Who is the maker, governor, and preserver of all men, of every condition, and of every nation; and equally wills the salvation of all.

And one mediator] The word μεσιτης, *mediator,* signifies, literally, a *middle person,* one whose office it is to reconcile two parties at enmity; and hence *Suidas* explains it by ειρηνοποιος, a *peace-maker.* God was offended with the crimes of men; to restore them to his peace, Jesus Christ was incarnated; and being God and man, both God and men met in and were re-

conciled by him. But this reconciliation required a *sacrifice* on the part of the peace-maker or mediator; hence what follows.

Verse 6. *Who gave himself a ransom*] The word λυτρον signifies a ransom paid for the *redemption of a captive;* and αντιλυτρον, the word used here, and applied to the death of Christ, signifies that ransom which consists in the *exchange of one person for another,* or the *redemption of life* by *life;* or, as *Schleusner* has expressed it in his translation of these words, *Qui morte sua omnes liberavit a vitiositatis vi et pœnis, a servitute quasi et miseria peccatorum.* "He who by his death has redeemed all from the power and punishment of vice, from the slavery and misery of sinners." As God is the God and father of all, (for there is but *one God,* ver. 5,) and Jesus Christ the mediator of all, so he gave himself a ransom for all; i. e., for all that God made, consequently for every human soul; unless we could suppose that there are human souls of which God is not the Creator; for the argument of the apostle is plainly this: 1. There is one God; 2. This God is the Creator of all; 3. He has made a revelation of his kindness to all; 4. He will have all men to be saved, and come unto the knowledge of the truth; and 5. He has provided a mediator for all, who has given himself a ransom for all. As surely as God has created all men, so surely has Jesus Christ died for all men. This is a truth which the nature and revelation of God unequivocally proclaim.

To be testified in due time.] The original words, το μαρτυριον καιροις ιδιοις, are not very clear, and have been understood variously. The most authentic copies of the *printed Vulgate* have simply, *Testimonium temporibus suis;* which CALMET translates: *Rendant ainsi temoignage au tems marqué;* "Thus rendering testimony at the appointed time." Dr. MACKNIGHT thus: *Of which the testimony is in its proper season.* WAKEFIELD thus: "That testimony *reserved* to *its* proper time." ROSENMULLER: *Hæc est doctrina, temporibus suis reservata.* "This is the doctrine which is reserved for its own times;" that is, adds he, *quæ suo tempore in omni terrarum orbe tradetur,* "the doctrine which in its own time shall be delivered to all the inhabitants of the earth." Here he translates μαρτυριον, *doctrine;* and contends that this, not *testimony,* is its meaning, not only in this passage, but in 1 Cor. i. 6; ii. 1, &c. Instead of μαρτυριον, *testimony,* one MS., Cod. Kk., vi. 4, in the public library, Cambridge, has, μυστηριον, *mystery;* but this is not acknowledged by any other MS., nor by any *version.* In D*FG the whole clause is read thus: ου το μαρτυριον

590 2

A. M. cir. 4069.
A. D. 64 or 65.
A. U. C. 818.
An. Imp. Neronis Cæs.
Aug. 12.

7 [p] Whereunto I am ordained
a preacher, and an apostle, [q] (I
speak the truth in Christ, *and*
lie not,) [r] a teacher of the Gentiles in faith and verity.

8 I will therefore that men
pray [s] everywhere, [t] lifting up
holy hands, without wrath and
doubting.

9 In like manner also, that [u] women adorn

A. M. cir. 4069
A. D. 64 or 65.
A. U. C. 818.
An. Imp. Neronis Cæs.
Aug. 12.

[p] Eph. iii. 7, 8; 2 Tim. i. 11.——[q] Rom. ix. 1.——[r] Rom. xi. 13; xv. 16; Gal. i. 16.

[s] Mal. i. 11; John iv. 21.——[t] Psalm cxxxiv. 2; Isaiah i. 15. [u] 1 Pet. iii. 3.

καιροις ιδιοις εδοθη· The testimony of which was given in its own times. This is nearly the reading which was adopted in the *first printed copies* of the *Vulgate.* One of them now before me reads the passage thus: *Cujus testimonium temporibus suis confirmatum est.* "The testimony of which is confirmed in its own times." This reading was adopted by Pope *Sixtus V*, in the *famous* edition published by him; but was corrected to the reading above, by *Pope Clement VIII.* And this was rendered literally by our *first* translator: **Whos witnessinge is confermyd in his tymis.** This appears to be the apostle's meaning: Christ gave himself a ransom for all. This, in the times which seemed best to the Divine wisdom, was to be testified to every nation, and people, and tongue. The apostles had begun this testimony; and, in the course of the Divine economy, it has ever since been gradually promulgated; and at present runs with a more rapid course than ever.

Verse 7. *I am ordained a preacher*] *I am set apart, ετεθην, appointed.* The word does not imply any *imposition of hands* by either *bishop* or *presbytery,* as is vulgarly supposed.

I speak the truth in Christ] As I have received my commission from him, so I testify his truth. I did not run before I was sent; and I speak nothing but what I have received.

A teacher of the Gentiles] Being *specially* commissioned to preach the Gospel, not to the *Jews,* but to the *nations* of the *world.*

In faith and verity.] *Faithfully* and *truly;* preaching the TRUTH, the *whole* TRUTH, and *nothing but* the TRUTH; and this *fervently, affectionately,* and *perseveringly.*

Instead of *εν πιστει, in faith,* the Cod. Alexand. has *εν πνευματι, in spirit.* "A teacher of the Gentiles in spirit and truth."

Verse 8. *I will therefore*] Seeing the apostle had his authority from Christ, and spoke nothing but what he received from him, his *βουλομαι, I will,* is equal to *I command.*

That men pray] That is, for the blessings promised in this testimony of God. For, although God has provided them, yet he will not give them to such as will not pray. See the note on verse 1, the subject of which is here resumed.

Everywhere] Εν παντι τοπῳ· *In every place.* That they should always have a praying heart, and this will ever find a praying place. This may refer to a Jewish superstition. They thought, at first, that no prayer could be acceptable that was not offered at the temple at Jerusalem; afterward this was extended to the Holy Land; but, when they became dispersed among the nations, they built oratories or places of prayer, principally by *rivers* and by the *seaside;* and *in these* they were obliged to allow that public prayer might be legally offered, but nowhere else. In opposition to this, the apostle, by the authority of Christ, commands men to pray *everywhere;* that *all places* belong to God's dominions; and, as he fills every place, in every place he may be worshipped and glorified. As to *ejaculatory* prayer, they allowed that this might be performed *standing, sitting, leaning, lying, walking by the way,* and during their *labour. Beracoth,* fol. xi. 1. And yet in some other places they teach differently. See *Schoettgen.*

Lifting up holy hands] It was a common custom, not only among the *Jews,* but also among the *heathens,* to *lift up* or *spread out* their *arms* and *hands* in prayer. It is properly the action of *entreaty* and *request;* and seems to be an effort to embrace the assistance requested. But the apostle probably alludes to the Jewish custom of *laying their hands on the head of the animal which they brought for a sin-offering, confessing their sins, and then giving up the life of the animal as an expiation for the sins thus confessed.* And this very notion is conveyed in the original term *επαιροντας,* from *αιρω, to lift up,* and *επι, upon* or *over.* This shows us how *Christians* should pray. *They* should come to the altar; set God before their eyes; humble themselves for their *sins;* bring as a sacrifice *the Lamb of God;* lay their hands on this sacrifice; and by faith offer it to God in their souls' behalf, expecting salvation through his meritorious death alone.

Without wrath] Having no vindictive feeling against any person; harbouring no unforgiving spirit, while they are imploring pardon for their own offences.

The *holy hands* refer to the Jewish custom of *washing* their hands before prayer; this was done to signify that they had *put away* all sin, and purposed to *live* a *holy life.*

And doubting.] *Διαλογισμου* or *διαλογισμων,* as in many MSS., *reasonings, dialogues.* Such as are often felt by distressed penitents and timid believers; faith, hope, and unbelief appearing to hold a disputation and controversy in their own bosoms, in the issue of which *unbelief* ordinarily triumphs. The apostle therefore *wills* them to *come,* implicitly relying on the promises of God, and the sacrifice and mediation of Jesus Christ.

Verse 9. *In like manner also*] That is, he *wills* or *commands* what follows, *as* he had commanded what went before.

That women adorn themselves] *Και τας γυναικας εν καταστολῃ κοσμιῳ.* The apostle seems to refer here to different parts of the Grecian and Roman dress. The *στολη, stola,* seems to have been originally very simple. It was a long piece of cloth, doubled in the middle, and sewed up on both sides, leaving room only for the arms; at the top, a piece was cut out, or a slit made,

A. M. cir. 4069.
A. D. 64 or 65.
A. U. C. 818.
An. Imp. Neronis Cæs.
Aug. 12.

themselves in modest apparel, with shame-facedness and sobriety; not with ^v broidered hair, or gold, or pearls, or costly array;

___

^v Or, *plaited.*

___

10 ^w But (which becometh women professing godliness) with good works.

11 Let the woman learn in silence with all subjection.

A. M. cir. 4069.
A. D. 64 or 65.
A. U. C. 818.
An. Imp. Neronis Cæs.
Aug. 12.

___

^w 1 Pet. iii. 4.

___

through which the head passed. It hung down to the feet, both before and behind, and was girded with the *zona* round the body, just under the breasts. It was sometimes made with, sometimes without, sleeves; and, that it might sit the better, it was gathered on each shoulder with a *band* or *buckle.* Some of the Greek women wore them *open* on each side, from the bottom up above the knee, so as to discover a part of the *thigh.* These were termed φαινομηριδες, *showers* (*discoverers*) *of the thigh;* but it was, in general, only *young girls* or *immodest* women who wore them thus.

The κατασολη seems to have been the same as the *pallium* or *mantle,* which, being made nearly in the form of the *stola,* hung down to the *waist,* both in back and front, was gathered on the shoulder with a band or buckle, had a hole or slit at top for the head to pass through, and hung loosely over the *stola,* without being confined by the *zona* or *girdle.* Representations of these dresses may be seen in LENS' *Costume des Peuples de l'Antiquité,* fig. 11, 12, 13, and 16. A more modest and becoming dress than the Grecian was never invented; it was, in a great measure, revived in England about the year 1805, and in it, simplicity, decency, and elegance were united; but it soon gave place to another mode, in which frippery and nonsense once more prevailed. It was too rational to last long; and too much like religious simplicity to be suffered in a land of shadows, and a world of painted outsides.

With shame-facedness and sobriety] The *stola, catastola, girdle, &c.,* though simple in themselves, were often highly ornamented both with *gold* and *precious stones;* and, both among the Grecian and Roman women, the *hair* was often *crisped* and *curled* in the most variegated and complex manner. To this the apostle alludes when he says : Μη εν πλεγμασιν, η χρυσῳ, η μαργαριταις, η ιματισμῳ πολυτελει· *Not with plaited hair, or gold, or pearls, or costly raiment.* The *costly raiment* might refer to the *materials* out of which the raiment was made, and to the *workmanship;* the *gold* and *pearls,* to the *ornaments* on the raiment.

With shame-facedness or *modesty,* μετα αιδους. This would lead them to avoid every thing *unbecoming* or *meretricious* in the mode or *fashion* of their dress.

With sobriety, μετα σωφροσυνης. Moderation would lead them to avoid all unnecessary expense. They might follow the *custom* or *costume of the country* as to the dress itself, for nothing was ever more becoming than the Grecian *stola, catastola,* and *zona;* but they must not imitate the extravagance of those who, through *impurity* or *littleness of mind,* decked themselves merely to attract the eye of admiration, or set in lying action the tongue of flattery. Woman has been invidiously defined : *An animal fond of dress.* How long will they permit themselves to be thus degraded?

Those beautiful lines of *Homer,* in which he speaks of the death of Euphorbus, who was slain by Menelaus, show how anciently the Grecians plaited and adorned their hair :—

Αντικρυ δ' απαλοιο δι' αυχενος ηλυθ' ακωκη·
Δουπησεν δε πεσων, αραβησε δε τευχε' επ' αυτῳ.
Αιματι οι δευοντο κομαι, Χαριτεσσιν ομοιαι,
Πλοχμοι θ' οι χρυσῳ τε και αργυρῳ εσφηκωντο.

Il. xvii., ver. 49.

Wide through the neck appears the ghastly wound ;
Prone sinks the warrior, and his arms rebound.
The *shining circlets* of his *golden hair,*
Which e'en the Graces might be proud to wear,
Instarr,d with gems and *gold* bestrew the shore,
With dust dishonour'd, and deform'd with gore.

POPE.

Or thus, more literally :—

Sounding he fell ; loud rang his batter'd arms.
His locks, which e'en the Graces might have own'd,
Blood sullied; and his *ringlets wound about*
With twine of *gold* and *silver,* swept the dust.

COWPER.

The extravagance to which the Grecian and Asiatic women went in their ornaments might well be a reason for the apostle's command.

Kypke, however, denies that any particular article of dress is intended here, and says that κατασολη is to be understood as coming from καταστελλω, to *restrain, repress;* and he refers it to that *government* of the *mind,* or *moderation* which women should exercise over their dress and demeanour in general, and every thing that may fall under the observation of the senses. All this, undoubtedly, the apostle had in view.

When either women or men spend much time, cost, and attention on decorating their persons, it affords a painful proof that *within* there is little excellence, and that they are endeavoring to supply the want of *mind* and *moral good* by the feeble and silly aids of dress and ornament. Were *religion* out of the question, *common sense* would say in all these things : Be decent; but be moderate and modest.

Verse 10. *But (which becometh, &c.*] That is : *Good works* are the only *ornaments* with which women professing *Christianity* should seek to be adorned. The Jewish matrons were accustomed to cry to the *bride:* "There is no need of paint, no need of antimony, no need of braided hair; she herself is most beautiful." The eastern women use a preparation of antimony, which they apply both to the eyes and eyelids, and by which the eye itself acquires a wonderful lustre.

Verse 11. *Let the woman learn in silence*] This is generally supposed to be a prohibition of women's preaching. I have already said what I judge neces-

A. M. cir. 4069.
A. D. 64 or 65.
A. U. C. 818.
An. Imp. Ne-
ronis Cæs.
Aug. 12.

12 But ˣ I suffer not a woman to teach, ʸ nor to usurp
authority over the man, but to
be in silence.

13 ᶻ For Adam was first formed, then Eve.

14 And ᵃ Adam was not deceived ; but the

woman being deceived, was in
the transgression.

15 ᵇ Notwithstanding she shall
be saved in ᶜ child-bearing, if
they continue in faith and charity and holiness
with sobriety.

A. M. cir. 4069.
A. D. 64 or 65.
A. U. C. 818.
An. Imp. Ne-
ronis Cæs.
Aug. 12.

ˣ 1 Cor. xiv. 34.——ʸ Eph. v. 24.——ᶻ Gen. i. 27 ; ii. 18, 22 ;
1 Cor. xi. 8, 9.——ᵃ Gen. iii. 6 ; 2 Cor. xi. 3.

ᵇ Gen. iii. 16 ; Luke i. 42 ; Exod. i. 19.——ᶜ Gen. iv. 1, 25 ; Ezek.
xviii. 3 ; Acts xiv. 22.

---

sary on this subject in the notes on 1 Cor. xi. 5, &c.,
and xiv. 34, 35 ; to which places I beg leave to refer
the reader.

Verse 12. *Nor to usurp authority*] A woman
should attempt nothing, either in public or private,
that belongs to man as his peculiar function. This
was prohibited by the Roman laws : *In multis juris
nostri articulis deterior est conditio fœminarum quam
masculorum ; l.* 9, Pap. Lib. 31, Quæst. *Fœminæ
ab omnibus officiis civilibus vel publicis remotæ sunt ;
et ideo nec judicis esse possunt, nec magistratum
gerere, nec postulare, nec pro alio invenire, nec procu-
ratores existere ; l.* 2, *de Reg. Juris.* Ulp. Lib. i.
ad Sab.—-Vid. Poth. *Pand. Justin.,* vol. i. p. 13.

"In our laws the condition of *women* is, in many
respects, worse than that of *men.* Women are precluded from all public offices ; therefore they cannot
be judges, nor execute the function of magistrates ;
they cannot *sue, plead,* nor act in any case as *proxies.*"
They were under many other disabilities, which may
be seen in different places of the *Pandects.*

But to be in silence.] It was lawful for *men* in
public assemblies to ask questions, or even interrupt
the speaker when there was any matter in his speech
which they did not understand ; but this liberty was
not granted to *women.* See the note on 1 Cor. xiv.
34, 35.

Verse 13. *For Adam was first formed, then Eve.*]
And by this very act God designed that he should have
the *pre-eminence.* God fitted man, by the robust construction of his body, to live a *public life,* to contend
with difficulties, and to be capable of great exertions.
The structure of woman's body plainly proves that she
was never designed for those exertions required in
public life. In this the chief part of the *natural inferiority* of woman is to be sought.

Verse 14. *Adam was not deceived*] It does not
appear that Satan attempted the man ; the woman
said : *The serpent beguiled me, and I did eat.* Adam
received the fruit from the hand of his wife ; *he knew
he was transgressing,* he was not *deceived ;* however,
she led the way, and in consequence of this she was
subjected to the domination of her husband : *Thy desire
shall be to thy husband, and he shall rule over thee ;*
Gen. iii. 16. There is a Greek verse, but it is not
English law, that speaks a language nearly similar to
that above :——

Γυναικι δ' αρχειν ου διδωσιν ἡ φυσις.

For nature suffers not a woman's rule.

God has not only rendered her unfit for it, but he has
subjected her, expressly, to the government of the man.

Verse 15. *She shall be saved in child-bearing*]

Σωθησεται δε δια της τεκνογονιας· *She shall be saved
through child-bearing*—she shall be saved by means,
or through the instrumentality, of child-bearing or of
bringing forth a child. Amidst the different opinions
given of the meaning of this very singular text, that
of Dr. Macknight appears to me the most probable,
which I shall give in his *paraphrase* and *note.*

"However, though Eve was first in the transgression, and brought death on herself, her husband, and
all her posterity, the *female sex shall be saved* (equally
with the male) *through child-bearing*—through bringing forth the Saviour, *if they live in faith, and love,
and chastity, with* that *sobriety* which I have been
recommending.

"The word σωθησεται, *saved,* in this verse refers to
ἡ γυνη, *the woman,* in the foregoing verse, which is
certainly Eve. But the apostle did not mean to say
that *she* alone was to be saved through child-bearing,
but that all her posterity, whether male or female, are
to be saved through the child-bearing of a woman ;
as is evident from his adding, *If they live in faith and
love and holiness, with sobriety.* For *safety* in child-
bearing does not depend on that condition at all ; since
many *pious* women die in child-bearing, while others
of a *contrary character* are preserved. The salvation
of the human race, through child-bearing, was intimated in the sentence passed on the serpent, Gen. iii.
15 : *I will put enmity between thee and the woman,
and between thy seed and her seed. It shall bruise
thy head.* Accordingly, the Saviour being conceived
in the womb of his mother by the power of the Holy
Ghost, he is truly the *seed of the woman* who was to
bruise the head of the serpent ; and a woman, by
bringing *him* forth, has been the occasion of our salvation." This is the most consistent sense, for in the
way in which it is commonly understood it does not
apply. There are innumerable instances of women
dying in child-bed who have lived in faith and charity
and holiness, with sobriety ; and equally numerous instances of worthless women, slaves to different kinds
of vices, who have not only been saved in child-bearing, but have passed through their travail with comparatively little pain ; hence that is not the sense in
which we should understand the apostle. Yet it must
be a matter of great consolation and support, to all
pious women labouring of child, to consider that, by
the holy virgin's child-bearing, salvation is provided
for them and the whole human race ; and that, whether
they die or live, though their own child-bearing can
contribute nothing to their salvation, yet *he* who was
born of a woman has purchased *them* and the whole
human race by his blood.

If they continue] Εαν μεινωσιν is rightly translated, *if they live ;* for so it signifies in other passages, particularly Phil. i. 25. The change in the *number* of the verb from the *singular* to the *plural,* which is introduced here, was *designed* by the apostle to show that he does not speak of *Eve,* nor of any *particular woman,* but of the whole sex. See *Macknight.*

Without *faith* it is impossible to please God, or to be saved ; and without *love* it will be impossible to *obey.* Faith and love are essentially necessary to *holiness* and *sobriety ;* and unless both men and women *live in these,* they cannot, scripturally, expect to dwell with God for ever. Some foolish women have supposed, from this verse, that the very act of bringing forth children shall entitle them to salvation ; and that all who die in childbed infallibly go to glory! Nothing can be more unfounded than this ; faith, love, holiness, and sobriety, are as absolutely requisite for the salvation of every *daughter of Eve,* as they are for the salvation of every *son of Adam.* Pain and *suffering* neither purify nor make atonement. On the mercy of God, in Christ, dispensing remission of sins and holiness, both men and women may confidently rely for salvation ; but on nothing else. Let *her* that readeth understand.

On the subject of *dress* I will conclude in the words of a late writer : " What *harm* does it do to adorn ourselves with gold, or pearls, or costly array, suppose we can afford it ? The first harm it does is, it engenders *pride ;* and, where it is already, increases it. Nothing is more natural than to think ourselves better because we are dressed in better clothes. One of the old heathens was so well apprised of this, that when he had a spite to a poor man, and had a mind to turn his head, he made him a present of a suit of fine clothes.

    Eutrapelus cuicunque *nocere* volebat,
      Vestimenta dabat *pretiosa.*

He could not then but imagine himself to be as much better, as he was finer, than his neighbour ; inferring the superior value of his person from the value of his clothes."—Rev. *J. Wesley's* Sermons.

CHAPTER III.

Concerning bishops, their qualifications and work, 1–7. *Of deacons, and how they should be proved,* 8–10. *Of their wives and children, and how they should be governed,* 11–13. *How Timothy should behave himself in the Church,* 14, 15. *The great mystery of godliness,* 16.

A. M. cir. 4069.
A. D. 64 or 65.
A. U. C. 818.
An. Imp. Neronis Cæs.
Aug. 12.

THIS [a] *is* a true saying, If a man desire the office of a [b] bishop, he desireth a good [c] work.

2 [d] A bishop then must be blameless, [e] the husband of one wife, vigilant, sober, [f] of good behaviour, given to hospitality, [g] apt to teach ;

A. M. cir. 4069.
A. D. 64 or 65.
A. U. C. 818.
An. Imp. Neronis Cæs.
Aug. 12.

---

[a] Chap. i. 5——[b] Acts xx. 28 ; Phil. i. 1.——[c] Eph. iv. 12.
[d] Tit. i. 6, &c.——[e] Chap. v. 9.——[f] Or, *modest.*——[g] 2 Tim. ii. 24.

NOTES ON CHAP. III.

Verse 1. *This* is *a true saying*] Πιστος ὁ λογος· *This is a true doctrine.* These words are joined to the last verse of the preceding chapter by several of the Greek fathers, and by them referred to the doctrine there stated.

The office of a bishop] Επισκοπης· The *episcopacy, overseership* or *superintendency.* The word ορεγεται, which we translate *desire,* signifies *earnest, eager, passionate desire ;* and επιθυμει, which we translate *desire,* also signifies *earnestly to desire* or *covet.* It is strange that the episcopacy, in those times, should have been an object of *intense desire* to any man ; when it was a place of danger, and exposure to severe labour, want, persecution, and death, without any secular emolument whatsoever. On this ground I am led to think that the Spirit of God designed these words more for the ages that were to come, than for those which were then ; and in reference to after ages the whole of what follows is chiefly to be understood.

A good work.] A *work* it then was ; heavy, incessant, and painful. There were no unpreaching prelates in those days, and should be none now. *Episcopacy* in the *Church* of God is of Divine appointment, and should be maintained and respected. Under God, there should be supreme governors in the *Church* as well as in the *state.* The *state* has its *monarch,* the *Church* has its *bishop ;* one should govern according to the *laws of the land,* the other according to the *word of God.*

What a *constitutional king should be,* the principles of the *constitution* declare ; what a *bishop* should be, the following verses particularly show.

Verse 2. *A bishop then must be blameless*] Our term *bishop* comes from the Anglo-Saxon biɼceop, which is a mere corruption of the Greek επισκοπος, and the Latin *episcopus ;* the former being compounded of επι, over, and σκεπτομαι, to *look* or *inspect,* signifies one who has the *inspection* or *oversight* of a place, persons, or business ; what we commonly term a *superintendent.* The New Testament writers have borrowed the term from the *Septuagint,* it being the word by which they translate the פקיד *pakid* of the Hebrew text, which signifies a *visiter,* one that *personally inspects* the people or business over which he presides. It is given by St. Paul to the elders at Ephesus, who had the *oversight* of Christ's flock, Acts xx. 28 ; and to such like persons in other places, Phil. i. 1 ; 1 Tim. iii. 2, the place in question ; and Tit. i. 7.

Let us consider the *qualifications* of a Christian bishop, and then we shall soon discover *who* is fit for the office.

First.—This Christian bishop must be *blameless ;*

A. M. cir. 4069.
A. D. 64 or 65.
A. U. C. 818.
An. Imp. Ne-
ronis Cæs.
Aug. 12.

3 ^hNot given to wine, ^kno striker, ^lnot greedy of filthy lucre; but ^mpatient, not a brawler, not covetous;

4 One that ruleth well his own house, ⁿhaving his children in subjection with all gravity;

A. M. cir. 4069
A. D. 64 or 65.
A. U. C. 818.
An. Imp. Ne-
ronis Cæs.
Aug. 12.

^h Ver. 8; Tit. i. 7.——ⁱ Or, *not ready to quarrel, and offer wrong, as one in wine.*

^k 1 Tim. ii. 24.——^l 1 Pet. v. 2.——^m 2 Tim. ii. 24.——ⁿ Tit. i. 6; 1 Sam. ii. 22, &c.

ανεπιληπτον, a person *against whom no evil can be proved;* one who is everywhere *invulnerable;* for the word is a metaphor, taken from the case of an expert and skilful pugilist, who *so defends every part of* his *body* that it is impossible for his antagonist to give one hit. So this Christian bishop is one that has so conducted himself, as to put it out of the reach of any person to prove that he is either *unsound* in a single article of the Christian *faith,* or *deficient* in the *fulfilment* of any *duty* incumbent on a Christian. He *must* be irreprehensible; for how can he reprove that in others which they can reprove in him?

Second.—He must be *the husband of one wife.* He should be a *married* man, but he should be no *polygamist;* and have only *one wife,* i. e. *one* at a *time.* It does *not mean* that, if he has been married, and his wife die, he should never marry another. Some have most foolishly spiritualized this, and say, that by *one wife* the *Church* is intended! This silly quibbling needs no refutation. The apostle's meaning appears to be this: that he should not be a man who has *divorced* his wife and married another; nor one that has *two wives* at a time. It does not appear to have been any part of the apostle's design to prohibit *second* marriages, of which some have made such a serious business. But it is natural for some men to tithe mint and cummin in religion, while they neglect the weightier matters of the law.

Third.—He must be *vigilant;* νηφαλεον, from νη, *not* and πιω, to *drink. Watchful;* for as one who drinks is apt to *sleep,* so he who abstains from it is more likely to *keep awake,* and attend to his *work* and *charge.* A bishop has to watch *over* the Church, and watch *for* it; and this will require all his care and circumspection. Instead of νηφαλεον, many MSS. read νηφαλιον· this may be the better *orthography,* but makes no alteration in the sense.

Fourth.—He must be *sober;* σωφρονα, *prudent,* or, according to the etymology of the word, from σως, *sound,* and φρην, *mind, a man of a sound mind;* having a good understanding, and the complete government of all his passions.

A bishop should be a man of *learning,* of an extensive and well cultivated mind, dispassionate, prudent, and sedate.

Fifth.—He must be *of good behaviour;* κοσμιον, orderly, decent, grave, and correct in the whole of his *appearance, carriage,* and *conduct.* The preceding term, σωφρονα, refers to the *mind;* this latter, κοσμιον, to the *external manners.* A clownish, rude, or boorish man should never have the rule of the Church of God; the sour, the sullen, and the boisterous should never be invested with a dignity which they would most infallibly disgrace.

Sixth.—He must be *given to hospitality;* φιλοξενον, literally, a *lover of strangers;* one who is ready to receive into his house and relieve every necessitous stranger. *Hospitality,* in those primitive times, was a great and necessary virtue; then there were few *inns,* or places of *public entertainment;* to those who were noted for benevolence the necessitous stranger had recourse. A Christian bishop, professing love to God and all mankind, preaching a religion, one half of the morality of which was included in, *Thou shalt love thy neighbour as thyself,* would naturally be sought to by those who were in distress and destitute of friends. To enable them to entertain such, the Church over which they presided must have furnished them with the *means.* Such a bishop as St. Paul, who was often obliged to labour with his hands for his own support, could have little to give away. But there is a considerable difference between an apostolical bishop and an ecclesiastical bishop : the one was generally itinerant, the other comparatively local; the former had neither house nor home, the latter had both; the apostolical bishop had charge of the Church of Christ universally, the ecclesiastical bishop of the Churches in a particular district. Such should be addicted to hospitality, or works of charity; especially in these modern times, in which, besides the *spiritualities,* they possess the *temporalities,* of the Church.

Seventh.—He should be *apt to teach;* διδακτικον, one *capable of teaching;* not only *wise* himself, but *ready* to communicate his wisdom to others. One whose delight is, to instruct the ignorant and those who are out of the way. He must be a *preacher;* an able, zealous, fervent, and assiduous preacher.

He is no bishop who has health and strength, and yet seldom or never preaches; i. e. if he *can* preach—if he have the necessary gifts for the office. In former times bishops wrote much and preached much; and their labours were greatly owned of God. No Church since the apostle's days has been more honoured in this way than the British Church. And although bishops are *here,* as elsewhere, appointed by the *state,* yet we cannot help adoring the good providence of God, that, taken as a body, they have been an honour to their function; and that, since the reformation of religion in these lands, the bishops have in general been men of great learning and probity, and the ablest advocates of the Christian system, both as to its *authenticity,* and the *purity* and *excellence* of its *doctrines* and *morality.*

CHAUCER's character of the *Clerke of Oxenford* is a good paraphrase on St. Paul's character of a primitive bishop :—

Of studie tookin he moste cure and hede,
Nought oo word spak he more than ther was nede,
And that was selde in forme and reverence,
And short, and quick, and full of high sentence;
Sowning in moral vertue was his speche,
And gladly wolde he lerne, and gladly teache.

2

A. M. cir. 4069.
A. D. 64 or 65.
A. U. C. 818.
An. Imp. Neronis Cæs.
Aug. 12.

5 (For if a man know not how to rule his own house, how shall he take care of ° the Church of God?)

6 Not ᴾ a novice, lest being lifted up with pride �𐞥 he fall into the condemnation of the devil.

A. M. cir. 4069.
A. D. 64 or 65.
A. U. C. 818.
An. Imp. Neronis Cæs.
Aug. 12.

° Acts xx. 28.——ᴾ Or, *one newly come to the faith.*

�𐞥 Isa. xiv. 12.

Verse 3. An *eighth* article in his character is, he must not be *given to wine*; μη παροινον. This word not only signifies one who is *inordinately attached to wine*, a *winebibber* or *tippler*, but also one who is *imperious*, *abusive*, *insolent*, whether through wine or otherwise. *Kypke* contends for this latter acceptation here. See his *proofs* and *examples*.

Ninth.—He must be *no striker*; μη πληκτην, not *quarrelsome*; not ready to *strike a person* who may displease him; no *persecutor* of those who may differ from him; not prone, as one wittily said,

"To prove his doctrine orthodox
By apostolic blows and knocks."

It is said of Bishop *Bonner*, of infamous memory, that, when examining the poor *Protestants* whom he termed *heretics*, when worsted by them in argument he was used to *smite them with his fists*, and sometimes *scourge* and *whip* them. But though he was a most ignorant and consummate savage, yet from such a scripture as this he might have seen the necessity of surrendering his mitre.

Tenth.—He must *not be greedy of filthy lucre*; μη αισχροκερδη, *not desirous of base gain*; not using *base* and *unjustifiable* methods to raise and increase his revenues; not trading or trafficking; for what would be honourable in a *secular* character, would be base and dishonourable in a bishop. Though such a trait should never appear in the character of a Christian prelate, yet there is much reason to suspect that the words above are not authentic; they are omitted by ADFG, many others, the *Syriac*, all the *Arabic*, *Coptic*, (and *Sahidic*,) *Æthiopic*, *Armenian*, later *Syriac*, (but it appears in the margin,) the *Vulgate* and *Itala*, and by most of the *Greek fathers*. *Griesbach* has left it out of the text, in which it does not appear that it ever had a legitimate place. The word *covetous*, which we have below, expresses all the meaning of this; and it is not likely that the apostle would insert in the same sentence two words of the same *meaning*, because they were different in *sound*. It appears to have been borrowed from verse 8.

Eleventh.—He must be *patient*; επιεικη, *meek*, *gentle*; the opposite to πληκτην, a quarrelsome person, which it immediately follows when the spurious word αισχροκερδη is removed. Where *meekness* and *patience* do not reign, *gravity* cannot exist, and the *love of God* cannot dwell.

Twelfth.—He must not be a *brawler*; αμαχον, not *contentious* or *litigious*, but *quiet* and *peaceable*.

Thirteenth.—He must not be *covetous*; αφιλαργυρον, *not a lover of money*; not desiring the *office* for the sake of its *emoluments*. He who loves money will stick at nothing in order to get it Fair and foul methods are to him alike, provided they may be equally productive. For the sake of reputation he may wish

to get all honourably; but if that cannot be, he will not scruple to adopt other methods. A brother heathen gives him this counsel: "Get money if thou canst by fair means; if not, get it by hook and by crook."

Verse 4. The *fourteenth* qualification of a Christian bishop is, that he *ruleth well his own house*; του ιδιου οικου καλως προϊσταμενον, one who *properly presides over* and *governs his own family*. One who has the *command*, of his *own house*, not by sternness, severity, and tyranny, but with all *gravity*; governing his household by *rule*, every one knowing his own *place*, and each doing his own *work*, and each work having the proper *time* assigned for its beginning and end. This is a maxim of common sense; no family can be prosperous that is not under subjection, and no person can govern a family but the *head* of it, the husband, who is, both by nature and the appointment of God, the *head* or *governor* of his own house. See the note on Eph. v. 22.

Verse 5. *For if a man know not*] *Method* is a matter of great importance in all the affairs of life. It is a true saying, *He that does little with his head must do much with his hands*; and even *then* the business is not half done for want of *method*. Now, he who has a proper method of doing business will show it in *every affair* of life, even the *least*. He who has a *disorderly* family has no *government* of that family; he probably has none because he has no *method*, no *plan*, of presiding. It was natural for the apostle to say, *If a man know not how to rule his own house, how shall he take care of the Church of God?* Look at a man's domestic arrangements; if they be not good, he should not be trusted with any branch of government, whether ecclesiastical or civil.

Verse 6. *Fifteenth.*—It is required that he be *not a novice*] Νεοφυτον· Not a *young plant*, not recently *ingrafted*, that is, one *not newly converted to the faith*; (old MS. Bible;) one who has been of considerable standing in the Christian Church, if he have the preceding qualifications, may be safely trusted with the government of that Church. It is impossible that one who is not long and deeply experienced in the ways of God can guide others in the way of life. Hence *presbyters* or *elders* were generally appointed to have the oversight of the rest, and hence *presbyter* and *bishop* seem to have been *two names* for the *same office*; yet all presbyters or elders certainly were not bishops, because all presbyters had not the qualifications marked above. But the apostle gives another reason: *Lest being lifted up with pride he fall into the condemnation of the devil*. It is natural for man to think himself of more importance than his fellows when they are intrusted to his government. The apostle's term τυφωθεις, *puffed up*, *inflated*, is a metaphor taken from a *bladder* when *filled with air* or *wind*. It is a *substance*, has a certain *size*, is *light*,

2

A. M. cir. 4069.
A. D. 64 or 65.
A. U. C. 818.
An. Imp. Ne-
ronis Cæs.
Aug. 12.

7 Moreover he must have a good report ʳ of them which are without; lest he fall into reproach ˢ and the snare of the devil.

8 Likewise *must* ᵗ the deacons *be* grave, not double-tongued, ᵘ not given to much wine, not greedy of filthy lucre;

ʳ Acts xxii. 12; 1 Cor. v. 12; 1 Thess. iv. 12.——ˢ Chap. vi. 9; 2 Tim. ii. 26.

9 ᵛ Holding the mystery of the faith in a pure conscience.

10 And let these also first be proved; then let them use the office of a deacon, being *found* blameless.

11 ʷ Even so *must their* wives *be* grave, not slanderers, sober, faithful in all things.

A. M. cir. 4069.
A. D. 64 or 65.
A. U. C. 818.
An. Imp. Ne-
ronis Cæs.
Aug. 12.

ᵗ A its vi. 3.——ᵘ Ver. 3; Lev. x. 9; Ezek. xliv. 21.——ᵛ Chap. i. 19.——ʷ Tit. ii. 3.

can be the sport of the *wind*, but has nothing in it but *air*. Such is the classical coxcomb; a mere *puff-ball*, a disgrace to his function, and despised by every intelligent man. Should we not say to those whom it may concern,

"From such apostles, O ye mitred heads,
Preserve the Church; and lay not careless hands
On skulls that *cannot teach*, and *will not learn.*"

From these words of the apostle we are led to infer that *pride* or *self-conceit* was the cause of the devil's downfall. In Ecclus. x. there are some excellent sayings concerning *pride:* "Pride is hurtful before God and man." "Why is earth and ashes proud?" "The beginning of pride is when one departeth from God." "For pride is the beginning of sin; and he that hath it shall pour out abomination." "PRIDE *was not made for* MEN." See verses 7, 9, 12, 13, and 18, of the above chapter.

Verse 7. The *sixteenth* requisite is, that he *should have a good report of them which are without*] That he should be one who had not been previously a profligate, or scandalous in his life. Such a person, when converted, may be a worthy private member of religious society; but I believe God *rarely* calls such to the work of the *ministry*, and *never* to the *episcopate. Them* that are *without* are the Jews, Gentiles, and the *unconverted* of all kinds. For the meaning of this term see the note on Col. iv. 5.

Lest he fall into reproach] For his former scandalous life.

And the snare of the devil.] Snares and temptations, such as he fell in and fell by before. This is called the *snare of the devil;* for, as he well knows the constitution of such persons, and what is most likely to prevail, he infers that what was effectual *before* to their transgressing may be so still; therefore on all suitable occasions he tempts them to their old sins. Backsliders in general fall by those sins to which they were addicted previously to their conversion. Former inveterate habits will revive in him who does not continue to deny himself, and watch unto prayer.

The snare of the devil.—Some would translate παγιδα του διαβολου, *the snare of the accuser;* and they give the same meaning to the word in verse 6, because it is evident that διαβολους has that meaning, verse 11, and our translators render it *slanderers.* Now, though διαβολος signifies an *accuser*, yet I do not see that it can, with any propriety, be restrained to this meaning in the texts in question, and especially as the word is emphatically applied to Satan himself; for he who, in Rev. xii. 10, is *called the accuser of the*

brethren, is, in verse 9, called *the great dragon, the old serpent,* the DEVIL, διαβολος, and *Satan.*

Verse 8. *Likewise* must *the deacons*] The term *deacon,* διακονος, simply signifies a *regular* or *stated servant:* from *δια, through* or *emphatic,* and κονεω, to *minister* or serve. See it explained in the note on Matt. xx. 26. As nearly the same qualifications were required in the *deacons* as in the *bishops,* the reader may consult what is said on the preceding verses.

Grave] Of a sedate and dignified carriage and conduct.

Not double-tongued] Speaking one thing to one person, and another thing to another, on the *same subject.* This is hypocrisy and deceit. This word might also be translated *liars.*

Not given to much wine] Neither a drunkard, tippler, nor what is called a *jovial companion.* All this would be inconsistent with *gravity.*

Not greedy of filthy lucre] See on verse 3.

Verse 9. *Holding the mystery of the faith*] Instead of της πιστεως, *the faith,* one MS. (the readings of which are found in the margin of a copy of Mill's Greek text in the Bodleian library, and which is marked 61 in *Griesbach*) reads αναστασεως, *of the resurrection.* This reading, like many others in this MS., is found nowhere else; and is worthy of little regard, but as expressing what appeared to the writer to be the apostle's *meaning.* One of the greatest mysteries of the faith was undoubtedly the *resurrection of the dead;* and this was held in a *pure conscience* when the person *so exercised himself* as to *have a conscience void of offence towards God and towards men.* See Acts xxiv. 16. What has been *since* called *Antinomianism,* that is, making void the *moral law,* by a pretended *faith* in the righteousness of Christ, is that which the apostle has here particularly in view.

Verse 10. *Let these—be proved*] Let them not be *young converts,* or persons lately brought to the knowledge of the truth. This is the same in spirit with what is required of the bishops, verse 6.

Let no man be put into an office in the Church till he has given full proof of his sincerity and steadiness, by having been for a considerable time a consistent private member of the Church.

Being found *blameless.*] Ανεγκλητοι οντες· Being irreproachable; persons against whom no evil can be proved. The same as in verse 2, though a different word is used. See the note there.

Verse 11. *Even so* must their *wives be* grave] I believe the apostle does not mean here the *wives* either of the *bishops* or *deacons* in particular, but the Christian *women* in general. The original is simply:

A. M. cir. 4069.
A. D. 64 or 65.
A. U. C. 818.
An. Imp. Ne-
ronis Cæs.
Aug. 12.

12 Let the deacons be the husbands of one wife, ruling their children and their own houses well.

13 For [x] they that have [y] used the office of a deacon well, purchase to themselves a good degree, and great boldness in the faith which is in Christ Jesus.

14 These things write I unto thee, hoping to come unto thee shortly;

15 But if I tarry long, that thou mayest know how thou oughtest to behave thyself [z] in the house of God, which is the Church of the living God, the pillar and [a] ground of the truth.

16 And without controversy, great is the mystery of godliness: [b] God was [c] manifest in the flesh, [d] justified in the Spirit, [e] seen of angels, [f] preached unto the Gentiles, [g] believed on in the world, [h] received up into glory.

A. M. cir. 4069.
A. D. 64 or 65.
A. U. C. 818.
An. Imp. Ne-
ronis Cæs.
Aug. 12.

---

[x] See Matt. xxv. 21.——[y] Or, *ministered.*——[z] Eph. ii. 21, 22; 2 Tim. ii. 20.——[a] Or, *stay.*——[b] John i. 14; 1 John i. 2,——[c] Gr. *manifested.*——[d] Matt. iii. 16; John i. 32, 33; xv. 26; xvi. 8, 9; Rom. i. 4; 1 Pet. iii. 18; 1 John v. 6, &c.——[e] Matt. xxviii. 2;

Mark xvi. 5; Luke ii. 13; xxiv. 4; John xx. 12; Eph. iii. 10; 1 Peter i. 12.——[f] Acts x. 34; xiii. 46, 48; Gal. ii. 8; Eph. iii. 5, 6, 8; Romans x. 18; Colossians i. 27, 28; Acts i. 19; 1 Peter iii. 22.

Γυναικας ὡσαυτως σεμνας· *Let the women likewise be grave.* Whatever is spoken here becomes women in general; but if the apostle had those termed *deaconesses* in his eye, which is quite possible, the words are peculiarly suitable to *them.* That there was such an *order* in the apostolic and primitive Church, and that they were appointed to their office by the *imposition of hands,* has already been noticed on Rom. xvi. 1. Possibly, therefore, the apostle may have had this *order* of *deaconesses* in view, to whom it was as necessary to give counsels and cautions as to the *deacons* themselves; and to prescribe their qualifications, lest improper persons should insinuate themselves into that office.

Not slanderers] Μη διαβολους· Literally, *not devils.* See on verse 7. This may be properly enough translated *slanderers, backbiters, tale-bearers,* &c., for all these are of their father, the devil, and his lusts they will do. Let all such, with the vast tribe of *calumniators* and *dealers in scandal,* remember that the apostle ranks them all with *malicious, fallen spirits;* a consideration which one would suppose might be sufficient to deter them from their injurious and abominable conduct.

Sober] See on verse 2.

Faithful in all things.] The deaconesses had much to do among the poor, and especially among poor women, in dispensing the bounty of the Church. They were not only *faithfully* to *expend all* they had got, and *for* the *purpose* for which they got it; but they must do this with *impartiality,* showing no *respect of persons,* the degree of *distress* being the only rule by which the distribution was to be regulated.

Verse 12. Let the deacons be the husbands of one wife] This is the same that is required of the *bishops.* See on verses 2, 4, and 5.

Verse 13. That have used the office of a deacon well] They who, having been *tried* or *proved,* ver. 10, have shown by their steadiness, activity, and zeal, that they might be raised to a higher office, are here said to have *purchased to themselves a good degree,* βαθμον καλον· for, instead of having to administer to the *bodies* and *bodily wants* of the poor, the faithful deacons were raised to minister in holy things; and, instead of ministering the *bread that perisheth,* they were raised to the *presbyterate* or *episcopate,* to minister the *bread of life* to immortal souls. And hence the apostle adds; *And great boldness in the faith;*

πολλην παρρησιαν, *great liberty of speech;* i. e. in teaching the *doctrines* of Christianity, and in expounding the Scriptures, and preaching. It seems to have been a practice dictated by common sense, that the most grave and steady of the *believers* should be employed as *deacons;* the most experienced and zealous of the *deacons* should be raised to the rank of *elders;* and the most able and pious of the *elders* be consecrated *bishops.* As to a *bishop of bishops,* that age did not know such. The *pope of Rome* was the first who took this title. The *same office,* but not with the same powers nor abuse, is found in the *patriarch* of the *Greek* Church, and the *archbishop* of the *Protestant* Church. As the *deacon* had many *private members* under his care, so the *presbyter* or *elder* had several *deacons* under his care; the *bishop,* several presbyters; and the *archbishop,* several *bishops.* But I speak now more of the *modern* than of the *ancient* Church. The *distinction* in some of these *offices* is not so apparent in ancient times; and some of the offices themselves are *modern,* or comparatively so. But *deacon, presbyter,* and *bishop,* existed in the *apostolic Church,* and may therefore be considered of *Divine origin.*

Verse 14. These things write I] That is: I write *only* these things; because *I hope to come unto thee shortly.*

Verse 15. But if I tarry long] That is: Notwithstanding I hope to come to thee shortly, and therefore do not feel the necessity of writing at large; yet, lest I should be delayed, I write what I judge necessary to direct thy conduct in the Church of God.

The house of God] This is spoken in allusion to the ancient tabernacle; which was God's house, and in which the symbol of the Divine Majesty dwelt. So the Christian Church is God's house, and every believer is a habitation of God through the Spirit.

The Church of the living God] The assembly in which God lives and works; each member of which is a living stone, all of whom, properly united among themselves, grow up unto a holy temple in the Lord.

The pillar and ground of the truth.] Never was there a greater variety of opinions on any portion of the sacred Scripture than has been on this and the following verse. Commentators and critics have given senses and meanings till there is no meaning to be seen. It would be almost impossible, after reading all that has been said on this passage, for any man to make up

2

his own mind. To what, or to whom, does *the pillar and ground of the truth* refer?

1. Some say to *Timothy*, who is called the *pillar*, &c., because left there to *support* and *defend* the truth of God against false doctrines and false teachers; and is so called for the same reason that Peter, James, and John, are said to be *pillars*, i. e. supporters of the truth of God. Gal. ii. 9.

2. Others suppose that *the pillar and ground of the truth* is spoken of God; and that ὁς εστι, *who is*, should be supplied as referring immediately to Θεος, God, just before. By this mode of interpretation the passage will read thus: *That thou mayest know how thou oughtest to behave thyself in the house of God, which is the Church of the living God,* WHO IS (ὁς εστι) *the pillar and ground of the truth.* How God may be fitly termed the pillar and ground of truth, requires no explanation.

3. Others think that the words should be understood of the CHURCH *of the living God;* and in this case the feminine relative ἡτις εστι, *which is,* must be repeated immediately after εκκλησια, the Church. *The house of God is the Church of the living God;* WHICH (Church) IS *the pillar and ground of the truth.* That is: The full revelation of God's truth is in the *Christian Church.* The great doctrines of that Church are *the truth* without error, metaphor, or figure. Formerly the *truth* was but *partially* revealed, much of it being shadowed with types, ceremonies, and comparatively dark prophecies; but *now* all is plain, and the full revelation given; and the foundation on which this truth rests are the grand *facts* detailed in the Gospel, especially those which concern the *incarnation, miracles, passion, death,* and *resurrection* of Christ, and the *mission* of the *Holy Spirit.*

4. *Lastly,* others refer the whole to το της ευσεβειας μυστηριον, *the mystery of godliness;* and translate the clause thus: *The mystery of godliness is the pillar and ground of the truth; and, without controversy, a great thing.* This gives a very good sense, but it is not much favoured by the arrangement of the words in the original.

Verse 16. *And, without controversy*] Και ὁμολογουμενως· *And confessedly, by general consent,* it is a thing which no man *can* or *ought to dispute;* any phrase of this kind expresses the meaning of the original.

God was manifest in the flesh] If we take in the whole of the 14th, 15th, and 16th verses, we may make a consistent translation in the following manner, and the whole paragraph will stand thus: *Hoping to see thee shortly; but should I tarry long, these things I now write unto thee, that thou mayest know how thou oughtest to behave thyself in the house of God, which is the Church of the living God. The mystery of godliness, which is the pillar and ground of the truth, is, without controversy, a great thing.* And then he proceeds to show what this mystery of godliness is, which he sums up in the *six* following particulars: 1. *God was manifest in the flesh;* 2. *Justified in the Spirit;* 3. *Seen of angels;* 4. *Preached unto the Gentiles;* 5. *Believed on in the world;* 6. *Received up into glory.*

Though all this makes a very plain and consistent

sense, yet we are perplexed by *various readings* on the first clause, Θεος εφανερωθη εν σαρκι, *God was manifest in the flesh';* for instead of Θεος, *God,* several MSS., versions, and fathers, have ὁς or ὁ, *who* or *which.* And this is generally referred to the word *mystery; Great is the mystery of godliness,* WHICH *was manifest in the flesh.*

The insertion of Θεος for ὁς, or ὁς for Θεος, may be easily accounted for. In ancient times the Greek was all written in *capitals,* for the common Greek character is comparatively of modern date. In these early times words of frequent recurrence were written *contractedly,* thus: for πατηρ, π̅ρ̅; Θεος, θ̅ς̅: Κυριος, κ̅ς̅; Ιησους, ι̅η̅ς̅, &c. This is very frequent in the oldest MSS., and is continually recurring in the *Codex Bezæ,* and *Codex Alexandrinus.* If, therefore, the *middle stroke* of the Θ, in Θ̅C̅, happened to be *faint,* or obliterated, and the *dash* above not very apparent, both of which I have observed in ancient MSS., then Θ̅C̅, the contraction for ΘΕΟC, *God,* might be mistaken for OC, *which* or *who;* and *vice versa.* This appears to have been the case in the *Codex Alexandrinus,* in this passage. To me there is ample reason to believe that the Codex Alexandrinus originally read Θ̅C̅, God, in this place; but the stroke becoming *faint* by length of time and injudicious handling, of which the MS. in this place has had a large proportion, some person has supplied the place, most reprehensibly, with a *thick black line.* This has destroyed the evidence of this MS., as now it can neither be quoted *pro* or *con,* though it is very likely that the person· who supplied the ink line, did it from a conscientious conviction that Θ̅C̅ was the original reading of this MS. I examined this MS. about thirty years ago, and this was the conviction that rested then on my mind. I have seen the MS. several times since, and have not changed my opinion. The enemies of the Deity of Christ have been at as much pains to destroy the evidence afforded by the common reading in support of this doctrine as if this text were the *only one* by which it can be supported; they must be aware that John i. 1, and 14, proclaim the same truth; and that in those verses there is no authority to doubt the genuineness of the reading. We read, therefore, *God was manifested in the flesh,* and I cannot see what good sense can be taken out of, the GOSPEL *was manifested in the flesh;* or, the *mystery of godliness was manifested in the flesh.* After seriously considering this subject in every point of light, I hold with the reading in the commonly received text.

Justified in the Spirit] By the miracles which were wrought by the apostle in and through the name of Jesus; as well as by his resurrection from the dead, through the energy of the Holy Ghost, by which he was proved to be the Son of God with power. Christ was justified from all the calumnies of the Jews, who crucified him as an impostor. All these miracles, being wrought by the power of God, were a full proof of his innocence; for, had he not been what he professed to be, God would not have borne such a decisive testimony to his Messiahship.

Seen of angels] By αγγελοι here, some understand not those celestial or infernal beings commonly called *angels*, but *apostles* and other persons who became messengers, to carry far and wide and attest the truth of his resurrection from the dead. If, however, we take the word *seen*, in its Jewish acceptation, for *made known*, we may here retain the term *angels* in its common acceptation; for it is certain that previously to our Lord's ascension to heaven, these holy beings could have little knowledge of the necessity, reasons, and economy of human salvation; nor of the nature of Christ as God and man. St. Peter informs us that the *angels desire to look into these things*, 1 Pet. i. 12. And St. Paul says the same thing, Eph. iii. 9, 10, when speaking of the revelation of the Gospel plan of salvation, which he calls *the mystery, which* FROM *the* BEGINNING OF THE WORLD *had been* HID *in God ;* and which was now published, that *unto the* PRINCIPALITIES *and* POWERS *in heavenly places might be* MADE KNOWN, *by the Church, the manifold wisdom of God*. Even those angelic beings have got an accession to their blessedness, by an increase of knowledge in the things which concern Jesus Christ, and the whole scheme of human salvation, through his incarnation, passion, death, resurrection, ascension, and glorification.

Preached unto the Gentiles] This was one grand part of the *mystery* which had been *hidden in God*, that the Gentiles should be made fellow heirs with the Jews, and be admitted into the kingdom of God. To the Gentiles, therefore, he was proclaimed as having *pulled down the middle wall of partition between them and the Jews ;* that, through him, God had granted unto them *repentance unto life ;* and that they also might have *redemption in his blood*, the *forgiveness of sins*.

Believed on in the world] Was received by mankind as the *promised Messiah*, the Anointed of God, and the only Saviour of fallen man. This is a most striking part of the *mystery of godliness*, that one who was crucified as a *malefactor*, and whose kingdom is not of this world, and whose doctrines are opposed to all the sinful propensities of the human heart, should, wherever his Gospel is preached, be acknowledged as the *only Saviour of sinners*, and the *Judge of quick and dead !* But some would restrict the meaning to the *Jews,* whose economy is often denominated עולם הזה *olam hazzeh*, this world, and which words both our Lord and the apostles often use in the same sense. Notwithstanding their prejudices, many even of the *Jews* believed on him; and a *great company of the priests* themselves, who were his crucifiers, *became obedient to the faith*. Acts vi. 7. This was an additional proof of Christ's innocence.

Received up into glory.] Even that *human nature* which he took of the Virgin Mary was raised, not only from the grave, but taken up into glory, and this in the most *visible* and *palpable* manner. This is a part of the mystery of godliness which, while we have every reasonable evidence to believe, we have not powers to comprehend. His *reception into glory* is of the utmost consequence to the Christian faith; as, in consequence, Jesus Christ in his human nature ever appears before the throne as our *sacrifice* and as our *Mediator*.

1. THE directions given in this chapter concerning *bishops* and *deacons* should be carefully weighed by every branch of the Christian Church. Not only the *offices* which are of Divine appointment, such as *bishop, presbyter*, and *deacon*, should be most religiously preserved in the Church; but, that they may have their full effect, the persons exercising them should be such as the apostle prescribes. Religion will surely suffer, when religious *order* is either contemned or neglected; and even the words of God will be treated with contempt, if ministered by unholy persons. Let *order*, therefore, be duly observed; and let those who fill these orders be not only wholly irreprehensible in their conduct, but also able ministers of the new covenant. A *wicked man* can neither have, nor communicate, *authority* to dispense heavenly mysteries; and a *fool*, or a *blockhead*, can never teach others the way of salvation. The highest abilities are not too great for a preacher of the Gospel; nor is it possible that he can have too much human learning. But all is nothing unless he can bring the grace and Spirit of God into all his ministrations; and these will never accompany him unless he live in the spirit of prayer and humility, fearing and loving God, and hating covetousness.

2. It is well known that almost every Church supposes itself to be THE *true Church ;* and some consider themselves the *only* Church, and deny salvation to all who are not of their communion. To such a Church the two last verses in this chapter have been confidently self-applied, as being *the pillar and ground of the truth*—the possessor and dispenser of all the mysteries of God. But, supposing that the words in verse 15 are spoken of the *Church*, it is the *Christian Church*, as defined under article the third above, that must be meant; and we may see from this the vanity of applying the words to any *particular Church*, as if *it* had all the truth without error, and none else could pretend either to *truth* or *ecclesiastical authority*. The *Christian Church* is a widely different thing; it is the whole system of Christianity as laid down in the New Testament; it is built on the great foundation of prophets and apostles, Jesus Christ himself being the chief corner stone. It is composed of all who hold the doctrines of Christianity; who acknowledge Jesus as their Teacher, Redeemer, and only Advocate; of all who love God with all their heart, soul, mind, and strength, and their neighbour as themselves; or who are labouring after this conformity to the mind and command of their Creator. It is not known by any particular *name ;* it is not distinguished by any particular *form* in its *mode* of worship; it is not exclusively *here* or *there*. It is the *house of God* —it is where God's Spirit dwells, where his precepts are obeyed, and where pure, unadulterated love to God and man prevails. It is not in the *creed* or religious *confessions* of any denomination of Christians; for, as all who hold the truth and live a holy life, acknowledging Jesus alone as the *head of the Church* and *Saviour* of the *world*, are members of his mystical body; (and such may be found in all sects and parties;) so the Church of Christ may be said to be everywhere, and to be confined nowhere; i. e. in whatever place Christianity is *credited* and *acknowledged*. The *wicked* of all sorts, no matter what their profession

may be, and all *persecutors of religious people,* who differ from them, are *without* the pale of this Church. *Essentially* must their *spirit* and *conduct* be changed, before the living Head of this spiritual building can acknowledge them as members of the heavenly family.

This text, therefore, will never apply to the Romish Church, till that Church be, both in doctrine and discipline, what the Christian Church should be. When it is the established religion of any country it gives no toleration to those who differ from it; and in Protestant countries its cry *for* toleration and secular authority is loud and long. I wish its partisans the full and free exercise of their religion, even to its superstitions and nonsense; but how can they expect toleration who give none? The Protestant Church tolerates it fully; it persecutes the Protestants to bonds and death when it has power; which then is the true Church of Christ?

CHAPTER IV.

Apostasy from the true faith predicted, and in what that apostasy should consist, 1–5. *Exhortations to Timothy to teach the truth,* 6. *To avoid old wives' fables; to exercise himself to godliness,* 7, 8. *To labour, command, and teach,* 9, 10, 11. *To act so that none might despise his youth,* 12. *To give attendance to reading and preaching,* 13, 14. *To give up himself wholly to the Divine work,* 15. *And so doing he should both save himself and them that heard him,* 16.

A. M. cir. 4069.
A. D. 64 or 65.
A. U. C. 818.
An. Imp. Neronis Cæs.
Aug. 12.

NOW the Spirit [a] speaketh expressly, that [b] in the latter times some shall depart from the faith, giving heed [c] to seducing spirits, [d] and doctrines of devils;

2 [e] Speaking lies in hypocrisy; [f] having their conscience seared with a hot iron;

3 [g] Forbidding to marry, [h] *and commanding* to abstain from meats, which

A. M. cir. 4069.
A. D. 64 or 65.
A. U. C. 818.
An. Imp. Neronis Cæs.
Aug. 12.

---

[a] John xvi. 13; 2 Thess. ii. 3; 2 Tim. iii. 1, &c.; 2 Pet. iii. 3; 1 John ii. 18; Jude 4, 18.——[b] 1 Pet. i. 20.——[c] 2 Tim. iii. 13; 2 Pet. ii. 1; Rev. xvi. 14.——[d] Dan. xi. 35, 37, 38; Rev. ix. 20.——[e] Matt. vii. 15; Rom. xvi. 18; 2 Pet. ii. 3.——[f] Eph. iv. 19.——[g] 1 Cor. vii. 28, 36, 38; Col. ii. 20, 21; Hebrews xiii. 4. [h] Rom. xiv. 3, 17; 1 Cor. viii. 8.

NOTES ON CHAP. IV.

Verse 1. *Now the Spirit speaketh expressly*] 'Ρητως· *Manifestly, openly.* It is very likely that the apostle refers here to a prophecy *then* furnished by the Holy Ghost, and probably immediately after he had written the words in the preceding verses; and as this prophecy contains things nowhere else spoken of in the sacred writings, and of the utmost moment to the Christian Church, we cannot hear or read them with too much reverence or respect.

In the latter times] This does not necessarily imply the last ages of the world, but any times consequent to those in which the Church then lived.

Depart from the faith] Αποστησονται—της πιστεως· *They will apostatize from the faith,* i. e. from Christianity; renouncing the whole system *in effect,* by bringing in doctrines which render its essential truths null and void, or denying and renouncing such doctrines as are essential to Christianity as a system of salvation. A man may hold all the truths of Christianity, and yet render them of none effect by holding other doctrines which counteract their influence; or he may apostatize by denying some essential doctrine, though he bring in nothing *heterodox.*

Giving heed to seducing spirits] Πνευμασι πλανοις· Many MSS. and the chief of the fathers have πνευμασι πλανης· *spirits of deceit;* which is much more emphatic than the common reading. Deception has her spirits, emissaries of every kind, which she employs to darken the hearts and destroy the souls of men. Pretenders to *inspiration,* and false teachers of every kind, belong to this class.

And doctrines of devils] Δαιμονιων· *Demons;* either meaning *fallen spirits,* or *dead men, spectres,* &c., or doctrines inspired by Satan relative to these, by which he secures his own interest, and provides for his own worship.

Verse 2. *Speaking lies in hypocrisy*] Persons pretending, not only to Divine inspiration, but also to extraordinary degrees of holiness, self-denial, mortification, &c., in order to accredit the *lies* and false doctrines which they taught. Multitudes of lies were framed concerning miracles wrought by the *relics* of departed *saints,* as they were termed. For, even in this country, Thomas a Becket was deemed a saint, his relics wrought numerous miracles; and his tomb was frequented by multitudes of pilgrims! However, as he works none now, we may rest assured that he never did work any. In 1305, King Edward I. was prevailed on by his clergy to write to Pope Clement V. to *canonize* Thomas de Cantelupo, bishop of Hereford, because a multitude of miracles had been wrought by his influence; *In tantum,* says the king, *quod ipsius meritis et intercessionibus gloriosis, lumen cæcis, surdis auditus, verbum mutis, et gressus claudis, et alia pleraque beneficia ipsius patrocinium implorantibus, cælesti dextra conferuntur.* "Insomuch that, by his glorious merits and intercessions, the blind receive their sight, the deaf hear, the dumb speak, and the lame walk; and many other benefits are conferred by the right hand of the Divine Being on those who implore his patronage." And therefore he prays that this dead bishop may be added to the calendar, "that he and his kingdom may enjoy his suffrages and merit his patronage in heaven, who had the benefit of his conversation on earth." *Nos attendentes, per Dei*

A. M. cir. 4069.
A. D. 64 or 65.
A. U. C. 818.
An. Imp. Ne-
ronis Cæs.
Aug. 12.

God hath created ⁱ to be received ^k with thanksgiving of them which believe and know the truth.

4 For ^l every creature of God *is* good, and nothing to be refused, if it be received with thanksgiving ;

5 For it is sanctified by the word of God and prayer.

6 If thou put the brethren in remembrance of these things, thou shalt be a good minister of Jesus Christ, ^m nourished up in the words of faith and of good doctrine, whereunto thou hast attained.

7 But ⁿ refuse profane and old wives' fables, and ^o exercise thyself *rather* unto godliness.

A. M. cir. 4069.
A. D. 64 or 65.
A. U. C. 818.
An. Imp. Ne-
ronis Cæs.
Aug. 12.

ⁱ Gen. i. 29; ix. 3.——^k Rom. xiv. 6; 1 Cor. x. 30.——^l Rom. xiv. 14, 20; 1 Cor. x. 25; Tit. i. 15.——^m 2 Tim. iii. 14, 15.——ⁿ Chap. i. 4; vi. 20; 2 Tim. ii. 16, 23 iv. 4; Tit. i. 14.——^o Heb. v. 14.

---

gratiam, fideles in Christo, nosque præcipue, et populum regni nostri, ejus posse suffragiis adjuvari, ut, quem familiarem habuimus in terris, mereamur habere patronum in cœlis. Fœdera, vol. i., p. 976. Edit. 1816.

Having their conscience seared with a hot iron] They bear the marks of their hypocrisy as evidently and as indelibly in their conscience in the sight of God, as those who have been *cauterized* for their crimes do in their bodies in the sight of men. It was customary in ancient times to mark those with a *hot iron* who had been guilty of great crimes, such as sacrilege, &c. And the heathens supposed that even in the other world they bear such marks; and by these the infernal judges knew the quantum of their vices, and appointed the degrees of their punishment. There is a saying much like that of the apostle in the invective of *Claudian* against *Rufinus*, whom he supposes to be thus addressed by Rhadamanthus, one of the infernal judges :—

Quid demens manifesta negas ? En pectus INUSTÆ *Deformant* MACULÆ *! vitiisque inolevit imago,*

Nec sese commissa tegunt.

" Thou fool, why dost thou deny what is so manifest ? Behold the *deep-burnt marks* deform thy conscience : the appearance of them has grown up with thy vices; neither can the crimes which thou hast committed hide themselves."

Verse 3. *Forbidding to marry*] These hypocritical priests pretending that a single life was much more favourable to devotion, and to the perfection of the Christian life. This sentiment was held by the *Essenes*, a religious sect among the Jews; and we know that it is a favourite opinion among the Romanists, who oblige all their clergy to live a single life by a *vow of continency*.

To abstain from meats] Both among the heathens, Jews, and Romanists, certain *meats* were prohibited; Some *always*, others at *particular times*. This the apostle informs us was directly contrary to the original design of God; and says that those *who know the truth*, know this.

Verse 4. *For every creature of God is good*] That is : Every creature which God has made for man's nourishment is good for that purpose, and to be thankfully received whenever necessary for the support of human life; and *nothing* of that sort is at any time to be refused, *ουδεν αποβλητον, rejected* or *despised*.

We find a saying very similar to this in *Lucian's Timon :* Ουτοι αποβλητα εισι δωρα τα παρα Διος. The *gifts which are from Jove ought not to be* DESPISED. This appears to have been a proverbial saying among the heathens.

Verse 5. *For it is sanctified by the word of God*] Δια λογου Θεου· *By the command of God ;* probably referring to Gen. i. 29 : *And God said, I have given you every herb—and every tree—to you it shall be for meat ;* and to chap. ix. 3 : *Every moving thing that liveth shall be meat for you; even as the green herb have I given you all things;* i. e. I have given you every animal that is proper for food, as I have given you every herb and fruit proper for nourishment. Therefore, all this was *sanctified, set apart,* and appropriated to this use by this command. And when man is about to use it, he is to *sanctify* or *set it apart* to that use by *prayer to God,* 1. That it may answer the end to us for which it was designed; 2. That we may use it with gratitude and moderation; 3. That all the strength derived from it may be devoted to God, in filling up the duties of those situations in which his providence has placed us. Those who thank not God for their food, and pray not for his blessing in the use of it, are unworthy even of a morsel of bread, and of the breath they breathe. Bishop Newton's opinion of this prophecy I have reserved to the end of this chapter.

Verse 6. *If thou put the brethren in remembrance of these things*] Show the Church that, even now, there is danger of this apostasy; put them on their guard against it; for the forewarned are half armed. Schoettgen supposes from this verse that what is spoken above refers to the *Jews* alone; and that there is no reference here to a Church which in after ages might apostatize from, or corrupt, the true doctrine of our Lord and Saviour. Bishop Newton and others are of a different opinion. See at the end of this chapter.

Nourished up in the words of faith] By acting as I command thee, thou wilt show that thou art a good minister of Jesus Christ, and that thou hast been nourished from thy youth up in the doctrines of faith. The apostle seems to allude here to Timothy's Christian education. See the preface to this epistle.

Whereunto thou hast attained.] Ἡ παρηκολουθηκας· Which thou hast *thoroughly understood.* For the meaning of this word, see the note on Luke i. 3.

Verse 7. *But refuse profane and old wives' fables*] This seems to refer particularly to the *Jews*, whose

A. M. cir. 4069.
A. D. 64 or 65.
A. U. C. 818.
An. Imp. Ne-
ronis Cæs.
Aug. 12.

8 For ᵖ bodily exercise profiteth �q little ; ʳ but godliness is
profitable unto all things, ˢ having promise of the life that now
is, and of that which is to come.

9 ᵗ This *is* a faithful saying, and worthy of
all acceptation.

10 For therefore ᵘ we both
labour and suffer reproach, because ᵛ we trust in the living
God, ʷ who is the Saviour of all
men, specially of those that believe.

A. M. cir. 4069.
A. D. 64 or 65.
A. U. C. 818.
An. Imp. Ne-
ronis Cæs.
Aug. 12.

11 ˣ These things command and teach.

12 ʸ Let no man despise thy youth ; but

ᵖ 1 Cor. viii. 8 ; Col. ii. 23.——�q Or, *for a little time.*——ʳ Ch.
vi. 6.——ˢ Psa. xxxvii. 4 ; lxxxiv. 11 ; cxii. 2, 3 ; cxlv. 19 ; Matt.
vi. 33 ; xix. 29 ; Mark x. 30 ; Rom. viii. 28.

ᵗ Chap. i. 15.——ᵘ 1 Cor. iv. 11, 12.——ᵛ Chap. vi. 17.——ʷ Psa.
xxxvi. 6 ; cvii. 2, 6, &c.——ˣ Chap. vi. 2.——ʸ 1 Cor. xvi. 11 ;
Tit. ii. 15.

Talmudical writings are stuffed with the most ridiculous and profane fables that ever disgraced the human
intellect. It may with equal propriety be applied to
the *legends* of the Romish Church. Let any man
read the *Aurea Legenda*, and he will find of profane
and old wives' fables what may stand, with considerable propriety, column for column with the Talmud.
See *Joseline's* Life of St. Patrick for miracles, without rhyme or reason, abundantly more numerous and
more stupendous than all the *necessary* ones wrought
by Jesus Christ and his apostles. This is enough to
persuade a man that the Spirit of God had these very
corruptions and this corrupt Church particularly in view.

Exercise thyself rather *unto godliness.*] To understand this expression it is necessary to know that the
apostle alludes here to the *gymnastic* exercises among
the Greeks, which were intended as a *preparation* for
their contests at the public *games.* They did this in
order to obtain a *corruptible* or *fading crown,* i. e. a
chaplet of leaves, which was the reward of those who
conquered in those games ; Timothy was to exercise
himself unto godliness, that he might be prepared for
the kingdom of heaven, and there receive a crown that
fadeth not away. See the notes on 1 Cor. ix. 24, &c.

Verse 8. *For bodily exercise profiteth little*] Προς
ολιγον εστιν ωφελιμος. Those gymnastic exercises, so
highly esteemed among the Greeks, are but *little
worth* ; they are but of *short duration* ; they refer only
to *this life,* and to the applause of men : but godliness
has the promise of this life, and the life to come ; it is
profitable for all things ; and for both time and eternity.

But godliness is profitable unto all things] By
godliness we are to understand every thing that the
Christian religion either *promises* or *prescribes :* the
life of God in the soul of man ; and the *glory of God*
as the *object* and *end* of that *life.* To receive the
first, a man must renounce his sins, deny himself, take
up his cross, and follow his Lord through evil and
through good report. To obtain the latter, a man
must *labour* to enter into that rest which remains for
the people of God.

Having promise of the life that now is] The man
that fears, loves, and serves God, has God's blessing
all through life. His religion saves him from all those
excesses, both in *action* and *passion,* which sap the
foundations of life, and render existence itself often a
burden. The peace and love of God in the heart produce a *serenity* and *calm* which cause the lamp of life
to burn clear, strong, and permanent. Evil and disorderly passions obscure and stifle the vital spark.
Every truly religious man extracts the uttermost good

out of life itself, and through the Divine blessing gets
the uttermost good that is in life ; and, what is better
than all, acquires a full preparation here below for an
eternal life of glory above. Thus godliness has the
promise of, and secures the blessings of, both worlds.

Verse 9. *This is a faithful saying*] The truth of
this doctrine none need doubt ; and every man has it
in his power to put this to the proof. See on chap.
i. 15.

Verse 10. *For therefore we both labour*] This verse
was necessary to explain what he had before said ;
and here he shows that his meaning was not that the
followers of God should enjoy *worldly prosperity* and
exemption from natural evils ; for, said he, it is because we exercise ourselves to godliness that we have
both labour and reproach, and we have these because
we trust in the living God : but still we have mental
happiness, and all that is necessary for our passage
through life ; for in the midst of persecutions and afflictions we have the peace of God that passeth knowledge, and have all our crosses and sufferings so sanctified to us that we consider them in the number of
our blessings.

Who is the Saviour of all men] Who has provided
salvation for the whole human race, and has freely
offered it to them in his word and by his Spirit.

Specially of those that believe.] What God intends
for ALL, he actually gives to *them* that believe in Christ,
who died for the sins of the world, and tasted death
for every man. As *all* have been purchased by his
blood so all may believe ; and consequently all may
be saved. Those that perish, perish through their
own fault.

Verse 11. *These things command and teach.*] Let
it be the sum and substance of thy preaching, that true
religion is profitable for both worlds ; that *vice* destroys
both body and soul ; that Christ tasted death for every
man ; and that he saves to the uttermost all them that
believe in his name.

Verse 12. *Let no man despise thy youth*] Act
with all the *gravity* and decorum which become thy
situation in the Church. As thou art in the place of
an *elder,* act *as* an *elder.* Boyish playfulness ill becomes a minister of the Gospel, whatever his age may
be. Concerning Timothy's age see the conclusion of
the preface to this epistle.

Be thou an example of the believers] It is natural
for the flock to follow the shepherd ; if *he* go wrong,
they will go wrong also.

" Himself a wanderer from the narrow way,
His silly sheep, no wonder if they stray."

2

A. M. cir. 4069.
A. D. 64 or 65.
A. U. C. 818.
An. Imp. Ne-
ronis Cæs.
Aug. 12.

z be thou an example of the believers, in word, in conversation, in
charity, in spirit, in faith, in purity.

13 Till I come, give attendance

to ᵃ reading, to exhortation, to
doctrine.

14 ᵇ Neglect not the gift that
is in thee, which was given thee

A. M. cir. 4069
A. D. 64 or 65.
A. U. C. 818.
An. Imp. Ne-
ronis Cæs.
Aug. 12.

ᶻ Tit. ii. 7; 1 Pet. v. 3.——ᵃ John v. 39;

chap. iii. 14; 2 Tim. iii. 15.——ᵇ 2 Tim. i. 6.

Though, according to the just judgment of God, they
who die in their sins have their blood on their own
head; yet, if they have either gone into sin or *continued* in it through the watchman's fault, their blood
will God require at *his* hand. How many have endeavoured to excuse their transgressions by alleging,
in vindication of their conduct, " Our minister does
so, and he is more wise and learned than we." What
an awful account must such have to give to the Head
of the Church when he appears!

In word] Εν λογω· *In doctrine;* teach nothing but
the truth of God, because nothing but that will save
souls.

In conversation] Εν αναστροφη· In the whole of
thy conduct in every department which thou fillest in
all thy domestic as well as public relations, *behave
thyself well.*

In charity] Εν αγαπη· *In love* to God and man;
show that this is the *principle* and *motive* of all thy
conduct.

In spirit] Εν πνευματι· In the *manner* and *disposition* in which thou dost all things. How often is
a *holy* or *charitable* work done in an *unholy, uncharitable,* and peevish spirit! To the doer, such work is
unfruitful.

These words are wanting in ACDFG, and several
others; both the *Syriac,* Erpen's *Arabic, Æthiopic,
Armenian, Vulgate,* and *Itala,* and many of the *fathers.* ⸳ Griesbach leaves them out of the text. They
have in all probability been added by a later hand.

In faith] Εν πιστει· This word πιστις is probably
taken here for *fidelity,* a sense which it often bears
in the New Testament. It cannot mean *doctrine,* for
that has been referred to before. Be *faithful* to thy
trust, to thy *flock,* to thy *domestics,* to the *public,*
to thy GOD. *Fidelity* consists in honestly keeping,
preserving, and delivering up when required, whatever is intrusted to our care; as also in *improving*
whatever is delivered in trust for that purpose. Lose
nothing that God gives, and improve every gift that he
bestows.

In purity.] Εν ἁγνεια· Chastity of body and mind;
a direction peculiarly necessary for a young minister,
who has more temptations to break its rules than
perhaps any other person. " *Converse sparingly
with women, and especially with young women,*" was
the advice of a very holy and experienced minister of
Christ.

Verse 13. *Give attendance to reading*] Timothy
could easily comprehend the apostle's meaning; but
at present this is not so easy. What *books* does the
apostle mean? The books of the Old Testament were
probably what he intended; these testified of Jesus,
and by these he could either *convince* or *confound* the
Jews. But, whether was the reading of these to be
public or *private?* Probably both. It was customary

to read the law and the prophets in the synagogue, and
doubtless in the assemblies of the Christians; after
which there was generally an exhortation founded upon
the subject of the prophecy. Hence the apostle says:
Give attendance to reading, to EXHORTATION, *to* DOC-
TRINE. Timothy was therefore to be diligent in reading the sacred writings at *home,* that he might be the
better qualified to read and expound them in the public assemblies to the Christians, and to others who
came to these public meetings.

As to *other books,* there were not many at that time
that could be of much use to a Christian minister. In
those days the great business of the preacher was to
bring forward the *grand facts* of Christianity, to prove
these, and to show that all had happened according to
the prediction of the prophets; and from these to show
the work of God in the *heart,* and the evidence of that
work in a *holy life.*

At present the truth of God is not only to be *proclaimed,* but defended; and many *customs* or *manners,*
and *forms of speech,* which are to us obsolete, must be
explained from the writings of the ancients, and particularly from the works of those who lived about the
same times, or nearest to them, and in the same or contiguous *countries.* This will require the knowledge
of those languages in which those works have been
composed, the chief of which are *Hebrew* and *Greek,*
the languages in which the Holy Scriptures of the Old
and New Testaments have been originally written.

Latin is certainly of the next consequence; a language in which some of the most *early comments* have
been written; and it is worth the trouble of being
learned, were it only for the sake of the works of *St.
Jerome,* who translated and wrote a commentary on
the whole of the Scriptures; though in many respects
it is both erroneous and superficial.

Arabic and *Syriac* may be added with great advantage: the *latter* being in effect the language in which
Christ and his apostles spoke and preached in Judea;
and the *former* being radically the same with the Hebrew, and preserving many of the *roots* of that language, the derivatives of which often occur in the
Hebrew Bible, but the *roots* never.

The works of various scholars prove of how much
consequence even the writings of heathen authors,
chiefly those of *Greece* and *Italy,* are to the illustration of the sacred writings. And he who is best acquainted with the sacred records will avail himself of
such helps, with gratitude both to God and man.
Though so many languages and so much reading are
not absolutely necessary to form a minister of the Gospel, (for there are many eminent ministers who have
not such advantages,) yet they are *helps* of the first
magnitude to those who have them and know how to
use them.

Verse 14. *Neglect not the gift that is in thee*] The

2

A. M. cir. 4069.
A. D. 64 or 65.
A. U. C. 818.
An. Imp. Ne-
ronis Cæs.
Aug. 12.

c by prophecy, d with the laying on of the hands of the presbytery.

15 Meditate upon these things ; give thyself wholly to them ; that thy profiting may appear e to all.

16 f Take heed unto thyself, and unto thy doctrine ; continue in them : for in doing this thou shalt both g save thyself and h them that hear thee.

A. M. cir. 4069.
A. D. 64 or 65.
A. U. C. 818.
An. Imp. Ne-
ronis Cæs.
Aug. 12.

---

c Chap. i. 18.——d Acts vi. 6; viii. 17; xiii. 3 ; xix. 6 ; chap. v. 22 ; 2 Tim. i. 6.——e Or, *in all things.* | f Acts xx. 28.——g Ezekiel xxxiii. 9.——h Rom. xi. 14 ; 1 Cor. ix. 22 ; James v. 20.

---

word χαρισμα here must refer to the *gifts* and *graces* of the *Divine Spirit*, which Timothy received when set apart to the work of an evangelist by the imposition of *St. Paul's hands*, 2 Tim. i. 6, and by that of the *presbytery* or *eldership ;* for it most evidently appears, from this verse and that above quoted, that he received this double *imposition*, not probably at *different* times, but on one and the same occasion. These very gifts and graces might be *improved ;* and we have reason to believe, if not improved, would be withdrawn by the great Head of the Church.

Given thee by prophecy] It has already been conjectured (see the *preface*, and the note on chap. i. 18) that there had been some remarkable *prediction* relative to the future destiny and usefulness of Timothy. And probably it was in consequence of this that he was set apart to the office of evangelist and bishop in the Church at Ephesus. When apostles laid their hands on men, they ordinarily received the Holy Spirit with this imposition. This may be what the apostle calls to' the remembrance of Timothy, and tells him not to neglect what he had received, nor the purpose for which he had received it.

Verse 15. Meditate upon these things] Ταυτα μελετα· Revolve them frequently in thy mind ; consider deeply their nature and importance ; get them deeply fastened in thy heart, and let all thy conduct flow from this inward feeling and conviction. Let the nature, reasons, and motives of thy ministry, be ever in the view of thy heart and conscience.

Give thyself wholly to them] Εν τουτοις ισθι· *Be thou in these things.* Horace has a similar expression : *Omnis in hoc sum.* "I am absorbed in this." Occupy thyself wholly with them ; make them not only thy *chief* but thy *sole* concern. Thou art called to save thy own soul, and the souls of them that hear thee ; and God has given thee the Divine *gifts* for this and *no other purpose.* To this let all thy reading and study be directed ; this is thy great business, and thou must perform it as the servant and steward of the Lord. *Bengel* has a good saying on this verse, which I will quote : In his qui est, *minus erit in sodalitatibus mundanis, in studiis alienis, in colligendis libris, conchis, nummis, quibus multi pastores notabilem ætatis partem insistentes conterunt ;* "*He* who is *wholly in these things* will be *little* in worldly company, in foreign studies, in collecting books, shells, and coins, in which many ministers consume a principal part of their life " Such persons are worthy of the deepest reprehension, unless all these studies, collections, &c., be formed with the *express view* of illustrating the sacred records ; and to such awful drudgery few Christian ministers are called. Many, when they have made such collections, seem to know nothing of their use ;

they only *see* them and *show* them, but can never bring them to their assistance in the work of the ministry. *These should be prayed for and pitied.*

That thy profiting may appear to all.] By being made a universal blessing ; convincing and converting sinners ; and building up the Church of God on its most holy faith.

Verse 16. *Take heed unto thyself*] See that the life of God remains and the work of God prospers in thine own soul. *Take heed to thy doctrine,* that the matter be pure and orthodox ; that thou teach nothing for truth but what God has revealed.

Continue in them] i. e., In *taking heed to thyself and to thy doctrine ;* for this must be thy continual study. Without this, the Divine influence shall recede from thy heart, and the Divine gift from thy intellect ; and, like Samson shorn of his strength, thou wilt soon become as another man, as any *common man ;* thy *power* will depart from thee, and thou shalt be no longer able to *persuade ;* the UNCTION shall depart from thee, and, destitute of spiritual *feeling* thyself, thou shalt not be able to cause others to *feel.* Take the apostle's advice, and thou shalt save thy own soul, and the souls of them that hear thee.

IN the course of the preceding notes I have referred to Bishop Newton's opinion and application of the prophecy contained in the first five verses. Not being fully persuaded in my own mind to what Church this, and the prophecy in the Epistle to the Thessalonians, should be applied, I produce an accredited author, who, for his Dissertations on the Prophecies, has a high and honoured name in the Church.

" I. The first thing to be considered is, the apostasy here predicted. ' Some shall depart, or rather *apostatize*, from the faith.' An *apostasy from the faith* may be either total or partial ; either when we renounce the whole, or when we deny some principal and essential article of it. It is not every error, or every heresy, that is apostasy from the faith. It is a revolt in a principal and essential article, when we worship God by any image or representation, or when we worship other beings besides God, and pray unto other mediators besides *the one Mediator between God and man, the man Christ Jesus.* This is the very essence of Christian worship, to worship the one true God, through the one true Christ ; and to worship any other god, or any other mediator, is apostasy and rebellion against God and against Christ. Such is the nature of *apostasy from the faith ;* and it is implied that this apostasy shall be general, and affect great numbers. For, though it be said only *some shall apostatize*, yet by *some*, here, *many* are understood The original word frequently signifies a *multitude* and there are abundant instances in Scripture where it is used in that sense, as the reader may perceive from John vi. 64–66 ; Rom. xi. 17 ; 1 Cor. x. 5, 6. This apostasy may be general and extensive, and include *many* but not *all*.

"II. It is more particularly shown wherein the apostasy should consist, in the following words : *Giving heed to seducing spirits and doctrines of devils ;* or rather : ' Giving heed to *erroneous* spirits and doctrines concerning *demons*.' *Spirits* seem to be much the same in sense as *doctrines*, the latter word may be considered as explanatory of the former ; and error sometimes signifying *idolatry*, *erroneous doctrines* may comprehend *idolatrous* as well as *false doctrines*. But it is still farther added, for explanation, that these doctrines should be *doctrines of devils* or *of demons*, where the genitive case is not to be taken actively, as if demons were the authors of these doctrines, but passively, as if demons were the subject of these doctrines. In Jer. x. 8 ; Acts xiii. 12 ; Heb. vi. 2, the genitive case is used in this manner ; and, by the same construction, *doctrines of demons* are doctrines *about* or *concerning demons*. This is, therefore, a prophecy that the idolatrous theology of demons, professed by the Gentiles, should be revived among Christians. Demons, according to the theology of the Gentiles, were middle powers between the gods and mortal men ; and were regarded as mediators and agents between the gods and men. Of these demons there were accounted two kinds : one kind were the souls of men deified or canonized after death ; the other kind were such as had never been the souls of men, nor ever dwelt in mortal bodies. These latter demons may be paralleled with angels, as the former may with canonized saints ; and as we Christians believe there are good and evil angels, so did the Gentiles that there were good and evil demons. It appears then as if the doctrine of demons, which prevailed so long in the heathen world, was to be revived and established in the Christian Church. And is not the worship of saints and angels now, in all respects, the same that the worship of demons was in former times ? The name only is different, the thing is essentially the same. The heathens looked upon their demons as mediators and intercessors between God and men ; and are not the saints and angels regarded in the same light by many professed Christians ? The promoters of this worship were sensible that it was the same, and that the one succeeded the other ; and as the worship is the same, so likewise it is performed with the same ceremonies. Nay, the very same temples, the very same images, the very same altars, which once were consecrated to Jupiter and the other demons, are now reconsecrated to the Virgin Mary and other saints. The very same titles and inscriptions are ascribed to both ; the very same prodigies and miracles are related of these as of those In short, the whole almost of paganism is converted and applied to popery , the one is manifestly formed upon the same plan and principles as the other

"III Such an *apostasy* as this—of reviving the *doctrines of demons*, and worshipping the dead—was not likely to take place immediately , it should prevail and prosper *in the latter days*. The phrase of the

latter times or *days*, or the *last times* or *days*, signifies any time yet to come ; but denotes more particularly the times of Christianity. The times of Christianity may properly be called the *latter times* or *days*, or the *last times* or *days*, because it is the last of all God's revelations to mankind. Heb. i. 1, 2 ; 1 Pet. i. 20.

"IV. Another remarkable peculiarity of this prophecy is, the solemn and emphatic manner in which it is delivered : *The Spirit speaketh expressly.* By the *Spirit* is meant the Holy Spirit of God, which inspired the prophets and apostles. The *Spirit speaking expressly*, may signify his speaking precisely and certainly, not obscurely and involvedly, as he is wont to speak in the prophets ; or it may be said, *The Spirit speaketh expressly*, when he speaks in express words in some place or other of Divine writ ; and the Spirit hath spoken the same thing in express words before in the prophecy of Daniel. Daniel has foretold, in express words, the worship of new demons or demi-gods ; Dan. xi. 38. The *mauzzim* of Daniel are the same as the *demons* of St. Paul ; gods protectors, or saints protectors, defenders and guardians of mankind. This, therefore, is a prophecy, not merely dictated by private suggestion and inspiration, but taken out of the written word. It is a prophecy not only of St. Paul's, but of Daniel's too ; or rather of Daniel, confirmed and approved by St. Paul.

"V. The apostle proceeds, ver. 2, to describe by what means and by what persons this apostasy should be propagated and established in the world : *Speaking lies in hypocrisy, &c. ;* or rather, *through* the hypocrisy of *liars*, having their conscience, &c.; for the preposition rendered *in*, frequently signifies *through* or *by*. *Liars* too, or *speaking lies*, cannot possibly be joined with the original word rendered *some*, and that rendered *giving heed*, because they are in the nominative case, and this is in the genitive. Neither can it well be joined in the construction with the word rendered *devils*, or *demons ;* for how can *demons*, or *devils*, be said *to speak lies in hypocrisy*, and *to have their conscience seared, &c.?* It is plain, then, that the great apostasy of the latter times was to prevail, *through the hypocrisy of liars, &c.* And has not the great idolatry of Christians, and the worship of the dead particularly, been diffused and advanced in the world by such instruments and agents ? by fabulous books, forged under the names of the apostles and saints ; by fabulous legends of their lives ; by fabulous miracles, ascribed to their relics ; by fabulous dreams and revelations ; and even by fabulous saints, who never existed but in imagination.

"VI. Verse 3. *Forbidding to marry, &c.*] This is a farther character of the promoters of this apostasy. The same hypocritical liars who should promote the worship of demons should also prohibit lawful marriage. The monks were the first who brought a *single life* into repute ; they were the first also who revived and promoted the worship of demons. One of the primary and most essential laws and constitutions of all monks was the profession of a single life, and it is equally clear that the monks had the principal share in promoting the worship of the dead. The monks then were the principal promoters of the worship of the dead in former times. And who are the great patrons and advocates of the same worship now? Are not their legitimate successors and descendants, the monks and priests and bishops of the Church of Rome? And do not they also profess and recommend a single life, as well as the worship of saints and angels? Thus have the worship of demons, and the prohibition of marriage, constantly gone hand in hand together; and as they who maintain one maintain the other, so it is no less remarkable that they who disclaim the one, disclaim the other.

" VII. The last mark and character of these men is : *Commanding to abstain from meats, &c.* The same lying hypocrites who should promote the worship of demons, should not only prohibit lawful marriage, but likewise impose unnecessary abstinence from meats; and these too, as indeed it is fit they should, usually go together as constituent parts of the same hypocrisy. It is as much the law of monks to abstain from meats, as from marriage. Some never eat any flesh ; others only certain kinds, on certain days. Frequent fasts are the rule and boast of their orders. So lived the monks of the ancient Church ; so live, with less strictness perhaps, but with greater ostentation, the monks and friars of the Church of Rome ; and these have been the principal propagators and defenders of the worship of the dead, both in former and in latter times. The worship of the dead is indeed so monstrously absurd as well as impious, that there was hardly any

probability of its ever prevailing in the world but by hypocrisy and lies. But that these particular sorts of hypocrisy—celibacy, under pretence of chastity ; and abstinence, under pretence of devotion—should be employed for this purpose, the Spirit of God alone could foresee and foretell. There is no necessary connection between the worship of the dead, *and forbidding to marry, and commanding to abstain from meats ;* and yet it is certain that the great advocates for this worship have, by their pretended purity and mortification, procured the greater reverence to their persons, and the readier reception to their doctrines. But this idle, popish, monkish abstinence is as unworthy of a *Christian* as it is unnatural to a *man*; it is preventing the purpose of nature, and *commanding to abstain from meats, which God hath created to be received with thanksgiving by believers, and them who know the truth.*" See Bishop *Newton's Dissertations on the Prophecies ;* and Dr. *Dodd's* notes.

Which mode of interpretation is best, I shall not attempt to say : to *determine* the *meaning* of prophecies is a difficult task ; and, in a case of this kind, I rather choose to trust to the judgment of others than to my own. It is to be deplored that all the preceding particulars apply but too well to the corruptions in the Romish Church, therefore to it they appear peculiarly applicable. But whether God had this Church alone in view, I dare not affirm.

CHAPTER V.

Rules to be observed in giving reproofs to the old and to the young, 1, 2. *Directions concerning widows,* 3–16. *Of elders that rule well,* 17, 18. *How to proceed against elders when accused, and against notorious offenders,* 19–21. *Directions concerning imposition of hands,* 22. *Concerning Timothy's health,* 23. *Reasons why no person should be hastily appointed to sacred offices,* 24, 25.

A. M. cir. 4069.
A. D. 64 or 65.
A. U. C. 818.
An. Imp. Neronis Cæs.
Aug. 12.

REBUKE [a] not an elder, but entreat *him* as a father ; *and* the younger men as brethren ;
2 The elder women as mothers ;
the younger as sisters, with all purity.
3 Honour widows [b] that are widows indeed.

A. M. cir. 4069.
A. D. 64 or 65.
A. U. C. 818.
An. Imp. Neronis Cæs.
Aug. 12.

[a] Lev. xix. 32.

[b] Ver. 5, 16.

NOTES ON CHAP. V.

Verse 1. *Rebuke not an elder*] That is, an elderly person ; for the word πρεσβυτερος is here taken in its natural sense, and signifies one advanced in years. At ver. 17, it is taken in what may be termed its ecclesiastical meaning, and signifies, an *officer* in the Church, what we commonly call a *presbyter* or *bishop ;* for sometimes these terms were confounded. There are but few cases in which it at all becomes a young man to reprove an old man, and especially one who is a father in the Church. If such a one does wrong, or gets out of the way, he should be *entreated* as a father, with great caution and respect. To this at least his age entitles him. The word επιπληξης signifies, do not *smite ;* i. e. do not treat them *harshly*, nor with *magisterial austerity.*

The younger men as brethren] Showing humility, and arrogating nothing to thyself on account of thy

office. Feel for them as thou oughtest to feel for thy own brethren.

Verse 2. *The elder women as mothers*] Treating them with the respect due to their age.

The younger as sisters] Feel for every member of the Church, old and young, male and female ; consider them as fathers, mothers, brothers, and sisters ; treat them all with gentleness ; and labour to keep them in, not to expel them from, the Church.

With all purity.] Εν παση αγνεια· With all chastity. See the note on chap. iv. 12.

There are some who seem to take a barbarous pleasure in expelling members from, the Church. They should be continued in as long as possible ; while they are in *the* Church—under its ordinances and discipline, there is some hope that their errors may be corrected ; but when once driven out again into the world, that hope must necessarily become extinct. As *judgment*

A. M. cir. 4069.
A. D. 64 or 65.
A. U. C. 818.
An. Imp. Ne-
ronis Cæs.
Aug. 12.

4 But if any widow have children or nephews, let them learn
first to show c piety at home,
and d to requite their parents :
e for that is good and acceptable before God.

5 f Now she that is a widow indeed, and
desolate, trusteth in God, and g continueth in
supplications and prayers h night and day.

6 i But she that liveth k in
pleasure is dead while she liveth.

7 l And these things give in
charge, that they may be blameless.

A. M. cir. 4069.
A. D. 64 or 65.
A. U. C. 818.
An. Imp. Ne
ronis Cæs.
Aug. 12.

8 But if any provide not for his own, m and
specially for those of his own n house, o he hath
denied the faith, p and is worse than an infidel.

9 Let not a widow be taken q into the num-

---

c Or, *kindness.*——d See Gen. xlv. 10, 11 ; Matt. xv. 4 ; Eph.
vi. 1, 2.——e Chapter ii. 3.——f 1 Cor. vii. 32.——g Luke ii. 37 ;
xviii. 1.——h Acts xxvi. 7.——i James v. 5.

k Or, *delicately.*——l Chap. i. 3 ; iv. 11 ; vi. 17.——m Isa. lviii. 7 ;
Gal. vi. 10.——n Or, *kindred.*——o 2 Timothy iii. 5 ; Titus i. 16.
p Matt. xviii. 17.——q Or, *chosen.*

---

is God's strange work, so *excommunication* should be
the strange, the last, and the most reluctantly performed
work of every Christian minister.

Verse 3. *Honour widows that are widows indeed.*]
One meaning of the word τιμαω, to *honour*, is to *support, sustain, &c.*, Matt. xv. 4, 5 ; and here it is most
obviously to be taken in this sense.　Provide for those
widows especially which are *widows indeed*—persons
truly destitute, being aged and helpless, and having
neither *children* nor *friends* to take care of them, and
who behave as becometh their destitute state.　But see
the note on verse 10.

Verse 4. *But if any widow have children or nephews*]
This shows that *widows indeed* are those that have
neither *children* nor *nephews*, i. e. no relatives that
either will or can help them, or no near relatives alive.

Let them learn first to show piety at home]　Let
these children and nephews provide for their aged or
helpless parents or relatives, and not burden the
Church with them while they are able to support them.

And to requite their parents]　Και αμοιβας αποδι-
δοναι τοις προγονοις·　Let them learn to *give benefit for
benefit.*　Your parents supported and nourished *you*
when you were young and helpless ; *you* ought therefore to support *them* when they are old and destitute.
This is called *showing piety;* and there is doubtless
an allusion to the fifth commandment : *Honour thy
father and thy mother*—provide for them in their old
age and afflictions ; God commands this.

Verse 5. *And desolate*]　Και μεμονωμενη·　*Left entirely alone*—having neither children nor relatives to
take care of her.

Trusteth in God]　Finding she has no other helper,
she *continues in prayer and supplication*, that she may
derive that from God which, in the course of his providence, he has deprived her of among men.

Verse 6. *But she that liveth in pleasure*]　Ἡ δε
σπαταλωσα·　*She that liveth delicately—voluptuously*
indulging herself with dainties ; it does not indicate
grossly criminal pleasures ; but simply means one who
indulges herself in *good eating and drinking*, pampering her body at the expense of her mind.　The word
is used in reference to what we term *petted* and *spoiled*
children ; and a remarkable passage is produced by
Kypke, from an epistle of *Theanus* to *Eubulus*, found
in *Opusc. Myth.* Galæi, page 741, where he says :
" What can be done with that boy, who, if he
have not food when and as he pleases, bursts out
into weeping ; and, if he eats, must have dainties
and sweetmeats ?　If the weather be hot he com-

plains of fatigue ; if it be cold, he trembles ; if
he be reproved, he scolds ; if every thing be not provided for him according to his wish, he is enraged.
If he eats not, he breaks out into fits of anger.　He
basely indulges himself in pleasure ; and in every
respect acts voluptuously and effeminately.　Knowing
then, O friend, ὁτι τα σπαταλωντα των παιδιων, ὁταν
ακμαση προς ανδρας, ανδραποδα γινεται, τας τοιαυτας
ἡδονας αφαιρει· that boys living thus *voluptuously*, when
they grow up are wont to become *slaves ;* take away,
therefore, such pleasures from them."　I have introduced this long quotation, the better to fix the meaning of the apostle, and to show that the *life of pleasure*
mentioned here does not mean *prostitution* or *uncleanness* of any kind, though such a life may naturally lead
to dissolute manners.

Is dead while she liveth.]　No purpose of life is
answered by the existence of such a person.　*Seneca,*
in *Epist.* 60, says of pleasure-takers, and those who
live a voluptuous life : *Hos itaque animalium loco nu-
mercmus, non hominum : quosdam vero ne animalium
quidem, sed mortuorum—mortem antecesserunt.* "We
rank such persons with brutes, not with men ; and some
of them not even with brutes, but with dead carcasses.
They anticipate their own death."　Such persons are,
as the apostle says elsewhere, *dead in trespasses, and
dead in sins.*

Verse 7. *That they may be blameless.*]　Charge the
whole *Church* to attend to these things, that *they* may
be blameless.　The words are not spoken of the widows
only, but of the Church or its officers ; it cannot be
restricted to the *widows*, for the adjective ανεπιληπτοι
is both of the *masculine* and feminine gender.

Verse 8. *But if any provide not for his own*]　His
own *people* or *relatives.*

Those of his own house]　That is, his own family,
or a poor widow or relative that lives under his roof.

Hath denied the faith]　The Christian religion,
which strongly inculcates love and benevolence to all
mankind.

Is worse than an infidel.]　For what are called the
dictates of nature lead men to feel for and provide for
their own families.　Heathen writers are full of
maxims of this kind ; Tacitus says : *Liberos cuique
ac propinquos* NATURA *carissimos esse voluit.* " Nature
dictates that to every one his own children and relatives should be most dear." And Cicero, in *Epist.*
ad Caption.: *Suos quisque debet tueri.* " Every man
should take care of his own family."

Verse 9. *Taken into the number*]　Let her not be

A. M. cir. 4069.
A. D. 64 or 65.
A. U. C. 818.
An. Imp. Ne-
ronis Cæs.
Aug. 12.

ber under threescore years old, [r] having been the wife of one man,

10 Well reported of for good works; if she have brought up children, if she have [s] lodged strangers, if she have [t] washed the saints' feet, if she have relieved the afflicted, if she have diligently followed every good work.

A. M. cir. 4069.
A. D. 64 or 65.
A. U. C. 818.
An. Imp. Ne-
ronis Cæs.
Aug. 12.

11 But the younger widows refuse: for when they have begun to wax wanton against Christ, they will marry;

12 Having damnation, because they have cast off their first faith.

13 [u] And withal they learn *to be* idle, wandering about from house to house; and not only idle, but tattlers also, and busybodies,

---

[r] Luke ii. 36; chap. iii. 2.——[s] Acts xvi. 15; Heb. xiii. 2; 1 Pet. iv. 9.

[t] Genesis xviii. 4; xix. 2; Luke vii. 38, 44; John xiii. 5, 14. [u] 2 Thess. iii. 11.

---

taken into the list of those for which the Church must provide. But some think that the apostle means the list of those who were *deaconesses* in the Church; and that no widow was to be admitted into that rank who did not answer to the following character. See on ver. 10.

Under threescore years] As it might be supposed that, previously to this age, they might be able to do something towards their own support. See on ver. 10.

Having been the wife of one man] Having lived in conjugal fidelity with her husband; or having had but one husband at a time; or, according to others, having never been but once married. But the former is the opinion of some of the most eminent of the Greek fathers, and appears to be that most consistent with the scope of the place, and with truth.

Verse 10. *Well reported of for good works*] Numbers being able to *bear testimony*, as the word implies, that she has not only avoided all sin, but that she has walked according to the testimony of God.

Brought up children] It was customary among the Gentiles to expose their children, when so poor that they were not able to provide for them. Pious and humane people took these up; and fed, clothed, and educated them. The words *brought up* may refer to the children of *others*, who were educated in the Christian faith by pious Christian women.

Lodged strangers] If she have been given to hospitality, freely contributing to the necessitous, when she had it in her power.

Washed the saints' feet] This was an office of humanity shown to all strangers and travellers in the eastern countries, who, either walking *barefoot*, or having only a sort of *sole* to defend the foot, needed washing when they came to their journey's end. Pious women generally did this act of kindness.

Relieved the afflicted] Visited and ministered to the sick.

Diligently followed every good work] In a word, if she have been *altogether* a *Christian*, living according to the precepts of the Gospel, and doing the Lord's work with all her heart, soul, and strength.

From the character given here of the *widow indeed*, it may be doubted whether χηρα, widow, was not in some cases the name of an *office*, which name it might have from being ordinarily filled by *widows*. It can hardly be supposed that any widow, unless she had considerable property, could have done the things enumerated in this verse, some of which would occasion

no small expense. The *widow indeed* may mean a person who was to be employed in some office in the Church; and Timothy is enjoined not to take any into that office unless she had been before remarkable for piety and humanity. Some think that the widows of whom the apostle speaks had been *deaconesses*, and wished now to be taken on what might be termed the *superannuated list*; and the apostle lays down *rules* for the admission of such, the sum of which is: Let none come on this superannuated list unless she be at least sixty years of age, and can bring proof of her having conscientiously discharged the office and duty of a *deaconess*.

Verse 11. *But the younger widows refuse*] Do not admit those into this office who are under sixty years of age. Probably those who were received into such a list *promised* to *abide* in their *widowhood*. But as young or comparatively young women might have both occasion and temptations to remarry, and so break their engagement to Christ, they should not be admitted. Not that the apostle condemns their remarrying as a crime in itself, but because it was contrary to their engagement. See on verse 14.

Wax wanton] Καταστρηνιασωσι· From κατα, intensive, and στρηνιαω, to act in a luxurious or wanton manner. The word is supposed to be derived from στερειν, to remove, and ἡνια, the rein; and is a metaphor taken from a pampered horse, from whose mouth the rein has been removed, so that there is nothing to check or confine him. The metaphor is plain enough, and the application easy.

Verse 12. *Having damnation*] In the sense in which we use this word I am satisfied the apostle never intended it. It is likely that he refers here to some promise or engagement which they made when taken on the list already mentioned, and now they have the *guilt* of having violated that promise; this is the κριμα, or condemnation, of which the apostle speaks.

They have cast off their first faith.] By pledging their *fidelity* to a husband they have cast off their *fidelity* to Christ, as a married life and their previous engagement are incompatible. Dr. *Macknight* translates these two verses thus: But the younger widows *reject*, for when they *cannot endure Christ's rein*, they will marry; *incurring condemnation*, because they have *put away* their first *fidelity*.

Verse 13. *And withal they learn* to be *idle*] They do not love work, and they will not work.

Wandering about from house to house] Gadding,

A. M. cir. 4069.
A. D. 64 or 65.
A. U. C. 818.
An. Imp. Ne-
ronis Cæs.
Aug. 12.

speaking things which they ought not.

14 [v] I will therefore that the younger women marry, bear children, guide the house, [w] give none occasion to the adversary [x] to speak reproachfully.

15 For some are already turned aside after Satan.

16 If any man or woman that believeth

have widows, let them relieve them, and let not the Church be charged; that it may relieve [y] them that are widows indeed.

A. M. cir. 4069.
A. D. 64 or 65.
A. U. C. 818.
An. Imp. Ne-
ronis Cæs.
Aug. 12.

17 [z] Let the elders that rule well [a] be counted worthy of double honour, especially they who labour in the word and doctrine.

18 For the Scripture saith, [b] Thou shalt not muzzle the ox that treadeth out the corn. And,

---

[v] 1 Cor. vii. 9.——[w] Chap. vi. 1; Tit. ii. 8.——[x] Gr. *for their railing.*——[y] Ver. 3, 5.——[z] Rom. xii. 8; 1 Cor. ix. 10, 14; Gal.

vi. 6; Phil. ii. 29; 1 Thess. v. 12, 13; Heb. xiii. 7, 17.——[a] Acts xxviii. 10.——[b] Deut. xxv. 4; 1 Cor. ix. 9.

---

gossiping; never contented with home; always visiting.

And not only idle] If it went no farther, this would be intolerable; but they are *tattlers*—tale-bearers; whisperers; light, trifling persons; all noise and no work.

Busybodies] Persons who meddle with the concerns of others; who mind every one's business but their own.

Speaking things which they ought not.] Lies, slanders, calumnies; backbiting their neighbours, and everywhere sowing the seed of dissension.

Verse 14. I will therefore that the younger women marry] As the preceding discourse has been about the younger widows, and this is an inference from it; it is most evident that by the *younger women* the apostle means the young *widows*. These he considers unfit for the office of the female *diaconate*, and therefore wills them to marry, educate children, and give themselves wholly up to *domestic affairs*. Here the apostle, so far from forbidding *second* marriages, positively enjoins or at least recommends them. And what man of sense could have done otherwise in the cases he mentions? It is no sin in any case to marry, bear children, and take care of a family; but it is a sin in every case to be idle persons, gadders about, tattlers, busybodies, sifting out and detailing family secrets, &c., &c. The good sentiment, put by an able poet and pious divine into the mouths of *little children*, cannot be ill applied to multitudes of women, mothers, and grandmothers :—

" See how the little busy bee
    Improves each shining hour,
And gathers honey all the day
    From every opening flower!
In works of labour or of skill,
    We should be busy too;
For Satan finds some mischief, still,
    For idle hands to do." DR. WATTS.

The adversary] Any person, whether Jew or Gentile, who might be watching for an occasion to reproach, through the misconduct of its professors, the cause of Christianity.

Verse 15. For some are already turned aside] Some of these young widows, for he appears to be still treating of them, are turned aside to *idolatry*, to follow Satan instead of Christ. Slight deviations, in the first instance, from a right line, may lead at last to an infinite distance from Christ.

Verse 16. If any man or woman that believeth] If any *Christian man* or *woman* have poor *widows*, which are their relatives, *let them relieve them*—provide them with the necessaries of life, and not *burden the Church* with their maintenance, that the funds may be spared for the support of those *widows* who were employed in its service, teaching children, visiting the sick, &c., &c. For the performing of such offices it is very likely that none but *widows* were employed; and these were chosen, other things being equal, out of the most indigent of the widows, and therefore called by the apostle, here and in ver. 3, αις οντως χηραι, *widows indeed*—widows desolate, without support, and without relatives. See the note on ver. 10.

Verse 17. Let the elders that rule well] Elder is probably here the name of an ecclesiastical officer, similar to what we now term *presbyter*. See on ver. 1. Dr. *Macknight* has remarked that, " in the first age, the name πρεσβυτερος, *elder*, was given to all who exercised any sacred office in the Church, as is plain from Acts xx. 28, where the persons are called επισκοποι, *bishops*, who, ver. 17, were called πρεσβυτεροι, *elders*. The same thing appears from Tit. i. 5, where those are called *elders* who, ver. 7, are named *bishops*; and from 1 Tim. iv. 14, where, collectively, all who held sacred offices in Lystra are called πρεσβυτεριον, the *presbytery* or *eldership*, and are said to have concurred with St. Paul in setting Timothy apart to the ministry."

Double honour] Διπλης τιμης. Almost every critic of note allows that τιμη here signifies *reward, stipend, wages*. Let him have a double or a larger salary who rules well; and why? Because in the discharge of his office he must be at expense, in proportion to his diligence, in visiting and relieving the sick, in lodging and providing for strangers; in a word, in his being given to *hospitality*, which was required of every bishop or presbyter.

Especially they who labour in the word and doctrine.] Those who not only preach publicly, but instruct privately, catechize, &c. Some think this refers to distinct ecclesiastical *orders*; but these technical distinctions were, in my opinion, a work of later times.

Verse 18. The Scripture saith, Thou shalt not muzzle the ox] This is a manifest proof that by τιμη, *honour*, in the preceding verse, the apostle means *salary* or *wages*: " Let the elders that rule well be accounted worthy of double honour," a *larger salary* than any of the *official widows* mentioned before, for

A. M. cir. 4069.
A. D. 64 or 65.
A. U. C. 818.
An. Imp. Neronis Cæs.
Aug. 12.

c The labourer *is* worthy of his reward.

19 Against an elder receive not an accusation, but d before e two or three witnesses.

20 f Them that sin rebuke before all, g that others also may fear.

21 h I charge *thee* before God, and the Lord Jesus Christ, and the elect angels, that thou

observe these things, i without preferring one before another, doing nothing by partiality.

22 k Lay hands suddenly on no man, l neither be partaker of other men's sins : keep thyself pure.

23 Drink no longer water, but use a little wine m for thy stomach's sake, and thine often infirmities.

A. M. cir. 4069.
A. D. 64 or 65.
A. U. C. 818.
An. Imp. Neronis Cæs.
Aug. 12.

---

c Lev. xix. 13; Deut. xxiv. 14,15; Matt. x. 10; Luke x. 7.
d Or, *under*.——e Deut. xix. 15.——f Gal. ii. 11, 14; Tit. i. 13.
g Deut. xiii. 11.

h Chap. vi. 13; 2 Tim. ii. 14; iv. 1.——i Or, *without prejudice*.
k Acts vi. 6; xiii. 3; chap. iv. 14; 2 Tim. i. 6.——l 2 John 11.
m Psa. civ. 15.

" the labourer is worthy of his hire." The maintenance of every man in the Church should be in proportion to his own labour, and the necessities of his family. He that does *no work* should have *no wages*. In the Church of Christ there never can be a *sinecure*. *They who minister at the altar* should *live by the altar ;* the *ox that treadeth out the corn should not be muzzled ; the labourer is worthy of his hire :* but the altar should not support him who *does not minister* at it ; if the ox *won't tread out the corn*, let him go to the *common* or be *muzzled ;* if the *man will not labour*, let him have *no hire*.

Verse 19. *Against an elder*] Be very cautious of receiving evil reports against those whose business it is to preach to others, and correct their vices. Do not consider an elder as guilty of any alleged crime, unless it be *proved* by *two* or *three* witnesses. This the law of Moses required in respect to all. Among the Romans, a *plebeian* might be condemned on the deposition of *one* credible witness ; but it required *two* to convict a *senator*. The reason of this difference is evident : those whose business it is to correct others will usually have many enemies ; great caution, therefore, should be used in admitting accusations against such persons.

Verse 20. *Them that sin rebuke before all*] That is, before the members of the Church ; which was the custom of the Jews in their synagogues. But, if the words refer to the elders alone, then the transgressing elder is to be reproved before his fellows, and be tried by them.

That others also may fear.] This is the grand object of Church censures, to reclaim the transgressors, and to give warning to others.

Verse 21. *I charge* thee *before God*] The apostle would have Timothy to consider that all he did should be done as in the sight of God, the Father of the spirits of all flesh ; in the sight of Christ, the Saviour of sinners, who purchased the Church with his own blood ; and in the sight of the most holy, approved, and eminent angels, whose office it was to minister to the heirs of salvation. The word εκλεκτοι, *elect*, applied to the angels here, is supposed to distinguish those who *stood*, when others fell from their first estate. The former were *elect*, or *approved ;* the latter *reprobate*, or *disapproved*. This is not an unfrequent sense of the word εκλεκτος, *elect*. Perhaps there is nothing else meant than the angels that are chosen out from

among others, by the Lord himself, to be ministering servants to the Church.

Without preferring one before another] Χωρις προ-κριματος· *Without prejudice*. Promote no man's cause ; make not up thy mind on any case, till thou hast weighed both sides, and heard both parties, with their respective witnesses ; and then act *impartially*, as the matter may appear to be *proved*. Do not treat any man, in religious matters, according to the rank he holds in life, or according to any personal attachment thou mayest have for him. Every man should be dealt with in the Church as he will be dealt with at the judgment-seat of Christ. A minister of the Gospel, who, in the exercise of discipline in the Church, is swayed and warped by *secular* considerations, will be a curse rather than a blessing to the people of God. Accepting the persons of the rich, in ecclesiastical matters, has been a source of corruption in Christianity. With some ministers the *show* of piety in a *rich* man goes farther than the *soundest Christian experience* in the *poor*. What account can such persons give of their stewardship ?

Verse 22. *Lay hands suddenly on no man*] Do not hastily appoint any person to the sacred ministry ; let the person be well proved before he receives the *imposition of hands*. Some understand this of laying hands on the sick.

Neither be partaker of other men's sins] It is a sin for any improper person to *thrust himself* into the sacred office ; and he partakes of that sin who introduces, helps him forward, or sanctions him in it. O, what an account will rash, undiscerning, and prejudiced bishops, presbyters, and others, have to render to God for their *ordinations !* Their laying rash or careless hands " on skulls that cannot teach, and will not learn ;" while probably they refuse inducting others well qualified for the Christian ministry.

Keep thyself pure.] From this and every other evil

Verse 23. *Drink no longer water, but use a little wine*] The whole of this verse seems, to several learned critics and divines, strangely inserted in this place ; it might have been, according to them, a note which the apostle inserted in the margin of his letter, on recollecting the precarious state of Timothy's health, and his great abstemiousness and self-denial. I believe the verse to be in its proper place ; and, for reasons which I shall adduce, not less necessary than the directions which precede and follow it. But it

2

A. M. cir. 4069.
A. D. 64 or 65.
A. U. C. 818.
An. Imp. Ne-
ronis Cæs.
Aug. 12.

24 [n] Some men's sins are open beforehand, going before to judgment; and some *men* they follow after.

25 Likewise also the good works *of some* are manifest beforehand; [o] and they that are otherwise cannot be hid.

A. M. cir. 4069.
A. D. 64 or 65.
A. U. C. 818.
An. Imp. Ne-
ronis Cæs.
Aug. 12.

[n] Gal. v. 19; Rev. xiv. 13.

[o] Matt. vii. 17–20.

may be necessary to inquire a little into the reasons of the advice itself. The priests under the *Mosaic law*, while performing sacred rites, were forbidden to drink wine : *Do not drink wine nor strong drink, thou, nor thy sons with thee, when ye go into the tabernacle of the congregation, lest ye die :* it shall be *a statute for ever through your generations ;* Lev. x. 9 ; Ezek. xliv. 21. It was the same with the Egyptian priests. It was forbidden also among the Romans, and particularly to *women* and *young persons.* PLATO, *De Legibus*, lib. ii., edit. Bip., vol. viii., page 86, speaks thus: Αρ' ου νομοθετησομεν, πρωτον μεν, τους παιδας μεχρις ετων οκτωκαιδεκα τοπαραπαν οινου μη γενεσθαι ;—μετα δε τουτο, οινου μεν δη γενεσθαι του μετριου, μεχρι τριακοντα ετων·—τετταρακοντα δε επιβαινοντα ετων, εν τοις ξυσσιτιοις ευωχηθεντα, κ. τ. λ. " Shall we not ordain by law, in the first place, that *boys* shall not, on any account, taste *wine* till they are *eighteen* years old ? In the next place, we should inform them that *wine* is to be used moderately till they are *thirty years* old. But when they have attained the *fortieth year*, then they may attend feasts ; for Bacchus has bestowed wine upon men as a remedy against the austerity of old age, της του γηρως αυστηροτητος εδωρησατο τον οινον φαρμακον, ωσт' ανηβαν ημας, και δυσθυμιας ληθην γιγνεσθαι, μαλακωτερον εκ σκληροτερου το της ψυχης ηθος, καθαπερ εις πυρ σιδηρον εντεθεντα, γιγνομενον· that through this we might acquire a second youth, forget sorrow, and the manners of the mind be rendered softer, as iron is softened by the action of the fire." But *wine*, accoıding to the assertions of some, was given to men as a *punishment*, that they might be rendered insane : Ὁ δε νυν λεγομενος ὑφ' ημων, φαρμακον επι τουναντιον φησιν αιδους μεν ψυχης κτησεως ενεκα δεδοσθαι, σωματος δε ὑγιεας τε και ισχυος· page 100. " But we have now said that it is, on the contrary, *medicine ;* and was given that the soul might acquire modesty, and the body health and vigour."

From Athenæus we learn that the *Greeks* often mingled their *wine* with *water ;* sometimes one part of wine to two of water ; three parts of water to one of wine ; and at other times three parts of water to two of wine. See his *Deipnosophistæ*, lib. ix. " Among the Locrians, if any one was found to have drunk *unmixed wine*, unless prescribed by a physician, he was punished with death ; the laws of Zaleucus so requiring. And among the Romans, no servant, nor free woman, ουτε των ελευθερων οι εφηβοι μεχρι τριακοντα ετων, nor youths of quality, drank any wine till they were thirty years of age." *Deipnosoph.*, lib. x. c. 7, p. 429. And it was a maxim among all, that continued *water-drinking* injured the stomach. Thus *Libanius*, Epist. 1578 : Πεπτωκε και ημιν ὁ στομαχος ταις συνεχεσιν ὑδροποσιαις· " *Our stomach is weakened by continual water-drinking.*"

From chap. iv. 12, we learn that Timothy was a

young man ; but as among the *Greeks* and *Romans* the state of *youth* or adolescence was extended to thirty years, and no respectable *young men* were permitted to drink wine before that time ; allowing that Timothy was about twenty when Paul had him circumcised, which was, according to Calmet, in the year of our Lord 51, and that this epistle was written about A. D. 64 or 65, then Timothy must have been about thirty-five when he received this epistle ; and as that was on the borders of *adolescence*, and as the Scripture generally calls that *youth* that is not *old age*, Timothy might be treated as a *young man* by St. Paul, as in the above text, and might still feel himself under the custom of his country relative to drinking wine, (for his father was a *Greek*, Acts xvi. 1,) and, through the influence of his Christian profession, still continue to abstain from wine, drinking *water only ;* which must have been very prejudicial to him, his weak state of health considered, the delicacy of his stomach, and the excess of his ecclesiastical labours.

As Timothy's life was of great consequence to the Church of God at Ephesus, it was not unworthy of the Spirit of God to give the direction in the text, and to mingle it immediately with what some have called more solemn and important advice. 1. It was necessary that the *work* should be done in the Church at Ephesus which the apostle appointed to Timothy. 2. There was no person at Ephesus fit to do this work but Timothy. 3. Timothy could not continue to do it if he followed his present mode of abstemiousness. 4. It was necessary, therefore, that he should receive direction from *Divine authority* relative to the preservation of his life, and consequently the continuation of his usefulness, as it is not likely that a minor authority would have weighed with him.

Verse 24. *Some men's sins are open beforehand*] In appointing men to sacred offices in the Church, among the candidates Timothy would find, 1. Some of whom he knew nothing, but only that they professed Christianity ; let such be tried before they are appointed. 2. Some of whose faith and piety he had the fullest knowledge, and whose usefulness in the Church was well known. 3. Some whose lives were not at all or but partially reformed, who were still unchanged in their hearts, and unholy in their lives. The sins of these latter were known to all ; *they go before to judgment ;* with them he could have no difficulty. With the first class he must have more difficulty ; there might have been hypocrites among them, whose sins could not be known till *after* they were brought into the sacred office. The characters of all should be fully investigated. The sins of some, before this investigation, might be so manifest as to lead at once εις κρισιν, to condemnation. The sins of others might be found out *after*, or in consequence of, this investigation ; and those that were otherwise could not be

2

long hid from his knowledge, or the knowledge of the Church. On all these accounts the exhortation is necessary : *Lay hands suddenly on no man.*

Verse 25. *Likewise also the good works* of some] Though those who are very holy and very useful in the Church cannot be unknown, yet there are others not less holy who need to be brought forward ; who do much good in private ; and their character and good works are not fully known till after diligent inquiry. These are they who do not let their left hand know what their right doeth.

1. AFTER so long and minute an examination of the subjects in this chapter, little remains to be said in the way of farther and more satisfactory explanation. The whole account concerning the *widows, who* they were, and *what* their *provision,* and what their *occupation,* and *how supported,* are to me questions of considerable difficulty. In the notes I have given the best account of the different subjects in my power. If the reader be satisfied and edified, I have gained my end.

2. On the subject of the *imposition of hands,* or what is vulgarly but improperly called *ordination,* I have not said much here, having given my views of the subject elsewhere in these notes. See on chap.

iii. **1,** &c. I must again state my conviction that what is said on this subject in this chapter, and indeed in the epistle, is rather to be understood *prophetically ;* and to have been intended for a much lower age of the Christian Church. That any person should, from *impure* or *secular motives,* desire to be appointed to the ministerial office at such a time, when poverty and persecution were the least they would reasonably expect, to me seems altogether inexplicable. But that many, after the Church got *accredited* and *established,* and an ample *revenue* appointed for its ministers by emperors and kings, should wish to get into the priesthood for its emoluments, is a melancholy truth, which every year's experience testifies. To those who have the authority from the state to appoint ministers for the Church, this chapter reads a solemn and awful lesson. And not to them only, but to all who have the appointment of ministers or preachers in every sect and party. How few are there who would kindle a fire on God's altar were there not *secular emoluments* attending it ! I am afraid the Scottish poet spoke the truth who said :—

" 'Tis *gow'd* maks sogers feight the fiercer,
Without *it, preaching* wad be scarcer."

Gold or *money* is the *primum mobile* through every department of life. *Proh dolor !*

CHAPTER VI.

Of the duty of servants, 1, 2. *Of false teachers, who suppose gain to be godliness,* 3–5. *Of true godliness, and contentment,* 6–8. *Of those, and their dangerous state, who determine to be rich ; and of the love of money,* 9, 10. *Timothy is exhorted to fight the good fight of faith, and to keep the charge delivered to him,* 11–14. *A sublime description of the majesty of God,* 15, 16. *How the rich should behave themselves ; and the use they should make of their property,* 17–19. *Timothy is once more exhorted to keep what was committed to his trust ; and to avoid profane babblings, through which some have erred from the faith,* 20, 21.

A. M. cir. 4069. A. D. 64 or 65. A. U. C. 818. An. Imp. Neronis Cæs. Aug. 12.	LET as many [a] servants as are under the yoke count their own masters worthy of all honour, [b] that the name of God and *his* doctrine be not blasphemed. 2 And they that have believing masters, let them not despise	A. M. cir. 4069. A. D. 64 or 65. A. U. C. 818. An. Imp. Neronis Cæs. Aug. 12.

[a] Eph. vi. 5 ; Col. iii. 22 ; Tit. ii. 9 ; 1 Pet. ii. 18. [b] Isa. lii. 5 ; Rom. ii. 24 ; Tit. ii. 5, 8.

NOTES ON CHAP. VI.

Verse 1 *Let as many servants as are under the yoke*] The word δουλοι here means slaves converted to the Christian faith ; and the ζυγον, or yoke, is the *state of slavery ;* and by δεσποται, *masters, despots,* we are to understand the heathen masters of those Christianized slaves. Even these, in such circumstances, and under such domination, are commanded to treat their masters with all honour and respect, that the name of God, by which they were called, and the doctrine of God, Christianity, which they had professed, might not be evilly spoken of in consequence of their improper conduct. Civil rights are never abolished by any communications from God's Spirit. The civil state in which a man was before his conversion is not altered by that

conversion ; nor does the grace of God absolve him from any claims which either the state or his neighbour may have on him. All these outward things continue unaltered. See the notes on Eph. vi. 5, &c. ; and 1 Cor. vii. 21, &c., and especially the observations at the end of that chapter.

Verse 2. *And they that have believing masters*] Who have been lately converted as well as themselves.

Let them not despise them] Supposing themselves to be their equals, because they are their brethren in Christ ; and grounding their opinion on this, that *in him there is neither male nor female, bond nor free ;* for, although all are equal as to their *spiritual privileges* and state, yet there still continues in the order of God's providence a great disparity in their *station :*

2   613

A. M. cir. 4069.
A. D. 64 or 65.
A. U. C. 818.
An. Imp. Ne-
ronis Cæs.
Aug. 12.

them, [c] because they arc brethren; but rather do *them* service,
because they are [d] faithful and
beloved, partakers of the benefit. [e] These things teach and exhort.

3 If any man [f] teach otherwise, and consent
[g] not to wholesome words, *even* the words of
our Lord Jesus Christ, [h] and to the doctrine
which is according to godliness;

4 He is [i] proud, [k] knowing nothing, but [l] doting about [m] questions and strifes of words, whereof cometh envy, strife, railings,
evil surmisings,

A. M. cir. 4069.
A. D. 64 or 65.
A. U. C. 818.
An. Imp. Ne-
ronis Cæs.
Aug. 12.

5 [n] Perverse [o] disputings of [p] men of corrupt
minds, and destitute of the truth, [q] supposing
that gain is godliness: [r] from such withdraw
thyself.

---

[c] Col. iv. 1.——[d] Or, *believing.*——[e] Chap. iv. 11.——[f] Chap.
i. 3.——[g] Chap. i. 10; 2 Tim. i. 13; iv. 3; Tit. i. 9.——[h] Tit. i. 1.
[i] Or, *a fool.*——[k] 1 Cor. viii. 2; chap. i. 7.——[l] Or, *sick.*

[m] Chap. i. 4; 2 Tim. ii. 23; Tit. iii. 9.——[n] 1 Cor. xi. 16; chap.
i. 6.——[o] Or, *gallings one of another.*——[p] 2 Tim. iii. 8.——[q] Tit.
i. 11; 2 Peter ii. 3.——[r] Rom. xvi. 17; 2 Tim. iii. 5.

---

the *master* must ever be in this sense *superior* to the
servant.

But rather do them *service*] Obey them the more
cheerfully, because they are *faithful* and *beloved; faithful* to God's grace, *beloved* by him and his true followers.

Partakers of the benefit.] Της ευεργεσιας αντιλαμβα-
νομενοι· *Joint partakers of the benefit.* This is generally understood as referring to the *master's* participation in the services of his slaves. *Because those who
are partakers of the benefit of your services are faithful and beloved;* or it may apply to the servants who
are partakers of many benefits from their Christian
masters. Others think that *benefit* here refers to the
grace of the *Gospel,* the *common salvation* of believing masters and slaves; but Dr. *Macknight* well observes that ευεργεσια is nowhere used to denote the
Gospel. One of *Uffenbach's* MSS. has εργασιας, *of
the service;* this reading is plainly a gloss; it is not
acknowledged by any other MS., nor by any version.
FG, and the Codex *Augustanus* 6, have ευσεβειας, *of
godliness;* a term by which the whole *Gospel doctrine*
is expressed, chap. iv. 7, 8, as also in the 6th verse
of this chapter.

Verse 3. If any man teach otherwise] It appears
that there were teachers of a different kind in the
Church, a sort of *religious levellers,* who preached
that the converted servant had as much right to the
master's service as the master had to his. Teachers
of this kind have been in vogue long since the days of
Paul and Timothy.

And consent not to wholesome words] Ὑγιαινουσι
λογοις *Healing doctrines*—doctrines which give *nourishment* and *health* to the soul, which is the true character of all the doctrines taught by our Lord Jesus
Christ; doctrines which are *according to godliness*—
securing as amply the honour and glory of God, as
they do the peace, happiness, and final salvation of man.

All this may refer to the general tenor of the Gospel; and not to any thing said, or *supposed to have
been said, by our Lord,* relative to the condition of
slaves. With political questions, or questions relative
to private *rights,* our Lord scarcely ever meddled; he
taught all men to *love one another;* to respect each
other's rights; to submit to each other; to show all
fidelity; to be obedient, humble, and meek; and to
know that his kingdom was not of this world.

Verse 4. He is proud] Τετυφωται· He is *blown up,*
or *inflated* with a vain opinion of his own knowledge;

whereas his knowledge is foolishness, for he knows
nothing.

Doting about questions] He is *sick, distempered,*
about these questions relative to the Mosaic law and
the traditions of the elders; for it is most evident that
the apostle has the *Judaizing teachers* in view, who
were ever, in questions of theology, straining out a
gnat, and swallowing a camel.

Strifes of words] Λογομαχιας· *Logomachies;* verbal
contentions; splitting hairs; producing *Hillel* against
Shammai, and *Shammai* against *Hillel,* relative to the
particular mode in which the punctilios of some rites
should be performed. In this sort of sublime nonsense
the works of the Jewish rabbins abound.

Whereof cometh envy, strife, &c.] How little good
have religious disputes ever done to mankind, or to the
cause of truth! Most controversialists have succeeded
in getting their own tempers *soured,* and in *irritating*
their opponents. Indeed, truth seems rarely to be the
object of their pursuit; they labour to accredit their
own party by abusing and defaming others; from *generals* they often descend to *particulars;* and then *personal* abuse is the order of the day. Is it not strange
that Christians either cannot or will not see this? Cannot any man support his own opinions, and give his own
views of the religion of Christ, without abusing and
calumniating his neighbour? I know not whether such
controversialists should not be deemed *disturbers of
the public peace,* and come under the notice of the civil
magistrate. Should not all Christians know that the
*wrath of man worketh not the righteousness of the
Lord?*

*Verse 5. Perverse disputings of men of corrupt
minds*] Disputations that cannot be settled, because
their partisans will not listen to the truth; and they
will not listen to the truth because their *minds* are corrupt. Both under the *law* and under the *Gospel* the
true religion was: *Thou shalt love the Lord thy God
with all thy heart, soul, mind, and strength; and thy
neighbour as thyself.* Where, therefore, the love of
God and man does not prevail, *there* there is no religion. Such corrupt disputers are as *destitute of the
truth* as they are of love to God and man.

Supposing that gain is godliness] Professing religion only for the sake of secular profit; defending
their own cause for the emoluments it produced; and
having no respect to another world.

From such withdraw thyself.] Have no religious

A. M. cir. 4069.
A. D. 64 or 65.
A. U. C. 818.
An. Imp. Ne-
ronis Cæs.
Aug. 12.

6 But ˢ godliness with contentment is great gain.

7 For ᵗ we brought nothing
into *this* world, *and it is* certain
we can carry nothing out.

8 And ᵘ having food and raiment, let us be
therewith content.

9 But ᵛ they that will be rich
fall into temptation ʷ and a snare,
and *into* many foolish and hurtful lusts, ˣ which drown men in
destruction and perdition.

10 ʸ For the love of money is the root of all
evil ; which while some coveted after, they'

A. M. cir. 4069.
A. D. 64 or 65.
A. U. C. 818.
An. Imp. Ne-
ronis Cæs.
Aug. 12.

ˢ Psa. xxxvii. 16; Prov. xv. 16; xvi. 8; Heb. xiii. 5.——ᵗ Job
i. 21; Psa. xlix. 17; Prov. xxvii. 24; Eccles. v. 15.——ᵘ Gen.
xxviii. 20; Heb. xiii. 5.

ᵛ Prov. xv. 27; xx. 21 ;ı xxviii. 20; Matt. xiii. 22; James v. 1.
ʷ Chapter iii. 7.——ˣ Chapter i. 19.——ʸ Exodus xxiii. 8; Deut
xvi. 19.

---

fellowship with such people. But this clause is wanting in AD*FG, some others, the *Coptic, Sahidic,
Æthiopic, Vulgate,* and *Itala,* one copy excepted. It
is probably spurious.

Verse 6. *But godliness with contentment is great
gain.*] The word *godliness,* ευσεβεια, here, and in several other places of this epistle, signifies the *true* religion, *Christianity ;* and the word *contentment,* αυταρ-
κεια, signifies a *competency,* a *sufficiency ;* that measure or portion of secular things which is necessary
for the support of life, while the great work of regeneration is carrying on in the soul. Not what this or
the other person may deem a *competency,* but what is
necessary for the mere purposes of life in reference to
another world; *food, raiment,* and *lodging.* See ver. 7.
So, if a man have the life of God in his soul, and
just a sufficiency of food and raiment to preserve and
not burden life, he has what God calls *great gain,* an
abundant portion.

It requires but little of this world's goods to satisfy
a man who feels himself to be a citizen of another
country, and knows that this is not his *rest.*

Verse 7. *We brought nothing into* this *world*]
There are some sayings in *Seneca* which are almost
verbatim with this of St. Paul : *Nemo nascitur dives;
quisquis exit in lucem jussus est lacte et panno esse
contentus ;* Epist. xx. " No man is born rich ; every
one that comes into the world is commanded to be
content with food and raiment." *Excutit natura re-
deuntem, sicut intrantem; non licet plus auferre, quam
intuleris ;* Epist., cap. ii. " Nature, in returning,
shakes off all incumbrances as in entering ; thou canst
not carry back more than thou broughtest in." Seneca
and St. Paul were contemporary ; but all the Greek
and Latin poets, and especially the *stoic philosophers,*
are full of such sentiments. It is a self-evident truth;
relative to it there can be no controversy.

Verse 8. *Having food and raiment, let us be therewith content.*] Αρκεσθησομεθα· Let us consider this
a *competency.* And it is evident that the apostle considers this a competency, and by these words explains
what he said verse 6.

The word σκεπασματα, which we translate *raiment,*
signifies *covering* in general; and here means *house*
or *lodging,* as well as *clothing.*

Verse 9. *But they that will be rich*] Οι δε βουλομενοι
πλουτειν. The words are *emphatic,* and refer to persons who are *determined* to get riches; who make this
their *object* and *aim* in life; who live to get money ;
who get all they can, save all they can, and keep all
they get ; and yet are apprehensive of no danger, be-

cause they seek to be rich by *honest means ;* for it is
likely that the apostle does not refer to those who wish
to get riches by *robbery, plunder, extortion,* &c.

By the term *rich* it is very likely that the apostle
refers to what he had said above : *Having food and
raiment, let us be therewith content.* He that has
more than these is *rich* in the sense in which the apostle uses the term.

Fall into temptation and a snare] Του διαβολου,
Of the devil, is added by D*FG, *Vulgate, Itala,* and
many of the *fathers.* It is in consequence of the
temptation of the devil that they have determined to be
rich ; this temptation once received, others quickly
succeed : and when they have swallowed down the
temptation to the *thing,* then they drink in a thousand
temptations to the *means ;* and all these lead them εις
παγιδα, into an unforeseen and concealed trap. Παγις
signifies a net, trap, gin, snare, springe, or pit dug in
the ground filled with sharp stakes, and slightly covered
over ; so that when a man, or any animal, steps upon
it, he tumbles in, and is taken or destroyed. Such a snare
is that into which those *who will be rich* must necessarily
fall. But who will believe this ? See on verse 10.

And into many foolish and hurtful lusts] The
whole conduct of such a person is a tissue of *folly ;*
scraping, gathering, and heaping up riches, and scarcely
affording to take the necessaries of life out of them
for himself. These lusts or desires are not only *foolish,* but they are *hurtful ;* the mind is debased and
narrowed by them ; benevolent and generous feelings
become extinct ; charity perishes ; and *selfishness,* the
last and lowest principle in mental degradation, absorbs
the soul ; for these *foolish* and *hurtful lusts drown men
in destruction and perdition*—the soul is *destroyed* by
them here, and brought through them into a state of
perdition hereafter. The apostle considers these persons like mariners in a storm ; by the concurrence of
winds, waves, and tide, they are violently driven among
the rocks, the vessel is dashed to pieces, and in a moment they are all ingulfed in the great deep ! Such
is the lot and unavoidable catastrophe of them *that will
be rich,* even though they should strive to accomplish
their desires by means the most rigidly honest.

In this place I beg leave to refer the reader to a
sermon on this text by the late Rev. JOHN WESLEY, in
which the whole of this subject is treated by the hand
of a master; and, for usefulness, the sermon is superior
to every thing of the kind ever published. It is entitled, *The Danger of Riches;* and is found in his WORKS,
Vol. 2, page 248, American edit.

Verse 10. *The love of money is the root of all evil*]

A. M. cir. 4069.
A. D. 64 or 65.
A. U. C. 818.
An. Imp. Ne-
ronis Cæs.
Aug. 12.

have ᶻ erred from the faith, and pierced themselves through with many sorrows.

11 ᵃ But thou, ᵇ O man of God, flee these things ; and follow after righteousness, godliness, faith, love, patience, meekness.

12 ᶜ Fight the good fight of faith, ᵈ lay hold on eternal life, whereunto thou art also called,

ᵉ and hast professed a good profession before many witnesses.

13 ᶠ I give thee charge in the sight of God, ᵍ who quickeneth all things, and *before* Christ Jesus, ʰ who before Pontius Pilate witnessed a good ⁱ confession ;

14 That thou keep *this* commandment with-

A. M. cir. 4069.
A. D. 64 or 65.
A. U. C. 818.
An. Imp. Ne-
ronis Cæs.
Aug. 12.

ᶻ Or, *been seduced.*——ᵃ 2 Tim. ii. 22.——ᵇ Deut. xxxiii. 1 ; 2 Tim. iii. 17.——ᶜ 1 Cor. ix. 25, 26 ; chap. i. 18 ; 2 Tim. iv. 7. ᵈ Phil. iii. 12, 14 ; ver. 19.

ᵉ Heb. xiii. 23.——ᶠ Chap. v. 21.——ᵍ Deut. xxxii. 39 ; 1 Sam. ii. 6 ; John v. 21.——ʰ Matt. xxvii. 11 ; John xviii. 37 ; Rev. i. 5 ; iii. 14.——ⁱ Or, *profession.*

Perhaps it would be better to translate παντων των κακων, *of all these evils* ; i. e. the evils enumerated above ; for it cannot be true that the love of money is the root of *all evil*, it certainly was not the root whence the transgression of Adam sprang, but it is the root whence all the evils mentioned in the preceding verse spring. This text has been often very incautiously quoted ; for how often do we hear, " The Scripture says, *Money is the root of all evil !*" No, the Scripture says no such thing. *Money* is the root of *no* evil, nor is it an evil of any kind ; but the *love* of it is the root of all the evils mentioned here.

While some coveted after] Ορεγομενοι· Insatiably desiring.

Have erred from the faith] Απεπλανηθησαν· Have *totally erred*—have made a most fatal and ruinous departure from the religion of Christ.

And pierced themselves through with many sorrows.] The word περιεπειραν signifies to be *transfixed in every part* ; and is an allusion to one of those *snares*, παγιδα, mentioned ver. 9, where a hole is dug in the earth, and filled full of sharp stakes, and, being slightly covered over with turf, is not perceived ; and whatever steps on it falls in, and is *pierced through and through with* these *sharp stakes*, the οδυναις πολλαις, the *many torments*, mentioned by the apostle. See on verse 9.

Verse 11. *But thou, O man of God*] Thou, who hast taken God for thy portion, and art seeking a city that hath foundations, whose builder is the living God, *flee these things.* Escape for thy life. Even *thou* art not out of the reach of the *love of money.* How many of the ministers of religion have been ruined by this ! And how much has religion itself suffered by *their* love of money !

Follow after righteousness] Justice and uprightness in all thy dealings with men. *Godliness*—a thorough conformity to the image of God and mind of Christ. *Faith* in Jesus, and in all that he has spoken ; and *fidelity* to the talents thou hast received, and the office with which thou art intrusted.

Love] To God and all mankind. *Patience* in all trials and afflictions.

Meekness.] Bearing up with an *even mind* under all adversities and contradictions.

Verse 12. *Fight the good fight of faith*] "Agonize the good agony." Thou hast a *contest* to sustain in which thy honour, thy life, thy soul, are at stake. Live the Gospel, and defend the cause of God. Unmask hypocrites, expel the profligate, purge and

build up the Church, live in the spirit of thy religion, and give thyself wholly to this work.

Lay hold on eternal life] All this is in allusion to the exercises in the public Grecian games : Fight, conquer, and seize upon the prize ; carry off the crown of eternal life !

Whereunto thou art also called] The allusion to the public games is still carried on : Thou hast been *called* into this palæstra ; thou hast been *accepted* as one proper to enter the lists with any antagonists that may offer ; in the *presence of many witnesses* thou hast taken the necessary *engagements* upon thee, and submitted to be governed by the laws of the *stadium* ; many eyes are upon thee, to see whether thou wilt fight manfully, and be faithful. Timothy's faith was undoubtedly tried by severe persecution. In Heb. xiii. 23, it is said : *Know ye that our brother Timothy is set at liberty.* Hence it appears that he was *imprisoned* for the testimony of Christ, and perhaps it was *then*, more than at his *ordination*, that he made the *good confession* here mentioned. He risked his life and conquered. If not a *martyr*, he was a *confessor.*

Verse 13. *I give thee charge*] This is similar to that in verse 21 of the preceding chapter, where see the note.

Who quickeneth all things] God, who is the fountain of life, and who is the resurrection ; and who will raise thee up at the last day to a life of ineffable glory, if thou be faithful unto death. And should thy life fall a sacrifice to the performance of thy duty, all will be safe ; for thy life is hid with Christ in God, and when he who is thy life shall appear, then shalt thou also appear with him in glory ! Thy kingdom is not of this world ; remember that this good confession was made by thy Master before Pilate. Keep disentangled from all earthly things, live to and for God, and all will be well.

A good confession] The confession made by Christ before Pontius Pilate is, that *he was Messiah the King* ; but that *his kingdom was not of this world* ; and *that hereafter he should be seen coming in the clouds of heaven to judge the quick and dead.* See John xviii. 36, 37 ; and Mark xiv. 61, 62.

Verse 14. *That thou keep* this commandment *without spot*] Two things are mentioned here : 1. That the *commandment* itself—the whole *doctrine of Christ*, should be kept *entire.* 2. That his *life* should be agreeable to that doctrine. Keep it *without spot*—

2

A. M. cir. 4069.
A. D. 64 or 65.
A. U. C. 818.
An. Imp. Ne-
ronis Cæs.
Aug. 12.

out spot, unrebukable, [k] until the appearing of our Lord Jesus Christ :

15 Which in his times he shall show, *who is* [1] the blessed and only Potentate, [m] the King of kings, and Lord of lords ;

16 [n] Who only hath immortality, dwelling in the light which no man can approach unto ; [o] whom no man hath seen, nor can see : [p] to whom *be* honour and power everlasting. Amen.

17 Charge them that are rich in this world,

A. M. cir. 4069.
A. D. 64 or 65.
A. U. C. 818.
An. Imp. Ne-
ronis Cæs.
Aug. 12.

[k] Phil. i. 6. 10 ; 1 Thess. iii. 13 ; v. 23.——[l] Chapter i. 11, 17. [m] Rev. xvii. 14 ; xix. 16.

[n] Chap. i. 17.——[o] Exod. xxxiii. 20 ; John vi. 46.——[p] Eph. iii. 21 ; Phil. iv. 20 ; Jude 25 ; Rev. i. 6 ; iv. 11 ; vii. 12.

let there be no *blot* on the sacred book ; *add* nothing *to* it ; *take* nothing *from it* ; *change* nothing *in* it. Deliver down to thy successors the truth as thou hast had it from God himself.

Unrebukable] Let there be nothing in thy *conduct* or *spirit* contrary to this truth. Keep the truth, and the truth will keep thee.

Until the appearing of our Lord] Hand it down pure, and let thy conduct be a comment on it, that it may continue in the world and in the Church till the coming of Christ.

Verse 15. *Which in his times he shall show*] Jesus will appear in the *most proper time ;* the time which the infinite God in his wisdom has appointed for the second coming of his Son.

The blessed and only Potentate] Δυναστης, *Potentate,* is applied to *secular governors ;* but none of these can be styled ὁ μακαριος και μονος, the *happy and only One ;* ὁ Βασιλευς των βασιλευοντων, *the King of kings,* or *the King over all kings ;* and Κυριος των κυριευοντων, *the Lord over all lords* or *rulers.* These are titles which could not be given to any mortals. This is made more specific by the verse following.

Verse 16. *Who only hath immortality*] All beings that are not *eternal* must be *mutable ;* but there can be only one eternal Being, that is God ; and he only can have *immortality.*

Dwelling in the light which no man can approach unto] All this is said by the apostle in three words : φως οικων απροσιτον, *inhabiting unapproachable light.* Such is the excessive glory of God, that neither angel nor man can approach it. It is indeed equally un-approachable to all created beings.

Whom no man hath seen, nor can see] Moses himself could only see the symbol of the Divine presence ; but the *face of God* no man could ever see. Because he is infinite and eternal, therefore he is *incomprehensible ;* and if incomprehensible to the *mind,* consequently invisible to the eye.

To whom] As the author of being, and the dispenser of all good, be ascribed *honour and power*—the sole authority of all-pervading, all-superintending, all-preserving, and everlasting might.

The words of St. Paul are inimitably sublime. It is a doubt whether human language can be carried much higher, even under the influence of inspiration, in a description of the supreme Being. It is well known that St. Paul had read the Greek poets. He quotes *Aratus, Epimenides,* and *Menander ;* this is allowed on all hands. But does he not quote, or refer to, *Æschylus* and *Sophocles* too ? Scarcely any person suspects this ; and yet there is such a complete similarity between the following quotations

from the above poets and the apostle's words, that we are almost persuaded he had them in his eye. But if so, he extends the thought infinitely higher, by language incomparably more exalted. I shall introduce and compare with the text the passages I refer to.

Verse 15. Ὁ μακαριος και μονος Δυναστης, ὁ Βασιλευς των βασιλευοντων, και Κυριος των κυριευοντων.

The supreme Being is also styled the King of kings, and the Blessed, by ÆSCHYLUS in his tragedy of the *Suppliants :*—

Αναξ ανακτων, μακαρων
Μακαρτατε, και τελεων
Τελειοτατον κρατος.

Ver. 520. Ed. Porson.

" O King of kings ! most Blessed of the blessed ! most Perfect of the perfect !"

Ver. 16. Ὁ μονος εχων αθανασιαν, φως οικων απροσιτον.

In the Antigone of SOPHOCLES there is a sublime address to Jove, of which the following is an extract :

Αγηρως χρονῳ Δυναστας,
Κατεχεις Ολυμπου
Μαρμαροεσσαν αιγλαν.

Ver. 608. Edit. Brunk.

"But thou, an ever-during Potentate, dost inhabit the refulgent splendour of Olympus !"

This passage is grand and noble ; but how insignificant does it appear when contrasted with the superior sublimity of the inspired writer ! The deity of Sophocles dwells in the dazzling splendour of heaven ; but the God of Paul inhabits light so dazzling and so resplendent that it is perfectly unapproachable !

Synesius, in his third hymn, has a fine idea on the mode of God's existence, which very probably he borrowed from St. Paul :—

Κεκαλυμμενε νου
Ιδιαις αυγαις.

"O intellectual Being ! veiled in thine own effulgence !"

And a few lines after, he says,—

Συ το κρυπτομενον
Ιδιαις αυγαις.

"Thou art He who art concealed by thy splendours."

All these are excellent, but they are *stars* of the twelfth magnitude before the apostolic SUN.

See a quotation from Euripides, 2 Tim. iv. 8.

Verse 17. *Charge them that are rich*] He had before, in verses 9, 10, given them a very awful lesson

2

A. M. cir. 4069.
A. D. 64 or 65.
A. U. C. 818.
An. Imp. Ne-
ronis Cæs.
Aug. 12.

that they be not high-minded, q nor trust in r uncertain s riches, but in the t living God, u who giveth us richly all things to enjoy;

18 That they do good, that v they be rich in good works, w ready to distribute, x willing y to communicate;

19 z Laying up in store for themselves a good foundation against the time to come, that they may a lay hold on eternal life.

20 O Timothy, b keep that which is committed to thy trust, c avoiding profane and vain babblings, and oppositions of science falsely so called:

21 Which some professing, d have erred concerning the faith. Grace be with thee. Amen

¶ The first to Timothy was written from Laodicea, which is the chiefest city of Phrygia Pacatiana.

A. M. cir. 4069.
A. D. 64 or 65.
A. U. C. 818.
An. Imp. Ne-
ronis Cæs.
Aug. 12.

---

q Job xxxi. 24; Psa. lii. 7; lxii. 10; Mark x. 24; Luke xii. 21.——r Gr. the uncertainty of riches.——s Proverbs xxiii. 5. t 1 Thess. i. 9; chap. iii. 15; iv. 10.——u Acts xiv. 17; xvii. 25. v Luke xii. 21; chap. v. 10; Tit. iii. 8; James ii. 5.——w Rom.

xii. 13.——x Or, sociable.——y Gal. vi. 6; Heb. xiii. 16.——z Matt. vi. 20; xix. 21; Luke xii. 33; xvi. 9.——a Ver. 12.——b 2 Tim. i. 24; Tit. i. 9; Rev. iii. 3.——c Chap. i. 4, 6; iv. 7; 2 Tim. ii. 14, 16, 23; Tit. i. 14; iii. 9.——d Chap. i. 6, 19; 2 Tim. ii. 18.

---

concerning their *obtaining riches*; and now he gives them one equally so concerning their *use* of them.

That they be not high-minded] That they do not value themselves on account of their wealth, for this adds nothing to mind or moral worth.

Nor trust in uncertain riches] Πλουτου αδηλοτητι· The uncertainty of riches; things which are never at a *stay*, are ever changing, and seldom continue long with one proprietor; therefore, as well as on many other accounts, they are not to be trusted in: they cannot give happiness, because they are not *fixed* and *permanent*; neither can they meet the wishes of an immortal spirit; *but in the living God*, who is the unchangeable fountain of perfection.

Who giveth us richly all things to enjoy] Who not only has all good, but dispenses it liberally for the supply of the wants of all his creatures; and he does not give merely what is *necessary*, but he gives what tends to render life *comfortable*. The *comforts* of life come from God, as well as the *necessaries*. He not only gives us a bare *subsistence*, but he gives us *enjoyments*. Were it not for the oppression and rapine of wicked men, every situation and state in life would be comparatively comfortable. God gives liberally; man divides it badly.

Verse 18. That they do good] That they relieve the wants of their fellow creatures, according to the abundance which God has given them. The highest luxury a human being can enjoy on this side of the grave.

Rich in good works] That their good works may be as abundant as their riches.

Ready to distribute] Ευμεταδοτους ειναι· That they give nothing through partiality or favour, but be guided in their distribution by the necessities of the objects presented to them; and that they confine not their charity at home, but scatter it abroad.

Willing to communicate] Κοινωνικους· Bringing every poor person into a state of *fellowship* with themselves.

Verse 19. Laying up in store for themselves a good foundation] St. Paul seems to have borrowed this form of speech from Tobit. See chap. iv. 8, 9: *If thou hast abundance, give alms accordingly: if thou hast but a little, be not afraid to give according to that little: for thou treasurest up a good reward for thyself against the day of necessity.* Θεμα γαρ

αγαθον θησαυριζεις σεαυτω εις ημεραν αναγκης. The apostle says: Αποθησαυριζοντας εαυτοις θεμελιον καλον εις το μελλον, ινα επιλαβωνται της αιωνιου ζωης "Treasuring up a good foundation to them for the future, that they may lay hold on eternal life." The sentiment is the same in both writers; the words nearly so; and the meaning is simply this, as it is judiciously paraphrased by Mr. J. Wesley in his note on this passage: "*Treasuring up for themselves a good foundation*, of an abundant reward by the free mercy of God, *that they may lay hold on eternal life.* This cannot be done by almsdeeds; yet, they *come up for a memorial before God*; Acts x. 4. And the lack even of *this* may be the cause why God will withhold grace and salvation from us." Christ has said: *Blessed are the merciful, for they shall obtain mercy.* They who have not been merciful according to their power, shall not obtain mercy; they that have, shall obtain mercy: and yet the eternal life which they obtain they look for from the mercy of God through Jesus Christ.

Verse 20. O Timothy, keep that which is committed to thy trust] This is another repetition of the apostolic charge. (See chap. i. 5, 18, 19; iv. 6, 7, 14, 15, 16; v. 21; vi. 13.) Carefully preserve that doctrine which I have delivered to thee. Nothing can be more solemn and affectionate than this charge.

Avoiding profane and vain babblings] See on chap. i. 4, and iv. 7.

And oppositions of science falsely so called] Και αντιθεσεις της ψευδωνυμου γνωσεως· *And oppositions of knowledge falsely so named.* Dr. Macknight's note here is worthy of much attention: "In the enumeration of the different kinds of inspiration bestowed on the first preachers of the Gospel, 1 Cor. xii. 8, we find the *word of knowledge* mentioned; by which is meant that kind of inspiration which gave to the apostles and superior Christian prophets the *knowledge of the true meaning of the Jewish Scriptures.* This inspiration the false teachers pretending to possess, dignified their misinterpretations of the ancient Scriptures with the name of *knowledge*, that is, *inspired* knowledge; for so the word signifies, 1 Cor. xiv. 6. And as by these interpretations they endeavoured to establish the efficacy of the Levitical atonements, the apostle very properly termed these interpretations *oppositions of knowledge*, because they were framed

2

to establish doctrines opposite to, and subversive of, the Gospel. To destroy the credit of these teachers, he affirmed that the *knowledge* from which they proceeded was *falsely called inspired knowledge;* for they were not inspired with the knowledge of the meaning of the Scriptures, but only pretended to it." Others think that the apostle has the *Gnostics* in view. But it is not clear that these heretics, or whatever they were, had any proper existence at this time. On the whole, Dr. Macknight's interpretation seems to be the best.

Verse 21. *Which some professing*] Which *inspired knowledge* some pretending to, have set up *Levitical rites* in opposition to the great *Christian sacrifice,* and consequently *have erred concerning the faith*—have completely mistaken the whole design of the Gospel. See chap. i. 6, 7.

Grace be with thee.] May the favour and influence of God be with thee, and preserve thee from these and all other errors !

Amen.] This word, as in former cases, is wanting in the most ancient MSS. In a majority of cases it appears to have been added by different transcribers nearly in the same way in which we add the word FINIS, simply to indicate the *end* of the work.

The *subscriptions* as usual are various. The following are the most remarkable afforded by the MSS. :—

The first to Timothy is completed ; the second to Timothy begins.—DE. The First Epistle to Timothy is completed ; the second to him begins.—G. The first to Timothy, written from Laodicea.—A. The first to Timothy, written from Ladikia.—CLAROMONT. Written from Laodicea, which is the metropolis of Phrygia.—The first to Timothy, written from Laodicea, which is the metropolis of Phrygia of Pacatiana.—*Common* GREEK TEXT, and several MSS. Instead of *Pacatiana,* some have *Pancatiana, Capatiana,* and *Paracatiana.*

The VERSIONS are not less discordant :—

The First Epistle to Timothy, which was written from Laodicea.—SYR.

The VULGATE has no subscription.

The end of the epistle. It was written from Laodicea, which is the metropolis of the cities of Phrygia. —ARAB.

To the man Timothy.—ÆTHIOPIC.

The First Epistle to Timothy, written from Athens. —ARABIC of *Erpenius.*

Written from Athens, and sent by Titus, his disciple.—COPTIC.

Written from Macedonia.—AUCTOR SYNOPS.

The First Epistle to Timothy is ended. It was written from Laodicea, the metropolis of Phrygia of Pacatiana.—PHILOXENIAN SYRIAC.

There is *one* authority in Griesbach, Mt. c., for its being written from NICOPOLIS. This is the opinion also of Dr. Macknight.

That the epistle was not written from *Laodicea* nor *Athens,* but from Macedonia, has been rendered probable by the arguments produced in the preface, to which the reader is referred for this and the date of the epistle itself.

In reviewing the whole of this epistle, I cannot help considering it of the first consequence to the Church of God. In it we see more clearly than elsewhere what the *ministers* of the Gospel should be, and what is the character of the *true Church. Bishops, presbyters,* and *deacons* are particularly described ; and their qualifications so circumstantially detailed, that it is impossible to be ignorant on this head. What the *Church* should be is also particularly stated ; it is the house of the living God ; the place where he lives, works, and manifests himself. The *doctrines* and *discipline* of the Church are not less specifically noted. All these subjects are considered at large in the notes, and here nothing need be added.

Should it be said, the apostle, in giving the qualifications of a bishop, "nowhere insists on *human learning,*" it may be answered in general, that no *ignorant person* in those times could have possibly got admittance into the Church as a teacher of Christianity. Every person, acknowledged as a teacher, was himself well taught in the word of God, and well taught by the Spirit of God ; and much teaching of the Divine Spirit was then necessary, as the New Testament Scriptures were not then completed ; and, if we were to allow the *earlier* date of this epistle, scarcely any part of the New Testament had then been written. The *gospels* had not come as yet into general circulation ; and only a few of St. Paul's epistles, viz. those to the Thessalonians, and that to the Galatians, and the first to the Corinthians, had been written before the year 56. At such times much must have been done by immediate revelations, and a frequent communication of miraculous powers.

It is natural for men to run into extremes ; and there is no subject on which they have run into wider extremes than that of the necessity of human learning ; for in order to a proper understanding of the sacred Scriptures, on one hand, all *learning* has been cried down, and the necessity of the inspiration of the Holy Spirit, as the sole interpreter, strongly and vehemently argued. On the other, all *inspiration* has been set aside, the *possibility* of it questioned, and all pretensions to it ridiculed in a way savouring little of Christian charity or reverence for God. That there is a middle way from which these extremes are equally distant, every candid man who believes the Bible must allow. That there is an inspiration of the Spirit which every conscientious Christian may claim, and without which no man can be a Christian, is sufficiently established by innumerable scriptures, and by the uninterrupted and universal testimony of the Church of God ; this has been frequently proved in the preceding notes. If any one, professing to be a preacher of the Gospel of Jesus, denies, speaks, or writes against this, he only gives awful proof to the Christian Church how utterly unqualified he is for his sacred function. *He* is not sent by God, and therefore he shall not profit the people at all. With such, human learning is all in all ; it is to be a substitute for the unction of Christ, and the grace and influences of the Holy Spirit.

But while we flee from such sentiments, as from the influence of a pestilential vapour, shall we join with those who decry learning and science, absolutely denying them to be of any service in the work of the ministry, and often going so far as to assert that they are dangerous and subversive of the truly Christian temper and spirit, engendering little besides pride, self-sufficiency, and intolerance?

That there have been *pretenders to learning*, proud and intolerant, we have too many proofs of the fact to doubt it; and that there have been *pretenders to Divine inspiration*, not less so, we have also many facts to prove. But such are only *pretenders*; for a truly learned man is ever humble and complacent, and one who is under the influence of the Divine Spirit is ever meek, gentle, and easy to be entreated. The proud and the insolent are neither Christians nor scholars. Both religion and learning disclaim them, as being a disgrace to both.

But what is that learning which may be a useful handmaid to religion in the ministry of the Gospel? Perhaps we may find an answer to this important question in one of the qualifications which the apostle requires in a Christian minister, 1 Tim. iii. 2: He should be *apt to teach*—capable of teaching others. See the note. Now, if he be capable of teaching others, he must be well instructed himself; and in order to this he will need all the learning that, in the course of the Divine providence, he is able to acquire. But it is not the ability merely to interpret a few *Greek* and *Latin* authors that can constitute a man a *scholar*, or qualify him to teach the Gospel. Thousands have this knowledge who are neither wise unto salvation themselves, nor capable of leading those who are astray into the path of life. *Learning* is a word of extensive import; it signifies *knowledge* and *experience*; the knowledge of God and of nature in general, and of man in particular; of man in all his relations and connections; his history in all the *periods* of his being, and in all the *places* of his existence; the means used by Divine providence for his support; the manner in which he has been led to employ the powers and faculties assigned to him by his Maker; and the various dispensations of grace and mercy by which he has been favoured. To acquire this *knowledge*, an acquaintance with some languages, which have long ceased to be vernacular, is often not only highly expedient, but in some cases indispensably necessary. But how few of those who pretend most to learning, and who have spent both much time and much money in seats of literature in order to obtain it, have got

this knowledge! All that many of them have gained is merely the *means* of acquiring it; with this they become satisfied, and most ignorantly call it *learning*. These resemble persons who carry large unlighted tapers in their hand, and boast how well qualified they are to give light to them who sit in darkness, while they neither emit light nor heat, and are incapable of kindling the taper they hold. Learning, in one proper sense of the word, is the means of acquiring knowledge; but multitudes who have the *means* seem utterly unacquainted with their *use*, and live and die in a *learned ignorance*. Human learning, properly applied and sanctified by the Divine Spirit, is of inconceivable benefit to a Christian minister in teaching and defending the truth of God. No man possessed more of it in his day than St. Paul, and no man better knew its use. In this, as well as in many other excellences, he is a most worthy pattern to all the preachers of the Gospel. By learning a man may acquire knowledge; by knowledge reduced to practice, experience; and from knowledge and experience *wisdom* is derived. The learning that is got from books or the study of languages is of little use to any man, and is of no estimation, unless practically applied to the purposes of life. He whose learning and knowledge have enabled him to do good among men, and who lives to promote the glory of God and the welfare of his fellow creatures, can alone, of all the literati, expect to hear in the great day: Well done, good and faithful servant! Enter thou into the joy of thy Lord.

How necessary learning is at present to interpret the sacred writings, any man may see who reads with attention; but none can be so fully convinced of this as he who undertakes to write a comment on the Bible. Those who despise helps of this kind are to be pitied. Without them they may, it is true, understand enough for the mere salvation of their souls; and yet even much of this they owe, under God, to the teaching of experienced men. After all, it is not a knowledge of *Latin* and *Greek* merely that can enable any man to understand the Scriptures, or interpret them to others; if the Spirit of God take not away the veil of ignorance from the heart, and enlighten and quicken the soul with his all-pervading energy, all the learning under heaven will not make a man wise unto salvation.

Finished correcting for a new edition, Dec. 22d, 1831.—A. C.

2

PREFACE

TO THE

SECOND EPISTLE OF PAUL THE APOSTLE

TO

TIMOTHY.

IN the preface to the *first* of these epistles, particular mention has been made of the parentage, country, and education of Timothy; his call to the evangelic office; and of his appointment to the presidency of the Church at Ephesus. And for every particular of this kind the reader is referred to that preface. What remains to be done in reference to the present epistle is to inquire into the *time* in which it was most probably written. The disagreement on this question among learned men is very great; some arguing that it was written about the year 61, others referring it to the year 66. Some asserting that it is the *first*, in order of time, of these two epistles; and that it was written on Paul's first imprisonment at Rome. Several of the most eminent critics are of this opinion; and they have supported their sentiments with arguments of no small weight. *Hammond, Lightfoot,* and *Lardner,* as well as several critics on the continent, contend for this earlier date. *Macknight* and *Paley* take the opposite side. Were I convinced that the weight of the argument lay with the former, I should have fixed its chronology accordingly; but the latter appearing to me to have the more direct and the most weighty evidence in their favour, I am led, from the reasons which they give, to adopt their opinion.

Dr. Paley observes, that it was the uniform tradition of the primitive Church that St. Paul visited Rome *twice,* and *twice* there suffered imprisonment; and that at the conclusion of his *second* imprisonment he was put to death; and he thinks that the opinion concerning these *two* journeys of St. Paul is confirmed by many hints and allusions in this epistle, compared with what St. Paul has said in other epistles, which are allowed to have been written from Rome. I shall give his principal reasons :—

" That this epistle was written while Paul was a *prisoner* is distinctly marked by the 8th verse of the first chapter : ' Be not thou therefore ashamed of the testimony of our Lord, nor of me his *prisoner.*' And that it was written whilst he was prisoner *at Rome* is proved by the 16th and 17th verses of the same chapter : ' The Lord give mercy to the house of Onesiphorus, for he often refreshed me, and was not ashamed of my *chain;* but when he was in *Rome,* he sought me out very diligently, and found me.' Since it appears from the former quotation that St. Paul wrote this epistle in confinement, it will hardly admit of doubt that the word *chain* in the latter quotation refers to that confinement—the *chain* by which he was then bound, the *custody* in which he was then kept. And if the word *chain* designate the author's confinement at the time of writing this epistle, the next words determine it to have been written from *Rome* : ' *He was not ashamed of my chain, but when he was in Rome, he sought me out very diligently.*'" Dr. Macknight thinks that Paul was now a *close* prisoner, very different in his circumstances from his first imprisonment, in which he was permitted to *dwell alone in his own hired house, and receive all that came to him,* and publicly to preach the Gospel, being guarded only by a single soldier. That he was in close confinement he argues from the circumstance that when Onesiphorus came to Rome he found that Paul was no longer that well-known public character which he had been while in his first imprisonment, but being closely confined he had some difficulty to find him out; and this appears to be fully implied in the apostle's words : Σπουδαιοτερον εζητησε με, και ευρε " He very diligently sought me out, and found me ;" chap. i. 17. And, that crimes were now laid to his charge widely different from those formerly alleged against him, appears from chap. ii. 9 : Κακοπαθω μεχρι δεσμων, ὡς κακουργος· " I suffer evil even to bonds as a malefactor ;" plainly implying that he was not only abridged of all liberty, but was *bound hands and feet* in a *close* dungeon. And this was probably on the pretence that he was one of those Christians whom Nero accused with having set Rome on fire. Hence the word *malefactor,* κακουργος, which may mean here that the apostle was treated as the worst of criminals.

That this epistle was not written during St. Paul's first imprisonment at Rome, or during the time in which the Epistles to the *Ephesians, Colossians, Philippians,* and *Philemon* were written, may be gathered, says Dr. Paley, with considerable evidence from a comparison of these several epistles with the present.

I. " In the former epistles the author confidently looked forward to his *liberation* from confinement, and his speedy departure from Rome. He tells the Philippians, chap. ii. 24 : ' I trust in the Lord that I also myself shall come shortly.' Philemon he bids *to prepare for him a lodging* ; ' for I trust (says he) that through your prayers I shall be given unto you ;' ver. 22. In the epistle before us he holds a language extremely different ' I am now ready to be offered, and the time of my departure is at hand. I have fought a good fight, I have finished my course, I have kept the faith; henceforth there is laid up for me a crown of righteousness, which the Lord, the righteous Judge, shall give me at that day;' chap. iv. 6–8."

Those who espouse the contrary opinion suppose that these words only express the *strong apprehensions* and *despair of life* which the apostle had when he was *first* imprisoned; but that afterwards, finding he was treated with kindness, he altered his language, and so strongly anticipated that he predicted his *enlargement*. This reflects little honour upon the apostle's character; it shows him to be a person subject to alarms, and presaging the *worst* from every gloomy *appearance*. The whole of St. Paul's conduct shows him to have been the reverse of what this opinion represents him.

II. "When the former epistles were written from Rome Timothy was *with* St. Paul, and is joined with him in writing to the Colossians, the Philippians, and Philemon; the present epistle implies that he was *absent*.

III. "In the former epistles *Demas* was *with* St. Paul at Rome: 'Luke the beloved physician, and Demas, greet you.' In the epistle now before us: 'Demas hath forsaken me, having loved this present world, and is gone to Thessalonica.'

IV. "In the former epistles *Mark* was *with* St. Paul, and joins in saluting the Colossians. In the present epistle Timothy is ordered to bring him *with him*, '*for he is profitable to me for the ministry*;' chap. iv. 11."

The circumstance of Demas being *with* St. Paul while he wrote the former epistles, which was certainly during his *first* imprisonment, and of his having *forsaken* him when he wrote this, is a strong proof of the posterior date of this epistle; nor can the feelings of the apostle, so contradictorily expressed in this and the preceding epistles, be ever cleared (on the supposition of their relating to the same time and circumstances) from *weakness* and *contradiction*.

Lewis Capellus has suggested the following considerations, which are still more conclusive:—

1. "In chap. iv., ver. 20, St. Paul informs Timothy that *Erastus abode at Corinth*, Εραστος εμεινεν εν Κορινθῳ· the form of expression (the verb being in the first aorist) implies that Erastus had stayed behind at Corinth when St. Paul left it: but this could not be meant of any journey from Corinth which St. Paul took prior to his first imprisonment at Rome; for when Paul departed from Corinth, as related in the 20th chapter of the Acts, Timothy was with him; and this was the last time the apostle left Corinth before his coming to Rome, because he left it on his way to proceed to Jerusalem soon after his arrival, at which place he was taken into custody, and continued in that custody till he was brought to Cæsar's tribunal.

There could be no need, therefore, to inform Timothy that *Erastus stayed behind at Corinth*, upon this occasion; because, if the fact were so, it must have been known to Timothy, who was *present* as well as St. Paul.

2. "In the same verse our epistle also states the following article: 'Trophimus have I left at Miletus sick.' When St. Paul passed through Miletus, on his way to Jerusalem, as related Acts xx., *Trophimus was not left behind*, but accompanied him to that city. He was indeed the occasion of the uproar at Jerusalem, in consequence of which St. Paul was apprehended: 'For they had seen,' says the historian, 'before with him in the city, Trophimus an Ephesian, whom they supposed that Paul had brought into the temple.' This was evidently the last time of Paul's being at Miletus before his first imprisonment; for, as has been said, after his apprehension at Jerusalem he remained in custody till he was sent to Rome.

"In these two articles we have a journey referred to, which must have taken place subsequent to the conclusion of St. Luke's history; and, of course, after St. Paul's liberation from his first imprisonment. The epistle, therefore, which contains this reference, since it appears from other parts of it to have been written while St. Paul was a prisoner at Rome, proves that he had *returned* to that city again, and undergone there a *second imprisonment*.

"These particulars," adds Dr. Paley, "I have produced, not merely for the support they lend to the testimony of the fathers concerning St. Paul's *second* imprisonment, but to remark their consistency and agreement with one another. They are all resolvable into one supposition, viz., that this epistle was not written during St. Paul's *first* residence at Rome, but in some future imprisonment in that city. The epistle touches upon *names* and *circumstances* connected with the *date* and with the *history* of the first imprisonment, and mentioned in letters during that imprisonment; and so touches upon them as to leave what is said of one consistent with what is said of others, and consistent also with what is said of them in different epistles."

From the whole, there seems the fullest evidence, 1. That this epistle was not written during St. Paul's *first imprisonment* at Rome. 2. That he was at *Rome* when he wrote *this* epistle. 3. That he was there a *prisoner*, and in such confinement as we know, from the Acts of the Apostles, he was not in during the time of his first imprisonment there. 4. That this must have been some subsequent imprisonment. 5. That as the general consent of all Christian antiquity states that St. Paul was *twice* imprisoned at Rome, and that from his *second* imprisonment he was never liberated, but was at its conclusion martyred; therefore this epistle must have been written while St. Paul was in his second imprisonment at Rome, and but a short time before his martyrdom. And as the Christian Church has generally agreed that this apostle's martyrdom took place on the 29th of June, A. D. 66, the Second Epistle to Timothy might have been written sometime towards the end of the *spring* or beginning of *summer* of that year. It is supposed that St. Paul went from Crete to Rome, about the end of the year 65, on hearing of the persecution which Nero was then carrying on against the Christians, on pretence that they had set Rome on fire: for, as he knew that the Church must be then in great tribulation, he judged that his presence would be necessary to comfort, support, and build it up. Like a true soldier of Jesus Christ, he was ever at the post of danger; and in *this* case he led on the *forlorn hope*.

Other matters relative to the state and circumstances of the apostle, and those of Timothy; and the Church at Ephesus, will be carefully brought before the reader in the course of the notes on this epistle.

THE

SECOND EPISTLE OF PAUL THE APOSTLE

TO

TIMOTHY.

Chronological Notes relative to this Epistle.

Year of the Constantinopolitan era of the world, or that used by the Byzantine historians, 5573.—Year of the Alexandrian era of the world, 5567.—Year of the Antiochian era of the world, 5557.—Year of the Julian period, 4775.—Year of the world, according to Archbishop Usher, 4069.—Year of the world, according to Eusebius, in his Chronicon, 4293.—Year of the minor Jewish era of the world, or that in common use, 3825.—Year of the Greater Rabbinical era of the world, 4424.—Year from the Flood, according to Archbishop Usher, and the English Bible, 2413.—Year of the Cali yuga, or Indian era of the Deluge, 3167. —Year of the era of Iphitus, or since the first commencement of the Olympic games, 1005.—Year of the era of Nabonassar, king of Babylon, 812.—Year of the CCXIth Olympiad, 1.—Year from the building of Rome, according to Fabius Pictor, 812.—Year from the building of Rome, according to Frontinus, 816.—Year from the building of Rome, according to the Fasti Capitolini, 817.—Year from the building of Rome, according to Varro, which was that most generally used, 818.—Year of the era of the Seleucidæ, 377.—Year of the Cæsarean era of Antioch, 113.—Year of the Julian era, 110.—Year of the Spanish era, 103.—Year from the birth of Jesus Christ according to Archbishop Usher, 69.—Year of the vulgar era of Christ's nativity, 65 or 66.—Year of Gessius Florus, governor of the Jews, 1.—Year of Vologesus, king of the Parthians, 16. —Year of L. C. Gallus, governor of Syria, 1.—Year of Matthias, high priest of the Jews, 3.—Year of the Dionysian period, or Easter Cycle, 66.—Year of the Grecian Cycle of nineteen years, or Common Golden Number, 9; or the first after the third embolismic.—Year of the Jewish Cycle of nineteen years, 6, or the second embolismic.—Year of the Solar Cycle, 18.—Dominical Letter, it being the first after the Bissextile, or Leap Year, F.—Day of the Jewish Passover, according to the Roman computation of time, the VIIth of the ides of April, or, in our common mode of reckoning, the seventh of April, which happened in this year on the day after the Jewish Sabbath.—Easter Sunday, the day after the ides of April, or the XVIIIth of the Calends of May, named by the Jews the 22d of Nisan or Abib; and by Europeans in general, the 14th of April.—Epact, or age of the moon on the 22d of March, (the day of the earliest Easter Sunday possible,) 28.—Epact, according to the present mode of computation, or the moon's age on New Year's day, or the Calends of January, 5.—Monthly Epacts, or age of the moon on the Calends of each month respectively, (beginning with January,) 5, 7, 6, 7, 8, 9, 10, 11, 12, 12, 14, 14.—Number of Direction, or the number of days from the twenty-first of March to the Jewish Passover, 17.—Year of the reign of Caius Tiberius Claudius Nero Cæsar, the fifth Roman emperor computing from Augustus Cæsar, 12.—Roman Consuls, A. Licinius Nerva Silanus, and M. Vestinius Atticus; the latter of whom was succeeded by Anicius Cerealis, on July 1st. Dr. Lardner and others suppose this epistle to have been written in A. D. 56, *i. e.* nine years earlier than is stated above. See the preface to the First Epistle to Timothy, where this point is largely considered, and also the general observations prefixed to the Acts of the Apostles.

CHAPTER I.

Paul's address to Timothy, and declaration of his affection for him, 1–4. His account of the piety of Timo-thy's mother and grandmother, and the religious education they had given their son, 5. He exhorts him to stir up the gift of God that is in him, and not to be ashamed of the testimony of the Lord, 6–8. How God has saved them that believe; and how Christ has brought life and immortality to light by the Gospel, 9, 10. The apostle's call to preach it, and the persecutions which he had been obliged in consequence to endure, 11, 12. Timothy is exhorted to hold fast the form of sound words, 13, 14. And is informed of the apostasy of several in Asia; and particularly of Phygellus and Hermogenes, 15. And of the great kindness of Onesiphorus to the apostle in his imprisonment, 16–18.

A. M. cir. 4069.
A. D. 65 or 66.
A. U. C. 818.
An. Imp. Ne-
ronis Cæs.
Aug. 12.

PAUL, [a] an apostle of Jesus Christ, by the will of God, according to [b] the promise of life which is in Christ Jesus,

2 [c] To Timothy, *my* dearly beloved son: Grace, mercy, *and* peace, from God the Father and Christ Jesus our Lord.

3 [d] I thank God, [e] whom I serve from *my*

A. M. cir. 4069.
A. D. 65 or 66.
A. U. C. 818.
An. Imp. Ne-
ronis Cæs.
Aug. 12.

forefathers with pure conscience, that [f] without ceasing I have re-membrance of thee in my prayers night and day;

4 [g] Greatly desiring to see thee, being mind-ful of thy tears, that I may be filled with joy;

5 When I call to remembrance [h] the un-feigned faith that is in thee, which dwelt first

---

[a] 2 Cor. i. 1.——[b] Eph. iii. 6; Tit. i. 2; Heb. ix. 15.——[c] 1 Tim. i. 2.——[d] Rom. i. 8; Eph. i. 16.——[e] Acts xxii. 3; xxiii. 1; xxiv.

14; xxvii. 23; Rom i. 9; Gal. i. 14.——[f] 1 Thess. i. 2; iii. 10. [g] Chap. iv. 9, 21.——[h] 1 Tim. i. 5; iv. 6.

NOTES ON CHAP. I.

Verse 1. *Paul an apostle*] St. Paul at once shows his *office*, the *authority* on which he held it, and the *end* for which it was given him. He was an *apostle* —an extraordinary ambassador from heaven. He had his apostleship by the *will of God*—according to the counsel and design of God's infinite wisdom and good-ness. And he was appointed that he might proclaim that *eternal life* which God had in view for mankind by the incarnation of his Son Jesus Christ, and which was the *end* of all the *promises* he had made to men, and the *commandments* he had delivered to all his pro-phets since the world began. The mention of this *life* was peculiarly proper in the apostle, who had now the sentence of death in himself, and who knew that he must shortly seal the truth with his blood. *His life* was hidden with Christ in God; and he knew that, as soon as he should be *absent* from the *body*, he should be *present* with the *Lord*. With these words he both comforted himself and his son Timothy.

Verse 2. *To Timothy, my dearly beloved son*] See the note on 1 Tim. i. 2.

Verse 3. *Whom I serve from* my *forefathers*] Be-ing born a *Jew*, I was carefully educated in the know-ledge of the true God, and the proper manner of wor-shipping him.

With pure conscience] Ever aiming to please him, even in the time when through ignorance I persecuted the Church.

Without ceasing I have remembrance of thee] The apostle thanks God that he has constant remembrance of Timothy in his prayers. It is a very rare thing now in the Christian Church, that a man particularly thanks God *that he is enabled to pray for* OTHERS. And yet that he can do this most must have an increase of that brotherly love which the second greatest com-mandment of God requires: *Thou shalt love thy neigh-bour as thyself*. It is also a great blessing to be able to maintain the spirit of a pure friendship, especially

through a considerable lapse of time and absence. He that can do so may well thank God that he is saved from that *fickleness* and *unsteadiness of mind* which are the bane of friendships, and the reproach of many once warm-hearted friends.

Verse 4. *Being mindful of thy tears*] Whether the apostle refers to the affecting parting with the Ephesian Church, mentioned Acts xx. 37, or to the deep impressions made on Timothy's heart when he instructed him in the doctrine of Christ crucified, or to some interview between themselves, it is not certainly known. The mention of this by the apostle is no small proof of his most affectionate regards for Timothy, whom he appears to have loved as a father loves his only son.

Verse 5. *The unfeigned faith that is in thee*] Timothy had given the fullest proof of the sincerity of his conversion, and of the purity of his faith.

Which dwelt first in thy grandmother Lois] In Acts xvi. 1, we are informed that Paul *came to Derbe and Lystra; and behold, a certain disciple was there, named Timotheus, the son of a certain woman, who was a Jewess, and believed; but his father was a Greek.* Luke, the historian, it appears, was not par-ticularly acquainted with the family; Paul evidently was. Luke mentions the same circumstance which the apostle mentions here; but in the apostle's account there are *particulars* which argue an intimate acquaint-ance with the family and its history. Luke says Timothy's father was a *Greek*, consequently we may believe him to have been then in his *heathen* state; Paul, in mentioning the *grandmother, mother*, and *son*, passes by the *father* in silence; which intimates that either the father remained in his *unconverted* state, or was now *dead*. Lois and Eunice are both Grecian, and indeed heathen names; hence we are led to con-clude that, although Timothy's mother was a *Jewess* according to St. Luke, yet she was a *Grecian* or *Hellenist* by birth. Lois, the grandmother, appears to

2

A. M. cir. 4069.
A. D. 65 or 66.
A. U. C. 818.
An. Imp. Ne-
ronis Cæs.
Aug. 12.

in thy grandmother Lois, and [i] thy mother Eunice ; and I am persuaded that in thee also.

6 Wherefore I put thee in remembrance [k] that thou stir up the gift of God, which is in thee by the putting on of my hands.

7 [l] For God hath not given us the spirit of fear ; [m] but of power, and of love, and of a sound mind.

A. M. cir. 4069.
A. D. 65 or 66.
A. U. C. 818.
An. Imp. Ne-
ronis Cæs.
Aug. 12.

8 [n] Be not thou therefore ashamed of [o] the testimony of our Lord, nor of me [p] his prisoner : [q] but be thou partaker of the afflictions of the Gospel according to the power of God.

9 [r] Who hath saved us, and [s] called *us* with a holy calling, [t] not according to our works, but [u] according to his own purpose and grace,

[i] Acts xvi. 1.——[k] 1 Thess. v. 19 ; 1 Tim. iv. 14.——[l] Romans viii. 15.——[m] Luke xxiv. 49 ; Acts i. 8.——[n] Romans i. 16. [o] 1 Tim. ii. 6 ; Rev. i. 2.——[p] Eph. iii. 1 ; Phil. i. 7.

[q] Col. i. 24 ; chapter iv. 5.——[r] 1 Timothy i. 1 ; Titus iii. 4. [s] 1 Thess. iv. 7 ; Heb. iii. 1.——[t] Rom. iii. 20 ; ix. 11 ; Tit. iii. 5. [u] Rom. viii. 28.

have been the *first* convert to Christianity : she instructed her daughter *Eunice*, and both brought up *Timothy* in the Christian faith ; so that he had a general knowledge of it before he met with St. Paul at Lystra. There, it appears the apostle was the instrument of the conversion of his *heart* to God ; for a man may be *well instructed* in Divine things, have a very orthodox creed, and yet his heart not be changed. Instruction precedes conversion ; conversion should follow it. To be brought up in the fear of God is a great blessing ; and a truly religious education is an advantage of infinite worth.

Verse 6. Stir up the gift of God, which is in thee] The gift which Timothy had received was the Holy Spirit ; and through him, a particular power to preach and defend the truth. This gift is represented here, under the notion of a *fire*, which, if it be not *frequently stirred up*, and *fresh fuel added* to it, will go out. This is the precise idea which the apostle had in his mind ; hence the term αναζωπυρειν, which signifies to *stir up the fire ; to add fresh fuel to it.* From this it plainly appears, that if Timothy had not continued to be a daily worker with God, he would have received the grace of God in vain. The *Latins* have a similar metaphor, *excitare igniculos ingenii, to stir up the sparks of genius.*

By the putting on of my hands.] See on 1 Tim. iv. 14.

Verse 7. God hath not given us the spirit of fear] Here is an allusion to the giving of the law on mount Sinai. This was communicated with such *terrible majesty* as to engender fear in all the Israelites : even Moses, on the occasion, *did exceedingly fear and tremble.* The Gospel was ushered in, in a much milder manner ; every thing was placed on a level with the human intellect ; and within reach of every human spirit. Nothing was *terrific*, nothing *forbidding* ; but all was *inviting.* The very spirit and genius of it was a spirit of power, of love, and of a sound mind.

Instead of δειλιας, *fear*, some MSS. and versions have δουλειας, *servitude* or *bondage* ; God hath not *given unto us the spirit of* BONDAGE—*but of power*, δυναμεως, to work miracles, to confound enemies, to support us in trials, and enable us to do that which is lawful and right in his sight. *And of love*, which enables us to hear, believe, hope, and endure all things ; and is the incentive to all obedience. *Of a sound mind*, σωφρονισμου, of *self-possession* and *government*, according to some. But a sound mind implies much

more ; it means a clear understanding, a sound judgment, a rectified will, holy passions, heavenly tempers ; in a word, the whole soul harmonized in all its powers and faculties ; and completely regulated and influenced so as to think, speak, and act aright in all things. The apostle says, God hath given the *spirit* of these things ; they are not *factitious* ; they are not *assumed* for *times and circumstances* ; they are *radical* powers and tempers ; each produced by its proper *principle.*

Verse 8. Be not—ashamed of the testimony] The testimony of Christ is the *Gospel* in general, which proclaims *Christ crucified*, and redemption *through his blood.* In the sight of the *world*, there appeared to be reason why a man should be ashamed of this ; ashamed of him who was crucified as a malefactor ; but, when this Gospel became the power of God to the salvation of every one that believed, it was a subject to exult in. Hence the apostle, Rom. i. 16, said, *I am not ashamed of the Gospel of Christ* ; where see the note.

Nor of me his prisoner] When our *friends* are in power and credit, we can readily acknowledge them, and take opportunities to show that we have such and such connections ; but when the person falls into disgrace or discredit, though we cannot pretend *not to know* him, yet we take care *not to acknowledge* him. This induced Cicero, in relation to friendships, to give for a maxim—*Amicus certus in re incertâ cernitur :* " A true friend is known in adverse circumstances ;" and from this we have borrowed our proverb, *A friend in need, is a friend indeed.*

Be thou partaker of the afflictions of the Gospel] No parent could love a child better than Paul loved Timothy ; and, behold ! he who could wish him nothing but what was *great, honourable*, and *good*, wishes him to be a *partaker of the afflictions of the Gospel!* Because, to suffer for Christ, and suffer with Christ, was the highest glory to which any human being in this state could arrive. The royal way to the crown of glory, is by the cross of Christ.

According to the power of God.] While thou hast no more affliction than thou hast grace to sustain thee under, thou canst have no cause to complain. And God will take care that if a faithful discharge of thy duty shall expose thee to afflictions, his power manifested in thee shall be in proportion to thy necessities. His load cannot be oppressive, who is strengthened to bear it by the *power of God.*

Verse 9. Who hath saved us] From sin ; the spiri-

A. M. cir. 4066.
A. D. 65 or 66.
A. U. C. 818.
An. Imp. Ne-
ronis Cæs.
Aug. 12.

which was given us in Christ Jesus, ^v before the world began;

10 But ^w is now made manifest by the appearing of our Saviour, Jesus Christ, ^x who hath abolished death, and hath brought life and immortality to light through the Gospel :

11 ^y Whereunto I am appointed a preacher, and an apostle, and a teacher of the Gentiles.

A. M. cir. 4069.
A. D. 65 or 66.
A. U. C. 818.
An. Imp. Ne-
ronis Cæs.
Aug. 12.

12 ^z For the which cause I also suffer these things : nevertheless I am not ashamed : ^a for I know whom I have ^b believed, and am persuaded that he is able to ^c keep that which I have committed unto him ^d against that day.

13 ^e Hold fast ^f the form of ^g sound words, ^h which thou hast heard of me, ⁱ in faith and love which is in Christ Jesus.

---

^v Rom. xvi. 25; 1 Cor. ii. 7; Gal. i. 26; Eph. i. 4; iii. 11; Tit. i. 2; 1 Peter i. 20.——^w Rom. xvi. 26; Eph. i. 9; Col. i. 26; Tit. i. 3; 1 Pet. i. 20.——^x 1 Cor. xv. 54, 55; Heb. ii. 14. ^y Acts ix. 15; Eph. iii. 7, 8; 1 Tim. ii. 7; chap. iv. 17.

^z Eph. iii. 1; chap. ii. 9.——^a 1 Pet. iv. 19.——^b Or, *trusted.* ^c 1 Tim. vi. 20.——^d Ver. 18; chap. iv. 8.——^e Chap. iii. 14; Tit. i. 9; Heb. x. 23; Rev. ii. 25.——^f Rom. ii. 20; vi. 17.——^g 1 Tim. i. 10; vi. 3.——^h Chap. ii. 2.——ⁱ 1 Tim. i. 14.

---

of bondage, and all tormenting fear. This is the design of the Gospel.

And called us with a holy calling] Invited us to holiness and comfort here; and to eternal glory hereafter.

Not according to our works] We have not *deserved* any part of the good we have received; and can never merit one moment of the exceeding great and eternal weight of glory which is promised. See the notes on the parallel passages.

Before the world began] Προ χρονων αιωνιων. Before the *Mosaic dispensation* took place, God purposed the salvation of the Gentiles by Christ Jesus; and the Mosaic dispensation was intended only as the introducer of the Gospel. *The law was our schoolmaster unto Christ*, Gal. iii. 24. See the parallel places, and the notes there.

Verse 10. *But is now made manifest*] This purpose of God to save the Gentiles as well as the Jews, and call them to the same state of salvation by Jesus Christ, was, previously to the manifestation of Christ, generally hidden; and what was revealed of it, was only through the means of types and ceremonies.

Who hath abolished death] Καταργησαντος μεν τον θανατον. Who has *counterworked death;* operated against his operations, destroyed his batteries, undersunk and destroyed his mines, and rendered all his instruments and principles of attack useless. By death here, we are not to understand merely natural death, but that corruption and decomposition which take place in consequence of it; and which would be naturally endless, but for the work and energy of Christ. By him alone, comes the *resurrection* of the body; and through him eternal life and glory are given to the souls of believers.

Brought life and immortality to light] The literal translation of the original is, *He hath illustrated life and incorruption by the Gospel.* Life eternal, or the doctrine of *life eternal,* even implying the resurrection of the body, was not unknown among the Jews. They expected this, for they found it in their prophets. It abounded among them long before the incarnation: and they certainly never borrowed any notion in it from the Christians; therefore the Gospel could not be stated as *bringing to light* what certainly was *in the light* before that time. But this doctrine was never *illustrated* and *demonstrated* before; it existed in *promise,* but had never been *practically exhibited.* Jesus Christ

died, and lay under the empire of death; he arose again from the dead, and thus *illustrated* the *doctrine of the resurrection :* he took the same *human body* up into heaven, in the sight of his disciples; and ever appears in the presence of God for us; and thus, has *illustrated* the doctrine of *incorruption.* In his death, resurrection, and ascension, the doctrine of eternal life, and the resurrection of the human body, and its final *incorruptibility,* are fully illustrated by *example,* and established by *fact.*

Verse 11. *Whereunto I am appointed a preacher*] Κηρυξ, a *herald.* See the notes at the end of Matt. chap. iii.

And an apostle] Sent immediately from God to man.

A teacher] One whose business it is to *instruct* men, and particularly the Gentiles, to whom he was especially sent; to proclaim the doctrines of eternal life, the resurrection and final incorruptibility of the human body; and, in a word, the salvation both of the body and soul of man by Christ Jesus.

Verse 12. *I am not ashamed*] Though I suffer for the Gospel, I am not ashamed of the Gospel; nor am I confounded in my expectation; his grace being at all times sufficient for me.

For I know whom I have believed] I am well acquainted with the goodness, mercy, and power of Christ; and know that I cannot confide in him in vain.

That which I have committed unto him] This is variously understood. Some think he means his *life,* which he had put, as it were, into the hands of Christ, in order that he might receive it again, in the resurrection, at the great day. Others think he means his *soul.* This he had also given into the hands of his faithful Creator, knowing that although wicked men might be permitted to take away his life, yet they could not destroy his soul, nor disturb its peace. Others think that he is speaking of the *Gospel,* which he knows will be carefully preserved by the great Head of the Church; for, though he shall be soon called to seal the truth with his blood, yet he knows that God will take care that the same truth shall be proclaimed to the world by others, whom God shall raise up for that very purpose.

Verse 13. *Hold fast the form of sound words*] The word υποτυπωσις signifies the *sketch, plan,* or *outline* of a building, picture, &c.; and here refers to the *plan of salvation* which the apostle had taught Timothy.

A. M. cir. 4069.
A. D. 65 or 66.
A. U. C. 818.
An. Imp. Ne-
ronis Cæs.
Aug. 12.

14 [k] That good thing which was committed unto thee, keep by the Holy Ghost [l] which dwelleth in us.

15 This thou knowest, that [m] all they which are in Asia be [n] turned away from me; of whom are Phygellus and Hermogenes.

16 The Lord [o] give mercy unto [p] the house of Onesiphorus; [q] for he oft refreshed me, and

[r] was not ashamed of [s] my chain:

17 But when he was in Rome, he sought me out very diligently, and found *me*.

18 The Lord grant unto him [t] that he may find mercy of the Lord [u] in that day: and in how many things he [v] ministered unto me at Ephesus, thou knowest very well.

A. M. cir. 4069.
A. D. 65 or 66.
A. U. C. 818.
An. Imp. Ne-
ronis Cæs.
Aug. 12.

---

[k] 1 Tim. vi. 20.——[l] Rom. viii. 11.——[m] Acts xix. 10.——[n] Chap. iv. 10, 16.——[o] Matt. v. 7.——[p] Chap. iv. 19.——[q] Philem. 7.

[r] Ver. 8.——[s] Acts xxviii. 20; Eph. vi. 20.——[t] Matt. xxv. 34. 40.——[u] 2 Thess. i. 10; ver. 12.——[v] Heb. vi. 10.

No man was left to *invent a religion* for his own use, and after his own mind. God alone knows that with which God can be pleased. If God did not give a revelation of himself, the inventions of man, in religious things, would be endless error, involving itself in contortions of unlimited confusion. God gives, in his mercy to man, a *form of sound words* or doctrines; a perfect *plan* and *sketch* of the original building; fair and well defined outlines of every thing which concerns the present and eternal welfare of man, and his own glory.

In faith and love] Faith credits the Divine doctrines. *Love* reduces them all to practice. *Faith* lays hold on Jesus Christ, and obtains that *love* by which every precept is cheerfully and effectually obeyed.

Verse 14. *That good thing*] The everlasting Gospel, *keep by the Holy Ghost;* for without a continual *spiritual energy* man can do nothing. This *indwelling Spirit* will make them effectual to thy own salvation, and enable thee to preach them to the salvation of the souls of others.

Verse 15. *All they which are in Asia*] It seems as if the apostle must refer to the Asiatic Christians which were then at Rome, or had been lately there. Finding the apostle in disgrace, and thinking it dangerous to own him or his cause, they neither visited him, nor confessed Christianity. He cannot be speaking of any general defection of the Asiatic *Churches*, but of those Asiatics who had professed a particular friendship for him.

Phygellus and Hermogenes.] These were two of the persons of whom he complains; but who they were, or what office they held, or whether they were any thing but private Christians who had for a time ministered to St. Paul in prison, and, when they found the state determined to destroy him, ceased to acknowledge him, we cannot tell.

Verse 16. *The Lord give mercy*] Onesiphorus had acknowledged him, and continued to do so; *he,* and his *house,* or *family,* ministered to him in prison, and were not ashamed of their imprisoned pastor, nor of the *cause* for which he was in disgrace and suffering. As *he* showed mercy to the apostle, the apostle prays the Lord to show mercy to him.

Verse 17. *When he was in Rome*] Onesiphorus was no doubt an Asiatic, (probably an Ephesian, see below,) who had frequent business at Rome; and when he came sought out the apostle, who, it is supposed, had been confined in some *close and private prison,* (see the *preface,*) so that it was with great difficulty

he could find him out. This man had entertained the apostle when he was at Ephesus, and now he sought him out at Rome. Pure love feels no loads. Here was a true friend, one that sticketh closer than a brother.

Verse 18. *The Lord grant—that he may find mercy of the Lord*] Some think that this is a prayer to God the Father to communicate grace to him, that he might find mercy in the great day at the hand of Jesus Christ the Judge. It is probably only a Hebraism for, God grant that he may here be so saved by Divine grace, that in the great day he may receive the mercy of the Lord Jesus Christ unto eternal life. See a similar form of expression, Gen. ix. 16; xix. 24; Exod. xxiv. 1, 2.

IT is impossible to read this chapter over without feeling deeply interested for this most noble and amiable of men. To what trials did God expose him! His life was a life of perils and tribulations, his labours were superabundant, and his success all but incredible. Wherever he went, he left a track of light and life behind him. To him, as the grand instrument of God, the Gentiles, the whole habitable world, owe their salvation. Yet see him, in his old age, neglected by his friends, apparently forsaken of God, and abandoned to the hands of ruthless men; in prison and in chains; triumphing over sufferings and death; perfectly unshaken, unstumbled, with the evils with which he is obliged to contend, having the fullest persuasion of the truth of the doctrines which he had preached, and the strongest and most encouraging anticipation of the glory that was about to be revealed. He felt no evil, and he feared none. Sin had lost its power, and death its sting; the grave its victory, and hell its horrors. He had the happiness which heathenism spoke of, but could not attain, because it knew not the great *Source* whence it must proceed. This God *he* knew, feared, loved, obeyed, and was happy. Who but the righteous man can sing:—

Felix, qui potuit rerum cognoscere causas;
Atque metus omnes et inexorabile fatum
Subjecit pedibus, strepitumque Acherontis avari!—
Illum non populi fasces, non purpura regum
Flexit, et infidos agitans discordia fratres;—
Non res Romanæ, perituraque regna.

VIRG. GEORG. ii. v. 490.

No murmur is heard from his heart; he is persuaded that all things work together for good to them that love God; the *miserable uncertainty of friend-*

2

ship, the defection of cowardly brethren, and the apostasy of once zealous professors, did not move *him.* As far as it is lawful, he courts death; knowing that to be absent from the body is to be present with the Lord. Glorious system of truth by which such an apostle was formed! and glorious *apostle* by whom this system was illustrated and confirmed! The character and conduct of St. Paul must make Christianity doubly amiable to believers and highly respectable even to its enemies.

CHAPTER II.

He exhorts Timothy to constancy, fidelity, and courage; and to acquit himself as a true soldier of Jesus Christ; and patiently expect the fruit of his labours, 1–7. What the apostle's doctrine was relative to Christ, 8. He mentions his own sufferings and consolations, 9–13. What Timothy is to preach, how he is to acquit himself, and what he is to shun, 14–16. Of Hymeneus and Philetus, and their errors, 17, 18. Of the foundation of God, and its security, 19. The simile of a great house and its utensils, 20, 21. Timothy is to avoid youthful lusts, and foolish and unlearned questions, 22, 23. How he is to act in reference to false teachers, 24–26.

A. M. cir. 4069.
A. D. 65 or 66.
A. U. C. 818.
An. Imp. Neronis Cæs.
Aug. 12.

THOU therefore, ª my son, ᵇ be strong in the grace that is in Christ Jesus.

2 ᶜ And the things that thou hast heard of me ᵈ among many witnesses, ᵉ the same commit thou to faithful men, who shall be ᶠ able to teach others also.

3 ᵍ Thou therefore endure hardness, ʰ as a good soldier of Jesus Christ.

4 ⁱ No man that warreth entangleth himself with the affairs of *this* life; that he may please him who hath chosen him to be a soldier.

5 And ᵏ if a man also strive for masteries,

A. M. cir. 4069.
A. D. 65 or 66.
A. U. C. 818.
An. Imp. Neronis Cæs.
Aug. 12.

ª 1 Tim. i. 2; chap. i. 2.——ᵇ Eph. vi. 10.——ᶜ Chap. i. 13; iii. 10, 14.——ᵈ Or, *by.*——ᵉ 1 Tim. i. 18.

ᶠ 1 Tim. iii. 2; Tit. i. 9.——ᵍ Chap. i. 8; iv. 5.——ʰ 1 Tim. i. 18. ⁱ 1 Cor. ix. 25.——ᵏ 1 Cor. ix. 25, 26.

NOTES ON CHAP. II.

Verse 1. *Be strong in the grace*] Though the genuine import of the word *grace* is *favour,* yet it often implies an *active principle* communicated from God; *light* directing how to act, and *power* enabling to act according to the light.

Verse 2. *The things that thou hast heard of me*] Those doctrines which I have preached the most publicly, and which many persons can attest. But he seems to refer here to the doctrines delivered to him when, in the *presence of many witnesses,* he laid his hands upon him; see 1 Tim. vi. 12. Then the apostle gave him the proper form of sound words which he was to teach; and now he tells him to commit those truths to faithful men in the same way that they were committed to him, that the truth might be preserved in the Church, and holy men appointed successively to preach it. These truths still continued in the Church, and still there are faithful men who proclaim them. But where is the *uninterrupted* apostolical succession? Who can tell? Probably it does not exist on the face of the world. All the pretensions to it by certain Churches are as stupid as they are idle and futile. He who appeals to this for his authority as a Christian minister, had best sit down till he has made it out; and this will be by the next Greek kalends.

Verse 3. *Endure hardness*] He considers a Christian minister under the notion of a *soldier,* not so much for his continual conflicts with the world, the devil, and the flesh, for these are in a certain sense common to all Christians, but for the hardships and difficulties to which he must be exposed who faithfully preaches the Gospel of Christ.

Verse 4. *No man that warreth entangleth, &c.*] It is well remarked by *Grotius,* on this passage, that the legionary soldiers among the Romans were not permitted to engage in husbandry, merchandise, mechanical employments, or any thing that might be inconsistent with their calling. Many *canons,* at different times, have been made to prevent ecclesiastics from intermeddling with secular employments. He who *will* preach the Gospel thoroughly, and wishes to give full proof of his ministry, had need to have *no other work.* He should *be wholly in this thing,* that his profiting may appear unto all. There are many who sin against this direction. They love the world, and labour for it, and are regardless of the souls committed to their charge. But what are they, either in number or guilt, compared to the immense herd of men professing to be Christian ministers, who neither read nor study, and consequently never improve? These are too conscientious to meddle with secular affairs, and yet have no scruple of conscience to *while away time,* be among the chief in *needless self-indulgence,* and, by their burdensome and monotonous ministry, become an incumbrance to the Church! Do you inquire: In what sect or party are these to be found? I answer: In ALL. Idle drones,—

Fruges consumere nati,

"Born to consume the produce of the soil,"

disgrace every department in the Christian Church. They cannot teach because they will not learn.

Verse 5. *If a man also strive for masteries*] Εαν δε και αθλη τις· *If a man contend in the public games* —the Olympic or Isthmian games among the Greeks, so often alluded to and particularly explained in the

2

A. M. cir. 4069.
A. D. 65 or 66.
A. U. C. 818.
An. Imp. Ne-
ronis Cæs.
Aug. 12.

yet is he not crowned, except he strive lawfully.

6 [l] The [m] husbandman that laboureth must be first partaker of the fruits.

7 Consider what I say; and the Lord give thee understanding in all things.

8 Remember that Jesus Christ, [n] of the seed of David, [o] was raised from the dead [p] according to my Gospel:

9 [q] Wherein I suffer trouble, as an evil doer, [r] *even* unto bonds; [s] but the word of God is not bound.

10 Therefore [t] I endure all things for the elect's sake, [u] that they may also obtain the salvation which is in Christ Jesus with eternal glory.

A. M. cir. 4069.
A. D. 65 or 66.
A. U. C. 818.
An. Imp. Ne-
ronis Cæs.
Aug. 12.

11 [v] *It is* a faithful saying: For [w] if we be dead with *him*, we shall also live with *him*:

12 [x] If we suffer, we shall also reign with *him*: if we [y] deny *him*, he also will deny us:

13 [z] If we believe not, *yet* he abideth faithful: [a] he cannot deny himself.

14 Of these things put *them* in remembrance, [b] charging *them* before the Lord [c] that they strive not about words to no profit, *but* to the subverting of the hearers.

---

[l] 1 Cor. ix. 10.——[m] Or, *The husbandman, labouring first, must be partaker of the fruits.*——[n] Rom. i. 3, 4; Acts ii. 30; xiii. 23. [o] 1 Cor. xv. 1, 4, 20.——[p] Rom. ii. 16.——[q] Acts ix. 16; chap. i. 12.——[r] Eph. iii. 1; Phil. i. 7; Col. iv. 3, 18.——[s] Acts xxviii. 31; Eph. vi. 19, 20; Phil. i. 13, 14.

[t] Eph. iii. 13; Col. i. 24.——[u] 2 Cor. i. 6.——[v] 1 Timothy i. 15. [w] Rom. vi. 5, 8; 2 Cor. iv. 10.——[x] Rom. viii. 17; 1 Pet. iv. 13. [y] Matt. x. 33; Mark viii. 38; Luke xii. 9.——[z] Rom. iii. 3; ix. 6.——[a] Num. xxiii. 19.——[b] 1 Tim. v. 21; vi. 13; chap. iv. 1. [c] 1 Tim. i. 4; vi. 4; Tit. iii. 9, 11.

---

notes on 1 Cor. ix. 24–26, to which the reader is referred for a full illustration of this verse.

Is he not crowned] Though he may have conquered, *except he strive lawfully*—unless he enter according to the rules of the athletæ, and act as these direct. No man, however zealous he may have been, is to expect the *Well done, good and faithful servant*, from Jesus Christ, unless he have *laboured in the word and doctrine*, preached the *truth as it is in Jesus, and built up the Church* upon HIM who is its *only* FOUNDATION.

Verse 6. *The husbandman that laboureth*] That is: The *husbandman* must *first* till his ground before he can expect a crop; and he must till it according to the proper *rules* of *agriculture*, else he cannot have a crop. The *combatant* must fight and conquer, and fight according to the laws of the *agones*, before he can be crowned; so the Christian minister must labour in the spiritual vineyard, and labour too under the eye and according to the direction of his Master, before he can expect that crown of righteousness that fadeth not away.

Verse 7. *Consider what I say*] Apply my metaphors and similitudes in a proper manner.

And the Lord give thee understanding] But instead of δῴη, *may he give*, ACDEFG, several others, besides *versions* and *fathers*, have δωσει, *he will give*. Consider thou properly, and God *will* give thee a proper understanding of all things that concern thy own peace, and the peace and prosperity of his Church. *Think* as well as *read*.

Verse 8. *Remember that Jesus Christ*] The apostle seems to say: Whatever tribulations or deaths may befall us, let us remember that Jesus Christ, who was slain by the Jews, rose again from the dead, and his resurrection is the proof and pledge of ours. We also shall rise again to a life of glory and blessedness.

According to my Gospel] The false teaching of Hymeneus and Philetus stated that the resurrection was past already. Paul preached the resurrection from the dead; and founded his doctrine on the resurrection and promise of Christ. This was *his* Gospel; the other was of a different nature.

Verse 9. *Wherein I suffer trouble, as an evil doer*] This verse contains one of the proofs that this epistle was written while St. Paul was a prisoner the *second time* at Rome. See the *preface*, where this is particularly considered.

Verse 10. *For the elect's sake*] For the sake of the *Gentiles*, elected by God's goodness to enjoy every privilege formerly possessed by the Jews, and, in addition to these, all the blessings of the Gospel; the salvation of Christ *here*, and eternal glory *hereafter*.

Verse 11. *If we be dead with* him] That is: As surely as Christ rose again from the dead, so surely shall we rise again; and if we die for him, we shall surely live again with him. This, says the apostle, is πιστος ὁ λογος, a true doctrine. This is properly the import of the word; and we need not seek, as Bp. Tillotson and many others have done, for some *saying* of Christ which the apostle is supposed to be here quoting, and which he learned from tradition.

Verse 12. *If we suffer*—*with* him] These are other parts of the *true doctrine*, which the apostle mentions above.

Verse 13. *If we believe not*] Should we deny the faith and apostatize, he is the same, as true to his threatenings as to his promises; *he cannot deny*—act contrary to, himself.

Verse 14. *That they strive not about words*] WORDS, not *things*, have been a most fruitful source of contention in the Christian world; and among religious people, the principal cause of animosity has arisen from the *different manner* of apprehending the same *term*, while, in *essence*, both meant the *same thing*. All preachers and divines should be very careful, both in speaking and writing, to explain the terms they use, and never employ them in any sense but that in which they have explained them.

The subverting of the hearers.] This is the general tendency of all polemical divinity and controversial preaching, when angry passions are called in to support the doctrines of the Gospel.

A. M. cir. 4069.
A. D. 65 or 66.
A. U. C. 818.
An. Imp. Ne-
ronis Cæs.
Aug. 12.

15 Study to show thyself approved unto God, a workman that needeth not to be ashamed, rightly dividing the word of truth.

16 But [d] shun profane *and* vain babblings; for they will increase unto more ungodliness.

17 And their word will eat as doth a [e] canker: of whom is [f] Hymeneus and Philetus;

18 Who [g] concerning the truth have erred, [h] saying that the resurrection is past already; and overthrow the faith of some.

A. M. cir. 4069.
A. D. 65 or 66.
A. U. C. 818.
An. Imp Ne-
ronis Cæs.
Aug. 12.

19 Nevertheless [i] the foundation of God standeth [k] sure, having this seal, The Lord [l] knoweth them that are his. And, Let every one that nameth the name of Christ depart from iniquity.

---

[d] 1 Tim. iv. 7; vi. 20; Tit. i. 14.——[e] Or, *gangrene.*——[f] 1 Tim. i. 20.——[g] 1 Tim. vi. 21.——[h] 1 Cor. xv. 12.

[i] Matt. xxiv. 24; Rom. viii. 35; 1 John ii. 19.——[k] Or, *steady.*
[l] Nah. i. 7; John x. 14, 27; see Num. xvi. 5.

Verse 15. *Study to show thyself approved unto God*] Endeavour so to cultivate and improve thy heart and mind, that thou mayest not be a reproach to him from whom thou professest to receive thy commission.

Rightly dividing the word of truth.] It is generally supposed that the apostle alludes here to the care taken to divide the sacrifices under the law; the priests studied, in dividing the victim down the spine, to do it so scrupulously that one half of the spinal marrow should be found on each side the backbone. Probably nothing was much farther from the apostle's thoughts than this view, which is now commonly taken of the subject. Indeed this scrupulously dividing does not appear to have been any *original* ordinance among the Jews; much stress was laid upon it in *later* times, but from the beginning it was not so. The word ορθοτομειν signifies, 1. Simply to *cut straight,* or to *rectify.* 2. To *walk in the right way;* it is thus used by Gregory Nazianzen, who, in *Orat. Apol. fugæ,* opposes ορθοτομειν to κακως οδενειν, *walking in a right way* to *walking in a bad way.* Thus, καινοτομειν signifies to *walk in a new way,* and κατευθυνειν to *walk in a straight way.* See *Kypke.* Therefore, by *rightly dividing the word of truth,* we are to understand his continuing in the true doctrine, and teaching *that* to every person; and, according to our Lord's simile, *giving each his portion of meat in due season* —milk to babes, strong meat to the *full grown,* comfort to the *disconsolate,* reproof to the *irregular* and *careless;* in a word, finding out the necessities of his hearers, and preaching so as to meet those necessities.

Verse 16. *Shun profane* and *vain babblings*] This is the character he gives of the preaching of the false teachers. Whatever was not agreeable to the *doctrine of truth* was, in the sight of God, *empty* and *profane babbling;* engendering nothing but *ungodliness,* and daily *increasing* in that.

Verse 17. *Their word will eat as doth a canker*] 'Ως γαγγραινα' As a gangrene; i. e. as a *mortification in the flesh,* where the circulation is entirely stopped, and putrefaction takes place, which continues to corrupt all the circumjacent flesh, spreading more and more till death takes place, unless stopped by a timely and judicious application of medicine. Such is the influence of *false doctrine;* it fixes its *mortal seed* in the soul, which continues to *corrupt* and *assimilate every thing to itself,* till, if not prevented by a timely application of the *word of life,* under the direction of the heavenly *Physician,* it terminates in the bitter pains of an *eternal death.* To such a *gangrene* the apostle compares the corrupt doctrines of *Hymeneus* and *Philetus.*

Verse 18. *Who concerning the truth have erred*] They had the *truth,* but *erred* or *wandered from it,* saying the resurrection was already past, and thus denying the resurrection of the body, and, by consequence, future rewards and punishments; and this necessarily sapped the foundation of all religion: and thus the gangrene had, in reference to their unhappy votaries, a rapid and unchecked operation.

Verse 19. *The foundation of God standeth sure*] The word θεμελιος signifies literally a *foundation,* and especially the *foundation* of a *building;* and metaphorically, the *building* itself, and often a *noble mansion* or *palace.* In this place the apostle compares the religion of Christ to a *great* or *noble mansion.* See ver. 20. And as this religion is *founded* on the *authority* and *power* of the *Almighty,* it necessarily must *stand sure* and be *permanent.* This house has an *inscription* on it, for so σφραγις, seal, is frequently understood; and this is evidently an allusion to the ancient temples. Above the door of the temple of Delphi there was the Greek word ει, *thou art,* on which Plutarch has written an express treatise. In many of the Mohammedan mosques the *walls are covered with inscriptions,* which are ordinarily sentences taken from the *Koran,* relative to the majesty of God, or the nature of his worship. And we know that there was an *inscription* on the mitre of the high priest among the Jews, viz: קדש ליהוה *kodesh laihovah,* "Holiness to the Lord;" Exod. xxviii. 36; xxxix. 30. See also Zech. xiv. 20. And this inscription may here be represented as being made with the *seal* of God, for he stamps this on all things belonging to himself and his worship.

But some suppose θεμελιος here to signify a *contract* or *covenant* by which two parties are bound to fulfil certain conditions and duties, the obligation to which each takes on him by *sealing* the instrument with his seal. Among the Asiatics, these seals have scarcely ever any *image* or *figure* on them, but always some very *expressive inscription.* I have seen many of these, and several of them are now before me. The *twofold* inscription, i. e. one on the seal of each party, may be here alluded to; that on God's seal is, Εγνω Κυριος τους οντας αυτου' *The Lord approveth of them that are his.* That on the seal of his followers is, Αποστητω απο αδικιας πας ο ονομαζων το ονομα Κυριου. *Let every one who nameth the name of the Lord* (every Christian) *depart from iniquity.* Thus each has his peculiar inscription.

Κυριου, Lord, instead of Χριστου, Christ, is the reading of almost all the MSS. of importance, and the principal versions.

   2

A. M. cir. 4069.
A. D. 65 or 66.
A. U. C. 818.
An. Imp. Neronis Cæs.
Aug. 12.

20 [m] But in a great house there are not only vessels of gold and of silver, but also of wood and of earth; [n] and some to honour, and some to dishonour.

21 [o] If a man therefore purge himself from these, he shall be a vessel unto honour, sanctified, and meet for the master's use, *and* [p] prepared unto every good work.

22 Flee also youthful lusts; but [q] follow righteousness, faith, charity, peace, with them that [r] call on the Lord [s] out of a pure heart.

23 But [t] foolish and unlearned questions avoid, knowing that they do gender strifes.

24 And [u] the servant of the Lord must not strive; but be gentle unto all *men*, [v] apt to teach, [w] patient.

25 [x] In meekness instructing those that oppose themselves; [y] if God peradventure will give them repentance [z] to the acknowledging of the truth;

26 And *that* they may [a] recover themselves [b] out of the snare of the devil, who [c] are taken captive by him at his will.

A. M. cir. 4069.
A. D. 65 or 66.
A. U. C. 818.
An. Imp. Neronis Cæs.
Aug. 12.

---

[m] 1 Timothy iii. 15.——[n] Romans ix. 21.——[o] See Isa. liii. 11
[p] Chap. iii. 17; Tit. iii. 1.——[q] 1 Tim. vi. 11.——[r] Acts ix. 14;
1 Cor. i. 2.——[s] 1 Tim. i. 5, iv. 12.——[t] 1 Tim. i. 4, iv. 7, vi.
4; ver 16; Tit. iii. 9.

[u] Tit. iii. 2.——[v] 1 Tim. iii. 2, 3; Tit. i, 9.——[w] Or, *forbearing.*——[x] Gal. vi. 1; 1 Tim. vi. 11; 1 Pet. iii. 15.——[y] Acts viii.
22.——[z] 1 Tim. ii. 4; chapter iii. 7; Titus i. 1.——[a] Gr. *awake.*
[b] 1 Tim. iii. 7.——[c] Gr. *taken alive.*

The Lord knoweth] i. e. Approves, watches over, and *provides for, them that are his* true followers. To this his followers most cheerfully subscribe, and say *Let every one that nameth this Lord avoid every appearance of evil.*

Verse 20. *But in a great house*] Here the apostle carries on the allusion introduced in the preceding verse As the *foundation of God* refers to God's *building,* i. e. the whole system of Christianity, so here the *great house* is to be understood of the same; and the different kinds of vessels mean the different teachers, as well as the different kinds of members. In this sacred house at Ephesus there were *vessels of gold and silver*—eminent, holy, sincere, and useful teachers and members, and also *vessels of wood and of earth*—false and heretical teachers, such as Hymeneus and Philetus, and their followers. There are also in such houses vessels employed, some in a more *honourable,* others in a *less honourable, office.* To these he seems also to compare the same persons.

Verse 21 *If a man therefore purge himself from these*] He that takes heed to his ways and to his doctrines, and walks with God, will separate himself, not only from all *false doctrine,* but from all *wicked men,* and thus be sanctified and proper to be employed by the Master in every good word and work The apostle has not made the application of these different similes, and it is very difficult to tell what he means.

Verse 22 *Flee also youthful lusts*] Not only all irregular and sensual desires, but *pride, ambition,* and, above all, *the lust of power,* to which most men will sacrifice all other propensities, their ease, pleasure, health, &c. This is the most bewitching passion in the human heart. Both in *Church* and *state* it is ruinous; but particularly so in the former Timothy was not between thirty and forty years of age, the very age in which *ambition* and the *love of power* most generally prevail. *Carnal pleasures* are the sins of *youth; ambition* and the *love of power* the sins of *middle age; covetousness* and *carking cares* the crimes of old age.

Follow righteousness] Flee from sin, pursue goodness. *Righteousness*—whatever is just, holy, and

innocent. *Faith*—fidelity both to God and man, improving that grace by which thy soul may be saved, and faithfully discharging the duties of thy office, that thou mayest save the souls of others. *Charity*—love to God and man. *Peace* among all the members of the Church, and as far as possible with all men; but especially among those who invoke the Lord out of a pure desire to glorify his name.

Verse 23. *Foolish and unlearned questions*] See the notes on 1 Tim. i. 4; iv. 7; and Tit. iii. 9.

Verse 24. *The servant of the Lord must not strive*] See on 1 Tim. iii. 2, 3.

Verse 25. *Those that oppose*] Αντιδιατιθεμενους. This seems to refer to those who opposed the apostle's *authority;* and hence the propriety of the allusion to the *rebellion* of Korah and his company. See observations at the end of the chapter.

If God peradventure] He was to use every means which he had reason to believe God might bless; and the apostle intimates that, bad as they were, they were not out of the reach of God's mercy.

Verse 26. *And that they may recover themselves*] The construction of this verse is extremely difficult, though the sense given by our translation is plain enough. I shall set down the original, and the principal English translations —

Και ανανηψωσιν εκ της του διαβολου παγιδος, εζωγρημενοι υπ' αυτου εις το εκεινου θελημα.

𝔄𝔫𝔡 𝔱𝔥𝔢𝔦 𝔯𝔦𝔰𝔢 𝔞𝔤𝔢𝔦𝔫 𝔣𝔯𝔬 𝔰𝔫𝔞𝔞𝔯𝔦𝔰 𝔬𝔣 𝔱𝔥𝔢 𝔡𝔢𝔟𝔶𝔩, 𝔬𝔣 𝔴𝔥𝔬𝔪𝔢 𝔱𝔥𝔢𝔦 𝔟𝔢𝔫 𝔥𝔬𝔩𝔡𝔢 𝔠𝔞𝔭𝔱𝔶𝔣𝔣𝔦𝔰 𝔞𝔱 𝔥𝔦𝔰 𝔴𝔦𝔩𝔩𝔢.—WICLIF, First *translation* into English, 1378.

And to turne agayne from the snare of devell, which are holden in prison of him at his will.—COVERDALE. First *printed* English Bible, 1535

That they may come to themselves agayne out of the snare of the devyll, which are now taken of him at hys will.—EDWARD VIth's Bible, by *Becke,* 1549.

And they may recover their senses to perform his will, after being rescued alive by the servant of the Lord out of the snare of the devil.—WAKEFIELD; who refers αυτου, *him,* to *the servant of the Lord,* verse 24.

2

And being caught alive by him out of the snare of the devil, they may awake to do his will.—MACKNIGHT; who remarks that αυτου, the relative, means the servant of the Lord; and εκεινου,· the demonstrative, refers to God, mentioned ver. 15.

I leave these different translations with the reader.

I HAVE referred, in the preceding notes, to *inscriptions* which appear on the buildings and coins of the Asiatics; such inscriptions are, in general, very curious, and carry with them a considerable show of piety to God, in the acknowledgment of his providence and mercy. I shall quote one merely as a curiosity, without supposing it to be immediately applicable to the illustration of the text.

There is extant a gold circular coin of the Great Mogul *Shah Jehan,* struck at Delhi, A. H. 1062, A. D. 1651, five inches and a half in diameter; on each side of this coin is a square, the angles of which touch the periphery; within this square, and in the segments, there are the following inscriptions:—

1. Within the square, on one side,

The bright star of religion, Mohammed (a second Sahib Kiran) Shah Jehan, the victorious emperor.

2. In the segment on the upper side of the square,

The impression upon this coin of 200 mohurs, was struck through the favour of God.

3. On the lateral segment to the left,

By the second Sahib Kiran, Shah Jehan, the defender of the faith.

4. On the bottom segment,

May the golden countenance from the sculpture of this coin enlighten the world.

5. On the lateral segment to the right,

As long as *the splendid face of the moon is illuminated by the rays of the sun!*

1. On the reverse, within the square,

There is no god but God; and Mohammed is the prophet of God. Struck in the capital of Shah Jehanabad, A. H. 1062.

2. On the top of the square,

Religion was illuminated by the truth of Abu Beker.

3. On the left hand compartment,

The faith was strengthened by the justice of Omar.

4. On the bottom compartment,

Piety was refreshed by the modesty and mildness of Othman.

5. On the right hand compartment,

The world was enlightened by the learning of Aly.

On these inscriptions it may be just necessary to observe that Abu Beker, Omar, Othman, and Aly, were the four *khalifs* who succeeded Mohammed. Abu Beker was the father of *Ayesha,* one of Mohammed's wives. *Othman* was son-in-law of Mohammed, having married his two daughters, *Rakiah,* and *Omal-Calthoom.* And *Aly,* son of *Abi Taleb,* Mohammed's uncle, was also one of the sons-in-law of Mohammed, having married *Fatima,* the daughter of his favourite wife, *Ayesha.* The Ottoman empire was not so called from *Othman,* the third khalif, but from Ottoman, the successful chief, who conquered a small part of the Grecian empire in Asia, and thus laid the foundation for the Turkish.

Grotius and others have supposed that the apostle alludes to the custom of putting an inscription on the foundation stone of a city or other building, giving an account of the time in which it was founded, built, &c. Sometimes engraved stones were placed over the principal gates of cities and fortresses, particularly in the east, specifying the date of erection, repairs, &c., and containing some religious sentiment or verse from the Koran. But I do not think it likely that the apostle refers to any thing of this kind. There appears to be an allusion here to the *rebellion* of Korah and his company against the *authority* of Moses, Num. xvi., where, ver. 5, it is said: *The Lord will show who are his:* here the words of the Septuagint are nearly the same that the apostle uses in this verse, εγνω ὁ Θεος τους οντας αυτου· God knoweth or approveth of them that are his. And the words in ver. 26, *Depart from the tents of these wicked men,* are similar to those of the apostle, *Let every one that nameth the name of the Lord depart from iniquity.* We may therefore take it for granted that those false teachers, the chief of whom were *Hymeneus* and *Philetus,* had risen up against the *authority* of St. Paul; and he, in effect, informs Timothy here that God will deal with *them* as he did with Korah, Dathan, and Abiram, and their company. And as the true Israelites were to *separate themselves from the tents of those wicked men,* so he and the believers at Ephesus were to hold no sort of communion with those workers of iniquity. This subject he farther illustrates by a contract between two parties, each of which sets his seal to the instrument, the seal bearing the motto peculiar to the party. This I conceive to be the meaning; but the common mode of interpretation will, it is probable, be most commonly followed.

CHAPTER III.

Dangerous times in the latter days, from the apostasy and wickedness of men, of whom an affecting description is given, 1–7. It shall happen to them as to Jannes and Jambres, who withstood Moses, 8, 9. The apostle speaks of his persecutions and sufferings, and shows that all those who will live a godly life must suffer persecution, 10–12, because evil men and seducers will wax worse and worse, 13. Timothy is exhorted to continue in the truths he had received, having known the Scriptures from a child, 14, 15. All Scripture is given by Divine inspiration, 16, 17.

     2

A. M. cir. 4069.
A. D. 65 or 66.
A. U. C. 818.
An. Imp. Ne-
ronis Cæs.
Aug. 12.

THIS know also, that [a] in the last days perilous times shall come.

2 For men shall be [b] lovers of their own selves, [c] covetous, [d] boasters, [e] proud, [f] blasphemers, [g] disobedient to parents, unthankful, unholy,

3 [h] Without natural affection, [i] truce-breakers, [k] false accusers, [l] incontinent, fierce, despisers of those that are good,

4 [m] Traitors, heady, high-minded, [n] lovers of pleasures more than lovers of God;

5 Having a form of godliness, but [o] denying

A. M. cir. 4069.
A. D. 65 or 66.
A. U. C. 818.
An. Imp. Ne-
ronis Cæs.
Aug. 12.

---

[a] 1 Tim. iv. 1; chap. iv. 3; 2 Pet. iii. 3; 1 John ii. 18; Jude 18.——[b] Phil. ii. 21.——[c] 2 Pet. ii. 3.——[d] Jude 16.——[e] 1 Tim. vi. 4.——[f] 1 Tim. i. 20; 2 Pet. ii. 12; Jude 10.

[g] Rom. i. 30.——[h] Rom. i. 31.——[i] Rom. i. 31; or, *makebates.* [k] Tit. ii. 3.——[l] 2 Pet. iii. 3.——[m] 2 Pet. ii. 10.——[n] Phil. iii. 19; 2 Pet. ii. 13, &c.; Jude 4, 19.——[o] 1 Tim. v. 8; Tit. i. 16.

NOTES ON CHAP. III.

Verse 1. In the last days] This often means the days of the Messiah, and is sometimes extended in its signification to the destruction of Jerusalem, as this was properly the *last days* of the Jewish state. But the phrase may mean any *future* time, whether *near* or *distant.*

Verse 2. For men shall be] The description in this and the following verses the Papists apply to the Protestants; the Protestants in their turn apply it to the Papists; *Schoettgen* to the *Jews*; and others to *heretics* in general. There have been both teachers and people in every age of the Church, and in every age of the world, to whom these words may be most legitimately applied. Both Catholics and Protestants have been lovers of their own selves, &c.; but it is probable that the apostle had some particular age in view, in which there should appear some very essential corruption of Christianity.

Lovers of their own selves] Φιλαυτοι· *Selfish*, studious of their own interest, and regardless of the welfare of all mankind.

Covetous] Φιλαργυροι· *Lovers of money*, because of the influence which riches can procure.

Boasters] Αλαζονες· Vainglorious: self-assuming; valuing themselves beyond all others.

Proud] Ὑπερηφανοι· Airy, light, trifling persons; those who love to make a show—who are all *outside;* from ὑπερ, *above*, and φαινω, *to show.*

Blasphemers] Βλασφημοι· Those who speak *impiously* of God and sacred things, and *injuriously* of men.

Disobedient to parents] Γονευσιν απειθεις· Headstrong children, whom their parents cannot *persuade.*

Unthankful] Αχαριστοι· Persons without grace, or gracefulness; who think they have a right to the services of all men, yet feel no obligation, and consequently no gratitude.

Unholy] Ανοσιοι· Without piety; having no heart reverence for God.

Verse 3. Without natural affection] Αστοργοι· Without that affection which *parents* bear to their *young*, and which the *young* bear to their *parents.* An affection which is common to every class of *animals*; consequently, men without it are worse than *brutes.*

Truce-breakers] Ασπονδοι· From *a, negative*, and σπονδη, a *libation*, because in making treaties *libations* both of *blood* and *wine* were poured out. The word means those who are bound by no promise, held by no engagement, obliged by no oath; persons who

readily promise any thing, because they never intend to perform.

False accusers] Διαβολοι· *Devils;* but properly enough rendered *false accusers*, for this is a principal work of the devil. Slanderers; striving ever to ruin the characters of others.

Incontinent] Ακρατεις· From *a, negative*, and κρατος, *power.* Those who, having sinned away their power of self-government, want strength to govern their appetites; especially those who are slaves to uncleanness.

Fierce] Ανημεροι· From *a, negative*, and ἡμερος, *mild* or *gentle.* Wild, impetuous, whatever is contrary to *pliability* and gentleness.

Despisers of those that are good] Αφιλαγαθοι· *Not lovers of good men.* Here is a remarkable advantage of the *Greek* over the *English* tongue, *one word* of the former expressing five or six of the latter. Those who *do not love the good* must be radically bad themselves.

Verse 4. Traitors] Προδοται· From προ, *before*, and διδωμι, *to deliver up.* Those who deliver up to an enemy the person who has put his life in their hands; such as the Scots of 1648, who *delivered up* into the hands of his enemies their unfortunate *countryman* and *king*, Charles the First; a stain which no lapse of ages can wipe out.

Heady] Προπετεις· From προ, *forwards*, and πιπτω, *to fall;* headstrong, precipitate, rash, inconsiderate.

High-minded] Τετυφωμενοι· From τυφος, *smoke;* the frivolously aspiring; those who are full of themselves, and empty of all good.

Lovers of pleasures more than lovers of God] This is nervously and beautifully expressed in the Greek, φιληδονοι μαλλον η φιλοθεοι, lovers of pleasure rather than lovers of God; i. e. pleasure, sensual gratification, is their god; and this they love and serve; God they do not.

Verse 5. Having a form of godliness] The original word μορφωσις signifies a *draught, sketch*, or *summary*, and will apply well to those who have all their religion in their creed, confession of faith, catechism, bodies of divinity, &c., while destitute of the life of God in their souls; and are not only destitute of this life, but deny that such life or power is *here* to be experienced or known. They have religion in their creed, but none in their hearts. And perhaps to their *summary* they add a decent round of religious observances. *From such turn away*—not only do not imitate them, but have no kind of fellowship with them; they are a dangerous people, and but seldom suspected, because their outside is fair.

2

A. M. cir. 4069.
A. D. 65 or 66.
A. U. C. 818.
An. Imp. Ne-
ronis Cæs.
Aug. 12.

the power thereof: ᵖ from such turn away.

6 For �q of this sort are they which creep into houses, and lead captive silly women laden with sins, led away with divers lusts,

7 Ever learning, and never able ʳ to come to the knowledge of the truth.

8 ˢ Now as Jannes and Jambres withstood Moses, so do these also resist the truth:

ᵗ men of corrupt minds, ᵘ reprobate ᵛ concerning the faith.

9 But they shall proceed no farther: for their folly shall be manifest unto all *men*, ʷ as theirs also was.

10 ˣ But ʸ thou hast fully known my doctrine, manner of life, purpose, faith, long-suffering, charity, patience,

11 Persecutions, afflictions, which came unto me ᶻ at Antioch, ᵃ at Iconium, ᵇ at Lystra,

A. M. cir. 4069.
A. D. 65 or 66.
A. U. C. 818.
An. Imp. Ne-
ronis Cæs.
Aug. 12.

ᵖ 2 Thess. iii. 6; 1 Tim. vi. 5.——q Matt. xxiii. 14; Tit. i. 11. ʳ 1 Tim. ii. 4.——ˢ Exod. vii. 11.——ᵗ 1 Tim. vi. 5.——ᵘ Rom. i. 28; 2 Cor. xiii. 5; Tit. i. 16.——ᵛ Or, *of no judgment*.

ʷ Exod. vii. 12; viii. 18; ix. 11.——ˣ Phil. ii. 22; 1 Tim. iv. 6.——ʸ Or, *thou hast been a diligent follower of.*——ᶻ Acts xiii. 45, 50.——ᵃ Acts xiv. 2, 5.——ᵇ Acts xiv. 19, &c.

Verse 6. *For of this sort are they*] He here refers to *false teachers* and their *insinuating manners*, practising upon weak women, who, seeing in them such a semblance of piety, entertain them with great eagerness, and at last become partakers with them in their impurities. Among the Jews there are remarkable cases of this kind on record, and not a few of them among the full fed monks of the Romish Church. But in what sect or party have not such teachers been occasionally found? yet neither *Judaism, Protestantism*, nor *Roman Catholicism* makes any provision for such men.

Verse 7. *Ever learning*] From their false teachers, *and never able to come to the knowledge of the truth*, because that teaching never leads to the *truth;* for, although there was a *form of godliness*, which gave them a sort of *authority* to teach, yet, as they denied the *power of godliness*, they never could bring their votaries to the knowledge of the saving power of Christianity.

There are many professors of Christianity still who answer the above description. They hear, repeatedly hear, it may be, good sermons; but, as they seldom meditate on what they hear, they derive little profit from the ordinances of God. They have no more grace *now* than they had *several years ago*, though hearing all the while, and perhaps not wickedly departing from the Lord. They do not meditate, they do not think, they do not reduce what they hear to practice; therefore, even under the preaching of an apostle, they could not become wise to salvation.

Verse 8. *Now as Jannes and Jambres withstood Moses*] This refers to the history of the Egyptian magicians, given in Exod. vii., where see the notes, and particularly the concluding observations at the end of that chapter, where several things are said concerning these two men.

Men of corrupt minds] It appears as if the apostle were referring still to some Judaizing teachers who were perverting the Church with their doctrines, and loudly calling in question the authority and doctrine of the apostle.

Reprobate concerning the faith.] Αδοκιμοι· Undiscerning or *untried;* they are base metal, unstamped; and should not pass current, because not standard. This metaphor is frequent in the sacred writings.

Verse 9. *But they shall proceed no farther*] Such

teaching and teachers shall never be able *ultimately* to prevail against the truth; for the foundation of God standeth sure.

Their folly shall be manifest] As the Scriptures, which are the only rule of morals and doctrine, shall ever be preserved; so, sooner or later, all false doctrines shall be tried by *them:* and the folly of men, setting up their wisdom against the wisdom of God, must become manifest to all. False doctrine cannot prevail long where the sacred Scriptures are read and studied. Error prevails only where the book of God is withheld from the people. The religion that fears the Bible is not the religion of God. Is *Popery* or *Protestantism* this religion?

Verse 10. *Thou hast fully known my doctrine*] And having had the opportunity of knowing me, the *doctrine* I preached, my *conduct* founded on these doctrines, the *object* I have in view by my preaching, my *fidelity* to God and to my trust, my *long-suffering* with those who walked disorderly, and opposed themselves to the truth, and did what they could to lessen my authority and render it suspected, my *love* to them and to the world in general, and my *patience* in all my adversities; thou art capable of judging between me and the false teachers, and canst easily discern the difference between their doctrines, conduct, motives, temper, spirit, &c., and mine.

Verse 11. *Persecutions—which came unto me at Antioch*] The *Antioch* mentioned here was Antioch in Pisidia, to which place Paul and Barnabas came in their first apostolic progress, and where Paul delivered that memorable discourse which is preserved in the 13th chapter of Acts, ver. 16–43. In this city, it is said, *the Jews stirred up the devout and honourable women, and the chief men of the city, and raised persecution against Paul and Barnabas, and expelled them out of their coasts; but they shook off the dust of their feet against them, and came to Iconium*, Acts xiii. 50, 51. Here *there was an assault made both of the Gentiles and also of the Jews with their rulers, to treat them despitefully, and to stone them*, and they fled unto *Lystra* and *Derbe; and there came thither certain Jews, who persuaded the people, and having stoned Paul, drew him out of the city, supposing he had been dead*. The historian informs us that his life was miraculously restored, and that he departed thence, and came to *Derbe*, and afterwards returned to

2

A. M. cir. 4069.
A. D. 65 or 66.
A. U. C. 818.
An. Imp. Ne-
ronis Cæs.
Aug. 12.

what persecutions I endured : but c out of *them* all the Lord delivered me.

12 Yea, and d all that will live godly in Christ Jesus shall suffer persecution.

13 e But evil men and seducers shall wax worse and worse, deceiving, and being deceived.

14 But f continue thou in the things which thou hast learned and hast been assured of,

A. M. cir. 4069.
A. D. 65 or 66.
A. U. C. 818.
An. Imp. Ne-
ronis Cæs.
Aug. 12.

knowing of whom thou hast learned *them* ;

15 And that from a child thou hast known g the Holy Scriptures, which are able to make thee wise unto salvation through faith which is in Christ Jesus.

16 h All Scripture *is* given by inspiration of God, i and *is* profitable for doctrine, for reproof, for correction, for instruction in righteousness ;

17 k That the man of God may be perfect, i throughly m furnished unto all good works.

---

c Psa. xxxiv. 19 ; 2 Cor. i. 10 ; chap. iv. 7.——d Psa. xxxiv. 19 ; Acts xiv. 22 ; Matt. xvi. 24 ; Josh. xvii. 14 ; 1 Cor. xv. 19 ; 1 Thess. iii. 3.

e 2 Thess. ii. 11 ; 1 Tim. iv. 1 ; chap. ii. 16.——f Chap. i. 13 ; ii. 2.——g John v. 39.——h 2 Peter i. 20, 21.——i Romans xv. 4. k 1 Tim. vi. 11.——l Or, *perfected.*——m Chap. ii. 21.

Lystra, Iconium, and *Antioch,* where they had lately been so grievously persecuted. See Acts xiv. 5, 6, 19-21. These are the persecutions, &c., to which the apostle alludes ; and we find that he mentions them here precisely in the same *order* in which, according to the relation of St. Luke, they occurred. Now it is said here that Timothy *fully knew all these things ;* and we may naturally suppose they could not be unknown to him, when it is evident he was either a native of, or resided in, those parts ; for when the apostle, sometime after the above, visited Derbe and Lystra, *behold, a certain disciple was there named Timotheus, well reported of by the brethren that were at Lystra and Iconium ;* Acts xvi. 1, 2. As these things happened in his own neighbourhood, Timothy must have known them ; for a person who had such a religious education as he had could not be unacquainted with these persecutions, especially as we may believe that his mother and grandmother had been converts to Christianity at that time. See several useful remarks in Dr. Paley's *Horæ Paulinæ,* on these circumstances, page 312.

Verse 12. *All that will live godly*] So opposite to the spirit and practice of the world is the whole of Christianity, that he who gives himself entirely up to God, making the Holy Scriptures the rule of his words and actions, will be less or more reviled and persecuted. " If religion gives no quarter to vice, the vicious will give no quarter to religion and its professors."

Verse 13. *Evil men and seducers shall wax worse*] They will yet get on for a season, deceiving themselves and deceiving others ; but, by and by, *their folly will become manifest to all,* ver. 9. The word γοητες, which we render *seducers,* signifies *jugglers, pretenders to magical arts ;* probably persons dealing in *false miracles,* with whom the Church in all ages has been not a little disgraced.

Verse 14. *But continue thou*] No man, however well instructed in the things of God, or grounded in Divine grace, is out of the reach of temptation, apostasy, and final ruin ; hence the necessity of watching unto prayer, depending upon God, continuing in the faith, and persevering unto the end.

Verse 15. *From a child thou hast known the Holy Scriptures*] The early religious education of Timothy has been already sufficiently noticed ; see chap. i. 5,

and the *preface* to the first epistle. St. Paul introduces this circumstance again here for the confirmation of Timothy's faith. He had learned the doctrines of Christianity from a genuine apostle ; and, as Christianity is founded on the law and the prophets, Timothy was able to compare its doctrines with all that had been *typified* and *predicted,* and consequently was *assured* that the Christian religion was true.

Able to make thee wise unto salvation] The apostle is here evidently speaking of the Jewish Scriptures ; and he tells us that *they are able to make us wise unto salvation* provided we have *faith in Jesus Christ.* This is the simple use of the *Old Testament.* No soul of man can be made wise unto salvation by it, but as he refers all to Christ Jesus. The Jews are unsaved though they know these Scriptures, because they believe not in Christ ; for Christ is the end of the law for the justification of all that believe.

Verse 16. *All Scripture is given by inspiration of God*] This sentence is not well translated ; the original πασα γραφη θεοπνευστος ωφελιμος προς διδασκαλιαν, κ. τ. λ. should be rendered : *Every writing Divinely inspired is profitable for doctrine, &c.* The particle και, *and,* is omitted by almost all the *versions* and many of the *fathers,* and certainly does not agree well with the text. The apostle is here, beyond all controversy, speaking of the writings of the *Old Testament,* which, because they came by Divine inspiration, he terms the *Holy Scriptures,* ver. 15 ; and it is of *them* alone that this passage is to be understood ; and although all the New Testament came by as direct an inspiration as the Old, yet, as it was not collected at that time, nor indeed complete, the apostle could have no reference to it.

The doctrine of the *inspiration of the sacred writings* has been a subject of much discussion, and even controversy, among Christians. There are two principal opinions on the subject : 1. That *every thought* and *word* were inspired by God, and that the writer did nothing but merely write as the Spirit dictated. 2. That God gave the whole *matter,* leaving the inspired writers to their *own language ;* and hence the great variety of style and different modes of expression. But as I have treated this subject at large in my *Introduction to the Four Gospels and Acts of the Apostles,* I must refer the reader to that work.

Is profitable for doctrine] To teach the *will of God*, and to point out Jesus Christ till he should come.

For reproof] To *convince* men of the truth ; and to *confound* those who should deny it, particularly the *Jews*.

For correction] Προς επανορθωσιν· For *restoring things* to their proper *uses* and *places*, correcting false notions and mistaken views.

Instruction in righteousness] Προς παιδειαν την εν δικαιοσυνη. For communicating all *initiatory* religious knowledge ; for *schooling mankind*. All this is perfectly true of the Jewish Scriptures ; and let faith in Christ Jesus be *added*, see ver. 15, and then all that is spoken in the following verse will be literally accomplished.

Verse 17. *That the man of God*] The preacher of righteousness, the minister of the Gospel, the person who derives his commission from God, and always appears as *his* herald and servant.

May be perfect] Αρτιος· From αρω, to *fit* or *adapt*. It properly signifies an *integer* or *whole number* in arithmetic, to which nothing needs to be added to make it complete.

Throughly furnished] Εξηρτισμενος· From εξ, *intensive*, and αρτιος, *complete* ; see above. Not only complete in himself as to his *integrity*, religious *knowledge*, *faith* in Jesus, and *love* to God and man ; but that he should have *all those qualifications* which are necessary to *complete* the *character*, and insure the success of a *preacher*, of the Gospel. Timothy was to teach, reprove, correct, and instruct others ; and was to be to them a pattern of good works.

From what the apostle says here concerning the qualifications of a Christian minister, we may well exclaim : Who is capable of these things ? Is it such a person as has not intellect sufficient for a common trade or calling ? No. A preacher of the Gospel should be a man of the soundest sense, the most cultivated mind, the most extensive experience, one who is deeply taught of God, and who has deeply studied man ; one who has prayed much, read much, and studied much ; one who takes up his work as from God, does it as before God, and refers all to the glory of God ; one who abides under the inspiration of the Almighty, and who has hidden the word of God in his heart, that he might not sin against him. No minister formed by *man* can ever be such as is required here. The *school of Christ*, and that alone, can ever form such a preacher.

CHAPTER IV.

The apostle charges Timothy to be diligent, incessant, and faithful in his preaching ; to watch, suffer patiently, and give full proof of his ministry, 1–5. He predicts his own approaching death, and expresses the strongest confidence of being eternally happy, 6–8. Desires Timothy to come and see him ; shows that several had forsaken him, that others were gone to different districts, and that he had only Luke with him, 9–12. Desires him to bring the cloak, book, and parchments, which he had left at Troas, 13. Of Alexander the coppersmith's opposition, 14, 15. Tells Timothy how he was deserted by all when obliged to make his first defence before Nero ; how God supported him, and the confidence with which he was inspired, 16–18. Salutations to different persons at Ephesus, and from different persons at Rome, 19–21. The apostolical benediction, 22.

A. M. cir. 4069.
A. D. 65 or 66.
A. U. C. 818.
An. Imp. Neronis Cæs.
Aug. 12.

I [a] CHARGE *thee* therefore before God, and the Lord Jesus Christ, [b] who shall judge the quick and the dead at his appearing and his kingdom ;

2 Preach the word ; be instant in season, out of season ; reprove, [c] rebuke, [d] exhort with all longsuffering and doctrine.

3 [e] For the time will come when they will

A. M. cir. 4069.
A. D. 65 or 66.
A. U. C. 818.
An. Imp. Neronis Cæs.
Aug. 12.

---

[a] 1 Tim. v. 21 ; vi. 13, chap. ii. 14.——[b] Acts x. 42.——[c] 1 Tim.

v. 20 ; Titus i. 13 ; ii. 15.——[d] 1 Tim. iv. 13.——[e] Chap. iii. 1.

NOTES ON CHAP. IV.

Verse 1. *I charge thee therefore before God*] Whose *herald* thou art ; and *before the Lord Jesus Christ*, whose salvation thou art to proclaim, and who is coming to *judge the world*—all that shall be found then *alive*, and all that have *died* from the foundation of the world.

Verse 2. *Preach the word*] Κηρυξον τον λογον· *Proclaim the doctrine*, the doctrine of Christ crucified, for the sins of the whole world ; the doctrine, that the Gentiles are invited to be fellow heirs with the Jews, and that for Jews and Gentiles there is no salvation but by faith in Christ.

Be instant in season, out of season] Επιστηθι ευκαιρως, ακαιρως. Be urgent whether the times be *prosperous* or *adverse*, whenever there is an *opportunity* ; and when there is *none*, strive to make *one*. The Judge is at the door, and to every man eternity is at hand ! Wherever thou meetest a sinner, speak to him the word of reconciliation. Do not be contented with *stated times* and *accustomed places* merely ; all *time* and *place* belong to God, and are proper for his work. Wherever it can be done, there it should be done. Satan will omit neither time nor place where he can destroy. Omit thou none where thou mayest be the instrument of salvation to any.

Reprove] Ελεγξον· *Confute*, the false teacher.

Rebuke] Επιτιμησον· Reprove *cuttingly* and *severely* those who will not abandon their sins.

Exhort] Παρακαλεσον· *Comfort* the feeble-minded, the diffident and the tempted.

A. M. cir. 4069.
A. D. 65 or 66.
A. U. C. 818.
An. Imp. Ne-
ronis Cæs.
Aug. 12.

not endure [f] sound doctrine; [g] but after their own lusts shall they heap to themselves teachers, having itching ears;

4 And they shall turn away *their* ears from the truth, and [h] shall be turned unto fables.

5 But watch thou in all things, [i] endure afflictions, do the work of [k] an evangelist, [l] make full proof of thy ministry.

6 For [m] I am now ready to be offered, and the time of [n] my departure is at hand.

7 [o] I have fought a good fight, I have finished *my* course, I have kept the faith:

8 Henceforth there is laid up for me [p] a crown of righteousness, which the Lord, the righteous Judge, shall give me [q] at that day: and not to

A. M. cir. 4069.
A. D. 65 or 66.
A. U. C. 818.
An. Imp. Ne-
ronis Cæs.
Aug. 12.

---

[f] 1 Tim. i. 10.——[g] Chap. iii. 6.——[h] 1 Tim. i. 4; iv. 7; Tit. i. 14.——[i] Chap. i. 8; ii. 3.——[k] Acts xxi. 8; Eph. iv. 11.——[l] Or, *fulfil*; Rom. xv. 19; Col. i. 25; iv. 17.——[m] Phil. ii. 17.

[n] Phil. i. 23; see 2 Pet. i. 14.——[o] 1 Cor. ix. 24, 25; Phil. iii. 14; 1 Tim. vi. 12; Heb. xii. 1.——[p] 1 Cor. ix. 25; James i. 12; 1 Pet. v. 4; Rev. ii. 10.——[q] Chap. i. 12.

With all long-suffering] In reference to *each* and *all* of these cases.

And doctrine.] The *different modes of teaching* suited to each.

Verse 3. For the time will come] There is a time coming to the Church when men will not hear the *practical* truths of the Gospel, when they will prefer speculative opinions, which either do no good to the soul, or corrupt and destroy it, to that wholesome doctrine of "deny thyself, take up thy cross and follow me," which Jesus Christ has left in his Church.

But after their own lusts] For *these* they will follow, and hate those *preachers* and that doctrine by which they are opposed.

Shall they heap to themselves teachers] They will add one teacher to another, run and gad about after all, to find out those who insist not on the necessity of bearing the cross, of being crucified to the world, and of having the mind that was in Jesus. In this disposition interested men often find their account; they set up for teachers, "and widen and strew with flowers the way, down to eternal ruin," taking care to soothe the passions and flatter the vices of a trifling, superficial people.

Having itching ears] Endless curiosity, an insatiable desire of *variety*; and they get their ears tickled with the *language* and *accent* of the person, abandoning the *good* and *faithful preacher* for the *fine speaker*.

Verse 4. And they shall turn away their *ears from the truth*] The truth strips them of their vices, sacrifices their idols, darts its lightnings against their easily besetting sins, and absolutely requires a conformity to a crucified Christ; therefore *they turn their ears away from it.*

And shall be turned unto fables.] Believe any kind of stuff and nonsense; for, as one has justly observed, "Those who reject the truth are abandoned by the just judgment of God to credit the most degrading nonsense." This is remarkably the case with most deists; their creed often exhibits what is grossly absurd.

Verse 5. But watch thou in all things] It is possible to be overtaken in a fault, to neglect one's duty, and to lose one's soul. Watching unto prayer prevents all these evils.

Endure afflictions] Let no sufferings affright thee; nor let the dread of them either cause thee to abandon the truth, or relax in thy zeal for the salvation of men.

Do the work of an evangelist] That is: Preach

Christ crucified for the sins of the whole world; for this, and this alone, is doing the work of an evangelist, or preacher of the glad tidings of peace and salvation by Christ. An angel from God was first sent to do the work of an evangelist, and how did *he* do it? *Behold*, said he, *I bring you good tidings of great joy*; Ιδου γαρ, ευαγγελιζομαι ὑμιν χαραν μεγαλην, ἡτις εσται παντι τῳ λαῳ. *Behold, I evangelize unto you great joy, which shall be to all people; to you is born a Saviour.* Those who do not proclaim Christ as having tasted death for every man, and who do not implicitly show that every human soul may be saved, do not perform the work of *evangelists*; they, God help them! limit the Holy One of Israel. Yet, *as far as* they preach the truth in sincerity, *so far* God acknowledges and blesses them and their labours; they do a *part* of the work, but not the *whole*.

Make full proof of thy ministry.] Push all thy principles to their utmost power of activity; carry them on to all their consequences; and try what God will do for thee, and by thee. Neglect no part of thy sacred function; perform faithfully all the duties of which it is composed; and do God's work in his own way and in his own spirit.

Verse 6. For I am now ready to be offered] Ηδη σπενδομαι· *I am already poured out as a libation.* See the note on Phil. ii. 17. He considers himself as on the eve of being sacrificed, and looks upon his blood as the libation which was poured on the sacrificial offering. He could not have spoken thus positively had not the sentence of death been already passed upon him.

Verse 7. I have fought a good fight] Every reader will perceive that the apostle, as was his very frequent custom, alludes to the contests at the Grecian games: Τον αγωνα τον καλον ηγωνισμαι· *I have wrestled that good wrestling*—I have struggled hard, and have overcome, in a most honourable cause.

I have finished my course] I have started for the prize, and have come up to the goal, outstripping all my competitors, and have gained this prize also.

I have kept the faith] As the *laws* of these games must be most *diligently observed* and *kept*, (for though a man overcome, yet is he not crowned, except he strive *lawfully*,) so I have *kept the rules* of the *spiritual combat* and *race*; and thus, having contended *lawfully*, and conquered in each exercise, I have a right to expect the prize.

Verse 8. Henceforth there is laid up for me a crown]

2

A. M. cir. 4069.
A. D. 65 or 66.
A. U. C. 818.
An. Imp. Ne-
ronis Cæs.
Aug. 12.

me only, but unto all them also that love his appearing.

9 Do thy diligence to come shortly unto me :

10 For ʳ Demas hath forsaken me, ˢ having loved this present world, and is departed unto

Thessalonica ; Crescens to Galatia, Titus unto Dalmatia.

11 ᵗ Only ᵘ Luke is with me. Take ᵛ Mark, and bring him with thee ; for he is profitable to me for the ministry.

A. M. cir. 4069.
A. D. 65 or 66.
A. U. C. 818.
An. Imp. Ne-
ronis Cæs.
Aug. 12.

ʳ Col. iv. 15 ; Philem. 24.——ˢ 1 John ii. 15.——ᵗ See chap. i. 15.

ᵘ Col. iv. 14 ; Philem. 24.——ᵛ Acts xii. 25 ; xv. 37 ; Col. iv. 10.

This I can claim as my due ; but the crown I expect is not one of *fading leaves,* but *a crown of righteousness ;* the reward which God, in his kindness, has promised to them who are faithful to the grace he has bestowed upon them.

The Lord, the righteous Judge] He alludes here to the *brabeus,* or umpire in the Grecian games, whose office it was to declare the victor, and to give the crown.

At that day] The day of judgment ; the morning of the resurrection from the dead.

Unto all them also that love his appearing.] All who live in expectation of the coming of Christ, who anticipate it with joyfulness, having buried the world and laid up all their hopes above. Here is a *reward,* but it is a reward not of *debt* but of *grace ;* for it is by the *grace* of God that even an *apostle* is *fitted* for glory. And this reward is *common to the faithful ;* it is given, not only to apostles, but *to all them that love his appearing.* This crown *is laid up*—it is *in view,* but not *in possession.* We must die first.

I have several times noted the allusions of St. Paul to the Greek poets, and such as seemed to argue that he quoted immediately from them. There is a passage in the *Alcestis* of *Euripides,* in which the very expressions used here by the apostle are found, and spoken on the occasion of a wife laying down her life for her husband, when both his parents had refused to do it.

Ουκ ηθελησας ουδ' ετολμησας θανειν
Του σου προ παιδος· αλλα την δ' ειασατε
Γυναικ' οθνειαν, ἡν εγω και μητερα
Πατερα τε γ' ενδικως αν ἡγοιμην μονην·
Και τοι καλον γ' αν τονδ' αγων' ηγωνισω,
Του σου προ παιδος κατθανων.   *Alcest.* v. 644.

" Thou wouldst not, neither darest thou to die for thy son ; but hast suffered this strange woman to do it, whom I justly esteem to be alone my father and mother : thou wouldst *have fought a good fight* hadst thou died for thy son."

See *Sophocles* and *Æschylus,* quoted 1 Tim. vi. 15. The καλος αγων, *good fight,* was used among the Greeks to express a contest of the *most honourable kind,* and in this sense the apostle uses it.

Verse 9. *Do thy diligence to come shortly unto me*] He appears to have wished Timothy to be present at his death, that he might have his faith confirmed by seeing how a Christian could die ; and, as he had but a short time to live, he begs Timothy to *hasten his visit,* and particularly so as he had scarcely now any companions.

Verse 10. *Demas hath forsaken me*] This is another proof of the posteriority of this epistle ; for

Demas was with the apostle in his first imprisonment, and joins in the salutations, see Col. iv. 14, which were written when Paul was a prisoner at Rome for the first time.

Having loved this present world] Αγαπησας τον νυν αιωνα Having preferred Judaism to Christianity ; or having loved the Jews, and having sought their welfare in preference to that of the Gentiles.

The עולם הזה words *olam hazzeh,* which answer to the Greek τον νυν αιωνα, are generally to be understood as signifying, either the Jewish people, or the system of Judaism. It was now become doubly dangerous to be a Christian ; and those who had not religion enough to enable them to burn, or in any other way to expose life for it, took refuge in that religion which was exposed to no persecution. This is a light in which the conduct of Demas may be viewed. It could not have been the love of *secular gain* which had induced Demas to abandon St. Paul ; he must have counted this cost before he became a Christian. See below.

Crescens to Galatia] Whether the departure of *Crescens* was similar to that of *Demas,* as intimated above, or whether he went on an *evangelical embassy,* we know not. Charity would hope the latter ; for we can hardly suppose that *Titus,* who is here said to have *departed to Dalmatia,* had abandoned his Cretan Churches, his apostolical office, and especially his *aged father and friend,* now about to seal the truth with his blood ! It is probable that both these persons had gone on sacred missions, and perhaps had been gone some time before the apostle was brought into such imminent danger. Even for *Demas,* as standing in this connection, something might be said. It is not intimated that he had denied the faith, but simply that he *had left the apostle and gone into Thessalonica ;* for which this reason is given, that *he loved the present world.* Now, if αγαπησας, *having loved,* can be applied to a *desire to save the souls of the Jews,* and that he went *into Thessalonica,* where they abounded, for this very purpose, then we shall find all three—Demas, Crescens, and Titus, one at Thessalonica, another at Galatia, and the third at Dalmatia, doing the work of evangelists, visiting the Churches, and converting both Jews and Gentiles. This interpretation I leave to the *charitable reader,* and must own that, with all the presumptive evidences against it, it has some fair show of probability. Demas has received little justice from interpreters and preachers in general. It is even fashionable to hunt him down.

Verse 11. *Only Luke is with me.*] This was *Luke* the evangelist, and writer of the Acts of the Apostles, who was always much attached to St. Paul, and it is supposed continued with him even to his martyrdom.

   2

A. M. cir. 4069.
A. D. 65 or 66.
A. U. C. 818.
An. Imp. Ne-
ronis Cæs.
Aug. 12.

12 And ^wTychicus have I sent to Ephesus.

13 The cloak that I left at Troas with Carpus, when thou comest, bring *with thee,* and the books, *but* especially the parchments.

14 ^x Alexander the coppersmith did me much evil : ^y the Lord reward him according to his works :

15 Of whom be thou ware also ; for he hath greatly withstood ^z our words.

A. M. cir. 4069.
A. D. 65 or 66.
A. U. C. 818.
An. Imp. Ne-
ronis Cæs.
Aug. 12.

16 At my first answer no man stood with me, ^a but all *men* forsook me : ^b*I pray God* that it may not be laid to their charge.

17 ^c Notwithstanding the Lord stood with me, and strengthened me ; ^d that by me the preaching might be fully known, and *that*

---

^w Acts xx. 4 ; Eph. vi. 21 ; Col. iv. 7 ; Tit. iii. 12.——^x Acts xix. 33 ; 1 Tim. i. 20.——^y 2 Sam. iii. 39 ; Psa. xxviii. 4 ; Rev. xviii. 6.

^z Or, *our preachings.*——^a Chapter i. 15.——^b Acts vii. 60. ^c Matt. x. 19 ; Acts xxiii. 11 ; xxvii. 23.——^d Acts ix. 15 ; xxvi. 17, 18 ; Eph. iii. 8.

Take Mark, and bring him with thee] This was *John Mark,* the sister's son of Barnabas, who, after having wavered a little at first, became a steady, zealous, and useful man ; his name and conduct have been often before the reader. See the parallel passages.

For he is profitable to me for the ministry.] Εις διακονιαν· *For service ;* that is, he would be very useful to the apostle, to minister to him in his present close confinement. Some think that the apostle means his *preaching the Gospel ;* but at this time, I should suppose, there was very little, if any, public preaching at Rome.

Verse 12. Tychicus have I sent to Ephesus.] For this person, see Acts xx. 4 ; Eph. vi. 21 ; Col. iv. 7. It is rather strange that the apostle should say, *I have sent Tychicus to Ephesus,* if Timothy was at Ephesus at this time ; but it is probable that Tychicus had been sent to Ephesus some time before this, and therefore the apostle might say, though writing now to Ephesus, *Tychicus have I sent, &c.*

Verse 13. The cloak that I left at Troas] Τον φελονην is by several translated *bag* or *portmanteau ;* and it is most likely that it was something of this kind, in which he might carry his clothes, books, and travelling necessaries. What the *books* were we cannot tell, it is most likely they were *his own writings ;* and as to the *parchments,* they were probably the *Jewish Scriptures* and a copy of the *Septuagint.* These he must have had at hand at all times. The books and parchments now sent for could not be for the apostle's own use, as he was now on the eve of his martyrdom. He had probably intended to bequeath them to the faithful, that they might be preserved for the use of the Church.

Verse 14. Alexander the coppersmith] We are not to understand this of any *tradesman,* but of some *rabbin ;* for it was not unusual for the Jews to apply the name of some *trade* as an epithet to their rabbins and literary men. He is, in all probability, the very same mentioned Acts xix. 33, where see the note ; and it is not unlikely that he may have been the same whom the apostle was obliged to excommunicate, 1 Tim. i. 20.

The Lord reward him] Αποδωη αυτω ὁ Κυριος· But instead of αποδωη, which has here the power of a solemn *imprecation,* αποδωσει, *he will reward,* is the reading of the very best MSS., several of the *versions,* and some of the chief Greek *fathers.* This makes the sentence *declaratory : The Lord* WILL *reward him according to his works.* This reading is most like the spirit and temper of this heavenly man. See ver. 16.

Verse 15. Of whom be thou ware also] It seems that this rabbin travelled about from place to place for the purpose of opposing the Gospel, *the Jews putting him forward,* as it is said, Acts xix. 33.

He hath greatly withstood our words.] Has been a constant opposer of the Christian doctrines.

Verse 16. At my first answer] Εν τη πρωτη μου απολογια· *At my first apology ;* this word properly signifies a *defence* or *vindication.* To his is the meaning of what we call the *apologies of the primitive fathers ;* they were vindications or *defences* of Christianity. It is generally allowed that, when St. Paul had been taken this second time by the Romans, he was examined immediately, and required to account for his conduct ; and that, so odious was Christianity through the tyranny of Nero, he could procure no person to plead for him. Nero, who had himself set fire to Rome, charged it on the Christians, and they were in consequence persecuted in the most cruel manner ; he caused them to be wrapped up in *pitched* clothes, and then, chaining them to a stake, he ordered them to be set on fire to give light in the streets after night ! *Tormenti genus !* To this *Juvenal* appears to allude. Sat i. v. 155.

Pone Tigellinum, tæda lucebis in illa,
Qua stantes ardent, qui fixo gutture fumant.

" If into rogues omnipotent you rake,
Death is your doom, *impaled upon a stake ;*
Smear'd o'er with wax, and set on blaze *to light*
The streets, and make a *dreadful fire by night.*"
                     DRYDEN.

I pray God that it may not be laid to their charge.] How much more simple, elegant, and expressive are the apostle's own words : Μη αυτοις λογισθειη· *let it not be placed to their account !* Let them not have to reckon for it with the supreme Judge at the great day !

Verse 17. The Lord stood with me] When all human help failed, God, in a more remarkable manner, interposed ; and thus the excellency plainly appeared to be of God, and not of man.

That by me the preaching might be fully known] When called on to make his *defence* he took occasion to *preach the Gospel,* and to show that the great God of heaven and earth had designed to illuminate the Gentile world with the rays of his light and glory. This must have endeared him to some, while others might consider him an opposer of their gods, and be the more incensed against him.

2

A. M. cir. 4069.
A. D. 65 or 66.
A. U. C. 818.
An. Imp. Ne-
ronis Cæs.
Aug. 12.

all the Gentiles might hear: and I was delivered ᵉ out of the mouth of the lion.

18 ᶠ And the Lord shall deliver me from every evil work, and will preserve *me* unto his heavenly kingdom: ᵍ to whom *be* glory for ever and ever. Amen.

19 Salute ʰ Prisca and Aquila, and ⁱ the household of Onesiphorus.

20 ᵏ Erastus abode at Corinth: but ˡ Trophimus have I left at Miletum sick.

21 ᵐ Do thy diligence to come before winter. Eubulus greeteth thee, and Pudens, and Linus, and Claudia, and all the brethren.

A. M. cir. 4069.
A. D. 65 or 66.
A. U. C. 818.
An. Imp. Ne-
ronis Cæs.
Aug. 12.

22 ⁿ The Lord Jesus Christ *be* with thy spirit. Grace *be* with you. Amen.

¶ The Second *Epistle* unto Timotheus, ordained the first bishop of the Church of the Ephesians, was written from Rome, when Paul was brought before ᵒ Nero the second time.

ᵉ Psa. xxii. 21 ; 2 Pet. ii. 9.——ᶠ Psa. cxxi. 7.——ᵍ Rom. xi. 36 ; Galatians i. 5 ; Hebrews xiii. 21.——ʰ Acts xviii. 2 ; Rom. xvi. 3. ⁱ 2 Tim. i. 16.

ᵏ Acts xix. 22 ; Rom. xvi. 23.——ˡ Acts xx. 4 ; xxi. 29.——ᵐ Ver. 9.——ⁿ Gal. vi. 18 ; Philem. 25.——ᵒ Gr. *Cæsar Nero,* or, *the Emperor Nero.*

I was delivered out of the mouth of the lion.] I escaped the imminent danger at that time. Probably he was seized in a tumultuous manner, and expected to be torn in pieces. The words εκ στοματος, or εκ βρυγμου λεοντος ρυεσθαι, *to be rescued from the mouth or jaws of the lion,* are a proverbial form of speech for deliverance from the most imminent danger. Several writers think *Nero* to be intended by the *lion,* because of his rage and oppressive cruelty. But *Helius Cæsarinus* was at this time prefect of the city ; Nero being in Greece. He was a bloody tyrant, and Nero had given him the power of life and death in his absence. The apostle may mean him, if the words be not proverbial.

Verse 18. *And the Lord shall deliver me from every evil work*] None of the evil designs formed against me to make me unfaithful or unsteady, to cause me to save my life at the expense of faith and a good conscience, shall succeed ; my life may go, but he will preserve me *unto his heavenly kingdom.* A continuance on earth the apostle expects not ; but he has *glory* full in view, and therefore he gives God glory for what he had done, and for what he had promised to do.

Verse 19. *Salute Prisca and Aquila*] Several MSS., *versions,* and *fathers* have *Priscilla* instead of Prisca : they are probably the same as those mentioned Acts xviii. 18, 26.

The household of Onesiphorus.] See chap. i. 16. Onesiphorus was probably at this time dead : his *family* still remained at Ephesus.

Verse 20. *Erastus abode at Corinth*] He was *treasurer* of that city, as we learn from Rom. xvi. 23. See the note there. The apostle had sent him and Timothy on a mission to Macedonia, Acts xix. 22, whence it is probable he returned to Corinth, and there became finally settled.

Trophimus have I left at Miletum sick.] Even the apostles could not work miracles *when they pleased ;* that power was but rarely given, and that for very special purposes. *Trophimus* was an Ephesian. See Acts xx. 4, and the note there.

Miletus was a maritime town of Ionia, not far from Ephesus ; but there was another Miletus, in Crete, which some learned men think to be intended here. It appears that St. Paul went from Macedonia to

Corinth, where he left Erastus ; from Corinth he proceeded to Troas, where he lodged with Carpus : from Troas he went to Ephesus, where he visited Timothy ; from Ephesus he went to Miletus, where he left Trophimus sick ; and having embarked at Miletus, he went by sea to Rome. See *Calmet.* It is most likely, therefore, that the *Miletus* of Ionia is the place intended.

Verse 21. *Come before winter.*] 1. Because the apostle's time was short and uncertain. 2. Because sailing in those seas was very dangerous in winter. Whether Timothy saw the apostle before he was martyred is not known.

Eubulus] This person is nowhere else mentioned in the New Testament.

Pudens] Of this person we have traditions and legends, but nothing certain. The Catholics make him bishop of Rome.

Linus] He also is made, by the same persons, bishop of Rome ; but there is no sufficient ground for these pretensions.

Claudia] Supposed to be the wife of *Pudens.* Some think she was a British lady, converted by St. Paul ; and that she was the first that brought the Gospel to Britain.

All the brethren.] All the Christians, of whom there were many at Rome ; though of Paul's *companions* in travel, only Luke remained there.

Verse 22. *The Lord Jesus Christ be with thy spirit.*] This is a prayer addressed to Christ by one of the most eminent of his apostles ; another proof of the untruth of the assertion, that prayer is never offered to Christ in the New Testament. He prays that Christ may be *with his spirit,* enlightening, strengthening, and confirming it to the end.

Grace be with you.] These words show that the epistle was addressed to the *whole Church,* and that it is not to be considered of a *private* nature.

Amen.] Omitted by ACFG and some others. See the note on this word at the end of the preceding epistle.

The principal subscriptions, both in the *versions* and MSS., are the following :—

The Second Epistle to Timothy was written from Rome.—SYRIAC.

To the man Timothy.—ÆTHIOPIC.

Nothing in the VULGATE.

End of the epistle; it was written from the city of Rome when Timothy had been constituted bishop over Ephesus; and when Paul had stood the second time in the presence of Nero Cæsar, the Roman emperor. Praise to the Lord of glory, perpetual, perennial, and eternal! Amen, Amen, Amen.—Arabic.

The Second Epistle to Timothy is ended, who was the first bishop of the Church of Ephesus. It was written from Rome when Paul had stood the second time before Nero, the Roman emperor.—Philoxenian Syriac.

Written from Rome, and sent by Onesimus.—Coptic.

The MSS. are also various :—

The Second Epistle to Timothy is finished; that to Titus begins.

The second to Timothy, written from Laodicea.—Codex Alexandrinus.

The Second Epistle of Paul the Apostle to Timothy, ordained the first bishop of the Church of the Ephesians, was written from Rome when Paul was brought the second time before Nero Cæsar.—Common Greek Text.

There are other slighter differences in the MSS., but they are unworthy of note.

That the epistle was written from *Rome*, about the year 65 or 66, and a little before St. Paul's martyrdom, is the general opinion of learned men. See the *preface.*

The reader has already been apprized that this is most probably the last epistle the apostle ever wrote; and it is impossible to see him in a more advantageous point of view than he now appears, standing on the verge of eternity, full of God, and strongly anticipating an eternity of glory. For farther observations, see the conclusion of the first epistle.

On verse 16 I have mentioned the *apologies* of the *primitive fathers*, or their *vindications* of Christianity against the aspersions and calumnies of the *Gentiles.* Several of these writings are still extant; of the whole I shall here give a short account in chronological order.

1. Quadratus. St. Jerome relates that this man was contemporary with the apostles, and one also of their disciples. There is only a fragment of his *apology* extant; it is preserved by *Eusebius*, in Hist. Eccles., lib. iv. c. 3, and was addressed to the Emperor *Adrian* about A. D. 126, on whom it is said to have had a good effect.

2. Aristides, according to *Eusebius*, was an Athenian philosopher, and contemporary with Quadratus; he wrote his *apology* for the Christians about the same time, (A. D. 126,) and addressed it to the same emperor. St. Jerome gives some remarkable particulars of him in his book *Of Illustrious Men.* "He was," says he, "a most eloquent philosopher, and after his conversion he continued to wear his former habit." His *apology* was extant in the days of St. Jerome, but is now utterly lost.

3. Justin Martyr flourished about A. D. 140, and presented his first *apology* for Christianity to the Emperor *Antoninus Pius* and the Roman senate, about A. D. 150; and his second *apology* was presented to *Marcus Antoninus* about A. D. 162 or 166. These two very important *apologies* are come down to us nearly entire, and are exceedingly useful and important.

4. Athenagoras wrote his *apology* for the Christians about the year 178. He is said to have sat down to write against the Christians; and that he might the better confute them he read over the Scriptures, and was so thoroughly converted by what he read, that he immediately wrote an *apology* for them, instead of an *invective against* them. This piece is still extant.

5. Tertullian, who flourished about A. D. 200, was the earliest, and one of the chief of the Latin fathers: he was born in Carthage, and was a presbyter of the Church in that city. His *apology* was written about A. D. 198, or, according to some, 200. It appears to have been addressed to the *governors of provinces*, and is allowed to be a work of extraordinary eminence, and a master piece of its kind. It is still extant.

6. Marcus Minucius Felix flourished towards the end of the reign of *Septimius Severus*, about A. D. 210. His *apology* for the Christian religion is written in the form of a *dialogue* between *Cæcilius Natalis*, a heathen, and *Octavius Januarius*, a Christian, in which *Minucius* sits as judge. "This work," says Dr. Lardner, "is a monument of the author's ingenuity, learning, and eloquence; and the conversion of a man of his great natural and acquired abilities to the Christian religion, and his public and courageous defence of it, notwithstanding the many worldly temptations to the contrary, which he must have met with at that time, as they give an advantageous idea of his virtue, so they likewise afford a very agreeable argument in favour of the truth of our religion." Works, vol. ii., p. 367.

To the above, who are properly the Christian *apologists* for the first 200 *years*, several add *Tatian's* book against the Gentiles; *Clemens Alexandrinus'* Exhortation to the Gentiles; *Origen's* eight books against *Celsus*; *Cyprian* Of the Vanity of Idols; *Arnobius'* seven books against the Gentiles; the Institutions of *Lactantius*, and *Julius Fermicus Maturnus* Of the Errors of Profane Religion. All these works contain much important information, and are well worthy the attention of the studious reader. The principal part of these writings I have *analyzed* in my *Succession of Sacred Literature*, and to this they who cannot conveniently consult the originals may refer.

As the word *apology* generally signifies now an *excuse for a fault*, or "something spoken rather in *extenuation of guilt* than to *prove innocence*," it is seldom used in its primitive sense; and for some hundreds of years no *defence* of Christianity has borne this title till that by the late bishop of Llandaff, intituled, *An Apology for the* Bible, *in a Series of Letters addressed to* Thomas Paine. This is a very masterly work, and a complete refutation of *Paine's* "Age of Reason," and of any thing that has yet appeared, or can appear, under the same form. Ever since the days of St. Paul God has raised up able *apologists* for the truth of Christianity, when it has been attacked by the most powerful partisans of the kingdom of darkness; and each *attack* and *apology* has been a new *triumph* for the religion of Christ.

Finished correcting for a new edition, Dec. 23, 1831.

PREFACE

TO THE

EPISTLE OF PAUL THE APOSTLE

TO

TITUS.

IT is strange, that of a person who must have attained considerable eminence in the Christian Church, and one to whom a canonical epistle has been written by the great apostle of the Gentiles, we should know so very little. That Titus was a frequent companion of St. Paul in his journeys we have evidence from his epistles; and although this was the case, he is not once mentioned in the book of the Acts of the Apostles! That he was a *Greek*, and brought up in *heathenism*, we learn from Gal. ii. 3: "But neither Titus, who *was* with me, being a GREEK, was compelled to be CIRCUMCISED." As he was *uncircumcised*, he was neither a *Jew* nor a *proselyte of justice*, and probably was a mere heathen till he heard the Gospel preached by St. Paul, by whose ministry he was converted to the Christian faith; chap. i. 4: "To Titus, my own son, (γνησιω τεκνω, *my genuine son*,) after the common faith;" which words sufficiently indicate that St. Paul alone had the honour of his conversion. That he was very highly, and consequently deservedly, esteemed by St. Paul, is evident from the *manner* in which he mentions him in different places: "I had no rest in my spirit till I found Titus, my brother;" 2 Cor. ii. 13. "Nevertheless, God, that comforteth those who are cast down, comforted us by the coming of Titus; and not by his coming only, but by the consolation wherewith he was comforted in you: therefore, we were comforted in your comfort: yea, and exceedingly the more joyed we for the joy of Titus, because his spirit was refreshed by you all; and his inward affection is more abundant toward you whilst he remembereth how with fear and trembling ye received him;" 2 Cor. vii. 6, 7, 13, 15. "But thanks be to God, who put the same earnest care into the heart of Titus for you. Whether *any do inquire* of Titus, *he is* my partner and fellow helper concerning you;" 2 Cor. viii. 16, 23. "Did Titus make a gain of you? Walked we not in the same spirit? *walked we* not in the same steps?" 2 Cor. xii. 18.

Though St. Paul's preaching the Gospel in Crete is not expressly mentioned anywhere, yet it may be plainly inferred from chap. i. 5: "For this cause left I thee in Crete, that thou shouldest set in order the things that are wanting, and ordain elders in every city." It is supposed that this was some time in the year 62, after the apostle was released from his first imprisonment in Rome. But not being able to spend much time in that island, he left the care of the Churches to Titus, and sailed into Judea in the beginning of 63, taking Timothy with him. Having spent some time in Jerusalem, he proceeded to Antioch, comforting and establishing the Churches whithersoever they went. From Antioch he set out on his fifth and last apostolical journey, in which he and Timothy travelled through Syria and Cilicia, and came to Colosse in Phrygia, early in the year 64. On this occasion it is supposed he wrote his Epistle to Titus, in which he desires him to meet him in Nicopolis, as he had intended to spend the winter there; Titus iii. 12. From Colosse he went with Timothy to Ephesus, where he left him to regulate and govern the Church; from thence he passed into Macedonia, and probably visited Philippi, and different Churches in that province, according to his intention, Phil. ii. 24; and thence to Nicopolis, where he intended to spend the winter, and where he had desired Titus to meet him. See above.

Whether Titus ever left Crete we know not; nor how, nor where, he died. Some traditions, on which little dependence can be placed, say he lived till he was 94 years of age, and died and was buried in Crete. He appears to have been a young man when intrusted with the care of the Churches in this island. In such an extensive district, an aged or infirm man would have been of little service.

Crete, where Titus was resident, to whom this epistle was sent, is the largest island in the Mediterranean Sea; it lies between 22° and 27° long. E., and between 35° and 36° lat. N. According to Strabo, it is 287 miles in length; Pliny makes it 270, and Scylax 312. Pliny also states that its greatest breadth is 55 miles; and, as its *length* was so disproportionate to its *breadth*, it is called, by Stephanus *Byzantinus*, the *long island*. It has the Archipelago to the north, the African sea to the south, the Carpathian to the east, and the Ionian to the west. It is now generally computed to be about 250 miles long, about 50 broad, and 600 in circumference. It was anciently called *Æria, Cthonia, Curete, Idæa,* and *Macaris;* but its most common name was Crete Of it Homer gives us the following description. Odyss., lib. xix. v. 172–179 :—

> Κρητη τις γαι' εστι, μεσφ ενι οινοπι ποντφ,
> Καλη και πιειρα, περιρρυτος· εν δ' ανθρωποι
> Πολλοι, απειρεσιοι, και εννηκοντα πολῃες.
> Αλλη δ' αλλων γλωσσα μεμιγμενη· εν μεν Αχαιοι,
> Εν δ' Ετεοκρητες μεγαλητορες, εν δε Κυδωνες,
> Δωριεες τε τριχαϊκες, διοι τε Πελασγοι.
> Τοισι δ' ενι Κνωσσος μεγαλη πολις· ενθα τε Μινως
> Εννεωρος βασιλευς Διος μεγαλου οαριστης·

> Crete awes the circling waves, a fruitful soil;
> And ninety cities crown the sea-born isle.
> Mix'd with her genuine sons, adopted names
> In various tongues avow their various claims.
> Cidonians, dreadful with the bended yew,
> And bold Pelasgi, boast a native's due :
> The Dorians plumed amidst the files of war,
> Her foodful glebe, with fierce Achaians, share.
> Cnossus, her capital of high command,
> Where sceptred Minos, with impartial hand,
> Divided right; each ninth revolving year
> By Jove received in council to confer.   Pope.

Though in the above quotation Homer attributes to this island only *ninety cities,* εννηκοντα πολῃες, yet in other places he gives it the epithet of ἑκατομπολις, *hundred cities.* And this number it is generally allowed to have had originally; but we must not let the term *city* deceive us, as in ancient times places were thus named which would rate with villages or hamlets only in these modern times. Few places in antiquity have been more celebrated than *Crete :* it was not only famous for its *hundred cities,* but for the arrival of *Europa* on a bull, or in the ship *Taurus,* from Phœnicia ; for the *Labyrinth,* the work of Dædalus ; for the *destruction* of the *Minotaur,* by Theseus ; for Mount *Ida,* where Jupiter was preserved from the jealousy of his father Saturn ; for *Jupiter's sepulchre ;* and above all, for its king, *Minos,* and the laws which he gave to his people ; the most pure, wholesome, and equal, of which antiquity can boast.

Their lawgiver, Minos, is said by Homer to have held a conference every *ninth* year with Jupiter, from whom he is reported to have received directions for the farther improvement of his code of laws ; though this be fable, it probably states a fact in disguise. Minos probably revised his laws every ninth year, and, to procure due respect and obedience to them, told the people that he received these improvements from Jupiter himself. This was customary with ancient legislators who had to deal with an ignorant and gross people, and has been practised from the days of Minos to those of Mohammed.

According to ancient authors, Crete was originally peopled from *Palestine.* Bochart has shown, *Canaan,* lib. i. c. 15, col. 420, that that part of Palestine which lies on the Mediterranean was by the Arabs called *Keritha,* and by the Syrians, *Creth ;* and the *Hebrews* called its inhabitants *Kerethi* כרתי or *Kerethim* כרתים, which the *Septuagint* have translated Κρητας. Thus Ezek. xxv. 16, we find והכרתי את כרתים *vehicratti eth Kerethin,* which we translate *I will cut off the Cherethims,* translated by the Septuagint και εξολοθρευσω Κρητας, *I will destroy the Cretans ;* and Zeph. ii. 5 : "Wo unto the inhabitants of the seacoast, the nation of the Cherethites, (גוי כרתים goi *Kerethim, The nation of the Kerethim ;*") παροικοι Κρητων, Sept., *The sojourners of the Cretans.* That these prophets do not speak of the *island* of *Crete* is plain from their joining the *Kerethim* with the *Pelishtim* as one and the same people. "Thus saith the Lord God, Behold I will stretch out my hand upon the Philistines, and will cut off the Cherethims, and destroy the remnant of the seacoast ;" Ezek. xxv. 16. "Wo unto the inhabitants of the seacoasts, the nation of the Cherethites ; the word of the Lord is against you : O Canaan, the land of the Philistines, I will even destroy thee ;" Zeph. ii. 5. Accordingly it appears that the *Kerethim* were a part of the *Philistines.* The Kerethim in Palestine were noted for *archery ;* and we find that some of them were employed by David as his life guards, 2 Sam. viii. 18 ; xv. 18 ; xx. 23 ; 1 Kings i. 38 ; 1 Chron. xviii. 17 ; in all which places they are called, in our translation, *Cherethites ;* but the Hebrew is כרתי *Kerethi,* which the Chaldee paraphrase renders קשתיא *kashtia,* or קשתייה *kashtaiyah, archers.* See the Targum of Rab. Joseph. It is very likely that the Kerethi or Kerethim of Palestine had their name from their *successful use* of their favourite instrument the *bow,* as by it they *destroyed* many ; for כרת *carath,* in Hebrew, signifies to *destroy* or lay *waste ;* and hence the paronomasia of the prophet, quoted above, Ezek. xxv. 16 : "I will cut off the Cherethims (והכרתי את כרתים) literally, *I will destroy the destroyers.*")

Idomeneus, who assisted Agamemnon in the Trojan war, was the last king of Crete. He left the regency of the island to his adopted son *Leucus,* who, in the absence of the king, usurped the empire ; the usurper was however soon expelled, and Crete became one of the *most celebrated republics* in antiquity. The

2

Romans at last, under *Quintus Metellus*, after an immense expenditure of blood and treasure, succeeded in subduing the island, on which he abolished the laws of Minos, and introduced the code of Numa Pompilius. Crete, with the small kingdom of Cyrene, became a Roman province; this was at first governed by a *proconsul*, next by a *quæstor* and *assistant*, and lastly by a *consul*. *Constantine* the Great, in the new division he made of the provinces of the empire, separated Crete from Cyrene, and left it, with Africa and Illyria, to his third son *Constans*. In the ninth century, in the reign of Michael II., it was attacked and conquered by the Saracens. About 965, the Emperor *Nicephorus Phocas*, in the following century, defeated and expelled the Saracens, and reunited the island to the empire, after it had been under the power of the infidels upwards of 100 years. It remained with the empire until the time of *Baldwin*, earl of Flanders, who, being raised to the throne, rewarded the services of *Boniface*, marquis of Montferrat, by making him king of Thessalonica, and adding to it the island of Crete. Baldwin, preferring a sum of gold to the government of the island, sold it to the Venetians, A. D. 1194, under whose government it was called *Candia*, from the Arabic كندق *Kandak*, a *fortification*, the name which the Saracens gave to the metropolis which they had built and strongly *fortified*. In 1645, in the midst of a profound peace, it was attacked by the Turks with a fleet of 400 sail, which had on board an army of 60,000 men, under the command of four pachas, to oppose whom the whole island could only muster 3,500 infantry, and a small number of cavalry; yet with these they held out against a numerous and continually recruited army, disputing every inch of ground, so that the whole Ottoman power was employed for nearly thirty years before they got the entire dominion of the island. In this long campaign against this brave people the Turks lost about 200,000 men! Since about the year 1675, the whole island has been under the government of the Turks.

The island of Crete is perhaps one of the most salubrious in the world. The soil is rich, and it produces no *ferocious* or *poisonous* animal. The present number of its inhabitants may amount to about 350,200, of whom about 200 are Jews, 150,000 Greeks, and 200,000 Turks. This is a large population for a place under Turkish despotism; but had it the blessings of a free government, it could support at least *treble* the number.

The island is divided into twelve bishops' sees, under the patriarch of Constantinople; but though the execrable Turks profess to allow to the Christians the free exercise of their religion, yet they will not permit them to repair their churches. It is only by the influence of large sums of gold, paid to the pachas, that they can keep their religious houses from total dilapidation. The Mohammedans have indeed converted most of the Christian temples into mosques. In *Candia*, the metropolis, they have left two churches to the *Greeks*, one to the *Armenians*, and a synagogue to the *Jews*. Candia is about five hundred miles from Constantinople. Is it not strange that the maritime powers of Europe have not driven those oppressors of the human race from this and every inch of Christian ground which they have usurped by treachery and violence, and which they continue to govern by despotism and cruelty?

Many have observed the *affinity* that subsists between the First Epistle to Timothy and this to Titus. Both epistles are directed to persons left by the writer to preside in their respective Churches during his absence. Both epistles are principally occupied in describing the qualifications of those who should be appointed to ecclesiastical offices; and the ingredients in this description are nearly the same in both epistles. Timothy and Titus are both cautioned against the same prevailing corruptions; the phrases and expressions in both letters are nearly the same; and the writer accosts his two disciples with the same salutations, and passes on to the business of his epistle with the same transition.

For example:—

Unto Timothy, *my own son in the faith*—as *I besought thee to abide still at Ephesus*, &c.; 1 Tim. i. 1, 2, 3.

To Titus, *my own son after the common faith*—for this cause *left I thee in Crete*; Tit. i. 4, 5.

If Timothy was not to *give heed to fables* and endless *genealogies* which minister *questions*, 1 Tim. i. 4; Titus was also to *avoid foolish questions* and *genealogies*, chap. iii. 9; *not giving heed to Jewish fables*, chap. i. 14.

If Timothy was to be a *pattern*, (τυπος,) 1 Tim. iv. 12; so was Titus, chap. ii. 7.

If Timothy was to *let no man despise his youth*, 1 Tim. iv. 12; Titus was also to *let no man despise him*, chap. ii. 15.

This verbal consent is also observable in some very peculiar expressions, which have no relation to the particular character of Timothy or Titus.

The phrase πιστος ὁ λογος, *it is a faithful saying*, occurs *thrice* in the First Epistle to Timothy, *once* in the second, and *once* in that to Titus; and in no other part of St. Paul's writings. These three epistles were probably written towards the close of his life, and are the only epistles written after his first imprisonment at Rome.

The same observation belongs to another singularity of expression, viz. the epithet *sound*, (ὑγιαινων,) as applied to words or doctrine. It is thus used *twice* in the First Epistle to Timothy, *twice* in the second, and *thrice* in the Epistle to Titus; besides two cognate expressions, ὑγιαινοντας τη πιστει, *sound in the faith*, and λογον ὑγιη, *sound speech*. And the word is not found in the same sense in any other part of the New Testament.

The phrase *God our Saviour* stands in the same predicament. It is repeated three times in the First Epistle to Timothy, and thrice in the Epistle to Titus; but does not occur in any other book of the New Testament, except once in the Epistle of Jude.

2

Similar terms, though intermixed with others, are employed in the two epistles, in enumerating the qualifications required in those who should be advanced to the station of authority in the Church ; compare 1 Tim. iii. 2–4 with Tit. i. 6–8.

The most natural accounts which can be given of these resemblances, is to suppose that the two epistles were written nearly at the same time, and whilst the same ideas and phrases dwelt in the writer's mind.

The journey of St. Paul to Crete, alluded to in this epistle, in which Titus was left in Crete to set in order the things which were wanting, must be carried to the period which intervened between his first and second imprisonment. For the history of the *Acts*, which reaches to the time of St. Paul's imprisonment, contains no account of his going to Crete, except upon his voyage as a prisoner to Rome ; and that this could not be the occasion referred to in this epistle, is evident from hence, that when St. Paul wrote this epistle he appears to have been at liberty ; whereas, after that voyage, he continued at least two years in confinement.

It is agreed that St. Paul wrote his First Epistle to Timothy from Macedonia ; and that he was in these parts, i. e. in the Peninsula, when he wrote the Epistle to Titus, is rendered probable by his directing Titus to come to him in Nicopolis. The most noted city of that name was in Epirus, near to Actium ; but the form of speaking, as well as the nature of the case, renders it probable that the writer was in the neighbourhood of this city when he dictated this direction to Titus.

Upon the whole, if we be allowed to suppose that St. Paul, after his liberation at Rome, sailed into Asia, taking Crete in his way ; and that from Asia, and from Ephesus its capital, he proceeded to Macedonia, and, crossing the Peninsula in his progress, came into the neighbourhood of Nicopolis ; we have a route which falls in with every thing. It executes the intention expressed by the apostle of visiting Colosse and Philippi, as soon as he should be set at liberty at Rome. It allows him to leave " Titus at Crete," and " Timothy at Ephesus, as he went into Macedonia ;" and he wrote to both not long after from the Peninsula of Greece, and probably the neighbourhood of Nicopolis ; thus bringing together the dates of these two epistles, and thereby accounting for that affinity between them, both in subject and language, which has been above pointed out. Though the journey thus traced out for St. Paul be in a great measure hypothetical, yet it is a species of consistency which seldom belongs to falsehood, to admit of an hypothesis which includes a great number of independent circumstances without contradiction. See Paley's Horæ Paulinæ, p. 321

2   645

THE

EPISTLE OF PAUL THE APOSTLE

TO

TITUS.

Chronological Notes relative to this Epistle.

Year of the Constantinopolitan era of the world, or that used by the Byzantine historians, 5573.—Year of the Alexandrian era of the world, 5567.—Year of the Antiochian era of the world, 5557.—Year of the Julian period, 4775.—Year of the world, according to Archbishop Usher, 4069.—Year of the world, according to Eusebius, in his Chronicon, 4293.—Year of the minor Jewish era of the world, or that in common use, 3825.—Year of the Greater Rabbinical era of the world, 4424.—Year from the Flood, according to Archbishop Usher, and the English Bible, 2413.—Year of the Cali yuga, or Indian era of the Deluge, 3167. —Year of the era of Iphitus, or since the first commencement of the Olympic games, 1005.—Year of the era of Nabonassar, king of Babylon, 812.—Year of the CCXIth Olympiad, 1.—Year from the building of Rome, according to Fabius Pictor, 812.—Year from the building of Rome, according to Frontinus, 816.—Year from the building of Rome, according to the Fasti Capitolini, 817.—Year from the building of Rome, according to Varro, which was that most generally used, 818.—Year of the era of the Seleucidæ, 377.—Year of the Cæsarean era of Antioch, 113.—Year of the Julian era, 110.—Year of the Spanish era, 103.—Year from the birth of Jesus Christ according to Archbishop Usher, 69.—Year of the vulgar era of Christ's nativity, 65 or 66.—Year of Gessius Florus, governor of the Jews, 1.—Year of Vologesus, king of the Parthians, 16. —Year of L. C. Gallus, governor of Syria, 1.—Year of Matthias, high priest of the Jews, 3.—Year of the Dionysian period, or Easter Cycle, 66.—Year of the Grecian Cycle of nineteen years, or Common Golden Number, 9; or the first after the third embolismic.—Year of the Jewish Cycle of nineteen years, 6, or the second embolismic.—Year of the Solar Cycle, 18.—Dominical Letter, it being the first after the Bissextile, or Leap Year, F.—Day of the Jewish Passover, according to the Roman computation of time, the VIIth of the ides of April, or, in our common mode of reckoning, the seventh of April, which happened in this year on the day after the Jewish Sabbath.—Easter Sunday, the day after the ides of April, or the XVIIIth of the Calends of May, named by the Jews the 22d of Nisan or Abib; and by Europeans in general, the 14th of April.—Epact, or age of the moon on the 22d of March, (the day of the earliest Easter Sunday possible,) 28.—Epact, according to the present mode of computation, or the moon's age on New Year's day, or the Calends of January, 5.—Monthly Epacts, or age of the moon on the Calends of each month respectively, (beginning with January,) 5, 7, 6, 7, 8, 9, 10, 11, 12, 12, 14, 14.—Number of Direction, or the number of days from the twenty-first of March to the Jewish Passover, 17.—Year of the reign of Caius Tiberius Claudius Nero Cæsar, the fifth Roman emperor computing from Augustus Cæsar, 12.—Roman Consuls, A. Licinius Nerva Silanus, and M. Vestinius Atticus; the latter of whom was succeeded by Anicius Cerealis, on July 1st.

2

CHAPTER I.

The apostle's statement of his character, his hope, and his function, 1–3. His address to Titus, and the end for which he left him in Crete, 4, 5. The qualifications requisite in those who should be appointed elders and bishops in the Church of God, 6–9. Of false teachers, 10, 11. The character of the Cretans, and how they were to be dealt with, 12–14. Of the pure, the impure, and false professors of religion, 15, 16.

A. M. cir. 4069.
A. D. 65 or 66.
A. U. C. 818.
An. Imp. Ne-
ronis Cæs.
Aug. 12.

PAUL, a servant of God, and an apostle of Jesus Christ, according to the faith of God's elect, and ᵃ the acknowledging of the truth ᵇ which is after godliness;

2 ᶜ In ᵈ hope of eternal life, which God, ᵉ that cannot lie, promised ᶠ before the world began;

3 ᵍ But hath in due times manifested his

A. M. cir. 4069.
A. D. 65 or 66.
A. U. C. 818.
An. Imp. Ne-
ronis Cæs.
Aug. 12.

ᵃ 2 Tim. ii. 25.——ᵇ 1 Tim. iii. 16; vi. 3.——ᶜ Or, *for.*——ᵈ 2 Tim. i. 1; chap. iii. 7.

ᵉ Num. xxiii. 19; 1 Tim. ii. 13.——ᶠ Rom. xvi. 25; 2 Tim. i. 9; 1 Pet. i. 20.——ᵍ 2 Tim. i. 10.

NOTES ON CHAP. I.

Verse 1. *Paul, a servant of God*] In several places of his other epistles St. Paul styles himself the *servant of Jesus Christ*, but this is the only place where he calls himself *the servant of God*. Some think that he did this to vindicate himself against the Jews, who supposed he had renounced God when he admitted the Gentiles into his Church. But if *thus* to vindicate himself was at all necessary, why was it not done in his Epistle to the Romans, the grand object of which was to prove that the Gentiles came legally into the Church on believing in Christ, without submitting to circumcision, or being laid under obligation to observe the rites and ceremonies of the Jewish law? This reason seems too fanciful. It is very likely that in the use of the phrase the apostle had no particular design; for, according to him, he who is the *servant of Christ* is the *servant of God*, and he who is *God's servant* is also the *servant of Christ*.

The faith of God's elect] The Christians, who were now chosen in the place of the Jews, who, for their obstinate rejection of the Messiah, were reprobated; i. e. cast out of the Divine favour.

The acknowledging of the truth] For the propagation of that truth, or system of doctrines, which is calculated to promote godliness, or a holy and useful life.

Verse 2. *In hope of eternal life*] In expectation of a state of *being* and *well being* which should last through eternity, when time should be no more. This includes, not only the *salvation of the soul* and its eternal *beatification*, but also the *resurrection of the body*. This was a point but ill understood, and not very clearly revealed, under the Mosaic law; but it was fully revealed under the Gospel, and the doctrine illustrated by the resurrection and ascension of Christ.

Which God, that cannot lie, promised] We have often seen that the phrase, *the foundation of the world*, means the Jewish economy; and, *before the foundation of the world*, the times antecedent to the giving of the law. This is evidently the meaning here. See 2 Tim. i. 9, 10, 11.

Supposing the word αιωνιων in this verse to signify *eternal*, says Dr. Macknight, the literal translation of προ χρονων αιωνιων would be, *before eternal times;*

but that being a contradiction in terms, our translators, contrary to the propriety of the Greek language, have rendered it *before the world began*, as Mr Locke observes on Rom. xvi. 25. The true literal translation is *before the secular times*, referring us to the Jewish *jubilees*, by which times were computed among the Hebrews, as among the Gentiles they were computed by *generations of men*. Hence, Col. i. 26, *The mystery which was kept hid* απο των αιωνων και απο των γενεων, *from the ages and from the generations*, signifies the mystery which was kept hid from the Jews and from the Gentiles.

Verse 3. *But hath in due times*] Καιροις ιδιοις· In its own times. See 1 Tim. ii. 6; Gal. iv. 4; Eph. i. 10; ii. 7. God caused the Gospel to be published in that time in which it could be published with the greatest effect. It is impossible that God should prematurely hasten, or causelessly delay, the accomplishment of any of his works. Jesus was manifested precisely at the time in which that manifestation could best promote the glory of God and the salvation of man.

Manifested his word] Τον λογον αυτου· His doctrine—the doctrine of eternal life, by the incarnation, passion, death, and resurrection of Jesus Christ.

Which is committed unto me] That is, to preach it among the Gentiles.

According to the commandment of God our Saviour] This evidently refers to the commission which he had received from Christ. See Acts ix. 15: "He is a chosen vessel unto me, to bear my name before the Gentiles." For, "I have appeared unto thee for this purpose, to make thee a minister and a witness both of these things which thou hast seen, and of those things in the which I will appear unto thee; delivering thee from the people and from the Gentiles, unto whom now I send thee; to open their eyes, to turn them from darkness to light," &c,; Acts xxvi. 16, &c. This is the commandment; and according to it he became the apostle of the Gentiles.

God our Saviour.—As the commission was given by Jesus Christ alone, the person whom he terms here *God our Saviour* must be Jesus Christ only; and this is another proof that St. Paul believed Jesus Christ to be God. This *eternal life* God had *promised* in a comparatively *obscure* way before the foundation of the world, the Jewish dispensation; but now under

A. M. cir. 4069.
A. D. 65 or 66.
A. U. C. 818.
An. Imp. Neronis Cæs.
Aug. 12.

word through preaching, which is committed unto me [i] according to the commandment of God our Saviour ;

4 To [k] Titus, [l] *mine* own son after [m] the common faith : [n] Grace, mercy, *and* peace, from God the Father and the Lord Jesus Christ our Saviour.

5 For this cause left I thee in Crete, that thou shouldest [o] set in order the things that are [p] wanting, and [q] ordain elders in every city, as I had appointed thee :

6 [r] If any be blameless, [s] the husband of one

wife, [t] having faithful children, not accused of riot, or unruly.

7 For a bishop must be blameless, as [u] the steward of God ; not self-willed, not soon angry, [v] not given to wine, no striker, [w] not given to filthy lucre ;

8 [x] But a lover of hospitality, a lover of [y] good men, sober, just, holy, temperate ;

9 [z] Holding fast [a] the faithful word, [b] as he hath been taught, that he may be able [c] by sound doctrine both to exhort and to convince the gainsayers.

A. M. cir. 4069
A. D. 65 or 66.
A. U. C. 818.
An. Imp. Neronis Cæs.
Aug. 12.

---

[h] 1 Thess. ii. 4 ; 1 Tim. i. 11.——[i] 1 Tim. i. 1 ; ii. 3 ; iv. 10. [k] 2 Cor. ii. 13 ; vii. 13 ; viii. 6, 16, 23 ; xii. 18 ; Galatians ii. 3. [l] 1 Tim. i. 2.——[m] Rom. i. 12 ; 2 Cor. iv. 13 ; 2 Pet. i. 1.——[n] Eph. i. 2 ; Col. i. 2 ; 1 Tim. i. 2 ; 2 Tim. i. 2.——[o] 1 Cor. xi. 34. [p] Or, *left undone.*——[q] Acts xiv. 23 ; 2 Timothy ii. 2.——[r] 1 Tim. iii. 2, &c.

[s] 1 Tim. iii. 12.——[t] 1 Timothy iii. 4, 12.——[u] Matt. xxiv. 45 ; 1 Cor. iv. 1, 2.——[v] Lev. x. 9 ; 1 Timothy iii. 3, 8 ; Eph. v. 18. [w] 1 Tim. iii. 3, 8 ; 1 Pet. v. 2.——[x] 1 Tim. iii. 2.——[y] Or, *good things.*——[z] 2 Thess. ii. 15 ; 2 Tim. i. 13.——[a] 1 Tim. i. 15 ; iv. 9 ; vi. 3 ; 2 Tim. ii. 2.——[b] Or, *in teaching.*——[c] 1 Tim. vi. 3 ; 2 Tim. iv. 3 ; chap. ii. 1.

---

the Gospel, he had *made it manifest*—produced it with all its brightness, illustrations, and proofs.

Verse 4. To Titus, mine *own son*] Him whom I have been the instrument of converting to the Christian faith ; and in whom, in this respect, I have the same right as any man can have in his own begotten son. See the preface ; and see on 1 Tim. i. 2.

Verse 5. For this cause left I thee in Crete] That St. Paul had been in Crete, though nowhere else intimated, is clear from this passage. That he could not have made such an important visit, and evangelized an island of the first consequence, without its being mentioned by his historian, Luke, had it happened during the period embraced in the Acts of the Apostles, must be evident. That the journey, therefore, must have been performed *after* the time in which St. Luke ends his history, that is, after St. Paul's first imprisonment at Rome, seems almost certain.

Set in order the things that are wanting] It appears from this that the apostle did not spend much time in Crete, and that he was obliged to leave it before he had got the Church properly organized. The supplying of this defect, he tells Titus, he had confided to him as one whose spiritual views coincided entirely with his own.

Ordain elders in every city] That thou mightest appoint, καταστησῃς, elders—persons well instructed in Divine things, who should be able to instruct others, and observe and enforce the discipline of the Church. It appears that those who are called *elders* in this place are the same as those termed *bishops* in ver. 7. We have many proofs that bishops and elders were of the same order in the apostolic Church, though afterwards they became distinct. Lord Peter King, in his view of the primitive Church, has written well on this subject.

In every city.—Κατα πολιν. This seems to intimate that the apostle had gone over the whole of the *hecatompolis* or *hundred cities* for which this island was celebrated. Indeed it is not likely that he would leave one in which he had not preached Christ crucified.

Verse 6. If any be blameless] See the notes on 1 Tim. iii. 2, &c.

Having faithful children] Whose family is converted to God. It would have been absurd to employ a man to govern the Church whose children were not in subjection to himself ; for it is an apostolic maxim, that he who cannot rule his own house, cannot rule the Church of God ; 1 Tim. iii. 5.

Verse 7. Not self-willed] Μη αυθαδη· Not one who is determined to have his own way in every thing ; setting up his own judgment to that of all others ; expecting all to pay homage to his understanding. Such a governor in the Church of God can do little good, and may do much mischief.

Not soon angry] Μη οργιλον· Not a choleric man ; one who is irritable ; who is apt to be inflamed on every opposition ; one who has not proper command over his own temper.

Verse 8. A lover of hospitality] Φιλοξενον· A lover *of strangers.* See the note on 1 Tim. iii. 2. Instead of φιλοξενον, one MS. has φιλοπτωχον, a lover *of the poor.* That minister who neglects the *poor*, but is frequent in his visits to the *rich*, knows little of his Master's work, and has little of his Master's spirit.

A lover of good men] Φιλαγαθον· A lover *of goodness* or of *good things* in general.

Sober] Prudent in all his conduct. *Just* in all his dealings. *Holy* in his heart. *Temperate*—self-denying and abstemious, in his food and raiment ; not too nice on points of honour, nor magisterially rigid in the exercise of his ecclesiastical functions. Qualifications rarely found in spiritual governors.

Verse 9. Holding fast the faithful word] Conscientiously retaining, and zealously maintaining, the true Christian doctrine, κατα την διδαχην, according to *the instructions*, or according to the *institutions, form of sound doctrine*, or *confession of faith*, which I have delivered to thee.

That he may be able by sound doctrine] If the doctrine be not *sound*, vain is the profession of it, and vain its influence. It is good to be zealously affected

2

A. M. cir. 4069.
A. D. 65 or 66.
A. U. C. 818.
An. Imp. Ne-
ronis Cæs.
Aug. 12.

10 For ᵈ there are many un-ruly and vain talkers and ᵉ de-ceivers, ᶠ specially they of the circumcision:

11 Whose mouths must be stopped, ᵍ who subvert whole houses, teaching things which they ought not, ʰ for filthy lucre's sake.

12 ⁱ One of themselves, *even a* prophet of their own, said, The Cretians *are* always liars, evil beasts, slow bellies.

13 This witness is true. ᵏ Wherefore re-buke them sharply; that they may be ˡ sound in the faith;

A. M. cir. 4069.
A. D. 65 or 66.
A. U. C. 818.
An. Imp. Ne-
ronis Cæs.
Aug. 12.

ᵈ 1 Tim. i. 6.——ᵉ Rom. xvi. 18.——ᶠ Acts xv. 1.——ᵍ Matt. xxiii. 14; 2 Tim. iii. 6.

ʰ 1 Tim. vi. 5.——ⁱ Acts xvii. 28.——ᵏ 2 Cor. xiii. 10; 2 Tim. iv. 2.——ˡ Chap. ii. 2.

in a good thing; but zeal for what is not of God will do no good to the souls of men, how sincere soever that zeal may be.

To exhort] Them to hold the faith, that they may persevere.

And to convince] Refute the objections, confound the sophistry, and convert the gainsayers; and thus defend the truth.

Verse 10. *There are many unruly*] Persons who will not receive the sound doctrine, nor come under wholesome discipline.

Vain talkers] Empty boasters of knowledge, rights, and particular privileges; all *noise*, empty parade, and no *work*.

Deceivers] Of the souls of men by their specious pretensions.

They of the circumcision] The Judaizing teachers, who maintained the necessity of circumcision, and of observing the rites and ceremonies of the Mosaic law, in order to the perfecting of the Gospel.

Verse 11. *Whose mouths must be stopped*] Unmask them at once; exhibit them to the people; make manifest their ignorance and hypocrisy; and let them be confounded before the people whom they are en-deavouring to seduce.

Subvert whole houses] Turn whole Christian fami-lies from the faith, attributing to the *broad way* what belongs only to the *strait gate*; ministering to disor-derly passions, and promising salvation to their prose-lytes, though not saved from their sins.

Verse 12. *One of themselves, even a prophet of their own*] This was *Epimenides*, who was born at *Gnossus*, in Crete, and was reckoned by many the *seventh wise man* of Greece, instead of *Periander*, to whom that honour was by them denied. Many fabulous things are related of this poet, which are not proper to be noticed here. He died about 538 years before the Christian era. When St. Paul calls him a *prophet of their own*, he only intimates that he was, by the *Cre-tans*, reputed a *prophet*. And, according to Plutarch, (*in Solone*,) the Cretans paid him divine honours after his death. *Diogenes Laertius* mentions some of his prophecies: beholding the fort of Munichia, which guarded the port of Athens, he cried out: "O igno-rant men! if they but knew what slaughters this fort shall occasion, they would pull it down with their teeth!" This prophecy was fulfilled several years after, when the king, Antipater, put a garrison in this very fort, to keep the Athenians in subjection. See *Diog. Laert.*, lib. i. p. 73.

Plato, *De Legibus*, lib. ii., says that, on the Athe-nians expressing great fear of the Persians, Epimenides

encouraged them by saying "that they should not come before *ten* years, and that they should return after having suffered great disasters." This predic-tion was supposed to have been fulfilled in the defeat of the Persians in the battles of Salamis and Marathon.

He predicted to the Lacedemonians and Cretans the captivity to which they should one day be reduced by the Arcadians. This took place under Euricrates, king of Crete, and Archidamus, king of Lacedemon; vide *Diog. Laert.*, lib. i. p. 74, edit. *Meibom*.

It was in consequence of these prophecies, whether true or false, that his countrymen esteemed him a *prophet*; that he was termed ανηρ αθειος, a divine man, by Plato; and that Cicero, *De Divin.*, lib. i., says he was *futura præsciens, et vaticinans per furorem*: "He knew future events, and prophesied under a di-vine influence." These things are sufficient to justify the epithet of *prophet*, given him here by St. Paul. It may also be remarked that *vates* and *poeta*, prophet and poet, were synonymous terms among the Romans.

The Cretians are always liars] The words quoted here by the apostle are, according to St. *Jerome*, So-crates, *Nicephorus*, and others, taken from a work of Epimenides, now no longer extant, entitled Περι χρησμων· *Concerning Oracles*. The words form a hexameter verse:—

Κρητες αει ψευσται, κακα θηρια, γαστερες αργαι.

The Cretans are always liars; destructive wild beasts; sluggish gluttons.

That the Cretans were reputed to be egregious liars, several of the ancients declare; insomuch that Κρη-τιζειν, to act like a Cretan, signifies *to lie*; and χρησθαι Κρητισμω, to deceive. The other Greeks reputed them liars, because they said that among them was the sepul-chre of Jupiter, who was the highest object of the Greek and Roman worship. By telling this *truth*, which all others would have to pass for a *lie*, the Cre-tans showed that the object of their highest admiration was only a *dead man*.

Evil beasts] Ferocious and destructive in their manners.

Slow bellies.] Addicted to voluptuousness, idleness, and gluttony; sluggish or hoggish men.

Verse 13. *This witness is true.*] What Epimenides said of them nearly 600 years before continued still to be true. Their original character had undergone no moral change.

Rebuke them sharply] Αποτομως· *Cuttingly, severely;* show no indulgence to persons guilty of such crimes.

That they may be sound in the faith] That they may receive the incorrupt doctrine, and illustrate it by a holy and useful life.

2   649

A. M. cir. 4069.
A. D. 65 or 66.
A. U. C. 818.
An. Imp. Ne-
ronis Cæs.
Aug. 12.

14 ^m Not giving heed to Jewish fables, and ⁿ commandments of men, that turn from the truth.

15 ^o Unto the pure all things *are* pure, but ^p unto them that are defiled and unbelieving

is nothing pure : but even their mind and conscience is defiled.

16 They profess that they know God ; but ^q in works they deny *him,* being abominable, and disobedient, ^r and unto every good work ^s reprobate.

A. M. cir. 4069.
A. D. 65 or 66.
A. U. C. 818.
An. Imp. Ne-
ronis Cæs.
Aug. 12.

---

^m 1 Timothy i. 4; iv. 7; 2 Timothy iv. 4.——ⁿ Isaiah xxix. 13; Matthew xv. 9; Colossians ii. 22.——^o Luke xi. 39, 40, 41; Romans xiv. 14, 20; 1 Cor. vi. 12; x. 23, 25; 1 Timothy

iv. 3, 4.——^p Romans xiv. 23.——^q 2 Timothy iii. 5; Jude 4. ^r Romans i. 28; 2 Timothy iii. 8.——^s Or, *void of judgment.*

Verse 14. *Not giving heed to Jewish fables*] See on 1 Tim. i. 4, and iv. 7.

Commandments of men] The injunctions of the scribes and Pharisees, which they added to the law of God.

That turn from the truth.] For such persons made the word of God of none effect by their traditions. Sometimes the verb αποστρεφομαι signifies to be *averse from, slight,* or *despise.* So, here, the persons in question despised the truth, and taught others to do the same.

Verse 15. *Unto the pure all things* are *pure*] This appears to have been spoken in reference to the Jewish distinctions of *clean* and *unclean meats.* To the genuine Christian every kind of meat proper for human nourishment is pure, is lawful, and may be used without scruple. This our Lord had long before decided. See on Luke xi. 39–41.

But unto them that are defiled] In their consciences, and *unbelieving,* απιστοις, *unfaithful* both to *offered* and *received* grace, *nothing is pure*—they have no part in Christ, and the wrath of God abides upon them. Their *mind* is contaminated with impure and unholy *images* and *ideas,* and *their conscience is defiled* with the *guilt of sins* already committed against God.

Verse 16. *They profess that they know God*] He still speaks concerning the unbelieving Jews, the seducing teachers, and those who had been seduced by their bad doctrine. None were so full of pretensions to the knowledge of the true God as the Jews. They would not admit that any other people could have this knowledge ; nor did they believe that God ever did or ever would reveal himself to any other people ; they supposed that to give the *law* and the *prophets* to the Gentiles would be a profanation of the words of God. Hence they became both proud, uncharitable, and intolerant ; and in this disposition they continue till the present day.

But in works they deny him] Their profession and practice were at continual variance. Full of a pretended faith, while utterly destitute of those *works* by which a genuine faith is accredited and proved. *Dio Cassius* represents Cæsar as saying of his mutinous soldiers : Ονομα 'Ρωμαιων εχοντας, εργα δε Κελτων δρων-τας. "Having the name of Romans, while they had the manners of the Gauls." How near are those words to the saying of the apostle !

Being abominable] Βδελυκτοι. This word sometimes refers to unnatural lusts.

And disobedient] Απειθεις· *Unpersuadable, unbelieving,* and consequently *disobedient.* Characters remarkably applicable to the Jews through all their generations.

Unto every good work reprobate.] Αδοκιμοι· *Adulterate ;* like bad coin, deficient both in the *weight* and *goodness* of the *metal,* and without the proper sterling *stamp ;* and consequently not *current.* If they did a good work, they did not do it in the spirit in which it should be performed. They had the name of God's people ; but they were counterfeit. The prophet said : *Reprobate silver shall men call them.*

1. Though the principal part of this chapter, and indeed of the whole epistle, may be found in nearly the same words in the *First* Epistle to Timothy, yet there are several circumstances here that are not so particularly noted in the other ; and every minister of Christ will do well to make himself master of both ; they should be carefully registered in his memory, and engraven on his heart.

2. The *truth,* which is *according to godliness,* in reference to *eternal life,* should be carefully regarded. The substantial knowledge of the truth must have *faith* for its foundation, *godliness* for its rule, and *eternal life* for its object and end. He who does not begin well, is never likely to finish fair. He who does not refer every thing to *eternity,* is never likely to live either well or happily in *time.*

3. There is one subject in this chapter not sufficiently attended to by those who have the authority to appoint men to ecclesiastical offices ; none should be thus appointed who is *not able, by sound doctrine, both to exhort and convince the gainsayers.* The powers necessary for this are partly *natural,* partly *gracious,* and partly *acquired.* 1. If a man have not good natural abilities, nothing but a miracle from heaven can make him a proper preacher of the Gospel ; and to make a man a Christian minister, who is unqualified for any function of *civil life,* is sacrilege before God. 2. If the *grace of God* do not communicate ministerial qualifications, no natural gifts, however splendid, can be of any avail. To be a successful Christian minister, a man must *feel the worth* of immortal souls in such a way as God only can show it, in order to spend and be spent in the work. He who has never passed through the travail of the soul in the work of regeneration in his own heart, can never make plain the way of salvation to others. 3. He who is employed in the Christian ministry should *cultivate his mind* in the most diligent manner ; he can neither learn nor know too much. If called of God to be a preacher, (and without such a call he had better be a galley slave,) he will be able to bring all his knowledge to the assistance and success of his ministry. If he have human learning, so much the better ; if he be accredited, and appointed by those who have authority in the

Church, it will be to his advantage; but no human learning, no ecclesiastical appointment, no mode of ordination, whether Popish, Episcopal, Protestant, or Presbyterian, can ever supply the *Divine unction,* without which he never can convert and build up the souls of men. The piety of the flock must be faint and languishing when it is not animated by the heavenly zeal of the pastor; *they* must be blind if *he* be not enlightened; and their faith must be wavering when he can neither encourage nor defend it.

4. In consequence of the appointment of improper persons to the Christian ministry, there has been, not only a decay of piety, but also a corruption of religion. No man is a true Christian minister who has not *grace, gifts,* and *fruit;* if he have the grace of God, it will appear in his holy life and godly conversation. If to this he add genuine abilities, he will give full proof of his ministry; and if he give full proof of his ministry, he will have *fruit;* the souls of sinners will be converted to God through his preaching, and believers will be built up on their most holy faith. How contemptible must that man appear in the eyes of common sense, who boasts of his clerical education, his sacerdotal *order,* his legitimate authority to preach, administer the Christian sacraments, &c., while no soul is benefited by his ministry! Such a person may have legal authority to take tithes, but as to an appointment from God, *he* has none; else his word would be with power, and his preaching the means of salvation to his perishing hearers.

CHAPTER II.

Sundry directions to aged men, 1, 2. *To aged women,* 3. *To young women,* 4, 5. *To young men* 6. *Directions to Titus, relative to his own conduct,* 7, 8. *Directions to servants,* 9, 10. *What the Gospel of the grace of God teaches all men,* 11, 12. *The glorious prospect held out by it; salvation from all sin, and final glory,* 13–15.

A. M. cir. 4069.
A. D. 65 or 66.
A. U. C. 818.
An. Imp. Neronis Cæs.
Aug. 12.

BUT speak thou the things which become [a] sound doctrine:

2 That the aged men be [b] sober, grave, temperate, [c] sound in faith, in charity, in patience.

3 [d] The aged women likewise, that *they* be in behaviour as becometh [e] holiness, not [f] false accusers, not given to much wine, teachers of good things;

4 That they may teach the young women

A. M. cir. 4069.
A. D. 65 or 66.
A. U. C. 818.
An. Imp. Neronis Cæs.
Aug. 12.

---

[a] 1 Tim. i. 10; vi. 3; 2 Tim. i. 13; chap. i. 9.——[b] Or, *vigilant.* [c] Chap. i. 13.

[d] 1 Tim. ii. 9, 10; iii. 11; 1 Peter iii. 3, 4.——[e] Or, *holy women.* [f] Or, *makebates;* 2 Tim. iii. 3.

NOTES ON CHAP. II.

Verse 1. But speak thou the things] This is a conclusion drawn from the preceding chapter: the Judaizing teachers not only taught a false doctrine, but they led an unholy life; Titus was to act directly opposite; he must teach a sacred doctrine, and the things which become it; he must proclaim the truth, and illustrate that truth. The people must not only be well instructed, but they must be holy in their lives. Principle and practice must go hand in hand.

Verse 2. That the aged men be sober] It is very likely that the word *aged* is to be taken here in its literal sense; that it refers to *advanced years,* and not to any *office* in the Church: the whole context seems to require this sense.

For an old man to be a drunkard, a light and trifling person, and a glutton, and not to be *sober, grave,* and *temperate,* is not only blamable but monstrous. Seneca has well said: *Luxuriosus adolescens peccat; senex insanit.* "A young man addicted to a life of luxury transgresses; an old man thus addicted runs mad."

Verse 3. The aged women likewise] I believe *elderly* women are meant, and not *deaconesses.*

That they be in behaviour] Εν καταστηματι ιεροπρεπεις· That they be in their *dress, gait,* and general *deportment,* such as their holy calling requires; that they be not like the world but like the Church, decent without, and adorned with holiness within.

Not false accusers] Μη διαβολους· Not devils; we have had the same expression applied in the same way, 1 Tim. iii. 11, where see the note.

Not given to much wine] Μη οινω πολλω δεδουλωμενας· Not *enslaved* by much wine, not habitual drunkards or tipplers; *habit* is a species of *slavery.* Both among the Greeks and Romans old women were generally reputed to be fond of much wine; hence the ancient scholiast on Homer, Il. vi., speaking of old women, says: Χαιρει τω οινω η ηλικια αυτη· *At this age they delight in wine;* which words Ovid seems to have translated literally: *Vinosior ætas hæc erat.* It is likely, therefore, that it was customary among the elderly women, both Greeks and Romans, to drink much wine; and because it was inconsistent with that *moderation* which the Gospel requires, the apostle forbids it: doubtless it was not considered criminal among them, because it was a common practice; and we know that the Greek philosophers and physicians, who denied wine to young persons, judged it to be necessary for the aged. See the note on 1 Tim. v. 23.

Verse 4. That they may teach the young women to be sober] That it was natural for the young to imitate the old will be readily allowed; it was therefore necessary that the old should be an example of

A. M. cir. 4069.
A. D. 65 or 66.
A. U. C. 818.
An. Imp. Neronis Cæs.
Aug. 12.

to be [g] sober, [h] to love their husbands, to love their children,
5 *To be* discreet, chaste, keepers at home, good, [i] obedient to
their own husbands, [k] that the word of God
be not blasphemed.
6 Young men likewise exhort to be [l] sober-
minded.
7 [m] In all things showing thyself a pattern
of good works: in doctrine *show-*
ing uncorruptness, gravity, [n] sincerity,
8 [o] Sound speech that cannot
be condemned; [p] that he that is of the contrary part [q] may be ashamed, having no evil
thing to say of you.
9 *Exhort* [r] servants to be obedient unto their
own masters, *and* to please *them* well [s] in

A. M. cir. 4069.
A. D. 65 or 66.
A. U. C. 818.
An. Imp. Neronis Cæs.
Aug. 12.

[g] Or, *wise.*——[h] 1 Tim. v. 14.——[i] 1 Cor. xiv. 34; Eph. v. 22; Col. iii. 18; 1 Tim. ii. 11; 1 Pet. iii. 1, 5.——[k] Romans ii. 24; 1 Tim. vi. 1.——[l] Or, *discreet.*——[m] 1 Timothy iv. 12; 1 Peter v. 3.

[n] Eph. vi. 24.——[o] 1 Tim. vi. 3.——[p] Neh. v. 9; 1 Tim. v. 14; 1 Pet. ii. 12, 15; iii. 16.——[q] 2 Thess. iii. 14.——[r] Eph. vi. 5, Col. iii. 22; 1 Timothy vi. 1, 2; 1 Peter ii. 18.——[s] Eph v. 24.

godly living to the young. St. Jerome, taking it for granted that *drunkenness* and *impurity* are closely connected, asks this serious question: *Quomodo potest docere anus adolescentulas castitatem, cum, si ebrietatem vetulæ mulieris adolescentula fuerit imitata, pudica esse non possit?* "How can an elderly woman teach young women chastity, when, if the young woman should imitate the drunkenness of the matron, it would be impossible for her to be chaste?"

To love their husbands] The duties recommended in this and the following verses are so plain as to need no comment; and so absolutely necessary to the character of a wife, that no one deserves the name who does not live in the practice of them.

Verse 5. *Keepers at home*] Οικουρους. A woman who spends much time in *visiting*, must neglect her family. The idleness, dirtiness, impudence, and profligacy of the children, will soon show how deeply criminal the mother was in rejecting the apostle's advice. Instead of *οικουρους*, *keepers of the house*, or *keepers at home*, ACD*EFG, and several of the *Itala*, have *οικουργους*, *workers at home;* not only *staying in the house* and *keeping* the *house*, but *working* in the *house*. A woman may keep the house very closely, and yet do little in it for the support or comfort of the family.

That the word of God be not blasphemed.] The enemies of the Gospel are quick-eyed to spy out imperfections in its professors; and, if they find women professing Christianity living an irregular life, they will not fail to decry the Christian doctrine on this account: "Behold your boasted religion! it professes to reform all things, and its very professors are no better than others! Our heathenism is as good as your Christianity." These are cutting reproaches; and much they will have to answer for who give cause for these blasphemies.

Verse 6. *Young men—exhort to be sober-minded.*] Reformation should begin with the old; they have the authority, and they should give the example. The young of both sexes must also give an account of themselves to God; *sober-mindedness* in young men is a rare qualification, and they who have it not plunge into excesses and irregularities which in general sap the foundation of their constitution, bring on premature old age, and not seldom lead to a fatal end.

Verse 7. *In all things showing thyself a pattern*] As the apostle had given directions relative to the conduct of *old men*, ver. 2, of *old women*, ver. 3, of *young women*, ver. 4, and of *young men*, ver. 6, the words *περι παντα*, which we translate *in all things*, should be rather considered in reference to the above persons, and the behaviour required in them: *showing thyself a pattern of good works to all these persons*—being, in *sobriety*, *gravity*, *temperance*, what thou requirest others to be.

In doctrine showing *uncorruptness*] Mixing nothing with the truth; taking nothing from it; adding nothing to it; and exhibiting it in all its connection, energy, and fulness.

Verse 8. *Sound speech*] Λογον ὑγιη· *Sound* or *healing doctrine.* Human nature is in a state of *dis ease;* and the doctrine of the Gospel is calculated to remove the disease, and restore all to perfect *health* and *soundness.* All false doctrines leave men under the influence of this spiritual disease; the unadulterated doctrine of the Gospel alone can *heal* men.

He that is of the contrary part] Whether this may refer to the Judaizing teachers in general, or to some *one* who might, by his false doctrine, have been disturbing the peace of the Churches in Crete, we cannot tell.

Having no evil thing to say of you.] Against a person who is sound in his doctrine, and holy in his life, no evil can be justly alleged. He who reports evil of such a person must be confounded when brought to the test. Instead of *περι ὑμων*, *of* YOU, *περι ἡμων*, *of* US, is the reading of CDEFG, and about forty others; with both the *Syriac*, all the *Arabic*, *Slavonic*, *Vulgate*, *Itala*, and several of the primitive *fathers*. This reading makes a better sense, and is undoubtedly genuine.

Verse 9. Exhort *servants to be obedient*] The apostle refers to those who were *slaves*, and the *property* of their masters; even these are exhorted to be obedient *ἰδιοις δεσποταις*, *to their own despots*, though they had no right over them on the ground of *natural justice*.

Please them *well in all* things] They were to endeavour to do this in all things, though they could not hope to succeed in every thing.

Not answering again] Μη αντιλεγοντας· *Not contradicting* or *gainsaying*. This is no part of a servant's duty; a servant is hired to do his master's work, and this his master has a right to appoint.

A. M. cir. 4069.
A. D. 65 or 66.
A. U. C. 818.
An. Imp. Ne-
ronis Cæs.
Aug. 12.

all *things;* not ^t answering again;

10 Not purloining, but show-ing all good fidelity; ^u that

they may adorn the doctrine of God our Saviour in all things.

11 For ^v the grace of God

A. M. cir. 4069.
A. D. 65 or 66.
A. U. C. 818.
An. Imp. Ne-
ronis Cæs.
Aug. 12.

---

^t Or, *gainsaying.*——^u Matt. v. 16; Phil. ii. 15.

^v Rom. v. 15; Col. i. 6; chap. iii. 4, 5; 1 Pet. v. 12.

Verse 10. *Not purloining*] Μη νοσφιζομενους· Nei-ther *giving away, privately selling,* nor in any way *wasting,* the master's goods. The word signifies, not only *stealing* but *embezzling* another's property; *keep-ing back a part of the price* of any commodity sold on the master's account. In Acts v. 2, we translate it, *to keep back part of the price;* the crime of which Ananias and Sapphira were guilty. It has been re-marked that among the heathens this species of fraud was very frequent; and servants were so noted for purloining and embezzling their master's property that *fur,* which signifies a *thief,* was commonly used to signify a *servant;* hence that verse in Virgil, Eclog. iii. 16 :——

Quid domini faciant, audent cum talia FURES?

" What may not masters do, when servants (thieves) are so bold?"

On which *Servius* remarks: *Pro* SERVO FUREM *posuit, furta enim specialiter servorum sunt. Sic Plautus de servo, Homo es trium literarum,* i. e. *fur.* "He puts *fur,* a thief, to signify a *servant,* because servants are commonly thieves. Thus Plautus, speaking of a *servant,* says: Thou art a man of three letters, i. e. *f-u-r,* a thief." And *Terence* denominates a number of ser-*vants, manipulus furum,* " a bundle of thieves." Eun. 4, 7, 6. The place in Plautus to which Servius refers is in *Aulul.,* act ii. scene iv. *in fine :——*

———*Tun', trium literarum homo, Me vituperas? F-u-r, etiam fur trifurcifer.*

" Dost thou blame me, thou man of three letters? Thou art a thief, and the most notorious of all knaves."

It was necessary, therefore, that the apostle should be so very particular in his directions to *servants,* as they were in general *thieves* almost by profession.

Verse 11. *The grace of God that bringeth salvation hath appeared to all men*] Επεφανη γαρ ἡ χαρις του Θεου ἡ σωτηριος πασιν ανθρωποις· Literally translated, the words stand thus: *For the grace of God, that which saves, hath shone forth upon all men.* Or, as it is expressed in the margin of our authorized version: *The grace of God, that bringeth salvation to all men, hath appeared.* As *God's grace* signifies God's *fa-vour,* any *benefit* received from him may be termed *God's grace.* In this place, and in Col. i. 6, the *Gos-pel,* which points out God's infinite mercy to the world, is termed the *grace of God;* for it is not only a *favour* of infinite worth in itself, but it announces that great-est gift of God to man, the incarnation and atoning sacrifice of Jesus Christ. Now it cannot be said, ex-cept in a very refined and spiritual sense, that this Gospel had then *appeared to all men;* but it may be well said that *it bringeth salvation to all men;* this is

its design; and it was *to taste death for every man* that its author came into the world. There is a beauty and energy in the word επεφανη, *hath shined out,* that is rarely noted; it seems to be a metaphor taken from the *sun.* As by his rising in the east and *shining out,* he enlightens, *successively,* the whole world; so the Lord Jesus, who is called *the Sun of righteous-ness,* Mal. iv. 2, arises on the whole human race with healing in his wings. And as the *light* and *heat* of the sun are denied to no nation nor individual, so the grace of the Lord Jesus, this also *shines out upon all;* and God designs that all mankind shall be as equally benefited by it in reference to their *souls,* as they are in respect to their bodies by the sun that shines in the firmament of heaven. But as all the parts of the earth are not *immediately* illuminated, but come into the so-lar light *successively,* not only in consequence of the earth's diurnal revolution round its own axis, but in consequence of its annual revolution round its whole orbit; so this Sun of righteousness, who has *shined out,* is bringing every part of the habitable globe into his Divine light; that light is shining more and more to the perfect day; so that *gradually* and *successively* he is enlightening every nation, and every man; and, when his *great year* is filled up, every nation of the earth shall be brought into the light and heat of this unspotted, uneclipsed, and eternal Sun of righteous-ness and truth. Wherever the Gospel comes, it brings *salvation*—it offers *deliverance from all sin* to every soul that hears or reads it. As freely as the sun dis-penses his genial influences to every inhabitant of the earth, so freely does Jesus Christ dispense the merits and blessings of his passion and death to every soul of man. From the influences of this spiritual Sun no soul is *reprobated* any more than from the influences of the natural sun. In both cases, only those who wilfully shut their eyes, and hide themselves in dark-ness, are deprived of the gracious benefit. It is no objection to this view of the subject, that whole nations have not yet received the Divine light. When the earth and the sun were created, every part of the globe did not come *immediately* into the light; to effect this purpose fully there must be a complete revolution, as has been marked above, and this could not be effected till the earth had not only revolved on its own axis, but passed successively through all the signs of the zodiac. When its *year* was completed, and not till then, every part had its due proportion of light and heat. God may, in his infinite wisdom, have deter-mined the *times* and the *seasons* for the full manifes tation of the Gospel to the nations of the world, as he has done in reference to the solar light; and when the Jews are brought in with the fulness of the Gen-tiles, then, and not till then, can we say that the *grand revolution of the important* YEAR *of the Sun of right-eousness is completed.* But, in the meantime, the

2

A. M. cir. 4069.
A. D. 65 or 66.
A. U. C. 818.
An. Imp. Ne-
ronis Cæs.
Aug. 12.

ʷ that bringeth salvation ˣ hath appeared to all men,

12 Teaching us, ʸ that, denying ungodliness ᶻ and worldly lusts, we should live soberly, righteously,

and godly, in this present world;

13 ᵃ Looking for that blessed ᵇ hope, and the glorious ᶜ appearing of the great God and our Saviour Jesus Christ;

A. M. cir. 4069
A. D. 65 or 66.
A. U. C. 818.
An. Imp. Ne-
ronis Cæs.
Aug. 12.

ʷ Or, *that bringeth salvation to all men, hath appeared.*——ˣ Luke iii. 6; John i. 9; 1 Tim. ii. 4.——ʸ Luke i. 75; Rom. vi. 19; Eph. i. 4; Col. i. 22; 1 Thess. iv. 7.——ᶻ 1 Pet. iv. 2; 1 John ii. 16.

ᵃ 1 Cor. i. 7; Phil. iii. 20; 2 Pet. iii. 12.——ᵇ Acts xxiv. 15; Col. i. 5, 23; chap. i. 2; iii. 7.——ᶜ Col. iii. 4; 2 Tim. iv. 1, 8; Heb. ix. 28; 1 Pet. i. 7; 1 John iii. 2.

---

unenlightened parts of the earth are not left in total darkness; as there was light

"————————ere the infant sun
Was rolled together, or had tried his beams
Athwart the gloom profound;"

light being created, and in a certain measure dispersed, at least three whole days before the *sun* was formed; (for his creation was a part of the *fourth* day's work;) so, previously to the incarnation of Christ, there was *spiritual light* in the world; for he diffused his *beams* while his *orb* was yet unseen. And even now, where by the preaching of his Gospel he is not yet manifested, he is that true light which enlightens every man coming into the world; so that the moral world is no more left to absolute darkness, where the Gospel is not yet preached, than the earth was the four days which preceded the creation of the sun, or those parts of the world are where the Gospel has not yet been preached. The *great year* is rolling on, and all the parts of the earth are coming successively, and now *rapidly*, into the light. The vast *revolution* seems to be nearly completed, and the whole world is about to be filled with the light and glory of God. A heathen poet, apparently under the inspiration of God (for God has his witnesses every where) speaks of those glorious times in *words* and *numbers* which nothing but the Spirit of God can equal. It gratifies myself to refer to them, and it will gratify my reader to find them entered here:—

Ultima Cumæi venit jam carminis ætas:
Magnus ab integro sæclorum nascitur ordo.—
Talia sæcla suis dixerunt, currite, fusis
Concordes stabili fatorum numine Parcæ.—
Aspice convexo nutantem pondere mundum,
Terrasque, tractusque maris, cœlumque profundum:
Aspice, venturo lætentur ut omnia sæclo!—

The last *great age*, foretold by sacred rhymes,
Renews its *finish'd course;* Saturnian times
Roll round again; and *mighty years*, begun
From their first orb, in radiant circles run.
Majestic months, with swift but steady pace,
Set out with him on their appointed race.—
The Fates, when they their happy web have spun,
Shall bless the clew, and bid it smoothly run.—
See labouring nature calls thee to sustain
The nodding frame of heaven and earth and main;
See, to their base restored, earth, seas, and air;
And joyful ages from behind appear
In crowding ranks.   DRYDEN.

Hasten the time, thou God of ages! Even so. Amen. Come, Lord Jesus!

Verse 12. *Teaching us, that, denying, &c.*] Παιδευουσα· Instructing us as *children* are instructed. Christ is the great teacher; and men, in order to learn, must become his *disciples*—must put themselves under his tuition, and learn of him.

Denying ungodliness] Ασεβειαν· All things contrary to God; whatever would lead us to doubt his being, deny any of his essential attributes; his providence or government of the world, and his influence on the souls of men. Every thing, also, which is opposed to his true worship; theoretical and practical atheism, deism, and irreligion in general.

Worldly lusts] Such desires, affections, and appetites, as men are governed by who have their portion in this life, and live without God in the world. Gluttony, drunkenness, lasciviousness, anger, malice, and revenge; together with the immoderate love of riches, power, and fame.

We should live soberly] Having every temper, appetite, and desire, under the government of *reason*, and reason itself under the government of the *Spirit of God*.

Righteously] Rendering to every man his due, injuring no person in his body, mind, reputation, or property; doing unto all as we would they should do to us; and filling up the duties of the particular stations in which it has pleased God to fix us, committing no sin, omitting no duty.

And godly] Ευσεβως. Just the reverse of what is implied in *ungodliness.* See above.

In this present world] Not supposing that any thing will be purified in the world to come that is not cleansed in this. The three words above evidently include our duty to God, to our neighbour, and to ourselves. 1. We are to live *soberly* in respect to *ourselves.* 2. *Righteously* in respect to our *neighbour.* And 3. *Godly*, or piously, in respect to our *Maker.*

Verse 13. *Looking for that blessed hope*] Expecting the grand object of our hope, *eternal life.* See chap. i. ver. 2. This is what the Gospel teaches us to expect, and what the grace of God prepares the human heart for. This is called a *blessed* hope; those who have it are *happy* in the sure prospect of that glory which shall be revealed.

The glorious appearing] Και επιφανειαν της δοξης του μεγαλου Θεου και σωτηρος ημων Ιησου Χριστου. This clause, literally translated, is as follows: And the appearing of the glory of the great God, even our Saviour Jesus Christ. On this passage I must refer the reader to the ESSAY ON THE GREEK ARTICLE, by H. S. Boyd, Esq., appended to the notes on the Epistle to the Ephesians, where both the *structure* and *doctrine* of this passage are explained at large.

A. M. cir. 4069.
A. D. 65 or 66.
A. U. C. 818.
An. Imp. Ne-
ronis Cæs.
Aug. 12.

14 ^d Who gave himself for us, that he might redeem us from all iniquity, ^e and purify unto himself ^f a peculiar people, ^g zealous of good works.

15 These things speak, and ^h exhort, and rebuke with all authority. ⁱ Let no man despise thee.

A. M. cir. 4069.
A. D. 65 or 66.
A. U. C. 818.
An. Imp. Ne-
ronis Cæs.
Aug. 12.

^d Gal. i. 4; ii. 20; Eph. v. 2; 1 Tim. ii. 6.——^e Heb. ix. 14.
^f Exod. xv. 16; xix. 5; Deut. vii. 6; xiv. 2; xxvi. 18; 1 Pet. ii.

9.——^g Eph. ii. 10; 1 Thess. v. 14; 1 Tim. vi. 2; 2 Tim. iv. 2; ver. 6, 9; chap. iii. 8.——^h 2 Tim. iv. 2.——ⁱ 1 Tim. iv. 12. -

Some think that the *blessed hope* and *glorious appearing* mean the same thing; but I do not think so. The *blessed hope* refers simply to eternal glorification in general; the *glorious appearing,* to the resurrection of the body; for when Christ appears he will change this vile body, and make it like unto his GLORIOUS BODY, according to the working by which he is able even to subdue all things to himself. See Phil. iii. 20, 21.

Verse 14. *Who gave himself for us*] Who gave his own life as a *ransom price* to redeem ours. This is evidently what is meant, as the words λυτρωσηται and λαον περιουσιον imply. The verd λυτροω signifies to *redeem* or *ransom by paying a price,* as I have often had occasion to observe; and περιουσιος signifies such a *peculiar property* as a man has in what he has *purchased* with *his own money.* Jesus gave his life for the world, and thus has purchased men unto himself; and, having purchased the *slaves* from their thraldom, he is represented as stripping them of their sordid vestments, *cleansing* and *purifying them unto himself* that they may become his *own servants,* and bringing them out of their *dishonourable* and *oppressive servitude,* in which they had no proper motive to *diligence* and could have no affection for the despot under whose authority they were employed. Thus redeemed, they now become his willing servants, and are *zealous of good works*—affectionately attached to that noble employment which is assigned to them by that Master whom it is an inexpressible honour to serve. This seems to be the allusion in the above verse.

Verse 15. *These things speak*] That is, *teach;* for λαλει, *speak,* has the same meaning here as διδασκε, *teach,* which, as being synonymous, is actually the reading of the *Codex Alexandrinus.*

And exhort] Παρακαλει· Repeat them again and again, and urge them on their attention and consciences.

And rebuke] Ελεγχε· *Demonstrate* the importance, utility, and necessity of them; and show them that God requires their obedience.

With all authority.] Μετα πασης επιταγης· With all that authority with which thy office invests thee, and which thou hast received from God.

Let no man despise thee.] That is: Act so that no person shall have any cause to despise thee, either for thy work, or the manner and spirit in which thou dost perform it.

1. FEW portions of the New Testament excel this chapter. It may well form the creed, system of ethics, and text book of every Christian preacher. Does any man inquire what is the duty of a Gospel minister? Send him to the second chapter of the Epistle to Titus for a complete answer. There he will find what he is to *believe,* what he is to *practise,* and what he is to *preach.* Even his *congregation* is parcelled out to him. The *old* and the *young* of both sexes, and those who are in their employment, are considered to be the objects of his ministry; and a plan of teaching, in reference to those different descriptions of society, is laid down before him. He finds here the *doctrine* which he is to preach to them, the *duties* which he is required to inculcate, the *motives* by which his exhortations are to be strengthened, and the *end* which both he and his people should have invariably in view.

2. The *Godhead* of Jesus Christ is here laid down in a most solemn and explicit manner: He is the great God our Saviour, ο μεγας Θεος και Σωτηρ· human language can go no higher, and the expressions are such, and are so placed, that it is impossible either to misunderstand or to misapply them. HE who is the *great God,* higher than the highest, is our *Saviour;* he who is our *Saviour* is the *great God;* but Jesus Christ is our Saviour, and Jesus Christ is here stated to be the great God.

3. The *extent* of human redemption is here also pointed out. The *saving grace* of this great God hath shone out upon every man; none has been passed by, none left uninfluenced, none without the first offer of *life eternal,* and a sufficiency of grace to qualify him for the state.

4. The *operation* of Divine grace in preparing the soul for glory is next referred to. It cleanses us from all unrighteousness, it purifies us unto God, and makes us fervent and abundant in good works. This system is worthy of God, and is properly suited to the state and necessities of man. These are truths which must be preached, which are not preached enough, and which cannot be preached too often. Awake, pastors! and do not the work of the Lord carelessly. Awake, people! and believe to the saving of your souls. How shall *he* who is styled a minister of the Gospel, and who neither knows, feels, nor heartily inculcates these things, give an account in the great day, of himself, his calling, and his flock, to God? And when this Gospel is preached faithfully and zealously, how shall the people escape who *neglect* so great a salvation? *Neglect,* in such a case, is the highest *contempt* which man can offer to his Maker. Surely such conduct must expect judgment without mixture of mercy. Reader, lay this to heart.

2

CHAPTER III.

The necessity of obedience to the civil powers, and of meek and gentle deportment towards all men, is to be diligently enforced, 1, 2. The wretched state of man, previously to the advent of Christ, 3. The wonderful change which the grace of God makes, and the means which it uses to bring men to glory, 4–7. The necessity of a holy life, and of avoiding things which produce strifes and contentions, and are unprofitable and vain, 8, 9. How to deal with those who are heretics, 10, 11. St. Paul directs Titus to meet him at Nicopolis, and to bring Zenas and Apollos with him, 12, 13. Concluding directions and salutations, 14, 15.

A. M. cir. 4069.
A. D. 65 or 66.
A. U. C. 818.
An. Imp. Neronis Cæs.
Aug. 12.

PUT them in mind ᵃ to be subject to principalities and powers, to obey magistrates, ᵇ to be ready to every good work,

2 ᶜ To speak evil of no man, ᵈ to be no brawlers, *but* ᵉ gentle, showing all ᶠ meekness unto all men.

3 For ᵍ we ourselves also were sometimes foolish, disobedient, deceived, serving divers lusts and pleasures,

A. M. cir. 4069.
A. D. 65 or 66.
A. U. C. 818.
An. Imp. Neronis Cæs.
Aug. 12.

ᵃ Rom. xiii. 1; 1 Pet. ii. 13.——ᵇ Col. i. 10; 2 Tim. ii. 21; Heb. xiii. 21.——ᶜ Eph. iv. 31.——ᵈ 2 Tim. ii. 24, 25.——ᵉ Phil. iv. 5.——ᶠ Eph. iv. 2; Col. iii. 12.——ᵍ 1 Cor. vi. 11; Eph. ii. 1; Col. i. 21; iii. 7; 1 Pet. iv. 3.

NOTES ON CHAP. III.

Verse 1. *Put them in mind to be subject to principalities,* &c.] By *principalities, αρχαις,* we are to understand the Roman *emperors,* or the supreme civil powers in any place.

By *powers, εξουσιαις,* we are to understand the *deputies* of the emperors, such as *proconsuls,* &c., and all such as are in authority under the supreme powers wherever we dwell. See the doctrine of obedience to the civil powers discussed at large in the notes on Rom. xiii. 1–7.

This doctrine of obedience to the civil powers was highly necessary for the Cretans, who were reputed a people exceedingly jealous of their civil privileges, and ready to run into a state of insurrection when they suspected any attempt on the part of their rulers to infringe their liberties. *Suidas,* under the word *ανεσειον, they stirred up,* gives the following fragment: Οἱ δε Κρητες, φοβουμενοι μη τι τιμωριας τυχωσιν, ανεσειον τα πληθη, παρακαλουντες την εξ αιωνος παραδεδομενην ελευθεριαν διαφυλαττειν. "But the Cretans, fearing lest they should be punished, stirred up the populace, exhorting them that they should carefully preserve that liberty which they had received from their ancestors." What part of the history of Crete this refers to I cannot tell; the words stand thus insulated in Suidas, without introduction or connection. To be jealous of our civil rights and privileges, and most strenuously to preserve them, is highly praiseworthy; but to raise a public tumult to avoid merited chastisement, under pretence that our civil privileges are in danger, is not the part of *patriots* but insurgents. For such advice as that given here the known character of the Cretans is a sufficient reason: "They were ever liars, ferocious wild beasts, and sluggish gluttons." Such persons would feel little disposition to submit to the wholesome restraints of law.

Verse 2. *To speak evil of no man*] Μηδενα βλασφημειν· To blaspheme no person, to reproach none, to speak nothing to any man's injury; but, on the contrary, bearing reproach and contumely with patience and meekness.

Verse 3. *For we ourselves*] All of us, whether Jews or Gentiles, were, before our conversion to Christ, foolish, disobedient, and deceived. There is no doubt that the apostle felt he could include himself in the above list, previously to his conversion. The manner in which he persecuted the Christians, to whose charge he could not lay one moral evil, is a sufficient proof that, though he walked according to the *letter* of the law, as to its ordinances and ceremonies, blameless, yet his heart was in a state of great estrangement from God, from justice, holiness, mercy, and compassion.

Foolish] Ανοητοι· *Without understanding*—ignorant of God, his nature, his providence, and his grace.

Disobedient] Απειθεις· *Unpersuaded, unbelieving,* obstinate, and *disobedient.*

Deceived] Πλανωμενοι· *Erring*—wandering from the right way in consequence of our ignorance, not knowing the right way; and, in consequence of our unbelief and obstinacy, not choosing to know it. It is a true saying, "There are none so blind as those who will not see." Such persons are proof against conviction, they will not be convinced either by God or man.

Serving divers lusts and pleasures] Δουλευοντες· Being in a state of continual *thraldom;* not *served* or *gratified* by our lusts and pleasures, but living, as *their slaves,* a life of misery and wretchedness.

Divers lusts—Επιθυμιαις· *Strong* and *irregular appetites* of every kind.

Pleasures—'Ηδοναις· *Sensual pleasures.* Persons intent only on the gratification of *sense,* living like the *brutes,* having no rational or spiritual object worthy the pursuit of an immortal being.

Living in malice and envy] Εν κακια και φθονω διαγοντες· *Spending our life in wickedness and envy*—not bearing to see the prosperity of others, because we feel ourselves continually wretched.

Hateful] Στυγητοι· *Abominable; hateful as hell* The word comes from Στυξ, *Styx,* the infernal river by which the gods were wont to swear; and he who (according to the mythology of the heathens) violated this oath, was expelled from the assembly of the gods, and was deprived of his nectar and ambrosia for a year; hence the river was hateful to them beyond all things, and the verb στυγεω, formed from this, signifies to shiver with horror.

It may be taken *actively,* says *Leigh,* as it is read, *hateful;* or else *passively,* and so may be read *hated,* that is, justly execrable and odious unto others, both God and man.

Hating one another.] Μισουντες αλληλους· This

2

A. M. cir. 4069.
A. D. 65 or 66.
A. U. C. 818.
An. Imp. Neronis Cæs.
Aug. 12.

living in malice and envy, hateful, *and* hating one another.

4 But after that [h] the kindness and [i] love of [k] God our Saviour toward man appeared,

5 [l] Not by works of righteousness which we have done, but according to his mercy he saved us, by [m] the washing of regeneration,

and renewing of the Holy Ghost;

6 [n] Which he shed on us [o] abundantly through Jesus Christ our Saviour;

7 [p] That, being justified by his grace, [q] we should be made heirs [r] according to the hope of eternal life.

A. M. cir. 4069.
A. D. 65 or 66.
A. U. C. 818.
An. Imp. Neronis Cæs.
Aug. 12.

---

[h] Eph. ii. 7; chap. ii. 11.——[i] Or, *pity*; Rom. v. 5; 1 John iii. 16; iv. 9.——[k] 1 Tim. ii. 3.——[l] Rom. iii. 20; ix. 11; xi. 6; Gal. ii. 16; Eph. ii. 4, 8, 9; 2 Tim. i. 9.——[m] John iii. 3, 5; Eph. v. 26; 1 Pet. iii. 21.

[n] Ezekiel xxxvi. 25; Joel ii. 28; John i. 16; Acts ii. 33; x. 45; Rom. v. 5.——[o] Gr. *richly.*——[p] Rom. iii. 24; Gal. ii. 16; chapter ii. 11.——[q] Romans viii. 23, 24.——[r] Chapter i. 2.

---

word is less expressive than the preceding : there was no brotherly love, consequently no kind offices ; they hated each other, and self-interest alone could induce them to keep up civil society. This is the true state of all unregenerate men. The words which the apostle uses in this place give a finished picture of the carnal state of man ; and they are not true merely of the *Cretans* and *Jews* that then were, but of all mankind in every age and country ; they express the wretched state of fallen man.

Some of the Greek moralists expressed a dissolute and sensual life by nearly the same expressions as those employed by the apostle. *Plutarch,* in *Præcept. Conjug.,* says: Σωματος εστι κηδεσθαι, μη δουλευοντα ταις ἡδοναις αυτου, και ταις επιθυμιαις· "We must take care of the body, that we may not be *enslaved* by its lusts and pleasures." And *Josephus,* speaking of *Cleopatra,* Antiq., lib. xv. cap. 4, says : Γυναικα πολυτελη, και δουλευουσαν ταις επιθυμιαις· "She was an expensive woman, enslaved to lusts."

Verse 4. *But after that the kindness and love of God*] By χρηστοτης we may understand the *essential goodness* of the Divine nature ; that which is the *spring* whence all kindness, mercy, and beneficence proceed.

Love toward man—Φιλανθρωπια· Philanthropy. It is to be regretted that this attribute of the Divine nature, as it stands in relation to man, should have been entirely lost by a paraphrastical translation. *Philanthropy* is a character which God gives here to himself ; while human nature exists, this must be a character of the Divine nature. *God loves man* ; he *delighted* in the *idea* when formed in his own infinite mind, he formed man according to that idea, and *rejoiced* in the work of his hands ; when man fell, the same *love* induced him to devise his redemption, and God the *Saviour* flows from God the *Philanthropist.* Where *love* is it will be active, and will show itself. So the philanthropy of God *appeared,* επεφανη, *it shone out,* in the incarnation of Jesus Christ, and in his giving his life for the life of the world.

Verse 5. *Not by works of righteousness*] Those who were foolish, disobedient, and deceived, serving divers lusts and pleasures, could not possibly have *works of righteousness* to plead ; therefore, if saved at all, they must be saved by *mercy.* See the note on Eph. ii. 8 ; and see a discourse entitled, *Salvation by Faith proved,* 8vo., 1816, in which I have examined every system invented by man for his restoration to the Divine favour and image ; and have demonstrated,

by mere reason, their utter insufficiency to answer the end for which they have been invented ; and have proved that the doctrine of salvation by faith is the only *rational* way of salvation.

By the washing of regeneration] Δια λουτρου παλιγγενεσιας· Undoubtedly the apostle here means *baptism,* the rite by which persons were admitted into the Church, and the *visible sign* of the cleansing, purifying influences of the Holy Spirit, which the apostle immediately subjoins. Baptism is only a *sign,* and therefore should never be separated from the *thing signified ;* but it is a *rite* commanded by God himself, and therefore the *thing signified* should never be expected without it.

By *the renewing of the Holy Ghost* we are to understand, not only the profession of being bound to *live a new life,* but the grace that *renews the heart,* and enables us thus to live ; so the *renewing influences* are here intended. Baptism changes nothing ; the grace signified by it cleanses and purifies. They who think *baptism* to be *regeneration,* neither know the Scriptures nor the power of God ; therefore they do greatly err.

Verse 6. *Which he shed on us abundantly*] Ου εξεχεεν· *Which he poured out* on us, as the water was poured out on them in baptism, to which there is here a manifest allusion ; but as this was sometimes only *sprinkled* on the person, the heavenly gift was *poured* out, not in *drops,* but πλουσιως, *richly,* in *great abundance.*

Through Jesus Christ] Baptism is nothing in itself ; and there had been no outpouring of the Holy Spirit had there been no *saving* and *atoning Christ.* Through him alone all good comes to the souls of men.

Verse 7. *That, being justified by his grace*] Being freed from sin ; for the term *justification* is to be taken here as implying the whole work of the grace of Christ on the heart, in order to its preparation for eternal glory.

Should be made heirs] The Gospel not only gave them the hope of an endless state of glory for their souls, but also of the *resurrection* and final *glorification* of their *bodies ;* and they who were *children* of God were to be made *heirs* of his glory. See the note on Gal. iv. 6, 7.

Verse 8. This is *a faithful saying*] Πιστος ὁ λογος· *This is the true doctrine ;* the doctrine that cannot *fail.*

And these things I will] Και περι τουτων βουλομαι σε διαβεβαιουσθαι· And I will, or desire, thee to maintain earnestly what concerns these points. The things to which the apostle refers are those of which he had just been writing, and may be thus summed up :—

1. The ruined state of man, both in soul and body.

A. M. cir. 4069.
A. D. 65 or 66.
A. U. C. 818.
An. Imp. Ne-
ronis Cæs.
Aug. 12.

8 [s] *This is* a faithful saying, and these things I will that thou affirm constantly, that they which have believed in God might be careful [t] to maintain good works. These things are good and profitable unto men.

9 But [u] avoid foolish questions, and genealo-

gies, and contentions, and strivings about the law ; [v] for they are unprofitable and vain.

10 A man that is a heretic, [w] after the first and second admonition, [x] reject ;

11 Knowing that he that is such is subverted, and sinneth, [y] being condemned of himself.

A. M. cir. 4069.
A. D. 65 or 66.
A. U. C. 818.
An. Imp. Ne-
ronis Cæs.
Aug. 12.

[s] 1 Tim. i. 15; chap. i. 9.——[t] Ver. 1, 14; chap. ii. 14.——[u] 1 Tim. i. 4; 2 Tim. ii. 23; chap. i. 14.——[v] 2 Tim. ii. 14.

[w] 2 Cor. xiii. 2.——[x] Matt. xviii. 17; Rom. xvi. 17; 2 Thess. iii. 6, 14; 2 Tim. iii. 5; 2 John 10.——[y] Acts xiii. 46.

2. The infinite goodness of God which devised his salvation.

3. The manifestation of this goodness, by the incarnation of Jesus Christ.

4. The justification which they who believed received through his blood.

5. The mission of the Holy Spirit, and the purification of the heart by his influence.

6. The hope of the resurrection of the body, and the final glorification of both it and the soul through all eternity.

7. The necessity of obedience to the will of God, and of walking worthy of the vocation wherewith they had been called.

8. And all these points he wills him to press continually on the attention of believers ; and to keep constantly in view, that all good comes from God's infinite kindness, by and through Christ Jesus.

They which have believed in God] All Christians ; for who can maintain good works but those who have the principle from which good works flow, for without faith it is impossible to please God.

These thing are good and profitable] They are good in themselves, and calculated to promote the well-being of men.

Verse 9. *Avoid foolish questions, and genealogies*] In these the Jews particularly delighted ; they abounded in the most frivolous questions ; and, as they had little piety *themselves*, they were solicitous to show that they had descended from *godly ancestors*.

Of their frivolous questions, and the answers given to them by the wisest and most reputable of their rabbins, the following is a specimen :—

Rabbi Hillel was asked : *Why have the Babylonians round heads ?* To which he answered : This is a difficult question, but I will tell the reason : *Their heads are round because they have but little wit.*

Q. *Why are the eyes of the Tarmudians so soft ?*—A. *Because they inhabit a sandy country.*

Q. *Why have the Africans broad feet?*—A. *Because they inhabit a marshy country.* See more in *Schoettgen.*

But ridiculous and trifling as these are, they are little in comparison to those solemnly proposed and most gravely answered by those who are called the *schoolmen.* Here is a specimen, which I leave the reader to translate :—

Utrum essent excrementa in Paradiso ? Utrum sancti resurgent cum intestinis ? Utrum, si deipara fuisset vir, potuisset esse naturalis parens Christi ?

These, with many thousands of others, of equal use to religion and common sense, may be found in their writings. See the *Summa* of Thomas Aquinas, *passim.* Might not the Spirit have these religious triflers in view, rather than the less ridiculous Jews? See the notes on 1 Tim. i. 4 ; 2 Tim. ii. 23.

Contentions, and strivings about the law] Of legal contentions, and different and conflicting decisions about the meaning of particular rites and ceremonies, the Talmud is full.

Verse 10. *A man that is a heretic*] Generally defined, one that is obstinately attached to an opinion contrary to the peace and comfort of society, and will neither submit to Scripture nor reason. Here it means a person who maintains Judaism in opposition to Christianity, or who insists on the necessity of circumcision, &c., in order to be saved. This is obviously the meaning of the word heretic in the only place in which it occurs in the sacred writings.

After the first and second admonition, reject] Labour to convince him of his error ; but if he will not receive instruction, if he have shut his heart against conviction, then—*burn him alive ?* No : even if demonstrably a heretic in any one sense of that word, and a disturber of the peace of the Church, God gives no man any other authority over him but to *shun him,* παραιτου. Do him no harm in body, soul, character, or substance ; hold no communion with him ; but leave him to God. See the notes on Acts v. 17, and xxiv. 14, where the word *heresy* is particularly explained.

Verse 11. *Is subverted*] Is turned out of the way in which he may be saved, and consequently *sinneth*— enters into that way that leads to destruction.

Being condemned of himself.] This refers to the Judaizing teacher, who maintained his party and opinions for filthy lucre's sake. He was conscious of his own insincerity ; and that he proclaimed not his system from a conscientious love of truth, but from a desire to get his livelihood. Were the Church in all countries, whether established by law or unestablished, strictly scrutinized, multitudes of *heretics* of this kind would be found. And perhaps this is the only bad sense in which the word should be understood.

Verse 12. *When I shall send Artemas—or Tychicus*] These were either deacons or presbyters, which the apostle intended to send to Crete, to supply the place of Titus. Who Artemas was we know not ; he is not mentioned in any other place in the New Testament. Tychicus was a native of Asia, as we learn from Acts xx. 4, where see the note.

Be diligent to come unto me to Nicopolis] Nicopolis was a city of Epirus, on the gulf of Ambracia, near to Actium, which Augustus built in commemoration of his victory over Mark Antony. There was another Nicopolis in Thrace, at the entrance of Macedonia, on the river Nessus ; but the former is supposed to be the place here intended.

For I have determined there to winter.] Hence the apostle was at *liberty*, seeing his spending the winter

A. M. cir. 4069.
A. D. 65 or 66.
A. U. C. 818.
An. Imp. Ne-
ronis Cæs.
Aug. 12.

12 When I shall send Artemas unto thee, or ᶻ Tychicus, be diligent to come unto me to Nicopolis : for I have determined there to winter.

13 Bring Zenas the lawyer and ᵃ Apollos on their journey diligently, that nothing be wanting unto them.

14 And let ours also learn ᵇ to ᶜ maintain

good works for necessary uses, that they be ᵈ not unfruitful.

15 All that are with me salute thee. Greet them that love us in the faith. Grace *be* with you all. Amen.

A. M. cir. 4069.
A. D. 65 or 66.
A. U. C. 818.
An. Imp. Ne-
ronis Cæs.
Aug. 12.

¶ It was written to Titus, ordained the first bishop of the Church of the Cretians, from Nicopolis of Macedonia.

ᶻ Acts xx. 4 ; 2 Tim. iv. 12.——ᵃ Acts xviii. 24.——ᵇ Ver. 8.
ᶜ Or, *profess honest trades* ; Eph. iv. 28.

ᵈ Romans xv. 28 ; Philippians i. 11 ; iv. 17 ; Colossians i. 10 ;
2 Peter i. 8.

---

at this or at any other practicable place depended on his *own determination.* It was probably now pretty late in the autumn, and the apostle was now drawing near to Nicopolis ; for he certainly was not yet arrived, else he would not have said, *I have determined* εκει, **THERE**, *to winter.*

Verse 13. *Bring Zenas the lawyer*] This person is only mentioned in this place ; whether he was a *Jewish, Roman,* or *Greek* lawyer, we cannot tell.

And Apollos] Of this person we have some valuable particulars in Acts xviii. 24 ; 1 Cor. i. 12 ; iii. 5, 6, and iv. 6. Either St. Paul had left these at Crete when he visited that island, or he had heard that, in their evangelical itinerancy, they were about to pass through it.

On their journey diligently] Afford them the *means* to defray their expenses. The Churches through which these evangelists passed bore their expenses from one to the other. See 3 John ver. 6.

Verse 14. *And let ours also learn to maintain good works*] There is something very remarkable in this expression. The words καλων εργων προϊστασθαι, which we translate *to maintain good works,* occur also in ver. 8 ; and some think they mean, *to provide for our own, and the necessities of others, by working at some honest occupation* ; and that this was necessary to be taught to the Cretans, *let* **OURS** *also learn, &c.,* who were naturally and practically *idle gluttons.* Kypke observes that the words mean, 1. To be employed in good works. 2. To defend good works, and to recommend the performance of them. 3. To promote and forward good works ; to be always first in them.

For necessary uses] That they may be able at all times to help the Church of God, and those that are in want.

That they be not unfruitful.] As they must be if they indulge themselves in their *idle, slothful* disposition.

Verse 15. *All that are with me*] He means his companions in the ministry

Salute thee.] Wish thee well, and desire to be affectionately remembered to thee.

Greet them that love us in the faith.] All that love us for Christ's sake, and all that are genuine Christians.

Grace be *with you*] May the Divine favour be your portion for ever.

Some MSS. read, *The grace of the Lord be with you all* ; others, *The grace of God be with you all* ; and one, *Grace be with* **THY** *spirit,* as if the greeting was

sent to *Titus* only, whereas the others send it to the *whole Church* at Crete.

Amen.] This is wanting in ACD, and some others.

The *subscriptions* are, as usual, various. Those of the **VERSIONS** are the following :——

The Epistle to Titus was written from Nicopolis ; and sent by the hands of Zena and Apollo.—SYRIAC.

To the man Titus.—ÆTHIOPIC.

The end of the epistle : it was written from Nicopolis. Incessant and eternal praise be to the God of glory. Amen.—ARABIC.

Written in Nicopolis, and sent by Artemas, his disciple.—COPTIC.

The Epistle to Titus is ended, who was the first bishop of the Church of the Cretans : and it was written from Nicopolis of Macedonia.—PHILOXENIAN SYRIAC.

There is no subscription in the VULGATE.

The MANUSCRIPTS are also various.

To Titus.—C, and *Clarom.*

That to Titus is completed : that to Philemon begins.—DEFG.

To Titus, written from Nicopolis.—A.

To Titus, written from Nicopolis of Macedonia.—of the Macedonians.—From Nicopolis, which is a province of Macedonia.

Paul the apostle's Epistle to Titus.

To Titus, ordained the first bishop of the Church of the Cretans : written from Nicopolis of Macedonia. —*Common Greek Text.*

To Titus, archbishop of Crete.—*One of the Vienna MSS., written* A. D. 1331.

THERE is not one of these subscriptions of any authority, and some of them are plainly ridiculous. We do not know that Titus was what we term *bishop,* much less that he was *ordained bishop of Crete,* as appointed to a particular see ; and still less that he was the *first* bishop there. As to his being *archbishop,* that is the fiction of a time of deep darkness. That the epistle was written from *some place near to Nicopolis,* of Epirus, is very probable. That it was *not* written *at* Nicopolis is evident ; and that this was *not* Nicopolis of Macedonia is also very probable. See the preface to this epistle for farther information on this point. And see a treatise by old Mr. Prynne entitled, The unbishoping of Timothy and Titus, 4to. Lond. 1636 and 1660, where, among many crooked things, there are some just observations.

PHILEMON

IT may be thought strange that a short letter, written entirely on a *private subject*, without reference to the proof or defence of any *doctrine* of the Gospel, should, by the general consent of the Church of God, from the highest Christian antiquity, have been received into the sacred canon, not only as a genuine production of St. Paul, but as a piece designed by the Holy Spirit for the edification of the Church. However, such is the fact; and we may add, that this very piece was held so sacred that even the ancient heretics did not attempt to impugn its authenticity or corrupt its matter, while making dangerously free with the four gospels, and all the other epistles!

Philemon, the person to whom it is addressed, was undoubtedly, at the time in which this epistle was sent, an inhabitant of Colosse, (concerning which city, see the preface to the Epistle to the Colossians,) and was probably a Colossian by birth, though some suppose that he was of Ephesus. It is evident, from ver. 19 of this epistle, that he was converted to the Christian faith by St. Paul; this is agreed on all hands; but as some suppose that the apostle had not visited Colosse previously to the writing of this epistle, they think it probable that he might have met with him at Ephesus, or in some other part of Asia Minor, where he formed an acquaintance with him, and became the means of his conversion. But there is no need for this supposition, as it is most probable that the apostle had not only visited *Colosse* prior to this, but that the Gospel was planted in that city, as in all other parts of *Phrygia*, by himself. See the preface to the Colossians, and the note on Col. ii. 1.

That Philemon was a person of some consideration in his own city, and in the Church in that place, is very evident from this epistle. He had a Church in his house, ver. 2, and was so opulent as to be extensive in works of charity, and in entertaining those Christians who from different quarters had occasion to visit Colosse. See ver. 5—7.

Whether he had any *office* in the Church is not clear: some think he was a bishop, others an *elder* or *deacon;* but of this there is no evidence. He was probably no more than a *private member*, whose house, hand, and property were consecrated to God, his Church, and the poor. He who, by the good *providence* of God, has *property* and *influence* thus to employ, and a *heart* to do it, need not envy the state of the highest ecclesiastic in the Church of Christ. Both the *heart* and the *means* to do secular good are possessed by few, whereas multitudes are found willing both to *teach* in and *govern* the Church.

The *occasion* of writing this letter was the following: *Onesimus*, a slave, had on some pretence or other run away from his master Philemon, and had come to Rome, where St. Paul was at that time in prison, though not in close confinement, for he dwelt in his own hired house, in which he assiduously preached the Gospel, being guarded only by one soldier. See Acts xxviii. 16, 23.

It appears that Onesimus sought out Paul, whose public preaching, both to Jews and Gentiles, had rendered him famous in the city; and it is very likely that he was led to visit the apostle from having formerly seen him at his master's house in Colosse, and the word of life, preached by the apostle, became the means of his conversion. Being thus brought back to God, he became affectionately attached to his spiritual father, and served him zealously as his son in the Gospel. Onesimus, being thus brought to the acknowledgment of the truth which is according to godliness, gave the apostle a full account of his elopement from his master, and no doubt intimated his wish to return and repair the breach which he had made. Though he was now both *dear* and *necessary* to St. Paul, yet, as justice required that reparation should be made, he resolved to send him back; and to remove all suspicion from the mind of Philemon, and to reconcile him to his once unfaithful servant, he wrote the following letter, in which, as Dr. Macknight expresses it, " with the greatest softness of expression, warmth of affection, and delicacy of address, he not only interceded for Onesimus's pardon, but urged Philemon to esteem him, and put confidence in him as a sincere Christian ; and because *restitution*, by repairing the injury that had been done, restores the person who did it to the character he had lost, the apostle, to enable Onesimus to appear in Philemon's family with some degree of reputation, bound himself in this epistle, by his handwriting, ver. 18, 19, not only to repay all that Onesimus owed to Philemon, but to make full reparation also for whatever injury he had done to him by running away."

It is generally thought that Onesimus had *robbed* his master ; but there is certainly nothing in the epistle from which this can be legitimately inferred ; the words, " If he hath wronged thee, or oweth thee aught, put that on mine account," ver. 18, certainly do not *prove* it ; they only state a possible case, that he might have wronged his master, or have been under some *pecuniary* obligation to him ; and the apostle, by appearing to assume this, greatly strengthened his own argument, and met the last objection which Philemon could be supposed capable of making. There is neither justice nor piety in making things worse than they appear to be, or in drawing the most unfavourable conclusions from premises which, without constraint, will afford others more consonant to the spirit of charity.

That this epistle was written about the same time with those to the *Philippians* and *Colossians* is proved by several coincidences. " As the letter to Philemon and that to the Colossians were written," says Dr. Paley, " at the same time, and sent by the same messenger, the one to a particular inhabitant, the other to the Church of Colosse, it may be expected that the same or nearly the same persons would be about St. Paul, and join with him, as was the practice, in the salutations of the epistle. Accordingly we find the names of *Aristarchus*, *Marcus*, *Epaphras*, *Luke*, and *Demas*, in both epistles. *Timothy*, who is joined with St. Paul in the superscription of the Epistle to the Colossians, is joined with him in this. *Tychicus* did not salute Philemon because he accompanied the epistle to Colosse, and would undoubtedly there see him." It will not be forgotten that Onesimus, the bearer of this epistle, was one of the bearers of that sent to the Colossians, Col. iv. 9 ; that when the apostle wrote that he was in *bonds*, Col. iv. 3, 18, which was his case also when he wrote this ; (see ver. 1, 10, 13, 23 ;) from which, and various other circumstances, we may conclude that they were written about the same time, viz. the ninth year of Nero, A. D. 62. Other particulars relative to this epistle will be pointed out in the course of the notes, and particularly the *uses* which the Church of God and the private Christian may derive from it.

2

THE

EPISTLE OF PAUL THE APOSTLE

TO

PHILEMON.

Chronological Notes relative to this Epistle.

Year of the Constantinopolitan era of the world, or that used by the Byzantine historians, 5570.—Year of the Alexandrian era of the world, 5563.—Year of the Antiochian era of the world, 5554.—Year of the Julian period, 4773.—Year of the world, according to Archbishop Usher, 4066.—Year of the world, according to Eusebius, in his Chronicon, 4290.—Year of the minor Jewish era of the world, or that in common use, 3822.—Year of the Greater Rabbinical era of the world, 4421.—Year from the Flood, according to Archbishop Usher, and the English Bible, 2410.—Year of the Cali yuga, or Indian era of the Deluge, 3164. —Year of the era of Iphitus, or since the first commencement of the Olympic games, 1002.—Year of the era of Nabonassar, king of Babylon, 809.—Year of the CCXth Olympiad, 2.—Year from the building of Rome, according to Fabius Pictor, 809.—Year from the building of Rome, according to Frontinus, 813.—Year from the building of Rome, according to the Fasti Capitolini, 814.—Year from the building of Rome, according to Varro, which was that most generally used, 815.—Year of the era of the Seleucidæ, 374.—Year of the Cæsarean era of Antioch, 110.—Year of the Julian era, 107.—Year of the Spanish era, 100.—Year from the birth of Jesus Christ according to Archbishop Usher, 66.—Year of the vulgar era of Christ's nativity, 62.—Year of Albinus, governor of the Jews, 1.—Year of Vologesus, king of the Parthians, 13.—Year of Domitus Corbulo, governor of Syria, 3.—Jesus, high priest of the Jews, 3.—Year of the Dionysian period, or Easter Cycle, 63.—Year of the Grecian Cycle of nineteen years, or Common Golden Number, 6; or the first after the second embolismic.—Year of the Jewish Cycle of nineteen years, 3, or the first embolismic. —Year of the Solar Cycle, 15.—Dominical Letter, it being the second after the Bissextile, or Leap Year, C.—Day of the Jewish Passover, according to the Roman computation of time, the IVth of the ides of April, or, in our common mode of reckoning, the tenth of April, which happened in this year on the day after the Jewish Sabbath.—Easter Sunday, the IIId of the ides of April, named by the Jews the 22d of Nisan or Abib; and by Europeans in general, the 11th of April.—Epact, or age of the moon on the 22d of March, (the day of the earliest Easter Sunday possible,) 25.—Epact, according to the present mode of computation, or the moon's age on New Year's day, or the Calends of January, 2.—Monthly Epacts, or age of the moon on the Calends of each month respectively, (beginning with January,) 2, 4, 3, 4, 5, 6, 7, 8, 9, 9, 11, 11.—Number of Direction, or the number of days from the twenty-first of March to the Jewish Passover, 20.—Year of the reign of Caius Tiberius Claudius Nero Cæsar, the fifth Roman emperor, computing from Augustus Cæsar, 9.—Roman Consuls, P. Marius Celsus and L. Asinius Gallus, who were succeeded by L. Annæus Seneca and Trebellius Maximus, on the 1st of July.

Paul's salutation to Philemon, and the Church at his house, 1–3. He extols his faith, love, and Christian charity, 4–7. Entreats forgiveness for his servant Onesimus, 8–14. Urges motives to induce Philemon to forgive him, 15–17. Promises to repair any wrong he had done to his master, 18, 19. Expresses his confidence that Philemon will comply with his request, 20, 21. Directs Philemon to prepare him a lodging. 22. Salutations and apostolical benediction, 23–25.

A. M. cir. 4066.
A. D. cir. 62.
A. U. C. 815.
An. Imp. Neronis Cæs.
Aug. 9.

PAUL, [a] a prisoner of Jesus Christ, and Timothy *our* brother, unto Philemon our dearly beloved, [b] and fellow labourer,

2 And to *our* beloved Apphia, and [c] Archippus [d] our fellow soldier, and to [e] the Church in thy house :

3 [f] Grace to you, and peace, from God our Father, and the Lord Jesus Christ.

A. M. cir. 4066.
A. D. cir. 62.
A. U. C. 815.
An. Imp. Neronis Cæs.
Aug. 9.

4 [g] I thank my God, making mention of thee always in my prayers,

5 [h] Hearing of thy love and faith, which thou has toward the Lord Jesus, and toward all saints ;

[a] Ephes. iii. 1; iv. 1; 2 Tim. i. 8; ver. 9.——[b] Philip. ii. 25.
[c] Col. iv. 17.——[d] Phil. ii. 25.

[e] Rom. xvi. 5; 1 Cor. xvi. 19.——[f] Eph. i. 2.——[g] Eph. i. 16; 1 Thess. i. 2; 2 Thess. i. 3.——[h] Eph. i. 15; Col. i. 4.

NOTES ON PHILEMON.

Verse 1. *Paul, a prisoner of Jesus Christ*] It has already been noted, in the preface, that Paul was a prisoner at Rome when he wrote this epistle, and those to the Colossians and Philippians. But some think that the term *prisoner* does not sufficiently point out the apostle's *state*, and that the original word δεσμιος should be translated *bound with a chain :* this is certainly its meaning ; and it shows us in some measure his circumstances—one arm was bound with a chain to the arm of the soldier to whose custody he had been delivered.

It has also been remarked that Paul does not call himself an *apostle* here, because the letter was a letter of *friendship*, and on *private concerns*. But the MSS. are not entirely agreed on this subject. Two MSS. have δουλος, a *servant ;* the *Codex Claromontanus* and the *Codex Sangermanensis,* both in the *Greek* and *Latin,* have αποστολος, *apostle ;* and *Cassiodorus* has αποστολος δεσμιος, Paul, *an imprisoned apostle of* Jesus Christ. They, however, generally agree in the omission of the word αποστολος.

Unto Philemon our dearly beloved] There is a peculiarity in the use of *proper names* in this epistle which is not found in any other part of St. Paul's writings. The names to which we refer are *Philemon, Apphia, Archippus,* and *Onesimus.*

PHILEMON, Φιλημων. *Affectionate* or *beloved,* from φιλημα, a *kiss ;* this led the apostle to say : *To Philemon our* DEARLY BELOVED.

Verse 2. APPHIA. Απφια. Under the word Απφα *Suidas* says : Αδελφης και αδελφου υποκορισμα· *Appha* is the affectionate address of a brother or sister ; or the diminutive of a brother and sister, used to express kindness and affection. Hence the apostle, referring to the meaning of the word, says : Και Απφια τη αδελφη αγαπητη· *And to Apphia the beloved sister.* Though αδελφη, *sister,* be not in our common text, it is found in AD*EFG, several others, the *Itala, Vulgate, Slavonic, &c. ;* and is undoubtedly genuine.

ARCHIPPUS, Αρχιππος. The *ruler* or *master of the horse ;* from αρχων, a *chief,* and ιππος, a *horse.* HEROES of old were, both among the Greeks and Trojans, celebrated for their skill in *managing* and *taming the horse,* and employing him in *war ;* this frequently

occurs in Homer. The import of the name of *Archippus* might suggest this idea to the apostle's mind, and lead him to say : *Archippus our* FELLOW SOLDIER.

Suidas mentions a person of this name, who was once *victor* at the games, in the *ninety-first* Olympiad.

There was one of the pupils of Pythagoras of this name ; and I introduce him here for the sake of a quotation from St. Jerome, (Apol. adv. Ruffin.,) relative to the doctrines taught by him and his fellow disciple, *Lysis :* Φευκτεον πανταπασι και εκκοπτεον ασθενειαν μεν του σωματος, απαιδευσιαν δε της ψυχης, ακολασιαν δε της γαστρος, στασιν δε της πολεως, την δε διαφωνιαν απο της οικιας, και κοινη απο παντων το ακρατες· "By all means and methods these evils are to be shunned and cut off : *effeminacy* from the *body ;* IGNORANCE from the *soul ; delicacies* from the *belly ; sedition* from the *city ; discord* from the *house ;* and, in general, *intemperance* from *all things.*" Vid. FAB. *Thes. Erud. Schol.*

ONESIMUS, Ονησιμος. *Useful* or *profitable ;* from ονημι, *to help.* The import of this name led the apostle to play upon the word thus : *I beseech thee for my son Onesimus—which in time past was to thee* UNPROFITABLE, *but now* PROFITABLE *to thee and me.*

To the Church in thy house] The congregation of Christians frequently assembling in Philemon's house ; for at this time the Christians had neither temples, churches, nor chapels. See the note on Rom. xvi. 5, and the reference there.

It is very probable that *Apphia* was the wife of Philemon, and Archippus, their son, the pastor of the Church at Philemon's house.

Verse 4. *I thank my God*] For all the good he has bestowed upon you, *making mention of thee always in my prayers,* that thou mayest hold fast all that thou hast got, and get all that thou dost farther need.

Verse 5. *Hearing of thy love and faith*] His *faith* in Christ Jesus, his *love* to the saints. Several excellent MSS. and some versions put *faith* before *love,* which makes a more natural reading. There is no figure of speech which would vindicate our saying *faith in the saints ;* so that, if we do not allow of the arrangement in the MSS. referred to, we shall be obliged to have recourse to the transposition, because *faith* must refer to *Jesus Christ,* and *love* to the *saints.*

2

A M. cir. 4066.
A. D. cir. 62.
A. U. C. 815.
An. Imp. Ne-
ronis Cæs.
Aug. 9.

6 That the communication of thy faith may become effectual [i] by the acknowledging of every good thing which is in you in Christ Jesus.

7 For we have great joy and consolation in thy love, because the bowels of the saints [k] are refreshed by thee, brother.

8 Wherefore, [l] though I might be much bold in Christ to enjoin thee that which is convenient,

9 Yet for love's sake I rather beseech *thee*, being such a one as Paul the aged, [m] and

A. M. cir. 4066.
A. D. cir. 62.
A. U. C. 815.
An. Imp. Ne
ronis Cæs.
Aug. 9.

---

[i] Phil. i. 9, 11.——[k] 2 Cor. vii. 13 ; 2 Tim. i. 16 ; ver. 20.   [l] 1 Thess. ii. 6.——[m] Ver. 1.

Verse 6. *That the communication of thy faith*] The words ἡ κοινωνια της πιστεως σου, the *fellowship* or *communication of thy faith*, may be understood as referring to the *work* of *love* towards the *saints*—the poor Christians, which his *faith* in Christ enabled him to perform, *faith* being taken here for its *effects*; and indeed the word κοινωνια itself is not unfrequently used to denote *liberality, almsgiving*; and this is very properly remarked by *Theophylact* here : Κοινωνιαν πιστεως ελεημοσυνην καλει, ὡς απο πιστεως πολλης γενομενην· "He terms *almsgiving* the *communication of faith*, because it is the fruit of much faith."

May become effectual] Dr. Macknight understands these words thus : "That the many good offices which thou dost to the saints *may become effectual* in bringing others *to the acknowledgment of every good disposition which is in you towards Christ Jesus, or towards his members.*"

Instead of ενεργης, *energetic* or *effectual*, the *Vulgate* and some of the *fathers*, as well as several Latin MSS., have read εναργης, *evident*. This makes a very good sense, and seems to agree best with the scope of the place.

Instead of εν ὑμιν, *in* you, εν ἡμιν, *in* us, is the reading of all the best MSS., as well as of several versions and fathers.

Verse 7. *For we have great joy*] This verse does not read harmoniously. The Greek authorizes the following arrangement : *For we have great joy and consolation in thy love, O brother, because the bowels of the saints are refreshed by thee.* The apostle speaks here of the works of charity in which Philemon abounded towards poor Christians.

Verse 8. *Wherefore, though I might be much bold*] It would be better to read : *Wherefore, although I have much authority through Christ, to command thee to do what is proper ; yet, on account of my love to thee, I entreat thee.*

The tenderness and delicacy of this epistle, says Dr. Paley, have long been admired : "Though I might be much bold in Christ to enjoin thee that which is convenient ; yet, for love's sake, I rather beseech thee, being such a one as Paul the aged, and now also a prisoner of Christ Jesus, I beseech thee for my son Onesimus, whom I have begotten in my bonds."

There is something certainly very melting and persuasive in this and every part of the epistle. Yet, in my opinion, the character of St. Paul prevails in it throughout. The warm, affectionate, authoritative teacher is interceding with an absent *friend* for a beloved *convert*. He urges his suit with an earnestness befitting, perhaps, not so much the occasion as the ardour and sensibility of his own mind. Here also, as everywhere, he shows himself conscious of the weight and dignity of his mission ; nor does he suffer Philemon, for a moment, to forget it : "I *might* be much bold in Christ, to enjoin thee that which is convenient." He is careful also to recall, though obliquely, to Philemon's memory, the sacred obligation under which he had laid him, by bringing him to the knowledge of Christ : "I do not say to thee, how thou owest to me even thine own self besides." Without laying aside, therefore, the apostolic character, our author softens the imperative style of his address, by mixing with it every sentiment and consideration that could move the heart of his correspondent. Aged, and in prison, he is content to supplicate and entreat. Onesimus was rendered dear to him by his conversation and his services ; the child of his affliction, and "ministering unto him in the bonds of the Gospel." This ought to recommend him, whatever had been his fault, to Philemon's forgiveness: "Receive him as myself, as my own bowels." Every thing, however, should be voluntary. St. Paul was determined that Philemon's compliance should flow from his own bounty ; "Without thy mind would I do nothing, that thy benefit should not be as it were of necessity, but willingly ;" trusting, nevertheless, to his gratitude and attachment for the performance of all that he requested, and for more : "Having confidence in thy obedience, I wrote unto thee, knowing that thou wilt also do more than I say."

St. Paul's discourse at Miletus ; his speech before Agrippa ; his Epistle to the Romans ; that to the Galatians, chap. iv. 11–20 ; to the Philippians, i. 29 ; ii. 2 ; the second to the Corinthians, vi. 1–13 ; and indeed some part or other of almost every epistle, exhibit examples of a similar application to the feelings and affections of the persons whom he addresses. And it is observable that these pathetic effusions, drawn for the most part from his own sufferings and situation, usually precede a *command*, soften a *rebuke*, or mitigate the *harshness* of some *disagreeable truth*. Horæ Paulinæ, p. 334.

Verse 9. *Paul the aged*] If we allow St. Paul to have been about 25 years of age at the utmost, in the year 31, when he was assisting at the martyrdom of Stephen, Acts vii. 58 ; as this epistle was written about A. D. 62, he could not have been at this time more than about 56 years old. This could not constitute him an *aged* man in our sense of the term ;

A. M. cir. 4066.
A. D. cir. 62.
A. U. C. 815.
An. Imp. Ne-
ronis Cæs.
Aug. 9.

now also a prisoner of Jesus Christ.

10 I beseech thee for my son [n] Onesimus, [o] whom I have begotten in my bonds:

11 Which in time past was to thee unprofitable, but now profitable to thee and to me:

12 Whom I have sent again: thou therefore receive him, that is, mine own bowels;

13 Whom I would have retained with me, [p] that in thy stead he might have ministered unto me in the bonds of the Gospel:

14 But without thy mind would I do nothing; [q] that thy benefit should not be as it were of necessity, but willingly.

15 [r] For perhaps he therefore departed for a season, that thou shouldest receive him for ever;

16 Not now as a servant, but above a servant, [s] a brother beloved, specially to me, but how much more unto thee, [t] both in the flesh and in the Lord?

17 If thou count me therefore [u] a partner, receive him as myself.

A. M. cir. 4066.
A. D. cir. 62.
A. U. C. 815.
An. Imp. Ne-
ronis Cæs.
Aug. 9.

---

[n] Col. iv. 9.——[o] 1 Cor. iv. 15; Gal. iv. 19.——[p] 1 Cor. xvi. 17; Phil. ii. 30.——[q] 2 Cor. ix. 7.

[r] So Gen. xlv. 5, 8.——[s] Matt. xxiii. 8; 1 Tim. vi. 2.——[t] Col. iii. 22.——[u] 2 Cor. viii. 23.

---

yet, when the whole length of his life is taken in, being martyred about four years after this, he may not improperly be considered an *aged* or *elderly man*, though it is generally allowed that his martyrdom took place in the 66th year of our Lord.

But the word πρεσβυς signifies, not only an *old man*, but also an *ambassador*; because *old* or *elderly* men were chosen to fulfil such an office, because of their experience and solidity; and πρεσβυτης, for πρεσβευτης, is used in the same sense and for the same reason by the Septuagint; hence some have thought that we should translate here, *Paul the ambassador.* This would agree very well with the scope and even the design of the place.

Verse 10. *I beseech thee for my son Onesimus*] It is evident from this that Onesimus was converted by St. Paul while he was prisoner at Rome, and perhaps not long before he wrote this epistle.

Verse 11. *Was to thee unprofitable*] Alluding to the meaning of Onesimus's name, as has been already noted; though the apostle uses a different Greek word to express the same idea.

Verse 12. *Whom I have sent again*] The Christian religion never cancels any civil relations; a *slave*, on being converted, and becoming a free man of Christ, has no right to claim, on that ground, emancipation from the service of his master. *Justice*, therefore, required St. Paul to send back Onesimus to his master, and *conscience* obliged Onesimus to agree in the propriety of the measure; but *love* to the *servant* induced the apostle to write this conciliating letter to the *master.*

Verse 13. *That in thy stead he might have ministered unto me*] As Philemon was one of Paul's converts, he became thereby his spiritual father, and had a right to his services when in need. This was a strong argument, not only to induce Philemon to forgive his servant, but to send him back to the apostle, that he might minister to him in his master's stead.

Verse 14. *That thy benefit should not be as it were of necessity*] If the apostle had kept Onesimus in his service, and written to Philemon to forgive him and permit him to stay, to this it is probable he would have agreed; but the *benefit* thus conceded

might have lost much of its real worth by the consideration that, had he been at Colosse, Philemon would not have sent him to Rome; but, being there and in the apostle's service, he could not with propriety order him home: thus the benefit to the apostle would have appeared to have been of *necessity.* The apostle, therefore, by sending him back again, gave Philemon the opportunity to do all as if *self-moved* to it. This is a very delicate touch.

Verse 15. *He—departed for a season*] This is another most delicate stroke. He departed thy *slave*, thy *unfaithful slave*; he departed *for a short time*; but so has the mercy of God operated in his behalf, and the providence of God in thine, that he now returns, not an unfaithful *slave*, in whom thou couldst repose no confidence, but as a *brother*, a *beloved brother in the Lord*, to be in the same heavenly family with thee for *ever.* Thou hast, therefore, reason to be thankful to God that he did depart, that he might be restored to thee again infinitely better than he was when he left thee. God has permitted his unfaithfulness, and overruled the whole both to his advantage and thine. The apology for Onesimus is very similar to that made by Joseph for his brethren, Gen. xlv. 5.

Verse 16. *Not now as a servant?*] Do not receive him merely as thy *slave*, nor treat him according to that condition; *but as a brother*—as a genuine Christian, and particularly dear to me.

Both in the flesh and in the Lord?] There is no reason to believe that Onesimus was of the *kindred* of Philemon; and we must take the term *flesh*, here, as referring to the *right* which Philemon had in him. He was a part of his *property* and of his *family*; as a *slave*, this was his condition; but he now stood in a twofold relation to Philemon: 1. According to the *flesh*, as above explained, he was one of his family. 2. *In the Lord*; he was now also a member of the *heavenly family*, and of the *Church* at Philemon's house. Philemon's interest in him was now doubled, in consequence of his conversion to Christianity.

Verse 17. *If thou count me therefore a partner*] If thou dost consider me as a *friend*; if I have still the place of a friend in thy affection, *receive him as*

2

A. M. cir. 4066.
A. D. cir. 62.
A. U. C. 815.
An. Imp. Ne-
ronis Cæs.
Aug. 9.

18 If he hath wronged thee, or oweth *thee* aught, put that on mine account;

19 I Paul have written *it* with mine own hand, I will repay *it;* albeit I do not say to thee how thou owest, unto me even thine own self besides

20 Yea, brother, let me have joy of thee in the Lord: ^v refresh my bowels in the Lord.

21 ^wHaving confidence in thy obedience, I wrote unto thee, knowing that thou wilt also do more than I say.

22 But withal prepare me also a lodging: for ^x I trust that ^y through your prayers I shall be given unto you.

23 There salute thee ^z Epaphras, my fellow prisoner in Christ Jesus;

A. M. cir. 4066.
A. D. cir. 62,
A. U. C. 815.
An. Imp. Ne-
ronis Cæs
Aug. 9.

---

^v Ver. 7.——^w 2 Cor. vii. 16.——^x Phil. i. 25; ii. 24.

^y 2 Cor. i. 11.——^z Col. i. 7; iv. 12.

---

myself; for, as I feel him as my own soul, in receiving *him* thou receivest *me.*

There is a fine model of recommending a friend to the attention of a great man in the epistle of *Horace* to *Claudius Nero,* in behalf of his friend *Septimius,* Epistolar. lib. i., Ep. 9, which contains several strokes not unlike some of those in the Epistle to Philemon. It is written with much art; but is greatly exceeded by that of St. Paul. As it is very short I shall insert it:—

> *Septimius, Claudi, nimirum intelligit unus,*
> *Quanti me facias; nam cum rogat, et prece cogit*
> *Scilicet, ut tibi se laudare, et tradere coner,*
> Dignum mente domoque legentis honesta Neronis,
> *Munere cum fungi proprioris censet amici;*
> *Quid possim videt, ac novit me valdius ipso.*
> *Multa quidem dixi, cur excusatus abirem:*
> Sed timui, mea ne finxisse minora putarer,
> Dissimulator opis propriæ, mihi commodus uni.
> Sic ego, majoris fugiens opprobria culpæ,
> Frontis ad urbanæ descendi præmia. *Quod si*
> *Depositum laudas,* ob amici jussa, *pudorem;*
> Scribe tui gregis hunc, et fortem crede bonumque.

"O Claudius Septimius alone knows what value thou hast for me; for he asks and earnestly entreats me to recommend him to thee, as a man worthy of the service and confidence of Nero, who is so correct a judge of merit. When he imagines that I possess the honour of being one of thy most intimate friends, he sees and knows me more particularly than I do myself. I said indeed many things to induce him to excuse me; but I feared lest I should be thought to dissemble my interest with thee, that I might reserve it all for my own advantage. Therefore, in order to shun the reproach of a greater fault, I have assumed all the consequence of a courtier, and have, at the request of my friend, laid aside becoming modesty; which if thou canst pardon, receive this man into the list of thy domestics, and believe him to be a person of probity and worth."

This is not only greatly outdone by St. Paul, but also by a letter of *Pliny* to his friend *Sabinianus,* in behalf of his servant, who, by some means, had incurred his master's displeasure. See it at the conclusion of these notes.

Verse 18. *If he hath wronged thee, or oweth thee aught*] Had the apostle been assured that Onesimus had *robbed* his master, he certainly would not have spoken in this hypothetical way; he only puts a pos-

sible case: If he have wronged thee, or owe thee aught, place all to my account; I will discharge all he owes thee.

Verse 19. *I Paul have written* it *with mine own hand*] It is likely that the whole of the letter was written by St. Paul himself, which was not his usual custom. See on 2 Thess. iii. 17. But by thus speaking he bound Philemon to do what he requested, as an act of common civility, if he could not feel a higher motive from what he had already urged.

Albeit I do not say to thee how thou owest unto me] I ask thee to do this thing to *oblige* me, though I will not say how much thou owest unto me; *even thine own self*, as having been the means of thy conversion.

Verse 20. *Yea, brother*] It is even so, that thou art thus indebted to me. *Let me have joy of thee*, in forgiving Onesimus, and receiving him into thy favour. In the words εγω σου οναιμην, which we should translate, *let me have* PROFIT *of thee*, there is an evident *paronomasia*, or play on the name of *Onesimus*. See on ver. 2 and 11.

Refresh my bowels] Gratify the earnest longing of my soul in this. I ask neither thy money nor goods; I ask what will *enrich*, not *impoverish*, thee to give.

Verse 21. *Having confidence in thy obedience*] I know that it will please thee thus to oblige thy friend, and I know that thou wilt do more than I request, because thou feelest the affection of a son to thy spiritual father. Some think that the apostle hints to Philemon that he should manumit Onesimus.

Verse 22. *But withal prepare me also a lodging*] Does not the apostle mention this as conferring an obligation on Philemon? I will begin to repay thee by taking up my abode at thy house, as soon as I shall be enlarged from prison. But some think he wished Philemon to *hire* him a house, that he might have a *lodging of his own* when he returned to Colosse.

For I trust that through your prayers] It is very likely that this epistle was written a short time before the liberation of the apostle from his first imprisonment at Rome. See Acts xxviii. 30, and Phil. ii. 24; and that he had that liberation now in full prospect.

Verse 23. *Epaphras, my fellow prisoner*] Epaphras was a Colossian, as we learn from Col. iv. 12: *Epaphras, who is one of you.* But there is no account there of his being in prison, though the not mentioning of it does not necessarily imply that he was not. Some time or other he had suffered imprisonment for the truth of the Gospel; and on that account St. Paul might, in a general way, call him his *fellow prisoner.*

2

A. M. cir. 4066.
A. D. cir. 62.
A. U. C. 815.
An. Imp. Neronis Cæs.
Aug. 9.

24 • [a] Marcus, [b] Aristarchus, [c] Demas, [d] Lucas, my fellow labourers.

25 [e] The grace of our Lord

Jesus Christ *be* with your spirit. Amen.

¶ Written from Rome to Philemon by Onesimus a servant.

A. M. cir. 4066.
A. D. cir. 62.
A. U. C. 815.
An. Imp. Ne ronis Cæs
Aug. 9.

[a] Acts xii. 12, 25.——[b] Acts xix. 29; xxvii. 2; Col. iv. 10.

[c] Col. iv. 14.——[d] 2 Tim. iv. 11.——[e] 2 Tim. iv. 22.

Verse 24. *Marcus, Aristarchus, &c.*] These were all acquaintances of Philemon, and probably Colossians; and may be all considered as joining here with St. Paul in his request for Onesimus. Some think that *Marcus* was either the evangelist, or *John Mark*, the nephew of Barnabas, Acts xii. 12, 25. *Aristarchus* was probably the same with him mentioned Acts xix. 29; xx. 4; xxvii. 2. See Col. iv. 10.

Demas] Is supposed to be the same who continued in his attachment to Paul till his last imprisonment at Rome; after which he left him for what is supposed to have been the *love of the world*, 2 Tim. iv. 10; but see the note.

Lucas] Is supposed to be *Luke* the *evangelist*, and *author* of the *Acts of the Apostles*. On these suppositions little confidence can be placed: they may be correct; they may be otherwise.

Verse 25. *The grace of our Lord Jesus Christ be with your spirit*] By using the *plural*, ὑμῶν, *your* the apostle in effect directs or addresses the epistle, not only to Philemon, but *to all the Church at his house*.

Amen.] Is wanting as usual in the best MSS.

The subscriptions are also various, as in preceding cases.

VERSIONS:

The Epistle to Philemon was writen at Rome, and sent by the hand of Onesimus.—SYRIAC.

Through the help of God the epistle is finished. It was written at Rome by the hand of Onesimus, servant to Philemon.—ARABIC.

To the man Philemon.—ÆTHIOPIC.

It was written at Rome, and sent by Onesimus.—COPTIC.

VULGATE, nothing.

The Epistle to Philemon, Apphia, and Archippus: the end of the Epistle to Philemon and Apphia, the master and mistress of Onesimus; and to Archippus, the deacon of the Church at Colosse: it was written from Rome by Onesimus, a servant.—PHILOXENIAN SYRIAC.

MANUSCRIPTS:

To Philemon.—To Philemon is finished.—To Philemon, written from Rome by Onesimus—Onesiphorus.—From Paul, by Onesimus, a servant.—From the presence of Paul and Timothy.—The Epistle of Paul the apostle to Philemon.—*The common Greek text has.* To Philemon, written from Rome by Onesimus, a servant.

As some have thought it strange that a private letter, of a particular business and friendship, should have got a place in the sacred canon, others have been industrious to find out the general *uses* which may be made of it. The following are those which seem to come most naturally from the text:—

1. In a religious point of view, all genuine Christian converts are on a level; Onesimus, the slave, on his conversion becomes the apostle's beloved *son*, and Philemon's *brother*.

2. Christianity makes no change in men's civil affairs; even a slave did not become a freeman by Christian baptism.

3. No servant should be either taken or retained from his own master, without the master's consent, verses 13, 14.

4. We should do good unto all men, and not be above helping the meanest slave when we have the opportunity.

5. *Restitution* is due where an injury has been done, unless the injured party freely forgive, ver. 18.

6. We should do all in our power to make up quarrels and differences, and reconcile those that are at variance.

7. We should be grateful to our benefactors, and be ready to compensate one good turn with another.

8. We should forgive the penitent who have offended us, and rejoice in the opportunity of being reconciled to them.

9. *Authority* is not always to be used; a prudent man who is possessed of it will rather use a mild and obliging manner, than have recourse to the authority of his office.

10. The ministers of the Gospel should learn to know the worth of an immortal soul, and be as ready to use their talents for the conversion of *slaves* and the *ignoble* as the *great* and *opulent*, and prize the converted *slave* as highly as the converted *lord*, showing no sinful respect of persons.

11. Christianity properly understood, and its doctrines properly applied, become the most powerful means of the melioration of men; the wicked and profligate, when brought under its influence, become useful members of society. It can transform a worthless slave into a pious, amiable, and useful man; and make him, not only happier and better in himself, but also a blessing to the community.

12. We should never despair of reclaiming the wicked. No man is out of the reach of God's mercy as long as he breathes. Pretending to say that such and such cases are *hopeless*, is only a colouring for our want of zeal, and a pretence to excuse our slothfulness.

13. The anxiety which the apostle showed for the welfare of Onesimus, in return for his affectionate services, could not fail to cherish good dispositions in the breast of Philemon. We do a man a great kindness when we even engage him in acts of mercy and benevolence.

14. From this epistle we learn what sort of man the apostle was in private life. He has here displayed qualities which are in the highest estimation among men; a noble spirit arising from a consciousness of his own dignity, consummate prudence, uncommon generosity, the warmest friendship, the most skilful address, and the greatest politeness, as well as purity of manners; qualities which are never found either in the enthusiast or impostor. See *Macknight* and *Dodd*.

2

There is extant an epistle of Pliny on the very same subject, directed to his friend *Sabinianus* in behalf of his manumitted slave who had offended him, and was consequently cast out of favour. Dr. Doddridge says that " that epistle, though penned by one who was allowed to excel in the epistolary style, and though it undoubtedly has many beauties, will be found by persons of taste much inferior to this animated composition of the Apostle Paul.

I have already introduced an epistle of Horace on a somewhat similar subject ; but that of *Pliny* is so exactly *parallel*, and so truly excellent, that I am sure its insertion will gratify every intelligent reader, and I insert it the rather because the works of Pliny are in but few hands, and his epistles are known to very few except the learned.

C. Plinius Sabiniano *suo*, S.

Libertus tuus, cui succensere te dixeras, venit ad me, advolutusque pedibus meis, tanquam tuis, hæsit. Flevit multum, multum rogavit, multum etiam tacuit : in summa, fecit mihi fidem pœnitentiæ. Vere credo emendatum, quia deliquisse se sentit. Irasceris scio ; et irasceris merito, id quoque scio : sed tunc præcipua mansuetudinis laus, cum iræ causa justissima est. Amasti hominem ; et, spero, amabis : interim sufficit, ut exorari te sinas. Licebit rursus irasci, si merueris : quod exoratus excusatius facies.

Remitte aliquid adolescentiæ ipsius ; remitte lachrymis ; remitte indulgentiæ tuæ : ne torseris illum, ne torseris etiam te. Torqueris enim, cum tam lenis irasceris. Vereor, ne videar non rogare, sed cogere, si precibus ejus meas junxero. Jungam tamen tanto plenius et effusius, quanto ipsum acrius severiusque corripui, districte minatus nunquam me postea rogaturum. Hoc illi, quem terreri oportebat ; tibi non idem. Nam fortasse iterum rogabo, impetrabo iterum : sit modo tale, ut rogare me, ut præstare te deceat. Vale.—Epistolar. lib. ix., Ep. 21.

" Caius Plinius *to* Sabinianus *his friend, health.*

" Thy freed man, with whom thou didst inform me thou wert incensed, came to me and threw himself at my feet, and grasped them as if they had been thine. He wept much, earnestly entreated, and yet said more by his silence. In short, he fully convinced me that he is a penitent. I do verily believe him reformed, because he feels his guilt. Thou art incensed against him I know, and I know that he has justly merited thy displeasure ; but then, clemency has its chief praise when there is the greatest cause for irritation. Thou didst once love the man, and I hope thou wilt love him again. In the meantime permit thyself to be entreated in his behalf. Should he again merit thy displeasure thou wilt have the stronger excuse for indulging it, shouldst thou pardon him now. Consider his youth, consider his tears, consider thy own gentleness of disposition. Do not torment him, do not torment thyself ; for, with thy mild disposition, thou must be tormented if thou suffer thyself to be angry. I fear, were I to join my prayers to his, that I should rather seem to compel than to supplicate. Yet I will unite them, and the more largely and earnestly too, as I have sharply and severely reproved him, solemnly threatening, should he offend again, never more to

intercede for him. This I said to *him*, it being necessary that I should alarm him ; but I do not say the same to *thee*, for probably I may entreat thee again, and command thee again, should there be a sufficient reason to induce *me* to request, and *thee* to concede Farewell."

Nothing on the subject can be finer than this ; but Paul has the advantage, because he had *Christian motives* to urge. If the energetic Roman had had these, we should have found it difficult to decide between his *Latin* and the apostle's *Greek*.

It may be now as' ed whether St. Paul's application in behalf of Onesimus was successful ? We have no direct answer to this question, but we may fairly suppose that such pleading could not be in vain. Philemon was a Christian, and owed too much to his God and Saviour, and too much to the apostle, as the instrument of his salvation, not to concede a favour which it is congenial to the very spirit of Christianity to grant.

The application of *Horace* in behalf of *Septimius* was successful, and both Claudius Nero and Augustus took him into their warmest confidence. But this was only a common case of recommendation, and had no difficulties in the way. But did the heathen Sabinianus yield to the entreaties of his friend, and forgive his slave ? He did ; and we have the record of it in another very elegant letter, in which Pliny expresses his obligation to his friend for his prompt attention to his request. I will transcribe it, and give a translation for the farther satisfaction of the reader.

C. Plinius Sabiniano *suo*, S.

Bene fecisti quod libertum aliquando tibi carum, reducentibus epistolis meis, in domum, in animum recepisti. Juvabit hoc te : me certe juvat ; primum quod te talem video, ut in ira regi possis : deinde quod tantum mihi tribuis, ut vel auctoritati meæ pareas, vel precibus indulgeas. Igitur, et laudo, et gratias ago. Simul in posterum moneo, ut te erroribus tuorum, etsi non fuerit, qui deprecetur, placabilem præstes. Vale.—Epistolar. lib. ix., Ep. 24.

" Caius Plinius *to his friend* Sabinianus, *health.*

" Thou hast done well, that, in compliance with my letter, thou hast received thy freed man both into thy house and into thy heart. This must be pleasing to thyself, and it is certainly pleasing to me ; first, because I find thee to be a person capable of being governed in thy anger ; and secondly, because thou showest so much regard for me, as either to yield this to my authority, or concede it to my entreaties. Therefore I both praise and return thee thanks. 'At the same time I admonish thee to be always ready to forgive the errors of thy servants, although there should be no one to intercede in their behalf. Farewell."

These letters contain such excellent lessons of instruction that it will be impossible to read them without profit. They are master pieces in their kind ; and no Christian need be ashamed to be indebted to them, whether in regulating his own conduct in respect to forgiveness of injuries, or whether in interceding for them who have fallen under the displeasure of others Reader, go thou and do likewise.

Finished correcting for a new edition, Dec. 23, 1831

INTRODUCTION

EPISTLE OF PAUL THE APOSTLE

TO THE

HEBREWS.

THE chief points in controversy, relative to the Epistle to the Hebrews, though discussed by many, have not in my opinion been treated so successfully by any writer as by Dr. Lardner; he has entered into the whole controversy, and brought his knowledge from far. I shall avail myself of his labours as the best on the subject, and generally use his own words.

"I shall," says he, "inquire, 1. To *whom* it was written. 2. In what *language*. 3. By *whom*. 4. The *time* and *place* of writing it.

"I. In the first place, let us consider to whom this epistle was written.

"Dr. *Lightfoot* thought that this epistle was sent by Paul to the believing Jews of Judea; 'a people,' says he, 'that had been much engaged to him, for his care of their poor, getting collections for them all along in his travels.' He adds, 'It is not to be doubted, indeed, that he intends the discourse and matter of this epistle to the Jews throughout their dispersion. Yet does he endorse it and send it chiefly to the Hebrews, or the Jews of Judea, the principal part of the circumcision, as the properest centre to which to direct it, and from whence it might be best diffused in time to the whole circumference of the dispersion.' *Whitby*, in his preface to the Epistle to the Hebrews, is of the same opinion, and argues much after the same manner as *Lightfoot*.

"So likewise *Mill*, *Pearson*, *Lewis Capellus*, and *Beza*, in his preface to this epistle, and *Beausobre* and *L'Enfant*, the editors of the French New Testament at Berlin, in their general preface to St. Paul's epistles, and in their preface to this epistle in particular.

"Of this Mr. Hallet had no doubt, who in his synopsis of the epistle, says, that this epistle was particularly designed for the Hebrew Christians, who dwelt in one certain place, and was sent thither, as appears from the apostle's saying, chap. xiii. 19, 23 : 'I beseech you the rather to do this, that I may be restored to you the sooner : I will see you.' And what particular place can this be supposed to be but Judea? There, the Christians were continually persecuted by the unbelieving Jews, as we read in the Acts of the Apostles ; and as St. Paul takes notice, 1 Thess. ii. 14; Heb. x. 32—36; xii. 4, 5. By these persecutions the Hebrew Christians were tempted to *apostatize* from Christianity, and to think there was strength in the arguments used by the persecutors in favour of Judaism. The apostle, therefore, sets himself to guard against both these dangers.

"This appears to me to be the most probable opinion : for, 1. It is the opinion of the ancient Christian writers who received this epistle. It may be taken for granted, that this was the opinion of *Clement* of *Alexandria*, and *Jerome*, and *Euthalius*, who supposed this epistle to have been first written in Hebrew, and afterwards translated into Greek. It may be allowed to have been also the opinion of many others who quote this epistle, to have been written to Hebrews, when they say nothing to the contrary. Nor do I recollect any of the ancients, who say it was written to Jews living *out* of Judea.

"*Chrysostom* says that the epistle was sent to the believing Jews of Palestine, and supposes that the apostle afterwards made them a visit. *Theodoret*, in his preface to the epistle, allows it to have been sent to the same Jews ; and *Theophylact*, in his argument of the epistle, expressly says, as *Chrysostom*, that it was sent to the Jews of Palestine. So that this was the general opinion of the ancients.

"There are in this epistle many things especially suitable to the believers in Judea ; which must lead us to think it was written to *them*. I shall select such passages.

"1. Heb. i. 2 : 'Has in these last days spoken unto us by his Son.'

"2. Chap. iv. 2 : 'For unto us was the Gospel preached, as well as unto them.'

"3. Chap. ii. 1–4 : 'Therefore we ought to give the more earnest heed to the things which we have heard : How then shall we escape if we neglect so great salvation, which at the first began to be spoken by the Lord, and was confirmed unto us by them that heard him ; God also bearing them witness with signs and wonders, and with divers miracles, and gifts of the Holy Ghost.'

" Does not this exhortation, and the reason with which it is supported, peculiarly suit the believers of Judea, where Christ himself first taught, and then his disciples after him; confirming their testimony with very numerous and conspicuous miracles ?

" 4. The people to whom this epistle is sent were well acquainted with our Saviour's sufferings, as they of Judea must have been. This appears in chap. i. 3 ; ii. 9, 18 ; v. 7, 8 ; ix. 14, 28 ; x. 11 ; xii. 2, 3 ; xiii. 12.

" 5. Chap. v. 12 : ' For when ye ought to be teachers of others,' and what follows, is most properly understood of Christians in Jerusalem and Judea, to whom the Gospel was first preached.

" 6. What is said, chap. vi. 4–6, and x. 26, 29, is most probably applicable to *apostates* in Judea.

" 7. Chap. x. 32–34 : ' But to call to remembrance the former days, in which, after ye were illuminated, ye endured a great fight of afflictions;' to the end of verse 34. This leads us to the Church of Jerusalem, which had suffered much, long before the writing of this epistle, even very soon after they had received the knowledge of the truth. Compare Acts viii. 1; ix. 1, 2 ; xi. 19 ; and 1 Thess. ii. 14. *Grotius* supposes as much.

" 8. Those exhortations, chap. xiii. 13, 14, must have been very suitable to the case of the Jews at Jerusalem, at the supposed time of writing this epistle ; a few years before the war in that country broke out.

" 9. The regard shown in this epistle to the rulers of the Church or Churches to which it is sent, is very remarkable. They are mentioned twice or thrice, first in chap. xiii. 7 : ' Remember your rulers, who have spoken unto you the word of God ; whose faith imitate, considering the end of their conversation.' These were dead, as Grotius observes. And Theodoret's note is to this purpose. He intends the saints that were dead—Stephen the proto-martyr, James the brother of John, and James called the Just. And there were many others who were taken off by the Jewish rage. Consider these, says he, and, observing their example, imitate their faith. Then again, at ver. 17 : ' Obey them that have the rule over you, and submit yourselves. For they watch for your souls.' And once more, ver. 24 : ' Salute all them that have the rule over you, and all the saints.' Upon which Theodoret says : This way of speaking intimates, that their rulers did not need such instruction ; for which reason he did not write to them, but to their disciples. That is a fine observation. And Whitby upon that verse says: Hence it seems evident that this epistle was not sent to the bishops or rulers of the Church, but to the whole Church, or the laity; and it may deserve to be considered whether this repeated notice of the rulers among them does not afford ground to believe that some of the *apostles* were still in Judea. Whether there be sufficient reason to believe that or not, I think these notices very proper and suitable to the state of the Jewish believers in Judea ; for I am persuaded, that not only James, and all the other apostles, had exactly the same doctrine with Paul, but that all the elders likewise, and all the understanding men among the Jewish believers, embraced the same doctrine. They were, as I understand, the multitude only, πληθος, *plebs*, or the men of lower rank among them, who were attached to the peculiarities of the Mosaic law and the customs of their ancestors. This may be argued from what James and the elders of Jerusalem say to Paul, Acts xxi. 20–22 : ' Thou seest, brother, how many thousands of Jews there are that believe ; and they are all zealous of the law. What is it, therefore ? The multitude must needs come together.' It is hence evident that the zeal for the law, which prevailed in the minds of many, was not approved by James or the elders. That being the case, these recommendations of a regard for their rulers, whether apostles or elders, were very proper in an epistle sent to the believers in Judea.

" For these reasons, I think that this epistle was sent to the Jewish believers at Jerusalem and in Judea. But there are objections which must be considered.

" *Obj.* 1 Chap. vi. 10 : ' God is not unrighteous to forget your work and labour of love—in that ye have ministered to the saints, and do minister.' Upon which Dr. *Wall* remarks : Here again we are put upon thinking to what Church or what Christians this is said ; for as to those of Jerusalem, we read much in Paul's former letters of their poverty, and of their being ministered to by the Gentile Christians of Galatia, Macedonia, and Corinth ; and in the Acts, by the Antiochians ; but nowhere of their ministering to other saints. This objection, perhaps, might be strengthened from Heb. xiii. 2 : ' Be not forgetful to entertain strangers.' And from ver. 16 : ' To do good, and to communicate, forget not.'

" *Ans.* But the poverty of the Jews in Judea, and the contributions of the Gentile Churches for their relief, are no reasons why such admonitions as these should not be sent to them. They are properly directed to all Christians, that they may be induced to exert themselves to the utmost. The Gentile Churches, among whom St. Paul made collections for the saints in Judea, were not rich. As he says, 1 Cor. i. 26 : ' For ye know your calling, brethren—not many mighty, not many noble, are called.' And of the Churches in Macedonia, he says, 2 Cor. viii. 2 : ' How that, in a great trial of affliction, the abundance of their joy, and their deep poverty, had abounded unto the riches of their liberality.' In like manner, there might be instances of liberality to the distressed among the believers in Judea. There is a very fine example recorded, Acts, ix. 36, 39 ; nor was there ever any city or country in the world to whom that exhortation, ' Be not forgetful to entertain strangers,' or, Be not unmindful of hospitality, της φιλοξενιας μη επιλανθανεσθε, could be more properly given, than Jerusalem and Judea. For the people there must have been much accustomed to it at their festivals, when there was a great resort thither from all countries ; and the writer of an epistle to the Christian inhabitants of Jerusalem and Judea would naturally think of such an admonition ; being desirous that they should not fall short of others in that respect. And we may here, not unfitly, recollect the history of St. Paul's going to Jerusalem; and how he and his fellow travellers were entertained at Cæsarea, in the house of Philip the evangelist, and at Jerusalem, in the house of Mnason, an old disciple, as related Acts xxi. 8–16.

"*Obj.* 2. Upon chap. xiii. 18, 19, the same Dr. *Wall* says : One would think that Paul should have prayed and purposed to go anywhere rather than to Jerusalem, where he had been so used, and where he fell into that five years' imprisonment, from which he was but just now delivered.

"*Ans.* But there is not any improbability that Paul might now desire to see his countrymen in Judea, if he might go thither with safety, as I think he might. Almost three years had now passed since he left Judea; and his trial, or apology, had been over two years; and he was now set at liberty by the emperor himself. No man, not very presumptuous, would admit a thought of disturbing him.

"*Obj.* 3. St. Peter's epistles were written to the Hebrew Christians, scattered in Asia and Pontus, Galatia, Cappadocia, and Bithynia. St. Paul must have written an epistle to those Hebrew Christians to whom St. Peter writes his two epistles. For St. Peter, 2 Epist. iii. 15, cites to them what *Paul had written unto them.* No epistle of Paul was written to the Hebrews particularly but this; so that these must be the Hebrews of the above named countries. To which I answer: That St. Peter's epistles were not sent to Jews, but to Gentiles, or to all Christians in general, in the places above mentioned, as will be clearly shown hereafter. When St. Peter says, *As Paul has written unto you,* he may intend Paul's Epistle to the Galatians, and some other epistles written to Gentiles. If he refers at all to this Epistle to the Hebrews, it is comprehended under that expression, verse 16. *As also in all his epistles.*

"*Obj.* 4 This Epistle to the Hebrews seems to have been written in *Greek.* But if it had been sent to the Jewish believers in Judea, it would have been written in *Hebrew.* To which I answer: That, allowing the epistle to have been written in Greek, it might be sent to the believers in Judea. If St. Paul wrote to the Jewish believers in Palestine he intended the epistle for general use—for all Christians, whether of Jewish or Gentile original. Many of the Jews in Judea understood Greek; few of the Jews out of Judea understood Hebrew. The Greek language was almost universal, and therefore generally used. *All* St Paul's epistles are in *Greek,* even that to the *Romans.* And are not both St. Peter's epistles in Greek And St. John's, and St. Jude's? Did not St. James likewise write in Greek, who is supposed to have resided in Jerusalem from the time of our Lord's ascension to the time of his own death? His epistle is inscribed *to the twelve tribes scattered abroad.* But I presume that they of the twelve tribes who dwelt in Judea are not excluded by him, but intended. Nor could he be unwilling that this epistle should be read and understood by those who were his especial charge. The epistle written by Barnabas, a Levite, or ascribed to him, was written in Greek; not now to mention any other Jewish writers who have used the Greek language.

"II. Thus we are unawares brought to the inquiry, In what *language* was this epistle written? For there have been doubts about it, among both ancients and moderns. Yet many learned and judicious moderns have been of opinion that *Greek,* and not *Hebrew,* was the original language of this epistle; *Beausobre, James Capellus, S. Basnage, Mill,* in his Prolegomena to the New Testament, and the late *Mr. Wetstein,* and also *Spanheim,* in his Dissertation concerning the author of this epistle, which well deserves to be consulted. One argument for this, both of *Spanheim* and *Wetstein,* is taken from the Greek paronomasias in the epistle, or the frequent concurrence of Greek words of like sound; which seem to be an argument not easy to be answered.

"Some ancient Christian writers were of opinion that the Epistle to the Hebrews was written in the *Hebrew* language, and translated into Greek by *Luke* or *Clement* of Rome. *Jerome,* in particular, seems to have supposed that this epistle was written in Hebrew; and *Origen* is also sometimes reckoned among those who were of this opinion. But I think I have shown it to be probable that he thought it was written in Greek. It seems likewise that they must have been of the same opinion who considered the elegance of the Greek language of this epistle as an objection against its having been written by St. Paul; for if the Greek epistle had been supposed to be a *translation,* the superior elegance of the style of this epistle above that of the other epistles of Paul, could have afforded no objection against his being the author of it. Indeed the ancients, as *Beausobre* said, formerly had no other reason to believe that St. Paul wrote in Hebrew, but that he wrote to the *Hebrews.* So, likewise, says *Capellus.* The title deceived them. And because it was written to *Hebrews,* they concluded it was written IN *Hebrew;* for none of the ancients appear to have seen a copy of this epistle in that language.

"III. I now proceed to the third inquiry, Who is the writer of this epistle? And many things offer in favour of the Apostle PAUL.

"I. It is ascribed to him by many of the ancients. Here I think myself obliged briefly to recollect the testimonies of ancient authors; and I shall rank them under two heads: First, the testimonies of writers who used the *Greek tongue;* then the testimonies of those who lived in that part of the Roman empire where the *Latin* was the vulgar language.

"There are some passages in the epistles of *Ignatius,* about the year 107, which may be thought, by some to contain allusions to the Epistle to the Hebrews. This epistle seems to be referred to by *Polycarp,* bishop of Smyrna, in his epistle written to the Philippians, in the year 108, and in the relation of his martyrdom, written about the middle of the second century. This epistle is often quoted as Paul's by *Clement of Alexandria,* about the year 194. It is received and quoted as Paul's by *Origen,* about 230. It was also received as the apostle's by *Dionysius,* bishop of Alexandria, in 247. It is plainly referred to by *Theognostus,* of

2

Alexandria, about 282. It appears to have been received by *Methodius* about 292; by *Pamphilius*, about 294; and by *Archelaus*, bishop in Mesopotamia, at the beginning of the *fourth* century; by the *Manichees* in the *fourth*; and by the *Paulicians*, in the *seventh* century. It was received and ascribed to Paul by *Alexander*, bishop of Alexandria, in the year 313; and by the *Arians*, in the *fourth* century. *Eusebius*, bishop of Cæsarea, about 315, says: 'There are fourteen epistles of Paul manifest and well known; but yet there are some who reject that to the Hebrews, alleging in behalf of their opinion, that it was not received by the Church of Rome as a writing of Paul.' It is often quoted by *Eusebius* himself as Paul's, and sacred Scripture. This epistle was received by *Athanasius*, without any hesitation. In his enumeration of St. Paul's fourteen epistles, this is placed next after the two to the Thessalonians, and before the Epistles to Timothy, Titus, and Philemon. The same order is observed in the *Synopsis of Scripture*, ascribed to him. This epistle is received as Paul's by *Adamantius*, author of a dialogue against the Marcionites, in 380; and by *Cyril* of Jerusalem, in 347; by the *council of Laodicea*, in 363; where St. Paul's epistles are enumerated in the same order as in *Athanasius* just noticed. This epistle is also received as Paul's by *Epiphanius*, about 368; by the *apostolical constitutions*, about the end of the *fourth* century; by *Basil*, about 370; by *Gregory Nazianzen*, in 370; by *Amphilochius* also. But he says it was not received by all as Paul's. It was received by *Gregory Nyssen*, about 370; by *Didymus*, of Alexandria, about the same time; by *Ephrem*, the Syrian, in 370, and by the *Churches of Syria*; by *Diodorus*, of Tarsus, in 378; by *Hierax*, a learned *Egyptian*, about the year 302; by *Serapion*, bishop of Thumis, in Egypt, about 347; by *Titus*, bishop of Bostria, in Arabia, about 362; by *Theodore*, bishop of Mopsuestia, in Cilicia, about the year 394; by *Chrysostom*, about the year 398; by *Severian*, bishop of Gabala, in Syria, in 401; by *Victor*, of Antioch, about 401; by *Palladius*, author of a Life of Chrysostom, about 408; by *Isidore*, of Pelusium, about 412; by *Cyril*, bishop of Alexandria, in 412; by *Theodoret*, in 423; by *Eutherius*, bishop of Tiana, in Cappadocia, in 431; by *Socrates*, the ecclesiastical historian, about 440; by *Euthalius*, in Egypt, about 458; and probably by *Dionysius*, falsely called the *Areopagite*, by the author of the *Quæstiones et Responsiones*, commonly ascribed to *Justin Martyr*, but rather written in the *fifth* century. It is in the *Alexandrian manuscript*, about the year 500; and in the Stichometry of *Nicephorus*, about 806; is received as Paul's by *Cosmas*, of Alexandria, about 535; by *Leontius*, of Constantinople, about 610; by *John Damascen*, in 730; by *Photius*, about 858; by *Œcumenius*, about the year 950; and by *Theophylact*, in 1070. I shall not go any lower.

"I shall now rehearse such authors as lived in that part of the Roman empire where the *Latin* was the vulgar tongue.

"Here, in the first place, offers *Clement*, in his Epistle to the Corinthians, written about the year 96, or as some others say, about the year 70. For though he wrote in *Greek*, we rank him among *Latin authors*, because he was *bishop of Rome*. In his epistle are many passages, generally supposed to contain allusions or references to the Epistle to the Hebrews. *Irenæus*, bishop of Lyons, about 178, as we are assured by *Eusebius*, alleged some passages out of this epistle, in a work now lost; nevertheless it does not appear that he received it as St. Paul's. By *Tertullian*, presbyter of Carthage, about the year 200, this epistle is ascribed to *Barnabas*. *Caius*, about 212, supposed to have been presbyter in the Church of Rome, reckoning up the epistles of St. Paul, mentions *thirteen* only, omitting that to the Hebrews. Here I place *Hippolytus*, who flourished about 220; but it is not certainly known where he was bishop, whether of *Porto*, in Italy, or of some place in the east: we have seen evidences that he did not receive the Epistle to the Hebrews as St. Paul's, and perhaps that may afford an argument that, though he wrote in Greek, he lived where the *Latin* tongue prevailed. This epistle is not quoted by *Cyprian*, bishop of Carthage about 248, and afterwards; nor does it appear to have been received by *Novatus*, otherwise called *Novation*, presbyter of Rome about 251. Nevertheless it was in after times received by his followers. It may be thought by some that this epistle is referred to by *Arnobius*, about 306, and by *Lactantius* about the same time. It is plainly quoted by another *Arnobius*, in the *fifth* century. It was received as Paul's by *Hilary*, of Poictiers, about 354, and by *Lucifer*, bishop of Cagliari, in Sardinia, about the same time, and by his followers: it was also received as Paul's by *C. M. Victorianus*. Whether it was received by *Optatus*, of Milevi, in Africa, about 370, is doubtful. It was received as Paul's by *Ambrose*, bishop of Milan, about 374; by the *Priscillianists*, about 378. About the year 380 was published a Commentary upon thirteen epistles of Paul only, ascribed to *Hilary*, deacon of Rome. It was received as Paul's by *Philaster*, bishop of Brescia, in Italy, about 380; but he takes notice that it was not then received by all. His successor, *Gaudentius*, about 387, quotes this epistle as Paul's; it is also readily received as Paul's by *Jerome*, about 392, and he says it was *generally received by the Greeks*, and *the Christians in the east*, but not by *all* the *Latins*. It was received as Paul's by *Rufinus*, in 397; it is also in the *Catalogue* of the *third council of Carthage*, in 397. It is frequently quoted by *Augustine* as St. Paul's. In one place he says: 'It is of doubtful authority with some; but he was inclined to follow the opinion of the Churches in the east, who received it among the canonical Scriptures. It was received as Paul's by *Chromatius*, bishop of Aquileia, in Italy, about 401; by *Innocent*, bishop of Rome, about 402; by *Paulinus*, bishop of Nola, in Italy, about 403. *Pelagias*, about 405, wrote a commentary upon thirteen epistles of Paul, omitting that to the Hebrews; nevertheless it was received by his *followers*. It was received by *Cassian*, about 424; by *Prosper*, of Aquitain, about 434, and by the *authors* of the works ascribed to him; by *Eucherius*, bishop of Lyons, in 434; by *Sedulius*, about 818; by *Leo*, bishop of Rome, in 440; by *Salvian*, presbyter of Marseilles, about 440; by *Gelatius*, bishop of Rome, about 496: by *Facundus*, an *African* bishop, about 540; by *Junilius*, an *African* bishop, about 556; by *Cassiodorus*, in 556, by the *author* of the *imperfect work* upon St. Matthew, about 560; by *Gregory*, bishop of Rome, about 590; by *Isidore*, of Seville, about 596; and by *Bede*, about 701, or the beginning of the *eighth century.*

" Concerning the *Latin writers*, it is obvious to remark, that this epistle is not expressly quoted as Paul's by any of them in the three first centuries; however, it was known by *Irenæus* and *Tertullian*, as we have seen, and possibly to others also. But it is manifest that it was received as an epistle of St. Paul by many Latin writers, in the *fourth, fifth, and following centuries.*

" The reasons of doubting about the genuineness of this epistle probably were the *want of a name at the beginning*, and the difference of argument or subject matter, and of the style, from the commonly received epistles of the apostle, as is intimated by *Jerome*. Whether they are sufficient reasons for rejecting this epistle will be considered in the course of our argument.

" 2. There is nothing in the epistle itself that renders it impossible or unlikely to be his; for the epistle appears to have been written before the destruction of Jerusalem, as was of old observed by *Chrysostom* and *Theodoret*, and has been argued also by many moderns. That the temple was still standing, and sacrifices there offered, may be inferred from chap. viii. 4: ' For if he were on earth, he should not be a priest, seeing that there are priests that offer according to the law;' and from chap. xiii. 10: ' We have an altar, whereof they have no right to eat, which serve the tabernacle.' If the temple had been destroyed, and the worship there abolished, the writer would not have failed to take some notice of it in support of his argument, and for abating the too great attachment of many to the rites of the Mosaic institution. To this purpose speaks *Spanheim*. It is also probable that those words, chap. iii. 13, ' While it is called to-day,' refer to the patience which God yet continued to exercise toward the Jewish nation; he seems to have had in view the approach, ing destruction of Jerusalem, which would put an end to that *to-day*, and finish the time which God gave to the Jews, as a nation, to *hear his voice.* And Lightfoot argues, from chap. xii. 4, ' Ye have not yet resisted unto blood,' that the epistle was written *before* the war in Judea was begun.

" Indeed, those words have been the ground of an objection against this epistle having been sent to the believing Jews in Judea, because there had been already several martyrdoms in that country. That difficulty I would now remove; and I have received from a learned friend the following observation, which may be of use: ' It seems to me,' says he, ' that the apostle here, as well as in the preceding context, alludes to the Grecian games or exercises; and he signifies that they to whom he writes had not been called out to the most dangerous combats, and had not run the immediate hazard of their lives; which, I suppose, might be said of them as a body or Church.' And I shall transfer hither M. *Beausobre's* note upon this place: ' There had been martyrs in Judea, as Stephen and the two James; but, for the most part, the Jews did not put the Christians to death for want of power; they were imprisoned and scourged; see Acts v. 40, and here, chap. xiii. 3. And they endured reproaches, and the loss of their substance, chap. x. 32, 34. These were the sufferings which they had met with. The apostle, therefore, here indirectly reproves the Hebrews, that though God treated them with more indulgence than he had done his people in former times, and even than his own Son, they nevertheless wavered in their profession of the Gospel. See ver. 12.'

" 3. There are many exhortations in this epistle much resembling some in the epistles of St. Paul. 1. Chap. xii. 3: ' Lest ye be wearied and faint in your minds.' Gal. vi. 9: ' And let us not be weary in well-doing; for in due season we shall reap, if we faint not.' And see 2 Thess. iii. 13, and Eph. iii. 13. 2. Chap. xii. 14: ' Follow peace with all men, and holiness, without which no man shall see the Lord.' An exhorta- tion very suitable to Paul, and to the Jewish believers in Judea; admonishing them not to impose the rituals of the law upon others, that is, the Gentile believers; and to maintain friendship with them, though they did not embrace the law. It has also a resemblance to Rom. xii. 18, but the words of the original are different. 3. Chap. xiii. 1: ' Let brotherly love continue,' and what follows to the end of ver. 3. Then, in ver. 4: ' Marriage is honourable; but fornicators and adulterers God will judge.' Here is an agreement with Eph. v. 2, 3, 4: ' And walk in love, as Christ also has loved us—but fornication, and all uncleanness, or covetous- ness, let it not once be named among you. For this ye know, that no fornicator, nor unclean person, nor covetous man—has any inheritance in the kingdom of God.' 4. Chap. xiii. 16: ' But to do good, and to communicate, forget not; for with such sacrifices God is well pleased.' That exhortation is very suitable to Paul's doctrine, and has an agreement with what he says elsewhere, as Phil. iv. 18: ' An odour of a sweet smell; a sacrifice acceptable, well pleasing to God.' . Moreover, as is observed by Grotius upon this text, the word *communicate* or *communion* is found in a like sense in the Acts, and in other epistles of St. Paul. See Acts ii. 42; Rom. xv. 26; 2 Cor. viii. 4; ix. 13.

" 4. In the next place, I observe some instances of agreement in the *style* or *phrases*, of the Epistle to the Hebrews, and the acknowledged epistles of St. Paul. 1. Chap. ii. 4: ' God also bearing them witness with signs and wonders, and divers miracles, and gifts of the Holy Ghost:'—*signs and wonders*, together, seldom occur in other books of the New Testament; but they are found several times in the Acts, and in St. Paul's epistles. The phrase is in Matt. xxiv. 24, and Mark xiii. 22, and once likewise in St. John's Gospel, chap. iv. 48; but it is several times in the Acts, chap. ii. 19; iv. 30; v. 12; vi. 8; viii. 13; xiv. 3; xv. 12. The most remarkable are these where there are three different words, Acts ii. 22: ' A man approved of God among you, by miracles, and wonders, and signs.' Rom. xv. 19: ' Through mighty signs and wonders, by the power of the Spirit of God.' 2 Cor. xii. 12: ' In signs, and wonders, and mighty deeds.' 2 Thess. ii. 9: ' With all power, and signs, and lying wonders.' 2. Chap. ii. 14: ' That, through death, he might destroy him who had the power of death.' The word καταργεω or καταργεομαι is, I think, nowhere used in the New Testament, except in Luke xiii. 7, and St. Paul's epistles, where it is several times; and is sometimes used in a sense resembling this place, particularly 2 Tim. i. 10 : 'Who has abolished death;' καταργησαντος μεν του θανατου, and 1 Cor. xv. 26. Compare Dr. *Doddridge's* Family Expositor, vol. iv., upon 1 Cor. xv. 24. 3. Chap. iii. 1 : 'Holy brethren, partakers of the heavenly calling.' Phil. iii. 14 : 'The prize of the high calling of God in Christ Jesus.' 2 Tim. i. 9 : 'Who has called us with a holy calling.' 4. Chap. v. 12 : 'And are become such as have need of milk, and not of strong meat.' 1 Cor. iii. 2 : 'I have fed you with milk, and not with meat.' However, in the original, there is no great agreement in the words, except that in both places *milk* is used for the first rudiments of the Christian doctrine. 5. Chap. viii. 1 : 'Who is set on the right hand of the throne of the Majesty on high.' Eph. i. 20 : 'And set him at his own right hand in the heavenly places.' 6. Chap. viii. 6 ; ix. 15 ; and xii. 24, Jesus Christ is styled *Mediator*. So likewise in Gal. iii. 19, 20 ; 1 Tim. ii. 5 ; and in no other books of the New Testament. 7. Chap. viii. 5 : 'Who serve unto the example and shadow of heavenly things;' και σκια των επουρανιων. Chap. x. 1 : 'For the law, having a shadow of good things to come, and not the very image of the things;' σκιαν εχων των μελλοντων αγαθων, ουκ αυτην την εικονα των πραγματων. Col. ii. 17 : 'Which are a shadow of things to come ; but the body is of Christ ;' ἁ εστι σκια των μελλοντων· το δε σωμα του Χριστου. 8. Chap. x. 33 : 'Whilst ye were made a gazing-stock, *or spectacle*, both by reproaches and afflictions;' ονειδισμοις τε και θλιψεσι θεατριζομενοι. 1 Cor. iv. 9 : 'For we are made a spectacle unto the world ;' ὁτι θεατρον εγενηθημεν τῳ κοσμῳ. 9. St. Paul, in his acknowledged epistles, often alludes to the exercises and games which were then very reputable and frequent in Greece and other parts of the Roman empire. There are many such allusions in this epistle, which have also great elegance. So chap. vi. 18 : 'Who have fled for refuge to lay hold of the hope set before us ;' or the reward of eternal life, proposed to animate and encourage us. And, chap. xii. 1, 2, 3 : 'Wherefore, seeing we also are compassed about with so great a cloud of witnesses, let us lay aside every weight, and the sin which does so easily beset us, and let us run with patience the race that is set before us. Looking unto Jesus—who, for the joy that was set before him, endured the cross. Lest ye be wearied and faint in your minds.' And, ver. 12 : 'Wherefore lift up the hands that hang down, and the feeble knees.' All these texts seem to contain allusions to the celebrated *exercises* and *games* of those times. And to these may be added, if I mistake not, the place before noticed, chap. xii. 4 : 'Ye have not yet resisted unto blood, striving against sin.' 10. Chap. xiii. 9 : 'Be not carried about with divers and strange doctrines;' διδαχαις ποικιλαις και ξεναις μη περιφερεσθε. Eph. iv. 14 : 'That we henceforth be no more children, tossed to and fro, and carried about with every wind of doctrine ;' κλυδωνιζομενοι και περιφερομενοι παντι ανεμῳ της διδασκαλιας. 11. Chap. xiii. 10 : 'We have an altar whereof they have no right to eat.' 1 Cor. ix. 13 : 'And they that wait at the altar are partakers with the altar.' And, x. 18 : 'Are not they which eat of the sacrifices partakers of the altar?' 12. Chap. xiii. 20, 21 : 'Now the God of peace make you perfect;' which is a title of the Deity nowhere found in the New Testament but in St. Paul's epistles, and in them it is several times, and near the conclusion, as here : so Rom. xv. 33 : 'Now the God of peace be with you all.' See likewise xvi. 20 ; Phil. iv. 9 ; and 1 Thess. v. 23 : 'And the very God of peace sanctify you wholly ;' and 2 Cor. xiii. 11 : 'And the God of love and peace shall be with you.'

" 5. The *conclusion* of this epistle has a remarkable agreement with the *conclusions* of St. Paul's epistles in several respects. 1. He here desires the Christians to whom he is writing to pray for him, chap. xiii. 18 : 'Pray for us.' So Rom. xv. 30; Eph. vi. 18, 19 ; Col. iv. 3 ; 1 Thess. v. 25 ; 2 Thess. iii. 1. 2. It is added in the same ver. 18 : 'For we trust we have a good conscience, in all things willing to live honestly;' which may well come from Paul, some of the Jewish believers not being well affected to him, or being even offended with him. So says *Theodoret* upon this place, and *Chrysostom* to the like purpose, very largely. To which might be added, ver. 22 : 'And I beseech you, brethren, to suffer the word of exhortation.' It is also observable that St. Paul makes a like profession of his sincerity in pleading against the Jews before Felix, Acts xxiv. 16. 3. Having desired the prayers of these Christians for himself, he prays for them, ver. 20, 21 : 'Now the God of peace make you perfect, through Jesus Christ; to whom be glory for ever and ever. Amen.' So Rom. xv. 30, 32, having asked their prayers for him, he adds, ver. 33 : 'Now the God of peace be with you all. Amen.' Compare Eph. vi. 19, 23, and 1 Thess. v. 23 ; 2 Thess. iii. 16. 4. Chap. xiii. 24 : 'Salute all them that have the rule over you, and all the saints. They of Italy salute you.' The like salutations are in many of St. Paul's epistles, Rom. xvi. ; 1 Cor. xvi. 19–21 ; 2 Cor. xiii. 13 ; Phil. iv. 21, 22 ; not to refer to any more. 5. The *valedictory benediction* at the end is that which Paul had made the token of the *genuineness* of his epistles ; 2 Thess. iii. 18. So here, chap. xiii. 25 : Grace be with you all. Amen.' Indeed, sometimes it is 'The grace of our Lord Jesus Christ be with you.' But at other times it is more contracted. So Col. iv. 18 : 'Grace be with you.' 1 Tim. vi. 21 : 'Grace be with thee.' See likewise, Eph. vi. 24 ; 2 Tim. iv. 22 ; Tit. iii. 15. The same observation is in *Theodoret.*

" 6. The circumstances of this epistle lead us to the Apostle Paul. 1. Chap. xiii. 24 : 'They of Italy salute you.' The writer, therefore, was then in *Italy*, whither we know Paul was sent a prisoner, and where he resided two years, Acts xxviii. ; where also he wrote several epistles still remaining. 2. Ver. 19 : He desires them *the rather to pray for him, that he might be restored to them the sooner.* Paul had been brought from Judea to Rome. And he was willing to go thither again, where he had been several times. And though the original words are not the same, there is an agreement between this and Philem., ver. 22 : 'I trust that through your prayers I shall be given unto you.' This particular is one of the arguments of *Euthalius*, that this epistle is Paul's, and written to the Jews of Palestine. 3. Ver. 23 : ' Know ye, that our brother Timothy is set at liberty ; with whom, if he come shortly, I will see you.' Timothy was with Paul during his imprisonment at Rome, as is allowed by all : for he is expressly mentioned at the beginning of the Epistles to the *Philippians, Colossians,* and *Philemon,* written when he was in *bonds.* He is mentioned again, Phil. ii. 19. When the apostle writes to Timothy, he calls him his *son,* or *dearly beloved son,* 1 Tim. i. 2 ; 2 Tim. i. 2. But when he mentions him to others, he calls him *brother ;* 2 Cor. i. 1 ; Col. i. 1 ; 1 Thess. iii. 2. In like manner Titus. Compare Titus i. 4 and 2 Cor. ii. 13.

" This mention of *Timothy* has led many, not only *moderns,* but *ancients* likewise, to think of Paul as writer of the epistle, particularly *Euthalius ;* and, undoubtedly, many others have been confirmed in that supposition by this circumstance.

" The original word απολελυμενον is ambiguous, being capable of two senses : one of which is, that of our translation, *set at liberty,* that is, from *imprisonment ;* the other is *dismissed, sent abroad on an errand.* In this last sense it was understood by *Euthalius,* who, in the place just cited, says : ' That scarcely any one can be thought of, besides Paul, who would send Timothy abroad upon any service of the Gospel.' And indeed this passage does put us in mind of what Paul says to the Philippians, chap. ii. 19 : ' But I trust in the Lord Jesus to send Timothy shortly unto you, that I also may be of good comfort, when I know your state. Him, therefore, I hope to send presently, so soon as I shall see how it will go with me ; but I trust in the Lord, that I also myself shall come shortly,' ver. 23, 24, which induced *Beausobre* to say in the preface to this epistle : ' The sacred author concludes with asking the prayers of the Hebrews, chap. xiii. 19, that he may be restored to them. These words intimate that he was still *prisoner,* but that he hoped to be set at liberty : therefore, he adds, in ver. 23, that he intended to come and see them, with Timothy, as soon as he should be returned. If this explication be right, this epistle was written at Rome, some time after the Epistle to the Philippians, and since the departure of Timothy for Macedonia.'

" All these considerations just mentioned, added to the testimony of many ancient writers, make out an argument of great weight, (though not decisive and demonstrative,) that the Apostle Paul is the writer of this epistle. An objection against this epistle being St. Paul's is, that it is supposed to have in it *an elegance superior to that of his other writings.* This has been judged, by *Grotius* and *Le Clerc,* sufficient to show that this was not written by Paul.

" The opinion of *Origen,* in his homilies upon this epistle, as cited by *Eusebius,* and by us from him, is, ' that the style of the Epistle to the Hebrews has not the apostle's rudeness of speech, but, as to the texture of it, is elegant Greek, as every one will allow who is able to judge of the differences of style.' Again, he says : ' The sentiments of the epistle are admirable, and not inferior to the acknowledged writings of the apostle. This will be assented to by every one who reads the writings of the apostle with attention.' Afterwards he adds : ' If I were to speak my opinion, I should say, that the sentiments are the apostle's, but the language and composition another's, who committed to writing the apostle's sense, and, as it were, reduced into commentaries the things spoken by his master,' &c.

" *Eusebius* himself, speaking of *Clement's* Epistle to the Corinthians, says : ' Paul having written to the Hebrews in their own language, some think that the Evangelist Luke, others, that this very *Clement* himself, translated it into Greek : which last is most likely, there being a great resemblance between the style of the epistle of *Clement* and the Epistle to the Hebrews : nor are the sentiments of those two writings very different This passage has been already twice quoted by us ; once in the chapter of *Clement,* bishop of Rome, and again in that of *Eusebius.'*

" *Philaster,* bishop of Brescia, about 380, says : ' There are some who do not allow the Epistle to the Hebrews to be Paul's, but say it is either an epistle of the Apostle *Barnabas,* or of *Clement,* bishop of Rome ; but some say it is an epistle of *Luke* the evangelist : moreover, some reject it, as more eloquent than the apostle's other writings.

" *Jerome,* about 392, in his article of St. Paul, in the book of *Illustrious Men,* says : ' The Epistle called to the Hebrews is not thought to be his, because of the difference of the argument and style ; but either *Barnabas's,* as *Tertullian* thought ; or the Evangelist *Luke's,* according to some others ; or *Clement's,* bishop of Rome ; who, as some think, being much with him, clothed and adorned Paul's sense in his own language. Moreover, he wrote as a Hebrew to the Hebrews, in pure Hebrew, it being his own language ; whence it came to pass that, being translated, it has more elegance in the Greek than his other epistles.'

" Some learned men of late times, as *Grotius* and *Le Clerc,* have thought this to be an insuperable objection. Of this opinion also was *Jacob Tollius ;* who, in his notes upon *Longinus,* of the sublime, has celebrated the sublimity of this epistle, and particularly the elegance of the beginning of it ; which alone he thinks sufficient to show that it was not Paul's.

" It remains, therefore, it seems to me, that if the epistle be Paul's, and was originally written in Greek, as we suppose, the apostle must have had some assistance in composing it ; so that we are led to the judgment of *Origen,* which appears to be as ingenious and probable as any. ' The sentiments are the apostle's, but the language and composition of some one else, who committed to writing the apostle's sense ; and, as it were, rendered into commentaries the things spoken by his master.' According to this account the epistle is St. Paul's, as to the *thoughts* and *matter ;* but the *words* are *another's.*

" *Jerome,* as may be remembered, says : ' He wrote as a Hebrew to the Hebrews, pure Hebrew ; it being his own language; whence it came to pass that, being *translated*, it has more elegance in the Greek than his other epistles.' My conjecture, which is not very different, if I may be allowed to mention it, is, that St. Paul dictated the epistle in Hebrew, and another, who was a great master of the Greek language, immediately wrote down the apostle's sentiments in his own elegant Greek. But who this assistant of the apostle was is altogether unknown.

" The ancients, besides Paul, have mentioned *Barnabas*, *Luke*, and *Clement*, as *writers* or *translators* of this epistle; but I do not know that there is any remarkable agreement between the style of the Epistle to the Hebrews and the style of the epistle commonly ascribed to *Barnabas*. The style of *Clement*, in his Epistle to the Corinthians, is verbose and prolix. St. *Luke* may have some words which are in the Epistle to the Hebrews; but that does not make out the same style. This epistle, as *Origen* said, as to the texture of the style, is *elegant Greek*; but that kind of texture appears not in *Luke*, so far as I can perceive; there may be more art and labour in the writings of Luke than in those of the other evangelists, but not much more elegance that I can discern. This Epistle to the Hebrews is bright and elegant from the beginning to the end, and surpasses as much the style of St. Luke as it does the style of St. Paul in his acknowledged epistles. In short, this is an admirable epistle, but singular in sentiments and language; somewhat different in both respects from all the other writings of the New Testament; and whose is the language seems to me altogether unknown; whether that of *Zenas*, or *Apollos*, or some other of the Apostle Paul's assistants and fellow labourers.

" There still remains one objection more against this epistle being written by St. Paul, which is, *the want of his name;* for to all the thirteen epistles, received as his, he prefixes his name, and generally calls himself apostle. This objection has been obvious in all ages; and the omission has been differently accounted for by the ancients who received this epistle as a genuine writing of St. Paul.

" *Clement* of Alexandria, in his Institutions, speaks to this purpose: 'The Epistle to the Hebrews,' he says, 'is Paul's, but he did not make use of that inscription *Paul the Apostle;* for which he assigns this reason: writing to the Hebrews, who had conceived a prejudice against him, and were suspicious of him, he wisely declined setting his name at the beginning lest he should offend them. He also mentions this tradition: 'forasmuch as the Lord was sent, as the apostle of almighty God, to the Hebrews, Paul, out of modesty, does not style himself the apostle to the Hebrews, both out of respect to the Lord, and that, being preacher and apostle of the Gentiles, he over and above wrote to the Hebrews.'

" *Jerome* also speaks to this purpose: 'That Paul might decline putting his name in the inscription on account of the Hebrews being offended with him;' so in the article of St. Paul, in his book of *Illustrious Men.* In his *Commentary* in the beginning of his Epistle to the Galatians, he assigns another reason: 'That Paul declined to style himself apostle at the beginning of the Epistle to the Hebrews, because he should afterwards call Christ the High Priest and Apostle of our profession,' chap. iii. 1.

" *Theodoret* says, that Paul was especially the apostle of the Gentiles; for which he alleges Gal. ii. 9, and Rom. xi. 13. 'Therefore writing to the Hebrews, who were not intrusted to his care, he barely delivered the doctrine of the Gospel without assuming any character of authority, for they were the charge of the other apostles.'

" *Lightfoot* says, 'Paul's not affixing his name to this, as he had done to his other epistles, does no more deny it to be his than the First Epistle of John is denied to be John's on that account.'

" *Tillemont* says, ' Possibly Paul considered it to be a book rather than a letter, since he makes an excuse for its brevity, (chap. xiii. 22,) for indeed it is short for a *book*, but long for a *letter*.'

" It is, I think, observable, that there is not at the beginning of this epistle any salutation. As there is no name of the writer, so neither is there any description of the people to whom it is sent. It appears, from the conclusion, that it was sent to some people at a certain place; and undoubtedly they to whom it was sent, and by whom it was received, knew very well from whom it came, nevertheless there might be reasons for omitting an inscription and a salutation at the beginning. This might arise from the circumstances of things; there might be danger of offence at sending at that time a long letter to Jews in Judea; and this omission might be in part owing to a regard for the bearer, who too is not named. The only person named throughout the epistle is *Timothy;* nor was he then present with the writer Indeed I imagine that the two great objections against this being an epistle of St. Paul—the *elegance of the style*, and the *want of a name* and *inscription*, are both owing to some particular circumstance of the writer, and the people to whom it was sent. The people to whom it was sent are plainly Jews in Judea; and the writer very probably is St. Paul, whose circumstances at the breaking up of his confinement at Rome, and his setting out upon a new journey, might be attended with some peculiar embarrassments, which obliged him to act differently from his usual method.

" IV. Thus we are brought to the *fourth* and *last* part of our inquiry concerning this epistle—the *time* and *place* of writing it. *Mill* was of opinion that this epistle was written by Paul, in the year 63, in some part of Italy, soon after he had been released from his imprisonment at Rome. Mr *Wetstein* appears to have been of the same opinion. *Tillemont* likewise places this epistle in 63, immediately after the apostle's being set at liberty, who, as he says, was still at Rome, or at least in Italy *Basnage* speaks of this epistle at the year 61, and supposes it to be written during the apostle's imprisonment, for he afterward speaks of the Epistle to the Ephesians, and says it was the last letter the apostle wrote during the time of his *bonds.* *L'Enfant* and *Beausobre*, in their general preface to St. Paul's epistles, observe, ' That in the subscription at the end of the epistle it is said to have been written *from Italy;* the only ground of which, as they add, is what is said chap. xiii. 24 : *They of Italy salute you.* This has made some think that the, apostle wrote to the Hebrews after he had been set at liberty, and when he had got into that part of Italy which borders upon Sicily, and in ancient times was called *Italy.* Nevertheless there is reason to doubt this. When he requests the prayers of the Hebrews, that *he might be restored to them the sooner,* he intimates that he was not yet set at liberty.' Accordingly *they* place this epistle in the year 62.

" There is not any great difference in any of these opinions concerning the *time* or *place* of this epistle, all supposing that it was written by the apostle either at *Rome* or *Italy*, near the end of his imprisonment at Rome, or soon after it was over, before he removed to any other country.

" I cannot perceive why it may not be allowed to have been written at *Rome*. St. Paul's First Epistle to the Corinthians was written at Ephesus ; nevertheless he says, chap. xvi. 19 : ' The Churches of Asia salute you.' So now he might send salutations from the Christians of *Italy*, not excluding, but including, those at Rome, together with the rest throughout that country. The argument of *L'Enfant* and *Beausobre*, that Paul was not yet set at liberty, because he requested the prayers of the *Hebrews that he might be restored to them the sooner*, appears to me not of any weight. Though Paul was no longer a prisoner, he might request the prayers of those to whom he was writing, that he might have a prosperous journey to them whom he was desirous to visit, and that all impediments of his intended journey might be removed ; and many such there might be, though he was no longer under confinement. Paul was not a prisoner when he wrote his Epistle to the Romans ; yet he was very fervent in his prayers to God, that he might have a prosperous journey, and come to them, Rom. i. 10.

" For determining the *time* of this epistle, it may be observed that, when the apostle wrote the Epistle to the Philippians, the Colossians, and Philemon, he had hopes of deliverance. At the writing of all these epistles Timothy was present with him; but now he was absent, as plainly appears from chap. xiii. 23. This leads us to think that this epistle was written after *them.* And it is not unlikely that the apostle had now obtained that liberty which he expected when they were written.

" Moreover, in the Epistle to the Philippians, he speaks of sending Timothy to them, chap. ii. 19–23 : ' But I trust in the Lord Jesus, to send Timothy shortly unto you, that I also may be of good comfort, when I know your state.' Timothy, therefore, if sent, was to come back to the apostle. ' Him, therefore, I hope to send presently, so soon as I shall see how it will go with me.'

" It is probable that Timothy did go to the Philippians, soon after writing the above mentioned epistles, the apostle having gained good assurance of being quite released from his confinement. And this Epistle to the Hebrews was written during the time of that absence; for it is said, chap. xiii. 23: 'Know ye that our brother Timothy is set at liberty, *or* has been sent abroad.' The word is capable of that meaning, and it is a better and more likely meaning, because it suits the coherence. And I suppose that Timothy did soon come to the apostle, and that they both sailed to Judea, and after that went to Ephesus, where Timothy was left to reside with his peculiar charge.

" Thus this epistle was written at Rome, or in Italy, soon after that Paul had been released from his confinement at Rome, in the beginning of the year 63. And I suppose it to be the last written of all St. Paul's epistles which have come down to us, or of which we have any knowledge."—*Dr. Lardner's* WORKS, vol. vi., p. 381.

After this able and most circumstantial investigation I think it would be a mere *actum agere* to enter farther into this discussion ; all that the *ancients*, both Grecian and Roman, and all that the most intelligent of the *moderns*, have produced, both for and against the argument stated above, has been both judiciously and candidly stated by Dr. Lardner ; and it is not going too far to say that few readers will be found who will draw conclusions different from those of Dr. Lardner, from the same premises.

As all the epistles of St. Paul have an evident *object* and *occasion*, it is natural to look for these in the Epistle to the Hebrews as well as in those to other Churches. We have already seen that it was most probably written to the *converted Jews in Judea*, who were then in a state of *poverty, affliction,* and *persecution;* and who, it appears, had been assailed by the strongest arguments to apostatize from the faith, and turn back to the poor elementary teaching furnished by Mosaic rites and ceremonies. That in such circumstances they might begin to *halt* and *waver*, will not appear strange to any considerate person ; and that the apostle should write to guard them against *apostasy,* by showing them that the religious system which they had embraced was the *completion* and *perfection* of all those which had preceded it, and particularly of the Mosaic, is what might be naturally expected. This he has done in the most effectual and masterly manner, and has furnished them with arguments against their opponents which must have given them a complete triumph.

His arguments against *backsliding* or *apostasy* are the most awful and powerful that can well be conceived, and are as *applicable now* to guard Christian believers against *falling from grace* as they were in the apostolic times, and, from the general *laxity* in which most professors of religion indulge themselves, not less *necessary.*

A late sensible writer, Mr. *Thomas Olivers,* in a discourse on chap. ii. 3 of this epistle, has considered this subject at large, and treated it with great cogency of reasoning. I shall borrow his *Analysis* of the different chapters, and a few of his concluding remarks , a perusal of the whole work will amply repay the serious reader. After one hundred and thirty-two pages of previous discussion he goes on thus :—

" I shall," says he, " sum up all that has been said upon this head by giving a brief account of the OCCASION and DESIGN of this epistle, and of the apostle's *manner* of reasoning therein.

2

"The Christian religion being so contrary to the corrupt principles and practices of the world, those who embraced and propagated it were, on those accounts, rendered very odious wherever they came. The consequence of this was, that heavy persecutions were raised against them in most places. The converted Hebrews, because they had turned their backs on the law of Moses, and embraced the religion of JESUS whom their rulers had crucified, were exceedingly persecuted by their countrymen. Sometimes the unconverted Hebrews persecuted their converted brethren *themselves*; at other times they stirred up the *heathen* who were round about to do it. By these means the believing Hebrews had *a great fight of afflictions*, chap. x. 32; and were *made gazing-stocks, both by reproaches and afflictions*, ver. 33; and experienced *the spoiling of their goods*, which for a while they took joyfully, ver. 34. But this was not all; for, as the Christian religion was then a new thing in the world, it is natural to suppose that the new converts had a great many scruples and reasonings in themselves concerning the lawfulness of what they had done in embracing it: and what added to these scruples was, the constant endeavour of the Judaizing teachers to lay stumbling blocks in the way of these Hebrews, which they too often effected by means of their divers and strange doctrines, mentioned chap. xiii. 9. The consequence of this opposition, both from within and without, was, that great numbers of the Hebrews *apostatized* from Christ and his Gospel, and went back to the law of Moses; while the fluctuating state of the rest gave the apostles too much reason to fear a general, if not *universal apostasy*. Now this apparent danger was the OCCASION of this epistle, and the DESIGN of it was to prevent the threatened evil if possible.

"That this account is true will fully appear from a more particular survey of the contents of the whole epistle.

"Chap. i. The apostle shows that all former dispensations were delivered to the world by *men* and *angels*, who were only *servants* in what they did; but that the Gospel salvation was delivered by *Christ*, who is the *Son of God*, and the *Heir* of all things. How naturally does he then infer the *superiority of the Gospel* over the *law*; and, of consequence, the great absurdity of leaving the former for the sake of the latter!

"Chap. ii. He obviates an objection which might be made to the superior excellency of Christ on account of his humiliation. To this end he shows that this humiliation was voluntary; that it was intended for many important purposes, *viz.* that we might be sanctified, ver. 11; that through his death we might be delivered from death, ver. 14, 15; and that Christ, by experiencing our infirmities in his own person, might become a *faithful and merciful High Priest*, ver. 17, 18. The inference then is, that his taking our nature upon him, and dying therein, is no argument of his inferiority either to the *prophets* or to the *angels*; and therefore it is no excuse for those who *apostatize* from the *Gospel* for the sake of the *law*.

"Chap. iii. Here *Christ* is particularly compared with *Moses*, and shown to be superior to him in many respects. As, 1. *Christ* is shown to be the *great Builder* of that house of which *Moses* is only a *small part*, ver. 3, 4. 2. *Christ* is as a *son* in his *own* house; but *Moses* was only as a *servant* in his *master's* house, ver. 5. Therefore *Christ* and his salvation are superior to *Moses* and his law, and ought not to be neglected on account of any thing inferior. From ver. 7 of this chapter to ver. 14 of chap. iv., the apostle shows the great danger of *apostatizing* from Christ, by the severe sentence which was passed on those who rebelled against *Moses*, and apostatized from his law.

"Chap. v. *Christ* is compared to *Aaron*, and preferred to him on several accounts. As, 1. *Aaron* offered for his *own*, as well as for the *sins* of the *people*; but *Christ* offered only for the *sins of others*, having none of his own to offer for, ver. 3. 2. Christ was not a *priest* after the order of *Aaron*, but after the order of *Melchisedec*, which was a *superior order*, ver. 10. Concerning *Melchisedec* and *Christ*, the apostle observed that, through the dulness of the *Hebrews*, there were some things which they could not easily understand, ver. 11—14.

"He therefore calls on them, chap. vi., to labour for a more perfect acquaintance therewith; withal promising them his farther assistance, ver. 1—3. The necessity of their doing this, of their thus *going on unto perfection*, he enforced by the following consideration, that, if they did not go forward, they would be in danger of *apostatizing* in such manner as would be irrecoverable, ver. 7, 8. From thence to the end of the chapter he encourages them to patience and *perseverance*, by the consideration of the *love, oath*, and *faithfulness* of GOD; and also by the *example* of their father *Abraham*.

"Chap. vii. The apostle resumes the parallel between *Melchisedec* and *Christ*, and shows that they agree in title and descent, ver. 1—3; and then, from instances wherein the priesthood of *Melchisedec* was preferable to the priesthood of *Aaron*, he infers the superiority of *Christ's* priesthood over that of *Aaron*, ver. 4—17. From thence to the end of the chapter, he shows that the priesthood of *Aaron* was only subservient to the priesthood of *Christ*, in which it was consummated and abolished; and of consequence, that all those legal obligations were thereby abolished. How naturally then did the apostle infer the absurdity of *apostatizing* from the Gospel to the law, seeing they who did this, not only left the *greater* for the *lesser*, but also left that which remained in *full force*, for the sake of that which was *disannulled*.

"Chap. viii. is employed partly in recapitulating what had been demonstrated before concerning the superior dignity of our great High Priest, ver. 1—5; and partly in showing the superior excellency of the new covenant, as established in Christ, and as containing better promises; ver. 6 to the end of the chapter. From this last consideration, the impropriety of going from the new covenant to the old is as naturally inferred as from any other of the afore-mentioned considerations.

"With the same view the apostle, chap. ix., compares *Christ* and his priesthood to the *tabernacle* of old,

2

and to what the high priest did therein on the *great day of atonement*, in all things giving *Christ* the preference; from ver. 1 to the end.

"Chap. x. The apostle sets down the difference between the legal sacrifices and the sacrifice of *Christ :* the legal sacrifices were *weak*, and could not *put away sin*, ver. 1–4 ; but the sacrifice of *Christ* was *powerful*, doing that which the other *could not do*, ver. 5–10.

"The next point of difference was between the legal priests who offered these sacrifices, and the High Priest of our profession. And *first*, the legal priests were *many ;* ours is *one. Secondly*, they *stood* when they presented their offerings to God ; CHRIST *sits* at the right hand of his Father. *Thirdly*, they offered *often ;* but CHRIST, *once for all. Fourthly*, they, with all their offerings, could not put away the smallest sin ; but *Christ*, by his one offering, put away all sin, ver. 11–18. Now, from all these considerations, the apostle infers the great superiority of the Gospel over the law ; and, consequently, the impropriety of leaving the former for the latter.

"The next thing that the apostle does is to improve his doctrine ; this he does by showing that, for the reasons above given, the Hebrews ought to cleave to *Christ*, to hold fast their profession, and *not to forsake the assembling themselves together*, ver. 19–25. And, as a farther inducement to cleave to *Christ*, and to *persevere unto the end*, he urges the consideration of the difficulties which they had already overcome, and also of the love which they had formerly shown towards *Christ* and his Gospel, ver. 32–34. He also encouraged them not to *cast away their confidence, seeing it had a great recompense of reward*, which they should enjoy if they *persevered* unto the end, ver. 35–37. Another consideration which he urged was, that they ought not to depart from *faith* to the *works* of the law, because it is by *faith* that a *just man liveth*, and not by the *works of the law ;* because God has no pleasure in those who draw back from faith in him ; and because every one who does this exposes himself to eternal perdition, ver. 36–39.

"Another inducement which he laid before them, to *continue* to expect salvation by *faith* and *patience*, was the consideration of the powerful effects of these graces as exemplified in the patriarchs of old, and the rest of the ancient worthies ; chap. xi. throughout. ' This chapter,' according to Mr. *Perkins*, ' depends on the former ; thus we may read in the former chapter that many Jews, having received the faith and given their names to *Christ*, did afterwards *fall away ;* therefore, towards the end of the chapter, there is a notable exhortation, tending to persuade the Hebrews to *persevere* in faith unto the end. Now in this chapter he continues the same exhortation ; and the whole chapter (*as I take it*) *is nothing else*, in substance, but one reason to urge the former exhortation to *perseverance* in faith, and the reason is drawn from the excellency of it ; for this chapter, in divers ways, sets down what an excellent *gift* of GOD faith is ; his *whole scope*, therefore, is manifest to be *nothing else* but to urge them to *persevere* and *continue* in *that faith*, proved at large to be so excellent a thing.'

"As a farther encouragement to patience and *perseverance* he adds the example of *Christ*, chap. xii. 1–3 ; and as to the afflictions they met with on the Gospel's account, he tells them they ought not to be discouraged and driven away from *Christ* on their account, seeing they were signs of the Divine favour, and permitted to come upon them merely for their good, ver. 4–11. He then exhorts them to encourage one another to *persevere* in *well-doing*, ver. 12–14. To watch over one another lest any of them *fall from the grace of God*, ver. 15–18. And, seeing they were then in possession of privileges, Gospel privileges, such as the law of *Moses* could not give, he exhorts them to *hold fast the grace* they had, that thereby they might serve God in such a manner as the great obligation they were under required, which alone would be acceptable to him ; and this they ought to do, the rather because, if they did not, they would find God to be as much more severe to *them* as his *Gospel* is superior to the *law ;* ver. 19 to the end of the chapter.

"Chap. xiii. He exhorts them, instead of *apostatizing*, to *continue* their brotherly affection one for another, ver. 1–3. To *continue* their purity of behaviour, their dependence on God, and their regard for their teachers, ver. 4–8. He exhorts them not to suffer themselves to be *carried about* (from Christ and his Gospel) by *divers and strange doctrines*, but rather to strive to be established in grace, which they would find to be of more service to them than running about after Jewish ceremonies, ver. 9. Again he exhorts them to *cleave to* and to follow JESUS *without the camp*, and continually to give praise to God through him, ver. 9–16. And instead of *turning away* after seducers, that they might avoid persecution and the scandal of the cross, he exhorts them to submit to and obey their own Christian teachers, and to pray for their success and welfare, ver. 17–19, concluding the whole with some salutations and a solemn benediction from ver. 20 to the end.

"Now, if we closely attend to these general contents of the epistle, we shall find that *every argument* and *mode of reasoning*, which would be *proper* in a treatise written professedly on the *sin* and *danger* of *apostasy*, is made use of in this epistle.

"For, 1. As great temptations to prefer the law of *Moses* to the Gospel of *Christ* was one circumstance which exposed them to the danger of apostasy, nothing could be more to the purpose than to show them that the Gospel is *superior to the law*. Now we have seen how largely this argument is prosecuted in chap. i., ii., iii., v., vii., viii., ix., x. If we reduce it to form, it runs as follows : No one ought to prefer that which is less excellent to that which is more so : but the law is less excellent than the Gospel ; therefore none ought to prefer the law to the Gospel, by apostatizing from the latter to the former.

"2. Another argument, equally proper on such an occasion, is that taken from the consideration of the *punishment* which all apostates are exposed to. This argument is urged chap. ii. 2, 3 ; iii. 7 to the end ;

iv. 1–14; vi. 4, 8; x. 26–31; xii. 25, 28, 29. In most of these places the apostle compares the punishment which will be inflicted on apostates from *Christ* and his Gospel to that which was inflicted on the apostate Israelites of old, and he frequently shows that the former will be far greater than the latter. This argument is as follows: You ought not to do that which will expose you to as great and greater punishment than that which God inflicted on the rebellious Israelites of old: but total and final apostasy from Christ will expose you to this; therefore you ought not to apostatize from Christ.

" 3. Another argument proper on such an occasion is that taken from the consideration of the *great reward* which God has promised to perseverance. This the apostle urges, chap. iii. 6–14; iv. 1–9; v. 9; vi. 9, 11; ix. 28; x. 35–39. This argument runs thus: You ought to be careful to do that which God has promised greatly to reward: but he has promised you this on condition of your perseverance in the Gospel of his Son; therefore you ought to be careful to persevere therein.

" 4. A fourth argument, which must operate powerfully on such an occasion, is taken from the consideration of losing their present privileges by apostatizing. This argument is insisted on, chap. ii. 11 to the end; iii. 1; iv. 3–16; vi. 18–20; vii. 19; viii. 10, 12; ix. 14, 15; x. 14, 22; xii. 22, 24, 28; xiii. 10, 14. This argument runs thus: You ought not to do that for which you will lose the Gospel privileges you now enjoy: but if you apostatize from Christ and his Gospel you will lose them; therefore you ought not to apostatize from *Christ* and his Gospel.

" 5. A fifth argument, very proper in such a work, is taken from the consideration of their former zeal and diligence in cleaving to *Christ*, and in professing his religion. This argument is handled chap. vi. 10; x. 32–34. The argument here is: Those who have formerly been zealous in well-doing ought not to grow weary, but rather to be steadfast therein unto the end; but you have formerly been zealous in your adherence to *Christ*, and in professing his religion; therefore you ought not to grow weary of adhering to *Christ*, or of professing his religion.

" 6. Another argument, proper on such an occasion, is taken from the example of such persons as are held in very high esteem. Now this argument is urged, chap vi. 12–15; ix. throughout; xii. 1–3. Here the argument is: Whatever you esteem as an excellency in the example of holy men of old you ought to imitate: but you esteem it as an excellency in their example that they were *steadfast*, and did not *apostatize* from God and his ways; therefore you ought to imitate their example in being steadfast, and in not apostatizing from *Christ* and his Gospel.

" From all that has been said in these several surveys of this epistle, it undeniably appears, 1. That the apostle apprehended these Hebrews to be in danger of total and final apostasy; 2. That he wrote this epistle to them on purpose to prevent it if possible; and 3. That it was total and final apostasy from Christ and his Gospel, of which the believing Hebrews were in danger, and which the apostle endeavours to prevent."

For other matters relative to this subject see the preface, and the notes on all the passages referred to.

PREFACE

TO THE

EPISTLE OF PAUL THE APOSTLE

TO THE

HEBREWS.

THE Epistle to the Hebrews, on which the reader is about to enter, is by far the most important and useful of all the apostolic writings; all the doctrines of the Gospel are in it embodied, illustrated, and enforced in a manner the most lucid, by references and examples the most striking and illustrious, and by arguments the most cogent and convincing. It is an *epitome* of the dispensations of God to man, from the foundation of the world to the advent of Christ. It is not only the sum of the GOSPEL, but the sum and completion of the LAW, on which it is also a most beautiful and luminous comment. *Without* this, the law of Moses had never been fully understood, nor God's design in giving it. *With* this, all is clear and plain, and the ways of God with man rendered consistent and harmonious. The apostle appears to have taken a portion of one of his own epistles for his text—CHRIST *is the* END *of the* LAW *for* RIGHTEOUSNESS *to them that* BELIEVE, and has most amply and impressively demonstrated his proposition. All the rites, ceremonies, and sacrifices of the Mosaic institution are shown to have had *Christ* for their *object* and *end*, and to have had neither *intention* nor *meaning* but in reference to *him*; yea, as a *system* to be without *substance*, as a *law* to be without *reason*, and its *enactments* to be both *impossible* and *absurd*, if taken out of this reference and connection. Never were *premises* more clearly stated; never was an *argument* handled in a more masterly manner; and never was a *conclusion* more legitimately and satisfactorily brought forth. The *matter* is everywhere the most interesting; the *manner* is throughout the most engaging; and the *language* is most beautifully adapted to the whole, everywhere appropriate, always nervous and energetic, dignified as is the subject, pure and elegant as that of the most accomplished Grecian orators, and harmonious and diversified as the music of the spheres.

So many are the *beauties*, so great the *excellency*, so instructive the *matter*, so pleasing the *manner*, and so exceedingly interesting the *whole*, that the work may be read a hundred times over without perceiving any thing of *sameness*, and with new and increased information at each reading. This latter is an excellency which belongs to the whole revelation of God; but to no part of it in such a peculiar and supereminent manner as to the Epistle to the Hebrews.

To explain and illustrate this epistle multitudes have toiled hard; and exhibited much industry, much learning, and much piety. I also will show my opinion; and ten thousand may succeed me, and still bring out something that is *new*. That it was written to *Jews*, naturally such, the whole structure of the epistle proves. Had it been written to the *Gentiles*, not one in ten thousand of them could have comprehended the argument, because unacquainted with the Jewish system; the knowledge of which the writer of this epistle everywhere supposes. He who is well acquainted with the Mosaic law sits down to the study of this epistle with double advantages; and he who knows the *traditions of the elders*, and the *Mishnaic illustrations* of the written, and pretended *oral law* of the Jews, is still more likely to enter into and comprehend the apostle's meaning. No man has adopted a more likely way of explaining its phraseology than *Schoettgen*, who has traced its peculiar diction to Jewish sources; and, according to him, the proposition of the whole epistle is this:—

JESUS OF NAZARETH IS THE TRUE GOD.

And in order to convince the Jews of the truth of this proposition, the apostle uses but *three arguments*: 1. Christ is superior to the *angels*. 2. He is superior to *Moses*. 3. He is superior to *Aaron*.

These arguments would appear more distinctly were it not for the improper division of the chapters; as he who divided them in the middle ages (a division to which we are still unreasonably attached) had but a superficial knowledge of the word of God. In consequence of this it is that one peculiar excellency of the apostle is not noticed, viz. his *application* of every argument, and the strong exhortation founded on it. *Schoettgen* has very properly remarked, that commentators in general have greatly misunderstood the apostle's meaning through their unacquaintance with the Jewish writings and their peculiar phraseology, to which the apostle is continually referring, and of which he makes incessant use. He also supposes, allowing for the immediate and direct inspiration of the apostle, that he had in view this remarkable saying of the rabbins, on Isa. lii. 13 : " Behold, my servant will deal prudently." *Rab. Tanchum*, quoting *Yalcut Simeoni*, part ii., fol. 53, says : זה כלך המשיח, " *This is the King Messiah*, who shall be greatly extolled, and elevated : he shall be elevated beyond *Abraham ;* shall be more eminent than *Moses ;* and more exalted than ממלאכי השרת, *the ministering angels.*" Or, as it is expressed in *Yalcut Kadosh*, fol. 144 : משיח גדול מן האבות ומן משה ומן כלאכי השרת Mashiach gadol min ha-aboth ; umin Mosheh ; umin Malakey hashshareth. " The Messiah is greater than the patriarchs ; than Moses ; and than the ministering angels." These sayings he shows to have been fulfilled in *our Messiah ;* and as he dwells on the superiority of our Lord to all these illustrious persons because they were at the very *top* of all *comparisons* among the Jews ; he, according to their opinion, who was greater than all these, must be greater than all created beings.

This is the point which the apostle undertakes to prove, in order that he may show the Godhead of Christ ; therefore, if we find him proving that Jesus was *greater* than the *patriarchs, greater* than *Aaron, greater* than *Moses,* and greater than the *angels,* he must be understood to mean, according to the Jewish phraseology, that Jesus is an uncreated Being, infinitely greater than all others, whether *earthly* or *heavenly.* For, as they allowed the greatest eminence (next to God) to *angelic beings,* the apostle concludes " that he who is greater than the angels is truly God : but Christ is greater than the angels ; therefore Christ is truly God." Nothing can be clearer than that this is the apostle's grand argument ; and the proofs and illustrations of it meet the reader in almost every verse.

That the apostle had a *plan* on which he drew up this epistle is very clear, from the close connection of every part. The grand divisions seem to be *three :—*

I. The *proposition,* which is very short, and is contained in chap. i. 1–3. The majesty and pre-eminence of Christ.

II The *proof* or *arguments* which support the proposition, viz.—

Christ is greater than the ANGELS.

1. Because he has a more excellent name than they, chap. i. 4, 5.
2. Because the *angels* of God *adore him,* ver. 6.
3. Because the *angels* were *created* by him, ver. 7.
4. Because, in his human nature, he was endowed with *greater gifts* than they, ver. 8, 9.
5. Because he is *eternal,* ver. 10, 11, 12.
6. Because he is more *highly exalted,* ver. 13.
7. Because the *angels* are only the *servants* of God ; he, the *Son,* ver. 14.

In the ·application of this argument he exhorts the Hebrews not to *neglect Christ,* chap. ii. 1, by arguments drawn,—

1. From the minor to the major, ver. 2, 3.
2. Because the preaching of Christ was confirmed by *miracles,* ver. 4.
3. Because, in the *economy* of the New Testament, angels are not the *administrators ;* but the *Messiah* himself, to whom all things are subject, ver. 5.

Here the apostle inserts a twofold *objection,* professedly drawn from Divine revelation :—

1. Christ is man, and is less than the angels. *What is man—thou madest him a little lower than the angels,* ver. 6, 7. Therefore he cannot be *superior* to them.

To this it is answered : 1. Christ as a mortal man, by his death and resurrection, overcame all enemies, and subdued all things to himself ; therefore he must be greater than the angels, ver. 9.

2. Though Christ died, and was in this respect inferior to the angels, yet it was necessary that he should take on him this mortal state, that he might be of the same nature with those whom he was to redeem ; and this he did without any prejudice to his Divinity, ver. 10–18.

Christ is greater than MOSES.

1. Because Moses was only a *servant ;* Christ, the *Lord,* chap. iii. 2–6.

The *application* of this argument he makes from Psa. xcv. 7–11, which he draws out at length, chap iii. 7–iv. 13

Christ is greater than AARON, and all the other high priests.

1. Because he has not gone through the *veil* of the tabernacle to make an atonement for sin, but ha entered for this purpose into *heaven* itself, chap. iv. 14
2. Because he is the *Son of God,* ver. 14
3 Because it is from him we are to implore grace and mercy, chap. iv. 15, 16, and ver. 1, 2, 3.
4. Because he was consecrated High Priest by God himself, chap. v. 4–10.

5. Because he is not a priest according to the *order* of Aaron, but according to the *order* of Melchisedec, which was much more ancient, and much more noble, chap. vii.   For the excellence and prerogatives of this order, see the notes.

6. Because he is not a *typical* priest, prefiguring good things to come, but the *real* Priest, of whom the others were but *types* and *shadows*, chap. viii. 1–ix. 11.   For the various reasons by which this argument is supported, see also the notes.

In this part of the epistle the apostle inserts a *digression*, in which he reproves the ignorance and negligence of the Hebrews in their mode of treating the sacred Scriptures.   See chap. v. 11, and chap. vi.

The *application* of this part contains the following exhortations :—

1. That they should carefully retain their faith in Christ as the true Messiah, chap. x. 19–23.

2. That they should be careful to live a godly life, ver. 24, 25.

3. That they should take care not to incur the punishment of disobedience, ver. 32–37, and chap. xii 3–12.

4. That they should place their whole confidence in God, live by faith, and not turn back to perdition chap. x. 38; xii. 2.

5. That they should consider and imitate the faith and obedience of their eminent ancestors, chap. xi.

6. That they should take courage, and not be remiss in the practice of the true religion, chap. xii. 12–24.

7. That they should take heed not to despise the Messiah, now speaking to them from heaven, chap. xii. 25–29.

III. *Practical* and *miscellaneous exhortations* relative to sundry duties, chap. xiii.

All these subjects, (whether immediately designed by the apostle himself, in this particular order, or not,) are pointedly considered in this most excellent epistle; in the whole of which the *superiority* of CHRIST, his *Gospel*, his *priesthood*, and his *sacrifice*, over *Moses*, the *law*, the *Aaronic priesthood*, and the various *sacrifices* prescribed by the law, is most clearly and convincingly shown.

Different writers have taken different views of the order in which these subjects are proposed, but most commentators have produced the same results.

For other matters relative to the *author* of the epistle, the *persons* to whom it was sent, the *language* in which it was composed, and the *time* and *place* in which it was written, the reader is referred to the *introduction*, where these matters are treated in sufficient detail.

THE

EPISTLE OF PAUL THE APOSTLE

TO THE

HEBREWS

Chronological Notes relative to this Epistle.

Year of the Constantinopolitan era of the world, or that used by the Byzantine historians, and other eastern writers, 5571.—Year of the Alexandrian era of the world, 5565.—Year of the Antiochian era of the world, 5555.—Year of the world, according to Archbishop Usher, 4067.—Year of the world, according to Eusebius, in his Chronicon, 4291.—Year of the minor Jewish era of the world, or that in common use, 3823.—Year of the Greater Rabbinical era of the world, 4422.—Year from the Flood, according to Archbishop Usher, and the English Bible, 2411.—Year of the Cali yuga, or Indian era of the Deluge, 3165. —Year of the era of Iphitus, or since the first commencement of the Olympic games, 1003.—Year of the era of Nabonassar, king of Babylon, 810.—Year of the CCXth Olympiad, 3.—Year from the building of Rome, according to Fabius Pictor, 810.—Year from the building of Rome, according to Frontinus, 814.—Year from the building of Rome, according to the Fasti Capitolini, 815.—Year from the building of Rome, according to Varro, which was that most generally used, 816.—Year of the era of the Seleucidæ, 375.—Year of the Cæsarean era of Antioch, 111.—Year of the Julian era, 108.—Year of the Spanish era, 101.—Year from the birth of Jesus Christ according to Archbishop Usher, 67.—Year of the vulgar era of Christ's nativity, 63.—Year of Albinus, governor of the Jews, 2.—Year of Vologesus, king of the Parthians, 14.—Year of Domitius Corbulo, governor of Syria, 4.—Year of Matthias, high priest of the Jews, 1.—Year of the Dionysian period, or Easter Cycle, 64.—Year of the Grecian Cycle of nineteen years, or Common Golden Number, 7; or the second after the second embolismic.—Year of the Jewish Cycle of nineteen years, 4, or the first after the first embolismic.—Year of the Solar Cycle, 16.—Dominical Letter, it being the third after the Bissextile, or Leap Year, B.—Day of the Jewish Passover, according to the Roman computation of time, the IIId of the calends of April, or, in our common mode of reckoning, the thirtieth of March, which happened in this year on the fourth day after the Jewish Sabbath.—Easter Sunday, the IIId of the nones of April, named by the Jews the 19th of Nisan or Abib; and by Europeans in general, the 3d of April.—Epact, or age of the moon on the 22d of March, (the day of the earliest Easter Sunday possible,) 6.—Epact, according to the present mode of computation, or the moon's age on New Year's day, or the Calends of January, 13.—Monthly Epacts, or age of the moon on the Calends of each month respectively, (beginning with January,) 13, 15, 14, 15, 16, 17, 18, 19, 20, 20, 22, 22.—Number of Direction, or the number of days from the twenty-first of March to the Jewish Passover, 9.—Year of the reign of Caius Tiberius Claudius Nero Cæsar, the fifth Roman monarch, computing from Octavianus, or Augustus Cæsar, properly the first Roman emperor, 10.—Roman Consuls, C. Memmius Regulus and L Verginius Rufus.

684   2

CHAPTER I.

Different discoveries made of the Divine will to the ancient Israelites by the prophets, 1. The discovery now perfected by the revelation of Jesus Christ, of whose excellences and glories a large description is given, 2–13. Angels are ministering spirits to the heirs of salvation, 14.

A. M. cir. 4067.
A. D. cir. 63.
An. Olymp.
cir. CCX. 3.
A. U. C. cir.
816.

GOD, who at sundry times and [a] in divers manners spake in time past unto the fathers by the prophets,

2 Hath [b] in these last days [c] spoken unto us by *his* Son, [d] whom he hath appointed heir of all things, [e] by whom also he made the worlds ;

A. M. cir. 4067.
A. D. cir. 63.
An. Olymp.
cir. CCX. 3.
A. U. C. cir.
816.

[a] Num. xii. 6, 8.——[b] Deut. iv. 30 ; Galatians iv. 4 ; Eph. i. 10.
[c] John i. 17 ; xv. 15 ; chap. ii. 3.

[d] Psa. ii. 8 ; Matt. xxi. 38 ; xxviii. 18 ; John iii. 35 ; Rom. viii.
17.——[e] John i. 3 ; 1 Cor. viii. 6 ; Col. i. 16.

NOTES ON CHAP. I.

Verse 1. *God, who at sundry times and in divers manners*] We can scarcely conceive any thing more dignified than the opening of this epistle ; the sentiments are exceedingly elevated, and the language, harmony itself. The infinite God is at once produced to view, not in any of those attributes which are essential to the Divine nature, but in the manifestations of his love to the world, by giving a revelation of his will relative to the salvation of mankind, and thus preparing the way, through a long train of years, for the introduction of that most glorious Being, his own Son. This Son, in the fulness of time, was manifested in the flesh that he might complete all vision and prophecy, supply all that was wanting to perfect the great scheme of revelation for the instruction of the world, and then die to put away sin by the sacrifice of himself. The description which he gives of this glorious personage is elevated beyond all comparison. Even in his *humiliation*, his suffering of death excepted, he is infinitely exalted above all the angelic host, is the object of their unceasing adoration, is permanent on his eternal throne at the right hand of the Father, and from him they all receive their commands to minister to those whom he has redeemed by his blood. In short, this first chapter, which may be considered the introduction to the whole epistle is, for importance of subject, dignity of expression, harmony and energy of language, compression and yet distinctness of ideas, equal, if not superior, to any other part of the New Testament.

Sundry times] Πολυμερως, from πολυς, *many*, and μερος, a *part ;* giving portions of revelation at different times.

Divers manners] Πολυτροπως, from πολυς, *many*, and τροπος, a *manner, turn*, or *form of speech ;* hence *trope*, a figure in rhetoric. *Lambert Bos* supposes these words to refer to that part of music which is denominated *harmony*, viz. that general consent or union of musical sounds which is made up of different parts ; and, understood in this way, it may signify the *agreement* or *harmony* of all the Old Testament writers, who with one consent gave testimony to Jesus Christ, and the work of redemption by him. *To him gave all the prophets witness, that, through his name, whosoever believeth in him shall receive remission of sins ;* Acts x. 43.

But it is better to consider, with *Kypke*, that the words are rather intended to point out the *imperfect*

state of Divine revelation under the Old Testament ; it was not *complete*, nor can it without the New be considered a sufficiently ample discovery of the Divine will. Under the Old Testament, revelations were made πολυμερως και πολυτροπως, at *various* times, by *various* persons, in *various* laws and forms of teaching, with *various* degrees of clearness, under *various* shadows, types, and figures, and with *various* modes of revelation, such as by angels, visions, dreams, mental impressions, &c. See Num. xii. 6, 8. But under the New Testament all is done ἁπλως, *simply*, by *one* person, i. e. JESUS, who has fulfilled the prophets, and completed prophecy ; who is the way, the truth, and the life ; and the founder, mediator, and governor of his own kingdom.

One great object of the apostle is, to put the *simplicity* of the Christian system in opposition to the *complex* nature of the Mosaic economy ; and also to show that what the law could not do because it was weak through the flesh, Jesus has accomplished by the merit of his death, and the energy of his Spirit.

Maximus Tyrius, Diss. 1, page 7, has a passage where the very words employed by the apostle are found, and evidently used nearly in the same sense : Τη του ανθρωπου ψυχη δυο οργανων οντων προς συνεσιν, του μεν ἁπλου, ὁν καλουμεν νουν, του δε ποικιλου και πολυμερους και πολυτροπου, ἁς αισθησεις καλουμεν. "The soul of man has two organs of intelligence : one *simple*, which we call *mind ;* the other *diversified*, and acting in *various modes* and *various ways*, which we term *sense*."

A similar form of expression the same writer employs in Diss. 15, page 171 : "The city which is governed by the mob, πολυφωνον τε ειναι και πολυμερη και πολυπαθη, is full of noise, and is divided by various factions and various passions."

The excellence of the *Gospel* above the *law* is here set down in three points : 1. God spake unto the faithful under the Old Testament by Moses and the prophets ; worthy *servants*, yet servants ; now the *Son* is much better than a servant, ver. 4. 2. Whereas the body of the Old Testament was long in compiling, being about a thousand years from Moses to Malachi ; and God spake unto the fathers by piecemeal ; one while raising up one prophet, another while another , now sending them one parcel of prophecy or history, then another but when Christ came, all was brought to perfection in one age ; the apostles and evangelists were alive, some of them, when every

2

A. M. cir. 4067.
A. D. cir. 63.
An. Olymp.
cir. CCX. 3.
A. U. C. cir.
816.

3 f Who being the brightness of *his* glory, and the express image of his person, and g upholding all things by the word

of his power, h when he had by himself purged our sins, i sat down on the right hand of the Majesty on high;

A. M. cir. 4067.
A. D. cir. 63.
An. Olymp.
cir. CCX. 3.
A. U. C. cir.
816.

f Wisd. vii. 26; John i. 14; xiv. 9; 2 Cor. iv. 4; Col. i. 15.   g John i. 4; Col. i. 17; Rev. iv. 11.

h Chap. vii. 27 ix. 12, 14, 16.——i Psa. cx. 1; Eph. i. 20; chap. viii. 1; x. 12; xii. 2; 1 Pet. iii. 22.

part of the New Testament was completely finished.
3. The *Old Testament* was delivered by God in divers manners, both in utterance and manifestation; but the delivery of the *Gospel* was in a more simple manner; for, although there are various penmen, yet the subject is the same, and treated with nearly the same phraseology throughout; James, Jude, and the Apocalypse excepted. See *Leigh.*

Verse 2. *Last days*] The Gospel dispensation, called the *last days* and the *last time*, because not to be followed by any other dispensation; or the conclusion of the Jewish Church and state now at their termination.

By his Son] It is very remarkable that the pronoun αὐτου, *his*, is not found in the text; nor is it found in any MS. or version. We should not therefore supply the pronoun as our translators have done; but simply read εν Υἱω, BY A SON, or IN A SON, *whom he hath appointed heir of all things.* God has many *sons* and daughters, for he is *the Father of the spirits of all flesh;* and he has many *heirs*, for *if sons, then heirs, heirs of God, and joint heirs with Jesus Christ;* but he has no Son who is *heir of all things*, none *by whom he made the worlds*, none *in* whom *he speaks*, and *by* whom he has delivered a complete revelation to mankind, but Jesus the Christ.

The apostle begins with the lowest state in which Christ has appeared: 1. His being a SON, born of a woman, and made under the law. He then ascends, 2. So his being an *Heir*, and an Heir of *all things.* 3. He then describes him as the *Creator* of all worlds. 4. As the *Brightness of the Divine glory.* 5. As the *express Image of his person*, or *character of the Divine substance.* 6. As sustaining the immense fabric of the universe; and this by the word of his power. 7. As having made an *atonement* for the sin of the world, which was the most stupendous of all his works.

> " 'Twas great to speak a world from nought;·
> 'Twas greater to redeem."

8. As being on the *right hand* of God, infinitely exalted above all created beings; and the object of *adoration* to all the angelic host. 9. As having an eternal throne, neither his *person* nor his *dignity* ever *changing* or decaying. 10. As continuing to *exercise dominion*, when the earth and the heavens are no more! It is only in God manifested in the flesh that all these excellences can possibly appear, therefore the apostle begins this astonishing *climax* with the simple *Sonship* of Christ, or his *incarnation*; for, on *this*, all that he is to man, and all that he has done for man, is built.

Verse 3. *The brightness of* his *glory*] Απαυγασμα της δοξης. The resplendent outbeaming of the essential glory of God. *Hesychius* interprets απαυγασμα by ἡλιου φεγγος, the *splendour of the sun.* The same form of expression is used by an apocryphal writer,

Wisdom chap. vii. 26, where, speaking of the uncreated wisdom of God, he says : " For she is the *splendour of eternal light*, απαυγασμα γαρ εστι φωτος αἰδιου, and the unsullied mirror of the energy of God, and the image of his goodness." The word αυγασμα is that which has splendour *in itself*, απαυγασμα is the splendour *emitted from it*; but the *inherent* splendour and the *exhibited* splendour are radically and essentially the same.

The express image of his person] Χαρακτηρ της ὑποστασεως αυτου· *The character* or *impression of his hypostasis* or *substance.* It is supposed that these words expound the former; *image* expounding *brightness*, and *person* or *substance*, *glory.* The *hypostasis* of God is that which is essential to him as God; and the *character* or *image* is that by which all the likeness of the original becomes manifest, and is a perfect *fac-simile* of the whole. It is a metaphor taken from sealing; the *die* or *seal* leaving the full impression of its every part on the wax to which it is applied.

From these words it is evident, 1. That the apostle states Jesus Christ to be of the *same essence* with the Father, as the απαυγασμα; or *proceeding splendour*, must be the same with the αυγασμα, or *inherent splendour.*

2. That Christ, though proceeding from the Father, is of the same essence; for if one αυγη, or *splendour*, produce another αυγη, or splendour, the produced splendour must be of the same essence with that which produces it.

3. That although Christ is thus of the same essence with the Father, yet he is a *distinct person* from the Father; as the splendour of the sun, though of the same essence, is distinct from the sun itself, though each is essential to the other; as the αυγασμα, or *inherent splendour*, cannot subsist without its απαυγασμα, or *proceeding splendour*, nor the *proceeding splendour* subsist without the *inherent splendour* from which it proceeds.

4. That Christ is *eternal* with the Father, as the proceeding splendour must necessarily be coexistent with the inherent splendour. If the one, therefore, be uncreated, the other is *uncreated*; if the one be *eternal*, the other is *eternal.*

Upholding all things by the word of his power] This is an astonishing description of the infinitely energetic and all pervading power of God. He *spake*, and all things were created; He *speaks*, and all things are sustained. The Jewish writers frequently express the perfection of the Divine nature by the phrases, *He bears all things, both above and below; He carries all his creatures; He bears his world; He bears all worlds by his power.* The Hebrews, to whom this epistle was written, would, from this and other circumstances, fully understand that the apostle believed Jesus Christ to be truly and properly God.

2

A. M. cir. 4067
A. D. cir. 63.
An. Olymp.
cir. CCX. 3.
A. U. C. cir.
816.

4 Being made so much better than the angels, as [k] he hath by inheritance obtained a more excellent name than they.

5 For unto which of the angels said he at any time, [l] Thou art my Son, this day have I begotten thee? And again, [m] I will be to

A. M. cir. 4067.
A. D. cir. 63.
An. Olymp.
cir. CCX. 3.
A. U. C. cir.
816.

[k] Eph. i. 21 ; Philip. ii. 9, 10.——[l] Psa ii 7 · Acts xiii. 33 ; chap. v 5.

[m] 2 Sam. vii. 14 ; 1 Chron. xxii. 10 ; xxviii. 6 ; Psa. lxxxix. 26, 27.

Purged our sins] There may be here some reference to the great transactions in the wilderness.

1. Moses, while in communion with God on the mount, was so impressed with the Divine glories that his face shone, so that the Israelites could not behold it. But Jesus is infinitely greater than Moses, for he is the splendour of God's glory ; and,

2. Moses found the government of the Israelites such a burden that he altogether sank under it. His words, Num. xi. 12, are very remarkable : *Have I conceived all this people ? Have I begotten them, that thou shouldest say unto me,* CARRY *them in thy* BOSOM— *unto the land which thou swearest unto their fathers ?* But Christ not only *carried* all the Israelites, and all mankind ; but *he upholds* ALL THINGS *by the word of his power.*

3. The Israelites murmured against Moses and against God, and provoked the heavy displeasure of the Most High ; and would have been consumed had not Aaron made an *atonement* for them, by offering *victims* and *incense.* But Jesus not only makes an atonement for Israel, but for the whole world ; not with the blood of bulls and goats, but with his own blood : hence it is said that *he purged our sins δι' αὑτοῦ, by himself,* his own body and life being the victim: It is very likely that the apostle had all these things in his eye when he wrote this verse ; and takes occasion from them to show the infinite excellence of Jesus Christ when compared with Moses ; and of his *Gospel* when compared with the *law.* And it is very likely that the Spirit of God, by whom he spoke, kept in view those maxims of the ancient Jews, concerning the Messiah, whom they represent as being infinitely greater than Abraham, the patriarchs, Moses, and the ministering angels So Rabbi Tanchum, on Isa. lii. 13, *Behold my servant shall deal prudently,* says, וה כלך הכישח *Zeh melek hammashiach,* this is the King Messiah , *and shall be exalted, and be extolled, and be very high.* " He shall be *exalted* above Abraham, and shall be *extolled* beyond Moses, and shall be more *sublime* than the ministering angels." See the preface.

The right hand of the Majesty on high] As it were associated with the supreme Majesty, in glory everlasting, and in the government of all things in time and in eternity ; for the *right hand* is the place of the greatest eminence, 1 Kings ii 19 The king himself, in eastern countries, sits on the throne ; the *next* to him in the kingdom, and the highest *favourite,* sits on his *right hand ;* and the third greatest personage, on his *left*

Verse 4. *So much better than the angels*] Another argument in favour of the Divinity of our Lord The Jews had the highest opinion of the transcendent excellence of angels ; they even associate them with God

in the creation of the world, and suppose them to be of the privy council of the Most High ; and thus they understand Gen. i. 26 : *Let us make man in our own image, in our own likeness ;* " And the Lord said to the ministering angels that stood before him, and who were created the second day, Let us make man," &c. See the Targum of *Jonathan ben Uzziel.* And they even allow them to be worshipped for the sake of their Creator, and as his representatives ; though they will not allow them to be worshipped for their own sake. As, therefore, the Jews considered them next to God, and none entitled to their adoration but God ; on their own ground the apostle proves Jesus Christ to be God, because God commanded all the angels of heaven to worship him. He, therefore, who is greater than the angels, and is the object of their adoration, is God. But Jesus Christ is greater than the angels, and the object of their adoration ; therefore Jesus Christ must be God.

By inheritance obtained] Κεκληρονομηκεν ονομα. The verb κληρονομειν signifies generally to *participate, possess, obtain,* or *acquire ;* and is so used by the purest Greek writers : Kypke has produced several examples of it from *Demosthenes.* It is not by *inheritance* that Christ possesses a more excellent name than angels, but as God : he has it *naturally* and *essentially ;* and, as God *manifested in the flesh,* he has it in consequence of his humiliation, sufferings, and meritorious death. See Phil. ii. 9.

Verse 5. *Thou art my Son, this day have I begotten thee*] These words are quoted from Psa. ii. 7, a psalm that seems to refer only to the Messiah ; and they are quoted by St. Paul, Acts xiii. 33, as referring to the *resurrection of Christ.* And this application of them is confirmed by the same apostle, Rom. i. 4, as by his resurrection from the dead he *was declared*—manifestly proved, *to be the Son of God with power ;* God having put forth his miraculous energy in raising that body from the grave which had truly died, and died a violent death, for Christ was put to death as a malefactor , but by his *resurrection* his innocence was demonstrated, as God could not work a miracle to raise a wicked man from the dead As Adam was *created* by God, and because no natural generation could have any operation in this case, therefore he was called the *son of God,* Luke iii. 38, and could never have seen *corruption* if he had not sinned so the human nature of Jesus Christ, formed by the energy of the eternal Spirit in the womb of the virgin, without any human intervention, was for this very reason called the Son of God, Luke i 35 ; and because it had not *sinned,* therefore it could not see corruption , nor was it even *mortal,* but through a miraculous display of God's infinite love, for the purpose of making a sacrificial atonement for the sin of the world ; and

2   687

A. M. cir. 4067.
A. D. cir. 63.
An. Olymp.
cir. CCX. 3.
A. U. C. cir.
816.

him a Father, and he shall be to me a Son?

6 ⁿ And again, when he bringeth in ᵒ the first-begotten into the

world, he saith, ᵖ And let all the angels of God worship him.

7 And ᑫ of the angels he saith, ʳ Who maketh his angels spirits,

A. M. cir. 4067
A. D. cir. 63.
An. Olymp.
cir. CCX. 3.
A. U. C. cir.
816.

ⁿ Or, *When he bringeth again.*——ᵒ Romans viii. 29; Col. i. 18; Rev. i. 5.

ᵖ Deut. xxxii. 43; LXX.; Psa. xcvii. 7; 1 Peter iii. 22. ᑫ Gr. *unto.*——ʳ Psa. civ. 4.

God, having raised this sacrificed human nature from the dead, declared that same Jesus (who was, as above stated, *the Son of God*) to be his Son, the promised Messiah; and as coming by the Virgin Mary, the right heir to the throne of David, according to the uniform declaration of all the prophets.

The words, *This day have I begotten thee*, must refer either to his *incarnation*, when he was miraculously conceived in the womb of the virgin by the power of the Holy Spirit; or to his *resurrection* from the dead, when God, by this sovereign display of his almighty energy, declared him to be his 'Son, vindicated his innocence, and also the purity and innocence of the blessed virgin, who was the mother of this son, and who declared him to be produced in her womb by the power of God. The *resurrection* of Christ, therefore, to which the words most properly refer, not only gave the fullest proof that he was an *innocent* and *righteous* man, but also that he had accomplished the purpose for which he died, and that his *conception* was miraculous, and his mother a pure and unspotted virgin.

This is a subject of infinite importance to the Christian system, and of the last consequence in reference to the conviction and conversion of the Jews, for whose use this epistle was sent by God. Here is the rock on which they split; they deny this *Divine Sonship* of Jesus Christ, and their blasphemies against *him* and his *virgin mother* are too shocking to be transcribed. The *certainty of the resurrection* of Jesus refutes their every calumny; proves his miraculous conception; vindicates the blessed virgin; and, in a word, *declares him to be the Son of God with power.*

This most important use of this saying has passed unnoticed by almost every Christian writer which I have seen; and yet it lies here at the foundation of all the apostle's proofs. If Jesus was not thus the Son of God, the whole Christian system is vain and baseless: but his *resurrection* demonstrates him to have been the Son of God; therefore every thing built on this foundation is more durable than the foundations of heaven, and as inexpugnable as the throne of the eternal King.

He shall be to me a Son?] As the Jews have ever blasphemed against the *Sonship* of Christ, it was necessary that the apostle should adduce and make strong all his proofs, and show that this was not a new revelation; that it was that which was chiefly intended in several scriptures of the Old Testament, which, without farther mentioning the places where found, he immediately produces. This place, which is quoted from 2 Sam. vii. 14, shows us that the *seed* which God promised to David, and who was to *sit upon his throne*, and whose *throne should be established*

for ever, was not Solomon, but Jesus Christ; and indeed he quotes the words so as to intimate that they were so understood by the Jews. See among the observations at the end of the chapter.

Verse 6. *And again, when he bringeth in the first-begotten*] This is not a correct translation of the Greek, Ὅταν δε παλιν εισαγαγη τον πρωτοτοκον εις την οικουμενην· *But when he bringeth again*, or *the second time, the first-born into the habitable world.* . This most manifestly refers to his *resurrection*, which might be properly considered a *second incarnation*; for as the human soul, as well as the fulness of the Godhead bodily, dwelt in the man Christ Jesus on and during his incarnation, so when he expired upon the cross, both the *Godhead* and the *human spirit* left his dead body; and as on his resurrection these were reunited to his revivified manhood, therefore, with the strictest propriety, does the apostle say that the resurrection was a *second bringing of him into the world.*

I have translated οικουμενη the *habitable world*, and this is its proper meaning; and thus it is distinguished from κοσμος, which signifies the *terraqueous globe*, independently of its inhabitants; though it often expresses both the inhabited and uninhabited parts. Our Lord's *first coming* into the world is expressed by this latter word, chap. x. 5: *Wherefore when he cometh into the world,* διο εισερχομενος εις τον κοσμον, and this simply refers to his being *incarnated*, that he might be capable of *suffering* and *dying* for man. But the word is changed on this *second coming*, I mean his *resurrection*, and then οικουμενη is used; and why? (fancy apart) because he was now *to dwell with man*; to send his Gospel everywhere to all the inhabitants of the earth, and to *accompany* that Gospel wherever he sent it, and to *be* wherever two or three should be gathered together in his name. Wherever the messengers of Jesus Christ go, preaching the kingdom of God, even to the farthest and most desolate parts of the earth where human beings exist, there they ever find Christ; he is not only in *them*, and with *them*, but he is in and among all who believe on him through their word.

Let all the angels of God worship him.] The apostle recurs here to his former assertion, that Jesus is higher than the angels, ver. 4, that he is none of those who can be called ordinary angels or messengers, but one of the most extraordinary kind, and the object of worship to all the angels of God. To worship any *creature* is idolatry, and God resents idolatry more than any other evil. Jesus Christ can be no creature, else the angels who worship him must be guilty of idolatry, and God the author of that idolatry, who commanded those angels to worship Christ.

    2

A. M. cir. 4067.
A. D. cir. 63.
An. Olymp.
cir. CCX. 3.
A. U. C. cir.
816.

and his ministers a flame of fire.

8 But unto the Son *he saith,* [s] Thy throne, O God, *is* for ever

and ever: a sceptre of [t] righteousness *is* the sceptre of thy kingdom.

9 [u] Thou hast loved righteous-

A. M. cir. 4067.
A. D. cir. 63.
An. Olymp.
cir. CCX. 3.
A. U. C. cir.
816.

---

[s] Psa. xlv. 6, 7.——[t] Gr. *rightness* or *straightness.*

[u] Psa. xlv. 7.

There has been some difficulty in ascertaining the place from which the apostle quotes these words; some suppose Psa. xcvii. 7 : *Worship him, all ye gods;* which the Septuagint translate thus : Προσκυνησατε αυτω, παντες αγγελοι αυτου· *Worship him, all ye angels;* but it is not clear that the Messiah is intended in this psalm, nor are the words precisely those used here by the apostle. Our marginal references send us with great propriety to the *Septuagint* version of Deut. xxxii. 43, where the passage is found *verbatim et literatim;* but there is nothing answering to the words in the present Hebrew text. The apostle undoubtedly quoted the *Septuagint,* which

had then been for more than 300 years a version of the highest repute among the Jews; and it is very probable that the copy from which the Seventy translated had the corresponding words. However this may be, they are now sanctioned by Divine authority; and as the verse contains some singular *additions,* I will set it down in a parallel column with that of our own version, which was taken immediately from the Hebrew text, premising simply this, that it is the last verse of the famous prophetic song of Moses, which seems to point out the *advent of the Messiah* to discomfit his enemies, purify the land, and redeem Israel from all his iniquities.

Deut. xxxii. 43, from the Hebrew.

. . . .
. . . . Rejoice, O ye nations, *with* his people; . . . .
. . . . for he will avenge the blood of his servants; . . . . and will render vengeance to his adversaries: . . and . . .
. will be merciful to his land and to his people.

Deut. xxxii. 43, from the Septuagint.

Rejoice, ye heaven, together with him; and let all the angels of God worship him. Rejoice, ye Gentiles, *with* his people; *and let the children of God be strengthened in him;* for he will avenge the blood of his children; he will avenge, and will repay judgment to his adversaries; *and those who hate him will he recompense:* and *the Lord* will purge the land of his people.

This is a very important verse; and to it, as it stands in the Septuagint, St. Paul has referred once before; see Rom xv. 10. This very verse, as it stands now in the Septuagint, thus referred to by an inspired writer, shows the great importance of this ancient version; and proves the necessity of its being studied and well understood by every minister of Christ. In Rom. iii. there is a large quotation from Psalm xiv., where there are six whole verses in the apostle's quotation which are not found in the present Hebrew text, but are preserved in the Septuagint! How strange it is that this venerable and important version, so often quoted by our Lord and all his apostles, should be so generally neglected, and so little known! That the common people should be ignorant of it, is not to be wondered at, as it has never been put in an English dress; but that the ministers of the Gospel should be unacquainted with it may be spoken to their shame.

Verse 7. *Who maketh his angels spirits*] They are so far from being superior to Christ, that they are not called God's sons in any *peculiar* sense, but his *servants,* as *tempests* and *lightnings* are. In many respects they may have been made inferior even to *man* as he came out of the hands of his Maker, for *he* was made in the *image* and *likeness* of *God;* but of the angels, even the highest order of them, this is never spoken. It is very likely that the apostle refers here to the opinions of the Jews relative to the angels. In *Pirkey R. Elieser,* c. 4, it is said : "The angels which were created the second day, when they minister before God, של אש נעשין *become fire."* In *Shemoth Rabba,* s. 25, fol. 123, it is said : "God is

named *the Lord of hosts,* because with his angels he doth whatsoever he wills : when he pleases, he makes them *sit down;* Judg. vi. 11 : *And the angel of the Lord came, and sat under a tree.* When he pleases, he causes them to *stand;* Isa. vi. 2 : *The seraphim stood.* Sometimes he makes them like *women;* Zech. v. 9 : *Behold there came two women, and the wind was in their wings.* Sometimes he makes them like *men;* Gen. xviii. 2 : *And, lo, three men stood by him.* Sometimes he makes them *spirits;* Psa. civ. 4 : *Who maketh his angels spirits.* Sometimes he makes them *fire;* ibid. *His ministers a flame of fire."*

In *Yalcut Simeoni,* par. 2, fol. 11, it is said : "The angel answered Manoah, I know not in whose image I am made, for God changeth us every hour: sometimes he makes us *fire,* sometimes *spirit,* sometimes *men,* and at other times *angels."* It is very probable that those who are termed *angels* are not confined to any specific form or shape, but assume various forms and appearances according to the nature of the work on which they are employed and the will of their sovereign employer. This seems to have been the ancient Jewish doctrine on this subject.

Verse 8. *Thy throne, O God, is for ever and ever*] If this be said of the Son of God, i. e. Jesus Christ, then Jesus Christ must be God; and indeed the design of the apostle is to prove this. The words here quoted are taken from Psa. xlv. 6, 7, which the ancient Chaldee paraphrast, and the most intelligent rabbins, refer to the Messiah. On the third verse of this Psalm, *Thou art fairer than the children of men,* the Targum says : "Thy beauty, מלכא משיחא *malca Meshicha,* O King Messiah, is greater than the children of men." *Aben*

A. M. cir. 4067.
A. D. cir. 63.
An. Olymp.
cir. CCX. 3.
A. U. C. cir.
816.

ness, and hated iniquity ; therefore God, *even* thy God, [v] hath anointed thee with the oil of gladness above thy fellows.

10 And, [w] Thou, Lord, in the beginning hast

laid the foundation of the earth ; and the heavens are the works of thine hands :

11 [x] They shall perish ; but thou remainest : and they all shall wax old as doth a garment ;

A. M. cir. 4067.
A. D. cir. 63.
An. Olymp.
cir. CCX. 3.
A. U. C. cir.
816.

---

[v] Isa. lxi. 1 ; Acts iv. 27 ; x. 38.——[w] Psa. cii. 25, &c.——[x] Isa.

xxxiv. 4 ; li. 6 ; Matt. xxiv. 35 ; 2 Peter iii. 7, 10 ; Rev. xxi. 1.

Ezra says : " This Psalm speaks of David, or rather of his son, the *Messiah*, for this is his name," Ezek. xxxiv. 24 : *And David my servant shall be a Prince over them for ever.* Other rabbins confirm this opinion.

This verse is very properly considered a proof, and indeed a strong one, of the Divinity of Christ ; but some late versions of the New Testament have endeavoured to avoid the evidence of this proof by translating the words thus : *God is thy throne for ever and ever ;* and if this version be correct, it is certain the text can be no proof of the doctrine. Mr. Wakefield vindicates this translation at large in his *History of Opinions ;* and ὁ Θεος, being the *nominative* case, is supposed to be a sufficient justification of this version. In answer to this it may be stated that the *nominative* case is often used for the *vocative*, particularly by the Attics ; and the whole scope of the place requires it should be so used here ; and, with due deference to all of a contrary opinion, the original Hebrew cannot be consistently translated any other way, כסאך אלהים עולם וער *kisaca Elohim olam vaed, Thy throne, O God, is for ever, and to eternity.* It is in both worlds ; and extends over all time ; and will exist through all endless duration. To this our Lord seems to refer, Matt. xxviii. 18 : *All power is given unto me, both in* HEAVEN *and* EARTH. My *throne,* i. e my *dominion,* extends from the creation to the consummation of all things. These I have made, and these I uphold ; and from the end of the world, throughout eternity, I shall have the same glory—sovereign, unlimited power and authority, which I had with the Father before the world began ; John xvii. 5. I may add that none of the ancient versions has understood it in the way contended for by those who deny the Godhead of Christ, either in the Psalm from which it is taken, or in this place where it is quoted. Aquila translates אלהים *Elohim,* by Θεε, O God, in the vocative case ; and the Arabic adds the sign of the vocative يا *ya,* reading the place thus : كرسي يا الله الى ابد الابد *korsee yallaho ila aba-dilabada,* the same as in our version. And even allowing that ὁ Θεος here is to be used as the nominative case, it will not make the sense contended for, without adding εστι to it, a reading which is not countenanced by any *version,* nor by any MS. yet discovered. Wiclif, Coverdale, and others, understood it as the nominative, and translated it so ; and yet it is evident that this nominative has the power of the vocative : torsothe to the sone God thi troone into the world of world : a gerde of equite the gerde of thi reume. I give this, pointing and all, as it stands in my old MS. Bible. *Wiclif* is nearly the same, but is evidently of a more modern cast : but to the sone he seith, God thy trone is into the world of world, a gherd of equyte is the gherd of thi reume. *Coverdale* translates it thus : *But*

unto the sonne he sayeth, God, thi seate endureth for ever and ever : the cepter of thi kyngdome is a right cepter. *Tindal* and others follow in the same way, all reading it in the *nominative* case, with the force ·of the *vocative ;* for none of them has inserted the word εστι, *is,* because not authorized by the original : a word which the opposers of the Divinity of our Lord 'are obliged to *beg,* in order to support their interpretation. See some farther criticisms on this at the end of this chapter.

A sceptre of righteousness] The sceptre, which was a sort of staff or instrument of various forms, was the ensign of government, and is here used for government itself. This the ancient Jewish writers understand also of the Messiah.

Verse 9. *Thou hast loved righteousness*] This is the characteristic of a just governor : he abhors and suppresses iniquity ; he countenances and supports righteousness and truth.

Therefore God, even *thy God*] The original, δια τουτο εχρισε σε ὁ Θεος, ὁ Θεος σου, may be thus translated : *Therefore, O God, thy God hath anointed thee.* The form of speech is nearly the same with that in the preceding verse ; but the sense is sufficiently clear if we read, *Therefore God, thy God, hath anointed thee, &c.*

With the oil of gladness] We have often had occasion to remark that, anciently, *kings, priests,* and *prophets* were consecrated to their several offices by anointing ; and that this signified the gifts and influences of the Divine Spirit. Christ, ὁ Χριστος, signifies *The Anointed One,* the same as the Hebrew Messias ; and he is here said to be *anointed with the oil of gladness above his fellows.* None was ever constituted *prophet, priest,* and *king,* but himself ; some were kings only, prophets only, and priests only ; others were kings and priests, or priests and prophets, or kings and prophets ; but none had ever the *three offices* in his own person but Jesus Christ, and none but himself can be a King over the universe, a Prophet to all intelligent beings, and a Priest to the whole human race. Thus he is infinitely exalted *beyond his fellows* —all that had ever borne the regal, prophetic, or sacerdotal offices.

Some think that the word μετοχους, *fellows,* refers to *believers* who are made partakers of the same Spirit, but cannot have its infinite plenitude. The first sense seems the best. *Gladness* is used to express the *festivities* which took place on the inauguration of kings, &c.

Verse 10. *And, Thou, Lord*] This is an address to the *Son* as the *Creator,* see ver. 2 ; for this is implied in *laying the foundation* of the earth. The heavens, which are the work of his hands, point out his infinite wisdom and skill.

Verse 11. *They shall perish*] Permanently fixed

A. M. cir. 4067.
A. D. cir. 63.
An. Olymp.
cir. CCX. 3.
A. U. C. cir.
816.

12 And as a vesture shalt thou fold them up, and they shall be changed: but thou art the same, and thy years shall not fail.

13 But to which of the angels said he at any time, [y] Sit on my right hand, until I make thine enemies thy footstool?

14 [z] Are they not all ministering spirits, sent forth to minister for them who shall be [a] heirs of salvation?

A. M. cir. 4067
A. D. cir. 63.
An. Olymp.
cir. CCX. 3.
A. U. C. cir.
816.

---

[y] Psa. cx. 1; Matthew xxii. 44; Mark xii. 36; Luke xx. 42; chapter x. 12; verse 3.——[z] Genesis xix. 16; xxxii. 1, 2, 24; Psa. xxxiv. 7; xci. 11; ciii. 20, 21; Daniel iii. 28; vii. 10; x. 11; Matthew xviii. 10; Luke i. 19; ii. 9, 13; Acts xii. 7, &c.; xxvii. 23.——[a] Romans viii. 17; Titus iii. 7; James ii. 5; 1 Pet. iii. 7.

---

as they seem to be, a time shall come when they shall be *dissolved*, and afterward *new heavens* and a *new earth* be formed, in which righteousness alone shall dwell. See 2 Peter iii. 10–13.

Shall wax old as doth a garment] As a garment by long using becomes unfit to be longer used, so shall all visible things; they shall *wear old*, and *wear out*; and hence the necessity of their being *renewed*. It is remarkable that our word *world* is a contraction of *wear old*; a term by which our ancestors expressed the sentiment contained in this verse. That the word was thus compounded, and that it had this sense in our language, may be proved from the most competent and indisputable witnesses. It was formerly written ꝩeoꞃolꝺ, *weorold*, and ꝩeꞃelꝺ, *wereld*. This *etymology* is finely alluded to by our excellent poet, *Spencer*, when describing the primitive age of innocence, succeeded by the age of depravity:—

" The lion there did with the lambe consort,
  And eke the dove sat by the faulcon's side;
  Ne each of other feared fraude or tort,
  But did in safe security abide,
  Withouten perill of the stronger pride:
  But when the WORLD *woxe old*, it woxe *warre old*,
  Whereof it *hight*, and having shortly tride
  The trains of wit, in wickednesse *woxe bold*,
  And dared of all sinnes, the secrets to unfold."

Even the heathen poets are full of such allusions. See *Horace*, Carm. lib. iii., od. 6; *Virgil*, Æn. viii., ver. 324.

Thou remainest] Instead of διαμένεις, some good MSS. read διαμενεῖς, the first, without the circumflex, being the present tense of the indicative mood; the latter, with the circumflex, being the *future*—thou *shalt remain*. The difference between these two readings is of little importance.

Verse 12. *And they shall be changed*] Not *destroyed* ultimately, or *annihilated*. They shall be *changed* and *renewed*.

But thou art the same] These words can be said of no being but God; all others are *changeable* or *perishable*, because temporal; only that which is *eternal* can continue *essentially*, and, speaking after the manner of men, *formally the same*.

Thy years shall not fail.] There is in the Divine duration no circle to be run, no space to be measured, no time to be reckoned. All is eternity—infinite—and onward.

Verse 13. *But to which of the angels*] We have already seen, from the opinions and concessions of the Jews, that, if Jesus Christ could be proved to be

greater than the angels, it would necessarily follow that he was God: and this the apostle does most amply prove by these various quotations from their own Scriptures; for he shows that while he is the supreme and absolute Sovereign, they are no more than his *messengers* and *servants*, and *servants* even to his *servants*, i. e. to mankind.

Verse 14. *Are they not all ministering spirits*] That is, *They are all* ministering spirits; for the Hebrews often express the strongest *affirmative* by an interrogation.

All the angels, even those of the highest order, are employed by their Creator to serve those who believe in Christ Jesus. What these services are, and how performed, it would be impossible to state. Much has been written on the subject, partly founded on Scripture, and partly on conjecture. They are, no doubt, constantly employed in *averting evil* and *procuring good*. If God help *man* by *man*, we need not wonder that he helps man by *angels*. We know that he needs none of those helps, for he can do all things himself; yet it seems agreeable to his infinite wisdom and goodness to use them. This is part of the economy of God in the government of the world and of the Church; and a part, no doubt, essential to the harmony and perfection of the whole. The reader may see a very sensible discourse on this text in vol. ii., page 133, of the Rev. John Wesley's works, American edition. Dr. Owen treats the subject at large in his comment on this verse, vol. iii., page 141, edit. 8vo., which is just now brought to my hand, and which appears to be a very learned, judicious, and important work, but by far too diffuse. In it the words of God are drowned in the sayings of man.

THE Godhead of Christ is a subject of such great importance, both to the faith and hope of a Christian, that I feel it necessary to bring it full into view, wherever it is referred to in the sacred writings. It is a prominent article in the apostle's creed, and should be so in ours. That this doctrine cannot be established on ver. 8 has been the assertion of many. To what I have already said on this verse, I beg leave to subjoin the following criticisms of a learned friend, who has made this subject his particular study.

BRIEF REMARKS ON HEBREWS, chap. i., ver. 8.

Ὁ θρόνος σου, ὁ Θεος, εἰς τοὺς αἰωνας.

It hath ever been the opinion of the most sound divines, that these words, which are extracted from the 45th Psalm, are addressed by God the Father unto God the Son. Our translators have accordingly ren-

2

dered the passage thus : " Thy throne, O God, is for ever." Those who deny the Divinity of Christ, being eager to get rid of such a testimony against themselves, contend that ὁ Θεος is here the nominative, and that the meaning is : " God is thy throne for ever." Now it is somewhat strange, that none of them have had critical acumen enough to discover that the words cannot possibly admit of this signification. It is a rule in the Greek language, that when a substantive noun is the subject of a sentence, and something is predicated of it, the article, if used at all, is prefixed to the subject, but omitted before the predicate. The Greek translators of the Old, and the authors of the New Testament, write agreeably to this rule. I shall first give some examples from the latter :—

Θεος ην ὁ Λογος.—" The Word was God." John i. 1.

Ὁ Λογος σαρξ εγενετο.—" The Word became flesh." John i. 14.

Πνευμα ὁ Θεος.—" God is a Spirit." John iv. 24.

Ὁ Θεος αγαπη εστι.—" God is love." 1 John iv. 8.

Ὁ Θεος φως εστι.—" God is light." 1 John i. 5.

If we examine the Septuagint version of the Psalms, we shall find, that in such instances the author sometimes places the article before the subject, but that his usual mode is to omit it altogether. A few examples will suffice :—

Ὁ Θεος κριτης δικαιος.—" God is a righteous judge." Psa. vii. 11.

Ὁ Θεος ἡμων καταφυγη και δυναμις.—" God is our refuge and strength." Psa. xlvi. 1.

Κυριος βοηθος μου.—" The Lord is my helper." Psa. xxviii. 7.

Κυριος στερεωμα μου και καταφυγη μου.—" The Lord is my firm support and my refuge." Psa. xviii. 2.

Θεος μεγας Κυριος.—" The Lord is a great God." Psa. xcv. 3.

We see what is the established phraseology of the Septuagint, when a substantive noun has something predicated of it in the same sentence. Surely, then, we may be convinced that if in Psa. xlv. 6, the meaning which they who deny our Lord's Divinity affix, had been intended, it would rather have been written θρονος σου, ὁ Θεος, or θρονος σου, Θεος. This our conviction will, if possible, be increased, when we examine the very next clause of this sentence, where we shall find that the article is prefixed to the subject, but omitted before the predicate.

Ῥαβδος ευθυτητος ἡ ῥαβδος της βασιλειας σου.—" The sceptre of thy kingdom is a sceptre of rectitude."

" But it may be doubted whether Θεος with the article affixed be ever used in the vocative case." Your doubt will be solved by reading the following examples, which are taken not promiscuously from the Septuagint, but all of them from the Psalms.

Κρινον αυτους, ὁ Θεος.—" Judge them, O God." Psa. v 10.

Ὁ Θεος, ὁ Θεος μου.—" O God, my God." Psa. xxii. 1.

Σοι ψαλω, ὁ Θεος μου.—" Unto thee will I sing, O my God." Psa. lix. 17.

Ὑψωσω σε, ὁ Θεος μου.—" I will exalt thee, O my God." Psa. cxlv. 1

Κυριε, ὁ Θεος μου.—" O Lord my God." Psa. civ. 1.

I have now removed the only objection which can, I think, be started. It remains, that the son of Mary is here addressed as the God whose throne endures for ever.

I know that a *pronoun* sometimes occurs with the article prefixed to its predicate ; but I speak only of *nouns substantive.*

I must not fail to observe, that the rule about the subject and predicate, like that of the Greek prepositive article, pervades all classes of writers. It will be sufficient, if I give three or four examples. The learned reader may easily collect more.

Προσκηνιον μεν ὁ ουρανος ἁπας, θεατρον δ' ἡ οικουμενη.— " The whole heaven is his stage, and the world his theatre." Chrysostom. We have here two instances in one sentence. The same is the case in the following examples : —

Βραχυς μεν ὁ ξυλλογος, μεγας δ' ὁ ποθος.—" Small indeed is the assembly, but great is the desire." Chrysostom.

Καλον γαρ το αθλον, και ἡ ελπις μεγαλη.—" For the prize is noble, and the hope is great." Plato.

Το τ' αισχρον εχθρον, και το χρηστον ευκλεες.—" That which is base is hateful; and that which is honest, glorious." Sophocles.

Having spoken of nouns substantive only, I ought to state that the rule applies equally to adjectives and to participles. Near the opening of the fifth of Matthew, we find eight consecutive examples of the rule. In five of these the subject is an adjective, and in the other three, a participle. Indeed one of them has two participles, affording an instance of the rule respecting the prepositive article, as well as of that which we are now considering. Μακαριοι οἱ πεινωντες και διψωντες.— " Blessed are they who hunger and thirst." In the Apocalypse there are four examples of the rule with participles, and in all these twelve cases the predicate is placed first. See the supplement to my Essay on the Greek Article, at the end of Dr. A. Clarke's commentary on Ephesians.

I am aware that an exception now and then occurs in the sacred writings ; but I think I may assert that there are no exceptions in the Septuagint version of the book of Psalms. As the words ὁ θρονος σου, ὁ Θεος, occur in the book of Psalms, the most important question is this : Does that book always support the orthodox interpretation ? With regard to the deviations which are elsewhere occasionally found, I think there can be little doubt that they are owing to the ignorance or carelessness of transcribers, for the rule is unquestionably genuine.—H. S. Boyd.

The preceding remarks are original, and will be duly respected by every scholar.

I have shown my reasons in the note on Luke i. 35, why I cannot close in with the common view of what is called the *eternal Sonship* of Christ. I am inclined to think that from this tenet *Arianism* had its origin. I shall here produce my authority for this opinion. Arius, the father of what is called Arianism, and who flourished in A. D. 300, was a presbyter of the Church of Alexandria, a man of great learning and eloquence, and of deeply mortified manners ; and he continued to edify the Church by his teaching and example till the circumstance took place which produced that unhappy change in his religious sentiments, which afterwards gave rise to so much distraction and division in the Christian Church. The circumstance to which I refer is related by *Socrates Scholasticus*, in his supplement to the History of Eusebius, lib. i., c. 5; and is in substance as follows: Alexander, having succeeded Achillas in the bishopric of Alexandria, self-confidently philosophizing one day in the presence of his presbyters and the rest of his clergy concerning the holy Trinity, among other things asserted that there was a Monad in the Triad, φιλοτιμοτερον περι της ἁγιας Τριαδος, εν Τριαδι Μοναδα ειναι φιλοσοφων εθεολογει. What he said on the derived nature or *eternal Sonship* of Christ is not related. Arius, one of his presbyters, a man of considerable skill in the science of logic, ανηρ ουκ αμοιρος της διαλεκτικης λεσχης, supposing that the bishop designed to introduce the dogmas of Sabellius, the Libyan, who denied the personality of the Godhead, and consequently the Trinity, sharply opposed the bishop, arguing thus: "If the Father begot the Son, *he* who was thus begotten had a beginning of his existence; and from this it is manifest, that there was a time in which the Son was not. Whence it necessarily follows, that he has his subsistence from what exists not." The words which Socrates quotes are the following, of which the above is as close a translation as the different idioms will allow: Ει ὁ Πατηρ εγεννηυε τον Ὑιον, αρχην ὑπαρξεως εχει·ὁ γεννηθεις· και εκ τουτου δηλον, ὁτι ην ὁτε ουκ ην ὁ υιος· ακολουθει τε εξ αναγκης, εξ ουκ οντων εχειν αυτον την ὑποστασιν. Now, it does not appear that this had been previously the doctrine of Arius, but that it was the *consequence* which he logically drew from the doctrine laid down by the bishop; and, although Socrates does not tell us what the bishop stated, yet, from the *conclusions* drawn, we may at once see what the *premises* were; and these must have been some incautious assertions concerning the *Sonship* of the *Divine nature* of Christ: and I have shown elsewhere that these are fair deductions from such premises. "But is not God called Father; and Father of our Lord Jesus Christ?" Most certainly. That God graciously assumes the name of *Father*, and acts in that character towards mankind, the whole Scripture proves; and that the title is given to him as signifying *Author, Cause, Fountain*, and *Creator*, is also sufficiently manifest from the same Scriptures. In this sense he is said to be the *Father of the rain*, Job xxxviii. 28; and hence also it is said, *He is the Father of spirits*, Heb. xii. 9; and he is the Father of men because he created them; and Adam, the first man, is particularly called *his son*, Luke iii. 38. But he is the Father of the *human nature* of our blessed Lord in a peculiar sense, because by his energy this was produced in the womb of the virgin. Luke i. 35, *The Holy Ghost shall come upon thee, and the power of the Highest shall overshadow thee;* THEREFORE also that HOLY THING WHICH SHALL BE BORN OF THEE *shall be called* THE SON OF GOD. It is in consequence of this that our blessed Lord is so frequently termed the *Son of God*, and that *God* is called *his Father.* But I know not any scripture, fairly interpreted, that states the *Divine nature* of our Lord to be *begotten* of God, or to be the *Son of God*. Nor can I see it possible that he could be *begotten* of the Father, in *this sense*, and be *eternal;* and if not eternal, he is not God But numberless scriptures give

him every attribute of Godhead; his own works demonstrate it; and the whole scheme of salvation requires this. I hope I may say that I have demonstrated his supreme, absolute, and unoriginated Godhead, both in my note on Col. i. 16, 17, and in my *Discourse on Salvation by Faith.* And having seen that the doctrine of the *eternal Sonship* produced *Arianism*, and Arianism produced Socinianism, and Socinianism produces a kind of *general infidelity*, or disrespect to the sacred writings, so that several parts of them are rejected as being uncanonical, and the inspirations of a major part of the New Testament strongly suspected; I find it necessary to be doubly on my watch to avoid every thing that may, even in the remotest way, tend to so deplorable a catastrophe.

It may be said: "Is not God called the *eternal Father?* And if so, there can be no eternal Father if there be no eternal Son." I answer: God is not called in any part of Scripture, as far as I can recollect, either the *eternal* or *everlasting Father* in reference to our blessed Lord, nor indeed in reference to any thing else; but this very title, strange to tell, is given to Jesus Christ himself: *His name shall be called the* EVERLASTING FATHER, Isa. ix. 6; and we may on this account, with more propriety, look for an *eternal filiation* proceeding from *him*, than from any other person of the most holy Trinity.

Should it be asked: "Was there no *trinity* of persons in the Godhead before the incarnation?" I answer: That a *trinity of persons* appears to me to belong *essentially* to the eternal Godhead, neither of which was *before, after*, or *produced* from another; and of this the Old Testament is full: but the distinction was not fully evident till the incarnation; and particularly till the baptism in Jordan, when on *him*, in whom dwelt all the fulness of the Godhead, the *Holy Ghost* descended in a *bodily shape*, like a dove; and a *voice* from *heaven* proclaimed *that baptized person* God's beloved Son: in which transaction there were *three persons* occupying *distinct places;* as the *person* of *Christ* in the *water*, the *Holy Spirit* in a *bodily shape*, and the *voice* from *heaven*, sufficiently prove; and to each of these *persons* various scriptures give all the essential attributes of God.

On the doctrine of the *eternal Sonship* of the Divine nature of Christ I once had the privilege of conversing with the late reverend John Wesley, about three years before his death; he read from a book in which I had written it, the argument against this doctrine, which now stands in the note on Luke i. 35. He did not attempt to reply to it; but allowed that, on the *ground* on which I had taken it, the argument was conclusive I observed, that the proper, essential Divinity of Jesus Christ appeared to me to be so absolutely necessary to the whole Christian scheme, and to the faith both of penitent sinners and saints, that it was of the utmost importance to set it in the clearest and strongest point of view; and that, with my present light, I could not credit it, if I must receive the common doctrine of the *Sonship of the Divine nature* of our Lord. He mentioned two eminent divines who were of the same opinion; and added, that the eternal Sonship of Christ had been a doctrine very generally received in the Christian Church; and he believed no one had ever expressed it better than his brother Samuel had done in the following lines :—

> "From whom, in one eternal *now*,
> The Son, thy offspring, flow'd ;
> An *everlasting Father* thou,
> An *everlasting God*."

He added not one word more on the subject, nor ever after mentioned it to me, though after that we *had* many interviews. But it is necessary to mention his own note on the text, that has given rise to these observations ; which shows that he held the doctrine as commonly received, when he wrote that note ; it is as follows :—

"*Thou art my Son*] God of God, Light of Light. *This day have I begotten Thee*—I have begotten Thee from eternity, which, by its unalterable permanency of duration, is one continued unsuccessive day." Leaving the point in dispute out of the question, this is most beautifully expressed ; and I know not that this great man ever altered his views on this subject, though I am certain that he never professed the opinion as many who quote his authority do ; nor would he at any time have defended what he did hold in *their way*. I beg leave to quote a fact. In 1781, he published in the fourth volume of the Arminian Magazine, p. 384, an article, entitled "An Arian Antidote ;" in this are the following words : "Greater or lesser in infinity, is not ; inferior Godhead shocks our sense ; Jesus was inferior to the Father as touching his manhood, John xiv. 28 ; he was a son given, and slain intentionally from the foundation of the world, Rev. xiii. 8, and the first-born from the dead of every creature, Col. i. 15, 18. But, our *Redeemer*, from everlasting (Isa. lxiii. 16) *had not the inferior name*

of *Son ;* in the beginning was the Word, and the Word was with God from eternity, and the Word, made flesh, was God," &c. This is pointedly against the *eternal Sonship* of the *Divine nature*. But why did Mr. W. *insert* this ? and if by haste, &c., why did he not correct this when he published in 1790, in the 13th vol. of the Magazine, eight tables of errata to the eight first volumes of that work ? Now, although he had carefully noticed the slightest errors that might affect the sense in those preceding volumes, yet no fault is found with the *reasoning* in the *Arian Antidote*, and the sentence, "But, our Redeemer, from everlasting, had not the inferior name of Son," &c., is passed by without the slightest notice ! However necessary this view of the subject may appear to me, I do not presume to say that others, in order to be saved, must view it in the same light : I leave both opinions to the judgment of the reader ; for on such a point it is necessary that every man should be clear in his own mind, and satisfied in his own conscience. Any opinion of mine my readers are at perfect liberty to receive or reject. I never claimed infallibility ; I say, with St. Augustine, *Errare possum ; hæreticus esse nolo.* Refined Arians, with some of whom I am personally acquainted, are quite willing to receive all that can be said of the dignity and glory of Christ's nature, provided we admit the doctrine of the eternal Sonship, and omit the word *unoriginated*, which I have used in my demonstration of the Godhead of the Saviour of men ; but, as far as it respects myself, I can neither *admit* the one, nor *omit* the other. The proper essential Godhead of Christ lies deep at the foundation of my Christian creed ; and I must sacrifice ten thousand *forms of speech* rather than sacrifice the *thing*. My opinion has not been formed on slight examination.

CHAPTER II.

The use we should make of the preceding doctrine, and the danger of neglecting this great salvation, 1–4. The future world is not put in subjection to the angels, but all is under the authority of Christ, 5–8. Jesus has tasted death for every man, 9. Nor could he accomplish man's redemption without being incarnated and without dying ; by which he destroys the devil, and delivers all that believe on him from the fear of death and spiritual bondage, 10–15. Christ took not upon him the nature of angels, but the nature of Abraham, that he might die, and make reconciliation for the sins of the people, 16–18.

A. M. cir. 4067. A. D. cir. 63. An. Olymp. cir. CCX. 3. A. U. C. cir. 816.

THEREFORE we ought to give the more earnest heed to the things which we have heard, lest at any time we should [a] let them slip.

2 For if the word [b] spoken by angels was steadfast, and [c] every transgression and disobedience received a just recompense of reward ;

A. M. cir. 4067. A. D. cir. 63. An. Olymp. cir. CCX. 3. A. U. C. cir. 816.

[a] Gr. *run out as leaking vessels.*——[b] Deut. xxxiii. 2 ; Psa. lxviii. 17 ; Acts vii. 53 ; Gal. iii. 19.

[c] Numbers xv. 30, 31 ; Deuteronomy iv. 3 ; xvii. 2, 5, 12 xxvii. 26.

NOTES ON CHAP. II.
Verse 1. *Therefore*] Because God has spoken to us by his Son ; and because that Son is so great and glorious a personage ; and because the subject which is addressed to us is of such infinite importance to our welfare.

We ought to give the more earnest heed] We should

hear the doctrine of Christ with care, candour, and deep concern.

Lest at any time we should let them *slip.*] Μή ποτε παραρρυωμεν· "Lest at any time we should *leak out*." This is a metaphor taken from unstanch vessels ; the staves not being close together, the fluid put into them leaks through the chinks and crevices.

A. M. cir. 4067
A. D. cir. 63.
An. Olymp.
cir. CCX. 3.
A. U. C. cir.
816.

3 [d] How shall we escape, if we neglect so great salvation; [e] which at the first began to be spoken by the Lord, and was [f] confirmed unto us by them that heard *him;*

4 [g] God also bearing *them* witness, [h] both with signs and wonders, and with divers miracles, and [i] gifts [k] of the Holy Ghost, [l] according to his own will ?

5 For unto the angels hath he not put in subjection [m] the world to come, whereof we speak:

A. M. cir. 4067.
A. D. cir. 63.
An. Olymp.
cir. CCX. 3.
A. U. C. cir.
816.

---

[d] Ch. x. 28, 29 ; xii. 25.——[e] Matt. iv. 17; Mark i. 14; ch. i. 2. [f] Luke i. 2.——[g] Mark xvi. 20 ; Acts xiv. 3 ; xix. 11 ; Rom. xv. 18, 19; 1 Cor. ii. 4.——[h] Acts ii. 22, 43.——[i] Or, *distributions.*——[k] 1 Cor. xii. 4, 7, 11.——[l] Eph. i. 5, 9.——[m] Chap. vi. 5 ; 2 Pet. iii. 13.

Superficial hearers lose the benefit of he word preached, as the unseasoned vessel does its fluid ; nor can any one hear to the saving of his soul, unless he give *most earnest heed,* which he will not do unless he consider the dignity of the speaker, the importance of the subject, and the absolute necessity of the salvation of his soul. St. Chrysostom renders it μη ποτε απολωμεθα, εκπεσωμεν, lest we perish, lest we fall away.

Verse 2. If the word spoken by angels] The law, (according to some,) which was delivered by the *mediation of angels,* God frequently employing these to communicate his will to men. See Acts vii. 53 ; and Gal. iii. 19. But the apostle probably means those particular messages which God sent by angels, as in the case of *Lot,* Gen. xix., and such like.

Was steadfast] Was so confirmed by the Divine authority, and so strict, that it would not tolerate any offence, but inflicted punishment on every act of *transgression,* every case in which the *bounds* laid down by the law, were *passed over;* and every act of *disobedience* in respect to the *duties* enjoined.

Received a just recompense] That kind and degree of punishment which the law prescribed for those who broke it.

Verse 3. How shall we escape] If they who had fewer privileges than we have, to whom God spoke in divers manners by angels and prophets, fell under the displeasure of their Maker, and were often punished with a sore destruction ; how shall we escape wrath to the uttermost if we neglect the salvation provided for us, and proclaimed to us by the Son of God? Their offence was *high;* ours, indescribably *higher.* The *salvation* mentioned here is the whole system of Christianity, with all the privileges it confers ; properly called a *salvation,* because, by bringing such an abundance of heavenly *light* into the world, it *saves* or *delivers* men from the kingdom of *darkness, ignorance, error, superstition,* and *idolatry;* and provides all the requisite means to *free* them from the *power, guilt,* and *contamination* of sin. This salvation is great when compared with that granted to the Jews : 1. The Jewish dispensation was provided for the *Jews* alone ; the Christian dispensation for all mankind. 2. The Jewish dispensation was full of significant types and ceremonies ; the Christian dispensation is the substance of all those types. 3. The Jewish dispensation referred chiefly to the *body* and *outward* state of man— washings and external cleansings of the flesh ; the Christian, to the inward state—purifying the heart and soul, and purging the conscience from dead works. 4. The Jewish dispensation promised *temporal happiness;* the Christian, *spiritual.* 5. The Jewish dispensation belonged chiefly to *time;* the Christian, to *eternity.* 6. The Jewish dispensation had its glory ; but that was nothing when compared to the exceeding glory of the Gospel. 7. Moses administered the former ; Jesus Christ, the Creator, Governor, and Saviour of the world, the latter. 8. This is a great salvation, infinitely beyond the Jewish ; but how great no tongue or pen can describe.

Those who *neglect* it, αμελησαντες, are not only they who *oppose* or *persecute* it, but they who *pay no regard* to it ; who do not *meddle with* it, do not *concern themselves* about it, do not lay it to heart, and consequently do not get their hearts changed by it. Now these cannot *escape* the coming judgments of God ; not merely because they oppose his will and commandment, but because they sin against the very *cause* and *means* of their deliverance. As there is but *one* remedy by which their diseased souls can be saved, so by refusing to apply that one remedy they must necessarily perish.

Which at the first began to be spoken] Though John the Baptist went before our Lord to prepare his way, yet he could not be properly said to preach the Gospel ; and even Christ's preaching was only a *beginning* of the great proclamation : it was his own Spirit in the apostles and evangelists, the men who heard him preach, that opened the whole mystery of the kingdom of heaven. And all this testimony had been so confirmed in the land of Judea as to render it indubitable ; and consequently there was no excuse for their unbelief, and no prospect of their *escape* if they should continue to *neglect* it.

Verse 4. God also bearing them *witness*] He did not leave the confirmation of these great truths to the testimony of *men;* he bore his *own* testimony to them by *signs, wonders, various miracles,* and *distributions of the Holy Ghost,* Πνευματος Αγιου μερισμοις. And all these were proved to come from *himself;* for no man could do those miracles at *his own pleasure,* but the power to work them was given according to God's *own will;* or rather, God himself wrought them, in order to accredit the ministry of his servants.

For the meaning of *signs, wonders,* &c., see the note on Deut. iv. 34.

Verse 5. The world to come] That עולם הבא olam *habba, the world to come,* meant the *days of the Messiah* among the Jews, is most evident, and has been often pointed out in the course of these notes ; and that the administration of this kingdom has not been intrusted to *angels,* who were frequently employed under the law, is also evident, for the government is on the shoulder of Jesus Christ ; he alone has the keys of death and hell ; he alone shuts, and no man opens ; opens, and no man shuts ; he alone has the residue of the Spirit ; he alone is the Governor of the universe,

A. M. cir. 4067.
A. D. cir. 63.
An. Olymp.
cir. CCX. 3.
A. U. C. cir.
816.

6 But one in a certain place testified, saying, ⁿ What is man, that thou art mindful of him? or the son of man, that thou visitest him?

7 Thou madest him ° a little lower than the angels; thou crownedst him with glory and

honour, and didst set him over the works of thy hands:

8 ᵖ Thou hast put all things in subjection under his feet. For in that he put all in subjection under him, he left nothing *that is* not put under him. But now

A. M. cir. 4067.
A. D. cir. 63.
An. Olymp.
cir. CCX. 3.
A. U. C. cir.
816.

ⁿ Job vii. 17; Psa. viii. 4, &c.; cxliv. 3.——° Or, *a little while inferior to.*

ᵖ Matthew xxviii. 18; 1 Corinthians xv. 27; Eph. i. 22; chapter i. 13.

---

the Spirit, Soul, Heart, and Head of the Church: all is in his authority, and under subjection to him.

But some think that the *world to come* means *future glory,* and suppose the words are spoken in reference to the *Angel of God's presence,* Exod. xxiii. 20, who introduced the Israelites into the *promised land,* which land is here put in opposition to the *heavenly inheritance.* And it is certain that in this sense also we have an entrance into the holiest *only* by the blood of Jesus. Dr. *Macknight* contends for this latter meaning, but the former appears more consistent with the Jewish phraseology.

Verse 6. *But one in a certain place*] This *one* is *David;* and the *certain place,* Psa. viii. 4, 5, 6. But why does the apostle use this indeterminate mode of quotation? Because it was common thus to express the testimony of any of the inspired writers: אמר ההוא כתב *amar hahu kethab,* thus saith a certain scripture. So *Philo, De Plant. Noe:* Ειπε γαρ που, *he saith somewhere;* ειπε γαρ τις, *a certain person saith.* Thus even the heathens were accustomed to quote *high authorities;* so *Plato,* Tim.: Ὡς εφη τις, *as a certain person saith,* meaning *Heraclitus.* See in *Rosenmüller.* It is such a mode of quotation as we sometimes use when we speak of a very eminent person who is well known; as *that very eminent person, that great philosopher, that celebrated divine, that inspired teacher of the Gentiles,* the *royal psalmist,* the *evangelical prophet,* hath said. The mode of quotation therefore implies, not *ignorance,* but *reverence.*

What is man] This quotation is verbatim from the *Septuagint;* and, as the Greek is not so emphatic as the Hebrew, I will quote the original: מה אנוש כי תזכרנו ובן אדם כי תפקדנו *mah enosh ki thizkerennu, uben Adam ki thiphkedennu; What is miserable man, that thou rememberest him? and the son of Adam, that thou visitest him?* The variation of the terms in the original is very emphatic. *Adam,* אדם, is the name given to man at his creation, and expresses his origin, and generic distinction from all other animals. *Enosh,* אנוש, which signifies *sick, weak, wretched,* was never given to him till after his fall. The *son of Adam* means here, any one or all of the fallen posterity of the first man. That God should *remember* in the way of mercy these *wretched* beings, is great condescension; that he should *visit* them, *manifest* himself to them, yea, even *dwell among* them, and at last *assume their nature,* and give up his *life* to ransom them from the bitter pains of eternal death, is mercy and love indescribable and eternal.

Verse 7. *Thou madest him a little lower than the angels*] We must again have recourse to the original from which this quotation is made: ותחסרהו מעט

מאלהים *vattechasserehu meat meelohim.* If this be spoken of *man* as he came out of the hands of his Maker, it places him at the *head* of all God's works; for literally translated it is: *Thou hast made him less than God.* And this is proved by his being made in the *image* and *likeness of God,* which is spoken of no other creature either in heaven or earth; and it is very likely that in his original creation he stood at the head of all the works of God, and the next to his Maker. This sentiment is well expressed in the following lines, part of a paraphrase on this psalm, by the Rev. C. Wesley:—

> " Him with glorious majesty
> 　　Thy grace vouchsafed to crown:
> Transcript of the One in Three,
> 　　He in thine image shone.
> Foremost of created things,
> 　　Head of all thy works he stood;
> Nearest the great King of kings,
> 　　And *little less than God.*"

If we take the words as referring to *Jesus Christ,* then they must be understood as pointing out the time of his humiliation, as in ver. 9; and the *little lower,* βραχυ τι, in both verses, must mean *for a short time,* or *a little while,* as is very properly inserted among our *marginal readings.* Adam was originally made higher than the angels, but by sin he is now brought *low,* and subjected to death; for the angelic nature is not *mortal.* Thus, taking the words in their common acceptation, man in his present state may be said to be *lessened below the angels.* Jesus Christ, as the eternal Logos, or God with God, could not *die,* therefore a *body* was prepared for him; and thus βραχυ τι, for *a short while,* he was *made lower than the angels,* that he might be capable of *suffering death.* And indeed the whole of the passage suits *him* better than it does any of the children of men, or than even Adam himself in a state of innocence; for it is only *under the feet of Jesus that all things are put in subjection,* and it was in consequence of his humiliation that he had *a name above every name, that at the name of Jesus every knee should bow, of things in heaven, and things in earth, and things under the earth,* Phil. ii 9-11. Therefore he must be infinitely *higher than the angels,* for they, as well as all the *things in heaven,* bow in subjection to him.

Thou crownedst him with glory and honour] This was strictly true of *Adam* in his state of innocence, for he was set over all things in this *lower world; all sheep and oxen, the beasts of the field, the fowl of the air, the fish of the sea,* and *whatsoever passeth over the paths of the seas,* Psa. viii. 7, 8. So far all this

2

A. M. cir. 4067.
A. D. cir. 63.
An. Olymp.
cir. CCX. 3.
A. U. C. cir.
816.

^q we see not yet all things put under him :

9 But we see Jesus, ^r who was made a little lower than the angels ^s for the suffering of death, ^t crowned

with glory and honour ; that he by the grace of God should taste death ^u for every man.

10 ^v For, it became him, ^w for whom *are* all things, and by whom *are* all

A. M. cir. 4067.
A. D. cir. 63.
An. Olymp.
cir. CCX. 3.
A. U. C. cir.
816.

---

^q 1 Cor. xv. 25.——^r Phil. ii. 7, 8, 9.——^s Or, *by.*——^t Acts ii. 33.——^u John iii. 16; xii. 32; Rom. v. 18; viii. 32; 2 Cor. v. 15; 1 Tim. ii. 6; 1 John ii. 2; Rev. v. 9.——^v Luke xxiv. 46. ^w Rom. xi. 36.

---

perfectly applies to Adam; but it is evident the apostle takes *all* in a much higher sense, that of *universal dominion* ; and hence he says, *he left nothing that is not put under him.* These verses, collated with the above passage from the Epistle to the Philippians, mutually illustrate each other. And the *crowning Christ with glory and honour* must refer to his *exaltation* after his resurrection, in which, as the victorious Messiah, he had all power given to him in heaven and earth. And although *we do not yet see all things put under him,* for evil men, and evil spirits, are only under the *subjection of control,* yet we look forward to that time when the whole world shall be bowed to his sway, and when the stone cut out of the mountain without hands shall become great, and fill the whole earth. What was never true of the first Adam, even in his most exalted state, is true of the second Adam, the Lord Jesus Christ ; and to him, and to him alone, it is most evident that the apostle applies these things; and thus he is higher than the *angels,* who never had nor can have such dominion and consequent glory.

Verse 9. *Should taste death for every man.*] In consequence of the fall of Adam, the whole human race became sinful in their *nature,* and in their *practice* added *transgression* to *sinfulness* of disposition, and thus became exposed to endless perdition. To redeem them Jesus Christ took on him the nature of man, and suffered the penalty due to their sins.

It was a custom in ancient times to take off criminals by making them *drink a cup of poison.* Socrates was adjudged to drink a cup of the juice of hemlock, by order of the Athenian magistrates : Πινειν το φαρμακον, αναγκαζοντων των Αρχοντων. The sentence was one of the most unjust ever pronounced on man. Socrates was not only innocent of every crime laid to his charge, but was the greatest benefactor to his country. He was duly conscious of the iniquity of his sentence, yet cheerfully submitted to his appointed fate ; for when the officer brought in the poison, though his friends endeavoured to persuade him that he had yet a considerable time in which he might continue to live, yet, knowing that every purpose of life was now accomplished, he refused to avail himself of a few remaining moments, seized the cup, and drank off the poison with the utmost cheerfulness and alacrity ; επισχομενος και μαλα ευχερως και ευκολως εξεπιε. *Plato,* Phæd. sub. fin. The reference in the text seems to point out the whole human race as being accused, tried, found guilty, and condemned, each having his own *poisoned cup* to drink ; and Jesus, the wonderful Jesus, takes the cup out of he hand of each, and cheerfully and with alacrity drinks off the dregs ! Thus having drunk every man's *poisoned cup,* he *tasted* that *death* which they must have endured, had not their *cup* been drunk by *another.*

Is not this the *cup* to which he refers, Matt. xxvi. 39 : *O my Father, if it be possible, let this cup pass from me ?* But without his drinking it, the salvation of the world would have been *impossible ;* and therefore he cheerfully drank it in the place of every human soul, and thus made atonement for the sin of the whole world : and this he did, χαριτι Θεου, by the grace, mercy, or infinite goodness of God. Jesus Christ, incarnated, crucified, dying, rising, ascending to heaven, and becoming our Mediator at God's right hand, is the full proof of God's infinite love to the human race.

Instead of χαριτι Θεου, by the grace of God, some MSS. and the Syriac have χωρις Θεου, *without God,* or *God excepted ;* i. e. the *manhood* died, not the *Deity.* This was probably a marginal gloss, which has crept into the text of many MSS., and is quoted by some of the chief of the Greek and Latin fathers. Several critics contend that the verse should be read thus : " But we see Jesus, who for a little while was made less than angels, that by the grace of God he might taste death for every man, for the suffering of death crowned with glory and honour." Howsoever it be taken, the sense is nearly the same : 1. Jesus Christ was incarnated. 2. He suffered death as an expiatory victim. 3. The persons in whose behalf he suffered were the whole human race ; *every man*—all human creatures. 4. This Jesus is now in a state of the highest glory and honour.

Verse 10. *For it became him*] It was suitable to the Divine wisdom, the requisitions of justice, and the economy of grace, to offer Jesus as a sacrifice, in order to bring many sons and daughters to glory.

For whom—and by whom] God is the *cause* of all things, and he is the *object* or *end* of them.

Perfect through sufferings.] Without *suffering* he could not have *died,* and without *dying* he could not have made an *atonement for sin.* The sacrifice must be *consummated,* in order that he might be qualified to be the *Captain* or *Author* of the *salvation* of men, and lead all those who become children of God, through faith in him, into eternal glory. I believe this to be the sense of the passage ; and it appears to be an answer to the grand objection of the Jews : " The Messiah is never to be conquered, or die ; but will be victorious, and endure for ever." Now the apostle shows that this is not the counsel of God ; on the contrary, that it was entirely *congruous* to the will and nature of God, *by whom,* and *for whom are all things,* to bring men to eternal glory through the suffering and death of the Messiah. This is the decision of the Spirit of God against their prejudices ; and on the Divine authority this must be our *conclusion.* Without the passion and death of Christ, the salvation of man would have been impossible.

Υ   697

A. M. cir. 4067.
A. D. cir. 63.
An. Olymp.
cir. CCX. 3.
A. U. C. cir.
816.

things, in bringing many sons unto glory, to make ˣ the Captain of their salvation ʸ perfect through sufferings.

11 For ᶻ both he that sanctifieth and they who are sanctified ᵃ *are* all of one : for which

cause ᵇ he is not ashamed to call them brethren,

A. M. cir. 4067.
A. D. cir. 63.
An. Olymp.
cir. CCX, 3.
A. U. C. cir.
816.

12 Saying, ᶜ I will declare thy name unto my brethren ; in the midst of the Church will I sing praise unto thee.

ˣ Acts iii. 15; v. 31; chap. xii. 2.——ʸ Luke xiii. 32; chap. v. 9.——ᶻ Chap. x. 10, 14.

ᵃ Acts xvii. 26.——ᵇ Matt. xxviii. 10; John xx. 17; Rom. viii. 29.——ᶜ Psa. xxii. 22, 25.

As there are many different views of this and some of the following verses, I shall introduce a paraphrase of the whole from Dr. Dodd, who gives the substance of what Doddridge, Pearce, and Owen, have said on this subject.

Verse 10. *For it became him, &c.*—" Such has been the conduct of God in the great affair of our redemption; and the beauty and harmony of it will be apparent in proportion to the degree in which it is examined ; *for*, though the Jews dream of a temporal Messiah as a scheme conducive to the Divine glory, *it well became him*—it was expedient, that, in order to act worthy of himself, he should take this method ; *Him, for whom are all things*, and *by whom are all things*—that glorious Being who is the first cause and last end of all, *in* pursuit of the great and important design he had formed, of *conducting many*, whom he is pleased to adopt as his *sons*, to the possession of that inheritance of *glory* intended for them, *to make* and constitute Jesus, his first-begotten and well beloved Son, the *Leader* and *Prince* of their salvation, and to make him *perfect*, or *completely fit* for the full execution of his office, *by* a long train of various and extreme *sufferings*, whereby he was, as it were, solemnly *consecrated* to it.   Verse 11. *Now*, in consequence of this appointment, Jesus, *the great Sanctifier*, who engages and *consecrates* men to the service of God, and *they who are sanctified*, (i. e. consecrated and introduced to God with such acceptance,) *are all of one* family—all the descendants of Adam, and in a sense the seed of Abraham ; *for which cause he is not ashamed to call them*, whom he thus redeems, and presents to the Divine favour, his *brethren.* Verse 12. *Saying*, in the person of David, who represented the Messiah in his sufferings and exaltation, *I will declare thy name to my brethren ; in the midst of the Church will I praise thee.* Verse 13. *And again*, speaking as a mortal man, exposed to such exercises of faith in trials and difficulties as others were, he says, in a psalm which sets forth his triumph over his enemies : *I will trust in him*, as other good men have done in all ages ; *and again*, elsewhere in the person of Isaiah : *Behold I, and the children which my God hath given me*, are for signs and for wonders. Verse 14. *Seeing then* those whom he represents in one place and another, as *the children* of the same family with himself, *were partakers of flesh and blood, he himself in like manner participated in them, that* thereby becoming capable of those sufferings to which, without such a union with flesh, this Divine Sanctifier could not have been obnoxious, *he might, by* his own voluntary and meritorious *death, abolish and depose him who*, by Divine permission, *had the empire of death*, and led it

in his train when he made the first invasion on mankind ; *that is, the devil*, the great artificer of mischief and destruction ; at the beginning the murderer of the human race ; who still seems to triumph in the spread of mortality, which is his work, and who may often, by God's permission, be the executioner of it.   Verse 15. But Christ, the great Prince of mercy and life, graciously interposed, that he *might deliver those* miserable captives of Satan—mankind in general, and the dark and idolatrous Gentiles in particular, *who, through fear of death, were*, or justly might have been, *all their lifetime, obnoxious to bondage ;* having nothing to expect in consequence of it, if they rightly understood their state, but future misery ; whereas now, changing their lord, they have happily changed their condition, and are, as many as have believed in him, the heirs of eternal life."

Verse 11. *For both he that sanctifieth*] The word ὁ ἁγιαζων does not merely signify one who sanctifies or makes holy, but one who makes atonement or reconciliation to God ; and answers to the Hebrew כפר *caphar*, to expiate. See Exod. xxix. 33–36. He that sanctifies is he that makes atonement ; and they who are sanctified are they who receive that atonement, and, being reconciled unto God, become his children by adoption, through grace.

In this sense our Lord uses the word, John xvii. 19: *For their sakes I sanctify myself ;* ὑπερ αυτων εγω ἁγιαζω εμαυτον, on their account I consecrate myself to be a sacrifice. This is the sense in which this word is used generally through this epistle.

Are *all of one*] Εξ ἑνος παντες. What this *one* means has given rise to various conjectures ; *father, family, blood, seed, race, nature,* have all been substituted ; *nature* seems to be that intended, see ver. 14 ; and the conclusion of this verse confirms it. Both the *Sanctifier* and the *sanctified*—both Christ and his followers, are all of the same nature ; for as the children were partakers of flesh and blood, i. e. of *human nature*, he partook of the same, and thus he was qualified to become a sacrifice for *man.*

He is not ashamed to call them brethren] Though, as to his Godhead, he is infinitely raised above men and angels ; yet as he has become incarnate, notwithstanding his dignity, he blushes not to acknowledge all his true followers as his *brethren.*

Verse 12. *I will declare thy name*] See Psalm xxii. 22. The apostle certainly quotes this psalm as referring to Jesus Christ, and these words as spoken by Christ unto the Father, in reference to his incarnation ; as if he had said : " When I shall be incarnated, I will declare thy perfections to mankind ; and among my disciples I will give glory to thee for thy

2

A. M. cir. 4067.
A. D. cir. 63.
An. Olymp.
cir. CCX. 3.
A. U. C. cir.
816.

13 And again, ^d I will put my trust in him. And again, ^e Behold I and the children ^f which God hath given me.

14 Forasmuch then as the children are par-

---

^d Psa. xviii. 2; Isa. xii. 2.——^e Isaiah viii. 18.——^f John xx. 29; xvii. 6, 9, 11, 12.

---

mercy to the children of men." See the fulfilment of this, John i. 18 : *No man hath seen God at any time ; the* ONLY-BEGOTTEN SON, *which is in the bosom of the Father,* HE HATH DECLARED HIM. Nor were the perfections of God ever properly *known* or *declared*, till the manifestation of Christ. Hear another scripture, Luke x. 21, 22 : *In that hour Jesus rejoiced in spirit, and said, I thank thee, O Father, Lord of heaven and earth, that thou hast hid these things from the wise and prudent, and hast revealed them unto babes, &c.* Thus he gave praise to God.

Verse 13. *I will put my trust in him.*] It is not clear to what express place of Scripture the apostle refers : words to this effect frequently occur ; but the place most probably is Psalm xviii. 2, several parts of which psalm seem to belong to the Messiah.

Behold I and the children which God hath given me.] This is taken from Isa. viii. 18. The apostle does not intend to say that the *portions* which he has quoted have any particular reference, taken by themselves, to the subject in question ; they are only *catchwords* of *whole paragraphs*, which, taken together, are full to the point : because they are prophecies of the Messiah, and are fulfilled in him. This is evident from the last quotation : *Behold I and the children whom the Lord hath given me* are *for signs and for wonders in Israel.* Jesus and his *disciples* wrought a multitude of the most stupendous *signs* and *wonders* in Israel. The expression also may include all genuine Christians ; they are for signs and wonders throughout the earth. And as to the 18th Psalm, the principal part of it seems to refer to *Christ's sufferings ;* but the miracles which were wrought at his crucifixion, the destruction of the Jewish state and polity, the *calling of the Gentiles,* and the establishment of the *Christian Church,* appear also to be intended. See among others the following passages : SUFFERINGS—*The sorrows of death compassed me—in my distress I called upon the Lord.* MIRACLES at the crucifixion— *The earth shook and trembled—and darkness was under his feet.* DESTRUCTION of the Jewish state— *I have pursued mine enemies and overtaken them ; they are fallen under my feet.* CALLING of the GENTILES—*Thou hast made me head of the heathen ; a people whom I have never known shall serve me ; as soon as they hear of me they shall obey me, &c., &c.* A principal design of the apostle is to show that such scriptures are prophecies of the Messiah ; that they plainly refer to his appearing in the flesh in Israel ; and that they have all been fulfilled in Jesus Christ, and the calling of the Gentiles to the privileges of the Gospel. To establish these points was of great importance.

Verse 14. *The children are partakers of flesh and blood*] Since those children of God, who have

takers of flesh and blood, he ^g also himself likewise took part of the same ; ^h that through death he might destroy him that had the power of death, that is, the devil ;

A. M. cir. 4067.
A. D. cir. 63.
An. Olymp.
cir. CCX. 3.
A. U. C. cir.
816.

---

^g John i. 14 ; Romans viii. 3 ; Phil. ii. 7.——^h 1 Cor. xv. 54, 55 ; Col. ii. 15 ; 2 Tim. i. 10.

---

fallen and are to be redeemed, are *human beings ;* in order to be qualified to redeem them by suffering and dying in their stead, *He himself likewise took part of the same*—he became *incarnate ;* and thus he who was *God* with *God*, became *man* with *men*. By the *children* here we are to understand, not only the *disciples* and all *genuine Christians*, as in ver. 13, but also the *whole human race ;* all Jews and all Gentiles ; so John xi. 51, 52 : *He prophesied that Jesus should die for that nation ; and not for that nation only, but also that he should gather together in one the* CHILDREN *of* GOD *that were scattered abroad ;* meaning, probably, all the *Jews* in every part of the earth. But collate this with 1 John ii. 2, where the evangelist explains the former words : *He is the propitiation for our sins,* (the *Jews,*) *and not for ours only, but for the sins of the* WHOLE WORLD. As the apostle was writing to the *Hebrews* only, he in general uses a Jewish phraseology, pointing out to them *their own* privileges ; and rarely introduces the *Gentiles*, or what the Messiah has done for the other nations of the earth.

That through death] That by the merit of his own death, making atonement for sin, and procuring the almighty energy of the Holy Spirit, he might *counterwork* καταργηση, or *render useless* and *ineffectual*, all the operations of him who *had* the *power*, κρατος, or *influence*, to bring death into the world ; so that *death*, which was intended by him who was a murderer from the beginning to be the final ruin of mankind, becomes the instrument of their exaltation and endless glory ; and thus the death brought in by Satan is *counterworked* and rendered *ineffectual* by the death of Christ.

Him that had the power of death] This is spoken in conformity to an opinion prevalent among the Jews, that there was a certain fallen angel who was called כלאך המות *malak hammaveth,* the *angel of death ;* i. e. one who had the *power* of separating the soul from the body, when God decreed that the person should die. There were two of these, according to some of the Jewish writers : one was the angel of death to the *Gentiles ;* the other, to the Jews. Thus *Tob haarets,* fol. 31 : " There are two angels which preside over death : one is over those who die out of the land of Israel, and his name is *Sammael ;* the other is he who presides over those who die in the land of Israel, and this is *Gabriel.*" Sammael is a common name for the devil among the Jews ; and there is a tradition among them, delivered by the author of *Pesikta rabbetha* in *Yalcut Simeoni,* par. 2, f. 56, that the angel of death should be destroyed by the Messiah ! " Satan said to the holy blessed God : *Lord of the world, show me the Messiah.* The Lord answered : *Come and see him.* And when he had seen him he was terrified, and his countenance fell, and he said : *Most certainly this is the Messiah who shall cast me and all the nations*

2

A. M. cir. 4067.
A. D. cir. 63.
An. Olymp.
cir. CCX. 3.
A. U. C. cir.
816.

15 And deliver them who through fear of death were all ⁱ their lifetime subject to bond-age.

16 For verily ^k he took not on *him the na-*

ture *of* angels ; but he took on *him* the seed of Abraham.

17 Wherefore in all things it behoved him ^l to be made like unto *his* brethren, that he might be ^m a mer-

A. M. cir. 4067.
A. D. cir. 63.
An. Olymp.
cir. CCX. 3.
A. U. C. cir.
816.

ⁱ Luke i. 74; Romans viii. 15; 2 Timothy i. 7.

^k Gr. *he taketh not hold of angels, but of the seed of Abraham he taketh hold.*——^l Phil. ii. 7.——^m Chap. iv. 15.; v. 1, 2.

into hell, as it is written Isa. xxv. 8, *The Lord shall swallow up death for ever."* This is a very remarkable saying, and the apostle shows that it is true, for the Messiah came to *destroy him who had the power of death.* Dr. Owen has made some collections on this head from other Jewish writers which tend to illustrate this verse ; they may be seen in his comment, vol. i., p. 456, 8vo. edition.

Verse 15. *And deliver them who through fear of death*] It is very likely that the apostle has the Gentiles here principally in view. As *they* had no *revelation,* and no certainty of *immortality,* they were continually in bondage to the fear of death. They preferred *life* in any state, with the most grievous evils, to *death,* because they had no hope beyond the grave. But it is also true that all men naturally fear death ; even those that have the fullest persuasion and certainty of a future state dread it : genuine Christians, who know that, if the earthly house of their tabernacle were dissolved, they have a house not made with hands, a building framed of God, eternal in the heavens, only *they* fear it not. In the assurance they have of God's love, the fear of death is removed ; and by the purification of their hearts through faith, the sting of death is extracted. The people who know not God are in continual torment through the fear of death, and they fear death because they fear something beyond death. They are conscious to themselves that they are wicked, and they are afraid of God, and terrified at the thought of *eternity.* By these fears thousands of sinful, miserable creatures are prevented from hurrying themselves into the unknown world. This is finely expressed by the poet :—

" To die,—to sleep,—
No more :—and, by a sleep, to say we end
The heartache, and the thousand natural shocks
That flesh is heir to,—'tis a consummation
Devoutly to be wished. To die,—to sleep,—
To sleep !—perchance to *dream ;*—ay, there's the rub ;
For in that sleep of death what dreams may come,
When we have shuffled off this mortal coil,
Must give us pause :—There's the respect
That makes calamity of so long life :
For who could bear the whips and scorns of time,
The oppressor's wrong, the proud man's contumely,
The pangs of despised love, the law's delay,
The insolence of office, and the spurns
That patient merit of the unworthy takes,
When he himself might his quietus make
With a bare bodkin ? Who would fardels bear
To grunt and sweat under a weary life ;
But that the *dread of something after death,*—
The *undiscovered country* from whose bourn

No traveller returns,—puzzles the will ;
And makes us rather bear those ills we have,
Than fly to others that we know not of ?
Thus conscience does make cowards of us all ;
And thus the native hue of resolution
Is sicklied o'er with the pale cast of thought ;
And enterprises of great pith and moment,
With this regard, their currents turn awry
And lose the name of action."

I give this long quotation from a poet who was well acquainted with all the workings of the human heart ; and one who could not have described scenes of distress and anguish of mind so well, had he not passed through them.

Verse 16. *For verily he took not on* him the nature of *angels*] Ου γαρ δηπου αγγελων επιλαμβανεται, αλλα σπερματος Αβρααμ επιλαμβανεται· *Moreover, he doth not at all take hold of angels ; but of the seed of Abraham he taketh hold.* This is the *marginal* reading, and is greatly to be preferred to that in the text Jesus Christ, intending not to redeem angels, but to redeem man, did not assume the angelic nature, but was made man, coming directly by the *seed* or *posterity of Abraham,* with whom the *original covenant* was made, that *in his seed all the nations of the earth should be blessed ;* and it is on this account that the apostle mentioned the *seed* of *Abraham,* and not the *seed* of *Adam ;* and it is strange that so many commentators should have missed so obvious a sense. The word itself signifies not only to *take hold of,* but to *help, succour, save from sinking,* &c. The rebel *angels,* who sinned and fell from God, were permitted to *fall downe, alle downe,* as one of our old writers expresses it, till they fell into perdition : *man* sinned and fell, and was falling *downe, alle downe,* but Jesus laid hold on him and prevented him from falling into endless perdition. Thus he *seized on the falling human creature,* and prevented him from falling into the bottomless pit ; but he did not *seize* on the falling angels, and they fell down into outer darkness. By assuming the nature of man, he prevented this final and irrecoverable fall of man ; and by making an atonement in human nature, he made a provision for its restoration to its forfeited blessedness. This is a fine thought of the apostle, and is beautifully expressed. Man was falling from heaven, and Jesus caught hold of the falling creature, and prevented its endless ruin. In this respect he prefers men to angels, and probably for this simple reason, that the *human nature* was *more excellent* than the *angelic ;* and it is suitable to the wisdom of the Divine Being to regard all the works of his hands in proportion to the dignity or excellence with which he has endowed them.

Verse 17. *Wherefore in all things*] Because he

A. M. cir. 4067.
A. D. cir. 63.
An. Olymp
cir. CCX 3.
A. U. C cir.
816.

ciful and faithful high priest in things *pertaining* to God, to make reconciliation for the sins of the people.

18 [n] For in that he himself hath suffered, being tempted, he is able to succour them that are tempted.

A. M. cir. 4067
A. D. cir. 63.
An. Olymp.
cir CCX. 3.
A. U. C. cir.
816.

[n] Chap. iv. 15, 16 ;   v. 2 ; vii. 25.

---

thus *laid hold* on man in order to redeem him, it was necessary that he should in all things become like to man, that he might suffer in his stead, and make an atonement in his nature.

That he might be a merciful and faithful high priest] 'Ινα ελεημων γενηται' *That he might be merciful*—that he might be affected with a feeling of our infirmities, that, partaking of our nature with all its innocent infirmities and afflictions, he might know how to *compassionate* poor, afflicted, suffering man. And that he might be a *faithful high priest in those things which relate to God*, whose justice requires the punishment of the transgressors, or a suitable expiation to be made for the sins of the people. The proper meaning of ιλασκεσθαι τας αμαρτιας is *to make propitiation* or *atonement for sins by sacrifice*. See the note on this word, Luke xviii. 13, where it is particularly explained. Christ is the *great High Priest* of mankind ; 1. He exercises himself in the *things pertaining* to God, taking heed that God's honour be properly secured, his worship properly regulated, his laws properly enforced, and both his justice and mercy magnified. Again, 2. He exercises himself in *things pertaining* to MEN, that he may make an *atonement for* them, apply this atonement *to* them, and liberate them thereby from the curse of a broken law, from the guilt and power of sin, from its inbeing and nature, and from all the evils to which they were exposed through it, and lastly that he might open their way into the holiest by his own blood ; and he has *mercifully* and *faithfully* accomplished all that he has undertaken.

Verse 18. For in that he himself hath suffered] The maxim on which this verse is founded is the following : A state of suffering disposes persons to be compassionate, and those who endure most afflictions

are they who feel most for others. The apostle argues that, among other causes, it was necessary that Jesus Christ should partake of human nature, exposed to trials, persecutions, and various sufferings, that he might the better feel for and be led to succour those who are afflicted and sorely tried. This sentiment is well expressed by a Roman poet :—

Me quoque per multos similis fortuna *labores*
Jactatam *hac demum voluit consistere terra :*
Non ignara mali, miseris succurere disco.
          VIRG. *Æn.* i., v. **632.**

" For *I myself, like you*, have been *distress'd*,
Till heaven afforded me this place of rest ;
Like you, an *alien* in a land unknown,
I learn to pity woes so like my own." DRYDEN.

" There are three things," says Dr. Owen, " of which tempted believers do stand in need : 1. Strength to withstand their temptations ; 2. Consolations to support their spirits under them ; 3. Seasonable deliverance from them. Unto these is the succour afforded by our High Priest suited ; and it is variously administered to them : 1. By his *word* or *promises* ; 2. By his *Spirit* ; (and, that, 1. By communicating to them *supplies of grace* or spiritual strength ; 2. Strong *consolation* ; 3. By *rebuking* their *tempters* and *temptations* ;) and 3. By his *providence* disposing of all things to their good and advantage in the issue." Those who are peculiarly tempted and severely tried, have an especial interest in, and claim upon Christ. They, particularly, may go with boldness to the throne of grace, where they shall assuredly obtain mercy, and find grace to help in time of need. Were the rest of the Scripture silent on this subject, this verse might be an ample support for every tempted soul.

CHAPTER III.

Jesus is the High Priest of our profession, 1. *And is counted worthy of more honour than Moses, as the Son is more worthy than the servant*, 2–6. *We should not harden our hearts against the voice of God, as the Israelites did, and were excluded from the earthly rest in Canaan*, 7–11. *We should be on our guard against unbelief*, 12. *And exhort each other, lest we be hardened through the deceitfulness of sin ; and we should hold fast the beginning of our confidence to the end, and not provoke God as the Israelites did, and who were destroyed in the wilderness*, 13–17. *They were promised the earthly rest, but did not enter because of unbelief*, 18, 19.

2

A. M. cir. 4067.
A. D. cir. 63.
An. Olymp.
cir. CCX. 3.
A. U. C. cir.
816.

WHEREFORE, holy bre-
thren, partakers of ᵃ the
heavenly calling, consider ᵇ the
Apostle and High Priest of our
profession, Christ Jesus;

2 Who was faithful to him that
ᶜ appointed him, as also ᵈ Moses
was faithful in all his house.

3 For this *man* was counted
worthy of more glory than Moses, inasmuch

A. M. cir. 4067
A. D. cir. 63.
An. Olymp.
cir. CCX. 3.
A. U. C. cir.
816.

ᵃ Rom. i. 7; 1 Cor. i. 2; Eph. iv. 1; Phil. iii. 14; 2 Thess. i.
11; 2 Tim. i. 9; 2 Peter i. 10.——ᵇ Rom. xv. 8; chap. ii. 17;

iv. 14; v. 5; vi. 20; viii. 1; ix. 11; x. 21.——ᶜ Gr. *made*; 1 Sam.
xii. 6.——ᵈ Num. xii. 7; ver. 5.

NOTES ON CHAP. III.

Verse 1. *Holy brethren*] Persons *consecrated to
God*, as the word literally implies, and called, in consequence, to be *holy in heart, holy in life*, and *useful
in the world*. The Israelites are often called a *holy
people, saints*, &c., because *consecrated* to God, and
because they were bound by their profession to be holy;
and yet these appellations are given to them in numberless instances where they were very *unholy*. The
not attending to this circumstance, and the not discerning between actual positive *holiness*, and the *call* to it,
as the *consecration* of the persons, has led many commentators and preachers into destructive mistakes.
Antinomianism has had its origin here : and as it was
found that many persons were called *saints*, who, in
many respects, were miserable sinners, hence it has
been inferred that they were called *saints* in reference
to a holiness which they had in *another;* and hence
the Antinomian imputation of Christ's righteousness to
unholy believers, whose hearts were abominable before
God, and whose lives were a scandal to the Gospel.
Let, therefore, a due distinction be made between persons by their *profession holy*, i. e. *consecrated to God;*
and persons who are *faithful* to that profession, and
are both *inwardly* and *outwardly holy*. They are
not all Israel who are of Israel: a man, by a literal
circumcision, may be a Jew outwardly; but the circumcision of the heart by the Spirit makes a man a
Jew inwardly. A man may be a Christian in profession, and not such in heart; and those who pretend
that, although they are *unholy in themselves*, they are
reputed *holy in Christ*, because his righteousness is
imputed to them, most awfully deceive their own souls.

Dr. *Owen* has spoken well on the necessity of personal holiness against the Antinomians of his day.
"If a man be not made holy he cannot enter into the
kingdom of God. It is this that makes them meet for
the inheritance of the saints in light; as without it
they are not meet for their duty, so are they not
capable of their reward. Yea, heaven itself, in the
true light and notion of it, is undesirable to an unsanctified person. Such a one neither can nor would
enjoy God if he might. In a word, there is no one
thing required of the sons of God that an unsanctified
person can do, and no one thing promised unto them
that he can enjoy.

"There is surely then a woful mistake in the world.
If Christ sanctify all whom he saves, many will appear
to have been mistaken in their expectations at another
day. It is grown amongst us almost an abhorrency to
all flesh to say, *the Church of God is to be holy*.
What! though God has promised that it should be so;
that Christ has undertaken to make it so? What! if
it be required to be so? What! if all the duties of it

be rejected of God, if it be not so? It is all one, if
men be baptized, whether they will or not, and outwardly profess the name of Christ, though not one of
them be truly sanctified, yet they are, it is said, the
Church of Christ. Why then let them be so; but
what are they the better for it? Are their persons or
their services therefore accepted with God? Are they
related or united to Christ? Are they under his conduct unto glory? Are they meet for the inheritance
of the saints in light? Not at all : not all nor any of
these things do they obtain thereby. What is it then
that they get by the furious contest which they make
for the reputation of this privilege? Only this : that,
satisfying their minds by it, resting if not priding themselves in it, they obtain many advantages to stifle all
convictions of their condition, and so perish unavoidably.
A sad success, and for ever to be bewailed! Yet is
there nothing at all at this day more contended for in
this world than that Christ might be thought to be a
captain of salvation to them, unto whom he is not a
sanctifier; that he may have an *unholy Church, a dead
body*. These things tend neither to the glory of
Christ, nor to the good of the souls of men. Let none
then deceive themselves; sanctification is a qualification indispensably necessary to them who will be under the conduct of the Lord Christ unto salvation; he
leads none to heaven but whom he *sanctifies* on earth.
The holy God will not receive unholy persons. This
living head will not admit of *dead members*, nor bring
men into possession of a glory which they neither love
nor like."

Heavenly calling] The Israelites had an earthly
calling; they were called out of Egypt to go into the
promised land : Christians have a heavenly calling;
they are invited to leave the bondage of sin, and go to
the kingdom of God. These were made partakers of
this calling; they had already embraced the Gospel,
and were brought into a state of salvation.

Apostle and High Priest of our profession] Among
the Jews the *high priest* was considered to be also *the
apostle of God;* and it is in conformity to this notion
that the apostle speaks. And he exhorts the Hebrews
to *consider* Jesus Christ to be both their *High Priest*
and *Apostle;* and to expect these offices to be henceforth fulfilled by him, and by him alone. This was
the fullest intimation that the Mosaic economy was at
an end, and the priesthood changed. By της ομολογιας
ημων, *our profession*, or *that confession of ours*, the
apostle undoubtedly means the *Christian religion*.
Jesus was the Apostle of the Father, and has given
to mankind the *new covenant;* and we are to consider
the whole system of Christianity as coming immediately from him. Every system of religion must have
a *priest* and a *prophet;* the one to *declare* the will of

      2

A. M. cir. 4067.
A. D. cir. 63.
An. Olymp.
cir. CCX. 3.
A. U. C. cir.
816.

as [e] he who hath builded the house hath more honour than the house.

4 For every house is builded by some *man ;* but [f] he

that built all things *is* God.

5 [g] And Moses verily *was* faithful in all his house, as [h] a

A. M. cir. 4067.
A. D. cir. 63.
An. Olymp.
cir. CCX. 3.
A. U. C. cir.
816.

---

[e] Zech. vi. 12; Matt. xvi. 18.——[f] Eph. ii. 10; iii. 9; chap. i. 2.——[g] Ver. 2.

[h] Exodus xiv. 31; Numbers xii. 7; Deut. iii. 24; Josh. i. 2. viii. 31.

God, the other to *minister* in holy things. Moses was the *apostle* under the old testament, and Aaron the *priest.* When Moses was removed, the prophets succeeded him; and the sons of Aaron were the priests after the death of their father. This system is now annulled; and Jesus is the *Prophet* who declares the Father's will, and he is the *Priest* who ministers in the things pertaining to God, see chap. ii. 17; as he makes atonement for the sins of the people, and is the Mediator between God and man.

Verse 2. *Who was faithful to him*] In Num. xii. 7, God gives this testimony to Moses: *My servant Moses—is faithful in all my house ;* and to this testimony the apostle alludes. *House* not only means the *place* where a *family dwells,* but also the *family* itself. The whole congregation of Israel was the *house* or *family of God,* and God is represented as *dwelling among them ;* and Moses was his *steward,* and was faithful in the discharge of his office ; strictly enforcing the Divine rights; zealously maintaining God's honour; carefully delivering the mind and will of God to the people; proclaiming his promises, and denouncing his judgments, with the most inflexible integrity, though often at the risk of his life. Jesus Christ has his *house*—the whole great *family of mankind,* for all of whom he offered his sacrificial blood to God; and the *Christian Church,* which is especially *his own household,* is composed of his own *children* and *servants, among* and *in* whom he lives and constantly resides. He has been *faithful* to the trust reposed in him as the apostle of God; he has faithfully proclaimed the will of the Most High ; vindicated the Divine honour against the corrupters of God's worship; testified against them at the continual hazard of his life; and, at last, not only died as a *victim* to cancel sin, but also as a *martyr* to his faithfulness. Christ's faithfulness, says *Leigh,* consists in this : " That he has as fully revealed unto us the doctrine of the Gospel, as Moses did that of the law ; and that he hath faithfully performed and fulfilled all the types of himself and all the things signified by Moses' ceremonies, as Moses hath faithfully and distinctly set them down."

But there is a sense given to the word נאמן *neeman,* Num. xii. 7, which we translate *faithful,* by several of the Jewish writers, which is well worthy of note : it signifies, say they, *" one to whom secrets are confided, with the utmost confidence of their being safely and conscientiously kept."* The secret of God was with Moses, but all the treasures of *wisdom* and *knowledge* were in Christ. Life and immortality were comparatively *secrets* till Christ revealed and illustrated them, and even the *Divine nature* was but little known, and especially the Divine *philanthropy,* till Jesus Christ came ; and it was Jesus alone who *declared* that GOD *whom no man had ever seen.* Moses received the secrets of God, and faithfully taught them

to the people ; Jesus revealed the *whole will of God to mankind.* Moses was thus *faithful* to a small part of mankind, viz. the Jewish people ; but in this sense Jesus was *faithful* to all mankind : for he was the light to enlighten the Gentiles, and the glory of his people Israel.

Verse 3. *For this* man *was counted*] As Jesus Christ, in the character of *apostle* and *high priest,* is here intended, the word *apostle,* or this *person* or *personage,* should have been supplied, if any, instead of *man.* Indeed, the pronoun οὗτος should have been translated *this person,* and this would have referred immediately to Jesus Christ, verse 1.

More glory than Moses] We have already seen that the apostle's design is to prove that Jesus Christ is *higher than the angels, higher than Moses,* and *higher than Aaron.* That he is higher than the *angels* has been already proved ; that he is *higher than Moses* he is now proving.

He who hath builded the house] There can be no doubt that a man who builds a house for his own accommodation is more honourable than the house itself ; but the *house* here intended is the *Church* of God. This Church, here called a *house* or *family,* is built by Christ ; he is the Head, Governor, Soul and Life of it ; he must therefore be *greater than Moses,* who was only a *member* and *officer* in that Church, who never put a stone in this spiritual building but was even himself put in it by the great Architect. Moses was in this house, and faithful in this house ; but the house was the house of God, and builded and governed by Christ.

Verse 4. *For every house is builded by some* man] The literal sense is plain enough : " Every structure plainly implies an architect, and an *end* for which it was formed. The architect may be employed by him for whose use the house is intended ; but the *efficient* cause of the erection is that which is here to be regarded." The word *house,* here, is still taken in a *metaphorical* sense as above, it signifies *family* or *Church.* Now the general meaning of the words, taken in this sense, is : " Every family has an author, and a head or governor. Man may found families, civil and religious communities, and be the head of these ; but God alone is the Head, Author, and Governor, of all the families of the earth ; he is the Governor of the universe. But the apostle has a more restricted meaning in the words τα παντα, *all these things;* and as he has been treating of the Jewish and Christian Churches, so he appears to have them in view here. Who could found the Jewish and Christian Church but God ? Who could support, govern, influence, and defend them, but himself ? Communities or societies, whether religious or civil, may be founded by *man ;* but God alone can build his own Church. Now as *all these things* could be builded only by God, so he must be God who has built all these things. But as Jesus is the Founder of the

2

A. M. cir. 4067. A. D. cir. 63. An. Olymp. cir. CCX. 3. A. U. C. cir. 816.	servant, [i] for a testimony of those things which were to be spoken after ; 6 But Christ as [k] a Son over	his own house ; [l] whose house are we, [m] if we hold fast the confidence and the rejoicing of the hope firm unto the end.	A. M. cir. 4067. A. D. cir. 63. An. Olymp. cir. CCX. 3. A. U. C. cir. 816.

[i] Deut. xviii. 15, 18, 19.——[k] Chapter i. 2.——[l] 1 Cor. iii. 16; vi. 19; 2 Cor. vi. 16; Eph. ii. 21, 22; 1 Tim. iii. 15; 1 Pet. ii.

5.——[m] Ver. 14; Matt. x. 22; xxiv. 13; Rom. v. 2; Col. i. 23; chapter vi. 11; x. 35.

Church, and the Head of it, the word GOD seems here to be applied to *him;* and several eminent scholars and critics bring this very text as a proof of the supreme Deity of Christ : and the apostle's argument seems to require this ; for, as he is proving that Christ is *preferred before Moses* because *he built this house,* which Moses could not do, where he to be understood as intimating that this house was built by *another,* viz. the *Father,* his whole argument would fall to the ground ; and for *all this,* Moses might be equal, yea, superior to Christ. On this ground Dr. Owen properly concludes : "This then is that which the apostle intends to declare ; namely, the ground and reason whence it is that the house was or could be, in that glorious manner, built by Christ, even because he is GOD, and so able to effect it ; and by this effect of his power, he is manifested so to be."

Verse 5. *As a servant*] The *fidelity* of Moses was the fidelity of a *servant ;* he was not the framer of that Church or house ; he was employed, under God, to arrange and order it : he was *steward* to the Builder and Owner.

For a testimony of those things] Every ordinance under the law was *typical ;* every thing bore a *testimony* to the things which were to be spoken after ; i. e. to Jesus Christ, his suffering, death, and the glory which should follow ; and to his Gospel in all its parts. The *faithfulness* of Moses consisted in his scrupulous attention to every ordinance of God ; his framing every thing according to the pattern showed him by the Lord ; and his referring all to that Christ of whom he spoke as the prophet who should come after him, and should be raised up from among themselves ; whom they should attentively hear and obey, on pain of being cut off from being the people of the Lord. Hence our Lord told the Jews, John v. 46 : *If ye had believed Moses, ye would have believed me, for he wrote of me ;* "namely ;" says Dr. Macknight, "in the figures, but especially in the prophecies, of the law, where the Gospel dispensation, the coming of its Author, and his character as Messiah, are all described with a precision which adds the greatest lustre of evidence to Jesus and to his Gospel."

Verse 6. *But Christ as a Son over his own house*] Moses was faithful as a *servant* IN the house ; Jesus was faithful, as the *first-born Son,* OVER the house of which he is the Heir and Governor. Here, then, is the conclusion of the argument in reference to Christ's superiority over Moses. Moses did not found the house or family, Christ did ; Moses was but *in* the house, or one of the family, Christ was *over* the house as its Ruler ; Moses was but *servant* in the house, Christ was the *Son* and *Heir ;* Moses was in the house of *another,* Christ in his *own house.*

It is well known to every learned reader that the pronoun αυτου, without an *aspirate,* signifies *his* sim-

ply ; and that with the *aspirate,* αὑτου, it signifies *his own :* the word being in this form a contraction, not uncommon, of ἑαυτου. If we read αυτου without the *aspirate,* then *his* must refer to *God,* ver. 4.

But Christ as a Son over his (that is, God's) *house :* if we read αὑτου, with the *aspirate,* as some editions do, then what is spoken refers to *Christ ;* and the words above convey the same sense as those words, Acts xx. 28 : *Feed the Church of God, which he hath purchased with his own blood.* Some editions read the word thus ; and it is evident that the edition which our translators used had the word αὑτου, *his own,* and not αυτου, *his.* The Spanish and London Polyglots have the same reading. From the most ancient MSS. we can get no help to determine which is to be preferred, as they are generally written without accents. The two first editions of the Greek Testament, that of *Complutum,* 1514, and that of *Erasmus,* 1516, have αυτου, *his ;* and they are followed by most other editions : but the celebrated edition of Robert *Stephens,* 1550, has αὑτου, *his own.* The reading is certainly important ; but it belongs to one of those difficulties in criticism which, if the context or collateral evidence do not satisfactorily solve it, must remain in doubt ; and every reader is at liberty to adopt which reading he thinks best.

Whose house are we] We Christians are his *Church* and *family ;* he is our Father, Governor, and Head.

If we hold fast the confidence] We are now his Church, and shall *continue* to be such, and be acknowledged by him IF we maintain our Christian profession, την παρρησιαν, *that liberty of access to God,* which we now have, and the *rejoicing of the hope,* i. e. of eternal life, which we shall receive at the resurrection of the dead. The word παρρησια, which is here translated *confidence,* and which signifies *freedom of speech, liberty of access,* &c., seems to be used here to distinguish an important Christian privilege. Under the old testament no man was permitted to *approach to God :* even the very *mountain* on which God published his laws must not be touched by man nor beast ; and only the high priest was permitted to enter the holy of holies, and that only once a year, on the great day of atonement ; and even then he must have the blood of the victim to propitiate the Divine justice. Under the Christian dispensation the way to the holiest is now laid open ; and we have παρρησιαν, *liberty of access,* even to the holiest, by the blood of Jesus. Having such access unto God, by such a Mediator, we may obtain all that grace which is necessary to fit us for eternal glory ; and, having the witness of his Spirit in our heart, we have a well grounded hope of endless felicity, and exult in the enjoyment of that hope. But IF we retain not the grace, we shall not inherit the glory.

2

A. M. cir. 4067.
A. D. cir. 63.
An. Olymp.
cir. CCX. 3.
A. U. C. cir.
816.

7 Wherefore (as [n] the Holy Ghost saith, [o] To-day, if ye will hear his voice,

8 Harden not your hearts, as

in the provocation, [p] in the day of temptation in the wilderness;

9 When your fathers tempted

A. M. cir. 4067.
A. D. cir. 63.
An. Olymp.
cir. CCX. 3.
A. U. C. cir.
816.

---

[n] 2 Sam. xxiii. 2; Acts i. 16.——[o] Ver. 15; Psa. xcv. 7.

[p] Deut. vi. 16; xxxiii. 8.

Verse 7. *Wherefore (as the Holy Ghost saith, To-day*] These words are quoted from Psa. xcv. 7; and as they were written by David, and attributed here to the Holy Ghost, it proves that David wrote by the inspiration of God's Holy Spirit. As these words were originally a warning to the Israelites not to provoke God, lest they should be excluded from that *rest* which he had promised them, the apostle uses them here to persuade the Christians in Palestine to hold fast their religious privileges, and the grace they had received, lest they should come short of that state of future glory which Christ had prepared for them. The words strongly imply, as indeed does the whole *epistle*, the *possibility of falling from the grace of God*, and *perishing everlastingly*; and without this supposition these words, and all such like, which make more than *two-thirds* of the whole of Divine revelation, would have neither sense nor meaning. Why should God entreat man to receive his mercy, if he have rendered this impossible? Why should he exhort a believer to persevere, if it be impossible for him to fall away? What contemptible quibbling have men used to maintain a false and dangerous tenet against the whole tenor of the word of God! Angels fell—Adam fell—Solomon fell—and multitudes of believers have fallen, and, for aught we know, rose no more; and yet we are told that *we* cannot finally lose the benefits of our conversion! Satan preached this doctrine to our first parents; they believed him, sinned, and fell; and brought a whole world to ruin!

Verse 8. *Harden not your hearts*] Which ye will infallibly do, if ye *will not* hear his voice.

Provocation] Παραπικρασμος· From παρα, signifying *intensity*, and πικραινω, to *make bitter*; the *exasperation*, or *bitter provocation*. "The Israelites provoked God *first* in the wilderness of Sin, (Pelusium,) when they murmured for want of bread, and had the manna given them, Exod. xvi. 4. From the wilderness of Sin they journeyed to Rephidim, where they provoked God a second time for want of water, and insolently saying, *Is the Lord God among us or not?* Exod. xvii. 2–9, on which account the place was called *Massah* and *Meribah*. See 1 Cor. x. 4, note 1. From Rephidim they went into the wilderness of Sinai, where they received the law, in the beginning of the third year from their coming out of Egypt. Here they provoked God again, by making the golden calf, Exod. xxxii. 10. After the law was given they were commanded to go directly to Canaan, and take possession of the promised land, Deut. i. 6, 7: *God spake unto us in Horeb, saying, Ye have dwelt long enough in this mount: turn you, and take your journey, and go to the mount of the Amorites, and unto all the places nigh thereunto, in the plain, in the hills, and in the vales, and in the south, and by the seaside, to the land of the Canaanites, and unto Le-*

banon, and unto the great river, the river Euphrates. The Israelites, having received this order, departed from Horeb, and went forward three days' journey, Num. x. 33, till they came to Taberah, Num. xi. 3, where they provoked God the fourth time, by murmuring for want of flesh to eat; and for that sin were smitten with a very great plague, ver. 33; this place was called *Kibroth-hattaavah*, because there they buried the people who lusted. From Kibroth-hattaavah they went to *Hazeroth*, Num. xi. 35, and from thence into the *wilderness of Paran*, Num. xii. 16, to a place called *Kadesh*, chap. xiii. 26. Their journey from Horeb to Kadesh is thus described by Moses, Deut. i. 19–21: *And when we departed from Horeb, we went through all that great and terrible wilderness, which you saw by the way of the mountain of the Amorites, as the Lord our God commanded us; and we came to Kadesh-barnea. And I said unto you, Ye are come unto the mountain of the Amorites, which the Lord our God doth give unto us. Behold, the Lord thy God hath set the land before thee; go up and possess it.* But the people proposed to Moses to send spies, to bring them an account of the land, and of its inhabitants, ver. 22. These after forty days returned to Kadesh; and, except Caleb and Joshua, they all agreed in bringing an evil report of the land, Num. xiii. 25–32; whereby the people were so discouraged that they refused to go up, and proposed to make a captain, and return into Egypt, Num. xiv. 4. Wherefore, having thus shown an absolute disbelief of God's promises, and an utter distrust of his power, he sware that not one of that generation should enter Canaan, except Caleb and Joshua, but should all die in the wilderness, Num. xiv. 20; Deut. i. 34, 35; and ordered them to *turn, and get into the wilderness, by the way of the Red Sea.* In that wilderness the Israelites, as Moses informs us, sojourned thirty-eight years, Deut. ii. 14: *And the space in which we came from Kadesh-barnea, until we were come over the brook Zereb,* was *thirty and eight years; until all the generation of the men of war were wasted out from among the host, as the Lord sware unto them.* Wherefore, although the Israelites provoked God to wrath in the wilderness, from the day they came out of the land of Egypt until their arrival in Canaan, as Moses told them, Deut. ix. 7, their greatest provocation, the provocation in which they showed the greatest degree of evil disposition, undoubtedly was their refusing to go into Canaan from Kadesh. It was therefore very properly termed *the bitter provocation* and the *day of temptation*, by way of eminence; and justly brought on them the oath of God, excluding them from his rest in Canaan. To distinguish this from the provocation at Rephidim, it is called *Meribah-Kadesh*," Deut. xxxii. 51. See Dr Macknight.

Verse 9. *When your fathers tempted me*] It would

A. M. cir. 4067.
A. D. cir. 63.
An. Olymp.
cir. CCX. 3.
A. U. C. cir.
816.

me, proved me, and saw my works q forty years.

10 Wherefore I was grieved with that generation, and said, They do alway err in *their* heart; and they have not known my ways.

11 So I sware in my wrath, r They shall not enter into my rest.)

12 Take heed, brethren, lest there be in any

of you an evil heart of unbelief, in departing from the living God.

13 But exhort one another daily, while it is called to-day; lest any of you be hardened through the deceitfulness of sin.

14 For we are made partakers of Christ, s if we hold the beginning of our confidence steadfast unto the end;

A. M cir. 4067.
A. D. cir. 63.
An. Olymp.
cir. CCX. 3.
A. U. C. cir.
816.

---

q Deut. xi. 2, 5; xxix. 5.

r Gr. *If they shall enter.*——s Ver. 6.

---

be better to translate *ou where* than *when*, as the Vulgate has done in its *ubi*; and this translation has been followed by *Wiclif, Coverdale, Tindal*, and our first translators in general. In my old MS. Bible the 7th, 8th, and 9th verses stand thus :—

Wherefore as the Holy Gost seith, to-day gif ghe han herde his boyce: nye ghe herden ghour hertis as in wrath-thinge, after the day of temptacioun in desert. Where ghoure fadris temptiden me: probyden and salden my werkis. Wherefore fourtye yeere I was offendid or wrothe to this generatioun.

In behalf of this translation, Dr. Macknight very properly argues: " The word WHEN implies that, at the time of the *bitter provocation*, the Israelites had seen God's works *forty* years; contrary to the *history*, which shows that the *bitter provocation* happened in the beginning of the *third* year after the Exodus : whereas the translation *where*, as well as the matter of fact, represents God as saying, by David, that the Israelites tempted God in the wilderness during forty years, notwithstanding all that time they had seen God's miracles."

Verse 10. *Wherefore I was grieved*] God represents himself as the *Father* of this great Jewish family, for whose comfort and support he had made every necessary provision, and to whom he had given every proof of *tenderness* and *fatherly affection;* and because they disobeyed him, and walked in that way in which they could not but be miserable, therefore he represents himself as grieved and exceedingly displeased with them.

They do alway err in their *heart*] Their affections are set on earthly things, and they do not acknowledge my ways to be *right*—holy, just, and good. They are radically evil ; and they are evil *continually*. They have every proof of my power and goodness, and lay nothing to heart. They might have been saved, but they would not. God was grieved on this account. Now, can we suppose that it would have grieved him if, by a decree of his own, he had rendered their salvation impossible ?

Verse 11. *So I sware in my wrath*] God's *grief* at their continued disobedience became *wrath* at their final impenitence, and therefore he excluded them from the promised rest.

Verse 12. *Take heed, brethren, lest there be in any of you*] Take warning by those disobedient Israelites; they were brought out of the house of bondage, and had the fullest promise of a land of prosperity

and rest. By their disobedience they came short of it, and fell in the wilderness. Ye have been brought from the bondage of sin, and have a most gracious promise of an everlasting inheritance among the saints in light ; through unbelief and disobedience they lost their rest, through the same ye may lose yours. An evil heart of unbelief will lead away from the living God. What was possible in *their* case, is possible in *yours*. The apostle shows here *five* degrees of apostasy : 1. Consenting to sin, being deceived by its solicitations. 2. Hardness of heart, through giving way to sin. 3. Unbelief in consequence of this hardness which leads them to call even the truth of the Gospel in question. 4. This unbelief causing them to speak evil of the Gospel, and the provision God has made for the salvation of their souls. 5. Apostasy itself, or falling off from the living God; and thus extinguishing all the light that was in them, and finally grieving the Spirit of God, so that he takes his flight, and leaves them to a seared conscience and reprobate mind. See *Leigh*. He who begins to give the least way to sin is in danger of final apostasy ; the best remedy against this is to get the evil heart *removed*, as *one* murderer in the house is more to be dreaded than *ten* without.

Verse 13. *But exhort one another daily*] This supposes a state of close Church fellowship, without which they could not have had access to each other.

While it is called to-day] Use time while you have it, for by and by there will be no more present time ; all will be future ; all will be eternity. *Daily* signifies time continued. *To-day*, all present time. Your fathers said : Let us make ourselves a captain, and return back unto Egypt, Num. xiv. 4. Thus *they* exhorted each other *to depart from the living God*. Be ye warned by their example ; let not that unbelieving heart be in *you* that was in *them*; exhort each other daily to cleave to the living God ; lest, if ye do not, *ye*, like *them*, may be hardened through the deceitfulness of sin.

Verse 14. *For we are made partakers of Christ*] Having believed in Christ as the promised Messiah, and embraced the whole Christian system, they were consequently made partakers of all its *benefits* in this life, and entitled to the fulfilment of all its exceeding great and precious promises relative to the glories of the eternal world. The former they actually possessed, the latter they could have only in case of their perseverance ; therefore the apostle says, *If we hold fast the beginning of our confidence steadfast unto the*

A. M. cir. 4067.
A. D. cir. 63.
An. Olymp.
cir. CCX. 3.
A. U. C. cir.
816.

15 While it is said, [t] To-day, if ye will hear his voice, harden not your hearts, as in the provocation.

16 [u] For some, when they had heard, did provoke : howbeit not all that came out of Egypt by Moses.

17 But with whom was he grieved forty years ? *was it* not with them that had sinned, [v] whose carcasses fell in the wilderness ?

18 And [w] to whom sware he that they should not enter into his rest, but to them that believed not ?

19 [x] So we see that they could not enter in because of unbelief.

A. M. cir. 4067
A. D. cir. 63.
An. Olymp.
cir. CCX. 3.
A. U. C. cir.
816.

[t] Ver. 7; Psa. xcv. 7, 8.——[u] Num. xiv. 2, 4, 11, 24, 30; Deut. i. 34, 36, 38.

[v] Numbers xiv. 22, 29, &c. ; xxvi. 65 ; Psa. cvi. 26 ; 1 Cor. x. 5 ; Jude 5.——[w] Num. xiv. 30 ; Deut. i. 34, 35.——[x] Ch. iv. 6.

end, i. e. of our life. For our participation of glory depends on our continuing steadfast in the faith, to the end of our Christian race.

The word ὑποστασις, which we here translate *confidence,* from ὑπο, *under,* and ἱστημι, *to place* or *stand,* signifies properly a *basis* or *foundation;* that on which something else is builded, and by which it is supported. Their *faith* in Christ Jesus was this *hypostasis* or *foundation;* on that all their peace, comfort, and salvation were builded. If this were not held fast to the end, Christ, in his saving influences, could not be held fast ; and no Christ, no heaven. He who has Christ in him, has the well-founded hope of glory ; and he who is found in the great day with Christ in his heart, will have an abundant entrance into eternal glory.

Verse 15. *While it is said, To-day*] You may see the necessity of perseverance from the saying, "To-day, if ye will hear his voice," therefore *harden not your hearts*—do not neglect so great a salvation ; hold fast what ye have obtained, and let no man take your crown. See on ver. 7, 8, 9, and 12.

Verse 16. *For some, when they had heard, did provoke*] There is a various reading here, which consists merely in the different placing of an *accent,* and yet gives the whole passage a different turn :—τινες, from τις, *who,* if read with the accent on the *epsilon,* τινὲς, is the plural indefinite, and signifies *some,* as in our translation ; if read with the accent on the *iota,* τίνες, it has an *interrogative* meaning ; and, according to this, the whole clause, τίνες γαρ ακουσαντες παρεπικραναν; *But who were those hearers who did bitterly provoke? αλλ' ου παντες οι εξελθοντες εξ Αιγυπτου δια Μωσεως; Were they not all they who came out of the land of Egypt by Moses?* Or, the whole clause may be read with one interrogation : *But who were those hearers that did bitterly provoke, but all those who came out of Egypt by Moses?* This mode of reading is followed by some *editions,* and by *Chrysostom* and *Theodoret,* and by several learned *moderns.* It is more *likely* that this is the true reading, as all that follows to the end of the 18th verse is a series of interrogations.

Should it be said that *all* did not provoke, for Joshua and Caleb are expressly excepted ; I answer, that the term *all* may be with great propriety used, when out of many *hundreds of thousands* only two persons were found who continued faithful. To these also we may add the *priests* and the whole tribe of *Levi,* who, it is very likely, did not provoke ; for, as Dr. Macknight very properly remarks, they were not of the number of those who were to fight their way into Canaan,

being entirely devoted to the service of the sanctuary. See Num. i. 3, 45, and 49. And therefore what remained of them after forty years, no doubt, entered Canaan ; for it appears from Num. xxxiv. 17, and Josh. xxiv. 33, that *Eleazar,* the son of Aaron, was one of those who did take possession of Canaan. Should it be still said our version appears to be most proper, because *all* did not provoke ; it may be answered, that the common reading, τινες, *some,* is too *contracted* in its meaning to comprehend the hundreds of thousands who did rebel.

Verse 17. *But with whom was he grieved forty years?*] I believe it was *Surenhusius* who first observed that "the apostle, in using the term forty years, elegantly alludes to the space of time which had elapsed since the ascension of our Lord till the time in which this epistle was written, which was about forty years." But this does not exactly agree with what appears to be the exact date of this epistle. However, God had now been a long time provoked by that race rejecting the manifested Messiah, as he was by the conduct of their forefathers in the wilderness ; and as that provocation was punished by a very signal judgment, so they might expect this to be punished also. The analogy was perfect in the crimes, and it might reasonably be expected to be so in the punishment. And was not the destruction of Jerusalem a proof of the heinous nature of their crimes, and of the justice of God's outpoured wrath ?

Whose carcasses fell] Ὡν τα κωλα επεσεν· *Whose members fell;* for τα κωλα properly signifies the members of the body, and here may be an allusion to the scattered, bleached bones of this people, that were a long time apparent in the wilderness, continuing there as a proof of their crimes, and of the judgments of God.

Verse 18. *To whom sware he*] God never acts by any kind of caprice ; whenever he pours out his judgments, there are the most positive reasons to vindicate his conduct.

Those whose carcasses fell in the wilderness were they who had sinned. And those who did not enter into his rest were those who *believed not.* God is represented here as *swearing* that *they should not enter in,* in order to show the *determinate nature* of his purpose, the reason on which it was founded, and the height of the *aggravation* which occasioned it.

Verse 19. *So we see that they could not enter in*] It was no *decree* of God that prevented them, it was no want of necessary *strength* to enable them, it was through no deficiency of *Divine counsel* to instruct

2

them; all these they had in abundance: but they chose to sin, and *would* not believe. *Unbelief* produced *disobedience,* and disobedience produced *hardness of heart* and blindness of mind; and all these drew down the judgments of God, and wrath came upon them to the uttermost.

1. This whole chapter, as the epistle in general, reads a most awful lesson against *backsliders, triflers,* and *loiterers* in the way of salvation. Every believer in Christ is in danger of *apostasy,* while any remains of the *evil heart of unbelief* are found in him. God has promised to purify the heart; and the blood of Christ cleanses from all sin. It is therefore the highest wisdom of genuine Christians to look to God for the complete purification of their souls; this they cannot have too soon, and for this they cannot be too much in earnest.

2. No man should defer his salvation to any future time. If God speaks *to-day,* it is *to-day* that he should be *heard* and *obeyed.* To defer reconciliation to God to any *future* period, is the most reprehensible and destructive presumption. It supposes that God will indulge us in our sensual propensities, and cause his mercy to tarry for us till we have consummated our iniquitous purposes. It shows that we prefer, at least for the present, the devil to Christ, sin to holiness, and earth to heaven. And can we suppose that God will be thus mocked? Can we suppose that it can at all consist with his *mercy* to extend foregiveness to such abominable provocation? What a man sows that shall he reap. If he sows to the flesh, he shall of the flesh reap corruption. Reader, it is a dreadful thing to fall into the hands of the living God.

3. *Unbelief* has generally been considered the *most damning of all sins.* I wish those who make this assertion would condescend to explain themselves. What is this *unbelief* that *damns* and *ruins mankind?* Their not *permitting their minds to be persuaded of the truths which God speaks.* Απιστια, from *a,* negative, and πιστις, *faith,* signifies *faithless* or to be *without faith.* And this is an *effect* from another *cause* In chap. iv. 11, these very people are said to

have *fallen through unbelief;* but there the word is απειθεια, from *a,* negative, and πειθω, to *persuade.* They heard the Divine instructions, they saw God's stupendous miracles; but they would not suffer themselves to be persuaded, that he who said and did such things would perform those other things which he had either threatened or promised: hence they had *no faith,* because they were *unpersuaded;* and their *unbelief* was the *effect* of their *unpersuaded* or *unpersuadable* mind. And their minds were not persuaded of God's truth, because they had ears open only to the dictates of the flesh; see on chap. iv. 2. Here then is the damning sin, the not inferring, from what God has said and done, that he will do those other things which he has either threatened or promised. And how few are there who are not committing this sin daily! Reader, dost *thou* in this state dream of heaven? Awake out of sleep!

4. Where there are so many snares and dangers it is impossible to be too watchful and circumspect. Satan, as a roaring lion, as a subtle serpent, or in the guise of an angel of light, is momentarily going about seeking whom he may deceive, blind, and devour; and, when it is considered that the human heart, till entirely renewed, is on his side, it is a miracle of mercy that any soul escapes perdition: no man is safe any longer than he maintains the spirit of *watchfulness* and *prayer;* and to maintain such a spirit, he has need of all the means of grace. He who neglects any of them which the mercy of God has placed in his power, tempts the devil to tempt him. As a preventive of backsliding and apostasy, the apostle recommends *mutual exhortation.* No Christian should live for himself alone; he should consider his fellow Christian as a member of the same body, and feel for him accordingly, and love, succour, and protect him. When this is carefully attended to in religious society, Satan finds it very difficult to make an inroad on the Church; but when coldness, distance, and a want of brotherly love take place, Satan can attack each *singly,* and, by successive victories over *individuals,* soon make an easy conquest of the *whole.*

CHAPTER IV.

As the Christian rest is to be obtained by faith, we should beware of unbelief, lest we lose it, as the Hebrews did theirs, 1. *The reason why they were not brought into the rest promised to them,* 2. *The rest promised to the Hebrews was a type of that promised to Christians,* 3–10. *Into this rest we should earnestly labour to enter,* 11. *A description of the word of God,* 12, 13. *Jesus is our sympathetic High Priest,* 15. *Through him we have confidence to come to God,* 16.

A. M. cir. 4067. A. D. cir. 63. An. Olymp. cir. CCX. 3. A. U. C. cir. 816.	LET ᵃ us therefore fear, lest, a promise being left *us* of entering into his rest, any of you should seem to come short of it.	2 For unto us was the Gospel preached, as well as unto them: but the ᵇ word preached did not profit them, ᶜ not being	A. M. cir. 4067. A. D. cir. 63. An. Olymp. cir. CCX. 3. A. U. C. cir. 816.

ᵃ Chap. xii. 15.——ᵇ Gr. *the word of hearing.*   ᶜ Or, *because they were not united by faith to.*

NOTES ON CHAP. IV.

Verse 1. *Let us therefore fear*] Seeing the Israelites lost the rest of Canaan, through obstinacy and

unbelief, let us be afraid lest we come short of the heavenly rest, through the same cause.

Should seem to come short of it.] *Lest any of us*

A. M. cir. 4067.
A. D. cir. 63.
An. Olymp.
cir. CCX. 3.
A. U. C. cir.
816.

mixed with faith in them that heard *it*.

3 ^d For we which have believed do enter into rest, as he said,

^e As I have sworn in my wrath, If they shall enter into my rest: although the works were finished from the foundation of the world.

A. M. cir. 4067.
A. D. cir. 63.
An. Olymp.
cir. CCX. 3.
A. U. C. cir.
816.

^d Chap. iii. 14.

^e Psa. xcv. 11 ; chap. iii. 11.

---

should actually come short of it ; i. e. miss it. See the note on the verb δοκειν, to *seem*, Luke viii. 18. What the apostle had said before, relative to the *rest*, might be considered as an allegory ; here he explains and applies that allegory, showing that Canaan was a type of the grand privileges of the Gospel of Christ, and of the glorious eternity to which they lead.

Come short] The verb ὑστερειν is applied here metaphorically ; it is an allusion, of which there are many in this epistle, to the *races* in the Grecian games : he that *came short* was he who was any distance, no matter how small, *behind* the winner. Will it avail any of us how near we get to heaven, if the door be shut before we arrive ? How dreadful the thought, to have only *missed* being eternally saved ! To *run* well, and yet to permit the devil, the world, or the flesh, to hinder in the few last steps ! Reader, watch and be sober.

Verse 2. *For unto us was the Gospel preached*] Και γαρ εσμεν ευηγγελισμενοι· *For we also have received good tidings as well as they.* They had a gracious promise of entering into an earthly rest ; we have a gracious promise of entering into a heavenly rest. God gave them every requisite advantage ; he has done the same to us. Moses and the elders spoke the word of God plainly and forcibly to them ; Christ and his apostles have done the same to us. They might have persevered ; so may we : they disbelieved, disobeyed, and fell : and so may we.

But the word preached did not profit them] Αλλ ουκ ωφελησεν ὁ λογος της ακοης εκεινους· *But the word of hearing did not profit them.* The word and promise to which the apostle most probably refers is that in Deut. i. 20, 21 : *Ye are come unto the mountain of the Amorites, which the Lord our God doth give unto us. Behold, the Lord thy God hath set the land before thee ; go up and possess it, as the Lord God of thy fathers hath said unto thee : fear not.* Many exhortations they had to the following effect : *Arise, that we may go up against them ; for we have seen the land, and, behold, it is very good : and are ye still? Be ye slothful to go, and to enter to possess the land ; for God hath given it into your hands ; a place where there is no want of any thing that is in the earth ;* Judg. xviii. 9, 10. But instead of attending to the word of the Lord by Moses, the whole congregation murmured against him and Aaron, *and said one to another, Let us make a captain, and let us return into Egypt*; Num. xiv. 2, 4. But they were dastardly through all their generations. They spoke evil of the pleasant land, and did not give credence to his word. Their minds had been debased by their Egyptian bondage, and they scarcely ever arose to a state of mental nobility.

Not being mixed with faith in them that heard] There are several various readings in this verse, and

some of them important. The principal are on the word συγκεκραμενος, *mixed ;* which in the common text refers to ὁ λογος, *the word mixed ;* but, in ABCD and several others, it is συγκεκραμενους, referring to, and agreeing with, εκεινους, and may be thus translated : *The word of hearing did not profit them, they not being mixed with those who heard it by faith.* That is, they were not of the same spirit with Joshua and Caleb. There are other variations, but of less importance ; but the common text seems best.

The word συγκεκραμενος, *mixed*, is peculiarly expressive ; it is a metaphor taken from the nutrition of the human body by mixing the aliment taken into the stomach with the saliva and gastric juice, in consequence of which it is concocted, digested, reduced into chyle, which, absorbed by the lacteal vessels, and thrown into the blood, becomes the means of increasing and supporting the body, all the solids and fluids being thus generated ; so that on this process, properly performed, depend (under God) strength, health, and life itself. Should the most nutritive aliment be received into the stomach, if not *mixed* with the above juices, it would be rather the means of *death* than of life ; or, in the words of the apostle, it would *not profit*, because not thus *mixed*. *Faith* in the word preached, in reference to that God who sent it, is the grand means of its becoming the power of God to the salvation of the soul. It is not likely that he who does not credit a *threatening*, when he comes to hear it, will be deterred by it from repeating the sin against which it is levelled ; nor can he derive comfort from a *promise* who does not believe it as a pledge of God's veracity and goodness. Faith, therefore, must be *mixed* with all that we hear, in order to make the word of God effectual to our salvation.

This very use of the word, and its explanation, we may find in *Maximus Tyrius*, in his description of *health*, Dissert. x., page 101. "Health," says he, "is a certain disposition ὑγρων και ξηρων και ψυχρων και θερμων δυναμεων, ἡ ὑπο τεχνης συγκραθεισων καλως, ἡ ὑπο φυσεως ἁρμοσθεισων τεχνικως, which consists in a *proper mixture* together of the wet and the dry, the cold and the hot, either by an artificial process, or by the skilful economy of nature."

Verse 3. *For we which have believed do enter into rest*] The great spiritual blessings, the forerunners of eternal glory, which were all typified by that earthly rest or felicity promised to the ancient Israelites, we Christians do, by believing in Christ Jesus, actually possess. We have peace of conscience, and joy in the Holy Ghost ; are saved from the guilt and power of sin ; and thus enjoy an inward rest.

But *this* is a rest differing from the *seventh day's* rest, or *Sabbath*, which was the original type of Canaan, the blessings of the Gospel, and eternal glory ; seeing God said, concerning the unbelieving Israelites

2

A. M. cir. 4067.
A. D. cir. 63.
An. Olymp.
cir. CCX. 3.
A. U. C. cir.
816.

4 For he spake in a certain place of the seventh *day* on this wise, f And God did rest the seventh day from all his works.

5 And in this *place* again, If they shall enter into my rest.

6 Seeing therefore it remaineth that some must enter therein, g and they to whom h it

was first preached entered not in because of unbelief:

A. M. cir. 4067.
A. D. cir. 63.
An. Olymp.
cir. CCX. 3.
A. U. C. cir.
816.

7 (Again, he limiteth a certain day, saying in David, To-day, after so long a time; as it is said, i To-day, if ye will hear his voice, harden not your hearts.

8 For if k Jesus had given them rest, then

---

f Genesis ii. 2; Exodus xx. 11; xxxi. 17.——g Chapter iii. 19.

h Or, *the Gospel was first preached.*——i Psa. xcv. 7; ch. iii. 7. k That is, *Joshua.*

---

in the wilderness, I have sworn in my wrath that they shall not enter into my rest, notwithstanding the *works* of creation *were finished,* and the seventh day's rest was instituted *from the foundation of the world;* consequently the Israelites *had entered* into that rest before the oath was sworn. See *Macknight.*

We who believe, Οἱ πιστευσαντες, is omitted by Chrysostom, and some few MSS. And instead of εισερχομεθα γαρ, *for we do enter,* AC, several others, with the Vulgate and Coptic, read εισερχωμεθα ουν, *therefore let us enter;* and thus it answers to φωβηθωμεν ουν, *therefore let us fear,* ver. 1; but this reading cannot well stand unless οἱ πιστευσαντες be omitted, which is acknowledged by every MS. and version of note and importance. The meaning appears to be this: We Jews, who have believed in Christ, do actually possess that rest—state of happiness in God, produced by peace of conscience and joy in the Holy Ghost—which was typified by the happiness and comfort to be enjoyed by the believing Hebrews, in the possession of the promised land. See before.

From the foundation of the world.] The foundation of the world, καταβολη κοσμου, means the *completion* of the work of creation in six days. In those days was the world, i. e. the whole system of mundane things, begun and perfected; and this appears to be the sense of the expression in this place.

Verse 4. For he spake in a certain place] This *certain place* or *somewhere,* που, is probably Gen. ii. 2; and refers to the completion of the work of creation, and the setting apart the *seventh day* as a day of *rest* for man, and a *type* of everlasting felicity. See the notes on Gen. ii. 1, &c., and see here on chap. ii. 6.

Verse 5. And in this place again] In the ninety-fifth Psalm, already quoted, ver. 3. This was a *second* rest which the Lord promised to the believing, obedient seed of Abraham; and as it was spoken of in the days of David, when the Jews actually possessed this long promised *Canaan,* therefore it is evident that *that* was not the rest which God intended, as the next verse shows.

Verse 6. It remaineth that some must enter therein] Why our translators put in the word *must* here I cannot even conjecture. I hope it was not to serve a system, as some have since used it: "Some *must* go to heaven, for so is the doctrine of the decree; and there *must* be certain persons *infallibly* brought thither as a reward to Christ for his sufferings; and in this the will of man and free agency can have no part," &c, &c. Now, supposing that even all this was true,

710

yet it does not exist either positively or by implication in the text. The words επει ουν απολειπεται τινας εισελθειν εις αυτην, literally translated, are as follows: *Seeing then it remaineth for some to enter into it;* or, *Whereas therefore it remaineth that some enter into it,* which is Dr. *Owen's* translation, *and they to whom it was first preached* (οἱ προτερον ευαγγελισθεντες, they to whom the promise was given; they who first received the good tidings; i. e. the Israelites, to whom was given the promise of entering into the rest of Canaan) *did not enter in because of* their *unbelief;* and the promise still continued to be repeated even in the days of David; therefore, some *other rest* must be intended.

Verse 7. He limiteth a certain day] The term *day* signifies not only *time* in general, but also *present time,* and a particular *space.* Day here seems to have the same meaning as *rest* in some other parts of this verse. The day or time of rest relative to the ancient Jews being over and past, and *a long time* having elapsed between God's displeasure shown to the disobedient Jews in the wilderness and the days of David, and the true rest not having been enjoyed, God in his mercy has *instituted another day*—has given *another dispensation* of mercy and goodness by Christ Jesus; and now it may be said, as formerly, *To-day, if ye will hear his voice, harden not your hearts.* God speaks now as he spoke *before;* his *voice* is in the *Gospel* as it was in the *law.* Believe, love, obey, and ye shall enter into this rest.

Verse 8. For if Jesus had given them rest] It is truly surprising that our translators should have rendered the Ιησους of the text *Jesus,* and not *Joshua,* who is most clearly intended. They must have known that the יהושע *Yehoshua* of the Hebrew, which we write *Joshua,* is everywhere rendered Ιησους, *Jesus,* by the Septuagint; and it is their reading which the apostle follows. It is true the Septuagint generally write Ιησους Ναυη, or Υιος Ναυη, *Jesus Nave,* or *Jesus, son of Nave,* for it is thus they translate נון בן יהושע *Yehoshua ben Nun,* Joshua the son of Nun; and this is sufficient to distinguish it from *Jesus, son of David.* But as Joshua, the captain general of Israel, is above intended, the word should have been written *Joshua,* and not *Jesus.* One MS., merely to prevent the wrong application of the name, has Ιησους ὁ του Ναυη, *Jesus the son of Nave.* *Theodoret* has the same in his comment, and one *Syriac* version has it in the text. It is *Joshua* in Coverdale's Testament, 1535; in Tindal's 1548; in that edited by Edmund Becke, 1549; in Richard Cardmarden's, Rouen, 1565; several

2

A. M. cir. 4067.
A. D. cir. 63.
An. Olymp.
cir. CCX. 3.
A. U. C. cir.
816.

would he not afterward have spoken of another day.

9 There remaineth therefore a ¹ rest to the people ᶠ God.

10 For he that is entered into his rest, he

also hath ceased from his own works, as God *did* from his.)

11 Let us labour therefore to enter into that rest, lest any man fall ᵐ after the same example of ⁿ unbelief.

12 For the word of God *is* ° quick, and

A. M. cir. 4067.
A. D. cir. 63.
An. Olymp.
cir. CCX. 3.
A. U. C. cir.
816.

---

¹ Or, *keeping of a Sabbath.*——ᵐ Chap. iii. 12, 18, 19.——ⁿ Or, *disobe-* dience.——° Isa. xlix. 2; Jer. xxiii. 29; 2 Cor. x. 4, 5; 1 Pet. i. 23.

---

modern translators, Wesley, Macknight, Wakefield, &c., read *Joshua*, as does our own in the *margin.* What a pity it had not been in the text, as all the smaller Bibles have no marginal readings, and many simple people are bewildered with the expression.

The apostle shows that, although Joshua did bring the children of Israel into the promised land, yet this could not be the intended rest, because *long after* this time the Holy Spirit, by David, speaks of this rest; the apostle, therefore, concludes,

Verse 9. *There remaineth therefore a rest to the people of God.*] It was not, 1. The rest of the *Sabbath*; it was not, 2. The *rest* in the *promised land*, for the psalmist wrote long after the days of Joshua; therefore there is *another rest*, a state of *blessedness*, for the people of God; and this is the *Gospel*, the blessings it procures and communicates, and the *eternal glory* which it prepares for, and has promised to, genuine believers.

There are two words in this chapter which we indifferently translate *rest*, καταπαυσις and σαββατισμος· the *first* signifying a *cessation from labour*, so that the weary body is *rested* and *refreshed*; the *second* meaning, not only a rest from labour, but a *religious rest*; *sabbatismus*, a rest of a sacred kind, of which both soul and body partake. This is true, whether we understand the rest as referring to *Gospel blessings*, or to *eternal felicity*, or to *both*.

Verse 10. *For he that is entered into his rest*] The man who has believed in Christ Jesus has entered into his rest; the state of happiness which he has provided, and which is the forerunner of *eternal glory*.

Hath ceased from his own works] No longer depends on the observance of Mosaic rites and ceremonies for his justification and final happiness. He rests from all these *works of the law* as fully as God has rested from his works of *creation*.

Those who restrain the word *rest* to the signification of *eternal glory*, say, that *ceasing from our own works* relates to the *sufferings, tribulations, afflictions*, &c., of this life; as in Rev. xiv. 13. I understand it as including *both*.

In speaking of the *Sabbath*, as typifying a state of blessedness in the other world, the apostle follows the opinions of the Jews of his own and after times. The phrase שבת עלאה ושבת תתאה *shabbath illaah, veshabbath tethaah*, the *sabbath above*, and the *sabbath below*, is common among the Jewish writers; and they think that where the plural number is used, as in Lev. xix. 30: *Ye shall keep my Sabbaths*, that the *lower* and *higher sabbaths* are intended, and that the one is prefigured by the other. See many examples in *Schoettgen*.

Verse 11. *Let us labour therefore*] The word

σπουδασωμεν implies every *exertion* of *body* and *mind* which can be made in reference to the subject. *Rebus aliis omissis, hoc agamus;* All things else omitted, this one thing let us do. We receive grace, improve grace, retain grace, that we may obtain eternal glory.

Lest any man fall] Lest he fall off from the grace of God, from the Gospel and its blessings, and perish everlastingly. This is the meaning of the apostle, who never supposed that a man might not make final shipwreck of faith and of a good conscience, as long as he was in a state of *probation*.

Verse 12. *For the word of God is quick, and powerful*] Commentators are greatly divided concerning the meaning of the phrase Ὁ λογος του Θεου, *the word of God*; some supposing the whole of *Divine revelation* to be intended; others, *the doctrine of the Gospel faithfully preached*; others, the *mind of God* or the *Divine intellect*; and others, the *Lord Jesus Christ*, who is thus denominated in John i. 1, &c., and Rev. xix. 13; the only places in which he is thus *incontestably* characterized in the New Testament. The disputed text, 1 John v. 7, I leave at present out of the question. In the introduction to this epistle I have produced sufficient evidence to make it very probable that St. Paul was the author of this epistle. In this sentiment the most eminent scholars and critics are now agreed. That Jesus Christ, the *eternal, uncreated* WORD, is not meant here, is more than probable from this consideration, that St. Paul, in no part of his thirteen acknowledged epistles, ever thus denominates our blessed Lord; nor is he thus denominated by any other of the New Testament writers except St. John. Dr. Owen has endeavoured to prove the contrary, but I believe to no man's conviction who was able to examine and judge of the subject. He has not been able to find more than two texts which even appeared to look *his* way. The *first* is, Luke i. 2: *Us, which—were eye witnesses, and ministers* του λογου, *of the word*; where it is evident the whole of our Lord's ministry is intended. The *second* is, Acts xx. 32: *I commend you to God, and to the word of his grace*; where nothing but the *gracious doctrine* of salvation by faith, the influence of the Divine Spirit, &c., &c., can be meant: nor is there any legitimate mode of construction with which I am acquainted, by which the words in either place can be *personally* applied to our Lord. That the phrase was applied to denominate the second subsistence in the glorious Trinity, by Philo and the rabbinical writers, I have already proved in my notes on John i., where such observations are alone applicable.

Calmet, who had read all that either the ancients or moderns have said on this subject, and who does not think that Jesus Christ is here intended, speaks

2

A M. cir. 4067.
A. D. cir. 63.
An. Olymp.
cir. CCX. 3.
A. U. C. cir.
816.

powerful, and P sharper than any q two-edged sword, piercing even to the dividing asunder of soul and spirit, and of the joints and marrow; and *is* r a discerner of the thoughts and intents of the heart.

13 s Neither is there any crea-

A M. cir. 4067.
A. D. cir. 63.
An. Olymp.
cir. CCX. 3.
A. U. C. cir.
816.

P Prov. v. 4.——q Eph. vi. 17; Rev. i. 16; ii. 16.——r 1 Cor. xiv. 24, 25.——s Psa. xxxiii. 13, 14; xc. 8; cxxxix. 11, 12.

thus: "None of the properties mentioned here can be denied to the Son of God, the eternal Word; he sees all things, knows all things, penetrates all things, and can do all things. He is the ruler of the heart, and can turn it where he pleases. He enlightens the soul, and calls it gently and efficaciously, *when* and *how* he wills. Finally, he punishes in the most exemplary manner the insults offered to his Father and himself by infidels, unbelievers, and the wicked in general. But it does not appear that the Divine Logos is here intended, 1. Because St. Paul does not use that term to express the Son of God. 2. Because the conjunction γαρ, *for*, shows that this verse is an inference drawn from the preceding, where the subject in question is concerning the eternal rest, and the *means* by which it is to be obtained. It is therefore more natural to explain the term of the *word*, *order*, and *will* of God, for the Hebrews represent the revelation of God as an *active* being, *living*, *all-powerful*, *illumined*, *executing vengeance*, *discerning* and *penetrating all things*. Thus Wisd. xvi. 26: 'Thy children, O Lord, know that it is not the growing of fruits that nourisheth man, but that it is *thy word* that preserveth them that put their trust in thee.' See Deut. viii. 3. That is, the sacred Scriptures point out and appoint all the *means of life*. Again, speaking of the Hebrews who were bitten with the fiery serpents, the same writer says, ver. 12: 'For it was neither herb nor mollifying plaster that restored them to health, but *thy word*, O Lord, which healeth all things;' i. e. which describes and prescribes the means of healing And it is very likely that the *purpose* of God, sending the destroying angel to slay the firstborn in Egypt, is intended by the same expression, Wisd. xviii. 15, 16: '*Thine almighty word* leaped down from heaven out of thy royal throne, *as a fierce man of war* into a land of destruction, and brought thine unfeigned commandment as a *sharp sword*, and, standing up, filled all things with death.' This however may be applied to the eternal Logos, or uncreated Word.

"And this mode of speech is exactly conformable to that of the Prophet Isaiah, lv. 10, 11, where to the word of God, spoken by his prophets, the same kind of powers are attributed as those mentioned here by the apostle: *For as the rain cometh down and the snow from heaven, and returneth not thither, but watereth the earth, and maketh it bring forth and bud, that it may give seed to the sower, and bread to the eater; so shall my* WORD BE *that* GOETH FORTH OUT OF MY MOUTH: *it shall not return unto me void; but it shall accomplish that which I please, and it shall prosper in the thing whereto I sent it.* The centurion seems to speak a similar language, Luke vii. 7: *But say in a word,* (αλλα ειπε λογῳ, *speak to thy word*,) *and my servant shall be healed.*" This is the sum of what this very able commentator says on the subject.

In Dr. Dodd's collections we find the following:—

"*The word of God*, which promises to the faithful an entrance into God's rest in David's time, and now to us, is not a thing which *died* or was *forgotten* us soon as it was uttered, but it *continues* one and the same to all generations; it is ζων, *quick* or *living*. So Isaiah says: *The word of our God shall stand for ever;* chap. xl. 8. Compare chap. li. 6; lv. 11; 1 Esdras iv. 38; John iii. 34; 1 Peter i. 23. *And powerful*, ενεργης, *efficacious, active;* sufficient, if it be not actually hindered, to produce its effects; *effectual*, Philem. 6. See 2 Cor. x. 4; 1 Thess. ii. 13. *And sharper than any two-edged sword;* τομωτερος ὑπερ, *more cutting than.* The word of God *penetrates deeper* into a man than any sword; it enters into the soul and spirit, into all our *sensations, passions, appetites*, nay, to our very *thoughts;* and sits as *judge* of the most *secret intentions, contrivances,* and *sentiments* of the *heart.* Phocylides has an expression very similar to our author, where he says, of *reason,* 'that it is a weapon which penetrates deeper into a man than a sword.' See also Isa. xl. 4; Eph. vi. 17; Rev. i. 16; ii. 16.

"*Piercing even to the dividing asunder of soul and spirit.*—When the *soul* is thus distinguished from the *spirit*, by the former is meant that *inferior faculty* by which we *think of* and *desire* what concerns our *present being* and *welfare.* By *spirit* is meant a *superior power* by which we *prefer future things* to present, by which we are directed to pursue *truth* and *right* above all things, and even to despise what is agreeable to our present state, if it stand in competition with, or is prejudicial to, our *future happiness.* See 1 Thess. v. 23. Some have thought that by the expression before us is implied that the *word of God* is able to bring *death*, as in the case of Ananias and Sapphira; for, say they, if the *soul* and *spirit*, or the *joints* and *marrow* are separated one from another, it is impossible that life can remain. But perhaps the meaning of the latter clause may rather be: 'It can divide the joints and divide the marrow; i. e. enter irresistibly into the soul, and produce some sentiment which perhaps it would not willingly have received; and sometimes discover and punish secret, as well as open wickedness.' Mr. *Pierce* observes that our author has been evidently arguing from a tremendous judgment of God upon the ancient Israelites, the ancestors of those to whom this epistle is directed; and in this verse, to press upon them that care and diligence he had been recommending, he sets before them the efficacy and virtue of the word of God, connecting this verse with the former by a *for* in the beginning of it; and therefore it is natural to suppose that what he says of the *word of God* may have a relation to somewhat remarkable in that sore punishment of which he had been speaking, particularly to the destruction of the people by *lightning*, or *fire from heaven.* See Lev. x. 1–5; Num. xi. 1–3,

2

A. M. cir. 4067.
A. D. cir. 63.
An. Olymp.
cir. CCX. 3.
A. U. C. cir.
816.

ture that is not manifest in his sight: but all things *are* naked [t] and opened unto the eyes of him with whom we have to do.

14 Seeing then that we have [u] a great high priest [v] that is passed into the heavens, Jesus the Son of God, [w] let us hold fast *our* profession.

A. M. cir. 4067
A. D cir. 63.
An. Olymp.
cir. CCX. 3.
A. U. C. cir.
816.

---

[t] Job xxvi. xxxiv. 21; Prov. xv. 11.

[u] Chap. iii. 1.——[v] Chap. vii. 26; ix. 12, 24.——[w] Chap. x. 23.

---

xvi. 35; Psa. lxxviii. 21. All the expressions in this view will receive an additional force, for nothing is more *quick* and *living*, more *powerful* and *irresistible*, *sharp* and *piercing*, than *lightning*. If this idea be admitted, the meaning of the last clause in this verse will be, ' That the word of God is a judge, to censure and punish the evil thoughts and intents of the heart.' And this brings the matter home to the exhortation with which our author began, chap. iii. 12, 13; for under whatever disguise they might conceal themselves, yet, from such tremendous judgments as God executed upon their fathers, they might learn to judge as Moses did, Num. xxxii. 23: *If ye will not do so, ye have sinned against the Lord; and be sure your sin will find you out."* See *Hammond, Whitby, Sykes,* and *Pierce.*

Mr. Wesley's note on this verse is expressed with his usual precision and accuracy :—

" *For the word of God*—preached, ver. 2, and armed with threatenings, ver. 3, *is living and powerful*—attended with the power of the living God, and conveying either life or death to the hearers; *sharper than any two-edged sword*—penetrating the heart more than this does the body; *piercing* quite through, and laying open, *the soul and spirit, joints and marrow*—the inmost recesses of the mind, which the apostle beautifully and strongly expresses by this heap of figurative words; *and is a discerner, not only of the thoughts,* but also of the *intentions.*"

The *law,* and the *word of God* in general, is repeatedly compared to a *two-edged sword* among the Jewish writers, חרב שתי פיפיות *chereb shetey piphiyoth,* the sword with the two mouths. *By this sword* the man *himself lives,* and by it he destroys his enemies. This is implied in its two edges. See also *Schoettgen.*

Is a discerner of the thoughts] Και κριτικος ενθυμησεων και εννοιων καρδιας· *Is a critic of the propensities and suggestions of the heart.* How many have felt this property of God's word where it has been *faithfully* preached! How often has it happened that a man has seen the whole of his own character, and some of the most private transactions of his life, held up as it were to public view by the preacher; and yet the parties absolutely unknown to each other! Some, thus exhibited, have even supposed that their neighbours must have privately informed the preacher of their character and conduct; but it was the *word of God,* which, by the direction and energy of the Divine Spirit, thus searched them out, was a *critical examiner* of the *propensities* and *suggestions of their hearts,* and had pursued them through all their public haunts and private ways. Every genuine minister of the Gospel has witnessed such effects as these under his ministry in repeated instances.

But while this effect of the word or true doctrine

of God is acknowledged, let it not be supposed that *it,* of *itself,* can produce such effects. The word of God is compared to a *hammer* that *breaks* the *rock in pieces,* Jer. xxiii. 29; but will a *hammer* break a *stone* unless it is applied by the *skill* and *strength* of some powerful *agent?* It is here compared to a *two-edged sword;* but will a *sword cut* or *pierce* to the dividing of joints and marrow, or separation of soul and spirit, unless some *hand push* and *direct* it? Surely, no. Nor can even the words and doctrine of God produce any effect but as directed by the experienced teacher, and applied by the Spirit of God. It is an *instrument* the most apt for the accomplishing of its work; but it will do nothing, can do nothing, but as used by the *heavenly workman.* To this is the reference in the next verse.

Verse 13. *Neither is there any creature that is not manifest*] God, from whom this word comes, and by whom it has all its *efficacy,* is infinitely *wise.* He well knew how to construct his word, so as to suit it to the state of all *hearts;* and he has given it that infinite fulness of meaning, so as to suit it to all *cases.* And so infinite is he in his *knowledge,* and so *omnipresent* is he, that the whole creation is constantly *exposed to his view;* nor is there a *creature* of the *affections, mind,* or *imagination,* that is not constantly under his eye. He marks every rising thought, every budding desire; and such as these are supposed to be the *creatures* to which the apostle particularly refers, and which are called, in the preceding verse, the *propensities* and *suggestions of the heart.*

But all things are *naked and opened*] Παντα δε γυμνα και τετραχηλισμενα. It has been supposed that the phraseology here is *sacrificial,* the apostle referring to the case of *slaying* and *preparing* a victim to be *offered* to God. 1. It is *slain;* 2. It is *flayed,* so it is *naked;* 3. It is *cut open,* so that all the intestines are exposed to view; 4. It is carefully *inspected* by the priest, to see that all is *sound* before any part is offered to him who has prohibited all *imperfect* and *diseased* offerings; and, 5. It is *divided* exactly into two equal parts, by being split down the chine from the nose to the rump; and so exactly was this performed, that the spinal marrow was cloven down the centre, one half lying in the divided cavity of each side of the backbone. This is probably the metaphor in 2 Tim. ii. 15, where see the note.

But there is reason to suspect that this is not the metaphor here. The verb τραχηλιζω, from which the apostle's τετραχηλισμενα comes, signifies to have the *neck bent back* so as to expose the face to full view, that every feature might be seen; and this was often done with *criminals,* in order that they might be better *recognized* and *ascertained.* To this custom *Pliny* refers in the very elegant and important panegyric which he delivered on the Emperor Trajan, about

2

A. M. cir. 4067.
A. D. cir. 63.
An. Olymp.
cir. CCX. 3.
A. U. C. cir.
816.

15 For ˣ we have not a high priest which cannot be touched with the feeling of our infirmities : but ʸ was in all points tempted like as *we are,* ᶻ yet without sin.

ˣ Isa. liii. 3 ; chap. ii. 18.——ʸ Luke xxii. 28.——ᶻ 2 Cor. v. 21 ; chap. vii. 26; 1 Pet. ii. 22 ; 1 John iii. 5.

16 ᵃ Let us therefore come boldly unto the throne of grace, that we may obtain mercy, and find grace to help in time of need.

A. M. cir. 4067.
A. D. cir. 63.
An. Olymp.
cir. CCX. 3.
A. U. C. cir.
816.

ᵃ Ephesians ii. 18 ; iii. 12; chapter x. 19, 21, 22.——John x. 9 ; xiv. 6 ;

A. D. 103, when the emperor had made him consul ; where, speaking of the great attention which Trajan paid to the public morals, and the care he took to extirpate informers, &c., he says : *Nihil tamen gratius, nihil sæculo dignius, quam quod contigit* desuper intueri *delatorum supina ora, retortasque cervices. Agnoscebamus et fruebamur, cum velut piaculares publicæ sollicitudinis victimæ, supra sanguinem noxiorum ad lenta supplicia gravioresque pœnas ducerentur. Plin.* Paneg., cap. 34. "There is nothing, however, in this age which affects us more pleasingly, nothing more deservedly, than to behold from above the supine faces and reverted necks of the informers. We thus knew them, and were gratified when, as expiatory victims of the public disquietude, they were led away to lingering punishments, and sufferings more terrible than even the blood of the guilty."

The term was also used to describe the action of *wrestlers* who, when they could, got their hand under the chin of their antagonists, and thus, by bending both the head and neck, could the more easily give them a fall ; this stratagem is sometimes seen in ancient monuments. But some suppose that it refers to the custom of *dragging them by the neck.* Diogenes the philosopher, observing one who had been victor in the Olympic games often fixing his eyes upon a *courtezan,* said, in allusion to this custom : Ιδε κριον αρειμανιον, ως υπο του τυχοντος κορασιου τραχηλιζεται. "See how this mighty champion (martial ram) *is drawn by the neck by a common girl.*" See Stanley, page 305.

With whom we have to do.] Προς ὁν ἡμιν ὁ λογος· *To whom we must give an account.* He is our *Judge,* and is well qualified to be so, as all our hearts and actions are *naked* and *open* to him.

This is the true meaning of λογος in this place ; and it is used in precisely the same meaning in Matt. xii. 36; xviii. 23 ; Luke xvi. 2. Rom. xiv. 12 : *So then every one of us* λογον *δωσει, shall give an account of himself to God.* And Heb. xiii. 17 : *They watch for your souls* ὡς λογον αποδωσοντες, *as those who must give account.* We translate the words, *With whom we have to do ;* of which, though the phraseology is *obsolete,* yet the meaning is nearly the same. 𝕿𝕠 𝖜𝖍𝖔𝖒 𝖆 𝖜𝖔𝖗𝖉𝖊 𝖙𝖔 𝖚𝖘, is the rendering of my old MS. and *Wiclif.* 𝕺𝖋 𝖜𝖍𝖔𝖒 𝖜𝖊 𝖘𝖕𝖊𝖆𝖐𝖊, is the version of our other early translators.

Verse 14. *Seeing then that we have a great high priest*] It is contended, and very properly, that the particle ουν, which we translate *seeing,* as if what followed was an immediate inference from what the apostle had been speaking, should be translated *now ;* for the apostle, though he had before mentioned Christ as the *High Priest of our profession,* chap. iii. 1, and as the *High Priest* who made *reconciliation for the sins of the people,* chap. ii. 17, does not attempt to prove

this in any of the preceding chapters, but now enters upon that point, and discusses it at great length to the end of chap. x.

After all, it is possible that this may be a resumption of the discourse from chap. iii. 6 ; the rest of that chapter, and the preceding thirteen verses of this, being considered as a parenthesis. These parts left out, the discourse runs on with perfect connection. It is very likely that the words, here, are spoken to meet an objection of those Jews who wished the Christians of Palestine to apostatize : "You have no tabernacle—no temple—no high priest—no sacrifice for sin. Without these there can be no religion ; return therefore to us, who have the perfect temple service appointed by God." To these he answers : *We have a High Priest who is passed into the heavens, Jesus, the Son of God ; therefore let us hold fast our profession.* See on chap. iii. 1, to which this verse seems immediately to refer.

Three things the apostle professes to prove in this epistle :—
1. That Christ is greater than the *angels*
2. That he is greater than *Moses.*
3. That he is greater than *Aaron,* and all *high priests*
The *two* former arguments, with their applications and illustrations, he has already despatched ; and now he enters on the *third.* See the *preface* to this epistle.
The apostle states, 1. That we have a *high priest.* 2. That this high priest is Jesus, the *Son of God ;* not a *son* or *descendant* of Aaron, nor coming in that way, but in a more transcendent line.
3. Aaron and his successors could only pass into the holy of holies, and that once a year ; but our High Priest has passed into the heavens, of which that was only the type. There is an allusion here to the high priest going into the holy of holies on the great day of atonement. 1. He left the congregation of the people. 2. He passed through the veil into the holy place, and was not seen even by the priests. 3. He entered through the second veil into the holy of holies, where was the symbol of the majesty of God. Jesus, our High Priest, 1. Left the people at large. 2. He left his disciples by ascending up through the visible heavens, the clouds, as a veil, screening him from their sight. 3. Having passed through these veils, he went immediately to be our Intercessor : thus *he passed* ουρανους, the visible or ethereal heavens, into the presence of the Divine Majesty ; *through the heavens,* διεληλυθοτα τους ουρανους, and the empyreum, or heaven of heavens.

Verse 15. *For we have not a high priest*] To the objection, "Your High Priest, if entered into the heavens, can have no participation with you, and no sympathy for you, because out of the reach of human feelings and infirmities," he answers : Ου γαρ εχομεν

       2

Αρχιερεα μη δυναμενον συμπαθησαι ταις ασθενειαις ημων· *We have not a high priest who cannot sympathize with our weakness.* Though he be the Son of God, as to his *human nature,* and equal in his *Divine nature* with God; yet, having partaken of human nature, and having submitted to all its trials and distresses, and *being in all points tempted like as we are, without* feeling or consenting to *sin;* he is able to succour them that are tempted. See chap. ii. 18, and the note there.

The words κατα παντα καθ' ὁμοιοτητα might be translated, *in all points according to the likeness,* i. e. as far as his human nature could bear affinity to ours; for, though he had a perfect human body and human soul, yet 'that body was perfectly tempered; it was free from all morbid action, and consequently from all *irregular movements.* His *mind,* or *human soul,* being free from all sin, being every way perfect, could feel no *irregular temper,* nothing that was inconsistent with infinite purity. In all these respects he was different from us; and cannot, as *man,* sympathize with us in any feelings of this kind: but, as *God,* he has provided support for the *body* under all its trials and infirmities, and for the *soul* he has provided an *atonement* and *purifying sacrifice;* so that he cleanses the heart from al' unrighteousness, and fills the soul with his Holy Spirit, and makes it his own temple and continual habitation. He took our flesh and blood, a human body and a human soul, and lived a human life. Here was the *likeness of sinful flesh,* Rom. viii. 5; and by *thus* assuming human nature, he was completely qualified to make an atonement for the sins of the world.

Verse 16. *Let us therefore come boldly unto the throne of grace*] The allusion to the high priest, and his office on the day of atonement, is here kept up. The *approach* mentioned here is to the כפרת *kapporeth,* ἱλαστηριον, the *propitiatory* or *mercy-seat.* This was the covering of the ark of the testimony or covenant, at each end of which was a cherub, and between them the *shechinah,* or symbol of the Divine Majesty, which appeared to, and conversed with, the high priest. Here the apostle shows the great superiority of the privileges of the new testament above those of the old; for *there* the high priest *only,* and he with *fear* and *trembling,* was permitted to approach; and that not without the blood of the victim; and if in any thing he transgressed, he might expect to be struck with death. The throne of grace in heaven answers to this propitiatory, but to *this* ALL may approach who feel their need of salvation; and they may approach μετα παρρησιας, *with freedom, confidence, liberty of speech,* in opposition to the *fear* and *trembling* of the Jewish high priest. Here, nothing is to be feared, provided the heart be right with God, truly sincere, and trusting alone in the sacrificial blood.

That we may obtain mercy] Ἱνα λαβωμεν ελεον· *That we may take mercy*—that we may receive the pardon of all our sins; there is mercy for the *taking.*

As Jesus Christ *tasted death* for *every man,* so *every man* may go to that propiatory, and take the mercy that is suited to his degree of guilt.

And find grace] *Mercy* refers to the pardon of sin, and being brought into the favour of God. *Grace* is that by which the soul is supported after it has received this mercy, and by which it is purified from all unrighteousness, and upheld in all trials and difficulties, and enabled to prove faithful unto death.

To help in time of need.] Εις ευκαιρον βοηθειαν· *For a seasonable support;* that is, *support when necessary,* and *as necessary,* and in *due proportion* to the necessity. The word βοηθεια is properly rendered *assistance, help,* or *support;* but it is an assistance in consequence of the *earnest cry* of the person in distress, for the word signifies to *run at the cry,* θειν εις βοην, or επι βοην θειν. So, even at the throne of grace, or great *propitiatory,* no help can be expected where there is no *cry,* and where there is no *cry* there is no *felt* necessity; for he that *feels* he is perishing will *cry aloud* for help, and to such a cry the compassionate High Priest will *run;* and the *time of need* is the time in which God will show mercy; nor will he ever delay it *when* it is *necessary.* We are not to cry *to-day* to be helped *to-morrow,* or at some *indefinite time,* or at the *hour of death.* We are to call for mercy and grace *when we need them;* and we are to expect to receive them *when we call.* This is a part of our *liberty* or *boldness;* we *come up* to the throne, and we *call aloud* for mercy, and God hears and dispenses the blessing we need.

That this exhortation of the apostle may not be lost on us, let us consider :—

1. That there is a *throne of grace,* i. e. a *propitiatory,* the place where God and man are to *meet.*

2. That this propitiatory or mercy-seat is sprinkled with the atoning blood of that *Lamb of God* which taketh away the sin of the world.

3. That we must *come up,* προσερχωμεθα, to this throne; and this implies *faith* in the efficacy of the sacrifice.

4. That we must *call aloud* on God for his mercy, if we expect him to *run* to our assistance.

5. That we must *feel* our spiritual necessities, in order to our *calling* with fervency and earnestness.

6. That calling thus we shall infallibly get what we want; for in Christ Jesus, as a sacrificial offering, God is ever well pleased; and he is also well pleased with all who take refuge in the atonement which he has made.

7. That thus coming, feeling, and calling, we may have the *utmost confidence;* for we have *boldness, liberty of access, freedom of speech;* may plead with our Maker without *fear;* and expect all that heaven has to bestow; because Jesus, who died, sitteth upon the throne! Hallelujah! the Lord God Omnipotent reigneth.

8. All these are reasons why we should persevere.

CHAPTER V.

The nature of the high priesthood of Christ ; his pre-eminence, qualifications, and order, 1–10. Imperfect state of the believing Hebrews, and the necessity of spiritual improvement, 11–14.

A. M. cir. 4067.
A. D. cir. 63.
An. Olymp,
cir. CCX. 3.
A. U. C. cir.
816.

FOR every high priest taken from among men [a] is ordained for men [b] in things *pertaining to* God, [c] that he may offer both gifts and sacrifices for sins :

2 [d] Who [e] can have compassion on the ignorant, and on them that are out of the way;

for that [f] he himself also is compassed with infirmity.

3 And [g] by reason hereof he ought, as for the people, so also for himself, to offer for sins.

4 [h] And no man taketh this honour unto himself, but he that is called of God, as [i] *was* Aaron.

A. M. cir. 4067.
A. D. cir. 63.
An. Olymp.
cir. CCX. 3.
A. U. C. cir.
816.

---

[a] Chap. iii. 3.——[b] Chap. ii. 17.——[c] Chapter viii. 3, 4; ix. 9; x. 11 ; xi 4.——[d] Chap. ii. 18; iv. 15.——[e] Or, *can reasonably bear with.*——[f] Chap. vii. 28.

[g] Lev. iv. 3; ix. 7; xvi. 6; xv. 16, 17; chapter vii. 27; ix. 7. [h] 2 Chron. xxvi. 18; John iii. 27.——[i] Exodus xxviii. 1; Num. xvi. 5, 40; 1 Chron. xxiii. 13.

NOTES ON CHAP. V.

Verse 1. *For every high priest taken from among men*] This seems to refer to Lev. xxi. 10, where it is intimated that the high priest shall .be taken מאחיו *meachaiv*, from his brethren; i. e. he shall be of the tribe of Levi, and of the family of Aaron.

Is ordained for men] Ὑπερ ανθρωπων καθισταται τα προς τον Θεον· Is appointed to preside over the Divine worship in those things which relate to man's salvation.

That he may offer both gifts and sacrifices for sins] God ever appeared to all his followers in two points of view : 1. As the author and dispenser of all temporal good. 2. As their lawgiver and judge. In reference to this twofold view of the Divine Being, his worship was composed of two different parts : 1. *Offerings* or *gifts.* 2. *Sacrifices.* 1. As the creator and dispenser of all good, he had *offerings* by which his *bounty* and *providence* were acknowledged. 2. As the *lawgiver* and *judge*, against whose injunctions offences had been committed, he had *sacrifices* offered to him to make atonement for sin. The δωρα, or *gifts*, mentioned here by the apostle, included every kind of *eucharistical* offering. The θυσιαι, *sacrifices*, included *victims* of every sort, or *animals* whose lives were to be offered in sacrifice, and their blood poured out before God, as an atonement for sins. The high priest was the mediator between God and the people; and it was his office, when the people had brought these gifts and sacrifices, to offer them to God in their behalf. The people could not legitimately offer their own offerings, they must be all brought to the priest, and he alone could present them to God. As we have a high priest over the house of God, to offer all *our gifts* and his *own sacrifice*, therefore we may come with boldness to the throne of grace. See above.

Verse 2. *Who can have compassion on the ignorant*] The word μετριοπαθειν signifies, not merely to have compassion, but to *act with moderation*, and to *bear with each* in *proportion* to his ignorance, weakness, and untoward circumstances, all taken into consideration with the offences he has committed : in a word, to *pity*, *feel for*, and *excuse*, as far as possible; and, when the provocation is at the highest, to *moderate one's passion* towards the culprit, and be *ready to pardon*; and when punishment must be administered, to do it in the *gentlest manner.*

Instead of αγνοουσι, *the ignorant*, one MS. only, but that of high repute, has ασθενουσι, *the weak.* Most men sin much through *ignorance*, but this does not excuse them if they have within reach the means of instruction. And the great majority of the human race sin through *weakness.* The principle of evil is *strong* in them; the occasions of sin are many; through their fall from God they are become exceedingly *weak*; and what the apostle calls, chap. xii. 1, that ευπεριστατον ἁμαρτιαν, *the well-circumstanced sin*, often occurs to every man. But, as in the above case, weakness itself is no excuse, when the means of strength and succour are always at hand. However, all these are circumstances which the Jewish high priest took into consideration, and they are certainly not less attended to by the High Priest of our profession.

The reason given why the high priest should be slow to punish and prone to forgive is, that he himself is also *compassed with weakness*; περικειται ασθενειαν, *weakness lies all around him*, it is his *clothing*; and as he feels his clothing, so should he feel *it*; and as he feels it, so he should deplore it, and compassionate others.

Verse 3. *And by reason hereof*] As he is also a transgressor of the commands of God, and unable to observe the law in its spirituality, he must offer sacrifices for sin, not only for the people, but for himself also : this must teach him to have a fellow feeling for others.

Verse 4. *This honour*] Την τιμην undoubtedly signifies here *the office*, which is one meaning of the word in the best Greek writers. It is here an *honourable office*, because the man is the high priest of God, and is appointed by God himself to that office.

But he that is called of God, as was Aaron.] God himself appointed the tribe and family out of which the high priest was to be taken, and Aaron and his sons were expressly chosen by God to fill the office of the high priesthood. As God alone had the right to appoint his own priest for the Jewish nation, and *man* had no authority here; so God alone could provide and appoint a high priest for the whole human race. Aaron was thus appointed for the Jewish people ; Christ, for all mankind.

Some make this " an argument for the *uninterrupted succession of popes and their bishops* in the Church,

2

A. M. cir. 4067.
A. D. cir. 63.
An. Olymp.
cir. CCX. 3.
A. U. C. cir.
816.

5 ^k So also Christ glorified not himself to be made a high priest; but he that said unto him, ^l Thou art my Son, to-day have I begotten thee.

A. M. cir. 4067
A. D. cir. 63.
An. Olymp.
cir. CCX. 3.
A. U. C. cir.
816.

6 As he saith also in another place, ^m Thou *art* a priest for ever, after the order of Melchisedec.

7 Who in the days of his flesh, when he

---

^k John viii. 54.——^l Psa. ii. 7 ; chap. i. 5.

^m Psa. cx. 4 ; chap. vii. 17, 21.

---

who alone have the authority to ordain for the sacerdotal office ; and whosoever is not thus appointed is, with them, illegitimate." It is idle to employ time in proving that there is no such thing as an *uninterrupted succession* of this kind ; it does not exist, it never did exist. It is a silly fable, invented by ecclesiastical tyrants, and supported by clerical coxcombs. But were it even true, it has nothing to do with the text. It speaks merely of the appointment of a high priest, the succession to be preserved in the tribe of Levi, and in the family of Aaron. But even this succession was *interrupted* and *broken*, and the office itself was to cease on the coming of Christ, after whom there could be no high priest ; nor can Christ have any successor, and therefore he is said to be *a priest for ever*, for he ever liveth the intercessor and sacrifice for mankind. The verse, therefore, has nothing to do with the *clerical office*, with preaching God's holy word, or administering the sacraments ; and those who quote it in this way show how little they understand the Scriptures, and how ignorant they are of the nature of their own office.

Verse 5. Christ glorified not himself] The man Jesus Christ, was also appointed by God to this most awful yet glorious office, of being the High Priest of the whole human race. The Jewish high priest represented this by the sacrifices of beasts which he offered ; the Christian High Priest must offer *his own life* : Jesus Christ did so ; and, rising from the dead, he ascended to heaven, and there ever appeareth in the presence of God for us. Thus he has *reassumed the sacerdotal office* ; and because he *never dies*, he can never have a *successor*. He can have no *vicars*, either in heaven or upon earth ; those who pretend to be such are impostors, and are worthy neither of respect nor credit.

Thou art my Son] See on chap. i. 5, and the observations at the end of that chapter. And thus it appears that God can have no high priest but his Son ; and to that office none can now pretend without blasphemy, for the Son of God is still the High Priest in his temple.

Verse 6. He saith also in another place] That is, in Psa. cx. 4, a psalm of extraordinary importance, containing a very striking prediction of the birth, preaching, suffering, death, and conquests of the Messiah. See the notes there. For the mode of quotation here, see the note on chap. ii. 6.

Thou art *a priest for ever*] As long as the sun and moon endure, Jesus will continue to be high priest to all the successive generations of men, as he was the Lamb slain from the foundation of the world. If he be a priest *for ever*, there can be no *succession of priests* ; and if he have all power in heaven and in earth, and if he be present wherever two or three

2

are gathered together in his name, he can have no *vicars* ; nor can the Church need one to act in *his place*, when he, from the necessity of his nature, fills all places, and is everywhere present. This one consideration nullifies all the pretensions of the Romish pontiff, and proves the whole to be a tissue of imposture

After the order of Melchisedec.] Who this person was must still remain a secret. We know nothing more of him than is written in Gen. xiv. 18, &c., where see the notes, and particularly the observations at the end of that chapter, in which this very mysterious person is represented as a type of Christ.

Verse 7. Who in the days of his flesh] The time of his incarnation, during which he took all the infirmities of human nature upon him, and was afflicted in his body and human soul just as other men are, irregular and sinful passions excepted.

Offered up prayers and supplications] This is one of the most difficult places in this epistle, if not in the whole of the New Testament. The labours of learned men upon it have been prodigious ; and even in *their* sayings it is hard to find the meaning.

I shall take a *general view* of this and the two following verses, and then examine the particular expressions.

It is probable that the apostle refers to something in the agony of our Lord, which the evangelists have not distinctly marked.

The Redeemer of the world appears here as simply man ; but he is the representative of the whole human race. He must make expiation for sin by *suffering*, and he can suffer only as *man*. *Suffering* was as necessary as *death* ; for man, because he has *sinned*, must *suffer*, and because he has *broken the law*, should *die*. Jesus took upon himself the nature of man, subject to all the trials and distresses of human nature. He is now making atonement ; and he begins with sufferings, as sufferings commence with human life ; and he terminates with death, as that is the *end* of human existence in this world. *Though he was the Son of God*, conceived and born without sin, or any thing that could render him *liable* to suffering or death, and only suffered and died through infinite condescension ; yet, to constitute him a complete Saviour, he must submit to whatever the law required ; and therefore he is stated to have *learned* OBEDIENCE *by the things which he suffered*, ver. 8, that is, *subjection* to all the requisitions of the law ; and being *made perfect*, that is, having *finished* the whole by *dying*, he, by these means, became the *author of eternal salvation to all them who obey him*, ver. 9 ; to them who, according to his own command, repent and believe the Gospel, and, under the influence of his Spirit, walk in holiness of life. " But he appears to be under the most dreadful apprehension of death ; for *he offered*

A. M. cir. 4067.
A. D. cir. 63.
An. Olymp.
cir. CCX. 3.
A. U. C. cir.
816.

had [n] offered up prayers and supplications, [o] with strong crying and tears, unto him [p] that was able to save him from death,

and was heard [q] in [r] that he feared ;

8 [s] Though he were a Son, yet learned he [t] obedience

A. M. cir. 4067
A. D. cir. 63.
An. Olymp.
cir. CCX. 3.
A. U. C. cir.
816.

---

[n] Matt. xxvi. 39, 42, 44 ; Mark xiv. 36, 39 ; John xvii. 1.——[o] Psa. xxii. 1 ; Matt. xxvii. 46, 50 ; Mark xv. 34, 37.——[p] Matt. xxvi. 53 ;

Mark xiv. 36.——[q] Or, *for his piety.*——[r] Matt. xxvi. 37 ; Mark xiv. 33 ; Luke xxii. 44 ; John xii. 27.——[s] Ch. iii. 6.——[t] Phil. ii. 8.

---

up prayers and supplications, with strong crying and tears, unto him that was able to save him from death, ver. 7." I shall consider this first in the common point of view, and refer to the subsequent notes. This fear of death was in Christ a widely different thing from what it is in men ; *they* fear death because of what *lies beyond* the grave ; *they* have *sinned,* and they are afraid to meet their *Judge.* Jesus could have no fear on these grounds : he was now suffering for man, and he felt as *their* expiatory victim ; and God only can tell, and perhaps neither men nor angels can conceive, how great the suffering and agony must be which, in the sight of infinite Justice, was requisite to make this atonement. *Death,* temporal and eternal, was the portion of man ; and now Christ is to *destroy death* by agonizing and dying ! The tortures and torments necessary to effect this destruction Jesus Christ alone could feel, Jesus Christ alone could sustain, Jesus Christ alone can comprehend. We are referred to them in this most solemn verse ; but the apostle himself only drops *hints,* he does not attempt to explain them : he prayed ; he supplicated with strong crying and tears ; and he was *heard* in reference to that *which he feared.* His prayers, as our *Mediator,* were answered ; and his sufferings and death were complete and effectual as our *sacrifice.* This is the glorious sum of what the apostle here states ; and it is enough. We may hear it with awful respect ; and adore him with silence whose grief had nothing common in it to that of other men, and is not to be estimated according to the measures of human miseries. It was

A weight of wo, more than whole worlds could bear.

I shall now make some remarks on particular expressions, and endeavour to show that the words may be understood with a shade of difference from the common acceptation.

Prayers and supplications, &c.] There may be an allusion here to the manner in which the Jews speak of prayer, &c. "Rabbi Yehudah said : All human things depend on repentance and the *prayers* which men make to the holy blessed God ; especially if *tears* be poured out with the prayers. There is no *gate* which *tears* will not pass through." *Sohar, Exod.,* fol. 5.

"There are three degrees of prayer, each surpassing the other in sublimity ; *prayer, crying,* and *tears :* prayer is made in silence ; crying, with a loud voice ; but tears surpass all." *Synops. Sohar,* p. 33.

The apostle shows that Christ made every species of prayer, and those especially by which they allowed a man must be successful with his Maker.

The word ικετηριας, which we translate *supplications,* exists in no other part of the New Testament.

Ικετης signifies a *supplicant,* from ικομαι, *I come* or *approach ;* it is used in this connection by the purest Greek writers. Nearly the same words are found in Isocrates, *De Pace :* Ικετηριας πολλας και δεησεις ποιουμενοι *Making many supplications and prayers.* Ικετηρια, says Suidas, καλειται ελαιας κλαδος, στεμματι εστεμμενος·——εστιν, ην οι δεομενοι κατατιθενται που, η μετα χειρας εχουσιν· " *Hiketeria* is a branch of olive, rolled round with wool——is what suppliants were accustomed to deposite in some place, or to carry in their hands." And ικετης, *hiketes,* he defines to be, ὁ δουλοπρεπως παρακαλων, και δεομενος περι τινος ὁτουουν· " He who, in the most humble and servile manner, entreats and begs any thing from another." In reference to this custom the Latins used the phrase *velamenta prætendere,* "to hold forth these covered branches," when they made supplication ; and *Herodian* calls them ικετηριας θαλλους, "branches of supplication." *Livy* mentions the custom frequently ; see lib. xxv. cap. 25 ; lib. xxix. c. 16 ; lib. xxxv. c. 34 ; lib. xxxvi. c. 20. The place in lib. xxix. c. 16, is much to the point, and shows us the full force of the word, and nature of the custom. " *Decem legati Locrensium, obsiti squalore et sordibus, in comitio sedentibus consulibus* velamenta supplicium, ramos oleæ (*ut Græcis mos est,*) porrigentes, *ante tribunal cum flebili vociferatione humi procubuerunt.*" " Ten delegates from the Locrians, squalid and covered with rags, came into the hall where the consuls were sitting, *holding out in their hands olive branches covered with wool,* according to the custom of the Greeks, and prostrated themselves on the ground before the tribunal, with weeping and loud lamentation." This is a remarkable case, and may well illustrate our Lord's situation and conduct. The Locrians, pillaged, oppressed, and ruined by the consul, Q. *Plemmius,* send their delegates to the Roman government to implore protection and redress ; they, the better to represent their situation, and that of their oppressed fellow citizens, take the *hiketeria,* or *olive branch wrapped round with wool,* and present themselves before the consuls in open court, and with wailing and loud outcries make known their situation. The senate heard, arrested Plemmius, loaded him with chains, and he expired in a dungeon. Jesus Christ, the representative of and delegate from the whole human race, oppressed and ruined by Satan and sin, with the *hiketeria,* or ensign of a most distressed suppliant, presents himself before the throne of God, with *strong crying and tears,* and prays against *death* and his ravages, in behalf of those whose representative he was ; and he *was heard in that he feared*—the evils were removed, and the oppressor cast down. Satan was bound, he was spoiled of his dominion, and is reserved in chains of darkness to the judgment of the great day.

     2

A. M. cir. 4067.
A. D. cir. 63.
An. Olymp.
cir. CCX. 3.
A. U. C. cir.
816.

by the things which he suffered;

9 And ᵘ being made perfect, he became the author of eternal

salvation unto all them that obey him;

10 Called of God a high priest, ᵛ after the order of Melchisedec.

A. M. cir. 4067.
A. D. cir. 63.
An. Olymp.
cir. CCX. 3.
A. U. C. cir.
816.

ᵘ Chap. ii. 10; xi. 40.

ᵛ Ver. 6; chap. vi. 20.

Every scholar will see that the words of the Roman historian answer exactly to those of the apostle; and the allusion in both is to the same custom. I do not approve of allegorizing or spiritualizing; but the allusion and similarity of the expressions led me to make this application. Many others would make more of this circumstance, as the allusion in the text is so pointed to this custom. Should it appear to any of my readers that I should, after the example of great names, have gone into this house of Rimmon, and bowed myself there, they will pardon their servant in this thing.

To save him from death] I have already observed that Jesus Christ was the *representative* of the human race; and have made some observations on the peculiarity of his sufferings, following the common acceptation of the words in the text, which things are true, howsoever the text may be interpreted. But here we may consider the pronoun *αυτον, him,* as implying the *collective body* of mankind; *the children who were partakers of flesh and blood,* chap. ii. 14; *the seed of Abraham,* ver. 16, *who through fear of death were all their life subject to bondage.* So he made *supplication with strong crying and tears to him who was able to save* THEM *from death;* for I consider the *τουτους, them,* of chap. ii. 15, the same or implying the same thing as *αυτον, him,* in this verse; and, thus understood, all the difficulty vanishes away. On this interpretation I shall give a paraphrase of the whole verse: *Jesus Christ, in the days of his flesh,* (for he was incarnated that he might redeem the *seed of Abraham,* the fallen race of man,) and in his expiatory sufferings, when representing the whole human race, *offered up prayers and supplications, with strong crying and tears, to him who was able to save* THEM *from death:* the intercession was prevalent, the passion and sacrifice were accepted, the sting of death was extracted, and Satan was dethroned.

If it should be objected that this interpretation occasions a very unnatural change of *person* in these verses, I may reply that the change made by my construction is not greater than that made between verses 6 and 7; in the first of which the apostle speaks of *Melchisedec,* who at the conclusion of the verse appears to be antecedent to the relative *who* in ver. 7; and yet, from the nature of the subject, we must understand Christ to be meant. And I consider, ver. 8, *Though he were a Son, yet learned he obedience by the things which he suffered,* as belonging, not only to Christ considered in his *human nature,* but also to him in his *collective capacity;* i. e., belonging to all the sons and daughters of God, who, by means of suffering and various chastisements, *learn submission, obedience* and *righteousness;* and this very subject the apostle treats in considerable detail in chap. xii. 2–11, to which the reader will do well to refer.

Verse 8. *Though he were a Son*] See the whole of the preceding note.

Verse 9. *And being made perfect*] Και τελειωθεις· And having *finished* all—having *died* and *risen again.* Τελειωθηναι signifies to have *obtained the goal;* to have *ended one's labour,* and enjoyed the fruits of it. Chap. xii. 23: *The spirits of just men made perfect,* πνευμασι δικαιων τετελειωμενων, means the souls of those who have gained *the goal,* and *obtained the prize.* So, when Christ had *finished* his course of tremendous sufferings, and consummated the whole by his death and resurrection, he became αιτιος σωτηριας αιωνιου, *the cause of eternal salvation unto all them who obey him.* He was consecrated both high priest and sacrifice by his offering upon the cross.

" In this verse," says Dr. Macknight, " *three things* are clearly stated: 1. That *obedience* to Christ is equally necessary to salvation with *believing* on him. 2. That he was made perfect as a high priest by offering himself a sacrifice for sin, chap. viii. 3. 3. That, by the merit of that sacrifice, he hath obtained pardon and eternal life for them who obey him." He *tasted death* for *every man;* but he is the *author* and *cause* of eternal salvation only to them who *obey him.* It is not merely *believers,* but obedient believers, that shall be finally saved. Therefore this text is an absolute, unimpeachable evidence, that it is not the imputed obedience of Christ that saves any man. Christ has bought men by his blood; and by the infinite merit of his death he has purchased for them an endless glory; but, in order to be prepared for it, the sinner must, through that grace which God withholds from no man, repent, turn from sin, believe on Jesus as being a sufficient ransom and sacrifice for his soul, receive the gift of the Holy Ghost, be a worker together with him, walk in conformity to the Divine will through this Divine aid, and continue faithful unto death, through him, out of whose fulness he may receive grace upon grace.

Verse 10. *Called of God a high priest*] Προσαγορευθεις· Being *constituted, hailed,* and *acknowledged* to be a high priest. In *Hesychius* we find προσαγορευει, which he translates ασπαζεται· hence we learn that one meaning of this word is *to salute;* as when a man was constituted or anointed king, those who accosted him would say, *Hail, king!* On this verse Dr. Macknight has the following note, with the insertion of which the reader will not be displeased: " As our Lord, in his conversation with the Pharisees, recorded Matt. xxii. 43, spake of it as a thing certain of itself, and universally known and acknowledged by the Jews, that David wrote the 110th Psalm by inspiration, concerning the Christ or Messiah; the apostle was well founded in applying the whole of that Psalm to Jesus. Wherefore, having quoted the fourth verse, *Thou art a priest for ever after the order of Mel-*

A. M. cir. 4067.
A. D. cir. 63.
An. Olymp.
cir. CCX. 3.
A. U. C. cir.
816.

11 Of whom ^w we have many things to say, and hard to be uttered, seeing ye are ^x dull of hearing.

12 For when for the time ye ought to be

teachers, ye have need that one teach you again which *be* ^y the first principles of the oracles of God; and are become such as have need of ^z milk, and not of strong meat.

A. M. cir. 4067.
A. D. cir. 63.
An. Olymp.
cir. CCX. 3.
A. U. C. cir.
816.

^w John xvi. 12; 2 Pet. iii. 16.——^x Matt. xiii. 15.

^y Chap. vi. 1.——^z 1 Cor. iii. 1, 2, 3.

chisedec, as directed to Messiah, David's Lord, he justly termed that speech of the Deity a *salutation* of Jesus, according to the true import of the word προσαγορευθεις, which properly signifies to *address* one by his *name*, or *title*, or *office;* accordingly *Hesychius* explains προσαγορευομαι by ασπαζομαι. Now, that the deep meaning of this *salutation* may be understood, I observe, *First*, that, by the testimony of the inspired writers, Jesus sat down at the right hand of God when he returned to heaven, after having finished his ministry upon earth; Mark xvi. 19; Acts vii. 56; Heb. i. 3; viii. 1; 1 Pet. iii. 22. Not, however, *immediately*, but *after* that he had offered the sacrifice of himself in heaven, by presenting his crucified body before the presence of God; Heb. i. 3; x. 10. *Secondly*, I observe, that God's *saluting* Messiah *a priest after the order of Melchisedec*, being mentioned in the psalm after God is said to have invited him *to sit at his right hand*, it is reasonable to think the salutation was given him after he had offered the sacrifice of himself, and had taken his seat at God's right hand. Considered in this order, the *salutation* of Jesus, as a priest *after the order of Melchisedec*, was a public declaration on the part of God that he accepted the sacrifice of himself, which Jesus then offered, as a sufficient atonement for the sin of the world, and approved of the whole of his ministrations on earth, and confirmed all the effects of that meritorious sacrifice. And whereas we are informed in the psalm that, after God had *invited* his Son, in the human nature, to sit at his right hand as Governor of the world, and foretold the blessed fruits of his government, he published the *oath* by which he made him *a Priest for ever*, before he sent him into the world to accomplish the salvation of mankind; and declared that he would never repent of that oath: *The Lord hath sworn, and will not repent; Thou art a Priest for ever after the similitude of Melchisedec.* It was, in effect, a solemn publication of the method in which God would pardon sinners; and a promise that the effects of his Son's government as a *King*, and of his ministrations as a *Priest*, should be eternal; see chap. vi. 20. Moreover, as this solemn declaration of the dignity of the Son of God, as a King and a Priest for ever in the human nature, was made in the hearing of the angelical hosts, it was designed for this instruction, that they might understand their subordination to God's Son, and pay him that homage that is due to him as Governor of the world, and as Saviour of the human race; Phil. ii. 9, 10; Heb. i. 6. The above explanation of the import of God's *saluting* Jesus a Priest for ever, is founded on the apostle's reasonings in the *seventh* and following chapters, where he enters into the deep meaning of the *oath* by which that salutation was conferred."

Verse 11. *Of whom we have many things to say*]

The words περι ου, which we translate *of whom*, are variously applied: 1. To *Melchisedec*; 2. To *Christ*; 3. To the *endless priesthood*. Those who understand the place of *Melchisedec*, suppose that it is in reference to this that the apostle resumes the subject in the *seventh* chapter, where much more is said on this subject, though not very difficult of comprehension; and indeed it is not to be supposed that the Hebrews could be more capable of understanding the subject when the apostle wrote the *seventh chapter* than they were when, a few hours before, he had written the *fifth*. It is more likely, therefore, that the words are to be understood as meaning *Jesus*, or that *endless priesthood*, of which he was a little before speaking, and which is a subject that carnal Christians cannot easily comprehend.

Hard to be uttered] Δυσερμηνευτος· *Difficult to be interpreted*, because Melchisedec was a *typical* person. Or if it refer to the *priesthood* of *Christ*, that is still more difficult to be explained, as it implies, not only his being *constituted a priest* after this *typical* order, but his paying down the *ransom* for the sins of the whole world; and his *satisfying the Divine justice* by this sacrifice, but also thereby opening the kingdom of heaven to all believers, and giving the whole world an entrance to the holy of holies by his blood.

Dull of hearing.] Νωθροι ταις ακοαις· Your souls do not *keep pace* with the doctrines and exhortations delivered to you. As νωθρος signifies a person *who walks heavily* and makes *little speed*, it is here elegantly applied to those who are called to the Christian race, have the road laid down plain before them, how to proceed specified, and the blessings to be obtained enumerated, and yet make *no exertions* to get on, but are always learning, and never able to come to the full knowledge of the truth.

Verse 12. *For when for the time*] They had heard the Gospel for *many years*, and had professed to be Christians for a *long time;* on these accounts they might reasonably have been expected to be well instructed in Divine things, so as to be able to instruct others.

Which be the first principles] Τινα τα στοιχεια· *Certain first principles* or *elements*. The word τινα is not the nominative plural, as our translators have supposed, but the accusative case, governed by διδασκειν· and therefore the literal translation of the passage is this: *Ye have need that one teach you a second time* (παλιν) *certain elements of the doctrines of Christ*, or *oracles of God;* i. e. the notices which the prophets gave concerning the *priesthood* of Jesus Christ, such as are found in Psa. cx., and in Isa. liii. By the *oracles of God* the writings of the *Old Testament* are undoubtedly meant.

And are become such] The words seem to intimate that they had once been better instructed, and

2

A. M. cir. 4067.
A. D. cir. 63.
An. Olymp.
cir. CCX. 3.
A. U. C. cir.
816.

13 For every one that useth milk [a] *is* unskilful in the word of righteousness ; for he is [b] a babe.
14 But strong meat belongeth

to them that are [c] of full age, *even* those who by reason [d] of use have their senses exercised [e] to discern both good and evil.

A. M. cir. 4067.
A. D. cir. 63.
An. Olymp.
cir. CCX. 3.
A. U. C. cir.
816.

---

[a] Gr. *hath no experience.*——[b] 1 Cor. xiii. 11 ; xiv. 20 ; Eph. iv. 14 ; 1 Pet. ii. 2.——[c] Or, *perfect* ; 1 Cor. ii. 6 ; Eph. iv. 13 ;

Phil. iii. 15.——[d] Or, *of a habit*, or, *perfection.*——[e] Isa. vii. 15 ; 1 Cor. ii. 14, 15.

---

had now forgotten that teaching ; and this was occasioned by their being *dull of hearing* ; either they had not *continued* to hear, or they had heard so *carelessly* that they were not profited by what they heard. They had probably totally omitted the preaching of the Gospel, and consequently forgotten all they had learned. Indeed, it was to reclaim those Hebrews from backsliding, and preserve them from total *apostasy,* that this epistle was written.

Such as have need of milk] *Milk* is a metaphor by which many authors, both sacred and profane, express the *first principles* of *religion* and *science* ; and they apply *sucking* to learning ; and every student in his novitiate, or commencement of his studies, was likened to an *infant* that derives all its nourishment from the breast of its mother, not being able to digest any other kind of food. On the contrary, those who had well learned all the first principles of religion and science, and knew how to apply them, were considered as *adults* who were capable of receiving στερεα τροφη, *solid food* ; i. e. the more difficult and sublime doctrines. The rabbins abound with this figure ; it occurs frequently in *Philo,* and in the Greek ethic writers also. In the famous Arabic poem called البردة *al Bordah,* written by Abi Abdallah Mohammed ben Said ben Hamad Albusiree, in praise of Mohammed and his religion, every couplet of which ends with the letter م *mim,* the first letter in *Mohammed's* name, we meet with a couplet that contains a similar sentiment to that of the apostle :—

و التغتش كالطفل ان تهمله شب علي
حب الرضاع وان تفطمه ينفطم

"The soul is like to a young infant, which, if permitted, will grow up to manhood in the love of sucking ; but if thou take it from the breast it will feel itself weaned."

Dr. Owen observes that there are two sorts of hearers of the Gospel, which are here expressed by an elegant metaphor or similitude ; this consists, 1. In the *conformity* that is between bodily food and the Gospel as preached. 2. In the *variety* of natural food as suited to the various states of them that feed on it, answered by the truths of the Gospel, which are of *various kinds* ; and, in exemplification of this metaphor, natural food is reduced to two kinds : 1. *milk* ; 2. *strong* or *solid meat* ; and those who feed on these are reduced to two sorts : 1. *children* ; 2. *men of ripe age.* Both of which are applied to hearers of the Gospel.

1. Some there are who are νηπιοι, babes or *infants,* and some are τελειοι, perfect or *full grown.*

2. These *babes* are described by a double property : 1. They are *dull of hearing* ; 2. They are *unskilful in the word of righteousness.*

In opposition to this, those who are *spiritually adult* are,

1. They who are *capable of instruction.*

2. Such as *have their senses exercised to discern both good and evil.*

3. The different means to be applied to these different sorts for their good, according to their respective conditions, are expressed in the terms of the metaphor : to the first, γαλα, *milk* ; to the others, στερεα τροφη, *strong meat.* All these are comprised in the following scheme :—

The hearers of the Gospel are,

I. Νηπιοι· BABES or INFANTS.	II. Τελειοι· PERFECT or ADULT
Who are	Who are
1. Νωθροι ταις ακοαις· *Dull of hearing.*	1. Φρονιμοι· *Wise and prudent.*
2. Απειροι λογου δικαιοσυνης· *Inexperienced in the doctrine of righteousness.*	2. Τα αισθητηρια γεγυμνασμενα εχοντες· *And have their senses properly exercised.*
These have need	These have need
Γαλακτος· Of *milk.*	Στερεας τροφης· Of *solid food.*

But all these are to derive their nourishment or spiritual instruction εκ των λογιων του Θεου, *from the oracles of God.* The word *oracle,* by which we translate the λογιον of the apostle, is used by the best Greek writers to signify a *divine speech,* or *answer of a deity to a question proposed.* It always implied a *speech* or *declaration* purely *celestial,* in which man had no part ; and it is thus used wherever it occurs in the New

Testament. 1. It signifies the LAW received from God by Moses, Acts vii. 38.

2. The *Old Testament* in general ; the holy men of old having spoken by the *inspiration* of the Divine Spirit, Rom. iii. 2, and in the text under consideration.

3. It signifies *Divine revelation* in general, because all delivered immediately from God, 1 Thess. ii. 13 ; 1 Pet. iv. 11. When we consider what respect was

paid by the heathens to their *oracles*, which were supposed to be delivered by those gods who were the objects of their adoration, but which were only *impostures*, we may then learn what respect is due to the *true oracles* of God.

Among the heathens the credit of oracles was so great, that in all doubts and disputes their determinations were held sacred and inviolable; whence vast numbers flocked to them for advice in the management of their affairs, and no business of any importance was undertaken, scarcely any war waged or peace concluded, any new form of government instituted or new laws enacted, without the advice and approbation of the oracle. *Crœsus*, before he durst venture to declare war against the Persians, consulted not only the most famous oracles of Greece, but sent ambassadors as far as Libya, to ask advice of Jupiter Ammon. *Minos*, the Athenian lawgiver, professed to receive instructions from Jupiter how to model his intended government; and *Lycurgus*, legislator of Sparta, made frequent visits to the Delphian Apollo, and received from him the platform of the Lacedemonian commonwealth. See *Broughton*.

What a reproach to Christians, who hold the Bible to be a collection of the oracles of God, and who not only do not consult it in the momentous concerns of either this or the future life, but go in direct opposition to it! Were every thing conducted according to these oracles, we should have neither war nor desolation in the earth; families would be well governed, and individuals universally made happy.

Those who consulted the ancient oracles were obliged to go to enormous expenses, both in *sacrifices* and in *presents* to the *priests*. And when they had done so, they received oracles which were so *equivocal*, that, howsoever the event fell out, they were capable of being interpreted *that way*.

Verse 13. *For every one that useth milk*] It is very likely that the apostle, by using this term, refers to the *doctrines of the law*, which were only the *rudiments* of religion, and were intended to lead us to Christ, that we might be justified by faith.

The word of righteousness] Λογου δικαιοσυνης· The *doctrine of justification*. I believe this to be the apostle's meaning. He that uses *milk*—rests in the ceremonies and observances of the law, *is unskilful in the doctrine of justification;* for this requires *faith* in the sacrificial death of the promised Messiah.

Verse 14. *But strong meat*] The high and sublime doctrines of Christianity; the atonement, justification by faith, the gift of the Holy Ghost, the fulness of Christ dwelling in the souls of men, triumph in and over death, the resurrection of the body, the glorification of both body and soul in the realms of blessedness, and an endless union with Christ in the throne of his glory. This is the *strong food* which the genuine Christian understands, receives, digests, and by which he grows.

By reason of use] Who, by constant hearing, believing, praying, and obedience, *use* all the graces of God's Spirit; and, in the faithful use of them, find every one improved, so that they daily grow in grace, and in the knowledge of Jesus Christ our Lord.

Have their senses exercised] The word αισθητηρια signifies the different organs of sense, as the *eyes, ears, tongue*, and *palate, nose*, and *finger ends*, and the nervous surface in general, through which we gain the sensations called *seeing, hearing, tasting, smelling*, and *feeling*. These organs of sense, being *frequently exercised* or employed on a variety of subjects, acquire the power to discern the various objects of sense: viz. all objects of *light* ; difference of *sounds* ; of *tastes* or *savours* ; of *odours* or *smelling* ; and of hard, soft, wet, dry, cold, hot, rough, smooth, and all other *tangible* qualities.

There is something in the soul that answers to all these senses in the body. And as universal *nature* presents to the other senses their different and appropriate *objects*, so *religion* presents to these interior senses the objects which are suited to them. Hence in Scripture we are said, even in spiritual things, to *see, hear, taste, smell*, and *touch* or *feel*. These are the means by which the soul is rendered comfortable, and through which it derives its happiness and perfection.

In the *adult Christian* these senses are said to be γεγυμνασμενα, *exercised*, a metaphor taken from the *athletæ* or *contenders* in the Grecian games, who were wont to employ all their powers, skill, and agility in mock fights, running, wrestling, &c., that they might be the better prepared for the actual contests when they took place. So these employ and improve all their powers, and in using grace get more grace; and thus, being able to discern good from evil, they are in little danger of being imposed on by false doctrine, or by the pretensions of hypocrites; or of being deceived by the subtleties of Satan. They feel that their security depends, under God, on this exercise—on the proper use which they make of the grace already given them by God. Can any reader be so dull as not to understand this?

CHAPTER VI.

We must proceed from the first principles of the doctrine of Christ unto perfection, and not lay the foundation a second time, 1–3. Those who were once enlightened, and have been made partakers of the Holy Ghost and the various blessings of the Gospel, if they apostatize from Christ, and finally reject him as their Saviour, cannot be renewed again to repentance, 4–6. The double similitude of the ground blessed of God, and bearing fruit; and of that ground which is cursed of God, and bears briers and thorns, 7, 8. The apostle's confidence in them, and his exhortation to diligence and perseverance, 9–12. God's promise and oath to Abraham, by which the immutability of his counsel is shown, in order to excite our hope, 13–18. Hope is the anchor of the soul, and enters within the veil, 19, 20.

A. M. cir. 4067.
A. D. cir. 63.
An. Olymp.
cir. CCX. 3.
A. U. C. cir.
816.

THEREFORE, [a] leaving [b] the principles of the doctrine of Christ, let us go on unto perfection; not laying again the foundation of repentance [c] from dead works, and of faith toward God,

2 [d] Of the doctrine of bap-

A. M. cir. 4067.
A. D. cir. 63.
An. Olymp.
cir. CCX. 3.
A. U. C. cir.
816.

---

[a] Phil. iii. 12, 13, 14 ; chap. v. 12.——[b] Or, *the word of the begin-*   *ning of Christ.*——[c] Chap. ix. 14.——[d] Acts xix. 4, 5.

NOTES ON CHAP. VI.

Verse 1. Therefore] Because ye have been so indolent, *slow of heart,* and have still so many advantages.

Leaving the principles of the doctrine of Christ] Ceasing to continue in the state of *babes,* who must be fed with *milk*—with the *lowest* doctrines of the Gospel, when ye should be capable of understanding the highest.

Let us go on unto perfection] Let us never rest till we are *adult Christians*—till we are saved from all sin, and are filled with the Spirit and power of Christ.

The words τον της αρχης του Χριστου λογον might be translated, *The discourse of the beginning of Christ,* as in the *margin;* that is, the account of his *incarnation,* and the different types and ceremonies in the law by which his advent, nature, office, and miracles were pointed out. The whole law of Moses pointed out *Christ,* as may be seen at large in my comment on the Pentateuch; and therefore the words of the apostle may be understood thus : Leave the *law,* and come to the *Gospel.* Cease from *Moses,* and come to the *Messiah.*

Let us go on unto perfection.—The original is very emphatic : Επι την τελειοτητα φερωμεθα· *Let us be carried on to this perfection.* God is ever ready by the power of his Spirit, to *carry us forward* to every degree of light, life, and love, necessary to prepare us for an eternal weight of glory. There can be little difficulty in attaining the *end* of our faith, the salvation of our souls from all sin, if God *carry us forward* to it ; and this he will do if we submit to be saved in his own way, and on his own terms. Many make a violent outcry against the doctrine of *perfection,* i. e. against the heart being cleansed from all sin in this life, and filled with love to God and man, because *they* judge it to be impossible ! Is it too much to say of these that *they know neither the Scripture nor the power of God ?* Surely the *Scripture* promises the thing ; and the *power* of God can *carry us on* to the possession of it.

Laying again the foundation of repentance] The phrase νεκρα εργα, *dead works,* occurs but once more in the sacred writings, and that is in chap. ix. 14 of this epistle ; and in both places it seems to signify *such works as deserve death*—works of those who were *dead in trespasses, and dead in sins ;* and *dead by sentence of the law,* because they had by these works broken the law. Repentance may be properly called the *foundation* of the work of God in the soul of man, because by it we forsake sin, and turn to God to find mercy.

Faith toward God] Is also a *foundation,* or fundamental principle, without which it is impossible to please God, and without which we cannot be saved. By *repentance* we *feel* the need of God's mercy, by *faith* we *find* that mercy.

But it is very likely that the apostle refers here to the *Levitical law,* which, in its painful observances, and awful denunciations of Divine wrath against every breach of that law, was well calculated to produce repentance, and make it a grievous and bitter thing to sin against God. And as to *faith in God,* that was essentially necessary, in order to see the *end* of the commandment ; for without faith in him who was to come, all that *repentance* was unavailable, and all ritual observances without profit.

Verse 2. Of the doctrine of baptisms] " There were two things," says Dr. Owen, " peculiar to the Gospel, the *doctrine* of it and the *gifts of the Holy Ghost.* Doctrine is called *baptism,* Deut. xxxii. 2 ; hence the people are said to be *baptized to Moses,* when they were initiated into his *doctrines,* 1 Cor. x. 2. The *baptism* of John was his *doctrine,* Acts xix. 3 ; and the *baptism* of Christ was the *doctrine of Christ,* wherewith he was to *sprinkle many nations,* Isa. lii. 15. This is the *first* baptism of the Gospel, even its *doctrine.* The *other* was the communication of the gifts of the Holy Ghost, Acts i. 5 ; and this alone is what is intended by the *laying on of hands;* and then the sense will be the foundation of the Gospel baptisms, namely *preaching* and the *gifts of the Holy Ghost.*"

I am afraid, with all this great man's learning, he has not hit the meaning of the apostle. As *teaching* is the means by which we are to obtain the gifts of the Holy Ghost, surely the apostle never designed to separate them, but to lead men immediately through the one to the possession of the other. Nor is the word *baptism* mentioned in the passage in Deuteronomy which he quotes ; nor, indeed, any word properly synonymous ; Neither βαπτισμος, *baptism,* ραντισμος, *sprinkling,* nor any verb formed from them, is found in the *Septuagint,* in that place. But the other proofs are sufficiently in point, viz. that by *baptism* in the other places referred to, *doctrine* or TEACHING is meant ; but to call TEACHING one baptism, and the *gifts* of THE HOLY GHOST *another baptism,* and to apply this to the explanation of the difficulty here, is very far from being satisfactory.

I am inclined to think that all the terms in *this verse,* as well as those in the *former,* belong to the *Levitical law,* and are to be explained on that ground.

Baptisms, or *immersions* of the body in water, *sprinklings,* and *washings,* were frequent as religious rites among the Hebrews, and were all emblematical of that purity which a holy God requires in his worshippers, and without which they cannot be happy here, nor glorified in heaven.

Laying on of hands] Was also frequent, especially in *sacrifices :* the person bringing the victim laid his hands on its head, confessed his sins over it, and then gave it to the priest to be offered to God, that it might make atonement for his transgressions. This also had respect to Jesus Christ, that *Lamb of God who takes away the sins of the world.*

The doctrine also of the *resurrection* of the *dead* and of *eternal judgment,* were both Jewish, but were

2

A. M. cir. 4067.
A. D. cir. 63.
An. Olymp.
cir. CCX. 3.
A. U. C. cir.
816.

tisms, [e] and of laying on of hands, [f] and of resurrection of the dead, [g] and of eternal judgment.

3 And this will we do, [h] if God permit.

4 For [i] *it is* impossible for those [k] who were

once enlightened, and have tasted of [l] the heavenly gift, and [m] were made partakers of the Holy Ghost,

5 And have tasted the good word of God, and the powers of [n] the world to come,

A. M. cir. 4067.
A. D. cir. 63.
An. Olymp.
cir. CCX. 3.
A. U. C. cir.
816.

---

[e] Acts viii. 14, 15, 16, 17; xix. 6.——[f] Acts xvii. 31, 32. [g] Acts xxiv. 25; Romans ii. 16.——[h] Acts xviii. 21; 1 Cor. iv. 19.

[i] Matt. xii. 31, 32; chapter x. 26; 2 Pet. ii. 20, 21; 1 John v. 16.——[k] Chapter x. 32.——[l] John iv. 10; vi. 32; Eph. ii. 8. [m] Gal. iii. 2, 5; chap. ii. 4.——[n] Chap. ii. 5.

---

only partially revealed, and then referred to the *Gospel*. Of the *resurrection of the dead* there is a fine proof in Isa. xxvi. 19, where it is stated to be the consequence of the *death* and *resurrection* of Christ, for so I understand the words, *Thy dead shall live; with my dead body shall they arise: awake and sing, ye that dwell in the dust; for thy dew is as the dew of herbs, and the earth shall cast out the dead.* The valley of *dry bones*, Ezek. xxxvii. 1, &c., is both an illustration and proof of it. And Daniel has taught both the *resurrection* and the *eternal judgment*, chap. xii. 2: *And many of them that sleep in the dust of the earth shall awake; some to everlasting life, and some to shame and everlasting contempt.*

Now the *foundation* of all these doctrines was laid in the Old Testament, and they were variously represented under the law, but they were all referred to the Gospel for their proof and illustration. The apostle, therefore, wishes them to consider the Gospel as holding forth these in their full spirit and power. It preaches, 1. *Repentance*, unto life. 2. *Faith* in God through Christ, by whom we receive the atonement. 3. The *baptism* by *water*, in the name of the holy Trinity; and the *baptism* of the *Holy Ghost*. 4. The *imposition* of *hands*, the true sacrificial system; and, by and through it, the communication of the various gifts of the *Holy Spirit*, for the instruction of mankind, and the edification of the Church. 5. The *resurrection* of the *dead*, which is both proved and illustrated by the resurrection of Christ. 6. The doctrine of the *eternal* or *future judgment*, which is to take place at the bar of Christ himself, God having committed all judgment to his Son, called here κριμα αιωνιον, *eternal* or *ever during judgment*, because the sentences then pronounced shall be irreversible. Some understand the whole of the *initiation* of persons into the Church, as the candidates for admission were previously *instructed* in those doctrines which contained the *fundamental* principles of Christianity. The Hebrews had already received these; but should they Judaize, or mingle the Gospel with the law, they would thereby exclude themselves from the Christian Church, and should they be ever again admitted, they must come through the same gate, or lay a *second time*, παλιν, this foundation. But should they totally *apostatize* from Christ, and finally reject him, then it would be *impossible to renew them again to repentance*—they could no more be received into the Christian Church, nor have any right to any blessing of the Gospel dispensation; and, finally rejecting the Lord who bought them, would bring on themselves and their land swift destruction. See the 4th and following verses, and particularly the notes on verses 8 and 9.

Verse 3. *And this will we do*] God being my helper, I will teach you all the sublime truths of the Gospel; and show you how all its excellences were typified by the law, and particularly by its sacrificial system.

Verse 4. *For it is impossible for those who were once enlightened*] Before I proceed to explain the different terms in these verses, it is necessary to give my opinion of their design and meaning: 1. I do not consider them as having any reference to any person *professing Christianity*. 2. They do not belong, nor are they applicable, to *backsliders* of any kind. 3. They belong to *apostates* from Christianity; to such as reject the whole *Christian system*, and its *author*, the Lord Jesus. 4. And to those of them only who join with the blaspheming Jews, call Christ an impostor, and vindicate his murderers in having crucified him as a malefactor; and thus they render their salvation impossible, by *wilfully* and *maliciously* rejecting the Lord that bought them. No man *believing in the Lord Jesus* as the great sacrifice for sin, and acknowledging *Christianity* as a *Divine revelation*, is here intended, though he may have unfortunately *backslidden* from any degree of the salvation of God.

The design of these solemn words is evidently, *First*, to show the Hebrews that apostasy from the highest degrees of grace was possible; and that those who were highest in the favour of God might sin against him, lose it, and perish everlastingly. *Secondly*, to warn them against such an awful state of perdition, that they might not be led away, by either the persuasions or persecutions of their countrymen, from the truth of the heavenly doctrine which had been delivered to them. And, *Thirdly*, to point out the destruction which was shortly to come upon the Jewish nation.

Once enlightened—Thoroughly instructed in the nature and design of the Christian religion, having received the knowledge of the truth, chap. x. 32; and being convinced of sin, righteousness, and judgment, and led to Jesus the Saviour of sinners.

Tasted of the heavenly gift] Having received *the knowledge of salvation by the remission of sins*, through the Day Spring which from on high had visited them; such having received *Christ*, the *heavenly gift* of God's infinite *love*, John iii. 16; the *living bread that came down from heaven*, John vi. 51; and thus *tasting that the Lord is gracious*, 1 Pet. ii. 3, and witnessing the full effects of the Christian religion.

Partakers of the Holy Ghost] The Spirit himself witnessing with their spirits that they were the children of God, and thus assuring them of God's mercy towards them, and of the efficacy of the atonement through which they had received such blessings.

Verse 5. *And have tasted the good word of God*]

A. M. cir. 4067.
A. D. cir. 63.
An. Olymp.
cir. CCX. 3.
A. U. C. cir.
816.

6 If they shall fall away, to renew them again unto repentance; ° seeing they crucify to themselves the Son of God

afresh, and put *him* to an open shame.

7 For the earth which drinketh in the rain that cometh oft upon

A. M. cir. 4067.
A. D. cir. 63.
An. Olymp.
cir. CCX. 3.
A. U. C. cir.
816.

° Hebrews, chap. x. 29.

Have had this proof of the excellence of the *promise* of God in sending the Gospel, the Gospel being itself the *good word* of a *good God*, the reading and preaching of which they find sweet to the taste of their souls. Genuine believers have an *appetite* for the word of God; they *taste* it, and then their *relish* for it is the more abundantly increased. The more they get, the more they wish to have.

The powers of the world to come] Δυναμεις τε μελλοντος αιωνος. These words are understood two ways:
1. *The powers of the world to come* may refer to the stupendous *miracles* wrought in confirmation of the Gospel, the Gospel dispensation being *the world to come* in the Jewish phraseology, as we have often seen; and that δυναμις is often taken for a *mighty work* or *miracle*, is plain from various parts of the gospels. The prophets had declared that the Messiah, when he came, should work many miracles, and should be as mighty in word and deed as was *Moses*; see Deut. xviii. 15–19. And they particularly specify the giving *sight* to the *blind*, *hearing* to the *deaf*, *strength* to the *lame*, and *speech* to the *dumb*; Isa. xxxv. 5, 6. All these miracles Jesus Christ did in the sight of this very people; and thus they had the highest evidence they could have that Jesus was this promised Messiah, and could have no pretence to *doubt* his mission, or apostatize from the Christian faith which they had received; and hence it is no wonder that the apostle denounces the most awful judgments of God against those who had apostatized from the faith, which they had seen thus confirmed.

2. The words have been supposed to apply to those *communications* and *foretastes* of *eternal blessedness*, or of the *joys of the world to come*, which they who are justified through the blood of the covenant, and walk faithfully with their God, experience; and to this sense the word γευσαμενους, have tasted, is thought more properly to apply. But γευομαι, *to taste*, signifies *to experience* or *have full proof* of a thing. Thus, *to taste death*, Matt. xvi. 28, is *to die*, to come under the *power of death*, fully to *experience* its destructive nature as far as the body is concerned. See also Luke ix. 27; John viii. 52. And it is used in the same sense in chap. ii. 9 of this epistle, where Christ is said to *taste death for every man*; for notwithstanding the *metaphor*, which the reader will see explained in the note on the above place, the word necessarily means that he did *actually die*, that he *fully experienced* death; and had the fullest proof of it and of its malignity he could have, independently of the corruption of his flesh; for over this death could have no power. And to *taste that the Lord is gracious*, 1 Pet. ii. 3, is to experience God's graciousness thoroughly, in being made *living stones, built up into a spiritual house*, constituted *holy priests to offer spiritual sacrifices acceptable to God*; see ver. 5. And

in this sense it is used by the purest Greek writers. See several examples in *Schleusner*.

It seems, therefore, that the first opinion is the best founded.

Verse 6. If they shall fall away] Και παραπεσοντας *And having fallen away.* I can express my own mind on this translation nearly in the words of Dr. Macknight: " The participles φωτισθεντας, *who were enlightened*, γευσαμενους, *have tasted*, and γενηθεντας, *were made partakers*, being *aorists*, are properly rendered by our translators in the *past time*; wherefore, παραπεσοντας, being an aorist, ought likewise to have been translated in the *past time*, HAVE *fallen away*. Nevertheless, our translators, following *Beza*, who without any authority from ancient MSS. has inserted in his version the word *si*, *if*, have rendered this clause, IF *they fall away*, that this text might not appear to contradict the doctrine of the *perseverance of the saints*. But as no translator should take upon him to add to or alter the Scriptures, for the sake of any favourite doctrine, I have translated παραπεσοντας in the *past* time, *have fallen away*, according to the true import of the word, as standing in connection with the other aorists in the preceding verses."

Dr. Macknight was a Calvinist, and he was a thorough scholar and an honest man; but, professing to give a *translation* of *the epistle*, he consulted not his creed but his candour. Had our translators, who were excellent and learned men, leaned less to their own peculiar creed in the present authorized version, the Church of Christ in this country would not have been agitated and torn as it has been with polemical divinity.

It appears from this, whatever sentiment may gain or lose by it, that there is a fearful possibility of *falling away from the grace of God*; and if this scripture did not say so, there are many that do say so. And were there no scripture express on this subject, the nature of the present state of man, which is a state of *probation* or *trial*, must necessarily imply it. Let him who most assuredly standeth, take heed lest he fall.

To renew them again unto repentance] As *repentance* is the *first* step that a sinner must take in order to return to God, and as sorrow for sin must be useless in itself unless there be a proper sacrificial offering, these having rejected the only available sacrifice, their repentance for sin, had they any, would be nugatory, and their salvation impossible on this simple account; and this is the very reason which the apostle immediately subjoins:—

Seeing they crucify to themselves the Son of God] They reject him on the ground that he was an impostor, and *justly* put to death. And thus they are said to *crucify him to themselves*—to do that in their present apostasy which the Jews did; and they show thereby that, had they been present when he was crucified, they would have joined with his murderers.

2

A. M. cir. 4067. A. D. cir. 63. An. Olymp. cir. CCX. 3. A. U. C. cir. 816.

it, and bringeth forth herbs meet
for them [p] by whom it is dressed, [q] receiveth blessing from
God:
8 [r] But that which beareth thorns and briers
is rejected, and *is* nigh unto
cursing; whose end *is* to be
burned.
9 But, beloved, we are per-
suaded better things of you, and things that

A. M. cir. 4067. A. D. cir. 63. An. Olymp. cir. CCX. A. U. C. ci 816.

[p] Or, *for*.—[q] Psa. lxv. 10.

[r] Isa. v. 6.

And put him to an open shame.] Παραδειγματιζοντας· *And have made* him *a public example*; or, *crucifying unto themselves and making the Son of God a public example*. That is, they show openly that they judge Jesus Christ to have been worthy of the death which he suffered, and was justly made a public example by being crucified. This shows that it is *final apostasy*, by the total rejection of the Gospel, and blasphemy of the Saviour of men, that the apostle has in view. See the note on ver. 4.

Verse 7. *For the earth which drinketh in the rain*] As much as if he had said: In giving up such apostates as utterly incurable, we act as men do in cultivating their fields; for as the ground, which drinketh in the rain by which the providence of God waters it, brings forth fruit to compensate the toil of the tiller, and continues to be cultivated, God granting his blessing to the labours of the husbandman; so,

Verse 8. *That which beareth thorns and briers* is *rejected*] That is: The land which, notwithstanding the most careful cultivation, receiving also in due times the early and latter rain, produces nothing but thorns and briers, or noxious weeds of different kinds, is rejected, αδοκιμος, is given up as unimprovable; *its briers, thorns, and brushwood burnt down;* and then *left to be pastured on by the beasts of the field.* This seems to be the custom in *husbandry* to which the apostle alludes. The nature of the case prevents us from supposing that he alludes to the custom of *pushing and burning*, in order to farther *fertilization*. This practice has been common from very early times:—

Sæpe etiam steriles incendere profuit agros;
Atque levem stipulam crepitantibus urere flammis.
VIRG. *Geor.* i., v. 84.

Long practice has a sure *improvement* found,
With *kindled fires* to *burn* the *barren ground;*
When the light stubble to the flames resign'd,
Is driven along, and crackles in the wind.
DRYDEN.

But this, I say the circumstances of the case prevent us from supposing to be intended.

Is *nigh unto cursing*] It is acknowledged, almost on all hands, that this epistle was written *before* the destruction of Jerusalem by the Romans. This verse is in my opinion a proof of it, and here I suppose the apostle refers to that *approaching destruction;* and perhaps he has this all along in view, but speaks of it *covertly*, that he might not give offence.

There is a *good sense* in which all these things may be applied to the Jews at large, who were favoured by our Lord's ministry and miracles. They were *enlightened* by his preaching; *tasted* of the benefits of the *heavenly gift*—the Christian religion established among them; saw many of their children and relatives *made partakers of the Holy Ghost; tasted the good word of God*, by the fulfilment of the promise made to Abraham; and saw the almighty *power* of God exerted, in working a great variety of *miracles*. Yet, after being convinced that never man spake as this man, and that none could do those miracles which he did, except God were with him; after having followed him in thousands, for three years, while he preached to them the Gospel of the kingdom of God; they *fell away* from all this, crucified him who, even in his sufferings as well as his resurrection, was demonstrated by miracles to be the Son of God; and then to vindicate their unparalleled wickedness, endeavoured to make him a *public example*, by reproaches and blasphemies. Therefore their state, which had received much moral cultivation from Moses, the prophets, Christ, and his apostles; and now bore nothing but the most vicious fruits, pride, unbelief, hardness of heart, contempt of God's word and ordinances, blasphemy, and rebellion; was *rejected*—reprobated, of God; was *nigh unto cursing*—about to be cast off from the Divine protection; and their city and temple were shortly to be *burnt up* by the Roman armies. Thus the apostle, under the case of *individuals*, points out the destruction that was to come upon this people *in general*, and which actually took place about *seven* years after the writing of this epistle! And this appears to be the very subject which the apostle has in view in the parallel solemn passages, chap. x. 26–31; and, viewed in this light, much of their obscurity and difficulty vanishes away.

Verse 9. *But, beloved*] Here he softens what he had before said; having given them the most solemn warning against apostasy, he now encourages them to persevere, commends the good that is in them, and excites them to watchfulness and activity.

Better things of you] Than that you shall resemble that *unfruitful ground* that can be improved by no tillage, and is thrown into *waste*, and is fit only for the beasts of the forests to roam in.

Things that accompany salvation] Τα εχομενα σωτηριας· *Things that are suitable to a state of salvation;* you give proofs still that *you* have not, whatever others have done, *departed from the living God* Several of your brethren have already apostatized, and the whole nation is in a state of rebellion against God; and, in consequence of their final rejection of Christ and his Gospel, are about to be finally rejected by God. *They* must meet with *destruction; they* have *the things that are suitable to, and indicative of, a state of reprobation;* the wrath of God will come upon them to the *uttermost;* but, while *they* meet with *destruction, you* shall meet with *salvation*. It is worthy of remark, that no *genuine Christian* perished in the destruction of Jerusalem; they all, previously to the siege by Titus, escaped to *Pella*, in

A. M. cir. 4067.
A. D. cir. 63.
An. Olymp.
cir. CCX. 3.
A. U. C. cir.
816.

accompany salvation, though we thus speak.

10 ˢ For ᵗ God *is* not unrighteous, to forget ᵘ your work and labour of love, which ye have showed toward his name, in that ye have ᵛ ministered to the saints, and do minister.

11 And we desire ʷ that every one of you do show the same diligence ˣ to the full assurance of hope unto the end:

12 That ye be not slothful, but followers of them who through faith and patience ʸ inherit the promises.

A. M. cir. 4067.
A. D. cir. 63.
An. Olymp.
cir. CCX. 3.
A. U. C. cir.
816.

ˢ Prov. xiv. 31; Matt. x. 42; xxv. 40; John xiii. 20.——ᵗ Rom. iii. 4; 2 Thess. i. 6, 7.——ᵘ 1 Thess. i. 3.

ᵛ Rom. xv. 25; 2 Cor. viii. 4; ix. 1, 12; 2 Tim. i. 18.——ʷ Ch. iii. 6, 14.——ˣ Col. ii. 2.——ʸ Chap. xiii. 36.

Cœlosyria; and it is as remarkable that not one *Jew* escaped! all either fell by the *sword*, perished by *famine*, or were led into *captivity!* According to their own imprecation, *His blood be upon us and our children,* God visited and avenged the innocent blood of Christ upon them and upon their posterity; and they continue to be monuments of his displeasure to the present day.

Verse 10. *God is not unrighteous*] God is only *bound* to men by his own *promise:* this promise he is not obliged to make; but, when once made, his *righteousness* or *justice* requires him to keep it; therefore, whatever he has promised he will certainly perform. But he has promised to reward every good work and *labour of love,* and he will surely reward yours; God's *promise* is God's *debt.*

Every good work must spring from *faith* in the *name,* being, and goodness of God; and every work that is truly good must have *love* for its *motive,* as it has God for its *end.*

The word τον κοπου, labour, prefixed to *love,* is wanting in almost every MS. and version of importance. Griesbach has left it out of the text.

Ministered to the saints] Have contributed to the support and comfort of the poor *Christians* who were suffering persecution in Judea. As they *had* thus ministered, and were *still* ministering, they gave full proof that they had a common cause with the others; and this was one of the *things* that proved them to be in a *state of salvation.*

Verse 11. *We desire*] Επιθυμουμεν, We *earnestly wish,* that each person among you may continue ενδεικνυσθαι, to *manifest, exhibit to full view,* the same diligence. There might be reason to suspect that some, through *fear of man,* might not wish the good they did to be *seen,* lest they also should suffer persecution. This would not comport with the generous, noble spirit of the Gospel; the man who is afraid to let his decided attachment to God be known, is not far from backsliding. He who is more afraid of *man* than he is of *God Almighty,* can have very little religion. As the Church of Christ required all those who in these times embraced the Gospel to be publicly baptized, those who submitted to this rite gave full proof that they were thoroughly convinced of the truths of Christianity; and they gave this as a *public pledge* that they would be faithful.

The same diligence] They had an *active faith* and a *labouring love,* and the apostle wishes them to persevere in both. They were diligent, very diligent, and he desires them to continue so.

To the full assurance of hope] Προς την πληροφο-

ριαν της ελπιδος. "The *full assurance of faith,*" says Mr. Wesley, "relates to present pardon; the *full assurance of hope,* to future glory: the former is the highest degree of *Divine evidence* that God is reconciled to me in the Son of his love; the latter is the same degree of *Divine evidence,* wrought in the soul by the same immediate inspiration of the Holy Ghost, of persevering grace, and of eternal glory. So much as *faith* every moment *beholds with open face,* so much, and no more, does *hope* see to all eternity. But this assurance of faith and hope is not an opinion, not a bare construction of Scripture, but is given immediately by the power of the Holy Ghost, and what none can have for another, but for himself only."

We must not misapprehend these excellent sayings of this eminent man. 1. The person who has this *full assurance of hope* is he who not only *knows* and *feels* that his sins are forgiven through Christ Jesus, but also that his *heart is purified from all unrighteousness,* that the whole body of sin and death is destroyed, and that he is fully made a partaker of the Divine nature. As without holiness, complete, entire holiness, no man can see God; so, without this, none can scripturally or rationally *hope* for eternal glory; it being a contradiction to profess to have the full assurance of hope to enjoy a state and place for which the soul is conscious it is *not* prepared. 2. All that is said here must be understood as still implying the absolute necessity of *continuing in the same degree* of grace from which this full assurance of hope is derived. This full assurance, therefore, does not imply that the man *will absolutely persevere* to the end; but that, if he do persevere in this same grace, he shall infallibly have an eternal glory. There is no unconditional perseverance in the Scripture, nor can there be such in a state of *probation.*

Verse 12. *That ye be not slothful*] This shows how the full assurance of hope is to be regulated and maintained. They must be *diligent;* slothfulness will deprive them both of hope and faith. That faith which worketh by love will maintain hope in its full and due exercise.

Followers of them] Μιμηται δε —— κληρονομουντων τας επαγγελιας· *That ye be mimics* or *imitators of them who are inheriting the promises.* And they inherited these promises by faith in him who is invisible, and who, they knew, could not lie; and they *patiently* endured, through difficulties and adversities of every kind, and persevered unto death. "The promises made to Abraham and to his seed were, 1. That Abraham should have a numerous seed by faith as well as by natural descent. 2. That God would be a God to

2

A. M. cir. 4067.
A. D. cir. 63.
An. Olymp.
cir. CCX. 3.
A. U. C. cir.
816.

13 For when God made promise to Abraham, because he could swear by no greater, ᶻ he sware by himself,

14 Saying, Surely blessing I will bless thee, and multiplying 1 will multiply thee.

15 And so, after he had patiently endured, he obtained the p omise.

ᶻ Gen. xxii. 16, 17; Psa. :v. 9; Luke i. 73.——ᵃ Exod. xxii. 11.

16 For men verily swear by the greater: and ᵃ an oath for confirmation *is* to them an end of all strife.

17 Wherein God, willing more abundantly to show unto ᵇ the heirs of promise ᶜ the immutability of his counsel, ᵈ confirmed *it* by an oath;

18 That by two immutable things, in which

A. M. cir 4067
A. D. cir. 63.
An. Olymp.
cir CCX. 3.
A. U. C. cir.
816.

ᵇ Ch. xi. 9.——ᶜ Rom. xi. 29.——ᵈ Gr. *interposed himself by an oath.*

him and to his seed in their generations, by being the object of their worship and their protector. 3. That he would give them the possession of Canaan. 4. That he would bless all the nations of the earth in him. 5. That he would thus bless the nations through Christ, Abraham's seed. 6. That through Christ, likewise, he would bless the nations with the Gospel revelation. Four of these promises the believing Gentiles were inheriting at the time the apostle wrote this letter. 1. They were become Abraham's seed by faith. 2. God was become the object of their worship and their protector. 3. They were enjoying the knowledge of God in the Gospel Church, and the gifts of the Spirit. Gal. iii. 4. All these blessings were bestowed upon them through Christ. By observing that the believing Gentiles were actually inheriting the promises; *i. e.* the four promised blessings above mentioned, the apostle appealed to an undeniable fact, in proof that the believing Gentiles, equally with the believing Jews, were heirs of the promises made to Abraham and his seed." See *Dr. Macknight.* The *promises* may be considered as referring to the *rest of faith* here, and the *rest of glory* hereafter.

Verse 13. *When God made promise to Abraham*] The promise referred to is that made to Abraham when he had offered his son Isaac on the altar, Gen. xxii. 16–18: " By myself have I sworn, saith the Lord; for because thou hast done this thing, and hast not withheld thy son, thy only son; that in blessing I will bless thee, and in multiplying I will multiply thy seed as the stars of the heaven, and as the sand which is upon the seashore; and thy seed shall possess the gate of his enemies; and in thy seed shall all the nations of the earth be blessed." Of this promise the apostle only quotes a part, as is generally the case, because he knew that his readers were well acquainted with the Scriptures of the Old Testament, and particularly with the law.

He sware by himself] He pledged his eternal power and Godhead for the fulfilment of the promise; there was no being superior to himself to whom he could make appeal, or by whom he could be bound, therefore he appeals to and pledges his immutable truth and Godhead.

Verse 14. *Saying, Surely blessing I will bless thee*] I will continue to bless thee.

Multiplying I will multiply thee.] I will continue to increase thy posterity. In the most literal manner God continues to fulfil this promise; genuine Christians are Abraham's seed, and God is increasing their number daily. See the notes on Gen. xxii. 12–18; and xxiii. 1.

Verse 15. *He obtained the promise.*] Isaac was supernaturally born; and in his birth God began to fulfil the promise: while he lived, he saw a provision made for the multiplication of his seed; and, having continued steadfast in the faith, he received the *end* of all the promises in the enjoyment of an eternal glory. And the inference from this is: If we believe and prove faithful unto death, we shall also inherit the promises; and this is what is implied in the apostle's exhortation, ver. 12: *Be not slothful, but followers of them, &c.*

Verse 16. *Men verily swear by the greater*] One who has greater authority; who can take cognizance of the obligation, and punish the breach of it.

An oath for confirmation] " This observation teaches us," says Dr. Macknight, " that both promissory oaths concerning things lawful and in our power, and oaths for the confirmation of things doubtful, when required by proper authority, and taken religiously, are allowable under the Gospel."

Verse 17. *The heirs of promise*] All the believing posterity of Abraham, and the nations of the earth or Gentiles in general.

The immutability of his counsel] His unchangeable purpose, to call the Gentiles to salvation by Jesus Christ; to justify every penitent by faith; to accept faith in Christ for justification in place of personal righteousness; and finally to bring every persevering believer, whether Jew or Gentile, to eternal glory.

Verse 18. *That by two immutable things*] The *promise* and *oath* of God: the *promise* pledged his faithfulness and justice; the *oath*, all the infinite perfections of his Godhead, for he sware by himself. There is a good saying in *Beraçoth* on Exod. xxxii. 13, fol. 32: *Remember Abraham, Isaac, and Israel, thy servants, to whom thou swarest by thine own self.* " What is the meaning of *by thine own self?* Rab. Eleazar answered, Thus said Moses to the holy blessed God, Lord of all the world If thou hadst sworn to them by the heavens and the earth, then I should have said, As the heavens and the earth shall pass away, so may thy oath pass away. But now thou hast sworn unto them by thy great name, which liveth, and which endureth for ever, and for ever and ever; therefore thy oath shall endure for ever, and for ever and ever."

This is a good thought; if God had sworn by any thing finite, that thing might fail, and then the obligation would be at an end. but he has sworn by what is infinite, and cannot fail; therefore his oath is of eternal obligation.

We might have a strong consolation] There appears to be an allusion here to the cities of refuge, and to the persons who fled to them for safety. As the per-

A. M. cir. 4067
A. D. cir. 63.
An. Olymp.
cir. CCX. 3.
A. U. C. cir
816.

it was impossible for God to lie, we might have a strong consolation, who have fled for refuge to lay hold upon the hope e set before us:

19 Which *hope* we have as an anchor of the

soul, both sure and steadfast, f and which entereth into that within the veil;

20 g Whither the forerunner is for us entered, *even* Jesus, h made a high priest for ever after the order of Melchisedec.

A. M. cir. 4067.
A. D. cir. 63.
An. Olymp.
cir. CCX. 3.
A. U. C. cir.
816.

e Chap. xii. 1.——f Lev. xvi. 15; chap. ix. 7.

g Chap. iv. 14; viii. 1; ix. 24.——h Chap. iii. 1; v. 6, 10; vii. 17.

son who killed his neighbour unawares was sure if he gained the city of refuge he should be safe, and had strong consolation in the hope that he should reach it, this hope animated him in his race to the city; he ran, he fled, knowing that, though in danger the most imminent of losing his life, yet, as he was now acting according to an ordinance of God, he was certain of safety provided he got to the place.

It is easy to apply this to the case of a truly penitent sinner. Thou hast sinned against God and against thy own life! The avenger of blood is at thy heels! Jesus hath shed his blood for thee, he is thy intercessor before the throne; flee to him! Lay hold on the hope of eternal life which is offered unto thee in the Gospel! Delay not one moment! Thou art never safe till thou hast redemption in his blood! God invites thee! Jesus spreads his hands to receive thee! God hath sworn that he willeth not the death of a sinner; then he cannot will *thy* death: take God's *oath*, take his *promise*, credit what he hath spoken and sworn! Take encouragement! Believe on the Son of God, and thou shalt not perish, but have everlasting life!

Verse 19. *Which hope we have as an anchor*] The apostle here changes the allusion; he represents the state of the followers of God in this lower world as resembling that of a vessel striving to perform her voyage through a troublesome, tempestuous, dangerous sea. At last she gets near the port; but the tempest continues, the water is shallow, broken, and dangerous, and she cannot get in: in order to prevent her being driven to sea again she heaves out her sheet anchor, which she has been able to get within the pier head by means of her boat, though she could not herself get in; then, swinging at the length of her cable, she rides out the storm in confidence, knowing that her anchor is sound, the ground good in which it is fastened, and the cable strong. Though agitated, she is safe; though buffeted by wind and tide, she does not drive; by and by the storm ceases, the tide flows in, her sailors take to the capstan, wear the ship against the anchor, which still keeps its bite or hold, and she gets safely into port. See on ver. 20.

The comparison of *hope* to an *anchor* is frequent among the ancient heathen writers, who supposed it to be as necessary to the support of a man in adversity, as the anchor is to the safety of the ship when about to be driven on a lee shore by a storm. "To ground *hope* on a false supposition," says *Socrates*, "is like trusting to a weak *anchor*." He said farther, ουτε ναυν εξ ενος αγκυριου, ουτε βιον εκ μιας ελπιδος ὁρμισεον· a ship ought not to trust to one *anchor*, nor life to one *hope*. *Stob.*, Serm. 109

The *hope* of *eternal life* is here represented as the soul's anchor; the *world* is the *boisterous, dangerous*

sea; the *Christian course*, the *voyage*; the *port*, everlasting *felicity*; and the *veil* or *inner road*, the *royal dock* in which that anchor was cast. The storms of life continue but a short time; the anchor, hope, if fixed by faith in the eternal world, will infallibly prevent all shipwreck; the soul may be strongly tossed by various temptations, but will not drive, because the anchor is in *sure* ground, and itself is *steadfast*; it does not *drag*, and it does not *break*; *faith*, like the *cable*, is the *connecting medium* between the *ship* and the *anchor*, or the *soul* and its *hope of heaven*; faith sees the haven, hope desires and anticipates the rest; faith works, and hope holds fast; and, shortly, the soul enters into the haven of eternal repose.

Verse 20. *Whither the forerunner*] The word προδρομος, *prodromos*, does not merely signify one that *goes* or *runs before* another, but also one who *shows the way*, he who *first does a particular thing*; also the *first fruits*. So in the *Septuagint*, Isa. xxviii. 4, προδρομος συκου signifies the *first fruits of the fig tree*, or the *first ripe figs.*

To this meaning of the word *Pliny* refers, *Hist. Nat.*, lib. xvi., c. 26: *Ficus et præcoces habet, quas Athenis* PRODROMOS (προδρομος,) *vocant.* "The fig tree produces some figs which are ripe before the rest, and these are called by the Athenians *prodromos*, forerunner." The word is interpreted in the same way by *Hesychius;* it occurs in no other part of the *New Testament*, but may be found in Ecclus. xii. 8, and in Isa. xxviii. 4, quoted above from the Septuagint. From this we may at once perceive the meaning of the phrase: Jesus is the *first fruits* of human nature that has entered into the heavenly kingdom; the first human body that was ripe for glory, and ripe long before the rest of the children who are partakers of flesh and blood. And he is entered *for us*, as the first fruits of all who have found redemption in his blood. Compare John xiv. 2; 1 Cor. xv. 20, 23; and the notes there.

The metaphorical allusion is to the person who carries the anchor within the pier head, because there is not yet water sufficient to carry the ship in; and to this I have already referred.

After the order of Melchisedec.] After a long digression the apostle resumes his explanation of Psa. cx. 4, which he had produced, chap. v. 6, 10, in order to prove the permanency of the high priesthood of Christ.

1. WE have in this chapter a very solemn warning against *backsliding* and *apostasy*, and that *negligence* and *sloth* which are their forerunners. A man cannot be careless about God and heaven, till he has lost his relish for sacred things; and this relish he cannot

2

lose while he is diligent and faithful. The slightest departure from *truth* and *purity* may ultimately lead to a denying, and even reviling, of the Lord who bought him.

2. Every obedient believer in Christ Jesus has both the oath and promise of God that he will make all grace abound towards him, for in blessing God will bless him ; he may be greatly agitated and distressed, but, while he continues in the obedience of faith, he will ride out the storm. His anchor is within the veil while his heart is right with God. Jesus is gone before to prepare a place for him ; and where the first fruits are, there will soon be the whole lump. He who perseveres unto death shall as surely see God as Jesus Christ now does. God's oath and promise cannot fail.

CHAPTER VII.

Concerning the greatness of Melchisedec, after whose order Christ is a high priest, 1–4. The Levites had authority to take tithes of the people ; yet Abraham, their representative, paid tithes to Melchisedec, 5–10. Perfection cannot come by the Mosaic law, else there could be no need for another priest after the order of Melchisedec, according to the prediction of David in Psalm cx., which priest is sprung from a tribe to which the priesthood, according to the law, did not appertain ; but Christ is a priest for ever, not according to the law, but after the power of an endless life, 11–17. The law, therefore, is disannulled, because of its unprofitableness and imperfection ; and Christ has an unchangeable priesthood, 18–24. He is therefore able always to save them that come unto him, being in every respect a suitable Saviour ; and he has offered up himself for the sins of the people, 25–27. The law makes those priests who have infirmity ; but he who is consecrated by the oath is perfect, and endures for ever, 28.

A. M. cir. 4067.
A. D. cir. 63.
An. Olymp.
cir. CCX. 3.
A. U. C. cir.
816.

FOR this [a] Melchisedec, king of Salem, priest of the most high God, who met Abraham returning from the slaughter of the kings, and blessed him ;

2 To whom also Abraham gave a tenth part of all ; first being, by interpretation, King of righteousness, and after that also, King of Salem, which is, King of peace ;

3 Without father, without mother, [b] without descent, [c] having neither beginning of days, nor

A. M. cir. 4067
A. D. cir. 63.
An. Olymp.
cir. CCX. 3.
A. U. C. cir.
816.

---

[a] Gen. xiv. 18, &c.——[b] Gr. *without pedigree.*

[c] Isa. liii. 8 ; Ezra ii. 62 ; Neh. vii. 64 ; Luke i. 34 ; iii. 23.

NOTES ON CHAP. VII.

Verse 1. *For this Melchisedec, king of Salem*] See the whole of this history largely explained in the notes on Gen. xiv. 18, &c., and the concluding observations at the end of that chapter.

The name Melchisedec, מלכי צדק, is thus expounded in *Bereshith Rabba*, sec. 43, fol. 42, מצדיק את יושביו, *matsdic eth Yoshebaiv*, "The Justifier of those who dwell in him ;" and this is sufficiently true of Christ, but false of *Jerusalem*, to which the rabbins apply it, who state that it was originally called *Tsedek*, and that it *justified its inhabitants.*

Salem is generally understood to be *Jerusalem* ; but some think that it was that city of Shechem mentioned Josh. xx. 7. St. Jerome was of this opinion.

Verse 2. *Gave a tenth part of all*] It was an ancient custom, among all the nations of the earth, to consecrate a part or *tenth* of the spoils taken in war to the objects of their worship. Many examples of this kind occur. This however was not according to any provision in law, but merely *ad libitum*, and as a eucharistic offering to those to whom they imagined they owed the victory. But neither Abraham's decimation, nor theirs, had any thing to do, either with tithes as *prescribed* under the Mosaic dispensation, or as *claimed* under the Christian.

Verse 3. *Without father, without mother*] The object of the apostle, in thus producing the example of Melchisedec, was to show, 1. That Jesus was the person prophesied of in the 110th Psalm ; which psalm the Jews uniformly understood as predicting the Messiah. 2. To answer the objections of the Jews against the legitimacy of the priesthood of Christ, taken from the stock from which he proceeded. The objection is this : If the Messiah is to be a true priest, he must come from a legitimate stock, as all the priests under the law have regularly done ; otherwise we cannot acknowledge him to be a priest : but Jesus of Nazareth has not proceeded from such a stock ; therefore we cannot acknowledge him for a priest, the antitype of Aaron. To this objection the apostle answers, that it was not necessary for the priest to come from a particular stock, for Melchisedec was a priest of the most high God, and yet was not of the stock, either of Abraham or Aaron, but a Canaanite. It is well known that the ancient Hebrews were exceedingly scrupulous in choosing their high priest ; partly by Divine command, and partly from the tradition of their ancestors, who always considered this office to be of the highest dignity. .1. God had commanded. Lev. xxi. 10, that the high priest should be chosen from among their brethren, *i. e.* from the family of Aaron ; 2. that he should marry a virgin ; 3. he must not marry a widow ; 4. nor a divorced person ; 5. nor a harlot ; 6. nor one of another nation. He who was found to have acted contrary to these requisitions was, *jure divino*, excluded from the pontificate. On the

2

A. M. cir. 4067.
A. D. cir. 63.
An. Olymp.
cir. CCX. 3.
A. U. C. cir.
816.

end of life; but, made like unto the Son of God, abideth a priest continually.

4 Now consider how great this

man *was*, ^d unto whom even the patriarch Abraham gave the tenth of the spoils.

5 And verily ^e they that are of

A. M. cir. 4067.
A. D. cir. 63.
An. Olymp.
cir. CCX. 3.
A. U. C. cir.
816.

---

^d Gen. xiv. 18–20.

^e Num. xviii. 21, 26.

---

contrary, it was necessary that he who desired this honour should be able to prove his descent from the family of Aaron; and if he could not, though even in the priesthood, he was cast out, as we find from Ezra ii. 62, and Neh. vii. 63.

To these Divine ordinances the Jews have added, 1. That no *proselyte* could be a priest; 2. nor a *slave;* 3. nor a *bastard;* 4. nor the *son of a Nethinim;* 5. nor one whose father exercised any *base trade.* And that they might be well assured of all this, they took the utmost care to preserve their genealogies, which were regularly kept in the archives of the temple. When any person aspired to the sacerdotal function, his genealogical table was carefully inspected; and, if any of the above blemishes were found in him, he was rejected.

He who could not support his pretensions by just genealogical evidences, was said by the Jews to be *without father.* Thus in *Bereshith Rabba,* sect. 18, fol. 18, on these words, *For this cause shall a man leave father and mother,* it is said: If a proselyte to the Jewish religion have married his own sister, whether by the same father or by the same mother, they cast her out according to *Rabbi Meir.* But the wise men say if she be of the *same mother,* they cast her out; but if of the *same father,* they retain her, שאין אב לגוי *shein ab legoi,* "for a Gentile *has no father;*" i. e. his father is not reckoned in the Jewish genealogies. In this way both Christ and Melchisedec were *without father* and *without mother;* i. e. were not descended from the original Jewish sacerdotal stock. Yet Melchisedec, who was a Canaanite, was a priest of the most high God. This sense Suidas confirms under the word Melchisedec, where, after having stated that, having reigned in Salem 113 years, he died a righteous man and a bachelor, Αγενεαλογητος ειρηται, παρα το μη υπαρχειν εκ του σπερματος Αβρααμ ὁλως, ειναι δε Χαναναιον το γενος, και εκ της επαρατου σπορας ὁρμωμενον, ὁθεν ουδε γενεαλογιας ηξιωτο, he adds, "He is, therefore, said to be *without descent* or *genealogy,* because he was not of the seed of Abraham, but of Canaanitish origin, and sprung from an accursed seed; therefore he is without the honour of a genealogy." And he farther adds, "That, because it would have been highly improper for him, who was the most righteous of men, to be joined in affinity to the most unrighteous of nations, he is said to be *απατορα και αμητορα, without father and without mother.*" This sort of phraseology was not uncommon when the genealogy of a person was unknown or obscure; so Seneca, in his 108th epistle, speaking of some of the Roman kings, says: *De Servii matre dubitatur; Anci pater nullus dicitur.* "Of the mother of Servius Tullus there are doubts; and Ancus Marcus is said to have *no father.*" This only signifies that the parents were either unknown or obscure. Titus Livius, speaking of Servius, says he was born of a slave, named *Cornicularia, de patre*

nullo, of no father, i. e. his father was *unknown.* Horace is to be understood in the same way:—

Ante potestatem Tulli, atque ignobile regnum,
Multos sæpe viros, NULLIS MAJORIBUS *ortos,*
Et vixisse probos, amplis et honoribus auctos.
 Serm. l. 1. Sat. vi., ver. 9.

Convinced that, long before the ignoble reign
And power of Tullius, from a *servile* strain
Full many rose, for virtue high renown'd,
By worth ennobled, and with honours crown'd.
 FRANCIS.

The *viri nullis majoribus orti,* men sprung from *no ancestors,* means simply men who were born of *obscure* or *undistinguished parents;* i. e. persons. who had never been famous, nor of any public account.

The old *Syriac* has given the true meaning by translating thus:—

ܘܠܐ ܐܡܐ ܐܝܬ ܠܗ ܕܠܐ ܐܒܘܗܝ

Dela abuhi vela. emeh ethcathebu besharbotho.

Whose father and mother are not inscribed among the genealogies.

The *Arabic* is nearly the same:—

لا اب له لا ام له غير محسوبة نسبتة

He had neither father nor mother; the genealogy not being reckoned.

The *Æthiopic:* He had neither father nor mother upon earth, nor is his genealogy known.

As this passage has been obscure and troublesome to many, and I have thought it necessary to show the meaning of such phraseology by different examples, I shall, in order to give the reader full information on the subject, add a few observations from Dr. Owen.

"It is said of Melchisedec in the first place that he was *απατωρ, αμητωρ, without father* and *without mother,* whereon part of the latter clause, namely, 'without beginning of days,' doth depend. But how could a mortal man come into the world without father or mother? '*Man that is born of a woman*' is the description of every man; what, therefore, can be intended? The next word declares he was αγενεαλογητος '*without descent,*' say we. But γενεαλογια is a generation, a descent, a *pedigree,* not absolutely, but *rehearsed, described, recorded.* Γενεαλογητος is he whose stock and descent is entered on record. And so, on the contrary, αγενεαλογητος is not he who has no descent, no genealogy; but he whose descent and pedigree is nowhere entered, recorded, reckoned up. Thus the apostle himself plainly expresses this word, ver. 6: ὁ μη γενεαλογουμενος εξ αυτων, 'whose descent is not counted;' that is, reckoned up in record. Thus was Melchisedec without father or mother, in that the Spirit of God, who so strictly and exactly recorded the genealogies of other patriarchs and types of Christ,

A. M. cir. 4067.
A. D. cir. 63.
An. Olymp.
cir. CCX. 3.
A. U. C. cir.
816.

the sons of Levi, who receive the office of the priesthood, have a commandment to take tithes of the people according to the law, that is, of their brethren, though they come out of the loins of Abraham :

6 But he, whose f descent is not counted from them, received tithes of Abraham, g and blessed h him that had the promises.

7 And without all contradiction the less is blessed of the better.

A. M. cir. 4067.
A. D. cir. 63.
An. Olymp.
cir. CCX. 3.
A. U. C. cir.
816.

---

f Or, *pedigree.*——g Gen. xiv. 19.

h Rom. iv. 13; Gal. iii. 16.

---

and that for no less an end than to manifest the truth and faithfulness of God in his promises, speaks nothing to this purpose concerning him. He is introduced as it were one falling from heaven, appearing on a sudden, reigning in Salem, and officiating in the office of priesthood to the high God.

" 2. On the same account is he said to be μητε αρχην ημερων, μητε ζωης τελος εχων, ' without beginning of days or end of life.' For as he was a mortal man he had both. He was assuredly born, and did no less certainly die than other men. But neither of these is recorded concerning him. We have no more to do with him, to learn from him, nor are concerned in him, but only as he is described in the Scripture ; and there is no mention therein of the beginning of his days, or the end of his life. Whatever therefore he might have in himself, he had none to us. Consider all the other patriarchs mentioned in the writings of Moses, and you shall find their descent recorded, who was their father, and so up to the first man ; and not only so, but the time of their birth, the beginning of their days, and the end of their life, are exactly recorded. For it is constantly said of them, such a one lived so long, and begat such a son, which fixed the time of birth. Then of him so begotten it is said, he lived so many years, which determines the end of his days. These things are expressly recorded. But concerning Melchisedec none of these things are spoken. No mention is made of father or mother ; no genealogy is recorded of what stock or progeny he was ; nor is there any account of his birth or death. So that all these things are wanting to him in his historical narration, wherein our faith and knowledge are alone concerned."

Made like unto the Son of God] Melchisedec was without father and mother, having neither beginning of days nor end of life. His genealogy is not recorded ; when he was born and when he died, is unknown. His priesthood, therefore, may be considered as perpetual. In these respects he was like to Jesus Christ, who, as to his *Godhead,* had neither father nor mother, beginning of time nor end of days ; and has an everlasting priesthood. The priesthood of Melchisedec is to abide continually on the same ground that he is said to be without father and mother ; i. e. there is no record of the *end* of his priesthood or life, no more than there is any account of his ancestry.

Verse 4. Consider how great this man was] There is something exceedingly mysterious in the person and character of this king of Salem ; and to find out the whole is impossible. He seems to have been a sort of *universal* priest, having none superior to him in all that region ; and confessedly superior even to Abra-

ham himself, the father of the faithful, and the source of the Jewish race. See ver. 7.

The patriarch Abraham] Ὁ πατριαρχης· Either from πατηρ, a *father,* and αρχη, a *chief* or *head ;* or from πατριας αρχη, *the head of a family.* But the title is here applied, by way of eminence, to him who was the *head* or *chief* of all the *fathers*—or patriarch of the patriarchs, and father of the faithful. The Syriac translates it ܪܝܫ ܐܒܗܬܐ *Rish Abahatha,* " head of the fathers." The character and conduct of Abraham place him, as a man, deservedly at the *head* of the human race.

Verse 5. They that are of the sons of Levi] The priests who are of the posterity of the Levites, and receive the priesthood in virtue of their descent from Aaron, have authority from the law of God to receive tithes from the people.

According to the law] That is, the Levites received a *tenth* from the people. The priests received a *tenth* of this *tenth* from the Levites, who are here called their brethren, because they were of the same tribe, and employed in the same sacred work. The apostle is proceeding to show that Melchisedec was greater even than Abraham, the head of the fathers, for to him Abraham gave tithes ; and as the Levites were the posterity of Abraham, they are represented here as paying tithes to Melchisedec through *him.* Yet Melchisedec was not of this family, and therefore must be considered as having a more honourable priesthood than even Aaron himself ; for he took the *tenth* from Abraham, not for his *maintenance,* for he was a *king,* but in virtue of his *office* as universal high priest of all that region.

Verse 6. Blessed him that had the promises.] This is a continuation of the same argument, namely, to show the superiority of Melchisedec ; and, in consequence, to prove the superiority of the priesthood of Christ beyond that of Aaron. As in the seed of Abraham all the nations of the earth were to be blessed, Abraham received a sacerdotal blessing from Melchisedec, who was the representative of the Messiah, the promised seed, to show that it was through him, as the high priest of the human race, that this blessing was to be derived on all mankind.

Verse 7. The less is blessed of the better.] That the *superior* blesses the *inferior* is a general proposition ; but Abraham was blessed of Melchisedec, therefore Melchisedec was greater than Abraham. "The blessing here spoken of," says Dr. Macknight, "is not the simple *wishing of good* to others, which may be done by inferiors to superiors ; but it is the action of a person *authorized* to declare *God's intention* to bestow good things on another. In this manner

2

A. M. cir. 4067.
A. D. cir. 63.
An. Olymp.
cir. CCX. 3.
A. U. C. cir.
816.

8 And here men that die receive tithes ; but there he *receiveth them,* [i] of whom it is witnessed that he liveth.

9 And as I may so say, Levi also, who receiveth tithes, payed tithes in Abraham.

10 For he was yet in the loins of his father, when Melchisedec met him.

---

[i] Chap. v. 6 ; vi. 20.

---

11 [k] If therefore perfection were by the Levitical priesthood, (for under it the people received the law,) what farther need *was there* that another priest should rise after the order of Melchisedec, and not be called after the order of Aaron ?

12 For the priesthood being changed, there

A. M. cir. 4067.
A. D. cir. 63.
An. Olymp.
cir. CCX. 3.
A. U. C. cir.
816.

---

[k] Gal. ii. 21 ; ver. 18, 19 ; chap. viii. 7.

Isaac and Jacob blessed their children under a prophetic impulse ; in this manner the priests under the law blessed the people ; in this manner, likewise, Melchisedec, the priest of the most high God, blessed Abraham."

Verse 8. *Here men that die receive tithes*] The apostle is speaking of the ecclesiastical constitution of the Jews, which was standing at the time this epistle was written. Under the Jewish dispensation, though the priests were successively removed by *death*, yet they were as duly replaced by others appointed from the same family, and the payment of tithes was never interrupted. But as there is no account of Melchisedec *ceasing to be a priest*, or of *his* dying, he is represented as still living, the better to point him out as a type of Christ, and to show his priesthood to be more excellent than that which was according to the law, as an *unchanging* priesthood must be more excellent than that which was continually *changing*.

But there he receiveth them] The ὧδε, *here*, in the first clause of this verse refers to *Mosaical institutions*, as then existing : the εκει, *there*, in this clause refers to the place in Genesis (chap. xiv. 20) where it is related that Abraham gave *tithes* to Melchisedec, who is still considered as being *alive* or without a *successor*, because there is no account of his *death*, nor of any termination of his priesthood.

Verse 9. *And as I may so say*] Και ως επος ειπειν· *And so to speak a word.* This form of speech, which is very frequent among the purest Greek writers, is generally used to *soften* some *harsh* expression, or to *limit* the meaning when the proposition might otherwise appear to be too *general.* It answers fully to our *so to speak—as one would say—I had almost said—in a certain sense.* Many examples of its use by Aristotle, Philo, Lucian, Josephus, Demosthenes, Æschines, and Plutarch, may be seen in *Raphelius* and *Kypke*.

Payed tithes in Abraham.] The Levites, who were descendants of Abraham, paid tithes to Melchisedec δια, *through*, Abraham, their progenitor and representative.

Verse 10. *For he was yet in the loins of his father*] That is : Levi was seminally included in Abraham, his forefather.

Verse 11. *If therefore perfection were by the Levitical priesthood*] The word τελειωσις, as we have before seen, signifies the *completing* or *finishing* of any thing, so as to leave *nothing imperfect*, and *nothing wanting.* Applied here to the Levitical priesthood, it signifies the accomplishment of that for which a

priesthood is established, viz. : giving the Deity an acceptable service, enlightening and instructing the people, pardoning all offences, purging the conscience from guilt, purifying the soul and preparing it for heaven, and regulating the conduct of the people according to the precepts of the moral law. This *perfection* never came, and never could come, by the Levitical law ; *it* was the shadow of good things to come, but was not the substance. *It* represented a perfect system, but was imperfect in itself. *It* showed that there was guilt, and that there was an absolute need for a sacrifical offering to atone for sin, and it typified that sacrifice ; but every sacrificial act under that law most forcibly proved that it was *impossible for the blood of* BULLS *and* GOATS *to take away sin.*

For under it the people received the law] That is, as most interpret this place, under the priesthood, ιερωσυνη being understood ; because, on the priesthood the whole Mosaical law and the Jewish economy depended : but it is much better to understand επ' αυτη *on account of it*, instead of *under it ;* for it is a positive fact that the law was given before any priesthood was established, for Aaron and his sons were not called nor separated to this office till Moses came down the second time from the mount with the tables renewed, after that he had broken them, Exod. xl. 12–14. But it was in *reference* to the great sacrificial system that the law was given, and on that law the priesthood was established ; for, why was a priesthood necessary, but because that law was *broken* and must be fulfilled ?

That another priest should rise] The law was given that the offence might abound, and sin appear exceeding sinful ; and to show the absolute necessity of the sacrifice and mediation of the great Messiah but it was neither perfect in itself, nor could it confer perfection, nor did it contain the *original priesthood* Melchisedec had a priesthood more than *four* hundred years (422) before the law was given ; and David prophesied, Psa. cx. 4, that another priest should arise after the order of Melchisedec, nearly *five* hundred years (476) after the law was given. The law, therefore, did not contain the original priesthood ; this existed *typically* in Melchisedec, and *really* in Jesus Christ.

Verse 12. *The priesthood being changed*] That is, The order of Aaron being now abrogated, to make way for that which had preceded it, the order of Melchisedec.

There is made of necessity a change also of the law.] The very essence of the Levitical law consisting

2

A. M. cir. 4067.
A. D. cir. 63.
An. Olymp.
cir. CCX. 3.
A. U. C. cir.
816.

is made of necessity a change also of the law.

13 For he of whom these things are spoken pertaineth to another tribe, of which no man gave attendance at the altar.

14 For *it is* evident that [1] our Lord sprang out of Juda; of which tribe Moses spake nothing concerning priesthood.

15 And it is yet far more evident: for that after the similitude of Melchisedec there ariseth another priest,

16 Who is made, not after the law of a carnal commandment, but after the power of an endless life.

A. M. cir. 4067.
A. D cir. 63.
An. Olymp.
cir. CCX. 3.
A. U. C. cir.
816.

17 For he testifieth, [m] Thou *art* a priest for ever after the order of Melchisedec.

18 For there is verily a disannulling of the commandment going before, for [n] the weakness and unprofitableness thereof.

19 For [o] the law made nothing perfect, [p] but the bringing in of [q] a better hope *did*; by the which we [r] draw nigh unto God.

---

[1] Isa. xi. 1; Matt. i. 3; Luke iii. 33; Romans i. 3; Rev. v. 5. [m] Psa. cx. 4; chap. v. 6, 10; vi. 20.——[n] Rom. viii. 3; Gal. iv. 9.——[o] Acts xiii. 39; Rom. iii. 20, 21, 28; viii. 3; Gal. ii. 16;

chap. ix. 9.——[p] Or, *but it was the bringing in;* Galatians ii. 24 [q] Chap. vi. 18; viii. 6.——[r] Rom. v. 2; Eph. ii. 18; iii. 12; ch iv. 16; x. 19.

---

ing in its *sacrificial offerings;* and as these could not confer *perfection,* could not *reconcile God to man,* purify the unholy heart, nor open the kingdom of heaven to the souls of men, consequently it must be abolished, according to the order of God himself; for he said, *Sacrifice and offering, and burnt-offering, and sacrifice for sin, he would not;* see Heb. **x.** 5–10, and with Psa. cx. 4, where it is evident God designed to change both the law and the priesthood, and to introduce Jesus as the only Priest and Sacrifice, and to substitute the Gospel system for that of the Levitical institutions. The priesthood, therefore, being changed, Jesus coming in the place of Aaron, the law of ordinances and ceremonies, which served only to point out the Messiah, must of necessity be changed also.

Verse 13. For he of whom these things are spoken] That is, Jesus the Messiah, spoken of in Psa. cx. 4, who came, not from the tribe of Levi, but from the tribe of Judah, of which tribe no priest ever ministered at a Jewish altar, nor could minister according to the law.

Verse 14. For it is evident] As the apostle speaks here with so much confidence, it follows that our Lord's descent from the tribe of Judah was incontrovertible. The genealogical tables, both in Matthew and Luke, establish this point; and whatever difficulties *we* may find in them now, there were none apprehended in those days, else the enemies of the Gospel would have urged these as a chief and unanswerable argument against Christ and his Gospel.

Verse 15. And it is yet far more evident] Και περισσοτερον ετι καταδηλον εστιν· *And besides, it is more abundantly strikingly manifest.* It is very difficult to translate these words, but the apostle's meaning is plain, viz., that God designed the Levitical priesthood to be changed, because of the oath in Psa. cx., where, addressing the Messiah, he says: *Thou art a Priest for ever after the order,* or ὁμοιοτητα, *similitude, of Melchisedec,* who was not only a *priest,* but also a *king.* None of the Levitical priests sustained this *double* office; but they both, with that of *prophet,* appear and were exercised in the person of our Lord, who is the Priest to which the apostle alludes.

Verse 16. Who is made] Appointed to this high

office by God himself, not succeeding one that was *disabled* or *dead, according to that law* or ordinance directed to *weak* and *perishing* men, who could not *continue by reason of death.*

This is probably all that the apostle intends by the words *carnal commandment,* εντολης σαρκικης· for *carnal* does not always mean *sinful* or *corrupt,* but *feeble, frail,* or what may be said of or concerning *man* in his present *dying condition.*

But after the power of an endless life.] Not dying, or ceasing through weakness to be a priest; but properly *immortal* himself, and having the power to confer life and immortality on others. HE ever lives, as Priest, to make intercession for men; and they who believe on him shall never perish, but have everlasting life.

Verse 17. For he testifieth] That is, either the *Scripture,* in the place so often quoted, or GOD by that Scripture.

Thou art a priest for ever] This is the proof that he was not appointed according to the carnal commandment, but according to the power of an endless life, because he is a priest *for ever;* i. e. one that never dies, and is never disabled from performing the important functions of his office; for if he be a priest for ever, he *ever lives.*

Verse 18. For there is verily a disannulling] There is a total abrogation, προαγουσης εντολης, *of the former law,* relative to the Levitical priesthood. See ver. 19.

For the weakness] It had no *energy;* it communicated none; it had no *Spirit* to minister; it required perfect obedience, but furnished no *assistance* to those who were under it.

And unprofitableness] No man was *benefited* by the mere observance of its precepts: it pardoned no sin, changed no heart, reformed no life; it found men dead in trespasses and sins, and it consigned them to eternal death. It was therefore weak in itself, and unprofitable to men.

The Jews, who still cleave to it, are a proof that it is both *weak* and *unprofitable;* for there is not a more miserable, distressed, and profligate class of men on the face of the earth.

Verse 19. For the law made nothing perfect] It

734

2

A. M. cir. 4067.
A. D. cir. 63.
An. Olymp.
cir. CCX. 3.
A. U. C. cir.
816.

20 And inasmuch as not without an oath *he was made priest;* 21 (For those priests were made ˢ without an oath; but this with an oath by him that said unto him, ᵗ The Lord sware and will not repent, Thou *art* a priest for ever after the order of Melchisedec :)

22 By so much ᵘ was Jesus made a surety of a better testament.

23 And they truly were many priests, because they were not suffered to continue by reason of death :

24 But this *man,* because he continueth ever, hath ᵛ an unchangeable priesthood.

A. M. cir. 4067.
A. D. cir. 63.
An. Olymp.
cir. CCX. 3.
A. U. C. cir.
816.

ˢ Or, *without swearing of an oath.*——ᵗ Psa. cx. 4.——ᵘ Ch. viii. 6; ix. 15; xii. 24.——ᵛ Or, *which passeth not from one to another.*

---

completed nothing; it was only the *outline* of a great plan, the *shadow* of a glorious substance; see on ver. 11. It neither pardoned sin, nor purified the heart, nor gave strength to obey the moral precepts. Ουδεν, *nothing,* is put here for ουδενα, *no person.*

But the bringing in of a better hope] The original is very emphatic, επεισαγωγη, the *superintroduction,* or the *after introduction;* and this seems to be put in opposition to the προαγουσα εντολη, the *preceding commandment,* or *former* Levitical *law,* of ver. 18. This *went before* to prepare the way of the Lord; to show the exceeding sinfulness of sin, and the strict justice of God. *The better hope,* which referred not to earthly but to spiritual good, not to temporal but eternal felicity, founded on the priesthood and atonement of Christ, was afterwards introduced for the purpose of doing what the law could not do, and giving privileges and advantages which the law would not afford. One of these privileges immediately follows:——

By the which we draw nigh unto God.] This is a sacerdotal phrase: the high priest alone could *approach* to the Divine presence in the holy of holies; but not without the blood of the sacrifice, and that only once in the year. But through Christ, as our high priest, all believers in him have an entrance to the holiest by his blood; and through him perform acceptable service to God. The *better hope* means, in this place, Jesus Christ, who is the author and object of the hope of eternal life, which all his genuine followers possess. He is called *our hope,* 1 Tim. i. 1; Col. i. 27.

Verse 20. *Not without an oath*] "The apostle's reasoning here is founded on this, that God never interposed his *oath,* except to show the *certainty* and *immutability* of the thing sworn. Thus he sware to *Abraham,* Gen. xxii. 16–18, that *in his seed all the nations of the earth should be blessed;* and to the rebellious *Israelites,* Deut. i. 34, 35, that *they should not enter into his rest;* and to *Moses,* Deut. iv. 21, that *he should not go into Canaan;* and to *David,* Psa. lxxxix. 4, that *his seed should endure for ever, and his throne unto all generations.* Wherefore, since Christ was made a priest, *not without an oath* that he should be *a priest for ever, after the similitude of Melchisedec,* that circumstance showed God's immutable resolution never to change or abolish his priesthood, nor to change or abolish the covenant which was established on his priesthood; whereas the Levitical priesthood and the law of Moses, being established *without an oath,* were thereby declared to be *changeable* at God's pleasure." This judicious note is from Dr. *Macknight.*

Verse 21. *Those priests*] The Levitical, *were made without an oath,* to show that the whole system was changeable, and might be abolished.

But this] The everlasting priesthood of Christ, *with an oath,* to show that the Gospel dispensation should never change, and never be abolished.

By him] God the Father, *that said unto him*——the promised Messiah, Psa. cx. 4, *The Lord sware,* to show the immutability of his counsel, *and will not repent*——can never change his mind nor purpose, *Thou art a priest for ever*——as long as time shall run, and the generations of men be continued on earth. Till the necessity of the mediatorial kingdom be superseded by the fixed state of eternity, till this kingdom be delivered up unto the Father, and God shall be all in all, shall this priesthood of Christ endure.

Verse 22. *By so much*] This solemn, unchangeable *oath* of God, *was Jesus made a surety,* εγγυος, a *mediator,* one who brings the two parties together, witnesses the contract, and offers the covenant sacrifice on the occasion. See at the end of the chapter.

A better testament.] Κρειττονος διαθηκης· *A better covenant;* called, in the title to the sacred books which contain the whole Christian code, Ἡ Καινη Διαθηκη, THE NEW COVENANT, thus contradistinguished from the *Mosaic,* which was the *old covenant;* and this is called the *new* and *better covenant,* because God has in it promised other blessings, to other people, on other conditions, than the old covenant did. The *new* covenant is *better* than the *old* in the following particulars: 1. God promised to the Jewish nation certain secular blessings, peculiar to that nation, on condition of their keeping the law of Moses; but under the new covenant he promises pardon of sin, and final salvation to all mankind, on condition of believing on Jesus Christ, and walking in his testimonies. 2. The Jewish priests, fallible, dying men, were mediators of the old covenant, by means of their sacrifices, which could not take away sin, nor render the comers thereunto perfect. But Jesus Christ, who liveth for ever, who is infinite in wisdom and power, by the sacrifice of himself has established this new covenant, and by the shedding of his blood has opened the kingdom of heaven to all believers.

Verse 23. *And they truly were many priests*] Under the Mosaic law it was necessary there should be a succession of priests, because, being mortal, they were not suffered to continue always by reason of death.

Verse 24. *But this*] Ὁ δε, *But he,* that is, Christ, *because he continueth ever*——is eternal, *hath an unchangeable priesthood,* απαραβατον ιερωσυνην, a priest-

A. M. cir. 4067.
A. D. cir. 63.
An. Olymp.
cir. CCX. 3.
A. U. C. cir.
816.

25 Wherefore he is able also to save them ^w to the uttermost that come unto God by him, seeing he ever liveth ^x to make intercession for them.

26 For such a high priest became us, ^y *who is* holy, harmless, undefiled, separate from sinners, ^z and made higher than the heavens;

A. M. cir. 4067.
A. D. cir. 63.
An. Olymp.
cir. CCX. 3.
A. U. C. cir.
816.

---

^w Or, *evermore.*——^x Rom. viii. 34; 1 Tim. ii. 5; ch. ix. 24; 1 John ii. 1.——^y Chap. iv. 15.——^z Eph. i. 20; iv. 10; chap. viii. 1.

---

hood that passeth not away from him; he lives for ever, and he lives a *priest* for ever.

Verse 25. *Wherefore*] Because he is an everlasting priest, and has offered the only available sacrifice, *he is able to save*, from the power, guilt, nature, and punishment of sin, *to the uttermost*, εις το παντελες, to all intents, degrees, and purposes; and always, and in and through all times, places, and circumstances; for all this is implied in the original word: but *in and through all times* seems to be the particular meaning here, because of what follows, *he ever liveth to make intercession for them;* this depends on the *perpetuity* of his *priesthood*, and the *continuance* of his *mediatorial* office. As Jesus was the Lamb of God slain from the foundation of the world, has an everlasting priesthood, and is a continual intercessor; it is in virtue of this that all who were saved from the foundation of the world were saved through him, and all that shall be saved to the end of the world will be saved through him. He ever was and ever will be the High Priest, Sacrifice, Intercessor, and Mediator of the human race. All successive generations of men are equally interested in him, and may claim the same privileges. But none can be saved by his grace that do not *come unto God through him;* i. e. imploring mercy through him as their sacrifice and atonement; confidently trusting that God can be just, and yet the justifier of them who thus come to him, believing on Christ Jesus.

The phrase εντυγχανειν τινι, *to make intercession* for a person, has a considerable latitude of meaning. It signifies, 1. To *come to* or *meet a person* on any cause whatever. 2. To *intercede, pray for*, or *entreat in the behalf of*, another. 3. To *defend* or *vindicate* a person. 4. To *commend*. 5. To furnish any kind of *assistance* or *help*. 6. And, with the preposition κατα, *against*, to *accuse* or *act against another* in a judicial way.

" The nature of the apostle's arguments," says Dr. Macknight, " requires that, by Christ's *always living*, we understand his always *living in the body;* for it is thus that he is an affectionate and sympathizing High Priest, who, in his intercession, pleads the merit of his death to procure the salvation of all who come unto God through him. Agreeably to this account of Christ's intercession, the apostle, in verse 27, mentions the sacrifice of himself, which Christ offered for the sins of the people as the foundation of his intercession. Now, as he offered that sacrifice in heaven, chap. viii. 2, 3, by presenting his crucified body there, (see chap. viii. 5, note,) and as he continually resides there in the body, some of the ancients were of opinion that his continual intercession consists in the *continual presentation of his humanity before his Father*, because it is a continual declaration of his earnest desire of the salvation of men, and of his having, in obedience to

his Father's will, made himself flesh, and suffered death to accomplish it. See Rom. viii. 34, note 3. This opinion is confirmed by the manner in which the Jewish high priest made intercession for the people on the day of atonement, and which was a type of Christ's intercession in heaven. He made it, not by offering of *prayers* for them in the most holy place, but by *sprinkling the blood of the sacrifices on the mercy-seat*, in token of their death. And as, by that action, he opened the earthly holy places to the prayers and worship of the Israelites during the ensuing year; so Jesus, by presenting his humanity continually before the presence of his Father, opens heaven to the prayers of his people in the present life, and to their persons after the resurrection."

Verse 26. *Such a high priest became us*] Such a high priest was in every respect *suitable* to us, every way qualified to accomplish the end for which he came into the world. There is probably here an allusion to the qualifications of the Jewish high priest :—

1. He was required to be *holy*, ὁσιος, answering to the Hebrew חסיד *chasid, merciful*. Holiness was his calling; and, as he was the representative of his brethren, he was required to be *merciful* and *compassionate*.

2. He was to be *harmless*, ακακος, *without evil*—holy without, and holy within; injuring none, but rather living for the benefit of others.

3. He was *undefiled*, αμιαντος, answering to the Hebrew בעל מום *baal mum, without blemish*—having no *bodily imperfection*. Nothing low, mean, base, or unbecoming in his conduct.

4. He was *separate from sinners*, κεχωρισμενος απο των ἁμαρτωλων. By his office he was *separated* from all men and worldly occupations, and entirely devoted to the service of God. And as to *sinners*, or *heathens*, he was never to be found in their society.

5. *Higher than the heavens*. There may be some reference here to the exceeding *dignity* of the high priesthood; it was the highest office that could be sustained by man, the high priest himself being the immediate representative of God.

But these things suit our Lord in a sense in which they cannot be applied to the high priest of the Jews.

1. He was *holy*, infinitely so; and *merciful*, witness his shedding his blood for the sins of mankind.

2. *Harmless*—perfectly without sin in his humanity, as well as his divinity.

3. *Undefiled*—contracted no sinful infirmity in consequence of his dwelling among men.

4. *Separate from sinners*—absolutely unblamable in the whole of his conduct, so that he could challenge the most inveterate of his enemies with, *Which of you convicteth me of sin?* Who of you can show in my conduct the slightest deviation from truth and righteousness ?

5. *Higher than the heavens*—more exalted than all

A. M. cir. 4067.
A. D. cir. 63.
An. Olymp.
cir. CCX. 3.
A. U. C. cir.
816.

27 Who needeth not daily, as those high priests, to offer up sacrifice, ᵃ first for his own sins, ᵇ and then for the people's : ᶜ for this he did once, when he offered up himself.

28 For the law maketh ᵈ men high priests which have infirmity; but the word of the oath, which was since the law, *maketh* the Son, ᵉ who is ᶠ consecrated for evermore.

A. M. cir. 4067.
A. D. cir. 63.
An. Olymp.
cir. CCX. 3.
A. U. C. cir.
816.

ᵃ Lev. ix. 7; xvi. 6, 11; chap. v. 3; ix. 7.——ᵇ Lev. xvi. 15. ᶜ Rom. vi. 10; chap. ix. 12, 26; x. 12.

ᵈ Chapter v. 1, 2.——ᵉ Chapter ii. 10; v. 9.——ᶠ Greek, *perfected.*

---

the angels of God, than all created beings, whether thrones, dominions, principalities, or powers, because all these were created by him and for him, and derive their continued subsistence from his infinite energy.

But how was a person of such infinite dignity *suitable* to us? His *greatness* is put in opposition to our meanness. HE was *holy;* WE, *unholy.* HE was *harmless;* WE, *harmful, injuring* both ourselves and others. HE was *undefiled;* WE, *defiled,* most *sinfully spotted* and impure. HE was *separate from sinners;* WE were *joined to sinners,* companions of the vile, the worthless, the profane, and the wicked. HE was *higher than the heavens;* WE, *baser* and *lower* than the earth, totally unworthy to be called the creatures of God. And had we not had such a Saviour, and had we not been redeemed at an infinite price, we should, to use the nervous language of *Milton* on another occasion, "after a shameful life and end in this world, have been thrown down eternally into the *darkest* and *deepest* gulf of *hell,* where, under the *despiteful control,* the trample and spurn, of all the other *damned,* and in the anguish of their *torture* should have no other ease than to exercise a raving and bestial *tyranny* over *us* as their *slaves,* we must have remained in that plight for ever, the *basest,* the *lowermost,* the most *dejected,* most *under-foot* and *downtrodden vassals of perdition.*" MILTON on *Reformation, in fine.*

Verse 27. *Who needeth not daily*] Though the high priest offered the great atonement only *once* in the year, yet in the Jewish services there was a daily acknowledgment of sin, and a daily sacrifice offered by the priests, at whose head was the high priest, for their own sins and the sins of the people. The Jews held that a priest who neglected his own expiatory sacrifice would be smitten with death. (*Sanhedr.,* fol. 83.) When they offered this victim, they prayed the following prayer: " O Lord, I have sinned, and done wickedly, and gone astray before thy face, I, and my house, and the sons of Aaron, the people of thy holiness. I beseech thee, for thy name's sake, blot out the sins, iniquities, and transgressions by which I have sinned, done wickedly, and gone astray before thy face, I, and my house, and the sons of Aaron, the people of thy holiness; as it is written in the law of Moses thy servant, (Lev. xvi. 30 :) *On that day shall he make an atonement for you, to cleanse you, that ye may be clean from all your sins before the Lord !*" To which the Levites answered : " Blessed be the name of the glory of thy kingdom, for ever and ever !"

This prayer states that the priest *offered a sacrifice, first for his own sins, and then for the sins of the people,* as the apostle asserts.

For this he did once] For *himself* he offered no

sacrifice; and the apostle gives the reason—he needed none, because he was holy, harmless, undefiled, and separate from sinners : and for the *people* he offered himself once for all, when he expired upon the cross.

It has been very properly remarked, that the sacrifice offered by Christ differed in four essential respects from those offered by the Jewish priests : 1. He offered no sacrifice for himself, but only for the people. 2. He did not offer that sacrifice *annually,* but once for all. 3. The sacrifice which he offered was not of calves and goats, but of himself. 4. This sacrifice he offered, not for *one* people, but for the *whole human race ;* for he tasted death for *every* man.

Verse 28. *For the law maketh men high priests*] The Jewish priests have need of these repeated offerings and sacrifices, because they are fallible, sinful men : *but the word of the oath* (still referring to Psa. cx. 4) *which was since the law ;* for David, who mentions this, lived nearly 500 years after the giving of the law, and consequently that oath, constituting another priesthood, abrogates the law; and by this the Son *is consecrated,* τετελειωμενον, *is perfected, for evermore.* Being a high priest without blemish, immaculately holy, every way perfect, immortal, and eternal, HE *is a priest* εις τον αιωνα, to ETERNITY.

I. THERE are several respects in which the apostle shows the priesthood of Christ to be more excellent than that of the Jews, which priesthood was typified by that of Melchisedec.

1. Being after the order of Melchisedec, there was no need of a rigorous examination of his *genealogy* to show his right.

2. He has an *eternal* priesthood; whereas theirs was but *temporal.*

3. The other priests, as a token of the dignity of their office, and their state of dependence on God, received tithes from the people. Melchisedec, a priest and king, after whose order Christ comes, *tithed* Abraham, δεδεκατωκε τον Αβρααμ, the father of the patriarchs ; Jesus, infinitely greater than all, having an absolute and independent life, needs none. He is no man's debtor, but all receive out of his fulness.

4. He alone can bless the people, not by *praying for their good* merely, but by communicating the good which is necessary.

5. As another priesthood, different from that of Aaron, was promised, it necessarily implies that the Levitical priesthood was insufficient ; the priesthood of Christ, being that promised, must be greater than that of Aaron.

6. That which God has appointed and consecrated with an *oath,* as to endure for ever, must be greater than that which he has appointed simply for a time :

but the priesthood of Christ is thus appointed ; therefore, &c.

7. All the Levitical priests were fallible and sinful men ; but Christ was holy and undefiled.

8. The Levitical priests were only by their office distinguished from the rest of their brethren, being equally frail, mortal, and corruptible ; but Jesus, *our high priest, is higher than the heavens.* The statements from which these differences are drawn are all laid down in this chapter.

II. As the word *surety,* εγγυος, in ver. 22, has been often abused, or used in an unscriptural and dangerous sense, it may not be amiss to inquire a little farther into its meaning. The Greek word εγγυος, from εγγυη, a *pledge,* is supposed to be so called from being lodged εν γυιοις, *in the hands* of the creditor. It is nearly of the same meaning with *bail,* and signifies an engagement made by *C.* with *A.* that *B.* shall fulfil certain conditions then and there specified, for which *C.* makes himself answerable ; if, therefore, *B.* fails, *C.* becomes wholly responsible to *A.* In such *suretiship* it is never *designed* that *C.* shall pay any debt or fulfil any engagement that belongs to *B.* ; but, if *B.* fail, then *C.* becomes responsible, because he had *pledged* himself for *B.* In this scheme *A.* is the person legally empowered to take the bail or pledge, *B.* the debtor, and *C.* the surety. The idea therefore of *B.* paying his own debt, is necessarily implied in taking the surety. Were it once to be supposed that the surety undertakes *absolutely* to pay the debt, his suretiship is at an end, and he becomes the debtor ; and the real debtor is no longer bound. Thus the nature of the transaction becomes entirely changed, and we find nothing but *debtor* and *creditor* in the case. In this sense, therefore, the word εγγυος, which we translate *surety,* cannot be applied in the above case, for Christ never became *surety* that, if men did not fulfil the conditions of this *better covenant,* i. e. repent of sin, turn from it, believe on the Son of God, and having received grace walk as children of the light, and be faithful unto death, he would do all these things for them himself ! This would be both absurd and impossible ; and hence the gloss of some here is both absurd and dangerous, viz., " That Christ was the surety of the first covenant to pay the debt ; of the second, to perform the duty." That it cannot have this meaning in the passage in question is sufficiently proved by Dr. Macknight ; and, instead of extending my own reasoning on the subject, I shall transcribe his note.

" The Greek commentators explain this word εγγυος very properly by μεσιτης, a *mediator,* which is its etymological meaning ; for it comes from εγγυς, *near,* and signifies one who draws near, or who causes another to draw near. Now, as in this passage a comparison is stated between Jesus as a high priest, and the Levitical high priests ; and as these were justly considered by the apostle as the mediators of the Sinaitic covenant, because through their mediation the Israelites worshipped God with sacrifices, and received from him, as their king, a political pardon, in consequence

of the sacrifices offered by the high priest on the day of atonement ; it is evident that the apostle in this passage calls Jesus the *High Priest,* or *Mediator of the better covenant,* because through his mediation, that is, through the sacrifice of himself which he offered to God, believers receive all the blessings of the better covenant. And as the apostle has said, ver. 19, that *by the introduction of a better hope,* εγγιζομεν, *we draw near to God ;* he in this verse very properly calls Jesus εγγυος, rather than μεσιτης, to denote the effect of his mediation. See ver. 25. Our translators indeed, following the *Vulgate* and *Beza,* have rendered εγγυος by the word *surety,* a sense which it has, Ecclus. xxix. 16, and which naturally enough follows from its etymological meaning ; for the person who becomes *surety* for the good behaviour of another, or for his performing something stipulated, brings that other *near to the party* to whom he gives the security ; he reconciles the two. But in this sense the word εγγυος is not applicable to the Jewish high priests ; for to be a *proper surety,* one must either have power to compel the party to perform that for which he has become his surety ; or, in case of his not performing it, he must be able to perform it himself. This being the case, will any one say that the Jewish high priests were sureties to God for the Israelites performing their part of the covenant of the law ? Or to the people for God's performing his part of the covenant ? As little is the appellation, *surety of the new covenant,* applicable to Jesus. For since the new covenant does not require perfect obedience, but only the obedience of faith ; if the obedience of faith be not given by men themselves, it cannot be given by another in their room ; unless we suppose that men can be saved without personal faith. I must therefore infer, that those who speak of Jesus as the surety of the new covenant, must hold that it requires perfect obedience ; which, not being in the power of believers to give, Jesus has performed for them. But is not this to make the covenant of grace a covenant of works, contrary to the whole tenor of Scripture ? For these reasons I think the Greek commentators have given the true meaning of the word εγγυος, in this passage, when they explain it by μεσιτης, *mediator."*

The chief difference lies here. The old covenant required perfect obedience from the very commencement of life ; this is impossible, because man comes into the world depraved. The new covenant declares God's righteousness for the remission of sins that are *past ;* and furnishes grace to enable all true believers to live up to all the requisitions of the moral law, as found in the gospels. But in this sense Christ cannot be called the *surety,* for the reasons given above ; for he does not perform the obedience of faith in behalf of any man. It is the highest privilege of believers to love God with all their hearts, and to serve him with all their strength ; and to remove their obligation to keep this moral law would be to deprive them of the highest happiness they can possibly have on this side heaven.

CHAPTER VIII.

The sum, or chief articles, of what the apostle has spoken concerning the eternal priesthood of Christ, 1–5. The excellency of the new covenant beyond that of the old, 6–9. The nature and perfection of the new covenant stated from the predictions of the prophets, 10–12. By this new covenant the old is abolished, 13.

A. M. cir. 4067.
A. D. cir. 63.
An. Olymp.
cir. CCX. 3.
A. U. C. cir.
816.

NOW of the things which we have spoken *this is* the sum : We have such a high priest, [a] who is set on the right hand of the throne of the Majesty in the heavens ;

2 A minister [b] of [c] the sanctuary, and of [d] the true tabernacle, which the Lord pitched, and not man.

A. M. cir. 4067
A. D. cir. 63.
An. Olymp.
cir. CCX. 3.
A. U. C. cir.
816.

3 For [e] every high priest is ordained to offer gifts and sacrifices : wherefore [f] *it is* of necessity that this man have somewhat also to offer.

4 For if he were on earth, he should not be a priest, seeing that [g] there are priests that offer gifts according to the law ;

---

[a] Eph. i. 20 ; Col. iii. 1 ; chap. i. 3 ; x. 12 ; xii. 2.——[b] Or, *of holy things.*——[c] Chap. ix. 8, 12, 24.

[d] Chap. ix. 11.——[e] Chapter v. 1.——[f] Eph. v. 2 ; chapter ix. 14. [g] Or, *they are priests.*

NOTES ON CHAP. VIII.

Verse 1. *Of the things which we have spoken* this is *the* sum] The word κεφαλαιον, which we translate *sum*, signifies the *chief*, the *principal*, or *head ;* or, as St. Chrysostom explains it, κεφαλαιον αει το μεγιστον λεγεται, "that which is greatest is always called *kephalaion*," i. e. the *head* or *chief.*

Who is set on the right hand of the throne] This is what the apostle states to be the *chief* or *most important point* of all that he had yet discussed. His sitting down at the right hand of the throne of God, proves, 1. That he is higher than all the high priests that ever existed. 2. That the sacrifice which he offered for the sins of the world was sufficient and effectual, and as such accepted by God. 3. That he has all power in the heavens and in the earth, and is able to save and defend to the uttermost all that come to God through him. 4. That he did not, like the Jewish high priest, depart out of the holy of holies, after having offered the atonement ; but abides there at the throne of God, as a continual priest, in the permanent act of offering his crucified body unto God, in behalf of all the succeeding generations of mankind. It is no wonder the apostle should call this sitting down at the right hand of the throne of the Divine Majesty, the *chief* or *head* of all that he had before spoken.

Verse 2. *A minister of the sanctuary*] Των αγιων λειτουργος· A public minister of the holy things or places. The word λειτουργος, from λειτος, *public*, and εργον, a *work* or *office*, means a person who officiated for the public, a public officer ; in whom, and his work, all the people had a common right : hence our word *liturgy*, the *public work* of prayer and praise, designed for the *people at large ;* all having a right to attend it, and each having an equal interest in it. Properly speaking, the Jewish priest was the servant of the public ; he transacted the business of the people with God. Jesus Christ is also the same kind of public officer ; both as *Priest* and *Mediator* he transacts the business of the whole human race with God. He performs the *holy things* or *acts* in the *true tabernacle,* HEAVEN, of which the Jewish tabernacle was the *type.* The tabernacle was the place among the Jews where God,

by the *symbol of his presence, dwelt.* This could only typify *heaven*, where God, in his *essential glory*, dwells, and is manifest to angels and glorified saints ; and hence heaven is called here the *true tabernacle*, to distinguish it from the *type.*

Which the Lord pitched] The Jewish tabernacle was *man's work*, though made by God's direction ; the heavens, this *true tabernacle*, the work of God alone, and infinitely more glorious that that of the Jews. The tabernacle was also a type of the *human nature* of Christ, John i. 14 : *And the word was made flesh, and dwelt among us*, και εσκηνωσεν εν ημιν, and *tabernacled among us ;* for, as the Divine presence dwelt in the tabernacle, so the fulness of the Godhead, bodily, dwelt in the man Christ Jesus. And this human body was the *peculiar work of God*, as it came not in the way of *natural generation.*

Verse 3. *Every high priest is ordained*] Καθισταται, *Is set apart*, for this especial work.

Gifts and sacrifices] Δωρα τε και θυσιας· Eucharistic offerings, and *sacrifices for sin.* By the *former*, God's government of the universe, and his benevolence to his creatures in providing for their support, were acknowledged. By the *latter*, the destructive and ruinous nature of sin, and the necessity of an atonement, were confessed.

Wherefore—of necessity] If Christ be a high priest, and it be essential to the office of a high priest to offer atoning sacrifices to God, Jesus must offer such. Now it is manifest that, as he is the *public minister*, officiating in the *true tabernacle* as high priest, he must make an atonement ; and his being at the right hand of the throne shows that he has offered, and continues to offer, such an atonement.

Verse 4. *For if he were on earth*] As the Jewish temple was standing when this epistle was written, the whole temple service continued to be performed by the legal priests, descendants of Aaron, of the tribe of Levi ; therefore if Christ had been then on earth, he could not have performed the office of a priest, being of the tribe of Judah, to which tribe the office of the priesthood did not appertain.

There are priests that offer gifts] This is an addi

A. M. cir. 4067.
A. D. cir. 63.
An. Olymp.
cir. CCX. 3.
A. U. C. cir.
816.

5 Who serve unto the example and [h] shadow of heavenly things, as Moses was admonished of God when he was about to make the tabernacle : [i] for, See, saith he, *that* thou make all things according to the pattern showed to thee in the mount.

6 But now [k] hath he obtained a more excellent ministry, by how much also he is the mediator of a better [l] covenant, which was established upon better promises.

7 [m] For if that first *covenant* had been faultless, then should no place have been sought for the second.

8 For finding fault with them, he saith, [n] Behold, the days come, saith the Lord, when I will make a new covenant with the house of Israel and with the house of Judah ;

9 Not according to the covenant that I made with their fathers, in the day when I took them by the hand to lead them out of the land

A. M. cir. 4067.
A. D. cir. 63.
An. Olymp.
cir. CCX. 3.
A. U. C. cir.
816.

---

[h] Col. ii. 17 ; chap. ix. 23 ; x. 1.——[i] Exodus xxv. 40 ; xxvi. 30 ; xxvii. 8 ; Num. viii. 4 ; Acts vii. 44.

[k] 2 Cor. iii. 6, 8, 9 ; chap. vii. 22.——[l] Or, *testament.*——[m] Chap. vii. 11, 18.——[n] Jer. xxxi. 31–34.

---

tional proof that this epistle was written before the destruction of Jerusalem. As the word θυσιαι, *sacrifices,* is not added here as it is in ver. 3, is it any evidence that bloody sacrifices had then ceased to be offered ? Or, are both kinds included in the word δωρα, *gifts?* But is δωρον, a *gift,* ever used to express a *bloody sacrifice ?* I believe the Septuagint never use it for זבח *zebach,* which signifies an *animal* offered to God in sacrifice.

Verse 5. *Who serve*] Οἱτινες λατρευουσι· Who perform Divine worship.

Unto the example and shadow] Ὑποδειγματι και σκια, WITH *the representation and shadow ;* this is Dr. Macknight's translation, and probably the true one.

The whole Levitical service was a representation and shadow of heavenly things ; it appears, therefore, absurd to say that the priests served UNTO *an example* or *representation* of heavenly things ; they served rather unto the *substance* of those things, WITH appropriate *representations* and *shadows.*

As Moses was admonished] Καθως κεχρηματισται Μωσης· As Moses was Divinely *warned* or *admonished of God.*

According to the pattern] Κατα τον τυπον· According to the *type, plan,* or *form.* It is very likely that God gave a regular plan and *specification* of the tabernacle and all its parts to Moses ; and that from this Divine plan the whole was constructed. See on Exod. xxv. 40.

Verse 6. *Now hath he obtained a more excellent ministry*] His office of priesthood is more excellent than the Levitical, because the covenant is better, and established on better promises : the old covenant referred to *earthly* things ; the new covenant, to *heavenly.* The old covenant had promises of *secular* good ; the new covenant, of spiritual and eternal blessings. As far as Christianity is preferable to Judaism, as far as Christ is preferable to Moses, as far as spiritual blessings are preferable to earthly blessings, and as far as the enjoyment of God throughout eternity is preferable to the communication of earthly good during time ; so far does the new covenant exceed the old

Verse 7. *If that first had been faultless*] This is nearly the same argument with that in chap. vii. 11. The simple meaning is : If the first covenant had made a provision for and actually conferred *pardon* and *purity,* and given a *title* to eternal life, then there could have been no need for a second ; but the first

covenant did not give these things, therefore a second was necessary ; and the covenant that gives these things is the Christian covenant.

Verse 8. *For finding fault with them*] The meaning is evidently this : God, in order to show that the first covenant was inefficient, saith to *them,* the Israelites, *Behold, the days come when I will make a new covenant,* &c. He *found fault* with the *covenant,* and addressed the *people* concerning his purpose of giving another covenant, that should be such as the necessities of mankind required. As this place refers to Jer. xxxi. 31–34, the words *finding fault with them* may refer to the *Jewish people,* of whom the Lord complains that they had broken his covenant *though he was a husband to them.* See below.

With the house of Israel and with the house of Judah] That is, with all the descendants of the twelve sons of Jacob. This is thought to be a promise of the conversion of all the Jews to Christianity ; both of the *lost tribes,* and of those who are known to exist in Asiatic and European countries.

Verse 9. *Not according to the covenant*] The new covenant is of a widely different nature to that of the old ; it was only temporal and earthly in itself, though it pointed out spiritual and eternal things. The new covenant is totally different from this, as we have already seen ; and such a covenant, or *system of religion,* the Jews should have been prepared to expect, as the Prophet Jeremiah had, in the above place, so clearly foretold it.

They continued not in my covenant] It should be observed that the word διαθηκη, which we translate *covenant,* often means *religion* itself, and its various precepts. The old covenant in general stated, on God's side, *I will be your God ;* on the Israelites' side, *We will be thy people.* This covenant they brake ; they served other gods, and neglected the precepts of that holy religion which God had delivered to them.

And I regarded them not] Καγω ημελησα αυτων· *And I neglected them* or *despised them ;* but the words in the Hebrew text of the prophet are ואנכי בעלתי בם *veanochi baalti bam,* which we translate, *although I was a husband to them.* If our translation be correct, is it possible to account for this most strange difference between the apostle and the prophet ? Could the Spirit of God be the author of such a strange, not to say *contradictory,* translation of the same words ? Let it

A. M. cir. 4067.
A. D. cir. 63.
An. Olymp.
cir. CCX. 3.
A. U. C. cir.
816.

of Egypt; because they continued not in my covenant, and I regarded them not, saith the Lord.

10 For º this *is* the covenant that I will make with the house of Israel after those days, saith the Lord; I will ᴘ put my laws into their mind, and write them �q in their hearts; and ʳ I will

be to them a God, and they shall be to me a people:

11 And ˢ they shall not teach every man his neighbour, and every man his brother, saying, Know the Lord: for all shall know me, from the least, to the greatest.

12 For I will be merciful to their unrighte-

A. M. cir. 4067
A. D. cir. 63.
An. Olymp.
cir. CCX. 3.
A. U. C. cir.
816.

º Chap. x. 16.——ᴘ Gr. *give*.——q Or, *upon*.——ʳ Zech. viii. 8.

ˢ Isa. liv. 13; John vi. 45; 1 John ii. 27.

---

be observed: 1. That the apostle quotes from the Septuagint; and in quoting a version accredited by and commonly used among the Jews, he ought to give the text as he found it, unless the Spirit of God dictated an extension of meaning, as is sometimes the case; but in the present case there seems to be no necessity to alter the meaning. 2. The Hebrew words will bear a translation much nearer to the Septuagint and the apostle than our translation intimates. The words might be literally rendered, *And I was Lord over them*, or *I lorded* or *ruled over them*; i. e., I chastised them for their transgressions, and punished them for their iniquities; ημελησα, *I took no farther care of them*, and gave them up into the hands of their enemies, and so they were carried away into captivity. This pretty nearly reconciles the Hebrew and the Greek, as it shows the act of God in reference to them is nearly the same when the proper meaning of the Hebrew and Greek words is considered.

Some suppose that the letter ע *ain* in בעלתי is changed for ח *cheth*, and that the word should be read בחלתי *bachaltı*, *I have hated* or *despised them*. An ancient and learned Jew, Rab. *Parchon*, has these remarkable words on this passage, "פ: ב׳ ואנכי בעלתי בם שאתים וזו העין מהחלפה בחית שנ׳ וגם נפשם בהלה בי: פ: ש שנאה אותי, *and I baalti baam*, translate, *I hated them*; for ע *ain* is here changed and stands for ח *cheth*, as it is said, *their soul bachalah bi*, translate, *hath hated me*." None of the Hebrew MSS. collated by *Kennicott* and *De Rossi* give any various reading on this word. Some of the versions have used as much latitude in their translations of the Hebrew as the Septuagint. But it is unnecessary to discuss this subject any farther; the word בעל *baal* itself, by the consent of the most learned men, signifies to *disdain* or *despise*, and this is pretty nearly the sense of the apostle's expression.

Verse 10. *This is the covenant*] This is the nature of that glorious system of religion which I shall publish among them *after those days*, i. e., in the times of the Gospel.

I will put my laws into their mind] I will influence them with the principles of law, truth, holiness, &c.; and their understandings shall be fully enlightened to comprehend them.

And write them in their hearts] All their affections, passions, and appetites, shall be purified and filled with holiness and love to God and man; so that they shall willingly obey, and feel that *love is the fulfilling of the law:* instead of being written on *tables of stone*, they shall be written on the *fleshly tables of their hearts.*

I will be to them a God] These are the two grand conditions by which the parties in this covenant or agreement are bound: 1. *I will be your God*. 2. *Ye shall be my people*. As the object of religious adoration to any man is that Being from whom he expects light, direction, defence, support, and happiness; so God, promising to be their God, promises in effect to give them all these great and good things. To be God's people implies that they should give God their whole hearts, serve him with all their light and strength, and have no other object of worship or dependence but himself. Any of these conditions broken, the covenant is rendered null and void, and the other party absolved from his engagement.

Verse 11. *They shall not teach every man his neighbour*] Under the old covenant, properly speaking, there was no public instruction; before the erection of synagogues all worship was confined at first to the tabernacle, afterwards to the temple. When synagogues were established they were used principally for the bare reading of the law and the prophets; and scarcely any such thing as a *public ministry* for the continual instruction of the *common people* was found in the land till the time of John the Baptist, our Lord, and his apostles. It is true there were *prophets* who were a sort of general teachers, but neither was *their* ministry extended through all the people; and there were *schools of the prophets* and *schools of the rabbins*, but these were for the instruction of *select persons*. Hence it was necessary that every man should do what he could, under that dispensation, to *instruct his neighbour* and *brother*. But the prophecy here indicates that there should be, under the Gospel dispensation, a profusion of Divine light; and this we find to be the case by the plentiful diffusion of the sacred writings, and by an abundant Gospel ministry: and these blessings are not confined to *temples* or *palaces*, but are found in every corner of the land; so that, literally, all the people, from the least to the greatest, know and acknowledge the only true God, and Jesus Christ whom he has sent. Almost every man, at least in this land, has a Bible, and can read it; and there is not a family that has not the opportunity of hearing the Gospel preached, explained, and enforced.

Some have thought that *from the least to the greatest* is intended to signify the order in which God proceeds with a work of grace; he generally begins with the poor, and through these the *great* and the *high* often hear the Gospel of Christ.

Verse 12. *I will be merciful to their unrighteousness*] In order to be their God, as mentioned under

A. M. cir. 4067.
A. D. cir. 63.
An. Olymp.
cir. CCX. 3.
A. U. C. cir.
816.

ousness, [t] and their sins and their iniquities will I remember no more.

13 [u] In that he saith, A new covenant, he hath made the first old. Now that which decayeth and waxeth old *is* ready to vanish away.

A. M. cir. 4067.
A. D. cir. 63.
An. Olymp.
cir. CCX. 3.
A. U. C. cir.
816.

---

[t] Rom. xi. 27; chap. x. 17.

[u] 2 Cor. v. 17.

---

the preceding verse, it is requisite that their iniquity should be pardoned; this is provided for by the immolation of Jesus Christ as the *covenant sacrifice.* By his blood, redemption has been purchased, and all who with penitent hearts believe on the Lord Jesus receive remission of sins, and God remembers their iniquities no more against them so as to punish them on that account. All spiritual evil against the nature and law of God is represented here under the following terms:—

1. *Unrighteousness,* αδικια, *injustice* or *wrong.* This is against God, his neighbour, and himself.

2. *Sin,* ἁμαρτια, deviation from the Divine law; MISSING THE MARK; aiming at happiness but never attaining it, because sought *out* of God, and *in* the breach of his laws.

3. *Iniquity,* ανομια, *lawlessness,* not having, knowing, or ·acknowledging, a law; having no law written in their hearts, and restrained by none in the conduct of their lives. All these are to be removed by God's *mercy;* and this is to be understood of his mercy in Christ Jesus.

Verse 13. He hath made the first old.] That is: He has considered it as *antiquated,* and as being no longer of any force.

That which decayeth and waxeth old] Here is an allusion to the ancient laws, which either had perished from the *tables* on which they were written through *old age,* or were fallen into *disuse,* or were *abrogated.*

Is *ready to vanish away.*] Εγγυς αφανισμον· *Is about to be abolished.* Dionysius of Halicarnassus, speaking of the laws of Numa, which had been written on *oak boards,* says: 'Ας αφανισθηναι συνεβη τω χρονῳ· " which had perished through old age." And the word αφανιζειν is used to express the *abolition of the law.* The apostle, therefore, intimates that the old covenant was just about to be abolished; but he expresses himself cautiously and tenderly, that he might not give unnecessary offence.

WHEN the apostle said, *All shall know the Lord, from the least to the greatest,* under the new covenant, he had copious authority for saying so from the rabbins themselves. In *Sohar Chadash,* fol. 42, it is said : " In the days of the Messiah knowledge shall be renewed in the world, and the law shall be made plain among all; as it is written, Jer. xxxi. 33, *All shall know me, from the least to the greatest.*" We find the following legend in *Midrash Yalcut Simeoni,* part 2, fol. 46 : " The holy blessed God shall sit in paradise and explain the law; all the righteous shall sit before him, and the whole heavenly family shall stand on their feet; and the holy blessed God shall sit, and the *new law,* which he is to give by *the Messiah,* shall be interpreted."

In *Sohar Genes.,* fol. 74, col. 291, we find these remarkable words : " When the days of the Messiah shall approach, even the little children in this world shall find out the hidden things of wisdom; and in that time all things shall be revealed to all men."

And in *Sohar Levit.,* fol. 24, col. 95 : " There shall be no time like this till the Messiah comes, and then the knowledge of God shall be found in every part of the world."

This day are all these sayings fulfilled in our ears : the word of God is multiplied; many run to and fro, and knowledge is increased; all the nations of the earth are receiving the book of God; and men of every clime, and of every degree—Parthians, and Medes, and Elamites; the dwellers in Mesopotamia, in Judea, in Cappadocia, in Pontus and Asia, Phrygia and Pamphylia, in Egypt, in Libya; strangers of Rome, Jews and proselytes; Cretes and Arabians; Americans, Indians, and Chinese—hear, in their own tongues, the wonderful works of God.

CHAPTER IX.

Of the first covenant, and its ordinances, 1. *The tabernacle, candlestick, table, show-bread, veil, holy of holies, censer, ark, pot of manna, Aaron's rod, tables of the covenant, cherubim of glory, and mercy seat, 2-5. How the priests served, 6, 7. What was signified by the service, 8-10. The superior excellency of Christ's ministry and sacrifice, and the efficacy of his blood, 11-26. As men must once die and be judged, so Christ was once offered to bear the sins of many, and shall come without a sin-offering, a second time, to them that expect him, 27, 28.*

2

A. M. cir. 4067.
A. D. cir. 63.
An. Olymp.
cir. CCX. 3.
A. U. C. cir.
816.

$\rm T$HEN verily the first *covenant* had also ^a ordinances of Divine service, and a ^b worldly sanctuary. 2 ^c For there was a tabernacle made; the first, ^d wherein *was* ^e the candlestick, ^f and the table, and the show-bread; which is called ^g the sanctuary.

A. M. cir. 4067.
A. D. cir. 63.
An. Olymp.
cir. CCX. 3.
A. U. C. cir.
816.

^a Or, *ceremonies.*——^b Exod. xxv. 8.——^c Exod. xxvi. 1.——^d Exod. xxvi. 35; xl. 4.

^e Exodus xxv. 31.——^f Exodus xxv. 23, 30; Lev. xxiv. 5, 6. ^g Or, *holy.*

NOTES ON CHAP. IX.

Verse 1. *The first* covenant *had also ordinances*] Our translators have introduced the word *covenant,* as if διαθηκη had been, if not originally in the text, yet in the apostle's mind. Several MSS., but not of good note, as well as printed *editions,* with the *Coptic* version, have σκηνη, *tabernacle;* but this is omitted by ABDE, several others, both the *Syriac, Æthiopic, Armenian, Vulgate,* some copies of the *Itala,* and several of the Greek fathers; it is in all probability a spurious reading, the whole context showing that *covenant* is that to which the apostle refers, as that was the subject in the preceding chapter, and this is a continuation of the same discourse.

Ordinances] Δικαιωματα· Rites and ceremonies.

A worldly sanctuary.] Ἁγιον κοσμικον. It is supposed that the term *worldly,* here, is opposed to the term *heavenly,* chap. viii. 5; and that the whole should be referred to the carnality or secular nature of the tabernacle service. But I think there is nothing plainer than that the apostle is speaking here in *praise* of this sublimely emblematic service, and hence he proceeds to enumerate the various things contained in the first tabernacle, which added vastly to its *splendour* and importance; such as the table of the show-bread, the golden candlestick, the golden censer, the ark of the covenant overlaid round about with gold, in which was the golden pot that had the manna, Aaron's rod that budded, and the two tables which God had written with his own finger : hence I am led to believe that κοσμικος is here taken in its proper, natural meaning, and signifies *adorned, embellished, splendid;* and hence κοσμος, *the world : Tota hujus universi machina, cœlum et terram complectens et quicquid utroque continetur, κοσμος dicitur, quod nihil ea est* mundius, pulchriùs, *et* ornatius. "The whole machine of this universe, comprehending the heavens and the earth, and whatsoever is contained in both, is called κοσμος, because nothing is more *beautiful,* more *fair,* and more *elegant.*" So Pliny, Hist. Nat., l. ii. c. 5 : *Nam quem* κοσμον *Græci nomine* ornamenti *appellaverunt, eum nos a* perfecta absolutaque elegantia, MUNDUM. " That which the Greeks call κοσμος, *ornament,* we, (the Latins,) from its perfect and absolute elegance call *mundum,* world." See on Gen. ii. 1.

The Jews believe that the tabernacle was an epitome of the world; and it is remarkable, when speaking of their city, that they express this sentiment by the same Greek word, in Hebrew letters, which the apostle uses here : so in *Bereshith Rabba,* s. 19, fol. 19 : כל קוזמיקון שלו שם הוא *col* kozmikon (κοσμικον) *shelo sham hu.* " All his world is placed there." Philo says much to the same purpose.

If my exposition be not admitted, the next most likely is, that God has a *worldly tabernacle* as well as a *heavenly one;* that he as truly *dwelt* in the Jewish tabernacle as he did in the heaven of heavens; the one being his *worldly house,* the other his *heavenly house.*

Verse 2. *For there was a tabernacle made; the first, wherein*] The sense is here very obscure, and the construction involved: leaving out all punctuation, which is the case with all the very ancient MSS., the verse stands thus : Σκηνη γαρ κατεσκευασθη ἡ πρωτη εν ᾗ ἥ τε λυχνια, κ. τ. λ. which I suppose an indifferent person, who understood the language, would without hesitation render, *For, there was the first tabernacle constructed, in which* were *the candlestick, &c.* And this tabernacle or dwelling may be called the *first* dwelling place which God had among men, to distinguish it from the *second* dwelling place, the temple built by Solomon; for tabernacle here is to be considered in its general sense, as implying a *dwelling.*

To have a proper understanding of what the apostle relates here, we should endeavour to take a concise view of the tabernacle erected by Moses in the wilderness. This tabernacle was the epitome of the Jewish temple; or rather, according to this as a model was the Jewish temple built. It comprised, 1. The court where the people might enter. 2. In this was contained the altar of burnt-offerings, on which were offered the sacrifices in general, besides offerings of bread, wine, and other things. 3. At the bottom or lower end of this court was the *tent* of the covenant; the two principal parts of the tabernacle were, the holy place and the holy of holies. In the temple built by Solomon there was a court for the Levites, different from that of the people; and, at the entrance of the holy place, a vestibule. But in the tabernacle built by Moses these parts were not found, nor does the apostle mention them here.

In the holy place, as the apostle observes, there were,

1. The golden candlestick of seven branches, on the *south.*

2. The golden altar, or altar of incense, on the *north.*

3. The altar, or table of the show-bread; or where the twelve loaves, representing the twelve tribes, were laid before the Lord. 1. In each branch of the golden candlestick was a lamp; these were lighted every evening, and extinguished every morning. They were intended to give light by night. 2. The altar of incense was of gold; and a priest, chosen by lot each week, offered incense every morning and evening in a golden censer, which he probably left on the altar after the completion of the offering. 3. The table of the show-bread was covered with plates of gold; and on this, every Sabbath, they placed *twelve* loaves in two piles, six in each, which continued there all the week till the next Sabbath, when they were removed, and fresh loaves put in their place. The whole of this may be seen in all its details in the book of Exodus, from chap. xxxv. to xl. See *Calmet* also.

2

A. M. cir. 4067.
A. D. cir. 63.
An. Olymp.
cir. CCX. 3.
A. U. C. cir.
816.

3 [h] And after the second veil, the tabernacle which is called the Holiest of all ;

4 Which had the golden censer, and [i] the ark of the covenant overlaid round about with gold, wherein *was* [k] the golden pot that had manna, and [l] Aaron's rod that budded, and [m] the tables of the covenant ;

5 And [n] over it the cherubims of glory shadowing the mercy-seat ; of which we cannot now speak particularly.

6 Now when these things were thus ordained, [o] the priests went always into the first tabernacle, accomplishing the service *of God :*

A. M. cir. 4067.
A. D. cir. 63.
An. Olymp.
cir. CCX. 3.
A. U. C. cir.
816.

[h] Exod. xxvi. 31, 33 ; xl. 3, 21 ; ch. vi. 19.——[i] Exod. xxv. 10 ; xxvi. 33 ; xl. 3, 21.——[k] Exodus xvi. 33, 34.——[l] Numbers xvii. 10.

[m] Exod. xxv. 16, 21 ; xxxiv. 29 ; xl. 20 ; Deut. x. 2, 5 ; 1 Kings viii. 9, 21 ; 2 Chron. v. 10.——[n] Exod. xxv. 18, 22 ; Lev. xvi. 2 ; 1 Kings viii. 6, 7.——[o] Num. xxviii. 3 ; Dan. viii. 11.

Which is called the sanctuary.] Ἥτις λεγεται ἁγια· *This is called holy.* This clause may apply to any of the nouns in this verse, in the nominative case, which are all of the feminine gender ; and the adjective ἁγια, *holy,* may be considered here as the nominative singular feminine, agreeing with ἥτις. Several *editions* accent the words in reference to this construction. The word σκηνη, *tabernacle,* may be the proper antecedent ; and then we may read ἁγία, instead of ἁγια : but these niceties belong chiefly to grammarians.

Verse 3. And after the second veil] The first veil, of which the apostle has not yet spoken, was at the entrance of the holy place, and separated the temple from the court, and prevented the people, and even the Levites, from seeing what was in the holy place.

The *second* veil, of which the apostle speaks here, separated the holy place from the holy of holies.

The tabernacle, which is called the Holiest of all] That is, that part of the tabernacle which is called the holy of holies.

Verse 4. Which had the golden censer] It is evident that the apostle speaks here of the tabernacle built by Moses, and of the state and contents of that tabernacle as they were during the lifetime of Moses. For, as Calmet remarks, in the temple which was afterwards built there were many things *added* which were not in the tabernacle, and *several* things *left out.* The ark of the covenant and the two tables of the law were never found after the return from the Babylonish captivity. We have no proof that, even in the time of Solomon, the golden pot of manna, or the rod of Aaron, was either in or near the ark. In Solomon's temple the holy place was separated from the holy of holies by a solid *wall,* instead of a veil, and by strong wooden doors, 1 Kings vi. 31–33. In the same temple there was a large vestibule before the holy place ; and round about this and the holy of holies there were many chambers in three stories, 1 Kings vi. 5, 6. But there was nothing of all this in the Mosaic tabernacle ; therefore, says Calmet, we need not trouble ourselves to reconcile the various scriptures which mention this subject ; some of which refer to the tabernacle, others to Solomon's temple, and others to the temple built by Zorobabel ; which places were very different from each other.

The apostle says that the *golden censer* was in the holy of holies ; but this is nowhere mentioned by Moses. But he tells us that the high priest went in, once every year, with the golden censer to burn incense ; and Calmet thinks this censer was *left there* all the year, and

that its place was supplied by a new one, brought in by the priest the year following. Others think it was left just within the veil, so that the priest, by putting his hand under the curtain, could take it out, and prepare it for his next entrance into the holiest.

The ark of the covenant] This was a sort of chest overlaid with plates of gold, in which the two tables of the law, Aaron's rod, the pot of manna, &c., were deposited. Its top, or lid, was the propitiatory or mercy-seat.

Verse 5. And over it the cherubims of glory] Cherubim is the plural of *cherub,* and it is absurd to add our plural termination (*s*) to the plural termination of the Hebrew. The *glory* here signifies the *shechinah* or symbol of the Divine presence.

Shadowing the mercy-seat] One at each end of the ark, with their faces turned toward each other, but looking down on the cover or propitiatory, ἱλαστηριον, here called the *mercy-seat.*

Of which we cannot now speak particularly.] The apostle did not judge any farther account of these to be necessary ; and I may be excused from considering them particularly here, having said so much on each in the places where they occur in the Pentateuch. What these point out or signify is thus explained by St. Cyril : Christus licet unus sit, multifariam tamen a nobis intelligitur : Ipse est *Tabernaculum* propter carnis tegumentum : Ipse est *Mensa,* quia noster cibus est et vita : Ipse est *Arca* habens legem Dei reconditam, quia est Verbum Patris : Ipse est *Candelabrum,* quia est lux spiritualis : Ipse est *Altare incensi,* quia est odor suavitatis in sanctificationem : Ipse est *Altare holocausti,* quia est hostia pro totius mundi vita in cruce oblata. " Although Christ be but one, yet he is understood by us under a variety of forms. He is the *Tabernacle,* on account of the human body in which he dwelt. He is the *Table,* because he is our Bread of life. He is the *Ark* which has the law of God enclosed within, because he is the Word of the Father. He is the *Candlestick,* because he is our spiritual light. He is the *Altar* of incense, because he is the sweet-smelling odour of sanctification. He is the *Altar of burnt-offering,* because he is the victim, by death on the cross, for the sins of the whole world." This father has said, in a few words, what others have employed whole volumes on, by refining, spiritualizing, and allegorizing.

Verse 6. When these thing were thus ordained] When the tabernacle was made, and its furniture placed in it, according to the Divine direction.

2

A. M. cir. 4067.
A. D. cir. 63.
An. Olymp. cir. CCX. 3.
A. U. C. cir. 816.

7 But into the second *went* the
high priest alone [p] once every
year, not without blood, [q] which
he offered for himself, and *for*
the errors of the people:
8 [r] The Holy Ghost this signifying, that
[s] the way into the holiest of all was not yet
made manifest, while as the first tabernacle
was yet standing:

9 Which *was* a figure for the
time then present, in which were
offered both gifts and sacrifices,
[t] that could not make him that did
the service perfect, as pertaining to the conscience;
10 *Which stood* only in [u] meats and drinks,
and [v] divers washings, [w] and carnal [x] ordinances,
imposed *on them* until the time of reformation.

A. M. cir 4067.
A. D. cir. 63.
An. Olymp. cir. CCX. 3.
A. U. C. cir. 816.

[p] Exodus xxx. 10; Lev. xvi. 2, 11, 12, 15, 34; verse 25.——[q] Chapter v. 3; vii. 27.——[r] Chapter x. 19, 20.——[s] John xiv. 6.

[t] Gal. iii. 21; chap. vii. 18, 19; x. 1, 11.——[u] Lev. xi. 2; Col. ii. 16.——[v] Num. xix. 7, &c.——[w] Eph. ii. 15; Col. ii. 20; chap. vii. 16.——[x] Or, *rites* or *ceremonies.*

The priests went always into the first tabernacle] That is, into the *first part* of the tabernacle, or holy place, into which he went *every day twice, accomplishing the services*, τας λατρειας επιτελουντες, which included his burning the incense at the morning and evening sacrifice, dressing the lamps, removing the old show-bread and laying on the new, and sprinkling the blood of the sin-offerings before the veil, Lev. iv. 6; and for these works he must have *constant access to* the place.

Verse 7. *But into the second*] That is, the holy of holies, or *second part* of the tabernacle, *the high priest alone*, once every year, that is, on one day in the year only, which was the day on which the general atonement was made. The high priest could enter into this place only on one day in the year; but on that day he might enter several times. See Lev. xvi.

Not without blood] The day prescribed by the law for this great solemnity was the *tenth of the month Tisri*, in which the high priest brought in the incense or perfumes, which he placed on the golden censer; he brought also the blood of the bullock, and sprinkled some portion of it seven times before the ark, and the veil which separated the holy place from the holy of holies. See Lev. xvi. 14. He then came out, and, taking some of the blood of the goat which had been sacrificed, he sprinkled it between the veil and the ark of the covenant, ver. 15.

Which he offered for himself, and for *the errors of the people*] Ὑπερ των του λαου αγνοηματων· For transgressions of which they were not conscious: there were so many niceties in the ritual worship of the Jews, and so many ways in which they might offend against the law and incur guilt, that it was found necessary to institute sacrifices to atone for these sins of *ignorance*. And as the high priest was also clothed with infirmity, he required to have an interest in the same sacrifice, on the same account. This was a national sacrifice; and by it the people understood that they were absolved from all the errors of the past year, and that they now had a renewed right of access to the mercy-seat.

Verse 8. *The Holy Ghost this signifying*] These services were divinely appointed, and by each of them the Holy Spirit of God is supposed to speak.

The way into the holiest] That full access to God was not the *common privilege* of the people, while the Mosaic economy subsisted. That the apostle means that it is only by Christ that any man and every man can approach God, is evident from chap. x. 19–22; and it is about this, and not about the tabernacle of this world, that he is here discoursing.

I have already observed that the apostle appears to use the word σκηνη, or *tabernacle*, in the general sense of a *dwelling place;* and therefore applies it to the *temple*, which was reputed the *house* or *dwelling place* of God, as well as the ancient *tabernacle.* Therefore, what he speaks here concerning the *first tabernacle,* may be understood as applying with propriety to the then Jewish *temple*, as well as to the ancient tabernacle, which, even with all their sacrifices and ceremonies, could not make the way of holiness plain, nor the way to God's favour possible.

Verse 9. *Which*] Tabernacle and its services, was *a figure*, παραβολη, a dark enigmatical representation, *for the time then present*—for that age and dispensation, and for all those who lived under it.

In which, καθ' ὁν, *during which*, time or dispensation *were offered both gifts and sacrifices*—*eucharistic* offerings and *victims* for sin, *that could not make him that did the service*, whether the *priest* who made the offering, or the *person* who brought it in the behalf of his soul, *perfect as pertaining to the conscience*—could not take away guilt from the mind, nor purify the conscience from dead works. The whole was a *figure*, or dark representation, of a spiritual and more glorious system: and although a *sinner*, who made these offerings and sacrifices according to the law, might be considered as having done his duty, and thus he would be exempted from many ecclesiastical and legal disabilities and punishments; yet his *conscience* would ever tell him that the guilt of sin was still remaining, and that it was *impossible for the blood of bulls and goats to take it away.* Thus even he that did the service best continued to be *imperfect*—had a guilty conscience, and an unholy heart.

The words καθ' ὁν, *in which*, referred in the above paraphrase to τον καιρον, *the time*, are read καθ' ἡν by ABD, and several others, one copy of the *Slavonic*, the *Vulgate*, and some of the *fathers*, and thus refer to την σκηνην, *the tabernacle;* and this is the reading which our translators appear to have followed. Griesbach places it in his *margin*, as a very probable reading; but I prefer the other.

Verse 10. *In meats and drinks, and divers washings*] He had already mentioned eucharistic and sacrificial offerings, and nothing properly remained but the different kinds of clean and unclean animals

A. M. cir. 4067
A. D. cir. 63.
An. Olymp.
cir. CCX. 3.
A. U. C. cir.
816.

11 But Christ being come [y] a high priest [z] of good things to come, [a] by a greater and more perfect tabernacle, not made with hands, that is to say, not of this building;

12 Neither [b] by the blood of goats and calves, but [c] by his own blood, he entered in [d] once into the holy place, [e] having

obtained eternal redemption *for us.*

13 For if [f] the blood of bulls and of goats, and [g] the ashes of a heifer sprinkling the unclean, sanctifieth to the purifying of the flesh;

14 How much more [h] shall the blood of Christ, [i] who through the eternal Spirit [k] offered

A. M. cir. 4067
A. D. cir. 63.
An. Olymp.
cir. CCX. 3.
A. U. C. cir.
816.

---

[y] Chap. iii. 1.——[z] Chap. x. 1.——[a] Chap. viii. 2.——[b] Chap. x. 4.——[c] Acts xx. 28; Eph. i. 7; Col. i. 14; 1 Pet. i. 19; Rev. i. 5; v. 9.——[d] Zech. iii. 9; ver. 26, 28; chap. x. 10.——[e] Dan. ix. 24.

[f] Lev. xvi. 14, 16.——[g] Num. xix. 2, 17, &c.——[h] 1 Pet. i. 19; 1 John i. 7; Rev. i. 5.——[i] Rom. i. 4; 1 Pet. iii. 18.——[k] Eph. ii. 5; Tit. ii. 14; chap. vii. 27.

---

which were used, or forbidden to be used, as articles of food; together with the different kinds of drinks, washings, βαπτισμοις, *baptisms,* immersions, sprinklings and washings of the body and the clothes, and *carnal ordinances,* or things which had respect merely to the body, and could have no *moral influence* upon the soul, unless considered in reference to that of which they were the similitudes, or figures.

Carnal ordinances] Δικαιωματα σαρκος· Rites and ceremonies pertaining merely to the *body.* The word *carnal* is not used here, nor scarcely in any part of the New Testament, in that catachrestical or *degrading* sense in which many preachers and professors of Christianity take the liberty to use it.

Imposed on them *until the time of reformation.*] These rites and ceremonies were enacted, by Divine authority, as proper representations of the Gospel system, which should reform and rectify all things.

The time of reformation, καιρος διορθωσεως, *the time of rectifying,* signifies the Gospel dispensation, under which every thing is set *straight;* every thing referred to its proper purpose and end; the ceremonial law fulfilled and abrogated; the moral law exhibited and more strictly enjoined; (see our Lord's sermon upon the mount;) and the spiritual nature of God's worship taught, and grace promised to purify the heart: so that, through the power of the eternal Spirit, all that was *wrong* in the soul is *rectified;* the affections, passions, and appetites purified; the understanding enlightened; the judgment corrected; the will refined; in a word, all things made *new.*

Verse 11. *But Christ being come a high priest of good things*] I think this and the succeeding verses not happily translated: indeed, the *division* of them has led to a wrong translation; therefore they must be taken together, thus: *But the Christ, the high priest of those good things* (or *services*) *which were to come, through a greater and more perfect tabernacle, not made with hands, that is, not of the same workmanship, entered once for all into the sanctuary; having obtained eternal redemption* for us, *not by the blood of goats and calves, but by his own blood,* ver. 13. *For if the blood of* GOATS, *and bulls, and calves, and a heifer's ashes, sprinkled on the unclean, sanctifieth to the cleansing of the flesh,* (ver. 14,) *how much more shall the blood of Christ, who, through the eternal Spirit, offered himself without spot to God, cleanse your consciences from dead works, in order to worship* (or *that ye may worship*) *the living God?*

In the above translation I have added, in ver. 13,

τραγων, *of goats,* on the authority of ABDE, three others, the *Syriac,* the *Arabic* of Erpen, *Coptic, Vulgate,* two copies of the *Itala,* and *Theodoret.* And I have rendered εις το λατρευειν, (ver. 14,) IN ORDER *to worship,* or THAT YE MAY *worship;* for this is the meaning of these particles εις το in many parts of the New Testament. I shall now make a few observations on some of the principal expressions.

High priest of good things] Or *services, to come,* των μελλοντων αγαθων. He is the High Priest of Christianity; he officiates in the behalf of all mankind; for by him are all the prayers, praises, and services of mankind offered to God; and he ever appears in the presence of God for us.

A greater and more perfect tabernacle] This appears to mean our Lord's *human nature.* That, in which dwelt all the fulness of the Godhead bodily, was fitly typified by the tabernacle and temple, in both of which the majesty of God dwelt.

Not made with hands] Though our Lord's body was a perfect human body, yet it did not come in the way of natural generation; his *miraculous conception* will sufficiently justify the expressions used here by the apostle.

Verse 12. *But by his own blood*] Here the redemption of man is attributed to the *blood of Christ;* and this blood is stated to be shed in a *sacrificial* way, precisely as the blood of bulls, goats, and calves was shed under the law.

Once] *Once for all,* εφαπαξ, in opposition to the *annual* entering of the high priest into the holiest, with the blood of the *annual* victim.

The holy place] Or *sanctuary,* τα αγια, signifies *heaven,* into which Jesus entered with his own blood, as the high priest entered into the holy of holies with the blood of the *victims* which he had sacrificed.

Eternal redemption] Αιωνιαν λυτρωσιν· A redemption price which should stand good *for ever,* when once offered; and an *endless redemption* from sin, in reference to the pardon of which, and reconciliation to God, there needs no other sacrifice: it is *eternal* in its *merit* and *efficacy.*

Verse 13. *Sanctifieth to the purifying of the flesh*] Answers the end proposed by the law; namely, to remove legal disabilities and punishments, having the *body* and its interests particularly in view, though adumbrating or typifying the soul and its concerns.

Verse 14. *Who through the eternal Spirit*] This expression is understood two ways: 1. Of the Holy Ghost himself. As Christ's *miraculous conception*

A. M. cir. 4067.
A. D. cir. 63.
An. Olymp.
cir. CCX. 3.
A. U. C. cir.
816.

himself without [1] spot to God, [m] purge your conscience [n] from dead works [o] to serve the living God ?

15 [p] And for this cause [q] he is the Mediator of the new testament, [r] that by means of death, for the redemption of the transgressions *that were* under the first testament, [s] they which

are called might receive the promise of eternal inheritance.

16 For where a testament *is,* there must also of necessity [t] be the death of the testator.

17 For [u] a testament *is* of force after men are dead: otherwise it is of no strength at all while the testator liveth.

A. M. cir. 4067.
A. D. cir. 63.
An. Olymp.
cir. CCX. 3.
A. U. C. cir.
816.

---

[1] Or, *fault.*——[m] Chap. i. 3; x. 22.——[n] Chap. vi. 1.——[o] Luke i. 74; Rom. vi. 13, 22; 1 Pet. iv. 2.——[p] 1 Tim. ii. 5.

[q] Chap. vii. 22; viii. 6; xii. 24.——[r] Rom. iii. 25; v. 6; 1 Pet. iii. 18.——[s] Chap. iii. 1.——[t] Or, *be brought in.*——[u] Gal. iii. 15.

---

was by the *Holy Spirit,* and he wrought all his *miracles* by the *Spirit* of God, so his *death* or final offering was made through or by the *eternal Spirit ;* and by that *Spirit* he was *raised from the dead,* 1 Peter iii. 18. Indeed, through the whole of his life he was *justified by the Spirit ;* and we find that in this great work of human redemption, the Father, the Son, and the Holy Spirit were continually employed: therefore the words may be understood of the Holy Spirit properly. 2. Of the *eternal Logos* or Deity which dwelt in the man Christ Jesus, through the energy of which the offering of his humanity became an infinitely meritorious victim; therefore the Deity of Christ is here intended. But we cannot well consider one of these distinct from the other ; and hence probably arose the various readings in the MSS. and versions on this article. Instead of δια Πνευματος αιωνιου, *by the* ETERNAL *Spirit,* δια Πνευματος 'Αγιου, *by the* HOLY *Spirit,* is the reading of D*, and more than twenty others of good note, besides the *Coptic, Slavonic, Vulgate,* two copies of the *Itala, Cyril, Athanasius* sometimes, *Damascenus, Chrysostom,* and some others. But the common reading is supported by ABD**, and others, besides the *Syriac,* all the *Arabic, Armenian, Æthiopic, Theodoret, Theophylact,* and *Ambrosius.* This, therefore, is the reading that should be preferred, as it is probable that the *Holy Ghost,* not the *Logos,* is what the apostle had more immediately in view. But still we must say, that the *Holy Spirit,* with the *eternal Logos,* and the *almighty Father,* equally concurred in offering up the sacrifice of the human nature of Christ, in order to make atonement for the sin of the world.

Purge your conscience] Καθαριει την συνειδησιν· *Purify your conscience.* The term *purify* should be everywhere, both in the translation of the Scriptures, and in preaching the Gospel, preferred to the word *purge,* which, at present, is scarcely ever used in the sense in which our translators have employed it.

Dead works] Sin in general, or acts to which the *penalty of death* is annexed by the law. See the phrase explained, chap. vi. 1.

Verse 15. And for this cause] Some translate δια τουτο, *on account of this* (blood.) Perhaps it means no more than a mere inference, such as *therefore,* or *wherefore.*

He is the Mediator of the new testament] There was no proper reason why our translators should render διαθηκη by *testament* here, when in almost every other case they render it *covenant,* which is its proper ecclesiastical meaning, as answering to the Hebrew

ברית *berith,* which see largely explained, Gen. xv. 10, and in other places of the Pentateuch.

Very few persons are satisfied with the translation of the following verses to the 20th, particularly the 16th and 17th; at all events the word *covenant* must be retained. He—Jesus Christ, *is Mediator ;* the μεσιτης, or *mediator,* was the person who witnessed the contract made between the two contracting parties, slew the victim, and sprinkled each with its blood.

Of the new testament] The *new contract* betwixt God and the whole human race, by *Christ Jesus* the Mediator, distinguished here from the *old covenant* between God and the *Israelites,* in which *Moses* was the mediator.

That by means of death] His own death upon the cross.

For the redemption of the transgressions] To make atonement for the transgressions which were committed under the old covenant, which the blood of bulls and calves could not do ; so the death of Jesus had respect to all the time antecedent to it, as well as to all the time afterward till the conclusion of the world.

They which are called] The GENTILES, *might receive the promise*—might, by being brought into a covenant with God, have an equal right with the *Jews,* not merely to an inheritance such as the promised land, but to an *eternal inheritance,* and consequently infinitely superior to that of the Jews, inasmuch as the new covenant is superior in every point of view to the old.

How frequently the *Gentiles* are termed οι κλητοι and οι κεκλημενοι, *the called,* all St. Paul's writings show. And they were thus termed because they were *called* and *elected* in the place of the Jews, the ancient *called* and *elect,* who were now *divorced* and *reprobated* because of their disobedience.

Verse 16. For where a testament is] A learned and judicious friend furnishes me with the following translation of this and the 17th verse :—

" For where there is a covenant, it is necessary that the death of the appointed *victim* should be exhibited, because a covenant is confirmed over dead *victims,* since it is not at all valid while the appointed *victim* is alive."

He observes, " There is no word signifying *testator,* or *men,* in the original. Διαθεμενος is not a substantive, but a participle, or a participial adjective, derived from the same root as διαθηκη, and must have a substantive understood. I therefore render it *the disposed* or *appointed* victim, alluding to the manner of *disposing*

2

A. M. cir. 4067.
A. D. cir. 63.
An. Olymp.
cir. CCX 3.
A. U. C. cir
816.

18 ᵛ Whereupon neither the first *testament* was ʷ dedicated without blood.

19 For when Moses had spoken every precept to all the people according to the law, ˣ he took the blood of calves and of goats, ʸ with water, and ᶻ scarlet wool, and hyssop, and sprinkled both the book, and all the people,

20 Saying, ᵃ This *is* the blood of the testament which God hath enjoined unto you.

---

v Exod. xxiv. 6, &c.——w Or, *purified.*——x Exod. xxiv. 5, 6,
6. Lev. xvi. 14, 15, 18.——y Lev. xiv. 4, 6, 7, 49, 51, 52.——z Or, *purple.*

A. M. cir. 4067.
A. D. cir. 63.
An. Olymp.
cir. CCX. 3.
A. U. C. cir.
816.

21 Moreover, ᵇ he sprinkled likewise with blood both the tabernacle, and all the vessels of the ministry.

22 And almost all things are by the law purged with blood; and ᶜ without shedding of blood is no remission.

23 *It was* therefore necessary that ᵈ the patterns of things in the heavens should be purified with these; but the heavenly things themselves with better sacrifices than these.

---

a Exod. xxiv. 8; Matt. xxvi. 28.——b Exod. xxix. 12, 36; Lev. viii. 15, 19; xvi. 14, 15, 16, 18, 19.——c Lev. xvii. 11.——d Chap. viii. 5.

or *setting apart* the pieces of the victim, when they were going to ratify a covenant; and you know well the old custom of ratifying a covenant, to which the apostle alludes. I refer to your own notes on Gen. vi '18, and xv. 10.—J. C."

Mr. Wakefield has translated the passage nearly in the same way.

"For where a covenant *is*, there must be necessarily introduced *the* death of that which establisheth the covenant; because a covenant *is* confirmed over dead things, and is of no force at all whilst that which establisheth the covenant is alive." This is undoubtedly the meaning of this passage; and we should endeavour to forget that *testament* and *testator* were ever introduced, as they totally change the apostle's meaning. See the observations at the end of this chapter.

Verse 18. *Whereupon*] 'Οθεν, *Wherefore*, as a *victim* was required for the ratification of every covenant, the first covenant made between God and the Hebrews, by the mediation of Moses, *was not dedicated*, εγκεκαινισται, renewed or solemnized, *without blood*—without the death of a victim, and the aspersion of its blood.

Verse 19. *When Moses had spoken every precept*] The place to which the apostle alludes is Exod. xxiv. 4–8, where the reader is requested to consult the notes.

And sprinkled both the book] The sprinkling of the *book* is not mentioned in the place to which the apostle refers, (see above,) nor did it in fact take place. The words αυτο τε το βιβλιον, *and the book itself*, should be referred to λαβων, *having taken*, and not to ερραντισε, *he sprinkled*; the verse should therefore be read thus: *For after every commandment of the law had been recited by Moses to all the people, he took the blood of the calves, and of the goats, with water and scarlet wool, and the book itself, and sprinkled all the people.* The rite was performed thus: Having received the blood of the calves and goats into basins, and mingled it with water to prevent it from coagulating, he then took a bunch of *hyssop*, and having bound it together with *thread* made of *scarlet wool*, he dipped this in the basin, and sprinkled the blood and water upon the people who were nearest to him, and who might be considered on this occasion the representatives of all the rest; for it is impossible that he should have had blood enough to have sprinkled the whole of the congregation.

Some think that the blood was actually sprinkled *upon the book itself*, which contained the written covenant, to signify that the covenant itself was ratified by the blood.

Verse 20. *This* is *the blood of the testament*] (*covenant.*) Our Lord refers to the conduct of Moses here, and partly quotes his words in the institution of the eucharist: *This is my blood of the new covenant, which is shed for many for the remission of sins*, Matt. xxvi. 28. And by thus using the words and applying them, he shows that *his* sacrificial blood was intended by the blood shed and sprinkled on this occasion, and that by it alone the remission of sins is obtained.

Verse 21. *He sprinkled—with blood—all the vessels of the ministry.*] To intimate that every thing used by sinful man is polluted, and that nothing can be acceptable in the sight of a holy God that has not in effect the sprinkling of the atoning blood.

Verse 22. *And almost all things are—purged with blood*] The apostle says *almost*, because in some cases certain vessels were purified by *water*, some by *fire*, Num. xxxi. 23, and some with the *ashes* of the *red heifer*, Num. xix. 2–10, but it was always understood that every thing was at *first* consecrated by the blood of the victim.

And without shedding of blood is no remission.] The apostle shows fully here what is one of his great objects in the whole of this epistle, viz. that there is no salvation but through the sacrificial death of Christ, and to prefigure this the law itself would not grant any remission of sin without the blood of a victim. This is a maxim even among the Jews themselves, אין כפרה אלא בדם *ein capparah ella bedam*, "There is no expiation but by blood." *Yoma*, fol. 5, 1; *Menachoth*, fol. 93, 2. Every sinner has forfeited his *life* by his transgressions, and the law of God requires his *death*; the blood of the victim, which is its *life*, is shed as a *substitute* for the *life* of the sinner. By these victims the sacrifice of Christ was typified. He gave his *life* for the *life* of the world; human life for human life, but a life infinitely dignified by its union with God.

Verse 23 *The patterns of things in the heavens*] That is: The tabernacle and all its utensils, services, &c., must be purified *by these*, viz.: *The blood of*

A. M. cir. 4067.
A. D. cir. 63.
An. Olymp.
cir. CCX. 3.
A. U. C. cir.
816.

24 For [e] Christ is not entered into the holy places made with hands, *which are* the figures of [f] the true ; but into heaven itself, now [g] to appear in the presence of God for us :

25 Nor yet that he should offer himself often, as [h] the high priest entereth into the holy place every year with blood of others ;

26 For then must he often have suffered since the foundation of the world : but now

A. M. cir. 4067
A. D. cir. 63.
An. Olymp.
cir. CCX. 3
A. U. C cir
816.

[i] once [k] in the end of the world hath he appeared, to put away sin by the sacrifice of himself.

27 [l] And as it is appointed unto men once to die, [m] but after this the judgment ;

28 So [n] Christ was once [o] offered to bear the sins [p] of many : and unto them that [q] look for him shall he appear the second time, without sin, unto salvation.

---

[e] Chap. vi. 20.——[f] Chap. viii. 2.——[g] Rom. viii. 34 ; chapter vii. 25 ; 1 John ii. 1.——[h] Ver. 7.——[i] Ver. 12 ; chap. vii. 27 ; x. 10 ; 1 Pet. iii. 18.——[k] 1 Cor. x. 11 ; Galatians iv. 4 ; Eph. i. 10.

[l] Gen. iii. 19 ; Eccles. iii. 20.——[m] 2 Cor. v. 10 ; Rev. xx. 12, 13. [n] Rom. vi. 10 ; 1 Peter iii. 18.——[o] 1 Peter ii. 24 ; 1 John iii. 5. [p] Matt. xxvi. 28 ; Rom. v. 15.——[q] Tit. ii. 13 ; 2 Pet. v. 12.

---

calves and goats, and the sprinkling of the blood and water with the bunch of hyssop bound about with scarlet wool. These are called *patterns,* ὑποδειγματα, *exemplars,* earthly things, which were the representatives of heavenly things. And there is no doubt that every thing in the tabernacle, its parts, divisions, utensils, ministry, &c., as appointed by God, were representations of *celestial matters ;* but how *far* and in *what way* we cannot now see.

Purification implies, not only cleansing from defilement, but also *dedication* or *consecration.* All the utensils employed in the tabernacle service were thus *purified* though incapable of any moral pollution.

But the heavenly things themselves] Some think this means *heaven* itself, which, by receiving the sacrificed body of Christ, which appears in the presence of God for us, may be said to be *purified,* i. e. *set apart* for the reception of the souls of those who have found redemption in his blood. 2. Others think the *body of Christ* is intended, which is the *tabernacle* in which his Divinity dwelt ; and that this might be said to be *purified* by its own sacrifice, as he is said, John xvii. 19, to *sanctify himself ;* that is, to *consecrate* himself unto God as a sin-offering for the redemption of man. 3. Others suppose the *Church* is intended, which he is to *present to the Father without spot* or *wrinkle* or *any such thing.* 4. As the *entrance* to the holy of holies must be made by the sprinkling of the blood of the sacrifice, and as that holy of holies represented *heaven,* the apostle's meaning seems to be that there was and could be no entrance to the holiest but through his blood ; and therefore, when by a more perfect tabernacle, ver. 11, 12, he passed into the heavens, not with the blood of bulls and goats, but by his own blood, he thus purified or laid open the entrance to the holiest, by a more valuable sacrifice than those required to open the entrance of the holy of holies. *It was necessary,* therefore, for God had appointed it so, that the *tabernacle* and its *parts,* &c., which were *patterns of things in the heavens,* should be *consecrated* and *entered* with such sacrifices as have already been mentioned ; but the heaven of heavens into which Jesus entered, and whither he will bring all his faithful followers, must be propitiated, consecrated, and entered, by the infinitely *better sacrifice* of his own body and blood. That this is the meaning appears from the following verse.

Verse 24. *Christ is not entered into the holy places*

made with hands] He is not gone into the *holy of holies* of the *tabernacle* or *temple,* as the Jewish high priest does once in the year with the blood of the victim, to sprinkle it before the mercy-seat there ; but *into heaven itself,* which he has thus opened to all believers, having made the propitiatory offering by which both he and those whom he represents are entitled to enter and enjoy eternal blessedness. And hence we may consider that Christ, appearing in his crucified body before the throne, is a real offering of himself to the Divine justice in behalf of man ; and that there he continues in the constant act of being offered, so that every penitent and believer, coming unto God through him, find him their ever ready and available sacrifice, officiating as the High Priest of mankind in the presence of God.

Verse 25. *Nor yet that he should offer himself often*] The sacrifice of Christ is not like that of the Jewish high priest ; his must be offered every year, Christ has offered himself *once for all :* and this sacrificial act has ever the same efficacy, his crucified body being still a powerful and infinitely meritorious sacrifice before the throne.

Verse 26. *For then must he often have suffered*] In the counsel of God Christ was considered the *Lamb slain from the foundation of the world,* Rev. xiii. 8, so that all believers *before* his advent were equally interested in his sacrificial death with those who have lived *since* his coming. Humanly speaking, the virtue of the annual atonement could not last long, and must be repeated ; Christ's sacrifice is ever the same ; his life's blood is still considered as in the act of being *continually poured out.* See Rev. v. 6.

The end of the world] The conclusion of the Jewish dispensation, the Christian dispensation being that which shall continue till the end of time.

To put away sin] Εις αθετησιν ἁμαρτιας· *To abolish the sin-offerings ;* i. e. to put an end to the *Mosaic economy* by his one offering of himself. It is certain that, after Christ had offered himself, the typical sin-offerings of the law ceased ; and this was expressly foretold by the Prophet Daniel, chap. ix. 24. Some think that the expression should be applied to the *putting away the guilt, power,* and *being* of sin from the souls of believers.

Verse 27. *As it is appointed*] Αποκειται· It is *laid before them* by the Divine decree : *Dust thou art, and unto dust thou shalt return.* Unto men generally,

2

during the course of the present world, not *all men* as some falsely quote; for Enoch and Elijah have not died, and those that shall be alive at the day of judgment shall not *die*, but be *changed*.

But after this the judgment] They *shall die* but *once*, and be *judged* but *once*, therefore there is no *metempsychosis*, no *transmigration from body to body*; judgment succeeds to dying; and as they shall be *judged* but *once*, they can *die* but *once*.

Verse 28. *So Christ was once offered*] He shall die no more; he has borne away the sins of many, and what he has done *once* shall stand good for ever. Yet *he will appear a second time without sin, χωρις ἁμαρτιας, without a sin-offering;* THAT he has already made.

Unto salvation.] To deliver the *bodies* of believers from the *empire of death*, to reunite them to their purified souls, and bring both into his eternal glory. This is *salvation*, and the very highest of which the human being is capable. Amen! Even so, come Lord Jesus! Hallelujah!

1. In the preceding notes I have given my reasons for dissenting from our translation of the 15th, 16th, and 17th verses. Many learned men are of the same opinion; but I have not met with one who appears to have treated the whole in a more satisfactory manner than Dr. *Macknight,* and for the edification of my readers I shall here subjoin the substance of what he has written on this point.

"Verse 15. *Mediator of the new covenant.* See Heb. viii. 7. The word διαθηκη, here translated *covenant,* answers to the Hebrew word *berith,* which all the translators of the Jewish Scriptures have understood to signify *a covenant.* The same signification our translators have affixed to the word διαθηκη, as often as it occurs in the writings of the evangelists and apostles, except in the history of the institution of the supper, and in 2 Cor. iii. 6: and Heb. vii. 22, and in the passage under consideration; in which places, copying the Vulgate version, they have rendered διαθηκη by the word *testament.* Beza, following the Syriac Version, translates διαθηκη everywhere by the words *fœdus, pactum,* except in the 16th, 17th, and 20th verses of this chapter, where likewise following the Syriac version, he has *testamentum.* Now if καινη διαθηκη, *the new testament,* in the passages above mentioned, means the Gospel covenant, as all interpreters acknowledge, παλαια διαθηκη, *the old testament,* 2 Cor. iii. 14, and πρωτη διαθηκη, *the first testament,* Heb. ix. 15, must certainly be the *Sinaitic covenant* or *law of Moses,* as is evident also from Heb. ix. 20. On this supposition it may be asked, 1. In what sense the Sinaitic covenant or law of Moses, which required perfect obedience to all its precepts under penalty of death, and allowed no mercy to any sinner, however penitent, can be called a *testament,* which is a deed conferring something valuable on a person who may accept or refuse it, as he thinks fit? Besides, the transaction at Sinai, in which God promised to continue the Israelites in Canaan, on condition they refrained from the wicked practices of the Canaanites, and observed his statutes, Lev. xviii., can in no sense be called a testament. 2. If the law of Moses be a testament, and if, to render that testament

valid, the death of the testator be necessary, as the English translators have taught us, ver. 16, I ask who it was that made the testament of the law? Was it God or Moses? And did either of them die to render it valid? 3. I observe that even the Gospel covenant is improperly called *a testament,* because, notwithstanding all its blessings were procured by the death of Christ, and are most freely bestowed, it lost any validity which, as a testament, it is thought to have received by the death of Christ, when he revived again on the third day. 4. The things affirmed in the common translation of ver. 15 concerning *the new testament,* namely, that it has a Mediator; that that Mediator is the Testator himself; that there were transgressions of a former testament, for the redemption of which the Mediator of the new testament died; and, ver. 19, that the first testament was made by sprinkling the people in whose favour it was made with blood; are all things quite foreign to a testament. For was it ever known in any nation that a testament needed a mediator? Or that the testator was the mediator of his own testament? Or that it was necessary the testator of a new testament should die to redeem the transgressions of a former testament? Or that any testament was ever made by sprinkling the legatees with blood? These things however were usual in covenants. They had mediators who assisted at the making of them, and were sureties for the performance of them. They were commonly ratified by sacrifices, the blood of which was sprinkled on the parties; withal, if any former covenant was infringed by the parties, satisfaction was given at the making of a second covenant. 5. By calling Christ *the Mediator of the new testament* our thoughts are turned away entirely from the view which the Scriptures give us of his death as a sacrifice for sin; whereas, if he is called *the Mediator of the new covenant,* which is the true translation of διαθηκης καινης μεσιτης, that appellation directly suggests to us that the new covenant was procured and ratified by his death as a sacrifice for sin. Accordingly Jesus, on account of his being made a priest by the oath of God, is said to be *the Priest* or *Mediator of a better covenant* than that of which the Levitical priests were the mediators. I acknowledge that in classical Greek διαθηκη commonly signifies *a testament.* Yet, since the Seventy have uniformly translated the Hebrew word *berith,* which properly signifies a *covenant,* by the word διαθηκη, in writing Greek the Jews naturally used διαθηκη for συνθηκη as our translators have acknowledged by their version of Heb. x. 16. To conclude: Seeing in the verses under consideration διαθηκη may be translated *a covenant*; and seeing, when so translated, these verses make a better sense, and agree better with the scope of the apostle's reasoning than if it were translated *a testament*; we can be at no loss to know which translation of διαθηκη in these verses ought to be preferred. Nevertheless, the absurdity of a phraseology to which readers have been long accustomed, without attending distinctly to its meaning, does not soon appear.

"*He is the Mediator.* Here it is remarkable that Jesus is not called διαθεμενος, *the Testator,* but μεσιτης, the *Mediator,* of the new covenant; first, because he procured the new covenant for mankind, in which the pardon of sin is promised; for, as the apostle tells us, his death, as a sacrifice for sin, is the consideration on account of which the pardon of the transgressions of the first covenant is granted. Secondly, because the new covenant having been ratified as well as procured by the death of Christ, he is fitly called *the Mediator* of that covenant in the same sense that God's oath is called, Heb. vi. 17, the *mediator*, or *confirmer, of his promise.* Thirdly, Jesus, who died to procure the new covenant, being appointed by God the high priest thereof, to dispense his blessings, he is on that account also called, Heb. viii. 6, *the mediator of* that *better covenant.*

" Verse 16. *For where a covenant* [is made by sacrifice,] there is a necessity that the death of the appointed sacrifice be produced. This elliptical expression must be completed, if, as is probable, the apostle had now in his eye the covenant which God made with Noah and Abraham. His covenant is recorded, Gen. viii. 20, where we are told, that on coming out of the ark *Noah offered a burnt-offering of every clean beast and fowl. And the Lord smelled a sweet savour. And the Lord said in his heart, I will not again curse the ground, neither will I again smite any more every living thing as I have done.* This promise or declaration God called *his covenant with men, and with every living creature.* Gen. ix. 9, 10. In like manner God made a covenant with Abraham by sacrifice, Gen. xv. 9, 18, and with the Israelites at Sinai, Exod. xxiv. 8. See also Psa. l. 5. By making his covenants with men in this manner, God taught them that his intercourses with them were all founded on an expiation afterwards to be made for their sins by the sacrifice of the seed of the woman, *the bruising of whose heel,* or death, was foretold at the fall. On the authority of these examples, the practice of making covenants by sacrifice prevailed among the Jews; Jer. xxxiv. 18; Zech. ix. 11; and even among the heathens; for they had the knowledge of these examples by tradition. *Stabant et cæsa jungebant fœdera porca;* Virgil, Æneid, viii. 611. Hence the phrases, *fœdus ferire* and *percutere, to strike* or *kill the covenant.*

" There is a necessity that the death των διαθεμενου, *of the appointed.* Here we may supply either the word θυματος, *sacrifice,* or ζωον, *animal,* which might be either a calf, a goat, a bull, or any other animal which the parties making the covenant chose. Διαθεμενου is the participle of the second aorist of the middle voice of the verb διατιθημι, *constituo, I appoint.* Wherefore its primary and literal signification is, *of the appointed.* Our translators have given the word this sense, Luke xxii. 29 : Καγω διατιθεμαι ὑμιν, καθως διετιθετο μοι ὁ Πατηρ μου, βασιλειαν *And I appoint to you a kingdom, as my Father hath appointed to me a kingdom.*

" *Be brought in;* θανατον αναγκη φερεσθαι του διαθεμενου, Elsner, vol ii., p. 381, has shown that the word φερεσθαι is sometimes used in a forensic sense for what is *produced,* or *proved,* or made apparent in a court of judicature. Wherefore the apostle's meaning is, that it is necessary the death of the appointed sacrifice be brought in, or produced, at the making of the covenant. In the margin of our Bibles

this clause is rightly translated, *be brought in.* See Acts xxv. 7, where φεροντες is used in the forensic sense.

" Verse 17. *A covenant is firm over dead sacrifices;* Επι νεκροις. Νεκροις being an adjective, it must have a substantive agreeing with it, either expressed or understood. The substantive understood in this place, I think, is θυμασι, *sacrifices;* for which reason I have supplied it in the translation. Perhaps the word ζωοις, *animals,* may be equally proper; especially as, in the following clause, διαθεμενος is in the gender of the animals appointed for the sacrifice. Our translators have supplied the word ανθρωποις, *men,* and have translated επι νεκροις, *after men are dead,* contrary to the propriety of the phrase.

" *It never hath force whilst the appointed liveth;* Ὁτε ζη ὁ διαθεμενος. Supply μοσχος, or τραγος, or ταυρος· *whilst the calf,* or *goat,* or *bull, appointed for the sacrifice of ratification, liveth.* The apostle having, in verse 15, showed that Christ's death was necessary as ὁ Μεσιτης, *the Mediator,* that is, *the procurer,* and *ratifier* of the new covenant, he in the 16th and 17th verses observes that, since God's covenants with men were all ratified by sacrifice to show that his intercourses with men are founded on the sacrifice of his Son, it was necessary that the new covenant itself should be ratified by his Son's actually dying as a sacrifice.

" The faultiness of the common translation of the 15th, 16th, 17th, 18th, and 20th verses of this chapter having been already shown in the notes, nothing needs be added here, except to call the reader's attention to the propriety and strength of the apostle's reasoning, as it appears in the translation of these verses which I have given, compared with his reasoning as represented in the common version."

2. It is supposed that in verse 28, the apostle, in speaking about Christ's bearing the sins of many, alludes to the ceremony of the *scape goat.* This mysterious sacrifice was to be presented to God, Lev. xvi. 7, and the sins of the people were to be confessed over the head of it, ver. 21, and after this the goat was dismissed into a land uninhabited, laden, as the institution implied, with the sins of the people; and this the word ανενεγκειν, *to bear* or *carry away,* seems to imply. So truly as the goat did metaphorically bear away the sins of the many, so truly did Christ literally bear the punishment due to our sins; and in reference to every believer, has so *borne them away* that they shall never more rise in judgment against him.

3. In Christ's coming, or *appearing the second time,* it is very probable, as Dr. Doddridge and others have conjectured, that there is an allusion to the return of the high priest from the inner tabernacle; for, after appearing there in the presence of God, and making atonement for the people in the plain dress of an ordinary priest, Lev. xvi. 23, 24, he came out arrayed in his magnificent robes, to bless the people, who waited for him in the court of the tabernacle of the congregation. " But there will be this difference," says Dr. Macknight, " between the return of Christ to bless his people, and the return of the high priest to bless the congregation. The latter, after coming out of the most holy place, made a new atonement in his pontifical robes for himself and for the people, Lev. xvi. 24, which showed that the former atonement was not

2

real but *typical.* Whereas Jesus, after having made atonement, [and presented himself in heaven, before God,] will not return to the earth for the purpose of making himself a sacrifice the second time; but having procured an eternal redemption for us, by the sacrifice of himself once offered, he will return for the purpose of declaring to them who wait for him that they are accepted, and of bestowing on them the great blessing of eternal life. This reward he, being surrounded with the glory of the Father, Matt. xvi. 27, will give them in the presence of an assembled universe, both as their *King* and their *Priest.* This is the great salvation which Christ came to preach, and which was confirmed to the world by them who heard him: Heb. ii. 3." Reader, lay this sincerely to heart!

4. The *form* in which the high priest and the ordinary priests were to bless the people, after burning the incense in the tabernacle, is prescribed, Num. vi. 23–26. Literally translated from the Hebrew it

is as follows, and consists of three parts or benedictions :—

1. May Jehovah bless thee, and preserve thee!
2. May Jehovah cause his face to shine upon thee, and be gracious unto thee!
3. May Jehovah lift up his faces upon thee, and may he put prosperity unto thee! (See my notes on the place.)

We may therefore say that Christ, our High Priest, came to *bless* each of us, by turning us away from our iniquity. And let no one ever expect to see him at his second coming with joy, unless he have, in this life, been turned away from *his* iniquity, and obtained remission of all his sins, and that holiness without which none can see God. Reader, the time of his reappearing is, to thee, at hand! Prepare to meet thy God!

On the word *conscience,* which occurs so often in this chapter, and in other parts of this epistle, see the observations at the end of chap. xiii.

CHAPTER X.

The insufficiency of the legal sacrifices to take away sin, 1–4. The purpose and will of God, as declared by the Psalmist, relative to the salvation of the world by the incarnation of Christ; and our sanctification through that will, 5–10. Comparison between the priesthood of Christ and that of the Jews, 11–14. The new covenant which God promised to make, and the blessings of it, 15–17. The access which genuine believers have to the holiest by the blood of Jesus, 18–20. Having a High Priest over the Church of God, we should have faith, walk uprightly, hold fast our profession, exhort and help each other, and maintain Christian communion, 21–25. The danger and awful consequences of final apostasy, 26–31. In order to our perseverance, we should often reflect on past mercies, and the support afforded us in temptations and afflictions; and not cast away our confidence, for we shall receive the promise if we patiently fulfil the will of God, 32–37. The just by faith shall live; but the soul that draws back shall die, 38. The apostle's confidence in the believing Hebrews, 39.

A. M. cir. 4067.
A. D. cir. 63.
An. Olymp.
cir. CCX. 3.
A U. C. cir.
816.

FOR the law having a ª shadow ᵇ of good things to come, *and* not the very image of the things, ᶜ can never with those

sacrifices which they offered year by year continually make the comers thereunto ᵈ perfect.

A. M. cir. 4067.
A. D. cir. 63.
An. Olymp.
cir. CCX. 3.
A. U. C. cir.
816.

ª Col. ii. 17; chap. viii. 5; ix. 23.——ᵇ Chap. ix. 11. ᶜ Chap. ix. 9.——ᵈ Ver. 14.

NOTES ON CHAP. X.

Verse 1. *The law, having a shadow of good things to come*] A shadow, σκια, signifies, 1. *Literally,* the shade cast from a body of any kind, interposed between the place on which the shadow is projected, and the sun or light; the rays of the light not shining on that place, because intercepted by the opacity of the body, through which they cannot pass. 2. It signifies, *technically,* a sketch, rude plan, or imperfect draught of a building, landscape, man, beast, &c. 3. It signifies, *metaphorically,* any faint adumbration, symbolical expression, imperfect or obscure image of a thing; and is opposed to σωμα, *body,* or the *thing* intended to be thereby defined. 4. It is used *catachrestically* among the Greek writers, as *umbra* is among the Latins, to signify any thing *vain, empty, light,* not *solid;* thus Philostratus, Vit. Soph., lib. i. cap. 20: Ὅτι σκια και ονειρατα αἱ ἡδοναι πασαι· *All pleasures are but* SHADOWS *and dreams.* And Cicero,

in Pison., cap. 24: *Omnes umbras falsæ gloriæ consectari.* "All pursue the SHADOWS of FALSE GLORY." And again, *De Offic.,* lib. iii. cap. 17: *Nos veri juris germanæque justitiæ solidam et expressam effigiem nullam tenemus;* umbra *et* imaginibus *utimur.* "We have no solid and express effigy of true law and genuine justice, but we employ shadows and images to represent them."

And *not the very image*] Εικων, *image,* signifies, 1. A simple *representation,* from εικω, *I am like.* 2. The *form* or particular fashion of a thing. 3. The *model* according to which any thing is formed. 4. The *perfect image* of a thing as opposed to a faint representation. 5. *Metaphorically,* a *similitude,* agreement, or conformity.

The law, with all its ceremonies and sacrifices, was only a *shadow* of spiritual and eternal good. The Gospel is the *image* or *thing itself,* as including every spiritual and eternal good.

A. M. cir. 4067.
A. D. cir. 63.
An. Olymp.
cir. CCX. 3.
A. U..C. cir.
816.

2 For then ^e would they not have ceased to be offered ? because that the worshippers once purged should have had no more conscience of sins.

3 ^f But in those *sacrifices there is* a remembrance again *made* of sins every year.

4 For ^g *it is* not possible that the blood of bulls and of goats should take away sins.

5 Wherefore, when he cometh into the world, he saith, ^h Sacrifice and offering thou wouldest not, but a body ⁱ hast thou prepared me :

A. M. cir. 4067.
A. D. cir. 63.
An. Olymp.
cir. CCX. 3.
A. U. C. cir.
816.

e Or, *they would have ceased to be offered, because,* &c.——f Lev. xvi. 21; chap. ix. 7.——g Mic. vi. 6, 7; chap. ix. 13; ver. 11.

h Psa. xl. 6, &c.; l, 8, &c.; Isa. i. 11; Jer. vi. 20; Amos v. 21, 22.——i Or, *thou hast fitted me.*

We may note *three* things here : 1. The *shadow* or general outline, limiting the size and proportions of the thing to be represented. 2. The *image* or *likeness* completed from this shadow or general outline, whether represented on paper, canvass, or in statuary. 3. The *person* or *thing* thus represented in its actual, natural state of existence ; or what is called here the *very image of the things*, αυτην την εικονα των πραγματων. Such is the *Gospel*, when compared with the *law* ; such is *Christ*, when compared with *Aaron* ; such is his *sacrifice*, when compared with the *Levitical offerings* ; such is the *Gospel remission of sins* and *purification*, when compared with those afforded by the law ; such is the *Holy Ghost*, ministered by the Gospel, when compared with its types and shadows in the Levitical service ; such the *heavenly rest*, when compared with the *earthly Canaan*. Well, therefore, might the apostle say, *The law was only the shadow of good things to come.*

Can never—make the comers thereunto perfect.] Cannot remove guilt from the conscience, or impurity from the heart. I leave *preachers* to improve these points.

Verse 2. *Would they not have ceased to be offered?*] Had they made an effectual reconciliation for the sins of the world, and contained in their once offering a plenitude of permanent merit, they would have ceased to be offered, at least in reference to any individual who had once offered them ; because, in such a case, his conscience would be satisfied that its guilt had been taken away. But no Jew pretended to believe that even the annual atonement cancelled his sin before God ; yet he continued to make his offerings, the law of God having so enjoined, because these sacrifices pointed out that which was to come. They were offered, therefore, not in *consideration* of their own efficacy, but as referring to Christ ; see on chap. ix. 9.

Verse 4. *For it is not possible*] Common sense must have taught them that shedding the blood of bulls and goats could never satisfy Divine justice, nor take away guilt from the conscience ; and God intended that they should understand the matter so : and this the following quotation from the Psalmist sufficiently proves.

Verse 5. *When he* (the Messiah) *cometh into the world*] Was about to be incarnated, *He saith* to God the Father, *Sacrifice and offering thou wouldest not*—it was never thy *will* and design that the sacrifices under thy own law should be considered as making atonement for sin, they were only designed to point out my incarnation and consequent sacrificial death, and therefore *a body hast thou prepared me*, by a mira-

culous conception in the womb of a virgin, according to thy word, *The seed of the woman shall bruise the head of the serpent.*

A body hast thou prepared me] The quotation in this and the two following verses is taken from Psalm xl., 6th, 7th, and 8th verses, as they stand now in the *Septuagint*, with scarcely any variety of reading ; but, although the general meaning is the same, they are widely different in verbal expression in the Hebrew. David's words are, אזנים כרית לי *oznayim- caritha li*, which we translate, *My ears hast thou opened* ; but they might be more properly rendered, *My ears hast thou bored*, that is, thou hast made me *thy servant for ever*, to dwell in thine own house ; for the allusion is evidently to the custom mentioned, Exod. xxi. 2, &c. : "If thou buy a Hebrew servant, six years he shall serve, and in the seventh he shall go out free ; but if the servant shall positively say, I love my master, &c., I will not go out free, then his master shall bring him to the door post, and shall bore his ear through with an awl, and he shall serve him for ever."

But how is it possible that the Septuagint and the apostle should take a meaning so totally different from the sense of the Hebrew ? Dr. Kennicott has a very ingenious conjecture here : he supposes that the Septuagint and apostle express the meaning of the words as they stood in the copy from which the Greek translation was made ; and that the present Hebrew text is corrupted in the word אזנים *oznayim*, ears, which has been written through carelessness for אז גוה *az gevah*, THEN A BODY. The first syllable אז, THEN, is the same in both ; and the latter נים, which joined to אז, makes אזנים *oznayim*, might have been easily mistaken for גוה *gevah*, BODY ; נ *nun*, being very like ג *gimel* ; י *yod*, like ו *vau* ; and ה *he*, like final ם *mem* ; especially if the line on which the letters were written in the MS. happened to be blacker than ordinary, which has often been a cause of mistake, it might have been easily taken for the under stroke of the *mem*, and thus give rise to a corrupt reading : add to this the root כרה *carah*, signifies as well to *prepare* as to *open, bore*, &c. On this supposition the ancient copy, translated by the Septuagint, and followed by the apostle, must have read the text thus : אז גוה כרית לי *az gevah caritha li*, σωμα δε κατηρτισω μοι, *then a body thou hast prepared me* : thus the Hebrew text, the version of the Septuagint, and the apostle, will agree in what is known to be an indisputable fact in Christianity, namely, that Christ was *incarnated* for the sin of the world.

The *Æthiopic* has nearly the same reading ; the *Arabic* has both, *A body hast thou prepared me, and*

A. M. cir. 4067.
A. D. cir. 63.
An. Olymp.
cir. CCX. 3.
A. U. C. cir.
816.

6 In burnt-offerings and *sacrifices* for sin thou hast had no pleasure :

7 Then said I, Lo, I come (in the volume of the book it is written of me) to do thy will, O God.

8 Above, when he said, Sacrifice and offering and burnt-offerings and *offering* for sin thou wouldest not, neither hadst pleasure *therein ;* which are offered by the law ;

9 Then said he, Lo, I come to do thy will, O God. He taketh away the first,

that he may establish the second.

10 [k] By the which will we are sanctified, [l] through the offering of the body of Jesus Christ once *for all.*

11 And every priest standeth [m] daily ministering and offering oftentimes the same sacrifices, [n] which can never take away sins :

12 [o] But this man, after he had offered one sacrifice for sins, for ever sat down on the right hand of God ;

13 From henceforth expecting [p] till his

A. M. cir. 4067.
A. D. cir. 63.
An. Olymp.
cir. CCX. 3.
A. U. C. cir.
816.

---

[k] John xvii. 19 ; chapter xiii. 12.——[l] Chap. ix. 12.——[m] Num. xxviii. 3 ; chap. vii. 27.——[n] Ver. 4.

[o] Chapter i. 3 ; Col. iii. 1.——[p] Psa. cx. 1 ; Acts ii. 35 ; 1 Cor. xv. 25 ; chap. i. 13.

---

mine ears thou hast opened. But the *Syriac,* the *Chaldee,* and the *Vulgate,* agree with the present Hebrew text ; and none of the MSS. collated by *Kennicott* and *De Rossi* have any various reading on the disputed words.

It is remarkable that all the offerings and sacrifices which were considered to be of an atoning or cleansing nature, offered under the law, are here enumerated by the psalmist and the apostle, to show that *none* of them nor *all* of them could take away sin, and that the grand sacrifice of Christ was that alone which could do it.

Four kinds are here specified, both by the psalmist and the apostle, viz. : SACRIFICE, זבח *zebach,* θυσια· OFFERING, מנחה *minchah,* προσφορα· BURNT-OFFERING, עולה *olah,* ὁλοκαυτωμα· SIN-OFFERING, חטאה *chataah,* περι ἁμαρτιας. Of all these we may say, with the apostle, it was impossible that the blood of bulls and goats, &c., should take away sin.

Verse 6. *Thou hast had no pleasure.*] Thou couldst never be pleased with the victims under the law ; thou couldst never consider them as atonements for sin ; as they could never satisfy thy justice, nor make thy law honourable.

Verse 7. *In the volume of the book*] במגלת כפר *bimgillath sepher,* " in the *roll* of the book." Anciently, books were written on skins and rolled up. Among the Romans these were called *volumina,* from *volvo, I roll ;* and the Pentateuch, in the Jewish synagogues, is still written in this way. There are two wooden rollers ; on one they roll *on,* on the other they roll *off,* as they proceed in reading. The *book* mentioned here must be the *Pentateuch,* or five books of Moses ; for in David's time no other part of Divine revelation had been committed to writing. This whole book speaks about Christ, and his accomplishing the *will* of God ; not only in, *The seed of the woman shall bruise the head of the serpent,* and, *In thy seed shall all the nations of the earth be blessed,* but in all the *sacrifices* and sacrificial rites mentioned in the law.

To do thy will] God *willed* not the sacrifices under the law, but he *willed* that a human victim of infinite merit should be offered for the redemption of mankind. That there might be *such a victim,* a *body* was prepared for the eternal Logos ; and in that body *he came* to do the *will of God,* that is, to suffer and die for the sins of the world.

Verse 9. *He taketh away the first*] The offerings, sacrifices, burnt-offerings, and sacrifices for sin, which were prescribed by the *law.*

That he may establish the second.] The offering of the *body of Jesus* once for all. It will make little odds in the meaning if we say, he taketh away the first *covenant,* that he may establish the second *covenant ;* he takes away the first *dispensation,* that he may establish the second ; he takes away the *law,* that he may establish the *Gospel.* In all these cases the sense is nearly the same : I prefer the *first.*

Verse 10. *By the which will we are sanctified*] Closing in with this so solemnly declared WILL of God, that there is no name given under heaven among men, by which we can be saved, but Jesus the Christ, we believe in him, find redemption in his blood, and are sanctified unto God through the sacrificial *offering of his body.*

1. Hence we see that the sovereign WILL of God is, that Jesus should be incarnated ; that he should suffer and die, or, in the apostle's words, *taste death for every man ;* that all should believe on him, and be saved from their sins : for this is the WILL of God, our *sanctification.*

2. And as the apostle grounds this on the words of the psalm, we see that it is the WILL *of God* that that system shall end ; for as the essence of it is contained in its *sacrifices,* and God says he *will not* have these, and has prepared the *Messiah* to do his will, *i. e.* to *die for men,* hence it necessarily follows, from the psalmist himself, that the introduction of the Messiah into the world is the abolition of the law, and that his sacrifice is that which shall last for ever.

Verse 11. *Every priest standeth*] The office of the Jewish priest is here compared with the office of our High Priest. The Jewish priest *stands* daily at the altar, like a servant ministering, *repeating* the same sacrifices ; our High Priest offered himself once for all, and *sat down* at the right hand of God, as the only-begotten Son and Heir of all things, ver. 12. This *continual* offering argued the *imperfection* of the sacrifices. Our Lord's *once* offering, proves his was *complete.*

Verse 13. *Till his enemies be made his footstool.*] Till all that oppose his high priesthood and sacrificial offering shall be defeated, routed, and confounded ; and

A. M. cir. 4067.
A. D. cir. 63.
An. Olymp.
cir. CCX. 3.
A. U. C. cir.
816.
enemies be made his footstool.

14 For by one offering q he hath perfected for ever them that are sanctified.

15 *Whereof* the Holy Ghost also is a witness to us : for after that he had said before,

16 r This *is* the covenant that I will make with them after those days, saith the Lord, I will put my laws into their hearts, and in their minds will I write them ;

17 s And their sins and iniquities will I remember no more.

18 Now where remission of these *is, there is* no more offering for sin.

19 Having therefore, brethren, t boldness u to enter v into the holiest by the blood of Jesus,

20 By w a new and living way, which he hath x consecrated for us, y through the veil, that is to say, his flesh ;

A. M. cir. 4067.
A. D. cir. 63.
An. Olymp.
cir. CCX. 3.
A. U. C. cir.
816.

---

q Ver. 1.——r Jer. xxxi. 33, 34 ; chap. viii. 10, 12.——s Some copies have, *Then he said, And their.*——t Rom. v. 2 ; Eph. ii. 18 ;

iii. 12.——u Or, *liberty.*——v Chapter ix. 8, 12.——w John x. 9 ; xiv. 6 ; chap. ix. 8.——x Or, *new made.*——y Chap. ix. 3.

---

acknowledge, in their punishment, the supremacy of his power as universal and eternal King, who refused to receive him as their *atoning* and *sanctifying Priest.* There is also an oblique reference here to the destruction of the Jews, which was then at hand ; for Christ was about to *take away the second* with an overwhelming flood of desolations.

Verse 14. For by one offering] His death upon the cross.

He hath perfected for ever] He has procured remission of sins and holiness ; for it is well observed here, and in several parts of this epistle, that τελειοω, *to make perfect,* is the same as αφεσιν αμαρτιων ποιεω, *to procure remission of sins.*

Them that are sanctified.] Τους αγιαζομενους· Them that have received the sprinkling of the blood of this offering. These, therefore, receiving redemption through that blood, have no need of any other offering ; as this was a complete atonement, purification, and title to eternal glory.

Verse 15. The Holy Ghost—is a witness to us] The words are quoted from Jer. xxxi. 33, 34, and here we are assured that Jeremiah spoke by the inspiration of the Spirit of God.

Had said before] See chap. viii. 10, 12, and the notes there.

Verse 18. Now where remission of these is] In any case, where sin is once pardoned, there is no farther need of a sin-offering ; but every believer on Christ has his sin blotted out, and therefore needs no other offering for that sin.

"If," says Dr. Macknight, "after remission is granted to the sinner, there is no need of any more sacrifice for sin ; and if Christ, by offering himself once, has *perfected for ever the sanctified,* ver: 14, the *sacrifice of the mass,* as it is called, about which the Romish clergy employ themselves so incessantly, and to which the *papists* trust for the pardon of their sins, has no foundation in Scripture. Nay, it is an evident impiety, as it proceeds upon the supposition that the offering of the body of Christ *once* is not sufficient to procure the pardon of sin, but must be *frequently* repeated. If they reply that their mass is only the representation and commemoration of the sacrifice of Christ, they give up the cause, and renounce an article of their faith, established by the council of Trent, which, in session xxii. can. 1, 3, declared *the sacrifice of the*

mass to be a true and propitiatory sacrifice for sin. I say, give up the cause ; for the *representation* and *commemoration* of a sacrifice is not a sacrifice. Farther, it cannot·be affirmed that the body of Christ is offered in the mass, unless it can be said that, as often as it is offered, *Christ has suffered death* ; for the apostle says expressly, Heb. ix. 25, 26, that if Christ offered himself often, *he must often have suffered since the foundation of the world.*" Let him disprove this who can.

Verse 19. Having therefore, brethren, boldness] The apostle, having now finished the doctrinal part of his epistle, and fully shown the superiority of Christ to all men and angels, and the superiority of his priesthood to that of Aaron and his successors, the absolute inefficacy of the Jewish sacrifices to make atonement for sin, and the absolute efficacy of that of Christ to make reconciliation of man to God, proceeds now to show what influence these doctrines should have on the hearts and lives of those who believe in his merits and death.

Boldness to enter] Παρρησιαν εις την εισοδον· *Liberty, full access to the entrance of the holy place,* των αγιων· This is an allusion to the case of the high priest going into the holy of holies. He went with fear and trembling, because, if he had neglected the smallest item prescribed by the law, he could expect nothing but death. Genuine believers can come even to the throne of God with confidence, as they carry into the Divine presence the infinitely meritorious blood of the great atonement ; and, being justified through that blood, they have a right to all the blessings of the eternal kingdom.

Verse 20. By a new and living way] It is a *new* way ; no *human* being had ever before entered into the heaven of heavens ; Jesus in human nature was the *first,* and thus he has opened the way to heaven to mankind, his own resurrection and ascension to glory being the proof and pledge of ours.

The way is called οδον προσφατον και ζωσαν, *new* or *fresh, and living.* This is evidently an allusion to the blood of the victim *newly shed, uncoagulated,* and consequently proper to be used for *sprinkling.* The blood of the Jewish victims was fit for sacrificial purposes only so long as it was *warm and fluid,* and might be considered as yet possessing its *vitality* ; but when it grew *cold,* it *coagulated,* lost its *vitality,*

2

A. M. cir. 4067.
A. D. cir. 63.
An. Olymp.
cir. CCX. 3.
A. U. C. cir.
816.

21 And *having* [z] a high priest over [a] the house of God;

22 [b] Let us draw near with a true heart, [c] in full assurance of faith, having our hearts sprinkled [d] from an evil conscience, and [e] our bodies washed with pure water.

23 [f] Let us hold fast the profession of *our* faith without wavering; (for [g] he *is* faithful that promised;)

A. M. cir. 4067.
A. D. cir. 63.
An. Olymp.
cir. CCX. 3.
A. U. C. cir.
816.

---

[z] Chap. iv. 14.——[a] 1 Tim. iii. 15.——[b] Chap. iv. 16.——[c] Eph. iii. 12; James i. 6; 1 John iii. 21.——[d] Chap. ix. 14.

[e] Ezek. xxxvi. 25; 2 Cor. vii. 1.——[f] Chap. iv. 14.——[g] 1 Cor. i. 9; x. 13; 1 Thess. v. 24; 2 Thess. iii. 3; chap. xi. 11.

---

and was no longer proper to be used sacrificially. Christ is here, in the allusion, represented as *newly slain*, and yet *living*; the blood ever considered as *flowing* and giving life to the world. The *way* by the old covenant neither gave life, nor removed the liability to death. The way to peace and reconciliation, under the old covenant, was through the dead bodies of the animals slain; but Christ is living, and ever liveth, to make intercession for us; therefore he is a new and *living* way.

In the Choephoræ of Æschylus, ver. 801, there is an expression like this of the apostle:—

Αγετε, των παλαι πεπραγμενων
Λυσασθ' αιμα προσφατοις δικαις.

Agite, olim venditorum
Solvite sanguinem recenti vindicta.

This way, says Dr. Owen, is *new*, 1. Because it was but newly made and prepared. 2. Because it belongs unto the new covenant. 3. Because it admits of no decays, but is always new, as to its efficacy and use, as in the day of its first preparation. 4. The way of the tabernacle waxed old, and so was prepared for a removal; but the Gospel way of salvation shall never be altered, nor changed, nor decay; it is always *new*, and remains for ever.

It is also called ζωσαν, *living*, 1. In opposition to the way into the holiest under the tabernacle, which was by *death;* nothing could be done in it without the blood of a victim. 2. It was the cause of death to any who might use it, except the high priest himself; and he could have access to it only one day in the year. 3. It is called *living*, because it has a spiritual *vital* efficacy in our access to God. 4. It is *living* as to its effects; it leads to life, and infallibly brings those who walk in it unto *life eternal*.

Through the veil] As the high priest lifted up or drew aside the veil that separated the holy from the most holy place, in order that he might have access to the Divine Majesty; and as the veil of the temple was rent from the top to the bottom at the crucifixion of Christ, to show that the way to the holiest was then laid open; so we must approach the throne through the mediation of Christ, and through his sacrificial death. His pierced side is the way to the holiest. Here the veil—his humanity, is rent, and the kingdom of heaven opened to all believers.

Verse 21. *A high priest over the house of God*] The *house* or family of God is the Christian Church, or all true believers in the Lord Jesus. Over this Church, house, or family, Christ is the High Priest—in their behalf he offers his own blood, and their prayers and praises; and as the high priest had the ordering of all things that appertained to the house

and worship of God, so has Christ in the government of his Church. This government he never gave into other hands. As none can govern and preserve the world but God, so none can govern and save the Church but the Lord Jesus: He is *over* the house; He is its *President;* he instructs, protects, guides, feeds, defends, and saves the flock. Those who have such a President may well have *confidence;* for with him is the fountain of life, and he has all power in the heavens and in the earth.

Verse 22. *Let us draw near*] Let us come with the blood of our sacrifice to the throne of God: the expression is sacrificial.

With a true heart] Deeply convinced of our need of help, and truly in earnest to obtain it.

In full assurance of faith] Being fully persuaded that God will accept us for the sake of his Son, and that the sacrificial death of Christ gives us full authority to expect every blessing we need.

Having our hearts sprinkled] Not our *bodies*, as was the case among the Hebrews, when they had contracted any pollution, for they were to be *sprinkled with the water of separation*, see Num. xix. 2–10; but our *hearts*, sprinkled by the cleansing efficacy of the blood of Christ, without which we cannot draw nigh to God.

From an evil conscience] Having that deep sense of guilt which our conscience felt taken all away, and the peace and love of God shed abroad in our hearts by the Holy Ghost given unto us.

Our bodies washed with pure water.] The high priest, before he entered into the inner tabernacle, or put on his holy garments, was to wash his flesh in water, Lev. xvi. 4, and the Levites were to be cleansed the same way, Num. viii. 7. The apostle probably alludes to this in what he says here, though it appears that he refers principally to *baptisms*, the washing by which was an emblem of the purification of the soul by the grace and Spirit of Christ; but it is most likely that it is to the Jewish baptisms, and not the Christian, that the apostle alludes.

Verse 23. *Let us hold fast the profession of our faith*] The word ὁμολογια, from ὁμου, *together*, and λογος, *a word*, implies that general consent that was among Christians on all the important articles of their faith and practice; particularly their acknowledgment of the truth of the Gospel, and of Jesus Christ, as the only victim for sin, and the only Saviour from it. If the word *washed* above refer to Christian baptism in the case of adults, then the profession is that which the baptized then made of their faith in the Gospel; and of their determination to live and die in that faith.

The various readings on this clause are many in the MSS., &c. Της ελπιδος την ὁμολογιαν, the confession

9

A. M. cir. 4067.
A. D. cir. 63.
An. Olymp.
cir. CCX. 3.
A. U. C. cir.
816.

24 And let us consider one another to provoke unto love and to good works:

25 [h] Not forsaking the assembling of ourselves together, as the manner of some *is;* but exhorting *one another:* and [i] so much the more, as ye see [k] the day approaching.

26 For [1] if we sin wilfully [m] after that we have received the knowledge of the truth, there remaineth no more sacrifice for sins,

27 But a certain fearful looking for of judgment, and [n] fiery indignation, which shall devour the adversaries.

A. M. cir. 4067
A. D. cir. 63
An. Olymp
cir. CCX. 3.
A. U. C. cir
816.

[h] Acts ii. 42; Jude 19.——[i] Rom. xiii. 11.——[k] Phil. iv. 5; 2 Pet. iii. 9, 11, 14.——[1] Num. xv. 30; chap. vi. 4.

[m] 2 Peter ii. 20, 21.——[n] Ezekiel xxxvi. 5; Zeph. i. 18; iii. 8; 2 Thess. i. 8; chap. xii. 29.

of our HOPE; D*, two of the *Itala, Vulgate,* Erpen's *Arabic,* and the *Æthiopic.* Ὁμολογιαν της πιστεως, *the confession of* FAITH; one of the Barberini MSS. and two others. This is the reading which our translators have followed; but it is of very little authority. Την επαγγελιαν της ελπιδος, *the promise of* HOPE; St. Chrysostom. Την ελπιδα της ὁμολογιας, *the* HOPE *of* our PROFESSION; one of Petavius's MSS. But among all these, the *confession* or *profession of* HOPE is undoubtedly the genuine reading. Now, among the primitive Christians, the *hope* which they professed was the *resurrection of the body, and everlasting life;* every thing among these Christians was done and believed in reference to a future state; and for the joy that this set before them, they, like their Master, endured every cross, and despised all shame: they *expected* to be with God, through Christ; this *hope* they *professed to have;* and they *confessed* boldly and publicly the *faith* on which this hope was built. The apostle exhorts them to *hold fast* this *confession without wavering*—never to doubt the declarations made to them by their Redeemer, but having the *full assurance of faith* that their hearts were sprinkled from an evil conscience, that they had found redemption in the blood of the Lamb, they might expect to be glorified with their living Head in the kingdom of their Father.

He is *faithful that promised*] The eternal life, which is the *object* of your *hope,* is promised to you by him who cannot lie; as he then is *faithful* who has given you this *promise, hold fast the profession of* your *hope.*

Verse 24. *And let us consider one another*] Κατανοωμεν· Let us *diligently* and *attentively* consider each other's trials, difficulties, and weaknesses; feel for each other, and *excite* each other to an increase of *love* to God and man; and, as the proof of it, to be fruitful in *good works.* The words εις παροξυσμον, *to the provocation,* are often taken in a *good sense,* and signify *excitement, stirring up,* to do any thing laudable, useful, honourable, or necessary. Xenophon, *Cyrop.,* lib. vi., page 108, speaking of the conduct of Cyrus towards his officers, says: Και τουτους επαινων τε, παρωξυνε, και χαριζομενος αυτοις ὁ τι δυναιτο. "He by praises and gifts *excited* them as much as possible." See the note on Acts xv. 39, where the subject is farther considered.

Verse 25. *Not forsaking the assembling of ourselves*] Επισυναγωγην ἑαυτων. Whether this means *public* or *private* worship is hard to say; but as the word is but once more used in the New Testament, (2 Thess. ii. 1,) and there means the *gathering together* of the redeemed of the Lord at the day of judgment, it is as likely that

it means here *private* religious meetings, for the purpose of mutual exhortation: and this sense appears the more natural here, because it is evident that the Church was now in a state of persecution, and therefore their meetings were most probably held in *private.* For fear of persecution, it seems as if some had deserted these meetings, καθως εθος τισιν, *as the custom of certain persons is.* They had given up these strengthening and instructive means, and the others were in danger of following their example.

The day approaching.] Την ἡμεραν· *That day*— the time in which God would come and pour out his judgments on the Jewish nation. We may also apply it to the day of death and the day of judgment. Both of these are approaching to every human being. He who wishes to be found ready will carefully use every means of grace, and particularly the communion of saints, if there be even but *two* or *three* in the place where he lives, who statedly meet together in the name of Christ. Those who relinquish Christian communion are in a backsliding state; those who backslide are in danger of *apostasy.* To prevent this latter, the apostle speaks the awful words following. See at the end of this chapter.

Verse 26. *For if we sin wilfully*] If we deliberately, for fear of persecution or from any other motive, renounce the *profession of the Gospel* and the *Author* of that Gospel, after having received the knowledge of the truth so as to be convinced that Jesus is the promised Messiah, and that he had sprinkled our hearts from an evil conscience; for such *there remaineth no sacrifice for sins;* for as the Jewish sacrifices are abolished, as appears by the declaration of God himself in the fortieth Psalm, and Jesus being now the only sacrifice which God will accept, those who reject him have *none other;* therefore their case must be utterly without remedy. This is the meaning of the apostle, and the case is that of a *deliberate apostate*—one who has utterly rejected Jesus Christ and his atonement, and renounced the whole Gospel system. It has nothing to do with *backsliders* in our common use of that term. A man may be overtaken in a fault, or he may deliberately go into sin, and yet neither renounce the Gospel, nor deny the Lord that bought him. His case is dreary and dangerous, but it is not *hopeless;* no case is *hopeless* but that of the deliberate *apostate,* who rejects the whole Gospel system, after having been saved by grace, or convinced of the truth of the Gospel. To him there remaineth no *more sacrifice for sin;* for there was but the ONE, Jesus, and this he has utterly rejected.

Verse 27. *A certain fearful looking for of judg-*

2

A. M. cir. 4067.
A. D. cir. 63.
An. Olymp.
cir. CCX. 3.
A. U. C. cir.
816.

28 ° He that despised Moses' law died without mercy, ᵖ under two or three witnesses :

29 �q Of how much sorer punishment, suppose ye, shall he be thought worthy, who hath trodden under foot the Son of God, and ʳ hath counted the blood of the covenant, wherewith he was sanctified, an unholy thing, ˢ and hath done despite unto the Spirit of grace ?

30 For we know him that hath said, ᵗ Vengeance *belongeth* unto me, I will recompense, saith the Lord. And again, �u The Lord shall judge his people.

31 ᵛ *It is* a fearful thing to fall into the hands of the living God.

32 But ʷ call to remembrance the former days, in which, ˣ after ye were illuminated, ye endured ʸ a great fight of afflictions ;

A. M. cir. 4067.
A. D. cir. 63.
An. Olymp.
cir. CCX. 3.
A. U. C. cir.
816.

° Chap. ii. 2.——ᵖ Deut. xvii. 2, 6; xix. 15; Matt. xviii. 16; John viii. 17; 2 Cor. xiii. 1.——q Chap. ii. 3; xii. 25.——ʳ 1 Cor. xi. 29; chap. xiii. 20.——ˢ Matt. xii. 31, 32; Eph. iv. 30.

ᵗ Deut. xxxii. 35; Rom. xii. 19.——u Deut. xxxii. 36; Psa. l 4; cxxxv. 14.——ᵛ Luke xii. 5.——ʷ Gal. iii. 4; 2 John 8. ˣ Chap. vi. 4.——ʸ Phil. i. 29, 30; Col. ii. 1.

---

ment] From this it is evident that God will pardon no man without a sacrifice for sin; for otherwise, as Dr. Macknight argues, it would not follow, from there remaining to apostates no more sacrifice for sin, that there must remain to them a dreadful expectation of judgment.

And fiery indignation] Και πυρος ζηλος· A *zeal,* or *fervour of fire ;* something similar to the fire that came down from heaven and destroyed Korah and his company ; Num. xvi. 35.

Probably the apostle here refers to the case of the unbelieving Jews in general, as in chap. vi. to the dreadful judgment that was coming upon them, and the burning up their temple and city with fire. These people had, by the preaching of Christ and his apostles, received the knowledge of the truth. It was impossible that they could have witnessed his miracles and heard his doctrine without being convinced that he was the Messiah, and that their own system was at an end; but they rejected this only sacrifice at a time when God abolished their own : to that nation, therefore, *there remained no other sacrifice for sin ;* therefore the dreadful judgment came, the fiery indignation was poured out, and they, as *adversaries,* were *devoured* by it.

Verse 28. He that despised Moses' law] Αθετησας· He that rejected it, *threw it aside,* and denied its Divine authority by presumptuous sinning, *died without mercy*—without any extenuation or mitigation of punishment ; Num. xv. 30.

Under two or three witnesses] That is, when convicted by the testimony of two or three respectable witnesses. See Deut. xvii. 6.

Verse 29. Of how much sorer punishment] Such offences were trifling in comparison of this, and in justice the punishment should be proportioned to the offence.

Trodden under foot the Son of God] Treated him with the utmost contempt and blasphemy.

The blood of the covenant—an unholy thing] The blood of the covenant means here the sacrificial death of Christ, by which the new covenant between God and man was ratified, sealed, and confirmed. And counting this *unholy,* or common, κοινον, intimates that they expected nothing from it in a sacrificial or atoning way. How near to those persons, and how near to their destruction, do they come in the present day who

reject the atoning blood, and say, " that they expect no more benefit from the blood of Christ than they do from that of a cow or a sheep !" Is not this precisely the crime of which the apostle speaks here, and to which he tells us God would show no mercy ?

Despite unto the Spirit of grace ?] Hath *insulted* the Spirit of grace. The apostle means the Holy Spirit, whose gifts were bestowed in the first age on believers for the confirmation of the Gospel. See chap. vi. 4–6. Wherefore, if one apostatized in the first age, after having been witness to these miraculous gifts, much more after having possessed them himself, he must, like the scribes and Pharisees, have ascribed them to *evil spirits ;* than which a greater indignity could not be done to the Spirit of God. *Macknight.* This is properly the sin against the Holy Ghost, which has no forgiveness.

Verse 30. Vengeance belongeth unto me] This is the saying of God, Deut. xxxii. 35, in reference to the idolatrous Gentiles, who were the enemies of his people ; and is here with propriety applied to the above apostates, who, being enemies to God's ordinances, and Christ's ministry and merits, must also be enemies to Christ's people ; and labour for the destruction of them, and the cause in which they are engaged.

The Lord shall judge his people.] That is, he shall execute judgment *for* them ; for this is evidently the sense in which the word is used in the place from which the apostle quotes, Deut. xxxii. 36 : *For the Lord shall judge his people, and repent himself for his servants, when he seeth that their power is gone.* So God will avenge and vindicate the cause of Christianity by destroying its enemies, as he did in the case of the Jewish people, whom he destroyed from being a nation, and made them a proverb of reproach and monuments of his wrathful indignation to the present day.

Verse 31. It is *a fearful thing to fall into the hands of the living God.*] To fall into the hands of God is to fall under his *displeasure ;* and he who *lives for ever* can punish *for ever.* How dreadful to have the displeasure of an *eternal, almighty* Being to rest on the soul for ever ! Apostates, and all the persecutors and enemies of God's cause and people, may expect the heaviest judgments of an incensed Deity ; and these, not for a *time,* but through *eternity.*

Verse 32. *But call to remembrance*] It appears

2

A. M. cir. 4067.
A. D. cir. 63.
An. Olymp.
cir. CCX. 3.
A. U. C. cir.
816.

33 Partly, whilst ye were made ^z a gazing-stock both by reproaches and afflictions; and partly, whilst ^a ye became companions of them that were so used.

34 For ye had compassion of me ^b in my

bonds, and ^c took joyfully the spoiling of your goods, knowing ^d in yourselves that ^e ye have in heaven a better and an enduring substance.

A. M. cir. 4067.
A. D. cir. 63.
An. Olymp.
cir. CCX. 3.
A. U. C. cir.
816.

35 Cast not away therefore your confidence, ^f which hath great recompense of reward.

---

z 1 Corinthians iv. 9.——a Phil. i. 7; iv. 14; 1 Thess. ii. 14.
b Phil. i. 7; 2 Tim. i. 16.——c Matt. v. 12; Acts v. 41; James i. 2.

d Or, *that ye have in yourselves,* or *for yourselves.*——e Matt. vi 20; xix. 21; Luke xii. 33; 1 Timothy vi. 19.——f Matt. v. 12; x. 32.

---

from this, and indeed from some parts of the Gospel history, that the first believers in Judea were greatly persecuted; our Lord's crucifixion, Stephen's martyrdom, the persecution that arose after the death of Stephen, Acts viii. 1, Herod's persecution, Acts xii. 1, in which James was killed, and the various persecutions of St. Paul, sufficiently show that this disposition was predominant among that bad people.

A great fight of afflictions] Πολλην αθλησιν παθηματων· *A great combat* or *contention of sufferings.* Here we have an allusion to the combats at the Grecian games, or to exhibitions of gladiators at the public spectacles; and an intimation how *honourable* it was to contend for the faith once delivered to the saints, and to overcome through the blood of the Lamb, and their own testimony.

Verse 33. Ye were made a gazing-stock] Θεατριζομενοι· Ye were exhibited as wild beasts and other shows at the theatres. See the note on 1 Cor. iv. 9, where all this is illustrated.

Companions of them that were so used.] It appears, from 1 Thess. ii. 14, 15, that the Churches of God in Judea were greatly persecuted, and that they behaved with courage and constancy in their persecutions. When any victim of persecuting rage was marked out, the rest were prompt to take his part, and acknowledge themselves believers in the same doctrine for which he suffered. This was a noble spirit; many would have slunk into a corner, and put off the marks of Christ, that they might not be exposed to affliction on this account.

Verse 34. Ye had compassion of me in my bonds] Συνεπαθησατε· Ye suffered with me, ye sympathized *with me,* when bound for the testimony of Jesus. This probably refers to the sympathy they showed towards him, and the help they afforded him, during his long imprisonment in Cæsarea and Jerusalem. But instead of τοις δεσμοις μου, *my bonds,* τοις δεσμιοις, *the prisoners,* is the reading of AD, and several others, both the *Syriac,* the *Arabic* of Erpen, the *Coptic, Armenian, Vulgate,* some of the *Itala,* and several of the Greek *fathers.* This reading appears to be so well supported, that *Griesbach* has admitted it into the text. If it be genuine, it shows that there had been, and perhaps were *then,* several bound for the testimony of Jesus, and that the Church in Judea had shown its attachment to Christ by openly acknowledging these prisoners, and ministering to them.

Took joyfully the spoiling of your goods] They were deprived of their inheritances, turned out of their houses, and plundered of their goods; they wandered about in sheepskins and goatskins, being destitute,

afflicted, tormented. To suffer such persecution patiently was great; to endure it without a murmur was greater; to rejoice in it was greatest of all. But *how* could they do all this? The next clause informs us.

Knowing in yourselves] They had the fullest evidence that they were the children of God, the Spirit itself bearing this witness to their spirits; and if *children* then *heirs,* heirs of God and joint heirs with Christ. They knew that heaven was their *portion,* and that to it they had a sure right and indefeasible title by Christ Jesus. This accounts, and this alone can account, for their *taking joyfully the spoiling of their goods:* they had Christ in their hearts; they knew that they were his children, and that they had a kingdom, but that kingdom was not of this world. They had the support they needed, and they had it in the time in which they needed it most.

Verse 35. Cast not away therefore your confidence] Την παρρησιαν υμων· Your liberty of access to God; your *title* and *right* to approach his throne; your *birthright* as his sons and daughters; and the *clear evidence* you have of his favour, which, if you be not steady and faithful, you must lose. *Do not throw it away,* μη αποβαλητε· neither men nor devils can take it from you, and God will never deprive you of it if you continue faithful. There is a reference here to cowardly soldiers, who throw away their shields, and run away from the battle. This is your shield, your faith in Christ, which gives you the *knowledge of salvation;* keep it, and it will keep you.

The Lacedemonian women, when they presented the shields to their sons going to battle, were accustomed to say: Η ταν, η επι τας· "Either bring this back, or be brought back upon it;" alluding to the custom of bringing back a slain soldier on his own shield, a proof that he had preserved it to the last, and had been faithful to his country. They were accustomed also to excite their courage by delivering to them their fathers' shields with the following short address. Ταυτην ο πατηρ σοι αει εσωζε· και συ ουν ταυταν σωζε, η μη εσο· "This shield thy father always preserved; do thou preserve it also, or perish;" *Lacænarum Apophthegmata,* PLUT. OPERA, a *Wittenbach,* vol. i. p. 682. Thus spake the Lacedemonian mothers to their sons; and what say the oracles of God to us? Μη αποβαλητε την παρρησιαν υμων· *Cast not away your confession of faith.* This is your *shield;* keep it, and it will ever be your sure defence; for by it you will quench every fiery dart of the wicked one. The Church of Christ speaks this to all her sons, and especially to those employed in the work of the ministry.

A. M. cir. 4067.
A. D. cir. 63.
An. Olymp.
cir. CCX. 3.
A. U. C. cir.
816.

36 g For ye have need of patience, that, after ye have done the will of God, h ye might receive the promise.

37 For yet a little while, and k he that shall come will come, and will not tarry.

g Luke xxi. 19; Gal. vi. 9; chap. xii. 1.——h Col. iii. 24; chap. ix. 15; 1 Pet. i. 9.——i Luke xviii. 8; 2 Pet. iii. 9.

38 Now ¹ the just shall live by faith : but if *any man* draw back, my soul shall have no pleasure in him.

A. M. cir. 4067
A. D. cir. 63.
An. Olymp.
cir. CCX. 3.
A. U. C. cir.
816.

39 But we are not of them m who draw back unto perdition; but of them that n believe to the saving of the soul.

k Hab. ii. 3, 4.——l Rom. i. 17; Gal. iii. 11.——m 2 Peter ii. 20. 21.——n Acts xvi. 30, 31; 1 Thess. v. 9; 2 Thess. ii. 14.

Of *this shield*, of this glorious system of *salvation by Jesus Christ*, illustrated and defended in this work, I say to each of my children : Ταυτην ὁ πατηρ σοι αει εσωζε· και συ ουν ταυταν σωζε, η μη εσο· This faith, thy father, by the grace of God, hath always kept; keep thou it also, or thou must expect to perish ! May this be received both as a warning and encouragement !

Great recompense of reward.] No less than God's continual approbation ; the peace that passeth all understanding ruling the heart here ; and the glories of heaven as an eternal portion. Conscientiously keep the *shield*, and all these shall be thine. This will be thy *reward;* but remember that it is the *mercy* of God that gives it.

Verse 36. *Ye have need of patience*] Having so great a fight of sufferings to pass through, and they of so long continuance. God furnishes the *grace ;* you must exercise it. The grace or principle of patience comes from God ; the use and exercise of that grace is of yourselves. Here ye must be workers together with God. *Patience* and *perseverance* are nearly the same.

Have done the will of God] By keeping the faith, and patiently suffering for it.

Verse 37. *For yet a little while*] Ετι γαρ μικρον ὁσον· *For yet a very little time.* In a very short space of time the Messiah will come, and execute judgment upon your rebellious country. This is determined, because they have filled up the measure of their iniquity, and their destruction slumbereth not. The apostle seems to refer to Hab. ii. 3, 4, and accommodates the words to his own purpose.

Verse 38. *Now the just shall live by faith*] Ὁ δε δικαιος εκ πιστεως ζησεται· *But the just by faith,* i. e. he who is justified by faith, *shall live*—shall be preserved when this overflowing scourge shall come. See this meaning of the phrase vindicated, Rom. i. 17. And it is evident, both from this text, and Gal. iii. 11, that it is in this sense that the apostle uses it.

But if any man *draw back*] Και εαν ὑποστειληται· *But if he draw back ;* he, the *man who is justified by faith ;* for it is of *him,* and none other, that the text speaks. The insertion of the words *any man,* if done to serve the pupose of a *particular creed,* is a wicked perversion of the words of God. They were evidently intended to turn away the *relative* from the *antecedent,* in order to save the doctrine of final and *unconditional* perseverance ; which doctrine this text destroys.

My soul shall have no pleasure in him.] My very heart shall be opposed to him who makes shipwreck of faith and a good conscience. The word ὑποστελλειν signifies, not only to *draw back,* but to *slink away and*

hide through fear. In this sense it is used by the very best Greek writers, as well as by *Josephus* and *Philo.* As dastards and cowards are hated by all men, so those that *slink away* from Christ and his cause, for fear of persecution or secular loss, God must despise ; in them he cannot delight ; and his Spirit, grieved with their conduct, must desert their hearts, and lead them to *darkness* and *hardness.*

Verse 39. *But we are not of them who draw back*] Ουκ εσμεν ὑποστολης—, αλλα πιστεως· "We are not the cowards, but the courageous." I have no doubt of this being the meaning of the apostle, and the form of speech requires such a translation ; it occurs more than once in the New Testament. So, Gal. iii. 7 : Οἱ εκ πιστεως, *they who are of the faith,* rather *the faithful,* the *believers ;* Rom. iii. 26 : Ὁ εκ πιστεως, *the believer ;* Rom. ii. 8 : Οἱ εξ εριθειας, *the contentious ;* in all which places the learned reader will find that the form of speech is the same. We are not cowards who slink away, and notwithstanding meet *destruction ;* but we are *faithful,* and have our souls saved alive. The words περιποιησις ψυχης signify the *preservation of the life.* See the note, Eph. i. 14. He intimates that, notwithstanding the persecution was hot, yet they should escape with their *lives.*

1. IT is very remarkable, and I have more than once called the reader's attention to it, that not one Christian life was lost in the siege and destruction of Jerusalem. Every *Jew* perished, or was taken captive ; all those who had *apostatized,* and slunk away from Christianity, perished with them : all the genuine *Christians* escaped with their lives. This very important information, which casts light on many passages in the New Testament, and manifests the grace and providence of God in a very conspicuous way, is given both by *Eusebius* and *Epiphanius.* I shall adduce their words : " When the whole congregation of the Church in Jerusalem, according to an oracle given by revelation to the approved persons among them before the war, κατα τινα χρησμον τοις αυτοθι δοκιμοις δι' αποκαλυψεως δοθεντα προ του πολεμου, μεταναστηναι της πολεως, και τινα της περαιας πολιν οικειν κεκελευσμενον, Πελλαν αυτην ονομαζουσιν, were commanded to depart from the city, and inhabit a certain city which they call Pella, beyond Jordan, to which, when all those who believed in Christ had removed from Jerusalem, and when the saints had totally abandoned the royal city which is the metropolis of the Jews ; then the Divine vengeance seized them who had dealt so wickedly with Christ and his apostles, and utterly destroyed that wicked and abominable gene

ration." Euseb. *Hist. Eccles.*, l. iii. c. v. vol. i. p. 93. Edit. a *Reading.*

St. Epiphanius, in *Hæres. Nazaren*, c. 7, says : " The Christians who dwelt in Jerusalem, being forewarned by Christ of the approaching siege, removed to Pella."

The same, in his book *De Ponderibus et Mensuris*, says : " The disciples of Christ being warned by an angel, removed to Pella ; and afterwards, when Adrian rebuilt Jerusalem, and called it after his own name, *Ælia Colonia*, they returned thither." As those places in Epiphanius are of considerable importance, I shall subjoin the original : Εκειθεν γαρ ἡ αρχη γεγονε μετα την απο των Ἰεροσολυμων μεταστασιν, παντων των μαθητων των εν Πελλη ᾠκηκοτων, Χριστου φησαντος καταλειψαι τα Ἰεροσολυμα, και αναχωρησαι, επειδη ημελλε πασχειν πολιορκιαν. Epiph. *adver. Hæres.*, l. i. c. 7, vol. i. p. 123. Edit. Par. 1622. The other place is as follows : Ἡνικα γαρ εμελλεν ἡ πολις ἁλισκεσθαι ὑπο των Ῥωμαιων, προεχρηματισθησαν ὑπο Αγγελου παντες οἱ μαθηται μεταστηναι απο της πολεως, μελλουσης αρδην απολλυσθαι. Οἱ τινες και μετανασται γενομενοι ᾠκησαν εν Πελλη—περαν του Ιορδανου, ἡ τις εκ Δεκαπολεως λεγεται ειναι. Ibid. *De Pon. et Mens.*, vol. ii. p. 171.

These are remarkable testimonies, and should be carefully preserved. Pella, it appears, was a city of Cœlesyria, beyond Jordan, in the district of Decapolis. Thus it is evident that these Christians held fast their faith, preserved their shields, and continued to believe to the *saving of their lives* as well as to the *saving* of their *souls.* As the apostle gives several hints of the approaching destruction of Jerusalem, it is likely that this is the true sense in which the words above are to be understood.

2. I have already said a little, from verse 25, on the importance of *social worship.* Public *worship* is not of less consequence. Were it not for *public*, private worship would soon be at an end. To this, under God, the Church of Christ owes its being and its continuance. Where there is no public worship there is no *religion.* It is by this that God is acknowledged ; and he is the *universal Being ;* and by his

bounty and *providence* all live ; consequently, it is the duty of every intelligent creature *publicly* to acknowledge him, and offer him that worship which himself has prescribed in his word. The ancient Jews have some good maxims on this subject which may be seen in Schoettgen. I shall quote a few.

In *Berachoth*, fol. 8, it is written : " Rabbi Levi said, He who has a synagogue in his city, and does not go thither to pray, shall be esteemed a bad citizen," or a bad neighbour. And to this they apply the words of the prophet, Jer. xii. 14 : *Thus saith the Lord against all my evil neighbours—behold, I will pluck them out of their land.*

In *Mechilta*, fol. 48 : " Rabbi Eliezer, the son of Jacob, said," speaking as from God, " If thou wilt come to my house, I will go to thy house ; but if thou wilt not come to my house, I will not enter thy house. The place that my heart loveth, to that shall my feet go." We may safely add, that those who do not frequent the house of God can never expect his presence or blessing in their own.

In *Taanith*, fol. 11, it is said that " to him who separates himself from the congregation shall two angels come, and lay their hands upon his head and say, This man, who separates himself from the congregation, shall not see the comfort which God grants to his afflicted Church." The wisest and best of men have always felt it their duty and their interest to worship God in public. As there is nothing more necessary, so there is nothing more reasonable ; he who acknowledges God in all his ways may expect all his steps to be directed. The public worship of God is one grand line of distinction between the atheist and the believer. He who uses not public worship has either no God, or has no right notion of his being ; and such a person, according to the rabbins, is a *bad neighbour ;* it is dangerous to live near him, for neither he nor his can be under the protection of God. No man should be forced to attend a particular place of worship, but every man should be obliged to attend some place ; and he who has any fear of God will not find it difficult to get a place to his mind.

CHAPTER XI.

A definition of faith, 1, 2. *What are its immediate objects*, 3. *What are its effects, instanced in Abel*, 4 *In Enoch*, 5, 6. *In Noah*, 7. *In Abraham*, 8–10. *In Sara*, 11. *In their righteous posterity*, 12–16 *In Abraham's offering of his son Isaac*, 17–19. *In Isaac*, 20. *In Jacob*, 21. *In Joseph*, 22. *In Moses*, 23–28. *In the Israelites in the wilderness*, 29. *In the fall of Jericho*, 30. *In Rahab*, 31. *In several of the judges, and in David, Samuel, and the prophets*, 32–34. *The glorious effects produced by it in the primitive martyrs*, 35–40.

| A. M. cir. 4067. A. D. cir. 63. An. Olymp. cir. CCX. 3. A. U. C. cir. 816. | NOW faith is the [a] substance of things hoped for, the evidence [b] of things not seen. | 2 For [c] by it the elders obtained a good report. 3 Through faith we understand that [d] the worlds were framed | A. M. cir. 4067. A. D. cir. 63. An. Olymp. cir. CCX. 3. A. U. C. cir. 816. |

[a] Or, *ground ;* or, *confidence.*——[b] Romans viii. 24, 25 ; 2 Cor. iv. 18 ; v. 7.——[c] Ver. 39.

[d] Genesis i. 1 ; Psa. xxxiii. 6 ; John i. 3 ; chapter i. 2 ; 2 Peter iii. 5.

NOTES ON CHAP. XI.

Verse 1. *Faith is the substance of things hoped for*] Εστι δε πιστις ελπιζομενων ὑποστασις· *Faith is the*

SUBSISTENCE *of things hoped for ;* πραγματων ελεγχος ου βλεπομενων· *The* DEMONSTRATION *of things not seen.* The word ὑποστασις, which we translate *substance,*

A. M. cir. 4067.
A. D. cir. 63.
An. Olymp.
cir. CCX. 3.
A. U. C. cir.
816.

by the word of God, so that things which are seen were not made of things which do appear.

4 By faith ᵉ Abel offered unto God a more excellent sacrifice than Cain, by which he obtained witness that he was righteous,

A. M. cir. 4067.
A. D. cir. 63.
An. Olymp.
cir. CCX. 3.
A. U. C. cir.
816.

ᵉ Gen. iv. 4;   1 John iii. 12.

---

signifies *subsistence*, that which becomes a *foundation* for another thing to stand on. And ελεγχος signifies such a *conviction* as is produced in the mind by the *demonstration* of a *problem*, after which demonstration no doubt can remain, because we see from it that the thing *is*; that it *cannot but be*; and that it cannot be *otherwise* than as it is, and is proved to be. Such is the faith by which the soul is justified; or rather, such are the effects of justifying faith: on it subsists the peace of God which passeth all understanding; and the love of God is shed abroad in the heart where it lives, by the Holy Ghost. At the same time the Spirit of God witnesses with their spirits who have this faith that their sins are blotted out; and this is as fully manifest to their judgment and conscience as the axioms, "A whole is greater than any of its parts;" "Equal lines and angles, being placed on one another, do not exceed each other;" or as the deduction from prop. 47, book i., Euclid: "The square of the base of a right-angled triangle is equal to the difference of the squares of the other two sides." Ελεγχος is defined by logicians, *Demonstratio quæ fit argumentis certis et rationibus indubitatis, qua rei certitudo efficitur.* "A demonstration of the certainty of a thing by sure arguments and indubitable reasons." Aristotle uses it for a mathematical demonstration, and properly defines it thus: Ελεγχος δε εστιν ὁ μη δυνατος αλλως εχειν, αλλ' ούτως ὡς ἡμεις λεγομεν, "Elenchos, or Demonstration, is that which cannot be otherwise, but is so as we assert." Rhetor. ad Alexand., cap. 14, περι ελεγχου. On this account I have adduced the above theorem from *Euclid.*

Things hoped for] Are the peace and approbation of God, and those blessings by which the soul is prepared for the kingdom of heaven. A *penitent* hopes for the pardon of his sins and the favour of his God; faith in Christ puts him in possession of this pardon, and thus the thing that was hoped for is enjoyed by faith. When this is received, a man has the fullest conviction of the truth and reality of all these blessings; though *unseen* by the *eye*, they are *felt* by the *heart*; and the man has no more doubt of God's approbation and his own free pardon, than he has of his being.

In an extended sense the *things hoped for* are the resurrection of the body, the new heavens and the new earth, the introduction of believers into the heavenly country, and the possession of eternal glory.

The *things unseen*, as distinguished from the things hoped for, are, in an extended sense, the creation of the world from nothing, the destruction of the world by the deluge, the miraculous conception of Christ, his resurrection from the dead, his ascension to glory, his mediation at the right hand of God, his government of the universe, &c., &c., all which we as firmly believe on the testimony of God's word as if we had seen them. See *Macknight.* But this faith has particular

respect to the being, goodness, providence, grace, and mercy of God, as the subsequent verses sufficiently show.

Verse 2. For by it the elders obtained a good report.] By the *elders* are meant *ancestors, forefathers,* such as the patriarchs and prophets, several of whom he afterwards particularly names, and produces some fact from the history of their lives.

It is very remarkable that among the whole there is not one word concerning poor Adam and his wife, though both *Abraham* and *Sarah* are mentioned. There was no *good report* concerning *them*; not a word of their repentance, faith, or holiness. Alas! alas! did ever such bright suns set in so thick a cloud? Had there been any thing praiseworthy in their life after their fall, any act of faith by which they could have been distinguished, it had surely come out here; the mention of their second son Abel would have suggested it. But God has covered the whole of their spiritual and eternal state with a *thick* and *impenetrable veil.* Conjectures relative to their state would be very precarious; little else than *hope* can be exercised in their favour: but as to them the promise of Jesus was given, so we may believe they found redemption in that blood which was shed from the foundation of the world. Adam's rebellion against his Maker was too great and too glaring to permit his name to be ever after mentioned with honour or respect.

The word εμαρτυρηθησαν, which we translate *obtained a good report,* literally signifies, *were witnessed of;* and thus leads us naturally to GOD, who by his word, as the succeeding parts of the chapter show, *bore testimony* to the faith and holiness of his servants. The apostle does not mention one of whom an account is not given in the Old Testament. This, therefore, is God's witness or testimony concerning them.

Verse 3. Through faith we understand] By *worlds,* τους αιωνας, we are to understand the *material fabric of the universe;* for αιων can have no reference here to *age* or any measurement of time, for he speaks of the *things which are* SEEN; *not being made out of the things which do* APPEAR; this therefore must refer to the *material creation:* and as the word is used in the *plural* number, it may comprehend, not only the earth and visible heavens, but the whole planetary system; the different worlds which, in our system at least, revolve round the sun. The apostle states that these things were *not made* out of a *pre-existent matter;* for if they were, that matter, however extended or *modified,* must *appear* in that thing into which it is compounded and modified, consequently it could not be said that the things which are *seen* are not made of the things that *appear;* and he shows us also, by these words, that the present mundane fabric was not formed or *re-formed* from *one* anterior, as some suppose. According to Moses and the apostle we believe that God made

A. M. cir. 4067.
A. D. cir. 63.
An. Olymp.
cir. CCX. 3.
A. U. C. cir.
816.

God testifying of his gifts : and by it he, being dead, ^f yet ^g speaketh.

5 By faith ^h Enoch was translated that he should not see death ; and was not found, because God had translated him : for before his translation he had this testimony, that he pleased God.

6 But without faith *it is* impossible to please *him :* for he that cometh to God must believe that he is, and *that* he is a rewarder of them that diligently seek him.

7 By faith ⁱ Noah, being warned of God of things not seen as yet, ^k moved with fear, ^l prepared an ark to the saving of his house .

A. M. cir. 4067
A. D. cir. 63.
An. Olymp.
cir. CCX. 3.
A. U. C. cir.
816.

^f Gen. iv. 10 ; Matt. xxiii. 25 ; chap. xii. 24.——^g Or, *is yet spoken of.*——^h Gen. v. 22, 24 ; Wisd. iv. 10 ; Eccles. xliv. 16 ; xlix. 14.——ⁱ Gen. vi. 13, 22 ; Eccles. iv. 17.——^k Or, *being wary.* ^l 1 Pet. iii. 20.

all things out of *nothing.* See the notes on Gen. i. 1, &c.

At present we see trees of different kinds are produced from trees ; beasts, birds, and fishes, from others of the same kind ; and man, from man : but we are necessarily led to believe that there was a *first man,* who owed not his being to man ; first there were *beasts,* &c., which did not derive their being from others of the same kind ; and so of all manner of *trees, plants,* &c. God, therefore, made all these out of *nothing ;* his word tells us so, and we credit that word.

Verse 4. *By faith Abel offered—a more excellent sacrifice*] Πλειονα θυσιαν· *More sacrifice ;* as if he had said : Abel, by faith, made *more* than *one* offering ; and hence it is said, God testified of his GIFTS, τοις δωροις. The plain state of the case seems to have been this : Cain and Abel both brought offerings to the altar of God, probably the altar erected for the *family worship.* As Cain was a *husbandman,* he brought a *mincha,* or *eucharistic offering,* of the fruits of the ground, by which he acknowledged the being and providence of God. Abel, being a *shepherd* or a feeder of cattle, brought, not only the *eucharistic offering,* but also of the produce of his flock as a *sin-offering* to God, by which he acknowledged his own *sinfulness,* God's *justice* and *mercy,* as well as his *being* and *providence.* Cain, not at all apprehensive of the demerit of sin, or God's holiness, contented himself with the *mincha,* or *thank-offering :* this God could not, consistently with his holiness and justice, receive with complacency ; the other, as referring to him who was the Lamb slain from the foundation of the world, God could receive, and did particularly testify his approbation. Though the *mincha,* or *eucharistic offering,* was a very proper offering in its place, yet this was not received, because there was no *sin-offering.* The rest of the history is well known.

Now by this faith, thus exercised, in reference to an atonement, he, Abel, *though dead, yet speaketh ;* *i. e.* preacheth to mankind the necessity of an atonement, and that God will accept no sacrifice unless connected with this. See this transaction explained at large in my notes on Gen. iv. 3, &c.

Verse 5. *By faith Enoch was translated*] It is said, in Gen. v. 24, that Enoch walked with God, and *he was not, for God took him.* Here the apostle explains what God's taking him means, by saying that *he was translated that he should not see death ;* from which we learn that he did not die, and that God took him to a state of blessedness without obliging him to pass

through death. See his history explained at large in the above place, in Gen. v. 22–24.

Verse 6. *He that cometh to God*] The man who professes that it is his duty to worship God, must, if he act rationally, do it on the conviction that there is such a Being infinite, eternal, unoriginated, and self-existent ; the cause of all other being ; on whom all being depends ; and by whose energy, bounty, and providence, all other beings exist, live, and are supplied with the means of continued existence and life. He must believe, also, that he rewards them that diligently seek him ; that he is not indifferent about his own worship ; that he *requires* adoration and religious service from men ; and that he blesses, and especially protects and saves, those who in simplicity and uprightness of heart seek and serve him. This requires *faith,* such a faith as is mentioned above ; a faith by which we can *please God ;* and now that we have an abundant revelation, a faith *according* to that revelation ; a faith in God through Christ the great sin-offering, without which a man can no more please him, or be accepted of him, than Cain was. As the knowledge of the being of God is of infinite importance in religion, I shall introduce at the end of this chapter a series of propositions, tending to prove the being of God, 1st, *a priori ;* and 2dly, *a posteriori ;* omitting the proofs that are generally produced on those points, for which my readers may refer to works in general circulation on this subject : and 3dly, I shall lay down some *phenomena* relative to the heavenly bodies, which it will be difficult to account for without acknowledging the infinite skill, power, and *continual energy* of God.

Verse 7. *By faith Noah*] See the whole of this history, Gen. vi. 13.

Warned of God] Χρηματισθεις. As we know from the history in Genesis that *God* did warn Noah, we see from this the real import of the verb χρηματιζω, as used in various parts of the New Testament ; it signifies to *utter oracles,* to *give Divine warning.*

Moved with fear] Ευλαβηθεις· Influenced by *religious fear* or *reverence towards God.* This is mentioned to show that he acted not from a fear of losing his life, but from the fear of God ; and hence that fear is here properly attributed to *faith.*

He condemned the world] HE credited God, *they* did not ; *he* walked in the way God had commanded, *they* did not ; *he* repeatedly admonished them, 1 Pet. iii. 20, *they* regarded it not ; this aggravated their crimes, while it exalted his faith and righteousness

2

A. M. cir. 4067.
A. D. cir. 63.
An. Olymp.
cir. CCX. 3.
A. U. C. cir.
816.

by the which he condemned the world, and became heir of [m] the righteousness which is by faith.

8 By faith [n] Abraham, when he was called to go out into a place which he should after receive for an inheritance, obeyed; and he went out, not knowing whither he went.

9 By faith he sojourned in the land of promise, as *in* a strange country, [o] dwelling in tabernacles with Isaac and Jacob, [p] the heirs with him of the same promise:

10 For he looked for a [q] city which hath foundations, [r] whose builder and maker *is* God.

11 Through faith also [s] Sara herself received

strength to conceive seed, and [t] was delivered of a child when she was past age, because she judged him [u] faithful who had promised.

12 Therefore sprang there even of one, and him [v] as good as dead, [w] so many as the stars of the sky in multitude, and as the sand which is by the seashore innumerable.

13 These all died [x] in faith, [y] not having received the promises, but [z] having seen them afar off, and were persuaded of *them*, and embraced *them*, and [a] confessed that they were strangers and pilgrims on the earth.

14 For they that say such things [b] de-

A. M. cir. 4067.
A. D. cir. 63.
An. Olymp.
cir. CCX. 3.
A. U. C. cir.
816.

---

[m] Rom. iii. 22; iv. 13; Phil. iii. 9.——[n] Gen. xii. 1, 4; Acts vii. 2, 3, 4.——[o] Gen. xii. 8; xiii. 3, 18; xviii. 1, 9.——[p] Chap. vi. 17.——[q] Chap. xii. 22; xiii. 14.——[r] Chap. iii. 4; Rev. xxi. 2, 10.——[s] Gen. xvii. 19; xviii. 11, 14; xxi. 2.——[t] See Luke i. 36.

[u] Rom. iv. 21; chap. x. 23.——[v] Rom. iv. 19.——[w] Gen. xxii. 17; Romans iv. 18.——[x] Gr. *according to faith.*——[y] Verse 39. [z] Verse 27; John viii. 56.——[a] Gen. xxiii. 4; xlvii. 9; 1 Chron. xxix. 15; Ps. xxxix. 12; cxix. 19; 1 Pet. i. 17; ii. 11.——[b] Ch. xiii. 14.

" His faith and obedience condemned the world, *i. e.* the *unbelievers*, in the same sense in which every good man's virtues and exhortations condemn such as will not attend to and imitate them." *Dodd.*

Became heir of the righteousness] He became entitled to that justification which is by faith; and his temporal deliverance was a pledge of the salvation of his soul.

Verse 8. *Abraham, when he was called*] See on Gen. xii. 1—4.

Not knowing whither he went.] Therefore his *obedience* was the fullest proof of his *faith* in God, and his faith was an *implicit* faith; he obeyed, and went out from his own country, having no prospect of any good or success but what his implicit faith led him to expect from God, *as the rewarder of them that diligently seek him.* In all the preceding cases, and in all that follow, the apostle keeps this maxim· fully in view.

Verse 9. *By faith he sojourned in the land of promise*] It is remarkable that Abraham did not acquire any right in Canaan, except that of a *burying place;* nor did he build any house in it; his faith showed him that it was only a *type* and *pledge* of a better country, and he kept that better country continually in view: he, with Isaac and Jacob, who were heirs of the same promise, were contented to dwell in tents, without any *fixed* habitation.

Verse 10. *For he looked for a city which hath foundations*] He knew that earth could afford no permanent residence for an immortal mind, and he looked for that heavenly building of which God is the architect and owner; in a word, he lost sight of earth, that he might keep heaven in view. And all who are partakers of his faith possess the same spirit, walk by the same rule, and mind the same thing.

Whose builder and maker is God.] The word τεχνιτης signifies an *architect,* one who *plans, calculates,* and *constructs* a building. The word δημιουργος signifies the *governor of a people;* one who *forms them by institutions* and *laws;* the framer of a *politi-*

cal constitution. God is here represented the *Maker* or *Father* of all the heavenly inhabitants, and the *planner* of their *citizenship* in that heavenly country. See *Macknight.*

Verse 11. *Through faith also Sara*] Her history, as far as the event here is concerned, may be seen Gen. xvii. 19, and xxi. 2. Sarah at first treated the Divine message with ridicule, judging it to be absolutely impossible, not knowing then that it was from God; and this her age and circumstances justified, for, humanly speaking, such an event was impossible: but, when she knew that it was God who said this, it does not appear that she doubted any more, but implicitly believed that what God had promised he was able to perform.

Verse 12. *Him as good as dead*] According to nature, long past the time of the procreation of children. The birth of Isaac, the circumstances of the father and mother considered, was entirely supernatural; and the people who proceeded from this birth were a supernatural people; and were and are most strikingly singular through every period of their history to the present day.

Verse 13. *These all died in faith*] That is, Abraham, Sarah, Isaac, and Jacob, continued to believe, to the *end of their lives,* that God would· fulfil this promise; but they neither saw the numerous seed, nor did they get the promised rest in Canaan.

Strangers and pilgrims] Strangers, ξενοι, persons who are out of their own country, who are in a foreign land: *pilgrims,* παρεπιδημοι, sojourners only for a time; not intending to take up their abode in that place, nor to get naturalized in that country.

How many use these expressions, professing to be strangers and pilgrims here below, and yet the whole of their conduct, spirit, and attachments, show that they are *perfectly at home !* How little consideration and weight are in many of our professions, whether they relate to earth or heaven!

Verse 14. *Declare plainly that they seek a country.*] A man's *country* is that in which he has constitutional

2

A. M. cir. 4067.
A. D. cir. 63.
An. Olymp.
cir. CCX. 3.
A. U. C. cir.
816.

clare plainly that they seek a country.

15 And truly, if they had been mindful of that *country* from whence they came out, they might have had opportunity to have returned :

16 But now they desire a better *country*, that is, a heavenly : wherefore God is not ashamed ᶜ to be called their God ; for ᵈ he hath prepared for them a city.

17 By faith ᵉ Abraham, when he was tried,

offered up Isaac : and he that had received the promises ᶠ offered up his only-begotten *son*,

18 ᵍ Of whom it was said, ʰ That in Isaac shall thy seed be called :

19 Accounting that God ⁱ *was* able to raise him up, even from the dead ; from whence also he received him in a figure.

20 By faith ᵏ Isaac blessed Jacob and Esau concerning things to come.

21 By faith Jacob, when he was a dying,

A. M. cir. 4067.
A. D. cir. 63.
An. Olymp.
cir. CCX. 3.
A. U. C. cir.
816.

ᶜ Exod. iii. 6, 15 ; Matt. xxii. 32 ; Acts vii. 32.——ᵈ Phil. iii. 20 ; chap. xiii. 14.——ᵉ Gen. xxii. 1, 9.

ᶠ James ii. 21.——ᵍ Or, *To.*——ʰ Genesis xxi. 12 ; Romans ix. 7. ⁱ Rom. iv. 17, 19, 21.——ᵏ Gen. xxvii. 27, 39.

---

rights and privileges ; no stranger or sojourner has any such rights in the country where he sojourns. These, by declaring that they felt themselves strangers and sojourners, professed their faith in a heavenly country and state, and looked beyond the grave for a place of happiness. No intelligent Jew could suppose that Canaan was all the *rest* which God had promised to his people.

Verse 15. *If they had been mindful of that* country] They considered their right to the promises of God as dependent on their utter renunciation of Chaldea ; and it was this that induced Abraham to cause his steward Eliezer to *swear* that he would not carry his son Isaac to Chaldea ; see Gen. xxiv. 5–8. There idolatry reigned ; and God had called them to be the patriarchs and progenitors of a people among whom the knowledge of the true God, and the worship required by him, should be established and preserved.

Verse 16. *But now they desire a better*] They all expected *spiritual blessings,* and a *heavenly inheritance ;* they sought God as their *portion,* and in such a way and on such principles that he is not *ashamed to be called their God ;* and he shows his affection for them by preparing for them a city, to wit, *heaven,* as themselves would seek no city on earth ; which is certainly what the apostle has here in view. And from this it is evident that the patriarchs had a proper notion of the immortality of the soul, and expected a place of residence widely different from Canaan. Though to Abraham, Isaac, and Jacob, the promises were made in which Canaan was so particularly included, yet God did not give them any inheritance in that country, *no, not so much as to set a foot on ;* Acts vii. 5. Therefore, if they had not understood the promises to belong to *spiritual things,* far from enduring, as seeing him who is invisible, they must have considered themselves deceived and mocked. The apostle therefore, with the highest propriety, attributes their whole conduct and expectation to *faith.*

Verse 17. *Abraham, when he was tried*] See the history of this whole transaction explained at large in the notes on Gen. xxii. 1–9.

Offered up his only-begotten] Abraham did, *in effect,* offer up Isaac ; he built an altar, bound his son, laid him upon the altar, had ready the incense, took the knife, and would immediately have slain him had he not been prevented by the same authority by which

the sacrifice was enjoined. Isaac is here called *his only-begotten,* as he was the *only son* he had by his legitimate wife, who was heir to his property, and heir of the promises of God. The man who proved faithful in such a trial, deserved to have his faith and obedience recorded throughout the world.

Verse 19. *To raise* him *up, even from the dead*] Abraham staggered not at the promise through unbelief, but was strong in faith, giving glory to God. The resurrection of the dead must have been a doctrine of the patriarchs ; they expected a heavenly inheritance, they saw they died as did other men, and they must have known that they could not enjoy it but in consequence of a resurrection from the dead.

He received him in a figure.] Εν παραβολη· In my discourse on *parabolical writing* at the end of Matt. xiii., I have shown (signification 9) that παραβολη sometimes means a *daring exploit,* a *jeoparding of the life ;* and have referred to this place. I think it should be so understood here, as pointing out the very imminent danger he was in of losing his life. The clause may therefore be thus translated : " Accounting that God was able to raise him up from the dead, from whence he had received him, he being in the most imminent danger of losing his life." It is not, therefore, the natural deadness of Abraham and Sarah to which the apostle alludes, but the death to which Isaac on this occasion was exposed, and which he escaped by the immediate interference of God.

Verse 20. *By faith Isaac blessed Jacob and Esau*] He believed that God would fulfil his promise to his posterity ; and God gave him to see what would befall them in their future generations. The apostle does not seem to intimate that one should be an object of the *Divine hatred,* and the other of *Divine love,* in reference to their *eternal* states. This is wholly a *discovery* of later ages. For an ample consideration of this subject, see the notes on Gen. xxvii.

Verse 21. *Blessed both the sons of Joseph*] That is, Ephraim and Manasseh. See the account and the notes. Gen. xlviii. 5, &c.

Worshipped, leaning *upon the top of his staff.*] This subject is particularly considered in the note on Gen. xlvii. 31.

It appears, that at the time Joseph visited his father he was very weak, and generally confined to his couch, having at hand his *staff ;* either that with which he

2

A. M. cir. 4067.
A. D. cir. 63.
An. Olymp.
cir. CCX. 3.
A. U. C. cir.
816.

[l] blessed both the sons of Joseph.; and [m] worshipped, *leaning* upon the top of his staff.

22 By faith [n] Joseph, when he died, [o] made mention of the departing of the children of Israel; and gave commandment concerning his bones.

23 By faith [p] Moses, when he was born, was hid three months of his parents, because they saw *he was* a proper child; and they were not afraid of the king's [q] commandment.

24 By faith [r] Moses, when he was come to ·years, refused to be called the son of Pharaoh's daughter ;

A. M. cir. 4067
A. D. cir. 63.
An. Olymp.
cir. CCX. 3.
A. U. C. cir.
816.

25 [s] Choosing rather to suffer affliction with the people of God, than to enjoy the pleasures of sin for a season ;

26 Esteeming [t] the reproach [u] of Christ greater riches than the treasures in Egypt: for he had respect unto [v] the recompense of the reward.

---

[l] Gen. xlviii. 5, 16, 20.——[m] Gen. xlvii. 31.——[n] Gen. l. 24, 25 ; Exod. xiii. 19.——[o] Or, *remembered.*——[p] Exod. ii. 2 ; Acts vii. 20.

[q] Exodus i. 16, 22.——[r] Exodus ii. 10, 11.——[s] Psa. lxxxiv. 10.——[t] Chap. xiii. 13.——[u] Or, *for Christ.*——[v] Chap. x. 35.

---

usually supported his feeble body, or that which was the *ensign* of his office, as *patriarch* or *chief* of a very numerous family. The ancient chiefs, in all countries, had this staff or sceptre continually at hand. See Homer throughout. It is said, Gen. xlviii. 2, that when Joseph came to see his father Jacob, who was then in his last sickness, *Israel strengthened himself, and sat upon the bed.* Still I conceive he had his staff or sceptre at hand; and while sitting upon the bed, with his feet on the floor, he supported himself with his staff. When Joseph sware to him that he should be carried up from Egypt, he *bowed himself on his bed's head,* still supporting himself with his staff, which probably with this last act he laid aside, *gathered up his feet,* and reclined wholly on his couch. It was therefore indifferent to say that he worshipped or bowed himself on his staff or on his bed's head. But as שחה *shachah* signifies, not only to *bow,* but also to *worship,* because acts of adoration were performed by *bowing* and *prostration ;* and as מטה *mittah,* a *bed,* by the change of the vowel points becomes *matteh,* a *staff,* hence the *Septuagint* have translated the passage Και προσεκυνησεν Ισραηλ επι το ακρον της ραβδου αυτου· *And Israel bowed* or *worshipped on the head of his staff.* This reading the apostle follows here *literatim.*

Wretched must that cause be which is obliged to have recourse to what, at best, is an equivocal expression, to prove and support a favourite opinion. The Romanists allege this in favour of *image worship.* This is too contemptible to require confutation. To make it speak this language the Rheims version renders the verse thus : *By faith Jacob dying, blessed every one of the sons of Joseph, and adored the top of his rod.* A pretty object of adoration, indeed, for a dying patriarch ! Here the preposition επι, *upon,* answering to the Hebrew על *al,* is wholly suppressed, to make it favour the corrupt reading of the Vulgate. This preposition is found in the *Hebrew text,* in the *Greek version* of the *Seventy,* the *printed Greek text* of the New Testament, and in *every* MS. yet discovered of this epistle. It is also found in the *Syriac, Æthiopic, Arabic,* and *Coptic :* in which languages the connection necessarily shows that it is not an idle particle : and by no mode of construction can the text be brought to support *image worship,* any more than it can to support *transubstantiation.*

Verse 22. *Joseph, when he died*] Τελευτων, When

he was dying, gave commandment concerning his bones. On this subject I refer the reader to the notes on Gen. l. 23. And I have this to add to the account I have given of the *sarcophagus* now in the *British Museum,* vulgarly called *Alexander's coffin,* that it is more probably the *coffin of Joseph* himself ; and, should the time ever arrive in which the hieroglyphics on it shall be interpreted, this conjecture may appear to have had its foundation in truth.

Verse 23. *By faith Moses, &c.*] See the notes on Exod. ii. 2, and Acts vii. 20. We know that Moses was bred up at the Egyptian court, and *there* was considered to be the son of Pharaoh's daughter ; and probably might have succeeded to the throne of Egypt: but, finding that God had visited his people, and given them a promise of *spiritual and eternal blessings,* he chose rather to take the lot of this people, i. e. God as his portion for ever, than to *enjoy the pleasures of sin,* which, however gratifying to the animal senses, could only be προσκαιρον, *temporary.*

After the 23d verse, there is a whole clause added by DE, two copies of the *Itala,* and some copies of the *Vulgate.* The clause is the following : Πιστει μεγας γενομενος Μωϋσης ανειλεν τον Αιγυπτιον, κατανοων την ταπεινωσιν των αδελφων αυτου. *By faith Moses, when he was grown up, slew the Egyptian, considering the oppression of his own brethren.* This is a remarkable addition, and one of the largest in the whole New Testament. It seems to have been collected from the history of Moses as given in Exodus, and to have been put originally into the margin of some MS., from which it afterwards crept into the text.

Verse 26. *The reproach of Christ*] The *Christ* or *Messiah* had been revealed to Moses ; of him he prophesied, Deut. xviii. 15 ; and the *reproach* which God's people. had, in consequence of their decided opposition to idolatry, may be termed the *reproach of Christ,* for they refused to become one people with the Egyptians, because the *promise of the rest* was made to them, and in this *rest* CHRIST and his *salvation* were included : but, although it does not appear these things were known to the Hebrews *at large,* yet it is evident that there were sufficient intimations given to Moses concerning the Great Deliverer, (of whom himself was a type,) that determined his conduct in the above respect ; as he fully understood that he must renounce his interest in the promises, and in the life eternal to

2

A. M. cir. 4067.
A. D. cir. 63.
An. Olymp.
cir. CCX. 3.
A. U. C. cir.
816.

27 By faith ʷ he forsook Egypt, not fearing the wrath of the king : for he endured, as ˣ seeing him who is invisible.

28 Through faith ʸ he kept the passover, and the sprinkling of blood, lest he that destroyed the first-born should touch them.

29 By faith ᶻ they passed through the Red Sea as by dry *land :* which the Egyptians assaying to do, were drowned.

30 By faith ᵃ the walls of Jericho fell down,

after they were compassed about seven days.

31 By faith ᵇ the harlot Rahab perished not with them ᶜ that believed not, when ᵈ she had received the spies with peace.

32 And what shall I more say ? for the time would fail me to tell of ᵉ Gedeon, and *of* ᶠ Barak, and *of* ᵍ Samson, and *of* ʰ Jephthae ; *of* ⁱ David also, and ᵏ Samuel, and *of* the prophets :

A. M. cir. 4067.
A. D. cir. 63.
An. Olymp.
cir. CCX. 3.
A. U. C. cir.
816.

ʷ Exodus x. 28, 29; xii. 37; xiii. 17, 18.——ˣ Verse 13. ʸ Exod. xii. 21, &c.——ᶻ Exodus xiv. 22, 29.——ᵃ Josh. vi. 20. ᵇ Josh. vi. 23; James ii. 25.——ᶜ Or, *that were disobedient.*

ᵈ Josh. ii. 1.——ᵉ Judg. vi. 11.——ᶠ Judg. iv. 6.——ᵍ Judg. xiii. 24.——ʰ Judg. xi. 1; xii. 7.——ⁱ 1 Sam. xvi. 1, 13 ; xvii. 45. ᵏ 1 Sam. i. 20 ; xii. 20.

---

which they led, if he did not obey the Divine call in the present instance. Many have been stumbled by the word ὁ Χριστος, *Christ,* here ; because they cannot see how Moses should have any knowledge of him. It may be said that it was just as easy for God Almighty to reveal Christ to *Moses,* as it was for him to reveal him to *Isaiah,* or to the *shepherds,* or to *John Baptist ;* or to manifest him in the *flesh.* After all there is much reason to believe that, by του Χριστου, here, of *Christ* or the *anointed,* the apostle means the whole body of the Israelitish or Hebrew people ; for, as the word signifies the *anointed,* and anointing was a consecration to God, to serve him in some particular office, as prophet, priest, king, or the like, all the Hebrew people were considered thus *anointed* or *consecrated ;* and it is worthy of remark that Χριστος is used in this very sense by the Septuagint, 1 Sam. ii. 35 ; Psa. cv. 15 ; and Hab. iii. 13 ; where the word is necessarily restrained to .his meaning.

He had respect unto the recompense] Απεβλεπε· He *looked attentively* to it ; his eyes were *constantly directed* to it. This is the import of the original word ; and the whole conduct of Moses was an illustration of it.

Verse 27. *He forsook Egypt*] He believed that God would fulfil the promise he had made ; and he cheerfully changed an *earthly* for a *heavenly* portion.

Not fearing the wrath of the king] The apostle speaks here of the departure of Moses *with the Israelites,* not of his *flight to Midian,* Exod. ii. 14, 15 ; for he was then in great fear : but when he went to Pharaoh with God's authority, to demand the dismission of the Hebrews, he was without fear, and acted in the most noble and dignified manner ; he then feared nothing but God.

As seeing him who is invisible.] He continued to act as one who had the judge of his heart and conduct always before his eyes. By calling the Divine Being *the invisible,* the apostle distinguishes him from the gods of Egypt, who were *visible, corporeal, gross,* and *worthless.* The Israelites were worshippers of the *true God,* and this worship was not tolerated in Egypt. His pure and spiritual worship could never comport with the adoration of *oxen, goats, monkeys, leeks,* and *onions.*

Verse 28. *He kept the passover*] God told him that

he would destroy the first-born of the Egyptians, but would spare all those whose doors were *sprinkled with the blood* of the paschal lamb. Moses believed this, kept the passover, and *sprinkled the blood.* See the notes on Exod. xii. One of the Itala adds here, *Fide prædaverunt Ægyptios exeuntes.* "By faith, when they went out, they spoiled the Egyptians." This is any thing but *genuine.*

Verse 29. *By faith they passed through the Red Sea*] See the notes on Exod. xiv. 22. The Egyptians thought they could walk through the sea as well as the Israelites ; they tried, and were drowned ; while the former passed in perfect safety. The one walked by *faith,* the other by *sight ;* one perished, the other was saved.

Verse 30. *The walls of Jericho fell down*] This is particularly explained Josh. vi. 1, &c. God had promised that the walls of Jericho should fall down, if they compassed them about seven days. They *believed,* did as they were commanded, and the promise was fulfilled.

Verse 31. *The harlot Rahab perished not*] See this account Josh. ii. 1, 9, 11, and vi. 23, where it is rendered exceedingly probable that the word זונה *zonah* in Hebrew, and πορνη in Greek, which we translate *harlot,* should be rendered *innkeeper* or *tavernkeeper,* as there is no proper evidence that the person in question was such a woman as our translation represents her. As to her having been a *harlot* before and converted afterwards, it is a figment of an idle fancy. She was afterwards married to *Salmon,* a Jewish prince ; see Matt. i. 5. And it is extremely incredible that, had she been what we represent her, he would have sought for such an alliance.

Received the spies with peace.] Μετ' ειρηνης· The same as בשלום *beshalom,* giving them a *kind welcome, good fare,* and *protection.* After these words the *Slavonic* adds : Και ετερᾳ ὁδῳ εκβαλουσα, *and sent them out another way.*

Verse 32. *Time would fail me*] Με διηγουμενον ὁ χρονος. A very usual mode of expression with the best Greek writers, when they wish to intimate that much important intelligence remains to be com.municated on the subject already in hand, which must be omitted because of other points which have not yet been handled.

2

A. M. cir. 4067.
A. D. cir. 63.
An. Olymp.
cir. CCX. 3.
A. U. C. cir.
816.

33 Who through faith subdued kingdoms, wrought righteousness, [1] obtained promises, [m] stopped the mouths of lions,

34 [n] Quenched the violence of fire, [o] escaped the edge of the sword, [p] out of weakness were made strong, waxed valiant in fight,

[q] turned to flight the armies of the aliens.

35 [r] Women received their dead raised to life again: and others were [s] tortured, not accepting deliverance; that they might obtain a better resurrection:

A. M. cir. 4067
A. D. cir. 63.
An. Olymp.
cir. CCX. 3.
A. U. C. cir.
816.

---

[1] 2 Sam. vii. 11, &c.——[m] Judg. xiv. 5, 6; 1 Sam. xvii. 34, 35; Dan. vi. 22.——[n] Dan. iii. 25.——[o] 1 Sam. xx. 1; 1 Kings xix. 3; 2 Kings vi. 16.——[p] 2 Kings xx. 7, &c.; Job xlii. 10; Psa. vi. 8.——[q] Judg. xv. 8, 15; 1 Sam. xiv. 13, &c.; xvii. 51, 52; 2 Samuel viii. 1, &c.——[r] 1 Kings xvii. 22; 2 Kings iv. 35. [s] 2 Mac. vi. 19, 28; vii. 7, &c.; Acts xxii. 25.

Gedeon] Who by faith in God, with 300 men, destroyed a countless multitude of Midianites and Amalekites, and delivered Israel from oppression and slavery. Judg. vi., vii., viii.

Barak] Who overthrew Jabin, king of Canaan, and delivered Israel from servitude. Judg. iv.

Samson] Who was appointed by God to deliver Israel from the oppressive yoke of the *Philistines;* and, by extraordinary assistance, discomfited them on various occasions. Judg. xiii.-xvi.

Jephthae] Who, under the same guidance, defeated the Ammonites, and delivered Israel. Judg. xi., xii.

David] King of Israel, whose whole life was a life of faith and dependence on God; but whose character will be best seen in those books which contain an account of his reign, and the book of Psalms, to which, and the notes there, the reader must be referred. It is probable he is referred to here for that act of faith and courage which he showed in his combat with Goliah. See 1 Sam. xvii.

Samuel] The last of the Israelitish *judges,* to whom succeeded a race of *kings,* of whom Saul and David were the two first, and were both anointed by this most eminent man. See his history in the *first* book of *Samuel.*

All these are said to have performed their various exploits *through faith.* 1. The faith of *Gideon* consisted in his throwing down the altar of Baal, and cutting down his grove, in obedience to the command of God. 2. The faith of *Barak* consisted in his believing the revelation made to Deborah, and the command to go against Jabin's numerous army. 3. *Samson's* faith consisted in his obeying the various impulses produced by the Spirit of God in his own mind. 4. *Jephthae's* faith consisted particularly in his believing the promise made to Abraham and his posterity, that they should possess the land of Canaan; and in his resolutely fighting against the Ammonites, that they might not deprive the Israelites of the land between Arnon and Jabbok. It may be observed, here, that the apostle does not produce these in *chronological order;* for Barak lived before Gideon, and Jephthae before Samson, and Samuel before David. He was not producing facts in their chronological order, but instances of the power of God exerted in the behalf of men who had strong confidence in him.

Verse 33. *Who through faith subdued kingdoms*] As *Joshua,* who subdued the seven Canaanitish nations; and *David,* who subdued the Moabites, Syrians, Ammonites, and Edomites. 2 Sam. viii., &c.

Wrought righteousness] Did a great variety of works indicative of that faith in God without which it is impossible to do any thing that is good.

Obtained promises] This is supposed to refer to *Joshua* and *Caleb,* who, through their faith in God, obtained the promised land, while all the rest of the Israelites were excluded; to Phineas also, who, for his act of *zealous faith* in slaying *Zimri* and *Cosbi,* got the promise of an *everlasting priesthood;* and to *David,* who, for his *faith* and *obedience,* obtained the kingdom of Israel, and had the promise that from his seed the Messiah should spring.

Stopped the mouths of lions] Daniel, who, though cast into a den of lions for his fidelity to God, was preserved among them unhurt, and finally came to great honour.

Verse 34. *Quenched the violence of fire*] As in the case of the three faithful Hebrews, *Shadrach, Meshach,* and *Abed-nego,* who, for their steady attachment to God's worship, were cast into a fiery furnace, in which they were preserved, and from which they escaped unhurt. Dan. iii.

Escaped the edge of the sword] Moses, who escaped the sword of Pharaoh, Exod. xviii. 4; *Elijah,* that of Jezebel; and *David,* that of Saul: and many others.

Out of weakness were made strong] Were miraculously restored from *sickness,* which seemed to threaten their life; as *Hezekiah,* Isa. xxxviii. 21.

Waxed valiant in fight] Like *Gideon,* who overthrew the camp of the Midianites, and *Jonathan,* that of the Philistines, in such a way as must have proved that God was with them.

Verse 35. *Women received their dead*] As did the widow of *Zarephath,* 1 Kings xvii. 21, and the *Shunammite,* 2 Kings iv. 34. What other cases under all the above heads the apostle might have in view, we know not.

Others were tortured] Ετυμπανισθησαν. This is a word concerning the meaning of which the critics are not agreed. Τυμπανον signifies a stick, or *baton,* which was used in *bastinadoing* criminals. And τυμπανιζω signifies to *beat violently,* and is thus explained by the best lexicographers. After considering what others have written on this subject, I am inclined to think that the *bastinado* on the *soles of the feet* is what is here designed. That this was a most torturing and dangerous punishment, we learn from the most authentic accounts; and it is practised among the *Turks* and other *Mohammedans* to the present day. Mr. *Antes,* of Fulnek, in Yorkshire, twenty years a resident in Egypt, furnishes the latest account I have met with; he himself was the unhappy subject

2

A. M. cir. 4067.
A. D. cir. 63.
An. Olymp.
cir. CCX. 3.
A. U. C. cir.
816.

36 ᵗ And others had trial of cruel mockings and scourgings, yea, moreover, ᵘ of bonds and imprisonment:

37 ᵛ They were stoned, they were sawn asun-der, were tempted, were slain with the sword : ʷ they wandered about ˣ in sheepskins and goatskins; being destitute, afflicted, tormented ;

38 (Of whom the world was not worthy :)

A. M. cir. 4067.
A. D. cir. 63.
An. Olymp.
cir. CCX. 3.
A. U. C. cir.
816.

ᵗ 2 Mac. vii. 1, 7.——ᵘ Genesis xxxix. 20 ; Jeremiah xx. 2 ; xxxvii. 15.

ᵛ 1 Kings xxi. 13 ; 2 Chron. xxiv. 21 ; Acts. vii. 58 ; xiv. 19. ʷ 2 Kings i. 8 ; Matt. iii. 4.——ˣ Zech. xiii. 4.

---

of his own description. See at the end of this chapter, article 4.

Not accepting deliverance] This looks very like a reference to the case of the mother and her seven sons, mentioned 2 Mac. vii. 1, &c.

Verse 36. *Had trial of* cruel *mockings and scourgings*] We do not know the cases to which the apostle refers. The *mockings* here can never mean such as those of Ishmael against Isaac, or the youths of Bethel against Elisha. It is more probable that it refers to public exhibitions of the people of God at idol feasts and the like ; and Samson's case before Dagon, when the Philistines had put out his eyes, is quite in point: As to *scourgings*, this was a common way of punishing minor culprits : and even those who were to be punished *capitally* were first scourged. See the case of our Lord.

Bonds and imprisonment] Joseph was cast into prison ; Jeremiah was cast into a dungeon full of mire, chap. xxxvii. 16, and xxxviii. 6 ; and the Prophet Micaiah was imprisoned by Ahab, 1 Kings xxii. 27.

Verse 37. *They were stoned*] As Zechariah, the son of Barachiah or Jehoida, was, between the altar and the temple ; see the account, 2 Chron. xxiv. 21 ; and see the notes on Matt. xxiii. 35. And as Naboth the Jezreelite, who, on refusing to give up his father's inheritance to a covetous king, because it had respect to the promise of God, was falsely accused and stoned to death ; 1 Kings xxi. 1–14.

They were sawn asunder] There is a tradition that the Prophet Isaiah was thus martyred. In *Yevamoth*, fol. 49, 2, it is thus written : " Manasseh slew Isaiah ; for he commanded that he should be slain with a wooden saw. They then brought the saw, and cut him in two, and when the saw reached his mouth, his soul fled forth." St. Jerome and others mention the same thing ; and among the Jews the tradition is indubitable.

Were tempted] Επειρασθησαν. I believe this word has vexed the critics more than any other in the New Testament. How being *tempted* can be ranked among the *heavy sufferings* of the primitive martyrs and confessors is not easy to discern, because *to be tempted* is the common lot of every godly man. This difficulty has induced learned men to mend the text by conjecture : Beza proposes επυρωθησαν, *they were branded*. Junius, Piscator, and others, propose επυρασθησαν, *they were burnt alive*. Gataker thinks επρησθησαν, a word of the same import, should be preferred. Tanaquil Faber gives the preference to επηρωθησαν, *they were mutilated*—had different parts of their bodies *lopped off*. Sir *Norton Knatchbull* contends for επαρθησαν, *they were transfixed*, or *pierced*

through. Alberti thinks the original reading was εσπειρασθησαν, *they were strangled*. About as many more differences have been proposed by learned men, all bearing a very near resemblance to the words now found in the Greek text. By three MSS. the word is entirely *omitted ;* as also by the *Syriac, Arabic* of Erpen, the *Æthiopic*, and by *Eusebius* and *Theophylact*. Of all the conjectures, that of *Knatchbull* appears to me to be the most probable : *they were transfixed* or *impaled ;* and even the present reading might be construed in this sense.

Were slain with the sword] As in the case of the eighty-five priests slain by Doeg, see 1 Sam. xxii. 18 ; and the *prophets*, of whose slaughter by the sword Elijah complains, 1 Kings xix. 10. Probably the word means being *beheaded*, which was formerly done with a *sword*, and not with an *axe ;* and in the east is done by the sword to the present day.

They wandered about in sheepskins] Μηλωταις *Sheepskins* dressed with the wool on. This was probably the sort of mantle that Elijah wore, and which was afterwards used by Elisha ; for the Septuagint, in 2 Kings ii. 8, 13, expressly say : Και ελαβεν Ηλιας την μηλωτην αυτου· *and Elijah took his* SHEEPSKIN (mantle.) Και υψωσε την μηλωτην Ηλιου, ἡ επεσεν επανωθεν αυτου· *And he* (Elisha) *took the* SHEEPSKIN *of Elijah which had fallen from off him*. It was most probably on this account, as Dr. Macknight conjectures, that Elijah was called a *hairy man*, 2 Kings i. 8 ; and not on account of having a preposterously *long beard*, as those marrers of all the unities of time, place, circumstances, and common sense, the *painters*, represent him. And it is likely that the prophets themselves wore such garments, and that the false prophets imitated them in this, in order that they might gain the greater credit. *And it shall come to pass in that day, that the prophets shall be ashamed every one of his vision—neither shall they wear a rough garment to deceive*, Zech. xiii. 4 ; δερριν τριχινην, a hairy skin, SEPT., probably the *goatskins* mentioned above. In general, this was an *upper garment ;* but, in the cases to which the apostle alludes, the *sheepskin* and *goatskin* seem to have been the *only covering*.

Being destitute] Ὑστερουμενοι· *In want* of all the *comforts* and *conveniences* of life, and often of its *necessaries*.

Afflicted] In consequence of enduring such privations.

Tormented] Κακουχουμενοι· *Maltreated, harassed*, variously persecuted by those to whom they brought the message of salvation.

Verse 38. *Of whom the world was not worthy*] Yet they were obliged to wander by day in *deserts* and *mountains*, driven from the society of men, and often

A. M. cir. 4067.
A. D. cir. 63.
An. Olymp.
cir. CCX. 3.
A. U. C. cir.
816.

they wandered in deserts, and in mountains, and ʸ in dens and caves of the earth.

39 And these all, ᶻ having obtained a good report through

A. M. cir. 4067.
A. D. cir. 63.
An. Olymp.
cir. CCX. 3.
A. U. C. cir.
816.

faith, received not the promise :

40 God having ᵃ provided ᵇ some better thing for us, that they without us should not ᶜ be made perfect.

ʸ 1 Kings xviii. 4; xix. 9.——ᶻ Ver. 2, 13.——ᵃ Or, *foreseen.*

ᵇ Chap. vii. 22; viii. 6.——ᶜ Chap. v. 9; xii. 23; Rev. vi. 11.

---

obliged to hide by night in dens and caves of the earth, to conceal themselves from the brutal rage of men. Perhaps he refers here principally to the case of Elijah, and the hundred prophets hidden in caves by Obadiah, and fed with bread and water. See 1 Kings xviii. 4. David was often obliged thus to hide himself from Saul; 1 Sam. xxiv. 3, &c.

Verse 39. *Having obtained a good report* (having been witnessed to; see ver. 2) *through faith*] It was *faith in God* which supported all those eminent men who, in different parts of the world, and in different ages, were persecuted for righteousness' sake.

Received not the promise] They all heard of the promises made to Abraham of a heavenly rest, and of the promise of the *Messiah*, for this was a constant tradition; but they died without having seen this *Anointed of the Lord.* Christ was not in any of their times manifested in the flesh; and of him who was the expectation of all nations, they heard only by the hearing of the ear. This must be the promise, without receiving of which the apostle says *they died.*

Verse 40. *God having provided some better thing for us*] This is the dispensation of the Gospel, with all the privileges and advantages it confers.

That they without us should not be made perfect.] Believers before the flood, after the flood, under the law, and since the law, make but one Church. The Gospel dispensation is the last, and the Church cannot be considered as *complete* till the believers under all dispensations are gathered together. As the Gospel is the last dispensation, the preceding believers cannot be consummated even in glory till the Gospel Church arrive in the heaven of heavens.

There are a great variety of meanings put on this place, but the above seems the most simple and consistent. See Rev. vi. 11. "White robes were given unto every one of them; and it was said unto them, that they should rest yet for a little season, until their fellow servants also, and their brethren, that should be killed as they were, should be fulfilled." This time, and its blessings, are now upon the wing.

OBSERVATIONS ON THE BEING OF A GOD.

DEDUCED FROM A CONSIDERATION OF HEB. xi. 6 : *He that cometh unto God must believe that he is, and that he is the rewarder of them who diligently seek him.*

I. METAPHYSICIANS and philosophers, in order to prove the existence of God, have used two modes of argumentation :—

1. *A priori*, proofs drawn from the necessity that such a being as God is must exist: arguments of this kind do not produce any thing in evidence which is *derived* from his works.

2. *A posteriori*, proofs of the being and perfections of God, drawn from his own works

PROPOSITIONS A PRIORI.

PROP I. If there be no one being in the universe but such as might possibly *not have existed*, it would follow that there might possibly have been *no existence* at all; and if that could be so, it would be also possible that the present existence might have arisen from total *nonexistence*, which is absurd : therefore it is not possible that there might have been no existence at all. Consequently, an impossibility of not existing must be found somewhere; there must have been a being whose nonexistence is impossible.

II. The *whole nature* of an unoriginated being, or *aggregate* of his attributes, must be *unoriginated*, and necessarily what it is. A being cannot produce its own attributes; for this would suppose it acted before it existed. There is nothing in the nature of this being that is *contingent*, or could have been *otherwise* than it is; for whatever is *contingent*, must have a cause to determine its mode of existence.

III. The attributes of an unoriginated being must be possessed by it *unlimitedly*; for to possess an attribute *imperfectly*, or only in a *certain degree*, must suppose some cause to have *modified* this being so as to make him incapable of having that attribute in any other than an *imperfect degree*. But no cause can be admitted in this case, because this is the First of all beings, and the Cause of all things. Farther, an imperfect attribute, or any one that is not in its *highest degree*, must be capable of improvement by exercise and experience; which would imply that the unoriginated being must be originally imperfect, and that he was deriving farther degrees of perfection from the exercise of his own powers, and acquaintance with his own works.

IV. The unoriginated being must exist *everywhere*, in the same manner he does *anywhere*; for if he did not, it would suppose some *cause* by which his presence was limited; but there can be no cause to limit that presence. See above.

V. This unoriginated being must be a *simple un compounded* substance, identically the same everywhere; not consisting of *parts*, for these must be distinct and independent; nor of *whole*, for this is the aggregate of parts; nor of *magnitude* or *quantity*, for these signify a composition of parts. This being must be as truly *one* and omnipresent, as the present moment of time is indivisibly *one* in all places at once; and can no more be limited or measured by *time*, than the present moment can by duration.

Hence this being cannot be *matter* or *body*, because to these belong *extension, divisibility, figurability*, and *mobility*, which imply *limitation*. God and matter have essentially contrary properties.

God is not *material*. It has already been shown that there necessarily must exist one infinite, un-originated, and eternal being. Now this being must be a *thinking* being; for it is as impossible to conceive that *unthinking* matter could produce a *thinking* intelligent being, as it is to conceive that *nothing* could produce *matter*.

Let us suppose any parcel of matter to be *eternal*, we shall find it, in itself, unable to produce any thing. Let us suppose its *parts* firmly at rest together; if there were no other being in the world, must it not eternally remain so, a dead, inactive lump? Is it possible to conceive that it can add motion to itself, or produce it in other portions of matter? Matter, therefore, by its own strength, cannot produce in itself so much as *motion*. The motion it has must also be from eternity, or else added to matter by some other being more powerful than itself.

But let us suppose motion eternal too; yet matter, unthinking matter, and motion, could never produce *thought*. Knowledge will still be as far beyond the *power* of *motion* and *matter* to produce, as matter is beyond the power of nothing to produce. Divide matter into as minute parts as you will, vary the figure and motion of it as much as you please, it will operate no other ways upon other bodies of proportionate bulk than it did before this division. The minutest particles of matter strike, impel, and resist one another, just as the greater do; and that is all that they can do. So that if we will suppose *nothing* eternal, *matter* can never begin to be. If we suppose bare matter, without motion, eternal, then motion can never begin to be. If we suppose only *matter* and *motion* eternal, then *thought* can never begin to be. For it is impossible to conceive that matter, either with or without motion, could have originally, in and from itself, sense, perception, and knowledge, as is evident from hence, that sense, perception, and knowledge, must be properties eternally separate from matter, and every particle of it.

Since, therefore, whatsoever is the first eternal being must necessarily be a *thinking* being, and whatsoever is first of all things must necessarily contain in it and actually have, at least, all the perfections that can ever after exist, it necessarily follows that the first eternal being cannot be matter.

VI. This being must possess *intelligence* and *power* unlimited, and all other attributes that are in themselves absolute perfections.

Attributes are divided into *natural* and *moral*, or *primary* and *secondary*. The first are those which essentially belong to the *nature* of a being considered in *itself*; the second in its *manner of acting* toward *others*. All the attributes of God, being *uncontingent*, must be unlimited; and therefore his knowledge must extend to every thing that *can be known*, and his power to every thing that *can be done*.

VII. There cannot be in the universe more than *one* unoriginated being; for as this being is possessed of infinite attributes, let us suppose a *second* unoriginated being; he must possess the same: for both these beings are eternal, and necessarily the same, every

where alike present, without any possible difference or distinction, and therefore one and the same. *Two* such cannot subsist; and the supposition of a *second* such being is only a mental repetition of the being and attributes of the *first*.

VIII. All things owe their existence to their first cause, operating according to its own free will. Absolute power does not act of necessity, but freely: the power may exist without exertion; if it did not, then it acts by *necessity*; and if so, *necessity* is the agent, and not the free power, of the independent God. He can do what he will, but he will do only what is right, &c.

The like may be said of his *omniscience*. He knows himself, and what he has formed, and what he can do; but is not *necessitated* to *know* as certain what himself has made *contingent*. If God *must* continually act because he is omnipotent, and know because he is omniscient, then he must be constantly employed in doing or undoing whatever is possible to be done or undone, and knowing all that is, and all that can be, and what cannot be; which is absurd.

IX. God is a being of infinite *goodness, wisdom, mercy, justice*, and *truth*, and all other perfections which become the Framer and Governor of the universe.

GOODNESS consists in being pleased with communicating happiness to others.

WISDOM, in making a right or beneficent use of knowledge or power; for no being, howsoever intelligent or powerful, is said to act *wisely*, but that which makes a *good* or *beneficent* use of knowledge and power. Hence *wisdom* and *goodness* must be ever conjoined to make any act of power perfect. As he is *wise*, he *knows* what is best to be done; *powerful*, he *can* do it; *good*, he *will* do it. Justice, mercy, truth, or faithfulness, are not distinct attributes, but denominations given to his power and wisdom, in their various operations on different occasions, in reference to his creatures.

God's *liberty of acting* His power and wisdom being infinite, he cannot be prevented by any outward cause; his nature being essentially good, he can have no opposition from *within*. His power and all his other attributes, being infinite, eternal, and consequently unlimited, can have no opposition from *without*. And his liberty consists in his being free to act or not act, or infinitely or limitedly to vary his operations according to his own wisdom, goodness, and truth. See also the late *bishop of Ossory, Chevalier Ramsay, Dr. S. Clarke*, and others, on this subject.

SKETCHES OF PROOFS A POSTERIORI.

Recapitulation of the preceding Propositions

II. In the argument *a priori*, in order to demonstrate the being of a GOD, it was attempted to prove that there must have been a being whose nonexistence is impossible. In arguing on this subject it has been shown,—

1. That this being was unoriginated.
2. That all his attributes must also be unoriginated.
3. That these attributes must be unlimited and absolutely perfect.

4. That this being must exist everywhere in the same manner he does anywhere.

5. That he is simple and uncompounded, not consisting of *parts*, nor of *whole*, nor of *magnitude*, nor of *quantity*.

6. That he must possess intelligence and power unlimited, and all other attributes that are in themselves absolute perfections.

7. That there cannot be in the universe any more than one such unoriginated, simple, and infinite being.

8. That all things owe their existence to this first cause, operating, not according to any kind of *necessity*, but according to its own *free will*.

9. That as, in all his operations, all his attributes must concur and combine, so all the works of his hands must bear the impress of wisdom and goodness; of that *wisdom* which consists in making a right use of *knowledge* and *power*, i. e. using both beneficially; of that *goodness* which consists in being pleased with communicating happiness to others.

Hence may be deduced CREATION, the plan of which proceeded from his *wisdom*, the execution from his *power*, and the result a proof of his *goodness*.

From these data we might proceed to prove the being of a God, and his beneficence and moral government of the world, *a posteriori*, i. e. arguing from the *effects* to the *cause*.

And first, a being of infinite wisdom must be expected to form his works so as to evidence that wisdom in their multiplicity, variety, internal structure, arrangement, connections, and dependencies; and, consequently, that these works must be in many respects inscrutable to man. And this, as they are his works, must be one of their characteristics.

Whether there be any other kind of beings than *spiritual* and *material*, and such as are of a *mixed nature*, we cannot tell; but we have no ideas of any other kinds, nor can we conceive the possibility of the existence of any other; as we have no ideas of any figure that is not formed of *straight* or *curved* lines, or a *mixture* of both.

God, the uncreated Spirit, manifests himself by material substances. Created spirits must be manifested in the same way; and though matter may exist without spirit, and spirit without matter, yet without the latter, spirit cannot become manifest. Hence matter appears to have been created for the use of spirit or intellectual beings.

Creation in general demonstrates the being of a God.

The SOLAR SYSTEM and plurality of worlds, magnitude, distances, velocity and gravity, of the celestial bodies, projectile and centripetal forces, centre of gravity, ellipsis, double and treble motion, attraction, all demonstrate the wisdom, power, and goodness of God.

VEGETATION. Plants, trees, circulation of nutritious juices, composition of ligneous fibres, dissolution and regeneration of terrestrial productions.

PRESERVATION of genera and species, demonstrations of infinite skill, and of the wisest and most beneficent providence

MAN. Life, nutrition, sleep, the senses, particularly vision and muscular motion; each furnishes a series of irresistible arguments.

The HEART and the *circulation of the blood* afford the most striking proofs; and on this point let the reader particularly fix his attention.

In a healthy state the heart makes *eighty* pulsations in a minute, and it is calculated that from two ounces to two ounces and a half of blood are expelled into the *aorta* at each pulsation; consequently at least nine thousand six hundred ounces will be thrown into the *aorta* in *an hour*, which would amount to one thousand four hundred and forty pounds in one *day!*

At each pulsation this quantum of blood is propelled *eight inches*, which amounts to *fifty feet* in a *minute!* The quantity of blood in a human body is, on an average, about *thirty pounds*, and passes through the heart about *twenty-three* times in the space of one *hour!*

A weight of fifty pounds hung to the foot, the leg laid across the opposite knee, was raised by the action of the popliteal artery. Allowing for the distance from the centre of motion, this proves that the heart must possess a power of at least *four hundred pounds!*

The blood circulates by pressure from behind, occasioned by the action of the heart, which pressure having propelled it, according to the laws of gravity to the extremities, reconducts it, contrary to those laws, back to the heart. How is this effected? It has been supposed that the ARTERIES contribute much to the circulation of the blood; were it even so, it would be comparatively useless, as they cease where such an auxiliary power is most wanting, at the extremities, where their anastomosis with the veins takes place, and the veins are not supposed to possess any such propelling power.

But that the arteries possess no such power *Bichat* has proved by the following experiment: he took the arm of a dead man, placed it in warm water, inserted one end of a tube in the brachial artery, and the other end in the carotid artery of a living dog; the blood circulated in the dead arm, the pulse of which beat regularly by the action of the heart of the living animal. Is there not a wondrous and especial providence of God by which this is effected?

Others have attributed the pulsation of the heart itself to the stimulating nature of the blood. *Bichat* has disproved this by the following experiments:—

1. Expose the heart of an animal and empty it, apply a stimulus to its muscles, and it will dilate, and contract, as if it were full.

2. Puncture all the large vessels connected with the heart, so as to empty it entirely, and the alternate contractions and dilations will continue for some time, notwithstanding the total absence of the blood.

3. Remove two hearts of equal bulk from two living animals, place the fingers in the ventricles of the one, and grasp the other in the opposite hand, and it will be found that the effort of the latter in its dilation is as forcible as the other in its contraction.

Incessant action of the heart. Its unweariedness. What exhausts all other muscles appears to increase its action and its force! Can any person conceive how it is possible that a muscle can be in incessant action for threescore, fourscore, or a hundred years, without any kind of weariness? There is nothing in nature that can well explain this. Over its motion the mind has no power. This is wisely ordered, as many, in momentary fits of caprice, despair, and passion, would suspend the circulation, and thus put an end to their lives.

Providence, or the economical government of God in the provision for men and animals. Never too much, never too little; the produce of the earth being ever in proportion to the consumers, and the consumers to that produce.

Redemption. 1. As all things are intimately known to God, he must know wherein their happiness consists, and may from his goodness be expected to make every provision for that happiness.

2. Every sentient creature is capable of happiness or misery.

3. No creature can choose a state of misery for itself, because no creature can desire to be unhappy.

4. If any being could choose that state for another, he must be led to it by some motive which may make it eligible or desirable; and this must spring from his envy, jealousy, fear, or a conviction that the wretchedness of the other will contribute to his own happiness. None of these can exist in God the Creator, consequently he must be supposed to have made man for happiness. His counsels never change, and therefore when man had fallen he provided him a Saviour; this might be naturally expected from his infinite benevolence.

The moral changes made in sinners, proofs of the being, agency, goodness, and presence of God.

Man's existence is a proof of the being of God; he feels himself to be the *effect* of a cause, and that cause to be wise, powerful, and good. There is evidently no cause in nature capable of producing such an effect, for no operation of nature can produce *mind* or *intellect;* the wonderful structure of the body, and the astonishing powers of the *mind*, equally prove that God is our Maker, and that in him we live, move, and have our being.

III. Astronomical phenomena very difficult to be accounted for upon natural principles, which are strong evidences of the being and continual agency of God.

PHENOMENON I.

The motion of a planet in an elliptic orbit is truly wonderful, and incapable of a physical demonstration in all its particulars. From its aphelion, or greatest distance from the sun or body round which it revolves, to its perihelion or least distance, its motion is continually accelerated; and from its perihelion to its aphelion as constantly retarded. From what source has the planet derived that power which it opposes to the solar attraction, in such a manner that, when passing from aphelion to perihelion by a continued acceleration, it is prevented from making a nearer approach to the sun? And on the other hand, what prevents the planet, after it has passed by a continued retardation from perihelion to aphelion, from going altogether out of the solar attraction, and causes it to return again to perihelion? In Sir Isaac Newton's demonstration that this phenomenon is a necessary result of the laws of gravity and projectile forces, it is worthy of observation that, to account for a planet's moving in an elliptic orbit, little differing from a circle, and having the sun in the lower focus, the projectile force of the planet, or the power by which it would move for ever

in a straight line if not acted upon from without, is assumed to be nearly sufficient to counterbalance the planet's gravitating power, or, which is the same thing, the attraction of the central body; for the demonstration, the particulars of which are too complicated to be here detailed, puts us in possession of the following facts: If a planet be projected in a direction exactly perpendicular to that of the central body, with a velocity equal to what it would acquire by falling half way to the centre by attraction alone, it will describe a circle round the central body. If the velocity of projection be greater than this, but not equal to what the planet would acquire in falling to the centre, it will move in an elliptical orbit more or less eccentric according to the greater or less degree of projectile force. If the velocity of projection be equal to that which the planet would acquire in falling to the central body, it will move in a parabola; if greater than this, in a hyperbola. Now it cannot be demonstrated, upon physical principles, that a planet should have a certain projectile force and no other, or that it should have any at all; for it is a law of nature, ably demonstrated by Newton in his *Principia*, that all bodies have such an indifference to rest or motion that, if once at rest, they must remain eternally so, unless acted upon by some power sufficient to move them; and that a body once put in motion will proceed of itself ever after in a straight line, if not diverted out of this rectilinear course by some influence. Every planetary body has a certain projectile force, therefore some previously existing cause must have communicated it. The planets have not only a projectile force, but this power is at the same time nearly a counterbalance to its gravitation, or the attraction of the central body; so that, by virtue of these powers thus harmoniously united, the planets perform their revolutions in orbits nearly circular with the greatest regularity. It hence follows that the cause, which has communicated just so much projectile force as to produce so near an equilibrium in the centrifugal and centripetal powers, is infinitely intelligent; therefore this cause must be God.

As all the planets move in orbits more or less elliptical, when they could have been made to move in circles by a particular adjustment of the attractive and projectile forces, the Divine purpose must be best answered by the eccentric orbit. The habitable earth evidently derives very great advantage from the elliptical orbit; for, in consequence of it, the sun is seven or eight days of every year longer on the northern side of the equator than he is on the southern; *i. e.* from the 21st of March, when he crosses the equator northward, to the 23d of September, when he again returns to the equator, there are 186 days; but from the 23d of September, or autumnal equinox, to the 21st of March, or vernal equinox, there are only 179 days. From this circumstance the northern hemisphere, which it has pleased God should contain by far the greatest portion of land, is considerably warmer towards the polar regions than in similar latitudes towards the south pole, where an equal degree of temperature is not needed. Circumnavigators have not yet been able, because of the great cold of the south polar regions, to proceed beyond seventy-two or seventy-three degrees of south latitude, or, which is the same thing, to approach the south pole nearer than about 1200 miles; but the northern frigid zone, possessing a greater temperature, has been explored to within about 600 miles of the pole, *i. e.* to nearly eighty-two degrees of north latitude.

PHENOMENON II.

The *double motion* of a primary planet, namely, its *annual* revolution and *diurnal* rotation, is one of the greatest wonders the science of astronomy presents to our view. The laws which regulate the latter of these motions are so completely hid from man, notwithstanding his present great extension of philosophic research, that the times which the planets employ in their rotations can only be determined by observation. How is it that two motions, so essentially different from each other, should be in the same body at the same time, without one interfering at all with the other? The astonishing accuracy with which celestial observations have been conducted within the last one hundred years, has enabled astronomers to demonstrate that the neighbouring planets very sensibly affect the figure of the earth's orbit, and consequently its motion in its orbit. Of this every one may be convinced who examines the calculus employed in ascertaining for any particular point of time the sun's place in the heavens; or, which is the same thing, the point of the earth's orbit which is exactly opposed to the place of the earth in this orbit. Thus the maximum that the earth is affected by Venus is nine seconds and seven-tenths of a degree; by Mars, six seconds and seven-tenths; and by Jupiter, eight seconds, two-thirds, &c. But no astronomer, since the foundation of the world, has been able to demonstrate that the earth's motion in the heavens is at all accelerated or retarded by the diurnal rotation; or, on the other hand, that the earth's motion on its axis experiences the least irregularity from the annual revolution. How wonderful is this contrivance! and what incalculable benefits result from it! The uninterrupted and equable diurnal rotation of the earth gives us day and night in their succession, and the annual revolution causes all the varied scenery of the year. If one motion interfered with the other, the return of day and night would be irregular, and the change of seasons attended with uncertainty to the husbandman. These two motions are therefore harmoniously impressed upon the earth, that the gracious promise of the great Creator might be fulfilled: "While the earth remaineth, seed time and harvest, and cold and heat, and summer and winter, and day and night, shall not cease." The double motion of a secondary planet is still more singular than that of its primary; for, (taking the moon for an example,) besides its particular revolution round the earth, which is performed in twenty-seven days, seven hours, forty-three minutes, four seconds and a half; it is carried round the sun with the earth once every year. Of all the planetary motions with which we have a tolerable acquaintance, that of the moon is the most intricate: upwards of twenty equations are necessary, in the great majority of cases, to reduce her mean to her true place; yet not one of them is derivable from the circumstance that she accompanies the earth in its revolution round the sun. They depend on the different distances of the earth from the sun in its annual revolution, the position of the lunar nodes, and various other causes, and not on the annual revolution itself; a motion which of all others might be expected to cause greater irregularities in her revolution round the earth, than could be produced in that of the latter by the planetary attractions. Who can form an adequate conception of that influence of the earth which thus draws the moon with it round the sun, precisely in the same manner as if it were a part of the earth's surface, notwithstanding the intervening distance of about two hundred and forty thousand miles; and at the same time leaves undisturbed the moon's proper motion round the earth? And what beneficent purposes are subserved by this harmony! In consequence of it we have the periodical returns of new and full moon; and the ebbing and flowing of the sea, which depend on the various lunar phases with respect to the sun and earth, (as is demonstrable from each of these phases being continually contemporaneous with a particular phenomenon of the tides,) always succeed each other with a regularity necessarily equal to that of the causes which produce them

PHENOMENON III.

The impression of an inconceivably rapid motion upon the earth, without disturbing in the smallest degree any thing upon its surface, or in the atmosphere which surrounds it, is another instance of the infinite wisdom of God. That with which God has endued the celestial bodies, in order to accomplish this end, is called gravity or attraction. The existence of this influence is easily demonstrable from the curious law which pervades all the bodies in the solar system, and probably every other body in the whole compass of space. This law, *viz.* that the squares of the periodic times of the planets are to each other as the cubes of their mean distances from the central body, was first discovered by Kepler, and afterwards demonstrated by Sir Isaac Newton. Thus, if the distance of but one planet from the sun is known, and the periodic revolutions of the whole, the distance of each from the sun is easily ascertained. The mean distance of the earth from the sun has been found, by the transits of Venus in 1761 and 1769, to be about ninety-five and a half millions of English miles; and the periodic times of all the planets are known by direct observation. Thus, to find the distance of Jupiter from the sun, nothing more is necessary than first to square the period of the earth, 365 days, 5 hours, $48\frac{3}{4}$ minutes; and that of Jupiter, 11 years, 315 days, 14 hours and a half; and divide the greater product by the less to find the proportion one bears to the other; then to cube the earth's mean distance from the sun, $95\frac{1}{2}$ millions, and multiply the cube by the proportion between the periodic times already found, and the cube root of the last product will be the distance required. By this means it was that the distances of the different planets from the sun, and of the satellites from the primaries, (for this law extends to the satellites,) have been calculated. See the Table of the Periodic Revolutions, &c., of the Planets, in the notes on the first chapter of Genesis. From this law it is evident, to every one that deeply considers this subject, that the planets revolve in orbits

2

by an influence emanating from the sun; for the nearer a planet is to the sun, the swifter is its motion in its orbit, and *vice versa.* (See the Tables already referred to.) The singular phenomenon of a planet's describing equal areas in equal times results from gravitation combined with the projectile power; or, in other words, from the union of the centripetal and centrifugal forces. Thus, if a planet describe in twenty-four hours any given arc of its orbit, and the area contained between two straight lines, drawn from the extremities of this arc and meeting in the sun, be ascertained, it will be precisely equal to what the planet will describe in any other twenty-four hours, the greater or less quantity of the arc described being continually compensated by the less or greater extent of the straight lines including the respective areas. We also find that, by virtue of these laws, the motion of a planet in its orbit is not decreased in arithmetical proportion to the increase of the distance from the central body; for the hourly orbitical motion of the Georgium Sidus, for example, is only about five times slower than that of the earth, though its distance from the sun is full nineteen times greater.

Every man may convince himself of the existence of gravity, by observing the phenomena attending falling bodies. Why is it that the velocity of a falling body is continually accelerated till it arrives on the earth? We answer, that the earth continually attracts it; consequently, its velocity must be continually increasing as it falls. It is also observable, that the nature of the influence on falling bodies is precisely the same with that which retains the planets in their orbits. By numerous experiments it is found that, if the falling body descends towards the earth 16 feet in the first second, (a statement very near the truth,) it will fall through three times this space, or 48 feet, in the next second; five times this space, or 80 feet, in the third second; seven times this space, or 112 feet, in the fourth second; nine times this space, or 144 feet, in the fifth second, &c. Hence the spaces fallen through are as the squares of the times of falling, *i. e.* in the first second the body falls 16 feet, and in the next second, 48 feet; consequently the body falls as many feet in the two first seconds as is equal to the sum of these two numbers, *viz.* 64, which is 16 multiplied by 4, the square of 2, the number of seconds it took up in falling through the first 64 feet. See Exley's new theory of physics, page 469.

The above is but a very brief account of the influence of this wonderful principle, which is universally diffused through nature, and capable of attracting every particle of matter under all its possible modifications, and of imparting to each substance, from the lightest gas to the most ponderous metal, that property which constitutes one body specifically heavier or lighter than another. To detail all the benefits which result from it, would be almost to give a history of the whole material creation. But it may be asked, What is gravity? To the solution of this question natural philosophy is unable to lead us. Suffice it to say, all we know of gravity is its *mode* of operation, and that it is, like its great Creator, an all pervading and continued energy. Therefore, that *it is,* and not in *what it consists,* is capable of demonstration.

All these things prove, not only that there is a God infinitely powerful and intelligent, but also kind and merciful, working all according to the counsel of his will, and causing all his operations to result in the benefit of his creatures. They prove, also, that God is continually present, supporting all things by his energy; and that, while his working is manifest, his ways are past finding out. Yet, as far as he may be known, we should endeavour to know him; for, *he that cometh unto God must know that he is.* Without this it is not likely that any man will serve him; for those alone who know him seek him, and they only who put their trust in him can testify *he is the rewarder of them who diligently seek him.*

A short account of the BASTINADO, *supposed to be referred to in* ver. 35.

IV. On the 15th of Nov. 1779, Mr. Antes, returning from a short country excursion to Grand Cairo, was seized by some of the attendants of *Osman Bey,* a Mamaluke chief; and after stripping him of his clothes, they demanded money, which he not having about him, they dragged him before the bey, telling him that he was a European, from whom he might get something. In order to extort money from him, the bey ordered him to be bastinadoed. They first threw him down flat on his face, and then bent up his legs, so that the soles of his feet were horizontal; they then brought a strong staff, about six feet long, with an iron chain fixed to it at both ends. This chain they threw round both feet above the ancles, and twisted them together; and two fellows on each side, provided with what they call a *corbage,* held up the soles of the feet by means of the stick. When thus placed, an officer whispered in his ear, "Do not suffer yourself to be beaten; give him a thousand dollars, and he will let you go." Mr. Antes, not willing to give up the money which he had received for the goods of other merchants, refused; the two men then began to beat the soles of his feet, at first moderately; but when a second application for money was refused, and then the demand was two thousand dollars, they began to lay on more roughly, and *every stroke felt like the application of a red hot poker.* Finding they could get no money, supposing he might have some choice goods, a third application was made to him by the officer; he told them he had a fine silver-mounted blunderbuss at his lodging which he would give. The bey asked what he offered; the officer sneered, and said, *bir carabina,* i. e. "one blunderbuss;" on which the bey said, *ettrup il kulp,* "beat the dog." They then began to *lay on with all their might.* "At first," says Mr. Antes, "the pain was excruciating; but after some time my feeling grew numb, and it was like beating a bag of wool." Finding that nothing was to be got from him, and knowing that he had done nothing to deserve punishment, the bey ordered them to let him go. One of the attendants anointed his feet, and bound them up with some rags, put him on an ass, and conducted him to his house in Cairo, and laid him on his bed, where he was confined *for six weeks before he could walk, even with crutches;* and *for more than three years his feet and ancles were very much swelled;* and, *though twenty years had elapsed* when he published this account, *his feet and ancles were so affected that, on any strong exertion, ·they· were accustomed to swell.*

He mentions instances of the bastinado having been applied for three days successively, and, if the person survived, *the feet were rendered useless for life;* but in general, he observes, when they have received *between five and six hundred strokes, the blood gushes from their mouth and nose, and they die either under or soon after the operation.*

How he felt his mind affected on this distressing occasion, he thus piously describes : " I at once gave up myself for lost, well knowing that my life depended on the caprice of a brute in human shape ; and, having heard and seen such examples of unrelenting cruelty, I could not expect to fare better than others had done before me ; I had therefore nothing left *but to cast myself on the mercy of God, commending my soul to him ;* and indeed I must in gratitude confess, that I experienced his support most powerfully ; so that all fear of death was taken from me ; and if I could have bought my life for one halfpenny, I should, I believe, have hesitated to accept the offer."—*Observations on* the *Manners, &c., of the Egyptians,* by J. Antes, Esq. 12mo., *Dublin,* 1801, p. 146.

If this be the punishment to which the apostle alludes, it may justly rank with the *most severe ;* and, all circumstances considered, this appears to be what is intended in the original word ετυμπανισθησαν, which we, not knowing what was meant by it, render *they were tortured.* •These holy men needed no mercy from man ; and they received no *justice.* The case above is a specimen of Mohammedan justice, and Mamaluke cruelty ; and to rescue such wretches from the government of the French we spent torrents of British blood ! It would have been a mercy to man to have left them in the hands of any power that might abate their pride, assuage their malice, and confound their devices. As to their being corrupted by French manners, that is impossible ; the Mohammedans in general, and the Turks and Mamalukes of Egypt in particular, are too bad for the devil himself to corrupt. Pity, that political considerations rendered it necessary to restore that corrupt and abominable government. Reader, there is an infinite difference between the *Bible* and the *Koran ;* the one is from heaven, the other from earth and hell. " Thanks be to God for his holy Gospel !"

CHAPTER XII.

Having so many incitements to holiness, patience, and perseverance, we should lay aside every hinderance, and run with patience the race that is set before us, taking our blessed Lord for our example, 1–4. *These sufferings are to be considered as fatherly chastisements from God, and to be patiently submitted to on account of the benefits to be derived from them,* 5–11. *They should take courage and go forward,* 12, 13. *Directions to follow peace with all men, and to take heed that they fall not from the grace of God,* 14, 15. *References to the case of Esau,* 16, 17. *The privileges of Christians, compared with those of the Jews, by which the superior excellence of Christianity is shown,* 18–24. *They must take care not to reject Jesus, who now addressed them from heaven, and who was shortly to be their Judge,* 25–27. *As they were called to receive a kingdom, they should have grace, whereby they might serve God acceptably,* 28, 29.

A. M. cir. 4067.
A. D. cir. 63.
An. Olymp.
cir. CCX. 3.
A. U. C. cir.
816.

WHEREFORE, seeing we also are compassed about with so great a cloud of witnesses, [a] let us lay aside every weight, and the sin which doth so easily beset *us,* and [b] let us run [c] with patience the race that is set before us,

A. M cir. 4067.
A. D. cir. 63.
An. Olymp.
cir. CCX. 3.
A. U. C. cir.
816.

[a] Col. iii. 8 ; 1 Pet. ii. 1. —[b] 1 Cor. ix. 24 ; Phil. iii. 13, 14.   [c] Rom. xii. 12 ; chap. x. 36.

NOTES ON CHAP. XII.

Verse 1. Wherefore] This is an inference drawn from the examples produced in the preceding chapter, and on this account both should be read in connection.

Compassed about] Here is another allusion to the *Olympic games :* the *agonistæ,* or contenders, were often greatly animated by the consideration that the eyes of the *principal men* of their country were fixed upon them ; and by this they were induced to make the most extraordinary exertions.

Cloud of witnesses] Νεφος μαρτυρων. Both the *Greeks* and *Latins* frequently use the term *cloud,* to express a *great number* of persons or things ; so in *Euripides,* Phœniss. ver. 257 : νεφος ασπιδων πυκνον, a *dense cloud of shields ;* and *Statius,* Thebiad., lib. ix., ver. 120 : *jaculantum nubes,* a cloud of spearmen. The same metaphor frequently occurs.

Let us lay aside every weight] As those who ran in the Olympic races would throw aside every thing that might impede them in their course ; so Christians, professing to go to heaven, must throw aside every thing that might hinder them in their Christian race. Whatever weighs down our hearts or affections to earth and sense is to be carefully avoided ; for no man, with the love of the world in his heart, can ever reach the kingdom of heaven.

The sin which doth so easily beset] Ευπεριστατον αμαρτιαν· *The well circumstanced sin ;* that which has every thing in its favour, *time,* and *place,* and *opportunity ;* the *heart* and the *object ;* and a sin in which all these things frequently occur, and consequently the transgression is frequently committed. Ευπεριστατος is derived from εν, *well,* περι, *about,* and ιστημι, *I stand ;* the sin that stands well, or is favourably situated, ever

A. M cir. 4067
A. D. cir. 63.
An. Olymp.
cir. CCX. 3.
A. U. C. cir.
816.

2 Looking unto Jesus, the ^d author and finisher of *our* faith; ^e who, for the joy that was set before him, endured the cross, despising the shame, and ^f is set down at the right hand of the throne of God.

A. M. cir. 4067.
A. D. cir. 63.
An. Olymp.
cir. CCX. 3.
A. U. C. cir.
816.

3 ^g For consider him that endured such contradiction of sinners against himself, ^h lest ye be wearied and faint in your minds.

4 ⁱ Ye have not yet resisted unto blood, striving against sin.

---

^d Or, *beginner.*——^e Luke xxiv. 26; Phil. ii. 8, &c.; 1 Pet. i. 11. ^f Psa. cx. 1; chap. i. 3, 13; viii. 1; 1 Pet. iii. 22.

^g Matt. x. 24, 25; John xv. 20.——^h Gal. vi. 9.——ⁱ 1 Cor. x. 13; chap. x. 32, 33, 34.

---

surrounding the person and soliciting his acquiescence. What *we* term the *easily besetting sin* is the sin of our constitution, the sin of our trade, that in which our worldly honour, secular profit, and sensual gratification are most frequently felt and consulted. Some understand it of *original* sin, as that by which we are inveloped in body, soul, and spirit. Whatever it may be, the word gives us to understand that it is what meets us at every turn; that it is always presenting itself to us; that as a pair of compasses describe a circle by the revolution of one leg, while the other is at rest in the centre, so this, springing from that point of corruption within, called the *carnal mind*, surrounds us in every place; we are *bounded* by it, and often hemmed in on every side; it is a circular, well fortified wall, over which we must leap, or through which we must break. The man who is addicted to a particular species of sin (for every sinner has *his way*) is represented as a prisoner in this strong fortress.

In laying aside the weight, there is an allusion to the long garments worn in the eastern countries, which, if not laid aside or tucked up in the girdle, would greatly incommode the traveller, and utterly prevent a man from running a race. The easily besetting sin of the Hebrews was an aptness to be drawn aside from their attachment to the Gospel, for fear of persecution.

Let us run with patience the race] Τρεχωμεν τον προκειμενον ἡμιν αγωνα· Let us *start*, *run on*, and *continue running*, till we get to the goal. This figure is a favourite among the Greek writers; so *Euripides, Alcest.,* ver. 489 : Ου τον δ' αγωνα πρωτον αν δραμοιμ' εγω· *This is not the first race that I shall run.* Id. Iphig. in Aulid., ver. 1456 : Δεινους αγωνας δια σε κεινον δει δραμειν· *He must run a hard race for thee.* This is a race which is of infinite moment to us : the prize is ineffably great ; and, if we lose it, it is not a simple loss, for the whole soul perishes.

Verse 2. *Looking unto Jesus*] Αφορωντες· Looking *off* and *on,* or *from* and *to;* looking *off* or *from* the world and all secular concerns *to* Jesus and all the spiritual and heavenly things connected with him. This is still an allusion to the Grecian games : those who ran were to keep their eyes fixed on the mark of the prize ; they must keep the goal in view. The exhortation implies, 1. That they should place all their hope and confidence in Christ, as their sole helper in this race of faith. 2. That they should consider him their leader in this contest and imitate his example.

The author and finisher of—faith] Αρχηγος, translated here *author,* signifies, in general, captain or leader, or the first inventor of a thing ; see chap. ii. 10. But the reference seems to be here to the βραβευς, or judge in the games, whose business it was to admit the contenders, and to give the prize to the conqueror. Jesus is here represented as this officer ; every Christian is a contender in this race of life, and for eternal life. The heavenly course is *begun* under Jesus ; and under him it is *completed.* He is the finisher, by awarding the prize to them that are faithful unto death. Thus he is the *author* or the judge under whom, and by whose permission and direction, according to the rules of the heavenly race, they are permitted to enter the lists, and commence the race, and he is the finisher, τελειωτης, the *perfecter,* by awarding and giving the prize which consummates the combatants at the end of the race.

Who, for the joy that was set before him] The joy of fulfilling the will of the Father, Psa. xl. 6, &c., in tasting death for every man ; and having endured the cross and despised the shame of this ignominious death, He is set down at the right hand of God, ever appearing in the presence of God for us, and continuing his exhibition of himself as our Sacrifice, and his intercession as our Mediator. See the notes on chap. x. 5, &c. There are different other explanations given of this clause, but I think *that* here offered is the most natural. It never can, in any sense, be said of Jesus that he endured the cross, &c., in the prospect of gaining an everlasting glory ; when he had the fulness of that glory with the Father before the world began ; John xvii. 5.

Verse 3. *For consider him*] Αναλογισασθε—ἱνα μη καμητε, ταις ψυχαις—εκλυομενοι· Attentively observe and analyze every part of his conduct, enter into his spirit, examine his motives and object, and remember that, as he acted, ye are called to act ; he will furnish you with the same Spirit, and will support you with the same strength. He bore a continual opposition of sinners against himself ; but he conquered by meekness, patience, and perseverance : he has left you an example that ye should follow his steps. If ye trust in him, ye shall receive strength ; therefore, howsoever great your opposition may be, ye shall not *be weary :* if ye confide in and attentively look to him, ye shall have continual *courage* to go on, and never *faint* in your minds.

Here is a continued allusion to the contenders in the Grecian games, who, when exhausted in bodily strength and courage, yielded the palm to their opponents, and were said καμνειν, to be weary or exhausted ; εκλυεσθαι, to be dissolved, disheartened, or to have lost all bravery and courage.

Verse 4. *Ye have not yet resisted unto blood*] Many of those already mentioned were martyrs for the truth ; they persevered unto death, and lost their lives in bearing testimony to the truth. Though you have

2

A. M. cir. 4067.
A. D. cir. 63.
An. Olymp.
cir. CCX. 3.
A. U. C. cir.
816.

5 And ye have forgotten the exhortation which speaketh unto you as unto children, [k] My son, despise not thou the chastening of the Lord, nor faint when thou art rebuked of him:

6 For [l] whom the Lord loveth he chasteneth, and scourgeth every son whom he receiveth.

7 [m] If ye endure chastening, God dealeth with you as with sons; for what son is he whom the father chasteneth not?

8 But if ye be without chastisement, [n] whereof all are partakers, then are ye bastards, and not sons.

9 Furthermore, we have had fathers of our flesh which corrected *us*, and we gave *them* reverence: shall we not much rather be in subjection unto [o] the Father of spirits, and live?

A. M. cir. 4067
A. D. cir. 63.
An. Olymp.
cir. CCX. 3.
A. U. C. cir.
816.

---

[k] Job v. 17; Prov. iii. 11.——[l] Psa. xciv. 12; cxix. 75; Prov. iii. 12; James i. 12; Rev. iii. 19.——[m] Deut. viii. 5; 2 Sam. vii. 14; Prov. xiii. 24; xix. 18; xxiii. 13.

[n] Psa. lxxiii. 1; 1 Pet. v. 9.——[o] Numbers xvi. 22; xxvi. 16; Job xii. 10; Eccles. xii. 7; Isaiah xlii. 5; lvii. 16; Zech. xii. 1.

---

had opposition and persecution, yet you have not been called, in bearing your testimony against sin and sinners, to seal the truth with your blood.

Striving against sin.] Προς την ἁμαρτιαν ανταγωνιζομενοι· An allusion to *boxing* at the Grecian games. In the former passages the apostle principally refers to the foot races.

Verse 5. And ye have forgotten] Or, have ye forgotten the exhortation? This quotation is made from Prov. iii. 11, 12, and shows that the address there, which at first sight appears to be from Solomon to his son, or from some fatherly man to a person in affliction, is properly from *God himself* to any person in persecution, affliction, or distress.

Despise not thou the chastening] Μη ολιγωρει παιδειας Κυριου· *Do not neglect the correction of the Lord.* That man neglects correction, and profits not by it, who does not see the hand of God in it; or, in other words, does not fear the rod and him who hath appointed it, and, consequently, does not humble himself under the mighty hand of God, deplore his sin, deprecate Divine judgment, and pray for mercy.

Nor faint] Do not be discouraged nor despair, for the reasons immediately alleged.

Verse 6. For whom the Lord loveth he chasteneth] Here is the *reason* why we should neither *neglect* correction, nor *faint* under it: it is a proof of the fatherly love of God Almighty, and shows his most gracious designs towards us; from which we may be fully convinced that the affliction will prove the means of good to our souls, if we make a proper use of it.

And scourgeth every son whom he receiveth.] Μαστιγοι δε παντα υιον, ὁν παραδεχεται. This is a quotation, literatim from the Septuagint, of Prov. iii. 12, of which place our version is *Even as the father the son* in whom *he delighteth*. But, howsoever near this may appear to be the Hebrew, it bears scarcely any affinity to the apostle's words. The Hebrew text is as follows: וכאב את־בן ירצה *uchab eth-ben yirtseh*. Now, וכאב may be a *noun*, compounded of the conjunction ו *vau*, "and," the *comparative* particle כ *ke*, "as" or "like;" and אב *ab*, "a father:" or it may be the third person preterite kal of כאב *caab*, "he spoiled, wasted, marred, ulcerated," compounded with the conjunction ו *vau*, "and." And in this sense the *Septuagint* most evidently understood it; and it is so understood by the *Arabic*; and both readings seem to be combined by the *Syriac* and *Chaldee* versions. And as to רצה *ratsah*, one of its prime meanings is to *accept*, to *receive graciously*, to *take into favour*; the translation, therefore, of the Septuagint and apostle is perfectly consonant to the Hebrew text, and our version of Prov. iii. 12 is wrong.

Verse 7. If ye endure chastening] If ye submit to his authority, humble yourselves under his hand, and pray for his blessing, you will find that he deals with you as beloved children, correcting you that he may make you partakers of his holiness.

God dealeth with you as with sons] He acknowledges by this that you belong to the *family*, and that he, as your *Father*, has you under proper discipline. It is a maxim among the Jewish rabbins that "the love which is not conjoined with reproof is not genuine."

Verse 8. Then are ye bastards] This proceeds on the general fact, that *bastards* are neglected in their manners and education; the fathers of such, feeling little affection for, or obligation to regard, their spurious issue. But *all* that are legitimate children *are partakers* of chastisement or discipline; for the original word παιδεια does not imply *stripes* and *punishments*, but the whole discipline of a child, both at home and at school.

Verse 9. We have had fathers of our flesh] The fathers of our flesh, i. e. our natural parents, were correctors; and we reverenced them, notwithstanding their corrections often arose from whim or caprice: but *shall we not rather be in subjection to the Father of spirits*; to him from whom we have received both body and soul; who is our Creator, Preserver, and Supporter; to whom both we and our parents owe our life and our blessings; and who corrects us only for our profit; that we may *live* and be *partakers of his holiness?* The apostle in asking, *Shall we not much rather be in subjection to the Father of spirits, and live?* alludes to the punishment of the *stubborn* and *rebellious son*, Deut. xxi. 18—21: "If a man have a stubborn and rebellious son, who will not obey the voice of his father, or the voice of his mother, and that, when they have chastened him, will not hearken unto them; then shall his father and mother lay hold on him and bring him to the elders of the city, and they shall say, This our son is stubborn and rebellious; he will not obey our voice: and all the men of the city shall stone him with stones that he DIE." Had he been

2

A. M. cir. 4067.
A. D. cir. 63.
An. Olymp.
cir. CCX. 3.
A. U. C. cir.
816.

10 For they verily for a few days chastened *us* ᴾ after their own pleasure ; but he for *our* profit �q that *we* might be partakers of his holiness.

11 Now, no chastening for the present seemeth to be joyous, but grievous : nevertheless, afterward it yieldeth ʳ the peaceable fruit of righteousness unto them which are exercised thereby.

12 Wherefore ˢ lift up the hands which hang down, and the feeble knees ;

13 ᵗ And make ᵘ straight paths for your feet, lest that which is lame be turned out of the way ; ᵛ but let it rather be healed.

14 ʷ Follow peace with all *men*, and holiness, ˣ without which no man shall see the Lord :

15 ʸ Looking diligently, ᶻ lest any man ᵃ fail of the grace of God ; ᵇ lest any root of bitterness springing up trouble *you*, and thereby many be defiled ;

A. M. cir. 4067.
A. D. cir. 63.
An. Olymp.
cir. CCX. 3.
A. U. C. cir.
816.

ᴾ Or, as seemed *good* or *meet* to them.——q Lev. xi. 44 ; xix. 2 ; 1 Pet. i. 15, 16.——ʳ James iii. 18.——ˢ Job iv. 3, 4 ; Isa. xxxv. 3 ; see Ecclus. xxv. 23.——ᵗ Proverbs iv. 26, 27.——ᵘ Or, *even*. ᵛ Gal. vi. 1.

ʷ Psa. xxxiv. 14 ; Romans xii. 18 ; xiv. 9 ; 2 Timothy ii. 22. ˣ Matt. v. 8 ; 2 Cor. vii. 1 ; Eph. v. 5.——ʸ 2 Cor. vi. 1. ᶻ Galatians v. 4.——ᵃ Or, *fall from*.——ᵇ Deut. xxix. 18 ; chapter iii. 12.

---

subject to his earthly parents, he would have *lived ;* because not subject, he *dies.* If we be subject to our heavenly Father, we shall LIVE, and be partakers of his holiness ; if not, we shall DIE, and be treated as *bastards* and not *sons.* This is the sum of the apostle's meaning ; and the *fact* and the *law* to which he alludes.

Verse 10. *For—a few days*] The chastisement of our earthly parents lasted only a *short time ;* that of our heavenly Father will also be but a *short time,* if we submit : and as our parents ceased to correct when we learned obedience ; so will our heavenly Father when the end for which he sent the chastisement is accomplished. God delights not in the rod ; judgment is his strange work.

Verse 11. *No chastening for the present seemeth to be joyous*] Neither correction, wholesome restraint, domestic regulations, nor gymnastic discipline, are pleasant to them that are thus exercised ; but it is by these means that *obedient children, scholars,* and *great men* are made. And it is by God's discipline that *Christians* are made. He who does not bear the yoke of Christ is good for nothing to others, and never gains rest to his own soul.

The peaceable fruit of righteousness] *i. e.* The joyous, prosperous fruits ; those fruits by which we gain much, and through which we are made happy.

Exercised thereby.] Γεγυμνασμενοις· *To the trained.* There is still an allusion to the Grecian games ; and in the word before us to those *gymnastic exercises* by which the candidates for the prizes were trained to the different kinds of exercises in which they were to contend when the games were publicly opened.

Verse 12. *Wherefore lift up the hands*] The apostle refers to Isa. xxxv. 3. The words are an address to persons almost 'worn out with sickness and fatigue, whose hands hang down, whose knees shake, and who are totally discouraged. These are exhorted to exert themselves, and take courage, with the assurance that they shall infallibly conquer if they persevere.

Verse 13. *Make straight paths for your feet*] That is, Take the straight path that is before you, do not go in crooked or rough ways, where are stones, briers, and thorns, by which you will be inevitably lamed, and so totally prevented from proceeding in the way ;

whereas, if you go in the even, proper path, though you have been wounded by getting into a wrong way, that which was wounded will *be healed* by moderate, equal exercise, all impediments being removed. The application of all this to a correct, holy deportment in religious life, is both natural and easy.

Verse 14. *Follow peace with all* men] Cultivate, as far as you possibly can, a good understanding, both with Jews and Gentiles. Ειρηνην διωκετε, *pursue peace* with the same care, attention, and diligence, as *beasts* do their *game* ; follow it through all places ; trace it through all winding circumstances ; and have it with all men, if you can with a safe conscience.

And holiness] Τον ἁγιασμον· That *state* of continual *sanctification,* that life of *purity* and *detachment* from the *world* and all its lusts, without which detachment and sanctity *no man shall see the Lord*—shall never enjoy his presence in the world of blessedness. *To see God,* in the Hebrew phrase, is to *enjoy him ;* and without holiness of heart and life this is impossible. No soul can be fit for heaven that has not suitable dispositions for the place.

Verse 15. *Looking diligently*] Επισκοπουντες· *Looking about, over,* and *upon ;* being constantly on your guard.

Lest any man fail of the grace of God] Μη τις ὑστερων απο της χαριτος του Θεου· *Lest any person should come behind,* or *fall off from, this grace* or GIFT *of God ;* this *state* of salvation, viz. the *Gospel system* or *Christianity ;* for this is most evidently the meaning of the apostle. It is not the *falling from a work of grace in their own souls,* but from the *Gospel,* to apostatize from which they had now many temptations ; and to guard them against this, the whole epistle was written.

Lest any root of bitterness springing up] A root of bitterness signifies a *poisonous plant.* The Hebrews call every species of poison a *bitter,* and with considerable propriety, as most plants are poisonous in proportion to the quantum of the bitter principle they possess. The *root of bitterness* is here used metaphorically for a *bad man,* or a man holding *unsound doctrines,* and endeavouring to spread them in the Church.

Trouble you] This alludes to the effects of poison

A. M. cir. 4067.
A. D. cir. 63.
An. Olymp.
cir. CCX. 3.
A. U. C. cir.
816.

16 c Lest there *be* any fornicator, or profane person, as Esau, d who for one morsel of meat sold his birthright.

17 For ye know how that afterward, e when he would have inherited the blessing, he was rejected : f for he found no g place of repentance, though he sought it carefully with tears.

18 For ye are not come unto the h mount that might be touched, and that burned with

fire, nor unto blackness, and darkness, and tempest,

19 And the sound of a trumpet, and the voice of words ; which *voice* they that heard i entreated that the word should not be spoken to them any more :

20 (For they could not endure that which was commanded, k And if so much as a beast touch the mountain, it shall be stoned, or thrust through with a dart :

21 l And so terrible was the sight, *that*

A. M. cir. 4067.
A. D. cir. 63.
An. Olymp.
cir. CCX. 3.
A. U. C. cir
816.

---

c Eph. v. 3 ; Col. iii. 5 ; 1 Thess. iv. 3.——d Genesis xxv. 33.
e Gen. xxvii. 34, 36, 38.——f Chap. vi. 6.——g Or, *way to change his mind.*

h Exod. xix. 12, 18, 19 ; xx. 18 ; Deut. iv. 11 ; v. 22 ; Rom. vi. 14 ; viii. 15 ; 2 Tim. i. 7.——i Exod. xx. 19 ; Deut. v. 5, 25 ; xviii. 16.——k Exod. xix. 13.——l Exod. xix. 16.

---

taken into the body : the whole animal system is disturbed ; sometimes violent retchings, great disturbances through the whole alimentary canal, together with the most fatal changes in the whole sanguineous system, are the consequences of poison taken into the stomach. The *blood* itself (the principle, under God, of life) becomes putrescent ; and probably to this the intelligent apostle alludes when he says, *and thereby many be defiled,* μιανθωσι, *corrupted* or *contaminated.*

Bad example and false teaching have corrupted thousands, and are still making desolation in the *world* and in the *Church.*

Verse 16. *Lest there* be any *fornicator*] Any licentious person who would turn the Gospel of the grace of God into lasciviousness.

Or profane person, as Esau] It is not intimated that Esau was a *fornicator ;* and the disjunctive η, *or,* separates the *profane person* from the *fornicator.* And Esau is here termed *profane,* because he so far disregarded the spiritual advantages connected with his rights of primogeniture, that he alienated the whole for a single mess of pottage. See the note on Gen. xxv. 34. The word βεβηλος, which we translate *profane,* is compounded of βε, which in composition has a *negative* signification, and βηλος, *the threshold of a temple* or *sacred edifice ;* and was applied to those who were not *initiated* into the sacred mysteries, or who were *despisers* of *sacred things,* and consequently were to be denied *admittance* to the *temple,* and were not permitted to *assist at holy rites.* Indeed, among the Greeks βεβηλος signified any thing or person which was *not consecrated to the gods.* Hence, in the opening of their worship, they were accustomed to proclaim,

    Procul, O procul, este profani !   VIRG.

    " Hence ! O hence ! ye profane."

And,

    Odi profanum vulgus, et arceo.   HOR.

    " I abominate the profane vulgar, and drive them from the temple."

The Latin *profanus,* from which we have our word, is compounded of *procul a fano,* " far from the temple," properly an *irreligious man.*

Sold his birthright.] *The first-born,* in patriarchal times, 1. Had a right to the priesthood, Exod. xxii. 29. 2. And a double portion of all the father's possessions, Deut. xxi. 17. 3. And was *lord over his brethren,* Gen. xxvii. 29, 37 ; xlix. 3. 4. And in the family of Abraham the first-born was the very *source* whence the *Messiah* as the Redeemer of the world, and the Church of God, were to spring. Farther, 5. The first-born had the right of conveying especial blessings and privileges when he came to die. See the case of Isaac and his two sons, Jacob and Esau, in the history to which the apostle alludes, Gen. xxvii ; and that of Jacob and his twelve sons, Gen. xlix. In short, the rights of primogeniture were among the most noble, honourable, and spiritual in the ancient world.

Verse 17. *When he would have inherited the blessing*] When he wished to have *the lordship over the whole family conveyed to him,* and sought it earnestly with tears, he found no place for a *change* in his *father's mind* and counsel, who now perceived that it was the will of God that Jacob should be made *lord of all.*

Repentance] Here μετανοια is not to be taken in a theological sense, as implying *contrition* for sin, but merely *change of mind* or *purpose ;* nor does the word refer here to *Esau* at all, but to his *father,* whom Esau could not, with all his tears and entreaties, persuade to reverse what he had done. *I have blessed him,* said he, *yea, and he must be blessed ;* I cannot reverse it now. See the whole of this transaction largely considered and explained in the notes on Gen. xxv. 29, &c., and xxvii. 1, &c. Nothing spoken here by the apostle, nor in the history in Genesis to which he refers, concerns the *eternal* state of either of the two brothers. The use made of the transaction by the apostle is of great importance : Take heed lest, by apostatizing from the Gospel, ye forfeit all right and title to the heavenly birthright, and never again be able to retrieve it ; because they who reject the Gospel reject the only means of salvation.

Verses 18—21. *For ye are not come unto the mount that might be touched*] I believe the words ψηλαφωμενω ορει should be translated *to a palpable* or *material mountain ;* for that it was not a mountain that on this occasion *might be touched,* the history, Exod.

A. M. cir. 4067.
A. D. cir. 63.
An. Olymp.
cir. CCX 3.
A. U. C. cir.
816.

Moses said, I exceedingly fear and quake :)

22 But ye are come ᵐ unto mount Sion, ⁿ and unto the city of the living God, the heavenly Jerusalem, and

º to an innumerable company of angels,

23 To the general assembly and Church of ᵖ the first-born �q which are ʳ written in heaven, and to God

A. M. cir. 4067.
A. D. cir. 63.
An. Olymp.
cir. CCX. 3.
A. U. C. cir.
816.

ᵐ Gal. iv. 26; Rev. iii. 12; xxi. 2, 10.——ⁿ Phil. iii. 20.
º Deut. xxxiii. 2; Psa. lxviii. 17; Jude 14.

ᵖ Exod. iv. 22; James i 18, Rev. xiv. 4.——q Luke x. 20; Phil.
iv. 3; Rev xiii 8.——ʳ Or, *enrolled.*

xix. 12, 13, shows ; and the apostle himself, in ver. 20, confirms. It is called here a *palpable* or *material* mount, to distinguish it from that *spiritual* mount Sion, of which the apostle is speaking. Some contend that it should be translated *tacto de cœlo,* thunder-struck ; this sense would agree well enough with the scope of the place. The apostle's design is to show that the dispensation of the law engendered terror ; that it was most awful and exclusive ; that it belonged only to the Jewish people ; and that, even to them, it was so terrible that they *could not endure that which was commanded,* and entreated that God would not communicate with them in his own person, but by the ministry of Moses : and even to Moses, who held the highest intimacy with Jehovah, the revealed glories, the burning fire, the blackness, the darkness, the tempest, the loud-sounding trumpet, and the voice of words, were so terrible that he said, *I exceedingly fear and tremble.*

These were the things which were exhibited on that *material* mountain ; but the Gospel dispensation is one grand, copious, and interesting display of the infinite love of God. It is all encouragement ; breathes nothing but mercy ; is not an exclusive system ; embraces the whole human race ; has Jesus, the sinner's friend, for its mediator ; is ratified by his blood ; and is suited, most gloriously suited, to all the wants and wishes of every soul of man.

Verse 22. *But ye are come unto mount Sion*] In order to enter fully into the apostle's meaning, we must observe, 1. That the Church, which is called here the *city of the living God,* the heavenly Jerusalem, and mount Sion, is represented under the notion of a CITY. 2. That the great assembly of believers in Christ is here opposed to the congregation of the Israelites assembled at Mount Sinai. 3. That the *innumerable company of angels* is here opposed to those angels by whom the law was ushered in, Acts vii. 53 ; Gal. iii. 19. 4. That the Gospel *first-born, whose names are written in heaven,* are here opposed to the *enrolled first-born* among the Israelites, Exod. xxiv. 5, xix. 22. 5 That the *mediator* of the new covenant, the Lord *Jesus,* is here opposed to *Moses,* the mediator of the old. 6. And that the *blood of sprinkling,* of Christ, our High Priest, refers to the act of Moses, Exod xxiv. 8 : "And Moses took the blood, and sprinkled it on the people, and said, Behold the blood of the covenant, which the Lord hath made with you concerning all these words."

1 The description in these verses does not refer to a *heavenly state ;* for the *terrible nature* of the *Mosaic dispensation* is never opposed to *heaven* or *life eternal,* but to the economy of the New Testament. 2. In heaven there is no need of a *mediator,*

or *sprinkling of blood ;* but these are mentioned in the state which the apostle describes.

The heavenly Jerusalem] This phrase means the Church of the New Testament, as *Schoettgen* has amply proved in his dissertation on this subject.

To an innumerable company of angels] Μυριασιν αγγελων· *To myriads, tens of thousands, of angels.* These are represented as the attendants upon God, when he manifests himself in any external manner to mankind. When he gave the law at Mount Sinai, it is intimated that myriads of these holy beings attended him. " The chariots of the Lord are twenty thousand, even thousands of angels ; the Lord is among them as in Sinai, in the holy place ;" Psa. lxviii. 17. And when he shall come to judge the world, he will be attended with a similar company. " Thousand thousands ministered unto him, and ten thousand times ten thousand stood before him ;" Dan. vii. 10. In both these cases, as in several others, these seem to be, speaking after the manner of men, the *body guard* of the Almighty. Though angels make a part of the inhabitants of the New Jerusalem, yet they belong also to the Church below. Christ has in some sort incorporated them with his followers, for " they are all ministering spirits, sent forth to minister to them that shall be heirs of salvation," and they are all ever considered as making a part of God's subjects.

Verse 23. *To the general assembly*] Πανηγυρει. This word is joined to the preceding by some of the best MSS., and is quoted in connection by several of the fathers : *Ye are come—to the general assembly of innumerable angels ;* and this is probably the true connection.

The word πανηγυρις is compounded of παν, *all,* and αγυρις, an *assembly ;* and means, particularly, an assembly collected on *festive* occasions. It is applied to the assembly of the *Grecian states* at their national games, Olympic, Isthmian, &c. ; and hence a speech pronounced in *favour* of any person at such festive assemblies was called πανηγυρικος λογος, *a panegyrical discourse ;* and hence our word *panegyric.*

The first-born] Those who first received the Gospel of Christ, and who are elsewhere termed the *first fruits.* this is spoken in allusion to the first-born among the Israelites, who were all considered as the Lord's property, and were dedicated to him. The Jews gave the title בכור *bechor,* first-born, to those who were very eminent or excellent ; what we would term the *head* or *top of his kin.* The Church of the *first-born* is the assembly of the *most excellent.*

Which are written in heaven] Who are enrolled as citizens of the New Jerusalem, and are entitled to all the rights, privileges, and immunities of the Church here, and of heaven above. This is spoken in allusion

2

A. M. cir. 4067.
A. D. cir. 63.
An. Olymp.
cir. CCX. 3.
A. U. C. cir.
816.

ˢ the Judge of all, and to the spirits of just men ᵗ made perfect,

24 And to Jesus ᵘ the me-

diator of the new ᵛ covenant, and to ʷ the blood of sprinkling, that speaketh better things ˣ than *that* of Abel.

A. M. cir. 4067.
A. D. cir. 63.
An. Olymp.
cir. CCX. 3.
A. U. C. cir.
816.

ˢ Gen. xviii. 25 ; Psa. xciv. 2.——ᵗ Phil. iii. 12 ; chap. xi. 40.
ᵘ Chap. viii. 6 ; ix. 15.

ᵛ Or, *testament.*——ʷ Exod. xxiv. 8 ; chap. x. 22 ; 1 Peter i. 2.
ˣ Gen. iv. 10 ; chap. xi. 4.

---

to the custom of enrolling or writing on tables, &c., the names of all the citizens of a particular city ; and all those thus registered were considered as having a right to live there, and to enjoy all its privileges. All genuine believers are denizens of heaven. That is their country, and there they have their rights, &c. And every member of Christ has a right to, and can demand, every ordinance in the Church of his Redeemer ; and wo to him who attempts to prevent them !

God the Judge of all] The supreme God is ever present in this general assembly : *to* him they are all gathered ; *by* him they are admitted to all those rights, &c. ; under his inspection they continue to act ; and it is he alone who erases from the register those who act unworthily of their citizenship. *Judge* here is to be taken in the Jewish use of the term, i. e. one who exercises *sovereign rule* and *authority.*

The spirits of just men made perfect] We cannot understand these terms without the assistance of Jewish phraseology. The Jews divide mankind into three classes :—

1. The JUST PERFECT, צדיקים גמורים *tsaddikim gemurim.*

2. The wicked perfect, רשעים גמורים *reshaim gemurim.*

3. Those between both, בינוניים *beinoniyim.*

1. The *just perfect* are those, 1. Who have conquered all brutal appetites and gross passions. 2. Who have stood in the time of strong temptation. 3. Who give alms with a sincere heart. 4. Who worship the true God only. 5. Who are not invidious. 6. Those from whom God has taken יצר הרע *yetser hara*, evil concupiscence, and given יצר טוב *yetser tob*, the good principle.

2. The *wicked perfect* are those, 1. Who never repent. 2. They receive their portion in this life, because they can have none in the life to come, and are under the influence of יצר הרע *yetser hara*, the evil principle.

3. The *intermediate* are those who are influenced partly by the evil principle, and partly by the good.— See *Schoettgen.*

In several parts of this epistle τελειος, *the just man*, signifies one who has a *full knowledge* of the Christian system, who is justified and saved by Christ Jesus ; and the τετελειωμενοι are the *adult Christians*, who are opposed to the νηπιοι, or *babes in knowledge* and *grace.* See chap. v. 12—14 ; viii. 11 ; and Gal. iv. 1–3. *The spirits of the just men made perfect*, or the *righteous perfect*, are the full grown Christians ; those who are justified by the blood and sanctified by the Spirit of Christ. Being *come* to such, implies that spiritual union which the disciples of Christ have with each other, and which they possess how far soever separate ; for they are *all joined in one spirit*,

Eph. ii. 18 ; they are *in the unity of the spirit*, Eph. iv. 3, 4 ; and of *one soul*, Acts iv. 32. This is a *unity* which was never possessed even by the Jews themselves in their best state ; it is peculiar to real Christianity : as to *nominal* Christianity, wars and desolations between man and his fellows are quite consistent with *its* spirit. See at the end of the chapter.

Verse 24. And to Jesus the mediator of the new covenant] The old covenant and its mediator, Moses, are passed away. See chap. viii. 13. The new covenant, i. e. the Gospel, is now in force, and will be to the end of the world ; and Jesus, the Son of God, the brightness of the Father's glory, the Maker and Preserver of all things, the Saviour and the Judge of all men, is its mediator. Both the covenant and its mediator are infinitely superior to those of the Jews, and they are very properly set down here among the superior benefits and glories of Christianity.

To the blood of sprinkling] This is an allusion, as was before observed, to the sprinkling of the blood of the covenant sacrifice upon the people, when that covenant was made upon Mount Sinai ; to the sprinkling of the blood of the sin-offerings before the mercyseat ; and probably to the sprinkling of the blood of the paschal lamb on their houses, to prevent their destruction by the destroying angel. But all these sprinklings were *partial* and inefficacious, and had no meaning but as they referred to this ; the blood of sprinkling under the new covenant is ever ready ; all may have it applied ; it continues through ages ; and is the highest glory of Christianity, because by it we draw nigh to God, and through it get our hearts sprinkled from an evil conscience ; and, in a word, have an entrance unto the holiest by the blood of Jesus.

Better things than that of Abel.] God accepted Abel's sacrifice, and was well pleased with it ; for Abel was a righteous man, and offered his sacrifice by *faith* in the great promise. But the blood of Christ's sacrifice was infinitely more precious than the blood of Abel's sacrifice, as Jesus is infinitely greater than Abel ; and the blood of Christ avails for the sins of the *whole world*, whereas the blood of Abel's sacrifice could avail only for *himself.*

Many have supposed that the *blood of Abel* means here the blood that was shed by Cain in the murder of this holy man, and that the blood of Jesus *speaks better things than it does*, because the blood of Abel *called for vengeance*, but the blood of Christ *for pardon* ; this interpretation reflects little credit on the understanding of the apostle. To say that the blood of Christ *spoke better things than that of Abel* is saying little indeed ; it might speak very little good to any soul of man, and yet speak *better things* than *that* blood of Abel which spoke no kind of good to any human creature, and only called for vengeance against him

2

A. M. cir. 4067.
A. D. cir. 63.
An. Olymp.
cir. CCX. 3.
A. U. C. cir.
816.

25 See that ye refuse not him that speaketh. For ʸ if they escaped not who refused him that spake on earth, much more *shall not* we *escape,* if we turn away from him that *speaketh* from heaven :

26 ᶻ Whose voice then shook the earth: but now he hath promised, saying, ᵃ Yet once more I shake not the earth only, but also heaven.

27 And this *word,* Yet once more, signifieth ᵇ the removing of those things that ᶜ are shaken, as of things that are made, that those things which cannot be shaken may remain.

28 Wherefore we receiving a kingdom which cannot be moved, ᵈ let us have grace, whereby we may serve God acceptably with reverence and godly fear :

29 For ᵉ our God *is* a consuming fire.

A. M. cir. 4067.
A. D. cir. 63.
An. Olymp.
cir. CCX. 3.
A. U. C. cir.
816.

ʸ Ch. ii. 2, 3; iii. 17; x. 28, 29.——ᶻ Exod. xix. 18.——ᵃ Hag. ii. 6.——ᵇ Psa. cii. 26; Matt. xxiv. 35; 2 Pet. iii. 10; Rev. xxi. 1.——ᶜ Or, *may be shaken.*

ᵈ Or, *let us hold fast.*——ᵉ Exod. xxiv. 17; Deut. iv. 24; ix. 3; Psa. l. 3; xcvii. 3; Isa. lxvi. 15; 2 Thess. i. 8; chapter x. 27.

---

that shed it. The truth is, the *sacrifice* offered by Abel is that which is intended; that, as we have already seen, was pleasing in the sight of God, and was accepted in behalf of him who offered it : but the blood of Christ is infinitely more acceptable with God; it was shed for the whole human race, and cleanses all who believe from all unrighteousness.

Verse 25. See] Βλεπετε· *Take heed, that ye refuse not him*—the Lord Jesus, the mediator of the new covenant, who now speaketh *from heaven,* by his Gospel, to the Jews and to the Gentiles, having in his incarnation come down from God.

Him that spake on earth] Moses, who spoke on the part of God to the Hebrews, every transgression of whose word received a just recompense of reward, none being permitted to *escape* punishment; consequently, if ye turn away from Christ, who speaks to you from heaven, you may expect a much sorer punishment, the offence against God being so much the more heinous, as the privileges slighted are more important and glorious.

Verse 26. Whose voice then shook the earth] Namely, at the giving of the law on Mount Sinai; and from this it seems that it was the voice of *Jesus* that then shook the earth, and that it was he who came down on the mount. But others refer this simply to God the Father giving the law.

Not the earth only, but also heaven.] Probably referring to the approaching destruction of Jerusalem, and the total abolition of the political and ecclesiastical constitution of the Jews; the one being signified by the *earth,* the other by *heaven;* for the Jewish state and worship are frequently thus termed in the prophetic writings. And this seems to be the apostle's meaning, as he evidently refers to Haggai ii. 6, where this event is predicted. It may also remotely refer to the final dissolution of all things.

Verse 27. The removing of those things that are shaken] The whole of the *Jewish polity,* which had been in a *shaken state* from the time that Judea had fallen under the power of the Romans.

As of things that are made] That is, subjects intended to last only for a time. God never designed that the Jewish religion should become general, nor be permanent.

Those things which cannot be shaken] The whole *Gospel system,* which cannot be *moved* by the power of man.

May remain.] Be permanent; God designing that this shall be the *last dispensation* of his grace and mercy, and that it shall continue till the earth and the heavens are no more.

Verse 28. We receiving a kingdom] The Gospel dispensation, frequently termed the *kingdom of God* and the *kingdom of heaven,* because in it God reigns among men, and he reigns in the hearts of them that believe, and his kingdom is righteousness, peace, and joy in the Holy Ghost.

Which cannot be moved] Which never can fail, because it is the last dispensation.

Let us have grace] Εχωμεν χαριν· *Let us have, keep,* or *hold fast, the benefit* or *gift,* that is, the heavenly kingdom which God has given us. This is the meaning of the word, 2 Cor. viii. 4, and is so rendered by our translators; and it is only by this *heavenly gift* of the Gospel that we can serve God acceptably, for he can be pleased with no service that is not performed according to the Gospel of his Son.

If we prefer the common meaning of the word *grace* it comes to the same thing; without the *grace*—the especial *succour* and *influence of Christ,* we cannot serve, λατρευωμεν, pay religious worship to God; for he receives no *burnt-offering* that is not kindled by fire from his own altar.

Acceptably] Ευαρεστως· In such a way as to *please* him well. And the offering, with which he is *well pleased,* he will *graciously accept;* and if he accept our service, his Spirit will testify in our conscience that our ways please him. When *Abel* sacrifices, God is well pleased; where *Cain* offers, there is no approbation.

Reverence] Αιδους· With *shamefacedness* or *modesty.*

Godly fear] Ευλαβειας· *Religious fear.* We have boldness to enter into the holiest by the blood of Jesus, but let that boldness be ever tempered with *modesty* and *religious fear;* for we should never forget that *we have sinned,* and that *God is a consuming fire.* Instead of αιδους και ευλαβειας, modesty and religious fear, ACD*, several others, with the Slavonic and Chrysostom, have ευλαβειας και δεους, and others have φοβου και τρομου, *fear and trembling;* but the sense is nearly the same.

Verse 29. For our God is a consuming fire.] The apostle quotes Deut. iv. 24, and by doing so he teaches us this great truth, that sin under the Gospel is as abominable in God's sight as it was under the law; and

2

that the man who does not labour to serve God with the principle and in the way already prescribed, will find that fire to consume *him* which would otherwise have consumed his *sin*.

Additional remarks on verses 22-24.

On the whole, I think the description in these verses refers to the state of the Church *here below*, and not to any *heavenly state*. Let us review the particulars: 1. As the law was given on Mount *Sinai*, so the Gospel was given at Mount *Sion*. 2. As *Jerusalem* was the city of the living God while the Jewish dispensation lasted, (for *there* was the temple, its services, sacrifices, &c.,) the Christian Church is now called the *heavenly Jerusalem*, the city of the living God. In it is the great sacrifice, in it that spiritual worship, which God, the infinite Spirit, requires. 3. The ministry of angels was used under the *old covenant*, but that was *partial*, being granted only to particular persons, such as Moses, Joshua, Manoah, &c., and only to a few before the law, as Abraham, Jacob, &c. It is employed under the *new covenant* in its utmost latitude, not to a few peculiarly favoured people, but to all the followers of God in general; so that in this very epistle the apostle asserts that they are all ministering spirits, sent forth to minister to them that shall be heirs of salvation. 4. At the giving of the law, when the Church of the old covenant was formed, there was a *general assembly* of the *different tribes* by their representatives; in the Gospel Church all who believe in Christ, of every nation, and kindred, and tongue, form one grand aggregate body. Believers of all nations, of all languages, of all climates, however differing in their colour or local habits, are one in Christ Jesus; one body, of which he is the head, and the Holy Spirit the soul. 5. The *first-born* under the old dispensation had exclusive privileges; they had authority, emolument, and honour, of which the other children in the same family did not partake: but under the new, all who believe in Christ Jesus, with a heart unto righteousness, are equally children of God, are all entitled to the same privileges; for, says the apostle, ye are all children of God by faith in Christ, and to them that received him he gave authority to become the children of God; so that through the whole of this Divine family all have *equal rights* and *equal privileges*, all have GOD for their *portion*, and *heaven* for their *inheritance*. 6. As those who had the rights of citizens were *enrolled*, and their names *entered on tables*, &c., so that it might be known who were *citizens*, and who had the rights of such; so all the faithful under the new covenant are represented as having their names written in heaven, which is another form of speech for, *have a right to that glorious state*, and all the blessings it possesses; *there* are their possessions, and there are their rights. 7. Only the high priest, and he but one day in the year, was permitted to *approach God* under the Old Testament dispensation; but under the New, every believer in Jesus can *come even to the throne*, each has liberty to enter into the holiest by the blood of Jesus, and to real Christians alone it can be said, *Ye are come—to God the Judge of all*—to him ye have constant access, and from him ye are continually receiving grace upon grace. 8. We have already seen that the *righteous perfect*, or the *just men made perfect*, is a Jewish phrase, and signified those who had made the farthest advances in moral rectitude. The apostle uses it here to point out those in the Church of Christ who had received the highest degrees of grace, possessed most of the mind of Christ, and were doing and suffering most for the glory of God; those who were most deeply acquainted with the things of God and the mysteries of the Gospel, such as the apostles, evangelists, the primitive teachers, and those who presided in and over different Churches. And these are termed the *spirits* δικαιων τετελειωμενων, *of the just perfected*, because they were a *spiritual* people, forsaking *earth*, and living in reference to that *spiritual rest* that was typified by Canaan. In short, all genuine Christians had communion with each other, through God's Spirit, and even with those whose faces they had not seen in the flesh. 9. Moses, as the servant of God, and *mediator of the old covenant*, was of great consequence in the Levitical economy. By his laws and maxims every thing was directed and tried; and *to him* the whole Hebrew people *came* for both their civil and religious ordinances: but Christians *come* to Jesus, the mediator of the new covenant; he not only stands immediately between God and man, but reconciles and connects both. From him we receive the Divine law, by his maxims our conversation is to be ruled, and he gives both the light and life by which we walk; these things Moses could not do, and for such *spirituality* and *excellence* the old covenant made no provision; it was therefore a high privilege to be able to say, *Ye are come—to Jesus the mediator of the new covenant.* 10. The Jews had their blood of sprinkling, but it could not satisfy as touching things which concerned the conscience; it took away no guilt, it made no reconciliation to God: but the blood of sprinkling under the Christian covenant purifies from all unrighteousness; for the blood of the new covenant was shed for the remission of sins, and by its infinite merit it still continues to sprinkle and cleanse the unholy. All these are privileges of infinite consequence to the salvation of man; privileges which should be highly esteemed and most cautiously guarded; and because they are so great, so necessary, and so unattainable in the Levitical economy, therefore we should lay aside every weight, &c., and run with perseverance the race that is set before us. I see nothing therefore in these verses which determines their sense to the heavenly state; all is suited to the state of the Church of Christ militant here on earth; and some of these particulars cannot be applied to the Church triumphant on any rule of construction whatever.

CHAPTER XIII.

Exhortations to hospitality to strangers, 1, 2. *Kindness to those in bonds,* 3. *Concerning marriage,* 4. *Against covetousness,* 5, 6. *How they should imitate their teachers,* 7, 8. *To avoid strange doctrines,* 9. *Of the Jewish sin-offerings,* 10, 11. *Jesus suffered without the gate, and we should openly confess him and bear his reproach,* 12, 13. *Here we have no permanent residence ; and while we live we should devote ourselves to God, and live to do good,* 14—16. *We should obey them that have the rule over us,* 17. *The apostle exhorts them to pray for him, that he might be restored to them the sooner,* 18, 19. *Commends them to God in a very solemn prayer,* 20, 21. *Entreats them to bear the word of exhortation, mentions Timothy, and concludes with the apostolical benediction,* 22—25.

A. M. cir. 4067.
A. D. cir. 63.
An. Olymp.
cir. CCX. 3.
A. U. C. cir.
816.

LET ᵃ brotherly love continue.

2 ᵇ Be not forgetful to entertain strangers : for thereby ᶜ some have entertained angels unawares.

3 ᵈ Remember them that are in bonds, as bound with them ; *and* them which suffer adversity, as being yourselves also in the body.

4 Marriage *is* honourable in all, and the bed undefiled : ᵉ but whoremongers and adulterers God will judge.

5 *Let your* conversation *be* without covetousness ; *and* ᶠ *be* content with such things as ye have : for he hath said, ᵍ I will never leave thee, nor forsake thee.

A. M. cir. 4067.
A. D. cir. 63.
An. Olymp.
cir. CCX. 3.
A. U. C. cir
816.

ᵃ Rom. xii. 10; 1 Thess. iv. 9 ; 1 Pet. i. 22 ; ii. 17 ; iii. 8 ; iv. 3 ; 2 Pet. i. 7 ; 1 John iii. 11, &c. ; iv. 7, 20, 21.——ᵇ Matt. xxv. 35 ; Rom. xii. 13 ; 1 Tim. iii. 2 ; 1 Pet. iv. 9.——ᶜ Gen. xviii. 3 ; xix. 2.——ᵈ Matt. xxv. 36 ; Rom. xii. 15 ; 1 Cor. xii. 26 ; Col.

iv. 18 ; 1 Pet. iii. 8.——ᵉ 1 Cor. vi. 9 ; Gal. v. 19, 21 ; Eph. v 5 ; Col. iii. 5, 6 ; Rev. xxii. 15.——ᶠ Matt. vi. 25, 34 ; Phil. iv. 11, 12 ; 1 Tim. vi. 6, 8.——ᵍ Gen. xxviii. 15 ; Deut. xxxi. 6, 8 ; Josh. i. 5 ; 1 Chron. xxviii. 20 ; Psa. xxxvii. 25.

NOTES ON CHAP. XIII.

Verse 1. *Let brotherly love continue.*] Be all of one heart and one soul. Feel for, comfort, and support each other ; and remember that he who professes to love God should love his brother also. They had this brotherly love among them ; they should take care to retain it. As God is remarkable for his φιλανθρωπια, *philanthropy,* or love to man, so should they be for φιλαδελφια, or *love to each other.* See the note on Titus iii. 4.

Verse 2. *To entertain strangers*] In those early times, when there were scarcely any public inns or houses of entertainment, it was an office of charity and mercy to receive, lodge, and entertain travellers ; and this is what the apostle particularly recommends.

Entertained angels] Abraham and Lot are the persons particularly referred to. Their history, the angels whom they entertained, not knowing them to be such, and the good they derived from exercising their hospitality on these occasions, are well known ; and have been particularly referred to in the notes on Gen. xviii. 3 ; xix. 2.

Verse 3. *Remember them that are in bonds*] He appears to refer to those Christians who were suffering imprisonment for the testimony of Jesus.

As bound with them] Feel for them as you would wish others to feel for you were you in their circumstances, knowing that, being in the body, you are liable to the same evils, and may be called to suffer in the same way for the same cause.

Verse 4. *Marriage is honourable in all*] Let this state be highly esteemed as one of God's own instituting, and as highly calculated to produce the best interests of mankind. This may have been said against the opinions of the *Essenes,* called *Therapeutæ,* who held marriage in little repute, and totally abstained from it themselves as a state of comparative imperfection. At the same time it shows the absurdity of

the popish tenet, that marriage in the clergy is both dishonourable and sinful ; which is, in fact, in opposition to the apostle, who says marriage is honourable in ALL ; and to the institution of God, which evidently designed that every male and female should be united in this holy bond ; and to nature, which in every part of the habitable world has produced men and women in due proportion to each other.

The bed undefiled] Every man cleaving to his own wife, and every wife cleaving to her own husband, because *God will judge,* i. e. punish, all *fornicators* and *adulterers.*

Instead of δε, *but,* γαρ, *for,* is the reading of AD*, one other, with the *Vulgate, Coptic,* and one of the *Itala ;* it more forcibly expresses the *reason* of the prohibition : *Let the bed be undefiled,* FOR *whoremongers and adulterers God will judge.*

Verse 5. *Let your conversation*] That is, the whole tenor of your conduct, τροπος, the *manner of your life,* or rather the *disposition* of your hearts in reference to all your secular transactions ; for in this sense the original is used by the best Greek writers.

Be without covetousness] Desire nothing more than what God has given you ; and especially covet nothing which the Divine Providence has given to another man, for this is the very *spirit of robbery.*

Content with such things as ye have] Αρκουμενοι τοις παρουσιν· *Being satisfied with present things.* In one of the sentences of *Phocylides* we have a sentiment in nearly the same words as that of the apostle : Αρκεισθαι παρεουσι, και αλλοτριων απεχεσθαι· *Be content with present things, and abstain from others.* The covetous man is ever running out into futurity with insatiable desires after secular good ; and, if this disposition be not checked, it increases as the subject of it increases in years. Covetousness is the vice of old age.

I will never leave thee, nor forsake thee.] These words were, in sum, spoken to Joshua, chap. i. 5 : " As

A. M. cir. 4067
A. D. cir. 63.
An. Olymp.
cir. CCX. 3.
A. U. C. cir.
816.

6 So that we may boldly say, [h] The Lord *is* my helper, and I will not fear what man shall do unto me.

7 [i] Remember them which [k] have the rule over you, who have spoken unto you the word of God : [l] whose faith follow, considering the end of *their* conversation :

8 Jesus Christ [m] the same yesterday, and to-day, and forever.

9 [n] Be not carried about with divers and strange doctrines. For *it is* a good thing that the heart be established with grace, [o] not with meats, which have not profited them that have been occupied therein.

A. M. cir. 4067.
A. D. cir. 63.
An. Olymp.
cir. CCX. 3.
A. U. C. cir.
816.

---

[h] Psa. xxvii. 1 ; lvi. 4, 11, 12 ; cxviii. 6.——[i] Ver. 17.——[k] Or, *are the guides.*——[l] Chap. vi. 12.——[m] John viii. 59 ; chap. i. 12 ;

[n] Eph. iv. 14 ; v. 6 ; Col. ii. 4, 8 ; 1 John iv. 1.
[o] Rom. xiv. 17 ; Col. ii. 16 ; 1 Tim. iv. 3.

I was with Moses, so will I be with thee ; *I will not fail thee, nor forsake thee.*" They were spoken also by David to Solomon, 1 Chron. xxviii. 20 : " David said to Solomon his son, Be strong and of good courage, and do it: fear not, nor be dismayed ; for the Lord God, even my God, will be with thee ; *he will not fail thee, nor forsake thee.*" The apostle, in referring to the same promises, feels authorized to strengthen the expressions, as the Christian dispensation affords more consolation and confidence in matters of this kind than the old covenant did. The words are peculiarly emphatic : Ου μη σε ανω, ουδ' ου μη σε εγκαταλιπω. There are no less than *five negatives* in this short sentence, and these connected with two verbs and one pronoun twice repeated. To give a literal translation is scarcely possible ; it would run in this way : " No, I will not leave thee ; no, neither will I not utterly forsake thee." Those who understand the genius of the Greek language, and look at the manner in which these negatives are placed in the sentence, will perceive at once how much the meaning is strengthened by them, and to what an emphatic and energetic affirmative they amount.

This promise is made to those who are patiently bearing affliction or persecution for Christ's sake ; and may be applied to any faithful soul in affliction, temptation, or adversity of any kind. Trust in the Lord with thy whole heart, and never lean to thy own understanding ; for he hath said, " No, I will never leave thee ; not I : I will never, never cast thee off."

Verse 6. *So that we may boldly say*] We, in such circumstances, while cleaving to the Lord, may confidently apply to ourselves what God spake to Joshua and to Solomon ; and what he spake to David, " The Lord is my helper, I will not fear what man can do." God is omnipotent, man's power is limited ; howsoever strong he may be, he can do nothing against the Almighty.

Verse 7. *Remember them which have the rule over you*] This clause should be translated, *Remember your guides,* των ἡγουμενων, *who have spoken unto you the doctrine of God.* Theodoret's note on this verse is very judicious : " He intends the saints who were dead, Stephen the first martyr, James the brother of John, and James called the Just. And there were many others who were taken off by the Jewish rage. ' Consider these, (said he,) and, observing their example, imitate their faith.' " This remembrance of the dead saints, with admiration of their virtues, and a desire to imitate them, is, says Dr. Macknight, the only worship which is due to them from the living.

Considering the end of their conversation] Ὡν

αναθεωρουντες την εκβασιν της αναστροφης· " The issue of whose course of life most carefully consider." They lived to get good and do good ; they were faithful to their God and his cause ; they suffered persecution ; and for the testimony of Jesus died a violent death. God never left them ; no, he never forsook them ; so that they were happy in their afflictions, and glorious in their death. Carefully consider this ; act as they did ; keep the faith, and God will keep you.

Verse 8. *Jesus Christ the same yesterday*] In all past times there was no way to the holiest but through the blood of Jesus, either actually shed, or significantly typified. *To-day*—he is the lamb newly slain, and continues to appear in the presence of God for us. *For ever*—to the conclusion of time, he will be the way, the truth, and the life, none coming to the Father but through him ; and throughout eternity, εις τους αιωνας, it will appear that all glorified human spirits owe their salvation to his infinite merit. This Jesus was thus witnessed of by your guides, who are already departed to glory. Remember HIM ; remember *them ;* and take heed to *yourselves.*

Verse 9. *Be not carried about*] Μη περιφερεσθε· *Be not whirled about.* But ABCD, and almost every other MS. of importance, with the *Syriac, Coptic, Arabic, Vulgate,* and several of the Greek fathers, have μη παραφερεσθε, *be not carried away,* which is undoubtedly the true reading, and signifies here, *do not apostatize;* permit not yourselves to be carried off from Christ and his doctrine.

Divers and strange doctrines.] Διδαχαις ποικιλαις· *Variegated doctrines ;* those that blended the law and the Gospel, and brought in the Levitical sacrifices and institutions in order to perfect the Christian system. Remember the old covenant is abolished; the *new* alone is in force.

Strange doctrines, διδαχαις ξεναις, foreign doctrines ; such as have no *apostolical* authority to recommend them.

That the heart be established with grace] It is well to have the heart, the mind, and conscience, fully satisfied with the truth and efficacy of the *Gospel;* for so the word χαρις should be understood here, which is put in opposition to βρωμασιν, meats, signifying here the Levitical institutions, and especially its *sacrifices,* these being emphatically termed *meats,* because the offerers were permitted to *feast* upon them after the blood had been poured out before the Lord. See Lev. vii. 15 ; Deut. xii. 6, 7.

Which have not profited them] Because they neither took away guilt, cleansed the heart, nor gave power over sin.

(50**)

A. M. cir. 4067.
A. D. cir. 63.
An. Olymp.
cir. CCX. 3.
A. U. C. cir.
816.

10 [p] We have an altar, whereof they have no right to eat which serve the tabernacle.

11 For [q] the bodies of those beasts, whose blood is brought into the sanctuary by the high priest for sin, are burned without the camp.

12 Wherefore Jesus also, that he might sanctify the people with his own blood, [r] suffered without the gate.

13 Let us go forth therefore unto him without the camp, bearing [s] his reproach:

14 [t] For here have we no continuing city, but we seek one to come.

15 [u] By him therefore let us offer [v] the sacrifice of praise to God continually, that is, [w] the fruit of *our* lips, [x] giving thanks to his name.

16 [y] But to do good and to communicate

A. M. cir. 4067.
A. D. cir. 63.
An. Olymp.
cir. CCX. 3.
A. U. C. cir.
816.

---

[p] 1 Cor. ix. 13 ; x. 18.——[q] Exod. xxix. 14 ; Lev: iv. 11, 12, 21 ; vi. 30 ; ix. 11 ; xvi. 27 ; Num, xix. 3.——[r] John xix. 17, 18 ; Acts vii. 58.——[s] Chap. xi. 26 ; 1 Pet. iv. 14.——[t] Mic. ii. 10 ;

Phil. iii, 20 ; chap. xi. 10, 16 ; xii. 22.——[u] Eph. v. 20 ; 1 Pet. ii. 5.——[v] Lev. vii. 12 ; Psa. l. 14, 23 ; lxix. 30, 31 ; cvii. 22 ; cxvi. 17.——[w] Hos. xiv. 2.——[x] Or, *confessing to.*——[y] Rom. xii. 13.

Verse 10. *We have an altar*] The altar is here put for the sacrifice on the altar ; the Christian altar is the Christian sacrifice, which is Christ Jesus, with all the benefits of his passion and death. To these privileges they had no right who continued to offer the Levitical sacrifices, and to trust in them for remission of sins.

Verse 11. *For the bodies of those beasts*] Though in making covenants, and in some victims offered according to the law, the flesh of the sacrifice was eaten by the offerers ; yet the flesh of the *sin-offering* might no man eat : when the blood was sprinkled before the holy place to make an atonement for their souls, the skins, flesh, entrails, &c., were carried without the camp, and there entirely consumed by fire ; and this entire consumption, according to the opinion of some, was intended to show that sin was not pardoned by such offerings. For, as *eating* the other sacrifices intimated they were made *partakers* of the benefits procured by those sacrifices, so, not being permitted to eat of the sin-offering proved that they had no benefit from it, and that they must look to the Christ, whose sacrifice is pointed out, that they might receive that real pardon of sin which the shedding of his blood could alone procure. While, therefore, they continued offering those sacrifices, and refused to acknowledge the Christ, they had no right to any of the blessings procured by him, and it is evident they could have no benefit from their own.

Verse 12. *That he might sanctify the people*] That he might consecrate them to God, and make an atonement for their sins, he *suffered without the gate* at Jerusalem, as the sin-offering was consumed *without the camp* when the tabernacle abode in the wilderness. Perhaps all this was typical of the abolition of the Jewish sacrifices, and the termination of the whole Levitical system of worship. He left the city, denounced its final destruction, and abandoned it to its fate ; and suffered without the gate to bring the Gentiles to God.

Verse 13. *Let us go forth therefore unto him*] Let us leave this city and system, devoted to destruction, and take refuge in Jesus alone, bearing his reproach— being willing to be accounted the refuse of all things, and the worst of men, for his sake who bore the contradiction of sinners against himself, and was put to death as a malefactor.

Verse 14. *For here have we no continuing city*] Here is an elegant and forcible allusion to the approaching destruction of Jerusalem. The Jerusalem that was *below* was about to be burnt with fire, and erased to the ground ; the Jerusalem that was *from above* was that alone which could be considered to be μενουσαν, *permanent.* The words seem to say : " Arise, and depart ; for this is not your rest : it is polluted." About seven or eight years after this, Jerusalem was wholly destroyed.

Verse 15. *By him therefore let us offer the sacrifice of praise*] He has now fulfilled all vision and prophecy, has offered the last bloody sacrifice which God will ever accept ; and as he is the gift of God's love to the world, let us through him offer the sacrifice of praise to God continually, this being the substitute for all the Levitical sacrifices.

The Jews allowed that, in the time of the Messiah, all sacrifices, except the sacrifice of praise, should cease. To this maxim the apostle appears to allude ; and, understood in this way, his words are much more forcible. In *Vayikra Rabba,* sect. 9, fol. 153, and Rabbi *Tanchum,* fol. 55 : " Rabbi Phineas, Rabbi Levi, and Rabbi Jochanan, from the authority of Rabbi Menachem of Galilee, said, *In the time of the Messiah all sacrifice shall cease, except the sacrifice of praise.*" This was, in effect, quoting the authority of one of their own maxims, that *now* was the time of the Messiah ; that Jesus was that Messiah ; that the Jewish sacrificial system was now abolished ; and that no sacrifice would now be accepted of God, except the sacrifice of praise for the gift of his Son.

That is, the fruit of our *lips*] This expression is probably borrowed from Hos. xiv. 2, in the version of the Septuagint, καρπον χειλεων, which in the Hebrew text is פרים שפתינו *parim sephatheinu,* " the heifers of our lips." This may refer primarily to the *sacrifices, heifers, calves,* &c., which they had *vowed* to God ; so that the *calves of their lips* were the sacrifices which they had *promised.* But how could the Septuagint translate פרים *parim, calves,* by καρπον, *fruit ?* Very easily, if they had in their copy פרי *peri,* the *mem* being omitted ; and thus the word would be literally *fruit,* and not *calves.* This reading, however, is not found in any of the MSS. hitherto collated.

Verse 16. *But to do good and to communicate*] These are continual sacrifices which God requires, and

A. M. cir. 4067.
A. D. cir. 63.
An. Olymp.
cir. CCX. 3.
A. U. C. cir
816.

forget not; for [z] with such sacrifices God is well pleased.

17 [a] Obey them that [b] have the rule over you, and submit yourselves: for [c] they watch for your souls, as they that must give account, that they may do it with joy, and not with grief: for that *is* unprofitable for you.

18 [d] Pray for us: for we trust we have [e] a good conscience, in all things willing to live honestly.

19 But I beseech *you* [f] the rather to do this, that I may be restored to you the sooner.

20 Now [g] the God of peace, [h] that brought again from the dead our Lord Jesus, [i] that great Shepherd of the sheep, [k] through the blood of the everlasting [l] covenant,

A. M. cir. 4067
A. D. cir. 63.
An. Olymp.
cir. CCX. 3.
A. U. C. cir
816.

---

[z] 2 Cor. ix. 12 ; Phil. iv. 18 ; chap. vi. 10.——[a] Phil. ii. 29 ; 1 Thess. v. 12 ; 1 Tim. v. 17 ; ver. 7.——[b] Or, *guide.*——[c] Ezek. iii. 17 ; xxxiii. 2, 7 ; Acts xx. 26, 28.——[d] Romans xv. 30 ; Eph. vi. 19 ; Col. iv. 3 ; 1 Thess. v. 25 ; 2 Thess. iii. 1.——[e] Acts xxiii. 1 ; xxiv. 16 ; 2 Cor. i. 12.——[f] Philem. 22.

[g] Rom. xv. 33 ; 1 Thess. v. 23.——[h] Acts ii. 24, 32 ; Rom. iv. 24 ; viii. 11 ; 1 Cor. vi. 14 ; xv. 15 ; 2 Cor. iv. 14 ; Gal. i. 1 ; Col. ii. 12 ; 1 Thess. i. 10 ; 1 Pet. i. 21.——[i] Isa. xl. 11 ; Ezek. xxxiv. 23 ; xxxvii. 24 ; John x. 11, 14 ; 1 Peter ii. 25 ; v. 4. [k] Zech. ix. 11 ; chap. x. 22.——[l] Or, *testament.*

---

which will spring from a sense of God's love in Christ Jesus. Praise to God for his unspeakable gift, and acts of kindness to men for God's sake. No reliance, even on the infinitely meritorious sacrifice of Christ, can be acceptable in the sight of God if a man have not love and charity towards his neighbour. Praise, prayer, and thanksgiving to God, with works of charity and mercy to man, are the sacrifices which every genuine follower of Christ must offer : and they are the proofs that a man belongs to Christ ; and he who does not bear these fruits gives full evidence, whatever his *creed* may be, that he is no Christian.

Verse 17. *Obey them that have the rule over you*] Obey your *leaders,* τοις ἡγουμενοις. He is not fit to *rule* who is not capable of *guiding.* See on ver. 7. In the former verse the apostle exhorts them to remember those who had been their leaders, and to imitate their faith ; in this he exhorts them to obey the leaders they now had, and to submit to their authority in all matters of doctrine and discipline, on the ground that they *watched for their souls,* and should have to give an account of their conduct to God. If this conduct were improper, they must give in their report before the great tribunal with *grief;* but *in* it must be given : if holy and pure, they would give it in with *joy.* It is an awful consideration that many pastors, who had loved their flocks as their own souls, shall be obliged to accuse them before God for either having *rejected* or *neglected* the great salvation.

Verse 18. *Pray for us*] Even the success of apostles depended, in a certain way, on the prayers of the Church. Few Christian congregations feel, as they ought, that it is their bounden duty to pray for the success of the Gospel, both among themselves and in the world. The Church is weak, dark, poor, and imperfect, because it prays little.

We trust we have a good conscience] We are persuaded that we have a conscience that not only acquits us of all fraud and sinister design, but assures us that in simplicity and godly sincerity we have laboured to promote the welfare of you and of all mankind.

To live honestly.] Ἐν πασι καλως θελοντες αναστρεφεσθαι· *Willing in all things to conduct ourselves well*—to behave with decency and propriety.

Verse 19. *The rather to do this*] That is, pray for us, that, being enabled to complete the work which God has given us *here* to do, we may be the sooner

enabled to visit *you.* It is evident, from this, that the people to whom this epistle was written knew well who was the author of it ; nor does there appear, in any place, any design in the writer to conceal his name , and how the epistle came to lack a name it is impossible to say. I have sometimes thought that a part of the beginning might have been lost, as it not only begins without a name, but begins very abruptly.

Verse 20. *Now the God of peace*] We have often seen that *peace* among the Hebrews signifies *prosperity* of every kind. *The God of peace* is the same as the God of all blessedness, who has at his disposal all temporal and eternal good ; who loves mankind, and has provided them a complete salvation.

Brought again from the dead our Lord] As our Lord's sacrificial death is considered as an atonement offered to the Divine justice, God's acceptance of it as an atonement is signified by his raising the human nature of Christ from the dead ; and hence this raising of Christ is, with the utmost propriety, attributed to *God the Father,* as this proves his acceptance of the sacrificial offering.

That great Shepherd of the sheep] This is a title of our blessed Lord, given to him by the prophets ; so Isa. xl. 11 ; *He shall feed his flock like a shepherd; he shall gather the lambs with his arms, and carry them in his bosom, and shall gently lead those which are with young :* and Ezek. xxxiv. 23 ; *I will set up one shepherd over them, and he shall feed them ; even my servant David,* (*i. e.* the beloved, viz. Jesus,) and *he shall feed them, and be their shepherd :* and Zech. xiii. 7 ; *Awake, O sword, against my shepherd—smite the shepherd, and the flock shall be scattered.* In all these places the term *shepherd* is allowed to belong to our blessed Lord ; and he appropriates it to himself, John x. 11, by calling himself *the good Shepherd, who lays down his life for the sheep.*

Through the blood of the everlasting covenant] Some understand this in the following way, that "God brought back our Lord from the dead on account of his having shed his blood to procure the everlasting covenant." Others, that "the Lord Jesus became the great Shepherd and Saviour of the sheep by shedding his blood to procure and ratify the everlasting covenant." The sense, however, will appear much plainer if we connect this with the following verse : " Now the God of peace, who brought again from the dead

2

A. M. cir. 4067.
A. D. cir. 63.
An. Olymp.
cir. CCX. 3.
A. U. C. cir.
816.

21 ^m Make you perfect in every good work to do his will, ⁿ working ^o in you that which is well pleasing in his sight, through Jesus Christ, ^p to whom *be* glory for ever and ever. Amen.

22 And I beseech you, brethren, suffer the word of exhortation: for I ^q have written a letter unto you in few words.

23 Know ye that ^r *our* brother Timothy ^s is set at liberty; with whom, if he come shortly, I will see you.

24 Salute all them ^t that have the rule over you, and all the saints. They of Italy salute you.

25 ^u Grace *be* with you all. Amen.

¶ Written to the Hebrews from Italy by Timothy.

---

^m 2 Thess. ii. 17; 1 Pet. v. 10.——ⁿ Or, *doing.*——^o Phil. ii. 13. ^p Gal i. 5; 2 Tim. iv. 18; Rev. i. 6.——^q 1 Pet. v. 12.——^r 1 Thess. iii. 2.——^s 1 Tim. vi. 12.——^t Ver. 7, 17.——^u Tit. iii. 15.

---

our Lord Jesus, that great Shepherd of the sheep, make you, through the blood of the everlasting covenant, perfect in every good work to do his will." The Christian system is termed the *everlasting covenant,* to distinguish it from the *temporary covenant* made with the Israelites at Mount Sinai; and to show that it is the *last* dispensation of grace to the world, and shall endure to the end of time.

Verse 21. *Make you perfect*] Καταρτισαι υμας· Put you completely *in joint.* See the note on 2 Cor. xiii. 9, where the meaning of the original word is largely considered. From the following terms we see what the apostle meant by the *perfection* for which he prays. They were to do the will of God in every good work, from God working in them that which is well pleasing in his sight. 1. This necessarily implies a complete change in the whole soul, that God may be *well pleased* with whatsoever he sees in it; and this supposes its being cleansed from all sin, for God's *sight* cannot be *pleased* with any thing that is unholy. 2. This complete *inward purity* is to produce an outward conformity to God's will, so they were to be *made perfect in every good work.* 3. The *perfection within* and the *perfection without* were to be produced *by the blood of the everlasting covenant;* for although God is love, yet it is not consistent with his justice or holiness to communicate any good to mankind but through his Son, and through him as having died for the offences of the human race.

To whom be glory for ever.] As God does all *in, by,* and *through* Christ Jesus, to him be the honour of his own work ascribed through time and eternity. Amen.

Verse 22. *Suffer the word of exhortation*] Bear the word or doctrine of this exhortation. This seems to be an epithet of this whole epistle: and as the apostle had in it shown the insufficiency of the Levitical system to atone for sin and save the soul; and had proved that it was the design of God that it should be abolished; and had proved also that it was now abolished by the coming of Christ, whom he had shown to be a greater priest than Aaron, higher than all the angels, the only Son of God as to his human nature, and the Creator, Governor, and Judge of all; and that their city was shortly to be destroyed; he might suppose that they would feel prejudiced against him, and thus lose the benefit of his kind intentions toward them; therefore he entreats them to bear the exhortation which, notwithstanding the great extent of the subject, he had included in a short compass.

I have written a letter unto you in few words.] Perhaps it would be better to translate δια βραχεων επεστειλα υμιν, I have written to you briefly, as επιστελλειν often signifies simply *to write,* and this appears to be its meaning here.

Verse 23. *Know ye that* our *brother Timothy*] The word. ἡμων, our, which is *supplied* by our translators, is very probably genuine, as it is found in ACD*, ten others, the *Syriac,* Erpen's *Arabic,* the *Coptic, Armenian, Slavonic,* and *Vulgate.*

Is set at liberty] Απολελυμενον· *Is sent away;* for there is no evidence that Timothy had been imprisoned. It is probable that the apostle refers here to his being sent into Macedonia, Phil. ii. 19–24, in order that he might bring the apostle an account of the affairs of the Church in that country. In none of St. Paul's epistles, written during his confinement in Rome, does he give any intimation of Timothy's *imprisonment,* although it appears from Phil. i. 1; Col. i. 1; Philem. 1; that he was with Paul during the greatest part of the time.

With whom, if he come shortly, I will see you.] Therefore Paul himself, or the writer of this epistle, was now at liberty, as he had the disposal of his person and time in his own power. Some suppose that Timothy did actually visit Paul about this time, and that both together visited the Churches in Judea.

Verse 24. *Salute all them that have the rule over you*] *Salute all your leaders* or *guides,* τους ἡγουμενους ὑμων. See on verses 7 and 17.

And all the saints.] All the *Christians;* for this is the general meaning of the term in most parts of St. Paul's writings. But a *Christian* was then a *saint,* i. e. by profession a holy person; and most of the primitive Christians were actually such. But in process of time the term was applied to all that bore the Christian name; as *elect, holy people, sanctified,* &c., were to the nation of the Jews, when both their piety and morality were at a very low ebb.

They of Italy salute you.] Therefore it is most likely that the writer of this epistle was then in some part of Italy, from which he had not as yet removed after his being released from prison. By *they of Italy* probably the apostle means the Jews there who had embraced the Christian faith. These salutations show what a brotherly feeling existed in every part of the Christian Church; even those who had not seen each other yet loved one another, and felt deeply interested for each other's welfare.

Verse 25. *Grace be with you all.*] May the Divine

favour ever rest upon you and among you; and may you receive, from that source of all good, whatsoever is calculated to make you wise, holy, useful, and happy! And may you be enabled to *persevere* in the truth to the end of your lives! Amen. May it be so! May God seal the prayer by giving the blessings!

THE subscriptions to this epistle are, as in other cases, various and contradictory.

The VERSIONS are as follow :—

The Epistle to the Hebrews was written from Roman Italy, and sent by the hand of Timothy.—SYRIAC.

VULGATE nothing, in the present printed copies.

It was written from Italy by Timothy: with the assistance of God, disposing every thing right, the fourteen epistles of the blessed Paul are completed, according to the copy from which they have been transcribed. May the Lord extend his benedictions to us. Amen.—ARABIC.

The Epistle to the Hebrews is completed. The end.—ÆTHIOPIC.

Written in Italy, and sent by Timothy.—COPTIC.

The MANUSCRIPTS, and *ancient editions* taken from MSS., are not more to be relied on.

To the Hebrews, written from Rome.—CODEX ALEXANDRINUS.

The epistles of Saint Paul the apostle are finished.—COLOPHON, at the end of this epistle; in one of the first printed Bibles; and in an ancient MS. of the Vulgate in my own collection.

The end of the Epistle to the Hebrews.—GREEK TEXT of the COMPLUTENSIAN EDITION.

The Epistle of the blessed Paul to the Hebrews is finished.—LATIN TEXT of ditto.

To the Hebrews.—The Epistle of Paul the apostle to the Hebrews.—The Epistle to the Hebrews, written from Italy.—From Athens.—From Italy by Timothy.—Written in the Hebrew tongue, &c.—Various MSS.

Written to the Hebrews from Italy by Timothy.—COMMON GREEK TEXT.

That it was neither written from *Athens*, nor in the Hebrew tongue, is more than probable; and that it was not sent by *Timothy*, is evident from chap. xiii. 23. For the author, time, place, and people to whom sent, see the INTRODUCTION.

I. On the term "conscience," as frequently occurring in this epistle, I beg leave to make a few observations.

Conscience is defined by some to be " that judgment which the rational soul passes on all her actions;" and is said to be a faculty of the soul itself, and consequently natural to it. Others state that it is a ray of Divine light. Milton calls it "God's umpire;" and Dr. Young calls it a "god in man." To me it seems to be no other than a *faculty capable of receiving light and conviction from the Spirit of God*; and answers the end in spiritual matters to the soul, that the eye does to the body in the process of vision. The *eye* is not *light* in itself, nor is it capable of discerning any object, but by the instrumentality of solar or artificial light; but it has organs properly adapted to the reception of the rays of light, and the various images of the objects which they exhibit. When *these* are

present to an eye the organs of which are perfect, then there is a *discernment* of those objects which are within the sphere of vision; but when the light is absent, there is no *perception* of the shape, dimensions, size, or colour of any object, howsoever entire or perfect the optic nerve and the different humours may be.

In the same manner (comparing spiritual things with natural) the Spirit of God enlightens that eye of the soul which we call *conscience*; it penetrates it with its effulgence; and (speaking as human language will permit on the subject) it has powers properly adapted to the reception of the Spirit's emanations, which, when received, exhibit a real view of the situation, state, &c., of the soul, as it stands in reference to God and eternity. Thus the Scripture says, "The Spirit itself bears witness with our spirit," &c., i. e. it shines into the conscience, and reflects throughout the soul a conviction, proportioned to the degree of light communicated, of *condemnation* or *acquittance*, according to the end of its coming.

The late Mr. J. Wesley's definition of conscience, taken in a *Christian* sense, is nearly the same with the above: "It is," says he, "that *faculty* of the soul which, by the *assistance of the grace of God*, sees at one and the same time, 1. Our own tempers and lives; the real nature and quality of our thoughts, words and actions. 2. The *rule* whereby we are to be directed. And 3. The *agreement* or *disagreement* therewith. To express this a little more largely: Conscience implies, *first*, the *faculty* a man has of knowing himself; of discerning, both in general and in particular, his temper, words, thoughts, and actions: but this is not possible for him to do, *without the assistance of the Spirit of God*; otherwise self-love, and indeed every other irregular passion, would disguise and wholly conceal him from himself. It implies, *secondly*, a *knowledge* of the rule whereby he is to be directed in every particular, which is no other than the written word of God. Conscience implies, *thirdly*, a knowledge that all his thoughts, and words, and actions are *conformable* to that rule. In all these offices of conscience, the *unction of the holy One* is indispensably needful. Without this, neither could we clearly discern our lives and tempers, nor could we judge of the rule whereby we are to walk, nor of our conformity or disconformity to it. A *good* conscience is a Divine consciousness of walking in all things according to the written word of God. It seems, indeed, that there can be no conscience that has *not a regard to God*. I doubt whether the words *right* and *wrong*, according to the Christian system, do not imply, *in the very idea of them*, agreement and disagreement to the will and word of God. And if so, there is no such thing as conscience in a Christian, *if we leave God out of the question*." Sermon on Conscience, page 332.

Some of the Greek fathers seem to consider it as an especial gift of God; a principle implanted immediately by himself. So *Chrysostom*, on Psa. vii., speaking of conscience, says: Φυσικον γαρ εστι, και παρα του Θεου ἡμιν παρα την αρχην εντεθεν· *It is a natural thing, but is planted in us by our God from our birth.* In his homily on Isa. vi. 2, he explains himself more particularly: Θειον γαρ εστι, και παρα

Θεου ταις ημετεραις ενιδρυμενον ψυχαις· *It is a Divine principle, and is by God himself implanted in our souls.* It is allowed on all hands that it is a recorder and judge of human actions, which cannot be corrupted, or be induced to bear a false testimony. Every sense of the body, and every faculty of the mind, may be weakened, obstructed, or impaired, but conscience; all other powers may be deceived or imposed on, but conscience. "No man," says *Chrysostom,* "can flee from the judgment of his own conscience, which can-not be shunned. It cannot be corrupted; it cannot be terrified; it cannot be flattered or bribed; nor can its testimony be obscured by any lapse of time." *Epist. ad Olymp.* This strongly argues its Divine nature; and, *while* the Spirit of God strives with man, conscience has its full influence, and is ever alert in the performance of its office. *Cicero,* in his oration for Milo, describes the power of conscience well in a few words: *Magna est vis conscientiæ in utramque partem, ut neque timeant qui nihil commiserint, et pænam semper ante oculos versari putent qui peccarint.* "Great is the power of conscience in both cases; they fear nothing who know they have committed no evil; on the contrary, they who have sinned live in continual dread of punishment." One of our poets has said, "'Tis conscience that makes cowards of us all." And had we been sure that Shakspeare was a scholar, we might have supposed that he had borrowed the thought from Menander.

'Ο συνιστορων αυτω τι, καν η θρασυτατος,
'Η συνεσις αυτον δειλοτατον ειναι ποιει.

If a man be conscious of any crime, although he were the most undaunted of mankind,
His conscience makes him the most timid of mortals.
Apud Stobæum, Serm. xxiv., p. 192.

Conscience is sometimes said to be *good, bad, tender, seared,* &c.: *good,* if it acquit or approve; *bad,* if it condemn or disapprove; *tender,* if it be alarmed at the least approach of evil, and severe in scrutinizing the actions of the mind or body; and *seared,* if it feel little alarm, &c., on the commission of sin. But these epithets can scarcely belong to it if the common definition of it be admitted; for how can it be said there is a "tender light," a "dark or hardened light," a "bad god," &c., &c.? But on the other definition these terms are easily understood, and are exceedingly proper; *e. g.* "a *good* conscience" is one *to* which the Spirit of God has brought intelligence of the pardon of all the sins of the soul, and its reconciliation to God through the blood of Christ; and this good conscience *retained,* implies God's *continued* approbation of such a person's conduct; see Acts xxiii. 1; 1 Tim. i. 5, 19; and here, chap. xiii. 18. "A *bad* or evil conscience" supposes a charge of guilt brought against the soul by the Holy Spirit, for the breach of the Divine laws; and which he makes known to it by conscience, as a *medium* of conveying his own light to the mind; see chap. x. 22; 1 Tim. iv. 2; Tit. i. 3. "A *tender* conscience" implies one fully irradiated by the light of the Holy Ghost, which enables the soul to view the good as *good,* and the evil as *evil,* in every important respect; which leads it to abomi-nate the latter, and cleave to the former; and, if at any time it act in the smallest measure opposite to these views, it is severe in its reprehensions, and bitter in its regret. "A *darkened* or *hardened* conscience" means one that has little or none of this Divine light; consequently, the soul feels little or no self-reprehension for acts of transgression, but runs on in sin, and is not aware of the destruction that awaits it, heedless of counsel, and regardless of reproof. This state of the soul St. Paul calls by the name of a "seared conscience," or one cauterized by repeated applications of sin, and resistings of the Holy Ghost; so that, being grieved and quenched, he has withdrawn his light and influence from it.

The word conscience itself ascertains the above explication with its deductions, being compounded of *con, together,* or *with,* and *scio,* to *know,* because it *knows* or convinces *by* or *together* with the Spirit of God. The Greek word συνειδησις, which is the only word used for *conscience* through the whole New Testament, has the very same meaning, being compounded of συν, *together* or *with,* and ειδω, to *know.* This is the same as συνειδος, which is the word generally used among ecclesiastical writers.

From the above view of the subject I think we are warranted in drawing the following inferences:—

1. All men have what is called conscience; and conscience plainly supposes the light or Spirit of God. 2. The Spirit of God is given to enlighten, convince, strengthen, and bring men back to God. 3. Therefore all men may be saved who attend to and coincide with the light and convictions communicated; for the God of the Christians does not give men his Spirit to enlighten, &c., merely to leave them without excuse; but that it may direct, strengthen, and lead them to himself, that they may be finally saved. 4. That this spirit comes from the *grace* of God is demonstrable from hence: it is a "good and perfect gift," and St. James says all such come from the Father of lights. Again, it cannot be merited, for as it implies the influence of the Holy Spirit, it must be of an infinite value; yet it is GIVEN; *that* then which is *not merited* and yet is *given* must be of *grace;* not *ineffectual grace,* there is no such principle in the Godhead.

Thus it appears all men are partakers of the grace of God, for all acknowledge that conscience is common to *all;* and this is but a recipient faculty, and necessarily implies the spirit of grace given by Jesus Christ, not that the world might be thereby condemned, but that it might be saved. Nevertheless, multitudes, who are partakers of this heavenly gift, sin against it, lose it, and perish everlastingly, not through the deficiency of the gift, but through the abuse of it. I conclude that conscience is not a power of the soul, acting *by* or *of itself;* but a *recipient faculty,* in which that *true light that lighteth every man that cometh into the world* has its especial operation.

II. In this chapter the apostle inculcates the duty of hospitality, particularly in respect to entertaining *strangers;* i. e. persons of whom we know nothing, but that they are now in a state of distress, and require the necessaries of life. Some, says the apostle, have entertained angels without knowing them; and some, we may say, have entertained great men, kings, and emperors, without knowing them. By exercising this virtue many have *gained*; few have ever *lost*.

God, in many parts of his own word, is represented as the stranger's friend; and there is scarcely a duty in life which he inculcates in stronger terms than that of hospitality to strangers. The heathen highly applauded this virtue; and among them the person of a stranger was sacred, and supposed to be under the particular protection of Jove. Homer gives the sentiment in all its beauty when he puts the following words into the mouth of Eumæus, when he addressed Ulysses, who appeared a forlorn stranger, and, being kindly received by him, implored in his behalf a Divine blessing:—

Ζευς τοι δοιη, Ξεινε, και αθανατοι θεοι αλλοι
'Οττι μαλιστ' εθελεις, οτι με προφρων ὑπεδεξο.
Τον δ' απαμειβομενος προσεφης, Ευμαιε συβωτα·
Ξειν', ου μοι θεμις εστ', ουδ' ει κακιων σεθεν ελθοι,
Ξεινον ατιμησαι· προς γαρ Διος εισιν ἁπαντες
Ξεινοι τε, πτωχοι τε· δοσις δ' ολιγη τε φιλη τε
Γιγνεται ἡμετερη.   ODYSS., lib. xiv., v. 53.

My gentle host, Jove grant thee, and the gods
All grant thee, for this deed thy best desire!
To whom the herd Eumæus thus replied:
My *guest*, it were unjust to treat with scorn
The *stranger*, though a poorer should arrive
Than even thou; for all the poor that are,
And all the *strangers*, are the care of Jove.
Little, and with good will, is all that lies
Within my scope.   COWPER.

The scriptures which more particularly recommend this duty are the following: *He doth execute the judgment of the fatherless and widow, and loveth the stranger, in giving him food and raiment. Love ye, therefore, the stranger; for ye were strangers in the land of Egypt*; Deut. x. 18, 19. *I was a stranger, and ye took me in. Come, ye blessed of my Father*, Matt. xxv. 35. *Given to hospitality*; Rom. xii. 13. *Neglect not to entertain strangers*; Heb. xiii. 2. "The entertaining of unknown strangers," says Dr. Owen, "which was so great a virtue in ancient times, is almost driven out of the world by the wickedness of it. The false practices of some, with wicked designs, under the habit and pretence of strangers, on the one hand, and pretences for sordid covetousness on the other, have banished it from the earth. And there are enough who are called Christians who never once thought it to be their duty." But it is vain to inculcate the duty where the spirit of it is not found; and we shall never find the spirit of it in any heart where the love of God and man does not rule.

Benevolent wishes of *Be ye warmed* and *Be ye clothed* are frequent enough; these cost nothing, and therefore can be readily used by the most parsimonious. But to draw out a man's soul to the hungry, to draw out his warmest affections, while he is drawing out, in order to divide with the destitute, the contents of his purse, belongs to the man of genuine feel-

ing; and this can scarcely be expected where the compassionate mind that was in Christ does not rule. One bountiful meal to the poor may often be a preventive of death; for there are times in which a man may be brought so low for want of proper nourishment that, if he get not a timely supply, after-help comes in vain, nature being too far exhausted ever to recover itself, though the vital spark may linger long. One wholesome meal in time may be the means of enabling nature to contend successfully with after privations; and he who has afforded this meal to the destitute has saved a life. "But most who go about seeking relief are idle persons and impostors, and it would be sinful to relieve them." When you *know* the applicant to be such, then refuse his suit; but if you have nothing but suspicion, which suspicion generally arises from an uncharitable and unfeeling heart, then beware how you indulge it. If, through such suspicion, a man should lose his life, God will require his blood at your hand.

Reader, permit me to relate an anecdote which I have heard from that most eminent man of God, the reverend *John Wesley*; it may put thee in mind to entertain *strangers* "At Epworth, in Lincolnshire, where (says he) I was born, a poor woman came to a house in the market-place and begged a morsel of bread, saying, *I am very hungry*. The master of the house called her *a lazy jade*, and bade her *be gone*. She went forward, called at another house, and asked for a little small-beer, saying, *I am very thirsty*. Here she was refused, and told to *go into the workhouse*. She struggled on to a third door and begged a little water, saying, *I am faint*. The owner drove her away, saying, *He would encourage no common beggars*. It was winter, and the snow lay upon the ground. The boys, seeing a poor ragged creature driven away from door to door, began to throw snow-balls at her. She went to a little distance, sat down on the ground, lifted up her eyes to heaven, reclined on the earth, and expired!" Here was a stranger; had the first to whom she applied relieved her with a morsel of bread, he would have saved her life, and not been guilty of blood. As the case stood, the woman was murdered; and those three householders will stand arraigned at the bar of God for her death. Reader, fear to send any person empty away. If you know him to be an *impostor*, why then give him nothing. But if you only *suspect* it, let not your suspicion be the rule of your conduct; give something, however little; because that little may be sufficient to preserve him, if in real want, from present death. If you know him not to be a knave, to you he may be an *angel*. God may have *sent* him to exercise your charity, and try your faith. It can never be a matter of regret to you that you gave an alms for God's sake, though you should afterwards find that the person to whom you gave it was both a hypocrite and impostor. Better to be imposed on by ninety-nine hypocrites out of a hundred applicants, than send *one*, like the poor *Epworth woman*, empty away.

Finished correcting this epistle for a new edition, Dec. 30. 1831.—A. C

PREFACE

TO

THE GENERAL EPISTLE

OF

JAMES.

THERE have been more doubts, and more diversity of opinion, concerning the *author* of this epistle, and the *time* in which it was written, than about most other parts of the New Testament. To enter at large into a discussion of the opinions of ancient and modern writers on this subject would tend but little to the establishment of truth, or to the edification of the reader. Lardner, Michaelis, and Macknight, have entered considerably into the controversy relative to the author, the time, and the canonical authority of this book; and to them the reader who wishes to see the difficulties with which the subject is pressed may have recourse.

This epistle, with those of Peter, John, and Jude, is termed *catholic*, καθολικη, from κατα, *through*, and ὁλος, *the whole*; for the application of which term Œcumenius, in cap. i. Jacobi, gives the following reason: Καθολικαι λεγονται αυται, οἱονει εγκυκλιοι· ου γαρ αφωρισμενως εθνει ἑνι η πολει, αλλα καθολου τοις πιστοις· "These epistles are called catholic, universal, or *circular*, because they were not written to one nation or city, but to believers *everywhere*."

Yet, as these epistles had some difficulty at first to get into general circulation, but at last were everywhere received, it is more likely that they obtained the term *catholic* from the circumstance of their being at last *universally* acknowledged as *canonical*; so that the word *catholic* is to be understood here in the same sense as *canonical*.

Who the writer of the epistle in question was, is difficult to say; all that we know *certainly* is, from his own words, that his name was *James*, and that he was a servant of God, and of the Lord Jesus. Two persons of this name are mentioned in the New Testament; James the son of Zebedee, called also James the elder; and James του μικρου, *the less* or the *little one*, called the *son of Alpheus*, and *brother of our Lord*: but whether one of these, or if one of them, *which*, or whether one of the same name different from both, are points that cannot be satisfactorily determined. Michaelis, who has examined the subject with his usual ability, leaves the matter in doubt; but leans to the opinion that *James* the *son of Zebedee* was the author, and that this epistle was written *before* any of those in the New Testament. Other great authorities ascribe it to *James*, called the *brother of our Lord*, who was president, or bishop, of the Church in Jerusalem. Even allowing this opinion to be correct, it is not agreed in what sense James is called our *Lord's brother*, there being *four* or *five* different opinions concerning the meaning of this term. From Matt. xiii. 55, 56, we learn that there were four persons called brethren of our Lord: "Is not this the carpenter's son? Is not his mother called Mary? And his brethren *James*, and *Joses*, and *Simon*, and *Judas?* And his sisters, are they not all with us?" Now, it is generally allowed that the James here is the author of this epistle, and the *Jude* or *Judas*, mentioned with him, the author of that which stands last in this collection. But with respect to the meaning of the term *brother*, as here used, it will be necessary to state the opinions of learned men:—

1. It is supposed that these were children of Joseph, by a former marriage; this is a very ancient opinion; as there is nothing improbable in the supposition that Joseph was a *widower* when he married the blessed virgin.

2. They are supposed to have been children of Joseph and his wife Mary; all born after the birth of our Lord. This is an opinion extremely probable: see some reasons for it in the note on Matt. xiii. 56; see also on Matt. i. 25.

3. That they were called our *Lord's brethren*, because children of Joseph by the wife of one of his brothers, who had died childless, and whose widow Joseph took, according to the Mosaic law, to raise up seed to his

deceased brother. This is very unlikely, because, in this case, it would have been only requisite for Joseph to have had one male by his brother's wife ; but here we find *four*, besides several *sisters*.

4. That Cleophas, called also Alpheus, married a sister of the blessed virgin, called also *Mary*, by whom he had the above issue ; and that these were called brethren of our Lord, from the common custom among the Hebrews, to term all the more immediately cognate branches of the same family, *brothers'* and *sisters' children*, i. e. cousins-german, *brethren*. These, therefore, being aunt's children of our Lord, are, according to this usage, called his *brethren*. The first and second of these opinions appear to me the most probable ; though most modern writers are of the latter opinion.

That of the two James's, *James the less* was the author of this epistle, Dr. Macknight thinks, following Lardner and others, is incontestable : I shall quote his abridgment of Lardner's arguments ; but the point in question is not, in my opinion, made out by any of these writers.

" In the catalogue of the apostles, Matt. x. 2 ; Mark iii. 17 ; Luke vi. 14 ; Acts i. 13 ; we find two persons of the name of James ; the first was the son of *Zebedee*, Matt. x. 2 ; the second in all the catalogues is called the son of *Alpheus* : one of these apostles is called, Gal. i. 19, *the Lord's brother*. Wherefore, as there were only *twelve* apostles, and as James the son of Zebedee, so far as we know, was in no respect related to our Lord, the apostle called *James, the Lord's brother*, must have been *James the son of Alpheus*, called also *James the less or younger*, whose relation to Christ will appear by comparing Mark xv. 40, with John xix. 25. In the former passage, *Mark*, speaking of the women who were present at the crucifixion, says : ' There were also women looking on afar off, among whom were Mary Magdalen, and Mary the mother of James the less and of Joses, and Salome.' In the latter passage, John, speaking of the same women, says : ' There stood by the cross of Jesus, his mother, and his mother's sister, Mary, the wife of Cleophas, and Mary Magdalen :' wherefore, *our Lord's mother's sister*, *Mary the wife of Cleophas*, mentioned by John, is in all probability the person whom Mark calls *Mary the mother of James the less, and of Joses* ; consequently, her sons, *James and Joses*, were our Lord's cousins-german by his mother. And as the Hebrews called all near relations *brethren*, it is more than probable that James the son of Alpheus, who was our Lord's cousin-german, is *James the Lord's brother*, mentioned Gal. i. 19. Three circumstances confirm this opinion : 1. James and Joses, the sons of Mary, our Lord's mother's sister, are expressly called *the brethren* of Jesus, Matt. xiii. 55 ; Mark vi. 3. 2. James, the son of our Lord's mother's sister, being distinguished from another James by the appellation of *the less*, Mark xv. 40, there is good reason to suppose that he is the James whom Mark, in his catalogue, distinguishes from *James the son of Zebedee*, by the appellation of the *son of Alpheus*. It is true, Mary the mother of James and of Joses, is called the *wife of Cleophas*, John xix. 25 : but *Cleophas* and *Alpheus* are the same name differently pronounced.; the one according to the Hebrew, and the other according to the Greek, orthography. 3. Of the persons called the *brethren of Jesus*, Matt. xiii. 55, there are three mentioned in the catalogue as APOSTLES ; *James*, and *Simon*, and *Judas*. They, I suppose, are the brethren of the Lord, who are said, as apostles, to have had a right to lead about a sister or a wife, &c.; 1 Cor. ix. 5. Jerome likewise thought *James the Lord's brother* was so called because he was the son of Mary, our Lord's mother's sister; Art. *Jacobus*. Lardner, Canon., vol. iii. p. 63, says : ' Jerome seems to have been the *first* who said our Lord's brethren were the sons of his mother's sister ; and this opinion was at length embraced by *Augustine*, and has prevailed very much of late, being the opinion of the *Romanists* in general, and of Lightfoot, Witsius, Lampe, and many of the *Protestants*. On the other hand, *Origen*, *Epiphanius*, and other ancient writers, both Greeks and Latins, were of opinion that James, the Lord's brother, was not the son of the virgin's sister, but of Joseph, our Lord's reputed father, by a *former wife*, who died before he espoused the virgin. Of the same opinion were *Vossius, Basnage*, and *Cave*, among the Protestants ; and *Valesius* among the Romanists. Epiphanius and Theophylact supposed that Joseph's first wife was the widow of Alpheus, who, being Joseph's brother, Joseph married her to raise up seed to him ; and therefore James, the issue of that marriage, was fitly called the *son of Alpheus*, and *brother of our Lord*.' But these suppositions might have been spared, if the ancients and moderns had recollected that near *relations* were called *brethren* by the Hebrews, and that Alpheus and Cleophas are the same names differently written : James the less, the son of Alpheus, being not only the Lord's near relation, but an *apostle*, whom, as is generally supposed, he honoured in a particular manner, by appearing to him *alone*, after his resurrection ; 1 Cor. xv. 7. These circumstances, together with his own personal merit, rendered him of such note among the apostles that they appointed him to reside at Jerusalem, and to superintend the Church there. This appointment, Lardner says, was made soon after the martyrdom of Stephen ; and, in support of this opinion, observes, ' that Peter always speaks first, as president among the apostles, until after the choice of the seven deacons. Every thing said of St. James, after that, implies his presiding in the Church at Jerusalem.' Canon., vol. iii. p. 28. For example, when the apostles and elders at Jerusalem came together to consider whether it was needful to circumcise the Gentiles, after there had been much disputing, Peter spake, Acts xv. 7, then Barnabas and Paul, ver. 12. And when they had ended, James summed up the whole, and proposed the terms on which the Gentiles were to be received into the Church, ver. 19, 20, 21 ; to which the whole assembly agreed, and wrote letters to the Gentiles, conformably to the opinion of James, ver. 22–29. From this it is inferred, that James presided in the council of Jerusalem, because he was president of the Church in that city.

" Chrysostom, in his Homily on Acts xv., says : ' James was bishop of Jerusalem, and therefore spoke last.' In the time of this council, Paul communicated the Gospel which he preached among the Gentiles to

PREFACE TO THE EPISTLE OF ST. JAMES.

three of the apostles, whom he calls *pillars*; and tells us that, when they perceived the inspiration and miraculous powers which he possessed, they gave him the right hand of fellowship, mentioning James first, Gal. ii. 9 : 'And knowing the grace that was bestowed on me, James, Cephas, and John, who were pillars, gave to me and Barnabas the right hand of fellowship.' This implies that James, whom, in the first chapter, he had called *the Lord's brother*, was not only an *apostle*, but the presiding apostle in the Church at Jerusalem. In the same chapter, Paul, giving an account of what happened after the council, says, ver. 11 : 'When Peter was come to Antioch, before that certain came from James, he did eat with the Gentiles; but when they were come he withdrew, and separated himself, fearing them who were of the circumcision.' This shows that James resided at Jerusalem, and presided in the Church there, and was greatly respected by the Jewish believers. The same circumstance appears from Acts xxi. 17, where, giving an account of Paul's journey to Jerusalem, with the collections from the saints in Judea, Luke says, ver. 18 : 'Paul went in with us to James, and all the elders were present.' Farther, the respect in which James was held by the apostles appears from two facts recorded by Luke : the first is, when Paul came to Jerusalem, three years after his conversion, Barnabas took him, and brought him to Peter and James, as the chief apostles. Compare Acts ix. 27 with Gal. i. 19. The second fact is, after Peter was miraculously delivered out of prison, about the time of the passover, in the year 44, 'he came to the house of Mary—where many were gathered together praying; (Acts xii. 12 ;)—and when he had declared to them how the Lord had brought him out of the prison, he said, Go, show these things to James, and to the brethren ;' ver. 17. These particulars are mentioned by Lardner, and before him by Whitby and Cave, to show that James, the Lord's brother, was really an *apostle*, in the strict acceptation of the word; consequently, that Eusebius was mistaken when he placed him among the seventy disciples ; E. H., lib. vii. c. 12.

"That the Epistle of James was early esteemed an inspired writing, is evident from the following fact : that while the Second Epistle of Peter, the second and third of John, the Epistle of Jude, and the Revelation, are omitted in the first Syriac translation of the New Testament, (the *Peshito*,) which was made in the beginning of the second century for the use of the converted Jews ; the Epistle of James has found a place in it, equally with the books which were never called in question. This is an argument of great weight ; for certainly the Jewish believers, to whom that epistle was addressed and delivered, were much better judges of its authenticity than the converted Gentiles, to whom it was not sent, and who perhaps had no opportunity of being acquainted with it till long after it was written. Wherefore its being received by the Jewish believers is an undeniable proof that they knew it to be written by James the apostle; whereas the ignorance of the Gentile believers, concerning this epistle, is not even a presumption against its authenticity.

"That the converted Gentiles had little knowledge of the Epistle of James in the first ages, may have been owing to various causes ; such as, that it was addressed to the *Jews*, and that the matters contained in it were personal to the Jews. For on these accounts the Jewish believers may have thought it not necessary to communicate it to the Gentiles. And when it was made known to them, they may have scrupled to receive it as an inspired writing for the following reasons : 1. The writer does not, in the inscription, take the title of an apostle, but calls himself simply *James, a servant of God, and of the Lord Jesus Christ.* 2. Many of the ancients, by calling the writer of this epistle *James the Just*, have rendered his apostleship doubtful. 3. As they have done, likewise, by speaking of him commonly as *bishop of Jerusalem*, and not as an apostle of Christ. It is little wonder, therefore, that this epistle was not received generally by the converted Gentiles ; consequently it is little that it was not often quoted by them in their writings. But afterwards, when it was considered that this epistle was from the beginning received by the Jewish believers, and that it was translated into the Syriac language for their use ; and that Paul, though an apostle, sometimes contented himself with the appellation of *a servant of Christ*, Phil. i. 1; Philem. ver. 1; and sometimes took no appellation but his own name ; 1 Thess. i. 1; 2 Thess. i. 1; and that the apostle John did not, in any of his epistles, call himself an *apostle*; the title which the author of the Epistle of James had to be an apostle was no longer doubted, but he was generally acknowledged to be *James, the son of Alpheus, and the Lord's brother*; and his epistle, after an accurate examination, was received as an inspired writing. So *Estius* tells us, who affirms that after the *fourth century* no Church nor ecclesiastical writer is found who ever doubted of the authority of this epistle ; but, on the contrary, all the catalogues of the books of Scripture published, whether by general or provincial councils, or by Roman bishops, or other orthodox writers, since the fourth century, constantly number it among the *canonical* Scriptures.

"With respect to what is remarked by Eusebius, that there are not many ancient writers who have quoted the Epistle of James, learned men have observed that *Clement* of Rome has quoted it four several times; and so does *Ignatius* in his genuine Epistle to the Ephesians, sec. 10, 12, 17, 30 ; and *Origen* in his thirteenth Homily on Genesis, sec. 5. That it was not more generally quoted by the ancients, besides the things already mentioned, may have been owing to the following reasons : 1. Being written to the whole Jewish nation to correct the errors and vices which prevailed among them, the Gentiles may have thought themselves little concerned with it, and may have been at no pains to procure copies of it ; by which means it was not so generally known among them as some other books of Scripture. 2. The seeming opposition of the doctrine of this epistle to the doctrine of Paul, concerning *justification by faith without the works of the law*, may have occasioned it to be less regarded by the most ancient writers ; just as it was in later times, on the same account, rejected by Luther, who, to show his contempt of it, called it (*epistola straminea*) a *strawy* or *chaffy epistle*.

2

795

"To conclude, the authority of the Epistle of James, as an inspired writing, is abundantly established, in Mill's opinion, by the Apostles Paul and Peter, who have in their writings many sentiments and expressions similar to those contained in this epistle ; for example :—

1 Pet. i. 3 : Who hath begotten us again to a living hope through the resurrection of Jesus Christ.

James i. 18 : Having willed it, he hath begotten us by the word.

Rom. v. 3, 4 : Knowing that affliction worketh out patience ; and patience experience.

James i. 3 : Knowing that the proving of your faith worketh out patience.

Rom. ii. 13 : That the hearers of the law are not just before God, but the doers of the law shall be justified.

James i. 22 : And be ye doers of the law, and not hearers only, deceiving yourselves by false reasoning.

Rom. vii. 23 : I see another law in my members, warring against the law of my mind.

James iv. 1 : Come they not hence, even from your lusts, which war in your members ?

1 Pet. ii. 11 : Lusts which war against the soul.

1 Pet. v. 8, 9 : Your adversary the devil ; whom resist, steadfast in the faith.

James iv. 7 : Resist the devil, and he will flee from you.

1 Pet. v. 6 : Be humbled under the mighty hand of God, that he may exalt you.

James iv. 10 : Be humbled in the presence of God, and he will lift you up.

Rom. xiv. 4 : Who art thou that condemnest another man's household servant ?

James iv. 12 : Thou, who art thou that condemnest another ?

1 Pet. iv. 8 : Love covereth a multitude of sins.

James v. 20 : Will cover a multitude of sins."

See *Macknight's* preface.

That James the less may have been our Lord's cousin-german, or even our Lord's brother by a former wife of Joseph, or even by the virgin, is perfectly possible ; and that he was an *apostle*, and an eminent man among both Jews and Christians, may be readily credited ; and that he was author of this epistle, is also possible : but I must still assert that we have neither decisive nor satisfactory evidence on this subject : and that it is arguing in a circle to deduce the evidence of its authenticity from the apostleship of James the less, because this person is not proved to be its author. The chief and proper evidence of its being *canonical* must be taken from the fact that it was universally received by the Church of Christ, and without scruple incorporated with those writings, which were, on all hands, allowed to have been given by the inspiration of God.

Before I conclude, I shall mention the opinion of *Michaelis* relative to the author of this epistle. "All things considered," says he, "I see no ground for the assertion that James, the son of Zebedee, was not the author of this epistle. One circumstance affords, at least, a presumptive argument in favour of the opinion that it was really written by the elder James, and at a time when the Gospel had not been propagated among the Gentiles ; namely, that it contains no exhortations to harmony between the Jewish and Gentile converts, which, after the time that the Gentiles were admitted into the Church, became absolutely necessary. Had it been written after the apostolic council of Jerusalem, mentioned Acts xv., and by the younger James, we might have expected that, at least, some allusion would be made in it to the decree of that council, which was propounded by the younger James in favour of the Gentile converts ; and that the epistle would contain an admonition to the Jewish converts, to consider the Gentile converts as their brethren."—*Introduction to the New Testament.*

The epistle itself is entirely different in its complexion from all those in the sacred canon ; the style and manner are more that of a Jewish prophet than a Christian apostle. It scarcely touches on any subject purely Christian. Our blessed Lord is only mentioned twice in it, chap. i. 1 ; ii. 1 ; but it has nothing of his miracles or teaching, of his death or resurrection, nor of any redemption by him. It begins without any apostolical salutation, and ends without any apostolical benediction. In short, had it not been for the two slight notices of our blessed Lord, we had not known it was the work of any Christian writer. It may be considered a sort of connecting link between Judaism and Christianity, as the ministry of John Baptist was between the old covenant and the new. There is neither plan nor arrangement in it ; but it contains many invaluable lessons which no serious person can read without profit.

James the less was martyred at Jerusalem about A. D. 62 : and the epistle is supposed to have been written a short time before his death. Though I believe it to be the work of an unknown author, not long after the ascension of our Lord, I shall follow the usual chronology, and date it in the year 61 ; not because I think that to be the true date, but because it is what is generally adopted.

THE GENERAL EPISTLE

OF

JAMES

Chronological Notes relative to this Epistle.

Year of the Constantinopolitan era of the world, or that used by the Byzantine historians, and other eastern writers, 5569.—Year of the Alexandrian era of the world, 5563.—Year of the Antiochian era of the world, 5553.—Year of the world, according to Archbishop Usher, 4065.—Year of the world, according to Eusebius, in his Chronicon, 4289.—Year of the minor Jewish era of the world, or that in common use, 3821.—Year of the Greater Rabbinical era of the world, 4420.—Year from the Flood, according to Archbishop Usher, and the English Bible, 2409.—Year of the Cali yuga, or Indian era of the Deluge, 3163. —Year of the era of Iphitus, or since the first commencement of the Olympic games, 1001.—Year of the era of Nabonassar, king of Babylon, 810.—Year of the CCXth Olympiad, 1.—Year from the building of Rome, according to Fabius Pictor, 808.—Year from the building of Rome, according to Frontinus, 812.—Year from the building of Rome, according to the Fasti Capitolini, 813.—Year from the building of Rome, according to Varro, which was that most generally used, 814.—Year of the era of the Seleucidæ, 373.—Year of the Cæsarean era of Antioch, 109.—Year of the Julian era, 106.—Year of the Spanish era, 99.—Year from the birth of Jesus Christ according to Archbishop Usher, 65.—Year of the vulgar era of Christ's nativity, 61.—Year of Porcius Festus, governor of the Jews, 1.—Year of Vologesus, king of the Parthians, 12.— Year of Domitius Corbulo, governor of Syria, 2.—Jesus, high priest of the Jews.—Year of the Dionysian period, or Easter Cycle, 62.—Year of the Grecian Cycle of nineteen years, or Common Golden Number, 5; or the second embolismic.—Year of the Jewish Cycle of nineteen years, 2, or the year before the first embolismic.—Year of the Solar Cycle, 14.—Dominical Letter, it being the first after the Bissextile, or Leap Year, D.—Day of the Jewish Passover, according to the Roman computation of time, the XIth of the calends of April, or, in our common mode of reckoning, the twenty-second of March, which happened in this year on the day after the Jewish Sabbath.—Easter Sunday, the IVth of the Calends of April, named by the Jews the 22d of Nisan or Abib; and by Europeans in general, the 29th of March.—Epact, or age of the moon on the 22d of March, (the day of the earliest Easter Sunday possible,) 14.—Epact, according to the present mode of computation, or the moon's age on New Year's day, or the Calends of January, 22.—Monthly Epacts, or age of the moon on the Calends of each month respectively, (beginning with January,) 22, 24, 22, 23, 24, 25, 26, 27, 28, 28, 0, 0—Number of Direction, or the number of days from the twenty-first of March to the Jewish Passover, 1.—Year of the reign of Caius Tiberius Claudius Nero Cæsar, the fifth Roman monarch, computing from Octavianus, or Augustus Cæsar, properly the first Roman emperor, 8.—Roman Consuls, C. Cæsonius Pætus and C. Petronius Turpilianus.

2

CHAPTER I.

He addresses the dispersed of the twelve tribes, 1. Shows that they should rejoice under the cross, because of the spiritual good which they may derive from it; especially in the increase and perfecting of their patience, 2–4. They are exhorted to ask wisdom of God, who gives liberally to all, 5. But they must ask in faith, and not with a doubting mind, 6–8. Directions to the rich and the poor, 9–11. The blessedness of the man that endures trials, 12. How men are tempted and drawn away from God, 13–15. God is the Father of lights, and all good proceeds from him, 16–18. Cautions against hasty words and wrong tempers, 19–21. We should be doers of the word, and not hearers merely, lest we resemble those who, beholding their natural face in a glass, when it is removed forget what manner of persons they were, 22–24. We should look into the perfect law of liberty, and continue therein, 25. The nature and properties of pure religion, 26, 27.

A. M. cir. 4065.
A. D. cir. 61.
An. Olymp.
cir. CCX. 1.
A. U. C. cir.
814.

JAMES, [a] [b] a servant of God and of the Lord Jesus Christ, [c] to the twelve tribes [d] which are scattered abroad, greeting.

2 My brethren, [e] count it all joy [f] when ye fall into divers temptations;

3 [g] Knowing *this*, that the try-

A. M. cir. 4065.
A. D. cir. 61.
An. Olymp.
cir. CCX. 1.
A. U. C. cir.
814.

[a] Acts xii. 17; xv. 13; Gal. i. 19; ii. 9; Jude 1.——[b] Tit. i. 1. [c] Acts xxvi. 7.——[d] Deut. xxxii. 26; John vii. 35; Acts ii. 5; viii. 1; 1 Pet. i. 1.——[e] Matt. v. 12; Acts v. 41; Heb. x. 34; 1 Pet. iv. 13, 16.——[f] 1 Pet. i. 6.——[g] Rom. v. 3.

NOTES ON CHAP. I.

Verse 1. *James, a servant of God*] For an account of this person, or rather for the conjectures concerning him, see the *preface.* He neither calls himself an *apostle*, nor does he say that he was the *brother of Christ*, or *bishop of Jerusalem*; whether he was *James the elder*, son of Zebedee, or *James the less*, called our Lord's brother, or some other person of the same name, we know not. The assertions of writers concerning these points are worthy of no regard. The Church has always received him as an *apostle* of Christ.

To the twelve tribes—scattered abroad] To the Jews, whether converted to Christianity or not, who lived out of Judea, and sojourned among the Gentiles for the purpose of trade or commerce. At this time there were Jews partly *travelling*, partly *sojourning*, and partly *resident* in most parts of the civilized world; particularly in Asia, Greece, Egypt, and Italy. I see no reason for restricting it to Jewish believers only; it was sent to all whom it might concern, but particularly to those who had received the faith of our Lord Jesus Christ; much less must we confine it to those who were scattered abroad at the persecution raised concerning Stephen, Acts viii. 1, &c.; xi. 19, &c. That the twelve tribes were in actual existence when James wrote this epistle, Dr. Macknight thinks evident from the following facts : " 1. Notwithstanding Cyrus allowed all the Jews in his dominions to return to their own land, many of them did not return. This happened agreeably to God's purpose, in permitting them to be carried captive into Assyria and Babylonia; for he intended to make himself known among the heathens, by means of the knowledge of his being and perfections, which the Jews, in their dispersion, would communicate to them. This also was the reason that God determined that the ten tribes should never return to their own land, Hos. i. 6; viii. 8; ix. 3, 15–17. 2. That, comparatively speaking, few of the twelve tribes returned in consequence of Cyrus's decree, but continued to live among the Gentiles, appears from this : that in the days of Ahasuerus, one of the successors of Cyrus, who reigned from India to Æthiopia, over one hundred and twenty-seven provinces, Esther

iii. 8, *The Jews were dispersed among the people in all the provinces of his kingdom, and their laws were diverse from the laws of all other people, and they did not keep the king's laws;* so that, by adhering to their own usages, they kept themselves distinct from all the nations among whom they lived. 3. On the day of pentecost, which happened next after our Lord's ascension, Acts ii. 5, 9, *There were dwelling at Jerusalem Jews, devout men, out of every nation under heaven; Parthians, Medes, and Elamites,* &c.; so numerous were the Jews, and so widely dispersed through all the countries of the world. 4. When Paul travelled through Asia and Europe, he found the Jews so numerous, that in all the noted cities of the Gentiles they had synagogues in which they assembled for the worship of God, and were joined by multitudes of proselytes from among the heathens, to whom likewise he preached the Gospel. 5. The same apostle, in his speech to King Agrippa, affirmed that the twelve tribes were then existing, and that they served God day and night, in expectation of the promise made to the fathers, Acts xxvi. 6. 6. Josephus, Ant. i. 14, cap. 12, tells us that one region could not contain the Jews, but they dwelt in most of the flourishing cities of Asia and Europe, in the islands and continent, not much less in number than the heathen inhabitants. From all this it is evident that the Jews of the dispersion were more numerous than even the Jews in Judea, and that James very properly inscribed this letter to the *twelve tribes which were in the dispersion*, seeing the twelve tribes really existed then, and do still exist, although not distinguished by separate habitations, as they were anciently in their own land.

Greeting.] Χαιρειν· *Health* ; a mere expression of benevolence, a wish for their prosperity; a common form of salutation; see Acts xv. 23; xxiii. 26; 2 John, 11.

Verse 2. *Count it all joy*] The word πειρασμος, which we translate *temptation*, signifies affliction, persecution, or *trial* of any kind; and in this sense it is used here, not intending diabolic suggestion, or what is generally understood by the word temptation.

Verse 3. *The trying of your faith*] Trials put religion, and all the graces of which it is composed, to

798

2

A. M. cir. 4065.
A. D. cir. 61.
An. Olymp.
cir. CCX. 1.
A. U. C. cir.
814.

ing of your faith worketh patience.

4 But let patience have *her* perfect work, that ye may be perfect and entire, wanting nothing.

5 [h] If any of you lack wisdom, [i] let him ask of God, that giveth to all *men* liberally, and upbraideth not; and [k] it shall be given him.

6 [l] But let him ask in faith, nothing waver-

ing. For he that wavereth is like a wave of the sea driven with the wind and tossed.

A. M. cir. 4065.
A. D. cir. 61.
An. Olymp.
cir. CCX. 1.
A. U. C. cir.
814.

7 For let not that man think that he shall receive any thing of the Lord.

8 [m] A double-minded man *is* unstable in all his ways.

9 Let the brother of low degree [n] rejoice in that he is exalted:

---

[h] 1 Kings iii. 9, 11, 12; Prov. ii. 3.——[i] Matt. vii. 7; xxi. 22; Mark xi. 24; Luke xi. 9; John xiv. 13; xv. 7; xvi. 23.

[k] Jer. xxix. 12; 1 John v. 14, 15.——[l] Mark xi. 24; 1 Tim. ii. 8. [m] Chap. iv. 8.——[n] Or, *glory.*

---

proof; the man that *stands* in such trials gives proof that his religion is sound, and the evidence afforded to his own mind induces him to take courage, bear *patiently,* and *persevere.*

Verse 4. *Let patience have* her *perfect work*] That is, Continue faithful, and your patience will be *crowned* with its full reward; for in this sense is εργον, which we translate *work,* to be understood. It is any *effect* produced by a cause, as *interest* from *money, fruit* from *tillage, gain* from *labour,* a *reward* for *services performed;* the *perfect work* is the *full reward.* See many examples in *Kypke.*

That ye may be perfect and entire] Τελειοι, *Fully instructed,* in every part of the doctrine of God, and in his whole will concerning you. 'Ολοκληροι, having all your *parts, members,* and *portions;* that ye may have *every grace* which constitutes the mind that was in Christ, so that your knowledge and holiness may be complete, and bear a proper proportion to each other. These expressions in their present application are by some thought to be borrowed from the Grecian games: the man was τελειος, *perfect,* who in any of the athletic exercises had got the victory; he was ὁλοκληρος, *entire,* having *every thing complete,* who had the victory in the *pentathlon,* in each of the *five* exercises. Of this use in the last term I do not recollect an example, and therefore think the expressions are borrowed from the *sacrifices* under the law. A victim was τελειος, *perfect,* that was perfectly sound, having no *disease;* it was ὁλοκληρος, *entire,* if it had all its *members,* having nothing *redundant,* nothing *deficient.* Be then to the Lord what he required his sacrifices to be; let your whole heart, your body, soul, and spirit, be sanctified to the Lord of hosts, that he may fill you with all his fulness.

Verse 5. *If any of you lack wisdom*] Wisdom signifies in general *knowledge of the best end,* and *the best means of attaining it;* but in Scripture it signifies the same as *true religion,* the thorough practical knowledge of God, of one's self, and of a Saviour.

Let him ask of God] Because God is the only teacher of this wisdom.

That giveth to all men *liberally*] Who has all good, and gives all necessary good to every one that asks fervently. He who does not ask thus does not feel his need of Divine teaching. The ancient Greek maxim appears at first view strange, but it is literally true:—

Αρχη γνωσεως της αγνοιας ἡ γνωσις.

"The knowledge of ignorance is the beginning of knowledge."

In knowledge we may distinguish these four things:—

1. INTELLIGENCE, the object of which is *intuitive truths.*

2. WISDOM, which is employed in finding out the *best end.*

3. PRUDENCE, which *regulates* the whole *conduct* through life.

4. ART, which provides infallible rules to reason by.

Verse 6. *Let him ask in faith*] Believing that God IS; that he has all good; and that he is ever ready to impart to his creatures whatever they need.

Nothing wavering.] Μηδεν διακρινομενος· *Not judging otherwise;* having no doubt concerning the truth of these grand and fundamental principles, never supposing that God will permit him to ask in vain, when he asks sincerely and fervently. Let him not hesitate, let him not be *irresolute;* no man can believe too much good of God.

Is like a wave of the sea] The man who is not thoroughly persuaded that if he ask of God he shall receive, resembles a wave of the sea; he is in a state of continual agitation; driven by the wind, and tossed: now *rising* by *hope,* then *sinking* by *despair.*

Verse 7. *Let not that man think*] The man whose mind is divided, who is not properly persuaded either of his own wants or God's sufficiency. Such persons may pray, but having no faith, they can get no answer.

Verse 8. *A double-minded man*] Ανηρ διψυχος· The man of two souls, who has one for earth, and another for heaven; who wishes to secure both worlds; he will not give up earth, and he is loth to let heaven go. This was a usual term among the Jews, to express the man who attempted to worship God, and yet retained the love of the creature. Rabbi *Tanchum,* fol. 84, on Deut. xxvi. 17, said: "Behold, the Scripture exhorts the Israelites, and tells them when they pray, לא יהיה להם שתי לבבות *lo yiyeh lahem shetey lebaboth,* that they should not have two hearts, one for the holy blessed God, and one for something else." A man of this character is continually distracted; he will neither let earth nor heaven go, and yet he can have but *one.* Perhaps St. James refers to those Jews who were endeavoring to incorporate the law with the Gospel, who were divided in their minds and affections, not willing to give up the Levitical rites, and yet unwilling to renounce the Gospel. Such persons could make no progress in Divine things.

A. M. cir. 4065. A. D. cir. 61. An. Olymp. cir. CCX. 1. A. U. C. cir. 814.

10 But the rich, in that he is
made low: because [o] as the
flower of the grass he shall pass
away.
11 For the sun is no sooner risen with a
burning heat, but it withereth the grass, and
the flower thereof falleth, and the grace of the
fashion of it perisheth: so also shall the rich
man fade away in his ways.
12 [p] Blessed *is* the man that
endureth temptation: for when
he is tried, he shall receive [q] the
crown of life, [r] which the Lord
hath promised to them that love him.
13 Let no man say when he is tempted, I
am tempted of God: for God cannot be tempted with [s] evil, neither tempteth he any man;
14 But every man is tempted, when he is

[o] Job xiv. 2; Psa. xxxvii. 2; xc. 5, 6; cii. 11; ciii. 15; Isa. xl. 6; 1 Cor. vii. 31; chap. iv. 14; 1 Pet. i. 24; 1 John ii. 17.—[p] Job v. 17; Proverbs iii. 11, 12; Hebrews xii. 5; Rev. iii. 19.—[q] 1 Cor. ix. 25; 2 Tim. iv. 8; chap. ii. 5; 1 Pet. v. 4; Rev. ii. 10.—[r] Matthew x. 22; xix. 28, 29; chapter ii. 5.—[s] Or, *evils*.

Verse 9. *Let the brother of low degree*] The poor, destitute Christian may *glory* in the cross of Christ, and the blessed hope laid up for him in heaven; for, being a child of God, he is an heir of God, and a joint heir with Christ.

Verse 10. *But the rich, in that he is made low*] Εν τῃ ταπεινωσει· *In his humiliation*—in his being brought to the foot of the cross to receive, as a poor and miserable sinner, redemption through the blood of the cross: and especially let him rejoice in this, because all outward glory is only as the flower of the field, and, like that, will wither and perish.

Verse 11. *For the sun is no sooner risen*] We need not pursue this metaphor, as St. James' meaning is sufficiently clear: All human things are transitory; *rise* and *fall*, or *increase* and *decay*, belong to all the productions of the earth, and to all its inhabitants. This is unavoidable, for in many cases the very cause of their growth becomes the cause of their decay and destruction. The sun by its genial heat nourishes and supports all plants and animals; but when it arises with a *burning heat*, the atmosphere not being tempered with a sufficiency of moist vapours, the juices are exhaled from the plants; the earth, for lack of moisture, cannot afford a sufficient supply; vegetation becomes checked; and the plants soon wither and die. Earthly possessions are subject to similar mutations. God gives and resumes them at his pleasure, and for reasons which he seldom explains to man. He shows them to be uncertain, that they may never become an object of confidence to his followers, and that they may put their whole trust in God. If for righteousness' sake any of those who were in affluence suffer loss, or spoiling of their goods, they should consider that, while they have gained that of infinite worth, they have lost what is but of little value, and which in the nature of things they must soon part with, though they should suffer nothing on account of religion.

Verse 12. *Blessed* is *the man that endureth temptation*] This is a mere Jewish sentiment, and on it the Jews speak some excellent things. In *Shemoth Rabba*, sec. 31, fol. 129, and in Rab. *Tanchum*, fol. 29, 4, we have these words: "Blessed is the man שהיה עומד בנסיונו *shehayah omed benisyono* who stands in his temptation; for there is no man whom God does not *try*. He tries the *rich*, to see if they will open their hands to the poor. He tries the *poor*, to see if they will receive affliction and not murmur. If, therefore, the rich *stand in his temptation*, and give alms to the poor, he shall enjoy his riches in this world, and his horn shall be exalted in the world to come, and the holy blessed God shall deliver him from the punishment of hell. If the poor *stand in his temptation*, and do not repine, (kick back,) he shall have double in the world to come." This is exactly the sentiment of James. Every man is in this life in a state of temptation or trial, and in this state he is a candidate for another and a better world; he that *stands* in his trial shall receive the crown of life, which the Lord hath promised to them that love him. It is only *love to God* that can enable a man to endure the trials of life. Love feels no loads; all practicable things are possible to him who loveth.

There may be an allusion here to the contests in the Grecian games. He is crowned who conquers, and none else.

Verse 13. *Let no man say*] Lest the former sentiment should be misapplied, as the word *temptation* has two grand meanings, *solicitation to sin*, and trial from *providential situation* or *circumstances*, James, taking up the word in the former sense, after having used it in the latter, says: *Let no man say, when he is tempted*, (solicited to sin,) *I am tempted of God;* for God cannot be tempted with evil, *neither tempteth he* (thus) *any man*. Thus the author has explained and guarded his meaning.

Verse 14. *But every man is tempted*] Successfully solicited to sin, when *he is drawn away of his own lust*—when, giving way to the evil propensity of his own heart, he does that to which he is solicited by the enemy of his soul.

Among the rabbins we find some fine sayings on this subject. In *Midrash hanaalam*, fol. 20, and *Yalcut Rubeni*, fol. 17, it is said: "This is the custom of evil concupiscence, יצר הרע *yetser hara:* To-day it saith, Do this; to-morrow, Worship an idol. The man goes and worships. Again it saith, Be *angry*."

"Evil concupiscence is, at the beginning, like the thread of a spider's web; afterwards it is like a cart rope." *Sanhedrim*, fol. 99.

In the words, *drawn away by his own lust and enticed*, ὑπο της ιδιας επιθυμιας εξελκομενος και δελεαζομενος, there is a double metaphor; the first referring to the *dragging a fish* out of the water by a *hook* which it had swallowed, because *concealed by a bait;* the second, to the *enticements* of impure women, who draw away the unwary into their snares, and involve them in their ruin. Illicit connections of this kind the

A. M. cir. 4065.
A. D. cir. 61.
An. Olymp.
cir. CCX. 1.
A. U. C. cir.
814.

drawn away of his own lust, and enticed.

15 Then [t] when lust hath conceived, it bringeth forth sin : and sin, when it is finished, [u] bringeth forth death.

16 Do not err, my beloved brethren.

17 [v] Every good gift and every perfect gift is from above, and cometh down from the Father of lights, [w] with whom is no variableness, neither shadow of turning.

18 [x] Of his own will begat he us with the

A. M. cir. 4065.
A. D. cir. 61.
An. Olymp.
cir. CCX. 1.
A. U. C. cir.
814.

---

[t] Job xv. 35 ; Psa. vii. 14.——[u] Rom. vi. 21, 23.——[v] John iii. 27 ; 1 Cor. iv. 7.

[w] Num. xxiii. 19 ; 1 Samuel xv. 29 ; Mal. iii. 6 ; Rom. xi. 29.   [x] John i. 13 ; iii. 3 ; 1 Cor. iv. 15 ; 1 Pet. i. 23.

---

writer has clearly in view ; and every word that he uses refers to something of this nature, as the following verse shows.

Verse 15. *When lust hath conceived*] When the evil propensity works unchecked, *it bringeth forth sin* —the evil act between the parties is perpetrated.

And sin, when it is finished] When this breach of the law of God and of innocence has been a sufficient time completed, it *bringeth forth death*—the spurious offspring is the fruit of the criminal connection, and the evidence of that *death* or *punishment* due to the transgressors.

Any person acquainted with the import of the verbs συλλαμβανειν, τικτειν, and αποκυειν, will see that this is the metaphor, and that I have not exhausted it. Συλλαμβανω signifies concipio sobolem, *quæ comprehenditur utero* ; concipio fœtum ;—τικτω, pario, genero, efficio ;—αποκυεω, *ex απο et κυω, prægnans sum,* in utero gero. *Verbum proprium prægnantium, quæ fœtum maturum emittunt. Interdum etiam* gignendi *notionem habet.*—MAIUS, *Obser. Sacr.,* vol. ii., page 184. *Kypke* and *Schleusner.*

Sin is a small matter in its commencement ; but by indulgence it grows great, and multiplies itself beyond all calculation. To use the rabbinical metaphor lately adduced, *it is, in the commencement, like the thread of a spider's web*—almost *imperceptible* through its extreme *tenuity* or *fineness,* and as *easily broken,* for it is as yet but a *simple irregular imagination ; afterwards it becomes like a cart rope*—it has, by being indulged produced *strong desire and delight ;* next *consent ;* then, time, place, and opportunity serving, that which was *conceived* in the *mind,* and *finished* in the *purpose,* is consummated by *act.*

"The *soul,* which the Greek philosophers considered as the seat of the appetites and passions, is called by *Philo* το θηλυ, the *female* part of our nature ; and the *spirit* το αρρεν, the *male* part. In allusion to this notion, James represents men's *lust* as a *harlot ;* which entices their understanding and will into its impure embraces, and from that conjunction *conceives* sin. Sin, being *brought forth,* immediately acts, and is nourished by frequent repetition, till at length it gains such strength that in its turn it *begets* death. This is the true *genealogy* of sin and death. *Lust* is the *mother* of sin, and *sin* the *mother* of *death,* and the *sinner* the *parent* of both." See *Macknight.*

Verse 16. *Do not err*] By supposing that God is the author of sin, or that he impels any man to commit it.

Verse 17. *Every good gift and every perfect gift is from above*] Whatever is good is from God ; whatever is evil is from man himself. As from the sun,

which is the *father* or fountain of *light,* all light comes ; so from GOD, who is the infinite Fountain, Father, and *Source of good,* all good comes. And whatever can be called *good,* or *pure,* or *light,* or *excellence* of any kind, must necessarily spring from him, as he is the only source of all goodness and perfection.

With whom is no variableness] The *sun,* the fountain of light to the whole of our system, may be obscured by clouds ; or the different bodies which revolve round him, and particularly the earth, may from time to time suffer a diminution of his light by the intervention of other bodies *eclipsing* his splendour, and his apparent *tropical variation, shadow of turning ;* when, for instance, in our winter, he has declined to the *southern tropic,* the tropic of Capricorn, so that our days are greatly shortened, and we suffer in consequence a great diminution both of *light* and *heat.* But there is nothing of this kind with God ; he is never affected by the changes and chances to which mortal things are exposed. He occupies no *one* place in the universe ; he fills the *heavens* and the *earth,* is *everywhere present,* sees all, pervades all, and shines upon all ; dispenses his blessings equally to the universe ; hates nothing that he has made ; is loving to every man ; and his tender mercies are over all his works : therefore he is not *affected with evil,* nor does he *tempt,* or influence to sin, *any man.* The sun, the source of light, rises and sets with a continual *variety* as to the *times* of both, and the *length* of the time in which, in the course of three hundred and sixty-five days, five hours, forty-eight minutes, and forty-eight seconds, it has its revolution through the ecliptic, or rather the earth has its revolution round the sun ; and by which its light and heat are, to the inhabitants of the earth, either constantly *increasing* or *decreasing :* but God, the Creator and Preserver of all things, is eternally the same, dispensing his *good* and *perfect gifts*—his *earthly* and *heavenly* blessings, to all his creatures, ever unclouded in himself, and ever *nilling* EVIL and *willing* GOOD. Men may hide themselves from his light by the works of darkness, as owls and bats hide themselves in dens and caves of the earth during the prevalency of the solar light : but his good will to his creatures is permanent : he wills not the death of a sinner, but rather that he may come unto him and live ; and no man walks in wretchedness or misery but he who *will not come unto God that he may have life.* See diagram and notes at the end of this chapter

Verse 18. *Of his own will begat he us*] God's *will* here is opposed to the *lust of man,* verse 15 ; his *truth,* the means of human salvation, to the *sinful means* referred to in the above verse ; and the *new*

A. M. cir. 4065.
A. D. cir. 61.
An. Olymp.
cir. CCX. 1.
A. U. C. cir.
814.

word of truth, ʸ that we should be a kind of ᶻ first fruits of his creatures.

19 Wherefore, my beloved brethren, ᵃ let every man be swift to hear, ᵇ slow to speak, ᶜ slow to wrath:

20 For the wrath of man worketh not the righteousness of God.

ʸ Eph. i. 12.——ᶻ Jer. ii. 3; Rev. xiv. 4.——ᵃ Eccles. v. 1.
ᵇ Prov. x. 19; xvii. 27; Eccles. v. 2.——ᶜ Prov. xiv. 17; xvi. 32;
Eccles. vii. 9.——ᵈ Col. iii. 8; 1 Pet. ii. 1.——ᵉ Acts xiii. 26;

---

creatures, to the *sin conceived* and *brought forth,* as above. As the *will* of God is essentially *good,* all its productions must be *good* also; as it is infinitely *pure,* all its productions must be *holy.* The *word* or *doctrine* of *truth,* what St. Paul calls *the word of the truth of the Gospel,* Col. i. 5, is the *means* which God uses to convert souls.

A kind of first fruits] By *creatures* we are here to understand the *Gentiles,* and by *first fruits* the *Jews,* to whom the Gospel was first sent; and those of them that believed were the *first fruits* of that astonishing *harvest* which God has since reaped over the whole Gentile world. See the notes on Rom. viii. 19, &c. There is a remarkable saying in *Philo* on this subject, *De Allegoris,* lib. ii. p. 101: *God begat Isaac, for he is the father of the perfect nature,* σπειρων εν ταις ψυχαις, *sowing seed in souls, and begetting happiness.*

Verse 19. *Swift to hear*] *Talk little and work much,* is a rabbinical adage.—*Pirkey Aboth,* cap. i. 15.

The righteous speak little, and do much; the wicked speak much, and do nothing.—*Bava Metzia,* fol. 87.

The son of Sirach says, cap. v. 11: Γινου ταχυς εν τῃ ακροασει σου, και εν μακροθυμια φθεγγου αποκρισιν. " Be swift to hear, and with deep consideration give answer."

Slow to wrath] " There are *four* kinds of dispositions," says the *Midrash hanaalam,* cap. v. 11: " *First,* Those who are easily incensed, and easily pacified; these *gain* on one hand, and *lose* on the other. *Secondly,* Those who are not easily incensed, but are difficult to be appeased; these *lose* on the one hand, and *gain* on the other. *Thirdly,* Those who are difficult to be incensed, and are easily appeased; these are the *good.* *Fourthly,* Those who are easily angered, and difficult to be appeased; these are the *wicked.*"

Those who are hasty in speech are generally of a peevish or angry disposition. A person who is careful to consider what he says, is not likely to be soon angry.

Verse 20. *The wrath of man*] A furious zeal in matters of religion is detestable in the sight of God; he will have no sacrifice that is not consumed by fire from his own altar. The zeal that made the Papists persecute and burn the Protestants, was kindled in hell. This was *the wrath of man,* and did not work any *righteous act* for *God;* nor was it the means of working righteousness in others; the bad fruit of a bad tree. And do they still vindicate these cruelties? Yes: for still they maintain that no faith is to be kept with heretics, and they acknowledge the *inquisition.*

802

A. M. cir. 4065.
A. D. cir. 61.
An. Olymp.
cir. CCX. 1.
A. U. C. cir.
814.

21 Wherefore, ᵈ lay apart all filthiness and superfluity of naughtiness, and receive with meekness the ingrafted word, ᵉ which is able to save your souls.

22 But ᶠ be ye doers of the word, and not hearers only, deceiving your own selves.

23 For ᵍ if any be a hearer of the word, and

Romans i. 16; 1 Cor. xv. 2; Eph. i. 13; Tit. ii. 11; Heb. ii. 3
1 Pet. i. 9.——ᶠ Matt. vii. 21; Luke vi. 46; xi. 28; Rom. ii. 13·
1 John iii. 7.——ᵍ Luke vi. 47, &c.; see chap. ii. 14, &c.

Verse 21. *All filthiness*] Πασαν ρυπαριαν. This word signifies any impurity that cleaves to the body; but applied to the mind, it implies all impure and unholy affections, such as those spoken of ver. 15, which pollute the soul; in this sense it is used by the best Greek writers.

Superfluity of naughtiness] Περισσειαν κακιας· The *overflowing of wickedness.* Perhaps there is an allusion here to the part cut off in circumcision, which was the emblem of impure desire; and to lessen that propensity, God, in his mercy, enacted this rite. Put all these evil dispositions aside, for they blind the soul, and render it incapable of receiving any good, even from that ingrafted word of God which otherwise would have saved their souls.

The ingrafted word] That doctrine which has already been *planted among you,* which has brought forth fruit in all them that have *meekly* and humbly received it, and is as *powerful to save your souls* as the souls of those who have already believed. I think this to be the meaning of εμφυτον λογον, the *ingrafted word* or *doctrine.* The seed of life had been sown in the land; many of them had received it to their salvation; others had partially credited it, but not so as to produce in them any saving effects. Besides, they appear to have taken up with other doctrines, from which they had got no salvation; he therefore exhorts them to receive the doctrine of Christ, which would be the means of saving them unto eternal life. And when those who were Jews, and who had been originally planted by God as altogether a right vine, received the faith of the Gospel, it is represented as being ingrafted on that right stock, the pure knowledge of the true God and his holy moral law. This indeed was a good stock on which to implant *Christianity.* This appears to be what the apostle means by the ingrafted word, which is able to save the soul.

Verse 22. *But be ye doers of the word*] They had heard this doctrine; they had believed it; but they had put it to no practical use. They were downright *Antinomians,* who put a sort of stupid, inactive faith in the place of all moral righteousness. This is sufficiently evident from the second chapter.

Deceiving your own selves.] Παραλογιζομενοι εαυτους· Imposing on your own selves by sophistical arguments; this is the meaning of the words. They had reasoned themselves into a state of carnal security, and the object of St. James is, to awake them out of their sleep.

Verse 23. *Beholding his natural face in a glass*]

(51**)

A. M. cir. 4065.
A. D. cir. 61.
An. Olymp.
cir. CCX. 1.
A. U. C. cir.
814.

not a doer, he is like unto a man beholding his natural face in a glass:

24 For he beholdeth himself, and goeth his way, and straightway forgetteth what manner of man he was.

25 But [h] whoso looketh into the perfect [i] law of liberty, and continueth *therein*, he being not a forgetful hearer, but a doer of the work, [k] this man shall be blessed in his [l] deed.

A. M. cir. 4065
A. D. cir. 61.
An. Olymp.
cir. CCX. 1.
A. U. C. cir.
814.

26 If any man among you seem to be reli-

---

[h] 2 Cor. iii. 18.——[i] Chap. ii. 12.

[k] John xiii. 17.——[r] Or, *doing*.

This metaphor is very simple, but very expressive. A man wishes to see his own face, and how, in its natural state, it appears; for this purpose he looks into a mirror, by which his real face, with all its blemishes and imperfections, is exhibited. He is affected with his own appearance; he sees deformities that might be remedied; spots, superfluities, and impurities, that might be removed. While he *continues to look* into the mirror he is affected, and wishes himself different to what he appears, and forms purposes of doing what he can to render his countenance agreeable. On going away he soon forgets what manner of person he was, because the mirror is now removed, and his face is no longer reflected to himself; and he no longer recollects how disagreeable he appeared, and his own resolutions of improving his countenance. The *doctrines* of God, faithfully preached, are such a *mirror;* he who hears cannot help discovering his own character, and being affected with his own deformity; he sorrows, and purposes amendment; but when the preaching is over, the mirror is removed, and not being careful to examine the records of his salvation, the *perfect law of liberty*, ver. 25, or *not continuing to look therein*, he soon forgets what manner of man he was; or, reposing some unscriptural trust in God's mercy, he reasons himself out of the necessity of repentance and amendment of life, and thus deceives his soul.

Verse 25. *But whoso looketh into the perfect law*] The word παρακυψας, which we translate *looketh into*, is very emphatic, and signifies that deep and attentive consideration given to a thing or subject which a man cannot bring up to his eyes, and therefore must *bend his back and neck, stooping down*, that he may see it to the greater advantage. The *law of liberty* must mean the *Gospel;* it is a *law*, for it *imposes obligations* from God, and prescribes a *rule of life;* and it *punishes* transgressors, and *rewards* the obedient. It is, nevertheless, a law that gives *liberty* from the guilt, power, dominion, and influence of sin; and it is *perfect*, providing a *fulness of salvation* for the soul: and it may be called *perfect* here, in opposition to the *law*, which was a system of types and representations of which the Gospel is the sum and substance. Some think that the word τελειον, *perfect*, is added here to signify that the *whole* of the Gospel must be considered and received, not a *part;* all its threatenings with its promises, all its precepts with its privileges.

And continueth] Παραμεινας· Takes time to see and examine the state of his soul, the grace of his God, the extent of his duty, and the height of the promised glory. The metaphor here is taken from those females who spend much time at their glass, in order that they may decorate themselves to the greatest advantage, and

not leave one hair, or the smallest ornament, out of its place.

He being not a forgetful hearer] This seems to be a reference to Deut. iv. 9: "Only take heed to thyself, and keep thy soul diligently, lest thou forget the things which thine eyes have seen, and lest they depart from thy heart all the days of thy life." *He who studies and forgets is like to a woman who brings forth children, and immediately buries them.* Aboth R. Nathan, cap. 23.

Shall be blessed in his deed.] In *Pirkey Aboth*, cap. v. 14, it is said: "There are four kinds of men who visit the synagogues, 1. He who enters but does not work. 2. He who works but does not enter. 3. He who enters and works. 4. He who neither enters nor works. The first two are indifferent characters; the *third* is the righteous man; the *fourth* is wholly evil."

As the path of duty is the way of *safety*, so it is the way of *happiness;* he who obeys God from a loving heart and pure conscience, will infallibly find continual blessedness.

Verse 26. *Seem to be religious*] The words θρησκος and θρησκεια, which we translate *religious* and *religion*, (see the next verse,) are of very uncertain etymology. *Suidas*, under the word θρησκευει, which he translates θεοσεβει· υπηρετει τοις θεοις, he *worships* or *serves the gods*, accounts for the derivation thus: "It is said that Orpheus, a *Thracian*, instituted the mysteries (or religious rites) of the Greeks, and called the worshiping of God θρησκευειν *threskeuein*, as being a *Thracian* invention." Whatever its derivation may be, the word is used both to signify *true religion*, and *superstition* or *heterodoxy*. See Hesychius, and see on verse 27.

Bridleth not his tongue] He who speaks not according to the oracles of God, whatever pretences he makes to religion, only shows, by his want of scriptural knowledge, that his religion is *false*, ματαιος, or *empty* of solid truth, profit to others, and profit to himself. Such a person should *bridle his tongue*, put the *bit in his mouth;* and particularly if he be a professed *teacher* of religion; no matter where he has studied, or what else he has learned, if he have not learned *religion*, he can never teach it. And religion is of such a nature that no man can learn it but by *experience;* he who does not feel the doctrine of God to be the power of God to the salvation of his soul, can neither teach religion, nor act according to its dictates, because he is an unconverted, unrenewed man. If he be *old*, let him retire to the desert, and pray to God for light; if he be in the *prime of life*, let him turn his attention to some honest calling; if he be *young*, let him tarry at Jericho till his beard grows.

2

A. M. cir. 4065.
A. D. cir. 61.
An. Olymp.
cir. CCX. 1.
A. U. C. cir.
814.

gious, and [m] bridleth not his tongue, but deceiveth his own heart, this man's religion *is* vain.

27 Pure religion, and undefiled

before God and the Father, is this, [n] To visit the fatherless and widows in their affliction, [o] *and* to keep himself unspotted from the world.

A. M. cir. 4065.
A. D. cir. 61.
An. Olymp.
cir. CCX. 1.
A. U. C. cir.
814.

[m] Psa. xxxiv. 13; xxxix. 1; 1 Pet. iii. 10.——[n] Isa. i. 16, 17;

lviii. 6, 7; Matt. xxv. 36.——[o] Rom. xii. 2; ch. iv. 4; 1 John v. 18.

Verse 27. *Pure religion, and undefiled*] Having seen something of the etymology of the word θρησκεια, which we translate *religion,* it will be well to consider the etymology of the word *religion* itself.

In the 28th chapter of the ivth book of his *Divine Instructions,* LACTANTIUS, who flourished about A. D. 300, treats of *hope, true religion,* and *superstition;* of the two latter he gives Cicero's definition from his book *De Natura Deorum,* lib. ii. c. 28, which with his own definition will lead us to a correct view, not only of the *etymology,* but of the *thing* itself.

" *Superstition,*" according to that philosopher, " had its name from the custom of those who offered daily prayers and sacrifices, that their children might SURVIVE THEM; *ut sui sibi liberi* superstites essent. Hence they were called *superstitiosi,* superstitious. On the other hand, religion, *religio,* had its name from those who, not satisfied with what was commonly spoken concerning the nature and worship of the gods, searched into the whole matter, and *perused the writings* of past times; hence they were called *religiosi,* from *re,* again, and *lego,* I read."

This definition Lactantius ridicules, and shows that religion has its name from *re,* intensive, and *ligo,* I bind, because of that *bond of piety* by which it *binds* us to God; and this he shows was the notion conceived of it by *Lucretius,* who laboured to *dissolve* this bond, and make men atheists.

Primum quod magnis doceo de rebus, et ARCTIS
RELIGIONUM *animos* NODIS EXSOLVERE *pergo.*

For first I teach great things in lofty strains,
And *loose* men from *religion's* grievous chains.
Lucret., lib. i., ver. 930, 931

As to *superstition,* he says it derived its name from those who paid religious veneration to the memory of the dead, (*qui superstitem memoriam defunctorem colunt,*) or from those who, *surviving* their parents, worshipped their images at home, as household gods; *aut qui, parentibus suis superstites, colebant imagines eorum domi, tanquam deos penates. Superstition,* according to others, refers to novel rites and ceremonies in religion, or to the worship of new gods. But by *religion* are meant the *ancient forms* of worship belonging to those gods, which had long been received. Hence that saying of Virgil :——

Vana superstitio veterumque ignara deorum.

" Vain superstition not knowing the ancient gods."

Here Lactantius observes, that as the ancient gods were consecrated precisely in the same way with *these new ones,* that therefore it was nothing but *superstition* from the beginning. Hence he asserts, the *superstitious* are those who worship many and false gods, and the *Christians* alone are *religious,* who worship and supplicate the one true God only. St. James' definition rather refers to the *effects* of *pure religion* than to its

nature. The *life of God in the soul of man,* producing *love to God* and *man,* will show itself in the acts which St. James mentions here. It is *pure* in the *principle,* for it is Divine truth and Divine love. It is *undefiled* in all its operations: it can produce nothing *unholy,* because it ever acts in the *sight of God;* and it can produce no *ungentle* word nor *unkind* act, because it comes from the *Father.*

The words καθαρα και αμιαντος, pure and undefiled, are supposed to have reference to a *diamond* or *precious stone,* whose perfection consists in its being *free from flaws;* not *cloudy,* but of a *pure water.* True religion is the *ornament* of the soul, and its *effects,* the ornament of the *life.*

To visit the fatherless and widows in their affliction] Works of *charity* and *mercy* are the proper fruits of religion; and none are more especially the objects of charity and mercy than the *orphans* and *widows* False religion may perform acts of mercy and charity; but its *motives* not being *pure,* and its principle being *defiled,* the *flesh,* self, and hypocrisy, *spot* the man, and *spot* his acts. True religion does not merely *give* something for the *relief* of the distressed, but it *visits them,* it takes *the oversight of them,* it takes them under its care; so επισκεπτεσθαι means. It goes to their houses, and speaks to their hearts; it relieves their wants, sympathizes with them in their distresses, instructs them in Divine things, and recommends them to God. And all this it does for the Lord's sake. This is the religion of Christ. The religion that does not prove itself by works of charity and mercy is not of God. Reader, what religion hast thou? Has thine ever led thee to cellars, garrets, cottages, and houses, to find out the distressed? Hast thou ever fed, clothed, and visited a destitute representative of Christ?

The subject in verse 11 suggests several reflections on the mutability of human affairs, and the end of all things.

1. Nature herself is subject to mutability, though by her secret and inscrutable exertions she effects her renovation from her decay, and thus *change* is prevented from terminating in *destruction.* Yet nature herself is tending, by continual *mutations,* to a final destruction; or rather to a fixed state, when *time,* the place and sphere of mutability, shall be absorbed in eternity. Time and nature are coeval; they began and must terminate together. All *changes* are efforts to arrive at destruction or renovation; and destruction must be the *term* or bound of all created things, had not the Creator purposed that his works should endure for ever. According to his promise, we look for a new heaven and a new earth; a fixed, permanent, and endless state of things; an everlasting sabbath to all the works of God.

I shall confirm these observations with the last verses of that incomparable poem, the *Faery Queene,* of our much neglected but unrivalled poet, *Edmund Spenser* :——

"When I bethink me on that speech whylear,
Of *mutability*, and well it weigh ;
Me seems, that though she all unworthy were
Of the *heaven's rule ;* yet very sooth to say,
In *all things else she bears the greatest sway ;*
Which makes me loath this state of life so tickle,
And love of things so vain to cast away ;
Whose *flow'ring pride*, so *fading* and so *fickle*,
Short Time shall soon cut down with his consuming sickle.

Then gin I think on that which *Nature* sayd,
Of that same time when *no more change* shall be,
But *stedfast* rest of all things, firmly stayd
Upon the pillours of eternity,
That is contrayr to *mutability :*
For all that *moveth*, doth in *change* delight :
But thenceforth all shall rest eternally
With him that is the God of Sabaoth hight :
O that great Sabaoth God, grant me that Sabaoth's sight !"

When this is to be the glorious *issue*, who can regret the speedy lapse of time ? Mutability shall end in permanent perfection, when time, the destroyer of all things, shall be absorbed in eternity. And what has a righteous man to fear from that " wreck of matter and that crush of worlds," which to him shall usher in the glories of an eternal day ? A moralist has said, " Though heaven shall vanish like a vapour, and this firm globe of earth shall crumble into dust, the righteous man shall stand unmoved amidst the shocked depredations of a crushed world; for he who hath appointed the heavens and the earth to fail, hath said unto the virtuous soul, Fear not ! for *thou* shalt neither perish nor be wretched."

Dr. *Young* has written most nervously, in the spirit of the highest order of poetry, and with the knowledge and feeling of a sound divine, on this subject, in his Night Thoughts. Night vi. *in fine.*

Of man *immortal* hear the lofty style :——

"If so decreed, th' Almighty will be done.
Let earth dissolve, yon ponderous orbs descend
And grind us into dust : the *soul* is safe ;
The *man* emerges ; mounts above the wreck,
As towering flame from nature's funeral pyre ;
O'er desolation, as a gainer, smiles ;
His charter, his inviolable rights,
Well pleased to learn from thunder's impotence,
Death's pointless darts, and hell's defeated storms."

After him, and borrowing his *imagery* and *ideas*, another of our poets, *in canticis sacris facile princeps*, has expounded and improved the whole in the following hymn on the *Judgment.*

"Stand the Omnipotent decree,
    Jehovah's will be done !
Nature's end we wait to see,
    And hear her final groan.
Let this earth dissolve, and blend
    In death the wicked and the just ;
Let those ponderous orbs descend
    And grind us into dust.

Rests secure the righteous man ;
    At his Redeemer's beck,
Sure to emerge, and rise again,
    And mount above the wreck.
Lo ! the heavenly spirit towers
    Like flames o'er nature's funeral pyre ;
Triumphs in immortal powers,
    And claps her wings of fire.

Nothing hath the just to lose
    By worlds on worlds destroy'd ;
Far beneath his feet he views,
    With smiles, the flaming void ;
Sees the universe renew'd ;
    The grand millennial reign begun ;
Shouts with all the sons of God
    Around th' eternal throne."   WESLEY

One word more, and I shall trouble my reader no farther on a subject on which I could wear out my pen and drain the last drop of my ink. The learned reader will join in the wish.

" Talia sæcla suis dixerunt, currite, fusis
Concordes stabili fatorum numine Parcæ.
Aggredere O magnos (aderit jam tempus !) honores,
Cara Deum soboles, magnum Jovis incrementum.
Aspice convexo nutantem pondere mundum,
Terrasque, tractusque maris, cœlumque profundum :
Aspice, venturo lætentur ut omnia sæclo.
O mihi tam longæ maneat pars *ultima* vitæ,
Spiritus, et quantum sat erit tua dicere facta !"
    VIRG. *Eclog.* iv.

There has never been a translation of this, worthy of the poet ; and to such a piece I cannot persuade myself to append the hobbling verses of Mr. Dryden.

2. Taken in every point of view, the 17th verse is one of the most curious and singular in the New Testament. It has been well observed, that the first words make a regular *Greek hexameter verse*, supposed to be quoted from some Greek poet not now extant; and the last clause of the verse, with a very little change, makes another hexameter :——

Πασα δοσις αγαθη, και παν δωρημα τέλειον,
Εστ' απο των φωτων Πατρος καταβαινον ανωθεν.

" Every goodly gift, and every perfect donation,
    Is from the Father of lights, and from above it descendeth."

The first line, which is incontestably a *perfect hexameter*, may have been designed by St. James, or in the course of composition may have originated from accident, a thing which often occurs to all good writers ; but the sentiment itself is immediately from heaven, I know not that we can be justified by sound criticism in making any particular distinction between δοσις and δωρημα· our translators have used the same word in rendering both. They are often synonymous ; but sometimes we may observe a shade of difference, δοσις signifying a *gift* of any kind, here probably meaning *earthly blessings* of all sorts, δωρημα signifying a *free gift*—one that comes without constraint, from the mere *benevolence* of the giver ; and here it may signify all *spiritual and eternal blessings.* Now all these *come from above ;* God is as much the AUTHOR of our *earthly good*, as he is of our *eternal salvation.* Earthly blessings are simply *good;* but they are *imperfect,* they perish in the using. The blessings of *grace* and *glory* are supreme goods, they are permanent and perfect; and to the *gift* that includes these the term τελειον, *perfect,* is here properly added by St. James. There is a sentiment very similar to this in the ninth Olympic Ode of Pindar, l. 41:—

—————————Αγαθοι δε
Και σοφοι κατα Δαιμον' ανδρες.

Man, boast of naught: whate'er thou hast is given;
Wisdom and virtue are the gifts of Heaven.

But how tame is even Pindar's verse when compared with the energy of James!

3. In the latter part of the verse, παρ ᾧ ουκ ενι παραλλαγη, η τροπης αποσκιασμα, which we translate, *with whom is no variableness, neither shadow of turning,* there is an allusion to some of the most abstruse principles in astronomy. This is not accidental, for every word in the whole verse is astronomical. In his Πατηρ των φωτων, *Father of lights,* there is the most evident allusion to the SUN, who is the *father, author,* or *source* of all the *lights* or luminaries proper to our system. It is not only his light which *we* enjoy by day, but it is his light also which is reflected to us, from the moon's surface, by *night.* And it is demonstrable that all the *planets*—*Mercury, Venus, the Earth,* the *Moon, Mars, Ceres, Pallas, Juno, Vesta, Jupiter, Saturn,* Saturn's *Rings,* and *Herschel,* or the *Georgium Sidus,* with the *four* satellites of Jupiter, the *seven* satellites of Saturn, and the *six* satellites of the Georgium Sidus, thirty-one bodies in all, besides the *comets,* all derive their light from the sun, being perfectly *opaque* or *dark* in themselves; the sun being the only luminous body in our system; all the rest being *illumined* by him.

The word παραλλαγη, which we translate *variableness,* from παραλλαττω, *to change alternately, to pass from one change to another,* evidently refers to *parallax* in astronomy. To give a proper idea of what astronomers mean by this term, it must be premised that all the diurnal motions of the heavenly bodies from east to west are only *apparent,* being occasioned by the rotation of the earth upon its axis in an opposite direction in about twenty-four hours. These diurnal motions are therefore performed *uniformly* round the axis or polar diameter of the earth, and not round the place of the spectator, who is upon the earth's surface. Hence every one who observes the apparent motion of the heavens from this surface will find that this motion is not even, equal arches being described in unequal times; for if a globular body, such as the earth, describe equally the circumference of a circle by its rotatory motion, it is evident the equality of this motion can be seen in no other points than those in the axis of the circle, and therefore any object viewed from the centre of the earth will appear in a different place from what it does when observed from the surface. This difference of place of the same object, seen at the same time from the earth's centre and surface, is called its *parallax.*

As I shall make some farther use of this point, in order to make it plain to those who are not much acquainted with the subject, to which I am satisfied St. James alludes, I shall introduce the following diagram :

Let the circle OKNS, in the annexed figure, represent the *earth,* E its *centre,* O the *place* of an *observer* on its surface, whose *visible* or *sensible horizon* is OH, and the line EST, parallel to OH, the *rational, true,* or *mathematical horizon.* Let ZDFT be considered a portion of a *great circle* in the heavens, and A the *place* of an *object* in the visible *horizon.* Join EA by a line produced to C : then C is the *true* place of the object, and H is its *apparent* place; and the angle CAH is its *parallax;* and, because the object is in the horizon, it is called its *horizontal parallax.* As OAE, the angle which the earth's radius or semidiameter subtends to the object, is necessarily equal to its opposite angle CAH, hence the *horizontal parallax* of an object is defined to be the angle which the earth's semidiameter subtends at that object.

The whole effect of parallax is in a *vertical* direction; for the parallactic angle is in the *plane* passing through the *observer* and the *earth's centre,* which plane is necessarily *perpendicular* to the *horizon,* the earth being considered as a *sphere.* The more *elevated* an object is above the horizon, the *less* the *parallax,* the distance from the earth's centre continuing the same. To make this sufficiently clear, let B represent an object at any given altitude above the visible horizon OAH; then the angle DBF, formed by the straight lines OB and EB produced to F and D, will be the parallax of the object at the given altitude, and is less than the parallax of the same object when in the visible horizon OAH, for the angle DBF is less than the angle CAH. Hence the horizontal parallax is the greatest of all diurnal parallaxes; and when the object is in the *zenith,* it has no *parallax,* the visual ray passing perpendicularly *from* the *object* through the *observer* to the earth's *centre,* as in the line ZOE.

The quantity of the horizontal parallax of any object is in proportion to its distance from the place of observation, being greater or less as the object is nearer to or farther removed from the spectator. In illustration of this point, let I be the place of an object in the sensible horizon; then will LIH be its horizontal parallax, which is a smaller angle than CAH, the horizontal parallax of the nearer object A.

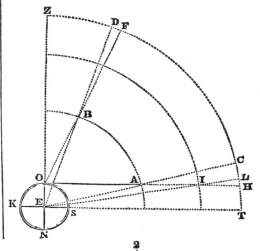

The horizontal parallax being given, the distance of the object from the earth's centre, EA or EI, may be readily found in semidiameters of the earth by the resolution of the right-angled triangle OEA, in which we have given the angle OAE, the horizontal parallax, the side OE, the semidiameter of the earth, considered as unity, and the right angle AOE, to find the side EA, the distance of the object from the earth's centre. The proportion to be used in this case is : The sine of the horizontal parallax is to unity, the semidiameter of the earth, as radius, *i. e.* the right angle AOE, the sine of ninety degrees being the radius of a circle, is to the side EA. This proportion is very compendiously wrought by logarithms as follows : Subtract the logarithmic sine of the horizontal parallax from 10, the radius, and the remainder will be the logarithm of the answer.

Example. When the moon's horizontal parallax is a degree, what is her distance from the earth's centre in semidiameters of the earth?

From the radius,	- -	10·0000000
Subtract the sine of 1 degree		8·2418553

Remainder the logarithm of 57·2987 1·7581447

Which is the distance of the moon in semidiameters of the earth, when her horizontal parallax amounts to a degree. If 57·2987 be multiplied by 3977, the English miles contained in the earth's semidiameter, the product, 227876·9, will be the moon's distance from the earth's centre in English miles.

The sun's horizontal parallax is about *eight seconds* and *three-fifths*, as is evident from the phenomena attending the transits of Venus, of 1761 and 1769, as observed in different parts of the world : a method of obtaining the solar parallax abundantly less liable to be materially affected by error of observation than that of Hipparchus, who lived between the 154th and 163d Olympiad, from lunar eclipses ; or than that of Aristarchus the Samian, from the moon's dichotomy ; or even than that of modern astronomers from the parallax of Mars when in opposition, and, at the same time, in or near his perihelion. The sun's horizontal parallax being scarcely the four hundred and eighteenth part of that of the moon given in the preceding example, if 227876·9, the distance of the moon as found above, be multiplied by 418·6, (for the horizontal parallax decreases nearly in proportion as the distance increases,) the product will be the distance of the sun from the earth's centre, which will be found to be upwards of *ninety-five millions* of English *miles.*

When we know the horizontal parallax of any object, its magnitude is easily determined. The apparent diameter of the sun, for example, at his mean distance from the earth, is somewhat more than *thirty-two minutes of a degree*, which is at least a hundred and eleven times greater than the double of the sun's horizontal parallax, or the apparent diameter of the earth as seen from the sun ; therefore, the real solar diameter must be at least a *hundred and eleven* times greater that that of the earth; *i. e.* upwards of 880,000 English miles. And as spherical bodies are to each other as the cubes of their diameters, if 111 be cubed, we shall find that the magnitude of the sun is more than *thirteen hundred thousand* times greater than that of the earth.

The whole effect of parallax being in a *vertical circle*, and the circles of the sphere not being in this direction, the parallax of a star will evidently change its true place with respect to these different circles ; whence there are *five* kinds of diurnal parallaxes, *viz.* the parallax of *longitude*, parallax of *latitude*, parallax of *ascension* or *descension*, parallax of *declination*, and parallax of *altitude*, the last of which has been already largely explained ; and the meaning of the first four, simply, is the *difference* between the *true* and *visible* longitude, latitude, right ascension, and declination of an object. Besides these, there is another kind of parallax, called by modern astronomers the *parallax* of the *earth's* ANNUAL ORBIT, by which is meant the difference between the places of a planet as seen from the sun and the earth at the same time, the former being its *true* or *heliocentric* place, and the latter its *apparent* or *geocentric* place. The ancient astronomers gave the term *parallax* only to the diurnal apparent inequalities of motion in the moon and planets ; Ptolemy, who lived in the second century, calling *prosaphæresis orbis* what is now named the *parallax* of the *great* or *annual orbit*. This parallax is more considerable than the diurnal parallax, as the earth's annual orbit is more considerable than the earth's semidiameter. This parallax, when greatest, amounts in Mars, the nearest superior planet, to upwards of *forty-seven* degrees ; in Jupiter to near *twelve* degrees ; in Saturn to more than *six* degrees, &c. In the region of the nearest fixed stars, *i. e.* those new ones of 1572 and 1604, *double* the *radius* of the earth's orbit does not subtend an angle of a *single minute* of a degree ; whence it is evident the nearest fixed stars are at least *hundreds of times* more distant from us than the Georgium Sidus is, whose greatest annual parallax amounts to upwards of *three* degrees. The annual parallaxes of the fixed stars are, in general, *too minute* to be measured ; hence their distances from the earth must be inconceivably great.

Any farther description of parallax would be useless in reference to the subject to be illustrated.

The words τροπης αποσκιασμα, *shadow of turning*, either refer to the darkness in which the earth is involved in consequence of its *turning round its axis* once in every twenty-four hours, by means of which one hemisphere, or half of its surface, is involved in darkness, being hidden from the sun by the opposite hemisphere ; or to the different portions of the earth which come gradually into the solar light by its revolution round its *orbit*, which, in consequence of the pole of the earth being inclined nearly twenty-three degrees and a half to the plane of its orbit, and keeping its *parallelism* through every part of its revolution, causes all the *vicissitudes of season*, with all the increasing and decreasing proportions of light and darkness, and of cold and heat.

Every person who understands the images will see with what propriety St. James has introduced them ; and through this his great object is at once discernible. It is evident from this chapter that there were persons, among those to whom he wrote, that held

2

very erroneous opinions concerning the Divine nature; *viz.* that God tempted or influenced men to sin, and, consequently, that he was the author of all the evil that is in the world; and that he withholds his light and influence when necessary to convey truth and to correct vice. To destroy this error he shows that though the sun, for its *splendour, genial heat,* and *general utility* to the globe and its inhabitants, may be a fit emblem of God, yet in several respects the metaphor is very *imperfect;* for the sun himself is liable to repeated obscurations; and although, as to his mass, he is the *focus of the system,* giving light and heat to all, yet he is not everywhere present, and both his light and heat may be intercepted by a great variety of opposing bodies, and other causes. St. James refers particularly to the Divine *ubiquity* or omnipresence. Wherever his light and energy are, there is he *himself;* neither his *word* nor his *Spirit* gives false or inconsistent views of his nature and gracious purposes. He has no *parallax,* because he is equally present everywhere, and intimately *near* to all his creatures; HE is never *seen where* he *is not,* or *not seen* where he *is. He is the God and Father of all; who is* ABOVE *all, and* THROUGH *all, and* IN *all;* " in the wide waste, as in the city full;" nor can any thing be hidden from his light and heat. There can be no opposing bodies to prevent him from sending forth his light and truth, because he is everywhere *essentially* present. He suffers no *eclipses;* he *changes* not in his nature; he varies not in his designs; he is ever a full, free, and eternal fountain of mercy, goodness, truth, and good will, to all his intelligent offspring. Hallelujah, the Lord God Omnipotent reigneth! Amen.

IN concluding these observations, I think it necessary to refer to Mr. Wakefield's translation of this text, and his vindication of that translation: *Every good gift, and every perfect kindness, cometh down from above, from the Father of lights, with whom is no parallax, nor tropical shadow.* "Some have affected," says he, "to ridicule my translation of this verse; if it be obscure, the author must answer for that, and not the translator. Why should we impoverish the sacred writers, by *robbing* them of the learning and science they display? Why should we *conceal* in *them* what we should *ostentatiously point out* in *profane authors?* And if any of these wise, learned, and judicious critics think they understand the phrase *shadow of turning,* I wish they would condescend to explain it." Yes, if such a sentiment were found in *Aratus,* or in any other *ancient* astronomical writer, whole pages of commentary would be written on it, and the subtle doctrine of the parallactic angle proved to be well known in itself, and its use in determining the distances and magnitudes of the heavenly bodies, to the ancients some hundreds of years before the Christian era.

The sentiment is as elegant as it is just, and forcibly points out the *unchangeableness* and *beneficence* of God. He is the Sun, not of a system, but of all worlds; the great Fountain and Dispenser of light and heat, of power and life, of order, harmony, and perfection. In him all live and move, and from him they have their being. There are no *spots* on his disk; all is unclouded splendour. Can he who dwells in this unsufferable and unapproachable light, in his own eternal self-sufficiency, concern himself with the affairs of mortals? Yes, *for we are his offspring;* and it is one part of his perfection to delight in the welfare of his intelligent creatures. He is loving to every man: he hates nothing that he has made; and his praise endureth for ever!

CHAPTER II.

We should not prefer the rich to the poor, nor show any partiality inconsistent with the Gospel of Christ, 1—4. God has chosen the poor, rich in faith, to be heirs of his kingdom, even those whom some among their brethren despised and oppressed, 5, 6. They should love their neighbour as themselves, and have no respect of persons, 7—9. He who breaks one command of God is guilty of the whole, 10, 11. They should act as those who shall be judged by the law of liberty; and he shall have judgment without mercy, who shows no mercy, 12, 13. Faith without works of charity and mercy is dead; nor can it exist where there are no good works, 14—20. Abraham proved his faith by his works, 21—24. And so did Rahab, 25. As the body without the soul is dead, so is faith without good works, 26.

A. M. cir. 4065. A. D. cir. 61. An. Olymp. cir. CCX. I. A. U. C. cir. 814.		A. M. cir. 4065. A. D. cir. 61. An. Olymp. cir. CCX. I. A. U. C. cir. 814.

MY brethren, have not the faith of our Lord Jesus Christ, [a] *the Lord* of glory, with [b] respect of persons.

2 For if there come unto your [c] assembly a man with a gold ring, in goodly apparel, and there come in also a poor man in vile raiment;

---

[a] 1 Cor. ii. 8.——[b] Lev. xix. 15; Deut. i. 17; xvi. 19; Prov. xxiv. 23; xxviii. 21; Matt. xxii. 16; ver. 9; Jude 16.——[c] Gr. *synagogue.*

NOTES ON CHAP. II.

Verse 1. *My brethren, have not*] This verse should be read interrogatively: *My brethren, do ye not make profession of the faith or religion of our glorious Lord Jesus Christ with acceptance of persons?* That is, preferring the rich to the poor merely because of their riches, and not on account of any moral excellence, personal piety, or public usefulness. Πιστις, *faith,* is put here for religion; and της δοξης, *of glory,* should, according to some critics, be construed with it as the Syriac and Coptic have done. Some connect it with *our Lord Jesus Christ—the religion of our glorious*

A. M. cir. 4065.
A. D. cir. 61.
An. Olymp.
cir. CCX. 1.
A. U. C. cir.
814.

3 And ye have respect to him that weareth the gay clothing, and say unto him, Sit thou here ^din a good place; and say to the poor, Stand thou there, or sit here under my footstool:

4 Are ye not then partial in yourselves, and are become judges of evil thoughts?

5 Hearken, my beloved brethren, ^eHath not God chosen the poor of this world ^frich in faith, and heirs of ^gthe kingdom ^hwhich he

hath promised to them that love him?

A. M. cir. 4065.
A. D. cir. 61.
An. Olymp.
cir. CCX. 1.
A. U. C. cir.
814.

6 But ⁱye have despised the poor. Do not rich men oppress you, ^kand draw you before the judgment-seats?

7 Do not they blaspheme that worthy name by the which ye are called?

8 If ye fulfil the royal law according to the scripture, ^lThou shalt love thy neighbour as thyself, ye do well;

---

^d Or, *well; or, seemly.*——^e John vii. 48; 1 Cor. i. 26, 28.
^f Luke xii. 21; 1 Tim. vi. 18; Rev. ii. 9.——^g Or, *that.*——^h Exod.
xx. 6; 1 Sam. ii. 30; Prov. viii. 17; Matt. v. 3; Luke vi. 20;

xii. 32; 1 Cor. ii. 9; 2 Tim. iv. 8; chap. i. 12.——ⁱ 1 Cor. xi.
22.——^k Acts xiii. 50; xvii. 6; xviii. 12; chap. v. 6.——^l Lev.
xix. 18; Matt. xxii. 39; Rom. xiii. 8, 9; Gal. v. 14; vi. 2.

Lord Jesus Christ. Others translate thus, *the faith of the glory of our Lord Jesus.* There are many various readings in the MSS. and versions on this verse: the meaning is clear enough, though the connection be rather obscure.

Verse 2. *If there come unto your assembly*] Εις την συναγωγην· *Into the synagogue.* It appears from this that the apostle is addressing *Jews* who frequented their synagogues, and carried on their worship there and judicial proceedings, as the Jews were accustomed to do. Our word *assembly* does not express the original; and we cannot suppose that these synagogues were at this time occupied with Christian worship, but that the Christian Jews continued to frequent them for the purpose of hearing the law and the prophets read, as they had formerly done, previously to their conversion to the Christian faith. But St. James may refer here to proceedings in a court of justice.

With a gold ring, in goodly apparel] The ring on the finger and the splendid garb were proofs of the man's opulence; and his *ring* and his *coat*, not his *worth*, moral good qualities, or the righteousness of his cause, procured him the respect of which St. James speaks.

There come in also a poor man] In ancient times petty courts of judicature were held in the synagogues, as *Vitringa* has sufficiently proved, *De Vet. Syn.* l. 3, p. 1, c. 11; and it is probable that the case here adduced was one of a judicial kind, where, of the two *parties*, one was *rich* and the other *poor;* and the master or ruler of the synagogue, or he who presided in this court, paid particular deference to the rich man, and neglected the poor man; though, as *plaintiff* and *defendant*, they were equal in the eye of justice, and should have been considered so by an impartial judge.

Verse 3. *Sit here under my footstool*] Thus evidently prejudging the cause, and giving the poor man to see that he was to expect no impartial administration of justice in his cause.

Verse 4. *Are ye not then partial*] Ου διεκριθητε· *Do ye not make a distinction,* though the case has not been heard, and the law has not decided?

Judges of evil thoughts?] Κριται διαλογισμων πονηρων· *Judges of evil reasonings;* that is, *judges who reason wickedly;* who, in effect, say in your hearts, **we will** espouse the cause of the *rich,* because they

can befriend us; we will neglect that of the poor, because they cannot help us, nor have they power to hurt us.

Verse 5. *Hath not God chosen the poor of this world*] This seems to refer to Matt. xi. 5: *And the poor have the Gospel preached to them.* These believed on the Lord Jesus, and found his salvation; while the *rich* despised, neglected, and persecuted him. These had that faith in Christ which put them in possession of the *choicest spiritual blessings*, and gave them a *right* to the *kingdom of heaven.* While, therefore, they were despised of men, they were highly prized of God.

Verse 6. *Do not rich men oppress you*] The administration of justice was at this time in a miserable state of corruption among the Jews; but a *Christian* was one who was to expect no justice any where but from his God. The words καταδυναστευουσιν, *exceedingly oppress,* and ἑλκουσιν εις κριτηρια, *drag you to courts of justice,* show how grievously oppressed and maltreated the Christians were by their countrymen the Jews, who made *law* a pretext to afflict their bodies, and spoil them of their property.

Verse 7. *Blaspheme that worthy name*] They took every occasion to asperse the *Christian* name and the Christian faith, and have been, from the beginning to the present day, famous for their blasphemies against Christ and his religion. It is evident that these were *Jews* of whom St. James speaks; no *Christians* in these early times could have acted the part here mentioned.

Verse 8. *The royal law*] Νομον βασιλικον. This epithet, of all the New Testament writers, is peculiar to James; but it is frequent among the Greek writers in the sense in which it appears St. James uses it. Βασιλικος, *royal,* is used to signify any thing that is of general concern, is suitable to all, and necessary for all, as brotherly love is. This commandment, *Thou shalt love thy neighbour as thyself,* is a *royal law,* not only because it is ordained of God, and proceeds from his *kingly* authority over men, but because it is so *useful, suitable,* and *necessary* to the present state of man; and as it was given us particularly by Christ himself, John xiii. 34; xv. 12, who is our *King,* as well as Prophet and Priest, it should ever put us in mind of his *authority* over us, and our *subjection to*

3

A. M. cir. 4065.
A. D. cir. 61.
An. Olymp.
cir. CCX. 1.
A. U. C. cir.
814.

9 But ^m if ye have respect to persons, ye commit sin, and are convinced of the law as transgressors.

10 For whosoever shall keep the whole law, and yet offend in one *point*, ⁿ he is guilty of all.

11 For ^o he that said, ^p Do not commit adultery, said also, Do not kill. Now if thou com-

mit no adultery, yet if thou kill, thou art become a transgressor of the law.

12 So speak ye, and so do, as they that shall be judged by ^q the law of liberty,

13 For ^r he shall have judgment without mercy, that hath showed no mercy; and ^s mercy ^t rejoiceth against judgment.

A. M. cir. 4065.
A. D. cir. 61.
An. Olymp.
cir. CCX. 1.
A. U. C. cir.
814.

^m Ver. 1.——ⁿ Deut. xxvii. 26 ; Matt. v. 19 ; Gal. iii. 10.
^o Or, *that law which said.*——^p Exod. xx. 13, 14.——^q Chap. i. 25.

^r Job xxii. 6, &c. ; Prov. xxi. 13 ; Matt. vi. 15 ; xviii. 35 ; xxv. 41, 42.——^s 1 John iv. 17, 18.——^t Or, *glorieth.*

him. As the *regal state* is the most excellent for secular dignity and civil utility that exists among men, hence we give the epithet *royal* to whatever is excellent, noble, grand, or useful.

Verse 9. *But if ye have respect to persons*] In judgment, or in any other way; *ye commit sin* against God, and against your brethren, and are *convinced*, ελεγχομενοι, and are *convicted*, *by the law ;* by this royal law, Thou shalt love thy neighbour as thyself; *as transgressors*, having shown this sinful acceptance of persons, which has led you to refuse *justice* to the *poor man*, and uphold the *rich* in his oppressive conduct.

Verse 10. *For whosoever shall keep the whole law, &c.*] This is a rabbinical form of speech. In the tract *Shabbath*, fol. 70, where they dispute concerning the thirty-nine works commanded by Moses, Rabbi Yochanan says: *But if a man do the whole, with the omission of one, he is guilty of the whole, and of every one.* In *Bammidbar rabba*, sec. 9, fol. 200, and in *Tanchum*, fol. 60, there is a copious example given, how an *adulteress*, by that one crime, *breaks all the ten commandments*, and by the same mode of proof any one sin may be shown to be a breach of the whole decalogue. The truth is, any sin is against the Divine authority; and he who has committed one transgression is guilty of death; and by his one deliberate act dissolves, as far as he can, the sacred connection that subsists between all the Divine precepts and the obligation which he is under to obey, and thus casts off in effect his allegiance to God. For, if God should be obeyed in any one instance, he should be obeyed in all, as the authority and reason of obedience are the same in every case; he therefore who breaks one of these laws is, in effect, if not in fact, guilty of the whole. But there is scarcely a more *common form of speech* among the rabbins than this, for they consider that any one sin has the seeds of all others in it. See a multitude of examples in *Schoettgen*.

Verse 11. *For he that said*] That is, the authority that gave one commandment gave also the rest; and he who breaks one resists this authority; so that the breach of any one commandment may be justly considered a breach of the whole law. It was a maxim also among the Jewish doctors that, if a man kept any one commandment carefully, though he broke all the rest, he might assure himself of the favour of God; for while they taught that "He who transgresses all the precepts of the law has broken the yoke, dis-

solved the covenant, and exposed the law to contempt, and so has he done who has broken even one precept," (*Mechiltá*, fol. 5, *Yalcut Simeoni*, part 1, fol. 59,) they also taught, "that he who observed any *principal* command was equal to him who kept the whole law ;" (*Kiddushin*, fol. 39 ;) and they give for example, "If a man abandon idolatry, it is the same as if he had fulfilled the whole law," (*Ibid.*, fol. 40.) To correct this false doctrine James lays down that in the 11th verse. Thus they *did* and *undid*.

Verse 12. *So speak ye, and so do*] Have respect to every commandment of God, for this the *law of liberty*—the Gospel of Jesus Christ, particularly requires; and this is the law by which all mankind, who have had the opportunity of knowing it, shall be judged. But all along St. James particularly refers to the precept, *Thou shalt love thy neighbour as thyself.*

Verse 13. *For he shall have judgment*] He who shows no mercy to man, or, in other words, he who does not exercise himself in works of charity and mercy to his needy fellow creatures, shall receive no mercy at the hand of God; for he hath said, *Blessed are the merciful, for they shall obtain mercy.* The unmerciful therefore are *cursed*, and they shall obtain no mercy.

Mercy rejoiceth against judgment.] These words are variously understood. 1. *Mercy*, the merciful man, the abstract for the concrete, exults over judgment, that is, he is not afraid of it, having acted according to the law of liberty, *Thou shalt love thy neighbour as thyself.* 2. Ye shall be exalted by mercy above judgment. 3. For he (God) exalts mercy above judgment. 4. A merciful man rejoices rather in opportunities of showing mercy, than in acting according to strict justice. 5. In the great day, though justice might condemn every man according to the rigour of the law, yet God will cause mercy to triumph over justice in bringing those into his glory who, for his sake, had fed the hungry, clothed the naked, ministered to the sick, and visited the prisoners. See what our Lord says, Matt. xxv. 31—46.

In the MSS. and versions there is a considerable variety of readings on this verse, and some of the senses given above are derived from those readings. The spirit of the saying may be found in another scripture, *I will have mercy and not sacrifice*—I prefer works of charity and mercy to every thing else, and especially to all acts of worship. The ROYAL LAW, *Thou shalt love thy neighbour as thyself*, should par-

2

A. M. cir. 4065.
A. D. cir. 61.
An. Olymp.
cir. CCX. 1.
A. U. C. cir.
814.

14 [u] What *doth it* profit, my brethren, though a man say he hath faith, and have not works ? Can faith save him ?

15 [v] If a brother or sister be naked, and destitute of daily food,

16 And [w] one of you say unto them, Depart in peace, be *ye* warmed and filled; notwithstanding ye give them not those things which are needful to the body ; what *doth it* profit ?

17 Even so faith, if it hath not works, is dead, being [x] alone.

18 Yea, a man may say, Thou hast faith,

A. M. cir. 4065
A. D. cir. 61
An. Olymp.
cir. CCX. 1.
A. U. C. cir.
814.

---

[u] Matt. vii. 26 ; chap. i. 23.——[v] See Job xxxi. 19, 20; Luke iii. 11.——[w] 1 John iii. 18.——[x] Gr. *by itself.*

---

ticularly prevail among *men,* because of the miserable state to which all are reduced by sin, so that each particularly needs the help of his brother.

Verse 14. *What doth it profit—though a man say he hath faith*] We now come to a part of this epistle which has appeared to some eminent men to contradict other portions of the Divine records. In short, it has been thought that James teaches the doctrine of *justification by the merit of good works,* while Paul asserts this to be insufficient, and that man is *justified by faith.* Luther, supposing that James did actually teach the doctrine of justification by works, which his good sense showed him to be absolutely insufficient for salvation, was led to condemn the epistle *in toto,* as a production unauthenticated by the Holy Spirit, and consequently worthy of no regard ; he therefore termed it *epistola straminea, a chaffy epistle,* an *epistle of straw,* fit only to be burnt. Learned men have spent much time in striving to reconcile these two writers, and to show that St. Paul and St. James perfectly accord ; one teaching the pure doctrine, the other guarding men against the abuse of it. Mr. *Wesley* sums the whole up in the following words, with his usual accuracy and precision : " From chap. i. 22 the apostle has been enforcing Christian practice. He now applies to those who neglect this under the pretence of faith. St. Paul had taught that *a man is justified by faith without the works of the law.* This some already began to wrest to their own destruction. Wherefore St. James, purposely repeating, ver. 21, 23, 25, the same phrases, testimonies, and examples which St. Paul had used, Rom. iv. 3 ; Heb. xi. 17, 31, refutes not the doctrine of St. Paul, but the error of those who abused it. There is therefore no contradiction between the apostles ; they both delivered the truth of God, but in a different manner, as having to do with different kinds of men. This verse is a summary of what follows : *What profiteth it,* is enlarged on, ver. 15—17; *though a man say,* ver. 18, 19; *can that faith save him ?* ver. 20. It is not *though he have faith,* but *though he say, I have faith.* Here therefore true living faith is meant. But in other parts of the argument the apostle speaks of a dead imaginary faith. He does not therefore teach that true faith *can,* but that it *cannot,* subsist without works. Nor does he oppose *faith* to *works,* but that empty name of faith to real faith working by love. *Can that faith which is without works save him ?* No more than it can profit his neighbour."—*Explanatory notes.*

That St James quotes the same scriptures, and uses the same phrases, testimonies, and examples which St. Paul has done, is fully evident ; but it does not follow that he wrote *after* St. Paul. It is *possible* that one had seen the epistle of the other ; but if so, it is strange that neither of them should quote the other. That St. Paul might write to correct the abuses of St. James' doctrine is as possible as that James wrote to prevent St. Paul's doctrine from being abused ; for there were *Antinomians* in the Church in the time of St. James, as there were *Pharisaic persons* in it at the time of St. Paul. I am inclined to think that James is the elder writer, and rather suppose that neither of them had ever seen the other's epistle. Allowing them both to be inspired, God could teach each what was necessary for the benefit of the Church, without their having any knowledge of each other. See the preface to this epistle.

As the Jews in general were very strenuous in maintaining the *necessity of good works* or *righteousness* in order to justification, wholly neglecting the doctrine of *faith,* it is not to be wondered at that those who were converted, and saw the absolute necessity of *faith* in order to their justification, should have gone into the contrary extreme.

Can faith save him ?] That is, his profession of faith ; for it is not said that he *has faith,* but that *he says,* I have faith. St. James probably refers to that faith which simply took in the being and unity of God. See on ver. 19, 24, 25.

Verse 15. *If a brother or sister be naked*] That is, ill-clothed ; for γυμνος, *naked,* has this meaning in several parts of the New Testament, signifying bad clothing, or the want of some particular article of dress. See Matt. xxv. 36, 38, 43, 44, and John xxi. 7. It has the same *comparative* signification in most languages.

Verse 16. *Be ye warmed and filled*] Your saying so to them, while you give them nothing, will just profit them as much as your professed faith, without those works which are the genuine fruits of true faith, will profit you in the day when God comes to sit in judgment upon your soul.

Verse 17. *If it hath not works, is dead*] The faith that does not produce works of charity and mercy is without the living principle which animates all true faith, that is, *love to God* and *love to man.* They had faith, such as a man has who credits a well-circumstanced relation that it has all the appearance of truth ; but they had nothing of that faith that a sinner convinced of his sinfulness, God's purity, and the strictness of the Divine laws, is obliged to exert in the Lord Jesus, in order to be saved from his sins.

Verse 18. *Show me thy faith without thy works*] Your pretending to have faith, while you have no works of charity or mercy, is utterly vain : for as *faith,* which is a principle in the mind, cannot be dis-

A. M. cir. 4065
A. D. cir. 61.
An. Olymp.
cir. CCX. 1.
A. U. C. cir.
814.

and I have works : show me thy faith ʸ without thy works, ᶻ and I will show thee my faith by my works.

19 Thou believest that there is one God ; thou doest well : ᵃ the devils also believe, and tremble.

20 But wilt thou know, O vain man, that faith without works is dead ?

21 Was not Abraham our father justified by works, ᵇ when he had offered Isaac his son upon the altar ?

22 ᶜ Seest thou ᵈ how faith wrought with his

works, and by works was faith made perfect ?

A. M. cir. 4065
A. D. cir. 61.
An. Olymp.
cir. CCX. 1.
A. U. C. cir.
814.

23 And the scripture was fulfilled which saith, ᵉ Abraham believed God, and it was imputed unto him for righteousness : and he was called ᶠ the friend of God

24 Ye see then how that by works a man is justified, and not by faith only.

25 Likewise also ᵍ was not Rahab the harlot justified by works, when she had received the messengers, and had sent *them* out another way ?

26 For as the body without the ʰ spirit is dead, so faith without works is dead also.

ʸ Some copies read, *by thy works.*——ᶻ Chap. iii. 13.——ᵃ Matt. viii. 29 ; Mark i. 24 ; v. 7 ; Luke iv. 34 ; Acts xvi. 17 ; xix. 15. ᵇ Gen. xxii. 9, 12.——ᶜ Or, *Thou seest.*

ᵈ Heb. xi. 17.——ᵉ Genesis xv. 6 ; Rom. iv. 3 ; Gal. iii. 6. ᶠ 2 Chron. xx. 7 ; Isaiah xli. 8.——ᵍ Josh. ii. 1 ; Hebrews xi. 31. ʰ Or, *breath.*

---

cerned but by the *effects*, that is, *good works ;* he who has no good works has, presumptively, no faith.

I will show thee my faith by my works.] My works of charity and mercy will show that I have faith ; and that it is the living tree, whose root is love to God and man, and whose fruit is the good works here contended for.

Verse 19. *Thou believest that there is one God*] This is the faith in which these persons put their hope of pleasing God, and of obtaining eternal life. Believing in the *being and unity of God* distinguished them from all the nations of the world ; and having been circumcised, and thus brought into the covenant, they thought themselves secure of salvation. The insufficiency of this St. James immediately shows.

The devils also believe, and tremble.] It is well to believe there is one only true God ; this truth universal nature proclaims. Even the *devils* believe it ; but far from *justifying* or *saving* them, it leaves them in their damned state, and every act of it only increases their torment ; φρισσουσι, *they shudder with horror*, they believe and tremble, are increasingly tormented ; but they can neither *love* nor *obey.*

Verse 20. *But wilt thou know*] Art thou willing to be instructed in the nature of true saving faith ? Then attend to the following examples.

Verse 21. *Was not Abraham our father*] Did not the conduct of Abraham, in offering up his son Isaac on the altar, sufficiently prove that *he believed in God*, and that it was his *faith* in him that led him to this extraordinary act of obedience ?

Verse 22. *Seest thou how faith wrought*] Here is a proof that faith cannot exist without being active in works of righteousness. His faith in God would have been of no avail to him, had it not been manifested by works ; for *by works*—by his obedience to the commands of God, *his faith was made perfect*—it dictated obedience, he obeyed ; and thus faith ετελειωθη, *had its consummation.* Even *true faith* will soon die, if its possessor do not live in the spirit of *obedience.*

Verse 23. *The scripture was fulfilled*] He believed God ; this faith was never inactive, it was accounted to him for righteousness ; and, being justified by thus be-

lieving, his life of obedience showed that he had not received the grace of God in vain. See the notes on Gen. xv. 6 ; Rom. iv. 3 ; Gal. iii. 6 ; where this subject is largely explained.

The friend of God.] The highest character ever given to man. As among friends every thing is in common ; so God took Abraham into intimate communion with himself, and poured out upon him the choicest of his blessings : for as God can never be in want, because he possesses all things ; so Abraham his friend could never be destitute, because God was his friend.

Verse 24. *Ye see then how*] It is evident from this example that Abraham's faith was not merely *believing that there is a God ;* but a principle that led him to credit God's promises relative to the future Redeemer, and to implore God's mercy : this he received, and was justified by faith. His faith now began to work by love, and therefore he was found ever obedient to the will of his Maker. He brought forth the fruits of righteousness ; and his works *justified*— proved the genuineness of his faith ; and he continued to enjoy the *Divine approbation*, which he could not have done had he not been thus obedient ; for the Spirit of God would have been grieved, and his principle of faith would have perished. Obedience to God is essentially requisite to maintain faith. Faith lives, under God, by works ; and works have their being and excellence from faith. Neither can subsist without the other, and this is the point which St. James labours to prove, in order to convince the Antinomians of his time that their faith was a delusion, and that the hopes built on it must needs perish.

Verse 25 *Rahab the harlot*] See the notes on Joshua ii. 1, &c., and Heb. xi. 31, &c. Rahab had the *approbation* due to genuine faith, which she actually possessed, and gave the fullest proof that she did so by her conduct. As justification signifies, not only the pardon of sin, but receiving the *Divine approbation*, James seems to use the word in this latter sense. God *approved* of them, because of their obedience to his will ; and he *approves* of no man who is not *obedient.*

2

Verse 26. *For as the body without the spirit is dead*] There can be no more a *genuine faith* without *good works*, than there can be a living human body without a soul.

WE shall never find a series of disinterested godly living without true faith. And we shall never find true faith without such a life. We may see works of apparent benevolence without faith: their principle is *ostentation;* and, as long as they can have the reward (human applause) which they seek, they may be continued. And yet the experience of all mankind shows how *short-lived* such works are; they want both *principle* and *spring;* they endure for a time, but soon wither away. Where true faith is, there is God; his *Spirit* gives *life,* and his *love* affords *motives* to righteous actions. The *use* of any Divine principle leads to its *increase.* The more a man exercises faith in Christ, the more he is enabled to believe; the more he believes, the more he receives; and the more he receives, the more able he is to work for God. Obedience is

his delight, because love to God and man is the element in which his soul lives. Reader, thou professest to believe; show thy faith, both to God and man, by a life conformed to the *royal law,* which ever gives *liberty* and confers *dignity.*

"Some persons, known to St. James, must have taught that men are justified by merely believing in the one true God; or he would not have taken such pains to confute it. Crediting the unity of the Godhead, and the doctrine of a future state, was that faith through which both the Jews in St. James' time and the Mohammedans of the present day expect justification. St. James, in denying this faith to be of avail, if unaccompanied with good works, has said nothing more than what St. Paul has said, in other words, Rom. ii., where he combats the same Jewish error, and asserts that not the hearers but the doers of the law will be justified, and that a knowledge of God's will, without the performance of it, serves only to increase our condemnation."—*Michaelis.*

CHAPTER III.

They are exhorted not to be many masters, 1. And to bridle the tongue, which is often an instrument of much evil, 2-12. The character and fruits of true and false wisdom, 13-18.

A. M. cir. 4065.
A. D. cir. 61.
An. Olymp.
cir. CCX. 1.
A. U. C. cir.
814

MY brethren, [a] be not many masters, [b] knowing that we shall receive the greater [c] condemnation

2 For [d] in many things we offend all. [e] If any man offend not in word, [f] the same *is* a perfect man, *and* able also to bridle the whole body.

A. M. cir. 4065.
A. D. cir. 61.
An. Olymp.
cir. CCX. 1.
A. U. C. cir.
814

[a] Matt. xxiii. 8, 14; Rom. ii. 20, 21; 1 Pet. v. 3.——[b] Luke vi. 37.
[c] Or, *judgment.*——[d] 1 Kings viii. 46; 2 Chron. vi. 36; Prov. xx.

9; Eccles. vii. 20; 1 John i. 8.——[e] Psa. xxxiv. 13; Ecclus. xiv. 1; xix. 16; xxv. 8; chap. i. 26; 1 Pet. iii. 10.——[f] Matt. xii. 37.

NOTES ON CHAP. III.

Verse 1. *Be not many masters*] Do not affect the *teacher's* office, for many wish to be teachers who have more need to learn. There were many teachers or *rabbins* among the Jews, each affecting to have THE truth, and to draw disciples after him. We find a caution against such persons, and of the same nature with that of St. James, in *Pirkey Aboth,* c. i. 10: *Love labour, and hate the rabbin's office.*

This caution is still necessary; there are multitudes, whom God has never called, and never can call, because he has never qualified them for the work, who earnestly wish to get into the priest's office. And of this kind, in opposition to St. James, *we* have *many masters*—persons who undertake to show us the way of salvation, who know nothing of that way, and are unsaved themselves. These are found among *all descriptions* of Christians, and have been the means of bringing the ministerial office into contempt. Their case is awful; *they shall receive greater condemnation* than common sinners; they have not only sinned in thrusting themselves into that office to which God has never called them, but through their *insufficiency* the flocks over whom they have assumed the *mastery* perish for lack of knowledge, and their blood will God require at the watchman's hand. A man may have this *mastery* according to the *law* of the land, and yet

not have it according to the *Gospel;* another may affect to have it according to the *Gospel,* because he dissents from the religion of the *state,* and not have it according to Christ. Blockheads are common, and knaves and hypocrites may be found everywhere.

Verse 2. *In many things we offend all.*] Πταιομεν απαντες· *We all stumble* or *trip.* Dr. Barrow very properly observes: "As the general course of life is called a *way,* and particular actions *steps,* so going on in a regular course of right action is *walking uprightly;* and acting amiss, *tripping* or *stumbling.*" There are very few who walk so closely with God, and inoffensively with men, as never to stumble; and although it is the privilege of every follower of God *to be sincere and without offence to the day of Christ,* yet few of them are so. Were this *unavoidable,* it would be useless to make it a subject of regret; but as every man may receive grace from his God to enable him to walk in every respect *uprightly,* it is to be deplored that so few live up to their privileges. Some have produced these words as a *proof* that "no man can live without sinning against God; for James himself, a holy apostle speaking of himself, all the apostles, and the whole Church of Christ, says, *In many things we offend all.*" This is a very bad and dangerous doctrine; and, pushed to its consequences, would greatly affect the credibility of the whole Gospel system. Besides, were

A. M. cir. 4065.
A. D. cir. 61.
An. Olymp.
cir. CCX. 1.
A. U. C. cir.
814.

3 Behold, ᵍ we put bits in the horses' mouths, that they may obey us ; and we turn about their whole body.

4 Behold also the ships, which though *they be* so great, and *are* driven of fierce winds, yet are they turned about with a very small

helm, whithersoever the governor listeth.

5 Even so ʰ the tongue is a little member, and ⁱ boasteth great things. Behold, how great ᵏ a matter a little fire kindleth !

6 And ˡ the tongue *is* a fire, a world of ini-

A. M. cir. 4065.
A D. cir. 6
An. Olymp.
cir. CCX. 1.
A. U. C. cir.
814.

ᵍ Psa. xxxii. 9.——ʰ Prov. xii. 18 ; xv. 2.

ⁱ Psa. xii. 3 ; lxxiii. 8, 9.——ᵏ Or, *wood.*——ˡ Prov. xvi. 27.

---

the doctrine as true as it is dangerous and false, it is foolish to ground it upon such a text ; because St. James, after the common mode of all teachers, includes himself in his addresses to his hearers. And were we to suppose that where he appears by the use of the *plural pronoun* to include himself, he means to be thus understood, we must then grant that himself was one of those *many teachers* who were to *receive a great condemnation*, ver. 1 ; that he was a *horse-breaker*, because he says, " *we* put bits in the horses' mouths, that they may obey *us*;" ver. 3 ; that *his* tongue was a world of iniquity, and set on fire of hell, for he says, " so is the tongue among *our* members," ver. 6 ; that he cursed men, " wherewith curse *we* men, ver. 9. No man possessing common sense could imagine that James, or any man of even tolerable morals, could be guilty of those things. But some of those were thus guilty to whom he wrote ; and to soften his reproofs, and to cause them to enter the more deeply into their hearts, he appears to include himself in his own censure ; and yet not one of his readers would understand him as being a brother delinquent.

Offend not in word, the same is a perfect man] To understand this properly we must refer to the caution St. James gives in the preceding verse : *Be not many masters* or *teachers*—do not affect that for which you are not qualified, because in your *teaching*, not knowing the heavenly doctrine, ye may *sin* against the *analogy of faith*. But, says he, *if any man offend not*, ου πταιει, *trip not*, εν λογω, *in doctrine*, teaching the truth, the whole truth, and nothing but the truth, *the same is* τελειος ανηρ, *a man fully instructed* in Divine things: How often the term λογος, which we render *word*, is used to express *doctrine*, and the *doctrine of the Gospel*, we have seen in many parts of the preceding comment. And how often the word τελειος, which we translate *perfect*, is used to signify an *adult Christian*, one *thoroughly instructed* in the doctrines of the Gospel, may be seen in various parts of St. Paul's writings. See among others, 1 Cor. ii. 6 ; xiv. 20 ; Eph. iv. 13 ; Phil. iii. 15 ; Col. iv. 12 ; Heb. v. 14. The man, therefore, who advanced no false doctrine, and gave no imperfect view of any of the great truths of Christianity ; that man proved himself thereby to be *thoroughly instructed* in Divine things ; to be no novice, and consequently, among the *many teachers*, to be a *perfect master*, and worthy of the sacred vocation.

Able also to bridle the whol body.] Grotius, by *body*, believed that the Church of Christ was intended ; and this the view we have taken of the preceding clauses renders very probable. But some think the *passions* and *appetites* are intended ; yet these persons

understand *not offending in word* as referring simply to well guarded speech. Now how a man's cautiousness in *what he says* can be a proof that he has *every passion* and *appetite under control*, I cannot see. Indeed, I have seen so many examples of a contrary kind, that I can have no doubt of the impropriety of this exposition. But it is objected " that χαλιναγωγεω signifies to *check*, *turn*, or *rule with a bridle* ; and is never applied to the government of the Church of Christ." Probably not : but St. James is a very peculiar writer ; his phraseology, metaphors, and diction in general, are different from all the rest of the New Testament writers, so as to have scarcely any thing in common with them, but only that he writes in Greek. The sixth verse is supposed to be a proof against the opinion of *Grotius* ; but I conceive that verse to belong to a different subject, which commences ver. 3.

Verse 3. *Behold, we put bits in the horses' mouths*] In order to show the necessity of regulating the tongue, to which St. James was led by his exhortation to them who wished to thrust themselves into the teacher's office, supposing, because they had the *gift of a ready flow of speech*, that therefore they might commence teachers of Divine things ; he proceeds to show that the tongue must be bridled as the horse, and governed as the ships ; because, though it is small, it is capable of ruling the whole man, and of irritating and offending others.

Verse 5. *Boasteth great things.*] That is, *can do great things*, whether of a *good* or *evil* kind. He seems to refer here to the powerful and all commanding eloquence of the Greek orators : they could carry the great mob whithersoever they wished ; calm them to peaceableness and submission ; or excite them to furious sedition.

Behold, how great a matter] See what a flame of discord and insubordination one man, merely by his persuasive tongue, may kindle among the common people.

Verse 6. *The tongue is a fire*] It is often the instrument of producing the most desperate contentions and insurrections.

A world of iniquity] This is an unusual form of speech, but the meaning is plain enough ; WORLD signifies here a *mass*, a *great collection*, an *abundance*. We use the term in the same sense—a *world of troubles*, a *world of toil*, a *world of anxiety* ; for *great* troubles, *oppressive* toil, *most distressing* anxiety. And one of our lexicographers calls his work a *world of words* ; i. e. a vast collection of words : so we also say, a *deluge of wickedness*, a *sea of troubles* ; and the Latins, *oceanus malorum*, an ocean of evils. I do not recollect an example of this use of the word among

2

A. M. cir. 4065.
A. D. cir. 61.
An. Olymp.
cir. CCX. 1.
A. U. C. cir.
814.

quity: so is the tongue among our members, that ^m it defileth the whole body, and setteth on fire the ⁿ course of nature; and it is set on fire of hell.

7 For every ^o kind of beasts, and of birds, and of serpents,

A. M. cir. 4065.
A. D. cir. 61.
An. Olymp.
cir. CCX. 1.
A. U. C. cir.
814.

---

^m Matt. xv. 11, 18, 19, 20; Mark vii. 15, 20, 23.

ⁿ Gr. *wheel.*——^o Gr. *nature.*

---

the Greek writers; but in this sense it appears to be used by the Septuagint, Prov. xvii. 6 : Του πιστου ὁλος ὁ κοσμος των χρηματων, του δε απιστου ουδε οβολος, which may be translated, " The faithful has a *world of riches,* but the unfaithful not a penny." This clause has nothing answering to it in the *Hebrew* text. Some think that the word is thus used, 2 Pet. ii. 5 : *And brought the flood, κοσμῳ ασεβων, on the multitude of the ungodly.* Mr. *Wakefield* translates the clause thus : The tongue is the *varnisher of injustice.* We have seen that κοσμος signifies adorned, elegant, beautiful, &c., but I can scarcely think that this is its sense in this place. The *Syriac* gives a curious turn to the expression : *And the tongue is a fire ; and the world of iniquity is like a wood.* Above, the same version has : *A little fire burns great woods.* So the world of iniquity is represented as inflamed by the wicked tongues of men ; the world being *fuel,* and the tongue a *fire.*

So is the tongue among our members] I think St. James refers here to those well known speeches of the rabbins, *Vayikra Rabba,* sec. 16, fol. 159. " Rabbi Eleazar said, Man has one hundred and forty-eight members, some confined, others free. The tongue is placed between the jaws ; and from under it proceeds a fountain of water, (the great sublingual salivary gland,) and it is folded with various foldings. Come and see *what a flame the tongue kindles !* Were it one of the unconfined members, what would it not do ?" The same sentiment, with a little variation, may be found in *Midrash, Yalcut Simeoni,* par. 2, fol. 107 ; and in *Erachin,* fol. xv. 2, on Psa. cxx. 3 : *What shall be given unto thee, or what shall be done unto thee, thou false tongue ?* " The holy blessed God said to the tongue : All the rest of the members of the body are *erect,* but thou *liest down ;* all the rest are *external,* but thou art *internal.* Nor is this enough : I have built *two walls* about thee ; the one *bone,* the other *flesh : What shall be given unto thee, and what shall be done unto thee, O thou false tongue ?"

Setteth on fire the course of nature] Φλογιζουσα τον τροχον της γενεσεως· *And setteth on fire the wheel of life.* I question much whether this verse be in general well understood. There are three different interpretations of it : 1. St. James does not intend to express the whole circle of human affairs, so much affected by the tongue of man ; but rather the *penal wheel* of the Greeks, and not unknown to the Jews, on which they were accustomed to extend criminals, to induce them to confess, or to punish them for crimes ; under which *wheels, fire* was often placed to add to their torments. In the book, *De Maccabæis,* attributed to Josephus, and found in *Haverkamp's* edition, vol. ii., p. 497–520, where we have the account of the martyrdom of seven Hebrew brothers, in chap. ix, speaking of the death of the eldest, it is said : Ανεβαλον αυτον επι τον τροχον·—περι ὁν κατατεινομενος· " They cast him

on the *wheel,* over which they extended him ; πυρ ὑπεστρωσαν και διηρεθισαν τον τροχον προσεπικατατεινοντες· they put *coals* under it, and strongly agitated the wheel." And of the martyrdom of the sixth brother it is said, cap. 11 : Παρηγον επι τον τροχον, εφ' ου κατατεινομενος εκμελως και εκσφονδυλιζομενος ὑπεκαιετο. και οβελισκους δε οξεις πυρωσαντες, τοις νοτοις ᾖπροσεφερον, και τα πλευρα διαπειραντες αυτου, και τα σπλαγχνα διεκαιον· " They brought him to the *wheel,* on which having distended his limbs, and broken his joints, they *scorched* him with the *fire* placed underneath ; and with sharp spits *heated in the fire,* they pierced his sides, and burned his bowels.

The *fire* and the *wheel* are mentioned by *Achilles Tatius,* lib. 7, p. 449. " Having stripped me of my garments, I was carried aloft, των μεν μαστιγας κομιζοντων, των δε πυρ και τροχον, some bringing scourges, others the *fire* and the *wheel.*" Now as γενεσις often signifies *life,* then the *wheel of life* will signify the miseries and torments of life. To *set on fire the wheel of life* is to increase a man's torments ; and to be *set on fire from hell* implies having these miseries rendered more active by diabolic agency ; or, in other words, bad men, instigated by the devil, through their *lies* and *calumnies,* make life burdensome to the objects of their malicious tongues. The *wheel* and the *fire,* so pointedly mentioned by St. James, make it probable that this sort of punishment might have suggested the idea to him. See more in *Kypke.*

2. But is it not possible that by the *wheel of life* St. James may have the *circulation of the blood* in view ? Angry or irritating language has an astonishing influence on the circulation of the blood : the heart beats high and frequent ; the blood is hurried through the arteries to the veins, through the veins to the heart, and through the heart to the arteries again, and so on ; an extraordinary degree of *heat* is at the same time engendered ; the eyes become more prominent in their sockets ; the capillary vessels suffused with blood ; the face flushed ; and, in short, the whole *wheel of nature* is *set on fire of hell.* No description can be more natural than this : but it may be objected that this intimates that the *circulation of the blood* was known to St. James. Now supposing it does, is the thing impossible ? It is allowed by some of the most judicious medical writers, that Solomon refers to this in his celebrated *portraiture of old age,* Eccles. xii., particularly in ver. 6 : " Or ever the silver cord be loosed, or the golden bowl be broken, or the *pitcher be broken at the fountain,* or the *wheel broken at the cistern.*" Here is the very *wheel of life* from which St. James might have borrowed the idea ; and the different times evidently refer to the *circulation of the blood,* which might be as well known to St. James as the doctrine of the *parallax of the sun.* See on chap. i. 17.

3. It is true, however, that the rabbins use the

A. M. cir. 4065. A. D. cir. 61. An. Olymp. cir. CCX. 1. A. U. C. cir. 814.

and of things in the sea, is tamed, and hath been tamed of [p] mankind:

8 But the tongue can no man tame; *it is* an unruly evil, [q] full of deadly poison.

9 Therewith bless we God, even the Father; and therewith curse we men, [r] which are made after the similitude of God.

10 Out of the same mouth proceedeth blessing and cursing. My brethren, these things ought not so to be.

A. M. cir. 4065. A. D. cir. 61. An. Olymp. cir. CCX. 1. A. U. C. cir. 814.

11 Doth a fountain send forth at the same [s] place sweet *water* and bitter?

12 Can the fig tree, my brethren, bear olive berries? either a vine, figs? so *can* no fountain both yield salt water and fresh.

p Gr. *nature of man*.——q Psa. cxl, 3.

r Gen. i, 26; v. 1; ix. 6.——s Or, *hole*.

term נלגל תולדות *gilgal toledoth*, "the wheel of generations," to mark the successive generations of men: and it is possible that St. James might refer to this; as if he had said: "The tongue has been the instrument of confusion and misery through all the ages of the world." But the other interpretations are more likely.

Verse 7. *Every kind of beasts*] That is, every *species* of wild beasts, *πασα φυσις θηριων*, *is tamed*, i. e. brought under man's power and dominion. Beasts, birds, serpents, and some kinds of fishes have been *tamed* so as to be domesticated; but every kind, particularly *των εναλιων*, of *sea monsters*, has not been *thus* tamed; but all have been subjected to the power of man; both the *shark* and *whale* become an easy prey to the skill and influence of the human being. I have had the most credible information, when in the Zetland Isles, of the *seals* being domesticated, and of one that would pass part of his time on shore, receive his allowance of milk, &c., from the servants, go again to sea, and return, and so on.

Verse 8. *But the tongue can no man tame*] No cunning, persuasion, or influence has ever been able to silence it. Nothing but the grace of God, *excision*, or *death*, can bring *it* under subjection.

It is *an unruly evil*] *Ακατασχετον κακον*· An *evil* that *cannot* be *restrained;* it cannot be *brought* under any kind of government; it breaks all bounds.

Full of deadly poison.] He refers here to the tongues of serpents, supposed to be the means of conveying their poison into wounds made by their teeth. Throughout the whole of this poetic and highly declamatory description, St. James must have the tongue of the *slanderer*, *calumniator*, *backbiter*, *whisperer*, and *tale-bearer*, particularly in view. Vipers, basilisks, and rattlesnakes are not more dangerous to *life*, than these are to the peace and reputation of men.

Verse 9. *Therewith bless we God*] The tongue is capable of rehearsing the praises, and setting forth the glories, of the eternal King: what a pity that it should ever be employed in a contrary work! It can proclaim and vindicate the truth of God, and publish the Gospel of peace and good will among men: what a pity that it should ever be employed in falsehoods, calumny, or in the cause of infidelity!

And therewith curse we men] In the true Satanic spirit, many pray to God, the *Father*, to destroy those who are objects of their displeasure! These are the *common swearers*, whose mouths are generally full of direful imprecations against those with whom they are offended.

The consideration that *man is made after the image of God* should restrain the tongue of the swearer; but there are many who, while they pretend to *sing the high praises of God*, are ready to wish the direst imprecations either on those who offend them, or with whom they choose to be offended.

Verse 10. *Out of the same mouth*] This saying is something like that, Prov. xviii. 21: *Death and life are in the power of the tongue;* and on this, for an illustration of St. James' words, hear *Vayikra Rabba*, sec. 33: "Rabbi Simeon, the son of Gamaliel, said to his servant Tobias, Go and bring me some *good food* from the market: the servant went, and he bought *tongues*. At another time he said to the same servant, Go and buy me some *bad food:* the servant went, and bought *tongues*. The master said, What is the reason that when I ordered thee to buy me *good* and *bad* food, thou didst bring *tongues?* The servant answered, From the *tongue* both *good* and *evil* come to man: if it be *good*, there is nothing *better;* if *bad*, there is nothing *worse*."

A saying very like that of St. James is found in *Rabbi Tanchum*, fol. 10, 4: "The mouth desires to study in the law, and to speak good words; to praise God, to glorify him, and to celebrate him with hymns: but it can also slander, blaspheme, reproach, and swear falsely." See *Schoettgen*.

To find a man who officiates in sacred things to be a common swearer, a slanderer, &c., is truly monstrous; but there have been many cases of this kind, and I have known several. Let me say to all such, *My brethren, these things ought not so to be.*

Verse 11. *Doth a fountain send forth—sweet* water *and bitter?*] In many things *nature* is a sure guide to man; but no such inconsistency is found in the natural world as this blessing and cursing in man. No fountain, at the same opening, sends forth sweet water and bitter; no fig tree can bear olive berries; no vine can bear figs; nor can the sea produce salt water and fresh from the same place. These are all contradictions, and indeed impossibilities, in nature. And it is depraved man alone that can act the monstrous part already referred to.

Verse 12. *So can no fountain both yield salt water and fresh.*] For the reading of the common text, which is *ουτως ουδεμια πηγη ἁλυκον και γλυκυ ποιησαι ὑδωρ, so no fountain can produce salt water and sweet*, there are various other readings in the MSS. and versions. The word *ουτως*, *so*, which makes this a continuation of the comparison in ver. 11, is wanting in ABC, one other, with the *Armenian* and ancient *Syriac;* the later *Sy-*

A. M. cir. 4065.
A. D. cir. 61.
An. Olymp.
cir. CCX. 1.
A. U. C. cir.
814.

13 [t] Who *is* a wise man and endued with knowledge among you ? let him show out of a good conversation [u] his works [v] with meekness of wisdom.

14 But if ye have [w] bitter envying and strife in your hearts, [x] glory not, and lie not against the truth.

15 [y] This wisdom descendeth not from above, but *is* earthly, [z] sensual, devilish.

A. M. cir 4065
A. D. cir. 61.
An. Olymp.
cir. CCX. 1.
A. U. C. cir.
814.

16 For [a] where envying and strife *is*, there *is* [b] confusion and every evil work.

17 But [c] the wisdom that is from above is first pure, then peaceable, gentle, *and* easy to be entreated, full of mercy and good fruits, [d] without partiality, [e] and without hypocrisy.

18 [f] And the fruit of righteousness is sown in peace of them that make peace.

---

[t] Gal. vi. 4.——[u] Chap. ii. 18.——[v] Chap. i. 21.——[w] Rom. xiii. 13.——[x] Rom. ii. 17, 23.——[y] Chap. i. 17 ; Phil. iii. 19.——[z] Or, *natural ;* Jude 19.——[a] 1 Cor. iii. 3 ; Gal. v. 20.——[b] Gr. *tumult,* or *unquietness.*——[c] 1 Cor. ii. 6, 7.——[d] Or, *without wrangling.* [e] Rom. xii. 9 ; 1 Pet. i. 22 ; ii. 1 ; 1 John iii. 18.——[f] Prov. xi. 18 ; Hos. x. 12 ; Matt. v. 9 ; Phil. i. 11 ; Heb. xii. 11.

---

riac has it in the margin with an asterisk. ABC, five others, with the *Coptic, Vulgate,* one copy of the *Itala,* and *Cyril,* have ουτε ἁλυκον γλυκυ ποιησαι ὑδωρ, *neither can salt water produce sweet.* In the *Syriac* and the *Arabic* of Erpen, it is, *So, likewise, sweet water cannot become bitter ; and bitter water cannot become sweet.* The true reading appears to be, *Neither can salt water produce sweet,* or, *Neither can the sea produce fresh water ;* and this is a new comparison, and not an inference from that in ver. 11. This reading *Griesbach* has admitted into the text ; and of it Professor *White,* in his *Crisews,* says, *Lectio indubie genuina,* " a reading undoubtedly genuine." There are therefore, *four* distinct comparisons here : 1. A fountain cannot produce sweet water and bitter. 2. A fig tree cannot produce olive berries. 3. A vine cannot produce figs. 4. Salt water cannot be made sweet. That is, according to the ordinary operations of nature, these things are impossible. Chemical analysis is out of the question.

Verse 13. *Who is a wise man*] One truly religious ; who, although he can neither bridle nor tame other men's tongues, can restrain his own.

And endued with knowledge] Και επιστημων· And qualified to teach others.

Let him show] Let him by a holy life and chaste conversation show, through meekness and gentleness, joined to his Divine information, that he is a Christian indeed ; his works and his spirit proving that God is in him of a truth ; and that, from the fulness of a holy heart, his feet walk, his hands work, and his tongue speaks. We may learn from this that *genuine wisdom* is ever accompanied with *meekness* and *gentleness.* Those *proud, overbearing,* and *disdainful men,* who pass for *great scholars* and *eminent critics,* may have *learning,* but they have not *wisdom.* Their learning implies their correct knowledge of the *structure of language,* and of *composition in general ;* but *wisdom* they have none, nor any *self-government.* They are like the blind man who carried a lantern in daylight to keep others from jostling him in the street. That *learning* is not only *little worth,* but *despicable,* that does not teach a man to *govern his own spirit,* and to be humble in his conduct towards others.

Verse 14. *If ye have bitter envying and strife*] If ye be under the influence of an *unkind, fierce,* and *contemptuous* spirit, even while attempting or pretending to defend true religion, *do not boast* either of your *exertions* or *success* in silencing an adversary ; ye have *no religion,* and no *true wisdom ;* and to profess either is *to lie against the truth.* Let all writers on what is called *polemic* (fighting, warring) *divinity* lay this to heart. The pious Mr. Herbert gives excellent advice on this subject :—

" Be calm in arguing, for *fierceness* makes
   Error a fault, and *truth discourtesy ;*
Why should I feel another man's mistakes
   More than his *sickness* or his *poverty ?*
In *love* I should ; but *anger* is not *love,*
Nor *wisdom* neither ; therefore g-e-n-t-l-y m-o-v-e."

Verse 15. *This wisdom descendeth not from above*] God is not the author of it, because it is *bitter*—not *meek.* See at the end of this chapter.

Is *earthly*] Having *this* life only in view.

Sensual] Ψυχικη· *Animal*—having for its object the *gratification* of the *passions* and *animal propensities.*

Devilish.] Δαιμονιωδης· *Demoniacal*—inspired by demons, and maintained in the soul by their indwelling influence.

Verse 16. *For where envying and strife is*] Ζηλος και εριθεια· *Zeal*—fiery, inflammatory passion, and *contention*—altercations about the different points of the law, of no use for edification ; such as those mentioned, Tit. iii. 9. The *Jews* were the most intolerant of all mankind ; it was a maxim with them to kill those who would not conform to their law ; and their salvation they believed to be impossible. This has been the spirit of *Popery,* and of the Romish Church at large ; in vain do they attempt to deny it ; they have written it in characters of *blood* and *fire* even in this country, (England,) when they were possessed of political power. With them it is still an established maxim, that out of their Church there is no redemption ; and fire and faggot have been in that Church legal means of *conversion* or *extinction.* In the short popish reign of *Mary* in this country, besides multitudes who suffered by fine, imprisonment, confiscation, &c., two hundred and seventy-seven were *burnt alive,* among whom were *one* archbishop, *four* bishops, *twenty-one* clergymen, *eight* lay gentlemen, *eighty-four* tradesmen, *one* hundred husbandmen, *fifty-five* women, and *four* children ! O earth ! thou hast not drunk their *blood ;* but their *ashes* have been strewed on the face of the field.

Verse 17. *The wisdom that is from above*] The pure religion of the Lord Jesus, bought by his blood, and infused by his Spirit. See the rabbinical meaning of this phrase at the end of this chapter.

Is first pure] 'Αγνη· *Chaste, holy*, and *clean*.

Peaceable] Ειρηνικη· Living in peace with others, and promoting peace among men.

Gentle] Επιεικης· *Meek, modest*, of an *equal mind*, taking every thing in good part, and putting the best construction upon all the actions of others.

Easy to be entreated] Ευπειθης· Not stubborn nor obstinate ; of a yielding disposition in all indifferent things ; obsequious, docile.

Full of mercy] Ready to pass by a transgression, and to grant forgiveness to those who offend, and performing every possible act of kindness.

Good fruits] Each temper and disposition producing fruits suited to and descriptive of its nature.

Without partiality] Αδιακριτος· *Without making a difference*—rendering to every man his due ; and being never swayed by self-interest, worldly honour, or the fear of man ; knowing no man after the flesh. One of the *Itala* has it *irreprehensible*.

Without hypocrisy.] Ανυποκριτος· *Without dissimulation ;* without *pretending to be what it is not ;* acting always in *its own character ;* never *working under a mask.* Seeking nothing but God's glory, and using no other means to attain it than those of his own prescribing.

Verse 18. *And the fruit of righteousness is sown*] The whole is the *principle* of righteousness in the soul, and all the above virtues are the *fruits* of that righteousness.

Is sown in peace] When the peace of God rules the heart, all these virtues and graces grow and flourish abundantly.

Of them that make peace.] The peace-makers are continually recommending this wisdom to others, and their own conduct is represented as *a sowing of heavenly seed*, which brings forth Divine fruit. Perhaps *sowing in peace* signifies *sowing prosperously*—being very successful. This is not only the proper disposition for every *teacher* of the Gospel, but for every professed follower of the Lord Jesus.

Some render this verse, which is confessedly obscure, thus : *And the peaceable fruits of righteousness are sown for the practisers of peace. He who labours to live peaceably shall have peace for his reward.*

1. ALMOST the whole of the preceding chapter is founded on maxims highly accredited in the *rabbinical* writings, and without a reference to those writings it would have been impossible, in some cases, to have understood St. James' meaning. There is one phrase, the rabbinical meaning and use of which I have reserved for this place, viz. . *The wisdom that is from above.* This is greatly celebrated among them by the terms חכמה עליונה *chocmah elyonah*, the *supernal wisdom.* This they seem to understand to be a *peculiar inspiration of the Almighty*, or a teaching communicated immediately by the angels of God. In *Sohar, Yalcut Rubeni,* fol. 19, *Rabbi Chiya* said : " *The wisdom from above* was in Adam more than in the supreme angels, and he knew all things."

In *Sohar Chadash,* fol. 35, it is said concerning *Enoch,* " That the angels were sent from heaven, and taught him the *wisdom that is from above.*" *Ibid.* fol. 42, 4 : " Solomon came, and he was perfect in all things, and strongly set forth the praises of the *wisdom that is from above.*" See more in *Schoettgen.* St. James gives us the *properties* of this wisdom, which are not to be found in such detail in any of the rabbinical writers. It is another word for the *life of God in the soul of man,* or *true religion ;* it is the *teaching of God in the human heart,* and he who has this not is not a *child* of God ; for it is written, *All thy children shall be taught of the Lord.*

2. To enjoy the peace of God in the conscience, and to live to promote peace among men, is to answer the end of our creation, and to enjoy as much happiness ourselves as the present state of things can afford. They who are in continual broils live a wretched life ; and they who *love* the life of the salamander must share no small portion of the demoniacal nature. In *domestic society* such persons are an *evil disease ;* therefore a *canker* in the *Church*, and a pest in the *state.*

CHAPTER IV.

The origin of wars and contentions, and the wretched lot of those who are engaged in them, 1, 2. *Why so little heavenly good is obtained,* 3. *The friendship of the world is enmity with God,* 4, 5. *God resists the proud,* 6. *Men should submit to God, and pray,* 7, 8. *Should humble themselves,* 9, 10. *And not speak evil of each other,* 11, 12. *The impiety of those who consult not the will of God, and depend not on his providence,* 13–15. *The sin of him who knows the will of God, and does not do it,* 16, 17.

A. M. cir. 4065. A. D. cir. 61. An. Olymp. cir. CCX. 1. A. U. C. cir. 814.	FROM whence *come* wars and [a] fightings among you ? *come they* not hence, *even* of your [b] lusts [c] that war in your members ?	2 Ye lust, and have not : ye [d] kill, and desire to have, and cannot obtain : ye fight and war, yet ye have not, because ye ask not.	A. M. cir. 4065. A. D. cir. 61. An. Olymp. cir. CCX. 1. A. U. C. cir. 814.

---

[a] Or, *brawlings.*——[b] Or, *pleasures ;* so ver. 3.

[c] Rom. vii. 23 ; Gal. v. 17 ; 1 Pet. ii. 11.——[d] Or, *envy.*

NOTES ON CHAP. IV.

Verse 1. *From whence* come *wars and fightings*] About the time in which St. James wrote, whether we

follow the *earlier* or the *later date* of this epistle, we find, according to the accounts given by Josephus, *Bell. Jud.* lib. ii. c. 17, &c., that the Jews, under pre-

A. M. cir. 4065.
A. D. cir. 61.
An. Olymp.
cir. CCX. 1.
A. U. C. cir.
814.

3 ᵉ Ye ask, and receive not, ᶠ because ye ask amiss, that ye may consume *it* upon your ᵍ lusts.

4 ʰ Ye adulterers and adulteresses, know ye

not that the ⁱ friendship of the world is enmity with God? ᵏ whosoever therefore will be a friend of the world, is the enemy of God.

5 Do ye think that the scripture saith in vain,

A. M. cir. 4065.
A. D. cir. 61.
An. Olymp.
cir. CCX. 1.
A. U. C. cir.
814.

ᵉ Job xxvii. 9; xxxv. 12; Psa. xviii. 41; Prov. i. 28; Isa. i 15; Jer. xi. 11; Mic. iii. 4; Zech. vii. 13.——ᶠ Psa. lxvi. 18.

l John iii. 22; v. 14.——ᵍ Or, *pleasures.*——ʰ Psa. lxxiii. 27 ⁱ 1 John ii. 15.——ᵏ John xv. 19; xvii. 14; Gal. i. 10.

---

tence of defending their religion, and procuring that liberty to which they believed themselves entitled, made various insurrections in Judea against the Romans, which occasioned much bloodshed and misery to their nation. The *factions* also, into which the Jews were split, had violent contentions among themselves, in which they massacred and plundered each other. In the provinces, likewise, the Jews became very turbulent; particularly in Alexandria, and different other parts of Egypt, of Syria, and other places, where they made war against the heathens, killing many, and being massacred in their turn. They were led to these outrages by the opinion that they were bound by their law to extirpate idolatry, and to kill all those who would not become proselytes to Judaism. These are probably the *wars* and *fightings* to which St. James alludes; and which they undertook rather from a principle of *covetousness* than from any sincere desire to convert the heathen. See *Macknight.*

Come they *not hence—of your lusts*] This was the principle from which these Jewish contentions and predatory wars proceeded, and the principle from which all the wars that have afflicted and desolated the world have proceeded. One nation or king *covets* another's *territory* or *property;* and, as *conquest* is supposed to *give right* to all the possessions gained by it, they kill, slay, burn, and destroy, till one is overcome or exhausted, and then the other makes his own terms; or, several neighbouring potentates fall upon one that is weak; and, after murdering one half of the people, partition among themselves the fallen king's territory; just as the *Austrians, Prussians,* and *Russians* have done with the kingdom of *Poland!*—a stain upon their justice and policy which no lapse of time can ever wash out.

These *wars* and *fightings* could not be attributed to the Christians in that time; for, howsoever fallen or degenerate, they had no power to raise *contentions;* and no political consequence to enable them to resist their enemies by the edge of the sword, or resistance of any kind.

Verse 2. *Ye lust, and have not*] Ye are ever covetous, and ever poor.

Ye kill, and desire to have] Ye are constantly engaged in insurrections and predatory wars, and never gain any advantage.

Ye have not, because ye ask not.] Ye get no especial blessing from God as your fathers did, because ye do not pray. Worldly good is your god; ye leave no stone unturned in order to get it; and as ye ask nothing from God but to *consume it upon your evil desires and propensities,* your prayers are not heard.

Verse 3. *Ye ask, and receive not*] Some think that this refers to their prayers for the conversion of the

heathen; and on the pretence that they were not converted thus, they thought it lawful to extirpate them and possess their goods.

Ye ask amiss] Κακως αιτεισθε· Ye ask evilly, wickedly. Ye have not the proper *dispositions* of prayer, and ye have an improper *object.* Ye ask for worldly prosperity, that ye may employ it in riotous living. This is properly the meaning of the original, ινα εν ταις ἡδοναις ὑμων δαπανησητε, That ye may expend it upon your pleasures. The rabbins have many good observations on *asking amiss* or *asking improperly,* and give examples of different kinds of this sort of prayer; the phrase is *Jewish,* and would naturally occur to St. James in writing on this subject. Whether the *lusting* of which St. James speaks were their desire to make proselytes, in order that they might increase their power and influence by means of such, or whether it were a desire to cast off the Roman yoke, and become independent; the *motive* and the *object* were the same, and the prayers were such as God could not hear.

Verse 4. *Ye adulterers and adulteresses*] The Jews, because of their *covenant* with God, are represented as being *espoused* to him; and hence their idolatry, and their iniquity in general, are represented under the notion of *adultery.* And although they had not since the Babylonish captivity been guilty of *idolatry,* according to the *letter;* yet what is intended by idolatry, having their hearts estranged from God, and seeking their portion in this life and out of God, is that of which the Jews were then notoriously guilty. And I rather think that it is in this sense especially that St. James uses the words. "Lo! they that are far from thee shall perish; thou hast destroyed all them that *go a whoring* from thee." But perhaps something more than spiritual adultery is intended. See ver. 9.

The friendship of the world] The world was their god; here they committed their *spiritual adultery;* and they cultivated this friendship in order that they might gain this end.

The word μοιχαλιδες, *adulteresses,* is wanting in the Syriac, Coptic, Æthiopic, Armenian, Vulgate, and one copy of the *Itala.*

Whosoever—will be a friend of the world] How strange it is that people professing Christianity can suppose that with a worldly spirit, worldly companions, and their lives governed by worldly maxims, they can be in the favour of God, or ever get to the kingdom of heaven! When the *world* gets into the *Church,* the Church becomes a painted sepulchre; its spiritual vitality being extinct.

Verse 5. *Do ye think that the scripture saith in vain*] This verse is exceedingly obscure. We can-

2

A. M. cir. 4065.
A. D. cir. 61.
An. Olymp.
cir. CCX. 1.
A. U. C. cir.
814.

[1] The spirit that dwelleth in us lusteth [m] to envy?

6 But he giveth more grace. Wherefore he saith, [n] God resisteth the proud, but giveth grace unto the humble.

7 Submit yourselves therefore to God. [o] Re-

sist the devil, and he will flee from you.

8 [p] Draw nigh to God, and he will draw nigh to you. [q] Cleanse *your* hands, *ye* sinners; and [r] purify *your* hearts, *ye* [s] double-minded.

9 [t] Be afflicted, and mourn, and weep: let

A. M. cir. 4065.
A. D. cir. 61.
An. Olymp.
cir. CCX. 1.
A. U. C. cir.
814.

---

[l] See Gen. vi. 5; viii. 21; Num. xi. 29; Prov. xxi. 10.——[m] Or, *enviously.*——[n] Job xxii. 29; Psa. cxxxviii. 6; Prov. iii. 34; xxix. 23; Matt. xxiii. 12; Luke i. 52; xiv. 11; xviii. 14; 1 Pet.

[v. 5.——[o] Eph. iv. 27; vi. 11; 1 Pet. v. 9.——[p] 2 Chron. xv. 2 [q] Isa. i. 16.——[r] 1 Pet. i. 22; 1 John iii. 3.——[s] Chapter i. 8 [t] Matt. v. 4.

---

not tell what scripture St. James refers to; many have been produced by learned men as that which he had particularly in view. Some think Gen. vi. 5: "Every *imagination* of the thoughts of his heart was *only evil* continually." Gen. viii. 21: "The *imagination* of man's heart is evil from his youth." Num. xi. 29: "Moses said unto him, *Enviest thou* for my sake?" and Prov. xxi. 10: "The soul of the wicked *desireth evil.*" None of these scriptures, nor any others, contain the precise words in this verse; and therefore St. James may probably refer, not to any particular portion, but to the spirit and design of the Scripture in those various places where it speaks against *envying, covetousness, worldly associations,* &c., &c.

Perhaps the word in this and the two succeeding verses may be well paraphrased thus: "Do ye think that concerning these things the *Scripture speaks falsely,* or that the *Holy Spirit which dwells in us* can *excite us to envy* others instead of being contented with the state in which the providence of God has placed us? Nay, far otherwise; for *He gives us more grace* to enable us to bear the ills of life, and to lie in deep humility at his feet, knowing that his Holy Spirit has said, Prov. iii. 34: *God resisteth the proud, but giveth grace to the humble.* Seeing these things are so, *submit yourselves to God; resist the devil,* who would tempt you to envy; and *he will flee from you; draw nigh to God and he will draw nigh to you.*

I must leave this sense as the best I can give, without asserting that I have hit the true meaning. There is not a critic in Europe who has considered the passage that has not been puzzled with it. I think the 5th verse should be understood as giving a contrary sense to that in our translation. Every genuine Christian is a habitation of the Holy Ghost, and that Spirit προς φθονον επιποθει, *excites strong desires against envy*; a man must not suppose that he is a Christian if he have an *envious* or *covetous* heart.

Verse 6. *But he giveth more grace*] Μειζονα χαριν, A *greater benefit,* than all the goods that the world can bestow; for he gives genuine happiness, and this the world cannot confer. May this be St. James' meaning?

God resisteth the proud] Αντιτασσεται· Sets himself *in battle array* against him.

Giveth grace unto the humble.] The sure way to please God is to submit to the dispensations of his grace and providence; and when a man acknowledges him in all his ways, he will direct all his steps. The covetous man grasps at the *shadow,* and loses the *substance.*

Verse 7. *Submit—to God*] Continue to bow to all his decisions, and to all his dispensations.

Resist the devil] He cannot conquer you if you continue to resist. Strong as he is, God never permits him to conquer the man who continues to resist him. he cannot *force* the human will. He who, in the *terrible name* of Jesus, opposes even the devil himself, is sure to have a speedy and glorious conquest. He flees from that *name,* and from his conquering blood.

Verse 8. *Draw nigh to God*] Approach Him, in the name of Jesus, by faith and prayer, and *he will draw nigh to you*—he will *meet* you at your coming. When a soul sets out to seek God, God sets out to meet that soul; so that while we are drawing near to him, he is drawing near to us. The *delicacy* and *beauty* of these expressions are, I think, but seldom noted.

Cleanse your *hands, ye sinners*] This I think to be the beginning of a new address, and to different persons; and should have formed the commencement of a new verse. Let your whole conduct be changed; cease to do evil learn to do well. *Washing* or *cleansing the hands* was a token of innocence and purity.

Purify your *hearts*] *Separate* yourselves from the world, and consecrate yourselves to God: this is the true notion of sanctification. We have often seen that to sanctify signifies to separate a thing or person from profane or common use, and consecrate it or him to God. This is the true notion of קרש *kadash,* in Hebrew, and ἁγιαζω in Greek. The person or thing thus consecrated or separated is considered to be *holy,* and to be God's property; and then God hallows it to himself. There are, therefore, two things implied in a man's sanctification: 1. That he separates himself from evil ways and evil companions, and devotes himself to God. 2. That God separates guilt from his conscience, and sin from his soul, and thus makes him internally and externally *holy.*

This double sanctification is well expressed in Sohar, Levit. fol. 33, col. 132, on the words, *be ye holy, for I the Lord am holy*: אדם מקרש עצמו כלמטה מקדישין אותו מלמעלה, *a man sanctifies himself on the earth, and then he is sanctified from heaven.* As a man is a *sinner,* he must have his *hands cleansed* from wicked works; as he is *double-minded,* he must have his *heart sanctified.* Sanctification belongs to the *heart,* because of *pollution of mind; cleansing* belongs to the *hands,* because of *sinful acts.* See the note on chap. i. 8 for the signification of *double-minded.*

Verse 9. *Be afflicted, and mourn*] Without true and deep repentance ye cannot expect the mercy of God.

Let your laughter be turned to mourning] It ap-

2

A. M. cir. 4065.
A. D. cir. 61.
An. Olymp.
cir. CCX. 1.
A. U. C. cir.
814.

your laughter be turned to mourning, and *your* joy to beaviness.

10 ^u Humble yourselves in the sight of the Lord, and he shall lift you up.

11 ^v Speak not evil one of another, brethren. He that speaketh evil of *his* brother, ^wand judgeth his brother, speaketh evil of the law, and judgeth the law : but if thou judge the law,

thou art not a doer of the law, but a judge.

A. M. cir. 4065.
A. D. cir. 61.
An. Olymp.
cir. CCX. 1.
A. U. C. cir.
814.

12 There is one lawgiver, ^x who is able to save and to destroy : ^y who art thou that judgest another ?

13 ^z Go to now, ye that say, To-day, or to morrow, we will go into such a city, and con tinue there a year, and buy and sell, and get gain :

---

^u Job xxii. 29 ; Matt. xxiii. 12 ; Luke xiv. 11 ; xviii. 14 ; 1 Pet. v. 6.———^v Eph. iv. 31 ; 1 Pet. ii. 1.———^w Matt. vii. 1 ; Luke vi. 37 ; Rom. ii. 1 ; 1 Cor. iv. 5.———^x Matt. x. 28.———^y Rom. xiv 4, 13.———^z Prov. xxvii. 1 ; Luke xii. 18, &c.

---

pears most evidently that many of those to. whom St. James addressed this epistle had lived a very *irregular* and *dissolute life.* He had already spoken of their *lust,* and *pleasures,* and he had called them *adulterers* and *adulteresses ;* and perhaps they were so in the *grossest* sense of the words. He speaks here of their *laughter* and their *joy ;* and all the terms taken together show that a *dissolute life* is intended. What a strange view must he have of the nature of primitive Christianity, who can suppose that these words can possibly have been addressed to people professing the *Gospel of Jesus Christ,* who were few in number, without wealth or consequence, and were persecuted and oppressed both by their brethren the Jews and by the Romans !

Verse 10. *Humble yourselves in the sight of the Lord*] In ver. 7 they were exhorted to *submit* to God ; here they are exhorted to *humble themselves in his sight.* Submission to God's authority will precede *humiliation* of soul, and genuine repentance is performed as in the *sight* of God ; for when a sinner is truly awakened to a sense of his guilt and danger, he seems to see, whithersoever he turns, the *face* of a justly incensed God turned against him.

He shall lift you up.] Mourners and penitents lay on the ground, and rolled themselves in the dust. When comforted and pardoned, they arose from the earth, shook themselves from the dust, and clothed themselves in their better garments. God promises to raise these from the dust, when sufficiently humbled.

Verse 11. *Speak not evil one of another*] Perhaps this exhortation refers to evil speaking, slander, and backbiting in general, the writer having no particular persons in view. It may, however, refer to the *contentions* among the *zealots,* and different *factions* then prevailing among this wretched people, or to their calumnies against those of their brethren who had embraced the Christian faith.

He that speaketh evil of his *brother*] It was an avowed and very general maxim among the rabbins, that " no one could speak evil of his brother without denying God, and becoming an atheist." They consider detraction as the devil's crime originally : he calumniated God Almighty in the words, " He doth know that in the day in which ye eat of it, your eyes shall be opened, and ye shall be like God, knowing good and evil ;" and therefore insinuated that it was through *envy* God had prohibited the tree of knowledge.

Speaketh evil of the law] The law condemns all

evil speaking and *detraction.* He who is guilty of these, and allows himself in these vices, in effect judges and condemns the law ; *i. e.* he considers it unworthy to be kept, and that it is no sin to break it.

Thou art not a doer of the law, but a judge.] Thou rejectest the law of God, and settest up thy own mischievous conduct as a rule of life ; or, by allowing this *evil speaking* and *detraction,* dost intimate that the law that condemns them is improper, imperfect, or unjust.

Verse 12. *There is one lawgiver*] Και κριτης, *And judge,* is added here by AB, about *thirty* others, with both the *Syriac,* Erpen's *Arabic,* the *Coptic, Armenian, Æthiopic, Slavonic, Vulgate,* two copies of the *Itala, Cyril* of Antioch, *Euthalius, Theophylact,* and *Cassiodorus.* On this evidence Griesbach has received it into the text.

The man who breaks the law, and teaches others so to do, thus in effect sets himself up as a *lawgiver* and *judge.* But there is only one such lawgiver and judge—God Almighty, who is *able to save* all those who obey him, and *able to destroy* all those who trample under feet his testimonies.

Who art thou that judgest another ?] Who art thou who darest to usurp the office and prerogative of the supreme Judge ? But what is that *law* of which St. James speaks ? and who is this *lawgiver* and *judge ?* Most critics think that the *law* mentioned here is the same as that which he elsewhere calls the *royal law* and *the law of liberty,* thereby meaning the *Gospel ;* and that *Christ* is the person who is called the *lawgiver and judge.* This, however, is not clear to me. I believe James means the *Jewish law ;* and by the *lawgiver* and *judge,* God Almighty, as acknowledged by the Jewish people. I find, or think I find, from the closest examination of this epistle, but few references to Jesus·Christ or his Gospel. His Jewish creed, forms, and maxims, this writer keeps constantly in view ; and it is proper he should, considering the persons to whom he wrote. Some of them were, doubtless, *Christians ;* some of them certainly *no Christians ;* and some of them *half Christians* and *half Jews.* The two latter descriptions are those most frequently addressed.

Verse 13. *Go to now*] Αγε νυν· *Come now,* the same in meaning as the Hebrew הבה *habah, come,* Gen. xi. 3, 4, 7. *Come,* and *hear what I have to say, ye that say,* &c.

To-day, or to-morrow, we will go] This presumption on a precarious life is here well reproved : and the

A. M. cir. 4065.
A. D. cir. 61.
An. Olymp.
cir. CCX. 1.
A. U. C. cir.
814.

14 Whereas ye know not what *shall be* on the morrow. For what *is* your life? [a] It is even a [b] vapour, that appeareth for a little time, and then vanisheth away.

15 For that ye *ought* to say, [c] If the Lord

will, we shall live, and do this, or that.

16 But now ye rejoice in your boastings: [d] all such rejoicing is evil.

17 Therefore [e] to him that knoweth to do good, and doeth *it* not, to him it is sin.

A. M. cir. 4065.
A. D. cir. 61.
An. Olymp.
cir. CCX. 1.
A. U. C. cir
814.

---

[a] Or, *for it is.*——[b] Job vii. 7; Psa. cii. 3; chap. i. 10; 1 Pet. i. 24; 1 John ii. 17.——[c] Acts xviii. 21; 1 Cor. iv. 19; xvi. 7;

Heb. vi. 3.——[d] 1 Cor. v. 6.——[e] Luke xii. 47; John ix. 41; xv. 22; Rom. i. 20, 21, 32; ii. 17, 18, 23.

---

ancient Jewish rabbins have some things on the subject which probably St. James had in view. In *Debarim Rabba,* sec. 9, fol. 261, 1, we have the following little story: "Our rabbins tell us a story which happened in the days of Rabbi Simeon, the son of Chelpatha. He was present at the circumcision of a child, and stayed with its father to the entertainment. The father brought out wine for his guests that was seven years old, saying, *With this wine will I continue for a long time to celebrate the birth of my new-born son.* They continued supper till midnight. At that time Rabbi Simeon arose and went out, that he might return to the city in which he dwelt. On the way he saw the angel of death walking up and down. He said to him, Who art thou? He answered, I am the messenger of God. The rabbin said, Why wanderest thou about thus? He answered, I slay those persons who say, *We will do this, or that,* and *think not how soon death may overpower them:* that man with whom thou hast supped, and who said to his guests, *With this wine will I continue for a long time to celebrate the birth of my new-born son,* behold the end of his life is at hand, for he shall die within thirty days." By this parable they teach the necessity of considering the shortness and uncertainty of human life; and that God is particularly displeased with those

"Who, counting on long years of pleasure here,
Are quite unfurnished for a world to come."

And continue there a year, and buy and sell] This was the custom of those ancient times; they traded from city to city, carrying their goods on the backs of camels. The Jews traded thus to *Tyre, Sidon, Cæsarea, Crete, Ephesus, Philippi, Thessalonica, Corinth, Rome, &c.* And it is to this kind of itinerant mercantile life that St. James alludes. See at the end of this chapter.

Verse 14. *Whereas ye know not*] This verse should be read in a parenthesis. It is not only impious, but grossly absurd, to speak thus concerning futurity, when ye know not what a day may bring forth. Life is utterly precarious; and God has not put it within the power of all the creatures he has made to *command one moment of what is future.*

It is even a vapour] Ατμις γαρ εστιν· *It is a smoke,* always fleeting, uncertain, evanescent, and obscured with various trials and afflictions. This is a frequent metaphor with the Hebrews; see Psa. cii. 11; *My days are like a shadow:* Job viii. 9; *Our days upon earth are a shadow:* 1 Chron. xxix. 15; *Our days on the earth are a shadow, and there is no abiding. Quid tam circumcisum, tam breve, quam hominis vita*

longissima? Plin. l. iii., Ep. 7. "What is so circumscribed, or so short, as the longest life of man?" "All flesh is grass, and all the goodliness thereof is as the flower of the field. The grass withereth, and the flower fadeth, because the breath of the Lord bloweth upon it. Surely the people is like grass." St. James had produced the same figure, chap. i. 10, 11. But there is a very remarkable saying in the book of *Ecclesiasticus,* which should be quoted: "As of the green leaves of a thick tree, some fall and some grow; so is the generation of flesh and blood. one cometh to an end, and another is born." Ecclus. xiv. 18.

We find precisely the same image in *Homer* as that quoted above. Did the apocryphal writer borrow it from the *Greek* poet?

Οιη περ φυλλων γενεη, τοιηδε και ανδρων·
Φυλλα τα μεν τ' ανεμος χαμαδις χεει, αλλα δε θ' ὑλη
Τηλεθοωσα φυει, εαρος δ' επιγιγνεται ὡρη·
Ὡς ανδρων γενεη, ἡ μεν φυει, ἡ δ' απολητει.
Il. l. vi., ver. 146.

Like leaves on trees the race of man is found,
Now green in youth, now withering on the ground
Another race the following spring supplies;
They fall successive, and successive rise.
So generations in their course decay;
So flourish *these,* when *those* are pass'd away.
Pope.

Verse 15. *For that ye* ought *to say*] Αντι τοι λεγειν ὑμας· *Instead of saying,* or *instead of which ye should say,*

If the Lord will, we shall live] I think St. James had another example from the rabbins in view, which is produced by *Drusius, Gregory, Cartwright,* and *Schoettgen,* on this clause: "*The bride went up to her chamber, not knowing what was to befall her there.*" On which there is this comment: "No man should ever say that he *will do this or that,* without the condition IF GOD WILL. A certain man said, 'To-morrow shall I sit with my bride in my chamber, and there shall rejoice with her.' To which some standing by said, אם גוזר השם *im gozer hashshem,* 'If the Lord will.' To which he answered, 'Whether the Lord will or not, to-morrow will I sit with my bride in my chamber.' He did so; he went with his bride into his chamber, and at night they lay down; but they both died, *antequam illam cognosceret.*" It is not improbable that St. James refers to this case, as he uses the same phraseology.

On this subject I shall quote another passage which I read when a schoolboy, and which even then taught me a lesson of caution and of respect for the providence of God. It may be found in *Lucian*, in the piece entitled, Χαρων, η επισκοπουντες, c. 6 : Επι δειπνον, οιμαι, κληθεις υπο τινος των φιλων ες την υστεραιαν, μαλιστα ηξω, εφη· και μεταξυ λεγοντος, απο του τεγους κεραμις επιπεσουσα, ουκ οιδ' οτου κινησαντος, απεκτεινεν αυτον· εγελασα ουν, ουκ επιτελεσαντος την υποσχεσιν. "A man was invited by one of his friends to come the next day to supper. *I will certainly come*, said he. In the mean time a tile fell from a house, I knew not who threw it, and killed him. I therefore laughed at him for not fulfilling his engagement." It is often said *Fas est et ab hoste doceri,* "we should learn even from our enemies." Take heed, Christian, that this heathen buffoon laugh thee not out of countenance.

Verse 16. *But now ye rejoice in your boastings*] Ye glory in your proud and self-sufficient conduct, exulting that ye are free from the trammels of *superstition,* and that ye can live independently of God Almighty. *All such boasting is wicked,* πονηρα εστιν, is impious. In an old English work, entitled, *The godly man's picture drawn by a Scripture pencil,* there are these words: "Some of those who despise religion say, *Thank God we are not of this holy number!* They who thank God for their unholiness had best go ring the bells for joy that they shall never see God."

Verse 17. *To him that knoweth to do good*] As if he had said: After this warning none of you can plead *ignorance ;* if, therefore, any of you shall be found to act their ungodly part, not acknowledging the Divine providence, the uncertainty of life, and the necessity of standing every moment prepared to meet God—as you will have the greater sin, you will infallibly get the greater punishment. This may be applied to all who know better than they act. He who does not the Master's will because he does *not know* it, will be beaten with few stripes ; but he who knows it and does not do it, shall be beaten with many ; Luke xii. 47, 48. St. James may have the *Christians* in view who were converted from Judaism to Christianity. They had much more light and religious knowledge than the Jews had ; and God would require a proportionable improvement from them.

1. SAADY, a celebrated Persian poet, in his *Gulistan,* gives us a remarkable example of this going from city to city to buy and sell, and get gain. "I knew," says he, "a merchant who used to travel with a hundred camels laden with merchandise, and who had forty slaves in his employ. This person took me one day to his warehouse, and entertained me a long time with conversation good for nothing. 'I have,' said he, 'such a partner in Turquestan ; such and such property

in India ; a bond for so much cash in such a province ; a security for such another sum.' Then, changing the subject, he said, 'I purpose to go and settle at Alexandria, because the air of that city is salubrious.' Correcting himself, he said, 'No, I will not go to Alexandria ; the African sea (the Mediterranean) is too dangerous. But I will make another voyage ; and after that I will retire into some quiet corner of the world, and give up a mercantile life.' I asked him (says Saady) what voyage he intended to make. He answered, 'I intend to take *brimstone* to *Persia* and *China,* where I am informed it brings a good price ; from *China* I shall take *porcelian* to *Greece ;* from *Greece* I shall take *gold tissue* to *India ;* from *India* I shall carry *steel* to *Haleb* (Aleppo ;) from *Haleb* I shall carry *glass* to *Yemen* (Arabia Felix ;) and from *Yemen* I shall carry *printed goods* to *Persia.* When this is accomplished I shall bid farewell to the mercantile life, which requires so many troublesome journeys, and spend the rest of my life in a shop.' He said so much on this subject, till at last he wearied himself with talking ; then turning to me he said, 'I entreat thee, Saady, to relate to me something of what thou hast seen and heard in thy travels.' I answered, Hast thou never heard what a traveller said, who fell from his camel in the desert of Joor ? *Two things only can fill the eye of a covetous man—contentment,* or the *earth* that is cast on him when laid in his grave."

This is an instructive story, and is taken from *real life.* In this very way, to those same places and with the above specified goods, trade is carried on to this day in the Levant. And often the same person takes all these journeys, and even more. We learn also from it that a covetous man is restless and unhappy, and that to avarice there are no bounds. This account properly illustrates that to which St. James refers : *To-day or to-morrow we will go into such a city, and continue there a year, and buy and sell, and get gain.*

2. Providence is God's government of the world : he who properly trusts in Divine providence trusts in God ; and he who expects God's direction and help must walk uprightly before him ; for it is absurd to expect God to be our *friend* if we continue to be his *enemy.*

3. That man walks most safely who has the least confidence in himself. True *magnanimity* keeps God continually in view. He appoints it its work, and furnishes discretion and power ; and its chief excellence consists in being a resolute worker together with him. Pride ever sinks where humility swims ; for that man who abases himself God will exalt. To *know* that we are dependent creatures is well ; to *feel* it, and to act suitably, is still better.

CHAPTER V.

The profligate rich are in danger of God's judgments, because of their pride, fraudulent dealings, riotous living, and cruelty, 1-6. *The oppressed followers of God should be patient, for the Lord's coming is nigh ; and should not grudge against each other,* 7-9. *They should take encouragement from the example of the prophets, and of Job,* 10, 11. *Swearing forbidden,* 12. *Directions to the afflicted,* 13-15. *They should confess their faults to each other,* 16. *The great prevalence of prayer instanced in Elijah,* 17, 18. *The blessedness of converting a sinner from the error of his way,* 19, 20.

A. M. cir. 4065.
A. D. cir. 61.
An. Olymp.
cir. CCX. 1.
A. U. C. cir.
814.

GO ^a to now, *ye* rich men, weep and howl for your miseries that shall come upon *you.*

2 Your riches are corrupted, and ^b your garments are moth-eaten.

3 Your gold and silver is cankered; and the rust of them shall be a witness against you, and shall eat your flesh as it were fire. ^c Ye have heaped treasure together for the last days.

4 Behold, ^d the hire of the labourers who have reaped down your fields, which is of you kept back by fraud, crieth: and ^e the cries of them which have reaped are entered into the ears of the Lord of sabaoth.

5 ^f Ye have lived in pleasure on the earth, and been wanton; ye have nourished your hearts, as in a day of slaughter.

A. M. cir. 4065.
A. D. cir. 61.
An. Olymp.
cir. CCX. 1.
A. U. C. cir.
814.

---

^a Prov. xi. 28; Luke vi. 24; 1 Tim. vi. 9.——^b Job xiii. 28; Matt. vi. 20; chap. ii. 2.——^c Rom. ii. 5.——^d Lev. xix. 13; Job xxiv. 10, 11; Jer. xxii. 13; Mal. iii. 5; Eccles. xxxiv. 21, 22.——^e Deut. xxiv. 15.——^f Job xxi. 13; Amos vi. 1, 4; Luke xvi. 19, 25; 1 Tim. v. 6.

NOTES ON CHAP. V.

Verse 1. *Go to now*] See on chap. iv. 13.

Weep and howl for your miseries] St. James seems to refer here, in the spirit of prophecy, to the destruction that was coming upon the Jews, not only in Judea, but in all the provinces where they sojourned. He seems here to assume the very air and character of a *prophet;* and in the most dignified language and peculiarly expressive and energetic images, foretells the desolations that were coming upon this bad people.

Verse 2. *Your riches are corrupted*] Σεσηπε· Are *putrefied.* The term πλουτος, *riches,* is to be taken here, not for *gold,* *silver,* or *precious stones,* (for these could not *putrefy,*) but for the produce of the fields and flocks, the different stores of grain, wine, and oil, which they had laid up in their granaries, and the various changes of raiment which they had amassed in their wardrobes.

Verse 3. *Your gold and silver is cankered*] Instead of helping the poor, and thus honouring God with your substance, ye have, through the principle of covetousness, kept all to yourselves.

The rust of them shall be a witness against you] Your putrefied stores, your moth-eaten garments, and your tarnished coin, are so many proofs that it was not for want of property that you assisted not the poor, but through a principle of avarice; *loving money,* not for the sake of what it could procure, but for its *own sake,* which is the genuine principle of the *miser.* This was the very character given to this people by our Lord himself; he called them φιλαργυροι, *lovers of money.* Against this despicable and abominable disposition, the whole of the xiith chapter of St. Luke is levelled; but it was their easily besetting sin, and is so to the present day.

Shall eat your flesh as it were fire.] This is a very bold and sublime figure He represents the rust of their coin as becoming a canker that should produce gangrenes and phagedenous ulcers in their flesh, till it should be eaten away from their bones.

Ye have heaped treasure together] This verse is variously *pointed.* The word ὡς, *like as,* in the preceding clause, is left out by the *Syriac,* and some others; and πυρ, *fire,* is added here from that clause; so that the whole verse reads thus: "Your gold and your silver is cankered; and the rust of them shall be a witness against you, and shall consume your flesh. Ye have treasured up FIRE against the last days." This is a bold and fine image: instead of the *treasures of*

corn, wine, and *oil,* rich *stuffs,* with *silver* and *gold,* which ye have been laying up, ye shall find a *treasure,* a *magazine* of *fire,* that shall burn up your city, and consume even your temple. This was literally true; and these solemn denunciations of Divine wrath were most completely fulfilled. See the notes on Matt. xxiv., where all the circumstances of this tremendous and final destruction are particularly noted.

By the *last days* we are not to understand the *day of judgment,* but the *last days* of the *Jewish commonwealth,* which were not long distant from the date of this epistle, whether we follow the *earlier* or *later* computation, of which enough has been spoken in the preface.

Verse 4. *The hire of the labourers*] The law, Lev. xix. 13, had ordered: *The wages of him that is hired shall not abide with thee all night until the morning,* every day's labour being paid for as soon as ended. This is more clearly stated in another law, Deut. xxiv. 15: *At his day thou shalt give him his hire; neither shall the sun go down upon it;—lest he cry against thee unto the Lord, and it be sin unto thee.* And that God particularly resented this defrauding of the hireling we see from Mal. iii. 5: *I will come near to you in judgment, and will be a swift witness against those who oppress the hireling in his wages.* And on these laws and threatenings is built what we read in *Synopsis Sohar,* p. 100, 1 45 "When a poor man does any work in a house, the vapour proceeding from him, through the severity of his work, ascends towards heaven. Wo to his employer if he delay to pay him his wages." To this James seems particularly to allude, when he says: *The cries of them who have reaped are entered into the ears of the Lord of hosts;* and the rabbins say, "The vapour arising from the sweat of the hard-worked labourer *ascends up before God.*" Both images are sufficiently expressive.

The Lord of sabaoth.] St. James often conceives in *Hebrew* though he writes in *Greek.* It is well known that יהוה צבאות *Yehovah tsebaoth,* Lord of hosts, or Lord of armies, is a frequent appellation of God in the Old Testament; and signifies his uncontrollable power, and the infinitely numerous means he has for governing the world, and defending his followers, and punishing the wicked.

Verse 5 *Ye have lived in pleasure*] Ετρυφησατε. *Ye have lived luxuriously;* feeding yourselves without fear, pampering the flesh.

And been wanton] Εσπαταλησατε· *Ye have lived*

A. M. cir. 4065
A. D. cir. 61.
An. Olymp.
cir. CCX. 1.
A. U. C. cir.
814.

6 �g Ye have condemned *and* killed the just; *and* he doth not resist you.

7 ʰ Be patient, therefore, brethren, unto the coming of the Lord. Behold, the husbandman waiteth for the precious fruit of the earth, and hath long patience for it, until he receive ⁱ the early and latter rain.

8 Be ye also patient; stablish your hearts: ᵏ for the coming of the Lord draweth nigh.

9 ˡ Grudge ᵐ not one against another, brethren,

lest ye be condemned; behold, the judge ⁿ standeth before the door.

10 ° Take, my brethren, the prophets, who have spoken in the name of the Lord, for an example of suffering affliction, and of patience.

11 Behold, ᵖ we count them happy which endure. Ye have heard of �۹ the patience of Job, and have seen ʳ the end of the Lord; that ˢ the Lord is very pitiful, and of tender mercy.

A. M. cir. 4065
A. D. cir. 61.
An. Olymp.
cir. CCX. 1.
A. U. C. cir.
814.

ᵍ Chap. ii. 6.——ʰ Or, *Be long patient; or, Suffer with long patience.*——ⁱ Deut. xi. 14; Jer. v. 24; Hosea vi. 3; Joel ii. 23; Zech. x, 1.——ᵏ Phil. iv. 5; Hebrews x. 25, 37; 1 Peter iv. 7. ˡ Chap. iv. 11.

ᵐ Or, *Groan; or, Grieve not.*——ⁿ Matt. xxiv. 33; 1 Cor. iv. 5 ° Matt. v. 12; Heb. xi. 35, &c.——ᵖ Psa. xciv. 12; Matt. v. 10, 11; x. 22.——۹ Job i. 21, 22; ii. 10.——ʳ Job xlii. 10, &c ˢ Num. xiv. 18; Psa. ciii. 8.

---

lasciviously.** Ye have indulged all your sinful and sensual appetites to the uttermost; and your lives have been scandalous.

Ye have nourished your hearts] Εθρεψατε· Ye have *fattened your hearts,* and have rendered them incapable of *feeling, as in a day of slaughter,* ἡμερᾳ σφαγης, *a day of sacrifice,* where many victims are offered at once, and where the people feast upon the sacrifices; many, no doubt, turning, on that occasion, a holy ordinance into a riotous festival.

Verse 6. *Ye have condemned* and *killed the just; and he doth not resist you.*] Several by τον δικαιον, *the just one,* understand Jesus Christ, who is so called, Acts iii. 14; vii. 52; xxii. 14; but the structure of the sentence, and the connection in which it stands, seem to require that we should consider this as applying to the *just* or *righteous in general,* who were persecuted and murdered by those oppressive rich men; and their death was the consequence of their *dragging them before the judgment seats,* chap. ii. 6, where, having no influence, and none to plead their cause, they were unjustly condemned and executed.

And he doth not *resist you.*—In this, as in τον δικαιον, *the just,* there is an *enallege* of the *singular* for the *plural* number. And in the word ουκ αντιτασσεται, he doth not *resist,* the idea is included of *defence in a court of justice.* These poor righteous people had none to plead their cause; and if they had it would have been useless, as their oppressors had all power and all influence, and those who sat on these judgment seats were lost to all sense of justice and right. Some think that *he doth not resist you* should be referred to Gᴏᴅ; as if he had said, God permits you to go on in this way at present, but he will shortly awake to judgment, and destroy you as enemies of truth and righteousness.

Verse 7. *Be patient, therefore*] Because God is coming to execute judgment on this wicked people, therefore be patient till he comes. He seems here to refer to the coming of the Lord to execute judgment on the Jewish nation, which shortly afterwards took place.

The husbandman waiteth] The *seed* of your deliverance is already sown, and by and by the harvest of your salvation will take place. God's counsels will ripen in due time.

The early and latter rain.] The rain of *seed time;* and the rain of ripening before *harvest:* the first fell in Judea, about the beginning of *November,* after the seed was sown; and the second towards the end of *April,* when the ears were filling, and this prepared for a full harvest. Without these two rains, the earth would have been unfruitful. These God had promised: *I will give you the rain of your land in his due season, the first rain and the latter rain, that thou mayest gather in thy corn, and thy wine, and thy oil,* Deut. xi. 14. But for these they were not only to *wait patiently,* but also to *pray,* Ask ye of the Lord rain *in the time of the latter rain; so shall the Lord make bright clouds, and give them showers of rain, to every one grass in the field;* Zech. x. 1.

Verse 8. *Be ye also patient*] Wait for God's deliverance, as ye wait for his bounty in providence.

Stablish your hearts] Take courage; do not sink under your trials.

The coming of the Lord draweth nigh.] Ηγγικε· Is at hand. He is already *on his way* to destroy this wicked people, to raze their city and temple, and to destroy their polity for ever; and this judgment will soon take place.

Verse 9. *Grudge not*] Μη στεναζετε· Groan not; grumble not; do not murmur through impatience; and let not any ill treatment which you receive, induce you to vent your feelings in imprecations against your oppressors. Leave all this in the hands of God.

Lest ye be condemned] By giving way to a spirit of this kind, you will get under the condemnation of the wicked.

The judge standeth before the door.] His eye is upon every thing that is *wrong in you,* and every *wrong that is done to you;* and he is now entering into judgment with your oppressors.

Verse 10. *Take—the prophets*] The prophets who had spoken to their forefathers by the authority of God, were persecuted by the very people to whom they delivered the Divine message; but they suffered affliction and persecution with patience, commending their cause to him who judgeth righteously; therefore, imitate their example.

Verse 11. *We count them happy which endure.*] According to that saying of our blessed Lord, *Blessed are ye when men shall persecute and revile you—for*

A. M. cir. 4065.
A. D. cir. 61.
An. Olymp.
cir. CCX. 1.
A. U. C. cir.
814.

12 But above all things, my brethren, ^t swear not, neither by heaven, neither by the earth, neither by any other oath : but let your yea be yea ; and *your* nay, nay ; lest ye fall into condemnation.

13 Is any among you afflicted ? let him pray. Is any merry ? ^u let him sing psalms.

14 Is any sick among you ? let him call for the elders of the Church ; and let them pray over him, ^v anointing him

A. M. cir. 4065.
A. D. cir. 61.
An. Olymp.
cir. CCX. 1.
A. U. C. cir.
814.

^t Matt. v. 34, &c.——^u Eph. v. 19 ; Col. iii. 16.

^v Mark vi. 13 ; xvi. 18.

so persecuted they the prophets which were before you. Matt. v. 11, &c.

Ye have heard of the patience of Job] Stripped of all his worldly possessions, deprived at a stroke of all his children, tortured in body with sore disease, tempted by the devil, harassed by his wife, and calumniated by his friends, he nevertheless held fast his integrity, resigned himself to the Divine dispensations, and charged not God foolishly.

And have seen the end of the Lord] The *issue* to which God brought all his afflictions and trials, giving him children, increasing his property, lengthening out his life, and multiplying to him every kind of spiritual and secular good. This was *God's end* with respect to him ; but the *devil's end* was to drive him to despair, and to cause him to blaspheme his Maker. This mention of *Job* shows him to have been a real person ; for a fictitious person would not have been produced as an example of any virtue so highly important as that of patience and perseverance. *The end of the Lord is a Hebraism* for the *issue to which God brings any thing or business.*

The Lord is very pitiful, and of tender mercy.] Instead of πολυσπλαγχνος, which we translate *very pitiful,* and which might be rendered *of much sympathy,* from πολυς, *much,* and σπλαγχνον, *a bowel,* (because any thing that affects us with commiseration causes us to feel an indescribable emotion of the bowels,) several MSS. have πολυευσπλαγχνος, from πολυς, *much,* ευ, *easily,* and σπλαγχνον, *a bowel,* a word not easy to be translated ; but it signifies *one whose commiseration* is *easily excited,* and whose commiseration is *great* or *abundant.*

Verse 12. *Above all things—swear not*] What relation this exhortation can have to the subject in question, I confess I cannot see. It may not have been designed to stand in any connection, but to be a separate piece of advice, as in the several cases which immediately follow. That the Jews were notoriously guilty of *common swearing* is allowed on all hands ; and that swearing by *heaven, earth, Jerusalem,* the *temple,* the *altar,* different parts of the *body,* was not considered by them as *binding oaths,* has been sufficiently proved. Rabbi Akiba taught that " a man might swear with his *lips,* and annul it in his *heart ;* and then the oath was not binding." See the notes on Matt. v. 33, &c., where the subject is considered in great detail.

Let your yea be yea, &c.] Do not pretend to say *yea* with your *lips,* and annul it in your *heart ;* let the *yea* or the *nay* which you *express* be *bonâ fide* such. Do not imagine that any mental reservation can cancel any such *expressions* of obligation in the sight of God.

Lest ye fall into condemnation.] Ἱνα μη ὑπο κρισιν πεσητε· *Lest ye fall under judgment.* Several MSS. join ὑπο and κρισιν together, ὑποκρισιν, and prefix εις, *into,* which makes a widely different reading : *Lest ye fall into hypocrisy.* Now, as it is a fact, that the Jews did teach that there might be *mental reservation,* that would *annul the oath,* how solemnly soever it was taken ; the object of St. James, if the last reading be genuine, and it is supported by a great number of excellent MSS., some *versions,* and some of the most eminent of the *fathers,* was to guard against that *hypocritical* method of taking an oath, which is subversive of all moral feeling, and must make conscience itself callous.

Verse 13. *Is any among you afflicted ? let him pray*] The Jews taught that the meaning of the ordinance, Lev. xiii. 45, which required the leper to cry, *Unclean ! unclean !* was, " that thus *making known* his calamity, the people might be led to offer up prayers to God in his behalf ;" *Sota,* page 685, ed. Wagens. They taught also, that when any sickness or affliction entered a family, they should go to the wise men, and implore their prayers. *Bava bathra,* fol. 116, 1.

In *Nedarim,* fol. 40, 1, we have this relation : " Rabba, as often as he fell sick, forbade his domestics to mention it for the first day ; if he did not then begin to get well, he told his family to go and publish it in the highways, that they who hated him might rejoice, and they that loved him might intercede with God for him."

Is any merry ? let him sing psalms.] These are all general but very useful directions. It is natural for a man to *sing* when he is *cheerful* and *happy.* Now no subject can be more noble than that which is Divine : and as God alone is the author of all that good which makes a man *happy,* then his praise should be the subject of the *song* of him who is merry. But where persons rejoice in iniquity, and not in the truth, God and sacred things can never be the subject of their song.

Verse 14. *Is any sick among you ? let him call for the elders*] This was also a Jewish maxim. Rabbi Simeon, in *Sepher Hachaiyim,* said : " What should a man do who goes to visit the sick ? *Ans.* He who studies to restore the health of the body, should first lay the foundation in the health of the soul. The wise men have said, No healing is equal to that which comes from the *word of God* and *prayer.* Rabbi Phineas, the son of Chamma, hath said, ' When sickness or disease enters into a man's family, let him apply to a *wise man,* who will implore mercy in his behalf.' " See *Schoettgen.*

A. M. cir. 4065.
A. D. cir. 61.
An. Olymp.
cir. CCX. 1.
A. U. C. cir.
814.

with oil in the name of the Lord :

15 And the prayer of faith shall save the sick, and the Lord shall raise him up ; w and if he have committed sins, they shall be forgiven him.

16 Confess *your* faults one to

A. M. cir. 4065.
A. D. cir. 61.
An. Olymp.
cir. CCX. 1.
A. U. C. cir.
814.

w Isa. xxxiii. 24 ;   Matt. ix. 2.

St. James very properly sends all such to the elders of the Church, who had power with God through the great Mediator, that they might pray for them.

Anointing him with oil] That St. James neither means any kind of *incantation*, any kind of *miracle*, or such *extreme unction* as the Romish Church prescribes, will be sufficiently evident from these considerations : 1. He was a holy man, and could prescribe nothing but what was holy. 2. If a *miracle* was intended, it could have been as well wrought *without the oil*, as *with* it. 3. It is not intimated that even this unction is to save the sick man, but the prayer of faith, ver. 15. 4. What is here recommended was to be done as a natural means of restoring health, which, while they used prayer and supplication to God, they were not to neglect. 5. *Oil* in Judea was celebrated for its *sanative* qualities ; so that they scarcely ever took a journey without carrying oil with them, (see in the case of the Samaritan,) with which they anointed their bodies, healed their wounds, bruises, &c. 6. *Oil* was and is frequently used in the east as a means of cure in very dangerous diseases ; and in Egypt it is often used in the cure of the *plague*. Even in Europe it has been tried with great success in the cure of *dropsy*. And *pure olive oil* is excellent for recent wounds and bruises : and I have seen it tried in this way with the best effects. 7. But that it was the custom of the Jews to apply it as a means of healing, and that St. James refers to this custom, is not only evident from the case of the wounded man ministered to by the good Samaritan, Luke x. 34, but from the practice of the Jewish rabbins. In *Midrash Koheleth*, fol. 73, 1, it is said : " Chanina, son of the brother of the Rabbi Joshua, went to visit his uncle at Capernaum ; he was taken ill ; and Rabbi Joshua went to him and *anointed him with oil, and he was restored.*" They had, therefore, recourse to this as a *natural* remedy ; and we find that the disciples used it also in this way to heal the sick, not exerting the miraculous power but in cases where natural means were ineffectual. *And they cast out many devils, and anointed with oil many that were sick, and healed* them ; Mark vi. 13. On this latter place I have supposed that it might have been done *symbolically*, in order to prepare the way for a miraculous cure : this is the opinion of many commentators ; but I am led, on more mature consideration, to doubt its propriety, yet dare not decide. In short, *anointing the sick with oil*, in order to their recovery, was a constant practice among the Jews. See *Lightfoot* and Wetstein on Mark vi. 13. And here I am satisfied that it has no other meaning than as a *natural means* of restoring health ; and that St. James desires them to use *natural means* while looking to God for an especial blessing. And no wise man would direct otherwise. 8. That the *anointing* recommended here by St. James cannot be such as the Romish Church prescribes, and it is on this passage principally

that they found their sacrament of *extreme unction*, is evident from these considerations : 1. St. James orders the sick person to be *anointed* in reference to *his cure* ; but they anoint the sick in the *agonies of death*, when there is *no prospect of his recovery* ; and never administer that *sacrament*, as it is called, while there is *any hope of life*. 2. St James orders this *anointing* for the cure of the *body*, but they apply it for the cure of the *soul* ; in reference to which use of it St. James gives no directions : and what is said of the *forgiveness of sins*, in ver. 15, is rather to be referred to *faith* and *prayer*, which are often the means of restoring lost health, and preventing premature death, when *natural means*, the most skilfully used, have been useless. 3. The *anointing with oil*, if ever used as a means or *symbol* in *working miraculous cures*, was only applied in *some cases*, perhaps *very few*, if any ; but the Romish Church uses it in *every case* ; and makes it *necessary* to the salvation of every departing soul. Therefore, St. *James' unction*, and the *extreme unction* of the Romish Church, are essentially different. See below.

Verse 15. And the prayer of faith shall save the sick] That is, God will often make these the means of a sick man's recovery ; but there often are cases where *faith* and *prayer* are both ineffectual, because God sees it will be prejudicial to the patient's salvation to be restored ; and therefore all faith and prayer on such occasions should be exerted on this ground : " If it be most for thy glory, and the eternal good of this man's soul, let him be restored ; if otherwise, Lord, pardon, purify him, and take him to thy glory."

The Lord shall raise him up] Not the *elders*, how faithfully and fervently soever they have prayed.

And if he have committed sins] So as to have occasioned his present malady, *they shall be forgiven him* ; for being the *cause* of the affliction it is natural to conclude that, if the *effect* be to cease, the *cause* must be removed. We find that in the miraculous restoration to health, under the powerful hand of Christ, the sin of the party is generally said to be *forgiven*, and this also *before* the miracle was wrought on the *body* : hence there was a maxim among the Jews, and it seems to be founded in *common sense* and *reason*, that God never restores a man miraculously to health till he has pardoned his sins ; because it would be incongruous for God to exert his miraculous power in saving a *body*, the *soul* of which was in a state of condemnation to eternal death, because of the crimes it had committed against its Maker and Judge. Here then it is God that *remits the sin*, not in reference to the *unction*, but in reference to the *cure of the body*, which he is miraculously to effect.

Verse 16. Confess your faults one to another] This is a good general direction to Christians who endeavour to maintain among themselves the communion of saints. This social confession tends much to humble

2

A. M. cir. 4065.
A. D. cir. 61.
An. Olymp.
cir. CCX. 1.
A. U. C. cir.
814.

another, and pray one for another, that ye may be healed. [x] The effectual fervent prayer of a righteous man availeth much.

17 Elias was a man [y] subject to like passions as we are, and [z] he prayed [a] earnestly tnat it might not rain; [b] and it rained not on the earth by the space of three years and six months.

18 And [c] he prayed again, and the heaven gave rain, and the earth brought forth her fruit.

19 Brethren, [d] if any of you do err from the truth, and óne convert him :

20 Let him know, that he which converteth the sinner from the error of his way [e] shall save a soul from death, and [f] shall hide a multitude of sins.

A. M. cir. 4065.
A. D. cir. 61.
An. Olymp.
cir. CCX. 1.
A. U. C. cir.
814.

---

[x] Gen. xx. 17; Num. xi. 2; Deut. ix. 18, 19, 20; Josh. x. 12; 1 Sam. xii. 18; 1 Kings xiii. 6; 2 Kings iv. 33; xix. 15, 20; xx. 2, 4, &c.; Psa. x. 17; xxxiv. 15; cxlv. 18; Prov. xv. 29; xxviii. 9; John ix. 31; 1 John iii. 22.

[y] Acts xiv. 15.——[z] 1 Kings xvii. 1.——[a] Or, *in prayer.* [b] Luke iv. 25.——[c] 1 Kings xviii. 42, 45.——[d] Matt. xviii. 15. [e] Rom. xi. 14; 1 Cor. ix. 22; 1 Tim. iv. 16.——[f] Prov. x. 12; 1 Pet. iv. 8.

---

the soul, and to make it watchful. We naturally wish that our friends in general, and our religious friends in particular, should think well of us; and when we confess to them offences which, without this confession, they could never have known, we feel humbled, are kept from self-applause, and induced to watch unto prayer, that we may not increase our offences before God, or be obliged any more to undergo the painful humiliation of acknowledging our weakness, fickleness, or infidelity to our religious brethren.

It is not said, *Confess your faults to the* ELDERS *that they may forgive them,* or prescribe *penance* in order to forgive them. No; the members of the Church were to *confess their faults to each other;* therefore *auricular confession* to a priest, such as is prescribed by the Romish Church, has no foundation in this passage. Indeed, had it any foundation here it would prove more than they wish, for it would require the *priest* to *confess his sins* to the *people,* as well as the people to confess theirs to the priest.

And pray one for another] There is no instance in *auricular confession* where the *penitent* and the *priest* pray together for pardon; but here the people are commanded to pray for each other that they may be healed.

The effectual fervent prayer of a righteous man availeth much.] The words δεησις ενεργουμενη signify *energetic supplication,* or such a prayer as is *suggested* to the *soul* and *wrought in it by a Divine energy.* When God designs to do some particular work in his *Church* he pours out on his followers the spirit of grace and supplication; and this he does sometimes when he is about to do some especial work for an *individual.* When such a power of prayer is granted, faith should be immediately called into exercise, that the blessing may be given : the spirit of prayer is the proof that the power of God is present to heal. *Long prayers* give no particular evidence of *Divine inspiration:* the following was a maxim among the ancient Jews, שתפלת צדיקים קצרה *the prayers of the righteous are short.* This is exemplified in almost every instance in the Old Testament.

Verse 17. *Elias was a man subject to like passions*] This was *Elijah,* and a consistency between the *names* of the same persons as expressed in the Old and the New Testaments should be kept up.

The word ὁμοιοπαθης signifies of *the same constitution,* a human being just as ourselves are. See the

same phrase and its explanation in Acts xiv. 15, and the note there. There was some reason to apprehend that because Elijah was *translated,* that therefore he was more *than human,* and if so, his example could be no pattern for us ; and as the design of St. James was to excite men to pray, expecting the Divine interference whenever that should be necessary, therefore he tells them that *Elijah was a man like themselves, of the same constitution, liable to the same accidents,* and *needing the same supports.*

And he prayed earnestly] Προσευχῃ προσηυξατο· *He prayed with prayer ;* a Hebraism for, he *prayed fervently.*

That it might not rain] See this history, 1 Kings xvii. 1, &c.

And it rained not on the earth] Επι της γης· *On that land,* viz. the land of Judea ; for this drought did not extend elsewhere.

Three years and six months.] This is the term mentioned by our Lord, Luke iv. 25 ; but this is not specified in the original history. In 1 Kings xviii. 1, it is said, *In the third year the word of the Lord came to Elijah,* that is, concerning the *rain ;* but this *third year* is to be computed from the time of his going to live at Zarephath, which happened many days after the *drought began,* as is plain from this, that he remained at the *brook Cherith* till it was dried up, and then went to Zarephath, in the country of Zidon ; 1 Kings xvii. 7–9. Therefore the *three years* and *six months* must be computed from his denouncing the drought, at which time that judgment commenced. *Macknight.*

Verse 18. *And he prayed again*] This *second* prayer is not mentioned in the history in express words, but as in 1 Kings xvii. 42, it is said, *He cast himself down upon the earth, and put his face between his knees ;* that was probably the time of the second praying, namely, that rain might come, as this was the proper posture of prayer.

Verse 19. *Err from the truth*] Stray away from the Gospel of Christ ; *and one convert him*—reclaim him from his error, and bring him back to the fold of Christ.

Verse 20. *Let him know*] Let him duly consider, for his encouragement, that he who is the instrument of converting a sinner shall save a soul from eternal death, and a body from ruin, *and shall hide a multitude of sins ;* for in being the means of his conversion we bring him back to God, who, in his infinite mercy, *hides* or *blots out* the numerous sins which he had committed during the time of his backsliding. It is not the man's sins who is the means of his conversion, but the sins of the backslider, which are here said to be *hidden.* See more below.

1. MANY are of opinion that the *hiding a multitude of sins* is here to be understood of the person who converts the backslider : this is a dangerous doctrine, and what the Holy Spirit never taught to man. Were this true it would lead many a sinner to endeavour the reformation of his neighbour, that himself might continue under the influence of his own beloved sins; and *conversion to a particular creed* would be put in the place of *conversion to God,* and thus the substance be lost in the shadow. Bishop *Atterbury,* (Ser. vol. i. p. 46,) and *Scott,* (Christian Life, vol. i. p. 368,) contend " that the *covering a multitude of sins* includes also that the *pious action* of which the apostle speaks engages God to look with *greater indulgence* on the character of the person that performs it, and to be *less severe in marking what he has done amiss.*" See *Macknight.* This from such authorities may be considered doubly dangerous; it argues however great ignorance of God, of the nature of Divine justice, and of the sinfulness of sin. It is besides completely *anti-evangelical;* it teaches in effect that something besides the *blood of the covenant* will render God propitious to man, and that the performance of *a pious action* will induce God's justice to show *greater indulgence* to the person who performs it, and to be *less severe in marking what he has done amiss.* On the ground of this doctrine we might confide that, had we a certain quantum of *pious acts,* we might have all the sins of our lives forgiven, independently of the *sacrifice of Christ;* for if *one pious act* can procure pardon for a *multitude of sins,* what may not be expected from many?

2. The *Jewish* doctrine, to which it is possible St. James may allude, was certainly more *sound* than that taught by these *Christian divines.* They allowed that the man who was the means of converting another had done a work highly pleasing to God, and which should be rewarded; but they never insinuate that this would *atone* for sin. I shall produce a few examples :—

In *Synopsis Sohar,* p. 47, n. 17, it is said : *Great is his excellence who persuades a sick person to turn from his sins.*

Ibid, p. 92, n. 18 : *Great is his reward who brings back the pious into the way of the blessed Lord.*

Yoma, fol. 87, 1 : *By his hands iniquity is not committed, who turns many to righteousness;* i. e. God does not permit him to fall into sin. *What is the reason?* Ans. *Lest those should be found in paradise, while their instructer is found in hell.*

This doctrine is both innocent and godly in comparison of the other. It holds out a *motive* to diligence and zeal, but nothing farther. In short, if we allow any thing to *cover our sins* beside the *mercy of God* in *Christ Jesus,* WE *shall err* most dangerously *from the truth,* and add this moreover to the *multitude of* OUR *sins,* that we maintained that the gift of God could be purchased by our puny acts of comparative righteousness.

3. As one immortal soul is of more worth than all

the material creation of God, every man who knows the worth of his own should labour for the salvation of others. To be the means of depriving hell of her expectation, and adding even one soul to the Church triumphant, is a matter of infinite moment; and he who is such an instrument has much reason to thank God that ever he was born. He who lays out his accounts to do good to the souls of men, will ever have the blessing of God in his own. Besides, God will not suffer him to labour in vain, or spend his strength for naught. At first he may see little fruit; but the bread cast upon the waters shall be found after many days : and if he should never see it in this life, he may take for granted that whatsoever he has done for God, in simplicity and godly sincerity, has been less or more effectual.

After the last word of this epistle ἁμαρτιων, *of sins,* some versions add *his,* others *theirs;* and one MS. and the later *Syriac* have *Amen.* But these additions are of no authority.

The *subscriptions* to this epistle, in the VERSIONS, are the following : The end of the Epistle of James the apostle.—SYRIAC. The catholic Epistle of James the apostle is ended.—SYRIAC PHILOXENIAN. The end.—ÆTHIOPIC. Praise be to God for ever and ever; and may his mercy be upon us. Amen.—ARABIC. The Epistle of James the *son of Zebedee,* is ended. —ITALA, one copy. Nothing.—COPTIC. Nothing.— Printed VULGATE. The Epistle of James is ended.— *Bib.* VULG. Edit. *Eggestein.* The Epistle of St. James the apostle is ended.—*Complutensian.*

In the MANUSCRIPTS : Of James.—Codex *Vaticanus,* B. The Epistle of James.—Codex *Alexandrinus.* The end of the catholic Epistle of James.— Codex *Vaticanus,* 1210. The catholic Epistle of James the apostle.—A *Vienna* MS. The catholic Epistle of the holy Apostle James.—An ancient MS. in the library of the *Augustins,* at Rome. The end of the Epistle of the holy Apostle James, the *brother of God.*—One of *Petavius's* MSS., written in the *thirteenth century.* The same is found in a *Vatican* MS. of the *eleventh* century. The most ancient MSS. have little or no subscription.

Two opinions relative to the author are expressed in these MSS. One copy of the *Itala,* the *Codex Corbejensis,* at Paris, which contains this epistle only, attributes it to *James, the son of Zebedee;* and two, comparatively *recent,* attribute it to James, *our Lord's brother.* The former testimony, taken in conjunction with some internal evidences, led Michaelis, and some others, to suppose it probable that *James the elder,* or the *son of Zebedee,* was the author. I should give it to this apostle, in preference to the other, had I not reason to believe that a *James,* different from either, was the author. But *who* or *what* he was, at this distance of time, it is impossible to say. Having now done with all comments on the text, I shall conclude with some particulars relative to *James,* our Lord's brother, and some general observations on the structure and importance of this epistle.

I have entered but little into the history of this James, because I was not satisfied that he is the author of this epistle : however, observing that the current of

modern authors are decided in their opinion that he
was the author, I perceive I may be blamed unless I
be more particular concerning his life; as some of the
ancients have related several circumstances relative to
him that are very remarkable, and, indeed, singular.
Dr. Lardner has collected the whole; and, although
the same authors from whom he has taken his accounts
are before me, yet, not supposing that I can at all
mend either his selections or arrangement, I shall take
the accounts as he states them.

" I should now proceed," says this learned man,
" to write the history of this person (*James*) from
ancient authors; but that is a difficult task, as I have
found, after trying more than once, and at distant
spaces of time. I shall therefore take DIVERS passages
of Eusebius and others, and make such reflections as
offer for finding out as much truth as we can.

" Eusebius, in his chapter concerning our Saviour's
disciples, (Eccl. Hist. lib. i., cap. 12,) speaks of James,
to whom our Lord showed himself after his resurrection, 1 Cor. xv. 7, as being one of the seventy disciples.

" The same author has another chapter, (Hist. Eccl.,
lib. ii., cap. 1,) entitled, Of Things constituted by the
Apostles after our Saviour's Ascension, which is to this
purpose:—

" The first is the choice of Matthias, one of Christ's
disciples, into the apostleship, in the room of Judas;
then the appointment of the seven deacons, one of
whom was Stephen, who, soon after his being ordained, was stoned by those who had killed the Lord, and
was the first martyr for Christ; then James, called the
Lord's brother, because he was the son of Joseph, to
whom the Virgin Mary was espoused. This James,
called by the ancients the just, on account of his eminent virtue, is said to have been appointed the first
bishop of Jerusalem; and Clement, in the sixth book
of his Institutions, writes after this manner: That after
our Lord's ascension, Peter, and James, and John,
though they had been favoured by the Lord above the
rest, did not contend for honour, but chose James the
just to be bishop of Jerusalem; and in the seventh
book of the same work he says, that after his resurrection the Lord gave to James the just, and Peter,
and John, the gift of knowledge; and they gave it to
the other apostles, and the other apostles gave it to the
seventy, one of whom was Barnabas: for there were
two named James, one the just, who was thrown down
from the battlement of the temple and killed by a fuller's staff; the other is he who was beheaded. Of
him who was called the just, Paul also makes mention, saying, Other of the apostles saw I none, save
James the Lord's brother.

" I would now take a passage from Origen, in the
tenth vol. of his Commentaries upon Matt. xiii. 55, 56:
*Is not this the carpenter's son? Is not his mother
called Mary? And his brethren, James, and Joses,
and Simon, and Judas? And his sisters, are they not
all with us?* They thought, says Origen, that he was
the son of Joseph and Mary. The brethren of Jesus,
some say, upon the ground of tradition, and particularly of what is said in the gospel according to Peter,
or the book of James, were the sons of Joseph by a
former wife, who cohabited with him before Mary.
They who say this are desirous of maintaining the

honour of Mary's virginity to the last, (or her perpetual
virginity,) that the body chosen to fulfil what is said,
*The Holy Ghost shall come upon thee, and the power
of the Highest shall overshadow thee,* Luke i. 35,
might not know man after that: and I think it very
reasonable that, as Jesus was the first fruits of virginity among men, Mary should be the same among
women; for it would be very improper to give that
honour to any besides her. This James is he whom
Paul mentions in his Epistle to the Galatians, saying,
*Other of the apostles. saw I none, save James the
Lord's brother.* This James was in so great repute
with the people for his virtue, that Josephus, who
wrote twenty books of the Jewish antiquities, desirous
to assign the reason of their suffering such things, so
that even their temple was destroyed, says that those
things were owing to the anger of God for what they
did to James, the brother of Jesus, who is called
Christ. And it is wonderful that he, who did not believe our Jesus to be the Christ, should bear such a
testimony to James. He also says that the people
thought they suffered those things on account of
James. Jude, who wrote an epistle, of a few lines
indeed, but filled with the powerful word of the heavenly grace, says, at the beginning, *Jude, a servant
of Jesus Christ, and brother of James.* Of Joses and
Simon we know nothing.

" Origen, in his books against Celsus, quotes Josephus again as speaking of James, to the like purpose;
but there are not now any such passages in Josephus,
though they are quoted as from him by Eusebius also.
As the death of James has been mentioned, I shall now
immediately take the accounts of it which are in Eusebius, and I will transcribe a large part of the twenty-
third chapter of the second book of his Ecclesiastical
History: ' But when Paul had appealed to Cæsar, and
Festus had sent him to Rome, the Jews being disappointed in their design against him, turned their rage
against James, the Lord's brother, to whom the apostles
had consigned the episcopal chair of Jerusalem, and in
this manner they proceeded against him: having laid
hold of him, they required him, in the presence of all
the people, to renounce his faith in Christ; but he,
with freedom and boldness beyond expectation, before
all the multitude declared our Lord and Saviour Jesus
Christ to be the Son of God. They, not enduring the
testimony of a man who was in high esteem for his
piety, laid hold of the opportunity when the country
was without a governor to put him to death; for Festus
having died about that time in Judea, the province had
in it no procurator. The manner of the death of James
was shown before in the words of Clement, who said
that he was thrown off the battlement of the temple,
and then beat to death with a club. But no one has
so accurately related this transaction as Hegesippus, a
man in the first succession of the apostles, in the fifth
book of his Commentaries, whose words are to this
purpose: James, the brother of our Lord, undertook,
together with the apostles, the government of the
Church. He has been called the just by all, from
the time of our Saviour to ours: for many have been
named James; but he was holy from his mother's
womb. He drank neither wine nor strong drink, nor
did he eat any animal food; there never came a razor

830   2

upon his head; he neither anointed himself with oil, nor did he use a bath. To him alone was it lawful to enter the holy place. He wore no woollen, but only linen garments. He entered into the temple alone, where he prayed upon his knees; insomuch that his knees were become like the knees of a camel by means of his being continually upon them, worshipping God, and praying for the forgiveness of the people. Upon account of his virtue he was called the just, and Oblias, that is, the defence of the people, and righteousness. Some, therefore, of the seven sects which were among the Jews, of whom I spoke in the former part of these Commentaries, asked him, Which is the gate of Jesus? or, What is the gate of salvation? and he said, Jesus is the Saviour, or the way of salvation. Some of them therefore believed that Jesus is the Christ. And many of the chief men also believing, there was a disturbance among the Jews and among the scribes and Pharisees, who said there was danger lest all the people should think Jesus to be the Christ. Coming therefore to James they said, We beseech thee to restrain the error of this people; we entreat thee to persuade all who come hither at the time of passover to think rightly concerning Jesus, for all the people and all of us put confidence in thee. Stand therefore on the battlement of the temple, that being placed on high thou mayest be conspicuous, and thy words may be easily heard by all the people; for because of the passover all the tribes are come hither, and many Gentiles. Therefore the scribes and Pharisees before named placed James upon the battlement of the temple, and cried out to him, and said, O Justus, whom we ought all to believe, since the people are in an error, following Jesus, who was crucified, tell us what is the gate of Jesus. And he answered with a loud voice, Why do you ask me concerning the Son of man? He even sitteth in the heaven, at the right hand of the great Power, and will come in the clouds of heaven. And many were fully satisfied and well pleased with the testimony of James, saying, Hosanna to the Son of David! But the same scribes and Pharisees said one to another, We have done wrong in procuring such a testimony to Jesus. Let us go up and throw him down, that the people may be terrified from giving credit to him. And they went up presently, and cast him down, and said, Let us stone James the just: and they began to stone him because he was not killed by the fall. But he turning himself, kneeled, saying, I entreat thee, O Lord God the Father, forgive them, for they know not what they do. As they were stoning him, one said, Give over. What do ye? The just man prays for you. And one of them, a fuller, took a pole, which was used to beat clothes with, and struck him on the head. Thus his martyrdom was completed. And they buried him in that place; and his monument still remains near the temple. This James was a true witness, both to Jews and Gentiles, that Jesus is the Christ. Soon after Judea was invaded by Vespasian, and the people were carried captive.' So writes Hegesippus at large, agreeably to Clement. For certain, James was an excellent man, and much esteemed by many for his virtue; insomuch that the most thoughtful men among the Jews were of opinion that his death was the cause of the siege of Jerusalem,

which followed soon after his martyrdom; and that it was owing to nothing else but the wickedness committed against him. And Josephus says the same in these words: 'These things befell the Jews in vindication of James the just, who was brother of Jesus, called the Christ. For the Jews killed him, who was a most righteous man.'

"The time of the death of James may be determined without much difficulty; he was alive when Paul came to Jerusalem at the pentecost, in the year of Christ 58, and it is likely that he was dead when St. Paul wrote the Epistle to the Hebrews at the beginning of the year 63. Theodoret, upon Heb. xiii. 7, supposes the apostle there to refer to the martyrdoms of Stephen, James the brother of John, and James the just. According to Hegesippus, the death of James happened about the time of passover, which might be that of the year 62; and if Festus was then dead, and Albinus not arrived, the province was without a governor. Such a season left the Jews at liberty to gratify their licentious and turbulent disposition, and they were very likely to embrace it."

I have said but little relative to the controversy concerning the *apostleship* of James, our Lord's brother; for, as I am still in doubt whether he was the author of this epistle, I do not judge it necessary to enter into the question. I proceed now to some general observations on the epistle itself, and the evidence it affords of the learning and science of its author.

1. I have already conjectured that this epistle ranks among the *most ancient* of the Christian writings; its total want of reference to the great facts which distinguish the early history of the Church, viz., the calling of the Gentiles, the disputes between them and the Jews, the questions concerning circumcision, and the obligation of the law in connection with the Gospel, &c., &c., shows that it must have been written *before* those things took place, or that they must have been wholly unknown to the author; which is incredible, allowing him to have been a *Christian* writer.

2. The *style* of this epistle is much more elevated than most other parts of the New Testament. It abounds with figures and metaphors, at once bold, dignified, just, and impressive. Many parts of it are in the genuine prophetic style, and much after the manner of the Prophet *Zephaniah*, to whom there is a near resemblance in several passages.

3. An attentive reader of this epistle will perceive the author to be a man of *deep thought* and *considerable learning*. He had studied the Jewish prophets closely, and imitated their style; but he appears also to have read the *Greek poets:* his *language* is such as we might expect from one who had made them his study, but who avoided to quote them. We find a perfect *Greek hexameter* in chap. i. 17, and another may be perceived in chap. iv. 4; but these are probably not borrowed, but are the spontaneous, undesigned effort of his own well cultivated mind. His *science* may be noted in several places, but particularly in chap. i. 17, on which see the note and the diagram, and its explanation at the end of the chapter. Images from *natural history* are not unfrequent; and that in chap. i. 14, 15 is exceedingly correct and appropriate, but will not bear a closely literal translation.

4. His constant attention and reference to the *writings and maxims of his own countrymen* is peculiarly observable. Several of his remarks tend to confirm the antiquity of the *Talmud;* and the parallel passages in the different *tracts* of that work cast much light on the allusions of St. James. Without constant reference to the ancient Jewish rabbins, we should have sought for the meaning of several passages in vain.

5. St. James is in many places *obscure;* this may arise partly from his own deep and strong conceptions, and partly from allusions to *arts* or *maxims* which are not come down to us, or which lie yet undiscovered in the *Mishna* or *Talmud.* To elucidate this writer I have taken more than common pains, but dare not say that I have been always successful, though I have availed myself of all the help within my reach. To *Schoettgen's* Horæ Hebraicæ I am considerably indebted, as also to Dr. *Macknight, Kypke, Rosenmüller,* &c., but in many cases I have departed from all these, and others of the same class, and followed my own light.

6. On the controversy relative to the *doctrine of justification,* as taught by Paul and James, I have not entered deeply; I have produced in the proper places what appeared to me to be the most natural method of reconciling those writers. I believe St. James not to be in opposition to St. Paul, but to a corrupt doctrine taught among his *own countrymen* relative to this important subject. The *doctrine of justification by faith in Christ Jesus,* as taught by St. Paul, is *both* rational and true. St. James shows that a *bare belief in the God of Israel* justifies no man; and that the *genuine faith* that justifies works by love, and produces obedience to all the precepts contained in the moral law; and that this obedience is the evidence of the sincerity of that faith which professes to have put its possessor in the enjoyment of the peace and favour of God.

7. This epistle ends *abruptly,* and scarcely appears to be a finished work. The author probably intended to have added more, but may have been prevented by death. James, our Lord's brother, was murdered by the Jews, as we have already seen. James, the son Zebedee, had probably a short race; but whether either of these were its author we know not. The work was probably *posthumous,* not appearing till after the author's death; and this may have been one reason why it was so little known in the earliest ages of the primitive Church.

8. The spirit of *Antinomianism* is as dangerous in the Church as the spirit of *Pharisaism;* to the *former* the Epistle of James is a most *powerful antidote;* and the Christian minister who wishes to improve and guard the morals of his flock will bring its important doctrines, in due proportion, into his public ministry It is no proof of the improved state of public morals that many, who call themselves *evangelical teachers,* scarcely ever attempt to instruct the public by texts selected from this epistle.

For other particulars, relative to the *time* of writing this epistle, the *author,* his *inspiration, apostleship,* &c., I must refer to Michaelis and Lardner, and to the *preface.*

Millbrook, Dec. 9, 1816

Finished correcting this epistle for a new edition, Dec. 31, 1831.

832

2

PREFACE

TO

THE FIRST AND SECOND EPISTLES

OF

PETER.

DR. LARDNER and Professor Michaelis have done much to remove several difficulties connected with the *person* of St. Peter, the *people* to whom he wrote, the *places* of their dispersion, and the *time* of writing. I shall extract what makes more immediately for my purpose.

"The land of Palestine, says Cave, at and before the coming of our blessed Saviour, was distinguished into three several provinces, Judea, Samaria, and Galilee. In the upper, called also Galilee of the Gentiles, within the division belonging to the tribe of Naphtali, stood Bethsaida, formerly an obscure and inconsiderable village, till lately re-edified and enlarged by Philip the Tetrarch; and, in honour of Julia, daughter of Augustus, called by him Julias. It was situated upon the banks of the sea of Galilee, called also the lake of Tiberias, and the lake of Gennesareth, which was about forty furlongs in breadth, and a hundred in length; and had a wilderness on the other side called the desert of Bethsaida, whither our Saviour used often to retire.

"At this place was born *Simon*, surnamed *Cephas*, or *Petros*, *Petrus*, *Peter*, signifying a *stone*, or fragment of a rock. He was a fisherman upon the forementioned lake or sea, as was also in all probability his father Jonas, Jonah, or John. He had a brother named Andrew: which was the eldest of the two is not certain; for, concerning this, there were different opinions among the ancients. Epiphanius supposed Andrew to be the elder; but, according to Chrysostom, Peter was the first-born. So likewise Bede and Cassian, who even make Peter's age the ground of his precedence among the apostles; and Jerome himself has expressed himself in like manner, saying, 'that the keys were given to all the apostles alike, and the Church was built upon all of them equally; but, for preventing dissension, precedency was given to one. John might have been the person, but he was too young; and Peter was preferred on account of his age.'

"The call of Andrew and Peter to a stated attendance on Jesus is recorded in three evangelists. Their father Jonas seems to have been dead; for there is no mention of him, as there is of Zebedee, when his two sons were called. It is only said of Andrew and Peter that, when Jesus called them, *they left their nets and followed him. Follow me*, said he, *and I will make you fishers of men.*

"Simon Peter was married when called by our Lord to attend upon him; and upon occasion of that alliance, it seems, had removed from Bethsaida to Capernaum, where was his wife's family. Upon her mother our Saviour wrought a great miracle of healing. And, I suppose, that when our Lord *left Nazareth, and came and dwelled at Capernaum*, he made Peter's house the place of his usual abode when he was in those parts. I think we have a proof of it in the history just noticed. When Jesus came out of the synagogue at Capernaum, he *entered into Simon's house*, Luke iv. 38. Compare Mark i. 29, which is well paraphrased by Dr. Clarke: 'Now when Jesus came out of the synagogue, he went home to Peter's house;' and there it was that the people resorted unto him.

"Some time after this, when our Lord had an opportunity of private conversation with the disciples, he inquired of them what men said of him; and then whom they thought him to be. 'Simon Peter answered and said, Thou art the Christ, the Son of the living God;' Matt. xvi. 13–16. So far likewise in Mark viii. 27–29, and Luke ix. 18–20. Then follows, in Matt. xvi. 17–19: 'And Jesus answered and said unto him, Blessed art thou, Simon Bar-Jona, for flesh and blood hath not revealed it unto thee, but my Father which is in heaven:' that is, 'it is not a partial affection for me, thy Master, nor a fond and inconsiderate regard for the judgments of others for whom thou hast a respect, that has induced thee to think thus of me; but it is a just persuasion formed in thy mind by observing the great works thou hast seen me do by the power of God in the confirmation of my mission and doctrine.' 'And I say unto thee, thou art Peter, and upon this rock will I build my Church—and I will give unto thee the keys of the kingdom of heaven.' By which many of our interpreters suppose that our Lord promised to Peter that he should have the honour of beginning to preach the Gospel after his resurrection to Jews and Gentiles, and of receiving them into the Church; if so that is personal. Nevertheless, what follows, ' And whatsoever thou shalt bind on earth, shall be bound in heaven; and whatsoever thou shalt loose on earth, shall be loosed in heaven;' this, I say, must have been the privilege of all the apostles, for the like things are expressly said to them, Luke xxii. 29, 30; John xx. 21–23. Moreover, all the apostles concurred with Peter in the first preaching both to Jews and Gentiles. As he was president in the college of the apostles, it was very fit, and a thing of course, that he should be primarily concerned in the first opening of things. The confession now particularly before us was made by him; but it was in answer to a question that had been put to all; and he spoke the sense of all the apostles, and in their name. I suppose this to be as true in this instance, as in the other before mentioned, which is in John vi. 68, 69. In the account which St. John has given us of our Saviour's washing the disciples' feet, Peter's modesty and fervour are conspicuous. When the Jewish officers were about to apprehend our Lord, ' Peter, having a sword, drew it, and smote a servant of the high priest, and cut off his right ear.' Our Lord having checked Peter, touched the servant's ear, and healed him. So great is Jesus everywhere! They that laid hold of Jesus led him away to the house of Caiaphas; the rest of the disciples now forsook him and fled; ' but Peter followed him afar off, unto the high priest's palace; and went in and sat with the servants to see the end.' Here Peter thrice disowned his Lord, peremptorily denying that he was one of the disciples, or had any knowledge of him, as related by all the evangelists; for which he soon after humbled himself, and wept bitterly. We do not perceive that Peter followed our Lord any farther; or that he at all attended the crucifixion. It is likely that he was under too much concern of mind to appear in public; and that he chose retirement, as most suitable to his present temper and circumstances.

" On the first day of the week, early in the morning, when Mary Magdalene and other women came to the sepulchre, bringing sweet spices which they had prepared, 'they saw an angel, who said unto them, Be not affrighted; ye seek Jesus who was crucified: he is not here, for he is risen: Go quickly, and tell his disciples that he is risen from the dead.' As in Matthew, ' Tell his disciples and Peter.' As in Mark, ' Behold he goeth before you into Galilee.' That was a most gracious disposal of Providence to support the disciples, Peter in particular, in their great affliction.

" Our Lord first showed himself to Mary Magdalene, and afterwards to some other women. On the same day likewise on which he arose from the dead, he showed himself to Peter, though the circumstances of this appearance are nowhere related. And it has been observed, that as Mary Magdalene was the first woman, so Peter was the first man, to whom Jesus showed himself after he was risen from the dead.

" We have nowhere any distinct account of this apostle's travels: he might return to Judea, and stay there a good while after having been at Antioch, at the time spoken of by St. Paul in the Epistle to the Galatians. However, it appears from Epiphanius that Peter was often in the countries of Pontus and Bithynia; and by Eusebius we are assured that Origen, in the third tome of his Exposition of the Book of Genesis, writes to this purpose: ' Peter is supposed to have preached to the Jews of the dispersion in Pontus, Galatia, Bithynia, Cappadocia, and Asia; who, at length coming to Rome, was crucified with his head downwards, himself having desired it might be in that manner.' For the time of Peter's coming to Rome, no ancient writer is now more regarded by learned moderns than Lactantius, or whoever is the author of the book of the Deaths of Persecutors; who says that Peter came thither in the time of Nero. However, it appears to me very probable that St. Peter did not come to Rome before the year of Christ 63 or 64, nor till after St. Paul's departure thence at the end of his two years' imprisonment in that city. The books of the New Testament afford a very plausible, if not certain, argument for it. After our Lord's ascension we find Peter, with the rest of the apostles, at Jerusalem. He and John were sent by the apostles from Jerusalem to Samaria, whence they returned to Jerusalem. When Paul came to Jerusalem, three years after his conversion, he found Peter there. Upon occasion of the tranquillity of the Churches in Judea, Galilee, and Samaria, near the end of the reign of Caligula, Peter left Jerusalem, and visited the Churches in several parts of that country, particularly at Lydda and Joppa, where he tarried many days. Thence he went to Cæsarea, by the seaside, where he preached to Cornelius and his company. Thence he returned to Jerusalem, and sometime afterwards was imprisoned there by Herod Agrippa. This brings down the history of our apostle to the year 44. A few years after this he was present at the council of Jerusalem; nor is there any evidence that he came there merely on that occasion. It is more probable that he had not yet been out of Judea: soon after that council he was at Antioch, where he was reproved by St. Paul.

" The books of the New Testament afford no light for determining where Peter was for several years after that. But to me it appears not unlikely that he returned after a short time to Judea from Antioch, and that he stayed in Judea a good while before he went thence any more; and it seems to me that, when he left Judea, he went again to Antioch, the chief city of Syria. Thence he might go to other parts of the continent, particularly Pontus, Galatia, Cappadocia, Asia, and Bithynia, which are expressly mentioned in the beginning of his first epistle. In those countries he might stay a good while; and it is very likely that he did so; and that he was well acquainted with the Christians there, to whom he afterwards wrote two epistles. When he left those parts, I think he went to Rome, but not till after Paul had been in that city and was gone from it. Several of St. Paul's epistles furnish out a cogent argument of Peter's absence from Rome for a considerable space of time. St. Paul, in the last chapter of his Epistle to the Romans, written, as we suppose, in the beginning of the year 58, salutes many by name, without mentioning Peter; and the whole tenor of the epistle makes it reasonable to think that the Christians there had not yet had the benefit of the apostle's presence and instructions. During his two years' confinement at Rome, which ended, as we suppose, in the spring of the year 63, St. Paul wrote four or five epistles; those to the Ephesians, the Second Epistle to Timothy, to the Philippians, the Colossians, and Philemon; in none of which is any mention of Peter, nor is any thing said or hinted whence it can be concluded that he had ever been there. I think, therefore, that Peter did not come to Rome before the year 63, or perhaps 64. And, as I suppose, obtained the crown of martyrdom in the year 64 or 65; consequently, St. Peter could not reside very long at Rome before his death.

"Cave likewise, in his life of St. Peter, written in English in 1676, places his death in 64 or 65: nor was his mind much altered when he published his Historia Literaria in 1688; for there also he supposes that St. Peter died a martyr at Rome, in the year of Christ 64, at the beginning of Nero's persecution; and indeed he expresses himself with a great deal of assurance and positiveness. Jerome concludes his article of St. Peter saying, ' He was buried at Rome, in the Vatican, near the triumphal way; and is in veneration all over the world.'

"It is not needful to make any remarks upon this tradition; but it is easy to observe it is the general, uncontradicted, disinterested testimony of ancient writers, in the several parts of the world, Greeks, Latins, and Syrians. As our Lord's prediction concerning the death of Peter is recorded in one of the four gospels, it is very likely that Christians would observe the accomplishment of it, which must have been in some place, and about this place there is no difference among Christian writers of ancient times; never any other place was named besides Rome; nor did any other city ever glory in the martyrdom of Peter. There were, in the second and third centuries, disputes between the bishop of Rome and other bishops and Churches about the time of keeping Easter, and about the baptism of heretics; yet none denied the bishop of Rome what they called the chair of Peter. It is not for our honour or interest, either as Christians or Protestants, to deny the truth of events ascertained by early and well attested tradition. If any make an ill use of such facts, we are not accountable for it. We are not, from the dread of such abuses, to overthrow the credit of all history, the consequences of which would be fatal. Fables and fictions have been mixed with the account of Peter's being at Rome; but they are not in the most early writers, but have been added since: and it is well known that fictions have been joined with histories of the most certain and important facts.*

"Having written the history of the Apostle Peter, I now proceed to his epistles; concerning which three or four things are to be considered by us: their genuineness, the persons to whom they were sent, the place where, and the time when, they were written.

"The first epistle was all along considered, by catholic Christians, as authentic and genuine; this we learn from Eusebius, who says: ' Of the controverted books of the New Testament, yet well known and approved by many, are that called the Epistle of James, and that of Jude, and the second and third of John.' And in another place, ' One epistle of Peter, called the first, is universally received.' This the presbyters of ancient times have quoted in their writings as undoubtedly genuine; but that called his second, we have been informed, (by tradition,) has not been received as a part of the New Testament; nevertheless, appearing to many to be useful, it has been carefully studied with other scriptures.' By which, I think, we may be assured that a great regard was shown to this epistle by many Christians in the time of our learned ecclesiastical historian. Jerome says, ' Peter wrote two epistles called catholic, the second of which is denied by many to be his, because of the difference of the style from the former.' And Origen before them, in his commentaries upon the gospel of St. Matthew, as cited by Eusebius, says, ' Peter, on whom the Church is built, has left one epistle universally acknowledged: let it be granted that he also wrote a second, for this has been doubted.'

"What those learned writers of the third and fourth centuries say of those two epistles, we have found agreeable to the testimony of more ancient writers, whom we have consulted: for the first epistle seems to be referred to by Clement of Rome; it is plainly referred to by Polycarp several times; it is also referred to by the martyrs at Lyons; it was received by Theophilus, bishop of Antioch; it was quoted by Papias; it is quoted in the remaining writings of Irenæus, Clement of Alexandria, and Tertullian: consequently it was all along received. But we do not perceive the second epistle to be quoted by Papias, nor by Irenæus, (though in Grabe's edition this epistle is twice quoted,) nor Tertullian, nor Cyprian. However, both these epistles were generally received in the fourth and following centuries by all Christians, except the Syrians: for they were received by Athanasius, Cyril of Jerusalem, the council of Laodicea, Epiphanius, Jerome, Rufin, Augustine, and others.

"The first epistle being allowed to be St. Peter's, we can argue in favour of the other also, in this manner: It bears in the inscription the name of the same apostle; for so it begins, ' Simon Peter, a servant and an apostle of Jesus Christ.' And in chap. i. 14 are these words: ' Knowing that I must shortly put off this my tabernacle, even as our Lord Jesus Christ has showed me.'

"The writer of this epistle may have had a particular revelation concerning the time of his death, not long before writing this. But it is probable that here is a reference to our Lord's prediction concerning St. Peter's

* I commend Dr. Lardner for his candour, and thank him for his advice; but I must think, on the evidence before me, that there is as much danger in believing too much as in believing too little. To me there is not the slightest evidence that St. Peter ever saw Rome; much less that he was first or indeed any bishop of that city. Those who mention his having been there, give us no evidence that they had any fact or history to vouch for their belief, but a sort of uncertain report that never attempts to show its origin or vouch for its truth. The New Testament, by direct inference, is totally against the tradition.

death, and the manner of it, which are recorded in John xxi. 18, 19. From chap. i. 16, 17, 18, it appears that the writer was one of the disciples who were with Jesus in the mount, when he was transfigured in a glorious manner. This certainly leads us to Peter, who was there, and whose name the epistle bears in the inscription, chap. iii. 1: 'This second epistle, beloved, I now write unto you; in both which I stir up your pure minds by way of remembrance;' plainly referring to the former epistle, which has been always acknowledged to be Peter's. These words are express. But it might have been argued, with some degree of probability, from chap. i. 12, 15, that he had before written to the same persons. Once more, chap. iii. 15, 16, he calls Paul brother, and otherwise so speaks of him and his epistles as must needs be reckoned most suitable to an apostle. The writer, therefore, is the Apostle Peter, whose name the epistle bears in the inscription. We are led here to the observation which Wall placed at the head of his notes upon this second epistle: 'It is,' says he, 'a good proof of the cautiousness of the ancient Christians in receiving any book for canonical, that they not only rejected all those pieces forged by heretics under the name of apostles; but also if any good book, affirmed by some men or some Churches to have been written and sent by some apostle, were offered to them, they would not, till fully satisfied of the fact, receive it into their canon.' He adds: 'There is more hazard in denying this to be Peter's, than in denying some other books to be of that author to whom they are by tradition ascribed. For they, if they be not of that apostle to whom they are imputed, yet may be of some other apostle, or apostolical man; but this author is either the apostle, or else by setting his name, and by other circumstances, he does designedly personate him, which no man of piety and truth would do.' And then he concludes: 'This epistle being written by him but a little before his death, chap. i. 14, and perhaps no more than one copy sent, it might be a good while before a number of copies, well attested, came abroad to the generality of the Christian Churches.'

"Certainly these epistles, and the discourses of Peter, recorded in the Acts, together with the effects of them, are monuments of Divine inspiration, and of the fulfilment of the promise which Christ made to him, when he saw him and his brother Andrew employed in their trade, and casting a net into the sea; *Follow me, and I will make you fishers of men*, Matt. iv. 19.

"Concerning the *persons* to whom these epistles were sent, there have been different opinions among both ancients and moderns. Mr. Wetstein argues from divers texts that the first epistle was sent to the Gentiles. Mr. Hallett, in his learned introduction to the Epistle to the Hebrews, observes, 'Some go upon the supposition that St. Peter's epistles were written to the Jews, but it seems to me more natural to suppose that they were written to Gentile Christians, if we consider many passages of the epistles themselves:' where he proceeds to allege many passages, and in my opinion, very pertinently; some of which will be also alleged by me by and by.

"To me it seems that St. Peter's epistles were sent to all Christians in general, Jews and Gentiles, living in Pontus, Galatia, Cappadocia, Asia, and Bithynia; the greatest part of whom must have been converted by Paul, and had been before involved in ignorance and sin, as all people in general were till the manifestation of the Gospel of Christ. That St. Peter wrote to all Christians in those countries is apparent, from the valedictory blessing or wish at the end of the epistle, 1 Epis. v. 14: *Peace be with you all that are in Christ Jesus*. Lewis Capellus, who thought that St. Peter's first epistle was written to Jewish believers, allows that the second epistle was written to all Christians in general, and particularly to Gentiles, induced thereto by the comprehensiveness of the address at the beginning of that epistle, *To them that have obtained like precious faith with us*. He should have concluded as much of the first epistle likewise, for they were both sent to the same people, as is evident from St. Peter's own words, 2 Epis. iii. 1. Moreover, the inscription of the first epistle seems to be as general as that of the second. Let us observe it distinctly: to the elect, εκλεκτοις, says Wall upon the place: 'He uses the word εκλεκτοι, *choice ones*, just as St. Paul does the word ἁγιοι, *saints*, for the word *Christians*: and as St. Paul directs almost all his epistles *to the saints*, that is, the *Christians* of such a place; so St. Peter here, *to the elect* or *choice ones*, that is, *Christians*, sojourning in the dispersions of Pontus, Galatia, and Bithynia. *Strangers*, παρεπιδημοις· good men, though at home, are strangers, especially if they meet with opposition, trouble, and affliction, as those Christians did to whom St. Peter is here writing; for he speaks of their trials and temptations, chap. i. 6, 7, and exhorts them, ii. 11, *as sojourners and strangers*, ὡς παροικους και παρεπιδημους, *to abstain from fleshly lusts*. Says Œcumenius upon chap. i. 1, 2: 'He calls them *strangers*, either on account of their dispersion, or because all that live religiously are called *strangers* on this earth; as David also says, 'I am a sojourner with thee, and a stranger, as all my fathers were,' Psa. xxxix. 12. *Scattered throughout Pontus*, or *of the dispersion of Pontus, Galatia;* so he calls them, not because they had been driven out from their native country, but because he writes to the Christians of divers countries, who also were but a few or a small number in every place where they dwelt. I shall now show that these Christians were, for the most part, of the Gentile stock and original. 1 Pet. i. 14: 'As obedient children, not fashioning yourselves according to the former lusts in your ignorance.' This might be very pertinently said to men converted from Gentilism to Christianity; but no such thing is ever said by the apostle concerning the Jewish people, who had been favoured with Divine revelation, and had the knowledge of the true God. And ver. 20, 21, he says, that 'through Christ they did now believe in God;' therefore they were not worshippers till they were acquainted with the Christian revelation. In like manner, chap. ii. 9, St. Peter speaks of those to whom he writes as having been 'called out of darkness into God's marvellous light.' Moreover, they were not once God's people; ver. 10: 'Which in times past were not a people, but are now the people of God; which had not obtained mercy, but now have obtained mercy.'

Words resembling those of St. Paul, Rom. ix. 24, 25, where he is unquestionably speaking of Gentile converts. There are also other expressions which plainly show that these persons had been Gentiles, and had lived in the sins of Gentilism; chap. i. 18 : 'Forasmuch as ye know that ye were redeemed from your vain conversation, received by tradition from your fathers.' And chap. iv. 3 : 'For the time past may suffice us to have wrought the will of the Gentiles; when we walked in lasciviousness, lusts, excess of wine, revellings, banquetings, and abominable idolatries.' St. Peter does not charge himself with such things, but they to whom he writes had been guilty in those respects ; and, by way of condescension, and for avoiding offence, and for rendering his argument more effectual, he joins himself with them. And more, when St. Peter represents the dignity of those to whom he writes, upon account of their Christian vocation, chap. ii. 9, as 'a chosen generation, a peculiar people, a royal priesthood;' certainly the expressions are most pertinent and emphatical, if understood of such as had been brought from Gentilism to the faith of the Gospel, as indeed they plainly were. For he there says, ' they were to show forth the praises of Him who had called them out of darkness into his marvellous light.' To all which might be added, what was hinted before, that the persons to whom Peter writes were for the most part the Apostle Paul's converts. This must be reckoned probable from the accounts which we have in the Acts of St. Paul's travels and preaching. Whence we know that he had been in Galatia, and the other countries mentioned by St. Peter at the beginning of his first epistle. Moreover he observes, 2 Epis. iii. 15, that 'his beloved brother Paul had written unto them.' We may reasonably suppose that he thereby intends St. Paul's Epistles to the Galatians, the Ephesians, and Colossians, all in those countries, and for the most part Gentile believers. Nor do I see reason to doubt that Peter had, before now, seen and read St. Paul's Epistles to Timothy; and if we should add them, as here intended also, it would be no prejudice to our argument. For those epistles likewise were designed for the use and benefit of the Churches in those parts. To me these considerations appear unanswerable ; I shall, therefore, take notice of but one objection, which is grounded upon 1 Epis. ii. 12 : 'Having your conversation honest among the Gentiles ; that whereas they speak against you as evil doers, they may by your good works, which they shall behold, glorify God in the day of visitation.' Upon the first clause in that verse Beza says, that this place alone is sufficient to show that this epistle was sent to Jews. But I think not. From St. Paul may be alleged a text of the like sort, 1 Cor. x. 32 : 'Give no offence, neither to the Jews, nor to the Gentiles, (καὶ Ἕλλησι,) nor to the Church of God.' It might be as well argued from that text that the Corinthians were by descent neither Jews nor Greeks, as from this, that the persons to whom St. Peter wrote were not originally Gentiles. In the text of St. Paul just quoted, by Jews, and Gentiles or Greeks, are intended such as were unbelievers. So it is likewise in the text of St. Peter which we are considering, as is apparent from the latter part of the verse above transcribed at large. St. Peter had a right to distinguish those to whom he writes from the Gentile people among whom they lived, as he had at the beginning of the epistle called them *elect*, or *choice ones*, and *strangers*; and they likewise went by the name of Christians, as we perceive from chap. iv. 16.

" St. Peter's two epistles, then, were sent to all Christians in general, living in those countries, the greatest part of whom had been converted from Gentilism or heathenism.

" Our next inquiry is concerning *where* these epistles were written.

" At the end of the first epistle St. Peter says : 'The *Church that is* at Babylon, elected together with you, saluteth you ;' which text, understood literally, has been thought by some to denote, 1. Babylon in Assyria ; or, 2. Babylon in Egypt. 3. By others it is interpreted figuratively, and is supposed to denote Jerusalem ; or, 4. Rome. So that there are four opinions concerning the place where this epistle was written.

" If St. Peter had read St. Paul's Epistle to the Romans before he wrote his first epistle, it was written after St. Paul's journey from Corinth to Jerusalem, described in Acts xx., xxi. ; for the Epistle to the Romans was written from Corinth. How much later than the time of this journey the First Epistle of Peter was written it is very difficult, for want of sufficient data, to determine. The epistle itself has hardly any marks which can guide us in deciding the year of its composition ; and we know nothing of the history of St. Peter from the time of the apostolic council at Jerusalem, Acts xv., which is the last place where St. Luke mentions him, till his arrival many years afterwards at Rome, where, according to the accounts of ecclesiastical writers, he suffered martyrdom. However, a comparison of the first with the second epistle of St. Peter will enable us to form at least an opinion on this subject. St: Peter says, in his second epistle, chap. iii. 1 : Ταύτην ἤδη, ἀγαπητοί, δευτέραν ὑμῖν γράφω ἐπιστολήν· whence we may conclude that his first epistle was written to the same persons as the second. But if the second epistle was written fifteen or twenty years after the first, they who received the one were not the same persons as they who received the other ; and we might rather expect that in this case St. Peter would have called his first epistle an epistle which he had written to their fathers. It appears, then, that the interval between the dates of the two epistles could not have been very long ; and as the second epistle was written shortly before St. Peter's death, we may infer that the first epistle was written either not long before, or not long after, the year 60. On the other hand, Lardner assigns this epistle too late a date ; for he is of opinion that it was written between 63 and 65. This reason for supposing that it was not written till after 63 is, that an earlier date cannot be assigned for St. Peter's arrival at Rome ; and as he takes the word Babylon, whence St. Peter dates his epistle, not in its proper but in a mystical sense, as denoting Rome, he concludes that the epistle was not written before the time above mentioned. But if we take Babylon in its proper sense, the argument not only proves not what Lardner intended, but the very reverse ; for if St. Peter's arrival in Rome is to be dated about the year 63, an epistle written by St. Peter, in Babylon, must have a date prior to that year.

"St. Peter, in the close of his epistle, sends a salutation from the Church in Babylon, which, consequently, is the place where he wrote his epistle. But commentators do not agree in regard to the meaning of the word Babylon, some taking it in its literal and proper sense, others giving it a figurative and mystical interpretation. Among the advocates for the latter sense have been men of such learning and abilities, that I was misled by their authority in the younger part of my life to subscribe to it ; but at present, as I have more impartially examined the question, it appears to me very extraordinary that, when an apostle dates his epistle from Babylon, it should ever occur to any commentator to ascribe to this work a mystical meaning, instead of taking it in its literal and proper sense. For, in the first century, the ancient Babylon, on the Euphrates, was still in existence ; and there was likewise a city on the Tigris, Seleucia, not far distant from the ancient Babylon, to which the name of modern Babylon was given ; but through some mistake it has been supposed that the ancient Babylon, in the time of St. Peter, was no longer in being ; and in order to furnish a pretence for a mystical interpretation, it has been denied that Seleucia was ever so called.

"It is true that the ancient Babylon, in comparison of its original splendour, might be called in the first century a desolated city ; yet it was not wholly a heap of ruins, nor wholly destitute of inhabitants. This appears from the account which Strabo, who lived in the time of Tiberius, has given of it : for he says that Alexander (who died at Babylon, and who intended, if he had lived, to have made it the place of his residence) proposed to rebuild there a pyramid, which was a stadium in length, in breadth, and in height ; but that his successors did not put the design into execution : that the Persians destroyed a part of Babylon, and that the Macedonians neglected it ; but that Babylon had suffered the most from the building of Seleucia, by Seleucus Nicator, at the distance of three hundred stadia from it, because Seleucia then became the capital of the country, and Babylon was drained of its inhabitants. Strabo then adds : at present Seleucia is greater than Babylon, which last city has been desolated, so that one may say of it, what the comic poet said of Megalopolis in Arcadia : 'A great city is become a great desert.' If this be not sufficient proof that Babylon was still in existence in the first century, the reader may consult Cellarii Geographia, tom. ii., page 747 ; and Assemani Bibliotheca Orientalis, tom. iii., par. ii., page 7.

"It will be objected, perhaps, that if Babylon still existed in the time of St. Peter, it was yet in such a state of decay that an apostle would hardly have gone to preach the Gospel there. But I can see no reason why he should not ; especially as Babylon was at that time so far from being literally destitute of inhabitants that Strabo draws a parallel between this city and Seleucia, saying, at present Babylon is not so great as Seleucia, which was then the capital of the Parthian empire, and, according to Pliny, contained six hundred thousand inhabitants. To conclude therefore that Babylon, whence St. Peter dates this epistle, could not have been the ancient Babylon, because this city was then in a state of decay ; and thence to argue that St. Peter used the word mystically to denote Rome, is nearly the same as if, on the receipt of a letter dated from Ghent or Antwerp, in which mention was made of a Christian community there, I concluded that, because these cities are no larger than what they were in the sixteenth century, the writer of the epistle meant a spiritual Ghent or Antwerp, and that the epistle was really written from Amsterdam.

"It is, therefore, at least possible that St. Peter wrote his first epistle in the ancient Babylon, on the Euphrates. But before we conclude that he really did write there, we must first examine whether he did not mean Seleucia on the Tigris, which was sometimes called the modern Babylon. According to Strabo, Seleucia was only three hundred stadia distant from the ancient Babylon ; and it was separated by the Tigris from Ctesiphon, the winter residence of the Parthian kings. At present it is not called Bagdad, as some have supposed, which is a very different city ; but, in conjunction with Ctesiphon, is named by Syrian and Arabic writers Medinotho, Medain, Madáin, under which name it appears in D'Anville's maps in the latitude of 33° 7½.

"Since, then, the name of Babylon was given actually to Seleucia, it is not impossible that St. Peter thus understood the word Babylon, and that his first epistle therefore was written at Seleucia on the Tigris. But I have shown in the preceding part of this section that there is likewise a possibility of its having been written in Babylon, properly so called, or in the ancient Babylon on the Euphrates. The question therefore is, which of these two senses shall we ascribe to the word Babylon ? For one of these two we must ascribe to it, unless we give it, without any reason, a mystical interpretation. In the two last editions of this introduction I preferred the former sense ; but after a more mature consideration, I think it much more probable, at present, that St. Peter meant the ancient Babylon. It is true that Lucan, Sidonius Apollinaris, and Stephanus Byzantinus, gave the name of Babylon to Seleucia ; but the two last of these writers lived so late as the fifth century ; and therefore their authority is perhaps not sufficient to prove that Seleucia was called Babylon in the first century. Lucan, indeed, was a contemporary with St. Peter ; but then he uses this word in an epic poem, in which a writer is not bound by the same rules as in prose : and it is not improbable that he selected the word Babylon, because, partly, its celebrity added pomp to his diction ; and, partly, because neither Ctesiphon nor Seleucia would have suited the verse. The writer of an epistle, on the contrary, can allow himself no such latitude ; and perspicuity requires that in the date of his epistle, he should use no other name for the town where he writes than that which properly belongs to it. If, therefore, St. Peter had really written at Seleucia, he would have hardly called this city by the name of Babylon, though this name was sometimes applied to it : consequently, it is most probable that St. Peter wrote his first epistle in ancient Babylon on the Euphrates.

"Before I conclude this section, I must take notice of a passage in Josephus, which not only confutes all notions of a spiritual or mystical Babylon, but throws a great light on our present inquiry; and this passage is of so much the more importance, because Josephus was a historian who lived in the same age with St. Peter; and the passage itself relates to an event which took place thirty-six years before the Christian era, namely, the delivery of Hyrcanus, the Jewish high priest, from imprisonment, by order of Phraates, king of Parthia, with permission to reside in Babylon, where there was a considerable number of Jews. This is recorded by Josephus, Antiq. xv. c. 2, in the following words : Δια τουτο δεσμων μεν αφηκεν, εν Βαβυλωνι δε καταγεσθαι παρειχεν, ενθα και πληθος ην Ιουδαιων. Josephus then adds, that both the Jews in Babylon, and all who dwelt in that country, as far as the Euphrates, respected Hyrcanus, as high priest and king. Now the word Babylon in this passage of Josephus evidently means a city in the east ; and it cannot possibly be interpreted in a mystical manner either of Jerusalem or Rome. The only question is, whether he meant the ancient Babylon on the Euphrates, or Seleucia on the Tigris. The former is the most obvious interpretation; and is warranted by the circumstance that, in other places where Josephus speaks of Seleucia on the Tigris, he calls it by its proper name Seleucia.

"The first argument in favour of a mystical and against a literal interpretation of the word Babylon is, that in the whole country of Babylonia there were no Jews in the time of St. Peter ; and thence it is inferred that he could not have gone to preach the Gospel there. Now in this argument both the premises and inference are false. The inference is false, because even if there had been no Jews in the whole country of Babylonia, St. Peter might have gone to preach the Gospel there ; for he preached to the uncircumcised at Caesarea, and he himself declared that it was ordained by God that the Gentiles, by his mouth, should hear the word of the Gospel and believe. The premises themselves are also totally unfounded ; for if we except Palestine, there was no country in the world where the Jews were so numerous and so powerful as in the province of Babylonia, in which they had their two celebrated seats of learning, Nehardea and Susa.

"The second argument in favour of a mystical interpretation of the word Babylon is, that almost all the ancient fathers have explained it in this manner, and have asserted that St. Peter used it to denote Rome. But we must recollect that an assertion of this kind is not testimony to a fact, but a mere matter of opinion, in which the ancients were as liable to mistake as we are. Nor is it true that all the ancient ecclesiastical writers have ascribed to the word Babylon a mystical meaning ; for though the Greek and Latin fathers commonly understood Rome, yet the Syriac and Arabic writers understood it literally, as denoting a town in the east ; and if we are to be guided by opinion, an oriental writer is surely as good authority, on the present question, as a European.

"The third argument on which Lardner particularly insists is, that, in the accounts which we have on record relative to St. Peter's history, no mention is made of a journey to Babylon. Now this argument would prove nothing, even if our knowledge of St. Peter's life and transactions were more perfect than it really is. Let us suppose an instance of some eminent man in modern times, in the history of whose life no mention is made that, during his travels, he paid a visit to Vienna, but that among his letters to his friends, one of them, notwithstanding the silence of his biographer, is dated from Vienna. In this case, unless we had reason to suppose that the whole epistle was a forgery, or that the author had used a false date, we should immediately conclude, on the bare authority of this single epistle, that he had actually been at Vienna ; and we should hardly think of a mystical or spiritual Vienna. Lardner himself has argued in this very manner with respect to Paul, though his history is infinitely better known than that of St. Peter, and has inferred from the single passage, Tit. i. 5, 'For this cause left I thee in Crete,' that St. Paul made a voyage into Crete in the year 56, though this voyage is mentioned neither by St. Luke nor by any other historian. No reason therefore can be assigned why we should refuse to argue in the same manner with respect to St. Peter. In fact, Lardner's argument could nowhere have been more unfortunately applied than in the present instance.

"From the time of the apostolic council at Jerusalem, in the year 49, at which St. Peter was present, till the time of his [supposed] arrival in Rome, which Lardner acknowledges was not before 63, there is an interval of fourteen years, during which we have no history of him whatsoever. How then can we form a judgment of his transactions during that period except from his own writings ? And how can the silence of history, in respect to his journey to Babylon, afford an argument that he was never there, in contradiction to his own epistle, when the fact is, we have no history at all of St. Peter during this period ! We cannot therefore talk of its silence in respect to any one particular transaction, since every transaction of St. Peter, throughout the whole of this interval, is unrecorded. Lardner indeed conjectures, as the epistle is addressed to the inhabitants of Pontus, Galatia, &c., that St. Peter spent a part of his time in these countries, though he denies that St. Peter ever was in Babylon, whence the epistle is dated. Now this mode of arguing is nearly the same as if I concluded, from a letter dated from Vienna, and addressed to a person in Venice, that the writer of that letter had been in Venice, but that he never was at Vienna. Lardner supposes also that St. Peter spent a part of this time in Jerusalem. Now it is impossible for us to determine what stay St. Peter made in Jerusalem after the holding of the apostolic council, or whether he remained there at all ; but this I think is certain, that he was not at Jerusalem when St. Paul returned thither for the last time, since St. Luke makes particular mention of St. James, and describes him as the head of the Christian community at Jerusalem, but says nothing of St. Peter, whom he would hardly have passed over in perfect silence if he had been there. Now St. Paul's last

2

visit to Jerusalem happened in the year 60 ; and since I have shown that the First Epistle of St. Peter was written about this time, it is not at all improbable that St. Peter, who was absent from Jerusalem, was then engaged in preaching the Gospel to the Babylonians.

" The last argument in favour of the opinion that the Babylon where Peter wrote was not Babylon properly so called, is derived from chap. ii. 13, where St. Peter commands obedience to the king, and from chap. ii. 17, where he says, ' Honour the king.' Hence Lardner concludes that St. Peter must have written in a place which was subject to the same king or emperor as the people to whom he sent the epistle. But these were subject to the Roman emperor, whereas Babylon, with its whole territory, was then subject, not to the Romans, but the Parthians , and therefore, according to Lardner, could not have been the place where St. Peter wrote. Now this argument rests on a supposition which is contradicted by the common usage of every language , the expression, ' the king,' in a letter from a person in one country to a person in another country, may, according to circumstances, denote the king to which the reader is subject as well as the king to which the writer is subject.

" It appears, then, that the arguments which have been alleged to show that St. Peter did not write his first epistle in the country of Babylonia are devoid of foundation , and consequently the notion of a mystical Babylon, as denoting either Jerusalem or Rome, loses its whole support. For in itself the notion is highly improbable, and therefore the bare possibility that St. Peter took a journey to Babylon, properly so called, renders it inadmissible. The plain language of epistolary writing does not admit of the figures of poetry , and, though it would be very allowable, in a poem written in honour of Göttingen, to style it another Athens, yet if a professor of this university should, in a letter written from Göttingen, date it Athens, it would be a greater piece of pedantry than ever was laid to the charge of the learned. In like manner, though a figurative use of the word Babylon is not unsuitable to the animated and poetical language of the Apocalypse, yet St. Peter, in a plain and unadorned epistle, would hardly have called the place where he wrote by any other appellation than that which literally and properly belonged to it."

That many persons both of learning and eminence have been of a different opinion from Professor Michaelis, the intelligent reader is well aware, but Dr. Lardner, of all others, has written most argumentatively in vindication of the mystical Babylon, i. e. Rome, as being the place from which the apostle wrote this epistle His weightiest arguments however are here answered by Michaelis, and to me it appears that there is a great balance in favour of the opinion that *Babylon* on the Euphrates is the place intended The decision of this question, although not an article of faith, is nevertheless of some importance. I am still of opinion that St. Peter did not write from Rome ; that he was neither bishop of Rome nor martyred at Rome ; in a word, that he never saw Rome.

840   2

THE FIRST GENERAL EPISTLE

OF

PETER.

Chronological Notes relative to this Epistle.

Year of the Constantinopolitan era of the world, or that used by the Byzantine historians, and other eastern writers, 5568.—Year of the Alexandrian era of the world, 5562.—Year of the Antiochian era of the world, 5552.—Year of the world, according to Archbishop Usher, 4064.—Year of the world, according to Eusebius, in his Chronicon, 4288.—Year of the minor Jewish era of the world, or that in common use, 3820.—Year of the Greater Rabbinical era of the world, 4419.—Year from the Flood, according to Archbishop Usher, and the English Bible, 2408.—Year of the Cali yuga, or Indian era of the Deluge, 3162.—Year of the era of Iphitus, or since the first commencement of the Olympic games, 1000.—Year of the era of Nabonassar, king of Babylon, 809.—Year of the CCIXth Olympiad, 4.—Year from the building of Rome, according to Fabius Pictor, 807.—Year from the building of Rome, according to Frontinus, 811.—Year from the building of Rome, according to the Fasti Capitolini, 812.—Year from the building of Rome, according to Varro, which was that most generally used, 813.—Year of the era of the Seleucidæ, 372.—Year of the Cæsarean era of Antioch, 108.—Year of the Julian era, 105.—Year of the Spanish era, 98.—Year from the birth of Jesus Christ, according to Archbishop Usher, 64.—Year of the vulgar era of Christ's nativity, 60.—Year of Claudius Felix, governor of the Jews, 8.—Year of Vologesus, king of the Parthians, 11.—Jesus, high priest of the Jews, 1.—Year of the Dionysian period, or Easter Cycle, 61.—Year of the Grecian Cycle of nineteen years, or Common Golden Number, 4; or the second after the first embolismic.—Year of the Jewish Cycle of nineteen years, 1; or two years before the first embolismic.—Year of the Solar Cycle, 13.—Dominical Letter, it being Bissextile, or Leap Year, FE.—Day of the Jewish Passover, the second of April, which happened in this year on the fourth day after the Jewish Sabbath.—Easter Sunday, the sixth of April.—Epact, or age of the moon on the 22d of March, (the day of the earliest Easter Sunday possible,) 3.—Epact, according to the present mode of computation, or the moon's age on New Year's day, or the Calends of January, 11.—Monthly Epacts, or age of the moon on the Calends of each month respectively, (beginning with January,) 11, 13, 12, 13, 14, 15, 16, 17, 19, 19, 21, 21.—Number of Direction, or the number of days from the twenty-first of March to the Jewish Passover, 12.—Year of the reign of Caius Tiberius Claudius Nero Cæsar, the fifth Roman monarch, computing from Octavianus, or Augustus Cæsar, properly the first Roman emperor, 7.—Roman Consuls, the Emperor Nero Augustus, the fourth time, and Cossus Cornelius Lentulus.

CHAPTER I.

Of the persons to whom this epistle was directed, and their spiritual state, 1, 2. He describes their privileges, and thanks God for the grace by which they were preserved faithful in trials and difficulties, 3–5. The spiritual benefit they were to receive out of their afflictions, 6, 7. Their love to Christ, 8. And the salvation they received through believing, 9. This salvation was predicted by the prophets, who only saw it afar off, and had only a foretaste of it, 10–12. They should take encouragement, and be obedient and holy, 13–16. They should pray, and deeply consider the price at which they were purchased, that their faith and hope might be in God, 17–21. As their souls had been purified by obeying the truth through the Spirit, they should love each other with a pure and fervent love, 22, 23. The frailty of man, and the unchangeableness of God, 24, 25.

A. M. cir. 4064.
A. D. cir. 60.
An. Olymp.
cir. CCIX. 4.
A. U. C. cir.
813.

PETER, an apostle of Jesus Christ, to the strangers ᵃ scattered throughout Pontus, Galatia, Cappadocia, Asia, and Bithynia,

2 ᵇ Elect ᶜ according to the foreknowledge of God the Father, ᵈ through sanctification of the Spirit, unto obedience and

A. M. cir. 4064.
A. D. cir. 60.
An. Olymp.
cir. CCIX. 4.
A. U. C. cir.
813.

ᵃ John vii. 35; Acts ii. 5, 9, 10; James i. 1.——ᵇ Eph. i. 4; chap. ii. 9.——ᶜ Rom. viii. 29; xi. 2.——ᵈ 2 Thess. ii. 13.

NOTES ON CHAP. I.

Verse 1. *Peter, an apostle*] Simon Peter, called also *Kephas:* he was a fisherman, son of *Jonah*, brother of *Andrew*, and born at Bethsaida; and one of the first disciples of our Lord. See the *preface.*

The strangers scattered throughout] Jews first, who had believed the Gospel in the different countries here specified; and converted *Gentiles* also. Though the word *strangers* may refer to all truly religious people, see Gen. xlvii. 9; Psa. xxxix. 12, in the Septuagint, and Heb. xi. 13, yet the inscription may have a special reference to those who were driven by persecution to seek refuge in those heathen provinces to which the influence of their persecuting brethren did not extend.

Pontus] An ancient kingdom of Asia Minor, originally a part of *Cappadocia;* bounded on the east by *Colchis*, on the west by the river *Halys*, on the north by the *Euxine Sea*, and on the south by *Armenia Minor.* This country probably derived its name from the *Pontus Euxinus*, on which it was partly situated. In the time of the Roman emperors it was divided into three parts: 1. *Pontus Cappadocius;* 2. *Pontus Galaticus;* and, 3. *Pontus Polemoniacus.* The *first* extended from the Pontus Polemoniacus to Colchis, having *Armenia Minor* and the upper stream of the *Euphrates* for its southern boundary. The *second* extended from the river *Halys* to the river *Thermodon.* The *third* extended from the river Thermodon to the borders of the Pontus Cappadocius.

Six kings of the name of *Mithridates* reigned in this kingdom, some of whom are famous in history. The last king of this country was *David Comnenus*, who was taken prisoner, with all his family, by *Mohammed* II. in the year 1462, and carried to Constantinople; since which time this country (then called the empire of *Trebizond*, from *Trapezus*, a city founded by the Grecians, on the uttermost confines of Pontus) has continued under the degrading power of the Turks.

Galatia] The ancient name of a province of *Asia Minor*, now called *Amasia.* It was called also *Gallogræcia*, and *Gallia Parva.* It was bounded on the east by *Cappadocia*, on the south by *Pamphylia*, on the north by the *Euxine Sea*, and on the west by *Bithynia.* See the preface to the Epistle to the Galatians.

Cappadocia] An ancient kingdom of Asia, comprehending all the country lying between Mount Taurus and the Euxine Sea.

Asia] This word is taken in different senses: It signifies, 1. One of the three general divisions of our continent, and one of the *four* of the whole earth. It is separated from Europe by the Mediterranean Sea, the Archipelago, the Black Sea, the *Palus Mæotis*, the rivers *Don* and *Dwina;* and from Africa by the Arabic Gulf, or Red Sea: it is everywhere else surrounded by water. It is situated between latitude 2° and 77° N., and between longitude 26° E. and 170° W.; and is about 7,583 miles in length, and 5,200 miles in breadth.

2. Asia Minor, that part of Turkey in Asia, now called *Natolia*, which comprehends a great number of province situated between the Euxine, Mediterranean, and Archipelago.

3. That province of Asia Minor of which Ephesus was the capital. It appears, says Calmet, that it is in this latter sense that it is used here by St. Peter, because *Pontus, Galatia*, and *Bithynia*, are comprised in the provinces of *Asia Minor.* See *Calmet.*

Bithynia] An ancient kingdom of Asia, formerly called *Mysia, Mygdonia, Bebrycia*, and *Bithonia.* It was bounded on the west by the *Bosphorus, Thracius*, and part of the *Propontis*, on the south by the river *Rhyndacus*, and Mount *Olympus*, on the north by the *Euxine Sea*, and on the east by the river *Parthenius.* This place is in some sort rendered infamous by the conduct of *Prusias*, one of its kings, who delivered up Hannibal, who had fled to him for protection, into the hands of the Romans. *Nicomedes* IV. bequeathed it to the Romans; and it is now in the hands of the Turks.

Verse 2. *Elect according to the foreknowledge of God*] If the apostle had directed his letter to persons *elected to eternal life*, no one, as Drs. Lardner and Macknight properly argue, could have received such a letter, because no one could have been sure of his election in this way till he had arrived in heaven. But

A. M. cir. 4064.
A. D. cir. 60.
An. Olymp.
cir. CCIX. 4.
A. U. C. cir.
813.

e sprinkling of the blood of Jesus Christ : f Grace unto you, and peace, be multiplied.

3 g Blessed *be* the God and

Father of our Lord Jesus Christ, which h according to his i abundant mercy k hath begotten us again unto a lively hope l by the

A. M. cir. 4064
A. D. cir. 60.
An. Olymp.
cir. CCIX. 4.
A. U. C. cir.
813.

---

e Hebrews x. 22 ; xii. 24.——f Romans i. 7 ; 2 Pet. i. 2 ; Jude 2.
g 2 Cor. i. 3 ; Eph. i. 3.

h Titus iii. 5.——i Gr. *much.*——k John iii. 3, 5 ; James i. 18.
l 1 Cor. xv. 20 ; 1 Thess. iv. 14 ; chap. iii. 21.

---

the persons to whom the apostle wrote were all, with propriety, said to be *elect according to the foreknowledge of God ;* because, agreeably to the original purpose of God, discovered in the prophetical writings, Jews and Gentiles, indiscriminately, were called to be the visible Church, and entitled to all the privileges of the people of God, on their believing the Gospel. In this sense the word *elected* is used in other places of Scripture ; see 1 Thess. i. 4, and the note there.

The Rev. J. Wesley has an excellent note on this passage, which I shall transcribe for the benefit of those of my readers who may not have his works at hand.

" Strictly speaking, there is no *foreknowledge,* no more than *afterknowledge,* with God ; but all things are known to him as *present,* from eternity to eternity. *Election,* in the scriptural sense, is God's doing any thing that our merit or power has no part in. The true predestination or foreappointment of God is, 1. He that believeth shall be saved from the guilt and power of sin. 2. He that endureth to the end shall be saved eternally. 3. They who receive the precious gift of faith thereby become the sons of God ; and, being sons, they shall receive the Spirit of holiness, to walk as Christ also walked. Throughout every part of this appointment of God, *promise* and *duty* go hand in hand. All is free gift ; and yet, such is the gift, that it depends in the final issue on our future obedience to the heavenly call. But other predestination than this, either to life or death eternal, the Scripture knows not of : moreover, 1. It is cruel respect of persons ; an unjust regard of one, and an unjust disregard of another : it is mere *creature partiality,* and not *infinite justice.* 2. It is not *plain* Scripture doctrine, (if true,) but rather inconsistent with the express written word that speaks of God's universal offers of grace ; his invitations, promises, threatenings, being all *general.* 3. We are bid to choose life, and reprehended for not doing it. 4. It is inconsistent with a state of *probation* in those that *must* be saved, or *must* be lost. 5. It is of fatal consequence ; all men being ready, on very slight grounds, to *fancy* themselves of the elect number. But the doctrine of predestination is entirely changed from what it formerly was : *now* it implies neither faith, peace, nor purity ; it is something that will do *without* them all. Faith is no longer, according to the modern predestination scheme, a Divine *evidence of things not seen* wrought in the soul by the immediate power of the Holy Ghost ; not an *evidence* at all, but a *mere notion :* neither is faith made any longer a means of holiness, but something that will do without it. Christ is no more a Saviour *from sin,* but a defence and a countenancer of it. He is no more a fountain of spiritual life in the souls of believers, but leaves his elect inwardly *dry,* and outwardly *unfruitful ;* and is made little more than

a refuge from the image of the heavenly, even from righteousness, peace, and joy in the Holy Ghost."

Through sanctification of the Spirit—through the renewing and purifying influences of his Spirit on their souls, *unto obedience*—to engage and enable them to yield themselves up to all holy obedience, the foundation of all which is the *sprinkling of the blood of Jesus Christ*—the atoning blood of Jesus Christ which was typified by the sprinkling of the blood of sacrifices under the law, in allusion to which it is called the *blood of sprinkling.*

Verse 3. *Blessed* be *the God and Father*] Ευλογητος ὁ Θεος και Πατηρ· *Blessed be God even the Father,* or *blessed* be God, the Father of our Lord Jesus Christ. The και, *and,* is omitted by the *Syriac,* Erpen's *Arabic,* and the *Æthiopic.* But if we translate και, *even,* a meaning which it frequently has in the New Testament, then we have a very good sense : Let that God have praise who is the Father of our Lord Jesus Christ, and who deserves the praise of every human being for his infinite mercy to the world, in its redemption by Christ Jesus.

Begotten us again unto a lively hope] I think the apostle has a reference here to his own case, and that of his fellow apostles, at the time that Christ was taken by the Jews and put to death. Previously to this time they had strong confidence that he was the Messiah, and *that it was he who should redeem Israel ;* but when they found that he actually expired upon the cross, and was buried, they appear to have *lost all hope of the great things which before they had in prospect.* This is feelingly expressed by the two disciples whom our Lord, after his resurrection, overtook on the road going to Emmaus, see Luke xxiv. 13–24. And the hope, that with them, *died with their Master,* and seemed to be *buried in his grave,* was restored by the *certainty* of his *resurrection.* From Christ's preaching, miracles, &c., they had a *hope of eternal life,* and all other blessings promised by him ; by his *death* and *burial* this hope became nearly, if not altogether, *extinct ;* but by his *resurrection* the hope was *revived.* This is very properly expressed here by being *begotten again to a living hope,* εις ελπιδα ζωσαν· or, as some MSS. and versions have it, εις ελπιδα ζωης, *to the hope of life ;* which one copy of the *Itala,* with *Augustine, Gildas, Vigilius* of *Tapsum,* and *Cassiodorus,* have considered as meaning *eternal life,* agreeably to the context ; and therefore they read *vitæ æternæ.*

The expressions, however, may include more particulars than what are above specified ; as none can *inherit* eternal life except those who are *children* in the heavenly *family,* and none are *children* but those who are *born again :* then St. Peter may be considered as laying *here* the foundation of the hope of eternal life in the *regeneration of the soul ;* for none can *legally* inherit but the children, and none are chil-

2

A. M. cir. 4064.
A. D. cir. 60.
An. Olymp.
cir. CCIX. 4.
A. U. C. cir.
813.

resurrection of Jesus Christ from the dead,

4 To an inheritance incorruptible, and undefiled, [m] and that fadeth not away, [n] reserved in heaven [o] for you,

5 [p] Who are kept by the power of God

through faith unto salvation, ready to be revealed in the last time :

6 [q] Wherein ye greatly rejoice, though now [r] for a season, if need be, [s] ye are in heaviness through manifold temptations :

A. M. cir. 4064.
A. D. cir. 60.
An. Olymp.
cir. CCIX. 4.
A. U. C. cir.
813.

---

[m] Chapter v. 4.——[n] Col. i. 5 ; 2 Timothy iv. 8.——[o] Or, *for us.*
[p] John x. 28, 29 ; xvii. 11, 12, 15 ; Jude 1.

[q] Matt. v. 12 ; Romans xii. 12 ; 2 Cor. vi. 10 ; chapter iv. 13.
[r] 2 Cor. iv. 17 ; chap. v. 10.——[s] James i. 2.

---

dren of God till they are spiritually *begotten* and born *again.*

It is the Gospel alone that gives the well-grounded hope of eternal life ; and the ground on which this hope rests is the *resurrection of Christ* himself. The certainty of our Lord's resurrection is the *great seal* of the Gospel. Without this what is vision, what is prophecy, what is promise, what are even miracles, to that unbelief which is natural to man on such a subject as this ? But the resurrection of the human nature of Christ, the incontestable proofs of this resurrection, and the ascension of our nature to heaven in his person, are such evidences of the possibility and certainty of the thing, as for ever to preclude all doubt from the hearts of those who believe in him.

Verse 4. *To an inheritance*] Called an *inheritance* because it belongs to the *children* of God. Eternal life cannot be a gift to any but *these ;* for, even in heaven, the *lot* is dealt out according to *law :* if *children,* then *heirs ;* if *not children,* then *not heirs.*

Incorruptible] Αφθαρτον· It has no principles of *dissolution* or *decay* in it ; and, therefore, must be totally different from this earth.

Undefiled] Αμιαντον· Nothing *impure* can enter it ; it not only has no principles or seeds of *dissolution* in itself, but it can never admit any ; therefore its deterioration is impossible.

Fadeth not away] Αμαραντον· *It cannot wither,* it is always in *bloom ;* a metaphor taken from those flowers that never lose their *hue* nor their *fragrance.* From the Greek αμαραντος we have our flowers called *amaranths,* because they preserve their hue and odour for a long time.

Reserved in heaven] Such a place as that described above is not to be expected on *earth ;* it is that which was typified by the earthly Canaan, and in reference to which the patriarchs endured all trials and difficulties in this life, as seeing Him who is *invisible.*

Verse 5. *Who are kept*] Φρουρουμενους· Who are *defended as in a fortress* or *castle.* There is a remarkable correspondence between the two verbs used in this sentence : the verb τηρεω, signifies to *keep, watch, guard ;* and τηρησις, is a *place of custody* or *prison.* And φρουρεω, from φρουρος, a *sentinel,* signifies to *keep as under a military guard.* See on Gal. iii. 22, 23. The true disciples of Christ are under the continual watchful care of God, and the inheritance is *guarded* for them. In some countries military posts are constantly kept on the *confines,* in order to prevent irruptions from a neighbouring people ; and, in many cases, *heirs,* while in their *minority,* are kept in *fortified places* under military guards.

By the power of God] Εν δυναμει Θεου· By the

mighty and *miracle-working power of God ;* for nothing less is necessary to keep and preserve, in this state of continual trial, a soul from the contagion that is in the world. But this *power of God* is interested in the behalf of the soul by *faith ;* to believe is our work, the exertion of the almighty power is of God. No *persevering* without the *power,* and no power without *faith.*

Ready to be revealed] Or rather, *Prepared to be revealed.* The inheritance is *prepared* for you ; but its glories will not be revealed till the *last time*—till ye have done with life, and passed through your probation, having held fast faith and a good conscience. Some by *salvation* understand the deliverance of the Christians from the sackage of Jerusalem, the end of the Jewish polity being called the *last time ;* others suppose it to refer to the *day of judgment,* and the glorification of the body and soul in heaven.

Verse 6. *Wherein ye greatly rejoice*] Some refer *wherein,* εν ᾧ, to the *salvation* mentioned above ; others, to the *last time,* καιρῳ εσχατῳ, in ver. 5 ; others think that it applies to the *being kept by the power of God through faith ;* and others, that it refers to all the preceding advantages and privileges. It was in the present salvation of God that they rejoiced or gloried, though not without having an eye to the great recompense of reward.

Though now for a season] Ολιγον αρτι· *A little while yet*—during your pilgrimage here below, which is but a *point* when compared with *eternity.*

If need be] Ει δεον εστι· *If it be necessary*—if your situation and circumstances be such that you are exposed to trials and persecutions which you cannot avoid, unless God were to work a miracle for your deliverance, which would not be for your ultimate good, as he purposes to turn all your trials and difficulties to your advantage.

Sometimes there is a kind of necessity that the followers of God should be afflicted ; when they have no trials they are apt to get careless, and when they have secular prosperity they are likely to become worldly-minded. "God," said a good man, "can neither trust me with health nor money ; therefore I am both poor and afflicted." But the disciples of Christ may be very happy in their souls, though grievously afflicted in their bodies and in their estates. Those to whom St. Peter wrote rejoiced greatly, *danced for joy,* αγαλλιασθε, while *they were grieved,* λυπηθεντες, with *various trials.* The verb λυπεω signifies to *grieve, to make sorrowful :* perhaps *heaviness* is not the best rendering of the original word, as this can scarcely ever consist with *rejoicing ;* but to be *sorrowful* on account of something external to our

A. M. cir. 4064.
A. D. cir. 60.
An. Olymp.
cir. CCIX. 1.
A. U. C. cir.
813.

7 That ^t the trial of your faith, being much more precious than of gold that perisheth, though ^u it be tried with fire, ^v might be found unto praise and honour and glory at the appearing of Jesus Christ:

8 ^w Whom having not seen, ye love; ^x in whom, though now ye see *him* not, yet believ-

t James i. 3, 12; chap. iv. 12.——u Job xxiii. 10; Psa. lxvi. 10; Prov. xvii. 3; Isa. xlviii. 10; Zech. xiii. 9; 1 Cor. iii. 13. v Rom. ii. 7, 10; 1 Cor. iv. 5; 2 Thess. i. 7–12.

selves, and yet exulting in God from a sense of his goodness to us, is quite compatible: so that we may say with St. Paul, *always sorrowing, yet still rejoicing.*

Verse 7. *That the trial of your faith, being much more precious than of gold*] As by the action of fire gold is separated from all alloy and heterogeneous mixtures, and is proved to be gold by its enduring the action of the fire without losing any thing of its nature, weight, colour, or any other property, so genuine faith is proved by adversities, especially such as the primitive Christians were obliged to pass through. For the word was then, "Renounce Jesus and live," "Cleave to him and die;" for every Christian was in continual danger of losing his life. He then who preferred Christianity to his life gave full proof, not only of his own sincerity, but also of the excellency of the principle by which he was influenced; as his religion put him in possession of greater blessings, and more solid comforts, than any thing the earth could afford.

Though it be tried with fire] That is: Though gold will bear the action of the fire for any given time, even millions of years, were they possible, without losing the smallest particle of weight or value, yet even gold, in process of time, will wear away by continual use; and the earth, and all its works, will be burnt up by that *supernatural* fire whose action nothing can resist. But on that day the faith of Christ's followers will be found brighter, and more glorious. The earth, and universal nature, shall be dissolved; but he who doeth the will of God shall abide for ever, and his faith shall then be found to the *praise* of God's grace, the *honour* of Christ, and the *glory* or glorification of his own soul throughout eternity. God himself will *praise* such faith, angels and men will hold it in *honour*, and Christ will crown it with *glory*. For some remarks on the nature and properties of gold see at the end of the chapter.

Verse 8. *Whom having not seen, ye love*] Those to whom the apostle wrote had never seen Christ in the flesh; and yet, such is the *realizing* nature of faith, they loved him as strongly as any of his disciples could, to whom he was *personally known*. For faith in the Lord Jesus brings him into the heart; and by his indwelling all his virtues are proved, and an excellence discovered beyond even that which his disciples beheld, when conversant with him upon earth. In short, there is an equality between believers in the present time, and those who lived in the time of the incarnation; for Christ, to a believing soul, is the same *to-day* that he was *yesterday* and will be *for ever.*

ing, ye rejoice with joy unspeakable and full of glory:

9 Receiving ^y the end of your faith, *even* the salvation of *your* souls.

10 ^z Of which salvation the prophets have inquired and searched diligently, who prophesied of the grace *that should come* unto you:

11 Searching what, or what manner of time

A. M. cir. 4064.
A. D. cir. 60.
An. Olymp.
cir. CCIX. 4.
A. U. C. cir.
813.

w 1 John iv. 20.——x John xx. 29; 2 Cor. v. 7; Heb. xi. 1, 27. y Rom. vi. 22.——z Gen. xlix. 10; Dan. ii. 44; Hag. ii. 7; Zech. vi. 12; Matt. xiii. 17; Luke x. 24; 2 Pet. i. 19, 20, 21.

Ye rejoice with joy unspeakable] Ye have unutterable happiness through believing; and ye have the fullest, clearest, strongest evidence of eternal glory. Though they did not see him on earth, and men could not see him in glory, yet by that faith which is the evidence of things not seen, and the subsistence of things hoped for, they had the very highest persuasion of their acceptance with God, their relation to him as their Father, and their sonship with Christ Jesus.

Verse 9. *Receiving the end of your faith*] Ye are put in possession of the salvation of your souls, which was the thing presented to your faith, when ye were called by the Gospel of Christ. Your faith has had a proper issue, and has been crowned with a proper recompense. The word τελος, end, is often used so as to imply the *issue* or *reward* of any labour or action.

Salvation of your *souls.*] The object of the Jewish expectations in their Messiah was the salvation or deliverance of their bodies from a foreign yoke; but the true Messiah came to save the soul from the yoke of the devil and sin. This glorious salvation these believers had already received.

Verse 10. *Of which salvation the prophets have inquired*] The incarnation and suffering of Jesus Christ, and the redemption procured by him for mankind, were made known, in a general way, by the prophets; but they themselves did not know the time when these things were to take place, nor the people among and by whom he was to suffer, &c.; they therefore *inquired accurately* or *earnestly*, εξεζητησαν, and *searched diligently*, εξηρευνησαν, *inquiring* of others who were then under the same inspiration, and *carefully searching* the writings of those who had, before their time, spoken of these things. The prophets plainly saw that the grace which was to come under the Messiah's kingdom was vastly superior to any thing that had ever been exhibited under the law; and in consequence they made all possible inquiry, and searched as after grains of gold, hidden among sand or compacted with ore, (for such is the meaning of the original word,) in order to ascertain the time, and the signs of that time, in which this wondrous display of God's love and mercy to man was to take place; but all that God thought fit to instruct them in was what is mentioned ver. 12.

Verse 11. *The glory that should follow.*] Not only the glory of his resurrection, ascension, exaltation, and the effusion of his Spirit; but that grand manifestation of God's infinite love to the world in causing the Gospel of his Son to be everywhere preached, and

A. M. cir. 4064.
A. D. cir. 60.
An. Olymp.
cir. CCIX. 4.
A. U. C. cir.
813.

^a the Spirit of Christ which was in them did signify, when it testified beforehand ^b the sufferings of Christ, and the glory that should follow.

12 ^c Unto whom it was revealed, that ^d not unto themselves, but unto us, they did minister the things which are now reported unto you by them that have preached the Gospel unto you, with ^e the Holy Ghost sent down from heaven; ^f which things the angels desire to look into.

A. M. cir. 4064.
A. D. cir. 60.
An. Olymp.
cir. CCIX. 4.
A. U. C. cir.
813.

13 Wherefore ^g gird up the loins of your mind, ^h be sober, and hope ⁱ to the end for the grace that is to be brought unto you ^k at the revelation of Jesus Christ;

14 As obedient children, ^l not fashioning yourselves according to the former lusts ^m in your ignorance:

15 ⁿ But as he which hath called you is

---

^a Chap. iii. 19; 2 Pet. i. 21.——^b Psa. xxii. 6; Isa. liii. 3, &c.; Dan. ix. 26; Luke xxiv. 25, 26, 44, 46; John xii. 41; Acts xxvi. 22, 23.——^c Dan. ix. 24; xii. 9, 13.——^d Hebrews xi. 13, 39, 40. ^e Acts ii. 4.——^f Exod. xxv. 20; Dan. viii. 13; xii. 5, 6; Eph. iii. 10.——^g Luke xii. 35; Eph. vi. 14.

^h Luke xxi. 34; Rom. xiii. 13; 1 Thess. v. 6, 8; chap. iv. 7; v. 8.——ⁱ Gr. *perfectly.*——^k Luke xvii. 30; 1 Cor. i. 7; 2 Thess. i. 7.——^l Rom. xii. 2; chap. iv. 2.——^m Acts xvii. 30; 1 Thess. iv. 5.——ⁿ Luke i. 74, 75; 2 Cor. xii. 1; 1 Thess. iv. 3, 4, 7; Heb. xii. 14; 2 Pet. iii. 11.

---

the glorious moral changes which should take place in the world under that preaching, and the final glorification of all them who had here received the report, and continued faithful unto death. And we may add to this the ineffable glorification of the human nature of Jesus Christ, which, throughout eternity, will be the glorious Head of his glorified body, the Church.

Verse 12. *Unto whom it was revealed*] We may presume that, in a great variety of cases, the prophets did not understand the meaning of their own predictions. They had a general view of God's designs; but of particular circumstances, connected with those great events, they seem to have known nothing, God reserving the explanation of all particulars to the time of the issue of such prophecies. When they wished to find out the times, the seasons, and the circumstances, God gave them to understand that it *was not for themselves, but for us, that they did minister the things which are now reported unto us by the preaching of the Gospel.* This was all the satisfaction they received in consequence of their earnest searching; and this was sufficient to repress all needless curiosity, and to induce them to rest satisfied that the Judge of all the earth would do right. If all succeeding interpreters of the prophecies had been contented with the same information relative to the predictions still unaccomplished, we should have had fewer books, and more wisdom.

Angels desire to look into.] Παρακυψαι· *To stoop down to;* the posture of those who are earnestly intent on finding out a thing, especially a *writing* difficult to be read; they bring it to the light, place it so that the rays may fall on it as collectively as possible, and then *stoop down* in order to examine all the parts, that they may be able to make out the whole. There is evidently an allusion here to the attitude of the cherubim who stood at the ends of the ark of the covenant, in the inner tabernacle, with their faces turned towards the mercy-seat or propitiatory in a bending posture, as if *looking attentively*, or, as we term it, *poring* upon it. Even the holy angels are struck with astonishment at the plan of human redemption, and justly wonder at the incarnation of that infinite object of their adoration. If then these things be objects of deep consideration to the *angels* of God, how much more so should they be to us; in them angels can have no such interest as human beings have.

We learn from the above that it was the *Spirit of Christ* in the Jewish prophets that prophesied of Christ; it was that Spirit which revealed him; and it is the same Spirit which takes of the things of Christ, and shows them unto us. Christ was never known by prophecy, but through his own Spirit; and he never was known, nor can be known, to the salvation of any soul, but by a revelation of the same Spirit. It is he alone that bears witness with our spirits that we are the children of God.

Verse 13. *Gird up the loins of your mind*] Take courage from this display of God's love now made known to you; and though you must expect trials, yet fortify your minds with the consideration that he who has given you his Son Jesus will withhold from you no manner of thing that is good. The allusion here is to the *long robes* of the Asiatics, which, when they were about to perform any active service, they tucked in their girdles: this they did also when they waited on their superiors at meals.

Hope to the end for the grace] Continue to expect all that God has promised, and particularly that utmost salvation, that glorification of body and soul, which ye shall obtain at the revelation of Christ, when he shall come to judge the world.

But if the apostle alludes here to the approaching revelation of Christ to inflict judgment on the Jews for their final rebellion and obstinacy, then the *grace*, χαριν, *benefit*, may intend their *preservation* from the evils that were coming upon that people, and their *wonderful escape* from Jerusalem at the time that the Roman armies came against it.

Verse 14. *Not fashioning yourselves*] As the *offices* of certain perons are known by the *garb* or *livery* they wear, so are transgressors: where we see the *world's livery* we see the *world's servants*; they *fashion* or *habit* themselves according to their *lusts*, and we may guess that they have a *worldly mind* by their conformity to *worldly fashions*.

Verse 15. *But as he which hath called you*] Heathenism scarcely produced a god whose example was not the most abominable; their greatest gods, especially, were paragons of impurity; none of their philosophers could propose the objects of their adoration as

2

A. M. cir. 4064.
A. D. cir. 61.
An. Olymp.
cir. CCIX. 4.
A. U. C. cir.
813.

holy, so be ye holy in all manner of conversation ;

16 Because it is written, ᵒ Be ye holy ; for I am holy.

17 And if ye call on the Father, ᵖ who without respect of persons judgeth according to every man's work, ᑫ pass the time of your ʳ sojourning *here* in fear :

A. M. cir. 4064.
A. D. cir. 60.
An. Olymp.
cir. CCIX. 4.
A. U. C. cir.
813.

18 Forasmuch as ye know ˢ that ye were not redeemed with corruptible things, *as* silver and gold, from your vain conversation ᵗ *received* by tradition from your fathers ;

19 But ᵘ with the precious blood of Christ, ᵛ as of a lamb without blemish and without spot

20 ʷ Who verily was foreordained before

ᵒ Lev. xi. 44; xix. 2; xx. 7.——ᵖ Deut. x. 17; Acts x. 34; Rom. ii. 11.——ᑫ 2 Cor. vii. 1; Phil. ii. 12; Heb. xii. 28. ʳ 2 Cor. v. 6; Heb. xi. 13; chap. ii. 11.——ˢ 1 Cor. vi. 20; vii. 23. ᵗ Ezek. xx. 18; chap. iv. 3.

ᵘ Acts xx. 28; Eph. i. 7; Heb. ix. 12, 14; Rev. v. 9.——ᵛ Exod. xii. 5; Isa. liii. 7; John i. 29, 36; 1 Cor. v. 7.——ʷ Rom. iii. 25 ; xvi. 25, 26; Eph. iii. 9, 11; Col. i. 26; 2 Tim. i. 9, 10; Tit. i. 2, 3; Rev. xiii. 8.

---

objects of imitation. Here Christianity has an infinite advantage over heathenism. *God is holy,* and he calls upon all who believe in him to *imitate his holiness ;* and the reason why they should be holy is, that *God who has called them is holy,* ver. 15.

Verse 17. *And if ye call on the Father*] Seeing ye invoke the Father of our Lord Jesus Christ, and your Father through Christ, and profess to be *obedient children,* and *sojourners* here below for a short time only, see that ye maintain a godly *reverence* for this Father, walking in all his testimonies blameless.

Who without respect of persons] God is said to be *no respecter of persons* for this reason among many others, that, being infinitely righteous, he must be infinitely impartial. He cannot prefer one to another, because he has nothing to *hope* or *fear* from any of his creatures. All *partialities* among men spring from one or other of these two principles, *hope* or *fear ;* God can feel neither of them, and therefore God can be no *respecter of persons.* He approves or disapproves of men according to their *moral character.* He pities all, and provides salvation for all, but he loves those who resemble him in his holiness ; and he loves them in proportion to that resemblance, *i. e.* the more of his image he sees in any, the more he loves him ; and *e contra.* And every *man's work* will be the *evidence* of his conformity or nonconformity to God ; and according to this evidence will God judge him. Here, then, is no *respect of persons ;* God's judgment will be according to a *man's work,* and a *man's work* or *conduct* will be according to the moral state of his mind. No *favouritism* can prevail in the day of judgment ; nothing will pass there but *holiness* of *heart* and *life.* A righteousness imputed, and not possessed and practised, will not avail where God *judgeth according to every man's work.* It would be well if those *sinners* and *spurious believers* who fancy themselves safe and complete in the righteousness of Christ, while impure and unholy in themselves, would think of this testimony of the apostle.

Verse 18. *Ye were not redeemed with corruptible things*] To *redeem,* λυτρόω, signifies to procure life for a captive or liberty for a slave by *paying a price,* and the *precious blood of Christ* is here stated to be the *price* at which the souls of both Jews and Gentiles were redeemed ; it was a *price* paid down, and a price which God's righteousness required.

Corruptible things mean here any thing that man usually gives in exchange for another ; but the term necessarily includes all created things, as all these are

corruptible and perishing. The meaning of the apostle is, evidently, that created things could not purchase the souls of men, else the sacrifice of Christ had not been offered ; could any thing less have done, God would not have given up his only-begotten Son. Even *silver* and *gold,* the most valuable medium of commerce among men, bear no proportion in their value to the souls of a lost world, for there should be a congruity between the *worth* of the thing *purchased* and the *valuable consideration* which is *given for it ;* and the laws and customs of nations require this : on this ground, *perishable things,* or things the value of which must be infinitely less than the worth of the souls of men, cannot purchase those souls. Nothing, therefore, but such a *ransom price* as God provided could be a sufficient ransom, oblation, and satisfaction, for the sins of the world.

Vain conversation] Empty, foolish, and unprofitable conduct, full of vain hopes, vain fears, and vain wishes.

Received by tradition from your fathers] The Jews had innumerable burdens of empty ceremonies and useless ordinances, which they received *by tradition* from their fathers, rabbins, or doctors. The *Gentiles* were not less encumbered with such than the Jews ; all were wedded to their *vanities,* because they received them from their *forefathers,* as *they* had done from *theirs.* And this *antiquity* and *tradition* have been the ground work of many a vain ceremony and idle pilgrimage, and of numerous doctrines which have nothing to plead in their behalf but this mere antiquity. But such persons seem not to consider that *error* and *sin* are nearly *coeval* with the world itself.

Verse 19. *The precious blood of Christ*] Τιμίω αἵματι· The valuable blood ; *how valuable* neither is nor could be stated.

As of a lamb] Such as was required for a *sin-offering* to God ; and ᴛʜᴇ *Lamb of God that takes away the sin of the world.*

Without blemish] In himself, and *without spot* from the world ; being perfectly *pure* in his *soul,* and *righteous* in his *life.*

Verse 20. *Who verily was foreordained*] Προεγνωσμένου· Foreknown; appointed in the Divine purpose to be sent into the world, because infinitely approved by the Divine justice.

Before the foundation of the world] Before the law was given, or any sacrifice prescribed by it. Its whole sacrificial system was appointed in reference

A. M. cir. 4064.
A. D. cir. 60.
An. Olymp.
cir. CCIX. 4.
A. U. C. cir.
813.

the foundation of the world, but was manifest [x] in these last times for you,

21 Who by him do believe in God, [y] that raised him up from the dead, and [z] gave him glory; that your faith and hope might be in God.

22 Seeing ye [a] have purified your souls in obeying the truth through the Spirit unto unfeigned [b] love of the brethren, *see that ye* love one another with a pure heart fervently:

23 [c] Being born again, not of corruptible seed, but of incorruptible, [d] by the word of God, which liveth and abideth for ever.

24 [e] For [f] all flesh *is* as grass, and all the glory of man as the flower of grass. The grass withereth, and the flower thereof falleth away:

25 [g] But the word of the Lord endureth for ever. [h] And this is the word which by the Gospel is preached unto you.

A. M. cir. 4064.
A. D. cir. 60.
An. Olymp.
cir. CCIX. 4.
A. U. C. cir.
813.

---

[x] Gal. iv. 4; Eph. i. 10; Heb. i. 2; ix. 26.——[y] Acts ii. 24.
[z] Matt. xxviii. 18; Acts ii. 33; iii. 13; Eph. i. 20; Phil. ii. 9;
Heb. ii. 9; chap. iii. 22.——[a] Acts xv. 9.——[b] Rom. xii. 9, 10;
1 Thess. iv. 9; 1 Tim. i. 5; Heb. xiii. 1; chap. ii. 17; iii. 8;
iv. 8; 2 Pet. i. 7; 1 John iii. 18; iv. 7, 21.——[c] John i. 13; iii.
5.——[d] James i. 18; 1 John iii. 9.——[e] Or, *For that.*——[f] Psa.
ciii. 15; Isa. xl. 6; li. 12; James i. 10.——[g] Psa. cii. 12, 26;
Isa. xl. 8; Luke xvi. 17.——[h] John i. 1, 14; 1 John i. 1, 3.

---

to this *foreappointed Lamb,* and consequently from him derived all its significance and virtue. The phrase καταβολη κοσμου, *foundation of the world,* occurs often in the New Testament, and is supposed by some learned men and good critics to signify the *commencement of the Jewish state.* Perhaps it may have this meaning in Matt. xiii. 35; Luke xi. 50; Eph. i. 4; Heb. iv. 3; and ix. 26. But if we take it here in its common signification, the *creation of universal nature,* then it shows that God, foreseeing the fall and ruin of man, appointed the remedy that was to cure the disease. It may here have a reference to the opinion of the Jewish doctors, who maintain that *seven* things existed before the creation of the world, one of which was the *Messiah.*

Last times] The Gospel dispensation, called the *last times,* as we have often seen, because never to be succeeded by any other.

Verse 21. *Who by him do believe in God*] This is supposed to refer to the *Gentiles,* who never knew the true God till they heard the preaching of the Gospel: the Jews had known him long before, but the Gentiles had every thing to learn when the first ▴ teachers of the Gospel arrived amongst them.

Gave him glory] Raised him to his right hand, where, as a Prince and a Saviour, he gives repentance and remission of sins.

That your faith] In the fulfilment of all his promises, and *your hope* of eternal glory, *might be in God,* who is unchangeable in his counsels, and infinite in his mercies.

Verse 22. *Seeing ye have purified your souls*] Having purified your souls, *in obeying the truth*—by believing in Christ Jesus, *through* the influence and teaching of *the Spirit;* and giving full proof of it by *unfeigned love* to the *brethren;* ye *love one another,* or *ye will love each other, with a pure heart fervently.* These persons, *First,* heard the *truth,* that is, the *Gospel;* thus called in a great variety of places in the New Testament, because it contains THE *truth* without mixture of error, and is the *truth* and substance of all the preceding dispensations by which it was typified. *Secondly,* they *obeyed* that *truth,* by believing on Him who came into the world to save sinners. *Thirdly,* through this believing on the Son

of God, their hearts were purified by the word of truth applied to them by the Holy Spirit. *Fourthly,* the love of God being shed abroad in their hearts by the Holy Ghost, they loved the brethren with pure hearts fervently, εκτενως, *intensely* or *continually;* the full proof that their *brotherly love* was *unfeigned,* φιλαδελφιαν ανυποκριτον, a *fraternal affection without hypocrisy.*

Verse 23. *Being born again*] For being born of Abraham's seed will not avail to the entering of the kingdom of heaven.

Not of corruptible seed] By no human generation, or earthly means; *but of incorruptible*—a Divine and heavenly principle which is not liable to decay, nor to be affected by the changes and chances to which all sublunary things are exposed.

By the word of God] Δια λογου ζωντος Θεου· By the *doctrine of the living God,* which *remaineth for ever;* which doctrine shall never change, any more than the source shall whence it proceeds.

Verse 24. *For all flesh is as grass*] Earthly seeds, earthly productions, and earthly generations, shall fail and perish like as the grass and flowers of the field; for the *grass withereth,* and the *flower falleth off,* though, in the ensuing spring and summer, they may put forth new verdure and bloom.

Verse 25. *But the word of the Lord*] The doctrine delivered by God concerning Christ endureth for ever, having, at *all times* and in *all seasons,* the same excellence and the same efficacy.

And this is the word] To ρημα, *What is spoken,* by the Gospel preached unto you. "This is a quotation from Isa. xl. 6–8, where the preaching of the Gospel is foretold; and recommended from the consideration that every thing which is merely human, and, among the rest, the noblest races of mankind, with all their glory and grandeur, their honour, riches, beauty, strength, and eloquence, as also the arts which men have invented, and the works they have executed, shall decay as the flowers of the field. But the Gospel, called by the prophet *the word of the Lord,* shall be preached while the world standeth."—*Macknight.* All human schemes of salvation, and plans for the melioration of the moral state of man, shall come to naught; and the doctrine of Christ crucified, though a stumbling block to the Jews, and foolishness to the Gentiles, shall be alone the power of God for salvation to every soul that believeth.

As the apostle, on ver. 7, mentions *gold*, and gold chemically examined and tried ; and as this figure frequently occurs in the sacred writings ; I think it necessary to say something here of the nature and properties of that metal.

Gold is defined by chemists to be the most perfect, the most ductile, the most tenacious, and the most unchangeable of all metals. Its specific *gravity* is about 19·3. A cubic foot of pure gold, cast and not hammered, weighs 1348*lbs*. In its native state, without mixture, it is *yellow*, and has no perceptible *smell* nor *taste*. When exposed to the action of the fire it becomes *red hot* before it melts, but in melting suffers no alteration ; but if a strong heat be applied while in fusion, it becomes of a beautiful green colour. The continual action of any furnace, howsoever long applied, has no effect on any of its properties. It has been kept in a state of fusion for *several months*, in the furnace of a glass house, without suffering the smallest *change*. The *electric* and *galvanic* fluids inflame and convert it into a *purple oxide*, which is volatilized in the form of smoke. In the focus of a very powerful burning glass it becomes *volatilized*, and partially *vitrified ;* so that we may say with the apostle, that, though *gold is tried by the fire*—abides the action of all culinary fires, howsoever applied, yet *it perisheth* by the *celestial fire* and the *solar influence ;* the rays of the sun collected in the focus of a powerful burning glass, and the application of the electric fluid, destroy its colour, and alter and impair all its properties. This is but a late discovery ; and previously to it a philosopher would have ridiculed St. Peter for saying, *gold that perisheth.*

Gold is so very *tenacious* that a piece of it drawn into wire, one-tenth of an inch in diameter, will sustain a weight of 500*lbs*. without breaking.

One grain of gold may be so extended, by its great malleability, as to be easily divided into *two millions* of parts ; and a *cubic inch* of gold into *nine thousand, five hundred and twenty-three millions, eight hundred and nine thousand, five hundred and twenty-three parts ;* each of which may be *distinctly seen* by the naked eye!

A *grain and a half* of gold may be beaten into leaves of one inch square, which, if intersected by parallel lines, drawn at right angles to each other, and distant only the 100th part of an inch, will produce *twenty-five millions* of *little squares*, each of which may be distinctly seen without the help of glasses!

The surface of any given quantity of gold, according to Mr. *Magellan*, may be extended by the hammer 159,092 times!

Eighty books, or *two thousand* leaves, of what is called leaf gold, each leaf measuring 3·3 inches square,

viz. each leaf containing 10·89 square inches, weigh less than 384 grains ; each book, therefore, or *twenty-five* leaves, is equal to 272·25 inches, and weighs about 4·8 grains ; so that *each grain* of gold will produce 56·718, or nearly *fifty-seven* square inches !

The *thickness* of the metal thus extended appears to be no more than the *one* 282·020th of an inch ! One pound, or *sixteen* ounces of gold, would be sufficient to gild a silver wire, sufficient in length to encompass the whole terraqueous globe, or to extend 25,000 miles !

Notwithstanding this extreme degree of *tenuity*, or *thinness*, which some carry much higher, no *pore* can be discerned in it by the strongest magnifying powers ; nor is it pervious to the particles of light, nor can the most subtile fluids pass through it. Its *ductility* has never yet been carried to the uttermost pitch, and to human art and ingenuity is probably unlimited.

Sulphur, in the state of a *sulphuret*, dissolves it ; *tin* and *lead* greatly impair its tenacity ; and *zinc* hardens and renders it very brittle. *Copper* heightens its colour, and renders it harder, without greatly impairing its *ductility*. It readily unites with *iron*, which it *hardens* in a remarkable manner.

The *oxigenated muriatic* acid, and the *nitro-muriatic* acid, dissolve gold. In this state it is capable of being applied with great success to the *gilding of steel*. The process is very simple, and is instantaneously performed, viz. :—

To a solution of gold in the *nitro-muriatic* acid add about twice the quantity of *sulphuric ether*. In order to gild either iron or steel, let the metal be *well polished*, the higher the better : the *ether* which has taken up the gold may be applied by a camel hair pencil, or small brush ; the ether then evaporates, and the gold becomes strongly attached to the surface of the metal. I have seen *lancets, penknives*, &c., gilded in a moment, by being dipped in this solution. In this manner all kinds of figures, letters, mottoes, &c., may be delineated on steel, by employing a pen or fine brush.

The *nitro-muriatic* acid, formerly called *aqua regia*, is formed by adding *muriatic* acid, vulgarly *spirit of salt*, to the *nitric* acid, formerly *aqua fortis*. *Two parts* of the *muriatic* acid to *one* of the *nitric* constitute this solvent of gold and platina, which is called the *nitro-muriatic* acid.

Gold was considered the *heaviest* of all metals till the year 1748, when the knowledge of *platina* was brought to Europe by *Don Antonio Ulloa*: this, if it be a *real* metal, is the *hardest* and *weightiest* of all others. The specific gravity of gold is, as we have seen, 19·3 ; that of platina is from 20·6 to 23 : but *gold* will ever be the most valuable of all metals, not merely from its *scarcity*, but from its *beautiful colour* and great *ductility*, by which it is applicable to so many uses, and its power of preserving its hue and polish without suffering the least tarnish or oxidation from the action of the air.

CHAPTER II.

We should lay aside all evil dispositions, and desire the sincere milk of the word, that we may grow thereby, 1–3. And come to God to be made living stones, and be built up into a spiritual temple, 4, 5. The prophecy of Christ as chief corner stone, precious to believers, but a stumbling stone to the disobedient, 6–8. True believers are a chosen generation, a royal priesthood, &c., 9, 10. They should abstain from fleshly lusts, 11. Walk uprightly among the Gentiles, 12. Be obedient to civil authority, according to the will of God, 13–15. Make a prudent use of their Christian liberty, 16. Fear God and honour the king, 17. Servants should be subject to their masters, and serve them faithfully, and suffer indignities patiently, after the example of Christ, 18–23. Who bore the punishment due to our sins in his own body upon the tree, 24. They were formerly like sheep going astray, but are now returned unto the Shepherd and Bishop of their souls, 25.

A. M. cir. 4064.
A. D. cir. 60.
An. Olymp.
cir. CCIX. 4.
A. U. C. cir.
813.

WHEREFORE, [a] laying aside all malice, and all guile, and hypocrisies, and envies, and all evil speakings,

2 [b] As new-born babes, desire the sincere [c] milk of the word, that ye may grow thereby, (*unto salvation :*)

3 If so be ye have [d] tasted that the Lord *is* gracious.

4 To whom coming, *as unto* a living stone,

A. M. cir. 4064.
A. D. cir. 60.
An. Olymp.
cir. CCIX. 4.
A. U. C. cir.
813.

---

[a] Eph. iv. 22, 25, 31 ; Col. iii. 8 ; Heb. xii. 1 ; James i. 21 ; v. 9 ; chap. iv. 2.——[b] Matt. xviii. 3 ; Mark x. 15 ; Rom. vi. 4 ;

[l] Cor. xiv. 20 ; chap. i. 23.——[c] 1 Cor. iii. 2 ; Heb. v. 12, 13. [d] Psa. xxxiv. 8 ; Heb. vi. 5.

NOTES ON CHAP. II.

Verse 1. *Wherefore, laying aside*] This is in close connection with the preceding chapter, from which it should not have been separated ; and the subject is continued to the end of the 10th verse.

Laying aside all malice] See the notes on Eph. iv. 22–31. These tempers and dispositions must have been common among the Jews, as they are frequently spoken against : Christianity can never admit of such ; they show the mind, not of Christ, but of the old murderer.

Verse 2. *As new-born babes*] In the preceding chapter, ver. 23, the apostle states that they had been *born again ;* and as the new-born infant desires that aliment which nature has provided for it, so they, being *born again*—born from above, should as earnestly require that heavenly nourishment which is suited to their new nature ; and this the apostle calls the *sincere milk of the word, το λογικον αδολον γαλα,* or, as some translate, *the rational unadulterated milk ; i. e.* the pure doctrines of the Gospel, as delivered in the epistles and gospels, and as preached by the apostles and their successors. The rabbins frequently express *learning to know the law,* &c., by the term *sucking,* and their disciples are often denominated *those that suck the breast.* The figure is very expressive : as a child newly born shows an immediate desire for that nourishment, and that only, which is its most proper food ; so they, being just *born of God,* should show that the incorruptible seed abides in them, and that they will receive nothing that is not suited to that new nature : and, indeed, they can have no spiritual growth but by the pure doctrines of the Gospel.

That ye may grow thereby] Εις σωτηριαν, *Unto salvation,* is added here by ABC, and about forty others ; both the *Syriac,* the *Arabic* of Erpen, *Coptic, Æthiopic, Armenian, Slavonic, Vulgate,* and several of the ancient *fathers.* The reading is undoubtedly *genuine,* and is very important. It shows why they were regenerated, and why they were to desire the unadulterated doctrines of the Gospel ; viz. : that they

might *grow up unto salvation.* This was the *end* they should always have in view ; and nothing could so effectually promote this end as continually receiving the pure truth of God, claiming the fulfilment of its promises, and acting under its dictates.

Verse 3. *If so be ye have tasted*] Ειπερ εγευσασθε· *Seeing ye have tasted.* There could be no *doubt* that they had tasted the goodness of Christ *who were born again of incorruptible seed,* and whose *hearts were purified by the truth,* and who *had like precious faith* with the apostles themselves.

That the Lord is gracious.] 'Οτι χρηστος ὁ Κυριος. From the similarity of the letters, many MSS. and several of the *fathers* have read, Χριστος ὁ κυριος, *the Lord is Christ,* or *Christ is the Lord.* This seems to refer to Psa. xxxiv. 8 : *O taste and see that the Lord is good ;* Γευσασθε και ιδετε οτι χρηστος ὁ Κυριος, *Sept.* And there is still a reference to the *sucking child* that, having once tasted its mother's milk, ever after desires and longs for it. As they were born of God, and had tasted his goodness, they would naturally desire the same pure unadulterated milk of the word.

Verse 4. *To whom coming, as unto a living stone*] This is a reference to Isa. xxviii. 16 : *Behold, I lay in Zion for a foundation a stone, a tried stone, a precious corner stone, a sure foundation.* Jesus Christ is, in both the prophet and apostle, represented as the *foundation* on which the Christian Church is built, and on which it must continue to rest : and the *stone* or *foundation* is called here *living,* to intimate that he is the source of life to all his followers, and that it is in union with him that they live, and answer the end of their regeneration ; as the stones of a building are of no use but as they occupy their proper places in a building, and rest on the foundation.

Disallowed indeed of men] That is, rejected by the Jews. This is a plain reference to the prophecy, Psa. cxviii. 22 : *The stone which the builders refused is become the head stone of the corner.*

Chosen of God] To be the Saviour of the world,

A. M. cir. 4064.
A. D. cir. 60.
An. Olymp
cir. CCIX. 4.
A. U. C. cir
813.

[e] disallowed indeed of men, but chosen of God, *and* precious,

5 [f] Ye also, as lively stones, [g] are built up [h] a spiritual house, [f] a holy priesthood, to offer up [k] spiritual sacrifices, [l] acceptable to God by Jesus Christ.

6 Wherefore also it is contained in the Scripture; [m] Behold, I lay in Sion a chief corner stone, elect, precious : and he that believeth on him shall not be confounded.

A. M. cir. 4064
A. D. cir. 60.
An. Olymp.
cir. CCIX. 4.
A. U. C. cir.
813.

---

[e] Psa. cxviii. 22 ; Matt. xxi. 42; Acts iv. 11.——[f] Eph. ii. 21, 22. [g] Or, *be ye built.*——[h] Heb. iii. 6.——[i] Isa. lxi. 6; lxvi. 21; ver. 9.

[k] Hos. xiv. 2 ; Mal. i. 11; Rom. xii. 1; Heb. xiii. 15, 16 [l] Phil. iv. 18; chap. iv. 11.——[m] Isa. xxviii. 16 ; Rom. ix. 33.

---

and the Founder of the Church, and the foundation on which it rests. As Christ is the *choice* of the Father, we need have no doubt of the efficacy and sufficiency of all that he has suffered and done for the salvation of a lost world. God can never be mistaken in his *choice ;* therefore he that chooses Christ for his portion shall never be confounded.

Precious] Εντιμον· *Honourable.* Howsoever despised and rejected by men, Jesus, as the sacrifice for a lost world, is infinitely honourable in the sight of God ; and those who are united by faith to him partake of the same honour, being *members* of that great and glorious *body* of which he is the *head,* and *stones* in that superb *building* of which he is the *foundation.*

Verse 5. *Ye also, as lively stones*] Λιθοι ζωντες· *Living stones ;* each being instinct with the principle of life, which proceeds from him who is the foundation, called above λιθον ζωντα, a living stone.

The metaphor in this and the following verse is as bold as it is singular ; and commentators and critics have found it difficult to hit on any *principle* of explanation. In all metaphors there is something in the natural image that is illustrative of some chief moral property in the thing to be represented. But what analogy is there between the *stones* of a building and a multitude of *human beings?* We shall soon see. The Church of Christ, it is true, is represented under the figure of a *house,* or rather *household ;* and as a *household* or *family* must have a *place* of residence, hence, by a *metonymy,* the *house* itself, or *material building,* is put for the *household* or *family* which occupies it, the *container* being put for the *contained.* This point will receive the fullest illustration if we have recourse to the Hebrew : in this language, בית *beith* signifies both a *house* and a *family ;* בן *ben* a son ; בת *bath* a daughter ; and אבן *eben* a stone. Of all these nouns, בנה *banah,* he built, is, I believe, the common *root.* Now as בית *beith,* a house, is built of אבנים *abanim,* stones, hence בנה *banah,* he built, is a proper radix for both *stones* and *building ;* and as בית *beith,* a family or *household* (Psa. lxviii. 6) is constituted or made up of בנים *banim,* sons, and בנות *bánoth;* daughters, hence the same root בנה *banah,* he built, is common to all ; for sons and daughters *build up* or constitute a *family,* as *stones* do a *building.* Here, then, is the ground of the metaphor : the *spiritual house* is the *holy* or *Christian family* or *household,* this *family* or *household* is composed of the *sons* and *daughters* of God Almighty ; and hence the propriety of *living stones,* because this is the *living house* or *spiritual family.* As a building *rests* upon a *foundation,* and this foundation is its *support ;* so a *family* or *household* rests on the *father,* who is properly con-

sidered the *foundation* or *support* of the building. But as every father is *mortal* and *transitory,* none can be called a *living stone,* foundation, or support, but He who *liveth for ever,* and has *life independent ;* so none but Jesus, who hath *life in himself,* i. e. *independently,* and who is the *Way, the Truth,* and the LIFE, can be a *permanent* foundation or support to the whole spiritual house. And as all the stones—sons and daughters, that constitute the spiritual building are made partakers of the *life* of Christ, consequently, they may with great propriety be called *living stones,* that is, *sons and daughters of God,* who *live by Christ Jesus,* because *he lives in them.* Now, following the metaphor; these various *living stones* become one grand *temple,* in which God is *worshipped,* and in which he manifests himself as he did in the temple of old. Every stone—son and daughter, being a spiritual sacrificer or priest, they all offer up praise and thanksgiving to God through Christ ; and such sacrifices, being offered up in the name and through the merit of his Son, are all acceptable in his sight.

This is the true metaphor, and which has not, as far as I know, ever been properly *traced out.* To talk of " stones being said to be *alive* as long as they are not cut out of the quarry, but continue to partake of that nourishment which circulates from vein to vein," is as unsatisfactory as it is unphilosophical ; the other is the true metaphor, and explains every thing.

Verse 6. *Behold, I lay in Sion*] This intimates that the foundation of the Christian Church should be laid at Jerusalem ; and *there* it was laid, for there Christ suffered, and there the preaching of the Gospel commenced.

A chief corner stone] This is the same as the foundation stone ; and it is called here the *chief corner stone* because it is laid in the foundation, at an angle of the building where its two sides form the ground work of a *side* and *end* wall. And this migh probably be designed to show that, in Jesus, both Jews and Gentiles were to be *united ;* and this is probably the reason why it was called a *stone of stumbling, and rock of offence ;* for nothing stumbled, nothing offended the Jews so much as the calling of the Gentiles into the Church of God, and admitting them to the same privileges which had been before peculiar to the Jews.

Elect, precious] *Chosen* and *honourable.* See on ver. 4.

Shall not be confounded.] These words are quoted from Isa. xxviii. 16 ; but rather more from the Septuagint than from the Hebrew text. The latter we translate, *He that believeth shall not make haste*—he who comes to God, through Christ, for salvation, shall

A.M. cir. 4064.
A. D. cir. 60.
An. Olymp.
cir. CCIX. 4.
A. U. C. cir.
813.

7 Unto you therefore which believe *he is* [n] precious: but unto them which be disobedient, [o] the stone which the builders disallowed, the same is made the head of the corner,

8 [p] And a stone of stumbling, and a rock of offence, [q] *even to them* which stumble at the word, being disobedient: [r] whereunto also they were appointed.

9 But ye *are* [s] a chosen generation, [t] a royal priesthood, [u] a holy nation, [v] a [w] peculiar peo-

A. M. cir. 4064.
A. D. cir. 60.
An. Olymp.
cir. CCIX. 4.
A. U. C. cir.
813.

---

[n] Or. *an honour.*——[o] Psa. cxviii. 22 ; Matt. xxi. 42 ; Acts iv. 11.
[p] Isaiah viii. 14 ; Luke ii. 34 ; Romans ix. 33.——[q] 1 Cor. i. 23.
[r] Exod. ix. 16 ; Rom. ix. 22 ; 1 Thess. v. 9 ; Jude 4.——[s] Deut.
x. 15 ; chap. i. 2.

[t] Exod. xix. 5, 6 ; Rev. i. 6 ; v. 10.——[u] John xvii. 19 ; 1 Cor.
iii. 17 ; 2 Tim. i. 9.——[v] Deut. iv. 20 ; vii. 6 ; xiv. 2 ; xxvi. 18,
19 ; Acts xx. 28 ; Ephesians i. 14 ; Tit. ii. 14.——[w] Or,
a purchased people.

---

never be confounded ; he need not *haste* to flee away, for no enemy shall ever be able to annoy him.

Verse 7. *Unto you therefore which believe*] You, both Jews and Gentiles.

He is *precious*] Ὑμιν ουν ἡ τιμη τοις πιστευουσιν· *The honour is to you who believe ;* i. e. the honour of being in this building, and of having your souls saved through the blood of the Lamb, and becoming sons and daughters of God Almighty.

Them which be disobedient] The *Jews,* who continue to reject the Gospel ; that very person whom they reject is *head of the corner*—is Lord over all, and has all power in the heavens and the earth.

Verse 8. *A stone of stumbling*] Because in him all Jews and Gentiles who believe are united ; and because the latter were admitted into the Church, and called by the Gospel to enjoy the same privileges which the Jews, as the peculiar people of God, had enjoyed for two thousand years before ; therefore they rejected the Christian religion, they would have no partakers with themselves in the salvation of God. This was the true cause why the Jews rejected the Gospel ; and they rejected Christ because he did not come as a *secular* prince. In the *one case* he was a *stone of stumbling*—he was *poor,* and affected no worldly pomp ; in the other he was a *rock of offence,* for his Gospel called the Gentiles to be a peculiar people whom the Jews believed to be everlastingly reprobated, and utterly incapable of any spiritual good.

Whereunto also they were appointed.] Some good critics read the verse thus, carrying on the sense from the preceding : *Also a stone of stumbling, and a rock of offence : The disobedient stumble against the word,* (or doctrine,) *to which verily they were appointed.*— Macknight.

Mr. Wakefield, leaving out, with the *Syriac,* the clause, *The stone which the builders disallowed, the same is made the head of the corner,* reads the 7th and 8th verses thus : *To you therefore who trust* thereon, this stone is *honourable ; but to those who are not persuaded,* (απειθουσι,) *it is a stone to strike upon and to stumble against, at which they stumble who believe not the word ; and unto this indeed they were appointed :* that is, they who *believe not the word* were appointed to stumble and fall by it, not to disbelieve it ; for the word of the Lord is either a *savour of life unto life,* or *death unto death,* to all them that hear it, according as they *receive* it by *faith,* or *reject* it by *unbelief.* The phrase τιθεναι τινα εις τι is very frequent among the purest Greek writers, and signifies *to attribute any thing to another,* or *to speak a thing of them ;* of which *Kypke* gives several examples from *Plutarch ;* and

paraphrases the words thus : *This stumbling and offence, particularly of the Jews, against Christ, the corner stone, was long ago asserted and predicted by the prophets, by Christ, and by others ;* compare Isa. viii. 14, 15 ; Matt. xxi. 42, 44 ; Luke ii. 34 ; and Rom. ix. 32, 33. Now this interpretation of Kypke is the more likely, because it is evident that St. Peter refers to Isa. viii. 14, 15 : *And he shall be for a sanctuary ; but for a stone of stumbling and for a rock of offence to both the houses of Israel, for a gin and for a snare to the inhabitants of Jerusalem : and many among them shall stumble, and fall, and be broken, &c.* The *disobedient,* therefore, being appointed to stumble against the word, or being *prophesied of* as persons that should stumble, necessarily means, from the connection in which it stands, and from the passage in the prophet, that their *stumbling, falling,* and *being broken,* is the consequence of their disobedience or unbelief ; but there is no intimation that they were *appointed* or *decreed to disobey,* that they might stumble, and fall, and be broken. They stumbled and fell through their *obstinate unbelief ;* and thus their stumbling and falling, as well as their unbelief, were of themselves ; in consequence of this they were *appointed* to be *broken ;* this was God's work of judgment. This seems to be the meaning which our Lord attaches to this very prophecy, which he quotes against the chief priests and elders, Matt. xxi. 44. On the whole of these passages, see the notes on Matt. xxi. 42-44.

Verse 9. *Ye are a chosen generation*] The titles formerly given to the whole Jewish Church, i. e. to all the Israelites without exception, all who were in the covenant of God by circumcision, whether they were holy persons or not, are here given to Christians in general in the same way ; i. e. to all who believed in Christ, whether Jews or Gentiles, and who received baptism in the name of the Father, and of the Son, and of the Holy Ghost.

The Israelites were a *chosen* or *elected* race, to be *a special people unto the Lord their God, above all people that were upon the face of the earth,* Deut. vii. 6.

They were also a *royal priesthood,* or what Moses calls *a kingdom of priests,* Exod. xix. 6. For all were called to sacrifice to God ; and he is represented to be the *King* of that people, and *Father* of those of whom he was king ; therefore they were all *royal.*

They were a *holy nation,* Exod. xix. 6 ; for they were separated from all the people of the earth, that they might worship the one only true God, and abstain from the abominations that were in the heathen world.

They were also a *peculiar people,* λαος εις περιποιησιν, a *purchased people ;* סגלה *segullah,* a *private pro-*

A. M. cir. 4064.
A. D. cir. 60.
An. Olymp.
cir. CCIX. 4.
A. U. C. cir.
813.

ple; that ye should show forth the [x] praises of him who hath called you out of [y] darkness into his marvellous light:

10 [z] Which in time past *were* not a people, but *are* now the people of God: which had not obtained mercy, but now have obtained mercy.

11 Dearly beloved, I beseech *you* [a] as

strangers and pilgrims, [b] abstain from fleshly lusts, [c] which war against the soul;

12 [d] Having your conversation honest among the Gentiles; that [e] whereas they speak against you as evil doers, [f] they may by *your* good works, which they shall behold, glorify God [g] in the day of visitation.

A. M. cir. 4064.
A. D. cir. 60.
An. Olymp.
cir. CCIX. 4.
A. U. C. cir.
813.

---

[x] Or, *virtues.*——[y] Acts xxvi. 18; Eph. v. 8; Col. i. 13; 1 Thess. v. 4, 5.——[z] Hos. i. 9, 10; ii. 23; Rom. ix. 25.——[a] 1 Chron. xxix. 15; Psa. xxxix. 12; cxix. 19; Heb. xi. 13; chap. i. 17.

[b] Rom. xiii. 14; Gal. v. 16.——[c] James iv. 1.——[d] Rom. xii, 17; 2 Cor. viii. 21; Phil. ii. 15; Titus ii. 8; chapter iii. 16. [e] Or, *wherein.*——[f] Matt. v. 16.——[g] Luke xix. 44.

---

perty, belonging to God Almighty, Deut. vii. 6; none other having any *right* in them, and they being under obligation to God alone. All these things the apostle applies to the Christians, to whom indeed they belong, in their spirit and essence, in such a way as they could not belong to the Hebrews of old. But they were called to this state of salvation *out of darkness*—idolatry, superstition, and ungodliness, *into his marvellous light*—the Gospel dispensation, which, in reference to the discoveries it had made of God, his nature, will, and gracious promises towards mankind, differed as much from the preceding dispensation of the Jews, as the light of the meridian *sun* from the faint twinkling of a *star.* And they had these privileges *that they might show forth the praises of Him who had* thus *called them;* αρετας, *the virtues,* those perfections of the wisdom, justice, truth, and goodness of God, that shone most illustriously in the Christian dispensation. These they were to exhibit in a holy and useful life, being transformed into the image of God, and walking as Christ himself walked.

Verse 10. *Which in time past* were *not a people*] This is a quotation from Hosea i. 9, 10, and ii. 23, where the *calling of the Gentiles,* by the preaching of the Gospel, is foretold. From this it is evident, that the people to whom the apostle now addresses himself had been *Gentiles,* covered with ignorance and superstition, and now had obtained mercy by the preaching of the Gospel of Christ.

Verse 11. *As strangers and pilgrims*] See the note on Heb. xi. 13. These were *strangers* and *pilgrims* in the most literal sense of the word, see chap. i. 1, for they were *strangers* scattered through Asia, Pontus, &c.

Abstain from fleshly lusts] As ye are *strangers* and *pilgrims,* and profess to seek a heavenly country, do not entangle your affections with earthly things. While others spend all their time, and employ all their skill, in acquiring earthly property, and totally neglect the salvation of their souls; *they* are not *strangers,* they are here *at home;* they are not *pilgrims,* they are seeking an *earthly possession:* Heaven is *your home,* seek *that;* God is your *portion,* seek *him.* All kinds of earthly desires, whether those of the *flesh* or of the *eye,* or those included in the *pride of life,* are here comprised in the words *fleshly lusts.*

Which war against the soul] Αἱτινες στρατευονται κατα της ψυχης· Which are *marshalled* and *drawn up in battle array,* to fight against the soul; either to slay

it, or to bring it into captivity. This is the object and operation of every earthly and sensual desire. How little do those who indulge them think of the ruin which they produce!

Verse 12. *Having your conversation honest*] Living in such a manner among the Gentiles, in whose country ye sojourn, as becomes the Gospel which ye profess.

That whereas they speak against you as evil doers] In all the heathen countries, in the first age of the Church, the Christians and the Jews were confounded together; and as the latter were everywhere exceedingly troublesome and seditious, the Christians shared in their blame, and suffered no small measure of obloquy and persecution on this very account. It was doubly necessary, therefore, that the Christians should be exceedingly cautious; and that their conduct should prove that, although many of them were of the same nation, yet they who had embraced Christianity differed widely in their spirit and conduct from those, whether Jews or Gentiles, who had *not* received the faith of Christ.

In the day of visitation.] I believe this refers to the time when God should come to execute judgment on the disobedient Jews, in the destruction of their civil polity, and the subversion of their temple and city. God did at that time put a remarkable difference between the Jews and the Christians: *all the former* were either destroyed or carried into slavery; *not one of the latter:* nor did they deserve it; for not one of them had joined in the sedition against the Roman government. That the *day of visitation* means a time in which punishment should be inflicted, is plain from Isa. x. 3: *And what will ye do in the* DAY *of* VISITATION, *and in the desolation which shall come from afar? To whom will ye flee for help? And where will ye leave your glory?* Some think that by the phrase in this place is meant the time in which they should be brought before the heathen magistrates, who, after an impartial examination, should find them innocent, and declare them as such; by which God would be glorified, the work appearing to be his own. Others think that it signifies the time in which God should make them the offer of mercy by Jesus Christ. The words, however, may refer to the time in which the Christians should be called to suffer for the testimony of Christ; the heathens, seeing them bear their sufferings with unconquerable patience, were constrained to confess that God was with them; and not a few, from being *spectators* of their sufferings, became *converts to* Christianity.

A. M. cir. 4064.
A. D. cir. 60.
An. Olymp.
cir. CCIX. 4.
A. U. C. cir.
813.

13 [h] Submit yourselves to every ordinance of man for the Lord's sake : whether it be to the king, as supreme ;

14 Or unto governors, as unto them that are sent by him [i] for the punishment of evil doers, and [k] for the praise of them that do well.

15 For so is the will of God, that [l] with well-

doing ye may put to silence the ignorance of foolish men :

16 [m] As free, and not [n] using *your* liberty for a cloak of maliciousness, but as [o] the servants of God.

17 [p] Honour [q] all *men.* [r] Love the brotherhood. [s] Fear God. Honour the king.

18 [t] Servants, *be* subject to *your* masters

A. M. cir. 4064.
A. D. cir. 60.
An. Olymp.
cir. CCIX. 4.
A. U. C. cir.
813.

[h] Matt. xxii. 21 ; Rom. xiii. 1 ; Tit. iii. 1.——[i] Rom. xiii. 4. [k] Rom. xiii. 3.——[l] Tit. ii. 8 ; ver. 12.——[m] Gal. v. 1. 13.——[n] Gr. *having.*——[o] 1 Cor. vii. 22.——[p] Rom. xii. 10 ; Phil. ii. 3.

[q] Or, *esteem.*——[r] Heb. xiii. 1 ; chap. i. 22.——[s] Proverbs xxiv. 21 ; Matt. xxii. 21 ; Rom. xiii. 7.——[t] Eph. vi. 5 ; Col. iii. 22 ; 1 Tim. vi. 1 ; Tit. ii. 9.

Verse 13. *Submit yourselves to every ordinance of man*] In every settled state, and under every form of political government, where the laws are not in opposition to the laws of God, it may be very soundly and rationally said : " Genuine Christians have nothing to do with the laws but to obey them." Society and civil security are in a most dangerous state when the people take it into their heads that they have a right to remodel and change the laws. See the whole of this subject fully handled in the notes on Rom. xiii. 1, &c., to which I beg every reader, who may wish to know the political sentiments of this work, to have recourse.

The words πασῃ ανθρωπινῃ κτισει literally signify, not *every ordinance of man,* but *every human creature ;* yet κτιζειν signifies sometimes to *arrange, order,* as well as to *create,* and therefore our translation may do : but as the apostle is evidently speaking here of *magistracy,* or *legislative* authority, and as the appointment of magistrates was termed a creating of them, it is better to understand the words thus, All the constituted authorities. So, *Decem tribunos plebis per pontificem creaverunt ;* Cor. Nep. " They created ten tribunes of the plebeians, by the high priest." *Carthagine quotannis annui bini reges creabantur ;* Cæsar. " They created two kings every year at Carthage." *Consules creantur Cæsar et Servilius ;* Sallust. " Cæsar and Servilius are created consuls." *Creare ducem gerendo bello.* " To create a general to conduct the war." The meaning of St. Peter appears to be this : the Jews thought it unlawful to obey any ruler that was not of *their own stock ;* the apostle tells them they should obey the civil magistrate, let him be of what stock he may, whether a Jew or a Gentile, and let him exercise the government in whatsoever *form.* This is the general proposition : and then he instances *emperors* and their *deputies ;* and, far from its being unlawful for them to *obey a heathen magistrate,* they were to do it *for the Lord's sake,* δια τον Κυριον, *on account of the Lord,* whose *will* it was, and who *commanded* it.

Verse 14. *Or unto governors*] By *king as supreme,* the Roman *emperor* is meant ; and by *governors,* ἡγεμοσιν, are meant, leaders, governors, presidents, proconsuls, and other chief magistrates, sent by him into the provinces dependent on the Roman empire.

For the punishment of evil doers] This was the object of their mission ; they were to punish delinquents, and encourage and protect the virtuous.

Verse 15. *For so is the will of God*] God, as their supreme governor, shows them that it is his will that they should act uprightly and obediently at all

times, and thus confound the ignorance of foolish men, who were ready enough to assert that their religion made them bad subjects. The word φιμουν, which we translate *put to silence,* signifies to *muzzle.* i. e., stop their mouths, leave them nothing to say ; let them *assert,* but ever be unable to bring proof to support it.

Verse 16. *As free*] The Jews pretended that they were a free people, and owed allegiance to God alone ; hence they were continually rebelling against the Roman government, to which God had subjected them because of their rebellion against him : thus they *used their liberty for a cloak of maliciousness*—for a *pretext* of rebellion, and by it endeavoured to vindicate their seditious and rebellious conduct.

But as the servants of God.] These were *free* from sin and Satan, but they were the *servants of God*—bound to obey him ; and, as he had made it their duty to obey the civil magistrate, they served God by submitting to every ordinance of man for the Lord's sake.

Verse 17. *Honour all men.*] That is, Give honour to whom honour is due, Rom. xiii. 7. Respect every man as a fellow creature, and as one who may be a fellow heir with you of eternal life ; and therefore be ready to give him every kind of succour in your power.

Love the brotherhood.] All true Christians, who form one great family of which God is the head.

Fear God.] Who gives you these commandments ; lest he punish you for disobedience.

Honour the king.] Pay that respect to the *emperor* which his high authority requires, knowing that civil power is of God ; that the authority with which he, in the course of his providence, has invested him, must be respected in order to its being obeyed ; and that if the man be even bad, and as a man be worthy of no reverence, yet he should be respected on account of his *office.* If respect be banished, subordination will flee with it, and anarchy and ruin will rise up in their place. Truly *religious* persons are never found in seditions. *Hypocrites* may join themselves with *any* class of the workers of iniquity, and say, *Hail, brethren !*

Verse 18. *Servants, be subject*] See the notes on Eph. vi. 5 ; Col. iii. 22 ; and Tit. ii. 9.

With all fear] With all submission and reverence.

The good and gentle] Those who are ever just in their commands, never requiring more work than is necessary or proper, and always allowing sufficient food and sufficient time.

The froward.] Σκολιοις· The crooked, perverse,

      2

A. M. cir. 4064.
A. D. cir. 60.
An. Olymp.
cir. CCIX. 4.
A. U. C. cir.
813.

with all fear; not only to the good and gentle, but also to the froward.

19 For this *is* ᵘ thankworthy, ᵛ if a man for conscience toward God endure grief, suffering wrongfully.

20 For ʷ what glory *is it*, if, when ye be buffeted for your faults, ye shall take it patiently? but if, when ye do well, and suffer *for it*, ye take it patiently, this *is* ˣ acceptable with God.

21 For ʸ even hereunto were ye called: because ᶻ Christ also suffered ᵃ for us, ᵇ leaving us an example, that ye should follow his steps:

22 ᶜ Who did no sin, neither was guile found in his mouth:

A. M. cir. 4064
A. D. cir. 60,
An. Olymp.
cir. CCIX. 4.
A. U. C. cir.
813.

23 ᵈ Who, when he was reviled, reviled not again; when he suffered, he threatened not; but ᵉ committed ᶠ *himself* to him that judgeth righteously:

24 ᵍ Who his own self bare our sins in his own body ʰ on the tree, ¹ that we, being dead to sins, should live unto righteousness: ᵏ by whose stripes ye were healed.

25 For ¹ ye were as sheep going astray; but are now returned ᵐ unto the Shepherd and Bishop of your souls.

ᵘ Or, *thank*; Luke vi. 32; ver. 20.——ᵛ Matt. v. 10; Rom. xiii. 5; chap. iii. 14.——ʷ Chap. iii. 14; iv. 14, 15.——ˣ Or, *thank*, ʸ Matt. xvi. 24; Acts xiv. 22; 1 Thess. iii. 3; 2 Tim. iii. 12. ᶻ Chap. iii. 18.——ᵃ Some read, *for you*.——ᵇ John xiii. 15; Phil. ii. 5; 1 John ii. 6.——ᶜ Isa. liii. 9; Luke xxiii. 41; John viii. 46; 2 Cor. v. 21; Heb. iv. 15.

ᵈ Isa. liii. 7; Matt. xxvii. 39; John viii. 48, 49; Heb. xii. 3. ᵉ Luke xxiii. 46.——ᶠ Or, *committed* his cause.——ᵍ Isa. liii. 4, 5, 6, 11; Matt. viii. 17; Heb. ix. 28.——ʰ Or, *to*.——¹ Rom. vi. 2, 11; vii. 6.——ᵏ Isa. liii. 5.——¹ Isa. liii. 6; Ezek. xxxiv. 6. ᵐ Ezek. xxxiv. 23; xxxvii. 24; John x. 11, 14, 16; Heb. xiii. 20; chap. v. 4.

---

unreasonable, morose, and austere. Your time belongs to your master; obey him in every thing that is not sinful; if he employs you about unreasonable or foolish things, let him answer for it. He may waste your time, and thus play the fool with his own property; you can only fill up your time: let him assign the work; it is your duty to obey.

Verse 19. *For this is thankworthy*] If, in a conscientious discharge of your duty, you suffer evil, this is in the sight of God thankworthy, pleasing, and proper; it shows that you prefer his authority to your own ease, peace, and emolument; it shows also, as Dr. Macknight has well observed, that they considered their obligation to relative duties not to depend on the character of the person to whom they were to be performed, nor on their performing the duties they owed to their servants, but on the unalterable relations of things established by God.

Verse 20. *For what glory is it*] It appears from this that the poor Christians, and especially those who had been converted to Christianity while in a state of slavery, were often grievously abused; they were *buffeted* because they were Christians, and because they would not join with their masters in idolatrous worship.

Verse 21. *Hereunto were ye called*] Ye were called to a state of suffering when ye were called to be Christians; for the world cannot endure the yoke of Christ, and they that will live godly in Christ must suffer persecution; they will meet with it in one form or other.

Christ also suffered for us] And left us the example of his meekness and gentleness; for when he was reviled, he reviled not again. Ye cannot expect to fare better than your master; imitate his example, and his Spirit shall comfort and sustain you. Many MSS. and most of the versions, instead of *Christ also suffered for us, leaving us,* &c., read, *suffered for you, leaving you,* &c. This reading, which I think is genuine, is noticed in the *margin*.

Verse 22. *Who did no sin*] He suffered, but not on account of any evil he had either *done or said*.

In *deed* and *word* he was immaculate, and yet he was exposed to suffering; expect the same, and when it comes bear it in the same spirit. It is very likely that the apostle mentions *guile*, because those who do wrong generally strive to screen themselves by prevarication and lies. These words appear to be a quotation from Isa. liii. 9.

Verse 23. *But committed* himself] Though he could have inflicted any kind of punishment on his persecutors, yet to give *us*, in this respect also, an example that we should follow his steps, *he committed his cause* to him who is the *righteous Judge*. To avoid evil tempers, and the uneasiness and danger of avenging ourselves, it is a great advantage in all such cases to be able to refer our cause to God, and to be assured that the Judge of all the earth will do right.

The *Vulgate*, one copy of the *Itala*, St. *Cyprian*, and *Fulgentius*, read, *Tradebat autem judicanti se injuste;* " He delivered himself to him who judged unrighteously;" meaning Pontius Pilate. Some critics approve of this reading, but it has not sufficient evidence to recommend it as genuine.

Verse 24. *Who his own self*] Not *another* in his place, as some anciently supposed, because they thought it impossible that the Christ should suffer.

Bare our sins in his own body] Bore the punishment due to our sins. In no other sense could Christ bear them. To say that they were so *imputed* to him as if they had been *his* own, and that the Father beheld him as *blackened with imputed sin*, is monstrous, if not blasphemous.

That we, being dead to sins] Ἵνα ταῖς ἁμαρτίαις ἀπογενομενοι· That we, being *freed from sin*—delivered out of its power, and from under its tyranny.

Should live unto righteousness] That *righteousness* should be our *master* now, as *sin* was before. He is speaking still to *servants* who were under an oppressive yoke, and were cruelly used by their masters, scourged, buffeted, and variously maltreated.

By whose stripes ye were healed.] The apostle refers here to Isa. liii. 4—6; and he still keeps the

2

case of these persecuted servants in view, and encourages them to suffer patiently by the example of Christ, who was *buffeted* and *scourged*, and who bore all this that the deep and inveterate *wounds,* inflicted on their souls by sin, *might be healed.*

Verse 25. *For ye were as sheep going astray*] Formerly ye were not in a better moral condition than your oppressors; ye were like *stray sheep*, in the wilderness of ignorance and sin, till Christ, the true and merciful Shepherd, called you back from your wanderings, by sending you the Gospel of his grace.

Bishop of your souls.] Unless we consider the word *bishop* as a corruption of the word επισκοπος, *episcopos*, and that this literally signifies an *overseer*, an *inspector*, or *one that has the oversight*, it can convey to us no meaning of the original. Jesus Christ is the *Overseer of souls;* he has them continually under

his eye; he knows their wants, wishes, dangers, &c., and provides for them. As their *shepherd*, he leads them to the best pastures, defends them from their enemies, and guides them by his eye. Jesus is the *good Shepherd that laid down his life for his sheep.* All human souls are inexpressibly dear to him, as they are the purchase of his blood. He is still supreme *Bishop* or *Overseer* in his Church. He alone is *Episcopus episcoporum,* "the Bishop of bishops;" a title which the Romish pontiffs have blasphemously usurped. But this is not the only attribute of Jesus on which they have laid sacrilegious hands. And besides this, with force and with cruelty have they ruled the *sheep:* but the Lord is breaking the staff of their pride, and delivering the nations from the bondage of their corruption. Lord, let thy kingdom come!

CHAPTER III.

The duty of wives to their husbands, how they are to be adorned, and be in subjection as Sarah was to Abraham, 1–6. The duty of husbands to their wives, 7. How to obtain happiness, and live a long and useful life, 8–11. God loves and succours them that do good; but his face is against the wicked, 12, 13. They should suffer persecution patiently, and be always ready to give a reason of the hope that is in them; and preserve a good conscience, though they suffered for righteousness, 14–17. Christ suffered for us, and was put to death in the flesh, but quickened by the Spirit, 18. How he preached to the old world while Noah was preparing the ark, 19, 20. The salvation of Noah and his family a type of baptism, 21 Christ is ascended to heaven, all creatures being subject to him, 22.

A. M. cir. 4064. A. D. cir. 60. An. Olymp. cir. CCIX. 4. A. U. C. cir. 813.		A. M. cir. 4064. A. D. cir. 60. An. Olymp. cir. CCIX. 4. A. U. C. cir. 813.

LIKEWISE, [a] ye wives, *be in* subjection to your own husbands; that if any obey not the word, [b] they also may without the word [c] be won by the conversation of the wives;

2 [d] While they behold your chaste conversation *coupled* with fear.

3 [e] Whose adorning let it not be that outward *adorning* of plaiting the hair,

---

[a] 1 Cor. xiv. 34; Eph. v. 22; Col. iii. 18; Tit. ii. 5.——[b] 1 Cor. vii. 16.

[c] Matt. xviii. 15; 1 Cor. ix, 19–22.——[d] Chap. ii. 12.——[e] 1 Tim ii. 9; Tit. ii. 3, &c.

NOTES ON CHAP. III.

Verse 1. *Ye wives, be in subjection*] Consider that your husband is, by God's appointment, the head and ruler of the house; do not, therefore, attempt to usurp his government; for even though he *obey not the word*—is not a *believer in the Christian doctrine*, his rule is not thereby impaired; for Christianity never alters civil relations: and your affectionate, obedient conduct will be the most likely means of convincing him of the truth of the doctrine which you have received.

Without the word] That your hóly conduct may be the means of begetting in them a reverence for Christianity, the preaching of which they will not hear. See the notes on 1 Cor. xiv. 34, and the other places referred to in the margin.

Verse 2. *Chaste conversation—with fear.*] While they see that ye join modesty, chastity, and the purest manners, to the fear of God. Or perhaps *fear,* φοβος, is taken, as in Eph. v. 33, for the *reverence* due to the husband.

Verse 3. *Whose adorning*] Κοσμος. See the note on Heb. ix. 1, where the word κοσμος, *world* or *ornament,* is defined; and also the note on Gen. ii. 1.

Plaiting the hair, and of wearing of gold] Plaiting the hair, and variously folding it about the head, was the most ancient and most simple mode of disposing of this chief ornament of the female head. It was practised anciently in every part of the east, and is so to the present day in India, in China, and also in Barbary. It was also prevalent among the Greeks and Romans, as ancient gems, busts, and statues, still remaining, sufficiently declare. We have a remarkable instance of the plaiting of the hair in a statue of Agrippina, wife of Germanicus, an exact representation of which may be seen in a work of *Andrè Lens,* entitled *Le Costume de Peuple de l' Antiquité*, pl. 33. Many plates in the same work show the different modes of dressing the hair which obtained among the Egyptians, Greeks, Romans, Persians, and other na tions. Thin *plates of gold* were often mixed with the hair, to make it appear more ornamental by the reflection of light and of the solar rays. Small golden *buckles* were also used in different parts; and among the Roman ladies, *pearls* and precious stones of different colours. *Pliny* assures us, *Hist. Nat.*, l. ix. c. 35 that these latter ornaments were not introduced among the Roman women till the time of Sylla, about 110

A. M. cir. 4064.
A. D. cir. 60.
An. Olymp.
cir. CCIX. 4.
A. U. C. cir.
813.

and of wearing of gold, or of putting on of apparel ;

4 But *let it be* ⁶ the hidden man of the heart, in that which is not corruptible, *even the ornament* of a

⁶ Psa. xlv. 13 ; Rom. ii. 29 ; vii. 22 ;

meek and quiet spirit, which is in the sight of God of great price.

5 For after this manner, in the old time the holy women also, who trusted in

A. M. cir. 4064
A. D. cir. 60.
An. Olymp.
cir. CCIX. 4.
A. U. C. cir.
813.

2 Cor. iv. 16.

years before the Christian era. But it is evident, from many remaining monuments, that in numerous cases the *hair* differently plaited and curled was the *only* ornament of the head. Often a simple *pin*, sometimes of *ivory*, pointed with gold, seemed to connect the plaits. In monuments of antiquity the *heads* of the *married* and *single* women may be known, the former by the hair being *parted* from the forehead over the middle of the top of the head, the latter by being quite close, or being plaited and curled all in a general mass.

There is a remarkable passage in Plutarch, *Conjugalia Præcept.*, c. xxvi., very like that in the text : Κοσμος γαρ εστιν, ὡς ελεγε Κρατης, το κοσμουν· κοσμει δε το κοσμιωτεραν γυναικα ποιουν· ποιει δε ταυτην ου χρυσος, ουτε σμαραγδος, ουτε κοκκος, αλλ' ὁσα σεμνοτητος, ευταξιας, αιδους εμφασιν περιτιθησιν. *Opera a Wyttenb.*, vol. i., page 390. "An *ornament*, as Crates said, is that which *adorns*. The proper ornament of a woman is that which becomes her best. This is neither gold, nor pearls, nor scarlet ; but those things which are an evident proof of gravity, regularity, and modesty." The wife of *Phocion*, a celebrated Athenian general, receiving a visit from a lady who was elegantly adorned with *gold* and *jewels*, and her *hair with pearls*, took occasion to call the attention of her guest to the elegance and costliness of her dress, remarking at the same time, "*My* ornament is my husband, now for the twentieth year general of the Athenians." *Plut.*, in *vit. Phoc.* How few Christian women act this part ! Women are in general at as much pains and cost in their dress, as if by it they were to be recommended both to God and man. It is, however, in every case, the argument either of a *shallow mind*, or of a *vain* and *corrupted heart*.

Verse 4. *The hidden man of the heart*] Ὁ κρυπτος της καρδιας ανθρωπος. This phrase is of the same import with that of St. Paul, Rom. vii. 22, ὁ εσω ανθρωπος, the *inner man* ; that is, the *soul*, with the whole system of affections and passions. Every part of the Scripture treats man as a compound being : the *body* is the *outward* or *visible man* ; the *soul*, the *inward*, *hidden*, or *invisible man*. The term ανθρωπος, man, is derived, according to the best etymologists, from ανα τρεπων ωπα, *turning the face upward*. This derivation of the word is beautifully paraphrased by *Ovid*. The whole passage is beautiful ; and, though well known, I shall insert it. After speaking of the creation and formation of all the irrational animals, he proceeds thus :—

" Sanctius his animal, mentisque capacius altæ
Deerat adhuc, et quod dominari in cætera posset.
Natus HOMO est : sive hunc divino semine fecit
Ille opifex rerum, mundi melioris origo ;
Sive recens tellus, seductaque nuper ab alto
Æthere, cognati retinebat semina cœli.—
Pronaque cum spectent animalia cætera terram,

Os homini sublime dedit ; cœlumque tueri
Jussit, et erectos ad sidera tollere vultus."

METAM, lib. i. ver. 76.

" A creature of a more exalted kind
Was wanting yet, and then was MAN design'd ;
Conscious of thought, of more capacious breast,
For empire form'd, and fit to rule the rest.
Whether with particles of heavenly fire
The God of nature did his soul inspire,
Or earth but new divided from the sky,
Which still retain'd th' ethereal energy.—
Thus, while the mute creation *downward* bend
Their sight, and to their earthly mother tend,
Man *looks aloft*, and with *erected eyes*
Beholds his own hereditary skies."   DRYDEN.

The word ανθρωπος, man, is frequently applied to the *soul*, but generally with some epithet. Thus ὁ εσω ανθρωπος, the *inner man*, Rom. vii. 22, to distinguish it from the *body*, which is called ὁ εξω ανθρωπος, *the outer man*, 2 Cor. iv. 16 ; ὁ κρυπτος ανθρωπος, *the hidden man*, as in the text ; ὁ καινος ανθρωπος, *the new man*, the soul renewed in righteousness, Eph. ii. 15, to distinguish him from ὁ παλαιος ανθρωπος, *the old man*, that is, man unregenerate or in a state of sin, Rom. vi. 6. And the *soul* is thus distinguished by the Greek philosophers.

A meek and quiet spirit] That is, a mind that will not give provocation to others, nor receive irritation by the provocation of others. *Meekness* will prevent the first ; *quietness* will guard against the last.

Great price.] All the ornaments placed on the head and body of the most illustrious female, are, in the sight of God, of no worth ; but a *meek and silent spirit* are, in his sight, invaluable, because proceeding from and leading to himself, being incorruptible, surviving the ruins of the *body* and the ruins of *time*, and enduring eternally.

Verse 5. *For after this manner*] Simplicity reigned in primitive times ; *natural ornaments* alone were then in use. Trade and commerce brought in luxuries ; and luxury brought *pride*, and all the *excessive nonsense* of DRESS. No female head ever looks so well as when adorned with its own hair alone. This is the ornament appointed by God. To cut it off or to cover it is an unnatural practice ; and to exchange the hair which God has given for hair of some other colour, is an insult to the Creator. How the *delicacy* of the female character can stoop to the use of *false hair*, and especially when it is considered that the chief part of this kind of hair was once the *natural* property of some ruffian soldier, who fell in battle by many a ghastly wound, is more than I can possibly comprehend. See the notes on 1 Cor. xi. 14—16 ; and 1 Tim. ii. 9.

Who trusted in God] The women *who trust* NOT

A. M. cir. 4064.
A. D. cir. 60.
An. Olymp.
cir. CCIX. 4.
A. U. C. cir.
813.

God, adorned themselves, being in subjection unto their own husbands:

6 Even as Sara obeyed Abraham, [g] calling him lord: whose [h] daughters ye are, as long as ye do well, and are not afraid with any amazement.

7 [i] Likewise, ye husbands, dwell with *them* according to knowledge, giving honour unto the wife, [k] as unto the weaker vessel, and as being

heirs together of the grace of life; [l] that your prayers be not hindered.

A. M. cir. 4064.
A. D. cir. 60.
An. Olymp.
cir. CCIX. 4.
A. U. C. cir.
813.

8 Finally, [m] *be ye* all of one mind, having compassion one of another; [n] love [o] as brethren, [p] *be* pitiful, *be* courteous:

9 [q] Not rendering evil for evil, or railing for railing: but contrariwise blessings; knowing that ye are thereunto called, [r] that ye should inherit a blessing.

---

[g] Gen. xviii. 12.——[h] Gr. *children.*——[i] 1 Cor. vii. 3 ; Eph. v. 25 ; Col. iii. 19.——[k] 1 Cor. xii. 23 ; 1 Thess. iv. 4.——[l] See Job xlii. 8 ; Matt. v. 23, 24 ; xviii. 19.——[m] Rom. xii. 16 ; xv. 5 ; Phil. iii. 16.

[n] Rom. xii. 10 ; Heb. xiii. 1 ; chap. ii. 17.——[o] Or, *loving to the brethren.*——[p] Col. iii. 12 ; Eph. iv. 32.——[q] Prov. xvii. 13 ; xx. 22 ; Matt. v. 39 ; Rom. xii. 14, 17 ; 1 Cor. iv. 12 ; 1 Thess. v. 15.——[r] Matt. xxv. 34.

---

in God are fond of *dress* and *frippery ;* those *who trust in God* follow *nature* and *common sense.*

Being in subjection unto their own husbands] It will rarely be found that women who are *fond of dress,* and extravagant in it, have any subjection to their husbands but what comes from *mere necessity.* Indeed, their dress, which they *intend* as an attractive to the eyes of *others,* is a sufficient proof that they have neither *love* nor *respect* for their own husbands. Let them who are concerned refute the charge.

Verse 6. *Even as Sara obeyed*] Almost the same words are in *Rab. Tanchum,* fol. 9, 3 : "The wife of Abraham reverenced him, and called him lord, as it is written, Gen. xviii. 12 : *And my lord is old.*" The words of the apostle imply that she acknowledged his superiority, and her own subjection to him, in the order of God.

Whose daughters ye are] As Abraham is represented the *father* of all his male *believing descendants,* so Sara is represented as the *mother* of all her believing female posterity. A *son of Abraham* is a true believer ; a *daughter of Sarah* is the same.

As long as ye do well] For you cannot maintain your relationship to her longer than ye *believe ;* and ye cannot *believe* longer than ye continue to *obey.*

And are not afraid with any amazement.] It is difficult to extract any sense out of this clause. The original is not very easy ; Μη φοβουμεναι μηδεμιαν πτοησιν may be rendered, *And not fearing with any terror.* If ye do well, and act conscientiously your part as *faithful wives,* ye will at no time live under the *distressing apprehension* of being *found out,* or terrified at every appearance of the discovery of *infidelities,* or improper conduct. Being not guilty of these, you will not have occasion to fear *detection.* On this subject a learned man has quoted these words, which I have produced elsewhere, Eph. vi. 14 :—

———————— *hic murus aheneus esto,*

Nil conscire sibi, *nulla* pallescere *culpa.*

" Let this be my brazen wall, to be *self-convicted* of no private delinquency, nor to *change colour* at being charged with a fault."

Happy is the *wife,* and happy is the *husband,* who can *conscientiously* adopt the saying.

Verse 7. *Dwell with* them *according to knowledge*] Give your wives, by no species of unkind carriage, any

excuse for delinquency. How can a man expect his wife to be faithful to him, if he be unfaithful to her ? and *vice versa.*

Giving honour unto the wife] Using your superior strength and experience in her behalf, and thus *honouring* her by becoming her protector and support. But the word τιμη, *honour,* signifies *maintenance* as well as *respect ;*—maintain, *provide for* the wife.

As—the weaker vessel] Being more delicately, and consequently more slenderly, constructed. *Roughness* and *strength* go hand in hand ; so likewise do *beauty* and *frailty.* The female has what the man wants—beauty and delicacy. The male has what the female wants—courage and strength. The one is as good in its place as the other : and by these things God has made an equality between the man and the woman, so that there is properly very little superiority on either side. See the note on 1 Thess. iv. 4.

Being heirs together] Both the man and woman being equally called to eternal glory : and as *prayer* is one great means of obtaining a meetness for it, it is necessary that they should live together in such a manner as to prevent all family contentions, that they may not be prevented, by disputes or misunderstandings, from uniting daily in this most important duty—family and social prayer.

Verse 8. Be ye *all of one mind*] Unity, both in the family and in the Church, being essentially necessary to *peace* and *salvation.* See on Rom. xii. 16, and xv. 5.

Having compassion] Συμπαθεις· Being *sympathetic ;* feeling for each other ; bearing each other's burdens.

Love as brethren] Φιλαδελφοι· *Be lovers of the brethren.*

Pitiful] Ευσπλαγχνοι· *Tender-hearted ;* let your *bowels yearn* over the distressed and afflicted.

Courteous] Φιλοφρονες· Be *friendly-minded ;* acquire and cultivate a friendly disposition. But instead of this word, ταπεινοφρονες, be *humble-minded,* is the reading of ABC, more than twenty others, with the *Syriac, Arabic* of Erpen, *Coptic, Armenian, Slavonic,* and some of the *fathers.* This is probably the true reading, and *Griesbach* has admitted it into the text.

Verse 9. *Not rendering evil for evil*] Purposing, saying, doing nothing but *good ;* and invariably returning good for evil.

Ye are thereunto called] This is your *calling—*

A. M. cir. 4064.
A. D. cir. 60.
An. Olymp.
cir. CCIX. 4.
A. U. C. cir.
813.

10 For ^s he that will love life, and see good days, ^t let him refrain his tongue from evil, and his lips that they speak no guile :

11 Let him ^u eschew evil, and do good ; ^v let him seek peace, and ensue it.

12 For the eyes of the Lord *are* over the righteous, ^w and his ears *are open* unto their

prayers : but the face of the Lord *is* ^x against them that do evil.

A. M. cir. 4064.
A. D. cir. 60.
An. Olymp.
cir. CCIX. 4.
A. U. C. cir.
813.

13 ^y And who *is* he that will harm you, if ye be followers of that which is good ?

14 ^z But and if ye suffer for righteousness' sake, happy *are ye :* and ^a be not afraid of their terror, neither be troubled ;

15 But sanctify the Lord God in your hearts :

---

^s Psa. xxxiv. 12, &c.——^t James i. 26; chap. ii. 1, 22; Rev. xiv. 5.——^u Psa. xxxvii. 27 : Isa. i. 16, 17 ; 3 John 11.——^v Rom. xii. 18; xiv. 19 ; Heb. xii. 14.

^w John ix. 31 : James v. 16.——^x Gr. *upon.*——^y Prov. xvi. 7 ; Tobit xii. 7 ; Rom. viii. 28.——^z Matt. v, 10, 11, 12 ; chap. ii. 19 ; iv. 14 ; James i. 12.——^a Isa. viii. 12, 13 ; Jer. i. 8 ; John xiv. 1, 27.

---

your *business in life,* to do good, and to do good for evil, and to implore God's *blessing* even on your worst enemies. And this is not only your *duty,* but your *interest ;* for in so doing you shall obtain God's blessing, even life for evermore.

Verse 10. *For he that will love life*] This is a quotation from Psa. xxxiv. 12–16, as it stands in the Septuagint ; only the aorist of the imperative is changed from the second into the third person, &c. He who wishes to live long and prosperously, must act as he is here directed. 1. He must refrain from *evilspeaking, lying,* and *slandering.* 2. He must avoid *flattery* and fair speeches, which cover *hypocritical* or wicked *intentions.* 3. He must *avoid evil,* keep *going away* εκκλινατω, from evil. 4. He must *do good* ; he must walk in the way of righteousness. 5. He must live *peaceably* with all men ; *seek peace* where it has been lost ; *restore* it where it has been broken, and *pursue it* where it seems to be flying away. He who lives thus must live happy in himself. And as *excess* in *action* and *passion* always tends to the shortening of life, and nothing preys on the constitution more than disorderly passions, he must live not only happiest but longest who avoids them. It is an edifying story that is told in the book *Mussar,* chap. i., quoted by Rosenmüller " A certain person, travelling through the city, continued to call out, *Who wants the elixir of life ?* The daughter of Rabbi Joda heard him, and told her father He said, Call the man in. When he came in, the rabbi said, What is that elixir of life thou sellest ? He answered, Is it not written, *What man is he that loveth life, and desireth to see good days, let him refrain his tongue from evil, and his lips from speaking* guile ? This is the elixir of life, and is found in the mouth of man."

Verse 12. *The eyes of the Lord* are *over the righteous*] That is, He is continually under God's notice and his care ; God continually watches *for* him and watches *over* him, and he is *under* his constant protection.

And his ears are open *unto their prayers*] The original is very emphatic *The eyes of the Lord* are *upon the righteous, and his ears to their prayers.* The righteous man ever attracts the Divine notice, and wherever he is, there is the ear of God ; for, as every righteous man is a *man of prayer,* wherever he prays, there is the ear of God, into which the prayer, as soon **as** formed, enters.

But the face of the Lord] Far from his eye being

upon *them,* or his ear open to their requests, (for *prayer* they have none,) his *face,* his *approbation,* his *providence* and *blessing,* are turned away from them ; and he only looks upon them to abhor them, and to turn the arm of his justice against them.

Verse 13. *Who* is *he that will harm you*] Is it possible that a man can be wretched who has God for his friend ? " All the devices which the devil or wicked men work against such must be brought to naught, and by the providence of his goodness be dispersed."

If ye be followers, &c.] Εαν Του Αγαθου μιμηται γενησθε· *If ye be imitators of the good One, i. e. of* God. 'Ο Αγαθος, *the good One,* is one of God's prime epithets, see Matt. xix. 17, and Satan is distinguished by the reverse, ὁ πονηρος, the EVIL one, Matt. xxiii. 19, where see the notes. Instead of μιμηται, *followers,* or rather *imitators,* ζηλωται, *zealous* of what is good, is the reading of ABC, fifteen others, both the *Syriac,* Erpen's *Arabic,* the *Coptic, Æthiopic, Armenian* and *Vulgate,* with some of the *fathers.* This is a very probable reading, and *Griesbach* has placed it in the *margin* as a candidate for the place of that in the text.

Verse 14. *But and if ye suffer*] God may permit you to be tried and persecuted for righteousness' sake, but this cannot *essentially harm you ;* he will press even this into your service, and make it work for your good.

Happy are ye] This seems to refer to Matt. v. 10, &c. *Blessed* or *happy, are ye when men persecute you,* &c. It is a happiness to suffer for Christ ; and it is a happiness, because if a man were not *holy* and *righteous* the world would not persecute him . so he is happy in the very *cause* of his sufferings.

Be not afraid of their terror] Τον δε φοβον αυτων μη φοβηθητε· *Fear not their fear ;* see Isa. viii. 12. Sometimes *fear* is put for the *object of a man's religious worship ;* see Gen. xxxi. 42 ; Prov. i. 26, and the place in *Isaiah* just quoted. The exhortation may mean, *Fear not their gods,* they can do you no hurt ; and supposing that they curse you by them, yet *be not troubled ;* " He who fears God need have no other fear."

Verse 15. *But sanctify the Lord God in your hearts*] To sanctify God may signify to offer him the *praises* due to his grace, but as to *sanctify* literally signifies to *make holy,* it is impossible that God should be thus sanctified. We have often already seen that αγιαζω signifies to *separate from earth,* that is, from any *common* use or purpose, that the *thing* or *person* thus *sepa*

A. M. cir. 4064.
A. D. cir. 60.
An. Olymp.
cir. CCIX. 4.
A. U. C. cir.
813.

and [b] *be* ready always to *give* an answer to every man that asketh you a reason of the hope that is in you with meekness and [c] fear:

16 [d] Having a good conscience ; [e] that, whereas they speak evil of you, as of evil-doers, they may be ashamed that

A. M. cir. 4064.
A. D. cir. 60.
An. Olymp.
cir. CCIX. 4.
A. U. C. cir.
813.

---

[b] Psa. cxix. 46; Acts iv. 8; Col. iv. 6; 2 Tim. ii. 25.

[c] Or, *reverence.*——[d] Heb. xiii. 18.——[e] Tit. ii. 8; chap. ii. 12.

---

rated may be *devoted to a sacred use.* Perhaps we should understand Peter's words thus : Entertain just notions of God; of his nature, power, will, justice, goodness, and truth. Do not conceive of him as being actuated by such *passions* as *men ; separate him in your hearts* from every thing *earthly, human, fickle, rigidly severe,* or *capriciously merciful.* Consider that he can neither be like man, feel like man, nor act like man. Ascribe no *human passions* to him, for this would *desecrate* not *sanctify* him. Do not *confine* him in your conceptions to place, space, vacuity, heaven, or earth ; endeavour to think worthily of the *immensity* and *eternity* of his nature, of his *omniscience, omnipresence,* and *omnipotence.* Avoid the error of the heathens, who bound even their *Dii Majores,* their *greatest gods,* by *fate,* as many well-meaning Christians do the true God by *decrees ;* conceive of him as infinitely *free to act* or *not act,* as he pleases. Consider the *goodness* of his nature ; for *goodness,* in every possible state of perfection and infinitude, belongs to him. Ascribe no *malevolence* to him ; nor any work, purpose, or decree, that implies it : this is not only a human passion, but a passion of *fallen* man. Do not suppose that he can do evil, or that he can *destroy* when he might *save ;* that he ever did, or ever can, *hate* any of those whom he made in his own image and in his own likeness, so as by a positive decree to doom them, unborn, to everlasting perdition, or, what is of the same import, *pass them by* without affording them the means of salvation, and consequently rendering it impossible for them to be saved. Thus endeavour to conceive of him ; and, by so doing, you *separate him* from all that is *imperfect, human, evil, capricious, changeable,* and *unkind.* Ever remember that he has wisdom without error, power, without limits, truth without falsity, love without hatred, holiness without evil, and justice without rigour or severity on the one hand, or capricious tenderness on the other. In a word, that he neither can *be, say, purpose,* or *do,* any thing that is not infinitely just, holy, wise, true, and gracious ; that he hates nothing that he has made ; and has so loved the world, the whole human race, as to give his only-begotten Son to die for them, that they might not perish, but have everlasting life. Thus *sanctify the Lord God in your hearts,* and you will ever be *ready to give a reason of the hope that is in you* to every serious and candid inquirer after truth. Most religious systems and creeds are incapable of rational explanation, because founded on some misconception of the Divine nature.

 " They set at odds heaven's jarring attributes,
 And with one excellence another wound."

The system of *humanizing* God, and making him, by our unjust conceptions of him, to act as *ourselves* would in certain circumstances, has been the bane of both religion and piety ; and on this ground infidels

have laughed us to scorn. It is high time that we should no longer *know God after the flesh ;* for even if we have known Jesus Christ after the flesh, we are to know him so no more.

What I have written above is not against any particular creed of religious people, it is against any or all to whom it may justly apply, it may even be against some portions of *my own ;* for even in this respect I am obliged daily to labour to sanctify the Lord God in my heart, to *abstract* him from every thing *earthly* and *human,* and apprehend him as far as possible in his own essential nature and attributes through the light of his Spirit and the medium of his own *revelation.* To act thus requires no common effort of soul : and just apprehensions of this kind are not acquired without much prayer, much self-reflection, much time, and much of the grace and mercy of God.

Instead of τον Θεον, God, ABC, four others, both the *Syriac,* Erpen's *Arabic,* the *Coptic, Vulgate,* and *Armenian,* with *Clement* and *Fulgentius,* read τον Χριστον, Christ. *Sanctify Christ in your hearts.* This reading is at least equal to the other in the authorities by which it is supported ; but *which* was written by St. Peter we know not.

A reason of the hope] An *account* of your *hope of the resurrection of the dead* and eternal life in God's glory. This was the great object of their *hope,* as Christ was the grand *object* of their *faith.*

The word απολογια, which we translate *answer,* signifies a *defence ;* from this we have our word *apology,* which did not originally signify an *excuse* for an act, but a *defence of that act.* The *defences of Christianity* by the primitive fathers are called *apologies.* See the note on Acts xxi. 1.

With meekness and fear] Several excellent MSS. add the word αλλα, *but,* here, and it improves the sense considerably : *Be ready always to give an answer to every man that asketh you a reason of the hope that is in you,* BUT *with meekness and fear.* Do not permit your *readiness to answer,* nor the *confidence* you have in the goodness of your cause, to lead you to answer *pertly* or *superciliously* to any person ; defend the truth with all possible *gentleness* and *fear,* lest while you are doing it you should forget his presence whose cause you support, or say any thing unbecoming the dignity and holiness of the religion which you have espoused, or inconsistent with that heavenly temper which the Spirit of your indwelling Lord must infallibly produce.

Verse 16. *Having a good conscience*] The testimony of God in your own soul, that in simplicity and godly sincerity you have your conversation in the world. See on the term *conscience* at the end of Hebrews.

Whereas they speak evil of you] See the same sentiment in chap. ii. 11, and the note there.

2

A. M. cir. 4064.
A. D. cir. 60.
An. Olymp.
cir. CCIX. 4.
A. U. C. cir.
813.

falsely accuse your good conversation in Christ.

17 For *it is* better, if the will of God be so, that ye suffer for well-doing, than for evil-doing.

18 For Christ also hath [f] once suffered for

sins, the just for the unjust, that he might bring us to God, [g] being put to death [h] in the flesh, but [i] quickened by the Spirit:

19 By which also he went and [k] preached unto the spirits [l] in prison;

A. M. cir. 4064
A. D. cir. 60.
An. Olymp.
cir. CCIX. 4.
A. U. C. cir.
813.

---

[f] Rom. v. 6 ; Heb. ix. 26, 28 ; chapter ii. 21 ; iv. 1.——[g] 2 Cor. xiii. 4.——[h] Col. i. 21, 22.

[i] Rom. i. 4 ; viii. 11.——[k] Chapter i. 12 ; iv. 6.——[l] Isa. xlii. 7 ; xlix. 9 ; lxi. 1.

Verse 17. *For it is better*] See on chap. ii. 19, 20.

Verse 18. *Christ also hath once suffered*] See the notes on Rom. v. 6 ; Heb. ix. 28.

Put to death in the flesh] In his human nature.

But quickened by the Spirit] That very dead body revived by the power of his Divinity. There are various opinions on the meaning of this verse, with which I need not trouble the reader, as I have produced that which is most likely.

Verse 19. *By which*] Spirit, his own Divine energy and authority.

He went and preached] By the ministry of Noah, one hundred and twenty years.

Unto the spirits in prison] The inhabitants of the antediluvian world, who, having been *disobedient*, and convicted of the most flagrant transgressions against God, were sentenced by his just law to destruction. But their punishment was delayed to see if they would *repent* ; and *the long-suffering of God waited* one hundred and twenty years, which were granted to them for this purpose ; during which time, as criminals tried and convicted, they are represented as being *in prison* ——detained under the arrest of Divine justice, which *waited* either for their *repentance* or the expiration of the *respite*, that the punishment pronounced might be inflicted. This I have long believed to be the sense of this difficult passage, and no other that I have seen is so consistent with the whole scope of the place. That the *Spirit of God* did *strive* with, convict, and reprove the antediluvians, is evident from Gen. vi. 3 : *My Spirit shall not always strive with man, forasmuch as he is flesh ; yet his days shall be one hundred and twenty years.* And it was by this Spirit that Noah became a *preacher of righteousness,* and *condemned that* ungodly *world,* Heb. xi. 7, who would not believe till wrath——Divine punishment, came upon them to the uttermost. The word πνευμασι, *spirits*, is supposed to render this view of the subject improbable, because this must mean *disembodied* spirits ; but this certainly does not follow, for the *spirits of just men made perfect,* Heb. xii. 23, certainly means *righteous men,* and men *still in the Church militant ;* and the *Father of spirits,* Heb xii. 9, means *men still in the body ;* and *the God of the spirits of all flesh,* Num. xvi. 22, and xxvii. 16, means *men not in a disembodied state.*

But even on this word there are several various readings ; some of the Greek MSS. read πνευματι, *in spirit*, and one Πνευματι Ἁγιῳ, in the *Holy Spirit.* I have before me one of the first, if not the very *first edition* of the *Latin Bible ;* and in it the verse stands thus : *In quo et hiis, qui in carcere erant,* SPIRITUALITER *veniens prædicavit ;* "by which he came *spiritually,* and preached to them that were in prison."

In two very ancient MSS. of the Vulgate before me, the clause is thus : *In quo et his qui in carcere erant* SPIRITU *venient prædicavit ;* "in which, coming *by the Spirit,* he preached to those who were in prison." This is the reading also in the *Complutensian Polyglot.*

Another ancient MS. in my possession has the words nearly as in the printed copy : *In quo et hiis qui in carcere* CONCLUSI *erant* SPIRITUALITER *veniens prædicavit ;* "in which, coming *spiritually,* he preached to those who were SHUT UP in prison."

Another MS., written about A. D. 1370, is the same as the printed copy.

The common *printed Vulgate* is different from all these, and from all the MSS. of the Vulgate which I have seen, in reading *spiritibus,* "to the spirits."

In my old MS. Bible, which contains the first translation into English ever made, the clause is the following : Ӡn whiche thing and to hem that weren closed togyder in prison, hi commynge in Spirit, prechhe. The copy from which this translation was taken evidently read *conclusi erant,* with one of the MSS. quoted above, as closed togyder proves.

I have quoted all these authorities from the most authentic and correct copies of the Vulgate, to show that from them there is no ground to believe that the text speaks of Christ's going to hell to preach the Gospel to the damned, or of his going to some feigned place where the souls of the patriarchs were detained, to whom he preached, and whom he delivered from that place and took with him to paradise, which the Romish Church holds as an article of faith.

Though the judicious *Calmet* holds with his Church this opinion, yet he cannot consider the text of St. Peter as a proof of it. I will set down his own words : *Le sentiment qui veut que Jesus Christ soit descendu aux enfers, pour annoncer sa venue aux anciens patriarches, et pour les tirer de cette espece de prison, ou ils l'attendoient si long tems, est indubitable ; et nous le regardons comme un article de notre foi : mais on peut douter que ce soit le sens de Saint Pierre en cet endroit.* "The opinion which states that Jesus Christ descended into hell, to announce his coming to the ancient patriarchs, and to deliver them from that species of prison, where they had so long waited for him, is incontrovertible ; and we (the Catholics) consider it as an article of our faith : but we may doubt whether this be the meaning of St. Peter in this place."

Some think the whole passage applies to the preaching of the Gospel to the *Gentiles ;* but the interpretation given above appears to me, after the fullest consideration, to be the most consistent and rational, as I have already remarked.

2

A. M. cir. 4064.
A. D. cir. 60.
An. Olymp.
cir. CCIX. 4.
A. U. C. cir
813.

20 Which sometime were disobedient, [m] when once the long-suffering of God waited in the days of Noah, while [n] the ark was a preparing, [o] wherein few, that is, eight souls, were saved by water.

21 [p] The like figure whereunto *even* baptism doth also now save us (not the putting away

of [q] the filth of the flesh, but [r] the answer of a good conscience toward God,) [s] by the resurrection of Jesus Christ :

A. M. cir. 4064
A. D. cir. 60.
An. Olymp.
cir. CCIX. 4
A. U. C. cir.
813.

22 Who is gone into heaven, and [t] is on the right hand of God ; [u] angels and authorities and powers being made subject unto him.

---

[m] Gen. vi. 3, 5, 13.——[n] Heb. xi. 7.——[o] Gen. vii. 7; viii. 18;
2 Pet. ii. 5.——[p] Eph. v. 26.——[q] Tit. iii. 5.——[r] Rom. x. 10.

[s] Chap. i. 3.——[t] Psa. cx. 1 ; Rom. viii. 34 ; Eph. i. 20 ; Col. iii.
1 ; Heb. i. 3.——[u] Rom. viii. 38 ; 1 Cor. xv. 24 ; Eph. i. 21.

Verse 20. *When once the long-suffering of God waited*] In *Pirkey Aboth*, cap. v. 2, we have these words : " There were ten generations from Adam to Noah, that the *long-suffering* of God might appear ; for each of these generations provoked him to anger, and went on in their iniquity, till at last the deluge came."

Were saved by water.] While the ark was preparing, only Noah's family believed ; these amounted to *eight persons ;* and these only were saved from the deluge δι' ὕδατος, *on the water :* all the rest perished *in the water ;* though many of them, while the rains descended, and the waters daily increased, did undoubtedly humble themselves before God, call for mercy, and receive it ; but as they had not repented at the preaching of Noah, and the ark was now closed, and the fountains of the great deep broken up, they lost their lives, though God might have extended mercy to their souls.

Verse 21. *The like figure whereunto, &c.*] Dr. Macknight has translated this verse so as to make the meaning more clear : *By which* (water) *the antitype baptism* (*not the putting away of the filth of the flesh, but the answer of a good conscience towards God*) *now saveth us also, through the resurrection of Jesus Christ.*

He remarks that the relative ᾧ being in the neuter gender, its antecedent cannot be κιβωτος, *the ark,* which is feminine, but ὕδωρ, *water,* which is neuter.

There are many difficulties in this verse ; but the simple meaning of the place may be easily apprehended. Noah believed in God, walked uprightly before him, and found grace in his sight ; he obeyed him in building the ark, and God made it the means of his salvation from the waters of the deluge. *Baptism* implies a consecration and dedication of the soul and body to God, the Father, Son, and Holy Spirit. He who is faithful to his baptismal covenant, taking God through Christ, by the eternal Spirit, for his portion, is saved here from his sins ; and *through the resurrection of Christ from the dead,* has the well-grounded hope of eternal glory. This is all plain ; but was it the *deluge,* itself, or the *ark,* or the *being saved* by that ark from the deluge, that was the *antitype* of which St. Peter speaks ? Noah and his family were *saved by water ; i. e.* it was the instrument of their being saved through the good providence of God. So the water of *baptism,* typifying the regenerating influence of the Holy Spirit, is the means of salvation to all those who receive this Holy Spirit in its quickening, cleansing efficacy. Now as the waters of the flood could not have saved Noah and his family, had they not made use of the ark ; so the water of baptism

saves no man, but as it is the means of his getting his heart purified by the Holy Spirit, and typifying to him that purification. The ark was not *immersed* in the water ; had it been so they must all have perished ; but it was *borne up on the water,* and *sprinkled* with the *rain* that fell from heaven. This text, as far as I can see, says nothing in behalf of *immersion* in baptism ; but is rather, from the circumstance mentioned above, in favour of *sprinkling.* In either case, it is not the sprinkling, washing, or cleansing the body, that can be of any avail to the salvation of the soul, *but the answer of a good conscience towards God—* the internal evidence and external proof that the soul is purified in the laver of regeneration, and the person enabled to walk in newness of life. We are therefore strongly cautioned here, not to rest in the *letter,* but to look for the *substance.*

Verse 22. *Who is gone into heaven*] Having given the fullest proof of his resurrection from the dead, and of his having accomplished the end for which he came into the world.

On the right hand of God] In the place of the highest dignity, honour, and influence.

The Vulgate, one copy of the Itala, Augustine, Fulgentius, Cassiodorus, and Bede, have the following remarkable addition after the above words : *Deglutiens mortem, ut vitæ æternæ hæredes efficeremur.* " Having abolished (swallowed down) death, that we might be made heirs of eternal life." But this addition is found in no Greek copy, nor in any other of the ancient versions.

Angels and authorities and powers] That is, all creatures and beings, both in the heavens and in the earth, are put under subjection to Jesus Christ. He has all power in the heavens and in the earth. He alone can save ; and he alone can destroy. None need fear who put their trust in him, as he can do whatsoever he will in behalf of his followers, and has good and evil spirits under his absolute command. Well may his enemies tremble, while his friends exult and sing. He can raise the dead, and save to the uttermost all that come unto the Father through him.

If he have all power, if angels and authorities and powers be subject to him, then he can do *what* he will, and employ *whom* he will. To raise the dead can be no difficulty to him, because he has power over all things. He created the world ; he can destroy it, and he can create it anew. We can conceive nothing too difficult for Omnipotence. This same omnipotent Being is the friend of man. Why then do we not come to him with confidence, and expect the utmost salvation of which our souls and bodies are capable ?

    2

CHAPTER IV.

We should suffer patiently, after the example of Christ, 1.   *And no longer live according to our former custom, but disregard the scoffs of those who are incensed against us because we have forsaken their evil ways, who are shortly to give account to God for their conduct,* 2–5.   *How the Gospel was preached to Jews and Gentiles,* 6.   *As the end of all things was at hand, they should be sober, watchful, charitable, benevolent, good stewards of the bounty of Providence; and, when called to instruct others, speak as the oracles of God,* 7–11.   *Of the persecutions and trials which were coming upon them, and how they were to suffer so as not to disgrace their Christian character,* 12–16.   *Judgment was about to begin at the house of God, and even the righteous would escape with difficulty from the calamities coming upon the Jews; but they must continue in well-doing, and thus commit the keeping of their souls to their faithful Creator,* 17–19.

A. M. cir. 4064.
A. D. cir. 60.
An. Olymp.
cir. CCIX. 4.
A. U. C. cir.
813.

FORASMUCH then [a] as Christ hath suffered for us in the flesh, arm yourselves likewise with the same mind: for [b] he that hath suffered in the flesh hath ceased from sin;

2 [c] That he no longer [d] should live the rest of *his* time in the flesh to the lusts of men, [e] but to the will of God.

3 [f] For the time past of *our* life may suffice

us [g] to have wrought the will of the Gentiles, when we walked in lasciviousness, lusts, excess of wine, revellings, banquetings, and abominable idolatries:

4 Wherein they think it strange that ye run not with *them* to the same excess of riot, [h] speaking evil of *you:*

5 Who shall give account to him that is ready [i] to judge the quick and the dead.

A. M. cir. 4064.
A. D. cir. 60.
An. Olymp.
cir. CCIX. 4.
A. U. C. cir.
813.

[a] Chap. iii. 18.——[b] Romans vi. 2, 7; Gal. v. 24; Col. iii. 3, 5. [c] Rom. xiv. 7; chap. ii. 1.——[d] Gal. ii. 20; chap. i. 14.——[e] John 1. 13; Rom. vi. 11; 2 Cor. v. 15; James i. 18.——[f] Ezek. xliv. 6; xlv. 9; Acts xvii. 30. [g] Eph. ii. 2; iv. 17; 1 Thess. iv. 5; Tit. iii. 3; chap. i. 14. [h] Acts xiii. 45; xviii. 6; chap. iii. 16.——[i] Acts x. 42; xvii. 31; Romans xiv. 10, 12; 1 Cor. xv. 51, 52; 2 Tim. iv. 1; James v. 9.

NOTES ON CHAP. IV.

Verse 1. *As Christ hath suffered*] He is your proper pattern; have the same disposition he had; the same forgiving spirit, with meekness, gentleness, and complete self-possession.

He that hath suffered in the flesh, hath ceased from sin] This is a general maxim, if understood literally: The man who suffers generally reflects on his ways, is humbled, fears approaching death, loathes himself because of his past iniquities, and ceases from them; for, in a state of suffering, the mind loses its relish for the sins of the flesh, because they are embittered to him through the apprehension which he has of death and judgment; and, on his application to God's mercy, he is delivered from his sin.

Some suppose the words are to be understood thus: " Those who have *firmly resolved*, if called to it, to *suffer death* rather than *apostatize* from Christianity, have consequently *ceased from*, or are *delivered* from, the sin of *saving* their *lives* at the expense of their faith." Others think that it is a parallel passage to Rom. vi. 7, and interpret it thus: " He that hath mortified the flesh, hath ceased from sin." Dr. Bentley applies the whole to our redemption by Christ: *He that hath suffered in the flesh hath died for our sins.* But this seems a very constrained sense.

Verse 2. *That he no longer should live—in the flesh*] Governed by the base principle of giving up his faith to save his life; *to the lusts of men*—according to the will of his idolatrous persecutors; *but to the will of God*; which will of God is, that he should retain the truth, and live according to its dictates, though he should suffer for it.

Verse 3. *The time past of* our *life*] This is a complete epitome of the Gentile or heathen state, and a proof that those had been Gentiles to whom the apostle wrote.

1. They *walked in lasciviousness,* εν ασελγειαις· every species of lechery, lewdness, and impurity.

2. In *lusts,* επιθυμιαις· strong irregular appetites, and desires of all kinds.

3. In *excess of wine,* οινοφλυγιαις· from οινος, *wine,* and φλυω, *to be hot,* or *to boil ;* to be inflamed with wine; they were in continual debauches.

4. In *revellings,* κωμοις· lascivious feastings, with drunken songs, &c. See the note on Rom. xiii. 13.

5. In *banquetings,* ποτοις· *wine feasts, drinking matches,* &c.

6. In *abominable idolatries,* αθεμιτοις ειδωλολατρειαις· that is, the abominations practised at their idol feasts, where they not only worshipped the idol, but did it with the most impure, obscene, and abominable rites. This was the general state of the Gentile world; and with this monstrous wickedness Christianity had everywhere to struggle.

Verse 4. *They think it strange*] Ξενιζονται· They *wonder* and are *astonished* at you, that ye can renounce these gratifications of the flesh for a spiritual something, the good of which *they* cannot see.

Excess of riot] Ασωτιας αναχυσιν· *Flood of profligacy;* bearing down all rule, order, and restraints before it.

Speaking evil of you] Βλασφημουντες· Literally, *blaspheming;* i. e. speaking *impiously* against *God,* and *calumniously* of you.

Verse 5. *To judge the quick and the dead.*] They

2

A. M. cir. 4064.
A. D. cir. 60.
An. Olymp.
cir. CCIX. 4.
A. U. C. cir.
813.

6 For this cause ^k was the Gospel preached also to them that are dead, that they might be judged according to men in the flesh, but live according to God in the spirit.

7 But ^l the end of all things is at hand: ^m be ye therefore sober, and watch unto prayer.

8 ⁿ And above all things have fervent charity among your-selves : for ^o charity ^p shall cover the multitude of sins.

9 ^q Use hospitality one to another ^r without grudging.

10 ^s As every man hath received the gift,

A. M. cir. 4064.
A. D. cir. 60.
An. Olymp.
cir. CCIX. 4.
A. U. C. cir.
813.

k Chap. iii. 19.——l Matt. xxiv. 13, 14 ; Rom. xiii. 12 ; Phil. iv. 5 ; Heb. x. 25 ; James v. 8 ; 2 Pet. iii. 9, 11 ; 1 John ii. 18.——m Matt. xxvi. 41 ; Luke xxi. 34 ; Col. iv. 2 ; chap. i. 13 ; v. 8.——n Heb. xiii. 1 ; Col. iii. 14.——o Prov. x. 12 ; 1 Cor. xiii. 7 ; James v. 20. P Or, *will.*——q Rom. xii. 13 ; Heb. xiii. 2.——r 2 Cor. ix 7 ; Phil. ii. 14 ; Philem. 14.——s Rom. xii. 6 ; 1 Cor. iv. 7.

shall give account of these irregularities to Him who is prepared to judge both the Jews and the Gentiles. The *Gentiles*, previously to the preaching of the Gospel among them, were reckoned to be *dead in trespasses and sins*, Eph. ii. 1–5 ; under the sentence of *death, because* they had sinned. The Jews had at least, by their religious profession, a name to live ; and by that profession were bound to live to God.

Verse 6. *Was the Gospel preached also to them that are dead*] This is a most difficult verse ; the best translations I have seen of it are the following :—

"For this indeed was *the effect* of the preaching of the Gospel to *the* dead, (the unconverted Gentiles,) that *some* will be punished as carnal men ; but *others*, (those converted to Christianity,) lead a spiritual life unto God."—WAKEFIELD.

"For this purpose hath the Gospel been preached even to the dead, (i. e. the Gentiles,) that although they might be condemned, indeed, by men in the flesh, (their persecutors,) yet they might live eternally by God in the Spirit."—MACKNIGHT.

"For this cause was the Gospel preached to them that were dead ; that they who live according to men in the flesh, may be condemned ; but that they who live according to God in the Spirit, may live."—KNATCHBULL.

There are as many different translations of this verse, and comments upon it, as there are translators and commentators. That of Sir Norton Knatchbull, could the Greek text bear it, appears the most simple ; but that of Dr. Macknight, which is nearly the sense given by Mr. Wesley in his *Paraphrase*, is more likely to be the true one among those already proposed.

But if the apostle had the same fact in view which he mentions, chap. iii. 19, 20, then the *antediluvians* are the persons intended : *For this cause*—that Christ is *prepared to judge the quick and the dead*, and to dispense righteous judgment in consequence of having afforded them every necessary advantage, *was the Gospel preached* by Noah *to them also who are dead*—the antediluvian world, then dead in trespasses and sins, and condemned to death by the righteous judgment of God ; but in his great compassion he afforded them a respite, *that though they were condemned as men in the flesh*, (for this was their character ; *my Spirit will not always strive with man, forasmuch as he is* FLESH, Gen. vi. 3,) yet, hearing this Gospel by Noah, they may believe, *and live according to God in the Spirit*—live a blessed life in eternity according to the mercy of God, who sent his *Spirit* to strive with them. This appears to me to be the most consistent sense ; especially as the apostle seems to refer to what he had

said of the Spirit of Christ in Noah preaching to the spirits in prison—the rebellious that lived before the flood. See the notes on chap. iii. 19, 20.

Verse 7. *But the end of all things is at hand*] I think that here also St. Peter keeps the history of the deluge before his eyes, finding a parallel to the state of the Jews in his own time in that of the antediluvians in the days of Noah. In Gen. vi. 13, God said unto Noah, The end of all flesh is come before me. This was spoken at a time when God had decreed the destruction of the world by a flood. Peter says, *The end of all things is at hand* ; and this he spoke when God had determined to destroy the Jewish people and their polity by one of the most signal judgments that ever fell upon any nation or people.

In a very few years after St. Peter wrote this epistle, even taking it at the lowest computation, viz., A. D. 60 or 61, Jerusalem was destroyed by the Romans. To this destruction, which was literally *then at hand*, the apostle alludes when he says, *The end of all things is at hand* ; the end of the temple, the end of the Levitical priesthood, the end of the whole Jewish economy, was then at hand.

If these words could be taken in any general sense, then we might say to every present generation, *The end of all things is at hand* ; the end of all the *good* which the *wicked* enjoy, and the end of all the *evil* which the *righteous* suffer.

Be—sober, and watch unto prayer.] *Be sober*—make a prudent and moderate use of all you possess ; and *watch* against all occasions of sin ; and *pray* for the supporting hand of God to be upon you for good, that ye may escape the destruction that is coming upon the Jews, and that ye may be saved from among them when the scourge comes.

Verse 8. *Have fervent charity*] Αγαπην εκτενη· *Intense love* ; *for love shall cover a multitude of sins.* A loving disposition leads us to pass by the faults of others, to forgive offences against ourselves, and to excuse and lessen, as far as is consistent with truth, the transgressions of men. It does not mean that our love to others will induce God to pardon our offences. See the note on James v. 20.

Verse 9. *Use hospitality*] Be ever ready to divide your bread with the *hungry*, and to succour the *stranger*. See on Heb. xiii. 2.

Without grudging.] Ανευ γογγυσμων· *Without grumblings.* Do nothing merely because it is commanded, but do it from love to God and man ; then it will be *without grumbling.*

Verse 10. *Hath received the gift*] Χαρισμα· *A gift*; any blessing of *providence* or *grace*. I cannot think

A. M. cir. 4064.
A. D. cir. 60.
An. Olymp.
cir. CCIX. 4.
A. U. C. cir.
813.

even so minister the same one to another, [t] as good stewards of [u] the manifold grace of God.

11 [v] If any man speak, *let him speak* as the oracles of God ; [w] if any man minister, *let him do it* as of the ability which God giveth : that [x] God in all things may be glorified through Jesus Christ : [y] to whom be praise and dominion for ever and ever. Amen.

12 Beloved, think it not strange concerning [z] the fiery trial which is to try you, as though

some strange thing happened unto you :

A. M. cir. 4064.
A. D. cir. 60.
An. Olymp.
cir. CCIX. 4.
A. U. C. cir.
813.

13 [a] But rejoice, inasmuch as [b] ye are partakers of Christ's sufferings ; [c] that, when his glory shall be revealed, ye may be glad also with exceeding joy.

14 [d] If ye be reproached for the name of Christ, happy *are ye;* for the Spirit of glory and of God resteth upon you : [e] on their part he is evil spoken of, but on your part he is glorified.

---

[t] Matt. xxiv. 45 ; xxv. 14, 21 ; Luke xii. 42 ; 1 Cor. iv. 1, 2 ; Titus i. 7.——[u] 1 Cor. xii. 4 ; Eph. iv. 11.——[v] Jer. xxiii. 22. [w] Rom. xii. 6, 7, 8 ; 1 Cor. iii. 10.——[x] Eph. v. 20 ; chap. ii. 5. [y] 1 Tim. vi. 16 ; chapter v. 11 ; Rev. i. 6.——[z] 1 Cor. iii. 13 ;

chap. i. 7.——[a] Acts v. 41 ; James i. 2.——[b] Rom. viii. 17 ; 2 Cor. i. 7 ; iv. 10 ; Phil. iii. 10 ; Col. i. 24 ; 2 Tim. ii. 12 ; chap. v. 1, 10 ; Rev. i. 9.——[c] Chap. i. 5, 6.——[d] Matt. v. 11 ; 2 Cor. xii. 10 ; James i. 12 ; chap. ii. 19, 20 ; iii. 14.——[e] Chap. ii. 12 ; iii. 16.

---

that the word means here the *Holy Ghost,* or any of his supernatural gifts or influences ; it may include those, but it signifies any thing given by the mere mercy and bounty of God : but perhaps in this place it may signify some or any *office* in the Church : and this sense, indeed, the connection seems to require.

Stewards of the manifold grace] Whatever gifts or endowments any man may possess, they are, properly speaking, not his own ; they are the Lord's property, and to be employed in his work, and to promote his glory.

Verse 11. *If any man speak*] In order to explain or enforce God's word, and edify his neighbour, let him do it as those did to whom the *living oracles* were committed : they spoke as they were inspired by the Holy Ghost. Those, therefore, at Pontus, &c., who undertook to teach others, should speak by the same influence ; or, if not under this immediate influence, should speak *as* or *according to* the oracles already delivered, grounding all their exhortations and doctrines on some portion of that revelation already given. This command is sent to every man upon earth in *holy orders,* in *pretended holy orders,* or *pretending to holy orders.* Their teaching should be what the oracles of God, the Holy Scriptures, teach and authenticate.

Of the ability which God giveth] Perhaps the *ministering* here may refer to the *care of the poor,* and the *ability* is the *quantum of means* which God may have placed in their hands ; and they are to minister this as coming immediately *from God,* and lead the minds of the poor to consider *him* as their benefactor, *that he in all things may be glorified through Christ Jesus.* This is implied in the *essence* of any charitable act : the *actor* is not the *author,* God is the author ; and the poor man should be taught to consider *him* as his immediate *benefactor.* Those who give any thing *as from themselves,* rob God ; for to him the *praise* for all good, and the *dominion* over all men and things, belong *for ever and ever.*

Verse 12. *Think it not strange concerning the fiery trial*] Πυρωσει· *The burning.* The metaphor is old, but noble ; it represents the Christians at Pontus as having *fire* cast upon them for the *trying* of their faith, as *gold* is tried by fire, chap. i. 7, to which the apostle alludes.—*Macknight.*

St. Peter returns here to what he had often touched upon in this epistle, namely, to exhort the Christians to behave with patience and integrity under their present severe persecution ; to which purpose he uses the following arguments :—

First, He intimates that it was not a *strange* or *unusual* thing for the people of God to be persecuted.

Secondly, That if they suffered here as *Christ did,* they should hereafter be glorified with *him.*

Thirdly, Besides the prospect of that future glory, they had at present the *Spirit of God* for their support and comfort.

Fourthly, That it was an honour for any of them to suffer, not as a *malefactor,* but as a *Christian.*

Fifthly, Though the afflictions began with the Christians, yet the weight of the storm would fall upon the unbelievers. From these considerations he exhorted them to persevere in their duty, and trust all events with God. See *Dodd.*

Verse 14. *If ye be reproached for the name of Christ*] To be reproached for the *name of Christ* is to be reproached for being a *Christian,* that is, for being *like Christ.* This is the highest honour to which any man can arrive in this world, and therefore the apostle says to such, *Happy* are ye.

The Spirit of glory and of God resteth upon you] As this Divine Spirit *rested* upon Jesus, so does it rest upon his persecuted followers. There is a various reading here, και δυναμεως, *and of power,* which is found in some of the chief MSS., (the *Codex Alexandrinus,* and above twenty others,) the later *Syriac,* all the *Arabic,* Coptic, Æthiopic, Armenian, Vulgate, some copies of the *Itala,* Athanasius, Theophylact, Cyprian, and Cassiodorus ; and in them the whole verse reads thus : *If ye be reproached for the name of Christ, happy* are ye ; *for the Spirit of glory,* AND OF POWER, *and of God, resteth upon you.* This is agreeable to our Lord's words, Matt. v. 11, 12. So that what constituted them *unhappy* in the sight of the *world* was their *chief happiness* in the sight of *God;* they carried Christ the fountain of *blessedness* in their heart, and therefore could not be unhappy.

On their part he is evil spoken of] Κατα μεν αυτους βλασφημειται, κατα δε υμας δοξαζεται· *By them he is blasphemed, by you he is honoured.*

A. M. cir. 4064.
A. D. cir. 60.
An. Olymp.
cir. CCIX. 4.
A. U. C. cir.
813.

15 But f let none of you suffer as a murderer, or *as* a thief, or *as* an evil-doer, g or as a busybody in other men's matters.

16 Yet if *any man suffer* as a Christian, let him not be ashamed; h but let him glorify God on this behalf.

17 For the time *is* come i that judgment must begin at the house of God: and k if *it*

first *begin* at us, l what shall the end *be* of them that obey not the Gospel of God.

18 m And if the righteous scarcely be saved, where shall the ungodly and the sinner appear?

19 Wherefore, let them that suffer according to the will of God n commit the keeping of their souls *to him* in well-doing, as unto a faithful Creator.

A. M. cir. 4064
A. D. cir. 60.
An. Olymp.
cir. CCIX. 4.
A. U. C. cir.
813.

---

f Chap. ii. 20.——g 1 Thess. iv. 11; 1 Tim. v. 13.——h Acts v. 41.——i Isa. x. 12; Jer. xxv. 29; xlix. 12; Ezek. ix. 6; Mal.

iii. 5.——k Luke xxiii. 31.——l Luke x. 12, 14.——m Prov. xi. 31; Luke xxiii. 31.——n Psa. xxxi. 5; Luke xxiii. 46; 2 Tim. i. 12

Verse 15. *But let none of you suffer—as a busybody in other men's matters*] Αλλοτριοεπισκοπος· *The inspector of another;* meddling with other people's concerns, and forgetting their own; such persons are hated of all men. But some think that meddling with those in *public office* is here intended, as if he had said: Meddle not with the affairs of state, leave public offices and public officers to their own master, strive to live peaceably with all men, and show yourselves to be humble and unaspiring.

Verse 16. *Yet if—as a Christian*] If he be persecuted because he has embraced the *Christian* faith, let him not be *ashamed*, but let him rather glorify God on this very account. Christ suffered by the Jews because he was *holy*; Christians suffer because they resemble him.

The word Χριστιανος, *Christian*, is used only here and in Acts xi. 26; xxvi. 28. See the note on the former passage.

Verse 17. *Judgment must begin at the house of God*] Our Lord had predicted that, previously to the destruction of Jerusalem, his own followers would have to endure various calamities; see Matt. xxiv. 9. 21, 22; Mark xiii. 12, 13; John xvi. 2, &c. Here his true disciples are called *the house* or *family of God.* That the converted Jews suffered much from their own brethren, the *zealots,* or *factions* into which the Jews were at that time divided, needs little proof; and some interpreters think that this was in conformity to the purpose of God, (Matt. xxiii. 35: *That on you may come all the righteous blood shed from the foundation of the world,*) "that the Jewish Christians were to be involved in the general punishment; and that it was proper to begin at *them* as a part of the devoted Jewish nation, notwithstanding they were now become the house of God, because the justice of God would thereby be more illustriously displayed." See *Macknight.* But probably the word κριμα, which we here translate *judgment,* may mean no more than affliction and distress; for it was a Jewish maxim that, when God was about to pour down some general judgment, he began with afflicting his *own people* in order to correct and amend them, that they might be prepared for the overflowing scourge. In *Bava Kama,* fol. 60, 1, we have the same sentiment, and in nearly the same words, as in Peter, viz.: "God never punishes the world but because of the wicked, but he always begins with the righteous first. The destroyer makes no

difference between the just and the unjust, only he begins first with the righteous." See Ezek. ix. 1–7, where God orders the destroyer to slay both old and young in the city: *But,* said he, *begin at my sanctuary.*

And if it *first* begin *at us*] Jews, who have repented, and believed on the Son of God; *what shall the end* be *of them*—the Jews who continue impenitent, and *obey not the Gospel of God?* Here is the plainest reference to the above Jewish maxim; and this, it appears, was founded upon the text which St. Peter immediately quotes.

Verse 18. *And if the righteous scarcely be saved*] If it shall be with *extreme difficulty* that the *Christians* shall escape from Jerusalem, when the Roman armies shall come against it with the full commission to destroy it, *where shall the ungodly and the sinner appear?* Where shall the proud *Pharisaic boaster* in his own outside holiness, and the *profligate transgressor* of the laws of God, *show themselves,* as having escaped the Divine vengeance? The Christians, though with difficulty, did escape, every man; but not one of the Jews escaped, whether found in Jerusalem or elsewhere.

It is rather strange, but it is a fact, that this verse is the Septuagint translation of Prov. xi. 31: *Behold, the righteous shall be recompensed in the earth; much more the wicked and the sinner.* For this the Septuagint and *St. Peter* have, *If the righteous scarcely be saved, where shall the ungodly and the sinner appear?* Such a latitude of construction can scarcely be accounted for. The original is this: הן צדיק בארץ ישלם אף כי רשע וחוטא *hen tsaddik baarets yeshullam, aph ki rasha vechote:* "Behold, to the righteous it shall be returned on the earth; and also to the wicked and the transgressor."

The *Chaldee* paraphrast has given this a different turn: *Behold, the righteous shall be strengthened in the earth; but the ungodly and the sinners shall be consumed from the earth.*

The *Syriac* thus: *If the righteous scarcely live, the ungodly and the sinner where shall he stand?*

The *Arabic* is nearly the same as the *Septuagint* and the *apostle;* the *Vulgate* follows the Hebrew.

I have on several occasions shown that, when *Cestius Gallus* came against Jerusalem, many Christians were shut up in it; when he strangely raised the siege the Christians immediately departed to *Pella* in Cœlesyria, into the dominions of King Agrippa, who was an ally of the Romans, and there they were in safety;

and it appears, from the ecclesiastical historians, that they had but *barely time* to leave the city before the Romans returned under the command of Titus, and never left the place till they had destroyed the temple, razed the city to the ground, slain upwards of a million of those wretched people, and put an end to their civil polity and ecclesiastical state.

Verse 19. *Suffer according to the will of God*] A man suffers according to the will of God who suffers for righteousness' sake; and who, being reviled, reviles not again.

Commit the keeping of their souls] Place their *lives* confidently in his hand, who, being their *Creator*, will also be their preserver, and keep that safely which is committed to his trust. God is here represented as *faithful*, because he will always *fulfil his promises*, and withhold no good thing from them that walk uprightly.

But they had no reason to hope that he would care for their *lives* and *souls* unless they continued in *well-doing*. He who is employed in God's work will have God's protection. The path of duty ever was, and ever will be, the only way of safety.

1. THE apostle recommends *fervent charity*—unfeigned love both to God and man. It is well said of this grace that it is a universal virtue which ought to precede, accompany, and follow, all others. A charity which has God for its principle, and Jesus Christ for its pattern, never faileth. If our *charity* be extensive enough to *cover* all the defects of our neighbour in bearing with them; that of God is sufficient to cover all the sins of a sincere penitent by blotting them out. If we ought to be charitable to all, it is after the example of our heavenly Father, who is loving to every man, and hateth nothing that he has made.

2. The difficulty of escaping the corruption that is in the world is great; and, consequently, the danger of losing our souls. In this great work, watchfulness prayer, faith, and obedience, are indispensably necessary. He who does not walk with God here cannot see nor enjoy him hereafter.

CHAPTER V.

Directions to the elders to feed the flock of God, and not to be lords over God's heritage, that when the chief Shepherd does appear, they may receive a crown of glory, 1–4. The young are to submit themselves to the elder, and to humble themselves under the mighty hand of God, and cast all their care upon him, 5–7. They should be sober and watchful, because their adversary the devil is continually seeking their destruction, whom they are to resist, steadfast in the faith, 8, 9. They are informed that the God of all grace had called them to his eternal glory, 10, 11. Of Silvanus, by whom this epistle was sent, 12. Salutations from the Church at Babylon, 13. The apostolic benediction, 14.

A. M. cir. 4064.
A. D. cir. 60.
An. Olymp.
cir. CCIX. 4.
A. U. C. cir.
813.

THE elders which are among you I exhort, who am also [a] an elder, and [b] a witness of the sufferings of Christ, and also [c] a partaker of the glory that shall be revealed:

2 [d] Feed the flock of God [e] which is among you; taking the

A. M. cir. 4064.
A. D. cir. 60.
An. Olymp.
cir. CCIX. 4.
A. U. C. cir.
813.

---

[a] Philem. 9.——[b] Luke xxiv. 48; Acts i. 8, 22; v. 32; x. 39. [c] Rom. viii: 17; 18; Rev. i. 9.

[d] John xxi. 15, 16, 17; Acts xx. 28.——[e] Or, *as much as in you is.*

NOTES ON CHAP. V.

Verse 1. *The elders which are among you*] In this place the term πρεσβυτεροι, elders or *presbyters* is the name of an office. They were as *pastors* or *shepherds* of the flock of God, the Christian people among whom they lived. They were the same as *bishops, presidents, teachers* and *deacons*, Acts xiv. 23; 1 Tim. v. 17. And that these were the same as *bishops* the next verse proves.

Who am also an elder] Συμπρεσβυτερος· *A fellow elder*; one on a level with yourselves. Had he been what the popes of Rome say he was—*the prince of the apostles*; and *head of the Church*, and what *they* affect to be—mighty *secular* lords, binding the kings of the earth in chains, and their nobles in fetters of iron; could he have spoken of himself as he here does? It is true that the Roman pontiffs, in all their bulls, each style themselves *servus servorum Dei*, servant of the servants *of God*, while each affects to be *rex regum*, king of kings, and vicar of Jesus Christ. But the *popes* and the *Scriptures* never agree.

A witness of the sufferings of Christ] He was with Christ in the *garden*, he was with him when he was *apprehended*, and he was with him in the *high priest's hall*. Whether he followed him to the *cross* we know not; probably he did not, for in the hall of the high priest he had denied him most shamefully; and, having been deeply convinced of the greatness of his crime, it is likely he withdrew to some private place, to *humble himself* before God, and to implore mercy. He could, however, with the strictest propriety, say, from the above circumstances, that he was a *witness of the sufferings of Christ.*

A partaker of the glory] He had a *right* to it through the blood of the Lamb; he had a blessed *anticipation* of it by the power of the Holy Ghost; and he had the *promise* from his Lord and Master that he should be with him in heaven, to behold his glory; John xvii. 21, 24.

Verse 2. *Feed the flock*] Do not *fleece* the flock.

Taking the oversight] Επισκοπουντες· Discharging the office of *bishops* or *superintendents*. This is an-

2

A. M. cir. 4064.
A. D. cir. 60.
An. Olymp.
cir. CCIX. 4.
A. U. C. cir.
813.
oversight *thereof,* f not by constraint, but willingly; g not for filthy lucre, but of a ready mind;

3 Neither as h being i lords over k *God's* heritage, but l being ensamples to the flock.

---

f 1 Cor. ix. 17.——g 1 Tim. iii. 3, 8 ; Tit. i. 7.——h Or, *overruling.*——i Ezek. xxxiv. 4 ; Matt. xx. 25, 26 ; 1 Cor. iii. 9 ; 2 Cor. i. 24.——k Psa. xxxiii. 12 ; lxxiv. 2.

---

other proof that *bishop* and *presbyter* were the same order in the *apostolic* times, though *afterwards* they were made distinct.

Not by constraint] The office was laborious and dangerous, especially in these times of persecution ; it is no wonder then that even those who were best qualified for the office should strive to excuse themselves with a genuine *Nolo episcopari,* " I 'am unwilling to be a bishop."

Not for filthy lucre] Could the office of a *bishop,* in those early days, and in the time of persecution, be a *lucrative* office ? Does not the Spirit of God lead the apostle to speak these things rather for *posterity* than for that time ? See the notes on 1 Tim. iii. 3.

But of a ready mind] Doing all for Christ's sake, and through love to immortal souls.

Verse 3. *Neither as being lords over* God's *heritage*] This is the voice of St. Peter in his *catholic epistle* to the *catholic Church!* According to him there are to be no lords over God's heritage, the bishops and presbyters who are appointed by the head of the Church are to *feed the flock,* to *guide* and to *defend* it, not to *fleece* and *waste* it ; and they are to look for their reward in another world, and in the approbation of God in their consciences. And in humility, self-abasement, self-renunciation, and heavenly-mindedness, they are to be *ensamples,* τυποι, *types,* to the flock, *moulds* of a heavenly form, into which the spirits and lives of the flock may be *cast,* that they may come out after a perfect pattern. We need not ask, Does the Church that arrogates to itself the exclusive title of *Catholic,* and do its *supreme pastors,* who affect to be the successors of Peter and the vicars of Jesus Christ, act in this way ? They are in every sense the reverse of this. But we may ask, Do the other Churches, which profess to be *reformed* from the abominations of the above, keep the advice of the apostle in their eye ? Have they *pastors according to God's own heart, who feed them with knowledge and understanding?* Jer. iii. 15. Do they feed *themselves,* and not the *flock?* Are they *lords over the heritage of Christ,* ruling with a high ecclesiastico-secular hand, disputing with their flocks about penny-farthing *tithes* and *stipends,* rather than contending for the faith once delivered to the saints ? Are *they* heavenly *moulds,* into which the spirits and conduct of their flocks may be cast ? I leave those who are concerned to answer these questions ; but I put them, in the name of God, to all the preachers in the land. How many among them properly care for the flock ? Even among those reputed *evangelical* teachers, are there not some who, on their first coming to a parish or a congregation, make it their *first* business to *raise the tithes* and the *stipends,*

4 And when m the chief Shepherd shall appear, ye shall receive n a crown of glory o that fadeth not away.

5 Likewise, ye younger, submit yourselves unto the elder. Yea, p all *of you* be subject
A. M. cir. 4064.
A. D. cir. 60.
An. Olymp.
cir. CCIX. 4.
A. U. C. cir.
813.

---

l Phil. iii. 17; 2 Thess. iii. 9 ; 1 Timothy iv. 12 ; Titus ii. 7 m Heb. xiii. 20.——n 1 Cor. ix. 25 ; 2 Tim. iv. 8 ; James i. 12. o Chap. i. 4.——p Rom. xii. 10 ; Eph. v. 21 ; Phil. ii. 3.

---

where, in all good conscience, there was before enough, and more than enough, to provide them and their families with not only the *necessaries,* but all the *conveniences* and *comforts* of life ! conveniences and comforts which neither Jesus Christ nor his servant Peter ever enjoyed. And is not the great concern among ministers to seek for those *places, parishes,* and *congregations,* where the provision is the most ample, and the work the smallest ? Preacher or minister, whosoever thou art, who readest this, apply not the word to thy *neighbour,* whether he be state-appointed, congregation-appointed, or self-appointed ; take all to thyself ; *mutato nomine de* TE *fabula narratur.* See that thy own heart, views, and conduct be right with God ; and then proceed to the next verse.

Verse 4. *When the chief Shepherd*] That is, the Lord Jesus Christ, whose is the flock, and who provides the pasture, and from whom, if ye are legally called to the most awful work of preaching the Gospel, ye have received your commission ; when he *shall appear* to judge the world in righteousness, ye who have fed his flock, who have taken the *superintendency* of it, not by *constraint,* nor for *filthy lucre's sake,* not as *lords over the heritage,* but with a *ready mind,* employing body, soul, spirit, time and talents, in endeavouring to pluck sinners as brands from eternal burnings, and build up the Church of Christ on its most holy faith ; YE shall *receive a crown of glory* that *fadeth not away,* an eternal nearness and intimacy with the ineffably glorious God ; so that ye who have turned many to righteousness shall shine, not merely as *stars,* but as *suns* in the kingdom of your Father ! O ye heavenly-minded, diligent, self-denying pastors after God's own heart, whether ye be in the *Church* established by the *state,* or in those *divisions* widely separated from, or *nearly* connected with it, take courage ; preach Jesus; press through all difficulties in the faith of your God ; fear no evil while meditating nothing but good. Ye are stars in the right hand of Jesus, who walks among your golden candlesticks, and has lighted that lamp of life which ye are appointed to trim ; fear not, *your* labour in the Lord cannot be in vain ! Never, never can ye preach one sermon in the spirit of your office, which the God of all grace shall permit to be unfruitful ; ye carry and sow the seed of the kingdom by the command and on the authority of your God ; ye sow it, and the heavens shall drop down dew upon it. Ye may go forth weeping, though bearing this precious seed ; but ye shall doubtless come again with rejoicing, bringing your sheaves with you. Amen, even so, Lord Jesus !

Verse 5. *Likewise, ye younger*] Νεωτεροι probably means here *inferiors,* or those not in sacred offices ;

                   2

A. M. cir. 4064.
A. D. cir. 60.
An. Olymp.
cir. CCIX. 4.
A. U. C. cir.
813.

one to another, and be clothed with humility : for � God resisteth the proud, and ʳ giveth grace to the humble.

6 ˢ Humble yourselves therefore under the mighty hand of God, that he may exalt you in due time :

A. M. cir. 4064
A. D. cir. 60.
An. Olymp.
cir. CCIX. 4.
A. U. C. cir.
813.

7 ᵗ Casting all your care upon him ; for he careth for you.

8 ᵘ Be sober, be vigilant ; because ᵛ your adversary the devil, as a roaring lion, walketh about, seeking whom he may devour :

9 ʷ Whom resist steadfast in the faith,

ᵠ James iv. 6.——ʳ Isa. lvii. 15; lxvi. 2.——ˢ James iv. 10.
ᵗ Psa. xxxvii. 5; lv. 22; Wisd. xii. 13; Matt. vi. 25; Luke xii. 11, 22; Phil. iv. 6; Heb. xiii. 5.

ᵘ Luke xxi. 34, 36 ; 1 Thess. v. 6; chap. iv. 7.——ᵛ Job i. 7; ii. 2 ; Luke xxii. 31; Rev. xii. 12.——ʷ Eph. vi. 11, 13 ; James iv. 7.

and may be understood as referring to the *people* at large who are called to obey them that have the rule over them in the Lord. In this sense our Lord, it appears, uses the word, Luke xxii. 26.

Be subject one to another] Strive all to serve each other ; let the pastors strive to serve the people, and the people the pastors ; and let there be no contention, but who shall do most to oblige and profit all the rest.

Be clothed with humility] To be. *clothed with a thing* or *person* is a Greek mode of speech for *being that thing* or *person* with which a man is said *to be clothed.* Be ye *truly humble ;* and let your *outward garb* and *conduct* be a proof of the humility of your hearts. Εγκομβωμα, from the original word εγκομβω-σασθε, signifies often an outward ornamental garment, tied in different places with *knots* or *bows,* probably ornamented all over with bows or knots of different coloured ribands, silk twist, &c. But it also signifies the outward garment worn by *servants, slaves, girls,* and *shepherds,* which was rather intended to be the *guard* of the other garments than an *ornament* to those thus dressed : and I am rather inclined to take it in this sense than in the former ; for as the apostle calls upon them to be *subject* to each other, he desires them to put on *humility,* as the *encomboma* or *servant's dress,* that they may appear to be such as were *ready to serve ;* and that he cannot refer to this article of clothing as an *ornament* the next words sufficiently prove : *God resisteth the* PROUD, *and giveth grace to the* HUMBLE—the *proud,* with all their *ornaments,* God *resists ;* while those who are clothed with the humble garment he *adorns.*

Verse 6. *Humble yourselves*] Those who submit patiently to the dispensations of God's providence he lifts up ; those who lift themselves up, God thrusts down.

If we humble not ourselves under God's *grace,* he will humble us under his *judgments.* Those who patiently submit to him, he exalts in due time ; if his hand be *mighty to depress,* it is also *mighty to exalt.*

Verse 7. *Casting all your care*] Την μεριμναν· Your *anxiety,* your *distracting care,* on him, *for he careth for you,* ὁτι αυτω μελει περι ὑμων, *for he meddles* or *concerns himself, with the things that interest you.* Whatever things concern a follower of God, whether they be spiritual or temporal, or whether in themselves great or small, God concerns himself with them ; what affects them affects him ; in all their afflictions he is afflicted. He who knows that God cares for him, need have no anxious cares about himself. This is a

plain reference to Psa. lv. 22 : *Cast thy burden upon the Lord, and he will sustain thee.* He will bear both thee and thy burden.

Verse 8. *Be sober*] Avoid *drunkenness* of your *senses,* and *drunkenness* in your *souls ;* be not *over-charged* with the concerns of the world.

Be vigilant] Awake, and keep awake ; be always *watchful ;* never be off your guard ; your enemies are alert, they are never off theirs.

Your adversary the devil] This is the reason why ye should be sober and vigilant ; ye have an ever active, implacable, subtle enemy to contend with. He *walketh about*—he has access to you everywhere ; he knows your feelings and your propensities, and informs himself of all your circumstances ; only God can know more and do more than he, therefore your care must be cast upon God.

As a roaring lion] Satan tempts under *three* forms : 1. The *subtle serpent ;* to beguile our senses, pervert our judgment, and enchant our imagination. 2. As an *angel of light ;* to deceive us with *false views* of spiritual things, *refinements* in religion, and presumption on the providence and grace of God. 3. As a *roaring lion ;* to bear us down, and destroy us by *violent opposition, persecution,* and *death.* Thus he was acting towards the followers of God at Pontus, &c., who were now suffering a grievous persecution.

Walketh about] Traversing the earth ; a plain reference to Job ii. 2, which see.

Seeking whom he may devour] Τινα καταπιη· *Whom he may gulp down.* It is not *every one* that he can *swallow down :* those who are *sober and vigilant* are proof against him, these he MAY NOT *swallow down ;* those who are *drunken* with the cares of this world, &c., and are *unwatchful,* these he MAY *swallow down.* There is a beauty in this verse, and a striking apposition between the *first* and *last words,* which I think have not been noticed : *Be sober,* νηψατε, from νη, *not,* and πιειν, to *drink ; do not drink, do not swallow down :* and the word καταπιη, from κατα, *down,* and πιειν, to *drink.* If you swallow strong drink down, the devil will swallow you down. Hear this, ye drunkards, topers, tipplers, or by whatsoever name you are known in society, or among your fellow sinners. Strong drink is not only the way to the devil, but the devil's way into you ; and YE are such as the devil particularly MAY *swallow down.*

Verse 9. *Whom resist*] Stand against him, αντιστητε. Though *invulnerable,* he is not *unconquerable :* the weakest follower of God can confound and overpower him, if he continue *steadfast in the faith*—believing

A. M. cir. 4064.
A. D. cir. 60.
An. Olymp.
cir. CCIX. 4.
A. U. C. cir.
813.

ˣ knowing that the same afflictions are accomplished in your brethren that are in the world.

10 But the God all grace, ʸ who hath called us unto his eternal glory by Christ Jesus, after that ye have suffered ᶻ a while, ᵃ make you perfect, ᵇ stablish, strengthen, settle *you*.

11 ᶜ To him *be* glory and dominion for ever and ever. Amen.

12 ᵈ By Silvanus, a faithful brother unto you, as I suppose, I have ᵉ written briefly, exhorting, and testifying ᶠ that this is the true grace of God wherein ye stand.

A. M. cir. 4064.
A. D. cir. 60.
An. Olymp.
cir. CCIX. 4.
A. U. C. cir.
813.

ˣ Acts xiv. 22 ; 1 Thess. iii. 3 ; 2 Tim. iii. 12 ; chapter ii. 21.
ʸ 1 Cor. i. 9 ; 1 Timothy vi. 12.——ᶻ 2 Cor. iv. 17 ; chapter i. 6.
ᵃ Heb. xiii. 21 ; Jude 24.

ᵇ 2 Thess. ii. 17 ; iii. 3.——ᶜ Chap. iv. 11 ; Rev. i. 6.
ᵈ 2 Cor. i. 19.——ᵉ Heb. xiii. 22.——ᶠ Acts xx. 24 ; 1 Cor. xv. 1 ;
2 Peter i. 12.

---

on the Son of God, and walking uprightly before him. To a soul thus engaged he can do no damage.

The same afflictions are accomplished in your brethren] It is the lot of all the disciples of Christ to suffer persecution. The *brotherhood, αδελφοτης,* the *Christian Church,* everywhere is exposed to the assaults of men and devils ; you are persecuted by the *heathen* among whom ye live, and from among whom ye are gathered into the fold of Christ : but even those who profess the same faith with you, and who are resident among the *Jews,* (for so I think *εν κοσμω, in the world,* is here to be understood,) are also persecuted, both *heathens* and *Jews* being equally opposed to the pure and holy doctrines of the Gospel. Any man who has read the Greek Testament with any attention must have observed a vast number of places in which the word *κοσμος,* which we translate *world,* means the *Jewish people* and the *Jewish state,* and nothing else.

Verse 10. But the God of all grace] The Fountain of infinite compassion, mercy, and goodness. *Mohammed* has conveyed this fine description of the Divine Being in the words with which he commences every surat or chapter of his *Koran,* two excepted ; viz. :—

بسم الله الرحمن الرحيم

Bismillahi arrahmani arraheemi.

Of which the best translation that can be given is that of the apostle, *In the name of the God of all grace ;* the God who is the most merciful and the most compassionate, who is an exuberant Fountain of love and compassion to all his intelligent offspring.

Who hath called us] By the preaching of the Gospel.

Unto his eternal glory] To the infinite felicity of the heavenly state.

By Christ Jesus] Through the *merit* of his *passion* and *death,* by the *influence* of his *Holy Spirit,* by the *precepts* of his *Gospel,* and by the *splendour* of his own *example.*

After that ye have suffered a while] Ολιγον παθοντας· *Having suffered a little time ;* that is, while ye are enduring these persecutions, God will cause all to work together for your good.

Make you perfect] Καταρτισει, στηριξει, σθενωσει, Θεμελιωσει· All these words are read in the *future* tense by the best MSS. and versions.

He will make you perfect.—Καταρτισει· Put you in *complete joint* as the timbers of a building.

Stablish] Στηριξει· Make you *firm* in every part ;

adapt you strongly to each other, so that you may be mutual supports, the whole building being *one* in the Lord.

Strengthen] Σθενωσει· Cramp and bind every part, so that there shall be no danger of warping, splitting, or falling.

Settle] Θεμελιωσει· Cause all to rest so *evenly* and *firmly* upon the best and surest foundation, that ye may grow together to a holy temple in the Lord : in a word, that ye may be *complete* in all the mind that was in Christ ; *supported* in all your trials and difficulties ; *strengthened* to resist and overcome all your enemies ; and after all *abide,* firmly *founded,* in the truth of grace. All these phrases are *architectural ;* and the apostle has again in view the fine image which he produced chap. ii. 5. where see the notes.

Verse 11. To him] The God of all grace, *be glory*—all honour and praise be ascribed, and *dominion*—the government of heaven, earth, and hell, *for ever*—through time, *and ever*—through eternity. *Amen*—so be it, so let it be, and so it shall be. Amen and Amen !

Verse 12. By Silvanus, a faithful brother unto you, as I suppose] To say the least of this translation, it is extremely obscure, and not put together with that elegance which is usual to our translators. I see no reason why the clause may not be thus translated : *I have written to you, as I consider, briefly, by Silvanus, the faithful brother.* On all hands it is allowed that this *Silvanus* was the same as *Silas,* Paul's faithful companion in travel, mentioned Acts xv. 40 ; xvi. 19 ; and, if he were the same, Peter could never say *as I suppose* to *his* faith and piety : but he might well say this to the shortness of his epistle, notwithstanding the many and important subjects which it embraced. See the *Syriac, Vulgate,* &c. If the words be applied to *Silvanus,* they must be taken in a sense in which they are often used : "I *conclude* him to be a trustworthy person ; one by whom I may safely send this letter ; who will take care to travel through the different regions in Asia, Pontus, Galatia, and Bithynia ; read it in every Church ; and leave a copy for the encouragement and instruction of Christ's flock." And in such a state of the Church, in such countries, no ordinary person could have been intrusted with such a message.

Exhorting] Calling upon you to be faithful, humble, and steady.

And testifying] Επιμαρτυρων, *Earnestly witnessing,* that it *is the true grace*—the genuine Gospel of Jesus

2

A. M. cir. 4064.
A. D. cir. 60.
An. Olymp.
cir. CCIX. 4.
A. U. C. cir.
813.

13 The *Church that is* at Babylon, elected together with *you,* saluteth you; and *so doth* g Marcus my son.

14 h Greet ye one another with a kiss of charity. i Peace be with you all that are in Christ Jesus. Amen.

A. M. cir. 4064.
A. D. cir. 60.
An. Olymp.
cir. CCIX. 4.
A. U. C. cir.
813.

g Acts xii. 12, 25.——h Rom. xvi. 16; 1 Cor. xvi. 20 ;

2 Cor. xiii. 12; 1 Thess. v. 26.——i Eph. vi. 23.

Christ, *in which ye stand,* and in which ye should persevere to the end.

Verse 13. *The* Church that is *at Babylon*] After considering all that has been said by learned men and critics on this place, I am quite of opinion that the apostle does not mean Babylon in *Egypt,* nor *Jerusalem,* nor *Rome* as *figurative* Babylon, but the ancient celebrated Babylon in Assyria, which was, as Dr. Benson observes, the metropolis of the eastern dispersion of the Jews; but as I have said so much on this subject in the *preface,* I beg leave to refer the reader to that place.

Instead of *Babylon,* some MSS. mentioned by *Syncellus* in his Chronicon have Ιοππη, *Joppa;* and one has Ρωμη, *Rome,* in the margin, probably as the meaning, according to the writer, of the word *Babylon.*

Elected together with you] Συνεκλεκτη· *Fellow elect,* or *elected jointly* with you. Probably meaning that they, and the believers at Babylon, received the Gospel about the same time. On the *election* of those to whom St. Peter wrote, see the notes on chap. i. 2.

And—Marcus my son.] This is supposed to be the same person who is mentioned Acts xii. 12, and who is known by the name of *John Mark;* he was sister's son to Barnabas, Col. iv. 10, his mother's name was Mary, and he is the same who wrote the gospel that goes under his name. He is called here *Peter's son,* i. e. according to the *faith,* Peter having been probably the means of his conversion. This is very likely, as Peter seems to have been intimate at his mother's house. See the account, Acts xii. 6–17.

Verse 14. *Greet ye one another with a kiss of charity.*] See the notes on Rom. xvi. 16, and on 1 Cor. xvi. 20. In the above places the kiss is called *a holy kiss;* here, φιλημωτι αγαπης, *a kiss of* LOVE; i. e. as a mark of their love to each other, in order that misunderstandings might be prevented. But ten or twelve MSS., with the *Syriac, Arabic, Armenian,* and *Vulgate,* have αγιω, *holy; salute one another with a* HOLY *kiss* The difference is not great.

Peace be *with you all*] May all *prosperity,* spiritual and temporal, be with all *that are in Christ Jesus*—that are truly converted to him, and live in his Spirit obedient to his will.

Amen.] Is wanting, as usual, in some of the principal MSS. and versions.

The *subscriptions* are, as in other cases, various.

In the VERSIONS :

The end of the First Epistle of the Apostle Peter.—SYRIAC.

The First Catholic Epistle of Peter the apostle is ended.—SYRIAC PHILOXENIAN.

The end of the Epistle of St. Peter; may his supplication preserve us! Amen. Praise be to the Lord of never ending and eternal glory! Amen.—ARABIC.

The First Epistle of Peter is completed; may his intercession be with us! Amen, and Amen.—ÆTHIOPIC.

Nothing in the COPTIC.

Nothing in the printed VULGATE.

The end of the First Epistle of St. Peter.—COMPLUTENSIAN *Polyglott.*

The First Epistle of St. Peter is ended.—BIR VULGAT. Edit. *Princ.*

In the MANUSCRIPTS :

The First of Peter.—Codex *Alexand.* and Codex *Vatican.*

Written from Rome.—A MS. of the twelfth century.

The end of the First Catholic Epistle of Peter, written from Rome.—A MS. of the thirteenth century.

These later subscriptions are of little value; nor do any of them help to ascertain the *place* where the epistle was written. The word *Rome* is only the supposed interpretation of the word *Babylon,* as in ver. 14, which see.

As the true Church of Christ has generally been in a state of *suffering,* the epistles of St. Peter have ever been most highly prized by all believers. That which we have just finished is an admirable letter, containing some of the most important maxims and consolations for the Church in the wilderness. No Christian can read it without deriving from it both light and life. Ministers, especially, should study it well, that they may know how to comfort their flocks when in persecution or adversity. He never speaks to good effect in any spiritual case who is not furnished out of the Divine treasury. God's words invite, solicit, and command assent; on them a man may confidently rely. The words of man may be *true,* but they are not *infallible.* This is the character of God's word alone

I SHALL sum up the contents of this chapter in the words of a good commentator : " Because the knowledge and good behaviour of the people depend, in a great measure, upon the kind of instruction which they receive from their teachers, the apostle in this chapter addressed the *elders,* that is, the bishops, pastors, rulers, and deacons among the brethren of Pontus, &c., ver. 1, exhorting the bishops in particular to feed the flock of God committed to their care faithfully, and to exercise their episcopal office, not as by constraint, but willingly; not from the love of gain, but from love to their Master and to the flock, ver. 2 ; and not to lord it over God's heritage, but to be patterns of humility and disinterestedness to the people, ver. 3. This exhortation to bishops to feed Christ's flock was given with much propriety by Peter, who had himself been appointed by Christ to feed his lambs and his sheep. Next, because the faithful performance of the bishop's office was, in that age, attended with great difficulty and danger, the apostle, to encourage the

2

bishops, assured them that, when the chief Shepherd shall appear, they shall receive a crown of glory that fadeth not away, ver. 4.   The distinguished reward which Christ is to bestow on those who have suffered for his sake being a favourite topic with our apostle, he introduces it often in this epistle.

"Having thus exhorted the pastors, the apostle turned his discourse to the people, charging them to be subject to their elders, and to one another ; that is, to be of a teachable disposition, and to receive instruction from every one capable of giving it, and to do all the duties which they could to each other, according to their different stations and relations, ver. 5.   But especially to be subject to God, by humbly submitting themselves to the judgments which were coming upon them, that God might exalt them in due time, ver. 6. Casting all their anxious care on God, because he cared for them, ver. 7.   And to watch against the devil, who went about as a roaring lion, seeking to destroy them by instigating the wicked to persecute them, and drive them into apostasy, ver. 8.   But they were to resist that terrible enemy by steadfastness in the faith, and not to think themselves hardly dealt with when persecuted, knowing that their brethren everywhere were exposed to the same temptations of the devil, ver. 9.   In the meantime, to give them all the assistance in his power, the apostle prayed earnestly to God to stablish and strengthen them, ver. 10. And ended his prayer with a doxology to God, expressive of his supreme dominion over the universe, and all the things it contains.

"The apostle informed the brethren of Pontus that he had sent this letter to them by Silvanus, whom he praised for his fidelity to Christ, ver. 12.   Then, giving them the salutation of the Church in Babylon, where it seems he was when he wrote this letter, he added the salutation of Mark, whom he called *his son,* either because he had converted him, or on account of the great attachment which Mark bore to him, ver. 13.   And having desired them to salute one another, he concluded with giving them his apostolical benediction, ver. 14."   See Dr. *Macknight.*

Finished correcting this epistle for a new edition, Dec. 31, 1831.—A. C.

INTRODUCTION

TO

THE SECOND EPISTLE

OF

PETER.

AS the preface to the preceding epistle embraces the question of the authenticity of both epistles, and also considers several matters common to both, I need not take up the subject here afresh; but simply consider those matters which are peculiar to the epistle before me, and which have not been examined in the foregoing preface.

"This epistle, as appears from chap. iii. 1, (says *Michaelis*,) was written to the same communities as the first epistle; and the author gives us thus to understand, that he was the person who wrote the first epistle; that is, the Apostle Peter. He calls himself likewise, chap. i. 1, Συμεων Πετρος, δουλος και αποστολος Ιησου Χριστου, *Symeon Peter, a servant and apostle of Jesus Christ*; and chap. i. 16—18 says that he was present at the transfiguration of Christ on the mount. The notion therefore entertained by Grotius, that this epistle was written by a bishop of Jerusalem of the name of Simeon, is absolutely inadmissible; and we have no other alternative than this: either it was written by the Apostle St. Peter, or it is a forgery in his name.

"The ancients entertained very great doubts whether St. Peter was really the author. Eusebius, in his chapter where he speaks of the books of the New Testament in general, reckons it among the αντιλεγομενα, those *not canonical*. He says that tradition does not reckon, as a part of the New Testament, the second epistle ascribed to Peter; but that, as in the opinion of most men, it is useful, it is therefore much read. Origen had said, long before, that Peter had left behind him one epistle universally received, and perhaps a second, though doubts are entertained about it.

"The old Syriac version, though it contains the Epistle of St. James, which Eusebius likewise reckons among the αντιλεγομενα, does not contain the Second Epistle of St. Peter. Now it cannot be said that the other books of the New Testament were translated into Syriac before St. Peter's second epistle was written; for St. Paul's Second Epistle to Timothy was written certainly as late, and yet is contained in this very version. And if an epistle, addressed only to an individual, was known to the Syriac translator, it may be thought that a circular epistle addressed to communities dispersed in several countries in Asia, would hardly have escaped his notice. The circumstance, therefore, that the old Syriac translator did not translate the Second Epistle of St. Peter as well as the first, may be used as an argument against its antiquity, and of course against its authenticity.

"It appears then that, if the authenticity of this epistle were determined by external evidence, it would have less in its favour than it would have against it. But, on the other hand, the internal evidence is greatly in its favour; and indeed so much so, that the epistle gains in this respect more than it loses in the former. Wetstein, indeed, says that since the ancients themselves were in doubt, the moderns cannot expect to arrive at certainty, because we cannot obtain more information on the subject in the eighteenth, than ecclesiastical writers were able to obtain in the third and fourth, centuries. Now this is perfectly true as far as relates to historical knowledge, or to the testimony of others in regard to the matter of fact, whether St. Peter was the author or not. But when this question is to be decided by an examination of the epistle itself, it is surely possible that the critical skill and penetration of the moderns may discover in it proofs of its having been written by St. Peter, though these proofs escaped the notice of the ancients. After a diligent comparison of the First Epistle of St. Peter with that which is ascribed to him as his second, the agreement between them appears to me to be such, that, if the second was not written by St. Peter as well as the first, the person who forged it not only possessed the power of imitation in a very unusual degree, but understood likewise the design of the first epistle, with which the ancients do not appear to have been acquainted. Now, if this be true, the supposition that the second epistle was not written by St. Peter himself, involves a contradiction. Nor is it credible that a pious impostor of the first or second century should have imitated St. Peter so successfully as to betray no marks of a forgery; for the spurious productions of those ages, which were sent into

2

the world in the name of the apostles, are for the most part very unhappy imitations, and discover very evident marks that they were not written by the persons to whom they were ascribed. Other productions of this kind betray their origin by the poverty of their materials, or by the circumstance that, instead of containing original thoughts, they are nothing more than a rhapsody of sentiments collected from various parts of the Bible, and put together without plan or order.

"This charge cannot possibly be laid to the Second Epistle of Peter, which is so far from containing materials derived from other parts of the Bible, that the third chapter exhibits the discussion of a totally new subject. Its resemblance to the Epistle of Jude will hardly be urged as an argument against it; for no doubt can be made that the Second Epistle of St. Peter was, in respect to the Epistle of St. Jude, the original, and not the copy. Lastly, it is extremely difficult, even for a man of the greatest talents, to forge a writing in the name of another, without sometimes inserting what the pretended author either would not or could not have said; and support the imposture in so complete a manner as to militate, in not a single instance, either against his character or against the age in which he lived. Now, in the Second Epistle of St. Peter, though it has been a subject of examination full seventeen hundred years, nothing has hitherto been discovered which is unsuitable either to the apostle or the apostolic age. Objections, indeed, have been made on account of its style; but the style of the second epistle, when compared with that of the first, warrants rather the conclusion that both were written by the same person. We have no reason, therefore, to believe that the Second Epistle of St. Peter is spurious, especially as it is difficult to comprehend what motive could have induced a Christian, whether orthodox or heretic, to attempt the fabrication of such an epistle, and then falsely ascribe it to St. Peter.

"Having shown that the supposition that this epistle is spurious is without foundation, I have, in the next place, to show that there are positive grounds for believing it to be genuine. The arguments in favour of its genuineness are of two kinds, being founded on the similarity of the two epistles, either in respect to their *materials*, or in respect to their *style*. The arguments of the former kind are as follow:—

"The design of the first epistle was to assure the uncircumcised Christians that they stood in the grace of God. Now it was not generally known that this was the design of it; and therefore we cannot suppose that any person whose object was to forge an epistle in St. Peter's name should have observed it. But the design of the second epistle was certainly the same as that of the first, as appears from the address, chap. i. 1: Τοις ισοτιμον ἡμιν λαχουσι πιστιν εν δικαιοσυνη του Θεου· *To them who have obtained like precious faith with us, through the righteousness of God.* If we explain *ἡμιν*, as denoting 'us apostles,' the address will imply what was wholly unnecessary, since no one could doubt that the faith of other Christians might be as good as the faith of the apostles; and it will sound likewise rather haughty and assuming; but if we explain *ἡμιν* as denoting 'us who were born Jews,' and consider that the second epistle, as well as the first, was directed to persons who were born heathens, the address becomes clear and consistent: δικαιοσυνη του Θεου, will then signify the impartiality of God in estimating the faith of native heathens as highly as the faith of native Jews, which St. Peter has extolled in other places. We shall likewise be able to explain chap. i. 8–10, which appears to contain the tautology that those who are diligent in good works are not idle; whereas, if this epistle be explained from the design of the first, we shall perceive the meaning of the passage to be this, that they who are diligent in good works need not fear the reproach that they observe not the Levitical law, since their good works, which are the fruit of their religious knowledge, will be the means of making their calling and election sure. (See the note on this place.)

"The deluge, which is not a common subject in the apostolic epistles, is mentioned both in 1 Peter iii. 20, and in 2 Peter ii. 5; and in both places the circumstance is noted, that eight persons only were saved; though in neither place does the subject require that the number should be particularly specified. Now it is true that St. Peter was not the only apostle who knew how many persons were saved in the ark; but he only, who by habit had acquired a familiarity with the subject, would ascertain the precise number, where his argument did not depend upon it. The author of the first epistle had read St. Paul's Epistle to the Romans; and the author of the second epistle speaks in express terms, chap. iii. 15, 16, of the epistles of St. Paul. Now, no other writer of the New Testament has quoted from the New Testament; consequently, we have in these epistles a criterion from which we may judge that they were written by the same author.

"Before I consider the arguments which are derived from the *style* of these epistles, I must observe that several commentators have on the contrary contended that the style is very different; and hence have inferred that they were written by different authors; but it is extremely difficult to form from a single epistle so complete a judgment of the author's style and manner as to enable us to pronounce with certainty that he was *not* the author of another epistle ascribed to him. The style of the same writer is not always the same at every period of his life, especially when he composes not in his native, but in a foreign, language.

"From what has been said in the course of this section, it appears that even the second chapter of the second epistle has some resemblance both in style and contents to the first epistle. This is to be particularly noted, because even the advocates for the second epistle have in general granted that the style of this chapter is not the usual style of St. Peter. Bishop Sherlock, for instance, acknowledges it; nor, though I contend that there is some similarity, as in ver. 5–7, will I assert that there is no difference. But it will not therefore follow that the whole epistle was not written by St. Peter: and if it is allowable to draw a conclusion from one or two passages, it will be no other than this, that the second chapter is spurious, because the style of it is said to be as different from the first and third chapters as it is from the first epistle. This conclusion, however, no one will draw who has examined the connection of the whole epistle; in fact the difference in question

2

is rather of a negative kind; for though I am unable to discover any remarkable *agreement* in style between the first epistle and the second chapter of the second epistle, I do not perceive any remarkable *difference*. This second chapter has indeed several words which are unusual in other parts of the New Testament, but the same may be said of the first epistle: and some of the expressions which to us appear extraordinary were borrowed perhaps from the Gnostics, whose doctrines are here confuted; for it is not unusual in combatting the opinions of a particular sect to adopt their peculiar terms. Thus in 2 Peter ii. 17, the Gnostics are called 'clouds, agitated by a tempest;' and we know that the Manicheans, who had many doctrines in common with the Gnostics, taught that there were five good and five bad elements, and that one of the latter was called 'tempest.' In like manner they frequently speak of darkness under the name of ζοφος, which occurs more than once in this chapter. The Epistle of St. Jude has a still greater number of unusual figurative expressions; and it is not impossible that these also were borrowed from the Gnostics. The Second Epistle of St. Peter must have been written only a short time before his death; for he says, chap. i. 14, 'shortly I must put off this my tabernacle, even as our Lord Jesus Christ hath showed me.' St. Peter here alludes to his conversation with Christ after the resurrection, recorded in John xxi. 18–22, where Christ had foretold his death in the following manner: 'When thou shalt be old thou shalt stretch forth thy hands, and another shall gird thee and carry thee whither thou wouldest not.' Hence St. Peter might very easily conclude that he would not survive the coming of Christ to judge Jerusalem. But Christ has declared that Jerusalem would be destroyed before one generation passed away. St. Peter, therefore, after a lapse of thirty years, that is, in the year 64, necessarily considered his death as an event not far distant. As to the design of this epistle, it appears that St. Peter wrote against certain persons who, though members of the Church, denied the doctrine of a general judgment and a dissolution of the world. They inferred that this event, because it had been long delayed, would never take place; to which objection St. Peter replies by saying, That one day is with the Lord as a thousand years, and a thousand years as one day: that the Lord is not slack concerning his promise, as some men count slackness; but is long-suffering, not willing that any man should perish, but that all should come to repentance. Farther, St. Peter argues, that as the earth has already undergone a great revolution at the deluge, another revolution equally great is not incredible; and that since the former event was at the time when it happened as unexpected as the latter will be, we ought to believe in God's declaration, that the world will one day be totally destroyed. This destruction, St. Peter says, will be effected, not by water, as at the deluge, but by fire. 'The elements shall melt with fervent heat, the earth also, and the works that are therein, shall be burned up.' Now, a general conflagration will be more easily admitted by those who are unacquainted with the state of the earth, than a universal deluge; for though it may be difficult to comprehend whence a sufficient quantity of water could be brought to cover the whole earth, yet no one can deny that the bowels of the earth abound with inflammable matter, and that fiery eruptions may spread themselves throughout the surface of the globe. (See the notes on chap. iii. 9–11.)

"It must be observed that St. Peter's appeal to the deluge in the time of Noah implies that the adversaries whom he combats admitted that the Mosaic account of it was true, since it would have been useless to have argued from a fact which they denied. This must be kept in view, because it will assist us in determining who these adversaries were.

"St. Peter describes these false teachers, chap. ii. 10, 11, 12, as *calumniators of the angels*; which the apostle highly censures, even though the calumny should be directed against the fallen angels, since some respect is due to their former greatness and power. St. Peter says, 'angels themselves, which are greater in power and might, bring not railing accusation against them before the Lord; but these as natural brute beasts, made to be taken and destroyed, speak evil of the things which they understand not.' Here we have a description of these false teachers, which points them out more distinctly than any of the preceding accounts, and shows they were *Gnostics*. For the *ecclesiastical* history furnishes many examples of improper adoration paid to the angels. I know of no sect which calumniated them, except that of the Gnostics. Now the Gnostics *calumniated the angels* by their doctrine in respect to the creation of the world. They raised certain angels to the rank of creators; but described the creation as very imperfect, and the authors of it as wicked and rebellious against the supreme Being.

"Having thus shown that St. Peter in his second epistle combats the opinion of a *Gnostic* sect, I will now venture to go a step farther, and attempt to determine the *name* which the orthodox gave to this particular sect in the first century. St. Peter describes them, chap. ii. 15, as *following the way of Balaam*, that is, as following the *religious doctrine of Balaam*. The doctrine of Balaam, as St. John says, Apoc. ii. 14, was *to eat things sacrificed to idols*, and *to commit fornication*. And since *Nicolaus*, in Greek, has the same meaning as *Balaam* in Hebrew, the followers of Balaam are called by St. John, Apoc. ii. 15, *Nicolaitans*. Now it is well known that the Nicolaitans were *a sect of the Gnostics*; and therefore it was probable that this was the sect against which St. Peter wrote. To this opinion it has been objected, that if St. Peter had meant the *Nicolaitans*, he would have called them, not *followers of Balaam*, but by their proper name, *Nicolaitans*; first, because in general proper names are retained and not translated; and, secondly, because in the present instance, no one before *Cocceius* observed the analogy between the *Hebrew* word *Balaam* and the *Greek* word *Nicolaus*. But neither of these reasons are true. For to say nothing of the general custom which once prevailed among the literati of Germany, of translating their names into Greek or Latin; I could produce examples of such translations amongst the Jews, of which it will be sufficient to mention that which occurs in Acts ix. 36. And the derivation of the *Nicolaitans* from *Balaam* must have been long known, at least in Asia; for in the

Arabic version published by *Erpenius*, we find an instance of it in Apoc. ii. 6, where τα εργα των Νικολαιτων is rendered اعمال الشعوب that is, 'works of the Shuaibites.' Now the Arabic word شعيب (*Shuaib*) is equivalent to the Hebrew *Balaam*. Shuaib is mentioned in the *Koran* (Surat vii. 86; xxvi. 176, and in other places) as the prophet of the *Midianites*. Some suppose that by *Shuaib* is meant *Jethro*; but in my opinion no other person is meant but *Balaam*, who was sent for by the Midianites as well as by the Moabites. At least I cannot comprehend how the Nicolaitans, or any other heretics, could be considered as *followers of Jethro*. The Arabic verb شعب *shaaba*, signifies *he destroyed*, and the noun شعب *shaabon*, the *people*. It is not improbable, therefore, that the Arabs adopted the word شعيب *shuaib*, as corresponding to the Hebrew word בלעם *Balaam*, which is compounded of בלע *bala*, *he swallowed up* or *destroyed*, and עם *am*, the *people*. So Νικολαος, *Nicolas*, is from νικαω, to *overcome*, and λαος, the *people*."—See *Michaelis's Introduction.*

I shall not attempt to dispute the propriety of these derivations and etymologies; but I must make one remark on the Shuaibites. In general, the Arabic writers say that *Shuaib* was Jethro, the father-in-law of Moses, and that God had sent him, according to the Koran, to preach pure morality to the Midianites; but I do not remember to have met with a sect of idolaters or heretics called *Shuaibites*. In both the places of the Koran mentioned above, *Shuaib* is spoken of with respect. But the conjecture that *Shuaib* and *Balaam* are the same is exceedingly probable; and this makes the etymology the more likely.

We may safely conclude from all the evidence before us, 1. That St. Peter, the apostle, was the author of this, as well as of the other, epistle. 2. That it was written to the same persons. 3. That they were in a state of persecution, and had also to contend with *Gnostics* or other heretics in the Church. 4. That it was written a short time after the first epistle, and not long before St. Peter's martyrdom; but the precise year cannot be ascertained.

THE

SECOND GENERAL EPISTLE

OF

PETER.

Chronological Notes relative to this Epistle.

Year of the Constantinopolitan era of the world, or that used by the Byzantine historians, and other eastern writers, 5568.—Year of the Alexandrian era of the world, 5562.—Year of the Antiochian era of the world, 5552.—Year of the world, according to Archbishop Usher, 4064.—Year of the world, according to Eusebius, in his Chronicon, 4288.—Year of the minor Jewish era of the world, or that in common use, 3820.—Year of the Greater Rabbinical era of the world, 4419.—Year from the Flood, according to Archbishop Usher, and the English Bible, 2408.—Year of the Cali yuga, or Indian era of the Deluge, 3162. —Year of the era of Iphitus, or since the first commencement of the Olympic games, 1000.—Year of the era of Nabonassar, king of Babylon, 809.—Year of the CCIXth Olympiad, 4.—Year from the building of Rome, according to Fabius Pictor, 807.—Year from the building of Rome, according to Frontinus, 811.—Year from the building of Rome, according to the Fasti Capitolini, 812.—Year from the building of Rome, according to Varro, which was that most generally used, 813.—Year of the era of the Seleucidæ, 372.—Year of the Cæsarean era of Antioch, 108.—Year of the Julian era, 105.—Year of the Spanish era, 98.—Year from the birth of Jesus Christ, according to Archbishop Usher, 64.—Year of the vulgar era of Christ's nativity, 60.—Year of Claudius Felix, governor of the Jews, 8.—Year of Vologesus, king of the Parthians, 11.— Jesus, high priest of the Jews, 1.—Year of the Dionysian period, or Easter Cycle, 61.—Year of the Grecian Cycle of nineteen years, or Common Golden Number, 4; or the second after the first embolismic. —Year of the Jewish Cycle of nineteen years, 1; or two years before the first embolismic.—Year of the Solar Cycle, 13.—Dominical Letter, it being the Bissextile, or Leap Year, FE.—Day of the Jewish Passover, the second of April, which happened in this year on the fourth day after the Jewish Sabbath.— Easter Sunday, the sixth of April.—Epact, or age of the moon on the 22d of March, (the day of the earliest Easter Sunday possible,) 3.—Epact, according to the present mode of computation, or the moon's age on New Year's day, or the Calends of January, 11.—Monthly Epacts, or age of the moon on the Calends of each month respectively, (beginning with January,) 11, 13, 12, 13, 14, 15, 16, 17, 19, 19, 21, 21.— Number of Direction, or the number of days from the twenty-first of March to the Jewish Passover, 12.— Year of the reign of Caius Tiberius Claudius Nero Cæsar, the fifth Roman monarch, computing from Octavianus, or Augustus Cæsar, properly the first Roman emperor, 7.—Roman Consuls, the Emperor Nero Augustus, the fourth time, and Cossus Cornelius Lentulus.

2

CHAPTER I.

The apostolical address, and the persons to whom the epistle was sent described by the state into which God had called, and in which he had placed, them, 1–4. What graces they should possess in order to be fruitful in the knowledge of God, 5–8. The miserable state of those who either have not these graces, or have fallen from them, 9. Believers should give diligence to make their calling and election sure, 10, 11. The apostle's intimations of his speedy dissolution, and his wish to confirm and establish those Churches in the true faith, 12–15. The certainty of the Gospel, and the convincing evidence which the apostle had of its truth from being present at the transfiguration, by which the word of prophecy was made more sure, 16–19. How the prophecies came, and their nature, 20, 21.

A. M. cir. 4064.
A. D. cir. 60.
An. Olymp.
cir. CCIX. 4.
A. U. C. cir.
813.

[a] SIMON PETER, a servant and an apostle of Jesus Christ, to them that have obtained [b] like precious faith with us, through the righteousness [c] of God and our Saviour Jesus Christ.

2 [d] Grace and peace be multiplied unto you through the knowledge of God, and of Jesus our Lord,

3 According as his Divine power hath given unto us all things that *pertain* unto life and

A. M. cir. 4064.
A. D. cir. 60.
An. Olymp.
cir. CCIX. 4.
A. U. C. cir.
813.

---

[a] Or, *Symeon*; Acts xv. 14.——[b] Rom. i. 12; 2 Cor. iv. 13; Eph. iv. 5; Tit. i. 4.

[c] Gr. *of our God and Saviour*; Tit. ii. 13.——[d] Dan. iv. 1; vi. 25; 1 Pet. i. 2; Jude 2.

NOTES ON CHAP. I.

Verse 1. *Simon Peter*] *Symeon*, Συμεων, is the reading of almost all the versions, and of all the most important MSS. And this is the more remarkable, as the surname of Peter occurs upwards of seventy times in the New Testament, and is invariably read Σιμων, *Simon*, except here, and in Acts xv. 14, where James gives him the name of *Symeon*. Of all the versions, only the *Armenian* and *Vulgate* have *Simon*. But the *edit. princ.*, and several of my own MSS. of the Vulgate, write *Symon*; and Wiclif has *Symont*.

A servant] Employed in his Master's work.

And an apostle] Commissioned immediately by Jesus Christ himself to preach to the Gentiles, and to write these epistles for the edification of the Church. As the writer was an *apostle*, the epistle is therefore necessarily *canonical*. All the MSS. agree in the title *apostle*; and of the *versions*, only the *Syriac* omits it.

Precious faith] Ισοτιμον πιστιν· *Valuable faith;* faith worth a great price, and faith which cost a great price. The word *precious* is used in the *low* religious phraseology for *dear, comfortable, delightful*, &c.; but how much is the dignity of the subject let down by expressions and meanings more proper for the nursery than for the noble science of salvation! It is necessary however to state, that the word *precious* literally signifies *valuable, of great price, costly;* and was not used in that *low* sense in which it is now employed when our translation was made. That *faith* must be of infinite value, the grace of which Christ purchased by his blood; and it must be of infinite value also when it is the very instrument by which the soul is saved unto eternal life

With us] God having given to *you*—believing *Gentiles*, the same faith and salvation which he had given to *us*—believing *Jews*.

Through the righteousness of God] Through his *method* of bringing a lost world, both Jews and Gentiles, to salvation by Jesus Christ; through his gracious impartiality, providing for Gentiles as well as Jews. See the notes on Rom. iii. 21–26.

Of God and our Saviour Jesus Christ] This is

not a proper translation of the original του Θεου ημων και σωτηρος Ιησου Χριστου, which is literally, *Of our God and Saviour Jesus Christ;* and this reading, which is indicated in the *margin*, should have been received into the text; and it is an absolute proof that St. Peter calls Jesus Christ GOD, even in the properest sense of the word, with the *article* prefixed. It is no evidence against this doctrine that one MS. of little authority, and the *Syriac* and two *Arabic* versions have Κυριου, *Lord*, instead of Θεου, *God*, as all other MSS. and versions agree in the other reading, as well as the fathers. See in *Griesbach*.

Verse 2. *Grace*] God's favour; *peace*—the effects of that favour in the communication of spiritual and temporal blessings.

Through the knowledge of God] Εν επιγνωσει· *By the acknowledging of God, and of Jesus our Lord.* For those who acknowledge him in all their ways, he will direct their steps. Those who know Christ, and do not acknowledge him before men, can get no multiplication of grace and peace.

Verse 3. *As his Divine power*] His power, which no power can resist, because it is *Divine*—that which properly belongs to the infinite Godhead.

Hath given unto us] Δεδωρημενης· *Hath endowed us with the gifts;* or, hath *gifted us*, as Dr. *Macknight* translates it, who observes that it refers to the gifts which the Holy Spirit communicated to the apostles, to enable them to bring men to *life and godliness;* which were, 1. A complete knowledge of the doctrines of the Gospel. 2. Power to preach and defend their doctrines in suitable language, which their adversaries were not able to gainsay or resist. 3. Wisdom to direct them how to behave in all cases, *where* and *when* to labour; and the *matter* suitable to all different cases, and every variety of persons. 4. Miraculous powers, so that on all proper and necessary occasions they could work miracles for the confirmation of their doctrines and mission.

By *life* and *godliness* we may understand, 1. a *godly life;* or, 2. eternal life as the end, and godliness the way to it; or, 3. what was essentially necessary

　　　　2

A. M. cir. 4064.
A. D. cir. 60.
An. Olymp.
cir. CCIX. 4.
A. U. C. cir.
813.

godliness, [e] through the knowledge of him [f] that hath called us [g] to glory and virtue :

4 [h] Whereby are given unto us exceeding great and precious promises ;

that by these ye might be [i] partakers of the Divine nature, [k] having escaped the corruption that is in the world through lust.

A. M. cir. 4064.
A. D. cir. 60.
An. Olymp.
cir. CCIX. 4.
A. U. C. cir.
813.

---

[e] John xvii. 3.——[f] 1 Thess. ii. 12; iv. 7; 2 Thess. ii. 14; 2 Tim. i. 9; 1 Pet. ii. 9; iii. 9.

[g] Or, *by.*——[h] 2 Cor. vii. 1.——[i] 2 Cor. iii. 18; Eph. iv. 24; Heb. xii. 10; 1 John iii. 2.——[k] Chap. ii. 18, 20.

---

for the *present life*, food, raiment, &c., and what was requisite for the life to come. As they were in a suffering state, and most probably many of them *strangers* in those places. one can scarcely say that they had *all things that* pertained *to life;* and yet so had God worked in their behalf, that none of them perished, either through lack of food or raiment. And as to what was *necessary for godliness*, they had that from the *Gospel ministry*, which it appears was still continued among them, and the *gifts of the Holy Spirit* which were not withdrawn ; and what was farther necessary in the way of personal caution, comfort, and instruction, was supplied by means of these *two epistles.*

That hath called us to glory and virtue] To *virtue* or *courage* as the *means;* and *glory*—the kingdom of heaven, as the *end.* This is the way in which these words are commonly understood, and this sense is plain enough, but the construction is harsh. Others have translated δια δοξης και αρετης, *by his glorious benignity,* a Hebraism for δια της ενδοξου αρετης· and read the whole verse thus : *God by his own power hath bestowed on us every thing necessary for a happy life and godliness, having called us to the knowledge of himself, by his own infinite goodness.* It is certain that the word αρετη, which we translate *virtue* or *courage*, is used, 1 Pet. ii. 9, to express the *perfection* of the Divine nature : *That ye may show forth τας αρετας, the virtues* or PERFECTIONS, *of him who hath called you from darkness into his marvellous light.*

But there is a various reading here which is of considerable importance, and which, from the authorities by which it is supported, appears to be genuine : Του καλεσαντος ημας ιδια δοξη και αρετη, through the knowledge of him who hath called us *by his own glory and power,* or *by his own glorious power.* This is the reading of AC, several others ; and, in effect, of the *Coptic, Armenian, Syriac, Æthiopic, Vulgate, Cyril, Cassiodorus, &c.*

Verse 4. *Whereby are given unto us*] By his own glorious power he hath *freely given unto us exceeding great and invaluable promises.* The Jews were distinguished in a very particular manner by the *promises* which they received from God ; the promises to Abraham, Isaac, Jacob, Moses, and the prophets. God promised to be their God ; to protect, support, and save them ; to give them what was emphatically called the promised land ; and to cause the Messiah to spring from their race. St. Peter intimates to these *Gentiles* that God had also given unto them exceeding great promises ; indeed all that he had given to the Jews, the mere settlement in the promised land excepted ; and this also he had given in all its *spiritual* meaning and force. And besides τα μεγιστα επαγγελματα, these

superlatively great promises, which distinguished the Mosaic dispensation, he had given them τα τιμια επαγγελματα; the *valuable* promises, those which came through the great *price;* enrolment with the Church of God, redemption in and through the blood of the cross, the continual indwelling influence of the Holy Ghost, the resurrection of the body, and eternal rest at the right hand of God It was of considerable consequence to the comfort of the Gentiles that these promises were made to *them,* and that salvation was not exclusively of the Jews.

That by these ye might be partakers] The object of all God's promises and dispensations was to bring fallen man back to the *image of God*, which he had lost. This, indeed, is the sum and substance of the religion of Christ. We have partaken of an *earthly*, *sensual*, and *devilish* nature ; the design of God by Christ is to remove this, and to make us *partakers of the Divine nature ;* and save us from all the *corruption* in principle and fact *which is in the world ;* the source of which is *lust*, επιθυμια, irregular, unreasonable, inordinate, and impure desire ; desire to have, to do, and to be, what God has prohibited, and what would be ruinous and destructive to us were the desire to be granted.

Lust, or irregular, impure desire, is the *source* whence all the corruption which is in the world springs. Lust conceives and brings forth sin ; sin is finished or brought into act, and then brings forth death. This destructive principle is to be rooted out ; and love to God and man is to be implanted in its place. This is every Christian's privilege ; God has promised to purify our hearts by faith ; and that as sin hath reigned unto death, even so shall grace reign through righteousness unto eternal life ; that here we are to be delivered out of the hands of all our enemies, and have even " the thoughts of our hearts so cleansed by the inspiration of God's Holy Spirit, that we shall perfectly love him, and worthily magnify his holy name."

This blessing may be expected by those who are continually escaping, αποφυγοντες, *flying from*, the corruption that is in the world and in themselves. God purifies no heart in which sin is *indulged.* Get pardon through the blood of the Lamb ; feel your need of being purified in heart ; seek that with all your soul ; plead the exceeding great and invaluable promises that refer to this point ; abhor your inward self ; abstain from every appearance of evil ; flee from self and sin to God ; and the very God of peace will sanctify you through body, soul, and spirit, make you burning and shining lights here below, (a proof that he can save to the uttermost all that come to him by Christ,) and afterwards, having guided you by his counsel through life, will receive you into his eternal glory.

A. M. cir. 4064.
A. D. cir. 60.
An. Olymp.
cir. CCIX. 4.
A. U. C. cir.
813.

5 And beside this, [1] giving all diligence, add to your faith, virtue; and to virtue, [m] knowledge;

6 And to knowledge, temperance; and to temperance, patience; and to patience, godliness;

7 And to godliness, brotherly kindness; and [n] to brotherly, kindness charity.

8 For if these things be in you, and abound, they make *you that ye shall* neither *be* [o] barren [p] nor unfruitful in the knowledge of our Lord Jesus Christ.

9 But he that lacketh these things [q] is blind, and cannot see afar off, and hath forgotten that he was [r] purged from his old sins.

A. M. cir. 4064.
A. D. cir. 60.
An. Olymp.
cir. CCIX. 4.
A. U. C. cir.
813.

---

[1] Chap. iii. 18.——[m] 1 Pet. iii. 7.——[n] Gal. vi. 10; 1 Thess. iii. 12; v. 15; 1 John iv. 21.——[o] Gr. *idle.*

[p] John xv. 2; Tit. iii. 14.——[q] 1 John ii. 9, 11.——[r] Eph. v. 26; Heb. ix. 14; 1 John i. 7.

Verse 5. *And beside this*] Notwithstanding what God hath done for you, in order that ye may not receive the grace of God in vain;

Giving all diligence] Furnishing all *earnestness* and *activity:* the original is very emphatic.

Add to your faith] Επιχορηγησατε· *Lead up hand in hand;* alluding, as most think, to the *chorus* in the Grecian dance, who danced with joined hands. See the note on this word, 2 Cor. ix. 10.

Your faith—That faith in Jesus by which ye have been led to embrace the whole Gospel, and by which ye have the evidence of things unseen.

Virtue] Αρετην· *Courage* or *fortitude*, to enable you to profess the faith before men, in these times of persecution.

Knowledge] True wisdom, by which your faith will be increased, and your courage directed, and preserved from degenerating into *rashness.*

Verse 6. *Temperance*] A proper and limited use of all earthly enjoyments, keeping every sense under proper restraints, and never permitting the animal part to subjugate the rational.

Patience] Bearing all trials and difficulties with an even mind, enduring in all, and persevering through all.

Godliness] Piety towards God; a deep, reverential, religious fear; not only worshipping God with every becoming *outward* act, but adoring, loving, and magnifying him in the heart: a disposition indispensably necessary to salvation, but exceedingly rare among professors.

Verse 7. *Brotherly kindness*] Φιλαδελφιαν· *Love of the brotherhood*— the strongest attachment to Christ's flock; feeling each as a member of your own body.

Charity] Αγαπην· *Love* to the whole human race, even to your persecutors: love to God and the brethren they had; love to all *mankind* they must also have. True religion is neither selfish nor insulated; where the love of God is, bigotry cannot exist. Narrow, selfish people, and people of a party, who scarcely have any hope of the salvation of those who do not believe as they believe, and who do not follow with them, have scarcely any religion, though in their own apprehension none is so truly orthodox or religious as themselves.

After αγαπην, *love*, one MS. adds these words, εν δε τη αγαπη την παρακλησιν, *and to this love consolation;* but this is an idle and useless addition.

Verse 8. *For if these things be in you and abound*] If ye possess all these graces, and they increase and abound in your souls, *they will make*—show, you to be neither αργους, *idle*, nor ακαρπους, *unfruitful, in the acknowledgment of our Lord Jesus Christ.* The common translation is here very unhappy: *barren* and *unfruitful* certainly convey the same ideas; but *idle* or *inactive*, which is the proper sense of αργους, takes away this tautology, and restores the sense. The graces already mentioned by the apostle are in themselves active principles; he who was possessed of them, and had them *abounding* in him, could not be *in active*; and he who is not *inactive* in the way of life, must be *fruitful*. I may add, that he who is thus active, and consequently fruitful, will ever be ready at all hazard to acknowledge his Lord and Saviour, by whom he has been brought into this state of salvation.

Verse 9. *But he that lacketh these things*] He, whether Jew or Gentile, who professes to have FAITH in God, and has not added to that FAITH *fortitude, knowledge, temperance, patience, godliness, brotherly kindness,* and universal *love;* is *blind*—his understanding is darkened, *and cannot see afar off,* μυωπαζων, *shutting his eyes against the light, winking*, not able to look truth in the face, nor to behold that God whom he once knew was reconciled to him: and thus it appears he is *wilfully blind*, and *hath forgotten that he was purged from his old sins*—has at last, through his nonimprovement of the grace which he received from God, his faith ceasing to work by love, lost the evidence of things not seen; for, having grieved the Holy Spirit by not showing forth the virtues of him who called him into his marvellous light, he has lost the testimony of his sonship; and then, darkness and hardness having taken place of *light* and *filial confidence*, he first calls all his former experience into doubt, and questions whether he has not put enthusiasm in the place of religion. By these means his darkness and hardness increase, his memory becomes indistinct and confused, till at length he forgets the work of God on his soul, next denies it, and at last asserts that the knowledge of salvation, by the remission of sins, is impossible, and that no man can be saved from sin in this life. Indeed, some go so far as to deny the Lord that bought them; to renounce Jesus Christ as having made atonement for them; and finish their career of apostasy by utterly denying his Godhead. Many cases of this kind have I known; and they are all the consequence of believers not continuing to be workers together with God, after they had experienced his pardoning love.

3

A. M. cir. 4064.
A. D. cir. 60.
An. Olymp.
cir. CCIX. 4.
A. U. C. cir.
813.

10 Wherefore the rather, brethren, give diligence ˢ to make your calling and election sure : for if ye do these things, ᵗ ye shall never fall :

11 For so an entrance shall be ministered unto you abundantly into the everlasting kingdom of our Lord and Saviour Jesus Christ.

12 Wherefore ᵘ I will not be negligent to put you always in remembrance of these things,

ᵛ though ye know *them*, and be established in the present truth.

13 Yea, I think it meet, as ʷ long as I am in this tabernacle, ˣ to stir you up by putting *you* in remembrance ;

14 ʸ Knowing that shortly I must put off *this* my tabernacle, ᶻ even as our Lord Jesus Christ hath showed me.

15 Moreover, I will endeavour that ye may

A. M. cir. 4064.
A. D. cir. 60.
An. Olymp.
cir. CCIX. 4.
A. U. C. cir.
813.

ˢ 1 John iii. 19.——ᵗ Chap. iii. 17.——ᵘ Rom. xv. 14, 15 ; Phil. iii. 1 ; chap. iii. 1 ; 1 John ii. 21 ; Jude 5.——ᵛ 1 Pet. v. 12 ; ch.

iii. 17.——ʷ 2 Cor. v. 1, 4.——ˣ Chap. iii. 1.——ʸ See Deut. iv 21, 22 ; xxxi. 14 ; 2 Tim. iv. 6.——ᶻ John xxi. 18, 19.

Reader, see that the light that is in thee become not darkness ; for if it do, *how great a darkness !*

Verse 10. *Wherefore*] Seeing the danger of apostasy, and the fearful end of them who obey not the Gospel, and thus receive the grace of God in vain ; *give all diligence, σπουδασατε,* hasten, be deeply careful, labour with the most intense purpose of soul,

To make your calling] From deep Gentile darkness into the marvellous light of the Gospel.

And election] Your being *chosen*, in consequence of obeying the heavenly *calling*, to be the people and Church of God. Instead of κλησιν, calling, the *Codex Alexandrinus* has παρακλησιν, *consolation*.

Sure] Βεβαιαν· Firm, solid. For your calling to believe the Gospel, and your *election* to be members of the Church of Christ, will be ultimately unprofitable to you, unless you hold fast what you have received by adding to your faith virtue, knowledge, temperance, &c.

For if ye do these things] If ye be careful and diligent to work out your own salvation, through the grace which ye have already received from God ; *ye shall never fall*, ου μη πταισητε ποτε, ye shall at no time *stumble* or *fall ;* as the Jews have done, and lost their election, Rom. xi. 11, where the same word is used, and as apostates do, and lose their peace and salvation. We find, therefore, that they who *do not* these things *shall fall ;* and thus we see that there is nothing absolute and unconditional in their *election*. There is an addition here in some MSS. and versions which should not pass unnoticed : the *Codex Alexandrinus*, nine others, with the *Syriac*, Erpen's *Arabic, Coptic, Æthiopic, Armenian,* later *Syriac* with an asterisk, the *Vulgate*, and *Bede*, have ινα δια των καλων (υμων) εργων, THAT BY (*your*) GOOD WORKS *ye may make your calling and election firm.* This clause is found in the edition of *Colinæus,* Paris, 1534 ; and has been probably omitted by more recent editors on the supposition that the edition does not make a very *orthodox* sense. But on this ground there need be no alarm, for it does not state that the good works thus required merit either the *calling* and *election*, or the *eternal glory*, of God. He who does not by good works *confirm* his *calling* and *election*, will soon have *neither ;* and although no good works ever did purchase or ever can purchase the kingdom of God, yet no soul can ever scripturally expect to see God who has them not. *I was hungry, and ye gave me no meat ; thirsty, and ye gave me no drink : go, ye cursed. I was hungry, and ye gave me meat ; &c., &c. ; come, ye blessed.*

Verse 11. *For so an entrance shall be ministered*] If ye *give diligence ;* and do *not fall*, an abundant, free, honourable, and triumphant entrance shall be ministered to you into the everlasting kingdom. There seems to be here an allusion to the *triumphs* granted by the Romans to their generals who had distinguished themselves by putting an end to a war, or doing some signal military service to the state. (See the whole account of this military pageant in the note on 2 Cor. ii. 14.) "Ye shall have a triumph, in consequence of having conquered your foes, and led captivity captive."

Instead of *everlasting kingdom,* αιωνιον βασιλειαν, two MSS. have επουρανιον, *heavenly kingdom ;* and several MSS. omit the word και Σωτηρος, and Saviour.

Verse 12. *Wherefore I will not be negligent*] He had already written *one* epistle, this is the *second ;* and probably he meditated more should he be spared. He plainly saw that there was no way of entering into eternal life but that which he described from the 5th to the 10th verse ; and although they knew and were established in the present truth, yet he saw it necessary to bring these things frequently to their recollection.

Verse 13. *As long as I am in this tabernacle*] By *tabernacle* we are to understand his *body ;* and hence several of the versions have σωματι, *body*, instead of σκηνωματι, *tabernacle*. Peter's mode of speaking is very remarkable : as long as I AM in this *tabernacle ;* so then the *body* was not *Peter*, but *Peter* dwelt in that *body*. Is not this a proof that St. Peter believed his soul to be very distinct from his body ? As a man's house is the place where he dwells, so the body is the house where the soul dwells.

Verse 14. *Knowing that shortly I must put off*] St. Peter plainly refers to the conversation between our Lord and himself, related John xxi. 18, 19. And it is likely that he had now a particular intimation that he was *shortly* to seal the truth with his blood. But as our Lord told him that his death would take place when he should be *old*, being aged now he might on this ground fairly suppose that his departure was at hand.

Verse 15. *Moreover, I will endeavour*] And is not this endeavour seen in these two epistles ? By leaving these among them, even after his decease, they had *these things* always in remembrance.

After my decease] Μετα την εμην εξοδον· *After my going out*, i. e. of his *tabernacle*. The real Peter was not open to the eye, nor palpable to the touch ; he

A. M. cir. 4064.
A. D. cir. 60.
An. Olymp.
cir. CCIX. 4.
A. U. C. cir.
813.

be able after my decease to have these things always in remembrance.

16 For we have not followed [a] cunningly devised fables, when we made known unto you the power and coming of our Lord Jesus Christ, but [b] were eye witnesses of his majesty.

17 For he received from God the Father ho-

nour and glory, when there came such a voice to him from the excellent glory, [c] This is my beloved Son, in whom I am well pleased.

18 And this voice which came from heaven we heard, when we were with him in [d] the holy mount.

19 We have also a more sure word of pro

A. M. cir. 4064.
A. D. cir. 60.
An. Olymp.
cir. CCIX. 4.
A. U. C. cir.
813.

---

[a] 1 Cor. i. 17; ii. 1, 4; 2 Cor. ii. 17; iv. 2.——[b] Matt. xvii. 1, 2; Mark ix. 2; John i. 14; 1 John i. 1; iv. 14.——[c] Matt. iii.

17; xvii. 5; Mark i. 11; ix. 7; Luke iii. 22; ix. 35.——[d] See Exod. iii. 5; Josh. v. 15; Matt. xvii. 1.

---

was concealed in that *tabernacle* vulgarly supposed to be *Peter.* There is a thought very similar to this in the last conversation of Socrates with his friends. As this great man was about to drink the poison to which he was condemned by the Athenian judges, his friend CRITO said, " But how would you be buried ?—SOCRATES : Just as you please, *if you can but catch me,* and I do not elude your pursuit. Then, gently smiling, he said : I cannot persuade Crito, ως εγω ειμι ουτος ὁ Σωκρατης ὁ νυνι διαλεγομενος, that *I* AM *that Socrates who now converses with you;* but he thinks that *I am he,* ὁν οψεται ολιγον ὑστερον νεκρον, και ερωτα πως εδι με θαπτειν, *whom he shall shortly see dead;* and he asks how I would be buried ? I have asserted that, after I have drunk the poison, *I should no longer remain with you, but shall depart to certain felicities of the blessed.*" PLATONIS *Phædo,* Oper., vol. i., edit. Bipont., p. 260.

Verse 16. *Cunningly devised fables*] Σεσοφισμενοις μνθοις. I think, with Macknight and others, from the apostle's using εποπται, *eye witnesses,* or rather *beholders,* in the end of the verse, it is probable that he means those *cunningly devised fables* among the heathens, concerning the *appearance of their gods on earth in human form.* And to gain the greater credit to these fables, the priests and statesmen instituted what they called the *mysteries* of the gods, in which the fabulous appearance of the gods was represented in mystic *shows.* But one particular *show* none but the fully initiated were permitted to *behold;* hence they were entitled εποπται, *beholders.* This *show* was probably some resplendent image of the god, imitating life, which, by its *glory,* dazzled the eyes of the beholders, while their ears were ravished by hymns sung in its praise ; to this it was natural enough for St. Peter to allude, when speaking about the transfiguration of Christ. Here the indescribably resplendent majesty of the great God was *manifested,* as far as it could be, in conjunction with that human body in which the fulness of the Divinity dwelt. *And we,* says the apostle, *were* εποπται, *beholders,* της εκεινου μεγαλειοτητος, *of his own majesty.* Here was no *trick,* no feigned show ; we saw him in his glory whom thousands saw before and afterwards ; and we have made known to you the *power and coming,* παρουσιαν, the appearance and presence, of our Lord Jesus ; and we call you to feel the exceeding greatness of this power in your conversion, and the glory of this appearance in his revelation by the power of his Spirit to your souls. These things we have witnessed, and these things ye have experienced ; and therefore we can confidently say

that neither you nor we have followed cunningly devised fables, but that blessed Gospel which is the power of God to the salvation of every one that believes.

Verse 17. *For he received—honour and glory*] In his transfiguration our Lord received from the Father *honour* in the *voice* or declaration which said, *This is my Son, the beloved One, in whom I have delighted.* And he received *glory,* when, penetrated with, and involved in, that *excellent glory,* the *fashion of his countenance was altered,* for his face did shine as the sun, and his raiment was white and glistering exceeding white like snow ; which most glorious and *preternatural appearance* was a *confirmation* of the *supernatural voice,* as the *voice* was of this *preternatural appearance :* and thus his Messiahship was *attested* in the most complete and convincing manner.

Verse 18. *And this voice—we heard*] That is, himself, James, and John heard it, and saw this glory ; for these only were the εποπται, *beholders,* on the holy mount. It is worthy of remark that our blessed Lord, who came to give a *new law* to mankind, appeared on this *holy mount* with *splendour* and *great glory,* as God did when he came on the *holy mount, Sinai,* to give the *old law* to Moses. And when the voice came from the excellent glory, *This is my Son, the beloved One, in whom I have delighted ; hear him :* the authority of the old law was taken away. Neither *Moses* nor *Elijah,* the law nor the prophets, must *tabernacle* among men, as teaching the whole way of salvation, and affording the means of eternal life ; these things they had *pointed out,* but these things they did not *contain ;* yet the fulfilment of their types and predictions rendered their declarations more *firm* and incontestable. See below.

Verse 19. *We have also a more sure word of prophecy*] Εχομεν βεβαιοτερον τον προφητικον λογον· *We have the prophetic doctrine more firm* or more *confirmed ;* for in this sense the word βεβαιοω is used in several places in the New Testament. See 1 Cor. i. 6 : *Even as the testimony of Christ* εβεβαιωθη, *was* CONFIRMED, *among you.* 2 Cor. i. 21 : *Now he which stablisheth us,* ὁ δε βεβαιων ἡμας, *who* CONFIRMETH *us.* Col. ii. 7 : *Rooted and built up in him, and established in the faith,* βεβαιουμένοι, CONFIRMED *in the faith.* Heb. ii. 3 : *How shall we escape if we neglect so great salvation* ἡτις εβεβαιωθη, *which was* CONFIRMED *to us.* Heb. vi. 16 : *And an oath,* εις βεβαιωσιν, *for* CONFIRMATION. This is the literal sense of the passage in question ; and this sense removes that ambiguity from the text which has given rise to so many differ-

A. M. cir. 4064.
A. D. cir. 60.
An. Olymp.
cir. CCIX. 4.
A. U. C. cir.
813.

phecy; whereunto ye do well that ye take heed, as unto ^e a light that shineth in a dark place, until the day dawn, and ^f the day star arise in your hearts:

20 Knowing this first, that ^g no prophecy of the Scripture is of any private interpretation.

21 For ^h the prophecy came not ⁱ in old time by the will of man: ^k but holy men of God spake *as they were* moved by the Holy Ghost.

A. M. cir. 4064.
A. D. cir. 60.
An. Olymp.
cir. CCIX 4.
A. U. C. cir.
813.

---

e Psa. cxix. 105; John v. 35.——f Rev. ii. 28; xxii. 16; see 2 Cor. iv. 4, 6.——g Rom. xii. 6.

h 2 Tim. iii. 16; 1 Pet. i. 11.——i Or, *at any time.*——k 2 Sam. xxiii. 2; Luke i. 70; Acts i. 16; iii. 18.

---

ent interpretations. Taken according to the common translation, it seems to say that *prophecy* is a surer evidence of Divine revelation than *miracles ;* and so it has been understood. The meaning of the apostle appears to be this: The law and the prophets have spoken concerning Jesus Christ, and Isaiah has particularly pointed him out in these words : *Behold my servant whom I uphold, my* CHOSEN IN WHOM MY SOUL DELIGHTETH ; *I have put my Spirit upon him, and he shall bring forth judgment to the Gentiles ; to open the blind eyes, to bring out the prisoners from the prison, and* THEM THAT SIT IN DARKNESS *out of the prison house,* Isa. xlii. 1, 7. Now both at his *baptism,* Matt. iii. 17, and at his *transfiguration,* Jesus Christ was declared to be this *chosen person, God's only Son, the beloved One in* WHOM HE DELIGHTED. The voice, therefore, from heaven, and the miraculous transfiguration of his person, have confirmed the prophetic doctrine concerning him. And to this doctrine, thus confirmed, ye do well to take heed; for it is *that* light that *shines in the dark place*—in the Gentile world, as well as among the Jews ; giving light to them that *sit in darkness, and bringing the prisoners out of the prison house :* and this ye must continue to do till the *day* of his second, last, and most glorious appearing to judge the world comes ; and the *day star,* φωσφορος, *this light-bringer, arise in your hearts*— manifest himself to your eternal *consolation.* Or perhaps the latter clause of the verse might be thus understood : The prophecies concerning Jesus, which have been so signally confirmed to us on the holy mount, have always been as a *light shining in a dark place,* from the time of their delivery to the time in which the *bright day* of Gospel light and salvation dawned forth, and the Son of righteousness has arisen in our souls, with healing in his rays. And to this all who waited for Christ's appearing have taken heed. The word φωσφορος, *phosphorus,* generally signified the planet *Venus,* when she is the *morning star ;* and thus she is called in most European nations.

Verse 20. *Knowing this first*] Considering this as a *first principle, that no prophecy of the Scripture,* whether that referred to above, or any other, is of any *private interpretation*—proceeds from the prophet's *own knowledge* or *invention,* or was the offspring of *calculation* or *conjecture.* The word επιλυσις signifies also *impetus, impulse ;* and probably this is the best sense here : not by the mere private impulse of his own mind.

Verse 21. *For the prophecy came not in old time*] That is, in any former time, *by the will of man*—by a man's own searching, conjecture, or calculation ; *but holy men of God*—persons separated from the world,

and devoted to God's service, *spake, moved by the Holy Ghost.* So far were they from *inventing* these prophetic declarations concerning Christ, or any future event, that they were φερομενοι, *carried away,* out of themselves and out of the whole region, as it were, of human knowledge and conjecture, by the Holy Ghost, who, without their knowing any thing of the matter, dictated to them what to speak, and what to write ; and so far above their knowledge were the words of the prophecy, that they did not even know the *intent* of those words, but *searched what, or what manner of time the Spirit of Christ which was in them did signify, when it testified beforehand the sufferings of Christ, and the glory that should follow.* See 1 Pet. i. 11, 12, and the notes there.

1. As the writer of this epistle asserts that he was on the holy mount with Christ when he was transfigured, he must be either *Peter, James,* or *John,* for there was no other person present on that occasion except *Moses* and *Elijah,* in their glorious bodies. The epistle was never attributed to *James* nor *John ;* but the uninterrupted current, where its Divine inspiration was granted, gave it to *Peter* alone. See the *preface.*

2. It is not unfrequent for the writers of the New Testament to draw a comparison between the Mosaic and Christian dispensations ; and the comparison generally shows that, *glorious* as the former was, it had no glory in comparison of the glory that excelleth. St. Peter seems to touch here on the same point ; the Mosaic dispensation, with all the light of prophecy by which it was illustrated, was only as a *lamp shining in a dark place.* There is a propriety and delicacy in this image that are not generally noticed : a lamp in the dark gives but a very small portion of light, and only to those who are *very near to it ;* yet it always gives light enough to make *itself visible,* even at a *great distance ;* though it enlightens not the space between it and the beholder, it is still literally the *lamp shining in a dark place.* Such was the Mosaic dispensation ; it gave a little light to the Jews, but shone not to the Gentile world, any farther than to make itself *visible.* This is compared with the Gospel under the emblem of *daybreak,* and the *rising of the sun.* When the sun is even eighteen degrees below the horizon *daybreak* commences, as the rays of light begin then to diffuse themselves in our atmosphere, by which they are reflected upon the earth. By this means a whole *hemisphere* is enlightened, though but in a partial degree ; yet this increasing every moment, as the sun approaches the horizon, prepares for the full manifestation of his resplendent

orb : so the ministry of John Baptist, and the initiatory ministry of Christ himself, prepared the primitive believers for his full manifestation on the day of pentecost and afterwards. Here the sun rose in his strength, bringing light, heat, and life to all the inhabitants of the earth. So far, then, as a *lantern* carried in a *dark night* differs from and is inferior to the beneficial effects of *daybreak*, and the *full light* and *heat of a meridian sun ;* so far was the Mosaic dispensation, in its beneficial effects, inferior to the Christian dispensation.

3. Perhaps there is scarcely any point of view in which we can consider *prophecy* which is so satisfactory and conclusive as that which is here stated ;

that is, far from *inventing* the subject of their own predictions, the ancient prophets did not even *know* the meaning of what themselves wrote. They were *carried beyond themselves* by the influence of the *Divine Spirit*, and after ages were alone to discover the object of the prophecy ; and the fulfilment was to be the absolute proof that the prediction was of God, and that it was of no *private invention*—no *discovery* made by *human sagacity* and *wisdom*, but by the especial revelation of the all-wise God. This is sufficiently evident in all the prophecies which have been already fulfilled, and will be equally so in those yet to be fulfilled ; the events will point out the prophecy, and the prophecy will be seen to be fulfilled in that event.

CHAPTER II.

False teachers foretold, who shall bring in destructive doctrines and shall pervert many, but at last be destroyed by the judgments of God, 1–3. *Instances of God's judgments in the rebellious angels,* 4. *In the antediluvians,* 5. *In the cities of Sodom and Gomorrha,* 6–8. *The Lord knoweth how to deliver the godly, as well as to punish the ungodly,* 9. *The character of those seducing teachers and their disciples ; they are unclean, presumptuous, speak evil of dignities, adulterous, covetous, and cursed,* 10–14. *Have forsaken the right way, copy the conduct of Balaam, speak great swelling words, and pervert those who had escaped from error,* 15–19. *The miserable state of those who, having escaped the corruption that is in the world, have turned back like the dog to his vomit, and the washed swine to her wallowing in the mire,* 20–22.

A. M. cir. 4064.
A. D. cir. 60.
An. Olymp.
cir. CCIX. 4.
A. U. C. cir.
813.

BUT [a] there were false prophets also among the people, even as [b] there shall be false teachers among you, who privily shall bring in damnable heresies, even [c] denying the Lord [d] that bought them, [e] and bring upon themselves swift destruction.

2 And many shall follow their [f] pernicious ways ; by reason of whom the

A. M. cir. 4064.
A. D. cir. 60.
An. Olymp.
cir. CCIX. 4.
A. U. C. cir.
813.

---

[a] Deut. xiii. 1.——[b] Matt. xxiv. 11 ; Acts xx. 30 ; 1 Cor. xi. 19 ; 1 Tim. iv. 1 ; 2 Timothy iii. 1, 5 ; 1 John iv. 1 ; Jude 18. [c] Jude 4.

[d] 1 Cor. vi. 20 ; Gal. iii. 13 ; Eph. i. 7 ; Heb. x. 29 ; 1 Pet. i. 18 ; Rev. v. 9.——[e] Phil. iii. 19.——[f] Or, *lascivious ways*, as some copies read.

NOTES ON CHAP. II.

Verse 1. *But there were false prophets*] There were not only holy men of God among the Jews, who prophesied by Divine inspiration, but there were also false prophets, whose prophecies were from their own imagination, and perverted many.

As there shall be false teachers among you] At a very early period of the Christian Church many heresies sprung up ; but the chief were those of the Ebionites, Cerinthians, Nicolaitans, Menandrians, and Gnostics, of whom many strange things have been spoken by the primitive fathers, and of whose opinions it is difficult to form any satisfactory view. They were, no doubt, bad enough, and their opponents in general have doubtless made them worse. By what name those were called of whom the apostle here speaks, we cannot tell. They were probably some sort of apostate Jews, or those called the Nicolaitans. See the *preface.*

Damnable heresies] Αἱρεσεις απωλειας· *Heresies of destruction ;* such as, if followed, would lead a man to perdition. And these παρεισαξουσιν, they will *bring in privately*—cunningly, without making much noise, and as covertly as possible. It would be better to translate *destructive heresies* than *damnable.*

Denying the Lord that bought them] It is not certain whether God the Father be intended here, or our Lord Jesus Christ ; for God is said to have *purchased* the Israelites, Exod. xv. 16, and to be the *Father that had bought them*, Deut. xxxii. 6, and the words may refer to these or such like passages ; or they may point out Jesus Christ, who had *bought them with his blood ;* and the *heresies*, or *dangerous opinions*, may mean such as opposed the Divinity of our Lord, or his meritorious and sacrificial death, or such opinions as bring upon those who hold them swift destruction. It seems, however, more natural to understand the Lord that bought them as applying to *Christ*, than otherwise ; and if so, this is another proof, among many, 1. That none can be saved but by Jesus Christ. 2. That through their own wickedness some may perish for whom Christ died.

Verse 2. *Many shall follow*] WILL follow, because determined to gratify their sinful propensities.

Pernicious ways] Ταις απωλειαις· *Their destructions ;* i. e. the *heresies of destruction*, or *destructive opinions*, mentioned above. But instead of απωλειαις, *destructions*, ασελγειαις, *lasciviousnesses* or *uncleannesses*, is the reading of ABC, and upwards of *sixty others*, most of which are among the most ancient,

2

A. M. cir 4064.
A. D. cir. 60.
An. Olymp.
cir. CCIX. 4.
A. U. C. cir.
813.

way of truth shall be evil spoken of.

3 And ^g through covetousness shall they with feigned words ^h make merchandise of you: ⁱ whose judgment

now of a long time lingereth not, and their damnation slumbereth not.

4 For if God spared not ^k the angels ^l that sinned, but ^m cast *them* down to hell, and delivered *them* into

A. M. cir. 4064.
A. D. cir. 60.
An. Olymp.
cir. CCIX. 4.
A. U. C. cir.
813.

---

^g Rom. xvi. 18; 2 Cor. xii. 17, 18; 1 Timothy vi. 5; Tit. i. 11.
^h 2 Cor. ii. 17; chap. i. 16.——ⁱ Deut. xxxii. 35; Jude 4, 15.

^k Job iv. 18; Jude 6.——^l John viii. 44; 1 John iii. 8.
^m Luke viii. 31; Rev. xx. 2, 3.

---

correct, and authentic. This is the reading also of both the *Syriac,* all the *Arabic,* the *Coptic, Æthiopic, Armenian, Slavonic, Vulgate, Chrysostom, Theophylact, Œcumenius,* and *Jerome.* A very few, and those of little repute, have the word in the text.

The word *lasciviousnesses* is undoubtedly the true reading, and this points out what the nature of the heresies was: it was a sort of Antinomianism; they pampered and indulged the lusts of the flesh; and, if the Nicolaitans are meant, it is very applicable to them, for they taught the community of wives, &c. Griesbach has received this reading into the text.

By reason of whom] These were persons who professed *Christianity;* and because they were called Christians, and followed such abominable practices, the *way of truth*—the Christian religion, βλασφημη-θησεται, was *blasphemed.* Had they called themselves by any name but that of *Christ,* his religion would not have suffered.

Verse 3. *And through covetousness*] That they might get money to spend upon their lusts, *with feigned words,* πλαστοις λογοις, with *counterfeit tales, false narrations,* of pretended facts, *lying miracles, fabulous legends.* "In this single sentence," says Dr. Macknight, "there is a clear prediction of the iniquitous practices of those great merchants of souls, the Romish clergy, who have rated all crimes, even the most atrocious, at a fixed price; so that if their doctrine be true, whoever pays the price may commit the crime without hazarding his salvation." How the popish Church has made merchandise of souls, needs no particular explanation here. It was this abominable doctrine that showed to some, then in that Church, the absolute necessity of a reformation.

Whose judgment now of a long time] From the beginning God has condemned sin, and inflicted suitable punishments on transgressors; and has promised in his word, from the earliest ages, to pour out his indignation on the wicked. The punishment, therefore, *so long ago predicted,* shall fall on these impure and incorrigible sinners; and the *condemnation* which is denounced against them *slumbers not*—it is alert, it is on its way, it is hurrying on, and must soon overtake them.

Verse 4. *For if God spared not the angels*] The angels were originally placed in a state of probation; some having fallen and some having stood proves this. How long that probation was to last to them, and what was the particular *test* of their fidelity, we know not; nor indeed do we know what was their *sin;* nor *when* nor *how* they fell. St. Jude says *they kept not their first estate, but left their own habitation;* which seems to indicate that they got *discontented* with their lot, and aspired to higher honours, or perhaps to celestial

domination. The tradition of their fall is in all countries and in all religions, but the accounts given are various and contradictory; and no wonder, for we have no direct revelation on the subject. *They kept not their first estate,* and *they sinned,* is the sum of what we know on the subject; and here curiosity and conjecture are useless.

But cast them down to hell, and delivered them into chains of darkness] Αλλα σειραις ζοφου ταρταρωσας παρεδωκεν εις κρισιν τετηρημενους· *But with chains of darkness confining them in Tartarus, delivered them over to be kept to judgment;* or, *sinking them into Tartarus, delivered them over into custody for punishment, to chains of darkness.* Chains of darkness is a highly poetic expression. Darkness binds them on all hands; and so dense and strong is this darkness that it cannot be broken through; they cannot deliver themselves, nor be delivered by others.

As the word *Tartarus* is found nowhere else in the *New Testament,* nor does it appear in the *Septuagint,* we must have recourse to the Greek writers for its meaning. Mr. *Parkhurst,* under the word ταρταροω, has made some good collections from those writers, which I here subjoin.

"The Scholiast on Æschylus, *Eumen.,* says: *Pindar* relates that *Apollo* overcame the *Python* by force; wherefore the earth endeavoured ταρταρωσαι, *to cast* him *into Tartarus. Tzetzes* uses the same word, ταρταροω, for *casting* or *sending into Tartarus;* and the compound verb καταταρταροω is found in *Apollodorus;* in *Didymus'* Scholia on *Homer;* in *Phurnutus,* De Nat. Deor., p. 11, edit. *Gale;* and in the book Περι Ποταμων, which is extant among the works of *Plutarch.* And those whom Apollodorus styles καταταρταρωθεντας, he in the same breath calls ῥιφθεντας εις Ταρταρον, *cast into Tartarus.* Thus the learned *Windet,* in *Pole's* Synopsis. We may then, I think, safely assert that ταρταρωσας, in St. Peter, means not, as *Mede* (Works, fol., p. 23) interprets it, *to adjudge to,* but *to cast into, Tartarus;* ῥιπτειν εις Ταρταρον, as in *Homer,* cited below. And in order to know what was the precise intention of the apostle by this expression, we must inquire what is the accurate import of the term Ταρταρος. Now, it appears from a passage of *Lucian,* that by Ταρταρος was meant, in a *physical* sense, *the bounds* or *verge of this material system;* for, addressing himself to ΕΡΩΣ, Cupid or *Love,* he says: Συ γαρ εξ αφανους και κεχυμενης αμορφιας ΤΟ ΠΑΝ εμορφωσας, κ. τ. λ. 'Thou formedst the *universe* from its confused and chaotic state; and, after separating and dispersing the circumfused chaos, in which, as in one common sepulchre, the *whole world* lay buried, thou drovest it to the confines or recesses of outer *Tartarus*—

A. M. cir. 4064.
A. D. cir. 60.
An. Olymp.
cir. CCIX. 4.
A. U. C. cir,
813.

chains of darkness, to be reserved unto judgment;

5 And spared not the old world, but saved ⁿ Noah the eighth *person,* ᵒ a preacher of righteousness, ᵖ bringing in the flood upon the world of the ungodly;

ⁿ Gen. vii. 1, 7, 23 ; Heb. xi. 7 ; 1 Pet. iii. 20.——ᵒ 1 Pet. iii. 19.——ᵖ Chap. iii. 6.

' Where iron gates and bars of solid brass
Keep it in durance irrefrangible,
And its return prohibit.'

" The ancient Greeks appear to have received, by tradition, an account of the punishment of the ' fallen angels,' and of bad men after death ; and their poets did, in conformity I presume with that account, make *Tartarus* the place where the giants who rebelled against *Jupiter,* and the souls of the wicked, were confined. 'Here,' saith *Hesiod,* Theogon., lin. 720, 1, ' the rebellious *Titans* were bound in penal chains.'

Τοσσον ενερθ' ὑπο γης, ὁσον ουρανος εστ' απο γαιης.
Ισον γαρ τ' απο γης ες ΤΑΡΤΑΡΟΝ ηεροεντα.

'As far beneath the earth as earth from heaven ;
For such the distance thence to *Tartarus.*'

" Which description will very well agree with the proper sense of Tartarus, if we take the earth for the centre of the material system, and reckon from our zenith, or the extremity of the heavens that is over our heads. But as the Greeks imagined the earth to be of a boundless depth, so it must not be dissembled that their poets speak of *Tartarus* as *a vast pit* or *gulf in the bowels of it.*— Thus Hesiod in the same poem, lin. 119, calls it—

ΤΑΡΤΑΡΑ τ' ηεροεντα μυχῳ χθονος ευρυοδειης·

'Black Tartarus, within earth's spacious womb.'

" And Homer, Iliad viii., lin. 13, &c., introduces Jupiter threatening any of the gods who should presume to assist either the Greeks or the Trojans, that he should either come back wounded to heaven, or be sent to *Tartarus.*

Η μιν ἑλων ῥιψω ες ΤΑΡΤΑΡΟΝ ηεροεντα,
Τηλε μαλ', ἡχι βαθιστον ὑπο χθονος εστι βερεθρον,
Ενθα σιδηρειαι τε πυλαι, και χαλκεος ουδος,
Τοσσον ενερθ' αἰδεω, ὁσον ουρανος εστ' απο γαιης.

' Or far, O far, from steep *Olympus* thrown,
Low in the deep *Tartárean* gulf shall groan.
That gulf which iron gates and brazen ground
Within the earth inexorably bound ;
As deep beneath th' infernal centre hurl'd,
As from that centre to the ethereal world.'
POPE.

' Where, according to *Homer's* description, Iliad viii., lin. 480, 1,—

———— Ουτ' αυγης ὑπεριονος ηελιοιο
Τερπουτ', ουτ' ανεμοισι· βαθυς δε τε ΤΑΡΤΑΡΟΣ αμφις.

' No sun e'er gilds the gloomy horrors there,
No cheerful gales refresh the lazy air,
But murky *Tartarus* extends around.' POPE.
886

6 And, ᑫ turning the cities of Sodom and Gomorrha into ashes, condemned *them* with an overthrow, ʳ making *them* an ensample unto those that after should live ungodly;

A. M. cir. 4064.
A. D. cir. 60.
An. Olymp.
cir. CCIX. 4.
A. U. C. cir.
813.

ᑫ Genesis xix. 24 ; Deut. xxix. 23 ; Jude 7.——ʳ Numbers xxvi. 10.

" Or, in the language of the old Latin poet, (cited by Cicero, Tuscul., lib. i. cap. 15,)

Ubi rigida constat crassa caligo inferum.

" On the whole, then, ταρταρουν, in St. Peter, is the same as ῥιπτειν ες Ταρταρον, *to throw into Tartarus,* in *Homer,* only rectifying the poet's mistake of *Tartarus* being in the bowels of the earth, and recurring to the original sense of that word above explained, which when applied to *spirits* must be interpreted *spiritually ;* and thus ταρταρωσας will import that God cast the apostate angels out of his presence *into that ζοφος του σκοτους, blackness of darkness,* (2 Pet. ii. 17 ; Jude, ver. 13,) where they will be for ever banished *from the light of his countenance,* and from the *beatifying influence of the ever blessed Three,* as truly as a person plunged into the *torpid boundary of this created system* would be from the *light of the sun* and the *benign operations of the material heavens.*"

By *chains of darkness* we are to understand a *place of darkness* and *wretchedness,* from which it is *impossible for them to escape.*

Verse 5. *Spared not the old world*] The apostle's argument is this : If God spared not the rebellious angels, nor the sinful antediluvians, nor the cities of Sodom and Gomorrha, he will not spare those wicked teachers who corrupt the pure doctrines of Christianity.

Saved Noah the eighth] Some think that the words should be translated, *Noah the eighth preacher of righteousness ;* but it seems most evident, from 1 Pet. iii. 20, that *eight persons* are here meant, which were the whole that were saved in the ark, *viz.* Shem, Ham, Japhet, and their three wives, six ; Noah's wife seven ; and Noah himself the *eighth.* The form of expression, ογδοον Νωε, *Noah the eighth,* i. e. Noah and *seven* more, is most common in the Greek language. So in APPIAN, *Bell. Pun.,* p. 12, Τριτος δε ποτε εν σπηλαιω κρυπτομενος ελαθε, sometimes *he the third* (i. e. he with two others) *lay hid in a cave.* ANDOCIDES, *Orat.* iv. p. 295 : Αἱρεθεις επι τουτῳ δεκατος αυ-ος, *he himself the tenth* (i. e. he and nine others) *were chosen to this.* See a number of other examples in *Kypke.*

World of the ungodly] A whole race *without God*— without any pure *worship* or rational religion.

Verse 6. *The cities of Sodom and Gomorrha*] See the notes on Gen. xix. for an account of the sin and punishment of these cities.

Making them an ensample] These three words, ὑποδειγμα, παραδειγμα, and δειγμα, are used to express the same idea ; though the former may signify an *example to be shunned,* the second an *example to be*

A. M. cir. 4064.
A. D. cir. 60.
An. Olymp.
cir. CCIX. 4.
A. U. C. cir.
813.

7 And ⁸ delivered just Lot, vexed with the filthy conversation of the wicked :

8 (ᵗ For that righteous man dwelling among them, ᵘ in seeing and hearing, vexed *his* righteous soul from day to day with *their* unlawful deeds :)

9 ᵛ The Lord knoweth how to deliver the godly out of temptations, and to reserve the unjust unto the day of judgment to be punished :

10 But chiefly ʷ them that walk after the flesh in the lust of uncleanness, and despise

---

ˣ government. ʸ Presumptuous *are they*, self-willed, they are not afraid to speak evil of dignities.

11 Whereas ᶻ angels, which are greater in power and might, bring not railing accusation ᵃ against them before the Lord.

12 But these, ᵇ as natural brute beasts, made to be taken and destroyed, speak evil of the things that they understand not, and shall utterly perish in their own corruption ;

13 ᶜ And shall receive the reward of unright-

A. M. cir. 4064.
A. D. cir. 60.
An. Olymp.
cir. CCIX. 4.
A. U. C. cir.
813.

ˢ Gen. xix. 16.——ᵗ Wisd. xix. 17.——ᵘ Psa. cxix. 139, 158; Ezek. ix. 4.——ᵛ Psa. xxxiv. 17, 19 ; 1 Cor. x. 13.——ʷ Jude 4,

7, 8, 10, 16.——ˣ Or, *dominion*.——ʸ Jude 8.——ᶻ Jude 9.——ᵃ Some read, *against themselves*.——ᵇ Jer. xii. 3 ; Jude 10.——ᶜ Phil. iii. 19.

---

followed, and the third a *simple exhibition*. But these differences are not always observed.

Verse 7. *Vexed with the filthy conversation*] Καταπονουμενον ὑπο της των αθεσμων εν ασελγεια αναστροφης· *Being exceedingly pained with the unclean conduct of those lawless persons.* What this was, see in the history, Gen. xix., and the notes there.

Verse 8. *That righteous man dwelling among them*] Lot, after his departure from Abraham, A. M. 2086, lived at Sodom till A. M. 2107, a space of about twenty years ; and, as he had a *righteous soul*, he must have been *tormented* with the abominations of that people *from day to day*.

The word εβασανιζεν, *tormented*, is not less emphatic than the word καταπονουμενον, *grievously pained*, in the preceding verse, and shows what this man must have felt in dwelling so long among a people so abandoned.

Verse 9. *The Lord knoweth how to deliver the godly*] The preservation and deliverance of Lot gave the apostle occasion to remark, that God knew as well to *save* as to *destroy ;* and that his *goodness* led him as forcibly to save righteous Lot, as his *justice* did to destroy the rebellious in the instances already adduced. And the design of the apostle in producing these examples is to show to the people to whom he was writing that, although God would destroy those false teachers, yet he would powerfully save his faithful servants from their contagion and from their destruction. We should carefully observe, 1. That the godly man is not to be preserved *from* temptation. 2. That he will be preserved *in* temptation. 3. That he will be delivered *out* of it.

Verse 10. *But chiefly them that walk*] That is, God will in the most signal manner punish them that walk after the flesh—addict themselves to sodomitical practices, and the *lust of pollution ;* probably alluding to those most abominable practices where men abuse themselves and abuse one another.

Despise government.] They brave the power and authority of the civil magistrate, practising their abominations so as to keep out of the reach of the letter of the law ; and they *speak evil of dignities*—they blaspheme civil government, they abhor the restraints laid upon men by the laws, and would wish all governments destroyed that they might live as they list.

Presumptuous are they] Τολμηται· They are bold and daring, headstrong, regardless of fear.

Self-willed] Αυθαδεις· Self-sufficient ; presuming on themselves ; following their own opinions, which no authority can induce them to relinquish.

Are not afraid to speak evil of dignities.] They are lawless and disobedient, spurn all human authority, and speak contemptuously of all legal and civil jurisdiction. Those in general despise governments, and speak evil of dignities, who wish to be under no control, that they may act as freebooters in the community.

Verse 11. *Whereas angels, &c.*] This is a difficult verse, but the meaning seems to be this : The holy angels, who are represented as bringing an account of the actions of the fallen angels before the Lord in judgment, simply state the facts without exaggeration, and without permitting any thing of a bitter, reviling, or railing spirit, to enter into their accusations. See Zech. iii. 1, and Jude 9 ; to the former of which St. Peter evidently alludes. But these persons, not only speak of the actions of men which they conceive to be wrong, but do it with untrue colourings, and the greatest malevolence. Michael, the archangel, treated a damned spirit with courtesy ; he only said, *The Lord rebuke thee, Satan !* but these treat the rulers of God's appointment with disrespect and calumny.

Before the Lord.] Παρα Κυριω is wanting in a number of MSS. and most of the *versions*.

Verse 12. *But these, as natural brute beasts*] Ὡς αλογα ζωα φυσικα· As those natural animals void of reason, following only the gross instinct of nature, being governed neither by reason nor religion,

Made to be taken and destroyed] Intended to be taken with nets and gins, and then destroyed, because of their fierce and destructive nature ; so these false teachers and insurgents must be treated ; first incarcerated, and then brought to judgment, that they may have the reward of their doings. And thus, by *blaspheming what they do not understand*, they at last *perish in their own corruption ; i. e.* their corrupt doctrines and vicious practices.

Verse 13. *They that count it pleasure to riot in the day time.*] Most sinners, in order to practise their abominable pleasures, seek the secrecy of the night ; but these, bidding defiance to all decorum, decency,

2

A. M. cir. 4064.
A. D. cir. 60.
An. Olymp.
cir. CCIX. 4.
A. U. C. cir.
813.

eousness, *as they that count it* pleasure [d] to riot in the day time. [e] Spots *they are* and blemishes, sporting themselves with their own deceivings while [f] they feast with you :

14 Having eyes full of [g] adultery, and that cannot cease from sin; beguiling unstable souls : [h] a heart they have exercised with covetous practices; cursed children :

15 Which have forsaken the right way, and are gone astray, following the way of [i] Balaam *the son* of Bosor, who loved the wages of unrighteousness;

16 But was rebuked for his iniquity; the dumb ass, speaking with man's voice, forbade the madness of the prophet.

17 [k] These are wells without water, clouds

A. M. cir. 4064.
A. D. cir. 60.
An. Olymp.
cir. CCIX. 4.
A. U. C. cir.
813.

---

[d] See Romans xiii. 13.——[e] Jude 12.——[f] 1 Cor. xi. 20, 21. [g] Gr. *an adulteress.*

[h] Jude 11.——[i] Num. xxii. 5, 7, 21, 23, 28 ; Jude 11.——[k] Jude 12, 13.

---

and shame, take the open day, and thus proclaim their impurities to the sun.

Spots—and blemishes] They are a disgrace to the Christian name.

Sporting themselves] Forming opinions which give license to sin, and then acting on those opinions; and thus rioting in their own deceits.

With their own deceivings] Εν ταις απαταις. But instead of this, AB, and almost all the versions and several of the fathers, have εν ταις αγαπαις, *in your love feasts,* which is probably the true reading.

While they feast with you] It appears they held a kind of communion with the Church, and attended sacred festivals, which they desecrated with their own unhallowed opinions and conduct.

Verse 14. *Having eyes full of adultery*] Μοιχαλιδος· *Of an adulteress;* being ever bent on the gratification of their sensual desires, so that they are represented as having *an adulteress constantly before their eyes,* and that their eyes can take in no other object but *her.* But instead of μοιχαλιδος, of an *adulteress,* the Codex *Alexandrinus,* three others, with the *Coptic, Vulgate,* and one copy of the *Itala,* together with several of the *fathers,* have μοιχαλιας, of *adultery.*

Cannot cease from sin] *Which cease not from sin;* they might cease from sin, but they do not ; they love and practise it. Instead of ακαταπαυστους, *which cannot cease,* several MSS. and versions have ακαταπαυστου, and this requires the place to be read, *Having eyes full of adultery and incessant sin.* The images of sinful acts were continually floating before their disordered and impure fancy. This figure of speech is very common in the Greek writers; and *Kypke* gives many instances of it, which indeed carry the image too far to be here translated.

Beguiling unstable souls] The metaphor is taken from adulterers seducing unwary, inexperienced, and light, trifling women ; so do those false teachers seduce those who are not established in righteousness.

Exercised with covetous practices] The metaphor is taken from the *agonistæ* in the Grecian games, who exercised themselves in those feats, such as *wrestling, boxing, running, &c.,* in which they proposed to contend in the public games. These persons had their hearts schooled in nefarious practices; they had *exercised themselves* till they were perfectly *expert* in all the arts of seduction, overreaching, and every kind of fraud.

Cursed children] Such not only live under God's curse here, but they are heirs to it hereafter.

Verse 15. *Which have forsaken the right way*] As Balaam did, who, although God showed him the right way, took one contrary to it, preferring the reward offered him by Balak to the approbation and blessing of God.

The way of Balaam] Is the *counsel* of Balaam. He counselled the Moabites to give their most beautiful young women to the Israelitish youth, that they might be enticed by them to commit *idolatry.* See the notes on Num. xxii. 5, &c., and xxiii. 1, &c.

The son of Bosor] Instead of Βοσορ, Βοσορ two ancient MSS. and some of the versions have Βεωρ, *Beor,* to accommodate the word to the Hebrew text and the Septuagint. The difference in this name seems to have arisen from mistaking one letter for another in the Hebrew name, בעור *Beor,* for בצור *Betsor* or *Bosor;* *tsaddi* צ and *ain* ע, which are very like each other, being interchanged.

Verse 16. *The dumb ass, speaking with man's voice*] See the note on Num. xxii. 28.

The madness of the prophet.] Is not this a reference to the speech of the ass, as represented in the Targums of Jonathan ben Uzziel and Jerusalem? " Wo to thee, Balaam, thou sinner, thou madman : there is no wisdom found in thee." These words contain nearly the same expressions as those in St. Peter.

Verse 17. *These are wells without water*] Persons who, by their *profession,* should furnish *the water of life* to souls athirst for salvation ; but they have not this water; they are *teachers* without *ability* to *instruct;* they are *sowers,* and have no *seed* in their basket. Nothing is more cheering in the deserts of the east than to meet with a *well of water;* and nothing more distressing, when parched with thirst, than to meet with a well that contains no water.

Clouds that are carried with a tempest] In a time of great *drought,* to see *clouds* beginning to cover the face of the heavens raises the expectation of rain ; but to see these *carried off* by a sudden *tempest* is a dreary disappointment. These false teachers were equally as unprofitable as the empty well, or the light, dissipated cloud.

To whom the mist of darkness is reserved] That is, an eternal separation from the presence of God, and the glory of his power. They shall be thrust into *outer darkness,* Matt. viii. 12 ; into the utmost degrees of misery and despair. False and corrupt teachers will be sent into the lowest hell ; and be " the most downcast, underfoot vassals of perdition."

It is scarcely necessary to notice a various reading here, which, though very different in sound, is nearly

2

A. M. cir. 4064.
A. D. cir. 60.
An. Olymp.
cir. CCIX. 4.
A. U. C. cir.
813.

that are carried with a tempest; to whom the mist of darkness is reserved for ever.

18 For when [1] they speak great swelling *words* of vanity, they allure through the lusts of the flesh, *through much* wantonness, those that [m] were [n] clean escaped from them who live in error.

19 While they promise them [o] liberty, they themselves are [p] the servants of corruption : for of whom a man is overcome, of the same is he brought in bondage.

20 For [q] if after they [r] have escaped the pol-

lutions of the world, [s] through the knowledge of the Lord and Saviour Jesus Christ, they are again entangled therein, and overcome, the latter end is worse with them than the beginning.

21 For [t] it had been better for them not to have known the way of righteousness, than, after they have known *it*, to turn from the holy commandment delivered unto them.

22 But it is happened unto them according to the true proverb, [u] The dog *is* turned to his own vomit again; and the sow that was washed to her wallowing in the mire.

A. M. cir. 4064.
A. D. cir. 60.
An. Olymp.
cir. CCIX. 4.
A. U. C. cir.
813.

---

[1] Jude 16.——[m] Acts ii. 40; chap. i. 4; verse 20.——[n] Or, *for a little ; or, a while ;* as some read.——[o] Gal. v. 13 ; 1 Pet. ii. 16. [p] John viii. 34 ; Rom. vi. 16.

[q] Matt. xii. 45 ; Luke xi. 26 ; Hebrews vi. 4, &c. ; x. 26, 27. [r] Chap. i. 4 ; ver. 18.——[s] Chapter i. 2.——[t] Luke xii. 47, 48 ; John ix. 41 ; xv. 22.——[u] Prov. xxvi. 11.

---

the same in sense. Instead of νεφελαι, *clouds*, which is the common reading, και ὁμιχλαι, *and mists*, or perhaps more properly *thick darkness*, from ὁμου, *together*, and αχλυς, *darkness*, is the reading in ABC, sixteen others, Erpen's *Arabic*, later *Syriac*, *Coptic*, *Æthiopic*, and *Vulgate*, and several of the *fathers*. This reading Griesbach has admitted into the text.

Verse 18. *They speak great swelling* words *of vanity*] The word ὑπερογκα signifies things of great magnitude, grand, superb, sublime ; it sometimes signifies *inflated, tumid, bombastic*. These false teachers spoke of great and high things, and no doubt promised their disciples the greatest privileges, as they themselves pretended to a high degree of illumination ; but they were all false and vain, though they tickled the fancy and excited the desires of the flesh ; and indeed this appears to have been their object. And hence some think that the impure sect of the Nicolaitans is meant. See the *preface*.

Those that were clean escaped] Those who, through hearing the doctrines of the Gospel, had been converted, were perverted by those false teachers.

Verse 19. *While they promise them liberty*] Either to live in the highest degrees of spiritual good, or a freedom from the Roman yoke ; or from the yoke of the law, or what they might term needless restraints. Their own conduct showed the falsity of their system ; for they were slaves to every disgraceful lust.

For of whom a man is overcome] This is an allusion to the ancient custom of selling for slaves those whom they had conquered and captivated in war. The ancient law was, that a man might either kill him whom he overcame in battle, or *keep him* for a slave. These were called *servi*, slaves, from the verb *servare*, to *keep* or *preserve*. And they were also called *mancipia*, from *manu capiuntur*, they are taken captive by the hand of their enemy. Thus the person who is overcome by his lusts is represented as being the slave of those lusts. See Rom. vi. 16, and the note there.

Verse 20. *The pollutions of the world*] *Sin* in general, and particularly superstition, idolatry, and lasciviousness. These are called μιασματα, *miasmata*, things that *infect, pollute,* and *defile*. The word was

anciently used, and is in use at the present day, to express those noxious particles of effluvia proceeding from persons infected with contagious and dangerous diseases ; or from dead and corrupt bodies, stagnant and putrid waters, marshes &c., by which the sound and healthy may be infected and destroyed.

The world is here represented as one large, putrid marsh, or corrupt body, sending off its destructive *miasmata* everywhere and in every direction, so that none can escape its contagion, and none can be healed of the great epidemic disease of sin, but by the mighty power and skill of God. St. Augustine has improved on this image : " The whole world," says he, " is one great diseased man, lying extended from east to west, and from north to south ; and to heal this great sick man, the almighty Physician descended from heaven." Now, it is by the *knowledge* of *the Lord and Saviour Jesus Christ*, as says St. Peter, that we *escape* the destructive influence of these contagious *miasmata*. But if, *after having been* healed, and *escaped* the death to which we were exposed, we get *again entangled*, εμπλακεντες, *enfolded, enveloped* with them; then *the latter end will be worse than the beginning* : forasmuch as we shall have sinned against more light, and the soul, by its conversion to God, having had all its powers and faculties greatly improved, is now, being repolluted, more capable of iniquity than before, and can bear more expressively the image of the earthly.

Verse 21. *For it had been better for them not to have known*] For the reasons assigned above ; because they have sinned against more mercy, are capable of more sin, and are liable to greater punishment.

The holy commandment] The whole religion of Christ is contained in this one commandment, " Thou shalt love the Lord thy God with all thy heart, with all thy soul, with all thy mind, and with all thy strength ; and thy neighbour as thyself." He who obeys this great commandment, and this by the grace of Christ is possible to every man, is saved from sinning either against his God or against his neighbour. Nothing less than this does the religion of Christ require.

Verse 22. *According to the true proverb*] **This**

seems to be a reference to Prov. xxvi. 11: כְּכֶלֶב שָׁב עַל קֵאוֹ *kekeleb shab al keo; as the dog returneth to his vomit, so a fool repeateth his folly.* In substance this proverb is found among the rabbins; so Midrash Ruth, in Sohar Chadash, fol. 62 : *Orphah is returned to her mire, Ruth persevered in spirit;* and again, Ibid. fol. 64 : " *Orphah, which is* נֶפֶשׁ הַבְּהֵמִית *nephesh habbehemith,* the bestial soul, is returned to her mire.''

The Greeks have something like it; so *Arrian,* Dissert. Epict. l. iv. c. 11, says : Απελθε και χοιρῳ διαλεγου, ιν' εν βορβορῳ μη κυλιηται, " Go and reason with the swine, lest he be rolled in the mire.'' This is called a *true proverb*: for it is a *fact* that a dog will eat up his own vomit; and the swine, howsoever carefully washed, will again wallow in the mire. As applied here it is very expressive : the poor sinner, having heard the Gospel of Christ, was led to *loathe* and *reject* his sin; and, on his application to God for mercy, was *washed* from his unrighteousness. But he is here represented as *taking up again* what he had before *rejected,* and *defiling* himself in that from which he had been *cleansed.*

Here is a sad proof of the possibility of falling from grace, and from very high degrees of it too. These had *escaped from the contagion that was in the world;* they had had true repentance, and *cast* up "their soursweet morsel of sin ;'' they had been *washed* from all their filthiness, and this must have been through the blood of the Lamb; yet, after all, they went back, got *entangled* with their old sins, *swallowed down* their formerly *rejected* lusts, and rewallowed in the mire of corruption. It is no wonder that God should say, *the latter end is worse with them than the beginning :* reason and nature say it *must* be so; and Divine justice says it *ought* to be so; and the person himself must confess that it is *right* that it *should* be so. But how dreadful is this state ! How dangerous when the person has abandoned himself to his old sins ! Yet it is not said that it is impossible for him to return to his Maker; though his case be deplorable, it is not utterly hopeless; the leper may yet be made clean, and the dead may be raised. Reader, is thy backsliding a grief and burden to thee ? Then thou art not far from the kingdom of God; believe on the Lord Jesus, and thou shalt be saved,

---

CHAPTER III.

The apostle shows his design in writing this and the preceding epistle, 1, 2. *Describes the nature of the heresies which should take place in the last times,* 3–8. *A thousand years with the Lord are but as a day,* 9. *He will come and judge the world as he has promised, and the heavens and the earth shall be burnt up,* 10. *How those should live who expect these things,* 11, 12. *Of the new heavens and the new earth, and the necessity of being prepared for this great change,* 13, 14. *Concerning some difficult things in St. Paul's epistles,* 15, 16. *We must watch against the error of the wicked, grow in grace, and give all glory to God,* 17, 18.

A. M. cir. 4064.
A. D. cir. 60.
An. Olymp.
cir. CCIX. 4.
A. U. C. cir.
813.

THIS second epistle, beloved, I now write unto you; in *both* which [a] I stir up your pure minds by way of remembrance :

2 That ye may be mindful of the words which were spoken before by the holy prophets, [b] and of the commandment of us the apostles of the Lord and Saviour :

3 [c] Knowing this first, that there shall come in the last days scoffers, [d] walking after their own lusts,

A. M. cir. 4064.
A. D. cir. 60.
An. Olymp.
cir. CCIX. 4.
A. U. C. cir.
813.

---

[a] Chap. i. 13.——[b] Jude 17.   [c] 1 Tim. iv. 1; 2 Tim. iii. 1; Jude 18.——[d] Chap. ii. 10.

NOTES ON CHAP. III.

Verse 1. *This second epistle*] In order to guard them against the seductions of false teachers, he calls to their remembrance the doctrine of the ancient prophets, and the commands or instructions of the apostles, all founded on the same basis.

He possibly refers to the prophecies of *Enoch,* as mentioned by *Jude,* ver. 14, 15; of *David,* Psa. l. 1, &c.; and of *Daniel,* xii. 2, relative to the coming of our Lord to judgment : and he brings in the instructions of the apostles of Christ, by which they were directed how to prepare to meet their God.

Verse 3. *Knowing this first*] Considering this in an *especial* manner, that those prophets predicted the coming of false teachers : and their being now in the Church proved how clearly they were known to God, and showed the Christians at Pontus the necessity of having no intercourse or connection with them.

There shall come—scoffers] Persons who shall endeavour to turn all religion into ridicule, as this is the most likely way to depreciate truth in the sight of the giddy multitude. The scoffers, having no solid argument to produce against revelation, endeavour to make a scaramouch of some parts; and then affect to laugh at it, and get superficial thinkers to laugh with them.

Walking after their own lusts] Here is the true *source* of all infidelity. The Gospel of Jesus is *pure* and *holy,* and requires a *holy heart* and *holy life.* They wish to follow their own *lusts,* and consequently cannot brook the restraints of the Gospel : therefore they labour to prove that it is not true, that they may get rid of its injunctions, and at last succeed in persuading themselves that it is a forgery; and then throw the reins on the neck of their evil propensities. Thus their opposition to revealed truth began and ended in their own *lusts.*

A. M. cir. 4064.
A. D. cir. 60.
An. Olymp.
cir. CCIX. 4.
A. U. C. cir.
813.

4 And saying, [e] Where is the promise of his coming? for since the fathers fell asleep, all things continue as *they were* from the beginning of the creation.

5 For this they willingly are ignorant of, that

A. M. cir. 4064.
A. D. cir. 60.
An. Olymp.
cir. CCIX. 4.
A. U. C. cir.
813.

[f] by the word of God the heavens were of old, and the earth [g] standing [h] out of the water and in the water:

6 [i] Whereby the world that then was, being overflowed with water, perished:

---

[e] Isa. v. 19; Jer. xvii. 15; Ezek. xii. 22, 27; Matt. xxiv. 48; Luke xii. 45.——[f] Gen. i. 6, 9; Psa. xxxiii. 6; Heb. xi. 3.——[g] Gr.

consisting.——[h] Psa. xxiv. 2; cxxxvi. 6; Col. i. 17.——[i] Gen. vii. 11, 21, 22, 23; chap. ii. 5.

There is a remarkable *addition* here in almost every MS. and *version* of note: *There shall come in the last days*, IN MOCKERY, εν εμπαιγμονη, *scoffers walking after their own lusts.* This is the reading of ABC, eleven others, both the *Syriac*, all the *Arabic, Coptic, Æthiopic, Vulgate,* and several of the *fathers.* They come *in mockery;* this is their *spirit* and *temper;* they have no desire to find out *truth;* they take up the Bible merely with the design of *turning it into ridicule.* This reading Griesbach has received into the text.

The last days] Probably refer to the conclusion of the Jewish polity, which was then at hand.

Verse 4. *Where is the promise of his coming?*] Perhaps the false teachers here referred to were such as believed in the *eternity of the world:* the prophets and the apostles had foretold its destruction, and they took it for granted, if this were true, that the terrestrial machine would have begun long ago to have shown some symptoms of decay; but they found that since the patriarchs died all things remained as they were from the foundation of the world; that is, men were propagated by natural generation, one was born and another died, and the course of nature continued regular in the seasons, succession of day and night, generation and corruption of animals and vegetables, &c.; for they did not consider the power of the Almighty, by which the whole can be annihilated in a moment, as well as created. As, therefore, they saw none of these changes, they presumed that there *would be none,* and they intimated that there *never had been any.* The apostle combats this notion in the following verse.

Verse 5. *For this they willingly are ignorant of*] They shut their eyes against the light, and refuse all evidence; what does not answer their purpose *they will not know.* And the apostle refers to a *fact* that militates against their hypothesis, with which they refused to acquaint themselves; and their ignorance he attributes to their unwillingness to learn the true state of the case.

By the word of God the heavens were of old] I shall set down the Greek text of this extremely difficult clause: Ουρανοι ησαν εκπαλαι, και γη εξ ύδατος και δι' ύδατος συνεστωσα, τω του Θεου λογω· translated thus by Mr. *Wakefield:* "A heaven and an earth formed out of water, and by means of water, by the appointment of God, had continued from old time." By Dr. *Macknight* thus: "The heavens were anciently, and the earth of water: and through water the earth consists by the word of God." By *Kypke* thus: "The heavens were of old, and the earth, which is framed, by the word of God, from the waters, and between the waters.". However we take the words, they seem to refer to the origin of the earth. It was the opinion

of the remotest antiquity that the earth was formed out of *water,* or a primitive *moisture* which they termed ύλη, hulé, a *first matter* or *nutriment* for all things; but *Thales* pointedly taught αρχην δε των παντων ύδωρ ειναι, that all things derive their existence from water, and this very nearly expresses the sentiment of Peter, and nearly in his own terms too. But is this doctrine true? It must be owned that it appears to be the doctrine of Moses: *In the beginning,* says he, *God made the heavens and the earth; and the earth was without form and void; and darkness was upon the face of the deep.* Now, these *heavens* and *earth* which God made in the beginning, and which he says were at first *formless* and *empty,* and which he calls the *deep,* are in the very next verse called *waters;* from which it is evident that Moses teaches that the earth was made out of some *fluid substance,* to which the name of *water* is properly given. And that the earth was at first in a *fluid* mass is most evident from its *form;* it is not *round,* as has been demonstrated by measuring some *degrees* near the north *pole,* and under the *equator;* the result of which proved that the figure of the earth was that of an *oblate spheroid,* a figure nearly resembling that of an *orange.* And this is the form that any *soft* or elastic body would assume if whirled rapidly round a centre, as the earth is around its axis. The measurement to which I have referred shows the earth to be *flatted* at the *poles,* and *raised* at the *equator.* And by this measurement it was demonstrated that the diameter of the earth at the *equator* was *greater* by about twenty-five miles than at the *poles.*

Now, considering the earth to be thus formed εξ ύδατος, of *water,* we have next to consider what the apostle means by δι' ύδατος, variously translated by *out of, by means of,* and *between, the water.*

Standing out of the water gives no sense, and should be abandoned. If we translate *between the waters,* it will bear some resemblance to Gen. i. 6, 7: *And God said, Let there be a firmament in the midst of,* בתוך *bethoch,* between, *the waters; and let it divide the waters from the waters: and God divided the waters which were under the firmament from the waters which were above the firmament;* then it may refer to the whole of the *atmosphere,* with which the earth is everywhere surrounded, and which contains all the *vapours* which belong to our globe, and without which we could neither have animal nor vegetative life. Thus then the *earth,* or *terraqueous globe,* which was originally formed *out of water,* subsists *by water;* and by *means* of that very water, the water compacted with the earth—the *fountains of the great deep,* and the waters in the atmosphere—*the windows of heaven,* Gen. vii. 11, the antediluvian earth was *destroyed,* as

2

A. M. cir. 4064.
A. D. cir. 60.
An. Olymp.
cir. CCIX. 4.
A. U. C. cir.
813.

7 But *k* the heavens and the earth which are now, by the same word are kept in store, reserved unto [1] fire against the day of judgment and perdition of ungodly men.

8 But, beloved, be not ignorant of this one thing, that one day *is* with the Lord as a thousand years, and *m* a thousand years as one day.

k Ver. 10.——[1] Matt. xxv. 41 ; 2 Thess. i. 8.——*m* Psa. xc. 4.
n Hab. ii. 3 ; Heb. x. 37.——*o* Isa. xxx. 18 ; 1 Pet. iii. 20 ; ver. 15.——*p* Ezek. xviii. 23, 32 ; xxxiii. 11.——*q* Rom. ii. 4 ; 1 Tim.

A. M. cir. 4064.
A. D. cir. 60.
An. Olymp.
cir. CCIX. 4.
A. U. C. cir.
813.

9 *n* The Lord is not slack concerning his promise, as some men count slackness ; but *o* is long-suffering to us-ward, *p* not willing that any should perish, but *q* that all should come to repentance.

10 But *r* the day of the Lord will come as a thief in the night ; in the which *s* the heavens shall pass away with a great noise, and the ele-

ii. 4.——*r* Matt. xxiv. 43 ; Luke xii. 39 ; 1 Thess. v. 2 ; Rev. iii. 3 ; xvi. 15.——*s* Psa. cii. 26 ; Isa. li. 6 ; Matt. xxiv. 35 ; Mark xiii. 31 ; Romans viii. 20 ; Heb. i. 11 ; Rev. xx. 11 ; xxi. 1.

St. Peter states in the next verse : the terraqueous globe, which was formed originally of water or a fluid substance, the *chaos* or *first matter*, and which was suspended in the *heavens*—the atmosphere, enveloped with water, by means of which water it was preserved ; yet, because of the wickedness of its inhabitants, was destroyed by those very same waters out of which it was originally made, and by which it subsisted.

Verse 7. *But the heavens and the earth, which are now*] The present earth and its atmosphere, which are liable to the same destruction, because the same *means* still exist, (for there is still *water* enough to drown the earth, and there is *iniquity* enough to induce God to destroy it and its inhabitants,) are nevertheless *kept in store*, τεθησαυρισμενοι, *treasured up*, kept in God's storehouse, to be destroyed, not by *water*, but by *fire* at the day of judgment.

From all this it appears that those *mockers* affected to be ignorant of the *Mosaic account* of the formation of the earth, and of its destruction by the waters of the deluge ; and indeed this is implied in their stating that *all things continued as they were from the creation*. But St. Peter calls them back to the Mosaic account, to prove that this was false ; for the earth, &c., which were then formed, had perished by the *flood ;* and that the present earth, &c., which were formed out of the preceding, should, at the day of judgment, perish by the *fire* of God's wrath.

Verse 8. *Be not ignorant*] Though *they* are wilfully ignorant, neglect not *ye* the means of instruction.

One day is *with the Lord as a thousand years*] That is : All time is as nothing before him, because in the *presence* as in the *nature* of God all is *eternity ;* therefore nothing is *long*, nothing *short*, before him ; no *lapse* of ages impairs his purposes, nor need he *wait* to find convenience to execute those purposes. And when the *longest period* of time has passed by, it is but as a *moment* or indivisible *point* in comparison of *eternity*. This thought is well expressed by PLUTARCH, *Consol. ad Apoll. :* " If we compare the time of life with eternity, we shall find no difference between *long* and *short*. Τα γαρ χιλια, και τα μυρια ετη, στιγμη τις εστιν αοριστος, μαλλον δε μοριον τι βραχυτατον στιγμης· for a *thousand* or *ten thousand years* are but a certain *indefinite point*, or rather the *smallest part of a point*." The words of the apostle seem to be a quotation from Psa. xc. 4.

Verse 9. *The Lord is not slack*] They probably in their *mocking* said, " Either God had made no such

promise to judge the world, destroy the earth, and send ungodly men to perdition ; or if he had, he had forgotten to fulfil it, or had not convenient time or leisure." To some such *mocking* the apostle seems to refer ; and he immediately shows the reason why deserved punishment is not inflicted on a guilty world.

But is long-suffering] It is not *slackness, remissness*, nor want of due *displacence* at sin, that induced God to prolong the respite of ungodly men ; but his long-suffering, his *unwillingness* that any should perish : and therefore he spared them, that they might have additional offers of grace, and *be led to repentance*—to deplore their sins, implore God's mercy, and find redemption through the blood of the Lamb.

As God is *not willing that any should perish*, and as he is *willing that all should come to repentance*, consequently he has never devised nor decreed the damnation of any man, nor has he rendered it impossible for any soul to be saved, either by *necessitating* him to do evil, that he might die for it, or *refusing him the means* of recovery, without which he could not be saved.

Verse 10. *The day of the Lord will come*] See Matt. xxiv. 43, to which the apostle seems to allude.

The heavens shall pass away with a great noise] As the *heavens* mean here, and in the passages above, the whole *atmosphere*, in which all the terrestrial vapours are lodged ; and as *water* itself is composed of two gases, eighty-five parts *in weight* of oxygen, and fifteen of hydrogen, or two parts *in volume* of the latter, and one of the former ; (for if these quantities be put together, and several electric sparks passed through them, a chemical union takes place, and water is the product ; and, *vice versa*, if the galvanic spark be made to pass through water, a portion of the fluid is immediately decomposed into its two constituent gases, oxygen and hydrogen ;) and as the *electric* or *ethereal fire* is that which, in all likelihood, God will use in the general conflagration ; the noise occasioned by the application of this fire to such an immense *congeries* of *aqueous* particles as float in the atmosphere, must be terrible in the extreme. Put a drop of water on an anvil, place over it a piece of iron red hot, strike the iron with a hammer on the part above the drop of water, and the report will be as loud as a musket ; when, then, the whole strength of those opposite agents is brought together into a state of conflict, the *noise*, the *thunderings*, the *innumerable explosions*, (till every particle of water on the earth and in the atmosphere is, by the action of the fire, reduced into its component gaseous

A. M. cir. 4064.
A. D. cir. 60.
An. Olymp.
cir. CCIX. 4.
A. U. C. cir.
813.

ments shall melt with fervent heat, the earth also, and the works that are therein, shall be burned up.

11 *Seeing* then *that* all these things shall be dissolved, what manner *of persons* ought ye to be ᵗ in *all* holy conversation and godliness,

12 ᵘ Looking for and ᵛ hasting unto the com-

ing of the day of God, wherein the heavens being on fire, shall ʷ be dissolved, and the elements shall ˣ melt with fervent heat?

A. M. cir. 4064.
A. D. cir. 60.
An. Olymp.
cir. CCIX. 4.
A. U. C. cir.
813.

13 Nevertheless we, according to his promise, look for ʸ new heavens and a new earth, wherein dwelleth righteousness.

14 Wherefore, beloved, seeing that ye look

ᵗ 1 Pet. i. 15.——ᵘ 1 Cor. i. 7; Tit. i. 13.——ᵛ Or, *hasting the coming.*——ʷ Psa. l. 3 ; Isa. xxxiv. 4.

ˣ Mic. i. 4 ; ver. 10.——ʸ Isaiah lxv. 17; lxvi. 22; Rev xxi. 1.

---

parts,) will be *frequent, loud, confounding,* and *terrific,* beyond every comprehension but that of God himself.

The elements shall melt with fervent heat] When the *fire* has conquered and decomposed the *water,* the elements, στοιχεια, the *hydrogen* and *oxygen* airs or gases, (the former of which is most highly inflammable, and the latter an eminent supporter of all combustion,) will occupy *distinct* regions of the atmosphere, the hydrogen by its very great levity ascending to the top, while the oxygen from its superior specific gravity will keep *upon* or *near* the surface of the earth ; and thus, if different substances be once ignited, the fire, which is supported in this case, not only by the oxygen which is one of the constituents of atmospheric air, but also by a great additional quantity of oxygen obtained from the decomposition of all aqueous vapours, will rapidly seize on all other substances, on all terrestrial particles, and the whole frame of nature will be necessarily torn in pieces, and *thus the earth and its works be burned up.*

Verse 11. *All these things shall be dissolved*] They will all be *separated,* all *decomposed ;* but none of them *destroyed.* And as they are the original matter out of which God formed the terraqueous globe, consequently they may enter again into the *composition* of a *new system ;* and therefore the apostle says, ver. 13 : *we look for new heavens and a new earth*—the others being *decomposed,* a new system is to be formed out of their materials. There is a wonderful philosophic propriety in the words of the apostle in describing this most awful event.

What manner of persons *ought ye to be*] Some put the note of interrogation at the end of this clause, and join the remaining part with the 12th verse, thus : *Seeing then that all these things shall be dissolved, what manner of persons ought ye to be ? By holy conversation and godliness, expecting and earnestly desiring the coming of the day of God, &c.* Only those who walk in holiness, who live a godly and useful life, can contemplate this most awful time with joy.

The word σπευδοντας, which we translate *hasting unto,* should be rendered *earnestly desiring,* or *wishing for ;* which is a frequent meaning of the word in the best Greek writers.

Verse 12. *The heavens being on fire*] See on ver. 10. It was an ancient opinion among the heathens, that the earth should be burnt up with fire ; so OVID, *Met.,* lib. i. v. 256.

Esse quoque in fatis reminiscitur, adfore tempus,
Quo mare, quo tellus, correptaque regia cœli
Ardeat ; et mundi moles operosa laboret.

"Remembering in the fates a time when fire
   Should to the battlements of heaven aspire,
And all his blazing world above should burn,
And all the inferior globe to cinders turn."

DRYDEN.

Minucius Felix tells us, xxxiv. 2, that it was a common opinion of the Stoics that, the moisture of the earth being consumed, the whole world would catch fire. The *Epicureans* held the same sentiment ; and indeed it appears in various authors, which proves that a tradition of this kind has pretty generally prevailed in the world. But it is remarkable that none have fancied that it will be destroyed by *water.* The tradition, founded on the declaration of God, was against this ; therefore it was not received.

Verse 13. *We, according to his promise, look for new heavens*] The promise to which it is supposed the apostle alludes, is found Isa. lxv. 17 : *Behold, I create new heavens and a new earth ; and the former shall not be remembered, nor come into mind ;* and chap. lxvi. 22 : *For as the new heavens and the new earth which I will make shall remain before me, saith the Lord, so shall your seed, &c.* Now, although these may be interpreted of the *glory of the Gospel dispensation,* yet, if St. Peter refer to them, they must have a more *extended* meaning.

It does appear, from these promises, what the apostle says here, and what is said Rev. xxi. 27; xxii. 14, 15, that the present earth, though destined to be burned up, will not be *destroyed,* but be *renewed* and *refined, purged* from all *moral* and *natural imperfection,* and made the endless abode of blessed spirits. But this state is certainly to be expected *after the day of judgment ;* for on this the apostle is very express, who says the conflagration and renovation are to take place at *the judgment of the great day ;* see ver. 7, 8, 10, and 12. That such an event *may* take place is very *possible ;* and, from the terms used by St. Peter, is very *probable.* And, indeed, it is more *reasonable* and *philosophical* to conclude that the earth shall be *refined* and *restored,* than finally *destroyed.* But this has nothing to do with what some call the *millennium state ;* as this shall take place when *time,* with the present state and order of things, shall be no more.

Verse 14. *Seeing that ye look for such things*] As ye profess that such a state of things shall take place, and have the expectation of enjoying the blessedness of it, *be diligent* in the use of every means and influence of grace, *that ye may be found of him*—the Lord Jesus, the Judge of quick and dead, *without spot*—any contagion of sin in your souls, *and blameless*—being not only *holy* and *innocent,* but *useful* in your lives.

A. M. cir. 4064.
A. D. cir. 60.
An. Olymp.
cir. CCIX. 4.
A. U. C. cir.
813.

for such things, be diligent ᶻ that ye may be found of him in peace, without spot, and blameless :

15 And account *that* ᵃ the long-suffering of our Lord *is* salvation ; even as our beloved brother Paul also, according to the wisdom given unto him, hath written unto you ;

16 As also in all *his* epistles, ᵇ speaking in them of these things ; in which are some things hard to be understood, which they that are unlearned and unstable wrest, as *they do* also the other scriptures, unto their own destruction.

A. M. cir. 4064
A. D. cir. 60.
An. Olymp.
cir. CCIX. 4.
A. U. C. cir.
813.

ᶻ 1 Cor. i. 8 ; xv. 58 ; Phil. i. 10 ; 1 Thessalonians iii. 13 ; v. 23.

ᵃ Rom. ii. 4 ; 1 Pet. iii. 20 ; ver. 9.——ᵇ Rom. viii. 19 ; 1 Cor. xv. 24 ; 1 Thess. iv. 15.

Verse 15. *And account* that *the long-suffering of our Lord*] Conclude that God's long-suffering with the world is a proof that he designs men to be saved ; *even as our beloved brother Paul.* "This epistle being written to those to whom the *first epistle* was sent, the persons to whom the Apostle Paul wrote concerning the *long-suffering* of God were the Jewish and Gentile Christians in Pontus, Galatia, Cappadocia, Asia, and Bithynia. Accordingly, we know he wrote to the *Ephesians,* (chap. ii. 3, 4, 5,) to the *Colossians,* (chap. i. 21,) and to *Timothy,* (1 Epist., chap. ii. 3, 4,) things which imply that God's bearing with sinners is intended for their salvation. The persons to whom Peter's epistles were sent were, for the most part, Paul's converts."—*Macknight.*

According to the wisdom given unto him] That is, according to the measure of the Divine inspiration, by which he was qualified for the Divine work, and by which he was so capable of entering into the deep things of God. It is worthy of remark that Paul's epistles are ranked among the *Scriptures ;* a term applied to those writings which are divinely inspired, and to those only.

Verse 16. *As also in all* his *epistles, speaking in them of these things*] Paul, in all his epistles, says Dr. *Macknight,* has spoken of the things written by Peter in this letter. For example, he has spoken of *Christ's coming to judgment ;* 1 Thess. iii. 13 ; iv. 14–18 ; 2 Thess. i. 7–10 ; Titus ii. 13. And of the *resurrection of the dead,* 1 Cor. xv. 22 ; Phil. iii. 20, 21. And of the *burning of the earth ;* 2 Thess. i. 8. And of the *heavenly country ;* 2 Cor. v. 1–10. And of the *introduction of the righteous into that country ;* 1 Thess. iv. 17 ; Heb. iv. 9 ; xii. 14, 18, 24. And of the *judgment of all mankind by Christ ;* Rom. xiv. 10.

In which are some things hard to be understood] Δυσνοητα τινα· That is, if we retain the common reading εν οις, *in* or *among which things,* viz., what he says of the day of judgment, the resurrection of the body, &c., &c., there are some things difficult to be comprehended, and from which a wrong or false meaning may be taken. But if we take the reading of AB, twelve others, with both the *Syriac,* all the *Arabic,* and *Theophylact,* εν αις, the meaning is more general, as εν αις must refer to επιστολαις, *epistles,* for this would intimate that there were difficulties in all the epistles of St. Paul ; and indeed in what ancient writings are there not difficulties ? But the papists say that the decision of all matters relative to the faith is not to be expected from the Scriptures on this very account, but must be received from the Church ; *i. e.* the Popish or Romish Church. But what evidence have we that Church can infallibly solve any of those difficulties ? We have none ! And till we have an express, unequivocal revelation from heaven that an unerring spirit is given to that Church, I say, for example, to the present Church of Rome, with the pope called *Pius VII.* at its head, we are not to receive its pretensions. Any Church may pretend the same, or any number of equally learned men as there are of *cardinals* and *pope* in the conclave ; and, after all, it would be but the opinion of so many men, to which no absolute certainty or infallibility could be attached.

This verse is also made a pretext to deprive the common people of reading the word of God ; because the *unlearned* and *unstable* have sometimes *wrested this word to their own destruction :* but if it be human learning, and stability in any system of doctrine, that qualifies men to judge of these difficult things, then we can find many thousands, even in Europe, that have as much learning and stability as the whole college of cardinals, and perhaps ten thousand times more ; for that conclave was never very reputable for the learning of its members : and to other learned bodies we may, with as much propriety, look up as infallible guides, as to this *conclave.*

Besides, as it is only the *unlearned* and the *unestablished* (that is, young Christian converts) that are in danger of wresting such portions ; the *learned,* that is, the *experienced* and the *established* in the knowledge and life of God, are in no such danger ; and to such we may safely go for information : and these abound everywhere, especially in *Protestant* countries ; and by the labours of learned and pious men on the sacred writings there is not one difficulty relative to the things which concern our salvation left unexplained. If the members of the Romish Church have not these advantages, let them go to those who have them ; and if their teachers are afraid to trust them to the instruction of the Protestants, then let them who pretend to have *infallibly* written their exposition of these *difficult places,* also put them, with a wholesome text in the vulgar language, into the hands of their people, and then the appeal will not lie to *Rome,* but to the *Bible ;* and those interpretations will be considered according to their worth. being weighed with other scriptures, and the expositions of equally learned and equally *infallible* men.

We find, lastly, that those who wrest such portions, are those who wrest the *other scriptures* to their destruction ; therefore they are no patterns, nor can such form any precedent for withholding the Scriptures from the common people, most of whom, instead of wresting them to their *destruction,* would become *wise*

A. M. cir. 4064.
A. D. cir. 60.
An. Olymp.
cir. CCIX. 4.
A. U. C. cir.
813.

17 Ye therefore, beloved, ^c see-ing ye know *these things* before, ^d beware lest ye also, being led away with the error of the wicked, fall from your own steadfastness.

18 ^e But grow in grace, and *in* the knowledge of our Lord and Saviour Jesus Christ. ^f To him *be* glory both now and for ever. Amen.

A. M. cir. 4064.
A. D. cir. 60.
An. Olymp.
cir. CCIX. 4.
A. U. C. cir.
813.

^c Mark. xiii. 23 ; ch. i. 12.——^d Eph. iv. 14 ; chap. i. 10, 11 ; ii. 18.

^e Eph. iv. 15 ; 1 Pet. ii. 2.——^f 2 Tim. iv. 18 ; Rev. i. 6.

unto salvation by reading them. We may defy the Romish Church to adduce a single instance of any soul that was perverted, destroyed, or damned, by reading of the Bible ; and the insinuation that they may is blasphemous. I may just add that the verb στρεβλοω, which the apostle uses here, signifies to *distort*, to *put to the rack*, to *torture*, to *overstretch* and *dislocate the limbs* ; and hence the persons here intended are those who proceed according to no fair plan of interpretation, but *force unnatural* and *sophistical meanings* on the word of God : a practice which the common simple Christian is in no danger of following. I could illus-trate this by a multitude of interpretations from popish writers.

Verse 17. *Seeing ye know—before*] Seeing that by prophets and apostles you have been thus forewarned, *beware*, φυλασσεσθε, *keep watch*, be on *your guard* ; cleave to God and the word of his grace, *lest ye be led away* from the truth delivered by the prophets and apostles, *by the error of the wicked*, αθεσμων, *of the lawless*—those who wrest the Scriptures to make them countenance their lusts, exorbitant exactions, and law-less practices.

Fall from your own steadfastness.] From that faith in Christ which has put you in possession of that *grace* which *establishes the heart.*

Verse 18. *But grow in grace*] Increase in the image and favour of God ; every grace and Divine influence which ye have received is a seed, a heavenly seed, which, if it be watered with the dew of heaven from above, will endlessly increase and multiply itself. He who continues to *believe, love*, and *obey*, will grow in grace, and continually increase in the knowledge of Jesus Christ, as his sacrifice, sanctifier, counsellor, preserver, and final Saviour. The life of a Christian is a *growth*; he is at first *born of God*, and is a *little child*; becomes a *young man*, and a *father* in Christ. Every *father* was once an *infant*; and had he not grown, he would have never been a *man*. Those who content themselves with the grace they received when *converted to God*, are, at best, in a continual state of *infancy*: but we find, in the order of nature, that the *infant* that does not *grow*, and grow daily, too, is sickly and soon dies ; so, in the order of grace, those who do not *grow up* into Jesus Christ are sickly, and will soon die, die to all sense and influence of heavenly things.

There are many who boast of the grace of their conversion ; persons who were never more than *babes*, and have long since lost even that grace, because they did not *grow* in it. Let him that readeth understand.

To him] The Lord Jesus, *be* glory—all honour and excellency attributed, *both now—*in this present state, *and for ever*, εις ημεραν αιωνος, *to the day of eternity—*that in which death, and misery, and trial, and dark-ness, and change, and time itself, are to the righteous for ever at an end : it is *eternity*; and this eternity is

one unalterable, interminable, unclouded, and unchange-able DAY !

Amen.] So let it be ! and so it shall be ! Though this word is wanting in some reputable MSS., yet it should be retained, as it has here more than usual au-thority in its support.

Subscriptions to this epistle in the VERSIONS :
The end of the Second Epistle of Peter the apostle. —SYRIAC.
The Second Epistle of Peter the apostle is ended.—SYRIAC PHILOXENIAN.
Nothing in the printed VULGATE.
The end of the epistles of blessed Peter the apostle, the rock of the faith.—ARABIC.
The Second Epistle of Peter is ended ; and glory be to God for ever and ever !—ÆTHIOPIC.
Nothing in the COPTIC.
The end of the Second catholic Epistle of St. Pe-ter.—COMPLUTENSIAN POLYGLOT.
The end of the Second Epistle of St. Peter.—BIB. LAT., edit. antiq.

Subscriptions in the MANUSCRIPTS ;
Of the second of Peter.—CODEX ALEXANDRINUS, and CODEX VATICANUS.
Of the catholic epistle of Peter.—CODEX EPHREM.
The Second Epistle of the holy Apostle Peter.—Other MSS.

WE have now passed over all the canonical writings of Peter that are extant ; and it is worthy of remark that, in no place of the two epistles already examined, nor in any of this apostle's sayings in any other parts of the sacred writings do we find any of the *peculiar* tenets of the Romish Church : not one word of *his* or the *pope's supremacy* ; not one word of those who affect to be his *successors* ; nothing of the *infallibility* claimed by those pretended successors ; nothing of *purgatory, penances, pilgrimages, auricular confes-sion, power* of the *keys, indulgences, extreme unction, masses*, and *prayers for the dead* ; and not one word on the most essential doctrine of the Romish Church, *transubstantiation.* Now, as all these things have been considered by themselves most essential to the being of that Church ; is it not strange that *he*, from whom they profess to derive all their power, authority, and influence, in spiritual and secular matters, should have said nothing of these most necessary things ? Is it not a proof that they are all *false* and *forged* ; that the holy apostle knew nothing of them ; that they are no *part* of the doctrine of God ; and, although they distinguish the *Church of Rome*, do not belong to the *Church of Christ* ? It is no wonder that the rulers of this Church endeavour to keep the *Scriptures* from the common people ; for, were they permitted to con-sult these, the imposture would be detected, and the solemn, destructive cheat at once exposed.

2

AS the author of this epistle is the same who wrote the gospel, I need not detain the reader with any particulars of his life, having taken up the subject pretty much at large in my preface to his gospel, to which I must refer for that species of information.

Two questions have been urged relative to this epistle, which are very difficult to be solved : 1. *When* was it written ? 2. To *whom* was it sent ? The precise year it is impossible to determine ; but it was probably written before the destruction of Jerusalem ; and perhaps about the year 68 or 69, though some think not before 80. The second question *Michaelis* answers thus :—

" This question is still more difficult to decide than the preceding. In the Latin version it was formerly called *The Epistle of St. John to the Parthians* ; and this title was adopted by some of the ancient fathers, and in modern times has been defended by Grotius. But if St. John had intended this epistle for the use of the Parthians, he would hardly have written it in Greek, but would have used either the language of the country, or, if he was unacquainted with it, would have written at least in Syriac, which was the language of the learned in the Parthian empire, and especially of the Christians. We know, from the history of Manes, that even the learned in that country were for the most part unacquainted with the Greek language ; for to Manes, though he united literature with genius, his adversaries objected that he understood only the barbarous Syriac. That a Grecian book would not have been understood in the Parthian empire, appears from what Josephus says in the preface to his History of the Jewish War, where he declares that a work intended for Parthian Jews must be written, not in Greek, but Hebrew. However, it is worth while to examine whence the superscription 'ad Parthos' took its rise. Whiston conjectures that an ancient Greek superscription of this epistle was προς παρθενους, (to virgins,) because this epistle is chiefly addressed to uncorrupted Christians, and that this title was falsely copied προς Παρθανς, whence was derived the Latin superscription, ' ad Parthos.' But this conjecture is without foundation ; for since the faithful are not called in a single instance throughout the whole epistle by the name of παρθενους, it is very improbable that the title προς παρθενους was ever affixed to it. I would rather suppose, therefore, that the frequent use in this epistle of the words 'light' and 'darkness,' which occur in the Persian philosophy, and on the same occasions as those on which St. John has used them, gave rise to the opinion that St. John wrote it with a view of correcting the abuses of the Persian philosophy ; whence it was inferred that he designed it for the use of the Christians in the Parthian empire. That St. John really designed his epistle as a warning to those Christians who were in danger of being infected with Zoroastrian principles, is very probable, though the language of the epistle will not permit us to place St. John's readers in a country to the east of the Euphrates.

" LAMPE, who appeals to Theodoret, contends that it was not designed for any particular community, but that it was written for the use of Christians of every denomination ; and this is really the most probable opinion, since the epistle contains no reference to any individual Church. The only difficulty attending this opinion lies in the name 'epistle,' because the frequent use in an epistle of the terms 'light and darkness,' taken in the Persian sense of these words, seems to imply that it was written to persons of a particular description. But if we call it a treatise, this difficulty will cease ; and in fact, the name 'epistle' is improperly applied to it, since it has nothing which entitles it to this appellation. It does not begin with the salutation which is used in Greek epistles, and with which St. John himself begins his two last epistles ; nor does it contain any salutations, though they are found in almost all the epistles of the apostles. It is true that St. John addresses his readers in the second person ; but this mode of writing is frequently adopted in books, and especially in prefaces : for instance, in Wolfe's Elements of Mathematics, the reader is addressed throughout in the second person. I therefore consider that which is commonly called the First Epistle of

St. John as a book or treatise, in which the apostle declared to the whole world his disapprobation of the doctrines maintained by Cerinthus and the Gnostics. However, as I do not think it worth while to dispute about words, I have retained the usual title, and have called it the First Epistle of St. John.

"That the design of this epistle was to combat the doctrine delivered by certain false teachers, appears from chap. ii. 18–26; iii. 7; iv. 1–3: and what this false doctrine was may be inferred from the counter doctrine delivered by St. John, chap. v. 1–6. The apostle here asserts that 'Jesus is the Christ,' and that he was the Christ, 'not by water only, but by water and blood.' Now these words, which are not in themselves very intelligible, become perfectly clear if we consider them as opposed to the doctrine of Cerinthus, who asserted that Jesus was by birth a mere man; but that the Æon, Christ, descended on him at his baptism, and left him before his death. But if what St. John says, chap. v. 1–6, was opposed to Cerinthus, the Antichrists of whom he speaks, chap. ii. 18, 19, and who, according to ver. 22, denied that Jesus was the Christ, as also the false prophets, mentioned chap. iv. 1, 3, must be Cerinthians, or at least Gnostics. That they were neither Jews nor heathens may be inferred from chap. ii. 19, where St. John says, 'They went out from us.' Farther, he describes them, chap. ii. 18, as persons who had lately appeared in the world. But this description suits neither Jews nor heathens, who, when this epistle was written, had not lately begun to deny that Jesus was the Christ. Lastly, in the same verse, he describes them as tokens of the last time, saying, 'As ye have heard that Antichrist shall come, even now there are many Antichrists, *whereby* we know that it is the last time.' But this inference could not be drawn from the refusal of the Jews to acknowledge that Jesus was the Messiah. Now, as soon as we perceive that the position, 'Jesus is the Christ,' is a counter position against Cerinthus, we may infer, as I have already observed, that the Antichrists who denied that Jesus was the Christ, or who denied that Christ had appeared in the flesh, were Cerinthians; or perhaps the latter were Docetes. It is, therefore, highly probable that the whole epistle, which in various places discovers an opposition to false teachers, was written against Cerinthians, or at least against Gnostics and Magi. A proposition can never be completely understood, unless we know the author's design in delivering it. For instance, 'God is light, and in him is no darkness,' appears to contain a tautology, if we consider it as a detached dogma; and if it be considered as an admonitory proposition, it may be thought to contain a severe reproof; but if we regard it in a polemical view, it will present itself under a very different form. This epistle abounds with exhortations; but no man who wishes to understand it will be satisfied without asking the following questions: Why did St. John give these admonitions? Why has he so frequently repeated them? Why has he admonished, if he thought admonition necessary, merely in general terms, to holiness and brotherly love? And why has he not sometimes descended to particulars, as other apostles have done? An answer to these questions will throw great light on the epistle; and this light I will endeavour to procure for the reader, by pointing out the several propositions which, in my opinion, are laid down in opposition to Gnostic errors.

"1. In the first chapter the four first verses are opposed to the following assertion of the Gnostics: 'That the apostles did not deliver the doctrine of Jesus as they had received it, but made additions to it, especially in the commandments which were termed legal; whereas they themselves (the Gnostics) retained the genuine and uncorrupted mystery.' St. John therefore says: 'That he declared that which was from the beginning, which he himself had seen and heard;' that is, that he taught the doctrine of Christ as it was originally delivered, as he had heard it from Christ's own mouth, whose person he had seen and felt; and that he made no additions of his own, but only reported as a faithful witness. In like manner he appeals, chap. ii. 13, 14, to the elder Christians, whom he calls fathers, 'because they knew him who was from the beginning;' that is, because they knew how Christ had taught from the beginning; and ver. 24, he says: 'Let that abide in you which ye have heard from the beginning.' Farther he says, chap. ii. 7: 'Brethren, I write no new commandment unto you, but an old commandment, which ye had from the beginning.' In the next verse he adds: 'Again a new commandment I write unto you, which thing is true in him and in you, because the darkness is past, and the light now shineth.' Now Christ himself had given his disciples a commandment which he called a new commandment, and this was, 'that they should love one another.' The term 'new commandment,' therefore, St. John borrowed from Christ; but in the present instance he appears to have applied it to a different subject, because the special command which Christ gave to his disciples, that they should love one another, and which he called a new commandment, could not well be called an old commandment, being very different from the general commandment, that we should love our neighbour. St. John, therefore, very probably meant that the commandment of love and sanctification was no new commandment, as the Gnostics contended, but the old commandment which the Christians had heard from the beginning. It was, indeed, become a new commandment, in consequence of the false doctrines which then prevailed; or rather, it appeared to be so, because the Gnostics had endeavoured to banish it from their system of theology. But whether a new or an old commandment, St. John thought proper to enforce it.

"2. The Gnostics, who contended that those commandments which were legal were not given by Christ, but were added by the apostles without his authority, counteracted, by so doing, the whole doctrine of sanctification. St. John, therefore, devotes the greatest part of his epistle to the confirmation and enforcement of this doctrine. In chap. i. 5, 7, he asserts, as a principal part of the message which he had heard from Christ, that no one who does not walk in the light has fellowship with God. In the three following verses he limits this proposition in such a manner as was necessary in arguing with an adversary; and chap. ii. 1, 2, he removes the objection, that, according to his doctrine, a Christian who was guilty of wilful sins lost thereby all hopes of salvation. He then maintains, ver. 3–5, and apparently in allusion to the word γνωσις, knowledge, the favourite term of the Gnostics, that he who boasted of profound knowledge, and at the same time rejected the commandments of Christ, had not a real but only a pretended knowledge ; and that in him only the love of God is perfected, τετελειωται, who keeps God's word. The expression τετελειωται is a term which was used in the schools of the philosophers, and applied to the scholars called esoterici, who had made a considerable progress in the inner school. Now the Gnostics were, in their own opinion, scholars of this description ; but since they, whose imaginary system of theology annuls the commands of God, are so far from being perfect that they are not even beginners in the science, St. John very properly refuses to admit their pretensions, and opposes to them others who were perfect in a different way, and who were more justly entitled to the appellation. With respect to the expressions, 'keeping the commandments of God,' or 'not keeping his commandments,' it must be observed that, when used in a polemical work, they denote, not merely the observance or violation of God's commands in our own practice, but the teaching of others that they are to be observed or rejected. What St. John says, ver. 7, 8, has been already explained in the preceding paragraph.

"The whole of the third chapter, and part of the fourth, is devoted to the doctrine of sanctification, on which I have to make the following remarks. When St. John says, chap. iii. 7, 'Let no man deceive you ; he who doeth righteousness is righteous,' he probably intends, not merely to deliver a precept, but to oppose the doctrine of those who asserted that a man, though he sinned, might be righteous in respect to his spiritual soul, because sin proceeded only from the material body. A similar observation may be applied to ver. 4 : 'Whosoever committeth sin transgresseth also the law ;' which, considered by itself, appears to be an identical proposition ; but when considered as an assertion opposed to the Gnostics, it is far from being superfluous, because, evident as it appears to be, they virtually denied it. From the passage above quoted from the works of Irenæus, we have seen that they rejected the legal commandments as parts of the Christian religion which were not warranted by the authority of Christ ; consequently, they denied that sin was a transgression of the law. Farther, it was consistent with their principles to regard sins as diseases ; for they believed in a metempsychosis, and imagined that the souls of men were confined in their present bodies as in a prison, and as a punishment for having offended in the region above. According to this system, the violent and irregular passions of anger, hatred, &c., were tortures for the soul ; they were diseases, but not punishable transgressions of the law. I will not assert that all who believed in a transmigration of souls argued in this manner, but some of them certainly did so ; and against these it was not superfluous to write, 'Whosoever committeth sin transgresseth also the law, for sin is the transgression of the law.'

"The love of the brethren, which St. John enforced as a chief commandment, is generally understood of that special love which Christ commanded his disciples to have towards each other. But I rather think that St. John means the love of our neighbour in general, which Christ commanded, as comprehending the half of the law ; for this general love St. John might very properly call the love of our brother, since God has created us all, and is our common Father. Besides, as St. John calls Cain Abel's brother, he could not intend to signify by this term a person of the same religious sentiments. Nor would it have been consistent with candour to have censured the Gnostics for not having Christian brotherly love towards St. John and other true believers, for in this particular sense they were not brethren ; and St. John himself, in his second epistle, ver. 10, forbids the exercise of Christian brotherly love towards those who teach false doctrines. I believe, therefore, that the brotherly love of which St. John speaks in the third chapter of this epistle, is not confined to that special love which we owe to those who are allied to us by religion, but denotes the love of our neighbour in general. Nor do I except even the 16th verse, where some think that St. John would require too much, if he meant brotherly love in general, or charity toward all men. But are there not certain cases in which it is our duty to hazard and even sacrifice our lives, in order to rescue our neighbour ? Is not this duty performed by the soldier ? And is it not performed by him who visits those who are infected with contagious diseases ? It is true that this is not a duty which every man owes in all cases to his neighbour ; but then, on the other hand, is it not a duty which every man owes to his spiritual brother ? Nor was it St. John's design so much to enforce this duty, and to recommend the exercise of it, as to argue from the acknowledgment of this duty in certain cases, to the necessity of performing the less painful duty of supporting our brethren in distress, by a participation of our temporal possessions. But though I believe that in the third chapter St. John speaks of the love of our neighbour in general, I do not mean to affirm that he nowhere understands that special love which Christians owe one to another, of which we meet with an instance in chap. v. 1, 2.

"With respect to the moral conduct of the Gnostics, against whom St. John wrote, we may infer, therefore, that the apostle found more reason to censure them for their want of charity toward their neighbours, than for dissoluteness or debauchery. This want of charity they probably displayed by a hatred of the true believers.

"What St. John says, chap. v. 3, that 'God's commandments are not grievous,' appears in the clearest light when we consider it as opposed to the Gnostics, to whom the Divine commandments, as delivered by the apostles, appeared to be too legal.

"St. John declares, chap. i. 5, as the message which he had heard from Christ, that 'God is light, and in him is no darkness at all.' Now if this proposition had been then as generally admitted as it is at present, there could have been no necessity for declaring it at the very beginning of the epistle, with so much energy, to be the grand message of Christ. We may reasonably infer, therefore, that it was opposed to certain persons who delivered a contrary doctrine. Farther, the words 'light' and 'darkness,' which are here applied to the Deity in a manner which is not usual in the Bible, remind us of the technical terms used by the Persian Magi, and afterwards by the Manicheans. It is true that in the Bible we meet with the expressions 'works of the light,' 'children of the light,' 'to walk in the light,' and others of the same kind; but in these instances the term 'light' is not synonymous with 'holiness;' works of the light denoting nothing more than works which no man need be ashamed to perform openly, and in the face of the whole world. This explanation of the word 'light' is inapplicable in the proposition 'God is light,' because there would be an impropriety in representing God either as fearing or not fearing to act in the face of the whole world. St. John, therefore, uses the term 'light' as equivalent to holiness.

"Now, the Gnostics admitted that the supreme Being was perfectly holy and pure light; but they denied that the supreme Being was the God whom the Jews and the Christians worshipped. For the Jews and the Christians worshipped the Creator of the world; and the Gnostics asserted that the Creator of the world was either a spirit of darkness, or, if he was a spirit of light, that he was not free from darkness.

"From chap. ii. 23, where St. John says, that 'he who denies the Son, rejects also the Father,' it appears that his adversaries did not deny the Father in positive terms, since the apostle argues only that they virtually did so by denying the Son. Now, the Gnostics did not positively deny the Father of Christ, whom they allowed to be the supreme Being, but then they did not allow that he was the Creator. The terms, therefore, 'God' and the 'Father of Christ,' though they denote in reality the same person, must not be considered as having precisely the same import; since the adversaries of St. John admitted that the Father of Christ was the supreme Being, and pure light; but denied that the Creator, who is in fact God, was light without darkness.

"4. In some places, especially chap. iv. 2, 3, St. John opposes false teachers of another description, namely, those who denied that Christ was come in the flesh. Now they who denied this were not Cerinthians, but another kind of Gnostics, called Docetes. For as, on the one hand, Cerinthus maintained that Jesus was a mere and therefore real man, the Docetes on the other hand contended that he was an incorporeal phantom, in which the Æon, Christ, or Divine nature, presented itself to mankind. Chap. i. 1: 'Our hands have handled,' appears likewise to be opposed to this error of the Docetes.

"The doctrines which St. John has delivered in this epistle he has not supported, either by arguments drawn from reason, or by quotations from the Old Testament; for neither of them are necessary, since the bare assertion of an apostle of Christ is sufficient authority. It is true that, in one respect, this epistle has less energy than St. John's gospel, because in his gospel he warrants his doctrines by the speeches of Christ. But then, on the other hand, St. John declares in this epistle, chap. iii. 24; iv. 4; v. 14, 16, that God sent his Spirit to the apostolic Church, and heard their prayers. And it is evident that St. John alludes to the extraordinary gifts of the Holy Ghost, and to the miraculous powers obtained by prayer.

"The close of this epistle, 'Keep yourselves from idols,' has no immediate connection with the preceding discourse. I am therefore in doubt whether St. John meant to warn his readers against taking part in heathen sacrifices, which was allowed by these Gnostics, who are called Nicolaitans in the Apocalypse; or whether he meant to describe the system of the Gnostics in general as a system of idolatry, which in fact it was."

Dr. *Macknight* has some judicious observations on the authenticity of this epistle, from the similarity of the style to that of the gospel of John.

"The authenticity of any ancient writing is established, first, by the testimony of contemporary and succeeding authors, whose works have come down to us; and who speak of that writing as known to be the work of the person whose name it bears. Secondly, by the suitableness of the things contained in such writing to the character and circumstances of its supposed author, and by the similarity of its style to the style of the other acknowledged writings of that author. The former of these proofs is called the *external evidence* of the authenticity of a writing; the latter, its *internal evidence*. When these two kinds of evidence are found accompanying any writing, they render its genuineness indubitable.

"The external evidence of the authenticity of John's first epistle has been amply detailed by Dr. Lardner, who shows that the earliest and best Christian writers have all, with one consent, and without any hesitation, ascribed the first epistle to him. And their testimony is confirmed by this circumstance, that the Syriac translator, who omitted the Second Epistle of Peter, the Second and Third Epistles of John, and the Epistle of Jude, because some doubts were entertained concerning them in the first age, or perhaps because they had not come to his knowledge, has translated John's first epistle, as an apostolical writing of which there never was any doubt in that or in any other Christian Church.

"In this preface, therefore, we shall state the internal evidence of the authenticity of John's first epistle, by showing, *first*, that, in respect of its matter, and, *secondly*, in respect of its style, it is perfectly suitable to the character and circumstances of its supposed author. In respect of the matter or subject of the epistle under consideration, the writer of it has discovered himself to be John the apostle, by introducing a number of sentiments and expressions found in the gospel, which all Christians from the beginning have acknowledged to be the work of John the apostle.

EPISTLE.	GOSPEL.
Chap. i. 1. That which was from the beginning— ὁ εθεασαμεθα, which we have contemplated, concerning the living Word.	Chap. i. 1. In the beginning was the Word: ver. 14; And εθεασαμεθα, we beheld his glory: ver. 4; In him was light: ver. 14; The Word was made flesh.

EPISTLE.

Chap. ii. 5. Whosoever keepeth his word truly, in that man the love of God is perfected.

Chap. ii. 6. He who saith he abideth in him, ought himself also so to walk, even as he walked. See chap. iii. 24; iv. 13–16.

Chap. ii. 8. I write to you a new commandment.

Chap. iii. 11. This is the message which ye heard from the beginning, that ye should love one another.

Chap. ii. 8. The darkness passeth away, and the light which is true now shineth.

Ver. 10. Abideth in the light, and there is no stumbling block to him.

Chap. ii. 13. Young children, I write to you, because ye have known the Father.

Ver. 14. Because ye have known him from the beginning.

Chap. iii. 8, 9. Every one who worketh righteousness is begotten of God. See also chap. v. 1.

Chap. iii. 1. Behold how great love the Father hath bestowed on us, that we should be called the sons of God!

Chap. iii. 2. We shall be like him, for we shall see him as he is.

Chap. iii. 8. He who worketh sin is of the devil; for the devil sinneth from the beginning.

Chap. iii. 13. Do not wonder, my brethren, that the world hateth you.

Chap. iv. 9. By this the love of God was manifested, that God sent his Son, the only begotten, into the world, that we might live through him.

Chap. iv. 12. No man hath seen God at any time.

Chap. v. 13. These things I have written to you, who believe on the name of the Son of God, that ye may know that ye have eternal life; and that ye may believe in the name of the Son of God.

Chap. v. 14. If we ask any thing according to his will, he heareth us.

Chap. v. 20. The Son of God is come, and hath given us an understanding, that we may know him that is true, and we are in him that is true, even in his Son Jesus Christ. This is the true God, and eternal life.

GOSPEL.

Chap. xiv. 23. If a man love me he will keep my words, and my Father will love him.

Chap. xv. 4. Abide in me, and I in you. As the branch cannot bring forth fruit of itself, except it abide in the vine; no more can ye, except ye abide in me.

Chap. xiii. 34. A new commandment I give unto you,

That ye love one another, as I have loved you

Chap. i. 5. The light shineth in darkness.

Ver. 9. That was the true light.

Chap. xi. 10. If a man walk in the night he stumbleth, because there is no light in him.

Chap. xvii. 3. This is the eternal life, that they might know thee, the only true God,

And Jesus Christ, whom thou hast sent.

Chap. iii. 3. Except a man be begotten again: ver. 5; Except a man be begotten of water and of the Spirit.

Chap. i. 12. To them he gave power to become the sons of God, even to them who believe on his name.

Chap. xvii. 24. Be with me where I am, that they may behold my glory.

Chap. viii. 44. Ye are of your father the devil; he was a murderer from the beginning.

Chap. xv. 20. If they have persecuted me, they will also persecute you.

Chap. iii. 16. God so loved the world that he gave his only begotten Son, that whosoever believeth on him might not perish, but have eternal life.

Chap. i. 18. No man hath seen God at any time.

Chap. xx. 31. These things are written that ye might believe that Jesus is the Christ, the Son of God; and that believing ye might have life through his name.

Chap. xiv. 14. If ye shall ask any thing in my name, I will do it.

Chap. xvii. 2. Thou hast given him power over all flesh, that he might give eternal life to as many as thou hast given him. Ver. 3: And this is the eternal life, that they might know thee, the only true God, and Jesus Christ whom thou hast sent.

"From the above comparison of the first epistle of John with his gospel, there appears such an exact agreement of sentiment in the two writings, that no reader who is capable of discerning what is peculiar in an author's turn of thinking, can entertain the least doubt of their being the productions of one and the same writer. Farther, since John has not mentioned his own name in his gospel, the want of his name in the epistle is no proof that it was not written by him; but rather a presumption that it is his; especially as he has sufficiently discovered himself to be an apostle, by affirming, in the beginning of the epistle, that he was an eye and an ear witness of the things he has written concerning the living Word.

"The style of this epistle being the same with the style of the gospel of John, it is, by that internal mark likewise, denoted to be his writing. In his gospel, John does not content himself with simply affirming or denying a thing; but, to strengthen his affirmation, he denies the contrary. In like manner, to strengthen his denial of a thing, he affirms its contrary. See John i. 20; iii. 36; v. 22. The same manner of expressing things strongly, is found in this epistle; for example, chap. ii. 4: 'He who saith, I have known him, and doth not keep his commandments, is a liar, and the truth is not in him.' Ver. 27: 'The same unction teacheth you concerning all things, and is truth, and is no lie.' Chap. iv. 2: 'Every spirit which confesseth that Jesus Christ hath come in the flesh, is from God.' Ver. 3: 'And every spirit which doth not confess that Jesus Christ hath come in the flesh, is not from God.'

"In his gospel likewise, John, to express things emphatically, frequently uses the demonstrative pronoun *this.* Chap. i. 19: Αὐτη· 'This is the testimony.' Chap. iii. 19: Αὐτη· 'This is the condemnation, that light,' &c.   Chap. vi. 29 : Τοῦτο· 'This is the work of God.'   Ver. 40 : Τοῦτο· 'This is the will of him.' Ver. 50 : Οὗτος· 'This is the bread which cometh down from heaven.'   Chap. xvii. 3 : Αὕτη· 'This is the eternal life.'   In the epistle the same emphatical manner of expression is found, chap. i. 5 ; ii. 25 : 'This is the promise.'   Chap. iii. 23 : Αὕτη· 'This is the commandment.'   Chap. v. 3 : Αὕτη· 'This is the love of God.'   Ver. 4 : 'This is the victory.'   Ver. 6 : Οὗτος· 'This is he who came by water.'   Ver. 14 : Αὕτη· 'This is the boldness which we have with him.'

"Such is the internal evidence on which all Christians, from the beginning, have received the First Epistle of John as really written by him, and of Divine authority, although his name is not mentioned in the inscription, nor in any part of the epistle."

On the term *epistle*, as applied to this work of St. John, it may be necessary to make a few remarks. There is properly nothing of the *epistolary style* in this work : it is addressed neither to any particular *person*, nor to any *Church*.

The writer does not mention himself either in the beginning or ending ; and, although this can be no objection against its *authenticity*, yet it is some proof that the work was never intended to be considered in the light of an *epistle*.

1. Is it a *tract* or *dissertation* upon the more sublime parts of Christianity ?   2. Is it a *polemical discourse* against *heretics*, particularly the Gnostics, or some of their teachers, who were disturbing the Churches where John dwelt ?   3. Is it a *sermon*, the subject of which is God's love to man in the mission of Jesus Christ ; from which our obligations to love and serve him are particularly inferred ?   4. Or is it a *collection* of Christian *aphorisms*, made by John himself ; and put together as they occurred to his mind, without any intended *order* or *method* ?   Much might be said on all these heads of inquiry ; and the issue would be, that the idea of its being an *epistle* of any kind must be relinquished ; and yet *epistle* is its general denomination through all antiquity.

It is a matter, however, of little importance what its *title* may be, or to what species of literary composition it belongs ; while we know that it is the genuine work of St. John ; of the holiest man who ever breathed ; of one who was most intimately acquainted with the doctrine and mind of his Lord ; of one who was admitted to the closest fellowship with his Saviour ; and who has treated of the deepest things that can be experienced or comprehended in the Christian life.

As to *distinct heads of discourse*, it does not appear to me that any were intended by the apostle ; he wrote just as the subjects occurred to his mind, or rather as the Holy Spirit gave him utterance ; and, although *technical order* is not here to be expected, yet nothing like disorder or confusion can be found in the whole work.

As Professor Michaelis has considered it in the light of a *polemical treatise*, written against the *Gnostics*, and other false teachers of that time, I have thought it right to give his view of the work considered in this light ; but as I, in general, pursue another plan of interpretation in the *notes*, I have inserted his elucidations in the preceding pages of this preface.

On the controverted text of the three heavenly Witnesses I have said what truth and a deep and thorough examination of the subject have obliged me to say.   I am satisfied that it is not genuine, though the *doctrine* in behalf of which it has been originally introduced into the epistle is a doctrine of the highest importance, and most positively revealed in various parts both of the Old and New Testament.   The stress which has been laid on the testimony of this text in behalf of the doctrine of the Trinity has done much evil ; for when its own authenticity has come to be critically examined, and has been found to rest on no sure foundation, the adversaries of the doctrine itself have thought they had full cause for triumph, and have in effect said, " If this text be to the epistle, and to the doctrine in question, what the sun is in the world, what the heart is in man, and what the needle is in the mariner's compass, then the doctrine is spurious, for the text is a most manifest forgery."   I would just observe, that incautious or feeble defences of any doctrine do not affect the doctrine itself but in the view of superficial minds.   The *proof* that this text is an interpolation which, first existing as an illustrative marginal note, has afterwards been unfortunately introduced into the text, has " demolished *no strong hold* of the orthodox, has taken away *no pillar* from the Christian faith."   The grand defences of the doctrine of the Trinity, brought down to us from the highest Christian antiquity, stand still in all their force ; not one of them was built upon this text, because the text, as a supposed part of St. John's work, did not then exist ; therefore neither *evidence, prop*, nor *pillar* of the grand doctrine is injured.   We have what we ever had in this respect, and we may make the same *illustrating use* of the words in reference to this doctrine which many Latin writers, since the time of St. Cyprian, made ; and which was proper enough in its own place, but became useless when incorporated with the sure sayings of God.

No man, it is hoped, will be so obstinate, perverse, or disingenuous, as to say or insinuate that the man who gives up this text is unsound in the faith ; it would be as reasonable to assert, on the other hand, that he who understands the mass of evidence that is against the authenticity of this verse, and who nevertheless *will contend* for its continuance in the sacred canon, is a Deist in his heart, and endeavours to discredit the truth by mixing it with error and falsehood.   Those whose doubts are not removed by the dissertation at the end of this epistle had better read the late Professor *Porson's* Answer to Dean *Travis*, where it is presumed they will receive the fullest satisfaction.

2

THE

FIRST GENERAL EPISTLE

OF

JOHN.

Chronological Notes relative to this Epistle.

Year of the Constantinopolitan era of the world, or that used by the Byzantine historians, and other eastern writers, 5577.—Year of the Alexandrian era of the world, 5571.—Year of the Antiochian era of the world, 5561.—Year of the world, according to Archbishop Usher, 4073.—Year of the world, according to Eusebius, in his Chronicon, 4297.—Year of the minor Jewish era of the world, or that in common use, 3829.—Year of the Greater Rabbinical era of the world, 4428.—Year from the Flood, according to Archbishop Usher, and the English Bible, 2417.—Year of the Cali yuga, or Indian era of the Deluge, 3171. —Year of the era of Iphitus, or since the first commencement of the Olympic games, 1009.—Year of the era of Nabonassar, king of Babylon, 818.—Year of the CCXIIth Olympiad, 1.—Year from the building of Rome, according to Fabius Pictor, 816.—Year from the building of Rome, according to Frontinus, 820.—Year from the building of Rome, according to the Fasti Capitolini, 821.—Year from the building of Rome, according to Varro, which was that most generally used, 822.—Year of the era of the Seleucidæ, 381.—Year of the Cæsarean era of Antioch, 117.—Year of the Julian era, 114.—Year of the Spanish era, 107.—Year from the birth of Jesus Christ, according to Archbishop Usher, 73.—Year of the vulgar era of Christ's nativity, 69.—Year of Vologesus, king of the Parthians, 20.——Year of the Dionysian period, or Easter Cycle, 70.—Year of the Grecian Cycle of nineteen years, or Common Golden Number, 13; or the fifth embolismic.—Year of the Jewish Cycle of nineteen years, 10; or the year before the fourth embolismic.—Year of the Solar Cycle, 22.—Dominical Letter, it being the first year after the Bissextile, or Leap Year, A.— Day of the Jewish Passover, the twenty-fourth of March, which happened in this year on the sixth day after the Jewish Sabbath.—Easter Sunday, the twenty-sixth of March.—Epact, or age of the moon on the 22d of March, (the day of the earliest Easter Sunday possible,) 12.—Epact, according to the present mode of computation, or the moon's age on New Year's day, or the Calends of January, 20.—Monthly Epacts, or age of the moon on the Calends of each month respectively, (beginning with January,) 20, 22, 21, 22, 23, 24, 25, 27, 27, 28, 0, 0, 2, 2.—Number of Direction, or the number of days from the twenty-first of March to the Jewish Passover, 3.—In this year reigned four Roman emperors, viz., Galba, from Jan. 1 to Jan. 15, Otho ninety days, Vitellius eight months, and Vespasian for the remainder of the year.—Roman Consuls, Servius Sulpicius Galba Augustus, the second time, and Titus Vinius Rufinus, from Jan. 1 to the death of Galba, Jan. 15; Salvius Otho Augustus, and L. Salvius Otho Titianus, from Jan. 15 to March 1; L. Virginius Rufus, and Vopiscus Pompeius Silvanus, from March 1 to May 1; Titus Arrius Antoninus and P. Marius Celsus, the second time, from May 1 to Sept. 1; C. Fabius Valens and Aulus Alienus Cœcina, from Sept. 1, the former holding the Consulship to Nov. 1, the latter being succeeded by Roscius Regulus, on Oct. 31; Cn. Cæcilius Simplex and C. Quintius Atticus, from Nov. 1, to the end of the year.

CHAPTER I.

The testimony of the apostle concerning the reality of the person and doctrine of Christ ; and the end for which he bears this testimony, 1–4. God is light, and none can have fellowship with him who do not walk in the light ; those who walk in the light are cleansed from all unrighteousness by the blood of Christ, 5–7. No man can say that he has not sinned ; but God is faithful and just to cleanse from all unrighteousness them who confess their sins, 8–10.

A. M. cir. 4073.
A. D. cir. 69.
Impp. Galba,
Othone, Vitel.
et Vespa-
siano.

THAT [a] which was from the beginning, which we have heard, which we have seen with our eyes, [b] which we have looked upon, and [c] our hands have handled, of the Word of life ;

2 (For [d] the Life [e] was manifested, and we have seen *it*, [f] and bear witness, [g] and show unto you that eternal Life, [h] which was with the Father, and was manifested unto us ;)

3 [i] That which we have seen and heard declare we unto you, that ye also may have fellowship with us : and truly [k] our fellowship *is* with the Father, and with his Son Jesus Christ.

A. M. cir. 4073.
A. D. cir. 69.
Impp. Galba,
Othone, Vitel.
et Vespa-
siano.

4 And these things write we unto you, [l] that your joy may be full.

5 [m] This then is the message which we have heard of him, and declare unto you, that [n] God

---

[a] John i. 1 ; chap. ii. 13.——[b] John i. 14 ; 2 Pet. i. 16 ; chap. iv. 14.——[c] Luke xxiv. 39 ; John xx. 27.——[d] John i. 4 ; xi. 25 ; xiv. 6.——[e] Romans xvi. 26 ; 1 Timothy iii. 16 ; chapter iii. 5.

[f] John xxi. 24 ; Acts ii. 32.——[g] Chap. v. 20.——[h] John. i. 1, 2.——[i] Acts i. 20.——[k] John xvii. 11 ; 1 Cor. i. 9 ; chap. ii. 24 ; [l] John xv. 11 ; xvi. 24 ; 2 John 12.——[m] Chap. iii. 11.——[n] John i. 9 ; viii. 12 ; ix. 5 ; xii. 35, 36.

NOTES ON CHAP. I.

Verse 1. *That which was from the beginning*] That glorious personage, JESUS CHRIST *the* LORD, who was from *eternity* ; him, being *manifested in the flesh, we have heard* proclaim the *doctrine of eternal life* ; with *our* own *eyes have we seen him*, not transiently, for we have *looked upon him* frequently ; and *our hands have handled*—frequently touched, his person ; and we have had every proof of the identity and reality of this glorious being that our senses of *hearing*, ὁ ακηκοαμεν, *seeing*, ὁ ἑωρακαμεν τοις οφθαλμοις ἡμων, and *feeling*, και αἱ χειρες ἡμων εψηλαφησαν could possibly require.

Verse 2. *For the Life was manifested*] The Lord Jesus, who is the creator of all things, and the *fountain of life* to all sentient and intellectual beings, and from whom *eternal life* and *happiness* come, *was manifested* in the flesh, and we *have seen him*, and in consequence *bear witness* to him as the fountain and author of eternal life ; for he who *was from eternity with the Father was manifested unto us* his apostles, and to the whole of the Jewish nation, and preached that doctrine of eternal life which I have before delivered to the world in my gospel, and which I now farther confirm by this epistle.

Verse 3. *That which we have seen and heard*] We deliver nothing by hearsay, nothing by tradition, nothing from conjecture ; we have had the fullest certainty of all that we write and preach.

That ye also may have fellowship with us] That ye may be preserved from all false doctrine, and have a real *participation* with us apostles of the grace, peace, love, and life of God , which communion we have *with God* the Father, who hath loved us, and given his Son Jesus Christ to redeem us ; and *with his Son Jesus Christ*, who laid down his life for the life of the world, and *through* whom, being God manifested in the flesh, we have union with God, are made partakers of the Divine nature, and dwell in God, and God in us.

Verse 4. *That your joy may be full.*] Ye have already *tasted* that the Lord is good ; but I am now going to show you the height of your Christian calling, that your *happiness may be complete*, being thoroughly cleansed from all sin, and filled with the fulness of God.

Verse 5. *This then is the message*] This is the *grand principle* on which all depends, *which we have heard of* απ' αυτου, FROM *him* ; for neither Moses nor the prophets ever gave that full instruction concerning God and communion with him which Jesus Christ has given, for the only-begotten Son, who was in the bosom of the Father, has alone declared the fulness of the truth, and the extent of the blessings, which believers on him are to receive. See John i. 18.

God is light] The source of wisdom, knowledge, holiness, and happiness ; and *in him is no darkness at all*—no ignorance, no imperfection, no sinfulness, no misery. And from him wisdom, knowledge, holiness, and happiness are received by every believing soul. This is the grand message of the Gospel, the great principle on which the happiness of man depends. LIGHT implies every essential excellence, especially wisdom, holiness, and happiness. DARKNESS implies all imperfection, and principally *ignorance, sinfulness, and misery*. LIGHT is the purest, the most subtile, and the most diffusive of all God's creatures ; it is, therefore, a very proper emblem of the *purity, perfection*, and *goodness* of the Divine nature. God is to human souls what the light is to the world ; without the latter all would be dismal and uncomfortable, and terror and death would universally prevail : and without an indwelling God what is religion ? Without his all-penetrating and diffusive light, what is the soul of man ? Religion would be an empty science, a dead letter, a system unauthorited and uninfluencing ; and the soul a trackless wilderness, a howling waste, full of evil, of terror and dismay, and ever racked with

2

A. M. cir. 4073.
A. D. cir. 69.
Impp. Galba,
Othone, Vitel.
et Vespa-
siano.

is light, and in him is no dark-ness at all.

6 °If we say that we have fellowship with him, and walk in darkness, we lie, and do not the truth :

7 But if we walk in the light, as he is in the light, we have fellowship one with another, and ᵖ the blood of Jesus Christ his Son cleanseth us from all sin.

A. M. cir. 4073
A. D. cir. 69.
Impp. Galba,
Othone, Vitel,
et Vespa-
siano.

8 �q If we say that we have no sin, we deceive ourselves, ʳ and the truth is not in us.

9 ˢ If we confess our sins, he is faithful and just to forgive us *our* sins, and to ᵗ cleanse us from all unrighteous-ness.

10 If we say that we have not sinned, we make him a liar, and his word is not in us.

�q 2 Cor. vi. 14 ; chap. ii. 4.——ᵖ 1 Cor. vi. 11 ; Eph. i. 7 ; Heb. ix. 14 ; 1 Peter i. 19 ; chap. ii. 2 ; Rev. i. 5 ——�q 1 Kings viii. 46 ; 2 Chron. vi. 36 ; Job ix. 2 ; xv. 14 ; xxv. 4 ; Prov. xx. 9 ;

Eccles. vii. 20 ; James iii 2.——ʳ Chapter ii. 4.——ˢ Psalm xxxii. 5 ; Proverbs xxviii. 13.——ᵗ Verse 7 ; Psalm li. 2.

---

realizing anticipations of future, successive, permanent, substantial, and endless misery. No wonder the apostle lays this down as a first and grand principle, stating it to be the essential message which he had received from Christ to deliver to the world.

Verse 6. *If we say that we have fellowship*] Having fellowship, κοινωνια, communion, with God, necessarily implies a *partaking of the Divine nature.* Now if a man profess to have such communion, and *walk in darkness*—live an irreligious and sinful life, *he lies,* in the profession which he makes, and *does not the truth* —does not walk according to the directions of the Gospel, on the grace of which he holds his relation to God, and his communion with him.

The *Gnostics,* against whose errors it is supposed this epistle was written, were great pretenders to *knowledge,* to the highest degrees of the Divine illumination, and the nearest communion with the fountain of holiness, while their manners were excessively corrupt.

Verse 7. *But if we walk in the light*] If, having received the principle of holiness from him, we live a holy and righteous life, deriving continual light, power, and life from him, then *we have fellowship one with another ;* that is, we have communion with God, and God condescends to hold communion with us. This appears to be the intention of the apostle ; and so he was understood by some versions and MSS., which, instead of μετ' αλληλων, *with each other,* have μετ' αυτου, *with him.* Those who are deeply experienced in Divine things converse with God, and God with them. What John says is no *figure ;* God and a holy heart are in continual correspondence.

The blood of Jesus Christ] The meritorious efficacy of his passion and death has purged our consciences from dead works, *and cleanseth us,* καθαριζει ημας, *continues to cleanse us,* i. e., to *keep clean* what it has made clean, (for it requires the same merit and energy to preserve holiness in the soul of man, as to produce it,) or, as several MSS. and some versions read, καθαριει and καθαρισει, *will cleanse ;* speaking of those who are already justified, and are expecting *full redemption* in his blood.

And being cleansed from all sin is what every believer should look for, what he has a right to expect, and what he must have *in this life,* in order to be prepared to meet his God. Christ is not a *partial Saviour ;* he saves to the uttermost, and he cleanses from ALL *sin.*

Verse 8. *If we say that we have no sin*] This is tantamount to ver. 10 : *If we say that we have not sinned.* All have sinned, and come short of the glory of God ; and therefore every man needs a *Saviour,* such as Christ is. It is very likely that the heretics, against whose evil doctrines the apostle writes, denied that they had any sin, or needed any Saviour. Indeed, the *Gnostics* even denied that Christ suffered : the Æon, or Divine Being that dwelt in the man Christ Jesus, according to them, left him when he was taken by the Jews ; and he, being but a common man, his sufferings and death had neither merit nor efficacy.

We deceive ourselves] By supposing that we have no guilt, no sinfulness, and consequently have no need of the blood of Christ as an atoning sacrifice : this is the most dreadful of all deceptions, as it leaves the soul under all the guilt and pollution of sin, exposed to hell, and utterly unfit for heaven.

The truth is not in us.] We have no *knowledge* of the *Gospel* of Jesus, the whole of which is founded on this most awful truth—all have sinned, all are guilty, all are unholy ; and none can redeem himself. Hence it was necessary that Jesus Christ should become incarnated, and suffer and die to bring men to God.

Verse 9. *If we confess our sins*] If, from a deep sense of our guilt, impurity, and helplessness, we humble ourselves before God, acknowledging our iniquity, his holiness, and our own utter helplessness, and implore mercy for his sake who has died for us ; *he is faithful,* because to such he has *promised* mercy, Psa. xxxii. 5 ; Prov. xxviii. 13 ; *and just,* for Christ has died for us, and thus made an atonement to the Divine justice ; so that God can now be just, and yet the justifier of him who believeth in Jesus.

And to cleanse us from all unrighteousness.] Not only to *forgive the sin,* but to *purify the heart.*

OBSERVE here, 1. Sin exists in the soul after two modes or forms : (1.) In *guilt,* which requires *forgiveness* or *pardon.* (2.) In *pollution,* which requires *cleansing.*

2. *Guilt,* to be forgiven, must be *confessed ;* and *pollution,* to be cleansed, must be also *confessed.* In order to *find mercy,* a man must *know* and *feel* himself to be a *sinner,* that he may fervently apply to God for pardon ; in order to get a *clean heart,* a man must know and feel its depravity, acknowledge and deplore it before God, in order to be *fully sanctified.*

904

2

3. Few are pardoned, because they do not feel and confess their sins; and few are sanctified or cleansed from all sin, because they do not feel and confess their own sore, and the plague of their hearts.

4. As the blood of Jesus Christ, the merit of his passion and death, applied by faith, purges the conscience from *all dead works,* so the same *cleanses the heart* from *all unrighteousness.*

5. As all unrighteousness is *sin,* so he that is cleansed from all unrighteousness is cleansed from all sin. To attempt to evade this, and plead for the continuance of sin in the heart through life, is ungrateful, wicked, and even blasphemous; for as he who *says he has not sinned,* ver. 10, *makes God a liar,* who has

declared the contrary through every part of his revelation; so he that says the *blood of Christ* either *cannot* or *will not cleanse us from* all *sin* in this life, gives also the lie to his Maker, who has declared the contrary, and thus shows that the *word*—the doctrine *of God is not in him.*

Reader, it is the birthright of every child of God to be cleansed from all sin, to keep himself unspotted from the world, and so to live as never more to offend his Maker. All things are possible to him that believeth; because all things are possible to the infinitely meritorious blood and energetic Spirit of the Lord Jesus. See the notes on the parallel passages in the margin; and particularly in St. John's gospel, chap. i.

CHAPTER II.

He exhorts them not to sin; yet encourages those who may have fallen, by the hope of mercy through Christ, who is a propitiation for the sins of the whole world, 1, 2. He who knows God keeps his commandments; and he who professes to abide in Christ ought to walk as Christ walked, 3–6. The old and new commandment, that we should walk in the light, and love the brethren, 7–11. The apostle's description of the different states in the family of God; little children, young men, and fathers; and directions to each, 12–15. A statement of what prevails in the world, 16, 17. Cautions against antichrists, 18–23. Exhortations to persevere in what they had received, and to continue to follow that anointing of the Divine Spirit, by which they could discern all men, and know all things necessary to their salvation, and proper to prepare them for eternal glory, 24–29.

| A. M. cir. 4073. A. D. cir. 69. Impp. Galba, Othone, Vitel. et Vespasiano. | MY little children, these things write I unto you, that ye sin not. And if any man sin, [a] we have an advocate with the | Father, Jesus Christ the righteous: 2 And [b] he is the propitiation for our sins: and not for ours | A. M. cir. 4073 A. D. cir. 69. Impp. Galba, Othone, Vitel. et Vespasiano. |

[a] Rom. viii. 34; 1 Tim. ii. 5; Heb. vii. 25; ix. 24.   [b] Rom. iii. 25; 2 Cor. v. 18; chap. i. 7; iv. 10.

NOTES ON CHAP. II

Verse 1. *My little children*] Τεκνια μου· *My beloved children;* the address of an affectionate father to children whom he tenderly loves. The term also refers to the apostle's *authority* as their spiritual father, and their *obligation* to obey as his spiritual children.

That ye sin not.] This is the language of the whole Scripture; of every dispensation, ordinance, institution, doctrine, and word of God. *Sin not*—do not run into ruin; live not so as to promote your own misery; be happy, for it is the will of God that ye should be so; therefore he wills that ye should be holy: *holiness* and *happiness* are inseparable; *sin* and *misery* are equally so.

And if any man sin] If, through ignorance, inexperience, the violence of temptation, unwatchfulness, &c., ye have fallen into sin, and grieved the Spirit of God, do not continue in the sin, nor under the guilt; do not despair of being again restored to the favour of God; your case, it is true, is deeply deplorable, but not desperate; there is still hope, for—

We have an advocate with the Father] We still have him before the throne who died for our offences, and rose again for our justification; and *there* he makes intercession for us. He is the *righteous;* he who suffered, the JUST for the *unjust,* that he might

bring us to God. Do not, therefore, despair, but have immediate recourse to God through him.

Verse 2. *And he is the propitiation*] Ἱλασμος· The *atoning sacrifice* for our sins. This is the proper sense of the word as used in the *Septuagint,* where it often occurs; and is the translation of אשם *asham,* an *oblation for sin,* Amos viii. 14. חטאת *chattath,* a *sacrifice for sin,* Ezek. xliv. 27. כפור *kippur,* an *atonement,* Num. v. 8. See the note on Rom. iii. 25, and particularly the note on Luke xviii. 13. The word is used only here and in chap. iv. 10.

And not for ours only] It is not for us *apostles* that he has died, nor exclusively for the *Jewish people,* but περι ὁλου του κοσμου, *for the whole world,* Gentiles as well as Jews, all the descendants of Adam. The apostle does not say that he died for any select *part* of the inhabitants of the earth, or for *some out of every nation, tribe,* or *kindred;* but for ALL MANKIND: and the attempt to limit this is a violent outrage against God and his word.

For the meaning of the word παρακλητος, which we here translate *advocate,* see the note on John xiv. 16.

From these verses we learn that a poor backslider need not despair of again finding mercy; this passage holds out sufficient encouragement for his hope. There is scarcely another such in the Bible; and why? That sinners might not *presume* on the mercy of God. And

A. M. cir. 4073.
A. D. cir. 69.
Impp. Galba,
Othone, Vitel.
et Vespa-
siano.

only, but ᶜ also for *the sins of* the whole world.

3 And hereby we do know that we know him, if we keep his commandments.

4 He ᵈ that saith, I know him, and keepeth not his commandments, ᵉ is a liar, and the truth is not in him.

5 But ᶠ whoso keepeth his word, ᵍ in him verily is the love of God perfected : ʰ hereby know we that we are in him.

6 ⁱ He that saith he abideth in him ᵏ ought

himself also so to walk, even as he walked.

A. M. cir. 4073.
A. D. cir. 69.
Impp. Galba,
Othone, Vitel.
et Vespa-
siano.

7 Brethren, ¹ I write no new commandment unto you, but an old commandment ᵐ which ye had from the beginning. The old commandment is the word which ye have heard from the beginning,

8 Again ⁿ a new commandment I write unto you, which thing is true in him and in you : ᵒ because the darkness is past, and ᵖ the true light now shineth.

ᶜ John i. 29 ; iv. 42 ; xi. 51, 52 ; chap. iv. 14.——ᵈ Chapter i. 6 ; iv. 20.——ᵉ Chap. i. 8.——ᶠ John xiv. 21, 23.——ᵍ Chap. iv. 12. ʰ Chap. iv. 13.——ⁱ John xv. 4, 5.——ᵏ Matt. xi. 29 ; John xiii.

15 ; 1 Pet. ii. 21.——¹ 2 John 5.——ᵐ Chapter iii. 11 ; 2 John 5. ⁿ John xiii. 34 ; xv. 12.——ᵒ Rom. xiii. 12 ; Eph. v. 8 ; 1 Thess. v. 5, 8.——ᵖ John i. 9 ; viii. 12 ; xii. 35.

---

why this *one ?* That no backslider might utterly despair. Here, then, is a guard against presumption on the one hand, and despondency on the other.

Verse 3. *And hereby we do know that we know him*] If we keep the commandments of God, loving him with all our heart, and our neighbour as ourselves, we have the fullest proof that we have the true saving knowledge of God and his Christ. The *Gnostics* pretended to much *knowledge*, but their knowledge left them in possession of all their bad passions and unholy habits ; they, therefore, gave no proof that they had known either God or his Son Jesus ; nor is any man properly acquainted with God, who is still under the power of his sins.

Verse 4. *He that saith, I know him*] This is a severe blow against those false teachers, and against all pretenders to religious knowledge, who live under the power of their sins ; and against all Antinomians, and false boasters in the righteousness of Christ as a covering for their personal unholiness. They are all *liars*, and no *truth of God* is in them.

Verse 5. *But whoso keepeth his word*] Conscientiously observes his doctrine, the spirit and letter of the religion of Christ.

Is the love of God perfected] The design of God's love in sending Jesus Christ into the world to die for the sin of man τετελειωται, *is accomplished*, in that man who receives the doctrine, and applies for the salvation provided for him. This seems to be the meaning of the apostle.

That we are in him.] That we have entered into his spirit and views, received his salvation, have been enabled to walk in the light, and have communion with him by the Holy Spirit.

Verse 6. *Abideth in him*] He who not only professes to have known Christ, but also that he has communion with him, and abides in his favour, should prove the truth of his profession by walking as Christ walked ; living a life of devotion and obedience to God, and of benevolence and beneficence to his neighbour. Thus Christ walked ; and he has left us an example that we should follow his steps.

To *be in Christ*, ver. 5, is to be converted to the Christian faith, and to have received the remission of sins. To *abide in Christ*, ver. 6, is to *continue* in

that state of salvation, growing in grace, and in the knowledge of our Lord Jesus Christ.

Verse 7. *Brethren, I write no new commandment*] There seems a contradiction between this and the next verse. But the apostle appears to speak, not so much of any difference in the *essence* of the precept itself, as in reference to the *degrees* of light and grace belonging to the Mosaic and Christian dispensations. It was *ever* the command of God that men should receive his light, walk by that light, and love him and one another. But this commandment was *renewed* by Christ with much latitude and spirituality of meaning ; and also with much additional *light* to see its extent, and *grace* to observe it. It may therefore be called the OLD *commandment*, which was from the beginning ; and also a NEW *commandment* revealed afresh and illustrated by Christ, with the important addition to the meaning of *Thou shalt love thy neighbour as thyself*, ye shall love the brethren so as to lay down your lives for each other. See the note on John xiii. 34.

Instead of αδελφοι, *brethren*, ABC, thirteen others, with both the *Syriac*, Erpen's *Arabic*, *Coptic*, *Sahidic*, *Armenian*, *Slavonic*, and *Vulgate*, with several of the *fathers*, have αγαπητοι, *beloved*. This is without doubt the *true reading*.

Verse 8. *Which thing is true in him and in you*] It is true that Christ loved the world so well as to lay down his life for it ; and it was true in them, in all his faithful followers at that time, who were ready to lay down their lives for the testimony of Jesus. There is a saying in *Synopsis* Sohar, p. 94, n. 51, that may cast some light on this passage : *That way in which the just have walked, although it be* OLD, *yet may be said to be* NEW *in the love of the righteous.* The love that the righteous bear to God and to each other is a *renewal* of the commandment.

The darkness is past] The total thick darkness of the heathen world, and the comparative darkness of the Mosaic dispensation, are now *passing away ;* and the pure and superior light of Christianity is now diffusing its beams everywhere. He does not say that the darkness was *all gone by*, but παραγεται, *it is passing away ;* he does not say that the *fulness* of the *light* had appeared, but ηδη φαινει, it is *now shining*, and will shine more and more to the perfect day ; for the darkness

2

A. M. cir. 4073.
A. D. cir. 69.
Impp. Galba,
Othone, Vitel.
et Vespa-
siano.

9 q He that saith he is in the light, and hateth his brother, is in darkness even until now.

10 r He that loveth his brother, abideth in the light, and s there is none t occasion of stumbling in him.

11 But he that hateth his brother is in darkness, and u walketh in darkness, and knoweth not whither he goeth, because that darkness hath blinded his eyes.

12 I write unto you, little children, because v your sins are forgiven you for his name's sake.

A. M. cir. 4073.
A. D. cir. 69.
Impp. Galba,
Othone, Vitel.
et Vespa-
siano.

13 I write unto you, fathers, because ye have known him w *that is* from the beginning. I write unto you, young men. because ye have overcome the wicked one. I write unto you, little children, because ye have known the Father.

---

q 1 Cor. xiii. 2; 2 Pet. i. 9; chap. iii. 14, 15.——r Chap. iii. 14. s 2 Pet. i. 10.——t Gr. *scandal.*

u John xii. 35.——v Luke xxiv. 47; Acts iv. 12; x. 43; xiii. 38; chap. i. 7.——w Chap. i. 1.

---

passes away in proportion as the light shines and increases.

Verse 9. *He that saith he is in the light*] He that professes to be a convert to Christianity, even in the lowest degree; *and hateth his brother*—not only does not love him, but wills and does him evil, as the Jews did the Gentiles; *is in darkness*—has received no saving knowledge of the truth; and, whatever he may pretend, is in heathen ignorance, or even worse than heathen ignorance, to the present time, notwithstanding the clear shining of the light of the Gospel.

Verse 10. *He that loveth his brother*] That is, his neighbour, his fellow creature, whether Jew or Gentile, so as to bear him continual good will, and to be ready to do him every kind office; *abideth in the light*—not only gives proof that he has received Christ Jesus the Lord, but that he walks in him, that he *retains* the grace of his justification, and grows therein.

And there is none occasion of stumbling in him.] Και σκανδαλον εν αυτω ουκ εστιν· *And there is no stumbling block in him;* he neither *gives* nor *receives offence:* love prevents him from giving any to his neighbour; and love prevents him from receiving any from his neighbour, because it leads him to put the best construction on every thing. Besides, as he walks in the light, he sees the stumbling blocks that are in the way, and avoids them; every part of his path being illuminated. Many fall into sin because they do not see the snares that are in the way; and they do not see the snares because they either have not received, or do not abide in, the light.

Verse 11. *But he that hateth his brother is in darkness*] He is still in his heathen or unconverted state; and *walketh in darkness*, his conduct being a proof of that state; *and knoweth not whither he goeth*—having no proper knowledge of God or eternal things; and *cannot tell whether he is going to heaven or hell, because that darkness has blinded his eyes*—darkened his whole soul, mind, and heart.

Verse 12. *I write unto you, little children*] Τεκνια· *Beloved children,* (see on ver. 1,) those who were probably the apostle's own converts, and members of the Church over which he presided. But it may be applied to young converts in general; those who can call God *Abba, Father,* by the Holy Spirit: therefore he says of them, that *their sins were forgiven them for his name's sake;* i. e. on account of *Jesus,* the *Saviour,*

who had died for them, and was now their Mediator at the right hand of God.

Verse 13. *I write unto you, fathers*] By fathers it is very likely that the apostle means persons who had embraced Christianity on its first promulgation in Judea and in the Lesser Asia, some of whom had probably seen Christ in the flesh; for this appears to be what is meant by, *Ye have known him from the beginning.* These were the *elders* and *eye witnesses,* who were of the longest standing in the Church, and well established in the truths of the Gospel, and in Christian experience. But τον απ' αρχης, *him who is from the beginning,* may mean Jesus Christ in the eternity of his nature, see John i. 1, 2; but the sense is the same.

I write unto you, young men] These were confirmed disciples of Christ; persons who were well-grounded in the truth, had been thoroughly exercised in the Christian warfare, were no longer agitated by doubts and fears, but had arrived at the abiding testimony of the Spirit of God in their consciences; hence they are said to have *overcome the wicked one,* ver. 14. They were persons in the prime of life, and in the zenith of their faith and love.

I write unto you, little children] Παιδια, a very different term from that used in the 12th verse, τεκνια, which means *beloved* children, as we have already seen. This is another *class,* and their state is differently described: *Ye have known the Father.* If the apostle does not use these two words indifferently, *four* states instead of *three,* are here described:—

1. FATHERS, πατερες· those who had been converted at the very commencement of Christianity, and had seen the eternal Word manifested in the flesh.

2. YOUNG MEN, νεανισκοι· youths in the prime of their spiritual life, *valiant soldiers,* fighting under the banner of Christ, who had confounded Satan in his wiles, and overcome him by the blood of the Lamb.

3. LITTLE CHILDREN, παιδια· disciples of Christ, not of very long standing in the Church, nor of much experience, but who had *known the Father;* i. e. persons who had been made sons: God had sent the Spirit of his Son into their hearts, whereby they cried *Abba, Father!*

4. BELOVED CHILDREN, τεκνια· the most recent converts, and particularly those among *young men* and *women* who, from their youth, simplicity, openheartedness, and affectionate attachment to God and

A. M. cir. 4073.
A. D. cir. 69.
Impp. Galba,
Othone, Vitel.
et Vespa-
siano.

14 I have written unto you, fathers, because ye have known him *that is* from the beginning. I have written unto you, young men, because ˣ ye are strong, and the word of God abideth in you, and ye have overcome the wicked one.

15 ʸ Love not the world, neither the things *that are* in the world. ᶻ If any man love the world, the love of the Father is not in him.

A. M. cir. 4073.
A. D. cir. 69.
Impp. Galba,
Othone, Vitel.
et Vespa-
siano.

16 For all that *is* in the world, the lust of the flesh, ᵃ and the lust of the eyes, and the pride of life, is not of the Father, but is of the world.

17 And ᵇ the world passeth away, and the lust thereof: but he that doeth the will of God abideth for ever.

ˣ Eph. vi. 10.——ʸ Rom. xii. 2.——ᶻ Matt. vi. 24; Gal. i. 10; James iv. 4.

ᵃ Eccles. v. 11.——ᵇ 1 Cor. vii. 31; James i. 10; iv. 14; 1 Pet. i. 24.

---

his cause, were peculiarly dear to this aged apostle of Jesus Christ. These are represented as having their *sins forgiven them on account of his name,* δια το ονομα αυτου, that is, for the sake of Jesus, or on account of his merit or worthiness.

These *four classes* constituted the household or family of God; each class, in ascending gradation, seems to have had more light, experience, and holiness than the other. 1. The τεκνια, *beloved children,* or *infants,* are those who are just born into the heavenly family. 2. The παιδια, *little children,* are those who are able to walk and speak; they know their heavenly Father, and can call him by that name. 3. The νεανισκοι, *young men,* are such as are grown up to man's estate; these perform the most difficult part of the labour, and are called to fight the battles of the Lord. 4. The πατερες, *fathers,* are those who are at the foundation of the spiritual family, and have known the whole economy of the work of God in themselves and in others. These have the largest stock of spiritual wisdom and religious experience. All these answer to the component members of a perfect human family. 1. There is the *beloved infant* dandled on the knees of its parents. 2. There are the *little children* that can speak a little, run about, answer to their own names, distinguish and call on their father and mother, and are now put under *instruction.* 3. There are the *youths,* those who are grown up to man's estate, are *strong* to labour, *retain* the instructions they have received, act upon them, and are occasionally called upon to *defend* their family, property, and country, against spoilers and oppressors. 4. There are the *parents,* the *father* and *mother,* from whom the family sprang, and who are the governors and directors of the household. To these *four* classes, in a perfect family, the apostle appears to allude; and we see, considered in this light, with what delicacy and propriety he uses these images.

Verse 14. *The word of God abideth in you*] Ye have not only thoroughly known and digested the Divine doctrine, but your hearts are moulded into it; ye know it to be the truth of God from the *power* and happiness with which it inspires you, and from the constant abiding testimony of the Spirit of that truth which lives and witnesses wherever that truth lives and predominates.

Verse 15. *Love not the world*] Though these several classes were so well acquainted with Divine things, and had all tasted the powers of the world to come; yet so apt are men to be drawn aside by sen-

sible things, that the Holy Spirit saw it necessary to caution these against the love of the world, the inordinate desire of earthly things. *Covetousness* is the predominant vice of old age: *Ye fathers, love not the world.* The things which are in the world, its profits, pleasures, and honours, have the strongest allurements for *youth;* therefore, ye *young men, little children,* and *babes,* love not the things of this world. Let those hearts abide faithful to God who have taken him for their portion.

The love of the Father is not in him.] The love of God and the love of earthly things are incompatible. If you give place to the love of the world, the love of God cannot dwell in you; and if you have not his love, you can have no peace, no holiness, no heaven.

Verse 16. *For all that is in the world*] All that it can boast of, all that it can promise, is only sensual, transient gratification, and even this promise it cannot fulfil; so that its warmest votaries can complain loudest of their disappointment.

The lust of the flesh] Sensual and impure desires which seek their gratification in women, strong drink, delicious viands, and the like.

Lust of the eyes] Inordinate desires after *finery* of every kind, gaudy dress, splendid houses, superb furniture, expensive equipage, trappings, and decorations of all sorts.

Pride of life] Hunting after honours, titles, and pedigrees; boasting of ancestry, family connections, great offices, honourable acquaintance, and the like.

Is not of the Father] Nothing of these inordinate attachments either comes from or leads to God. They are of this world; here they begin, flourish, and end. They deprave the mind, divert it from Divine pursuits, and render it utterly incapable of spiritual enjoyments.

Verse 17. *The world passeth away*] All these things are continually fading and perishing; and the very *state* in which they are possessed is changing perpetually; and the earth and its works will be shortly burnt up.

And the lust thereof] The men of this world, their vain pursuits, and delusive pleasures, are passing away in their successive generations, and their very memory perishes; *but he that doeth the will of God*—that seeks the pleasure, profit, and honour that comes from above, shall abide for ever, always happy through time and eternity, because God, the unchangeable source of felicity, is his portion.

2

A. M. cir. 4073.
A. D. cir. 69.
Impp. Galba,
Othone, Vitel.
et Vespa-
siano.

18 c Little children, d it is the last time : and as ye have heard that e antichrist shall come, f even now are there many antichrists ; whereby we know g that it is the last time.

19 h They went out from us, but they were

not of us ; for i if they had been of us, they would *no doubt* have continued with us : but *they went out,* k that they might be made manifest that they were not all of us.

20 But l ye have an unction m from the

A. M. cir. 4073.
A. D. cir. 69.
Impp. Galba,
Othone, Vitel
et Vespa-
siano.

---

c John xxi. 5.——d Heb. i. 2.——e 2 Thess. ii. 3, &c. ; 2 Pet. ii. 1 ; chap. iv. 3.——f Matt. xxiv. 5, 24 ; 2 John 7.——g 1 Tim. iv. 1 ; 2 Tim. iii. 1.——h Deut. xiii. 13 ; Psa. xli. 9 ; Acts xx. 30.

i Matt. xxiv. 24 ; John vi. 37 ; x. 28, 29 ; 2 Tim. ii. 19.——k 1 Cor. xi. 19.——l 2 Cor. i. 21 ; Heb. i. 9 ; verse 27.——m Mark i. 24 ; Acts iii. 14.

Verse 18. *Little children, it is the last time*] This place is variously understood. This is the *last dispensation* of grace and mercy to mankind ; the *present age* is the *conclusion* of the Jewish state, as the temple and holy city are shortly to be destroyed. But as there are many who suppose that this epistle was written after the destruction of Jerusalem, consequently the words cannot, on that supposition, refer to this. Others think that εσχατη ωρα should be translated, a most *difficult, perilous,* and *wretched time* ; a time in which all kinds of vices, heresies, and pollutions shall have their full reign ; that time which our Lord predicted, Matt. vii. 15, when he said, *Beware of false prophets.* And xxiv. 11, 12 : *Many false prophets shall arise, and shall deceive many ; and because iniquity shall abound, the love of many shall wax cold.* And verse 24 : *There shall arise false Christs and false prophets, and shall show great signs and wonders.* And verse 25 : *Behold, I have told you before.* Now the apostle may allude to these predictions of our Lord ; but all these refer to a time antecedent to the destruction of Jerusalem. I am therefore inclined to think, whatever may be here the precise meaning of the *last time,* that the epistle before us was written while Jerusalem yet stood. See what is said in the preface on this head.

Antichrist shall come] Who is this αντιχριστος, antichrist ? Is he the Emperor *Domitian,* the *Gnostics, Nicolaitans, Nazareans, Cerinthians, Romish pontiffs,* &c., &c. ? Ans. Any *person, thing, doctrine, system of religion, polity,* &c., which is *opposed* to *Christ,* and to the spirit and spread of his Gospel, is antichrist. We need not look for this imaginary being in any of the above exclusively. Even *Protestantism* may have its antichrist as well as *Popery.* Every *man* who opposes the spirit of the Gospel, and every *teacher* and *writer* who endeavours to lower the Gospel standard to the spirit and taste of the world, is a genuine *antichrist,* no matter *where* or *among whom* he is found. The heresies which sprang up in the days of St. John were the *antichrist* of that time. As there has been a succession of oppositions to Christianity in its spirit and spread through every age since its promulgation in the world, so there has been a succession of *antichrists.* We may bring this matter much lower ; every enemy of Christ, every one who opposes his reign in the world, in others, or in himself, is an *antichrist* ; and consequently every *wicked man* is an antichrist. But the name has been generally applied to whatever *person* or *thing systematically* opposes Christ and his religion.

Many antichrists] Many false prophets, false Messiahs, heretics, and corrupters of the truth.

Whereby we know that it is the last time.] That time which our Lord has predicted, and of which he has warned us.

Verse 19. *They went out from us*] These heretics had belonged to our Christian assemblies, they professed Christianity, and do so still ; but we apostles did not commission them to preach to you, for they have disgraced the Divine doctrine with the most pernicious opinions ; they have given up or explained away its most essential principles ; they have mingled the rest with heathenish rites and Jewish glosses. While, therefore, we acknowledge that they once belonged to us, we assert that they are not of us. They are not Christians ; we abhor their conduct and their creed. We never sent them to teach.

They were not of us] For a considerable time before they left our assemblies they gave proofs that they had departed from the faith ; *for if they had been of us*—if they had been apostles, and continued in the firm belief of the Christian doctrines, they would not have departed from us to form a sect of themselves.

That they were not all of us.] They were not expelled from the Christian Church ; they were not sent out by us ; but they separated from it and us. None of them had been inspired as we apostles were, though they pretended to a very high teaching ; but their separating from us *manifested* that they were not taught, as we were, by the Spirit of God. These false teachers probably drew many sincere souls away with them ; and to this it is probable the apostle alludes when he says, they were not ALL *of us.* Some *were ;* others *were not.*

Verse 20. *But ye have an unction*] The word χρισμα signifies not an *unction,* but an *ointment,* the very thing itself by which *anointing* is effected ; and so it was properly rendered in our former translations. Probably this is an allusion to the holy anointing oil of the law, and to Psa. xlv. 7 : *God hath anointed thee with the oil of gladness*—he hath given thee the *plenitude of the Spirit,* which none of thy *fellows*—none of the prophets, ever received in such abundance. By this it is evident that not only the gifts of the Spirit, but the Holy Spirit himself, is intended. This Spirit dwelt at that time in a peculiar manner in the Church, to teach apostles, teachers, and all the primitive believers, every thing requisite for their salvation ; and to make them the instruments of handing down to posterity that glorious system of truth which is contained in the New Testament. As *oil* was used among the Asiatics for the inauguration of persons into important offices, and this oil was acknowledged to be an emblem of the *gifts* and *graces of the Holy Spirit,* without which the duties of those offices could not be dis-

2

A. M. cir. 4073.
A. D. cir. 69.
Impp. Galba,
Othone, Vitel.
et Vespa-
siano.

Holy One, and [n] ye know all things.

21 I have not written unto you because ye know not the truth, but because ye know it, and that no lie is of the truth.

22 [o] Who is a liar but he that denieth that Jesus is the Christ? He is anti-christ, that denieth the Father and the Son.

23 [p] Whosoever denieth the Son, the same hath not the Father: *but* [q] he that acknowledgeth the Son hath the Father also.

A. M. cir. 4073.
A. D. cir. 69.
Impp. Galba,
Othone, Vitel.
et Vespa-
siano.

---

[n] John x. 4, 5; xiv. 26; xvi. 13; verse 27.——[o] Chapter iv. 3; 2 John 7.

[p] John xv. 23; 2 John 9.——[q] John xiv. 7, 9, 10; chapter iv. 15.

---

charged; so it is put here for the Spirit himself, who presided in the Church, and from which all gifts and graces flowed. The χρισμα, *chrism* or *ointment* here mentioned is also an allusion to the *holy anointing ointment* prescribed by God himself, Exod. xxx. 23–25, which was composed of fine *myrrh*, sweet *cinnamon*, sweet *calamus*, *cassia lignea*, and *olive oil*. This was an emblem of the gifts and graces of the Divine Spirit. See the notes on the above place. And for the *reason* of this anointing see the note on Exod. xxix. 7.

Ye know all things.] Every truth of God necessary to your salvation and the salvation of man in general, and have no need of that knowledge of which the Gnostics boast.

But although the above is the sense in which this verse is generally understood, yet there is reason to doubt its accuracy. The adjective παντα, which we translate *all things*, is most probably in the accusative case singular, having ανθρωπον, *man*, or some such substantive, understood. The verse therefore should be translated: *Ye have an ointment from the Holy One, and ye know or discern* EVERY MAN. This inter-pretation appears to be confirmed by των πλανωντων in ver. 26, *those who are deceiving* or *misleading you*; and in the same sense should παντων, ver. 27, be understood: *But as the same anointing teacheth you* παντων, not *of all things*, but *of* ALL MEN. It is plain, from the whole tenor of the epistle, that St. John is guarding the Christians against seducers and deceivers, who were even then disturbing and striving to corrupt the Church. In consequence of this he desires them *to try the spirits whether they were of God*, chap. iv. 1. But how were they to try them? Principally by that *anointing*—that *spiritual light* and *discernment* which they had received from God; and also by comparing the doctrine of these men with *what they had heard from the beginning*. The *anointing* here mentioned seems to mean the spirit of illumination, or great knowledge and discernment in spiritual things. By this they could readily distinguish the false apostles from the true.

Verse 21. *I have not written, &c.*] It is not because ye are *ignorant* of these things that I write to you, but because you *know them*, and can by these judge of the doctrines of those false teachers, and clearly perceive that they are *liars*; for they contradict the *truth* which ye have already received, and consequently their doc-trine is a lie, and no lie can be of the truth, *i. e.* con-sistent with Christianity.

Verse 22. *Who is a liar but he that denieth that*

Jesus is the Christ?] Here we see some of the false doctrines which were then propagated in the world. There were certain persons who, while they acknow-ledged Jesus to be a *Divine teacher*, denied him to be the *Christ*, i. e. the MESSIAH.

He is antichrist, that denieth the Father and the Son.] He is antichrist who denies the supernatural and miraculous birth of Jesus Christ, who denies Jesus to be the *Son of God*, and who denies God to be the *Father* of the Lord Jesus; thus he denies the Father and the Son. The Jews in general, and the Gnostics in particular, denied the *miraculous conception* of Jesus; with both he was accounted no more than a *common man*, the son of Joseph and Mary. But the Gnostics held that a Divine person, Æon, or angelical being, dwelt in him; but all things else relative to his mira-culous generation and Divinity they rejected. These were *antichrists*, who denied *Jesus* to be the Christ.

Verse 23. *Whosoever denieth the Son*] He who denies Jesus to be the Son of God, and consequently the Christ or Messiah, *he hath not the Father*—he can have no birth from above, he cannot be enrolled among the children of God, because none can be a child of God but by faith in Christ Jesus.

He that acknowledgeth the Son hath the Father also.] This clause is printed by our translators in Italics to show it to be of doubtful authority, as it was probably wanting in the chief of those MSS. which they consulted, as it was in Coverdale's Bible, printed 1535; Tindall's Text, printed 1548; and in all the early printed editions (which I have seen) previously to 1566; the Bible of *Richard Cardmarden*, printed in English at Rouen, where this clause is inserted in a different letter between brackets. But that the clause is genuine, and should be restored to the text without any mark of spuriousness, as I have done in the text of this work, is evident from the authorities by which it is supported. It is found in ABC, and in between twenty and thirty others of the best authority; as also in both the *Syriac*, Erpen's *Arabic*, *Coptic*, *Sahidic*, *Armenian*, and *Vulgate*. It is also quoted as a part of the text by *Origen*, *Meletius*, *Athanasius*, both the *Cyrils*, *Theophylact*, *Vigilius* of Tapsum, *Pelagius*, *Cerealis*, *Cassian*; and in substance by *Euthalius*, *Epiphanius*, *Cyprian*, *Hilary*, *Faustinus*, *Lucifer* of Cagliari, *Augustine*, and *Bede*. It is want-ing in the *Arabic*, in the Polyglot, in a MSS. in the *Harleian* library, and in some few others. It is doubt-less genuine, and Griesbach has with propriety restored it to the text, from which it never should have been separated.

A. M. cir. 4073.
A. D. cir. 69.
Impp. Galba,
Othone, Vitel.
et Vespa-
siano.

24 Let that therefore abide in you ʳ which ye have heard from the beginning. If that which ye have heard from the beginning shall remain in you, ˢ ye also shall continue in the Son, and in the Father.

25 ᵗ And this is the promise that he hath promised us, *even* eternal life.

26 These *things* have I written unto you ᵘ concerning them that seduce you.

27 But ᵛ the anointing which ye have received of him abideth in you, and ʷ ye need not that

A.M. cir. 4073
A. D. cir. 69.
Impp. Galba,
Othone, Vite
et Vespa-
siano.

any man teach you : but as the same anointing ˣ teacheth you of all things, and is truth, and is no lie, and even as it hath taught you, ye shall abide in ʸ him.

28 And now, little children, abide in him that, ᶻ when he shall appear, we may have confidence, ᵃ and not be ashamed before him at his coming.

29 ᵇ If ye know that he is righteous, ᶜ ye know that ᵈ every one that doeth righteousness is born of him.

ʳ 2 John 6.——ˢ John xvi. 23 ; chap. i. 3.——ᵗ John xvii. 3 ; chap. i. 2 ; v. 11.——ᵘ Chapter iii. 7 ; 2 John 7.——ᵛ Verse 20. ʷ Jer. xxxi. 33, 34 ; Heb. viii. 10, 11.

ˣ John xiv. 26 ; xvi. 13 ; ver. 20.——ʸ Or, *it.*——ᶻ Chap. iii. 2 ᵃ Chap. iv. 17.——ᵇ Acts xxii. 14.——ᶜ Or, *know ye.*——ᵈ Chap iii. 7, 10.

Verse 24. *Let that therefore abide in you*] Continue in the doctrines concerning the incarnation, passion, death, resurrection, ascension, and intercession of the Lord Jesus, which you have heard preached from the beginning by us his apostles.

Ye also shall continue in the Son, and in the Father.] Ye who are preachers shall not only be acknowledged as ministers of the Church of Christ, but be genuine children of God, by faith in the Son of his love ; and ye all, thus continuing, shall have fellowship with the Father and with the Son.

Verse 25. *This is the promise*] God has promised eternal life to all who believe on Christ Jesus. So they who receive his doctrine, and continue in communion with the Father and the Son, shall have this eternal life.

Verse 26. *These* things *have I written*] Either meaning the whole epistle, or what is contained in the preceding verses, from the beginning of the 18th to the end of the 25th.

Them that seduce you.] Περι των πλανωντων ὑμας· That is, the *deceivers that were among them*, and who were labouring to pervert the followers of Christ.

Verse 27. *But the anointing which ye have received*] That *ointment*, the gifts of the Holy Spirit, mentioned ver. 20, where see the note.

Ye need not that any man teach you] The *Gnostics*, who pretended to the highest illumination, could bring no proof that they were divinely taught, nor had they any thing in their teaching worthy the acceptance of the meanest Christian ; therefore they had no need of that, nor of any other teaching but that which *the same anointing teacheth*, the same Spirit from whom they had already received the light of the glory of God, in the face of Jesus Christ. Whatever that taught, they needed ; and whatever those taught whose teaching was according to this Spirit, they needed. St. John does not say that those who had once received the teaching of the Divine Spirit had no farther need of the ministry of the Gospel ; no, but he says they had no need of such teaching as their false teachers proposed to them ; nor of any other teaching that was different from *that anointing*, i. e. the teaching of the Spirit of God. No man, howsoever holy, wise, or pure, can ever be in such a state as to have no need of the Gospel ministry ; they who think so give the highest

proof that they have never yet learned of Christ or his Spirit.

And is truth] Because it is the Spirit of truth. John xvi. 13.

And is no lie] It has nothing like the fables of the Gnostics. It can neither deceive, nor be deceived.

Verse 28. *And now, little children*] Τεκνια, *Beloved children*, abide in him——in Christ Jesus. Let his word and spirit continually abide in you, and have communion with the Father and the Son.

That when he shall appear] To judge the world, *we may have confidence*, παρρησιαν, *freedom of speech, liberty of access, boldness*, from a conviction that our cause is good, and that we have had proper ground for exultation ; *and not be ashamed*——confounded, when it appears that those who were brought to Christ Jesus, have apostatized, and are no longer found in the congregation of the saints, and consequently are not our crown of rejoicing in the day of the Lord Jesus. Abide in him, that this may not be the case.

Verse 29. *If ye know that he is righteous*] That God is a holy God, *ye know* also, *that every one who doeth righteousness*——who lives a holy life, following the commandments of God, *is born of him*, BEGOTTEN *of him*——is made a partaker of the Divine nature, without which he could neither have a holy heart, nor live a holy life.

This verse properly belongs to the following chapter, and should not be separated from it. The subject is the same, and does not stand in any strict relation to that with which the 28th verse concludes.

THE *titles* bestowed on Christians in the New Testament have been misunderstood by many. *What belongs, strictly speaking, to the* PURE *and* HOLY, *is often applied to those who, though bound by their* PROFESSION *to be such, were very far from it.* This has been strongly denied by writers who should have known better. Dr. *Taylor* has handled this point well in his *Key to the Apostolic Writings*, from which I have given a copious extract in my preface to the Epistle to the Romans, from the conviction that the subject had been most dangerously misapprehended ; and that several of the worst heresies which disgrace religion had sprung from this misapprehension. With some, Dr. *Taylor's* being an *Arian* was sufficient to invalidate any testimony he might offer ; but it is no discovery of Dr. Taylor ; it is what every attentive, *unprejudiced* reader finds on reading the Old Testament in connection with the New. Perhaps the testimony of a judicious *Calvinist* may be better received, not that this truth needs the testimony of either, because it everywhere speaks for itself, but because those who have too little grace, sense, and candour to search for themselves, may be pleased that Dr. *Macknight* saves them the trouble.

After having remarked that the words *born of him*, εξ αυτου γεγεννηται, should be translated *hath been* BEGOTTEN *of him*, which is the literal signification of the word, from γενναω, *genero, gigno, I beget*, (BORN *of God* being nowhere found in the Scripture,) he goes on to say :—

" To understand the import of the high titles which in the New Testament are given to the disciples of Christ, viz. : *the begotten of God*, as here ; *children of God*, as in the next chapter ; *heirs of God*, Rom. viii. 17 ; *elect of God—adopted of God—saints—a royal priesthood—a holy nation—a peculiar people*, 1 Pet. ii. 9 ; the following observations may be of use.

" 1. These high titles were anciently given to the Israelites as a nation, because they were separated from mankind to be God's visible Church, for the purpose of preserving the knowledge and worship of him in the world, as the only true God.

" This appears from God's own words, Exod. xix. 3, &c. : *Tell the children of Israel ; Ye have seen what I did to the Egyptians, and how I bare you on eagles' wings, and brought you unto myself. Now therefore, if ye will obey my voice indeed, and keep my covenant, then ye shall be a peculiar treasure unto me above all people. And ye shall be unto me a kingdom of priests, and a holy nation.* Deut. xiv. 1, &c. . *Ye are the children of the Lord your God—for thou art a holy people to the Lord thy God.* In particular, the title of *God's Son, even his first-born*, was given to the *whole Israelitish nation* by God himself, Exod. iv. 22, chiefly because they were the descendants of Isaac, who was supernaturally begotten by Abraham, through the power which accompanied the promise, Gen. xviii. 10 : *Lo, Sarah shall have a son.* So St. Paul informs us, Rom. ix. 7 : *Neither because they are the seed of Abraham, are they all children ;* (namely of God ;) *but in Isaac shall a seed be to thee —the children of the flesh, these are not the children of God ; but the children of promise are counted for the seed.* The apostle's meaning is, that Ishmael and his posterity, whom Abraham procreated by his own natural strength, being children of the flesh, were not children of God ; that is, they were not made the visible Church and people of God. But Isaac and his descendants, whom Abraham procreated through the strength which accompanied the promise, being more properly procreated by GOD than by *Abraham*, were *the children of God, i. e.* were made the visible Church and people of God, because, by their supernatural generation and title to inherit Canaan, they were a fit image to represent the catholic invisible Church of God, consisting of believers of all ages and nations, who, being regenerated by the Spirit of God, are the true

children of God, and heirs of the heavenly country of which Canaan was a type.

" 2. As the promise, *Lo, Sarah shall have a son*, which was given to Abraham when he was a hundred years old, and Sarah was *ninety*, implied that that son was to be supernaturally procreated ; so the promise given to Abraham, Gen. xvii. 5, *A father of many nations have I constituted thee*, implied that the many nations of believers who, by this promise, were given to Abraham for a seed, were to be *generated by the operation of the Spirit of God*, producing in them faith and obedience, similar to those for which Abraham was constituted the father of all believers. This higher generation, by which believers have the moral image of God communicated to them, is well described, John i. 12 : *As many as received him, to them gave he power to be called the sons of God, even to them who believe on his name ;* οι εγεννηθησαν, *who were* BEGOTTEN, *not of blood, nor of the will of the flesh, nor of the will of man, but of God.* That is : Men become the true sons of God, not by their being naturally descended from this or that father, nor by their being called the *sons of God* by men like themselves, but by God's bestowing on them that high appellation on account of their faith and holiness," (which were produced in them by their regeneration through the Spirit of God.)

" 3. If the Israelites, of whom the ancient visible Church and people of God were composed, were all called the *sons of God* because Isaac, from whom they were descended, was supernaturally begotten by the power of God ; certainly the believers of all ages and nations, of whom the visible Church is composed, may with much greater propriety be called *the sons of God*, since they are begotten of God, and possess his moral nature.

" 4. Thus it appears that the high titles above mentioned, namely, the *sons of God, the children of God, the elect of God, the adoption of sons, the election, saints, holy nation, royal priesthood, peculiar people*, were anciently given to the Israelites AS A NATION, merely on account of their being the *visible* Church and people of God, without any regard to the *personal character* of the *individuals* of whom that nation was composed. It appears, also, that under the Gospel the same high titles were bestowed *on whole Churches*, merely on account of their *profession of Christianity*, without any regard to the *personal character* of the *individuals* who composed these Churches. But these high titles, with some others of greater importance, such as the *begotten of God, the heirs of God, the adoption*, were given in an *appropriated sense* to individuals likewise, on account of their faith and holiness. When given to *whole Churches*, these titles imported nothing more than that the society to which they were given was a *Church of Christ*, (i. e. professed Christianity,) and that the individuals of which that society was composed were entitled to all the privileges belonging to the visible Church of God. But when appropriated to *individuals*, these titles implied that the persons to whom they were given were really partakers of the nature of God ; and that they were the objects of his paternal love, and heirs of his glory.

" Wherefore, in reading the Scriptures, by attending to the different foundations of these titles, and by considering whether they are applied to *Churches* or *individuals*, we shall easily understand their true import. Thus, when St. Paul, writing to the Thessalonians, says, 1 Thess. i. 4, *Knowing, brethren, beloved of God, your election,* he could not mean their election to eternal life, since many of them were living disorderly, 2 Thess. iii. 11, but their election to be the visible Church of God under the Gospel; whereas, when John, in the verse before us, says, *Every one who doeth righteousness hath been begotten of God,* by restricting the title to a specific character he teaches us that the persons of whom he speaks are the *sons of God* in the highest sense, and heirs of eternal glory." How forcible are right words! See also the introduction to the Epistle to the Romans.

CHAPTER III.

The extraordinary love of God towards mankind, and the effects of it, 1–3. Sin is the transgression of the law, and Christ was manifested to take away our sins, 4–6. The children of God are known by the holiness of their lives, the children of the devil by the sinfulness of theirs, 7–10. We should love one another, for he that hateth his brother is a murderer; as Christ laid down his life for us, so we should lay down our lives for the brethren, 11–16. Charity is a fruit of brotherly love; our love should be active, not professional merely, 17, 18. How we may know that we are of the truth, 19–21. They whose ways please God, have an answer to all their prayers, 22. The necessity of keeping the commandment of Christ, that he may dwell in us and we in him by his Spirit, 23, 24.

A. M. cir. 4073.
A. D. cir. 69.
Impp. Galba,
Othone, Vitel.
et Vespasiano.

BEHOLD, what manner of love the Father hath bestowed upon us, that [a] we should be called the sons of God: therefore the world knoweth us not, [b] because it knew him not.

2 Beloved, [c] now are we the sons of God, and [d] it doth not yet appear what we shall be: but we know that, when he shall appear, [e] we shall be like him; for [f] we shall see him as he is.

A. M. cir. 4073
A. D. cir. 69.
Impp. Galba,
Othone, Vitel.
et Vespasiano.

---

[a] John i. 12.——[b] John xv. 18, 19; xvi. 3; xvii. 25.——[c] Isa. lvi. 5; Rom. viii. 15; Gal. iii. 26; iv. 6; chap. v. 1.——[d] Rom. viii. 18; 2 Cor. i. 17.

[e] Rom. viii. 29; 1 Cor. xv. 49; Phil. iii. 21; Col. iii. 4; 2 Pet. i. 4.——[f] Job xix. 26; Psa. xvi. 11; Matt. v. 8; 1 Cor. xiii. 12; 2 Cor. v. 7.

NOTES ON CHAP. III.

Verse 1. *Behold, what manner of love*] Whole volumes might be written upon this and the two following verses, without exhausting the extraordinary subject contained in them, viz., *the love of God to man.* The apostle himself, though evidently filled with God, and walking in the fulness of his light, does not attempt to describe it; he calls on the world and the Church to *behold it,* to *look upon* it, to *contemplate* it, and *wonder* at it.

What manner of love.—Ποταπην αγαπην· *What great love,* both as to *quantity* and *quality;* for these ideas are included in the original term. The length, the breadth, the depth, the height, he does not attempt to describe.

The Father hath bestowed] For we had neither *claim* nor *merit that we should be called,* that is, *constituted* or *made, the sons of God,* who were before children of the wicked one, animal, earthly, devilish; therefore, the love which brought us from such a depth of misery and degradation must appear the more extraordinary and impressive. After κληθωμεν, *that we might be called,* και εσμεν, *and we are,* is added by ABC, seventeen others, both the *Syriac,* Erpen's *Arabic, Coptic, Sahidic, Æthiopic, Slavonic,* and *Vulgate.*

Therefore the world] The Jews, and all who know not God, and are seeking their portion in this life; *knoweth us not*—do not *acknowledge, respect, love,* or *approve* of us. In this sense the word γινωσκειν is here to be understood. The *world* KNEW well enough that there were such persons; but they did not *approve* of them. We have often seen that this is a frequent use of the term *know,* both in *Hebrew* and *Greek,* in the Old Testament and also in the New.

Because it knew him not.] The Jews did not *acknowledge* Jesus; they neither *approved* of him, his doctrine, nor his manner of life.

Verse 2. *Now are we the sons of God*] He speaks of those who are *begotten* of God, and who work righteousness. See the preceding chapter.

And it doth not yet appear what we shall be] Ουπω εφανερωθη· *It is not yet manifest;* though we *know* that we are the children of God, we do not know that state of glorious excellence to which, as such, we shall be raised.

When he shall appear] Εαν φανερωθη· *When he shall be manifested;* i. e., when he comes the second time, and shall be manifested in his glorified human nature to judge the world.

We shall be like him] For our vile bodies shall be made like unto his glorious body; *we shall see him as he is,* in all the glory and majesty both of the Divine and human nature. See Phil. iii. 21; and John xvii. 24: *Father, I will that they also whom thou hast given me be with me where I am, that they may behold my glory.* John had seen his glory on the mount when he was transfigured; but even this must have been ineffably grand; but even this must have been partially obscured, in order to enable the disciples to bear the sight, for they were not then *like him.* But when they shall be like him, they shall see him *as he is*—in all the splendour of his infinite majesty.

A. M. cir. 4073.
A. D. cir. 69.
Impp. Galba,
Othone, Vitel.
et Vespa-
siano.

3 ⁵ And every man that hath this hope in him purifieth himself, even as he is pure.

4 Whosoever committeth sin transgresseth also the law: for ʰ sin is the transgression of the law.

5 And ye know ¹ that he was manifested ᵏ to take away our sins; and ¹ in him is no sin.

6 Whosoever abideth in him sinneth not: ᵐ whosoever sinneth hath not seen him, neither known him.

A. M. cir. 4073
A. D. cir. 69.
Impp. Galba,
Othone, Vitel.
et Vespa-
siano.

⁵ Chap. i. 17.——ʰ Rom. iv. 15; chap. v. 17.——ⁱ Chapter i. 2.
ᵏ Isa. liii. 5, 6, 11; 1 Tim. i. 15; Heb. i. 3; ix. 26; 1 Peter ii.

24.——¹ 2 Cor. v. 21; Hebrews iv. 15; ix. 28; 1 Peter ii. 22.
ᵐ Chap. ii. 4; iv. 8; 3 John 11.

Verse 3. *And every man that hath this hope in him*] All who have the hope of seeing Christ as he is; that is, of *enjoying* him in his own glory; *purifieth himself*—abstains from all evil, and keeps himself from all that is in the world, viz., the lusts of the flesh, of the eye, and the pride of life. God having purified his heart, it is his business to *keep himself in the love of God, looking for the mercy of our Lord Jesus Christ unto eternal life.* The apostle does not here speak of any man purifying his own heart, because this is impossible; but of his *persevering* in the state of purity into which the Lord hath brought him. The words, however, may be understood of a man's anxiously using all the means that lead to purity; and imploring God for the sanctifying Spirit, to " cleanse the thoughts of his heart by its inspiration, that he may perfectly love him, and worthily magnify his name."

As he is pure.] Till he is as completely saved from his sins as Christ was free from sin. Many tell us that " this never can be done, for no man can be saved from sin in this life." Will these persons permit us to ask, How much sin may we be saved from in this life? Something must be *ascertained* on this subject: 1. That the soul may have some *determinate object* in view; 2. That it may not lose its time, or employ its faith and energy, in praying for what is *impossible* to be attained. Now, as he was manifested to take away our sins, ver. 5, to destroy the works of the devil, ver. 8; and as his blood cleanseth from all sin and unrighteousness, chap. i. 7, 9; is it not evident that God means that believers in Christ shall be saved from all sin? For if his blood cleanses from all sin, if he destroys the works of the devil, (and sin is the work of the devil,) and if he who is born of God does not commit sin, ver. 9, then he must be cleansed from all sin; and, while he continues in that state he lives without sinning against God, *for the seed of God remaineth in him, and he cannot sin because he is born, or begotten, of God*, ver. 9. How strangely warped and blinded by prejudice and system must men be who, in the face of such evidence as this, will still dare to maintain that no man can be saved from his sin in this life; but must daily commit sin, in thought, word, and deed, as the Westminster divines have asserted: that is, every man is laid under the *fatal necessity* of sinning as many ways against God as the devil does through his natural wickedness and malice; for even the devil himself can have no other way of sinning against God except by *thought, word,* and *deed.* And yet, according to these, and others of the same creed, " even the most regenerate sin thus against God as long as they live." It is a miserable salvo to say, they do not sin so much as they used to do; and they

do not sin *habitually*, only occasionally. Alas for this system! Could not the grace that saved them *partially* save them *perfectly*? Could not that power of God that saved them from *habitual* sin, save them from *occasional* or accidental sin? Shall we suppose that sin, how potent soever it may be, is as potent as the Spirit and grace of Christ? And may we not ask, If it was for God's glory and their good that they were *partially saved*, would it not have been *more* for God's glory and their good if they had been *perfectly saved*? But the letter and spirit of God's word, and the design and end of Christ's coming, is to save his people *from* their sins. Dr. Macknight having stated that ἁγνίζει, *purifieth*, is in the *present* tense, most ridiculously draws this conclusion from it: " In this life no one can attain to perfect purity; by this text, therefore, as well as by 1 John i. 8, those fanatics are condemned who imagine they are able to live without sin." Yes, doctor, the men you call *fanatics* do most religiously believe that, by the grace of Christ cleansing and strengthening them, they can love God with all their heart, soul, mind, and strength, and their neighbour as themselves; and live without grieving the Spirit of God, and without sinning against their heavenly Father. And they believe that, if they are not thus saved, it is *their own fault.* But a blind man must ever be a bad judge of colours.

Verse 4. *Sin is the transgression of the law.*] The spirit of the law as well as of the Gospel is, that " we should love God with all our powers, and our neighbour as ourselves." All disobedience is contrary to *love;* therefore *sin is the transgression of the law,* whether the act refers immediately to God or to our neighbour.

Verse 5. *And ye know that he was manifested to take away our sins*] He came into the world to destroy the power, pardon the guilt, and cleanse from the pollution of sin. This was the very *design* of his manifestation in the flesh. He was born, suffered, and died for this very purpose; and can it be supposed that he either *cannot* or *will not* accomplish the object of his own coming?

In him is no sin.] And therefore he is properly qualified to be the atoning sacrifice for the sins of men.

Verse 6. *Whosoever abideth in him*] By faith, love, and obedience.

Sinneth not] Because his heart is purified by faith, and he is a worker together with God, and consequently does not receive the grace of God in vain. See on ver. 3.

Hath not seen him] It is no unusual thing with this apostle, both in his gospel and in his epistles, to put occasionally the *past* for the *present*, and the

A. M. cir. 4073. A. D. cir 69. Impp. Galba, Othone, Vitel. et Vespasiano.

7 Little children, [n] let no man
deceive you: [o] he that doeth
righteousness is righteous, even
as he is righteous.
8 [p] He that committeth sin is of the devil; for
the devil sinneth from the beginning For this
purpose the Son of God was manifested, [q] that
he might destroy the works of the devil.
9 [r] Whosoever is born of God doth not commit sin; for [s] his seed remaineth in him: and
he cannot sin, because he is born of God.

10 In this the children of God
are manifest, and the children of
the devil: [t] whosoever doeth not
righteousness is not of God; [u] neither he that loveth not his brother.
11 For [v] this is the [w] message that ye heard
from the beginning, [x] that we should love one
another.
12 Not as [y] Cain, *who* was of that wicked
one, and slew his brother. And wherefore
slew he him? Because his own works

A. M. cir. 4073. A. D. cir. 69. Impp. Galba, Othone, Vitel. et Vespasiano.

[n] Chap. ii. 26 ——[o] Ezek. xviii 5-9; Rom ii. 13; chap. ii. 29. [p] Matt. xiii. 38; John viii 44.——[q] Gen. iii. 15; Luke x. 18; John xvi. 11; Heb ii. 14.——[r] Chap. v 18.——[s] 1 Pet. i. 23.

[t] Chap. ii. 29.——[u] Chap. iv. 8.——[v] Chap. i. 5; ii. 7.——[w] Or, *commandment*.——[x] John xiii. 34; xv. 12; ver. 23; chap. iv. 7, 21; 2 John 5.——[y] Gen. iv. 4, 8; Heb. xi. 4; Jude 11.

present for the *past* tense. It is very likely that here he puts, after the manner of the Hebrew, the *preterite* for the *present:* He who sins against God *doth not see him, neither doth he know him*—the eye of his faith is darkened, so that he cannot see him as he formerly did; and he has no longer the experimental *knowledge* of God as his Father and portion.

Verse 7. *Let no man deceive you*] Either by asserting that "you cannot be saved from sin in this life," or "that sin will do you no harm and cannot alter your state, if you are adopted into the family of God; for sin cannot annul this adoption." Hear God, ye deceivers! *He that doeth righteousness is righteous*, according to his state, nature, and the extent of his moral powers,

Even as he is righteous.] Allowing for the disparity that must necessarily exist between that which is *bounded*, and that which is *without limits*. As God, in the infinitude of his nature, is righteous; so they, being filled with him, are in their limited nature righteous.

Verse 8. *He that committeth sin is of the devil*] Hear this, also, ye who plead for Baal, and cannot bear the thought of that doctrine that states believers are to be saved from all sin in this life! *He who committeth sin is* a child *of the devil*, and shows that he has still the nature of the devil in him; *for the devil sinneth from the beginning*—he was the father of sin, brought sin into the world, and maintains sin in the world by living in the hearts of his own children, and thus leading *them* to transgression; and persuading *others* that they cannot be saved from their sins in this life, that he may secure a continual residence in their heart. He knows that if he has a place there throughout life, he will probably have it at death; and, if so, throughout eternity.

For this purpose] Εις τουτο· For *this very end*—with this *very design*, was Jesus manifested in the flesh, *that he might destroy*, ἱνα λυσῃ, *that he might loose*, the bonds of sin, and *dissolve* the power, influence, and connection of sin. See on ver. 3.

Verse 9. *Whosoever is born of God*] Γεγεννημενος, *Begotten* of God, *doth not commit sin:* "that is," say some, "as he used to do, he does not sin *habitually* as he formerly did." This is bringing the influence and privileges of the heavenly birth very low indeed.

We have the most indubitable evidence that many of the heathen philosophers had acquired, by mental discipline and cultivation, an entire ascendency over all their wonted vicious habits. Perhaps my reader will recollect the story of the physiognomist, who, coming into the place where Socrates was delivering a lecture, his pupils, wishing to put the principles of the man's science to proof, desired him to examine the face of their master, and say what his moral character was. After a full contemplation of the philosopher's visage, he pronounced him "the most gluttonous, drunken, brutal, and libidinous old man that he had ever met." As the character of Socrates was the reverse of all this, his disciples began to insult the physiognomist. Socrates interfered, and said, "The principles of his science may be very correct, *for such I was, but I have conquered it by my philosophy.*" O ye Christian divines! ye real or pretended Gospel ministers! will ye allow the influence of the grace of Christ a sway not even so extensive as that of the philosophy of a heathen who never heard of the true God?

Verse 10. *In this the children of God are manifest*] Here is a fearful text. Who is a child of the devil? *He that commits sin.* Who is a child of God? *He that works righteousness.* By this text we shall stand or fall before God, whatever our particular *creed* may say to the contrary.

Neither he that loveth not his brother.] No man is of God who is not ready on all emergencies to do any act of kindness for the comfort, relief, and support of any human being. For, as God made of one blood all the nations of men to dwell upon the face of the whole earth, so all are of *one family;* and consequently all are *brethren*, and should love as brethren.

Verse 11. *For this is the message*] See chap. i. 5. From the *beginning* God hath taught men that they should *love one another*. How essentially necessary this is to the comfort and well-being of man in this state of trial and difficulty, every sensible man must see. All are dependent upon all; all upon each, and each upon all. Mutual love makes this dependence pleasant and doubly profitable. Nothing can be more pleasing to an ingenuous and generous mind than to communicate acts of kindness.

Verse 12. *Not as Cain*] Men should not act to each other as Cain did to his brother Abel. He mur-

A. M. cir. 4073.
A. D. cir. 69
Impp. Galba,
Othone, Vitel.
et Vespa-
siano.

were evil, and his brother's righteous.

13 Marvel not, my brethren, if [z] the world hate you.

14 [a] We know that we have passed from death unto life, because we love the brethren. [b] He that loveth not *his* brother abideth in death.

---

[z] John xv. 18, 19; xvii. 14; 2 Tim. iii. 12.——[a] Chap. ii. 10. [b] Chap. ii. 9, 11.——[c] Matt. v. 21, 22; chap. iv. 20.——[d] Gal. v.

15 [c] Whosoever hateth his brother is a murderer: and ye know that [d] no murderer hath eternal life abiding in him.

16 [e] Hereby perceive we the love *of God* because he laid down his life for us: and we ought to lay down *our* lives for the brethren.

17 But [f] whoso hath this world's good, and

A. M. cir. 4073.
A. D. cir. 69.
Impp. Galba,
Othone, Vitel.
et Vespa-
siano.

21; Rev. xxi. 8.——[e] John iii. 16; xv. 13; Rom. v. 8; Eph. v. 2, 25; chap. iv. 9, 11.——[f] Deut. xv. 7; Luke iii. 11.

dered him because he was better than himself. But who was Cain? Εκ του πονηρου ην, *he was of the devil.* And who are they who, through pride, lust of power, ambition, gain, &c., murder each other in *wars* and political contentions? Εκ του πονηρου εισι. To attempt to justify the *principle*, and excuse the *instigators, authors, abettors, &c.*, of such wars, is as vain as it is wicked. They are opposed to the *nature of God*, and to that *message* which he has sent to man from the *beginning: Love one another. Love your enemies.* Surely this does not mean, *Blow out their brains*, or, *Cut their throats.* O, how much of the spirit, temper, and letter of the Gospel have the nations of the world, and particularly the nations of Europe, to learn!

And wherefore slew he him?] What could induce a brother to imbrue his hands in a brother's blood? Why, his brother was righteous, and he was wicked; and the seed of the wicked one which was in him induced him to destroy his brother, because the seed of God—the Divine nature, was found in him.

Verse 13. *Marvel not—if the world hate you.*] Expect no better treatment from unconverted Jews and Gentiles than Abel received from his wicked and cruel brother. This was a lesson to the Church, preparatory to *martyrdom.* Expect neither justice nor mercy from the men who are enemies of God. They are either full of malice and envy, hateful, hating one another, or they are specious, hollow, false, and deceitful.

" A *foe* to GOD was ne'er true *friend to* MAN."

Verse 14. *We know that we have passed from death unto life*] *Death* and *life* are represented here as two distinct *territories, states*, or *kingdoms*, to either of which the inhabitants of either may be removed. This is implied in the term μεταβεβηκαμεν, from μετα, denoting *change of place*, and βαινω, *I go.* It is the same figure which St. Paul uses, Col. i. 13: *Who hath delivered us from the power of darkness, and translated us into the kingdom of the Son of his love.* The believers to whom St. John writes had been once in the region and shadow of death, in the place where sin and death reigned, whose subjects they were; but they had left that kingdom of oppression, wretchedness, and wo, and had *come over* to the kingdom of *life*, whose king was the *Prince* and *Author of life;* where all was *liberty, prosperity*, and *happiness;* where *life* and *love* were universally prevalent, and *death* and *hatred* could not enter. *We know*, therefore, says the apostle, *that we are passed* over *from* the territory of *death* to the kingdom of *life, because we love the brethren*, which those who continue in the old kingdom—under the old

covenant, can never do; for *he that loveth not his brother abideth in death.* He has never changed his original residence. He is still an unconverted, unrenewed sinner.

Verse 15. *Whosoever hateth his brother is a murderer*] He has the same principle in him which was in Cain, and it may lead to the same consequences.

No murderer hath eternal life] Eternal life springs from an *indwelling God;* and God cannot dwell in the heart where *hatred* and *malice* dwell. This text has been quoted to prove that *no murderer can be saved.* This is not said in the text; and there have been many instances of persons who have been guilty of murder having had deep and genuine repentance, and who doubtless found mercy from his hands who prayed for his murderers, *Father, forgive them; for they know not what they do!* It is, however, an awful text for the consideration of those who shed human blood on frivolous pretences, or in those *wars* which have their origin in the worst passions of the human heart.

Verse 16. *Hereby perceive we the love* of God] This sixteenth verse of this third chapter of John's first epistle is, in the main, an exact counterpart of the sixteenth verse of the third chapter of St. John's gospel: *God so loved the world, that he gave his only-begotten Son*, &c. Here the apostle says, We perceive, εγνωκαμεν, *we have known*, the love of God, because he laid down his life for us. *Of God* is not in the text, but it is preserved in one MS., and in two or three of the *versions;* but though this does not establish its authenticity, yet του Θεου, *of God*, is necessarily understood, or του Χριστου, *of Christ*, as Erpen's *Arabic* has it; or αυτου εις ημας, *his love to us*, as is found in the Syriac. A higher proof than this of his love Christ could not have possibly given to the children of men.

We ought to lay down our *lives for the brethren.*] We should *risk* our life to save the lives of others; and we should be ready to lay down our lives to redeem their souls when this may appear to be a means of leading them to God.

Verse 17. *But whoso hath this world's good*] Here is a *test* of this love; if we do not *divide our bread* with the hungry, we certainly would not *lay down our life* for him. Whatever love we may pretend to mankind, if we are not charitable and benevolent, we give the lie to our profession. If we have not bowels of compassion, we have not the love of God in us; if we *shut up* our bowels against the poor, we shut Christ out of our hearts, and ourselves out of heaven.

This world's good.—Τον βιον του κοσμου· *The life*

A. M. cir. 4073.
A. D. cir. 69.
Impp. Galba,
Othone, Vitel.
et Vespa-
siano.

seeth his brother have need, and shutteth up his bowels *of compassion* from him, g how dwelleth the love of God in him?

18 My little children, h let us not love in word, neither in tongue; but in deed and in truth.

19 And hereby we know i that we are of the truth, and shall k assure our hearts before him.

20 l For if our heart condemn us, God is greater than our heart, and knoweth all things.

21 m Beloved, if our heart condemn us not,

n *then* have we confidence toward God.

22 And o whatsoever we ask, we receive of him, because we keep his commandments, p and do those things that are pleasing in his sight.

23 q And this is his commandment, That we should believe on the name of his Son Jesus Christ, r and love one another, s as he gave us commandment.

24 And t he that keepeth his commandments u dwelleth in him, and he in him. And v hereby we know that he abideth in us, by the Spirit which he hath given us.

A. D. cir. 4073
A. D. cir. 69.
Impp. Galba,
Othone, Vitel
et Vespa
siano.

---

g Chap. iv. 20.——h Ezek. xxxiii. 31; Rom. xii. 9; Eph. iv. 15; James ii. 15; 1 Pet. i. 22.——i John xviii. 37; chap. i. 8.——k Gr. *persuade.*——l 1 Cor. iv. 4.——m Job xxii. 26.——n Heb. x. 22; chap. ii. 28; iv. 17.——o Psa. xxxiv. 15; cxlv. 18, 19; Prov. xv. 29; Jer. xxix. 12; Matt. vii. 8; xxi. 22; Mark xi. 24; John xiv. 13; xv. 7; xvi. 23, 24; James v. 16; chap. v. 14.——p John viii. 29; ix. 31.——q John vi. 29; xvii. 3.——r Matt. xxii. 29; John xiii. 34; xv. 12; Eph. v. 2; 1 Thess. iv. 9; 1 Pet. iv. 8; verse 11; chap. iv. 21.——s Chap. ii. 8, 10.——t John xiv. 23; xv. 10; chap. iv. 12.——u John xvii. 21, &c.——v Rom. viii. 9; ch. iv. 13.

---

of this world, i. e. *the means of life;* for so βιος is often used. See Mark xii. 44; Luke viii. 43; xv. 12, 30; xxi. 4, and other places.

How dwelleth the love of God in him?] That is, it cannot possibly dwell in such a person. Hardheartedness and God's love never meet together, much less can they be associated.

Verse 18. *My little children*] Τεκνια μου, *My beloved children, let us not love in word*—in merely *allowing* the general *doctrine* of love to God and man to be just and right;

Neither in tongue] In making *professions* of love, and of a charitable and humane disposition, and resting there; *but in deed*—by humane and merciful acts;

And in truth.] Feeling the disposition of which we speak. There is a good saying in *Yalcut Rubeni,* fol. 145, 4, on this point: " If love consisted in *word only,* then love ceaseth as soon as the word is pronounced. Such was the love between Balak and Balaam. But if love consisteth not in *word,* it cannot be *dissolved;* such was the love of Abraham, Isaac, Jacob, and the rest of the patriarchs which were before them."

Verse 19. *Hereby we know that we are of the truth*] That we have the true religion of the Lord Jesus, *and shall assure our hearts*—be persuaded in our consciences, that we have the truth as it is in Jesus; as no man can *impose upon himself* by imagining he *loves* when he *does not:* he may make empty *professions* to *others,* but if he loves either God or man, he *knows* it because he *feels* it; and love *unfelt* is not love, it is *word* or *tongue.* This the apostle lays down as a *test* of a man's Christianity, and it is the strongest and most infallible test that can be given. He that loves *feels* that he does love; and he who *feels* that he loves God and man has true religion; and he who is careful to show the fruits of this love, in obedience to God and humane acts to man, gives *others* the fullest proof that he has the loving mind that was in Jesus.

Verse 20. *If our heart condemn us*] If we be con-

scious that our love is *feigned,* we shall feel inwardly condemned in professing to have what we have not. *And if our heart condemn us, God is greater than our heart,* for he knows every hypocritical winding and turning of the soul, he searches the heart, and tries the reins, and sees all the deceitfulness and desperate wickedness of the heart which we cannot see, and, if we could see them, could not comprehend them; and as he is the just Judge, he will condemn us more *strictly* and *extensively* than we can be by our own *conscience.*

Verse 21. *If our heart condemn us not*] If we be *conscious* to ourselves of our own sincerity, that we practise not deceit, and use no mask, then have *we confidence toward God*—we can appeal to him for our sincerity, and we can come with boldness to the throne of grace, to obtain mercy, and find grace to help in time of need. And therefore says the apostle,

Verse 22. *Whatsoever we ask*] In such a spirit, *we receive of him,* for he delights to bless the humble, upright, and sincere soul.

Because we keep his commandments] Viz., by loving him and loving our neighbour. These are the great commandments both of the old covenant and the new. And whoever is filled with this love to God and man will *do those things which are pleasing to him;* for *love* is the very soul and principle of obedience.

The word *heart* is used in the preceding verses for *conscience;* and so the Greek fathers interpret it, particularly Origen, Nicephorus, and Œcumenius; but this is not an unfrequent meaning of the word in the sacred writings.

Verse 23. *That we should believe on the name of his Son*] We are commanded to believe on Christ, that for the sake of his passion and death we may be justified from all things from which we could not be justified by the law of Moses; and being through him redeemed from the guilt of sin, restored to the Divine favour, and made partakers of the Holy Ghost, we are enabled to *love one another as he gave us commandment;* for without a renewal of the heart love to God and man is impossible, and this renewal comes by Christ Jesus.

Verse 24. Dwelleth in him] i. e. in God; *and he*—God, *in him*—the believer.

And hereby we know] We know by the Spirit which he hath given us that we dwell in God, and God in us. It was not by *conjecture* or *inference* that Christians of old knew they were in the favour of God, it was by the testimony of God's own Spirit in their hearts; and this testimony was not given in a *transient* manner, but was *constant* and *abiding* while they continued under the influence of that faith that worketh by love, Every good man is a temple of the Holy Ghost, and wherever he is, he is both *light* and *power*. By his *power* he *works*; by his *light* he makes both himself and his work *known*. Peace of conscience and joy in the Holy Ghost must proceed from the indwelling of that Holy Spirit; and those who have these blessings *must know that they have them*, for we can-

not have heavenly peace and heavenly joy without *knowing* that we have them. But this Spirit in the soul of a believer is not only manifest by its *effects*, but it *bears its own witness to its own indwelling*. So that a man not only knows that he has this Spirit from the *fruits* of the Spirit, but he knows that he has it from *its own direct witness*. It may be said, "How can these things be?" And it may be answered, By the power, light, and mercy of God. But that such things are, the Scriptures uniformly attest, and the experience of the whole genuine Church of Christ, and of every truly converted soul, sufficiently proves. As the wind bloweth where it listeth, and we cannot tell whence it cometh and whither it goeth, so is every one that is born of the Spirit: the thing is certain, and fully known by its effects; but *how* this testimony is given and confirmed is inexplicable. Every good man feels it, and knows he is of God by the Spirit which God has given him,

CHAPTER IV.

We must not believe every teacher who professes to have a Divine commission to preach, but try such, whether they be of God; and the more so because many false prophets are gone out into the world, 1. Those who deny that Jesus Christ is come in the flesh have the spirit of antichrist, 2, 3. The followers of God have been enabled to discern and overcome them, 4–6. The necessity of love to God and one another shown, from God's love to us, 7–11. Though no man hath seen God, yet every genuine Christian knows him by the spirit which God has given him, 12, 13. The apostles testified that God sent his Son to be the Saviour of the world; and God dwelt in those who confessed this truth, 14, 15. God is love, 16. The nature and properties of perfect love, 17, 18. We love him because he first loved us, 19. The wickedness of pretending to love God while we hate one another, 20, 21.

A. M. cir. 4073.
A. D. cir. 69.
Impp. Galba,
Othone, Vitel.
et Vespa-
siano.

BELOVED, [a] believe not every spirit, but [b] try the spirits whether they are of God: because [c] many false prophets are gone out into the world.

2 Hereby know ye the Spirit of God: [d] Every spirit that confesseth that Jesus Christ is come in the flesh, is of God:

3 And [e] every spirit that confesseth not that Jesus Christ is come in the flesh, is not of God: and this is that *spirit* of antichrist, whereof ye have heard that it should come; and

A. M. cir. 4073.
A. D. cir. 69.
Impp. Galba,
Othone, Vitel.
et Vespa-
siano.

[a] Jer. xxix. 8; Matt. xxiv. 4.——[b] 1 Cor. xiv. 29; 1 Thess. v. 21; Rev. ii. 2.——[c] Matt. xxiv. 5, 24; Acts xx. 30; 1 Tim. iv. 1; 2 Pet. ii. 1; chap. ii. 18; 2 John 7.——[d] 1 Cor. xii. 3; chap. v. 1.——[e] Chap. ii. 22; 2 John 7.

NOTES ON CHAP. IV.

Verse 1. Beloved, believe not every spirit] Do not be forward to believe every teacher to be a man sent of God. As in those early times every teacher professed to be *inspired* by the Spirit of God, because all the prophets had come thus accredited, the term *spirit* was used to express the man who pretended to *be* and *teach* under the Spirit's influence. See 1 Cor. xii. 1–12; 1 Tim. iv. 1.

Try the spirits] Δοκιμαζετε τα πνευματα· Put these teachers to the proof. Try them by that testimony which is known to have come from the Spirit of God, the word of revelation already given.

Many false prophets] Teachers not inspired by the Spirit of God, *are gone out into the world*—among the Jewish people particularly, and among them who are carnal and have not the Spirit.

Verse 2. Hereby know ye the Spirit of God] We know that the man who teaches that Jesus Christ is the promised Messiah, and that he is come in the flesh, *is of God*—is inspired by the Divine Spirit; for no man can call Jesus Lord but by the Holy Ghost.

Verse 3. Every spirit] Every teacher, *that confesseth not Jesus, is not of God*—has not been inspired by God. The words εν σαρκι εληλυθοτα, *is come in the flesh*, are wanting in AB, several others, both the Syriac, the Polyglot *Arabic, Æthiopic, Coptic, Armenian*, and *Vulgate*; in *Origen, Cyril, Theodoret, Irenæus*, and others. *Griesbach* has left them out of the text.

Spirit of antichrist] All the opponents of Christ' incarnation, and consequently of his *passion, death*, and *resurrection*, and the benefits to be derived from them.

A. M. cir. 4073.
A. D. cir. 69.
Impp. Galba,
Othone, Vitel.
et Vespa-
siano.

[f] even now already is it in the
world.
4 [g] Ye are of God, little children, and have overcome them:
because greater is he that is in you, than [h] he
that is in the world.
5 [i] They are of the world: therefore speak
they of the world, and [k] the world heareth
them.
6 We are of God: [l] he that knoweth God
heareth us; he that is not of God heareth not
us. Hereby know we [m] the spirit of truth,
and the spirit of error.
7 [n] Beloved, let us love one another: for love
is of God; and every one that
loveth is born of God, and knoweth God.
8 He that loveth not [o] knoweth
not God; for [p] God is love.
9 [q] In this was manifested the love of God
toward us, because that God sent his only-
begotten Son into the world, [r] that we might
live through him.
10 Herein is love, [s] not that we loved God,
but that he loved us, and sent his Son [t] *to be*
the propitiation for our sins.
11 Beloved, [u] if God so loved us, we ought
also to love one another.

A. M. cir. 4073
A. D. cir. 69.
Impp. Galba,
Othone, Vitel.
et Vespa-
siano.

[f] 2 Thess. ii. 7; chap. ii. 18, 22.——[g] Chap. v. 4.——[h] John xii. 31; xiv. 30; xvi. 11; 1 Cor. ii. 12; Eph. ii. 2; vi. 12. [i] John iii. 31.——[k] John xv. 19; xvii. 14.——[l] John viii. 47; x. 27; 1 Cor. xiv. 37; 2 Cor. x. 7.——[m] Isa. viii. 20; John xiv. 17.

[n] Chap. iii. 10, 11, 23.——[o] Chapter ii. 4; iii. 6.——[p] Ver. 16. [q] John iii, 16; Rom, v, 8; viii. 32; chap. iii. 16.——[r] Chap. v. 11.——[s] John xv. 16; Rom. v. 8, 10; Tit. iii. 4.——[t] Chap. ii. 2. [u] Matt. xviii. 33; John xv. 12, 13; chap. iii. 16.

Ye have heard that it should come] See 2 Thess. ii. 7.

Even now already is it in the world.] Is working powerfully both among the Jews and Gentiles.

Verse 4. *Ye are of God*] Ye are under the influence of the Divine Spirit, *and have overcome them*—your testimony, proceeding from the Spirit of Christ, has invalidated theirs which has proceeded from the influence of Satan; *for greater* is the Holy Spirit *which is in you, than* the spirit *which is in the world.*

Verse 5. *They are of the world*] They have no spiritual views, they have no spirituality of mind; they seek the present world and its enjoyments. Their conversation is worldly, and worldly men hear them in preference to all others. Thus they have their partisans.

Verse 6. *We are of God*] We, apostles, have the Spirit of God, and speak and teach by that Spirit. *He that knoweth God*—who has a truly spiritual discernment, *heareth us*—acknowledges that our doctrine is from God; that it is spiritual, and leads from earth to heaven.

Hereby know we the Spirit of truth] The *doctrine* and *teacher* most prized and followed by *worldly men*, and by the *gay*, *giddy*, and *garish multitude*, are not from God; they savour of the *flesh*, lay on no restraints, prescribe no cross-bearing, and leave every one in full possession of his heart's lusts and easily besetting sins. And by this, false doctrine and false teachers are easily discerned.

Verse 7. *Beloved, let us love one another*] And ever be ready to promote each other's welfare, both spiritual and temporal.

For love is of God] And ever acts like him; he loves man, and daily loads him with his benefits. *He that loveth most* has most of God in him; and he that loveth God and his neighbour, as before described and commanded, *is born of God*, *εκ του Θεου γεγεννηται*, *is begotten of God*—is a true child of his heavenly Father, for he is made a partaker of the Divine nature; and this his love to God and man proves.

Verse 8. *He that loveth not*] As already described, *knoweth not God*—has no experimental knowledge of him.

God is love.] An infinite fountain of benevolence and beneficence to every human being. He hates nothing that he has made. He cannot *hate*, because he is *love*. He causes his sun to rise on the evil and the good, and sends his rain on the just and the unjust. He has made no human being for perdition, nor ever rendered it impossible, by any necessitating decree, for any fallen soul to find mercy. He has given the fullest proof of his love to the whole human race by the incarnation of his Son, who tasted death for every man. How can a *decree* of absolute, unconditional *reprobation*, of the greater part or any part of the human race, stand in the presence of such a text as this? It has been well observed that, although God is holy, just, righteous, &c., he is never called *holiness*, *justice*, &c., in the *abstract*, as he is here called LOVE. This seems to be the essence of the Divine nature, and all other attributes to be only modifications of this.

Verse 9. *In this was manifested the love of God*] The mission of Jesus Christ was the fullest proof that God could give, or that man could receive, of his infinite love to the world.

That we might live through him.] The whole world was sentenced to *death* because of sin; and every individual was *dead in trespasses* and sins; and Jesus came to die in the stead of the world, and to *quicken* every believer, that all might live to him who died for them and rose again. This is another strong allusion to John iii. 16: *God so loved the world, that he gave his only-begotten Son, that whosoever believeth in him should not perish, but have everlasting life*; where the reader is requested to see the note.

Verse 10. *Not that we loved God*] And that he was thereby induced to give his Son *to be a propitiation for our sins*. No: we were enemies to God, and yet Christ died for our ungodly souls. (See Rom. v. 6–11, and the notes there.) So it was God's love, not our merit, that induced him to devise means that his banished might not be expelled from him.

Verse 11. *If God so loved us*] Without any reason or consideration on our part, and without any *desert* in us; *we ought also*, in like manner, *to love one another*,

A. M. cir. 4073.
A. D. cir. 69.
Impp. Galba,
Othone, Vitel.
et Vespa-
siano.

12 ᵛ No man hath seen God at any time. If we love one another, God dwelleth in us, and ʷ his love is perfected in us.

13 ˣ Hereby know we that we dwell in him, and he in us, because he hath given us of his Spirit.

14 And ʸ we have seen and do testify that ᶻ the Father sent the Son *to be* the Saviour of the world.

15 ᵃ Whosoever shall confess that Jesus is the Son of God, dwelleth in him, and he in God.

A. M. cir. 4073
A. D. cir. 69.
Impp. Galba,
Othone, Vitel.
et Vespa-
siano.

16 And we have known and believed the love that God hath to us. ᵇ God is love ; and ᶜ he that dwelleth in love dwelleth in God, and God in him.

17 Herein is ᵈ our love made perfect, that ᵉ we may have boldness in the day of judgment : ᶠ because as he is, so are we in this world.

18 There is no fear in love ; but perfect love casteth out fear : because fear hath torment. He that feareth is ᵍ not made perfect in love.

ᵛ John i. 18 ; 1 Tim. vi. 16 ; ver. 20.——ʷ Chap. ii. 5 ; ver. 18.——ˣ John xiv. 20 ; chap. iii. 24.——ʸ John i. 14 : chap. i. 1, 2. ᶻ John iii. 17.

ᵃ Rom. x. 9 ; chap. v. 1, 5.——ᵇ Ver. 8.——ᶜ Ver. 12 ; chap. iii. 24.——ᵈ Gr. *love with us.*——ᵉ James ii. 13 ; chap. ii. 28 ; iii. 19, 21.——ᶠ Chap. iii. 3.——ᵍ Ver. 12,

and not suspend our love to a fellow-creature. either on his *moral worth* or his *love to us.* We should love one another for *God's sake ;* and then, no unkind carriage of a brother would induce us to withdraw our love from him ; for if it have GOD for its *motive* and *model*, it will *never fail.*

Verse 12. *No man hath seen God at any time.*] The very words, with the change of ἑώρακε for τεθέαται, of this apostle in his gospel, chap. i. 18. We may *feel* him, though we cannot *see* him ; and if we love one another he *dwelleth in us,* and *his love is perfected in us*—it has then its full *accomplishment,* having moulded us according to its own nature.

Verse 13. *Hereby know we, &c.*] See the note on chap. iii. 24.

Verse 14. *And we have seen*] Jesus Christ manifested in the flesh ; see chap. i. 1, &c. ; *and do testify* —bear witness, in consequence of having the fullest conviction, *that the Father sent the Son to be the Saviour of the world.* We have had the fullest proof of this from his *doctrine* and *miracles,* which we *heard* and *saw* during the whole time that he sojourned among men.

Verse 15. *Whosoever shall confess*] Much stress is laid on this confession, because the false teachers denied the reality of the incarnation ; but this confession implied also such a belief in Christ as put them in possession of his pardoning mercy and indwelling Spirit.

Verse 16. *God is love*] See on ver. 8. *He that dwelleth in love*—he who is full of love to God and man is full of God, for God is love ; and where such love is, there is God, for he is the fountain and maintainer of it.

Verse 17. *Herein is our love made perfect*] By God dwelling in us, and we in him ; having cast out all the carnal mind that was *enmity* against himself, and filled the whole heart with the spirit of love and purity. Thus the love is made perfect ; when it thus fills the heart it has all its *degrees ;* it is all in all ; and all in every power, passion, and faculty of the soul.

May have boldness in the day of judgment] Παρρησίαν· Freedom of speech, and *liberty of access ;* seeing in the person of our Judge him who has died for us, regenerated our hearts, and who himself fills them.

As he is] Pure, holy, and loving ; *so are we in this world ;* being saved from our sins, and made like to himself in righteousness and true holiness. No man can contemplate the *day of judgment* with any comfort or satisfaction but on this ground, that the blood of Christ hath cleansed him from all sin ; and that he is *kept* by the power of God, through faith, unto salvation. This will give him boldness in the day of judgment.

Verse 18. *There is no fear in love*] The man who feels that he loves God with all his heart can never *dread* him as his *Judge.* As he is now made a partaker of his Spirit, and carries a sense of the Divine approbation in his conscience, he has nothing of that *fear* that produces *terror* or brings *torment.* The *perfect love*—that fulness of love, which he has received, *casteth out fear*—removes all terror relative to this day of judgment, for it is of this that the apostle particularly speaks. And as it is inconsistent with the gracious design of God to have his followers miserable, and as he cannot be unhappy whose heart is full of the love of his God, this love must necessarily exclude this fear or terror ; because that brings *torment,* and hence is inconsistent with that happiness which a man must have who continually enjoys the approbation of his God.

He that feareth] He who is still *uncertain* concerning his interest in Christ ; who, although he has many heavenly drawings, and often sits with Christ some moments on a throne of love, yet feels from the evils of his heart a dread of the day of judgment ; *is not made perfect in love*—has not yet received the abiding witness of the Spirit that he is begotten of God ; nor that fulness of love to God and man which excludes the *enmity* of the *carnal mind,* and which it is his privilege to receive. But is the case of such a man *desperate ?* No : it is neither *desperate* nor *deplorable ;* he is in the way of salvation, and not far from the kingdom of heaven. Let such earnestly seek, and fervently believe on the Son of God ; and he will soon give them another baptism of his Spirit, will purge out all the old leaven, and fill their whole souls with that love which is the fulfilling of the law. He who is not yet perfect in love may speedily become so, because

A. M. cir. 4073.
A. D. cir. 69.
Impp. Galba,
Othone, Vitel.
et Vespa-
siano.

19 We love him, because he first loved us.

20 [h] If a man say, I love God, and hateth his brother, he is a liar: for he that loveth not his brother whom

---

[h] Chap. ii. 4 ; iii. 17.——[i] Ver. 12.

A. M. cir. 4073.
A. D. cir. 69.
Impp. Galba
Othone, Vitel.
et Vespa-
siano.

he hath seen, how can he love God [i] whom he hath not seen?

21 And [k] this commandment have we from him, That he who loveth God love his brother also.

---

[k] Matt. xxii. 37, 39 ; John xiii. 34 ; xv. 12 ; chap. iii. 23.

God can say in a moment, *I will, be thou clean; and immediately his leprosy will depart.* Among men we find some that have neither love nor fear; others that have fear without love; others that have love and fear; and others that have love without fear.

1. Profligates, and worldly men in general, have neither the fear nor love of God.

2. Deeply awakened and distressed penitents have the fear or terror of God without his love.

3. Babes in Christ, or young converts, have often distressing fear mixed with their love.

4. Adult Christians have love without this fear; because fear hath torment, and they are ever happy, being filled with God. See Mr. *Wesley's* note on this place.

1. We must not suppose that the love of God shed abroad in the heart is ever *imperfect* in *itself*; it is only so in *degree.* There may be a *less* or *greater degree* of what is *perfect* in itself; so it is with respect to the love which the followers of God have; they may have *measures* or *degrees* of perfect love without its *fulness.* There is nothing *imperfect* in the love of God, whether it be considered as existing in himself, or as communicated to his followers.

2. We are not to suppose that the love of God casts out *every kind of fear* from the soul; it only casts out that which has *torment.* 1. A *filial fear* is consistent with the highest degrees of love; and even necessary to the preservation of that grace. This is properly its guardian; and, without this, love would soon degenerate into listlessness, or presumptive boldness. 2. Nor does it cast out that *fear* which is so necessary to the *preservation of life;* that fear which leads a man to *flee from danger* lest his life should be destroyed. 3. Nor does it cast out that *fear* which may be engendered by *sudden alarm.* All these are necessary to our well-being. But it destroys, 1. The fear of *want;* 2. The fear of *death;* and 3. The fear or terror of *judgment.* All these fears bring torment, and are inconsistent with this perfect love.

Verse 19. *We love him because he first loved us.*] This is the foundation of our love to God. 1. We love him because we find he has loved us. 2. We love him from a sense of obligation and gratitude. 3. We love him from the influence of his own love; from his love shed abroad in our hearts our love to him proceeds. It is the seed whence our love springs. The verse might be rendered, *Let us therefore love him, because he first loved us:* thus the *Syriac* and *Vulgate.*

Verse 20. *If a man say, I love God, and hateth his brother*] This, as well as many other parts of this epistle, seems levelled against the Jews, who pretended much love to God while they hated the *Gentiles;* and even some of them who were brought into the Christian Church brought this leaven with them. It required a miracle to redeem St. Peter's mind from the influence of this principle. See Acts x.

Whom he hath seen] We may have our love excited towards our brother, 1. By a consideration of his *excellences* or *amiable qualities.* 2. By a view of his *miseries* and *distresses.* The *first* will excite a love of *complacency* and *delight;* the *second,* a love of *compassion* and *pity.*

Whom he hath not seen?] If he love not his brother, it is a proof that the love of God is not in him; and if he have not the love of God, he cannot love God, for God can be loved only through the influence of his own love. See on ver. 19. The man who hates his fellow does not love God. He who does not love God has not the love of God in him, and he who has not the love of God in him can neither love God nor man.

Verse 21. *This commandment have we*] We should love one another, and love our neighbour as ourselves. The love of God and the love of man can never be separated; he who loves God will love his brother; he who loves his brother gives this proof that he loves God, because he loves with a measure of that love which, in its infinitude, dwells in God.

CHAPTER V.

He that believeth is born of God; loves God and his children; and keeps his commandments, which are not grievous, 1—3. Faith in Christ overcomes the world, 4, 5. The three earthly and heavenly witnesses, 6—9. He that believeth hath the witness in himself, 10. God has given unto us eternal life in his Son, 11, 12. The end for which St. John writes these things, 13—15. The sin unto death, and the sin not unto death, 16, 17. He that is born of God sinneth not, 18. The whole world lieth in the wicked one, 19. Jesus is come to give us an understanding, that we may know the true God, 20. All idolatry to be avoided, 21.

A. M. cir. 4073.
A. D. cir. 69.
Impp. Galba,
Othone, Vitel.
et Vespa-
siano.

WHOSOEVER [a] believeth that [b] Jesus is the Christ is [c] born of God: [d] and every one that loveth him that begat, loveth him also that is begotten of him.

2 By this we know that we love the children of God, when we love God, and keep his commandments.

3 [e] For this is the love of God, that we keep his commandments: and [f] his commandments are not grievous.

4 For [g] whatsoever is born of God overcometh the world: and this is the victory that overcometh the world, *even our faith.*

5 Who is he that overcometh the world, but [h] he that believeth that Jesus is the Son of God?

6 This is he that came [i] by water and blood,

A. M. cir. 4073.
A. D. cir. 69.
Impp. Galba,
Othone, Vitel.
et Vespa-
siano.

NOTES ON CHAP. V

Verse 1. *Whosoever believeth, &c.*] Expressions of this kind are to be taken in *connection with the subjects necessarily implied in them.* He that believeth that Jesus is the Messiah, and confides in him for the remission of sins, *is begotten of God;* and they who are pardoned and begotten of God love him in return for his love, and love all those who are his children.

Verse 2. *By this we know that we love the children of God*] Our love of God's followers is a *proof* that we love God. Our love to God is the *cause* why we love his children, and our *keeping the commandments of God* is the *proof* that we love *him.*

Verse 3. *For this is the love of God*] This the love of God necessarily produces. It is vain to pretend love to God while we live in opposition to his will.

His commandments] To love him with all our heart, and our neighbour as ourselves, *are not grievous*—are not burdensome; for no man is burdened with the duties which his own *love* imposes. The old proverb explains the meaning of the apostle's words, *Love feels no loads.* Love to God brings *strength* from God; through his *love* and his *strength,* all his commandments are not only easy and light, but pleasant and delightful.

On the love of God, as being the foundation of all religious worship, there is a good saying in *Sohar Exod.,* fol. 23, col. 91: "Rabbi Jesa said, how necessary is it that a man should love the holy blessed God! For he can bring no other worship to God than love; and whoever loves him, and worships him from a principle of love, him the holy blessed God calls his beloved."

Verse 4. *Whatsoever is born of God*] Παν το γεγεννημενον· Whatsoever (the neuter for the masculine) *is begotten of God overcometh the world.* "I understand by this," says *Schoettgen,* "the *Jewish Church,* or *Judaism,* which is often termed עולם הזה *olam hazzeh,* this world. The reasons which induce me to think so are, 1. Because this κοσμος, *world,* denied that the Messiah was come; but the Gentiles did not oppose this principle. 2. Because he proves the truth of the Christian religion against the *Jews,* reasoning according to the *Jewish manner;* whence it is evident that he contends, not against the *Gentiles,* but against the *Jews.* The sense therefore is, he who possesses the true Christian faith can easily convict the Jewish religion of falsity." That is, He can show the vanity of their expectations, and the falsity of their glosses and prejudices. Suppose we understand by *the world* the *evil principles* and *practices* which are among men, and in the human heart; then the influence of God in the soul may be properly said to *overcome* this; and by faith in the Son of God a man is able to overcome all that is in the world, viz., *the desire of the flesh, the desire of the eye,* and *the pride of life.*

Verse 5. *He that believeth that Jesus is the Son of God?*] That he is the promised Messiah, that he came by a supernatural generation; and, although truly *man,* came not *by man,* but by the power of the Holy Ghost in the womb of the Virgin Mary. The person who believes this has the privilege of applying to the Lord for the benefits of the incarnation and passion of Jesus Christ, and receives the blessings which the Jews cannot have, because they believe not the Divine mission of Christ.

Verse 6. *This is he that came by water and blood*] Jesus was attested to be the Son of God and promised Messiah by *water, i. e.* his *baptism,* when the Spirit of God came down from heaven upon him, and the voice from heaven said, *This is my beloved Son, in whom I am well pleased.* Jesus Christ came also by *blood.* He shed his blood for the sins of the world; and this was in accordance with all that the Jewish prophets had written concerning him. Here the apostle says that the Spirit witnesses this; that *he came not by water only*—being baptized, and baptizing men in his own name that they might be his followers and disciples; *but by blood also*—by his sacrificial death, without which the world could not be saved, and he could have had no disciples. As, therefore, the Spirit of God witnessed his being the Son of God at his baptism, and as the same Spirit in the prophets had witnessed that he should die a cruel, yet a sacrificial, death; he is said here to *bear witness,* because he is the *Spirit of truth.*

Perhaps St. John makes here a mental comparison between CHRIST, and *Moses* and *Aaron;* to both of whom he opposes our Lord, and shows his superior excellence. *Moses came by water*—all the Israelites were baptized unto him in the cloud and in the sea, and thus became his flock and his disciples; 1 Cor. x. 1, 2. *Aaron came by blood*—he entered into the holy of holies with the blood of the victim, to make atone-

A. M. cir. 4073.
A. D. cir. 69.
Impp. Galba,
Othone, Vitel.
et Vespasiano.

even Jesus Christ; not by water only, but by water and blood. ᵏ And it is the Spirit that beareth witness, because the Spirit is truth.

7 For there are three that bear record in heaven, the Father, ˡ the Word, and the Holy Ghost: ᵐ and these three are one.

A. M. cir. 4073.
A. D. cir. 69.
Impp. Galba,
Othone, Vitel.
et Vespasiano.

ᵏ John xiv. 17; xv. 26; xvi. 13; 1 Tim. iii. 16.

ˡ John i. 1; Rev. xix. 13.——ᵐ John x. 30.

---

ment for sin. Moses initiated the people into the covenant of God by bringing them *under the cloud* and *through the water*. Aaron confirmed that covenant by shedding the *blood*, sprinkling part of it upon them, and the rest before the Lord in the holy of holies. *Moses* came only by *water*, *Aaron* only by *blood;* and both came as *types*. But Christ came both by *water* and *blood*, not typically, but really; not by the authority of *another*, but by his own. Jesus initiates his followers into the Christian covenant by the baptism of water, and confirms and seals to them the blessings of the covenant by an application of the *blood* of the atonement; thus purging their consciences, and purifying their souls.

Thus, his religion is of infinitely greater efficacy than that in which Moses and Aaron were ministers. See *Schoettgen.*

It may be said, also, that the *Spirit* bears witness of Jesus by his *testimony* in the *souls of genuine Christians*, and by the *spiritual gifts* and *miraculous powers* with which he endowed the apostles and primitive believers. This is agreeable to what St. John says in his gospel, chap. xv. 26, 27: *When the Comforter is come, the Spirit of truth, which proceedeth from the Father, he shall testify of me; and ye also shall bear witness, because ye have been with me from the beginning.* This place the apostle seems to have in his eye; and this would naturally lead him to speak concerning the *three witnesses,* the Spirit, the water, and the blood, ver. 8.

Verse 7. *There are three that bear record*] The Father, who bears testimony to his Son; the Word or Λογος, *Logos*, who bears testimony to the Father; and the Holy Ghost, which bears testimony to the Father and the Son. And *these three* are one in essence, and *agree in* the *one* testimony, that Jesus came to die for, and give life to, the world.

But it is likely this verse is not genuine. It is wanting in every MS. of this epistle written *before* the invention of printing, one excepted, the *Codex Montfortii*, in Trinity College, Dublin: the others which omit this verse amount to *one hundred and twelve.*

It is wanting in both the *Syriac*, all the *Arabic*, *Æthiopic*, the *Coptic*, *Sahidic*, *Armenian*, *Slavonian*, &c., in a word, in all the ancient *versions* but the *Vulgate;* and even of this version many of the most ancient and correct MSS. have it not. It is wanting also in all the ancient Greek fathers; and in most even of the Latin.

The words, as they exist in all the Greek MSS. with the exception of the *Codex Montfortii*, are the following:—

" 6. This is he that came by water and blood, Jesus Christ; not by water only, but by water and blood. And it is the Spirit that beareth witness, because the

Spirit is truth. 7. For there are three that bear witness, the Spirit, the water, and the blood; and these three agree in one. 9. If we receive the witness of man, the witness of God is greater, &c."

The words that are omitted by all the MSS., the above excepted, and all the *versions*, the *Vulgate* excepted, are these:—

[In heaven, the Father, the Word, and the Holy Spirit, and these three are one. and there are three which bear witness in earth.]

To make the whole more clear, that every reader may see what has been *added*, I shall set down these verses, with the *inserted* words in brackets.

" 6. And it is the Spirit that beareth witness, because the Spirit is truth. 7. For there are three that bear record [in heaven, the Father, the Word, and the Holy Ghost, and these three are one. 8. And there are three that bear witness in earth,] the Spirit, and the water, and the blood, and these three agree in one. 9. If we receive the witness of men, the witness of God is greater, &c." Any man may see, on examining the *words*, that if those included in brackets, which are wanting in the MSS. and *versions*, be omitted, there is no want of *connection;* and as to the *sense*, it is complete and perfect without them; and, indeed much more so than with them. I shall conclude this part of the note by observing, with Dr. Dodd, " that there are some internal and accidental marks which may render the passage suspected; for the sense is complete, and indeed more clear and better preserved, without it. Besides, the Spirit is mentioned, both as a witness in heaven and on earth; so that the six witnesses are thereby reduced to five, and the equality of number, or antithesis between the witnesses in heaven and on earth, is quite taken away. Besides, what need of witnesses in *heaven?* No one there doubts that Jesus is the Messiah; and if it be said that Father, Son, and Spirit are witnesses on earth, then there are five witnesses on earth, and none in heaven; not to say that there is a little difficulty in interpreting how the Word or the Son can be a witness to himself."

It may be necessary to inquire how this verse stood in our earliest English Bibles. In Coverdale's Bible, printed about 1535, for it bears no date, the *seventh* verse is put in brackets thus —

𝔄𝔫𝔡 𝔦𝔱 𝔦𝔰 𝔱𝔥𝔢 𝔖𝔭𝔯𝔢𝔱𝔢 𝔱𝔥𝔞𝔱 𝔟𝔢𝔞𝔯𝔢𝔱𝔥 𝔴𝔶𝔱𝔫𝔢𝔰; 𝔣𝔬𝔯 𝔱𝔥𝔢 𝔖𝔭𝔯𝔢𝔱𝔢 𝔦𝔰 𝔱𝔥𝔢 𝔱𝔯𝔲𝔢𝔱𝔥. (𝔉𝔬𝔯 𝔱𝔥𝔢𝔯𝔢 𝔞𝔯𝔢 𝔱𝔥𝔯𝔢 𝔴𝔥𝔦𝔠𝔥 𝔟𝔢𝔞𝔯𝔢 𝔯𝔢𝔠𝔬𝔯𝔡𝔢 𝔦𝔫 𝔥𝔢𝔞𝔲𝔢𝔫: 𝔱𝔥𝔢 𝔉𝔞𝔱𝔥𝔢𝔯, 𝔱𝔥𝔢 𝔚𝔬𝔬𝔯𝔡𝔢, 𝔞𝔫𝔡 𝔱𝔥𝔢 𝔥𝔬𝔩𝔶 𝔊𝔬𝔬𝔰𝔱, 𝔞𝔫𝔡 𝔱𝔥𝔢𝔰𝔢 𝔱𝔥𝔯𝔢 𝔞𝔯𝔢 𝔬𝔫𝔢.) 𝔄𝔫𝔡 𝔱𝔥𝔢𝔯𝔢 𝔞𝔯𝔢 𝔱𝔥𝔯𝔢 𝔴𝔥𝔦𝔠𝔥 𝔟𝔢𝔞𝔯𝔢 𝔯𝔢𝔠𝔬𝔯𝔡𝔢 𝔦𝔫 𝔢𝔞𝔯𝔱𝔥: 𝔱𝔥𝔢 𝔖𝔭𝔯𝔢𝔱𝔢, 𝔴𝔞𝔱𝔢𝔯, 𝔞𝔫𝔡 𝔟𝔩𝔬𝔲𝔡𝔢 𝔞𝔫𝔡 𝔱𝔥𝔢𝔰𝔢 𝔱𝔥𝔯𝔢 𝔞𝔯𝔢 𝔬𝔫𝔢. 𝔎𝔣 𝔴𝔢 𝔯𝔢𝔠𝔢𝔭𝔥𝔢, &c.

Tindal was as critical as he was conscientious; and though he admitted the words into the text of the first edition of his New Testament printed in 1526, yet he distinguished them by a different letter, and put them in brackets, as *Coverdale* has done; and

A. M. cir. 4073.
A. D. cir. 69.
Impp. Galba,
Othone, Vitel.
et Vespa-
siano.

8 And there are three that bear witness in earth, the Spirit, and the water, and the blood; and these three agree in one.

9 If we receive ⁿ the witness of men, the witness of God is greater: ° for this is the witness of God, which he hath testified of his Son.

10 He that believeth on the Son of God

ᵖ hath the witness in himself: he that believeth not God, ᑫ hath made him a liar; because he believeth not the record that God gave of his Son.

11 ʳ And this is the record, that God hath given to us eternal life, and ˢ this life is in his Son.

12 ᵗ He that hath the Son hath life; *and he*

A. M. cir. 4073.
A. D. cir. 69.
Impp. Galba,
Othone, Vitel.
et Vespa-
siano.

ⁿ John viii. 17, 18.——° Matt. iii. 16, 17; xvii. 5.——ᵖ Rom. viii. 16; Gal. iv. 6.

ᑫ John iii. 33; v. 38.——ʳ Chap. ii. 25.——ˢ John i. 4; chap. iv. 9.——ᵗ John iii. 36; v. 24

---

also the words *in earth*, which stand in ver. 8, without proper authority, and which being excluded make the text the same as in the MSS., &c.

Two editions of this version are now before me; one printed in English and Latin, quarto, with the following title:—

𝔗𝔥𝔢 𝔑𝔢𝔴𝔢 𝔗𝔢𝔰𝔱𝔞𝔪𝔢𝔫𝔱, 𝔟𝔬𝔱𝔥 𝔦𝔫 𝔈𝔫𝔤𝔩𝔶𝔰𝔥𝔢 𝔞𝔫𝔡 𝔏𝔞𝔱𝔢𝔫, 𝔬𝔣 𝔐𝔞𝔶𝔰𝔱𝔢𝔯 𝔈𝔯𝔞𝔰𝔪𝔲𝔰 𝔱𝔯𝔞𝔫𝔰𝔩𝔞𝔱𝔦𝔬𝔫—𝔞𝔫𝔡 𝔦𝔪𝔭𝔯𝔦𝔫𝔱𝔢𝔡 𝔟𝔶 𝔚𝔦𝔩𝔩𝔦𝔞𝔪 𝔓𝔬𝔴𝔢𝔩𝔩—𝔱𝔥𝔢 𝔶𝔢𝔯𝔢 𝔬𝔣 𝔬𝔲𝔯 𝔏𝔬𝔯𝔡𝔢 M.CCCC.XLVII. 𝔄𝔫𝔡 𝔱𝔥𝔢 𝔣𝔶𝔯𝔰𝔱𝔢 𝔶𝔢𝔯𝔢 𝔬𝔣 𝔱𝔥𝔢 𝔨𝔶𝔫𝔤𝔢𝔰 (Edw. VI.) 𝔪𝔬𝔰𝔱𝔢 𝔤𝔯𝔞𝔠𝔦𝔬𝔲𝔰 𝔯𝔢𝔶𝔤𝔫𝔢.

In this edition the text stands thus:—

𝔄𝔫𝔡 𝔦𝔱 𝔦𝔰 𝔱𝔥𝔢 𝔖𝔭𝔦𝔯𝔦𝔱𝔢 𝔱𝔥𝔞𝔱 𝔟𝔢𝔞𝔯𝔢𝔱𝔥 𝔴𝔶𝔱𝔫𝔢𝔰, 𝔟𝔢𝔠𝔞𝔲𝔰𝔢 𝔱𝔥𝔢 𝔖𝔭𝔦𝔯𝔦𝔱𝔢 𝔦𝔰 𝔱𝔯𝔲𝔱𝔥 (𝔣𝔬𝔯 𝔱𝔥𝔢𝔯𝔢 𝔞𝔯𝔢 𝔱𝔥𝔯𝔢 𝔴𝔥𝔦𝔠𝔥𝔢 𝔟𝔢𝔞𝔯𝔢 𝔯𝔢𝔠𝔬𝔯𝔡𝔢 𝔦𝔫 𝔥𝔢𝔞𝔳𝔢𝔫, 𝔱𝔥𝔢 𝔉𝔞𝔱𝔥𝔢𝔯, 𝔱𝔥𝔢 𝔚𝔬𝔯𝔡𝔢, 𝔞𝔫𝔡 𝔱𝔥𝔢 𝔥𝔬𝔩𝔶 𝔊𝔥𝔬𝔰𝔱, 𝔞𝔫𝔡 𝔱𝔥𝔢𝔰𝔢 𝔱𝔥𝔯𝔢 𝔞𝔯𝔢 𝔬𝔫𝔢.) 𝔉𝔬𝔯 𝔱𝔥𝔢𝔯𝔢 𝔞𝔯𝔢 𝔱𝔥𝔯𝔢 𝔴𝔥𝔦𝔠𝔥𝔢 𝔟𝔢𝔞𝔯𝔢 𝔯𝔢𝔠𝔬𝔯𝔡𝔢, (𝔦𝔫 𝔢𝔞𝔯𝔱𝔥,) 𝔱𝔥𝔢 𝔖𝔭𝔦𝔯𝔦𝔱𝔢, 𝔴𝔞𝔱𝔢𝔯, 𝔞𝔫𝔡 𝔟𝔩𝔬𝔡𝔢, 𝔞𝔫𝔡 𝔱𝔥𝔢𝔰𝔢 𝔱𝔥𝔯𝔢 𝔞𝔯𝔢 𝔬𝔫𝔢. 𝔌𝔣 𝔴𝔢 𝔯𝔢𝔠𝔢𝔶𝔳𝔢, &c.

The other printed in London "by William Tylle, 4to; without the Latin of Erasmus in M.CCCC.XLIX. the thyrde yere of the reigne of our moost dreade Soverayne Lorde Kynge Edwarde the Syxte," has, with a small variety of spelling, the text in the same order, and the same words included in brackets as above.

The English Bible, with the book of Common Prayer, printed by *Richard Cardmarden*, at Rouen in Normandy, fol. 1566, exhibits the text faithfully, but in the following singular manner:—

𝔄𝔫𝔡 𝔦𝔱 𝔦𝔰 𝔱𝔥𝔢 𝔖𝔭𝔶𝔯𝔶𝔱𝔢 𝔱𝔥𝔞𝔱 𝔟𝔢𝔞𝔯𝔢𝔱𝔥 𝔴𝔦𝔱𝔫𝔢𝔰𝔰𝔢, 𝔟𝔢𝔠𝔞𝔲𝔰𝔢 𝔱𝔥𝔢 𝔖𝔭𝔶𝔯𝔶𝔱𝔢 𝔦𝔰 𝔱𝔯𝔲𝔱𝔥𝔢. (𝔣𝔬𝔯 𝔱𝔥𝔢𝔯𝔢 𝔞𝔯𝔢 𝔱𝔥𝔯𝔢𝔢 𝔴𝔥𝔦𝔠𝔥 𝔟𝔢𝔞𝔯𝔢 𝔯𝔢𝔠𝔬𝔯𝔡𝔢 𝔦𝔫 𝔥𝔢𝔞𝔳𝔢𝔫, 𝔱𝔥𝔢 𝔉𝔞𝔱𝔥𝔢𝔯, 𝔱𝔥𝔢 𝔚𝔬𝔬𝔯𝔡𝔢, 𝔞𝔫𝔡 𝔱𝔥𝔢 𝔥𝔬𝔩𝔶 𝔊𝔥𝔬𝔰𝔱; 𝔞𝔫𝔡 𝔱𝔥𝔢𝔰𝔢 𝔗𝔥𝔯𝔢𝔢 𝔞𝔯𝔢 𝔒𝔫𝔢) 𝔄𝔫𝔡 𝔱𝔥𝔯𝔢𝔢 𝔴𝔥𝔦𝔠𝔥 𝔟𝔢𝔞𝔯𝔢 𝔯𝔢𝔠𝔬𝔯𝔡𝔢* (in earth) 𝔱𝔥𝔢 𝔖𝔭𝔦𝔯𝔦𝔱𝔢, 𝔞𝔫𝔡 𝔴𝔞𝔱𝔢𝔯, 𝔞𝔫𝔡 𝔟𝔩𝔬𝔬𝔡𝔢; 𝔞𝔫𝔡 𝔱𝔥𝔢𝔰𝔢 𝔱𝔥𝔯𝔢𝔢 𝔞𝔯𝔢 𝔬𝔫𝔢.

The first English Bible which I have seen, where these *distinctions* were omitted, is that called The *Bishops' Bible*, printed by Jugge, fol. 1568. Since that time, all such distinctions have been generally disregarded.

Though a conscientious believer in the doctrine of the ever blessed, holy, and undivided Trinity, and in the proper and essential Divinity of our Lord Jesus Christ, which doctrines I have defended by many, and even new, arguments in the course of this work, I cannot help doubting the authenticity of the text in question; and, for farther particulars, refer to the *observations* at the end of this chapter.

Verse 8. *The Spirit, and the water, and the blood*]

This verse is supposed to mean " *the Spirit*—in the word confirmed by miracles; the *water*—in baptism, wherein we are dedicated to the Son, (with the Father and the Holy Spirit,) typifying his spotless purity, and the inward purifying of our nature; *and the blood* —represented in the Lord's Supper, and applied to the consciences of believers: and all these harmoniously agree in the same testimony, that Jesus Christ is the Divine, the complete, the only Saviour of the world."—Mr. *Wesley's* notes.

By the *written word*, which proceeded from the Holy Spirit, that Spirit is continually witnessing *upon earth*, that God hath given unto us eternal life.

By *baptism*, which points out our *regeneration*, and the renewing of the Holy Ghost, and which is still maintained as an initiatory rite in the Christian Church, we have another witness *on earth* of the truth, certainty, importance, and efficacy of the Christian religion. The same may be said of the *blood*, represented by the *holy eucharist*, which continues to show forth the death and atoning sacrifice of the Son of God till he comes. See the note on verse 6.

Verse 9. *If we receive the witness of men*] Which all are obliged to do, and which is deemed a sufficient testimony to truth in numberless cases; *the witness of God is greater*—he can neither be deceived nor deceive, but man may deceive and be deceived.

Verse 10. *He that believeth on the Son of God*] This is God's witness to a truth, the most important and interesting to mankind. God has witnessed that *whosoever believeth on his Son* shall be saved, and have *everlasting life*; and shall have the *witness* of it *in himself*, the Spirit bearing witness with his spirit that he is a child of God. To *know*, to *feel* his sin forgiven, to have the testimony of this in the heart from the Holy Spirit himself, is the privilege of every true believer in Christ.

Verse 11. *This is the record*] The great truth to which the *Spirit*, the *water*, and the *blood* bear testimony. *God hath given us eternal life*—a *right* to endless glory, and a *meetness* for it. *And this life is in his Son*; it comes *by* and *through* him; he is its *author* and its *purchaser*; it is only *in* and *through* HIM. No other scheme of salvation can be effectual; God has provided none other, and in such a case a man's invention must be vain.

Verse 12. *He that hath the Son hath life*] As the eternal life is given IN the Son of God, it follows that it cannot be enjoyed without him. No man can

A. M. cir. 4073.
A. D. cir. 69.
Impp. Galba,
Othone, Vitel.
et Vespa-
siano.

that hath not the Son of God hath not life.

13 [u] These things have I written unto you that believe on the name of the Son of God ; [v] that ye may know that ye have eternal life, and that ye may believe on the name of the Son of God.

14 And this is the confidence that we have

---

[u] John xx. 31.——[v] Chap. i. 1, 2.

A. M. cir. 4073.
A. D. cir. 69.
Impp. Galba,
Othone, Vitel.
et Vespa-
siano.

[w] in him, that, [x] if we ask any thing according to his will, he heareth us.

15 And if we know that he hear us, whatsoever we ask, we know that we have the petitions that we desired of him.

16 If any man see his brother sin a sin *which is* not unto death, he shall ask, and

---

[w] Or, *concerning him.*——[x] Chap. iii. 22.

---

have it without having Christ ; therefore *he that hath the Son hath life*, and he *that hath not the Son hath not life.* It is in vain to expect eternal glory, if we have not Christ in our heart. The indwelling Christ gives both a title to it, and a meetness for it. This is God's record. Let no man deceive himself here. An *indwelling Christ* and GLORY ; *no indwelling Christ*, NO *glory.* God's record must stand.

Verse 13.. *That ye may know that ye have eternal life*] I write to show your privileges—to lead you into this holy of holies—to show what believing on the Son of God is, by the glorious effects it produces : it is not a blind reliance *for*, but an actual enjoyment *of*, salvation ; Christ living, working, and reigning in the heart.

And that ye may believe] That is, continue to believe ; for Christ dwells in the heart *only by* FAITH, and *faith* lives only by LOVE, and *love* continues only by OBEDIENCE ; he who BELIEVES *loves*, and he who LOVES *obeys.* He who *obeys* loves ; he who *loves believes ;* he who *believes has* the *witness in himself :* he who has this witness has Christ in his heart, the hope of glory ; and he who believes, loves, and obeys, has Christ in his heart, and is a man of *prayer.*

Verse 14. *This is the confidence*] Παρρησια, The *liberty of access* and *speech, that if we ask any thing according to his will*, that is, which he has *promised* in his *word.* His word is a *revelation* of his *will*, in the things which concern the salvation of man. All that God has *promised* we are justified in expecting ; and what he has *promised*, and we *expect*, we should *pray for.* Prayer is the language of the children of God. He who is begotten of God *speaks* this language. He calls God Abba, Father, in the true spirit of supplication. *Prayer* is the language of dependence on God ; where the soul is *dumb*, there is neither life, love, nor faith. Faith and prayer are not boldly to advance *claims* upon God ; we must take heed that what we *ask* and *believe for* is agreeable to the *revealed will* of God. What we find *promised*, that we may *plead.*

Verse 15. *And if we know that he hear us*] Seeing we are satisfied that he hears the prayer of faith, requesting the things which himself has promised ; *we know*, consequently, *that we have the petitions*—the answer to the *petitions, that we desired of him ;* for he cannot deny himself ; and we may consider them *as sure* as *if we had them ;* and we shall have them *as soon* as we plead for and need them. We are not to ask *to-day* for mercy that we *now* need, and not receive it till *to-morrow*, or some *future* time. God gives it to him who prays, *when* it is needful.

Verse 16. *A sin* which is *not unto death*] This is an extremely difficult passage, and has been variously interpreted. What is the *sin not unto death*, for which we *should ask*, and life shall be given to him that commits it ? And what is the *sin unto death*, for which we *should not pray* ?

I shall note three of the chief opinions on this subject :—

1. It is supposed that there is here an allusion to a distinction in the Jewish law, where there was חטאה למיתה *chattaah lemithah*, " a sin unto death ;" and חטאה לא למיתה *chattaah lo lemithah*, " a sin not unto death ;" that is, 1. A *sin*, or transgression, to which the law had assigned the punishment of *death ;* such as idolatry, incest, blasphemy, breach of the Sabbath, and the like. And 2. A sin not unto death, i. e. transgressions of ignorance, inadvertence, &c., and such as, in their own nature, appear to be comparatively light and trivial. That such distinctions did exist in the Jewish synagogue both *Schoettgen* and *Carpzovius* have proved.

2. By the *sin not unto death*, for which intercession might be made, and *unto death*, for which prayer might not be made, we are to understand transgressions of the *civil law* of a particular place, some of which must be punished with *death*, according to the *statutes*, the crime admitting of *no pardon :* others *might* be punished with death, but the magistrate had the power of commuting the punishments, i. e. of changing *death* into *banishment*, &c., for reasons that might appear to him satisfactory, or at the *intercession* of powerful friends. To *intercede* in the *former* case would be useless, because the law would not relax, therefore they need *not pray for it ;* but *intercession* in the *latter* case *might be prevalent*, therefore they *might pray ;* and if they did not, the person might suffer the punishment of death. This opinion, which has been advanced by *Rosenmüller*, intimates that men should feel for each other's distresses, and use their influence in behalf of the wretched, nor ever abandon the unfortunate but where the case is utterly hopeless.

3. *The sin unto death* means a case of transgression, particularly of grievous backsliding from the life and power of godliness, which God determines to punish with *temporal death*, while at the same time he extends mercy to the penitent soul. The *disobedient prophet*, 1 Kings xiii. 1–32, is, on this interpretation, a case in point : many others occur in the history of the Church, and of every religious community. The *sin not unto death* is any sin which God does not choose *thus* to punish. This view of the subject is

A. M. cir. 4073.
A. D. cir. 69.
Impp. Galba,
Othone, Vitel.
et Vespa-
siano.

ʸ he shall give him life for them that sin not unto death. ᶻ There is a sin unto death : ᵃ I do not say that he shall pray for it.

17 ᵇ All unrighteousness is sin : and there is a sin not unto death.

18 We know that ᶜ whosoever is born of God sinneth not ; but he that is begotten of God ᵈ keepeth himself, and that wicked one toucheth him not.

19 *And* we know that we are of God, and

ᵉ the whole world lieth in wickedness.

20 And we know that the Son of God is come, ᶠ and hath given us an understanding, ᵍ that we may know him that is true, and we are in him that is true, *even* in his Son Jesus Christ. ʰ This is the true God, ⁱ and eternal life.

21 Little children, ᵏ keep yourselves from idols. Amen.

A. M. cir. 4073.
A. D. cir. 69.
Impp. Galba,
Othone, Vitel.
et Vespa-
siano.

ʸ Job xlii. 8 ; James v. 14, 15.——ᶻ Matt. xii. 31, 32 ; Mark iii. 29 ; Luke xii. 10 ; Heb. vi. 4, 6 : x. 26.——ᵃ Jer. vii. 16 ; xiv. 11 ; John xvii. 9.——ᵇ Chapter iii. 4.——ᶜ 1 Pet. i. 23 ; chap. iii. 9. ᵈ James i. 27.

ᵉ Gal. i. 4.——ᶠ Luke xxiv. 45.——ᵍ John xvii. 3.——ʰ Isa. ix. 6 ; xliv. 6 ; liv. 5 ; John xx. 28 ; Acts xx. 28 ; Rom. ix. 5 ; 1 Tim. iii. 16 ; Tit. ii. 13 ; Heb. i. 8.——ⁱ Ver. 11, 12, 13.——ᵏ 1 Cor. x. 14.

---

that taken by the late Rev. *J. Wesley*, in a sermon entitled, *A Call to Backsliders.*—Works, vol. ii., page 239.

I do not think the passage has any thing to do with what is termed *the sin against the Holy Ghost ;* much less with the popish doctrine of *purgatory ;* nor with sins committed *before* and *after* baptism, the *former* pardonable, the latter *unpardonable,* according to some of the fathers. Either of the last opinions (viz., 2 and 3) make a good sense ; and the *first* (1) is not unlikely : the apostle may allude to some *maxim* or *custom* in the Jewish Church which is not now distinctly known. However, this we know, that any penitent may find mercy through Christ Jesus ; for through him every kind of sin may be forgiven to man, except the sin against the Holy Ghost ; which I have proved no man can now commit. See the note on Matt. xii. 31, 32.

Verse 17. *All unrighteousness is sin*] Πασα αδικια, Every act contrary to *justice is sin—is a transgression of the law* which condemns all *injustice.*

Verse 18. *Whosoever is born of God sinneth not*] This is spoken of adult Christians ; *they* are *cleansed from all unrighteousness,* consequently from all *sin,* chap. i. 7–9.

Keepeth himself] That is, *in the love of God,* Jude 21, by building up himself on his most holy faith, and praying in the Holy Ghost ; *and that wicked one—*the devil, *toucheth him not—*finds nothing of his own nature in him on which he can work, Christ dwelling in his heart by faith.

Verse 19. *We know that we are of God*] Have the fullest proof of the truth of Christianity, and of our own reconciliation to God through the death of his Son.

The whole world lieth in wickedness.] Εν τω πονηρω κειται· *Lieth in the wicked one—*is embraced in the arms of the devil, where it lies fast asleep and carnally secure, deriving its heat and power from its infernal fosterer. What a truly awful state ! And do not the actions, tempers, propensities, opinions, and maxims of all worldly men prove and illustrate this ? " In this short expression," says Mr. Wesley, " the horrible state of the world is painted in the most lively colours ; a comment on which we have in the actions, conversations, contracts, quarrels and

friendships of worldly men." Yes, their ACTIONS are opposed to the law of God ; their CONVERSATIONS shallow, simulous, and false ; their CONTRACTS forced, interested, and deceitful ; their QUARRELS puerile, ridiculous, and ferocious : and their FRIENDSHIPS hollow, insincere, capricious, and fickle :—all, all the effect of their lying in the arms of the wicked one ; for thus they become instinct with his own spirit : and because they are of their father the devil, therefore his lusts they will do.

Verse 20. *We know that the Son of God is come*] In the flesh, and has made his soul an offering for sin : *and hath given us an understanding—*a more eminent degree of light than we ever enjoyed before ; for as he lay in the bosom of the Father, he hath declared him unto us ; and he hath besides given us a spiritual understanding, that we may know him who is true, even the TRUE GOD, and get eternal life from him through his Son, IN whom we are by faith, as the branches in the vine, deriving all our knowledge, light, life, love, and fruitfulness from him. And it is through this revelation of Jesus that we know the ever blessed and glorious Trinity ; and the Trinity, *Father, Word,* and *Holy Ghost,* in the eternal, undivided unity of the ineffable Godhead.

Verse 21. *Little children*] Τεκνια· *Beloved children ;* he concludes with the same affectionate feeling with which he commenced.

Keep yourselves from idols.] Avoid the idolatry of the heathens ; not only have no *false gods,* but have the *true God.* Have no idols in your *houses,* none in your *churches;* none in your *hearts.* Have no object of idolatrous worship ; no *pictures, relics, consecrated tapers, wafers, crosses,* &c., by attending to which your minds may be divided, and prevented from worshipping the infinite Spirit in spirit and in truth.

The apostle, says Dr. Macknight, cautioned his disciples against going with the heathens into the temple of their idol gods, to eat of their feasts upon the sacrifices they had offered to these gods ; and against being present at any act of worship which they paid them ; because, by being present, they participated of that worship, as is plain from what St. Paul has written on the subject, 1 Cor. viii. 10, where see the notes.

That is a man's *idol* or *god* from which he seeks his *happiness ;* no matter whether it be Jupiter, Juno,

Apollo, Minerva, Venus, or Diana; or pleasure, wealth, fame, a fine house, superb furniture, splendid equipage, medals, curiosities, books, titles, human friendships, or any earthly or heavenly thing, God, the supreme good, only excepted. That is a man's idol which prevents him from seeking and finding his ALL in God.

Wiclif ends his epistle thus: *My little sones, kepe ye you fro mawmitis*, i. e. *puppets, dolls*, and such like; for thus Wiclif esteemed all *images* employed in religious worship. They are the *dolls* of a spurious Christianity, and the drivellings of religion in *nonage* and *dotage*. *Protestants*, keep yourselves from such *mawmets!*

Amen.] So be it! So let it be! And so it shall be, God being our helper, for ever and ever!

Subscriptions in the VERSIONS :—

The end of the Epistle of the Apostle John.—SYRIAC.

The First Epistle of John the apostle is ended.—SYR. *Philoxenian.*

Nothing in either the COPTIC or VULGATE.

Continual and eternal praise be to God!—ARABIC.

The end.—ÆTHIOPIC:

In this version the epistle is thus introduced :—

In the name of the Father, and of the Son, and of the Holy Spirit, one God, the Epistle of John, the son of Zebedee, the evangelist and apostle of our Lord Jesus Christ; may his intercession be with us for ever and ever! Amen.

In the MANUSCRIPTS :—

The First of John.—AB.

The First Epistle of John the evangelist.

The First catholic Epistle of St. John the divine, written from Ephesus.

The Epistle to the Parthians.—See several Latin MSS.

The word *amen* is wanting in all the best MSS. and in most of the *versions*.

For other matters relative to the epistle itself see the *preface:* and for its heavenly doctrine and unction read the *text*, in the *original* if you can; if not, in our own excellent *translation*.

OBSERVATIONS ON THE TEXT OF THE THREE DIVINE WITNESSES,

Accompanied with a plate, containing two very correct fac-similes of 1 JOHN, *chap. v. ver. 7, 8, and 9, as they stand in the first edition of the New Testament, printed at Complutum, 1514, and in the Codex Montfortii, a manuscript marked G. 97, in the library of Trinity College, Dublin.*

Παντα δοκιμαζετε, το καλον κατεχετε. 1 Thess. v. 21.

The *seventh verse* of the *fifth chapter* of 1 JOHN, has given rise to more theological disputes than any other portion of the sacred writings. Advocates and antagonists have arisen in every quarter of the civilized world : but the dispute has been principally confined to the *Unitarians* of all classes, and those called *Ortho-*

dox; the former asserting that it is an *interpolation*, and the latter contending that it is a *part of the original text of St. John.* It is asserted that (one excepted, which shall be noticed by and by) all the Greek MSS. written *before the invention of printing* omit the passage in dispute. How the seventh and eighth verses stand in these may be seen in the following view, where the words included between brackets are those which are wanting in the MSS.

Ὅτι τρεις εισιν οἱ μαρτυρουντες [εν τῳ ουρανῳ, ὁ πατηρ, ὁ λογος, και το ἁγιον πνευμα· και οὗτοι οἱ τρεις ἑν εισι. Και τρεις εισιν οἱ μαρτυρουντες εν τῃ γῃ] το πνευμα, και το ὑδωρ, και το αἱμα· και οἱ τρεις εις το ἑν εισιν.

Of all the MSS. yet discovered which contain this epistle, amounting to *one hundred and twelve, three* only, two of which are of no authority, have the text, viz. :—

1. The *Codex Guelpherbytanus* G, which is demonstrably a MS. of the seventeenth century, (for it contains the Latin translation of Beza, written by the same hand,) and therefore of no use or importance in sacred criticism.

2. The *Codex Ravianus* or *Berolinensis*, which is a forgery, and only a copy of the Greek text in the *Complutensian Polyglot*, printed in 1514, and so close an imitation of it, that it copies even its typographical errors; hence, and from the similarity of the letters, it appears to have been forged that it might pass for the *original* MS. from which the Complutensian text was taken. In this MS. some various readings are inserted from the margin of Stevens' edition of 1550.

3. The *Codex Montfortii*, or *Codex Dubliniensis*, cited by Erasmus, under the title of *Codex Britannicus*, in Trinity College, Dublin. This may be said to be the only *genuine* MS. which contains this text; as no advocate of the sacred doctrine contained in the disputed passage would wish to lay any stress whatever on such evidence as the two preceding ones afford. *Michaelis* roundly asserts, vol. iv., page 417, of his *Introductory Lectures*, that this MS. was written after the year 1500. This, I scruple not to affirm, is a perfectly unguarded assertion, and what *no man can prove.* In 1790 I examined this MS. myself, and though I thought it to be comparatively modern, yet I had no doubt that it existed before the invention of printing, and was never written with an intention to deceive. I am rather inclined to think it the work of an unknown bold critic, who formed a text from one or more MSS. in conjunction with the Vulgate, and was by no means sparing of his own conjectural emendations; for it contains many various readings which exist in no other MS. yet discovered. But how far the writer has in any place faithfully copied the text of any ancient MS. is more than can be determined. To give the reader a fair view of this subject, I here subjoin what I hope I may call a perfect *fac-simile* of the seventh and eighth verses, as they exist in this MS., copied by the accurate hand of the Rev. Dr. Barrett, the present learned librarian of Trinity College.

2

FAC-SIMILE of 1 John v. 7, 8, and 9,

From the Codex Montfortii in Trinity College, Dublin.

ὅτι· τρεῖς ἐισὶν οἱ μαρτι··
ροῦντ ἐν τῳ ὀυ ω, πατρ, λόγος, καὶ πᾶ ἁγιον·
Καὶ οὗτοι οἱ τρῖς ἕν ἐσι· Καὶ τρεῖς ἐισιν οἱ μαρτυ
ροῦντ ἐν τῇ γῆς, πνᾶ, ὑδωρ, Καὶ αἷμα, ἐι τὴν
μαρτυρίαν τῶν ἀνων λαμβάνομεν, ἡ μαρτυρία τοῦ
θυ μεῖζων ἐστι· ὅτι αὕτη ἐστὶ ἡ μαρτυρία τοῦ θεοῦ, ὅτι·
μεμαρτύρηκε περὶ τοῦ ῦῦ ἀυτοῦ.

When I examined the original myself, though I took down a *transcript*, yet I neglected to take a *fac-simile*. That no mistake might be made in a matter of so much importance, I got a fac-simile, and after it was engraved, had it collated with the MS. by Dr. Barrett himself, and the plate finished according to his last corrections; so that I hope it may be said every jot and every tittle belonging to the text are here fairly and faithfully represented; nothing being *added*, and nothing *omitted*. I have examined this MS. since, and have not been able to detect any inaccuracy in my *fac-simile*. To it I have annexed a perfect *fac-simile* of the same words, as they stand in the *Complutensian Polyglot*, which the curious reader will be glad to see associated with the other, as they are properly the only *Greek authorities* on which the authenticity of the text of the Three Witnesses depends.

FAC-SIMILE of 1 John v. 7, 8, and 9,

From the Editio Princeps of the Greek Testament, printed at Complutum, in 1514.

ᵒὅτι ᶦτρεῖς ᵏει =
δίμ, οι ᶠμαρτυρουντες ᵐᵐεμ, τω ᵐᵐουρανω, ᵒ ᵖπα=
τηρ ᵖκαι, ο ᑫ λόγος ᵏκαι, το ˢἅγιον ᶜπνευμα , ᵐκαι
οι ᵐτρεις ᵏεις το ᵃεμ ᵉεισι, ᶠκαι τρεῖς ᵍεισιμ, οι ᶜμαρ
τυρούμτες ᵉεπι, της ᶦγης, το ᵏπνευμα ᵏκαι, το ᵏ ῦ
δωρ ᶠκαι, το ᵐαιμα, ᵐει, την ᵐαρτυρίαν, τωμ ᵖαμ
θρωπωμ ᶦλαμβάνομεμ, η ᵐμαρτυρία, του ᵗθεου
ᵗμειζωμ ᵘεστιμ, ᵒοτι, αυτη ᵉεστιμ, η ᵐμαρτυρία, του
ᵏθεου, ᶠηρ ᵖμεμαρτύρηκε ᶜπερι, του ᶠυιου, αυτου.

It may be necessary to observe,

First, That the *five* first lines of the fac-simile of the text in the Complutensian edition are at the top of the opposite page to that on which the other *four* lines are found. The *alphabetical letters*, mingled with the Greek text, are those which refer to the corresponding words in the Latin text, printed in a parallel column in the Complutensian Polyglot, and marked with the same letters to ascertain more easily the corresponding Greek and Latin words, for the benefit, I suppose, of learners. The column containing the Latin text, which is that of the *Vulgate*, is not introduced here, being quite unnecessary.

Second. The sixth and seventh lines of the *fac-simile* of the *Codex Montfortii* belong to the second page of that leaf on which the other *five* lines are written.

This MS. is a thick duodecimo, written on paper, without *folios.* There is an inscription in it in these words, *Sum Thomæ Clementis, olim fratris Froyhe.* On this inscription Dr. Barrett remarks: "It appears *Froyhe* was a *Franciscan;* and I find in some blank leaves in the book these words written (by the same hand, in my opinion, that wrote the MS.) Ιησους Μαρια Φραγκισκος; by the latter, I understand the founder of that order." If *St. Francis d'Assise* be here meant, who was the founder of the order of *Franciscans*, and the inscription be written by the same who wrote the MS., then the MS. could not have been written before the thirteenth century, as St. Francis founded his order in 1206, and died in 1226; and consequently proves that the MS. could not have been written in the eleventh century, as Mr. *Martin* of Utrecht, and several others, have imagined.

Much stress has been laid on the dots over the *i* and *ʋ* which frequently appear in this MS. Montfaucon has observed, *Palæographia Græca*, page 33, that such

2

dots were in use a thousand years ago; hence the advocates of the antiquity of the *Codex Montfortii* have inferred that this MS. must have been written at least in the tenth or eleventh century. But as these are found in *modern* MSS. (see *Palæog.* pages 324, 333,) they are therefore no proof of antiquity. In *Michaelis' Introduction*, vol. ii., page 286, where he is describing the MSS. of the Greek Testament, he gives the text in question *as it is supposed to exist* in the *Codex Montfortii*, in which two dots appear over *every iota* and *upsilon* in the whole five lines there introduced; but on comparing this of Michaelis with the *fac-simile* here produced, the reader will at once perceive that the *arrangement* is false, and the dotting egregiously inaccurate. Deceived by this false representation, Dr. *Marsh*, (bishop of Peterborough,) in his notes on the passage, page 754, observes, "that no MS. written in *small characters* before the twelfth century has these dots. That a MS. written in the twelfth century has these dots *sometimes* on the *iota*, but never on the *upsilon*; but MSS. written in the fourteenth century have these dots on *both letters*, but not in all cases. Now as these letters are *dotted always* in the *Codex Montfortianus*, but not always in the MSS. of the thirteenth and fourteenth centuries, and still less often in those of the twelfth century, we may infer that the *Codex Montfortianus* is at least as modern as the fifteenth century."

On this quotation I beg leave to make a few remarks. Dr. Marsh says, "that no MS. written in small letters previous to the twelfth century has these dots." This excellent critic has only to consult the *Palæographia Græca*, page 293, in which he will find No. 1, a *fac-simile* of one of the Colbert MSS. (No. 4954,) written A. D. 1022, where the *iota* appears thrice dotted; and in No. 2, on the same page, another *fac-simile* of a MS. written A. D. 1045, the iota is dotted in the word ιησου. *Ibid.*, page 283, (No. 7,) a MS. written in 986, has the iota *twice* dotted in the word Ιεμενει. *Ibid.*, page 275, (No. 2,) a MS. of the ninth or beginning of the tenth century, has the *iota* dotted in αχαιας˙ and in No. 3, a specimen of the *Codex Regius*, (No. 2271,) written A. D. 914, the *iota* is dotted in θεικην. *Ibid.*, page 271, (No. 4,) written about 890, the *iota* is dotted in ιερων˙ and in Spec. v. in the word ποιια. See also *Ibid.*, page 320, No. 3, another of the Colbert MSS. (4111,) written A. D. 1236, where the *iota* is dotted *seven* times. All these specimens are taken from MSS. written in *small characters*, and, as the dates show, (the last excepted,) long before the twelfth century. As to these dots being more frequent in manuscripts of the fifteenth than those of the twelfth, thirteenth, and fourteenth centuries, I cannot say much; it is certain they became more frequent towards the fourteenth century than they were in the twelfth, and yet this was not a general case. In two well-written manuscripts now before me, one of which I suppose to be of the fourteenth century, and the other of the fifteenth, these dots often occur, but they are by no means *regular*. I have noticed several pages in the oldest manuscript where they occur but *once*; and in other pages they may be met with ten or twelve times. On the contrary, in the more *recent* manuscript, *whole pages* occur without one of them; and where they do

occur, they are much less frequent than in the former. So that it rather appears from this evidence, that they began to disappear in the fifteenth century. Dr. Marsh, misled by the specimen in *Michaelis*, vol. ii. page 286, says: "The letters in question are *always* dotted in the *Codex Montfortianus.*" By referring to the fac-simile, the reader will be able at once to correct this mistake. The *iota* in the fac-simile occurs *thirty* times, and is dotted only in *five* instances; and the *upsilon* occurs *nineteen* times, and is dotted only in *seven*.

But arguments *for* or *against* the age of any MS., on account of such dots, are futile in the extreme; as the most ancient MSS. have them not only on the *iota* and *upsilon*, but upon several other letters, as may be seen in the *Codex Alexandrinus*, the *Codex Rescriptus*, published by Dr. *Barrett*, and the *Codex Bezæ*; in the latter of which they seem to occur more frequently than they do even in the *Codex Montfortii*.

On the evidence of these *dots*, Mr. *Martin* of Utrecht supposed the Dublin manuscript to be as old as the eleventh century; and on the same evidence Dr. *Marsh* argues, "that it is at least as modern as the *fifteenth*." Both these judgments are too hastily formed; *medio tutissimus ibis* is the best counsel in such a case; the manuscript is more likely to have been a production of the thirteenth than of either the eleventh or fifteenth. The former date is as much *too high* as the latter is *too low*; the zeal of the critics for and against this controverted text having carried them, in my opinion, much too far on either side.

In comparing the *writing* of the *Codex Montfortii*, with the different specimens given by *Montfaucon* in the *Palæographia Græca*, it appears to approach nearest to that on page 320, No. 4, which was taken from one of the Colbert manuscripts, (No. 845,) written in the year of our Lord 1272, which I am led to think may be nearly about the date of the *Codex Montfortii*; but on a subject of so much difficulty, where critics of the first rank have been puzzled, I should be sorry to hazard any more than an *opinion*, which the reader is at liberty to consider either correct or incorrect, as may seem best to his own judgment.

Though a conscientious advocate for the *sacred doctrine* contained in the disputed text, and which I think expressly enough revealed in several other parts of the sacred writings, I must own the passage in question stands on a most dubious foundation. All the Greek manuscripts (the Codex Montfortii alone excepted) omit the passage; so do *all the ancient versions*; the *Vulgate* excepted; but in many of the ancient MSS. even of this version it is wanting. There is one in the British Museum, of the tenth or eleventh century, where it is added by a more recent hand in the margin; for it is wanting in the text. It is also *variously written* in those manuscripts which retain it. This will appear more plainly by comparing the following extracts taken from four manuscripts of the Vulgate in my own possession :—

1. ——Quoniam tres sunt qui testimonium dant in cœlo, Pater, Verbum, et Spiritus Sanctus, et hii tres unum sunt. Et tres sunt qui testimonium dant in terra, spiritus, sanguis, et aqua. This is the same with the text in the Complutensian Polyglot, only *aqua* is placed before *sanguis*.

2. ——Quoniam tres sunt qui testimonium dant in terra, spiritus, aqua, et sanguis, et hii tres unum sunt. Et tres sunt qui testimonium dant in cœlo, Pater, Verbum, et Spiritus Sanctus, et hii tres unum sunt.

3. ——Quoniam tres sunt qui testimonium dant in cœlo, Pater, et Filius, et Spiritus Sanctus, et hii tres unum sunt. Et tres sunt qui testimonium dant in terra, spiritus, aqua, et sanguis.

4. ——Quoniam tres sunt qui testimonium dant in terra, spiritus, aqua, et sanguis, et hii tres unum sunt. Et tres sunt qui testimonium dant in cœlo, Pater, et Filius, et Spiritus Sanctus, et hii tres unum sunt.

5. ——Quoniam tres sunt qui testimonium dant in terra, spiritus, aqua, et sanguis, et tres sunt qui testimonium perhibent in cœlo, Pater, Verbum, et Spiritus Sanctus, et hi tres unum sunt.

This last I took from an ancient manuscript in Marsh's library, St. Patrick's, Dublin.

In what has been denominated the *Editio Princeps* of the Latin Bible, and supposed to have been printed between 1455 and 1468, the text stands thus : Quoniam tres sunt qui testimonium dant in cœlo, Pater, Verbum, et Spiritus Sanctus, et hii tres unum sunt. Et tres sunt qui testimonium dant in terra. Spiritus, aqua, et sanguis, et tres unum sunt."

In the Bible printed by *Fradin* and *Pinard*, Paris, 1497, fol., the text is the same with No. 2, only instead of *testimonium dant*, it reads *dant testimonium.*

The reader will observe that in Nos. 2, 4, and 5, the *eighth* verse is put *before* the *seventh*, and that 3 and 4 have *filius* instead of *verbum*. But both these readings are united in an ancient English manuscript of my own, which contains the Bible from the beginning of Proverbs to the end of the New Testament, written on thick strong vellum, and evidently prior to most of those copies attributed to Wiclif.

𝔣𝔬𝔯 𝔱𝔥𝔯𝔢𝔢 𝔟𝔢𝔫 𝔱𝔥𝔞𝔱 𝔤𝔢𝔟𝔢𝔫 𝔴𝔦𝔱𝔫𝔢𝔰𝔰𝔦𝔫𝔤 𝔦𝔫 𝔥𝔢𝔟𝔢𝔫 𝔱𝔥𝔢 𝔣𝔞𝔟𝔦𝔯, 𝔱𝔥𝔢 𝔚𝔬𝔯𝔡 𝔬𝔯 𝔖𝔬𝔫𝔢 𝔞𝔫𝔡 𝔱𝔥𝔢 𝔥𝔬𝔬𝔩𝔶 𝔊𝔬𝔬𝔰𝔱, 𝔞𝔫𝔡 𝔱𝔥𝔢𝔰𝔢 𝔱𝔥𝔯𝔢𝔢 𝔟𝔢𝔫 𝔬𝔬𝔫. 𝔄𝔫𝔡 𝔱𝔥𝔯𝔢𝔢 𝔟𝔢𝔫 𝔱𝔥𝔞𝔱 𝔤𝔢𝔟𝔢𝔫 𝔴𝔦𝔱𝔫𝔢𝔰𝔰𝔦𝔫𝔤 𝔦𝔫 𝔢𝔯𝔱𝔥𝔢, 𝔱𝔥𝔢 𝔖𝔭𝔦𝔯𝔦𝔱, 𝔚𝔞𝔱𝔢𝔯, 𝔞𝔫𝔡 𝔅𝔩𝔬𝔬𝔡, 𝔞𝔫𝔡 𝔱𝔥𝔢𝔰𝔢 𝔱𝔥𝔯𝔢𝔢 𝔟𝔢𝔫 𝔬𝔬𝔫.

As many suppose the Complutensian editors must have had a manuscript or manuscripts which contained this disputed passage, I judge it necessary to add the *note* which they subjoin at the bottom of the page, by which (though nothing is clearly expressed) it appears they either had such a manuscript, or *wished to have it thought they had such*. However, the note is curious, and shows us how this disputed passage was read in the most approved manuscripts of the Vulgate extant in the thirteenth century, when *St. Thomas Aquinas* wrote, from whom this note is taken. The following is the whole note *literatim :*—

" Sanctus Thomas in oppositione secunde Decretalis de suma Trinitate et fide Catholica, tractans istum passum contra Abbatem Joachim ; ut tres sunt qui testimonium dant in celo, Pater, Verbum, et Spiritus Sanctus ; dicet ad literam verba sequentia. Et ad insinuandam unitatem trium personarum subditur. Et hii tres unum sunt. Quodquidem dicitur propter essentie Unitatem. Sed hoc Joachim perverse trahere volens ad unitatem charitatis et consensus, inducebat consequentem auctoritatem. Nam subditur ibidem : et tres sunt qui testimonium dant in terra, S. Spiritus : Aqua :

et sanguis. Et in quibusdam libris additur : et hii tres unum sunt. Sed hoc in veris exemplaribus non habetur : sed dicitur esse appossitum ab hereticis arrianis ad pervertendum intellectum sanum auctoritatis premisse de unitate essentie trium personarum. Hec beatus Thomas ubi supra."

If the Complutensian editors *translated* the passage into Greek from the *Vulgate*, it is strange they made no mention of it in this place, where they had so fair an opportunity while speaking so very pointedly on the doctrine in question and forming a note for the occasion, which is indeed the only *theological* note in the whole volume. It is again worthy of note that, when these editors found an important various reading in any of their Greek manuscripts, they noted it in the margin: an example occurs 1 Cor. xiii. 3, and another, *ibid.* xvi. ; why was it then that they took no notice of so important an *omission* as the text of the three witnesses, if they really had no manuscript in which it was contained ? Did they intend to *deceive* the reader, and could they possibly imagine that the knavery could never be detected ? If they designed to deceive, they took the most effectual way to conceal the fraud, as it is supposed they destroyed the manuscripts from which they printed their text ; for the story of their being sold in 1749 to a *rocket-maker* (see *Michaelis*, vol. ii., page 440) is every way so exceptionable and unlike the truth, that I really wonder there should be found any person who would seriously give it credit. The substance of this story, as given by *Michaelis*, is as follows : " *Professor Moldenhawer*, who was in Spain in 1784, went to Alcala on purpose to discover these MSS., but was informed that a very illiterate librarian, about thirty-five years before, who *wanted room for some new books*, sold the ancient vellum MSS as *useless parchments*, to one *Toryo* who dealt in fireworks, as materials for making rockets." It is farther added that " *Martinez*, a man of learning, *heard of it soon after they were sold*, and *hastened* to save these treasures from destruction ; but it was too late, for they were already destroyed, except a few scattered leaves which are now in the library." On the whole of this account, it is natural to ask the following questions : Is it likely that the management of so important a trust should be in the hands of a person so ignorant that he could not know a *Hebrew* or *Greek* MS. from a piece of *useless parchment ?* Could such a person be intrusted to make a purchase of *new books* for the library, for which he wanted room ? or if they were purchased by the *trustees* of the library, is it likely they would leave the classification and arrangement of these to such a *Goth* as this librarian is said to be ? Would such a librarian, or indeed any other, be *permitted* to dispose of any part of the library which *he* might deem useless ? If Mr. Martinez heard of it *soon after* they were sold, and *hastened to rescue them*, is it likely that almost the whole should have been converted into rockets before he got to the place, when we are informed they were so many as to cost originally 4,000 aurei; and that even the price which the librarian sold them for was so considerable, that it had to be paid at *two different instalments ?* Was it possible that in so short a time the rocket-maker could have already consumed the whole ? The whole account is so improbable that

I cannot help saying, *Credat Judæus Apella; non ego.*

It is more likely the manuscripts were destroyed at first, or that they are still *kept secret,* to prevent the forgery (if it be one) of the text of the three witnesses from being detected ; or the librarian already mentioned may have converted them to *his own use.* If they were not destroyed by the Complutensian editors, I should not be surprised if the same manuscripts should come to light in some other part of the world, if not in the Alcala library itself.

It is worthy of remark that *Luther* never admitted the text of the three witnesses into any of the editions of his translation; it is true it was afterwards added, but never during his lifetime. On this Professor Michaelis makes the following observation.: " It is uncandid in the extreme for one Protestant to condemn another for rejecting 1 John v. 7, since it was rejected by the author of our Reformation." Any conscientious Trinitarian may *innocently hesitate* to receive the feebly supporting evidence of this disputed text, in confirmation of a doctrine which he finds it his duty and interest to receive on the unequivocal testimony of various other passages in the book of God.

Professor Griesbach, who does not appear to be an enemy to the doctrine, and who has carefully and critically examined all the evidences and arguments, pro and con., has given up the text as utterly defenceless, and thinks that to plead for its authenticity is dangerous. " For if," says he, " a few dubious, suspicious, and modern evidences, with such weak arguments as are usually adduced, are sufficient to demonstrate the authenticity of *a reading,* then there remains no longer any criterion by which the *spurious* may be distinguished from the *genuine;* and consequently the whole text of the New Testament is unascertained and dubious."

Much stress has been laid on *Bengel's* defence of this text: Michaelis has considered the strength of his arguments in a candid and satisfactory manner.

" The ancient writers which Bengel has produced in favour of 1 John v. 7, are all *Latin writers,* for he acknowledges that no *Greek father* has ever quoted it. Now, if no objection could be made to Bengel's witnesses, and the most ancient Latin fathers had quoted in express terms the whole of the controverted passage, their quotations would prove nothing more than that the passage stood in their manuscripts of the Latin version, and therefore that the Latin version contained it in a very early age. But it will appear upon examination that their evidence is very unsatisfactory. The evidence of Tertullian, the oldest Latin writer who has been quoted in favour of 1 John v. 7, is contained in the following passage of his treatise against Praxeas, book i., chap. 25 : *Ita connexus Patris in Filio et Filii in Paracleto, tres efficit cohærentes, alterum ex altero; qui tres unum sunt, non unus; quomodo dictum est: Ego et Pater unum sumus.* Hence it is inferred, that because *tres unum sunt* stand at present in the Latin version, 1 John v. 7, these words stood there likewise in the time of Tertullian, and that Tertullian borrowed them from the Latin version. But this inference is wholly without foundation; for Tertullian does not produce these words as a quotation,

and the bare circumstance of his using the expression *tres unum sunt* will not prove that he found that expression in the Bible. On the contrary, it is evident, from what immediately follows, that 1 John v. 7 was *not* contained in the Latin version when Tertullian wrote. For, in proof of this assertion, *qui tres unum sunt,* he immediately adds, *quomodo dictum est: Ego et Pater unum sumus,* which is a quotation from St. John's gospel, chap. x. 30. Now as this quotation relates only to the Father and the Son, and not to the Holy Ghost, surely Tertullian would not have proved the unity of the Trinity from this passage, if 1 John v. 7, which is much more to the purpose, had then been contained in any Latin manuscript with which he was acquainted. At any rate, the mere use of the words *tres unum sunt* affords no argument in favour of the controverted passage; and if any inference is to be deduced from their agreement with our present copies of the Latin version in 1 John v. 7; it is this : that the person who afterwards fabricated this passage retained an expression which had been sanctioned by the authority of Tertullian. So much for the evidence of this Latin father, the only writer of the *second* century to whom appeal has been made.

" Of the Latin fathers who lived in the *third* century, Cyprian alone has been produced as evidence in favour of 1 John v. 7. From the writings of Cyprian two passages have been quoted as proofs that 1 John v. 7 was contained in his manuscript of the Latin version. The one is from his epistle to Jubaianus; where Cyprian writes thus : *Si baptizari quis apud hæreticum potuit, utique et remissam consecutus est, et sanctificatus est, et templum Dei factus est; quæro cujus Dei? Si Creatoris; non potuit; qui in eum non credidit: si Christi, non hujus potest fieri templum, qui negat, Deum Christum : si Spiritus Sancti,* cum tres unum sint, *quomodo Spiritus Sanctus placatus esse et potest, qui aut Patris aut Filii inimicus est?* Here it must be observed, that the words *cum tres unum sint,* though inserted in the later editions of Cyprian's works, are *not* contained in that edition which was published by Erasmus; and even if they were genuine, they will prove nothing more than the same words just quoted from Tertullian. The other passage, which is much more to the purpose, is in Cyprian's treatise, *De Ecclesiæ Unitate,* where Cyprian writes thus : *Dicit Dominus: Ego et Pater unum sumus; et iterum de Patre et Filio, et Spiritu Sancto,* scriptum est : Et tres unum sunt. Now, admitting that the words *et tres unum sunt* were quoted by Cyprian from 1 John v. 7, I seriously ask every impartial judge whether a passage found in no ancient Greek manuscript, quoted by no Greek father, and contained in no other ancient version than the Latin, (and not in all copies of this,) is therefore to be pronounced genuine; merely because one Latin father of the three first centuries, who was bishop of Carthage, where the Latin version only was used, and where Greek was unknown; has quoted it? Under these circumstances, should we conclude that the passage stood originally in the Greek autograph of St. John! Certainly not; for the only inference which could be deduced from Cyprian's quotation would be this, that the passage had been introduced into the Latin version so early as the third century;

" The preceding answer is sufficient to invalidate Cyprian's authority in establishing the authenticity of 1 John v. 7, on the supposition that Cyprian really quoted it; but that he did so is more than any man can prove. The words *tres unum sunt* are contained not only in the seventh, but also in the eighth verse, which is a part of the ancient and genuine text of St. John; and therefore it is at least possible that Cyprian took them not from the seventh, but from the eighth verse. It is true that he says these words are written of the Father, Son, and Holy Ghost; whereas *tres unum sunt*, in the eighth verse, relates only to the spirit, the water, and the blood. But it must be observed that the Latin fathers interpreted *spiritus, aqua, et sanguis*, not literally, but mystically; and some of them really understood by these words, *Pater, Filius, et Spiritus Sanctus*, taking *aqua* in the sense of *Pater, sanguis* in the sense of *Filius*, and *spiritus* in the sense of *Spiritus Sanctus*.

" This is expressly asserted by Eucherius in his *Quæstiones N. T. difficiliores*; for after having quoted 1 John v. 8, thus: *Tria sunt, quæ testimonium perhibent, aqua, sanguis, et spiritus*, he adds, soon after, *plures tamen hic ipsam interpretatione mystica intelligere Trinitatem; aqua Patrem, sanguine Christum, spiritu Spiritum Sanctum manifestante*. But if Cyprian really thought that *aqua, sanguis, et spiritus*, 1 John v. 8, denoted *Pater, Filius, et Spiritus Sanctus*, he might say of *tres unum sunt*, ver. 8, that it was written, *de Patre, et Filio, et Spiritu Sancto*. And that he actually did so, that he quoted not ver. 7, but understood ver. 8, mystically, appears from the following passage of Facundus, who lived in the neighbourhood of Carthage, and consequently used the same Latin version as Cyprian. *Johannes Apostolus in epistola sua de Patre, et Filio, et Spiritu Sancto, sic dicit: Tres sunt qui testimonium dant in terra, spiritus, aqua, et sanguis, et hi tres unum sunt: in spiritu significans Patrem, &c.* Quod Johannis Apostoli testimonium beatus Cyprianus, in epistola, sive libro, quem de Trinitate scripsit, de Patre, Filio, et Spiritu Sancto, dictum intelligit." Facundus then quotes the words of Cyprian, which are the subject of our present inquiry. From the preceding passage it is manifest that 1 John v. 7 was unknown to Facundus; for he proves the doctrine of the Trinity by a mystical interpretation of ver. 8, and appeals to the authority of Cyprian, who, he says, gave the same interpretation. But if 1 John v. 7 was unknown to Facundus, who lived in the same country as Cyprian, used the same Latin version, and wrote almost three centuries later, it is incredible that 1 John v. 7 was already introduced in the Latin manuscripts which Cyprian used. Consequently we must conclude that the assertion of Facundus is true, and that the words of Cyprian contain, not a quotation from 1 John v. 7, but a mystical application of 1 John v. 8. This is farther confirmed by Augustine, who was likewise an African bishop, who lived a hundred years later than Cyprian, and still knew nothing of 1 John v. 7, for he has never quoted this passage, not even where he speaks of the Trinity, but he has mystically applied the eighth verse."—MICHAELIS, vol. vi. p. 420.

The Greek writers who have not quoted this verse, though several of them wrote professedly on the Deity of Christ, and on the Trinity, are the following:—

Irenæus.	Cyril of Alexandria.
Clemens Alexandrinus.	The Exposition of Faith
Dionysius Alexandrinus (or	in Justin Martyr's
the writer against Paul	works.
of Samosata under his	Cæsarius.
name.)	Proclus.
Athanasius.	The Council of Nice, as
The Synopsis of Scripture.	it is represented by Gelasius Cyzicenus.
The Synod of Sardica.	
Epiphanius.	Hippolytus.
Basil.	Andreas.
Alexander of Alexandria.	Six catenæ, quoted by
Gregory Nyssen.	Simon.
Gregory Nazianzen, with	The marginal scholia of
his two commentators,	three MSS.
Elias Cretensis and	Hesychius.
Nicetas.	John Damascenus.
Didymus *de Spiritu Sancto*.	Germanus of Constantinople.
Chrysostom.	
An author under his name,	Œcumenius.
de sancta et consubstantiali Trinitate.	Euthymius Zigabenus

LATIN AUTHORS.

Novatian.	Facundus.
Hilary.	Junilius.
Lucifer Calaritanus.	Cerealis.
Jerome.	Rusticus.
Augustine.	Bede.
Ambrose.	Gregory.
Faustinus.	Philastrius.
Leo Magnus.	Paschasius.
The author *de Promissis*.	Arnobius, junior
Eucherius.	Pope Eusebius.

The writers that have quoted it are comparatively recent or spurious, for those of any note which have been supposed, from certain expressions in their works, to have had reference to this verse, have been proved by learned men to have had no such text in view. A great and good man has said that " the seventh verse, in conjunction with the sixth and eighth, has been quoted by Tertullian, Cyprian, and an uninterrupted train of fathers." But a more incautious assertion was never made, as the preceding list will prove; and the evidence on the subject I have most carefully examined. *Bengel*, who was an excellent critic and a good man, endeavoured to defend it, but without success; and *Michaelis* demonstrated its spuriousness from Bengel's *five* concessions. *Knittel* has defended its authenticity with much critical acumen; *Hezelius* with great sagacity; *David Martin*, of Utrecht, with much honest simplicity; and Dean *Travis* with abundance of zeal, without much knowledge of the critical bearings of the subject. *Socinians* need not glory that it is indefensible, and that honest Trinitarians give it up; for the sacred *doctrine* which it appears to express is diffused through every part of the Scriptures, and is as inexpugnable as a rock of adamant, and will live and prevail in the Church of Christ while sun and moon endure, and till time shall be swallowed up in eternity.

SUMMARY *of the whole evidence relative to the* THREE HEAVENLY WITNESSES, 1 *John* v. 7.

1. ONE HUNDRED AND THIRTEEN *Greek* MSS. are extant, containing the First Epistle of John, and the text in question is wanting in 112. It only exists in the *Codex Montfortii,* (a comparatively recent MS.,) already described. The *Codex Ravianus,* in the Royal Library at Berlin, is a *transcript* taken from the *Complutensian* Polyglot.

2. All the GREEK *fathers* omit the verse, though many of them quote both ver. 6 and ver. 8, applying them to the Trinity, and Divinity of Christ and the Holy Spirit; yea, and endeavour to prove the doctrine of the *Trinity* from ver. 6 and ver. 8, without referring to any such verse as the 7th, which, had it existed, would have been a more positive proof, and one that could not have been overlooked.

3. The *first place* in which the verse appears in *Greek* is the Greek translation of the Acts of the *Council of Lateran,* held A. D. 1215.

4. Though it is found in many *Latin* copies, yet it does not appear that any written previously to the TENTH CENTURY contains it.

5. The LATIN *fathers* do not quote it, even where it would have greatly strengthened their arguments; and where, had it existed, it might have been most naturally expected.

6. *Vigilius,* bishop of *Tapsum,* at the conclusion of the fifth century, is the first who seems to have referred expressly to the three heavenly witnesses; but his quotation does not agree with the present text either in *words* or in *sense;* and besides, he is a writer of very little credit, nor does the place alleged appear to learned men to be genuine.

7. The *Latin writers* who do refer to the three heavenly witnesses vary greatly in their quotations, the more *ancient* placing the *eighth verse* before the *seventh,* and very many omitting, after the earthly witnesses, the clause *these three are one.* Others who insert *these three are one* add *in Christ Jesus;* others use different terms.

8. It is wanting in all the ancient VERSIONS, the *Vulgate* excepted; but the more ancient copies of this have it not; and those which have it vary greatly among themselves, as may be seen in the specimens already produced.

9. It is wanting in the *first edition* of Erasmus, A. D. 1516, which is properly the *editio princeps* of the Greek text.

It is wanting also in his *second* edition 1519, but he added it in the *third* from the *Codex Montfortii.*

It is wanting in the editions of *Aldus, Gerbelius, Cephalæus,* &c.

It is wanting in the *German* translation of LUTHER, and in *all the editions* of it published *during his lifetime.*

It is inserted in our early *English* translations, but with marks of *doubtfulness,* as has already been shown.

10. In short, it stands on no authority sufficient to authenticate any part of a revelation professing to have come from God.

See *Griesbach's* Dissertation on this verse at the end of the second volume of his Greek text. Halæ et Londini, 1806.

In defence of this verse see " Archdeacon *Travis'* Letters to *Gibbon;*" and on the other side, " Professor *Porson's* Answer to *Travis.*" The latter has left nothing farther to be said on the subject either in vindication or reply.

Finished the correction for a reimpression, Jan. 3, 1832.—A. C.

2

PREFACE

TO

THE SECOND EPISTLE

OF

JOHN.

THE authority of the *First* Epistle of John being established, little need be said concerning either the *second* or *third*, if we regard the *language* and the *sentiment* only, for these so fully accord with the *first*, that there can be no doubt that he who wrote *one*, wrote all the *three*. But it must not be concealed that there were doubts entertained in the primitive Church as to the two latter being *canonical*. And so late as the days of *Eusebius*, who lived in the fourth century, they were ranked among those writings which were then termed αντιλεγομενα, not received by all, or contradicted, because not believed to be the genuine productions of the Apostle John.

It is very likely that, being letters to *private* persons, they had for a considerable time been kept in the possession of the families to which they were originally sent; and only came to light perhaps long after the death of the apostle, and the death of the *elect lady* or *Kyria;* and *Gaius* or *Caius*, to whom they were addressed. When first discovered, all the immediate vouchers were gone; and the Church of Christ, that was always on its guard against imposture, and especially in relation to writings professing to be the work of apostles, hesitated to receive them into the number of canonical Scriptures, till it was fully satisfied that they were Divinely inspired. This extreme caution was of the utmost consequence to the Christian faith; for had it been otherwise, had any measure of what is called *credulity* prevailed, the Church would have been inundated with spurious writings, and the genuine faith greatly corrupted, if not totally destroyed.

The number of apocryphal *gospels, acts of apostles*, and *epistles*, which were offered to the Church in the earliest ages of Christianity, is truly astonishing. We have the names of at least *seventy-five* gospels which were offered to, and rejected by, the Church; besides *Acts of Peter, Acts of Paul and Thecla, Third Epistle to the Corinthians, Epistle to the Laodiceans, Book of Enoch, &c.*, some of which are come down to the present time, but are convicted of *forgery* by the *sentiment*, the *style*, and the *doctrine.*

The suspicion, however, of forgery, in reference to the Second Epistle of Peter, second and third of John, Jude, and the Apocalypse, was so strong, that in the third century, when the *Peshito Syriac* version was made, these books were omitted, and have not since been received into that version to the present day, which is the version still used in the Syrian Churches. But the *later Syriac* version, which was made A. D. 508, and is called the *Philoxenian*, from *Philoxenus*, bishop of Hierapolis, under whose direction it was formed from the Greek by his rural Bishop *Polycarp*, and was afterwards corrected and published by *Thomas of Charkel*, in 616, contains these, as well as all the other canonical books of the New Testament.

From the time that the language, sentiments, and doctrines of these two epistles were *critically* examined, no doubts were entertained of their authenticity; and at present they are received by the whole Christian Church throughout the world; for although they are not in the ancient Syriac version, they are in the Philoxenian; and concerning their authenticity I believe the Syrian Churches have at present no doubts.

Dr. Lardner observes that the first epistle was received and quoted by Polycarp, bishop of Smyrna, contemporary with the apostle; by Papias, who himself had been a disciple of St. John; by Irenæus; Clement of Alexandria; Origen, and many others. The *second* epistle is quoted by Irenæus, was received by Clement of Alexandria, mentioned by Origen and Dionysius of Alexandria, is quoted by Alexander, bishop of Alexandria. All the three epistles were received by Athanasius; by Cyril, of Jerusalem; by the council of Laodicea; by Epiphanius; by Jerome; by Ruffinus; by the third council of *Carthage;* by Augustine, and by all those authors who received the same canon of the New Testament that we do. All the epistles are in the Codex Alexandrinus, in the catalogues of Gregory of Nazianzen, &c., &c.

Thus we find they were known and quoted at a very early period; and have been received as genuine by the most respectable fathers, Greek and Latin, of the Christian Church. Their being apparently of a *private* nature might have prevented their more general circulation at the beginning, kept them for a considerable time unknown, and prevented them from being reckoned canonical. But such a circumstance as this cannot operate in the present times.

As to the *time* in which this epistle was written, it is very uncertain. It is generally supposed to have been written at Ephesus between A. D. 80 and 90, but of this there is no proof; nor are there any *data* in the epistle itself to lead to any probable conjecture relative to this point. I have placed it at A. D. 85, but would not wish to pledge myself to the correctness of that date.

2

THE SECOND EPISTLE

OF

JOHN.

Chronological Notes relative to this Epistle.

Year of the Constantinopolitan era of the world, or that used by the Byzantine historians, and other eastern writers, 5593.—Year of the Alexandrian era of the world, 5587.—Year of the Antiochian era of the world, 5577.—Year of the world, according to Archbishop Usher, 4089.—Year of the world, according to Eusebius, in his Chronicon, 4311.—Year of the minor Jewish era of the world, or that in common use, 3845.—Year of the Greater Rabbinical era of the world, 4444.—Year from the Flood, according to Archbishop Usher, and the English Bible, 2433.—Year of the Cali yuga, or Indian era of the Deluge, 3187. —Year of the era of Iphitus, or since the first commencement of the Olympic games, 1025.—Year of the era of Nabonassar, king of Babylon, 834.—Year of the CCXVIth Olympiad, 1.—Year from the building of Rome, according to Fabius Pictor, 832.—Year from the building of Rome, according to Frontinus, 836.—Year from the building of Rome, according to the Fasti Capitolini, 837.—Year from the building of Rome, according to Varro, which was that most generally used, 838.—Year of the era of the Seleucidæ, 397.—Year of the Cæsarean era of Antioch, 133.—Year of the Julian era, 130.—Year of the Spanish era, 123.—Year from the birth of Jesus Christ, according to Archbishop Usher, 89.—Year of the vulgar era of Christ's nativity, 85.—Year of Artabanus IV., king of the Parthians, 4.—Year of the Dionysian period, or Easter Cycle, 86.—Year of the Grecian Cycle of nineteen years, or Common Golden Number, 10; or the year before the fourth embolismic.—Year of the Jewish Cycle of nineteen years, 7; or the year before the third embolismic.—Year of the Solar Cycle, 10.—Dominical Letter, it being the first year after the Bissextile, or Leap Year, B.—Day of the Jewish Passover, the twenty-seventh of March, which happened in this year on the Jewish Sabbath.—Easter Sunday, the third of April.—Epact, or age of the moon on the 22d of March, (the day of the earliest Easter Sunday possible,) 9.—Epact, according to the present mode of computation, or the moon's age on New Year's day, or the Calends of January, 17.—Monthly Epacts, or age of the moon on the Calends of each month respectively, (beginning with January,) 17, 19, 18, 19, 20, 21, 22, 24, 24, 25, 27, 27.—Number of Direction, or the number of days from the twenty-first of March to the Jewish Passover, 6.—Year of the Emperor Flavius Domitianus Cæsar, the last of those usually styled the Twelve Cæsars, 5.—Roman Consuls, Domitianus Augustus Cæsar, the eleventh time, and T. Aurelius Fulvus or Fulvius.—The years in which Domitian had been consul before were, A. D. 71, 73, 74, 75, 76, 77, 80, 82, 83, and 84. It should be observed that the date of this epistle is very uncertain. The above is only upon the supposition that it was written about A. D. 85. See the *preface*.

The apostle's address to a Christian matron and her children, 1–3. He rejoices to find that certain of her family had received, and continued to adorn, the truth ; and he exhorts them to continue to love one another according to the commandment of Christ, 4–6. And particularly cautions them against deceivers, and to be watchful that they might not lose the benefit of what they had received, 7, 8. The necessity of abiding in the doctrine of Christ, 9. He cautions them against receiving, or in any way forwarding, those who did not bring the true doctrine of Christ, 10, 11. Excuses himself from writing more largely, and purposes to pay her and family a visit shortly, 12, 13.

A. M. cir. 4089.
A. D. cir. 85.
An. Imp. Flavii
Domitiani
Cæs. Augusti 5.

THE elder unto the elect lady and her children, a whom I love in the truth ; and not I only, but also all they that have known b the truth ;

2 For the truth's sake which dwelleth in us, and shall be with us for ever.

3 c Grace d be with you, mercy, *and* peace, from God the Father, and from the Lord Jesus Christ, the Son of the Father, e in truth and love.

A. M. cir. 4089.
A. D. cir. 85.
An. Imp. Flavii
Domitiani
Cæs. Augusti 5.

4 I rejoiced greatly that I found of thy children f walking in truth, as we have received a commandment from the Father.

5 And now I beseech thee, lady, g not as

---

a 1 John iii. 18 ; 3 John 1 ; ver. 3.——b John viii. 32 ; Gal. ii. 5, 14 ; iii. 1 ; v. 7 ; Col. i. 5 ; 2 Thess. ii. 13 ; 1 Timothy ii. 4 ;

Heb. x, 26.——c 1 Tim. i. 2.——d Greek, *shall be.*——e Verse 1. f 3 John 3.——g 1 John ii. 7, 8 ; iii. 11.

NOTES ON II. JOHN.

Verse 1. *The elder*] John the apostle, who was now a very old man, generally supposed to be about ninety, and therefore he uses the term ὁ πρεσβυτερος, presbyter or elder, not as the name of an *office*, but as designating his advanced age. He is allowed to have been the oldest of all the apostles, and to have been the only one who died a natural death.

This title led some of the ancients to attribute this epistle to a person called *John the Presbyter*, a member of the Church at Ephesus ; and not to John the apostle. But this is a groundless supposition.

The elect lady] Εκλεκτη Κυρια· As Κυρια, *kuria*, may be the feminine of Κυριος, *kurios*, lord, therefore it may signify *lady ;* and so several, both ancients and moderns, have understood it. But others have considered it the *proper name* of a woman, *Kyria ;* and that this is a very ancient opinion is evident from the *Peshita Syriac*, the oldest version we have, which uses it as a proper name ܟܘܪܝܐ *koureea*, as does also the Arabic كوريا *kooreea.*

Some have thought that *Eclecta* was the name of this matron, from the word εκλεκτη, which we translate *elect*, and which here signifies the same as *excellent, eminent, honourable*, or the like. Others think that a particular *Church* is intended, which some suppose to be the *Church at Jerusalem*, and that the *elect sister*, ver. 13, means the *Church at Ephesus ;* but these are conjectures which appear to me to have no good ground. I am satisfied that no *metaphor* is here intended ; that the epistle was sent to some eminent Christian matron, not far from Ephesus, who was probably *deaconess* of the Church, who, it is likely, had a Church at her house, or at whose house the apostles and travelling evangelists frequently preached, and were entertained. This will appear more probable in the course of the notes.

Whom I love in the truth] Whom I love as the Christian religion requires us to love one another.

And not I only] She was well known in the Churches ; many had witnessed or heard of her fidelity, and partook of her hospitality ; so that she had a good report of all Christians in that quarter.

Verse 2. *For the truth's sake*] On account of the Gospel.

Which dwelleth in us] By the grace which it has proclaimed.

And shall be with us] For God will preserve not only the Christian religion but its truth, all its essential doctrines for ever. And they that *abide in the truth* shall go whither that truth leads, *i. e.* to glory. The Armenian has a strange reading here : " For the truth's sake which dwelleth in us, *because it is also with you ; and ye shall be with us for ever.*" But this is supported by no other version, nor by any MS.

Verse 3. *Grace be with you*] This is addressed to *her*, her *household*, and probably that part of the *Church* which was more immediately under her care.

The Son of the Father] The apostle still keeps in view the *miraculous conception* of Christ ; a thing which the *Gnostics* absolutely denied ; a doctrine which is at the ground work of our salvation.

Verse 4. *That I found of thy children walking in truth*] I have already supposed this Christian matron to be *mother of a family*, probably a *widow*, for no mention is made of her husband ; and that she was also a *deaconess* in the Church, and one in whose house the travelling evangelists preached, and where they were entertained. The *children* mentioned here may either be *her own children*, or those *members of the Church* which were under her care, or some of *both*. The apostle was glad to *find*, probably by an epistle sent from herself to him, or from the information of some of the itinerant evangelists, that the work of God was prospering in the place where she lived, and also in her own household. He does not say that *all* were walking in the *truth*, but εκ των τεκνων, *some of her children ;* there was a growing and spreading work, and there were many adversaries who strove to pervert them who had already believed, and perhaps were successful in drawing several away from their simplicity.

Verse 5. *That which we had from the beginning*]

2

A. M. cir. 4089.
A. D. cir. 85.
An. Imp. Flavii
Domitiani
Cæs. Au-
gusti 5.
though I wrote a new commandment unto thee, but that which
we had from the beginning, [h] that
we love one another.

6 And [i] this is love, that we walk after his
commandments. This is the commandment,
That, [k] as ye have heard from the beginning,
ye should walk in it.

7 For [l] many deceivers are entered into the
world, [m] who confess not that Jesus Christ is
come in the flesh. [n] This is a deceiver and
an antichrist.

8 [o] Look to yourselves, [p] that
we lose not those things which
we have [q] wrought, but that we
receive a full reward.

A. M. cir. 4089.
A. D. cir. 85.
An. Imp. Flavii
Domitiani
Cæs. Au-
gusti 5.

9 [r] Whosoever transgresseth, and abideth not
in the doctrine of Christ, hath not God. He
that abideth in the doctrine of Christ, he hath
both the Father and the Son.

10 If there come any unto you, and bring
not this doctrine, receive him not into *your*
house, [s] neither bid him God speed :

11 For he that biddeth him God speed

---

[h] John xiii. 34; xv. 12; Eph. v. 2; 1 Pet. iv. 8; 1 John iii.
23.——[i] John xiv. 15, 21; xv. 10; 1 John ii. 5; v. 3.——[k] 1 John
ii. 24.——[l] 1 John iv. 1.——[m] 1 John iv. 2, 3.——[n] 1 John ii. 22;
iv. 3.——[o] Mark xiii. 9.

[p] Gal. iii. 4; Heb. x. 32, 35.——[q] Or, *gained;* some copies
read, *which ye have gained, but that ye receive,* &c.——[r] 1 John
ii. 23.——[s] Rom. xvi. 17; 1 Cor. v. 11; xvi. 22; Gal. i. 8, 9;
2 Tim. iii. 5; Tit. iii. 10.

The commandment *to love one another* was what they
had heard from the first publication of Christianity,
and what he wishes this excellent woman to inculcate
on all those under her care. The mode of address
here shows that it was a *person*, not a *Church*, to
which the apostle wrote.

Verse 6. *And this is love*] That is, our love is
shown and proved by our walking according to the
commandments of God; for love is the principle of
obedience.

Verse 7. *For many deceivers, &c.*] Of these he
had spoken before, see 1 Epistle, chap. iv. 1, &c.
And these appear to have been *Gnostics*, for they
denied that *Jesus was come in the flesh*. And this
doctrine, so essential to salvation, none could deny
but a *deceiver* and an *antichrist*. Instead of εισηλθον,
are entered in, many excellent MSS. and versions
have εξηλθον, *are gone out*. The sense is nearly the
same.

Verse 8. *Look to yourselves*] Be on your guard
against these seducers; watch, pray, love God and
each other, and walk in newness of life.

*That we lose not those things which we have
wrought*] That we apostles, who have been the means
of your conversion, may not be deprived of you as our
crown of rejoicing in the day of the Lord Jesus.

Instead of the *first person plural*, απολεσωμεν, &c.,
WE *lose*, &c., many MSS., *versions*, and *fathers*,
read the whole clause in the *second person* plural,
απολεσητε, YE *lose*, &c. *Take heed to yourselves that*
YE *lose not the things which* YE *have wrought, but
that* YE *receive a full reward*. This reading is more
consistent and likely, and is supported by at least as
good evidence as the other. We find that if these
persons did not *keep on their guard* they might lose
their salvation, and the apostles their rejoicing in the
day of the Lord Jesus. Even this intimation might
put them on their guard. Had the apostle said *ye
cannot finally fall*, what a different effect would it
have produced! Griesbach has placed these readings
in the margin as being very probable.

Verse 9. *Whosoever transgresseth*] Παραβαινων·
He who *passes over* the sacred enclosure, or *goes
beyond* the prescribed limits; *and abideth not in the*

doctrine—does not remain *within* these *holy limits*,
but indulges himself either in excesses of *action* or
passion; hath not God for his Father, nor the love of
God in his heart.

Hath both the Father and the Son.] He who abideth
in the doctrine of Christ, his body is a temple of the
Holy Trinity, and he has communion with the Father
as his Father, and *with the Son* as his Saviour and
Redeemer.

Verse 10. *If there come any unto you*] Under the
character of an apostle or evangelist, to preach in your
house; *and bring not this doctrine*, that Jesus is
come in the flesh, and has died for the redemption of
the world;

Receive him not into your *house*] Give him no
entertainment as an evangelical teacher. Let him
not preach under your roof.

Neither bid him God speed.] Και χαιρειν αυτω μη
λεγετε· And do not say, *Health to him*—do not salute
him with *Peace be to thee!* The usual salutation
among *friends* and those of the same religion in the
east is, ‏سلام عليكم‎ *Salam aleekum*, " Peace be to
you;" which those of the same religion will use
among themselves, but never to strangers, except in
very rare cases. This is the case to the present day;
and, from what John says here, it was a very ancient
custom. We have often seen that *peace* among the
Hebrews comprehended every spiritual and temporal
blessing. The words mean, according to the eastern
use of them, " Have no religious connection with him,
nor act towards him so as to induce others to believe
you acknowledge him as a brother."

Verse 11. *Is partaker of his evil deeds.*] He that
acts towards him as if he considered him a Christian
brother, and sound in the faith, puts it in his power
to deceive others, by thus apparently accrediting his
ministry. No sound Christian should countenance
any man as a *Gospel minister*, who holds and preaches
erroneous doctrines; especially concerning the *Lord
Jesus*. Nor can any Christian *attend the ministry of
such teachers without being criminal in the sight of
God*. He who attends their ministry is, in effect,
bidding them *God speed*; no matter whether such belong to an *established Church*, or to any congregation

A. M. cir. 4089.
A. D. cir. 85.
An. Imp. Flavii
Domitiani
Cæs. Augusti 5.

is partaker of his evil deeds.

12 ᵗ Having many things to write unto you, I would not *write* with paper and ink; but I trust to come

unto you, and speak ᵘ face to face, ᵛ that ᵂ our joy may be full.

13 ˣ The children of thy elect sister greet thee. Amen.

A. M. cir. 4089.
A. D. cir. 85.
An. Imp. Flavii
Domitiani
Cæs. Augusti 5.

ᵗ 3 John 13.——ᵘ Gr. *mouth to mouth.*

ᵛ John xvii. 13 ; 1 John i. 4.——ᵂ Or, *your.*——ˣ 1 Pet. v. 13.

---

of *dissenters* from it. But what St. John says here does not mean that we should deny such the common offices of humanity, charity, and mercy. No. In these offices we are equally bound to all men ; far less does it intimate that we should *persecute* such on account of their heretical or heterodox sentiments. No. This right has God given to no man, to no Church, to no state. They who persecute others, even for the worst heretical opinions, may expect the heaviest judgments of Almighty God.

There is a remarkable *addition* here in several MSS. of the *Vulgate*, and in some printed editions . *Ecce prædixi vobis, ut in diem Domini nostri Jesu Christi non confundamini.* "Behold, I have foretold this to you, that ye may not be confounded in the day of our Lord Jesus Christ."

This addition is found in the edition of *Pope Sixtus* the Fifth, and in the *Complutensian Polyglot ;* but it is not acknowledged by any of the *versions*, nor by any *Greek* MSS.

Verse 12. *Having many things to write*] That is, I have many things that I might write to thee, but I think it best not to commit them to paper, because I hope to visit thee shortly, and speak fully of those matters, which will be a means of increasing the comfort both of thee and thy family, as well as my own. There is more comfort in mutual *interviews* among friends than in epistolary correspondence.

Verse 13 *The children of thy elect sister*] Probably her *own sister*, who lived at Ephesus ; and, being acquainted with the apostle's writing, desired to be thus remembered to her. *Elect*, both in this and the first verse, signifies *excellent, eminent*, or *honourable.* See on verse 1

Amen is wanting in the most ancient MSS., and in most of the *versions ;* but ἡ χαρις μετα σου and μεθ ὑμων, *Grace be with thee*, or *with you*, is found in several MSS. and *versions.*

938

Subscriptions in the Versions ;—

The end of the Second Epistle.—Syriac.
The Second Epistle of John is ended.—*Philox.* Syriac.
Praise be to God for ever, Amen !—Arabic.

In the Manuscripts :—

The Second of John.—Codex Alexandrinus and Codex Vaticanus.
The Second of John to the Parthians.—One of *Colbert's* MSS.
The Second catholic Epistle of St. John the apostle and divine.
There are other subscriptions, but, like the above, they are worthy of little regard.

This epistle is more remarkable for the spirit of Christian love which it breathes than for any thing else. It contains scarcely any thing that is not found in the preceding ; and out of the thirteen verses there are at least *eight* which are found, either in so many words or in sentiment, precisely the same with those of the first epistle. The most remarkable part of it is the *tenth* and *eleventh* verses, relative to the orders concerning the *heretical teacher ;* and from them we see how such teachers were treated in the apostolic Church. They held no communion with them, afforded them no support, as *teachers ;* but *did not persecute* them.

On this model the conduct of all Christians should be formed, relative to the teachers of false doctrine in general. To go *thus far*, we have apostolical authority, to go *farther*, we have none. And let us still remember, in all cases it is our duty to love even our enemies, and consequently to do them any act of humanity and mercy.

2

THE THIRD EPISTLE

OF

JOHN.

Chronological Notes relative to this Epistle.

Year of the Constantinopolitan era of the world, or that used by the Byzantine historians, and other eastern writers, 5593.—Year of the Alexandrian era of the world, 5587.—Year of the Antiochian era of the world, 5577.—Year of the world, according to Archbishop Usher, 4089.—Year of the world, according to Eusebius, in his Chronicon, 4311.—Year of the minor Jewish era of the world, or that in common use, 3845.—Year of the Greater Rabbinical era of the world, 4444.—Year from the Flood, according to Archbishop Usher, and the English Bible, 2433.—Year of the Cali yuga, or Indian era of the Deluge, 3187. —Year of the era of Iphitus, or since the first commencement of the Olympic games, 1025.—Year of the era of Nabonassar, king of Babylon, 834.—Year of the CCXVIth Olympiad, 1.—Year from the building of Rome, according to Fabius Pictor, 832.—Year from the building of Rome, according t Frontinus, 836.—Year from the building of Rome, according to the Fasti Capitolini, 837.—Year from the building of Rome, according to Varro, which was that most generally used, 838.—Year of the era of the Seleucidæ, 397.—Year of the Cæsarean era of Antioch, 133.—Year of the Julian era, 130.—Year of the Spanish era, 123.—Year from the birth of Jesus Christ, according to Archbishop Usher, 89.—Year of the vulgar era of Christ's nativity, 85.—Year of Artabanus IV., king of the Parthians, 4.—Year of the Dionysian period, or Easter Cycle, 86.—Year of the Grecian Cycle of nineteen years, or Common Golden Number, 10; or the year before the fourth embolismic.—Year of the Jewish Cycle of nineteen years, 7; or the year before the third embolismic.—Year of the Solar Cycle, 10.—Dominical Letter, it being the first year after the Bissextile, or Leap Year, B.—Day of the Jewish Passover, the twenty-seventh of March, which happened in this year on the Jewish Sabbath.—Easter Sunday, the third of April.—Epact, or age of the moon on the 22d of March, (the day of the earliest Easter Sunday possible,) 9.—Epact, according to the present mode of computation, or the moon's age on New Year's day, or the Calends of January, 17.—Monthly Epacts, or age of the moon on the Calends of each month respectively, (beginning with January,) 17, 19, 18, 19, 20, 21, 22, 24, 24, 25, 27, 27.—Number of Direction, or the number of days from the twenty-first of March to the Jewish Passover, 6.—Year of the Emperor Flavius Domitianus Cæsar, the last of those usually styled the Twelve Cæsars, 5.—Roman Consuls, Domitianus Augustus Cæsar, the eleventh time, and T. Aurelius Fulvus or Fulvius.—The years in which Domitian had been consul before were, A. D. 71, 73, 74, 75, 76, 77, 80, 82, 83, and 84. It should be observed that the date of this epistle is very uncertain. The above is only upon the supposition that it was written about A. D. 85.

2

A. M. cir. 4089.
A. D. cir. 85.
An. Imp. Flavii
Domitiani
Cæs. Augusti 5.

THE elder unto the well-beloved Gaius, [a] whom I love [b] in the truth.

2 Beloved, I [c] wish above all things that thou mayest prosper and be in health, even as thy soul prospereth.

A. M. cir. 4089.
A. D. cir. 85.
An. Imp. Flavii
Domitiani
Cæs. Augusti 5.

3 For I rejoiced greatly, when

---

[a] 2 John 1.——[b] Or, *truly*.   [c] Or, *pray*.

This epistle being of nearly the same complexion with the former, and evidently written about the same time, and incontestably by the same person, it is not necessary to give it any particular preface; as the subject of the authenticity of all the three epistles has been treated already so much at large, not only in the introduction to them, but in the notes in general.

This and the preceding epistle are, by Dr. Lardner, supposed to have been written between A. D. 80 and 90. There are no *notes of time* in the epistles themselves to help us to fix any date, therefore all is conjecture concerning the time in which they were written: but to me it appears as likely that they were written *before* the destruction of Jerusalem as *after*; for it is scarcely to be supposed that so signal a display of the justice of God, and such a powerful argument in favour of Christianity and of the truth of Christ's predictions, could be passed unnoticed and unappealed to by any of the inspired persons who wrote after that event. However, where there is no positive evidence, conjecture is useless.

NOTES ON III. JOHN.

Verse 1. *The elder*] See on the first verse of the preceding epistle, and also the *preface*.

The well-beloved Gaius] Γαιος, Gaius, is the Greek mode of writing the Roman name *Caius*; and thus it should be rendered in European languages.

Several persons of the name of *Caius* occur in the New Testament.

1. In the Epistle to the Romans, chap. xvi. 23, St. Paul mentions a *Caius* who lived at Corinth, whom he calls his *host*, and *the host of the whole Church*.

2. In 1 Cor. i. 14, St. Paul mentions a *Caius* who lived at Corinth, whom he had baptized; but this is probably the same with the above.

3. In Acts xix. 29, mention is made of a *Caius* who was a native of Macedonia, who accompanied St. Paul, and spent some time with him at Ephesus. This is probably a different person from the preceding; for the description given of the *Caius* who lived at Corinth, and was the *host of the whole Church* there, does not accord with the description of the *Macedonian Caius*, who, in the very same year, travelled with St. Paul, and was with him at Ephesus.

4. In Acts xx. 4, we meet a *Caius of Derbe*, who was likewise a fellow traveller of St. Paul. This person cannot be the *Corinthian Caius*, for the host of the Church at Corinth would hardly leave that city to travel into Asia; and he is clearly distinguishable

from the *Macedonian Caius* by the epithet Δερβαιος, *of Derbe.*

5. And lastly, there is the *Caius* who is mentioned here, and who is thought by some critics to be different from all the above; for, in writing to him, St. John ranks him among *his children*, which seems, according to them, to intimate that he was converted by this apostle.

Now, whether this Caius was one of the persons just mentioned, or whether he was different from them all, is difficult to determine; because *Caius* was a very common name. Yet if we may judge from the similarity of character, it is not improbable that he was the Caius who lived at Corinth, and who is styled by St. Paul *the host of the whole Church;* for hospitality to his Christian brethren was the leading feature in the character of this Caius to whom St. John wrote, and it is on this very account that he is commended by the apostle. Besides, St. John's friend lived in a place where this apostle had in Diotrephes a very ambitious and tyrannical adversary; and that there were men of this description at Corinth is evident enough from the two epistles to the Corinthians, though St. Paul has not mentioned *their* names. See *Michaelis.*

The probability of this Caius being the same with the Corinthian Caius has suggested the thought that this epistle was sent to *Corinth;* and consequently that the second epistle was sent to some place in the neighbourhood of that city. But I think the distance between Ephesus, where St. John resided, and Corinth, was too considerable for such an aged man as St. John is represented to be to travel, whether by *land* or *water*. If he went by *land*, he must traverse a great part of Asia, go through Thrace, Macedonia, Thessaly, and down through Greece, to the Morea, a most tedious and difficult journey. If he went by *water*, he must cross the Ægean Sea, and navigate among the Cyclades Islands, which was always a dangerous voyage. Now as the apostle promises, both in the second and in this epistle, to see the persons shortly to whom he wrote, I take it for granted that they could not have lived at Corinth, or anywhere in the vicinity of that city. That St. John took such a voyage *Michaelis* thinks probable; "for since Corinth lay almost opposite to Ephesus, and St. John, from his former occupation, before he became an apostle, was accustomed to the sea, it is not improbable that the journey or voyage which he proposed to make was from Ephesus to Corinth."

2

A. M. cir. 4089.
A. D. cir. 85.
An. Imp. Flavii
Domitiani
Cæs. Augusti 5.
the brethren came and testified of the truth that is in thee, even as [d] thou walkest in the truth.

4 I have no greater joy than to hear that [e] my children walk in truth.

5 Beloved, thou doest faithfully whatsoever thou doest to the brethren, and to strangers ;

---

[d] 2 John 4.——[e] 1 Cor. iv. 15 ; Philem. 10.

In answer to this I would just observe, 1. That the voyage was too long and dangerous for a man at John's advanced age to think of taking. 2. That John had never been accustomed to any such *sea* as the *Ægean*, for the *sea of Galilee*, or *sea of Tiberias*, on which, as a fisherman, he got his bread, was only an inconsiderable fresh water lake ; and his acquaintance with it could give him very few advantages for the navigation of the *Ægean Sea*, and the danger of coasting the numerous islands dispersed through it.

Verse 2. I wish above all things] Περι παντων ευχομαι· Above all things I pray that thou mayest prosper, and be in health, και υγιαινειν· to which one MS. adds εν αληθεια, which gives it a different meaning, viz., *that thou mayest be sound in the truth.* The prayer of St. John for Caius includes *three* particulars: 1. Health of body ; 2. Health of soul; and 3. Prosperity in secular affairs. *That thou mayest* PROSPER *and be in* HEALTH, *as thy* SOUL PROSPERETH. These *three* things, so necessary to the comfort of life, every Christian may in a certain measure expect, and for them every Christian is authorized to pray ; and we should have more of all three if we devoutly prayed for them.

It appears from the last *clause* that the soul of Caius was in a very prosperous state.

Verse 3. When the brethren came] Probably the same of whom he speaks in the fifth and following verses, and who appear to have been itinerant evangelists.

The truth that is in thee] The soundness of thy faith and the depth of thy religion.

Verse 4. To hear that my children] From this it has been inferred that Caius was one of St. John's converts, and consequently not the Corinthian Caius, who was converted, most probably, by St. Paul. But the apostle might use the term *children* here as implying those who were immediately under his pastoral care, and, being an *old man*, he had a right to use such terms in addressing his juniors both in age and grace ; and there is much both of propriety and dignity in the appellation coming from such a person.

Verse 5. Thou doest faithfully] Πιστον ποιεις. *Kypke* thinks that πιστον is put here for πιστιν, and that the phrase signifies *to keep* or *preserve the faith*, or *to be bound by the faith*, or *to keep one's engagements. Thou hast acted as the faith*—the Christian religion, *required thee to act, in all that thou hast done, both to the brethren* at home, *and to the strangers*—the itinerant evangelists, who, in the course of their travels, have called at thy house. There is not a word here about the *pilgrims* and *penitential journeys* which the papists contrive to bring out of this text.

2

6 Which have borne witness of thy charity before the Church ; whom if thou bring forward on their journey [f] after a godly sort, thou shalt do well ;

7 Because that for his name's sake they went forth, [g] taking nothing of the Gentiles.

A. M. cir. 4089.
A. D. cir. 85.
An. Imp. Flavii
Domitiani
Cæs. Augusti 5.

---

[f] Gr. *worthy of God.*——[g] 1 Cor. ix. 12, 15.

Verse 6. Which have borne witness of thy charity] Of thy love and benevolence.

Before the Church] The believers at Ephesus; for to this Church the apostle seems to refer.

Whom if thou bring forward] If thou continue to assist such, as thou hast done, *thou shalt do well.*

The *brethren* of whom St. John speaks might have been *apostles* ; the *strangers*, assistants to these apostles, as John Mark was to Barnabas. Both were *itinerant evangelists.*

After a godly sort] Αξιως του Θεου· *Worthy of God*; and in such a way as he can approve. Let all Churches, all congregations of Christians, from whom their ministers and preachers can claim nothing by *law*, and for whom the state makes no provision, lay this to heart ; let them ask themselves, Do we deal with these in a manner *worthy of God*, and worthy of the profession we make ? Do we suffer them to lack the bread that perisheth, while they minister to us with no sparing hand the bread of life ? Let a certain class of religious people, who will find themselves out when they read this note, consider whether, when their preachers have ministered to them their certain or stated time, and are called to go and serve other Churches, *they send them forth* in a manner *worthy of God*, making a reasonable provision for the journey which they are obliged to take. In the itinerant ministry of the apostles it appears that each Church bore the expenses of the apostle to the next Church or district to which he was going to preach the word of life. So it should be still in the mission and itinerant ministry.

Verse 7. For his name's sake they went forth] For the sake of preaching the Gospel of the grace of God, and making known JESUS to the heathen.

Taking nothing of the Gentiles.] Receiving no emolument for their labour, but in every respect showing themselves to be truly disinterested. Sometimes, and on some special occasions, this may be necessary ; but *the labourer is worthy of his hire* is the maxim of the author of Christianity. And those congregations of Christians are ever found to prize the Gospel most, and profit most by it, who *bear all expenses incident to it*, and *vice versa.*

But some construe εξηλθον, *they went out*, with απο των εθνων, *from the Gentiles*, or rather *by the Gentiles*, and give the passage this sense : *They went out*, i. e., were *driven out by the Gentiles, taking nothing with them*, i. e., leaving all their property behind, so that they were in a state of great destitution. A curious reading here, εθνικων, *heathenish men*, for εθνων, *Gentiles*, which latter might imply those who were converted from among the Gentiles, while the sense of the other term seems to be restrained to those who

A. M. cir. 4089.
A. D. cir. 85.
An. Imp. Flavii
Domitiani
Cæs. Augusti 5.

8 We therefore ought to receive such, that we might be fellow helpers to the truth.

9 I wrote unto the Church: but Diotrephes, who loveth to have the pre-eminence among them, receiveth us not.

10 Wherefore, if I come, I will remember his deeds which he doeth, [h] prating against us with malicious words: and not content therewith, neither doth he himself receive the brethren, and forbiddeth them that would, and casteth *them* out of the Church.

11 Beloved, [i] follow not that which is evil, but that which is good. [k] He that doeth good is of God: but he that doeth evil hath not seen God.

12 Demetrius [l] hath good report of all *men,* and of the truth itself: yea, and we *also* bear record; [m] and ye know that our record is true.

13 [n] I had many things to write, but I will not with ink and pen write unto thee:

14 But I trust I shall shortly see thee, and we shall speak [o] face to face. Peace *be* to thee. Our friends salute thee. Greet the friends by name.

A. M. cir. 4089.
A. D. cir. 85.
An. Imp. Flavii
Domitiani
Cæs. Augusti 5.

[h] Prov. x. 8, 10.——[i] Psa. xxxvii. 27; Isa. i. 16, 17; 1 Pet. iii. 11.——[k] 1 John ii. 29; iii. 6, 9.   [l] 1 Tim. iii. 7.——[m] John xxi. 24.——[n] 2 John 12.——[o] Greek, *mouth to mouth.*

were still *unconverted,* may seem to strengthen the above interpretation; and although the construction seems rather harsh, yet it is not, on the whole, unlikely. The reading above referred to is that of the most ancient and reputable MSS. That *to be driven out* or *expelled* is one scriptural meaning of the verb εξερχομαι, see Matt. viii. 32: *And when they were come out,* οι δε εξελθοντες, *and when they were* DRIVEN OUT. Ib. xii. 43: *When the unclean spirit is gone out,* εξελθη, *is* DRIVEN OUT. See Mark v. 13, and vii. 29: *The devil is gone out of thy daughter,* εξεληλυθε, *is* EXPELLED. Ib. ix. 29: *This kind can come forth by nothing* εν ουδενι δυναται εξελθειν, *can be* DRIVEN OUT *by nothing, but by prayer and fasting.* Luke viii. 2: *Mary Magdalene, out of whom went,* αφ' ης δαιμονια επτα εξεληλυθει, *out of whom were* CAST *seven demons.* See also 1 John ii. 19; Rev. iii. 12; and *Schleusner,* in voc. εξερχομαι.

Verse 8. We therefore ought to receive such] Those who are persecuted for righteousness' sake, and have professed the truth at the hazard of their lives, and the loss of all their worldly substance. Instead of απολαμβανειν, *to receive,* the most ancient and reputable MSS. have υπολαμβανειν, *to take up, undertake for,* or *kindly receive.*

Fellow helpers to the truth] And thus encourage the persecuted, and contribute to the spread and maintenance of the Gospel.

Verse 9. I wrote unto the Church.] The Church where Caius was; *but Diotrephes, who loveth to have the pre-eminence,* φιλοπρωτευων, *who loves the presidency,* or *chief place* in the Church. He was doubtless an officer in the Church, at least a deacon, probably a bishop; and, being one, he magnified himself in his office; he loved such eminence, and behaved himself haughtily in it.

Receiveth us not.] Does not acknowledge the apostolical authority. As some MSS. supply αν after εγραψα, and several judicious critics believe it is implied, the translation will run thus: *I would have written to the Church to receive these men kindly, but Diotrephes, who affects the presidency, and into whose hands, if I wrote to the Church, my letter must come, receiveth us not*—would not acknowledge my authority to interfere with any of the matters of his Church;

and therefore I have written unto thee, whose love to the brethren and general hospitality are well known, that thou wouldst receive those strangers and persecuted followers of our common Lord.

Verse 10. If I come, I will remember] I will show him the authority which, as an apostle of Jesus Christ, I possess.

Prating against us] Diotrephes might have been a *converted Jew,* who was unwilling that the Gentiles should be received into the Church; or a *Judaizing Christian,* who wished to incorporate the *law* with the Gospel, and calumniated the apostles who taught otherwise. This haughty and unfeeling man would give no countenance to the converted Gentiles; so far from it, that he would not receive any of them himself, forbade others to do it, and excommunicated those who had been received into the Church by the apostles. This appears to be the meaning of *neither doth he himself receive the brethren, and forbiddeth them that would, and casteth them out of the Church.* He had the complete *dog in the manger* principle; he would neither do, nor let do; and when good was done that he did not approve, he endeavoured to undo it.

Verse 11. Follow not that which is evil] Μη μιμου το κακον. Do not imitate that wicked man, i. e., the conduct of Diotrephes; be merciful, loving, and kind. For whatever profession any man may make, it will ever appear that *he who doeth good is of God*—he alone is the person who uses rightly the grace received from God, and he alone shall enjoy the Divine approbation;

While *he that doeth evil*] He who is unfeeling, unmerciful, unkind, *hath not seen God*—has no proper knowledge of that God whose NAME is *mercy,* and whose NATURE is *love.*

Verse 12. Demetrius hath good report] Perhaps another member of the Church where Caius was; or he might have been one of those whom the apostle recommends to Caius; or, possibly, the *bearer of this letter* from John to Caius. He seems to have been an excellent person: all *testified* of his righteousness; the *truth*—Christianity, *itself bore testimony* to him; and the *apostles* themselves added theirs also.

Verse 13. I had many things to write] That is, I have many things that I might write; but having the

    2

hope of seeing thee shortly, I will not commit them to paper. *Ink* and *pen* are here mentioned; *paper* and *ink* in the preceding epistle.

Verse 14. *Peace be to thee.*] Mayest thou possess every requisite good, both of a spiritual and temporal kind.

Our *friends salute thee.*] Desire to be affectionately remembered to thee. *Greet the friends by name*—remember me to all those with whom I am acquainted, as if I had specified them by *name*. This is a proof to me that this epistle was not sent to Corinth, where it is not likely John ever was; and where it is not likely he had any particular acquaintances, unless we could suppose he had seen some of them when he was an exile in Patmos, an island in the Ægean Sea.

For other particulars concerning John, the reader is requested to refer to the preface to his gospel.

Instead of φιλοι and φιλους, *friends*, the Codex Alexandrinus and several others read αδελφοι and αδελφους, *brethren*. The former (*friends*) is a very singular appellation, and nowhere else found in Scripture; the latter is of frequent occurrence.

Subscriptions in the VERSIONS :—

In the ancient SYRIAC.—Nothing.
The Third Epistle of John the apostle is ended.—SYRIAC *Philoxenian*.
ÆTHIOPIC.—Nothing.

VULGATE.—Nothing.
The end of the epistles of the pure Apostle and Evangelist John.—ARABIC.
The Third Epistle of St. John the apostle is ended.—*Latin text* of the COMPLUTENSIAN.
The end of the Third catholic Epistle of St John.—DITTO, *Greek text*.

Subscriptions in the MANUSCRIPTS :—

The third of John.—CODD. ALEX. and VATICAN.
The Third catholic Epistle of John the evangelist and divine.
The third of John to Caius concerning Demetrius, of whom he witnesses the most excellent things.

I have already shown in the *preface* to those epistles termed *catholic*, that the word καθολικος is not to be taken here, and elsewhere in these epistles, as signifying *universal*, but *canonical*; for it would be absurd to call an epistle *universal* that was written to a private individual.

We seldom hear this epistle quoted but in the reproof of lordly tyrants, or prating troublesome fellows in the Church. And yet the epistle contains many excellent sentiments, which, if judiciously handled, might be very useful to the Church of God. But it has been the lot both of the *minor prophets* and the *minor epistles* to be generally neglected; for with many readers *bulk* is every thing; and, no *magnitude* no goodness.

This and the preceding epistle both read over in reference to a new edition, Jan. 3d, 1832.—A. C

IN the preface to the Epistle of James several things have been said relative to Jude the brother of James, the supposed author of this epistle ; and to that preface the reader is requested to refer. What is farther necessary to be said on the author and the authenticity of this epistle, I shall take the liberty to borrow principally from *Michaelis*.

"If James and Jude, whom the evangelists call brothers of Jesus, were in fact only cousins or relations, as some suppose, and were sons, not of Joseph, but of Alpheus, these two persons were the same as the two brothers James and Jude, who were apostles. And in this case Jude, the author of this epistle, was the same as the Apostle Jude, the brother of James who was son of Alpheus. On the other hand, if the James and the Jude, whom the evangelists call brothers of Jesus, were not the two brothers of this name who were apostles, but were the sons of Joseph, the reputed father of Jesus, we have then two different persons of the name of Jude, either of which might have written this epistle. And in this case we have to examine whether the epistle was written by an apostle of the name of Jude, or by Jude the brother-in-law of Christ.

" The author of the epistle himself has assumed neither the title of apostle of Jesus Christ, nor of brother of Jesus Christ, but calls himself only ' Jude, the servant of Jesus Christ, and brother of James.' Now, as the author distinguishes himself by the title 'brother of James,' and this was a common name among the Jews, he undoubtedly meant some eminent person of this name, who was well known at the time when he wrote, or the title ' brother of James' would have been no mark of distinction. We may infer, therefore, that the author of this epistle was the brother, either of the Apostle James the son of Alpheus, or of James, called the brother of Jesus, or of both, if they were one and the same person.

" The first question, therefore, to be asked is, Was the author of this epistle the Apostle Jude ? or was he brother of James, the son of Alpheus ? Now, I have already observed, that this question *must* be answered in the affirmative if James and Jude who were called brothers of Jesus, were the same as the two brothers James and Jude who were apostles. And it *may* be answered in the affirmative, even if they were different persons, for Jude, the author of this epistle, had in either case a brother of the name of James, and therefore might in either case call himself Jude the brother of James. I say the question *may* be answered in the affirmative, even if the Apostle Jude was a different person from Jude, called the brother of James. But whether it ought in this case to be answered in the affirmative, is another matter ; and I really believe that it ought not : for if the Jude who wrote this epistle had been himself an apostle, and brother of an apostle, he would hardly have called himself, in an epistle written to Christians, simply ' Jude, the brother of James,' without adding the title apostle. It is true that the Apostle Jude, who was brother of James, is called by St. Luke Ιουδας Ιακωβου ; but St. Luke gives him this title merely to distinguish him from another apostle of this name, who was called Iscariot. Now the author of this epistle could have no motive for distinguishing himself from Judas Iscariot, who had hanged himself many years before this epistle was written. The name of Jude was very common among the Jews ; and therefore the author of this epistle wished to distinguish himself from other persons who were so called. But James was likewise a very common name, and therefore if the author had been an apostle he surely would have preferred an appellation which would have removed all doubts to an appellation which left it at least uncertain whether he was an apostle or not ; I grant that the omission of this title does not necessarily prove that the author of this epistle was not an apostle, for Paul has omitted it in four of his epistles : in the Epistle to the Philippians, in both Epistles to the Thessalonians, and in that to Philemon. But St. Paul was sufficiently known without this title, whereas the author of the

2

epistle in question felt the necessity of a distinguishing appellation, as appears from the very title which he has given himself of ' brother of James.' Besides, at the time when this epistle was written, only one apostle of the name of James was then alive; for the elder James, the son of Zebedee, had been beheaded many years before. If then the author of this epistle had only given to his brother James the title of apostle, he would thus likewise have clearly ascertained who he himself was. But since he has no more given to his brother than to himself the title of apostle, I think it highly probable that neither of them were apostles.

" The next question to be asked, therefore, is, Was the Jude, who wrote this epistle, the same person as the Jude whom the evangelists call brother of Jesus? and who, according to the opinion which I think the most defensible, was in this sense brother of Jesus, that he was son of Joseph by a former wife, and therefore not his own brother, but only brother-in-law of Jesus. Now, that this epistle was written by a person of this description, appears to me highly probable; and on this supposition we may assign the reason why the author called himself ' brother of James;' for, if he was the brother-in-law of Jesus, his brother James was the person who, during so many years, had presided over the Church at Jerusalem, was well known both to Jews and Christians, and appears to have been more celebrated than either of the apostles called James. It will be objected, perhaps, that the very same reasons which I have alleged, to show that an apostle of the name of Jude would have assumed his proper title, will likewise show that a person who was called brother of Jesus would have done the same, and styled himself brother of Jesus. To this I answer, that if he was the son of Joseph, not by Mary but by a former wife, and Jude believed in the immaculate conception, he must have been sensible that though to all outward appearance he was brother-in-law to Jesus, since his own father was the husband of Jesus' mother, yet in reality he was no relation of Jesus. On the other hand, if Jude, called the brother of Jesus, was the son of Joseph, not by a former wife but by Mary, as Herder asserts, I do not see how the preceding objection can be answered; for if Jesus and Jude had the same mother, Jude might, without the least impropriety, have styled himself ' brother of Jesus,' or ' brother of the Lord;' and this would have been a much more remarkable and distinguishing title than that of brother of James. A third question still remains to be asked on this subject. The apostle whom St. Luke calls Jude is called Thaddæus by St. Matthew and St. Mark, as I have already observed. But the apostle of the Syrians, who first preached the Gospel at Edessa, and founded a Church there, was named Thaddæus or Adæus. It may be asked, therefore, whether the author of this epistle was Thaddæus, the apostle of the Syrians? But the answer is decisive: the old Syriac version does not contain this epistle; consequently it is highly probable that Adai or Adæus was not the author, for an epistle written by the great apostle of the Syrians would surely have been received into the canon of the Syrian Church."

The most accurate critics have been unable to determine the time *when*, and the persons to whom, this epistle was written; so that much concerning these points, as well as the author of the epistle, must remain undecided.

" I am really unable to determine," says Michaelis, " who the persons were to whom this epistle was sent; for no traces are to be discovered in it which enable us to form the least judgment on this subject; and the address with which this epistle commences is so indeterminate, that there is hardly any Christian community where Greek was spoken, which might not be denoted by it. Though this epistle has a very great similarity to the Second Epistle of Peter, it cannot have been sent to the same persons, namely, the Christians who resided in Pontus, &c., because no mention is made of them in this epistle. Nor can it have been sent to the Christians of Syria and Assyria, where Jude preached the Gospel, if he be the same person as the apostle of the Syrians; for in this case the epistle would not have been written in Greek, but in Syriac or Chaldee, and would certainly have been received into the old Syriac version.

" With respect to the date of this epistle, all that I am able to assert is, that it was written after the Second Epistle of Peter; but how many years after, whether between 64 and 66, as Lardner supposes, or between 70 and 75, as Beausobre and L'Enfant believe; or, according to Dodwell and Cave, in 71 or 72, or so late as the year 90, as is the opinion of Mill, I confess I am unable to determine, at least from any certain data. The expression, ' in the last time,' which occurs ver. 18, as well as in 2 Pet. iii. 3, is too indeterminate to warrant any conclusion respecting the date of this epistle; for though, on the one hand, it may refer to the approaching destruction of Jerusalem, it may, on the other hand, refer to a later period, and denote the close of the apostolic age; for in the First Epistle of St. John a similar expression occurs, which must be taken in this latter sense. The inference, therefore, that the Epistle of St. Jude was written before the destruction of Jerusalem, which some commentators have deduced from the above-mentioned expression, on the supposition that it alluded to that event then approaching, is very precarious, because it is drawn from premises which are themselves uncertain. However, there is some reason to believe, on other grounds, that this epistle was not written after the destruction of Jerusalem; for, as the author has mentioned, ver. 5–8, several well known instances of God's justice in punishing sinners, which Peter had already quoted in his second epistle to the same purpose, he would probably, if Jerusalem had been already destroyed at the time he wrote, have not neglected to add to his other examples this most remarkable instance of Divine vengeance, especially as Christ himself had foretold it.

" Lardner, indeed, though he admits the similarity of the two epistles, still thinks it a matter of doubt whether St. Jude had ever seen the Second Epistle of St. Peter; his reason is, that ' if St. Jude had formed a design of writing, and had met with an epistle of one of the apostles very suitable to his own thoughts and intentions, he would have forborne to write.'

" To this argument I answer :—

" 1. If the Epistle of St. Jude was inspired by the Holy Ghost, as Lardner admits, the Holy Ghost certainly knew, while he was dictating the epistle to St. Jude, that an epistle of St. Peter, of a like import, already existed. And if the Holy Ghost, notwithstanding this knowledge, still thought that an epistle of St. Jude was not unnecessary ; why shall we suppose that St. Jude himself would have been prevented writing by the same knowledge ?

" 2. The Second Epistle of St. Peter was addressed to the inhabitants of some particular countries ; but the address of St. Jude's.is general : St. Jude therefore might think it necessary to repeat for general use what St. Peter had written only to certain communities.

" 3. The Epistle of St. Jude is not a bare copy of the Second Epistle of St. Peter, for in the former, not only several thoughts are more completely unravelled than in the latter, but several additions are made to what St. Peter had said ; for instance ver. 4, 5, 9, 16.

" Eusebius, in his catalogue of the books of the New Testament, places the Epistle of St. Jude among the αντιλεγομενα, contradicted or apocryphal books, in company with the Epistle of St. James, the Second Epistle of St. Peter, and the Second and Third of John.

" But Origen, who lived in the third century, though he speaks in dubious terms of the Second Epistle of St. Peter, has several times quoted the Epistle of St. Jude, and has spoken of it as an epistle on which he entertained no doubt. In his commentary on St. Matthew, when he comes to chap. xiii. 55, where James, Joses, Simon, and Jude are mentioned ; he says Jude wrote an epistle of few lines indeed, but full of the powerful words of the heavenly grace, who at the beginning says, ' Jude, the servant of Jesus Christ, and brother of James.' This is a very clear and unequivocal declaration of Origen's opinion ; and it is the more remarkable because he says nothing of the Epistle of St. James, though the passage, Matt. xiii. 55, afforded him as good an opportunity of speaking of this epistle, as it did of the Epistle of St. Jude. Nay, Origen carries his veneration for the Epistle of Jude so far that, in his treatise *De Principiis, lib.* iii. *cap.* 2, he quotes an apocryphal book, called the Assumption of Moses, as a work of authority ; because a passage from this book had been quoted by St. Jude. In one instance, however, in his commentary on St. Matthew, Origen speaks in less positive terms, for there he says, ' If any one receive the Epistle of St. Jude,' &c. Tertullian, in whose works Lardner could discover no quotation from the Second Epistle of St. Peter, describes the Epistle of St. Jude as the work of an apostle ; for in his treatise *De cultu fœminarum,* chap. 3, he says, ' Hence it is that Enoch is quoted by the Apostle Jude.'

" Clement of Alexandria, in whose works likewise Lardner could find no quotation from the Second Epistle of St. Peter, has three times.quoted the Epistle of St. Jude without expressing any doubt whatever. It appears, then, that the three ancient fathers, Clement of Alexandria, Tertullian, and Origen, as far as we may judge from their writings which are now extant, preferred the Epistle of St. Jude to the Second Epistle of St. Peter. However, I think it not impossible that if all the writings of these authors were now extant, passages might be found in them which would turn the scale in favour of the latter ; and it may be owing to mere accident that in those parts of their works which have descended to us, more passages in which they speak decidedly of St. Jude are to be found, than such as are favourable to the Second Epistle of St. Peter. For I really cannot comprehend how any impartial man who has to choose between these two epistles, which are very similar to each other, can prefer the former to the latter, or receive the Epistle of St. Jude, the contents of which labour under great difficulties, and at the same time reject, or even consider as dubious, the Second Epistle of St. Peter, the contents of which labour under no such difficulties.

" But it is much more difficult to explain the ninth verse, in which the Archangel Michael is said to have disputed with the devil about the body of Moses. The history of this dispute, which has the appearance of a Jewish fable, it is not at present very easy to discover ; because the book from which it is supposed to have been taken by the author of this epistle is no longer extant ; but I will here put together such scattered accounts of it as I have been able to collect.

" Origen found in a Jewish Greek book called the Assumption of Moses, which was extant in his time, this very story related concerning the dispute of the Archangel Michael with the devil about the body of Moses. And from a comparison of the relation in his book with St. Jude's quotation, he was thoroughly persuaded that it was the book from which St. Jude quoted. This he asserts without the least hesitation ; and in consequence of this persuasion he himself has quoted the *Assumption of Moses* as a work of authority, in proof of the temptation of Adam and Eve by the devil. But as he quoted it merely for this purpose, he has given us only an imperfect account of what this book contained, relative to the dispute about the body of Moses. One circumstance, however, he has mentioned, which is not found in the Epistle of St. Jude, viz., that Michael reproached the devil with having possessed the serpent that seduced Eve. In what manner this circumstance is connected with the dispute about the body of Moses, will appear from the following consideration :—

" The Jews imagined the person of Moses was so holy that God could find no reason for permitting him to die ; and that nothing but the sin committed by Adam and Eve in paradise, which brought death into the world, was the cause why Moses did not live for ever. The same notions they entertained of some other very holy persons ; for instance, of Isaiah, who they say was delivered to the angel of death merely on account of the sins of our first parents, though he himself did not deserve to die. Now, in the dispute between Michael and the devil about Moses, the devil was the accuser, and demanded the death of Moses. Michael therefore

(60**)

replied to him that he himself was the cause of that sin, which alone could occasion the death of Moses. How very little such notions as these agree, either with the Christian theology, or with Moses' own writings, it is unnecessary for me to declare. Besides the account given by Origen, there is a passage in the works of Œcumenius, which likewise contains a part of the story related in the Assumption of Moses, and which explains the reason of the dispute which St. Jude has mentioned concerning Moses' body. According to this passage, Michael was employed in burying Moses; but the devil endeavoured to prevent it by saying that he had murdered an Egyptian, and was therefore unworthy an honourable burial. Hence it appears that some modern writers are mistaken, who have imagined that in the ancient narrative the dispute was said to have arisen from an attempt of the devil to reveal to the Jews the burial place of Moses, and to incite them to an idolatrous worship of his body.

" There is still extant a Jewish book, written in Hebrew, and intituled פטירת משה, that is, 'The Death of Moses,' which some critics, especially De La Rue, supposed to be the same work as that which Origen saw in Greek. Now if it were this Hebrew book, intituled ' Phetirath Mosheh,' it would throw a great light on our present inquiry ; but I have carefully examined it, and can assert that it is a modern work, and that its contents are not the same as those of the Greek book quoted by Origen. Of the Phetirath Mosheh we have two editions, which contain very different texts; the one was printed at Constantinople in 1518, and reprinted at Venice in 1544 and 1605, the other was published from a manuscript by Gilbert Gaulmyn, who added a translation of both texts, with notes."

To show that neither St. Jude, nor any inspired writer, nor indeed any person in his sober senses, could quote or in any way accredit such stuff and nonsense, I shall give the substance of this most ridiculous legend as extracted by Michaelis ; for as to the Phetirath Mosheh, I have never seen it.

" Moses requests of God, under various pretences, either that he may not die at all, or at least that he may not die before he comes into Palestine. This request he makes in so froward and petulant a manner as is highly unbecoming, not only a great prophet, but even any man who has expectations of a better life after this. In short, Moses is here represented in the light of a despicable Jew begging for a continuance of life, and devoid both of Christian faith and heathen courage ; and it is therefore not improbable that the inventor of this fable made himself the model after which he formed the character of Moses. God argues on the contrary with great patience and forbearance, and replies to what Moses had alleged relative to the merit of his own good works. Farther, it is God who says to Moses that he must die on account of the sin of Adam ; to which Moses answers, that he ought to be excepted, because he was superior in merit to Adam, Abraham, Isaac, &c. In the meantime Samael, that is, the angel of death, whom the Jews describe as the chief of the devils, rejoices at the approaching death of Moses : this is observed by Michael, who says to him, ' Thou wicked wretch, I grieve, and thou laughest.' Moses, after his request had been repeatedly refused, invokes heaven and earth, and all creatures around him to intercede in his behalf. Joshua attempts to pray for him, but the devil stops Joshua's mouth, and represents to him, really in scriptural style, the impropriety of such a prayer. The elders of the people, and with them all the children of Israel, then offered to intercede for Moses ; but their mouths are likewise stopped by a million eight hundred and forty thousand devils, which, on a moderate calculation, make three devils to one man. After this, God commands the angel Gabriel to fetch the soul of Moses ; but Gabriel excuses himself, saying, that Moses was too strong for him : Michael receives the same order, and excuses himself in the same manner, or, as other accounts say, under pretence that he had been the instructer of Moses, and therefore could not bear to see him die. But this latter excuse, according to the Phetirath Mosheh, was made by Zinghiel, the third angel who received this command. Samael, that is, the devil, then offers his services ; but God asks him how he would take hold of Moses, whether by his mouth, or by his hands, or by his feet, saying, that every part of Moses was too holy for him to touch. The devil, however, insists on bringing the soul of Moses ; yet he does not accuse him, for, on the contrary, he prizes him higher than Abraham, Isaac, or Jacob. The devil then approaches towards Moses, to execute this voluntary commission ; but as soon as he sees the shining countenance of Moses, he is seized with a violent pain, like that of a woman in labour : Moses, instead of using the oriental salutation, ' Peace be with thee,' says to him, in the words of Isaiah, (for in this work Moses frequently quotes Isaiah and the Psalms,) ' There is no peace to the wicked.' The devil replies that he was come, by the order of God, to fetch his soul ; but Moses deters him from the attempt by representing his own strength and holiness ; and saying, ' Go, thou wicked wretch, I will not give thee my soul,' he affrights the devil in such a manner that he immediately retires. The devil then returns to God, and relates what had passed, and receives an order to go a second time ; the devil answers that he would go everywhere God commanded him, even into hell, and into fire, but not to Moses. This remonstrance is, however, of no avail, and he is obliged to go back again ; but Moses, who sees him coming with a drawn sword, meets him with his miraculous rod, and gives him such a blow with it that the devil is glad to escape. Lastly, God himself comes ; and Moses, having then no farther hopes, requests only that his soul may not be taken out of his body by the devil. This request is granted him ; Zinghiel, Gabriel, and Michael then lay him on a bed, and the soul of Moses begins to dispute with God, and objects to its being taken out of a body which was so pure and holy that no fly dared to settle on it ; but God kisses Moses, and with that kiss extracts his soul from his body. Upon this God utters a heavy lamentation ; and thus the story in the Phetirath ends, without any mention of a dispute about the burial of Moses' body. This last scene, therefore, which was contained in the Greek book seen by Origen, is wanting in the Hebrew. But in both of these works Michael, as well as the devil, expresses the same sentiments in respect to Moses ; in both works the same spirit prevails; and the concluding scene, which was contained in the Greek book, is nothing more than a continuation of the same story which is contained in the Hebrew."

Had Jude quoted a work like the above, it would have argued no inspiration, and little common sense; and the man who could have quoted it must have done it with approbation, and in that case his own composition would have been of a similar stamp. But nothing can be more dissimilar than the Epistle of Jude and the Phetirath Mosheh: the former contains nothing but manly sense, expressed in pure, energetic, and often sublime language, and accompanied, most evidently, with the deepest reverence for God; while the latter is despicable in every point of view, even considered as the work of a *filthy dreamer*, or as the most *superannuated* of *old wives' fables*.

" Lastly," says Michaelis, " besides the quotation which St. Jude has made in the 9th verse relative to the dispute between Michael and the devil, he has another quotation, ver. 14, 15, likewise from an apocryphal book called the ' Prophecies of Enoch;' or, if not from any written book, from oral tradition. Now, should it be granted that Enoch was a prophet, though it is not certain that he was, yet as none of his prophecies are recorded in the Old Testament no one could possibly know what they were. It is manifest, therefore, that the book called the ' Prophecies of Enoch' was a mere Jewish forgery, and that too a very unfortunate one, since in all human probability the use of letters was unknown in the time of Enoch, and consequently he could not have left behind him any written prophecies. It is true that an inspired writer might have known, through the medium of Divine information, what Enoch had prophesied, without having recourse to any written work on this subject. But St. Jude, in the place where he speaks of Enoch's prophecies, does not speak of them as prophecies which had been made known to him by a particular revelation; on the contrary, he speaks of them in such a manner as implies that his readers were already acquainted with them."

From all the evidence before him, Michaelis concludes that the canonical authority of this epistle is extremely dubious; that its author is either unknown, or very uncertain; and he has even doubts that it is a forgery in the name of the Apostle Jude. Others have spoken of it in strains of unqualified commendation and praise, and think that its genuineness is established by the matters contained in it, which in every respect are suitable to the character of an inspired apostle of Christ. What has led to its discredit with many is the hasty conclusion that St. Jude quotes such a work as the Phetirath Mosheh; than which nothing can be more improbable, and perhaps nothing more false.

In almost all ages of the Church it has been assailed and defended; but it is at present generally received over the whole Christian world. It contains some very *sublime* and *nervous passages*, from the 10th to the 13th verse inclusive; the *description* of the false teachers is bold, happy, and energetic; the *exhortation* in verses 20 and 21, is both forcible and affectionate; and the *doxology*, in verses 24 and 25, is well adapted to the subject, and is peculiarly dignified and sublime.

I have done what I could, time and circumstances considered, to present the whole epistle to the reader in the clearest point of view; and now must commend him to God and the word of his grace, which is able to build him up, and give him an inheritance among them that are sanctified by faith in Jesus.

THE GENERAL EPISTLE

OF

J U D E.

Chronological Notes relative to this Epistle.

Year of the Constantinopolitan era of the world, or that used by the Byzantine historians, and other eastern writers, 5573.—Year of the Alexandrian era of the world, 5567.—Year of the Antiochian era of the world, 5557.—Year of the world, according to Archbishop Usher, 4069.—Year of the world, according to Eusebius, in his Chronicon, 4291.—Year of the minor Jewish era of the world, or that in common use, 3825.—Year of the Greater Rabbinical era of the world, 4424.—Year from the Flood, according to Archbishop Usher, and the English Bible, 2413.—Year of the Cali yuga, or Indian era of the Deluge, 3167. —Year of the era of Iphitus, or since the first commencement of the Olympic games, 1005.—Year of the era of Nabonassar, king of Babylon, 814.—Year of the CCXIth Olympiad, 1.—Year from the building of Rome, according to Fabius Pictor, 812.—Year from the building of Rome, according to Frontinus, 816.—Year from the building of Rome, according to the Fasti Capitolini, 817.—Year from the building of Rome, according to Varro, which was that most generally used, 818.—Year of the era of the Seleucidæ, 377.—Year of the Cæsarean era of Antioch, 113.—Year of the Julian era, 110.—Year of the Spanish era, 103.—Year from the birth of Jesus Christ, according to Archbishop Usher, 69.—Year of the vulgar era of Christ's nativity, 65.—Year of Gessius Florus, governor of the Jews, 1.—Year of Domitius Corbulo, governor of Syria, 5. —Year of Matthias, high priest of the Jews, 2.—Year of Vologesus, king of the Parthians, 16.—Year of the Dionysian period, or Easter Cycle, 66.—Year of the Grecian Cycle of nineteen years, or Common Golden Number, 9; or the year after the third embolismic.—Year of the Jewish Cycle of nineteen years, 6; or the second embolismic.—Year of the Solar Cycle, 18.—Dominical Letter, it being the first year after the Bissextile, or Leap Year, F.—Day of the Jewish Passover, the seventh of April, which happened in this year on the Jewish Sabbath.—Easter Sunday, the fourteenth of April.—Epact, or age of the moon on the 22d of March, (the day of the earliest Easter Sunday possible,) 28.—Epact, according to the present mode of computation, or the moon's age on New Year's day, or the Calends of January, 6.— Monthly Epacts, or age of the moon on the Calends of each month respectively, (beginning with January,) 6, 8, 7, 8, 9, 10, 11, 13, 13, 14, 16, 16.—Number of Direction, or the number of days from the twenty-first of March to the Jewish Passover, 17.—Year of the Emperor Caius Tiberius Claudius Nero Cæsar, 12. —Roman Consuls, A. Licinius Nerva Silanus, and M. Vestinius Atticus. Vestinius was succeeded by Anicius Cerealis on the first of July.

2

The address and apostolical benediction, 1, 2. The reasons which induced Jude to write this epistle, to excite the Christians to contend for the true faith, and to beware of false teachers, lest, falling from their stead-fastness, they should be destroyed after the example of backsliding Israel, the apostate angels, and the inhabitants of Sodom and Gomorrha, 3–7. Of the false teachers, 8. Of Michael disputing about the body of Moses, 9. The false teachers particularly described: they are like brute beasts, going the way of Cain, run after the error of Balaam, and shall perish, as did Korah in his gainsaying, 10, 11. Are impure, unsteady, fierce, shameless, &c., 12, 13. How Enoch prophesied of such, 14, 15. They are farther described as murmurers and complainers, 16. We should remember the cautions given unto us by the apostles who foretold of these men, 17–19. We should build up ourselves on our most holy faith, 20, 21. How the Church of Christ should treat such, 22, 23. The apostle's farewell, and his doxology to God, 24, 25.

A. M. cir. 4069.
A. D. cir. 65.
A. U. C. 818.
An. Olymp. CCXI. 1.

JUDE, the servant of Jesus Christ, and [a] brother of James, to them that are sanctified by God the Father, and [b] preserved in Jesus Christ, *and* [c] called:

2 Mercy unto you, and [d] peace, and love, be multiplied.

3 Beloved, when I gave all diligence to write unto you [e] of the common salvation, it was needful for me to write unto you, and exhort *you* that [f] ye should earnestly contend for the faith which was once delivered unto the saints.

4 [g] For there are certain men crept in una-wares, [h] who were before of old ordained to this

A. M. cir. 4069.
A. D. cir. 65.
A. U. C. 818.
An. Olymp. CCXI. 1.

---

[a] Luke vi. 16; Acts i. 13.——[b] John xvii. 11, 12, 15; 1 Pet. i. 5.——[c] Rom. i. 7.——[d] 1 Pet. i. 2; 2 Pet. i. 2.——[e] Titus i. 4.

[f] Phil. i. 27; 1 Tim. i. 18; vi. 12; 2 Tim. i. 13; iv. 7.——[g] Gal. ii. 4; 2 Pet. ii. 1.——[h] Rom. ix. 21, 22; 1 Pet. ii. 8.

NOTES ON THE EPISTLE OF JUDE.

Verse 1. *Jude, the servant of Jesus Christ*] Pro-bably Jude the apostle, who was surnamed *Thaddeus* and *Lebbeus*, was son to *Alpheus*, and brother to *James the less*, *Joses*, and *Simon*. See Matt. x. 3, and collate with Luke vi. 16; Matt. xiii. 55. See the *preface*.

Brother of James] Supposed to be *James the less*, bishop of Jerusalem, mentioned here, because he was an eminent person in the Church. See the preface to St. James.

To them that are sanctified by God] Instead of ἡγιασμένοις, *to the sanctified*, AB, several others, both the *Syriac*, Erpen's *Arabic*, *Coptic*, *Sahidic*, *Armenian*, *Æthiopic*, and *Vulgate*, with several of the *fathers*, have ἠγαπημένοις, *to them that are beloved*; and before εν τω Θεω, *in God*, some MSS., with the *Syriac* and *Armenian*, have εθνεσιν, *to the Gentiles*, *in God the Father*: but although the first is only a *probable* read-ing, this is much less so. St. Jude writes to *all believers* everywhere, and not to any particular Church; hence this epistle has been called a *general* epistle.

Sanctified signifies here *consecrated to God* through faith in Christ.

Preserved in (or *by*) *Jesus Christ*] Signifies those who continued unshaken in the Christian faith; and implies also, that none can be preserved in the faith that do not continue in union with Christ, by whose grace alone they can be *preserved* and *called*. This should be read consecutively with the other epithets, and should be rather, in a translation, read first than last, *to the saints in God the Father, called and pre-served by Christ Jesus. Saints* is the same as *Chris-tians;* to become such they were *called* to believe in Christ by the preaching of the Gospel, and having believed, were *preserved* by the grace of Christ in the life and practice of piety.

Verse 2. *Mercy unto you*] For even the *best* have no *merit*, and must receive every blessing and grace in the way of *mercy*.

Peace] With God and your consciences, *love* both to God and man, *be multiplied*—be unboundedly in-creased.

Verse 3. *When I gave all diligence*] This phrase, πασαν σπουδην ποιουμενος, is a Grecism for being ex-ceedingly intent upon a subject; *taking it up seriously with determination to bring it to good effect.* The meaning of the apostle seems to be this: " Beloved brethren, when I saw it necessary to write to you con cerning the common salvation, my mind being deeply affected with the dangers to which the Church is ex-posed from the false teachers that are gone out into the world, I found it extremely necessary to write and exhort you to hold fast the truth which you had re-ceived, and strenuously to contend for that only faith which, by our Lord and his apostles, has been delivered to the Christians."

Some think that St. Jude intimates that he had at *first* purposed to write to the Church at large, on the nature and design of the Gospel; but seeing the dangers to which the Churches were exposed, because of the false teachers, he changed his mind, and wrote pointedly against those false doctrines, exhorting them strenuously to contend for the faith.

The common salvation] The Christian religion, and the salvation which it brings. This is called *common* because it equally belongs to Jews and Gentiles; it is the saving grace of God which has appeared to every man, and equally offers to every human being that re-demption which is provided for the whole world.

Verse 4. *For there are certain men crept in un-awares*] Παρεισεδυσαν· They had got into the Church under *specious pretences;* and, when in, began to sow their bad seed.

Before of old ordained] Οἱ παλαι προγεγραμμενοι

       2

A. M. cir. 4069.
A. D. cir. 65.
A. U. C.
818.
An. Olymp.
CCXI. 1.

condemnation, ungodly men, [i] turning [k] the grace of our God into lasciviousness, and [l] denying the only Lord God, and our Lord Jesus Christ.

5 I will therefore put you in remembrance, though ye once knew this, how that [m] the Lord,

---

[i] 2 Peter ii. 10.——[k] Titus ii. 11; Heb. xii. 15.——[l] Titus i. 16; 2 Pet. ii. 1; 1 John ii. 22.——[m] 1 Cor. x. 9.

Such as were *long ago proscribed, and condemned in the most public manner ;* this is the import of the word προγραφειν in this place, and there are many examples of this use of it in the Greek writers. See *Kypke.*

To this condemnation] To a similar punishment to that immediately about to be mentioned.

In the sacred writings all such persons, false doctrines, and impure practices, have been *most openly proscribed* and *condemned ;* and the apostle immediately produces several examples, viz., the disobedient *Israelites,* the unfaithful *angels,* and the impure inhabitants of *Sodom* and *Gomorrha.* This is most obviously the apostle's meaning, and it is as ridiculous as it is absurd to look into such words for a decree of eternal reprobation, &c., such a doctrine being as far from the apostle's mind as from that of *Him* in whose name he wrote.

Turning the grace of our God into lasciviousness] Making the grace and mercy of God a covering for crimes ; intimating that men might sin safely who believe the Gospel, because in that Gospel *grace abounds.* But perhaps the *goodness* of God is here meant, for I cannot see how they could believe the Gospel in any way who denied the Lord Jesus Christ ; unless, which is likely, their denial refers to this, that while they acknowledged Jesus as the promised Messiah, they denied him to be the only Lord, Sovereign, and Ruler of the Church and of the world. There are many in the present day who hold the same opinion.

The only Lord God, and our Lord Jesus Christ.] Μονον Δεσποτην Θεον και Κυριον ἡμων Ιησουν Χριστον αρνουμενοι. These words may be translated, Denying the only sovereign God, even our Lord Jesus Christ. But Θεον, GOD, is omitted by ABC, sixteen others, with Erpen's *Arabic,* the *Coptic, Æthiopic, Armenian,* and *Vulgate,* and by many of the *fathers.* It is very likely that it was originally inserted as a gloss, to ascertain to whom the title of τον μονον Δεσποτην, the *only Sovereign,* belonged ; and thus make *two persons* where only *one* seems to be intended. The passage I believe belongs solely to Jesus Christ, and may be read thus: *Denying the only sovereign Ruler, even our Lord Jesus Christ.* The text is differently arranged in the *Complutensian Polyglot,* which contains the *first edition* of the Greek Testament : Και τον μονον Θεον και Δεσποτην, τον Κυριον ἡμων Ιησουν Χριστον αρνουμενοι· *Denying the only God and Sovereign, our Lord Jesus Christ.* This is a very remarkable position of the words, and doubtless existed in some of the MSS. from which these editors copied. The *Simonians, Nicolaitans,* and *Gnostics,* denied God to be the creator of the world ; and Simon is said to

having saved the people out of the land of Egypt, afterward [n] destroyed them that believed not.

A. M. cir. 4069.
A. D. cir. 65.
A. U. C.
818.
An. Olymp.
CCXI. 1.

6 And [o] the angels which kept not their [p] first estate, but left their own habitation, [q] he hath reserved in everlasting chains, under dark

---

[n] Num. xiv. 29, 37; xxvi. 64; Psa. cvi. 26; Hebrews iii. 17, 19 [o] John viii. 44.——[p] Or, *principality.*——[q] 2 Pet. ii. 4.

---

have proclaimed *himself* as FATHER to the *Samaritans,* as SON to the *Jews,* and as the HOLY GHOST to all other *nations.* All such most obviously denied both *Father, Son,* and *Spirit.*

Verse 5. *I will therefore put you in remembrance*] That is, how such persons were *proscribed,* and *condemned* to bear the punishment due to such crimes.

Though ye once knew this] The word ἁπαξ, here translated *once,* has greatly puzzled many interpreters. It has *two* meanings in the sacred writings, and indeed in the Greek writers also. 1. It signifies *once, one time,* as opposed to *twice,* or *several* times. 2. *Altogether, entirely, perfectly,* interpreted by Suidas αντι του διολου, ὁλοσχερως· and of this meaning he produces a proof from Josephus. This appears to be the sense of the word in Heb. vi. 4 : τους ἁπαξ φωτισθεντας· *those who were* FULLY *enlightened.* Heb. x. 2 : ἁπαξ κεκαθαρμενους· THOROUGHLY *cleansed.* See also ver. 3 of this epistle. Psa. lxii. 11 : ἁπαξ ελαλησεν ὁ Θεος. *God spoke* FULLY, *completely,* on the subject. St. Jude is to be understood as saying, *I will therefore put you in remembrance, though ye are* THOROUGHLY *instructed in this.*

Saved the people] Delivered them from the Egyptian bondage.

Afterward destroyed them] Because they neither believed his word, nor were obedient to his commands. This is the *first* example of what was mentioned ver. 4.

Verse 6. *The angels which kept not their first estate*] Την ἑαυτων αρχην *Their own principality.* The words may be understood of their having invaded the office or dignity of some others, or of their having by some means forfeited their own. This is spoken of those generally termed the *fallen angels ; but from what they fell,* or *from what cause* or *for what crime,* we know not. It is generally thought to have been *pride ;* but this is mere conjecture. One thing is certain ; the angels who fell must have been in a state of *probation,* capable of either standing or falling, as Adam was in paradise. They did not continue faithful, though they *knew the law* on which they stood ; they are therefore produced as the *second* example.

But left their own habitation] This seems to intimate that they had *invaded the office and prerogatives of others,* and attempted to seize on their place of residence and felicity.

He hath reserved in everlasting chains] That is, in a state of confinement from which they *cannot escape.*

Under darkness] Alluding probably to those *dungeons* or *dark cells* in prisons where the most flagitious culprits were confined.

The judgment of the great day.] The final judg-

2

A. M. cir. 4069.
A. D. cir. 65.
A. U. C.
818.
An. Olymp.
CCXI. 1.

ness, ʳ unto the judgment of the great day.

7 Even as ˢ Sodom and Gomorrha, and the cities about them in like manner, giving themselves over to fornication, and going after ᵗ strange flesh, are set forth for an example, suffering the vengeance of eternal fire.

8 ᵘ Likewise also these *filthy* dreamers defile the flesh, despise dominion, and ᵛ speak evil of dignities.

9 Yet ʷ Michael the archangel, when con-

A. M. cir. 4069.
A. D. cir. 65.
A. U. C.
818.
An. Olymp.
CCXI. 1.

ʳ Rev. xx. 10.——ˢ Gen. xix. 24 ; Deut. xxix. 23 ; 2 Peter ii. 6.
ᵗ Gr. *other.*

ᵘ 2 Peter ii. 10.——ᵛ Exod. xxii. 28.——ʷ Daniel x. 13 ; xii. 1 ;
Rev. xii. 7.

---

ment, when both angels and men shall receive their eternal doom. See on 2 Pet. ii. 4. In *Sohar Exod.*, fol. 8, c. 32 : "Rabbi Isaac asked : Suppose God should punish any of his heavenly family, how would he act ? R. Abba answered : He would send them into the flaming river, take away their dominion, and put others in their place." Some suppose that the *saints* are to occupy the places from which these angels, by transgression, fell.

Verse 7. *Even as Sodom and Gomorrha*] What their sin and punishment were may be seen in Gen. xix., and the notes there. This is the *third* example to illustrate what is laid down ver. 4.

Are set forth for an example] Both of what God will do to such transgressors, and of the position laid down in ver. 4, viz., that God has in the most *open and positive manner declared* that such and such sinners shall meet with the punishment due to their crimes.

Suffering the vengeance of eternal fire.] Subjected to such a punishment as an endless fire can inflict. Some apply this to the utter subversion of these cities, so that by the action of that fire which descended from heaven they were *totally* and *eternally destroyed ;* for as to their being *rebuilt*, that is impossible, seeing the very *ground* on which they stood is burned up, and the whole *plain* is now the immense *lake Asphaltites.* See my notes on Gen. xix.

The *first* sense applies to the *inhabitants* of those wicked cities ; the *second*, to the cities themselves : in either case the word πυρ αιωνιον signifies an *eternally destructive fire ;* it has no end in the punishment of the wicked Sodomites, &c. ; it has no end in the destruction of the cities ; they were totally burnt up, and never were and never can be rebuilt. In either of these senses the word αιωνιος, *eternal*, has its grammatical and proper meaning.

Verse 8. *Likewise also these* filthy *dreamers*] He means to say that these false teachers and their followers were as *unbelieving* and *disobedient* as the *Israelites* in the wilderness, as *rebellious* against the authority of God as the *fallen angels*, and as *impure* and *unholy* as the *Sodomites ;* and that consequently they must expect *similar punishment.*

Our translators, by rendering ενυπνιαζομενοι *filthy dreamers*, seem to have understood St. Jude to mean *les pollutions nocturnes et voluntaires de ces hommes impurs, qui se livrent sans scrupule à toutes sortes des pensées ; et salissant leur imagination par la vûe de toutes sortes d' objets, tombent ensuite dans les corruptions honteuses et criminelles.* See Calmet. In plain English, self-pollution, with all its train of curses and cursed effects on body, soul, and spirit. The *idea* of our translators seems to be confirmed by the words

σαρκα μεν μιαινουσι, *they indeed pollute the flesh.* See what is said at the conclusion of the thirty-eighth chapter of Genesis.

Despise dominion] Κυριοτητα δε αθετουσι· *They set all government at nought*—they will come under no restraints ; they despise all law, and wish to live as they list.

Speak evil of dignities.] Δοξας δε βλασφημουσιν· *They blaspheme* or *speak injuriously of supreme authority.* (See 2 Pet. ii. 10, 11.) They treat *governors* and *government* with contempt, and calumniate and misrepresent all Divine and civil institutions.

Verse 9. *Yet Michael the archangel*] Of this personage many things are spoken in the Jewish writings. "Rabbi Judah Hakkodesh says : Wherever *Michael* is said to appear, the glory of the Divine Majesty is always to be understood." *Shemoth Rabba*, sec. ii., fol. 104, 3. So that it seems as if they considered Michael in some sort as we do the Messiah manifested in the flesh.

Let it be observed that the word *archangel* is never found in the *plural* number in the sacred writings. There can be properly only one *archangel*, one chief or head of all the angelic host. Nor is the word *devil*, as applied to the great enemy of mankind, ever found in the *plural ;* there can be but one monarch of all fallen spirits. *Michael* is this *archangel*, and head of all the *angelic orders ;* the *devil*, great *dragon*, or *Satan*, is head of all the *diabolic* orders. When these two hosts are opposed to each other they are said to act under these two chiefs, as leaders ; hence in Rev. xii. 7, it is said : MICHAEL *and his angels fought against the* DRAGON *and his angels.* The word *Michael* מיכאל, seems to be compounded of מי *mi*, who, כ *ke*, like, and אל *El*, God ; *he who is like God ;* hence by this personage, in the Apocalypse, many understand the Lord Jesus.

Disputed about the body of Moses] What this means I cannot tell ; or from what source St. Jude drew it, unless from some tradition among his countrymen. There is something very like it in *Debarim Rabba*, sec. ii., fol. 263, 1 : "Samael, that wicked one, the prince of the satans, carefully kept the soul of Moses, saying : When the time comes in which Michael shall lament, I shall have my mouth filled with laughter. Michael said to him : Wretch, I weep, and thou laughest. *Rejoice not against me, O mine enemy, because I have fallen ; for I shall rise again : when I sit in darkness, the Lord is my light ;* Mic. vii. 8. By the words, *because I have fallen*, we must understand the *death* of Moses ; by the words, *I shall rise again*, the government of Joshua, &c." See the preface.

A. M. cir. 4069.
A. D. cir. 65.
A. U. C.
818.
An. Olymp.
CCXI. 1.

tending with the devil he disputed about the body of Moses, [x] durst not bring against him a railing accusation, but said, [y] The Lord rebuke thee.

10 [z] But these speak evil of those things which they know not : but what they know naturally, as brute beasts, in those things they corrupt themselves.

11 Wo unto them ! for they have gone in

the way [a] of Cain, and [b] ran greedily after the error of Balaam for reward, and perished [c] in the gainsaying of Core.

A. M. cir. 4069.
A. D. cir. 65.
A. U. C.
818.
An. Olymp.
CCXI. 1.

12 [d] These are spots in your [e] feasts of charity, when they feast with you, feeding themselves without fear : [f] clouds *they are* without water, [g] carried about of winds ; trees whose fruit withereth, without fruit, twice dead, [h] pluck ed up by the roots ;

---

[x] 2 Pet. ii. 11.——[y] Zech. iii. 2.——[z] 2 Pet. ii. 12.——[a] Gen. iv. 5 ; 1 John iii. 12.——[b] Num. xxii. 7, 21 ; 2 Pet. ii. 15.——[c] Num. xvi. 1, &c.——[d] 2 Pet. ii. 13.——[e] 1 Cor. xi. 21.——[f] Prov. xxv. 14 ; 2 Pet. ii. 17.——[g] Eph. iv. 14.——[h] Matt. xv. 13.

Another *contention* of Michael with Satan is mentioned in *Yalcut Rubeni*, fol. 43, 3 : " At the time in which Isaac was bound there was a contention between Michael and Satan. Michael brought a ram, that Isaac might be liberated ; but Satan endeavoured to carry off the ram, that Isaac might be slain."

The *contention* mentioned by Jude is not about the sacrifice of Isaac, nor the *soul* of Moses, but about the BODY of Moses ; but why or wherefore we know not. Some think the devil wished to show the Israelites *where* Moses was buried, knowing that they would then *adore* his *body ;* and that Michael was sent to resist this discovery.

Durst not bring against him a railing accusation] It was a Jewish maxim, as may be seen in *Synopsis Sohar*, page 92, note 6 : " It is not lawful for man to prefer ignominious reproaches, even against wicked spirits." See *Schoettgen*.

Dr. *Macknight* says : " In Dan. x. 13, 21 ; xii. 1, Michael is spoken of as one of the chief angels who took care of the Israelites as a nation ; he may therefore have been *the angel of the Lord* before whom Joshua the high priest is said, Zech. iii. 1, to have stood, *Satan being at his right hand to resist him ;* namely, in his design of restoring the *Jewish Church* and *state*, called by Jude the *body of Moses*, just as the Christian Church is called by Paul *the body of Christ.* Zechariah adds, *And the Lord*, that is, *the angel of the Lord*, as is plain from ver. 1, *said unto Satan, The Lord rebuke thee, O Satan ! even the Lord that hath chosen Jerusalem, rebuke thee !*" This is the most likely interpretation which I have seen ; and it will appear the more probable when it is considered that, among the Hebrews, גוף *guph*, BODY, is often used for *a thing itself.* So, in Rom. vii. 24, σωμα της ἁμαρτιας, the *body of sin*, signifies *sin* itself : so *the body of Moses*, גוף של משה *guph shel Mosheh*, may signify Moses himself ; or that in which he was particularly concerned, viz., his institutes, religion, &c

It may be added, that the Jews consider *Michael* and *Samael*, one as the *friend*, the other as the *enemy*, of Israel. Samael is their *accuser*, Michael their *advocate.* " Michael and Samael stand before the Lord ; Satan accuses, but Michael shows the merits of Israel. Satan endeavours to speak, but Michael silences him : Hold thy tongue, says he, and let us hear what the Judge determines : for it is written, *He will speak peace to his people, and to his saints ;* Psa. lxxxv. 9." *Shemoth Rabba*, sec. xviii., fol. 117, 3.

2

Verse 10. *Speak evil of those things which they know not*] They do not understand the origin and utility of civil government ; they revile that which ever protects their own persons and their property. This is true in most insurrections and seditions.

But what they know naturally] They are destitute of reflection ; their minds are uncultivated ; they follow *mere natural instinct*, and are slaves to their animal propensities.

As brute beasts] Ὡς τα αλογα ζωα· Like the irrational animals ; but, in the indulgence of their animal propensities, *they corrupt themselves*, beyond the example of the brute beasts. A fearful description ; and true of many in the present day.

Verse 11 *They have gone in the way of Cain*] They are *haters of their brethren*, and they that are such are *murderers ;* and by their false doctrine they corrupt and destroy the souls of the people.

The error of Balaam] For the sake of gain they corrupt the word of God and refine away its meaning, and let it down so as to suit the *passions* of the profligate. This was literally true of the *Nicolaitans*, who taught most impure doctrines, and followed the most lascivious practices.

Gainsaying of Core.] See the account of the rebellion of Korah, Dathan, and Abiram, and their company, in Num. xxii. It appears that these persons *opposed the authority of the apostles* of our Lord, as Korah and his associates did that of *Moses and Aaron ;* and St. Jude predicts them a similar punishment. In this verse he accuses them of murder, covetousness, and rebellion against the authority of God.

Verse 12. *Spots in your feasts of charity*] It appears that these persons, unholy and impure as they were, still continued to have outward fellowship with the Church ! This is strange : but it is very likely that their power and influence in that place had swallowed up, or set aside, the power and authority of the real ministers of Christ ; a very common case when worldly, time-serving men get into the Church.

The *feasts of charity*, the αγαπαι or *love feasts*, of which the apostle speaks, were in use in the primitive Church till the middle of the *fourth* century, when, by the council of Laodicea, they were prohibited to be held in the Churches ; and, having been abused, fell into disuse. In later days they have been revived, in all the purity and simplicity of the primitive institution, among the *Moravians* or *Unitas Fratrum*, and the people called *Methodists*.

A. M. cir. 4069.
A. D. cir. 65.
A. U. C.
818.
An. Olymp.
CCXI. 1.

13 [i] Raging waves of the sea, [k] foaming out their own shame; wandering stars, [l] to whom is reserved the blackness of darkness for ever.

A. M. cir. 4069.
A. D. cir. 65.
A. U. C.
818.
An. Olymp.
CCXI. 1.

14 And Enoch also, [m] the seventh from Adam, prophesied of these, saying, Behold, [n] the Lord cometh with ten thousand of his saints,

---

[i] Isa. lvii. 20.——[k] Phil. iii. 19.——[l] 2 Pet. ii. 17.——[m] Genesis v. 18.

[n] Deut. xxxiii. 2; Dan. vii. 10; Zech. xiv. 5; Matt. xxv. 31; 2 Thess. i. 7; Rev. i. 7.

Among the ancients, the richer members of the Church made an occasional general feast, at which all the members attended, and the poor and the rich ate together. The fatherless, the widows, and the strangers were invited to these feasts, and their eating together was a proof of their love to each other; whence such entertainments were called *love feasts.* The love feasts were at first celebrated *before* the Lord's Supper; in process of time they appear to have been celebrated *after* it. But they were never considered as the Lord's Supper, nor any substitute for it. See, for farther information, *Suicer,* in his *Thesaurus,* under the word Αγαπη.

Feeding themselves without fear] Eating, not to suffice nature, but to pamper appetite. It seems the provision was abundant, and they ate to gluttony and riot. It was this which brought the love feasts into disrepute in the Church, and was the means of their being at last wholly laid aside. This abuse is never likely to take place among the Methodists, as they only use *bread* and *water;* and of this the provision is not sufficient to afford the tenth part of a meal.

Instead of αγαπαις, love feasts, απαταις, deceits, is the reading of the *Codex Alexandrinus,* and the *Codex Ephrem,* two MSS. of the highest antiquity; as also of those MSS. collated by *Laurentius Valla,* and of some of those in the *Medicean* library. This reading appears to have been introduced in order to avoid the conclusion that some might be led to draw concerning the state of the Church; it must be very corrupt, to have in its communion such corrupt men.

Clouds—without water] The *doctrine* of God is compared to the *rain,* Deut. xxxii. 2, and *clouds* are the instruments by which the rain is distilled upon the earth. In arid or parched countries the very appearance of a cloud is delightful, because it is a token of refreshing showers; but when sudden winds arise, and disperse these clouds, the hope of the husbandman and shepherd is cut off. These false teachers are represented as *clouds;* they have the *form* and *office* of the teachers of righteousness, and from such *appearances* pure doctrine may be naturally expected: but these are *clouds without water*—they distil no refreshing showers, because they have none; they are *carried away* and *about* by their *passions,* as those *light fleecy clouds* are carried by the winds. See the notes on 2 Peter ii. 17.

Trees whose fruit withereth] Δενδρα φθινοπωρινα· Galled or *diseased trees;* for φθινοπωρον is, according to *Phavorinus,* νοσος φθινουσα οπωρας, *a disease* (in trees) *which causes their fruit to wither;* for although there are *blossoms,* and the *fruit shapes* or is *set,* the galls in the trees prevent the proper circulation of the sap, and therefore the fruit never comes to perfection. Hence the apostle immediately adds, *without fruit;*

i. e. the fruit never comes to maturity. This metaphor expresses the same thing as the preceding. They have the appearance of ministers of the Gospel, but they have no fruit.

Twice dead] *First, naturally* and *practically dead in sin,* from which they had been revived by the preaching and grace of the Gospel. *Secondly,* dead by *backsliding* or *apostasy* from the true faith, by which they lost the grace they had before received; and now likely to continue in that death, because *plucked up from the roots,* their roots of faith and love being no longer fixed in Christ Jesus. Perhaps the *aorist* is taken here for the *future: They* SHALL BE *plucked up from the roots* —God will exterminate them from the earth.

Verse 13. *Raging waves of the sea, foaming out their own shame*] The same metaphor as in Isa. lvii. 20: *The wicked are like the troubled sea, when it cannot rest, whose waters cast up mire and dirt.* These are like the sea in a storm, where the *swells* are like mountains; the *breakers* lash the shore, and sound like thunder; and the great deep, stirred up from its very bottom, rolls its muddy, putrid sediment, and deposits it upon the *beach.* Such were those proud and arrogant boasters, those headstrong, unruly, and ferocious men, who swept into their own vortex the souls of the simple, and left nothing behind them that was not indicative of their folly, their turbulence, and their impurity.

Wandering stars] Αστερες πλανηται· Not what we call *planets;* for although these differ from what are called the *fixed stars,* which never change their place, while the *planets* have their revolution round the sun; yet, properly speaking, there is no *irregularity* in their motions: for their appearance of *advancing, stationary,* and *retrograde,* are only in reference to an observer on the earth, viewing them in different parts of their orbits; for as to themselves, they ever continue a steady course through all their revolutions. But these are uncertain, anomalous meteors, *ignes fatui, wills-o'-the-wisp;* dancing about in the *darkness* which themselves have formed, and leading simple souls astray, who have ceased to walk in the *light,* and have no other guides but those oscillating and devious meteors which, if you run *after* them, will flee before you, and if you run *from* them will follow you.

The blackness of darkness] They are such as are going headlong into that *outer* darkness where there is wailing, and weeping, and gnashing of teeth. The whole of this description appears to have been borrowed from 2 Pet. ii., where the reader is requested to see the notes.

Verse 14. *Enoch also, the seventh from Adam*] He was the *seventh* patriarch, and is distinguished thus from *Enoch,* son of *Cain,* who was but the *third* from Adam; this appears plainly from the genealogy, 1 Chron. i. 1: Adam, Seth, Enosh, Kenan, Mahalaleel,

2

A. M. cir. 4069.
A. D. cir. 65.
A. U. C.
818.
An. Olymp.
CCXI. 1.

15 To execute judgment upon all, and to convince all that are ungodly among them of all their ungodly deeds which they have ungodly committed, and of all their ° hard *speeches* which ungodly sinners have spoken against him.

16 These are murmurers, complainers, walking after their own lusts ; and ᵖ their mouth speaketh great swelling *words,* ᑫ having men's

persons in admiration because of advantage.

17 ʳ But, beloved, remember ye the words which were spoken before of the apostles of our Lord Jesus Christ ;

18 How that they told you ˢ there should be mockers in the last time, who should walk after their own ungodly lusts.

19 These be they ᵗ who separate themselves, ᵘ sensual, having not the Spirit.

A. M. cir. 4069
A. D. cir. 65.
A. U. C.
818.
An. Olymp.
CCXI. 1.

° 1 Sam. ii. 3 ; Psa. xxxi. 18 ; xciv. 4 ; Mal. iii. 13.——ᵖ 2 Pet. ii. 18.——ᑫ Proverbs xxviii. 21 ; James ii. 1, 9.——ʳ 2 Peter iii. 2.

ˢ 1 Tim. iv. 1 ; 2 Tim. iii. 1 ; iv. 3 ; 2 Pet. ii. 1 ; iii. 3.—— ᵗ Prov. xviii. 1 ; Ezekiel xiv. 7 ; Hosea iv. 14 ; ix. 10 ; Hebrews x. 25. ᵘ 1 Cor. ii. 14 ; James iii. 15.

Jered, Henoch or *Enoch,* &c. Of the *book of Enoch,* from which this prophecy is thought to have been taken, much has been said ; but as the work is *apocryphal,* and of no authority, I shall not burden my page with *extracts.* See the *preface.*

Perhaps the word προεφητευσε, *prophesied,* means no more than *preached, spoke,* made *declarations,* &c., concerning these things and persons ; for doubtless he reproved the ungodliness of his own times. It is certain that a *book* of Enoch was known in the earliest ages of the primitive Church, and is quoted by *Origen* and *Tertullian ;* and is mentioned by St. *Jerome* in the *Apostolical Constitutions,* by *Nicephorus, Athanasius,* and probably by St. *Augustine.* See *Suicer's* Thesaurus, vol. i., col. 1131. Such a work is still extant among the *Abyssinians.*

Ten thousand of his saints] This seems to be taken from Dan. vii. 10.

Verse 15. *To execute judgment*] This was originally spoken to the antediluvians ; and the coming of the Lord to destroy that world was the thing spoken of in this prophecy or declaration. But as God had threatened this, it required no direct inspiration to foretell it. *To execute judgment,* &c. This is a very strange verse as to its composition, and is loaded with various readings ; the MSS. and *versions* being at little agreement among themselves on its phraseology. Αυτων, which we translate *among them,* is omitted by the best MSS. and *versions,* and is, in all probability, spurious. Many also omit ασεβειας after ργων, *ungodly deeds.* Many insert λογων, *words* or *speeches,* after σκληρων, *hard ;* and this word our translators have supplied. And instead of ἁμαρτωλοι, *sinners,* the *Sahidic* has ανθρωποι, *men.* There are others of less note ; but the frequent recurrence of ALL and UNGODLY makes the construction of the sentence very harsh.

Dr. *Macknight* supposes that Enoch's prophecy was common among the Jews ; for the first words in Hebrew are *Maranatha,* and these were used by them in that form of excommunication or cursing which they pronounced against irreclaimable offenders. The doctor forgets himself here ; the words *Maranatha* are not *Hebrew,* but *Syriac.* In Hebrew the form of execration begins with ארור אתה *arur attah,* "cursed art thou ;" or מחרם אתה *mochoram attah :* but the *Syriac* ܡܪܢ ܐܬܐ 121 *maran atha,* is literally, *our Lord is coming ;* see on 1 Cor. xvi. 22 ; but here, in the *Syriac,*

the words are ܡܪܝܐ ܐܬܐ 121 *atha moria,* "the Lord cometh." So it is doubtful whether this fancied analogy exists.

Verse 16. *These are murmurers*] Grudging and grumbling at all men, and at all things ; *complainers,* μεμψιμοιροι, *complainers of their fate* or *destiny*—finding fault with God and all his providential dispensations, making and governing worlds in their own way ; persons whom neither God nor man can please.

Walking after their own lusts] Taking their wild, disorderly, and impure passions for the rule of their conduct, and not the writings of the prophets and apostles.

Great swelling words] Ὑπεροχκα. See the explanation of this term in 2 Pet. ii. 18.

Having men's persons in admiration] Time-servers and flatterers ; persons who pretend to be *astonished* at the *greatness, goodness, sagacity, learning, wisdom,* &c., of *rich* and *great* men, hoping thereby to acquire money, influence, power, friends, and the like.

Because of advantage.] Ωφελειας χαριν· *For the sake of lucre.* All the flatterers of the rich are of this kind ; and especially those who profess to be *ministers* of the Gospel, and who, for the sake of a more advantageous *settlement* or *living,* will soothe the rich even in their sins. With such persons a *rich man* is *every thing ;* and if he have but a *grain* of grace, his *piety* is extolled to the skies ! I have known several ministers of this character, and wish them all to read the *sixteenth verse of Jude.*

Verse 17. *Remember—the words*] Instead of following those teachers and their corrupt doctrine, remember what Christ and his apostles have said ; for they foretold the coming of such false teachers and impostors.

Verse 18. *Mockers in the last time*] See the notes on 1 Tim. iv. 1 ; 2 Tim. iii. 1, &c. ; and particularly 2 Pet. iii. 2, 3, &c., to which Jude seems to refer.

The last time.—The conclusion of the Jewish polity.

Verse 19. *Who separate themselves*] From the true Church, which they leave from an affectation of *superior wisdom.*

Sensual] Ψυχικοι· *Animal*—living as brute beasts, guided simply by their *own lusts* and *passions,* their Bible being the manifold devices and covetousness of their own hearts ; for they *have not the Spirit*—they

A. M. cir. 4069.
A. D. cir. 65.
A. U. C. 818.
An. Olymp. CCXI. 1.

20 But ye, beloved, ᵛ building up yourselves on your most holy faith, ʷ praying in the Holy Ghost,

21 Keep yourselves in the love of God, ˣ looking for the mercy of our Lord Jesus Christ unto eternal life.

22 And of some have compassion, making a difference :

23 And others ʸ save with fear, ᶻ pulling

them out of the fire ; hating even ᵃ the garment spotted by the flesh.

A. M. cir. 4069
A. D. cir. 65.
A. U. C. 818.
An. Olymp. CCXI. 1.

24 ᵇ Now unto him that is able to keep you from falling, and ᶜ to present *you* faultless before the presence of his glory with exceeding joy,

25 ᵈ To the only wise God our Saviour, *be* glory and majesty, dominion and power, both now and ever. Amen.

ᵛ Col. ii. 7 ; 1 Tim. i. 4.——ʷ Rom. viii. 26 ; Eph. vi. 18. ˣ Titus ii. 13 ; 2 Peter iii. 12.——ʸ Romans xi. 14 ; 1 Timothy iv. 16.

ᶻ Amos iv. 11 ; 1 Cor. iii. 15 ; Zech. iii. 2.——ᵃ Zech. iii. 4, 5 ; Rev. iii. 4.——ᵇ Romans xvi. 25 ; Eph. iii. 20.——ᶜ Col. i. 22. ᵈ Rom. xvi. 27 ; 1 Tim. i. 17 ; ii. 3.

---

are not spiritually minded, and have no Holy Ghost, no inspiration from God.

Verse 20. Building up yourselves] Having the *most holy faith*—the *Gospel* of our *Lord Jesus*, and the *writings* of his *apostles*, for your foundation ; founding all your expectations on these, and seeking from the Christ who is their sum and substance all the grace and glory ye need.

Praying in the Holy Ghost] Holding fast the Divine influence which ye have received, and under that influence making prayer and supplication to God. The prayer that is not sent up through the influence of the Holy Ghost is never likely to reach heaven.

Verse 21. Keep yourselves in the love of God] By building up yourselves on your most holy faith, and praying in the Holy Ghost ; for without this we shall soon lose the love of God.

Looking for the mercy of our Lord] For although they were to build *themselves* up, and to *pray* in the Holy Ghost, and keep *themselves* in the love of God, yet this *building, praying,* and *keeping,* cannot *merit* heaven ; for, after all their diligence, earnestness, self-denial, watching, obedience, &c., they must look for the MERCY *of the Lord Jesus Christ,* to bring *them to* ETERNAL LIFE.

Verse 22. And of some have compassion, making a difference] The general meaning of this exhortation is supposed to be, " Ye are not to deal alike with all those who have been seduced by false teachers ; ye are to make a difference between those who have been led away by weakness and imprudence, and those who, in the pride and arrogance of their hearts, and their unwillingness to submit to wholesome *discipline*, have separated themselves from the Church, and become its inveterate enemies."

Instead of Και ους μεν ελεειτε διακρινομενοι, *and of some have compassion, making a difference*, many MSS., versions, and *fathers* have και ους μεν ελεγχετε διακρινομενους, *and some rebuke, after having judged them ;* or, *rebuke those that differ ;* or, *some that are wavering convince ;* or whatever else the reader pleases : for this and the following verse are all confusion, both in the MSS. and versions ; and it is extremely difficult to know what was the original text. Our own is as likely as any.

Verse 23. And others save with fear] " Some of them snatch from the fire ; but when they repent,

have mercy upon them in fear."—*Syriac.* " And some of them rebuke for their sins ; and on others have mercy when they are convicted ; and others save from the fire and deliver them."—*Erpen's Arabic.* Mr. Wesley's note has probably hit the sense. " Meantime watch over *others* as well as *yourselves ;* and give them such help as their various needs require. For instance, 1. *Some that are wavering* in judgment, staggered by others' or by their own evil reasoning, endeavour more deeply to *convince* of the truth as it is in Jesus. 2. *Some snatch* with a swift and strong hand *out of the fire* of sin and temptation. 3. *On others* show *compassion*, in a milder and gentler way ; though still *with* a jealous *fear*, lest you yourselves be infected with the disease you endeavour to cure. See therefore that, while ye love the sinners, ye retain the utmost abhorrence of their sins, and of any, the least, degree of or approach to them."

Having even the garment spotted by the flesh.] Fleeing from all *appearance of evil. Dictum sumptum, ut apparet, a mulieribus sanguine menstruo pollutis, quarum vestes etiam pollutæ censebantur :* or there may be an allusion to a case of *leprosy*, for that infected the garments of the afflicted person, and these garments were capable of conveying the contagion to others.

Verse 24. Now unto him that is able to keep you from falling] Who alone can preserve you from the contagion of sin, and preserve you from falling into any kind of error that might be prejudicial to the interests of your souls ; and thus to *present you faultless*, or, as many others read, ασπιλους, *without spot*, alluding to the *spotted garment* mentioned above.

Before the presence of his glory] Where nothing can stand that does not resemble himself, *with exceeding great joy*, in finding yourselves eternally out of the reach of the possibility of falling, and for having now arrived at an eternity of happiness.

Verse 25. To the only wise God] Who alone can *teach*, who alone has declared the *truth ;* that truth in which ye now stand. See on Rom, xvi. 27.

Our Saviour] Who has by his blood washed us from our sins, and made us kings and priests unto God the Father.

Be *glory*] Be ascribed all light, excellence, and splendour.

Majesty] All power, authority, and pre-eminence

Dominion] All rule and government in the world and in the Church, in earth and in heaven

And power] All energy and operation to every thing that is wise, great, good, holy, and excellent.

Both now] In the present state of life and things.

And ever.] Εις παντας τους αιωνας· To the end of all states, places, dispensations, and worlds; and to a state which knows no *termination*, being that ETERNITY in which this *glory, majesty, dominion,* and *power* ineffably and incomprehensibly dwell.

Amen.] So let it be, so ought it to be, and so it shall be.

After *to the only wise God our Saviour,* many excellent MSS. *versions,* &c., add διa Iησου Χριστου του Κυριου ἡμων, *by Jesus Christ our Lord;* and after *dominion and power* they add προ παντος του αιωνος, *before all time;* and both these readings Griesbach has received into the text. The text, therefore, may be read thus: *To the only wise God our Saviour, by Christ Jesus our Lord, be glory and majesty, dominion and power, before all time; and now, and through all futurity. Amen.* Let the whole creation join in one chorus, issuing in one eternal *Amen!*

Subscriptions to this epistle in the VERSIONS :—

The Epistle of Jude the apostle, whose intercession be ever with us, Amen. The end.—SYRIAC.

The Epistle of Jude, the brother of James is finished: and glory be to God for ever and ever, Amen.—ÆTHIOPIC.

Nothing in the VULGATE.

Nothing in the ARABIC.

" This epistle was written A. D. 64, by the Apostle Jude, the brother of James; who is also called Lebbeus and Thaddeus; and who preached (the Gospel) to the Armenians and to the Persians."—This is found at the end of the ARMENIAN Bible, printed in 1698.

The Epistle of Jude the son of Joseph, and brother of James, is ended.—A MS. copy of the SYRIAC.

The end of the catholic Epistle of St. Jude.—COMPLUTENSIAN.

The Epistle of Jude the apostle is ended.—IBID. Latin text.

In the MANUSCRIPTS :—

Jude.—*Codex Vaticanus,* B.

The Epistle of Jude.—*Codex Alexandrinus.*

The catholic Epistle of Jude.—*Codex Ephrem.*

The Epistle of the holy Apostle Jude.—*Codex G,* in Griesbach.

Of how little authority such subscriptions are, we have already had occasion to observe in various cases. Very few of them are ancient; and none of them coeval with the works to which they are appended. They are, in general, the opinions of the scribes who wrote the copies; or of the Churches for whose use they were written. No stress therefore should be laid on them, as if proceeding from Divine authority.

With the Epistle of Jude end all the apostolical epistles, and with it the canon of the New Testament, as to *gospels* and *epistles;* for the *Apocalypse* is a work *sui generis,* and can rank with neither. It is in general a collection of symbolic prophecies, which do not appear to be yet fully understood by the Christian world, and which can only be known when they are fulfilled.

Finished for a new impression, January 4th, 1832.—A. C.

INTRODUCTION

TO

THE REVELATION

OF

ST. JOHN THE DIVINE.

AS there has been much controversy concerning the authenticity of this book; and as it was rejected by many for a considerable time, and, when generally acknowledged, was received cautiously by the Church; it will be well to examine the testimony by which its authenticity is supported, and the arguments by which its claim to a place in the sacred canon is vindicated. Before, therefore, I produce my own sentiments, I shall beg leave to lay before the reader those of Dr. *Lardner*, who has treated the subject with much judgment.

"We are now come to the last book of the New Testament, the *Revelation*; about which there have been different sentiments among Christians; many receiving it as the writing of John the apostle and evangelist others ascribing it to John a presbyter, others to Cerinthus, and some rejecting it, without knowing to whom it should be ascribed. I shall therefore here rehearse the testimony of ancient Christians, as it arises in several ages.

"It is probable that Hermas read the book of the Revelation, and imitated it; he has many things resembling it. It is referred to by the martyrs at Lyons. There is reason to think it was received by Papias Justin Martyr, about the year 140, was acquainted with this book, and received it as written by the Apostle John; for, in his dialogue with Trypho, he expressly says: 'A man from among us, by name John, one of the apostles of Christ, in the revelation made to him, has prophesied that the believers in our Christ shall live a thousand years in Jerusalem; and after that shall be the general, and, in a word, the eternal resurrection and judgment of all together.' To this passage we suppose Eusebius to refer in his ecclesiastical history, when giving an account of Justin's works, he observes to this purpose. He also mentions the Revelation of John, expressly calling it the apostle's. Among the works of Melito, bishop of Sardis, one of the seven Churches of Asia, about the year 177, Eusebius mentions one entitled, 'Of the Revelation of John.' It is very probable that Melito ascribed this book to the apostle of that name, and esteemed it of canonical authority. Irenæus, bishop of Lyons in Gaul, about A. D. 178, who in his younger days was acquainted with Polycarp, often quotes this book as the Revelation of John, the apostle of the Lord. And in one place he says: 'It was seen not long ago, but almost in our age, at the end of the reign of Domitian.'

"Theophilus was bishop of Antioch about 181. Eusebius, speaking of a work of his against the heresy of Hermogenes, says: 'He therein made use of testimonies, or quoted passages, from John's Apocalypse.' The book of the Revelation is several times quoted by Clement of Alexandria, who flourished about 194; and once in this manner: 'Such a one, though here on earth he is not honoured with the first seat, shall sit upon the four and twenty thrones judging the people, as John says in the Revelation.' Tertullian, about the year 200, often quotes the Revelation, and supposes it to have been written by St. John, the same who wrote the First Epistle of John, universally received: 'Again, the Apostle John describes, in the Apocalypse, *a sharp two-edged sword coming out of the mouth of God.*' He also says: 'We have Churches that are the disciples of John. For though Marcion rejects the Revelation, the succession of bishops, traced to the original, will assure us that John is the author:' by John undoubtedly meaning the apostle.

"From Eusebius we learn that Apollonius, who wrote against the Montanists about 211, quoted the Revelation. By Caius, about 212, it was ascribed to Cerinthus: it was received by Hippolytus about 220, and by Origen about 230. It is often quoted by him. He seems not to have had any doubt about its genuineness. In his Commentary upon St. John's gospel, he speaks of it in this manner: 'Therefore John, the son of Zebedee, says in the Revelation.' Dionysius, bishop of Alexandria, about 247, or somewhat later, wrote a book against the Millenarians, in which he allows the Revelation to be written by John, a holy and divinely inspired man. But he says, 'He cannot easily grant him to be the apostle, the son of Zebedee, whose is the gospel

2

according to John, and the catholic epistle.' He rather thinks it may be the work of John an elder, who also lived at Ephesus in Asia, as well as the apostle. It also appears, from a conference which Dionysius had with some Millenarians, that the Revelation was, about 240 and before, received by Nepus, an Egyptian bishop, and by many others in that country; and that it was in great reputation. It was received by Cyprian, bishop of Carthage, about 248, and by the Church of Rome in his time, and by many Latin authors. The Revelation was received by Novatus and his followers, and by various other authors. It is also probable that it was received by the Manichees. It was received by Lactantius, and by the Donatists; by the latter Arnobius about 460, and by the Arians.

"In the time of Eusebius, in the former part of the fourth century, it was by some not received at all; and therefore it is reckoned by him among contradicted books. Nevertheless, it was generally received. Eusebius himself seems to have hesitated about it, for he says: 'It is likely the Revelation was seen by John the elder, if not by John the apostle.' It may be reckoned probable that the critical argument of Dionysius of Alexandria was of great weight with him and others of that time. The Revelation was received by Athanasius, and by Epiphanius; but we also learn from him that it was not received by all in his time. It is not in the catalogue of Cyril of Jerusalem, and seems not to have been received by him. It is also wanting in the catalogue of the Council of Laodicea, about 363.

"The Revelation is not in Gregory Nazianzen's catalogue; however, it seems to have been received by him. It is in the catalogue of Amphilochius; but he says it was not received by all. It is also omitted in Ebedjesus' catalogue of the books of Scripture received by the Syrians; nor is it in the ancient Syriac version.

"It was received by Jerome; but he says it was rejected by the Greek Christians. It was received by Rufin, by the third Council of Carthage, and by Augustine, but it was not received by all in his time. It is never quoted by Chrysostom, and probably was not received by him. It is in the catalogue of Dionysius, called the Areopagite, about 490. It is in the Alexandrian MS. It was received by Sulpicius Severus about 401; and by J. Damascenus, and by Œcumenius, and by many other authors. Andrew, bishop of Cæsarea, in Cappadocia, at the end of the fifth century, and Arethas, bishop of the same place, in the sixth century, wrote commentaries upon it. But it was not received by Severian, bishop of Gabala; nor, as it seems, by Theodoret. Upon the whole, it appears that this book has been generally received in all ages, though some have doubted of it, and rejected it; particularly the Syrians, and some other Christians in the east.

"Having thus represented the external evidence of the genuineness of the Book of the Revelation, or of its being written by St. John, I should proceed to consider the internal evidence. But I need not enlarge here, but merely take notice of a few things of principal note, which learned men insist upon as arguments that the Revelation has the same author with the gospel and epistles that go under the name of the Evangelist and Apostle John. Chap. i. ver. 1: 'The revelation of Jesus Christ, which God gave unto him, to show unto his servant things which must shortly come to pass. And he sent and signified it by his angel unto his servant John.'

"Hence it is argued, that John styles himself the *servant of Christ*, in a sense not common to all believers, but peculiarly to those who are especially employed by him. So Paul and other apostles call themselves *servants of God and of Christ*. Particularly Rom. i. 1: 'Paul, a servant of Jesus Christ.' James i. 1: 'James, a servant of God and of the Lord Jesus Christ.' 2 Peter i. 1: 'Simon Peter, a servant and an apostle of Jesus Christ.' Jude ver. 1: 'Jude, a servant of Jesus Christ.' So Moses is called 'the servant of God,' Num. xii. 7; and Heb. iii. 2; and in like manner many of the prophets. And in this very book, chap. x. 7, is the expression, 'as he has declared unto his servants, the prophets.'

"This observation may be of some weight for showing that the writer is an apostle, but it is not decisive; and in the same verse, whence this argument is taken, the phrase is used in its general sense: 'Which God gave unto him, to show unto his servants.' Verse 2: 'Who bare record of the word of God, and of the testimony of Jesus Christ, and of all things that he saw.'

"Some suppose the writer here refers to the written gospel of St. John, and should be understood to say that he had already *borne testimony concerning the word of God, and of Jesus Christ*. But these words may be understood of this very book, the Revelation, and the things contained in it. The writer says here, very properly at the beginning, and by way of preface, that he had performed his office in this book, having faithfully recorded in it the word of God which he had received from Jesus Christ. Certainly, if these words did clearly refer to a written gospel, they would be decisive; but they are allowed to be ambiguous, and other senses have been given of them. By some they have been understood to contain a declaration that the writer had already borne witness to Jesus Christ before magistrates. Moreover, I think that, if St. John had intended to manifest himself in this introduction, he would more plainly have characterized himself in several parts of this book than he has done. This observation therefore appears to me to be of small moment for determining who the writer is.

"Farther, it is argued, in favor of the genuineness of this book, that 'there are in it many instances of conformity, both of sentiment and expression, between the Revelation and the uncontested writings of St. John. Our Saviour says to his disciples, John xvi. 33: 'Be of good cheer, I have overcome the world.' Christian firmness under trials is several times represented by *overcoming, overcoming the world*, or *overcoming the wicked one*, in St. John's First Epistle, chap. ii. 13, 14; iv. 4; v. 4, 5. And it is language peculiar to St. John, being in no other books of the New Testament. And our Lord says, Rev. iii. 21: 'To him that overcometh will I grant to sit with me in my throne; even as I also overcame, and am set down with my Father in his throne." Compare chap. ii. 7, 11, 17, 26; iii. 5, 12, 21; and xxi. 7.

"Concerning the time of writing this book, I need not now say much. It is the general testimony of ancient authors that St. John was banished into Patmos in the time of Domitian, in the latter part of his reign, and restored by his successor Nerva. But the book could not be published till after John's release and return to Ephesus in Asia. As Domitian died in 96, and his persecution did not commence till near the end of his reign, the Revelation seems to be fitly dated in the year 95 or 96. Mill places the Revelation in the year of Christ 96, and the last year of the Emperor Domitian. At first he supposed that the Revelation was written at Patmos; but afterwards he altered his mind, and thought it was not written till after his return to Ephesus. He builds his opinion upon the words of Revelation i. 9. If so, I apprehend it might not be published before the year 97; or, at the soonest, near the end of 96. Basnage places the Revelation in 96. Le Clerc, likewise, who readily admits the genuineness of this book, speaks of it in the same year. Mr. Lowman supposes St. John to have had his visions in the Isle of Patmos, in 95; but Mr. Wetstein favours the opinion of those who have argued that the Revelation was written before the Jewish war. He also says that, if the Revelation was written before that war, it is likely that the events of that time should be foretold in it; to which I answer, that though some interpreters have applied some things in this book to those times, I cannot say whether they have done it rightly or not, because I do not understand the Revelation. But, to me, it seems that though this book was written before the destruction of Jerusalem, there was no necessity that it should be foretold here; because our blessed Lord had, in his own preaching, frequently spoken very plainly and intelligibly concerning the calamities coming upon the Jewish people in general, and the city and temple of Jerusalem in particular; and his plain predictions and symbolical prefigurations of those events were recorded by no less than three historians and evangelists before the war in Judea broke out.

"Grotius, who places this book in the reign of Claudius, was of opinion that the visions of this book were seen at different times, and afterwards joined together in one book, in the same way as the visions and prophecies of some of the prophets of the Old Testament.

"Concerning this opinion it is not proper for me to dispute; though there appears not any foundation for it in the book itself, as Vitringa has observed. But that the Book of the Revelation in its present form, sent as an epistle to the seven Churches of Asia, chap. i. 4, was not composed and published before the reign of Domitian, appears to me very probable, from the general and almost universally concurring testimony of the ancients, and from some things in the book itself.

"I shall now transcribe a part of L'Enfant's and Beausobre's Preface to the Revelation, at the same time referring to Vitringa, who has many like thoughts:—

"Having quoted Irenæus, Origen, Eusebius, and various other writers, placing St. John's banishment at Patmos in the latter part of the reign of Domitian, and saying, that he there saw the Revelation, they say 'To these incontestable witnesses it is needless to add a long list of others of all ages, and of the same sentiment, to whom the authority of Epiphanius is by no means comparable.' And they go on: 'We must add to so constant a tradition other reasons which farther show that the Revelation was not written till after Claudius and Nero. It appears from the book itself that there had been already Churches for a considerable space of time in Asia; forasmuch as St. John, in the name of Christ, reproves faults that happen not but after a while. The Church of Ephesus *had left her first love.* That of Sardis *had a name to live, but was dead.* The Church of Laodicea was fallen into lukewarmness and indifference. But the Church of Ephesus, for instance, was not founded by St. Paul before the last years of Claudius. When in 61 or 62, St. Paul wrote to them from Rome, instead of reproving their want of love, he commends their love and faith, chap. i. 15. It appears from the Revelation that the Nicolaitans made a sect when this book was written, since they are expressly named; whereas they were only foretold and described in general terms by St. Peter, in his second epistle, written after the year 60, and in St. Jude, about the time of the destruction of Jerusalem by Vespasian. It is evident from many places of the Revelation that there had been an open persecution in the provinces; St. John himself had been banished to the Isle of Patmos for the testimony of Jesus. The Church of Ephesus, or its bishops, is commended for their labour and patience, which seems to imply persecution. This is still more clear in the words directed to the Church of Smyrna, chap. ii. 9: *I know thy works and tribulation.* For the original word always denotes persecution in the scriptures of the New Testament, as it is also explained in the following verse. In the thirteenth verse of the same chapter mention is made of a martyr named Antipas, put to death at Pergamus. Though ancient ecclesiastical history gives us no information concerning this Antipas, it is nevertheless certain that, according to all the rules of language, what is here said must be understood literally. All that has been now observed concerning the persecution, of which mention is made in the first chapters of the Revelation, cannot relate to the time of Claudius, who did not persecute the Christians; nor to the time of Nero, whose persecution did not reach the provinces; and therefore it must relate to Domitian, according to ecclesiastical tradition.'

"The visions therefore here recorded, and the publication of them in this book, must be assigned, as far as I can see, to the years of Christ 95, and 96, or 97."

The reasoning of Dr. Lardner, relative to the *date* of this book, is by no means satisfactory to many other critics, who consider it to have been written *before* the destruction of Jerusalem; and in this opinion they are supported by the most respectable testimonies among the ancients, though the contrary was the more general opinion. *Epiphanius* says, that John was banished to Patmos by *Claudius Cæsar;* this would bring back the date to about A. D. 50. *Andreas,* (bishop of Cæsarea, in Cappadocia, about A. D. 500,) in his comment on this book, chap. vi. 16, says : " John received this Revelation under the reign of *Vespasian.*" This date also might place it *before* the final overthrow of the Jewish state ; though Vespasian reigned to A. D. 79. The *inscription* to this book, in the *Syriac version,* first published by *De Dieu,* in 1627, and, afterwards in the London Polyglot, is the following : " The Revelation which God made to John the evangelist, in the island of Patmos, to which he was banished by Nero Cæsar." This places it before the year of our Lord 69, and consequently *before* the destruction of Jerusalem. Of this opinion are many eminent writers, and among them *Hentenius, Harduin, Grotius, Lightfoot, Hammond,* Sir *Isaac Newton,* Bishop *Newton, Wetstein,* and others.

If the *date* could be settled, it would be of the utmost consequence to the right interpretation of the book ; but, amidst so many conflicting opinions, this is almost hopeless.

Dr. Lardner has given several proofs, from *internal* evidence, that the Revelation is the work of St. John ; as there are found in it the same forms of expression which are found in his gospel and epistles, and which are peculiar to this apostle. *Wetstein* gives a collection, which the reader may examine at his leisure. *E. g.* compare

Rev. i. 1.	with John xii. 33 ; xviii. 37 ; xxi. 19.	Rev. iii. 10.	with John xii. 27.
5.	1 John i. 7.	21.	1 John ii. 13, 14 ; iv. 4 ; v. 5.
7.	John xix. 37.	vi. 12.	John i. 29.
9.	1 John v. 10.	ix. 5.	John xviii. 26 ; iii. 17.
ii. 10.	John xx. 27.	xii. 9.	John xii. 31.
17.	John vi. 32.	xix. 13.	John i. 1.
iii. 4.	John vi. 66.	xxi. 6.	John vii. 37.
7, 9.	John xv. 20 ; xvii. 6 ; 1 John ii. 5.	xxii. 8, 10.	John vii. 51, 52, 55 ; xiv. 23, 24.
9.	John xi. 27.		

Dr. Lardner has considered several of these, with the addition of other *resemblances,* in his account of *Dionysius,* bishop of Alexandria, in A. D. 247, in the third volume of his works, pages 121–126. This mode of proof, as it applies to most of the above references, is not entirely satisfactory.

Dionysius argues that the *style* of the Revelation is totally different from that of John in his acknowledged writings ; and it seems strange to me that this should be contested by any man of learning. Nothing more *simple* and *unadorned* than the *narrative* of St. John in his GOSPEL ; nothing more *plain* and *natural* than his EPISTLES ; but the REVELATION, on the contrary, is *figurative, rhetorical, laboured,* and *elevated* to the highest degree. All that can be said here on this subject is, that if the Spirit of God choose to inspire the *words* and *style,* as well as the *matter,* of his communications, he may choose what *variety* he pleases ; and speak at different times, and *in divers manners,* to the same person. This, however, is not his usual way.

For other matters relative to this subject I must refer to the following *preface,* and to the writers quoted above.

PREFACE

TO

THE REVELATION

OF

ST. JOHN THE DIVINE.

AMONG the interpreters of the *Apocalypse*, both in ancient and modern times, we find a vast diversity of opinions, but they may be all reduced to *four* principal hypotheses, or modes of interpretation :—

1. The Apocalypse contains a prophetical description of the destruction of Jerusalem, of the Jewish war, and the civil wars of the Romans.

2. It contains predictions of the persecutions of the Christians under the heathen emperors of Rome, and of the happy days of the Church under the Christian emperors, from Constantine downwards.

3. It contains prophecies concerning the tyrannical and oppressive conduct of the Roman pontiffs, the true antichrist; and foretells the final destruction of popery.

4. It is a prophetic declaration of the schism and heresies of Martin Luther, those called Reformers, and their successors; and the final destruction of the Protestant religion.

The first opinion has been defended by Professor Wetstein, and other learned men on the continent.

The second is the opinion of the primitive fathers in general, both Greek and Latin.

The third was first broached by the Abbé *Joachim*, who flourished in the thirteenth century, was espoused by most of the Franciscans, and has been and still is the general opinion of the Protestants.

The fourth seems to have been invented by popish writers, merely by way of retaliation; and has been illustrated and defended at large by a Mr. *Walmsley*, (I believe,) titular dean of Wells, in a work called the History of the Church, under the feigned name of *Signior Pastorini.*

In this work he endeavours to turn every thing against Luther and the Protestants, which they interpreted of the pope and popery; and attempts to show, from a computation of the Apocalyptical numbers, that the total destruction of Protestantism in the world will take place in 1825! But this is not the first prophecy that has been invented for the sake of an event, the accomplishment of which was earnestly desired; and as a stimulus to excite general attention, and promote united exertion, when the time of the pretended prophecy was fulfilled. But 1825 is past by, and 1832 is come, and the Protestant Church is still in full vigour, while the Romish Church is fast declining.

The full title of the book which I quote is the following :—

" The General History of the Christian Church, from her birth to her final triumphant state in Heaven, chiefly deduced from the Apocalypse of St. John the Apostle. By SIG. PASTORINI.

'Blessed is he that readeth and heareth the words of this prophecy.'—APOCALYPSE, Chap. i. ver. 3.

Printed in the year M.DCC.LXXI." 8vo. No *place* nor *printer's* name mentioned.

The place where he foretells the final destruction of Protestantism is in pp. 249 and 262.

The Catholic college of *Maynooth*, in Ireland, have lately published a new edition of this work! in which the author kindly predicts the approaching overthrow of the whole Protestant system, both in Church and state; and in the meantime gives them, most condescendingly, *Abaddon* or the *devil* for their king!

Who the writer of the Apocalypse was, learned men are not agreed. This was a *question*, as well in ancient as in modern times. We have already seen that many have attributed it to the *Apostle John*; others, to a person called *John* the *presbyter*, who they say was an Ephesian, and totally different from John the apostle. And lastly, some have attributed it to *Cerinthus*, a contemporary of John the apostle. This hypothesis, however, seems utterly unsupportable; as there is no probability that the Christian Church would have so generally received a work which came from the hands of a man at all times reputed a very dangerous heretic; nor can the doctrines it contains ever comport with a Cerinthian creed.

Whether it was written by *John the apostle*, *John the presbyter*, or some *other* person, is of little importance if the question of its *inspiration* be fully established. If written by an *apostle* it is *canonical*; and should be received, without hesitation, as a work Divinely inspired. Every apostle acted under the inspiration of the Holy Spirit. John was an apostle, and consequently inspired; therefore, whatever he wrote was written by Divine inspiration. If, therefore, the *authenticity* of the work be established, *i. e.*, that it was written by John the apostle, all the rest necessarily follow.

As I have scarcely any opinion to give concerning this book on which I could wish any of my readers to rely, I shall not enter into any discussion relative to the author, or the meaning of his several visions and prophecies; but for general information refer to Dr. Lardner, Michaelis, and others.

Various attempts have been made by learned men to fix the *plan* of this work; but even in this few agree. I shall produce some of the chief of these: and first, that of *Wetstein*, which is the most singular of the whole.

He supposes the book of the Apocalypse to have been written a considerable time before the destruction of Jerusalem. The events described from the fourth chapter to the end he supposes to refer to the Jewish war, and to the civil commotions which took place in Italy while Otho, Vitellius, and Vespasian were contending for the empire. These contentions and destructive wars occupied the space of about three years and a half, during which Professor Wetstein thinks the principal events took place which are recorded in this book. On these subjects he speaks particularly in his notes, at the end of which he subjoins what he calls his Ανακεφα-λαιωσις, or synopsis of the whole work, which I proceed now to lay before the reader.

"This prophecy, which predicts the calamities which God should send on the enemies of the Gospel, is divided into two parts. The first is contained in the *closed book;* the second, in the *open book.*

I. The first concerns the *earth and the third part, i. e.,* Judea and the Jewish nation.

II. The second concerns *many peoples, and nations, and tongues, and kings,* chap. x. 11, *i. e.,* the Roman empire.

1. The *book written within and without, and sealed with seven seals,* chap. v. 1, is the bill of divorce sent from God to the Jewish nation.

2. The *crowned conqueror on the white horse armed with a bow,* chap. vi. 2, is Artabanus, king of the Parthians, who slaughtered multitudes of the Jews in Babylon.

3. The *red horse,* ver. 4. The Sicarii and robbers in Judea, in the time of the Proconsuls Felix and Festus.

4. The *black horse,* ver. 5. The famine under Claudius.

5. The *pale horse,* ver. 8. The plague which followed the robberies and the famine.

6. The *souls of those who were slain,* ver. 9. The Christians in Judea, who were persecuted, and were now about to be avenged.

7. The *great earthquake,* ver. 12. The commotions which preceded the Jewish rebellion.

8. The *servants of God from every tribe, sealed in their foreheads,* chap. vii. 3. The Christians taken under the protection of God, and warned by the prophets to flee immediately from the land.

9. The *silence for half an hour,* chap. viii. 1. The short truce granted at the solicitation of King Agrippa. Then follows the rebellion itself.

1. The *trees are burnt,* ver. 7. The fields and villages, and unfortified places of Judea, which first felt the bad effects of the sedition.

2. The *burning mountain cast into the sea which* in consequence *became blood,* ver. 8; and,

3. The *burning star falling into the rivers, and making the waters bitter,* chap. viii. 10, 11. The slaughter of the Jews at Cæsarea and Scythopolis.

4. The *eclipsing of the sun, moon, and stars,* ver. 12. The anarchy of the Jewish commonwealth.

5. The *locusts like scorpions hurting men,* chap. ix. 3. The expedition of Cestius Gallus, prefect of Syria.

6. The *army with arms of divers colours,* ver. 16, 17. The armies under Vespasian in Judea. About this time Nero and Galba died; after which followed the civil war, signified by *the sounding of the seventh trumpet,* chap. x. 7, 11; xi. 15.

1. The *two prophetic witnesses, two olive trees, two candlesticks,* chap. xi. 3, 4. Teachers in the Church, predicting the destruction of the Jewish temple and commonwealth.

2. The *death of the witnesses,* ver. 7. Their flight, and the flight of the Church of Jerusalem, to Pella, in Arabia.

3. The *resurrection of the witnesses, after three days and a half,* ver. 11. The predictions began to be fulfilled at a time in which their accomplishment was deemed impossible; and the doctrine of Christ begins to prevail over Judea, and over the whole earth.

4. The *tenth part of the city fell in the same hour, and seven thousand names of men slain,* ver. 13. Jerusalem seized by the Idumeans; and many of the priests and nobles, with Annas, the high priest, signified by *names of men, i. e. men of name,* slain by the Zealots.

5. The *woman clothed with the sun, the moon under her feet, and a crown of twelve stars on her head,* chap. xii. 1. The Christian Church.

6. The *great red dragon seen in heaven, with seven heads, seven diadems, and ten horns,* ver. 6 The six first Cæsars, who were all made princes at Rome, governing the armies and the Roman people with great authority; especially Nero, the last of them, who, having killed his mother, cruelly vexed the Christians. and afterwards turned his wrath against the rebellious Jews.

2

7. The *seven-headed beast from the sea, having ten horns surrounded with diadems*, chap. xiii. 1. Galba, Otho, and Vitellius, who were shortly to reign, and who were proclaimed emperors by the army.

8. This *beast, having a mouth like a lion, the body like a leopard, the feet like a bear*, ver. 2. Avaricious Galba; rash, unchaste, and inconstant Otho; Vitellius, cruel and sluggish, with the German army.

9. *One head, i. e., the seventh, cut off*, ver. 3. Galba.

10. *He who leadeth into captivity shall be led into captivity; he who killeth with the sword shall be killed with the sword*, ver. 10. Otho, who subdued the murderers of Galba, and slew himself with a dagger, Vitellius, who bound Sabinus with chains, and was himself afterwards bound.

11. *Another beast rising out of the earth, with two horns*, ver. 11. Vespasian and his two sons, Titus and Domitian, elected emperors at the same time in Judea.

12. The *number of the wild beast*, 666, *the number of a man*, TEITAN, Titan or Titus : T, 300. E, 5. I, 10. T, 300. A, 1. N, 50, making in the whole 666. [But some very respectable MSS. have 616 for the number; if the N be taken away from Teitan, then the letters in Teita make exactly the sum 616.]

13. A *man sitting upon a cloud, with a crown of gold upon his head, and a sickle in his hand*, chap. xiv. 14. Otho and his army, about to prevent supplies for the army of Vitellius.

14. An *angel of fire commanding another angel to gather the vintage; the winepress trodden whence the blood flows out 1600 furlongs*. The followers of Vitellius laying all waste with fire; and the Bebriaci conquering the followers of Otho with great slaughter.

Then follow the seven plagues :—

1. The *grievous sore*, chap. xvi. 2. The diseases of the soldiers of Vitellius through intemperance.

2. The *sea turned into blood*, ver. 3. The fleet of Vitellius beaten, and the maritime towns taken from them by the Flavii.

3. The *rivers turned into blood*, ver. 4. The slaughter of the adherents of Vitellius, at Cremona and elsewhere, near rivers.

4. The *scorching of the sun*, ver. 8. The diseases of the Vitellii increasing, and their exhausted bodies impatient of the heat.

5. The *seat of the beast darkened*, ver. 10. All Rome in commotion through the torpor of Vitellius.

6. *Euphrates dried up, and a way made for the kings of the east; and the three unclean spirits like frogs* The Flavii besieging Rome with a treble army; one part of which was by the bank of the Tiber.

The *shame of him who is found asleep and naked*. Vitellius, ver. 15. *Armageddon*, ver. 16. The prætorian camps.

7. The *fall of Babylon*, ver. 19. The sacking of Rome.

1. The *whore*, chap. xvii. 1. Rome.

2. The *seven kings*, ver. 10. Cæsar, Augustus, Tiberius, Caligula, Claudius, Nero, and Galba.

3. The *eighth, which is of the seven*, ver. 11. Otho, destined by adoption to be the son and successor of Galba.

4. The *ten horns*, ver. 12–16. The leaders of the Flavian factions.

5. The *merchants of the earth*, chap. xviii. 11; *i. e.*, of Rome, which was then the emporium of the whole world.

6. The *beast and the false prophet*, chap. xix. 20. Vespasian and his family, contrary to all expectation, becoming extinct in Domitian, as the first family of the Cæsars, and of the three princes, Galba, Otho, and Vitellius.

7. The *millennium, or a thousand years*, chap. xx. 2. Taken from Psa. xc. 4, a time appointed by God, including the space of *forty* years, from the death of Domitian to the Jewish war under Adrian.

8. *Gog and Magog, going out over the earth*, ver. 8. Barchochebas, the false Messiah, with an immense army of the Jews, coming forth suddenly from their caves and dens, tormenting the Christians, and carrying on a destructive war with the Romans.

9. The *New Jerusalem*, chap. xxi. 1, 2. The Jews being brought so low as to be capable of injuring no longer; the whole world resting after being expiated by wars; and the doctrine of Christ propagated and prevailing everywhere with incredible celerity.

Wetstein contends (and he is supported by very great men among the ancients and moderns) that " the book of the Revelation was written before the Jewish war, and the civil wars in Italy; that the important events which took place at that time, the greatest that ever happened since the foundation of the world, were worthy enough of the Divine notice, as the affairs of his Church were so intimately connected with them: that his method of exposition proves the whole book to be a well-connected, certain series of events; but the common method of interpretation, founded on the hypothesis that the book was written *after* the destruction of Jerusalem, is utterly destitute of certainty, and leaves every commentator to the luxuriance of his own fancy, as is sufficiently evident from what has been done already on this book; some interpreters leading the reader now to *Thebes*, now to *Athens*, and finding in the words of the sacred penman *Constantine* the Great; *Arius, Luther, Calvin*; the *Jesuits*; the *Albigenses*; the *Bohemians*; Chemnitius; *Elizabeth*, queen of England; *Cecil*, her treasurer; and who not !"—See *Wetslein's Gr. Test.*, vol. ii. p. 889.

Those who consider the Apocalypse as a *prophecy* and *scenical* exhibition of what shall happen to the Christian Church to the end of the world, lay this down as a proposition, which comprises the subject of the whole book : *The contest of Christ with his enemies; and his final victory and triumph over them.* See

2

1 Cor. xv. 25; Matt. xxiv.; Mark xiii.; Luke xxi. But what is but briefly hinted in the above scriptures, is detailed at large in the Apocalypse, and represented by various images, nearly in the following order :—

1. The *decrees* of the Divine providence, concerning what is to come, are declared to John.

2. The *manner* in which these decrees shall be executed is painted in the most vivid colours.

3. Then follow *thanksgivings* to God, the ruler and governor of all things, for these manifestations of his power, wisdom, and goodness.

After the *exordium*, and the *seven epistles* to the seven Churches of Asia Minor, to whose angels or bishops the book seems to be dedicated, (chap. i., ii., iii.,) the scene of the visions is opened in heaven, full of majesty; and John receives a promise of a *revelation* relative to the future state of the Church, chap. iv., v.

The enemies of the Church of Christ which the Christians had then most to fear were the *Jews*, the *heathens*, and the *false teachers*. All these are overcome by Christ, and over them he triumphs gloriously First of all, punishments are threatened to the enemies of the kingdom of Christ, and the preservation of his own followers in their greatest trials determined; and these determinations are accompanied with the praises and thanksgivings of all the heavenly inhabitants, and of all good men, chap. vi.–x.

The transactions of the Christian religion are next recorded, chap. xi.–xiv. 5. The Christians are persecuted,—

1. By the *Jews*; but they were not only preserved, but they increase and prosper.

2. By the *heathens*; but in vain do these strive to overthrow the kingdom of Christ, which is no longer confined within the limits of Judea, but spreads among the Gentiles, and diffuses itself over the whole Roman empire, destroying idolatry, and rooting out superstition, in every quarter, chap. xii., xiii., 1–10.

3. *False teachers* and *impostors* of various kinds, under the name of Christians, but enemies of the cross of Christ, more intent on promoting the interests of idolatry or false worship than the cause of true religion, chap. xiii. 11–18, exert their influence to corrupt and destroy the Church; but, notwithstanding, Christianity becomes more extended, and true believers more confirmed in their holy faith, chap. xiv. 1–5. Then new punishments are decreed against the enemies of Christ, both Jews and heathens: the calamities coming upon the Jewish nation before its final overthrow are pointed out, chap. xiv., xv. Next follows a prediction of the calamities which shall take place during the Jewish war; and the civil wars of the Romans during the contentions of Otho and Vitellius, chap. xvi. 1–16, who are to suffer most grievous punishments for their cruelties against the Christians, chap. xvii. The Jewish state being now finally overthrown, chap. xviii., the heavenly inhabitants give praise to God for his justice and goodness; Christ is congratulated for his victory over his enemies, and the more extensive progress of his religion, chap. xix. 1–10.

Opposition is, however, not yet totally ended: idolatry again lifts up its head, and new errors are propagated; but over these also Christ shows himself to be conqueror, chap. xix. 11–21. Finally, Satan, who had long reigned by the worship of false gods, errors, superstitions, and wickedness, is deprived of all power and influence; and the concerns of Christianity go on gloriously, chap. xx. 1–6. But towards the end of the world new enemies arise, and threaten destruction to the followers of Christ; but in vain is their rage, God appears in behalf of his servants, and inflicts the most grievous punishments upon their adversaries, chap. xx. 6–10. The last judgment ensues, ver. 11–15, all the wicked are punished, and the enemies of the truth are chained so as to be able to injure the godly no more; the genuine Christians, who had persevered unto death, are brought to eternal glory; and, freed from all adversities, spend a life that shall never end, in blessedness that knows no bounds, chap. xxi. and xxii. See *Rosenmüller*.

Eichhorn takes a different view of the *plan* of this book; though in substance not differing much from that above. According to this writer the whole is represented in the form of a *drama*, the parts of which are the following: I. The *title*, chap. i. 1–3. II. The *prologue*, chap. i. 4; iv. 22.; in which it is stated that the argument of the drama refers to the Christians; epistles being sent to the Churches, which, in the symbolic style, are represented by the number *seven*. Next follows the *drama* itself, the parts of which are :—

The *prolusio*, or *prelude*, chap. iv. 1; viii. 5; in which the scenery is prepared and adorned.

Act the first, chap. viii. 6; xii. 17. Jerusalem is taken, and Judaism vanquished by Christianity.

Act the second, chap. xii. 18; xx. 10. Rome is conquered, and heathenism destroyed by the Christian religion.

Act the third, chap. xx. 11; xxii. 5. The New Jerusalem descends from heaven; or the happiness of the life to come, and which is to endure for ever, is particularly described, chap. xxii. 6–11. Taken in this sense, *Eichhorn* supposes the work to be most exquisitely finished, and its author to have had a truly poetic mind, polished by the highest cultivation; to have been accurately acquainted with the history of all times and nations, and to have enriched himself with their choicest spoils.

My readers will naturally expect that I should either give a decided preference to some one of the opinions stated above, or produce one of my own; I can do neither, nor can I pretend to explain the book: I do not understand it; and in the things which concern so sublime and awful a subject, I dare not, as my predecessors, indulge in *conjectures*. I have read elaborate works on the subject, and each seemed right till another was examined. I am satisfied that no *certain* mode of interpreting the prophecies of this book has yet been found out, and I will not add another monument to the littleness or folly of the human mind by endeavouring to strike out a new course. I repeat it, I do not understand the book; and I am satisfied that not one who has written on the subject knows any thing more of it than myself. I should, perhaps, except *J. E. Clarke*, who has written on the *number of the beast*. His interpretation amounts nearly to demonstration; but that is but a small part of the difficulties of the Apocalypse : that interpretation, as the most probable ever yet offered to the public, shall be inserted in its proper place ; as also his illustration of the xiith, xiiith, and xviith chapters. As to other matters, I must leave them to God, or to those events which shall point out the prophecy ; and *then*, and probably *not till then*, will the sense of these visions be explained.

A conjecture concerning the *design* of the book may be safely indulged ; thus then it has struck me, that *the book of the Apocalypse may be considered as a* PROPHET *continued in the Church of God, uttering predictions relative to all times, which have their successive fulfilment as ages roll on ; and thus it stands in the Christian Church in the place of the* SUCCESSION *of* PROPHETS *in the Jewish Church ; and by this especial economy* PROPHECY *is* STILL CONTINUED, *is* ALWAYS SPEAKING ; *and yet a succession of prophets rendered unnecessary.* If this be so, we cannot too much admire the wisdom of the contrivance which still continues the voice and testimony of prophecy, by means of a very short book, without the assistance of any extraordinary messenger, or any succession of such messengers, whose testimony would at all times be liable to suspicion, and be the subject of infidel and malevolent criticism, howsoever unexceptionable to ingenuous minds the credentials of such might appear.

On this ground it is reasonable to suppose that several prophecies contained in this book have been already fulfilled, and that therefore it is the business of the commentator to point such out. It may be so ; but as it is impossible for me to *prove* that my *conjecture* is right, I dare not enter into proceedings upon it, and must refer to Bishop Newton, and such writers as have made this their particular study.

After having lived in one of the most eventful eras of the world ; after having seen a number of able pens employed in the illustration of this and other prophecies ; after having carefully attended to those facts which were supposed to be the incontestable proofs of the fulfilment of such and such *visions, seals, trumpets, thunders*, and *vials* of the Apocalypse ; after seeing the issue of that most terrible struggle which the French *nation*, the French *republic*, the French *consulate*, and the French *empire*, have made to regain and preserve their liberties, which, like arguing in a circle, have terminated where they began, without one political or religious advantage to them or to mankind ; and after viewing how the prophecies of this book were supposed to apply almost exclusively to these events, the writers and explainers of these prophecies keeping pace in their publications with the rapid succession of military operations, and confidently promising the most glorious issue, in the final destruction of superstition, despotism, arbitrary power, and tyranny of all kinds, nothing of which has been realized ; I say, viewing all these things, I feel myself at perfect liberty to state that, to my apprehension, all these prophecies have been misapplied and misapprehended ; and that the KEY to them is not yet intrusted to the sons of men. My readers will therefore excuse me from any exposure of my ignorance or folly by attempting to do what many, with much more wisdom and learning, have attempted, and what every man to the present day has failed in, who has preceded me in expositions of this book. I have no other *mountain* to heap on those already piled up ; and if I had, I have not strength to lift it : those who have courage may again make the trial ; already we have had a sufficiency of vain efforts.

> Ter sunt conati imponere Pelio Ossam
> Scilicet, atque Ossæ frondosum involvere Olympum :
> Ter Pater extructos disjecit fulmine montes.   VIRG., G. i. 281.
>
> With mountains piled on mountains thrice they strove
> To scale the steepy battlements of Jove ;
> And thrice his lightning and red thunder play'd,
> And their demolish'd works in ruin laid.   DRYDEN

I had resolved, for a considerable time, not to meddle with this book, because I foresaw that I could produce nothing satisfactory on it : but when I reflected that the *literal sense* and *phraseology* might be made much plainer by the addition of *philological* and *critical* notes ; and that, as the diction appeared in many places to be purely *rabbinical*, (a circumstance to which few of its expositors have attended,) it might be rendered plainer by examples from the ancient Jewish writers ; and that several parts of it spoke *directly* of the work of God in the soul of man, and of the conflicts and consolations of the followers of Christ, particularly in the beginning of the book, I changed my resolution, and have added short notes, principally *philological*, where I thought I understood the meaning.

I had once thought of giving a *catalogue* of the writers and commentators on this book, and had begun a collection of this kind ; but the question of *Cui bono?* *What good end is this likely to serve?* not meeting with a satisfactory answer in my own mind, caused me to throw this collection aside. I shall notice *two* only.

1. The curious and learned work entitled, "A plaine Discovery of the whole Revelation of St. John," written by Sir *John Napier*, inventor of the logarithms, I have particularly described in the general preface to the Holy Scriptures, prefixed to the Book of Genesis, to which the reader is requested to refer.

2. Another work, not less singular, and very rare, entitled, "The Image of both Churches, after the most wonderfull and heavenly Revelation of Sainct John the Evangelist, containing a very fruitfull exposition or *paraphrase* upon the same: wherein it is conferred with the other scriptures, and most auctorised histories. Compyled by John Bale, an exyle also in thys lyfe for the faithful testimony of Jesu." Printed at London by *Thomas East*, 18mo., *without date*.

966   2

PREFACE TO THE REVELATION OF ST. JOHN.

The author was at first a Carmelite, but was afterwards converted to the Protestant religion. He has turned the whole of the Apocalypse against the Romish Church; and it is truly astonishing to see with what address he directs every image, metaphor, and description, contained in this book, against the corruptions of this Church. He was made bishop of Ossory, in Ireland; but was so persecuted by the papists that he narrowly escaped with his life, five of his domestics being murdered by them. On the accession of Mary he was obliged to take refuge in the Low Countries, where it appears he compiled this work. As he was bred up a *papist*, and was also a *priest*, he possessed many advantages in attacking the strongest holds of his adversaries. He knew all their secrets, and he uncovered the whole; he was acquainted with all their rites, ceremonies, and superstitions, and finds all distinctly marked in the Apocalypse, which he believes was written to point out the abominations, and to foretell the final destruction of this corrupt and intolerant Church. I shall make a few references to his work in the course of the following notes. In chap. xvii. 1, the author shows his opinion, and speaks something of himself: *Come hither, I will show thee the judgment of the great whore, &c.* " Come hither, friende John, I will show thee in secretnesse the tirrible judgement of the great whore, or counterfaite Church of hypocrites. Needs must this whore be Rome, for that she is the great citie which reigneth over the kings of the earth. Evident it is both by Scriptures and Cronicles that in John's dayes Rome had dominion over all the whole world : and being infected with the abominations of all landes, rightly is shee called Babylon, or Citie of Confusion. And like as in the Scriptures ofte tymes under the name of Jerusalem is ment the whole kingdom of Juda, so under the name of Rome here may be understanded the unyversall worlde, with all their abominations and divilleshnesses, their idolatryes, witchcraftes, sectes, superstitions, papacyes, priesthoodes, relygions, shavings, anointings, blessings, sensings, processions, and the divil of all such beggeryes. For all the people since Christes assencion, hath this Rome infected with hir pestilent poisons gathered from all idolatrous nations, such time as she held over them the monarchial supremit. At the wryting of this prophecy felt John of their cruiltie, being exiled into Pathmos for the faithfull testimony of Jesu. And so did I, poore creature, with my poore wife and children, at the gatheringe of this present commentary, flying into Germanye for the same," &c.

Shall I have the reader's pardon if I say that it is my firm opinion that the expositions of this book have done great disservice to religion: almost every commentator has become a *prophet;* for as soon as he began to explain he began also to prophesy. And what has been the issue? *Disappointment laughed at hope's career*, and superficial thinkers have been led to despise and reject prophecy itself. I shall sum up all that I wish to say farther in the words of GRASERUS : *Mihi tota Apocalypsis valde obscura videtur; et talis, cujus explicatio citra periculum vix queat tentari. Fateor me hactenus in nullius Scripti Biblici lectione minus proficere, quam in hoc obscurissimo Vaticinio.*

3

THE REVELATION

OF

ST. JOHN THE DIVINE.

Chronological Notes relative to this Book.

Year of the Constantinopolitan era of the world, or that used by the Byzantine historians, and other eastern writers, 5604.—Year of the Alexandrian era of the world, 5598.—Year of the Antiochian era of the world, 5588.—Year of the world, according to Archbishop Usher, 4100.—Year of the world, according to Eusebius, in his Chronicon, 4322.—Year of the minor Jewish era of the world, or that in common use, 3856.—Year of the Greater Rabbinical era of the world, 4455.—Year from the Flood, according to Archbishop Usher, and the English Bible, 2444.—Year of the Cali yuga, or Indian era of the Deluge, 3198. —Year of the era of Iphitus, or since the first commencement of the Olympic games, 1036.—Year of the era of Nabonassar, king of Babylon, 845.—Year of the CCXVIIIth Olympiad, 4.—Year from the building of Rome, according to Fabius Pictor, 843.—Year from the building of Rome, according to Frontinus, 847.—Year from the building of Rome, according to the Fasti Capitolini, 848.—Year from the building of Rome, according to Varro, which was that most generally used, 849.—Year of the era of the Seleucidæ, 408.—Year of the Cæsarean era of Antioch, 144.—Year of the Julian era, 141.—Year of the Spanish era, 134.—Year from the birth of Jesus Christ, according to Archbishop Usher, 100.—Year of the vulgar era of Christ's nativity, 96.—Year of Pacorus II , king of the Parthians, 6.—Year of the Dionysian period, or Easter Cycle, 97. —Year of the Grecian Cycle of nineteen years, or Common Golden Number, 2; or the first embolismic. —Year of the Jewish Cycle of nineteen years, 18; or the year before the seventh embolismic.—Year of the Solar Cycle, 21.—Dominical Letters, it being the Bissextile, or Leap Year, CB.—Day of the Jewish Passover, the twenty-fifth of March, which happened in this year on the day before the Jewish Sabbath. —Easter Sunday, the twenty seventh of March.—Epact, or age of the moon on the 22d of March, (the day of the earliest Easter Sunday possible,) 11.—Epact, according to the present mode of computation, or the moon's age on New Year's day, or the Calends of January, 19.—Monthly Epacts, or age of the moon on the Calends of each month respectively, (beginning with January,) 19, 21, 20, 21, 22, 23, 24, 26, 26, 27, 29, 29.—Number of Direction, or the number of days from the twenty-first of March to the Jewish Passover, 4.—Year of the Emperor Flavius Domitianus Cæsar, the last of those usually styled The Twelve Cæsars, 15 : Nerva began his reign in this year.—Roman Consuls, C. Antistius Vetus, and C. Manlius Valens.

CHAPTER I.

The preface to this book, and the promise to them who read it, 1–3. John's address to the seven Churches of Asia, whose high calling he particularly mentions ; and shows the speedy coming of Christ, 4–8. Mentions his exile to Patmos, and the appearance of the Lord Jesus to him, 9–11. Of whom he gives a most glorious description, 12–18. The command to write what he saw, and the explanation of the seven stars and seven golden candlesticks, 19, 20.

A. M. cir. 4100.
A. D. cir. 96.
Impp. Flavio
Domitiano
Cæs. Aug. et
Nerva.

THE Revelation of Jesus Christ, [a] which God gave unto him, to show unto his servants things which [b] must shortly come to pass ; and [c] he sent and signified *it* by his angel unto his servant John.

2 [d] Who bare record of the word of God, and of the testimony of Jesus Christ, and of all things [e] that he saw.

3 [f] Blessed *is* he that readeth, and they that hear the words of this prophecy, and keep those things which are written therein : for [g] the time *is* at hand.

A. M. cir. 4100.
A. D. cir. 96.
Impp. Flavio
Domitiano
Cæs. Aug. et
Nerva.

4 JOHN to the seven Churches which are in Asia : Grace *be* unto you, and peace, from him [h] which is, and [i] which was, and which is to come ; [k] and from the seven

---

[a] John iii. 32.; viii. 26 ; xii. 49.——[b] Chapter iv. 1 ; verse 3. [c] Chap. xxii. 16.——[d] 1 Cor. i. 6 ; chap. vi. 9 ; xii. 17 ; ver. 9. [e] 1 John i. 1.——[f] Luke xi. 28 ; chap. xxii. 7.

[g] Rom. xiii. 11 ; James v. 8 ; 1 Pet. iv. 7 ; chapter xxii. 10. [h] Exod. iii. 14 ; ver. 8.——[i] John i. 1.——[k] Zech. iii. 9 ; iv. 10 ; chap. iii. 1 ; iv. 5 ; v. 6.

NOTES ON CHAP. I.

The Revelation of St. John the divine. To this book the *inscriptions* are various. "The Revelation.—The Revelation of John.—Of John the divine.—Of John the divine and evangelist.—The Revelation of John the apostle and evangelist.—The Revelation of the holy and glorious apostle and evangelist, the beloved virgin John the divine, which he saw in the island of Patmos.—The Revelation of Jesus Christ, given to John the divine." These several inscriptions are worthy of little regard ; the first verse contains the *title* of the book.

Verse 1. *The Revelation of Jesus Christ*] The word Αποκαλυψις, from which we have our word *Apocalypse*, signifies literally, a *revelation*, or *discovery* of what was *concealed* or *hidden*. It is here said that this *revelation*, or *discovery* of hidden things, was given by GOD to *Jesus Christ ;* that Christ gave it to his *angel ;* that this angel showed it to JOHN ; and that John sent it to the CHURCHES. Thus we find it came from God to Christ, from Christ to the angel, from the angel to John, and from John to the Church. It is properly, therefore, *the Revelation of God,* sent by these various agents *to his servants* at large ; and this is the proper title of the book.

Things which must shortly come to pass] On the mode of interpretation devised by *Wetstein,* this is plain ; for if the book were written *before* the destruction of Jerusalem, and the prophecies in it relate to that destruction, and the civil wars among the Romans, which lasted but *three* or *four years,* then it might be said the *Revelation* is of things which *must shortly come to pass.* But if we consider the book as referring to the state of the Church in all ages, the words here, and those in ver. 3, must be understood of the *commencement* of the events predicted ; as if he had said : In a short time the train of these visions will be put in motion.

———— *et incipient magni procedere menses.*

"And those times, pregnant with the most stupendous events, will begin to roll on."

Verse 2. *Who bare record of the word of God*] Is there a reference here to the first chapter of John's gospel, *In the beginning was the Word, and the Word was with God, &c.* ? Of this *Word* John did bear record. Or, does the writer mean the *fidelity* with which he noted and related the *word*—doctrines or prophecies, which he received at this time by revelation from God ? This seems more consistent with the latter part of the verse.

Verse 3. *Blessed is he that readeth*] This is to be understood of the happiness or security of. the persons who, reading and hearing the prophecies of those things which were to come to pass shortly, took proper measures to escape from the impending evils.

The time is at hand.] Either in which they shall be all fulfilled, or *begin* to be fulfilled. See the note on ver. 1.

These three verses contain the *introduction ;* now the *dedication* to the seven Churches commences.

Verse 4. *John to the seven Churches*] The apostle begins thus much in the manner of the Jewish prophets. They often name themselves in the messages which they receive from God to deliver to the people ; *e. g.* "The vision of ISAIAH, the son of Amoz, which he saw concerning Judah and Jerusalem." "The words of JEREMIAH, the son of Hilkiah ; to whom the word of the Lord came." "The word of the Lord came expressly unto EZEKIEL, the priest." "The word of the Lord that came unto HOSEA, the son of Beeri." "The word of the Lord that came to JOEL." "The words of AMOS, who was among the herdsmen of Tekoa." "The vision of OBADIAH ; thus saith the Lord." "The word of the Lord came unto JONAH." So, "The revelation of Jesus Christ, which he sent and signified to his servant JOHN." "JOHN to the seven Churches," &c.

The *Asia* here mentioned was what is called *Asia*

A. M. cir. 4100.
A. D. cir. 96.
Impp. Flavio
Domitiano
Cæs. Aug. et
Nerva.

Spirits which are before his throne ;

5 And from Jesus Christ, [1] *who is* the faithful witness, *and the* [m] first-begotten of the dead, and [n] the prince of the kings of the earth. Unto him [o] that

loved us, [p] and washed us from our sins in his own blood,

6 And hath [q] made us kings and priests unto God and his Father ; [r] to him *be* glory and dominion for ever and ever. Amen.

A. M. cir. 4100.
A. D. cir. 96.
Impp. Flavio
Domitiano
Cæs. Aug. et
Nerva.

---

[1] John viii. 14 ; 1 Tim. vi. 13 ; chap. iii. 14.——[m] 1 Cor. xv. 20 ; Col. i. 18.——[n] Eph. i. 20 ; chap. xvii. 14 ; xix. 16.——[o] John xiii. 44 ; xv. 9 ; Gal. ii. 20.

[p] Heb. ix. 14 ; 1 John i. 7.——[q] 1 Pet. ii. 5, 9 ; chap. v. 10 ; xx. 6.——[r] 1 Timothy vi. 16 ; Hebrews xiii. 21 ; 1 Peter iv. 11 ; v. 11.

Minor, or the *Lydian* or *Proconsular Asia ;* the *seven Churches* were those of *Ephesus, Smyrna, Pergamos, Thyatira, Sardis, Philadelphia,* and *Laodicea.* Of these as they occur. We are not to suppose that they were the only Christian Churches then in Asia Minor ; there were several others then in Phrygia, Pamphylia, Galatia, Pontus, Cappadocia, &c., &c. But these *seven* were those which lay nearest to the apostle, and were more particularly under his care ; though the message was sent to the Churches in general, and perhaps it concerns the whole Christian world. But the number *seven* may be used here as the *number of perfection ;* as the Hebrews use the *seven* names of the *heavens*, the *seven* names of the *earth*, the *seven patriarchs*, seven suns, seven kings, seven years, seven months, seven days, &c., &c. ; in which the rabbins find a great variety of mysteries.

Grace be unto you] This form of apostolical benediction we have often seen in the preceding epistles.

From him which is, and which was, and which is to come] This phraseology is purely Jewish, and probably taken from the Tetragrammaton, יהוה YEHOVAH; which is supposed to include in itself all time, *past, present,* and *future.* But they often use the phrase of which the ὁ ων, και ὁ ην, και ὁ ερχομενος, of the apostle, is a literal translation. So, in *Sohar Chadash*, fol. 7, 1 : " Rabbi Jose said, By the name Tetragrammaton, (*i. e.* יהוה Yehovah,) the higher and lower regions, the heavens, the earth, and all they contain, were perfected ; and they are all before him reputed as nothing ; והוא היה הוה והוא יהיה *vehu hayah, vehu hoveh, vehu yihyeh* ; and HE WAS, and HE IS, and HE WILL BE. So, in *Shemoth Rabba,* sec. 3, fol. 105, 2 : " The holy blessed God said to Moses, tell them— אני שהייתי ואני הוא עכשיו ואני הוא לעתיד לבוא *ani she-hayithi, veani hu achshaiv, veani hu laathid labo ;* I WAS, I NOW AM, and I WILL BE IN FUTURE."

In *Chasad Shimuel*, Rab. Samuel ben David asks : " Why are we commanded to use *three hours of prayer ?* Answer : These hours point out the holy blessed God ; שהוא היה הוה ויהיה *shehu hayah, hoveh, veyihyeh* ; he who WAS, who IS, and who SHALL BE. The MORNING prayer points out him who WAS before the foundation of the world ; the NOONDAY prayer points out him who IS ; and the EVENING prayer points out him who IS TO COME." This phraseology is exceedingly appropriate, and strongly expresses the *eternity* of God ; for we have no other idea of *time* than as *past*, or *now existing*, or *yet to exist* ; nor have we any idea of *eternity* but as that duration called by some *æternitas a parte ante*, the eternity that was before time, and *æternitas a parte post*, the endless duration

that shall be when time is no more. That which WAS, is the eternity *before time ;* that which IS, is *time itself ;* and that which IS TO COME, is the eternity which shall be when *time is no more.*

The seven Spirits—before his throne] The ancient Jews, who represented the throne of God as the *throne of an eastern monarch*, supposed that there were *seven ministering angels* before this throne, as there were *seven ministers* attendant on the throne of a Persian monarch. We have an ample proof of this, *Tobit* xii. 15 : *I am Raphael, one of the* SEVEN HOLY ANGELS *which present the prayers of the saints, and which go in and out before the glory of the Holy One.* And in *Jonathan ben Uzziel's* Targum, on Gen. xi. 7 : *God said to the* SEVEN ANGELS *which stand before him, Come now,* &c.

In *Pirkey Eliezer*, 4 and vii : " The angels which were first created minister before him without the veil." Sometimes they represent them as *seven cohorts* or *troops of angels*, under whom are *thirty* inferior orders.

That *seven* ANGELS are here meant, and not the *Holy Spirit*, is most evident from the *place*, the *number*, and the *tradition*. Those who imagine the *Holy Ghost* to be intended suppose the number *seven* is used to denote his manifold *gifts* and *graces.* That these *seven spirits* are *angels*, see chap. iii. 1 ; iv. 5 ; and particularly v. 6, where they are called *the seven spirits of God* SENT FORTH INTO ALL THE EARTH.

Verse 5. *The faithful witness*] The true teacher, whose testimony is infallible, and whose sayings must all come to pass.

The first-begotten of the dead] See the note on Col. i. 18.

The prince of the kings] Ὁ αρχων, The *chief* or *head*, of all earthly potentates ; who has them all under his dominion and control, and can dispose of them as he will.

Unto him that loved us] This should begin a new verse, as it is the commencement of a new subject. Our salvation is attributed to the love of God, who gave his Son ; and to the love of Christ, who died for us. See John iii. 16.

Washed us from our sins] The redemption of the soul, with the remission of sins, and purification from unrighteousness, is here, as in all the New Testament, attributed to the *blood of Christ shed on the cross for man.*

Verse 6. *Kings and priests*] See on 1 Pet. ii. 5, 9 But instead of βασιλεις και ιερεις, *kings and priests* the most reputable MSS., versions, and fathers, have βασιλειαν ιερεις, *a kingdom* and *priests* ; *i. e.* a kingdom of priests, or a royal priesthood. The *regal* and

2

A. M. cir. 4100.
A. D. cir. 96.
Impp. Flavio
Domitiano
Cæs. Aug. et
Nerva.

7 ^s Behold, he cometh with clouds ; and every eye shall see him, and ^t they *also* which pierced him : and all kindreds of the earth shall wail because of him. Even so, Amen.

8 ^u I am Alpha and Omega, the beginning and the ending, saith the Lord, ^v which is,

and which was, and which is to come, the Almighty.

9 I John, who also am your brother, and ^w companion in tribulation, and ^x in the kingdom and patience of Jesus Christ, was in the isle that is called Patmos, ^y for the word of God, and for the testimony of Jesus Christ.

A. M. cir. 4100.
A. D. cir. 96.
Impp. Flavio
Domitiano
Cæs. Aug. et
Nerva.

---

* Dan. vii. 13 ; Matt. xxiv. 30 ; xxvi. 64 ; Acts i. 11.——t Zech. xii. 10 ; John xix. 37.——u Isa. xli. 4 ; xliv. 6 ; xlviii. 12 ; ver. 17 ; chap. ii. 8 ; xxi. 6 ; xxii. 13 ; ver. 11.

v Verse 4 ; chap. iv. 8 ; xi. 17 ; xvi. 5.——w Phil. i. 7 ; iv. 14. 2 Tim. i. 8.——x Rom. viii. 17 ; 2 Tim. ii. 12.——y Chapter vi 9 ; ver. 2.

---

sacerdotal dignities are the two highest that can possibly exist among men ; and these two are here mentioned to show the glorious prerogatives and state of the children of God.

To him be *glory*] That is, to Christ ; for it is of him that the prophet speaks, and of none other.

For ever and ever] Εις τους αιωνας των αιωνων· To ages of ages ; or rather, *through all indefinite periods* ; *through all time*, and *through eternity.*

Amen.] A word of *affirmation* and *approbation ;* so it *shall* be, and so it *ought* to be.

Verse 7. *Behold, he cometh with clouds*] This relates to his coming to execute judgment on the enemies of his religion ; perhaps to his coming to destroy Jerusalem, as he was to be particularly manifested to them that *pierced him*, which must mean the incredulous and rebellious Jews.

And all kindreds of the earth] Πασαι αι φυλαι της γης· *All the tribes of the land.* By this the *Jewish people* are most evidently intended, and therefore the whole verse may be understood as predicting the destruction of the Jews ; and is a presumptive proof that the Apocalypse was written *before* the final overthrow of the Jewish state.

Even so, Amen.] Ναι, αμην· *Yea, Amen. It is true, so be it.* Our Lord will come and execute judgment on the Jews and Gentiles. This the Jews and Romans particularly felt.

Verse 8. *I am Alpha and Omega*] I am from eternity to eternity. This mode of speech is borrowed from the Jews, who express the *whole compass of things* by א *aleph* and ת *tau*, the *first* and *last* letters of the *Hebrew* alphabet ; but as St. John was writing in *Greek*, he accommodates the whole to the *Greek* alphabet, of which A *alpha* and Ω *omega* are the first and last letters. With the rabbins ת וער 'מא *mealeph vead tau*, " *from aleph to tau*," expressed the whole of a matter, *from the beginning to the end.* So in *Yalcut Rubeni*, fol. 17, 4 : *Adam transgressed the whole law from aleph to tau ;* i. e., from the beginning to the end.

Ibid., fol. 48, 4 : *Abraham observed the law, from aleph to tau ;* i. e., he kept it *entirely*, from *beginning to end.*

Ibid., fol. 128, 3 : *When the holy blessed God pronounced a blessing on the Israelites, he did it from aleph to tau ;* i. e., he did it *perfectly.*

The beginning and the ending] That is, as *aleph* or *alpha* is the *beginning* of the alphabet, so am I the author and cause of all things ; as *tau* or *omega* is the *end* or last letter of the alphabet, so am I the end of

all things, the destroyer as well as the establisher of all things. This clause is wanting in almost every MS. and version of importance. It appears to have been added first as an explanatory note, and in process of time crept into the text. Griesbach has left it out of the text. It is worthy of remark, that as the union of א *aleph* and ת *tau* in Hebrew make את *eth*, which the rabbins interpret of the *first matter* out of which all things were formed, (see on Gen. i. 1 ;) so the union of A *alpha* and Ω *omega*, in Greek, makes the verb *αω, I breathe*, and may very properly, in such a symbolical book, point out Him in whom we *live*, and *move*, and have our *being ;* for, having formed man out of the dust of the earth, he *breathed* into his nostrils the *breath* of life, and he became a *living soul ;* and it is by the *inspiration* or *inbreathing* of his Spirit that the souls of men are quickened, made alive from the dead, and fitted for life eternal. He adds also that he is the *Almighty*, the *all-powerful framer of the universe*, and the *inspirer of men.*

Verse 9. *Your brother*] A Christian, begotten of God, and incorporated in the heavenly *family.*

Companion in tribulation] Suffering under the persecution in which you also suffer.

In the kingdom] For we are a kingdom of priests unto God.

And patience of Jesus] Meekly bearing all indignities, privations, and sufferings, for the sake and after the example of our Lord and Master.

The isle that is called Patmos] This island is one of the *Sporades*, and lies in the *Ægean Sea*, between the island of *Icaria*, and the promontory of *Miletus.* It is now called *Pactino, Patmol*, or *Palmosa.* It has derived all its celebrity from being the place to which St. John was banished by one of the Roman emperors ; whether *Domitian*, *Claudius*, or *Nero*, is not agreed on, but it was most probably the latter. The island has a convent on a well fortified hill, dedicated to John the apostle ; the inhabitants are said to amount to about three hundred men, and about twenty women to one man. It is very barren, producing very little grain, but abounding in partridges, quails, turtles, pigeons, snipes, and rabbits. It has many good harbours, and is much infested by pirates. *Patmos*, its capital and chief harbour, lies in *east* LONG. 26° 24′, *north* LAT. 37° 24′. The whole island is about thirty miles in circumference.

For the testimony of Jesus Christ.] For preaching Christianity, and converting heathens to the Lord Jesus

2

A. M. cir. 4100.
A. D. cir. 96.
Impp. Flavio
Domitiano
Cæs. Aug. et
Nerva.

10 ˣ I was in the Spirit on ᵃ the Lord's day, and heard behind me ᵇ a. great voice, as of a trumpet,

11 Saying, ᶜ I am Alpha and Omega, ᵈ the first and the last: and, What thou seest, write in a book, and send *it* unto the seven Churches

which are in Asia; unto Ephesus, and unto Smyrna, and unto Pergamos, and unto Thyatira, and unto Sardis, and unto Philadelphia, and unto Laodicea.

12 And I turned to see the voice that spake with me. And being turned, ᵉ I

A. M. cir. 4100.
A. D. cir. 96.
Impp. Flavio
Domitiano
Cæs. Aug. et
Nerva.

ˣ Acts x. 10; 2 Cor. xii. 2; chap. iv. 2; xvii. 3; xxi. 10.
ᵃ John xx. 26; Acts xx. 7; 1 Cor. xvi. 2.

ᵇ Chap. iv. 1; x. 8.——ᶜ Ver. 8.——ᵈ Ver. 17.——ᵉ Ver. 20; Exod: xxv. 37; Zech. iv. 2.

Verse 10. *I was in the Spirit*] That is, I received the Spirit of prophecy, and was under its influence when the first vision was exhibited.

The Lord's day] The first day of the week, observed as the Christian Sabbath, because on it Jesus Christ rose from the dead; therefore it was called *the Lord's day*, and has taken place of the Jewish Sabbath throughout the Christian world.

And heard behind me a great voice] This voice came *unexpectedly* and *suddenly*. He felt himself under the Divine afflatus; but did not know what scenes were to be represented.

As of a trumpet] This was calculated to call in every wandering thought, to fix his attention, and solemnize his whole frame. Thus God prepared Moses to receive the law. See Exod. xix. 16, 19, &c.

Verse 11. *I am Alpha and Omega, the first and the last: and*] This whole clause is wanting in ABC, thirty-one others; some editions; the *Syriac, Coptic, Æthiopic, Armenian, Slavonic, Vulgate, Arethas, Andreas,* and *Primasius. Griesbach* has left it out of the text.

Saying—What thou seest, write in a book] Carefully note down every thing that is represented to thee. John had the visions from heaven; but he described them in his own language and manner.

Send it *unto the seven Churches*] The names of which immediately follow. *In Asia.* This is wanting in the principal MSS. and *versions. Griesbach* has left it out of the text.

Ephesus] This was a city of Ionia, in Asia Minor, situated at the mouth of the river *Cayster*, on the shore of the Ægean Sea, about fifty miles south of *Smyrna*. See *preface* to the Epistle to the *Ephesians*.

Smyrna] Now called also *Ismir*, is the largest and richest city of Asia Minor. It is situated about one hundred and eighty-three miles west by south of *Constantinople*, on the shore of the Ægean Sea. It is supposed to contain about one hundred and forty thousand inhabitants, of whom there are from fifteen to twenty thousand Greeks, six thousand Armenians, five thousand Roman Catholics, one hundred and forty Protestants, eleven thousand Jews, and fifteen thousand Turks. It is a beautiful city, but often ravaged by the plague, and seldom two years together free from earthquakes. In 1758 the city was nearly desolated by the plague; scarcely a sufficient number of the inhabitants survived to gather in the fruits of the earth. In 1688 there was a terrible earthquake here, which overthrew a great number of houses; in one of the shocks, the rock on which the castle stood opened, swallowed up the castle and five thousand persons! On these ac-

counts, nothing but the *love of gain*, so natural to man, could induce any person to make it his residence; though, in other respects, it can boast of many advantages. In this city the *Turks* have nineteen mosques; the *Greeks*, two churches; the *Armenians*, one; and the *Jews*, eight synagogues; and the *English* and *Dutch* factories have each a chaplain. Smyrna is one hundred miles north of the island of Rhodes, long. 27° 25′. E., lat. 38° 28′ N.

Pergamos] A town of Mysia, situated on the river *Caicus*. It was the royal residence of *Eumenes*, and the kings of the race of the *Attali*. It was anciently famous for its library, which contained, according to Plutarch, two hundred thousand volumes. It was here that the *membranæ Pergameniæ*, Pergamenian skins, were invented; from which we derive our word *parchment*. Pergamos was the birthplace of *Galen*; and in it *P. Scipio* died. It is now called *Pergamo* and *Bergamo*, and is situated in long. 27° 0′ E., lat. 39° 13′ N.

Thyatira] Now called *Akissat* and *Ak-kissar*, a city of Natolia, in Asia Minor, seated on the river *Hermus*, in a plain eighteen miles broad, and is about fifty miles from *Pergamos;* long. 27° 49′ E., lat. 38° 15′ N. The houses are chiefly built of earth, but the mosques are all of marble. Many remarkable ancient inscriptions have been discovered in this place.

Sardis] Now called *Sardo* and *Sart*, a town of Asia, in Natolia, about forty miles east from Smyrna. It is seated on the side of mount *Tmolus*, and was once the capital of the *Lydian kings*, and here *Crœsus* reigned. It is now a poor, inconsiderable village. Long. 28° 5′ E., lat. 37° 51′ N.

Philadelphia] A city of Natolia, seated at the foot of mount *Tmolus*, by the river *Cogamus*. It was founded by *Attalus Philadelphus*, brother of *Eumenes*, from whom it derived its name. It is now called *Alah-sheker*, and is about forty miles ESE. of Smyrna. Long. 28° 15′ E., lat. 38° 28′ N.

Laodicea] A town of Phrygia, on the river *Lycus;* first called *Diospolis*, or the city of Jupiter. It was built by Antiochus Theos, and named after his consort *Laodice.* See the note on Col. ii. 1. And, for a very recent account of these seven Churches, see a letter from the Rev. *Henry Lindsay*, inserted at the end of chap. iii.

Verse 12. *And I turned*] For he had heard the voice *behind* him. *To see the voice;* i. e., the person from whom the voice came.

Seven golden candlesticks] Ἑπτα λυχνιας χρυσας· *Seven golden lamps.* It is absurd to say, a golden silver, or brazen candle*stick*. These seven lamps re-

2

A. M. cir. 4100.
A. D. cir. 96.
Impp. Flavio
Domitiano
Cæs. Aug. et
Nerva.

saw seven golden candle-sticks;

13 [f] And in the midst of the seven candlesticks [g] *one* like unto the Son of man, [h] clothed with a garment down to the foot, and [i] girt about the paps with a golden girdle.

14 His head and [k] *his* hairs *were* white like

wool, as white as snow; [l] and his eyes *were* as a flame of fire;

15 [m] And his feet like unto fine brass, as if they burned in a furnace; and [n] his voice as the sound of many waters.

16 [o] And he had in his right hand seven stars; [p] and out of his mouth went a sharp

A. M. cir. 4100.
A. D. cir. 96.
Impp. Flavio,
Domitiano
Cæs. Aug. et
Nerva.

---

[f] Chap. ii. 1.——[g] Ezek. i. 26; Dan. vii. 13; x. 16; chap. xiv. 14.——[h] Dan. x. 5.——[i] Chap. xv. 6.——[k] Dan. vii. 9.——[l] Dan. x. 6; chap. ii. 18; xix. 12.——[m] Ezek. i. 7; Dan. x. 6; ch. ii. 18.

[n] Ezek. xliii. 2; Dan. x. 6; chap. xiv. 2; xix. 6.——[o] Ver. 20; chap. ii. 1; iii. 1.——[p] Isa. xlix. 2; Eph. vi. 17; Heb. iv. 12; chap. ii. 12, 16; xix. 15, 21.

---

presented the *seven Churches*, in which the *light* of God was continually *shining*, and the *love* of God continually *burning*. And they are here represented as *golden*, to show how *precious* they were in the sight of God. This is a reference to the temple at Jerusalem, where there was a *candlestick* or *chandelier* of *seven branches;* or rather six branches; three springing out on either side, and *one* in the centre. See Exod. xxxvii. 17–23. This reference to the temple seems to intimate that the temple of Jerusalem was a type of the whole Christian Church.

Verse 13. *Like unto the Son of man*] This seems a reference to Dan. vii. 13. This was our blessed Lord himself, ver. 18.

Clothed with a garment down to the foot] This is a description of the *high priest*, in his sacerdotal robes. See these described at large in the notes on Exod. xxviii. 4, &c., Jesus is our high priest, even in heaven. He is still discharging the sacerdotal functions before the throne of God.

Golden girdle.] The emblem both of *regal* and *sacerdotal* dignity.

Verse 14. *His head and his hairs were white like wool*] This was not only an emblem of his *antiquity*, but it was the evidence of his *glory;* for the *whiteness* or splendour of his head and hair doubtless proceeded from the *rays of light* and glory which encircled his head, and darted from it in all directions. The *splendour* around the head was termed by the Romans *nimbus,* and by us a *glory;* and was represented round the heads of gods, deified persons, and saints. It is used in the same way through almost all the nations of the earth.

His eyes were as a flame of fire] To denote his omniscience, and the all-penetrating nature of the Divine knowledge.

Verse 15. *His feet like unto fine brass*] An emblem of his *stability* and *permanence, brass* being considered the most durable of all metallic substances or compounds.

The original word, χαλκολιβανον, means the famous *aurichalcum,* or factitious metal, which, according to *Suidas,* was ειδος ηλεκτρου, τιμιωτερον χρυσου, "a kind of amber, more precious than gold." It seems to have been a composition of gold, silver, and brass, and the same with the *Corinthian brass,* so highly famed and valued; for when Lucius Mummius took and burnt the city of Corinth, many statues of these three metals, being melted, had run together, and formed the composition already mentioned, and which was held in as

high estimation as gold. See *Pliny,* Hist. Nat., lib. 34, c. 2; *Florus,* lib. 2, c. 16. It may however mean no more than *copper* melted with *lapis calaminaris,* which converts it into brass; and the flame that proceeds from the metal during this operation is one of the most intensely and unsufferably *vivid* that can be imagined. I have often seen several furnaces employed in this operation, and the flames bursting up through the earth (for these furnaces are under ground) always called to remembrance this description given by St. John: His feet of fine brass, *as if they burned in a furnace;* the propriety and accuracy of which none could doubt, and every one must feel who has viewed this most dazzling operation.

His voice as the sound of many waters.] The same description we find in Ezek. xliii. 2: *The glory of the God of Israel came from the way of the east;* and his voice was like the noise of many waters: *and the earth shined with his glory.*

Verse 16. *In his right hand seven stars*] The *stars* are afterwards interpreted as representing the *seven angels,* messengers, or bishops of the *seven Churches.* Their being in the *right hand* of Christ shows that they are under his special care and most powerful protection. See below.

Out of his mouth went a sharp two-edged sword] This is no doubt intended to point out the *judgments* about to be *pronounced* by Christ against the rebellious *Jews* and persecuting *Romans;* God's judgments were just now going to fall upon *both.* The *sharp two-edged sword* may represent the *word of God* in general, according to that saying of the apostle, Heb. iv. 12: *The word of God is quick and powerful, sharper than any two-edged sword, piercing even to the dividing asunder of soul and spirit, &c.* And the *word of God* is termed *the sword of the Spirit,* Eph. vi. 17.

And his countenance was as the sun shineth in his strength.] His face was like the disk of the sun in the brightest summer's day, when there were no clouds to abate the splendour of his rays. A similar form of expression is found in Judges v. 31: *Let them that love him be as the sun when he* GOETH FORTH IN HIS MIGHT. And a similar description may be found, *Midrash in Yalcut Simeoni,* part I., fol. 55, 4: " When Moses and Aaron came and stood before Pharaoh, they appeared like the *ministering angels;* and their stature, like the cedars of Lebanon; וגלגלי עיניהם דומים לגלגלי חמה *vegalgilley eyneyhem domim legalgilley chammah, and the pupils of their eyes were like the wheels of the sun;* and their beards were as the grape

2

A. M. cir. 4100.
A. D. cir. 96.
Impp. Flavio
Domitiano
Cæs. Aug. et
Nerva.

two-edged sword: ⁹ and his countenance *was* as the sun shineth in his strength.

17 And ʳ when I saw him, I fell at his feet as dead. And ˢ he laid his right hand upon me, saying unto me, Fear not; ᵗ I am the first and the last:

18 ᵘ *I am* he that liveth, and was dead; and, behold, ᵛ I am alive for evermore, Amen; and ʷ have the keys of hell and of death.

A. M. cir. 4100.
A. D. cir. 96.
Impp. Flavio
Domitiano
Cæs. Aug. et
Nerva.

19 Write ˣ the things which thou hast seen, ʸ and the things which are, ᶻ and the things which shall be hereafter.

20 The mystery ᵃ of the seven stars which thou sawest in my right hand, and ᵇ the seven golden candlesticks. The seven stars are ᶜ the angels of the seven Churches: and ᵈ the seven candlesticks which thou sawest are the seven Churches.

---

⁹ Acts xxvi. 13; chap. x. 1.——ʳ Ezek. i. 28.——ˢ Dan. viii. 18; x. 10.——ᵗ Isa. xli. 4; xliv 5; xlviii. 12; chap. ii. 8; xxii. 13; ver. 11.——ᵘ Rom. vi. 9.——ᵛ Chap. iv. 9; v. 14.

ʷ Psa. lxviii. 20; chap. xx. 1.——ˣ Ver. 12, &c.——ʸ Chap. ii. 1, &c.——ᶻ Chap. iv. 1, &c.——ᵃ Ver. 16.——ᵇ Ver. 12.——ᶜ Mal. ii. 7; chap. ii. 1, &c.——ᵈ Zech. iv. 2; Matt. v. 15; Phil. ii. 15.

---

of the palm trees; זיו פניהם כזיו חמה *veziv peneyhem keziv chammah, and the* SPLENDOUR *of* THEIR FACES *was as the* SPLENDOUR *of the* SUN."

Verse 17. *I fell at his feet as dead.*] The appearance of the *glory* of the Lord had the same effect upon Ezekiel, chap. i. 28: and the appearance of Gabriel had the same effect on Daniel, chap. viii. 17. The terrible splendour of such majesty was more than the apostle could bear, and he fell down deprived of his senses, but was soon enabled to behold the vision by a communication of strength from our Lord's right hand.

Verse 18. I am *he that liveth, and was dead*] I am Jesus the Saviour, who, though the fountain of life, have died for mankind; and being raised from the dead I shall die no more, the great sacrifice being consummated. *And have the keys of death and the grave,* so that I can destroy the living and raise the dead. The *key* here signifies the *power* and authority over life, death, and the grave. This is also a rabbinical form of speech. In the Jerusalem *Targum,* on Gen. xxx. 22, are these words: "There are four KEYS in the hand of God which he never trusts to angel or seraph. 1. The *key* of the *rain;* 2. The *key* of *provision;* 3. The *key* of the *grave;* and 4. The *key* of the *barren womb.*"

In *Sanhedrin,* fol. 113, 1, it is said: "When the son of the woman of Sarepta died, Elijah requested that to him might be given the *key* of the *resurrection of the dead.* They said to him, there are *three* KEYS which are not given into the hand of the apostle, the *key* of *life,* the *key* of the *rain,* and the *key* of the *resurrection of the dead.*" From these examples it is evident that we should understand ᾅδης, *hades,* here, not as *hell,* nor the place of *separate spirits,* but merely as the *grave;* and the *key* we *find* to be merely the emblem of *power* and *authority.* Christ can both *save* and *destroy,* can *kill* and make *alive.* Death is still under his dominion, and he can recall the dead whensoever he pleases. He is the resurrection and the life.

Verse 19. *Write the things which thou hast seen*] These visions and prophecies are for general instruction, and therefore every circumstance must be faithfully recorded. What he *had seen* was to be written; what he *was about* to see, relative to the seven Churches, must be also written; and what he was *to see afterwards,* concerning other Churches and states, was to be recorded likewise.

Verse 20. *The mystery*] That is, the *allegorical* explanation of the *seven stars* is the *seven angels* or ministers of the Churches; and the allegorical meaning of the *seven golden lamps* is the *seven Churches* themselves.

1. IN the *seven stars* there may be an allusion to the *seals* of different *offices* under potentates, each of which had its *own particular seal,* which verified all instruments from that office; and as these seals were frequently set in *rings* which were worn on the fingers, there may be an allusion to those *brilliants* set in rings, and worn επι της δεξιας, UPON *the right hand.* In Jer. xxii. 24, Coniah is represented as a *signet* on the *right hand of the Lord;* and that such signets were in *rings* see Gen. xxxviii. 18, 25; Exod. xxviii. 11; Dan. vi. 17; Hag. ii. 23. On close examination we shall find that all the *symbols* in this book have their foundation either in *nature, fact, custom,* or *general opinion.* One of the cutchery seals of the late *Tippoo Saib,* with which he stamped all the commissions of that office, lies now before me; it is cut on *silver,* in the *Taaleck* character, and the piece of silver is set in a large *gold ring,* heavy, but roughly manufactured.

2. The *Churches* are represented by these lamps; they hold the *oil* and the *fire,* and dispense the *light.* A lamp is not *light in itself,* it is only the *instrument* of dispensing light, and it must receive both *oil* and *fire* before it can dispense any; so no Church has in itself either *grace* or *glory,* it must receive all from Christ its head, else it can dispense neither light nor life.

3. The ministers of the Gospel are *signets* or *seals* of Jesus Christ; he uses them to *stamp* his truth, to *accredit* it, and give it *currency.* But as a seal can mark nothing of itself unless applied by a proper hand, so the ministers of Christ can do no good, *seal no truth, impress no soul,* unless the great owner condescend to use them.

4. How careful should the Church be that it have the *oil* and the *light,* that it continue to *burn* and send forth Divine knowledge! In vain does any Church pretend to be a Church of Christ if it dispense no light; if souls are not enlightened, quickened, and converted in it. If Jesus walk in it, its light will shine both **clearly** and **strongly,** and sinners will be con-

verted unto him; and the members of that Church will be children of the light, and walk as children of the light and of the day, and there will be no occasion of stumbling in them.

5. How careful should the ministers of Christ be that they *proclaim* nothing as *truth*, and *accredit* nothing as *truth*, but what comes from their master!

They should also take heed lest, after having preached to others, themselves should be cast-aways; lest God should say unto them as he said of Coniah, *As I live, saith the Lord, though Coniah, the son of Jehoiakim, were the* SIGNET UPON MY RIGHT HAND, *yet would I pluck thee thence.*

On the other hand, if they be faithful, their labour shall not be in vain, and their safety shall be great. He that toucheth them toucheth the apple of God's eye, and none shall be able to pluck them out of his hand. They are the angels and ambassadors of the Lord; their persons are sacred; they are the messengers of the Churches, and the glory of Christ. Should they lose their lives in the work, it will be only a *speedier* entrance into an eternal glory.

The *rougher* the way, the *shorter* their stay,
    The troubles that rise
Shall gloriously *hurry* their souls to the skies.

CHAPTER II.

The epistle to the Church of Ephesus, commending their labour and patience, 1–3. *And, reprehending their having left their first love, exhorting them to repent, with the promise of the tree of life,* 4–7. *The epistle to the Church of Smyrna, commending their piety, and promising them support in their tribulation,* 8–11. *The epistle to the Church of Pergamos, commending their steadfastness in the heavenly doctrine,* 12, 13. *And reprehending their laxity in ecclesiastical discipline, in tolerating heretical teachers in the Church,* 14, 15. *The apostle exhorts them to repent, with the promise of the white stone and a new name,* 16, 17. *The epistle to the Church of Thyatira, with a commendation of their charity, faith, and patience,* 18, 19. *Reprehending their toleration of Jezebel, the false prophetess, who is threatened with grievous punishment,* 20–23. *Particular exhortations and promises to this Church,* 24–29.

A. M. cir. 4100.
A. D. cir. 96.
Impp. Flavio
Domitiano
Cæs. Aug. et
Nerva.

UNTO the angel of the Church of Ephesus write; These things saith [a] he that holdeth the seven stars in his right hand, [b] who walketh in the midst of the seven golden candlesticks;

2 [c] I know thy works, and thy labour, and thy patience, and how

A. M. cir. 4100.
A. D. cir. 96.
Impp. Flavio
Domitiano
Cæs. Aug. et
Nerva.

---

[a] Chap. i. 16, 20.——[b] Chap. i. 13.

[c] Psa. i. 6; ver. 9, 13, 19; chap. iii. 1, 8, 15.

NOTES ON CHAP. II.

I must here advertise my readers, 1. That I do not perceive any metaphorical or allegorical meaning in the epistles to these Churches. 2. I consider the Churches as real; and that their spiritual state is here really and literally pointed out; and that they have no reference to the state of the Church of Christ in all ages of the world, as has been imagined; and that the notion of what has been termed the Ephesian state, the Smyrnian state, the Pergamenian state, the Thyatirian state, &c., &c., is unfounded, absurd, and dangerous; and such expositions should not be entertained by any who wish to arrive at a sober and rational knowledge of the Holy Scriptures. 3. I consider the angel of the Church as signifying the messenger, the pastor, sent by Christ and his apostles to teach and edify that Church. 4. I consider what is spoken to this angel as spoken to the whole Church; and that it is not *his* particular state that is described, but the states of the *people* in general under his care.

The epistle to the Church at Ephesus.

Verse 1. *Unto the angel of the Church of Ephesus*] By αγγελος, angel, we are to understand the *messenger* or person sent by God to preside over this Church; and to him the epistle is directed, not as pointing out his state, but the state of the Church

under his care. *Angel of the Church* here answers exactly to that officer of the synagogue among the Jews called צבור שליח *sheliach tsibbur*, the messenger of the Church, whose business it was to *read, pray,* and *teach* in the synagogue. The Church at Ephesus is *first* addressed, as being the place where John chiefly resided; and the city itself was the metropolis of that part of Asia. The angel or bishop at this time was most probably *Timothy*, who presided over that Church before St. John took up his residence there, and who is supposed to have continued in that office till A. D. 97, and to have been martyred a short time before St. John's return from Patmos.

Holdeth the seven stars] Who particularly preserves, and guides, and upholds, not only the ministers of those seven Churches, but all the genuine ministers of his Gospel, in all ages and places.

Walketh in the midst of the seven golden candlesticks] Is the supreme Bishop and Head, not only of those seven Churches, but of all the Churches or congregations of his people throughout the world.

Verse 2. *I know thy works*] For the eyes of the Lord are throughout the earth, beholding the evil and the good; and, being omnipresent, all things are continually open and naked before him. It is worthy of remark, that whatsoever is *praiseworthy* in any of these Churches is *first* mentioned; thereby intimating that

2

A. M. cir. 4100.
A. D. cir. 96.
Impp. Flavio
Domitiano
Cæs. Aug. et
Nerva.

thou canst not bear them which are evil: and ^d thou hast tried them ^e which say they are apostles, and are not, and hast found them liars:

3 And hast borne, and hast patience, and for my name's sake hast laboured, and hast ^f not fainted.

4 Nevertheless I have *somewhat* against thee,

because thou hast left thy first love.

A. M. cir. 4100.
A. D. cir. 96.
Impp. Flavio
Domitiano
Cæs. Aug. et
Nerva.

5 Remember therefore from whence thou art fallen, and repent, and do the first works; ^g or else I will come unto thee quickly, and will remove thy candlestick out of his place, except thou repent.

6 But this thou hast, that thou hatest the deeds of ^h the Nicolaitanes, which I also hate.

---

^d 1 John iv. 1.——^e 2 Cor. xi. 13; 2 Pet. ii. 1.

^f Gal. vi. 9; Heb. xii. 3, 5.——^g Matt. xxi. 41, 43.——^h Ver. 15

God is more intent on finding out the good than the evil in any person or Church; and that those who wish to reform such as have fallen or are not making sufficient advances in the Divine life, should take occasion, from the good which yet remains, to encourage them to set out afresh for the kingdom of heaven. The fallen or backsliding who have any tenderness of conscience left are easily discouraged, and are apt to think that there is no seed left from which any harvest can be reasonably expected. Let such be told that there is still a seed of godliness remaining, and that it requires only watching and strengthening the things which *remain*, by prompt application to God through Christ, in order to bring them back to the full enjoyment of all they have lost, and to renew them in the spirit of their mind. Ministers continually harping on *Ye are dead, ye are dead; there is little or no Christianity among you*, &c., &c., are a contagion in a Church, and spread desolation and death wheresoever they go. It is far better to say, in such cases, "Ye have *lost ground*, but ye have not lost *all* your *ground*; ye might have been much farther advanced, but through mercy ye are still in the *way*. The Spirit of God is grieved by you, but it is evident he has not forsaken you. Ye have not walked in the light as ye should, but your candlestick is not yet removed, and still the light shines. Ye have not *much* zeal, but ye have a *little*. In short, God still strives with you, still loves you, still waits to be gracious to you; take courage, set out afresh, come to God through Christ; believe, love, obey, and you will soon find days more blessed than you have ever yet experienced." Exhortations and encouragements of this kind are sure to produce the most blessed effects; and under such the work of God infallibly revives.

And thy labour] He knew their *works* in general. Though they had left their *first love*, yet still they had so much love as excited them to *labour*, and enabled them to *bear* persecution *patiently*, and to keep the faith; for they could not tolerate *evil men*, and they had put fictitious *apostles* to the *test*, and had found them to be *liars*, pretending a Divine commission while they had none, and teaching false doctrines as if they were the truths of God.

Verse 3. *And hast borne*] The same things mentioned in the preceding verse, but in an *inverted* order, the particular reason of which does not appear; perhaps it was intended to show more *forcibly* to this Church that there was no good which they had done, nor evil which they had suffered, that was forgotten before God.

And hast not fainted.] They must therefore have had a considerable portion of this love remaining, else they could not have thus acted.

Verse 4. *Nevertheless I have* somewhat *against thee*] The clause should be read, according to the Greek, thus: *But I have against thee that thou hast left thy first love.* They did not retain that strong and ardent affection for God and sacred things which they had when first brought to the knowledge of the truth, and justified by faith in Christ.

Verse 5. *Remember*] Consider the state of grace in which you once stood; the happiness, love, and joy which you felt when ye received remission of sins; the zeal ye had for God's glory and the salvation of mankind; your willing, obedient spirit, your cheerful self-denial, your fervour in private prayer, your detachment from the world, and your heavenly-mindedness. *Remember*—consider, all these.

Whence thou art fallen] Fallen from all those blessed dispositions and gracious feelings already mentioned. Or, *remember what a loss you have sustained;* for so εκπιπτειν is frequently used by the best Greek writers.

Repent] Be deeply humbled before God for having so carelessly guarded the Divine treasure.

Do the first works] Resume your former zeal and diligence; watch, fast, pray, reprove sin, carefully attend all the ordinances of God, walk as in his sight, and rest not till you have recovered all your lost ground, and got back the evidence of your acceptance with your Maker.

I will come unto thee quickly] In the way of judgment.

And will remove thy candlestick] Take away my ordinances, remove your ministers, and send you a famine of the word. As there is here an allusion to the candlestick in the tabernacle and temple, which could not be removed without suspending the whole Levitical service, so the threatening here intimates that, if they did not repent, &c., he would *unchurch* them; they should no longer have a pastor, no longer have the word and sacraments, and no longer have the presence of the Lord Jesus.

Verse 6. *The deeds of the Nicolaitanes*] These were, as is commonly supposed, a sect of the *Gnostics*, who taught the most impure doctrines, and followed the most impure practices. They are also supposed to have derived their origin from Nicolas, one of the seven deacons mentioned Acts vi. 5, where see the note. The *Nicolaitanes* taught the community

3

A. M. cir. 4100.
A. D. cir. 96.
Impp. Flavio
Domitiano
Cæs. Aug. et
Nerva.

7 ⁱHe that hath an ear, let him hear what the Spirit saith unto the Churches; To him that overcometh will I give ^k to eat of ^l the tree of life, which is in the midst of the paradise of God.

8 And unto the angel of the Church in Smyrna write; These things saith ^m the first

and the last, which was dead, and is alive;

9 ⁿI know thy works, and tribulation, and poverty, (but thou art ^o rich,) and *I know* the blasphemy of ^p them which say they are Jews and are not, ^q but *are* the synagogue of Satan.

10 ^r Fear none of those things which thou

A. M. cir. 4100.
A. D. cir. 96.
Impp. Flavio
Domitiano
Cæs. Aug. et
Nerva.

ⁱ Matt. xi. 15; xiii. 9, 43; ver. 11. 17, 29; chap. iii. 6, 13, 22; xiii. 9.——^k Chap. xxii. 2, 14.——^l Gen. ii. 9.——^m Chapter i. 8, 17, 18.——ⁿ Ver. 2.——^o Luke xii. 21; 1 Tim. vi. 18; James ii. 5.——^p Rom. ii. 17, 28, 29; ix. 6.——^q Chap. iii. 9.——^r Matt. x. 22.

---

of wives, that adultery and fornication were things indifferent, that eating meats offered to idols was quite lawful; and mixed several pagan rites with the Christian ceremonies. Augustine, Irenæus, Clemens Alexandrinus, and Tertullian, have spoken largely concerning them. See more in my preface to 2d Peter, where are several particulars concerning these heretics.

Verse 7. *He that hath an ear*] Let every intelligent person, and every Christian man, attend carefully to what the Holy Spirit, in this and the following epistles, says to the Churches. See the note on Matt. xi. 15, where the same form of speech occurs.

To him that overcometh] To him who continues steadfast in the faith, and uncorrupt in his life; who faithfully confesses Jesus, and neither imbibes the doctrines nor is led away by the error of the wicked; *will I give to eat of the tree of life.* As he who conquered his enemies had, generally, not only great *honour*, but also a *reward*; so here a great reward is promised τῷ νικῶντι, *to the conqueror*: and as in the Grecian games, to which there may be an allusion, the conqueror was crowned with the leaves of some *tree*; here it is promised that they should *eat of the fruit of the tree of life, which is in the midst of the paradise of God*; that is, that they should have a happy and glorious immortality. There is also here an allusion to Gen. ii. 9, where it is said, *God made the tree of life to grow out of the midst of the garden*; and it is very likely that by eating the fruit of this tree the immortality of Adam was secured, and on this it was made dependent. When Adam transgressed, he was expelled from this garden, and no more permitted to eat of the tree of life; hence he became necessarily mortal. This tree, in all its sacramental effects, is secured and restored to man by the incarnation, death, and resurrection of Christ. The *tree of life* is frequently spoken of by the rabbins; and by it they generally mean the immortality of the soul, and a final state of blessedness. See many examples in *Schoettgen.* They talk also of a *celestial* and *terrestrial paradise.* The former, they say, "is for the reception of the souls of the *just perfect*; and differs as much from the earthly paradise as light from darkness."

The Epistle to the Church at Smyrna.

Verse 8. *Unto the angel*] This was probably the famous Polycarp. See below.

These things saith the first and the last] He who is *eternal*; from whom all things come, and to whom all things must return. *Which was dead*, for the

redemption of the world; *and is alive* to die no more for ever, his glorified humanity being enthroned at the Father's right hand.

Verse 9. *I know thy works*] As he had spoken to the preceding Church, so he speaks to this : I know all that ye have *done*, and all that ye have *suffered.* The *tribulation* here mentioned must mean persecution, either from the Jews, the heathens, or from the heretics, who, because of their flesh-pampering doctrine, might have had many partisans at Smyrna.

And poverty] Stripped probably of all their temporal possessions, because of their attachment to the Gospel.

But thou art rich] Rich in faith, and heir of the kingdom of Christ.

The blasphemy of them which say they are Jews] There were persons there who professed *Judaism*, and had a synagogue in the place, and professed to worship the true God; but they had no genuine religion, and they served the devil rather than God. They applied a sacred name to an unholy thing: and this is one meaning of the word *blasphemy* in this book.

Verse 10. *Fear none of those things which thou shalt suffer*] This may be addressed particularly to *Polycarp*, if he was at that time the bishop of this Church. He had much to suffer; and was at last burnt alive at Smyrna, about the year of our Lord 166. We have a very ancient account of his martyrdom, which has been translated by *Cave*, and is worthy of the reader's perusal. That account states that the *Jews* were particularly active in this martyrdom, and brought the fagots, &c., by which they were consumed. Such persons must indeed have been of *the synagogue of Satan.*

Ten days] As the *days* in this book are what is commonly called *prophetic days*, each answering to a *year*, the *ten days* of tribulation may denote *ten years of persecution*; and this was precisely the duration of the persecution under *Diocletian*, during which all the Asiatic Churches were grievously afflicted. Others understand the expression as implying *frequency* and *abundance*, as it does in other parts of Scripture. Gen. xxxi. 7, 41 : *Thou hast changed my wages* TEN TIMES; i. e. thou hast *frequently* changed my wages. Num. xiv. 22 : *Those men have tempted me now these* TEN TIMES; i. e. they have *frequently* and grievously tempted and sinned against me. Neh. iv. 12 : *The Jews that dwelt by them came and said unto us* TEN TIMES, i. e. they were *frequently* coming and informing us, that our adversaries intended to attack us. Job xix. 3 ; *These* TEN TIMES *have ye reproached me*; i. e. ye have

A. M. cir. 4100.
A. D. cir. 96.
Impp. Flavio
Domitiano
Cæs. Aug. et
Nervа.
shalt suffer: behold, the devil shall cast *some* of ycu into prison, that ye may be tried; and ye shall have tribulation ten days: [s] be thou faithful unto death, and I will give thee [t] a crown of life.

11 [u] He that hath an ear, let him hear what the Spirit saith unto the Churches; He that overcometh shall not be hurt of [v] the second death.

12 And to the angel of the Church in Pergamos write; These things saith [w] he which hath the sharp sword with two edges,

---

[s] Matt. xxiv. 13.——[t] James i. 12; chap. iii. 11.——[u] Ver. 7; chapter xiii. 19.——[v] Chapter xx. 14; xxi. 8.——[w] Chapter i. 16. [x] Ver. 2.——[y] Ver. 9.

---

13 [x] I know thy works, and where thou dwellest, *even* [y] where Satan's seat *is:* and thou holdest fast my name, and hast not denied my faith, even in those days wherein Antipas *was* my faithful martyr, who was slain among you, where Satan dwelleth.

14 But I have a few things against thee, because thou hast there them that hold the doctrine of [z] Balaam, who taught Balac to cast a stumbling-block before the children of Israel, [a] to eat things sacrificed unto idols, [b] and to commit fornication.

A. M. cir. 4100.
A. D. cir. 96.
Impp. Flavio
Domitiano
Cæs. Aug. et
Nerva.

---

[z] Num. xxiv. 14; xxv. 1; xxxi. 16; 2 Pet. ii. 15; Jude 11. [a] Ver. 20; Acts xv. 29; 1 Cor. viii. 9, 10; x. 19, 20.——[b] 1 Cor. vi. 13, &c.

---

loaded me with *continual* reproaches. Dan. i. 20: *In all matters of wisdom, he found them* TEN TIMES *better than all the magicians;* i. e. the king frequently consulted Daniel and his companions, and found them *more abundantly informed* and *wise* than all his counsellors.

Some think the *shortness* of the affliction is here intended, and that the ten days are to be understood as in Terence, *Heaut.*, Act v., scen. 1, ver. 36, *Decem dierum vix mi est familia.* " I have enjoyed my family but a *short* time."

Be thou faithful unto death] Be firm, hold fast the faith, confess Christ to the last, and at all hazards, and thou shalt have *a crown of life*—thou shalt be crowned with life, have an eternal happy existence, though thou suffer a temporal death. It is said of *Polycarp* that when brought before the judge, and commanded to abjure and blaspheme Christ, he firmly answered, "Eighty and six years have I served him, and he never did me wrong, how then can I blaspheme my king who hath saved me!" He was then adjudged to the flames, and suffered cheerfully for Christ his Lord and Master.

Verse 11. *He that overcometh*] The *conqueror* who has stood firm in every trial, and vanquished all his adversaries.

Shall not be hurt of the second death.] That is, an eternal separation from God and the glory of his power; as what we commonly mean by *final perdition*. This is another rabbinical mode of speech in very frequent use, and by it they understand the punishment of hell in a future life.

The Epistle to the Church at Pergamos.

Verse 12. *The angel of the Church in Pergamos*] See the description of this place, chap. i. 2.

Which hath the sharp sword] See on chap. i. 16. The *sword of the Spirit, which is the word of God*, cuts every way; it convinces of sin, righteousness, and judgment; pierces between the joints and the marrow, divides between the soul and spirit, dissects the whole mind, and exhibits a regular anatomy of the soul. It not only reproves and exposes sin, but it slays the ungodly, pointing out and determining the punishment

they shall endure. Jesus has the sword with the two edges, because he is the Saviour of sinners, and the Judge of quick and dead.

Verse 13. *Where Satan's seat* is] Ὅπου ὁ θρονος του Σατανα· *Where Satan has his throne*—where he *reigns* as king, and is universally obeyed. It was a maxim among the Jews, that where the law of God was *not* studied, there Satan dwelt; but he was obliged to leave the place where a synagogue or academy was established.

Thou holdest fast my name] Notwithstanding that the profession of *Christianity* exposed this Church to the bitterest persecution, they held fast the name of *Christian*, which they had received from Jesus Christ, and *did not deny his faith;* for when brought to the trial they openly professed themselves disciples and followers of their Lord and Master.

Antipas was *my faithful martyr*] Who this *Antipas* was we cannot tell. We only know that he was a *Christian*, and probably bore some office in the Church, and became illustrious by his martyrdom in the cause of Christ. There is a work extant called *The Acts of Antipas*, which makes him bishop of Pergamos, and states that he was put to death by being enclosed in a burning brazen bull. But this story confutes itself, as the Romans, under whose government Pergamos then was, never put any person to death in this way. It is supposed that he was murdered by some mob, who chose this way to vindicate the honour of their god *Æsculapius*, in opposition to the claims of our Lord Jesus.

Verse 14. *I have a few things against thee*] Their *good deeds* are first carefully sought out and commended; what was *wrong* in them is touched with a gentle but effectual hand.

The followers of Balaam, the Nicolaitanes, and the Gnostics, were probably all the same kind of persons; but see on ver. 6. What the doctrine of Balaam was, see the notes on Num. xxiv., xxv., and xxxi. It appears that there were some then in the Church at Pergamos who held eating things offered to idols in honour of those idols, and fornication, indifferent things. They associated with idolaters in the heathen temples, and partook with them in their religious festivals.

A. M. cir. 4100.
A. D. cir. 96.
Impp. Flavio
Domitiano
Cæs. Aug. et
Nerva.

15 So hast thou also them that hold the doctrine ^c of the Nicolaitanes, which thing I hate.

16 Repent; or else I will come unto thee quickly, ^d and will fight against them with the sword of my mouth.

17 ^e He that hath an ear, let

A. M. cir. 4100.
A. D. cir. 96.
Impp. Flavio
Domitiano
Cæs. Aug. et
Nerva.

---

^c Ver. 6.——^d Isa. xi. 4; 2 Thess. ii. 8; chap. i. 16; xix. 15, 21.

^e Ver. 7, 11.

Verse 15. *The doctrine of the Nicolaitanes*] See on ver. 6.

Verse 16. *Will fight against them with the sword of my mouth.*] See on ver. 12. He now speaks for their edification and salvation; but if they do not repent, he will shortly declare those judgments which shall unavoidably fall upon them.

Verse 17. *The hidden manna*] It was a constant tradition of the Jews that the ark of the covenant, the tables of stone, Aaron's rod, the holy anointing oil, and the pot of manna, were *hidden* by King Josiah when Jerusalem was taken by the Chaldeans; and that these shall all be restored in the days of the Messiah. This *manna* was *hidden*, but Christ promises to give it to him that is conqueror. Jesus is the ark, the oil, the rod, the testimony, and the manna. He who is partaker of his grace has all those things in their spiritual meaning and perfection.

And will give him a white stone] I. It is supposed that by the white stone is meant *pardon* or *acquittance*, and the evidence of it; and that there is an allusion here to the custom observed by judges in ancient times, who were accustomed to give their suffrages by *white* and *black* pebbles; those who gave the former were for *absolving* the culprit, those who gave the latter were for his *condemnation*. This is mentioned by Ovid, Metam. lib. xv., ver. 41:

Mos erat antiquus, niveis atrisque lapillis,
His damnare reos, illis absolvere culpa.
Nunc quoque sic lata est sententia tristis.

"A custom was of old, and still remains,
Which life or death by suffrages ordains:
White stones and *black* within an *urn* are cast,
The *first absolve*, but *fate* is in the *last*."
              DRYDEN.

II. Others suppose there is an allusion here to conquerors in the public games, who were not only conducted with great pomp into the city to which they belonged, but had a *white stone* given to them, with their name inscribed on it; which badge entitled them, during their whole life, to be maintained at the public expense. See *Pind.*, *Olymp.* vii. 159, and the *Scholia* there; and see the collections in *Wetstein*, and *Rosenmüller's* note. These were called *tesseræ* among the Romans, and of these there were several kinds.

1. *Tesseræ conviviales*, which answered exactly to our *cards of invitation*, or tickets of admission to a public feast or banquet; when the person invited produced his *tessera* he was admitted. The mention of the *hidden manna* here may seem to intimate that there is a reference to these *convivial tesseræ*, whether given to the victor in the public games, entitling him to be fed at the public expense, or to a particular friend, inviting him to a family meal or to a public banquet.

2 There were *tesseræ* inscribed with different kinds of things, such as provisions, garments, gold or silver vessels, horses, mares, slaves, &c. These were sometimes thrown by the Roman emperors among the crowd in the theatres, and he that could snatch one; and on producing it he received that, the name of which was inscribed on it. But from *Dio Cassius* it appears that those *tesseræ* were small wooden balls, whereas the *tesseræ* in general were *square*, whence they had their name, as having *four sides, angles,* or *corners*. *Illi* τεσσαρην, *vel* τεσσαραν, *vocabant figuram quamvis* quadratam, *quæ* quatuor angulos *haberet;* and these were made of *stone, marble, bone,* or *ivory, lead, brass,* or other metal. See *Pitiscus*.

3. *Tesseræ frumentariæ*, or tickets to receive grain in the public distributions of corn; the *name* of the person who was to receive, and the *quantum* of grain, being both *inscribed* on this badge or ticket. Those who did not need this public provision for themselves were permitted to sell their ticket, and the *bearer* was entitled to the quantum of grain mentioned on it.

4. But the most remarkable of these instruments were the *tesseræ hospitales*, which were given as badges of *friendship* and *alliance*, and on which some device was engraved, as a testimony that a contract of friendship had been made between the parties. A small oblong square piece of wood, bone, stone, or ivory, was taken and divided into two equal parts, on which each of the parties wrote his own name, and then interchanged it with the other. This was carefully preserved, and handed down even to posterity in the same family; and by producing this when they travelled, it gave a mutual claim to the bearers of kind reception and hospitable entertainment at each other's houses.

It is to this custom that *Plautus* refers in his PŒNULUS, act. v., scen. 2, ver. 80, in the interview between *Agorastocles*, and his unknown uncle *Hanno*.

HANNO.—O mi popularis, salve!
AGORASTOCLES.—— —— Et tu edepol, quisquis es,
Et si quid opus est, quæso, dic atque impera,
Popularitatis caussa.
HAN.—— —— Habeo gratiam.
Verum ego hic hospitium habeo: Antidamæ filium
Quæro; commonstra, si novisti, Agorastoclem.
Ecquem adolescentem tu hic novisti Agorastoclem?
AGOR.—Siquidem tu Antidamarchi quæris adoptatitium,
Ego sum ipsus, quem tu quæris.
HAN.—— —— Hem! quid ego audio?
AGOR.—Antidamæ me esse.
HAN.—— —— si ita est, *tesseram*
Conferre si vis *hospitalem*, eccam adtuli.
AGOR.—Agedum huc ostende; est par probe: nam habeo domi.
HAN.—O mi hospes, salve multum! nam mihi tuus pater,

A. M. cir. 4100.
A. D. cir. 96.
Impp. Flavio
Domitiano
Cæs. Aug. et
Nerva.

him hear what the Spirit saith unto the Churches; To him that overcometh will I give to eat of the hidden manna, and will give him a white stone, and in the stone f a new name written, which no man knoweth saving he that receiveth *it.*

f Chap. iii. 12; xix. 12.

18 And unto the angel of the Church in Thyatira write; These things saith the Son of God, g who hath his eyes like unto a flame of fire, and his feet *are* like fine brass;

19 h I know thy works, and charity, and service, and faith, and thy patience, and thy

A. M. cir. 4100
A. D. cir. 96.
Impp. Flavio
Domitiano
Cæs. Aug. et
Nerva.

g Chap. i. 14, 15.——h Ver. 2.

Pater tuus ergo, hospes Antidamas fuit.
Hæc mihi *hospitalis tessera* cum illo fuit.

AGOR.——Ergo hic apud me hospitium tibi præbebitur.

Nam haud repudio hospitium, neque Carthaginem: Inde sum oriundus.

HAN.—— —— Di dent tibi omnes quæ velis.

HANNO.——Hail, my countryman!

AGORASTOCLES.——I hail thee also, in the name of Pollux, whosoever thou art. And if thou have need of any thing, speak, I beseech thee; and thou shalt obtain what thou askest, for civility's sake.

HANNO.——I thank thee, but I have a lodging here; I seek the son of Antidamas. Tell me if thou knowest Agorastocles. Dost thou know in this place the young Agorastocles?

AGORASTOCLES.——If thou seek the adopted son of Antidamarchus, I am the person whom thou seekest.

HANNO.——Ha! What do I hear?

AGORASTOCLES.——Thou hearest that *I am* the son of Antidamas.

HANNO.——If it be so, compare, if thou pleasest, the *hospitable tessera;* here it is, I have brought it with me.

AGORASTOCLES.——Come then, reach it hither: it is the exact counterpart; I have the other at home.

HANNO.——O my friend, I am very glad to see thee, for thy father was my friend; therefore Antidamas thy father was my guest. I divided *this hospitable tessera* with him.

AGORASTOCLES.——Therefore, a lodging shall be provided for thee with me; I reverence hospitality, and I love Carthage, where I was born.

HANNO.——May all the gods grant thee whatsoever thou wishest!

The *tessera* taken in this sense, seems to have been a kind of *tally;* and the two parts were compared together to ascertain the truth. Now it is very probable that St. John may allude to this; for on this mode of interpretation every part of the verse is consistent. 1. The word ψηφος does not necessarily signify a *stone* of any kind, but a suffrage, sentence, decisive vote; and in this place seems answerable to the *tessera.* The tessera which Hanno had, he tells us in his *Punic* language, was inscribed with the image or name of his god. "Sigillum hospitii *mei est tabula sculpta, cujus sculptura* est Deus meus.' This is the interpretation of the Punic words at the beginning of the above 5th act of the *Pœnulus,* as given by *Bochart.* 2. The person who held it had a right to entertainment in the house of him who originally gave it; for it was in reference to this that the *friendly contract* was made. 3. The *names* of the contracting persons, or

some *device,* were written on the tessera, which commemorated the friendly contract; and as the *parts* were *interchanged, none could know* that *name* or *device,* or the *reason* of the contract, *but he who received it.* 4. This, when produced, gave the bearer a right to the offices of hospitality; he was accommodated with food, lodging, &c., as far as these were necessary; and to this the *eating of the hidden manna* may refer.

But what does this mean in the language of Christ? 1. That the person is taken into an intimate state of friendship with him. 2. That this contract is witnessed to the party by some especial token, sign, or seal, to which he may have recourse to support his claim, and identify his person. This is probably what is elsewhere called the *earnest of the Spirit;* see the note on Eph. i. 14, and the places there referred to. He then who has received and retains the witness of the Spirit that he is *adopted* into the *heavenly family,* may humbly claim, in virtue of it, his support of the bread and water of life; the *hidden manna*—every grace of the Spirit of God; and the *tree of life*—immortality, or the final glorification of his body and soul throughout eternity. 3. By this state of grace into which he is brought he acquires a *new name,* the name of *child of God;* the earnest of the Spirit, the *tessera,* which he has received, shows him this new name. 4. And this name of child of God *no man can know* or understand, but he who has received the *tessera* or Divine witness. 5. As his Friend and Redeemer may be found everywhere, because he fills the heavens and the earth, everywhere he may, on retaining this *tessera,* claim direction, succour, support, grace, and glory; and therefore the privileges of him who overcometh are the greatest and most glorious that can be imagined.

For a farther account of the *tessera* of the ancients, as well as for engravings of several, see *Grævii Thesaur.; Pitisci* Lexic.; and *Poleni* Supplement; and the authors to whom these writers refer.

The Epistle to the Church at Thyatira.

Verse 18. *These things saith the Son of God*] See the notes on chap. i. 14, 15.

Verse 19. *I know thy works*] And of these he first sets forth their *charity,* την αγαπην, their *love* to God and each other; and particularly to the *poor* and *distressed:* and hence followed their *faith,* την πιστιν, their *fidelity,* to the grace they had received; and *service,* την διακονιαν, and ministration; properly pious and benevolent service to widows, orphans, and the poor in general.

And thy patience] Την υπομονην σου· Thy *perseverance* under *afflictions* and *persecutions,* and thy

A. M. cir. 4100
A. D. cir. 96.
Impp. Flavio
Domitiano
Cæs. Aug. et
Nerva.

works; and the last *to be* more than the first.

20 Notwithstanding I have a few things against thee, because thou sufferest that woman ^i Jezebel, which calleth herself a prophetess, to teach and to seduce my servants ^k to commit fornication, and to eat things sacrificed unto idols.

21 And I gave her space ^l to repent of her fornication; and she repented not.

A. M. cir. 4100.
A. D. cir. 96.
Impp. Flavio
Domitiano
Cæs. Aug. et
Nerva.

22 Behold, I will cast her into a bed, and them that commit adultery with her into great tribulation, except they repent of their deeds.

23 And I will kill her children with death; and all the Churches shall know that ^m I am he which searcheth the reins and hearts; and ^n I will give unto every one of you according to your works.

---

^i 1 Kings xvi. 31; xxi. 25; 2 Kings ix. 7.——^k Exod. xxxiv. 15; Acts xv. 20, 29; 1 Cor. x. 19, 20; ver. 14.——^l Rom. ii. 4; chap. ix. 20.——^m 1 Sam. xvi. 7; 1 Chron. xxviii. 9; xxix. 17;

2 Chron. vi. 30; Psa. vii. 9; Jer. xi. 20; xvii. 10; xx. 12; John ii. 24, 25; Acts i. 24; Rom. viii. 27.——^n Psa. lxii. 12; Matt. xvi. 27; Rom. ii. 6; xiv. 12; 2 Cor. v. 10; Gal. vi. 5; ch. xx. 12.

---

continuance in well-doing. I put *faith* before *service* according to the general consent of the best MSS. and versions.

Thy works] The continued labour of love, and thorough obedience.

The last to be *more than the first*.] They not only *retained* what they had received at first, but *grew* in grace, and in the knowledge and love of Jesus Christ. This is a rare thing in most Christian Churches: they generally lose the power of religion, and rest in the forms of worship; and it requires a powerful *revival* to bring them to such a state that their last works shall be more than their first.

Verse 20. *That woman Jezebel*] There is an allusion here to the history of Ahab and Jezebel, as given in 2 Kings ix., x.; and although we do not know who this Jezebel was, yet from the allusion we may take it for granted she was a woman of power and influence in Thyatira, who corrupted the true religion, and harassed the followers of God in that city, as Jezebel did in Israel. Instead of *that woman Jezebel*, την γυναικα Ιεζαβηλ, many excellent MSS., and almost all the ancient versions, read την γυναικα σου Ιεζαβηλ, THY WIFE *Jezebel;* which intimates, indeed asserts, that this bad woman was the wife of the bishop of the Church, and his criminality in suffering her was therefore the greater. This reading Griesbach has received into the text. She called herself a prophetess, i. e., set up for a teacher; taught the Christians that fornication, and eating things offered to idols, were matters of indifference, and thus they were seduced from the truth. But it is probable that by *fornication* here is meant *idolatry* merely, which is often its meaning in the Scriptures. It is too gross to suppose that the wife of the bishop of this Church could teach fornication literally. The messenger or bishop of this Church, probably her *husband, suffered* this: he had power to have cast her and her party out of the Church, or, as his *wife*, to have restrained her; but he did not do it, and thus she had every opportunity of seducing the faithful. This is what Christ had *against* the messenger of this Church.

Verse 21. *I gave her space to repent*] "This alludes to the history of Jezebel. God first sent Elijah to Ahab to pronounce a severe judgment upon him; upon which Ahab showed tokens of repentance, and so God put off his punishment. By these means the

like punishment pronounced against Jezebel was also put off. Thus God gave *her* time to repent, which she did not, but instead of that seduced *her sons* to the same sins. See 1 Kings xxi. According to the Mosaical law, the punishment of idolatrous seducers was not to be delayed at all, but God sometimes showed mercy; and now much more under the Christian dispensation, though that mercy is often abused, and thus produces the contrary effect, as in the case of this Jezebel. See Eccles. viii. 11.

Verse 22. *Behold, I will cast her into a bed*] "This again alludes to the same history. Ahaziah, son of Ahab and Jezebel, by his mother's ill instruction and example, followed her ways. God punished him by making him fall down, as is supposed, from the top of the terrace over his house, and so to be bedridden for a long time under great anguish, designing thereby to give him time to repent; but when, instead of that, he sent to consult Baalzebub, Elijah was sent to pronounce a final doom against his impenitence. Thus the *son of Jezebel*, who had committed idolatry with and by her advice, was long *cast into the bed of affliction*, and not repenting, died: in the same manner his brother Jehoram succeeded likewise. All this while Jezebel had *time* and warning enough to *repent;* and though she did not prevail with Jehoram to continue in the idolatrous worship of Baal, yet she persisted in her own way, notwithstanding God's warnings. The sacred writer, therefore, here threatens the *Gnostic Jezebel* to make that wherein she delighteth, as adulterers in the bed of lust, to be the very place, occasion, and instrument, of her greatest torment. So in Isaiah, the *bed* is made a symbol of *tribulation*, and *anguish* of body and mind. See Isa xxviii. 20; Job xxxiii. 19.

Verse 23. *And I will kill her children with death*] "That is, I will certainly destroy her offspring and memory, and thereby ruin her designs. Jezebel's two sons, being both kings were both slain; and after that, all the seventy sons of Ahab; (2 Kings x. 1;) in all which the hand of God was very visible. In the same manner God predicts the destruction of the heretics and heresies referred to; see ver. 16. It should seem by the expression, *I am he which searcheth the reins and the hearts*, that these heretics lurked about, and sowed their pernicious doctrines *secretly*. But our Saviour tells them that it was in vain, for he had

A. M. cir. 4100.
A. D. cir. 96.
Impp. Flavio
Domitiano
Cæs. Aug. et
Nerva.

24 But unto you I say, and unto the rest in Thyatira, as many as have not this doctrine, and which have not known the depths of Satan, as they speak; ° I will put upon you none other burden.

25 But ᵖ that which ye have *already,* hold fast till I come.

26 And he that overcometh, and keepeth ᑫ my works unto the end, ʳ to him will

I give power over the na-tions :

27 ˢ And he shall rule them with a rod of iron ; as the vessels of a potter shall they be broken to shivers : even as I received of my Father.

28 And I will give him ᵗ the morning star.

29 ᵘ He that hath an ear, let him hear what the Spirit saith unto the Churches.

A. M. cir. 4100.
A. D. cir. 96.
Impp. Flavio
Domitiano
Cæs. Aug. et
Nerva.

° Acts xv. 28.——ᵖ Chap. iii. 11.——ᑫ John vi. 29 ; 1 John iii. 23.——ʳ Matt. xix. 28; Luke xxii. 29, 30 ; 1 Cor. vi. 3 ; chap. iii. 21 ; xx. 4.——ˢ Psa. ii. 8, 9 ; xlix. 14; Dan. vii. 22 ; chap. xix. 15 ; xii. 5.——ᵗ 2 Pet. i. 19 ; chap. xxii. 16.——ᵘ Ver. 7.

---

power to bring their deeds to light, having that Divine power of searching into the wills and affections of men ; and hereby he would show both them and us that he is, according to his title, *The Son of God ;* and hath such *eyes* to pry into their actions, that, like a *fire,* they will search into every thing, and burn up the chaff which cannot stand his trial ; so that the *depths of Satan,* mentioned in the next verse, to which this alludes, (Christ assuming here this title purposely,) shall avail nothing to those who think by their secret craft to undermine the Christian religion ; he will not only bring to light but baffle all their evil intentions. See chap. xvii. 9.

Verse 24. *But unto you I say, and unto the rest*] " But unto the rest, &c. This is the reading of the Complutensian, and seems preferable to the common one, as it evidently shows that the rest of the epistle wholly concerns the faithful, who have not received the former doctrine of error. *I will put upon you none other burden* is a commendation of the sound part of the Church, that they have no need of any new exhortation or charge to be given them, no new advice but to persevere as usual. See Rom. xv. 14, 15. The expression of *burden* is taken from the history of Ahab, 2 Kings ix. 25 : *The Lord laid this burden on him ;* a word often used by the prophets to signify a prophecy threatening heavy things to be suf-fered. See on Isa. xiii. 1, and Num. iv. 19." See Dodd's Notes.

It is worthy of remark that the Gnostics called their doctrine *the depths of God,* and *the depths of Bythos,* intimating that they contained the most *pro-found secrets* of Divine wisdom. Christ here calls them the *depths of Satan,* being master pieces of his *subtlety.* Perhaps they thought them to be of God, while all the time they were deceived by the devil.

Verse 25. *That which ye have*] That is, the pure doctrine of the Gospel, *hold fast till I come*—till I come to execute the judgments which I have threatened.

Verse 26. *Power over the nations*] Every wit-ness of Christ has power to confute and confound all the false doctrines and maxims of the nations of the world, for Christianity shall at last rule over all ; the kingdom of Christ will come, and the kingdoms of this world become the kingdoms of our God and of his Christ.

Verse 27. *He shall rule them with a rod of iron*] He shall restrain vice by the *strictest administration of justice ;* and those who finally despise the word and rebel shall be *broken* and destroyed, so as never more to be able to make head against the truth. This seems to refer to the *heathen* world ; and perhaps Constan-tine the Great may be intended, who, when he over-came Licinius, became the instrument in God's hand of destroying *idolatry* over the whole Roman empire ; and it was so effectually *broken* as to be ever after like the fragments of an *earthen vessel,* of no use in them-selves, and incapable of being ever united to any good purpose.

Verse 28. *And I will give him the morning star.*] He shall have the brightest and most glorious empire, next to that of Christ himself. And it is certain that the Roman empire under Constantine the Great was the brightest emblem of the latter day glory which has ever yet been exhibited to the world. It is well known that *sun, moon,* and *stars* are emblems, in pro-phetic language, of *empires, kingdoms,* and *states.* And as the *morning star* is that which immediately precedes the rising of the sun, it probably here intends an empire which should usher in the universal sway of the kingdom of Christ.

Ever since the time of Constantine the light of true religion has been increasingly diffused, and is shining more and more unto the perfect day.

Verse 29. *He that hath an ear*] Let every Chris-tian pay the strictest regard to these predictions of Christ ; and let them have a suitable influence on his heart and life.

       2

CHAPTER III.

The epistle to the Church of Sardis, 1–6. The epistle to the Church of Philadelphia, 7–13. The epistle to the Church of Laodicea, 14–22.

A. M. cir. 4100.
A. D. cir. 96.
Impp. Flavio
Domitiano
Cæs. Aug. et
Nerva.

AND unto the angel of the Church in Sardis write; These things saith he [a] that hath the seven Spirits of God, and the seven stars; [b] I know thy works, that thou hast a name that thou livest, [c] and art dead.

2 Be watchful, and strengthen the things which remain, that are ready to die : for I have not found thy works perfect before God.

3 [d] Remember therefore how thou hast received and heard ; and hold fast, and [e] repent. [f] If therefore thou shalt not watch, I will come on thee as a thief, and thou shalt not know what hour I will come upon thee.

A. M. cir. 4100.
A. D. cir. 96.
Impp. Flavio
Domitiano
Cæs. Aug. et
Nerva.

4 Thou hast [g] a few names even in Sardis which have not [h] defiled their garments ; and they shall walk with me [i] in white : for they are worthy.

5 He that overcometh, [k] the same shall be clothed in white raiment ; and I will not [l] blot out his name out of the [m] book of life, but [n] I will confess his name before my Father, and before his angels.

---

[a] Chap. i. 4, 16 ; iv. 5 ; v. 6.——[b] Chap. ii. 2.——[c] Eph. ii. 1, 5 ; 1 Tim v. 6.——[d] 1 Tim. vi. 20 ; 2 Tim. i. 13 ; verse 11. [e] Ver. 19.——[f] Matt. xxiv. 42, 43 ; xxv. 13 ; Mark xiii. 33 ; Luke xii. 39, 40 ; 1 Thess. v. 2, 6 ; 2 Pet. iii. 10 ; chap. xvi. 15.

[g] Acts i. 15.——[h] Jude 23.——[i] Chap. iv. 4 ; vi. 11 ; vii. 9, 13. [k] Chap. xix. 8.——[l] Exod. xxxii. 32 ; Psa. lxix. 28.——[m] Phil. iv. 3 ; chap. xiii. 8 ; xvii. 8 ; xx. 12 ; xxi. 27.——[n] Matt. x. 32 ; Luke xii. 8.

NOTES ON CHAP. III.

Epistle to the Church at Sardis.

Verse 1. *The seven Spirits, of God*] See the note on chap. i. 4, 16, &c.

Thou hast a name that thou livest] Ye have the reputation of Christians, and consequently of being alive to God, through the quickening influence of the Divine Spirit; but ye *are dead*—ye have not the life of God in your souls, ye have not walked consistently and steadily before God, and his Spirit has been grieved with you, and he has withdrawn much of his light and power.

Verse 2. *Be watchful*] Ye have lost ground by carelessness and inattention. Awake, and keep awake !

Strengthen the things which remain] The convictions and good desires, with any measure of the fear of God and of a tender conscience, which, although still subsisting, are about to perish, because the Holy Spirit, who is the author of them, being repeatedly grieved, is about finally to depart.

Thy works perfect] Πεπληρωμενα· *Filled up.* They performed duties of all kinds, but no duty *completely.* They were constantly beginning, but never brought any thing to a proper end. Their resolutions were languid, their strength feeble, and their light dim. They probably maintained their reputation *before men*, but their works were not perfect *before God.*

Verse 3. *Remember*] Enter into a serious consideration of your state.

How thou hast received] With what joy, zeal, and gladness ye heard the Gospel of Christ when first preached to you.

Hold fast] Those good desires and heavenly influences which still remain.

And repent.] Be humbled before God, because ye have not been workers together with him, but have received much of his grace in vain.

If therefore thou shalt not watch] If you do not consider your ways, watching against sin, and for opportunities to receive and do good.

I will come on thee as a thief] As the thief comes when he is not expected, so will I come upon you if ye be not watchful, and cut you off from life and hope.

Verse 4. *Thou hast a few names even in Sardis*] A few *persons, names* being put for those who bore them. And as the members of the Church were all *enrolled*, or their names entered in a book, when admitted into the Church or when baptized, *names* are here put for the *people* themselves. See ver. 5.

Have not defiled their garments] Their *souls.* The Hebrews considered holiness as the *garb* of the soul, and evil actions as *stains* or *spots* on this garb. So in *Shabbath*, fol. 152, 2 : " A certain king gave royal garments to his servants : those who were prudent folded them up, and laid them by in a chest ; those who were foolish put them on, and performed their daily labour in them. After some time the king asked for those royal robes ; the wise brought theirs white and clean, the foolish brought theirs spotted with dirt. With the former the king was well pleased ; with the latter he was angry. Concerning the former he said : Let those garments be laid up in my wardrobe, and let the persons go home in peace. Of the latter he said : Let the garments be put into the hands of the fuller, and cast those who wore them into prison." This parable is spoken on these words of Ecclesiastes, chap. xii. 7 : *The spirit shall return to God who gave it.*

They shall walk with me in white] They shall be raised to a state of eternal glory, and shall be for ever with their Lord.

Verse 5. *I will not blot out his name*] This may be an allusion to the custom of registering the names of those who were admitted into the Church in a book kept for that purpose, from which custom our

2

A. M. cir. 4100.
A. D. cir. 96.
Impp. Flavio Domitiano Cæs. Aug. et Nerva.

6 [o] He that hath an ear, let
him hear what the Spirit saith
unto the Churches.
7 And to the angel of the
Church in Philadelphia write; These things
saith [p] he that is holy, [q] he that is true, he that
hath [r] the key of David, [s] he that openeth,
and no man shutteth; and [t] shutteth, and no
man openeth;
8 [u] I know thy works: behold, I have set
before thee [v] an open door, and no man can
shut it: for thou hast a little
strength, and hast kept my word,
and hast not denied my name.
9 Behold, I will make [w] them
of the synagogue of Satan, which say they are
Jews, and are not, but do lie; behold, [x] I will
make them to come and worship before thy
feet, and to know that I have loved thee.
10 Because thou hast kept the word of my
patience, [y] I also will keep thee from the hour
of temptation, which shall come upon [z] all the

A. M. cir. 4100.
A. D. cir. 96.
Impp. Flavio. Domitiano Cæs. Aug. et Nerva.

[o] Chap. ii. 7.——[p] Acts iii. 14.——[q] 1 John v. 20; ver. 14; chap. i. 5; vi. 10; xix. 11.——[r] Isa. xxii. 22; Luke i. 32; chapter i. 18. [s] Matt. xvi. 19.

[t] Job xii. 14.——[u] Ver. 1.——[v] 1 Cor. xvi. 9; 2 Cor. ii. 12. [w] Chapter ii. 9.——[x] Isaiah xlix. 23; lx. 14.——[y] 2 Peter ii. 9. [z] Luke ii. 1.

baptismal registers in Churches are derived. These are properly *books of life*, as there those who were born unto God were registered; as in the latter those who were born in that parish were enrolled. Or there may be allusions to the *white raiment* worn by the priests, and the erasing of the name of any priest out of the sacerdotal list who had either sinned, or was found not to be of the seed of Aaron. In *Middoth*, fol. 37, 2: "The great council of Israel sat and judged the priests. If in a priest any vice was found they stripped off his white garments and clothed him in *black*, in which he wrapped himself, went out, and departed. Him in whom no vice was found they clothed in *white*, and he went and took his part in the ministry among his brother priests."

I will confess his name] I will acknowledge that this person is my true disciple, and a member of my mystical body. In all this there may also be an allusion to the custom of registering citizens. Their names were entered into books, according to their condition, tribes, family, &c.; and when they were dead, or had by unconstitutional acts forfeited their right of citizenship, the name was *blotted out*, or erased from the registers. See the note on Exod. xxxii. 32.

Verse 6. *He that hath an ear*] The usual caution and counsel carefully to attend to the things spoken to the members of that Church, in which every reader is more or less interested.

Epistle to the Church at Philadelphia,

Verse 7. *He that is holy*] In whom holiness essentially dwells, and from whom all holiness is derived.

He that is true] He who is the fountain of truth; who cannot lie nor be imposed on; from whom all truth proceeds; and whose veracity in his *Revelation* is unimpeachable.

He that hath the key of David] See this metaphor explained, Matt. xvi. 19. *Key* is the emblem of authority and knowledge; *the key of David* is the regal right or authority of David. David could *shut* or *open* the kingdom of Israel to whom he pleased. He was not bound to leave the kingdom even to his eldest son. He could choose whom he pleased to succeed him. The kingdom of the Gospel, and the kingdom of heaven, are at the disposal of Christ. He can *shut* against whom he will; he can *open* to whom he pleases. If he *shuts*, no man can *open*; if he *opens*, no man can *shut*. His determinations all stand fast, and none can reverse them. This expression is an allusion to Isa. xxii. 22, where the prophet promises to Eliakim, under the symbol of the key of the house of David, the government of the whole nation; i. e., all the power of the king, to be executed by him as his deputy; but the words, as here applied to Christ, show that *He* is absolute.

Verse 8. *I have set before thee an open door*] I have opened to thee a door to proclaim and diffuse my word; and, notwithstanding there are many adversaries to the spread of my Gospel, yet none of them shall be able to prevent it.

Thou hast a little strength] Very little political authority or influence; yet thou *hast kept my word*—hast kept the true *doctrine; and hast not denied my name*, by taking shelter in heathenism when Christianity was persecuted. The *little strength* may refer either to the smallness of the numbers, or to the littleness of their grace.

Verse 9. *I will make them*] Show them to be, *of the synagogue of Satan, who say they are Jews*, pretending thereby to be of the synagogue of God, and consequently his true and peculiar children.

I will make them to come and worship] I will so dispose of matters in the course of my providence, that the Jews shall be obliged to seek unto the Christians for toleration, support, and protection, which they shall be obliged to sue for in the most *humble* and *abject* manner.

To know that I have loved thee.] That the love which was formerly fixed on the Jews is now removed, and transferred to the Gentiles.

Verse 10. *The word of my patience*] The doctrine which has exposed you to so much trouble and persecution, and required so much patience and magnanimity to bear up under its attendant trials.

The hour of temptation] A *time* of sore and peculiar trial which might have proved too much for their strength. He who is faithful to the grace of God is often hidden from trials and difficulties which fall without mitigation on those who have been unfaithful in his covenant. Many understand by the *hour of temptation* the persecution under *Trajan*, which was greater and more extensive than the preceding ones under *Nero* and *Domitian*.

To try them] That is, such persecutions will be

A. M. cir. 4100.
A. D. cir. 96.
Impp. Flavio
Domitiano
Cæs. Aug. et
Nerva.

world, to try them that dwell [a] upon the earth.

11 Behold, [b] I come quickly : [c] hold that fast which thou hast, that no man take [d] thy crown.

12 Him that overcometh will I make [e] a pillar in the temple of my God, and he shall go no more out : and [f] I will write upon him the name of my God, and the name of the city of my God, *which is* [g] new Jerusalem, which cometh down out of heaven from my God : [h] and *I will write upon him* my new name.

13 [i] He that hath an ear, let him hear what the Spirit saith unto the Churches.

14 And unto the angel of the Church [k] of the Laodiceans write ; [l] These things saith the Amen, [m] the faithful and true witness, [n] the beginning of the creation of God ;

15 [o] I know thy works, that thou art neither cold nor hot : I would thou wert cold or hot.

16 So then because thou art lukewarm, and neither cold nor hot, I will spue thee out of my mouth.

A. M. cir. 4100.
A. D. cir. 96.
Impp. Flavio
Domitiano
Cæs. Aug. et
Nerva.

---

[a] Isa. xxiv. 17.——[b] Phil. iv. 5 ; chap. i. 3 ; xxii. 7, 12, 20. [c] Ver. 3 ; chap. ii. 25.——[d] Chapter ii. 10.——[e] 1 Kings vii. 21 ; Gal. ii. 9.——[f] Chap. ii. 17 ; xiv. 1 ; xxii. 4.

[g] Gal. iv. 26 ; Heb. xii. 22 ; chap. xxi. 2, 10.——[h] Chap. xxii. 4.——[i] Chapter ii. 7.——[k] Or, *in Laodicea.*——[l] Isa. lxv. 16 [m] Ch. i. 5 ; xix. 11 ; xxii. 6 ; ver. 7.——[n] Col. i. 15.——[o] Ver. 1.

---

the means of trying and proving those who profess Christianity, and showing who were sound and thorough Christians and who were not.

Verse 11. Behold, I come quickly] These things will shortly take place ; and I am coming with *consolations* and *rewards* to my faithful followers, and with *judgments* to my adversaries.

Take thy crown.] God has provided mansions for you ; let none through your fall occupy those seats of blessedness.

Verse 12. A pillar in the temple] There is probably an allusion here to the *two pillars* in the temple of Jerusalem, called *Jachin* and *Boaz*, stability and strength. The *Church* is the *temple ;* CHRIST is the *foundation* on which it is built ; and his *ministers* are the PILLARS by which, under him, it is adorned and supported. St. Paul has the same allusions, Gal. ii. 9.

I will write upon him the name of my God] That is, I will make upon him a *priest* unto myself. The priest had written on his forehead קורש ליהוה *kodesh laihovah,* "Holiness to the Lord."

And the name of the city of my God] As the high priest had on his breastplate the names of the twelve tribes engraved, and these constituted the *city* or *Church of God ;* Christ here promises that in place of them the twelve apostles, representing the *Christian Church,* shall be written, which is called the *New Jerusalem,* and which God has adopted in place of the *twelve Jewish tribes.*

My new name.] The *Saviour* of ALL ; the *light* that *lightens* the GENTILES ; the CHRIST ; the Anointed One ; the only GOVERNOR of his Church ; and the *Redeemer* of ALL mankind.

There is here an intimation that the Christian *Church* is to endure for ever ; and the Christian *ministry* to last as long as time endures : *He shall go no more out for ever.*

Epistle to the Church of the Laodiceans.

Verse 14. These things saith the Amen] That is, He who is true or faithful ; from אמן *aman,* he was true ; immediately interpreted, *The faithful and true witness.* See chap. i. 5.

The beginning of the creation of God] That is, the head and governor of all creatures ; the king of the

creation. See on Col. i. 15. By his *titles,* here, he prepares them for the humiliating and awful truths which he was about to declare, and the *authority* on which the declaration was founded.

Verse 15. Thou art neither cold nor hot] Ye are neither heathens nor Christians—neither good nor evil —neither led away by false doctrine, nor thoroughly addicted to that which is true. In a word, they were listless and indifferent, and seemed to care little whether heathenism or Christianity prevailed. Though they felt little zeal either for the salvation of their own souls or that of others, yet they had such a general conviction of the truth and importance of Christianity, that they could not readily give it up.

I would thou wert cold or hot] That is, ye should be decided ; adopt some part or other, and be in earnest in your attachment to it. If ever the words of Mr. Erskine, in his Gospel Sonnets, were true, they were true of this Church :—

"To good and evil equal bent,
I'm both a devil and a saint."

They were too *good* to go to *hell,* too *bad* to go to *heaven.* Like Ephraim and Judah, Hos. vi. 4 : *O Ephraim, what shall I do unto thee ? O Judah, what shall I do unto thee ? for your goodness is as a morning cloud, and as the early dew it passeth away.* They had *good* dispositions which were captivated by evil ones, and they had *evil* dispositions which in their turn yielded to those that were good ; and the Divine justice and mercy seem puzzled to know what to do *to* or *with* them. This was the state of the Laodicean Church ; and our Lord expresses here in this apparent wish, the same that is expressed by *Epictetus,* Ench., chap. 36 : Ἕνα σε δει ανθρωπον, η αγαθον, η κακον, ειναι. "Thou oughtest to be one kind of man, either a good man or a bad man."

Verse 16. Because thou art lukewarm] Irresolute and undecided.

I will spue thee out of my mouth.] He alludes here to the known effect of *tepid water* upon the *stomach ;* it generally produces a *nausea.* I will cast thee off. Thou shalt have no interest in me. Though thou hast been near to my heart, yet now I must pluck thee thence, because slothful, careless, and indolent ; thou art not in earnest for thy soul.

2

A. M. cir. 4100.
A. D. cir. 96.
Impp. Flavio,
Domitiano
Cæs. Aug. et
Nerva.

17 Because thou sayest, [p] I am rich, and increased with goods, and have need of nothing; and knowest not that thou art wretched, and miserable, and poor, and blind, and naked:

18 I counsel thee [q] to buy of me gold tried in the fire, that thou mayest be rich; and [r] white raiment, that thou mayest be clothed, and *that* the shame of thy nakedness do not appear; and anoint thine eyes with eye-salve, that thou mayest see.

19 [s] As many as I love, I rebuke and chasten: be zealous therefore, and repent.

A. M. cir. 4100.
A. D. cir. 96.
Impp. Flavio
Domitiano
Cæs. Aug. et
Nerva.

20 Behold, [t] I stand at the door, and knock: [u] if any man hear my voice, and open the door, [v] I will come in to him, and will sup with him, and he with me.

21 To him that overcometh [w] will I grant to sit with me in my throne, even as I also overcame, and am set down with my Father in his throne.

22 [x] He that hath an ear, let him hear what the Spirit saith unto the Churches.

[p] Hos. xii. 8; 1 Cor. iv. 8.——[q] Isa. lv. 1; Matt. xiii. 44; xxv. 9.——[r] 2 Cor. v. 3; chap. vii. 13; xvi. 15; xix. 8.——[s] Job v. 17; Prov. iii. 11, 12; Heb. xii. 5, 6; James i. 12.

[t] Cant. v. 2.——[u] Luke xii. 37.——[v] John xiv. 23.——[w] Matt. xix. 28; Luke xxii. 30; 1 Cor. vi. 2; 2 Tim. ii. 12; chap. ii. 26, 27.——[x] Chap. ii. 7.

Verse 17. *I am rich*] Thou supposest thyself to be in a safe state, perfectly sure of final salvation, because thou hast begun well, and laid the right foundation. It was this most deceitful conviction that cut the nerves of their spiritual diligence; they rested in what they had already received, and seemed to think that *once in grace* must be *still in grace.*

Thou art wretched] Ταλαιπωρος· *Most wretched.* "The word signifies," according to Mintert, "being worn out and fatigued with grievous labours, as they who labour in a *stone quarry*, or are condemned to the *mines.*" So, instead of being children of God, as they supposed, and infallible heirs of the kingdom, they were, in the sight of God, in the condition of the most abject *slaves.*

And miserable] Ὁ ελεεινος· Most deplorable, to be pitied by all men.

And poor] Having no *spiritual riches*, no *holiness* of heart. *Rich* and *poor* are sometimes used by the rabbins to express the *righteous* and the *wicked.*

And blind] The eyes of thy understanding being darkened, so that thou dost not see thy state.

And naked] Without the image of God, not clothed with holiness and purity. A more deplorable state in spiritual things can scarcely be imagined than that of this Church. And it is the true picture of many *Churches*, and of innumerable individuals.

Verse 18. *I counsel thee*] O fallen and deceived soul, hear Jesus! Thy case is not *hopeless. Buy of me.*

Gold tried in the fire] Come and receive from me, without money and without price, *faith* that shall stand in every trial: so *gold tried in the fire* is here understood. But it may mean pure and undefiled *religion*, or that *grace* or *Divine influence* which produces it, which is more valuable to the soul than the purest gold to the body. They had before *imaginary riches;* this alone can make them *truly* rich.

White raiment] Holiness of heart and life.

Anoint thine eyes] Pray for, that ye may receive, the enlightening influences of my Spirit, that ye may be convinced of your true state, and see where your help lies.

Verse 19. *As many as I love*] So it was the love he still had to them that induced him thus to reprehend and thus to counsel them.

Be zealous] Be in *earnest*, to get your souls saved. They had no zeal; this was their bane. He now stirs them up to diligence in the use of the means of grace and repentance for their past sins and remissness.

Verse 20. *Behold, I stand at the door and knock*] There are many sayings of this kind among the ancient rabbins; thus in *Shir Hashirim Rabba*, fol. 25, 1: "God said to the Israelites, My children, open to me one *door* of repentance, even so wide as the eye of a needle, and I will open to you *doors* through which calves and horned cattle may pass."

In *Sohar Levit*, fol. 8, col. 32, it is said: "If a man *conceal* his sin, and do not open it before the holy King, although he ask mercy, yet the *door* of repentance shall not be *opened* to him. But if he *open* it before the holy blessed God, God spares him, and mercy prevails over wrath; and when he laments, although *all the doors* were *shut*, yet they shall be *opened* to him, and his prayer shall be heard."

Christ *stands*—waits long, at the *door* of the sinner's heart; he *knocks*—uses judgments, mercies, reproofs, exhortations, &c., to induce sinners to repent and turn to him; he lifts up his *voice*—calls loudly by his word, ministers, and Spirit.

If any man hear] If the sinner will seriously consider his state, and attend to the voice of his Lord.

And open the door] This must be his *own act*, receiving power for this purpose from his offended Lord, who will not *break open* the door; he will make no *forcible entry.*

I will come in to him] I will manifest myself to him, heal all his backslidings, pardon all his iniquities, and love him freely.

Will sup with him] Hold communion with him, feed him with the bread of life.

And he with me.] I will bring him at last to dwell with me in everlasting glory.

Verse 21. *To sit with me in my throne*] In every case it is to him that *overcometh*, to the *conqueror*, that the final promise is made. He that *conquers* not is not *crowned*, therefore every promise is here made to him that is *faithful unto death.* Here is a most remarkable expression: Jesus has conquered, and is set down with the FATHER upon the Father's *throne;* he who conquers through Christ sits down with Christ upon his *throne* : but Christ's throne and the throne of the Father is the same ; and it is on this *same throne* that those who are faithful unto death are finally to sit ! How astonishing is this state of exaltation ! The dignity and grandeur of it who can conceive ?

This is the worst of the seven Churches, and yet the most eminent of all the promises are made to it, showing that the worst may repent, finally conquer, and attain even to the highest state of glory.

Verse 22. *He that hath an ear, let him hear*] Mr. Wesley has a very judicious note on the conclusion of this chapter, and particularly on this last verse, *He that hath an ear,* &c. " This (counsel) stands in *three* former letters *before* the promise, in the *four* latter *after* it ; clearly dividing the seven into *two parts,* the first containing *three,* the last *four* letters. The titles given our Lord in the *three former* letters peculiarly respect his power after his resurrection and ascension, particularly over his Church ; those in the *four latter,* his Divine glory and unity with the Father and the Holy Spirit. Again, this word being placed *before the promises* in the *three former letters* excludes the false apostles at Ephesus, the false Jews at Smyrna, and the partakers with the heathens at Pergamos, from having any share therein. In the *four latter,* being placed *after* them, it leaves the promises immediately joined with Christ's address to the angel of the Church, to show that the fulfilling of these was near ; whereas the others reach beyond the end of the world. It should be observed that the *overcoming* or *victory* (to which alone these *peculiar* promises are annexed) is not the ordinary victory obtained by *every believer,* but a special victory obtained over great and peculiar temptations, by those that are strong in faith."

The latest account we have of the state of the *seven Asiatic Churches* is in a letter from the Rev. *Henry Lindsay,* chaplain to the British embassy at Constantinople, to a member of the *British and Foreign Bible Society,* by which society Mr. Lindsay had been solicited to distribute some copies of the New Testament in modern Greek among the Christians in Asia Minor. The following is his communication, dated

" *Constantinople, January* 10, 1816.

" When I last wrote to you, I was on the point of setting out on a short excursion into Asia Minor. Travelling hastily, as I was constrained to do from the circumstances of my situation, the information I could procure was necessarily superficial and unsatisfactory. As, however, I distributed the few books of the society which I was able to carry with me, I think it necessary to give some account of the course I took :

" 1. The regular intercourse of England with SMYRNA will enable you to procure as accurate intelligence of its present state as any I can pretend to offer. From the conversations I had with the Greek bishop and his clergy, as well as various well-informed individuals, I am led to suppose that, if the population of Smyrna be estimated at *one hundred and forty thousand* inhabitants, there are from *fifteen* to *twenty*

thousand Greeks, *six thousand* Armenians, *five thousand* Catholics, *one hundred and forty* Protestants, and *eleven thousand* Jews.

" 2. After Smyrna, the first place I visited was EPHESUS, or rather (as the site is not quite the same) Aiasalick, which consists of about fifteen poor cottages. I found there but *three* Christians, two brothers who keep a small shop, and a gardener. They are all three Greeks, and their ignorance is lamentable indeed. In that place, which was blessed so long with an apostle's labours, and those of his zealous assistants, are Christians who have not so much as heard of that apostle, or seem only to recognize the name of Paul as one in the calendar of their saints. One of them I found able to read a little, and left with him the New Testament, in ancient and modern Greek, which he expressed a strong desire to read, and promised me he would not only study it himself, but lend it to his friends in the neighbouring villages.

" 3. My next object was to see LAODICEA ; in the road to this is Guzel-hisar, a large town, with one church, and about *seven hundred* Christians. In conversing with the priests here, I found them so little acquainted with the Bible, or even the New Testament in an entire form, that they had no distinct knowledge of the books it contained beyond the four gospels, but mentioned them indiscriminately with various idle legends and lives of saints. I have sent thither three copies of the modern Greek Testament since my return. About three miles from Laodicea is Denizli, which has been styled (but I am inclined to think erroneously) the ancient Colosse ; it is a considerable town, with about *four hundred* Christians, Greeks, and Armenians, each of whom has a church. I regret however to say that here also the most extravagant tales of miracles, and fabulous accounts of angels, saints, and relics, had so usurped the place of the Scriptures as to render it very difficult to separate in their minds Divine truths from human inventions. I felt that here that unhappy time was come when men should 'turn away their ears from the truth, and be turned unto fables.' I had with me some copies of the gospels in ancient Greek which I distributed here, as in some other places through which I had passed. Eski-hisar, close to which are the remains of ancient Laodicea, contains about fifty poor inhabitants, in which number are but two Christians, who live together in a small mill ; unhappily neither could read at all ; the copy therefore of the New Testament, which I intended for this Church, I left with that of Denizli, the offspring and poor remains of Laodicea and Colosse. The prayers of the mosque are the only prayers which are heard near the ruins of Laodicea, on which the threat seems to have been fully executed in its utter rejection as a Church.

" 4. I left it for PHILADELPHIA, now Alah-shehr. It was gratifying to find at last some surviving fruits of early zeal ; and here, at least, whatever may be the loss of the *spirit* of Christianity, there is still the *form* of a Christian Church ; this has been kept from the 'hour of temptation,' which came upon all the Christian world. There are here about *one thousand* Christians, chiefly Greeks, who for the most part speak only Turkish; there are twenty-five places of public worship, five of which are large regular churches; to these there is a resident bishop, with twenty inferior clergy. A copy of the modern Greek Testament was received by the bishop with great thankfulness.

"5. I quitted Alah-shehr, deeply disappointed at the statement I received there of the Church of SARDIS. I trusted that in its utmost trials it would not have been suffered to perish utterly, and I heard with surprise that not a vestige of it remained. With what satisfaction then did I find on the plains of Sardis a small Church establishment; the few Christians who dwell around modern Sart were anxious to settle there and erect a church, as they were in the habit of meeting at each other's houses for the exercise of religion. From this design they were prohibited by Kar Osman Oglu, the Turkish governor of the district; and in consequence, about five years ago they built a church upon the plain, within view of ancient Sardis, and there they maintain a priest. The place has gradually risen into a little village, now called Tatar-keny; thither the few Christians of Sart, who amount to *seven*, and those in its immediate vicinity, resort for public worship, and form together a congregation of about forty. There appears then still a remnant, 'a few names even in Sardis,' which have been preserved. I cannot repeat the expressions of gratitude with which they received a copy of the New Testament in a language with which they were familiar. Several crowded about the priest to hear it on the spot, and I left them thus engaged.

"6. Ak-hisar, the ancient THYATIRA, is said to contain about *thirty thousand* inhabitants, of whom *three thousand* are Christians, all Greeks except about *two hundred* Armenians. There is, however, but one Greek church and one Armenian. The superior of the Greek Church to whom I presented the Romaic Testament esteemed it so great a treasure that he earnestly pressed me, if possible, to spare another, that one might be secured to the Church and free from accidents, while the other went round among the people for their private reading. I have, therefore, since my return hither, sent him four copies.

"7. The Church of PERGAMOS, in respect to numbers, may be said to flourish still in Bergamo. The town is less than Ak-hisar, but the number of Christians is about as great, the proportion of Armenians to Greeks nearly the same, and each nation also has one church. The bishop of the district, who occasionally resides there, was at that time absent, and I experienced with deep regret that the resident clergy were totally incapable of estimating the gift I intended them; I therefore delivered the Testament to the lay vicar of the bishop at his urgent request, he having assured me that the bishop would highly prize so valuable an acquisition to the Church. He seemed much pleased that the benighted state of his nation had excited the attention of strangers.

"Thus, sir, I have left at least one copy of the unadulterated word of God at each of the seven Asiatic Churches of the Apocalypse, and I trust they are not utterly thrown away; but whoever may plant, it is God only who can give the increase, and from his goodness we may hope they will in due time bring forth fruit, 'some thirty, some sixty, and some a hundred fold.'

"HENRY LINDSAY."

In my note on Acts xix. 24 I have given an account of the celebrated temple of Diana at *Ephesus*, to which building, called one of the *seven wonders* of the world, St. Paul is supposed to allude in his epistle to this Church, particularly at chap. iii. 18, where I have again given the measurement of this temple.

CHAPTER IV.

John sees the throne of God in heaven surrounded by twenty-four elders; and four living creatures, full of eyes; which all join in giving glory to the Almighty, 1–11.

A. M. cir. 4100.
A. D. cir. 96.
Impp. Flavio Domitiano Cæs. Aug. et Nerva.

AFTER this I looked, and, behold, a door *was* opened in heaven: and [a] the first voice which I heard *was* as it were of a trumpet talking with me; which said, [b] Come up hither, [c] and I will show thee things which must be hereafter.

2 And immediately [d] I was in the Spirit: and, behold, [e] a throne was set in heaven, and *one* sat on the throne.

3 And he that sat was to look upon like a jasper and a sardine stone: [f] and *there was* a rainbow round about the throne, in sight like unto an emerald.

A. M. cir. 4100
A. D. cir. 96.
Impp. Flavio Domitiano Cæs. Aug. et Nerva.

---

[a] Chap. i. 10.——[b] Chapter xi. 12.——[c] Chapter i. 19; xxii. 6. [d] Chap. i. 10; xvii. 3; xxi. 10.

[e] Isa. vi. 1; Jer. xvii. 12; Ezekiel i. 26; x. 1; Daniel vii. 9. [f] Ezek. i. 28.

NOTES ON CHAP. IV.

Verse 1. *A door* was *opened in heaven*] This appears to have been a visible aperture in the sky over his head.

Verse 2. *I was in the Spirit*] Rapt up in an ecstasy.

Verse 3. *And he that sat*] There is here no description of the Divine Being, so as to point out any

A. M. cir. 4100.
A D. cir. 96.
Impp. Flavio
Domitiano
Cæs. Aug. et
Nerva.

4 ᵍ And round about the throne *were* four and twenty seats : and upon the seats I saw four and twenty elders sitting, ʰ clothed in white raiment ; ⁱ and they had on their heads crowns of gold.

5 And out of the throne proceeded ᵏ lightnings and thunderings and voices : ˡ and *there were* seven lamps of fire burning before the throne, which are ᵐ the seven Spirits of God.

6 And before the throne *there was* ⁿ a sea of glass, like unto crystal : ᵒ and in the midst of the throne, and round about the throne, *were* four beasts, full of eyes before ᵖ and behind.

ᵍ Chap. xi. 16.——ʰ Chap. iii. 4, 5 ; vi. 11 ; vii. 9, 13, 14 ; xix. 14.——ⁱ Ver. 10.——ᵏ Chap. viii. 5 ; xvi. 18.——ˡ Exod. xxxvii. 23 ; 2 Chron. iv. 20 ; Ezek. i. 13 ; Zech. iv. 2.——ᵐ Chap. i. 4 ; iii. 1 ; v. 6.

---

7 ᑫ And the first beast *was* like a lion, and the second beast like a calf, and the third beast had a face as a man, and the fourth beast *was* like a flying eagle.

A. M. cir. 4100.
A. D. cir. 96.
Impp. Flavio
Domitiano
Cæs. Aug. et
Nerva.

8 And the four beasts had each of them ʳ six wings about *him ;* and *they were* full of eyes ˢ within : and ᵗ they rest not day and night, saying, ᵘ Holy, holy, holy, ᵛ Lord God Almighty, ʷ which was, and is, and is to come.

9 And when those beasts give glory and honour and thanks to him that sat on the throne, ˣ who liveth for ever and ever,

---

ⁿ Exod. xxxviii. 8 ; chap. xv. 2.——ᵒ Ezek. i 5.——ᵖ Ver. 8. ᑫ Num. ii. 2, &c. ; Ezek. i. 10 ; x. 14.——ʳ Isa. vi. 2.——ˢ Ver. 6.——ᵗ Gr. *they have no rest.*——ᵘ Isa. vi. 3.——ᵛ Chapter i. 8. ʷ Chap. i. 4.——ˣ Chap. i. 18 ; v. 14 ; xv. 7.

---

similitude, shape, or *dimensions.* The description rather aims to point out the surrounding *glory* and *effulgence* than the *person* of the almighty King. See a similar description Num. xxiv. 10, &c., and the notes there.

Verse 4. *Four and twenty elders*] Perhaps this is in reference to the smaller *Sanhedrin* at Jerusalem, which was composed of twenty-three elders ; or to the *princes of the twenty-four courses* of the Jewish priests which ministered at the tabernacle and the temple, at first appointed by David.

Clothed in white raiment] The garments of the priests.

On their heads crowns of gold.] An emblem of their *dignity.* The Jewish writers represent human souls as being created first ; and before they enter the body, each is taken by an angel into paradise, where it sees the righteous sitting in glory with crowns upon their heads. *Rab. Tanchum,* fol. 39, 4.

Verse 5. *Seven lamps of fire*] Seven angels, the attendants and ministers of the supreme King. See chap. i. 4, and the note there.

Verse 6. *Four beasts*] Τεσσαρα ζωα· *Four living creatures* or *four animals.* The word *beast* is very improperly used here and elsewhere in this description. *Wiclif* first used it, and translators in general have followed him in this uncouth rendering. A *beast* before the throne of God in heaven sounds oddly.

Verse 7. *The first beast* was *like a lion*] It is supposed that there is a reference here to the *four standards* or *ensigns* of the *four divisions* of the tribes in the Israelitish camp, as they are described by Jewish writers.

The first living creature was like a *lion ;* this was, say the rabbins, the standard of JUDAH on the *east,* with the two tribes of *Issachar* and *Zabulon.* The second, like a *calf* or *ox,* which was the emblem of EPHRAIM who pitched on the *west,* with the two tribes of *Manasseh* and *Benjamin.* The third, with the *face* of a *man,* which, according to the rabbins, was the standard of REUBEN who pitched on the *south,* with the two tribes of *Simeon* and *Gad.* The fourth,

which was like a *flying* (spread) *eagle,* was, according to the same writers, the emblem on the ensign of DAN who pitched on the *north,* with the two tribes of *Asher* and *Naphtali.* This traditionary description agrees with the *four faces* of the cherub in Ezekiel's vision. See my *notes* and *diagrams* on Num. ii.

Christian tradition has given these creatures as emblems of the *four* evangelists. To *John* is attributed the EAGLE ; to *Luke* the ox, to *Mark* the LION, and to *Matthew* the MAN, or *angel* in human form. As the former represented the *whole Jewish Church* or *congregation,* so the latter is intended to represent the *whole Christian Church.*

Verse 8. *The four beasts had each of them six wings*] I have already observed, in the *preface* to this book, that the *phraseology* is *rabbinical ;* I might have added, and the *imagery* also. We have almost a counterpart of this description in *Pirkey Elieser.* chap. 4. I shall give the substance of this from *Schoettgen.* " Four troops of ministering angels praise the holy blessed God : the first is *Michael,* at the right hand ; the next is *Gabriel,* at the left ; the third is *Uriel,* before ; and the fourth is *Raphael,* behind him. The *shechinah* of the holy, blessed God is *in the midst,* and he himself *sits upon a throne* high and elevated, hanging in the air ; and his magnificence is as *amber* חשמל, (chashmal,) *in the midst of the fire,* Ezek. i. 4. On his head is placed a *crown* and a *diadem,* with the incommunicable name (יהוה *Yehovah*) inscribed on the front of it. His *eyes* go throughout the whole earth ; a part of them is *fire,* and a part of them *hail.* At his right hand stands *Life,* and at his left hand *Death ;* and he has a fiery sceptre in his hand. Before him is the *veil* spread, that *veil* which is between the *temple* and the *holy of holies ;* and *seven angels* minister before him within that *veil :* the veil and his footstool are like *fire* and *lightning ;* and *under the throne of glory* there is a shining like fire and *sapphire,* and *about his throne* are *justice* and *judgment.*

" The place of the throne are the *seven clouds of glory ;* and the *chariot wheels,* and the *cherub,* and the *living creatures* which *give glory* before his face. The throne

A. M. cir. 4100.
A. D. cir. 96.
Impp. Flavio
Domitiano
Cæs. Aug. et
Nerva.

10 y The four and twenty elders fall down before him that sat on the throne, z and worship him that liveth for ever and ever, a and cast their crowns before the throne, saying,

11 b Thou art worthy, O Lord, to receive glory and honour and power : c for thou hast created all things, and for thy pleasure they are and were created.

A. M. cir. 4100.
A. D. cir. 96.
Impp. Flavio
Domitiano
Cæs. Aug. et
Nerva.

y Chap. v. 8, 14.——z Ver. 9.——a Ver. 4.——b Chap. v. 12.

c Gen. i. 1 ; Acts xvii. 24 ; Eph. iii. 9 ; Col. i. 16 ; chap. x. 6.

is in similitude like *sapphire* ; and at the four feet of it are *four living creatures*, each of which has *four faces* and *four wings*. When God speaks from the *east*, then it is from between the two cherubim with the *face of a* MAN ; when he speaks from the *south*, then it is from between the two cherubim with the *face of a* LION ; when from the *west*, then it is from between the two cherubim with the *face of an* ox ; and when from the *north*, then it is from between the two cherubim with the *face of an* EAGLE. " And the *living creatures stand before the throne of glory* ; and they stand in fear, in trembling, in horror, and in great agitation ; and from this agitation a *stream of fire* flows before them. Of the two *seraphim* one stands at the right hand of the holy blessed God, and one stands at the left ; and each has *six wings* : with *two they cover their face* lest they should see the face of the *shechina* ; with *two they cover their feet* lest they should find out the footstool of the shechinah ; and *with two they fly*, and sanctify his great name. And they answer each other, saying *Holy, holy, holy, Lord God of hosts* ; the whole earth is full of his glory. And the *living creatures* stand near his glory, yet they do not know the place of his glory ; but wheresoever his glory is, they cry out and say, *Blessed be the glory of the Lord in his place*." In *Shemoth Rabba*, sec. 23, fol. 122, 4, Rabbi

Abin says : " There are *four* which have principality in this world : among *intellectual creatures*, MAN ; among *birds*, the EAGLE ; among *cattle*, the ox ; and among *wild beasts*, the LION : each of these has a kingdom and a certain magnificence, and they are placed *under the throne of glory*, Ezek. i. 10, to show that no creature is to exalt itself in this world, and that the kingdom of God is over all." These creatures may be considered the representatives of the whole creation.

Verse 10. *Cast their crowns before the throne*] Acknowledge the infinite supremacy of God, and that they have derived their being and their blessings from him alone. This is an allusion to the custom of prostrations in the east, and to the homage of petty kings acknowledging the supremacy of the emperor.

Verse 11. *Thou art worthy, O Lord, to receive*] Thus all creation acknowledges the supremacy of God ; and we learn from this song that he *made all things for his pleasure* ; and through the same motive he *preserves*. Hence it is most evident, that he hateth nothing that he has made, and could have made no intelligent creature with the design to make it eternally miserable. It is strange that a contrary supposition has ever entered into the heart of man ; and it is high time that the benevolent nature of the Supreme God should be fully vindicated from aspersions of this kind.

CHAPTER V.

The book sealed with seven seals, which no being in heaven or earth could open, 1–3. Is at last opened by the Lion of the tribe of Judah, 4–8. He receives the praises of the four living creatures and the twenty-four elders, 9, 10. And afterwards of an innumerable multitude, who acknowledge that they were redeemed to God by his blood, 11, 12. And then, of the whole creation, who ascribe blessing, honour, glory, and power to God and the Lamb for ever, 13, 14.

A. M. cir. 4100.
A. D. cir. 96.
Impp. Flavio
Domitiano
Cæs. Aug. et
Nerva.

AND I saw in the right hand of him that sat on the throne a a book written within and on the back side, b sealed with seven seals.

2 And I saw a strong angel proclaiming with a loud voice, Who is worthy to open the book, and to loose the seals thereof ?

A. M. cir. 4100.
A. D. cir. 96.
Impp. Flavio
Domitiano
Cæs. Aug. et
Nerva.

a Ezek. ii. 9, 10.

b Isa. xxix. 11 ; Dan. xii. 4.

NOTES ON CHAP. V.

Verse 1. *A book written within and on the back side*] That is, the book was full of solemn contents *within*, but it was *sealed* ; and on the *back side* was a *superscription* indicating its contents. It was a *labelled* book, or one written on each side of the skin, which was not usual.

Sealed with seven seals.] As seven is a number of *perfection*, it may mean that the book was so sealed

that the seals could neither be *counterfeited* nor *broken*; i. e., the matter of the book was *so obscure* and *enigmatical*, and the work it enjoined and the facts it predicted so difficult and stupendous, that they could neither be known nor performed by human wisdom or power.

Verse 2. *A strong angel*] One of the *chief* of the angelic host.

Proclaiming] As the *herald* of God.

2

A. M. cir. 4100.
A. D. cir. 96.
Impp. Flavio
Domitiano
Cæs. Aug. et
Nerva.

3 And no man ᶜ in heaven, nor in earth, neither under the earth, was able to open the book, neither to look thereon.

4 And I wept much, because no man was found worthy to open and to read the book, neither to look thereon.

5 And one of the elders saith unto me, Weep not : behold, ᵈ the Lion of the tribe of Juda, ᵉ the Root of David, hath prevailed to open the book, and ᶠ to loose the seven seals thereof.

6 And I beheld, and lo, in the midst of the throne and of the four beasts, and in the midst of the elders, stood ᵍ a Lamb as it had been slain, having seven horns and ʰ seven eyes, which are ⁱ the seven Spirits of God sent forth into all the earth.

A. M. cir. 4100.
A. D. cir. 96.
Impp. Flavio
Domitiano
Cæs. Aug. et
Nerva.

7 And he came and took the book out of the right hand ᵏ of him that sat upon the throne.

8 And when he had taken the book, ˡ the four beasts and four *and* twenty elders fell down before the Lamb, having every one of them ᵐ harps, and golden vials, full of ⁿ odours, ᵒ which are the prayers of saints.

ᶜ Ver. 13.——ᵈ Gen. xlix. 9, 10; Heb. vii. 14.——ᵉ Isa. xi. 1, 10; Rom. xv. 12; ch. xxii. 16.——ᶠ Ver. 1; ch. vi. 1.——ᵍ Isa. liii. 7; John i. 29, 36; 1 Pet. i. 19; chap. xiii. 8; ver. 9, 12.

ʰ Zech. iii. 9; iv. 10.——ⁱ Ch. iv. 5.——ᵏ Ch. iv. 2.——ˡ Chap. iv. 8, 10.——ᵐ Chap. xiv. 2; xv. 2.——ⁿ Or, *incense.*——ᵒ Psa. cxli. 2; chap. viii. 3, 4.

To open the book, and to loose the seals] To loose the seals that he may open the book. Who can tell what this book contains? Who can open its mysteries? The book may mean the purposes and designs of God relative to his government of the world and the Church; but we, whose habitation is in the dust, know nothing of such things. We are, however, determined to *guess.*

Verse 3. *And no man*] Ουδεις· No *person* or *being.*

In heaven] Among all the angels of God.

Nor in the earth] No *human* being.

Neither under the earth] No *disembodied spirit,* nor any *demon.* Neither *angels, men,* nor *devils,* can fathom the decrees of God.

Neither to look thereon.] None can *look* into it unless it be, opened, and none can *open* it unless the *seals* be unloosed.

Verse 4 *I wept much*] Because the world and the Church were likely to be deprived of the knowledge of the contents of the book.

Verse 5. *The Lion of the tribe of Juda*] Jesus Christ, who sprang from this tribe, as his genealogy proves; see on Matt. i. and Luke iii. There is an allusion here to Gen. xlix. 9, *Judah is a lion's whelp;* the *lion* was the emblem of this tribe, and was supposed to have been embroidered on its ensigns.

The Root of David] See Isa. xi. 1. Christ was the *root* of David as to his *Divine nature;* he was a *branch out of the stem of Jesse* as to his *human nature.*

Hath prevailed] By the merit of his incarnation, passion, and death.

To open the book] To *explain* and *execute* all the purposes and decrees of God, in relation to the government of the world and the Church.

Verse 6. *Stood a Lamb*] Christ, so called because he was a sacrificial offering; αρνιον signifies a *little* or *delicate* lamb.

As it had been slain] As if now *in the act of being offered.* This is very remarkable; so important is the sacrificial offering of Christ in the sight of God that he is still represented as being in the very act of pouring out his blood for the offences of man. This gives great advantage to faith; when any soul comes to the throne of grace, he finds a sacrifice there provided for him to offer to God. Thus all succeeding generations find they have the *continual* sacrifice ready, and the newly-shed blood to offer.

Seven horns] As *horn* is the emblem of *power,* and *seven* the number of *perfection,* the *seven horns* may denote the all-prevailing and infinite *might* of Jesus Christ. He *can* support all his *friends;* he can destroy all his *enemies;* and he *can* save to the uttermost all that come unto God through him.

Seven eyes] To denote his infinite knowledge and wisdom: but as these *seven eyes* are said to be the *seven Spirits of God,* they seem to denote rather his *providence,* in which he often employs the ministry of *angels;* therefore, these are said to be *sent forth into all the earth.* See on chap. i. 4.

Verse 7. *He came and took the book*] This verse may be properly explained by John, chap. i. 18. *No man hath seen God at any time; the only-begotten Son, which is in the bosom of the Father, he hath* DECLARED *him.* With Jesus alone are all the counsels and mysteries of God.

Verse 8. *The four beasts—fell down before the Lamb*] The whole Church of God, and all his children in heaven and earth, acknowledge that Jesus Christ is alone worthy and able to unfold and execute all the mysteries and counsels of God. See on verse 9.

Having every one of them harps] There were harps and vials; and each of the elders and living creatures had one.

Odours, which are the prayers of saints.] The frankincense and odours offered at the tabernacle were emblems of the prayers and praises of the Lord. That *prayers* are compared to *incense,* see Psa. cxli. 2: *Let my* PRAYER *be set forth before thee as* INCENSE. Hence that saying in *Synopsis Sohar,* p. 44, n. 37: "The odour of the prayers of the Israelites is equal to *myrrh* and *frankincense;* but on the Sabbath it is preferred to the scent of all kinds of perfumes." The words *which are the prayers of saints* are to be understood as *this is my body,* this signifies or *represents* my body; these odours *represent* the prayers of the saints.

2   991

A. M. cir. 4100.
A. D. cir. 96.
Impp. Flavio
Domitiano
Cæs. Aug. et
Nerva.

9 And ᵖ they sung a new song, saying, ᑫ Thou art worthy to take the book, and to open the seals thereof: ʳ for thou wast slain, and ˢ hast redeemed us to God by thy blood ᵗ out of every kindred, and tongue, and people, and nation;

10 ᵘ And hast made us unto our God kings and priests: and we shall reign on the earth.

11 And I beheld, and I heard the voice of many angels ᵛ round about the throne and the beasts and the elders; and the number of them was ʷ ten thousand times ten thousand, and thousands of thousands;

12 Saying with a loud voice, ˣ Worthy is the Lamb that was slain to receive power, and riches, and wisdom, and strength, and honour, and glory, and blessing.

13 And ʸ every creature which is in heaven, and on the earth, and under the earth, and such as are in the sea, and all that are in them, heard I saying, ᶻ Blessing, and honour, and glory, and power, be unto him ᵃ that sitteth upon the throne, and unto the Lamb for ever and ever.

14 ᵇ And the four beasts said, Amen. And the four and twenty elders fell down and worshipped him ᶜ that liveth for ever and ever.

A. M. cir. 4100.
A. D. cir. 96.
Impp. Flavio
Domitiano
Cæs. Aug. et
Nerva.

ᵖ Psa. xl. 3; chap. xiv. 3.——ᑫ Chapter iv. 11.——ʳ Verse 6.
ˢ Acts xx. 28; Rom. iii. 24; 1 Cor. vi. 20; vii. 23; Eph. i. 7;
Col. i. 14; Heb. ix. 12; 1 Pet. i. 18, 19; 2 Pet. ii. 1; 1 John i.
7; chap. xiv. 4.——ᵗ Dan. iv. 1; vi. 25; chapter vii. 9; xi. 9;
xiv. 6.

ᵘ Exod. xix. 6; 1 Pet. ii. 5, 9; chapter i. 6; xx. 6; xxii. 5.
ᵛ Chap. iv. 4, 6.——ʷ Psa. lxviii. 17; Dan. vii. 10; Heb. xii. 22.
ˣ Chap. iv. 11.——ʸ Phil. ii. 10; ver. 3.——ᶻ 1 Chron. xxix. 11;
Rom. ix. 5; xvi. 27; 1 Tim. vi. 16; 1 Pet. iv. 11; v. 11; chap.
i. 16.——ᵃ Ch. vi. 16; vii. 10.——ᵇ Ch. xix. 4.——ᶜ Ch. iv. 9, 10.

Verse 9. *A new song*] Composed on the matters and blessings of the Gospel, which was just now opened on earth. But *new song* may signify a *most excellent song*; and by this the Gospel and its blessings are probably signified. The Gospel is called a *new song*, Psa. xcvi. 1. And perhaps there is an allusion in the *harps* here to Psa. cxliv. 9: *I will sing a* NEW SONG *unto thee, O God: upon a* PSALTERY, *and an* INSTRUMENT OF TEN STRINGS, &c. The same form of speech is found, Isa. xlii. 10: *Sing unto the Lord a* NEW SONG, &c.; and there the prophet seems to have the *Gospel dispensation* particularly in view.

Thou—hast redeemed us to God—out of every—nation] It appears, therefore, that the *living creatures* and the *elders* represent the *aggregate* of the followers of God; or the *Christian Church* in all nations, and among all kinds of people, and perhaps through the whole compass of time: and all these are said to be redeemed by Christ's *blood*, plainly showing that his *life* was a *sacrificial offering* for the sins of mankind.

Verse 10. *Kings and priests*] See Exod. xix. 6; 1 Pet. ii. 5, 9, and the notes there.

Verse 11. *The voice of many angels*] These also are represented as joining in the chorus with *redeemed mortals*.

Ten thousand times ten thousand] "Myriads of myriads and chiliads of chiliads;" that is, an infinite or innumerable multitude. This is in reference to Dan. vii. 10.

Verse 12. *To receive power*] That is, Jesus Christ is worthy *to take*, λαβειν, to have ascribed to him, *power*—omnipotence; *riches*—beneficence; *wisdom*—omniscience; *strength*—power in prevalent exercise; *honour*—the highest reputation for what he has done; *glory*—the praise due to such actions; *and blessing*—the thankful acknowledgments of the whole creation. Here are seven different species of praise; and this is exactly agreeable to the rabbinical forms, which the author of this book keeps constantly in view. See *Sepher Rasiel*, fol. 39, 2: "To thee belongs כבוד

cabod, *glory*; גדולה gedulah, *magnitude*; גבורה geburah, *might*; הממלכה hammamlakah, *the kingdom*; התפארת hattiphereth, *the honour*; הנצח hannetsach, *the victory*; וההוד vehahod, and *the praise*."

Verse 13. *Every creature*] All parts of the creation, animate and inanimate, are represented here, by that figure of speech called *prosopopœia* or *personification*, as giving praise to the Lord Jesus, because by him *all things were created*. We find the whole creation gives precisely the *same praise*, and in the *same terms*, to Jesus Christ, who is undoubtedly meant here by the *Lamb just slain* as they give to God who *sits upon the throne*. Now if Jesus Christ were not properly God this would be *idolatry*, as it would be giving to the *creature* what belongs to the *Creator*.

Verse 14. *The four beasts said, Amen.*] Acknowledged that what was attributed to Christ was his due.

The four and twenty elders] The word εικοσιτεσσαρες, *twenty-four*, is wanting in the most eminent MSS. and versions.

Fell down and worshipped] Επεσαν και προσεκυνησαν· Fell down on their knees, and then *prostrated themselves* before the throne. This is the eastern method of *adoration*: first, the person worshipping fell down on his knees; and then, bowing down touched the earth with his forehead. This latter act was *prostration*.

Him that liveth for ever] This clause is wanting in ABC, thirty-seven others, *Syriac, Arabic, Coptic, Æthiopic*, some copies of the *Slavonic, Itala*, and *Vulgate*; and in *Andreas*, and *Arethas*, ancient commentators on this book. It is also wanting in some editions, and is undoubtedly spurious. Griesbach has left this and the above *twenty-four* out of the text.

Now follow the least intelligible parts of this mysterious book, on which so much has been written, and so much in vain. It is natural for man to desire to be wise; and the more difficult the subject the more it is

2

studied; and the hope of finding out something by which the world and the Church might be profited, has caused the most eminently learned men to employ their talents and consume their time on these abstruse prophecies. But of what use has all this learned and well-meant labour been to mankind? Can *hypothesis* explain *prophecy*, and *conjecture* find a *basis* on which *faith* can rest? And what have we better in all attempts hitherto made to explain the mysteries of this book?

CHAPTER VI.

What followed on the opening of the seven seals. The opening of the first *seal; the* white horse, 1, 2. *The opening of the* second *seal; the* red horse, 3, 4. *The opening of the* third *seal; the* black horse and the famine, 5, 6. *The opening of the* fourth *seal; the* pale horse, 7, 8. *The opening of the* fifth *seal; the* souls of men under the altar, 9–11. *The opening of the* sixth *seal; the* earthquake, the darkening of the sun *and* moon, *and* falling of the stars, 12–14. *The* terrible consternation of the kings and great men of the earth, 15–17.*

A. M. cir. 4100.
A. D. cir. 96.
Impp. Flavio
Domitiano
Cæs. Aug. et
Nerva.

AND [a] I saw when the Lamb opened one of the seals; and I heard, as it were the noise of thunder, [b] one of the four beasts, saying, Come and see.

2 And I saw, and behold [c] a white horse; [d] and he that sat on him had a bow; [e] and a crown was given unto him: and he went forth conquering, and to conquer.

3 And when he had opened the second seal, [f] I heard the second beast say, Come and see.

4 [g] And there went out another horse *that*

was red: and *power* was given to him that sat thereon to take peace from the earth, and that they should kill one another: and there was given unto him a great sword.

5 And when he had opened the third seal, [h] I heard the third beast say, Come and see. And I beheld, and lo [i] a black horse; and he that sat on him had a pair of balances in his hand.

6 And I heard a voice in the midst of the four beasts say, [k] A measure of wheat for a

A. M. cir. 4100
A. D. cir. 96
Impp. Flavio
Domitiano
Cæs. Aug. et
Nerva.

---

[a] Chap. v. 5, 6, 7.——[b] Chap. iv. 7.——[c] Zech. vi. 3; chapter xix. 11.——[d] Psa. xlv. 4, 5; LXX.——[e] Zech. vi. 11; chapter xiv. 14.——[f] Chap. iv. 7.

[g] Zech. vi. 2.——[h] Chap. iv. 7.——[i] Zech. vi. 2.——[k] The word *chœnix* signifieth a measure containing one wine quart, and the twelfth part of a quart.

NOTES ON CHAP. VI.

Verse 1. *When the Lamb opened one of the seals*] It is worthy of remark that the opening of the seals is not merely a declaration of what God will do, but is the exhibition of a purpose then accomplished; for whenever the seal is opened, the sentence appears to be *executed*. It is supposed that, from chap. vi. to xi. inclusive, the calamities which should fall on the enemies of Christianity, and particularly the Jews, are pointed out under various images; as well as the preservation of the Christians under those calamities.

One of the four beasts] Probably that with the face of a *lion*. See chap. iv. 7.

Come and see.] Attend to what is about to be exhibited. It is very likely that all was exhibited before his eyes as in a *scene*; and he saw every *act* represented which was to take place, and all the *persons* and *things* which were to be the chief *actors*.

Verse 2. *A white horse*] Supposed to represent the *Gospel system*, and pointing out its excellence, swiftness, and purity.

He that sat on him] Supposed to represent *Jesus Christ*.

A bow] The *preaching of the Gospel*, darting conviction into the hearts of sinners.

A crown] The emblem of the *kingdom* which Christ was to establish on earth.

Conquering, and to conquer.] Overcoming and

confounding the *Jews* first, and then the *Gentiles*; spreading more and more the doctrine and influence of the cross over the face of the earth.

Verse 3. *The second beast*] That which had the face of an *ox*.

Verse 4. *Another horse—red*] The emblem of *war*; perhaps also of *severe persecution*, and the *martyrdom* of the saints.

Him that sat thereon] Some say, *Christ*; others. *Vespasian*; others, the *Roman armies*; others, *Artabanus*, king of the Parthians, &c., &c.

Take peace from the earth] To deprive Judea of all tranquillity.

They should kill one another] This was literally the case with the *Jews*, while besieged by the Romans.

A great sword.] Great influence and success, producing terrible carnage.

Verse 5. *The third beast*] That which had the face of a *man*.

A black horse] The emblem of *famine*. Some think that which took place under *Claudius*. See Matt. xxiv. 7; the same which was predicted by *Agabus*, Acts xi. 28.

A pair of balances] To show that the *scarcity* would be such, that every person must be put under an *allowance*.

Verse 6. *A measure of wheat for a penny*] The

A. M. cir. 4100.
A. D. cir. 96.
Impp. Flavio
Domitiano
Cæs. Aug. et
Nerva.

penny, and three measures of barley for a penny; and [l] see thou hurt not the oil and the wine.

7 And when he had opened the fourth seal, [m] I heard the voice of the fourth beast say, Come and see.

8 [n] And I looked, and behold, a pale horse: and his name that sat on him was Death, and hell followed with him. And power was given [o] unto them over the fourth part of the earth, [p] to kill with sword, and with hunger, [q] and with death, [r] and with the beasts of the earth.

9 And when he had opened the fifth seal, I

saw under [s] the altar [t] the souls of them that were slain [u] for the word of God, and for [v] the testimony which they held:

10 And they cried with a loud voice, saying, [w] How long, O Lord, [x] holy and true, [y] dost thou not judge and avenge our blood on them that dwell on the earth?

11 And [z] white robes were given unto every one of them; and it was said unto them, [a] that they should rest yet for a little season, until their fellow servants also and their brethren, that should be killed as they *were,* should be fulfilled.

A. M. cir. 4100.
A. D. cir. 96.
Impp. Flavio
Domitiano
Cæs. Aug. et
Nerva.

---

[l] Chap. ix. 4.——[m] Ch. iv. 7.——[n] Zech. vi. 3.——[o] Or, *to him.* [p] Ezek. xiv. 21.——[q] 2 Esdr. xv. 5.——[r] Lev. xxvi. 22.——[s] Ch. viii. 3; ix. 13; xiv. 18.——[t] Chap. xx. 4.

[u] Chap. i. 9.——[v] 2 Tim. i. 8; chap. xii. 17; xix. 10.——[w] See Zech. i. 12.——[x] Ch. iii. 7.——[y] Ch. xi. 18; xix. 2.——[z] Chap. iii. 4, 5; vii. 9, 14.——[a] Heb. xi. 40; chap. xiv. 13.

---

chœnix here mentioned was a measure of *dry* things; and although the *capacity* is not exactly known, yet it is generally agreed that it contained as much as one man could consume in a day; and a *penny,* the Roman *denarius,* was the ordinary pay of a labourer. So it appears that in this scarcity each might be able to obtain a bare subsistence by his daily labour; but a man could not, in such cases, provide for a *family.*

Three measures of barley] This seems to have been the *proportion of value* between the wheat and the barley. Barley was allowed to afford a poor aliment, and was given to the Roman soldiers instead of wheat, by way of *punishment.*

Hurt not the oil and the wine.] Be sparing of these: use them not as *delicacies,* but for *necessity;* because neither the *vines* nor the *olives* will be productive.

Verse 7. *The fourth beast*] That which had the face of an *eagle.*

Verse 8. *A pale horse*] The symbol of *death. Pallida mors, pale death,* was a very usual poetic epithet; of this symbol there can be no doubt, because it is immediately said, *His name that sat on him was* Death.

And hell followed with him.] The *grave,* or *state of the dead,* received the *slain.* This is a very elegant *prosopopœia,* or personification.

Over the fourth part of the earth] One fourth of mankind was to feel the desolating effects of this seal.

To kill with sword] War; *with hunger*—famine; *with death*—pestilence; *and with the beasts of the earth*—lions, tigers, hyænas, &c., which would multiply in consequence of the devastations occasioned by *war, famine,* and *pestilence.*

Verse 9. *The fifth seal*] There is no *animal* nor any other *being* to introduce this seal, nor does there appear to be any new event predicted; but the whole is intended to comfort the followers of God under their persecutions, and to encourage them to bear up under their distresses.

I saw under the altar] A symbolical vision was exhibited, in which he saw an *altar;* and under it the *souls of those who had been slain for the word of God*—martyred for their attachment to Christianity, are represented as being newly slain as victims to idolatry and superstition. The altar is upon earth, not in heaven.

Verse 10. *And they cried with a loud voice*] That is, their *blood,* like that of Abel, cried for vengeance; for we are not to suppose that there was any thing like a vindictive spirit in those happy and holy souls who had shed their blood for the testimony of Jesus. We sometimes say *Blood cries for blood;* that is, in the order of Divine justice, every murderer, and every murdering persecutor, shall be punished.

O Lord] Ὁ Δεσποτης· Sovereign Lord, supreme Ruler; one having and exercising unlimited and uncontrolled authority.

Holy] In thy own nature, hating iniquity;

And true] In all thy promises and threatenings;

Dost thou not judge] The persecutors;

And avenge our blood] Inflict signal punishment;

On them that dwell on the earth?] Probably meaning the persecuting *Jews;* they dwelt επι της γης, *upon that land,* a form of speech by which *Judea* is often signified in the New Testament.

Verse 11. *White robes*] The emblems of purity, innocence, and triumph.

They should rest yet for a little season] This is a declaration that, when the cup of the iniquity of the Jews should be full, they should then be punished in a mass. They were determined to proceed farther, and God permits them so to do; reserving the fulness of their punishment till they had filled up the measure of their iniquity. If this book was written *before* the destruction of Jerusalem, as is most likely, then this destruction is that which was to fall upon the *Jews;* and the *little time* or *season* was that which elapsed between their martyrdom, or the date of this book, and the final destruction of Jerusalem by the Romans, under

A. M. cir. 4100.
A. D. cir. 96.
Impp. Flavio
Domitiano
Cæs. Aug. et
Nerva.

12 And I beheld when he had opened the sixth seal, b and lo, there was a great earthquake; and c the sun became black as sackcloth of hair, and the moon became as blood;

13 d And the stars of heaven fell unto the earth, even as a fig tree casteth her e untimely figs, when she is shaken of a mighty wind.

14 f And the heaven departed as a scroll when it is rolled together; and g every mountain and island were moved out of their places.

15 And the kings of the earth, and the great men, and the rich men, and the chief captains, and the mighty men, and every bondman, and every freeman, h hid themselves in the dens and in the rocks of the mountains;

A. M. cir. 4100.
A. D. cir. 96.
Impp. Flavio
Domitiano
Cæs. Aug. et
Nerva.

16 i And said to the mountains and rocks, Fall on us, and hide us from the face of him that sitteth on the throne, and from the wrath of the Lamb:

17 k For the great day of his wrath is come; l and who shall be able to stand?

---

b Chap. xvi. 18.——c Joel ii. 10, 31; iii. 15; Matt. xxiv. 29; Acts ii. 20.——d Ch. viii. 10; ix. 1.——e Or, *green figs.*——f Psa. cii. 26; Isa. xxxiv. 4; Heb. i. 12, 13.

g Jer. iii. 21; iv. 24; chap. xvi. 20.——h Isa. ii. 19.——i Hos. x. 8; Luke xxiii. 30; chap. ix. 6.——k Isa. xiii. 6, &c.; Zeph i. 14, &c.; chap. xvi. 14.——l Psa. lxxvi. 7.

Vespasian and his son Titus, about A. D. 70. What follows may refer to the destruction of the heathen Roman empire.

Verse 12. *The sixth seal*] This seal also is opened and introduced by Jesus Christ alone.

A great earthquake] A most stupendous change in the civil and religious constitution of the world. If it refer to Constantine the Great, the change that was made by his conversion to Christianity might be very properly represented under the emblem of an *earthquake*, and the other symbols mentioned in this and the following verses.

The *sun*—the ancient *pagan government* of the Roman empire, was totally darkened; and, like a *black hair sackcloth*, was degraded and humbled to the dust.

The *moon*—the ecclesiastical state of the same empire, became as *blood*—was totally ruined, their sacred rites abrogated, their priests and religious institutions desecrated, their altars cast down, their temples destroyed, or turned into places for Christian worship.

Verse 13. *The stars of heaven*] The gods and goddesses, demi-gods, and deified heroes, of their poetical and mythological *heaven*, were prostrated indiscriminately, and lay as useless as the figs or fruit of a tree shaken down before ripe by a *tempestuous wind.*

Verse 14. *And the heaven departed as a scroll*] The whole system of pagan and idolatrous worship, with all its spiritual, secular, and superstitious influence, was blasted, shrivelled up, and rendered null and void, as a parchment scroll when exposed to the action of a strong fire.

And every mountain] All the props, supports, and dependencies of the empire, whether *regal allies, tributary kings, dependent colonies,* or *mercenary troops,* were all moved out of their places, so as to stand no longer in the same relation to that empire, and its worship, support, and maintenance, as they formerly did.

And island] The heathen temples, with their *precincts* and *enclosures, cut off* from the common people, and into which none could come but the *privileged,* may be here represented by *islands,* for the same reasons.

Verse 15. *The kings of the earth, &c.*] All the secular powers who had endeavoured to support the

pagan worship by authority, influence, riches, political wisdom, and military skill; with *every bondman*—all *slaves,* who were in life and limb addicted to their masters or owners.

And every freeman] Those who had been *manumitted,* commonly called *freedmen,* and who were attached, through gratitude, to the families of their liberators. All *hid themselves*—were astonished at the total overthrow of the heathen empire, and the revolution which had then taken place.

Verse 16. *Said to the mountains and rocks*] Expressions which denote the strongest perturbation and alarm. They preferred any kind of death to that which they apprehended from this most awful revolution.

From the face of him that sitteth on the throne] They now saw that all these terrible judgments came from the *Almighty;* and that *Christ,* the author of Christianity, was now judging, condemning, and destroying them for their cruel persecutions of his followers.

Verse 17. *For the great day of his wrath*] The decisive and manifest time in which he will execute judgment on the oppressors of his people.

Who shall be able to stand?] No might can prevail against the might of God. All these things may literally apply to the final destruction of Jerusalem, and to the revolution which took place in the Roman empire under Constantine the Great. Some apply them to the *day of judgment;* but they do not seem to have that awful event in view. These two events were the greatest that have ever taken place in the world, from the *flood* to the eighteenth century of the Christian era; and may well justify the strong figurative language used above.

THOUGH I do not pretend to say that my remarks on this chapter point out its true signification, yet I find others have applied it in the same way. Dr. *Dodd* observes that the fall of Babylon, Idumea, Judah, Egypt, and Jerusalem, has been described by the prophets in language equally pompous, figurative, and strong. See Isa. xiii. 10; xxxiv. 4, concerning *Babylon* and *Idumea;* Jer. iv. 23, 24, concerning *Judah;*

2

Ezek. xxxii. 7, concerning *Egypt*; Joel ii. 10, 31, concerning *Jerusalem*; and our Lord himself, Matt. xxiv. 29, concerning the same city. " Now," says he, " it is certain that the fall of any of these cities or kingdoms was not of greater concern or consequence to the world, nor more deserving to be described in pompous figures, than the fall of the *pagan Roman empire*, when the great lights of the heathen world, *the sun, moon, and stars*, the powers civil and ecclesiastical, were·all eclipsed and obscured, the heathen emperors and Cæsars were slain, the heathen priests and augurs were extirpated, the heathen officers and magistrates were removed, the temples were demolished, and their revenues 'were devoted to better uses. It is customary with the prophets, after they have described a thing in the most symbolical and figurative manner, to represent the same again in plainer lan-

guage; and the same method is observed here, ver. 15, 16, 17 : *And the kings of the earth, &c.* That is, Maximin, Galerius, Maxentius, Licinius, &c., with all their adherents and followers, were so routed and dispersed that *they hid themselves in dens, &c.*; expressions used to denote the utmost terror and confusion. This is, therefore, a triumph of Christ over his heathen enemies, and a triumph after a severe persecution ; so that the time and all the circumstances, as well as the series and order of the prophecy, agree perfectly with this interpretation. *Galerius, Maximin,* and *Licinius,* made even a public confession of their guilt, recalled their decrees and edicts against the Christians, and acknowledged the just judgments of God and of Christ in their own destruction." See *Newton, Lowman, &c.,* and Dr. *Dodd* on this chapter, with the works of several more recent authors.

CHAPTER VII.

The four angels holding the four winds of heaven, 1. *The angel with the seal of the living God, and sealing the servants of God out of the twelve tribes, whose number amounted to one hundred and forty-four thousand,* 2–8. *Besides these, there was an innumerable multitude from all nations, who gave glory to God and the Lamb,* 9–12. *One of the elders shows who these are, and describes their most happy state,* 13–17.

A. M. cir. 4100.
A. D. cir. 96.
Impp. Flavio
Domitiano
Cæs. Aug. et
Nerva.

AND after these things I saw four angels standing on the four corners of the earth, [a] holding the four winds of the earth, [b] that the wind should not blow on the earth, nor on the sea, nor on any tree.

2 And I saw another angel ascending from the east, having the seal of the living God : and he cried with a loud voice to the four

angels, to whom it was given to hurt the earth and the sea,

3 Saying, [c] Hurt not the earth, neither the sea, nor the trees, till we have [d] sealed the servants of our God [e] in their foreheads.

4 [f] And I heard the number of them which were sealed : *and there were* sealed [g] a hundred *and* forty *and* four thousand of

A. M. cir. 4100
A. D. cir. 96.
Impp Flavio
Domitiano
Cæs. Aug. et
Nerva.

---

[a] Daniel vii. 2.——[b] Chapter ix. 4.——[c] Chapter vi. 6 ; ix. 4.

[d] Ezek. ix. 4 ; chap. xiv. 1.——[e] Chap. xxii. 4.——[f] Chapter ix. 16.——[g] Chap. xiv. 1.

NOTES ON CHAP. VII.

Verse 1. And after these things] Immediately after the preceding vision.

I saw four angels] Instruments which God employs in the dispensation of his providence ; we know not what.

On the four corners of the earth] On the extreme parts of the land of *Judea*, called ἡ γη, the land, or *earth*, by way of eminence.

Holding the four winds] Preventing evil from every quarter. *Earth—sea, nor on any tree*; keeping the whole of the land free from evil, till the Church of Christ should wax strong, and each of his followers have time to prepare for his flight from Jerusalem, previously to its total destruction by the Romans.

Verse 2. The seal of the living God] This angel is represented as the chancellor of the supreme King, and as *ascending from the east*, απο ανατολης ἡλιου, *from the rising of the sun.* Some understand this of Christ, who is called ανατολη, the *east*, Luke i. 78.

Four angels, to whom it was given to hurt] Parti-

cular *agents* employed by Divine providence in the management of the affairs of the earth ; but whether *spiritual* or *material* we know not.

Verse 3. Till we have sealed the servants of our God] There is manifestly an allusion to Ezek. ix. 4 here. By *sealing* we are to understand *consecrating* the persons in a more especial manner to God, and showing, by this mark of God upon them, that they were under his more immediate protection, and that nothing should hurt them. It was a custom in the *east*, and indeed in the *west* too, to stamp with a hot iron the name of the owner upon the *forehead* or *shoulder* of his slave.

It is worthy of remark that not one Christian perished in the siege of Jerusalem ; all had left the city, and escaped to Pella. This I have often had occasion to notice.

Verse 4. I heard the number of them which were sealed] In the number of 144,000 are included all the *Jews* converted to Christianity ; 12,000 out of each of the twelve tribes : but this must be only a certain

A. M. cir. 4100.
A. D. cir. 96.
Impp. Flavio
Domitiano
Cæs. Aug. et
Nerva.

all the tribes of the children of Israel.

5 Of the tribe of Juda *were* sealed twelve thousand. Of the tribe of Reuben *were* sealed twelve thousand. Of the tribe of Gad *were* sealed twelve thousand.

6 Of the tribe of Aser *were* sealed twelve thousand. Of the tribe of Nephthalim *were* sealed twelve thousand. Of the tribe of Manasses *were* sealed twelve thousand.

7 Of the tribe of Simeon *were* sealed twelve thousand. Of the tribe of Levi *were* sealed twelve thousand. Of the tribe of Issachar *were* sealed twelve thousand.

8 Of the tribe of Zabulon *were* sealed twelve thousand. Of the tribe of Joseph *were* sealed twelve thousand. Of the tribe of Benjamin *were* sealed twelve thousand.

9 After this I beheld, and lo, [h] a great multitude, which no man could number, [i] of all nations, and kindreds, and people, and tongues, stood before the throne, and before the Lamb,

[k] clothed with white robes, and palms in their hands;

10 And cried with a loud voice, saying, [l] Salvation to our God [m] which sitteth upon the throne, and unto the Lamb.

A. M. cir. 4100.
A. D. cir. 96.
Impp. Flavio
Domitiano
Cæs. Aug. et
Nerva.

11 [n] And all the angels stood round about the throne, and *about* the elders and the four beasts, and fell before the throne on their faces, and worshipped God,

12 [o] Saying, Amen: Blessing, and glory, and wisdom, and thanksgiving, and honour, and power, and might, *be* unto our God for ever and ever. Amen.

13 And one of the elders answered, saying unto me, What are these which are arrayed in [p] white robes? and whence came they?

14 And I said unto him, Sir, thou knowest. And he said unto me, [q] These are they which came out of great tribulation, and have [r] washed their robes, and made them white in the blood of the Lamb.

15 Therefore are they before the throne of God, and serve him day and night in his

---

[h] Rom. xi. 25.——[i] Chap. v. 9.——[k] Chap. iii. 5, 18; iv. 4; vi. 11; ver. 14.——[l] Psa. iii. 8; Isa. xliii. 11; Jer. iii. 23; Hos. xiii. 4; chap. xix. 1.——[m] Chap. v. 13.

[n] Chap. iv. 6.——[o] Chap. v. 13, 14.——[p] Ver. 9.——[q] Chap. vi. 9; xvii. 6.——[r] Isa. i. 18; Heb. ix. 14; 1 John i. 7; chap. 1. 5; see Zech. iii. 3, 4, 5.

---

for an uncertain number; for it is not to be supposed that *just* 12,000 were converted out of *each* of the *twelve tribes.*

Verses 5–8. *Of the tribe of Juda,* &c.] *First,* we are to observe that the tribe of *Levi* is here mentioned, though that tribe had no inheritance in Israel; but they now belonged to the spiritual priesthood. *Secondly,* That the tribe of *Dan,* which had an inheritance, is here *omitted;* as also the tribe of *Ephraim. Thirdly,* That the tribe of *Joseph* is here *added* in the place of *Ephraim. Ephraim* and *Dan,* being the principal promoters of idolatry, are left out in this enumeration.

Verse 9. *A great multitude*] This appears to mean the Church of Christ among the *Gentiles,* for it was different from that collected from the *twelve tribes;* and it is here said to be *of all nations, kindreds, people,* and *tongues.*

Clothed with white robes] As emblems of *innocence* and *purity.* With *palms in their hands,* in token of victory gained over the world, the devil, and the flesh.

Verse 10. *Salvation to our God*] That is, God alone is the author of the salvation of man; and this salvation is procured for and given to them through the *Lamb,* as their propitiatory sacrifice.

Verse 11. *All the angels,* &c.] As there is joy in the presence of God among these holy spirits when one sinner repents, no wonder that they take such an

interest in the gathering together of such innumerable multitudes who are fully saved from their sins.

Verse 12. *Saying, Amen*] Giving their most cordial and grateful *assent* to the praises attributed to God and the Lamb.

Blessing, and glory, &c.] There are here *seven* different species of praise attributed to God, as in chap. v. 12, where see the note.

Verse 13. *One of the elders answered*] A Hebraism for *spoke.* The question is here asked, that the proposer may have the opportunity of answering it.

Verse 14. *Sir, thou knowest*] That is, I do not know, but thou canst inform me.

Came out of great tribulation] Persecutions of every kind.

And have washed their robes] Have obtained their pardon and *purity,* through the *blood of the Lamb.*

Their *white robes* cannot mean the *righteousness of Christ,* for this cannot be washed and made white in his own blood. This *white linen* is said to be *the righteousness of the saints,* chap. xix. 8, and this is the righteousness in which they stand *before the throne;* therefore it is not Christ's righteousness, but it is a righteousness wrought in them by the merit of his blood, and the power of his Spirit.

Verse 15. *Therefore*] Because they are washed in the blood of the Lamb, *are they before the throne*—admitted to the immediate presence, *of God.*

And serve him day and night] Without ceasing;

A. M. cir. 4100.
A. D. cir. 96.
Impp. Flavio
Domitiano
Cæs. Aug. et
Nerva.

temple : and he that sitteth on the throne shall [s] dwell among them.

16 [t] They shall hunger no more, neither thirst any more , [u] neither shall the sun light on them, nor any heat.

[s] Isa. iv. 5, 6 ; chap. xxi. 3.——[t] Isa. xlix. 10.——[u] Psa. cxxi. 6 ; chap. xxi. 4.

A. M. cir. 4100.
A. D. cir. 96.
Impp. Flavio
Domitiano
Cæs. Aug. et
Nerva.

17 For the Lamb which is in the midst of the throne [v] shall feed them, and shall lead them unto living fountains of waters : [w] and God shall wipe away all tears from their eyes.

[v] Psa. xxiii. 1 ; xxxvi. 8 ; John x. 11, 14.——[w] Isa. xxv. 8 ; ch. iv. 21.

being filled with the spirit of prayer, faith, love, and obedience.

Shall dwell among them.] He lives in his own Church, and in the heart of every true believer.

Verse 16. *They shall hunger no more*] They shall no longer be deprived of their religious ordinances, and the blessings attendant on them, as they were when in a state of persecution.

Neither shall the sun light on them] Their *secular rulers*, being converted to God, became nursing fathers to the Church.

Nor any heat.] Neither persecution nor affliction of any kind. These the Hebrews express by the term *heat, scorching,* &c.

Verse 17. *The Lamb*] The Lord Jesus, enthroned with his Father in ineffable glory.

Shall feed them] Shall communicate to them every thing calculated to secure, continue, and increase their happiness.

Living fountains of water] A *spring* in the Hebrew phraseology is termed *living water*, because constantly boiling up and running on. By these *perpetual fountains* we are to understand *endless sources* of comfort and happiness, which Jesus Christ will open out of his own infinite plenitude to all glorified souls. These eternal living fountains will make an infinite *variety* in the enjoyments of the blessed. There will be no

sameness, and consequently no *cloying* with the perpetual enjoyment of the same things ; every moment will open a *new source* of pleasure, instruction, and improvement ; they shall make an eternal progression into the fulness of God. And as God is infinite, so his attributes are infinite ; and throughout infinity more and more of those attributes will be discovered ; and the discovery of each will be a *new fountain* or *source* of pleasure and enjoyment. These sources must be *opening* through all eternity, and yet, through all eternity, there will still remain, in the absolute perfections of the Godhead, an infinity of them to be opened ! This is one of the finest images in the Bible.

God shall wipe away] In the most affectionate and fatherly manner, *all tears from their eyes*—all causes of distress and grief. They shall have pure, unmixed happiness. Reader, this is the happiness of those who are washed from their sins. Art thou washed ? O, rest not till thou art prepared to appear before God and the Lamb.

IF these saints had not met with troubles and distresses, in all likelihood they had not excelled so much in righteousness and true holiness. When all avenues of worldly comfort are shut up, we are obliged to seek our all in God ; and there is nothing sought from him that is not found in him.

CHAPTER VIII.

The opening of the seventh seal, 1. The seven angels with the seven trumpets, 2–6. The first sounds, and there is a shower of hail, fire, and blood, 7. The second sounds, and the burning mountain is cast into the sea, 8, 9. The third sounds, and the great star Wormwood falls from heaven, 10, 11. The fourth sounds, and the sun, moon, and stars are smitten ; and a threefold wo is denounced against the inhabitants of the earth, because of the three angels who are yet to sound, 12, 13.

A. M. cir. 4100.
A. D. cir. 96.
Impp. Flavio
Domitiano
Cæs. Aug. et
Nerva.

AND [a] when he had opened the seventh seal, there was silence in heaven about the space of half an hour.

[a] Chap. vi. 1.——[b] Tobit xii. 15 ; Matt. xviii. 10 ; Luke i. 19.

A. M. cir. 4100.
A. D. cir. 96.
Impp. Flavio
Domitiano
Cæs. Aug. et
Nerva.

2 [b] And I saw the seven angels which stood before God ; [c] and to them were given seven trumpets.

[c] 2 Chron. xxix. 25–28.

NOTES ON CHAP. VIII.

Verse 1. *The seventh seal*] This is ushered in and opened only by the Lamb.

Silence in heaven] This must be a mere *metaphor*, *silence* being put here for the deep and solemn *expectation* of the stupendous things about to take place, which the opening of this seal had produced. When any thing prodigious or surprising is expected, all is

silence, and even the breath is scarcely heard to be drawn.

Half an hour.] As *heaven* may signify the *place* in which all these representations were made to St. John, the *half hour* may be considered as the time during which no representation was made to him ; the time in which God was preparing the august exhibition which follows.

A. M. cir. 4100.
A. D. cir. 96.
Impp. Flavio
Domitiano
Cæs. Aug. et
Nerva.

3 And another angel came and stood at the altar, having a golden censer; and there was given unto him much incense, that he should ^d offer *it* with ^e the prayers of all saints upon ^f the golden altar which was before the throne.

4 And ^g the smoke of the incense, *which came* with the prayers of the saints, ascended up before God out of the angel's hand.

5 And the angel took the censer, and filled it with fire of the altar, and cast *it* ^h into the earth: and ⁱ there were voices, and thunderings, and lightnings, ^k and an earthquake.

A. M. cir. 4100.
A. D. cir. 96.
Impp. Flavio
Domitiano
Cæs. Aug. et
Nerva.

6 And the seven angels which had the seven trumpets prepared themselves to sound.

7 The first angel sounded, ^l and there followed hail and fire mingled with blood, and they were cast ^m upon the earth: and the third part ⁿ of trees was burnt up, and all green grass was burnt up.

8 And the second angel sounded, ^o and as it

---

^d Or, *add it to the prayers.*——^e Chap. v. 8.——^f Exod. xxx. 1; chapter vi. 9.——^g Psa. cxli. 2; Luke i. 10.——^h Or, *upon.*
ⁱ Chap. xvi. 18.

^k 2 Samuel xxii. 8; 1 Kings xix. 11; Acts iv. 31.——^l Ezek. xxxviii. 22.——^m Ch. xvi. 2.——ⁿ Isa. ii. 13; ch. ix. 4.——^o Jer. li. 25; Amos vii. 4.

There is here, and in the following verses, a strong allusion to different parts of the *temple worship;* a presumption that the temple was still standing, and the regular service of God carried on. The *silence* here refers to this fact—while the priest went in to burn incense in the holy place, all the people continued in silent mental prayer without till the priest returned. See Luke i. 10. The angel mentioned here appears to execute the office of priest, as we shall by and by see.

Verse 2. *The seven angels which stood before God* Probably the same as those called *the seven Spirits which are before his throne,* chap. i. 4, where see the note. There is still an allusion here to the seven ministers of the Persian monarchs. See Tobit, chap. xii. 15.

Verse 3. *Another angel*] About to perform the office of *priest.*

Having a golden censer] This was a preparation peculiar to the *day of expiation.* " On other days it was the custom of the priest to *take fire* from the *great altar* in a *silver censer,* but on the *day of expiation* the high priest took the fire from the *great altar* in a *golden censer;* and when he was come down from the great altar, he took incense from one of the priests, who brought it to him, and went with it to the *golden altar;* and while he offered the incense the people prayed without in silence, which is the *silence in heaven for half an hour.*" See Sir Isaac Newton.

Much incense, that he should offer it] Judgments of God are now about to be executed; the *saints*—the genuine Christians, *pray* much to God for protection. The angelic priest comes with *much incense,* standing between the living and those consigned to death, and offers his incense to God WITH *the prayers of the saints.*

Verse 4. *The smoke of the incense—with the prayers*] Though incense itself be an emblem of the prayers of the saints, Psa. cxli. 2; yet here *they* are said to *ascend before God,* as well as the *incense.* It is not said that the angel presents these prayers. He presents the incense, and the *prayers* ascend WITH IT. The *ascending* of the *incense* shows that the prayers and offering were accepted.

Verse 5. *Cast* it *into the earth*] That is, upon the land of Judea; intimating the judgments and desolations which were now coming upon it, and which appear to be farther opened in the sounding of the seven trumpets.

There were voices] All these seem to point out the confusion, commotions, distresses, and miseries, which were coming upon these people in the *wars* which were at hand.

Verse 6. *Prepared themselves to sound.*] Each took up his trumpet, and stood prepared to blow his blast. *Wars* are here indicated; the *trumpet* was the emblem of *war.*

Verse 7. *Hail and fire mingled with blood*] This was someting like the *ninth* plague of Egypt. See Exod. ix. 18–24: " The Lord sent thunder and hail —and fire mingled with the hail—and the fire ran along upon the ground." In the *hail* and *fire mingled with blood,* some fruitful imaginations might find *gunpowder* and *cannon balls,* and *canister shot* and *bombs.*

They were cast upon the earth] Εις την γην· *Into that land;* viz., Judea, thus often designated.

And the third part of trees] Before this clause the *Codex Alexandrinus,* thirty-five others, the *Syriac, Arabic, Æthiopic, Armenian, Slavonic, Vulgate, Andreas, Arethas,* and some others, have και το τριτον της γης κατεκαη· *And the third part of the land was burnt up.* This reading, which is undoubtedly genuine, is found also in the *Complutensian* Polyglot. Griesbach has received it into the text.

The *land* was wasted; the *trees*—the chiefs of the nation, were destroyed; and the *grass*—the *common people,* slain, or carried into captivity. High and low, rich and poor, were overwhelmed with one general destruction. This seems to be the meaning of these figures.

Many eminent men suppose that the irruption of the barbarous nations on the Roman empire is here intended. It is easy to find coincidences when fancy runs riot. Later writers might find here the irruption of the *Austrians* and *British,* and *Prussians, Russians,* and *Cossacks,* on the French empire!

Verse 8. *A great mountain burning with fire*] Supposed to signify the powerful nations which invaded the Roman empire. *Mountain,* in prophetic language, signifies a *kingdom;* Jer. li. 25, 27, 30, 58

2

A. M. cir. 4100.
A. D. cir. 96.
Impp. Flavio
Domitiano
Cæs. Aug. et
Nerva.

were a great mountain burning with fire was cast into the sea : P and the third part of the sea q became blood;

9 r And the third part of the creatures which were in the sea, and had life, died; and the third part of the ships were destroyed.

10 And the third angel sounded, s and there fell a great star from heaven, burning as it were a lamp, t and it fell upon the third part of the rivers, and upon the fountains of waters;

11 u And the name of the star is called Wormwood : v and the third part of the waters became wormwood; and many men died of

the waters, because they were made bitter.

12 w And the fourth angel sounded, and the third part of the sun was smitten, and the third part of the moon, and the third part of the stars; so as the third part of them was darkened, and the day shone not for a third part of it, and the night likewise.

13 And I beheld, x and heard an angel flying through the midst of heaven, saying with a loud voice, y Wo, wo, wo to the inhabiters of the earth, by reason of the other voices of the trumpet of the three angels, which are yet to sound!

A. M. cir. 4100.
A. D. cir. 96.
Impp. Flavio
Domitiano
Cæs. Aug. et
Nerva.

---

p Chap. xvi. 3.——q Ezek. xiv. 19.——r Chapter xvi. 3.——s Isa. xiv. 12; chap. ix. 1.——t Chap. xvi. 4.——u Ruth i. 20.

v Exod. xv. 23; Jer. ix. 15; xxiii. 15.——w Isa. xiii. 10; Amos viii. 9.——x Chap. xiv. 6; xix. 17.——y Chap. ix. 12; xi. 14.

Great disorders, especially when kingdoms are moved by hostile invasions, are represented by *mountains* being *cast into the midst of the sea*, Psa. xlvi. 2. *Seas* and *collections of waters* mean *peoples*, as is shown in this book, chap. xvii. 15. Therefore, great commotions in kingdoms and among their inhabitants may be here intended, but to *whom*, *where*, and *when* these happened, or are to happen, we know not.

The third part of the sea became blood] Another allusion to the Egyptian plagues, Exod. vii. 20, 21. *Third part* is a rabbinism, expressing a considerable number. "When Rabbi Akiba prayed, wept, rent his garments, put off his shoes, and sat in the dust, the world was struck with a curse; and then the *third part* of the olives, the *third part* of the wheat, and the *third part* of the barley, was smitten," Rab. Mardochæus, in Notitia Karaeorum, p. 102.

Verse 9. *The third part of the ships were destroyed.*] These judgments seem to be poured out upon some *maritime nation*, destroying much of its population, and much of its traffic.

Verse 10. *There fell a great star from heaven*] This has given rise to various conjectures. Some say the star means *Attila* and his Huns; others, Genseric with his Vandals falling on the city of Rome; others,

Eleazer, the son of Annus, spurning the emperor's victims, and exciting the fury of the Zealots; others, Arius, infecting the pure Christian doctrine with his heresy, &c., &c. It certainly cannot mean *all these*; and probably *none* of them. Let the reader judge.

Verse 11. *The star is called Wormwood*] So called from the *bitter* or *distressing effects* produced by its influence.

Verse 12. *The third part of the sun—moon—stars, was smitten*] Supposed to mean *Rome*, with her *senates, consuls*, &c., eclipsed by *Odoacer*, king of the Heruli, and *Theodoric*, king of the Ostrogoths, in the fifth century. But all this is uncertain.

Verse 13. *I—heard an angel flying*] Instead of αγγελου πετωμενου, an angel *flying*, almost every MS. and version of note has αετου πετωμενου, an eagle *flying*. The *eagle* was the symbol of the Romans, and was always on their ensigns. The *three woes* which are here expressed were probably to be executed by this people, and upon the Jews and their commonwealth. Taken in this sense the symbols appear consistent and appropriate; and the reading *eagle* instead of *angel* is undoubtedly genuine, and Griesbach has received it into the text.

CHAPTER IX.

The fifth angel sounds, and a star falls from heaven to earth, 1. *The bottomless pit is opened, and locusts come out upon the earth,* 2, 3. *Their commission,* 4–6. *Their form,* 7–10. *Their government,* 11, 12. *The sixth angel sounds, and the four angels bound in the Euphrates are loosed,* 13–15. *The army of horsemen, and their description,* 16–19. *Though much evil is inflicted upon men for their idolatry, &c., they do not repent,* 20, 21.

3

A. M. cir. 4100.
A. D. cir. 96.
Impp. Flavio
Domitiano
Cæs. Aug. et
Nerva.

AND the fifth angel sounded, [a] and I saw a star fall from heaven unto the earth: and to him was given the key of [b] the bottomless pit.

2 And he opened the bottomless pit; [c] and there arose a smoke out of the pit, as the smoke of a great furnace; and the sun and the air were darkened by reason of the smoke of the pit.

3 And there came out of the smoke [d] locusts upon the earth: and unto them was given power, [e] as the scorpions of the earth have power.

4 And it was commanded them [f] that they should not hurt [g] the grass of the earth, neither any green thing, neither any tree; but only those men which have not [h] the seal of God in their foreheads.

A. M. cir. 4100.
A. D. cir. 96.
Impp. Flavio
Domitiano
Cæs. Aug. et
Nerva.

5 And to them it was given that they should not kill them, [i] but that they should be tormented five months: and their torment *was* as the torment of a scorpion, when he striketh a man.

6 And in those days [k] shall men seek death, and shall not find it; and shall desire to

---

[a] Luke x. 18; chap. viii. 10.——[b] Luke viii. 31; chap. xvii. 8; xx. 1; ver. 2, 11.——[c] Joel ii. 2, 10.——[d] Exod. x. 4; Judg. vii. 12.——[e] Ver. 10.

[f] Chap. vi. 6; vii. 3.——[g] Chap. viii. 7.——[h] Chap. vii. 3; see Exod. xii. 23; Ezek. ix. 4.——[i] Chap. xi. 7; ver. 10.——[k] Job iii. 21; Isa. ii. 19; Jer. viii. 3; chap. vi. 16.

NOTES ON CHAP. IX.

Verse 1. *A star fall from heaven*] An angel encompassed with light suddenly descended, and seemed like a *star* falling from heaven.

The key of the bottomless pit.] Power to inundate the earth with a flood of temporal calamities and moral evils.

Verse 2. *He opened the bottomless pit*] Το φρεαρ της αβυσσου· *The pit of the bottomless deep.* Some think the angel means *Satan,* and the bottomless pit *hell.* Some suppose *Mohammed* is meant; and Signior *Pastorini* professes to believe that *Luther* is intended!

There arose a smoke] False doctrine, obscuring the true light of heaven.

Verse 3. *Locusts*] Vast hordes of military troops: the description which follows certainly agrees better with the *Saracens* than with any other people or nation, but may also apply to the Romans.

As the scorpions of the earth have power.] Namely, to hurt men by *stinging* them. Scorpions may signify *archers;* and hence the description has been applied to *Cestius Gallus,* the Roman general, who had many *archers* in his army.

Verse 4. *They should not hurt the grass*] Neither the common people, the men of middling condition, nor the nobles. However, this appears rather to refer to the prudent counsels of a military chief, not to destroy the *crops* and *herbage* of which they might have need in their campaigns.

Which have not the seal of God] All false, hypocritical, and heterodox Christians.

Verse 5. *To them it was given*] That is, they were *permitted.*

That they should be tormented five months] Some take these months *literally,* and apply them to the conduct of the Zealots who, from *May* to *September,* in the year of the siege, produced dreadful contests among the people; or to the afflictions brought upon the Jews by *Cestius Gallus,* when he came against Jerusalem, before which he lay one whole summer, or nearly five months.—See *Joseph.,* Bell. Jud., l. ii. c. 19.

Others consider the *months* as being *prophetical* months, each *day* being reckoned for a *year;* therefore this period must amount to one hundred and fifty

years, counting thirty days to each month, as was the general custom of the Asiatics.

Their torment was as the torment of a scorpion] The phraseology here is peculiar, and probably refers to the warlike weapon called a *scorpion,* several of which, or men armed with them, Cestius Gallus brought with him in his army.

Isidore describes this *scorpion* thus: *Scorpio est sagitta venenata arcu vel tormentis excussa, quæ, dum ad hominem venerit, virus qua figit infundit; unde et scorpio nomen accepit.* "The scorpion is a poisoned arrow shot from a bow or other instrument, which, when it wounds a man, deposits the poison with which it is covered in the wound; whence it has the name of scorpion." *Seneca,* in his *Hercules Œtæus,* act iv., ver. 1218, describes the torment which is occasioned by this species of poisoned arrow:—

> Heu qualis intus *scorpius,* quis fervida
> Plaga revulsus cancer infixus meas
> Urit medullas?

Verse 6. *In those days shall men seek death*] So distressing shall be their sufferings and torment that they shall long for death in *any form,* to be rescued from the evils of life. There is a sentiment much like this in *Maximianus,* Eleg. i., ver. 111, commonly attributed to *Cornelius Gallus:*—

> Nunc quia longa mihi gravis est et inutilis ætas,
> Vivere cum nequeam, sit mihi posse mori?
> O quam dura premit miseros conditio vitæ!
> Nec mors humano subjacet arbitrio.
> *Dulce mori miseris; sed mors optata recedit:*
> At cum tristis erit, præcipitata venit.

"Seeing that long life is both useless and burdensome
When we can no longer live comfortably, shall we be
permitted to die?
O how hard is the condition on which we hold life!
For death is not subjected to the will of man.
To die is sweet to the wretched; but *wished-for* death
flees away.
Yet when it is not desired, it comes with the hastiest
strides."

A. M. cir. 4100.
A. D. cir. 96.
Impp. Flavio
Domitiano
Cæs. Aug. et
Nerva.

die, and death shall flee from them.

7 And ¹ the shapes of the locusts *were* like unto horses prepared unto battle ; ᵐ and on their heads *were* as it were crowns like gold, ⁿ and their faces *were* as the faces of men.

8 And they had hair as the hair of women, and ° their teeth were as *the teeth* of lions.

9 And they had breastplates, as it were breastplates of iron ; and the sound of their wings *was* ᵖ as the sound of chariots of many horses running to battle.

10 And they had tails like unto scorpions, and there were stings in their tails : ۹ and their power *was* to hurt men five months.

11 ʳ And they had a king over them, *which*

is ˢ the angel of the bottomless pit, whose name in the Hebrew tongue *is* Abaddon, but in the Greek tongue hath *his* name ᵗ Apollyon.

12 ᵘ One wo is past ; *and,* behold, there come two woes more hereafter.

13 And the sixth angel sounded, and I heard a voice from the four horns of the golden altar which is before God,

14 Saying to the sixth angel which had the trumpet, Loose the four angels which are bound ᵛ in the great river Euphrates.

15 And the four angels were loosed, which were prepared ʷ for an hour, and a day, and a month, and a year, for to slay the third part of men.

16 And ˣ the number of the army ʸ of the horsemen *were* two hundred thousand thou-

A. M. cir. 4100.
A. D. cir. 96.
Impp. Flavio
Domitiano
Cæs. Aug. et
Nerva.

---

¹ Joel ii. 4.——ᵐ Nah. iii. 17.——ⁿ Dan. vii. 8.——° Joel i. 6.
ᵖ Joel ii. 5, 6, 7.——۹ Ver. 5.——ʳ Eph. ii. 2.——ˢ Ver. 1.——ᵗ That
is to say, a destroyer.——ᵘ Ch. viii. 13.——ᵛ Ch. xvi. 12.——ʷ Or,
at.——ˣ Psa. lxiii. 17 ; Dan. vii. 10.——ʸ Ezek. xxxviii. 4.

Job expresses the same sentiment, in the most plaintive manner :—

> Why is light given to the miserable,
> And life to the bitter of soul ?
> Who wait for death, but it is not;
> And dig for it more than hid treasures.
> They rejoice for it, and are glad,
> And exult when they find the grave.
> Ch. iii. 20—22.

Verse 7. *The locusts were like unto horses*] This description of the locusts appears to be taken from Joel ii. .4. The whole of this symbolical description of an overwhelming military force agrees very well with the troops of Mohammed. The Arabs are the most expert horsemen in the world : they live so much on horseback that the horse and his rider seem to make but one animal. The *Romans* also were eminent for their cavalry.

Crowns like gold] Not only alluding to their costly *tiaras* or *turbans,* but to the extent of their conquests and the multitude of powers which they subdued.

Their faces were *as the faces of men.*] That is, though locusts symbolically, they are really *men.*

Verse 8. *Hair as the hair of women*] No razor passes upon their flesh. Their *hair long,* and their *beards unshaven.*

Their teeth were as the teeth *of lions,*] They are ferocious and cruel.

Verse 9. *They had breastplates—of iron*] They seemed to be invulnerable, for no force availed against them.

The sound of their wings] Their hanging weapons and military trappings, with the clang of their shields and swords when they make their fierce onsets. This simile is borrowed from Joel ii. 5—7.

Verse 10. *They had tails like unto scorpions*] This may refer to the consequences of their victories. They infected the conquered with their pernicious doctrines.

Their power was *to hurt men five months.*] The locusts make their principal ravages during the *five* summer *months.* But probably these may be *prophetic months,* as above, in ver. 5—150 years.

Ver. 11. *A king over them*] A supreme head; some think Mohammed, some think Vespasian.

The angel of the bottomless pit] The chief envoy of Satan.

Abaddon] From אבד *abad,* he destroyed.

Apollyon.] From απο, intensive, and ολλυω, to destroy. The meaning is the same both in the Hebrew and Greek.

Verse 12. *One wo is past*] That is, the wo or desolation by the symbolical scorpions.

There came two woes more] In the trumpets of the sixth and seventh angels.

Verse 13. *The four horns of the golden altar*] This is another not very obscure indication that the Jewish temple was yet standing.

Verse 14. *Loose the four angels*] These four angels *bound*—hitherto restrained, in the Euphrates, are by some supposed to be the Arabs, the Saracens, the Tartars, or the Turks ; by others, Vespasian's four generals, one in Arabia, one in Africa, one in Alexandria, and one in Palestine.

Verse 15. *For an hour, and a day, and a month, and a year*] We have in this place a year resolved into its component parts. Twenty-four *hours* constitute a *day,* seven *days* make a *week,* four *weeks* make a *month,* and twelve *months* make a *year.* Probably no more is meant than that these four angels were *at all times* prepared and permitted to inflict evil on the people against whom they had received their commission. There are some who understand these divisions of time as prophetical periods, and to these I must refer, not professing to discuss such uncertainties.

Verse 16. *Two hundred thousand thousand*] Δυο μυριαδες μυριαδων· *Two myriads of myriads; that is, two hundred millions;* an army that was never yet got together from the foundation of the world, and could not find *forage* in any part of the earth. Per-

2

A. M. cir. 4100.
A. D. cir. 96.
Impp Flavio
Domitiano
Cæs. Aug. et
Nerva.

sand: ᶻ and I heard the number of them.

17 And thus I saw the horses in the vision, and them that sat on them, having breastplates of fire, and of jacinth, and brimstone : ᵃ and the heads of the horses *were* as the heads of lions ; and out of their mouths issued fire, and smoke, and brimstone.

18 By these three was the third part of men killed, by the fire, and by the smoke, and by the brimstone, which issued out of their mouths.

19 For their power is in their mouth, and in

their tails : ᵇ for their tails *were* like unto serpents, and had heads, and with them they do hurt.

20 And the rest of the men which were not killed by these plagues ᶜ yet repented not of the works of their hands, that they should not worship ᵈ devils, ᵉ and idols of gold, and silver, and brass, and stone, and of wood: which neither can see, nor hear, nor walk :

21 Neither repented they of their murders, ᶠ nor of their sorceries, nor of their fornication, nor of their thefts.

A. M. cir. 4100.
A. D. cir. 96.
Impp. Flavio
Domitiano
Cæs. Aug. et
Nerva.

ᶻ Chap. vii. 4.——ᵃ 1 Chron. xii. 8 ; Isa. v. 28, 29.——ᵇ Isa. ix. 15.——ᶜ Deut. xxxi. 29.

ᵈ Lev. xvii. 7 ; Deut. xxxii. 17 ; Psalm cvi. 37 ; 1 Cor. x. 20 ᵉ Psa. cxv. 4 ; cxxxv. 15 ; Dan. v. 23.——ᶠ Chap. xxii. 15.

---

haps it only means *vast numbers, multitudes without number.* Such a number might be literally true of the *locusts.* Those who will have their particular system supported by the images in this most obscure book, tell us that the number here means all the soldiers that were employed in this war, from its commencement to its end ! Those who can receive this saying let them receive it.

Verse 17. *Breastplates of fire—jacinth, and brimstone*] That is, *red, blue,* and *yellow ;* the first is the colour of *fire,* the second of *jacinth,* and the third of *sulphur.*

And the heads of the horses] Is this an allegorical description of great *ordnance ?* Cannons, on the mouths of which horses' heads were formed, or the mouth of the cannon cast in that form ? *Fire, smoke,* and *brimstone,* is a good allegorical representation of *gunpowder.* The Ottomans made great use of heavy artillery in their wars with the Greeks of the lower empire.

Verse 18. *By these three was the third part of men killed*] That is, By these was great carnage made.

Verse 19. *Their power is in their mouth*] From these the destructive *balls* are projected ; *and in their tails,* the *breech* where the *charge* of gunpowder is lodged.

Their tails were *like unto serpents, and had heads*] If *cannons* are intended, the description, though allegorical, is plain enough ; for *brass ordnance* especially are frequently thus ornamented, both at their *muzzles* and at their *breech.*

Verse 20. *Yet repented not*] The commission which these horsemen had was against idolaters ; and though multitudes of them were destroyed, yet the residue continued their senseless attachment to dumb idols, and therefore heavier judgments might be ex-

pected. These things are supposed to refer to the desolation brought upon the Greek Church by the *Ottomans,* who entirely ruined that Church and the Greek empire. The Church which was then remaining was the *Latin* or western Church, which was not at all corrected by the judgments which fell upon the eastern Church, but continued its senseless adoration of angels, saints, relics, &c., and does so to the present day. If, therefore, God's wrath be kindled against such, this Church has much to fear.

Verse 21. *Neither repented they of their murders*] Their cruelties towards the genuine followers of God the Albigenses, and Waldenses, and others, against whom they published crusades, and hunted them down, and butchered them in the most shocking manner. The innumerable murders by the horrible *inquisition* need not be mentioned.

Their sorceries] Those who apply this also to the Romish Church understand by it the various *tricks, sleights of hand,* or *legerdemain,* by which they impose on the common people in causing images of Christ to bleed, and the various pretended *miracles* wrought at the tombs, &c., of pretended saints, holy wells, and such like.

Fornication] Giving that honour to various creatures which is due only to the Creator.

Their thefts.] Their exactions and impositions on men for *indulgences, pardons,* &c. These things *may* be intended, but it is going too far to say that this is the true interpretation. And yet to express any doubt on this subject is with some little else than heresy. If such men can see these things so clearly in such obscure prophecies, let them be thankful for their sight, and indulgent to those who still sit in darkness.

CHAPTER X.

The description of a mighty angel with a little book in his hand, 1, 2. The seven thunders, 3, 4. The angel swears that there shall be time no longer, 5—7. John is commanded to take the little book and eat it ; he does so, and receives a commission to prophesy to many peoples, 8—11.

A. M. cir. 4100.
A. D. cir. 96.
Impp. Flavio
Domitiano
Cæs. Aug. et
Nerva.

AND I saw another mighty angel come down from heaven, clothed with a cloud; [a] and a rainbow *was* upon his head, and [b] his face *was* as it were the sun, and [c] his feet as pillars of fire:

2 And he had in his hand a little book open: [d] and he set his right foot upon the sea, and *his* left *foot* on the earth,

3 And cried with a loud voice, as *when* a lion roareth: and when he had cried, [e] seven thunders uttered their voices.

4 And when the seven thunders had uttered their voices, I was about to write: and I heard a voice from heaven saying unto me, [f] Seal up those things which the seven thunders uttered, and write them not.

5 And the angel which I saw stand upon the sea and upon the earth [g] lifted up his hand to heaven,

6 And sware by him that liveth for ever and ever, [h] who created heaven, and the things that therein are, and the earth, and the things that therein are, and the sea, and the things which are therein, [i] that there should be time no longer:

7 But [k] in the days of the voice of the seventh angel, when he shall begin to sound, the mystery of God should be finished, as he hath declared to his servants the prophets.

8 And [l] the voice which I heard from heaven spake unto me again, and said, Go *and* take the little book which is open in the hand of the angel which standeth upon the sea and upon the earth.

9 And I went unto the angel, and said unto him, Give me the little book. And he said unto me, [m] Take *it*, and eat it up; and it shall make thy belly bitter, but it shall be in thy mouth sweet as honey.

10 And I took the little book out of the angel's hand, and ate it up; [n] and it was in my mouth sweet as honey: and as soon as I had eaten it, [o] my belly was bitter.

11 And he said unto me, Thou must prophesy again before many peoples, and nations, and tongues, and kings.

A. M. cir. 4100.
A. D. cir. 96.
Impp. Flavio
Domitiano
Cæs. Aug. et
Nerva.

---

a Ezek. i. 28.——b Matt. xvii. 2; chap. i. 16.——c Chap. i. 15. d Matt. xxviii. 18.——e Chap. viii. 5.——f Dan. viii. 26; xii. 4, 9——g Exod. vi. 8; Dan. xii. 7.

h Neh. ix. 6; chap. iv. 11; xiv. 7.——i Dan. xii. 7; chap. xvi. 17.——k Chap. xi. 15.——l Ver. 4.——m Jer. xv. 16; Ezek. ii. 8; iii. 1, 2, 3.——n Ezek. iii. 3.——o Ezek. ii. 10.

NOTES ON CHAP. X.

Verse 1. *Another mighty angel*] Either Christ or his representative; *clothed with a cloud;* a symbol of the Divine majesty.

A rainbow was *upon his head*] The token of God's merciful covenant with mankind.

His face was *as it were the sun*] So intensely glorious that it could not be looked on.

His feet as pillars of fire] To denote the rapidity and energy of his motions, and the stability of his counsels.

Verse 2. *A little book open*] Meaning probably some *design* of God long concealed, but now about to be made manifest. But who knows what it means?

His right foot upon the sea, and his *left—on the earth*] To show that he had the command of each, and that his power was universal, all things being under his feet.

Verse 3. *Seven thunders*] Seven being a number of perfection, it may here mean many, great, loud, and strong peals of thunder, accompanied with distinct voices; but what was said St. John was not permitted to reveal, ver. 4.

Verse 5. *Lifted up his hand to heaven*] As one making an appeal to the supreme Being.

Verse 6. *By him that liveth for ever and ever*] The eternal, self-existent Jehovah, the Maker of all things.

That there should be time no longer] That the great counsels relative to the events already predicted should be immediately fulfilled, and that there should be no longer *delay.* This has no reference to the day of judgment.

Verse 7. *The mystery of God should be finished*] What this mystery refers to who knows? Nor have we more knowledge concerning the sounding of the seventh angel. On these points there is little agreement among learned men. Whether it mean the destruction of Jerusalem, or the destruction of the papal power, or something else, we know not. And yet with what confidence do men speak of the meaning of these hidden things!

Declared to his servants the prophets.] It is most likely, therefore, that this trumpet belongs to the *Jewish* state.

Verse 8. *Take the little book which is open*] Learn from this angel what should be published to the world.

Verse 9. *Take* it, *and eat it up*] Fully comprehend its meaning; study it thoroughly.

Verse 10. *It was in my mouth sweet as honey*] There was in it some pleasing, some unpleasing, intelligence. I read of the consolations and protection of the true worshippers of God, and did *rejoice;* I read of the persecutions of the Church, and was *distressed.*

Verse 11. *Thou must prophesy again*] Thou must write, not only for the instruction of the Jews in Palestine, but of those in the different provinces, as well as the heathens and heathen emperors and potentates in general.

THE reader will find, on comparing this chapter with Dan. viii. and xii., and Ezek. ii. and iii., that there are several things similar in both ; and the writer of the Apocalypse appears to keep these two prophets continually in view. I must once more say that I do not understand these prophecies, therefore I do not take upon me to explain them. I see with regret how many learned men have mistaken their way here. Commentators, and even some of the *most modern*, have strangely trifled in these solemn things; all trumpets, vials, woes, &c., are perfectly easy to *them ;* yet from their descriptions, none get wise either to common sense or to the things that make for their peace.

On the same ground I cannot admit the interpretation that is given of the word χρονος, translated *time* in ver. 6, which some have construed into an artificial period of **1,111** years, which they term *chronos ;* hence we have the *chronos, half-chronos,* and *non-chronos.* Bengel has said much on these points, but to very little purpose ; the word in the above place seems to signify *delay* simply, and probably refers to the long-suffering of God being ended in reference to Jerusalem ; for I all along take for probable that his book was written *previously* to the destruction of that city.

CHAPTER XI.

The command to measure the temple, 1, 2. *The two witnesses which should prophesy* twelve hundred ana sixty *days,* 3. *The description, power, and influence of these witnesses,* 4–6. *They shall be slain by the beast which shall arise out of the bottomless pit; and shall arise again after three days and a half, and ascend to heaven,* 7–12. *After which shall be a great earthquake,* 13. *The introduction to the third wo,* 14. *The sounding of the seventh angel, and the four and twenty elders give glory to God,* 15–19.

A. M. cir. 4100.
A. D. cir. 96.
Impp. Flavio
Domitiano
Cæs. Aug. et
Nerva.

AND there was given me [a] a reed like unto a rod : and the angel stood, saying, [b] Rise, and measure the temple of God, and the altar, and them that worship therein.

2 But [c] the court which is without the temple [d] leave out, and measure it not ; [e] for it is given unto the Gentiles : and the holy city shall they [f] tread under foot [g] forty *and* two months.

3 And [h] I will give *power* unto my two [i] witnesses, [k] and they shall prophesy [l] a thousand two hundred *and* threescore days, clothed in sackcloth.

A. M. cir. 4100
A. D. cir. 96.
Impp. Flavio
Domitiano
Cæs. Aug. et
Nerva.

4 These are the [m] two olive trees, and the two candlesticks standing before the God of the earth.

5 And if any man will hurt them, [n] fire proceedeth out of their mouth, and devoureth their enemies ; [o] and if any man will hurt them, he must in this manner be killed.

6 These [p] have power to shut heaven, that it rain not in the days of their prophecy ; and [q] have power over waters to turn them to blood, and to smite the earth with all plagues, as often as they will.

---

[a] Ezek. xl. 3, &c. ; Zech. ii. 1, chapter xxi. 15.——[b] Num. xxiii. 18.——[c] Ezek. xl. 17, 20.——[d] Gr. *cast out.*——[e] Psa. lxxix. 1 ; Luke xxi. 24.——[f] Dan viii. 10 ; 1 Mac. iii. 51.——[g] Chap. xiii. 5.——[h] Or, *I will give unto my two witnesses that they may*

prophesy.——[i] Chap. xx. 4.——[k] Chap. xix 10.——[l] Chap. xii. 6. [m] Psa. lii. 8 ; Jer. xi. 16, Zech. iv 3, 11, 14.——[n] 2 Kings i. 10, 12; Jer. i. 10 ; v. 14; Ezek. xliii. 3 ; Hos. vi. 5.——[o] Num. xvi 29.——[p] 1 Kings xvii. 1 ; James v. 16, 17.——[q] Exod. vii. 19.

NOTES ON CHAP. XI.

Verse 1. *And there was given me a reed*] See Ezek. xl. 3, &c.

Measure the temple of God] This must refer to the temple of Jerusalem ; and this is another presumptive evidence that it was yet standing.

Verse 2. *But the court—is given unto the Gentiles*] The measuring of the temple probably refers to its approaching *destruction*, and the *termination* of the whole *Levitical service ;* and this we find was to be done by the Gentiles, (Romans,) who were to tread it down forty-two months ; *i. e.,* just *three years and a half,* or *twelve hundred and* sixty days. This must be a symbolical period.

Verse 3. *My two witnesses*] This is extremely obscure ; the conjectures of interpreters are as unsatisfactory as they are endless on this point. *Conjec-*

turas conjecturis superstruunt, parum verosimiles, says Rosenmüller : *quorum sententias enarrare, meum non est.* I say the same. Those who wish to be amused or bewildered, may have recourse both to ancients and moderns on this subject.

Verse 4. *These are the two olive trees*] Mentioned Zech. iv. 14, which there represent *Zerubbabel* and *Joshua* the high priest. The whole account seems taken from Zech. iv. 1–14. Whether the prophet and the apostle mean the same things by these emblems, we know not.

Verse 5. *Fire proceedeth out of their mouth*] That is, they are commissioned to denounce the judgments of God against all who would attempt to prevent them from proceeding in their ministry.

Verse 6. *These have power to shut heaven*] As *Elijah* did, 1 Kings xvii. and xviii.

A. M. cir. 4100.
A. D. cir. 96.
Impp. Flavio
Domitiano
Cæs. Aug. et
Nerva.

7 And when they ʳ shall have finished their testimony, ˢ the beast that ascendeth ᵗ out of the bottomless pit ᵘ shall make war against them, and shall overcome them, and kill them.

8 And their dead bodies *shall lie* in the street of ᵛ the great city, which spiritually is called Sodom and Egypt, ʷ where also our Lord was crucified.

9 ˣ And they of the people, and kindreds, and tongues, and nations, shall see their dead bodies three days and a half, ʸ and shall not suffer their dead bodies to be put in graves.

10 ᶻ And they that dwell upon the earth shall rejoice over them, and make merry, ᵃ and shall send gifts one to another; ᵇ because these two prophets tormented them that dwelt on the earth.

A. M. cir. 4100.
A. D. cir. 96.
Impp. Flavio
Domitiano
Cæs. Aug. et
Nerva.

11 ᶜ And after three days and a half ᵈ the spirit of life from God entered into them, and they stood upon their feet; and great fear fell upon them which saw them.

12 And they heard a great voice from heaven saying unto them, Come up hither. ᵉ And they ascended up to heaven ᶠ in a cloud; ᵍ and their enemies beheld them.

13 And the same hour ʰ was there a great earthquake, ⁱ and the tenth part of the city fell, and in the earthquake were slain ᵏ of men seven thousand: and the remnant were affrighted, ˡ and gave glory to the God of heaven.

14 ᵐ The second wo is past; *and,* behold, the third wo cometh quickly.

15 And ⁿ the seventh angel sounded: ᵒ and there were great voices in heaven, saying,

---

ʳ Luke xiii. 32.——ˢ Chap. xiii. 1, 11; xvii. 8.——ᵗ Chap. ix. 2.——ᵘ Dan. vii. 21; Zech. xiv. 2.——ᵛ Chap. xiv. 8; xvii. 1, 5; xviii. 10.——ʷ Heb. xiii. 12; chap. xviii. 24.——ˣ Chap. xvii. 15.——ʸ Psa. lxxix. 2, 3.——ᶻ Chap. xii. 12; xiii. 8.——ᵃ Esther ix. 19, 22.——ᵇ Chap. xvi. 10.——ᶜ Ver. 9.

ᵈ Ezek. xxxvii. 5, 9, 10, 14.——ᵉ Isa. xiv. 13; chap. xii. 5. ᶠ Isa. lx. 8; Acts i. 9.——ᵍ 2 Kings ii. 1, 5, 7.——ʰ Chap. vi. 12. ⁱ Chap. xvi. 19.——ᵏ Gr. *names of men*; chap. iii. 4.——ˡ Josh. vii. 19; chap. xiv. 7; xv. 4.——ᵐ Chap. viii. 13; ix. 12; xv. 1. ⁿ Chap. x. 7.——ᵒ Isa. xxvii. 13; chap. xvi. 17; xix. 6.

To turn them to blood] As *Moses* did, Exod. vii. They shall have power to afflict the land with plagues, similar to those which were inflicted on the Egyptians.

Verse 7. *The beast that ascendeth out of the bottomless pit*] This may be what is called *antichrist;* some power that is opposed to genuine Christianity. But *what* or *whence,* except *from the bottomless pit,* i. e., under the influence and appointment of the devil, we cannot tell; nor do we know by what name this power or being should be called. The conjectures concerning the *two witnesses* and the *beast* have been sufficiently multiplied. If the whole passage, as some think, refer to the persecution raised by the *Jews* against the *Christians,* then some *Jewish power* or *person* is the *beast* from the bottomless pit. If it refer to the early ages of Christianity, then the *beast* may be one of the persecuting *heathen emperors.* If it refer to a later age of Christianity, then the *beast* may be the *papal power,* and the *Albigenses* and *Waldenses* the *two witnesses,* which were nearly extinguished by the horrible persecutions raised up against them by the Church of Rome. Whatever may be *here* intended, the earth has not yet covered *their* blood.

Verse 8. *The great city*] Some say *Rome,* which may be spiritually called *Sodom* for its *abominations, Egypt* for its *tyrannous cruelty,* and the *place where our Lord was crucified,* because of its persecution of the members of Christ; but *Jerusalem* itself may be intended. All these things I must leave to others.

Verse 9. *Shall not suffer their dead bodies to be put in graves.*] They shall be treated with the greatest *barbarity.* Refusal of burial to the dead was allowed to be the sum of brutality and cruelty. In popish lands they will not suffer a Protestant to have *Christian burial,* or to have a grave in a churchyard! Contemptible wretches!

Verse 10. *Shall send gifts*] This was a custom in days of public rejoicing. They sent gifts to each other, and gave portions to the poor. See Esther ix. 19, 22.

Verse 11. *They stood upon their feet*] Were restored to their primitive state.

Verse 12. *They ascended up to heaven*] Enjoyed a state of great peace and happiness.

Verse 13. *A great earthquake*] Violent commotions among the persecutors, and revolutions of states.

Slain of men seven thousand] Many perished in these popular commotions.

The remnant were affrighted] Seeing the hand of God's judgments so remarkably stretched out.

Gave glory] Received the pure doctrines of the Gospel, and glorified God for *his* judgments and *their* conversion.

Verse 14. *The second wo is past*] That which took place under the *sixth trumpet,* and has been already described.

The third wo cometh] Is about to be described under the *seventh trumpet,* which the angel is now prepared to sound.

Of the *three woes* which were denounced, chap. viii. 13, the first is described, chap. ix. 1—12; the second, chap. ix. 13—21. These woes are supposed by many learned men to refer to the destruction of Jerusalem. *The first wo*—the seditions among the Jews themselves. *The second wo*—the besieging of the city by the Romans. *The third wo*—the taking and sacking of the city, and burning the temple. This was the greatest of all the woes, as in it the city and temple were destroyed, and nearly a million of men lost their lives.

Verse 15. *There were great voices in heaven*] All the heavenly host—angels and redeemed human spirits,

2

A. M. cir. 4100.
A. D. cir. 96.
Impp. Flavio
Domitiano
Cæs. Aug. et
Nerva.

[p] The kingdoms of this world are become *the kingdoms* of our Lord, and of his Christ; [q] and he shall reign for ever and ever.

16 And [r] the four and twenty elders, which sat before God on their seats, fell upon their faces, and worshipped God,

17 Saying, We give thee thanks, O Lord God Almighty, [s] which art, and wast, and art to come; because thou hast taken to thee thy great power, [t] and hast reigned.

18 [u] And the nations were angry, and thy wrath is come, [v] and the time of the dead, that they should be judged, and that thou shouldest give reward unto thy servants the prophets, and to the saints, and them that fear thy name, [w] small and great; [x] and shouldest destroy them which [y] destroy the earth.

19 And [z] the temple of God was opened in heaven, and there was seen in his temple the ark of his testament: and [a] there were lightnings, and voices, and thunderings, and an earthquake, [b] and great hail.

A. M. cir. 4100,
A. D. cir. 96.
Impp. Flavio
Domitiano
Cæs. Aug. et
Nerva.

---

[p] Chap. xii. 10.——[q] Dan. ii. 44; vii. 14, 18, 27.——[r] Chap. iv. 4; v. 8; xix. 4.——[s] Chap. i. 4, 8; iv. 8; xvi. 5.——[t] Chap. xix. 6.——[u] Ver. 2, 9.

[v] Dan. vii. 9, 10; chap. vi. 10.——[w] Chap. xix. 5.——[x] Chap. xiii. 10; xviii. 6.——[y] Or, *corrupt.*——[z] Chap. xv. 5, 8.——[a] Ch. viii. 5; xvi. 18.——[b] Chap. xvi. 21.

---

joined together to magnify God, that he had utterly discomfited his enemies, and rendered his friends glorious. This will be truly the case when the kingdoms of this world become the kingdoms of God and of his Christ. But *when* shall this be? Some say, what is meant by these words has already taken place in the destruction of the Jewish state, and sending the Gospel throughout the Gentile world. Others say that it refers to the millennium, and to the consummation of all things.

Verse 16. *The four and twenty elders*] The representatives of the universal Church of Christ. See on chap. v. 8–10.

Verse 17. *O Lord God Almighty, which art*] This gives a proper view of God in his eternity; all *times* are here comprehended, the *present*, the *past*, and the *future*. This is the infinitude of God.

Hast taken to thee] Thou hast *exercised* that power which thou ever hast; and thou hast broken the power of thy enemies, and exalted thy Church.

Verse 18. *The nations were angry*] Were enraged against thy Gospel, and determined to destroy it.

Thy wrath is come] The time to avenge thy servants and to destroy all thy enemies.

The time of the dead, that they should be judged] The word κρινειν, *to judge*, is often used in the sense of *to avenge.* The dead, here, may mean those who were *slain for the testimony of Jesus*, and the *judging* is the *avenging* of their blood.

Give reward unto thy servants] Who have been faithful unto death.

The prophets] The faithful *teachers* in the Church *the saints*—the Christians.

And them that fear thy name] All thy sincere followers.

Destroy them which destroy the earth.] All the authors, fomenters, and encouragers of bloody wars.

Verse 19. *The temple of God was opened in heaven*] The true worship of God was established and performed in the Christian Church; this is the true temple, that at Jerusalem being destroyed.

And there were lightnings, and voices, and thunderings, and an earthquake, and great hail.] These great commotions were intended to introduce the following vision; for the 12th chapter is properly a continuation of the 11th, and should be read in strict connection with it.

I NOW come to a part of this book that is deemed of the greatest importance by the Protestant Church, but is peculiarly difficult and obscure. I have often acknowledged my own incapacity to illustrate these prophecies. I might have availed myself of the labours of others, but I know not who is right; or whether any of the writers on this book have hit the sense is more than I can assert, and more than I think. The illustration of the xiith, xiiith, and xviith chapters, which I have referred to in the *preface*, drawn up and displayed with great industry and learning, I shall insert in its place, as by far the most probable I have yet seen; but I leave the learned author responsible for his own particular views of the subject.

CHAPTER XII.

The woman clothed with the sun, and in travail, 1, 2. The great red dragon waiting to devour the child as soon as born, 3, 4. The woman is delivered of a son, who is caught up unto God; and she flees to the wilderness, 5, 6. The war in heaven between Michael and the dragon, 7, 8. The dragon and his angels are overcome and cast down to the earth; whereupon the whole heavenly host give glory to God, 9–11. The dragon, full of wrath at his defeat, persecutes the woman, 12, 13. She flees to the wilderness, whither he attempts to pursue her; and he makes war with her seed, 14–17.

2

A. M. cir. 4100.
A. D. cir. 96.
Impp. Flavio
Domitiano
Cæs. Aug. et
Nerva.

AND there appeared a great ª wonder in heaven; a woman clothed with the sun, and the moon under her feet, and upon her head a crown of twelve stars:

2 And she being with child cried, ᵇ travailing in birth, and pained to be delivered.

3 And there appeared another ᶜ wonder in heaven; and behold ᵈ a great red dragon, ᵉ having seven heads and ten horns, ᶠ and seven crowns upon his heads.

4 And ᵍ his tail drew the third part ʰ of the stars of heaven, ⁱ and did cast them to the earth: and the dragon stood ᵏ before the woman which was ready to be delivered, ˡ for to devour her child as soon as it was born.

5 And she brought forth a man child, ᵐ who was to rule all nations with a rod of iron: and

A. M. cir. 4100.
A. D. cir. 96.
Impp. Flavio
Domitiano
Cæs. Aug. et
Nerva.

her child was caught up unto God, and *to* his throne.

6 And ⁿ the woman fled into the wilderness, where she hath a place prepared of God, that they should feed her there ᵒ a thousand two hundred *and* threescore days.

7 And there was war in heaven: ᵖ Michael and his angels fought ᑫ against the dragon; and the dragon fought and his angels,

8 And prevailed not; neither was their place found any more in heaven.

9 And ʳ the great dragon was cast out, ˢ that old serpent, called the Devil, and Satan, ᵗ which deceiveth the whole world: ᵘ he was cast out into the earth, and his angels were cast out with him.

10 And I heard a loud voice saying in

ª Or, *sign.*——ᵇ Isaiah lxvi. 7; Gal. iv. 19.——ᶜ Or, *sign.*
ᵈ Chap. xvii. 3.——ᵉ Chap. xvii. 9, 10.——ᶠ Ch. xiii. 1.——ᵍ Ch. ix. 10, 19.——ʰ Chap. xvii. 18.——ⁱ Dan. viii. 10.——ᵏ Verse 2.
ˡ Exod. i. 16.

ᵐ Psa. ii. 9; chap. ii. 27; xix. 15.——ⁿ Ver. 4.——ᵒ Chapter xi. 3.——ᵖ Dan. x. 13, 21; xii. 1.——ᑫ Ver. 3; chapter xx. 2.
ʳ Luke x. 18; John xii. 31.——ˢ Gen. iii. 1, 4; chapter xx. 2.
ᵗ Chap. xx. 3.——ᵘ Chap. ix. 1.

NOTES ON CHAP. XII.

Before I introduce the comment mentioned at the close of the preceding chapter, I think it necessary to state that the *phraseology* of the whole chapter is peculiarly *rabbinical*, and shall insert a few selections which may serve to illustrate some of the principal *figures*.

In *Sohar Exod.*, fol. 47, col. 187, we find a mystical interpretation of Exod. xxi. 22: *If men strive, and hurt a woman with child, so that her fruit depart—he shall be surely punished, as the woman's husband will lay upon him.* " If men strive, i. e. Michael and Samael, and hurt a woman with child, i. e. *the Israelitish Church*, so that her fruit depart, *hoc fit in exilio*, he shall surely be punished, i. e., Samael. As the *woman's husband*, that is, the holy and blessed God."

Verse 5. *And her child was caught up unto God, and to his throne.*] In *Yalcut Rubeni* are these words: " Rachael, the niece of Methusala, was pregnant, and ready to be delivered in Egypt. They trod upon her, and the child came out of her bowels, and lay under the bed; *Michael descended, and took him up to the throne of glory.* On that same night the first-born of Egypt were destroyed."

Verse 7. *There was war in heaven*] In the same treatise, fol. 87, 2, on Exod. xiv. 7, *Pharaoh took six hundred chariots*, we have these words: " There was war among those *above* and among those *below*; והמלחמה היתה חזקה בשמים vehammilchamah, hayethah chazakah bashshamayim, *and there was great war in heaven.*"

Of *Michael* the rabbins are full. See much in *Schoettgen*, and see the note on Jude, ver 9.

The dragon—and his angels] The same as *Rab. Sam. ben David*, in *Chasad Shimuel*, calls כמאל וחייילותיו Samael vechayilothaiv, " *Samael and his troops*;" fol. 28, 2.

Verse 9. *That old serpent*] The rabbins speak much of this *being*, sometimes under the notion of

יצר הרע yetser hara, *the evil principle*, and sometimes *Samael*.

He was cast out into the earth, and his angels were cast out with him.] This is very like a saying in the book *Bahir*, in *Sohar Gen.*, fol. 27, col. 107: " *And God cast out Samael and his troops from the place of their holiness.*"

Verse 10. *The accuser of our brethren*] There is scarcely any thing more common in the rabbinical writings than *Satan as the accuser of the Israelites*. And the very same word κατηγορος, *accuser*, or, as it is in the *Codex Alexandrinus*, κατηγωρ, is used by them in Hebrew letters, קטיגור katigor; e. gr., *Pirkey Eliezer*, c. 46, speaking of the day of expiation: " And the holy blessed God hears their testimony *from their accuser*, מן הקטיגור *min hakkatigor;* and expiates the altar, the priests, and the whole multitude, from the greatest to the least."

In *Shemoth Rabba*, sec. 31, fol. 129, 2, are these words: " If a man observes the precepts, and is a son of the law, and lives a holy life, then *Satan stands and accuses him.*"

" *Every day*, except the day of expiation, *Satan is the accuser of men.*"—*Vayikra Rabba*, sec. 21, fol. 164.

" The holy blessed God said to the seventy princes of the world, Have ye seen him *who always accuses my children ?*"—*Yalcut Chadash*, fol. 101, 3.

" The devil *stands always as an accuser* before the King of Israel."—*Sohar Levit.*, fol. 43, col. 171. See much more in *Schoettgen*.

NOTES ON CHAP. XII., BY J. E. C.

Verse 1. *There appeared a great wonder in heaven; a woman clothed with the sun*] That the woman here represents the true Church of Christ most commentators are agreed. In other parts of the Apocalypse, the pure Church of Christ is evidently portrayed by

A. M. cir. 4100.
A. D. cir. 96.
Impp. Flavio
Domitiano
Cæs. Aug. et
Nerva.

heaven, ᵛ Now is come salvation, and strength, and the kingdom of our God, and the power of his Christ : for the accuser of our brethren is cast down, ʷ which accused them before our God day and night.

11 And ˣ they overcame him by the blood of the Lamb, and by the word of their testimony; ʸ and they loved not their lives unto the death.

12 Therefore ᶻ rejoice, *ye* heavens, and ye that dwell in them. ᵃ Wo to the inhabiters of the earth, and of the sea ! for the devil is come down unto you, having great wrath, ᵇ because he knoweth that he hath but a short time.

13 And when the dragon saw that he was cast unto the earth, he persecuted ᶜ the woman which brought forth the man *child.*

14 ᵈ And to the woman were given two wings of a great eagle, ᵉ that she might fly ᶠ into the wilderness, into her place; where she is nourished ᵍ for a time, and times ; and half a time, from the face of the serpent.

A. M. cir. 4100
A. D. cir. 96.
Impp. Flavio
Domitiano
Cæs. Aug. et
Nerva.

15 And the serpent ʰ cast out of his mouth water as a flood after the woman, that he might cause her to be carried away of the flood.

16 And the earth helped the woman, and the earth opened her mouth, and swallowed up the flood which the dragon cast out of his mouth.

17 And the dragon was wroth with the woman, ⁱ and went to make war with the remnant of her seed, ᵏ which keep the commandments of God, and have ˡ the testimony of Jesus Christ.

ᵛ Chapter xi. 15; xix. 1.——ʷ Job i. 9; ii. 5; Zech. iii. 1. ˣ Rom. viii. 33, 34, 37; xvi. 20.——ʸ Luke xiv. 26.——ᶻ Psalm xcvi. 11 ; Isa. xlix. 13; chap. xviii. 20.——ᵃ Chap. viii. 13; xi. 10.——ᵇ Chap. x. 6.——ᶜ Ver. 5.

ᵈ Exod. xix. 4 ; 1 Mac. ii. 29, 30, 31.——ᵉ Ver. 6.——ᶠ Chap xvii. 3.——ᵍ Dan. vii. 25 ; xii. 7.——ʰ Isa. lix. 15; chap. xi. 7; xiii. 7 ——ᵏ Chapter xiv. 12.——ˡ 1 Cor. ii. 1 ; 1 John v. 10 ; chap. i. 2, 9 ; vi. 9 ; xx. 4.

---

a woman. In chap. xix., ver. 7, a great multitude are represented as saying, " Let us be glad and rejoice, and give honour to him ; for the marriage of the Lamb is come, and his WIFE hath made herself ready." In chap. xxi. 9, an angel talks with St. John, saying, ".. Come hither, I will show thee the BRIDE, the Lamb's wife." That the Christian Church is meant will appear also from her being *clothed with the sun,* a striking emblem of Jesus Christ, the Sun of righteousness, the light and glory of the Church ; for the countenance of the Son of God is *as the sun shineth in his strength.* The woman has

The moon under her feet.] Bishop Newton understands this of the Jewish typical worship ; and indeed the Mosaic system of rites and ceremonies could not have been better represented, for it was the *shadow of good things to come.* The moon is the less light, ruling over the night, and deriving all its illumination from the sun ; in like manner the Jewish dispensation was the bright moonlight night of the world, and possessed a portion of the glorious light of the Gospel. At the rising of the sun the night is ended, and the lunar light no longer necessary, as the sun which enlightens her shines full upon the earth ; exactly in the same way has the whole Jewish system of types and shadows been superseded by the birth, life, crucifixion, death, resurrection, ascension, and intercession of Jesus Christ. Upon the head of the woman is

A crown of twelve stars.] A very significant representation of the *twelve apostles,* who were the first founders of the Christian Church, and by whom the Gospel was preached in great part of the Roman empire with astonishing success. " They that be wise shall shine as the brightness of the firmament ; and they that turn many to righteousness, as the STARS for ever and ever." Dan. xii. 3.

Verse 2. *And she being with child cried, travailing in birth, &c.*] This, when taken in connection with the following verses, is a striking figure of the great persecution which the Church of Christ should suffer under the heathen Roman emperors, but more especially of that long and most dreadful one under Diocletian. The woman is represented as BEING *with child,* to show that the time would speedily arrive when God's patient forbearance with the heathen would be terminated, and that a *deliverer* should arise in the Christian world who would execute the Divine vengeance upon paganism.

Verse 3. *There appeared another wonder—a great red dragon*] The dragon here is a symbol, not of the *Roman empire* in general, but of the HEATHEN *Roman empire.* This great pagan power must have, therefore, been thus represented from the religion which it supported. But what is a dragon ? An entirely fabulous beast of antiquity, consequently, in this respect, a most proper emblem of the heathen worship, which consisted in paying adoration to numerous imaginary beings, termed gods, goddesses, &c. The very foundation of the heathen religious system is mostly built upon fable ; and it is very difficult to trace many of their superstitions to any authentic original ; and even those which appear to derive their origin from the sacred writings are so disguised in fable as literally to bear no more resemblance to the truth than the dragon of the ancients does to any animal with which we are acquainted. But it may be asked why the Spirit of God should represent the heathen Roman empire by a *dragon,* rather than by any other of the fabulous animals with which the mythology of the ancient Romans abounded. The answer is as follows : In the eighth chapter of the Prophet Daniel, God has represented the kingdom of the Greeks by a *he-goat,* for no other apparent reason than this, that it was the national military standard of the Grecian monarchy; we may therefore expect that the pagan Roman empire is called a DRAGON on a similar account. In confirmation of this point it is very remarkable that the *dragon* was the principal standard of the Romans next to the eagle, in the *second, third, fourth,* and *fifth* centuries of the Christian era. Of this we have abundant evidence in the writings of both heathens and Christians. Arrian is the earliest writer who has mentioned that dragons were used as military standards among the Romans. See his Tactics, c. 51. Hence Schwebelius supposes that this standard was introduced after Trajan's conquest of the Daci. See *Vegetius de Re Militari a Schwebelio,* p. 191, Argentorati, 1806; and *Grævii* Thesaur., Antiq. Roman., tom. x., col. 1529. Vegetius, who flourished about A. D. 386, says, lib. ii. c. 13 : *Primum signum totius legionis est aquila, quam aquilifer portat.* DRACONES *etiam per singulas cohortes a draconariis feruntur ad prælium.* "The first standard of the whole legion is the eagle, which the aquilifer carries. DRAGONS are also borne to battle by the Draconarii." As a legion consisted of ten cohorts, there were therefore *ten* draconarii to *one* aquilifer; hence, from the great number of draconarii in an army, the word *signarii* or *signiferi,* standard-bearers, came at last to mean the carriers of the dragon standards only, the others retaining the name of *aquiliferi.*—See *Veget.,* lib. ii. c. 7, and his commentators. The heathen Roman empire is called *a* RED *dragon;* and accordingly we find from the testimony of ancient writers that the dragon standards of the Romans were painted *red.* We read in Ammianus Marcellinus, lib. xvi., c. 12, of PURPUREUM *signum draconis,* "the purple standard of the dragon." See also *Claudianus* in Rufinum, lib. ii., l. 177, 178. *Pitiscus,* in his Lexicon Antiq. Rom., and *Ducange,* in his Glossarium Mediæ et Infimæ Latinitatis, sub voc. *Draco,* have considered this subject at great length, especially the latter writer, who has made several quotations from Claudianus, Sidonius, Prudentius, and others, in which not only the standard, but also the image of the dragon itself, is stated to be of a *red* or *purple* colour. Of what has been said above respecting the dragon, this is then the sum : a *huge fabulous* beast is shown to St. John, by which some GREAT PAGAN *power* is symbolically represented; and *the* RED *dragon* is selected from among the numerous imaginary animals which the fancies of mankind have created to show that this great pagan power is the *heathen* ROMAN *empire.*

Having seven heads] As the dragon is an emblem of the heathen Roman power, its *heads* must denote *heathen forms of government.*—See the note on chap. xvii. 10, where the heads of the beast are explained in a similar way. These were exactly *seven,* and are enumerated by Tacitus (Annal., lib. i., in *principio*) in words to the following effect : "The city of Rome was originally governed by *kings.* L. Brutus instituted liberty and the *consulate.* The *dictatorship* was only occasionally appointed; neither did the *decemviral power* last above two years; nor the *consular power of the military tribunes* was not of long continuance. Neither had Cinna nor Sylla a long domination; the

1010

power of Pompey and Crassus was also soon absorbed in that of Cæsar; and the arms of Lepidus and Antony finally yielded to those of Augustus." From this passage it is evident to every person well acquainted with the Roman history, that the seven forms of government in the heathen Roman world were, 1. The regal power; 2. The consulate; 3. The dictatorship; 4 The decemvirate; 5. The consular power of the military tribunes; 6. The triumvirate; and, 7. The imperial government.

It is singular that commentators in general, in their citation of this passage, have taken no notice of *the triumvirate,* a form of government evidently as distinct from any of the others as *kings* are from *consuls,* or *consuls* from *emperors.* For the triumvirate consisted in the division of the Roman republic into three parts, each governed by an officer possessed with consular authority in his own province; and all three united together in the regulation of the whole Roman state. Consequently, it differed entirely from *the imperial power,* which was the entire conversion of the Roman state from a republic to a monarchy.

And ten horns] That these ten horns signify as many kingdoms is evident from the seventh chapter of Daniel, where the angel, speaking of the fourth beast, says, that "the ten horns out of this kingdom are ten kings that shall arise;" and in this view of the passage many commentators are agreed, who also admit that the ten kingdoms are to be met with "amid the broken pieces of the Roman empire." And it is evident that nothing less than the dismemberment of the Roman empire, and its division into ten independent kingdoms, can be intended by the angel's interpretation just quoted. If, therefore, the ten horns of Daniel's fourth beast point out as many kingdoms, for the very same reason must the horns of the dragon have a similar meaning. But the Roman empire was not divided into several independent kingdoms till a considerable time after it became Christian. In what sense then can it be said that the different kingdoms into which the Roman empire was divided by the barbarous nations are horns of the dragon? They were so because it was the Roman monarchy, *in its seventh* DRACONIC *form of government,* which was dismembered by the barbarians. For though the Roman empire was not completely dismembered till the fifth century, it is well known that the depression of the heathen idolatry, and the advancement of Christianity to the throne, effected not the least change in the *form* of government : the Romans continued still to be under subjection to the imperial power; and, consequently, when the heathen barbarous nations divided the Roman empire among themselves, they might very properly be denominated *horns of the dragon,* as it was by means of their incursions that the *imperial power,* FOUNDED by the heathen Cæsars, was abolished. Machiavel and Bishop Lloyd enumerate the horns of the dragon thus :— 1. The kingdom of the Huns; 2. The kingdom of the Ostrogoths; 3 The kingdom of the Visigoths; 4. The kingdom of the Franks; 5. The kingdom of the Vandals; 6. The kingdom of the Sueves and Alans; 7. The kingdom of the Burgundians; 8. The kingdom of the Heruli, Rugii, Scyrri, and other tribes which composed the Italian kingdom of Odoacer; 9. The kingdom of the Saxons; and 10. The kingdom of the Lombards.

And seven crowns upon his head.] In the seven Roman forms of government already enumerated, heathenism has been the *crowning* or *dominant religion.*

Verse 4. *And his tail drew the third part of the stars of heaven*] It is not unusual in Scripture, as Dr. Mitchell observes, to call the hindmost of an enemy the *tail,* as in Josh. x. 19 : *Ye shall cut off the hindmost of them,* which is literally in Hebrew, וזנבתם אותם "Ye shall cut off their *tail.*" See also Deut. xxv. 18. It is also observable that the word ουρα, in this verse, has been used by the Greeks in the same sense with the Hebrew word זנב already referred to. Thus ουρα στρατου, which we would translate the *rear of an army,* is literally the *tail* of an army. See the Thesaurus of Stephens, in loc. The *tail* of the dragon is therefore the heathen Roman power in its *seventh* or *last* form of government, viz., *the imperial power;* and is not, as Dr. Mitchell supposes, to be restricted to the *last* heathen Roman emperors. The heathen imperial power is said to draw *the third part of the stars of heaven,* by which has generally been understood that the Roman empire subjected the third part of the princes and potentates of the earth. But that this is not a correct statement of the fact is evident from the testimony of ancient history. The Roman empire was always considered and called *the empire of the world* by ancient writers. See *Dionys. Halicar.,* Antiq. Rom. lib. i., prope principium ; *Pitisci* Lexicon Antiq. Roman., sub voc. imperium ; *Ovidii* Fast., lib. ii. l. 683 ; *Vegetius* de Re Militari, lib. i. c. 1., &c., &c. And it is even so named in Scripture, for St. Luke, in the second chapter of his gospel, informs us that *there went out a decree from Cæsar Augustus that* THE WHOLE WORLD *should be taxed,* by which is evidently meant *the Roman empire.* The whole mystery of this passage consists in the misapprehension of its symbolical language. In order therefore to understand it, the symbols here used must be examined. By *heaven* is meant the *most eminent* or *ruling part* of any nation. This is evident from the very nature of the symbol, for " *heaven* is God's throne ;" they therefore who are advanced to the supreme authority in any state are very properly said to be *taken up into heaven,* because they are raised to this eminence by the favour of the Lord, and are *ministers of his to do his pleasure.* And the calamity which fell upon Nebuchadnezzar was to instruct him in this important truth, that *the heavens do rule ;* that is, that all monarchs possess their kingdoms by Divine appointment, and that no man is raised to power by what is usually termed the chances of war, but that " the Most High ruleth in the kingdom of men, and giveth it to whomsoever he will, and setteth up over it the basest of men." The meaning of *heaven* being thus ascertained, it cannot be difficult to comprehend the meaning of *earth,* this being evidently its opposite, that is, every thing in subjection to the *heaven* or *ruling part.* *Stars* have already been shown to denote *ministers of religion ;* and this is more fully evident from chap. i. of this book, where *the seven stars* which the Son of God holds in his right hand are explained to signify *the seven angels* (or messengers) *of the seven Churches,* by whom must be

meant the *seven pastors* or *ministers* of these Churches. The resemblance of ministers to stars is very striking ; for as the stars give light upon the earth, so are ministers the lights of the cause they advocate ; and their position in *heaven,* the symbol of domination, very fitly betokens the spiritual authority of priests or ministers over their flocks. Hence, as the woman, or Christian Church, has upon her head a *crown* of twelve stars, which signifies that she is under the *guidance* of the twelve apostles, who are the twelve principal lights of the Christian world, so has the dragon also his *stars* or *ministers.* The stars therefore which the dragon draws with his tail must represent the whole body of pagan priests, who were the *stars* or *lights* of the heathen world. But in what sense can it be said that the heathen Roman empire, which ruled over the whole known world, only draws a *third part* of the stars of heaven? The answer is : The religious world in the time of St. John was divided into three grand branches, viz., the Christian world, the Jewish world, and the heathen and pagan world. consequently, as *a dragon,* a fabulous animal, is an emblem of a civil power supporting *a religion founded in fable ;* it necessarily follows that the *stars* or *ministers* of the Jews and Christians cannot be numbered among those which he draws with his tail, as they were not the advocates of his idolatry, but were ministers of a religion founded by the God of heaven, and consequently formed no part of the pagan world, though they were in subjection in secular matters to the pagan Roman empire. The tail of the dragon therefore draweth after him *the whole heathen world.*

And did cast them to the earth] That is, reduced all the pagan priests under the Roman yoke. The words of the prophecy are very remarkable. It is said the tail of the dragon *draweth,* (for so ουρει should be translated,) but it is added, *and* HATH CAST *them upon the earth,* to show that at the time the Apocalypse was written the world was divided into the three grand religious divisions already referred to ; but that the tail of the dragon, or the pagan Roman power under its *last* form of government, had brought the whole heathen world (which was a third part of the religious world in the apostolic age) into subjection previously to the communication of the Revelation to St. John. It is the dragon's *tail* that draws the third part of the stars of heaven, therefore it was during the dominion of his *last* form of government that Christianity was introduced into the world ; for in the time of the six preceding draconic forms of government, the world was divided religiously into only two grand branches, Jews and Gentiles. That the sense in which the *third part* is here taken is the one intended in the prophecy is put beyond all controversy, when it is considered that this very division is made in the first and third verses, in which mention is made of the *woman clothed with the sun*—the Christian Church, *the moon under her feet,* or Jewish Church, and the *dragon,* or heathen power. Thus the *heathen* IMPERIAL *government* is doubly represented, first, by *one of the seven* draconic heads, to show that it was one of those seven heathen forms of government which have been successively at the *head* of the Roman state ; and secondly, by the dragon's *tail,* because it was the *last* of those seven. For a justification of this method of interpretation, see on the angel's double explanation of the heads of the beast, chap. xvii. 9, 10, 16.

And the dragon stood before the woman, &c.] Constantius Chlorus, the father of Constantine, abandoned the absurdities of paganism, and treated the Christians with great respect. This alarmed the pagan priests, whose interests were so closely connected with the continuance of the ancient superstitions, and who apprehended that to their great detriment the Christian religion would become daily more universal and triumphant throughout the empire. Under these anxious fears they moved Diocletian to persecute the Christians. Hence began what is termed the *tenth* and last general persecution, which was the most severe of all, and continued nearly ten years; (see *Mosheim's* Ecclesiastical History of the Third Century;) and as it was the Divine pleasure that, at this time, a great deliverer should be raised up in behalf of his suffering people, the *woman*, or Christian Church, is very appropriately represented as overtaken with the pangs of labour, *and ready to be delivered.* Before the death of Constantius, the heathen party, aware that Constantine would follow the example of his father, who so much favoured the Christians, beheld him with a watchful and malignant eye. Many were the snares that, according to Eusebius, were laid for him by Maximin and Galerius : he relates the frequent and dangerous enterprises to which they urged him, with the design that he might lose his life. When Galerius heard of the death of Constantius, and that he had appointed Constantine his successor, he was filled with the most ungovernable rage and indignation, notwithstanding he did not dare to take any steps contrary to the interest of Constantine. The dread of the armies of the west, which were mostly composed of Christians, was a sufficient check to all attempts of that kind. Thus the dragon, or heathen power, stood before the woman, or Christian Church, to devour her son, or deliverer, as soon as he was born. See Dr. *Mitchell's* Exposition of the Revelation, in loc.

Verse 5. *And she brought forth a man child*] The Christian Church, when her full time came, obtained a *deliverer*, who, in the course of the Divine providence, was destined

To rule all nations] The heathen Roman empire,

With a rod of iron] A strong figure to denote the *very great restraint* that should be put upon paganism, so that it should not be able longer to persecute the Christian Church. The *man child* mentioned in this verse is *the dynasty of Christian emperors*, beginning with Constantine's public acknowledgment of his belief in the divinity of the Christian religion, which happened in the latter part of A. D. 312, after the defeat of the Emperor Maxentius.

And her child was caught up unto God, and to his throne.] A succession of Christian emperors was raised up to the Church ; for the Roman throne, as Bishop Newton observes, is here called the throne of God, because there is no power but of God : *the powers that be are ordained of God.*

Verse 6. *And the woman fled into the wilderness*] The account of the woman's flying into the wilderness immediately follows that of her child being caught up

to the throne of God, to denote the great and *rapid* increase of heresies in the Christian Church after the time that Christianity was made the religion of the empire.

Where she hath a place prepared of God] See on ver. 14.

Ver. 7. *And there was war in heaven*] As *heaven* means here the *throne* of the Roman empire, the war in heaven consequently alludes to the breaking out of civil commotions among the governors of this empire.

Michael and his angels fought against the dragon] Michael was the man child which the woman brought forth, as is evident from the context, and therefore signifies, as has been shown already, the dynasty of Christian Roman emperors. This dynasty is represented by Michael, because he is " the great prince which standeth for the children of God's people." Dan. xii. 1.

And the dragon fought and his angels] Or ministers.

Verse 8. *And prevailed not*] Against the cause of Christianity.

Neither was their place found any more in heaven.] The advocates of the heathen idolatry were prevented from having any farther share in the government of the empire. The wonderful success of Constantine over all his enemies, and his final triumph over Licinius, correspond exactly to the symbolical language in this verse.

Verse 9. *And the great dragon was cast out, &c.*] By the terms *Devil* and *Satan* mentioned in this verse, Pareus, Faber, and many other commentators, understand literally the great spiritual enemy of mankind. But this view of the passage cannot be correct, from the circumstance that it is the *dragon* which is thus called. Now, if by the *dragon* be meant the *devil*, then we are necessarily led to this conclusion, that the great apostate spirit is a monster, having seven heads and ten horns ; and also that he has a *tail*, with which he drags after him the third part of the stars of heaven. The appellations, *old serpent, devil*, and *Satan*, must, therefore, be understood figuratively. The heathen power is called *that old serpent which deceiveth the whole world*, from its subtlety against the Christians, and its causing the whole Roman world, as far as it was in its power to embrace the absurdities of paganism. It is called the *devil*, from its continual false accusations and slanders against the true worshippers of God, for the devil is *a liar from the beginning* ; and it is also called *Satan*, שטן, which is a Hebrew word signifying *an adversary*, from its frequent persecutions of the Christian Church. The dragon and his angels are said to be cast out, which is more than was said in the preceding verse. There mention is made of his being found no longer in *heaven*, or on the throne of the Roman empire, here he is entirely cast out from all offices of trust in the empire ; his religion is first only tolerated, and then totally abolished, by the imperial power. This great event was not the work of a reign ; it took up many years, for it had to contend with the deep-rooted prejudices of the heathen, who to the very last endeavoured to uphold their declining superstition. Paganism received several mortal strokes in the time of Constantine and his sons Constans and Constantius. It was farther reduced by the great zeal of Jovian, Valentinian, and Valens; and was finally suppressed by the edicts of Gratian, Theodosius I., and his successors. It was not till A. D. 388 that Rome itself, the residence of the emperor, was generally reformed from the absurdities of paganism; but the total suppression of paganism soon followed the conversion of the metropolitan city, and about A. D. 395 the dragon may be considered, in an eminent sense, to have been *cast into the earth*, that is, into a state of utter subjection to the ruling dynasty of Christian emperors.

Verse 10. *And I heard a loud voice, saying,—Now is come salvation, &c.*] This is a song of triumph of the Christian Church over the heathen idolatry, and is very expressive of the great joy of the Christians upon this most stupendous event. The loud voice of triumph is said to be heard in *heaven*, to show that the Christian religion was now exalted to the *heaven* or *throne* of the Roman empire. " It is very remarkable," as Bishop Newton observes, " that Constantine himself, and the Christians of his time, describe his conquests under the image of a *dragon*, as if they had understood that this prophecy had received its accomplishment in him. Constantine himself, in his epistle to Eusebius and other bishops concerning the re-edifying and repairing of the churches, saith that ' liberty being now restored, and that the *dragon* being removed from the administration of public affairs, by the providence of the great God and by my ministry, I esteem the great power of God to have been made manifest to all.' Moreover, a picture of Constantine was set up over the palace gate, with the cross over his head, and under his feet the great enemy of mankind, who persecuted the Church by means of impious tyrants, *in the form of a dragon*, transfixed with a dart through the midst of his body, and falling headlong into the depth of the sea." See *Eusebius* de Vita Constantini, lib. ii. c. 46; and lib. iii. c. 3, and *Socratis* Hist. Eccles., lib. i. c. 9. Constantine added to the other Roman ensigns the *labarum*, or standard of the cross, and constituted it the principal standard of the Christian Roman empire. To this *labarum* Prudentius refers, when speaking of the Christian soldiers, in his first hymn π

ερι στεφανων,

Cæsaris vexilla linquunt, eligunt SIGNUM CRUCIS,
Proque ventosis Draconum, quæ gerebant, palliis,
Proferunt INSIGNE LIGNUM, quod Draconem subdidit.

" They leave the ensigns of Cæsar; they choose the standard of the cross; and instead of the dragon flags which they carried, moved about with the wind, they bring forward the illustrious wood that subdued the dragon."

When the apostle saw the woman in *heaven*, well might he call it, in the spirit of prophecy, *a great wonder*.

Verse 11. *And they overcame him by the blood of the Lamb*] Here is given the reason why the followers of Christ prevailed at this time against all their adversaries. It was because they fought against the dragon in the armour of God. *They overcame him by the blood of the Lamb*—by proclaiming salvation to sinners through Christ crucified, and by their continual

intercession at the throne of grace for the conversion of the heathen world.

And by the word of their testimony] By constantly testifying against the errors and follies of mankind.

And they loved not their lives unto the death.] They regarded not their present temporal estate, but even gladly delivered up their lives to the fury of their persecutors, and thus sealed the truth of what they spake with their blood.

Verse 12. *Therefore rejoice, ye heavens, and ye that dwell in them.*] Let the Christians, who are now partakers of the present temporal prosperity, and advanced to places of trust in the empire, praise and magnify the Lord who has thus so signally interfered in their behalf. But it is added,

Wo to the inhabiters of the earth, and of the sea! for the devil is come down unto you] By *the inhabiters of the earth* are meant the people in subjection to the Roman empire; and by the *sea*, those parts of the Roman dominions appear to be intended that were reduced to a state of anarchy by the incursions of the barbarous nations. It is not without precedent to liken great hosts of nations combined together to the sea. See Ezek. xxvi. 3. Here then is a wo denounced against the whole Roman world which will be excited by the devil, the father of lies, the heathen party being thus denominated from the method they pursued in their endeavours to destroy the religion of Jesus. See on ver. 15.

Having great wrath, because he knoweth that he hath but a short time.] The Christian religion, the pagan party see with great regret, is rapidly gaining ground everywhere; and, if not timely checked, must soon brave all opposition.

Verse 13. *And when the dragon saw that he was cast unto the earth*] When the heathen party saw that they were no longer supported by the civil power,

He persecuted the woman which brought forth the man child.] The heathens persecuted the Christian Church in the behalf of which Divine Providence had raised up a dynasty of Christian Roman emperors.

Verse 14. *And to the woman were given two wings of a great eagle*] Του αετου του μεγαλου· Of THE great eagle. The great eagle here mentioned is an emblem of the Roman empire in general, and therefore differs from the *dragon*, which is a symbol of *the* HEATHEN ROMAN *empire* in particular. The Roman power is called an *eagle* from its legionary standard, which was introduced among the Romans in the second year of the consulate of C. Marius; for before that time minotaurs, wolves, leopards, horses, boars, and eagles were used indifferently, according to the humour of the commander. The Roman eagles were figures in relievo of silver or gold, borne on the tops of pikes, the wings being displayed, and frequently a thunderbolt in their talons. Under the eagle, on the pike, were piled bucklers, and sometimes crowns. The two wings of the great eagle refer to the *two grand independent divisions* of the Roman empire, which took place January 17, A. D. 395, and were given to the woman, Christianity being the established religion of both empires.

That she might fly into the wilderness, into her place, &c.] The apparent repetition here of what is said in ver. 6 has induced Bishop Newton to consider the former passage as introduced by way of *prolepsis* or *anticipation;* for, says he, the woman did not fly into the wilderness till several years after the conversion of Constantine. But that there is no such prolepsis as the bishop imagines is evident from the ecclesiastical history of the fourth century ; for the woman, or true Church, *began* to flee into the wilderness a considerable time before the division of the great Roman empire into two independent monarchies. The word translated *fled* is not to be taken in that peculiar sense as if the woman, in the commencement of her flight, had been furnished with *wings*, for the original word is εφυγεν. The meaning therefore of verses 6 and 14, when taken in connection with their respective contexts, is, that the woman began to make rapid strides towards the desert almost immediately after her elevation to the *heaven* or *throne* of the Roman empire, and *in the course of her flight* was furnished with the *wings* of the great eagle ἱνα πετηται, *that she might* FLY, into *that* place prepared of God, where she should be fed a thousand two hundred and threescore days. It is said here that the period for which the woman should be nourished in the wilderness would be *a time, times, and a half;* consequently this period is the same with the *twelve hundred and sixty days* of ver. 6. But in no other sense can they be considered the same than by understanding a *time* to signify a *year;* times, *two years;* and *half a time, half a year;* i. e., *three years and a half.* And as each prophetic year contains *three hundred and sixty* days, so three years and a half will contain precisely *twelve hundred and sixty* days. The Apocalypse being highly symbolical, it is reasonable to expect that its periods of time will also be represented symbolically, that the prophecy may be homogeneous in all its parts. The Holy Spirit, when speaking of *years* symbolically, has invariably represented them by *days,* commanding, *e. gr.,* the Prophet Ezekiel to lie upon his left side *three hundred and ninety days,* that it might be a *sign* or *symbol* of the house of Israel bearing their iniquity as many years ; and *forty days* upon his right side, to represent to the house of Judah in a symbolical manner, that they should bear their iniquity *forty* years. The one thousand two hundred and threescore days, therefore, that the woman is fed in the wilderness, must be understood *symbolically,* and consequently denote as many natural years. The wilderness into which the woman flies is the Greek and Latin worlds, for she is conveyed into her place by means of the two wings of the great eagle. We must not understand the phrase *flying into her place* of her removing from one part of the habitable world into another, but of her speedy declension from a state of great prosperity to a forlorn and desolate condition. The woman is nourished for one thousand two hundred and threescore years *from the face of the serpent.* The empires in the east and west were destined, in the course of the Divine providence, to support the Christian religion, at least nominally, while the rest of the world should remain in pagan idolatry or under the influence of the dragon, here called the *serpent,* because he deceiveth the whole world. The words of the prophecy are very remarkable. The Christian Church is said to be supported by the eastern and western

empires, *two mighty dominations;* and at the same time situated in *the wilderness,* strongly denoting that, though *many* professed Christianity, there were but *very few* who " kept the commandments of God, and had the testimony of Jesus Christ."

Verse 15. *And the serpent cast out of his mouth water as a flood*] The water here evidently means *great multitudes of nations and peoples* in chap. xvii. 15, the interpreting angel says, *The waters which thou sawest—are peoples, and multitudes, and nations, and tongues.* This water, then, which the dragon cast out of his mouth, must be an inundation of heathen barbarous nations upon the Roman empire ; and the purpose which the dragon has in view by this inundation is, that he might cause the woman, or Christian Church,

To be carried away of the flood.] Entirely swept away from the face of man. Dr. Mosheim, in the commencement of his second chapter upon the fifth century, observes " that the Goths, the Heruli, the Franks, the Huns, and the Vandals, with other fierce and warlike nations, for the most part strangers to Christianity, had invaded the Roman empire, and rent it asunder in the most deplorable manner. Amidst these calamities the Christians were grievous, nay, we may venture to say the principal, sufferers. It is true these savage nations were much more intent upon the acquisition of wealth and dominion than upon the propagation or support of the pagan superstitions, nor did their cruelty and opposition to the Christians arise from any religious principle, or from an enthusiastic desire to ruin the cause of Christianity ; it was merely *by the* INSTIGATION *of the pagans who remained yet in the empire,* that they were excited to treat with such severity and violence the followers of Christ." Thus the wo which was denounced, ver. 12, against *the inhabiters of the earth and of the sea,* came upon the whole Roman world ; for, in consequence of the excitement and malicious misrepresentations of the pagans of the empire, " a transmigration of a great swarm of nations" came upon the Romans, and ceased not their ravages till they had desolated the eastern empire, even as far as the gates of Byzantium, and finally possessed themselves of the western empire. " If," says Dr. Robertson, in the introduction to his History of Charles V., vol. i., pp. 11, 12, edit. Lond. 1809, " a man was called to fix upon the period in the history of the world, during which the condition of the human race was most calamitous and afflicted, he would, without hesitation, name that which elapsed from the death of Theodosius the Great to the establishment of the Lombards in Italy, a period of *one hundred and seventy-six years.* The contemporary authors who beheld that scene of desolation, labour and are at a loss for expressions to describe the horror of it. *The scourge of God, the destroyer of nations,* are the dreadful epithets by which they distinguish the most noted of the barbarous leaders ; and they compare the ruin which they had brought on the world to the havoc occasioned by earthquakes, conflagrations, or deluges, the most formidable and fatal calamities which the imagination of man can conceive." But the subtle design which the serpent or dragon had in view, when he vomited out of his mouth a flood of waters, was most providentially frustrated ; for

Verse 16. *The earth helped the woman*] "Nothing, indeed," as Bishop Newton excellently observes, "was more likely to produce the ruin and utter subversion of the Christian Church than the irruptions of so many barbarous nations into the Roman empire. But the event proved contrary to human appearance and expectation: *the earth swallowed up the flood;* the barbarians were rather swallowed up by the Romans, than the Romans by the barbarians; the heathen conquerors, instead of imposing their own, submitted to the religion of the conquered Christians; and they not only embraced the religion, but affected even the laws, the manners, the customs, the language, and the very name, of Romans, so that the victors were in a manner absorbed and lost among the vanquished." See his Dissertations on the Prophecies, in loc.

Verse 17. *And the dragon was wroth with the woman*] The heathen party, foiled in their subtle attempt to destroy Christianity, were greatly enraged, and endeavoured to excite the hatred of the multitude against the religion of Jesus. "They alleged that before the coming of Christ the world was blessed with peace and prosperity; but that since the progress of their religion everywhere, the gods, filled with indignation to see their worship neglected and their altars abandoned, had visited the earth with those plagues and desolations which increased every day." See Mosheim's Ecclesiastical History, cent. V., part 1, and other works on this subject.

Went to make war with the remnant of her seed] The dragon απηλθε, departed, i. e., into the wilderness, whither the woman had fled; and in another form commenced a new species of persecution, directed *only* against *the remnant of her seed, who keep the commandments of God, and have the testimony of Jesus Christ.* See on verse 13 of the following chapter for an illustration of this remarkable passage.

CHAPTER XIII.

The beast rising out of the sea with seven heads, ten horns, and ten crowns, 1. *His description, power, blasphemy, cruelty, &c.,* 2–10. *The beast coming out of the earth with two horns, deceiving the world by his false miracles, and causing every one to receive his mark in their right hand,* 11–17. *His number,* 666, 18.

A. M. cir. 4100.
A. D. cir. 96.
Impp. Flavio
Domitiano
Cæs. Aug. et
Nerva.

AND I stood upon the sand of the sea, and saw ª a beast rise up out of the sea, ᵇ having seven heads and ten horns, and upon his horns ten crowns, and upon his heads the ᶜ name of blasphemy.

2 ᵈ And the beast which I

A. M. cir. 4100.
A. D. cir. 96.
Impp. Flavio
Domitiano
Cæs. Aug. et
Nerva.

ª Dan. vii. 2, 7.——ᵇ Chap. xii. 3; xvii. 3, 9, 12.   ᶜ Or, *names;* chap. xvii. 3.——ᵈ Dan. vii. 6.

NOTES ON CHAP. XIII., BY J. E. C.

Verse 1. *And I stood upon the sand of the sea, and saw a beast rise up out of the sea*] Before we can proceed in the interpretation of this chapter, it will be highly necessary to ascertain the meaning of the prophetic symbol *beast,* as the want of a proper understanding of this term has probably been one reason why so many discordant hypotheses have been published to the world. In this investigation it is impossible to resort to a higher authority than Scripture, for the Holy Ghost is his own interpreter. What is therefore meant by the term *beast* in any one prophetic vision, the same species of *thing* must be represented by the term whenever it is used in a similar manner in any other part of the sacred oracles. Having therefore laid this foundation, the angel's interpretation of the last of Daniel's four beasts need only be produced, an account of which is given in the seventh chapter of this prophet. Daniel being very desirous to "know the truth of the *fourth beast which was diverse from all the others, exceeding dreadful,* and of the *ten horns* that were on his head," the angel thus interprets the vision "The fourth beast shall be the fourth kingdom upon earth, which shall be diverse from all kingdoms, and shall devour the whole earth, and shall tread it down, and break it in pieces. And the ten horns out of this kingdom are ten kings that shall arise," &c.

In this scripture it is plainly declared that the *fourth beast* should be the *fourth kingdom* upon earth; consequently, the *four beasts* seen by Daniel are *four kingdoms:* hence the term *beast* is the prophetic symbol for a *kingdom.*

As to the nature of the kingdom which is represented by the term *beast,* we shall obtain no inconsiderable light in examining the most proper meaning of the original word חיה *chaiyah.* This Hebrew word is translated in the Septuagint by the Greek word θηριον, and both words signify what we term a *wild beast;* and the latter is the one used by St. John in the Apocalypse. Taking up the Greek word θηριον in this sense, it is fully evident, if a power be represented in the prophetical writings under the notion of *a wild beast,* that the power so represented must partake of the nature of *a wild beast.* Hence an earthly *belligerent* power is evidently designed. And the comparison is peculiarly appropriate; for as several species of wild beasts carry on perpetual warfare with the animal world, so most governments, influenced by ambition, promote discord and depopulation. And, also, as the carnivorous wild beast acquires its strength and magnitude by preying upon the feebler animals; so most earthly monarchies are raised up by the sword, and derive their political consequence from the unsuccessful resistance of the contending nations. The kingdom of God, on

2

| A. M. cir. 4100. A. D. cir. 96. Impp. Flavio Domitiano Cæs. Aug. et Nerva. | saw was like unto a leopard, [e] and his feet were as *the feet* of a bear, [f] and his mouth as the mouth of a lion : and [g] the dragon | gave him his power, [h] and his seat, [i] and great authority. 3 And I saw one of his heads [k] as it were [l] wounded to death ; | A. M. cir. 4100. A. D. cir. 96. Impp. Flavio Domitiano Cæs. Aug. et Nerva. |

e Dan. vii. 5.——f Dan. vii. 4.——g Chap. xii. 9.　　　h Ch. xvi. 10.——i Ch. xii. 4.——k Ver. 12, 14.——l Gr. *slain.*

the other hand, is represented as "a stone cut out of the mountain without hands ;" and is never likened to a *beast,* because it is not raised up by the sword as all other secular powers are, but sanctifies the persons under its subjection ; in which last particular it essentially differs from all other dominations.

This beast is said to *rise up out of the sea,* in which particular it corresponds with the four beasts of Daniel ; the *sea* is therefore the symbol of a *great multitude of nations,* as has already been proved ; and the meaning is, that every mighty empire is raised upon the ruins of a great number of nations, which it has successfully contended against and incorporated with its dominions. The *sea,* here, is doubtless the same against the inhabiters of which a wo was denounced, chap. xii. 12 ; for St. John was standing *upon the sand of the sea* when the vision changed from the *woman* and the *dragon* to that recorded in this chapter. It therefore follows that the kingdom or empire here represented by the *beast,* is that which sprung up out of the ruins of *the* WESTERN *Roman empire.*

Having seven heads and ten horns, and upon his horns ten crowns] The beast here described is the Latin empire, which supported the Romish or Latin Church ; for it has *upon his horns ten crowns,* i. e., is an empire composed of ten distinct monarchies in the interest of the Latin Church. See the *heads and horns* fully explained in the notes on chap. xvii. 10, 12, 16.

As the phrases *Latin Church, Latin empire,* &c., are not very generally understood at present, and will occur frequently in the course of the notes on this and the xviith chapter, it will not be improper here to explain them. During the period from the division of the Roman empire into those of the east and west, till the final dissolution of the western empire, the subjects of both empires were equally known by the name of *Romans.* Soon after this event the people of the west lost almost entirely the name of Romans, and were denominated after their respective kingdoms which were established upon the ruins of the western empire. But as the eastern empire escaped the ruin which fell upon the western, the subjects of the former still retained the name of *Romans,* and called their dominion Ἡ Ῥωμαϊκη βασιλεια, *the Roman empire ;* by which name this monarchy was known among them till its final dissolution in 1453, by Mohammed II., the Turkish sultan. But the subjects of the eastern emperor, ever since the time of Charlemagne or before, (and more particularly in the time of the crusades and subsequently,) called the western people, or those under the influence of the Romish Church, *Latins,* and their Church the *Latin Church.* And the western people, in return, denominated the eastern Church *the Greek Church,* and the members of it *Greeks.* Hence the division of the Christian Church into those of the *Greek* and *Latin.* For a confirmation of what has just been said the reader may consult the Byzantine writers, where he will

find the appellations Ῥωμαιοι and Λατινοι, Romans and Latins, used in the sense here mentioned in very numerous instances. The members of the Romish Church have not been named *Latins* by the Greeks alone ; this term is also used in the public instruments drawn up by the general popish councils, as may be instanced in the following words, which form a part of a decree of the council of Basil, dated Sept. 26, 1437 : *Copiosissimam subventionem pro unione* GRÆCORUM *cum* LATINIS, "A very great convention for the union of the Greeks with the Latins." Even in the very papal bulls this appellation has been acknowledged, as may be seen in the edict of Pope Eugenius IV., dated Sept. 17, 1437, where in one place mention is made of *Ecclesiæ* LATINORUM *quæsita unio,* "the desired union of the Church of the Latins ;" and in another place we read, *Nec superesse modum alium prosequendi operis tam pii, et servandi* LATINÆ ECCLESIÆ *honoris,* "that no means might be left untried of prosecuting so pious a work, and of preserving the honour of the Latin Church." See Corps Diplomatique, tom. iii., pp. 32, 35. In a bull of the same pontiff, dated Sept., 1439, we have *Sanctissima* LATINORUM *et* GRÆCORUM *unio,* "the most holy union of the Greeks with the Latins." See Bail's Summa Conciliorum, *in loc.* By *the Latin empire* is meant the whole of the powers which support the Latin Church

And upon his heads the name of blasphemy.] Ονομα βλασφημιας· *A name of blasphemy.* This has been variously understood. Jerome and Prosper give it as their opinion that the name of blasphemy consists in the appellation *urbs æterna,* eternal city, applied to Rome ; and modern commentators refer it to the idolatrous worship of the Romans and papists. Before we attempt to ascertain the meaning of this passage, it must be first defined what the Holy Spirit means by *a name of blasphemy.* Blasphemy, in Scripture, signifies *impious speaking* when applied to GOD, and *injurious speaking* when directed against our *neighbour.* A name of blasphemy is the prostitution of a sacred name to an unholy purpose. This is evident from the 9th verse of the second chapter of the Apocalypse, where God says, "I know the blasphemy of them which say they are Jews, and are not, but are the synagogue of Satan." These wicked men, by calling themselves Jews, blasphemed the name, *i. e.,* used it in an injurious sense ; for he ONLY *is a Jew who is one inwardly.* Hence the term *Jews* applied to the synagogue of Satan is *a name of blasphemy, i. e.* a sacred name blasphemed. *A name of blasphemy,* or a blasphemous appellation, is said to be upon all the seven heads of the beast. To determine what this name is, the meaning of the seven heads in this place must be ascertained. If the reader refer to the notes on chap. xvii. 9, 10, 11, he will find that the heads are explained to have a double meaning, *viz.,* that they signify the *seven electorates of the German empire,* and also *seven forms of Latin*

A. M. cir. 4100.
A. D. cir. 96.
Impp. Flavio
Domitiano
Cæs. Aug. et
Nerva.

and his deadly wound was healed : and [m] all the world wondered after the beast.

4 And they worshipped the

dragon which gave power unto the beast : and they worshipped the beast, saying, [n] Who *is* like unto the beast ? who

A. M. cir. 4100
A. D. cir. 96.
Impp. Flavio
Domitiano
Cæs. Aug. et
Nerva.

---

[m] Chap. xvii. 8.

[n] Chap. xviii. 18.

---

government. As this is the first place in which the heads of the beast are mentioned with any description, it is reasonable to expect that that signification of the heads which is first in order in the angel's interpretation, chap. xvii. 9, must be what is here intended. This is, " the seven heads are seven mountains on which the woman sitteth ;" the name of blasphemy will consequently be found upon the seven electorates of Germany. This, therefore, can be no other than that which was common, not only to the electorates but also to the whole empire of Germany, or that well known one of Sacrum Imperium Romanum, " The Sacred (or Holy) Roman Empire." Here is a sacred appellation *blasphemed* by its application to the principal power of the beast. No kingdom can properly be called *holy* but that of Jesus; therefore it would be blasphemy to unite this epithet with any other power. But it must be horridly blasphemous to apply it to the German empire, the grand supporter of antichrist from his very rise to temporal authority. Can that empire be *holy* which has killed the saints, which has professed and supported with all its might an idolatrous system of worship ? It is impossible. Therefore its assumption of *sacred* or *holy* (which appellation was originally given to the empire from its being the main support of what is termed the *holy* catholic Church, the emperor being styled, on this account, Christ's temporal vicar upon earth : see *Cæsarini Fürstenerii* Tractatus De Suprematu Principum Germaniæ, cc. 31, 32) is, in the highest sense the word can be taken, *a name of blasphemy.* The name of blasphemy is very properly said to be upon the seven heads of the beast, or seven electorates of the German empire, because the electors are styled Sacri *Imperii Principes Electores,* Princes, Electors of the Holy Empire ; Sacri *Romani Imperii Electores,* Electors of the Holy Roman Empire

Verse 2. *And the beast which I saw was like unto a leopard*] This similitude of the beast to a leopard appears to be an allusion to the third beast of Daniel, which is well known to represent the empire of the Greeks. The Latin empire greatly resembled the modern empire of the Greeks; for that the power of the Greeks was still said to be like a leopard, even after its subjugation by the Romans, is evident from Dan. vii. 12 : " As concerning the rest of the beasts, they had their dominion taken away ; yet their lives were prolonged for a season and time." The Latin empire was, in the first place, like to its contemporary, because both adhered to an idolatrous system of worship, professedly Christian, but really antichristian ; and it is well known that the Greek and Latin Churches abound in monstrous absurdities. *Secondly,* Both empires were similar in their opposition to the spread of pure Christianity ; though it must be allowed that the Latins far outstripped the Greeks in this particular. *Thirdly,* Both empires were similar in respect to the civil authority being powerfully depressed by the ecclesiastical; though

it must be granted the authority of the Latin Church was more strongly marked, and of much longer continuance. The excommunication of the Greek emperor by the Patriarch Arsenius, and the consequences of that excommunication, afford a remarkable example of the great power of the Greek clergy. But the beast of St. John, though in its general appearance it resembles a leopard, yet differs from it in having feet like those *of a bear.* The second beast of Daniel was likened to a bear, and there can be no doubt that the kingdom of the Medes and Persians was intended ; and it is very properly likened to this animal, because it was one of the most inhuman governments that ever existed, and a *bear* is the well known Scripture emblem of *cruelty.* See 2 Sam. xvii. 8, and Hos. xiii. 8. Is not *cruelty* a striking characteristic of the papal Latin empire ? Have not the subjects of this empire literally trampled to death all those in their power who would not obey their idolatrous requisitions ? In Fox's Book of Martyrs, and other works which treat upon this subject, will be found a melancholy catalogue of the horrid tortures and most lingering deaths which they have obliged great numbers of Christians to suffer. In this sense the feet of the beast *were as the feet of a bear.* Another particular in which the beast differed from a leopard was, in having a mouth like a lion. " It is," says Dr. More, " like the Babylonish kingdom (the first beast of Daniel, which is likened to a lion) in its *cruel decrees* against such as will not obey their idolatrous edicts, nor worship the golden image that Nebuchadnezzar had set up. Their stubbornness must be punished by a hot fiery furnace ; fire and fagot must be prepared for them that will not submit to this new Roman idolatry."

And the dragon gave him his power, and his seat, and great authority.] It was said of the dragon, in chap. xii. 8, that his place was found *no more* in heaven ; the dragon here cannot therefore be the heathen Roman empire, as this was abolished previously to the rising up of the beast. It must then allude to the restoration of one of the Draconic heads of the beast, as will be seen in the explanation of the following verse, and more fully in the notes on chap. xvii.

Verse 3. *And I saw one of his heads as it were wounded to death*] This is the second and last place where the heads of the beast are mentioned with any description ; and therefore the meaning here must be *forms of government,* as these were noticed last in the angel's double explanation. The head that was wounded to death can be no other than the seventh draconic head, which was the sixth head of the beast, viz., *the imperial power;* for " this head," as Bishop Newton observes, " was, as it were, wounded to death when the Roman empire was overturned by the northern nations, and an end was put to the very name of emperor in Momyllus Augustulus." It was

2

A. M. cir. 4100. A. D. cir. 96. Impp. Flavio Domitiano Cæs. Aug. et Nerva.

is able to make war with
him?
5 And there was given unto
him [o] a mouth speaking great
things and blasphemies; and
power was given unto him [p] to
continue [q] forty *and* two months.
6 And he opened his mouth in

[o] Dan. vii. 8, 11, 25; xi. 36.

[p] Or *to make war*.——[q] Chap. xi. 2; xii. 6.

so wounded that it was wholly improbable that it could ever rise again to considerable power, for the western empire came into the possession of several barbarous nations of independent interests.

And his deadly wound was healed] This was effected by Charlemagne, who with his successors assumed all the marks of the ancient emperors of the west, with the titles of Semper Augustus, Sacred Majesty, First Prince of the Christian World, Temporal Chief of the Christian People, and Rector or Temporal Chief of the Faithful in Germany; Mod. Universal History, vol. xxxii., p. 79. But it is said in ver. 2 that the dragon gave the beast *his power*, δυναμιν, *his armies* or *military strength*; i. e., he employed all his imperial power in defence of the Latin empire, which supported the Latin Church. He also gave *his seat*, θρονον, literally *his throne*, to him: that is, his whole empire formed an integral part of the Latin empire, by its conversion to the Roman Catholic faith. He also gave him *great authority*. This is literally true of the Roman empire of Germany, which, by its great power and influence in the politics of Europe, extended the religion of the empire over the various states and monarchies of Europe, thus incorporating them as it were in one vast empire, by uniting them in one common faith.

And all the world wondered after the beast.] Ὁλη ἡ γη· *All the earth.* As the original word signifies *earth*, and not *world* as in our translation, the Latin world, which is the *earth* of the beast, is here intended; and the meaning of the passage consequently is, that the whole body of the Roman Catholics were affected with great astonishment at the mighty sway of the Latin empire, considering it as a great and holy power.

Verse 4. *And they worshipped the dragon*] *Worshipping* the dragon here evidently means the voluntary religious subjection of the members of the Latin Church to the revived western empire, because of the eminent part it has taken in the support of their faith.

And they worshipped the beast] Not only the dragon or revived western empire was worshipped; the beast, the *whole* Latin empire, is a partaker in the adoration. The manner in which it is worshipped consists in the subjects of it—

Saying, Who is *like unto the beast?*] Is it not the only holy power in the universe? Is it possible for any person not a subject of it to be saved?

Who is able to make war with him?] Can any nation successfully fight with it? Is not the Roman empire, which is its principal bulwark, *invictissimum*, most invincible? *Invictissimus*, most invincible, was the peculiar attribute of the emperors of Germany. See modern Universal History, vol. xxxii., p. 197.

Verse 5. *And there was given unto him a mouth speaking great things*] That is, There was given to the rulers of the Latin empire, who are the *mouth* of the beast, (and particularly the Roman emperors of Germany,) power to assume great and pompous titles, indicative of their mighty sway over many subjugated countries, (see the imperial instruments of the middle centuries in the Corps Diplomatique,) and also to utter against their opponents the most terrible edicts.

And blasphemies] The system of worship supported by the beast is a system of blasphemy, as there will be occasion to show presently.

And power was given unto him to continue forty and *two months.*] As these forty-two months are prophetic, they must mean so many *years* as there are *days* contained in them; *viz.*, 1260, each month containing 30 days. The beast, therefore, will continue in existence at least 1260 years; but when the termination of this period will take place is difficult to say, as the beginning cannot be at present indubitably ascertained.

Verse 6. *And he opened his mouth in blasphemy against God, to blaspheme his name*] The Latin empire is here represented as a blasphemous power in three respects. *First*, he blasphemes the *name* of God. This has been most notoriously the case with the different popish princes, who continually blaspheme the sarced names of God by using them in their idolatrous worship. The mouth of blasphemy against God cannot be more evident than in the following impious words which form a part of the *Golden Bull* published by Charles IV. in January, 1356: "But thou, envy, how often hast thou attempted to ruin by division the Christian empire, which God hath founded upon the three cardinal virtues, faith, hope, and charity, as upon a holy and indivisible Trinity, vomiting the old venom of discord among the seven electors, who are the pillars and seven principal members of the holy empire; by the brightness of whom the holy empire ought to be illuminated as by seven torches, the light of which is reinforced by the seven gifts of the Holy Spirit!"

And his tabernacle] Tabernacle is any kind of dwelling place, and in an eminent sense among the Jews was a kind of tent to take up and down as occasion required, which was as it were the palace of the Most High, the dwelling of the God of Israel. It was divided into two partitions, one called the holy place, and the other the most holy place, in the latter of which, before the building of the temple, the ark of the covenant was kept, which was a symbol of God's gracious presence with the Jewish Church. All this the author of the Epistle to the Hebrews, in the eighth and ninth chapters, explains to prefigure the human nature of Christ. The beast's blasphemy of the tabernacle of God is,

A. M. cir. 4100.
A. D. cir. 96.
Impp. Flavio
Domitiano
Cæs. Aug. et
Nerva.

blasphemy against God, to blaspheme his name, [r] and his tabernacle, and them that dwell in heaven.

7 And it was given unto him [s] to make war with the saints, and to overcome them : [t] and power was given him over all kindred, and tongues, and nations.

8 And all that dwell upon the earth shall worship him, [u] whose names are not written in the book of life of the Lamb slain [v] from the foundation of the world.

A. M. cir. 4100.
A. D. cir. 96.
Impp. Flavio
Domitiano
Cæs. Aug. et
Nerva.

9 [w] If any man have an ear, let him hear.

---

[r] John i. 14 ; Col. ii. 9.——[s] Daniel vii. 21 ; chap. xi. 7 ; xii. 17. [t] Chap. xi. 18 ; xvii. 15.

[u] Exod. xxxii. 32 ; Dan. xii. 1 ; Phil. iv. 3 ; chap. iii. 5 ; xx. 12, 15 ; xxi. 27.——[v] Chap. xvii. 8.——[w] Chap. ii. 7.

---

therefore, as Dr. More and others properly observe, his impious doctrine of transubstantiation, in which it is most blasphemously asserted that the substance of the *bread* and *wine* in the sacrament is literally converted by the consecration of the priest, into the very *body* and *blood* of Jesus Christ! This doctrine was first advanced among the Latins in the tenth century ; and in 1215, fully received as an article of the Roman Catholic faith. It is for the pages of ecclesiastical history to record the incredible numbers which have been martyred by the papists for their non-reception of this most unscriptural and antichristian doctrine.

And them that dwell in heaven.] By *heaven* is here meant the throne of God, and not the throne of the beast, because it is *against God* the beast blasphemes. This must therefore allude to his impious adoration of the saints and angels, whose residence is in heaven. He blasphemes against God by paying that adoration to the celestial inhabitants which belongs to God alone. That this sort of worship has been and still is kept up among the Roman Catholics, their mass book is a sufficient evidence.

Verse 7. *And it was given unto him to make war with the saints, and to overcome them*] "Who can make any computation," says Bishop Newton, " or even frame any conception, of the numbers of pious Christians who have fallen a sacrifice to the bigotry and cruelty of Rome? Mede upon the place hath observed, from good authorities, that in the war with the Albigenses and Waldenses there perished of these poor creatures in France alone *a million.* From the first institution of the Jesuits to the year 1580, that is, in little more than thirty years, nine hundred thousand orthodox Christians were slain, and these all by the common executioner. In the space of scarce thirty years the inquisition destroyed, by various kinds of torture, a hundred and fifty thousand Christians. Sanders himself confesses that an innumerable multitude of Lollards and Sacramentarians were burnt throughout all Europe, who yet, he says, were not put to death by the pope and bishops, but by the civil magistrates." The dragon in a new shape, or Roman empire of Germany, acted a very conspicuous part in this nefarious warfare against the remnant of the woman's seed, who kept the commandments of God, and had the testimony of Jesus Christ. See the imperial edict of Frederic II. against heretics, in Limborch's History of the Inquisition.

And power was given him over all kindreds, and tongues, and nations.] As the book of the Revelation is a prophecy of all that should come upon the Christian world till the end of time, *all kindreds, and tongues, and nations,* must imply *the whole Christian world.* That the Latin empire in the course of its reign has had the extensive power here spoken of, is evident from history. It is well known that the profession of Christianity was chiefly confined within the limits of the Greek and Latin empires, till the period of the Reformation. By means of the crusades the Latins extended their empire over several provinces of the Greeks. In 1097 Baldwin extended his conquests over the hills of Armenia and the plain of Mesopotamia, and founded the first principality of the Franks or Latins, which subsisted fifty-four years, beyond the Euphrates. In 1204 the Greeks were expelled Constantinople by the Latins, who set up an empire there which continued about fifty-seven years. The total overthrow of the Latin states in the east soon followed the recovery of Constantinople by the Greeks ; and in 1291 the Latin empire in the east was entirely dissolved. Thus the Latins have had power over the whole world professedly Christian : but it is not said that the whole world was in utter subjection to him, for we read in the following verse,

Verse 8. *And all that dwell upon the earth shall worship him, whose names are not written in the book of life of the Lamb*] The *earth* here is the *Latin world,* as has been observed before in similar cases. The meaning therefore is, that all the corrupt part of mankind who are inhabitants of the Latin world shall submit to the religion of the empire, except, as Bishop Newton expresses it, "those faithful few whose names, as citizens of heaven, were enrolled in the registers of life."

Slain from the foundation of the world.] That is, of the Christian world ; for this has been shown to be the meaning of *all kindreds, and tongues, and nations.* The year of the crucifixion is properly the commencement of Christianity, as the apostles then first began to promulgate the religion of Christ with the Holy Ghost sent down from heaven. But as Jesus Christ was in the Divine purpose appointed from the foundation of the world to redeem man by his blood, he therefore is, in a very eminent sense, the Lamb slain from the foundation of the world, i. e., from the creation.

Verse 9. *If any man have an ear, let him hear.*] These words are evidently introduced to impress the reader with the awfulness of what has just been spoken—*all shall worship him whose names are not written in the book of life,* as well as to fix his attention upon the following words :—

2

A. M. cir. 4100.
A. D. cir. 96.
Impp. Flavio
Domitiano
Cæs. Aug. et
Nerva.

10 ˣ He that leadeth into captivity shall go into captivity : ʸ he that killeth with the sword must be killed with the sword.

ᶻ Here is the patience and the faith of the saints.

11 And I beheld another beast ᵃ coming up out of the earth ; and he had two horns like a lamb, and he spake as a dragon.

12 And he exerciseth all the power of the

A. M. cir. 4100
A. D. cir. 96.
Impp. Flavio
Domitiano
Cæs. Aug. et
Nerva.

ˣ Isa. xxxiii. 1.——ʸ Gen. ix. 6 ; Matt. xxvi. 52.

ᶻ Chap. xiv. 12.——ᵃ Chap. xi. 7.

Verse 10. *He that leadeth into captivity shall go into captivity*] The Latin empire here spoken of must *go into captivity*, because it has led into captivity, by not only propagating among the various nations its abominable antichristian system, but also in compelling them to embrace it under the penalty of forfeiting the protection of the empire.

He that killeth with the sword must be killed with the sword.] The Latin empire must be also broken to pieces by the sword, because it has killed the saints of God. This prophecy will not receive its full accomplishment till *the kingdoms of this world become the kingdoms of our Lord and of his Christ.*

Here is the patience and the faith of the saints.] By these words, as Dr. Mitchell observes, " God calls upon his saints to keep in view, under all their persecutions, his retributive justice ; there is no violence that has been exercised upon them but what shall be retaliated upon the cruel and persecuting government and governors of the Latin empire."

Verse 11. *And I beheld another beast coming up out of the earth*] As a *beast* has already been shown to be the symbol of a *kingdom* or *empire*, the rising up of this second beast must consequently represent the rising up of *another empire*. This beast comes up *out of the earth* ; therefore it is totally different from the preceding, which rose up out of the *sea*. *Earth* here means the *Latin world*, for this word has been shown to import this already in several instances ; the rising up of the beast out of *this earth* must, consequently, represent the springing up of some power out of a state of subjection to the Latin empire : therefore the beast, here called *another beast*, is *another* LATIN *empire*. This beast is the spiritual Latin empire, or, in other words, the Romish hierarchy ; for with no other power can the prophetic description yet to be examined be shown to accord. In the time of Charlemagne the ecclesiastical power was in subjection to the civil, and it continued to be so for a long time after his death ; therefore the beast, whose deadly wound was healed, ruled over the whole Latin world, both clergy and laity ; these, consequently, constituted but one beast or empire. But the Latin clergy kept continually gaining more and more influence in the civil affairs of the empire, and in the tenth century their authority was greatly increased. In the subsequent centuries the power of the Romish hierarchy ascended even above that of the emperors, and led into captivity the kings of the whole Latin world, as there will be occasion to show in commenting upon the following verses. Thus the Romish hierarchy was at length entirely exempted from the civil power, and constituted *another beast*, as it became entirely independent of the secular Latin empire. And this beast came up out of *the earth* ; that is, the Latin clergy, which

composed a part of the *earth* or *Latin world*, raised their authority against that of the secular powers, and in process of time wrested the superintendence of ecclesiastical affairs from the secular princes.

And he had two horns] As the seven-headed beast is represented as having *ten horns*, which signify so many kingdoms leagued together to support the Latin Church, so the beast which rises out of the earth has also *two horns*, which must consequently represent two kingdoms ; for if *horns of a beast* mean *kingdoms* in one part of the Apocalypse, *kingdoms* must be intended by this symbol whenever it is used in a similar way in any other part of this book. As the second beast is the spiritual Latin empire, the two horns of this beast denote that the empire thus represented is composed of two distinct spiritual powers These, therefore, can be no other, as Bishop Newton and Faber properly observe, than the two grand independent branches of the Romish hierarchy, viz., the Latin clergy, REGULAR and SECULAR. " The first of these comprehends all the various monastic orders, the second comprehends the whole body of parochial clergy." These two grand branches of the hierarchy originally constituted but one dominion, as the monks as well as the other clergy were in subjection to the bishops : but the subjection of the monks to their diocesans became by degress less apparent ; and in process of time, through the influence and authority of the Roman pontiffs, they were entirely exempted from all episcopal jurisdiction, and thus became a spiritual power, entirely independent of that of the secular clergy.

Like a lamb] As *lamb*, in other parts of the Apocalypse, evidently means Christ, who is *the Lamb of God which taketh away the sin of the world*, it must have a similar import in this passage ; therefore the meaning here is evidently that the two horns of the beast, or the regular and secular clergy, profess to be the ministers of Christ, to be like him in meekness and humility, and to teach nothing that is contrary to godliness. The two-horned beast, or spiritual Latin empire, has in reality the name, and in the eyes of the Latin world the appearance, of *a* CHRISTIAN *power*. But he is only so in appearance, and that alone among his deluded votaries ; for when he spake,

He spake as a dragon.] The doctrines of the Romish hierarchy are very similar to those contained in the old heathen worship ; for he has introduced " a new species of idolatry, nominally different, but essentially the same, the worship of angels and saints instead of the gods and demi-gods of antiquity."

Verse 12. *And he exerciseth all the power of the first beast before him*] In the preceding verse the two-horned beast was represented as rising out of the earth, that is, obtaining gradually more and more influ-

2

A. M. cir. 4100.
A. D. cir. 96.
Impp. Flavio
Domitiano
Cæs. Aug. et
Nerva.

first beast before him, and causeth the earth and them which dwell therein to ^b worship the first beast, ^c whose deadly wound was healed.

13 And ^d he doeth great wonders, ^e so that he maketh fire come down from heaven on the earth in the sight of men,

14 And ^f deceiveth them that dwell on the

A. M. cir. 4100
A. D. cir. 96.
Impp. Flavio.
Domitiano
Cæs. Aug. e\
Nerva.

^b Ver. 4.——^c Ver. 3.——^d Deut. xiii. 1, 2, 3 ; Matt. xxiv. 24 ; 2 Thess. ii. 9 ; chap. xvi. 14.——^e 1 Kings xviii. 38 ; 2 Kings i. 10, 12.——^f Chapter xii. 9 , xix. 20.

ence in the civil affairs of the Latin world. Here he is represented as having obtained the direction and management of all the power of the first beast or secular Latin empire *before him, ενωπιον αυτου, in his presence.* That the Romish hierarchy has had the extensive power here spoken of, is evident from history ; for the civil power was in subjection to the ecclesiastical. The parochial clergy, one of the horns of the second beast, have had great secular jurisdiction over the whole Latin world. Two-thirds of the estates of Germany were given by the three Othos, who succeeded each other, to ecclesiastics ; and in the other Latin monarchies the parochial clergy possessed great temporal power. Yet extraordinary as the power of the secular clergy was in all parts of the Latin world, it was but feeble when compared with that of the monastic orders, which constituted another horn of the beast. The mendicant friars, the most considerable of the regular clergy, first made their appearance in the early part of the thirteenth century. These friars were divided by Gregory X., in a general council which he assembled at Lyons in 1272, into the four following societies or denominations, viz., the Dominicans, the Franciscans, the Carmelites, and the Hermits of St. Augustine. " As the pontiffs," observes Mosheim, " allowed these four mendicant orders the liberty of travelling wherever they thought proper, of conversing with persons of all ranks, of instructing the youth and the multitude wherever they went ; and as these monks exhibited, in their outward appearance and manner of life, more striking marks of gravity and holiness than were observable in the other monastic societies ; they arose all at once to the very summit of fame, and were regarded with the utmost esteem and veneration throughout all the countries of Europe. The enthusiastic attachment to these sanctimonious beggars went so far that, as we learn from the most authentic records, several cities were divided, or cantoned out, into four parts, with a view to these four orders ; the first part was assigned to the Dominicans, the second to the Franciscans, the third to the Carmelites, and the fourth to the Augustinians. The people were unwilling to receive the sacraments from any other hands than those of the mendicants, to whose churches they crowded to perform their devotions while living, and were extremely desirous to deposit there also their remains after death ; all which occasioned grievous complaints among the ordinary priests, to whom the cure of souls was committed, and who considered themselves as the spiritual guides of the multitude. Nor did the influence and credit of the mendicants end here : for we find in the history of this (thirteenth century) and the succeeding ages, that they were employed, not only in spiritual matters, but also in temporal and political affairs of the greatest

consequence ; in composing the differences of princes, concluding treaties of peace, concerting alliances, presiding in cabinet councils, governing courts, levying taxes, and other occupations not only remote from, but absolutely inconsistent with, the monastic character and profession. We must not, however, imagine that all the mendicant friars attained to the same degree of reputation and authority ; for the power of the Dominicans and Franciscans surpassed greatly that of the two other orders, and rendered them singularly conspicuous in the eyes of the world. During three centuries these two fraternities governed, with an almost universal and absolute sway, both state and Church ; filled the most eminent posts, ecclesiastical and civil ; taught in the universities and churches with an authority before which all opposition was silent ; and maintained the pretended majesty and prerogatives of the Roman pontiffs against kings, princes, bishops, and heretics, with incredible ardour and equal success. The Dominicans and Franciscans were, before the Reformation, what the Jesuits have been since that happy and glorious period, the very soul of the hierarchy, the engines of state, the secret springs of all the motions of the one and the other, and the authors and directors of every great and important event in the religious and political world." Thus the Romish hierarchy has *exercised all the power of the first beast in his sight*, both temporal and spiritual ; and therefore, with such astonishing influence as this over secular princes, it was no difficult matter for him to cause

The earth and them which dwell therein to worship the first beast, whose deadly wound was healed.] That is, he causes the whole Latin world to submit to the authority of the Latin empire, with the revived western empire at its head, persuading them that such submission is beneficial to their spiritual interests, and absolutely necessary for their salvation. Here it is observable that both beasts have dominion over the same *earth* ; for it is expressly said that the second beast *causeth* THE EARTH *and them that dwell therein, to worship the first beast* ; therefore it is, as Bishop Newton and others have observed, *imperium in imperio,* " an empire within an empire." We have, consequently, the fullest evidence that the two beasts consist in the division of the great Latin empire, by the usurpation of the Latin clergy, into two distinct empires, the one secular, the other spiritual, and both united in one antichristian design, viz., to diffuse their most abominable system of idolatry over the whole *earth*, and to extend the sphere of their domination. Here we have also an illustration of that remarkable passage in chap. xvi. 10, *the kingdom of the beasts*, i. e., the kingdom of the Latin kingdom ; which is apparently a solecism, but in reality expressed with wonderful precision. The

A. M. cir. 4100.
A. D. cir. 96.
Impp. Flavio
Domitiano
Cæs. Aug. et
Nerva.

earth ᵍ by *the means of* those miracles which he had the power to do in the sight of the beast; saying to them that dwell on the earth, that they should make an image to the beast, which had the wound by a sword, ʰ and did live.

15 And he had power to give ⁱ life unto the image of the beast, that the image of the beast should both speak,

A. M. cir. 4100.
A. D. cir. 96.
Impp. Flavio
Domitiano
Cæs. Aug. et
Nerva.

ᵍ 2 Thess. ii. 9, 10.——ʰ 2 Kings xx. 7.   ⁱ Gr. *breath.*

---

fifth vial is poured out *upon the throne of the beast, and* HIS KINGDOM *is darkened*, i. e., the Latin kingdom in subjection to the Latin kingdom or the secular Latin empire.

Verse 13. *And he doeth great wonders*] That we may have the greatest assurance possible that the two-horned beast is the spiritual Latin empire, it is called in chap. xix. 20, a passage illustrative of the one now under consideration, *the false prophet,* "than which," as Bishop Newton observes, "there cannot be a stronger or plainer argument to prove that false doctors or teachers were particularly designed;" for *prophet*, in the Scripture style, is not unfrequently used for a *preacher* or *expounder* of God's word. See 1 Cor. xiv. It hence follows that the two-horned beast is an empire of false doctors or teachers.

In order to establish the Latin Church upon a foundation that can never fail, the false prophet *doth great wonders*—he attempts the most wonderful and prodigious exploits, and is crowned with incredible success. He has the art to persuade his followers that the clergy of the Church of Rome are the only true ministers of Christ; that they have such great influence in the court of heaven as to be able not only to forgive sins, but also to grant indulgences in sin, by paying certain stipulated sums. He persuades them too that they can do works of supererogation. He pretends that an incredible number of miracles have been wrought and are still working by the Almighty, as so many evidences of the great sanctity of the Latin Church; and the false prophet has such an astonishing influence over his flock, as to cause them to believe all his fabulous legends and lying wonders. He pretends also (and is believed!) that his power is not confined to this world; that he is able by his prayers to deliver the souls of the deceased from what he calls purgatory, a place which he has fabled to exist for the purification of sinful souls after their departure from this world. His wonderful exploits, in being able to induce men possessed of reasoning faculties to believe his monstrous absurdities, do not end here; he even

Maketh fire come down from heaven—in the sight of men] *Fire*, in Scripture, when it signifies *wrath*, represents that species of indignation which is attended with the destruction of whatever is the cause of it. Thus the *wrath* of God is likened to *fire*, Psa. xviii. 7, 8; Jer. iv. 4. Therefore the *fire* which the false prophet bringeth down from *heaven* upon the *earth*, is the *fiery indignation* which he causes to come down from the *heaven* or *throne* of the Latin empire upon all those of the *earth* or *Latin world* who rebel against his authority. All this has been fulfilled in the Romish hierarchy; the Latin clergy have denominated all those that oppose their authority heretics, they have instituted tribunals to try the cause of heresy, and all

those that would not submit to their idolatry they have condemned to various kinds of tortures and deaths. It is said of the false prophet that he bringeth *fire* FROM HEAVEN upon the earth; that is to say, he will only try the cause of heresy, and pass the sentence of condemnation; he will not suffer an ecclesiastic tᵥ *execute* the sentence of the court; *the destroying fire* he causeth to come down from the *heaven* or *throne* of the Latin empire; secular princes and magistrates must execute the sentence of death upon all that are capitally condemned by the spiritual power. *He* MAKETH *fire come down from heaven; he compels* secular princes to assist him against heretics; and if any rebel against his authority he immediately puts them under the ban of the anathema, so that they are deprived of their offices, and exposed to the insults and persecution of their brethren. Thus the false prophet deceives the Latin world *by the means of those miracles which he had power to do in the sight of the beast.* Under the appearance of great sanctity he persuades men to believe all his lying doctrines, and enforces his canons and decretals with the sword of the civil magistrate.

Verse 14. *Saying to them that dwell on the earth, that they should make an image to the beast, which had the wound by a sword, and did live.*] The *image of the beast* must designate a person who represents in himself the whole power of the Latin empire, therefore it cannot be the emperor; for though he was, according to his own account, *supremum caput Christianitatis*, the supreme head of Christendom, yet he was only the chief of the Germanic confederation, and consequently was only sovereign of the principal power of the Latin empire. The image of the beast must be the supreme ruler of the Latin empire, and as it is through the influence of the false prophet that this image is made for the first beast, this great chief must be an ecclesiastic. Who this is has been ably shown by Bishop Newton in his comment on the following verse.

Verse 15. *And he had power to give life unto the image of the beast, that the image of the beast should both speak, and cause that as many as would not worship the image of the beast should be killed.*] I would just observe that the *Brahmins*, by ascribing incantations, profess to give *eyes* and a *soul* to an image recently made, before it is worshipped; afterwards, being supposed to be the *residence* of the god or goddess it represents, it has a *legal* right to *worship*. On this verse the learned bishop observes: " The influence of the two-horned beast, or corrupted clergy, is farther seen in persuading and inducing mankind *to make an image to the beast which had the wound by a sword, and did live.* This image and representative of the beast is the *pope.* He is properly the *idol of*

2

A. M. cir. 4100.
A. D. cir. 96.
Impp. Flavio
Domitiano
Cæs. Aug. et
Nerva.

k and cause that as many as would not worship the image of the beast should be killed.

16 And he caused all, both small and great, rich and poor, free and bond, l to m receive a mark in their right hand, or in their foreheads :

A. M. cir. 4100.
A. D. cir. 96.
Impp. Flavio
Domitiano
Cæs. Aug. et
Nerva.

---

k Chap. xvi. 2; xix. 20; xx. 4.

l Chap. xiv. 9; xix. 20; xx. 4.——m Gr. *to give them.*

---

the Church. He represents in himself the whole power of the beast, and is the head of all authority, temporal as well as spiritual. He is nothing more than a private person, without power and without authority, till the two-horned beast or corrupted clergy, by choosing him pope, give life unto him, and enable him to speak and utter his decrees, and to persecute even to death as many as refuse to submit to him and to worship him. As soon as he is chosen pope he is clothed with the pontifical robes, and crowned and placed upon the altar, and the cardinals come and kiss his feet, which ceremony is called *adoration.* They first elect and then they worship him, as in the medals of Martin V., where two are represented crowning the pope, and two kneeling before him, with this inscription, *Quem creant adorant;* 'Whom they create they adore.' He is THE PRINCIPLE OF UNITY TO THE TEN KINGDOMS OF THE BEAST, and causeth, as far as he is able, all who will not acknowledge his supremacy to be put to death." The great ascendency which the popes have obtained over the kings of the Latin world by means of the Romish hierarchy is sufficiently marked in the history of Europe. As long as the great body of the people were devoted to the Roman Catholic idolatry, it was in vain for the kings of the different Roman Catholic countries to oppose the increasing usurpations of the popes. They ascended, in spite of all opposition, to the highest pinnacle of human greatness ; for even the authority of the emperors themselves was established or annulled at their pleasure. The high sounding tone of the popes commenced in Gregory VII., A. D. 1073, commonly known by the name of Hildebrand, who aimed at nothing less than universal empire. He published an anathema against all who received the investiture of a bishopric or abbacy from the hands of a layman, as also against those by whom the investiture should be performed. This measure being opposed by Henry IV., emperor of Germany, the pope deposed him from all power and dignity, regal or imperial See Corps Diplomatique, tom. i. p. 53. Great numbers of German princes siding with the pope, the emperor found himself under the necessity of going, (in January, 1077,) to the bishop of Rome to implore his forgiveness, which was not granted him till he had fasted three days, standing from morning to evening barefooted, and exposed to the inclemency of the weather ! In the following century the power of the pope was still farther increased ; for on the 23d of September, 1122, the Emperor Henry V. gave up all right of conferring the regalia by the ceremony of the ring and crosier, so that the chapters and communities should be at liberty to fill up their own vacancies. In this century the election of the Roman pontiffs was confined by Alexander III. to the college of cardinals. In the thirteenth century the popes (Dr. Mosheim observes) " inculcated that pernicious maxim, that the bishop of Rome is *the supreme lord of the universe,*

and that neither princes nor bishops, civil governors nor ecclesiastical rulers, have any lawful power in Church or state but what they derive from him. To establish their authority both in civil and ecclesiastical matters upon the firmest foundation, they assumed to themselves the power of disposing of the various offices of the Church, whether of a higher or more subordinate nature, and of creating bishops, abbots, and canons, according to their fancy. The first of the pontiffs who usurped such an extravagant extent of authority was Innocent III., (A. D. 1198-1216,) whose example was followed by Honorius III., (A. D. 1216,) Gregory IX., (A. D. 1227,) and several of their successors." Thus the plenitude of the papal power (as it is termed) was not confined to what was spiritual ; the Romish bishops " dethroned monarchs, disposed of crowns, absolved subjects from the obedience due to their sovereigns, and laid kingdoms under interdicts. There was not a state in Europe which had not been disquieted by their ambition. There was not a throne which they had not shaken, nor a prince who did not tremble at their presence." The point of time in which the Romish bishops attained their highest elevation of authority was about the commencement of the fourteenth century. Boniface VIII., who was pope at this time, outstripped all his predecessors in the high sounding tone of his public decrees. According to his famous bull *Unam Sanctam,* published Nov. 16, 1302, " the secular power is but a simple emanation from the ecclesiastical ; and the double power of the pope, founded upon Holy Scripture, is even an article of faith. God," said he, " has confided to Saint Peter, and to his successors, two swords, the one spiritual, the other temporal. The first ought to be exercised by the Church itself ; and the other, by secular powers for the service of the Church, and according to the will of the pope. The latter, that is to say, the temporal sword, is in subjection to the former, and the temporal authority depends indispensably on the spiritual power which judges it, while God alone can judge the spiritual power. Finally," he adds, " it is necessary to salvation for every human creature to be in subjection to the Roman pontiff." The false prophet SAID " to them that dwell upon the earth, that they should make an image to the beast that had the wound by a sword, and did live ;" that is, the Romish priesthood PREACHED UP the pope's supremacy over temporal princes ; and, through their astonishing influence on the minds of the people, the bishop of Rome at last became the supreme sovereign of the secular Latin empire, and thus was at the head of all authority, temporal and spiritual.

The papists have in their various superstitions professed to worship God. But they are said, in the unerring words of prophecy, to *worship* the dragon, beast, and image of the beast, and to *blaspheme* God ; for they received as holy those commandments of men that stand in direct opposition to the sacred Scriptures,

A. M. cir. 4100.
A. D. cir. 96.
Impp. Flavio
Domitiano
Cæs. Aug. et
Nerva.

17 And that no man might buy or sell, save he that had the mark, or ⁿ the name of the beast, ᵒ or the number of his name.

18 ᵖ Here is wisdom. Let him that hath

understanding count �q the number of the beast: ʳ for it is the number of a man; and his number *is* Six hundred threescore *and* six.

A. M. cir. 4100
A. D. cir. 96.
Impp. Flavio
Domitiano
Cæs. Aug. et
Nerva.

ⁿ Chap. xiv. 11.——ᵒ Chap. xv. 2.——ᵖ Chap. xvii. 9.   q Chap. xv. 2.——ʳ Chap. xxi. 17.

and which have been imposed on them by the Romish bishops, aided by the secular powers. "God is a Spirit, and they who worship him must worship him in SPIRIT and in TRUTH."

Verse 16. *And he caused all, both small and great, rich and poor, free and bond, to receive a mark*] To ascertain the meaning of the *mark* which the two-horned beast causes all orders and degrees of men in the Latin world to receive, we need only refer to chap. xiv. 11, where the mark imposed by the two-horned beast is called *the mark of his name*. The *name of the beast* is *the Latin empire*: the *mark of his name* must therefore be *his* LATIN *worship*: for this very reason, that it is the two-horned beast, or false prophet, who causes all descriptions of persons to receive it. Now it is well known that the continual employment of the Latin clergy is to enforce the Latin idolatry upon their flocks. The mass and offices of the Church, which are in Latin, and contain the sum and substance of their idolatrous worship, are of different kinds, and abound in impious prayers to the Virgin Mary, and the saints and angels. In a word, *the* LATIN *worship* is the universal badge of distinction of *the* LATIN *Church*, from all other Churches on the face of the earth; and is therefore the only infallible MARK by which a genuine papist can be distinguished from the rest of mankind. But the two-horned beast causes all to receive this mark—

In their right hand, or in their foreheads] *Right hand* in Scripture language, when used figuratively, represents the physical power of the person of whom it is spoken; and when applied to God designates a signal manifestation of Divine power against his enemies, and in behalf of his people. See Psa. xvii. 7; xx 6; xxi. 8; xlv. 3, 4, &c. The reception of the mark in the right hand must therefore mean, that all so receiving it devote the whole powers of their mind and body to the propagation of the Latin worship, and to the eradication of all they denominate heresies out of their Church. But some receive the mark *in their foreheads*. By any thing being impressed upon *the forehead*, is meant the public profession of whatever is inscribed or marked upon it. See chap. ix. 4; xiv. 1; xxii. 4, &c. The mark of the beast being received on the *forehead*, therefore, means that all those so marked make a public profession of *the Latin worship*; whereby it is evident to all that they form a part of the Latin Church. Many may be marked in the right hand who are also marked on their foreheads, but it does not follow that those marked on their foreheads are also marked in their right hand; that is to say, it is not every individual that complies with the Latin worship who, to the utmost of his power, endeavours to propagate his religious system. Hence the propriety of the words, "He causeth all—to receive a mark in their right hand, OR in their foreheads."

Verse 17. *And that no man might buy or sell, save he that had the mark*] "If any," observes Bishop Newton, "dissent from the stated and authorized forms, they are condemned and excommunicated as heretics; and in consequence of that they are no longer suffered to *buy or sell*; they are interdicted from traffic and commerce, and all the benefits of civil society. So Roger Hoveden relates of William the Conqueror, that he was so dutiful to the pope that he would not permit any one in his power to buy or sell any thing whom he found disobedient to the apostolic see. So the canon of the council of Lateran, under Pope Alexander III., made against the Waldenses and Albigenses, enjoins, upon pain of anathema, that no man presume to entertain or cherish them in his house or land, or exercise traffic with them. The synod of Tours, in France, under the same pope, orders, under the like intermination, that no man should presume to receive or assist them, no, not so much as hold any communion with them, *in selling or buying*; that, being deprived of the comfort of humanity they may be compelled to repent of the error of their way." In the tenth and eleventh centuries the severity against the excommunicated was carried to so high a pitch, that nobody might come near them, not even their own wives, children, or servants; they forfeited all their natural legal rights and privileges, and were excluded from all kinds of offices. The form of excommunication in the Romish Church is to take lighted torches, throw them upon the ground with curses and anathemas, and trample them out under foot to the ringing of the bells. It is in this and similar ways that the false prophet has terrified the Latin world, and kept it in subjection to the secular and spiritual powers. Those interdicted by the two-horned beast from all offices of civil life are also such as have not—

The name of the beast, or the number of his name.] See on the following verse.

Verse 18. *Here is wisdom. Let him that hath understanding count the number of the beast; for it is the number of a man; and his number* is *Six hundred threescore and six.*] In this verse we have the very name of the beast given under the symbol of the number 666. Before the invention of figures by the Arabs, in the tenth century, letters of the alphabet were used for numbers. The Greeks in the time of Homer, or soon after, are thought by some to have assigned to their letters a numerical value corresponding to their order in the alphabet: thus, *a* was 1, because the first letter; and ω 24, being the last. It is in this manner that the books of the Iliad and Odyssey are numbered, which have been thus marked by Homer himself, or by some person who lived near his time. A system of representing numbers of great antiquity was used by the Greeks, very much resembling that afterwards adopted by the Romans. This consisted in assigning to the initial letter of the name of the number a value equal to the number. Thus X, the initial of χιλια, stood for a thousand ; Δ, the initial of δεκα, for ten ; Π, the initial of πεντε, for five, &c. Herodotus, the grammarian, is the only writer of antiquity who has noticed this system, and the chronological table of remarkable events on the Arundelian marbles the only work extant in which this method of representing numbers is exhibited. The system now in use cannot be traced to any very ancient source. What can be proved is, that it was in use before the commencement of the Christian era. Numerical letters, denoting the year of the Roman emperor's reign, exist on great numbers of the Egyptian coins, from the time of Augustus Cæsar through the succeeding reigns. See *Numi Ægyptii Imperatorii, a Geo. Zoega,* edit. Rom. 1787. There are coins extant marked of the 2d, 3d, 14th, 30th, 35th, 38th, 39th, 40th, 41st, and 42d years of Augustus Cæsar, with the numerical letters preceded by L or Λ, for λυκαβας, *year,* thus : LB, LΓ, LIΔ, ΛΑ, LΑΕ, LΛΗ, LΛΘ, LM, LMA, and LMB. The following is the Greek alphabet, with the numerical value of each letter affixed, according to the generally received system :—

α	 1	ι	 10	ρ	 100
β	 2	κ	 20	σ	 200
γ	 3	λ	 30	τ	 300
δ	 4	μ	 40	υ	 400
ε	 5	ν	 50	φ	 500
ζ	 7	ξ	 60	χ	 600
η	 8	ο	 70	ψ	 700
ϑ	 9	π	 80	ω	 800

The method just described of representing numbers by letters of the alphabet, gave rise to a practice among the ancients of representing names also by numbers. Examples of this kind abound in the writings of heathens, Jews, and Christians. When the practice of counting the number in names or phrases began first to be used, cannot be ascertained ; it is sufficient for the illustration of the passage under consideration, if it can be shown to have been in existence in the apostolic age. Seneca, who was contemporary with St. Paul, informs us, in his eighty-eighth epistle, that Apion, the grammarian, maintained Homer to have been the author of the division of his poems of the Iliad and Odyssey into forty-eight books ; for a proof of which Apion produces the following argument: that the poet commenced his Iliad with the word μηνιν, that the two first letters, whose sum is 48, might indicate such division. Leonidas of Alexandria, who flourished in the reigns of Nero, Vespasian, &c., carried the practice of computing the number in words so far as to construct equinumeral distichs ; that is, epigrams of four lines, whose first hexameter and pentameter contain the same number with the other two. We will only notice two examples ; the first is addressed to one of the emperors, the other to Poppæa, the wife of Nero.

> Θυει σοι τοδε γραμμα γενεθλιακαισιν εν ωραις,
> Καισαρ, Νειλαιη Μουσα Λεωνιδεω.
> Καλλιοπης γαρ ακαπνον αει θνος· εις δε νεωτα
> Ην εθελης, θυσει τουδε περισσοτερα.

"The muse of Leonidas of the Nile offers up to thee, O Cæsar, this writing, at the time of thy nativity ; for the sacrifice of Calliope is always without smoke : but in the ensuing year he will offer up, if thou wilt, better things than this."

From the numerical table already given, the preceding epigram may be shown to contain equinumeral distichs, as follows : Θυει contains 424, i. e., ϑ 9, υ 400, ε 5, ι 10 ; in all 424 : σοι contains 280, i. e., σ 200, ο 70, ι 10. In like manner τοδε will be found to contain 379, γραμμα 185, γενεθλιακαισιν 404, εν 55, ωραις 1111, Καισαρ 332, Νειλαιη 114, Μουσα 711, Λεωνιδεω 1704. The sum of all these is 5699, the number in the first distich. In the second distich, Καλλιοπης contains 449, γαρ 104, ακαπνον 272, αει 16, θνος 679, εις 215, δε 9, νεωτα 1156, Ην 58, εϑελης 267, (the subscribed *iota* being taken into the account,) θυσει 624, τουδε 779, περισσοτερα 1071. The sum of all 5699, which is precisely the same with that contained in the first distich.

> Ουρανιον μειμημα γενεθλιακαισιν εν ωραις
> Τουτ' απο Νειλογενους δεξο Λεωνιδεω,
> Ποππαια, Διος ευνι, Σεβαστιας· εναδε γαρ σοι
> Δωρα, τα και λεκτρων αξια και σοφιης.

"O Poppæa, wife of Jupiter (Nero) Augusta, receive from Leonidas of the Nile a celestial globe on the day of thy nativity ; for gifts please thee which are suited to thy imperial dignity and wisdom."

In this epigram each of the distichs contains the number 6422, viz., Ουρανιον 751, (i. e., ο 70, υ 400, ρ 100, α 1, ν 50, ι 10, ο 70, ν 50, the sum of which is 751,) μειμημα 144, γενεθλιακαισιν 404, εν 55, ωραις 1111, τουτ' 1070, απο 151, Νειλογενους 893, δεξο 139, Λεωνιδεω 1704 ; the sum of all 6422. The numbers corresponding to the words of the second distich are, respectively, 322, 284, 465, 919, 415, 104, 280, 905, 301, 31, 1305, 72, 31, 988 ; the sum of which is also 6422.

This poet did not restrict himself to the construction of equinumeral distichs. The following is one of his distichs in which the hexameter line is made equal in number to its corresponding pentameter :—

> Εις προς ενα ψηφοισιν ισαζεται, ου δυο δοιοις,
> Ου γαρ ετι στεργω την δολιχογραφιην.

"One line is made equal in number to one, not two to two ; for I no longer approve of long epigrams."

In this distich the words of the hexameter line contain, respectively, the numbers 215, 450, 56, 1548, 534, 470, 474, and 364 ; the sum of which is 4111. The numbers corresponding to the words of the pentameter line are, respectively, 470, 104, 315, 1408, 358, and 1456 ; the sum of which is also 4111. The equinumeral distichs of Leonidas are contained in the second volume of Brunck and Jacob's edition of the Greek Anthology. It appears from ancient records that some of the Greeks in the early part of the second century, if not in the apostolic age, employed themselves in counting the numbers contained in the verses of Homer to find out what two consecutive lines were ισοψηφοι or equinumeral. Aulus Gellius, the grammarian, who lived in the reigns of Hadrian and Antoninus Pius, gives us an account (lib. xiv., cap. 6) of a person who presented him with a book filled with a variety of information collected from numerous sources, of which he was at liberty to avail himself in writing his Attic Nights. Among the subjects treated of in this book, we are informed by Gellius, was that of Homeric equinumeral verses. None of the examples are given by the grammarian; but Labbeus says, in his Bibl. Nov. MSS., p. 284, that the equinumeral verses are marked in the Codex 2216, in the French king's library. Gronovius, in his notes on Gellius, p. 655, has copied what he found in a MS. (No. 1488) upon this subject, viz., two examples out of the Iliad, and one in the Odyssey. The examples in the Iliad are lines 264 and 265 of book vii., each line containing 3508; and lines 306 and 307 of book xix., each containing 2848. The verses in the Odyssey (ω, 110, 111) stated to be equinumeral in the MS. cited by Gronovius have not now this property, owing possibly to some corruption that may have taken place in the lines from frequent transcription.

For other examples of the computation of the number in words or phrases, the reader is referred to the Oneirocritica of Artemidorus, lib. ii. c. 75 ; lib. iii. c. 34 : and lib. iv. c. 26. See also Martiani Minei Felicis Capelhæ Africarthaginensis, De Nuptiis Philologiæ et Mercurii, lib. ii. and vii. ; Irenæus adversus Hæreses, lib. i., ii., and v. ; Tertullian. de Præscriptionibus Hæret., tom. ii., p. 487; Wirceburgi, 1781; Sibyll. Oracul., lib. i., &c.

Having thus shown that it was a practice in the apostolic age, and subsequently, to count the number in words and phrases, and even in whole verses, it will be evident that what is intended by 666 is, that the Greek name of the beast (for it was in the Greek language that Jesus Christ communicated his revelation to St. John) contains this number. Many names have been proposed from time to time as applicable to the beast, and at the same time containing 666. We will only notice one example, viz., that famous one of Irenæus, which has been approved of by almost all commentators who have given any sort of tolerable exposition of the Revelation. The word alluded to is Λατεινος, the letters of which have the following numerical values : λ 30, α 1, τ 300, ε 5, ι 10, ν 50, ο 70, ς 200 ; and if these be added together, the sum will be found to be equivalent to the number of the beast. This word was applied by Irenæus, who lived in the second century, to the then existing Roman empire ; " for," says he, " they are LATINS who now reign." Though it is evident, from the notes on the preceding part of this chapter, that the conjecture of Irenæus respecting the number 666 having some way or other a reference to *the empire of the Latins* is well founded ; yet his production of the word Λατεινος, as containing 666, is not a proof that it has any such reference. Bellarmin the Jesuit objected against Λατεινος being the name intended in the prophecy from its orthography ; for, says he, it should be written Λατινος. That the objection of the learned Jesuit has very great force is evident from every Greek writer extant, who has used the Greek word for *Latinus*, in

all of whom it is uniformly found without the dipthong. See Hesiod, Polybius, Dionysius of Halicarnassus, Strabo Plutarch, Dio Cassius, Photius, the Byzantine historians, &c., &c. It hence follows that if the Greek word for *Latinus* had been intended, the number contained in Λατινος, and not that in Λατεινος, would have been called *the number of the beast.* We have already observed that the beast is *the Latin kingdom* or *empire* ; therefore, if this observation be correct, the Greek words signifying *the Latin kingdom* must have this number. The most concise method of expressing this among the Greeks was as follows, Ἡ Λατινη βασιλεια, which is thus numbered :—

H	=	8	THE
Λ	=	30	
α	=	1	
τ	=	300	
ι	=	10	LATIN
ν	=	50	
η	=	8	
B	=	2	
α	=	1	
σ	=	200	
ι	=	10	
λ	=	30	KINGDOM.
ε	=	5	
ι	=	10	
α	=	1	

666

No other kingdom on earth can be found to contain 666. This is then ἡ σοφια, *the wisdom* or *demonstration.* A *beast* is the symbol of a *kingdom* ; THE *beast* has been *proved*, in the preceding part of this chapter, to be *the* LATIN *kingdom* ; and Ἡ Λατινη βασιλεια, being shown to contain, exclusively, the number 666, is the *demonstration.*

Having demonstrated that Ἡ Λατινη βασιλεια, *The Latin kingdom*, is the *name* of the beast, we must now examine what is intended by the phrase in the 17th verse, *the name of the beast, or the number of his name.* Bishop Newton supposes that *the name of the beast,* and *the number of his name,* mean the same thing ; but this opinion is totally irreconcilable with chap. xv. 2, where St. John informs us that he " saw as it were a sea of glass mingled with fire, and them that had gotten the victory over the beast, and over his image, and over the number of his name, stand upon the sea of glass, having the harps of God." In this passage it is evident that the beast, his image, and the number of his name, are perfectly distinet ; and therefore no two of them can mean the same thing. Hence what is meant by *the name of the beast* is entirely different from that intended by *the number of his name.* But how can this be, when it is expressly declared that the number of the beast is 666, which number is declared to be *that* of his name? The solution of the whole mystery is as follows : Both beasts of the Apocalypse, we have already shown, have the same appellation ; that is to say, the name of the first and second beast is equally Ἡ Λατινη βασιλεια, the Latin kingdom; therefore, by *the name of the beast* is meant *the Latin kingdom*, and by *the number of his name* is also meant *the Latin kingdom*. Hence only one of the beasts is numbered; the name of that which is not numbered is termed *the name of the beast*, and the numbered Latin empire is denominated *the number of his name*, or 666, exactly agreeable to an ancient practice already noticed, of representing names by the numbers contained in them. Therefore the meaning of the whole passage is, that those whom the false prophet does not excommunicate, or put out of the pale of his Church, have the *mark* of the beast, that is, are genuine papists, or such as are actively or passively obedient to his Latin idolatry. Those also escape his ecclesiastical interdicts who have *the name of the beast*, or *the number of his name*. By a person having the name of the beast is evidently meant his being *a Latin*, i. e., in subjection to the Latin empire, and, consequently an individual of the Latin world; therefore those that have the name of the beast, or the number of his name, are those that are subjects of the Latin empire, or of the numbered Latin empire, viz., who are in subjection to the Latin empire, *secular* or *spiritual*. All that were in subjection to the secular or spiritual power were not papists in heart; hence the propriety of distinguishing those which have *the mark* from those which *have the name of the beast* or *the number of his name*. But which of the two beasts it is which God has numbered has been not a little contested. That it is the first beast which is numbered has been the prevailing opinion. On this side are Lord Napier, Whiston, Bishop Newton, Faber, and others. Among those that have supposed the second beast to be the one which is numbered are, Dr. Henry More, Pyle, Kershaw, Galloway, Bicheno, Dr. Hales, &c. Drs. Gill and Reader assert that both beasts have the same number, and that the name is Λατεινος. Though it has been demonstrated that the *name* of the beast is the Latin kingdom, it is impossible from the mere name to say whether it is the Latin empire, SECULAR OR SPIRITUAL; hence the necessity of determining which of the two beasts God has computed. That it is the second beast which is numbered is evident from three different passages in the Apocalypse. The first is in chap. xiii. 17, where it is said, " that no man might buy or sell, save he that had the mark, or the name of the beast, or the number of his name." Here *the name of the beast* is mentioned before *the number of his name*, which is a presumptive evidence that *the name of the beast* refers to the first beast, and *the number of his name* to the second. The second passage is in chap. xv. 2, where mention is made of " them that had gotten the victory over the beast, and over his image,

and over the number of his name." That here styled *the beast* is evidently *the secular Latin empire*, for it was to *this* that the two-horned beast made an image; consequently there can be no doubt that *the number of his name*, or *the numbered Latin empire*, is the two-horned beast or false prophet. To feel the full force of this argument, it must be considered that the saints of God are represented as getting the victory over *the beast* as well as over *the number of his name*, which is a proof that two distinct antichristian empires are here spoken of, for otherwise it would be tautology. That the two-horned beast is the one which is numbered, is farther evident from a comparison of this passage with chap. xix. 20. In the latter passage the words are : " And the beast was taken, and with him the false prophet that wrought miracles before him, with which he deceived them that had received the mark of the beast, and them that worshipped his image." Here nothing is said of the *number of his name*, which is so particularly mentioned in chap. xv. 2, and in that chapter nothing is mentioned of the *false prophet*, the reason of which can only be, that what is termed in one passage *the number of his name*, is in its parallel one called *the false prophet*. Hence the two-horned beast, or false prophet, is also designated by the phrase *the number of his name;* and consequently it is *this beast* which is numbered. But what adds the last degree of certainty to this argument is the passage in chap. xiii. 18 : " Here is wisdom. Let him that hath a mind count the number of the beast; for it is the number of a man : and his number is six hundred threescore and six." Here is the solution of this mystery : *let him that hath a mind* for investigations of this kind, find out a kingdom which contains precisely the number 666, for this must be infallibly the *name* of the beast. Ἡ Λατινη βασιλεια, THE LATIN KINGDOM, has exclusively this number. But both beasts are called by this name; which is, therefore, the one that is numbered? It is said *the number of the beast* is *the number of a man;* consequently the numbered beast must be A MAN, that is, it must be represented elsewhere in the Revelation under this emblem, for in no other sense can *an empire* be denominated *a man*. Therefore, it is not the ten-horned beast, for this is uniformly styled *The Beast* in every part of the Apocalypse where there has been occasion to mention this power. It can therefore be no other than the two-horned beast, or Romish hierarchy; which, on account of its *preaching* to the world its most antichristian system of doctrines, and calling it Christianity, is likewise named in chap. xvi. 13; xix. 20; and xx. 10, THE FALSE PROPHET.

JOHN EDWARD CLARKE.

CHAPTER XIV.

The Lamb on mount Sion, and his company and their character, 1–5. The angel flying in the midst of heaven, with the everlasting Gospel, 6, 7. Another angel proclaims the fall of Babylon, 8. A third angel denounces God's judgments against those who worship the beast or his image, 9–11. The patience of the saints, and the blessedness of them who die in the Lord, 12, 13. *The man on the white cloud, with a sickle, reaping the earth,* 14–16. *The angel with the sickle commanded by another angel, who had power over fire, to gather the clusters of the vines of the earth,* 17, 18. *They are gathered and thrown into the great winepress of God's wrath, which is trodden without the city, and the blood comes out* 1600 *furlongs,* 19, 20.

A. M. cir. 4100.
A. D. cir. 96.
Impp. Flavio
Domitiano
Cæs. Aug. et
Nerva.

AND I looked, and lo, [a] a Lamb stood on the mount Sion, and with him [b] a hundred forty *and* four thousand, [c] having his Father's name written in their foreheads.

2 And I heard a voice from heaven, [d] as the voice of many waters, and as the voice of a great thunder : and I heard the voice of [e] harpers harping with their harps :

3 And [f] they sung as it were a new song before the throne, and before the four beasts, and the elders : and no man could learn that song [g] but the hundred *and* forty *and* four thousand, which were redeemed from the earth.

A. M. cir. 4100.
A. D. cir. 96.
Impp. Flavio
Domitiano
Cæs. Aug. et
Nerva.

4 These are they which were not defiled with women ; [h] for they are virgins. These are they [i] which follow the Lamb whithersoever he goeth. These [k] were [l] redeemed from among men, [m] *being* the first fruits unto God and to the Lamb.

5 And [n] in their mouth was found no guile : for [o] they are without fault before the throne of God.

6 And I saw another angel [p] fly in the midst of heaven, [q] having the everlasting Gospel to

---

[a] Chap. v. 5.——[b] Chap. vii. 4.——[c] Chapter vii. 3 ; xiii. 16.
[d] Chap. i. 15 ; xix. 6.——[e] Chap. v. 8.——[f] Chapter v. 9 ; xv. 3.
[g] Ver. 1.——[h] 2 Cor. xi. 2.——[i] Chap. iii. 4 ; vii. 15, 17 ; xvii. 14.

[k] Gr. *were bought.*——[l] Chap. v. 9.——[m] James i. 18.——[n] Psa. xxxii. 2 ; Zeph. iii. 13.——[o] Eph. v. 27 ; Jude 24.——[p] Chapter viii. 13.——[q] Eph. iii. 9, 10, 11 ; Tit. i. 2.

NOTES ON CHAP. XIV.

Verse 1. *A Lamb stood on the mount Sion*] This represents Jesus Christ in his *sacrificial office ; mount Sion* was a type of the Christian Church.

And with him a hundred and *four thousand*] Representing those who were converted to Christianity from among the *Jews.* See chap. vii. 4.

His Father's name written in their foreheads.] They were professedly, openly, and practically, the children of God, by faith in Christ Jesus. Different *sects* of idolaters have the *peculiar mark* of their god on their foreheads. This is practised in the east to the present day, and the mark is called the *sectarial mark.* Between eighty and ninety different figures are found on the foreheads of different Hindoo deities and their followers.

Almost every MS. of importance, as well as most of the *versions* and many of the *fathers,* read this clause thus : *Having* HIS NAME *and his Father's name written upon their foreheads.* This is undoubtedly the true reading, and is properly received by *Griesbach* into the text.

Verse 2. *The voice of many waters*] That is, of multitudes of various nations.

The voice of harpers] Though the sounds were many and apparently confused, yet both *harmony* and *melody* were preserved.

Verse 3. *They sung—a new song*] See on chap. v. 9.

No man could learn that song] As none but genuine Christians can worship God acceptably, because they approach him through the only Mediator, so none can understand the deep things of God but such ; nor can others know the cause why true believers exult so much in God through Christ, because they know not the communion which such hold with the Father and the Son through the Holy Ghost.

Verse 4. *These are they which were not defiled with women*] They are pure from idolatry, and are presented as unspotted *virgins* to their Lord and

Saviour Christ. See 2 Cor. xi. 2. There may be an allusion here to the Israelites committing idolatry, through the means of their criminal connection with the Midianitish women. See Num. xxv. 1–4, and xxxi. 16.

Follow the Lamb whithersoever he goeth] They go through good and through evil report, bear his reproach, and love not their lives even to the death.

The first fruits unto God] The reference appears to be to those *Jews* who were the *first converts to* Christianity.

Verse 5. *In their mouth was found no guile*] When brought before kings and rulers they did not dissemble, but boldly confessed the Lord Jesus.

Verse 6. *Another angel fly in the midst of heaven, having the everlasting Gospel*] Whether this angel mean any more than a particular dispensation of providence and grace, by which the Gospel shall be rapidly sent throughout the whole world ; or whether it mean any especial messenger, order of preachers, people, or society of Christians, whose professed object it is to send the Gospel of the kingdom throughout the earth, we know not. But the vision seems truly descriptive of a late institution, entitled THE BRITISH AND FOREIGN BIBLE SOCIETY, whose object it is to print and circulate the Scriptures of the Old and New Testaments, through all the habitable world, and in all the languages spoken on the face of the earth. Already they have been the instruments, by actually printing (or by affording the means to different nations to print for themselves) the Bible in a vast number of languages and dialects, so that it has been sent in hundreds of thousands of copies, in whole or in part, to almost every part of the globe : *viz.,* in their native language to the *Welsh ;* in *Erse* to the *Irish ;* in *Gaelic* to the *Highlands* of Scotland ; in *Manks* to the *Isle of Man ;* in *French, Italian, Portuguese,* and *Spanish,* to those countries and *Switzerland ;* in *Low Dutch* to *Holland, &c. ;* in *High Dutch* to *Germany, Prussia, &c*

A. M. cir. 4100.
A. D. cir. 96.
Impp. Flavio
Domitiano
Cæs. Aug. et
Nerva.

preach unto them that dwell on the earth, [r] and to every nation, and kindred, and tongue, and people,

7 Saying with a loud voice, [s] Fear God, and give glory to him ; for the hour of his judgment is come : [t] and worship him that made heaven, and earth, and the sea, and the fountains of waters.

8 And there followed another angel, saying, [u] Babylon is fallen, is fallen, [v] that great city, because she made all nations drink of the wine of the wrath of her fornication.

9 And the third angel followed them, saying with a loud voice, [w] If any man worship the

beast and his image, and receive *his* mark in his forehead, or in his hand,

A. M. cir. 4100.
A. D. cir. 96.
Impp. Flavio
Domitiano
Cæs. Aug. et
Nerva.

10 The same [x] shall drink of the wine of the wrath of God, which is [y] poured out without mixture into [z] the cup of his indignation ; and [a] he shall be tormented with [b] fire and brimstone in the presence of the holy angels, and in the presence of the Lamb :

11 And [c] the smoke of their torment ascendeth up for ever and ever : and they have no rest day nor night, who worship the beast and his image, and whosoever receiveth the mark of his name.

12 [d] Here is the patience of the saints :

---

[r] Chap. xiii. 7.——[s] Chap. xi. 18 ; xv. 4.——[t] Neh. ix. 6 ; Psa. xxxiii. 6 ; cxxiv. 8 ; cxlvi. 5, 6 ; Acts xiv. 15 ; xvii. 24.——[u] Isa. xxi. 9 ; Jer. li. 8 ; chap. xviii. 2.——[v] Jer. li. 7 ; chap. xi. 8 ; xvi. 19 ; xvii. 2, 5 ; xviii. 3, 10, 18, 21 ; xix. 2.

[w] Chap. xiii. 14, 15, 16.——[x] Psa. lxxv. 8 ; Isa. li. 17 ; Jer. xxv. 15.——[y] Chap. xviii. 6.——[z] Chap. xvi. 19.——[a] Chap. xx. 10.——[b] Chapter xix. 20.——[c] Isa. xxxiv. 10 ; chap. xix. 3. [d] Chap. xiii. 10.

Through them a similar society has been established at St. Petersburgh, by which the Bible has been sent in *Slavonic* to the Russians ; and in different dialects to the people of that vast empire ; besides the *Turkish*, *Tartaric*, and *Calmuck.* They have also sent the Holy Scriptures in *ancient* and *modern* Greek to *Asia Minor* and the different *isles* of the *Mediterranean Sea* ; in *Arabic* and *Æthiopic* to *Egypt* and *Abyssinia* ; in *Syriac* to the *Holy Land*, and to the *Christians* at *Travancore.* They have also greatly and effectually assisted a very worthy society in the East Indies, whose indefatigable and incomparable missionaries, the Rev. Messrs. Carey, Marshman, and Ward, have translated the Scriptures into the principal languages of India ; and they have furnished the means of printing a complete translation of the New Testament in the Chinese language at Canton, by the Rev. Mr. Morrison. In short, almost every nation in the universe has, through this society, *directly* or *indirectly* received, or is receiving, the words of eternal life ; so that it appears to answer the description of the Apocalyptic " angel, flying in the midst of heaven, having the everlasting Gospel to preach unto them that dwell on the earth, and to every nation, and kindred, and tongue, and people."

Verse 7. *Fear God, and give glory to him*] This is the general language of the sacred writings. Worship the true God, the creator and governor of all things ; and give *him* glory, for to him alone, not to idols or men, all glory and honour belong.

Verse 8. *Babylon is fallen, is fallen*] This is generally understood to be a prediction concerning *Rome ;* and it is certain that *Rome*, in the rabbinical writings, is termed *Babylon.*

That great city] Among the same writers this city is styled קרתא רבתא karta rabbetha, *the great city ;* and רומי רבתא Romi rabbetha, *the great Rome.* But *which* Rome is meant ? *Pagan* or *Papal* Rome ? Some parts of the description apply best to the former.

The wine of the wrath of her fornication.] There is an allusion here to a custom of impure women, who

give *philtres* or *love potions* to those whom they wish to seduce and bind to their will ; and these potions are generally of an *intoxicating* nature, greatly inflaming the blood, and disturbing the intellect.

Fornication and *adultery* are frequently used in Scripture as emblems of idolatry and false worship.

The wine of the wrath is another expression for the *envenomed* or *poisoned cup* given by such women.

No nation of the earth spread their *idolatries* so far as the *ancient Romans ;* they were as extensive as their conquests. And *papal Rome* has been not less active in disseminating her superstitions. She has given her *rituals*, but not the *everlasting Gospel*, to most nations of the earth.

Verse 9. *And the third angel followed*] Bishop Bale considers these three angels as three descriptions of preachers, who should bear their testimony against the corruptions of the *papal Church.*

The beast and his image] See the notes on chap. xiii.

Mark in his forehead] Such as the *sectarial marks* of the idolatrous Hindoos, as has been observed before.

Verse 10. *The wine of the wrath of God*] As they have drunk the intoxicating wine of idolatry or spiritual fornication, they shall now drink the wine of God's wrath, which is poured out into the cup of his indignation. This is an allusion to the *poisoned cup*, which certain criminals were obliged to drink, on which ensued speedy death. See on Heb. ii. 9.

Shall be tormented with fire and brimstone] An allusion to the punishment of *Sodom* and *Gomorrha* for their unnatural crimes.

Presence of the holy angels, and—of the Lamb] These being the *instruments* employed in their destruction ; the *Lamb*—the Lord Jesus Christ, acting as judge.

Verse 11. *The smoke of their torment*] Still an allusion to the destruction of Sodom and Gomorrha.

Verse 12. *Here is the patience of the saints*] Here the faith of the true Christians shall be proved ; they *will* follow the Lamb whithersoever he goeth, they

A. M. cir. 4100.
A. D. cir. 96.
Impp. Flavio
Domitiano
Cæs. Aug. et
Nerva.

e here *are* they that keep the commandments of God, and the faith of Jesus.

13 And I heard a voice from heaven saying unto me, Write, f Blessed *are* the dead g which die in the Lord h from henceforth : Yea, saith the Spirit,

A. M. cir. 4100.
A. D cir. 96.
Impp. Flavio
Domitiano
Cæs. Aug. et
Nerva.

---

e Chapter xii. 17.——f Ecclesiastes iv. 1, 2; chapter xx. 6.

g 1 Cor. xv. 18 ; 1 Thess. iv. 16.——h Or, *from henceforth saith the Spirit, Yea.*

---

keep the commandments of God, and are steadfast in the faith of our Lord Jesus Christ.

Sometimes ἡ ὑπομονη, *patience* or *perseverance,* is taken for the *reward* of these virtues; the text therefore may be thus understood : Here is the reward of the perseverance of the true Christians ; for although they die for the testimony of Jesus, yet they shall be unutterably blessed. See the next verse.

Verse 13. *I heard a voice from heaven*] As the information now to be given was of the utmost importance, it is solemnly communicated by a voice from heaven ; and the apostle is commanded to write or record what is said.

Blessed are *the dead*] Happy are they. They are *happy* in two respects : 1. They do not see the evil that shall come upon the world, and are exempted from any farther sufferings. 2. They actually and conscientiously enjoy happiness in a state of blessedness.

In the first sense, *Happy are the dead !* is a proverb frequently to be met in the Greek and Roman poets. *Ex. gr.*

Τρις μακαρες Δαναοι και τετρακις, οἱ τοτ' ολοντο
Τροιῃ εν ευρειῃ, χαριν Ατρειδῃσι φεροντες.
'Ως δη εγωγ' οφελον θανεειν και ποτμον επισπειν
Ἡματι τῳ, ὁτε μοι πλειστοι χαλκηρεα δουρα
Τρωες επερριψαν περι Πηλειωνι θανοντι.

Odyss., lib. v. ver. 306.

Happy, thrice happy, who, in battle slain,
Press'd, in. Atrides' cause, the Trojan plain :
O, had I died before that well fought wall ;
Had some distinguish'd day renown'd my fall,
Such as was that when showers of javelins fled,
From conquering Troy, around Achilles dead.

Pope.

Thus imitated by the prince of the Roman poets :—

Extemplo Æneæ solvuntur frigore membra.
Ingemit, et, duplices tendens ad sidera palmas,
Talia voce refert : O terque quaterque beati,
Queis ante ora patrum Trojæ sub mœnibus altis
Contigit oppetere ! O Danaum fortissime gentis
Tydide, mene Iliacis occumbere campis
Non potuisse ! tuaque animam hanc effundere dextra ?
Sævus ubi Æacidæ telo jacet Hector, ubi ingens
Sarpedon : ubi tot Simois correpta sub undis
Scuta virum, galeasque, et fortia corpora volvit.

Virg., Æn. i., ver. 93.

"In horror fix'd the Trojan hero stands,
He groans, and spreads to heaven his lifted hands.
Thrice happy those whose fate it was to fall,
Exclaims the chief, before the Trojan wall !
O, 'twas a glorious fate to die in fight !
To die so bravely in their parents' sight !
O, had I there, beneath Tydides' hand,
That bravest hero of the Grecian band,
Pour'd out this soul, with martial glory fired,
And in the plain triumphantly expired,

Where Hector fell, by fierce Achilles' spear,
And great Sarpedon, the renown'd in war ;
Where Simois' stream, encumber'd with the slain,
Rolls shields and helms and heroes to the main."

Pitt.

Which die in the Lord] These are the only *glorious* dead. They die, not in the field of battle, in either what are called *lawful* or *unlawful wars* against their fellow men ; but they die in the cause of God, they die under the smile and approbation of God, and they die to live and reign with God for ever and ever.

From henceforth] Απαρτι· *From this time ; now ; immediately.* This word is joined to the following by many MSS. and some *versions.* It was a maxim among the Jews, that as soon as the souls of the just departed from this life they ascended *immediately* to heaven.

Yea, saith the Spirit] The Holy Spirit confirms the declaration from heaven, and assigns the reasons of it.

That they may rest from their labours] Have no more tribulation and distress.

And their works do follow them.] Εργα αυτων ακολουθει μετ' αυτων· *And their works follow* with *them.* They are in *company.* Here is an elegant prosopopœia or personification ; their good works, sufferings, &c., are represented as so many *companions* escorting them on their way to the kingdom of God.

There are some good and pertinent things in the Jewish writers on this subject. "*Rabbi Jonathan* taught, If a man perform one righteous action in this life, *it goes before him* into the world to come. But if a man commit one crime, it *cleaves* to him, and *drags him to the day of judgment.*" *Sota,* fol. 3, 2. *Avoda Sara,* fol. 5, 1.

" Come and see, If any man observe a precept, that work ascends to God, and says, *Such a one performed me.* But if a man transgress the law, that sin ascends to the holy blessed God, and says, *I came from* such a one, *who has performed me.*" *Sohar Levit.,* fol. 34, col. 136. Here the same personification is observed as that in the text.

" In that hour in which a man passes from this life into eternity, *all his works precede him ;* and there they say unto him, 'This and that thou hast done in such a place on such a day.' This he shall acknowledge. They shall require that he shall subscribe this with his own hand, as it is written, Job xxxvii. 7 ; each man shall subscribe with his own hand ; and not only this, but he shall acknowledge that the sentence brought against him is most just." *Taanith,* fol. 11, 1

The following elegant similitude *Schoettgen* gives from *Sepher Hachayim,* Part II., fol. 47, 1, 2. "A certain man had three friends, *two* of whom he loved ; but the *third* he did not highly esteem. On a time the king commanded him to be called before him ; and being alarmed, he sought to find an advocate. He

A. M. cir. 4100.
A. D. cir. 96.
Impp. Flavio
Domitiano
Cæs. Aug. et
Nerva.

[i] that they may rest from their labours; and their works do follow them.

14 And I looked, and behold a white cloud, and upon the cloud *one* sat [k] like unto the Son of man, [l] having on his head a golden crown, and in his hand a sharp sickle.

15 And another angel [m] came out, of the temple, crying with a loud voice to him that sat on the cloud, [n] Thrust in thy sickle, and reap: for the time is come for thee to reap; for the harvest [o] of the earth is [p] ripe.

16 And he that sat on the cloud thrust in his sickle on the earth; and the earth was reaped.

17 And another angel came out of the tem-

ple which is in heaven, he also having a sharp sickle.

A. M. cir. 4100
A. D. cir. 96.
Impp. Flavio
Domitiano
Cæs. Aug. et
Nerva.

18 And another angel came out from the altar, [q] which had power over fire; and cried with a loud cry to him that had the sharp sickle, saying, [r] Thrust in thy sharp sickle, and gather the clusters of the vine of the earth; for her grapes are fully ripe.

19 And the angel thrust in his sickle into the earth, and gathered the vine of the earth, and cast *it* into [s] the great winepress of the wrath of God.

20 And [t] the winepress was trodden [u] without the city, and blood came out of the winepress, [v] even unto the horse bridles, by the space of a thousand *and* six hundred furlongs.

---

[i] 2 Thess. i. 7; Heb. iv. 9, 10; chap. vi. 11.——[k] Ezek. i. 26; Dan. vii. 13; chap. i. 13.——[l] Chap. vi. 2.——[m] Chap. xvi. 17. [n] Joel iii. 13; Matt. xiii. 39.

[o] Jer. li. 33; chap. xiii. 12.——[p] Or, *dried.*——[q] Chapter xvi. 8 [r] Joel iii. 13.——[s] Chapter xix. 15.——[t] Isa. lxiii. 3; Lam. i. 15 [u] Chap. xi. 8; Heb. xiii. 12.——[v] Chap. xix. 14.

---

went to that *friend* whom he loved most, but he utterly refused to go with him. The *second* offered to go with him as far as the door of the king's palace, but refused to speak a word in his behalf. The *third*, whom he loved least, not only went with him, but pleaded his cause so well before the king, that he was cleared from all blame. In like manner, every man has three friends, when he is cited by death to appear before God. The *first* friend, whom he loved most, viz., his *money*, cannot accompany him at all. His *second*, viz., his *relations* and *neighbours*, accompanied him only to the *grave*, and then returned; but could not deliver him from the Judge. The *third* friend, whom he held but in little esteem, viz., the law and his good works, *went with him* to the king, and delivered him from judgment." The meaning of this most plainly is, that nothing except the *deeds* of good and evil men shall accompany them to the judgment-seat of God, and that a man's lot will be in the other world as his conduct has been in this; *Their works follow with them.*

Verse 14. *A white cloud*] It is supposed that, from this verse to the end of the chapter, the *destruction* of Rome is represented under the symbols of *harvest* and *vintage*; images very frequent among the ancient prophets, by which they represented the destruction and excision of nations. See Joel iii. 12–14; Isa. xvii. 5; lxiii. 1; and Matt. xiii. 37.

A golden crown] In token of victory and regal power.

Verse 15. *Thrust in thy sickle*] Execute the judgments which God has decreed.

For the harvest of the earth is ripe.] The cup of the people's iniquity is full.

Verse 16. *The earth was reaped.*] The judgments were executed. But *where*, or on *whom*, who can tell?

Verse 18. *Power over fire*] Probably meaning the same angel which is mentioned, chap. viii. 3; ix. 13, who stood by the *altar of burnt-offering*, having autho-

rity over its fire to offer that incense to God which represents the prayers of the saints.

Verse 19. *The great winepress of the wrath of God.*] The *place* or *kingdom* where God executes his judgments on the workers of iniquity, whether pagans or persecuting Christians; Rome *pagan*, or Rome *papal*.

Verse 20. *Even unto the horse bridles*] A hyperbolical expression, to denote a *great effusion of blood.* The Jews said, "When Hadrian besieged the city called Bitter, he slew so many that the horses waded in blood up to their mouths." The same kind of hyperbole with that above. See Wetstein on this verse.

The space of a thousand and six hundred furlongs.] It is said that the *state of the Church*, or St. Peter's patrimony, extends from Rome to the Po, *two hundred Italian miles*, which make exactly *one thousand six hundred furlongs!* If this be really so, the coincidence is certainly surprising, and worthy of deep regard.

On these two last verses pious Quesnel thus speaks: "As the favourable sickle of Jesus Christ reaps his wheat when ripe for heaven, so that of the executioners of his justice cuts off from this life the tares which are only fit for the fire of hell. Then shall the blood of Christ cease to be trampled on by sinners; and that of the wicked shall be eternally trodden down in hell, which is the *winepress of the wrath of God.*

"*And the winepress was trodden without the city*, eternally without the city of the heavenly Jerusalem, and far from the presence of God; eternally crushed and trodden down by his justice; eternally tormented in body and soul, without any hope either of living or dying! This is the miserable lot and portion of those who shall have despised the law of God, and died in impenitence. My God, pierce my heart with a salutary dread of thy judgments!"

Whatever these passages may mean, this is a prudent and Christian use of them.

CHAPTER XV.

The seven angels with the seven last plagues, 1. The sea of glass, and those who had a victory over the beast, 2. The song of Moses and the Lamb, 3, 4. The temple in heaven opened, 5. Seven angels come out of the temple, who receive from one of the four living creatures seven golden vials full of the wrath of God, 6-8.

A. M. cir. 4100.
A. D. cir. 96.
Impp. Flavio
Domitiano
Cæs. Aug. et
Nerva.

AND [a] I saw another sign in heaven, great and marvellous, [b] seven angels having the seven last plagues; [c] for in them is filled up the wrath of God.

2 And I saw as it were [d] a sea of glass [e] mingled with fire ; and them that had gotten the victory over the beast, [f] and over his image, and over his mark, *and* over the number of his name, stand on the sea of glass, [g] having the harps of God.

3 And they sing [h] the song of Moses the servant of God, and the song of the Lamb, saying, [i] Great and marvellous *are* thy works, Lord God Almighty ; [k] just and true *are* thy ways, thou King of [l] saints.

4 [m] Who shall not fear thee, O Lord, and glorify thy name ? for *thou* only *art* holy : for [n] all nations shall come and worship before thee ; for thy judgments are made manifest.

A. M. cir. 4100.
A. D. cir. 96.
Impp. Flavio
Domitiano
Cæs. Aug. et
Nerva.

5 And after that I looked, and, behold, [o] the temple of the tabernacle of the testimony in heaven was opened :

6 [p] And the seven angels came out of the temple, having the seven plagues, [q] clothed in pure and white linen, and having their breasts girded with golden girdles.

7 [r] And one of the four beasts gave unto the seven angels seven golden vials full of the wrath of God, [s] who liveth for ever and ever.

---

[a] Chap. xii. 1, 3.——[b] Chap. xvi. 1 ; xxi. 9.——[c] Chap. xiv. 10. [d] Chap. iv. 6 ; xxi. 18.——[e] Matt. iii. 11.——[f] Chap. xiii. 15, 16, 17.——[g] Chap. v. 8 ; xiv. 2.——[h] Exod. xv. 1 ; Deut. xxxi. 30 ; ch xiv. 3.——[i] Deut. xxxii. 4 ; Psa. cxi. 2 ; cxxxix. 14.——[k] Psa.

cxlv. 17 ; Hos. xiv. 9 ; chap. xvi. 7.——[l] Or, *nations, or ages.* [m] Exod. xv. 14, 15, 16 ; Jer. x. 7.——[n] Isa. lxvi. 22.——[o] Ch. xi. 19 ; see Num. i. 50.——[p] Ver. 1.——[q] Exod. xxviii. 6, 8 ; Ezek. xliv. 17, 18 ; ch. i. 13.——[r] Ch. iv. 6.——[s] 1 Thess. i. 9 ; ch. iv. 9 ; x. 6.

NOTES ON CHAP. XV.

Verse 1. *Seven angels having the seven last plagues*] Under the emblems of *harvest* and *vintage* God's judgments on the enemies of his Church have already been pointed out ; but these are farther signified by the *seven vials*, which are called the seven last plagues of God. The seven last plagues appear to fall under the seventh and last *trumpet.* As the *seventh seal* contained the *seven trumpets*, so the seventh trumpet contains the *seven vials.* And as seven angels sounded the seven trumpets, so seven angels are appointed to pour out the seven vials, angels being always the ministers of Providence. This chapter contains the opening vision which is preparatory to the pouring out of the vials.

The Targum of Jonathan on Isa. li. 17, *Awake, awake, stand up, O Jerusalem, which hast drunk at the hand of the Lord the cup of his fury*, uses the same words employed by the evangelist here : " Jerusalem, thou hast received from the face of the Lord the cup of his wrath ; ית פילי כסא דלוטא *yath pailey casa dilvata*, " the PHIALS of the cup of malediction." And again on ver. 22 : *I will take out of thy hand the cup of malediction*; ית פילי כסא רחמתי *yath* PAILEY *casa dechemti*, " the PHIALS of the cup of my indignation."

Verse 2. *A sea of glass*] A spacious lucid plain around the throne, from which fiery coruscations were continually emitted : or, the reflection of the light upon this lucid plain produced the prismatic colours of the most vivid *rainbow.*

Over the beast, and over his image] See the notes on chap. xiii.

Verse 3. *They sing the song of Moses*] That which Moses sang, Exod. xv. 1, when he and the Israelites, by the miraculous power of God, had got safely through the Red Sea, and saw their enemies all destroyed.

And the song of the Lamb] The same song adapted to the state of the suffering, but now delivered Christians.

Great and marvellous are thy works] God's works are descriptive of his *infinite power* and *wisdom.*

Lord God Almighty] Nearly the same as *Jehovah, God of hosts.*

Just and true are thy ways] Every step God takes in grace or providence is according to *justice*, and he carefully accomplishes all his *threatenings* and all his *promises* ; to this he is bound by his truth.

Verse 4. *Who shall not fear thee*] That is, *All should fear* and worship this true God, because he is just and true and holy ; and his *saints* should love and obey him, because he is their *King* ; and they and all men *should* acknowledge his judgments, because they are *made manifest.*

Verse 5. *The temple of the tabernacle of the testimony*] The *temple* which succeeded the *tabernacle*, in which was the *testimony*, viz., the two tables, Aaron's rod, pot of manna, holy anointing oil, &c. All bearing *testimony* to the *truth* of God and his miraculous interposition in their behalf.

Verse 6. *The seven angels came out of the temple*] To show that they were sent from God himself

A. M. cir. 4100.
A. D. cir. 96.
Impp. Flavio
Domitiano
Cæs. Aug. et
Nerva.

8 And [t] the temple was filled with smoke [u] from the glory of God, and from his power ; and no man was able to enter into the temple, till the seven plagues of the seven angels were fulfilled.

A. M. cir. 4100.
A. D. cir. 96.
Impp. Flavio
Domitiano
Cæs. Aug. et
Nerva.

[t] Exod. xl. 34 ; 1 Kings viii. 10 ; 2 Chron. v. 14 ; Isa. vi. 4.

[u] 2 Thess. i. 9.

Clothed in pure and white linen] Habited as *priests.* For these habits see Exod. xxviii. 6, 8 ; and see the note on chap. i. ver. 13.

Verse 8. *The temple was filled with smoke*] So was the tabernacle when consecrated by Moses, Exod. xl. 34, 35, and the temple when consecrated by Solomon, 1 Kings viii. 10, 11 ; 2 Chron. v. 14. See Isa. vi. 4. This account seems at least partly copied from those above.

When the high priest entered into the holy of holies, and the ordinary priest into the holy place, they always carried with them a great deal of *smoking incense,* which filled those places with smoke and darkness, which prevented them from considering too attentively the parts and ornaments of those holy places, and thus served to produce an air of majesty in the temple, which none dared to approach without the deepest reverence. To this *Calmet* thinks the allusion may be here

---

CHAPTER XVI.

The angels are commanded to pour out their vials upon the earth, 1. *The first pours out his vial on the earth, by which a grievous sore is produced,* 2. *The second angel pours out his vial on the sea, and it is turned into blood,* 3 *The third angel pours out his vial on the* rivers *and fountains, and they are turned also into blood,* 4–7. *The fourth angel pours out his vial on the* sun, *and men are scorched with fire,* 8, 9. *The fifth angel pours out his vial on the* throne of the beast, 10, 11. *The sixth angel pours out his vial on the* river Euphrates, 12. *Three unclean spirits come out of the mouth of the beast, dragon and false prophet : and go forth to gather all the kings of the world to battle, in the place called Armageddon,* 13–16. *The seventh angel pours out his vial on the* air, *on which followed thunders, lightnings, earthquakes, and extraordinary hail,* 17–21.

A. M. cir. 4100.
A. D. cir. 96.
Impp. Flavio
Domitiano
Cæs. Aug. et
Nerva.

AND I heard a great voice out of the temple, saying [a] to the seven angels, Go your ways, and pour out the vials [b] of the wrath of God upon the earth.

2 And the first went and poured out his vial [c] upon the earth ; and [d] there fell a noisome and grievous sore upon the men [e] which had the mark of the beast, and *upon* them [f] which worshipped his image.

3 And the second angel poured out his vial [g] upon the sea ; and [h] it became as the blood of a dead *man :* [i] and every living soul died in the sea.

4 And the third angel poured out his vial [k] upon the rivers and fountains of waters ; [l] and they became blood.

5 And I heard the angel of the waters say, [m] Thou art righteous, O Lord, [n] which art,

A. M. cir. 4100.
A. D. cir. 96.
Impp. Flavio
Domitiano
Cæs. Aug. et
Nerva.

[a] Chap. xv. 1.——[b] Chapter xiv. 10 ; xv. 7.——[c] Chap. viii. 7. [d] Exod. ix. 9, 10, 11.——[e] Chap. xiii. 16, 17.——[f] Chap. xiii. 14. [g] Chap. viii. 8.

[h] Exod. vii. 17, 20.——[i] Chapter viii. 9.——[k] Chapter viii. 10. [l] Exod. vii. 20.——[m] Chapter xv. 3.——[n] Chapter i. 4, 8 ; iv. 8 ; xi. 17.

NOTES ON CHAP. XVI.

Verse 1. *Go your ways, and pour out*] These ministers of the Divine justice were ready to execute vengeance upon transgressors, having full power ; but could do nothing in this way till they received *especial commission.* Nothing can be done without the *permission* of God ; and in the manifestation of justice or mercy by Divine agency, there must be positive command.

Verse 2. *A noisome and grievous sore*] This is a reference to the *sixth* Egyptian plague, *boils and blains,* Exod. ix. 8 &c.

Verse 3. *As the blood of a dead* man] Either meaning blood in a state of *putrescency,* or an effusion of blood in *naval conflicts ;* even the sea was tinged with the blood of those who were slain in these wars.

This is most probably the meaning of this vial. These engagements were so sanguinary that both the conquerors and the conquered were nearly destroyed ; *every living soul died in the sea.*

Verse 4. *Upon the rivers and fountains of waters*] This is an allusion to the *first* Egyptian plague, Exod. vii. 20 ; and to those plagues in general there are allusions throughout this chapter. It is a sentiment of the rabbins that " whatever plagues God inflicted on the Egyptians in former times, he will inflict on the enemies of his people in all later times." See a long quotation on this subject from *Rabbi Tanchum* in *Schoettgen.*

Verse 5. *The angel of the waters*] The rabbins attribute angels, not only to the four elements so called, but to almost every thing besides. We have already seen the *angel* of the *bottomless pit,* chap. ix. 11,

A. M. cir. 4100.
A. D. cir. 96.
Impp. Flavio
Domitiano
Cæs. Aug. et
Nerva.

and wast, and shall be, because thou hast judged thus :

6 For [o] they have shed the blood [p] of saints and prophets, [q] and thou hast given them blood to drink ; for they are worthy.

7 And I heard another out of the altar say, Even so, [r] Lord God Almighty, [s] true and righteous *are* thy judgments.

8 And the fourth angel poured out his vial [t] upon the sun ; [u] and power was given unto him to scorch men with fire.

9 And men were [v] scorched with great heat, and [w] blasphemed the name of God, which hath power over these plagues : [x] and they repented not [y] to give him glory.

10 And the fifth angel poured out his vial [z] upon the seat of the beast ; [a] and his kingdom was full of darkness ; [b] and they gnawed their tongues for pain,

11 And [c] blasphemed the God of heaven because of their pains and [d] their sores, [e] and repented not of their deeds.

12 And the sixth angel poured out his vial [f] upon the great river Euphrates ; [g] and the water thereof was dried up, [h] that the way of the kings of the east might be prepared.

13 And I saw three unclean [i] spirits like frogs *come* out of the mouth of [k] the dragon, and out of the mouth of the beast, and out of the mouth of [l] the false prophet.

A. M. cir. 4100
A. D. cir. 96.
Impp. Flavio
Domitiano
Cæs. Aug. et
Nerva.

---

[o] Matt. xxiii. 34, 35 ; chap. xiii. 15.——[p] Chap. xi. 18 ; xviii. 20.——[q] Isa. xlix. 26.——[r] Chap. xv. 3.——[s] Chap. xii. 10 ; xiv. 10 ; xix. 2.——[t] Chap. viii. 12.——[u] Chapter ix. 17, 18 ; xiv. 18. [v] Or, *burned.*——[w] Ver. 11, 21.——[x] Dan. v. 22, 23 ; chap. ix. 20.

[y] Chap. xi. 13 ; xiv. 7.——[z] Chap. xiii. 2.——[a] Chap. ix. 2. [b] Ch. xi. 10.——[c] Ver. 9, 21.——[d] Ver. 2.——[e] Ver. 9.——[f] Ch. ix. 14.——[g] See Jer. l. 38 ; li. 36.——[h] Isa. xli. 2, 25.——[i] 1 John iv. 1, 2, 3.——[k] Chap. xii. 3, 9.——[l] Chap. xix. 20 ; xx. 10.

---

and *the angel of the fire,* chap. xiv. 18. The *angel of the earth* is spoken of in *Yalcut Rubeni,* fol. 13, 2, and is called *Admael.* They have also an *angel* that presides over the *grass ;* another that presides over the *cattle* which feed upon the grass.

They say that God employed the *angel of the sea* to swallow up the waters at the creation, that the dry land might appear. He disobeyed, and God slew him ; the name of the angel of the sea is *Rahab.* See *Baba bathra,* fol. 74, 2. It is plain from several places that the writer of the Apocalypse keeps these notions distinctly in view.

Verse 6. *Thou hast given them blood to drink*] They thirsted after blood and massacred the saints of God ; and now they have got blood to drink ! It is said that when *Tomyris,* queen of the Scythians, had vanquished Cyrus, she cut off his head and threw it into a vessel of blood, saying these words : *Satia te sanguine, quem sitisti, cujusque insatiabilis semper fuisti ;* "Satisfy thyself with blood, for which thou hast thirsted, and for which thy desire has been insatiable." See *Justin.* Hist., lib. i. c. 8. This figure of speech is called *sarcasm* in rhetoric.

" *Sarcasmus* with this biting taunt doth kill :

Cyrus, thy thirst was blood ; now drink thy fill."

Verse 8. *Poured out his vial upon the sun*] . Mr. Robert Fleming, more than *one hundred* years ago, in his *View of Scripture Prophecy,* supposed that the *sun* here meant the *French empire,* and conjectured that this vial would be poured out on that empire about the year 1794. And it is remarkable that in 1793 the French king was beheaded by the National Assembly ; and great and unparalleled miseries fell upon the French nation, which nearly extinguished all their nobility, and brought about a war that lasted twenty-three years, and nearly ruined that country and all the nations of Europe.

Verse 9. *They repented not*] No moral national

amendment has taken place in consequence of the above calamities in that unhappy country, nor indeed any of those nations engaged against her in that long and ruinous contest, which has now terminated, (1817,) without producing one political, moral, or religious advantage to herself or to Europe.

Verse 10. *The seat of the beast*] Επι τον θρονον του θηριου· *Upon the throne of the wild beast.* The regal family was smitten by the fourth vial ; they did not repent : then the fifth angel pours out his vial on the throne of the wild beast, or antichristian idolatrous power.

Was full of darkness] Confusion, dismay, and distress.

Verse 11. *Blasphemed the God of heaven*] Neither did they repent ; therefore other judgments must follow. Some think that the *sun* was *Vitellius,* the Roman emperor, and that his *throne* means *Rome ;* and the darkening refers to the injuries she sustained in her political consequence by the civil wars which then took place, from which she never entirely recovered. Others apply it all to *papal Rome,* and in this respect make out a very clear case ! Thus have men conjectured, but how much nearer are we to the truth ?

Verse 12. *Upon the great river Euphrates*] Probably meaning the people in the vicinity of this river ; though some think that the *Tiber* is intended.

The water thereof was dried up] The *people* discomfited, and all impediments removed.

The kings of the east] There seems to be an allusion here to the ruin of Babylon by Cyrus, predicted by the Prophet Jeremiah, chap. l. and li. But what city or people is pointed out by this Babylon it is in vain to conjecture.

Verse 13. *Three unclean spirits*] Perhaps *false teachers,* called afterwards *spirits of devils,* which persuade the kings of the earth by *lying miracles* to come forth to the place of general slaughter, ver. 14, 16.

        2

A. M. cir. 4100.
A. D. cir. 96.
Impp. Flavio
Domitiano
Cæs. Aug. et
Nerva.

14 [m] For they are the spirits of devils, [n] working miracles, *which* go forth unto the kings of the earth, [o] and of the whole world, to gather them to [p] the battle of that great day of God Almighty.

15 ¶ [q] Behold, I come as a thief. Blessed *is* he that watcheth, and keepeth his garments, [r] lest he walk naked, and they see his shame.

16 [s] And he gathered them together into a place called in the Hebrew tongue Armageddon.

17 And the seventh angel poured out his vial into the air; and there came a great voice out of the temple of heaven, from the throne, saying, [t] It is done.

18 And [u] there were voices, and thunders, and lightnings; [v] and there was a great earthquake, [w] such as was not since men were upon the earth, so mighty an earthquake, *and* so great.

19 And [x] the great city was divided into three parts, and the cities of the nations fell: and great Babylon [y] came in remembrance before God, [z] to give unto her the cup of the wine of the fierceness of his wrath.

20 And [a] every island fled away, and the mountains were not found.

21 [b] And there fell upon men a great hail out of heaven, *every stone* about the weight of a talent: and [c] men blasphemed God because of [d] the plague of the hail; for the plague thereof was exceeding great.

A. M. cir. 4100.
A. D. cir. 96.
Impp. Flavio
Domitiano
Cæs. Aug. et
Nerva.

---

[m] 1 Tim. iv. 1; James iii. 15.——[n] 2 Thess. ii. 9; chap. xiii. 13, 14; xix. 20.——[o] Luke ii. 1.——[p] Chap. xvii. 14; xix. 19; xx. 8.——[q] Matt. xxiv. 43; 1 Thess. v. 2; 2 Pet. iii. 10; chap. iii. 3.——[r] 2 Cor. v. 3; chap. iii. 4, 18.——[s] Chap. xix. 19.

[t] Chap. xxi. 6.——[u] Chap. iv. 5; viii. 5; xi. 19.——[v] Chap. xi. 13.——[w] Dan. xii. 1.——[x] Chap. xiv. 8; xvii. 18.——[y] Ch. xviii. 5.——[z] Isa. li. 17, 23; Jer. xxv. 15, 16; ch. xiv. 10.——[a] Ch. vi. 14.——[b] Ch. xi. 19.——[c] Ver. 9, 11.——[d] See Exod. ix. 23, 24, 25.

Some good critics apply this to *Vespasian,* and his pretended *miracles.* See the account in Tacitus, lib. iv. c. 81.

Verse 15. *Behold, I come as a thief.*] Here is a sudden but timely warning to put every man on his guard, when this sudden and generally unexpected tribulation should take place.

Keepeth his garments, lest he walk naked] Here is a plain allusion to the office of him who was called the *prefect* or *overseer, of the mountain of the temple.* His custom was to go his rounds during the watches of the night; and if he found any of the Levites sleeping on his watch, he had authority to beat him with a stick, and burn his vestments. See *Middoth,* fol. 34, 1, and *Tamid.* fol. 27, 2; 28, 1. Such a person being found on his return home *naked,* it was at once known that he had been found *asleep at his post,* had been *beaten,* and his *clothes burnt;* thus his *shame* was seen—he was reproached for his infidelity and irreligion.

Verse 16. *Armageddon.*] The original of this word has been variously formed, and variously translated. It is הר־מגדון *har-megiddon,* "the mount of the assembly;" or חרמה גדהון *chormah gedehon,* "the destruction of their army;" or it is הר־מגדו *har-megiddo,* "Mount Megiddo," the valley of which was remarkable for two great slaughters: one of the Israelites, 2 Kings xxiii. 29, the other of the Canaanites, Judg. iv. 16; v. 19. But *Mount Megiddo,* that is Carmel, is the place, according to some, where these armies should be collected.

But what is the *battle of Armageddon?* How ridiculous have been the conjectures of men relative to this point! Within the last twenty years this battle has been fought at various places, according to our purblind seers and self-inspired prophets! At one time it was *Austerlitz,* at another *Moscow,* at another *Leipsic,* and now *Waterloo!* And thus they have gone on, and will go on, confounding and being confounded.

Verse 17. *Poured out his vial into the air*] To signify that this plague was to be widely diffused, and perhaps to intimate that pestilences and various deaths would be the effect of this vial. But possibly *air* in this place may have some emblematical meaning.

It is done.] It is said, chap. x. 7, that in the days of the seventh trumpet *the mystery of God should be finished;* so here we find it *completed.* Γεγονε· All's over! Fuimus Troes! Ilium fuit! Once there were Trojans, and they had a city; but now all are extinct.

Verse 18. *A great earthquake*] Most terrible commotions, both civil and religious. Or a convulsion, shaking, or revolution.

Verse 19. *The great city*] Some say Jerusalem, others *Rome pagan,* others *Rome papal.*

The cup of the wine of the fierceness of his wrath.] Alluding to the mode of putting certain criminals to death, by making them drink a cup of poison. See on Heb. ii. 9.

Verse 20. *Every island fled away*] Probably meaning the capture of seaport towns, and fortified places.

Verse 21. *A great hail—about the weight of a talent*] Has this any reference to *cannon balls* and *bombs?* It is very doubtful; we are all in the dark in these matters.

The words ὡς ταλαντιαια, *as a talent,* are used to express something *great, excessively oppressive;* as νοσηματων ταλαντιαιων, *terrible diseases,* not diseases of the *weight* of a *talent.* See *Rosenmüller.*

CHAPTER XVII.

The judgment of the great whore, which sits on many waters, 1, 2. Her description, name, and conduct, 3–6.
The angel explains the mystery of the woman, of the beast, &c., 7–18.

A. M. cir. 4100.
A. D. cir. 96.
Impp. Flavio
Domitiano
Cæs. Aug. et
Nerva.

A. M. cir. 4100.
A. D. cir. 96.
Impp. Flavio
Domitiano
Cæs. Aug. et
Nerva.

AND there came ᵃ one of the seven angels which had the seven vials, and talked with me, saying unto me, Come hither; ᵇ I will show unto thee the judgment of ᶜ the great whore ᵈ that sitteth upon many waters :

2 ᵉ With whom the kings of the earth have committed fornication, and ᶠ the inhabitants of the earth have been made drunk with the wine of her fornication.

3 So he carried me away in the spirit ᵍ into the wilderness : and I saw a woman sit ʰ upon a scarlet-coloured beast, full of ⁱ names of blasphemy, ᵏ having seven heads and ˡ ten horns.

4 And the woman ᵐ was arrayed in purple and scarlet colour, ⁿ and º decked with gold, and precious stones, and pearls, ᵖ having a golden cup in her hand ۹ full of abominations and filthiness of her fornication :

5 And upon her forehead *was* a name

ᵃ Chap. xxi. 9.——ᵇ Ch. xvi. 19 : xviii. 16, 17, 19.——ᶜ Nah. iii. 4 ; chap. xix. 2.——ᵈ Jer. li. 13 ; ver. 15.——ᵉ Chap. xviii. 3.——ᶠ Jer. li. 7 ; chap. xiv. 8 ; xviii. 3.——ᵍ Chap. xii. 6, 14.

ʰ Chap. xii. 3.——ⁱ Chap. xiii. 1.——ᵏ Ver. 9.——ˡ Ver. 12. ᵐ Ch. xviii. 12, 16.——ⁿ Dan. xi. 38.——º Gr. *gilded.*——ᵖ Jer. li. 7 ; chap. xviii. 6.——۹ Chap. xiv. 8.

This chapter is, on several accounts, very important, and particularly as it appears to explain several of the most remarkable symbols in the book. The same author who has written so largely on the twelfth and thirteenth chapters, has also obliged me with his interpretation of this chapter. Not pretending to explain these things myself, I insert this as the most elaborate and learned exposition I have yet seen, leaving my readers at perfect liberty to reject it, and adopt any other mode of interpretation which they please. God alone knows all the secrets of his own wisdom.

NOTES ON CHAP. XVII., by J. E. C.

Verse 1. *And there came one of the seven angels which had the seven vials, and talked with me, saying unto me, Come hither ; I will show unto thee the judgment of the great whore that sitteth upon many waters*] That idolatrous worship is frequently represented in Scripture under the character of *a whore* or *whoredom,* is evident from numerous passages which it is unnecessary to quote. See 1 Chron. v. 25 ; Ezek. xvi., xxiii., &c. The woman mentioned here is called *a great whore,* to denote her excessive depravity, and the awful nature of her idolatry. She is also represented as *sitting upon many waters,* to show the vast extent of her influence. See on ver. 13.

Verse 2. *With whom the kings of the earth have committed fornication, and the inhabitants of the earth have been made drunk with the wine of her fornication.*] What an awful picture this is of the state of the religion of the world in subjection to this whore ! Kings have committed spiritual fornication with her, and their subjects have drunk deep, dreadfully deep, into the doctrine of her abominable errors.

Verse 3. *So he carried me away in the spirit into the wilderness*] This wilderness into which the apostle was carried is the desolate state of the true Church of Christ, in one of the wings of the once mighty Roman empire. It was a truly awful sight, a terrible

desert, a waste howling wilderness ; for when he came hither he—

Saw a woman sit upon a scarlet-coloured beast, full of names of blasphemy, having seven heads and ten horns.] No doubt can now be entertained that this woman is the Latin Church, for she sits upon the beast with seven heads and ten horns, which has been already proved to be the Latin empire, because this empire alone contains the number 666. See on chap. xiii. This is a representation of the Latin Church in her highest state of antichristian prosperity, for she sits upon the scarlet-coloured beast, a striking emblem of her *complete domination* over the secular Latin empire. The state of the Latin Church from the commencement of the fourteenth century to the time of the Reformation may be considered as that which corresponds to this prophetic description in the most literal and extensive sense of the words ; for during this period she was at her highest pitch of worldly grandeur and temporal authority. The beast is *full of names of blasphemy ;* and it is well known that the nations, in support of the Latin or Romish Church, have abounded in blasphemous appellations, and have not blushed to attribute to themselves and to their Church the most sacred titles, not only blaspheming by the improper use of sacred names, but even by applying to its bishop those names which alone belong to God ; for God hath expressly declared that he *will not give his glory to another, neither his praise to graven images.*

Verse 4. *And the woman was arrayed in purple and scarlet colour, and decked with gold, and precious stones, and pearls, having a golden cup in her hand full of abominations and filthiness of her fornication*] This strikingly represents the most pompous and costly manner in which the Latin Church has held forth to the nations the rites and ceremonies of its idolatrous and corrupt worship.

Verse 5. *And upon her forehead was a name written, Mystery, Babylon the Great, the Mother of Harlots, and Abominations of the Earth.*] This inscription

2

A. M. cir. 4100.
A. D. cir. 96.
Impp. Flavio
Domitiano
Cæs. Aug. et
Nerva.

written, ʳ MYSTERY, BABY-LON ˢ THE GREAT, ᵗ THE MOTHER OF ᵘ HARLOTS AND ABOMINATIONS OF THE EARTH.

6 And I saw ᵛ the woman drunken ʷ with the blood of the saints, and with the blood of ˣ the martyrs of Jesus : and when I saw her,

I wondered with great admiration.

7 And the angel said unto me, Wherefore didst thou marvel? I will tell thee the mystery of the woman, and of the beast that carrieth her, which hath the seven heads and ten horns.

8 The beast that thou sawest was, and is

A. M. cir. 4100.
A. D cir. 96.
Impp. Flavio
Domitiano
Cæs. Aug. et
Nerva:

ʳ 2 Thess. ii. 7.——ˢ Chap. xi. 8 ; xiv. 8 ; xvi. 19 ; xviii. 2, 10, 21. ᵗ Chap. xviii. 9 ; xix. 2.

ᵘ Or, *fornications.*——ᵛ Chap. xviii. 24.——ʷ Chap. xiii. 15 ; xvi. 6.——ˣ Chap. vi. 9, 10 ; xii. 11.

---

being written upon her forehead is intended to show that she is not ashamed of her doctrines, but publicly professes and glories in them before the nations : she has indeed *a whore's forehead, she has refused to be ashamed.* The inscription upon her forehead is exactly the portraiture of the Latin Church. This Church is, as Bishop Newton well expresses it, A MYSTERY *of iniquity.* This woman is also called *Babylon the Great ;* she is the exact antitype of the ancient Babylon in her idolatry and cruelty, but the ancient city called Babylon is only a drawing of her in miniature. This is indeed *Babylon* THE GREAT. " She affects the style and title of *our* HOLY MOTHER, *the* CHURCH ; but she is, in truth, the *mother* of harlots and abominations of the earth."

Verse 6. *And I saw the woman drunken with the blood of the saints, and with the blood of the martyrs of Jesus : and when I saw her, I wondered with great admiration.*] How exactly the cruelties exercised by the Latin Church against all it has denominated heretics correspond with this description, the reader need not be informed.

Verse 7. *And the angel said unto me, Wherefore didst thou marvel ? I will tell thee the mystery of the woman, and of the beast that carrieth her, which hath the seven heads and ten horns.*] The apostle was greatly astonished, as well he might be, at the woman's being *drunk with the blood of the saints,* when the beast which carried her abounded with sacred appellations, such as *holy, most holy, most Christian, sacred, most sacred.* The angel undertakes to explain to St. John the vision which had excited in him so great astonishment ; and the explication is of such great importance, that, had it not been given, the mystery of the dragon and the beast could never have been satisfactorily explained in all its particulars. The angel begins with saying,

Verse 8. *The beast that thou sawest was, and is not ; and shall ascend out of the bottomless pit, and go into perdition*] The beast is the Latin kingdom ; (Ἡ Λατινη βασιλεια ;) consequently the beast *was,* that is, was in existence previously to the time of St. John ; (for Latinus was the first king of the Latins, and Numitor the last ;) *is not* now, because the Latin nation has ceased long ago to be an independent power, and is now under the dominion of the Romans ; but *shall ascend out of the bottomless pit,* that is, the Latin kingdom, the antichristian power, or that which ascendeth out of the abyss or bottomless pit, is yet in futurity. But it is added,

And they that dwell on the earth shall wonder, whose names were not written in the book of life from the foundation of the world, when they behold the beast that was, and is not, and yet is.] By the *earth* is here meant *the Latin world ;* therefore the meaning is, that all who dwell in the Latin world shall adhere to the idolatrous and blasphemous religion of the Latin Church, which is supported by the Latin empire, except those who abide by the *sacred Scriptures,* receiving them as the only rule of faith and practice. These believe in the true Sacrifice, and keep themselves unspotted from the corruption that is in the world. But the inhabitants of the Latin world, under the dominion of the Romish religion, shall wonder when they behold the beast, or Latin empire ; that is, as Lord Napier remarks, " shall have in great admiration, reuerence, and estimation, this great monarchie." They shall wonder at it, by considering it the most sacred empire in the world, that in which God peculiarly delights ; but those that so wonder have not their names written in the book of life, but are such as prefer councils to Divine revelation, and take their religion from *missals, rituals,* and *legends,* instead of the sacred oracles : hence they are corrupt and idolatrous, and *no idolater hath inheritance in the kingdom of God.* In the preceding part of the verse the beast is considered in *three* states, as that which *was,* and *is not, and shall ascend out of the bottomless pit ;* here a fourth is introduced, *and yet is.* This is added to show that, though the Latins were subjugated by the Romans, nevertheless the Romans themselves were Latins ; for Romulus, the founder of their monarchy, was a Latin ; consequently that denominated in St. John's days the *Roman empire* was, in reality, *the Latin kingdom ;* for the very language of the empire was the Latin, and the Greek writers, who lived in the time of the Roman empire, expressly tell us that those formerly called Latins are now named Romans. The meaning of the whole verse is therefore as follows : The corrupt part of mankind shall have in great admiration the Latin empire yet in futurity, which has already been, but is now extinct, the Romans having conquered it ; and yet is still in being ; for, though the Latin nation has been subjugated, its conquerors are themselves Latins. But it may be objected against the interpretation here given, that these phrases are spoken of the beast upon which the apostle saw the woman, or Latin Church, sit ; for the angel says, *The beast that* THOU SAWEST *was, and is not,* &c. ; what reference, therefore, can the Latin empire, which

A. M. cir. 4100.
A. D. cir. 96.
Impp. Flavio
Domitiano
Cæs. Aug. et
Nerva.

not; and ʸ shall ascend out of the bottomless pit, and ᶻ go into perdition : and they that dwell on the earth ᵃ shall wonder, ᵇ whose names were not written in the book of life from the foundation of the world, when

they behold the beast that was, and is not, and yet is.

A. M. cir. 4100.
A. D. cir. 96.
Impp. Flavio
Domitiano
Cæs. Aug. et
Nerva.

9 And ᶜ here *is* the mind which hath wisdom. ᵈ The seven heads are seven mountains, on which the woman sitteth.

ʸ Chap. xi. 7 ; xiii. 1.——ᶻ Chap. xiii. 10 ; ver. 11.

ᵃ Ch. xiii. 3.——ᵇ Ch. xiii. 8.——ᶜ Ch. xiii. 18.——ᵈ Ch. xiii. 1.

---

supports the Latin Church, have to the Latin kingdom which subsisted before St. John's time, or to the Roman empire which might properly be so denominated? This objection has very great weight at first sight, and cannot be answered satisfactorily till the angel's explanation of the heads and horns of the beast have been examined ; therefore it is added,

Verse 9. *Here is the mind which hath wisdom.*] It was said before, chap. xiii. 18, *Here is wisdom. Let him that hath* A MIND, *or understanding,* (νουν,) *count the number of the beast. Wisdom,* therefore, here means a correct view of what is intended by the number 666 ; consequently the parallel passage, *Here is* THE MIND *which hath* WISDOM, is a declaration that the number of the beast must first be understood, before the angel's interpretation of the vision concerning the whore and the beast can admit of a satisfactory explanation.

The seven heads are seven mountains, on which the woman sitteth.] This verse has been almost universally considered to allude to the seven hills upon which Rome originally stood. But it has been objected that modern Rome is not thus situated, and that, consequently, pagan Rome is intended in the prophecy. This is certainly a very formidable objection against the generally received opinion among Protestants, that papal Rome is the city meant by the woman sitting upon seven mountains. It has been already shown that *the woman* here mentioned is an emblem of *the Latin Church* in her highest state of antichristian prosperity ; and therefore the city of Rome, seated upon seven mountains, is not at all designed in the prophecy. In order to understand this scripture aright, the word *mountains* must be taken in a figurative and not a literal sense, as in chap. vi. 14, and xvi. 20. See also Isa. ii. 2, 14 ; Jer. li. 25 ; Dan. ii. 35, &c. ; in which it is unequivocally the emblem of *great and mighty power.* The mountains upon which the woman sitteth must be, therefore, *seven great powers* ; and as the mountains are *heads* of the beast, they must be the *seven* GREATEST *eminences* of the Latin world. As no other power was acknowledged at the head of the Latin empire but that of Germany, how can it be said that the beast has *seven* heads? This question can only be solved by the feudal constitution of the late Germanic league, the history of which is briefly as follows : At first kings alone granted fiefs. They granted them to laymen only, and to such only who were free ; and the vassal had no power to alienate them. Every freeman, and particularly the feudal tenants, were subject to the obligation of military duty, and appointed to guard their sovereign's life, member, mind, and right honour. Soon after, or perhaps a little before, the extinction of the Carlovingian dynasty in

France, by the accession of the Capetian line, and in Germany by the accession of the house of Saxony, fiefs, which had been entirely at the disposal of the sovereign, became hereditary. Even the offices of duke, count, margrave, &c., were transmitted in the course of hereditary descent ; and not long after, the right of primogeniture was universally established. The crown vassals usurped the sovereign property of the land, with civil and military authority over the inhabitants. The possession thus usurped they granted out to their immediate tenants ; and these granted them over to others in like manner. Thus the principal vassals gradually obtained every royal prerogative ; they promulgated laws, exercised the power of life and death, coined money, fixed the standard of weights and measures, granted safeguards, entertained a military force, and imposed taxes, with every right supposed to be annexed to royalty. In their titles they styled themselves dukes, &c., *Dei gratia,* by the grace of God ; a prerogative avowedly confined to sovereign power. It was even admitted that, if the king refused to do the lord justice, the lord might make war upon him. The tenants, in their turn, made themselves independent of their vassal lords, by which was introduced an ulterior state of vassalage. The king was called *the sovereign lord,* his immediate vassal was called *the suzereign,* and the tenants holding of him were called the *arrere* vassals. See *Butler's* Revolutions of the Germanic Empire, pp. 54–66. Thus the power of the emperors of Germany, which was so very considerable in the ninth century, was gradually diminished by the means of the feudal system ; and during the anarchy of the long interregnum, occasioned by the interference of the popes in the election of the emperors, (from 1256 to 1273,) the imperial power was reduced almost to nothing. Rudolph of Hapsburg, the founder of the house of Austria, was at length elected emperor, because his territories and influence were so inconsiderable as to excite no jealousy in the German princes, who were willing to preserve the forms of constitution, the power and vigour of which they had destroyed. See *Robertson's* Introduction to his History of Charles V. Before the dissolution of the empire in 1806, Germany "presented a complex association of principalities more or less powerful, and more or less connected with a nominal sovereignty in the emperor, as its supreme feudal chief." "There were about three hundred princes of the empire, each sovereign in his own country, who might enter into alliances, and pursue by all political measures his own private interest, as other sovereigns do ; for if even an imperial war were declared he might remain neuter, if the safety of the empire were not at stake. Here then was an empire of a construction, without excep-

A. M. cir. 4100.
A. D. cir. 96.
Impp. Flavio
Domitiano
Cæs. Aug. et
Nerva.

10 And there are seven kings : five are fallen, and one is, *and* the other is not yet come ; and when he cometh,

he must continue a short space.

11 And the beast that was, and is not, even he is the eighth, and

A. M. cir. 4100.
A. D. cir. 96.
Impp. Flavio
Domitiano
Cæs. Aug. et
Nerva.

tion, the most singular and intricate that ever appeared in the world ; for the emperor was only the chief of the Germanic confederation." Germany was, therefore, speaking in the figurative language of Scripture, a country abounding in *hills*, or containing an immense number of distinct principalities. But the different German states (as has been before observed) did not each possess an equal share of power and influence ; some were more eminent than others. Among them were also a few which might, with the greatest propriety, be denominated *mountains*, or states possessing a very high degree of political importance. But the seven mountains on which the woman sits must have their elevations above all the other eminences in the whole Latin world ; consequently, they can be no other than the SEVEN ELECTORATES of the German emipre. These were, indeed, mountains of vast eminence ; for in their sovereigns was vested the sole power of electing the head of the empire. But this was not all ; for besides the power of electing an emperor, the electors had a right to capitulate with the new head of the empire, to dictate the conditions on which he was to reign, and to depose him if he broke those conditions. They actually deposed Adolphus of Nassau in 1298, and Wenceslaus in 1400. They were sovereign and independent princes in their respective dominions, had the *privilegium de non appellando illimitatum*, that of making war, coining, and exercising every act of sovereignty ; they formed a separate college in the diet of the empire, and had among themselves a particular covenant or league called *Kur verein ;* they had precedence of all the other princes of the empire, and even ranked with kings. The heads of the beast understood in this way, is one of the finest emblems of the German constitution which can possibly be conceived; for as the Roman empire of Germany had the precedence of all the other monarchies of which the Latin empire was composed, *the seven mountains* very fitly denote the *seven* PRINCIPAL *powers* of what has been named the holy Roman empire. And also, as each electorate, by virtue of its union with the Germanic body, was more powerful than any other Roman Catholic state of Europe not so united ; so was each electorate, in the most proper sense of the word, one of the highest elevations in the Latin world. The time when the seven electorates of the empire were first instituted is very uncertain. The most probable opinion appears to be that which places their origin some time in the *thirteenth* century. The uncertainty, however, in this respect, does not in the least weaken the evidence of the mountains being the seven electorates, but rather confirms it ; for, as we have already observed, the representation of the woman sitting upon the beast is a figure of the Latin Church in the period of her greatest authority, spiritual and temporal ; this we know did not take place before the commencement of the *fourteenth* century, a period subsequent to the institution of the seven electorates. Therefore the

woman sits upon the seven mountains, or the German empire in its elective aristocratical state ; she is said to sit upon them, to denote that she has the whole German empire under her direction and authority, and also that it is her chief support and strength. Supported by Germany, she is under no apprehension of being successfully opposed by any other power : she sits upon the seven mountains, therefore she is higher than the seven highest eminences of the Latin world ; she must therefore have the secular Latin empire under her complete subjection. But this state of eminence did not continue above two or three centuries ; the visible declension of the papal power in the fourteenth and fifteenth centuries, occasioned partly by the removal of the papal see from Rome to Avignon, and more particularly by the great schism from 1377 to 1417, though considered one of the remote causes of the Reformation, was at first the means of merely transferring the supreme power from the pope to a general council, while the dominion of the Latin Church remained much the same. At the council of Constance, March 30, 1415, it was decreed " that the synod being lawfully assembled in the name of the Holy Ghost, which constituted the general council, and represented the whole Catholic Church militant, had its power immediately from Jesus Christ ; and that every person, of whatsoever state or dignity, EVEN THE POPE HIMSELF, is obliged to obey it in what concerns the faith, the extirpation of schism, and the general reformation of the Church in its head and members." The council of Basil of 1432 decreed " that every one of whatever dignity or condition, NOT EXCEPTING THE POPE HIMSELF, who shall refuse to obey the ordinances and decrees of this general council, or any other, shall be put under penance, and punished. It is also declared that the pope has no power to dissolve the general council without the consent and decree of the assembly." See the third tome of *Du Pin's* Ecclesiastical History. But what gave the death blow to the temporal sovereignty of the Latin Church was the light of the glorious reformation which first broke out in Germany in 1517, and in a very few years gained its way, not only over several of the great principalities in Germany, but was also made the established religion of other popish countries. Consequently, in the sixteenth century, the woman no longer sat upon the seven mountains, the electorates not only having refused to be ruled by her, but some of them having also despised and abandoned her doctrines. The changes, therefore, which were made in the seventeenth, eighteenth, and nineteeth centuries, in the number of the electorates, will not affect in the least the interpretation of the seven mountains already given. The seven electors were the archbishops of *Mentz, Cologne,* and *Triers,* the *count palatine of the Rhine,* the *duke of Saxony,* the *marquis of Brandenburgh,* and the *king of Bohemia.* But the heads of the beast have a double signification ; for the angel says,—

2   1039

A. M. cir. 4100.
A. D. cir. 96.
Impp. Flavio
Domitiano
Cæs. Aug. et
Nerva.

is of the ᵉ seven, ᶠ and goeth into perdition.

12 And ᵍ the ten horns which thou sawest are ten kings, which

have received no kingdom as yet; but receive power as kings one hour with the beast.

13 These have one mind, and

A. M. cir. 4100.
A. D. cir. 96.
Impp. Flavio
Domitiano
Cæs. Aug. et
Nerva.

ᵉ Ver. 10.——ᶠ Ver. 8.

ᵍ Dan. vii. 20; Zech. i. 18, 19, 21; chap. xiii. 1.

Verse 10. *And there are seven kings*] Και βασιλεις επτα εισιν· *They are also seven kings.* Before, it was said, *they are seven mountains;* here, *they are also seven kings,* which is a demonstration that *kingdoms* are not here meant by *mountains :* and this is a farther argument that the seven electorates are represented by seven mountains, for though the sovereigns of these states ranked with kings, they were not kings : that is to say, they were not absolute and sole lords of the territories they possessed, independently of the emperor, for their states formed a part of the Germanic body. But the seven heads of the beast are also seven kings, that is to say, the Latin empire has had seven supreme forms of government; for *king* is used in the prophetical writings for any supreme governor of a state or people, as is evident from Deut. xxxiii. 5, where Moses is called a king. Of these seven kings, or supreme forms of Latin government, the angel informs St. John——

Five are fallen, and one is] It is well known that the first form of Latin government was that of *kings,* which continued after the death of Latinus 428 years, till the building of Rome, B. C. 753. After Numitor's decease the Albans or Latins instituted the form of a republic, and were governed by *dictators.* We have only the names of two, viz. Cluilius and Metius Fufetius or Suffetius ; but as the *dictatorship* continued at least eighty-eight years, there might have been others, though their names and actions are unknown. In the year before Christ 665 *Alba,* the metropolis· of the Latin nation, was destroyed by Tullus Hostilius, the third king of the Romans, and the inhabitants carried to Rome. This put an end to the monarchical republic of the Latins ; and the Latins elected two annual magistrates, whom Licinius calls *dictators,* but who are called *prætors* by other writers. This form of government continued till the time of P Decius Mus, the Roman consul ; for Festus, in his fourteenth book, informs us " that the Albans enjoyed prosperity till the time of King Tullus ; but that, Alba being then destroyed, the consuls, till the time of P. Decius Mus, held a consultation with the Latins at the head of Ferentina, and the empire was governed by the council of both nations." The Latin nation was entirely subjugated by the Romans B. C. 336, which put an end to the government by *prætors,* after it had continued upwards of three hundred years. The Latins from this time ceased to be a nation, as it respects the name ; therefore the three forms of government already mentioned were those which the Latins had during that period which the angel speaks of, when he says, *The beast which thou sawest* WAS. But as five heads, or forms of government, had fallen before St. John's time, it is evident that the two other forms of government which had fallen must be among those of the Romans; first, because though the Latin nation so called, was deprived of all authority by the Romans, yet the Latin power continued to exist, for the very

conquerors of the Latin nation were *Latins ;* and, consequently the Latins, though a conquered people, continued to have a LATIN government. Secondly, the angel expressly says, when speaking to St. John, that *one is,* that is, the sixth head, or Latin form of government, was then in existence ; which could be no other than the *imperial power,* this being the only independent form of Latin government in the apostolic age. It therefore necessarily follows, that the Roman forms of government by which Latium was ruled must be the remaining heads of the beast. Before the subjugation of the Latins by the Romans four of the Roman or draconic forms of government had fallen, the *regal power,* the *dictatorship,* the *decemvirate,* and the *consular power* of the military tribunes, the last of which was abolished about 366 years before the commencement of the Christian era ; none of these, therefore, ruled over the WHOLE *Latin nation.* But as the Latins were finally subdued about 336 B. C., the *consular government* of the Romans, which was then the supreme power in the state, must be the *fourth* head of the beast. This form of government continued, with very little interruption, till the rising up of the *triumvirate,* the fifth head of the beast, B. C. 43. The *dictatorship* of Sylla and Julius Cæsar could not be considered a new head of the beast, as the Latins had already been ruled by it in the persons of Cluilius and Fufetius. The *sixth* head of the beast, or that which existed in the time of St. John, was consequently, as we have already proved, the *imperial power* of the heathen Cæsars, or the seventh draconic form of government.

And the other is not yet come] Bishop Newton considers *the Roman dutchy,* under the eastern emperor's lieutenant, the exarch of Ravenna, the *seventh* head of the beast. But this cannot be the form of government signified by the seventh head, for *a head of the beast* as we have already shown, *is a supreme, independent form of Latin government ;* consequently the Roman dutchy cannot be the seventh head, as it was dependent upon the exarchate of Ravenna ; and the exarchate cannot be the head, as it was itself in subjection to the Greek empire. The Rev. G Faber has ascertained the truth exactly in denominating the *Carlovingian patriciate* the seventh head of the beast. That this was a supreme, independent form of government, is evident from history. Gibbon, in speaking of the patriciate, observes that " the decrees of the senate and people successively invested Charles Martel and his posterity with the honours of *patrician of Rome.* The leaders of a powerful nation would have disdained a servile title and subordinate office ; but the reign of the Greek emperors was suspended, and in the vacancy of the empire they derived a more glorious commission from the pope and the republic. The Roman ambassadors presented these patricians with the keys of the shrine of St Peter as a pledge and symbol of sove-

A. M. cir. 4100.
A. D. cir. 96.
Impp. Flavio
Domitiano
Cæs. Aug. et
Nerva.

shall give their power and strength unto the beast.

14 ^h These shall make war with the Lamb, and the Lamb

shall overcome them: ⁱ for he is Lord of lords, and King of kings: ^k and they that are with him *are* called, and chosen, and faithful.

A. M. cir. 4100.
A. D. cir. 96.
Impp. Flavio
Domitiano
Cæs. Aug. et
Nerva.

---

^h Chap. xvi. 14 ; ix. 19.——ⁱ Deut. x. 17 ; 1 Tim. vi. 15 ; chap. xix. 16.——^k Jer. l. 44, 45 ; chap. xiv. 4.

---

reignty, and with a holy banner, which it was their right and duty to unfurl in defence of the Church and city In the time of Charles Martel and of Pepin, the interposition of the Lombard kingdom covered the freedom, while it threatened the safety of Rome ; and the patriciate represented only the title, the service, the alliance, of these distant protectors. The power and policy of Charlemagne annihilated an enemy, and imposed a master In his first visit to the capital he was received with all the honours which had formerly been paid to the exarch, the representative of the emperor ; and these honours obtained some new decorations from the joy and gratitude of Pope Adrian I. In the portico Adrian expected him at the head of his clergy ; they embraced as friends and equals ; but in their march to the altar, the king, or patrician, assumed the right hand of the pope Nor was the Frank content with these vain and empty demonstrations of respect In the twenty-six years that elapsed between the conquest of Lombardy and his imperial coronation, Rome, which had been delivered by the sword, was subject, as his own, to the sceptre of Charlemagne. The people swore allegiance to his person and family, in his name money was coined and justice was administered, and the election of the popes was examined and confirmed by his authority. Except an original and self-inherent claim of sovereignty, there was not any prerogative remaining which the title of *emperor* could add to the *patrician of Rome*." The seven heads of the beast are therefore the following : The *regal power*, the *dictatorship*, the power of the *prætors*, the *consulate*, the *triumvirate*, the *imperial* power, and the *patriciate*.

And when he cometh, he must continue a short space.] The seventh form of government was only to remain a short time, which was actually the case ; for from its first rise to independent power to its utter extinction, there passed only about forty-five years, a short time in comparison to the duration of several of the preceding forms of government ; for the primitive regal government continued at least four hundred and twenty-eight years, the dictatorship was in power about eighty-eight years, the power of the prætors was in being for upwards of three hundred years, the consulate lasted about two hundred and eighty years, and the imperial power continued upwards of five hundred years.

Verse 11 *And the beast, that was, and is not, even he is the eighth, and is of the seven, and goeth into perdition.*] That is to say, the Latin kingdom that has already been, but is now no longer nominally in existence, shall immediately follow the dissolution of the seventh form of Latin government ; and this dominion is called ογδοος, *an eighth*, because it succeeds to the seventh. Yet it is not an eighth *head* of the beast, because the beast has only *seven* heads ; for to constitute a new head of the beast the form of government must not only differ in *nature*, but also in *name*.

This head of the beast is, therefore, εκ των επτα, ONE *of the seven*. Consequently the form of government represented by this head is the restoration of one of the preceding seven. The restored head can be therefore no other than the regal state of the Latins, or in other words *the Latin kingdom*, ('Η Λατινη βασιλεια,) which followed the patriciate or seventh head of Latin government. But the beast in his eighth state, or under his first head restored, *goeth into perdition*. No other form of Latin government shall succeed ; but the beast in his last or antichristian condition shall be taken together with the false prophet that wrought miracles in his sight, " and cast alive into a lake of fire burning with brimstone."

It is observable that the eighth Latin power is called by the angel *the beast*, and also *one* of his heads This apparent discordance arises from the double signification of the heads, for if we take the beast upon which the woman sits to be merely a representation of that secular power which supports the Latin Church, then the seven heads will represent the seven electorates of the Germanic empire ; but if by the beast we understand the general Latin empire from first to last, then what is, according to the angel's first interpretation of the heads, called *the beast*, is in this case only *one* of his heads. See on ver. 18.

Verse 12. *And the ten horns which thou sawest are ten kings, which have received no kingdom as yet ; but receive power as kings one hour with the beast.*] The meaning of *horns* has already been defined when speaking of those of the dragon. The meaning is therefore as follows : Though the Latin empire be now in existence, the ten horns refer to ten Latin kingdoms yet in futurity, and consequently they have received no dominion AS YET ; for that part of the Latin domination now in power is the *sixth* head, or imperial government of the heathen Cæsars. But the ten states of the Latins receive dominion as monarchies μιαν ωραν, one time, (as it may be properly translated,) *i. e.*, at the same time with the beast, or that which ascendeth out of the bottomless pit ; consequently, the Latin empire here intended is the one which was in futurity in the apostolic age.

Verse 13. *These have one mind, and shall give their power and strength unto the beast.*] Therefore the ten horns must constitute the principal strength of the Latin empire ; that is to say, this empire is to be composed of the dominions of ten monarchs independent of each other in every other sense except in their implicit obedience to the Latin Church. The *beast* in this and the preceding verse is distinguished from its *horns*, as the WHOLE Latin empire is distinguished in history from its constituent powers. See on ver. 16.

Verse 14. *These shall make war with the Lamb, and the Lamb shall overcome them ; for he is Lord of lords, and King of kings : and they that are with him are called, and chosen, and faithful.*] The ten

A. M. cir. 4100.
A. D. cir. 96.
Impp. Flavio
Domitiano
Cæs. Aug. et
Nerva.

15 And he saith unto me, ¹ The waters which thou sawest, where the whore sitteth, ᵐ are peoples, and multitudes, and nations, and tongues.

16 And the ten horns which thou sawest

upon the beast, ⁿ these shall hate the whore, and shall make her desolate ᵒ and naked, and shall eat her flesh, and ᵖ burn her with fire.

17 ᑫ For God hath put in their hearts to

A. M. cir. 4100.
A. D. cir. 96.
Impp. Flavio
Domitiano
Cæs. Aug. et
Nerva.

---

¹ Isa. viii. 7 ; ver. 1.——ᵐ Chap. xiii. 7.——ⁿ Jer. l. 41, 42 ; ch. xvi. 12.

ᵒ Ezekiel xvi. 37–44 ; chapter xviii. 16.——ᵖ Chapter xviii. 8
ᑫ 2 Thess. ii. 11.

---

powers of the beast must compose the secular kingdom of antichrist, for they make war *with the Lamb,* who is Christ Jesus. This is perfectly true of all popish states, for they have constantly opposed, as long as they have had any secular power, the progress of pure Christianity. They make war with the Lamb by persecuting his followers ; *but the Lamb shall overcome them, for he is the Lord of lords, and King of kings*—all lords have their authority from him, and no king can reign without him ; therefore the ten Latin kings are God's ministers to execute his vengeance upon the idolatrous nations. But when these antichristian monarchies have executed the Divine purpose, those that are with the Lamb—the called, the chosen, and the faithful, those who have kept THE TRUTH in the love of it, shall prevail against all their adversaries, because their battles are fought by the Lamb, who is their God and Deliverer. See chap. xix. 19, 20.

Verse 15. *And he saith unto me, The waters which thou sawest, where the whore sitteth, are peoples, and multitudes, and nations, and tongues.*] "So many words," Bishop Newton observes, "in the plural number, fitly denote the great extensiveness of her power and jurisdiction. She herself glories in the title of the *Catholic* Church, and exults in the number of her votaries as a certain proof of the true religion. Cardinal Bellarmin's first note of the true Church is, *the very name of the Catholic Church ;* and his fourth note is, *amplitude, or multitude, and variety of believers ;* for the truly Catholic Church, says he, ought not only to comprehend all ages, but likewise all *places,* all *nations,* all *kinds* of men."

Verse 16. *And the ten horns which thou sawest upon the beast, these shall hate the whore, and shall make her desolate and naked, and shall eat her flesh, and burn her with fire.*] Here is a clew to lead us to the right interpretation of *the horns of the beast.* It is said the TEN *horns* shall *hate* the whore ; by which is evidently meant, when connected with what follows, that *the whole* of the ten kingdoms in the interest of the Latin Church shall finally despise her doctrines, be reformed from popery, assist in depriving her of all influence and in exposing her follies, and in the end consign her to utter destruction. From this it follows that no Roman Catholic power which did not exist so late as the Reformation can be numbered among the horns of the beast ; the horns must, therefore, be found among the great states of Europe at the commencement of the Reformation. These were exactly ten, viz., *France, Spain, England, Scotland, The Empire, Sweden, Denmark, Poland, Hungary,* and *Portugal.* In these were comprehended most of the

minor states not styled monarchies, and which, from their first rise to the period of the Reformation, had been subdued by one or more of the ten grand Roman Catholic powers already named. Consequently, these ten constituted *the power and strength of the beast ;* and each minor state is considered a part of that monarchy under the authority of which it was finally reduced previously to the Reformation.

But it may be asked, How could *the empire,* which was the revived *head* of the beast, have been at the same time one of its *horns ?* The answer is as follows : *Horns of an animal,* in the language of prophecy, represent the powers of which that empire or kingdom symbolized by the animal is composed. Thus the angel, in his interpretation of Daniel's vision of the ram and he-goat expressly informs us that " the ram with two horns are the kings of Media and Persia." One of the horns of the ram, therefore, represented the kingdom of Media, and the other the kingdom of Persia ; and their union in one animal denoted the united kingdom of Media and Persia, viz., the Medo-Persian empire. In like manner the beast with ten horns denotes that the empire represented by the beast is composed of ten distinct powers, and the ten horns being united in *one beast* very appropriately show that the monarchies symbolized by these horns are united together to form *one empire ;* for we have already shown, in the notes on chap. xiii. 1, that *a beast* is the symbol of *an empire.* Therefore, as the *horns* of an animal, agreeably to the angel's explanation, (and we can have no higher authority,) represent *all* the powers of which that domination symbolized by the animal is composed, the Roman empire of Germany, as one of those monarchies which gave their power and strength to the Latin empire, must consequently have been A HORN *of the beast.* But the Germanic empire was not only a LATIN power, but at the same time was acknowledged by all Europe to have *precedency* of all the others. Therefore, as it is not possible to express these *two* circumstances by *one* symbol, it necessarily follows, from the nature of symbolical language, that what has been named the holy Roman empire must have a *double* representation. Hence the influence the empire, as *one* of the powers of the Latin monarchy, was *a horn* of the beast, and in having *precedency* of all the others was its revived *head.* See a similar explanation of the tail of the dragon in the notes on chap. xii., ver. 4.

Verse 17. *For God hath put in their hearts to fulfil his will, and to agree, and give their kingdom unto the beast, until the words of God shall be fulfilled.*] Let no one imagine that these ten Latin kingdoms, because they support an idolatrous worship, have been

A. M. cir. 4100.
A. D. cir. 96.
Impp. Flavio
Domitiano
Cæs. Aug. et
Nerva.
fulfil his will, and to agree, and give their kingdom unto the beast, [r] until the words of God shall be fulfilled.

[r] Chap. x. 7.——[s] Chap. xvi. 19.

18 And the woman which thou sawest [s] is that great city, [t] which reigneth over the kings of the earth.

A. M. cir. 4100.
A. D. cir. 96.
Impp. Flavio
Domitiano
Cæs. Aug. et
Nerva.

[t] Chap. xii. 4.

raised up merely by the power of man or the chances of war. No kingdom or state can exist without the will of God; therefore let the inhabitants of the world tremble when they see a wicked monarchy rise to power, and let them consider that it is raised up by the Lord to execute his vengeance upon the idolatries and profligacies of the times. It is said of the kings in communion with the Church of Rome, that *God hath put in their hearts to fulfil his will.* How is this Divine will accomplished? In the most awful and afflictive manner! In causing ten Latin kings to unite their dominions into one mighty empire for the defence of the Latin Church. Here is a dreadful dispensation of Jehovah; but it is such as the nations have most righteously deserved, because when they had *the truth* they lived not according to its most holy requisitions, but loved darkness rather than light, because their deeds were evil. Therefore hath "the Lord sent them strong delusion that they should believe a lie, that they might all be damned who believe not the truth, but have pleasure in unrighteousness." But this deplorable state of the world is not perpetual, it can only continue till every word of God is fulfilled upon his enemies; and when this time arrives, (which will be that of Christ's second advent,) then shall the Son of God slay that wicked "with the spirit of his mouth, and shall consume him with the brightness of HIS COMING."

Verse 18. *And the woman which thou sawest is that great city, which reigneth over the kings of the earth.*] It has already been shown that the woman sitting upon the seven-headed beast is a representation of the Latin Church; here we have the greatest assurance that it is so, because the woman is called *a city,* which is a much plainer emblem of *a Church,* as the word is used unequivocally in this sense in so many parts of Scripture that we cannot well mistake its meaning. See chap. iii. 12; xi. 2; xxi. 10; xxii. 19; and also Psa. xlvi. 4; lxxxvii. 3; Heb. xii. 22, &c. The *woman* therefore must be *the Latin Church;* and as the apostle saw her *sitting* upon the beast, this must signify that ἡ εχουσα βασιλειαν, she hath A KINGDOM *over the kings of the earth,* i. e., over the kings of the Latin world, for that this is the meaning of *earth* has been shown before in numerous instances. That KINGDOM which the woman has over the kings of the Latin world, or secular Latin empire, or in other words THE KINGDOM of the Latin Church, is the numbered Latin kingdom or Romish hierarchy. See on chap. xiii. 18. The woman is also called *a* GREAT *city,* to denote the very great extent of her jurisdiction; for she has comprehended within her walls the subjects of the mighty dominations of France, Spain, England, Scotland, The Empire, Sweden, Denmark, Poland, Hungary, and Portugal. What an extensive city was this! Surely such as to justify the prophetic denomination, *that* GREAT *city.*

HAVING now gone through the whole of the angel's interpretation of St. John's vision of a whore sitting upon the seven-headed and ten-horned beast, it will be essentially necessary to examine a little more attentively the eighth verse of this chapter. It has already been shown that the phrases, *was, is not, shall ascend out of the bottomless pit, and yet is,* refer to the Latin kingdom which existed before the building of Rome, to the Roman empire in the time of St. John, and to the Latin empire which was in futurity in the apostolic age. But as the words *was, is not,* &c., are spoken of the beast upon which the apostle saw the woman, or Latin Church, sit; how can it be said of *this beast* that it had an existence before the date of the Apocalypse, when the woman whom it carried was not in being till long after this period? And what connection has the Latin empire of the middle ages with that which derived its name from Latinus, king of the Aborigines, and was subjugated by the ancient Romans; or even with that which existed in the time of the apostle? The answer is as follows: St. John saw the beast upon which the woman sat with *all* his seven heads and ten horns. Consequently, as the angel expressly says that *five* of these seven heads had already fallen in the time of the vision, it therefore necessarily follows that the apostle must have seen that part of the Latin empire represented by the seven-headed beast which had already been under the emblem of *five* heads. Therefore the woman sat upon the *beast that* WAS. But it is plain from the angel's interpretation that the whole of the seven heads fell, before the beast upon which the woman sat arose; and yet the woman is represented as sitting upon the seven-headed beast to denote, as we have before observed, that it is the Latin kingdom in its last estate, or under one of its heads restored, which is the secular kingdom of antichrist. The beast is also said not to have any existence in the time of the vision; from which it is evident that the monarchy of the *Latins,* and not that of the *Romans,* is here intended; because the latter *was* in the time of the vision. Again, the beast which St. John saw had not ascended out of the bottomless pit in his time; consequently the whole seven heads and ten horns were in futurity, for all these heads and horns rose up out of the abyss *at the same time* with the beast. How is this apparent contradiction reconciled? In the most plain and satisfactory manner, by means of the angel's double interpretation of the heads; for if the seven heads be taken in the sense of *seven mountains,* (*head* in the Scripture style being a symbol of *precedency* as well as *supremacy,*) then the beast with all its heads and horns was altogether in futurity in the apostle's time, for the seven heads are the seven electorates of the German empire, and the ten horns the ten monarchies in the interest of the Latin Church. Finally, the beast is said to exist in the time of the vision; therefore the Roman empire, which governed the world, must be here alluded to; and consequently the phrase *and yet is* is a proof that, as the beast is the Latin kingdom, and *this beast* is said to have an existence in the time of the apostle, the empire of the Cæsars, though generally known by the name of *the Roman*, is in a very proper sense *the Latin kingdom*, as the Latin was the language which prevailed in it. Hence the seven-headed and ten-horned beast is at once the representation of the ancient Latin power, of the Roman empire which succeeded it, and of the Latin empire which supports the Latin Church. Here is then the connection of the ancient Latin and Roman powers with that upon which the woman sits. She sits upon the beast *that was and is not*, because three of his heads represent the three forms of government which the ancient Latins had before they were subjugated by the Romans, viz., the regal power, the dictatorship, and the power of the prætors. She sits upon the beast which SHALL ASCEND *out of the bottomless pit*, because all his seven heads, taken in the sense of *mountains* were in futurity in the apostolic age. She sits upon the beast that *yet is*, because four of his heads represent four forms of government of the Roman or Latin empire now in existence, viz., the consulate, the triumvirate, the imperial power, and the patriciate. It is hence evident that *the beast*, in the largest acceptation of this term, is a symbol of the *Latin* power in general, from its commencement in Latinus to the end of time; his seven heads denoting seven kings or supreme forms of Latin government, during this period, *king* or *kingdom*, as we have already observed, being a general term in the prophetical writings for any kind of supreme governor or government, no matter by

what particular name such may have been designated among men. Thus the Latin power from the time of Latinus to the death of Numitor was the beast under the dominion of his *first* head; from the death of Numitor to the destruction of Alba it was the beast under the dominion of his *second* head; from the destruction of Alba to the final subjugation of the Latins by the Romans the beast under the dominion of his *third* head. And as the four Roman forms of government which were subsequent to the final conquest of the Latins, were also *Latin* dominations, the Latin power under these forms of government was the beast under the dominion of his *fourth*, *fifth*, *sixth* and *seventh* heads. The beast of the bottomless pit, which followed the fall of all the heads of the sea beast or general Latin empire, is, according to the angel's interpretation, ογδοος, (βασιλευς,) an EIGHTH king, i. e., an eighth species of Latin power, or, in other words, a supreme form of Latin government essentially differing from all the foregoing; yet, as it is *nominally* the same with one of the preceding seven, it is not accounted an eighth *head* of the beast. The first beast of chap. xiii. is a description of the *eighth* or *last* condition of *the* GENERAL *Latin empire*, and is said to arise εκ της θαλασσης, *out of the sea*, because the heads are there taken in a double sense, *sea* being a general term to express the origin of every great empire which is raised up by the sword; but when (as in ver. 11) one of the heads of the sea beast (viz., that secular power which is still in being, and has supported the Latin Church for more than a thousand years) is peculiarly styled *The Beast*, the Holy Ghost, speaking of *this* secular Latin empire exclusively, declares it to be εκ της αβυσσου, FROM *the bottomless pit*.

JOHN EDWARD CLARKE.

CHAPTER XVIII.

A luminous angel proclaims the fall of Babylon, and the cause of it, 1–3. *The followers of God are exhorted to come out of it, in order to escape her approaching punishment*, 4–8. *The kings of the earth lament her fate*, 9, 10. *The merchants also bewail her*, 11. *The articles in which she trafficked enumerated*, 12–16. *She is bewailed also by shipmasters, sailors*, &c., 17–19. *All heaven rejoices over her fall, and her final desolation is foretold*, 20–24.

A. M. cir. 4100.
A. D. cir. 96.
Impp. Flavio Domitiano Cæs. Aug. et Nerva.

AND [a] after these things I saw another angel come down from heaven, having great power; [b] and the earth was lightened with his glory.

2 And he cried mightily with a strong voice, saying, [c] Babylon the great is fallen, is fallen, and [d] is become the habitation of devils, and the hold of every foul spirit, and

A. M. cir. 4100.
A. D. cir. 96.
Impp. Flavio Domitiano Cæs. Aug. et Nerva.

---

[a] Chap. xvii. 1.——[b] Ezekiel xliii. 2.——[c] Isa. xiii. 19; xxi. 9; Jer. li. 8; chap. xiv. 8.

[d] Isaiah xiii. 21; xxi. 8; xxxiv. 14; Jeremiah l. 39; li. 37.

NOTES ON CHAP. XVIII.

Verse 1. *The earth was lightened with his glory.*] This may refer to some extraordinary messenger of the everlasting Gospel, who, by his *preaching* and *writings*, should be the means of diffusing the light of truth and true religion over the earth.

Verse 2. *Babylon the great is fallen, is fallen*] This

is a quotation from Isa. xxi. 9: *And he said, Babylon is fallen, is fallen; and all the graven images of her gods he hath broken unto the ground.* This is applied by some to Rome *pagan*; by others to Rome *papal*; and by others to *Jerusalem*.

Is become—the hold of every foul spirit] See the parallel passages in the margin. The figures here

2

A. M. cir. 4100.
A. D. cir. 96.
Impp. Flavio
Domitiano
Cæs. Aug. et
Nerva.

[e] a cage of every unclean and hateful bird.

3 For all nations [f] have drunk of the wine of the wrath of her fornication, and the kings of the earth have committed fornication with her, [g] and the merchants of the earth are waxed rich through the [h] abundance of her delicacies.

4 And I heard another voice from heaven, saying, [i] Come out of her, my people, that ye be not partakers of her sins, and that ye receive not of her plagues.

5 [k] For her sins have reached unto heaven, and [l] God hath remembered her iniquities.

6 [m] Reward her even as she rewarded you, and double unto her double according to her works: [n] in the cup which she hath filled, [o] fill to her double.

7 [p] How much she hath glorified herself, and lived deliciously, so much torment and

sorrow give her: for she saith in her heart, I sit a [q] queen, and am no widow, and shall see no sorrow.

A. M. cir. 4100.
A. D. cir. 96.
Impp. Flavio
Domitiano
Cæs. Aug. et
Nerva.

8 Therefore shall her plagues come [r] in one day, death, and mourning, and famine; and [s] she shall be utterly burned with fire: [t] for strong *is* the Lord God who judgeth her.

9 And [u] the kings of the earth, who have committed fornication and lived deliciously with her, [v] shall bewail her, and lament for her, [w] when they shall see the smoke of her burning.

10 Standing afar off for the fear of her torment, saying, [x] Alas, alas! that great city Babylon, that mighty city! [y] for in one hour is thy judgment come.

11 And [z] the merchants of the earth shall weep and mourn over her; for no man buyeth their merchandise any more:

---

[e] Isa. xiv. 2-; xxxiv. 11; Mark v. 2, 3.——[f] Chapter xiv. 8; xvii. 2.——[g] Ver. 11, 15; Isa. xlvii. 15.——[h] Or, *power.*——[i] Isa. xlviii. 20; lii. 11; Jer. l. 8; li. 6, 45; 2 Cor. vi. 17.——[k] Gen. xviii. 20, 21; Jer. li. 9; Jonah i. 2.——[l] Ch. xvi. 19.——[m] Psa. cxxxvii. 8; Jer. l. 15, 29; li. 24, 49; 2 Tim. iv. 14; chap. xiii. 10.——[n] Chap. xiv. 10.

[o] Chap. xvi. 19.——[p] Ezek. xxviii. 2, &c.——[q] Isa. xlvii. 7, 8, Zeph. ii. 15.——[r] Isa. xlvii. 9; ver. 10.——[s] Chapter xvii. 16 [t] Jer. l. 34; chap. xi. 17.——[u] Ezek. xxvi. 16, 17; chap. xvii. 2; ver. 3.——[v] Jer. l. 46.——[w] Ver. 18; chap. xix. 3.——[x] Isa. xxi 9; chapter xiv. 8.——[y] Ver. 17, 19.——[z] Ezekiel xxvii. 27-36; ver. 3.

---

point out the most *complete destruction.* A city utterly sacked and ruined, never to be rebuilt.

Verse 3. *The wine of the wrath*] The punishment due to her transgressions, because they have partaken with her in her sins. See the note on chap. xiv. 8.

Verse 4. *Come out of her, my people*] These words appear to be taken from Isa. xlviii. 20; Jer. i. 8; li. 6, 45. The poet Mantuanus expresses this thought well:—

Vivere qui sancte cupitis, discelite; Romæ
Omnia quum liceant, non licet esse bonum.

" Ye who desire to live a godly life, depart; for, although all things are lawful at Rome, yet to be *godly* is unlawful.

Verse 5. *Her sins have reached unto heaven*] They are become so great and enormous that the long-suffering of God must give place to his justice.

Verse 6. *Reward her even as she rewarded you*] These words are a prophetic declaration of what shall take place: God will deal with her as she dealt with others.

Verse 7. *How much she hath glorified herself*] By every act of transgression and sinful pampering of the body she has been preparing for herself a suitable and proportionate punishment.

Verse 8. *Therefore shall her plagues come*] *Death,* by the sword of her adversaries; *mourning* on account of the slaughter; and *famine,* the fruits of the field being destroyed by the hostile bands.

Utterly burned with fire] Of what *city* is this spoken? Rome *pagan* has never been thus treated; Alaric and Totilas burnt only some parts with fire. Rome *papal* has not been thus treated; but this is true of Jerusalem, and yet Jerusalem is not generally thought to be intended.

Verse 9. *The kings of the earth*] Those who copied her superstitions and adopted her idolatries.

Verse 10. *Standing afar off*] Beholding her desolations with wonder and astonishment, utterly unable to afford her any kind of assistance.

Verse 11. *The merchants of the earth*] These are represented as mourning over her, because their traffic with her was at an end.

Bishop Bale, who applies all these things to the Church of Rome, thus paraphrases the principal passages:—

" The mighty *kinges* and potentates *of the earth,* not havinge afore their eyes the love and feare of God, have committed with this whore moste vile filthynesse; abusinge themselves by many straunge or uncom maunded worshippings, and bynding themselves by othe to observe hyr lawes and customs. At the examples, doctrines, counsels, and perswasions of hyr holy whoremongers, have they broken the covenaunts of peace; battailed, oppressed, spoyled, ravished, tyrannously murthered innocents; yea, for vain foolish causes, and more vaine titles, as though there were neither heaven nor hel, God nor accounts to be made.

" And her mitred *marchantes,* hyr shorne souldiers, hir massemongers, hyr soulesellers, and hir martbrokers, waxed very riche, through the sale of hir oyles,

| A. M. cir. 4100. A. D. cir. 96. Impp. Flavio Domitiano Cæs. Aug. et Nerva. | 12 [a] The merchandise of gold, and silver, and precious stones, and of pearls, and fine linen, and purple, and silk, and scarlet, | and all [b] thyine wood, and all manner vessels of ivory, and all manner vessels of most precious wood, and of brass, and iron, and marble, | A. M. cir. 4100. A. D. cir. 96. Impp. Flavio Domitiano Cæs. Aug. et Nerva. |

----

[a] Chap. xvii. 4.   [b] Or, *sweet.*

----

creme, salt, water, bread, orders, hallowings, house-linges, ashes, palme, waxe, frankensence, beades, crosses, candlesticks, copes, belles, organes, images, reliques, and other pedlary wares.

"They have gotten in unto them pallaces and princely houses, fat pastors and parkes, meadowes and warrens, rivers and pondes, villages and townes, cities and whole provinces, with the divill and all els; besides other men's wives, daughters, mayde servantes, and children, whom they have abhominably corrupted. What profites they have drawen unto them also by the sale of great bishopricks, prelacies, promocions, benefices, *tot quoties,* pardons, pilgrymages, confessions, and purgatory; besides the yearely rents of cathedrall churches, abbayes, colleges, covents, for sutes and suche other.—Specially shal they be sore discontented with the matter, which have with hir committed the whordom of the spyrite, by many externe worshipings of drye waffer cakes, oyles, roods, relyques, ladyes, images, sculles, bones, chippes, olde ragges, showes, (shoes,) bootes, spurres, hattes, breches, whodes, night capes, and such like.

"And they that have *lived wantonly* with hir, (ver. 9,) in following hir idle observacions, in mattenses, houres, and masses; in sensinges, halowings, and font halowing; in going processions with canapye, crosse, and pyx; with banneres, stremers, and torche light; with such other gaudes to folish for children.

"*Alas, alas, that great cyty* (ver. 10) that beautiful *Babilon,* that blessed holy mother the Church, which somtime had so many popes pardons, so many bishoppes blessinges, so many holye stacions, so many cleane remissions *a pena et culpa,* so many good ghostly fathers, so many religious orders, so much holy water for spirites, and Saint John's gospel, with the five woundes and the length of our Lord for drowning, is nowe decayed for ever!

"Alas, alas, who shall pray for us now? Who shall singe dirges and trentoles? Who shal spoile us of our sinnes? Who shal give us ashes and palmes? Who shal blesse us with a spade, and singe us out of purgatory when we are deade? If we lacke these things we are like to want heaven. These are the desperate complaints of the wicked."

Verse 12. *The merchandise of gold, and silver, &c.*] The same author, *Bishop Bale,* who was once a priest of the Romish Church, goes on to apply all these things to that Church; and whether the text have this meaning or not, they will show us something of the religious usages of his time, and the *real mockery* of this intolerant and superstitious Church. Speaking in reference to the *Reformation,* and the general light that had been diffused abroad by the word of God, which was then translated into the vulgar tongue, and put into the hands of the people at large, he says:—

"They will pay no more *money* for the housell sippings, bottom blessings; nor for 'seest me and seest me not,' above the head and under of their chalices, which in many places be of fine *gold.* Neyther regarde they to kneele anye more downe, and to kisse their pontificall rings which are of the same metal. They will be no more at coste to have the ayre beaten, and the idols perfumed with their sensers at pryncipall feastes; to have their crucifixes layde upon horses, or to have them solemply borne aloft in their gaddings abroade; with the religious occupyings of their paxes, cruettes, and other jewels which be of *silver.*

"Neyther passe they greatly to beholde precyous stones any more in their two-horned miters, whan they hollow their churches, give theyr whorishe orders, and tryumphantly muster in processions. Nor in costuous pearles in theyr copes perrours, and chysibilles, whan they be in their prelately pompous sacrifices. Men, knowing the worde of God, supposeth that their ornaments of *silk,* wherewith they garnishe their temples and adorne their idolles, is very blasphemous and divillish. They thinke also, that their fayre white rockets of raynes, or fine linnen cloath; their costly gray amices, of calaber and cattes tayles; theyr fresh purple gownes, whan they walke for their pleasures; and their read scarlet frockes, whan they preach lyes in the pulpit, are very superfluous and vayne.

"In their *thynen wood* (whom some men call *algume trees,* some *basill,* some *corall*) may be understande all theyr curious buildings of temples, abbeys, chappels, and chambers; all shrines, images, church stooles, and pews that are well payed for; all banner staves, paternoster scores, and peeces of the holy crosse.

"The *vessels of ivory* comprehendeth all their maundye dyshes, their offring platters, their relique chestes, their god boxes, their drinking horns, their sipping cuppes for the hiccough, their tables whereupon are charmed their chalises and vestiments; their standiches, their combes, their muske balles, their pomaunder pottes, and their dust boxes, with other toyes.

"The *vessels of precious stone;* which after some interpretours, are of precious stone, or after some are *of most precious wood;* betokeneth their costuous cuppes, or cruses of jasper, jacinct, amel, and fine beral; and their alabaster boxes, wherwith they annointe kinges, confirme children, and minister their holy whorish orders. Their pardon masers, or drinking dishes, as St. Benit's bole, St. Edmond's bole, St. Giles's bole, St. Blythe's bole, and Westminster bole, with such other holy re-liques.

"Of *brasse,* which containeth latten, copper, alcumine, and other harde metals, are made all their great candlesticks, holy water kettles, lampes, desks, pyllers, butterasses, bosses, bels, and many other thinges more.

"Of strong *yron* are the braunches made that holde up the lightes before their false gods; the tacks that sustayne them for fallinge; the lockes that save them from the robberye of thieves; their fyre pans,

A. M. cir. 4100.
A. D. cir. 96.
Impp. Flavio
Domitiano
Cæs. Aug. et
Nerva.

13 And cinnamon, and odours, and ointments, and frankincense, and wine, and oil, and fine flour, and wheat, and beasts, and sheep, and horses, and chariots, and ᶜ slaves, and ᵈ souls of men.

14 And the fruits that thy soul lusted after are departed from

A. M. cir. 4100.
A. D. cir. 96.
Impp. Flavio
Domitiano
Cæs. Aug. et
Nerva.

ᶜ Or, *bodies.*

ᵈ Ezek. xxvii. 13.

bars, and poolyes, with many other straunge ginnes besides.

"With *marble* most commonlye pave they their temples, and build strong pillers and arches in their great cathedrale churches and monastries ; they make thereof also their superalities, their tumbs, and their solemne grave-stones ; besides their other buildinges, with free-stone, flint, ragge, and brick, comprehended in the same.

Verse 13. *And cinnamon*] "By the sinamon is ment all maner of costly spyces, wherewith they bury their byshops and founders, lest they shoulde stinke when they translate them agayne to make them saintes for advauntage.

"By the smellynge *odours,* the swete herbes that they strewe abrode at theyr dedications and burials ; besydes the damaske waters, bawmes, muskes, pomaunder, civet, and other curious confections they yet bestow upon theyr owne precious bodyes.

"The *oyntments* are such oyles as they mingle with rose water, aloes, and spike, with other mery conceits, wherwith they anoynt their holy savours and roods, to make them to sweat, and to smell sweete when they are borne abrod in procession upon their high feastfull dayes.

"*Frankinsence* occupye they ofte as a necessarie thinge in the sensyng of their idols, hallowinge of their paschal, conjuringe of their ploughes ; besydes the blessing of their palmes, candles, ashes, and their dead men's graves, with *requiescant in pace.*

"With *wine* synge they theyr masses for money, they housell the people at Easter, they wash their aultar stones upon Maundy Thursday ; they fast the holy imber dayes, besydes other banketinges all the whole yeare, to kepe theyr flesh chaste.

"With *oyle* smere they yonge infantes at baptisme and bishopping ; they grease their massmongers, and geve them the mark of madian ; they anele their cattell that starveth ; and do many other feates els.

"*Fyne floure* is suche a merchandyse of theirs as far excedeth all other, and was first geven them by Pope Alexander the first, thinkinge Christes institution not sufficient, nor comly in using the common breade in that ministerie. For that ware hath brought them in their plentifull possessions, their lordshippes, fatte benifices, and prebendaries, with innumerable plesures els.

"*Wheat* have thei of their farms, whereof they make pardon bread and cakes, to draw people to devocion towardes them.

"*Cattell* receive they, offered unto their idols by the idiots of the countries, for recover of sondrye diseases ; besides that they have of their tithes.

"*Shepe* have they, sometime of their owne pastures, sometime of begginge, sometime of bequestes for the dead, to cry them out of their feareful purgatorye, when they be asleepe at midnight.

"Great *horses* have they, for mortuaries, for offices, for favers, giftes, and rewardes, to be good lords unto them, that they may holde still their farmes, and to have saunder waspe their sonne and their heire a priest ; or to admitte him unto a manerly benefice, that he may be called ' maister person,' and suche lyke.

"*Charets* have they also, or *horse litters,* of al manner of sorts, specially at Rome, with foote men runninge on both sides of them, to make roome for the holy fathers. Of whom some carye their owne precious bodyes, some theyr treasure, some the blessed sacramente, some holy reliques and ornamentes, some their whores, and some their bastardes. The *bodyes of men* must needes be judged to be at their pleasure, so long as Christen provinces be tributaries unto them, princes obediente, people subject, and their lawes at their commaundement to slea and to kyll. And to make this good, who hath not in England payd his Peter peny, sometime to acknowledge hymselfe a *bondman* of theirs, at the receit of his yerely howsell ? Furthermore yet, besides their market muster of monkes, fryars, and priestes, they have certayne *bondmen,* of whom some they sell to the *Venicians,* some to the *Genues,* some to the *Portingales,* and some to the *Turks,* to row in their galleis. And laste of all, to make up their market, least any thing should escape theyr hands, these unmercifull bribers maketh marchaundise of the *soules of men,* to deprive Christe of his whole right, sending many unto hell, but not one unto heaven, (unlesse they maliciously murther them for the truths sake,) and all for mony. After many other sortes els, abuse they these good creatures of God, whom the Holy Ghost heere nameth. Much were it to shew here by the cronicles severally of what Pope they have received authorytie, power, and charge, to utter these wares to advauntage, and how they came firste by the old idolatrous."

Several of the most reputable MSS. *versions,* and some of the *fathers,* after *cinnamon,* add και αμωμον, *and amomum.* What this shrub was is not easy to say, though mentioned and partially described by *Pliny* and *Dioscorides.* Some think it was a species of *geranium ;* others, the *rose of Jericho.* It was an odoriferous plant supposed to be a native of Assyria ; and is thus mentioned by *Virgil,* Eclog. iv., ver. 25 :

——— *Assyrium vulgo nascetur amomum.*

" The Assyrian amomum shall grow in every soil."

This is translated by some *spikenard ;* by others *lady's rose.*

Thyine wood] The *Thyne* or *Thyin* is said to be a tree whose boughs, leaves, stalks, and fruit, resemble the cypress. It is mentioned by *Homer,* Odyss. lib. v., ver. 60 ; by *Theophrastes,* Hist. Plant. v. 5 ; and

A. M. cir. 4100.
A. D. cir. 96.
Impp. Flavio
Domitiano
Cæs. Aug. et
Nerva.
thee, and all things which were dainty and goodly are departed from thee,· and thou shalt find them no more at all.

15 'e The merchants of these things, which were made rich by her, shall stand afar off for the fear of her torment, weeping and wailing,

16 And saying, Alas, alas! that great city, f that was clothed in fine linen, and purple, and scarlet, and decked with gold, and precious stones, and pearls!

17 g For in one hour so great riches is come to naught. And h every shipmaster, and all the company in ships, and sailors, and as many as trade by sea, stood afar off,

18 i And cried, when they saw the smoke

of her burning, saying, k What city is like unto this great city!

19 And l they cast dust on their heads, and cried, weeping and wailing, saying, Alas! alas, that great city, wherein were made rich all that had ships in the sea by reason of her costliness! m for in one hour is she made desolate.

20 n Rejoice over her, *thou* heaven, and *ye* holy apostles and prophets; for o God hath avenged you on her.

21 And a mighty angel took up a stone like a great millstone, and cast *it* into the sea, saying, p Thus with violence shall that great city Babylon be thrown down, and q shall be found no more at all.

A. M. cir. 4100
A. D. cir. 96.
Impp. Flavio
Domitiano
Cæs. Aug. et
Nerva.

---

e Ver. 3, 11.——f Chap. xvii. 4.——g Verse 10.——h Isa. xxiii. 14; Ezek. xxvii. 29.——i Ezek. xxvii. 30, 31; ver. 9.——k Ch. xiii. 4.——l Josh. vii. 6; 1 Sam. iv. 12; Job ii. 12; Ezek. xxvii. 30.

m Ver. 8.——n Isa. xliv. 23; xlix. 13;· Jer. li. 48.——o Luke xi. 49, 50; chapter xix. 2.——p Jer. li. 64.——q Chapter xii. 8; xvi. 20.

---

by *Pliny*, Hist. Nat. lib. xiii. c. 16. How much the different articles mentioned in the 12th and 13th verses were in request among the ancients, and how highly valued, every scholar knows.

Slaves] Σωματων· *The bodies of men;* probably distinguished here from ψυχας, *souls of men*, to express *bondmen* and *freemen*.

Verse 14. *And the fruits that thy soul lusted after.*] και ἡ οπωρα της επιθυμιας της ψυχης σου. As οπωρα signifies *autumn*, any and all kinds of *autumnal fruits* may be signified by the word in the above clause.

Dainty and goodly] Τα λιπαρα· *Delicacies* for the *table*. Τα λαμπρα, what is *splendid* and *costly* in apparel.

Verse 15. *Stand afar off*] See ver. 10.

Verse 16. *Clothed in fine linen, and purple, &c.*] The verb περιβαλλεσθαι, which we here translate *clothed*, signifies often *to abound, be enriched, laden with*, and is so used by the best Greek writers; see many examples in *Kypke*. These articles are not to be considered here as *personal ornaments*, but as articles of trade or merchandise, in which this city trafficked.

Verse 17. *Every shipmaster*] Captains of vessels; some think *pilots* are meant, and this is most likely to be the meaning of the original word κυβερνητης. This description appears to be at least partly taken from Ezek. xxvii. 26–28.

And all the company in ships] Και πας επι των πλοιων ὁ ὁμιλος· *The crowd or passengers aboard.* But the best MSS. and versions have και πας ὁ επι τοπον πλεων, *those who sail from place to place*, or such as *stop at particular places* on the coast, without performing the *whole voyage*. This sufficiently marks the traffic on the coast of the Mediterranean Sea. Some might debark (in sailing from Rome) at the island of *Sicily*, others at different ports in *Greece*; some at *Corinth*, others at *Crete*, or the various islands of the *Ægean Sea*; some at *Rhodes, Pamphylia*, &c., &c.; as in those times in which the compass was un-

known, every voyage was performed *coastwise*, always keeping, if possible, within sight of the land.

Verse 18. *What city is like unto this great city!*] Viz. in magnitude, power, and luxury.

Verse 19. *They cast dust on their heads*] They showed every sign of the sincerest grief. The lamentation over this great ruined city, from ver. 9 to 19, is exceedingly strong and well drawn. Here is no dissembled sorrow; all is real to the mourners, and affecting to the spectators.

Verse 20. *Rejoice over her, thou heaven*] This is grand and sublime; the fall of this bad city was cause of grief to bad men. But as this city was a *persecutor of the godly*, and an *enemy* to the *works of God*, angels, apostles, and prophets are called to rejoice over her fall.

Verse 21. *Thus with violence shall that great city Babylon be thrown down*] This action is finely and forcibly expressed by the original words: Ουτως ὁρμηματι βληθησεται Βαβυλων ἡ μεγαλη πολις. The millstone will in falling have not only an accelerated force from the law of gravitation, but that force will be greatly increased by the projectile force impressed upon it by the power of the destroying angel.

Shall be found no more at all.] In her government, consequence, or influence. This is true of ancient *Babylon*; we are not certain even of the *place* where it stood. It is also true of *Jerusalem*; her government, consequence, and influence are gone. It is not true of *Rome pagan*; nor, as yet, of *Rome papal*: the latter still exists, and the former is most intimately blended with it; for in her religious service Rome papal has retained her language, and many of her heathen temples has she dedicated to *saints* real or reputed, and incorporated many of her superstitions and absurdities in a professedly *Christian* service. It is true also that many idols are now restored under the names of Christian saints!

Verse 22. *The voice of harpers, &c.*] This seems

A. M. cir. 4100.
A. D. cir. 96.
Impp. Flavio
Domitiano
Cæs. Aug. et
Nerva.

22 [r] And the voice of harpers, and musicians, and of pipers, and trumpeters, shall be heard no more at all in thee; and no craftsman, of whatsoever craft *he be,* shall be found any more in thee; and the sound of a millstone shall be heard no more at all in thee;

23 [s] And the light of a candle shall shine

no more at all in thee; [t] and the voice of the bridegroom and of the bride shall be heard no more at all in thee: for [u] thy merchants were the great men of the earth; [v] for by thy sorceries were all nations deceived.

24 And [w] in her was found the blood of prophets, and of saints, and of all that [x] were slain upon the earth.

A. M. cir. 4100.
A. D. cir. 96.
Impp. Flavio
Domitiano
Cæs. Aug. et
Nerva.

---

[r] Isa. xxiv. 8; Jer. vii. 34; xvi. 9; xxv. 10; Ezekiel xxvi. 13.
[s] Jer. xxv. 10.——[t] Jer. vii. 34; xvi. 9; xxv. 10; xxxiii. 11.

[u] Isa. xxiii. 8.——[v] 2 Kings ix. 22; Nah. iii. 4; chap. xvii. 2, 5.——[w] Chap. xvii. 6.——[x] Jer. li. 49.

---

to indicate not only a total destruction of influence, &c., but also of *being.* It seems as if this city was to be *swallowed up by an earthquake,* or *burnt up by fire from heaven.*

Verse 23. *By thy sorceries*] Political arts, state tricks, counterfeit miracles, and deceptive manœuvres of every kind. This may be spoken of many great cities of the world, which still continue to flourish!

Verse 24. *In her was found the blood of prophets, &c.*] She was the persecutor and murderer of prophets and of righteous men.

And of all that were slain upon the earth.] This refers to her *counsels* and *influence,* exciting other nations and people to persecute and destroy the real followers of God. There is no city to which *all* these things are yet applicable, therefore we may presume that the prophecy remains yet to be fulfilled.

Bishop Bale, who applies this, as before, to the Romish Church, has, on ver. 22, given some information to the curious *antiquary.*

" But be certaine," says he, " and sure, thou myserable Church, that thou shalt no longer enjoy the commodious pleasures of a free cittye.—The merry noyes of them that play upon *harpes, lutes,* and *fidels;* the sweet voice of musicians that sing with *virginals, vials,* and *chimes;* the armony of them that *pipe in recorders, flutes,* and *drums;* and the shirle showt of *trumpets, waits,* and *shawmes,* shall no more be heard in thee to the delight of men. Neyther shall the sweet *organs* containing the melodious noyse of all maner of *instruments* and *byrdes* be plaied upon, nor the great *belles* be rong after that, nor yet the *fresh discant, prick-song, counter-point,* and *faburden* be called for in thee, which art the very sinagog of Sathan. Thy lascivious armonye, and delectable musique, much provoking the weake hartes of men to meddle in thy abhominable whordom, by the wantonnes of idolatry in that kinde, shall perish with thee for ever. No cunning *artificer, carver, paynter,* nor *gilder, embroderer, goldsmith,* nor *silk-worker;* with such other like of what occupacion soever they be, or have bene

to thy commodity, shall never more be found so agayne.

" Copes, cruettes, candelstickes, miters, crosses, sensers, crismatoris, corporasses, and chalices, which for thy whorishe holines might not somtime be touched, will than for thy sake be abhorred of all men. Never more shall be builded for marchants of thi livery and mark, palaces, temples, abbeys, collages, covents, chauntries, fair houses, and horcherds of plesure. The clapping noise of neyther wyndmil, horsemil, nor watermil, shal any more be heard to the gluttenous feeding of thy puffed up porklings, for the maintenaunce of thine idle observacions and ceremonies. For thy mitred marchaunts were sumtimes princes of the earth, whan they reigned in their roialty. Thy shorn shavelinges were lordes over the multitude whan they held their priestly authority over the soules and bodies of men. Yea, and with thy privy legardemain, with thy juggling castes, with thy craftes and inchauntmentes of thy subtile charmes, were all nacions of the world deceyved."

This is very plain language, and thus on all hands a monstrous system of superstition and idolatry was attacked by our Reformers; and with these unfurbished weapons, directed by the Spirit of the living God, popery was driven from the *throne,* from the *bench,* from the *universities,* and from the *churches* of this favoured kingdom. And by a proper application of Scripture, and by the universal diffusion of the word of God, it may be soon driven from the face of the universe. And when the inventions of men are separated from that Church, and it becomes truly regenerated, (and of this it is highly capable, as, among its monstrous errors and absurdities, it contains all the essential truths of God,) it will become a praise and a glory in the earth. Protestants wish not its *destruction,* but its *reformation.*

Some there may be, who, in their zeal for truth, would pull the whole edifice to pieces; but this is not God's method: he destroys what is evil, and saves what is good. It is *reformation,* not *annihilation,* that this Church needs.

2

CHAPTER XIX.

The whole heavenly host give glory to God, because he has judged the great whore, and avenged the blood of his saints, 1–6. The marriage of the Lamb and his bride, 7–9. John offers to worship the angel, but is prevented, 10. Heaven is opened, and Jesus the Word of God appears on a white horse; he and his armies described, 11–16. An angel in the sun invites all the fowls of heaven to come to the supper of the great God, 17, 18. The beast, the false prophet, and the kings of the earth, gather together to make war with him who sits on the white horse; but they are all discomfited, and utterly destroyed, 19–21.

A. M. cir. 4100.
A. D. cir. 96.
Impp. Flavio
Domitiano
Cæs. Aug. et
Nerva.

AND after these things a I heard a great voice of much people in heaven, saying, Alleluia; b Salvation, and glory, and honour, and power, unto the Lord our God:

2 For c true and righteous *are* his judgments; for he hath judged the great whore, which did corrupt the earth with her fornication, and d hath avenged the blood of his servants at her hand.

3 And again they said, Alleluia. And e her smoke rose up for ever and ever.

·4 And f the four and twenty elders, and the four beasts, fell down and worshipped God that sat on the throne, saying, g Amen; Alleluia.

A. M. cir. 4100.
A. D. cir. 96.
Impp. Flavio
Domitiano
Cæs. Aug. et
Nerva.

5 And a voice came out of the throne, saying, h Praise our God, all ye his servants, and ye that fear him, i both small and great.

6 k And I heard as it were the voice of a great multitude, and as the voice of many waters, and as the voice of mighty thunderings, saying, Alleluia: for l the Lord God Omnipotent reigneth.

7 Let us be glad and rejoice, and give honour to him: for m the marriage of the Lamb is come, and his wife hath made herself ready.

8 And n to her was granted that she should be arrayed in fine linen, clean and o white:

---

a Chap. xi. 15.——b Chap. iv. 11; vii. 10, 12; xii. 10.——c Ch. xv. 3; xvi. 7.——d Deut. xxxii. 43; chap. vi. 10; xviii. 20. e Isa. xxxiv. 10; chap. xiv. 11; xviii. 9, 18.——f Chap. iv. 4, 6, 10; v. 14.——g 1 Chron. xvi. 36; Neh. v. 13; viii. 6; chap. v. 14.——h Psa. cxxxiv. 1; cxxxv. 1.

i Chap. xi. 18; xx. 12.——k Ezek. i. 24; xliii. 2; chap. xiv. 2. l Chapter xi. 15, 17; xii. 10; xxi. 22.——m Matt. xxii. 2; xxv. 10; 2 Cor. xi. 2; Eph. v. 32; chapter xxi. 2, 9.——n Psa. xlv. 13, 14; Ezekiel xvi. 10; chapter iii. 18.——o Or, *bright*.

NOTES ON CHAP. XIX.

Verse 1. *I heard a great voice of much people in heaven*] The idolatrous city being destroyed, and the blood of the martyred saints being avenged, there is a universal joy among the redeemed of the Lord, which they commence with the word יה הללו Hallelu-Yah, *praise ye Jah* or *Jehovah;* which the *Septuagint,* and St. John from them, put into Greek letters thus: Αλληλουϊα, *Allelou-ia,* a form of praise which the heathens appear to have borrowed from the Jews, as is evident from their *pæans,* or hymns in honour of Apollo, which began and ended with ελελευ ιη, *eleleu ie;* a mere corruption of the Hebrew words. It is worthy of remark that the *Indians of North America* have the same word in their religious worship, and use it in the same sense. " In their places of worship, or *beloved square,* they dance sometimes for a whole night always in a bowing posture, and frequently singing *halleluyah Ye ho wah;* praise ye Yah, Ye ho vah :" probably the true pronunciation of the Hebrew יהוה, which we call *Jehovah.* See Adair's History of the American Indians.

Salvation] He is the sole author of *deliverance from sin;* the *glory* of this belongs to him, the *honour* should be ascribed to him, and his *power* is that alone by which it is effected.

Verse 2. *For true and righteous*] His judgments displayed in supporting his followers, and punishing his enemies, are *true*—according to his *predictions;* and *righteous,* being all according to infinite *justice* and *equity.*

Verse 3. *Her smoke rose up*] There was, and shall

be, a *continual evidence* of God's judgments executed on this *great whore* or *idolatrous city;* nor shall it ever be restored.

Verse 4. *The four and twenty elders*] The true Church of the Lord Jesus converted from among the Jews. See chap. iv. 10; v. 14.

Verse 5. *Praise our God, &c.*] Let all, whether redeemed from among *Jews* or *Gentiles,* give glory to God.

Verse 6. *The voice of a great multitude*] This is the catholic or universal Church of God gathered from among the *Gentiles.*

The Lord God Omnipotent reigneth.] Εβασιλευσε Κυριος ο Θεος ο παντοκρατωρ. Many excellent MSS., most of the *versions,* with *Andreas* and *Arethas,* the two most ancient commentators on this book, add ημων, *our,* after ο Θεος· and according to this the text reads emphatically thus. OUR Lord God, *the Almighty, reigneth.* What consolation to every genuine Christian that HIS *Lord* and *God* is the *Almighty,* and that this Almighty never trusts the reins of the government of the universe out of his hands! What therefore has his Church to fear?

Verse 7. *The marriage of the Lamb is come*] The meaning of these figurative expressions appears to be this: After this overthrow of idolatry and superstition, and the discomfiture of antichrist, there will be a more glorious state of Christianity than ever was before.

Verse 8. *Arrayed in fine linen*] A prediction that the Church should become more *pure* in her *doctrines,* more *pious* in her *experience,* and more *righteous* in her *conduct,* than she had ever been from her formation.

2

A. M. cir. 4100.
A. D. cir. 96.
Impp. Flavio
Domitiano
Cæs. Aug. et
Nerva.

ᵖ for the fine linen is the righteousness of saints.

9 And he saith unto me, Write, ᑫ Blessed *are* they which are called unto the marriage supper of the Lamb. And he saith unto me, ʳ These are the true sayings of God.

10 And ˢ I fell at his feet to worship him. And he said unto me, ᵗ See *thou do it* not : I am thy fellow servant, and of thy brethren ᵘ that have the testimony of Jesus : worship God : for the testimony of Jesus is the spirit of prophecy.

11 ᵛ And I saw heaven opened, and behold

A. M. cir. 4100
A. D. cir. 96.
Impp. Flavio
Domitiano
Cæs. Aug. et
Nerva.

ʷ a white horse ; and he that sat upon him *was* called ˣ Faithful and True ; and ʸ in righteousness he doth judge and make war.

12 ᶻ His eyes *were* as a flame of fire, ᵃ and on his head *were* many crowns ; ᵇ and he had a name written, that no man knew but he himself :

13 ᶜ And he *was* clothed with a vesture dipped in blood : and his name is called ᵈ The Word of God.

14 ᵉ And the armies *which were* in heaven followed him upon white horses, ᶠ clothed in fine linen, white and clean.

15 And ᵍ out of his mouth goeth a sharp

ᵖ Psa. cxxxii. 9.——ᑫ Matthew xxii. 2, 3 ; Luke xiv. 15, 16. ʳ Chap. xxi. 5 ; xxii. 6.——ˢ Chap. xxii. 8.——ᵗ Acts x. 26 ; xiv. 14, 15 ; chap. xxii. 9.——ᵘ 1 John v. 10 ; chap. xii. 17.——ᵛ Chap. xv. 5.——ʷ Chap. vi. 2.——ˣ Chap. iii. 14.——ʸ Isa. xi. 4.

ᶻ Chap. i. 14 ; ii. 18.——ᵃ Chap. vi. 2.——ᵇ Chap. ii. 17 ; ver. 16.——ᶜ Isa. lxiii. 2, 3.——ᵈ John i. 1 ; 1 John v. 7.——ᵉ Chap. xiv. 20.——ᶠ Matt. xxviii. 3 ; chap. iv. 4 ; vii. 9.——ᵍ Isa. xi. 4 ; 2 Thess. ii. 8 ; chap. i. 16 ; ver. 21.

The fine linen here spoken of is not the *righteousness of Christ imputed to believers*, for it is here called *the righteousness of the saints*—that which the grace and Spirit of Christ has wrought in them.

Verse 9. *Blessed are they which are called unto the marriage supper*] This is an evident allusion to the *marriage of the king's son*, Matt. xxii. 2, &c., where the incarnation of our Lord, and the calling of Jews and Gentiles, are particularly pointed out. See the notes there. *Blessed* are all they who hear the Gospel, and are thus invited to lay hold on everlasting life.

Verse 10. *I fell at his feet to worship him.*] Great as this angel was, St. John could not mistake him either for Jesus Christ, or for God the Father ; nor was his prostration intended as an act of *religious worship*. It was merely an act of that sort of reverence which any *Asiatic* would pay to a *superior*. His mistake was, the considering that he was under obligation to the angel for the information which he had now received. This mistake the angel very properly corrects, showing him that it was from God alone this intelligence came, and that to him alone the praise was due.

I am thy fellow servant] No higher in dignity than thyself ; employed by the same God, on the same errand, and with the same testimony ; and therefore not entitled to thy prostration : *worship God*—prostrate thyself to him, and to him give thanks.

The testimony of Jesus is the spirit of prophecy.] As this is a *reason* given by the angel why he should not worship him, the meaning must be this : I, who have received this *spirit of prophecy*, am not superior to thee who hast received the *testimony of Christ*, to preach him among the Gentiles ; for the *commission* containing such a testimony is equal to the *gift of the spirit of prophecy*. Or, the spirit of prophecy is a general testimony concerning Jesus, for he is the *scope* and *design* of the whole *Scripture ; to him gave all the prophets witness*. Take Jesus, his grace, Spirit, and religion out of the Bible, and it has neither *scope*, *design*, *object*, nor *end*.

Verse 11. *A white horse*] This is an exhibition of the triumph of Christ after the destruction of his enemies. The white horse is the emblem of this, and FAITHFUL and TRUE are characters of Christ. See chap. iii. 14.

In righteousness he doth judge and make war.] The wars which *he* wages are from no principle of ambition, lust of power, or extension of conquest and dominion ; they are *righteous* in their *principle* and in their *object*. And this is perhaps what no earthly potentate could ever say.

Verse 12. *His eyes were as a flame of fire*] To denote the piercing and all-penetrating nature of his wisdom.

On his head were many crowns] To denote the multitude of his conquests, and the extent of his dominion.

A name written, that no man knew] This is a reference to what the rabbins call the *shem hammephorash*, or *tetragrammaton*, יהוה YHVH ; or what we call *Jehovah*. This name the Jews never attempt to pronounce : when they meet with it in the Bible, they read אדני *Adonai* for it ; but, to a man, they all declare that *no man can pronounce it ;* and that the *true pronunciation* has *been lost*, at least since the Babylonish captivity ; and that *God alone knows its true interpretation and pronunciation*. This, therefore, is *the name which no man knew but he himself*.

Verse 13. *He was clothed with a vesture dipped in blood*] To show that he was just come from recent slaughter. The description is taken from Isa. lxiii. 2, 3, where Judas Maccabæus, or some other conqueror, is described.

The Word of God.] Written in the Targum, and in other Jewish writings, מימרא דיי *meimera daiya*, " the word of Jehovah ;" by which they always mean a *person*, and not a *word spoken*. See the notes on John i. 1, &c.

Verse 14. *The armies which were in heaven*] Angels and saints over whom Jesus Christ is *Captain*.

Clothed in fine linen] All holy, pure, and righteous.

Verse 15. *Out of his mouth goeth a sharp sword*]

A. M. cir. 4100.
A. D. cir. 96.
Impp. Flavio.
Domitiano
Cæs. Aug. et
Nerva.

sword, that with it he should smite the nations: and [h] he shall rule them with a rod of iron: and [i] he treadeth the winepress

of the fierceness and wrath of Almighty God.

16 And [k] he hath on *his* vesture and on his thigh a name written,

A. M. cir. 4100
A. D. cir. 96.
Impp. Flavio.
Domitiano
Cæs. Aug. et
Nerva.

---

[h] Psa. ii. 9; chap. ii. 27; xii. 5. —— [i] Isa. lxiii. 3; chap. xiv. 19, 20.——[k] Ver. 12.

See on chap. i. 16. This appears to mean the word of the Gospel, by which his enemies are confounded, and his friends supported and comforted.

With a rod of iron] He shall execute the severest judgment on the opposers of his truth.

He treadeth the winepress] As the grapes are trodden to express the juice, so his enemies shall be bruised and beaten, so that their life's blood shall be poured out.

Verse 16. *On* his *vesture and on his thigh a ,name written*] Dr. Dodd has well observed on this passage, that " it appears to have been an ancient custom among several nations to adorn the images of their deities, princes, victors at public games, and other eminent persons, with *inscriptions*, expressing either the character of the persons, their names, or some other circumstance which might contribute to their honour; and to that custom the description here given of Christ may possibly have some allusion.

" There are several such images yet extant, with an inscription written either on the *garment*, or on one of the *thighs*, or on that part of the garment which was over the thigh; and probably this is the meaning of the apostle. And as these inscriptions are placed on the *upper garment*, Grotius seems very justly to have explained the words επι το ιματιον, by *his imperial robe*, that his power in this victory might be conspicuous to all. But as a farther confirmation of this sense of the passage it may not be improper here to describe briefly several remarkable figures of this sort, which are still extant." This description I shall give from my own examination.

1. HERODOTUS, Euterpe, lib. ii. p. 127, edit. *Gale*, speaking of the actions of *Sesostris*, and of the images he set up in the countries which he conquered, has the following words: Εισι δε περι Ιωνιην δυο τυποι εν πετρησι εγκεκολαμμενοι τουτου του ανδρος, κ. τ. λ. " Two images likewise of this man are seen in Ionia, on the way that leads from Ephesus to Phocæa, and from Sardis to Smyrna. The figure is five palms in height; in his right hand he holds a *dart*, in his left a *bow*, armed after the manner of the Egyptians and Ethiopians. On a line drawn across the breast, from one shoulder to the other, are these words, written in Egyptian hieroglyphics: Εγω τηνδε την χωρην ωμοισι τοισι εμοισι εκτησαμην· 'I obtained this country by these my shoulders;'" i. e., by my own power.

2. In the *Etruria Regalis* of Dempster, in the appendix at the end of vol. ii., there is a beautiful female figure of brass, about twelve inches high, the hair gracefully plaited, and the head adorned with a diadem. She has a *tunic* without sleeves, and over that a sort of *pallium*. On the outside of the *right thigh*, close to the tunic, and probably *on* it, in the original, is an *inscription* in Etruscan characters. What these import I cannot say. Dempster has given a general explanation of the *image* in the appendix to the above

volume, p. 108. The plate itself is the eighty-third of the work.

3. There are two other images found in the same author, vol. i., p. 91, tab. xxiv.; the first is *naked*, with the exception of a short loose jupe, or petticoat, which goes round the loins, and over the left arm. On the *left thigh* of this image there is an *inscription* in Etruscan characters. The second has a similar jupe, but much longer, which extends to the calf of the leg, and is supported over the bended left arm. Over the *right thigh*, on this vesture, there is an Etruscan *inscription* in two lines.

4. MONTFAUCON, *Antiquité Expliquée*, vol. iii., part 2, p. 268, has introduced an account of two fine images, which are represented tab. CLVII. The first is a warrior entirely naked, except a collar, one bracelet, and boots. On his *left thigh*, extending from the groin to a little below the knee, is an *inscription* in very ancient Etruscan characters, in two lines, but the import is unknown.

The second is a small figure of brass, about six inches long, with a loose tunic, which is suspended from the left shoulder down to the calf of the legs. On this tunic, *over the left thigh*, is an *inscription* (perhaps) in very ancient *Latin* characters, but in the *Etruscan* language, as the learned author conjectures. It is in one line, but what it means is equally unknown.

5. In the same work, p. 269, tab. CLVIII., another Etruscan *warrior* is represented entirely naked; on the *left thigh* is the following words in uncial Greek letters, ΚΑΦΙΣΟΔΩΡΟΣ, and on the *right thigh*, ΑΙΣ-ΧΛΑΜΙΟΥ, *i. e.*, " Kaphisodorus, the son of Aischlamius." All these inscriptions are written *longitudinally* on the thigh.

6. GRUTER, vol. iii., p. DCCCCLXXXIX, sub. tit. *Affectus Servorum et Libertinorum inter se, et in suos*, gives us the figure of a naked warrior, with his left hand on an axe, the end of whose helve rests on the ground, with the following *inscription* on the inside of his *left thigh*, longitudinally written, as in all other cases:—

A. POBLICIUS. D. L. ANTIOC.
TI. BARBIUS. Q. P. L. TIBER.

7. The *rabbins* say, that " God gave to the Israelites a *sword*, on which the *ineffable name* יהוה *Yehovah* was *inscribed*; and as long as they held that sword the angel of death had no power over them." *Shemoth Rabba*, sec. 51, fol. 143, 2. *Bemidbar Rabba*, sec. 12, fol. 214, 2.

In the latter tract, sec. 16, fol. 232, 3, and in *Rab. Tanchum*, fol. 66, mention is made of the *guardian angels* of the Israelites, who were *clothed with purple vestments*, on which was *inscribed* שם המפורש *shem hammephorash*, the ineffable name. See more in *Schoettgen*.

8. But what comes nearer to the point, in reference to the *title* given here to Christ, is what is re-

2

A. M. cir. 4100.
A. D. cir. 96.
Impp. Flavio
Domitiano
Cæs. Aug. et
Nerva.

[1] KING of KINGS, and LORD of LORDS.

17 And I saw an angel standing in the sun; and he cried with a loud voice, saying [m] to all the fowls that fly in the midst of heaven, [n] Come and gather yourselves together unto the supper of the great God ;

18 [o] That ye may eat the flesh of kings, and the flesh of captains, and the flesh of mighty men, and the flesh of horses, and of them that sit on them, and the flesh of all *men, both* free and bond, both small and great.

19 [p] And I saw the beast, and the kings of the earth, and their armies, gathered together to make war against him that sat on the horse, and against his army.

A. M. cir. 4100.
A. D. cir. 96.
Impp. Flavio
Domitiano
Cæs. Aug. et
Nerva.

20 [q] And the beast was taken, and with him the false prophet that wrought miracles before him, with which he deceived them that had received the mark of the beast, and [r] them that worshipped his image. [s] These both were cast alive into a lake of fire [t] burning with brimstone.

21 And the remnant [u] were slain with the sword of him that sat upon the horse, which *sword* proceeded out of his mouth : [v] and all the fowls [w] were filled with their flesh.

---

[l] Dan. ii. 47; 1 Tim. vi. 15; chapter xvii. 14.——[m] Ver. 21. [n] Ezek. xxxix. 17.——[o] Ezek. xxxix. 18, 20.——[p] Chap. xvi. 16; xvii. 13, 14.——[q] Chap. xvi. 13, 14.

[r] Chap. xiii. 12, 15.——[s] Chapter xx. 10; see Daniel vii. 11. [t] Chap. xiv. 10; xxi. 8.——[u] Ver. 15.——[v] Ver. 17, 18.——[w] Ch. xvii. 16.

---

lated of *Sesostris* by Diodorus *Siculus,* lib. i. c. 55, p. 166, edit. *Bipont,* of whom he says : " Having pushed his conquests as far as Thrace, he erected pillars, on which were the following words in Egyptian hieroglyphics : Τηνδε την χωραν ὁπλοις κατεστρεψατο τοις ἑαυτου Βασιλευς Βασιλεων, και Δεσποτης Δεσποτων, Σεσοωσις·" *This province, Sesoosis,* (Sesostris,) King of kings and Lord of lords, *conquered by his own arms.* This inscription is conceived almost in the *words* of St. John. Now the Greek historian did not *borrow* the words from the apostle, as he died in the reign of Augustus, about the time of our Lord's incarnation. This cannot be the same inscription mentioned above by *Herodotus,* the one being in Ionia, the other in Thrace ; but as he erected several of those pillars or images, probably a nearly similar inscription was found on each.

9. This custom seems to have been common among the ancient *Egyptians.* Inscriptions are frequently found on the images of *Isis, Osiris, Anubis,* &c., at the *feet,* on the *head,* on the *back,* on the *girdle,* &c., &c. Eight of those ancient images in my own collection abound with these inscriptions.

1. *Osiris,* four inches and a quarter high, standing on a throne, all covered over with *hieroglyphics* exquisitely engraved.

2. *Anubis,* six inches high, with a tiara, on the back of which is cut ΛΕΓΟΡΝΥΘ, in uncial Greek characters.

3. The *Cercopithecus,* seven inches long, sitting on a pedestal, and at his feet, in the same characters, CAΔEO.

4. An *Isis,* about eight inches high, on her back ΔΡΥΓΟ.

5. Ditto, seven inches, beautifully cut, standing, holding a serpent in her left hand, and at her feet ΕΤΑΠΥΓΙ.

6. Ditto, five inches and a quarter, round whose girdle is ΠΙΕΥCVΔΙ ; but part of this inscription appears to be hidden under her arms, which are extended by her side.

7. Ditto, five inches high, hooded, with a loose stola, down the *back* of which are seven lines of Greek uncial characters, but nearly obliterated.

8. Ditto, four inches high, with a *girdle* going round the back immediately under the arms, the front of which is hidden under a sort of a stomacher ; on the part that appears are these characters, CENΔΔ. These may be all intended as a kind of *abrasaxas* or tutelary deities ; and I give this notice of them, and the inscriptions upon them, partly in illustration of the text, and partly to engage my learned and antiquarian readers in attempts to decipher them. I would have given the *Etruscan* characters on the other images described above, but have no method of imitating them except by an engraving.

As these kinds of inscriptions on the *thigh,* the *garments,* and *different parts of the body,* were in use among different nations, to express character, conduct, qualities, and *conquests,* we may rest assured that to them St. John alludes when he represents our sovereign Lord with an *inscription upon his vesture* and *upon his thigh ;* and had we not found it a custom among other nations, we should have been at a loss to account for its introduction and meaning here.

Verse 17. *An angel standing in the sun*] Exceedingly luminous ; every part of him emitting rays of light. From this representation, Milton has taken his description of *Uriel,* the angel of the sun. Paradise Lost, b. iii. l. 648 :—

" The Archangel Uriel, one of the *seven*
Who, in God's presence, nearest to his throne
Stands ready at command, and are his eyes
That run through all the heavens, or down to the earth
Bears his swift errands over moist and dry,
Over sea and land."

All the fowls that fly] The carcasses of God's enemies shall be food for all the fowls of heaven. This is according to a Jewish tradition, *Synopsis Sohar,* p. 114, n. 25 : " In the time when God shall execute vengeance for the people of Israel, he shall feed all the

2

beasts of the earth for twelve months with their flesh; and all the fowls for seven years." It is well known that both beasts and birds of prey are accustomed to frequent fields of battle, and live upon the slain.

Verse 18. *That ye may eat the flesh of kings*] There shall be a universal destruction; the kings, generals, captains, and all their host, shall be slain.

Verse 19. *I saw the beast*] See the notes on chapters xii., xiii., and xvii.

Verse 20. *And the beast was taken, and—the false prophet*] See the notes on chap. xvii. 8, &c.

That worshipped his image.] The *beast* has been represented as the *Latin empire*; the *image of the beast*, the *popes of Rome*; and the *false prophet*, the *papal clergy*.

Were cast alive into a lake of fire] Were discomfited when *alive*—in the zenith of their power, and destroyed with an utter destruction.

Verse 21. *With the sword of him that sat upon the horse*] He who sat on the white horse is Christ; and his *sword* is his *word*—the unadulterated *Gospel*.

CHAPTER XX.

An angel binds Satan a thousand years, and shuts him up in the bottomless pit, 1–3. They who were beheaded for the testimony of Jesus, who have part in the first resurrection, and shall reign with Christ a thousand years, 4–6. When the thousand years are expired, Satan shall be loosed out of his prison, shall go forth and deceive the nations, and shall gather Gog and Magog from the four corners of the earth, 7, 8. These shall besiege the holy city; but fire shall come down from heaven and consume them, and they and the devil be cast into a lake of fire, 9 10. The great white throne, and the dead, small and great, standing before God, and all judged according to their works, 11, 12. The sea, death, and hades, give up their dead, and are destroyed; and all not found in the book of life are cast into the lake of fire, 13–15.

A. M. cir. 4100.
A. D. cir. 96.
Impp. Flavio
Domitiano
Cæs. Aug. et
Nerva.

AND I saw an angel come down from heaven, [a] having the key of the bottomless pit and a great chain in his hand.

2 And he laid hold on [b] the dragon, that old serpent, which is the Devil, and Satan, [c] and bound him a thousand years,

3 And cast him into the bottomless pit, and shut him up, and [d] set a seal upon

A. M. cir. 4100.
A. D. cir. 96.
Impp. Flavio
Domitiano
Cæs. Aug. et
Nerva.

---

[a] Chap. i. 18; ix. 1.——[b] Ch. xii. 9; see 2 Pet. ii. 4; Jude 6.——[c] Tobit viii. 3.——[d] Dan. vi. 17.

NOTES ON CHAP. XX.

Verse 1. *An angel came down from heaven*] One of the executors of the Divine justice, who receives criminals, and keeps them in prison, and delivers them up only to be tried and executed.

The *key* of the prison and the *chain* show who he is; and as the *chain* was *great*, it shows that the culprit was impeached of no ordinary crimes.

Verse 2. *The dragon*] See the notes on chap. xii. 9.

That old serpent, which is the Devil, and Satan] He who is called the *old serpent* is the DEVIL—the *calumniator*, and SATAN—the *opposer*. He who supposes that the term *old serpent* here plainly proves that the creature that tempted our first parents was actually a *snake*, must enjoy his opinion; and those who can receive such a saying, why let them receive it. *Selah.*

A thousand years] In what this *binding* of Satan consists, who can tell? How many visions have been seen on this subject both in ancient and modern times! This, and what is said ver. 3, 4, and 5, no doubt refers to a time in which the influence of Satan will be greatly restrained, and the true Church of God enjoy great prosperity, which shall endure for a long time. But it is not likely that the number, a thousand years, is to be taken literally here, and *year* symbolically and figuratively in all the book beside. The doctrine of the *millennium*, or of the saints reigning on earth a thousand years, with Christ for their head, has been illustrated and defended by many Christian writers, both among the ancients and moderns. Were I to give a collection of the conceits of the primitive fathers on this subject, my readers would have little reason to applaud my pains. It has long been the idle expectation of many persons that the millennium, in *their* sense, was at hand; and its commencement has been expected in every century since the Christian era. It has been fixed for several different years, during the short period of my own life! I believed those predictions to be vain, and I have lived to see them such. Yet there is no doubt that the earth is in a state of progressive moral improvement; and that the light of true religion is shining more copiously everywhere, and will shine more and more to the perfect day. But *when* the religion of Christ will be at its meridian of light and heat, we know not. In each believer this may speedily take place; but probably no such time shall ever appear, in which evil shall be wholly banished from the earth, till after the day of judgment, when the earth having been burnt up, a new heaven and a new earth shall be produced out of the ruins of the old, by the mighty power of God: righteousness alone shall dwell in them. The phraseology of the apostle here seems partly taken from the ancient prophets, and partly *rabbinical*; and it is from the Jewish use of those terms that we are to look for their interpretation.

Verse 3. *He should deceive the nations no more*] Be unable to blind men with superstition and idolatry as he had formerly done.

A. M. cir. 4100.
A. D. cir. 96.
Impp. Flavio
Domitiano
Cæs. Aug. et
Nerva.

him, e that he should deceive the nations no more, till the thousand years should be fulfilled : and after that he must be loosed a little season.

4 And I saw f thrones, and they sat upon them, and g judgment was given unto them : and *I saw* h the souls of them that were beheaded for the witness of Jesus, and for the word of God, and i which had not worshipped the beast, k neither his image, neither had received *his* mark upon their foreheads, or in

their hands ; and they lived and l reigned with Christ a thousand years.

5 But the rest of the dead lived not again until the thousand years were finished. This *is* the first resurrection.

6 Blessed and holy *is* he that hath part in the first resurrection : on such m the second death hath no power, but they shall be n priests of God and of Christ, o and shall reign with him a thousand years.

7 And when the thousand years are expired,

A. M. cir. 4100.
A. D. cir. 96.
Impp. Flavio
Domitiano
Cæs. Aug. et
Nerva.

---

e Chap. xvi. 14, 16 ; ver. 8.——f Dan. vii. 9, 22, 27 ; Matt. xix. 28 ; Luke xxii. 30.——g 1 Cor. vi. 2, 3.——h Chapter vi. 9. i Chap. xiii. 12.

k Chap. xiii. 15, 16.——l Rom. viii. 17 ; 2 Tim. ii. 12 ; chap. v. 10.——m Chap. ii. 11 ; xxi. 8.——n Isa. lxi. 6 ; 1 Pet. ii. 9 ; chap. i. 6 ; v. 10.——o Ver. 4.

Verse 4. *I saw thrones*] Christianity established in the earth, the kings and governors being all Christians.

Reigned with Christ a thousand years.] I am satisfied that this period should not be taken *literally*. It may signify that there shall be a long and undisturbed state of Christianity ; and so universally shall the Gospel spirit prevail, that it will appear as if Christ reigned upon earth ; which will in effect be the case, because his Spirit shall rule in the hearts of men ; and in this time the martyrs are represented as living again ; their testimony being revived, and the truth for which they died, and which was confirmed by their blood, being now everywhere prevalent. As to the term *thousand years*, it is a mystic number among the Jews. *Midrash Tillin*, in Psa. xc. 15, *Make us glad according to the days* wherein *thou hast afflicted us*, adds, " by Babylon, Greece, and the Romans ; and in the days of the Messiah. How many are the days of the Messiah? Rab. *Elieser*, the son of R. Jose, of Galilee, said, The days of the Messiah are *a thousand years.*"

Sanhedrin, fol. 92, 1, cited by the *Aruch*, under the word ארק says : " There is a tradition in the house of Elias, that the righteous, whom the holy blessed God shall raise from the dead, shall not return again to the dust ; but for the space of *a thousand years*, in which the holy blessed God shall renew the world, they shall have wings like the wings of eagles, and shall fly above the waters." It appears therefore that this phraseology is purely rabbinical. Both the Greeks and Latins have the same form of speech in speaking on the state of the righteous and wicked after death. There is something like this in the *Republic of Plato*, book x., p. 322, edit. Bip., where, speaking of *Erus, the son of Armenius*, who came to life after having been dead twelve days, and who described the states of departed souls, asserting " that some were obliged to make a long peregrination under the earth before they arose to a state of happiness, ειναι δε την πορειαν χιλιετη, *for it was a journey of a thousand years,*" he adds, " that, as the life of man is rated at a hundred years, those who have been wicked suffer in the other world a *tenfold* punishment, and therefore their punishment lasts *a thousand years.*"

A similar doctrine prevailed among the Romans ; whether they borrowed it from the Greeks, or from the rabbinical Jews, we cannot tell.

Thus *Virgil*, speaking of the punishment of the wicked in the infernal regions, says :——.

Has omnes, ubi MILLE *rotam volvere per annos*,
Lethæum ad fluvium Deus evocat agmine magno :
Scilicet immemores supera ut convexa revisant,
Rursus et incipiant in corpora velle reverti
                         ÆN., lib. vi., 748.

" But when a *thousand rolling years* are past,
So long their dreary punishment shall last,
Whole droves of spirits, by the driving god,
Are led to drink the deep Lethean flood
In large, forgetful draughts, to sleep the cares
Of their past labours and their irksome years ;
That, unremembering of its former pain,
The soul may clothe itself with flesh again."

How the apostle applies this general tradition, or in what sense he may use it, who can tell?

Verse 5. *The rest of the dead lived not again*] It is generally supposed from these passages that all who have been *martyred* for the truth of God shall be raised a thousand years before the other dead, and reign on earth with Christ during that time, after which the dead in general shall be raised ; but this also is very doubtful.

Verse 6. *Blessed*] Μακαριος· Happy. *And holy ;* he *was* holy, and therefore he suffered for the testimony of Jesus in the time when nothing but *holiness* was called to such a trial.

The first resurrection] Supposed to be that of the *martyrs*, mentioned above.

The second death] Punishment in the eternal world ; such is the acceptation of the phrase among the ancient Jews.

Hath no power] Ουκ εχει εξουσιαν· Hath no authority—no dominion over him. This is also a rabbinical mode of speech. In *Erubin*, fol. 19, 1 ; *Chagiga*, fol. 27, 1 : " Res Lakish said, The *fire of hell* hath *no power* over an Israelite who sins. Rab. Elioser says, The *fire of hell* hath *no power* over the disciples of the wise men."

Verse 7. *Satan shall be loosed*] How can this

A. M. cir. 4100.
A. D. cir. 96.
Impp. Flavio
Domitiano
Cæs. Aug. et
Nerva.

[p] Satan shall be loosed out of his prison,

8 And shall go out [q] to deceive the nations which are in the four quarters of the earth, [r] Gog and Magog, [s] to gather them together to battle: the number of whom *is* as the sand of the sea.

9 [t] And they went up on the breadth of the earth, and compassed the camp of the saints about, and the beloved city: and fire came down from God out of heaven, and devoured them.

10 [u] And the devil that deceived them was cast into the lake of fire and brimstone, [v] where

the beast and the false prophet *are,* and [w] shall be tormented day and night for ever and ever.

A. M. cir. 4100
A. D. cir. 96.
Impp. Flavio
Domitiano
Cæs. Aug. et
Nerva.

11 And I saw a great white throne, and him that sat on it, from whose face [x] the earth and the heaven fled away; [y] and there was found no place for them.

12 And I saw the dead, [z] small and great, stand before God; [a] and the books were opened: and another [b] book was opened, which is *the book* of life: and the dead were judged out of those things which were written in the books, [c] according to their works.

---

[p] Ver. 2.——[q] Ver. 3, 10.——[r] Ezek. xxxviii. 2; xxxix. 1.
[s] Chap. xvi. 14.——[t] Isa. viii. 8; Ezek. xxxviii. 9, 16.——[u] Ver. 8.——[v] Chap. xix. 20.——[w] Chap. xiv. 10, 11.——[x] 2 Pet. iii. 7, 10, 11; chap. xxi. 1.

[y] Dan. ii. 35.——[z] Chap. xix. 5.——[a] Dan. vii. 10.——[b] Psa. lxix. 28; Dan. xii. 1; Phil. iv. 3; chap. iii. 5; xiii. 8; xxi. 27. [c] Jer. xvii. 10; xxxii. 19; Matt. xvi. 27; Rom. ii. 6; chap. ii. 23; xxii. 12; ver. 13.

---

bear any kind of *literal* interpretation? Satan is bound a thousand years, and the earth is in peace; righteousness flourishes, and Jesus Christ alone reigns. This state of things may continue for ever if the imprisonment of Satan be *continued.* Satan, however, is loosed at the end of the thousand years, and goes out and deceives the nations, and peace is banished from the face of the earth, and a most dreadful war takes place, &c., &c. These can be only symbolical representations, utterly incapable of the sense generally put upon them.

Verse 8. *Gog and Magog*] This seems to be almost literally taken from the *Jerusalem Targum,* and that of *Jonathan ben Uzziel,* on Num. xi. 26. I shall give the words at length: "And there were two men left in the camp, the name of the one was Eldad, the name of the other was Medad, and on them the spirit of prophecy rested. Eldad prophesied and said, 'Behold, Moses the prophet, the scribe of Israel, shall be taken from this world; and Joshua the son of Nun, captain of the host, shall succeed him.' Medad prophesied and said, 'Behold quails shall arise out of the sea, and be a stumbling block to Israel.' Then they both prophesied together, and said, 'In the very end of time Gog and Magog and their army shall come up against Jerusalem, and they shall fall by the hand of the King Messiah; and for seven whole years shall the children of Israel light their fires with the wood of their warlike engines, and they shall not go to the wood nor cut down any tree.'" In the Targum of *Jonathan ben Uzziel,* on the same place, the same account is given; only the latter part, that is, the conjoint prophecy of Eldad and Medad, is given more *circumstantially,* thus "And they both prophesied together, and said, 'Behold, a king shall come up from the land of Magog in the last days, and shall gather the kings together, and leaders clothed with armour, and all people shall obey them; and they shall wage war in the land of Israel against the children of the captivity, but the hour of lamentation has been long prepared for them, for they shall be slain by the *flame of fire which shall proceed from under the throne of glory,* and their

dead carcasses shall fall on the mountains of the land of Israel; and all the wild beasts of the field, and the wild fowl of heaven, shall come and devour their carcasses; and afterwards *all the dead of Israel shall rise again* to life, and shall enjoy the delights prepared for them from the beginning, and shall receive the reward of their works.'"

This account seems most evidently to have been copied by St. John, but how he intended it to be applied is a question too difficult to be solved by the skill of man; yet both the account in the rabbins and in St. John is founded on Ezek. chap. xxxviii. and xxxix. The rabbinical writings are full of accounts concerning *Gog* and *Magog,* of which *Wetstein* has made a pretty large collection in his notes on this place. Under these names the enemies of God's truth are generally intended.

Verse 9. *The beloved city*] Primarily, Jerusalem, typically, the Christian Church.

Verse 10. *And the devil—was cast into the lake*] Before Satan was *bound,* that is, his power was curtailed and restrained; now, he is *cast into the lake of fire,* his power being *totally* taken away.

Verse 11. *A great white throne*] Refulgent with glorious majesty.

Him that sat on it] The indescribable Jehovah.

From whose face the earth and the heaven fled away] Even the brightness of his countenance dissolved the universe, and annihilated the laws by which it was governed. This is a very majestic figure, and finely expressed.

There was found no place for them.] The glorious majesty of God filling all things, and being all in all.

Verse 12. *The dead, small and great*] All ranks, degrees, and conditions of men. This description seems to refer to Dan. vii. 9, 10.

And the books were opened] See Dan. xii. 1. "Rab Jehuda said: All the actions of men, whether good or bad, *are written in a book,* and of all they shall give account."—*Sohar* Gen., fol. 79, col. 298. "How careful should men be to shun vice, and to act uprightly before the holy blessed God, seeing there are

2

A. M. cir. 4100.
A. D. cir. 96.
Impp. Flavio
Domitiano
Cæs. Aug. et
Nerva.

13 And the sea gave up the dead which were in it; and ^d death and ^e hell delivered up the dead which were in them; ^f and they were judged every man according to their works.

14 And ^g death and hell were cast into the lake of fire. ^h This is the second death.

15 And whosoever was not found written in the book of life ⁱ was cast into the lake of fire.

A. M. cir. 4100.
A. D. cir. 96.
Impp. Flavio
Domitiano
Cæs. Aug. et
Nerva.

---

^d Chap. vi. 8.——^e Or, *the grave.*——^f Ver. 12.

^g 1 Cor. xv. 26, 54, 55.——^h Ver. 6; ch. xxi. 8.——ⁱ Ch. xix. 20.

---

so many which go throughout the earth, see the works of men, testify of them, and *write them in a book !*"—Ibid., fol. 105, col. 417.

" In the first day of the new year the holy blessed God sits that he may judge the world; and all men, without exception, give an account of themselves; and *the books of the living and the dead are opened.*"— *Sohar Chadash,* fol. 19, 1.

The books mentioned here were the books of the *living* and the *dead,* or the *book of life* and the *book of death :* that is, the account of the good and evil actions of men; the former leading to *life,* the latter to *death.* St. John evidently alludes here to Dan. vii. 10, on which the rabbinical account of the books appears to be founded. The expressions are *figurative* in both.

According to their works.] And according to their *faith* also, for their *works* would be the proof whether their *faith* were *true* or *false;* but faith exclusively could be no rule in such a procedure.

Verse 13. *The sea gave up the dead*] Those who had been drowned in it; and those millions slain in naval contests, who had no other grave.

And death] All who died by any kind of *disease.* Death is here *personified,* and represented as a keeper of defunct human beings; probably no more than *earth* or the *grave* is meant, as properly belonging to the empire of death.

And hell] Ἅιδης, *Hades,* the place of separate spirits. The *sea* and *death* have the *bodies* of all human beings; *hades* has their *spirits.* That they may be judged, and punished or rewarded according to their works, their bodies and souls must be reunited;

hades, therefore, gives up the *spirits;* and the *sea* and the *earth* give up the *bodies.*

Verse 14. *And death and hell were cast into the lake*] Death himself is now abolished, and the *place* for separate spirits no longer needful. All dead bodies and separated souls being rejoined, and no more separation of bodies and souls by death to take place, consequently the existence of these things is no farther necessary.

This is the second death.] The *first death* consisted in the separation of the soul from the body for a season; the second death in the separation of body and soul from God for ever. The first death is that from which there may be a resurrection; the second death is that from which there can be no recovery. By the first the *body* is *destroyed* during *time;* by the second, *body* and *soul* are *destroyed* through *eternity.*

Verse 15. *Written in the book of life*] Only those who had continued faithful unto death were taken to heaven. All whose names were not found in the public registers, who either were not citizens, or whose names had been *erased* from those registers because of crimes against the state, could claim none of those emoluments or privileges which belong to the citizens; so those who either did not belong to the new and spiritual Jerusalem, or who had forfeited their rights and privileges by sin, and had died in that state, *were cast into the lake of fire.*

THIS is the way in which God, at the day of judgment, will proceed with sinners and apostates. Reader, see that thy name be written in the sacred register; and, if written in, see that it never be blotted out.

CHAPTER XXI.

The new heaven and the new earth, 1. *The new Jerusalem,* 2. *God dwells with men; the happy state of his followers,* 3–7. *The wretched state of the ungodly,* 8. *An angel shows John the holy city, the New Jerusalem,* 9, 10. *Her light, wall, gates, and foundations, described,* 11–21. *God and the Lamb are the temple and light of it,* 22, 23. *The nations and kings of the earth bring their glory and honour to it; the gates shall never be shut, nor shall any defilement enter into it,* 24–27.

A. M. cir. 4100.
A. D. cir. 96.
Impp. Flavio
Domitiano
Cæs. Aug. et
Nerva.

AND ^a I saw a new heaven and a new earth: ^b for the first heaven and the first earth were passed away;

and there was no more sea.

2 And I John saw ^c the holy city, new Jerusalem, coming

A. M. cir. 4100.
A. D. cir. 96.
Impp. Flavio
Domitiano
Cæs. Aug. et
Nerva.

---

^a Isaiah lxv. 17; lxvi. 22; 2 Peter iii. 13.——^b Chapter xx. 11.

^c Isa. lii. 1; Gal. iv. 26; Heb. xi. 10; xii. 22; xiii. 14; chap iii. 12 : ver. 10.

NOTES ON CHAP. XXI.

Verse 1. *A new heaven and a new earth*] See the notes on 2 Pet. iii. 13. The ancient Jews believed

that God would renew the heavens and the earth at the end of seven thousand years. The general supposition they founded on Isa. lxv. 17.

A. M. cir. 4100.
A. D. cir. 96.
Impp. Flavio
Domitiano
Cæs. Aug. et
Nerva.

down from God out of heaven, prepared ^d as a bride adorned for her husband.

3 And I heard a great voice out of heaven, saying, Behold, ^e the tabernacle of God *is* with men, and he will dwell with them, and they shall be his people, and God himself shall be with them, *and be* their God.

4 ^f And God shall wipe away all tears from their eyes ; ^g and there shall be no more death, ^h neither sorrow, nor crying, neither shall there be any more pain : for the former things are passed away.

A. M. cir. 4100.
A. D. cir. 96.
Impp. Flavio
Domitiano
Cæs. Aug. et
Nerva.

5 And ⁱ he that sat upon the throne said, ^k Behold, I make all things new. And he said unto me, Write : for ^l these words are true and faithful.

6 And he said unto me, ^m It is done. ⁿ I am Alpha and Omega, the beginning and the end. ^o I will give unto him that is athirst of the fountain of the water of life freely.

7 He that overcometh shall inherit ^p all things ; and ^q I will be his God, and he shall be my son.

8 ^r But the fearful, and unbelieving, and the abominable, and murderers, and whoremongers,

---

^d Isa. liv. 5 ; lxi. 10 ; 2 Cor. xi. 2.——^e Lev. xxvi. 11, 12 ; Ezek. xliii. 7 ; 2 Cor. vi. 16 ; chap. vii. 15.——^f Isa. xxv. 8 ; chap. vii. 17.——^g 1 Cor. xv. 26, 54 ; chapter xx. 14.——^h Isa. xxxv. 10 ; lxi. 3 ; lxv. 19.——ⁱ Chap. iv. 2, 9 ; v. 1 ; xx. 11.——^k Isa. xliii. 19 ; 2 Cor. v. 17.

^l Chap. xix. 9.——^m Chap. xvi. 17.——ⁿ Chap. i. 8 ; xxii. 13. ^o Isa. xii. 3 ; lv. 1 ; John iv. 10, 14 ; vii. 37 ; chapter xxii. 17. ^p Or, *these things.*——^q Zech. viii. 8 ; Heb. viii. 10.——^r 1 Cor. vi. 9, 10 ; Gal. v. 19, 20, 21 ; Eph. v. 5 ; 1 Tim. i. 9 ; Heb. xii. 14 ; chap. xxii. 15.

There was no more sea.] The *sea* no more appeared than did the first *heaven* and *earth.* All was made *new ;* and probably the new sea occupied a different position and was differently distributed, from that of the old sea.

However, with respect to these subjects as they stand in this most figurative book, I must express myself in the words of Calmet : *Vouloir dire quels seront ce nouveau ciel, et cette nouvelle terre, quels seront leurs ornamens et leur qualité, c'est à mon avis la plus grande de toutes les presomptions. En general, ces manieres de parler marquent de très grands changemens dans l'univers.* "To pretend to say what is meant by this new heaven and new earth, and what are their ornaments and qualities, is in my opinion the greatest of all presumptions. In general these figures of speech point out great alternations in the universe."

Verse 2. And I John] The writer of this book ; whether the evangelist and apostle, or John the Ephesian presbyter, has been long doubted in the Church.

New Jerusalem] See the notes on Gal. iv. 24—27. This doubtless means the Christian Church in a state of great prosperity and purity ; but some think eternal blessedness is intended.

Coming down from God] It is a maxim of the ancient Jews that both the tabernacle, and the temple, and Jerusalem itself, came down from heaven. And in *Midrash Hanaalem, Sohar* Gen. fol. 69, col. 271, Rab. Jeremias said, "The holy blessed God shall renew the world, and build Jerusalem, and shall cause it to descend from heaven." Their opinion is, that there is a spiritual temple, a spiritual tabernacle, and a spiritual Jerusalem ; and that none of *these* can be destroyed, because they subsist in their spiritual representatives. See *Schoettgen.*

Verse 3. The tabernacle of God is with men] God, in the most especial manner, dwells among his followers, diffusing his light and life everywhere.

Verse 4. There shall be no more death] Because there shall be a general resurrection. And this is the inference which St. Paul makes from his doctrine of

a general resurrection, 1 Cor. xv. 26, where he says, "The last enemy that shall be destroyed is death." But death cannot be *destroyed* by there being simply no farther death ; death can only be *destroyed* and *annihilated* by a *general resurrection ;* if there be no general resurrection, it is most evident that death will still retain his empire. Therefore, the fact that *there shall be no more death* assures the fact that there shall be a *general resurrection ;* and this also is a proof that, after the resurrection, *there shall be no more death.* See the whole of the note on 1 Cor. xv. 27.

Verse 5. Behold, I make all things new.] As the creation of the world at the beginning was the work of God alone, so this new creation.

These words are true and faithful.] *Truth* refers to the *promise* of these changes ; *faithfulness,* to the *fulfilment* of these promises.

Verse 6. It is done.] All is determined, and shall be fulfilled in due time. The great drama is finished, and what was intended is now completed ; referring to the period alluded to by the angel.

I am Alpha and Omega] See on chap. i. 8.

The fountain of the water of life] See on John iv. 10, 14 ; vii. 37, &c.

The rabbins consider *the fountain of the world to come* as one of the particular blessings of a future state In *Sanhedrim, Aboth R. Nathan,* c. 31, it is said, "He will show them the excellency of the *fountain of the future world,* that they may accurately see and consider, and say, Wo to us ! what good have we lost! and our race is cut off from the face of the earth."

Verse 7. Inherit all things] Here he had no inheritance ; there he shall inherit the kingdom of heaven, and be with God and Christ, and have every possible degree of blessedness.

Verse 8. But the fearful] Δειλοις· Those who, for *fear* of losing *life* or their *property,* either refused to receive the Christian religion, though convinced of its truth and importance ; or, having received it, in times of persecution fell away, not being willing to risk their lives.

And unbelieving] Those who resist against full

A. M. cir. 4100.
A. D. cir. 96.
Impp. Flavio
Domitiano
Cæs. Aug. et
Nerva.

and sorcerers, and idolaters, and all liars, shall have their part in ˢ the lake which burneth with fire and brimstone : which is the second death.

9 And there came unto me one of ᵗ the seven angels, which had the seven vials full of the seven last plagues, and talked with me, saying, Come hither, I will show thee ᵘ the bride, the Lamb's wife.

10 And he carried me away ᵛ in the spirit to a great and high mountain, and showed me ʷ that great city, the holy Jerusalem, descending out of heaven from God,

11 ˣ Having the glory of God : and her light

A. M. cir. 4100
A. D. cir. 96.
Impp. Flavio
Domitiano
Cæs. Aug. et
Nerva.

was like unto a stone most precious, even like a jasper stone, clear as crystal;

12 And had a wall great and high, *and* had ʸ twelve gates, and at the gates twelve angels, and names written thereon, which are *the names* of the twelve tribes of the children of Israel.

13 ᶻ On the east three gates ; on the north three gates ; on the south three gates ; and on the west three gates.

14 And the wall of the city had twelve foundations, and ᵃ in them the names of the twelve apostles of the Lamb.

15 And he that talked with me ᵇ had a golden

ˢ Chap. xx. 14, 15.——ᵗ Chap. xv. 1, 6, 7.——ᵘ Chap. xix. 7 ; ver. 2.——ᵛ Ch. i. 10; xvii. 3.——ʷ Ezek. xlviii. ; ver. 2.——ˣ Ch. xxii. 5 ; ver. 23.

ʸ Ezek. xlviii. 31-34.——ᶻ Ezek. xlviii. 31-34.——ᵃ Matt. xvi. 18; Gal. ii. 9 ; Eph. ii. 20.——ᵇ Ezek. xl. 3 ; Zech. ii. 1 ; chap. xi. 1.

---

evidence. *And* sinners, και ἁμαρτωλοις, is added here by about thirty excellent MSS., and is found in the *Syriac, Arabic*, some of the *Slavonic*, and in *Andreas* and *Arethas*. On this evidence Griesbach has admitted it into the text.

The abominable] Εβδελυγμενοις· Those who are polluted with unnatural lust.

And murderers] Φονευσι· Those who take away the life of man for any cause but the murder of another, and those who hate a brother in their heart.

And whoremongers] Πορνοις· Adulterers, fornicators, whores, prostitutes, and rakes of every description.

Sorcerers] Φαρμακοις· Persons who, by *drugs, philtres, fumigations*, &c., pretend to produce supernatural effects, chiefly by spiritual agency.

Idolaters] Ειδωλολατραις· Those who offer any kind of worship or religious reverence to any thing but God. All *image worshippers* are idolaters in *every sense* of the word.

And all liars] Και πασι τοις ψευδεσι· Every one who speaks contrary to the truth when he knows the truth, and even he who speaks the truth with the *intention to deceive* ; i. e., to persuade a person that a thing is different from what it really is, by telling only a part of the truth, or suppressing some circumstance which would have led the hearer to a different and to the true conclusion. All these shall have their *portion, το μερος*, their *share*, what *belongs to them*, their right, *in the lake which burneth with fire and brimstone. This is the second death*, from which there is no recovery.

Verse 9. *The bride, the Lamb's wife*] The pure and holy Christian Church.

Verse 10. *To a great and high mountain*] That, being *above* this city, he might see every street and lane of it.

The holy Jerusalem] See on ver. 2.

Verse 11. *Having the glory of God*] Instead of the sun and moon, it has the splendour of God to enlighten it.

Unto a stone most precious, even like a jasper stone, clear as crystal.] Among precious stones there are

some even of the same species more valuable than others : for their value is in proportion to their being free from *flaws*, and of a *good water*, i. e., a uniform and brilliant transparency. A *crystal* is perfectly *clear*, the oriental *jasper* is a beautiful *sea-green*. The stone that is here described is represented as a perfectly transparent jasper, being as unclouded as the brightest crystal, and consequently the *most precious* of its species. Nothing can be finer than this description : the light of this city is ever intense, equal, and splendid ; but it is tinged with this *green hue*, in order to make it agreeable to the sight. Nothing is so friendly to the eye as *blue* or *green* ; all other colours fatigue; and, if very intense, injure the eye. These are the colours of the earth and sky, on which the eye of man is to be constantly fixed. To these colours the structure of the eye is adapted ; and the general appearance of the earth and the sky is adapted to this structure.

Verse 12. *Had a wall great and high*] An almighty defence.

Twelve gates] A gate for every tribe of Israel, in the vicinity of which gate that tribe dwelt ; so that in coming in and going out they did not mix with each other. This description of the city is partly taken from Ezek. xlviii. 30-35.

In *Synopsis Sohar*, p. 115, n. 27, it is said : " In the palace of the world to come there are twelve gates, each of which is inscribed with one of the twelve tribes, as that of Reuben, of Simeon, &c. : he, therefore, who is of the tribe of Reuben is received into none of the twelve gates but his own ; and so of the rest."

Verse 13. *On the east three gates*] The city is here represented as standing to the four cardinal points of heaven, and presenting one side to each of these points.

Verse 14. *The wall—had twelve foundations*] Probably twelve stones, one of which served for a *foundation* or *threshold* to each gate ; and on these were inscribed the names of the twelve apostles, to intimate that it was by the *doctrine of the apostles* that souls enter into the Church, and thence into the New Jerusalem.

Verse 15. *Had a golden reed*] Several excellent

2

A. M. cir. 4100.
A. D. cir. 96.
Impp. Flavio
Domitiano
Cæs. Aug. et
Nerva.

reed to measure the city, and the gates thereof, and the wall thereof.

16 And the city lieth four-square, and the length is as large as the breadth: and he measured the city with the reed, twelve thousand furlongs. The length, and the breadth, and the height of it are equal.

17 And he measured the wall thereof, a hundred *and* forty *and* four cubits, *according to* the measure of a man, that is, of the angel.

18 And the building of the wall of it was *of* jasper: and the city *was* pure gold, like unto clear glass.

19 c And the foundations of the wall of the

A. M. cir. 4100.
A. D. cir. 96.
Impp. Flavio
Domitiano
Cæs. Aug. et
Nerva.

---

c Isaiah liv. 11.

MSS. add μετρον, a *measure ;* he had a *measuring rod made of gold.* This account of measuring the city seems to be copied, with variations, from Ezek. xl. 3, &c.

Verse 16. *The city lieth foursquare*] Each side was equal, consequently the length and breadth were equal ; and its *height* is here said to be equal to its length. It is hard to say how this should be understood. It cannot mean the height of the *buildings,* nor of the *walls,* for neither houses nor walls could be twelve thousand furlongs in height; some think this means the distance from the plain country to the place where the city stood. But what need is there of attempting to determine such measures in such a visionary representation ? The quadrangular form intimates its perfection and stability, for the *square* figure was a figure of perfection among the Greeks ; ανηρ τετραγωνος, the *square* or *cubical man,* was, with them, a man of *unsullied integrity,* perfect in all things.

Verse 17. *The wall—a hundred* and *forty* and *four cubits*] This is *twelve,* the number of the apostles, multiplied by itself : for *twelve times twelve* make *one hundred and forty-four.*

The measure of a man, that is, of the angel.] The *cubit,* so called from *cubitus,* the *elbow,* is the measure from the tip of the elbow to the tip of the middle finger, and is generally reckoned at *one foot and a half,* or eighteen inches ; though it appears, from some measurements at the pyramids of Egypt, that the *cubit* was, at least in some cases, twenty-one inches.

By the cubit of a man we may here understand the *ordinary cubit,* and that this was the angel's cubit who appeared in the form of a man. Or suppose we understand the *height* of the man as being here intended, and that this was the length of the measuring rod. Now allowing this *height* and rod to be *six feet,* and that this was intended to have some kind of symbolical reference to the *twelve tribes,* mentioned ver. 12, represented by the twelve gates ; and to the *twelve apostles,* represented by the twelve thresholds or foundations ; then twenty-four, the number of the tribes and apostles, multiplied by *six,* make precisely the number one hundred and forty-four.

Verse 18. *The building of the wall of it was of jasper*] The oriental jasper is exceedingly hard, and almost indestructible. Pillars made of this stone have lasted some thousands of years, and appear to have suffered scarcely any thing from the tooth of time.

Pure gold, like unto clear glass.] Does not this imply that the walls were made of some beautifully bright yellow stone, very highly polished ? This description has been most injudiciously applied to *heaven ;* and in some public discourses, for the comfort and edi-

fication of the pious, we hear of heaven with its *golden walls, golden pavements, gates of pearl,* &c., &c., not considering that nothing of this description was ever intended to be literally understood ; and that gold and jewels can have no place in the spiritual and eternal world. But do not such descriptions as these tend to keep up a fondness for gold and ornaments ? In symbols they are proper ; but construed into realities, they are very improper.

The ancient Jews teach that " when Jerusalem and the temple shall be built, they will be all of *precious stones,* and *pearls,* and *sapphire,* and with *every species of jewels.*"—*Sepher Rasiel Haggadol,* fol. 24, 1.

The same authors divide paradise into seven parts or houses ; the *third* they describe thus : " The third house is built of gold and pure silver, and all *kinds of jewels and pearls.* It is very spacious, and in it all kinds of the good things, either in heaven or earth, are to be found. All kinds of precious things, perfumes, and spiritual virtues, are there planted. In the midst of it is the tree of life, the height of which is five hundred years ; (*i. e.,* it is equal in height to the journey which a man might perform in five hundred years;) and under it dwell Abraham, Isaac, Jacob, the twelve patriarchs, and all that came out of Egypt, and died in the wilderness. Over these Moses and Aaron preside, and teach them the law," &c.—*Yalcut Rubeni,* fol. 13, 4. In the same tract, fol. 182, 1, we find these words : " Know that we have a tradition, that when the Messiah, with the collected captivity, shall come to the land of Israel, in that day the dead in Israel shall rise again ; and in that day the fiery walls of the city of Jerusalem shall descend from heaven, and in that day the temple shall be builded of *jewels and pearls.*"

Verse 19. *The foundations of the wall*] Does not this mean the foundations or *thresholds* of the *gates ?* The gates represented the twelve tribes, ver. 12 ; and these foundations or thresholds, the twelve apostles, ver. 14. There was no entrance into the city but *through those gates,* and none through the gates but *over these thresholds.* The whole of the Mosaic dispensation was the preparation of the Gospel system : without it the Gospel would have no *original ;* without the Gospel, it would have no *reference* nor proper *object.* Every part of the *Gospel* necessarily supposes the *law* and the *prophets.* They are the *gates,* it is the *threshold ;* without the Gospel no person could enter through those gates. The doctrine of Christ crucified, preached by the apostles, gives a solid foundation to stand on ; and we have an *entrance* into the holiest by the blood of Jesus, Heb. x. 19, &c. And

2

A. M. cir. 4100.
A. D. cir. 96.
Impp. Flavio
Domitiano
Cæs. Aug. et
Nerva.

city *were* garnished with all manner of precious stones. The first foundation *was* jasper ; the second, sapphire ; [d] the third, a chalcedony ; the fourth, an emerald ;

20 The fifth, sardonyx ; the sixth, sardius ; the seventh, chrysolyte ; the eighth, beryl ; the ninth, a topaz ; the tenth, a chrysoprasus ; the eleventh, a jacinth ; the twelfth, an amethyst.

21 And the twelve gates *were* twelve pearls ; every several gate was of one pearl : [e] and the

street of the city *was* pure gold, as it were transparent glass.

22 [f] And I saw no temple therein : for the Lord God Almighty and the Lamb are the temple of it.

23 [g] And the city had no need of the sun, neither of the moon, to shine in it : for the glory of God did lighten it, and the Lamb *is* the light thereof.

24 [h] And the nations of them which are saved shall walk in the light of it : and the kings of

A. M. cir. 4100.
A. D. cir. 96.
Impp. Flavio
Domitiano
Cæs. Aug. et
Nerva.

---

[d] Exod. xxiv. 10 ; Ezek. i. 26.——[e] Chapter xxii. 2.——[f] John iv. 23.

[g] Isa. xxiv. 23 ; lx. 19, 20 ; chap. xxii. 5 ; ver. 11.——[h] Isa. lx. 3, 5, 11 ; lxvi. 12 ; Tobit xiii. 11.

---

in reference to this we are said to be *built on the* FOUNDATION *of the* APOSTLES *and prophets, Jesus Christ himself being the chief corner stone,* Eph. ii. 20.

The first foundation was *jasper*] A stone very hard, some species of which are of a *sea-green* colour ; but it is generally a bright reddish brown.

The second, sapphire] This is a stone of a fine blue colour, next in hardness to the diamond.

The third, a chalcedony] A genus of the semipellucid gems, of which there are four species :—

1. A *bluish white;* this is the most common sort.

2. The *dull milky veined;* this is of little worth.

3. The *brownish black;* the least beautiful of all.

4. The *yellow and red;* the most beautiful, as it is the most valuable of all. Hitherto this has been found only in the East Indies.

The fourth, an emerald] This is of a *bright green* colour without any mixture, and is one of the most beautiful of all the gems. The true oriental emerald is very scarce, and said to be found only in the kingdom of *Cambay.*

Verse 20. *The fifth, sardonyx*] The onyx is an accidental variety of the agate kind ; it is of a dark horny colour, in which is a plate of a bluish white, and sometimes of red. When on one or both sides of the white there happens to lie also a plate of a reddish colour, the jewellers call the stone a *sardonyx.*

The sixth, sardius] The *sardius, sardel,* or *sardine stone,* is a precious stone of a *blood-red* colour.

The seventh, chrysolite] The *gold stone.* It is of a *dusky green* with a cast of *yellow.* It is a species of the *topaz.*

The eighth, beryl] This is a pellucid gem of a *bluish green* colour.

The ninth, a topaz] A *pale dead green,* with a mixture of *yellow.* It is considered by the mineralogists as a variety of the *sapphire.*

The tenth, a chrysoprasus] A variety of the *chrysolite,* called by some the *yellowish green and cloudy topaz.* It differs from the *chrysolite* only in having a *bluish* hue.

The eleventh, a jacinth] A precious stone of a *dead red* colour, with a mixture of *yellow.* It is the same as the hyacenet or cinnamon stone.

The twelfth, an amethyst.] A gem generally of a *purple* or *violet* colour, composed of a strong *blue* and *deep red.*

These stones are nearly the same with those on the breastplate of the high priest, Exod. xxviii. 17, &c., and probably were intended to express the meaning of the Hebrew words there used. See the notes on the above passages, where these gems are particularly explained.

Verse 21. *The twelve gates* were *twelve pearls*] This must be merely figurative, for it is out of all the order of nature to produce a *pearl* large enough to make a *gate* to such an immense city. But St. John may refer to some relations of this nature among his countrymen, who talk much of most prodigious pearls. I shall give an example : " When Rabbi Juchanan (John) once taught that God would provide *jewels* and *pearls, thirty cubits* every way, ten of which should exceed in height *twenty cubits,* and would place them in the gates of Jerusalem, according to what is said Isa. liv. 12, *I will make thy windows of agates, and thy gates of carbuncles,* one of his disciples ridiculed him, saying, Where can such be found, since at present there is none so large as a pigeon's egg ? Afterwards, being at sea in a ship, he saw the ministering angels cutting gems and pearls ; and he asked them for what purpose they were preparing those. They answered, to place them in the gates of Jerusalem. On his return he found Rabbi Juchanan teaching as usual ; to whom he said, Explain, master, what I have seen. He answered, Thou knave, unless thou hadst *seen,* thou wouldst not have *believed;* wilt thou not receive the saying of the wise men ? At that moment he fixed his eyes upon him, and he was reduced into a heap of bones."—*Bava bathra,* fol. 77, 1, and *Sanhedrim,* fol. 100, 1, page 393. Edit. *Cocceii.* See *Schoettgen.*

Verse 22. *I saw no temple*] There was no need of a *temple* where God and the Lamb were manifestly present.

Verse 23. *No need of the sun*] This is also one of the traditions of the ancient Jews, that " in *the world to come* the Israelites shall have no need of the *sun by day,* nor the *moon by night.*"—*Yalcut Rubeni,* fol. 7, 3. God's light shines in this city, and in the Lamb that light is concentrated, and from him everywhere diffused.

Verse 24. *The nations of them which are saved*] This is an illusion to the promise that the Gentiles should bring their riches, glory, and excellence, to the

A. M. cir. 4100.
A. D. cir. 95.
Impp. Flavio
Domitiano
Cæs. Aug. et
Nerva.

the earth do bring their glory and honour into it.

25 [i] And the gates of it shall not be shut at all by day: for [k] there shall be no night there.

26 [l] And they shall bring the glory and

honour of the nations into it.

27 And [m] there shall in nowise enter into it any thing that defileth, neither *whatsoever* worketh abomination, or *maketh* a lie; but they which are written in the Lamb's [n] book of life.

A. M. cir. 4100.
A. D. cir. 96.
Impp. Flavio
Domitiano
Cæs. Aug. et
Nerva.

---

[i] Isa. lx. 11.——[k] Isa lx. 20; Zech. xiv. 7; chap. xxii. 5. [l] Ver. 24.

[m] Isa. xxxv. 8; lii. 1; lx. 21; Joel iii. 17; chapter xxii. 14, 15. [n] Phil. iv 3; chap. iii. 5; xiii. 8; xx. 12.

---

temple at Jerusalem, after it should be rebuilt. See ver. 26.

Verse 25. *The gates of it shall not be shut at all*] The Christian Church shall ever *stand open* to receive sinners of all sorts, degrees, and nations.

There shall be no night there.] No more idolatry, no intellectual darkness; the Scriptures shall be everywhere read, the pure word everywhere preached, and the Spirit of God shall shine and work in every heart.

Verse 26. *The glory and honour of the nations into it.*] Still alluding to the declarations of the prophets, (see the passages in the margin, ver. 24, &c.,) that the Gentiles would be led to contribute to the riches and glory of the temple by their gifts, &c.

Verse 27. *There shall in nowise enter into it any thing that defileth*] See Isa. xxxv. 8; lii. 1. Neither an *impure person*—he who turns the grace of God into lasciviousness, *nor a liar*—he that holds and propagates false doctrines.

But they which are written] The acknowledged persevering members of the true Church of Christ shall enter into heaven, and only those who are saved from their sins shall have a place in the Church militant.

ALL Christians are bound by their baptism to renounce the devil and all his works, the pomps and vanities of this wicked world, and all the sinful lusts of the flesh; to keep God's holy word and commandments; and to walk in the same all the days of their life. This is the generation of them that seek thy face, O God of Jacob! Reader, art thou of this number? Or art thou expecting an eternal glory while living in sin? If so, thou wilt be fearfully disappointed. Presuming on the mercy of God is as ruinous as despairing of his grace. Where God gives power both to will and to do, the individual should work out his salvation with fear and trembling.

CHAPTER XXII.

The river of the water of life, 1. The tree of life, 2. There is no curse nor darkness in the city of God, 3-5. The angel assures John of the truth of what he has heard, and states that the time of the fulfilment is at hand, 6, 7. He forbids John to worship him, 8, 9. Again he states that the time of the fulfilment of the prophecies of this book is at hand, 10-12. Christ is Alpha and Omega, 13. The blessedness of those who keep his commandments; they enter through the gates into the city, 14. All the unholy are excluded, 15. Christ sent his angel to testify of those things in the Churches, 16. The invitation of the Spirit and the bride, 17. A curse denounced against those who shall either add to or take away from the prophecies of this book, 18, 19 Christ cometh quickly, 20. The apostolical benediction, 21

A. M. cir. 4100.
A. D. cir. 96.
Impp. Flavio
Domitiano
Cæs. Aug. et
Nerva.

AND he showed me [a] a pure river of water of life, clear as crystal, proceeding out of the throne of God and of the Lamb.

2 [b] In the midst of the street of it, and on either side of the river, *was there* [c] the tree of life, which bare twelve *manner of*

A. M. cir. 4100.
A. D. cir. 96.
Impp. Flavio
Domitiano
Cæs. Aug. et
Nerva.

---

[a] Ezek. xlvii. 1; Zech. xiv. 8.

[b] Ezek. xlvii. 12; chap. xxi. 21.——[c] Gen. ii. 9; chap. ii. 7

NOTES ON CHAP. XXII.

Verse 1. *Pure river of water of life*] This is evidently a reference to the *garden of paradise*, and the river by which it was watered; and there is also a reference to the account, Ezek. xlvii. 7–12. *Water of life*, as we have seen before, generally signifies *spring* or *running water*; here it may signify incessant communications of happiness proceeding from God.

Verse 2. *In the midst of the street of it*] That is, of the city which was described in the preceding chapter.

The tree of life] An allusion to Gen. ii. 9. As

this tree of life is stated to be in the *streets* of the city, and *on each side of the river, tree* must here be an *enallage* of the singular for the plural number, *trees of life*, or trees which yielded fruit whereof life was preserved. The account in Ezekiel is this. "And by the river, upon the bank thereof, on this side and on that side, shall grow all trees for meat, whose leaf shall not fade—it shall bring forth new fruit, according to his months—and the fruit thereof shall be for meat, and the leaf thereof for medicine;" chap. xlvii. 12.

Twelve manner of *fruits*] Καρπους δωδεκα· *Twelve fruits*; that is, fruit twelve times in the year, as is

1062   2

A. M. cir. 4100.
A. D. cir. 96.
Impp. Flavio Domitiano Cæs. Aug. et Nerva.

fruits, *and* yielded her fruit every month: and the leaves of the tree *were* [d] for the healing of the nations.

3 And [e] there shall be no more curse: [f] but the throne of God and of the Lamb shall be in it; and his servants shall serve him.

4 And [g] they shall see his face; and [h] his name *shall be* in their foreheads.

5 [i] And there shall be no night there; and they need no candle, neither light of the sun; for [k] the Lord God giveth them light: [l] and they shall reign for ever and ever.

6 And he said unto me, [m] These sayings *are* faithful and true: and the Lord God of the holy prophets [n] sent his angel to show unto his servants the things which must shortly be done.

7 [o] Behold, I come quickly: [p] blessed *is* he that keepeth the sayings of the prophecy of this book.

8 And I John saw these things, and heard *them*. And when I had heard and seen, [q] I fell down to worship before the feet of the angel which showed me these things.

A. M. cir. 4100.
A. D. cir. 96.
Impp. Flavio Domitiano Cæs. Aug. et Nerva.

9 Then saith he unto me, [r] See *thou do it* not: for I am thy fellow servant, and of thy brethren the prophets, and of them which keep the sayings of this book: worship God.

10 [s] And he saith unto me, Seal not the sayings of the prophecy of this book: [t] for the time is at hand.

11 [u] He that is unjust, let him be unjust still: and he which is filthy, let him be filthy still: and he that is righteous, let him be righteous still: and he that is holy, let him be holy still.

12 [v] And behold, I come quickly; and [w] my reward *is* with me, [x] to give every man according as his work shall be.

---

[d] Chapter xxi. 24.—[e] Zech. xiv. 11.—[f] Ezekiel xlviii. 35. [g] Matt. v. 8; 1 Cor. xiii. 12; 1 John iii. 2.—[h] Chap. iii. 12; xiv. 1.—[i] Chapter xxi. 23, 25.—[k] Psa. xxxvi. 9; lxxxiv. 11. [l] Dan. vii. 27; Rom. v. 17; 2 Tim. ii. 12; ch. iii. 21.—[m] Ch. xix. 9; xxi. 5.

[n] Chap. i. 1.—[o] Chap. iii. 11; ver. 10, 12, 20.—[p] Chapter i. 3.—[q] Chap. xix. 10.—[r] Chap. xix. 10.—[s] Dan. viii. 26; xii. 4, 9; chap. x. 4.—[t] Chap. i. 3.—[u] Ezek. iii. 27; Dan. xii. 10; 2 Tim. iii. 13.—[v] Ver. 7.—[w] Isa. xl. 10; lxii. 11. [x] Rom. ii. 6; xiv. 12; chap. xx. 12.

---

immediately explained, *yielded her fruit every month.* As this was a great and spacious city, one fountain was not sufficient to provide water for it, therefore a river is mentioned; a great river, by which it was sufficiently watered. Some think that by this *tree of life* the *Gospel* is indicated; the *twelve fruits* are the *twelve apostles;* and the *leaves* are *Gospel doctrines* by which the nations—the *Gentiles*, are healed of the disease of *sin*. But this seems to be a fanciful interpretation.

Verse 3. *No more curse*] Instead of καταναθεμα, *curse*, the best MSS., versions, &c., read καταθεμα, *cursed person*. As there shall be no more sinning against God, so there shall be no more curse of God upon the people; for they shall be all his *servants*, and *serve him*. Our first parents came under the curse by sinning against their Maker in paradise; these shall never apostatize, therefore neither *they* nor the *earth* shall be *cursed*.

Verse 4. *See his face*] Enjoy what is called the beatific vision; and they shall exhibit the fullest evidence that they belong entirely to him, for *his name* shall be *written on their foreheads.*

Verse 5. *There shall be no night there*] See the 23d and 25th verses of the preceding chapter.

Verse 6. *These sayings* are *faithful and true*] See the preceding chapter, ver. 5. From this verse to the end of the chapter is reckoned the *epilogue* of this book. 1. The angel affirms the truth of all that had been spoken, ver. 6–11. 2. Jesus Christ confirms what has been affirmed, and pledges himself for the fulfilment of all the prophecies contained in it, ver. 12–17. 3. John cautions his readers against adding or diminishing, and concludes with the apostolical blessing, ver. 18–21.

The things which must shortly be done.] There are many sayings in this book which, if taken *literally*, would intimate that the prophecies delivered in the whole of the Apocalypse were to be fulfilled in a *short* time after their delivery to John; and this is a strong support for the scheme of Wetstein, and those who maintain that the prophecies of this book all referred to those times in which the apostle lived, and to the disturbances which then took place, not only among the *Jews*, but in the *Roman* empire. What they all mean, and when and how they are to be fulfilled, God in heaven alone knows.

Verse 8. *I fell down to worship*] I prostrated myself before him as before a superior being, to express my gratitude, and give him thanks for the communications he had made. See on chap. xix. 10.

Verse 10. *Seal not the sayings*] Do not lay them up for future generations; they concern the present times; *they must shortly come to pass, for the time is at hand.* See above, ver. 6. What concerned the Jews was certainly *at hand*.

Verse 11. *He that is unjust, let him be unjust still*] The time of fulfilment will come so *suddenly* that there will be but little space for repentance and amendment. What is done must be done instantly; and let him that is holy persevere, and hold fast what he has received.

Verse 12. *Behold, I come quickly*] I come to establish my cause, comfort and support my followers, and punish the wicked.

A. M. cir. 4100.
A. D. cir. 96.
Impp. Flavio
Domitiano
Cæs. Aug. et
Nerva.

13 ʸ I am Alpha and Omega, the beginning and the end, the first and the last.

14 ᶻ Blessed *are* they that do his commandments, that they may have right ᵃ to the tree of life, ᵇ and may enter in through the gates into the city.

15 For ᶜ without *are* ᵈ dogs, and sorcerers, and whoremongers, and murderers, and idolaters, and whosoever loveth and maketh a lie.

16 ᵉ I Jesus have sent mine angel to testify unto you these things in the Churches. ᶠ I am the root and the offspring of David, *and* ᵍ the bright and morning star.

17 And the Spirit and ʰ the bride say, Come. And let him that heareth say, Come. ⁱ And let him that is athirst come. And whosoever

will, let him take the water of life freely.

A. M. cir. 4100.
A. D. cir. 96.
Impp. Flavio
Domitiano
Cæs. Aug. et
Nerva.

18 For I testify unto every man that heareth the words of the prophecy of this book, ᵏ If any man shall add unto these things, God shall add unto him the plagues that are written in this book:

19 And if any man shall take away from the words of the book of this prophecy, ˡ God shall take away his part ᵐ out of the book of life, and out of ⁿ the holy city, and *from* the things which are written in this book.

20 He which testifieth these things saith, ᵒ Surely I come quickly; ᵖ Amen. ᑫ Even so, come, Lord Jesus.

21 ʳ The grace of our Lord Jesus Christ *be* with you all. Amen.

ʸ Isa. xli. 4; xliv. 6; xlviii. 12; chapter i. 8, 11; xxi. 6.
ᶻ Dan. xii. 12; 1 John iii. 24.——ᵃ Ver. 2; chap. ii. 7.——ᵇ Ch. xxi. 27.——ᶜ 1 Cor. vi. 9, 10; Gal. v. 19, 20, 21; Col. iii. 6; ch. ix. 20, 21; xxi. 8.——ᵈ Phil. iii. 2.——ᵉ Ch. i. 1.——ᶠ Ch. v. 5. ᵍ Num. xxiv. 17; Zech. vi. 12; 2 Pet. i. 19; chap. ii. 28.

ʰ Chap. xxi. 2, 9.——ⁱ Isa. lv. 1; John vii. 37; chap. xxi. 6. ᵏ Deut. iv. 2; xii. 32; Prov. xxx. 6.——ˡ Exod. xxxii. 33; Psa. lxix. 28; chap. iii. 5; xiii. 8.——ᵐ Or, *from the tree of life.* ⁿ Ch. xxi. 2.——ᵒ Ver. 12.——ᵖ John xxi. 25.——ᑫ 2 Tim. iv. 8. ʳ Rom. xvi. 20, 24; 2 Thess. iii. 18.

Verse 13. *I am Alpha and Omega*] See on chap. i. 8, 18.

Verse 14. *Blessed* are *they that do his commandments*] They are happy who are obedient.

That they may have right to the tree of life] The original is much more expressive, Ἰνα εσται ἡ εξουσια αυτων επι το ξυλον της ζωης· *That they may have authority over the tree of life;* an *authority* founded on *right*, this *right* founded on *obedience* to the commandments of God, and that *obedience* produced by the *grace* of God working in them. Without *grace* no *obedience;* without *obedience* no *authority* to the tree of life; without *authority* no *right;* without *right* no *enjoyment:* God's *grace* through Christ produces the good, and then rewards it as if all had been our *own.*

Verse 15. *Without* are *dogs*] All those who are *uncircumcised* in heart. The Jews call all the uncircumcised *dogs.* "Who is a dog? Ans. He who is not circumcised." *Pirkey Elieser*, chap. 29.

And sorcerers] See the note on chap xxi. 8.

Verse 16. *I Jesus*] The Maker, the Redeemer, and Judge of all men.

Have sent mine angel] An especial messenger from heaven.

I am the root and the offspring of David] Christ is the *root* of David as to his *Divine nature;* for from that all the human race sprang, for *he is the Creator of all things,* and *without him was nothing made which is made.* And he is the *offspring* of David as to his *human nature;* for that he took of the stock of David, becoming thereby heir to the Jewish throne, and the only heir which then existed; and it is remarkable that the whole regal family terminated in Christ: and as ʜᴇ *liveth for ever,* he is the alone true David and everlasting King.

The bright and morning star.] I am splendour and glory to my kingdom; as the *morning star* ushers

in the sun, so shall I usher in the unclouded and eternal glories of the everlasting kingdom.

Verse 17. *The Spirit and the bride*] All the *prophets* and all the *apostles;* the Church of God under the Old Testament, and the Church of Christ under the New.

Say, Come.] Invite men to Jesus, that by him they may be saved and prepared for this kingdom.

Let him that heareth] Let all who are privileged with *reading* and *hearing* the word of God, join in the general invitation to *sinners.*

Him that is athirst] He who feels his need of salvation, and is longing to drink of the living fountain.

And whosoever will] No soul is excluded: Jesus died for every man; every man may be saved; therefore let him who *wills,* who *wishes* for salvation, come and take the *water of life freely*—without money or price!

Verse 18. *If any man shall add*] Shall give any other meaning to these prophecies, or any other application of them, than God intends, *he,* though not originally intended, shall have the plagues threatened in this book for his portion.

Verse 19. *If any man shall take away*] If any man shall lessen this meaning, curtail the sense, explain away the spirit and design, of these prophecies, *God shall take away his part out of the book of life,* &c. Thus Jesus Christ warns all those who consider this book to beware of indulging their own conjectures concerning it. I confess that this warning has its own powerful influence upon my mind, and has prevented me from indulging my own conjectures concerning its meaning, or of adopting the conjectures of others. These visions and threatenings are too delicate and awful a subject to trifle with, or even to treat in the most solemn manner, where the meaning is obscure. I must leave these things to *time* and *event,* the surest interpreters. No jot or tittle of Christ's word shall fall to the ground; all shall have its fulfilment in due time.

This is termed a *revelation*, but it is a revelation of *symbols;* an exhibition of *enigmas*, to which no particular solution is given, and to which God alone can give the solution.

Verse 20. Surely I come quickly] This may be truly said to every person in every age; Jesus the Judge is at the door!

Even so, come, Lord Jesus.] The wish and desire of the suffering Church, and of all the followers of God, who are longing for the coming of his kingdom.

Verse 21. The grace of our Lord Jesus Christ] May the favour and powerful influence of Jesus Christ *be with you all; you* of the seven Churches, and the whole Church of Christ in every part of the earth, and through all the periods of time.

Instead of παντων ὑμων, *you all*, the most excellent MSS. and versions have παντων των ἁγιων, *all the saints.* This reading Griesbach has received into the text as indisputably *genuine.*

Amen.] So be it! and so shall it be for ever and ever. The opinion of Dr. Priestley, concerning the *authenticity* of this book, and the *manner* in which it is written, should not be withheld from either the learned or pious reader. "I think it impossible for any intelligent and candid person to peruse this book without being struck in the most forcible manner with the peculiar dignity and sublimity of its composition, superior to that of any other writing whatever; so as to be convinced that, considering the age in which it appeared, none but a person *divinely inspired* could have written it. These prophecies are also written in such a *manner* as to satisfy us that the events announced to us were really foreseen, being described in such a manner as no person writing without that knowledge could have done. This requires such a mixture of *clearness* and *obscurity* as has never yet been imitated by any forgers of prophecy whatever. Forgeries, written of course after the events, have always been *too plain.* It is only in the Scriptures, and especially in the book of *Daniel*, and this of the *Revelation*, that we find this happy mixture of clearness and obscurity in the accounts of future events."—*Notes on Revelation.*

The *Subscriptions* to this book are both few and unimportant :—

The CODEX ALEXANDRINUS has simply—The Revelation of John.

The SYRIAC doubles the *Amen.*

The ÆTHIOPIC.—Here is ended the vision of John, the Apocalypse; Amen: this is, as one might say, the vision which he saw in his life; and it was written by the blessed John, the evangelist of God.

VULGATE and COPTIC nothing.

ANCIENT ARABIC.—By the assistance of our Lord Jesus Christ, the vision of John, the apostle and evangelist, the beloved of the Lord, is finished : this is the Apocalypse which the Lord revealed to him for the service of men. To Him be glory for ever and ever.

HAVING now brought my short notes on this very obscure book to a conclusion, it may be expected that, although I do not adopt any of the theories which have been delivered concerning it, yet I should give the most plausible *scheme* of the ancients or moderns which has come to my knowledge. This I would gladly do if I had any scheme to which I could give a decided preference. However, as I have given in the *preface* the *scheme* of *Professor Wetstein*, it is right that I should, at the *conclusion*, give the scheme of Mr. *Lowman*, which is nearly the same with that of *Bishop Newton*, and which, as far as I can learn, is considered by the most rational divines as being the most consistent and probable.

The scheme of the learned and pious *Bengel* may be found in the late Rev. *John Wesley's* notes on this book; that of Mr. *Lowman*, which now follows, may be found at the end of Dr. *Dodd's* notes.

Among other objections to this and all such schemes, I have this, which to me appears of vital consequence; its dates are too late. I think the book was written *before* the *destruction* of Jerusalem, and not in 95 or 96, the date which I follow in the margin; which date I give, not as my own opinion, but the opinion of others.

SCHEME AND ORDER OF THE PROPHECIES IN THE APOCALYPSE.

CHAP. I.	INTRODUCTION.	A. D.
1–19.	A prophetic vision in the Isle of Patmos, representing Christ; his care of the Churches; promising a revelation; with cautions and exhortations suitable to the then state of the Church, and to its future state in after ages; to encourage patience and constancy in the faith.	95
	FIRST PART of the *Apocalypse*, relating to the *things that are*, or to the *then state of the Church.*	
II.	*Seven epistles* to the seven Churches of Asia Minor, describing their *present state.*	

CHAP.		A. D.
IV.	SECOND PART of the Apocalypse, relating to the things which *shall be hereafter;* or to the state of the Church in the ages to come after the time of the vision; with cautions and exhortations suitable to it.	
	Scene of the visions: the throne of God; the consistory above and heavenly Church, representing God's power, majesty, authority, providence, and sure event of all his purposes.	
	A sealed book, containing a revelation of the state of the Church in after ages, given to the Lamb to open,	

2

CHAP.   A. D.

IV. or to Jesus Christ to reveal for the good of the Church by St. John.

Ver. 8. Chorus of angels and saints, or the whole heavenly Church, sings a psalm of praise to the Lamb.

VI. The revelation begins by opening the sealed book, which describes the future state of the Church in seven successive periods.

SEVEN PERIODS.

First period, showing the state of the Church under the heathen *Roman* emperors, from about the year 95 to about the year 323; the seals of the book opened in order.   95   323

Seven Seals.

1. First seal represents a white horse; the rider with a crown, going forth to conquer, signifying the kingdom of Christ, or Christian religion, prevailing against the opposition of *Jews* and heathens.

2. Second seal represents a red horse; power given to the rider to take peace from the earth, signifying the first memorable judgment on the persecutors of Christianity in the destruction of the Jews under Trajan and Hadrian.   100   138

3. Third seal represents a black horse; the rider with a balance to measure corn, signifying great scarcity of provisions, near to famine, in the time of the Antonines.   138   139

4. Fourth seal represents a pale horse; the name of the rider Death, signifying great mortality and pestilence, wherewith the empire was punished in the reigns of Maximin and Valerian.   193   270

5. Fifth seal represents the souls of the martyrs under the altar; their reward and deliverance in a short time, signifying the severe persecution in the reign of Diocletian, with an encouragement to constancy suitable to such times of difficulty.   270   304

6. Sixth seal represents earthquakes, sun darkened, stars falling from heaven; signifying great commotions in the empire, from Maximin to Constantine the Great, who put a period to the persecution of Rome heathen.   304   323

VII. Interval between the first and second periods, representing an angel sealing 144,000 with the seal of the living God; signifying great numbers forsaking the idolatrous worship of the heathen Roman empire,

1066

VII. and embracing the profession of Christianity.

Ver. 9. Chorus of the heavenly Church blessing God for his salvation. One of the elders shows unto St. John the happiness of those who were faithful and constant to true religion in the great trial of so grievous persecution.

PERIOD II.

VIII. *Second period* reveals the state of the Church and providence in times following the reign of Constantine, during the invasion of the empire by the northern nations; the rise and first progress of the Mohammedan imposture till the stop put to it in the western empire, which reaches from about the year 337 to 750. Seven angels receive seven trumpets to sound.   337   370

Seven Trumpets.

1. First trumpet represents hail and fire mingled with blood cast on the earth; signifying great storms of war to fall on the empire, and the blood that was shed in the reigns of the Constantine family, and their successors, till things were settled under Theodosius.   337   379

2. Second trumpet represents a mountain burning with fire, cast into the sea, whereby it became blood; signifying the invasion of Italy by the northern nations, and taking the city of Rome by Alaric.   379   412

3. Third trumpet represents a burning star falling upon the rivers, which became bitter; signifying the ravages in Italy, putting an end to the Roman empire, and founding a kingdom of Goths in Italy itself.   412   493

4. Fourth trumpet represents a part of the sun and moon darkened; signifying the wars in Italy between Justinian's generals and the Goths, whereby the exarchate of Ravenna was erected, and all remaining power and authority of Rome quite suppressed.   493   568

IX. 5. Fifth trumpet represents the bottomless pit opened, and locusts coming out of it; signifying the rise of the Mohammedan religion and empire, and the great progress of both, till a stop was put to them by a contention for the succession.   568   675

6. Sixth trumpet represents four angels loosed which were bound in the river Euphrates; signifying the reunion of the divided Saracen power, the invasion of Europe by   675   750

2

CHAP.		A. D.
IX.	them, and threatening the conquest of it, till defeated by Charles Martel.	

PERIOD III.

Third period of the vials reveals the state of the Church and providence in the times of the last head of Roman government, represented by the beast, for 1260 years to its final overthrow, from about the year 756 **[756 / 2016]**

X. to about the year 2016. An angel or nuncius brings a little book, the remainder of the sealed book opened by the Lamb, and gives it to St. John to eat; signifying a farther revelation of what was to follow in order of time to the end of the world.

Three general descriptions of this period :—

XI. 1. First general description represents the temple measured, part given to the Gentiles, two witnesses prophesy in sackcloth 1260 days; signifying the corrupt state of the Church, and the constancy of some faithful witnesses to the truth, though under severe persecutions, during this whole period.

XII. 2. Second general description represents a woman forced to fly into the wilderness for safety, and protected there 1260 days; signifying the persecution and preservation of the Church during the same period.

XIII. 3. Third general description represents a monstrous wild beast rising out of the sea, with seven heads, ten horns, as many crowns, and titles of blasphemy, who was to continue forty and two months; signifying that new Roman power, which should use its authority to promote idolatrous worship, and to persecute all who would not submit to it, and should be supported by another power like unto its own form and constitution, during the same period.

XIV. Chorus of the heavenly Church celebrates, in a hymn, the happiness of those who remain faithful and constant.

A nuncius or angel comes down from heaven to declare the certain and severe punishment of the enemies of truth and pure religion, in this period.

XV. Seven angels receive seven cups, full of the wrath of God; signifying that the enemies of truth and pure religion in this period shall be se-

CHAP.		A. D.
XV.	verely punished in the *course* of it; and that they shall be utterly destroyed in *the end*.	
XVI.	The oracle gives orders to the seven angels to pour out their vials or cups.	

Seven Vials.

First vial poured on the earth; a grievous sore upon the worshippers of the beast; signifying the great commotions throughout the whole empire, under the family of *Charles* the Great, by which that family becomes extinct, and by which both the empire and crown of France are transferred to other families. **[830 / 988]**

2. Second vial poured on the sea; it becomes as the blood of a dead man; signifying the great bloodshed of the holy war to recover Jerusalem from the Saracens. **[1040 / 1190]**

3. Third vial poured on the rivers and fountains; they become blood; signifying the bloody civil wars between the Guelphs and the Gibbelines, the papal and imperial factions, when the popes were driven out of Italy into France. **[1200 / 1371]**

4. Fourth vial poured on the sun, which has power given it to scorch men; signifying the long wars in Italy, Germany, France, and Spain, occasioned by a long schism in the papacy. Turks take Constantinople, and put an end to the eastern empire. Pestilential diseases occasioned by intemperate heat. **[1378 / 1530]**

5. Fifth vial poured on the seat of the beast, or his throne; signifying the Reformation, and the confirmation of it by the principal states of Europe, notwithstanding all opposition from the pope, and in opposition to the papal authority. **[1560 / 1650]**

6. Sixth vial poured on the river Euphrates, makes way for the kings of the east. This seems in the order of the prophecies to be yet future; but may likely mean some invasion of the pope's dominions from its eastern boundary or the Adriatic. **[1670 / 1850]**

7. Seventh vial poured on the air, the seat of Satan's empire, describes the utter ruin of this persecuting idolatrous Roman government, or mystical Babylon at the end of this period. **[1850 / 2016]**

XVII. Mentions an angel interpreter who fully explains the character of this idolatrous persecuting power, which should corrupt the Church, and persecute the faithful during this period.

PRINCIPLES

WHICH, ON CAREFULLY READING AND STUDYING THE SACRED WRITINGS, I THINK I FIND UNEQUIVOCALLY REVEALED THERE.

1. That there is but one uncreated, unoriginated, infinite, and eternal Being; the Creator, Preserver, and Governor of all things.

2. That there is in this Infinite Essence a *plurality* of what are commonly called *persons*, not separately subsisting, but essentially belonging to the Godhead; which *persons* are commonly termed FATHER, SON, and HOLY GHOST; or GOD, the LOGOS, and the HOLY SPIRIT: and these are generally named the TRINITY, which term, though not found in the New Testament, seems properly enough applied, as we never read of more than *three* persons in the Godhead.

3. That the sacred Scriptures, or holy books which form the Old and New Testaments, contain a full revelation of the will of God in reference to man; and are alone sufficient for every thing relative to the faith and practice of a Christian; and were given by the inspiration of God.

4. That man was created in righteousness and true holiness, without any moral imperfection or any kind of propensity to sin; but free to stand or fall.

5. That he fell from this state, became morally corrupt in his nature, and transmitted his moral defilement to all his posterity.

6. That, to counteract the evil principle, and bring man into a salvable state, God, from his infinite love, formed the *purpose* of redeeming man from his lost estate by Christ Jesus, and in the interim sent his Holy Spirit to enlighten, strive with, and convince men of sin, righteousness, and judgment.

7. That in due time the Divine Logos, called afterwards Jesus the Christ, the Son of God, the Saviour, &c., became incarnated, and sojourned among men, teaching the purest truth, and working the most stupendous and beneficent miracles.

8. That this Divine Person, foretold by the prophets, and described by evangelists and apostles, is *really* and *properly* GOD; having, by the inspired writers, assigned to him every attribute essential to the Deity; being one with him who is called God, Jehovah, &c.

9. That he is also *perfect man* in consequence of his incarnation, and in that man or manhood dwelt all

the fulness of the Godhead bodily; so that his nature is twofold—Divine and human, or God manifested in the flesh.

10. That his human nature is derived from the blessed Virgin Mary, through the creative energy of the Holy Ghost; but his Divine nature, because God, infinite and eternal, is uncreated, underived, and *unbegotten;* which, were it otherwise, he could not be God in *any proper sense of the word;* but as he IS GOD, the doctrine of the *eternal Sonship* must be *false.*

11. That, as he took upon him the nature of man, he *died* for the whole human race, without respect of persons; equally for all, and for every man.

12. That on the third day after his crucifixion and burial he rose from the dead; and after showing himself many days to his disciples and others, he ascended to heaven, where, as God manifest in the flesh, he continues and shall continue to be the Mediator of the human race, till the consummation of all things.

13. That there is no salvation but through him; and that throughout the Scriptures his passion and death are considered as *sacrificial,* pardon and salvation being obtained by the shedding of his blood.

14. That no human being since the fall either has or can have *merit* or *worthiness* of or by himself, and therefore has nothing to *claim* from God, but in the way of his mercy through Christ; therefore pardon, and every other blessing promised in the Gospel, have been purchased by his sacrificial death, and are given to men, not on account of any thing they have done or suffered, or can do or suffer, but for his sake, or through his merit alone.

15. That these blessings are received by *faith,* because not of works, nor of sufferings.

16. That the *power to believe,* or grace of faith, is the free gift of God, without which none can believe; but that the *act of faith,* or actually *believing,* is the act of the soul, under the influence of that power. But this power to believe, like all other gifts of God, may be slighted, not used, or misused; in consequence of which is that declaration, " He that believeth shall be saved; but he that believeth not shall be damned."

17. That justification, or the pardon of sin, is an instantaneous act of God's infinite mercy in behalf of a penitent soul, trusting only in the merits of Jesus Christ; that this act is absolute in respect of all past sin, all being forgiven where any is forgiven.

18. That the souls of all believers may be purified from all sin in this life; and that a man may live under the continual influence of the grace of Christ, without sinning against his God, all evil tempers and sinful propensities being destroyed, and his heart filled with pure love both to God and man.

19. That unless a believer live and walk in the spirit of obedience, he will fall from the grace of God, and forfeit all his Christian privileges and rights; in which state of backsliding he may persevere, and, if so, perish everlastingly.

20. That the whole period of human life is a *state of probation,* in every part of which a sinner may repent and turn to God, and in every part of it a believer may give way to sin and fall from grace; and that this

possibility of rising, and liability to falling, are essential to a state of trial or probation.

21. That all the promises and threatenings of the word of God are conditional, as they regard man in reference to his being here and hereafter; and that on this ground alone the sacred writings can be consistently interpreted or rightly understood.

22. That man is a free agent, never being impelled by any necessitating influence either to do evil or good, but has it continually in his power to choose the life or death that is set before him; on which ground he is an accountable being, and answerable for his own actions; and on this ground also he is alone capable of being rewarded or punished.

23. That his free will is a necessary constituent of his rational soul, without which man must be a mere machine, either the sport of blind chance, or the mere *patient* of an irresistible necessity; and, consequently, not accountable for any acts to which he was irresistibly impelled.

24. That every human being has his freedom of will, with a sufficiency of light and power to direct its operations; and that this powerful light is not inherent in any man's nature, but is graciously bestowed by Him who is the true light that lighteneth every man that cometh into the world.

25. That, as Christ has made, by his once offering himself upon the cross, a sufficient sacrifice, oblation, and satisfaction for the sins of the whole world; and that, as his gracious Spirit strives with and enlightens all men, thus putting them in a salvable state; therefore every human soul may be saved, if it be not his own fault.

26. That Jesus Christ has instituted, and commanded to be perpetuated in his Church, two sacraments; baptism (sprinkling, washing with, or immersion in water) in the name of the holy and ever blessed Trinity, as a sign of the cleansing and regenerating influences of the Holy Ghost, producing a death unto sin, and a new birth unto righteousness; and the eucharist, or Lord's Supper, as commemorating the sacrificial death of Christ. That by the first, once administered, every person may be initiated into the visible Church; and by the second, frequently administered, all believers may be kept in mind of the foundation on which their salvation is built, and receive grace to enable them to adorn the doctrine of God their Saviour in all things.

27. That the soul is immaterial and immortal, and can subsist independently of the body.

28. That there will be a general resurrection of the dead, both of the just and unjust; that the souls of both shall be reunited to their respective bodies; and that both will be immortal, and live eternally.

29. That there will be a day of judgment, after which all shall be punished or rewarded, according to the deeds done in the body; the wicked being sent to hell, and the righteous taken into heaven.

30. That these states of reward and punishment shall have no end, forasmuch as the time of probation or trial is for ever terminated, and the succeeding state must necessarily be fixed and unalterable.

31. That the origin of human salvation is found in the infinite *philanthropy* of God; and that on this

2

principle the unconditional reprobation of any soul is absolutely impossible.

32. The SACRED WRITINGS are a system of pure, un-sophisticated *reason*, proceeding from the immaculate mind of God ; in many places, it is true, vastly elevated *beyond* what the reason of man could have devised or found out, but in no case *contrary* to human reason ; they are addressed, not to the passions, but to the reason of man ; every *command* is urged *with reasons of obedience,* and every *promise* and *threatening* founded on the most evident *reason* and propriety. The whole, therefore, are to be rationally understood and rationally interpreted. He who would discharge reason from this, its noblest province, is a friend in his heart to the antichristian maxim, " Ignorance is the mother of devotion." Revelation and reason go hand in hand : faith is the servant of the former, and the friend of the latter ; while the Spirit of God, which gave the *revelation,* improves and exalts *reason,* and gives energy and effect to faith.

To conclude : the doctrines or principles which I have stated above, and defended in this work, I believe to be the truths of God. Those against which I have argued I believe to be either false or unproved. The doctrine which cannot stand the test of rational investigation cannot be true. The *doctrines* or *principles* already enumerated have stood this test ; and those which shrink from such a test are not doctrines of Divine revelation. We have gone too far when we have said, " Such and such doctrines should not be subjected to rational investigation, being doctrines of pure revelation." I know no such doctrines in the Bible. The doctrines of this book are doctrines of *eternal reason,* and they are *revealed* because they are *such.* Human reason could not have found them out ; but when revealed, reason can both apprehend and comprehend them. It sees their perfect harmony among themselves, their agreement with the perfections of the Divine nature, and their sovereign suitableness to the nature and state of man ; thus reason approves and applauds. Some men, it is true, cannot reason ; and therefore *they* declaim against reason, and proscribe it in the examination of religious truth. Were all the nation of this mind, *Mother Church* might soon reassume her ascendency, and " feed us with Latin masses and a wafer god."

Men may incorporate their doctrines in *creeds* or articles of faith, and sing them in *hymns,* and this may be all both useful and edifying if the doctrine be *true;* but in every question which involves the eternal interests of man, the *Holy Scriptures* must be appealed to, in union with *reason,* their great commentator. He who forms his *creed* or *confession of faith* without these, may believe any thing or nothing, as the cunning of others, or his own caprices, may dictate. Human creeds and confessions of faith have been often put in the place of the Bible, to the disgrace both of revelation and reason. Let *those* go away, let *these* be retained, whatever be the consequence. *Fiat justitia : ruat cœlum.*

No man either can or should believe a doctrine that *contradicts* reason ; but he may safely credit (in any thing that concerns the nature of God) what is *above* his reason, and even this may be a reason why he should believe it. I cannot comprehend the Divine nature, therefore I adore it : if I could comprehend I could not adore, forasmuch as the nature or being which can be comprehended by my mind must be less than that by which it is comprehended, and therefore unworthy of its homage. The more knowledge increases, the more we shall see that *reason* and *learning,* sanctified by piety towards God, are the best interpreters of the sacred oracles.

O Thou, who dwellest between the cherubim, shine forth, and in thy light we shall see light !

I have but *two words* more to add at the conclusion of this long and severe work ; one concerning *myself :*

Ὥσπερ ξενοι χαιροντες ιδειν πατριδα γαιαν,
Οὕτως δε οἱ γραφοντες ιδειν Βιβλιου τελος.

Like travellers, when they see their native soil,
Writers rejoice to terminate their toil.

And one to my readers :

Hic labor extremus, longarum hæc meta viarum :
Hinc me digressum vestris DEUS appulit oris.

My latest labour's end at length is gain'd
My longest journey's welcome goal obtain'd,
By GOD's assistance has the work been wrought,
By his direction to your dwellings brought.
ADAM CLARKE.

MILLBROOK, *July 26th,* 1817.

Finished correcting for a new edition, Jan. 9, 1832.—A. C.

END OF THE NEW TESTAMENT.